THE NEW GROVE
DICTIONARY OF MUSIC AND MUSICIANS

Volume Sixteen

The New GROVE

Dictionary

of Music and

Musicians

EDITED BY

Stanley Sadie

16

Riegel – Schusterfleck

MACMILLAN PUBLISHERS LIMITED, LONDON
GROVE'S DICTIONARIES OF MUSIC INC., WASHINGTON, DC
PENINSULA PUBLISHERS LIMITED, HONG KONG

First Edition of *A Dictionary of Music and Musicians*, planned and edited by SIR GEORGE GROVE, DCL, in
four volumes, with an Appendix edited by J. A. Fuller Maitland, and an Index by Mrs Edmond
Wodehouse, 1878, 1880, 1883, 1890.
Reprinted 1890, 1900

Second Edition, edited by J. A. FULLER MAITLAND, in five volumes, 1904–10

Third Edition, edited by H. C. COLLES, in five volumes, 1927

Fourth Edition, edited by H. C. COLLES, in five volumes, with Supplementary Volume, 1940

Fifth Edition, edited by ERIC BLOM, in nine volumes, 1954: with Supplementary Volume, 1961
Reprinted 1961, 1973, 1975

American Supplement, edited by WALDO SELDEN PRATT, in one volume, 1920
Reprinted, with new material, 1920, 1928, 1935, 1952

The New Grove Dictionary of Music and Musicians,
edited by STANLEY SADIE, in twenty volumes, 1980

Published by Macmillan Publishers Limited, London. This edition is distributed outside the United
Kingdom and Europe by Peninsula Publishers Limited, Hong Kong, a member of the Macmillan
Publishers Group, and by its appointed agents. In the United States of America and Canada, Peninsula
Publishers have appointed Grove's Dictionaries of Music Inc., Washington, DC, as sole distributor.

Text keyboarded, corrected, page-made-up and filmset by
Richard Clay (The Chaucer Press) Ltd, Bungay, Suffolk, England

Illustrations originated by Fletcher & Son Ltd, Norwich, England

Music examples processed by Halstan & Co. Ltd, Amersham, England

Printed and bound in the United States of America by Kingsport Press Inc.

British Library Cataloguing in Publication Data

The New Grove dictionary of music and
musicians.
  1. Music – Dictionaries
  I. Sadie, Stanley
  780′.3   ML100

ISBN 0–333–23111–2

Library of Congress Cataloging in Publication Data
Main entry under title:

The New Grove dictionary of music and musicians.
  Includes bibliographies.
  1. Music – Dictionaries.
  2. Music – Bio-bibliography.
  I. Grove, George, Sir, 1820–1900.
  II. Sadie, Stanley.
  ML100.N48   780′.3   79–26207

ISBN 0–333–23111–2

Contents

General Abbreviations

A	alto, contralto [voice]	Bte	Benedicite
a	alto [instrument]	Bucks.	Buckinghamshire (GB)
AB	see BA	Bulg.	Bulgarian
ABC	American Broadcasting Company; Australian Broadcasting Commission	BVM	Blessed Virgin Mary
Abt.	Abteilung [section]	BWV	Bach-Werke-Verzeichnis [Schmieder, catalogue of J. S. Bach's works]
acc.	accompaniment, accompanied by		
AD	anno Domini		
add, addl	additional		
add, addn	addition	c	circa [about]
ad lib	ad libitum	Calif.	California (USA)
Ag	Agnus Dei	CanD	Cantate Domino
all	alleluia	carn.	Carnival
AM	see MA	CBC	Canadian Broadcasting Corporation
a.m.	ante meridiem [before noon]	CBE	Commander of the Order of the British Empire
amp	amplified		
AMS	American Musicological Society	CBS	Columbia Broadcasting System (USA)
Anh.	Anhang [appendix]	CBSO	City of Birmingham Symphony Orchestra
anon.	anonymous(ly)	CeBeDeM	Centre Belge de Documentation Musicale
ant	antiphon	cel	celesta
appx	appendix	CEMA	Council for the Encouragement of Music and the Arts [now the Arts Council of Great Britain]
arr	arrangement, arranged by/for		
ASCAP	American Society of Composers, Authors and Publishers		
attrib.	attribution, attributed to	cf	confer [compare]
Aug	August	c.f.	cantus firmus
aut	autumn	CH	Companion of Honour
		chap.	chapter
		Chin.	Chinese
		chit	chitarrone
		Cie	Compagnie
B	bass [voice]	cimb	cimbalom
B	Brainard catalogue [Tartini]	cl	clarinet
b	bass [instrument]	clvd	clavichord
b	born	cm	centimetre(s)
BA	Bachelor of Arts	CNRS	Centre National de la Recherche Scientifique (F)
Bar	baritone [voice]		
bar	baritone [instrument]	Co.	Company; County
BBC	British Broadcasting Corporation	Cod.	Codex
BC	British Columbia (Canada)	col.	column
BC	before Christ	coll.	collected by
bc	basso continuo	collab.	in collaboration with
Bd.	Band [volume]	comm	communion
Berks.	Berkshire (GB)	conc.	concerto
Berwicks.	Berwickshire (GB)	cond.	conductor, conducted by
bk	book	Conn.	Connecticut (USA)
BLitt	Bachelor of Letters/Literature	cont	continuo
BM	British Museum	Corp.	Corporation
BMI	Broadcast Music Inc. (USA)	c.p.s.	cycles per second
BMus	Bachelor of Music	Cr	Credo, Creed
bn	bassoon	CSc	Candidate of Historical Sciences
Bros.	Brothers	Ct	countertenor
Bs	Benedictus	Cz.	Czech

D	Deutsch catalogue [Schubert]; Dounias catalogue [Tartini]	GmbH	Gesellschaft mit beschränkter Haftung [limited-liability company]
d.	denarius, denarii [penny, pence]	govt.	government [district in USSR]
d	died	grad	gradual
Dan.	Danish	GSM	Guildhall School of Music and Drama, London
db	double bass		
DBE	Dame Commander of the Order of the British Empire	gui	guitar
dbn	double bassoon		
DC	District of Columbia (USA)	H	Hoboken catalogue [Haydn]; Helm catalogue [C. P. E. Bach]
Dec	December		
ded.	dedication, dedicated to	Hants.	Hampshire (GB)
DeM	Deus misereatur	Heb.	Hebrew
Dept	Department	Herts.	Hertfordshire (GB)
Derbys.	Derbyshire (GB)	HMS	His/Her Majesty's Ship
dir.	director, directed by	HMV	His Master's Voice
diss.	dissertation	hn	horn
DLitt	Doctor of Letters/Literature	Hon.	Honorary; Honourable
DMus	Doctor of Music	hpd	harpsichord
DPhil	Doctor of Philosophy	HRH	His/Her Royal Highness
DSc	Doctor of Science/Historical Sciences	Hung.	Hungarian
		Hunts.	Huntingdonshire (GB)
		Hz	Hertz [c.p.s.]
ed.	editor, edited (by)		
edn.	edition		
e.g.	exempli gratia [for example]	IAML	International Association of Music Libraries
elec	electric, electronic		
EMI	Electrical and Musical Industries	ibid	ibidem [in the same place]
Eng.	English	i.e.	id est [that is]
eng hn	english horn	IFMC	International Folk Music Council
ens	ensemble	Ill.	Illinois (USA)
esp.	especially	IMS	International Musicological Society
etc	et cetera [and so on]	Inc.	Incorporated
ex., exx.	example, examples	inc.	incomplete
		incl.	includes, including
		Ind.	Indiana (USA)
f, ff	following page, following pages	inst	instrument, instrumental
f., ff.	folio, folios	int	introit
f	forte	IPEM	Institute for Psycho-acoustics and Electronic Music, Brussels
facs.	facsimile		
fasc.	fascicle	ISCM	International Society for Contemporary Music
Feb	February		
ff	fortissimo	ISM	Incorporated Society of Musicians (GB)
fff	fortississimo	ISME	International Society of Music Educators
fig.	figure [illustration]	It.	Italian
fl	flute		
fl	floruit [he/she flourished]		
fp	fortepiano	Jan	January
Fr.	French	Jap.	Japanese
frag.	fragment	*Jb*	Jahrbuch [yearbook]
FRAM	Fellow of the Royal Academy of Music, London	Jg.	Jahrgang [year of publication/volume]
		jr	junior
FRCM	Fellow of the Royal College of Music, London	Jub	Jubilate
FRCO	Fellow of the Royal College of Organists, London		
		K	Kirkpatrick catalogue [D. Scarlatti]; Köchel catalogue [Mozart; no. after / is from 6th edn.]
FRS	Fellow of the Royal Society, London		
		kbd	keyboard
Gael.	Gaelic	KBE	Knight Commander of the Order of the British Empire
Ger.	German		
Gk.	Greek	KCVO	Knight Commander of the Royal Victorian Order
Gl	Gloria		
Glam.	Glamorgan (GB)	kHz	kilohertz
glock	glockenspiel	km	kilometre(s)
Glos., Gloucs.	Gloucestershire (GB)	Ky	Kyrie
		Ky.	Kentucky (USA)

£	libra, librae [pound, pounds sterling]	Oct	October
L	Longo catalogue [D. Scarlatti]	off	offertory
Lancs.	Lancashire (GB)	OM	Order of Merit
Lat.	Latin	Ont.	Ontario (Canada)
Leics.	Leicestershire (GB)	op., opp.	opus, opera
lib	libretto	op cit	opere citato [in the work cited]
Lincs.	Lincolnshire (GB)	opt.	optional
lit	litany	orch	orchestra, orchestral
LittD	Doctor of Letters/Literature	orchd	orchestrated (by)
LlB	Bachelor of Laws	org	organ
LlD	Doctor of Laws	orig.	original(ly)
LP	long-playing record	ORTF	Office de Radiodiffusion-Télévision Française
LPO	London Philharmonic Orchestra		
LSO	London Symphony Orchestra	OUP	Oxford University Press
Ltd	Limited	ov.	overture

M.	Monsieur	P	Pincherle catalogue [Vivaldi]
MA	Master of Arts	p.	pars (1p. = *prima pars*, etc)
Mag	Magnificat	p., pp.	page, pages
mand	mandolin	*p*	piano
mar	marimba	p.a.	per annum
Mass.	Massachusetts (USA)	PC	number of chanson in A. Pillet and H.
MBE	Member of the Order of the British Empire		Carstens: *Bibliographie der Troubadours* (Halle, 1933)
Mez	mezzo-soprano	Penn.	Pennsylvania (USA)
mf	mezzo-forte	perc	percussion
mic	microphone	perf.	performance, performed (by)
Mich.	Michigan (USA)	pf	piano
Minn.	Minnesota (USA)	PhD	Doctor of Philosophy
Mlle	Mademoiselle	pic	piccolo
mm	millimetre(s)	pl.	plate; plural
Mme	Madame	p.m.	post meridiem [after noon]
MMus	Master of Music	PO	Philharmonic Orchestra
mod	modulator	Pol.	Polish
Mon.	Monmouthshire (GB)	Port.	Portuguese
movt	movement	posth.	posthumous(ly)
MP	Member of Parliament (GB)	POW	prisoner of war
mp	mezzo-piano	*pp*	pianissimo
MS	manuscript	*ppp*	pianississimo
MSc	Master of Science(s)	pr.	printed
Mt	Mount	PRO	Public Record Office, London
MusB,	Bachelor of Music	prol	prologue
MusBac		PRS	Performing Right Society (GB)
MusD,	Doctor of Music	Ps	Psalm
MusDoc		ps	psalm
MusM	Master of Music	pseud.	pseudonym
		pt.	part
		ptbk	partbook
NBC	National Broadcasting Company (USA)	pubd	published
n.d.	no date of publication	pubn	publication
NJ	New Jersey (USA)		
no.	number		
Nor.	Norwegian	qnt	quintet
Northants.	Northamptonshire (GB)	qt	quartet
Notts.	Nottinghamshire (GB)		
Nov	November		
n.p.	no place of publication	R	[in signature] editorial revision
nr.	near	R.	number of chanson in G. Raynaud: *Bibliographie des chansonniers français des XIIIe et XIVe siècles* (Paris, 1884) and H. Spanke: *G. Raynauds Bibliographie des altfranzösischen Liedes* (Leiden, 1955)
NSW	New South Wales (Australia)		
Nunc	Nunc dimittis		
NY	New York State (USA)		
		R	response
ob	oboe	R	Ryom catalogue [Vivaldi]
obbl	obbligato	*R*	photographic reprint
OBE	Officer of the Order of the British Empire	*r*	recto

RAF	Royal Air Force
RAI	Radio Audizioni Italiane
RAM	Royal Academy of Music, London
RCA	Radio Corporation of America
RCM	Royal College of Music, London
re	response
rec	recorder
recit	recitative
red.	reduction, reduced for
repr.	reprinted
Rev.	Reverend
rev.	revision, revised (by/for)
RIdIM	Répertoire International d'Iconographie Musicale
RILM	Répertoire International de Littérature Musicale
RISM	Répertoire International des Sources Musicales
RMCM	Royal Manchester College of Music
RNCM	Royal Northern College of Music, Manchester
RO	Radio Orchestra
Rom.	Romanian
RPO	Royal Philharmonic Orchestra (GB)
RSFSR	Russian Soviet Federated Socialist Republic
RSO	Radio Symphony Orchestra
Rt Hon.	Right Honourable
RTE	Radio Telefís Eireann (Ireland)
Russ.	Russian
RV	Ryom catalogue [Vivaldi]
S	San, Santa, Santo, São [Saint]; soprano [voice]
S.	south, southern
$	dollars
s	soprano [instrument]
s.	solidus, solidi [shilling, shillings]
SACEM	Société d'Auteurs, Compositeurs et Editeurs de Musique (F)
San	Sanctus
Sask.	Saskatchewan (Canada)
sax	saxophone
Sept	September
seq	sequence
ser.	series
sf, sfz	sforzando, sforzato
sing.	singular
SJ	Societas Jesu (Society of Jesus)
SO	Symphony Orchestra
SPNM	Society for the Promotion of New Music (GB)
spr.	spring
SS	Saints
Ss	Santissima, Santissimo
SSR	Soviet Socialist Republic
St	Saint, Sint, Szent
Staffs.	Staffordshire (GB)
Ste	Sainte
str	string(s)
sum.	summer
Sup	superius
suppl.	supplement, supplementary
Swed.	Swedish
sym.	symphony, symphonic
synth	synthesizer

T	tenor [voice]
t	tenor [instrument]
TeD	Te Deum
Tenn.	Tennessee (USA)
timp	timpani
tpt	trumpet
Tr	treble [voice]
tr	tract; treble [instrument]
trans.	translation, translated by
transcr.	transcription, transcribed by/for
trbn	trombone
U.	University
UHF	ultra-high frequency
UK	United Kingdom of Great Britain and Northern Ireland
unacc.	unaccompanied
unattrib.	unattributed
UNESCO	United Nations Educational, Scientific and Cultural Organization
unperf.	unperformed
unpubd	unpublished
US	United States [adjective]
USA	United States of America
USSR	Union of Soviet Socialist Republics
V	versicle
v, vv	voice, voices
v., vv.	verse, verses
v	verso
va	viola
vc	cello
vcle	versicle
VEB	Volkseigener Betrieb [people's own industry]
Ven	Venite
VHF	very high frequency
vib	vibraphone
viz	videlicet [namely]
vle	violone
vn	violin
vol.	volume
W.	west, western
Warwicks.	Warwickshire (GB)
Wilts.	Wiltshire (GB)
wint.	winter
Wisc.	Wisconsin (USA)
WoO, woo	Werke ohne Opuszahl [works without opus number]
Worcs.	Worcestershire (GB)
WQ	Wotquenne catalogue [C. P. E. Bach]
ww	woodwind
xyl	xylophone
Yorks.	Yorkshire (GB)
z	Zimmerman catalogue [Purcell]

Bibliographical Abbreviations

All bibliographical abbreviations used in this dictionary are listed below, following the typography used in the text of the dictionary. Broadly, *italic* type is used for periodicals and for reference works; roman type is used for anthologies, series etc (titles of individual volumes are italicized).

Full bibliographical information is not normally supplied in the list below if it is available elsewhere in the dictionary. Its availability is indicated as follows: D – in the article 'Dictionaries and encyclopedias of music'; E – in the article 'Editions, historical'; and P – in the list forming §III of the article 'Periodicals' (in this case the number in that list of the periodical concerned is added, in brackets). For other items, in particular national (non-musical) biographical dictionaries, basic bibliographical information is given here; and in some cases extra information is supplied to clarify the abbreviation used.

Festschriften and congress reports are not, in general, covered in this list. Although Festschrift titles are usually shortened in the dictionary, sufficient information is always given for unambiguous identification (dedicatee; occasion, if the same person is dedicatee of more than one Festschrift; place and date of publication; and where the dedicatee has an entry the editor's name may be found); for fuller information on musical Festschriften up to 1967 see W. Gerboth: *An Index to Musical Festschriften and Similar Publications* (New York, 1969). The only congress report series listed below are those of the international and the German musicological associations; for others cited in the dictionary, sufficient information is always given for identification (society or topic; place; date of occurrence); full information may be found in J. Tyrrell and R. Wise: *A Guide to International Congress Reports in Music, 1900–1975* (London, 1979).

AcM	*Acta musicologica* P [Intl 5]
ADB	Allgemeine deutsche Biographie (Leipzig, 1875–1912)
AM	*Antiphonale monasticum pro diurnis horis* (Paris, Tournai and Rome, 1934)
AMe (AMeS)	Algemene muziekencyclopedie (and suppl.) D
AMf	*Archiv für Musikforschung* P [D776]
AMI	L'arte musicale in Italia E
AMP	Antiquitates musicae in Polonia E
AMw	*Archiv für Musikwissenschaft* P [D552]
AMZ	*Allgemeine musikalische Zeitung* P [D32, 154, 170]
AMz	*Allgemeine Musik-Zeitung* P [D203]
AnM	*Anuario musical* P [E91]
AnMc	Analecta musicologica (some vols. in series Studien zur italienisch-deutschen Musikgeschichte), Veröffentlichungen der Musikabteilung des Deutschen historischen Instituts in Rom (Cologne, 1963–)
AnnM	*Annales musicologiques* P [F638]
AntMI	Antiquae musicae italicae E
AR	*Antiphonale sacrosanctae romanae ecclesiae pro diurnis horis* (Paris, Tournai and Rome, 1949)
AS	*Antiphonale sarisburiense*, ed. W. H. Frere (London, 1901–25/R1967)
Baker 5, 6	*Baker's Biographical Dictionary of Musicians* (5/1958 and 1971 suppl., 6/1978) D
BAMS	*Bulletin of the American Musicological Society* P [US540]
BeJb	*Beethoven-Jahrbuch* [1953–] P [D925]
BJb	*Bach-Jahrbuch* P [D434]
BMB	Biblioteca musica bononiensis E
BMw	*Beiträge zur Musikwissenschaft* P [D1013]
BNB	*Biographie nationale* [belge] (Brussels, 1866–)
BordasD	*Dictionnaire de la musique* (Paris: Bordas, 1970–76) D
Bouwsteenen: JVNM	Bouwsteenen: jaarbuch der Vereeniging voor Nederlandsche muziekgeschiedenis P [NL20]
BrownI	H. M. Brown: *Instrumental Music Printed before 1600: a Bibliography* (Cambridge, Mass., 2/1967)
BSIM	*Bulletin français de la S[ociété] I[nternationale de] M[usique]* [previously *Le Mercure musical*; also other titles] P [F364]
BUCEM	*British Union-catalogue of Early Music*, ed. E. Schnapper (London, 1957)
BurneyH	C. Burney: *A General History of Music from the Earliest Ages to the Present* (London, 1776–89) [p. nos. refer to edn. of 1935/R1957]
BWQ	*Brass and Woodwind Quarterly* P [US756]
CaM	Catalogus musicus E
CEKM	Corpus of Early Keyboard Music E
CEMF	Corpus of Early Music in Facsimile E
CHM	Collectanea historiae musicae (in series Biblioteca historiae musicae cultores) (Florence, 1953–)
CM	Le choeur des muses E
CMc	*Current Musicology* P [US747]
CMI	I classici musicali italiani E
CMM	Corpus mensurabilis musicae E
CMz	*Cercetări de muzicologie* P [R29]
CS	E. de Coussemaker: *Scriptorum de musica medii aevi nova series* (Paris, 1864–76/R1963)
ČSHS	*Československý hudebni slovnik* D
CSM	Corpus scriptorum de musica E
CSPD	*Calendar of State Papers* (*Domestic*) (London, 1856–1972)
Cw	Das Chorwerk E
DAB	*Dictionary of American Biography* (New York, 1928–)
DAM	*Dansk aarbog for musikforskning* P [DK88]
DBF	*Dictionnaire de biographie française* (Paris, 1933–)
DBI	*Dizionario biografico degli italiani* (Rome, 1960–)
DBL	*Dansk biografisk leksikon* (Copenhagen, 1887–1905, 2/1933–)
DBP	*Dicionário biográfico de musicos portuguezes* D
DČHP	*Dějiny české hudby v příkladech* E
DDT	Denkmäler deutscher Tonkunst E
DHM	Documenta historicae musicae E
DJbM	*Deutsches Jahrbuch der Musikwissenschaft* P [D980]
DM	Documenta musicologica E
DNB	*Dictionary of National Biography* (London, 1885–1901, suppls.)
DTB	Denkmäler der Tonkunst in Bayern E
DTÖ	Denkmäler der Tonkunst in Österreich E

EDM	Das Erbe deutscher Musik E
EECM	Early English Church Music E
EIT	*Ezhegodnik imperatorskikh teatrov* P [USSR17]
EitnerQ	R. Eitner: *Biographisch-bibliographisches Quellen-Lexikon* D
EitnerS	R. Eitner: *Bibliographie der Musik-Sammelwerke des XVI. und XVII. Jahrhunderts* (Berlin, 1877)
EKM	English (later Early) Keyboard Music E
EL	The English Lute-songs
EM	The English Madrigalists E
EM	*Ethnomusicology* P [US664]
EMDC	*Encyclopédie de la musique et dictionnaire du Conservatoire* D
EMN	Exempla musica neerlandica E
EMS	The English Madrigal School E
ES	*Enciclopedia dello spettacolo* D
ESLS	The English School of Lutenist-songwriters E
FAM	*Fontes artis musicae* P [Intl 16]
FasquelleE	*Encyclopédie de la musique* (Paris: Fasquelle, 1958–61) D
FCVR	Florilège du concert vocal de la renaissance E
FétisB (*FétisBS*)	F.-J. Fétis: *Biographie universelle des musiciens* (2/1860–65) (and suppl.) D
GerberL	R. Gerber: *Historisch-biographisches Lexikon der Tonkünstler* D
GerberNL	R. Gerber: *Neues historisch-biographisches Lexikon der Tonkünstler* D
GfMKB	*Gesellschaft für Musikforschung Kongressbericht* [1950–]
GMB	*Geschichte der Musik in Beispielen*, ed. A. Schering (Leipzig, 1931) E
GR	*Graduale sacrosanctae romanae ecclesiae* (Tournai, 1938)
Grove 1(–5)	G. Grove, ed.: *A Dictionary of Music and Musicians*, 2nd–5th edns. as *Grove's Dictionary of Music and Musicians* D
Grove 6	*The New Grove Dictionary of Music and Musicians* D
GS	*Graduale sarisburiense*, ed. W. H. Frere (London, 1894/*R*1967)
GS	M. Gerbert: *Scriptores ecclesiastici de musica sacra* (St Blasien, 1784/*R*1963)
GSJ	*The Galpin Society Journal* P [GB415]
HAM	*Historical Anthology of Music*, ed. A. T. Davison and W. Apel, i (Cambridge, Mass., 1946, rev. 2/1949); ii (Cambridge, Mass., 1950) E
HawkinsH	J. Hawkins: *A General History of the Science and Practice of Music* (London, 1776) [p. nos. refer to edn. of 1853/*R*1963]
HJb	*Händel-Jahrbuch* P [D712, 968]
HM	Hortus musicus E
HMT	*Handwörterbuch der musikalischen Terminologie* D
HMw	Handbuch der Musikwissenschaft, ed. E. Bücken (Potsdam, 1927–) [monograph series]
HMYB	*Hinrichsen's Musical Year Book* P [GB381]
HPM	Harvard Publications in Music E
HR	*Hudební revue* P [CS80]
HRo	*Hudební rozhledy* P [CS176]
HV	*Hudební věda* P [CS204]
IIM	*Izvestiya na Instituta za muzïka* P [BG14]
IMa	Instituta et monumenta E
IMi	Istituzioni e monumenti dell'arte musicale italiana E
IMSCR	*International Musicological Society Congress Report* [1930–]
IMusSCR	*International Musical Society Congress Report* [1906–11]
IRASM	*International Review of the Aesthetics and Sociology of Music* P [Intl 32]
IRMO	S. L. Ginzburg: *Istoriya russkoy muzïki v notnïkh obraztsakh* D
IRMAS	*The International Review of Music Aesthetics and Sociology* P [Intl 32]
IZ	*Instrumentenbau-Zeitschrift* P [D806]
JAMS	*Journal of the American Musicological Society* P [US613]

JbMP	*Jahrbuch der Musikbibliothek Peters* P [D336]
JEFDSS	*The Journal of the English Folk Dance and Song Society* P [GB341]
JFSS	*Journal of the Folk-song Society* P [GB183]
JIFMC	*Journal of the International Folk Music Council* P [Intl 10]
JMT	*Journal of Music Theory* P [US683]
JRBM	*Journal of Renaissance and Baroque Music* P [US590]
JRME	*Journal of Research in Music Education* P [US665]
JVNM	see *Bouwsteenen: JVNM* P [NL20]
KJb	*Kirchenmusikalisches Jahrbuch* P [D284]
KM	*Kwartalnik muzyczny* P [PL35, 64]
LaborD	*Diccionario de la música Labor* D
LaMusicaD	*La musica: dizionario* D
LaMusicaE	*La musica: enciclopedia storica* D
LM	*Lucrări de muzicologie* P [R27]
LSJ	*The Lute Society Journal* P [GB487]
LU	*Liber usualis missae et officii pro dominicis et festis duplicibus cum cantu gregoriano* (Solesmes, 1896; many later edns., incl. Tournai, 1963)
MA	*The Musical Antiquary* P [GB240]
MAB	Musica antiqua bohemica E
MAM	Musik alter Meister E
MAP	Musica antiqua polonica E
MAS	[publications of the British] Musical Antiquarian Society E
MB	Musica britannica E
MC	Musica da camera E
MD	*Musica disciplina* P [US590]
ME	*Muzïkal'naya entsiklopediya* D
MEM	Mestres de l'escolania de Montserrat E
Mf	*Die Musikforschung* P [D839]
MGG	*Die Musik in Geschichte und Gegenwart* D
MH	Musica hispana E
MJb	*Mozart-Jahrbuch des Zentralinstituts für Mozartforschung* [1950–] P [A254]
ML	*Music and Letters* P [GB280]
MLMI	Monumenta lyrica medii aevi italica E
MM	*Modern Music* P [US488]
MMA	*Miscellanea musicologica* [Australia] P [AUS19]
MMB	Monumenta musicae byzantinae E
MMBel	Monumenta musicae belgicae E
MMC	*Miscellanea musicologica* [Czechoslovakia] P [CS191]
MME	Monumentos de la música española E
MMFTR	Monuments de la musique française au temps de la renaissance E
MMg	*Monatshefte für Musikgeschichte* P [D188]
MMI	Monumenti di musica italiana E
MMN	Monumenta musicae neerlandicae E
MMP	Monumenta musicae in Polonia E
MMR	*The Monthly Musical Record* P [GB75]
MMRF	Les maîtres musiciens de la renaissance française E
MMS	Monumenta musicae svecicae E
MO	*Musical Opinion* P [GB90]
MQ	*The Musical Quarterly* P [US447]
MR	*The Music Review* P [GB376]
MRM	Monuments of Renaissance Music E
MRS	Musiche rinascimentali siciliane E
MS	*Muzïkal'nïy sovremennik* P [USSR37]
MSD	Musicological Studies and Documents, ed. A. Carapetyan (Rome, 1951–)
MT	*The Musical Times* P [GB33]
MVH	Musica viva historica E
MVSSP	Musiche vocali strumentali sacre e profane E
Mw	Das Musikwerk E
MZ	*Muzikološki zbornik* P [YU37]
NA	*Note d'archivio per la storia musicale* P [I186]
NBJb	*Neues Beethoven-Jahrbuch* P [D636]
NBL	*Norsk biografisk leksikon* (Oslo, 1921–)
NDB	*Neue deutsche Biographie* (Berlin, 1953–)
NM	Nagels Musikarchiv E
NNBW	*Nieuw Nederlandsch biografisch woordenboek* (Leiden, 1911–37)
NÖB	*Neue österreichische Biographie* (Vienna, 1923)

NOHM	*The New Oxford History of Music*, ed. E. Wellesz, J. A. Westrup and G. Abraham (London, 1954–)
NRMI	*Nuova rivista musicale italiana* P [I 282]
NZM	*Neue Zeitschrift für Musik* P [D75, 1088]
OHM	*The Oxford History of Music*, ed. W. H. Hadow (Oxford, 1901–5, enlarged 2/1929–38)
OM	*Opus musicum* P [CS222]
ÖMz	*ÖsterreichischeMusikzeitschrift* P [A233]
PalMus	Paléographie musicale (Solesmes, 1889–) [see entry SOLESMES]
PAMS	*Papers of the American Musicological Society* P [US543]
PÄMw	Publikationen älterer praktischer und theoretischer Musikwerke E
PBC	Publicaciones del departamento de música de la Biblioteca de Catalunya E
PG	*Patrologiae cursus completus*, ii: Series graeca, ed. J.-P. Migne (Paris, 1857–1912)
PGfM	Publikationen der Gesellschaft für Musikforschung E
PIISM	Pubblicazioni dell'Istituto italiano per la storia della musica E
PL	*Patrologiae cursus completus*, i: Series latina, ed. J.-P. Migne (Paris, 1844–64)
PM	Portugaliae musica E
PMA	*Proceedings of the Musical Association* P [GB80]
PMFC	Polyphonic Music of the Fourteenth Century E
PNM	*Perspectives of New Music* P [US724]
PRM	*Polski rocznik muzykologiczny* P [PL85]
PRMA	*Proceedings of the Royal Musical Association* P [GB80]
PSB	*Polskich słownik biograficzny* (Kraków, 1935)
PSFM	Publications de la Société française de musicologie E
Quaderni della RaM	*Quaderni della Rassegna musicale* P [I 272]
Rad JAZU	*Rad Jugoslavenske akademije znanosti i umjetnosti* (Zagreb, 1867–)
RaM	*La rassegna musicale* P [I 197]
RBM	*Revue belge de musicologie* P [B126]
RdM	*Revue de musicologie* P [F462]
ReM	*La revue musicale* [1920–] P [F475]
RHCM	*Revue d'histoire et de critique musicales* [1901]; *La revue musicale* [1902–10] P [F320]
RicordiE	*Enciclopedia della musica* (Milan: Ricordi, 1963–4) D
RiemannL 12	*Riemann Musik Lexikon* (12/1959–75) D
RIM	*Rivista italiana di musicologia* P [I 280]
RISM	*Répertoire international des sources musicales* [see entry under this title]
RMARC	*R[oyal] M[usical] A[ssociation] Research Chronicle* P [GB496]
RMFC	*Recherches sur la musique française classique* P [F677]
RMG	*Russkaya muzïkal'naya gazeta* P [USSR19]
RMI	*Rivista musicale italiana* P [I 84]
RMS	Renaissance Manuscript Studies E
RN	*Renaissance News* P [see US590]
RRMBE	Recent Researches in the Music of the Baroque Era E
RRMR	Recent Researches in the Music of the Renaissance E
SartoriB	C. Sartori: *Bibliografia della musica strumentale italiana stampata in Italia fino al 1700* (Florence, 1952–68)
SBL	*Svenska biografiskt leksikon* (Stockholm, 1918–)
SchmidlD (SchmidlDS)	C. Schmidl: *Dizionario dei musicisti* (and suppl.) D
SCMA	Smith College Music Archives E
SeegerL	H. Seeger: *Musiklexikon* D
SEM	[University of California] Series of Early Music E
SH	*Slovenská hudba* P [CS192]
SIMG	*Sammelbände der Internationalen Musik-Gesellschaft* P [Intl 2]
SM	*Studia musicologica Academiae scientiarum hungaricae* P [H49]
SMA	*Studies in Music* [Australia] P [AUS20]
SMd	Schweizerische Musikdenkmäler E
SML	*Schweizer Musiker Lexikon* D
SMM	Summa musicae medii aevi E
SMN	*Studia musicologica norvegica* P [N45]
SMP	*Słownik muzyków polskich* D
SMw	*Studien zur Musikwissenschaft* P [D536]
SMz	*Schweizerische Musikzeitung/Revue musicale suisse* P [CH4]
SOB	Süddeutsche Orgelmeister des Barock E
SovM	*Sovetskaya muzïka* P [USSR66]
STMf	*Svensk tidskrift för musikforskning* P [S46]
TCM	Tudor Church Music E
TM	Thesauri musici E
TVNM	*Tijdschrift van de Vereniging voor Nederlandse muziekgeschiedenis* P [NL26]
UVNM	Uitgaven der Vereniging voor Nederlandse muziekgeschiedenis E
VMPH	Veröffentlichungen der Musik-Bibliothek Paul Hirsch E
VMw	*Vierteljahrsschrift für Musikwissenschaft* P [D282]
VogelB	E. Vogel: *Bibliothek der gedruckten weltlichen Vocalmusik Italiens, aus den Jahren 1500 bis 1700* (Berlin, 1892); rev., enlarged, by A. Einstein (Hildesheim, 1962); further addns in *AnMc*, nos.4, 5, 9 and 12; further rev. by F. Lesure and C. Sartori as *Bibliografia della musica italiana vocale profana pubblicata dal 1500 al 1700* (?Geneva, 1978)
WaltherML	J. G. Walther: *Musicalisches Lexicon oder Musicalische Bibliothec* D
WDMP	Wydawnictwo dawnej muzyki polskiej E
WE	Wellesley Edition E
WECIS	Wellesley Edition Cantata Index Series E
YIFMC	*Yearbook of the International Folk Music Council* P [Intl 31]
ZfM	*Zeitschrift für Musik* P [D75]
ZHMP	Zrodła do historii muzyki polskiej E
ZI	*Zeitschrift für Instrumentenbau* P [D249]
ZIMG	*Zeitschrift der Internationalen Musik-Gesellschaft* P [Intl3]
ZL	*Zenei lexikon* D
ZMw	*Zeitschrift für Musikwissenschaft* P [D556]

Library Sigla

The system of library sigla in this dictionary follows that used in its publications (Series A) by Répertoire International des Sources Musicales, Kassel, by permission. Below are listed the sigla to be found; a few of them are additional to those in the published RISM lists, but have been established in consultation with the RISM organization. Some original RISM sigla that have now been changed are retained here.

In the dictionary, sigla are always printed in *italic*. In any listing of sources a national sigillum applies without repetition until it is contradicted. For German sigla, the intermediate *brd* and *ddr* are excluded; the list below shows in which part of Germany or Berlin each library is located.

Within each national list, entries are alphabetized by sigillum, first by capital letters (showing the city or town) and then by lower-case ones (showing the institution or collection).

A: AUSTRIA

Ee	Eisenstadt, Esterházy-Archiv
Eh	——, Haydn Museum
Ek	——, Stadtpfarrkirche
F	Fiecht, Benediktinerordensstift St Georgenberg
Gd	Graz, Diözesan Archiv
Gk	——, Hochschule für Musik und Darstellende Kunst
Gl	——, Steiermärkische Landesbibliothek am Joanneum
Gmi	——, Musikwissenschaftliches Institut der Universität
Gu	——, Universitätsbibliothek
GÖ	Furth bei Göttweig, Benediktinerstift
GÜ	Güssing, Franziskaner Kloster
H	Herzogenburg, Chorherrenstift
HE	Heiligenkreuz, Zisterzienserstift
Ik	Innsbruck, Konservatorium
Imf	——, Museum Ferdinandeum
Imi	——, Musikwissenschaftliches Institut der Universität
Iu	——, Universitätsbibliothek
Iw	——, Prämonstratenser-Chorherrenstift Wilten
KN	Klosterneuburg, Augustiner-Chorherrenstift
KR	Kremsmünster, Benediktinerstift
L	Lilienfeld, Zisterzienser-Stift
LA	Lambach, Benediktinerstift
LEx	Leoben, Pfarrbibliothek St Xaver
LIm	Linz, Oberösterreichisches Landesarchiv
LIs	——, Bundesstaatliche Studienbibliothek
M	Melk an der Donau, Benediktinerstift
MB	Michaelbeuern, Benediktinerabtei
MÖ	Mödling, Pfarrkirche St Othmar
MZ	Mariazell, Benediktiner-Priorat
N	Neuburg, Pfarrarchiv
NS	Neustift, Pfarrarchiv
R	Rein, Zisterzienserstift
Sca	Salzburg, Museum Carolino Augusteum
Sd	——, Dom-Musikarchiv
Sk	——, Kapitelbibliothek
Sm	——, Internationale Stiftung Mozarteum
Smi	——, Musikwissenschaftliches Institut der Universität
Sn	——, Nonnberg, Benediktiner-Frauenstift
Ssp	——, St Peter Benediktiner-Erzabtei
SB	Schlierbach, Stift
SCH	Schlägl, Prämonstratenser-Stift
SE	Seckau, Benediktinerabtei
SEI	Seitenstetten, Benediktinerstift
SF	St Florian, Augustiner-Chorherrenstift
SH	Solbad Hall, Franziskaner-Kloster
SL	St Lambrecht, Benediktiner-Abtei
SP	St Pölten, Diözesanarchiv
SPL	St Paul, Stift
ST	Stams, Zisterzienserstift
STE	Steyr, Stadtpfarrarchiv
TU	Tulln, Pfarrkirche St Stephan
Wd	Vienna, Stephansdom
Wdo	——, Zentralarchiv des Deutschen Ordens
Wdtö	——, Gesellschaft zur Herausgabe von Denkmälern der Tonkunst in Österreich
Wgm	——, Gesellschaft der Musikfreunde
Wh	——, Pfarrarchiv Hernals
Whb	——, Hauptverband des Österreichischen Buchhandels
Wk	——, Pfarrkirche St Karl Borromäus
Wkann	——, Hans Kann, private collection
Wkh	——, Kirche am Hof
Wkm	——, Kunsthistorisches Museum
Wl	——, Archiv für Niederösterreich (Landesarchiv)
Wm	——, Minoritenkonvent
Wmg	——, Pfarre, Maria am Gestade
Wmi	——, Musikwissenschaftliches Institut der Universität
Wmk	——, Akademie für Musik und Darstellende Kunst
Wn	——, Österreichische Nationalbibliothek, Musiksammlung
Wögm	——, Österreichische Gesellschaft für Musik
Wp	——, Musikarchiv, Piaristenkirche Maria Treu
Wph	——, Wiener Philharmoniker, Archiv und Bibliothek
Wps	——, Priesterseminar
Ws	——, Schottenstift
Wsa	——, Stadtarchiv
Wsp	——, St Peter, Musikarchiv
Wst	——, Stadtbibliothek, Musiksammlung
Wu	——, Universitätsbibliothek
Ww	——, Pfarrarchiv Währing
Wweinmann	——, Alexander Weinmann, private collection
Wwessely	——, Othmar Wessely, private collection
WAY	Waydhofen an der Ybbs, Pfarre
WE	Wels, Stift
WIL	Wilhering, Zisterzienserstift
Z	Zwettl, Zisterzienserstift

B: BELGIUM

Aa	Antwerp, Stadsarchief
Aac	——, Archief en Museum voor het Vlaamse Culturleven
Ac	——, Koninklijk Vlaams Muziekconservatorium
Ak	——, Onze-Lieve-Vrouwkathedraal
Amp	——, Museum Plantijn–Moretus
Apersoons	——, Guido Persoons, private collection
As	——, Stadsbibliotheek
Asa	——, Kerkebestuur St-Andries
Asj	——, Collegiale en Parochiale Kerk St-Jacob
Averwilt	——, F. Verwilt, private collection
AN	——, Anderlecht, St-Guiden Kerk
Ba	Brussels, Archives de la Ville
Bc	——, Conservatoire Royal de Musique
Bcdm	——, Centre Belge de Documentation Musicale [CeBeDeM]
Bg	——, Eglise de Ste Gudule
Bi	——, Institut de Psycho-acoustique et de Musique Electronique

Br	——, Bibliothèque Royale Albert 1er/Koninklijke Bibliotheek Albert I	*GLtschudi*	Glarus, A. Tschudi, private collection
Brtb	——, Radiodiffusion-Télévision Belge	*Lmg*	Lucerne, Allgemeine Musikalische Gesellschaft
Bsp	——, Société Philharmonique	*Ls*	——, Stiftsarchiv St Leodegar
BRc	Bruges, Stedelijk Muziekconservatorium	*Lz*	——, Zentralbibliothek
D	Diest, St Sulpitiuskerk	*LAc*	Lausanne, Conservatoire de Musique
Gar	Ghent [Gent, Gand], Stadsarchief	*LAcu*	——, Bibliothèque Cantonale et Universitaire
Gc	——, Koninklijk Muziekconservatorium	*LU*	Lugano, Biblioteca Cantonale
Gcd	——, Culturele Dienst Province Ost Vlaanderen	*Mbernegg*	Maienfeld, Sprecher von Bernegg, private collection
Geb	——, St Baafsarchief med Bibliotheek Van Damme	*MO*	Morges, Bibliothèque de la Ville
Gu	——, Rijksuniversiteit, Centrale Bibliotheek	*MÜ*	Müstair, Frauenkloster
K	Kortrijk, St Martinskerk	*N*	Neuchâtel, Bibliothèque Publique
Lc	Liège, Conservatoire Royal de Musique	*R*	Rheinfelden, Christkatholisches Pfarramt
Lu	——, Université de Liège	*S*	Sion, Bibliothèque Cantonale du Valais
LIc	Lier, Conservatoire	*Sa*	——, Staatsarchiv
LIg	——, St Gummaruskerk	*Sk*	——, Kathedrale
LV	Louvain, Dominikanenklooster	*SA*	Sarnen, Bibliothek des Kollegiums
LVu	——, Université de Louvain	*SAf*	——, Frauenkloster
M	Mons, Conservatoire Royal de Musique	*SCH*	Schwyz, Kantonsbibliothek
MA	Morlanwelz-Mariemont, Musée de Mariemont	*SGs*	St Gall, Stiftsbibliothek
MEa	Mechelen, Archief en Stadsbibliotheek	*SGv*	——, Stadtbibliothek
MEs	——, Stedelijke Openbare Bibliotheek	*SH*	Schaffhausen, Stadtbibliothek
OU	Oudenaarde, Parochiale Kerk	*SM*	St Maurice, Bibliothèque de l'Abbaye
Tc	Tournai, Chapitre de la Cathédrale	*SO*	Solothurn, Zentralbibliothek, Musiksammlung
Tv	——, Bibliothèque de la Ville	*TH*	Thun, Stadtbibliothek
TI	Tienen, St Germanuskerk	*W*	Winterthur, Stadtbibliothek
Z	Zoutleeuw, St Leonarduskerk	*Wpeer*	——, Peer private collection
		Zi	Zurich, Israelitische Kulturgemeinde
	BR: BRAZIL	*Zjacobi*	——, Erwin R. Jacobi, private collection
Rem	Rio de Janeiro, Escola de Música, Universidade Federal do Rio de Janeiro	*Zk*	——, Konservatorium und Musikhochschule
Rn	——, Biblioteca Nacional	*Zma*	——, Schweizerisches Musik-Archiv
		Zms	——, Musikwissenschaftliches Seminar der Universität
	C: CANADA	*Zp*	——, Pestalozzianum
E	Edmonton, University of Alberta	*Zz*	——, Zentralbibliothek
Fc	Fredericton, Christ Church Cathedral	*ZG*	Zug, Stadtbibliothek
Ku	Kingston, Queens University, Douglas Library	*ZO*	Zofingen, Stadtbibliothek
Lu	London, University of Western Ontario, Lawson Memorial Library	*ZU*	Zuoz, Gemeindearchiv
Mc	Montreal, Conservatoire de Musique et d'Art Dramatique		*CO*: COLOMBIA
		B	Bogotá, Catedral
Mfisher	——, Sidney T. Fisher, private collection [in *Tu*]		
Mm	——, McGill University, Faculty and Conservatorium of Music and Redpath Libraries		*CS*: CZECHOSLOVAKIA
		Bb	Brno, Klášter Milosrdných Bratří [in *Bm*]
On	Ottawa, National Library of Canada	*Bm*	——, Ústav Dějin Hudby Moravského Musea, Hudebněhistorické Oddělení
Qc	Quebec, Cathédrale de la Sainte-Trinité		
Qul	——, Université Laval	*Bu*	——, Státní Vědecká Knihovna, Universitní Knihovna
SAu	Sackville, Mt Allison University	*BA*	Bakov nad Jizerou, pobočka Státní Archívu v Mladé Boleslavi
SJm	St John, New Brunswick Museum		
Tb	Toronto, Canadian Broadcasting Corporation	*BEL*	Bělá pod Bezdězem, Městské Muzeum
Tm	——, Royal Ontario Museum	*BER*	Beroun, Okresní Archív
Tolnick	——, Harvey J. Olnick, private collection	*BRa*	Bratislava, Okresní Archív
Tp	——, Toronto Public Library, Music Branch	*BRe*	——, Evangelícka a. v. Cirkevná Knižnica
Tu	——, University of Toronto, Faculty of Music	*BRhs*	——, Knižnica Hudebného Seminara Filosofickej Fakulty University Komenského
Vu	Vancouver, University of British Columbia Library, Fine Arts Division		
		BRnm	——, Slovenské Národné Muzeum, Hudobné Oddělenie
W	Winnipeg, University of Manitoba		
		BRsa	——, Štátny Ústredný Archív Slovenskej Socialistickej Republiky
	CH: SWITZERLAND		
A	Aarau, Aargauische Kantonsbibliothek	*BRsav*	——, Slovenská Akadémia Vied
AShoboken	Ascona, Anthony van Hoboken, private collection	*BRu*	——, Univerzitná Knižnica
Bchristen	Basle, Werner Christen, private collection	*BREsi*	Březnice, Děkanský Kostel Sv Ignáce
Bm	——, Musikakademie der Stadt	*BSk*	Banská Štiavnica, Farský Rímsko-Katolícky Kostol, Archív Chóru
Bmi	——, Musikwissenschaftliches Institut der Universität		
Bu	——, Öffentliche Bibliothek der Universität, Musiksammlung	*CH*	Cheb, Okresní Archív
		CHOd	Choceň, Děkanský Úřad
BA	Baden, Historisches Museum (Landvogtei-Schloss)	*CHOm*	——, Městské Muzeum
BEk	Berne, Konservatorium	*H*	Hronov, Muzeum Aloise Jiráska
BEl	——, Schweizerische Landesbibliothek	*HK*	Hradec Králové, Muzeum
BEms	——, Musikwissenschaftliches Seminar der Universität	*HOm*	Hořice, Vlastivědné Muzeum
		J	Jur pri Bratislave, Okresní Archív, Bratislava-Vidick
BEsu	——, Stadt- und Universitätsbibliothek; Bürgerbibliothek	*JIa*	Jindřichův Hradec, Státní Archív
		JIm	——, Vlastivědné Muzeum
BI	Biel, Stadtbibliothek	*K*	Český Krumlov, Pracoviště Státního Archívu Třeboň, Hudební Sbírka
C	Chur, Kantonsbibliothek Graubünden		
D	Disentis, Stift	*KL*	Klatovy, Okresní Archív
E	Einsiedeln, Benediktinerkloster	*KO*	Košice, Městsky Archív
EN	Engelberg, Stift	*KOL*	Kolín, Děkanský Chrám
Fcu	Fribourg, Bibliothèque Cantonale et Universitaire	*KRa*	Kroměříž, Státní Zámek a Zahrady, Historicko-Umělecké Fondy, Hudební Archív
Ff	——, Franziskaner-Kloster		
Fk	——, Kapuziner-Kloster	*KRA*	Králíky, Děkanský Úřad
Fsn	——, Kapitel St Nikolaus	*KRE*	Kremnica, Městsky Archív
FF	Frauenfeld, Thurgauische Kantonsbibliothek	*KU*	Kutná Hora, Oblastní Muzeum
Gamoudruz	Geneva, Emile Amoudruz, private collection	*KVd*	Karlovy Vary, Děkanský Úřad
Gc	——, Conservatoire de Musique	*KVso*	——, Karlovarský Symfonický Orchestr
Gpu	——, Bibliothèque Publique et Universitaire	*L*	Levoča, Rímsko-Katolícky Farský Kostol
		LIa	Česká Lípa, Okresní Archív

LIT	Litoměřice, Státní Archív
LO	Loukov, Farní Úřad
Mms	Martin, Matica Slovenská, Oddělenie Hudobných Pamiatok
Mnm	——, Slovenské Národné Muzeum, Archív
MB	Mladá Boleslav, Okresní Archív
ME	Mělník, Okresní Archív
MH	Mnichovo Hradiště, Vlastivědné Muzeum
N	Nitra, Státní Archív
ND	Nové Dvory, Farní Úřad
NM	Nové Mesto nad Váhom, Rímsko-Katolický Farský Kostol
OLa	Olomouc, Státní Oblastní Archív v Opava
OLu	——, Státní Vědecká Knihovna, Universitní Knihovna
OP	Opava, Slezské Muzeum
OS	Ostrava, Československý Rozhlas, Hudební Archív
OSE	Osek, Klášter
Pa	Prague, Státní Ústřední Archív
Pak	——, Archív Metropolitní Kapituly
Pdobrovského	——, Knihovna Josefa Dobrovského
Ph	——, Československá Církev Holešovice
Pis	——, Československo Hudební Informační Středisko
Pk	——, Archív Státní Konservatoře v Praze
Pnm	——, Národní Muzeum, Hudební Oddělení
Pp	——, Archív Pražského Hradu
Ppp	——, Památník Národního Písemnictví na Strahově
Pr	——, Československý Rozhlas, Hudební Archív Různá Provenience
Pra	——, Rodinní Archív Karla Kovařovice
Ps	——, Strahovská Knihovna [in *Ppp*]
Psf	——, Kostel Sv Franciscus
Psj	——, Kostel Sv Jakuba
Pu	——, Státní Knihovna ČSSR, Universitní Knihovna
PLa	Plzeň, Městsky Archív
PLm	——, Západočeské Muzeum
PLA	Plasy, Okresní Archív
POa	Poděbrady, pobočka Státní Archívu Nymburk
POm	——, Helichovo Muzeum
PR	Příbram, Okresný Muzeum
PRE	Prešov, Rímsko-Katolický Farský Kostol
RA	Rakovník, Státní Archív
RAJ	Rajhrad, Klášter [in *Bm*]
RO	Rokycany, Okresný Muzeum
ROZ	Rožnava, Biskupskí Archív
RY	Rychnov, Muzeum Orlicka
Sk	Spišská Kapitula, Katedrálny Rímsko-Katolický Kostol, Knižnica Spišskej Kapituly
SNV	Spišská Nová Ves, Rímsko-Katolický Farský Kostol
SO	Sokolov, Státní Archív
TC	Třebíč, Městsky Archív
TN	Trenčín, Okresní Archív
TR	Trnava, Dóm Sv Mikuláša
TRB	Třebenice, Klášter
TRE	Třebőň, Státní Archív
TU	Turnov, Okresný Muzeum
VE	Velenice, Farní Úřad
VM	Vysoké Mýto, Okresný Muzeum
ZA	Zámrsk, Státní Archív

CU: CUBA

Hn	Havana, Biblioteca Nacional
Hse	——, Biblioteca de la Sociedad Económica de Amigos del País

D: GERMANY

Aa	Augsburg, BRD, Kantoreiarchiv St Annen
Af	——, Bibliothek der Fuggerschen Domänenkanzlei
Ahk	——, Dominikanerkloster Heilig-Kreuz
As	——, Staats- und Stadtbibliothek
Asa	——, Stadtarchiv
AAd	Aachen, BRD, Bischöfliche Diözesanbibliothek
AAg	——, Kaiser Karl-Gymnasium, Lehrerbibliothek
AAm	——, Domarchiv
AAst	——, Stadtbibliothek
AB	Amorbach, BRD, Fürstlich Leiningische Bibliothek, private collection
ABG	Annaberg-Buchholz, DDR, Pfarramt, Kirchenbibliothek
ABGa	——, Kantoreiarchiv St Annen
AD	Adolfseck bei Fulda, BRD, Schloss Fasanerie, Bibliothek der Kurhessischen Hausstiftung
ALa	Altenburg, DDR, Landesarchiv (Historisches Staatsarchiv)
ALs	——, Stadtarchiv

ALt	——, Bibliothek des Landestheaters
AM	Amberg, BRD, Staatliche Provinzialbibliothek
AN	Ansbach, BRD, Regierungsbibliothek
AÖ	Altötting, BRD, Kapuziner-Kloster St Konrad
ARk	Arnstadt, DDR, Kirchenbibliothek
ARsk	——, Stadt- und Kreisbibliothek
ARsm	——, Schlossmuseum
ASh	Aschaffenburg, BRD, Hofbibliothek
ASm	——, Stadtbücherei
ASsb	——, Stiftsbibliothek
B	Berlin, Staatsbibliothek Preussischer Kulturbesitz [W]
Ba	——, Amerika-Gedenkbibliothek (Berliner Zentralbibliothek) [W]; Deutsche Akademie der Künste [E]
Bch	——, Musikbücherei Charlottenburg [W]
Bdhm	——, Deutsche Hochschule für Musik Hanns Eisler [E]
Bds	——, Deutsche Staatsbibliothek (formerly Königliche Bibliothek; Preussische Staatsbibliothek; Öffentliche Wissenschaftliche Bibliothek), Musikabteilung [E]
Bdso	——, Deutsche Staatsoper [E]
Be	——, Institut für Musikerziehung der Humboldt-Universität [E]
Bgk	——, Streit'sche Stiftung [in *Bs*] [E]
Bhbk	——, Staatliche Hochschule für Bildende Kunst [W]
Bhesse	——, A. Hesse, private collection [E]
Bhm	——, Staatliche Hochschule für Musik und Darstellende Kunst [W]
Bim	——, Staatliches Institut für Musikforschung Preussischer Kulturbesitz [W]
Bk	——, Staatliche Museen Preussischer Kulturbesitz [W]
Bko	——, Komische Oper [E]
Blk	——, Bezirks-Lehrerbibliothek Kreuzberg [W]
Bm	——, Marienkirche [E]
Bmb	——, Internationale Musikbibliothek, Verband Deutscher Komponisten und Musikwissenschaftler [E]
Bmi	——, Musikwissenschaftliches Institut der Freien Universität [W]; Musikwissenschaftliches Institut der Humboldt-Universität [E]
Bmm	——, Märkisches Museum [E]
Bn	——, Nikolaikirche [E]
Bp	——, Pädagogisches Zentrum [W]
Br	——, Deutscher Demokratischer Rundfunk, Notenarchiv [E]
Bs	——, Berliner Stadtbibliothek [E]
Bst	——, Stadtbücherei, Hauptstelle Berlin-Wilmersdorf [W]
Btu	——, Universitätsbibliothek der Technischen Universität [W]
Btum	——, Lehrstuhl für Musikgeschichte der Technischen Universität [W]
Bu	——, Universitätsbibliothek der Freien Universität [W]
Buh	——, Universitätsbibliothek der Humboldt-Universität [E]
BAa	Bamberg, BRD, Staatsarchiv
BAf	——, Franziskaner-Kloster
BAs	——, Staatsbibliothek
BAL	Ballenstedt, DDR, Stadtbibliothek
BAR	Bartenstein, BRD, Fürst zu Hohenlohe-Bartensteinsches Archiv, private collection
BAUd	Bautzen, DDR, Domstift und Bischöfliches Ordinariat
BAUk	——, Stadt- und Kreisbibliothek
BB	Benediktbeuren, BRD, Pfarrkirche
BD	Brandenburg an der Havel, DDR, Domstift
BDH	Bad Homburg von der Höhe, BRD, Stadtbibliothek
BE	Berleburg, BRD, Fürstlich Sayn-Wittgenstein-Berleburgsche Bibliothek, private collection
BEU	Beuron, BRD, Benediktiner-Erzabtei
BEV	Bevensen, BRD, Superintendantur, Ephoratsbibliothek und Bibliothek Sursen
BFa	Burgsteinfurt, BRD, Gymnasium Arnoldinum
BFb	——, Fürstlich Bentheimsche Bibliothek [in *MÜu*]
BG	Beuerberg über Wolfratshausen, BRD, Pfarramt, Stiftskirche
BGD	Berchtesgaden, BRD, Katholisches Pfarramt
BH	Bayreuth, BRD, Stadtbücherei
BI	Bielefeld, BRD, Städtisches Ratsgymnasium
BIB	Bibra, DDR, Pfarrarchiv
BIR	Birstein über Wächtersbach, BRD, Fürst von Ysenburgisches Archiv und Schlossbibliothek, private collection

Sigla	Library
BIT	Bitterfeld, DDR, Kreismuseum
BK	Bernkastel-Kues, BRD, Cusanusstift
BKÖ	Bad Köstritz, DDR, Pfarrarchiv
BMek	Bremen, BRD, Bücherei der Bremer Evangelischen Kirche
BMs	——, Staats- und Universitätsbibliothek
BNba	Bonn, BRD, Beethoven-Haus und Beethoven-Archiv
BNek	——, Gemeindeverband der Evangelischen Kirche
BNms	——, Musikwissenschaftliches Seminar der Universität
BNu	——, Universitätsbibliothek
BO	——, Bollstedt, Pfarramt
BOCHb	Bochum, BRD, Bergbaumuseum
BOCHmi	——, Musikwissenschaftliches Institut der Ruhr-Universität
BOCHs	——, Stadtbibliothek, Musikbücherei
BORp	Borna, DDR, Pfarrkirche
BS	Brunswick, BRD, Stadtarchiv und Stadtbibliothek
BTH	Barth, DDR, Kirchenbibliothek
BÜ	Büdingen, BRD, Fürstlich Ysenburg- und Büdingisches Archiv und Schlossbibliothek
BW	Burgwindheim über Bamberg, BRD, Katholisches Pfarramt
Cl	Coburg, BRD, Landesbibliothek
Cm	——, Moritzkirche
Cv	——, Kunstsammlung der Veste Coburg
CA	Castell, BRD, Fürstlich Castell'sche Bibliothek
CD	Crottendorf, DDR, Kantoreiarchiv
CR	Crimmitschau, DDR, Stadtkirche St Laurentius
CZ	Clausthal-Zellerfeld, BRD, Kirchenbibliothek
CZu	——, Universitätsbibliothek
Dhm	Dresden, DDR, Hochschule für Musik Carl Maria von Weber
Dkh	——, Katholische Hofkirche
Dl	——, Bibliothek und Museum Löbau [in *Dlb*]
Dla	——, Staatsarchiv
Dlb	——, Sächsische Landesbibliothek
Dmb	——, Musikbibliothek
Ds	——, Staatstheater
DB	Dettelbach über Kitzingen, BRD, Franziskanerkloster
DEl	Dessau, DDR, Universitäts- und Landesbibliothek
DEs	——, Stadtarchiv, Rathaus
DI	Dillingen an der Donau, BRD, Kreis- und Studienbibliothek
DIp	——, Bischöfliches Priesterseminar
DIN	Dinkelsbühl, BRD, Katholisches Pfarramt St Georg
DIP	Dippoldiswalde, DDR, Evangelisch-Lutherisches Pfarramt
DL	Delitzsch, DDR, Museum und Bibliothek
DM	Dortmund, BRD, Stadt- und Landesbibliothek
DO	Donaueschingen, BRD, Fürstlich Fürstenbergische Hofbibliothek, private collection
DÖ	Döbeln, DDR, Pfarrbibliothek St Nikolai
DÖF	Döffingen über Bölingen, BRD, Pfarrbibliothek
DS	Darmstadt, BRD, Hessische Landes- und Hochschulbibliothek
DSim	——, Internationales Musikinstitut
DSk	——, Kirchenleitung der Evangelischen Kirche in Hessen und Nassau
DT	Detmold, BRD, Lippische Landesbibliothek
DÜgg	Düsseldorf, BRD, Staatliches Görres-Gymnasium
DÜha	——, Hauptstaatsarchiv
DÜk	——, Goethe-Museum
DÜl	——, Landes- und Stadtbibliothek
DÜmb	——, Stadtbüchereien, Musikbücherei
DÜR	Düren, BRD, Stadtbücherei, Leopold-Hoesch-Museum
Ek	Eichstätt, BRD, Kapuzinerkloster
Es	——, Staats- und Seminarbibliothek
Ew	——, Benediktinerinnen-Abtei St Walburg
EB	Ebrach, BRD, Katholisches Pfarramt
EBS	Ebstorf, BRD, Kloster
EF	Erfurt, DDR, Wissenschaftliche Bibliothek der Stadt
EFd	——, Dombibliothek
EFs	——, Stadt- und Bezirksbibliothek
EIa	Eisenach, DDR, Stadtarchiv
EIb	——, Bachhaus und Bachmuseum
EIl	——, Landeskirchenrat
EIHp	Eichtersheim, BRD, Pfarrbibliothek
EL	Eisleben, DDR, Andreas-Bibliothek
EM	Emden, BRD, Grosse Kirche
EMM	Emmerich, BRD, Staatliches Gymnasium
EN	Engelberg, BRD, Franziskanerkloster
ERms	Erlangen, BRD, Musikwissenschaftliches Seminar der Universität
ERu	——, Universitätsbibliothek
ES	Essen, BRD, Musikbücherei der Stadtbücherei
EU	Eutin, BRD, Kreisbibliothek
F	Frankfurt am Main, BRD, Stadt- und Universitätsbibliothek
Fkm	——, Museum für Kunsthandwerk
Fmi	——, Musikwissenschaftliches Institut der Johann Wolfgang von Goethe-Universität
Fsg	——, Philosophisch-Theologische Hochschule St Georgen
Fsm	——, Bibliothek für Neuere Sprachen und Musik
FBa	Freiberg, DDR, Stadtarchiv
FBb	——, Bergakademie, Bücherei
FBo	——, Geschwister-Scholl-Oberschule, Historische Bibliothek
FBsk	——, Stadt- und Kreisbibliothek
FF	Frankfurt an der Oder, DDR, Stadt- und Bezirksbibliothek
FG	Freyburg, DDR, Pfarrarchiv
FLa	Flensburg, BRD, Stadtarchiv
FLs	——, Staatliches Gymnasium
FRcb	Freiburg im Breisgau, BRD, Collegium Borromaeum
FRms	——, Musikwissenschaftliches Seminar der Universität
FRu	——, Universitätsbibliothek
FRIs	Friedberg, BRD, Stadtbibliothek
FRIts	——, Theologisches Seminar der Evangelischen Kirche in Hessen und Nassau
FS	Freising, BRD, Dombibliothek
FUf	Fulda, BRD, Kloster Frauenberg
FUl	——, Hessische Landesbibliothek
FUp	——, Bischöfliches Priesterseminar, Bibliothek der Philosophisch-Theologischen Hochschule
Ga	Göttingen, BRD, Staatliches Archivlager
Gb	——, Johann Sebastian Bach-Institut
Gms	——, Musikwissenschaftliches Seminar der Universität
Gs	——, Niedersächsische Staats- und Universitätsbibliothek
GA	Gaussig bei Bautzen, DDR, Schlossbibliothek
GAH	Gandersheim, BRD, Stiftsbibliothek
GAM	Gau-Algesheim, BRD, Stadtarchiv
GAR	Gars am Inn, BRD, Philosophisch-Theologische Ordenshochschule der Redemptoristen
GBB	Grossbrembach, DDR, Pfarrarchiv
GBR	Grossbreitenbach bei Arnstadt, DDR, Pfarrbibliothek
GD	Gaesdonck über Goch, BRD, Collegium Augustinianum
GE	Gelenau, DDR, Pfarrarchiv
GERk	Gera, DDR, Kirchenarchiv
GERs	——, Stadtmuseum
GERsb	——, Stadt- und Bezirksbibliothek
GEY	Geyer, DDR, Kirchenbibliothek
GF	Grossfahrer, DDR, Pfarrarchiv Starcklof-Eschenberger
GHk	Geithain, DDR, Evangelisch-Lutherisches Pfarramt
GHNa	Grossenhain, DDR, Archiv
GHNk	——, Kirche
GI	Giessen, BRD, Justus Liebig-Universität
GL	Goslar, BRD, Marktkirchenbibliothek
GLA	Glashütte, DDR, Pfarrarchiv
GM	Grimma, DDR, Göschenhaus, Johannes Sturm, private collection
GMl	——, Landesschule
GO	Gotha, DDR, Evangelisch-Lutherische Stadtkirchengemeinde
GOa	——, Augustinerkirche
GOg	——, Gymnasium
GOl	——, Forschungsbibliothek [former Landesbibliothek]
GOs	——, Stadtarchiv
GOsk	——, Stadt- und Kreisbibliothek
GÖp	Görlitz, DDR, Evangelischer Parochialverband
GÖs	——, Stadtbibliothek
GÖsp	——, Pfarramt St Peter
GOL	Goldbach bei Gotha, DDR, Pfarrarchiv
GRim	Greifswald, DDR, Institut für Musikwissenschaft
GRk	——, Konsistorialbibliothek
GRu	——, Ernst-Moritz-Arndt-Universität
GRÜ	Grünhain, DDR, Pfarramt
GÜ	Güstrow, DDR, Heimatmuseum
GZ	Greiz, DDR, Stadt- und Kreisbibliothek
GZbk	——, Staatliche Bücher- und Kupferstichsammlung

GZmb	——, Städtische Musikbibliothek
GZsa	——, Historisches Staatsarchiv
Ha	Hamburg, BRD, Staatsarchiv
Hch	——, Gymnasium Christianeum
Hhm	——, Harburg, Helmsmuseum
Hj	——, Gelehrtenschule des Johanneum
Hkm	——, Kunstgewerbemuseum
Hmb	——, Musikbücherei der Hamburger Öffentlichen Bücherhallen
Hmg	——, Museum für Hamburgische Geschichte
Hmi	——, Musikwissenschaftliches Institut der Universität
Hs	——, Staats- und Universitätsbibliothek
Hsa	——, Senatsarchiv
Hth	——, Universität, Theatersammlung
HAf	Halle an der Saale, DDR, Hauptbibliothek und Archiv der Franckeschen Stiftungen [in *HAu*]
HAh	——, Händel-Haus
HAmi	——, Institut für Musikwissenschaft der Martin-Luther-Universität
HAmk	——, Marienbibliothek
HAs	——, Stadt- und Bezirksbibliothek
HAu	——, Universitäts- und Landesbibliothek Sachsen-Anhalt
HAI	Hainichen, DDR, Heimatmuseum
HB	Heilbronn, BRD, Stadtarchiv
HCHs	Hechingen, BRD, Stiftskirche
HD	Hermsdorf, DDR, Pfarrarchiv
HEk	Heidelberg, BRD, Evangelisches Kirchenmusikalisches Institut
HEms	——, Musikwissenschaftliches Seminar der Universität
HEu	——, Universitätsbibliothek
HER	Herrnhut, DDR, Archiv der Brüder-Unität
HEY	Heynitz, DDR, Pfarrbibliothek
HG	Havelberg, DDR, Museum
HHa	Hildburghausen, DDR, Stadtarchiv
HIb	Hildesheim, BRD, Beverin'sche Bibliothek
HIm	——, St Michaelskirche
HIp	——, Bischöfliches Priesterseminar
HL	Haltenbergstetten, BRD, Schloss über Niederstetten, Fürst zu Hohenlohe-Jagstberg'sche Bibliothek, private collection
HLN	Hameln, BRD, Stadtbücherei des Schiller-Gymnasiums
HN	Herborn, BRD, Evangelisches Theologisches Seminar
HO	Hof an der Saale, BRD, Jean Paul-Gymnasium
HOr	——, Stadtarchiv, Ratsbibliothek
HOE	Hohenstein-Ernstthal, DDR, Kantoreiarchiv der Christophorikirche
HOG	Hofgeismar, BRD, Predigerseminar
HOR	Horst, BRD, Evangelisch-Lutherisches Pfarramt
HR	Harburg über Donauwörth, BRD, Fürstlich Oettingen-Wallerstein'sche Bibliothek, private collection
HSj	Helmstedt, BRD, Juleum
HSk	——, Kantorat zu St Stephani [in *W*]
HSm	——, Kloster Marienberg
HSwandersleb	——, Bibliothek Pastor Wandersleb
HTa	Halberstadt, DDR, Stadtarchiv
HTd	——, Dombibliothek
HTg	——, Gleimhaus
HVh	Hanover, BRD, Staatliche Hochschule für Musik und Theater
HVk	——, Arbeitsstelle für Gottesdienst und Kirchenmusik der Evangelisch-Lutherischen Landeskirche
HVl	——, Niedersächsische Landesbibliothek
HVs	——, Stadtbibliothek
HVsa	——, Staatsarchiv
HVth	——, Technische Hochschule
HX	Höxter, BRD, Kirchenbibliothek St Nikolaus
Iek	Isny, BRD, Evangelische Kirche St Nikolai
Iq	——, Fürstlich Quadt'sche Bibliothek, private collection
ILk	Ilmenau, DDR, Kirchenbibliothek
ILs	——, Stadtarchiv
IN	Indersdorf über Dachau, BRD, Katholisches Pfarramt
Jmb	Jena, DDR, Ernst Abbe-Bücherei, Musikbücherei
Jmi	——, Musikwissenschaftliches Institut der Friedrich-Schiller-Universität
Ju	——, Universitätsbibliothek der Friedrich-Schiller-Universität
JA	Jahnsdorf bei Stollberg, DDR, Pfarrarchiv
JE	Jever, BRD, Marien-Gymnasium
Kdma	Kassel, BRD, Deutsches Musikgeschichtliches Archiv
Kl	——, Murhardsche Bibliothek der Stadt und Landesbibliothek
Km	——, Musikakademie
Ksp	——, Louis-Spohr-Gedenk- und Forschungsstätte
KA	Karlsruhe, BRD, Badische Landesbibliothek
KAsp	——, Pfarramt St Peter
KAu	——, Universitätsbibliothek
KAL	Kaldenkirchen, BRD, Pfarrbibliothek
KARj	Karl-Marx-Stadt, DDR, Jacobi-Kirche
KARr	——, Ratsarchiv
KARs	——, Stadt- und Bezirksbibliothek
KBs	Koblenz, BRD, Stadtbibliothek
KBEk	Koblenz-Ehrenbreitstein, BRD, Provinzialat der Kapuziner
KFm	Kaufbeuren,BRD, Stadtpfarrkirche St Martin
KFs	——, Stadtbücherei
KIl	Kiel, BRD, Schleswig-Holsteinische Landesbibliothek
KImi	——, Musikwissenschaftliches Institut der Christian-Albrecht Universität
KIu	——, Universitätsbibliothek
KIN	Kindelbrück, DDR, Pfarrarchiv, Evangelisches Pfarramt
KMk	Kamenz, DDR, Evangelisch-Lutherische Hauptkirche
KMl	——, Lessingmuseum
KMs	——, Stadtarchiv
KNd	Cologne, BRD, Erzbischöfliche Diözesan- und Dombibliothek
KNh	——, Staatliche Hochschule für Musik
KNhi	——, Joseph Haydn-Institut
KNmi	——, Musikwissenschaftliches Institut der Universität
KNu	——, Universitäts- und Stadtbibliothek
KÖ	Köthen, DDR, Heimatmuseum
KPk	Kempten, BRD, Kirchenbibliothek, Evangelisch-Lutherisches Pfarramt St Mang
KPs	——, Stadtbücherei
KPsl	——, Stadtpfarrkirche St Lorenz
KR	Kleinröhrsdorf über Bischofswerda, DDR, Pfarrkirchenbibliothek
KT	Klingenthal, DDR, Kirchenbibliothek
KU	Kulmbach, BRD, Stadtarchiv
KZa	Konstanz, BRD, Stadtarchiv
KZr	——, Rosgarten-Museum
KZs	——, Städtische Wessenberg-Bibliothek
Lm	Lüneburg, BRD, Michaelisschule
Lr	——, Ratsbücherei
LA	Landshut, BRD, Historischer Verein für Niederbayern
LAU	Laubach, BRD, Gräflich Solms-Laubach'sche Bibliothek
LB	Langenburg, BRD, Fürstlich Hohenlohe-Langenburg'sche Schlossbibliothek, private collection
LCH	Lich, BRD, Fürstlich Solms-Lich'sche Bibliothek, private collection
LEb	Leipzig, DDR, Bach-Archiv
LEbh	——, Breitkopf & Härtel, Verlagsarchiv
LEdb	——, Deutsche Bücherei, Musikaliensammlung
LEm	——, Musikbibliothek der Stadt
LEmh	——, Hochschule für Musik
LEmi	——, Musikwissenschaftliches Institut der Karl-Marx-Universität
LEsm	——, Museum für Geschichte der Stadt
LEt	——, Thomasschule
LEu	——, Universitätsbibliothek der Karl-Marx-Universität
LFN	Laufen an der Salzach, BRD, Stiftsarchiv
LHD	Langhennersdorf über Freiberg, DDR, Pfarramt
LI	Lindau, BRD, Stadtbibliothek
LIM	Limbach am Main, BRD, Pfarramt
LL	Langula über Mühlhausen, DDR, Pfarramt
LM	Leitheim über Donauwörth, BRD, Schlossbibliothek Freiherr von Tucher
LO	Loccum über Wunstorf, BRD, Klosterbibliothek
LÖ	Lössnitz, DDR, Pfarrarchiv
LR	Lahr, BRD, Lehrerbibliothek des Scheffel-Gymnasiums
LST	Lichtenstein, DDR, Kantoreiarchiv von St Laurentius
LÜd	Lübeck, BRD, Distler Archiv
LÜh	——, Bibliothek der Hansestadt
LUC	Luckau, DDR, Nikolaikirche
Ma	Munich, BRD, Franziskanerkloster St Anna
Mb	——, Benediktinerabtei St Bonifaz
Mbm	——, Metropolitankapitel
Mbn	——, Bayerisches Nationalmuseum
Mbs	——, Bayerische Staatsbibliothek

Mcg	———, Georgianum, Herzogliches Priesterseminar
Mdm	———, Deutsches Museum
Mh	———, Staatliche Hochschule für Musik
Ml	———, Evangelisch-Lutherisches Landeskirchenamt
Mmb	———, Städtische Musikbibliothek
Mms	———, Musikwissenschaftliches Seminar der Universität
Msl	———, Süddeutsche Lehrerbücherei
Mth	———, Theatermuseum der Clara-Ziegler-Stiftung
Mu	———, Universitätsbibliothek
Mwg	———, Wilhelms-Gymnasium, Lehrerbibliothek
MAk	Magdeburg, DDR, Kulturhistorisches Museum, Klosterbibliothek
MAkon	———, Konsistorialbibliothek
MAl	———, Landeshauptarchiv
MAs	———, Stadt- und Bezirksbibliothek
MB	Marbach an der Neckar, BRD, Schiller-Nationalmuseum
MBG	Miltenberg am Main, BRD, Franziskanerkloster
MCH	Maria Laach über Andernach, BRD, Benediktinerabtei
ME	Meissen, DDR, Stadt- und Kreisbibliothek
MEIk	Meiningen, DDR, Evangelisch-Lutherische Kirchengemeinde
MEIl	———, Staatsarchiv
MEIo	———, Opernarchiv
MEIr	———, Staatliche Museen mit Reger-Archiv
MEL	Meldorf, BRD, Joachimsche Bibliothek, Dithmarsches Landesmuseum
MERa	Merseburg, DDR, Domstift
MERr	———, Regierungsbibliothek
MERs	———, Stadt- und Kreisbibliothek
MERz	———, Deutsches Zentral-Archiv, Historische Abteilung
MFL	Münstereifel, BRD, St Michael-Gymnasium
MGmi	Marburg an der Lahn, BRD, Musikwissenschaftliches Institut der Philipps-Universität
MGs	———, Staatsarchiv und Archivschule
MGu	———, Universitätsbibliothek der Philipps-Universität
MH	Mannheim, BRD, Wissenschaftliche Stadtbibliothek und Universitätsbibliothek
MHrm	———, Reiss-Museum
MHR	Mülheim, BRD, Stadtbibliothek
MI	Michelstadt, BRD, Evangelisches Pfarramt West
MK	Markneukirchen, DDR, Gewerbemuseum
MLHb	Mühlhausen, DDR, Blasiuskirche
MLHr	———, Ratsarchiv im Stadtarchiv
MMm	Memmingen, BRD, Evangelisch-Lutherisches Pfarramt St Martin
MMs	———, Stadtbibliothek
MÖ	Mölln, BRD, Evangelisch-Lutherische Kirchengemeinde St Nikolai
MOSp	Mosbach, BRD, Pfarrbibliothek
MR	Marienberg, DDR, Kirchenbibliothek
MS	Münsterschwarzach über Kitzingen am Main, BRD, Abtei
MT	Metten über Deggendorf, BRD, Abtei
MÜd	Münster, BRD, Bischöfliches Diözesanarchiv
MÜms	———, Musikwissenschaftliches Seminar der Universität
MÜp	———, Bischöfliches Priesterseminar und Santini-Sammlung
MÜrt	———, Seminar für Reformierte Theologie
MÜs	———, Santini-Bibliothek [in *MÜp*]
MÜsa	———, Staatsarchiv
MÜu	———, Universitätsbibliothek
MÜG	Mügeln, DDR, Pfarrarchiv
MWR	Marienweiher über Kulmbach, BRD, Franziskanerkloster
MZfederhofer	Mainz, BRD, Hellmut Federhofer, private collection
MZgm	———, Gutenberg-Museum
MZgottron	———, Adam Gottron, private collection
MZmi	———, Musikwissenschaftliches Institut der Universität
MZp	———, Bischöfliches Priesterseminar
MZs	———, Stadtbibliothek und Stadtsarchiv
MZsch	———, Musikverlag B. Schotts Söhne
MZu	———, Universitätsbibliothek der Johannes-Gutenberg-Universität
Ngm	Nuremberg, BRD, Germanisches National-Museum
Nla	———, Landeskirchliches Archiv
Nst	———, Stadtbibliothek
NA	Neustadt an der Orla, DDR, Pfarrarchiv
NAUs	Naumburg, DDR, Stadtarchiv
NAUw	———, Wenzelskirche
NBsb	Neuburg an der Donau, BRD, Staatliche Bibliothek
NBss	———, Studienseminar
NEhz	Neuenstein, BRD, Hohenlohe-Zentral-Archiv
NEschumm	———, Karl Schumm, private collection
NERk	Neuenrade, BRD, Kirchenbibliothek
NEZp	Neckarelz, BRD, Pfarrbibliothek
NGp	Neckargemünd, BRD, Pfarrarchiv
NIw	Nieheim über Bad Driburg, BRD, Weberhaus
NL	Nördlingen, BRD, Stadtarchiv, Stadtbibliothek und Volksbücherei
NLk	———, Kirchenbibliothek St Georg
NM	Neumünster, BRD, Schleswig-Holsteinische Musiksammlung der Stadt [in *Kll*]
NO	Nordhausen, DDR, Humboldt-Oberschule
NS	Neustadt an der Aisch, BRD, Evangelische Kirchenbibliothek
NSg	———, Gymnasialbibliothek
NT	Neumarkt-St Veit, BRD, Pfarrkirche
NW	Neustadt an der Weinstrasse, BRD, Heimatmuseum
OB	Ottobeuren, BRD, Benediktiner-Abtei
OF	Offenbach am Main, BRD, Verlagsarchiv André
OH	Oberfrankenhain, DDR, Pfarrarchiv
OLl	Oldenburg, BRD, Landesbibliothek
OLns	———, Niedersächsisches Staatsarchiv
OLH	Olbernhau, DDR, Pfarrarchiv
ORB	Oranienbaum, DDR, Landesarchiv–Historisches Staatsarchiv
OS	Oschatz, DDR, Ephoralbibliothek
OSa	Osnabrück, BRD, Niedersächsisches Staatsarchiv
OSm	———, Städtisches Museum
Pg	Passau, BRD, Gymnasialbibliothek
Pk	———, Bischöfliches Klerikalseminar
Po	———, Bischöfliches Ordinariat
Ps	———, Staatliche Bibliothek
PA	Paderborn, BRD, Erzbischöfliche Akademische Bibliothek
PI	Pirna, DDR, Stadtarchiv
POh	Potsdam, DDR, Pädagogische Hochschule
PR	Pretzschendorf über Dippoldiswalde, DDR, Pfarrarchiv
PU	Pulsnitz, DDR, Nikolaikirche
PW	Pesterwitz bei Dresden, DDR, Pfarrarchiv
Q	Quedlinburg, DDR, Stadt- und Kreisbibliothek
QUh	Querfurt, DDR, Heimatmuseum
QUk	———, Stadtkirche
Rim	Regensburg, BRD, Institut für Musikforschung [in *Ru*]
Rp	———, Bischöfliche Zentralbibliothek
Rs	———, Staatliche Bibliothek
Rtt	———, Fürstlich Thurn und Taxis'sche Hofbibliothek, private collection
Ru	———, Universitätsbibliothek
RAd	Ratzeburg, BRD, Domarchiv
RB	Rothenburg ob der Tauber, BRD, Stadtarchiv und Rats- und Konsistorialbibliothek
RE	Reutberg bei Schaftlach, BRD, Franziskanerinnen-Kloster
REU	Reuden, DDR, Pfarrarchiv
RH	Rheda, BRD, Fürst zu Bentheim-Tecklenburgische Bibliothek [in *MH* and *MÜu*]
RIE	Riesa, DDR, Heimatmuseum
RL	Reutlingen, BRD, Stadtbücherei
RMmarr	Ramelsloh über Winsen, BRD, G. Marr, private collection
ROmi	Rostock, DDR, Institut für Musikwissenschaft der Universität
ROs	———, Stadt- und Bezirksbibliothek
ROu	———, Universitätsbibliothek
RÖ	Röhrsdorf über Meissen, DDR, Pfarrbibliothek
RÖM	Römhild, DDR, Pfarrarchiv
ROT	Rotenburg, BRD, Predigerseminar
ROTTd	Rottenburg an der Neckar, BRD, Diözesanbibliothek
ROTTp	———, Bischöfliches Priesterseminar
RT	Rastatt, BRD, Friedrich-Wilhelm-Gymnasium
RUh	Rudolstadt, DDR, Hofkapellarchiv
RUl	———, Staatsarchiv
RÜ	Rüdenhausen über Kitzingen, BRD, Fürst Castell-Rüdenhausen Bibliothek
Seo	Stuttgart, BRD, Bibliothek und Archiv des Evangelischen Oberkirchenrats
Sh	———, Staatliche Hochschule für Musik und Darstellende Kunst
Sl	———, Württembergische Landesbibliothek
SAh	Saalfeld, DDR, Heimatmuseum
SAAmi	Saarbrücken, BRD, Musikwissenschaftliches Institut der Universität

SAAu	——, Universitätsbibliothek
SBg	Straubing, BRD, Johannes Turmair-Gymnasium
SBj	——, Kirchenbibliothek St Jakob
SBk	——, Karmeliter-Kloster
SCHhv	Schwäbisch Hall, BRD, Historischer Verein für Württembergisch-Franken
SCHm	——, Archiv der St Michaelskirche
SCHr	——, Ratsbibliothek im Stadtarchiv
SCHEY	Scheyern über Pfaffenhofen, BRD, Benediktinerabtei
SCHM	Schmölln, DDR, Archiv der Stadtkirche
SCHMI	Schmiedeberg bei Dresden, DDR, Pfarramt
SCHWherold	Schwabach, BRD, Herold collection
SCHWk	——, Kirchenbibliothek
SDF	Schlehdorf, BRD, Katholische Pfarrkirche
SF	Schweinfurt-Oberndorf, BRD, Kirchen- und Pfarrbibliothek des Evangelisch-Lutherischen Pfarramts
SFsj	——, Pfarramt St Johannis, Sakristei-Bibliothek
SGh	Schleusingen, DDR, Heimatmuseum
SHk	Sondershausen, DDR, Stadtkirche
SHs	——, Stadt- und Kreisbibliothek
SHsk	——, Schlosskirche
SI	Sigmaringen, BRD, Fürstlich Hohenzollernsche Hofbibliothek, private collection
SLk	Salzwedel, DDR, Katharinenkirche
SLm	——, J. F. Danneil-Museum
SLmk	——, Marienkirche
SNed	Schmalkalden, DDR, Evangelisches Dekanat
SNh	——, Heimatmuseum Schloss Wilhelmsburg
SO	Soest, BRD, Stadtbibliothek im Stadtarchiv
SÖNp	Schönau bei Heidelberg, BRD, Pfarrbibliothek
SPlb	Speyer, BRD, Pfälzische Landesbibliothek, Musikabteilung
SPlk	——, Bibliothek des Protestantischen Landeskirchenrats der Pfalz
SPF	Schulpforta, DDR, Heimoberschule
SSa	Stralsund, DDR, Bibliothek des Stadtarchivs
ST	Stade, BRD, Predigerbibliothek [in *ROT*]
STO	Stolberg, DDR, Bibliothek
SUa	Sulzenbrücken, DDR, Pfarrarchiv
SUH	Suhl, DDR, Stadt- und Bezirksbibliothek Martin Andersen Nexö
SWl	Schwerin, DDR, Wissenschaftliche Allgemeinbibliothek [former Mecklenburgische Landesbibliothek]
SWs	——, Stadt- und Bezirksbibliothek, Musikabteilung
SWsk	——, Schlosskirchenchor
SWth	——, Mecklenburgisches Staatstheater
SZ	Schleiz, DDR, Stadtkirche
Tes	Tübingen, BRD, Evangelisches Stift
Tl	——, Schwäbisches Landesmusikarchiv [in *Tmi*]
Tmi	——, Musikwissenschaftliches Institut der Eberhard-Karls-Universität
Tu	——, Universitätsbibliothek
Tw	——, Bibliothek des Wilhelmstiftes
TAB	Tabarz, DDR, Pfarrarchiv, Evangelisch-Lutherisches Pfarramt
TEG	Tegernsee, BRD, Pfarrkirche, Katholisches Pfarramt
TEI	Teisendorf, BRD, Katholisches Pfarramt
TH	Themar, DDR, Pfarramt
TIT	Tittmoning, BRD, Kollegiatstift
TO	Torgau, DDR, Johann-Walter-Kantorei
TOek	——, Evangelische Kirchengemeinde
TOs	——, Stadtarchiv
TRb	Trier, BRD, Bistumarchiv und Dombibliothek
TRp	——, Priesterseminar
TRs	——, Stadtbibliothek
Us	Ulm, BRD, Stadtbibliothek
Usch	——, Von Schermar'sche Familienstiftung
UDa	Udestedt über Erfurt, DDR, Pfarrarchiv, Evangelisch-Lutherisches Pfarramt
V	Villingen, BRD, Städtische Sammlung
VI	Viernau, DDR, Pfarramt
W	Wolfenbüttel, BRD, Herzog August Bibliothek
Wa	——, Niedersächsisches Staatsarchiv
WA	Waldheim, DDR, Stadtkirche St Nikolai
WAB	Waldenburg, DDR, Kirchenmusikalische Bibliothek von St Bartholomäus
WB	Weissenburg, BRD, Stadtbibliothek
WBB	Walberg, BRD, Albertus-Magnus-Akademie, Bibliothek St Albert
WD	Wiesentheid, BRD, Musiksammlung des Grafen von Schönborn-Wiesentheid, private collection
WE	Weiden, BRD, Pfannenstiel'sche Bibliothek, Evangelisch-Lutherisches Pfarramt
WEH	Weierhof, BRD, Mennonitische Forschungsstelle
WEL	Weltenburg, BRD, Benediktinerkloster
WER	Wernigerode, DDR, Heimatmuseum, Harzbücherei
WERk	Wertheim am Main, BRD, Evangelisches Pfarramt
WERl	——, Fürstlich Löwenstein'sche Bibliothek, private collection
WEY	Weyarn, BRD, Pfarrkirche [in *FS*]
WF	Weissenfels, DDR, Heimatmuseum
WFg	——, Heinrich-Schütz-Gedenkstätte
WGk	Wittenberg, DDR, Stadtkirche
WGl	——, Reformationsgeschichtliches Museum, Lutherhalle
WGp	——, Evangelisches Predigerseminar
WH	Windsheim, BRD, Stadtbibliothek
WIl	Wiesbaden, BRD, Hessische Landesbibliothek
WILd	Wilster, BRD, Stadtarchiv (Doos'sche Bibliothek)
WL	Wuppertal, BRD, Wissenschaftliche Stadtbibliothek
WM	Wismar, DDR, Stadtarchiv
WO	Worms, BRD, Stadtbibliothek
WRdn	Weimar, DDR, Deutsches Nationaltheater
WRgm	——, Goethe-National-Museum
WRgs	——, Goethe–Schiller-Archiv und Franz-Liszt-Museum
WRh	——, Franz-Liszt-Hochschule
WRhk	——, Herderkirche
WRiv	——, Institut für Volksmusikforschung
WRl	——, Landeshauptarchiv
WRs	——, Stadtbücherei, Musikbücherei
WRtl	——, Thüringische Landesbibliothek, Musiksammlung
WRz	——, Zentralbibliothek der Deutschen Klassik
WS	Wasserburg am Inn, BRD, Chorarchiv St Jakob, Pfarramt
WÜms	Würzburg, BRD, Musikwissenschaftliches Seminar der Universität
WÜsa	——, Stadtarchiv
WÜu	——, Universitätsbibliothek
X	Xanten, BRD, Stifts- und Pfarrbibliothek
Z	Zwickau, DDR, Ratsschulbibliothek
Zmk	——, Domkantorei der Marienkirche
Zsch	——, Robert-Schumann-Haus
ZE	Zerbst, DDR, Stadtarchiv
ZEo	——, Bücherei der Erweiterten Oberschule
ZGh	Zörbig, DDR, Heimatmuseum
ZGsj	——, Pfarramt St Jacobi
ZI	Zittau, DDR, Stadt- und Kreisbibliothek
ZIa	——, Stadtarchiv
ZL	Zeil, BRD, Fürstlich Waldburg-Zeil'sches Archiv, private collection
ZW	Zweibrücken, BRD, Bibliotheca Bipontina, Wissenschaftliche Bibliothek am Herzog-Wolfgang-Gymnasium
ZZ	Zeitz, DDR, Heimatmuseum
ZZs	——, Stiftsbibliothek

DK: DENMARK

A	Århus, Statsbiblioteket
Dschoenbaum	Dragør, Camillo Schoenbaum, private collection
Hfog	Hellerup, Dan Fog, private collection
Kc	Copenhagen, Carl Claudius Musikhistoriske Samling
Kh	——, Københavns Kommunes Hovedbiblioteket
Kk	——, Det Kongelige Bibliotek
Kmk	——, Det Kongelige Danske Musikkonservatorium
Km(m)	——, Musikhistorisk Museum
Ks	——, Samfundet til Udgivelse af Dansk Musik
Kt	——, Teaterhistorisk Museum
Ku	——, Universitetsbiblioteket 1. Afdeling
Kv	——, Københavns Universitet, Musikvidenskabeligt Institut
Ol	Odense, Landsarkivet for Fyen, Karen Brahes Bibliotek
Ou	——, Universitetsbibliothek
Rk	Ribe, Stifts- og Katedralskoles Bibliothek
Sa	Sorø, Sorø Akademis Bibliothek

E: SPAIN

Ac	Ávila, Catedral
Asa	——, Monasterio de S Ana (Real Monasterio de Encarnación)
Ast	——, Monasterio del S Tomás, Archivo de la Iglesia
AL	Alquezar, Colegiata
ALB	Albarracín, Colegiata
AS	Astorga, Catedral
Ba	Barcelona, Real Academia de Ciencias y Artes
Bac	——, Corona de Aragón

Bc	——, Biblioteca de Cataluña
Bca	——, Catedral
Bcapdevila	——, Felipe Capdevila Rovira, private collection
Bcm	——, Conservatorio Superior Municipal de Música
Bih	——, Instituto Municipal de Historia (formerly Archivo Histórico de la Ciudad)
Bim	——, Instituto Español de Musicología
Bit	——, Instituto del Teatro (formerly Museo del Arte Escénico)
Boc	——, Biblioteca Orfeó Catalá
Bsm	——, S María del Mar
Bu	——, Biblioteca del Universidad
BA	Badajoz, Catedral
BUa	Burgos, Catedral
BUlh	——, Monasterio de Las Huelgas
BUm	——, Museo Arqueológico
BUp	——, Biblioteca Provincial
BUse	——, Parroquia de S Esteban
C	Córdoba, Catedral
CA	Calahorra, Catedral
CAL	Calatayud, Colegiata de S María
CAR	Cardona, Archivo Comunal
CU	Cuenca, Catedral
CUi	——, Instituto de Música Religiosa
CZ	Cádiz, Archivo Capitular
E	El Escorial, Real Monasterio de S Lorenzo
G	Gerona, Biblioteca Catedralicia
Gm	——, Museo Diocesano
Gp	——, Biblioteca Pública
Gs	——, Seminario Gerundense
GRc	Granada, Catedral
GRcr	——, Capilla Real
GU	Guadalupe, Real Monasterio de S María
H	Huesca, Catedral
J	Jaca, Catedral
JA	Jaén, Catedral
LPA	Las Palmas, Catedral de Canarias
La	León, Catedral
Lc	——, Colegiata de S Isidoro
Lp	——, Biblioteca Pública Provincial
LEc	Lérida, Catedral
LEm	——, Museo Diocesano
Ma	Madrid, Real Academia de Bellas Artes de S Fernando
Mah	——, Archivo Histórico Nacional (Real Academia de la Historia)
Mam	——, Biblioteca Musical Circulante
Mat	——, Museo-Archivo Teatral
Mc	——, Conservatorio Superior de Música
Mca	——, Casa de Alba, private collection
Mcns	——, Congregación de Nuestra Señora
Mic	——, Instituto de Cultura Hispánica, Sección de Música
Mit	——, Ministerio de Información y Turismo
Mlg	——, Fundación Lazaro Galdiano
Mm	——, Biblioteca Municipal
Mmc	——, Casa Ducal de Medinaceli, Bartolomé March Servera, private collection
Mn	——, Biblioteca Nacional
Mp	——, Palacio Real
Mpm	——, Patronato Marcelino Menéndez y Pelayo del Consejo Superior de Investigaciones Científicas
Mrt	——, Radio Nacional de España-Televisión
Msa	——, Sociedad General de Autores de España
Msi	——, Ciudad Universitaria, Facultad de Filosofía y Letras, Biblioteca de S Isidoro
MA	Málaga, Catedral
MO	Montserrat, Monasterio de S María
MON	Mondoñedo, Catedral
OL	Olot, Biblioteca Popular
OR	Orense, Catedral
ORI	Orihuela, Catedral
OS	Osma, Catedral
OV	Oviedo, Catedral Metropolitana
P	Plasencia, Catedral
PAc	Palma de Mallorca, Catedral
PAp	——, Biblioteca Provincial
PAMc	Pamplona, Catedral
PAMm	——, Museo Sarasate
PAS	Pastrana, Iglesia Parroquial
RO	Roncesvalles, Monasterio de S María
Sc	Seville, Catedral
Sco	——, Biblioteca Capitular Colombina [in Sc]
SA	Salamanca, Catedral
SAcalo	——, José López-Calo, private collection
SAu	——, Universidad Pontificia, Biblioteca Universitaria

SAuf	——, Universidad Pontificia, Facultad de Filosofía y Letras
SAN	Santander, Biblioteca de Menéndez y Pelayo
SC	Santiago de Compostela, Catedral
SCu	——, Biblioteca Universitaria
SD	Santo Domingo de la Calzada, Archivo
SE	Segovia, Catedral
SEG	Segorbe, Catedral
SI	Silos, Monasterio Benedictino (Abadía) de S Domingo
SIG	Sigüenza, Catedral
SIM	Simancas, Archivo General
SO	Soria, Biblioteca Pública
Tc	Toledo, Archivo Capitular
Tp	——, Biblioteca Pública Provincial y Museo de la Santa Cruz
TAc	Tarragona, Catedral
TAp	——, Biblioteca Pública
TO	Tortosa, Catedral
TU	Tudela, Colegiata (formerly Catedral) de S María
TZ	Tarazona, Catedral
U (also SU)	Seo de Urgel, Catedral
V	Valladolid, Catedral
Vp	——, Parroquia de Santiago
VAa	Valencia, Archivo, Biblioteca y Museos Municipales
VAc	——, Catedral
VAcm	——, Conservatorio Superior de Música
VAcp	——, Colegio y Seminario del Corpus Christi del Patriarca
VAim	——, Instituto Valenciano de Musicología
VAu	——, Biblioteca Universitaria
VI	Vich, Museo Episcopal
VIT	Vitoria, Catedral
Zac	Saragossa, Archivo de Música del Cabildo
Zcc	——, Colegio Calasanci
Zfm	——, Facultad de Medicina
Zp	——, Biblioteca Pública
Zs	——, Biblioteca Capitular de la Seo
Zsc	——, Seminario de S Carlos
Zu	——, Biblioteca Universitaria
Zvp	——, Iglesia Metropolitana [in Zac]
ZA	Zamora, Catedral

EIRE: IRELAND

C	Cork, University College
Da	Dublin, Royal Irish Academy
Dam	——, Royal Irish Academy of Music
Dcb	——, Chester Beatty Library
Dcc	——, Christ Church Cathedral
Dm	——, Marsh's Library
Dmh	——, Mercer's Hospital
Dn	——, National Library and Museum of Ireland
Dpc	——, St Patrick's Cathedral
Dtc	——, Trinity College
Duc	——, University College

ET: EGYPT

S	Mt Sinai

F: FRANCE

A	Avignon, Bibliothèque Municipale, Musée Calvet
Aa	——, Archives Départementales de Vaucluse
AB	Abbeville, Bibliothèque Municipale
AG	Agen, Archives Départementales de Lot-et-Garonne
AI	Albi, Bibliothèque Municipale
AIXc	Aix-en-Provence, Conservatoire
AIXm	——, Bibliothèque Municipale, Bibliothèque Méjanes
AIXmc	——, Maîtrise de la Cathédrale
AL	Alençon, Bibliothèque Municipale
AM	Amiens, Bibliothèque Municipale
AN	Angers, Bibliothèque Municipale
ANG	Angoulême, Bibliothèque Municipale
ANN	Annecy, Bibliothèque Municipale
APT	Apt, Cathédrale Ste Anne
AR	Arles, Bibliothèque Municipale
AS	Arras, Bibliothèque Municipale
ASO	Asnières-sur-Oise, François Lang, private collection
AU	Auxerre, Bibliothèque Municipale
AUT	Autun, Bibliothèque Municipale
AV	Avallon, Société d'Etudes d'Avallon
AVR	Avranches, Bibliothèque Municipale
B	Besançon, Bibliothèque Municipale
Ba	——, Bibliothèque de l'Archevêché
Be	——, Ecole Nationale de Musique
BD	Bar-le-Duc, Bibliothèque Municipale
BE	Beauvais, Bibliothèque Municipale
BER	Bernay, Bibliothèque Municipale

BG	Bourg-en-Bresse, Bibliothèque Municipale et Musée de l'Ain	*NO*	Noyon, Bibliothèque Municipale
BL	Blois, Bibliothèque Municipale	*NS*	Nîmes, Bibliothèque Municipale
BO	Bordeaux, Bibliothèque Municipale	*NT*	Niort, Bibliothèque Municipale
BOI	Boisguillaume, Musée Boieldieu	*O*	Orleans, Bibliothèque Municipale
BOU	Bourbourg, Bibliothèque Municipale	*Pa*	Paris, Bibliothèque de l'Arsenal
BR	Brest, Bibliothèque Municipale	*Pal*	——, American Library in Paris
BS	Bourges, Bibliothèque Municipale	*Pbf*	——, Centre de Documentation Benjamin Franklin
BSM	Boulogne-sur-Mer, Bibliothèque Municipale	*Pc*	——, Conservatoire National de Musique [in *Pn*]
C	Carpentras, Bibliothèque Inguimbertine et Musée de Carpentras	*Pcf*	——, Comédie-Française, Bibliothèque
CA	Cambrai, Bibliothèque Municipale	*Pcrs*	——, Centre National de la Recherche Scientifique
CAc	——, Cathédrale	*Pe*	——, Schola Cantorum (Ecole Supérieure de Musique, Danse et Art Dramatique)
CAD	Cadouin, Bibliothèque de l'Abbaye	*Pgérard*	——, Yves Gérard, private collection
CAH	Cahors, Bibliothèque Municipale	*Pi*	——, Bibliothèque de l'Institut
CAL	Calais, Bibliothèque Municipale	*Pim*	——, Institut de Musicologie de l'Université, Bibliothèque Pierre Aubry
CC	Carcassonne, Bibliothèque Municipale	*Pis*	——, Institut Supérieur de Musique Liturgique
CF	Clermont-Ferrand, Bibliothèque Municipale et Universitaire, Section Centrale et Section Lettres	*Pm*	——, Bibliothèque Mazarine
		Pma	——, Musée National des Arts et Traditions Populaires
CH	Chantilly, Musée Condé	*Pmeyer*	——, André Meyer, private collection
CHA	Châteauroux, Bibliothèque Municipale	*Pmg*	——, Musée Guimet
CHE	Cherbourg, Bibliothèque et Archives Municipales	*Pmh*	——, Musée de l'Homme
CHM	Chambéry, Bibliothèque Municipale	*Pn*	——, Bibliothèque Nationale
CHR	Chartres, Bibliothèque Municipale	*Po*	——, Bibliothèque–Musée de l'Opéra
CN	Caen, Bibliothèque Municipale	*Pphon*	——, Phonothèque Nationale, Bibliothèque et Musée
CNc	——, Conservatoire National de Musique	*Ppincherle*	——, Marc Pincherle, private collection [dispersed 1975]
CO	Colmar, Bibliothèque Municipale		
COs	——, Consistoire de l'Eglise de la Confession d'Augsbourg à Colmar	*Ppo*	——, Bibliothèque Polonaise de Paris
		Prothschild	——, Germaine, Baronne Edouard de Rothschild, private collection
COUm	Coutances, Bibliothèque Municipale	*Prt*	——, Office de Radiodiffusion-Télévision Française
COUs	——, Grand Séminaire	*Psc*	——, Société des Auteurs et Compositeurs Dramatiques
CSM	Châlons-sur-Marne, Bibliothèque Municipale		
CV	Charleville, Bibliothèque Municipale	*Pse*	——, Société des Auteurs, Compositeurs et Editeurs de Musique
Dc	Dijon, Bibliothèque du Conservatoire		
Dm	——, Bibliothèque Municipale (Bibliothèque Publique)	*Psg*	——, Bibliothèque Ste Geneviève
		Pshp	——, Bibliothèque de la Société d'Histoire du Protestantisme
DI	Dieppe, Bibliothèque Municipale		
DO	Dôle, Bibliothèque Municipale	*Psi*	——, Séminaire Israélite de France
DOU	Douai, Bibliothèque Municipale	*Pthibault*	——, Geneviève Thibault, private collection
E	Epinal, Bibliothèque Municipale	*PAU*	Pau, Bibliothèque Municipale
EP	Epernay, Bibliothèque Municipale	*PE*	Périgueux, Bibliothèque Municipale
EV	Evreux, Bibliothèque Municipale	*PO*	Poitiers, Bibliothèque Municipale
F	Foix, Bibliothèque Municipale	*POu*	——, Faculté des Lettres de l'Université de Poitiers, Section de Musicologie
G	Grenoble, Bibliothèque Municipale		
Ge	——, Ecole Régionale de Musique, de Danse et d'Art Dramatique	*Rc*	Rouen, Conservatoire
		R(m)	——, Bibliothèque Municipale
GAP	Gap, Archives Départementales des Hautes-Alpes	*RE*	Rennes, Bibliothèque Municipale
H	Hyères, Bibliothèque Municipale	*RO*	Roanne, Bibliothèque Municipale
Lc	Lille, Conservatoire	*RSc*	Rheims, Bibliothèque de la Cathédrale
Lfc	——, Facultés Catholiques	*Sc*	Strasbourg, Conservatoire
Lm	——, Bibliothèque Municipale	*Sg(sc)*	——, Grand Séminaire (Séminaire Catholique)
LA	Laon, Bibliothèque Municipale	*Sim*	——, Institut de Musicologie de l'Université
LB	Libourne, Bibliothèque Municipale	*Sm*	——, Archives et Bibliothèque Municipale
LG	Limoges, Bibliothèque Municipale	*Sn*	——, Bibliothèque Nationale et Universitaire
LH	Le Havre, Bibliothèque Municipale	*Ssa*	——, Société des Amis des Arts de Strasbourg
LM	Le Mans, Bibliothèque Municipale	*Ssp*	——, Séminaire Protestant
LO	Louviers, Bibliothèque Municipale	*SA*	Salins, Bibliothèque Municipale
LP	Le Puy-en-Velay, Bibliothèque Municipale	*SAU*	Saumur, Bibliothèque Municipale
LR	La Rochelle, Bibliothèque Municipale	*SCL*	St-Claude, Bibliothèque Municipale
LV	Laval, Bibliothèque Municipale	*SDE*	St-Denis, Bibliothèque Municipale
LYc	Lyons, Conservatoire National de Musique	*SDI*	St-Dié, Bibliothèque Municipale
LYm	——, Bibliothèque Municipale	*SE*	Sens, Bibliothèque Municipale
Mc	Marseilles, Conservatoire de Musique et de Déclamation	*SEL*	Sélestat, Bibliothèque Municipale
		SERRANT	Serrant, Château
Mm	——, Bibliothèque Municipale	*SO*	Solesmes, Abbaye St-Pierre
MAC	Mâcon, Bibliothèque Municipale	*SOI*	Soissons, Bibliothèque Municipale
MD	Montbéliard, Bibliothèque Municipale	*SQ*	St-Quentin, Bibliothèque Municipale
MEL	Melun, Bibliothèque Municipale	*T*	Troyes, Bibliothèque Municipale
MH	Mulhouse, Bibliothèque Municipale	*TH*	Thiers, Bibliothèque Municipale
MIL	Millau, Bibliothèque Municipale	*TLc*	Toulouse, Conservatoire
MIR	Mirecourt, Bibliothèque Municipale	*TLd*	——, Musée Dupuy
ML	Moulins, Bibliothèque Municipale	*TLm*	——, Bibliothèque Municipale
MLN	Montluçon, Bibliothèque Municipale	*TO*	Tours, Bibliothèque Municipale
MO	Montpellier, Faculté de Médecine de l'Université	*TOgs*	——, Grand Séminaire
MOv	——, Bibliothèque de la Ville et du Musée Fabre	*TOul*	——, Bibliothèque Universitaire, Section Lettres
MON	Montauban, Bibliothèque Municipale	*TOur*	——, Centre d'Etudes Supérieures de la Renaissance
MZ	Metz, Bibliothèque Municipale	*TOU*	Toulon, Ecole Nationale de Musique
Nd	Nantes, Bibliothèque du Musée Dobrée	*TOUm*	——, Bibliothèque Municipale
Ne	——, Ecole Nationale de Musique, d'Art Dramatique et de Danse	*TOUs*	——, Société des Amis du Vieux Toulon
		TU	Tulle, Bibliothèque Municipale
Nm	——, Bibliothèque Municipale	*V*	Versailles, Bibliothèque Municipale
NAc	Nancy, Conservatoire	*VA*	Vannes, Bibliothèque Municipale
NAm	——, Bibliothèque Municipale	*VAL*	Valenciennes, Bibliothèque Municipale
NAR	Narbonne, Bibliothèque Municipale	*VE*	Vesoul, Bibliothèque Municipale
NI	Nice, Bibliothèque Municipale	*VN*	Verdun, Bibliothèque Municipale
NIc	——, Conservatoire de Musique		

GB: GREAT BRITAIN

A	Aberdeen, University Library, King's College
AB	Aberystwyth, National Library of Wales
AM	Ampleforth, Abbey and College Library, St Lawrence Abbey
Bp	Birmingham, Public Libraries
Bu	——, University of Birmingham, Barber Institute of Fine Arts
BA	Bath, Municipal Library
BEas	Bedford, Bedfordshire Archaeological Society
BEcr	——, Bedfordshire County Record Office
BEp	——, Public Library Music Department
BENcoke	Bentley (Hants.), Gerald Coke, private collection
BEV	Beverley, East Yorkshire County Record Office
BO	Bournemouth, Central Library
BRb	Bristol, Baptist College Library
BRp	——, Public Libraries, Central Library
BRu	——, University of Bristol Library
Ccc	Cambridge, Corpus Christi College
Cchc	——, Christ's College
Cclc	——, Clare College
Cfm	——, Fitzwilliam Museum
Cgc	——, Gonville and Caius College
Cjc	——, St John's College
Cjec	——, Jesus College
Ckc	——, Rowe Music Library, King's College
Cmc	——, Magdalene College
Cp	——, Peterhouse
Cpc	——, Pembroke College
Cpl	——, Pendlebury Library of Music
Ctc	——, Trinity College
Cu	——, University Library
Cumc	——, University Music Club
Cus	——, Cambridge Union Society
CA	Canterbury, Cathedral
CAR	Carlisle, Cathedral
CDp	Cardiff, Public Libraries, Central Library
CDu	——, University College of South Wales and Monmouthshire
CF	Chelmsford, Essex County Record Office
CH	Chichester, Diocesan Record Office
CHc	——, Cathedral
DRc	Durham, Cathedral
DRu	——, University Library
DU	Dundee, Public Libraries
En	Edinburgh, National Library of Scotland
Enc	——, New College Library
Ep	——, Public Library, Central Public Library
Er	——, Reid Music Library of the University of Edinburgh
Es	——, Signet Library
Eu	——, University Library
EL	Ely, Cathedral
EXc	Exeter, Cathedral
EXcl	——, Central Library
EXed	——, East Devon Area Record Office
EXu	——, University Library
Ge	Glasgow, Euing Music Library
Gm	——, Mitchell Library
Gsma	——, Scottish Music Archive
Gtc	——, Trinity College
Gu	——, University Library
GL	Gloucester, Cathedral
H	Hereford, Cathedral
HAdolmetsch	Haslemere, Carl Dolmetsch, private collection
Lam	London, Royal Academy of Music
Lbbc	——, British Broadcasting Corporation
Lbc	——, British Council
Lbm	——, British Library, Reference Division (formerly British Museum) (= *Lbl*)
Lcm	——, Royal College of Music
Lco	——, Royal College of Organists
Lcs	——, Vaughan Williams Memorial Library (Cecil Sharp Library)
Ldc	——, Dulwich College
Lgc	——, Gresham College (Guildhall Library)
Lkc	——, University of London, King's College
Llp	——, Lambeth Palace
Lmic	——, British Music Information Centre
Lmp	——, Marylebone Public Library
Lpro	——, Public Record Office
Lsc	——, Sion College
Lsm	——, Royal Society of Musicians of Great Britain
Lsp	——, St Paul's Cathedral
Ltc	——, Trinity College of Music
Lu	——, University of London, Music Library

Lva	——, Victoria and Albert Museum
Lwa	——, Westminster Abbey
Lwcm	——, Westminster Central Music Library
LA	Lancaster, District Central Library
LAu	——, University Library
LEbc	Leeds, University of Leeds, Brotherton Collection
LEc	——, Leeds Public Libraries, Music Department, Central Library
LF	Lichfield, Cathedral
LI	Lincoln, Cathedral
LVp	Liverpool, Public Libraries, Central Library
LVu	——, University Music Department
Mch	Manchester, Chetham's Library
Mcm	——, Royal Northern College of Music
Mp	——, Central Public Library, Henry Watson Music Library
Mr	——, John Rylands University Library, Deansgate Branch
Mrothwell	——, Evelyn Rothwell, private collection
Mu	——, John Rylands University Library
NO	Nottingham, University Library
NW	Norwich, Central Library
NWr	——, Norfolk and Norwich Record Office
Ob	Oxford, Bodleian Library
Obc	——, Brasenose College
Och	——, Christ Church
Ojc	——, St John's College
Olc	——, Lincoln College
Omc	——, Magdalen College
Onc	——, New College
Ooc	——, Oriel College
Oqc	——, Queen's College
Ouf	——, University, Faculty of Music
Oumc	——, University Music Club and Union
P	Perth, Sandeman Music Library
R	Reading, University, Music Library
RI	Ripon, Cathedral
RO	Rochester, Cathedral
SA	St Andrews, University Library
SB	Salisbury, Cathedral
SH	Sherborne, Sherborne School Library
SHR	Shrewsbury, Shropshire County Record Office
SOp	Southampton, Public Library
SR	Studley Royal, Fountains Abbey MS 23 [in *LEc*]
STb	Stratford-on-Avon, Shakespeare's Birthplace Trust
STm	——, Shakespeare Memorial Library
T	Tenbury, St Michael's College [Toulouse–Philidor collection now largely in *F-Pn*, *V*]
W	Wells, Cathedral
WB	Wimborne, Minster
WC	Winchester, Chapter Library
WCc	——, Winchester College
WI	Wigan, Public Library
WO	Worcester, Cathedral
WRch	Windsor, St George's Chapter Library
WRec	——, Eton College
Y	York, Minster
Yi	——, Borthwick Institute of Historical Research

GR: GREECE

Ae	Athens, Ethnike Biblioteke tes Hellados
AT	Mt Athos, Koutloumousi Monastery
ATSch	——, Chilandari Monastery
ATSdionision	——, Dionision Monastery
ATSgreat lavra	——, Monastery of the Great Lavra
ATSiviron	——, Iviron Monastery
ATSserbian	——, Serbian Monastery
ATSvatopedi	——, Vatopedi Monastery
LA	Lavra
P	Patmos

H: HUNGARY

Ba	Budapest, Magyar Tudományos Akadémia Régi Könyvek Tára és Kézirattár
Ba(mi)	——, Magyar Tudományos Akadémia Zenetudományi Intézet Könyvtára
Bb	——, Bartók Béla Zeneművészeti Szakközépiskola Könyvtára
Bev	——, Evangélikus Országos Könyvtár
Bf	——, Belvárosi Főplébániatemplom Kottatára
Bj	——, Józsefvárosi Evangélikus Egyházközség Kottatára
Bl	——, Liszt Ferenc Zeneművészeti Főiskola Könyvtára
Bm	——, Budavári Nagyboldogasszony Templom Kottatára

Bn	——, Országos Széchényi Könyvtára
Bo	——, Állami Operaház
Bp	——, Piarista Gimnázium Könyvtára
Br	——, Ráday Gyűjtemény, Könyvtár és Levéltár
Bs	——, Központi Szemináriumi Könyvtár
Bst	——, Szent István Bazilika Kottatára
Bu	——, Egyetemi Könyvtár
BA	Bártfa, church of St Aegidius [in *Bn*]
CSg	Csurgó, Csokonai Vitéz Mihály Gimnázium Könyvtára
DR	Debrecen, Tiszántúli Református Egyházkerület Nagykönyvtára
DRm	——, Déri Múzeum
DRu	——, Kossuth Lajos Tudományegyetem Könyvtára
Ea	Esztergom, Komárom Megyei Levéltár
Efko	——, Főszékesegyházi Kottatár
Efkö	——, Főszékesegyházi Könyvtár
Em	——, Keresztény Múzeum Könyvtára
EG	Eger, Főegyházmegyei Könyvtár
EGb	——, Bazilika Kottatára
Gc	Győr, Püspöki Papnevelő Intézet Könyvtára
Gk	——, Székesgyházi Kottatár
Gm	——, Xántus János Múzeum
Gz	——, Zeneművészeti Szakközépiskola Könyvtára
GGn	Gyöngyös, Országos Széchényi Könyvtár, Bajza József Müemlékkönyvtár
GYm	Gyula, Múzeum
KE	Keszthely, Országos Széchényi Könyvtár Helikon Könyvtára
KI	Kiskunhalas, Református Egyházközség Könyvtára
KŐ	Kőszeg, Plébániatemplom Kottatára
KŐm	——, Jurisich Múzeum
MOp	Mosonmagyaróvár, 1. sz Plébániatemplom Kottatára
NY	Nyiregyháza, Református Városi Egyházközség Könyvtára
P	Pécs, Székesgyházi Kottatár
PA	Pápa, Dunántuli Református Egyházkerület Könyvtára
PH	Pannonhalma, Szent Benedekrend Központi Főkönyvtára
Se	Sopron, Evangélikus Egyházközség Könyvtára
Sg	——, Berzsenyi Dániel Gimnázium Könyvtára
Sl	——, Liszt Ferenc Múzeum
Sp	——, Szentlélekröl és Szent Mihályról Nevezett Városplébánia Kottatára
Sst	——, Storno Gyűjtemény
SA	Sárospatak, Tiszáninneni Református Egyházkerület Nagykönyvtára
SD	Szekszárd, Balogh Ádám Megyei Múzeum
SFk	Székesfehérvár, Püspöki Könyvtár
SFm	——, István Király Múzeum
SFs	——, Székesgyházi Kottatár
SG	Szeged, Somogyi Könyvtár
SGm	——, Móra Ferenc Múzeum
SGu	——, Szegedi Orvostudományi Egyetem Könyvtára
SY	Szombathely, Püspöki Könyvtár
SYb	——, Berzsenyi Dániel Megyei Könyvtár
SYm	——, Smidt Múzeum
T	Tata, Plébániatemplom Kottatára
V	Vác, Székesgyházi Kottatár
VE	Veszprém, Püspöki Könyvtár
VEs	——, Székesgyházi Kottatár

I: ITALY

Ac	Assisi, Biblioteca Comunale
Ad	——, Cattedrale S Rufino
Af	——, S Francesco
AC	Acicatena, Biblioteca Comunale
AG	Agrigento, Biblioteca Lucchesiana
AGI	Agira, Biblioteca Comunale
AGN	Agnone, Biblioteca Emidiana
AL	Albenga, Cattedrale
ALEa	Alessandria, Archivio di Stato
ALEi	——, Istituto Musicale Antonio Vivaldi
AN	Ancona, Biblioteca Comunale
ANcap	——, Biblioteca Capitolare
ANd	——, Archivio della Cappella del Duomo
AO	Aosta, Seminario Maggiore
AP	Ascoli Picena, Biblioteca Comunale
AQ	Aquileia, Archivio della Basilica
ARc	Arezzo, Biblioteca Consorziale
ARd	——, Duomo
ASc(d)	Asti, Archivio Capitolare (Duomo)
ASi	——, Istituto Musicale Giuseppe Verdi
ASs	——, Seminario Vescovile

AT	Atri, Museo della Basilica Cattedrale, Biblioteca Capitolare
Baf	Bologna, Accademia Filarmonica
Bam	——, Biblioteca della Casa di Risparmio (Biblioteca Ambrosini)
Bas	——, Archivio di Stato
Bc	——, Civico Museo Bibliografico Musicale
Bca	——, Biblioteca Comunale dell'Arciginnasio
Bl	——, Conservatorio di Musica G. B. Martini
Bof	——, Oratorio dei Filippini
Bpm	——, Facoltà di Magistero dell'Università degli Studi, Scuola di Perfezionamento in Musicologia
Bsd	——, Convento di S Domenico
Bsf	——, Convento di S Francesco
Bsm	——, Biblioteca Conventuale S Maria dei Servi
Bsp	——, Basilica di S Petronio
Bu	——, Biblioteca Universitaria
BAca	Bari, Biblioteca Capitolare
BAcp	——, Conservatorio di Musica Nicola Piccinni
BAgiovine	——, Alfredo Giovine, private collection
BAn	——, Biblioteca Nazionale Sagarriga Visconti-Volpi
BAR	Barletta, Biblioteca Comunale Sabino Loffredo
BDG	Bassano del Grappa, Biblioteca Civica
BE	Belluno, Biblioteca del Seminario
BEc	——, Biblioteca Civica
BGc	Bergamo, Biblioteca Civica Angelo Mai
BGi	——, Civico Istituto Musicale Gaetano Donizetti
BI	Bitonto, Biblioteca Comunale Vitale Giordano
BRa	Brescia, Ateneo di Scienze, Lettere ed Arti
BRd	——, Duomo
BRi	——, Istituto Musicale A. Venturi
BRp	——, Archivio di S Maria della Pace
BRq	——, Biblioteca Civica Queriniana
BRs	——, Seminario Vescovile
BRsg	——, S Giovanni Evangelista (Cappella del Ss Sacramento)
BRsmg	——, Madonna delle Grazie
BRss	——, S Salvatore
BRE	Bressanone, Seminario Vescovile Vicentinum
BRI	Brindisi, Biblioteca Pubblica Arcivescovile Annibale de Leo
BV	Benevento, Archivio Capitolare
BVa	——, Archivio di Stato
BVam	——, Biblioteca e Archivio Storico Provinciale Antonio Mellusi
BVT	Borgo Val di Toro, Biblioteca Comunale Manara
BZa	Bolzano, Archivio di Stato
BZc	——, Conservatorio di Musica Claudio Monteverdi
BZd	——, Duomo
BZf	——, Biblioteca dei Minori Francescani
BZtoggenburg	——, Count Toggenburg, private collection
CAc	Cagliari, Biblioteca Comunale
CAcon	——, Conservatorio di Musica Giovanni Pierluigi da Palestrina
CAsm	——, Cattedrale S Maria
CAu	——, Biblioteca Universitaria
CAP	Capua, Museo Provinciale Campano
CARcc	Castell'Arquato, Chiesa Collegiata
CARc(p)	——, Archivio Capitolare (Archivio Parrochiale)
CATa	Catania, Archivio di Stato
CATc	——, Biblioteche Riunite Civica e Antonio Ursino Recupero
CATm	——, Museo Belliniano
CATss	——, Società di Storia Patria per la Sicilia Orientale
CC	Città di Castello, Duomo
CCc	——, Biblioteca Comunale
CDA	Codogna, Biblioteca Civica Popolare L. Ricca
CEb(sm)	Cesena, Badia S Maria del Monte
CEc	——, Biblioteca Comunale Malatestiana
CEN	Cento, S Biagio
CF	Cividale del Friuli, Archivio Capitolare
CFm	——, Museo Archeologico Nazionale
CHR	Chieri, Facoltà Teologica dei Gesuiti
CHT	Chieta, Biblioteca Provinciale Angelo Camillo de Meis
CHV	Chiavenna, Biblioteca Capitolare Laurenziana
CLE	Corleone, Biblioteca Comunale Francesco Bentivegna
CLO	Corlono, Chiesa della Reggia Ducale
CMac	Casale Monferrato, Archivio Capitolare
CMbc	——, Biblioteca Civica
CMs	——, Seminario Vescovile
CMI	Camogli, Biblioteca Comunale Nicolo Cueno
CMO	Camerino, Biblioteca Valentiniana e Comunale
COc	Como, Biblioteca Comunale
COd	——, Duomo

CORc	Correggio, Biblioteca Comunale	*LOcl*	——, Biblioteca Comunale Laudense
COS	Cosenza, Biblioteca Civica	*LT*	Loreto, Archivio Storico della Cappella Lauretana
CPa	Carpi, Archivio Paolo Guaitoli della Commissione di Storia Patria de Carpi	*LU*	Lugo, Biblioteca Comunale Fabrizio Trisi
CPc	——, Biblioteca Comunale	*Ma*	Milan, Biblioteca Ambrosiana
CR	Cremona, Biblioteca Statale	*Malfieri*	——, Trecani degli Alfieri, private collection
CRd	——, Duomo	*Mb*	——, Biblioteca Nazionale Braidense
CRE	Crema, Biblioteca Comunale	*Mc*	——, Conservatorio di Musica Giuseppe Verdi
CREi	——, Istituto Musicale L. Folcioni	*Mca*	——, Archivio della Curia Arcivescovile
CT	Cortona, Biblioteca Comunale e dell'Accademia Etrusca	*Mcap(d)*	——, Cappella Musicale del Duomo
CZorizio	Cazzago S Martino, Orizio private collection	*Mcom*	——, Biblioteca Comunale
DO	Domodossola, Biblioteca e Archivio dei Rosminiani di Monte Calvaro	*Md*	——, Archivio della Cappella Musicale del Duomo
		Mdonà	——, Mariangelo Donà, private collection
E	Enna, Biblioteca Comunale	*Mr*	——, Archivio Storico Ricordi (Casa Editrice)
Fa	Florence, Ss Annunziata	*Ms*	——, Biblioteca Teatrale Livia Simoni
Faq	——, Pius XII Institute, Graduate School of Fine Arts, Aquinas Library	*Msartori*	——, Claudio Sartori, private collection
		Mt	——, Biblioteca Trivulziana
Fas	——, Archivio di Stato	*Mvidusso*	——, Carlo Vidusso, private collection
Fc	——, Conservatorio di Musica Luigi Cherubini	*MAa*	Mantua, Archivio di Stato
Fd	——, Duomo	*MAad*	——, Archivio Storico Diocesano
Ffabbri	——, M. Fabbri, private collection	*MAav*	——, Accademia Virgiliana di Scienze, Lettere ed Arti
Fl	——, Biblioteca Medicea-Laurenziana	*MAc*	——, Biblioteca Comunale
Fm	——, Biblioteca Marucelliana	*MAi*	——, Istituto Musicale Lucio Campiani
Fn	——, Biblioteca Nazionale Centrale	*MAp*	——, Duomo S Pietro
Folschki	——, Olschki private collection	*MAs*	——, Seminario Vescovile
Fr	——, Biblioteca Riccardiana e Moreniana	*MAC*	Macerata, Biblioteca Comunale Mozzi-Borgetti
Fs	——, Seminario Arcivescovile Maggiore	*MACa*	——, Archivio di Stato
Fsa	——, Biblioteca Domenicana, Chiesa S Maria Novella	*MC*	Monte Cassino, Biblioteca dell'Abbazia
Fsm	——, Convento S Marco	*ME*	Messina, Biblioteca Universitaria
Fu	——, Università degli Studi, Facoltà di Lettere e Filosofia	*MEmeli*	——, Alfonso Meli, private collection
		MEnicotra	——, Arturo Nicotra, private collection
FA	Fabriano, Biblioteca Comunale	*MEs*	——, Biblioteca Painiana del Seminario Arcivescovile
FAd	——, Duomo	*MFc*	Molfetta, Biblioteca Comunale Giovanni Panunzio
FAN	Fano, Biblioteca Comunale Federiciana	*MFsr*	——, Pontificio Seminario Regionale Pio XI
FBR	Fossombrone, Biblioteca Civica Passionei	*MFsv*	——, Seminario Vescovile
FEbonfigliuoli	Ferrara, Bonfigliuoli private collection	*MOa*	Modena, Accademia Nazionale di Scienze, Lettere ed Arti
FEc	——, Biblioteca Comunale Ariostea		
FEd	——, Duomo	*MOd*	——, Duomo
FEmichelini	——, Bruto Michelini, private collection	*MOdep*	——, Deputazione di Storia Patria per le Antiche Province Modenesi
FELc	Feltre, Biblioteca Comunale		
FELd	——, Duomo	*MOe*	——, Biblioteca Estense
FELm	——, Museo Civico	*MOf*	——, Archivio Ferni
FEM	Finale Emilia, Biblioteca Comunale	*MOl*	——, Liceo Musicale Orazio Vecchi
FERc	Fermo, Biblioteca Comunale	*MOs*	——, Archivio di Stato
FERd	——, Duomo	*MTventuri*	Montecatini-Terme, Antonio Venturi, private collection
FERl	——, Liceo Musicale Girolamo Frescobaldi		
FERmichelini	——, Bruno Michelini, private collection	*MV*	Montevergine, Biblioteca del Santuario
FOc	Forlì, Biblioteca Comunale Aurelio Saffi	*MZ*	Monza, Insigne Basilica di S Giovanni Battista
FOd	——, Duomo	*MZc*	——, Biblioteca Civica
FOG	Foggia, Biblioteca Provinciale	*Na*	Naples, Archivio di Stato
FOLc	Foligno, Biblioteca Comunale	*Nc*	——, Conservatorio di Musica S Pietro a Majella
FOLd	——, Duomo	*Nf*	——, Biblioteca Oratoriana dei Filippini
FOSc	Fossano, Biblioteca Civica	*Nlp*	——, Biblioteca Lucchesi-Palli [in *Nn*]
FZac(d)	Faenza, Archivio Capitolare (Duomo)	*Nn*	——, Biblioteca Nazionale Vittorio Emanuele III
FZc	——, Biblioteca Comunale	*Ns*	——, Seminario Arcivescovile
FZsavini	——, Ino Savini, private collection	*Nsn*	——, Società Napoletana di Storia Patria
Gc	Genoa, Biblioteca Civica Berio	*Nu*	——, Biblioteca Universitaria
Gf	——, Biblioteca Franzoniana	*NO*	Novacello, Biblioteca dell'Abbazia
Ggrasso	——, Lorenzina Grasso, private collection	*NON*	Nonantola, Seminario Abbaziale
Gi(l)	——, Conservatorio di Musica Nicolò Paganini	*NOVc*	Novara, Biblioteca Civica
Gim	——, Istituto Mazziniano	*NOVd*	——, Archivio Musicale Classico del Duomo
Gsc	——, S Caterina	*NOVg*	——, Archivio e Biblioteca di S Gaudenzio
Gsmb	——, S Maria della Castagna	*NOVi*	——, Civico Istituto Musicale Brera
Gsmd	——, S Maria di Castello, Biblioteca dei Domenicani	*NOVsg*	——, Archivio Musicale di S Gaudenzio
Gu	——, Biblioteca Universitaria	*NT*	Noto, Biblioteca Comunale
GA	Ganna, Badia Benedittina	*Oc*	Orvieto, Biblioteca Comunale Luigi Fumi
GE	Gemona, Duomo	*Od*	——, Biblioteca dell'Opera del Duomo
GN	Giulianova, Biblioteca Comunale Vincenzo Bindi	*OR*	Oristano, Seminario Arcivescovile
GO	Gorizia, Seminario Teologico Centrale	*ORT*	Ortona, Biblioteca Comunale
GR	Grottaferrata, Badia Greca	*OS*	Ostiglia, Biblioteca Musicale Greggiati
GUA	Guastalla, Biblioteca Municipale Maldotti	*OSI*	Osimo, Biblioteca Comunale
GUBsp	Gubbio, Biblioteca Comunale Sperelliana	*Pbonelli*	Padua, E. Bonelli, private collection
I	Imola, Biblioteca Comunale	*Pc*	——, Biblioteca Capitolare
IE	Iesi, Archivio Comunale	*Pca*	——, Biblioteca Antoniana, Basilica del Santo
IV	Ivrea, Biblioteca Capitolare	*Pci*	——, Museo Civico, Biblioteca Civica e Archivio Comunale
La	Lucca, Archivio di Stato		
Lc	——, Biblioteca Capitolare Feliniana	*Pi(l)*	——, Istituto Musicale Cesare Pollini
Lg	——, Biblioteca Statale	*Ppapafava*	——, Novello Papafava dei Carreresi, private collection
Li	——, Istituto Musicale Luigi Boccherini		
Ls	——, Seminario Vescovile	*Ps*	——, Seminario Vescovile
LA	L'Aquila, Biblioteca Provinciale Salvatore Tommasi	*Pu*	——, Biblioteca Universitaria
LE	Lecce, Biblioteca Provinciale Nicola Bernardini	*PAac*	Parma, Archivio Capitolare
LI	Livorno, Biblioteca Comunale Labronica Francesco Domenico Guerrazzi	*PAas*	——, Archivio di Stato
		PAc	——, Conservatorio di Musica Arrigo Boito
		PAi	——, Istituto di Studi Verdiani
LOc	Lodi, Biblioteca Capitolare	*PAsg*	——, S Giovanni Evangelista
		PAst	——, Madonna della Steccata

PAt	——, Teatro Regio
PAL	Palestrina, Biblioteca Comunale Fantoniana
PAVc	Pavia, S Maria del Carmine
PAVi	——, Civico Istituto Musicale Franco Vittadini
PAVs	——, Seminario Vescovile
PAVsm	——, S Michele
PAVsp	——, S Pietro in Ciel d'Oro
PAVu	——, Biblioteca Universitaria
PCa	Piacenza, Collegio Alberoni
PCc	——, Biblioteca Comunale Passerini Landi
PCcon	——, Conservatorio di Musica G. Nicolini
PCd	——, Duomo
PCsa	——, Biblioteca e Archivio Capitolare di S Antonino
PCsm	——, S Maria di Campagna
PEc	Perugia, Biblioteca Comunale Augusta
PEd	——, Cattedrale
PEl	——, Conservatorio di Musica Francesco Morlacchi
PEsp	——, S Pietro
PEA	Pescia, Biblioteca Comunale Carlo Magnani
PESc	Pesaro, Conservatorio di Musica Gioacchino Rossini
PEScerasa	——, Amadeo Cerasa, private collection [now *VTcerasa*]
PESd	——, Duomo
PESo	——, Biblioteca Oliveriana
PIa	Pisa, Archivio di Stato
PIarc	——, Biblioteca Arcivescovile Cardinale Pietro Maffi
PIc	——, Museo Nazionale di S Matteo
PIca	——, Biblioteca Cateriniana
PIcc	——, Archivio e Biblioteca Certosa di Calci
PIp	——, Archivio Musicale dell'Opera della Primaziale
PIr	——, Biblioteca Raffaelli
PIraffaelli	——, Raffaelli private collection
PIs	——, Fondo Simoneschi
PIst	——, Chiesa dei Cavalieri di S Stefano
PIN	Pinerolo, Biblioteca Comunale Camillo Allinudi
PLa	Palermo, Archivio di Stato
PLcom	——, Biblioteca Comunale
PLcon	——, Conservatorio Vincenzo Bellini
PLd	——, Duomo
PLi	——, Istituto di Storia della Musica, Facoltà di Lettere, Università degli Studi
PLm	——, Teatro Massimo
PLn	——, Biblioteca Nazionale
PLpagano	——, Roberto Pagano, private collection
PLs	——, Baron Pietro Emanuele Sgadari di Lo Monaco, private collection [in Casa di Lavoro e Preghiera Padre Massini]
PLsd	——, Archivio Storico Diocesano
PO	Potenza, Biblioteca Provinciale
POa	——, Archivio di Stato
POd	——, Duomo
PR	Prato, Duomo
PS	Pistoia, Cattedrale
PSc	——, Biblioteca Comunale Forteguerriana
Ra	Rome, Biblioteca Angelica
Rac	——, Accademia di Francia
Raf	——, Accademia Filarmonica Romana
Ras	——, Archivio di Stato
Rc	——, Biblioteca Casanatense
Rcg	——, Curia Generalizia dei Padri Gesuiti; Pontificio Collegio Germano-Ungarico
Rchristoff	——, Boris Christoff, private collection
Rcns	——, Archivio della Chiesa Nazionale Spagnuola
Rco	——, Congregazione dell'Oratorio
Rcsg	——, Oratorio di S Girolamo della Cantà
Rdi	——, Discoteca di Stato
Rdp	——, Archivio Doria-Pamphili, private collection
Rf	——, Archivio dei Filippini
Rgiazotto	——, Remo Giazotto, private collection
Ria	——, Istituto Nazionale di Archeologia e Storia dell'Arte
Rif	——, Istituto di Fisiologia dell'Università
Rig	——, Istituto Storico Germanico
Rims	——, Pontificio Istituto di Musica Sacra
Rla	——, Biblioteca Lancisiana
Rli	——, Accademia Nazionale dei Lincei e Corsiniana
Rlib	——, Basilica Liberiana
Rn	——, Biblioteca Nazionale Centrale Vittorio Emanuele III
Rp	——, Biblioteca Pasqualini [in *Rsc*]
Rps	——, Pio Sodalizio de' Piceni
Rsc	——, Conservatorio di Musica S Cecilia
Rsg	——, S Giovanni in Laterano
Rsgf	——, Arciconfraternità di S Giovanni dei Fiorentini
Rslf	——, S Luigi de' Francesi
Rsm	——, Archivio Capitolare di S Maria Maggiore [in *Rvat*]
Rsmm	——, S Maria di Monserrato
Rsmt	——, S Maria in Trastevere
Rsp	——, Santo Spirito in Sassia
Rss	——, S Sabina (Venerabile Convento)
Rv	——, Biblioteca Vallicelliana
Rvat	——, Biblioteca Apostolica Vaticana
RA	Ravenna, Duomo
RAc	——, Biblioteca Comunale Classense
RAs	——, Seminario Arcivescovile dei Ss Angeli Custodi
REas	Reggio Emilia, Archivio di Stato
REc	——, Archivio e Biblioteca Capitolare del Duomo
REd	——, Archivio Capitolare del Duomo
REm	——, Biblioteca Municipale
REsp	——, Archivio Capitolare di S Prospero
RIM	Rimini, Biblioteca Civica Gambalunga
RO	Rosate, S Stefano
RVE	Rovereto, Biblioteca Civica Girolamo Tartarotti
RVI	Rovigo, Accademia dei Concordi
Sac	Siena, Accademia Musicale Chigiana
Sas	——, Archivio di Stato
Sc	——, Biblioteca Comunale degli Intronati
Sd	——, Archivio Musicale dell'Opera del Duomo
Smo	——, Biblioteca annessa al Monumento Nazionale di Monte Oliveti Maggiore
SA	Savona, Biblioteca Civica Anton Giulio Barrili
SAL	Saluzzo, Archivio del Duomo
SAS	Sassari, Biblioteca Universitaria
SDF	San Daniele del Friuli, Biblioteca Civica Guarneriana
SE	Senigallia, Biblioteca Comunale Antonelliana
SI	Siracusa, Biblioteca Comunale
SML	Santa Margherita Ligure, Biblioteca Comunale Francesco Domenico Costa
SO	Sant'Oreste, Collegiata di S Lorenzo
SON	Sondrio, Biblioteca Civica Pio Rajna
SPc	Spoleto, Biblioteca Comunale
SPd	——, Duomo
SPE	Spello, Collegiata S Maria Maggiore
ST	Stresa, Biblioteca Rosminiana
SUsb	Subiaco, Biblioteca S Benedetto
SUss	——, Monumenta Nazionale dell'Abbazia di S Scolastica
Ta	Turin, Archivio di Stato
Tb	——, Convento di Benevagienna
Tci	——, Biblioteca Civica Musicale Andrea della Corte
Tco	——, Conservatorio Statale di Musica Giuseppe Verdi
Td	——, Duomo
Tf	——, Accademia Filarmonica
Ti	——, Istituto Salesiano Valsalice
Tmc	——, Museo Civico
Tn	——, Biblioteca Nazionale Universitaria
Tr	——, Biblioteca Reale
Trt	——, Archivio Musicale Radiotelevisione Italiana
TE	Terni, Istituto Musicale G. Briccialdi
TEc	——, Biblioteca Comunale
TI	Termini-Imerese, Biblioteca Liciniana
TLP	Torre del Lago Puccini, Museo di Casa Puccini
TOD	Todi, Biblioteca Comunale Lorenzo Feoni
TOL	Tolentino, Biblioteca Comunale Filelfica
TRa	Trent, Archivio di Stato
TRc	——, Biblioteca Comunale
TRmd	——, Museo Diocesano
TRmn	——, Museo Nazionale
TRmr	——, Museo del Risorgimento
TRE	Tremezzo, Count Gian Ludovico Sola-Cabiati, private collection
TRN	Trani, Biblioteca Comunale G. Bovio
TRP	Trapani, Biblioteca Fardelliana
TSci(com)	Trieste, Biblioteca Civica
TScm	——, Civici Musei di Storia ed Arte
TScon	——, Conservatorio di Musica G. Tartini
TSmt	——, Civico Museo Teatrale di Fondazione Carlo Schmidl
TSsc	——, Fondazione Giovanni Scaramangà de Altomonte
TSsg	——, Archivio della Cappella della Cattedrale S Giusto
TVca(d)	Treviso, Biblioteca Capitolare (Duomo)
TVco	——, Biblioteca Comunale
Us	Urbino, Cappella del Sacramento (Duomo)
Usf	——, S Francesco [in *Uu*]
Uu	——, Biblioteca Universitaria
UD	Udine, Duomo
UDa	——, Archivio di Stato

UDc	——, Biblioteca Comunale Vincenzo Joppi
UDi	——, Istituto Musicale Jacopo Tomadini
URBc	Urbania, Biblioteca Comunale
URBcap	——, Biblioteca Capitolare (Duomo)
Vas	Venice, Archivio di Stato
Vc	——, Conservatorio di Musica Benedetto Marcello
Vcg	——, Biblioteca Casa di Goldoni
Vgc	——, Biblioteca e Istituto della Fondazione Giorgio Cini
Vlevi	——, Fondazione Ugo Levi
Vmarcello	——, Andrighetti Marcello, private collection
Vmc	——, Museo Civico Correr
Vnm	——, Biblioteca Nazionale Marciana
Vqs	——, Accademia Querini-Stampalia
Vs	——, Seminario Patriarcale
Vsf	——, Conventuale di S Francesco
Vsm	——, Procuratoria di S Marco
Vsmc	——, S Maria della Consolazione detta Della Fava
Vt	——, Teatro la Fenice
VAa	Varese, Archivio Prepositurale di S Vittore
VAc	——, Biblioteca Civica
VCc	Vercelli, Biblioteca Civica
VCd	——, Duomo (Biblioteca Capitolare)
VCs	——, Seminario Vescovile
VD	Viadana, Biblioteca Civica
VEaf	Verona, Società Accademia Filarmonica
VEas	——, Archivio di Stato
VEc	——, Biblioteca Civica
VEcap	——, Biblioteca Capitolare (Cattedrale)
VEs	——, Seminario Vescovile
VEsg	——, S Giorgio in Braida
VG	Voghera, Collegiata di S Lorenzo
VIb	Vicenza, Biblioteca Civica Bertoliana
VId	——, Duomo
VImc	——, Museo Civico
VImr	——, Museo del Risorgimento
VIs	——, Seminario Vescovile
VIGsa	Vigévano, Duomo S Ambrogio
VIGsi	——, S Ignazio
VIM	Vimercate, S Stefano
VO	Volterra, Biblioteca Guarnacci
VTc	Viterbo, Biblioteca Comunale degli Ardenti
VTcarosi	——, Attilio Carosi, private collection
VTcerasa	——, Amadeo Cerasa, private collection
VTp	——, Biblioteca Pio XII, Pontificio Seminario Regionale
VTs	——, Seminario Diocesano
VTM	Ventimiglia, Civica Biblioteca Aprosiana

IL: ISRAEL

J	Jerusalem, Jewish National and University Library
Jp	——, Patriarchal Library
S	Mt Sinai
SS	St Sabas, Monastery

IS: ICELAND

Rn	Reykjavik, National Library

J: JAPAN

Tm	Tokyo, Musashino Ongaku Daigaku
Tma(Tmc)	——, Bibliotheca Musashino Academia Musicae
Tn	——, Nanki Music Library, Ohki private collection

N: NORWAY

Bo	Bergen, Offentlige Bibliotek
Bu	——, Universitetsbiblioteket
Oic	Oslo, Norwegian Music Information Centre
Oim	——, Institutt for Musikkvitenskap, Universitet
Ok	——, Musik-Konservatoriet
Onk	——, Norsk Komponistforening
Or	——, Norsk Rikskringkastings
Ou	——, Universitetsbiblioteket
Oum	——, Universitetsbiblioteket, Norsk Musikksamling
T	Trondheim, Kongelige Norske Videnskabers Selskab
Tmi	——, Musikkvitenskapelig Institutt

NL: THE NETHERLANDS

Ad	Amsterdam, Stichting Donemus
At	——, Toonkunst-Bibliotheek
Au	——, Universiteitsbibliotheek
Avnm	——, Bibliotheek der Vereniging voor Nederlandse Muziekgeschiedenis [in *At*]
AN	Amerongen, Archief van het Kasteel der Graven Bentinck, private collection

BI	Bilthoven, Stichting Gaudeamus
D	Deventer, Stads- of Athenaeumbibliotheek
DHa	The Hague, Koninklijk Huisarchief
DHgm	——, Gemeentemuseum
DHk	——, Koninklijke Bibliotheek
DHmw	——, Rijksmuseum
G	Groningen, Universiteitsbibliotheek
Hs	Haarlem, Stadsbibliotheek
HIr	Hilversum, Radio Nederland
L	Leiden, Gemeentearchief
Lml	——, Museum Lakenhal
Lt	——, Bibliotheca Thysiana [in *Lu*]
Lu	——, Bibliotheek der Rijksuniversiteit
Lw	——, Bibliothèque Wallonne
LE	Leeuwarden, Provinciale Bibliotheek van Friesland
R	Rotterdam, Gemeentebibliotheek
'sH	's-Hertogenbosch, Archief van de Illustre Lieve Vrouwe Broederschap
Uim	Utrecht, Instituut voor Muziekwetenschap der Rijksuniversiteit
Usg	——, St Gregorius Vereniging, Bibliotheek [in *Uim*]
Uu	——, Bibliotheek der Rijksuniversiteit

NZ: NEW ZEALAND

Ap	Auckland, Public Library
Au	——, University Library
Dp	Dunedin, Public Library
Wt	Wellington, Alexander Turnbull Library

P: PORTUGAL

AN	Angra do Heroismo, Biblioteca Pública e Arquivo Distrital
AR	Arouca, Museu Regional de Arte Sacra do Mosteiro de Arouca
AV	Aveiro, Museu de Aveiro, Mosteiro de Jesus
BA	Barreiro, Biblioteca Municipal
BRp	Braga, Biblioteca Pública e Arquivo Distrital
BRs	——, Sé de Braga
C	Coimbra, Biblioteca Geral da Universidade
Cm	——, Biblioteca Municipal
Cmn	——, Museu Nacional de Machado de Castro
Cs	——, Sé Nova
Cug	——, Biblioteca Geral da Universidade
Cul	——, Faculdade de Letras da Universidade
CA	Cascais, Museu-Biblioteca Condes de Castro Guimarães
Em	Elvas, Biblioteca Pública Hortênsia
EVc	Évora, Arquivo da Sé
EVp	——, Biblioteca Pública e Arquivo Distrital
F	Figueira da Foz, Biblioteca Pública Municipal Pedro Fernandes Tomás
G	Guimaraes, Arquivo Municipal Alfredo Pimenta
La	Lisbon, Palácio Nacional da Ajuda
Laa	——, Academia de Amadores de Musica (Conservatorio Municipal)
Lac	——, Academia das Ciências
Lan	——, Arquivo Nacional de Torre do Tombo
Lc	——, Conservatorio Nacional
Lcg	——, Fundação Calouste Gulbenkian
Lf	——, Fábrica da Sé Patriarcal
Lif	——, Instituto de Franca
Ln	——, Biblioteca Nacional
Lr	——, Emissora Nacional de Radiodifusão
Ls	——, Sociedade de Escritores e Compositores Portugueses
Lt	——, Teatro Nacional de S Carlos
LA	Lamego, Biblioteca da Sé
LE	Leiria, Biblioteca Erudita e Arquivo Distrital (Biblioteca Pública)
Mp	Mafra, Palácio Nacional
Pa	Oporto, Ateneu Comercial
Pc	——, Conservatorio de Musica
Pcom	——, Biblioteca Comunale
Peh	——, Museu de Etnografia e Historia
Pf	——, Clube Fenianos Portuenses
Pm	——, Biblioteca Pública Municipal
PD	Ponta Delgada, Biblioteca Pública e Arquivo Distrital
PL	Ponte de Lima, Arquivo da Misericórdia
PO	Portalegre, Arquivo da Sé
Va	Viseu, Arquivo Distrital
Vm	——, Museu Grão Vasco
Vs	——, Arquivo da Sé
VV	Vila Viçosa, Casa da Bragança, Museu-Biblioteca

PL: POLAND

B	Bydgoszcz, Biblioteka Miejska
BA	Barczew, Archiwum Kościoła Parafialnego
Cb	Cieszyn, Biblioteka Śląska, Oddział Cieszyn
Cp	——, Biblioteka Tschammera w Kościele Ewangelickim
CZp	Częstochowa, Klasztor OO. Paulinów na Jasnej Górze
GD	Gdańsk, Biblioteka Polskiej Akademii Nauk
GNd	Gniezno, Archiwum Archidiecezjalne
GR	Grodzisk, Klasztor OO. Cystersów
Kc	Kraków, Biblioteka Czartoryskich
Kcz	——, Biblioteka Czapskich
Kd	——, Klasztor OO. Dominikanów
Kj	——, Biblioteka Jagiellońska
Kk	——, Kapituła Metropolitalna
Kp	——, Biblioteka Polskiej Akademii Nauk
Kpa	——, Archiwum Państwowe
Kz	——, Biblioteka Czartoryskich
KA	Katowice, Biblioteka Śląska
KO	Kórnik, Polska Akademia Nauk, Biblioteka Kórnicka
Lk	Lublin, Biblioteka Katolickiego Uniwersytetu
Lw	——, ——, Biblioteka Wojewódzka i Miejska im. H. Łopacińskiego
ŁA	Łancut, Muzeum
ŁO	Łowicz, Biblioteka Seminarium
MO	Mogiła, Klasztor OO. Cystersów
OB	Obra, Klasztor OO. Cystersów
Pa	Poznań, Biblioteka Archidiecezjalna
Pr	——, Miejska Biblioteka Publiczna im. Edwarda Raczyńskiego
Pu	——, Biblioteka Uniwersytecka
PE	Pelplin, Biblioteka Seminarium Duchownego
PŁp	Płock, Biblioteka Towarzystwa Naukowego
R	Raków, Archiwum Kościelne
SA	Sandomierz, Seminarium Duchownego
SZ	Szalowa, Archiwum Parafialne
Tu	Toruń, Biblioteka Uniwersytecka
TA	Tarnów, Archiwum Archidiecezjalne
Wm	Warsaw, Biblioteka Muzeum Narodowego
Wn	——, Biblioteka Narodowa
Wp	——, Biblioteka Publiczna
Ws	——, Biblioteka Synodalna Ewangelicka
Wtm	——, Biblioteka Warszawskiego Towarzystwa Muzycznego
Wu	——, Biblioteka Uniwersytecka
WL	Wilanów, Biblioteka, Oddział Muzeum Narodowego Warszawy
WRol	Wrocław, Biblioteka Ossolineum Leopoldiensis
WRu	——, Biblioteka Uniwersytecka

R: ROMANIA

Ab	Aiud, Biblioteca Documentară Bethlen
Ba	Bucharest, Biblioteca Academiei Republicii Socialiste România
Bc	——, Biblioteca Centrală de Stat
BRm	Braşov, Biblioteca Municipală
Sb	Sibiu, Muzeul Brukenthal
TMt	Tîrgu Mureş, Biblioteca Documentară Teleki

S: SWEDEN

A	Arvika, Folkliga Musikskolan
E	Enköping, Samrealskolans Arkiv
ES	Eskilstuna, Stadsbiblioteket
Gem	Göteborg, Etnografiska Museet
Ghl	——, Hvitfeldtska Högre Allmänna Läroverket
Gu	——, Universitetsbiblioteket (formerly Stadsbiblioteket)
GÄ	Gävle, Vasaskolans Bibliotek
Hfryklund	Hälsingborg, D. Daniel Fryklund, private collection [in *Skma*]
Hs	——, Stadsbiblioteket
J	Jönköping, Per Brahegymnasiet
K	Kalmar, Stifts- och Gymnasiebiblioteket
KA	Karlstad, Stadsbiblioteket
KAT	Katrineholm, Stadsbiblioteket
KH	Karlshamn, Museums Biblioteket
L	Lund, Universitetsbiblioteket
Lbarnekow	——, Barnekow private collection
LB	Leufsta Bruk, De Geer private collection
LI	Linköping, Stifts- och Landsbiblioteket
M	Malmö, Stadsbiblioteket
N	Norrköping, Stadsbiblioteket
Ö	Örebro, Karolinska Skolans Bibliotek
ÖS	Östersund, Jämtlands Läns Bibliotek
Sdt	Stockholm, Drottningholms Teatermuseum
Sic	——, Stims Informationscentral för Svensk Musik
Sk	——, Kungliga Biblioteket
Skma	——, Kungliga Musikaliska Akademiens Bibliotek
Sm	——, Musikmuseet
Smf	——, Stiftelsen Musikkulturens Främjande
Sn	——, Nordiska Museet
Ssr	——, Sveriges Radio
St	——, Kungliga Teaterns Bibliotek
SK	Skara, Stifts- och Landsbiblioteket
STd	Strängnäs, Domkyrkobiblioteket
STr	——, Roggebiblioteket
Uifm	Uppsala, Institutionen för Musikforskning vid Uppsala Universitetet
Uu	——, Universitetsbiblioteket
V	Västerås, Stadsbiblioteket
VIl	Visby, Landsarkivet
VIs	——, Stadsbiblioteket
VX	Växjö, Landsbiblioteket

SF: FINLAND

A	Turku [Åbo], Sibelius Museum Musikvetenskapliga Institutionen vid Åbo Akademi, Bibliotek & Arkiv
Aa	——, Åbo Akademis, Bibliotek
Hko	Helsinki, Helsingin Kaupunginorkester
Hmt	——, Musiikin Tiedotuskeskus
Hr	——, Oy Yleisradio AB, Nuotisto
Hs	——, Sibelius-Akatemian Kirjasto
Hy	——, Helsingin Yliopiston Kirjasto
Hyf	——, Helsingin Yliopiston Kirjasto, Department of Finnish Music
TA	Tampere, Tampereen Yliopiston Kansanperinteen Laitos

US: UNITED STATES OF AMERICA

AA	Ann Arbor, University of Michigan Music Library
AB	Albany, New York State Library
AL	Allentown (Penn.), Muhlenberg College, John A. W. Haas Library
AM	Amherst (Mass.), Amherst College, Robert Frost Building
ATu	Atlanta (Georgia), Emory University Library
AU	Aurora (NY), Wells College Library
AUS	Austin, University of Texas
Ba	Boston, Athenaeum Library
Bbs	——, Bostonian Society
Bc	——, New England Conservatory of Music
Bco	——, American Congregational Society, Congregational Library
Bfa	——, Fine Arts Museum
Bge	——, School of Fine Arts, General Education Library
Bh	——, Harvard Musical Association
Bhh	——, Handel and Haydn Society
Bhs	——, Massachusetts Historical Society
Bl	——, Grand Lodge of Masons in Massachusetts, A. F. and A. M. Library
Bm	——, University, Mugar Memorial Library
Bp	——, Public Library, Music Department
Bth	——, University, School of Theology
BAep	Baltimore, Enoch Pratt Free Library, Fine Arts and Music Department
BAhs	——, Maryland Historical Society
BApi	——, City Library, Peabody Institute
BAu	——, Johns Hopkins University Libraries
BAw	——, Walters Art Gallery
BAT	Baton Rouge, Louisiana State University Library
BE	Berkeley, University of California, Music Library
BER	Berea (Ohio), Baldwin-Wallace College, Ritter Library of the Conservatory
BETm	Bethlehem (Penn.), Archives of the Moravian Church in Bethlehem
BETu	——, Lehigh University, Lucy Packer Lindeman Memorial Library
BG	Bangor (Maine), Public Library
BK	Brunswick (Maine), Bowdoin College, Department of Music
BLl	Bloomington, Indiana University, Lilly Library
BLu	——, Indiana University, School of Music Library
BO	Boulder, University of Colorado Music Library
BRc	Brooklyn, Brooklyn College Music Library
BRp	——, Public Library
BU	Buffalo, Buffalo and Erie County Public Library
Charding	Chicago, W. N. H. Harding, private collection [in GB-Ob]
Chs	——, Chicago Historical Society Library
Cn	——, Newberry Library

Cu	——, University Music Library
CA	Cambridge, Harvard University Music Libraries
CAR	Carlisle (Penn.), Dickinson College
CDhs	Concord, New Hampshire Historical Society
CDs	——, New Hampshire State Library
CG	Coral Gables (Florida), University of Miami Music Library
CHua	Charlottesville, University of Virginia, Alderman Library
CHum	——, University of Virginia Music Library
CHH	Chapel Hill, University of North Carolina Music Library
CIhc	Cincinnati, Hebrew Union College
CIu	——, University of Cincinnati College-Conservatory of Music
CLm	Cleveland, Museum of Art, Cantatorium
CLp	——, Public Library, Fine Arts Department
CLwr	——, Western Reserve University, Freiberger Library and Music House Library
COu	Columbus, Ohio State University Music Library
CR	Cedar Rapids, Iowa Masonic Library
Dp	Detroit, Public Library, Music and Performing Arts Department
DB	Dearborn (Mich.), Henry Ford Museum and Greenfield Village
DE	Denver (Colorado), Public Library, Art and Music Division
DM	Durham (North Carolina), Duke University Libraries
DN	Denton, North Texas State University Music Library
DO	Dover (New Hampshire), Public Library
Eg	Evanston (Ill.), Garrett Theological Seminary
Eu	——, Northwestern University, Music Library
ECstarr	Eastchester (NY), Saul Starr, private collection
EXd	Exeter (New Hampshire), Phillips Exeter Academy, Davis Library
EXp	——, Public Library
FW	Fort Worth, Southwest Baptist Theological Seminary
G	Gainesville, University of Florida Library, Rare Book Collection
GA	Gambier (Ohio), Kenyon College Divinity School, Colburn Library
GB	Gettysburg, Lutheran Theological Seminary
GR	Granville (Ohio), Denison University Library
GRE	Greenville (Delaware), Eleutherian Mills Historical Library
Hhs	Hartford, Connecticut Historical Society Library
Hm	——, Case Memorial Library, Hartford Seminary Foundation
Hp	——, Public Library, Art and Music Department
Hs	——, Connecticut State Library
Hw	——, Trinity College, Watkinson Library
HA	Hanover (New Hampshire), Dartmouth College, Baker Library
HB	Harrisonburg (Virginia), Eastern Mennonite College, Menno Simons Historical Library and Archives
HG	Harrisburg, Pennsylvania State Library
HO	Hopkinton, New Hampshire Antiquarian Society
HU	Huntingdon (Penn.), Juniata College, L. A. Beechly Library
I	Ithaca (NY), Cornell University Music Library
IO	Iowa, University of Iowa Music Library
K	Kent (Ohio), Kent State University Library
Lu	Lawrence, University of Kansas Libraries
LAu	Los Angeles, University of California, Walter H. Rubsamen Music Library
LAuc	——, University of California, William Andrews Clark Memorial Library
LAusc	——, University of Southern California School of Music
LB	Lewisburg (Penn.), Bucknell University, Ellen Clark Bertrand Library
LChs	Lancaster (Penn.), Lancaster County Historical Society
LCm	——, Lancaster Mennonite Historical Library and Archives
LCts	——, Theological Seminary of the United Church of Christ
LEX	Lexington, University of Kentucky, Margaret I. King Library
LOs	Louisville (Ky.), Southern Baptist Theological Seminary, James P. Boyce Centennial Library
LOu	——, University, School of Music Library
LU	Lincoln University (Penn.), Vail Memorial Library
M	Milwaukee, Public Library, Art and Music Department
MI	Middletown (Conn.), Wesleyan University, Olin Memorial Library
MORduncan	Morgantown, Richard E. Duncan, private collection
MSp	Minneapolis, Public Library
MSu	——, University of Minnesota Music Library
MV	Mt Vernon (Virginia), Mt Vernon Ladies Association of the Union Collection
Nf	Northampton (Mass.), Forbes Library
Nsc	——, Smith College, Werner Josten Music Library
NAZ	Nazareth (Penn.), Moravian Historical Society
NBs	New Brunswick, Theological Seminary, Gardner A. Sage Library
NBu	——, Rutgers University Library
NEm	Newark (NJ), Newark Museum
NEp	——, Public Library
NH	New Haven, Yale University, School of Music Library
NORts	New Orleans, Theological Seminary
NORtu	——, Tulane University, Howard Tilton Memorial Library
NP	Newburyport (Mass.), Public Library
NYcc	New York, City College Library, Music Library
NYcu	——, Columbia University Music Library
NYfo	——, Fordham University Library
NYfuld	——, James J. Fuld, private collection
NYgo	——, University, Gould Memorial Library
NYgr	——, Grolier Club
NYhc	——, Hunter College Library
NYhs	——, New York Historical Society
NYhsa	——, Hispanic Society of America
NYj	——, Juilliard School of Music
NYlateiner	——, Jacob Lateiner, private collection
NYma	——, Mannes College of Music, Clara Damrosch Mannes Memorial Library
NYmc	——, City Museum, Theatre and Music Department
NYmm	——, Metropolitan Museum of Art, Thomas J. Watson Library
NYp	——, Public Library at Lincoln Center, Library and Museum of the Performing Arts
NYpm	——, Pierpont Morgan Library
NYq	——, Queens College of the City University, Paul Klapper Library, Music Library
NYts	——, Union Theological Seminary
OA	Oakland (Calif.), Public Library
OAm	——, Mills College, Margaret Prall Music Library
OB	Oberlin, Oberlin College Conservatory of Music
Pc	Pittsburgh, Carnegie Library
Pfinney	——, Theodore M. Finney, private collection [in *Pu*]
Ps	——, Theological Seminary, Clifford E. Barbour Library
Pu	——, University of Pittsburgh, Theodore Finney Music Library
PD	Portland, Maine Historical Society
PER	Perryville (Missouri), St Mary's Seminary
PHbo	Philadelphia, St Charles Borromeo Theological Seminary
PHbs	——, William Bacon Stevens Library
PHchs	——, American Catholic Historical Society of Philadelphia
PHci	——, Curtis Institute of Music
PHem	——, Eric Mandell Collection of Jewish Music
PHf	——, Free Library of Philadelphia
PHhs	——, Historical Society of Pennsylvania
PHkm	——, Lutheran Theological Seminary
PHlc	——, Library Company of Philadelphia
PHma	——, Musical Academy
PHphs	——, Presbyterian Historical Society
PHps	——, American Philosophical Society
PHr	——, Philip H. and A. S. W. Rosenbach Foundation
PHtr	——, Trinity Lutheran Church of Germantown
PHts	——, Westminster Theological Seminary
PHu	——, University of Pennsylvania, Otto E. Albrecht Music Library
PIlevy	——, Pikesville (Maryland), Lester S. Levy, private collection
PL	Portland (Oregon), Library Association of Portland, Music Department
PO	Poughkeepsie, Vassar College, George Sherman Dickinson Music Library
PRs	Princeton, Theological Seminary
PRu	——, University, Harvey S. Firestone Memorial Library

PROhs	Providence, Rhode Island Historical Society
PROu	——, Brown University Libraries
R	——, Rochester, University, Eastman School of Music, Sibley Music Library
RI	Richmond, Virginia State Library
Sp	Seattle, Public Library
Su	——, University of Washington Music Library
SA	Salem (Mass.), Essex Institute, James Duncan Phillips Library
SB	Santa Barbara, University of California, Library
SFp	San Francisco, Public Library, Fine Arts Department, Music Division
SFs	——, Sutro Library
SFsc	——, San Francisco State College Library, Frank V. de Bellis Collection
SHE	Sherman (Texas), Austin College, Arthur Hopkins Library
SLc	St Louis, Concordia Seminary
SLf	——, Fontbonne College
SLkrohn	——, Ernst C. Krohn, private collection
SLug	——, Washington University, Gaylord Music Library
SLC	Salt Lake City, University of Utah Library
SM	San Marino (Calif.), Henry E. Huntington Library and Art Gallery
SPmoldenhauer	Spokane (Washington), Hans Moldenhauer, private collection
STu	Stanford, University, Division of Humanities and Social Sciences, Music Library
SW	Swarthmore (Penn.), Swarthmore College Library
SY	Syracuse, University Music Library and George Arents Research Library
Tm	Toledo, Toledo Museum of Art
TA	Tallahassee, Florida State University, Robert Manning Strozier Library
U	Urbana, University of Illinois Music Library
Ufraenkel	——, Fraenkel collection
UP	University Park, Pennsylvania State University Library
Wc	Washington, DC, Library of Congress, Music Division
Wca	——, Cathedral
Wcu	——, Catholic University of America Music Library
Wgu	——, Georgetown University Libraries
Ws	——, Folger Shakespeare Libraries
Wsc	——, Scottish Rite Masons, Supreme Council
Wsi	——, Smithsonian Institution, Music Library
WA	Watertown (Mass.), Perkins School for the Blind
WC	Waco (Texas), Baylor University Music Library
WE	Wellesley (Mass.), Wellesley College Library
WELhartzler	Wellman (Iowa), J. D. Hartzler, private collection
WGc	Williamsburg (Virginia), College of William and Mary
WGw	——, Colonial Williamsburg Research Department, historical collection
WI	Williamstown (Mass.), Williams College, Chapin Library
WM	Waltham (Mass.), Brandeis University Library, Music Library, Goldfarb Library
WOa	Worcester (Mass.), American Antiquarian Society
WS	Winston-Salem (North Carolina), Moravian Music Foundation

USSR: UNION OF SOVIET SOCIALIST REPUBLICS

J	Jelgava, Muzei
Kan	Kiev, Tsentral'naya Naukova Biblioteka, Akademiya Nauk URSR
Kk	——, Biblioteka Gosudarstvennoy Konservatoriy imeni P. I. Chaykovskovo
KA	Kaliningrad, Oblastnaya Biblioteka
KAg	——, Gosudarstvennaya Biblioteka
KAu	——, Universitetskaya Biblioteka

KI	Kishinev, Biblioteka Gosudarstvennoy Konservatoriy imeni G. Muzichesku
Lan	Leningrad, Biblioteka Akademii Nauk SSSR
Lia	——, Gosudarstvennïy Tsentral'nïy Istoricheskïy Arkhiv
Lil	——, Institut Russkoy Literaturï
Lit	——, Leningradsky Gosudarstvennïy Institut Teatra, Muzïki i Kinematografii
Lk	——, Biblioteka Leningradskoy Gosudarstvennoy Konservatoriy imeni N. A. Rimskovo-Korsakova
Lph	——, Muzïkal'naya Biblioteka Leningradskoy Gosudarstvennoy Filarmonii
Lsc	——, Gosudarstvennaya Ordena Trudovovo Krasnovo Znameni Publichnaya Biblioteka imeni M. E. Saltïkova-Shchedrina
Lt	——, Leningradskiy Gosudarstvennïy Teatral'nïy Muzey
Ltob	——, Tsentral'naya Muzïkal'naya Biblioteka Gosudarstvennovo Teatra Operï i Baleta imeni S. M. Kirova
LV	L'vov, Biblioteka Gosudarstvennoy Konservatoriy imeni N. V. Lysenko
Mcl	Moscow, Gosudarstvennïy Tsentral'nïy Literaturnïy Arkhiv
Mcm	——, Gosudarstvennïy Tsentral'nïy Muzey Muzïkal'noy Kul'turï imeni M. I. Glinki
Mk	——, Gosudarstvennaya Konservatoriya imeni P. I. Chaykovskovo, Nauchnaya Muzïkal'naya Biblioteka imeni S. I. Taneyeva
Ml	——, Gosudarstvennaya Ordena Lenina Biblioteka SSSR imeni V. I. Lenina
Mm	——, Gosudarstvennïy Istoricheskïy Muzei
Mt	——, Gosudarstvennïy Teatral'nïy Muzei imeni A. Bakhrushina
MI	Minsk, Biblioteka Belorusskoy Gosudarstvennoy Konservatoriy
O	Odessa, Biblioteka Gosudarstvennoy Konservatoriy imeni A. V. Nezhdanovoy
R	Riga, Biblioteka Gosudarstvennoy Konservatoriy Latviyskoy imeni J. Vitola
TAu	Tartu, Universitetskaya Biblioteka
TAL	Tallinn, Biblioteka Gosudarstvennoy Konservatoriy
TB	Tbilisi, Biblioteka Gosudarstvennoy Konservatoriy imeni V. Saradzhisvili
V	Vilnius, Biblioteka Gosudarstvennoy Konservatoriy Litovskoy SSR

YU: YUGOSLAVIA

Bn	Belgrade, Narodna Biblioteka N. R. Srbije
Dsd	Dubrovnik, Knjižnica Samostana Dominikanaca
Dsmb	——, Franjevački Samostan Mala Braća
La	Ljubljana, Knjižnica Akademije za Glasbo
Lf	——, Knjižnica Frančiškanskega Samostana
Ls	——, Škofijski Arhiv in Biblioteka
Lsa	——, Slovenska Akademija Znanosti in Umjetnosti
Lsk	——, Arhiv Stolnega Kora
Lu	——, Narodna in Univerzitetna Knjižnica
MAk	Maribor, Glazbeni Arhiv Katedrale
MAs	——, Knjižnica Škofijskega Arhiva
NM	Novo Mesto, Knjižnica Frančiskanškega Samostana
NMc	——, Glazbeni Arhiv Katedrale
O	Ohrid, Narodno Museum
Sk	Split, Glazbeni Arhiv Katedrale
Ssf	——, Knjižnica Samostana Sv Frane
Za	Zagreb, Jugoslavenska Akademija Znanosti i Umjetnosti
Zda	——, Državni Arhiv
Zha	——, Hrvatski Glazbeni Zavod
Zk	——, Glazbeni Arhiv Katedrale
Zs	——, Glazbeni Arhiv Bogoslovnog Sjemeništa
Zu	——, Nacionalna i Sveučilišna Biblioteka

Riegel – Schusterfleck

A Note on the Use of the Dictionary

This note is intended as a short guide to the basic procedures and organization of the dictionary. A fuller account will be found in the Introduction, vol.1, pp.xi–xx.

Abbreviations in general use in the dictionary are listed on pp.vii–x; bibliographical ones (periodicals, reference works, editions etc) are listed on pp.xi–xiii.

Alphabetization of headings is based on the principle that words are read continuously, ignoring spaces, hyphens, accents, bracketed matter etc, up to the first comma; the same principle applies thereafter. 'Mc' and 'M'' are listed as 'Mac', 'St' as 'Saint'.

Bibliographies are arranged chronologically (within section, where divided), in order of year of first publication, and alphabetically by author within years.

Cross-references are shown in small capitals, with a large capital at the beginning of the first word of the entry referred to. Thus 'The instrument is related to the BASS TUBA' would mean that the entry referred to is not '**Bass tuba**' but '**Tuba, bass**'.

Work-lists are normally arranged chronologically (within section, where divided). Italic symbols used in them (like *D-Dlb* or *GB-Lbm*) refer to the libraries holding sources, and are explained on pp. xiv–xxx; each national sigillum stands until contradicted.

R

CONTINUED

Riegel. *See* RIGEL family.

Rieger. Austrian firm of organ builders. It was founded in 1845 by Franz Rieger (1812–85) at Jägerndorf (now Krnov), Silesia; his sons Otto the elder (1847–1903) and Gustav (1848–1905) took it over in 1873, and Otto's son, Otto the younger (1880–1920), became head of the firm in 1904. In 1920 control passed to Josef Edler von Glatter-Götz senior (1880–1948), a trained engineer. He bought the firm in 1922, and in 1936 took into partnership his sons, Egon (1911–40) and Josef Karl Maria (*b* Vienna, 15 Dec 1914), who were also qualified engineers. After World War II, the elder Josef moved the factory to Schwarzach. In 1948 the younger, who had served as technical director of the firm from 1937, succeeded his father as sole proprietor. He has an outstanding reputation as a designer. In 1939 the firm had more than 340 employees, and 4000 organs had been built; the staff was reduced to 40, who only build organs with slider-chests and mechanical actions (about 250 stops per year), mainly for Germany, Switzerland and the USA. Both tonally and mechanically, Rieger organs have always been among the best. Their many instruments include those for: Burgbergkirche, Jägerndorf (1845); St Paul, Oslo (1879); St Stephen, Prague (1887); Church of the Holy Sepulchre, Jerusalem (1896); Catholic Church, Nizhniy Novgorod (1896); St Cecilia's, Rome (1904); Concert Hall of the Musikverein, Vienna (1907; four manuals, 67 stops); Konzerthaus, Vienna (1912; five manuals, 109 stops; special music for its inauguration was composed by Richard Strauss); Mozarteum, Salzburg (1914; four manuals, 80 stops); St Matthew's, Łódz (1928; three manuals, 60 stops); Martin Agricola church, Helsinki (1934; four manuals, 73 stops); Prague radio (1935; three manuals, 64 stops); St Elisabeth's, Stuttgart (1957; four manuals, 55 stops); Friedenskirche, Krefeld (1960; four manuals, 66 stops); Mönchengladbach Minster (1961; three manuals, 45 stops); Neanderkirche, Düsseldorf (1966; three manuals, 47 stops); Presbyterian Church, Bryn Mawr (1974; four manuals, 68 stops); and Ratzeburg Cathedral (1977; four manuals, 60 stops).

BIBLIOGRAPHY

W. E. Ehrenhofer: *Taschenbuch des Orgelbau-Revisors* (Graz and Vienna, 1909)

J. K. M. von Glatter-Götz: 'Die physikalischen und physiologischen Grundlagen der mechanischen Spieltraktur', *Altbayrische Orgeltage* (Berlin, 1958), 34

R. Quoika: 'Rieger, Gebrüder', *MGG*

'Who's Who?', *ISO Information*, i (1969), 7

HANS KLOTZ

Rieger, Gottfried (*b* Opavice, 1 May 1764; *d* Brno, 13 Oct 1855). Moravian teacher and composer. The son of a musician, he began his career at the age of 13 in the service of Count Sedlnitzky. He quickly became proficient on several instruments and also began composing. He studied theory with Antonín Damasus Brosmann and then left the service of Sedlnitzky in 1787 to make a career in Brno. He soon won a reputation as a teacher and was appointed music director of the Brno theatre, for which he wrote several Singspiels. From 1804 to 1808 he was Kapellmeister to Count Haugwitz at Náměšti nad Orlici; he then returned permanently to Brno, where he resumed his teaching activities and conducted many oratorio and symphony concerts. Probably his most important achievement was the founding of the music institute in Brno in 1828. Under his guidance the institute produced many fine musicians; his teachings there were published in his *Theoretisch-praktische Anleitung die Generalbass und Harmonielehre in 6 Monaten gründlich und leicht zu erlernen* (Vienna, 1833).

Besides writing for the Brno theatre, Rieger was a prolific composer of sacred music, including 19 masses and a number of smaller pieces. His dramatic cantatas were popular, and were occasionally staged; some of these have a patriotic flavour, e.g. *Mährens Brüderbund* and *Svatopluk*. His instrumental music includes three piano trios, two piano concertos and a symphony. But his position in Brno isolated him from prevailing musical trends, and it is on his pioneering of musical life and education in Moravia, rather than on his compositions, that his reputation now rests.

BIBLIOGRAPHY

R. Vetterl: 'J. Rieger a jeho doba' [G. Rieger and his times], *Časopis moravského musea* (Brno, 1929–30), 45–86, 435–500

J. Racek: 'Moravská hudební kultura v době příchodu Pavla Křížkovského' [Moravian musical culture at the time of Křížkovsky's arrival], *Selský sborník*, xlviii (1950), 25

R. Quoika: *Die Musik der Deutschen in Böhmen und Mähren* (Berlin, 1956)

ADRIENNE SIMPSON

Riegger, Wallingford (*b* Albany, Georgia, 29 April 1885; *d* New York, 2 April 1961). American composer.

1. LIFE. Riegger was born into a musical family and started to play both the piano and the violin at an early age. When the family moved to New York in 1900, it was decided that young Riegger should learn the cello so that the family could have its own string quartet. He entered the Institute of Musical Art as a cello student, and there also began his first formal study of com-

1

Wallingford Riegger

position with Percy Goetschius. He was a member of the institute's first graduating class in 1907. A year later he went to Germany for further study of the cello with Robert Haussmann and Anton Hekking, and of composition with Max Bruch and Edgar Stillman-Kelley. In 1910 he made his début as conductor with the Blüthner Orchestra in Berlin.

On returning to the USA, Riegger took a position as cellist with the St Paul (Minnesota) SO, remaining there for three years. In 1911 he married Rose Schramm, and in 1914 he was offered a post as assistant conductor in the Stadttheater of Würzburg. He spent the next few years in Germany, returning to Berlin in 1916–17 to appear again as conductor of the Blüthner Orchestra. In 1917 he returned to the USA to accept a post as cello teacher at Drake University in Iowa. It was at this time that he turned seriously to composition rather than performance or conducting. His first major work, the Piano Trio, was completed in 1920. This was a thoroughly conservative work, but written with the skill of one who had obviously mastered his craft. The Trio won the Paderewski Prize and was published as Riegger's op.1 by the Society for the Publication of American Music. His début was thus not inauspicious, and he enjoyed some success in the next few years with other compositions in a traditional vein, but in 1923 he came to the conclusion that composing in the manner of the past could lead nowhere. Between 1923 and 1926 he composed nothing, devoting his time to teaching and to the serious reconsideration of his musical positions and beliefs. He came to feel that he had not resolved the conflict between the old and the new.

Riegger had returned to New York in 1922 and taught for a short time at the Institute of Musical Art. In the years following he became acquainted with some of the pioneer figures in modern music in America, including Varèse, Ives, Cowell and Ruggles. With them, he became active in the Pan-American Association of Composers, a society for the encouragement and performance of what was then known as 'ultra-modern' music. By this time Riegger had already committed himself to a new style, the result of his three years of self-examination and study. This style was foreshadowed in his Rhapsody for Orchestra op.5, and appeared almost fully realized in the *Study in Sonority* of 1926–7. This work, together with *Dichotomy* (1931–2), served to establish him as a new and distinct voice of originality and power. But performances were few and far between, and for many years Riegger was forced to support himself by doing editorial hack work and making commercial arrangements under a variety of pseudonyms. His composition from 1933 to 1941 was limited to works for the modern dance, in which he had become interested, and for which his music, with its driving and forceful rhythms, was particularly suitable. All of these were flexibly scored, according to available resources, but relied principally on piano and percussion. Among those for whom Riegger wrote were Martha Graham, José Limon, Doris Humphrey, Hanya Holm and most of the leaders of the modern dance movement at that time.

Outside this limited world, Riegger's name was little known. But abruptly, in 1941, he ceased working with and for dancers, and returned to composing chamber music and orchestral works. This was the most productive period of his life; for the next 20 years he continued to compose steadily, and although he could never be called a prolific or facile composer, he had produced 75 works by the time of his death. The works beginning with the First String Quartet (1938–9) began to attract some attention, although Riegger did not create a real stir, or achieve wide recognition, until his Third Symphony of 1946–7. This work was written to a commission from the Alice M. Ditson Fund of Columbia University, the first important commission he had received. The symphony was first performed in 1948, and from that time Riegger received a steady stream of performances and commissions, as well as invitations to teach or lecture.

2. WORKS. Riegger's most important work can perhaps best be described as freely atonal. At no time did he rely on the doctrinaire application of a system or a method. He continued throughout his life to write in several well-differentiated styles, which he described as 'non-dissonant (mostly)', 'impressionist', 'partly dissonant' and 'dissonant'. Although most of his later works were atonal and sharply dissonant, some being written in his own version of dodecaphonic technique, others were more or less tonal and traditional. His strict early training gave him a great and lasting technical assurance. As a rule he wrote slowly, revised extensively, edited his works with care, and felt strongly the need for control and clarity. His achievement was that of combining, especially in his later works, an advanced harmonic and rhythmic idiom with traditional structures. Basically Riegger's music, despite its wealth of invention and the depth of its technical vocabulary, is uncomplicated. It is usually direct and concise. He strove for clarity and logic, and felt that the enlargement of the tonal vocabulary in the 20th century was not a licence to greater freedom for the composer, but on the contrary imposed an ever greater need for discipline. In this sense his use

of established forms acted as an integrating factor binding his work to a tradition from which, at first hearing, it might appear remote.

His independence as a composer was evident from his first mature works, the *Study in Sonority* and *Dichotomy*. The *Study in Sonority*, written for ten violins or any multiple thereof, is a bitingly dissonant work using two invented harmonies more or less as tonic and dominant. *Dichotomy* uses two 'rows', one of 11 and one of ten notes, and jagged, almost brutally percussive rhythms. It owes nothing to Schoenberg, with whose works Riegger was not then familiar. And although in later works, he did indeed use 12-note series, and became, on acquaintance, an enthusiastic admirer of Schoenberg, Riegger's approach to atonality or dodecaphony remained entirely his own, and even his most strictly written 12-note works, such as the First String Quartet of 1938–9, cannot be mistaken for music of the Second Viennese School. Riegger used series when he wished to, normally as sources for motivic material which he could then manipulate in a more or less traditional manner. He also made considerable use of clusters, notably in the Music for Brass Choir op.45 (1948–9), the Nonet for Brass op.49 (1951) and occasionally in vocal works.

Riegger was a skilled contrapuntist, and apart from the many canonic and fugato passages that occur in his work, there are also straightforward traditional forms such as the passacaglia or fugue. Of his non-dissonant works, the Canon and Fugue for Strings op.33 (1941) has a neo-Baroque grandeur that contrasts strongly with the propulsive, dissonant and percussive character of his other works written at about the same time.

Belonging to no school, Riegger pursued his career independently and in relative isolation. He enjoyed no patronage of consequence, and until his last years received neither financial rewards nor honorary distinctions. He accepted a few pupils, but cannot be said to have been highly influential as a teacher. But his music eventually made a significant impression on his contemporaries, and the body of his work constitutes an important expression of originality and maturity in American music.

WORKS
(selective list)

op.   ORCHESTRAL AND LARGE ENSEMBLE
5   Rhapsody, orch, 1926
7   Study in Sonority, 10 vn or any multiple thereof, 1926–7
10   Fantasy and Fugue, orch, org, 1930–31
12   Dichotomy, chamber orch, 1931–2
13   Scherzo, chamber orch, 1932
18b New Dance (Finale only), orch, 1935
33   Canon and Fugue, str, 1941
33a Canon and Fugue, orch, 1941
34   Passacaglia and Fugue, band, 1942
34a Passacaglia and Fugue, orch, 1942
42   Symphony no.3, 1946–7
45   Music for Brass Choir, 10 tpt, 8 hn, 10 trbn, 2 tubas, perc, 1948–9
49   Nonet for Brass, 1951
50   Music for Orchestra, 1951
54   Variations, pf, orch, 1953
56   Suite for Younger Orchestras, 1954
58   Dance Rhythms, orch, 1955
63   Symphony no.4, 1957
68   Festival Overture, 1957
71   Variations, vn, orch, 1959
72   Quintuple Jazz, ens, 1959
73   Sinfonietta, orch, 1959
74   Introduction and Fugue, vc, wind, 1960
75   Duo, pf, orch, 1960

CHAMBER
1   Piano Trio, b, 1919–20
8   Suite, fl, 1929

9   Canons for Woodwinds, fl, ob, cl, bn, 1931
15   Divertissement, fl, harp, vc, 1933
23   Music for Voice and Flute, 1936
30   String Quartet no.1, 1938–9
35   Duos for Three Woodwinds, fl, ob, cl, 1943
39   Sonatina, vn, pf, 1947
43   String Quartet no.2, 1948
47   Piano Quintet, 1951
51   Woodwind Quintet, 1952
53   Concerto, pf, wind qnt, 1952
57   Variations, vn, va, 1956
66   Movement, 2 tpt, trbn, pf, 1957

DANCE
11   Bacchanale, pf duet, 1930
16   Frenetic Rhythms, pf, fl, cl, drums, 1933
17   Evocation, pf duet, 1933
18   New Dance, pf duet, drums, ens, 1935; arrs. of Finale, opp.18a–f
19   Theatre Piece, pf, ens, 1935
20   With my Red Fires, pf, ens, 1936
21   Chronicle, pf, ens, 1936
22   The Cry, pf duet, 1935
24   Candide, pf, drums, ens, 1937
25   Trend, pf, drums, ens, 1937
26   Trojan Incident, pf, drums, ens, 1938
27   Case History, pf, drums, ens, 1937
28   Machine Ballet, pf, orch, 1938
29   Pilgrims' Progress, pf, 1941

OTHER WORKS
4   La belle dame sans merci, 4 solo vv, 8 insts, 1923
32a Eternity (E. Dickinson), SSA, fl, 2 hn, db, 1942
32b From Some Far Shore, SATB, 1946
32c Easter Passacaglia, SATB, org, 1946
44   Who can Revoke (C. R. Harris), SATB, pf, 1951
46   In Certainty of Song, cantata, chorus, chamber orch, 1951
48   Non vincit malitia, 2 antiphonal choruses, 1951

Pf works, songs

Principal publishers: Associated, H. Flammer, Peer

BIBLIOGRAPHY
R. F. Goldman: 'The Music of Wallingford Riegger', *MQ*, xxxvi (1950)
E. Carter: 'Wallingford Riegger', *Bulletin of American Composers Alliance*, ii/1 (1952), 3
H. Cowell: 'A Note on Wallingford Riegger', *Juilliard Review*, ii (1955)
J. B. Schmoll: *An Analytical Study of the Principal Instrumental Compositions of Wallingford Riegger* (diss., Northwestern U., 1955)
R. F. Goldman: 'Wallingford Riegger, Composer and Pedagogue', *The Etude*, lxxiv (1956)
——: 'Wallingford Riegger', *HiFi/Stereo Review*, xx (1968)
D. D. Gatwood jr.: *Wallingford Riegger: a Biography and Analysis of Selected Works* (diss., George Peabody College for Teachers, 1970)
RICHARD FRANKO GOLDMAN

Riegler, Franz Paul [Franz Xaver, François Sav., František Pavel]. *See* RIGLER, FRANZ PAUL.

Riehm, Rolf (*b* Saarbrücken, 15 June 1937). German composer. He studied school music in Frankfurt (1958–61) and composition with Fortner in Freiburg (1961–3). In 1968 he was appointed to teach theory and aural training at the Rheinische Musikhochschule in Cologne, and in 1974 he became professor of composition at the Frankfurt Musikhochschule. With Hans Ulrich Humpert he is a member of the Gruppe 8 of Cologne. His essay 'Was ist moderne Musik?' appears in L. Zenetti's *Heisse (W)Eisen* (Munich, 1966).

WORKS
(selective list)

Zentrifuge, pf, 1961; Finish (Benn), Bar, pf, 1961; Ungebräuchliches, ob, 1964; In einer Landschaft (theatre piece), 1968; Der Seefahrer (stereo radio piece), vv, 1969; Studien, 3 solo vv, actress, eng hn, pf, tape, projections, 1970; Gebräuchliches, a rec, 1972; Leonce, Alban und andere, S, T, Bar, orch, 1972; Der Freie und der Unfreie, pf, 1973; O quam dulce et suave est diligere, chorus, 1974

Riemann, (Karl Wilhelm Julius) Hugo (*b* Gross-Mehlra, nr. Sondershausen, 18 July 1849; *d* Leipzig, 10 July 1919). German musicologist. He was first taught music by his father, Robert, a landowner and civil servant and a talented amateur musician, whose opera *Bianca*

Siffredi was performed in Sondershausen in 1881. His theory instructors were Heinrich Frankenberger, the Sondershausen Kapellmeister, and the pianists August Bartel and Theodor Ratzenberger (a Liszt pupil). He attended the gymnasiums at Sondershausen and Arnstadt, studied classical languages and literature in the Klosterschule at Rossleben and in 1868 went to the University of Berlin to read law, German philology and history. Since he was also in military service, he could not devote himself completely to his studies, but while still in the army he studied philosophy in Tübingen. In his spare time he wrote poetry, as he had done assiduously from the age of nine; only the Franco-Prussian War prevented publication of a two-volume edition of his poems. He fought at Beaumont and Sedan and for five months took part in the siege of Paris, during which he managed to find time to play the piano. He attended many regimental band rehearsals, and it was then that he decided to devote himself to music. In the autumn of 1871 he entered the Leipzig Conservatory and the University of Leipzig, studying harmony with Jadassohn and the piano and composition with Reinecke. In the same year he became acquainted with Oettingen's *Harmoniesystem in dualer Entwickelung*; this book influenced him greatly and he took it upon himself to continue the theoretical reforms suggested by Oettingen. As early as 1872, under the name of Hugibert Ries, he had published articles on musical logic and tonality in the *Neue Zeitschrift für Musik*. He took the doctorate of philosophy at the University of Göttingen with the dissertation *Über das musikalische Hören* (1873). During the years in which he wrote his harmony books Riemann was first a teacher in Bielefeld (1876–8), then lecturer at the University of Leipzig (1878) and then a teacher in Bromberg (where he began his *Musik-Lexikon*). From 1881 to 1890 he taught the piano and theoretical subjects at the Hamburg Conservatory, and, after three months at Sondershausen, he was appointed to the conservatory at Wiesbaden, where he taught for five years. In 1895 he returned to the University of Leipzig and resumed his lectures; in 1901 he was made professor and in 1908 appointed director of the newly founded Collegium Musicum. In 1914 he was made director of the Forschungsinstitut für Musikwissenschaft. He was an honorary member of numerous institutions, including the Accademia di S Cecilia and the Musical Association of London. He was granted an honorary doctorate from the University of Edinburgh in 1899.

Riemann was one of the outstanding music researchers of his time. The underlying goal of his prodigious investigations was a philosophical theory of musical perception, which he hoped to derive from his systematic analyses of the melodic, harmonic and rhythmic elements in musical works.

From the moment I determined to devote myself to the study of music, it was my greatest wish to co-ordinate the advances in musical composition with the most recent discoveries in acoustics and the physiology of the ear.

Riemann contrasted the theory of tonal sensations (*Tonempfindungen*) with that of tonal concepts (*Tonvorstellungen*). His reconstruction of the theory of harmony turned away from the principles of thoroughbass, with its chords based on the interval of the 3rd and its corresponding figures based on the distance of the notes in the chord from the fundamental note. He replaced this theory of fundamental notes, as represented by Sechter and the Viennese school, with a theory of functions, in which function refers to the dependent relationship of a particular harmony to one or several other harmonies. Understood in this way, the tonic triad is dependent on its dominant and subdominant; every chordal structure can thus be traced back to these functional triads and each triad can be represented by one of its constituent pitches or intervals (*Klangvertretung*). This system of functional tonality makes possible every kind of modulation or other alteration of the harmonic function of a chord.

Metre in Riemann's system refers to the differences in position and stress of the individual beats and beat groups (bars), while rhythm refers to the relative duration of notes. Riemann developed counterpoint initially from the theory of harmony as 'harmonic figuration', in which the part-writing is merely harmony composed out, and conversely, harmony merely the accidental result of the part-writing. Later he expanded his notion of counterpoint into a self-contained theory of successive part-invention in polyphonic composition. He was able to see the success of his methods in the works of such famous pupils as Reger and Pfitzner. The individual branches of Riemann's musical theories were gathered into his monumental *Grosse Kompositionslehre*.

The basic categories of music already mentioned, together with the categorical distinctions between theme and motif, motif and phrase, of thematic and non-thematic sections of a composition, form the basis of Riemann's theory of phrasing, or the subdivision of a musical composition. He compared literary punctuation with musical punctuation (phrasing). As with the spoken word, phrasing can give significance to an otherwise indistinct passage: 'incorrect punctuation can render the performance of a musical idea unclear, or even false'. Among those who shared in the widespread contemporary interest shown in the phrasing theory were Bülow and Nietzsche.

Although at first Riemann was chiefly concerned with the systematic development of music theory, his interest in music history later became more apparent:

I think it is the true purpose of [music] historical research to uncover the basic laws common to all ages, which govern all perception and forms of artistic expression.

Although he never became a rigorous, academic historian, he did concern himself with the biographies of the great masters and began to analyse music on the basis of his principles of style, genres and forms, resulting in the ideas under the headings 'Problems in Music History' and 'The Study of Music History'. This led him to the discovery of virtually forgotten periods, musical genres and masters; among his many editions, especially notable is the three-volume collection of symphonies of the Mannheim School in the Denkmäler deutscher Tonkunst in Bayern, and a volume of the selected works of Johann Schobert in the Denkmäler deutscher Tonkunst. Through his efforts he was the first to reawaken public interest in the Mannheim school and the German variation-suite of Schein, and he rediscovered the *Mödlinger Tänze* (1819) of Beethoven. He recognized, in the Johann Schobert group at Mannheim, the creators of ensemble music with keyboard accompaniment. Late in his career, he transcribed the Byzantine notation of the 10th to 15th centuries into modern notation. He was the first to perceive Florence around the year 1300 as the cradle of the instrumentally accompanied art song, and the first to make a stylistic analysis of the works of Dunstable. Riemann's enormous productivity throughout his life is clearly evident in the Festschrift for his 60th birthday, which lists 58 important books and 209 other publications, and original compositions numbering to op.68. His celebrated *Musik-Lexikon* alone, first published in 1882, might well have been the life's work of a less industrious man. He was a true 'Systematiker der Musikwissenschaft'; without neglecting historical research, he directed his view to the overriding problem of order within music. He was not interested in the individual case as such, but rather in discerning its typicality and its place in the entire system. He was a genius of method and one of the most original and creative scholars and teachers of modern musicology.

See also ANALYSIS, §§II, 3, and III, 1, 5, and fig.27.

WRITINGS

HISTORICAL AND THEORETICAL

Über das musikalische Hören (diss., U. of Göttingen, 1873; Leipzig, 1874) [also pubd as *Musikalische Logik* (Leipzig, 1873)]
Die objektive Existenz der Untertöne in der Schallwelle (Berlin, 1877)
Studien zur Geschichte der Notenschrift (Leipzig, 1878)
Die Entwickelung unserer Notenschrift, Sammlung musikalischer Vorträge, xxviii (Leipzig, 1881)
Musik-Lexikon (Leipzig, 1882, 8/1916, 9–11/1919–29, ed. A. Einstein; 12/1959–, ed. W. Gurlitt, C. Dahlhaus and H. H. Eggebrecht; Eng. trans., 1893–7, 4/1908/R)
Die Natur der Harmonik, Sammlung musikalischer Vorträge, xl (Leipzig, 1882)
Der Ausdruck in der Musik, Sammlung musikalischer Vorträge, l (Leipzig, 1883)
Musikalische Dynamik und Agogik: Lehrbuch der musikalischen Phrasierung (Hamburg, 1884)
Opern-Handbuch (Leipzig, 1887, 2/1893/R1979 with suppl. by F. Stieger)
Wie hören wir Musik?: drei Vorträge (Leipzig, 1888, 5/1921)
Katechismus der Musikinstrumente (Instrumentationslehre) (Leipzig, 1888, 8/1923 as *Handbuch der Musikinstrumente*; Eng. trans., 1888)
Katechismus der Musikgeschichte (Leipzig, 1888, 5/1914; Eng. trans., 1892)
Katechismus der Orgel (Orgellehre) (Leipzig, 1888, 2/1901, 6/n.d. as *Handbuch der Orgel*)
Katechismus der Musik (Allgemeine Musiklehre) (Leipzig, 1888, 8/1922; Eng. trans., n.d.)
Grundlinien der Musik-Ästhetik (Wie hören wir Musik?) (Leipzig, 1890, 3/1911 as *Katechismus der Musikästhetik*; Eng. trans., 1895)
Präludien und Studien: gesammelte Aufsätze zur Ästhetik, Theorie und Geschichte der Musik, i (Frankfurt am Main, 1895/R1967), ii–iii (Leipzig, 1900–01/R1967)
'Notenschrift und Notendruck: bibliographisch-typographische Studie', *Röder Festschrift* (Leipzig, 1896)
Geschichte der Musiktheorie im IX.–XIX. Jahrhundert (Leipzig, 1898, 2/1921; Eng. trans., 1962/R1974)
Die Elemente der musikalischen Ästhetik (Berlin, 1900)
'Epochen und Heroen der Musikgeschichte', *Spemanns goldenes Buch der Musik* (Berlin and Stuttgart, 1900)
Geschichte der Musik seit Beethoven (1800–1900) (Berlin and Stuttgart, 1901)
Beethovens Streichquartette (Berlin, 1903)
System der musikalischen Rhythmik und Metrik (Leipzig, 1903)
Handbuch der Musikgeschichte, i/1 (Leipzig, 1904, 2/1919, 3/1923), i/2 (Leipzig, 1905, 2/1920), ii/1 (Leipzig, 1907, 2/1920), ii/2, ed. A. Einstein (Leipzig, 1912, 3/1921), ii/3, ed. A. Einstein (Leipzig, 1913, 2/1922)
Das Problem des harmonischen Dualismus: ein Beitrag zur Ästhetik der Musik (Leipzig, 1905)
'Verloren gegangene Selbstverständlichkeiten der Musik des 15. und 16. Jahrhunderts', *Musikalisches Magazin*, xvii (Langensalza, 1907)
Kleines Handbuch der Musikgeschichte mit Periodisierung nach Stilprinzipien und Formen (Leipzig, 1908, 7/1947)
Grundriss der Musikwissenschaft (Leipzig, 1908, 4/1928, ed. J. Wolf)
Die byzantinische Notenschrift im 10. bis 15. Jahrhundert (Leipzig, 1909)
'Kompendium der Notenschriftkunde', *Kirchenmusik*, ed. K. Weinmann, iv–v (Regensburg, 1910)
Musikgeschichte in Beispielen, 3 vols. (Leipzig, 1911–12, 2–4/1921–9, ed. A. Schering)
Neue Beiträge zur Lösung der Probleme der byzantinischen Notenschrift (Leipzig, 1915)
Folkloristische Tonalitätsstudien, i (Leipzig, 1916)

L. van Beethovens sämtliche Klaviersolosonaten: ästhetische und formal-technische Analyse (Berlin, 1918–19, 4/1920)
'Kurze Erklärung der musikalischen Kunstausdrücke' [completed by R. Raillard] and 'Kurzgefasste Harmonielehre und Tabelle zur Musikgeschichte', *Musik-Taschenbuch für den täglichen Gebrauch* (Leipzig, n.d.)

PRACTICAL AND PEDAGOGICAL

Vademecum für den ersten Klavierunterricht, op.24 (Leipzig, 1876)
Musikalische Syntaxis: Grundriss einer harmonischen Satzbildungslehre (Leipzig, 1877/R1971)
Die Hilfsmittel der Modulation (Berlin, 1877)
Skizze einer neuen Methode der Harmonielehre (Leipzig, 1880, 2/1887 as *Handbuch der Harmonielehre*, 5/1912)
Elementar-Musiklehre (Hamburg, 1883)
Neue Schule der Melodik: Entwurf einer Lehre des Kontrapunkts nach einer neuen Methode (Hamburg, 1883)
Vergleichende theoretisch-praktische Klavier-Schule (Hamburg, 1883, 2/1890)
Systematische Modulationslehre als Grundlage der musikalischen Formenlehre (Hamburg, 1887)
Lehrbuch des einfachen, doppelten und imitierenden Kontrapunkts (Leipzig, 1888, 3/1915; Eng. trans., 1904)
Katechismus des Klavierspiels (Leipzig, 1888, 7/1922; Eng. trans., 1892)
Katechismus der Kompositionslehre (Musikalische Formenlehre) (Leipzig, 1889, 3/1905 as *Grundriss der Kompositionslehre*; Eng. trans., n.d.)
Katechismus des Generalbass-Spiels (Harmonie-Übungen am Klavier) (Leipzig, 1889, 2/1903)
Katechismus des Musik-Diktats (Systematische Gehörsbildung) (Leipzig, 1889, 2/1904 as *Handbuch des Musikdiktats*, 6/1923)
Katechismus der Harmonie- und Modulationslehre (Leipzig, 1890, 9/1923–4 as *Handbuch der Harmonielehre*)
with C. Fuchs: *Katechismus der Phrasierung (Praktische Anleitung zum Phrasieren)* (Leipzig, 1890, 2/1900 as *Vademecum der Phrasierung*, 8/1912 as *Handbuch der Phrasierung*)
Katechismus der Fugen-Komposition (Leipzig, 1890–94, 2/1906 as *Handbuch der Fugen-Komposition*; Eng. trans., 1925) [J. S. Bach analyses]
Katechismus der Gesangskomposition (Leipzig, 1891, 3/1923 as *Handbuch der Gesangskomposition*)
Vereinfachte Harmonielehre oder die Lehre von den tonalen Funktionen der Akkorde (London and New York, 1893, 2/1903; Eng. trans., 1896)
Anleitung zum Partiturspiel (Leipzig, 1902; Eng. trans., 1903, 2/1905)
Katechismus der Orchestrierung (Anleitung zum Instrumentieren) (Leipzig, 1902, 4/1923 as *Handbuch der Orchestrierung*; Eng. trans., 1903)
Grosse Kompositionslehre, i: *Der homophone Satz* (Berlin and Stuttgart, 1902, 2/1912); ii: *Der polyphone Satz* (Berlin and Stuttgart, 1903, 2/1912); iii: *Der Orchestersatz und der dramatische Gesangstil* (Berlin and Stuttgart, 1913)
Elementar-Schulbuch der Harmonielehre (Leipzig, 1906, 5/1918)
Normal-Klavierschule für Anfänger (Leipzig, 1906)

BIBLIOGRAPHY

RiemannL 11, 12
Riemann-Festschrift (Leipzig, 1909) [with complete list of writings pubd to 1909]
E. Kurth: *Die Voraussetzungen der theoretischen Harmonik* (Berne, 1913)
'Hugo Riemann zum 70. Geburtstag', *ZMw*, i (1918–19), 569–628 [incl. essays on Riemann's work by W. Altmann, G. Becking, A. Einstein, W. Gurlitt, R. Steglich]
H. Grabner: *Die Funktionstheorie Hugo Riemanns und ihre Bedeutung für die praktische Analyse* (Munich, 1923)
F. Blume: 'Hermann Abert und die Musikwissenschaft', *Gedenkschrift für Hermann Abert* (Halle, 1928), 18ff
W. Gurlitt: 'Aus den Briefen Max Regers an Hugo Riemann', *JbMP 1936*, 68
H. L. Denecke: *Die Kompositionslehre Hugo Riemanns* (diss., U. of Kiel, 1937)
G. Sievers: *Die Grundlagen Hugo Riemanns bei Max Reger* (diss., U. of Hamburg, 1949; Wiesbaden, 1967)
W. Gurlitt: 'Hugo Riemann: 1849–1919', *Abhandlungen der Akademie der Wissenschaft der Literatur Mainz*, xxv (Wiesbaden, 1951)
G. Wienke: *Voraussetzungen der 'musikalischen Logik' bei Hugo Riemann: Studien zur Musikästhetik in der 2. Hälfte des 19. Jahrhunderts* (diss., U. of Freiburg, 1952)
H. C. Wolff: 'Hugo Riemann: der Begründer der systematischen Musikbetrachtung', *Festschrift Max Schneider* (Leipzig, 1955), 265
H. Federhofer: 'Die Funktionstheorie Hugo Riemanns und die Schichtenlehre Heinrich Schenkers', *Kongressbericht: Wien Mozartjahr 1956*, 183
W. Kahl: 'Der "obscure" Riemann: ein Brief Fr. Chrysanders (1876 an

H. Deiters)', *Studien zur Musikgeschichte des Rheinlands: Festschrift zum 80. Geburtstag von Ludwig Schiedermair* (Cologne, 1956), 54

C. Dahlhaus: 'Untersuchen über die Entstehung der harmonischen Tonalität', *Saarbrücker Studien zur Musikwissenschaft*, ii (Kassel, 1967)

P. Rummenhöller: *Musiktheoretisches Denken im 19. Jahrhundert: Versuch einer Interpretation erkenntnistheoretischer Zeugnisse in der Musiktheorie* (Regensburg, 1967)

R. Heinz: *Geschichtsbegriff und Wissenschaftscharakter der Musikwissenschaft in der zweiten Hälfte des 19. Jahrhunderts: philosophische Aspekte einer Wissenschaftsentwicklung* (Regensburg, 1968)

W. C. Mickelsen: *Hugo Riemann's History of Harmonic Theory with a Translation of Harmonielehre* (diss., Indiana U., 1971)

W. Seidel: *Über Rhythmustheorien der Neuzeit* (Berne and Munich, 1975)

MARK HOFFMAN

Riemann, Jacob. *See* RICHMANN, JACOB.

Riemenschneider, (Charles) Albert (*b* Berea, Ohio, 31 Aug 1878; *d* Akron, Ohio, 20 July 1950). American organist, conductor, scholar and librarian. His father Karl H. Riemenschneider, president from 1893 to 1908 of the Methodist Episcopal Deutsches Wallace Kollegium in Berea, first taught him music, and he was a piano, organ and theory pupil of James H. Rogers of Cleveland (1896–1902). He became piano and organ instructor at the Kollegium (1896) and director of its music department (1897). He subsequently studied the piano with Hugo Reinhold and composition with Robert Fuchs in Vienna (1902–3), the organ with Charles Clemens in Cleveland (1903) and with Alexander Guilmant, and composition with Widor in Paris in 1904–5 and five successive summer sessions. In Paris Riemenschneider developed lifelong friendships with Dupré and Schweitzer. Meanwhile he continued his work at the Kollegium, which in 1913 was amalgamated with Baldwin University to form the Baldwin–Wallace College; their music departments merged to form the Baldwin–Wallace College Conservatory of Music, with Riemenschneider continuing as director until his retirement in 1947. In 1933, emulating the Bach Festivals in Bethlehem, Pennsylvania, he established the annual Baldwin–Wallace College Bach Festival, whose programmes included all Bach's major choral works in four-year cycles. He was president of the Ohio Music Teachers' Association (1930–31) and the Music Teachers' National Association (1933), and in 1949 served as acting president of Baldwin–Wallace College. He received an honorary DMus degree from the Sherwood School of Music in Chicago in 1939.

In 1951 Riemenschneider's Bach collection, begun in the 1920s, was presented to the college as the Emilie and Karl Riemenschneider Memorial Bach Library. The Riemenschneider Bach Institute, founded in 1969 to administer the library, publishes a quarterly journal, *Bach*, and sponsors a biannual symposium–concert series. Riemenschneider's publications include an essay on Bach's use of the flute, and editions of Bach's *Orgelbüchlein*, *Clavier-Übung* part iii, organ chorales and *371 Harmonized Chorales and 69 Chorale Melodies with Figured Bass* (New York, 1941).

RODNEY H. MILL

Riemenschneider, Johann Gottfried. *See* RIEMSCHNEIDER, JOHANN GOTTFRIED.

Riemer, Otto (*b* Badeleben, 2 Sept 1902; *d* Waibstadt, 26 June 1977). German writer on music. After a classical education in Magdeburg, he went to the universities of Marburg, Leipzig and Halle from 1921. He studied musicology with Stephani, Abert, Blume, Schering and Moser, with philosophy and education as secondary subjects. He received his doctorate in Halle in 1927 with a dissertation on Erhard Bodenschatz. He then worked as a music critic, first in Görlitz (1929–33), later in Magdeburg (1933–43) and Heidelberg (1949–72). At the same time he taught at the Volkshochschulen in Görlitz and Magdeburg. In his many articles, mostly in *Musica* (from 1947), he wrote chiefly about 18th- and 19th-century, as well as contemporary, music.

WRITINGS

Erhard Bodenschatz und sein Florilegium Portense (diss., U. of Halle, 1927; Leipzig, 1928)

'Heinrich Grimm: ein mitteldeutscher Musiker', *Festschrift Arnold Schering* (Berlin, 1937), 180

Musik und Musiker in Magdeburg (Magdeburg, 1937)

Chorklang im Zeitgeist: Geschichte des Heidelberger Bachvereins (Heidelberg, 1955)

Einführung in die Geschichte der Musikerziehung (Wilhelmshaven, 1970)

HANS HEINRICH EGGEBRECHT

Riemschneider [Riemenschneider], Johann Gottfried (*fl* 1720–40). German bass and composer. He was the son of Gebhard Riemenschneider (1657–1701), Kantor of the Marienkirche at Halle, and is said to have been a schoolfellow of Handel's. He enjoyed some success at Hamburg, in concerts and operas, from about 1720, and in 1726 sang there with his brother Gebhard Julius, also a bass, in Keiser's *Der lächerliche Printz Jodelet*. In spring 1729 Handel engaged him for the following London season at a salary of £300, the lowest in the company. He made his début at the King's Theatre on 2 December as Clodomiro in *Lotario*, and sang in a revival of *Giulio Cesare* (Achilla) on 17 January 1730, the new opera *Partenope* (Ormonte) on 24 February and the pasticcio *Ormisda* on 4 April. According to Rolli his voice was 'more of a natural contralto than a bass. He sings sweetly in his throat and nose, pronounces Italian in the Teutonic manner, acts like a sucking-pig, and looks more like a valet than anything'. The fact that Handel gave him three arias in *Lotario*, two (of the original three) in *Giulio Cesare* and only one in *Partenope* suggests no great confidence in his powers. His voice was a high baritone with a compass of *A* to *g'*. In 1730 Riemschneider returned to Hamburg, where he was later appointed Kantor and musical director at the cathedral; he held those posts until his death. An oratorio by him was performed there on Christmas Day 1737.

WINTON DEAN

Riemsdijk, Johan Cornelis Marius van (*b* Maastricht, 16 Dec 1841; *d* Utrecht, 30 June 1895). Dutch music scholar. Of noble birth (*jonkheer*), a doctor of law and by profession the chief officer of the state railways, he was also an active and enthusiastic amateur musician. He studied the violin with J. H. Kufferath in Utrecht (from 1854) and later with Léonard at the conservatory in Brussels and with Bargheer in Detmold. From 1860 he played in the municipal orchestra of Utrecht, where he came to appreciate the music of Brahms, whose influence is evident in his Piano Variations in B minor (1882). As board member of Utrecht's music school and of its section of the Maatschappij tot Bevordering der Toonkunst, he was an important figure in the city's musical life. He also conducted an *a cappella* choir which performed early Netherlands polyphony. A board member of the Vereeniging voor Nederlandsche Muziekgeschiedenis from 1880 onwards, he was in charge of many of its editions; among the most significant of his studies is the work on old Dutch folksong and its most authoritative source, Valerius's *Gedenck-clanck* (Haarlem, 1626[14]) which he wrote in collaboration with A. D. Loman and J. P. N. Land.

WRITINGS
Het Stadsmuziekcollege te Utrecht 1631–1881 (Utrecht, 1881)
J. J. H. Verhulst (Haarlem, 1886)
'De twee eerste musyckboekskens van Tielman Susato', *TVNM*, iii (1888)
Articles on historical concerts in Brussels, on Sweelinck, Reinken and Dutch folksongs, in *TVNM*

EDITIONS
Oud-nederlandsche danswijzen, UVNM, x (1882)
J. A. Reinken: Hortus musicus, UVNM, xiii (1886)
24 liederen uit de 15e en 16e eeuw met geestelijken en wereldlijken tekst, UVNM, xvi (1890)
with A. D. Loman: *Oud-nederlandsche liederen uit den 'Nederlandtschen Gedenck-clanck'* (Amsterdam, 1893)
with D. de Lange and G. Kalff: *Nederlandsch volksliederenboek* (Amsterdam, 1897)

BIBLIOGRAPHY
H. Viotta, ed.: 'Riemsdijk, Johan Cornelis Marius van', *Lexicon der toonkunst*, (Amsterdam, 1881–5)
J. D. C. van Dokkum: *Honderd jaar muziekleven in Nederland 1829–1929* (Amsterdam, 1929)

JAN TEN BOKUM

Riepel [Ipleer, Leiper, Perile], **Joseph** (*b* Hörschlag, Upper Austria, 22 Jan 1709; *d* Regensburg, 23 Oct 1782). Austrian theorist, composer and violinist. He attended the Lateinschulen in Linz and Graz, and studied philosophy at the University of Graz. He entered music late, about 1740, and was largely self-taught while living in Dresden (1740–45) and Poland. During his last 30 years he held various posts as a violinist, composer and music director in the chapel of the Count of Thurn and Taxis at Regensburg.

Riepel's *Anfangsgründe*, of which five treatises were published between 1752 and 1768, are his most important contributions to the theory of composition (see Twittenhoff, pp.47–115, for a summary of Riepel's extant theoretical works). His concern with teaching a student how to compose lends the works a strong didactic flavour, strengthened by his colloquial style of writing, the many topical references and the Fuxian dialogue between master and pupil. Riepel's method is based largely upon the *ars combinatoria*, which deals with the number of arrangements (combinations and permutations) possible among a given number of factors (this method had been used earlier by Mersenne, Kircher, Prinz and Ziegler). A rubric in the *Grundregeln* table of contents explains the approach: 'The unique *ars permutatoria*, by which one can invent many more than 99 themes in one day, is at least 99 times more healthy for musical composition than the above-mentioned mathematical speculations' (i.e. measurements, ratios etc). The minuet and symphony are used as basic formats; for Riepel the composition of a minuet was little different from that of an aria or symphony. The eight-bar section, with its component two- or four-bar phrases, is taken as a norm. Phrase syntax is examined closely, with many examples of irregular and extended structure. In both the minuet and symphony models, many alternative arrangements of melodic figures, cadences and harmonic layouts are given, each with specific comments on coherence and taste. Of particular interest are Riedel's key schemes in *Grundregeln*: (*i*) a circular

system of keys, as in earlier 18th-century concertos and fugues, with charts and examples covering every possible arrangement of keys closely related to C (pp.111–27); and (*ii*) a tonic–dominant modulation leading to a mediant (or submediant)–tonic one, which later became standard in Classical music (pp.65ff).

Riepel represents a stylistic turning-point: his melodic material is typical of the earlier 18th century, with courtly minuets and Italian sinfonias, but his sytematic treatment points to the structural clarity and symmetry of the later 18th century. His work received favourable comment from Hiller, Gerber, Schubart, Choron and Fétis, and had a strong influence on Koch, the most important theorist of the later 18th century; his pupils included J. C. Vogel, J. C. Schubarth, F. F. Cavallo, J. C. Kaffka, F. X. Pokorny, P. C. Steiglehner and Sebastian Prixner.

Riepel's extant compositions include three violin concertos with string quartet accompaniment (Ulm, n.d.), and symphonies, canons, divertimentos and other works in manuscript (mostly in *D-Rtt*; for a thematic catalogue see Merkl).

See also ANALYSIS, §II, 2

THEORETICAL WORKS
Anfangsgründe zur musikalischen Setzkunst, nicht zwar nach altmathematischer Einbildungsart der Zirkel-Harmonisten, sondern durchgehends mit sichtbaren Exempeln abgefasset, i: *De rhythmopoeia oder Von der Taktordnung* (Regensburg and Vienna, 1752, 2/1754); ii: *Grundregeln der Tonordnung insgemein* (Frankfurt and Leipzig, 1755); iii: *Gründliche Erklärung der Tonordnung insbesondere, zugleich aber für die mehresten Organisten insgemein* (Frankfurt and Leipzig, 1757); iv: *Erläuterung der betrüglichen Tonordnung* (Augsburg, 1765); v: *Unentbehrliche Anmerkungen zum Kontrapunkt* (Regensburg, 1768)
Harmonisches Silbenmass, Dichtern melodischer Werke gewidmet und angehenden Singkomponisten zur Einsicht mit platten Beispielen gesprächweise abgefasst, i–ii (Regensburg, 1776); iii (MS, *D-Bds*)
Basschlüssel, das ist Anleitung für Anfänger und Liebhaber der Setzkunst, ed. J. C. Schubarth (Regensburg, 1786)
Writings on counterpoint and fugue, *D-Bds*, and on canon, lost

BIBLIOGRAPHY
FétisB; *GerberL*; *GerberNL*
W. Twittenhoff: *Die musiktheoretischen Schriften Joseph Riepels* (Berlin, 1935/*R*1971)
F. Schwarzmaier: *Die Takt- und Tonordnung Joseph Riepels* (Wolfenbüttel, 1936)
J. Merkl: *Joseph Riepel als Komponist* (Kallmünz, 1937) [incl. thematic catalogue]
A. Feil: *Satztechnische Fragen in den Kompositionslehren von F. E. Niedt, J. Riepel, und H. Chr. Koch* (Heidelberg, 1955)
P. Benary: *Die deutsche Kompositionslehre des 18. Jahrhunderts* (Leipzig, 1961)
F. Ritzel: *Die Entwicklung der 'Sonatenform' im musiktheoretischen Schrifttum des 18. und 19. Jahrhunderts* (Wiesbaden, 1968)
L. G. Ratner: 'Ars combinatoria', *Studies in Eighteenth-century Music: a Tribute to Karl Geiringer* (New York and London, 1970), 343

LEONARD G. RATNER

Riepp, Karl Joseph (*b* Eldern, Ottobeuren, 24 Jan 1710; *d* Dijon, 5 May 1775). German organ builder. He probably learnt the craft with J. G. Hofer of Ottobeuren (*d* 1731). In 1732 he went to Strasbourg, where he was refused work by Andreas Silbermann; later he lived in Dôle and from 1742 or 1743 in Dijon. In 1747 he and his brother Rupert (*b* 1711; *d* between 1747 and 1750), who worked with him, took French citizenship. Karl Joseph was well known to Bédos de Celles, J. A. Silbermann and F.-H. Clicquot. Besides his organ-building interests he had a profitable wine business. His organs include those in Sainte Chapelle, Dijon (1741; four manuals, 36 stops); Dijon Cathedral (1743; four manuals, 44 stops); Autun Cathedral (1745–8; four manuals, 34 stops); Notre Dame, Beaune (1754–6; four manuals, 35 stops); Ottobeuren Abbey (two organs, both extant: 1757–66; two manuals, 27 stops, and four manuals, 48½ stops); Notre Dame, Dijon (1759–60); Salem Abbey (three organs: 1766–74; three manuals, c46 stops, three manuals, c45 stops, and two manuals, c19 stops; cases extant). Riepp's French organs correspond closely to the Parisian type, following Clicquot's style (rather than that of Thierry) in their late Classical form, which includes additional Bombardes, Trumpets, Clairons and Cornets. In the organs he built in Upper Swabia, Riepp added a number of stops of German origin, such as Quintaden, Viola da gamba, Salicional, Querflöte, Blockflöte, Waldflöte and Schalmei, and made the Pedal complete (in German fashion), basing it on 16′ pitch and including mixtures and soft stops. His mixtures, like those of Andreas Silbermann, Bédos de Celles and F.-H. Clicquot, have low dispositions. Riepp's organs at Ottobeuren are among the best-preserved of the 18th century, and their materials, workmanship and tonal qualities are outstanding. Bédos de Celles had great respect for Riepp, and especially praised his 'probité' and 'capacité'. In 1775 Riepp's business passed to the control of his nephew and pupil Joseph Rabiny (1732–1813); Rabiny was joined in 1787 by his son-in-law François Callinet (1754–1820), father of Joseph (1795–1857) and Claude Ignace Callinet (1803–74). Another of Riepp's pupils was Johann Nepomuk Holzhay.

BIBLIOGRAPHY
H. Klotz: Über die Orgelkunst der Gotik, der Renaissance und des Barock (Kassel, 1934, 2/1974), 274ff, 320ff, 345ff, 356ff
N. Dufourcq: Documents inédits relatifs à l'orgue français, ii (Paris, 1935), 425ff
H. Meyer: Karl Joseph Riepp, der Orgelbauer von Ottobeuren (Kassel, 1938)
J. Wörsching: Der Orgelbauer Karl Riepp (Mainz, 1940)
W. Supper: 'Riepp', MGG
P. Meyer-Siat: 'Die Orgelbauerfamilie Callinet', Acta organologica, ii (1968), 82

HANS KLOTZ

Ries. German family of musicians.

(1) **Johann Ries** (b Bensheim am Rhein, 1723; d Cologne, 1784). Instrumentalist. He was appointed court trumpeter to the Elector of Cologne at Bonn on 2 May 1747 with a salary of 192 thaler, and as a violinist to the court chapel on 5 March 1754.

(2) **Anna Maria Ries** (b Bonn, c1745; d after 1794). Singer, daughter of (1) Johann Ries. She was appointed soprano at the electoral court at Bonn on 27 April 1764. In 1774 she married Ferdinand Drewer, a violinist in the court orchestra, and they remained in Bonn until 1794, when the elector's establishment was dissolved by the French.

(3) **Franz (Anton) Ries** (b Bonn, 10 Nov 1755; d Godesberg, 1 Nov 1846). Violinist, son of (1) Johann Ries. He was a child prodigy on the violin, being taught by J. P. Salomon, and was able to take his father's place in the orchestra at the age of 11. In 1779 he visited Vienna, enjoying a great success as a solo violinist and quartet player. Rather than settle there, he chose to stay at Bonn on a poor salary. There he taught Beethoven and remained very close to the family, especially during the difficult years after the death of Beethoven's mother. He received an appointment from Elector Maximilian on 2 May 1779.

When the French dissolved the electoral court in 1794, Franz Anton remained in Bonn. He was promised a post in the court after the invasion, but when that came to nothing he was obliged to earn a meagre living from various minor positions and some violin teaching. He received the Order of the Red Eagle and an honorary doctorate from Bonn University. He was present at the unveiling of Beethoven's statue in 1845. He had five daughters and five sons. Three of his sons are noted below; his others were Jean Batist and Franz Joseph, the latter a piano maker in Vienna from about 1820.

(4) **Ferdinand Ries** (b Bonn, baptized 28 Nov 1784; d Frankfurt am Main, 13 Jan 1838). Pianist, composer and copyist, eldest son of (3) Franz (Anton) Ries and the most celebrated member of the family. He was taught the piano and the violin by his father and the cello by B. H. Romberg from the age of five. Because of the dissolution of the electoral court in 1794 Ferdinand failed to receive a promised position in the orchestra. Instead he spent most of the next seven years at home studying with his father, apart from a fruitless nine-month period in Arnsberg about 1797 studying with a man to whom he ended up teaching the violin. In 1801 he studied in Munich with Peter von Winter for a short time, earning money by copying music at about 3d. a sheet. With this he kept himself, paid his fees and saved enough to go to Vienna in October of that year, armed with a letter of introduction from Franz Anton. Beethoven received his old teacher's son well, and gave him much help.

The next three years were spent in Vienna studying with Beethoven and often acting as his secretary and copyist. Beethoven taught him the piano, but sent him to Albrechtsberger for composition. Beethoven also secured him an appointment as pianist to Count Browne in Baden in 1802, and with Prince Lichnowsky for the summer of 1805. Ferdinand made his début as Beethoven's pupil on 1 August 1804 at the Augarten. He performed Beethoven's C minor Concerto with his own cadenza, playing a most difficult passage against Beethoven's advice and, to his master's delight, succeeding. When he became liable for conscription into the French army in September 1805, being a citizen of Bonn, he returned to Koblenz by way of Prague, Dresden and Leipzig. Because he had lost an eye (in childhood, through smallpox), he was rejected, so he went on to Paris, where he lived in poor circumstances for two years. On 27 August 1808, described as 'musical composer from Bonn', he arrived in Vienna, where a misunderstanding over the post of Kapellmeister to Jérôme Buonaparte, King of Westphalia, caused a temporary rift with Beethoven. He stayed in Vienna for nearly a year.

For four years from summer 1809, Ries seems to have been constantly on tour; first to Kassel, then to Hamburg, Copenhagen and Stockholm, where he was in September 1810. This was a lucrative period. In St Petersburg he renewed his acquaintance with Bernhard Romberg, and together they toured Russia extensively. By February 1813 he was back in Stockholm, where he was made a member of the Swedish Royal Academy of Music. About the end of April he arrived in London, where he stayed for 11 years. There he met Sir George Smart and his father's aging teacher J. P. Salomon, who introduced him to the Philharmonic Concerts. He made his first appearance there on 14 March 1814, and his works appeared frequently in the programme. He married, on 25 July 1814, 'an English lady of great merit and possessing many personal charms'; this was Harriet Mangean (1796–1863). The 'Memoir of Ferdinand Ries' in the *Harmonicon* expressed the high regard in which London audiences held him as a pianist:

> Mr. Ries is justly celebrated as one of the finest piano-performers of the present day. His hand is powerful, and his execution is certain, – often surprising. But his playing is most distinguished from that of all others by its romantic wildness. . . . He produces an effect upon those who enter his style, which can only be compared to that arising from the most unexpected combinations and transitions of the Aeolian harp.

Beethoven is reported to have made the most damaging remark about him ('he imitates me too much'), which, though probably apocryphal, is only partly fair.

By 1824 Ferdinand had made enough money to retire, and he left London for his native Rhineland, living for nearly three years in Godesberg before moving to Frankfurt am Main. He did much for the Lower Rhine Music Festivals, composing several works and conducting for a number of years. He was appointed head of the town orchestra and the Singakademie of Aachen in 1834. He collaborated with F. G. Wegeler in *Biographische Notizen über Ludwig van Beethoven* (Koblenz, 1838, rev. 3/1906 by A. C. Kalischer), one of the most important early biographies of Beethoven.

WORKS
(woo numbers from Hill, 1977)

PIANO SOLO

14 sonatas: 2 as op.1; 2 as op.5 'Sonatinas'; 2 as op.9; 2 as op.11; op.26 'L'infortunée'; op.45; op.114; op.141; op.176; woo11 (1805)
39 rondos: op.43 'Que veut-il dire?'; op.50, on a Russian sailor's song; op.54 no.2; 2 as op.64; op.67 no.1, on Russian themes, no.2, on an Irish melody; op.78 no.2, with march; op.84 no.1, on Bishop's 'When the wind blows', no.3, on a Hibernian air, no.4, on 'The Emerald Isle'; op.85 no.2, on Irish themes; op.88 no.1, on Boieldieu's 'Gentille Annette', no.2, on Rossini's 'Una voce poco fa', no.3, on Mozart's 'Al bascia si faccia onore'
Op.98 no.1, on Rossini's 'Di piacer mi balza il cor', no.2, on Mozart's 'Mon ami bouvons'; op.102 no.1, on 'O for an & twenty, Tam', no.2, on 'O Kenmures on and awa, Willie', no.3, on 'There grows a bonnie briar bush'; op.104 no.1, on the Polacca from Rossini's Tancredi, no.2, on Bishop's 'As it fell upon a day', no.3, on Bishop's 'When in disgrace'; op.106 no.1, on 'When love was a child', no.2, no.3 'Bacchanale in the Form of a Rondo'; op.122 'élégant'; op.127 no.1, on 'Comin' thro' the rye', no.2, on Horsley's 'When shall we three meet again'
Op.139; op.153 no.1, on Haydn's Mermaid Song, no.2, on the Barcarole from Auber's Masaniello, no.3, on the Market Chorus from Auber's La muette di Portici; op.158 no.1, no.2 'alla tedesca'; op.161; op.182 no.1, on 'Sehnsucht nach der Heimat', no.2, on 'Kühreihen der Oberländer'; op 184 'alla zingaresco'
3 rondolettos: op.54 no.1; op.78 no.1; op.127 no.3 ('Rondino')
49 variation sets: op.15, on a Hungarian theme; op.33 no.1, on a theme by Méhul, no.2, on a Cossack song, no.3, on a theme by Beethoven; op.39, on a Russian theme; op.40 no.1, on a Cossack dance, no.2, on a Russian air, no.3, on a German song; op.46, on a theme by Méhul; op.51, on Mozart's 'Non più andrai'; op.56, on an air of Little Russia; op.65 no.1, on a theme by Bishop, no.2, on Braham's 'Said a smile', no.3 on Bishop's 'Stay, prithee'
Op.66 no.1, on Mozart's 'Amanti costanti', no.2, on the French air 'Malbrouk', no.3, on Mazzinghi's ''Tis merry'; op.73 no.1, on a Russian air, no.2, on a Basque air; op.75, on a Rhenish song; op.82 no.1, on an air from Paer's Griselda, no.2, on a Venetian air, no.3, on a French air; op.96 no.1, on the March from Tancredi, no.2, on Bishop's 'Grindoff et Claudine', no.3, on Bishop's 'The Dashing White Sergeant', no.4, on Braham's 'Nelson'; op.101 no.1, on 'We're a noddin' ', no.2, on 'O Logie, o Buchan, no.3, on 'O saw ye my father'
Op.105 no.1, on 'La sentinelle', no.2, on 'The old highland laddie', no.3, on Bishop's 'When meteor lights', no.4, on a Moldavian air; op.118 no.1, on Blangini's 'Il faut partir', no.2, on Welsh's 'The night is rainy', no.3, on Shield's 'The Streamlet'; op.147 no.1, on 'Vive Henry IV', no.2, on a German air; op.149 no.1, on a Danish song, no.2, on a German song; op.159 no.1, on a chorus from Die Räuberbraut, no.2, on an Austrian air, no.3 'du vieux capitaine'
Op.165 no.1, on C. Fischer's 'The Melting Snow', no.2, on a Rhenish peasant air; op.185 no.1, on a theme from Les Huguenots; woo49, on the Tarantella romana (1833); woo58, on Handel's Staffordshire Conservative Election Song (1835); woo64, on a theme from Liska (1836); woo91, on an Austrian song
15 fantasias: 2 as op.77, both on themes from Figaro; op.85 no.1, on 2 Irish airs, pf/harp; op.92 no.1, on Bishop's 'And has she then failed',

no.2, on Bishop's 'Come live with me'; op.97 'à la mode'; op.109, after Schiller's Resignation; op.121, on themes from Rossini's Zelmira; op.131, on themes from Der Freischütz; op.134 no.1, on themes from Rossini's Semiramide, no.2, on 'The wealth of the cottage'; op.163 on 'La parisienne'; op.185 no.2, on themes from Les Huguenots; woo87, ? for pf
22 waltzes: 8 as woo4 (1800); 6 (with an écossaise), pf/small orch as woo18 (1810); 5 as woo21 (1811–13); 2 as woo32 (1823); woo33 (1823)
4 marches: op.53 no.3, pf/harp/military band; 2 as op.61, no.2 for pf/pf 4 hands; op.78 no.2, with rondo
Other: 6 Exercises, op.31; The Dream, op.49; 12 Trifles, op.58; 40 Preludes, op.60; 2 polonaises, op.84 no.2, op.158 no.3, from Die Räuberbraut; 2 Allegri di bravura, op.99; Allegro eroica, op.103; 3 divertimenti, opp.117, 130, 137 'Grand Military Divertimento'; 15 easy pieces, op.124; Die Räuberbraut, ballet music, arr. pf, op.168; Kölner Carnavalstanz, op.178; Prelude woo41 (1831); 3 untitled pieces, woo47 (1833), woo67 (1837), woo90 (1837); Cotillon, woo68, pf/? orch ad lib; 6 Studies, woo78

PIANO FOUR HANDS

3 sonatas, op.6 'Sonatina', op.47, op.160
11 variation sets: op.14, on a Russian theme; op.108 no.1, on 'Flow on, thou shining river', no.2, on 'Those evening bells'; op.136, no.1, on 'Oft in the stilly night', no.2, on 'Hark, the vesper hymn is stealing'; op.148, no.1, on the March from Mayseder's Aline, no.2, on a Rhenish carnival air; op.155, no.1, on a German dance, no.2, on a German song, no.3, on an air from Die Räuberbraut, woo28, on Rossini's 'Di tanti palpiti' (1820)
5 polonaises, opp.41, 93, 138, 140, 175
11 marches: 3 as op.4; 3 as op.12; 3 as op.22; op.53 no.1 'Grand Triumphal March', no.2 'The Return of the Troops', pf/military band/orch

PIANO AND ONE INSTRUMENT

For 2 pf: Grand Introduction and Rondo, op.135
For harp, pf or 2 pf: Rondo, op.57; Rondo and Mazurka, op.79
For vn, pf: 28 sonatas, 2 as op.3, 2 as op.8, op.10, 3 as op.16 [vn/fl], op.18, op.19, 3 as op.30, 3 as op.38, 2 as op.59 [vn/fl], op.69, op.71, 2 as op.81, op.83, 3 as op.86 [vn/fl], woo5 (1800), woo7 (1804); 2 variation sets, op.111, on a fandango, woo3 (1799)
For vc, pf: 4 sonatas, opp.20, 21, 125 [all vc/vn], woo2 (1799); Variations on Russian airs, op.72 [vc/vn]; Rondo, on a Russian dance, op.113 no.1 [vc/vn]
For fl, pf: 5 sonatas, op.48, 2 as op.76, op.87, op.169 [fl/cl]; Divertimento, op.62; Rondo on 'Le garçon volage', op.85 no.2; Nocturne, op.89; Polonaise, op.119; 2 Fantasias, op.134, no.1 on themes from Armida, no.2 on themes from Mosè in Egitto; 2 Variations, op.152, no.1 on a Portuguese hymn, no.2 on Himmel's 'An Alexis'
Other: Sonata, cl/vn, pf, op.29; Sonata, hn/vc, pf, op.34; Rondo, on Stansbury's 'She smiled and I could', hn/vc, pf, op.113 no.2

CHAMBER MUSIC WITH PIANO

6 trios: op.2, op.143, woo86, with vn, vc; op.28, with cl/vn, vc; op.63, with fl, vc; op.95, with harp, pf 2
3 qts, op.13, 17, 129, all with vn, va, vc
Quintet, op.74, with vn, va, vc, db; Variations and March, woo77, with harp, 2 hn, db
3 sextets: op.100, with 2 vn, va, vc, db; op.142, with harp/pf 2, cl, hn, bn, db [also arr. for pf, harp/pf 2, vn, va, vc]; woo76, with vn, 2 va, vc, db
Septet, op.25, with cl, 2 hn, vn, vc, db; also arr. as pf qnt
Octet, op.128, with cl, hn, bn, bn, va, vc, db

CHAMBER MUSIC WITHOUT PIANO

3 trios: 2 as woo70, for vn, va, vc; woo82, for 2 vn, vc/db
26 str qts: 3 as woo70, 3 as op.126, 3 as op.150, 2 as op.166, 3 as woo1 (1798), woo6 (1803), woo10 (1805), woo34 (1825), woo36 (1826), woo37 (1827), woo48 (1833), woo71, woo72, 3 as woo73, woo74
6 qts, fl, vn, va, vc: 3 as op.145, 3 as woo35 (1826–30)
8 qnts: opp.37, 68, 167, 171, woo75, for 2 vn, 2 va, vc; op.107, for fl, vn, 2 va, vc; op.183 'Souvenir d'Italie', woo62 (1836), for 2 vn, va, 2 vc
Sextet, 2 vn, 2 va, 2 vc, woo63 (1836); 2 nocturnes, fl, 2 cl, hn, 2 bn: woo50 (1834), woo60 (1836)

ORCHESTRAL

8 syms.: op.23, op.80, op.90, op.110, op.112, op.146, op.181, woo30 (1822)
5 ovs.: op.94 'Don Carlos'; op.162 'Die Braut von Messina'; op.172, with triumphal march; woo24 'bardique' (1815); woo61 'L'apparition' (1836)
Vn Conc. (Conc. no.1), op.24; 8 pf concs. (numbered 2–9), op.42, op.55, op.115, op.120, op.123, op.132 'Farewell to London', op.151 'Salut au Rhin', op.177; Concertino, pf, orch, woo88; 3 variation sets, pf, orch: op.52, on Swedish national airs, op.116, on 'Rule, Britannia', op.170 'brillantes'; 2 rondos, pf, orch, op.144 'brillant',

woo54 (1835); Polonaise, pf, orch, op.174; Conc., 2 hn, orch, woo19 (1811)

VOCAL

Stage: Die Räuberbraut, opera, op.156, Frankfurt am Main, 1828; Liska, oder Die Hexe von Gyllensteen, opera, op.164, London, 1831; Iphigenie aus Aulis, scena, S, orch, woo17 (1810); Die Nacht auf dem Libanon, opera, woo51 (1834); Die Zigeunerin, melodrama, woo53 (1835)

Secular choral, partsongs, duets: Der Morgen, cantata, S, A, T, B, orch, op.27; 6 German Partsongs, 4 male vv, 1/2 pf, op.173; En ce beau jour de fête, 4 S, pf, woo14 (1809); Zu deinem Namensfeste, 4 S, pf, woo15 (1809); Bei Eröffnung der Tafellegen, 1v, male chorus, str qt, woo16 (1810); 7 canons, woo25 (1819), woo26 (1820), woo45 (1833), woo46 (1833), 2 as woo59 (1836), 1 as woo83; 3 nocturnes, 2vv, pf, woo42 'The gentle dew' (1832), woo65 'Wahre Liebe' (1836), woo66 'Weihnachten' (1836); Die Lebensfahrt, 1v, 3-part chorus, pf, woo44 (1833); Dir theuerster bester Vater, 4 S, pf, woo81

54 songs, 1v, pf: 6 German Songs, op.7; 6 Songs (Goethe), op.32; 6 German Songs, op.35; 6 German Songs, op.36; 4 English Songs, op.91; 6 German Songs, op.154; 4 Songs (Byron), op.179; 3 German Songs, op.180; Mein Mädchen, woo8 (1804); Absence, absence à l'exil condamnée, woo12 (1807); Das Lebewohl, woo13 (1808); Das Schiffchen, woo20 (1811); Die Sehensuch, woo22 (1812); The struggling pangs, woo27 (1820); Tis time, I feel, woo29 (1821); Nous (Corinne), romance, woo31 (1823); When shall we two now meet again?, woo43 (1832); Guten Morgen viel Liebchen, woo52 (1834); Romance pour le jour de fête de Mme E. Wergifosse, woo55 (1835); Totenstill, woo56 (1835); When shall we three meet again, woo57 (1835); Sia luminosa il fine di viver mio, scena, woo79; 6 German Songs, woo84; Historisch (after Mary Queen of Scots), woo85

Sacred: [3 pieces], op.44: Nun lasset uns den Leib begraben, S, male chorus, 2 hn, 2 bn, 2 va, vc/db, Das Fest der Maurer, T, male chorus, pf, Braasch's goldene Hochzeit, solo v, soprano chorus, pf; Der Sieg des Glaubens, oratorio, op.157; Die Könige in Israel, oratorio, op.186; Masonic Cantata, T, male chorus, orch, woo9 (1805); Requiem, 4vv, orch, woo23 (1815); Tantum ergo, S, 4vv, org, woo69

(5) (Pieter) Joseph Ries (b Bonn, 6 April 1791; d London, 6 April 1882). Amateur musician, second son of (3) Franz (Anton) Ries. He devoted his little spare time to teaching and playing. As a businessman he worked for the East India Co. and later as a foreign correspondent in the Broadwood house. After his elder brother (4) Ferdinand Ries left London in 1824, Joseph acted for him in dealings with London publishers, and numerous letters survive from that period.

(6) (Pieter) Hubert Ries (b Bonn, 1 April 1802; d Berlin, 14 Sept 1886). Violinist and composer, youngest son of (3) Franz (Anton) Ries. He first studied the violin with his father and afterwards with Spohr, receiving composition lessons from Moritz Hauptmann. He lived in Berlin from 1824, when he joined the Königstadt Theater orchestra, and became a member of the court orchestra in the following year. In 1835 he became director of the Berlin Philharmonic Society, and in 1836 was appointed leader. He had a distinguished career as a violinist, and was elected a fellow of the Royal Academy of Arts in 1839. He published two violin concertos, studies and duets for violin and some string quartets. But he was better known for his *Violin School* for beginners, which was published in an English edition in 1873.

(7) Louis Ries (b Berlin, 30 Jan 1830; d London, 3 Oct 1913). Violinist, eldest son of (6) (Pieter) Hubert Ries. He was taught by his father and by Vieuxtemps. In 1853 he settled in London, where he gained a reputation as a violinist and teacher. He was a member of the quartet of the Musical Union from 1855 to 1870, and also played second violin at the Monday Popular Concerts from their beginning in 1859 until his retirement in 1897.

(8) Adolph Ries (b Berlin, 20 Dec 1837; d April 1899). Pianist, second son of (6) (Pieter) Hubert Ries.

He was taught the piano by Theodor Kullak and composition by Boehmer. He worked in London as a piano teacher and published some songs and piano music. His daughter Marie Gertrude Ries (1880–1974), a pupil of Clara Schumann, emigrated to Australia, where she was a distinguished pianist.

(9) Franz Ries (b Berlin, 7 April 1846; d Naumburg, 20 Jan 1932). Violinist and music publisher, youngest son of (6) (Pieter) Hubert Ries. He studied the violin with his father and with Massart and Vieuxtemps in Paris. In 1870 he appeared at the Crystal Palace, but a promising career as a violinist was cut short in 1873 by nervous trouble. This prompted him to enter the music trade, and on 1 July 1881 he and Hermann Erler (1844–1918) jointly founded the publishing house of RIES & ERLER, of which his son Robert became proprietor in 1924. He wrote some orchestral and chamber music, and also edited works by Corelli, Schumann and others.

BIBLIOGRAPHY

'Memoir of Ferdinand Ries', *Harmonicon*, ii (1824), 33, 60

G. A. von Maltitz: *Denkmal, den berühmten musikalischen Künstlern* (Leipzig, 1835)

A. F. Schindler: *Biographie von Ludwig van Beethoven* (Münster, 1840, enlarged 2/1845, rev. 3/1860; Eng. trans., 1966 as *Beethoven as I Knew him*)

L. Überfeldt: *F. Ries' Jugendentwicklung* (Bonn, 1915)

E. Anderson: *The Letters of Beethoven* (London, 1961)

E. Forbes, ed.: *Thayer's Life of Beethoven* (Princeton, 1964, 2/1967)

D. W. McArdle: 'Beethoven and Ferdinand Ries', *ML*, xlvi (1965), 23

J. Schmidt-Görg and H. Schmidt: *Ludwig van Beethoven* (Hamburg, 1969; Eng. trans., 1970)

M. Cooper: *Beethoven: the Last Decade, 1817–1827* (London, 1970)

H. C. R. Landon: *Beethoven: a Documentary Study* (London, 1970)

C. Hill: 'Ferdinand Ries: a Preliminary List of Correspondence', *FAM*, xxiii (1976), 7

——: *The Music of Ferdinand Ries: a Thematic Catalogue* (Armidale, New South Wales, 1977)

CECIL HILL

Riesemann, (Bernhard) Oskar von (b Reval, 29 Feb 1880; d St Niklausen, nr. Lucerne, 28 Sept 1934). German writer on music and conductor. He read philology (1899–1900) and law (1900–04) at Moscow University, at the same time studying music and art history at Munich, Berlin (1901) and with Riemann in Leipzig (1903). He was awarded the doctorate at Moscow University in 1908 for a dissertation on ancient Russian notation. He worked in Moscow as a music critic and conductor, but left Russia after the 1917 Revolution, living first at Munich, then in Switzerland. His writings, regarded in their day as pioneering studies in Russian music, have largely been superseded by works based on more up-to-date, accurate information; some of the details in his biography of Rakhmaninov were refuted by the composer, although Riesemann had claimed in the preface that the facts 'need no verification and may, therefore, constitute the foundation of every future Rakhmaninov biography'. Of greater value are his German translations of Rimsky-Korsakov's autobiography and Sabaneyev's history of Russian music. He also composed some piano pieces.

WRITINGS

Die Notationen des altrussischen Kirchengesanges (diss., U. of Moscow, 1908; Leipzig, 1909)

'Zur Frage der Entzifferung altbyzantinischer Neumen', *Riemann-Festschrift* (Leipzig, 1909), 189

Monographien zur russischen Musik, i: *Die Musik in Russland vor Glinka: Michael Iwanowitsch Glinka, Alexander Sergejewitsch Dargomyschski, Alexander Nikolajewitsch Sseroff* (Munich, 1923/R1975); ii: *Modest Petrowitsch Mussorgski* (Munich, 1926/R1975; Eng. trans., 1929/R1971)

Geschichte der russischen Musik (Leipzig, 1926) [trans. of L. Sabaneyev: *Istoriya russkoy muzïki*, Moscow, 1924]
Chronik meines musikalischen Lebens (Stuttgart, 1928) [trans. of N.
Rimsky-Korsakov: *Letopis' moyey muzïkal'noy zhizni*, St Petersburg,
1909, 3/1928]
Rachmaninoff's Recollections told to Oskar von Riesemann (New York
and London, 1934) [trans. D. Rutherford]

BIBLIOGRAPHY
O. von Riesemann: *Rund um Südamerika* (Berlin, 2/1921)
——: *Fluchten* (Stuttgart, 1925, 3/1928)
G. Waldmann: 'Riesemann, Bernhard Oskar von', *MGG*
                                    GEOFFREY NORRIS

Ries & Erler. German firm of publishers. It was founded
in Berlin in 1881 by Franz Ries (*see* RIES family) and
Hermann Erler (*b* Radeberg, 3 June 1844; *d* Berlin, 13
Dec 1918). Ries started selling music in 1874 but in
1884 he sold his business (which also incorporated a
concert management agency) and entered publishing; he
had already made the first step in this direction in 1881,
when he became associated with the publishing
house that Erler had founded in Berlin in 1872. They acquired
the rights to the compositions of Heinrich Hofmann; in
1882 they took over the publication of educational
works (principally songs) from the firm of M. Schloss in
Cologne and the following year took over Voigt of
Kassel. They began to publish salon music, including
pieces by Ries himself. After Erler's death Ries acquired
the publishing rights to works by many composers,
including Humperdinck, Pfitzner and Reznicek; he also
published tutors by Carl Flesch, and the firm subsequently absorbed the R. Sulzer and Jatho houses.
   When Ries retired in 1924 the business was taken
over by his son Robert Ries (1889–1942), who extended the range of its publications, particularly of
orchestral music. In 1927 he was elected to the governing body of the Musikverleger-Verein, and was its
deputy chairman until 1929; also in 1927 he was
elected to the governing body of the Verband Deutscher
Musikverleger, of which he was president from 1930 to
1933. His particular interests were amateur and contemporary music, both of which he promoted vigorously. After his death the business was inherited by his
daughter Waltraud Ries, who rebuilt the firm in 1948
after its wartime destruction. Its present publications
consist mainly of symphonic and light orchestral music
by Theodor Berger, Dressel, Frommel, Genzmer,
Lothar and others, as well as solo instrumental, chamber
and vocal music and didactic and theoretical works.

based on *MGG* (xi, 494–5) by permission of Bärenreiter
                                    THOMAS-M. LANGNER

Rieter-Biedermann, Jakob Melchior (*b* Winterthur, 14
May 1811; *d* Winterthur, 25 Jan 1876). Swiss music
publisher. He was originally a part owner of his father's
spinning mill and engineering firm. In 1833 he studied
engineering design in Paris, where he met Berlioz and
Rossini; subsequently he was librarian and timpanist of
the Winterthur Musikkollegium (1835–48). His
enthusiasm for music led him to found a music shop and
publishing firm (1849), which had issued 900 items by
1876. The firm's publications included works by
Berlioz, Kirchner, Herzogenberg, Schumann and, after
1858, 22 works by Brahms, including opp.14, 15, 34,
39 and 45. Rieter-Biedermann's son-in-law Edmund
Astor (1845–1918) directed the branch established in
Leipzig (1862), which became the headquarters after the
original office closed in 1884. Rieter-Biedermann also
founded the *Leipziger Allgemeine musikalische Zeitung*,

which his firm published from 1866 to 1882. In 1917
C. F. Peters bought the company.

BIBLIOGRAPHY
Katalog des Musikalien-Verlags von J. Rieter-Biedermann (Leipzig,
1897)
*Verzeichniss der Compositionen von Johannes Brahms nebst ihren
Bearbeitungen aus dem Verlage von J. Rieter-Biedermann in Leipzig*
(Leipzig, 1898, 3/1908)
Katalog des Musikalien-Verlages von J. Rieter-Biedermann (Leipzig,
1909)
W. Altmann, ed.: *Johannes Brahms im Briefwechsel mit Breitkopf &
Härtel, Bartolf Senff, J. Rieter-Biedermann* (Berlin, 1920)
M. Fehr: '18 Briefe von H. Berlioz an den Winterthurer Verleger J.
Rieter-Biedermann', *Schweizerisches Jb für Musikwissenschaft*, ii
(1927), 90
——: *Das Musikkollegium Winterthur 1629–1837* (Winterthur,
1929)
                                    HANS-MARTIN PLESSKE

Rieti, Vittorio (*b* Alexandria, Egypt, 28 Jan 1898).
American composer of Italian descent. He studied
music with Frugatta in Milan (1912–17) as well as
economics at the University of Milan, where he obtained
a doctorate in 1917. After brief war service in the
Italian army, he completed his composition studies with
Respighi in Rome (until 1920). In the early 1920s he
was associated with Massarani and Labroca in a group
that called itself I Tre, in imitation of Les Six. His first
international success came at the ISCM Festival in
Prague in 1924 with his Concerto for wind and
orchestra, conducted by Casella, who continued to befriend his younger colleague. From 1925 to 1940 Rieti
divided his time between Rome and Paris, where he
formed close ties with Les Six. He wrote ballet music for
Dyagilev (*Barabau* being particularly successful) and
much incidental music for the Parisian theatre of Louis
Jouvet. He was also one of the founder-directors of the
Paris group La Sérénade, dedicated to modern chamber
music (1931–40). In 1940 he moved to the USA (he
became a citizen in 1944). There his ballet music was
choreographed by Balanchin, his orchestral music conducted by, among others, Toscanini and Mitropoulos.
He continued to be productive; on his 75th birthday a
number of new works were presented to the public. As a
teacher of composition, he was active at the Peabody
Conservatory (1948–9), the Chicago Musical College
(1950–53), Queens College (1955–60) and the New
York College of Music (1960–64).
   Rieti's musical style has been fairly consistent
throughout his long career. After early experiments with
atonality, he evolved an idiom akin to neo-classicism,
which remained his characteristic trait. He said in 1973:
'I maintain the same aesthetic assumptions I have
always had; I have kept evolving in the sense that one
keeps on perfecting the same ground'. His music has a
natural, unaffected fluency, elegant charm, controlled
feeling, sophisticated humour and impeccable technical
mastery; his textures are clear and limpid, his orchestration transparent and sensitive. Casella's praise (see
Cobbett) has lost none of its relevance; elsewhere he
wrote: 'Rieti's oeuvre stands apart in its specific clarity,
gaiety and sophistication of a kind only he possesses;
yet it hides a good deal of melancholia'.

WORKS
(selective list)

STAGE
Operas: Orfeo tragedia (Poliziano), 1928, withdrawn; Teresa nel bosco
(chamber opera, Rieti), 1933; Don Perlimplin (1), 1949; Viaggio
d'Europa (radio opera), 1954; The Pet Shop (1), 1957; The Clock (2),
1959–60; Maryam the Harlot (1), 1966
Ballets: L'arca di Noé, 1923, only orch suite extant; Robinson et

Vendredi, 1924, also orch suite; Barabau, 1925, also orch suite; Le bal, 1929; David triomphant, 1937; Hippolyte, 1937, also orch suite; The Night Shadow [on themes of Bellini], 1941; Waltz Academy [after Second Avenue Waltzes, 2 pf], 1944; The Mute Wife [on themes of Paganini], 1944; Trionfo di Bacco e Arianna (ballet-cantata), 1946–7 [contains material from Orfeo tragedia]; Native Dancer [after Sym. no.5], 1959; Conundrum, 1961; A Sylvan Dream, 1965; Scenes Seen, 1975
Incidental music

ORCHESTRAL

Conc., 5 wind, orch, 1923; 2 Pastorali, chamber orch, 1925; Pf Conc. no.1, 1926; Madrigale, 6 wind, pf, 5 str, 1927; Vn Conc. no.1 (Conc. napoletano), 1928, lost; Sym. no.1, 1929; Sym. no.2, 1930; Serenata, vn, 11 insts/chamber orch, 1931; Sym. no.3 (Sinfonietta), 1932; Vc Conc. no.1, vc, 12 insts, 1934; Pf Conc. no.2, 1930–37; Conc. du loup, 1938; Sym. no.4 (Sinfonia tripartita), 1942; Sym. no.5, 1945; Conc., 2 pf, orch, 1951; Hpd Conc., 1952–5, rev. 1972 [first drafted for harp, orch]; Introduzione e gioco delle ore, 1953; Vc Conc. no.2, 1953; Pf Conc. no.3, 1955; Dance Variations, str, 1956; La fontaine, suite, 1968; Vn Conc. no.2, 1969
Triple Conc., vn, va, pf, orch, 1971; Sym. no.6, 1973; Conc., str qt, orch, 1976; Sym. no.7 (1977)

VOCAL

Choral: Ulysses' Wandering, cantata, 1939; 3 Choral Songs, unacc., 1963; Missa brevis, vv, org, 1973
Songs: 2 Songs between 2 Waltzes (Yeats), 1957; 4 Songs (Lawrence), 1960; 5 Elizabethan Songs, 1967; 7 liriche saffiche, 1974

CHAMBER AND INSTRUMENTAL

For 3–8 insts: Sonata, fl, ob, bn, pf, 1924; 4 str qts, 1926, 1941, 1951, 1960; Partita, hpd, fl, ob, str qt, 1945; Quintet, ww, 1957; Concertino, fl, va, vc, harp, hpd, 1963; Variations on When from my Love, by John Bartlett (1606), fl, cl, va, vc, 1964; Pastorale and Fughetta, fl, va, pf, 1966; Sonata a 5, fl, ob, cl, bn, pf, 1966; Incisioni, brass qnt, 1967; Silografie, wind qnt, 1967; Octet, pf, 7 insts, 1971; Pf Trio, 1972; Pf Qt, 1973; Sestetto pro Gemini, fl, ob, pf qt, 1975
For 2 insts: Sonatina, fl, pf, 1920; Variations on a Chinese Theme, vn, pf, 1922; Capriccio, vn, pf, 1941; Rondo variato, vn, pf, 1945; Siciliana e tarantella, vc, pf, 1967; Sonata breve, vn, pf, 1967; Sonata concertante, vn, pf, 1970
For 2 pf: Second Avenue Waltzes, 1942; Chess Serenade, 1945; Suite champêtre, 1948; New Waltzes, 1956–7; Corale, variazioni e finale, 1969; 3 Vaudeville Marches, 1969; Valse fugitive, 1970; Scherzo-March, 1976
For pf: early pieces, 1920; Poema fiesolano, 1921; 2 studi, 1923; Sonatina, 1925; Suite, 1926; 3 preludi, 1931; 6 pezzi brevi, 1932; Sonata, A♭, 1938; 5 Little Recital Pieces [5 Pieces for Young Pianists], 1942; Sonata all'antica, pf/hpd, 1946; Academic Variations, 1950; Medieval Variations, 1962; Contrasti, 1967; Chironomes, suite, 1972

Principal publishers: Associated, Broude, General Music, Ricordi, Salabert, Universal

BIBLIOGRAPHY

G. Rossi-Doria: 'Giovani compositori italiani: Labroca, Massarani, Rieti', Il pianoforte, v (1924), 303
A. Casella: 'Neue Komponisten in Italien', Musikblätter des Anbruch, vii (1925), 399
——: 'Jeunes et indépendants: Vittorio Rieti', ReM, viii/3 (1927), 64
——: 'Vittorio Rieti', Cobbett's Cyclopedic Survey of Chamber Music (London, 1929–30, rev., enlarged 2/1963)
D. de' Paoli: La crisi musicale italiana (Milan, 1939), 168ff, 284f
C. Reis: Composers in America (New York, 4/1947)
J. C. G. Waterhouse: The Emergence of Modern Italian Music (up to 1940) (diss., U. of Oxford, 1968), 670, 679ff
Tributes to Rieti, New York Times (14, 19, 29 Jan 1973)

BORIS SCHWARZ

Rietsch [Löwy], Heinrich (b Falkenau an der Eger, 22 Sept 1860; d Prague, 12 Dec 1927). Austrian musicologist and composer. Rietsch studied law in Vienna and received a doctorate in law in 1883. At the same time he undertook music studies with Hanslick, Adler, F. Krems, E. Mandyczewski and R. Fuchs, and in 1895 completed his Habilitation in musicology at Vienna. He was appointed reader at the German University of Prague in 1900, succeeding Guido Adler. In 1909 he became full professor and founded the institute of musicology, which he directed until his death.

Rietsch was greatly influenced by Guido Adler's methods of style criticism. His principal areas of research were the music of the Baroque, the Viennese Classicists and the late 19th century; general music education; the aesthetics of music and the development of German monophonic song. In some of these areas, especially that of the German Minnesang, Rietsch made fundamental contributions with his editions. These and his writings show outstanding care, aesthetic sensitivity and concern for historical accuracy. Rietsch was also the composer of a short unpublished opera, Walther von der Vogelweide, orchestral and chamber music, lieder, choral pieces and works for piano.

WRITINGS

Die Tonkunst in der 2. Hälfte des 19. Jahrhunderts (Leipzig, 1900, 2/1906)
Die deutsche Liedweise: ein Stück positiver Ästhetik der Tonkunst (Vienna, 1905)
'Die kunstlerische Auslese in der Musik', JbMP 1906, 29
Die Grundlagen der Tonkunst (Leipzig, 1907, 2/1918)
'85 Variationen über Diabellis Walzer', BeethovenJb, i (1908), 28
'Kurze Betrachtungen zum deutschen Volkslied', Festschrift . . . Rochus Freiherrn von Liliencron (Leipzig, 1910), 215
'Zum Unterschied der älteren und neueren deutschen Volksweisen', JbMP 1911, 13
'Ein Sonatenthema bei Mozart', ZIMG, xiv (1912–13), 278
'Heinrich Isaac und das Innsbrucklied', JbMP 1917, 19
'Entlehnungen', AMw, ii (1920), 293
'Einige Leitsätze für das ältere deutsche einstimmige Lied', ZMw, vi (1923–4), 1
'Zur "Kunst der Fuge" von J. S. Bach', BJb, xxiii (1926), 1
'Mozarts G-Dur-Konzert für Geige', ZMw, x (1927–8), 198

EDITIONS

G. Muffat: Florilegium, DTÖ, ii, Jg. i/2 (1894/R); iv, Jg. ii/2 (1895/R)
with F. A. Mayer: Die Mondsee-Wiener Liederhandschrift und der Mönch von Salzburg (Berlin, 1896)
Gesänge von Frauenlob, Reinmar von Zweter und Alexander, DTÖ, xli, Jg. xx/2 (1913/R)
J. J. Fux: Concentus musico-instrumentalis, DTÖ, xlvii, Jg. xxiii/2 (1919/R)

BIBLIOGRAPHY

P. Nettl: 'Heinrich Rietsch: zum 22. September 1920', ZMw, ii (1919–20), 736 [contains complete list of writings and compositions up to 1920]
——: 'Heinrich Rietsch†', ZMw, x (1927–8), 193

BURKHARD KIPPENBERG

Rietz, Eduard (Theodor Ludwig) (b Berlin, 17 Oct 1802; d Berlin, 22 Jan 1832). German violinist and conductor. He studied the violin with his father Johann Christian Rietz (a violinist in the Berlin court orchestra, 1812–27) and with Rode (1813–20), and made his début in 1818. He joined the Berlin court orchestra in 1819 and became its leader, but personality clashes with Spontini led to his release in 1825. He founded the Berlin Philharmonic Society in 1826; though its orchestra was made up of amateurs, it was soon able to accompany the Singakademie in the performance of oratorios. Rietz was leader at Mendelssohn's historic performance of Bach's St Matthew Passion (1829), for which he and his brother Julius Rietz had copied out the parts. At the beginning of a promising career as a conductor, Rietz died of tuberculosis. He is remembered now as the teacher and friend of Mendelssohn. Together with his younger brother he played quartets with Mendelssohn as early as 1820; Mendelssohn studied the violin with him and dedicated his D minor Concerto, the Violin Sonata op.4 and the Octet op.20 to him. Both Mendelssohn and Rietz were fascinated by the music of Bach and were associated with C. F. Zelter at the Singakademie, where Rietz frequently sang solo tenor parts. Mendelssohn's letters reveal his affection for Rietz and his admiration of his violin playing; when Rietz died, Mendelssohn dedicated the Andante of the String Quintet op.18 to his friend's memory.

ALBERT MELL

Rietz, (August Wilhelm) Julius (*b* Berlin, 28 Dec 1812; *d* Dresden, 12 Sept 1877). German cellist, composer, conductor and editor, brother of Eduard Rietz. He studied the cello from the age of eight with Franz Schmidt, B. H. Romberg and Moritz Ganz. In 1829 he joined the orchestra of the Königstadt theatre. Refusing Spontini's offer of a post in the Berlin court orchestra, he went to Düsseldorf in 1834 to assist Mendelssohn at the Opera; though nominally only assistant conductor he did most of the conducting. When Mendelssohn left Düsseldorf, Rietz became the city's musical director. During the next 12 years he established a reputation as a conductor and a composer; more than two dozen works of his were published, including the music for Goethe's Singspiel *Jery und Bately*, a symphony, a cello concerto and several sets of lieder. He continued to play the cello in public, with Ferdinand Hiller and Ferdinand David among others. He assisted Mendelssohn at the Lower Rhine Music Festival of 1839, and was chief conductor at the festivals of 1845, 1856 and 1869.

In 1847 Rietz succeeded Stegmayr as conductor of the Leipzig Opera and the Singakademie. He became professor of composition at the conservatory and succeeded Gade as director of the Gewandhaus orchestra. He was also the secretary of the Bach Gesellschaft (1855–60), for which he edited the B minor Mass and the *St Matthew Passion*. He edited *Susanna* for the Händel Gesellschaft and prepared the scores of 14 Haydn symphonies for Breitkopf & Härtel. In 1859 he received an honorary doctorate from the University of Leipzig for his achievements as a composer, conductor and scholar. He succeeded Reissiger as musical director of the city of Dresden in 1860.

Rietz was more active as an administrator than as a composer, though he did write, among other works, a mass in F, a Te Deum and incidental music for *As You Like It* (1864). But his years in Dresden were disappointing, being marked by a decline in his prestige and in the respect accorded him by his colleagues. In his last years Rietz was again active as an editor. He prepared the scores of a number of Mozart operas, which were later incorporated into the Mozart Gesamtausgabe, and supervised the publication of the Mendelssohn Gesamtausgabe, which was completed in the year of his death.

BIBLIOGRAPHY
F. Pazdírek: *Universal-Handbuch der Musikliteratur* (Vienna, 1904–10) [incl. list of pubd works]
'Pauline Viardot-Garcia to Julius Rietz: Letters of Friendship', *MQ*, i (1915), 350
H. Zimmer: *Julius Rietz* (diss., Humboldt U., Berlin, 1943)
R. Sietz: 'Rietz, Julius', *Rheinische Musiker*, iii, ed. K. G. Fellerer (Cologne, 1964)
                                        ALBERT MELL

Rieu, Anselmo de. See REULX, ANSELMO DE.

Riff. In jazz, a short melodic ostinato, usually two to four bars long and with a small compass, which may at times be varied to accommodate an underlying harmonic pattern. Its origins are said to lie in the repetitive call-and-response patterns of west African music, and it has appeared in jazz solo and ensemble playing from earliest times. In the late 1920s and early 1930s the riff, especially as integrated with blues form, became an essential structural feature of 'Southwest' orchestral jazz, and at about the same time it was applied to a popular repertory in the orchestral scores of Don

Redman and Fletcher Henderson in New York. This led to it becoming a stock device of 1930s swing bands, both to accompany solo improvisation and as independent thematic material, and gave rise to 12- or 32-bar 'riff tunes', such as Glenn Miller's popular *In the Mood* or the many outstanding examples by Charlie Christian.

BIBLIOGRAPHY
G. Schuller: *Early Jazz* (New York, 1969), 28ff, 47ff
                              BRADFORD ROBINSON

Rifkin, Joshua (*b* New York, 22 April 1944). American musicologist, pianist, conductor and composer. He studied with Persichetti at the Juilliard School of Music (BS 1964), with Reese at New York University (1964–6), at the University of Göttingen (1966–7) and with Lockwood, Mendel, Babbitt and Oster at Princeton University (MFA, 1969); he also worked with Stockhausen at the Darmstadt summer courses of 1961 and 1965. He held various positions with Nonesuch Records in New York (1964–75) and in 1970 he joined the staff of Brandeis University; in 1972 he served as a visiting lecturer at Harvard. Rifkin's principal areas of research are Renaissance and Baroque music. As a pianist and conductor he has made several gramophone recordings and has contributed to the revival of interest in ragtime music. His compositions include chamber music and songs.

WRITINGS
'Ein unbekanntes Haydn-Zitat bei Mozart', *Haydn-Studien*, ii (1969–70), 317
'Schütz and Musical Logic', *MT*, cxiii (1972), 1067
Review of A. Dunning: *Die Staatsmotette 1480–1555* (Utrecht, 1970), *Notes*, xxviii (1971–2), 425
'Scribal Concordances for some Renaissance Manuscripts in Florentine Libraries', *JAMS*, xxvi (1973), 305
'The Chronology of Bach's Saint Matthew Passion', *MQ*, lxi (1975), 360
'Pietrequin Bonnel and Ms. 2794 of the Biblioteca Riccardiana', *JAMS*, xxix (1976), 284
'Ein römisches Messenrepertoire am bayerischen Hof: Bemerkungen zum Wolfenbütteler Chorbuch A Aug.fol. und zu seinem Umkreis', *Formen und Probleme der Überlieferung mehrstimmiger Musik im Zeitalter Josquins Desprez: Wolfenbüttel 1976*
                                    PAULA MORGAN

Riga [Rīga]. Capital of Latvia. Riga's musical history developed against a background of influence from both East and West. While the musical life of the rest of Latvia remained at the stage of folk culture until the 19th century, Riga, from its foundation in 1201, had a German culture, with some Polish and Russian influence from the 17th century. Many outstanding musicians visited Riga, including John Field (1805), Liszt (1842), Berlioz (1847) and Anton Rubinstein (first in 1849); Bach's pupil Müthel worked there (1753–88). Wagner was there from 1837 to 1839, and although this was a largely unproductive period for him because of domestic strife, he began work on *Rienzi* and conducted at the theatre. In the late 19th century Riga became the centre of Latvian musical development, then more strongly under Russian influence. As the capital of the independent Latvian republic (1919–40) it was the home of all the important Latvian musical institutions. From 1945 its significance as a European musical centre declined because of the shift of Western cultural exchange away from Latvia to the rest of the USSR.

The cathedral, converted into a concert hall in 1962, had a choir from 1240; the organ, with 125 stops and four manuals and built in 1884, attracts many virtuosos. In 1782 O. Fittinghof founded the German Riga City

Theatre, where most important operas were produced soon after their first performance: for example, *Die Entführung aus dem Serail* in 1785, *Fidelio* in 1818 and *Der Freischütz* in 1822. In 1919 the theatre became the state-owned National Opera, and after World War II the State Opera and Ballet Theatre of the Latvian SSR.

During the 17th century public concert life was promoted by the Collegium Musicum, and from 1760 for more than a century by the Musikalische Gesellschaft. Later, Latvian concerts were under the supervision of the Musical Commission of the Latvian Society of Riga (1888–1913). From 1941 concert life has been monopolized by the State Philharmonia of the Latvian SSR.

The first city symphony orchestra was organized in 1761 by the Musikalische Gesellschaft. The Broadcasting SO, which has become the main orchestra, was founded in 1926, a year after broadcasting began in Riga. Choral music was sponsored by the Rīgas Latviešu Dziedāšanas Biedrība ('Riga Latvian singing society') from 1879 to 1940. In Soviet Latvia professional choirs were established at the broadcasting station (1940) and the Philharmonia (1942). 14 of the 15 Latvian song festivals held between 1873 and 1973 took place in Riga. The impressive Schwarzhaupter Haus was used as a concert hall from the 18th century, but was destroyed in World War II; from 1946 the Lielā Ģilde ('Great guild') was used as the Philharmonic concert hall. Summer seasons have been held in the Dzintaru Koncertzāle ('Amber concert hall') on the Bay of Riga since the 1870s.

The first music school was begun in 1840 by P. Feigerl. Jāzeps Vītols founded the Latvian Conservatory in 1919 (now Jāzepa Vītola Valsts Konzervatorija), and a Folk Conservatory (from 1940 the Musical College) was started in 1929.

Professional associations, the German *Stadtmusikanten* guilds, are mentioned for the first time in 1443, and existed until the 18th century. From 1844 the instrument makers' guild was active for some 60 years. A Latvian composers' union (Skaņražu Kopa, 1923–40) was founded by Vītols, and the Composers' Union of the Latvian SSR was founded in 1944.

See also UNION OF SOVIET SOCIALIST REPUBLICS, §VI, 1.

BIBLIOGRAPHY

R. Behling: *100 Jahre der Musikalischen Gesellschaft zu Riga* (Riga, 1860)
M. Rudolph: *Rigaer Theater und Tonkunstler-Lexikon* (Riga, 1890)
N. Busch: 'Zur Geschichte des Rigaer Musiklebens im 17. Jahrhundert', *Gesellschaft für Geschichte und· Altertumskunde: Sitzungsberichte* (Riga, 1910), 25
J. Brauns: 'No latviešu instrumentālās mūzikas vēstures' [From the history of Latvian instrumental music], *Latviešu mūzika*, ii (Riga, 1962), 115
N. Grinfeld, ed.: *Latvijas Valsts Konzervatorija* (Riga, 1965)
E. Arro: 'Richard Wagners Rigaer Wanderjahre', *Musik des Ostens*, iii (1965), 123–68
S. Verinya: *Muzīkal'nie teatri Latvii i vozniknovenie Latishskoy nacio-nal'noy operi* (diss., Leningrad Conservatory, 1970)
J. Braun: 'Iz istorii Latishsko-Pol'skich muzikal'nich svjazey', *Ocherki muzīkal'noy kul'turi Sovetskoy Latvii*, ed. L. Karklin'sh (Leningrad, 1971), 117
S. Verinya: 'Russkaya opera v Latvii', *Ocherki muzīkal'noy kul'turi Sovetskoy Latvii*, ed. L. Karklin'sh (Leningrad, 1971), 97

JOACHIM BRAUN

Rigadon [rigadoon]. *See* RIGAUDON.

Rigatti, Giovanni Antonio (*b* Venice, 1615; *d* Venice, 25 Oct 1649). Italian composer and singer. He became a priest, serving at St Mark's and S Maria Formosa,

Venice. From September 1635 till March 1637 he was *maestro di cappella* at Udine Cathedral and was already considered one of the finest musicians of the Veneto. Later he sang in the choir of St Mark's and also taught singing at the Conservatorio degli Incurabili, Venice, where he had as a pupil Francesco Lucio, one of whose psalm settings he included in his 1646 collection. He was described in 1646 as *maestro di cappella* to the Patriarch of Venice.

The high esteem in which he was held at Udine at the age of only 20 is entirely consistent with his being, together with men such as Giovanni Rovetta and Gasparo Casati, one of the outstanding Italian composers of church music working in the 1630s and 1640s. Nine of his eleven surviving collections are of church music: two books of solo motets, three of small-scale concertato motets (one including a *messa breve*) and no fewer than four of psalm settings (three including a mass each). Most of this music includes parts for obbligato instruments, usually violins, and much of it is adaptable, either to an intimate chamber-like medium with solo voices and perhaps violins, or to grander occasions by the addition of a ripieno chorus and sometimes extra instruments. The 1640 *Messa e salmi*, dedicated to the Emperor Ferdinand III, is the most impressive collection. It maintains a consistently high level of invention and rivals Monteverdi's *Selva morale* of the same year in its comprehensive range of contents: one mass and several psalms in the grand concertato manner, psalms for smaller combinations of voices and instruments, and others marked 'da cappella' (denoting not the *stile antico* but the absence of soloists and the instrumental doubling of voices).

No matter how grand a texture he was writing for, Rigatti as a monodist was always capable of gracing his music with delightful, memorable melodies, vocal or instrumental (his violin ritornellos are often most attractive). This talent can be seen at its best in the second setting of *Nisi Dominus* (for SSB, two violins and continuo) in the 1640 volume. It is built almost entirely on a descending four-note ground bass (cf the love duet at the end of Monteverdi's *L'incoronazione di Poppea*). Its quite romantic expressiveness derives not only from the incredibly varied melodic writing over the anchoring bass, but also from the many tempo and dynamic changes specified by Rigatti himself and integral to his personal style – such markings are often found in his works. His church music is as inventive in other ways, for example in its coherent musical structures involving refrains, ritornellos and ground basses, in the occasional use of fugal exposition and in the often dramatic word-painting, which led him to introduce a 'toccata da guerra' in the *stile concitato* into the 'Fecit potentiam' verse of the *Magnificat* in the 1640 volume.

Ground basses are found too in the secular monodies of 1641; this volume also includes three cantatas – two examples of the now increasingly old-fashioned strophic-bass cantata and one of the new kind of chamber cantata in several contrasting sections, to words from Guarini's *Il pastor fido*. The madrigals of 1636 are Monteverdian in manner and include luscious duets, a canzonetta and a piece using the romanesca bass.

WORKS
(all except anthologies published in Venice)

SACRED

Primo parto de motetti, 2–4vv, con alcune cantilene, con suoi ripieni ad lib (1634)

Messa e salmi parte concertati, 3–8vv, 2 vn, other insts ad lib, e parte, 5vv (1640)

Messa e salmi ariosi, 3vv, concertati e parte con li ripieni ad lib (2/1643)

Motetti, 1v, bc (1643)

Salmi diversi di Compieta . . . 1–4vv, parte con istromenti e parte senza, con tutte le antiphone dell'anno (1646)

Motetti, 1v, bc (org/hpd/theorbo/other inst), libro II (1647)

Motetti, 2, 3vv, con una messa breve (1647)

Musiche diverse, 2vv, bc (1647)

Messa e salmi, 3vv, con 2 vn, 4 parti di ripieno ad lib, libro II (1648)

2 psalms repr. in 1646[4]; 1 mass repr. in 1671[1]

12 motets in 1646[4], 1649[1], 1653[1], 1659[3], *S-Uu*, *F-Pn*; other motets in *USSR-KA*; 1 mass in *S-Uu*; 2 psalms in *D-W*, *PL-WRu*

SECULAR

Musiche concertate cioe madrigali, 2–4vv, bc, libro I, op.2 (1636)

Musiche diverse, 1v, bc (1641)

BIBLIOGRAPHY

G. Vale: 'La cappella musicale del duomo di Udine', *NA*, vii (1930), 136, 150

H. A. Sander: 'Beiträge zur Geschichte der Barockmesse', *KJb*, xxviii (1933), 85, 89, 101, 110

J. L. A. Roche: *North Italian Liturgical Music in the Early 17th Century* (diss., U. of Cambridge, 1968)

——: 'Giovanni Antonio Rigatti and the Development of Venetian Church Music in the 1640s', *ML*, lvii (1976), 256

JEROME ROCHE

Rigaud, Louis de, Sieur de Fonlidon (*fl c*1623). French composer and lutenist. He was most probably in the service of the Maréchale de Thémines, to whom he dedicated his collection of *airs*. The *airs*, which are remarkable for their suppleness of style, were designed to please visitors to the maréchale's salon, who are known to have delighted in pieces such as the 'Ballet de Madame' and in the solo lute introduction to another *air*.

WORKS

Airs faits et mis en tablature de luth (Paris, 1623); 3 airs in *Airs de cour pour voix et luth* (*1603–43*), ed. A. Verchaly (Paris, 1961)

Libera me Domine, paraphrase, 5vv, cited by J. B. de la Borde (*Essai sur la musique ancienne et moderne*, Paris, 1780)

MARGARET M. McGOWAN

Rigaudon [rigadon, rigadoon]. A French folkdance, court dance and instrumental form popular in France and England in the 17th and 18th centuries. As a folkdance it was traditionally associated with southern France, especially the provinces of Vavarais, Languedoc, Dauphiné and Provence, although the term is now used to refer to a wide variety of folkdances from several regions. It is not certain that any of the folk rigaudons were related to the court dance that gained popularity during the reign of Louis XIV. A letter of Mme de Sévigné to her daughter, dated 1673, remarked that 'Mme Santa Cruz triumphs in the Rigadon'. The popularity of the dance seems to have spread quickly from Paris and Versailles to England and Germany. The rigaudon was especially popular in England, where at least one 'Rigadoon Royal' was composed by the famous dancing-master Isaac for Queen Anne's birthday in 1711. It was popular as a social dance for individual couples at balls, as a virtuoso theatre dance, and, in simplified form for several couples at once, as one of the many kinds of CONTREDANSE.

Like the bourrée, with which it was often compared (Mattheson, Quantz, Rousseau), the rigaudon was a 'gay' duple-metre dance in two or more strains characterized by four-bar phrases, usually with an upbeat. Apparently more than one type of rigaudon was known in England as several rigadoons in 6/8 metre appeared in George Bickham's *An Easy Introduction to Dancing* (1738). The duple rigaudon was used widely in French

ballets and operas, and occasionally somewhat stylized rigaudons were included in instrumental suites, usually after the sarabande movement along with one or more other 'popular' dances.

At least 26 choreographies with the title 'rigaudon' survive from the early 18th century (16 French and ten English); most are for social dancing, although a few were evidently for use in the theatre. The rigaudon was a courtship dance and was similar to the bourrée in that each dance represented a particular mixture of steps chosen from among many, including both the *pas de bourrée* and the *fleuret* (both characteristic of the BOURRÉE, involving a bend–rise–step–step combination). At least one step was peculiar to the rigaudon, the *pas de rigaudon*; this was a group of three movements (hop, step step, jump) done in place during three crotchets of music. Ex.1 shows the opening phrase of a popular early

Ex.1 *Le rigaudon de la paix*, dance by Feuillet, Paris, 1700

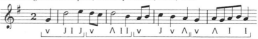

v = plié [bend]
∧ = élevé [rise]
I = plain step
J = jetté [leap]

18th-century court dance, the *Rigaudon de la paix*, as it appeared in Feuillet's *Recueil de dances* (1700). The *pas de rigaudon* is not shown here, but the second and fourth bars show the use of the *fleuret*; the combination of the rather restful *fleurets* in alternation with the activity of the first and third bars creates a rhythmic pattern of motion–repose–motion–repose for the phrase that was typical of the dance.

The heyday of the rigaudon was somewhat later than that of the bourrée. None of Lully's stage works includes pieces called 'rigaudon', although two *airs* from the pastorale *Acis et Galatée* were so labelled elsewhere. Lully's successors favoured it: Campra included two rigaudons in his ballet *L'Europe galant* (1697), both simple binary structures. The four-bar phrases begin with a rather static harmony and agogic emphasis on the first two downbeats, with both harmonic and rhythmic activity accelerating to the ends of phrases. Campra's rigaudon pair follows a brief shepherd's *air* that shares the rhythm and form of the dance, and the scene is followed by an instrumental passepied. Ex.2 shows the opening strain of the *air* and that of the first rigaudon.

A similar rhythmic and harmonic phrase structure appears in the one rigaudon in Desmarets' opera *Circé*

Ex.2 A. Campra: *L'Europe galant* (1697), Act 2 scene iii
(a) Air

Sou - pi - rons   tous,   sui - vons   l'A -

- mour sans nous con - train - dre

(b) Premier Rigaudon

Ex.4 Henry Purcell: *Musick's Hand-maid*, part 2, Rigadoon

(1694). Rameau seems to have been particularly fond of the rigaudon, using it in nearly all his operas. In *Hippolyte et Aricie* (Act 3) a pair of rigaudons, the first played da capo, frame a sailor's *air* in praise of a safe landing; the *air* borrows the opening rhythm of the second rigaudon. Ex.3 shows the beginnings of both the rigaudon and the *air* based on it; the harmonic rhythm of this rigaudon is similar to that of Campra's, beginning with almost no motion and gradually quickening; but the melodic rhythm does not give the agogic emphasis usually accompanying this motion. In the ballet *Platée* (1744), two passepieds and two rigaudons, both da capo, are played during a dance representing the mingling of peasants and satyrs. Both dramatic uses of the rigaudon confirm Mattheson's judgment (*Der vollkommene Capellmeister*, 1739) that the dance evoked a sense of sailing or of pastoral scenes.

Ex.3 Rameau: *Hippolyte et Aricie* (1733), Act 3 scene viii

L'a - mour com - me Nep - tu - ne In -

- vite   à   s'em - bar - quer

Many instrumental rigaudons for harpsichord and ensemble show the characteristic harmonic and melodic rhythms and clear phrase structure of the theatrical dance. Their form was usually either that of successive unrelated strains or, more typically in the 18th century, a rounded binary structure. Ex.4, a rigadoon by Purcell from the second part of *Musick's Hand-maid*, shows the adoption of a melodic rhythm like that in the Rameau example above, lacking the characteristic upbeat and long notes at the beginnings of phrases but retaining the harmonic shape of the phrase. A more typical keyboard rigaudon, adopting the rhythmic pattern of the Campra example above, is shown in ex.5, from Gottlieb Muffat's *Componimento musicale* (1726). Other keyboard composers who favoured the rigaudon were E.-C. Jacquet de la Guerre, Charles Daquin, J. C. F. Fischer, Johann Pachelbel, François Couperin and Rameau.

Ex.5 Gottlieb Muffat: *Componimento musicale*, 1726

etc

The rigaudon also found its way into Baroque orchestral and chamber music. J. J. Fux's *Concentus musicus* (1701) included two rigaudons, one linked with a trio bourrée that works out some rhythmic ideas introduced in the preceding rigaudon. The only significant difference between the rigaudon and the bourrée in this group is in the speed of harmonic change at the beginnings of phrases, for the rigaudon continues to have static openings accelerating to the ends of phrases. As a number of pieces called 'rigaudon' (see, for example, two in Muffat's *Componimento musicale*) give prominence to the crotchet–minim syncopation thought to be characteristic of the bourrée, and hence to be a distinguishing feature, the harmonic rhythm of rigaudon phrases may prove a useful distinction. Rigaudons were also included in instrumental suites by François Couperin (*4e concert royal*), Boismortier, Heudelinne, Lalande, Montéclair, J. C. F. Fischer, Telemann, Georg Böhm, J. C. Pez, Georg Muffat and Christoph Graupner, often, as in opera and ballet, followed by a passepied. Although the rigaudon gradually disappeared about the mid-18th century, a few later composers used it, including Grieg (*Holberg Suite*, 1884), Prokofiev, Saint-Saëns, MacDowell (*Air et rigaudon* for piano op.49 no.2) and Ravel (*Le tombeau de Couperin*, 1917).

BIBLIOGRAPHY
L. Horst: *Pre-classic Dance Forms* (New York, 1937/R1968)
V. Alford: 'The Rigaudon', *MQ*, xxx (1944), 277
P. Nettl: *The Story of Dance Music* (New York, 1947)
                                    MEREDITH ELLIS LITTLE

Rigel [Riegel]. German, later French, family of musicians. Only (2) Anton Riegel continued to use the original spelling of the family name. (1) Henri-Joseph Rigel, who settled permanently in France in about 1768, and his sons, who were born there, seem always to have used the spelling Rigel, as do all extant documents and first editions of their works.

(1) Henri-Joseph Rigel (*b* Wertheim, 9 Feb 1741; *d* Paris, 2 May 1799). Conductor, teacher and composer. He was the son of Georg Caspar Riegel, an intendant (from about 1725 to his death in 1754) for Prince Löwenstein. After Georg's death his widow Maria Anna petitioned the prince for the support of her under-aged children, and it is probable that he furthered the musical education of her sons. In 1767 the name Riegel appeared for the first time in the Breitkopf Catalogue, with incipits for seven symphonies and one violin concerto. According to La Borde (*Essai sur la musique*, 1780), Rigel studied with Jommelli in Stuttgart, was sent by F. X. Richter to France 'pour faire l'éducation d'une jeune personne', and then settled in Paris in 1768. From this statement, it could be inferred that he studied in Mannheim with Richter. However, La Borde's date for Rigel's arrival in the French capital is inexact. The French press places him in Paris early in 1767 with the announcement of his op.1, *Six sonates pour clavecin*, obtainable 'chez l'auteur, rue S. Marc, maison de M. Dupin de Francueil' (*Annonces*, 9 April 1767). The dedicatee, Mlle Dupin de Francueil (later George Sand's aunt), is possibly the 'jeune personne' referred to by La Borde. Rigel was probably first employed, about 1764–5, outside Paris on her father's estates. In 1768 he established his own residence in Paris, and that is also the probable date of his marriage; it was in these quarters that his sons were born in 1769 and 1772.

Before 1780 Rigel published his own music, 'chez l'auteur', with his wife as engraver. He even published at least one work by another composer: *Pièces de clavecin, harpe ou pianoforte . . . par M. de Chabanon, mis au jour par Rigel, 1775*. After his arrival in Paris, Rigel established a distinguished reputation in the musical life of that city. In 1772 he served as a principal judge, along with Duni and F.-A. Philidor, of an important contest for the best symphony and *symphonie concertante*; the winners of the valuable first and second prizes were Cannabich and Eichner. During the 1770s Rigel wrote numerous instrumental works (sonatas, quartets, concertos and symphonies) that were performed in Parisian concert rooms. On 2 February 1774 a symphony by Rigel first appeared on a programme at the Concert Spirituel. Two oratorios by him written during this period, *La sortie d'Egypte* (1774) and *La déstruction de Jéricho* (1778), enjoyed an immense success; the former was performed at the Concert Spirituel no fewer than 27 times from 1775 to 1786, and was performed in Paris as late as 1822. In about 1780 Rigel turned his attention from instrumental and sacred vocal composition to the writing of large-scale stage works. After 1780 his wife is no longer mentioned, and within the next two years, his younger brother (2) Anton Riegel came to live with him and act as his publisher until Boyer took over the sale and publication of his works in 1784. Between 1778 and his death in 1799, Rigel composed all of his 14 operatic works. He worked with a variety of librettists, composing operas for most of the prominent Parisian theatres, including the Comédie-Italienne, Théâtre Feydeau, Théâtre de l'Ambigu-Comique and the Opéra. In 1783 (and later) he was officially listed among the ten 'compositeurs de Concert Spirituel'. According to the *projet* of 1783 for the Ecole Royale de Chant, Rigel was appointed *maître de solfège*. The same source states that he was previously associated with the Paris Opéra. After the Revolution, when the school was reorganized as the Conservatoire, he remained as a professor *première classe* of the piano, a position he held for the rest of his life. Also in 1783 (and in 1787–8) Rigel is listed as *chef d'orchestre* of the Concert Spirituel. In the early 1790s works by him appeared frequently on programmes at the Cirque du Palais Royal and the Concert du Cirque National.

Henri-Joseph Rigel was one of the most respected musicians in Paris during the last quarter of the 18th century. His contemporaries praised the excellence of his teaching as well as the quality of his compositions. His oratorios and motets, all written for the Concert Spirituel, had remarkable records of performances. Although he composed 14 stage works (of which most of the music is lost), Rigel was less successful as an operatic composer; his talent was lyrical rather than dramatic. Of his most popular opera, *Rosanie* (1780), the editor of the *Mercure de France*, after reproaching the composer for interrupting the forward motion of his action with 'des airs à roulades', wrote the following: 'his style is pure; his workmanship is learned; his composition is full of ideas; his expression is true; his accompaniments well conceived, and his melodies of a fluent and graceful nature'. Rigel's principal contribution, however, was to instrumental music. His numerous works for the keyboard continued the tradition of the French piano school begun by Schobert. Except for the sonatas op.1 (1767), all his keyboard compositions are accompanied by a diversified assortment of instruments. Most are in two or three concise movements. Half of the *Six sonates* op.13 employ dance or dance-like movements: Scherzo, Allemande stirienne, Marcia maestoso a la polonese, etc. Despite their designation of both harpsichord and piano in the title, his works appear to have been conceived primarily for the piano, as evidenced by their wide range of dynamics and sonorities. The very nature of their settings, i.e. *Sonates de clavecin en quatuor* op.7, or *Second oeuvre de symphonies pour le clavecin ou piano-forte* op.17 (both with optional parts for two violins, two horns and a cello), indicates the composer's orchestral conception and treatment of the instrument. Similarly, half the solo sonatas show a strong influence of contemporary orchestral style: there are full, repeated chords in both hands at the opening of movements and important cadences, extended octave tremolos, and strongly contrasting second themes preceded by pauses. Rigel wrote more than 20 orchestral works, comprising symphonies, solo concertos, and an unusual *Concerto concertant* op.20 for keyboard and solo violin with orchestra. All are in three movements, except for the *Sinfonie pastorale* (op.21 no.4), which has an opening Andante preceding the usual fast–slow–fast movements. Frequent performances of this work were reported at the Concert Spirituel, Concert des Amateurs and the Concert de la Loge Olympique. The orchestral works are excellent examples of an internationalized style. The salient feature in Rigel's orchestral music, as pointed out by Sondheimer (1956, p.223), is its remarkable lyricism. Sondheimer distinguished two melodic types, the first of 'sweet grace and loveliness with every tone of touching affection [symbolizing] . . . feminine beauty. The second is in the minor and of a passionate and yearning disposition'. Rigel applied his lyrical gifts to many genres and styles with a great deal of success.

WORKS

OPERAS

(*first performed in Paris unless otherwise stated*)

Le savetier et le financier (opéra comique, 2, J.-B. Lourdet de Santerre), Marly, 23 Oct 1778 (Paris, 1778); ov. ed. R. Sondheimer (London, 1939)

Cora et Alonzo (grand opera, 4, P.-U. Dubuisson), commissioned by Opéra, 1779, not perf.

Rosanie (opéra comique, 3, A.-M.-D. Devismes), Comédie-Italienne, 24 July 1780; rev. as Azélie, 1790

Blanche et Vermeille (opéra comique, 3, J.-P. Florian), Comédie-

Italienne, 5 March 1781; rev. in 2 acts, 26 May 1781 (Paris, c1781); rev. in 1 act, 26 March 1782

L'automate (opéra comique, 1, Cuinet-Dorbeil), Comédie-Italienne, 20 Aug 1781 (Paris, 1781)

Les amours du Gros-Cailloux (opéra comique, 1, C.-J. Guillemain), Beaujolais, 10 April 1786

L'entrée du Seigneur (opéra comique, 1, Lebas), Beaujolais, 21 Oct 1786

Lucas et Babet (opéra comique, 1), Beaujolais, 15 June 1787

Alix de Beaucaire (drame lyrique, 3, M.-J. Boutillier), commissioned by Comédie-Italienne, 1787; perf. Montansier, 10 Nov 1791

Estelle et Némorin (mélodrame pastoral, 2, J.-L. Gabiot de Salins, after Florian), Ambigu-Comique, 25 June 1788 (Paris, 1788)

Aline et Zamorin (Aline et Dupré, ou Le marchand de marrons) (opéra comique, 2), Beaujolais, 9 Aug 1788

Le bon fermier (opéra comique, 1, Delvieu), Beaujolais, 18 May 1789

Pauline et Henri (comédie, 1, Boutillier), Feydeau, 9 Nov 1793 (Paris, 1794)

Le magot de la Chine (opéra comique, 1, L. J. H. Dancourt), Ambigu-Comique, 7 Aug 1800 [posth.]

OTHER VOCAL

Sacred (all perf. Paris, Concert Spirituel): La sortie d'Egypte, oratorio, 1774; La déstruction de Jéricho, oratorio, 1778; Regina coeli, motet, grand chorus, 1780; Ave verum, motet, 1783; Jepthé, oratorio, 1783; Les macchabées, oratorio

Revolutionary: Hymne sur l'enfance, ou Le devoir des mères (F. G. Desfontaines) (Paris, 1794); Hymne à la liberté, ou Hymne pour la Fête du 10 août (Baour-Lormian), 4vv (Paris, 1795), ed. C. Pierre, *Fêtes et cérémonies de la Revolution française* (Paris, 1899)

Many others pubd in collections and singly, incl. Le ménage comme il y a peu (Person) (Paris, 1793), L'amant trahi, ariette (Paris, c1778); some pubd in *Mercure de France*

INSTRUMENTAL

First published in Paris; many later edns. in Mannheim, Offenbach and Vienna, usually with different op. nos.; see DTB, xxviii, Jg.xvi (1915/R).

Syms.: 7 cited in Breitkopf catalogue of 1767 [1 pubd as op.12 no.1, 2 pubd as op.21 nos.3 and 5, 1 in CH-E, 3 lost]; 1, C, c1767, D-Rtt [listed under '?A. Riegel']; 6 sinfonies, op.12 (1774), nos.2, 4 ed. R. Sondheimer (London, 1938–9); 1, D, no.3 in 3 simphonies à grand orchestre: Gossec & Rigel (1782); 1, g, no.2 in 3 simphonies à grand orchestre: Rosetti, Rigel & Ditters (1783); 6 simphonies, op.21 (1786), no.2 ed. in B. S. Brook (1962)

Concs.: 1 for vn, G, cited in Breitkopf catalogue of 1767; 1er, hpd, op.2 (c1770); 2me, hpd, op.3 (c1770); 2 for hpd, op.11 (c1773); 1 for hpd, no.1 in Journal de pièces de clavecin, ?op.19 (1784); Concerto concertant, hpd, solo vn, no.36 of Journal de pièces de clavecin, op.20 (1786)

Chamber: 6 sonates, hpd, op.1 (1767); 6 quatuors dialogués, str qt, op.4 (c1770); Pièces de clavecin mêlées de préludes pour les commenceants, op.5 (c1770); Suite des pièces . . . mêlées de préludes, hpd, acc. vn ad lib, op.6 (c1771); Sonates de clavecin en quatuor, opt. acc. 2 vn, 2 hn, vc, op.7 (c1771); 6 sonates de clavecin en symphonie, op.8 (c1772); Sonates de clavecin en quatuor, op.9 (c1772); Second oeuvre de quatuors dialogués, str qt, op.10 (c1773); 6 sonates, hpd, acc. vn ad lib, op.13 (1777), march from no.4 ed. in G. de Saint-Foix (1924); 3 duos, pf/hpd, op.14 (c1777) [also pubd as qts, 2 vn, va, pf]; 3 sonates en symphonies, hpd/pf, op.16 (1783); Second oeuvre de symphonies, hpd/pf, op.17 (1783); 3 sonates, hpd/pf, op.18 (1784); other chamber and kbd pieces in 18th-century anthologies; various arrs.

(2) Anton Riegel [Antoine Rigel] (*b* Wertheim, ?c1745; *d* ?Mannheim, after 1807). Teacher and composer, brother of (1) Henri-Joseph Rigel. He appears to have travelled throughout Europe. His name is first mentioned in the Hummel Catalogue of 1771 with incipits of his six quartets op.1 for flute, violin, viola and bass (they were first advertised in January 1770). In the Breitkopf Catalogue of 1773 there is another listing for these quartets, as well as one for a flute concerto in C major by a Riegel, probably Anton. He may have arrived in Paris as early as 1776, when his op.1 quartets were published there by Le Menu & Boyer. In 1782 he was living in Paris with his older brother, Henri-Joseph; the *Almanach musical* of 1783 lists Anton as a teacher of the piano and the flute. During this period he published some of his brother's works (opp.16 and 18) as well as at least one of his own (op.6), and took up residence at the Cul de sac de la Corderie. His Parisian

publications, mainly accompanied keyboard works, ceased in 1787 with his op.7; he probably left the capital shortly thereafter. In the mid-1780s his works, including re-editions of Parisian prints, appeared in Offenbach, Amsterdam, Speyer, Mannheim and Heilbronn. At the end of the century he lived in Heilbronn, and after 1807 he was reported living in Mannheim. Anton Riegel enjoyed a modest if unfocussed career. He was a competent composer whose output consisted mainly of accompanied keyboard sonatas and chamber works.

WORKS

op.
1 Six quatuor, fl, vn, va, b (The Hague, 1770)
2 Six sonate en trio, hpd/pf (Paris, 1773)
3 Tre quattri, hpd, 2 vn, vc (Mannheim, before 1779)
4 Six sonates, hpd, acc. vn (Paris, 1782)
5 Six sonates, hpd/pf, acc. vn (Speyer, before 1781)
6 Deux sonates en symphonie, kbd, acc. 2 vn, 2 hn, vc (Paris, 1785)
7 Trois sonates, hpd, vn obbl (Paris, 1787)
8 Deux caprices, hpd, acc. vn (Offenbach, 1790)
9 Trois sonates faciles, hpd, acc. vn (Offenbach, 1790)

Works without op. nos.: Symphonie à grand orchestre, Eb, *F-Pc*; Sym., D, 2 ob, 2 fl, 2 hn, 2 tpt, timp, org, str, *US-Wc*; Sym., C, *D-Rtt* [doubtful; probably by Henri-Joseph Rigel]; Fl Conc., cited in Breitkopf catalogue of 1773; 6 trios, fl, vn, b, *KA*; Qt, d, fl, vn, va, vc, *B-Bc*

(3) Louis Rigel (*b* Paris, 1769; *d* Le Havre, 25 Feb 1811). Pianist, composer and teacher, son of (1) Henri-Joseph Rigel. He studied with his father and became an excellent pianist and teacher, as well as a fair performer on the violin. Louis was the first to publish piano arrangements (Paris, 1778; accompanied by two violins, a viola and a bass) of the six Paris Symphonies of Haydn. According to the title-page of these arrangements, he was a member of the Académie Royale de Musique (the Opéra). After the Revolution he settled in Le Havre, where he lived until his death. He left a number of unpublished works that his brother, Henri-Jean, proposed to publish but never did. His only other known publications are *romances* in *Feuilles de Terpsichore* (1786–7), and keyboard arrangements of trios by Pleyel and of various opera overtures.

(4) Henri-Jean Rigel (*b* Paris, 11 May 1772; *d* Abbeville, 16 Dec 1852). Pianist, teacher and composer, son of (1) Henri-Joseph Rigel. He first studied the piano and composition with his father, and then entered the Ecole Royale de Chant at its formation in 1784. In 1785, at the age of 13, he became a *sous-maître de solfège* there. After his first year he received official praise from F. J. Gossec, the school's director, for his great service in training the young, rehearsing choruses, and accompanying at the piano for both the theatre and the singing classes. On 9 April 1787 Henri-Jean made his début as a composer at the Concert Spirituel with a performance of a 'nouvelle scène française', possibly one of his cantatas (text by Vacherot). *Judith* and *Le retour de Tobie* (same librettist) were performed later that year at the Concert Spirituel. In 1788, the name Rigel *fils* appeared five times on programmes at the Concert Spirituel with performances of his *scène*, a *symphonie*, and the Duo with words by Vacherot. Choron and Fayolle, who apparently knew Rigel personally, list *Gédéon*, *Judith* and *Le retour de Tobie* as having been performed at the Concert Spirituel between 1787 and 1791. On 29 March 1790 scenes from *Judith* and *Le retour de Tobie* were performed at the Cirque du Palais Royal. None of these works was printed.

Rigel's first published work, *Trois sonates pour forte-*

piano op.1, appeared in 1794. During the post-Revolutionary period, he also published *Ode contre les émigrés* and transcribed a number of Revolutionary hymns and overtures by Catel, Méhul and Gossec for piano (1794–5). When the Ecole Royale de Chant was reorganized into the Conservatoire in 1795, Henri-Jean was retained as 'professeur de 2e classe', remaining there until 1797. In 1798 he was appointed by Napoleon to take part in an expedition to Egypt. In Cairo he was made a member of the Egyptian Institute of Sciences and Arts and was appointed music director of the newly formed French Theatre, for which he wrote *Les deux meuniers* (1799), an *opéra comique* in one act to a text by C. L. Balzac. After his return to France in 1800, he became known as one of the best professors of the piano in his time. Napoleon awarded him the title 'pianiste de la musique particulière de l'Empereur et Roi'. His career as teacher and accompanist was long and distinguished; he was later one of the teachers of César Franck. In addition to his teaching and performing, he continued conducting: on 28 September 1814 'M. Rigel de la musique du roi' conducted a solemn concert 'en l'honneur de la paix' at the church of Belleville, Paris. His reputation as a composer rivalled that of his father. He wrote a large number of works in many genres, including operas, cantatas, smaller vocal pieces, orchestral works and numerous sonatas, concertos and potpourris for the piano. From 1816 he was active as a member of the Société Académique des Enfants d'Apollon, serving as its Commissaire de Musique (1820) and as president (1825); a number of his works appear on the society's programme, and he was instrumental in reviving several of his father's works as well. He married Mlle Duval de Sorcourt and established his residence in Abbeville, where he died at the age of 80.

Henri-Jean's works have often been confused with his father's (in Eitner, Sondheimer, Riemann in DTB, xxviii, Jg.xvi etc). His publications reached op.50, but many appear to be lost, while works for which performances have been recorded in the contemporary press appear never to have been published. According to Choron and Fayolle's list, Rigel published the following works before 1811 (when their *Dictionnaire* appeared): three concertos, five sets of sonatas, nine fantasias or potpourris, a set of theme and variations dedicated to 'Dusseck', a Grand Duo for harp and piano dedicated to M. Naderman, three overtures for piano and large orchestra, three volumes (*cahiers*) of *romances*, several individual *romances* (among others, *Petits oiseaux*, which enjoyed much success), several *scènes italiennes* and a large piece for the panharmonicon, which was well received. He also composed many works that remain in manuscript, although he hoped to publish them. According to Choron and Fayolle, his compositions were esteemed for their good taste and 'regularité'.

WORKS

VOCAL

Les deux meuniers (opéra comique, 1, C.-L. Balzac), Cairo, 1799

Le duel nocturne (opéra comique, 1, Longchamps), Paris, Feydeau, 23 Dec 1805

Scènes françaises: Gédéon, Judith, Le retour de Tobie: all Concert Spirituel, 1787–91; Cantata in honour of Le Sueur, Abbeville, 5 Aug 1846

Romances (all pubd in Paris unless otherwise stated): Petits oiseaux (Balzac) (*c*1799); Recueil de 6 romances . . . déd. à Mme Bonaparte (?Paris, 1804), lost; 2me recueil de 3 nouvelles romances, op.18 (?Paris, 1805), lost; 3me recueil de 3 nouvelles romances, op.20 (?Paris, 1807), lost; La leçon de la rose (1807); Les souvenirs (1808),

lost; La bergère inquiète (1808), lost; Je t'aimerai (1809), lost; Fleur de beauté (Mme de Coupigny) (1811), lost; Autrefois dans ces prés fleuris (1811), lost; Le fleuve paisible (1811), lost; Limpides eaux dont le miroir (1811), lost; Revenez habiter mon coeur, tranquille paix (1811), lost; L'amitié (1812); Le jeune Hortense (1812); Regrets de l'absence (1812); Au Zéphir (1813); Le bouquet (1814); L'indifférence (1815), lost; Le barde au tombeau de sa bien-aimée (1815), lost

Others, incl. Duo (Vacherot), Concert Spirituel, 1788; Ode contre les émigrés (Crassous) (Paris, 1794)

Works known only through perfs. at Société Académique des Enfants d'Apollon: Hymne au soleil (recit, chorus), 11 May 1820; Scène italienne, songs and choruses from an oratorio, 31 May 1821; Rondo (Bouilly), couplets, Jan 1823; Scène et rondeau italiens, 24 May 1824; Invocation à Apollon, 3 solo vv, chorus, orch, 4 May 1826; Grande scène italienne, 21 May 1846

INSTRUMENTAL
(*printed works published in Paris unless otherwise stated*)

Orch: Simphonie à 15, *D-DS*; 1er concerto, pf (n.d.); 2me concerto, pf (n.d.); 3me concerto, pf (n.d.); 4me concerto, pf, op.28 (n.d.); Grande ouverture, D (n.d.); Ouverture à grand orchestre, Nov 1822, Ouverture pastorale (n.d.), 15 May 1828, Ouverture pour orchestre, 20 May 1830, L'héroïque, grand overture, 4 May 1845: all perf. at concerts of Société Académique des Enfants d'Apollon

Chamber: Sonates, pf, vn, op.7 (Paris and Offenbach, n.d.); Sonates, pf, vn, op.19 (Paris and Offenbach, n.d.); Partition du grand quintetto, 2 vn, va, vc, db/vc, op.49 (*c*1830); Quatuor, pf, vn, va, vc, op.50 (n.d.); Grand et brillant quintette, pf, vn, va, vc, db (n.d.); Trios, pf, harp, vn (n.d.); Divertimento, 2 harps (n.d.); Quintetto, 1826, Trio . . . sur l'air ancien 'Petits oiseaux', harp, pf, vn, Dec 1831, Quintetto, E♭, Dec 1839: all perf. at concerts of Société Académique des Enfants d'Apollon

Pf: 3 sonates, acc. vn ad lib [op.1] (1794); 3 sonates de différens genres, op.2 (*c*1795); 3 sonates, op.3 (n.d.); Nouveau mélange varié, op.16 (Paris and Zurich, n.d.); 2 grandes sonates, op.17 (n.d.); Pot-pourri varié . . . sur les airs d'Armide et Télémaque, pf, harp, op.35 (*c*1820); Rondo brillant, op.45 (n.d.), ?same as Rondeau, opt. acc. fl, 2 vn, va, b, db, op.45 (Leipzig, 1830); Grand morceau pattetico et brillant, 4 hands, op.48 (*c*1835); Duo, 4 hands (n.d.); Duo, 2 pf (n.d.); others, incl. rondos for 2 pf in *The Harmonicon* (1823–5); arrs. of works by Dalayrac, also of Revolutionary hymns and ov. by Méhul, Gossec etc, *c*1795

BIBLIOGRAPHY

EitnerQ; *FétisB*; *GerberL*; *GerberNL*

A. Choron and F. Fayolle: *Dictionnaire historique des musiciens* (Paris, 1810–11/*R*1971)

T. Lassabathie: *Histoire du Conservatoire impérial de musique et de déclamation* (Paris, 1860)

E. G. J. Gregoir: *Bibliothèque musicale populaire* (Brussels, 1877)

M. Decourcelle: *La Société académique des enfants d'Apollon* (Paris, 1881)

C. Pierre: *Le Magasin de musique* (Paris, 1895)

——: *Le Conservatoire national de musique et de déclamation: documents historiques et administratifs* (Paris, 1900)

——: *Les hymnes et chansons de la Révolution* (Paris, 1904)

G. de Saint-Foix: 'Les premiers pianistes Parisiens (III): Rigel (Henri-Joseph)', *ReM*, v/8 (1924), 192

H. Gougelot: *Catalogue des romances françaises parues sous la Révolution et l'Empire*, i: *Les recueils de romances* (Melun, 1937)

——: *La romance française sous la Révolution et l'Empire*, ii: *Etude historique et critique* (Melun, 1938)

E. Reeser: *De klaviersonate met vioolbegeleiding* (Rotterdam, 1939)

R. Sondheimer: *Haydn: a Historical and Psychological Study Based on his Quartets* (London, 1951)

——: 'Henri-Joseph Rigel', *MR*, xvii (1956), 221

B. S. Brook: *La symphonie française dans la seconde moitié du XVIIIe siècle* [incl. further bibliography, esp. early sources] (Paris, 1962)

——: 'Rigel', *MGG*

C. Pierre: *Histoire du Concert spirituel 1725–1790* (Paris, 1975)

BARRY S. BROOK, RICHARD VIANO

Righetti [Giorgi], **Geltrude** (*b* Bologna, 1793; *d* Bologna, 1862). Italian contralto. She studied in Bologna and gave her first public performance there in 1814. The next year she married Luigi Giorgi, a lawyer, and in September was invited by the Duke of Sforza Cesarini to sing, at the express wish of the composer, at the Teatro Argentina, Rome, in the première of *Il barbiere di Siviglia*. In 1817 she sang the lead in the première of *La Cenerentola* at the Teatro Valle, Rome. She had a brief career, retiring from the stage, probably for health reasons, in 1822. Her *Cenni d'una donna già cantante sopra il Maestro Rossini in risposta a ciò che ne scrisse nella state 1822 il giornalista inglese in Parigi e fu riportato in una gazzetta di Milano dello stesso anno* (Bologna, 1823), a reply to an article by Stendhal which he published under the pseudonym of Alceste in the *Revue mensuelle de Paris* (1822), gives an interesting account of the first performance of *Il barbiere di Siviglia.*

BRUNO CAGLI

Righi, Giovanni (*b* Carpi, 2 June 1577; *d* Carpi, 9 Aug 1613). Italian composer. A letter from Paolo Guaitoli to Angelo Catelani (printed in Gaspari) gives details of Righi's ecclesiastical career; he received the tonsure in December 1590, progressed slowly through minor and major orders and was finally ordained in April 1601. The Carpi Cathedral records show that he was *maestro di cappella* there on 10 June 1605, although according to Guaitoli's letter and the records he only held the post for a few days between 9 May and 27 June, and not for three years as Spinelli stated. It is evident from the dedication of his *Secondo libro* that he was then a canon and *maestro di cappella* at the collegiate church in Mirandola, a post which he still held in 1610 when his *Terzo libro* was published. On 9 January 1612 he was again elected *maestro di cappella* of Carpi Cathedral.

WORKS

SACRED

Psalmi omnes, 5vv (Venice, 1603)
Missa, motecta, psalmi, litaniae (Venice, 1606)
Completorium romanum . . . una cum litaniis, motectis et anthiphonis BVM, 8vv, bc (org) (Venice, 1610[8])
Compieta, 5vv, bc; lost, listed in *Indice*

SECULAR

Canzonette, libro primo, 3, 4vv (Venice, 1605)
Il secondo libro delle canzonette, 3vv (Venice, 1607)
Il terzo libro delle canzonette, 3, 4vv, con un madrigale, 6vv (Venice, 1610)

BIBLIOGRAPHY

Indice di tutte le opere di musica che si trovano nella Stampa della Pigna di Alessandro Vincenti in Venetia (Venice, 1621); repr. in *MMg*, xiv–xv (1882–3/*R*), suppl.
G. Gaspari: *Miscellanea musicale* (MS, *I-Bc* UU.12), iii, 329f
A. G. Spinelli: *Notizie spettanti alla storia della musica in Carpi* (Carpi, 1900), 271ff

PIER PAOLO SCATTOLIN

Righi, Giuseppe [Gioseffo] **Maria** (*fl* 1694–1717). Italian composer. He set to music *La Bernarda*, a 'dramma rusticale per musica' by T. Stanzani, performed at the Teatro Formagliari, Bologna, in Carnival 1694, and perhaps earlier at the church of S Paolo using marionettes. This work may be based on the prose 'commedia rusticale' of the same title by G. C. Allegri, in turn a translation into Bolognese dialect of the much adapted *La Tancia* by Michelangelo Buonarroti the younger. Righi also composed a *Regina coeli* for four voices (score in *I-Baf*) for his admission in 1707 (Schmidl gave 1702) to the Accademia Filarmonica, Bologna, of which he was elected *principe* in 1717.

BIBLIOGRAPHY

EitnerQ; *SchmidlD*
G. Mazzuchelli: *Gli scrittori d'Italia*, i (Brescia, 1753), 509
L. Allacci: *Drammaturgia* (Venice, enlarged 2/1755/*R*1961)
C. Ricci: *I teatri di Bologna nei secoli XVII e XVIII* (Bologna, 1888/*R*1965)
G. Gaspari: *Catalogo della biblioteca del Liceo musicale di Bologna*, v, ed. U. Sesini (Bologna, 1943/*R*1970)

THOMAS WALKER

Righini, Pietro (*b* Bologna, 31 July 1907). Italian horn player and specialist in physical acoustics. He studied the horn at the Bologna Liceo Musicale (diploma 1924) and physics and acoustics in Rome and Turin (1937–8), holding appointments in theatre orchestras in Bologna (Teatro Comunale, 1924–8), Turin (Teatro Regio, 1928–9) and Naples (San Carlo, 1929–32) and with the Italian radio orchestra (1932–51). He was professor of the horn at Turin Conservatory (1933–73) and on the staff of the sound-recording unit of RAI-TV, Direzione Tecnica (1951–68, director from 1961) and a member (1968–70) of the Council of Europe committee for the standardization of pitch. In 1973 he was appointed to teach the history of modern music theory at the Cremona Scuola Universitaria di Filologia e Paleografia Musicale. Righini believes that the study of acoustics is indispensable to a modern musical education. His book *Il suono* (written in collaboration with his son) in particular has indicated the contribution acoustic studies should make, not only to such related spheres as architectural acoustics, but also to such specifically musical topics as transcription, orchestration and performance.

WRITINGS

Acustica musicale generale e applicata agli strumenti ed alla strumentazione (Turin, 1942)
Acustica musicale (Turin, 1960)
'Quadro sinottico delle scale musicali', *Elettronica e telecomunicazione* (1963), no.4, p.2
'Transitori di attacco e di estinzione del suono e loro effetto sul timbro', *Elettronica e telecomunicazione* (1965), no.2, p.59
'Contributo per le ricerche sul linguaggio musicale originario dell'epoca monteverdiana', *Congresso internazionale sul tema Claudio Monteverdi e il suo tempo: Venezia, Mantova e Cremona 1968*, 539
with U. Leone: *Il diapason: storia della sua normalizzazione* (Turin, 1969)
Acustica per il musicista: i fondamenti fisici della musica (Padua, 1970)
Le scale musicali: leggende, pregiudizi e realtà (Padua, 1971)
with G. U. Righini: 'La memoria dell'altezza dei suoni e l'intonazione musicale', *Elettronica e telecomunicazione* (1971), no.4, p.147
'Attualità di una monografia quasi secolare: "The History of Musical Pitch" di A. J. Ellis', *RIM*, vii (1972), 277
Considerazioni sulla psicoacustica del cantante: risoluzioni del Comitato dei ministri del consiglio d'Europa sulla normalizzazione del diapason (Padua, 1972)
Il corno (Ancona, 1972)
Studio analitico sul ritmo musicale (Padua, 1972)
'Possibilità e limiti dell'analisi temporizzata dei parametri del suono musicale e significato delle misure per ricerche etnico-musicali', *L'etnomusicologia in Italia: 1° convegno sugli studi etnomusicologici in Italia: Rome 1973*, 141
'Psicologia e intonazione pratica degli intervalli musicali', *Elettronica e telecomunicazione* (1973), no.2, p.69
A difesa del Patricio: nel labirinto della musica greca (Padua, 1974)
Guida sonora attraverso i sistemi musicali antichi e moderni (Padua, 1974) [disc notes]
with G. Righini: *Il suono dalla fisica all'uomo, alla musica, alla macchina* (Milan, 1974)
Gli intervalli musicali e la musica (Padua, 1975)
Le basi tecniche della musica greca (Padua, 1975)

FERRUCCIO TAMMARO

Righini, Vincenzo (*b* Bologna, 22 Jan 1756; *d* Bologna, 19 Aug 1812). Italian composer, singing teacher and conductor. Because of his excellent voice he was soon made a choirboy at S Petronio in Bologna. According to his obituary in the *Allgemeine musikalische Zeitung*, he sang too much, so that his voice became somewhat husky and dull, and it is true that in later years he had little success as a singer. He is sometimes said to have been a composition pupil of Martini, but this was doubted even in his obituary. He certainly did not have singing lessons from Antonio Bernacchi (*d* 1756), but he was trained in the Bologna school of singing, which

Bernacchi had raised to its greatest heights. In 1775 Righini made his début as a tenor in Parma and in 1776 joined the Bustelli opera troupe in Prague, for which he wrote his first stage music – arias, scenes and whole operas. *Il convitato di pietra* (1776), his first opera, was successful and in the next few years was performed at Vienna (in both Italian and German), Eszterháza (through Haydn), Brunswick and Hanover. In 1780 Emperor Joseph II called him to Vienna to be singing master to Princess Elisabeth of Württemberg and director of the Italian Opera. In Vienna – and later in Berlin – Righini was a singing teacher much sought after by society, but he also trained a large number of professional singers. His *Exercices pour se perfectionner dans l'art du chant* (Paris, n.d.) were called by Gerber 'undoubtedly the most beautiful solfeggios we have' and were also highly praised by J. F. Reichardt. His Viennese operas show his thorough knowledge, not only of the voice, but also (as in the echo aria for coloratura soprano and clarinet in *Armida*) of instrumentation.

On 1 July 1787, through the offices of the Wallerstein court music director, Ignaz von Beecke, Righini became the first Italian to be appointed Kapellmeister at the electoral court in Mainz. His first important undertaking in this post was a performance of *Armida*, probably revised for the occasion, in Aschaffenburg (2 September 1788). Also in 1788 he married the contralto Anna Maria Lehritter (1762–93), a half-sister of the prebendary and court pianist Sterkel. Among the significant works of this period were the *azione teatrale Alcide al bivio* (1790), written for the Elector of Trier (Righini's correspondence with the elector reveals his attempts to increase the proportion of duets, trios, quartets and other ensemble pieces in the work), the oratorio *Der Tod Jesu*, and the *Missa solemnis* op.59, composed for the coronation of Leopold II in Frankfurt am Main (1790) and highly praised by critics for its nobility, polish and expressive depth. In 1793 Righini was appointed successor to Felice Alessandri as court Kapellmeister and director of the Italian Opera in Berlin, alongside J. F. Reichardt, who was succeeded in 1794 by Himmel. In 1793 he composed the opera *Arianna* for the wedding of the future King Friedrich Wilhelm III. He worked hard for the advancement of Italian opera in Berlin; he had a number of excellent singers at his disposal, among them the bass Ludwig Fischer, who as a pupil of Raaf had been trained in the Bologna school of singing. Righini's decisive effect on the development and cultivation of the bass aria resulted from his collaboration with Fischer.

In all contemporary accounts Righini is described as a straightforward, unpretentious and likable person who enjoyed general respect, so that on the death of Friedrich Wilhelm II in 1797, he was able to keep his post. In 1798 he visited Hamburg, where his second wife, the singer Henriette Kneisel (1767–1801) was engaged; he had married her in 1793 and was to divorce her in 1800. His activities in the years 1802–5 are not entirely clear. Reichardt (in the *Berliner musikalische Zeitung*, ii, 1806, p.100) stated that Righini composed his opera *La selva incantata* shortly before a journey to Italy and that because of an illness he was unable to conduct or hear it when it was first performed in January 1803. The following month the *Allgemeine musikalische Zeitung* reported that he was dangerously ill but did not say where he was at the time. In 1804 he visited Leipzig, Hamburg and Vienna, the last probably

on a second journey to Italy, during which he was at Bologna, Venice and Naples. He returned to Berlin with the singer Brizzi in November 1805. In 1806, following the outbreak of war, the Italian Opera was disbanded, but Righini remained in Berlin, and when the royal theatre was reorganized in 1811, he was by general consent appointed Kapellmeister, along with B. A. Weber. His last major work was a *Te Deum* for the return of the king and queen to Berlin in 1810. The unexpected death of his only son in 1810 is supposed to have brought on his fatal illness; in 1812 he went to Italy and died after an operation in Bologna.

The Berlin operas represent the peak of Righini's work, the direction which is already apparent in *Enea nel Lazio* (1793), which is defined as being 'con cori e balli analoghi'. The criticism that he sacrificed the dramatic concept by expanding the ballets misses the point: it is precisely in these ballets that he broke free from the traditional musical language and turned to a more dramatic expression. Criticism has also been levelled – and rightly – at Filistri's librettos, but as Filistri was court poet and (from 1797) also intendant of the royal theatres and had, through the Countess Lichtenau, considerable influence on the king, Righini was in no sense free in his choice of librettist. In spite of his limitations and of unfavourable comparisons – with Mozart, for example – Righini's operas were famous in their time and were praised for the way in which they combined expressive, authentically Italian vocal writing with German art and craftsmanship, but above all for their instrumentation, as in the 'sublime' horn, bassoon and cello trio in *Tigrane* (*AMZ*, iii, 1800, col.620). Gerber warmly remembered *Atalante* with its 'sublime music', and the author of Righini's obituary (in the *AMZ*) rightly stated that although his operas were really concert music, the best parts of them were among the most splendid music ever written for the voice. A thorough evaluation of Righini's work is still lacking, especially of his numerous songs and instrumental pieces, also popular in their day. In these the composer by no means followed the usual paths, as his songs with variations prove.

WORKS

STAGE

Il convitato di pietra, ossia Il dissoluto punito (Don Giovanni) (dramma tragicomico, 3, N. Porta), Prague, 1776; as Das steinerne Gastmahl, oder Der Ruchlose, Vienna, 1777

La bottega del cafè (commedia giocosa, 2, Goldoni), Prague, 1778

La vedova scaltra (dramma giocoso, 2, Goldoni), Prague, 1778

Armida (dramma, 2, M. Coltellini), Vienna, 1782; rev. (A. Filistri de Caramandani), Berlin, 1799; *D-Bds, DS, GB-Lbm*, vocal score (Bonn and Leipzig, *c*1799)

L'incontro inaspettato (dramma giocoso, 2, Porta), Vienna, 1785; *D-Bds*; as Die unvermutete Zusammenkunft, Berlin, 1793

Il Demogorgone, ovvero Il filosofo confuso (opera buffa, 2, Porta), Vienna, 1786; *Bds*

Antigono (dramma serio, Coltellini), Mainz, 1788

Alcide al bivio (azione teatrale, 1, Metastasio), Koblenz, 1790; as cantata, rev., Vienna, 1804; autograph *I-Bc*, copy *A-Wgm*

Vasco di Gama (opera), Berlin, 1792; pasticcio with music by Paisiello, Nasolini, Sarti, Neukomm, Jommelli etc

Enea nel Lazio (dramma eroi-tragico, 3, Filistri), Berlin, 1793; *Wgm, D-Bds, DS, GB-Lbm*, vocal score (Leipzig, n.d.)

Il trionfo d'Arianna (dramma, 3, Filistri), Berlin, 1793; *D-Bds*

Atalante e Meleagro (festa teatrale, 1, Filistri), Berlin, 1797; *Bds*

La Gerusalemme liberata, ossia Armida al campo de' franchi (dramma, 2), Berlin, 1799; *Bds, GB-Lbm*, vocal score (Leipzig, ?1802)

Tigrane (dramma eroico, 3), Berlin, 1800; ballets *Bds, DS*, excerpts (Leipzig, n.d.)

Minerva belebet die Statue des Dädalus (pantomimischer Tanz, Telle), Berlin, 1802; arr. pf (Berlin, ?1802)

La selva incantata (opera, Filistri), Berlin, 1803; *Bds, DS*, vocal score (Leipzig, ?1803); as Der Zauberwald, Berlin, 1811

OTHER WORKS

Cantatas and occasional works: La sopresa amorosa, cantata, 3vv, orch, Vienna, 1780; Il natal d'Apollo (Filistri), cantata, vv, orch, Vienna, 1789, *A-Wgm, D-Bds, Mbs*, perf. as opera, Berlin, 1794; Cantate avec choeurs et danses russes, vv, pf, Berlin, 1801, pubd; Cantata, Berlin, 1802; Eilt herbey zum heut'gen Feste, cantata, Berlin, ?1805; Divertissement, S, S, B, pf, for birthday of the Princess Royal, *Bds*; Fanta in solennitate, motet, 5vv, orch, *Bds*

Sacred: Der Tod Jesu, oratorio, *A-Wn*; Missa solemnis, SATB, orch, op.59 (Berlin, n.d.); Requiem, 4vv, autograph *D-Bds*; Te Deum, Berlin, 1810, autograph *I-Bc*; masses, others

Pedagogical· Exercices pour se perfectionner dans l'art du chant (Paris, n.d.; Ger. trans., n.d. as Übungen um sich in der Kunst des Gesanges zu vervollkommen, op.10)

Miscellaneous: numerous songs, ariettas, partsongs, pf pieces, many pubd

BIBLIOGRAPHY

EitnerQ; GerberNL; RiemannL 12

Obituary, *AMZ*, xiv (1812), col.687

G. Schilling: *Encyclopädie der gesammten musikalischen Wissenschaften oder Universal-Lexikon der Tonkunst* (Stuttgart, 1835–42/*R*1973)

C. von Ledebur: *Tonkünstler-Lexicon Berlin's* (Berlin, 1861/*R*1965)

H. Mendel and A. Reissmann: *Musikalisches Conversations-Lexikon* (Berlin, 1877)

M. Friedlaender: *Das deutsche Lied im 18. Jahrhundert* (Stuttgart and Berlin, 1902/*R*1970)

A. Weissmann: *Berlin als Musikstadt* (Berlin and Leipzig, 1911)

A. Gottron: *Tausend Jahre Musik in Mainz* (Berlin, 1941)

H. Fetting: *Die Geschichte der deutschen Staatsoper* (Berlin, 1955)

A. Gottron: *Mainzer Musikgeschichte von 1500–1800* (Mainz, 1959)

D. Bartha and L. Somfai: *Haydn als Opernkapellmeister* (Budapest and Mainz, 1960)

G. Tintori and W. Bollert: 'Righini, Vincenzo', *ES*

J. Harich: 'Das Repertoire des Opernkapellmeisters Joseph Haydn in Esterháza (1780–1790)', *Haydn Yearbook*, i (1962), 9–110

H. Engel: 'Righini, Vincenzo', *MGG* [incl. detailed list of songs and inst pieces]

G. Bereths: *Die Musikpflege am Kurtrierischen Hofe zu Koblenz-Ehrenbreitstein* (Mainz, 1964)

H. Federhofer: 'Vincenzo Righinis Opera *Alcide al bivio*', *Essays Presented to Egon Wellesz* (Oxford, 1966), 130

GUDRUN BECKER-WEIDMANN

Rigler [Riegler], **Franz Paul** [Franz Xaver, François Sav.] (*b* 1747 or 1748; *d* Vienna, 17 Oct 1796). Teacher, writer on music, pianist, organist and composer. He was probably Austrian by birth, but around 1775 moved to Pressburg (now Bratislava) and until 1791 was the music professor at the Hauptnazionalschule, mainly a training institution for teachers and Kantors. In this central position Rigler exerted considerable influence on the musical life of what was then northern Hungary. He was a performing keyboard artist until about 1785, when he developed a mental illness. Many music encyclopedias, beginning with Gerber (1792), mention him as one of the best keyboard players of his time. As a composer he showed early promise which was unfulfilled.

Rigler's most important work is the *Anleitung zum Gesange, und dem Klaviere* (1798), a compendium of information in virtually all areas of music: singing, keyboard playing, harmony, counterpoint, form and ornamentation. As he was one of the few theorists who worked in the sphere of the Viennese Classical masters his writings may reflect theories that influenced them, and are therefore an important source of late 18th-century tendencies in music theory and education, as well as a source for evaluating the relationship between the Viennese and the Hungarian and Slovak music cultures. Apart from the *Anleitung zum Gesange* Rigler left one smaller didactic work, several keyboard sonatas, character-pieces, rondos and songs.

WORKS

Hpd/pf: 2 sonate, pt.1 (Vienna, ?1778); 2 sonate, op.1 bk. 2 (Vienna, ?1782); 2 sonates (Vienna, ?1784); 3 rondos, op.6 (Vienna, ?1790); 18 pieces diverses petites et grandes (Bratislava, n.d.); 2 sonates, bk. 1, pt.3 (Vienna, n.d.), doubtful

Vocal: 12 Oden und Lieder (Vienna, ?1782), lost

PEDAGOGICAL WORKS

Anleitung zum Klavier für musikalischen Lehrstunden, i (Vienna, 1779, 2/1791, repr. 1791 as *Anleitung zum Klavier für musikalischen Privatlehrstunden*) [appx with 24 cadenzas, 6 kbd pieces]

Anleitung zum Gesange, und dem Klaviere oder die Orgel zu spielen, nebst den ersten Gründen zur Komposition (Budapest, 1798) [appxs: 33 church songs, 31 works of various composers, 4 org sonatas, 4 org fugues as samples, 25 practice pieces, 6 cadenzas]

BIBLIOGRAPHY

CSHS; GerberL

L. Munkachy: *Franz Paul Rigler as Theorist and Composer* (diss., U. of Pittsburgh, 1968) [incl. work-list and trans. of *Anleitung zum Gesange*]

LOUIS MUNKACHY

Rignold [Rignall], **Hugo (Henry)** (*b* Kingston-upon-Thames, 15 May 1905; *d* London, 30 May 1976). English conductor. At the RAM he studied the violin with Hans Wessely, the viola with Lionel Tertis and the oboe with Leon Goossens, and began his career as a freelance violinist in London. As a dance-band musician he worked with Jack Hylton, and also led his own band. In 1944, while serving with the RAF, he appeared as guest conductor with the Palestine SO, and he later fulfilled various other engagements in the Middle East. In 1947 he was appointed a conductor of the Sadler's Wells Ballet, and from 1948 to 1954 was musical director of the Liverpool PO. He returned to the Royal Ballet (as the Sadler's Wells Ballet was by then renamed) as musical director in 1957, but relinquished this post to become musical director of the City of Birmingham SO, 1960–68. He also appeared with various orchestras in South Africa, holding the appointment of resident guest conductor of the Cape Town SO in 1956, in 1971–2 and in 1973. He recorded with the London Philharmonic, Covent Garden and Birmingham orchestras, notably (with the Covent Garden orchestra) the two complete suites from Prokofiev's *Cinderella*.

ARTHUR JACOBS

Rigo (It.). STAFF.

Řihovský, Vojtěch [Adalbert] (*b* Dub na Moravě, north Moravia, 21 April 1871; *d* Prague, 15 Sept 1950). Czech composer. Between 1887 and 1892 he studied in Prague at the Organ School, the Jan Ludvík Lukes Singing Institute and the Arnošt Černý Music Institute. He then assisted the choir in his home town (where his father was teacher and choirmaster from 1892 to 1902), and directed the choirs in Chrudim (1902–14) and at St Ludmila, Prague-Vinohrady (1914–36). His activities also included performing (viola, violin and piano), directing the choir at the archbishop's seminary, acting as adviser to the Prague music publishing house of Mojmír Urbánek (from 1902) and contributing to the Prague periodicals *Dalibor* (which in 1920 he edited with Jaromír Borecký) and *Cyril*. His short compositions were printed as supplements to the journals *Hudebni květy* and *Česká hudba*. He also worked in the Cyrillic Association and played a part in the 'Cyrillic Movement', which aimed at a revival of Catholic church music.

For the most part Řihovský composed sacred music, producing almost 300 pieces in this field. The style is basically Romantic; the melodic invention and the refined polyphony do not depart from the norms established for liturgical music. His Christmas carols and organ compositions show the effect of his work on folksong, mainly in a stylized manner (e.g. the *Vánoční preludia*, 'Christmas prelude', for organ). In the sphere of secular music he wrote principally short vocal and instrumental pieces. Even in these he remained within the bounds of late Romanticism, and his style, affected by commercial demand, is sometimes eclectic. His educational works were important in their time.

WORKS
(selective list)

Sacred vocal: Cyrilmetodějská mše [Cyril and Methodius Mass], op.2; Missa loretta, op.3; Missa jubilaei solemnis, op.33; Missa pastoralis, op.48; Missa Sanctae Ludmilae, op.68; Missa Beatae Mariae de Lourdes, op.92; 31 other masses, 5 requiems, 50 graduals, 50 offertories, 11 litanies, 7 Te Deum, 120 Pange lingua etc

Secular vocal: 5 Pieces, op.10, female chorus; 3 Lyric Songs, op.30, chorus; Balada o starém hradě [Ballad of the old castle], op.37, male chorus

Chamber: Pohádka [Fairy tale], op.51, pf trio

Pf: Pieces, op.6; Prosté motivy [Simple motifs], op.52; Po různých stezkách [On diverse paths], op.60

Org: Vánoční preludia [Christmas prelude], op.69; Kniha preludií [Book of preludes], opp.81, 122

Educational: Malý Paganini [Young Paganini], vn, op.8; Albums for the Young, opp.22, 28, pf; Nálady [Moods], op.39, 4 vn; Sonatinas, op.50, pf; Studies, op.73, pf; Concertino, op.87, vn

Principal publishers: Česká Hudba, Promberger, Mojmír Urbánek

BIBLIOGRAPHY
C. Russ: *Řihovský als Kirchenkomponist* (Prague, 1913)
V. Balthasar: *Vojtěch Řihovský* (Prague, 1921) [with list of works]
J. Dušek: *Vojtěch Řihovský a jeho životní dílo* [Řihovský and his life's work] (Prague, 1933)

OLDŘICH PUKL

Rihtman, Cvjetko (*b* Rijeka, 4 May 1902). Yugoslav musicologist and composer. He studied music theory and composition at the conservatories in Leipzig and Prague under Křička and Metod Doležil, and composition and musicology at the Schola Cantorum in Paris under d'Indy and Gastoué. For a time he worked as an organist and choirmaster in Paris. Returning to Yugoslavia he worked as a choirmaster in Sarajevo and taught at a teacher-training college. From 1946 to 1947 he was the director of the Sarajevo Opera, in 1947 he founded the Institute for Folklore Studies at the Regional Museum of Bosnia and Hercegovina and became its first director. In 1955 he became professor of ethnomusicology at the Academy of Music in Sarajevo. He is a member of the Bosnian and Hercegovinian Academy of Arts and Sciences.

Rihtman has been very active as a conductor, teacher, administrator and above all researcher into the folk music of Bosnia and Hercegovina. During his numerous field trips he has recorded more than 7000 folksongs and built an impressive collection of tape recordings and transcriptions at the musicology department of the Academy of Music in Sarajevo. He was the first to undertake systematic research into the unique tradition of folk polyphony in Bosnia and has written authoritatively and extensively on this subject. He is largely responsible for the introduction of modern techniques of transcription, classification and description into Yugoslav ethnomusicology. His compositions have been strongly influenced by folk idiom.

WRITINGS
'Čičak Janja – narodni pjevač sa Kupresa' [Čičak Janja, folksinger from Kupres], *Bilten instituta za proučavanje folklora*, i (1951), 34
'Polifonici oblici u narodnoj muzičkoj tradiciji Bosne i Hercegovine' [Polyphonic forms in the folk music tradition of Bosnia and Hercegovina], ibid, i
'Narodna muzika jajačkog sreza' [Folk music of the county of Jajce], *Bilten instituta za proučavanje folklora*, ii (1953), 5
'Folk music: Yugoslavia', *Grove 5*
'Jugoslawien', §II, 5 *MGG*
'Muzička tradicija Neuma i okoline' [Musical tradition of Neum and the environs], *Glasnik Zemaljskog muzeja Sarajevo*, xiv (1959), 209
'Tradicionalna muzika Imljana', *Glasnik Zemaljskog muzeja Sarajevo*, xvii (1962), 227

'Tradicionalna muzika Lepenice', *Naučno društvo BiH: posebna izdanja*, iii (Sarajevo, 1963), 405
'Oblici kratkog napjeva u narodnoj tradiciji Bosne i Hercegovine' [Short-phrase forms in the folk tradition of Bosnia and Hercegovina], *Glasnik Zemaljskog muzeja Sarajevo*, xviii (1963), 61
'Die Hauptmerkmale der konstatierten Schichten in der traditionellen Musik und in den Musikinstrumenten Bosniens und der Herzegowina', *Naučno društvo BiH: radovi*, xxvi (Sarajevo, 1965), 213
'Orientalische Elemente in der traditionellen Musik Bosniens und der Herzegowina', *Das orientalische Element am Balkan: 2. Balkanologen-Tagung: Graz 1966*, 97
'Reforma obrednega petja srbske pravoslavne cerkve na začetku XIII stoletja' [The reform of the liturgical chant in the Serbian Orthodox Church in the early 13th century], *MZ*, ii (1966), 5
'O poreklu staroslovanskega obrednega petja na otoku Krku' [On the origins of the old Slavonic chant on the island of Krk], *MZ*, iv (1968), 34
'The Philosophy of Folk and Traditional Music Study in Yugoslavia', *Yugoslav-American Seminar on Music: Sveti Stefan 1968*, 143
'Le microton dans les aspects les plus anciens de la musique traditionelle en Bosnie-Herzégovine', *IIM*, xiii (1969), 293
Zbornik napjeva narodnih pjesama Bosne i Hercegovine, i: *Dječije pjesme* (Sarajevo, 1974)
Yugoslav Folk Music Instruments (Pittsburgh, 1976)

BOJAN BUJIĆ

Riisager, Knudåge (*b* Port Kunda, Estonia, 6 March 1897; *d* Copenhagen, 26 Dec 1974). Danish composer. Born of Danish parents abroad, he completed his school education in Denmark in 1915 and studied political science at the University of Copenhagen, graduating in 1921. He worked in the civil service until 1950, and was assistant secretary in the Ministry of Finance from 1939. His administrative abilities and training also benefited Danish and international musical life: he was, for example, chairman of the Dansk Komponistforening (1937–62), president of the Nordisk Komponistråd (1950–52), director of the Copenhagen Conservatory (1956–67) and president of the Society of European Conservatory Directors (1963–6). From 1957 he was a member of the adjudicating panel in composition at the Paris Conservatoire. In 1972 he was awarded an honorary doctorate at the University of Seattle, and the same year became an honorary citizen of the state of Washington.

As a composer Riisager was the most internationally orientated of Danish composers of his generation. Even in his first works he distinguished himself with his stylistic alternative to the predominantly national modernism of the Nielsen tradition of the years after 1920, although his music bears no trace of stylistic schism. He was taught theory and composition by Otto Malling and Peder Gram, and the violin by Peder Møller. His years of study in Paris (1921–3) were decisive for his development as a composer: he studied with Roussel and Le Flem, and came into contact with Les Six, French neo-classicism and the music of Stravinsky. In 1932 he stayed in Leipzig as a student of Grabner.

Riisager became the most prominent representative of the French-orientated trend in Danish music of the interwar years; his Trumpet Concertino op.29 (1933) is a major example of Danish neo-classicism. The main characteristics of his music became clarity and accessibility of form, transparent tonal structure in chamber music and, especially, virtuoso orchestration. His music often develops from small, marked rhythmic and melodic themes on a polytonal basis, and an orchestral work like Qarrtsiluni op.36 (1938), subsequently rewritten for a ballet, contains traces of both Stravinsky's and Ravel's knowing naivety. Riisager's international reputation rests particularly on the music he wrote for ballets by Harald Lander and Birgit

Cullberg, of which *Etude*, based on Czerny's music, has been the most successful. In some works from his later years, such as the Violin Concerto op.54, the *Canto dell'infinito* op.61 and the *Stabat mater* op.62, there is a lyrical and grave expression otherwise rare in his music.

WORKS
(selective list)

DRAMATIC

Opera: Susanna, op.49 (1, M. Lorentzen), Copenhagen, Royal Theatre, 1950

Ballets: Benzin, op.17 (E. Jørgen-Jensen), Copenhagen, Royal Theatre, 1930; Slaraffenland, op.33 [after orch work] (H. Lander), Copenhagen, Royal Theatre, 1942; Qarrtsiluni, op.36 [after orch work] (Lander), Copenhagen, Royal Theatre, 1942; Tolv med posten, op.37 (B. Ralov), Copenhagen, Royal Theatre, 1942; Fugl Fønix, op.44 (Lander), Copenhagen, Royal Theatre, 1946; Etude (Etudes) (Lander), Copenhagen, Royal Theatre, 1948; Månerenen, op.57 (B. Cullberg), Copenhagen, Royal Theatre, 1957; Fruen fra havet, op.59 (Cullberg), New York, Metropolitan, 1960; Galla-variationer (F. Flindt), Copenhagen, Royal Theatre, 1967; Svinedrengen (Flindt), Danish television, 1969

Incidental music: Darduse, op.32 (J. V. Jensen), Copenhagen, Royal Theatre, 1937, orch suite; Mascarade (L. Holberg), Copenhagen, Royal Theatre, 1954

Film scores

ORCHESTRAL

Erasmus Montanus, op.1, ov., 1920; Suite dionysiaque, op.6, chamber orch, 1924; Sym. no.1, op.8, 1925; Variationer over et thema af Mezangeau, op.12, 1926; Sym. no.2, op.14, 1927; Fastelavn, op.20, ov., 1929–30; Comoedie, op.21, ov., 1929–30; Conc. for Orch, op.24, 1931; Concertino, op.29, tpt, str, 1933; Primavera, op.31, ov., 1934; I anledning af, 1934; Sym. no.3, op.30, 1935; Slaraffenland, op.33, 1936; Partita, op.35, 1937; 3 danske peblin geviser, 1937

Qarrtsiluni, op.36, 1938; Sym. no.4 (Sinfonia gaia), op.38, 1940; Bellman-variationer, op.45, 1945; Sinfonietta, op.46, 1947; Chaconne, op.50, 1948; Archæopteryx, op.51, 1948; Sym. no.5 (Sinfonia serena), op.52, str, timp, 1949–50; Vn Conc., op.54, 1950–51; Pro fistulis et fidibus, op.56, 1952; Burlesk ouverture, op.60, 1964

OTHER WORKS

Choral orch: Dansk salme, op.41, 1942; Canto dell'infinito, op.61, 1964; Stabat mater, op.62, 1966

Other vocal works: unacc. choral pieces, songs with orch and pf

Chamber: 6 str qts, 1918, 1920, 1922, 1925–6, 1932, 1942–3; Wind Qnt, 1921; Sinfonietta, op.7, 8 wind insts, 1924; Divertimento, op.9, str qt, wind qnt, 1925; Musik, wind qnt, op.16, 1927; Concertino, op.28a, 5 vn, pf, 1933; many other pieces

Pf: 4 épigrammes, 1921; Sonata, op.22, 1931

Principal publisher: Hansen

WRITINGS

'Om principperne for den polytonale tonkunst', *Musik*, ix (1925), 19
'Stilprincipperne i nutidig musik', *Dansk musiktidsskrift*, ix (1934), 113, 186
Tanker i tiden (Copenhagen, 1952)
Det usynlige mønster (Copenhagen, 1957)

BIBLIOGRAPHY

J. Balzer: 'Knudåge Riisagers Qarrtsiluni', *Levende musik*, i (1942), 26
N. Schiørring: 'De tre Riisager-balletter (*Tolv med posten, Slaraffenland, Qarrtsiluni*)', *Dansk musiktidsskrift*, xvii (1942), 58
P. Debièvre: 'Un grand compositeur danois', *La vie musicale* (1959), Dec, 114
G. Cockshott: 'Knudåge Riisager', *Music in Education*, xxx (1966), 237
S. Berg and S. Bruhns: *Knudåge Riisagers kompositioner* (Copenhagen, 1967)

NIELS MARTIN JENSEN

Rijspoort, Jan (*fl* late 16th century). South Netherlands composer. He is known from a collection of four-and five-part *Moraele spreeckwoorden*, which exists in an incomplete copy (in the Plantin Museum, Antwerp). Only a damaged tenor part survives, with title-page and pages 5 and 6, 23 and 24, and 29 and 30 missing. From the quotation in De Jager (*Taalkundig magazijn*, iii, 1840, p.88), the missing title can be completed as follows: *Moraele spreeckwoorden op musyck gestelt door Jan Rijspoort*; the work was published in Antwerp by Phalèse in 1617. The volume contains 31 songs for four voices and 19 for five; the texts based on moral proverbs and popular sayings are uniformly written in five-verse stanzas, but are of little or no poetic value.

The problem of the identification of Jan Rijspoort with Jan Belle remains unsolved. Vander Straeten drew attention to the following item listed in the *Index de musica*, the catalogue of the music library of King John IV of Portugal: Jan Risport van Belle: *Madrigaes. Morale spreeckworden. Contem conversacoens moraes*. The *Index* was published in Lisbon in 1649 by Craesbeek, possibly a relative of the Antwerp painter Joos van Craesbeek. A 'Meester Jan Belle' is the author of six polyphonic songs in Phalèse's *Duytsch musyckboeck* (1572[11]); these rank among the finest works of the collection, and show first-rate command of contrapuntal techniques, e.g. *Int groene* and *O amoureusich mondeken root*.

Belle (now Bailleul) is a small village on the River Scheldt north of Tournai, in the province of Hainaut on the frontiers of the Dutch- and French-speaking communities. Bergmans mentioned that according to the record office in Ieper, a family Rijspoort was listed from 1575 to 1625 in both Bailleul and Ieper. A solution to the problem of identity is not aided by a stylistic comparison of the songs in the *Duytsch musyckboeck* with the *Moraele spreeckworden*, for the latter is too fragmentary; only a chance discovery of the complete book will provide an answer and presumably confirm the importance of Jan Belle as a composer of polyphonic songs.

BIBLIOGRAPHY

E. vander Straeten: *La musique aux Pays-Bas avant le XIXe siècle*, viii (Brussels, 1888/*R*1969)
P. Bergmans: 'Rijspoort, Jan', *BNB*
R. B. Lenaerts: *Het nederlands polifonies lied in de 16de eeuw* (Mechelen and Amsterdam, 1933), 43ff

R. B. LENAERTS

Riley, Dennis (*b* Los Angeles, 28 May 1943). American composer and teacher. He studied at the Universities of Colorado (1961–5), Illinois (1966–8) and Iowa (PhD 1974), his principal teachers being Storm Bull, Cecil Effinger and Crumb. Numerous awards have been made to him, including grants from the Guggenheim and Ford foundations, and in 1973 he was appointed to teach at California State University (Fresno). Within a sophisticated post-Webern style his music employs complex canons and intricate rhythms using clear and concise forms.

WORKS
(selective list)

Inst: 3 Pf Pieces: no.1 (6 Canonic Variations), 1963; no.2 (5 Little Movts), 1963; no.3, 1964; Theme and Variations, orch, 1965; Variations II, str trio, 1967; 3 Concertante Musics: 14 insts, 1970; 8 insts, 1972; va, orch, 1973; Variations III, va, 1972

Vocal: 5 Songs on Jap. Haiku, S, cl, vn, vc, 1963; Liebeslied (Rilke), chorus, 1964; Elegy for September 15, 1945 (Rilke), chorus, insts, 1965; Cantata I (D. H. Lawrence), Mez, T, sax, vib, vc, pf, 1966; Cantata II (Nashe), chorus, fl, pf, harp, 1966; Cantata III (Whitman), female chorus, orch, 1968

Tape: The Fragility of the Flower Unbruised Penetrates Space, 1970

Principal publisher: Peters

DON C. GILLESPIE

Riley, Terry (*b* Colfax, Calif., 24 June 1935). American composer and performer. He took the MA in composition at the University of California (Berkeley), and later moved to New York, where he was associated with Young and the Fluxus group of artists. From 1962 to 1964 he was in Europe, working in the ORTF recording studios, where he became interested in the effects of extended repetition of short phrases with regular pulses, using tape loops, and in building up layers of recorded sound combined in different phase relationships. An early piece of this kind is *Mescalin Mix*, built out of repetitions of recorded fragments, moving at a slow, dreamlike tempo. In subsequent compositions this repetition technique is transferred to instrumental playing. For example, in *Keyboard Studies* a four-note phrase is repeated over and over at a rapid tempo, and the downbeat is slowly shifted from one to another of the four pitches. The gradual change of stress creates a perceptual ambiguity similar to visual shifts in op art. *In C* (1964), a work for any number of melodic instruments, employs the same principles on a larger scale. Keeping in time with a pulse, each performer plays through a sequence of 53 motifs, repeating each one a freely chosen number of times, so that different combinations of the same and successive motifs occur, with constantly changing relationships between the parts. In this way an intricate texture of multiple canons and polyrhythmic combinations is created, each player deciding in the course of playing how to relate his part to the others. *Olson III*, for instruments and voices, commissioned by Swedish Radio in 1967, is another work of the same kind.

Riley has used recording techniques to produce similar effects of multiple overlapping in live performance. His 'time-lag accumulator', made up of a series of tape recorders with delayed playback, enables a solo performer to combine successively played sequences of motifs with each other. This technique of self-reduplication is used in a recording of *Dorian Reeds* (1965) for soprano saxophone (played by the composer), and in *A Rainbow in Curved Air* (1970), a largely improvised keyboard piece which is based on modal scales and uses a rhythmic cycle analogous to the tala in Indian music. Riley performs extended improvisations based on these principles, and has said that he prefers to create music directly in the act of playing.

His is music in which the quality of sound, rather than thematic development, is of primary interest. The apparently static nature of the material focuses attention on acoustical properties, on perceptual shifts and on microscopic changes in sound quality and execution. In using repetition to a much greater extent than is usual in European classical music, Riley's work draws on aspects of jazz and blues instrumental playing, and has parallels in oriental traditions. Since 1970, when together with Young he met the Indian classical singer Pandit Pran Nath and visited India to study with him, Riley has devoted much of his time to the study and performance of Indian music.

WORKS
(selective list)

Tape, 1962–3: She Moves; I Can't Stop, No; Mescalin Mix

Inst and vocal: Keyboard Studies, 1963; Dorian Reeds (Winds, Brass, Strings), melody inst/insts, tape recs, 1964; In C, melody insts, 1964; Olson III, vv, insts, 1967

Partly improvised works, sax, kbds, perc, multiple recording techniques: A Rainbow in Curved Air, 1970; Poppy Nogood's Phantom Band, 1970; Persian Surgery Dervishes, 1971

BIBLIOGRAPHY
L. Young and J. MacLow, ed.: *An Anthology* (New York, 1963)

K. Knox: 'The Parametric Music of Terry Riley', *Jazz Monthly*, xiii (1967), July, 9

K. and R. Knox: 'Relax and Fully Concentrate – the Time of Terry Riley', *Friends Magazine* (20 Feb 1970)

M. Nyman: *Experimental Music: Cage and Beyond* (London, 1974)
MICHAEL PARSONS

Rilling, Helmuth (*b* Stuttgart, 29 May 1933). German conductor, chorus master and organist. He studied the organ with Karl Gerock, composition with Johann Nepomuk David and choral conducting with Hans Grischkat at the Musikhochschule, Stuttgart (1952–5), and afterwards continued further organ studies with Fernando Germani in Rome (1955–7), and conducting with Bernstein in New York (1967). In 1954, while still a student, Rilling founded his first choir, the Gächinger Kantorei of some 40 voices, with whom he has made successful tours throughout the world. After his appointment in 1957 as organist and choirmaster at the Gedächtniskirche, Stuttgart, he built up the Figuralchor there; he re-formed the Spandauer Kantorei at Berlin while teaching choir training and organ at the Spandau Kirchenmusikschule (1963–6), and on his appointment as professor at the Frankfurt Musikhochschule in 1969 he succeeded Kurt Thomas as director of the Frankfurter Kantorei; he began recording a complete cycle of Bach cantatas with that choir, the Gächinger Kantorei and the Figuralchor of Stuttgart from 1972.

Rilling became internationally known during the 1960s first as an organist (making his London début in this capacity in 1963), and he recorded the complete *Orgelbüchlein* of Bach in the cycle of the church year. In 1965 he founded the Bach-Collegium of Stuttgart as an ensemble of instrumentalists to supplement the Gächingen choir, and he has successfully toured with these combined forces in other European countries, the USA (first in 1968), at English Bach Festival concerts in Oxford and London (1972) and Japan (1974). His performances of major choral works from Bach and Handel to Verdi and Reger, and of *a cappella* choral music of different centuries (including the complex *St Matthew Passion* of Ernst Pepping), are distinguished by intensity of expression, choral virtuosity in phrasing and articulation, and a style of conducting that combines sustained tension with expressive fluency.

WOLFRAM SCHWINGER

RILM. *See* RÉPERTOIRE INTERNATIONAL DE LITTÉRATURE MUSICALE.

Rimbault, Edward (Francis) (*b* London, 13 June 1816; *d* London, 26 Sept 1876). English musicologist. The son of a London organist, Stephen F. Rimbault (1773–1837), he received his first instruction in music from his father and then became a pupil of Samuel Wesley. At the age of 16 he was appointed organist of the Swiss Church, Soho. As a young man he directed his attention to the study of music history and literature, and in 1838 delivered a series of lectures on the history of music in England. In 1840 he took an active part in the formation of the Musical Antiquarian and Percy societies; he became secretary of both and edited several works for them, and in 1841 was made editor of the music publications of the Motett Society. In 1842 he was elected Fellow of the Society of Antiquaries and a member of the Swedish Royal Academy of Music, was awarded a doctorate by Göttingen University and was offered (but declined) the chair of music at Harvard University. He joined the committee of the Handel Society in 1844, and edited three of the society's volumes. He was extremely active for the rest of his life as a lecturer and in collecting, editing and writing about early music, particularly

English; but he still found time for composing and was organist of various London churches. He left an immense music library, which was sold by Sotheby's in July 1877. Not all his possessions were acquired by conventional means: in the early 1840s he helped himself to various items from the library of Christ Church, Oxford, which he subsequently sold to the British Museum.

Rimbault was a pioneer in English musicology, and his achievement should be measured not by the accuracy of his editions (for naturally they have been superseded several times over) but by the educational effect of his discoveries and revivals on the Victorian public: his work first gave the ordinary musician some awareness of the riches of England's musical past. He produced editions of the early settings of the Anglican liturgy, of Thomas East's Whole Book of Psalms and of countless early anthems and motets, which were eagerly seized on by church choirs in need of more inspiring material than the contemporary cathedral music. He also arranged many operas and other works, wrote many elementary books and articles for periodicals. The long list of his works in Brown and Stratton is by no means complete. His compositions, including an operetta *The Fair Maid of Islington* (1838), incidental music for *The Castle Spectre* (1839) and the cantata *Country Life* (published posthumously), are of slight importance.

WRITINGS
ed.: R. North: *Memoirs of Musick* (London, 1846)
Bibliotheca madrigaliana (London, 1847)
with E. J. Hopkins: *The Organ: its History and Construction* (London, 1855, enlarged 3/1877/R1965)
ed.: T. Overbury: *Works* (London, 1856)
The Harmonium: its Uses and Capabilities (London, 1857)
The Pianoforte: its Origin, Progress and Construction (London, 1860)
The Old Cheque-book, or Book of Remembrance of the Chapel Royal, Camden Society, new ser., iii (London, 1872/R1966)

EDITIONS
MAS – vol. no. in Musical Antiquarian Society publications
W. Byrd: *A Mass for Five Voices*, MAS, i (London, 1841)
T. Morley: *The First Set of Balletts*, MAS, v (London, 1842)
H. Purcell: *Bonduca*, MAS, vii (London, 1842); *Ode Composed for the Anniversary of St Cecilia's Day*, MAS, xix (London, 1847)
Anthems for Festivals, Services, Miscellaneous Anthems, Motett Society, i–iii (London, 1842–3)
S. Arnold: *Cathedral Music* (London, 1843)
O. Gibbons: *Fantasies in Three Parts*, MAS, ix (London, 1843)
E. Lowe: *A Short Direction for the Performance of Cathedral Service* (London, 1843)
The Order of Daily Service according to the Use of Westminster Abbey (London, 1843)
T. Tallis: *Responses* (London, 1843)
Cathedral Chants of the XVI, XVII and XVIII Centuries (London, 1844)
T. East: *The Whole Book of Psalms* (London, 1844)
A Collection of Anthems . . . from . . . MS Part Books formerly in the Evelyn Collection, MAS, xiv (London, 1845) [contains music by Bateson, M. East, Ford and Weelkes]
T. Bateson: *The First Set of Madrigals*, MAS, xvii (London, 1846)
Parthenia, MAS, xviii (London, 1847)
Musical Illustrations of Bishop Percy's Reliques of Ancient English Poetry, Percy Society (London, 1850)
G. F. Handel: *Messiah*, Handel Society, ix (London, 1850); *Samson*, ibid, xi (London, 1852); *Saul*, ibid, xiii (London, 1854)

BIBLIOGRAPHY
'The Late Dr. Rimbault', *Musical World*, liv (1876), 671 [D. Baptie], 707 [W. Chappell, C. Mackeson]
'Ancient Music', *Musical World*, lv (1877), 539 [account of sale of Rimbault's library]
Catalogue of the Music Library of Edward Francis Rimbault (London, 1877/R1975 with facs. of 1862 catalogue)
J. D. Brown and S. S. Stratton: *British Musical Biography* (Birmingham, 1897), 345f
'Christ Church Missing Books', *Times Literary Supplement* (11 Feb 1939)
P. A. Scholes: *The Mirror of Music* (London, 1947), 771 [on Rimbault's mythical LlD]
A. H. King: *Some British Collectors of Music, c1600–1960* (Cambridge, 1963)

W. H. HUSK/NICHOLAS TEMPERLEY

Rimonte [Ruimonte, Ruymonte], **Pedro** (*b* ?Saragossa, c1570; *d* after 1618). Spanish composer. Rimonte was probably taken to Brussels by the Infanta Isabella at the time of her marriage to Archduke Albert, Governor of the Netherlands, in 1598, though his name first appears as choirmaster on 18 September 1603. He held the position of master of chamber music from 1604 until at least 1611, when he took part in the mourning ceremonies for Marguerite of Austria, Queen of Spain. In 1614 he received a gift of 1500 Flemish pounds to return to Spain, and Diego Pontac said in his autobiography that in that year he was taught by Rimonte at Saragossa. A document cited by vander Straeten (ii, p.10), apparently from 1618, again names Rimonte as master of chamber music at Brussels.

Except for one MS motet, Rimonte's sacred music exists only in single partbooks. The madrigals in *El Parnaso español* are competently composed, often charming pieces in an old-fashioned style reminiscent of the period around 1550–60. They are mainly imitative, with a little word-painting and occasional chromaticisms. The villancicos are sharply distinguished by their refrain forms, use of 6/4 time and lively, intricate rhythms often including hemiola.

WORKS
Missae sex, 4–6vv (Antwerp, 1604), inc., 5 masses, 1 Requiem mass
Cantiones sacrae, . . . et Hieremiae Prophetae Lamentaciones, 4–7vv (Antwerp, 1607), inc., 12 motets, 1 set of Lamentations
El Parnaso español de madrigales y villancicos, 4–6vv (Antwerp, 1614), 9 madrigals, 8 villancicos (16 on Spanish texts, 1 on Italian); 1 villancico ed. J. Bal y Gay, *Trienta canciones de Lope de Vega* (Madrid, 1935), all madrigals, 3 villancicos ed. in Woldt
Motet: Sancta Maria, succurre miseris, 8vv, E-Zvp

BIBLIOGRAPHY
E. vander Straeten: *La musique aux Pays-Bas avant le XIX ᵉ siècle* (Brussels, 1867–88/R1969)
F. Pedrell: *Catàlech de la biblioteca musical de la Diputació de Barcelona* (Barcelona, 1908–9)
J. W. Woldt: *Spanish Madrigals: the Madrigals of Morales, Flecha, Valenzola, Brudieu, and Rimonte* (diss., U. of Rochester, NY, 1950)
R. Stevenson: 'Sixteenth and Seventeenth Century Resources in Mexico (Part I)', *FAM*, i (1954), 69
P. Calahorra Martínez: 'El maestro Pedro Ruimonte (1565–1627)', *AnM*, xxviii–xxix (1973–4), 155
E. Russel: 'Pedro Rimonte in Brussels (c. 1600–1614)', *AnM*, xxviii–xxix (1973–4), 181
——: 'The Villancicos in Pedro Rimonto's "Parnaso español" (1614)', *Festival Essays for Pauline Alderman* (Provo, Utah, 1976), 61

BARTON HUDSON

Rim shot. A technique of side-drumming; *see* DRUM, §3.

Rimskaya-Korsakova, Yuliya Lazarevna. *See* VEYSBERG, YULIYA LAZAREVNA.

Rimsky-Korsakov, Andrey Nikolayevich (*b* St Petersburg, 17 Oct 1878; *d* Leningrad, 23 May 1940). Russian musicologist, son of N. A. Rimsky-Korsakov, and husband of the composer Yuliya Veysberg (1880–1942). He had to abandon his studies in the faculty of St Petersburg University after participating in student disturbances, and in 1900 went abroad to study philosophy in Strasbourg and Heidelberg. On his return to St Petersburg he taught logic and the history of philosophy for a number of years in various classical Gymnasiums. His interest in music was encouraged from childhood: he played the cello in the family string quartet. He adopted music as a career in 1912 when he became music correspondent of the newspaper *Russkaya mol'ba*, and contributed to *Severnïye zapiski* and other publications. In 1915 he became editor of the new magazine *Muzïkal'nïy sovremennik* ('Musical contemporary', 1915–18), the first publication of its kind in Russia, covering not only concert life but also aspects of the history and theory of music. He contributed numerous articles, including studies on Musorgsky, Skryabin and Taneyev.

From 1918 until the end of his life Rimsky-Korsakov worked in the Saltïkov-Shchedrin Public Library in Leningrad as head of its music department. There he continued Stasov's work in cataloguing the library's vast collection of music manuscripts, and in 1938 produced a definitive guide to the collection. He also gave classes in music history at Leningrad University (1921–4) and was a member of the department of music history and theory at the Institute of Historical Studies (1923–8). He worked assiduously on behalf of his father's music, and helped set up the Rimsky-Korsakov Museum, attached to the Institute of Theatre and Music (now the Institute for the Theatre, Music and Cinematography). He wrote a five-volume study of the composer's life and works, and edited the third, fourth and fifth editions of the *Letopis' moyey muzïkal'noy zhizni* ('Chronicle of my musical life'); in the last years of his life he did much of the preparatory work for the publication of the correspondence between Rimsky-Korsakov and Tchaikovsky. He edited, with Maximilian Shteynberg, the first published volume (vol.xlv: songs) of the complete Soviet edition of Rimsky-Korsakov's works, and he also edited Glinka's memoirs and the collected letters of Musorgsky.

WRITINGS

'Boris Godunov M. P. Musorgskovo', *Muzïkal'nïy sovremennik* (1917), nos.5–6, pp.108–67
ed.: *Muzïkal'naya letopis': stat'i i materialï* [Musical chronicle: articles and materials] (Petrograd, 1922)
ed.: *N. A. Rimsky-Korsakov: Letopis' moyey muzïkal'noy zhizni, 1844–1906* [Chronicle of my musical life, 1844–1906] (Moscow, 3/1926, 4/1932, 5/1935)
with E. M. Braudo: *'Boris Godunov' Musorgskovo* (Moscow, 1927)
ed., with others: *V. G. Karatïgin: zhizn', deyatel'nost', stat'i i materialï* [Life, work, articles and materials] (Leningrad, 1927)
Maximilian Shteynberg (Moscow, 1928) [in Russ. and Eng.]
ed.: *M. I. Glinka: Zapiski* [Memoirs] (Moscow and Leningrad, 1930)
ed., with others: *M. P. Musorgsky: pis'ma i dokumentï* [Letters and documents] (Moscow and Leningrad, 1932)
N. A. Rimsky-Korsakov: zhizn' i tvorchestvo [Life and work] (Moscow, 1933–46) [vol.v, 1946, ed. V. Rimsky-Korsakov]
Muzïkal'nïye sokrovishcha rukopisnovo otdeleniya gosudarstvennoy publichnoy biblioteka imeni M. E. Saltïkova-Shchedrina: obzor muzïkal'nïkh rukopisnïkh [Musical treasures of the manuscript department of the Saltïkov-Shchedrin State Public Library: catalogue of music manuscripts] (Leningrad, 1938)

BIBLIOGRAPHY

P. Grachov: 'Pamyati A. N. Rimskovo-Korsakova' [In memory of A. N. Rimsky-Korsakov], *SovM* (1940), no.12, p.99

RITA McALLISTER

Rimsky-Korsakov, Georgy Mikhaylovich (*b* St Petersburg, 26 Dec 1901; *d* Leningrad, 10 Oct 1965). Russian composer and musicologist. A nephew of Nikolay Rimsky-Korsakov, he studied under Shteynberg, Sokolov, Lyapunov and Nikolayev at the Petrograd/Leningrad Conservatory until 1927. In the following year he took his *kandidat* degree at the Leningrad Institute of Theatre and Music, supervised by Finagin and Asaf'yev. He taught from 1927 at the Leningrad Conservatory, where he was Asaf'yev's assistant up to 1929; courses that he directed included acoustics, score

reading (from 1940) and orchestration (from 1953). In 1923 he founded a Petrograd society for quarter-tone music, and he made public appearances in concerts and lectures as the director of an ensemble for music of this type (1925–32). His compositions make use of the quarter-tone 'fisharmonium' and the 'emiriton', an electronic keyboard instrument constructed by A. A. Ivanov, A. V. Rimsky-Korsakov, V. L. Kreytser and V. P. Dzerzhkovich.

WORKS
(*selective list*)

Orch: Sym., F, 1925
Vocal: Myatezh [Uproar] (cantata, E. Barkharn, trans. V. Bryusov), 1927; Rumyanoy zareyu [Evening redness], 2 solo vv, pf, 1935; 3 vityaza [3 heroes] (Lermontov), 3 solo vv, pf, 1936; Parus [Sail] (Lermontov), 2 solo vv, pf, 1938; Morskaya pekhota [Sea infantry] (A. Barto), 1v, pf, 1941–5; other trios, duets and songs, c100 romances
Chamber: Qnt, cl, hn, str trio, 1925; 2 str qts, 1926, 1932; Octet, 2 emiritons, 2 cl, bn, str trio, 1932; Pieces, vn, pf, 1934–55; Poem, vc, pf, 1951; pieces for vc, pf and emiriton, pf; $\frac{1}{4}$-tone pieces for 2 pf, harp, fisharmonium, 2 harps, 1925–30
Pf: 24 preludes, 1922–55; 2 sonatas, 1924, 1932; 8 studies, 1932
Incidental music, film scores, folksong arrs.

WRITINGS

'Obosnovaniye chetvyortitonovoy muzïkal'noy sistemï' [Basis of the musical quarter-tone system], *De musica*, i (Leningrad, 1925)
'Rasshifrovka svetovoy stroki Skryabinskovo *Prometeya* [Deciphering the colour keyboard part in Skryabin's *Prometheus*], *De musica*, ii (Leningrad, 1926)
'O vïsote kombinatsionnïkh tonov' [The heights of combination tones], *De musica*, iii (Leningrad, 1927)
'Akusticheskoye obosnovaniye teorii ladovovo ritma' [The acoustic basis of the theory of key-rhythm], *Muzïkoznaniye* (1928), no.4
Evolyutsiya muzïkal'nïkh zvukoryadov [The evolution of musical tone rows] (diss., Leningrad Institute of Theatre and Music, 1928)
'Theorie und Praxis der Reintonsysteme', *Melos*, vii (1928), 15

DETLEF GOJOWY

Rimsky-Korsakov, Nikolay Andreyevich (*b* Tikhvin, Novgorod govt., 18 March 1844; *d* Lyubensk, St Petersburg govt., 21 June 1908). Russian composer.

1. 1844–71. 2. 1871–81. 3. 1881–93. 4. 1893–1908. 5. Works.

1. 1844–71. He came of a distinguished naval and military family, and his father had been civil governor of the Volïn government; but both his grandmothers were of humble origin, a priest's daughter and a peasant, and from them he claimed he had inherited his love of folksong and his love of religious ceremonies. In his *Chronicle of my Musical Life* he wrote:

The first signs of musical ability showed themselves in me very early. . . . Before I was two I could distinguish all the melodies my mother sang to me; at three or four I was an expert at beating time on a drum to my father's piano playing . . . I soon began to sing very accurately everything he played, and often sang with him; then I began to pick out the pieces with the harmonies for myself on the piano; and, having learned the names of the notes, would stand in another room and call them out when they were struck.

From the age of six he had piano lessons from various local teachers, learning for the most part easy fantasias on contemporary opera melodies, but his deepest musical impressions came from some numbers of Glinka's *Life for the Tsar*, which he found at home, and the music of Bortnyansky which he heard at the nearby monastery. Before long he was tempted to compose, one of his earliest essays being a piano 'overture' in progressively quicker tempos. But his heart was set not on music but on a career in the navy in emulation of his brother, 22 years older than himself. Accordingly at the end of July 1856 his father took him to St Petersburg to enter the College of Naval Cadets; he took the passing-out examination on 20 April 1862, a few months after his brother's appointment to the directorship.

While at the Cadet School, Rimsky-Korsakov continued to take piano lessons, but he was not interested in the instrument except as a means of recapturing the delights of opera. Family friends took him to the theatre to see and hear Rossini and Weber, Meyerbeer and (still his favourite) Glinka. His first opera, early in 1857, was Flotow's *Indra* but it was the orchestra that excited him most:

Dearest uncle, Imagine my joy, today I'm going to the theatre! I shall see *Lucia*! I shall hear the enormous orchestra and tam-tam! and I shall see how the conductor waves his little stick! In the orchestra 12 violins, 8 violas, 6 cellos, 6 double basses, 3 flutes, 8 clarinets, 6 horns, and all that sort of thing.

His real introduction to symphonic music came during the 1859–60 season, when he heard two of Beethoven's symphonies and Mendelssohn's *Midsummer Night's Dream* overture, though none of these 'dazzled' him as Glinka's *Jota aragonesa* did. At the same time (autumn 1859) he found a more inspiring piano teacher, Théodore Canille, who did much to form his taste, weaning him from the Italians, encouraging him to study Beethoven, Schumann, Mendelssohn, Chopin, and Bach's fugues, and sharing his love of Glinka. Canille helped the boy to harmonize chorales, to compose variations and even a sonata movement; his instruction was very unsystematic but even when the piano lessons stopped, as they did after a year, Canille invited his pupil to visit him weekly to play duets and talk about music. More important still, in December 1861 he introduced him to Balakirev, Cui and Musorgsky, all three in their early 20s but already known as composers.

Rimsky-Korsakov fell completely under the spell of Balakirev, who in turn detected the youth's talent. Shown 'a sort of beginning of a symphony in E♭ minor', he insisted that Rimsky-Korsakov should finish it; the first movement was completed in a month and the orchestration begun under Balakirev's guidance; the scherzo and finale were written during the early months of 1862. But a crisis came in April when Rimsky-Korsakov graduated as a midshipman and his brother reasonably refused to allow him to abandon his career in the service, as he now wished to do. Balakirev went to the Caucasus for the summer; the symphony came to a standstill; and on 2 November its composer sailed in the clipper *Almaz* for a cruise of two and a half years which took him to Gravesend (where he finished the slow movement of the symphony), the Baltic, New York, Rio de Janeiro and the Mediterranean. When he returned to Russia at the beginning of May 1865 he had become, in his own words, 'an officer-dilettante who sometimes enjoyed playing or listening to music'. He was rescued for music by renewed contact with Balakirev, who made him finish the symphony; the missing trio for the scherzo was composed in October. The entire symphony was reorchestrated under the supervision of Balakirev, who gave the first performance on 31 December at one of the concerts of the Free School of Music at St Petersburg which he had founded during Rimsky-Korsakov's absence. A second performance, under Konstantin Lyadov, father of the composer, followed in March 1866.

Rimsky-Korsakov's naval duties now occupied only two or three hours a day, and he had leisure for composition and for social life in a circle which now included Borodin, Dargomïzhsky, and an amateur singer, Sofiya Zotova, for whom he composed some of his earliest songs (op.2, published by Bernard in the summer of 1866). More songs (opp.3 and 4) followed and then another orchestral work, the Overture on Three Russian Themes modelled on Balakirev's folksong overtures (performed at a Free School concert, 23 December 1866). In lighter vein, he was also writing quadrilles on themes from *Martha* and *La belle Hélène*, which he played for dancing on Sunday evenings at his brother's, where he was considered a 'beautiful pianist'; by professional standards he was not, and he never dared to play before his musical friends.

The compositions of 1867 included the beginning of a symphony in B minor (too obviously influenced by the opening of Beethoven's Ninth), an orchestral Fantasia on Serbian Themes written in a great hurry for Balakirev's concert of pan-Slavonic music on 24 May, and a 'musical picture' based on the legend of the Novgorod merchant Sadko, completed on 12 October, in which the main influence was that of Liszt's *Mephisto Waltz*. Berlioz paid his last visit to Russia from November 1867 to February 1868; he was a sick man and, despite Stravinsky's story (*Conversations with Igor Stravinsky*; New York and London, 1959, p.29), Rimsky-Korsakov never met him; but the *Symphonie fantastique*, played on 7 December, and *Harold en Italie*, with which Berlioz ended his last concert on 8 February, were directly reflected in a programmatic symphony which Rimsky-Korsakov began on 21 January, *Antar*, based on an oriental tale by Osip Senkovsky (Baron Brambeus). All these orchestral works were scored for natural horns and trumpets, as described in Berlioz's *Traité de l'instrumentation*, and all were reorchestrated and sometimes drastically revised at least once in later years. Yet he was already recognized by Balakirev and his circle as a particularly gifted orchestrator, with the result that Balakirev asked him to score a Schubert march (D885) for a concert in May, Cui asked him to orchestrate the opening chorus of *William Ratcliff*, and the ailing Dargomïzhsky (who died in January 1869) bequeathed him the task of scoring *The Stone Guest*. At the same time he was giving a great deal of thought to an opera project of his own, based on Lev Mey's historical drama *Pskovityanka* ('The Maid of Pskov'); he had no sooner finished *Antar* (5 September 1868) than he began *The Maid of Pskov*, a month or two before his friend Musorgsky was to begin *Boris Godunov*. During the winter of 1871–2 the two composers shared a single room and worked on their operas at the same table and piano, Musorgsky in the morning, Rimsky-Korsakov in the afternoon.

2. 1871–81. Before he completed the full score of *The Maid of Pskov* with the overture, in January 1872, Rimsky-Korsakov had taken two important steps. In July 1871, despite his astonishing ignorance of elementary technicalities, he had accepted an invitation from Azanchevsky, the newly appointed director of the St Petersburg Conservatory, to become professor of practical composition and instrumentation and to direct the orchestral class with an annual salary of 1000 rubles; and in December he had become betrothed to Nadezhda Purgold, an excellent pianist and far better-trained musician than himself (they married on 12 July 1872 and enjoyed an extensive honeymoon in Switzerland and Italy). Nadezhda was beautiful, capable, and strong-minded; she was responsible for the published piano arrangements not only of her husband's works but of

some of those of his friends, and her influence on him was no less than Clara Schumann's on Robert.

In February 1872 *The Stone Guest* was produced, with Rimsky-Korsakov's orchestration, and (perhaps as a consequence) the director of the imperial theatres commissioned him to collaborate with Cui, Borodin and Musorgsky in the composition of an 'opera-ballet', *Mlada*, though this came to nothing and the collaborators used most of their music in other works. *The Maid of Pskov* was published by Bessel in vocal score and successfully produced at the Mariinsky Theatre on 13 January 1873. Four months later the composer was allowed to resign his commission; instead, his friend Krabbe, the Minister of Marine, created for him the special civil post of Inspector of Naval Bands, which carried a handsome salary. During the summer he wrote most of his Third Symphony, in C (*Antar* was reckoned as the second, only in 1897 being restyled 'symphonic suite'). But this marked the end of serious composition for several years. Rimsky-Korsakov embarked with zeal on the inspection of naval bands and on practical study of the various instruments, their mechanism and technique; he planned a great treatise on instrumentation, a project which he abandoned and returned to at various times in later life but left unfinished at his death; he taught himself harmony from Tchaikovsky's textbook and counterpoint from Cherubini and Bellermann with the success demonstrated in the six piano fugues of 1875 (published by Bessel as op.17) and the many fugal passages in a string quartet from the same year (op.12); and he began his not very successful career as a conductor on 2 March 1874 with a charity concert, the programme including his C major Symphony. In the following year he succeeded Balakirev as conductor of the Free School concerts, giving the first performance in Russia of arias from Bach's *St Matthew Passion* and, in 1876, excerpts from the B minor Mass and Handel's *Samson* (orchestrated by himself and some of his conservatory pupils). He made his first revisions of *Antar* and *The Maid of Pskov* (in the latter case a complete rewriting), compiled two collections of Russian folksongs, supplying them with piano accompaniments, and participated with Balakirev and Lyadov in the preparation of a new edition of Glinka's opera scores.

This intensive occupation with folk music and with Glinka's transparent orchestration had a cathartic effect: in February 1878 he began the composition of an opera in a folkish melodic idiom, harmonically and orchestrally modelled on Glinka's style, and very different from the 'grand opera' of *The Maid of Pskov*. This was *Mayskaya noch'* ('May Night'), based on one of Gogol's short stories of peasant life in the Ukraine, *Vecheri na khutore bliz Dikan'ki* ('Evenings on a Farm at Dikanka'), on which Tchaikovsky had already drawn for his *Vakula the Smith* (*Cherevichki*) and Musorgsky for *Sorochintsy Fair*. It was Rimsky-Korsakov's first essay in that blend of the fantastic with the comic in which he was to score most of his greatest successes. It was written directly in full score, completed (apart from the overture) in eight months, and produced at the Mariinsky Theatre on 21 January 1880, with Nápravník conducting and the part of the village headman sung by Fyodor Stravinsky.

Meanwhile, during the summer of 1879, Rimsky-Korsakov had composed a string quartet entirely based on Russian folktunes and begun what he described as 'an orchestral piece of fantastic character on Pushkin's prologue to *Ruslan and Lyudmila*' (in which the poet described all the characteristic figures of Russian folklore, such as the witch Baba-Yaga, whose name was at first given to the orchestral piece). The quartet was scrapped as such although the first three movements were later revised and orchestrated as the Sinfonietta on Russian Themes; the orchestral piece was completed in 1880 with the title *Skazka* ('Legend'). Immediately after the production of *May Night* Rimsky-Korsakov chanced to re-read Ostrovsky's fantastic play *Snegurochka* ('Snow Maiden') for which in 1873 Tchaikovsky had supplied incidental music. Previously Rimsky-Korsakov had not been attracted by it; now he 'fell deeply in love with it':

My mild interest in the ancient Russian customs and heathen pantheism flamed up. There seemed no better subject than this, no more poetic figures than Snegurochka, Lel or the Spring Fairy, no better realm than the kingdom of the Berendeys with their marvellous tsar, no better religion and philosophy of life than the worship of the Sun God, Yarilo.

Ostrovsky gave him permission to adapt the libretto and he spent the summer of 1880 in the depths of the Russian countryside, composing his opera in a state of extraordinary excitement, actually (as he confessed long afterwards)

praying to nature – to a crooked old tree-stump, to some willow or century-old oak, to the forest stream, to the lake . . . or at the cockcrow scattering the sorcery of the night. . . . It sometimes seemed to me that animals, birds, and even trees and flowers, know more of the magic and fantastic than human beings do; that they understand the language of nature far better. . . . I warmly believed in all this, as a child would . . . and in those minutes the world seemed to me nearer, more understandable, and I was somehow merged with it!

The whole of *Snow Maiden* was composed in short score in three months and, after the completion of the *Legend*, the full score of the opera (in which he at last abandoned natural brass) was finished in April 1881; it was produced on 10 February 1882.

3. 1881–93. After the completion of *Snow Maiden*, Rimsky-Korsakov was characteristically deflected from composition for nearly two years. Musorgsky died in March 1881 and his old friend took upon himself the colossal labour of setting in order his manuscripts and preparing them for publication, which in his view entailed the 'correction' of Musorgsky's innumerable harmonic 'solecisms' and 'improvement' of his melodies and part-writing. The worst part of the task was the chaotic score of the opera *Khovanshchina*, which occupied Rimsky-Korsakov mainly from December 1881 to July 1882, but there were also a number of songs (including the *Songs and Dances of Death*), choral pieces, orchestral pieces and piano pieces. The *Night on the Bare Mountain*, which Musorgsky had left in more than one version, temporarily baffled him and he compiled his well-known score only in 1886. Another distraction from composition had been the direction of the Free School of Music, which in September 1881 he persuaded Balakirev to resume. But the Musorgsky labours had not long been completed before he was more or less obliged to take another official post: in February 1883 Balakirev was appointed musical director of the imperial chapel, with Rimsky-Korsakov as his assistant (on the other hand, the Inspectorship of Naval Bands was abolished by a new minister in 1884). At nearly the same time he was beginning to be drawn into another circle soon involving other activities. This revolved about an extremely wealthy timber merchant, Mitrofan Petrovich Belyayev, an amateur viola player and passionate lover of chamber music at whose house young musicians (mostly Rimsky-Korsakov's ex-pupils, Lyadov, Glazunov and others) gathered on Friday evenings to play and hear string quartets, including their own compositions. Having printed their works at his own expense and hired orchestras and halls for their performance, Belyayev found himself becoming a music publisher and, in 1886, the backer of a regular series of 'Russian Symphony Concerts'; in both these undertakings Rimsky-Korsakov was his chief musical adviser. From then on, most of Rimsky-Korsakov's works were published by his firm. A further blow was the death of Borodin (February 1887), which presented Rimsky-Korsakov with what he conceived to be the duty of completing and orchestrating *Prince Igor*; this he proceeded to do with the help of Glazunov.

The mid-1880s were thus almost a complete blank creatively. From the beginning of 1883 came a one-movement piano concerto on a Russian theme, then nothing of any consequence for nearly four years. The First Symphony was revised, transposed to E minor and reorchestrated in 1884; the Third Symphony was also revised and reorchestrated (1886), but a fourth was no sooner begun than abandoned. Eight songs (opp.26 and 27, 1882–3), a very little church music (1883–4), a harmony textbook for the students of the imperial chapel (1884) and a movement for string quartet (1886) constituted his total original output. The Fantasia on Two Russian Themes for violin and orchestra at the end of 1886 was a more substantial though not a very important work, but it had important consequences, for

1. Nikolay Rimsky-Korsakov

a proposed companion piece on Spanish themes became in the summer of 1887 the popular *Kaprichchio na ispanskiye temï* ('Spanish Capriccio') for orchestra only. This was a study in virtuoso orchestration in which, as the composer insisted, the brilliant instrumental colouring is 'the very essence of the composition, not its mere dressing-up'. Work on *Prince Igor* precluded original composition for the time being, but during summer 1888 Rimsky-Korsakov produced two more major works in the same style as the *Spanish Capriccio*: the symphonic suite *Sheherazade* and *Svetlïy prazdnik* ('Russian Easter Festival'), an 'overture on liturgical themes'. In his autobiography, which he had already begun to write in a desultory way, he observed that the *Capriccio*, *Sheherazade* and the *Easter Festival* overture 'close a period of my work, at the end of which my orchestration had attained a considerable degree of virtuosity and warm sonority without Wagnerian influence, limiting myself to the normally constituted orchestra used by Glinka'. They were in fact his last important purely orchestral compositions; during the last 20 years of his life he wrote only a few occasional pieces for orchestra and suites or other concert arrangements from his operas.

The climacteric of Rimsky-Korsakov's creative life, after which he became almost exclusively an opera composer, was the visit to St Petersburg of Angelo Neumann's travelling 'Richard Wagner Theatre' which gave four cycles of the *Ring* under Karl Muck during March 1889. Rimsky-Korsakov attended all the rehearsals with Glazunov, following with the score and 'astonished by Wagner's handling of the orchestra' which soon began to influence his own. Just before the *Ring* experience, on the second anniversary of Borodin's death, the playing over of his contribution to the collective *Mlada* of 1872 had suggested to Rimsky-Korsakov not only that he should orchestrate it (which he did the following year) but that he should compose a complete *Mlada* of his own, revising and extending the original libretto himself. The composition of *Mlada* was interrupted by a visit to Paris to conduct the Colonne orchestra in two concerts of Russian music, including *Antar*, the Piano Concerto and *Spanish Capriccio*, at the Trocadéro on 22 and 29 June as part of the Universal Exhibition of 1889; yet the composition sketch of the opera was finished by the end of August. The orchestration, also interrupted by a visit to the west, to conduct in Brussels in April 1890, as well as by family troubles, took another year. *Mlada* was produced on 1 November 1892, but had no lasting success; the composer himself described it as 'cold – like ice' and prophesied that it would probably be his last composition, 'at any rate, the last important one'. Fearing that the end of his creative life was approaching, he set about winding up his affairs. He made yet a third version (published as the second) of his orchestral piece *Sadko* and, between April 1891 and April 1892, a third version of *The Maid of Pskov*, based in substance on the first and ignoring the second (1877). 'I closed my account with the past', he wrote. 'Not one of my major works of the period before *May Night* remained in its original form.'

Indeed in his current state of mind he found little satisfaction in anything he had written except *Snow Maiden*, in the music of his old friends or his new, younger ones, or for that matter in hardly any other music. He wrote to his wife in August 1891:

No music that I hear now pleases me. Beautiful harmony, texture, melodious phrases don't touch me, it all seems to me dry and cold. . . . A Beethoven quartet or symphony is another matter. There technique and working out are only the form; it is all pervaded with life and soul; of course it's the same with Chopin and Glinka and (just imagine) – the Italians with the sextet from *Lucia*, the quartet from *Rigoletto*, and all their melodies. That is where real life is. 'La donna è mobile' is music, but Glazunov is only technique and conventional acceptance of contemporary fashion and taste as beauty. I fancy that a great part of the Russian school is not music, but cold and brain-spun stuff.

The depression, perhaps brought on in the first place in 1890 by the dangerous illnesses of his wife and one of his sons, the deaths of his mother and youngest child, and the beginning of the prolonged and ultimately fatal illness of his second youngest child, deepened during 1891–3, a period in which one physical and intellectual crisis succeeded another. Having almost completely abandoned music – he hardly touched a piano for a whole year – he turned to vast programmes of reading aesthetics and philosophy and to writing on musical aesthetics; but these projects were continually interrupted by alarming physical symptoms: rushes of blood to the head and complete confusion of thoughts, frequent loss of memory and unpleasant obsessive ideas. The medical diagnosis was cerebro-spinal neurasthenia. He gave up the conducting of Belyayev's Russian Symphony Concerts and his post in the imperial chapel (though his resignation did not become official until January 1894).

4. 1893–1908. The turning-point came in December 1893 when Tchaikovsky's death stimulated Rimsky-Korsakov to conduct a Russian Symphony Concert of his friend's works (12 December); he went on to conduct the remaining concerts of the season. The death also removed a hindrance to the composition of an opera on a subject which had long attracted him: another of Gogol's stories, *Noch' pered Rozhdestvom* ('Christmas Eve'), on which Tchaikovsky had based *Vakula the Smith* (*Cherevichki*). For summer 1894 the Rimsky-Korsakovs found a new country home in most beautiful surroundings at Vechasha in the Luga district, to which they frequently returned, and in a letter of 4 July to Stasov announcing that he had embarked on an opera he gave two pieces of information; first he had

taken it into [his] head to connect Gogol's story with Kolyada and Ovsen. . . . I've long felt an obligation to them, since I dealt with 'Rusalka week' in *May Night*, Maslyanitsa and Yarilo in *Snow Maiden* and Kupala in *Mlada*. Now I shall have completed the whole solar cycle.

These pagan ritual figures connected with the winter solstice, the spring equinox, and midsummer are discussed at length in the preface to the opera. He added that the composition-sketch was already more than half finished. His second piece of news was that, as a result of a letter from the musical historian Findeyzen, he was contemplating an opera on the subject of Sadko, 'in which I shall make use, among other things, of the music of my symphonic picture'; with the help of a house-guest, Nikolay Shtrup, he had already worked out a detailed scenario which Shtrup would take to Stasov for his advice. Musical ideas for *Sadko* were already pouring into his head. But first of all *Christmas Eve* had to be finished, as indeed it was in sketch by the end of August despite the composer's paralysing consciousness that much of it was 'cold and brain-spun' and fears that he had lost his creative power for ever. *Sadko* restored his self-confidence; the greater part of the composition-sketch was completed during the summer of 1895, though additions to the plan suggested by a new friend Vladimir Bel'sky, who supplied the libretto for them,

were not composed until the following year. In the meantime Rimsky-Korsakov pressed ahead with the orchestration. He was so full of ideas that in October 1895 he wrote part of a libretto and sketched some of the music for the one-act *Bagdadskiy borodobrey* ('Barber of Baghdad'), from which the music of Nureddin's first aria was resuscitated as the Hymn to the Sun in *Zolotoy petushok* ('The Golden Cockerel').

The Barber of Baghdad was probably set aside in favour of preparations for the first performance of *Christmas Eve* on 10 December, from which Rimsky-Korsakov stayed away in protest at the absurd changes enforced by the imperial family. But still *Sadko* had to remain unfinished, for the composer was occupied from December until May 1896 with a task for which he has been bitterly censured, the rewriting and reorchestration of Musorgsky's *Boris Godunov*, some of which had been done desultorily during 1892–4. The full score of *Sadko* was completed in September 1896. But the play-through to Vsevolozhsky, the director of the imperial theatres, and his colleagues went badly; the production would obviously be complicated and difficult. Finally Nicholas II himself, on being told that the music was in the vein of *Mlada* and *Christmas Eve*, personally crossed *Sadko* from the list and instructed Vsevolozhsky to 'find something gayer' in its place. The consequent break with the imperial theatres, which lasted until Vsevolozhsky's supercession in 1899, would have had very serious consequences if private enterprise had not come to the rescue. The railway magnate Savva Mamontov, patron of music, painting and the theatre, financed what was called the Private Russian Opera in Moscow, with such singers as Shalyapin and Nadezhda Zabela-Vrubel (a remarkable lyric-coloratura soprano whom Rimsky-Korsakov regarded as the ideal type of opera singer); he had already put on the new version of *The Maid of Pskov* in the Solodovnikov Theatre with Shalyapin as Ivan the Terrible (24 December 1896). In June 1897 Mamontov's adviser, the critic Semyon Kruglikov, invited Rimsky-Korsakov to send him the score of *Sadko*, with the result that it was produced on 7 January 1898: a poor performance was redeemed by a very fine one two months later when the company gave a short season in the great hall of the St Petersburg Conservatory.

The period between the rejection of *Sadko* and its production by Mamontov, particularly summer 1897, was extraordinarily productive. Rimsky-Korsakov was now obsessed with vocal writing; he wrote no fewer than 40 songs, and also a miniature opera, a setting of Pushkin's 'little tragedy' *Mozart and Salieri*, in all of which the voice part was conceived first, and that of piano or orchestra afterwards, a complete reversal of his usual procedure before then. A cantata, *Switezianka*, dates from the same period and purely instrumental composition was not neglected; he composed a second string quartet in G and a piano trio in C minor, both of which he regarded as failures, and made yet another and much more drastic revision of *Antar*, which was now styled 'symphonic suite' instead of 'symphony'. This version was not published until 1913; the 'Nouvelle rédaction (1897)' of the miniature scores is nothing of the kind, but a minor revision (1903) of the 1875 version.

The compositions of 1898 included the Prologue to *The Maid of Pskov* omitted from the first and third versions and now completely reconstructed as a one-act opera, *Boyarïnya Vera Sheloga*, and a full-length opera also on a subject by Mey, *Tsarskaya nevesta* ('The Tsar's Bride'), in which the heroine's part was written specifically for Zabela-Vrubel. This was completely carried out, from first sketches to complete full score, between February and 6 October. Mamontov produced *Mozart and Salieri*, with Shalyapin as Salieri, on 7 December and *Vera Sheloga* on 27 December. *The Tsar's Bride* had to wait until 3 November 1899.

By that time Rimsky-Korsakov had nearly completed another opera, *Skazka o Tsare Saltane* (in its full title 'The Tale of Tsar Saltan, of his son the famous and mighty hero Prince Gvidon Saltanovich, and of the beautiful Swan Princess'), again with Zabela-Vrubel in mind as the heroine. Musically it was in some respects a return to the style of *Snow Maiden*. But its production (3 November 1900) almost marked the end of Rimsky-Korsakov's connection with the Moscow Private Opera. Shalyapin had deserted to the imperial theatres; Mamontov himself had disappeared from the scene after a railway financial scandal, leaving an artists' cooperative to carry on, while in St Petersburg a new director of imperial theatres opened the Mariinsky to Rimsky-Korsakov once more. Even Vsevolozhsky had made a conciliatory gesture by reviving *Snow Maiden* in December 1898; his successor put on *Sadko* with great success (8 February 1901) before the tsar and most of the imperial family.

But Rimsky-Korsakov's first new work on the Mariinsky stage, *Serviliya* (14 October 1902), a deliberate attempt to get away from Russian subjects, was a failure. Even before its production, he was contemplating, even beginning, other operatic experiments. One, on the Nausicaa episode from the *Odyssey*, had been in his mind since 1894; he wrote a 'prelude-cantata' *Iz Gomera* ('From Homer') and then abandoned the idea. He was also thinking of combining the legend of the invisible city of Kitezh with the story of St Fevroniya, though that too was laid aside for a while. But he finished the one-act *Kashchey bessmertnïy* ('Kaschchey the Immortal', produced by the former Mamontov company in Moscow, 25 December 1902), a Russian subject treated with unusual harmonic sophistication and little national colouring. By contrast, the full-length, melodramatic *Pan Voyevoda* (completed in 1903, and produced in St Petersburg, 16 October 1904, by another private company) is an extended (and unsuccessful) essay in a different national idiom, that of Poland; it was intended as a tribute to Chopin, to whose memory it is dedicated.

With *Kitezh*, taken up again in March 1903, Rimsky-Korsakov reverted to a profoundly Russian subject, underlaid by a pantheism much deeper than that of *Snow Maiden*, which stimulated his creative imagination to its highest level. But before he finished the full score, on 11 February 1905, he had become involved in distracting events. The long-simmering political discontents, naturally involving the students of the conservatory, had come to their first major crisis on 'Bloody Sunday' (22 January); Rimsky-Korsakov tried to calm the students but firmly supported their cause; on 18 February he publicly endorsed a letter to the press demanding political reforms which had been signed by Grechaninov, Taneyev, Rakhmaninov, Shalyapin and 25 other leading musicians; on 1 April, 'the conservatory being surrounded by foot and mounted police', he published an open letter to the director, his former pupil Bernhard, supporting the student strikers and

making a stinging attack on the 'circle of dilettanti' of the Russian Musical Society who really controlled the institution. The 'cowardly and tactless' Bernhard resigned, but on 5 April Rimsky-Korsakov was dismissed. Still more extraordinary events followed. On 9 April a student performance of *Kashchey*, conducted by Glazunov, was followed not by a short concert, as intended, but by a wild political demonstration of homage to the composer. As a result, the performance of his music was temporarily forbidden by the police.

Rimsky-Korsakov went to Vechasha for the summer, continued his autobiography (which he had resumed in 1904 after an 11-year break), began a thematic analysis of *Snow Maiden* and wrote a considerable part of his book on orchestration. He also pondered two opera subjects, an old one, Byron's *Heaven and Earth*, which came to nothing, and a new one, the 17th-century rebel Stenka Razin, in which he proposed to introduce tunes popular with the rebels of his own day. One of these, *Dubinushka* ('The little oak stick'), he orchestrated in October but *Sten'ka Razin* was abandoned in December. With Ziloti and others he had contemplated setting up a private school of music in St Petersburg, but in the end the conservatory was reopened with a freer constitution, the professors who had been dismissed or who had resigned in sympathy were invited to return and in December Glazunov was elected director.

Rimsky-Korsakov was partly occupied in 1906 with a new version of *Boris Godunov* in which he restored the cuts of 1896 (the next year he composed two additional passages for the Coronation Scene, for the Paris production). On 4 September, at Riva on Lake Garda, he completed his autobiography and not long after his return to Russia he noted down on 28 October the opening theme of *Zolotoy petushok* ('The Golden Cockerel'), an opera based on Pushkin's fairy-tale satire on stupid autocracy. Bel'sky, the librettist of *Sadko*, *Tsar Saltan* and *Kitezh*, skilfully augmented Pushkin's verses. Composition of the *Cockerel* went smoothly, although it was interrupted by the Mariinsky rehearsals of *Kitezh* (produced on 20 February 1907) and by a visit to Paris in May to conduct part of the Cinq Concerts Historiques Russes arranged by Dyagilev. The score of the *Cockerel* was finished on 11 September. But the libretto caused endless troubles with the censorship, which clouded the last three or four months of Rimsky-Korsakov's life and probably worsened the heart trouble (attacks of angina) of which he died on 21 June 1908. The *Cockerel* was first performed by the Zimin opera company at the Solodovnikov Theatre, Moscow, on 7 October 1909.

5. WORKS. Rimsky-Korsakov's operas far outweigh in importance his compositions in other fields. The purely orchestral works by which he is best known – *Sheherazade*, the *Spanish Capriccio* and the *Easter Festival* overture – are essentially brightly coloured mosaics; although the thematic ideas lack organic cohesion, they are often striking and piquant. The composer set them off by scoring which frequently involves the juxtaposition of 'pure' orchestral groups, as in the opening of the third movement of *Antar* where the melody is played by all the woodwind in octaves (with two horns which omit the ornamental notes) against a background of pure brass chords, with cymbals. Another example is the final tutti of *Sheherazade* where the theme on unison trombones is accompanied simul-

taneously by a combination of string patterns, another set of patterns, alternating with chromatic scales, on woodwind, and a third pattern of rhythms on percussion, with harp glissandos. But such passages can easily be matched in the operas; the procession of princes in *Mlada*, the harbour scene of *Sadko*, the wedding procession in *The Golden Cockerel*, are no less brilliant. And the operas give scope for a far wider variety of orchestral effect – fantastic, sensuous, grotesque or humorous.

Again, Rimsky-Korsakov's finest vocal writing is to be found in the operas, not in the solo songs with piano. He was a copious but not a great songwriter. His early songs tend to be declamatory, with the voice overshadowed by the piano part, while (conversely) the much more numerous later ones are more melodiously vocal but weakened by conventional piano figuration. (The solo piano compositions, which include some well-made fugues, are – like the handful of chamber works – negligible in value.) Even the best of the songs, beautiful as they are, never reach the level of Marfa's great aria in *The Tsar's Bride* or Fevroniya's music in *Kitezh*.

Yet as an opera composer Rimsky-Korsakov suffered from what might seem to be a crippling disability: lack of dramatic power, in particular the capacity to create characters in sound. In all his 15 operas there are no more than three or four solid characters realized in terms of music: Ivan the Terrible in *The Maid of Pskov*, the spiritually tormented drunken scoundrel Grishka Kuterma (his psychological masterpiece) in *Kitezh*, the saintly virgin Fevroniya in the same opera. He could provide a librettist's characters – the tenor lovers and the simple Russian heroines – with suitable, often lyrically beautiful music, but the music hardly ever seems to have grown out of the character's inner being. Rimsky-Korsakov's operas paradoxically succeed by being, in most cases, deliberately non-dramatic. As he repeatedly affirmed in the prefaces to the scores, he 'regarded an opera as first and foremost a *musical work*'. Instead of dramas, he created musico-scenic fairy tales; instead of characters, delightful fantastic puppets. In this field he is supreme, indeed unique. He even devised a type of short-breathed, rhythmically precise music suggesting the movements of puppets, which he associated, for instance, with the Tsar in *Snow Maiden* and with Tsar Saltan. And he employed a dual musical language: on the one hand diatonic and lyrical, shot through with the idioms of Russian folk music, sometimes actually quoting or closely imitating actual folk melodies, for the 'real' human characters; on the other, chromatic and highly artificial, often based on the whole-tone scale, a scale of alternate tones and semitones, even a scale invented by his librettist Bel'sky, or making play with harmonic ingenuities, e.g. alternat-

2. Autograph score from Act 3 of Rimsky-Korsakov's 'The Golden Cockerel', composed 1906–7 (USSR-Lsc)

ing chords hinged on the two notes common to two dominant 7ths an augmented 4th apart, for the 'unreal' magical beings. These puppets inhabit a world – the world of *May Night*, *Christmas Eve*, *Sadko*, *Tsar Saltan*, *The Golden Cockerel* – 'in which the commonplace and matter-of-fact are inextricably confused with the fantastic, naïveté with sophistication, the romantic with the humorous, and beauty with absurdity'. Even *Kitezh*, despite its mystical heights and psychological depths, belongs in some degree to the same world.

This duality in Rimsky-Korsakov's musical style is matched by strange contradictions in his personality: although cool and objective to an unusual degree, a religious sceptic, he not only delighted in depicting religious ceremonies but was capable of total surrender to the nature-mysticism which possessed him during the composition of *Snow Maiden*. He recognized this self-contradiction very clearly, as he recognized all his faults and weaknesses and limitations. Nothing annoyed him more than to be hailed as a 'genius' and he carried pitiless self-criticism to a point dangerously near

creative annihilation. In his writings and in conversation with friends he not only drew attention to, but exaggerated, his unconscious echoes of other composers' ideas and his adoption of their techniques. Neither his employment of leitmotifs nor his orchestration was deeply affected by Wagner after hearing the *Ring*. He had already devised a subtle and personal scheme of miniature motifs in *Snow Maiden* and his orchestral technique was only enriched, not deeply modified, by Wagner's.

His own style, pellucid and based on the bold use of primary instrumental colours over a framework of very clearly defined part-writing and harmony, was based on Glinka and Balakirev, Berlioz and Liszt. He transmitted it directly to two generations of Russian composers, from Lyadov (*b* 1855) and Glazunov (*b* 1865) to Myaskovsky (*b* 1881), Stravinsky (*b* 1882) and Prokofiev (*b* 1891), all of whom were his pupils, and his general influence is evident, if less pronounced, in the orchestral music of Ravel, Debussy, Dukas and Respighi.

WORKS

Edition: *N. Rimsky-Korsakov: Polnoye sobraniye sochineniy* [Complete edition of compositions], ed. A. Rimsky-Korsakov and others (Moscow, 1946–70) [RK]

STAGE

Moscow first performances at Solodovnikov Theatre, St Petersburg first performances at Mariinsky Theatre unless otherwise stated; * – full score; † – vocal score with pf acc.

op.	Title	Translation	Description	Libretto	Composed	Published	First performance	RK
—	Pskovityanka	The Maid of Pskov	opera, 4	Rimsky-Korsakov, after L. A. Mey				
	1st version				1868–72	†St Petersburg, 1872	St Petersburg, 13 Jan 1873	*1a, b †29a
	2nd version				1876–7	—	—	—
	3rd version				1891–2	St Petersburg, 1892	St Petersburg, Panayevsky, 18 April 1895	*1v, g †29b
	new Aria, act 3				1898			
—	Mlada, collab. Borodin, Cui, Musorgsky and Minkus; unfinished		opera-ballet, 4	V. A. Krïlov	1872	—	—	—
—	Mayskaya noch'	May Night	opera, 3	Rimsky-Korsakov, after Gogol	1878–9	Leipzig, 1893	St Petersburg, 21 Jan 1880	*2a, b †30
—	Pskovityanka	The Maid of Pskov	incidental music to Mey's play	—				
	1st version				1877	—	—	—
	2nd version				1882	Moscow, 1951	—	*19b
—	Snegurochka	Snow Maiden	opera, prol, 4	Rimsky-Korsakov, after A. N. Ostrovsky				
	1st version				1880–81	St Petersburg, 1881	St Petersburg, 10 Feb 1882	—
	2nd version				*c*1895	St Petersburg, 1898	—	*3a, b †31a, b
—	Mlada		opera-ballet, 4	Rimsky-Korsakov, after Krïlov	1889–90	Leipzig, 1891	St Petersburg, 1 Nov 1892	*4a, b †32
—	Noch' pered Rozhdestvom	Christmas Eve	opera, 4	Rimsky-Korsakov, after Gogol	1894–5	Leipzig, 1895	St Petersburg, 10 Dec 1895	*5a, b †33
—	Sadko		opera, 7 scenes	Rimsky-Korsakov, V. I. Bel'sky	1894–6	Leipzig, 1897	Moscow, 7 Jan 1898	*6a, b, v †34
—	Bagdadskiy borodobrey	The Barber of Baghdad	opera, 1, sketches	Rimsky-Korsakov	1895	—	—	—
48	Motsart i Sal'yeri	Mozart and Salieri	opera, 1	Pushkin	1897	Leipzig, 1898	Moscow, 7 Dec 1898	*7 †35
54	Boyarïnya Vera Sheloga [orig. prol to 2nd version of opera Pskovityanka, 1876–7]		opera, 1	Rimsky-Korsakov, after Mey	1898	St Petersburg, 1898	Moscow, 27 Dec 1898	*8 †36
—	Tsarskaya nevesta	The Tsar's Bride	opera, 4	after Mey; 1 scene, I. F. Tyumenev	1898	Leipzig, 1899	Moscow, 3 Nov 1899	*9a, b †37
	new Aria, act 3				1899			

op.	Title	Translation	Description	Libretto	Composed	Published	First performance	RK
—	Skazka o Tsare Saltane, o sïne evo slavnom i moguchem bogatïre knyaze Gvidone Saltanoviche i o prekrasnoy tsarevne lebedi	The Tale of Tsar Saltan, of his son the famous and mighty hero Prince Gvidon Saltanovich and of the beautiful Swan Princess	opera, prol, 4	Bel'sky, after Pushkin	1899–1900	St Petersburg, 1901	Moscow, 3 Nov 1900	*10a, b †38
—	Serviliya		opera, 5	Rimsky-Korsakov, after Mey	1900–01	St Petersburg, 1902	St Petersburg, 14 Oct 1902	*11a, b †39
—	Kashchey bessmertnïy [conclusion rewritten 1906]	Kashchey the Immortal	opera, 1	Rimsky-Korsakov, after E. M. Petrovsky	1901–2	St Petersburg, 1902	Moscow, 25 Dec 1902	*12 †40
—	Pan Voyevoda		opera, 4	Tyumenev	1902–3	St Petersburg, 1904	St Petersburg Conservatory, 16 Oct 1904	*13a, b †41
—	Skazaniye o nevidimom grade Kitezhe i deve Fevronii	Legend of the Invisible City of Kitezh and the Maiden Fevroniya	opera, 4	Bel'sky	1903–5	Leipzig, 1906	St Petersburg, 20 Feb 1907	*14a, b, suppl. †42
—	Zolotoy petushok	The Golden Cockerel	opera, 3	Bel'sky, after Pushkin	1906–7	Moscow, 1908	Moscow, 7 Oct 1909	*15a, b, v †43
—	Sten'ka Razin		opera, sketches	Bel'sky	1906	—	—	—
—	Zemlya i nebo	Heaven and Earth	opera, sketches	Byron	1906	—	—	—

CHORAL WORKS
(* full score; † vocal score with pf acc.)

op.	Title	Translation	Text	Forces	Composed	Published	RK
13	2 choruses:		Lermontov	3 female vv	1875	Leipzig, 1875	—
	1 Tuchki nebesnïya	Clouds in the sky					
	2 Nochevala tuchka zolotaya	The golden cloud had slept					
14	4 variations and fughetta on a Russian folksong, Nadoyeli nochi			4 female vv, pf/ harmonium ad lib	1875	Leipzig, 1875	—
16	6 choruses:					St Petersburg, 1876	—
	1 Na severe dikom	In the wild north		SATB	1875		
	2 Bakkhicheskaya pesn'	Bacchic song		TTBB	1875		
	3 Staraya pesnya: Iz lesov dremuchikh severnïkh	Old song: From the dense northern forests		SATB	1876		
	4 Mesyats plïvet i tikh i spokoyen	The moon floats peacefully		SATB	1876		
	5 Poslednyaya tucha razseyannoy buri	The last cloud of the storm		SSAA	1876		
	6 Molitva: Vladïko dney moikh	Prayer: Rule my days		SATB	1875		
18	2 choruses:			SATB	1876	St Petersburg, 1876	—
	1 Pred raspyat'yem	Before the Cross					
	2 Tatarskiy polon	The Tatar captivity					
23	4 choruses:			3 male vv, pf ad lib	1876	Leipzig, 1876	—
	1 Krest'yanskaya pirushka	The peasant feast					
	2 Voron k voron letit	Raven flies to raven					
	3 Plenivshis' rozoy solovey	Enslaved by the rose the nightingale					
	4 Dayte bokalï	Give me the goblet					
20	Stikh ob Alexeye Bozh'yem cheloveke	Poem about Alexey, the man of God		ATB, orch	1878	Leipzig, c1880	*24, 44
19	15 Russian folksongs:			mixed vv	1879	Moscow, 1879	—
	1 Iz za lesu, lesu temnovo	From the forest, the dark forest					
	2 Kak pri vechere	As at evening					
	3 A i gusto na beryoze list'ye	The leaves are thick on the birch tree					
	4 Zelyona grusha vo sadu	The green pear tree in the garden					
	5 Kak za rechoyu	As across the river					
	6 Vo luzyakh	In the meadows					
	7 Chto vilis'-to moi rus'ï kudri	When you waved my light brown curls					
	8 Poduy, poduy nepogodushka	Begone, begone bad weather					
	9 Akh, talan-li moy	Oh, my good fortune					

op.	Title	Translation	Text	Forces	Composed	Published	RK
	10 Tï vzoydi solntse krasnoye	Rise, red sun					
	11 Vzoydi tï, solntse, ni niizko, v'ïsoko	Rise, O sun, not low but high					
	12 Ay, vo pole lipen'ka	In the field there is a lime-tree					
	13 Zapletisya pleten'	Plait the wattle fencing					
	14 Posmotrite-ka dobrïye lyudi	Just see, good people					
	15 So v'yunom ya khozhu	With a youth I walk					
21	Slava	Be praised		SATB, orch	1879–90	—	*24
—	Tebe Boga khvalim	We praise thee O God	Greek chant	SATB	1883	St Petersburg, 1883	—
22	8 settings from the Liturgiya sv. Ioanna Zlatausta [Liturgy of St John Chrysostom]			SATB	1883	St Petersburg, 1884	—
22b	Traditional chants:			SATB	1884	St Petersburg, 1885–6	—
	1 Kheravimskaya pesnya	Song of the cherubim					
	2 Da molchit vsyakaya plot' chelovecha	Let all mortal flesh keep silent					
	3 Voskresnovo prichastnovo stikha	From the verses concerned with the Resurrection					
	4 Se zhenikh gryadet	See the bridegroom comes					
	5 Chertog tvoy vizhdu, Spase Moy	I enter thy hall, my Saviour					
	6 Psalm: Na rekakh Vavilonskikh	By the waters of Babylon					
44	Switezianka, cantata		L. A. Mey, after Mickiewicz	S, T, SATB, orch	1897	Leipzig, 1898	*24 †44
58	Pesn' o veshchem Olege	Song of Oleg the Wise	A. K. Tolstoy	T, B, TB, orch	1899	St Petersburg, 1901	*24 †44
60	Iz Gomera, prelude-cantata	From Homer	from the Odyssey	S, Mez, A, SA, orch	1901	Leipzig, 1905	*24 †44

ORCHESTRAL
(* – full score; † – composer's arr. pf 4 hands; ‡ – pf reduction of orch pt.)

op.	Title	Composed	Published	Remarks	RK
1	Symphony no.1				
	1st version	1861–5	Moscow, 1953		*16
	2nd version	1884	St Petersburg, 1885		*16
28	Overture on Russian themes				
	1st version	1866	Moscow, 1954		*20
	2nd version	1879–80	Leipzig, 1886		*20, †49b
6	Fantasia on Serbian themes				
	1st version	1867	Moscow, 1870		*19b, †49b
	2nd version	1886–7	Moscow, 1895		*19b
5	Sadko				
	1st version	1867	Moscow, 1951	entitled Epizod iz bïlinï o Sadko [Episode from the legend of Sadko]	*19a
	2nd version	1869	Moscow, 1870	entitled Muzïkal'naya kartina – Sadko [Musical picture – Sadko] in 2nd and 3rd versions	*19a
	3rd version	1892	Moscow, 1892		*19a
—	Symphony, b	1866–9	Moscow, 1970	sketches only; pt. of 2nd subject used in Mizgir's aria O lyubi menya, lyubi, in Snegurochka	*50
9	Symphony no.2 'Antar'				*17
	1st version	1868	—		
	2nd version	1875	St Petersburg, 1880	rev. 1903 (St Petersburg, 1903)	
	3rd version	1897	St Petersburg, 1913	described as Symphonic Suite	
32	Symphony no.3, C				
	1st version	1866–73	Moscow, 1959	scherzo composed 1866, trio 1870, other movts 1873	*18
	2nd version	1886	Leipzig, 1888		*18
—	Concerto, trbn, military band, B♭	1877	Moscow, 1950		*25
—	Variations, ob, military band, g	1878	Moscow, 1950	on Glinka's song Chto krasotka molodaya	*25
—	Concertstück, cl, military band, E♭	1878	Moscow, 1950		*25
29	Skazka [Legend]	1879–80	Leipzig, 1886	orig. title Baba-Yaga	*20, †49b
31	Sinfonietta on Russian Themes, a	1880–84	Leipzig, 1887	based on first 3 movts of str qt, 1878–9	*20
30	Pf concerto, c♯–D♭	1882–3	Leipzig, 1886		*26, ‡48
—	Symphony no.4	1884	Moscow, 1970	pf sketches for scherzo, d	50
33	Fantasia on Two Russian Themes, vn	1886–7	Leipzig, 1887		*26, ‡48
34	Kaprichchio na ispanskiye temï [Spanish capriccio]	1887	Leipzig, 1888	based on projected Fantasia on Spanish themes, vn, orch	*21, †49b
—	Malorossiyskaya fantaziya [Little Russian fantasia]	1887	Moscow, 1970	pf sketches only	50
35	Sheherazade, symphonic suite	1888	Leipzig, 1889		*22, †49b
—	Souvenir de trois chants polonais, vn	1888	‡Moscow, 1949	Polish themes used later in Pan Voyevoda; arr. pf, vn 1893	*26, ‡48

op.	Title	Composed	Published	Remarks	RK
36	Svetlïy prazdnik [Russian Easter Festival], ov.	1888	Leipzig, 1890	based on liturgical themes	*21
—	Variation no.4, A	1901	Leipzig, 1903	for Variations on a Russian theme, Uzh tï pole moye, collab. Artsïbushev, Vïtols, Lyadov, Sokolov and Glazunov	*23
—	Noch' na gore Triglave [Night on mount Triglav]	1899–1901	—	orch arr. of act 3 of opera Mlada	*4 suppl.
37	Serenade, vc	1903	—	orch arr. of Serenade, vc, pf, 1893	*26
57	Skazka o tsare Saltane [Tale of Tsar Saltan], musical pictures	1903	Leipzig, 1904	suite from the opera	—
59	Pan Voyevoda	1903	Leipzig, 1904	suite from the opera	—
—	Mlada	1903	Leipzig, 1904	suite from the opera	—
—	Noch' pered rozhdestvom [Christmas Eve], chorus ad lib	1903	Leipzig, 1904	suite from the opera	—
61	Nad mogiloy [On the tomb]	1904	Leipzig, 1905	in memory of M. P. Belyayev	*23, †49b
62	Dubinushka [The little oak stick]				
	1st version	1905	Moscow, 1966		*23
	2nd version, chorus ad lib	1906	Leipzig, 1907		*23, †49b
—	Zdravitsa [Greeting]	1906	Moscow, 1966	for Glazunov's jubilee, 1907	*23
63	Neapolitanskaya pesenka [Neapolitan song]	1907	Moscow, 1966	arr. of Denza: Funiculi, funicula	*23, †49b
—	Zolotoy petushok [The Golden Cockerel]	1907	—	concert arr. of introduction and wedding march to the opera	—
—	Skazka o rïbake i o rïbke [Tale of the fisherman and the fish], symphonic poem	1907	—	after Pushkin; sketches only	—

CHAMBER MUSIC

op.	Title	Composed	Published	Remarks	RK
12	String Quartet, F	1875	Moscow, c1875		27
—	String Sextet, A, 2 vn, 2 va, 2 vc	1876	Moscow, 1912		27
—	Quintet, B♭, fl, cl, hn, bn, pf	1876	Leipzig, 1911		28a
—	String Quartet on Russian themes:	1878–9	—	first 3 movts used later in Sinfonietta, op.31; last movt arr. pf 4 hands as V tserkvi	
	1 V pole [In the field]		—		—
	2 Na devichnike [At the wedding-eve party]		—		—
	3 V Khorovode [At Khorovod]		—		—
	4 U monastirya [At the monastery]		Moscow, 1955		27
—	4 variations on a chorale, g, str qt	1885	Moscow, 1955		27
—	String Quartet 'B–la–F'	1886	Leipzig, 1887	1st movt only, remainder by Lyadov, Glazunov and Borodin; arr. pf 4 hands	27
—	String Quartet 'Jour de fête'	1887	Leipzig, 1889	finale only, remainder by Glazunov and Lyadov	27
—	Nocturne, F, 4 hn	c1888	Moscow, 1955		27
—	2 Duets, F, 2 hn	?1883–94	Moscow, 1955		27
—	Canzonetta and Tarantella, 2 cl	?1883–94	Moscow, 1955		27
—	Serenade, vc, pf	1893	Leipzig, 1895	orchd 1903 as op.37	48
—	String Quartet, G	1897	Moscow, 1955		27
—	Trio, c, vn, vc, pf	1897	Moscow, 1970		28b
—	Theme and variation no.4, G, str qt	1898	Leipzig, 1899	for Variations on a Russian theme, Nadoyeli nochi nadoskuchili, collab. Artsïbushev, Skryabin, Glazunov, Lyadov, Vïtols, Blumenfeld, Ewald, Winkler and Sokolov	27
—	Allegro, B♭, str qt	1899	Leipzig, 1899	for collective qt 'Les vendredis', collab. Glazunov, Artsïbushev, Sokolov, Lyadov, Vïtols, Osten-Sacken, Blumenfeld, Borodin and Kopïlov	27

PIANO
(all for solo pf unless otherwise stated)

op.	Title	Composed	Published	Remarks	RK
—	Overture	1855	—	unfinished	—
—	Allegro, d	1859–60	—		—
—	Variations on a Russian theme	1859–60	—		—
—	Nocturne, d	1860	—		—
—	Funeral march, d	1860	—		—
—	Scherzo, c, pf 4 hands	1860	—		—
17	6 fugues, d, F, C, E, A, e	1875	St Petersburg, c1875		—
—	4-pt. fugue, C	1875	Moscow, 1951	arr. pf 4 hands 1875	49a
—	3 4-pt. fugues, C, e, g	1875	Moscow, 1951	nos.2 and 3 are double fugues; no.3 on B–A–C–H	49a
—	6 3-pt. fugues, G, F, E, A, d, D	1875	Moscow, 1951		49a
—	3 fughettas on Russian themes: 4-pt., g; 4-pt., d; 3-pt., g	1875	Moscow, 1951		49a
15	3 pieces: Valse, Romance, Fugue	1875–6	St Petersburg, c1880		49a
11	4 pieces: Impromptu, Novellette, Scherzino, Etude	1876–7	St Petersburg, 1878		49a

op.	Title	Composed	Published	Remarks	RK
10	6 variations on B–A–C–H: Valse, Intermezzo, Scherzo, Nocturne, Prelude, Fugue	1878	St Petersburg, 1878		49a
—	Chopsticks paraphrases	1878	St Petersburg, 1880	Variations nos.1, 2, 6, 11–13, 16, 19 and Berceuse, Fughetta on B–A–C–H, Tarantella, Minuet, Carillon and Grotesque March; remainder by Borodin, Cui, Lyadov, Liszt and Shcherbachev	49a
—	V tserkvi [In church], pf 4 hands	1879	Moscow, 1966	arr. of last movt of str qt, 1878–9	49b
—	Variations on a theme by Misha, pf 4 hands	?1878–9	Moscow, 1959	theme by Rimsky-Korsakov's eldest son, Mikhail	49a
—	Shutka kadril' [Joke quadrille]	1885	Leipzig, 1891	figure 6 (finale) only; remainder by Artsïbushev, Vïtols, Lyadov, Sokolov and Glazunov	49a
—	String quartet 'B–la–F', arr. pf 4 hands	1886	Moscow, 1966	1st movt only	49b
38	Prelude-impromptu, Mazurka	1894	St Petersburg, 1896	for Bessel's 25th jubilee album, collab. Artsïbushev, Cui, Glazunov, Lyadov and Sokolov	49a
—	Allegretto, C	1895	Moscow, 1959		49a
—	Prelude, G	1896	Moscow, 1959		49a
—	Fugal intermezzo, pf 4 hands	1897	—	intended for Motsart i Sal'yeri	—
—	Variation no.1, A	1899	Leipzig, 1900	for Variations on a Russian theme, collab. Winkler, Blumenfeld, Sokolov, Vïtols, Lyadov, Glazunov	49a
—	Pesenka [Song]	1901	St Petersburg, 1903	in the Dorian mode; melody later included as no.3 in Armenian collection Artsunker [Tears] (St Petersburg, 1907)	49a

SONGS

(unless otherwise stated, for 1v, pf acc. and in RK 45)

op.	Title	English version	Text	Composed	Published	Remarks
—	Babochka, duet	The butterfly	Anon.	1855	—	not in RK
—	Vikhodi ko mne, signora	Come out to me, signora	Anon.	1861	—	not in RK
—	V krovi gorit	My blood burns	Pushkin	1865	—	not in RK
2	4 songs:				St Petersburg, 1866	
	1 Shchekoyu k shcheke tï moyey prilozhis'	Lean thy cheek to mine	Heine, trans. M. Mikhaylov	1865		
	2 Plenivshis' rozoy, solovey	Enslaved by the rose, the nightingale	A. Kol'tsov	1866		
	3 Bayu, bayushki, bayu	Lullaby	L. Mey	1866		later used in 2nd version of Pskovityanka and in Boyarïnya Vera Sheloga
	4 Iz slyoz moikh	From my tears	Heine, trans. Mikhaylov	1866		
3	4 songs:			1866	St Petersburg, 1866	
	1 El' i pal'ma	The pine and the palm	Heine, trans. Mikhaylov			orchd 1888 (Leipzig, 1891), RK 23
	2 Yuzhnaya noch'	Southern night	N. Shcherbina			
	3 Nochevala tuchka zolotaya	The golden cloud had slept	Lermontov			
	4 Na kholmakh Gruzii	On the hills of Georgia	Pushkin			
4	4 songs:			1866	St Petersburg, 1866	
	1 Chto v imeni tebe moyem?	What is my name to thee?	Pushkin			
	2 Gonets	The messenger	Heine, trans. Mikhaylov			
	3 V temnoy roshche zamolk solovey	In the dark grove the nightingale is silent	I. Nikitin			nos.3 and 4 orchd 1891 (Moscow, 1922), RK 23
	4 Tikho vecher dogorayet	Quietly evening falls	A. Fet			
7	4 songs:			1867	St Petersburg, 1867	orig. op.5
	1 Moy golos dlya tebya i laskovïy, i tomnïy	My voice for thee is sweet and languid	Pushkin			
	2 Evreyskaya pesnya	Hebrew song	Mey			
	3 Switezianka	Switezianka	Mickiewicz, trans. Mey			later used in the choral setting, op.44
	4 Kak nebesa, tvoy vzor blistayet	Thy glance is radiant as the heavens	Lermontov			
8	6 songs:				Moscow, 1870	
	1 Gde tï, tam mïsl' moya letayet	Where thou art, my thought flies to thee	—	1870		
	2 Noch'	Night	Pleshcheyev	1868		orchd 1891 (Moscow, 1922), RK 23
	3 Tayna	The secret	After Chamisso	1868		
	4 Vstan', soydi!	Arise, come down!	Mey	1870		

op.	Title	English version	Text	Composed	Published	Remarks
	5 V tsarstvo rozï i vina	In the kingdom of roses and wine	Fet	1870		
	6 Ya veryu, ya lyubim	I believe I love	Pushkin	1870		
25	2 songs:		Heine, trans. Mikhaylov		St Petersburg, 1876	
	1 K moyey pesne	To my song		1870		
	2 Kogda glyazhu tebe v glaza	When I gaze into thy eyes		1876		
26	4 songs:			1882	St Petersburg, 1882	
	1 V porïve nezhnosti serdechnoy	In moment to delight devoted	Byron, trans. I. Kozlov			
	2 Zaklinaniye	Evocation	Pushkin			
	3 Dlya beregov otchiznï dal'noy	For the shores of thy far native land	Pushkin			
	4 Pesnya Zyuleyki	Zuleika's song	Byron, trans. Kozlov			
27	4 songs:			1883	St Petersburg, 1883	
	1 Gornimi tikho letela dusha nebesami	Softly the spirit flew up to Heaven	A. K. Tolstoy			
	2 Ekho	The echo	F. Coppée, trans. S. Andreyevsky			
	3 Tï i vï	Thou and you	Pushkin			
	4 Prosti! Ne pomni dney naden'ya	Forgive! Remember not these tearful days	N. Nekrasov			
39	4 songs:		A. K. Tolstoy	1897	Leipzig, 1897	
	1 O, eslib tï mogla	Oh, if thou couldst for one moment				
	2 Zapad gasnet v dali bledno-rozovoy	The west dies out in pallid rose				
	3 Na nivï zheltïye niskhodit tishina	Silence descends on the golden cornfields				
	4 Usni, pechal'nïy drug	Sleep, my poor friend				
40	4 songs:			1897	Leipzig, 1897	
	1 Kogda volnuyetsya zhelteyushchaya niva	When the golden cornfield waves	Lermontov			
	2 Po nebu polunochi	Across the midnight sky	Lermontov			
	3 O chem v tishi nochey	Of what I dream in the quiet night	A. Maykov			
	4 Ya v grote zhdal tebya v urochnïy chas	I waited for thee in the grotto at the appointed hour	Maykov			
41	4 songs:			1897	Leipzig, 1897	
	1 Nespyashchikh solntse	Sun of the sleepless	A. K. Tolstoy, after Byron			
	2 Mne grustno	I am unhappy	Lermontov			
	3 Lyublyu tebya, mesyats	I love thee, moon	Maykov			
	4 Posmotri v svoy vertograd	Look in thy garden	Maykov			
42	4 songs:			1897	Leipzig, ?1897	
	1 Shopot, robkoye dïkhan'ye	A whisper, a gentle breath	Fet			
	2 Ya prishol k tebe s privetom	I have come to greet thee	Fet			
	3 Redeyet oblakov letuchaya gryada	The clouds begin to scatter	Pushkin			
	4 Moya balovnitsa	My spoiled darling	Mickiewicz, trans. Mey			
43	Vesnoy [In spring]:			1897	Leipzig, 1898	
	1 Zvonche zhavoronka pen'ye	The lark sings louder	A. K. Tolstoy			
	2 Ne veter, veya s vïsotï	Not the wind, blowing from the heights	A. K. Tolstoy			
	3 Svezh i dushist tvoy roskoshnïy venok	Cool and fragrant is thy garland	Fet			
	4 To bïlo ranneyu vesnoy	Early spring	A. K. Tolstoy			
45	Poetu [To the poet]:				Leipzig, 1898	
	1 Ekho	The echo	Pushkin	1897		
	2 Iskusstvo	Art	Maykov	1897		
	3 Oktava	The octave	Maykov	1897		
	4 Somneniye	Doubt	Maykov	1897		
	5 Poet	The poet	Pushkin	1899		
46	U morya [By the sea]:		A. K. Tolstoy	1897	Leipzig, 1898	
	1 Drobitsya, i pleshchet, i brïzzhet volna	The wave breaks into spray				
	2 Ne penitsya more	Not a sound from the sea				
	3 Kolishetrya more	The sea is tossing				
	4 Ne ver' mne, drug	Do not believe me, friend				

op.	Title	English version	Text	Composed	Published	Remarks
	5 Vzdïmayutsya volnï	The waves rise up like mountains				
47	2 duets, Mez, Bar, or S, T:			1897	Leipzig, 1898	in RK 46a; orchd 1905 (Leipzig, 1906), RK 46a
	1 Pan	Pan	Maykov			
	2 Pesnya pesen	The song of songs	Mey			
49	2 songs, B:		Pushkin		Leipzig, 1898	
	1 Anchar	The upas tree		1882		rev. 1897; orchd 1906 (Leipzig, 1907), RK 23
	2 Prorok	The prophet		1897		orchd, with male vv ad lib, 1899 (Leipzig, 1899), RK 23
50	4 songs:		Maykov, after modern Greek poems		Leipzig, 1898	
	1 Deva i solntse	The maiden and the sun		1897		
	2 Pevets	The singer		1897		
	3 Tikho more goluboye	Quiet is the blue sea		1897		
	4 Eschcho ya poln, o drug moy milïy	I am still filled, dear friend		1898		
51	5 songs:		Pushkin	1897	Leipzig, 1898	
	1 Meditel'no vlekutsya dni moi	Slowly drag my days				
	2 Ne poy, krasavitsa, pri mne	Do not sing to me, o lovely one				
	3 Tsvetok zasokhshiy	Withered flower				
	4 Krasavitsa	The beauty				
	5 Nenastnïy den' potukh	The rainy day has waned				
52	2 duets:		Maykov		Leipzig, 1898	in RK 46a
	1 Gornïy kluch, S, Mez, or T, Bar	The mountain spring		1897		orchd as trio, S, Mez, A, op.52b, 1905 (Leipzig, 1906), RK 46a
	2 Angel i demon, S, Bar, or T, Mez	Angel and demon		1898		
53	Strekozï, 2 S, Mez	Dragonflies	A. K. Tolstoy	1897	Leipzig, 1898	in RK 46a; orchd, with female vv ad lib, 1897 (Leipzig, 1898), RK 46a
55	4 songs, T:				Leipzig, 1898	
	1 Probuzhden'ye	Awakening	Pushkin	1897		
	2 Grechanke	To a Grecian girl	Pushkin	1898		
	3 Snovideniye	The dream	Pushkin	1898		
	4 Ya umer ot schast'ya	I died from happiness	L. Uhland, trans. ?Zhukovsky	1898		
56	2 songs, S:		Maykov	1898	Leipzig, 1899	
	1 Nimfa	The nymph				orchd 1905 (Leipzig, 1908), RK 23
	2 Son v letnyuyu noch'	Summer night's dream				orchd 1906, ?unpubd, lost

FOLKSONG COLLECTIONS

op.	Title	Translation	Compiled	Published	Remarks	RK
—	40 narodnïkh pesen	40 folksongs	1875	Moscow, 1882	collab. T. I. Filippov	47
24	Sbornik 100 russkikh narodnïkh pesen	Collection of 100 Russian folksongs	1875–6	St Petersburg, 1877	—	47

WORK ON COMPOSITIONS BY OTHERS

Schubert: March for the Coronation of Nicholas I, orchd 1868
Cui: 1st number of William Ratcliff, orchd 1868
Dargomïzhsky: The Stone Guest, orchd 1869; 1st scene reorchd c1900, remainder reorchd and some passages rewritten 1902
Dargomïzhsky: Chorus of Maidens from Rogdana, orchd ?1873
Musorgsky: 2nd version of trio of Destruction of Sennacherib, orchd 1874; complete work orchd later
Handel: seven numbers from Samson, orchd 1875–6
Glinka: music for stage band in Ruslan and Lyudmila, 1878
Borodin: final chorus of Prince Igor, orchd 1879; prol and Act 1 scene i, rev. 1885; whole opera completed and orchd with Glazunov, 1887–8
Musorgsky: Persian dances from Khovanshchina, ed. and orchd 1879; whole opera rewritten, completed and orchd 1881–3
Musorgsky: miscellaneous orch and choral works, songs etc, ed. and orchd, 1881–3
Musorgsky: Dream Intermezzo from Sorochintsy Fair, rewritten and rescored for orch only as Night on the Bare Mountain, 1886
Glinka: excerpts from operas, arr. str qt 1884
Borodin: Nocturne from String Quartet no.2, arr. vn, orch 1887
Musorgsky: Polonaise from Boris Godunov, reorchd 1888; Coronation Scene, reorchd 1892; whole opera cut, rewritten and reorchd 1892–6; rewritten and reorchd with cuts restored 1906; two passages composed for the Coronation Scenes from Dyagilev's Paris production, 1907
Borodin: finale to Act 4 of collective Mlada, orchd 1890
Borodin: song The Sleeping Princess, orchd 1897
Borodin: song The Sea, orchd 1906
Musorgsky: The Marriage, rev. and partly orchd 1906

Musorgsky: songs Hopak, Gathering Mushrooms and Peasant Lullaby, orchd 1906
Musorgsky: song With Nurse, 'free musical rendering' 1908
Musorgsky: songs Night and The Field Marshal and pt. of Serenade, orchd 1908

TRANSCRIPTIONS FOR MILITARY BAND (1873–83)

Meyerbeer: Coronation March from Le prophète
Meyerbeer: Isabella's aria from Robert le diable, cl, military band
Meyerbeer: Conspiracy Scene from Les Huguenots
L. de Meyer: Berlioz's version of Marche marocaine
Schubert: March, b
Wagner: Prelude to Lohengrin
Mendelssohn: Nocturne and Wedding March from Midsummer Night's Dream
Beethoven: Overture Egmont

WRITINGS

Edition: *Polnoye sobraniye sochineniy: literaturnïye proizvedeniya i perepiska* [Complete edition of compositions: literary works and correspondence] (Moscow, 1955–) [RKL]

Uchebnik garmonii [Textbook of harmony] (St Petersburg, 1884–5, 2/1886 as *Prakticheskiy uchebnik garmonii*, 19/1949; Ger. trans., 1895; Fr. trans., 1910), RKL, iv, ed. V. V. Protopopov (Moscow, 1960), 7–387

Letopis' moyey muzïkal'noy zhizni [Chronicle of my musical life] (St Petersburg, 1909; Fr. trans., 1914; Eng. trans., 1924; enlarged 3/1926; Eng. trans., 1942/R1974), RKL, i, ed. A. V. Ossovsky and V. N. Rimsky-Korsakov (Moscow, 1955), 3–236

ed. N. Rimskaya-Korsakova: *Muzïkal'nïye stat'i i zametki 1869–1907* [Articles and notes on music 1869–1907] (St Petersburg, 1911)

ed. M. O. Shteynberg: *Osnovï orkestrovki* [Principles of orchestration] (St Petersburg, 1913, 2/1946; Fr. trans., 1914; Ger. trans., 1922; Eng. trans., 1922, 2/1964), RKL, iii, ed. A. N. Dmitriyev (Moscow, 1959)

ed. A. V. Ossovsky and V. N. Rimsky-Korsakov: *Dnevnik 1904–7* [Diary 1904–7; fragments only], RKL, i (Moscow, 1955), 237ff

ed. V. V. Protopopov: *Razbor Snegurochka* [An analysis of *Snow Maiden*], RKL, iv (Moscow, 1960), 381–426

ed. N. V. Shelkov: *Muzïkal'no-kriticheskiye stat'i* [Critical articles on music], RKL, ii (Moscow, 1963), 11–44

——: *Stat'i i materialï po voprosam istorii muzïki i estetiki* [Articles and materials on the history of music and aesthetics], RKL, ii (Moscow, 1963), 45ff

——: *Vïstupleniya v pechati* [Miscellaneous articles and letters], RKL, ii (Moscow, 1963), 235ff

BIBLIOGRAPHY

(RKL – see edn. of writings)

N. Findeyzen: *Nikolay Andreyevich Rimsky-Korsakov: ocherk evo muzïkal'noy deyatel'nosti* [Outline of his musical career] (St Petersburg, 1908)

V. V. Yastrebtsev: *Nikolay Andreyevich Rimsky-Korsakov: ocherk evo zhizni i deyatel'nosti* [Outline of his life and career] (Moscow, 1908)

I. I. Lapshin: *Filosofskiye motivi v tvorchestve N. A. Rimsko-Korsakova* [Philosophical motives in Rimsky-Korsakov's works] (St Petersburg, 1911)

V. V. Yastrebtsev: *Moi vospominaniya o Nikolaye Andreyeviche Rimskom-Korsakove* [My reminiscences of Rimsky-Korsakov] (Moscow, 1917) [incomplete; see Yastrebtsev (1959–60)]

N. van Gilse Van der Pals: *N. A. Rimsky-Korssakow. Opernschaffen nebst Skizzen über Leben und Wirken* (Paris and Leipzig, 1929)

A. N. Rimsky-Korsakov: *N. A. Rimsky-Korsakov: zhizn' i tvorchestvo* [Life and works] (Moscow, 1933–46)

I. Markévitch: *Rimsky-Korsakov* (Paris, 1934)

G. Abraham: 'Rimsky-Korsakov's First Opera', 'Rimsky-Korsakov's Gogol Operas', 'Snow Maiden', 'Sadko', 'The Tsar's Bride', 'Kitezh', 'The Golden Cockerel', *Studies in Russian Music* (London, 1935), 142–310

——: 'Rimsky-Korsakov's *Mlada* and *Tsar Saltan*', *On Russian Music* (London, 1939), 113

B. V. Asaf'yev: *Nikolay Andreyevich Rimsky-Korsakov (1844–1944)* (Moscow and Leningrad, 1944)

G. Abraham: *Rimsky-Korsakov: a Short Biography* (London, 1945)

M. O. Yankovsky: *Rimsky-Korsakov i revolyutsiya 1905 goda* [Rimsky-Korsakov and the 1905 revolution] (Moscow and Leningrad, 1950)

V. A. Kiselyov, ed.: *N. A. Rimsky-Korsakov: sbornik dokumentov* [Collection of documents] (Moscow and Leningrad, 1951)

V. V. Stasov: *Stat'i o Rimskom-Korsakove* [Articles on Rimsky-Korsakov], ed. V. A. Kiselyov (Moscow, 1953)

I. F. Belza: *Motsart i Sal'yeri, tragediya Pushkina: dramaticheskiye stsenï Rimskovo-Korsakova* [Mozart and Salieri, Pushkin's tragedy: Rimsky-Korsakov's dramatic scenes] (Moscow, 1953)

A. A. Solovtsov: *Simfonicheskiye proizvedeniya Rimskovo-Korsakova* [Rimsky-Korsakov's symphonic works] (Moscow, 1953)

M. O. Yankovsky and others, eds.: *Rimsky-Korsakov: issledovaniya, materialï, pis'ma* [Research, materials, letters] (Moscow, 1953–4)

M. F. Gnesin: *Mïsli i vospominaniya o N. A. Rimskom-Korsakove* [Thoughts and reminiscences about Rimsky-Korsakov] (Moscow, 1956)

A. A. Gozenpud: *N. A. Rimsky-Korsakov: temï i idei evo opernovo tvorchestva* [The themes and ideas in his operas] (Moscow, 1957)

V. A. Kiselyov, ed.: *Avtografï N. A. Rimskovo-Korsakova v fondakh gosudarstvennovo tsentral'novo muzeya muzïkal'noy kul'turï imeni M. I. Glinki: katalogspravochnik* [Rimsky-Korsakov's autographs in the collection of the State Central Glinka Museum of Musical Culture: a reference catalogue] (Moscow, 1958)

S. L. Ginzburg, ed.: *N. A. Rimsky-Korsakov i muzïkal'noye obrazovaniye* [Rimsky-Korsakov and musical education] (Leningrad, 1959)

V. V. Yastrebtsev: *Nikolay Andreyevich Rimsky-Korsakov: vospominaniya* [Reminiscences], ed. A. V. Ossovsky (Leningrad, 1959–60)

L. Danilevich: *Posledniye operï N. A. Rimskovo-Korsakova* [Rimsky-Korsakov's last operas] (Moscow, 1961)

Yu. A. Kremlyov: *Estetika prirodï v tvorchestve N. A. Rimskovo-Korsakova* [The aesthetics of nature in the works of Rimsky-Korsakov] (Moscow, 1962)

A. S. Lyapunova, ed.: *Perepiska N. A. Rimskovo-Korsakova* [Rimsky-Korsakov's correspondence, with Balakirev (1862–98), Borodin (1871–86), Cui (1862–1908), Musorgsky (1867–80), V. V. Stasov (1869–1906), D. V. Stasov (1866–1907), V. V. Vasil'yev (1870–72) and L. I. Shestakova (1878–89)], RKL, v (Moscow, 1963)

N. V. Shelkov: *Dokumentï i materialï, svyazannïye s deyatel'nost'yu v orkestrakh voyenno-morskovo flota* [Documents and materials in connection with Rimsky-Korsakov's activities in the naval military bands], RKL, ii (Moscow, 1963), 73–127

——: *Materialï, svyazannïye s deyatel'nost'yu v pridvornoy pevcheskoy kapelle* [Materials in connection with Rimsky-Korsakov's activities in the imperial chapel choir], RKL, ii (Moscow, 1963), 129–68

——: *Materialï, svyazannïye s deyatel'nost'yu v Peterburgskoy konservatorii* [Materials in connection with Rimsky-Korsakov's activities at the St Petersburg Conservatory], RKL, ii (Moscow, 1963), 169–222

——: *Materialï, svyazannïye s deyatel'nost'yu v Russkom muzïkal'nom obshchestve i v kachestve uchreditelya vïsshikh muzïkal'nïkh kursov* [Materials in connection with Rimsky-Korsakov's activities in the Russian Musical Society and in his role as the founder of higher education courses in music], RKL, ii (Moscow, 1963), 223ff

A. Solovtsov: *Zhizn' i tvorchestvo N. A. Rimskovo-Korsakova* [Life and works] (Moscow, 1964)

E. E. Yazovitskaya, ed.: *Perepiska N. A. Rimskovo-Korsakova* [Rimsky-Korsakov's correspondence, with Lyadov (1878–1908) and Glazunov (1882–1908)], RKL, vi (Moscow, 1965)

G. Abraham: '*Pskovityanka*: the Original Version of Rimsky-Korsakov's First Opera', *MQ*, liv (1968), 58

——: 'Rimsky-Korsakov as Self-critic', 'Rimsky-Korsakov's Songs', *Slavonic and Romantic Music* (London, 1968), 195

S. Feinberg: 'Rimsky-Korsakov's Suite from *Le coq d'or*', *MR*, xxx (1969), 47

E. Garden: 'Classic and Romantic in Russian Music', *ML*, l (1969), 153

A. Orlova and V. Rimsky-Korsakov, eds.: *Stranitsï zhizni Rimskovo-Korsakova* [Pages from Rimsky-Korsakov's life] (Leningrad, 1969)

S. Slonimsky: 'Die lebendige, moderne Kunst Rimski-Korsakovs', *Kunst und Literatur*, xvii (1969), 1307

S. Evseyev: *Rimsky-Korsakov i russkaya narodnaya pesnya* [Rimsky-Korsakov and Russian folksong] (Moscow, 1970)

G. Abraham: 'Satire and Symbolism in *The Golden Cockerel*', *ML*, lii (1971), 46

M. Smirnov: *Fortepiannïye proizvedeniya kompozitorov moguchey kuchki* [The piano works of the composers of the Mighty Handful] (Moscow, 1971)

G. Abraham: 'Arab Melodies in Rimsky-Korsakov and Borodin', *ML*, lvi (1975), 313

E. Garden: 'Three Russian Piano Concertos', *ML*, lx (1979), 166

GERALD ABRAHAM

Rinaldi, Margherita (*b* Turin, 12 Jan 1935). Italian soprano. She studied at Rovigo, winning a competition at Spoleto, where she made her début in 1958 as Lucia. After further study she appeared at Dublin in 1961, as

Carolina (*Il matrimonio segreto*) and Gilda, the role of her La Scala (1965) and American (Dallas, 1966) débuts. She has sung at Chicago, San Francisco, Barcelona, throughout Italy, and at Wexford. Her repertory includes Mozart (Ilia, Fiordiligi), Donizetti (Norina, Adina, *Linda di Chamounix*, Marie in *La fille du régiment*), Bellini (Giulietta, Amina, Elvira), Verdi (Violetta, Oscar, both Nannetta and Alice Ford) and Strauss (Sophie and the Marschallin). In 1974 she played the Marchesa del Poggio in Verdi's *Un giorno di regno* at Bregenz. The limpid quality of her voice and its agility make her a fine Bellini interpreter – Amina (*La sonnambula*) is among her most successful roles. In Italy she is also renowned as a concert singer. She has recorded Ilia under Colin Davis.

ELIZABETH FORBES

Rinaldo dall'Arpa (*b* late 16th century; *d* 2 Aug 1603). Italian harpist, singer and composer. He was a highly esteemed member of Gesualdo's retinue of musicians. He accompanied him to Ferrara in 1594, as is indicated by a letter from a courtier to Alfonso II, Duke of Ferrara, stating that Gesualdo 'hopes that Rinaldo will be able to join in the singing from time to time'. A letter written by the custodian of instruments at the court of Ferrara in December 1598 mentions that a 'Rainaldo detto la arppa' had taken a new harp to Rome and never returned it. Rinaldo dall'Arpa probably composed two keyboard pieces in *GB-Lbm* Add.30491 (edn., CEKM, xxiv, 1967).

BIBLIOGRAPHY
F. Vatielli: *Il principe di Venosa e Leonora d'Este* (Milan, 1941), 21
A. Newcomb: 'Carlo Gesualdo and a Musical Correspondence of 1594', *MQ*, liv (1968), 414

ROLAND JACKSON

Rinaldo di [da] **Capua** (*b* Capua or Naples, *c*1705; *d* ?Rome, *c*1780). Italian composer. Information about his life is scarce and sometimes unreliable. Burney (1771) described him as:

an old and excellent Neapolitan composer. He is the natural son of a person of very high rank in that country, and at first only studied music as an accomplishment; but being left by his father with only a small fortune, which was soon dissipated, he was forced to make it his profession. He was but seventeen when he composed his first opera at Vienna.

This last statement is enigmatic: if Burney was referring to *Ciro riconosciuto*, Rinaldo's first opera composed at Rome in 1737 to a libretto by Metastasio (already set by Caldara for Vienna), then Rinaldo would have been born in 1719 or 1720; but in that case, how could Burney have described him as 'old' and of 'long life' in 1770? Similarly, Capua could be Rinaldo's surname or, more likely, the name of the small town 30 km north of Naples where he was born; and the epithet 'Neapolitan' signifies both the composer's nationality and that he was professionally trained in the Neapolitan school, to which his musical style belongs (his name has not been found in lists of the pupils at the Naples conservatories).

It was at Rome, however, that Rinaldo mainly lived and worked. He made his début there in 1737 with a comic opera (title unknown) and with an *opera seria, Ciro riconosciuto*, which was performed at the Tor di Nona. The satirical opera *La commedia in commedia* was so outstanding a success at the Teatro Valle the following year that it was repeated in Florence (1741), London (1748), Venice (1749) and Munich (1749), and various versions of it were staged under other titles elsewhere. His most celebrated *opera seria* was *Vologeso re de' Parti*, first performed at the Teatro Argentina, Rome, in 1739. *La libertà nociva* (Teatro

Valle, 1740) enhanced his reputation as a composer of comic opera and, like *La commedia*, was repeated in various European cities. On 18 March 1740 Rinaldo set off with his wife for Portugal with a contract for 1000 scudi per annum. He composed two or three *opere serie* on libretto by Metastasio for the Rua dos Condes theatre at Lisbon. But by 1742 he was back in Rome, where all his later operas except *Gli impostori* and *Il capitano napoletano* were first produced. Eustachio Bambini's company of Italian *bouffons* performed *La donna superba* in Paris in 1752 and *La zingara* in 1753. The latter was extraordinarily successful; there were innumerable revivals and it played an important part in the Querelle des Bouffons. Rinaldo's last *opera seria*, *Adriano in Siria*, was given at the Teatro Argentina in 1758. From then on, he wrote only comic operas, and those infrequently. According to Dent, the last of them, *La Giocondina* (1778), was performed posthumously.

Rinaldo experienced 'various vicissitudes of fortune; sometimes in vogue, sometimes neglected'. Burney (1789) also said: 'He was living, or rather starving in 1770 at Rome'; and 'Lattila and Rinaldo di Capua, who are still living'. This last statement is doubtful; Rinaldo probably died about 1780. In his last years, 'the accumulated produce of his pen, had by a graceless son been sold for waste paper' (Burney, 1771).

32 stage works have been identified as by Rinaldo, of which two are doubtful. The problem of cataloguing is complicated by his tendency to present reworkings of his operas under new titles and by confusion with Marcello di Capua (Bernardini). Apart from a few dozen separate arias, the music of only six operas survives. In *Gli impostori* (1751) two of the 19 arias are in *ABA* form and ten in da capo form. The style is typical of Rinaldo, ranging from farcical caricature to lyrical and sentimental expression. The words are set to nimble figures and the declamation is clearly articulated. Accompanied recitative is rare, but the ensembles are expertly composed. The score reveals Rinaldo's favourite texture – three parts, generally for strings: the first violin doubles the vocal line, sometimes varying it; the second violin either doubles the first or follows it at a 3rd or 6th (it is rarely independent); the bass, doubled by the viola (which rarely has an independent part), provides an accompaniment, often in fast repeated notes. Of the 15 numbers in *La zingara*, six are reworkings from *Il cavalier Mignatta* (1751). After the performances by Bambini's *buffa* company in Paris in 1753, *La zingara* (an intermezzo) was translated into French as *La bohémienne* and adapted as an *opéra comique* by Favart in 1755. He cut out four numbers and added six others by various composers. *La bohémienne* is therefore a pasticcio (the aria 'Examinez sa grâce' is set to a motif from the celebrated 'Tre giorni son che Nina', which has been attributed at various times to Pergolesi, Rinaldo and Ciampi; the true composer remains unknown). A further version, arranged by Bambini, was performed in Pesaro in 1755. The rapid action of *La zingara* is carried along by the exceptionally felicitous inventiveness of the music; in the second intermezzo, the simple *buffo* style in which the work begins is expanded to embrace arias in *seria* style, a chorus and wind instruments. D'Orville wrote of the work:

La Bohémienne est plus gaie, plus folle que la *Servante maîtresse*, ce qui n'est pas un petit mérite au théâtre et dans le monde [. . .] son succès est indépendant du sujet; on doit l'attribuer aux charmes de la musique'.

I finti pazzi, which is in two parts, and *La donna*

vendicativa, of which only Act 1 survives, are lively little farces; *Il capitan Fracasso* is a short intermezzo in eight brisk numbers. Of Rinaldo's cantatas, only two are known, *La natività* and the allegorical, festive Cantata *a 5*; they each have a sinfonia and 11 numbers and resemble the operas in style.

The separate arias, which come mainly from *opere serie*, reaffirm Rinaldo's qualities – an architectonic expansiveness of form, a variety of style related to the expressive needs of the situation, a desire for contrast (especially between the two parts of da capo arias), and occasional bursts of virtuoso coloratura. Burney described the aria 'Ombra che pallida' from *Vologeso* as an 'example of the perfection to which dramatic music was brought in Italy'. Rinaldo's vocation as a dramatist is evident also in his boast that he was 'among the first who introduced long "ritornellos", or symphonies, into the recitatives of strong passion and distress, which express or imitate what it would be ridiculous for the voice to attempt'.

His qualities as an instrumental composer are revealed in his sinfonias, or *ouvertures*, in which he contributed to the development of the Classical symphony-sonata. The first movement departs from the old binary form of the Baroque period and tends towards bithematic structure, with signs of a 'subsidiary thematic group', and tripartite structure, with a sizable central development section. The second movement, formerly a short, unpretentious section, becomes a bipartite song form, and the third movement is normally a jig in binary form. Rinaldo's ability to compose solid, complex forms contradicts Burney's final judgment; although considering him 'a composer of great genius and fire', Burney seems also to have echoed the opinion of J. B. de La Borde: 'The science of this composer is not equal to his genius' (*Essai*, 1780).

WORKS
STAGE
(music lost unless otherwise stated)

Untitled comic opera, Rome, Valle, 1737
Ciro riconosciuto (opera seria, Metastasio), Rome, 19 Jan 1737
La commedia in commedia (dramma giocoso, G. Barlocci), Rome, Valle, 8 Jan 1738; as L'ambizione delusa, Venice, S Cassiano, carn. 1744; abridged as La donna superba (intermezzo), Paris, Académie royale de musique, 19 Dec 1752, parodied as La femme orgueilleuse, Paris, 1759; as Il vecchio amante (intermezzo), Pesaro, del Sole, Jan 1755
Farnace (opera seria, A. M. Lucchini), Venice, S Giovanni Grisostomo aut. 1739
Vologeso re de' Parti (opera seria, G. E. Luccarelli), Rome, Torre Argentina, carn. 1739, *US-NH*; facs. (New York, 1977)
La libertà nociva (dramma giocoso, G. Barlocci), Rome, Valle, 17 Jan 1740
? Ipermestra (opera seria, Metastasio), Lisbon, Rua dos Condes, 1741
? Didone abbandonata (opera seria, Metastasio), Lisbon, Rua dos Condes, 1741
Le nozze di Don Trifone (intermezzo, N. G. Neri), Rome, Torre Argentina, carn. 1743
Turno Heredonio Aricino (dramma per musica, S. Stampiglia), Rome, Capranica, 11 Dec 1743
Il bravo burlato (intermezzo, A. Pavoni), Rome, Pallacorda, carn. 1745; as Il capitan Fracasso, Stockholm, 1768, *S-St*
La forza del sangue (intermezzo), Rome, Pallacorda, 1746
Catone in Utica (opera seria, Metastasio), Milan, Regio Ducale, Jan, 1748 [? also Lisbon, 1740]
Il bravo e il bello (intermezzo), Rome, Granari, 1748
Mario in Numidia (opera seria, G. P. Tagliazucchi), Rome, della Dame, Jan 1749
Il ripiego in amore di Flaminia finta cameriera e Turco (intermezzo, A. Luigi), Rome, Valle, carn. 1751
Il cavalier Mignatta (intermezzo), Rome, Capranica, 1751 [6 arias rev. in La zingara]
Il Galoppino (intermezzo), Rome, Capranica, carn. 1751
Gli impostori (opera seria), Modena, Ducale, 1751, *I-MOe*
La forza della pace (intermezzo, G. Puccinelli/G. Aureli), Rome, della Pace, carn. 1752
La zingara (intermezzo), Paris, Académie royale de musique, 19 June 1753, *F-Pn, I-Fc*; rev. as La zingara, Pesaro, del Sole, Jan 1755; as La bohémienne (C. S. Favart), Paris, Comédie-Italienne, 28 July 1755, collab. others, *I-Mc*; parodied as La bohémienne (comédie), Paris, Foire St Laurent, 14 July 1756; copies also in *B-Bc, GB-Lbm, I-Bc, Tn, US-Bp, Wc*
L'amante deluso (farsa giocosa, A. Pavoni), Rome, Tor di Nona, May 1753
La serva sposa (intermezzo), Rome, Valle, carn. 1753
La chiavarina (intermezzo, G. Peruzzini and A. Luigi), Rome, Valle, carn. 1754
Attalo (opera seria, A. Papi ['Cleofante Doriano']), Rome, Capranica, Feb 1754
La smorfiosa (intermezzo), Rome, Valle, carn. 1756
Il capitano napoletano (comic opera), Florence, via del Cocomero, spring 1756
Adriano in Siria (opera seria, Metastasio), Rome, Torre Argentina, 2 Jan 1758
Le donne ridicole (intermezzo, Goldoni), Rome, Capranica, Jan 1759
Il caffè di campagna (farsetta, P. Chiari), Rome, della Pace, carn. 1764
I finti pazzi per amore (farsetta, T. Mariani), Rome, della Pace, carn. 1770, *I-Rdp*
La donna vendicativa e l'erudito spropositato (intermezzo, A. Pioli), Rome, della Pace, carn. 1771, *GB-Lbm, US-Wc* (both inc.)
La Giocondina, Rome, della Pace, 1778
Numerous single arias, many from the operas, in *A-Wgm, B-Bc, D-Dlb, Mbs, MÜp, F-Pn, GB-Lbm, I-Fc, Mc, Nc*

OTHER WORKS
Numerous oratorios; Per la natività della beatissima vergine, cantata, Rome, 1755, *D-MÜp*; Cantata a 5, *F-Pn*
Elia al Carmelo, Rome, 1761; Il roveto ardente, Rome, 1762; L'arca del Testamento, Rome, 1763; Eva riparata, Rome, 1765; L'angelo di Tobia, Rome, 1768: all lost
5 symphonies and numerous ovs. in *A-Wgm, B-Bc, D-Dlb*

BIBLIOGRAPHY
BurneyH
C. d'Orville: *Histoire de l'opéra bouffon*, i (Amsterdam, 1768), 66, 71
C. Burney: *The Present State of Music in France and Italy* (London, 1771/R1969), 283ff
P. Spitta: 'Rinaldo di Capua', *VMw*, iii (1887), 92
E. J. Dent: 'Ensembles and Finales in 18th-century Italian Opera', *SIMG*, xi (1909–10), 543; xii (1910–11), 112
E. Celani: 'Musica e musicisti in Roma (1750–1850)', *RMI*, xviii (1911), 1–63
R. Sondheimer: 'Die formale Entwicklung der vorklassischen Sinfonie', *AMw*, iv (1922), 85
A. Della Corte: *L'opera comica italiana nel '700* (Bari, 1923), i, 81ff
E. Sundström: 'Ett okänt Intermezzo av Rinaldo di Capua', *STMf*, xix (1937), 200
F. Walker: '"Tre giorni son che Nina", an Old Controversy Reopened', *MT*, xc (1949), 432
R. L. Bostian: *The Works of Rinaldo di Capua* (diss., U. of North Carolina, 1961)

CLAUDIO GALLICO

Rinck, Johann Christian Heinrich (*b* Elgersburg, Thuringia, 18 Feb 1770; *d* Darmstadt, 7 Aug 1846). German organist and composer. After early teaching from Abicht, J. A. Junghanss and H. C. Kirchner, he studied with Bach's pupil J. C. Kittel in Erfurt from 1786 to 1789. He became organist at Giessen in 1790. Having moved to Darmstadt in 1805, he was organist and teacher at the music school, also becoming organist (1813) and Kammermusiker (1817) to the Grand Duke Ludwig I. He toured with great success and received many honours, including an honorary doctorate from Giessen. He was also one of the best teachers of the day, widely respected and influential through both his music and his playing, and the founder of a distinguished line of pupils. Most of his music is for organ; he was brought up in the direct Bach organ tradition, but this is reflected chiefly in his technical mastery of the instrument's resources. His compositions include the *Praktische Orgel-Schule* (op.55), *Choralfreund* (7 vols. and 2 suppls., opp.101–27), *Theoretisch-praktische Anleitung zum Orgel-Spiel* (op.124), and a collection of chorale preludes (op.105), all for organ; he also wrote two masses, cantatas, motets etc and some keyboard works. His valuable library was bought in 1852 and given to Yale University.

BIBLIOGRAPHY
J. C. H. Rinck: *Selbstbiographie* (Breslau, 1833)
B. C. L. Natorp: *Über Rincks Präludien* (Essen, 1834)
G. Fölsing: *Züge aus dem Leben und Wirken des Dr. C. H. Rinck* (Erfurt, 1848)
K. G. Fellerer: *Beiträge zur Choralbegleitung und Choralverarbeitung in der Orgelmusik des ausgehenden 18. und beginnenden 19. Jahrhunderts* (Strasbourg, 1932)
F. W. Donat: *C. H. Rinck und die Orgelmusik seiner Zeit* (Bad Oeynhausen, 1933) [incl. list of works]
R. Caillet: 'Jean-Christian Rinck, organiste à Darmstadt', *L'orgue*, lxxxiii (1957), 127 [incl. list of works]
R. Sietz: 'Rinck, Johann Christian Heinrich', *MGG*
           HERBERT S. OAKELEY/JOHN WARRACK

Rinckart, Martin (*b* Eilenburg, nr. Leipzig, 24 April 1586; *d* Eilenburg, 8 Dec 1648). German poet, clergyman and ?composer. He went to the Thomasschule, Leipzig, and sang in its choir under Sethus Calvisius, rising to the position of prefect. From 1602 he also studied at the University of Leipzig where he took the bachelor's degree in 1609. In 1610 he became Kantor at St Nicolai, Eisleben, and thus also a teacher at the grammar school there. In 1611 he was appointed deacon at St Anna, Eisleben, and in 1613 priest at nearby Erdeborn. He was crowned poet laureate in 1615 and took the master's degree in 1616. Finally in 1617 he returned as a priest to Eilenburg, where he worked selflessly until his death, at times under very difficult conditions resulting from the Thirty Years War. He was particularly admired for his rehabilitation of the Eilenburg Kantoreigesellschaft, which had completely fallen into decline. He was highly regarded in his own day for his numerous literary works, among which seven Lutheran dramas are specially notable (see Liebsch's important, if one-sided, reassessment). Nowadays he is remembered only for *Nun danket alle Gott*, which is among the most popular Protestant hymns. Based closely on *Ecclesiasticus* 1.22–4, it originated in 1630 as a Tischlied. It is possible that Crüger's famous melody for it, first published in his *Praxis pietatis melica* (1647), derives to some extent from a melody by Rinckart himself. According to Eitner he published two motets, in 1645 and 1648 respectively. He published a sacred parody of *Il trionfo di Dori* (Venice, 1592[11]) as *Triumphi de Dorothea . . . das ist Geistliches musicalisches Triumph-Cräntzlein* (Leipzig, 1619[16]), which was apparently based on the expanded edition and translation, *Musicalisches Streitkränzlein* (1612–13), by JOHANN LYTTICH, who was briefly his successor at St Nicolai.

BIBLIOGRAPHY
EitnerQ
J. Linke: *Martin Rinckarts geistliche Lieder nebst einer . . . Darstellung des Lebens und der Werke des Dichters* (Gotha, 1886)
A. Werner: *Geschichte der Kantorei-Gesellschaften im Gebiete des ehemaligen Kurfürstentums Sachsen* (Leipzig, 1902)
——: 'Die Eilenburger Kantorei und Martin Rinckarts Verdienste um dieselbe', *Monatsschrift für Gottesdienst und Kirchliche Kunst*, vii (1902), 122
M. Brüssau: *Martin Rinckart und sein Lied 'Nun danket alle Gott'* (Leipzig, 1936)
Handbuch zum evangelischen Kirchengesangbuch, ii/1 and suppl. (Göttingen, 1957–8)
H. Liebsch: 'Die Reformationsdichtung Martin Rinckarts', *450 Jahre Reformation*, ed. E. Voigt and G. Brendler (Berlin, 1967), 286
           WALTER BLANKENBURG

Rinforzando (It.: 'strengthening', 'reinforcing'; gerund of *rinforzare*). A dynamic and expression mark, sometimes abbreviated as *R*, *rinf.*, *rf* or *rfz*. It implies a more sudden increase in volume than *crescendo*, and is often applied only to a short phrase or group of notes. In the 18th century, and particularly in the work of the Mannheim composers, it was used for a very short crescendo; and occasionally it was applied to a single note demanding an accent less extreme than is required by *sforzando* or *sforzato*. But consistency of usage is not easy to find: in the *Meistersinger* prelude Wagner has a *rinforzando* stretching over two bars.

See also TEMPO AND EXPRESSION MARKS.

           DAVID FALLOWS

Ringbom, Nils-Eric (*b* Turku, 27 Dec 1907). Finnish composer and critic. He studied at the Åbo Academy (1927–8, 1930–33, MA 1933) and at Helsinki University (1928–30, DMus 1955), his principal teachers being O. Andersson (theory and musicology) and Leo Funtek (violin and instrumentation). After playing the violin in the Turku SO (1927–8, 1930–32), he served as assistant manager (1938–42) and managing director (1942–70) of the Helsinki PO. He was also artistic director of the Sibelius Festival (1951–60), chairman of the Finnish section of the ISCM (1955–9) and chairman of the Helsinki Festival (1966–70); and he has served as music critic of the *Svenska pressen* (1933–44) and the *Nya pressen* (1945–70). His quite distinctive music makes moderate use of new techniques. The Wind Sextet was the first Finnish work performed at an ISCM Festival (1952).

WORKS
(*selective list*)
Orch: Little Suite, 1933, rev. 1946; 5 syms., 1938–9, 1943–4, 1948, 1962, 1970
Choral: Till livet [To life] (E. Therman), chorus, str orch, 1936; 2 Songs (Therman), 3vv, 1936; 2 Songs (E. Södergran), 1939; Hymn till Helsingfors (R. Enckell), chorus, orch, 1949
Solo vocal: Vandrerska [The wanderer] (L. Tegengren), S, orch, 1942; Ur en dagbok [From a diary] (K.-G. Hildebrand), S, pf, 1945; 4 Songs (G. Björling), Mez, orch, 1947; 3 Songs (E. Linde), Bar, pf, 1971–2
Inst: Antandino grazioso, pf, 1931; Tema con variazioni, pf, 1932; Andantino, vn, pf, 1935; Duo, vn, va, 1945; Sextet, ob, eng hn, cl, b cl, bn, hn, 1951; Str Qt 1952

WRITINGS
Helsingfors orkesterföretag 1882–1932 (Helsinki, 1932)
Säveltaide [The art of music] (Helsinki, 1945)
Sibelius (Stockholm, 1948; Ger. trans., 1950; Eng. trans., 1954)
Über die Deutbarkeit der Tonkunst (diss., U. of Helsinki, 1955; Helsinki and Wiesbaden, 1955)
'De två versionerna av Sibelius' tondikt "En saga"', *Acta Academiae Aboensis*, xxii/2 (1956)
Musik utan normer [Music without norms] (Helsinki, 1972)
           ERIK WAHLSTRÖM

Ringer, Alexander L(othar) (*b* Berlin, 3 Feb 1921). American musicologist of German birth. He was educated in Berlin and Amsterdam, where his teachers included Henk Badings, Felix de Nobel, Marius Flothuis and K. P. Bernet Kempers. After going to the USA he received his MA in 1949 from the New School for Social Research in New York and his PhD in 1955 from Columbia University, where he studied with Paul Henry Lang, Erich Hertzmann and William Mitchell. In 1948 he began teaching at the City College of New York. He held positions at Columbia University, Hebrew Union College–Jewish Institute of Religion, the University of Pennsylvania, the University of California at Berkeley and the University of Oklahoma. He joined the faculty of the University of Illinois in 1958.

Ringer has a wide range of musicological interests, including medieval organum, the music of the French Revolution, 19th-century music and contemporary American composers, such as George Rochberg, Leon Kirchner and Harrison Kerr. Other subjects which concern him are Dutch, Middle Eastern and Hebrew music, the aesthetics and sociology of music and music in education.

WRITINGS

'A French Symphonist at the Time of Beethoven: Etienne Nicolas Méhul', *MQ*, xxxvii (1951), 543
The Chasse: Historical and Analytical Bibliography of a Musical Genre (diss., Columbia U., 1955)
'Leon Kirchner', *MQ*, xliii (1957), 1
'Clementi and the Eroica', *MQ*, xlvii (1961), 454
'J.-J. Barthélemy and Musical Utopia in Revolutionary France', *Journal of the History of Ideas*, xxii (1961), 355
'Handel and the Jews', *ML*, xlii (1961), 17
'Musical Composition in Modern Israel', *MQ*, li (1965), 282
'On the Question of "Exoticism" in 19th-century Music', *SM*, vii (1965), 115
'The Art of the Third Guess: Beethoven to Becker to Bartók', *MQ*, lii (1966), 304
'The Music of George Rochberg', *MQ*, lii (1966), 409
'Salomon Sulzer, Joseph Mainzer and the Romantic a cappella Movement', *SM*, xi (1969), 355
'Mozart and the Josephian Era: some Socio-economic Notes on Musical Change', *CMc* (1969), no.9, p.158
'Cherubini's Médée and the Spirit of French Revolutionary Opera', *Essays in Musicology in Honor of Dragan Plamenac* (Pittsburgh, 1969), 281
ed.: *YIFMC*, i–ii (1969–70)
'Beethoven and the London Pianoforte School', *MQ*, lvi (1970), 742
'Schoenbergiana in Jerusalem', *MQ*, lix (1973), 1
'Musical Taste and the Industrial Syndrome', *IRASM*, v (1974), 139
PAULA MORGAN

Ring modulator. An electronic device much used in both recorded and live electronic music. It is a standard item in electronic music studios, and can appear as a free-standing unit connected to other electronic apparatus, or as a module within a synthesizer. The ring modulator takes its name from the characteristic ring formation of four diodes in its circuit (see illustration).

There are broadly two classes of instruments in an electronic music studio: sound generators and sound modifiers. The ring modulator is a sound modifier. It modifies the frequency components of a given sound (henceforward the 'signal'), according to definite laws, in relation to those of a second source, or 'carrier'. So a ring modulator has two inputs, the signal input and the carrier input, and one output. The modulator will function only if both inputs are present, and optimally when they are balanced, i.e. present at the same amplitude. The output consists of the sum and difference frequen-

cies of those at the inputs. For example, if sine waves (i.e. pure tones) of frequencies 1000 Hz and 400 Hz are present at the inputs, the output will consist of the two frequencies 1400 Hz and 600 Hz. In practice, it matters little which input is regarded as the signal and which the carrier, since it is only the modulation products that matter. These products are called 'sidebands'.

From a well-designed ring modulator, operating with balanced inputs, only the sum and difference frequencies will be heard. Unfortunately one often meets less than the best equipment in far from optimum conditions, and unwanted modulation products may be found to be present causing an unpleasant buzzing effect. In these circumstances the unwanted modulation products can usually be attenuated by passing the output through a low-pass filter. Another defect sometimes encountered is the leakage of one or both of the original input signals through to the output. This fault is usually attributable to poor design or to the incompatibility of the components in the device.

In the above example, where sine waves were the input signals, only two frequencies were contained in the output. If one of the inputs is changed to a more complex form, such as a square wave, then each of the harmonic partials contained within that input is modulated, and so the output is much more complex. Each harmonic generates a sideband not related to the harmonic series. This applies, of course, to any more complex sound at either of the inputs. Each instantaneous frequency component at one input is modulated with each instantaneous frequency component at the other input. With a varying input such as that often obtained in live electronic music from an instrumental source, the aural result is not precisely predictable.

Ring modulators may be used in studios to create new and complex sound mixtures, or to effect various transformations upon material. For example, a musical signal may be modulated with a low-frequency sine wave (say 5 Hz), to produce a strange amplitude-modulation effect. Related to this is the use of a pulse or any other very short carrier input to 'gate' the signal. Another characteristic result of the ring modulator is the creation of multiple glissandos when one of the input signals is varied in frequency.

It should be noted that, as in the 5 Hz example, the input signals need not be within the audio range. As long as at least some of the sidebands lie within it there will, of course, be an audible result. The device known as the 'frequency shifter' or 'Klangumwandler' exploits this. A double ring-modulation process heterodynes the signal into a higher frequency range and back again, isolating the upper or lower sideband. The signal is shifted in frequency by the amount of the frequency of the carrier, the direction of the shift depending on which sideband has been isolated.

Several works by Stockhausen can be cited as exemplifying the use of the ring modulator. In *Mixtur* the sounds of four groups of instrumentalists are picked up by microphones and fed into the signal inputs of four ring modulators. The carrier input of each is a full-range sine-wave oscillator operated by separate musicians. The frequencies of the carrier sine waves are varied throughout the composition, and the modulated sounds, amplified and reproduced through four loudspeakers, blend with the live orchestral sound. In *Mantra* the sounds of two pianos are presented to the signal inputs of two ring modulators, the carrier inputs again being

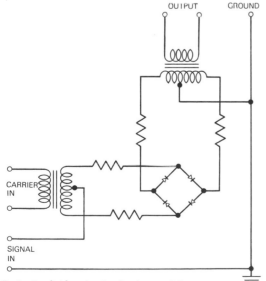

Basic ring bridge circuit of a ring modulator

sine waves. Ring-modulation techniques are applied to recorded materials in the tape compositions *Telemusik* and *Hymnen*.

BIBLIOGRAPHY

H. Bode: 'The Multiplier-type Ring Modulator', *Electronic Music Review* (1967), no.1, p.9

K. Stockhausen: *Texte zur Musik 1963–1970* (Cologne, 1971), 51ff, 66ff, 75ff

A. Strange: *Electronic Music: Systems, Techniques and Controls* (New York, 1972), 9ff

S. Emmerson: 'Ring Modulation and Structure', *Contact* (1977), no.17, p.14

RICHARD ORTON

Rinoldi, Antonio (*b* Milan; *fl* 1st half of the 17th century). Italian composer and organist. The title-pages of his two publications of 1627 – his only known music – show that he was organist of the collegiate church at S Martino in Rio, near Reggio Emilia. He is reported to have been organist at Tivoli Cathedral between 1646 and 1651. His publications are *Il primo libro de madrigali concertati a due, tre, et quattro voci* op.1 (Venice, 1627) which is incomplete and *Il primo libro de motetti concertati a due, tre, quattro, e cinque voci* op.2 (Venice, 1627). The motets show that he was a capable composer in both the monodic and concertato styles.

COLIN TIMMS

Rinuccini, Cino (*b* Florence, *c*1350; *d* Florence, 1417). Italian poet. He wrote many sonnets, ballatas, sestinas and at least one madrigal. But only one ballata, *Con gli occhi assai*, set to music by Francesco Landini, has been preserved.

BIBLIOGRAPHY

S. Bongi: *Rime di M. Cino Rinuccini fiorentino* (Lucca, 1858)

W. THOMAS MARROCCO

Rinuccini, Ottavio (*b* Florence, 20 Jan 1562; *d* Florence, 28 March, 1621). Italian librettist, poet and courtier. He came of a noble Florentine family prominent in cultural and diplomatic circles since the 13th century. His education was presumably that of a courtier – some classical training and enough exposure to the arts to have made him a lively participant in court entertainments in Florence, for which he began writing verses as early as 1579 (*Maschere d'Amazzoni*). The court chronicler Bastiano de' Rossi called him 'a very fine connoisseur' of music, and G. B. Doni suggested that Monteverdi relied on him greatly while setting his libretto for *Arianna*.

Already a member of the Accademia Fiorentina, Rinuccini in 1586 joined another Florentine academy, the Alterati – whose members were particularly interested in dramatic theory and music – and took the name 'Il Sonnacchioso' ('the somnolent one'). There is no evidence to affirm Rinuccini's connection with Giovanni de' Bardi's Camerata, but Bardi (like other musical humanists such as Girolamo Mei and Jacopo Corsi) was also a member of the Accademia degli Alterati and collaborated with Rinuccini on the 1589 *intermedi*, which he produced for the wedding celebrations of the Grand Duke Ferdinando I. Of the six *intermedi*, which are loosely unified by their dramatization of the marvellous powers of ancient music, Rinuccini was alone responsible for the text of three (nos.2, 3 and 6) and wrote the greater part of two more (nos.1 and 5), to which Bardi also contributed some verses. The third *intermedio*, which depicts the battle between Apollo and the dragon, later served Rinuccini as the basis for the opening scene of his first operatic text, *Dafne*, which he claimed to have written 'solely to test the power of music'. Thus Apollo, god of both music and the sun, by virtue of his power in vanquishing the irrational forces represented by the python, was his first aesthetic spokesman.

During the 1590s Rinuccini was associated with Corsi, who collaborated with Peri in setting *Dafne* to music in the newly invented recitative style. First performed at Corsi's home in 1598 and repeated in the following two years, *Dafne* was the first drama to be sung in its entirety 'in the manner of the ancients'. The innovations claimed by Rinuccini and Peri in their prefaces to *Euridice* (1600) inspired the rival claims of Cavalieri and Caccini, neither of whom, however, had written recitative as such before 1600.

Rinuccini adopted many conventions from the major lyric poets of the day, Tasso, Guarini and Chiabrera. His originality lay in his developing for *Dafne* a consistent and unique kind of verse well suited to Peri's recitative. This verse, a compromise between the blank verse typical of spoken tragedy and the uniform metres and close rhymes of traditional lyrical forms, consists of an irregular alternation of freely rhyming seven- and eleven-syllable lines, which, without precluding lyricism, allows for a musical setting designed to imitate the accents of speech. Moreover, by adopting Ovidian plots, which themselves reflect the power of art, and through the Prologue and happy ending of *Euridice*, Rinuccini established a link between the new art form and the tragi-comic genre, defended by Guarini as suitable for the purging of melancholy, rather than of pity and fear, as with the ancients. Thus Rinuccini's librettos must not be seen as unsuccessful imitations of classical tragedy but as highly appropriate vehicles through which 'modern' music might prove its power to move. That he called his next libretto, *Arianna* (1608), a 'tragedia' is more a reflection of its pathetic subject than a generic distinction, for it too follows Ovid and resorts at the end to a 'deus ex machina', with Ariadne being transported to the heavens.

Rinuccini's association with Monteverdi in Mantua also resulted in the *Ballo delle ingrate* (1608), which reflects the influence of the French court ballet and his periodic sojourns in France between 1600 and 1604 as one of Maria de' Medici's courtiers. Also in 1608 *Dafne* was revived in a new setting by Marco da Gagliano, whose Mantuan-based Accademia degli Elevati Rinuccini had joined. However, his last libretto, *Narciso*, dating from about the same period, did not find a willing composer, and he subsequently wrote only a few minor works in the pastoral vein and some sacred verses in addition to sonnets, canzoni and madrigals (including *Zefiro torna* and *Lamento della ninfa*, famous in Monteverdi's settings). His decline as a librettist was due perhaps more than anything else to the gradual shift of operatic activity before his death away from Florence and Mantua to Rome.

The texts of Rinuccini's principal works intended for musical setting appear in Solerti (1904–5, vol.ii).

BIBLIOGRAPHY

G. Mazzoni: 'Cenni sul Ottavio Rinuccini, poeta', *Commemorazione della riforma melodrammatica: atti dell'accademia del R. Istituto musicale di Firenze*, xxxiii (1895)

F. Raccamadoro-Ramelli: *Ottavio Rinuccini* (Fabriano, 1900)

A. Solerti: *Le origini del melodramma* (Turin, 1903/R1969)

——: *Gli albori del melodramma* (Milan, 1904–5/R1969)

——: *Musica, ballo e drammatica alla corte medicea dal 1600 al 1637* (Florence, 1905/*R*1969)

O. G. Sonneck: '*Dafne*, the First Opera: a Chronological Study', *SIMG*, xv (1913–14), 102

M. Schild: *Die Musikdramen O. Rinuccinis* (Würzburg, 1933)

O. Strunk: *Source Readings in Music History* (New York, 1950), 363ff

C. Calcaterra: *Poesie e canto: studi sulla poesia melica italiana e sulla favola per musica* (Bologna, 1951)

A. A. Abert: *Claudio Monteverdi und das musikalische Drama* (Lippstadt, 1954), 100ff, 105ff

W. V. Porter: 'Peri and Corsi's *Dafne*: some New Discoveries and Observations', *JAMS*, xviii (1965), 170

C. V. Palisca: 'The Alterati of Florence, Pioneers in the Theory of Dramatic Music', *New Looks at Italian Opera: Essays in Honor of Donald J. Grout* (Ithaca, NY, 1968), 9–38

N. Pirrotta: 'Early Opera and Aria', ibid, 39–107

——: 'Scelte poetiche di Monteverdi', *NRMI*, ii (1968), 10

——: 'Teatro, scene e musica nelle opere di Monteverdi', *Congresso internazionale sul tema Claudio Monteverdi e il suo tempo: Venezia, Mantova e Cremona 1968*, 45

B. R. Hanning: *The Influence of Humanist Thought and Italian Renaissance Poetry on the Formation of Opera* (diss., Yale U., 1968)

——: 'Apologia pro Ottavio Rinuccini', *JAMS*, xxvi (1973), 240

G. A. Tomlinson: 'Ancora su Ottavio Rinuccini', *JAMS*, xxviii (1975), 351

E. Strainchamps: 'New Light on the Accadamia degli Elevati of Florence', *MQ*, lxii (1976), 507

F. W. Sternfeld: 'The First Printed Opera Libretto', *ML*, lix (1978), 121

J. W. Hill: 'Oratory Music in Florence, I: *Recitar Cantando*, 1583–1655', *AcM*, li (1979), 108

B. RUSSANO HANNING

Rio de Janeiro. Chief port and former capital of Brazil. Since it became the capital in 1763 Rio de Janeiro has been a major centre of musical activities. Brazilian musicians of the 19th and 20th centuries sought to further their careers there. It was the seat of the Portuguese royal family from 1808 to 1821, of the Brazilian Empire from 1822 to 1889, and the administrative centre of the federal government until 1960. Important names associated with it include José Maurício Nunes Garcia, Marcos Portugal, Sigismund Neukomm, Francisco Manuel da Silva, Antônio Carlos Gomes, Alberto Nepomuceno, Villa-Lobos, Francisco Mignone and Claudio Santoro; distinguished visitors at various times included Sigismund Thalberg, Louis Moreau Gottschalk, Théodore Ritter, Enrico Tamberlick, Sarasate, Toscanini, Milhaud, R. Strauss and Stravinsky. From the 1930s the city has been on the South American itinerary of the major orchestras, chamber ensembles, opera companies, virtuosos and new music groups of the Western world. The library resources (National Library, library of the Escola de Música da Universidade Federal do Rio de Janeiro, Rio Cathedral Library) are considered some of the best on the continent.

1. Church music. 2. Opera. 3. Concert life. 4. Festivals, broadcasting. 5. Education, professional organizations.

1. CHURCH MUSIC. Nunes Garcia was *mestre de capela* of the cathedral from 1798. With the arrival of the Portuguese royal court in 1808 the Church of the Carmelites became the cathedral and royal chapel, to which Nunes Garcia was appointed *mestre de capela*. Marcos Portugal also held the post after his arrival (1811). Between 1810 and 1820 the chapel became one of the most remarkable centres of church music in South America, with a choir of about 50 singers, including some Italian castratos, and a large instrumental ensemble called 'magnificent' by European visitors. After Brazil became independent the chapel continued to exist as the imperial chapel. Francisco Manuel da Silva, one of its most dynamic members, was also secretary of the Real Irmandade de Santa Cecília, a celebrated associa-tion of professional musicians. In the 20th century establishments of sacred music lost their earlier importance, although composers continued to cultivate church music. The Franciscan friar Pedro Sinzig promoted the study of church music by editing the periodical *Música sacra* (Petrópolis) in the 1940s.

2. OPERA. The earliest known lyric theatre, Opera Velha (1767–70) was directed by a Father Ventura; the next, Opera Nova, opened in about 1776 under the direction of Manuel Luiz Ferreira. The presence of the royal family greatly stimulated opera and theatre life. The Teatro Régio, founded by Prince João VI, presented the first production in Rio (1811) of Portugal's *opera buffa L'oro non compra amore*. The Real Teatro de São João, founded in 1813, renamed the Imperial Teatro de São Pedro de Alcântara in 1824, produced mostly Italian operas, Rossini dominating the repertory until 1832, and Bellini and Donizetti after 1844. Opera companies usually included Italian artists living in Brazil, such as the celebrated prima donna Augusta Candiani, or visiting European singers, such as Rosine Stoltz and Enrico Tamberlick. A Verdi opera (*Ernani*) was first given in 1846, only two years after its première. The Teatro Provisório, renamed Teatro Lírico Fluminense in 1854, presented the most important seasons in the city until the end of the 19th century. Another theatre, the Teatro Ginásio Dramático, opened in 1855. Operettas were generally presented at the Teatro Fênix Dramática. Since its inauguration in 1909 the Teatro Municipal has been the chief venue for opera as well as other musical activities.

3. CONCERT LIFE. Regular concert life emerged in Rio during the second half of the 19th century. Concert societies and clubs founded at that time included the Clube Mozart (1867), the Clube Beethoven (1882), the Sociedade de Concertos Clássicos (1883) and the Sociedade de Concertos Populares (1896). Most concerts took place in the existing theatres; concert halls as such were not built until the 1960s when the Sala Cecília Meireles opened, although smaller halls, such as the Salão Leopoldo Miguez at the Escola de Música, were in use much earlier. Several orchestras and orchestral associations were founded early in the 20th century. The Sociedade de Concertos Sinfônicos do Rio de Janeiro (1912) had its own orchestra under the direction of Francisco Braga until 1932. Walter Burle Marx founded the short-lived Orquestra Filarmônica do Rio de Janeiro in 1931, and in the same year Villa-Lobos created his own orchestra which lasted until 1935, when the Orquestra do Teatro Municipal (1934), subsidized by the city government, became available to him. The best organized orchestra, the Orquestra Sinfônica Brasileira, was founded in 1940 by José Siqueira. In the late 1960s the orchestra was under the skilful management of the conductor Eleazar de Carvalho. More recently the broadcasting station of the Ministry of Education and Culture (MEC) established its own Orquestra Sinfônica Nacional and its own chamber orchestra and choir. Among the city's numerous choral groups the most important are the Associação de Canto Coral (at first known as Côro Feminino 'Pro Musica') under the direction of Cleofe Person de Mattos, and the choir of the Instituto Israelita Brasileiro de Cultura e Educação, directed by Henrique Morelenbaum. The choir of the Teatro Municipal performed mainly opera selections and oratorios. Earlier choral societies

included the Orfeão Carlos Gomes and the Côro Barroso Neto, both organized by the composer Barroso Neto. The Roberto de Regina Ensemble, established in the 1960s, specializes in medieval and Renaissance music. Among the several chamber ensembles that became active in the 1960s, the Rio de Janeiro Quartet, the Villa-Lobos Quintet and the quartet of the Escola de Música are particularly well known.

Concert promoting organizations have included the Associação Brasileira de Música (1930), the Cultura Artística do Rio de Janeiro (1933), the Associação Brasileira de Concertos (1947), the ABC-Pró Arte and the Associação Brasileira de Arte (ABRARTE). The Museu Villa-Lobos, founded by the Ministry of Education in 1960, has promoted numerous concerts and festivals of Villa-Lobos's music.

4. FESTIVALS, BROADCASTING. In the late 1950s Rio de Janeiro became a centre of national and international music festivals and contests, of which the most important have been the International Piano Contest (1958), the International Music Festival (1963), the International Singing Contests (from 1963), the International Music Festival of MEC Radio (1969), the Music Festival of Guanabara (the first was in 1969), the Villa-Lobos Festival (from 1966) with the International Competition of Villa-Lobos's String Quartets (1966), the International Guitar Competition (1971) and the Instrumental Ensembles Competition (1972).

The major broadcasting station, the Radio Ministério da Educação (PRA-2), has an extensive art-music programme, and counts among its personnel some of the best musicians in the country.

5. EDUCATION, PROFESSIONAL ORGANIZATIONS. The first official educational institution in Rio was the Conservatório Imperial de Música, founded in 1847 (active by 1848) by Francisco Manuel da Silva. Renamed the Instituto Nacional de Música by the republican government in 1890, it was incorporated into the University of Rio de Janeiro in 1931, and became the Escola Nacional de Música at the founding of the University of Brazil (1937). In the late 1960s it became known as the Escola de Música da Universidade Federal do Rio de Janeiro. The directors of the school since 1890 have included some of the best-known music teachers of the country. In 1936 the composer Lorenzo Fernândez founded the Conservatório Brasileiro de Música (officially recognized by the federal government in 1944). The Conservatório do Distrito Federal ceased to function in the early 1960s. Among the numerous private establishments the Academia de Música 'Lorenzo Fernândez', founded in 1953, has trained distinguished performing musicians.

The Academia Brasileira de Música was created by Villa-Lobos in Rio in July 1945. Of its 50 members, 30 are composers and 20 are musicologists, music critics and performers. The only professional union, Ordem dos Músicos do Brasil (1960), administered by a federal council, has its headquarters in Rio de Janeiro. Recently the federal council founded a Serviço de Documentação Musical, under the executive directorship of Marlos Nobre, for the dissemination of Brazilian new music.

BIBLIOGRAPHY
L. H. C. de Azevedo: 'Um jubileu', *Música viva*, i (1940)
L. M. Peppercorn: 'New Academy of Music founded in Rio', *Musical America*, lxv/16 (1945), 10
L. H. C. de Azevedo: *Música e músicos do Brasil* (Rio de Janeiro, 1950)
F. C. Lange: 'Estudios brasileños (Mauricinas) I: Manuscritos de la Biblioteca nacional de Rio de Janeiro', *Revista de estudios musicales*, i (1950), 99
——: 'Vida y muerte de Louis Moreau Gottschalk en Rio de Janeiro (1869): el ambiente musical en la mitad del segundo imperio', *Revista de estudios musicales*, ii (1950), 43, 97
G. Béhague: *Popular Musical Currents in the Art Music of the Early Nationalist Period in Brazil, ca. 1870–1920* (diss., Tulane U., 1966)
A. de Andrade: *Francisco Manuel da Silva e seu tempo, 1808–1865* (Rio de Janeiro, 1967)
For further bibliography see BRAZIL.

GERARD BÉHAGUE

Ríos, Álvaro de los (*b* c1580; *d* Madrid, 1623). Spanish composer and musician. In 1606 or earlier he composed some of the songs performed by two women and four instrumentalists in Tirso de Molina's play *El vergonçoso en palacio*, given alfresco at Toledo. In 1621 Tirso described him as unexcelled in the composition of tonos. He became a chamber musician to Queen Margherita on 10 August 1607 with an annual salary of 30,000 maravedis plus his keep. There are eight songs by him in the Sablonara cancionero of 1625 (in *D-Mbs*, ed. in Aroca). Six are duets that suffer from the loss of the instrumental accompaniment, but *Sin color anda la niña*, for three voices, is among the most poignant of the 75 songs in the collection in its portrayal of the sorrows of an abandoned maiden.

BIBLIOGRAPHY
Tirso de Molina [pseud. of G. Téllez]: *Cigarrales de Toledo* (Madrid, 1621; repr. Madrid, 1913)
J. Aroca: *Cancionero musical y poético del siglo XVII recogido por Claudio de la Sablonara* (Madrid, 1916), 333, 336
R. Mitjana: 'Comentarios y apostillas al "Cancionero poético y musical del siglo XVII", recogido por Claudio de la Sablonara', *Revista de filología española*, vi (1919), 258f
M. Penedo Rey: 'El fraile músico de Los Cigarrales de Toledo', *Estudios*, iii (1947), 384
A. Nougué: *L'oeuvre en prose de Tirso de Molina* (Toulouse, 1962), 170
R. A. Pelinski: *Die weltliche Vokalmusik Spaniens am Anfang des 17. Jahrhunderts* (Tutzing, 1971), 65

ROBERT STEVENSON

Riotte, Philipp Jakob (*b* St Wendel, Saar, 16 Aug 1776; *d* Vienna, 20 Aug 1856). German composer and conductor. He was a pupil of Anton André at Offenbach and in 1804 he appeared as pianist and composer at a concert in Frankfurt. In 1805 or 1806 he became music director at Gotha (so styled on the title-page of keyboard sonatas published by André in 1806 and 1807), and was subsequently at Danzig and Magdeburg. At the Erfurt Congress in 1808 he directed the French opera performances. He then went to Vienna where he worked at the court opera and, from 1818, as music director at the Theater an der Wien (1818–20 and 1824–6).

Although Riotte enjoyed success in his lifetime in every musical form then in favour, he was best known for his stage works and keyboard pieces (his contribution to Diabelli's *Vaterländischer Künstlerverein* is one of the longest); but the only score to outlive its composer was that written in 1827 for Raimund's *Moisasurs Zauberspruch*: only the songs survive (they were republished twice in the 1920s), but they are still sometimes used in performances of the play. Others of Riotte's Singspiels and stage scores (some 50 were given in the five principal Viennese theatres between 1809 and 1840) that were particularly successful in their day include the Horschelt pantomimes *Der Berggeist* (1818; 76 performances), *Elisene, Prinzessin von Bulgarien* (1819), *Die Wildschützen* (1820) and *Die Zaubernelke* (1821, the score partly by Gallenberg), all given in the Theater an der Wien; the Fenzl pantomime *Die*

Doppelgestalten (1834) for the Leopoldstadt Theatre; the Singspiel *Das Grenzstädtchen* (text by Kotzebue) given in the court theatres in April 1809, soon after Riotte's arrival in Vienna; a comic melodrama *Azondar* (*Azondai*) given in the Theater an der Wien in 1819; the operas *Euphemie von Avagora* (Kärntnertor Theatre, 1823) and *Nurredin, Prinz von Persien* (Theater an der Wien, 1825) and the Singspiel *Eine Prise Tobak* (Kärntnertor Theatre and Josefstadt Theatre, 1825).

Riotte also supplied music for many farces and plays; among his parody scores are *Staberl als Freischütz* (in collaboration with Röth), which had some 60 performances between 1826 and 1856, *Die geschwätzige Stumme von Nussdorf* (1830) and *Der Postillon von Stadl-Enzersdorf* (1840). He also wrote some large-scale orchestral works, a mass, chamber works and many piano pieces, including the once-popular 'characteristic tone painting' *Die Schlacht bei Leipzig*. In November 1852, after a long silence, he appeared before the Viennese public again and for the last time with the cantata *Der Sieg des Kreuzes*, which was favourably received. A large collection of his works in manuscript is held by the Gesellschaft der Musikfreunde, Vienna.

BIBLIOGRAPHY
P. J. Riotte: Autobiographical sketch, 1826, *A-Wgm* [with catalogue of works]
Obituary, *Neue Wiener Musik-Zeitung*, v (1856), 175
C. von Wurzbach: *Biographisches Lexikon des Kaiserthums Oesterreich*, xxvi (Vienna, 1874), 171 [with chronological work-list]
F. Hadamowsky: *Das Theater in der Wiener Leopoldstadt* (Vienna, 1934)
A. Bauer: *150 Jahre Theater an der Wien* (Zurich, 1952)
——: *Opern und Operetten in Wien* (Graz and Cologne, 1955)
——: *Das Theater in der Josefstadt zu Wien* (Vienna, 1957)
PETER BRANSCOMBE

Ripa (da Mantova), Alberto da [Rippe, Albert de] (*b* Mantua, *c*1500; *d* Paris, 1551). Italian lutenist and composer. He was in the service of Ercole Gonzaga, Cardinal of Mantua, on 12 February 1529, when he played before Henry VIII. Three months later he was in the service of François I; with the exception of a visit to Rome in 1531, he appears to have remained at the French court until his death. He was first an ordinary *jouer de lut*, then advanced to *valet de chambre du roi* in 1533. During most of his years at court he received the unusually large salary of 600 livres tournois; in addition, he was given occasional, often large gifts of money, granted the income from various properties and the sale of offices, and was named 'capitaine des Montils-sous-bois' near Blois in 1536, and 'seigneur de Carceys', (Carcois-en-Brie, near Fontainebleau) some time before 1545. Ripa's excellence on the lute is often mentioned in the literature of the time, and several poets, among them Bonaventure des Periers, Gabriello Simeoni, Clément Marot, Guy le Fevre de la Boderie, Olivier de Magny and Ronsard, addressed poems to him or wrote epitaphs after his death. Ripa was among the correspondents of the satirist Aretino.

His intabulations of chansons and motets are little more than short scores in tablature with a modicum of ornamentation (for a facsimile from *Quatriesme livre de tabulature de leut*, 1554, see NOTATION, fig.115). His dance pieces are simple and undistinguished. Several of the fantasias, however, are excellent examples of the full-textured, polyphonic (though not always imitative) lute style of the 1530s and 1540s, but many others are overlong, poorly organized and occasionally awkward pieces. Unfortunately the state in which his music survives is far from satisfactory. Like other virtuosos of the 16th century, he appears to have been reluctant to publish his music; according to Guillaume Morlaye, Ripa 'mettoit iournellement quelque cas par escript, qu'il estimoit pouvoir estre utile a ceulx qui le suivroyent'. Presumably the music edited by Morlaye and Le Roy came from Ripa's daily writings; hence the uneven quality of the music may be due as much to the conditions in which Ripa left his manuscripts as to the work of his editor. Clearly, although his reputation during his lifetime and afterwards rivalled that of Francesco da Milano, the surviving music rarely equals that of his illustrious compatriot.

WORKS
Edition: *A. de Rippe: Oeuvres*, ed. J.-M. Vaccaro, CM, *Corpus des luthistes français* (1972–5)

(*published in Paris by Fezandat*)
Premier livre de tabulature de leut, contenant plusieurs chansons et fantasies (1552³⁶)
Second livre de tabulature de leut, contenant plusieurs chansons, motetz et fantasies (1554³⁴)
Troisiesme livre de tabulature de leut, contenant plusieurs chansons, motetz et fantasies (1554³⁵)
Quatriesme livre de tabulature de leut, contenant plusieurs chansons, motetz et fantasies (1554³⁶)
Cinquiesme livre de tabulature de leut, contenant plusieurs chansons, fantasies, motetz, pavanes et gaillardes (1555³⁶)
Sixiesme livre de tabulature de leut, contenant plusieurs chansons, fantasies, motetz et gaillardes (1558)

(*published in Paris by Le Roy & Ballard*)
Premier livre de tabelature de luth contenant plusieurs fantasies (1562²⁵)
Second livre de tabelature de luth contenant plusieurs chansons (1562²⁶)
Tiers livre de tabelature de luth contenant plusieurs chansons (1562²⁷)
Quart livre de tabulature de luth contenant plusieurs fantasies, chansons, & pavanes (1553³⁶)
Cinquiesme livre de tabelature de luth contenant plusieurs motetz, & fantasies (1562²⁸)
Compositions from the above in 1536¹⁰, 1552³¹, 1563²¹, 1574¹²
2 fantasias attrib. 'Albert', 1552³³
MS sources of some printed pieces: *D-Mmb, EIRE-Dm, GB-Eu, S-Uu*

BIBLIOGRAPHY
BrownI
M. Brenet: 'Notes sur l'histoire du luth en France', *RMI*, v (1898), 637–76, esp. 646; pubd separately (Turin, 1899/R1973)
H. Prunières: 'La musique de la chambre de l'écurie sous le règne de François Ier 1516–1547', *L'année musicale*, i (1912), 219
J.-G. Prod'homme: 'Guillaume Morlaye, éditeur d'Albert de Ripe, et bourgeois de Paris', *RdM*, ix (1925), 157
L. Nordstrom: 'Albert de Rippe, joueur de luth du roy', *Early Music*, vii (1979), 378
JOHN M. WARD

Ripa (y Blanque), Antonio (*b* Tarazona, *c*1720; *d* Seville, 3 Nov 1795). Spanish composer. He was a choirboy in Tarazona Cathedral and such a prodigy that at 17 the chapter made him *maestro de capilla*. After graduating from the diocesan seminary and being ordained priest he served first as *maestro de capilla* of the Carmelite nuns' church at Saragossa and then (about 1756) of Cuenca Cathedral. On 13 December 1761, when he censured Antonio Soler's *Llave de la modulación*, he was *maestro de capilla* of Descalzas Reales convent at Madrid. He succeeded Rabassa as *maestro de capilla* of Seville Cathedral on 22 June 1768. In the 1770s his reputation was such that even as far away as Mexico City he was considered the leading Spanish composer of his epoch. Eslava y Elizondo, who edited a mass with orchestra and a *Stabat mater* setting by Ripa, both for eight voices, in Lira sacro-hispana (*Siglo XVIII*, ii/1, Madrid, 1869), concurred in this estimation.

As listed in the *Gazeta de Madrid* of November 1797 and confirmed in an advertisement in the *Diario de Madrid* of 21 February 1798, Ripa left for sale at his death a vast repertory of 12 orchestrally accompanied masses, 39 vesper psalms, ten *Miserere* settings, 11 Lamentations, five sets of responsories, 140 villancicos and 344 other works. Guatemala, Lima, Mexico City and Santiago de Chile cathedrals shared enthusiasm for his orchestrally accompanied polychoral music, Lima alone buying 32 villancicos and six Latin works, all of which are extant. A *Magnificat* for three voices is printed in Claro. Other works by him are at the Barcelona Biblioteca Central, Cuenca and Seville cathedrals, El Escorial and the monastery of Montserrat. Though Ripa was especially happy in local-colour gypsy villancicos, he came close to Haydn in the brilliance and profundity of his Latin music.

BIBLIOGRAPHY

C. J. de Benito: Catalogue of music at El Escorial (MS, *E-Mn*, 1875)
A. Lozano González: *La música popular, religiosa y dramática en Zaragoza* (Saragossa, 1895), 57
S. de la Rosa y López: *Los seises de la Catedral de Sevilla* (Seville, 1904), 328f
F. Pedrell: *Catàlech de la biblioteca musical de la Diputació de Barcelona* (Barcelona, 1908–9)
R. Navarro Gonzalo: *Catálogo musical del archivo de la Santa Iglesia Catedral Basílica de Cuenca* (Cuenca, 1965)
R. Stevenson: *Renaissance and Baroque Musical Sources in the Americas* (Washington, DC, 1970), 96, 126ff, 161, 342
S. Claro: *Antología de la música colonial en América del Sur* (Santiago de Chile, 1974), pp.xxxii f, xcix, 158
J. E. Ayarra Jarne: *La música en la catedral de Sevilla* (Seville, 1976), 64

ROBERT STEVENSON

Ripere [Ripert], Jean-Jacques. *See* RIPPERT, JEAN-JACQUES.

Ripieno (i) (It.: 'filled'). A term used to denote the tutti (or 'concerto grosso') in an orchestra performing music of the Baroque period, particularly the concerto repertory, in distinction to the solo group (the 'concertino'); it is more rarely applied to vocal music (as to the boys' choir in the first chorus of Bach's *St Matthew Passion*). The direction 'senza ripieni' requires all players except those at the leading desks to be silent; it is commonly found in Handel's extended vocal works. The term 'ripienista' designates an orchestral player who is not a leader or soloist. 'Ripieno' occurs in various corrupt forms ('ripiano', 'repiano') in band repertories, to denote players (particularly clarinettists and cornet players in military bands) not at the leading desk. *See* CONCERTO.

Ripieno (ii) (It.). An ORGAN STOP.

Ripin, Edwin M. (*b* New York, 21 April 1930; *d* New York, 12 Nov 1975). American musicologist. He studied at Williams College (BA 1952) and held editorial positions with various publishing firms (from 1956) before becoming a senior editor at Random House (1966–70). In 1970 he was appointed to the staff of the Metropolitan Museum of Art in New York, where he was assistant curator of musical instruments (1971–3). He taught at the State University of New York at Purchase (1973–4) and from 1974 until his death he was a member of the graduate faculty in the music department of New York University. Ripin's main interest was the study of instruments, particularly their restoration and relationship with the music written for them. His chief studies were of stringed keyboard instruments, musical iconography, instrument forgery and the development of new techniques in analysing instruments. At the time of his death he was working on a large-scale book on the history of keyboard instruments.

WRITINGS

Review of F. Hubbard: *Three Centuries of Harpsichord Building* (Cambridge, Mass., 1965), *MQ*, li (1965), 563
'The Early Clavichord', *MQ*, liii (1967), 518
'The French Harpsichord before 1650', *GSJ*, xx (1967), 43
'The Two-manual Harpsichord in Flanders before 1650', *GSJ*, xxi (1968), 33
'A Scottish Encyclopedist and the Piano Forte', *MQ*, lv (1969), 487
'Clavichord', 'Electronic Instruments', 'Piano', *Harvard Dictionary of Music* (Cambridge, Mass., 2/1969)
'The Couchet Harpsichord in the Crosby Brown Collection', *Metropolitan Museum Journal*, ii (1969), 169
'Antwerp Harpsichord-building: the Current State of Research', *Restauratieproblemen van Antwerpse Klavecimbels: Museum Vleeshuis 1970*, 12
'A Reassessment of the Fretted Clavichord', *GSJ*, xxiii (1970), 40
'A "Three-foot" Flemish Harpsichord', *GSJ*, xxiii (1970), 35
'Expressive Devices Applied to the Eighteenth-century Harpsichord', *Organ Yearbook*, i (1970), 65
ed.: *Keyboard Instruments: Studies in Keyboard Organology* (Edinburgh, 1971) [incl. 'On Joes Karest's Virginal and the Origins of the Flemish Tradition', 65]
'A Suspicious Spinet', *Metropolitan Museum of Art Bulletin*, new ser., xxx (1972), 196
'A "Five-foot" Flemish Harpsichord', *GSJ*, xxvi (1973), 135
'The Surviving Oeuvre of Girolamo Zenti', *Metropolitan Museum Journal*, vii (1973), 71
The Instrument Catalogues of Leopoldo Franciolini (Hackensack, NJ, 1974)
'The Norrlanda Organ and the Ghent Altarpiece', *Festschrift to Ernst Emsheimer* (Stockholm, 1974), 193
'Towards an Identification of the Chekker', *GSJ*, xxviii (1975), 11
'Keyboard Instruments', *Encyclopaedia britannica* (Chicago, 15/1974)
'Clavichord', 'Harpsichord', §§1–4, 'Pianoforte', §I, 1–2, 'Spinet', 'Virginal', Grove 6

PAULA MORGAN

Ripollés, Vicente (*b* Castellón de la Plana, 20 Nov 1867; *d* Rocafort, Valencia, 19 March 1943). Spanish composer. He studied solfège and the violin while a choirboy in his native town and then attended the Tortosa Seminary, where he was responsible for the chapel music. His best religious works were composed after studies with Giner in Valencia. Successively appointed *maestro de capilla* of Tortosa Cathedral (1893), the Real Colegio del Corpus Christi (1895) and Seville Cathedral, he wrote much church music, including a mass for seven voices and strings. His works were published by Musical Emporium and by the Institut d'Estudis Catalans.

WRITINGS

El drama liturgico (Valencia, 1928)
Músicos castellonenses (Castellón de la Plana, 1935)
El villancico y la cantata del siglo XVIII en Valencia (Barcelona, 1935)

CARLOS GÓMEZ AMAT

Ripon. English city, in North Yorkshire; *see* HARROGATE.

Riposta. *See* RISPOSTA.

Rippe, Albert de. *See* RIPA, ALBERTO DA.

Rippert [Ripert, Ripere], Jean-Jacques (*fl* 1696–1725). French maker of woodwind instruments. He worked in Paris and was perhaps also a composer. According to a document dated 14 February 1696 (now in *F-Pn*), Rippert was a 'maker of flutes' in Paris in 1696, and had already been established in that profession for a long time. Another document dated 21 August 1696 refers to him as 'Jean-Jacques Ripert master maker of wind instruments'. According to Sauveur, Rippert and the younger Jean Hotteterre were the two best woodwind instrument makers in Paris in 1701. Rippert was still active in 1715 although he was old at the time, according to Herr von Uffenbach, one of his customers. He apparently specialized in the making of recorders, since many of his make, ranging from sopranino to bass, still exist. Two important early one-keyed transverse flutes and a two-keyed oboe also survive. His instruments are marked with the name 'RIPPERT' and the sign of a dolphin.

On 26 June 1722 a Jean-Jacques Rippert took out a privilege to publish a collection of music. In the same year a 'M. R*' brought out the first entire book to appear in France of sonatas for solo transverse flute and continuo. Further books of pieces for two flutes by the same composer came out during the next few years, and since the titles of those that are extant correspond with the works listed under the name of 'Ripere' or 'Ripert' in various catalogues of music, it seems likely that this composer was Jean-Jacques Rippert. Whether it was the same Rippert who was the instrument maker cannot be said with certainty: possibly the craftsman, though old in 1715, decided to turn his attention to the field of composition; but it is also possible that the composer was another Jean-Jacques Rippert (perhaps a son of the craftsman).

WORKS
(all attrib. 'M.R', probably by Jean-Jacques Rippert)*
Sonates, fl, bc, op.1 (Paris, 1722)
3 books of pieces, 2 fl (Paris, before 1731), lost
2 books of brunettes, 2 fl (Paris, 1725, before 1731)
Symphonies polonoises (Paris, before 1742), lost

BIBLIOGRAPHY
F-Pn, fonds fr. 21732, f.106 and ff.220–23
J. Sauveur: *Principes d'acoustique et de musique, ou système général des intervalles des sons: inseré dans les Mémoires de 1701 de l'Académie royale des sciences* (?Paris, n.d.), 37
Catalogue général de musique, imprimée ou gravée en France (Paris, 1731), 16; (1737), 54
Catalogue général et alphabétique de musique, imprimée ou gravée en France (Paris, 1742)
C. Pierre: *Les facteurs d'instruments de musique: les luthiers et la facture instrumentale* (Paris, 1893), 75
M. Brenet: 'La librairie musicale en France de 1653 à 1790, d'après les registres de privilèges', *SIMG*, viii (1906–7), 427
E. Preussner: *Die musikalischen Reisen des Herrn von Uffenbach* (Kassel, 1949), 128
E. Halfpenny: 'A Seventeenth-century Flute d'Allemagne', *GSJ*, iv (1951), 42
L. G. Langwill: *An Index of Musical Wind-instrument Makers* (Edinburgh, 1960, rev. 4/1977), 131
P. Bate: *The Flute: a Study of its History, Development and Construction* (London, 1969), 83, plate 2
J. Bowers: *The French Flute School from 1700 to 1760* (diss., U. of California, Berkeley, 1971), 172, 370ff
R. Meylan: *La flûte* (Lausanne, 1974), 64   JANE M. BOWERS

Ripresa (It.). (1) A repeat or repetition in a general sense, including the repetition of an opera or play.

(2) The refrain of the 14th-century BALLATA and of the FROTTOLA.

(3) In the 16th and 17th centuries the term was applied to small instrumental units that appear, sometimes paired or in groups, before, after or between repetitions of the main music for a song or dance. The word first appears in Casteliono's *Intabolatura de leuto de diversi autori* (1536), and unmarked examples occur even earlier, in Attaingnant's *Dixhuit basses dances* (1530) and *Quatorze gaillardes* (1531), and possibly in Dalza's *Intabulatura de lauto, libro quarto* (1508). The name changed to 'ritornello' in Fabritio Caroso's *Il ballarino* (1581), but both terms were used during the first half of the 17th century (during which time 'ritornello' began to be used also in a different sense to refer

to an entire instrumental section alternating with other music).

The main music of a dance or song was based on certain fixed progressions of root position triads, which could be varied by activating the bass or upper voices melodically or by adding new chords that related to one of the framework chords as dominant or subdominant–dominant to tonic (*see* GROUND, §2). A *ripresa* is structurally a repeat or return of the final tonic chord of a main scheme, with this chord varied by the same technique of variation used in the scheme, but applied independently, so that the music is melodically and harmonically different from the main piece. Internal *riprese* (those between repetitions of the main chordal scheme) usually appear in pairs; concluding *riprese* (at the end of a dance or a pair of dances) consist of longer chains of as many as 20 or 30 phrases. Most occupy the time of two framework chords from the main scheme (the 'standard' type); others are twice as long ('double').

Ex.1 Riprese
   All the notes are roots of major triads, except the semibreves in bars 5–8 and the blackened one in bar 5 of f, which may be major or minor. In a, c, and f, a semibreve represents a framework chord, a blackened semibreve an alternative triad.

(a) One of the frameworks of the standard riprese

(b) The most common type of internal standard riprese

(c) Framework of the regular double riprese

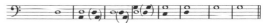

(d) An internal double riprese

(e) A concluding double riprese

(f) Framework of the double *B molle* riprese

The semibreves in ex.1a show one of the basic harmonic frameworks of the standard *ripresa* (other distributions of the two framework chords also occur). Alternative triads may be added to the framework as shown, resulting in a number of different progressions, the most common being that in ex.1b. Similarly, ex.1c shows the usual framework and some alternative chords for the double *ripresa*, ex.1d a specific internal example and ex.1e a concluding one in which the opening phrase is repeated a variable number of times. Most *riprese* are in triple metre, with each of the four structural chords occupying a single three-beat unit. Hemiola, however, is not uncommon, and duple metre is possible. During the 16th century most triads used in *riprese* were major, since chordal schemes for both modes ordinarily end with a major tonic chord or one without a 3rd. In the following century, however, pieces in the mode *per B molle* may end with a *ripresa* in which the bass line of ex.1*b* supports the progression subdominant (minor)–dominant–tonic (major or minor). Ex.1*f* shows a rare type of double *ripresa* based on the central chordal idea of the mode *per B molle*.

Riprese occur in music for lute, bandora, vihuela, cittern, stringed keyboard instruments, ensembles and guitar. The internal standard type is often attached to the French *gaillarde*, to the Italian saltarello or gagliarda paired with a passamezzo, to the romanesca, the folia and the *aria per cantare*. The usual type of internal double *ripresa* is found with the *passamezzo moderno* (the earliest example is by Hans Neusidler, 1540; in DTÖ, xxxvii, Jg.xviii/2, p.40), the English 'quadran' pavan on the same chordal scheme (by Byrd, Bull, Morley and others) and dances paired with them. Concluding double *riprese* occur in works by Mainerio (1578), Facoli (1588), Radino (1592) and Picchi (1621). The double *B molle ripresa* appears occasionally with the romanesca, as in Frescobaldi's *partite* of 1615 and 1637.

A sense of ostinato is sometimes established by repeating the opening half of ex.1*e*. Ostinato is more extensive, however, in the chains of standard *riprese* that conclude the saltarello or gagliarda paired with a passamezzo or pavana. There are also several independent sets of *riprese* (by Balletti, 1554), *reprinse* (M. Praetorius, 1612) and ritornellos (Castaldi, 1620). The characteristic procedure is to alternate from one harmonic formula to another within a single chain of *riprese*. Successive phrases may therefore differ markedly from one another. The ostinato, then, is rhythmic, in the sense that a short, four-bar phrase length is repeated; it may be harmonic if the composer wished to repeat one particular progression for several phrases, or used different formulae that all began or ended with the same chord; it may also be melodic, especially in the 17th century, if a composer chose to use the same bass line for successive phrases. The special sense of ostinato that characterizes this technique, however, comes from the random recurrence of formulae that were derived by the principles of construction prevailing in the Renaissance dance style and were selected by the composer from phrase to phrase according to his wishes. In this context, *see* PASSACAGLIA and CHACONNE.

BIBLIOGRAPHY

R. Hudson: 'The Ripresa, the Ritornello, and the Passacaglia', *JAMS*, xxiv (1971), 364–94

RICHARD HUDSON

Riquier, Guiraut (*b* Narbonne, *c*1230; *d c*1300). French troubadour poet and composer, usually considered the last of the troubadours. Although he is not mentioned in contemporary documents, and no Provençal *vida* exists for him, his life and career can be reconstructed in some detail through his poems and references to persons mentioned in them. In some sources, each of his 89 poems is assigned an exact date; these range from 1254 to 1292 and often specify a particular day or even time of day.

A brief notice preceding his works in one source describes him as 'Guiraut Riquier de Narbona', suggesting that he was born in that city (near the Spanish border). This assumption is confirmed by numerous references in his works to Amalrich IV, Viscount of Narbonne (1239–70), including *Ples de tristor*, a *planh*

on the occasion of Amalrich's death. After Amalrich's death, Guiraut entered the service of Alfonso X, the Wise, King of Castile, a fact supported by references in the poems, and also by a remarkable letter addressed to the king in 1274 in which Guiraut pleaded for an improvement in the lot of the troubadour and the jongleur. In 1279 he left Alfonso's court probably to enter the service of Henry II, Count of Rodez (1275–1302). Although he seems to have travelled after 1279, and was probably in Narbonne at least part of the time, Guiraut probably died in or around Rodez some time in the last decade of the 13th century.

The work of Guiraut Riquier is an invaluable document of the final flourishing of courtly song. No fewer than 48 of his 89 poems have survived with their melodies (more than twice the number preserved for any other troubadour). Equally remarkable is the fact that there is not a single contrafactum among them – striking evidence that, for Guiraut at least, the tradition of monophonic song was very much alive in the late 13th century. The notice preceding the poems in one source assures the reader that a songbook written by the author was used in preparing the edition ('libre escrig per la sua man'); this body of melody, therefore, is probably as close to an autograph as any that has survived from the period. The author's rubrics dating each song show him to have been a man convinced of his own importance and more than a little proud of his skill. He explained, for instance, that *Voluntiers faria* was composed in one afternoon, 13 March 1276.

Bar form was the one most used by Guiraut (29 examples), but there is considerable formal variety within the general type. Three songs are *retroenchas* (*No cugei, Pos astres*, and *Si chans*), the remainder are either through-composed (*Ab lo temps, Aissi pert, Anc non aigui, De far chanson, De midons, En tot, Los bes, Ogan no cugei, Ops m'agra*, and *Tant vei*) or employ some repetition scheme reminiscent of the *lai* (*Amors, pus, Be·m meravelh, Fis e verais, Qu·s tolgues*, and *Voluntiers faria*). Guiraut's songs are also clearly labelled in the sources as to type; 25 of those with music are called *cansos*, and 20 are labelled *vers*. The majority of the *vers* are set to music in some kind of bar form (17); the greater number of *cansos* (15) are either through-composed or set as some variety of *lai*-strophe.

WORKS

Editions: S. L. H. Pfaff: *Guiraut Riquier, Werke der Troubadours*, iv (Berlin, 1853) [P]
       H. Anglès: *Les melodies del trobador Guiraut Riquier* (Barcelona, 1926) [A]
    F. Gennrich: *Der musikalische Nachlass der Troubadours*, i Summa musica medii aevi, iii (Darmstadt, 1958) [G]
       U. Mölk: *Guiraut Riquier, los cansos* (Heidelberg, 1962) [M]

Ab lo temps agradiu gai, PC 281.1, A 39, G 185, P 12 (composed 1261)
Ab panc er decazutz, PC 248.2, A 44, G 186, M 62, P 19 (composed 1265)
Aissi cum selh, que francheman estai, PC 248.5, A 36, G 186, M 40, P 8 (composed 1258)
Aissi pert poder amors, PC 248.6, A 32, G 187, M 25, P 2 (composed 1255)
Aissi com es sobronada, PC 248.7, A 42, G 188, M 57, P 15 (composed 1263)
A mon dan sui esforcius, PC 248.8, A 38, G 189, M 48, P 11 (composed 1260)
Amors, pus a vos falh poders, PC 248.10, A 35, G 189, M 36, P 7 (composed 1257)
Anc mais per aital razo, PC 248.12, A 74, G 190, P 61 (composed 1284)
Anc non aigui nul temps de far chanso, PC 248.13, A 46, G 191, M 66, P 21 (composed 1266)

Be·m meravelh co non es envejos, PC 248.18, A 40, G 192, M 52, P 14 (composed 1260)

Be·m volgra d'amor partir, PC 248.19, A 43, G 192, P 17 (composed 1264)

Creire m'an fag mei dezir, PC 248.21, A 65, G 193, M 100, P 49 (composed 1277)

De far chanson sui marritz, PC 248.23, A 47, G 194, M 70, P 22 (composed 1268)

De midons e d'amor, PC 248.24, A 51, G 195, M 76, P 28 (composed 1271)

En re no·s melhura, PC 248·26, A 33, G 195, M 28, P 4 (composed 1256)

En tot quant qu'ieu saupes, PC 248.27, A 72, G 196, M 107, P 58 (composed Feb 1284)

Fis e verais e plus ferms que no suelh, PC 248.29, A 55, G 197, M 17, P 34 (composed 1275)

Fortz guerra fai tot lo mon guerreiar, PC 248.30, A 75, G 197, P 63 (composed Nov 1285)

Gauch ai, quar esper d'amor, PC 248.31, A 76, G 198, M 111, P 64 (composed Dec 1285)

Grans afans es ad home vergonhos, PC 248.33, A 54, G 199, P 32 (composed 1274)

Humils, forfaitz, repres e penedens, PC 248.44, A 54, G 200, P 31 (Marian song, composed 1273)

Jamais non er hom en est mon grazitz, PC 248.45, A 78, G 200, P 67 (composed Nov 1286)

Jhesus Cristz filh de Dieu viu, PC 248.46, A 56, G 201, P 35 (composed 1275)

Karitatz et Amors e fes, PC 248.48, A 58, G 202, P 38 (composed 1276)

Lo mons par enchantatz, PC 248.52, A 73, G 202, P 60 (composed March 1284)

Los bes, qu'ieu truep en amor, PC 248.53, A 61, G 203, M 96, P 43 (composed in one day, 11 March 1276)

Mentaugutz, PC 248.55, A 70, G 204, P 54 (composed Dec 1283)

Mout me tenc ben per pagatz, PC 248.56, A 52, G 204, M 79, P 30 (composed 1272)

No cugei mais d'esta razon chantar, PC 248.57, A 66, G 205, P 82 (composed Sept 1279)

No m sai d'amor si m'es mala o bona, PC 248.58, A 37, G 206, M 44, P 10 (composed 1259)

Ogan no cugei chantar, PC 248.60, A 57, G 206, M 85, P 37 (composed Jan 1276)

Ops m'agra que mos volers, PC 248.61, A 77, G 207, P 66 (composed Feb 1286)

Per proar si pro privatz, PC 248.62, A 69, G 208, P 53 (composed Nov 1283)

Ples de tristor, marritz e doloiros, PC 248.63, A 50, G 208, P 27, Gennrich, MGG (planh on the death of Amalrich IV, Viscount of Narbonne; composed 1270)

Pos astres no m'es donatz, PC 248.65, A 41, G 209, P 80 (composed 1262)

Pos sabers no.m val ni sens, PC 248.66, A 68, G 210, M 103, P 51 (composed April 1282)

Quar dregz ni fes, PC 248.67, A 49, G 211, P 25 (composed 1270)

Qui·m disses non a dos ans, PC 248.68, A 63, G 212, P 46 (composed 1276)

Qui·s tolgues, PC 248.69, A 71, G 212, P 56 (composed Jan 1284)

Razos m'adui voler qu'eu chan soven, PC 248.71, A 60, G 213, M 93, P 42 (composed in one day, 12 March 1276)

Si chans me pogues valensa, PC 248.78, A 45, G 214, P 81 (composed 1265)

S'ieu ja trobat mon agues, PC 248.79, A 67, G 214, P 50 (composed 1280)

Si ja·m deu mos chans valer, PC 248.80, A 48, G 215, M 73, P 24 (composed 1269)

Tan m'es plazens lo mals d'amor, PC 248.82, A 31, G 216, M 20, P 1 (composed 1254)

Tant vei, qu'es ab joi pretz mermatz, PC 248.83, A 34, G 216, M 33, P 6 (composed 1257)

Voluntiers faria, PC 248.85, A 59, G 217, M 88, P 40 (composed in one afternoon, 13 March 1276)

Xristias vei perillar, PC 248.87, A 62, G 218, P 44 (composed in one day, 10 March 1276)

Yverns no·m te de chantar embargat, PC 248.89, A 64, G 218, P 47 (composed 1277)

BIBLIOGRAPHY

J. Anglade: *Le troubadour Guiraut Riquier* (Paris, 1905)

A. Jeanroy: *La poésie lyrique des troubadours*, i (Toulouse and Paris, 1934), 280ff

F. Gennrich: 'Guiraut Riquier', *MGG* [incl. edn. of *Ples de tristor*]

For further bibliography see TROUBADOURS, TROUVÈRES.

ROBERT FALCK

Risinger, Karel (*b* Prague, 18 June 1920). Czech musicologist and composer. He began studying musicology and aesthetics at Prague University in 1939, continuing after the German occupation and taking the doctorate under Hutter in 1947 with a dissertation on the music-theory bases of intonation. In composition he was at first a private pupil of Řídký; later he studied at the Prague Conservatory (1941–7), attending Křička's advanced classes (1943–5) and Hába's microtonal department (1945–7). After teaching at the academy's music department and the music faculty of Prague University he joined the Institute of Musicology (now the Institute of the Theory and History of Art) of the Czechoslovak Academy of Sciences (1962), where he directed the department of theory (to 1971). In 1972 he was appointed lecturer at the music department of the academy. He gained the CSc in 1958 with a work on functional theory in contemporary tonal music, completed his *Habilitation* at the academy in 1966 with a study of leading personalities of modern Czech music theory and took the DSc in 1970 with a dissertation on the hierarchy of musical entities in contemporary European music.

Risinger concentrated on composition up to the early 1960s, writing a number of works for various combinations including large-scale vocal, instrumental and dramatic works, some of which have been performed. But severe self-criticism and a deepening interest in music theory led him away from composition. As a musicologist he has consistently directed his attention to theories of composition in 20th-century music; he has formulated a generalizing and systematic view of the evolution of contemporary composition from traditional melodic and harmonic approaches to a micro-interval system and 12-note technique.

WRITINGS

Hudebně teoretické základy intonace [The music-theory bases of intonation] (diss., U. of Prague, 1947)

Přehledná nauka o harmonii [A theory of harmony in outline] (Prague, 1955)

'O podstatě frygických a lydických funkcí' [The essence of Phrygian and Lydian functions], *MMC* (1956), no.1, p.127

Nástin obecného hudebního funkčního systému rozšířene tonality [An outline of a general system of functional harmony within extended tonality] (Prague, 1957)

Dvě kapitoly z funkčni teorie soudobé tonální hudby [Two chapters from the functional theory of contemporary tonal music] (diss., U. of Prague, 1958)

Základní harmonické funkce v soudobé hudbě [Basic harmonic functions in contemporary music] (Prague, 1958)

'Zvukový prostor a některé hudební problémy' [Space in sound and some musical problems], *HV 1961*, 86

'Úvod do problematiky hudební teorie' [Introduction to the problems of music theory], *HV 1962*, 83

'Atonalita a dodekafonie', *HV*, v (1968), 571

Hierarchie hudebních celků v novodobé evropské hudbě [The hierarchy of musical entities in present-day European music] (diss., U. of Prague, 1970; Prague, 1969)

Vývoj českých harmonických systémů po roce 1948 [The development of Czech systems of harmony after 1948] (Prague, 1969)

Intervalový mikrokosmos [The intervallic microcosm] (Prague, 1971)

'Die Hierarchie in Melodie, Harmonie und Akkordik', *De musica disputationes pragenses*, i (1972), 70

'Metodika výuky evropské harmonie 20. století' [A method of teaching European 20th-century harmony], *Živá hudba*, v (1973), 165

'Tektonické aspekty houslového koncertu Albana Berga' [Structural aspects of Berg's Violin Concerto], *HV*, x (1973), 56 [with Ger. summary]

'K současnému pojetí tonality' [The present day concept of tonality], *Současné hranice tonality*, ed. J. Válek (Prague, 1974), 13

BIBLIOGRAPHY

ČSHS [incl. list of compositions]

JOSEF BEK

RISM. See RÉPERTOIRE INTERNATIONAL DES SOURCES MUSICALES.

Risoluto (It.: 'dissolved', 'faded away', or 'resolved', 'decided'). Resolved, decisive. It appears in scores around 1800 as a tempo designation. But Beethoven preferred to use it as a qualification: his Piano Variations in D op.76 and the fugue of his Hammerklavier Sonata both begin *allegro risoluto*. Later it was used as an expression mark and was particularly favoured by Elgar and Bartók.

See also TEMPO AND EXPRESSION MARKS.

DAVID FALLOWS

Rispetto (It.). A stanzaic form of Italian poetry set by composers of the frottola and 16th-century madrigal, also known as STRAMBOTTO and *ottava rima*. Each stanza consists of eight lines of 11 syllables. *See* FROTTOLA, §2.

DON HARRÁN

Rispoli, Salvatore (*b* Naples, ?*c*1736–45; *d* Naples, 1812). Italian composer and teacher. He studied at the S Onofrio conservatory, Naples, under Cotumacci and Insanguine. In the 1770s he composed settings of some of Saverio Mattei's psalm translations, including, for the birth of the hereditary prince in 1777, Mattei's arrangement of Psalm lxxi as a cantata, *I voti di Davide per Salomone*. Mattei, in a note published in the 1770s in an edition of his psalms, praised Rispoli as 'a young man of rare ability and taste who joins to a solid study of old music all the brilliance of the modern' (Mattei's reference to Rispoli as a young man suggests that Fétis's birthdate for him, 1745, is closer to the true one than that given by Gerber, 1736). In 1781 Rispoli composed the music for Mattei's cantata on the death of Empress Maria Theresia; in the preface to the libretto Mattei repeated his praise of Rispoli (still calling him a young man) and added that through the 'happy disgrace' of not having had the opportunity to compose for the opera house he had avoided its corrupting influence. In 1782–7, however, Rispoli did have five operas, comic, serious and sacred, performed at Milan, Turin and the secondary theatres of Naples, but he never achieved the honour of being asked to compose for S Carlo. On 1 January 1793 he became *secondo maestro* at the S Onofrio conservatory, and on the death of Insanguine in 1795 he and Furno became joint *primi maestri*. In 1797, when the S Onofrio and Loreto conservatories merged, he was pensioned.

WORKS

OPERAS

Il trionfo de' pupilli oppressi (commedia, P. Mililotti), Naples, Fiorentini, 20 Jan 1782
Nitteti (dramma per musica, Metastasio), Turin, Regio, 26 Dec 1782
Ipermestra (dramma per musica, Metastasio), Milan, La Scala, 26 Dec 1785, *F-Pc*, aria *I-Mc*
Idalide (dramma per musica, F. Moretti), Turin, Regio, 26 Dec 1786
Il trionfo di Davide (dramma sacro), Naples, Fondo, Lent 1787, *I-Gi(l)*

Arias etc: *A-Wgm*, *CH-Zz*, *D-Dlb*, *I-Bsf*, *Gi(l)*, *Mc*

OTHER WORKS

Sacred: Requiem, 4vv, orch; I voti di Davide per Salomone (Ps lxxi, S. Mattei), for birth of hereditary prince, 1777; Duettini sacri sopra i salmi (Mattei); Laudate pueri, 5vv, orch: all *Nc*; Te Deum (It., Mattei); Salve regina, 2S, bc, *Mc*
Other vocal: Il salmista confuso (cantata, Mattei), on death of Maria Theresia, 4 solo vv, ?orch, Pavia, 1781; Gelosia, duetti, 2S, bc, ?*I-Nc*; Solfeggi, 2S/B, bc, *GB-Lbm*, *I-Mc*
Inst: Pastorale, org/hpd, *Mc*; toccatas, hpd, *Nc*

BIBLIOGRAPHY

FétisB; *GerberL*
F. Florimo: *La scuola musicale di Napoli e i suoi conservatorii* (Naples, 1880–82/*R*1969)
S. di Giacomo: *Il Conservatorio di Sant'Onofrio a Capuana e quello della Pietà dei Turchini* (Palermo, 1924)

DENNIS LIBBY (text), JAMES L. JACKMAN (work-list)

Risposta [riposta] (It.: 'reply'). In FUGUE, the ANSWER as opposed to the subject. The term gained currency in the writings on fugue of Italian theorists in the Baroque period; the term for the subject is *proposta*.

Risset, Jean-Claude (*b* Le Puy, 13 March 1938). French composer and technologist. He had lessons with Robert Trimaille (piano), Suzanne Demarquez (harmony and counterpoint) and Jolivet (composition) until 1963. The next year he moved to New York, where he began work on computer sound with Mathews and came in contact with Varèse. He pursued research with Mathews at the Bell Telephone Laboratories in 1964–5 and in 1967–9. Subsequently he held appointments as visiting professor of music at Stanford University (summer 1971) and *maître de conférences* at the music department of the Centre Universitaire de Marseille-Luminy (from 1971) before accepting the direction of the computer department at the Institut de Recherche et de Coordination Acoustique/Musique, Paris. His compositions include *Mutations I*, created with the assistance of the Music V programme, a piece that exploits different harmonic systems, tempered and continuous.

WORKS

Prelude, orch, 1963; Instantanés, pf, 1965; Neiz radenn, eng hn, pf, 1966; Little Boy (incidental music, P. Halet), orch, tape, 1968; Up-down/Bell Sirens, tape, 1968; Mutations I, tape, 1969; Mutations II, 4 insts, tape, film by L. Schwartz, 1973

WRITINGS

with M. V. Mathews: 'Analysis of Musical-instrument Tones', *Physics Today*, xxii/2 (1969), 23
An Introductory Catalogue of Computer-synthesized Sounds (Murray Hill, NJ, 1969)
'Synthèse des sons par ordinateur', *Musique et technologie* (Paris, 1971), 118
'X. Musique: ordinateur et création musicale', *Art et science: de la créativité* (Paris, 1972), 269

PAUL GRIFFITHS

Rist, Johann (*b* Ottensen, nr. Hamburg, 8 March 1607; *d* Wedel, 31 Aug 1667). German theologian, poet and composer. He studied theology, poetry, law and other subjects at the universities of Rinteln and Rostock and perhaps also in Leipzig and Holland. He worked briefly as a private tutor at Heide, Holstein, and in 1635 became pastor at Wedel, a position he held for the rest of his life. He was given the title of poet laureate in 1644 and was ennobled in 1653. He was admitted to the society known as the Fruchtbringende Gesellschaft, with the pseudonym 'Der Rüstige', in 1647, and he founded his own poets' academy, the Elbschwanenorden, in 1660.

Rist was a friend of many musicians, including Schütz and Christoph Bernhard (who wrote a motet for his funeral), and he worked closely with many minor Hamburg composers. Many of his poems were set to music in both sacred and secular collections edited by himself and others; he wrote the music of some of the songs but mostly relied on the talents of composers such as Hammerschmidt, Martin Köler, Peter Meier, Heinrich Pape, the elder Johann Schop and Selle. The secular poems treat typical pastoral subjects, and some are translations from Dutch, French or Italian. The sacred poems, many of them biblical translations or adaptations, were composed both for practical use in services and in teaching and for devotional use in the home. All the poems follow Opitz's reforms: they are usually strophic, with clear rhymes and regular metres. They are set syllabically, often with little rhythmic variety, for one voice with an unfigured (perhaps sung) bass accompaniment. In a few of his plays and ballets Rist included songs set to his own music or that of his Hamburg friends; they are important precursors of the works of the Hamburg school of opera composers.

WORKS
Edition: *J. Rist: Sämtliche Werke*, ed. E. Mannack (Berlin, 1967–).
For Rist's poetry, see K. Goedeke: *Grundriss zur Geschichte der deutschen Dichtung* (Dresden, 2/1887), iii, 79ff

SACRED
(all pubd in Lüneburg unless otherwise stated)
Himlische Lieder, 2 vols. (1641–3), music by J. Schop
Der . . . an das Kreutz geheftete Jesus Christus, 1v, bc (Hamburg, 1648, enlarged 2/1664 as Neue hochheilige Passions-Andachten), music by H. Pape, 2nd edn. with music by M. Köler
Neuer himlischer Lieder sonderbahres Buch (1651), music by Hammerschmidt, M. Jacobi, Kortkamp, P. Meier, Pape, Jacob Praetorius (ii), Scheidemann, J. Schultze, S. T. Staden
Sabbathische Seelenlust (1651), music by T. Selle
Neuer teutscher Parnass: see under 'Secular'
Frommer und Gottseliger . . . Haussmusik (1654), music by M. Jacobi, Schop
Neue musikalische Festandachten (1655), music by Selle
Neue musikalische Katechismus-Andachten, 1v, bc (1656), music by Hammerschmidt, M. Jacobi
Die verschmähte Eitelkeit, i, 1v, b (1658), music by Scheidemann
Die verlangete Seligkeit (1658), music by Scheidemann
Neue musikalische Kreutz-, Trost-, Lob- und Dank- Schule (1659), music by M. Jacobi
Neues musikalisches Seelenparadies, 2 vols. (1660–62), music by C. Flor
Neue hochheilige Passions-Andachten: see Der . . . an das Kreutz
Ander Theil. Die verschmähte Eitelkeit, 1v, bc (Frankfurt am Main, 1668)

SECULAR
(all pubd in Hamburg unless otherwise stated)
Musa teutonica (1634)
Poetischer Lustgarten (1638)
Des edlen Daphnis aus Cimbrien Galathee, 1, 2vv, bc (1642⁹, rev 2/1656), music by Pape, Rist, Schop and others
Friedensposaune (1646)
Des edlen Daphnis aus Cimbrien besungene Florabella, 2vv/1v, bc (1651), music by P. Meier
Neuer teutscher Parnass (Lüneburg, 1652); music by J. Jacobi, Pape, Rist, Schop, also includes sacred songs
10 poems in C. C. Dedekind: Aelbianische Musen-Lust (Dresden, 1657)
More than 30 stage works with songs, including Das Friedejauchzende Teutschland (Nuremburg, 1653), music by M. Jacobi

BIBLIOGRAPHY
W. Krabbe: *Johann Rist und das deutsche Lied* (diss., U. of Berlin, 1910)
K. Hortschansky: *Katalog der Kieler Musiksammlungen* (Basle, 1963), nos.18–48
R. H. Thomas: *Poetry and Song in the German Baroque* (Oxford, 1963)
J. H. Baron: *Foreign Influences on the German Secular Solo Continuo Lied in the Mid-Seventeenth Century* (diss., Brandeis U., Waltham, Mass., 1967)
H. Walter: *Musikgeschichte der Stadt Lüneburg: vom Ende des 16. bis zum Anfang des 18. Jahrhunderts* (Tutzing, 1967)

JOHN H. BARON

Ristenpart, Karl (*b* Kiel, 26 Jan 1900; *d* Lisbon, 24 Dec 1967). German conductor. After completing his studies at the Stern Conservatory in Berlin he took over the directorship of the Berlin Oratorio Choir, and then founded a chamber orchestra which gave concerts for many years in the town hall in Berlin-Zehlendorf. In 1946 he established the RIAS Chamber Orchestra with which he made many recordings, including the complete cantatas of Bach. In 1953 he moved to Saarbrücken

where he directed the Saar Radio chamber orchestra which quickly gained a wide reputation. Critics praised the stylistic authority and fervour of his interpretations, which were mainly devoted to German Baroque music.

HANS CHRISTOPH WORBS

Ristić, Milan (*b* Belgrade, 18 Aug 1908). Yugoslav composer. He studied privately in Paris and then at the Belgrade Music School with Milojević and Slavenski (composition), and Brezovšek (piano). In 1939 he attended Hába's microtone class at the Prague Conservatory, and in the next year he was appointed to the staff of Belgrade Radio, where he has sometimes acted as a piano accompanist. He was elected to corresponding membership of the Serbian Academy in 1961. In his first works, such as the Sinfonietta, the Symphony no.1 and the Violin Concerto, he was a follower of Schoenbergian atonal expressionism; he made use of quarter-tones in the Suite for four trombones, which was performed at the 1939 ISCM Festival. There followed a phase of works based on literature and on folk music, before he established himself as a neo-classical symphonist. The mature symphonies are masterfully orchestrated and increasingly free in form; in the Sixth and Seventh tonality is broadened with loose 12-note serial writing.

WORKS
(selective list)
Orch: 7 syms., 1941, 1951, 1961, 1966, 1967, 1968, 1972; Čovek i rat [Man and war], sym. poem, 1942; Vn Conc., 1944; Pf Conc., 1954; Suita giocosa, 1956; Burlesque, 1957; 7 Bagatelles, 1957; Conc., chamber orch, 1958; Music for Chamber Orch, 1962; Conc. for Orch, 1963; Cl Conc., 1964; 4 Movts, str, 1971
Chamber: Suite, 4 trbn, perf. 1939; Music for 4 Hn, 1971; 10 Epigrams, 10 insts, 1971; 5 Characters, 5 insts, 1972
Songs, film music

Principal publishers: Srpska Akademija Nauka i Umetnosti, Udruženje Kompozitora Srbije

STANA ĐURIĆ-KLAJN

Ristori, Giovanni Alberto (*b* ?Bologna, 1692; *d* Dresden, 7 Feb 1753). Italian composer. He was the son of Tommaso Ristori, a versatile musician and actor, and the director of a travelling company of Italian comedians which, shortly before Giovanni's birth, was in the service of the Saxon elector Johann Georg III at Dresden. But Giovanni's birthplace is variously given as Bologna by La Borde and Gerber, Vienna by a Saxon passport of 1715, and Venice in a score of his cantata *Verdi colli* (in *GB-Lbm*). His first opera, *Pallide trionfante in Arcadia*, had its première at the Obizzi theatre, Padua, in summer 1713, and in November his *Orlando furioso* was given in the Teatro S Angelo, Venice; both were revived in Venice the following year when, in addition, his *Euristeo* was performed in Venice and Bologna (see C. R. Mengelberg) and his *Pigmalione* in Rovigo.

In 1715 he and his wife Maria accompanied his parents to Dresden, but he held no official position there until 1717 when he was appointed composer to the Italian comic theatre managed by his father; at the same time he became director of the *cappella polacca*, Warsaw, with a salary of 600 thalers. The *cappella* consisted of a dozen musicians including the flautist J. J. Quantz and the violinist Franz Benda. Although Lotti was the resident opera composer at Dresden between 1717 and 1719, Ristori had *Cleonice*, his first opera for the court, staged on 15 August 1718. But Italian opera was severely curtailed soon afterwards, and Ristori and his father were among the few Italians not released from service in 1720. Ristori is not known to have composed any music for Dresden between 1718 and 1726 and the revival of *Cleonice* at Verona in 1723 suggests that he may have returned to Italy. The performance on 2 September 1726 of his comic opera *Calandro*, sometimes called the first Italian *opera buffa* written in Germany, indicates his presence at the Saxon court. It was followed in 1727 by another Italian comedy, *Un pazzo ne fà cento, ovvero Don Chisciotte*. When *Calandro* was revived in Carnival 1728, Frederick the Great attended a performance and requested a copy of the score.

In 1733 Ristori was demoted to the rank of chamber organist with a reduced salary, but by 1745 it had increased to 1200 thalers. Gerber's claim that, in 1740, Ristori became Kapellmeister to the court at St Petersburg has not been verified, but he spent some of 1731–2 in Russia in his father's troupe of Italian comedians. A serenata by him was performed in Moscow during summer 1731, and the revival of *Calandro* on 11 December is generally accounted the first performance of an Italian opera in Russia. After a short visit to St Petersburg in early 1732, Tommaso took his company to Poland, but Giovanni left them and went to Dresden to direct his oratorio *La deposizione della croce di nostro Signore* before returning to Warsaw, where he set the psalm *Lauda Jerusalem* in October 1732.

Most of the Italian comedians at Dresden were dismissed when the elector August I died in 1733. When Tommaso, aged 75, was pensioned off, improvised Italian comedy at the Dresden court came to an end, and serious opera, directed by Hasse the new Kapellmeister, dominated the Saxon stage. Ristori was probably in Warsaw between 1734 and August 1736 while the new Saxon elector was securing for himself the Polish throne. Sacred music and occasional secular works of 1735–6 indicate his close association with the court while Hasse was in Italy; he composed cantatas for birthdays and name days, a coronation opera *Le fate* performed on 10 August 1736, and *Arianna* for the elector's birthday on 7 October 1736.

Ristori probably did not supervise the première of his pasticcio *Didone abbandonata* at Covent Garden, London, on 13 April 1737, but he directed rehearsals and performances of his *Temistocle* and *Adriano in Siria* at S Carlo, Naples, in 1738 and 1739; he must have accompanied the Saxon princess Maria Amalia there following her marriage to Charles III, King of the Two Sicilies, in May 1738. By 1744 he had returned to Dresden, where, in that year, he composed three masses, including his finest one, in D; the quality of these and other choral works was acknowledged with his appointment as court *Kirchenkomponist* in 1746. Ristori also set several cantata texts by the Bavarian princess Maria Antonia soon after her marriage to the Saxon crown prince Friedrich Christian in 1747. In 1750 the elector again rewarded Ristori for his many years of service and outstanding music by naming him vice-Kapellmeister under Hasse. His last work, a Mass in C, is dated 1752. When he died the following year his widow was given a pension of 400 thalers and was paid for Ristori's collection of his own scores, some of which were lost in the bombardment of Dresden in 1760 and many others during World War II. A revival of *Arianna* at the Dresden court in 1756 is the last known per-

formance of a theatrical work by Ristori in the 18th century.

Despite C. R. Mengelberg's excellent study of Ristori's works, his music remains undervalued. He showed considerable competence in all the genres of his day except instrumental music, of which he wrote little. His best works are his chamber cantatas and his large sacred pieces, which reveal contrapuntal complexities beyond those of Hasse's works of the 1740s. But he did not match Hasse for breadth or melodic beauty. Only in his intermezzos does Ristori seem to equal his more famous colleague.

The early 18th-century priest Cosimo Ristori who composed oratorios for Florence is not known to have been related to Giovanni. His oratorios include *La fede trionfante di S Cresci* (1719), *L'incoronazione di Ester* (1720), and *David, ovvero L'innocenza difesa* (1721).

WORKS
OPERAS, ORATORIOS
d – *dramma per musica*

Pallide trionfante in Arcadia (dramma pastorale, 3, O. Mandelli), Padua, Obizzi, sum. 1713

Orlando furioso (d, 3, G. Braccioli), Venice, S Angelo, 7 Nov 1713; rev. Venice, 1714, *I-Tn*

Euristeo (d, 3), Venice and Bologna, 1714

Pigmalione (d, 3), Rovigo, 1714, *D-Dlb*

Cleonice (d, 3, A. Constantini), Moritzburg, 15 Aug 1718

Calandro (comic, 3, S. B. Pallavicini), Dresden, 2 Sept 1726, *Dlb*

Un pazzo ne fà cento, ovvero Don Chisciotte (comic, 3, Pallavicini), Dresden, 2 Feb 1727, *Dlb*

Le fate (d, 1, Pallavicini), Dresden, Hoftheater, 10 Aug 1736, *Dlb*

Didone abbandonata (pasticcio, 3, Metastasio), London, Covent Garden, 13 April 1737

Temistocle (d, 3, Metastasio), Naples, S Carlo, 19 Dec 1738, *Dlb*

Adriano in Siria (d, 3, Metastasio), Naples, S Carlo, 19 Dec 1739, *Dlb*, *I-Nc*

La liberalità di Numa Pompilio (serenata, 1, C. Pasquini), Dresden, 1746, *D-Dlb*

Diana vindicata (festa per musica, Pasquini), Dresden, 8 Dec 1746

I lamenti di Orfeo (festa da camera, 1, Pasquini), Dresden, 1749

Nicandro (d, 3); Ercole (d, 3): both formerly *Dlb*, lost in World War II

Intermezzos, probably 1st perf. Dresden: Delbo e Dorina; Despina, Simona e Trespolo; Fidelba ed Artabano; Lisandr. e Cast.; Serpilla e Perpello: all *Dlb*

Oratorios: La deposizione della croce di nostro Signore, Dresden, 1732; La sepoltura di Cristo, Dresden, 1744; La vergine annunziata, ?Dresden: all *Dlb*

CANTATAS AND OTHER SECULAR VOCAL

Verdi colli e spiagge amene, S, bc, Sept 1719, *GB-Lbm* (2 copies), *I-Nc*

Dovresti a mio core (serenata), 3vv, Moscow, for name day of the Saxon elector, 2 Aug 1731

Cantata, 4vv, for birthday of electress, 1735, *D-Dlb*

Versi cantate in Varsavia, for coronation of empress of Russia, 1736, *Dlb*

Componimento per musica, Warsaw, for name day of king, 1736, *Dlb*

Arianna (azione scenica, 1, Pallavicini), Hubertusburg, for birthday of elector, 7 Oct 1736, *Dlb*

Amore insuperabile (componimento drammatico, Pasquini), S, S, T, Dresden, 10 Feb 1747, *Dlb*

Didone abbandonata (Princess Maria Antonia), S, orch, Dresden, 1748, *Dlb*

Lavinia e Turno (Maria Antonia), S, ?orch, Dresden, 1748, *Dlb*

Nice e Tirsi (Maria Antonia), S, orch, Dresden, 1749, *Dlb*

Undated cantatas: La madonna in Villa, 2vv; Perdonati o cari amori, A, bc; La pesca, 7vv, orch; Suono di lieti canti, S, bc; Vaghi fiori vezzosi del bello, S, bc; Virtu e fortuna, S, S, T, ?orch: all *Dlb*

SACRED VOCAL
(*unless otherwise indicated, all in MS in D-Dlb and all for SATB*)

14 masses, C, 1752, C, C, C, D, 1744, D, D, D, F, F, G, 1744, g, 1749, A, Bb, 1744; 2 missa brevis, D, *D-Bds*, F; 2 Kyrie–Gloria, F, F; 3 Gloria, C, D, g; 2 Gloria brevis, D, Bb; Credo, F; Sanctus–Agnus, g; 3 Requiem, D, F, 1730, f

Psalms and psalm verses: Beati omnes, C; 2 Beatus vir, D, A; Confitebor, F, SAB; Confitemini Domino, *Bds*; Cum invocarem, C, 1738; 6 Dixit Dominus, C, 5vv, c, D, d, F, F; Ecce nunc benedicite, G; 2 In te Domine speravi, G, SB, G; Jubilate Deo, F; Lauda Jerusalem, A, 1732; 2 Laudate Dominum, A, 5vv, *LEt*, A; 2 Laudate pueri, B♭, B♭, SAB, another, *I-Pc*; 3 Miserere, c, c, 1748, E♭; 2 Nisi Dominus, A, SAB, a

Hymns: Concinnat plebs, D; Haec dies quam fecit, A; Iste confessor, D, T, orch; O lux beata; 2 Pange lingua, D, g; 3 Te Deum, C, D, 1745, D; Te lucis ante terminum, C

Solo motets: Ad sonos, ad jubila, A, tpt, timp, str; Alleluia, oh adesso si, A, bc; Care Joseph, S, orch; Cari affectus, S, orch; Casta columba, S, orch; Coelo tonanti, B, ob, tpt, str, bn; Domine non secundum, S, S, bc; Dormite, dormite, S, orch; Ite longe hostes crudeles, B, orch, *D-Bds*; Laeti campi, S, orch; Oh adesso si, A, orch; O intemerata, S, S, bc; O magnum pietatis, S, orch; Omnis fera sors, T, orch; Redemptionem misit Dominus, S, A, orch; Signum magnum, S, orch; Spirate zephiri, B, orch

Other motets: Afferento regi, SATB; Benedicta e venerabilis, SATB; O admirabile mysterium, S, S, A, A, 1748; Verbum caro, SATB, 1744

Marian antiphons: 6 Alma Redemptoris mater: C, 4vv; d, S; F, 4vv; G, 4vv, 1746; a, 4vv, 1749; 2 Ave regina coelorum, C, 4vv; G, 4vv; Regina coeli, A, 4vv; 6 Salve regina: c, 4vv; D, S; E♭, 4vv; G, S; G, SSA; B♭, 4vv

Litanies: 4 Litaniae lauretanae, c, 1746; D, 1733; A; B♭, 1746; Sub tuum praesidium, c; 2 Litaniae de V. Sacramento, F, g; 2 Litaniae di S. F. Xavier, E♭, F; Litaniae Ss Trinitatis, D: all SATB

5 Magnificat, D, E♭, e, 5vv, F, B♭; 2 Nunc dimittis, C, B♭; Lauda Sion salvatorem; 2 Stabat mater, C, 1736, B♭, 2vv; Veni Sancte Spiritus, C; 3 Domine ad adjuvandum, D; Misericordia Domini, F; 10 Lenten duets, S, A, org

OTHER WORKS

Ob conc., E♭, with str orch, *Dlb*
3 sinfonie, D, D, 1736, F, 1736, all for 2 hn, str, *Dlb*
Esercizi per l'accompanimento, *Dlb*

BIBLIOGRAPHY

EitnerQ; *FétisB*; *GerberL*; *SchmidlD*; *SchmidlDS*; *WaltherML*
J.-B. de La Borde: *Essai sur la musique ancienne et moderne* (Paris, 1780/*R*1972), iii, 228
M. Fürstenau: *Zur Geschichte der Musik und des Theaters am Hofe zu Dresden*, ii (Dresden, 1862/*R*1971), 119f, 162, 202f
C. Mennicke: *Hasse und die Brüder Graun als Symphoniker* (Leipzig, 1906), 385, 394, 411
A. Schering: *Geschichte des Oratoriums* (Leipzig, 1911/*R*1966), 215ff
E. Schmitz: *Geschichte der weltlichen Solokantate* (Leipzig, 1914, rev. 2/1955), 143
C. R. Mengelberg: *Giovanni Alberto Ristori* (Leipzig, 1916)
H. Schnoor: *Dresden: vierhundert Jahre deutsche Musikkultur* (Dresden, 1948), 72ff
R.-A. Mooser: *Annales de la musique et des musiciens en Russie*, i (Geneva, 1948), 39, 49ff, 67, 79f, 365, 373ff
R. Mengelberg: 'Ristori, Giovanni Alberto', *Grove 5*
D. Hartwig: 'Ristori, Giovanni Alberto', *MGG*
B. S. Brook, ed.: *The Breitkopf Thematic Catalogue, 1762–87* (New York, 1966), 174, 178, 332

SVEN HANSELL

Ritardando (It.: 'holding back', 'becoming slower'; gerund of *ritardare*). See RALLENTANDO. The form *tardando* also occasionally appears. Joseph Czerny (*Clavierschule*, 1825) gave a long list of contexts in which he considered *ritardando* admissible or appropriate and it is clear that in most of these he assumed an almost immediate return to the original tempo. The word tended to remain even where most Italian tempo marks had been rejected: see, for instance, Wagner's use of *etwas ritardierend* in Act 2 of *Lohengrin*.

For bibliography *see* TEMPO AND EXPRESSION MARKS.

DAVID FALLOWS

Ritchie, Margaret (Willard) (*b* Grimsby, 7 June 1903; *d* Ewelme, Oxfordshire, 7 Feb 1969). English soprano. She studied at the Royal College of Music and with Plunket Greene, Agnes Nicholls and Henry Wood. She first attracted attention as Pamina in a student performance of *Die Zauberflöte* at the RCM; and she soon became known (at first under the name of Mabel Ritchie) as a concert singer and as leading soprano of Frederick Woodhouse's Intimate Opera Company. In 1944 she joined the Sadler's Wells Opera Company,

distinguishing herself especially as Dorabella in *Così fan tutte*. In 1946 she sang Lucia in the first production, at Glyndebourne, of Britten's *Rape of Lucretia* and in the following year she joined the English Opera Group. The part of Miss Wordsworth, the prim and innocent schoolmistress in Britten's *Albert Herring*, displayed to perfection her musical qualities and delightful sense of comedy.

Margaret Ritchie's voice, though small, was clearly produced and of pure quality; she used it with an unfailing sense of style and showed unusual flexibility in the execution of florid passages. In her latter years she devoted much time to teaching, and in 1960 opened a summer school for singers at Oxford.

DESMOND SHAWE-TAYLOR

Ritenuto (It.: 'held back'; past participle of *ritenere*, to detain, withhold). Normally it is a more sudden and extreme slowing down than is implied by RALLENTANDO and *ritardando*; but strictly it is a firm change to a slower tempo, which is then maintained: bars 280–315 of the overture to *Die Fledermaus* (by Johann Strauss (ii)) have the tempo mark *tempo ritenuto*. *Ritenente*, the present participle, suggests something more gradual.

Ritornello (It.; Fr. *ritournelle*). A term, diminutive of the Italian *ritorno* ('return'), signifying a 'little return' or a short recurring passage (*see* REFRAIN; RIPRESA). It particularly signifies the tutti section of an aria or a concerto movement in the Baroque period, and the form of such movements is often known as 'ritornello form'. (For an account of the form and its development *see* ARIA; CONCERTO, §§2–4.)

The term was originally applied to folk verse, where it signified a form (alternatively known as *stornello*) proceeding in three-line verses with the outer two lines of each in rhyme; it may have influenced the *terza rima*. In the 14th-century Italian madrigal (*see* MADRIGAL, §I) and other forms, including the CACCIA, it applied to the last two lines of an 11- or eight-line verse otherwise arranged in threes (forming the pattern *aaab* or *aab*). It has been described as a coda, emphasizing that it was not, in spite of the meaning of the word, used as a refrain; possibly in forms other than the madrigal it was used elsewhere than at the end of a piece.

In the 17th century the term was applied to the instrumental prelude and its recurrences, complete or incomplete, in vocal items, or to short instrumental passages at the end of vocal ones. Pieces entitled 'ritornello' and 'sinfonia' were the only purely instrumental music in such works (their meaning is discussed by Praetorius, *Syntagma musicum*, iii, 1618, pp.108ff, 184ff); most of the recurring instrumental sections in Monteverdi's operas are entitled 'ritornello'. In his *Orfeo* (1607) the ritornello preceding and punctuating the prologue, sung by 'La musica', is prophetic of later developments: its recurrences are shortened by the telescoping of the middle phrase, except at the end of the prologue where it is exactly as at the opening; the same ritornello also introduces both Act 1 and Act 4, and is heard within Act 2. The term was used in other countries, for example by Purcell in England (sometimes in the form 'ritornel'), Krieger, Kindermann, Theile and others in Germany (notably in the German strophic song), and Lully and others in France, where the *ritournelle*, usually in triple time, came to signify a section to be danced following a song.

In its early forms, the music of the ritornello was distinct from the music that was to be sung, but later in the 17th century (for example in the works of Stradella, Pallavicino, Steffani, Purcell, Keiser etc) the same phrases often appeared both in the ritornello and in the vocal part that followed. By the 18th century, the ritornellos of formal arias in operas, cantatas and other works were often long and elaborate, sometimes stating the chief musical content of the aria at the outset. The ritornello normally recurred complete, in the tonic, only at the end of the aria, and, sometimes in slightly shorter form, in the dominant or relative major during its course (this procedure occurred twice in a full da capo aria); shorter ritornellos, often using only one idea or texture from the preludial statement, might punctuate the singer's sections and bravura passages. The vocal material might begin with new music, but it nearly always used the main ritornello idea at some point. The basic form was: opening ritornello (in the tonic); opening solo (moving to the dominant or relative major); ritornello in the new key; second solo (modulating, sometimes with brief appearances of the ritornello material, and ending with a cadence in the tonic); full ritornello in the tonic. In a da capo aria this entire pattern was repeated after a central section. The design of ritornello arias was far from stereotyped in the works of such major composers as Alessandro Scarlatti, Bach and Handel.

The same basic design was used in the Baroque concerto in the early 18th century, particularly in the music of the operatically inclined Venetian concerto composers such as Albinoni and Vivaldi. Here the solo instruments, usually violins, oboes or flutes, replaced the voice, and even in the orchestral concerto the same formal structure obtained. The first movement especially often had the lengthy statements and complex thematic relationships of elaborate arias. This form affected other music, as is seen particularly clearly in the works of Bach, for example in his choruses (those opening the B minor Mass and the *St Matthew Passion* are essentially in ritornello form), his organ sonatas, and indeed in some of his fugal movements like the second section of the overture of Suite no.3 in D and the last movement of Brandenburg Concerto no.4 where fugal expositions represent the ritornellos and episodes the solo sections.

In much expanded form, including contrasting material, the ritornello served in the mid-18th century and the Classical era, both in arias and in the concerto. Mozart's mature piano concertos, with their long processions of contrasting ideas in the initial statements (sometimes developed in symphonic style), show the most complex treatment of the ritornello ever to be devised for instrumental music. The concepts of the opening tutti or ritornello persisted in the concerto throughout the 19th century and into the 20th.

ARTHUR HUTCHINGS

Ritschel. German family of musicians of Austrian origin, active in the courts of Mannheim and Munich.

(1) **Georg Wenzel Ritschel** (*b* *c*1680; *d* Schwetzingen, 10 June 1757). Double bass player and violinist. With his brother (2) Franz Joseph Ritschel he accompanied the household of Duke Carl Philipp from Innsbruck via Heidelberg and Schwetzingen to Mannheim (1720)

when the duke succeeded as Elector Palatine. Ritschel was admitted as a supernumerary member of the court orchestra in 1713, and from the first court calendar in 1723 to the orchestral register of 1757 is recorded as a double bass player. The registration of his death in 1757 gives him as being 'in his late 70s'.

(2) **(Ignaz) Franz Joseph Ritschel** (*d* Schwetzingen, 4 July 1763). Organist, brother of (1) Georg Wenzel Ritschel. He is listed in the Mannheim court calendar as deputy organist in 1734, and from 1745 at the latest he was first organist. His salary in 1759 was higher than that of any other member of the already famous Mannheim musical establishment. In 1737 he married Maria Rosina Fränzl, the sister of the Mannheim violinist Ignaz Fränzl.

(3) **Johannes (Michael Ignaz) Ritschel** (*b* Mannheim, baptized 29 July 1739; *d* Mannheim, 25 March 1766). Violinist and composer son of (2) Franz Joseph Ritschel. At the age of 17 he was a violinist in the Mannheim orchestra. The Elector Karl Theodor encouraged his talent and on 8 October 1757 awarded him a three-year scholarship to Italy 'for his better perfection in music'. At the beginning of 1758 he began his studies with Padre Martini in Bologna. Three letters from his father now in the Biblioteca Musicale G. B. Martini in Bologna bear witness to the respect the teacher had for his pupil. In the spring of 1761 Ritschel was in Rome, and on 15 April wrote to Martini criticizing the local style of church music as superficial and 'Neapolitan'. All the same, later that year he went to Naples as a pupil of Gennaro Manna, and on 2 March 1762 wrote enthusiastically to Martini about two new operas by J. C. Bach, whom he probably met in Naples. At the age of 24 Ritschel was promoted to the position of *Protector Electoralis chori musici* in Mannheim, thereby ranking alongside Ignaz Holzbauer, 28 years his senior. His gratitude to the elector was expressed in the dedication to Carl Theodor of the oratorio *Gioas re di Giuda* (1763), his first composition on his return to Mannheim. Leopold Mozart, visiting Schwetzingen with his children in the summer of that year, mentioned 'Mr. Ritschel, Vice-Kapellmeister' as one of the most notable personalities in musical life at the electoral court, and in a letter of 11 December 1777 held him up as an example to his son. But by that time Ritschel was already dead, and his place taken by Vogler.

Considering the barely five-year period between his return from Italy and his early death, Ritschel must be reckoned among the most prolific and gifted of the second generation of Mannheim composers. His output, consisting predominantly of sacred music, includes the oratorio *Gioas*, several masses and numerous other church works. Stylistically his music stands between the restraint of Padre Martini and the more operatic Neapolitan manner. Eduard Schmitt remarked that 'the large-scale psalm settings and masses place Ritschel . . . on a par with Holzbauer and Richter'. Some student works dating from his time in Italy are in manuscript in the Biblioteca Musicale G. B. Martini in Bologna, his later Mannheim compositions in the Sächsische Landesbibliothek in Dresden.

WORKS

Gioas re di Giuda, oratorio, Good Friday, 1763, Mannheim, *D-Dlb*
5 masses with orch: Messa concertata, 4vv; 3 for 4vv; Messa breve, 8vv: *Dlb*
Other sacred: Nunc dimittis, 4vv, str qt, bc, 23 Jan 1760, Credo concertato, 4vv, 2 hn, str qt, bc, 27 May 1760: autograph, *I-Bc*; Miserere, 4vv, orch, 1764, Miserere, 4vv, orch, org, 1766, Te Deum,

4vv, orch, org, Dixit Dominus (Ps cx), 4vv, orch, Invitatorio della Resurezione, 4vv, orch, 8 motets, 1v, orch: *D-Dlb*
Other works: Exercises, 2vv, 21 April 1758; 9 fugues a 4, 1759: autograph, *I-Bc*

(4) Georg (Wenzel) Ritschel (*b* Mannheim, baptized 15 Sept 1744; *d* Munich, 1 July 1805). Violinist and composer, son of (2) Franz Joseph Ritschel. According to Walter he was a violinist in the Mannheim orchestra from 1757, but his name is first recorded in the court calendar in 1760 as a supernumerary. He went with the court on its removal to Munich in 1778 (see Leopold Mozart's letter of 10 September 1778) and was still a member of the orchestra in 1803, when he was principal second violin.

Ritschel's first published work was a keyboard piece included in the collection *Six Easy Lessons ... Book I* (London, *c*1765), and some flute quintets are said to have been published in Paris in 1780. Other chamber works, written for the court, concertos for flute, oboe and harpsichord and ballet music for Munich also survive (in *D-Mbs, Rtt*), and Gerber mentioned a set of *VI airs variés* for flute and bass (Paris, 1793). But as a composer Georg Ritschel was overshadowed by his brother Johannes.

BIBLIOGRAPHY
GerberL; GerberNL
F. Walter: *Geschichte des Theaters und der Musik am kurpfälzischen Hofe* (Leipzig, 1898/R1968)
W. Senn: *Musik und Theater am Hofe zu Innsbruck* (Innsbruck, 1954)
E. Schmitt: *Die kurpfälzische Kirchenmusik im 18. Jahrhundert* (diss., U. of Heidelberg, 1958)
W. A. Bauer and O. E. Deutsch, eds.: *Mozart: Briefe und Aufzeichnungen* (Kassel, 1962–75)
R. Würtz: 'Die Musikerfamilie Ritschel', *Mannheimer Hefte*, ii (1968), 40

ROLAND WÜRTZ

Ritson Manuscript (*GB-Lbm* Add.5665). See SOURCES, MS, §IX, 4.

Ritter. German family of musicians, probably of Bohemian origin.

(1) Georg Wenzel Ritter (*b* Mannheim, 7 April 1748; *d* Berlin, 16 June 1808). Bassoonist and composer. He was a member of the Mannheim orchestra from 1764 to 1778, then, after the removal of the court, second bassoonist in Munich until September 1788. From 1778 he was also one of the select group of chamber musicians there. Mozart made his acquaintance during his stay in Mannheim in 1777 and met him again in Paris, where in April 1778 he wrote for him the bassoon part of the *Sinfonia concertante* kAnh.9/297*B* (letter of 5 April 1778). From October 1788 Ritter was a member of the court orchestra in Berlin.

The *Musikalische Real-Zeitung* (Speyer, 1788, no.13) described Ritter as one of the greatest virtuosos of his instrument, and particularly stressed the exceptional salary of 1600 thalers paid to him in Berlin. The Paris publisher Bailleux issued two bassoon concertos and six quartets for bassoon and strings op.1 by Ritter. His portrait was engraved in 1805 by F. W. Bollinger (examples in *A-Wn* and Coburg Castle collection of engravings).

(2) Peter Ritter (*b* Mannheim, 2 July 1763; *d* Mannheim, 1 Aug 1846). Cellist and composer, nephew of (1) Georg Wenzel Ritter. After studying composition with G. J. Vogler he obtained in December 1783 a life appointment as cellist in the orchestra of the Mannheim theatre, became its Konzertmeister in 1801 and on 3 November 1803 Kapellmeister of the orchestra of the Grand Duchy of Baden under the director of music Ignaz Fränzl. It was Ritter's duty to direct the operas, which at first he conducted from his raised cello desk. In 1809 he declined an invitation to take up the post of Kapellmeister to the court at Karlsruhe. Until his retirement in 1823 he carried out his duties at the National Theatre in Mannheim, interrupted only by a few concert tours. A tireless supporter of the musical life of the city, he became chairman of the newly founded Mannheim Society of Arts in 1833. He was married to Katharina Baumann, the Mannheim actress admired by Schiller.

As early as 1780 Ritter announced six string quartets in G. J. Vogler's *Musicalische Monatsschrift* (Mainz, Jg.iii). In 1788 he dedicated six string quartets to the King of Prussia, Friedrich Wilhelm II, for which he received the king's personal thanks and a gift, although in a concert at the Berlin court in 1785 he could not stand comparison as a cellist with the older Duport. Of his stage works the most successful was the Singspiel *Der Zitherschläger*, which was praised by Weber on its first performance in Mannheim on 1 April 1810: 'an original German opera ... which certainly need not yield to any French work of its kind'. Ritter's Singspiel *Die lustigen Weiber von Windsor* was apparently the first musical setting of the Shakespearean subject. His song *Grosser Gott wir loben dich* of 1792 is still one of the most popular of German hymns.

WORKS
STAGE
(first performed in Mannheim unless otherwise stated)

Der Eremit auf Formentara (comic opera, 2, A. von Kotzebue), National, 14 Dec 1788, *D-Bhm*
Der Sklavenhändler (Singspiel, 2, C. F. Schwan), National, 11 April 1790 (Mannheim, n.d.)
Die Weihe (prol, G. Römer), 1792, *DS*
Die lustigen Weiber von Windsor (Singspiel, 3, Römer, after Shakespeare), National, 4 Nov 1794
Dilara oder Die schwarze Zauberin (Singspiel, 2, C. Gozzi), 1798
Die Geisterburg (Singspiel, 2, F. Hochkirch), 1799
Der Sturm oder Die bezauberte Insel (Singspiel, 2, J. W. Döring, after Shakespeare: The Tempest), 1799
Die lustigen Musikanten (incidental music, C. Brentano), Frankfurt am Main, 1803
Das neue Jahr in Famagusta (Singspiel, 2, Brentano), 1804
Salomons Urteil (opera, 3, L. C. Caigniez), 1808, *DS*
Das Fest im Olymp (prol), 1808
Marie von Montalban (opera, 2, K. Reger), Frankfurt am Main, 1810
Der Zitherschläger (Singspiel, 1, C. I. Seidel), Stuttgart, 1810 (Bonn, n.d.)
Das Tal von Barzelonetta oder Die beiden Eremiten (Singspiel, 1), 1811, *B-Bc*, Opernarchiv, Munich
Feodore (Singspiel, 1, Kotzebue), 1811, *DS*
Alexander in Indien (opera, 2, Metastasio), 1811
Das Kind des Herkules (pantomime, 1), 1812
Alfred (opera, 3, Kotzebue), 1820
Der Mandarin oder Die gefoppten Chinesen (Singspiel, 1), Karlsruhe, 1821 (Mannheim, n.d.)
Hoang-Puff oder Das dreifache Horoskop (Singspiel, 1), 1822
Bianca (opera, 2, Grimm), 1824
Der Talisman (Singspiel, 1, trans. from Fr.), 1824
Das Grubenlicht (opera, 2, L. Beck), 1833
Die Alpenhirtin, mentioned in *EitnerQ*
Vergönnen Sie mir (quodlibet)

OTHER WORKS
Sacred: Das verlorene Paradies (after Milton), oratorio, Mannheim, 1819; Die Geburt Jesu, cantata, Mannheim, 1832; Hymnus ambrosianus, chorus, org, orch, 1792; numerous smaller works
Inst: Pf Conc., *MH*; Vc Conc.; Str Qt (Mannheim, 1780); 6 quatuors, bn obbl (Paris, *c*1786); qt, vn, va, bn, b, *A-Wgm*; 6 duos concertants, 2 vc, op.1 (Paris, *c*1790); 6 quatuors concertants, str qt, op.1 (Paris, *c*1801) [autograph, 1788, *D-Bds*]; 6 sonatas, vc, bc, *Bds* [for thematic catalogue of chamber music, see DTB, xxviii, Jg.xvi (1915)]

MSS in *US-Wc*

(3) Heinrich Ritter (*fl* 1779–93). Brother of (2) Peter Ritter. He was described by Gerber as a 'splendid virtuoso and soloist on the violin'. Vogler mentioned a concert given by the two brothers Peter and Heinrich in 1779. From 1793 Heinrich was deputy Konzertmeister to Karl Wendling in Mannheim.

Other members of the Ritter family were also musicians. Heinrich Adam Ritter (*d* c1777) was a bassoonist in Mannheim from 1747 to 1772, and Georg Wilhelm Ritter (described by Marpurg in 1756 as 'a Bohemian') an oboist and violinist there from 1756 to 1802. The two violinists Jakob Ritter (Mannheim 1759–83) and Friedrich Ludwig Ritter (Mannheim 1772–8, thereafter in Munich) were also in the service of the Elector Palatine Carl Theodor. Karl Ritter, the son of (2) Peter Ritter, had a successful career as a singer and from 1839 was producer at the Mannheim National Theatre.

BIBLIOGRAPHY

GerberL; GerberNL

G. J. Vogler: *Betrachtungen der Mannheimer Tonschule*, ii (Mannheim, 1779/R1974)

W. Schulze: *Peter Ritter* (Berlin, 1895)

F. Walter: *Geschichte des Theaters und der Musik am kurpfälzischen Hofe* (Leipzig, 1898/R1968)

G. Schmidt: *Peter Ritter* (diss., U. of Munich, 1924)

F. Walter: 'Vom Liebhaberkonzert zur musikalischen Akademie', *150 Jahre Musikalische Akademie des Mannheimer Nationaltheater-Orchesters* (Mannheim, 1929)

E. Anderson, ed.: *The Letters of Mozart and his Family* (London, 1938, 2/1966)

E. Schmitt: *Die kurpfälzische Kirchenmusik im 18. Jahrhundert* (diss., U. of Heidelberg, 1958)

M. J. Gilveath: *The Violoncello Concertos of Peter Ritter* (diss., U. of North Carolina, Chapel Hill, 1961)

R. Würtz: *Ignaz Fränzl* (diss., U. of Mainz, 1970)

ROLAND WÜRTZ

Ritter, Alexander [Sascha] (*b* Narva, Estonia, 7 June 1833; *d* Munich, 12 April 1896). German composer and violinist. After his father's death the family moved in 1841 to Dresden, where Alexander entered the Gymnasium and became a violin pupil of Franz Schubert, the second Konzertmeister of the court orchestra. He and his older brother Karl became friends with Bülow and began a long association with Liszt and with Wagner, who became acquainted with the family shortly before he fled from Dresden in 1849. In subsequent years Ritter's mother Julie not only corresponded frequently with Wagner but also gave him regular financial support. Karl was for some time Wagner's protégé as a young, ultimately unsuccessful conductor in Zurich. Between 1849 and 1851 Ritter studied with Ferdinand David at the Leipzig Conservatory; on returning to Dresden he occasionally played in the court orchestra but devoted most of his time to composing. On 12 September 1854 he married the talented actress Franziska Wagner, a niece of the composer, and that year he accepted Liszt's invitation to become second Konzertmeister in the Weimar orchestra. Two years later he went to Stettin as Konzertmeister and music director of the city theatre, leaving after two years to return to Dresden and in the autumn of 1860 moving to Schwerin where his wife was engaged as an actress. In 1863 both he and his wife were engaged by the theatre in Würzburg, where they remained for the next 19 years. As an attempt to bolster his seriously depleted financial resources he opened a music shop in 1875; seven years later he was able to leave Würzburg with his family when he received Bülow's invitation to become second Konzertmeister in the Meiningen court orchestra.

In Meiningen Ritter met the young Richard Strauss, whom he strongly influenced, encouraging him to grow beyond the conservative compositional style of his early years. Strauss credited Ritter with introducing him to the music of Wagner, Liszt and Berlioz, and the writings of Schopenhauer, and urging him to write symphonic poems; when Strauss was engaged in 1886 as third conductor for the Munich court opera he persuaded Ritter also to settle there. Later, Strauss conducted the successful première in Weimar of Ritter's *Wem der Krone?* (1890) on a double bill with an earlier opera, *Der faule Hans* (1885), both set to his own texts. Ritter's poem *Tod und Verklärung*, a development of Strauss's scenario, was published with the score of the symphonic poem. As Wagner's nephew by marriage, Ritter frequently joined the Bayreuth circle, even playing more than once in the festival orchestra. Besides the two operas, his compositions include some 60 lieder, several tone poems, choral works, a string quartet and a piano quintet.

BIBLIOGRAPHY

S. von Hausegger: 'Alexander Ritter: ein Bild seines Charakters und Schaffens', *Die Musik*, ed. R. Strauss (Berlin, 1907)

W. Schuh, ed.: *Richard Strauss: Betrachtungen und Erinnerungen* (Zurich, 1949, enlarged 2/1957)

GEORGE J. BUELOW

Ritter, Christian (*b* probably between 1645 and 1650; *d* after 1717). German composer and organist. The earliest source of information about him is a manuscript copy of a work that is clearly an autograph and bears both the date 1666 and the description of him as 'chamber organist at Hall. [i.e. Halle]'. To have held such a post he must have been at least about 20: hence his probable date of birth above. The pattern of his later life seems to indicate that he came from the group of Dresden musicians headed by Schütz and Christoph Bernhard. His presence at Halle is confirmed by documents only from 1672, when he was a court musician; later he also became court organist. From 1681 he is recorded as organist at the Swedish court at Stockholm and he was soon appointed vice-Kapellmeister as well; that he wrote music for the funeral of the Swedish minister J. A. Rehnskiöld, who died on 12 October 1680, suggests that he arrived in Stockholm before 1681. He soon left, however, to take up a position at Dresden as vice-Kapellmeister and court organist in 1683. From 1688 to 1699 he was again working in Stockholm, where he is described variously as vice-Kapellmeister and musician. In fact he was probably in charge of the Hofkapelle, the position of Kapellmeister being held first, until 1690, by Gustaf Düben (i) and then nominally after his death by his son Gustaf (ii). There is no mention of his being in Stockholm after 1699. He was in Hamburg in 1704 according to what is probably an autograph composition of that date. He participated, through a letter published by Mattheson in 1725, in a controversy that Mattheson initiated in 1717. In it he called himself 'emeritus', but Mattheson referred to him as 'acting Kapellmeister to the King of Sweden'. Whatever his status he was clearly still alive in 1717 and from what Mattheson said could have been so in 1725 too.

The manuscript sources of Ritter's surviving works are concentrated in north Germany and especially in the Düben Collection (at *S-Uu*). Although they certainly do not account for his total output, the preponderance of vocal works may well have been a feature of it, for he was first and foremost a Kapellmeister and worked only temporarily as an organist. One of the two keyboard suites, that in C minor, is a lamento similar to those of Froberger; the Sonatina in D minor is, despite its title, somewhat in the style of the north German organ toccata, though the contrasts within it are not so great. The vocal works embrace a wide range of forms – sacred concerto, concertato motet and the early type of cantata – and the forces for which they are scored are very varied too. Only a few have mixed biblical and free texts, and there is still a preference for arioso and song-like solo movements rather than for recitatives and da capo arias. They show that Ritter was not only a sensitive composer with a flexible approach to form but one who, through expressive power and the use of rich sonorities, achieved a distinctive voice. By thus breaking away from the traditions of the Schütz school he made an individual contribution to Protestant church music before Bach.

WORKS
17 motets, 1–5vv, 3–7 insts, bc, *S-Uu*
4 motets, 1–8vv, 3–15 insts, bc, *D-B*
1 motet, 4vv, 3 insts, bc, 1706, *Lr*; ed. in Organum, i/9 (Leipzig, 1925)
1 suite, f♯, kbd, *LEm*, ed. R. Buchmayer, Aus historischen Klavierkonzerten, v (Leipzig, 1927)
1 sonatina, d, org, *LEm*, ed. R. Buchmayer, Aus historischen Klavierkonzerten, v (Leipzig, 1927); Organum, iv/5 (Leipzig, 1925)
1 suite, c, kbd, 1697, *B*

For 2 lost works, mentioned in inventories of Thomaskirche, Leipzig, and Rudolstadt court chapel, see Schering and Baselt

BIBLIOGRAPHY
WaltherML
J. Mattheson: *Das beschützte Orchestre* (Hamburg, 1717)
——: *Critica musica*, ii (Hamburg, 1725/*R*1964)
M. Fürstenau: *Beiträge zur Geschichte der Königlich Sächsischen musikalischen Kapelle* (Dresden, 1849)
——: *Zur Geschichte der Musik und des Theaters am Hofe zu Dresden*, i (Dresden, 1861/*R*1971)
R. Buchmayer: 'Christian Ritter, ein vergessener deutscher Meister des 17. Jahrhunderts', *Riemann Festschrift* (Leipzig, 1909), 354
T. Norlind: 'Zur Biographie Christian Ritter's', *SIMG*, xii (1910–11), 94
A. Schering: 'Die alte Chorbibliothek der Thomasschule zu Leipzig', *AMw*, i (1918–19), 275
W. Serauky: *Musikgeschichte der Stadt Halle*, ii/1 (Halle and Berlin, 1939/*R*1970)
T. Norlind: *Från tyska kyrkans glansdagar: bilder ur svenska musikens historia* (Stockholm, 1945)
F. Welter: *Katalog der Musikalien der Ratsbücherei Lüneburg* (Lippstadt, 1950)
C.-A. Moberg: 'Drag i östersjöområdets musikliv på Buxtehudes tid' [Sketch of musical life in the Österjö area in Buxtehude's day], *STMf*, xxxix (1957), 15–88
B. Baselt: 'Die Musikaliensammlung der Schwarzburg-Rudolstädtischen Hofkapelle unter Ph. H. Erlebach', *Wissenschaftliche Zeitschrift der Martin-Luther-Universität Halle-Wittenberg*, suppl.: *Traditionen und Aufgaben* (1963), 105–34
F. Krummacher: *Die Überlieferung der Choralbearbeitungen in der frühen evangelischen Kantate* (Berlin, 1965)
B. Grusnick: 'Die Dübensammlung: ein Versuch ihrer chronologischen Ordnung', *STMf*, xlvi (1964), 27–82; xlviii (1966), 63–186
H. Kümmerling: *Katalog der Sammlung Bokemeyer* (Kassel, 1970)
FRIEDHELM KRUMMACHER

Ritter, Hermann (*b* Wismar, Mecklenburg, 16 Sept 1849; *d* Würzburg, 25 Jan 1926). German viola player. He studied music at the Hochschule in Berlin and art and history at Heidelberg University. The history of musical instruments attracted him, and profiting by some practical hints in A. Bagatella's *Regole perla costruzione di violini* (Padua, 1786), he devoted some time to constructing a large viola. This new instrument was an exact enlargement of a violin based on the same acoustical properties (the normal viola being a com-

promise). For this *viola alta*, as he called it, he claimed improved resonance and a more brilliant tone. The history of the viola shows that there have always been two schools of thought, one favouring the more popular smaller viola with its slightly veiled tone and characteristic nasal quality, and the other favouring the larger model (*see* TERTIS, LIONEL). Ritter's *viola alta* was exhibited in 1876; Wagner was interested and asked Ritter to cooperate at the Bayreuth Festival. By 1889 five of Ritter's pupils were in the Bayreuth orchestra playing the *viola alta*. Ritter toured extensively throughout Europe writing and arranging a great deal of music for his instrument. In 1879 he was appointed professor of the viola and history of music at the music school in Würzburg. In 1905 he founded the Ritter Quartet. The Grand Duke of Mecklenburg appointed him court chamber virtuoso, and Ludwig II of Bavaria made him court professor. His book, *Die Geschichte der Viola alta* (Leipzig, 1885), traces the history of the instrument, which subsequently lost favour, possibly because of its unwieldy size; it is no longer played.

BIBLIOGRAPHY
G. Adema: *Hermann Ritter und seine Viola alta* (Würzburg, 1881, 2/1890)
WATSON FORBES

Ritter, Johann Christoph (*b* 1715; *d* Clausthal, 25 Jan 1767). German organist and composer. A pupil of J. S. Bach, Ritter was from 1744 until his death the organist of the Marktkirche in Clausthal, an important mining centre in the Harz mountains with a lively and independent cultural life. Around 1740 he prepared a complete copy of Bach's *Clavier-Übung*, i–ii (BWV825–30, 971, 831), which contains numerous interesting deviations from the printed versions of 1731 and 1735; this is the only extant MS copy of these works dating from before Bach's death. Another copy of the same works, known in Bach scholarship as P215, is also in Ritter's hand, but it was not written until after 1755. Barthold Fritz, the Brunswick builder of keyboard instruments, frequently mentioned him in his treatise on keyboard tuning as the consignee of clavichords 'for commission', and Ritter's numerous petitions to the Clausthal council regarding the disrepair of the organ show a comprehensive knowledge of and great experience in organ building. His only extant compositions are a set of *Drey Sonaten, denen Liebhabern des Claviers verfertiget . . . erster Theil* (1751), dedicated to the superintendent of mines, G. P. von Bülow, and published by Haffner of Nuremberg. These works, always interesting and full of good ideas, represent a historically important stage in the development of the early pre-Classical keyboard sonata.

BIBLIOGRAPHY
B. Fritz: *Anweisung, wie man Claviere, Clavecins und Orgeln . . . gleich rein stimmen könne* (Leipzig, 2/1757)
E. R. Jacobi: 'Johann Christoph Ritter (1715–1767), ein unbekannter Schüler J. S. Bachs, und seine Abschrift (etwa 1740) der 'Clavier-Übung' I/II', *BJb*, li (1965), 43
——: Foreword to *J. C. Ritter: Drei Sonaten für Cembalo* (Leipzig, 1968)
ERWIN R. JACOBI

Ritter, Johann Nikolaus (*b* 26 March 1702; *d* Erlangen, 28 Feb 1782). German organ builder. He was apprenticed to Christian Müller of Amsterdam. He was working for J. G. Schröter in about 1730 (in Erfurt), and from about 1732 for Gottfried Silbermann in Freiburg, where he met Graichen (1701–60). In 1736 he and Graichen worked for T. H. G. Trost on the construction of the organ in Altenburg Castle, and in 1739 they both settled at Hof, and in 1741 were appointed official organ builders and instrument makers at the court of the Prince of Brandenburg-Culmbach. They remained in partnership until Graichen's death. Organ cases of theirs survive at Berg bei Hof (1744; two manuals, 16 stops), Trebgast (1748–9; two manuals, 19 stops) and Baiersdorf (1755; one manual, 13 stops). Ritter's organ at the Reformed Church (formerly the French Reformed Church), Erlangen (1764; one manual, 15 stops), survives intact. Ritter was the most important organ builder of his time in east Franconia. Like Schröter, he could convey an impression of grandeur even with his small organs, by a judicious choice of specification; but unlike him, he favoured Silbermann's wide-scaled $2\frac{2}{3}'$, $1\frac{3}{5}'$ and $1'$ stops, with rather fewer foundation stops. In one-manual organs he often designed the quint and tierce ranks to draw in two halves, bass and treble. In contrast to Silbermann's practice, he tuned his organs to equal temperament (following the example of J. A. J. Ludwig). The Silbermann tradition in Franconia, founded by Ritter and Graichen, was carried on by Ritter's best pupil Friedrich Heidenreich (1741–1819) and his son Eberhard Friedrich (c1770–1830).

BIBLIOGRAPHY

G. A. Sorge: *Gespräch zwischen einem Musico theoretico und einem Studioso Musices von der Praetorianischen, Printzischen, Werckmeisterischen, Neidhardtischen und Silbermannischen Temperatur* (Lobenstein, 1748)

J. U. Sponsel: *Orgelhistorie* (Nuremberg, 1771)

E. Flade: *Der Orgelbauer Gottfried Silbermann* (Leipzig, 1926, 2/1953), 150f, 208f

H. Hofner: 'Die Silbermannschule im Markgrafentum Bayreuth', *ZI*, liii (1953), 301, 315, 331, 348

F. Krautwurst: 'Ludwig, Johann Adam Jacob', *MGG*

H. Hofner: 'Aus der Geschichte der Orgeln in der Stadtkirche zu Bayreuth', *Die Orgeln der Stadtkirche zu Bayreuth*, ed. V. Lukas (Bayreuth, 1961)

F. Krautwurst: 'Ritter', *MGG*

H. Fischer: 'Die Beziehungen Mainfrankens zu andern Orgellandschaften', *Acta organologica*, iii (1969), 13

H. Hofner: 'Der ostfränkische Orgelbau', *Archiv für Geschichte von Oberfranken*, lii (1972), 5–116

HANS KLOTZ

Ritter, Sascha. *See* RITTER, ALEXANDER.

Rittler [Ridler], Philipp Jakob (*b* c1637; *d* Olomouc, buried 16 Feb 1690). German composer and violinist active in Austria and Czechoslovakia. He was active in various capacities at the Jesuit college in Opava about 1660. It seems that he knew Vejvanovský and possibly also Biber. He was a priest and was court chaplain to Archduke Eggenberg in Graz between 1669 and 1673. In 1675 he appeared at the court of the Bishop of Olomouc, Karl Liechtenstein-Kastelkorn, at Kroměříž with the title of chaplain. In 1679 he became honorary vicar of the Olomouc Chapter and at the same time was employed as cathedral conductor and owned, among other instruments, five violins (one made by Jakob Stainer). Evidently he was already composing when at Opava. Up to 1675 only instrumental works by him survive, after 1675 only vocal works. With a few exceptions his sonatas were intended for church use. He must have been an accomplished violinist, judging from the technically very demanding solo passages in his works: some aspects of these suggest that he had mastered scordatura technique. During his lifetime his works were widely known, as is proved by records in music inventories at Český Krumlov, Slaný, Tovačov and Seitenstetten.

WORKS

The inventory of Karl Liechtenstein-Kastelkorn's orchestra lists 63 works by Rittler. The following works survive in MS, *CS-KRa* [listed in A. Breitenbacher: *Hudební archiv kolegiátního Kostela sv. Mořice v Kroměříži* (Olomouc, 1928)]

6 masses; 1 requiem; 14 sacred works; 5 dance suites; 10 sonate da chiesa, 1 incorrectly attrib. P. Vejvanovský, ed. in MAB, xlviii (1961)

BIBLIOGRAPHY

A. Neumann: 'Příspěvky k dějinám hudby a zpěvu při olomoucké katedrále (1614–1780)' [Contributions to the history of music and singing at Olomouc Cathedral (1614–1780)], *Hlídka*, xiii (1939), 39

H. Federhofer: 'Biographische Beiträge zu Georg Muffat und Johann Joseph Fux', *Mf*, xiii (1960), 140

J. Sehnal: 'Hudebníci 17. století v matrikách kostela sv. Petra a Pavla v Olomouci' [17th-century musicians in registers at SS Petr a Pavel, Olomouc], *Zprávy Vlastiv. ústavu v Olomouci* (1965), no.123, p.9

——: 'Die Musikkapelle des Olmützer Bischofs Karl Liechtenstein-Castelcorn in Kremsier', *KJb*, li (1967), 112

——: 'Die Kompositionen Heinrich Bibers in Kremsier', *Sborník prací filosofické fakulty brněnské university*, H5 (1970), 22, 25, 37

JIŘÍ SEHNAL

Riuwental, Neidhart von. *See* NEIDHART VON REUENTAL.

Riva, Giulio (*fl* 1663–70). Italian physician, formerly thought to have been a composer. The revisers of Allacci attributed to him the opera *L'Adelaide Regia Principessa di Susa* (to a libretto by G. B. Rodoteo), performed at Munich on 31 October 1669 in celebration of the birthday of Duke Ferdinand Maria of Bavaria and given at Venice the following year by a group of amateurs at the Accademia ai Saloni; the opera is now known to be by GIULIO ROSSONI, but it is not impossible that Riva had a hand in its revision.

BIBLIOGRAPHY

F. Sansovino: *Venetia città nobilissima e singolare . . . con aggiunta . . . da . . . Giustinian Martinioni* (Venice, 1663)

L. Allacci: *Drammaturgia* (Venice, enlarged 2/1755/R1961)

E. Thiel and G. Rohr: *Kataloge der Herzog-August-Bibliothek Wolfenbüttel, xiv: Libretti, Verzeichnis der bis 1800 erschienenen Textbücher* (Frankfurt am Main, 1970), 5

LORENZO BIANCONI

Rivafrecha [Ribafrecha, Rivaflecha], Martín de (*d* Palencia, 24 June 1528). Spanish composer. At the time of his appointment as *maestro de capilla* of Palencia Cathedral (1 December 1503) he was already a priest at S Domingo de la Calzada. On 26 June 1521 he resigned in favour of Gómez de Portillo, who had been in charge of the choirboys since 1504. He then held a singer's prebend in Calahorra Cathedral until just before Christmas 1523, when he returned to Palencia. On 27 January 1525 he resumed his former post there at the cathedral with the added responsibility of bringing up and educating the choirboys. He was so inept at this last chore that within a month the chapter deposed him and reinstated Gómez de Portillo. The chapter responded to Rivafrecha's appeal by granting him the income from a prebend, and on 30 December 1526 permitted him to collect on behalf of Palencia Cathedral the 21,000 maravedís bequeathed by Bishop Juan Rodríguez de Fonseca to endow a *Salve regina* and a mass. After his death the chapter paid him homage as 'unique in both practical and theoretical music, extremely learned, ingenious and wise', and honoured him with interment in the Capilla de la Santa Cruz at Palencia. Cristóbal de Villalón in *Ingeniosa comparación* (Valladolid, 1539) ranked him second only to Francisco de Peñalosa among Spanish composers of their time.

WORKS

Anima mea liquefacta est, 4vv, E-Sco 5-5-20 (probably by Rivafrecha)
Benedicamus Domino, 4vv, TZ 4
Quam pulchra es, 4vv, Bc 454
Salve regina, 4vv, Sco, ed. in Elústiza and Castrillo Hernández
Vox dilecti mei, 4vv, Sco, ed. in Elústiza and Castrillo Hernández

BIBLIOGRAPHY

J. B. de Elústiza and G. Castrillo Hernández, eds.: Antología musical (Barcelona, 1933)
R. Stevenson: Spanish Music in the Age of Columbus (The Hague, 1960), 190ff

ROBERT STEVENSON

Rivander, Paul (b Lössnitz, nr. Meissen, c1570; d after 1621). German composer and musician. According to his own account he was a student of the liberal arts. From 1613 to 1615 he was a musician in the Brandenburg Hofkapelle at Ansbach. Before that he was probably in Austria, since in the preface to the second part of his Prati musici (1613) he stated that the lost first part was published in Austria. It is possible that he went to Ansbach in the retinue of the Austrian Emperor Matthias, who was crowned at Frankfurt in 1612. From 1615 on he lived at Nuremberg. His four extant volumes of songs and dances (1613–21) illuminate the transition at that period from the polyphonic ensemble song to the Baroque continuo song, which had already been heralded by increasingly prevalent homophonic textures. The last collection at least was intended for students. In the preface to the second part of the Prati musici – in which he announced a subsequent third part that, like the first, is unknown – he showed that he was an intelligent musician who consciously adopted simple, up-to-date textures determined by the text, which could as a result be clearly heard. He also pointed out that the melody of a song ought not to be determined by the expressive content of the first verse of the poem alone. In the pieces without words he showed comparable precision by using a system of signs invented by himself to indicate loud and soft passages. Small individual details of melody, rhythm and phrasing and certain expressive contrasts testify to his efforts to find a language of his own.

WORKS

Prati musici ander Theil, darinnen newe weltliche Gesäng . . . benebens etlichen Paduanen, Intraden, Courrenten und Täntzen, 3–5, 8vv, viols/other insts (Ansbach, 1613); 3 ed. in Vetter, ii
Newe lustige Couranten, 4 vn/other insts (Ansbach, 1614)
Ein newes Quodlibet, 4vv (Nuremberg, 1615; B pubd separately, 1614)
Studenten Frewd, darinnen weltliche Gesänge . . . beneben Paduanen, 3–8vv (Nuremberg, 1621)

BIBLIOGRAPHY

W. Vetter: Das frühdeutsche Lied (Münster, 1928)
G. Schmidt: Die Musik am Hofe der Markgrafen von Brandenburg-Ansbach vom ausgehenden Mittelalter bis 1806 (Kassel, 1956)

LINI HÜBSCH-PFLEGER

Rivier, Jean (b Villemomble, Seine, 21 July 1896). French composer. His musical studies were interrupted by World War I; he volunteered, and his health was irrevocably impaired by the effects of mustard gas. After a period of convalescence, he entered the Paris Conservatoire in 1922, his most important teacher being Caussade. A string quartet written in 1924 attracted notice, and in 1926 he left the Conservatoire with premier prix in counterpoint and fugue. He quickly became one of the most progressive younger composers of the inter-war period, taking a leading part in the Groupe du Triton (1936–40). After World War II he was appointed professor of composition at the Conservatoire, at first jointly with Milhaud, later alone (1962–6). During this period he was also at the ORTF.

Rivier's music is characterized by solid and strong construction as much as by profound and sincere expression. His works contain nothing of the superficially pleasing or sensational; but equally, while using established forms and techniques, he avoids academicism. The triumphant grandness of his structures arises from a lack of decorative development and a concentration on a small number of thematic ideas. Of his several concertante works, the most noteworthy are the Piano Concerto (1940) and the Concerto for Brass, Timpani and Strings (1963).

WORKS
(selective list)

ORCHESTRAL

Rapsodie, vc, orch, 1927; Chant funèbre, 1927; 3 pastorales, 1928; Danse du Tchad, after Gide, 1929; Ouverture pour un Don Quichotte, 1929; Burlesque, vn, orch, 1929; Ouverture pour une opérette imaginaire, 1930; Adagio, str, 1930; 5 mouvements brefs, 1931; Le voyage d'Urien, 1931; Sym., D, 1932; Concertino, va, orch, 1935
Musiques nocturnes, 1936; Paysages pour une Jeanne d'Arc à Domrémy, 1936; Sym. no.2, C, 1937; Sym. no.3, G, 1938; Pf Conc. no.1, C, 1940; Sym. no.4, B, str, 1941; Vn Conc., 1942; Ballade des amants désespérés, 1945; Divertissement style d'opérette, 1947; Rapsodie provençale, 1947; Légende magache, 1947; Sym. no.5, 1950
Ouverture pour un drame, 1952; Conc. brève, pf, str, 1953; Conc., sax, tpt, str, 1954; Conc., fl, str, 1955; Nocturne, C, 1956; Musiques pour un ballet, 1957; Le déjeuner sur l'herbe, 1957; Sym. no.6, 1958; Conc., cl, str, 1958; Sym. no.7, 1960; Drames, 1961; Conc., brass, timp, str, 1963; Conc., ob, str, 1968; Conc., tpt, str, 1971

CHORAL

Psaume LVI, S, chorus, orch, 1937; Heureux ceux qui sont morts (in memoriam M. Jaubert) (Péguy), 1944; Les prophéties, n.d.; La marche des rois, 1944; Les litanies, n.d.; Offrande à un ange, 1950; Requiem, Mez, B, chorus, orch, 1953; 5 Choruses (Ronsard, Du Bellay), 1954; 4 Choruses (Nerval), female chorus, 1954; Dolor, mixed chorus, orch, 1974

CHAMBER

Piece, D, db, pf, 1920; Str Qt no.1, 1924; Rapsodie, vc, pf, 1927; Burlesque, vn, pf, 1929; Little Suite, ob, cl, bn, 1934; Str Trio, 1935; Concertino, va, pf, 1935; Oiseaux tendres, fl, 1935; Sonatine, vn, vc, 1937; Grave et presto, sax qt, 1938; Str Qt no.2, F, 1940; Improvisation et final, ob, pf, 1943; Sonatine, fl, pf, n.d.; Espagnole, vn, pf, n.d.; Duo, fl, cl, 1968; Capriccio, ww qnt, 1970; Brillances, brass septet, 1970; 3 silhouettes, fl, pf, 1973; Etude, gui, 1974

PIANO

5 mouvements brefs, 1931; Printemps, Les bouffons, Jeux, Tumultes, 1937–8; Tornade, 1950; 3 pointes sèches, 1952; Le petit gondolier, n.d.; Pour des mains amies, 1950–55; Stridences, 1956; Nocturne, C, 1956; Torrents, 1956; 4 fantasmes, 1966; Sonata, 1969; Alternances, 1975

SONGS

8 poèmes (Apollinaire), 1925–6, orchd, 1934–5; 3 poèmes, 1929; 3 mélodies, 1929–30, orchd, n.d.; 2 poèmes (Apollinaire), 1934–5; 3 mélodies, 1944; 3 poèmes (Ronsard, C. Marot), 1945; 4 poèmes (R. Chalupt), 1949; 3 poèmes (P. Gilson), 1956; Doloroso è giocoso, A, pf, 1969; Prière, v, org/pf, 1976

DRAMATIC

Vénitienne (comic opera), 1, R. Kerdyk), 1936
Radio scores for Henri IV (A. Obey), 1937; Henri IV (Zimmer), 1941; Marche des rois (L. del Vasto), 1941; Louis XIV (A. Obey), 1945; Tambour (Calderon), 1945; Le joueur de triangle, 1946; La première surprise de l'amour, 1947; Ligne no.9 (P. Descaves), 1948

Principal publishers: Salabert, Transatlantiques, Sofirad, Noel

ANNE GIRARDOT

Rivière & Hawkes. See BOOSEY & HAWKES.

Rivista (It.). REVUE.

Rivolgimento (It.). The inversion of the parts in double counterpoint (see INVERTIBLE COUNTERPOINT).

Rivoli [Riwoli], Ludwika (Tekla) (b Łęczyca, 3 March 1814; d Warsaw, 16 Oct 1878). Polish soprano, daughter of the actor and singer Wacław Rivoli. She studied at the opera school of the Warsaw Wielki Theatre, making her début in 1829 as an actress. She made her Warsaw stage début on 4 August 1830 in the comedy *Asmodeuszek*, and then appeared at Kraków. In 1832 she sang at Lublin, apparently with great success, and in August 1834 at Warsaw, where she appeared as Zerlina in *Fra Diavolo* and Księżniczka in Kurpiński's *Czaromysl*. She also sang in *Il barbiere di Siviglia*, *Robert le diable*, *Zampa* and various Polish works, continuing to appear in Warsaw as singer and actress until 1851. She was said to possess a strong and flexible voice. Her sister was the singer Paulina Rivoli.

BIBLIOGRAPHY
SMP
S. Dąbrowski, ed.: *Słownik biograficzny teatru polskiego* (Warsaw, 1973)
ELIZABETH FORBES

Rivoli [Riwoli], Paulina (*b* Vilnius, 22 July 1823 or 1817; *d* Warsaw, 12 Oct 1881). Polish soprano. Born into a family of itinerant actors, she studied at the opera school of the Wielki Theatre in Warsaw; she made her début there on 17 June 1837 in *L'italiana in Algeri*. She performed with much success in *Les Huguenots*, *La juive* and in operas by Weber, Auber, Cimarosa and Moniuszko. She was in Italy in 1851, and in 1858 sang the title role in the Warsaw première of *Halka*. Her lyrical voice was noted for its beauty of timbre. She retired in 1860.

BIBLIOGRAPHY
SMP
A. Sowiński: *Słownik muzyków polskich dawnych i nowoczesnych* [Dictionary of Polish musicians past and present] (Paris, 1874)
IRENA PONIATOWSKA

Rivortorto, Il. Nickname of FRANCESCO MARIA ANGELI.

Rivotorto. *See* DEANGELIS, ANGELO.

Rivulo, Franziscus de (*fl* Danzig [now Gdańsk], 1560–66). Netherlands composer resident in Germany. From at least 1560 until 1566 he worked at St Marien, Danzig, as Kapellmeister, Kantor and singer. As a composer he is known by a number of unpretentious four-part chorale arrangements (in *PL-GD*) in the style of the circle of Wittenberg composers surrounding Luther, some contrapuntal Latin festival motets in *RISM* 1564¹ and 1564³⁻⁵ and a few manuscript motets (in *D-AAm*, *Bds*, *GMl*, *Rp*, *Z* and *PL-WRu*, according to Eitner).

BIBLIOGRAPHY
EitnerQ
H. Rauschning: *Geschichte der Musik und Musikpflege in Danzig* (Danzig, 1931)
DIETER HÄRTWIG

Rīzhkin, Iosif Yakovlevich (*b* Moscow, 7 July 1907). Soviet musicologist. In 1930 he graduated from the Moscow Conservatory, where he studied piano with Alexander Gedike and music theory with Mikhail Gnesin and Nikolay Zhilyayev. He taught theory and music history at the conservatory from 1930 to 1944. In 1935 he was appointed senior lecturer, in 1940 professor, and from 1941 to 1944 he was dean of the faculty of history and theory. He was a professor at the Institute for Military Conductors (1944–9), and from 1966 taught at the State Institute of Culture in Moscow. He has worked at a number of research institutions, notably at the Institute for the History of the Arts, Moscow, where from 1948 to 1966 he was a senior

research fellow. At different times he has been an editor and consultant for music broadcasting. Rīzhkin's principal works are devoted to questions of musical aesthetics and theoretical musicology.

WRITINGS
with L. A. Mazel': *Ocherki po istorii teoreticheskovo muzĭkoznaniya* [Essays on the history of theoretical musicology] (Moscow, 1934–9)
'O natsional'nom voprose v istorii zapadno-evropeyskoy muzĭki' [The question of nationality in the history of west European music], *SovM* (1937), no.4, p.69
Betkhoven i klassicheskiy simfonizm [Beethoven and the Classical symphony] (Moscow, 1938)
'Ocherk o garmonii' [An essay on harmony], *SovM* (1940), no.3, p.47
'Vzaimootnosheniya obrazov v muzĭkal'nom proizvedenii i klassifikatsiya tak nazivayemĭkh muzĭkal'nĭkh form' [The interrelation of forms in musical composition and the classification of these so-called musical forms], *Voprosĭ muzĭkoznaniya*, ii, ed. A. S. Ogolevets and others (Moscow, 1955)
'Stil' i realizm' [Style and realism], *Voprosĭ estetiki*, i, ed. Institut Istorii Iskusstv, Moscow (Moscow, 1958)
'Val's-fantaziya Glinki' [Glinka's Valse-Fantaisie]; 'Ispanskiye uvertyurĭ Glinki' [Glinka's Spanish overtures], *Pamyati Glinki 1857–1957: issledovaniya i materialĭ*, ed. E. Gordeyeva (Moscow, 1958)
'Faustus XX veka i nepravĭy put' modernizma' [The 20th-century Faustus and the misguided path of modernism], *SovM* (1959), no.9, p.167
'M. F. Gnesin – chelovek, obshchestvennĭy deyatel, uchitel' [M. F. Gnesin: the man, public figure and teacher], *M. F. Gnesin: stat'i, vospominaniya, materialĭ*, ed. R. V. Glezer (Moscow, 1961)
'Sovremennaya muzĭka i gumanicheskiy ideal' [Contemporary music and the humanistic ideal], *Voprosĭ estetiki*, v, ed. Institut Istorii Iskusstv, Moscow (Moscow, 1962)
Naznacheniye muzĭki i eyo vozmozhnosti [The purpose and resources of music] (Moscow, 1962)
'Obraznaya kompozitsiya muzĭkal'novo proizvedeniya' [The formal composition of music], *Intonatsiya i muzĭkal'nĭy obraz*, ed. B. M. Yarustovsky (Moscow, 1965)
'Stanovleniye sovetskoy muzĭkal'noy estetiki' [The formation of the Soviet musical aesthetic], *Iz istorii sovetskoy esteticheskoy mĭsli*, ed. L. Denisov (Moscow, 1967)
'Sovetskoye teoreticheskoye muzĭkoznaniye: ocherk istoricheskovo razvitiya' [Soviet theoretical musicology: an essay on its historical development], *Voprosĭ teorii i istorii muzĭki*, vi–vii (Leningrad, 1968)
'Syuzhetnaya dramaturgiya betkhovenskovo simfonizma: pyataya i devyataya simfonii' [Beethoven's programmatic symphonies: the Fifth and Ninth], *Betkhoven: sbornik statey*, ii (Moscow, 1972)
YURY KELDĪSH

Rizza, Gilda dalla. *See* DALLA RIZZA, GILDA.

Rizzio [Riccio], David (*b* c1525; *d* Edinburgh, 9 March 1566). Italian musician. He is more important for his involvement in politics than for any musical achievement. From Piedmont he went to Scotland in 1561 in the service of the ambassador of Savoy, and there joined the court as bass singer and *valet de chambre* to Mary Queen of Scots. A Catholic, he rapidly rose in favour as Mary's confidant, and in 1564 was appointed her French secretary to the bitter resentment of the Scottish Protestant councillors. The more extreme of these under Lord Ruthven brutally murdered him in the queen's presence, an act that was to prove the tragic turning-point in Mary's career.

In the 18th century Rizzio acquired something of a reputation as a composer of Scots songs. This curious and groundless fiction seems to have started in William Thomson's *Orpheus Caledonius* (1725). The songs ascribed to Rizzio are all native airs and though some, like *An thou were my my ain thing*, can be traced back to the earliest (early 17th-century) surviving sources of Scots folk music, it is much more likely that Rizzio simply sang part-music of an international style, of which there was no lack at Mary's court. Thomson may have used Rizzio's name out of ignorance or for the sake of some sensational publicity.

BIBLIOGRAPHY
A. Fraser: *Mary Queen of Scots* (London, 1969)
I. B. Cowan: *The Enigma of Mary Stuart* (London, 1971)
KENNETH ELLIOTT

Rizzo, Giovanni Battista. *See* RICCIO, GIOVANNI BATTISTA.

RMA. *See* ROYAL MUSICAL ASSOCIATION.

Roach, Max [Maxwell] (*b* Brooklyn, NY, 10 Jan 1925). Black American jazz drummer and composer. He was associated with Charlie Parker from 1942, and participated in the early developments of the 'bop' school at Minton's club, New York. Influenced by the drummer Kenny Clarke, he was particularly important in establishing the practice of setting the fixed pulse in the ride cymbal instead of the bass drum, enabling a more flexible use of the other parts of the drum set and thereby a more polyrhythmic percussive texture. Roach's adept exploitation of timbral resources and his practice of carefully developing thematic ideas in his improvisations established him as one of the most outstanding and sought-after jazz drummers of his time. He played and recorded frequently with New York bop ensembles in the 1940s, particularly Parker's quintet (1947–9), and took part in Miles Davis's *Birth of the Cool* recordings (1948–9). In 1953 he formed his own quartet, and from 1954 to 1956 jointly led an important quintet with the trumpeter Clifford Brown, producing a number of seminal recordings. In the 1960s Roach composed several works for soloists, chorus and jazz ensemble, among them *Freedom Now Suite* (1960) with Oscar Brown jr. He has also written Broadway musicals and film scores, and has continued, with such recordings as *Drums Unlimited* (1966), to perform small-group jazz. He was married to the jazz singer Abbey Lincoln.

BIBLIOGRAPHY
I. Gitler: *Jazz Masters of the 40s* (New York, 1966), 183ff
J. Cooke: 'Max Roach', *Jazz on Record*, ed. A. McCarthy (London, 1968), 244
OLLY WILSON

Robb, John Donald (*b* Minneapolis, 12 June 1892). American composer. He was educated at Yale, Minneapolis and Harvard, and practised law until 1941, when he moved from New York to Albuquerque as professor and head of the music department at the University of New Mexico, from which posts he retired in 1957. His music studies have included work under Horatio Parker, Nadia Boulanger, Harris, Hindemith and Milhaud. A prolific composer, his works include an opera (*Little Jo*, 1947–9), three symphonies, other orchestral and chamber music, numerous songs, and electronic pieces. He is also a collector of folk music and has published *Hispanic Folk Songs of New Mexico* (Albuquerque, 1954/*R*1978) and *Hispanic Folk Music of New Mexico and the Southwest* (Norman, Oklahoma, 1980).

Robbins Landon, H(oward) C(handler). *See* LANDON, H. C. ROBBINS.

Robbio di San Rafaele. *See* SAN RAFAELE, BENVENUTO ROBBIO.

Roberday, François (*b* Paris, baptized 21 March 1624; *d* Auffargis, now in Seine-et-Oise, 13 Oct 1680). French composer and organist. Like his father he was a royal goldsmith. In 1659 he bought a privilege of 'Valet de chambre de la Reine', serving successively Anne of Austria, mother of Louis XIV, and Queen Marie-Thérèse. After a few years of affluence his fortunes were reversed and he was forced to retire, bankrupt, to Auffargis, where he died in an epidemic. It seems highly unlikely that he was organist to the order of Petits-Pères, as is suggested in *FétisB*. The possibility that he was one of Lully's teachers has not been clearly proved either.

Roberday's only extant work is the *Fugues, et caprices, à quatre parties* (Paris, 1660; ed. J. Ferrard, Le Pupitre, xliv, 1972). In his 'Avertissement' he mentioned the musicians who gave him the themes for the fugues: La Barre (?Pierre [iii]), Couperin (presumably Louis), Cambert, D'Anglebert (his brother-in-law), Froberger, Bertali and Cavalli. Three pieces are mere copies of works by Frescobaldi, Ebner and Froberger; until now only the fifth capriccio has been identified, as Froberger's Ricercar no.7. The music is in four parts. Seven of the nine fugues are followed by a capriccio, and each pair is linked by thematic unity. The rhythmic variations of the subjects, typical of Frescobaldi and Froberger, and the writing of the music in score denote a strong Italian influence. Indeed an Italian sense of rhythm and freedom, allied with a solid contrapuntal technique inherited from Titelouze, characterizes Roberday's most valuable music.

BIBLIOGRAPHY
P. Hardouin: 'François Roberday', *RdM*, xlvi (1960), 44
JEAN FERRARD

Robert, Frédéric [Wurmser, Frédéric Robert Léopold] (*b* Paris, 22 Feb 1932). French teacher and musicologist. He studied under Dufourcq at the Paris Conservatoire (1952–8), where he won a *premier prix* in music history (1955) and a *second prix* in musicology (1958). He began to produce radio broadcasts in 1951; from 1953 he worked for several non-specialist journals (*Lettres françaises*, *Europe*) and encyclopedias such as the *Larousse de la musique* (1957), *MGG* and the *Encyclopédie des musiques sacrées*. In 1966 he became professor of music history at the Montreuil, Drancy and Ivry conservatories.

He devoted his diploma in musicology to the *airs* in the periodical published by Ballard, *Recueil d'airs sérieux et à boire de différents auteurs* (1694–1724). His interests extend also to music for wind band (especially that of the French Revolution), and to two members of Les Six, Louis Durey and Germaine Tailleferre. His research has uncovered several little-known aspects of French music.

WRITINGS

Airs sérieux et airs à boire (diss., Paris Conservatoire, 1958)
'Une découverte musicologique: 3 quatuors op.7 de Marie-Alexandre Guénin (1744–1835)', *RMFC*, i (1960), 145
'La musique à travers le "Mercure galant" (1678)', *RMFC*, ii (1961–2), 173
La musique française au XIXe siècle (Paris, 1963, 2/1970)
'Scanderberg, le héros national albanais dans un opéra de Rebel et Francoeur', *RMFC*, iii (1963), 171
Georges Bizet: l'homme et son oeuvre (Paris, 1965)
'La musique française du classicisme au romantisme', *La musique, les hommes, les instruments, les oeuvres*, ii, ed. N. Dufourcq (Paris, 1965), 46
Louis Durey, l'aîné des 'Six' (Paris, 1968)
with D. Dondeyne: *Nouveau traité d'orchestration à l'usage des harmonies, fanfares et musiques militaires* (Paris, 1969)
Emmanuel Chabrier (Paris, 1970)
ed.: R. Dumesnil: *L'opéra et l'opéra comique* (Paris, 1971)
ed.: H. Berlioz: *Correspondance générale*, ii [1832–42] (Paris, 1975)

Germaine Tailleferre (in preparation)
La Marseillaise (in preparation)
EDITION
Airs sérieux et à boire à 2 et 3 voix [1694–1724] (Paris, 1968)
CHRISTIANE SPIETH-WEISSENBACHER

Robert, Pierre (*b* Louvres, nr. Paris, *c*1618; *d* Paris, buried at St Nicolas-des-Champs, 30 Dec 1699). French composer and ecclesiastic. Robert was trained at the Notre Dame choir school in Paris. No evidence supports Fétis's contention that he sang at Noyon Cathedral and, after 1637, at St Germain l'Auxerrois, Paris. In 1648 he was appointed *maître de chapelle* at Senlis Cathedral. From 1650 to 1652 he served in the same capacity at Chartres. On 28 April 1653 he returned to Notre Dame for ten years' service as *maître de chapelle*. In 1663 Louis XIV appointed four *sous-maîtres* for his royal chapel, each to serve for one quarter; Robert was assigned the quarter beginning in April. In 1669 Gobert and Expilly retired; Robert and Du Mont then divided the year between them, Robert taking the July and October quarters. Robert, along with Du Mont, was made *Compositeur de la musique de la chapelle et de la chambre du roi* after Gobert's death in 1672. He resigned from the royal chapel in 1683, receiving in December of that year a pension of 1500 livres. He left the king's service the next year. According to Fétis, Robert was ordained a priest as early as 1637. In 1671 he became abbot of Chambon in the diocese of Poitiers and in 1678 of St Pierre-de-Melun, positions that he retained until his death.

No secular music by Robert survives, although he spent 17 years as a musician attached to the king's chamber. His major contribution is the collection of *Motets pour la chapelle du Roy*. These 24 *grands motets*, printed 'by the express order of His Majesty', differ little in outward appearance from those of Lully and Du Mont. Both the *grand choeur* and orchestra have the five-part texture typical of the period in France. It is only in the *petit choeur* with its 'ensembles de récits' that the individuality of the composer is expressed. Choosing from eight possible solo voices, Robert contrasts sonorities by rapid and occasionally arbitrary alternation of vocal timbres.

In his *petits motets* Robert was more sensitive to the expressive power of dissonance and modulation: for example, the Italianate dialogue that closes *O flamma* with textual repetitions, melodic sequences and chromaticism is far removed from the often stiff *récits* of the *grands motets*.

WORKS
Motets pour la chapelle du Roy, 5, 6vv, bc (Paris, 1684), also quintet for vns; 2 ed. H. Charnassé (Paris, 1969) [incl. important preface]
10 pieces, 2–4vv, in Petits motets and Elévations de MM. Carissimi, de Lully, Robert, Daniélis et Foggia, *F-Pn* Vm.6 (dated 1688)
1 motet, Memorare dulcissime Jesu, 3vv, bc, in Motets de différens autheurs, *Pn* Vm.I.1175 bis
Splendor aeternae gloriae, 2vv, bc, *Pn* Vm.I.1176

BIBLIOGRAPHY
FétisB
P.-M. Masson: 'Le motet "Splendor aeternae gloriae" de Pierre Robert', *Musique et liturgie*, xxi (1938), 57
N. Dufourcq: 'Un document iconographique, le portrait présumé de Pierre Robert', *RdM*, xxxix (1957), 95
H. Charnassé: 'Contribution à l'étude du récitatif chez l'Abbé Pierre Robert', *RMFC*, i (1960), 61
——: 'Quelques aspects des "Ensembles de récits" chez l'Abbé Pierre Robert', *RMFC*, ii (1961–2), 61
D. Launay: 'Robert, Pierre', *MGG*

H. Charnassé: 'Contribution à l'étude des grands motets de Pierre Robert', *RMFC*, iii (1963), 49; iv (1964), 105
J. Anthony: *French Baroque Music from Beaujoyeulx to Rameau* (London, 1973, rev. 2/1978)
JAMES R. ANTHONY

Robert ap Huw. *See* AP HUW, ROBERT.

Robert de Blois. French trouvère poet, composer and author who was active in the 13th century. The five songs attributed to him in musical sources represent a minor aspect of his literary output, which includes a long narrative poem *Floris et Liriopé* based on Ovid, and the *Enseignements des dames*, a manual of instruction for noble ladies. Although he is known only through his works, one poem which has been attributed to him, *Li departis de douce contree*, refers to an abortive crusade of the year 1239. All of his songs are in the very common bar form, and two survive with more than one melody. While his larger works appear to have been well known, the songs are found in a very limited group of sources and none seems to have been imitated by other trouvères.

WORKS
Merveil moi que chanter puis, R.2077
Par trop celer mon courage, R.17
Puisque me sui de chanter entremis, R.1530
DOUBTFUL WORKS
Li departis de douce contree, R.499 (several melodies)
Tant com je fusse fors de ma contree, R.502 (several melodies)
BIBLIOGRAPHY
J. Ulrich: *Robert von Blois: Sämtliche Werke*, ii (Berlin, 1891)
G. Gröber: *Grundriss der romanischen Philologie*, ii/1 (Strasbourg, 1902), 832ff
For further bibliography *see* TROUBADOURS, TROUVÈRES.
ROBERT FALCK

Robert de Castel [du Chastel] (*fl* late 13th century). French trouvère poet and composer. He was one of a large group of trouvère poet-composers active around Arras in northern France in the late 13th century. The only datable reference to him is in the *Congés* of Baude Fastoul, written in 1272. He is addressed in the jeu-parti *Robert du Chastel, biaus sire* (R.1505) by Jehan Bretel (*d* 1272), a trouvère of Arras. Of the six songs attributed to Robert, only two seem to have enjoyed a wider popularity. *En loial amour* is designated as 'coronée' in one source, and *Se j'ai chanté* not only survives in a large number of sources, but was itself 'coronée' in the lost Chansonnier des Memses; it subsequently inspired a French religious contrafactum.

WORKS
Amours me mont me guerroie, R.1722
Bien ait l'amours qui m'a doné l'usage, R.43
En loial amour ai mis, R.1568
Nus fins amans ne se doit esmaier, R.1277
Pour ce se j'ain et je ne sui amés, R.913
Se j'ai chanté sans guerredon avoir, R.1789 [contrafactum: Anon., 'La volontés dont mes cuers est ravis', R.1607]
BIBLIOGRAPHY
J. Melander: 'Les poésies de Robert de Castel', *Studia neophilologica*, iii (1930), 17
For further bibliography *see* TROUBADOURS, TROUVÈRES.
ROBERT FALCK

Robert de Handlo (*fl* early 14th century). English music theorist. He may be connected with the De Handlo family, which took its name from the manor of Handlo (now Hadlow), near Tonbridge, Kent; this family produced a number of distinguished men in the 13th and 14th centuries, the most notable being Sir John de Handlo (*d* 1344). Robert de Handlo's one extant work

Regule cum maximis Magistri Franconis cum addition-ibus aliorum musicorum compilate a Roberto de Handlo (*CS*, i, 383–403) survives only in an excellent 18th-century transcription made for J. C. Pepusch from a manuscript (now *GB-Lbm* Cotton Tiberius B.IX) which soon afterwards was almost completely destroyed by a fire in Ashburnham House on 23 October 1731. Sir John Hawkins, who later owned the copy, presented it to the British Museum (*GB-Lbm* 4090). Handlo's *scholia* enjoyed a wide influence for almost three centuries after its compilation, for it formed the basis of John Hanboys's treatise about a century later (*CS*, i, 403). Moreover, he was mentioned by name in Thomas Morley's *A Plaine and Easie Introduction to Practicall Musicke* (1597), where there is also a citation of one of his interlocutors, Jacobus de Navernia.

According to its *explicit*, the treatise was completed in 1326, probably in England. It is entirely practical, using a clear didactic method of maxims and rules issuing from Handlo himself, as well as from Franco and the 'other musicians' of the title: Petrus de Cruce, Petrus Le Viser, Johannes de Garlandia, Admetus de Aureliana and Jacobus de Navernia. The author of each maxim and rule is identified at the beginning of each quotation, from which it is apparent that Franco of Cologne is the most frequently cited, although not directly, for his statements are mostly taken verbatim from the various compendia made from his teachings by Johannes Balox, and two anonymous authors (*CS*, i, 292; Anonymous II, 303; Anonymous III, 319). The treatise consists of 13 rubrics, each of which contains several rules with maxims, although they are not always clearly identified as such. The rules state specific principles and are always accompanied by music examples, whereas the maxims explicate, or add qualifications to, the rules, and sometimes give valuable information about performing practice not covered in the main rules; they do not have music examples.

In rubrics I–V the authors explained the single notes of mensural music, the most interesting aspects of which include a definition of the *longa erecta* and discussion of its performance, the use of points of division and the proportional division of semibreves in various combinations. In this last discussion Petrus Le Viser (*fl* c1290) stated three manners of performance: in *more longo*, semibreves are used in the Franconian manner among notes of longer note values; in *more mediocri*, two to five semibreves replace a breve and the point of division is implied as used by Petrus de Cruce; in *more lascivo*, either two unequal semibreves per breve may occur independently among other note values, or the pieces may be notated only in breves and semibreves, three of which may replace a breve. In this 'manner' duple rhythm is possible. Lastly, there is Johannes de Garlandia's (*fl* c1300) use of four different semibreves: *major* and *minorata*, which use the same sign (ex.1*a*), and *minor* and *minima*, which also use the same sign (ex.1*b*). A breve contains three *semibreves minores*, or one *semibrevis major* and one *semibrevis minor*; a *semibrevis minor* contains three *minimae*, or one *minorata* and one *minima*. The special sign shown in ex.1*c* (*signum rotundum*) is used as a point of division to distinguish *minoratae* and *minimae* from *semibreves majores* and *minores*, which use the normal dot of division.

Ex.1

(a) ♪   (b) ♦   (c) ○

In rubrics VI–VIII Handlo dealt with ligatures, following Franco's system, with one or two new forms, and in rubric IX he discussed the conjunction of semibreves with other semibreves and with ligatures. Here Admetus de Aureliana spoke of the practice of musicians in Navarre. In rubrics X–XI Handlo explained plicated ligatures and also granted the possibility of *conjuncturae* comprising runs of *semibreves minores* with an ascending *plica*. It is noteworthy that Handlo assigned the smaller portion of the division of a plicated note to the subsidiary note and the larger value to the main note. In rubric XII the six rests were explained according to Franco's system, including the immeasurable or final rest marking the end of a section. A small but important discussion of hockets by Jacobus de Navernia and Johannes de Garlandia concludes this section. The final rubric gives an account of Franco's system of five rhythmic modes, with the 1st mode in two divisions (conventional 1st and 5th modes). Each mode is illustrated by examples drawn from the contemporary motet repertory. Three motets cited are known only in this source and two others are known only by these and other theoretical citations. In the 3rd and 4th modes binary rhythm may be used. Handlo listed many types of composition which besides motets may use the 5th mode (conventional 6th mode), namely that mode which consists of faster note values: hockets, rondeaux, ballades, *coreae, cantifractus, estampies* and *floriturae* – a selection of secular songs and instrumental compositions that recalls that of Johannes de Grocheo. Certainly, Handlo must have been familiar with a wide range of sacred, secular and instrumental music.

Owing to Handlo's great reliance on Franco's teachings and his quotations from other sources, it is very difficult to identify his original contribution to theoretical codification, and how much of the theory given under his own name represents specific English musical practice at the turn of the 13th century. Possibly the three unica motet citations – one of them an adaptation of a hymn to St Magnus – represent compositions of English origin, while certain manuscripts (e.g. the Worcester and Westminster fragments) show many notational features parallel to those presented in his treatise. If Handlo did not contribute much that is original, he did give as a positive achievement a synoptic history of notation in the decisive period when the prolation of the semibreve was being formed, showing the development from Franconian notation to that of his own time and with his own peculiar English emphasis. His theoretical view was the last to embrace the theory of the rhythmic modes while they still continued to be a structural basis of contemporary polyphonic music.

BIBLIOGRAPHY

J. F. R. Stainer: 'Handlo, Robert de', *Grove 2*

H. Riemann: *Geschichte der Musiktheorie im IX.–XIX. Jahrhundert* (Berlin, 2/1920), 174, 213, 224; (Eng. trans., 1962)

H. Davey: *History of English Music* (London, 2/1921/*R*1969), 33

M. F. Bukofzer: Letter, *ML*, xxi (1940), 202

R. A. Harman, ed.: *Thomas Morley: A Plaine and Easie Introduction to Practicall Musicke* (London, 1952, 2/1963), 108, 112, 116

——: 'Handlo, Robert de', *MGG*

G. Reese: *Four Score Classics of Music Literature* (New York, 1957), 26

L. A. Dittmer, ed.: *Robert de Handlo: Rules*, Musical Theorists in Translation, ii (Brooklyn, 1959)

E. H. Sanders: 'Duple Rhythm and Alternate Third Mode in the 13th Century', *JAMS*, xv (1962), 249

GORDON A. ANDERSON

Robert de la Piere (*d* Arras, 1258). French trouvère

poet and composer. He was a member of a prominent bourgeois family of Arras whose earliest member is documented in the year 1212. Robert himself appears twice in archival documents: as a municipal magistrate (1255) and in his obituary (spring, 1258). In the jeux-partis which bear his name he debated with Jehan Bretel, Mahieu de Gant and Lambert Ferri among others, all of whom were mid- or late 13th-century poets from the north of France.

The nine songs and five jeux-partis attributed to him appear in a small number of northern French sources and seem not to have been particularly well-known. Only *Hé, Amours, je fui nouris* was recorded in a wider variety of sources and inspired two French contrafacta, one of them a Marian song. This song and *Joliement doi chanter* are both more often attributed to Gillebert de Berneville in their MSS. The remaining songs employ some variety of bar form with considerable freedom in the Abgesang section. Their melodies follow the same pattern, with a repeated two-part element at the beginning and a through-composed Abgesang.

WORKS

Cele que j'ain veut que je chant por li, R.1053
Chopart, uns clers que se veut marier, R.871 (jeu-parti)
C'il qui m'ont repris, R.1612
Contre le dous tens de mai, R.92
De ce, Robert de la Piere, R.1331 (jeu-parti)
Grieviler, un jugement, R.693 (jeu-parti)
J'ai chante mout liement, R.698
Je chantai de ma doulour, R.1976
Je ne cuidai mais chanter, R.823
Mahieu de Gant, respondés, A ce, R.945 (jeu-parti)
Mahieu de Gant, respondés, A moi, R.946 (jeu-parti)
Par maintes foi ai chanté liement, R.696

DOUBTFUL WORKS

Hé, Amours, je fui nouris, R.1573 [model for: Anon., 'Aucun gent m'out blasmé', R.405a; Anon., 'Mout sera cil bien mouris', R.1570; also attrib. Gillebert de Berneville]
Joliement doi chanter, R.803, Adler, i, 164 [also attrib. Gillebert de Berneville]

BIBLIOGRAPHY

G. Adler: *Handbuch der Musikgeschichte*, i (Berlin, 2/1930/R1961), 164
F. Gennrich: 'Robert de la Piere', *MGG*

For further bibliography *see* TROUBADOURS, TROUVÈRES.

ROBERT FALCK

Robert de Reins [Rains] **La Chievre.** French trouvère poet and composer from the Ile de France who was probably active in the 13th century. He may have been a member of the family called 'La Chievre' which is documented in Rheims in the 13th and 14th centuries. A 'Chievre de Reins' who may be identifiable with Robert is mentioned in the *Roman de Renart*, where a Tristan poem is attributed to him. Wilhelm Mann concluded from this that he was active before 1300, but others have maintained on linguistic grounds that his poems must be later. Of the nine works attributed to him, *Main s'est levée Aelis*, *Quant feuillisent li buisson* and *Quant voi le dous tens venir* are motets and *L'autrier de jouste un rivage* is constructed like a motet, although no tenor is extant. He is one of a very exclusive group of trouvères, including Richart de Fournival, who are associated with the early motet.

WORKS

CHANSONS

Bergier [= Tous] de vile champestre, R.957
Bien s'est amours honie, R.1163
Jamais pour tant con l'ame il cors me bate, R.383
Plaindre m'estuet de la bele en chantant, R.319
Qui bien veut amours descrive, R.1655
Tous [= Bergier] de vile champestre, R.957

MOTETS

L'autrier de jouste un rivage, R.35 (?motet)
Main s'est levée Aelis, 2vv, R.1510
Quant feuillisent li buisson, 2vv, R.1852
Quant voi le dous tens venir/En moi, quant rose est florie, 3vv, R.1485

BIBLIOGRAPHY

W. Mann: 'Die Lieder des Dichters Robert de Rains genannt La Chievre', *Zeitschrift für romanische Philologie*, xxiii (1899), 79–116
F. Gennrich: 'Trouvèrelieder und Motettenrepertoire', *ZMw*, ix (1926–7), 31, 34, 39
——, ed.: *Troubadours, Trouvères, Minnesang und Meistergesang*, Mw, ii (1951; Eng. trans., 1960), 37

For further bibliography *see* TROUBADOURS, TROUVÈRES.

ROBERT FALCK

Robert du Chastel. *See* ROBERT DE CASTEL.

Roberti, Girolamo Frigimelica. *See* FRIGIMELICA ROBERTI, GIROLAMO.

Roberti, Giulio (*b* Barge, Saluzzo, 14 Nov 1829; *d* Turin, 14 Feb 1891). Italian composer and teacher. Although he began as a lawyer, he studied music privately with Luigi Felice Rossi and soon turned to composition as a career. His first opera, *Piero de Medici* (1849), had some success, his second, *Petrarca alla corte d'amore* (1859), none. He wrote no more operas, concentrating on chamber, piano, sacred music and songs (which were considered of greater value than his theatrical pieces), as well as didactic and historical writings. In 1866 he settled in Florence as a singing teacher, founding a free singing school for the pupils of the Pia Casa di Lavoro; his method proved so successful that he was entrusted with establishing choral singing in the city schools. He also directed concerts of early Italian polyphony, in 1874 founding the Società di Coro 'Armonia Vocale', which made a tour of Germany. In 1879 he moved to Turin, where he directed vocal teaching in the elementary schools. He also served there as director of the Accademia Corale Stefano Tempia, which he conducted in the first Italian performance of Handel's *Judas Maccabaeus*.

MARVIN TARTAK

Robert le Pelé. *See* ROBINET DE LA MAGDALAINE.

Roberto [Roberti, Ruberti], **Costantino** (*b* Naples, 1700; *d* Naples, 17 March 1773). Italian violinist and composer. He began studies at the S Maria di Loreto Conservatory but was expelled in June 1717 'for the sake of quiet for the other students'. Although he is said to have studied counterpoint with the *maestro* of the school, Gaetano Veneziano, that seems doubtful since Gaetano, then an old man, died in 1716; more probably he worked with Gaetano's son Giovanni, *secondo maestro di cappella* from 1716. This perhaps appears the more likely since Giovanni was one of the pioneers in Neapolitan *opera buffa*, the field that Roberto was to enter. He also took lessons from the master violinist and friend of A. Scarlatti, G. C. Cailò, from whom he learnt enough to be called 'virtuoso'. Subsequently he made his living as a violinist, first in the orchestra of the Teatro di S Bartolomeo and, after the opening of the new theatre in 1737, at the S Carlo, where he remained until his old age; he was also a member of the orchestra of the royal chapel. None of his music is known to survive, but his comic operas are of historical interest, for it was just when he was writing, about 1725–35, that, in the hands of the librettists Mariani, Saddumene and Federico, the form underwent significant morphological changes, increasing the ratio of recitative to set numbers and decreasing the quantity of the latter while lengthening and elaborating them.

WORKS

OPERAS

(all comic; all for Naples)

La cantarina (A. Piscopo), Fiorentini, carn. 1728, Acts 2 and 3; Act 1 by M. Caballone

Lo cicisbeo coffeato (T. Mariani), Fiorentini, 1728

Lo Conte di Scrignano (Mariani), Fiorentini, 1729, collab. others

La Zita (G. A. Federico), Fiorentini, aut. 1731

Il Filippo (Federico), Nuovo, sum. 1735

BIBLIOGRAPHY

M. Scherillo: *L'opera buffa napoletana durante il settecento: storia letteraria* (Naples, 1883, 2/1917/Rc1969), 209ff, 214f

U. Prota-Giurleo: *La grande orchestra del R. teatro San Carlo nel settecento* (Naples, 1927), 7

——: *Nicola Logroscino: 'il dio dell'opera buffa'* (Naples, 1927), 56ff

S. di Giacomo: *I quattri antichi conservatorii musicali di Napoli*, ii (Milan and Naples, 1928), 218f, 235f, 239f

JAMES L. JACKMAN

Roberts, Charles Luckeyth. See ROBERTS, LUCKEY.

Roberts, Eleazer (*b* Pwllheli, North Wales, 15 Jan 1825; *d* Liverpool, 6 April 1912). Welsh musician. He was brought up in Liverpool, started work at 13 in a solicitor's office and eventually became chief assistant to the clerk to the stipendiary magistrate. He was elected JP in 1895, the year following his retirement. He contributed regularly to Welsh newspapers and journals, and his books included a biography of Henry Richard and a novel *Owen Rees*. Precentor at Netherfield Road Chapel, Liverpool, he was important in the early days of the Tonic sol-fa movement in Wales. After hearing John Curwen in Liverpool in 1860 he and John Edwards immediately started teaching the system in their Sunday school. He also travelled throughout Wales explaining Tonic sol-fa and setting up classes, and in 1861 brought out *Hymnau a thonau*, the first hymnbook in sol-fa notation published in Wales. His own hymn tunes include the popular 'O na bawn yn tyw tebyg i Iesu Grist yn byw'.

BIBLIOGRAPHY

R. D. Griffith: *Hanes canu cynulleidfaol Cymru* (Cardiff, 1948)

——: 'Roberts, Eleazer', *Dictionary of Welsh Biography* (London, 1959)

OWAIN EDWARDS

Roberts, Helen (Heffron) (*b* Chicago, 12 June 1888). American ethnomusicologist. After studying at Chicago Musical College (1907–9) and the American Conservatory of Music (1910–11) she studied anthropology under Franz Boas at Columbia University (1916–19, MA 1919) and subsequently did her first fieldwork, in Jamaica (1920–21) for the Vassar College Folklore Foundation. In 1923–4 she worked in Hawaii at the invitation of a government commission; she collected songs in northern and southern California (1926–8) and in Rio Grande Pueblos (1930). From about 1920 to 1936 she transcribed and analysed field recordings (her own and those of others) in New York and Washington (working with Fewkes) and at Yale (under Clark Wissler). She was a founder and later secretary (1934–7) of the American Society for Comparative Musicology. In 1936, when support for her work was discontinued, she abandoned her musical career, later becoming a nationally known gardening specialist.

Roberts was a pioneer ethnomusicologist and one of the best of her generation. Her transcriptions and analyses of songs collected in Jamaica and Hawaii and from the Nootka Indians, the Copper Eskimo and others put all ethnomusicologists in her debt, and her studies

based on her own Jamaican material (1925, 1926) are still important. Her best-known work is perhaps *Musical Areas in Aboriginal North America*, which has now been partly superseded by Nettl's *North American Indian Musical Styles* (1954). Problems of form particularly interested her (1932, 1933), and her account of the problem of variation in traditional music (1925) is regarded as a classic study. The collection of Hawaiian music is valued not only by scholars, but also by Hawaiians for its documentation of national traditions which have now disappeared.

WRITINGS

COLLECTIONS WITH ANALYSES

with H. Haeberlin: 'Some Songs of the Puget Sound Salish', *Journal of American Folklore*, xxxi (1918), 496

Jamaica Anansi Stories: Collected by Martha Warren Beckwith, with Music Recorded in the Field by Helen H. Roberts (New York, 1924)

with D. Jenness: *Songs of the Copper Eskimo* (Ottawa, 1925) [report of the Canadian Arctic expedition, 1913–18: Southern Party, 1913–16]

Ancient Hawaiian Music (Honolulu, 1926/R1967)

Jamaican Folk-lore: Collected by Martha Warren Beckwith, with Music Recorded in the Field by Helen H. Roberts (New York, 1928)

'Songs of the Nootka Indians of Western Vancouver Island: with a Section on the Language by Morris Swadesh', *Transactions of the American Philosophical Society*, new ser., xlv (1955), 199 [based on phonograph records and field notes by Edward Sapir, 1910–13]

STUDIES

'Study of Folk Song Variants Based on Field Work in Jamaica', *Journal of American Folklore*, xxxviii (1925), 149–216

'Possible Survivals of African Songs in Jamaica', *MQ*, xii (1962), 340

'Melodic Composition and Scale Foundations in Primitive Music', *American Anthropologist*, new ser., xxxiv (1932), 79

Form in Primitive Music: an Analytical and Comparative Study of the Melodic Form of some Ancient Southern California Indian Songs (New York, 1933)

Musical Areas in Aboriginal North America (New Haven, 1936/R1970)

BIBLIOGRAPHY

'Special Bibliography: Helen Heffron Roberts', *EM*, xi (1967), 228 [incl. references to unpubd MSS and to recordings and their present location]

BARBARA KRADER

Roberts, Henry (*fl* 1737–c1765). English engraver, active in London. From 1737 until about 1762 he kept a music and print shop in Holborn from which he issued several notable books of songs with pictorial embellishments heading each piece. The earliest, the two-volume *Calliope, or English Harmony*, was issued from 1737 by and for the engraver in periodical numbers of eight octavo pages each. The first volume of 25 numbers was completed in 1739; the parts of the second volume began to appear in the same year, though it was probably not finished until about 1746. A second issue of both volumes, appearing in 1746–7, was undertaken by the printer and publisher John Simpson. The plates later came into the possession of Longman & Broderip, who reprinted from them about 1780. Roberts's other famous work, *Clio and Euterpe, or British Harmony*, was similar in style, and issued by him in parts (from 1756) and in two volumes (1758–9). A later edition, dated 1762, had a third volume engraved by Roberts, and a fourth volume was added when John Welcker reissued the work about 1778.

Among other examples of Roberts's fine ornamental engraving are the dedicatory leaf in Giuseppe Sammartini's *XII sonate* op.3 (1743) and the title-page engraving of William Jackson's *Elegies* (c1762).

BIBLIOGRAPHY

F. Kidson: 'Some Illustrated Music-books of the Seventeenth and Eighteenth Centuries: English', *MA*, iii (1911–12), 195

C. Humphries and W. C. Smith: *Music Publishing in the British Isles* (London, 1954, 2/1970)

FRANK KIDSON/WILLIAM C. SMITH/
PETER WARD JONES

Roberts, John (i) (*fl* 1650–70). English composer. He was probably one of the many men who, according to Playford (*Musicall Banquet*, 1651), were teaching the harpsichord in London during the Commonwealth. He was one of the more important English harpsichord composers of this period, and a suite of his was published in *Melothesia* (1673). His music displays a particularly strong French influence, shown by his fondness for corants and his final cadences which, unlike those of most of his countrymen, never have a leading note added briefly to the last chord.

WORKS

Suite (5 movements), hpd, 1673[6]
Suite (3 movements), hpd, *GB-Och*
2 corants, hpd, *Och*, *US-NYp*
Saraband, hpd, *GB-Och*
10 other dance movements, hpd, *US-NYp*

B. A. R. COOPER

Roberts, John (ii) [Ieuan Gwyllt] (*b* nr. Aberystwyth, 27 Dec 1822; *d* nr. Caernarvon, 14 May 1877). Welsh writer, composer and conductor. After an indecisive start to his career Roberts (he used the name Ieuan Gwyllt till 1839) moved in 1852 to Liverpool to become sub-editor of the Welsh national newspaper *Yr Amserau*. Shortly afterwards he began preaching. Though a nonconformist, he came strongly under the influence of the Anglican style of church music while he was in Liverpool, and during this period he began work on his collection of hymn tunes. He moved to Aberdare to edit *Y Gwladgarwr* in 1858. The following year a new religious revival swept through Wales; he became a minister (but was not ordained until 1861) and published his *Llyfr Tonau Cynulleidfaol*. This hymn tune collection sold 17,000 copies in the first three years and its excellent preface, which emphasizes the importance of music in worship and exhorts churches to establish weekly 'singing meetings', was taken seriously. Roberts gave his energetic support to the Tonic sol-fa movement and edited among other newspapers and journals *Telyn y plant* (1859–61), *Y cerddor Cymreig* (1861–74), *Cerddor y tonic sol-ffa* (1869–72), and *Y Goleuad* (1871–2). He was prominent as an adjudicator at competitive eisteddfods and as a conductor at singing festivals. Many of his hymn tunes are still well known, his finest being 'Moab' and 'Liverpool'.

BIBLIOGRAPHY

R. D. Griffith: *Hanes canu cynulleidfaol Cymru* (Cardiff, 1948)
——: 'Roberts, John', *Dictionary of Welsh Biography* (London, 1959)
H. Williams: *Tonau a'u hawduron* (Caernarvon, 1967)

OWAIN EDWARDS

Roberts, John Henry [Pencerdd, Gwynedd] (*b* Mynydd Llandegai, Caernarvonshire, 31 March 1848; *d* Liverpool, 6 Aug 1924). Welsh composer and teacher. He started work as a boy in the Penrhyn slate quarry, Bethesda, but devoted his spare time to music. At the age of 20 he was appointed clerk at the Bryneglwys quarry, Abergynolwyn, and the choir which he founded and conducted sang in the 1868 Harlech Music Festival. His talent was recognized by S. S. Wesley, at whose instigation a fund was set up to enable him to study (1870–74) at the RAM. He also took the Cambridge MusB externally in 1882, and the FTSC diploma. On his appointment as organist of the Welsh Calvinistic Methodist Church in Chatham Street, Liverpool, in 1898 he started the Cambrian School of Music and a small music publishing company. Unlike most of his contemporaries in Welsh music, Roberts disliked pub-

licity. He seldom conducted and would not adjudicate at eisteddfods. A number of his partsongs (notably *Cwsg, Filwr, Cwsg*), anthems and hymn tunes became very popular: the hymn tunes 'Adelaide', 'Uxbridge' and 'Port Penrhyn' are still sung. He contributed regularly to *Y Cerddor*, published a rudiments book *Llyfr Elfennau Cerddoriaeth* (1890), edited a selection of Welsh anthems (1896) and either solely or jointly edited *Llawlyfr Moliant* (1880), *Hymnau yr Eglwys* (1893), *Hymnau a Thonau y Methodistiaid Calfinaidd* (1897) and *Llyfr Tonau ac Emynau* (1904).

BIBLIOGRAPHY

R. D. Griffith: 'Roberts, John Henry', *Dictionary of Welsh Biography* (London, 1959)
H. Williams: *Tonau a'u hawduron* (Caernarvon, 1967)

OWAIN EDWARDS

Roberts, Luckey [Charles Luckeyth (Luckeyeth)] (*b* Philadelphia, 7 Aug ?1887; *d* New York, 5 Feb 1968). Black American jazz pianist and composer. He was a child acrobat, and learnt the piano from about 1900. Some ten years later he had settled in New York, where in 1911 his first musical comedy, *My People*, was produced, and in 1913 his first published composition, *Junk Man Rag*, appeared. 13 further musical comedies followed in the next two decades. From the 1920s he was a popular band-leader at exclusive social functions in the eastern USA; he performed at Carnegie Hall in 1939, and from 1940 to 1954 owned the 'Rendezvous', a Harlem bar.

Roberts was of the post-ragtime 'stride' school of jazz pianism, and by reputation its most technically gifted member; but of the leading figures in that school he left the least trace of his work. He recorded a number of piano rolls in 1923, but made few gramophone recordings, and those late in his career. Among his compositions are *Pork and Beans* (1913), *Music Box Rag* (1914), *Ripples of the Nile* (popular as *Moonlight Cocktail* in 1941) and works for piano and orchestra.

BIBLIOGRAPHY

R. Blesh and H. Janis: *They all Played Ragtime* (New York, 1950, 4/1971)
L. Feather: *The New Handbook of Jazz* (New York, 1958), 145

J. R. TAYLOR

Roberts, (William Herbert) Mervyn (*b* Abergele, Denbighshire, 23 Nov 1906). Welsh composer. He read English and history at Trinity College, Cambridge (1925–8). In 1924–5 and intermittently between 1928 and 1939 he studied at the Royal College of Music where his teachers were Alexander for piano and Morris and Jacob for composition. He taught music at Clarendon School, Abergele (1953–6), and at Christ's Hospital (1963–7). A fastidious composer, he has produced his most important work for the piano. This, with its highly chromatic but fundamentally tonal idiom and its elegant, spacious keyboard writing, places him in the tradition of Bax and Ireland. The most important of his solo piano works is the Sonata, for which he was awarded the Edwin Evans Prize in 1950. There are also some substantial pieces for two pianos, written mainly for performance with his wife. The songs and choral works are on the whole more diatonic, often with a pronounced modal flavour. In addition to his activities as a composer Roberts has contributed to music journals, notably *Music in Education*.

WORKS
INSTRUMENTAL

Pf: Variations on an Original Theme, 2 pf, 1932, rev. 1942; Sonata, 1934, rev. 1939; Sonatina, 1936; 2 Chorales, 2 pf, 1936; Winter,

1937; Variations on a Scottish Melody, 2 pf, 1939, rev. 1960; 4 Preludes, 1944; Wind of Autumn, 1946; Ballad, 1950; Summer's Day, 1951; Cradle Song, 1951; A Christmas Prelude, pf duet, 1952; Romance, 1957; 2 Diversions, 1957; Elegy, 2 pf, 1958; Passacaglia, pf duet, 1960; 4 Folksong Studies, 1969; Rhapsody, 1969; Variations, A, 1970; In Friendship (4 Pieces), 1970; 5 Miniatures
Other works: 3 Pieces, vn, pf, 1946; 2 Pieces, cl, pf, 1948; Str Qt, 1949, withdrawn; Sonata, vn, pf, 1951, withdrawn; Aria, vn, pf, 1960; March for a Wedding, org, 1960; Sarabande, vn, pf, 1967

CHORAL

Y rhosyn (15th-century Ger., trans. T. G. Jones), SATB (1938); My Soul, there is a Country (Vaughan), SATB (1942); Love, which is here a care (Drummond of Hawthornden), SATB (1946); By Morning Twilight (Meredith), SATB (1949); To a Skylark (Meredith), TTBB, 1949; Violets (Meredith), SATB (1950); The Wind on the Lyre (Meredith), S, SATB, 1950; Dirge in the Woods (Meredith), SATB, 1950; Thou to me art such a spring (Meredith), SATB (1951); Magnificat and Nunc dimittis, SATB, org, 1962; Introit: Except the Lord Build the House (Psalm cxxvii), TTBB, 1964; The Flower of Humility, SATB, 1973, withdrawn

SONGS

2 Elegiac Songs (Nicias, Shelley), S, pf, 1935; St Govan (A. G. Prŷs-Jones), 1v, pf, 1935; Cyn cysgu (trad., trans. T. G. Jones), unison vv, pf (1938); 4 Songs of Innocence (Blake), 1v, pf, 1940, rev. 1972; Pilgrim Song (Bunyan), 2 solo vv, pf, 1942; There Comes a Galley (J. Tauler), unison vv, pf (1946); Egypt's Might is Fallen Down (M. Coleridge), unison vv, pf (1946); Christmas Day (A. Young), 1v, pf (1947); Put a rosebud on her lips (F. King), 1v, pf (1947)
Elsewhere (G. O. Warren), 1v, pf (1947); The Sentry (Warren), 1v, pf (1947); 3 Lyrics (E. Macdowell), S, pf, 1961; I like to see (J. Carter), unison vv, pf, 1961; Ble ganad y baban (D. Walters), unison vv, pf, 1964; The Shepherds Sing (Herbert), unison vv, pf, 1964; Prelude (Synge), 1v, pf, 1968; Song for Fine Weather (C. L. Skinner), unison vv, pf, 1971; At Delos (D. C. Scott), 1v, pf, 1972; 10 Short Songs, 2 solo vv, 1972; Old Song (F. R. Scott), 1v, pf, 1973; Invitation to Spring (L. A. Mackay), 1v, pf, 1973; Indian Summer (W. Campbell), 1v, pf, 1975

Principal publisher: Novello

BIBLIOGRAPHY

E. Davies: 'The Piano Music of Mervyn Roberts', *Welsh Music*, iv (1973), 14

PETER CROSSLEY-HOLLAND/MALCOLM BOYD

Robertsbridge Codex (*GB-Lbm* Add.28550). See SOURCES OF KEYBOARD MUSIC TO 1660, §2(vi), and TABLATURE, fig.1.

Robertson, Alec [Alexander] **(Thomas Parke)** (*b* Southsea, 3 June 1892). English writer on music. He was educated at Bradfield College and the Royal Academy of Music (1910–13), where he studied chiefly the organ, harmony and composition, and then was organist and choirmaster at Frensham parish church and briefly at Farnham. During World War I he served in India, Egypt and Palestine. In 1919 he was appointed music lecturer to London County Council evening institutes. In 1920 he joined the Gramophone Co.'s educational staff, first as a lecturer and later as its head. In 1930 he entered the Collegio Beda, Rome; he was ordained priest in 1934 and held an appointment at Westminster Cathedral. Though he returned to professional life in 1938 his experiences of Catholic church music, particularly Gregorian plainchant, led him to write a number of books on the subject. In 1940 he joined the Gramophone Department of the BBC, and after the war was appointed chief producer of music talks on the Home and Third Programmes. He developed a highly individual manner as a broadcaster and gave many illustrated talks, which he continued even after his retirement from the BBC in 1952. As an author and critic he reviewed records for *Gramophone* almost from its inception (1923) and was later its music editor (1952–72). His warmly personal style won him a wide public following. He was made FRAM in 1946.

WRITINGS

The Interpretation of Plainchant (London, 1937)
Brahms (London, 1939, 2/1974)

Dvořák (London, 1945, 2/1964)
'Schubert's Songs', *Schubert: a Symposium*, ed. G. Abraham (London, 1946), 149–97
Contrasts: the Arts and Religion (London, 1947/R1977)
How to Listen to Music (London, 1948)
Sacred Music (London, 1950)
ed.: *Chamber Music* (Harmondsworth, 1956, 4/1967)
ed., with D. Stevens: *Pelican History of Music* (Harmondsworth, 1960–68)
Christian Music (New York, 1961)
More than Music (London, 1961) [autobiography]
Music of the Catholic Church (London, 1961)
ed.: *G.B.S. on Music* (London, 1962)
Requiem: Music of Mourning and Consolation (London, 1967)
Church Cantatas of J. S. Bach (London, 1972)
Articles in *MT*, *ML*, *The Chesterian*, *Grove 5*

JULIAN HERBAGE

Robertson, Alexander. Scottish firm of music publishers, successors to PENSON, ROBERTSON & CO.

Robertson, Rae (*b* Ardersier, Inverness, 29 Nov 1893; *d* Los Angeles, 4 Nov 1956). Scottish pianist. He was educated at the RAM in London and the University of Edinburgh. At the former he won the Chappell Gold Medal, at the latter the Bucher Music Scholarship. After some years' experience as a solo pianist he and his wife, Ethel Bartlett (*b* London, 6 June 1900; *d* Santa Barbara, 17 April 1978), began to play music for two pianos. Their performances were characterized by great sensitivity to tone values and an unfailing unanimity of phrasing. From 1928 until Rae Robertson's death they toured extensively in Europe and North and South America with remarkable success. They made many arrangements of Classical and modern works, some of which were published in the Oxford Two Piano Series which they edited. Their achievements stimulated a number of British composers to write for two pianos. They gave the first performance of Britten's Scottish Ballad, composed for them, with the Cincinnati SO under Goossens.

H. C. COLLES/FRANK DAWES

Robertus de Anglia (*fl* 1460–75). English composer. He was witness to a deed of the Este family in 1454 in which he is called the son of Petrus Suchar, a name that cannot be traced and is probably corrupt. He went to Ferrara Cathedral in September 1460 to instruct the vicars in singing, and was still there a year later, perhaps staying until 1467 when he was enrolled by the chapter of S Petronio, Bologna, as *magister cantus*. There he remained until October 1474 when he returned to England. Apart from his two songs *O fallaze e ria Fortuna* and *El mal foco arda* (both in *P-Pm* 714 only), there is a poem *Iti caldi suspir e mente afflitta* by his Bolognese contemporary, Cesare Nappi, which appears with the annotation that it was set to music by 'Magister Robertus Anglia'. The music of *O fallaze e ria Fortuna* is in a style that suggests it may originally have had English text and could belong to a repertory similar to that represented in the Ritson Manuscript (*GB-Lbm* Add.5665).

BIBLIOGRAPHY

D. Fallows, ed.: *Galfridus and Robertus de Anglia: Four Italian Songs* (Newton Abbot, 1977) [complete edn., incl. Nappi's poem]
D. Fallows: 'Robertus de Anglia and the Oporto Song Collection', *Source Materials and the Interpretation of Music: a Memorial Volume to Thurston Dart* (London, in preparation)

DAVID FALLOWS

Robertus de Brunham [?Burnham], Frater. English cleric and musician. He was named by JOHN HANBOYS (*fl* 1470) in connection with three features of notation (*CS*, i, pp.431–2, 447). Brunham denoted altered semibreves in ligatures by using unusual shapes, some of which are defective according to the mensural system, or by writing a sign resembling an inverted 'v' above or below the note. This second method is used in the early 15th-century MS *GB-Lbm* Add.40011B, ff.9v–10, 13. Brunham also 'invented' three new rests for values not included in the normal symbols. In a theoretical MS of 1441, Torkesey's triangle (a diagram of mensural values) and the accompanying *declaratio* (CSM, xii, pp.9, 63) are ascribed to Brunham.

ANDREW HUGHES

Robertus de Sabilone, Magister (*fl* early 13th century). Teacher of music active in Paris. Anonymous IV (ed. Reckow, 1967, i, 46, 50), writing about 1275, clearly regarded him as the most significant figure since Pérotin: 'He taught most widely, and made the singing of music sound truly delicious'. The theorist also reported that 'the book of books of Pérotin were in use up to the time of Robertus de Sabilone in the choir of Notre Dame in Paris, and from his time up to the present day'. Niemann (1902) considered him to have been the first choirmaster of the new cathedral, and attempts have been made to identify him with one of two succentors at Notre Dame in the 12th century (Birkner). Despite this, he remains unidentified.

For bibliography *see* ORGANUM AND DISCANT: BIBLIOGRAPHY.

IAN D. BENT

Robeson, Paul (*b* Princeton, NJ, 9 April 1898; *d* Philadelphia, 23 Jan 1976). Black American bass-baritone and actor. He studied law at Columbia University, then appeared in an Eugene O'Neill play in 1921, establishing his reputation as an actor in *All God's Chillun got Wings* (1924) and *The Emperor Jones* (1925). He gave his first concert in 1925 and made his mark with his singing of negro spirituals. In 1926 he made a coast-to-coast tour of the USA with great success. Soon he became internationally known: he packed Drury Lane, London, by his majestic presence and his singing (especially of 'Ol' Man River') in *Show Boat* (1928) and was seen as Shakespeare's Othello both in London (1930) and later in the USA, the last time being at the Memorial Theatre, Stratford-on-Avon, in 1959. His many films included *The Emperor Jones* (1933), *Sanders of the River* (1935), *Show Boat* (1936) and *The Proud Valley* (1939). His embracing of communism in the 1940s after a tour of the USSR brought his American career to a halt. His voice was often listed as a baritone, but in reality it was a true bass of enveloping richness and earthy resonance: a great voice, but of limited compass. To hear him sing spirituals was a memorable experience.

BIBLIOGRAPHY
E. G. Robeson: *Paul Robeson: Negro* (New York, 1930)
S. Graham: *Paul Robeson: Citizen of the World* (New York, 1946)
P. Robeson: *Here I Stand* (London and New York, 1958) [autobiography]
M. Seton: *Paul Robeson* (London, 1958)
E. P. Hoyt: *Paul Robeson* (London, 1967)

MAX DE SCHAUENSEE

Robijns [Robyns], Jozef (*b* Meldert, 15 Aug 1920). Belgian musicologist. He studied music at the Lemmens Institute in Mechelen, where he obtained a performer's diploma. He took the doctorate in musicology in 1954 at the Catholic University of Louvain with a dissertation on Pierre de La Rue. In 1958 he became a deputy lecturer at Louvain and successively lecturer (1961) and professor (1963). For many years he was also librar-ian of the Bruges Conservatory and secretary of the Société Belge de Musicologie. His particular field of research is 15th- and 16th-century Netherlands polyphony. In his capacity as editorial secretary, he contributed numerous articles to the *Algemene muziekencyclopedie* (Amsterdam and Antwerp, 1957–63), to which as editor he added a seventh supplementary volume in 1972. In recognition of this achievement he was awarded the Dent Medal at the 11th congress of the IMS in Copenhagen (1972). He has unearthed some previously unknown music in old church archives; his musicological writings are thus supported by a thorough study of the source material.

WRITINGS
Pierre de la Rue (diss., Catholic U. of Louvain, 1954; Brussels, 1954)
'Pierre de la Rue als overgangsfiguur tussen middeleeuwen en renaissance', *RBM*, ix (1955), 122
'Eine Musikhandschrift des frühen 16. Jahrhunderts im Zeichen der Verehrung unserer lieben Frau der sieben Schmerzen', *KJb*, xliv (1960), 28
'Henricus Beauvarlet', *RBM*, xviii (1964), 32
ed.: *Renaissance-muziek 1400–1600: donum natalicium René Bernard Lenaerts* (Louvain, 1969) [incl. 'Professor Dr. René Bernard Lenaerts bij zijn 65ste verjaardag', p.7]

EDITIONS
with R. B. Lenaerts: *P. de La Rue: Missa de beata virgine; Missa de virginibus* (*O quam pulchra est*); *Missa de Sancta Anna*, MMBel, viii (1960)
H. Beauvarlet: Vier missen, MMBel, xi (1974)

BIBLIOGRAPHY
Jaarboek: Katholieke universiteit Leuven, xcii (1957–9), no.1, p.126, no.2, p.784; xciii (1960–61), no.1, p.133
Lovaniensia: academisch nieuws (van de) Katholieke universiteit Leuven (1965), no.1, p.37; (1967), no.1, p.82, no.3, p.90; (1968), no.1, p.73
J. Coppens: *Bibliographia academica (van de) Katholieke universiteit Leuven*, xii (1963–8), 352
Archief en Museum voor Vlaams cultuurleven (Antwerp), dossier R 5454

GODELIEVE SPIESSENS

Robineau, Abbé Alexandre-Auguste (*b* Paris, 23 April 1747; *d* Paris, 13 Jan 1828). French violinist, composer and painter. Son of the engraver and jeweller Jean-Charles Robineau and Madeleine-Charlotte Regnier, he became a choirboy at the Sainte-Chapelle in 1754 and also studied the violin with Gaviniès. Between about 1762 and 1767 he studied in Italy, first the violin and composition under Lolli at the conservatory of S Maria di Loreto in Naples, and later painting in Rome. In Naples his success was such that he was called 'Lollinelli' after his teacher. Returning to Paris, he made his début at the Concert Spirituel on 24 December 1767, and in the following year published his set of six brilliant sonatas 'in the style of six different masters'.

During the next two decades Robineau continued a double career as musician and painter, while simultaneously working as secretary to high government officials. In about 1774 he renounced his religious vows and married the singer Adélaïde Bertin. Six trips to England resulted in a number of important paintings there. Between 1778 and 1789 Robineau was listed in Parisian directories as a violin teacher, and from 1785 until the outbreak of the Revolution four years later he helped organize entertainments for the French court as *secrétaire des menus plaisirs*. His opera *Stratonice* (1791), never produced at the Opéra, was given privately in Paris. During this period Robineau was orchestral leader at the Théâtre Française (1789–92), and his paintings were exhibited at the Salon of 1791. In 1793, however, Robineau fled France, and, except for a brief visit in 1799 when he again exhibited at the Salon, he was an expatriate for the remainder of the Revolutionary and Napoleonic eras, embarking on picaresque travels during which he worked as a musician or painter at various courts in Spain, Germany and Russia.

Returning to Paris with the re-establishment of the monarchy in 1815, Robineau struggled to gain a musical position at court, but failed. His old age was spent in poverty, and lightened only by the publication of his autobiography and by a menial position playing among the violists at the Odéon.

WORKS

Stratonice (opera, ?F. B. Hoffman), Paris, 1791, lost

6 sonates, vn, b (Paris, 1768)
Concertos, vn, orch (Paris, 1770), lost
Cosaque walse, pf (Amsterdam, 1814)
Trio, ded. Duchesse de Polignac (Paris, n.d.), lost

WRITINGS

Les caprices de la fortune, ou Les deux muses en pèlerinage: extrait de la vie d'Auguste Robineau, peintre et musicien, encore existant, après avoir echappé aux quatre éléments (Paris, 1816) [extracts in Pincherle]

BIBLIOGRAPHY

L. de La Laurencie: *L'école française de violon de Lully à Viotti* (Paris, 1922–4/*R*1971)
——: 'A propos de l'abbé Robineau', *ReM*, vi (1925), 34
M. Pincherle: 'Le peintre-violiniste, ou Les aventures de l'abbé Robineau', *ReM*, vi (1925), 235 [also pubd with minor emendations in *Feuillets d'histoire du violon* (Paris, 1927), 22]

NEAL ZASLAW

Robinet de la Magdalaine [Robert le Pelé, Rubinus, Rubinet] (*b* Fouseran, diocese of Rouen, 30 March 1415; *d* 17 Sept 1478, buried abbey of Watten, diocese of St Omer). French composer. He is listed (*c*1508) by the poet Eloy d'Amerval as one of the 'grans musiciens' of the 15th century. He is apparently to be identified with 'Rubinet', named as the composer of six pieces in *I-Fn* Magl.XIX.59 and the 'Rubinus' who wrote a popular 15th-century chanson, *Entre Peronne et Saint Quentin* (also entitled *Environ laisant Valentin*), and *Der pawir schwantcz*.

Robinet was born Robert le Pelé in March 1415 and by the age of seven had been enrolled as a choirboy in the church of St Michel in Beauvais. He completed his training for the priesthood in 1438 and said his first Mass in Rouen in the monastery of the Magdalaine, from which he took his surname. In 1443 he travelled to England as a member of the chapel of the Archbishop of Rouen and then in 1446 was inscribed as a chorister in the chapel of Pope Nicolas V in Rome. By 1448 he had returned to Normandy to study theology, and it was from there that Philip the Good, Duke of Burgundy, called him to the Burgundian court to sing during Holy Week of 1448. Robinet's performance was judged satisfactory and he was retained in the ducal chapel. In 1462, at the request of Philip the Good, he was appointed provost of the monastery of Watten in the diocese of St Omer. Robinet seems to have been a raconteur and poet as well as a musician; he was apparently the author of one of the tales (no.65) in the *Cent nouvelles nouvelles* and he was elected 'prince' of a convocation of poets held in Brussels in 1460. He was buried in the abbey of Watten.

WORKS

Entre Peronne et Saint Quentin [Environ laisant Valentin], 3/4vv; edns. in EDM, 1st ser., iv (1936), 86, and Plamenac, 176
Je me plains de tant affanne, 3vv, *I-Fn* Magl.XIX.59
Je voy, 3vv, *Fn* Magl.XIX.59
Pour mieulx valoir, 3vv, *Fn* Magl.XIX.59
three textless pieces, 3vv, *Fn* Magl.XIX.59

BIBLIOGRAPHY

A. Leroy: 'Catalogue des prévosts du monastère de Watten', *Archives historiques et littéraires du Nord de la France*, new ser., vi (1847), 280
A. Pirro: 'Robinet de la Magdalaine', *Mélanges de musicologie offerts à M. Lionel de La Laurencie* (Paris, 1933), 15

J. Marix: *Histoire de la musique et des musiciens de la cour de Bourgogne sous le règne de Philippe le Bon* (Strasbourg, 1939), 202ff
D. Plamenac: 'The "Second" Chansonnier of the Biblioteca Riccardiana', *AnnM*, ii (1954), 113, 119, 134, 176

CRAIG WRIGHT

Robin et Marion. A play in courtly-popular style by Adam de la Halle, written about 1283; it survives in three manuscripts (*F-Pn* fr.25566, fr.1569, *AIXm* 572). The music for the play consists largely of traditional *refrains*.

For further information and bibliography *see* MEDIEVAL DRAMA, §III, 2 (iii).

JOHN STEVENS

Robinson (i). English family of musicians.

(1) John Robinson (*b* *c*1682; *d* Westminster, London, 30 April 1762). Keyboard player. He was a chorister of the Chapel Royal under Blow and his voice broke in the early part of 1704. In 1710 he became organist of St Laurence, near the Guildhall, London, a post that he retained after his appointment as organist of Westminster Abbey in 1727 in succession to Croft, whose deputy he had been. His first wife, whom he married on 6 September 1716, was the soprano Ann Turner (see (2) below).

Robinson happened to be the first person to play publicly on an English organ possessing a Swell manual when he opened the new organ in St Magnus's Church, London Bridge, built by the Jordans in 1713, and of which church it has also been suggested that he was organist. He is of no account as a composer, but was a popular performer on both the organ and the harpsichord, though reports of the style of his playing differ. Boyce remarked that he was 'a most excellent performer', and Hawkins (*General History of . . . Music*) said he was a 'florid and elegant performer on the organ' and 'highly cultivated as a master of the harpsichord'. But in his 'Memoir of Dr Boyce' prefixed to the second edition of Boyce's *Cathedral Music* (1788) the same writer accused Robinson of 'degrading' the organ and of 'tickling it with mere airs in two parts'.

(2) Ann Turner Robinson [née Turner] (*d* London, 5 Jan 1741). Soprano, the youngest daughter of the countertenor and composer WILLIAM TURNER (ii). She first sang in public at the King's Theatre on 5 April 1718, when she introduced a cantata by Ariosti composed 'purposely on this Occasion'. She repeated it on 21 March at a concert with the castrato Baldassari, and between October 1719 and March 1720 appeared several times at Drury Lane in Ariosti's serenata *Diana on Mount Latmos*. She had a benefit there on 17 May 1720. She was generally announced as 'Mrs Robinson, late Mrs Turner' or 'Mrs Turner Robinson', to distinguish her from Anastasia Robinson, who was singing at the same period and sometimes at the same theatre; but it is not always easy to tell which is meant. In the spring of 1720 both appeared together in the short first season of the Royal Academy of Music, in Porta's *Numitore* (2 April), Handel's *Radamisto* (27 April) and Domenico Scarlatti's *Narciso* (30 May). Ann Turner Robinson was the original Polissena in *Radamisto*, but missed the final performances of all three operas. She sang a Handel cantata at her Drury Lane benefit on 20 March 1723.

She was probably the Mrs Robinson who sang regularly between the acts at Drury Lane from December 1725 to December 1726, played in Carey's pantomime *Apollo and Daphne* from February 1726, and included seven Handel opera arias in her benefit programme on 28 April. She certainly had a benefit at Drury Lane on 26 March 1729, when she sang 14 Handel pieces, including two duets with Clarke; most of them had been composed for Cuzzoni or Faustina. She was in Handel's first London oratorio performances at the King's Theatre in May and June 1732, as an Israelite Woman in *Esther* and Clori in the bilingual *Acis and Galatea*. Her part in *Radamisto* shows that she was a capable singer with some brilliance at the top of her compass (*e'* to *a''*).

(3) **Robinson,** Miss [first name unknown] (*fl* 1733–45). Mezzo-soprano, the daughter of (1) John and (2) Ann Turner Robinson. She was probably the Miss Robinson who sang and played the harpsichord, having 'never appear'd before in Publick', for her own benefit at the New Haymarket Theatre on 29 March 1733, and possibly the one 'who never appeared on any stage before' in the pantomime *Harlequin Sorcerer* at Tottenham Court on 4 August 1741. (She cannot have been either of the Miss Robinsons who sang and danced constantly as children at Drury Lane in the mid-1720s, a period when the London theatre was peculiarly rich in Robinsons.) Handel engaged her for his last oratorio season at the King's Theatre in 1744–5, when she sang Barak in *Deborah* (October, one performance only), Ino in *Semele* (December), Dejanira in the first production of *Hercules* (5 January), Micah and an Israelite and Philistine Woman in *Samson* (Handel composed a new air, 'Fly from the cleaving mischief', for her), Phanor in *Joseph*, Daniel in the first production of *Belshazzar* (27 March), and in *Messiah*. She may have been in the March revival of *Saul*. She sang Handel airs and a part in the *Acis and Galatea* trio at the Musicians' Fund benefit at Covent Garden on 10 April, and again at her own benefit at the King's on 29 April. Handel paid her £210 from his Bank of England account on 4 May. If the magnificent part of Dejanira, which has a compass of *a* to *g♯''*, was composed for her, Handel must have held a high opinion of her vocal and dramatic ability. She was to have sung Cyrus (compass *b♭* to *f''*) in *Belshazzar*, but took over Mrs Cibber's part (raised in pitch) when the latter fell ill. The boy Robinson who sang alto in *Israel in Egypt* (April 1739), and possibly in the oratorios of the following season, may have been her brother.

WATKINS SHAW (1), WINTON DEAN (2, 3)

Robinson (ii). Irish family of musicians.

(1) **Francis Robinson** (*fl* Dublin, early 19th century). Teacher, administrator and baritone. He founded in 1810 the Sons of Handel, a large-scale concert-giving society. Of his seven children, six (four sons and two daughters) became professional musicians, the sons forming a vocal quartet which was the first to make known German partsongs in Ireland.

(2) **Francis James Robinson** (*b* Dublin, *c*1799; *d* Dublin, 21 Oct 1872). Tenor, organist and composer, son of (1) Francis Robinson. He was a chorister in Christ Church Cathedral, Dublin, and assistant organist from 1816 to 1841. He was also organist at St Patrick's Cathedral there (1828–9) and a tenor vicar-choral at Christ Church from 1833 until his death and at St Patrick's from 1843. In June 1834 he sang an important role at the Musical Festival in Westminster Abbey. He composed church music and songs, and was given an honorary MusD at Dublin in 1852.

(3) **William Robinson** (*b* Dublin, *c*1805). Bass, son of (1) Francis Robinson. He was a member of St Patrick's choir in 1845; he also sang in the choirs of Christ Church and Trinity College.

(4) **John Robinson** (*b* Dublin, *c*1812; *d* Dublin, 1844). Tenor and organist, son of (1) Francis Robinson. He was a chorister in Christ Church Cathedral and organist to both cathedrals (St Patrick's, 1829–43, and Christ Church, 1841–4) and to Trinity College (from 1834).

(5) **Joseph Robinson** (*b* Dublin, 16 Aug 1816; *d* Dublin, 23 Aug 1898). Baritone, conductor and composer, son of (1) Francis Robinson. He was a chorister at St Patrick's at the age of eight. In 1834 he founded the Antient Concert Society, which he conducted for 29 years. In 1837 he became conductor of the University Choral Society, founded by the students; at one of its concerts Mendelssohn's music for *Antigone* was given for the first time outside Germany. He conducted this Society for ten years. He conducted music for the opening of the Cork Exhibition in 1852, and the Dublin International Exhibition in 1853. In 1856 efforts were made to revive the Irish Academy of Music, founded in 1848 but languishing for want of funds and pupils. Robinson and his wife (6) Fanny Arthur joined as professors, and when, after 20 years, Robinson resigned, the institution had become stable and important. For the Handel centenary in 1859 he gave *Messiah*, with Lind and Belletti among the principals. In 1865 he conducted an orchestra and chorus of 700 when the Prince of Wales opened the large Exhibition Palace. In 1876 he established the Dublin Musical Society, a chorus which he trained. He wrote songs, concerted pieces and anthems. After Fanny Arthur's death he remarried in 1881.

(6) **Fanny Arthur** (*b* Sept 1831; *d* Dublin, 31 Oct 1879). English pianist, teacher and composer, wife of (5) Joseph Robinson. Having studied with Sterndale Bennett and Thalberg, she first appeared in Ireland on 19 February 1849. She was married to Joseph Robinson on 17 July 1849. Her first London appearance was at the Musical Union (26 June 1855) when she played Beethoven's op.24 with Ernst and was praised by Meyerbeer. In 1856 she played a Mendelssohn concerto at the New Philharmonic, and became professor at the IAM. She played at the Salle Erard in Paris, 4 Feb 1864. Her public life was often interrupted by illness. She wrote a cantata *God is Love*, piano pieces (*Song of the Mill-wheel, Elf-land, The Hunt* and *Village Fete*) and some songs.

BIBLIOGRAPHY
'Joseph Robinson', *MT*, xxxix (1898), 609
J. E. West: *Cathedral Organists* (London, 1921)

R. J. PASCALL

Robinson, Anastasia (*b* Italy, *c*1692; *d* Southampton, April 1755). English soprano, later contralto. She was the eldest daughter of Thomas Robinson, a portrait painter from Leicestershire who travelled and studied in Italy. Anastasia studied music with Croft and singing with Sandoni and the Baroness (Lindelheim). At first she exercised her talent in private, singing to her own accompaniment at weekly *conversazioni*, much patronized by society, in her father's house in Golden Square. When her father's sight failed she turned professional to support the family and began to give concerts at York Buildings and elsewhere. The solo soprano part in Handel's *Ode for Queen Anne's Birthday* was written

Anastasia Robinson: mezzotint (1727) by John Faber after a portrait (1723) by John Vanderbank

for her, and she presumably sang it in February 1714. On 9 June 1713 she had a benefit at the Queen's Theatre; on the 20th she introduced a new cantata there. She joined the opera company at the beginning of 1714, making her début in the pasticcio *Creso* on 27 January. She sang that spring in *Arminio* and *Ernelinda*, on several occasions with new songs, and met with immediate favour. The following season, in addition to her old parts, she played Almirena in the revival of Handel's *Rinaldo* (30 December 1714) and sang in the new pasticcio *Lucio Vero* (26 February). She created the part of Oriana in Handel's *Amadigi* on 25 May 1715, but retired after one performance owing to illness. In the 1715–17 seasons she was in A. Scarlatti's *Pirro e Demetrio*, the pasticcio *Clearte*, and revivals of *Rinaldo* and *Amadigi*. She had benefits in *Arminio* (1714), *Ernelinda* (1715) and twice in *Amadigi* (1716 and 1717); on the last occasion (21 March) Handel composed a new scene for her and Nicolini.

Although the opera closed in summer 1717, Robinson had benefits at the King's on 15 March 1718 and 21 February 1719. It must have been during this period that her voice dropped from soprano to contralto as the result of an illness. She sang at Drury Lane from October 1719 to March 1720, with a benefit on 2 February. On the foundation of the Royal Academy of Music she rejoined the opera company and sang in its first three productions in spring 1720: Porta's *Numitore* (2 April), Handel's *Radamisto* (Zenobia, 27 April) and Roseingrave's arrangement of Domenico Scarlatti's *Narciso* (30 May). A Hanoverian diplomat, de Fabrice, paid tribute to her performance in *Numitore*, ranking her in beauty in voice with the brilliant Durastanti. Robinson missed the opening of the autumn season, but returned in spring 1721 and sang in all the operas between then and summer 1724: the composite *Muzio Scevola* (Irene), Handel's *Floridante* (Elmira), *Ottone* (Matilda), *Flavio* (Teodata) and *Giulio Cesare* (Cornelia), Bononcini's *Crispo*, *Griselda*, *Erminia*, *Farnace* and *Calpurnia*, Ariosti's *Coriolano* and *Vespasiano*, and the pasticcios *Odio ed amore* and *Aquilio Consolo*. She appeared with the rest of the company in concerts and ridottos at the theatre in March

and June 1721 and February and March 1722; on the first occasion she took part in a serenata by A. Scarlatti. In June 1724 she retired from the stage, having secretly married the elderly Earl of Peterborough two years earlier; he did not acknowledge her publicly until shortly before his death in 1735. Her salary at the Royal Academy was reputed to be £1000, almost doubled by benefits and presents. In retirement she lived at Parson's Green (where she held a kind of musical academy at which Bononcini, Tosi, Greene and others performed) and, after Peterborough's death, at his seat near Southampton. She was on friendly terms with Bononcini, who had helped to advance her career, and obtained him a pension of £500 from the Duchess of Marlborough; he dedicated his *Farnace* to Peterborough. On 11 January 1723 she took part with Mrs Barbier, the opera orchestra and the Chapel Royal choir in a private performance at Buckingham House of Bononcini's choruses to the late Duke of Buckingham's play *Julius Caesar*, conducted by the composer. She was buried in Bath Abbey.

Robinson enjoyed great personal and artistic popularity. As a singer she was remarkable for charm and expressiveness rather than virtuosity; the care with which Handel supported and sometimes doubled her part in the orchestra suggests technical limitations. His richest part for her, Oriana, which offers many openings for pathos, belongs to her soprano period (compass d' to a''). From 1720 her range diminished (bb to e''), and Handel seldom taxed her with coloratura; but he gave her a highly emotional part in *Giulio Cesare* and an ironically humorous one in *Flavio*. She disliked playing termagants and found the role of Matilda in *Ottone* as first composed impossible to sing: 'a Patient Grisell by Nature', she was asked to play 'an abomminable Scold'. Afraid to face Handel, she enlisted the help of the diplomat Giuseppe Riva (and suggested approaching Lady Darlington, the king's mistress) to have it altered – apparently with success, for the aria to which she chiefly objected, 'Pensa, spietata madre', was replaced before performance. Robinson's letters to Riva in the Càmpori collection at Modena (*I-MOe*) show an attractive and generous character, though Lady Mary Wortley Montagu referred to her as 'at the same time a prude and a kept mistress'. Riva described her as 'of moderate beauty but of the highest spirit'. She was a woman of culture and social gifts, rare in an 18th-century singer, a friend of Pope and a Roman Catholic. The one blot on her memory is her destruction of Peterborough's memoirs after his death. There is a mezzotint of her by John Faber (1727; see illustration) after a portrait by John Vanderbank (1723), and an amusing caricature by A. M. Zanetti (1721) in the Cini collection (*I-Vgc*).

WINTON DEAN

Robinson, (Peter) Forbes (*b* Macclesfield, 21 May 1926). English bass. He studied at Loughborough College and at the training school of La Scala, joined the Covent Garden Opera in 1954 and made his début that year as Monterone. He has taken more than 60 roles with the company, the most important being the speaking part of Moses in Schoenberg's *Moses und Aron* (1965), the title role, which he created, in Tippett's *King Priam* (1962) and Claggart in *Billy Budd*. He has also sung frequently with the Welsh National Opera, notably as Don Giovanni, Boris Godunov, Fiesco and King Philip. In 1966 he appeared at the Teatro Colón, Buenos Aires. He is a notable oratorio singer, particularly of Handel and the solo in Walton's *Belshazzar's Feast*. Robinson has a dark, evenly produced, expressive voice and is capable of subtle characterization, especially in such roles as Claggart and Boris.

ALAN BLYTH

Robinson, Michael F(inlay) (*b* Gloucester, 3 March 1933). English musicologist. He was a music scholar at Rugby School (1946–51) before reading music at New College, Oxford (1953–60; BA 1956, BMus 1957). In 1958 he was an Italian government scholar and worked on Neapolitan opera, the topic of his doctoral dissertation (1963). He then held successive appointments as lecturer at Durham University (1961–5), assistant professor (1965) and associate professor (1967) at McGill University, Montreal, and lecturer at the University of Wales, Cardiff (1970). Robinson's research, which has centred on Neapolitan opera of the 18th century, is drawn together in his broad survey *Naples and Neapolitan Opera*, where the Neapolitan contribution to operatic history is surveyed and characterized. His earlier book *Opera before Mozart* provides a general picture of the rise of opera in the social and aesthetic circumstances of the 17th and early 18th centuries. Research on the Naples conservatories has led him towards a general interest in socio-musicological studies. His compositions include two string quartets, several instrumental works and songs.

WRITINGS

'The Aria in Opera Seria, 1725–80', *PRMA*, lxxxviii (1961–2), 31
Neapolitan Opera, 1700–1780 (diss., U. of Oxford, 1963)
Opera before Mozart (London, 1966, 2/1972)
'Porpora's Operas for London, 1733–1736', *Soundings*, ii (1971–2), 57–87
Naples and Neapolitan Opera (Oxford, 1972)
'The Governors' Minutes of the Conservatory S. Maria di Loreto, Naples', *RMARC*, x (1972), 1–97
'Anfossi, Pasquale'; 'Metastasio, Pietro'; 'Opera', §II, 3; 'Paisiello, Giovanni'; 'Porpora, Nicola', *Grove 6*

DAVID SCOTT

Robinson, Stanford (*b* Leeds, 5 July 1904). English conductor. He studied at the RCM in London, where he conducted his first opera performances, and in 1924 joined the BBC as chorus master, remaining a staff conductor until 1966. During the years 1924–8 he formed and trained the groups that later became the BBC Chorus, the BBC Singers and, as an amateur choir, the BBC Choral Society. He became conductor of the BBC Theatre Orchestra, 1932–46, and (concurrently from 1936) director of music productions, which gave him responsibility for studio opera and many distinguished broadcasts, including Massenet's *Manon* (1938), with Maggie Teyte, Heddle Nash and Dennis Noble. In 1946 he became associate conductor of the BBC SO, but returned to his former orchestra under its new name of BBC Opera Orchestra in 1949 until it was further changed into the BBC Concert Orchestra in 1952. After that, Robinson continued to conduct much radio and television opera without being attached to a specific orchestra.

He made his Covent Garden début with *Die Fledermaus* in 1937; he also directed the English Opera Group, and conducted the first London production of Alessandro Scarlatti's *Il trionfo dell'onore* (Fortune Theatre, 1951). From 1946, when he conducted opera and concerts in Budapest, he appeared occasionally abroad; he also made many records, especially with leading singers. His compositions include light orches-

tral pieces and songs, but his main achievement was in substantially helping to shape the BBC's choral and operatic policy and reputation. He married the soprano Lorely Dyer (*b* 1908). His younger brother Eric Robinson (1908–74) won success in presenting and conducting light music programmes on television.

ARTHUR JACOBS

Robinson, Thomas (*fl* 1589–1609). English lutenist, composer and teacher. From the dedication to James I in his *The Schoole of Musicke* (1603) we know that he was 'once thought (in Denmarke at Elsanure) the fittest to instruct your Majesties Queene'. It seems likely that this would have been before Anne's marriage to James in 1589. In the dedication of his second publication, *New Citharen Lessons* (1609), to 'Sir William Cecil . . . Sonne and Heire to the . . . Earle of Salisburie', he made it clear that both he and his father enjoyed the patronage of several members of the Cecil family. He wrote that he was 'sometime servant' to Thomas Cecil, Earl of Exeter, elder brother of Robert Cecil, Earl of Salisbury, whose 'comfortable liberalities' he had tasted, and that his father had been 'true and obedient servant' to 'your Lord and Grandfather', William Cecil, Lord Burghley.

Robinson's great importance lies in the clear exposition of his lute method set forth in *The Schoole of Musicke*. Before its publication it is likely that lute technique in England had, for some time, been based mainly on J. Alford's translation (*A Briefe and Easye Instru[c]tion*, 1568) of Le Roy's method (now lost), published in Paris in 1567. Robinson's method shows some important differences from Le Roy's, chiefly in his treatment of right-hand technique. He advocated the use of the thumb more consistently in passages on the lower courses where, according to earlier instruction books, alternating thumb and first finger would have been used; his use of the third finger in some passages of single notes on upper courses was a complete innovation. He explained with care the ornaments to be used in playing his music and included sections on playing the viol and on singing.

One other work of Robinson's, *Medulla Musicke*, was entered in the registers of the Stationers' Company in 1603, but no copy is now known. The full title of the work indicated that it contained his intabulations and arrangements for voices of the '40tie severall waies' by Byrd and Ferrabosco on *Miserere* (see WAYES).

Robinson's music is fresh, charming and often witty. Some of his best work is of outstanding quality.

WORKS

The Schoole of Musicke (London, 1603); ed. in CM (1971)
New Citharen Lessons (London, 1609)
Robinson's May, lute *GB-Cu* (2 versions); ed. I. Harwood, *Ten Easy Pieces for the Lute* (Cambridge, 1962)
Medulla Musicke, lost; licensed by Stationers' Company on 15 Oct 1603, see Fellowes

BIBLIOGRAPHY

O. Kinkeldey: 'Thomas Robinson's *Schoole of Musicke*', *BAMS*, i (1936), 7
T. Dart: 'The Cittern and its English Music', *GSJ*, i (1948), 46
M. Frost: *English and Scottish Psalm Tunes* (London, 1953)
W. S. Casey: *Printed English Lute Instruction Books 1568–1610* (diss., U. of Michigan, 1960) [incl. full transcr. of *The Schoole of Musicke*]
D. Poulton: 'Notes on the Spanish Pavan', *LSJ*, iii (1961), 5
D. Greer: ' "What if a Day": an Examination of the Words and Music', *ML*, xliii (1962), 304
C. M. Simpson: *The British Broadside Ballad and its Music* (New Brunswick, 1966)
F. Traficante: 'Music for the Lyra Viol: the Printed Sources', *LSJ*, viii (1966), 7

I. Harwood: 'Thomas Robinson's "General Rules" ', *LSJ*, xx (1978), 78

DIANA POULTON

Robinson, Sir **William Cleaver Francis** (*b* Rosmead, Co. Westmeeth, Ireland, 14 Jan 1834; *d* London, 2 May 1897). British civil administrator, music patron and composer. He had a distinguished career in the Colonial Office during which his posts included Governor of Prince Edward Island (1866), Governor of Western Australia (1874–7, 1880–83, 1890–95) and Governor of South Australia (1883–9). In his 20 years of vice-regal representation he acquired a popular reputation among musical and literary circles. He was patron of numerous societies including the Perth Musical Union (1882), Adelaide Quartet Club until 1886, and the Melbourne Metropolitan *Liedertafel* in 1883, besides lending his active support to numerous composers including Heuzenroeder, Julius Herz and Marshall-Hall, whose appointment to the Ormond Chair of Music at Melbourne University (1870), was largely due to Robinson's influence with Sir Charles Hallé and the London selection committee.

Unlike that of his predecessors, Robinson's influence on public concert-giving and musical taste in Australia stemmed from a personal commitment to music rather than social prestige. Having written partsongs and pieces for military band in London under the *nom de plume* 'Owen Hope', he composed several successful songs in Australia including *Remember me no more* (1885), *The Poet's Last Dream* (1890), *Severed* (1890) and *Unfurl the Flag* (1883), and collaborated with Herz in a two-act comic opera *Predatores* (F. Hart, 1892–4). His generosity extended to donating funds towards the establishment of a chair of music at Adelaide University (founded in 1885 as the Elder Chair). He was made CMG in 1873, KCMG in 1877 and GCMG in 1887.

BIBLIOGRAPHY

E. Scott: *A History of Melbourne University* (Melbourne, 1936), 142

A. Wentzel: *One Hundred Years of Music in Australia, 1788–1888* (diss., Sydney U., 1963), 94, 167

'Robinson, Sir William Cleaver Francis', *Australian Encyclopedia* (Sydney, 1965)

M. T. Radic: *Aspects of Organized Amateur Music in Melbourne, 1836–1890* (diss., U. of Melbourne, 1968), 501, 555

ELIZABETH WOOD

Robison [Nickrenz], **Paula** (*b* Nashville, Tenn., 8 June 1941). American flautist. She studied at the University of Southern California, and then at the Juilliard School, New York, where her principal teachers were Julius Baker and (for the violin) Louis Persinger. She trained further with Albert Tipton at the Aspen Music Festival and with Marcel Moyse at the Marlboro Music Festival. She made her New York recital début in 1961 under the auspices of the Young Concert Artists organization, and in 1966 she became the first American flautist to win the Geneva International Competition, an honour that led to her appearance as a soloist with L'Orchestre de la Suisse Romande.

A highly skilled performer, numbered among the élite of New York freelance musicians, Robison plays in a variety of ensembles, including the Chamber Music Society of Lincoln Center and the Orpheus Trio, and is often heard at festivals including those in Spoleto and Marlboro. Although not primarily committed to the newest music, she has given first performances of several pieces, among them Leon Kirchner's *Flutings for Paula* (1973).

GEORGE GELLES

Robjohn, W(illiam) J(ames) [Florio, Caryl] (*b* Tavistock, Devon, 2 Nov 1843; *d* Morganton, North Carolina, 21 Nov 1920). American composer and musician of English birth. His parents took him to New York in 1857 or 1858. Except for a few lessons as a child, he was self-taught in music. He was the first boy soloist in Trinity Church, New York, and later held many positions as organist and choirmaster. He became an actor in 1862, and touring in the northern states led to other musical jobs. Returning to New York in 1868, he became known as an accompanist, pianist in chamber music, choral and opera conductor, translator, teacher, critic and music editor. In 1870, his family opposing his musical career, he took the pseudonym Caryl Florio. In 1896 he took charge of the music at Biltmore, George Vanderbilt's estate near Asheville, North Carolina, where he remained for five years. After two more years in New York, he returned permanently to Asheville to teach and conduct choruses and church choirs. He never married.

Robjohn composed much but published little except church music. His MSS, diaries and notes for an auto-biography are in the New York Public Library. An inconsistent composer, he wrote some fresh, strong works between 1860 and 1879. However, his opera with spoken dialogue, *Uncle Tom's Cabin*, was a deserved failure in Philadelphia in 1882, and few later works were inspired.

WORKS
(selective list)

Trio in D, vn, vc, pf, 1866, *US-NYp*
Sonata no.2 in A♭, vn, pf, 1870, *NYp*
Revery and Scherzo, 2 cl, str orch, 1872, *PHf*
How the rain falls drearily, SATB, 1874, *NYp*
Quintet, pf, str, 1870s, *NYp*
Concerto in A♭, pf, orch, 1875, *PHf*
4 str quartets, 1872–96, *NYp*

BIBLIOGRAPHY

A. H. Messiter: *A History of the Choir and Music of Trinity Church, New York* (New York, 1906)

BARTON CANTRELL

Robledo, Juan Ruiz de. *See* RUIZ DE ROBLEDO, JUAN.

Robledo, Melchor (*b* c1520; *d* Saragossa, before 7 April 1587). Spanish composer. He was *maestro de capilla* at Tarragona Cathedral in 1549. He later spent some time in Rome, and on 2 July 1569 he was appointed *maestro de capilla* of La Seo, the main cathedral of Saragossa. On 12 January and 27 August 1571 respectively, the cathedral canons awarded him a prebend and a benefice in recognition of his outstanding service and in the expectation that he would enter the priesthood. A delay in his ordination, however, led to a break in his service in 1575 and to his temporary transfer to Calahorra. Early in 1581 Palencia Cathedral sought him, but by 10 February he had returned to La Seo with his annual salary increased to 100 libras. His output consists almost entirely of sacred music. His five-part mass is based on a recurrent head-motif used earlier by Morales in his *Missa cortilla* (fa, re, ut, fa, sol, la). Throughout the polytextual motet *Simile est/Inventa autem* (*I-Rvat*, copied in 1563) the quintus sings the antiphon *Veni sponsa Christi* in notes to the value of three semibreves. Robledo's music travelled as far as Mexico; his six-part *Salve regina* is in Puebla Cathedral, and a mass by Juan de Lienas, in a manuscript formerly at the Museo del Carmen, Mexico City, was closely modelled on his five-part mass.

WORKS

2 masses, 4, 5vv; 2 Magnificat, 4vv; Te Deum, 5vv; 28 psalms, 4vv; 4 motets (1 inc.), 4, 5vv; 2 Lat. hymns, 4, 6vv; 2 secular songs (inc.); several other works: *E-Bc, Boc, CA, TAc* (1 mass formerly *Tc,* see Trumpff), *TU V, Zac, I-Rvat*

4 psalms ed. H. Eslava y Elizondo, Lira sacro-hispana, siglo XVI, i/1 (Madrid, 1869); 1 motet ed. J. B. de Elústiza and G. Castrillo Hernández, *Antología musical* (Barcelona, 1933); 1 hymn ed. in *Polifonía española,* vi (Madrid, 1958); 1 Magnificat ed. S. Rubio, *Antología polifónica sacra,* ii (Madrid, 1956)

BIBLIOGRAPHY

R. Casimiri: 'Melchior Robledo, maestro a Saragozza; Juan Navarro, maestro ad Ávila nel 1574', *NA,* xi (1934), 203
H. Anglès: 'El archivo musical de la catedral de Valladolid', *AnM,* iii (1947), 85
G. A. Trumpff: 'Die Messen Cristobal de Morales', *AnM,* viii (1953), 121, 150
R. Stevenson: 'Sixteenth- and Seventeenth-century Resources in Mexico', *FAM,* i (1954), 69; ii (1955), 10
——: *Spanish Cathedral Music in the Golden Age* (Berkeley and Los Angeles, 1961), 325f

ROBERT STEVENSON

Robles, Marisa (*b* Madrid, 4 May 1937). Spanish harpist. After studying at the Madrid Conservatory, where she graduated in 1953, she made her début in Madrid in 1954 with the National Orchestra. In 1958 she briefly held the harp professorship at the Madrid Conservatory, but settled in Britain in 1959; almost immediately she began an extremely successful series of television appearances, in which the charm of her personality and the brilliant, quicksilver qualities of her playing soon endeared her to the public. She made her London début at the Festival Hall in 1963, and was appointed to teach at the RCM in 1971. She is much involved in chamber music (duo recitals with her husband, Christopher Hyde-Smith; the Robles Trio; and the Robles–Delmé Ensemble) and has made some solo recordings.

ANN GRIFFITHS

Robletti, Giovanni Battista (*fl* Rome, 1609–50). Italian printer. He usually published at his own expense at a time when printers were frequently financed either by a bookseller or the author or composer. However, he did occasionally print 'at the author's request' (e.g. Pugliaschi's *La gemma musicale,* 1618) or on behalf of booksellers, among them A. Poggioli (books 1, 4, 5 and 6 of Rontani's *Varie musiche,* 1620–23) and G. D. Franzini (Silvestri's *Florida verba* of 1648). Like other publishers of the time he published several anthologies of music he chose himself: two anthologies of sacred music (*Lilia campis, RISM* 1621³, and *Litanie,* 1622¹, both for voices and organ) and three of secular music (*Giardino musicale, RISM* 1621¹⁵, *Vezzosetti fiori,* 1622¹¹, and *Le risonanti sfere,* 1629⁹). He also published non-musical works.

Robletti's publications are accurate and clear, if not particularly elegant. A list of those extant shows that he catered for a wide range of styles and interests. He included many famous and lesser-known names in his output: G. F. Anerio (at least 16 volumes, 1609–29), Cifra (1609–20), Quagliati (1611–27) and Alessandro Capece (1615–25), as well as Frescobaldi, Landi, Nanino, Sabbatini, Soriano, Viadana, Agazzari, Falconieri, Fiorillo and d'India. Between 1631 and 1633, at the printing house of the Hospitio dei Letterati, Rome, he printed Agostino Diruta's *Messe concertate* for five voices, op.13, Serpieri's *Missa et vespertinum officium* and Sacchi's *Missarum liber primus.* Contemporary with these are F. Vitali's *Arie* for one to three voices and the *Varie musiche* for one to five voices

'concertate con il basso continuo' by Giulio Pasquali, which were published by a press of Robletti's in Orvieto.

Most of Robletti's output was produced in Rome, but he is known to have worked also in Tivoli, where a subsidy from the town granted in 1620 enabled him to print for almost 25 years, and in Rieti in 1636. His last publication is thought to be Giamberti's *Antiphonae et motecta* (1650).

BIBLIOGRAPHY

C. Sartori: *Dizionario degli editori musicali italiani* (Florence, 1958)

STEFANO AJANI

Robredo, Manuel Saumell. See SAUMELL ROBREDO, MANUEL.

Robson, Jean-Jacques (*b* Dendermonde, baptized 4 Dec 1723; *d* Tienen, 24 Oct 1785). South Netherlands composer and organist. He was singing at Notre-Dame in Dendermonde by 1734, and in 1749 became choir director of the collegiate church of St Germain in Tienen, a post which he held until 1783. The subscription lists appended to several of his works indicate that he held an important position in the musical life of his time. In 1772, with J. F. Krafft and Ignaz Vitzthumb, he served on a panel of adjudicators established to fill the post of organist of St Rombaut and bellringer of the town of Mechelen. It is known that he wrote bell pieces for this competition, but none have yet been discovered. Gregoir, who considered Robson one of the greatest organists of the period, claimed to be in possession of over 200 of his organ compositions, but his only known extant work for the organ is the *Préludes et versets* op.5; it reveals a technique orientated towards the harpsichord.

In Robson's early works an Italian influence seems prominent, though the language of Couperin and Rameau remains important. He gradually broke away from the ornamental French style but never achieved complete Classicism. His *Recueil de concert* is a model of the art of detail, of which he was undeniably a master.

Robson's brother, Sébastien-Joseph Robson (*b* Thuin, baptized 13 May 1734; *d* Turnhout, 3 July 1814), was the organist at St Pierre in Turnhout from 1754, and composed during the revolution in Brabant a *Marche des patriotes* which retained a regional popularity as *Turnhout verheven.* A later member of the family, Martin-Joseph Robson (*b* Turnhout, 18 Nov 1817; *d* Turnhout, 6 March 1884), was the organist at St Pierre from the age of 18, and later taught at Turnhout's Collège St Joseph; he also composed a *drame lyrique, Charles Quint,* as well as various motets and a mass.

WORKS

Hpd: Piesce de clavecin, op.1 (Liège, 1749), excerpts ed. in Elewyck (1877); Le divertissement du clavecin, vn acc., op.2 (Paris, n.d.); Sonates et concerts, acc. 2 vn, va, b, op.4 (before 1768); Recueil de concert (Brussels, n.d.)
Org: Préludes et versets dans les 8 différents tons, op.5 (before 1768)

BIBLIOGRAPHY

EitnerQ; FétisB
X. van Elewyck: *Matthias Van den Gheyn, le plus grand organiste et carillonneur belge du XVIII*ᵉ *siècle* (Paris, 1862)
E. Gregoir: *Galerie biographique des artistes-musiciens belges du XVIII*ᵉ *et du XIX*ᵉ *siècles* (Brussels, 1862)
X. van Elewyck: Preface to *Collection d'oeuvres composées par d'anciens et de célèbres clavecinistes flamands,* ii (Brussels, 1877)
E. vander Straeten: *La musique aux Pays-Bas avant le XIX*ᵉ *siècle,* iv (Brussels, 1878/R1969)
S. Clercx: 'Les clavecinistes belges et leur emprunts à l'art de François Couperin et de J. Ph. Rameau', *ReM* (1939), no.192, p.11

R. Vannes: *Dictionnaire des musiciens (compositeurs)* (Brussels, 1947)

S. Clercx: 'L'épanouissement au XVIIIe siècle', *La musique en Belgique du moyen âge à nos jours*, ed. E. Closson and C. van den Borren (Brussels, 1950), 201

K. De Schrijver: *Bibliografie der Belgische toonkunstenaars sedert 1800* (Louvain, 1958)

A. Billen: *J. J. Robson, zangmeester aan de kollegiale St. Germanus-kerk te Tienen* (diss., U. of Louvain, 1959)

TONY BILLEN

Robyns. This name appears on a page of 15th-century music (*GB-STb* Archer 2, f.1v) and has been assumed to apply to this setting in score of Kyrie *Deus Creator*. It is improbably located for an ascription. There is no evidence to support the existence of a composer of this name.

For bibliography *see* OLD HALL MS.

MARGARET BENT

Roca, Matheo Tollis de la. *See* TOLLIS DE LA ROCA, MATHEO.

Rocca, Giuseppe (*b* Barbaresco, Alba, 27 April 1807; *d* San Francesco d'Albaro, Genoa, 17 Jan 1865). Italian violin maker. He was a pupil of the well-known Turin violin maker Joannes Franciscus Pressenda, but probably not until after 1830. As the decade progressed Rocca's hand became ever more prominent in Pressenda's work, and two identical instruments dated 1839, one bearing Pressenda's original label and the other Rocca's, suggest that it was in that year that Rocca established himself independently. Over the following years his work was increasingly influenced by that of Stradivari, until by about 1845 there is little of Pressenda's influence to be seen. His best period is from then until about 1850, many of his instruments being strikingly handsome and excellent tonally. He used only two basic models, with almost no variation in such details as the set of the soundholes; one was based on Stradivari, the other on the Guarneri violin that belonged to the collector Tarisio and is now known as the 'Alard'. The wood is usually but not invariably of good appearance, sometimes American in origin and occasionally from a worm-affected plank said to have come from the old bridge at Turin. Violas and cellos are much rarer in his production than violins. In addition to the usual label Rocca sometimes branded the interiors with his initials. He achieved an accuracy of workmanship similar to that of French makers after his time – around 1880 – which has inevitably caused Rocca labels to be inserted in French instruments. His genuine violins are used by many fine players. About 1860 he moved his shop from Turin to Genoa, where certain of his productions lacked the finesse of earlier years.

Enrico Rocca (*b* Turin, 25 April 1847; *d* Turin, 7 June 1915) was Giuseppe's son and heir and for a brief period his pupil. He became, however, a woodworker in the naval shipyard at Genoa, and only in 1878 did he take up violin making, with the advantage of his father's designs, moulds and tools. Many of his instruments date from the early years of the 20th century. His production seems to have been much smaller than that of his father, whom he did not equal as a craftsman.

BIBLIOGRAPHY

R. Vannes: *Essai d'un dictionnaire universel des luthiers* (Paris, 1932, 2/1951/R1972 as *Dictionnaire universel des luthiers*, suppl. 1959)

CHARLES BEARE

Rocca, Lodovico (*b* Turin, 29 Nov 1895). Italian composer. He studied in Turin and under Giacomo Orefice

in Milan. From 1940 to 1966 he was director of the Turin Conservatory. His fame rests on his very successful third opera, *Il Dibuk*, in relation to which most of his other works may be regarded as preparations, by-products or postscripts. The first two operas are most interesting where they foreshadow *Il Dibuk* most strongly; the fourth, *Monte Ivnor*, uses an idiom very similar to that of its predecessor, but is less compelling and sometimes self-imitative (this decline in vitality continued in Rocca's postwar music, though the *Antiche iscrizioni* still show individuality). *Il Dibuk* is a difficult work to assess: it owes much to the striking libretto, while the music in itself often seems more an eclectic amalgam than a unified whole. The strange juxtapositions – of sombre Musorgskian or Pizzettian modality, Bloch-like orientalisms, sudden truculent outcrops of stark parallel 2nds, semitone clusters and other dissonances, and occasional sentimental reversions to a more traditional Italian operatic style – are disconcerting on paper; yet in the dramatic context these heterogeneous elements somehow cohere. Moreover, the orchestration, colourful and sometimes bizarre, even macabre, adds to the total effect, as does the Pizzetti-like power of the choral writing.

Rocca's non-theatrical works, too, may best be viewed in relation to *Il Dibuk*. The early songs, some notable in themselves, already point the way; and the *Interludio epico*, composed when the opera was in progress, is particularly close to it in style, successfully embodying some of its best qualities in compact form. In the *Proverbi di Salomone*, *Salmodia*, the *Schizzi francescani* and the relatively light *Storiella*, Rocca's taste for freakish instrumentation is carried to startling extremes. At their best these pieces recapture something of *Il Dibuk*'s poetry, but in their weaker moments (and this is already evident in the *Proverbi di Salomone*) they show that the devices deployed so tellingly in Rocca's best opera can too easily degenerate into mannerisms.

WORKS
(selective list)

Operas: La morte di Frine (E. Marco Senea [pseud. of C. Meano]), 1917–20, Milan, 1937; In terra di leggenda (La corona di re Gaulo) (Meano), 1922–3, Bergamo, 1936; Il Dibuk (R. Simoni, after S. An-Ski), 1928–30, Milan, 1934; Monte Ivnor (Meano, after Werfel; Die 40 Tage des Musa Dagh), 1936–8, Rome, 1939; L'uragano (E. Possenti, after Ostrovsky), 1942–51, Milan, 1952

Orch: Chiaroscuri, suite, 1920; La cella azzurra, 1924; Interludio epico, 1928; suites from In terra di leggenda, Il Dibuk and Monte Ivnor

Vocal with ens: Dittico, 1v, orch, 1921; Proverbi di Salomone, T, small female chorus, fl, bn, hn, tpt, harp, 2 pf, org, 14 perc, db, 1933; Salmodia (Psalm lvii), Bar, chorus, 3 hn, tpt, cel, pf, perc, 1934; Biribù, occhi di rana (N. Davicini), Mez/Bar, str qt, 1937; Schizzi francescani, T, ob, eng hn, cl, bn, pf, harp, hpd, 2 drums, 1939; Antiche iscrizioni (ancient Gk.), S, B, chorus, orch, 1952, choreographic version, Florence, 1955

Inst: Suite, vn, pf, 1928; Epitaffi, pf, 1928; Storiella, bn, 2 tpt, pf, harp, 1935

Songs: 8 cantilene su testi d'oriente, 1920; 4 melopee su epigrammi sepolcrali greci, 1921; Canti spenti, 1925; 2 sonetti francescani, 1926; 3 salmodie su fioretti di San Francesco, 1926; others

Principal publishers: Carisch, Ricordi, Suvini Zerboni

BIBLIOGRAPHY

C. Cordara: 'Un lirico della musica: Lodovico Rocca', *Pensiero musicale*, ix (Bologna, 1929), 40

F. Piccioli: 'Un musicista torinese: Lodovico Rocca', *Italia musicale*, v/6–8 (Genoa, 1932), 9

F. Abbiati: 'Lodovico Rocca e Il Dibuk', *Comoedia*, xvi/5 (Milan, 1934), 15

M. Mila: 'Compositori giovani: Lodovico Rocca', *Nuova antologia*, ccclxxvi (1934), 306

G. Rossi Doria: 'La stagione lirica a Roma: Il Dibuk', *Nuova antologia*, ccclxxxiii (1936), 351

R. Mariani: 'Musicisti del nostro tempo: Lodovico Rocca', *RaM*, xi (1938), 163
L. Colacicchi: 'Lodovico Rocca e *Monte Ivnor*', *Scenario*, ix (Rome, 1940), 40
R. Mariani: 'Ritorno di Rocca', *La Scala* (1952), no.27, p.41
G. Gavazzeni: 'Paragrafi su Lodovico Rocca', *La musica e il teatro* (Pisa, 1954), 261
F. L. Lunghi: 'Lodovico Rocca', *Santa Cecilia*, iii/2 (Rome, 1954), 54
R. Rossellini: 'Lodovico Rocca', *Polemica musicale* (Milan, 1962), 55
M. Bruni: *Lodovico Rocca* (Milan, 1963)
J. C. G. Waterhouse: *The Emergence of Modern Italian Music* (*up to 1940*) (diss., U. of Oxford, 1968), 643ff
G. Vigolo: 'Il temporale eclettico', *Il Dibuk*', *Mille e una sera all'opera e al concerto* (Florence, 1971), 153, 335
P. Caputo: 'L'operismo di Lodovico Rocca', *Rassegna musicale Curci*, xxviii/2–3 (1975), 48

JOHN C. G. WATERHOUSE

Rocchigiani, Giovanni Battista (*b* Orvieto; *d* ?Rieti, after 1632). Italian composer, anthologist and organist. When his op.3 was published in 1623 he was a musician at Orvieto Cathedral, but on 29 November in the same year he was appointed organist of Rieti Cathedral; he was confirmed in this position for five years in 1626 and again in 1631 for three, but there is no record of him after this latter date except for the publication of his op.7 in 1632. Most of his music is lost, and two of the three volumes that survive, opp.3 and 7, are anthologies. The latter includes a few of his own pieces, and it is likely that the first song in op.3 is also by him since it is a setting of a poem by him in praise of the volume's dedicatee. Of the eight monodies, seven duets and one trio (a dialogue) in op.3 only two monodies, Monteverdi's *Lamento d'Arianna* and Caccini's *Occhi soli d'amore*, have been identified; it is surprising that so famous a piece as Monteverdi's lament should have appeared anonymously. Some of the other pieces, notably the solo sonnet *Non dormo, no, non sogno*, are not unworthy companions for it.

WORKS
Il primo libro de' motetti, 1–4vv, bc, op.1 (Orvieto, 1620)
Il maggio fiorito: arie, sonetti, e madrigali de diversi autori, 1–3vv, bc, libro I, op.3 (Orvieto, 1623⁸), inc.
Dialogorum concentuum, 2–5vv, op.7 (Rome, 1632¹)

BIBLIOGRAPHY
A. Sacchetti-Sassetti: 'La cappella musicale del duomo di Rieti', *NA*, xvii (1940), 146
J. A. Westrup: 'Monteverdi's "Lamento d'Arianna"', *MR*, i (1940), 144

NIGEL FORTUNE

Roccia. Italian family of musicians, active mainly in Naples. Apart from the members discussed below, the family included Teseo, Geronimo, Nicandro and Aniello who served as singers at the Annunziata chapel between 1604 and 1621.

(1) **Aurelio Roccia** (*b* ?Venafro, ?*c*1540–50; *d* ?Naples, after 1571). Composer and instrumentalist. Both he and his brother Plinio (*b c*1540–50) were among the original members of a corporation of musicians formed in Naples in 1569. Both were musicians at the Naples court; Aurelio was employed there as a cornettist. In 1571 he published his *Primo libro de' madrigali à quattro voci* in Naples, settings of texts by Alamanni, Ariosto, L. Borra, L. Capilupi, F. M. Molza and Parabosco. One of his sons, Vespasiano (*b* Naples, ?*c*1570–80), is represented by four *laude* (in *RISM* 1599⁶).

(2) **Dattilo Roccia** (*b* ?Venafro, ?*c*1570–80; *d* ?Naples, after 1617). Singer and composer, son of (1) Aurelio Roccia. He was an alto in the chapel of the Annunziata in Naples from 1592 to 1594. Some time

before 1600 he dedicated his first book of five-voice madrigals (now lost) to Cardinal Innico d'Avalos d'Aragona and, on 2 August 1603, his *Secondo libro de madrigali à cinque voci* to Benedetto Giustiniano. His *Primo libro de madrigali a quattro voci* (Naples, 1608) and his *Libro terzo di madrigali à cinque voci* (Naples, 1617¹⁹) avoid the extreme dissonances and contrasts of the Neapolitan *seconda prattica* madrigal. One madrigal was printed in *RISM* 1609¹⁶.

(3) **Francesco Roccia** (*b* Naples, 5 Jan 1582; *d* ?Naples, after 1613). Composer and organist, son of Plinio Roccia. He is mentioned in Cerreto's *Della prattica musica* (1601) as an excellent composer and organist, but only four madrigals in *RISM* 1599⁶, 1609¹⁶, 1617¹⁹ and Dattilo's *Secondo libro* survive. On 3 January 1613 he was paid 20 ducats for giving singing lessons. In 1588 a Francesco Roccia was organist of the S Maria di Loreto Conservatory in Naples.

BIBLIOGRAPHY
U. Prota-Giurleo: 'I musici di Castelnuovo', *Corriere di Napoli* (5 April 1940)
——: 'Musica all'Annunziata', *Roma* (23 March 1950)
F. Strazzullo: 'Inediti per la storia della musica a Napoli', *Il fuidoro*, ii (1955), 107
U. Prota-Giurleo: 'Aggiunte ai "Documenti per la storia dell'arte a Napoli"', *Il fuidoro*, ii (1955), 273

KEITH A. LARSON

Rocha, Francisco Gomes da (*d* Vila Rica, 9 Feb 1808). Brazilian composer, singer and conductor, active in Minas Gerais during the colonial period. On 2 June 1768 he entered the Brotherhood of St Joseph of Coloured Men (St Joseph's was the church of the many mulattos in Vila Rica). In 1780 he was mentioned as a contralto in a document of the Royal Senate of the city of Vila Rica. About 1800 he succeeded the composer Lôbo de Mesquita as conductor for the Brotherhood of the Third Order of Carmo. The records of the Brotherhood of St Joseph mention him as kettledrummer in the local regiment of dragoons, an indication of the varied sources of income of many colonial musicians. His extant works are *Novena de Nossa Senhora do Pilar a 4* (1789), *Spiritus Domini a 8* (1795), *Popule meus a quatro vozes* and *Cum descendentibus in lacum para Sexta Feira da Paixão*. They reveal a thorough assimilation of Classical stylistic traits in the treatment of the chorus and in the concertato style of the instrumental accompaniment.

BIBLIOGRAPHY
F. C. Lange: 'La música en Vila Rica (Minas Gerais, siglo XVIII)', *Revista musical chilena* (1967), no.102, pp.8–55; (1968), no.103, pp.77–149
——: 'Os irmãos músicos da Irmandade de São José dos Homens Pardos, de Vila Rica', *Yearbook, Inter-American Institute for Musical Research*, iv (1968), 110
G. Béhague: 'Música "barrôca" mineira: problemas de fontes e estilística', *Universitas* (Revista de cultura da Universidade federal da Bahia), ii (1969), 133
——: 'Música colonial mineira à luz de novos manuscritos', *Barroco* (Revista de Ensaio e Pesquisa Universidade federal de Minas Gerais), iii (1971), 15

GERARD BÉHAGUE

Rochberg, George (*b* Paterson, NJ, 5 July 1918). American composer. After receiving the BA from Montclair State Teacher's College he attended the Mannes School (1939–42) to study counterpoint and composition with Weisse, Szell and Mannes. War service interrupted his studies, but on his return to the USA in 1945 he enrolled at the Curtis Institute, studied theory and composition with Scalero and Menotti, and obtained the

BMus in 1947. In the following year he obtained the MA from the University of Pennsylvania and joined the staff of the Curtis Institute, remaining there until 1954. In 1950, as a Fulbright and American Academy Fellow in Rome, he met Dallapiccola and was strongly impressed by the power of serial music. The next year he began his association with Presser as music editor and soon became director of publications, a post he held until he was appointed chairman of the music department at the University of Pennsylvania in 1960. He resigned the chairmanship in 1968 and has remained at that university as professor of music. The importance of his work as a composer and teacher has been recognized by appointments as guest composer at Buffalo as Slee Professor (1964), the Temple Institute of Music (1969), the Oberlin Festival of Contemporary Music (1970), Testimonium, Jerusalem (1970–71), and the Aspen Conference (1972).

The path of Rochberg's development as a composer is marked by a succession of intensive engagements with many of the major aesthetic issues of his time. At each stage he has produced a number of important compositions and essays that explore aesthetic problems. His music of the late 1940s reveals a vigorous temperament with strong affinities with the idioms of Stravinsky, Hindemith and, especially, Bartók (the Capriccio and the First String Quartet). Then in the early 1950s he plunged into Schoenbergian serialism and felt his imagination liberated at last by a language he took to be the inevitable culmination of historical developments. He mastered its technique and explored its expressive possibilities in such works as the 12 Bagatelles, the Chamber Symphony, *David the Psalmist* and the Second Symphony. In about 1957 he felt Webern's influence direct him to an increasingly refined serialism (*Cheltenham Concerto*), but he also became interested in the superposition of tempos in order to break down what he regarded as the temporal and gestural constraints imposed by serialism (*La bocca della verità* and *Time Span*). The most important work of this period, demonstrating these developments, is the Second String Quartet.

Rochberg's struggle to free himself from serialism continued into the early 1960s (his last serial piece is the Piano Trio) when he broadened his range to include tonal idioms. As a step towards assimilating traditional elements of style into a new and more universal language, he explored the technique of assemblage in such works as *Contra mortem et tempus* (where he quoted from Boulez, Berio, Varèse and Ives), *Music for the Magic Theater* (with inclusions from Mozart, Beethoven, Mahler, Webern, Varèse, Stockhausen and Rochberg himself) and *Nach Bach*. Quotation from the tonal repertory is replaced by a complete re-acquisition of earlier styles in later works, such as the Third String Quartet, which approaches Beethoven and Mahler in manner. Through this and other works he has challenged commonly held notions of 'traditional' and 'avant garde', and asserted his belief in the need for perceptibility of musical structure, for balance between reason and feeling, for transcendence over the ego and for universality.

WORKS
ORCHESTRAL
Night Music, 1949; Capriccio, 1949, rev. 1957; Chamber Sym., 9 insts, 1953; Cantio sacra, small orch, 1954; Sym. no.1, 1949–57, rev. 1971–; Sym. no.2, 1955–6; Cheltenham Conc., small orch, 1958; Time Span, 1962; Apocalyptica, band, 1964; Zodiac [orche-

stration of 12 Bagatelles], 1964–5; 3 Black Pieces, 1965; Music for the Magic Theater, 15 insts, 1965; Black Sounds, 1965, choreographed as The Act (A. Sokolow); Fanfares, brass, 1968; Sym. no.3, solo vv, chamber chorus, double chorus, orch, 1966–9; Imago mundi, 1973; Vn Conc., 1975

VOCAL
With orch/ens: David, the Psalmist, T, orch, 1954; Blake Songs, S, 8 insts, 1961; Passions According to the 20th Century, solo vv, chorus, insts, 1967; Music for The Alchemist (Jonson), S, 11 insts, 1966–8; Tableaux (P. Rochberg: Silver Talons of Piero Kostrov), S, 2 actors, small male chorus, 12 insts, 1968; Sacred Songs of Reconciliation (Mizmor l'Piyus), B-Bar, chamber orch, 1970; Phaedra (monodrama, R. Lowell, after Racine), Mez, orch, 1973–4
Unacc. choral: 3 Psalms, 1954
Songs for 1v, pf: Songs of Solomon, 1946; Book of [35] Songs, 1937–69; 3 cantes flamencos, high Bar, pf, 1969; Songs (P. Rochberg), 1969; [14] Songs in Praise of Krishna, 1970; 4 Fantasies (P. Rochberg, 1971)

CHAMBER AND INSTRUMENTAL
Chamber: Str Qt no.1, 1952; Duo concertante, vn, vc, 1955; Serenate d'estate, fl, harp, gui, str trio, 1955; Dialogues, cl, pf, 1957–8; La bocca della verità, ob, pf, 1958–9; Str Qt no.2 (Rilke), S, str qt, 1959–61; Pf Trio, 1963; Contra mortem et tempus, fl, cl, pf, vn, 1965; 50 Caprice-variations [after Paganini], vn, 1970; Str Qt no.3, 1972; Electrikaleidoscope, vn, vc, fl, cl, elec pf, 1972; Ukiyo-e, harp, 1974; Pf Qnt, 1975
Kbd: 12 Bagatelles, pf, 1952; Sonata-fantasia, pf, 1956; Arioso, pf, 1959; Bartokiana, pf, 1959; Nach Bach, fantasia, hpd/pf, 1966; Prelude on Happy Birthday, pf, 1969; Carnival Music, pf, 1971

Principal publisher: Presser

WRITINGS
The Hexachord and its Relation to the Twelve-tone Row (Bryn Mawr, 1955)
'The Harmonic Tendency of the Hexachord', *JMT*, iii (1959), 208
'Indeterminacy in the New Music', *The Score* (1960), no.27, p.9
'Duration in Music', *The Modern Composer and his World*, ed. J. Beckwith and U. Kasemets (Toronto, 1961), 56
'Webern's Search for Harmonic Identity', *JMT*, vii (1962), 109
'The New Image of Music', *PNM*, ii/1 (1963), 1
Review of G. Perle: *Serial Composition and Atonality, JAMS*, xvi (1963), 413
'Schoenberg's American Period', *International Cyclopedia of Music and Musicians* (New York, 9/1964), 1915
'The Avant Garde and the Aesthetics of Survival', *New Literary History*, iii (1971), 71
'Reflections on Renewal of Music', *CMc* (1972), no.13, p.75
'Reflections on Schoenberg', *PNM*, xi/2 (1973), 56

BIBLIOGRAPHY
A. Ringer: 'The Music of George Rochberg', *MQ*, lii (1966), 409
AUSTIN CLARKSON

Roche, Jerome (Lawrence Alexander) (*b* Cairo, 22 May 1942). British musicologist. He studied at Downside School (1956–9) before reading music at St John's College, Cambridge (1959–62, 1964–7; BA 1962, MusB 1963). He took the doctorate at Cambridge in 1968 with a dissertation on Italian 17th-century sacred music, supervised by Denis Arnold, in which he concentrated on the development of the sacred vocal duet. In 1967 he was appointed a lecturer at Durham University. He received a British Academy Scholarship to study at the Cini Foundation, Venice, in 1973. Italian studies have dominated Roche's research and through his work much Italian church music, particularly by Cavalli, Crivelli and Grandi (editions of whose music he published in 1968), has become more widely known. His monograph on Palestrina attempts to place the composer in a broad context. He has also published a concise study of the madrigal and edited *The Penguin Book of Four-part Italian Madrigals* (Harmondsworth, 1975).

WRITINGS
'Music at S. Maria Maggiore, Bergamo, 1614–1643', *ML*, xlvii (1966), 296
'The Duet in Early Seventeenth-century Italian Church Music', *PRMA*, xciii (1966–7), 33
North Italian Liturgical Music in the Early 17th Century (diss., U. of Cambridge, 1968)
'Monteverdi and the Prima Prattica', *The Monteverdi Companion*,

ed. D. Arnold and N. Fortune (London, 1968), 167
Palestrina (London, 1971)
'Monteverdi: an Interesting Example of Second Thoughts', *MR*, xxxiii (1971), 193
The Madrigal (London, 1972)
'Anthologies and the Dissemination of Early Baroque Italian Sacred Music', *Soundings*, iv (1974), 6
'Giovanni Antonio Rigatti and the Development of Venetian Church Music in the 1640's', *ML*, lvii (1976), 256
'Grandi, Alessandro (i)', 'Moscheles, Ignaz', 'Motet', §III, 2, *Grove 6*

DAVID SCOTT

Rochefort, Jean Baptiste (*b* Paris, 24 June 1746; *d* Paris, 1819). French composer and conductor. He was a choirboy at Notre Dame in Paris. In 1775 he joined the orchestra of the Paris Opéra as a double bass player, but left in 1780 to take charge of the French opera at the Landgrave of Hesse's court in Kassel. In 1785 he returned to the Opéra orchestra and shortly afterwards was appointed second conductor; he remained in the service of this institution until 1815. Apart from some chamber music, he composed mainly for the theatre, contributing additional music to other composers' works, arranging a pasticcio *Descente d'Orphée aux enfers* (1798) and a parody of Pasquale Anfossi's *L'incognita perseguitata* as *L'inconnue persécutée* (1776). His own works suggest his efficiency in meeting the demands of the ballet-masters rather than any pronounced individuality, although there are moments of originality in some of his major works, and his command of the orchestra is evident. *Bacchus et Ariane* (Paris Opéra, 11 December 1791) calls for a serpent, an instrument seldom explicitly named in scores of the period. His later works include several pieces of revolutionary sentiment, among them an (unfulfilled) 'prophétie', *La descente en Angleterre*, in which he attempted to depict in music the characteristics of the English and French peoples.

WORKS

STAGE

(first performed in Paris unless otherwise stated)

oc – *opéra comique*

Operas: La corbeille de mariage, ou La force du sang, 1775, *F-Pn*; Justine et Landri, ou Le bail à loyer (oc), 1780, *Pn*; Le temple de la postérité (intermède), Kassel, 1780; Daphnis et Florise (pastorale), Kassel, 1782, *Pn*; Les noces de Zerbine (oc), Kassel, ?1780–85; La pompe funèbre de Crispin (oc), Kassel, ?1780–85; Ariane (scène lyrique), 1788; Toulon soumis, 1793, *Pn*; La descente en Angleterre, 1797; La cassette (oc); Dorothée (oc); L'esprit de contradiction (oc); arr. P. Anfossi: L'incognita perseguitata as L'inconnue persécutée (oc), 1776

Melodramas: L'amour vengé, 1779; Pyrame et Thisbé, Kassel; Le lever de l'aurore (prologue), 1786–9; Echo et Narcisse, 1786–9

Ballets: L'enlèvement d'Europe (pantomime héroïque), 1776; Le fagot, ou Guillot et Guillemette (ballet pastoral), 1776; La pantoufle (ballet pantomime), 1779; Jérusalem délivrée, ou Renaud et Armide, 1780; Adélaide, ou L'innocence reconnue (pantomime) 1780; Hercule et Omphale (pantomime), 1787; La mort du Capitaine Cook (pantomime), 1788; Bacchus et Ariane, 1791; La mort d'Hercule (pantomime), 1796; La latière polonaise (pantomime), 1798; Kanko (pantomime), 1798; Descente d'Orphée aux Enfers (pantomime), 1798, pasticcio; Le mont terrible, ou Les amants piémontais (pantomime), 1799; La masque de fer, ou Le souterrain (pantomime); Diane enchaîné par l'Amour (comédie ballet); La Vestale (pantomime); La prise de Grenade, *Pn*

OTHER WORKS

(all printed works published in Paris)

Vocal: 3 motets, perf. Paris, Concert Spirituel, 1775; Prière à l'Etre suprême (n.d.); Prière à l'Eternel (1794); others, incl. airs, romances

Chamber: 6 str qts, op.1 (1778); 6 str qts, op.2 (1780); 6 duos dialogués, 2 vn, op.3 (1781)

BIBLIOGRAPHY

EitnerQ; *FétisB*
A. Choron and F. Fayolle: *Dictionnaire historique des musiciens* (Paris, 1810–11/*R*1971)

JULIAN RUSHTON

Rochester. American city in the state of New York, incorporated in 1834. The earliest accounts of music, dating from 1819, describe vocal recitals, hymn-singing, and concerts by town bands. German settlers added to the city's cultural life by the middle of the century. Touring virtuosos like Ole Bull and Jenny Lind shared their popularity with troupes of family singers, bell-ringers and minstrels. Church choirs performed oratorios as well as popular hymns.

By the beginning of the 20th century, four recital halls had been erected. Choral societies, bands, orchestras and an opera company were founded. Music was included in the curricula of the public schools in response to community demand. Teachers' institutes for vocal instruction, annual choral festivals and competitions were well attended. The impresario James E. Furlong, with an excellent artists' series, added to Rochester's importance as a concert centre in western New York.

In 1912 Herman Dossenbach, Alf Klingenberg and Oscar Gareissen opened the DKG Institute of Musical Art, later purchased by George Eastman to form the nucleus of the Eastman School of Music. The owner of the Eastman Kodak Company envisaged a cultural centre consisting of a professional school of music, a theatre for the performing arts, a cinema and a recital hall, all under one roof. In 1921 he presented the new building, with an endowment fund, to the University of Rochester. Today the Eastman Theatre (seating 3100) is the city's principal auditorium; Kilbourn Hall (seating 500) is a popular hall for recitals and chamber music. Rochester's other halls include Nazareth Arts Center, built 1967 (seating 1153), the Memorial Art Gallery Auditorium, built 1968 (seating 300), and Cutler Union (seating 700).

The Columbia Opera Company flourished briefly in the 1880s; the American Opera Company functioned from 1922 to 1929. The present Opera Theatre of Rochester (1962) engages guest stars, local singers, and the Rochester PO (founded 1922) to present standard repertory in Eastman Theatre. The Eastman School Opera Theatre (1947), directed by Leonard Treash, presents students in standard and new operas in Eastman Theatre. Since 1952 Opera Under the Stars (1952) has been part of a summer festival presented by the Eastman School of Music in cooperation with Monroe County and sponsored by the New York State Council of the Arts. Several operas produced by Daniel Patrylak are presented at Highland Park Bowl.

Eastman Theatre is the home of the Rochester PO, whose musical directors have included Albert Coates, Eugene Goossens, José Iturbi, Erich Leinsdorf, Theodore Bloomfield and László Somogyi. Under the patronage of the Rochester Civic Music Association, this professional orchestra has a regular season of 16 concerts, a chamber music series at Nazareth Arts Center, and many programmes for schools and factories. The Rochester Chamber Orchestra, founded in 1964, plays four annual concerts at Nazareth Arts Center under the direction of David Fetler.

The Rochester Oratorio Society, founded in 1945, a community chorus of 200 members conducted by Theodore Hollenbach, gives several major oratorios each season in addition to its annual performance of Handel's *Messiah*. Since 1955 the Bach Chorus, consisting of members of the Oratorio Society, has had a Baroque festival at Asbury First Methodist Church, assisted by guest soloists and the Rochester PO.

The University of Rochester's Eastman School of Music (founded 1921), with a faculty of 122 and student body of 600, offers a complete range of degrees in performance, composition, musicology, pedagogy and theory. The school supports two orchestras, a symphonic wind ensemble, chamber groups, choruses, an opera theatre, a collegium musicum and a jazz ensemble, as well as a Great Performers series of professional concerts in Kilbourn Hall. The director, Howard Hanson (emeritus since 1964), produced annual festivals of American music from 1925 to 1971. More than 250 works chosen from the programmes of these festivals have been recorded. The school's preparatory department trains 1000 pupils. Hanson was succeeded by Walter Hendl; in 1973 Robert S. Freeman became director.

Hochstein School (founded 1918) is a settlement music school with a faculty of 43 and a student body of 550. The Arts Council of Rochester (founded 1958) coordinates activities, publishes a bulletin, and issues a monthly calendar of cultural events.

BIBLIOGRAPHY

R. H. Lansing: 'Music in Rochester from 1817 to 1909', *Rochester Historical Society, Publication Fund Series*, ii (1923), 135–85

S. B. Sabin: 'A Retrospect of Music in Rochester', *Centennial History of Rochester, New York*, ii (1932), 45–90

B. McKelvey: *Rochester the Water Power City, 1812–1854* (Cambridge, Mass., 1945)

C. C. Riker: *The Eastman School of Music, 1921–1946* (Rochester, 1948)

B. McKelvey: *The Quest for Quality, 1890–1925* (Cambridge, Mass., 1956)

——: *An Emerging Metropolis, 1925–1961* (Cambridge, Mass., 1961)

C. C. Riker: *The Eastman School of Music, 1947–1962* (Rochester, 1963)

RUTH T. WATANABE

Rochetti, (Gaetano) Filippo (*fl* 1724–after 1750). Italian tenor. He joined Rich's company at Lincoln's Inn Fields as a singer between the acts in the autumn of 1724 (at a weekly salary of 5 guineas), making his first appearance 'on the British Stage' on 21 November, and remained there until the end of 1732. He then moved to Rich's new theatre at Covent Garden until 1735. He sang in many pantomimes and afterpieces, with music mostly by Galliard or Pepusch, a revival of the old pasticcio opera *Camilla* (November 1726), Purcell's *Dioclesian* (1731) and a one-act *Telemachus* with music by Alessandro Scarlatti (April 1732). He had a benefit every year, generally at Lincoln's Inn Fields but sometimes at the New Haymarket or Hickford's Room. The occasion of his 1731 benefit (Lincoln's Inn Fields, 26 March) was the first public performance of Handel's *Acis and Galatea*, in which he sang Acis and added the 'favourite hornpipe' 'Son confusa pastorella' from the new opera *Poro*, which had taken London by storm. Handel may have given his consent, but did not conduct the performance. In July 1733 Rochetti was a member of Handel's hastily assembled company at Oxford, singing in *Esther* (Harbonah and Israelite), the first performance of *Athalia* (Mathan), the bilingual *Acis and Galatea* (Dorindo) and perhaps *Deborah*. At Lincoln's Inn Fields in spring 1734 he played small parts for the Opera of the Nobility in Bononcini's *Astarto* (26 February) and Porpora's *Enea nel Lazio* (11 May), despite breaking his leg in between. He seems to have been out of London between April 1735 and March 1739, when he reappeared at Covent Garden in Pescetti's *Angelica e Medoro*. He sang there in a composite Purcell masque on 10 December, and from January to May 1740 was a member of Lord Middlesex's company at the New Haymarket, in a pasticcio and operas by Hasse (*Olimpia in Ebuda*) and Pescetti (*Busiri*). He appeared once at Covent Garden in January 1741, and on 16 May 1744 took part in a performance of Pergolesi's cantata *Orfeo* at Hickford's Room. He was singing at Edinburgh in the 1750s, having apparently settled permanently in Britain.

WINTON DEAN

Rochlitz, (Johann) Friedrich (*b* Leipzig, 12 Feb 1769; *d* Leipzig, 16 Dec 1842). German critic and editor. He was educated at the Thomasschule, Leipzig, and studied composition and counterpoint with the Thomas Kantor, J. F. Doles. He began composing at an early age and was 17 when his cantata *Die Vollendung des Erlösers* was first performed. It was perhaps the impression made on him by Mozart, whom he met in Leipzig in 1789, that caused him to doubt his own talent and abandon a musical career; on his father's advice he began studying theology, but in 1794 he chose the career of a writer, since his humble background prevented advancement in the Church. His time spent in theological studies had not been idle, though; he later worked on an edition of the *Heilige Schrift des Neuen Testaments* and, commissioned by the Leipzig city council, prepared a new adaptation of the text and music of the church hymnal. He also published many stories and dramatic works, as well as popular scientific articles, all of which found recognition in his lifetime. Goethe presented him at court in Weimar; he won much praise for his translation of Sophocles' *Antigone*; and his German text of Mozart's *Don Giovanni* was retained as the standard version in Germany for longer than any other contemporary translation. It was certainly these successes which prompted the publishers Breitkopf & Härtel to engage him in 1798 as editor of the newly founded journal *Allgemeine musikalische Zeitung*. This turned Rochlitz to a career of musical writing, and he quickly made an important name for himself. In 1818 he withdrew as the journal's editor, but he remained a contributor until 1835. As one of the directors of the Leipzig Gewandhaus Orchestra, he was able to affect directly the music of his time through the selection of music.

Rochlitz's influence was due not only to the fact that, during its life span of 50 years, the *Allgemeine musikalische Zeitung* greatly overshadowed other similar journals; it rested also on his comprehensive education and musical discrimination. Although Goethe did not consider himself particularly stimulated by Rochlitz, he held his friend of long standing in high esteem and treated him with distinction. Rochlitz procured for Goethe the carefully tested Streicher grand piano on which Mendelssohn and Hummel performed 'great and important concertos'. Goethe's friend C. G. Carus could picture Rochlitz only in 18th-century court dress, and it is true that Rochlitz was rather conservative even in his aesthetic views. He particularly admired the music of Handel, Haydn and Mozart, as well as that of J. S. Bach, although he also appreciated Weber and Spohr. (Both these composers set texts by Rochlitz, as did Schubert.)

Although he recognized Beethoven's genius, Rochlitz's attitude to his great contemporary was basically critical. The first issues of the *AMZ* contained quite severe appraisals of Beethoven's early works, and Schindler reported that Beethoven had often been decidedly annoyed with the 'Leipzig O[xen]'. These articles reveal the way in which Beethoven's works deviated from the prevailing theory of art, and clarify what was considered strange at the time. Beginning with the review of the violin sonatas opp.23 and 24 (May 1800) the *AMZ* critiques became benevolent. During a visit to Vienna in 1822, Rochlitz paid his respects to Beethoven and described the encounter in detail in his *Für Freunde der Tonkunst*. According to Schindler, Beethoven requested on his deathbed that Rochlitz compile his biography, but Rochlitz refused on grounds of ill-health. In his Mozart biography Jahn refuted what Rochlitz had reported after his meeting with Mozart, and similarly Thayer criticized Rochlitz's description of his visit to Beethoven. It therefore remains uncertain how accurately Rochlitz would have recounted the story of Beethoven's life and work; careful study of his remarks about Beethoven certainly raises doubt that he was able fully to appreciate Beethoven's character (Rochlitz saw him as having a disposition of 'childlike geniality'), though Rochlitz regarded him as the most important representative of the new German music. However, Beethoven certainly respected Rochlitz and supposedly showed no further interest in the *AMZ* after Rochlitz resigned as its editor. Indeed, the entire German-speaking world heeded Rochlitz's artistic judgments; Schindler lauded them as 'the only critical tribunal of generally recognized authority'.

WRITINGS
Edition: *Auswahl des Besten aus Friedrich Rochlitz' sämmtlichen Schriften*, ed. R. Rochlitz (Züllichau, 1821–2) [FR]

AESTHETIC AND BIOGRAPHICAL
Blick in das Gebiet der Künste und der praktischen Philosophie (Gotha, 1796)
Einige Ideen über die Anwendung des guten Geschmacks auf die religiösen Versammlungshäuser der Christen (Leipzig, 1796)
Für Freunde der Tonkunst (Leipzig, 1824, 3/1868, ed. A. Dörffel, with appx containing list of writings and biography) [3 essays on J. S. Bach repr. in *Wege zu Bach*, ed. J. M. Müller-Blattau (Augsburg, 1926)]
Essays, reviews, obituaries and biographical articles in *AMZ* and other journals, correspondence with Goethe and others

SETTINGS
Das Ende des Gerechten, oratorio, 1800, composed J. G. Schicht [FR, v]
Der erste Ton, cantata, 1800, composed Weber [FR, v]
Das Blumenmädchen, opera, 1802, composed G. B. Bierey [FR, ii]
In seiner Ordnung schafft der Herr, hymn, 1812, composed Weber
Die letzten Dinge, oratorio, 1825, composed Spohr
Des Heilands letzte Stunden [arr. from *Das Ende des Gerechten*], oratorio, 1835, composed Spohr

EDITIONS
Sammlung vorzüglicher Gesang-Stücke vom Ursprung gesetzmässiger Harmonie bis auf die Neuzeit (Leipzig, 1838–40)

BIBLIOGRAPHY
F. Rochlitz: 'Selbstbiographie', *AMZ*, xlv/7–12 (1843)
W. von Biedermann, ed.: *Goethes Briefwechsel mit Friedrich Rochlitz* (Leipzig, 1887)
H. Ehinger: *Friedrich Rochlitz als Musikschriftsteller* (Leipzig, 1929/R1976) [with a catalogue of Rochlitz's writings in *AMZ*]
J. M. Müller-Blattau: 'Friedrich Rochlitz und die Musikgeschichte', *Hans Albrecht in memoriam* (Kassel, 1962)
H. Ehinger: 'Rochlitz, (Johann) Friedrich', *MGG*
HORST LEUCHTMANN

Rochois, Marthe le. *See* LE ROCHOIS, MARTHE.

Rock. *See* POPULAR MUSIC, §III, 6.

Rock and roll. A style of popular music originating in the USA in the mid-1950s, and giving rise to 'rock' music. *See* POPULAR MUSIC, §III, 4, 6.

Röckel [Roeckel]. German family of musicians.

(1) **Joseph** [Josef] **(August) Röckel** (*b* Neunburg, Upper Palatinate, 28 Aug 1783; *d* Cöthen, 19 Sept 1870). Tenor. He was originally intended for the church, but in 1803 entered the diplomatic service. In 1804 he was engaged to sing in Vienna at the Theater an der Wien, where on 29 March 1806 he appeared as Florestan in the première of the second version of Beethoven's *Fidelio*. He subsequently taught singing at the Hofoper, where Henriette Sontag was among his pupils. After travelling to Mannheim, Trier, Bremen, Prague, Zagreb and Aachen, in 1830 he went to Paris, where he produced German operas with a German company. Encouraged by the success of this venture he remained in Paris until 1832, when he took his company to London and produced *Fidelio*, *Der Freischütz* and other German operas at the King's Theatre with such distinguished singers as Schröder-Devrient and Haitzinger. The company was conducted by Hummel, Röckel's brother-in-law. In 1835 he retired from operatic life, and in 1846 went to York as a music teacher, returning to Germany in 1853.

(2) **August Röckel** (*b* Graz, 1 Dec 1814; *d* Budapest, 18 June 1876). Conductor and composer, son of (1) Joseph Röckel. He was taught by his father, with whose travelling company he worked as a répétiteur, and later studied in Vienna (as a piano pupil of J. C. Kessler) and in Paris, where he was Rossini's assistant at the Théâtre-Italien. He became director of music at Bamberg (1838), Weimar (1839–43) and Dresden (1843–9), where he met Wagner. In 1839 he wrote an opera, *Farinelli*, which was later accepted for performance at Dresden, although Röckel withdrew it out of esteem for Wagner's genius. Like Wagner, he was involved in the Dresden Revolution of 1848, when he abandoned music and devoted himself entirely to politics. After 13 years in prison (1849–62) he became editor of various newspapers in Coburg, Frankfurt am Main, Munich and Vienna successively. It is for his correspondence with Wagner that he is chiefly remembered.

(3) **Eduard Röckel** (*b* Trier, 20 Nov 1816; *d* Bath, 2 Nov 1899). Pianist, son of (1) Joseph Röckel. He travelled with his father, and completed his studies in Weimar with his uncle, Hummel. He went to London in 1835 and gave his first concert the following year at the King's Theatre. He subsequently toured in Germany and performed with great success at the courts of Prussia, Saxony, Saxe-Weimar, Anhalt-Dessau and elsewhere. In 1848 he settled in Bath. He published a large amount of piano music.

(4) **Joseph Leopold Röckel** (*b* London, 11 April 1838; *d* Vittel, Vosges, 20 June 1923). Teacher and composer, son of (1) Joseph Röckel. He studied composition in Würzburg with Eisenhofer and orchestration with Götze in Weimar. Having settled in Bristol, he became well known as a teacher and a prolific composer of songs and cantatas.

BIBLIOGRAPHY
La Mara [pseud. of M. Lipsius], ed.: *Richard Wagners Briefe an August Röckel* (Leipzig, 1894, 2/1912; Eng. trans., 1897)
J. N. Burk, ed.: *Letters of Richard Wagner: the Burrell Collection* (London, 1951; Ger. edn., 1953)
R. Sietz: 'Röckel', *MGG*
WILLIAM BARCLAY SQUIRE/R

Rock gong. A LITHOPHONE consisting of a group of resonant boulders.

Rock harmonica. *See* LITHOPHONE.

Rock steady. Urban popular music and dance style of Jamaican origin. It succeeded 'ska' as the dominant indigenous type in the mid-1960s. By 1969–70 rock steady had undergone slight stylistic changes and became known as REGGAE.

Rockstro [Rackstraw], **William (Smith)** (*b* North Cheam, Surrey, 5 Jan 1823; *d* London, 2 July 1895). English pianist, composer and writer on music. His first teachers were the blind organist John Purkis and Sterndale Bennett; in 1845 he entered the Leipzig Conservatory and studied for a year with Mendelssohn (composition), Hauptmann (theory) and Louis Plaidy (piano). For some years after his return to England he was active in London as a teacher, performer and composer, and became the regular accompanist at the Wednesday Concerts. In the early 1860s he moved to Torquay, and from 1867 to 1891 was organist and honorary precentor at All Saints' Church, Babbacombe. During this time he produced successful textbooks on harmony (1881) and counterpoint (1882), as well as biographies of Handel and Mendelssohn and various books on music history. His interest in early music, on which he became one of the first authorities in England, led to the publication of a *Festival Psalter, adapted to the Gregorian Tones* (1863), in which he collaborated with T. F. Ravenshaw. In 1891 he returned to London and gave lectures in music history at the Royal Academy and the Royal College of Music, as well as instruction in piano and singing, in which his methods were remarkably successful. In the same year he collaborated with Scott Holland in writing a biography of his old friend, Jenny Lind.

As a composer Rockstro was too much influenced by others, especially Mendelssohn, to be truly original, though several of his songs have a certain charm, for example *Queen and Huntress*, perhaps his most popular work. As a teacher he was highly regarded, and as a historian he did useful and original work on early English music (e.g. his edition of *English Carols of the 15th Century*, 1891). His biographies and books on general history contain much of permanent value in spite of a tendency towards subjective evaluation of the music. His piano arrangements of classical and other operas in *The Standard Lyric Drama* (London, 1847–52) were among the first attempts to make such music more widely available.

WRITINGS
A History of Music (London, 1879, 2/c1885)
A Key to Practical Harmony (London, 1881)
Practical Harmony (London, 1881)
The Rules of Counterpoint (London, 1882)
The Life of G. F. Handel (London, 1883)
Mendelssohn (London, 1884)
A General History of Music (London, 1886)
with H. S. Holland: *Memoir of Jenny Lind-Goldschmidt* (London, 1891)
——: *Jenny Lind the Artist* (London, 1893)
Jenny Lind: a Record and Analysis (London, 1894)

BIBLIOGRAPHY
Obituary, *MT*, xxxvi (1895), 549

Rock-tom. *See* TOM-TOM.

Rococo. A term from decorative art that has been applied by analogy to music, especially French music, of the 18th century. It properly stands for a style of architectural decoration that originated in France during the last years of the 17th century, born of a relaxation of the rules of French classicism, not as a consequence of the Italian Baroque. The derivation of the term (*rocaille*, 'shellwork') is *post facto* and pejorative, like most critical descriptions of the style. Kimball, one of the first to establish its origins, described it as 'linear organization of surface through the transformation of the frame on the suggestion of the arabesque'. According to him the first phase, one of incomparable lightness and grace, lasted until about 1730 and is properly called 'style régence'; the main creative figure was Lepautre, who derived his inspiration from the painted arabesque of Bérain, the so-called prophet of Rococo. A second phase, the 'genre pittoresque' or 'style Louis XV', lasted until about 1760 and was an elaboration of the first in the direction of more exaggerated forms; Pineau was the main figure. The accompanying illustration, probably dating from the 1730s, shows the second phase. The style's caprices were criticized even during its heyday, by Voltaire and the architect Blondel (1738) among others. Its downfall was prepared with the neo-classical reaction, begun by French academicians in Rome working in collaboration with Piranesi; the 1750s marked the triumph of the neo-classical style in Paris, and in 1754 Cochin published an ironic obituary of Pineau saying 'everything that separates art from the antique taste may be said to owe its invention or perfection to Pineau'. In 1763 Grimm summarized the change in style: 'The forms of ancient times are much in favour. Taste has benefited thereby, and everything has become *à la Grècque*'. The demise of the older style was less complete or abrupt than he claimed; it was too ingrained and quintessentially French to disappear without leaving many traces. Several of the greatest artists, schooled in the playfulness of the Rococo, continued to draw delight from its manner, albeit in more refined and sober terms, for example Boquet, whose ethereal costumes and scenic designs set the style at the Opéra into the 1770s.

The Rococo style, in all its applications, spread rapidly, even as far as China, generally with a lag of a decade or so behind Paris. A Viennese equivalent evolved somewhat independently, starting from the same designs of Bérain. As 'the French style' it flowered briefly in England (e.g. Chippendale), whence it travelled to the American colonies. The most genial clients were in the southern, predominantly Catholic, parts of Germany. By the 1720s French artists, or their plans, were put to use at Bonn and Würzburg. The elder Cuvilliès, trained in Paris (1720–24), carried the style to Bavaria, where he worked under the lavish patronage of the electors for several decades, building several country houses and the theatre in the Munich residence (1751–3) which has been called the 'Jewel of the Rococo'. French architects dominated building at the courts of the two most important south German music centres, Mannheim (Pigage) and Stuttgart (Guépière). German artists fused Rococo ornament with traditional styles of church building, largely Italian-inspired, and achieved an architectural synthesis that is still much admired. The collision of an Italian-derived style with a French-derived one in south Germany and Austria has led to theories that the former yielded to the latter, temporally, producing the sequence Baroque–Rococo–neo-classicism within a few decades around the middle of the century. Hitchcock correctly regarded German Rococo as 'a sort of enclave in the Late Baroque rather than its successor'. He added that 'no inexorable stylistic sequence leads from the Baroque, through the Rococo, to the Neoclassic. The major historical break

Rococo stage design (c1730) by Jacques Lajoue in the Metropolitan Museum of Art, New York

... came not at the beginning but at the end of the Rococo'.

The concept of a Rococo in music has never been seriously elaborated. Critics have applied the term to a wide variety of musical phenomena, most of them more appropriately described by the 18th-century expression 'galant'. Pergolesi's *La serva padrona* has been called 'Italian Rococo', which illuminates neither artistic nor musical connections between France and Italy. The concept has been used just as dubiously about literature, even about the young Goethe. Prudence dictates that parallels with the Rococo be restricted to France, or to areas, geographic or artistic, where French culture was paramount. The ballet is such an area, being largely French-directed wherever encountered. At Paris itself preferences for the *opéra-ballet*, a lighter and less demanding spectacle than the *tragédie lyrique*, corresponded in time no less than in aim with the early Rococo. The *opéras-ballets* and pastorals of Destouches and Campra represented a considerable relaxation of tone compared with the solemnity and pathos of Lully's heroic tragedies. The first phase, or 'style régence', also corresponds with the maturity of François Couperin, who lightened the French style by further refinements in ornamentation while continuing the traditions of his 17th-century predecessors; the Rococo element is especially clear in his little character-pieces on pastoral subjects, a genre in which Daquin also excelled. The same period saw the emergence of the French flute school, of significance in helping to establish and further the *galant* style, which could also be described as a relaxing of the old rules. La Laurencie outlined a 'style rocaille ou galant' in connection with the French violin school (Leclair). The second phase (c1730–60) corresponds with the ascendancy of Rameau, whose works baffled many listeners because of their unexpected harmonic turns and complications. One contemporary commentator (Bricuaire de la Dixmérie, *Les deux âges du goût*, 1770) applied the term 'pittoresque' to Rameau's *Platée* (1745); Gardel attributed the perfection of dancing to Rameau, saying he created it by 'l'expression pitoresque' and the prodigious variety of his *airs de ballet* (Albert de Croix, *L'ami des arts*, 1776). Mondonville's new kind of keyboard sonata with string accompaniment, a fanciful and rather fussy genre, might also be compared with the 'genre pittoresque'. Even so, the clearest parallels between music and visual arts emerge when the Rococo was overthrown by Neo-classicism (*see* CLASSICAL, §3).

See also EMPFINDSAMKEIT; ENLIGHTENMENT; GALANT; STURM UND DRANG.

BIBLIOGRAPHY

L. de La Laurencie: *L'école française de violon de Lully à Viotti* (Paris, 1922–4/*R*1971)
E. Bücken: *Die Musik des Rokokos und der Klassik* (Potsdam, 1927)
F. Kimball: *The Creation of the Rococo* (Philadelphia, 1943; Fr. trans., enlarged, 1949, as *Le Style Louis XV*)
C. Cudworth: 'Baroque, Rococo, Galant, Classic', *MMR*, lxxxiii (1953), 172
P. de Colombier: *L'architecture française en Allemagne au xviiie siècle* (Paris, 1956)
H. A. Klaiber: *Der württembergische Oberbaudirektor Philip de la Guépière* (Stuttgart, 1959)
L. W. Böhm: *Das Mannheimer Schloss* (Karlsruhe, 1962) [on Pigage]
P. Minguet: *Esthétique du rococo* (Paris, 1966)
H. Sedlmayr and H. Bauer: 'Rococo', *Encyclopedia of World Art* (New York, 1966)
J. Harris: 'Legeay, Piranesi and International Neo-classicism in Rome 1740–1750', *Essays in the History of Architecture Presented to Rudolf Wittkower* (London, 1967), 189
F. Wolf: *François de Cuvilliés 1695–1768* (Munich, 1967)
H. R. Hitchcock: *Rococo Architecture in Southern Germany* (London, 1968)
S. Erikson: *Early Neo-classicism in France* (London, 1974)

DANIEL HEARTZ

Rocourt [Rocour, Roucourt], Pierre de (b ?Rocour, nr. Liège; fl 1540–50). South Netherlands composer. His name may indicate that he was from Rocour; it may, however, be a patronymic, which suggests that he could be related to Guillaume de Rocourt, who became chaplain at Furnes on 14 December 1545.

Rocourt's main work was printed by Jacques Bathenius in a book of motets (Louvain, 1546), and although the book is now lost, records of its title-page indicate that Rocourt was a priest and held a position as a singer at Liège Cathedral.

His few surviving works suggest that he was known essentially in the Low Countries, for they are found exclusively in publications brought out by Susato or in the famous Cambrai partbooks (compiled in Bruges in 1542). In his own country, however, Rocourt's reputation must have been a formidable one, for, along with Crecquillon and Manchicourt, he was among the first composers to be honoured by the publication in the Low Countries of a music book devoted solely to his works. Susato, moreover, placed him in the company of such important chanson composers as Certon, Claudin de Sermisy, Hesdin and Sandrin; his *Premier livre des chansons à deux ou à trois parties* of 1544 includes his arrangement of a piece by Rocourt along with similar arrangements of works by the most illustrious composers. Rocourt's chansons bridge the stylistic gap separating the Parisian from the Flemish idiom, for they combine a blend of genuine imitative writing on the one hand, and the chordal texture and melodic stereotypes of the Parisian chanson on the other.

WORKS
Motectorum, 4vv, liber primus (Louvain, 1546), lost
Adiutor meus in oportunit, 4vv, 1547[5]

Je me contenté sans avoir jouyssance, 4vv, 1543[16], *F-CA* 125–8, ed. R. J. van Maldeghem: Trésor musical: musique profane, xvi (Brussels, 1880), 32, with substitute text, Ce grand Dieu
O cueur ingrat, o fraulde terrienne, 4vv, 1543[16], ed. F. Commer: Collectio operum musicorum batavorum saeculi XVI, xii (Berlin, 1867)
Plaindre ny vault, ny moy desconforter, 4vv, 1549[29]

BIBLIOGRAPHY
FétisB
E. vander Straeten: *La musique aux Pays-Bas avant le XIXᵉ siècle* (Brussels, 1867–88/R1969)
A. Goovaerts: *Histoire et bibliographie de la typographie musicale dans les anciens Pays-Bas* (Antwerp and Brussels, 1880/R1963)
A. Auda: *La musique et les musiciens de l'ancien pays de Liège* (Liège, 1930)
L. Bernstein: 'The Cantus-firmus Chansons of Tylman Susato', *JAMS*, xxii (1969), 197–240

LAWRENCE F. BERNSTEIN

Roda, Cecilio de (b Albuñol, nr. Granada, 24 Oct 1865; d Madrid, 27 Nov 1912). Spanish writer on music. He studied law and philosophy at Madrid University. Together with F. Arteta and F. and J. Borrell, he founded the Sociedad Filarmónica of Madrid with the aim of fostering the performance of chamber works. He was a member of the Real Academia de Bellas Artes de San Fernando (1906) and director of music at the Madrid Conservatory (1910). Though he followed Barbieri and Pedrell in defending traditional Spanish music, including the *tonadilla*, his books and programme notes for the Sociedad Filarmónica did much to make foreign composers better known in Spain.

WRITINGS
Ilustraciones del Quijote: los instrumentos musicales y las danzas (Madrid, 1905)

Un cuaderno de autógrafos de Beethoven de 1825 (Madrid, 1905) [description of a Beethoven sketchbook for opp.130, 132 and 133]
Las sonatas para piano de Beethoven (Madrid, 1907)
Los cuartetos de Beethoven (Madrid, 1909)
Los instrumentos en España en el siglo XIII (Madrid, 1912)
'La música profana en el reinado de Carlos I', *Revista musical de Bilbao*, nos.5–11 (1912)

BIBLIOGRAPHY
F. Sopeña: *Historia de la música española contemporánea* (Madrid, 1958), 59, 63, 69, 71f

JACK SAGE

Rodan, Mendi (b Iaşi, 17 April 1929). Israeli conductor of Romanian birth. He studied the violin and conducting at the Bucharest Academy of Music (1945–7), then took a degree at the Arts Institute there (1947–9). He made his début with the Romanian Radio SO in 1953. He settled in Israel in 1961, conducted the Israel PO that year, and became chief conductor and music adviser to the Israel Broadcasting SO (1963–72), presenting new Israeli works and giving first performances in Israel of works in the international repertory. As a conductor he inclines towards post-Romantic and less extreme contemporary music. In 1965 he founded the Jerusalem Chamber Orchestra and, as its permanent conductor until 1969, toured with it to Europe, the Far East, Australia, South Africa and the USA. His recordings with this orchestra include a series with the harpsichordist Frank Pelleg of music by Bach and his sons. Rodan has appeared as a guest with various European orchestras and has frequently conducted at the Israel and the Artur Rubinstein festivals, with such soloists as Rubinstein himself, Barenboim, Rampal, Perlman and du Pré. In 1962 he began to teach at the Rubin Academy of Music, Jerusalem; in 1973 he received his professorship and was appointed head of department.

WILLIAM Y. ELIAS

Rode, (Jacques) Pierre (Joseph) (b Bordeaux, 16 Feb 1774; d Château de Bourbon, nr. Damazon, 25 Nov 1830). French violinist and composer. He began lessons when he was six with André-Joseph Fauvel, a violinist of solid reputation with whom he studied for eight years. At the age of 12, he was able to give successful performances of concertos in his native town. In 1787 Fauvel took his gifted pupil to Paris, where Rode attracted the attention of Viotti and soon became the master's favourite student. In 1790 Rode made his Paris début, playing Viotti's Concerto no.13. Since Viotti no longer played in public, he entrusted Rode with the first performances of his latest concertos, nos.17 and 18, given with immense success in the spring of 1792. All these concerts took place in the Théâtre de Monsieur of which Viotti was musical director; during those years (1789–92), Rode also occupied a modest place in the violin section of the orchestra.

On 22 November 1795, he was named professor of violin at the newly founded Conservatoire; however, he immediately took a long leave to give concerts in Holland and Germany. He also visited London but was not successful in his single appearance at a benefit concert. His reunion with his former teacher Viotti had a sad ending when both were exiled from England in February 1798, through political intrigues. Rode returned to Paris where he resumed his duties at the Conservatoire in 1799 and also served briefly as solo violinist at the Opéra. Towards the end of that year, he played in Madrid and became friends with Boccherini. It is said that Rode's Concerto no.6, dedicated to the Queen of Spain, profited from Boccherini's advice. In 1800, on his return to Paris, Rode was named solo violinist to Buonaparte, then first consul, and introduced his famous Seventh Concerto with great success.

In 1803, Rode decided to visit Russia; on the way, he played extensively in Germany. Spohr heard him in Brunswick and was captivated by his playing. From 1804 to 1808 Rode was solo violinist to the tsar in St Petersburg and enjoyed extraordinary popularity. However, his gifts as a performer seem to have suffered; at his reappearance in Paris on 22 December 1808, the public was unresponsive, and his latest concerto (no.10) was described as 'suffering from Russia's cold'. He resumed his European travels in 1811 and reached Vienna in December 1812 where he gave the first performance of Beethoven's Violin Sonata op.96, with the Archduke Rudolph at the piano. Although Beethoven had shaped the violin part to conform to Rode's style, the performance disappointed the composer. For a repeat performance, he decided to send Rode the violin part for further study, although he was afraid of offending him. Spohr, who heard Rode in Vienna, found that his skill had deteriorated.

In 1814 Rode settled in Berlin and married. On 26 April 1815 he gave a concert and introduced his Twelfth Concerto. Here he composed his Air varié no.6 and the famous 24 Caprices. Towards 1819 he returned with his family to France and settled in his native Bordeaux, visiting Paris only occasionally. Mendelssohn saw him there in 1825 and reported: 'Rode refuses to touch a violin'. However, he continued to compose for his instrument: he wrote his Concerto no.13, several string quartets and airs variés, and another set of 12 Studies. In 1828, he made an ill-advised attempt to play in Paris; the concert was a complete fiasco and undermined his health. He was stricken with paralysis and died soon afterwards.

At the height of his career, Rode was the most finished representative of the French violin school. Having assimilated Viotti's Classical approach, he imbued it with characteristically French verve, piquancy and a kind of nervous bravura. His artistic growth took place during the revolutionary decade, and it is not surprising that his music is akin to that of Cherubini and Méhul and the operas of the 1790s; there is declamatory pathos, martial dash and melting cantilena. Rode's best music is in his 13 concertos: they represent, to a greater degree than those of Viotti, the model of the French violin concerto, accepted as such by the entire generation and respected even by Beethoven. His airs variés, which led to the vogue of brief and brilliant violin pieces, enjoyed great popularity: one of them, the Variations in G major, became a repertory piece for voice, sung by Catalani, Malibran, Viardot-Garcia and other celebrities. Rode's virtuosity was always controlled by charm and taste and never served pure exhibitionism. He also composed a dozen string quartets (socalled 'quatuors brilliants' with a dominant first violin part), and 24 duos for two violins. He was co-author of the violin method (together with Baillot and Kreutzer) adopted by the Conservatoire (1803). His innate gifts as a teacher are demonstrated in his 24 Caprices, which balance the musical and technical needs of the student and have become an indispensable part of the violin curriculum.

BIBLIOGRAPHY
L. Spohr: Selbstbiographie (Kassel, 1860–61; Eng. trans., 1865)
A. Pougin: Notice sur Rode (Paris, 1874)
H. Ahlgrimm: Pierre Rode (diss., U. of Vienna, 1929)
B. Schwarz: French Instrumental Music between the Revolutions (1789–1830) (diss., Columbia U., 1950)
                                        BORIS SCHWARZ

Rode, Wilhelm (b Hanover, 17 Feb 1887; d Icking, nr. Munich, 2 Sept 1959). German baritone. He studied with Rudolf Moest in Hanover, and made his début in 1909 in Erfurt. He sang at Bremerhaven (1912–14), Breslau (1914–21), Stuttgart (1921–2), Munich (1922–30), Vienna (1930–32) and at the Deutsches Opernhaus, Berlin (1932–45), of which he became the general director in 1935. He sang Wotan at Covent Garden in 1928 and appeared in Spain, Holland, Prague, Budapest, Dresden and Paris. He had to retire in 1945, since his directorship was based on his Nazi sympathies. With Schorr and Bockelmann he was one of the leading Wagnerian baritones of the 1920s and 1930s, particularly as Hans Sachs and Wotan.

                                        LEO RIEMENS

Rodeheaver, Homer A(lvan) (b Cinco Hollow, Ohio, 4 Oct 1880; d Winona Lake, Indiana, 18 Dec 1955). American evangelistic song leader, composer and publisher. See GOSPEL MUSIC, §I. He wrote Twenty Years with Billy Sunday (Winona Lake, Ind., 1936).

Rodensteen [Rottenstein-Pock]. Dutch family of organ builders. Israel Rodensteen was apparently the first of the line; he built a new organ in St Petri, Utrecht (1507–8). Raphael (d between 26 Oct 1552 and 4 Sept 1554) obtained the citizenship of Vollenhove (Overijssel) in 1527, and lived in Bolsward (Friesland) from about 1535 to at least 1552. He was probably the builder of the organ in the Martinikirche at Bolsward (c1540; part of the casework survives). Raphael's son Hermann (d Weimar, buried 9 July 1583) worked in Denmark and Germany, and became a citizen of Zwickau in 1562. His new organs include those in Roskilde Cathedral (1553–5); the Castle Church, Copenhagen (1556); St Jakobi, Chemnitz (1559); Bautzen Cathedral (c1560); St Katharinen, Zwickau (1560–62); the Schlosskirche, Dresden (1563); St Michael, Vienna (c1567); Augustusburg, Schellenberg (1570); and the Stadtkirche, Bayreuth (1573). He also worked at Freiberg, Kronach, Leipzig (St Nikolai and St Thomas), Nuremberg (St Ägidien, St Lorenz and St Sebald), Oelsnitz, Schweinfurt, Vienna (St Stephen), Waldenburg, Weiden and Wunsiedel, and he entered into negotiations with the minster authorities at Ulm. Hermann's younger brother Gabriel worked with him at first, but later established an independent business.

Hermann Rodensteen was evidently by far the most important member of the family. His specifications were full of variety, with a good Principal chorus (Diapason, Principal, full Mixture and sharp Mixture); wide-scaled flue stops (Gedeckt, Flute, Nasard, Gemshorn, Quintflute and Sifflet); narrow-scaled flue stops (Quintaden, Schweizerpfeife, Querpfeife); and reeds (Trompete, Krummhorn, Regal). His set of registration instructions, which appeared in 1563, is among the most informative of the 16th century.

BIBLIOGRAPHY
H. Hofner: 'Eine Registrieranweisung aus der Zeitwende zwischen Renaissance und Barock', Zeitschrift für evangelische Kirchenmusik (1930), 152
E. Flade: 'Hermann Raphael Rottenstein-Pock: ein niederländischer

Orgelbaumeister des 16. Jahrhunderts in Zwickau in Sachsen', *ZMw*, xv (1932–3), 1

M. A. Vente: *Proeve van een repertorium van de archivalia betrekking hebbende op het Nederlandse orgel en zijn makers tot omstreeks 1630* (Brussels, 1956)

E. Flade: 'Literarische Zeugnisse zur Empfindung der Farbe und Farbigkeit bei der Orgel und beim Orgelspiel in Deutschland ca. 1500–1620', *AcM*, xxviii (1956), 176

N. Friis: *Roskilde domkirkes orgel i 400 aar* (Copenhagen, 1957)

M. A. Vente: *Die Brabanter Orgel: zur Geschichte der Orgelkunst in Belgien und Holland im Zeitalter der Gotik und der Renaissance* (Amsterdam, 1958, 2/1963)

——: 'Rodensteen', *MGG*

H. Hofner: 'Matthias Tretzscher, ein Kulmbacher Orgelbauer der Barockzeit', *Ars organi*, xxiii (1964), 655

U. Dähnert: 'Die Orgellandschaft Sachsen und Thüringen', *Acta organologica*, i (1967), 46

H. Fischer: 'Der mainfränkische Orgelbau bis zur Säkularisation', *Acta organologica*, ii (1968), 101

M. A. Vente: *Vijf eeuwen zwolse orgels* (Amsterdam, 1971)

H. Hofner: 'Der ostfränkische Orgelbau', *Archiv für Geschichte von Oberfranken*, lii (1972), 5–116

HANS KLOTZ

Röder, Carl Gottlieb (*b* Stötteritz, nr. Leipzig, 22 June 1812; *d* Gohlis, nr. Leipzig, 29 Oct 1883). German music printer. After a ten year apprenticeship as a music engraver and printer with Breitkopf & Härtel, he opened his own music engraving business in 1846. In 1863, after many attempts, he succeeded in adapting the lithographic mechanical press built by G. Sigl to the printing of music; his subsequent improvements to mechanical music printing processes were used for various musical editions (from 1867) and considerably furthered the development of German music publishing. The Röder printing works were among the most important of their kind and collaborated with the world's leading music publishers. In the 1870s Röder's two sons-in-law and later their successors (e.g. Carl Johannes Reichel) ensured the constant expansion of the firm. It became a joint stock company in 1930; having suffered severe damage in World War II, it was subsequently nationalized and as the 'Röderdruck' printing works has a considerable international reputation.

BIBLIOGRAPHY
Festschrift zur 50 jährigen Jubelfeier des Bestehens der Firma C. G. Röder, Leipzig (Leipzig, 1896)

W. von zur Westen: *Musiktitel aus vier Jahrhunderten: Festschrift anlässlich des 75 jährigen Bestehens der Firma C. G. Röder G.m.b.H.* (Leipzig, 1921)

O. Säuberlich: 'Leipzig als Hauptsitz des Notenstichs und Musikaliendrucks', *Archiv für Buchgewerbe und Gebrauchsgraphik*, lix (1922), 19

HANS-MARTIN PLESSKE

Röder, Johann Michael (*b* Berlin; *fl* 1713–45). German organ builder. He was first trained as a joiner, and then served a four-year organ builder's apprenticeship with Arp Schnitger, who held him in sufficient esteem to place him in charge of his business during his absence, but later tried to discredit him. In spite of Schnitger's well-established position, Röder managed to break away and, with the help of King Frederick I of Prussia, to set up his own independent business. In 1708 he was apparently still too young to take on a contract; he is last heard of in 1745. He is known to have worked on the following organs: Alte Garnisonkirche, Berlin (1713; two manuals, 23 stops); Alte Schloss- und Domkirche, Berlin (1720; two manuals, 31 stops); Marienkirche, Crossen (Oder) (1720–22; three manuals, 55 stops); St Maria Magdalena, Breslau (1721–5; three manuals, 55 stops); Gnadenkirche, Hirschberg (1727–9; three manuals, 50 stops); Frauenkirche, Liegnitz (1733–7; two manuals, 34 stops); Peter-Paulkirche, Liegnitz (1736; two manuals, 34 stops). Röder's specifications and organ cases were significantly different from those of his former master: his style more closely resembles that of M. Engler the younger. Röder was one of the most distinguished organ builders of J. S. Bach's time. Adlung described his large instrument at Breslau as a 'very valuable organ', and Röder himself as a 'famous master'.

BIBLIOGRAPHY
J. Mattheson: *Grundlage einer Ehren-Pforte* (Hamburg, 1740); ed. M. Schneider (Berlin, 1910/R1969)

J. Adlung: *Musica mechanica organoedi* (Berlin, 1768/R1961)

L. Burgemeister: *Der Orgelbau in Schlesien* (Strasbourg, 1925)

W. Kaufmann: *Die Orgeln des alten Herzogtums Oldenburg: Nordoldenburgische Orgeltopographie* (Oldenburg, 1962)

G. Fock: 'Röder', *MGG*

——: *Arp Schnitger und seine Schule* (Kassel, 1974)

HANS KLOTZ

Rodericus [S. Uciredor] (*fl* late 14th century). French composer. He is perhaps to be identified with the 'Rodriguet de la guitarra' who was sent to the Count of Foix in 1415; a Rodriguet was a member of the chapel at the court of Aragon under Alfonso V. However the only surviving piece attributed to Rodericus, *Angelorum psalat* (*F-CH* 564), seems to date from the 1390s. It displays proportional methods and a textual dichotomy (contrasting the harmony of the angelic spheres with Eve's sin) derived from the contemporary motet, though the piece is a ballade. Its notational complexity suggests the influence of Senleches.

BIBLIOGRAPHY
H. Anglès: 'La musica en la corte del rey Don Alfonso V de Aragón (1413–20)', *Spanische Forschungen der Görres-Gesellschaft*, 1st ser., viii (1939), 349

G. Reaney: 'The Manuscript Chantilly, Musée Condé 1047', *MD*, viii (1954), 78

N. Josephson: 'Rodericus, *Angelorum psalat*', *MD*, xxv (1971), 113

NORS S. JOSEPHSON

Rodgers, Jimmie [James] **(Charles)** (*b* Meridian, Mississippi, 8 Sept 1897; *d* New York, 26 May 1933). American country music performer. He worked on the railway for many years but retired because of ill health in 1925. In August 1927 he made his first recording, in Bristol, Tennessee. At his second session (November 1927) he recorded the first of his 12 blue yodels, *T for Texas*. He became the most popular of the early country singers and was perhaps the first of them to have an extravagant way of life that reflected his fame. Rodgers recorded 111 songs during his brief career and made personal appearances only in the southern USA, largely in Texas where he lived during his last years. His repertory encompassed almost every type of song with which rural and small-town southerners were familiar: sentimental tunes, rowdy or risqué songs, cowboy songs, Hawaiian tunes, railroad ballads and blues. Then known as the 'Father of Country Music', the 'Singing Brakeman' and 'America's Blue Yodeler'; he was widely imitated and had great influence, not only on singers who heard him, but on those such as Merle Haggard who know his music only through reissued recordings.

BIBLIOGRAPHY
C. Rodgers: *My Husband, Jimmie Rodgers* (Nashville, n.d.)

J. Greenway: 'Jimmie Rodgers: a Folksong Catalyst', *Journal of American Folklore*, lxx (1957), 231

B. C. Malone: *Country Music USA* (Austin, 1968)

C. Comber and M. Paris: 'Jimmie Rodgers', *Stars of Country Music*, ed. B. C. Malone and J. McCulloh (Urbana, Ill., 1975), 121

BILL C. MALONE

Rodgers, Richard (Charles) (*b* Hammels Station, Long Island, 28 June 1902; *d* New York, 30 Dec 1979). American composer. He studied the piano from the age of six; largely self-taught, he learnt to improvise and play by ear. In New York he was attracted to the operettas of Victor Herbert and the early musical comedies of Jerome Kern. While at Columbia University (1919–21) and the Institute of Musical Art (1921–3), where he studied with Henry Krehbiel and Percy Goetschius, he began writing music and lyrics for amateur musical productions and conducting some of his shows. In 1918 he met Lorenz Hart; they discussed the need for good poetry in place of the banal lyrics of current popular songs and agreed to collaborate. One of their first efforts (and Rodgers's first published song) was 'Any old place with you', used by the producer Lew Fields in *A Lonely Romeo* (1919); its lyrics were up-to-date and glib. They wrote Columbia's varsity show, *Fly with me* (1919), and seven songs for Fields's *Poor Little Ritz Girl* (1920). Their first success was a revue, *The Garrick Gaieties* (1925). In *Dearest Enemy* (1925) they moved away from the song-and-dance musical format towards the musical play, attempting to integrate song and drama in the context of serious subject matter and characters. Between 1926 and 1930 Rodgers and Hart were among the most popular American songwriters, producing 14 shows (including three for London) and numerous songs for other musicals and revues. They continued to experiment with the musical play; their programme for *Chee-Chee* (1928) announced that the musical numbers, some brief, were so closely linked with the story that they could not be listed, and in *Present Arms* (1928) Rodgers added transitional passages of music to strengthen the cohesion of the stage action.

In Hollywood (1930–34) Rodgers and Hart wrote songs and background music to spoken lines for films, but they were unsuccessful and returned to New York with a circus musical, *Jumbo* (1935). They began writing their own books as well as lyrics, and reverted to musical comedy, but in a more sophisticated form. *On your Toes* (1936) contains Rodgers's first extensive orchestral music for ballet sequences, including 'Slaughter on Tenth Avenue', choreographed by Balanchin, and one of his best songs, 'There's a small hotel'. *Babes in Arms* (1937) is one of their most varied scores, with songs that are lyrical ('My funny Valentine'), sophisticated ('The lady is a tramp') and strongly rhythmic ('Johnny one note'). Their most daring musical was *Pal Joey* (1940); its realistic, cynical and immoral story, unsavoury characters and suggestive lyrics ('Bewitched, bothered and bewildered') shocked audiences used to escapist musical comedy and the show was a failure, but a revival (1952) and a film version (1957) were highly successful. Hart's death in 1943 ended a collaboration that had produced nearly 30 stage musicals, as well as films and film versions of their stage shows. A film biography of their career, *Words and Music*, was made in 1948.

The partnership that Rogers formed with Oscar Hammerstein II in 1943 was even more remarkable. It led to a series of musicals that enjoyed unprecedented artistic, critical and financial success, beginning with *Oklahoma!* (1943), which is one of the masterpieces of the American musical stage and has been called the first American vernacular opera. More than any of its predecessors, it integrated song, dance and drama, the play and lyrics dictating the musical techniques. The chorus girls and 'production numbers' of musical comedy were replaced by ballet choreographed by Agnes de Mille and modelled on American square-dance. *Oklahoma!* won the Pulitzer Prize for drama in 1944, had 2248 performances on Broadway in five years and has continued to be performed throughout the USA, Europe (including London, 1947–50), Australia, South Africa and elsewhere.

In 1944 Rodgers and Hammerstein founded Williamson Music (a subsidiary of Chappell), which first published the score of *Oklahoma!*, and began producing plays and musicals in New York and, from 1950, in London. They contributed six songs to the film *State Fair* (1945) and wrote *Carousel* (1945) and *Allegro* (1947), musical plays choreographed by de Mille. *Carousel* includes an operatic soliloquy and several hit songs; *Allegro* is more like an experimental psychological drama and was less popular. *South Pacific* (1949) is another musical play that received international acclaim; it also won the Pulitzer Prize for drama (1950), and several of its songs (e.g. 'Some enchanted evening', 'I'm gonna wash that man right outa my hair') became very popular. *The King and I* (1951) and *The Sound of Music* (1959), Rodgers's and Hammerstein's last notable successes, furthered the integration of music and plot. After Hammerstein's death Rodgers continued composing, sometimes to his own lyrics, but with less success.

Besides musicals, Rodgers wrote *All Points West* (1936), a symphonic narrative performed by Paul Whiteman and the Philadelphia Orchestra; *Nursery Ballet*, a suite performed by Whiteman's orchestra at Carnegie Hall (25 December 1938); *Ghost Town*, an American folk ballet produced by the Ballets Russes at the Metropolitan Opera (12 November 1939); *Victory at Sea*, incidental music and a suite for a film and television documentary (1952); and music for a television series, *Winston Churchill, the Valiant Years* (1960). He helped to revise many of his musicals for stage revivals and for films. He was made a member of the National Institute of Arts and Letters (1955) and of several other professional societies and was presented with numerous honorary doctorates by American universities.

With Hart, Rodgers wrote songs largely on the model of Tin Pan Alley, with a limited vocal range, little ornamentation and simple harmonies, though more graceful and imaginative than most popular songs of the time. With Hammerstein, his song forms often expanded to meet the demands of the text, sometimes dispensing with the conventional juxtaposition of verse and chorus or the symmetry of four phrases in 32 bars. More than most theatre composers of the 1920s Rodgers used rhythms derived from popular dances influenced by jazz. Many of his most successful songs (e.g. 'Blue room', 'Bewitched, bothered and bewildered', 'The most beautiful girl in the world') are graceful and lyrical, their momentum being skilfully achieved by placing the longer notes and any unusual or colourful chord progressions on the second or third beats of the bar. But some of his livelier songs (e.g. 'Oklahoma!', 'Johnny one note') build up excitement through a held note on the first beat. In the tradition of Broadway, Rodgers relied throughout his career on orchestrators (particularly Robert Russell Bennett) to prepare his songs for the theatre.

Rodgers's daughter, Mary Rodgers (*b* New York, 11 Jan 1931), studied at Mannes College of Music, New

York (1943–8) and has composed musicals, including *Once upon a Mattress* (1967) and *The Mad Show* (1973).

WORKS
(selective list)

LH – L. Hart   OH – O. Hammerstein II   * – orchestrator

Collections: *The Rodgers and Hart Song Book* (New York, 1951)
       The Rodgers and Hammerstein Song Book, ed. H. Simon (New York, 1958, rev. 2/1968)

STAGE

All musical comedies unless otherwise stated; vocal scores or selections published. Dates and titles given are those of first New York performance unless otherwise stated. Authors are indicated as (book author; lyricist).

Fly with me (LH), 1919
Poor Little Ritz Girl (G. Campbell and L. Fields; LH), collab. S. Romberg, 28 July 1920
The Melody Man (H. Fields, Rodgers and LH), 13 May 1924, film 1930
The Garrick Gaieties (revue, LH and others), 17 May 1925
Dearest Enemy (Fields; LH), *E. Gerstenberger, 18 Sept 1925
The Fifth Avenue Follies (revue), Jan 1926
The Girl Friend (Fields; LH), *M. de Packh, 17 March 1926
The Garrick Gaieties (revue, LH and others), 10 May 1926
Lido Lady (G. Bolton, B. Kalmar, H. Ruby and R. Jeans; LH), London, 1 Dec 1926
Peggy-Ann (Fields, after E. Smith: Tillie's Nightmare; LH), *R. Webb, 27 Dec 1926
Betsy (I. Caesar, D. Freedman and A. Maguire; LH and others), 28 Dec 1926
One Dam Thing after Another (revue, Jeans; LH), London, 19 May 1927
A Connecticut Yankee (Fields, after S. Clemens [M. Twain]: A Connecticut Yankee in King Arthur's Court; LH), 3 Nov 1927
She's my Baby (Bolton, Kalmar and Ruby; LH), 3 Jan 1928
Present Arms (Fields; LH), 26 April 1928, film as Leathernecking, 1930
Chee-Chee (Fields, after C. Petit: The Son of the Grand Eunuch; LH), *Webb, 25 Sept 1928
Spring is Here (O. Davis; LH), 11 March 1929, film 1930
Heads Up! (J. McGowan and P. G. Smith; LH), *R. R. Bennett, 11 Nov 1929, film 1930
Simple Simon (E. Wynn and Bolton; LH), 18 Feb 1930
Evergreen (B. W. Levy; LH), London, 3 Dec 1930, film 1934
America's Sweetheart (Fields; LH), Feb 1931
Jumbo (B. Hecht and C. MacArthur; LH), *A. Deutsch, M. Cutter, J. Nussbaum, H. Spialek and C. Salinger, 16 Nov 1935, film 1962
On your Toes (G. Abbott, Rodgers and LH; LH), *Spialek, 11 April 1936, film 1939
Babes in Arms (Rodgers and LH; LH), *Spialek, 14 April 1937, film 1939
I'd Rather be Right (G. S. Kaufman and M. Hart; LH), *Spialek, 2 Nov 1937
I Married an Angel (Rodgers and LH, after J. Vaszary; LH), *Spialek, 11 May 1938, film 1942
The Boys from Syracuse (G. Abbott, after Shakespeare: A Comedy of Errors; LH), *Spialek, 23 Nov 1938, film 1940
Too Many Girls (G. Marion jr; LH), *Spialek, 18 Oct 1939, film 1940
Higher and Higher (G. Hurlbut and J. Logan, after I. Pincus; LH), *Spialek, 4 April 1940, film 1944
Pal Joey (J. O'Hara; LH), *Spialek, 25 Dec 1940, film 1957
By Jupiter (Rodgers and LH, after J. F. Thompson: The Warrior's Husband; LH), *D. Walker, 2 June 1942
Oklahoma! (musical play, OH, after L. Riggs: Green Grow the Lilacs), *Bennett, 31 March 1943, film 1955
Carousel (musical play, OH, after F. Molnar: Liliom), *Walker, 19 April 1945, film 1956
Allegro (musical play, OH), *Bennett, 10 Oct 1947
South Pacific (musical play, J. Logan and OH, after J. A. Michener: Tales of the South Pacific; OH), *Bennett, 7 April 1949, film 1958
The King and I (musical play, OH, after M. Landon: Anna and the King of Siam), *Bennett, 29 March 1951, film 1956
Me and Juliet (OH), *Walker, 28 May 1953
Pipe Dream (OH, after J. Steinbeck: Sweet Thursday), *Bennett, 30 Nov 1955
Flower Drum Song (musical play, J. Fields and OH, after C. Y. Lee; OH), *Bennett, 1 Dec 1958, film 1961
The Sound of Music (musical play, H. Lindsay and R. Crouse, after M. A. Trapp: The Trapp Family Singers; OH), *Bennett, 16 Nov 1959, film 1964
No Strings (S. Taylor; Rodgers), *R. Burns, 15 March 1962
Do I Hear a Waltz? (A. Laurents; S. Sondheim), *Burns, 18 March 1965
Two by Two (after C. Odets: The Flowering Peach; M. Charmin), Nov 1970
Rex (S. Yellen; S. Harnick), April 1976

OTHER WORKS

Films (only orig. scores): The Hot Heiress (LH), 1931; Love me Tonight (LH), 1932; The Phantom President (LH), 1932; Hallelujah I'm a Bum (LH), 1933; Hollywood Party (LH), collab. W. Donaldson, N. H. Brown, 1934; Mississippi (LH), 1935; Dancing Pirate (LH), 1936; Fools for Scandal (LH), 1938; They Met in Argentina (LH), 1941; 6 songs in State Fair (OH), *E. Powell, 1945; Words and Music (LH), *C. Salinger, 1948
Television musicals: Cinderella (OH, after C. Perrault), *Bennett, 31 March 1957; Androcles and the Lion (Rodgers, after Shaw), 1967
Songs (for other stage works), incl.: Any old place with you (LH), 1919; You are so lovely and I'm so lonely (LH), 1935; Rhythm (LH), 1936; I haven't got a worry in the world (OH), 1948
Other: All Points West (LH), 1v, orch, *A. Deutsch, 1936; Nursery Ballet, pf, *R. Bargy, 1938; Ghost Town (ballet), *H. Spialek, 1939; Victory at Sea (suite), *R. R. Bennett, 1952; Winston Churchill, the Valiant Years (television series), *R. E. Dolan, H. Kay and E. Sauter, 1960

BIBLIOGRAPHY

D. Taylor: *Some Enchanted Evenings* (New York, 1953/R1972)
Rodgers and Hammerstein Fact Book (New York, 1955, suppl. 1959–61)
D. Ewen: *Richard Rodgers* (New York, 1957, rev. 2/1963 as *With a Song in his Heart*)
S. Green: *The World of Musical Comedy* (New York, 1960, rev. 2/1968)
Richard Rodgers Fact Book (New York, 1965, suppl. 1968)
M. Kaye: *Richard Rodgers: a Comparative Analysis of his Songs with Hart and Hammerstein Lyrics* (diss., New York U., 1969)
A. Wilder: *American Popular Song: the Great Innovators, 1900–1950* (New York, 1972)

RONALD BYRNSIDE, DEANE L. ROOT

Rodio, Rocco (*b* Bari, Apulia, *c*1535; *d* Naples, after 1615). Italian composer and theorist. Both his volume of masses and the *Corona delle napolitane* (*RISM* 1570[18]) describe him as a native of Bari, and although the latter mentions that he had served Sigismund August of Poland he probably did not have a permanent post there. Kastner noted that Rodio's name does not appear in the surviving lists of Polish court musicians and suggested that his contacts with the Polish court originated with the marriage of Bona Sforza of Bari to Sigismund August. In his works printed after 1575 Rodio is described as 'Napolitano', and although it cannot be proved that he held a post either at the court or at the cathedral there he evidently cultivated the acquaintance of distinguished Neapolitan composers and performers. He was a member of Gesualdo's academy in Naples, and together with other musicians founded the Camerata di Propaganda per l'Affinamento del Gusto Musicale.

Rodio's sacred works display a command of counterpoint and his madrigals and canzoni contain progressive harmonic and melodic features. The *Regole di musica*, which was reprinted twice and widely circulated outside Italy, also contains advanced theoretical views. Rodio edited and contributed a piece to the *Aeri racolti* (*RISM* 1577[8]), which is an interesting demonstration of Neapolitan attempts to adapt *arie da cantare* to various poetic forms.

WORKS

Missarum decem liber primus, 4–6vv (Rome, 1562)
Libro di ricercate, a 4 (Naples, 1575); some ed. in Kastner
2 pieces, 1570[18]; 1 piece, 1577[8]; 2 motets, 1585[2]; 17 madrigals, 4vv, 1587[12]; 1 madrigal, 1591[18]
Il primo libro di madrigali; Duetti, 1589: lost

WRITINGS

Regole di musica di R. R. . . . tutti i canoni sopra il canto fermo (Naples, 1600)

BIBLIOGRAPHY

E. T. Ferand: *Die Improvisation in der Musik* (Zurich, 1938)
M. S. Kastner: *Note critiche ed illustrative di Rocco Rodio, cinque ricercate, una fantasia* (Padua, 1958)

JOSEF-HORST LEDERER

Rodolphe, Jean Joseph [Rudolph, Johann Joseph] (*b* Strasbourg, 14 Oct 1730; *d* Paris, 12 or 18 Aug 1812). Alsatian horn player, violinist and composer. A music pupil of his father, Theodor Peter Rudolph, he later studied with J. M. Leclair in Paris (*c*1745) and played the violin in Bordeaux and Montpellier. By 1754 he was probably a violinist in the orchestra of the Duke of Parma, where he was a counterpoint pupil of Tommaso Traetta from 1758. In 1760 or shortly thereafter he joined the court orchestra at Stuttgart as a chamber virtuoso and continued his studies with Jommelli. With J. G. Noverre as choreographer he composed several ballets at Stuttgart, including their most famous collaboration *Médée et Jason*, which was first performed after Act 1 of Jommelli's *Didone abbandonata* in 1763. In 1764 he played a horn concerto at the Concert Spirituel in Paris; his comic opera *Le mariage par capitulation* was performed at the Comédie-Italienne later that year. He must have left Stuttgart permanently at the end of 1766 or early in 1767 (perhaps due to Noverre's dismissal and the reduction of the ballet budgets), for he was in Prince Conti's orchestra in Paris by 1767. He played both the violin and the horn in the Opéra orchestra, and later became a member of the royal chapel; he composed *Isménor*, an *opéra-ballet* for the wedding of Count Artois (later Charles X) and Marie-Thérèse of Savoy in 1773. He again collaborated with Noverre in the ballet *Apelles et Campaspe* (1776) for Noverre's début as ballet-master at the Opéra, and rewrote his own *Médée et Jason* for a new production by Noverre in 1780. When Mozart visited Paris in 1778 Rodolphe befriended him and even tried to find a position for the young composer (letter of 14 May 1778). Rodolphe became a composition teacher at the new Ecole Royale de Chant et de Déclamation in 1784. He lost this position during the Revolution, but was reinstated at the newly named Conservatoire in 1798 as a solfège professor, a post he held until 1802.

Rodolphe was apparently an exceptionally fine horn player. It is likely that he independently developed a technique for hand-stopping, and was probably the first to introduce this innovation to Parisian audiences. By demonstrating the horn's virtuoso and expressive resources, including a tone so sweet it was said to resemble that of a flute, he persuaded Jommelli and other composers to treat it as a solo instrument. His ballets mainly adhered to the traditional French dance forms in the style of Rameau, with none of the German folksong influence found in the works of F. J. Deller, his colleague at Stuttgart. His two theory methods were widely used; in particular, his *Solfège ou Nouvelle méthode de musique* (1784) was more popular than any similar work, and was in use throughout the 19th century. He was probably the father of Anton Rudolph (*b c*1770), a violinist and possibly also a horn player in Regensburg, who published two sets of variations for solo violin with orchestral accompaniment in 1802.

For a portrait of Rodolphe, *see* HORN, fig.6.

WORKS

OPERAS

Le mariage par capitulation (opéra comique, 1, L. H. Dancourt), Paris, Comédie-Italienne, 3 Dec 1764
L'aveugle de Palmire (opéra comique, 2, F. G. Desfontaines), Paris, Comédie-Italienne, 5 March 1767 (Paris, 1768)
Isménor (opéra-ballet, 3, Desfontaines), Versailles, 17 Nov 1773

BALLETS

(*choreographers given in parentheses*)
Renaud et Armide (J. G. Noverre), Stuttgart, 11 Feb 1761; choreo-graphed by Lauchery, 1765; formerly in *D-DS*, ed. DDT, xliii–xliv (1913/*R*)
Psyche et l'Amour (Noverre), Stuttgart, 11 Feb 1762, lost
Médée et Jason (Noverre), Ludwigsburg, 11 Feb 1763; choreographed by Regnaud, Kassel, 1773; rev. Noverre, Paris, Opéra, 30 Jan 1780; *F-Po*, formerly *D-DS*, ed. in DDT, xliii–xliv (1913/*R*)
Apollon et Daphne (Lauchery), Kassel, *c*1764, collab. Deller, music lost; scenario (Kassel, *c*1764)
Titon et l'Aurore (Lauchery), Kassel, 1767, collab. Deller, music lost; scenario (Kassel, 1767)
Telephe et Isménie ou La mort d'Eurite (Lauchery), Kassel, 1768, collab. Deller, music lost; scenario (Kassel, *c*1768)
Apelles et Campaspe (Noverre), Paris, 1 Oct 1776
Spurious: La mort d'Hercule (Noverre), 1762 [by Deller]

OTHER WORKS

Ariette en simphonie (Paris, 1764)
Lauda Jerusalem, motet à grand choeur, perf. Paris, Concert Spirituel, 13 May 1779, lost
Other inst (all pubd Paris, n.d.): 1er concerto, hn (*c*1779); 2me concerto, hn; 24 fanfares, 3 hn; easy fanfares, 2 hn; vn duos, 3 vols.; vn études, 2 vols.

PEDAGOGICAL

Solfège ou Nouvelle méthode de musique (Paris, 1784, rev. 2/1790)
Théorie d'accompagnement et de composition (Paris, *c*1785)

BIBLIOGRAPHY

FétisB; *GerberL* ('Rudolph'); *GerberNL*
J. Uriot: *Description des fêtes données . . . à l'occasion du jour de naissance de . . . Monseigneur le duc regnant de Wurtemberge et Teck* (Stuttgart, 1763) [also pubd in Ger.]
Recueil des ballets exécutés sur les théâtres de Cassel depuis l'année 1764 jusqu'à la fin de l'année 1768 (Kassel, 1868)
J. Sittard: *Zur Geschichte der Musik und des Theaters am Württembergischen Hofe* (Stuttgart, 1890–91/*R*1970)
R. Krauss: *Das Stuttgarter Hoftheater von den ältesten Zeiten bis zur Gegenwart* (Stuttgart, 1908)
H. Abert.: Notes in DDT, xliii–xliv (1913/*R*)
R. Morley-Pegge: *The French Horn* (London, 1960)
E. Stiefel: 'Rudolph, Johann Joseph', *MGG*
                    FRIDERICA DERRA DE MORODA

Rodrigo, Joaquín (*b* Sagunto, 22 Nov 1901). Spanish composer. Blind from the age of three, he began his music education at an early age and took lessons in composition with Antich in Valencia. In 1924 the Valencia Orchestra performed his *Juglares* and in 1927 he entered the Schola Cantorum as a pupil of Dukas. During this period he received encouragement from Falla. Rodrigo married the Turkish pianist Victoria Kamhi in 1933, and in the following year he returned to Spain, immediately being awarded the Conde de Cartagena Grant which enabled him to return to Paris to study musicology with Emmanuel at the Conservatoire and with Pirro at the Sorbonne. During the Spanish Civil War (1936–9) he lived in Paris and Germany, returning finally to Madrid in 1939. In 1940 the *Concierto de Aranjuez* was given its highly successful première and Rodrigo was hailed as the leading postwar Spanish composer. The Manuel de Falla Chair was created for him at Madrid University in 1947. In 1949 he travelled to Buenos Aires for a festival of his music, and in 1950 he was elected to the San Fernando Fine Arts Academy, Madrid. During these years he also made several tours through Europe and America to attend first performances. The Spanish government awarded him the Cross of Alfonso X the Wise in 1953, and in 1959 tribute was paid to him at Aranjuez. In 1960 he was made an Officier des Arts et des Lettres by the French government. Other honours have included the Cross of the Légion d'honneur (1963), an honorary doctorate from the University of Salamanca (1963), the Grand Cross of Civil Merit (1966), the Gold Medal for Merit in Work (1966), membership of the Société Européenne de la Culture (1967) and of the Academy of the Latin World (1968), and honorary membership of the San Carlos Academy, Valencia (1969). In 1967 the town council of Sagunto instituted the Joaquín Rodrigo Prize for choral composition.

The passage of time has not brought any appreciable change in Rodrigo's compositional style, moulded partly by French music (in particular by that of Dukas) and partly by the examples of the Spanish nationalist composers. However, unlike Falla, Rodrigo has not attempted to enter deeply into the spirit of Spanish popular or art music. Rather, his aim has been to create a Spanish ambience, full of colour and agreeable tunes, where folklore is a picturesque element and references to art music of the past consist of distilled 18th-century mannerisms. In form, harmony, melody and rhythm Rodrigo's work might be broadly classified as neo-classical; in the post-Civil War context it was seen for a time as restoring traditional values after their disappearance in Spanish music immediately before the war. The success of the *Concierto de Aranjuez* persuaded Rodrigo to repeat the same concertante formula with other solo instruments, but without achieving the artistic results or the popular acclaim of the earlier piece. On the other hand, his guitar solos and the *Fantasía para un gentilhombre* for guitar and orchestra have been more frequently performed, though they have never had the resounding success of the first concerto. Rodrigo's influence was immense just after the Civil War, almost all of the Spanish composers of the period being affected in some way. Yet this was a transitory phenomenon, and Rodrigo has had no direct disciples. Indeed, some of his successors have seen him as an obstacle to the development of music in Spain, a retrogressive figure compared with such as Falla. Nonetheless, Rodrigo is the supreme representative of a particular phase in Spanish music.

WORKS
(selective list)
INSTRUMENTAL

Orch: Juglares, 1923; Zarabanda lejana y villancico, 1930; Per la flor del lliri blau, 1934; Concierto de Aranjuez, gui, orch, 1939; Concierto heróico, pf, orch, 1942; Concierto de estío, vn, orch, 1943; Concierto en modo galante, vc, orch, 1949; Concierto serenata, harp, orch, 1952; Fantasía para un gentilhombre, gui, orch, 1954; Música para un jardín, 1957; Concierto andaluz, 4 gui, orch, 1967; Concierto madrigal, 2 gui, orch, 1968

Suite, pf, 1923; Preludio al gallo mañanero, 1926; Siciliana, vc, pf, 1929; 4 piezas, pf, 1936; 5 sonatas de Castilla con toccata a modo de pregón, pf, 1951; 4 estampas andaluzas, pf, 1954; Tonadilla, 2 gui, 1960; Invocación y danza, gui, 1961; Sonata pimpante, vn, pf, 1966; Sonata a la española, gui, 1969

STAGE AND VOCAL

Pavana real (ballet, V. Kamhi), 1955; El hijo fingido (zarzuela, J. M. Valverde, after Lope de Vega), 1964; La azuzena de Quito (opera, J. M. Valverde), 1965

Cántico de la esposa, 1v, pf, 1934; Esta niña se lleva la flor, 1v, pf, 1934; Tríptico de Mosén Cinto, 1v, orch, 1935; 4 madrigales amatorios, 1v, pf Ausencias de Dulcinea, Bar, orch, 1948; 10 canciones españolas, 1v, pf, 1951; 3 villancicos, 1v, pf, 1951; 2 poemas (J. R. Jiménez), 1v, fl/pf, 1961; 4 canciones sefardíes, 1v, pf, 1963; Rosalina, 1v, orch, 1965; Con Antonio Machado, 1v, pf, 1970

Principal publishers: Chester, Eschig, Salabert, Schott, Unión Musical Española

BIBLIOGRAPHY

F. Sopeña: *Joaquín Rodrigo* (Madrid, 1946, rev. 2/1970)

A. Iglesias: *Joaquín Rodrigo: su música para piano* (Madrid, 1965)

M. G. Santos: *Españoles universales* (Madrid, 1969)

TOMÁS MARCO

Rodrigues Coelho, Manuel (*b* Elvas, *c*1555; *d* probably at Lisbon, *c*1635). Portuguese composer and organist. He probably began his musical studies at Elvas Cathedral about 1563 and may also have studied at Badajoz Cathedral, where he served as temporary organist from 1573 to 1577. During the 1580s he returned as organist to Elvas Cathedral, where he remained until in 1602 he became king's chaplain and organist at the Lisbon court. He retired on 13 October 1633.

Rodrigues Coelho is known through a single collection, *Flores de musica pera o instrumento de tecla & harpa* (Lisbon, 1620; ed. in PM, i, iii, 1959–61), the earliest surviving keyboard music printed in Portugal. Its contents span his creative life up to 1620. The most important are the 24 *tentos* (three for each tone), several of which are between 200 and 300 bars long. They are based on the imitative treatment of one or more themes in long notes, which are enhanced by much lively figuration with dotted and triplet figures sometimes repeated as many as 40 times consecutively. The themes are not related to each other. Dissonance is rare, and the broken-keyboard device (*medio registro*) common in Spanish music is not used. A second, larger group consists of 97 versets, most based on plainsong melodies richly elaborated with figuration; these include 35 for Kyries and 23 which have a verse of the *Magnificat* or *Nunc dimittis* sung to organ accompaniment. There are also four pieces based on the traditional Spanish melody *Pange lingua* and four intabulations of Lassus's chanson *Susanne ung jour*.

Rodrigues Coelho's musical style stems from that of Cabezón but is also indebted to Sweelinck and the English virginalists, who could have been known in Lisbon through residents such as Rinaldo del Mel and the elder Francis Tregian.

BIBLIOGRAPHY

S. Kastner: *Música hispânica: o estilo musical do Padre Manuel R. Coelho* (Lisbon, 1936)

——: 'Vestigios del arte de Antonio de Cabezón en Portugal', *AnM*, xxi (1966), 105

F. E. Kirby: *A Short History of Keyboard Music* (New York, 1966)

W. Apel: *Geschichte der Orgel- und Klaviermusik bis 1700* (Kassel, 1967; Eng. trans., rev. 1972)

BARTON HUDSON

Rodríguez, Vicente (*b* Onteniente, nr. Valencia; *d* Valencia, buried 16 Dec 1760). Spanish organist and composer. After the death of Cabanilles he was named interim organist of Valencia Cathedral on 1 June 1713 and was awarded the permanent post on 1 April 1715 after a competitive examination, retaining it until his death. His brother Félix Jorge Rodríguez (*d* 1748) was second organist and harpist there from 1703 until his death.

Rodríguez's masterpiece is a beautifully prepared manuscript, *Libro de tocatas para cimbalo repartidas por todos los puntos de un diapason* (E-Boc), which contains 30 harpsichord toccatas and a pastorela, arranged in ascending chromatic order through the available major and minor keys. These are actually sonatas (so called in the individual titles), some in several movements, but most in the single-movement bipartite form of Domenico Scarlatti and Soler. The style is animated and brilliant, with frequent hand-crossings. Textures are varied, including lively figuration, ornamented melody, full chords and occasional fugal passages. Sharp dissonance, chromaticism and a wide range of modulatory schemes occur. One of these works was published by Joaquín Nin (*Classiques espagnols du piano*, ii, Paris, 1928).

The organ works of Rodríguez include three colourful multi-movement toccatas in fanfare style (*de batalla*) and an incomplete *Pange lingua* (both at E-Bc). The style and type of notation of *Gran salmodia por Rodríguez* (*E-Bc*) indicate that it was composed by Vicente Rodríguez rather than the younger Felipe (1759–1814), whose works are also at the Biblioteca Central in Barcelona; among the 64 versets for the eight tones are a number of fugues with strikingly chromatic subjects. Two masses and two motets are at Valencia (*E-Vac*).

BIBLIOGRAPHY

J. Ruiz de Lihory: *La música en Valencia: diccionario biográfico y crítico* (Valencia, 1903)
S. Kastner: *Contribución al estudio de la música española y portuguesa* (Lisbon, 1941)
J. Piedra and J. Climent: 'Organistas valencianos de los siglos XVII y XVIII', *AnM*, xvii (1962), 192 [incl. further biographical data and Rodríguez's will]
W. S. Newman: *The Sonata in the Classic Era* (Chapel Hill, 1963, rev. 2/1972)

ALMONTE HOWELL

Rodríguez de Hita, Antonio (*b* *c*1724; *d* Madrid, 21 Feb 1787). Spanish composer and theorist. He served as *maestro de capilla* at Palencia Cathedral (*c*1740–*c*1757), and at the Madrid Convento Real de la Encarnación until his death. Known as a progressive, he helped to create a native Spanish opera, introduced more modern styles in church music, and helped to break down the rigidity of traditional Spanish theory. His successful stage works were written in collaboration with the popular dramatist Ramón de la Cruz. Their first production was *La Briseida* (1768), a 'zarzuela heroica' after the current style of Italian opera; they turned to contemporary subject matter and local colour in *Las segadoras de Vallecas* (1768) and their masterpiece, *Las labradoras de Murcia* (1769), which used peasant settings to introduce such native musical forms as a 'jota murciana' accompanied by popular instruments. After *Scipión en Cartagena* failed in 1770 Rodríguez apparently wrote no more for the stage.

Rodríguez was most prolific as a composer of choral works; the principal collection of these is at Montserrat and others are in the Madrid Biblioteca Nacional and various Spanish cathedrals. They consist of liturgical Latin works, Spanish villancicos and other partsongs for secular occasions or church festivals such as the Nativity and Corpus Christi. A few are for solo voice, but most are for one to three choirs in four to 12 parts; all require continuo and many call for a small orchestra. Composed in a transitional style ranging from late Baroque luxuriant counterpoint to the homophonic textures and figurations of the early Classical period, the music is dignified and noble in character, and avoids theatricalism. A collection of instrumental music by him at Palencia Cathedral was written for the *ministriles* (instrumentalists) to use in processions or interludes during the service.

Rodríguez's contribution as a theorist consists of his *Diapasón instructivo* of 1757. It begins with a lengthy eulogy to music, describing its many uses and the honour in which it was held throughout the ages. The brief main text, headed 'Consejos que daba a sus discípulos', has been listed by some writers as a separate publication of 1787, although apparently without foundation. In it he proposed a new approach to composition, and while recognizing the value of certain traditions, he attacked many of those still favoured in Spain, such as intricate imitation, thick textures and species counterpoint. In keeping with the new homophonic style of his time, he proposed much simpler rules and greater freedom, bas-

ing his approach upon chords ('diapasones') rather than rules of counterpoint. Unfortunately, the value of the book is lessened by the absence of musical examples. Antonio Roel del Rió published an attack upon it, entitled *Razón natural, i científica de la música* (1760).

WORKS

STAGE
(all 2-act zarzuelas; all in *E-Mm*)

La Briseida (R. de la Cruz), Madrid, Príncipe, 10 July 1768
Las segadoras de Vallecas (de la Cruz), Madrid, 13 Sept 1768
Las labradoras de Murcia (de la Cruz), Madrid, Príncipe, 16 Sept 1769
Scipión en Cartagena (A. Cordero), Madrid, 1770

OTHER WORKS
Música diatónico-enarmónica: música sinfónica, dividida en canciones, 1, 3–5 insts, 1751, in MH, ii, ser.C (1973)
Música mothética prática, *Mn* [23 pieces with Lat. texts incl. Lamentations, hymns, 1 mass, other works; most also in *MO*]
Música práctica de romance, *Mn* [25 pieces with Sp. texts incl. villancicos and diálogos; many also in *MO*]
172 other works incl. 10 masses, 14 Christmas responsories, other responsories, Lamentations, Magnificat settings, motets, hymns and villancicos: all in *MO*

THEORETICAL WORKS
Diapasón instructivo, consonancias músicas y morales, documentos a los profesores de música, carta a sus discipulos . . . sobre un breve, y facil méthodo de estudiar la composición, y nuevo modo de contrapunto para el nuevo estilo (Madrid, 1757)

BIBLIOGRAPHY
LaborD
E. Cotarelo y Mori: *Don Ramón de la Cruz* (Madrid, 1899)
R. Mitjana y Gordón: 'La musique en Espagne', *EMDC*, I/iv (1920), 2117, 2148, 2161
E. Cotarelo y Mori: *Historia de la zarzuela*, i (Madrid, 1934)
M. N. Hamilton: 'Music in Eighteenth Century Spain', *University of Illinois Studies in Language and Literature*, xxii (Urbana, 1937/R1971)
G. Chase: *The Music of Spain* (New York, 1941, 2/1959)
H. Anglès and J. Subirá: *Catálogo musical de la Biblioteca nacional de Madrid*, i–ii (Barcelona, 1946–9)
J. Subirá: *Historia de la música española e hispanoamericana* (Barcelona, 1953)
——: 'Repertorio teatral madrileño y resplandor transitorio de la zarzuela (años 1763 a 1771)', *Boletín de la Real academia española*, xxxix (1959), 429
F. J. León Tello: *La teoría española de la música en los siglos XVII y XVIII* (Madrid, 1974)
F. Bonastre: 'Estudio de la obra teórica y práctica del compositor Antonio Rodríguez de Hita', *Revista de musicología*, ii (1979), 47–86

ALMONTE HOWELL

Rodríguez de Ledesma, Mariano (*b* Saragossa, 14 Dec 1779; *d* Madrid, 28 March 1847). Spanish composer. While a choirboy at Saragossa Cathedral, he was taught music by F. J. García ('El Españoleto') and José Gil Palomar. From boyhood he was noted for his excellent voice and his extraordinary musicality. He also began conducting orchestras at an early age, in opera and sacred concerts, and won such a reputation that in 1800 he was made conductor of the opera company of Seville and in 1805 of the theatre of 'Los Caños del Peral' in Madrid. In 1807 the king named him a supernumerary tenor of the royal chapel with a substantial retainer. In 1811 he had to emigrate for political reasons and went to London, where he became so successful as a singing teacher that he was made an honorary member of the Philharmonic Society and, in 1814, taught Princess Charlotte, daughter of the prince regent. Also in 1814 the *Allgemeine musikalische Zeitung* warmly reviewed the first publication of his compositions in Germany by Breitkopf & Härtel. Later that year he was able to return to Spain, where he was named first tenor of the royal chapel and then singing master to the Princess Luisa Carlota. He wrote for her his most important pedagogical work, *Cuarenta ejercicios de vocalización*, prefaced by his 'Instrucciones teóricas o teoría del canto' and published in Madrid, Paris (1827) and London (under the title *A Collection of Forty Exercises, or Studies, of Vocalisation*, n.d.). In 1823, again because of the political situation, he returned to London, where he was remembered and welcomed with great enthusiasm. He was made a member of the Royal Academy of Music and, in 1825, director of its singing class. In spite of this prosperous position and his virtual adoption of England as a second home, he returned in 1831 to Spain, where he took up his post as tenor in the royal chapel until he was made its choirmaster in 1836, a position he held until his death.

Rodríguez de Ledesma's creative life was divided into two periods by his appointment as choirmaster of the royal chapel. In the first he composed only secular music – piano sonatas and, above all, vocal works (arias, *ariettes* and duets, accompanied by piano or orchestra). In the second he composed religious music almost exclusively, including three masses, an Office for the Dead, responsories for Epiphany, a None for the Ascension and motets. His best work is the nine Lamentations for Holy Week of 1838. The autographs of almost all the sacred works are in the music archives of the royal palace in Madrid. During his lifetime he did not enjoy in Spain a reputation commensurate with his worth, or the fame accorded some of his contemporaries. The most important reasons for this were his prolonged absences from the country and the many years spent as a singer rather than *maestro* in the royal chapel. But it may also have been because of his disregard of the musical style prevailing in Spain at that time. Although trained in the Italianate school of 'El Españoleto' and in the principles of the old Spanish polyphonic school by Gil Palomar, he was profoundly influenced by the German school – at first by the Classicism of Haydn and Mozart (he worked hard to make Mozart known in Madrid) and then especially by Weber, who fully converted him to Romanticism. He can almost be considered the first musical Romantic in Spain, though in a way very different from Adalid and the other great Spanish Romantics.

BIBLIOGRAPHY
R. Mitjana: *El maestro Rodríguez de Ledesma y sus Lamentaciones de Semana Santa: estudio crítico biográfico* (Málaga, 1909)
J. García Marcellán: *Catálogo del archivo de música de la real capilla de palacio* (Madrid, n.d.), 86f, 193f
JOSÉ LÓPEZ-CALO

Rodulfus St Trudonis. *See* RUDOLF OF ST TROND.

Rodwell, George (Herbert Bonaparte) (*b* London, 15 Nov 1800; *d* London, 22 Jan 1852). English composer and playwright. He was a pupil of Vincent Novello and Henry Bishop. His brother (James) Thomas Gooderham Rodwell was proprietor and manager of the Adelphi theatre, where his first musical stage piece (*Waverley*) was produced in 1824. In March 1825, on his brother's death, he succeeded to the proprietorship. In 1828 he became a professor of harmony and composition at the RAM, and in 1836 he was appointed director of the music at Covent Garden Theatre, where his most successful piece, *Teddy the Tiler*, had been produced in 1830. There he assisted in the Covent Garden policy of trying to anticipate the repertory of Drury Lane, as in the case of his version of Auber's *The Bronze Horse*. He wrote the words of many farces and melodramas (Nicoll lists 21 besides the ones for which he composed music),

and also a novel, *Memoirs of an Umbrella* (1846). He was musical instructor to Princess Victoria before her accession, and in this capacity composed three glees in honour of her 18th birthday (24 May 1837). He married the daughter of John Liston, the comedian. For many years he persistently advocated the establishment of a national opera.

Rodwell's songs, glees and stage pieces enjoyed a good deal of popularity in their day, but they scarcely outlived him, and to modern taste they have only a faint appeal.

WORKS
STAGE
Descriptions of works, taken from original sources, often omit 'grand'. No music survives, unless otherwise indicated. All first performances in London.

DL – *Drury Lane Theatre*   CG – *Covent Garden Theatre*
LY – *Lyceum Theatre (English Opera House)*
* – *partly adapted*

Waverley, or Sixty Years Since (melodramatic burletta, E. Fitzball, after Scott), Adelphi, 11 March 1824
The Flying Dutchman, or The Phantom Ship (nautical burletta, Fitzball), Adelphi, 4 Jan 1827
The Cornish Miners (melodrama, 2, R. B. Peake), LY, 2 July 1827
The Bottle Imp (operatic romance, Peake), LY, 7 July 1828
*The Mason of Buda (nautical burletta, J. R. Planché, after Scribe), Adelphi, 1 Oct 1828; after Auber's opera
The Earthquake, or The Spectre of the Nile (operatic spectacle or burletta, Fitzball), Adelphi, 15 Dec 1828, vocal score pubd
The Devil's Elixir, or The Shadowless Man (musical drama, Fitzball, after E. T. A. Hoffmann), CG, 20 April 1829, vocal score pubd
The Spring Lock (musical entertainment, Peake), LY, 18 Aug 1829
Teddy the Tiler (farce, Rodwell, after Pierre le Couvreur), CG, 8 Feb 1830
The Skeleton Lover (romantic musical drama), Adelphi, 16 July 1830, GB-Lbm
The Black Vulture, or The Wheel of Death (romantic burletta, Fitzball), Adelphi, 4 Oct 1830
The Evil Eye (musical drama, Peake), Adelphi, 18 Aug 1831
My Own Lover (operatic farce, Rodwell), DL, 11 Jan 1832
Don Quixote, the Knight of the Woful Countenance, or The Humours of Sancho Panza (romantic burletta, J. B. Buckstone, after Cervantes), Adelphi, 7 Jan 1833
The Lord of the Isles, or The Gathering of the Clans (romantic national opera, Fitzball, after Scott), Surrey, 20 Nov 1834, vocal score pubd
The Last Days of Pompeii, or Seventeen Hundred Years Ago (historical burletta, Buckstone, after E. L. Bulwer-Lytton), Adelphi, 15 Dec 1834
The Spirit of the Bell (comic opera, 2, J. Kenney), LY, 8 June 1835
Paul Clifford (musical drama, Fitzball, after Bulwer-Lytton), CG, 28 Oct 1835, vocal score pubd, collab. J. Blewitt
*The Bronze Horse, or The Spell of the Cloud King (musical drama, Fitzball, after Scribe), CG, 14 Dec 1835, vocal score pubd; after Auber's opera
*Quasimodo, or The Gipsy Girl of Notre Dame (operatic romance, Fitzball, after Hugo), CG, 2 Feb 1836; after Weber's Preciosa
The Sexton of Cologne, or The Burgomaster's Daughter (operatic romance, Fitzball), CG, 13 June 1836
Jack Sheppard (drama, Buckstone, after Ainsworth), Adelphi, 28 Oct 1839
The Seven Maids of Munich, or The Ghost's Tower (musical drama, Rodwell), Princess's, 19 Dec 1846

MISCELLANEOUS
29 trios and glees, 12 listed in Baptie (1895)
Songs of the Birds (London, 1827)
Songs of the Sabbath Eve (London, n.d.)
Many songs pubd singly

THEORETICAL WORKS
First Rudiments of Harmony (London, 1831)

BIBLIOGRAPHY
A. Bunn: *The Stage* (London, 1840), ii, 9f
E. Fitzball: *Thirty-five Years of a Dramatic Author's Life* (London, 1859)
D. Baptie: *Sketches of the English Glee Composers* (London, 1895), 129f
J. S. Curwen: *Music at the Queen's Accession* (London, 1897)
L. M. Middleton: 'Rodwell, George', *DNB*
A. Nicoll: *A History of English Drama, 1660–1900* (Cambridge, 1955), iv, 395, 608; v, 548
W. H. HUSK/NICHOLAS TEMPERLEY

Rodzinski, Artur (*b* Spalato [now Split], Dalmatia, 1 Jan 1892; *d* Boston, Mass., 27 Nov 1958). American conductor of Polish descent. In 1897, his father, an army surgeon, was transferred to Lwów, and it was there that he had his early training in music. At parental insistence he completed law studies in Vienna, but simultaneously studied composition with Marx and Schreker, conducting with Franz Schalk, and the piano with Sauer and Lalewicz. After military service he returned to Lwów, first as a choral conductor, then in 1920 at the Opera, making his début with *Ernani*. From 1921 he was also active in Warsaw, at the Opera (where he introduced *Der Rosenkavalier*, Wolf-Ferrari's *I gioielli della madonna*, and Ravel's *L'heure espagnole*) and at Philharmonic concerts.

Stokowski, impressed, invited him to Philadelphia, first as a guest conductor (November 1925), then as assistant (1926). At the same time he took charge of the opera and orchestral departments of the Curtis Institute. In 1929 he became conductor of the Los Angeles PO, and in 1933 of the Cleveland Orchestra, which then began its history as a front-rank virtuoso ensemble. The American première, on 31 January 1935, of Shostakovich's *Lady Macbeth of Mtsensk* was the single event that attracted the most attention during his ten-year stay in Cleveland. He was the most exciting of the younger conductors in the USA in the 1930s. He made a strong impression wherever he appeared as a guest, notably with the New York PO in 1934 and 1937 (his concert *Elektra* that year with Rosa Pauly is a landmark in the orchestra's history), in Salzburg in 1936, and in Vienna in 1937. Also in 1937, at Toscanini's request, the National Broadcasting Company engaged him to assemble and train its new symphony orchestra. He was a serious contender for the conductorship of the New York PO, which Toscanini had left in 1936; the appointment of Barbirolli to that post was the probable first cause of the bitterness that was to explode a decade later between Rodzinski and the Philharmonic's manager, Arthur Judson. In December 1942, Barbirolli having gone, the Philharmonic announced that Rodzinski would take over the following autumn. He began by dismissing 14 players, including the leader and several other first-desk men; there was general agreement that the orchestra played with a brilliance it had not shown in years. The major controversy, over matters of principle, policy and power, came in February 1947. Rodzinski demanded that the board choose between himself and Judson. They accepted Rodzinski's resignation, but his image was somewhat dimmed when it was revealed that he had all along been negotiating for the musical directorship of the Chicago SO. Chicago at once announced his appointment for 1947–8, but 11 months later dismissed him, charging him with 'last-minute program changes causing confusion in rehearsals, staging of operatic productions in place of regular concerts, exceeding the budget by $30,000 and attempting to secure a three-year contract'. For the public and the critics, however, Rodzinski's Chicago season was a brilliant success (one of the operas was a *Tristan* which was the occasion of Flagstad's return to the USA after the war).

After 1948, in reduced health, he was a guest conductor in Latin America and Europe, eventually settling in Italy. In Italy he had particular success in opera, conducting the first performance outside Russia of Prokofiev's *War and Peace* in Florence in May 1953.

Artur Rodzinski

His last performances, in November 1958, were of *Tristan* at the Chicago Lyric Opera.

Rodzinski was, above all, a great builder of orchestras. He made the Cleveland Orchestra, and he stunningly restored New York and Chicago, having inherited both in wretched condition. As an interpreter, he was ruggedly energetic, in no way eccentric or even strikingly individual, sometimes fiery, hardly ever poetic or delicate. He was generous, warm, impulsive, proud, reckless and much in the thrall of Frank Buchman and Moral Rearmament. It was characteristic of him that he chose for his Chicago SO farewell the 'Eroica' Symphony, *Ein Heldenleben*, and *The Stars and Stripes Forever*. The frictional surfaces he presented to the world in later years got in the way of a full realization of a potent musical and technical gift.

BIBLIOGRAPHY
D. Brook: *International Gallery of Conductors* (Bristol, 1951)
H. Rodzinski: *Our Two Lives* (New York, 1976)
MICHAEL STEINBERG

Roeckel. *See* RÖCKEL family.

Roel del Río, Antonio Ventura (*fl* 1748–64). Spanish theorist. A pupil of Pedro Rodrigo, *maestro de capilla* at Oviedo Cathedral, he served throughout his career as *maestro de capilla* of the cathedral at Mondoñedo. In his major work, *Institución harmonica* (1748), his stated purpose was to collect from past writers principles on which to base modern practice. The work summarizes the elementary theory and practice of plainsong and mensural music and contains a 'preliminary dissertation' treating the 'origin, progress and estimation of music' which draws upon the major Spanish theorists as well as a number of foreign theorists, historians and theologians. A defender of tradition, he published two later attacks upon the works of progressives. His *Razón natural* was directed against Rodríguez de Hita's *Diapasón instructivo* (1757), and claimed that the classical theorists offered sounder principles for composition than the modern Italian school; his *Reparos*, which attacked Soler's *Llave de la modulación* (1762) provoked a devastating reply by Soler in *Satisfacción a* *los reparos* (1765). A series of church pieces in Latin and Spanish which Roel del Río printed with his *Institución* show in their examples of recitative and aria and their Rococo melodic style, that he was more modern in practice than in theory.

WORKS

Institución harmonica, ò doctrina musical, theorica, y práctica, que trata del canto llano, y de órgano (Madrid, 1748)

Razón natural, i científica de la música en muchas de sus mas importantes materias: Carta a D. Antonio Rodríguez de Hita (Santiago, 1760)

Reparos músicos, precisos a la Llave de la modulación del P. Fr. Antonio Soler (Madrid, 1764)

BIBLIOGRAPHY

B. Saldoni: *Diccionario biográfico-bibliográfico de efemérides de músicos españoles*, iv (Madrid, 1881)

F. Pedrell: *Catàlech de la biblioteca musical de la Diputació de Barcelona*, i (Barcelona, 1908)

R. Mitjana y Gordón: 'La musique en Espagne', *EMDC*, I/iv (1920), 2117, 2120, 2141

H. Anglès and J. Subirá: *Catálogo musical de la Biblioteca nacional de Madrid*, ii (Barcelona, 1949)

J. Subirá: *Historia de la música española e hispanoamericana* (Barcelona, 1953)

F. J. León Tello: *La teoria española de la música en los siglos XVII y XVIII* (Madrid, 1974)

ALMONTE HOWELL

Roelstraete, Herman (*b* Lauwe, West Flanders, 20 Oct 1925). Belgian composer and organist. He studied at the Lemmens Institute (1942–6) with Durieux, De Jong, Van Nuffel, De Laet and Peeters, and at the conservatories of Brussels and Ghent (1946–51) with Weynandt, Maleingrau, Poot, Defossez, Bourguignon and Van Eechaute. Roelstraete was appointed director of the Izegem Academy of Music and teacher of singing at the Harelbeke Academy, acting at the same time as organist with the Schola Cantorum 'Cantemus Domino', a male chorus noted for its performance of plainsong and of Renaissance and contemporary Flemish polyphony. His music uses Gregorian modes together with the forms and counterpoint of the Baroque period.

WORKS

(selective list)

Orch: Sinfonia brevis, op.21, str, 1953; Sinfonia concertante, op.36/1, pf, str, 1957; Sinfonia concertante, op.36/2, tpt, str, 1957; Sym, op.39, 1958; Serenata per archi, op.41, 1961; Zomerdivertimento, op.63, 1967; Musica notturna, op.64, 1967; Variazioni, op.65, 1967; Sym. no.3, op.75, wind, 1969; Sym. no.4, op.82, 1971; Divertimento no.2, op.81, 1971; Partita piccola, op.88, ob, str, 1972

Vocal: Het aards bedrijf [The worldly business], op.18 (P. Devree), T, pf, 1951; Lichtbericht voor mensen, op.47 (J. Corijn), chorus, 1961; 15 oud-nederlandse liederen, op.17, 1943–62; 7 oud-nederlandse liederen, op.43, 1960–62; Kersthallel, op.48 (Albe), oratorio, A, T, vv, orch, 1963; Middeleeuwse triptiek, op.49, 3 male vv, 1962; De caritate Christo, op.54 (R. van Welan), oratorio, Mez, vv, insts, 1963; Missa de S Magdalena, op.52, 1963; Paul van Ostayen-triptiek, op.55, 1963; 4 oud-nederlandse kerstliederen, op.57, 1962–3; Psalm en lied voor de Heer, op.59 (H. Beex), vv, org, 1964–7; Paasmis, op.68 (G. Helderenberg) 1v, vv, org, 1967; 3 oud-nederlandse kerstliederen, op.72, SAT, 1968; Wij zingen in koor, op.78 (A. van Meirvenne), 2 children's vv, 1969; De memoria passionis, op.80 (A. Vernimmen), SAT, 1970; Lente, op.83 (Corijn), 1971; Cantiones sacrae, op.86 (G. van der Wiele), 1972; Missa pia, op.87, vv, org, 1972; Missa de Beata Maria, op.100, vv, org, 1973; Missa brevis, op.101, vv, org, 1973; Exodus, op.103, vv, org, 6 brass, 1973

Chamber: Terzet, op.44, str trio, 1961; Octet, op.60, 4 ww, 4 str, 1965; duos, sonatina etc

Org: 25 preambula pusilla, op.46, 1962; Sonata no.2, op.50, 1962; 3 Sonatinas, op.66, 1967; Sonata no.3, op.76, 1969; Studies in barok-stijl, op.79, 1969; Praeludium e passacaglia, op.84, 1971; 3 fantasias, op.95, 1972; 3 kantieken, op.110, 1975; Kleine suite, op.112, 1975

Other chamber pieces, songs etc

Principal publisher: De Monte
MSS in *B-Gcd*

CORNEEL MERTENS

Roeser, Valentin (*b* Germany, *c*1735; *d* Paris, probably 1782). German composer and clarinettist resident in Paris. The date of birth given above is an approximation based on the appearance of his first published works in 1762 and the publication of two instrumental works by his son, Charles Roeser, in 1775. Although his op.1 orchestral trios are modelled after Johann Stamitz, there is no evidence to support Riemann's assumption that he was Stamitz's pupil. Roeser arrived in Paris by 1762 at the latest. According to announcements in the *Mercure de France* (February 1762, p.155), his op.1 *Six sonates à trois ou à tout l'orchestre* was available for sale 'chez l'Auteur, rue de Varenne, à l'hotel de Matignon'. The work is dedicated to the Prince of Monaco, and its author is described on the title-page as a musician of the dedicatee. He lived and worked in Paris for the next two decades, during which time his name frequently appeared in the contemporary press and publishers' catalogues. In 1766 his title was given as *virtuoso di camera* to the Prince of Monaco. Three years later Roeser was in the service of the Duke of Orleans and had moved to the home of Lamy, a clockmaker in the rue Fromenteau. In 1775, still at that address, he was called 'musician and pensioner of the Duc d'Orléans'. After 1775 he was mentioned in press announcements primarily in connection with his publications. He was considered sufficiently important in 1780 for his name to be included in an advertisement for a harmony treatise by Mehrscheidt along with those of the Parisian composers Philidor, Gossec, Grétry and Rigel. The *Tablettes de renommée des musiciens* (1785) describe him as a 'celebrated composer known by a number of symphonic works, a clarinet quartet etc'. He probably died in 1782 as his name ceases to appear in the Paris press after that time; the 1785 description in *Tablettes* seems to be an error.

Roeser played an active role in the musical life of Paris, although he is not mentioned in the press as a solo clarinettist, a member of a Parisian orchestra, or as a *maître de clarinette*. His main activities were in pedagogy and composition. In 1764 he published the first of a series of eight didactic works, *Essai d'instruction à l'usage de ceux qui composent pour la clarinette et le cor*, the first true instrumentation treatise. Choron and Fayolle said he was responsible for the French translation of Marpurg's *Die Kunst das Clavier zu spielen* (1750), published anonymously under the title *L'art de toucher le clavecin selon la manière perfectionnée des modernes* and first announced by Le Menu in 1764. His name does appear, however, on methods for serpent, bassoon, clarinet, oboe and flute, as well as on the French translation of Leopold Mozart's *Violinschule*, published as *Méthode raisonnée pour apprendre à jouer du violon* (1770) with an additional 12 duos and a caprice; it is the work for which he is best known.

Roeser composed numerous original works ranging from clarinet duos to string trios that could 'also be played on the mandoline' and symphonies 'for grand orchestra' as well as a large number of instrumental arrangements. His extant works show him to be a competent composer of limited originality. In his earliest symphonic works, the orchestral trios op.1, the *Sinfonia périodique* no.2 (1762) and four of the six symphonies op.4 (1766), he imitated the style and four-movement framework of Johann Stamitz and the early Mannheim school. But his work lacks Stamitz's fire and abounds in clichés. After 1766 his symphonies follow French taste and employ the Parisian three-movement plan exclusively. Like his chamber works, many of which are limited to two movements, they never rise to great heights. Although he was so prolific, his importance lay primarily in his didactic works, his translations and his function as a conduit of German influences to Paris.

WORKS
(published in Paris unless otherwise indicated)

Syms: 6 sonates à trois ou à tout l'orchestre, op.1 (1762); Sinfonia périodique no.2 (1762), also as no.2 of 6 symphonies da vari autori, 4th collection by A. Bailleux (1762); Symphonie périodique no.34 (c1763), lost; 6 sinfonie, op.4 (1766), pubd separately as Symphonies périodiques nos.19–24; 6 simphonies, op.5 (c1772); 6 simphonies à grand orchestre, op.12 (1776)

Chamber: 6 sonates, vn, bc (n.d.); 6 sonates, 2 vn, op.2 (1766); 12 petit airs, 2 cl/vn, op.2 (n.d.); 6 sonates (2 vn, bc)/mand, op.3 (1770); Duos faciles, 2 vn, op.6 (1770); 12 duos, caprice, vns, in Fr. trans. by Roeser, Méthode raisonnée (1770), of L. Mozart: Violinschule; 12 sonates très faciles, hpd/pf, op.6 (1771); ?12 duo, 2 cl, op.8 (1773); 6 sonates . . . suivies de remarques sur les deux genres de polonaises, pf, op.10 (1774); 6 sonates, hpd, vn obbl, op.10 (Amsterdam, n.d.); 6 sonates . . . et 6 ariettes, pf, vn acc., op.11 (1775); 6 quatuor, cl/ob, vn, va, bc, op.12 (1775); Suite de duo de violon, op.13 (1775)

Sous les lois (M. H. de L.), romance, 1v, bc, in Mercure de France (June 1777)

Pedagogical: Gamme et 6 duo, cl (1769); Gamme et 12 duo, bn (1769); Gamme du serpent (1772); Gamme du hautbois et 12 duo (1777); Gamme pour la flûte traversière et 12 duo (1777)

Numerous collections and arrs. for 1v, kbd; kbd; ww; str; orch

WRITINGS

Essai d'instruction à l'usage de ceux qui composent pour la clarinette et le cor (Paris, 1764/R1972)

L'art de toucher le clavecin selon la manière perfectionnée des modernes (Paris, 1764) [trans. of F. W. Marpurg: Die Kunst das Clavier zu spielen (Berlin, 1750)]

Méthode raisonnée pour apprendre à jouer du violon (Paris, 1770) [trans. of L. Mozart: Violinschule (Augsburg, 1756), with 12 duos and 1 caprice]

BIBLIOGRAPHY

EitnerQ; FétisB; GerberL; GerberNL

A. Choron and F. Fayolle: Dictionnaire historique des musiciens (Paris, 1810–11/R1971)

E. vander Straeten: La musique aux Pays-Bas avant le XIXᵉ siècle, iv (Brussels, 1878/R1969)

C. Johansson: French Music Publishers' Catalogues of the Second Half of the Eighteenth Century (Stockholm, 1955)

B. S. Brook: La symphonie française dans la seconde moitié du XVIIIe siècle (Paris, 1962) [incl. list of primary sources]

H. Becker: Geschichte der Instrumentation (Cologne, 1964)

A. R. Rice: Valentin Roeser's Essay on the Clarinet (1764), Background and Commentary (diss., Claremont Graduate School, Calif., 1977)

BARRY S. BROOK, RICHARD VIANO

Roethinger. French firm of organ builders now at Schiltigheim, near Strasbourg. It was founded in 1895 by Edmond Alexandre Roethinger (b Strasbourg, 12 April 1866; d Strasbourg, 20 Feb 1953). The direction has passed to his son Max (b 2 Nov 1897) and his grandson André (b 9 Feb 1928). The firm has built organs at Ernstein (1914; 66 stops), Bischheim (1931; 50 stops), Mulhouse-Dornach (1932; 61 stops), Bourges Cathedral (1955; 54 stops), Gérardmer (1959; 42 stops), Immaculée-Conception, Schiltigheim (1960; 24 stops), Arras Cathedral (1963; 76 stops), Mont-Ste-Odile (1964; 21 stops), St Pierre-le-Vieux (1964; 49 stops) and Ste Madeleine, Strasbourg (1965; 48 stops). It has also restored the cathedral organs at Strasbourg, Amiens and Dijon, and organs at St Etienne, Mulhouse and Avenay.

BIBLIOGRAPHY

A. Bender: 'Restauration des deux orgues de la Cathédrale de Strasbourg', L'orgue (1960), no.94, p.51

N. Dufourcq: 'Echos-France', L'orgue (1962), no.104, p.123

M. Vanmackelberg: 'Les orgues de la Cathédrale d'Arras', L'orgue (1963), no.105, p.13

GUY OLDHAM

Roffredi, Guglielmo. See GUGLIELMO ROFFREDI.

Rogalski, Theodor (b Bucharest, 11 April 1901; d Zurich, 2 Feb 1954). Romanian composer, conductor and pianist. After studying with Gheorghe Cucu (theory), A. Castaldi (composition) and D. Cuclin (music history) at the Bucharest Conservatory (1919–20), he went on to study composition and conducting with Karg-Elert at the Leipzig Conservatory (1920–23) and then to take lessons at the Schola Cantorum, Paris (1924) with d'Indy (composition) and Ravel (orchestration). Rogalski was conductor of the Radio Bucharest SO (1930–51), making many hundreds of broadcasts and recordings of first performances of Romanian works; he was also conductor of the Romanian Railways SO and the Perinitza Folk Ensemble, and he ended his career as principal conductor of the George Enescu PO. He was professor of orchestration at the Bucharest Conservatory from 1950 to 1954. A sensitive piano accompanist, he was also engaged for a time as répétiteur at the Romanian Opera. He left a small body of polished works, notable above all for their lavish orchestral colouring, as in the Două schiţe simfonice ('Two symphonic sketches') and Trei dansuri româneşti ('Three Romanian dances'). Rogalski's use of instruments was always individual, although sometimes indebted to French impressionists, with a free handling of dissonant and polytonal harmonies and a close awareness of the potentialities of Romanian folk music.

WORKS
(selective list)

Orch: Allegro simfonic, 1923; 2 dansuri româneşti [2 Romanian dances], wind, perc, pf duet, 1926; 2 schiţe simfonice: Inmormîntare la Pătrunjel, Paparudele [2 symphonic sketches: Funeral at Pătrunjel, The rain makers], 1929; 2 capricii, 1932; 3 dansuri româneşti, 1950

Pf Sonata, 1920; Str Qt, 1925; Iancu Jianu, T, orch, 1940; Toma Alimoş, T, orch, 1940; Mihu Copilu, T, orch, 1940

Principal publishers: Editura muzicală, ESPLA

BIBLIOGRAPHY

G. Firca: 'Rogalski, Theodor', MGG

Z. Vancea: 'Theodor Rogalski', Muzica, v (Bucharest, 1966), 19

V. Cosma: Muzicieni români (Bucharest, 1970), 383f

VIOREL COSMA

Rogatis, Pascual de (b Teora, Italy, 17 May 1881). Argentinian composer of Italian birth. He studied the violin with Melani and Diaz Albertini and composition with Williams at the Buenos Aires Conservatory, where he won the first prize and gold medal for violin (1899), the first prize for all-round achievement (1902) and the major composition prize (1906). Thereafter he held a number of teaching posts, among them the professorship of chamber music at the Buenos Aires Conservatory of Music and Art for the Stage; and he was a member of the National Commission for Fine Arts. As a composer he was an initiator of Argentinian nationalism, most notably with the symphonic poem Zupay (1910), stimulated by popular tunes and by an indigenous legend, based on northern Argentinian vidalas (sad love-songs). The opera Huemac is based on a Mexican myth, but its harmony and orchestration are essentially European; the later La novia del hereje is set in colonial Lima and has traces of Inca influence. Rogatis also used the melodies and dances of native and peasant peoples in his chamber pieces, piano music and songs.

WORKS

(selective list)

Stage: Anfión y Zeto, incidental music, 1915, Colón, 1915; Huemac, lyric drama, 1, 1916, cond. Rogatis, Colón, 1916; La novia del hereje, opera, 4, 1935, Colón, 1935

Orch: Marko y el hada, 1905; Belkiss en la selva, 1906; Zupay, sym. poem, 1910; Suite americana, 1924; Atipac, 1931; La fiesta de Chiqui, 1935; Estampas argentinas, 1942; 16 other works

Choral music, songs, chamber works, pf pieces, school songs

BIBLIOGRAPHY

Compositores de América/Composers of the Americas, ed. Pan American Union, xii (Washington, DC, 1966)

SUSANA SALGADO

Rogé, Pascal (*b* Paris, 6 April 1951). French pianist. The third generation of a family of musicians, he received his first piano lessons from his mother, an organist. He was admitted to the Paris Conservatoire at the age of 11, and in the same year made his first public appearance with an orchestra in Paris. In 1966 he won *premiers prix* for the piano and chamber music at the Conservatoire, and began a three-year period of study with the American pianist Julius Katchen. In 1969 he gave his first recital in Paris and in London. After taking first prize in the Marguerite Long–Jacques Thibaud International Competition in 1971, Rogé was engaged to play with a number of European orchestras, and invited to give recitals in Holland, Luxembourg, Yugoslavia and Germany. He is widely admired as a young pianist of finesse and sensitivity, with a strong technique and a special sympathy for Romantic music. He has made several records.

DOMINIC GILL

Rogel, José (*b* Orihuela, 24 Dec 1829; *d* Cartagena, 25 Feb 1901). Spanish composer. At the age of nine he began composing waltzes and *pasodobles* while studying the piano and theory with Joaquín Cascales, organist of Orihuela Cathedral; in his early teens he conducted the town band. His father insisted on his studying law at Valencia, where he lived from 1845 to 1851, also studying composition, counterpoint and fugue with the cathedral organist Pascual Pérez Gascón (1802–64) and supporting himself by giving flute, piano, and solfège lessons. In 1852 he moved to Madrid, where he again taught the piano and singing, arranged zarzuelas for piano and began publishing dances and operatic fantasies. Between 1854 (when his zarzuela *Loa a la libertad* was first performed at the Teatro Lope de Vega) and 1875 he composed 81 zarzuelas, of which the most successful was the two-act *El joven Telémaco* (1865, Variedades), strongly influenced by Offenbach and with libretto by Eusebio Blasco. He also collaborated with F. A. Barbieri on *Revista de un muerte* (1865, Circo) and *La vuelta del mundo* (1875, Príncipe Alfonso); with Allú on *Las dos rosas*; with M. Fernández Caballero on *El criado de mi suegro, De verano* (1861, Eslava) and *La farsanta* (1861, Apolo); with Mariano Vásquez on *Por sorpresa* (1862, Zarzuela); with José Inzenga and Luis Cepeda on *Un cuadro, un melonar y dos bodas*; with Cristóbal Oudrid and Caballero on *Roquelaure* (1862, Zarzuela); and with Moderati on *El lago de las serpientes*.

BIBLIOGRAPHY

A. Peña y Goñi: *La ópera española y la música dramática en España en el siglo XIX* (Madrid, 1881)

ROBERT STEVENSON

Roger, Estienne (*b* Caen, 1665 or 1666; *d* Amsterdam, 7 July 1722). French music printer active in Amsterdam. He and his family, as Protestants, left Normandy after the revocation of the Edict of Nantes in 1685 and moved to Amsterdam, as is attested by Estienne Roger's registration as a member of the Walloon church there in February 1686. He soon went into the printing trade, apprenticed successively between 1691 and 1695 to Antoine Pointel and Jean-Louis de Lorme. On 11 August 1691, listed in the records as 'marchand', he married Marie-Suzanne de Magneville (*c*1670–1712). On 7 November 1695 he was on the rolls of the association of booksellers, printers and binders. By 1697 he was publishing music and other books (including histories, grammars and a dictionary of antiquities) under his own name.

Roger had two daughters. He designated the elder, Jeanne (1692–1722), as his successor in the business in a will dated 11 September 1716, and from that date he used her name alone on the titles of the books he printed. The younger daughter, Françoise (1694–1723), married Michel-Charles Le Cène in May 1716. Le Cène worked for his father-in-law for a few years after his marriage, but by 1720 was operating his own printing establishment.

After Roger's death Jeanne maintained her father's business with the help of a faithful employee, Gerrit Drinkman. But she soon fell ill, and died in December of the same year, after cutting Françoise out of her will (because, she said, her sister had left her ill and did not help her in her weakness), and leaving the business to Drinkman. Within a short time Drinkman was also dead. At this point Le Cène arranged to buy the printing firm from Drinkman's widow. In an advertisement in the *Gazette d'Amsterdam* of June 1723 he was able to announce that he was continuing 'the business of the late Mr Estienne Roger, his father-in-law, which had been interrupted since his demise'. His wife Françoise, the last of the Rogers, died two months later.

Le Cène carried on the business for 20 years more until his death in 1743. Although he was not as active as Roger, he added the works of many new composers to the house's roster. He frequently reprinted from Roger's plates, listing the firm's name then as 'Estienne Roger & Le Cène'. Music books for which Le Cène was the originator carried only his name. Since the earlier firm had used the names of 'Estienne Roger' and 'Jeanne Roger' there were then four names under which the business was identified.

After Le Cène's death his inventory was bought by the bookseller G. J. de la Coste, according to an advertisement in the *Nouvelles d'Amsterdam* of 18 October 1743. Shortly after this La Coste published a catalogue of 'the books of music, printed at Amsterdam, by Estienne Roger and Michel-Charles Le Cène'. There is no evidence that he was engaged in any printing activity; apparently he bought the books to add to his stock.

In the period from 1696 to 1743, 600 titles (not including reprints) were printed by the two firms. More than 500 of them were issued by Roger between 1696 and 1722 and less than 100 during Le Cène's regime, although Le Cène continued to republish and to have in stock most of Roger's output. Under both Roger and Le Cène the firm's music books were carefully edited and beautifully printed from copperplate engravings; they were valued for their quality.

Besides seeking new MSS through direct contacts with composers, Roger's practice from the beginning was to copy music of publishers in other countries and since there were no copyright laws he could do so with

Part of the Adagio from 'Sonata a violino e violone o cimbalo di Arcangelo Corelli' (Amsterdam, 3/1715), printed by Estienne Roger from engraved plates, showing the written-out embellishments claimed to be Corelli's own

impunity. While most other music printers had little distribution outside their own countries or even outside their own cities and printed the works of local composers only, Roger's distinction was that he could offer an international and not just a parochial repertory. Furthermore his distribution network was highly effective. At various times he had agents in Rotterdam, London, Cologne, Berlin, Liège, Leipzig, Halle, Brussels and Hamburg.

Early in the 18th century, as engraving superseded movable type, music printers discontinued the practice of dating their books. Roger was the first to use publishers' numbers, a practice soon imitated by others (such as Walsh and Balthasar Schmid) and one that continued to identify books through the 18th century and part of the 19th. In 1716 he assigned numbers to all the books in stock, without regard, however, to their chronological order of printing. The numbers after that time follow directly in chronological order.

Though the plate numbers of books printed before 1716 do not help in dating them, another of Roger's practices provides an approximation. From 1698 to 1716 he printed catalogues of his music books in the back of dated non-musical books. He also printed his music catalogues in advertisements in the Amsterdam and London papers over this period of time. Thus the listing of a new work in these sources serves as a *terminus ante quem*.

Roger's repertory was particularly strong in works by Italian composers. He printed the second editions of Vivaldi's opp.1 and 2, and beginning with op.3, *L'estro armonico*, the first editions of all Vivaldi's printed works but two were published by Roger or his successors. Roger also published all Corelli's works and although these were copied from Italian sources, the description of one of them from a catalogue of 1716 shows that the printer sometimes improved on the original editions as a result of his personal relations with the composer: 'Corelli opera quinta, new edition engraved in the same format as the four first works of Corelli, with the embellishments marked for the adagios, as Mr Corelli wants them played, and those who are curious to see the original of Mr Corelli with his letters written on this subject, can see them at Estienne Roger's' (see illustration). Other Italian composers in Roger's catalogues were Albicastro, Albinoni, Bassani, Bonporti, Caldara, Gentili, Marcello, C. A. Marino, Alessandro Scarlatti, Taglietti, Torelli, Valentini and Veracini. From Ballard in Paris he reprinted works by La Barre, Lebègue, Lully, Marais and Mouton, and Ballard's annual *Airs sérieux et à boire*. During Le Cène's time Geminiani, Handel, Locatelli (whom Le Cène evidently knew as a friend), Quantz, Tartini and Telemann, among others, were added to the catalogue.

Although Roger copied the music of others, he also had to defend himself against plagiarism of his own publications. There was an altercation with JOHN WALSH (i) of London around 1700, but the dispute was settled satisfactorily and later Walsh even became Roger's London agent. More serious was the threat from the Amsterdam printer Pierre Mortier, who copied many of Roger's books in 1708 and advertised them for sale at a lower price. This problem was only resolved with Mortier's death in 1711, when Roger bought his plates and later even issued some of Mortier's editions under his own name. The importance of the firm in the distribution of music in the first half of the 18th century cannot be overestimated.

BIBLIOGRAPHY

J. W. Enschede: 'Quelques mots sur E. Roger, marchand libraire à

Amsterdam', *Bulletin de la Commission de l'histoire des églises wallonnes* (1896), 209

C. Veerman: 'Estienne Roger, muziekuitgever te Amsterdam omstreaks 1700', *De muziek* (1932), May, 337

M. Pincherle: 'De la piraterie dans l'édition musicale aux environs de 1700', *RdM*, xiv (1933), 136

——: 'Note sur E. Roger et M. C. Le Cène', *RBM*, i (1946–7), 82

F. Lesure: 'Un épisode de la guerre des contrafaçons à Amsterdam: Estienne Roger et P. Mortier', *RdM*, xxxviii (1956), 35

C. G. Kneppers and A. J. Heuwekemeijer: 'De muziekuitgever E. Roger', *Ons Amsterdam* (1959), 187

A. Koole: 'Roger', *MGG*

F. Lesure: *Bibliographie des éditions musicales publiées par Estienne Roger et Michel-Charles Le Cène (Amsterdam 1696–1743)* (Paris, 1969)

SAMUEL F. POGUE

Roger, Gustave-Hippolyte (*b* Paris, 17 Dec 1815; *d* Paris, 12 Sept 1879). French tenor. He entered the Paris Conservatoire in 1836 as a pupil of Blès Martin and won *premiers prix* in singing and in *opéra comique* the following year. In 1838 he made his début as Georges in Halévy's *L'éclair* at the Opéra-Comique, where he subsequently created a number of roles written for him by Halévy, Auber and Thomas. His success rested on his considerable intelligence, fine bearing and pure tone. In 1846 he sang Faust in the first performance of Berlioz's *La damnation de Faust*, and in 1848 he moved from the Opéra-Comique to the Opéra, where, in 1849, he created the role of Jean de Leyde in Meyerbeer's *Le prophète*. Although his voice was too light for such parts, he had enormous success and continued to sing a number of leading tenor roles at the Opéra. He successfully toured Germany on several occasions. His most celebrated partners were Jenny Lind and Pauline Viardot, and he enjoyed the friendship of Berlioz, Meyerbeer and many literary figures. In 1859 he sang in Félicien David's *Herculanum* at the Opéra, but shortly afterwards he lost his right arm in a shooting accident. He continued to appear on stage with a mechanical arm, at the Opéra-Comique and in the provinces, for some years, and from 1868 until his death he was a professor of singing at the Conservatoire. His book *Le carnet d'un ténor* (1880) contains lively memories of his career, including an account of his visit to England in 1847 and 1848. In 1861 Berlioz orchestrated Schubert's *Erlkönig* for him.

BIBLIOGRAPHY

FétisB

A. Lajet: *Gustave-Hippolyte Roger: notice biographique* (Paris, 1865)

G.-H. Roger: *Le carnet d'un ténor* (Paris, 1880, 4/1880)

O. Fouque: *Les révolutionnaires de la musique* (Paris, 1882)

HUGH MACDONALD

Roger, Jeanne (*b* Amsterdam, 26 March 1692; *d* Amsterdam, 15 Dec 1722). Netherlands music printer, elder daughter of ESTIENNE ROGER whose printing business she inherited.

Roger, Victor (*b* Montpellier, 22 July 1853; *d* Paris, 2 Dec 1903). French composer and critic. He was the son of a musician, studied at the Ecole Niedermeyer and began his career as a composer of songs and operettas for the Eldorado music hall. It was with *Joséphine vendue par ses soeurs* (Bouffes-Parisiens, 1886), a work parodying Méhul's *Joseph*, that he really made his mark, confirming his success in France and abroad with *Les vingt-huit jours de Clairette* (1892) and *L'auberge du Tohu-Bohu* (1897); these are both examples of the slicker vaudeville-operettas in which he specialized. A Chevalier of the Légion d'honneur, he was critic for *La France*, edited the theatrical news in the *Petit journal*, and was general secretary of the balls at the Opéra. As a composer he showed melodic grace and charm and a flair for effective rhythms.

WORKS

All operettas and vaudevilles, unless otherwise stated first performed in Paris: most published in vocal score at time of original production.

BP – *Bouffes Parisiens*
FD – *Folies-Dramatiques*
MP – *Menus-Plaisirs*

Mademoiselle Louloute (1 act), 1882
Mademoiselle Irma (1, F. Carré), Trouville, Casino, 18 Aug 1883
Joséphine vendue par ses soeurs (3, P. Ferrier, Carré), BP, 20 March 1886
Balazi-Boumboum (1, J.-A. Praigneau), Eldorado, 23 March 1888
Le voyage en Écosse (1, Cottin, Lecomte), Lille, 17 May 1888
Oscarine (3, Nuitter, A. Guinon), BP, 15 Oct 1888
Cendrillonnette (4, Ferrier), BP, 24 Jan 1890, collab. G. Serpette
La fétiche (3, Ferrier, C. Clairville), MP, 13 March 1890
Mademoiselle Asmodée (3, Ferrier, Clairville), Renaissance, 23 Nov 1890, collab. P. Lacome
Samsonnet (3, Ferrier), Nouveautés, 26 Nov 1890
Les douze femmes de Japhet, Renaissance, 16 Dec 1890
Le coq (3, Ferrier, E. Depré), MP, 30 Oct 1891
Les vingt-huit jours de Clairette (4, H. Raymond, A. Mars), FD, 3 May 1892
Catinerette (1, Mars), Lunéville, 17 July 1893
Clary et Clara (3, Raymond, Mars), FD, 20 March 1894
Miss Nicol-Nick (4, Raymond, Mars, Duru), FD, 23 Jan 1895
La dot de Brigitte (3, Ferrier, Mars), BP, 6 May 1895, collab. Serpette
Le voyage de Corbillon (4, Mars), Cluny, 30 Jan 1896
Sa majesté l'Amour (3, M. Hennequin, Mars), Eldorado, 24 Dec 1896
L'auberge du Tohu-Bohu (3, M. Ordonneau), FD, 10 Feb 1897
Les fêtards (3, Mars, Hennequin), Palais-Royal, 28 Dec 1897
L'agence Crook et Cie (4, Ordonneau), FD, 22 Jan 1898
La petite tache (3, Carré), BP, 26 March 1898
Les quatre filles Aymon (Liorat, Fonteny), FD, 20 Sept 1898, collab. Lacome
La poule blanche (4, Hennequin, Mars), Cluny, 13 Jan 1899
Le jockey malgré lui (P. Gavault, Ordonneau), BP, 4 Dec 1902
Also a few other operettas, 2 ballets-pantomimes, some salon pieces

For bibliography *see* OPERETTA.

ANDREW LAMB

Roger, William (*d* Lauder Bridge, Scotland, 22 July 1482). English courtier and musician active in Scotland. According to Ferrerio he was one of an embassy sent to Scotland by Edward IV to negotiate a 20 years' peace; he was so delighted with the music there that he remained in Scotland for the rest of his life. He was perhaps the William Roger Esquire 'of the realm of Scotland' who on 13 November 1470 was granted a safe conduct pass to come and go between England and Scotland for a year. Roger found favour at the court of James III, and was awarded lands at Traquair in November 1469. As one of the king's familiars, he would have had an official position in the royal household; he was probably the clerk of spices whose own clerk was paid for receiving spices in 1472–3. In 1476 dissident nobles, jealous of James's favourites, forced Roger to give up his lands, and in 1482 hanged him and others off Lauder Bridge.

Ferrerio described Roger as 'musicus rarissimus ex Anglia' and wrote that in 1529 there were numerous distinguished men who claimed to have been taught by him. It is possible that, in his privileged position, Roger advised James on the disposition of his proposed royal chapel in Stirling (described by Pitscottie) but there is no evidence to support this.

BIBLIOGRAPHY

G. Ferrerio: *Scotorum historiae . . . libri xix . . . continuatio per Ioannem Ferrerium* (Paris, 1575), f.391*v*–392*r*

R. Lindsay of Pitscottie: *The Historie and Cronicles of Scotland*, i, ed. Scottish Text Society (Edinburgh, 1899), 200

MARGARET MUNCK

Roger-Ducasse, Jean (Jules Aimable) (*b* Bordeaux, 18 April 1873; *d* Taillan-Médoc, Gironde, 19 July 1954). French composer. At the Paris Conservatoire he studied composition with Fauré, and in 1910 he became inspector general for the teaching of singing in schools of the Ville de Paris. Later in his career he succeeded Paul Dukas as professor of composition at the Conservatoire, a post from which he resigned in 1940, after the fall of France.

As a composer Roger-Ducasse began in the tradition of Fauré but soon developed a more elaborate style, with a distinct personal quality. His first real attempt to break away from Fauré and establish his individuality came in 1901, with *Au jardin de Marguerite*. This is a work of large proportions, for soloists, much-divided chorus and orchestra, and it occupied him for four years. The text was his own, a new aspect of the Faust legend, set in a flexible, expansive musical style, and including some imaginative and unusual choral effects. The *Suite française* (1907) shows technical assurance; it is succinct and logical, displaying a wit rather like Chabrier's. A warmer, more varied content, showing Debussy's influence, was developed in the String Quartet (1909), whose scherzo has a very personal humour. A Sarabande for orchestra and voices starts from a simple 'classical' theme, in Spanish style, and gradually builds and elaborates to a climax of high emotional intensity. The 'mimodrame lyrique' *Orphée* is an ingenious combination of pantomime, choreography and 'pure' music in a series of tableaux devised by the composer.

These examples indicate a composer who was seeking new and individual paths, but on a firm classical basis. Romantic excesses were avoided, but an exploratory spirit often led Roger-Ducasse into abstract and complex writing, strongly disciplined but always sensitive. The *Variations plaisantes sur un thème grave* integrates the solo harp into the orchestral textures, exploring its technical and expressive possibilities, but never falling into empty virtuosity. The same is true of the piano music, which is often complex and technically very demanding. The polyphonic writing in the five movements of *Salve regina* is an attempt at a new type of fervent religious expression. In all, the melodic, contrapuntal, rhythmic and harmonic aspects of composition are developed along individual lines in Roger-Ducasse's work: a well-integrated style and a genuine dramatic quality are evident in his important four-act opera *Cantegril*, which was first produced in Paris, with success, in 1931.

WORKS
(*selective list*)

Stage: Orphée (mimodrame lyrique), 1913, Paris, Opéra, 1926; Cantegril (comédie lyrique, 4), Paris, Opéra-Comique, 1931
Orch: Suite française, 1907; Marche française, 1914; Nocturne de printemps, 1920; Epithalame, 1923; Nocturne d'hiver, 1931; Variations plaisantes sur un thème grave, harp, orch
Choral orch: Au jardin de Marguerite (Roger-Ducasse), 1901–5; Sarabande, 1910; Ulysse et les sirènes, triptyque, 1937
Other works: motets, songs, Pf Qt, 2 str qts, pf pieces

Principal publisher: Durand

BIBLIOGRAPHY
L. Ceillier: *Roger-Ducasse* (Paris, 1920)

DAVID COX

Rogeri, Giovanni Baptista (*fl c*1670–*c*1705). Italian violin maker. He was a native of Bologna and a pupil of Nicolo Amati. By 1675 he was in Brescia and his violins of that period reflect an awareness of the Amati system of design and construction and great neatness. The wood for his backs, sides and scrolls was at first mostly the narrow-flamed variety found locally; and perhaps not surprisingly he sought in certain of his violins to introduce features of Maggini, his predecessor in Brescia half a century earlier.

By 1690 Rogeri's work achieved a visual elegance exceeded by few of his contemporaries, and he was no doubt already assisted by his son, Pietro Giacomo (*fl c*1690–1720), though no instruments by the latter dated earlier than 1705 are known. Pietro Giacomo was a much finer craftsman than is usually appreciated, with a preference for hooked and almost clubby corners: in that detail and in others, such as the rather heavy, flatly carved scrolls, he exaggerated the taste of his father. Wood of the handsomest figure was often used, but there are also instruments less refined in appearance, many with unpurfled backs. Tonally some Rogeri instruments compare with the best of the Amatis, particularly the violins with 'grand pattern' dimensions. The many cellos offer a good blend of incisiveness and Cremonese quality.

Since Pietro Giacomo Rogeri at times spelt his name 'Ruggerius' it has been suggested that the family may have been related to Francesco Rugeri, who worked at Cremona, but their workmanship is quite dissimilar, and is seldom confused.

BIBLIOGRAPHY
W. H., A. F. and A. E. Hill: *Antonio Stradivari: his Life and Work* (*1644–1737*) (London, 1902, 2/1909)

CHARLES BEARE

Rogers. English firm of piano makers. George Rogers, a fine craftsman, founded the firm in London in 1843 as George Rogers & Sons. Shortly after World War I Rogers and the firm of Hopkinson amalgamated and became the Vincent Manufacturing Co. Ltd, after which Rogers and Hopkinson pianos – grand and upright – were made under the same roof. In 1963 H. B. Lowry and I. D. Zender took over and Lowry redesigned the string scales and casework of the pianos. Manufacture of grand pianos then ceased and the firm began specializing in uprights, establishing a considerable reputation for quality and durability.

MARGARET CRANMER

Rogers, Benjamin (*b* Windsor, baptized 2 June 1614; *d* Oxford, June 1698). English organist and composer. He was the son of a lay clerk of St George's Chapel, Windsor, where he himself was a chorister. In 1638 he became acting organist, then organist, of Christ Church Cathedral, Dublin, but returned to Windsor as lay clerk in 1641. In 1653, during the Commonwealth, while the choral services at St George's were suspended, he became a clerk (singing man) of Eton College. There he was befriended by Nathaniel Ingelo, at whose instance Cambridge University, on instructions from Cromwell, granted him the degree of MusB in 1653. In 1660 Rogers became joint organist of Eton College, and was sole organist from 1661 to 1664. In October 1662 he was again appointed a lay clerk of St George's Chapel, being allowed extra pay 'in consideration of his being able to play upon the organs and cornett'. It was arranged that he should deputize for the organist, William Child, who was to pay him a further £1 monthly when Rogers acted for him. In July 1664 he was appointed organist and *Informator choristarum* of Magdalen College, Oxford, entering on his duties in January 1665 with the generous stipend of £60 a year and rooms in the college. On the opening of the Sheldonian Theatre in July 1669 he received the Oxford degree of DMus.

He was dismissed from Magdalen in January 1686 because of noisy talk in the organ loft and complaints from the choir that he would not play services 'as they were willing and able to sing, but out of a thwarting humour would play nothing but Canterbury tune'; there was also scandal surrounding his daughter, who was with him in college rooms. He continued to live in Oxford on an annual pension of £30 which the college granted him.

Rogers was a close acquaintance of Anthony Wood, who, both in his *Fasti* and in his manuscript notes (*GB-Ob*, Wood D.19[4]) gave exceptionally full and, no doubt, favourably biassed information about him, stating that during the Commonwealth Rogers's instrumental music was well received by the future Emperor Leopold, Queen Christina of Sweden, and the States-General of Holland, and that his setting of Ingelo's 'Hymnus eucharisticus' for 12 voices and instruments was performed at King Charles II's civic reception at Guildhall, London in July 1660.

Rogers's instrumental music is a debased form of the earlier English fantasia. His church music is sober and undistinguished. It was at his hands that the short service first sank into the dull foursquare manner which prevailed in the 18th century. His unadventurous, mainly homophonic style is only slightly redeemed by a faint melodiousness. The convenience that a number of his anthems are for soprano, alto, tenor and bass only led to a slight revival of his music among surpliced parish church choirs of the 19th century, but today his name is chiefly kept alive by his Short Service in A minor. The 'Hymnus eucharisticus' (not the setting already mentioned) sung annually on the morning of May Day from the tower of Magdalen College comes from his setting of the college grace.

WORKS

Editions: *Cathedral Music*, ed. W. Boyce (London, 1760–73) [B]
  B. Rogers: Complete Keyboard Works, ed. R. Rastall, EKM, xxix (London, 1972) [R]
Principal sources: *GB-Cfm, Cu, Lbm, Lcm, Ob, Och, T, Y*; others given below and in Daniel and le Huray

VOCAL

Service, a (Mag, Nunc)
Service, D, B i, 170
3 Services, e, F, G (attrib. P. Rogers in *Lsp* and by Rimbault)
Anthems: Behold how good and joyful; Behold I bring you glad tidings; Behold now, praise the Lord, B ii, 102; Bow down thine ear; How long will thou forget me; I beheld, and lo; If the Lord himself; I will magnify thee; Let God arise, inc., *WO*; Lord, who shall dwell, ed. J. Page, *Harmonia sacra* (London, 1800), iii, 79; O clap your hands; O give thanks; O Lord our governor, inc., *CAR*; O pray for the peace of Jerusalem; O sing unto the Lord; O that the salvation; Praise the Lord, O my soul; Rejoice in the Lord; Save me O God; Teach me, O Lord, B ii, 105; Who shall ascend; 17 ed. in White
7 songs, 1674[2]
Other inc. anthems listed in Daniel and le Huray

Laudate Dominum; Te Deum patrem colimus (for Magdalen College)
Laudate Dominum, omnes gentes (for the Oxford Act)
4 pieces, 1673[4]; 1 song, 1683[5]

INSTRUMENTAL

15 pieces, hpd; 2, org: R
Consort music, 1655[5], 1662[8], *D-Hs, GB-Ob, Och, S-Uu*

BIBLIOGRAPHY

R. Rastall: 'Benjamin Rogers (1614–98): Some Notes on his Instrumental Music', *ML*, xlvi (1965), 237
R. T. Daniel and P. le Huray: *The Sources of English Church Music, 1549–1660*, EECM, suppl.i (1972)
J. P. White: *The Life and Vocal Music of Benjamin Rogers (1614–1698)* (diss. Iowa U., 1973) [incl. edns. of 17 anthems]

WATKINS SHAW

Rogers, Bernard (*b* New York, 4 Feb 1893; *d* Rochester, NY, 24 May 1968). American composer and teacher. He began piano studies at the age of 12 and left school at 15 to work for Carrère and Hastings, attending evening classes in architecture at Columbia University. Ambitious to become an artist, he obtained permission to copy paintings at the Metropolitan Museum of Art in New York. Throughout his life he painted as a hobby, and his interest in art, particularly in Japanese prints, continued to influence his music. He developed as well a strong liking for poetry, which was also reflected in his compositions. Rogers studied music theory with Hans van den Berg, composition with Farwell and harmony and composition with Bloch before enrolling at the Institute of Musical Art (now the Juilliard School) in 1921 to study with Goetschius. For several years he was on the editorial staff of *Musical America*, and in 1922–3 he was at the Cleveland Institute of Music, also serving as music critic for the *Cleveland Commercial*. In 1923, returning to New York, he resumed his work with *Musical America*. He taught at the Julius Hartt School of Music in 1926–7, and from 1927 to 1929 he held a Guggenheim Fellowship, which enabled him to study with Bridge in England and Boulanger in Paris. Returning to the USA, he joined the staff of the Eastman School, where, at the time of his retirement in 1967, he was chairman of the composition department, and where he taught many students who became prominent composers. Among the awards he received were a Pulitzer Travel Scholarship for the orchestral dirge *To the Fallen*, given its first performance by the New York PO in 1919, the David Bispham Medal for the opera *The Marriage of Aude*, and the Alice Ditson Award for opera for *The Warrior*. He also received honorary degrees from Valparaiso (1959) and Wayne State (1962) universities.

Rogers was often inspired by biblical themes, particularly in larger works and choral pieces; and poetry, notably that of Whitman, provided texts or points of departure for several works. Japanese prints, which he admired, influenced his orchestral colour as well as his subject matter. His sensitivity to possibilities of instrumentation informs his treatise *The Art of Orchestration* (New York, 1951), a standard work. His compositions can be striking, stark and majestic, or else witty, delicate and full of gossamer-like effects.

WORKS

(selective list)

OPERAS AND CHORAL

Operas: Deirdre, 1922; The Marriage of Aude (C. Rodda, after the Chanson de Roland), 1931; The Warrior (N. Corwin), 1944; The Veil (R. Lawrence), 1950; The Nightingale (Rogers), 1954
Choral orch: The Raising of Lazarus (L. Rogers), 1929; The Exodus (Rodda), 1931; The Passion (Rodda), oratorio, 1942; A Letter from Pete (Whitman), cantata, 1947; The Prophet Isaiah, cantata, 1950; The Light of Man, 1964
Other choral works: Psalm xcix, chorus, org, 1945; Response to Silent Prayer, 1945; Hear my Prayer, o Lord, S, chorus, org, 1955; Psalm xviii, male vv, pf, 1963; Psalm lxxxix, Bar, chorus, pf, 1963; Faery Song (Keats), female 4vv, 1965; Dirge for Two Veterans (Whitman), chorus, pf, 1967; Psalm cxiv, chorus, pf, 1968

ORCHESTRAL

Syms.: no.1 'Adonais', 1926; no.2, A♭, 1928; no.3 'On a Thanksgiving Song', 1936; no.4, g, 1940; no.5 'Africa', 1959
Large orch: To the Fallen, 1918; The Faithful, ov., 1922; In the Gold Room, 1924; Fuji in the Sunset Glow, 1925; Hamlet, prelude, 1925; 3 Japanese Dances, 1933; The Supper at Emmaus, 1937; The Song of the Nightingale, suite, 1939; The Colors of War, 1939; The Dance of Salome, 1940; The Sailors of Toulon, 1942; Invasion, 1943; Anzacs, 1944; Elegy in Memory of Franklin D. Roosevelt, 1945; Amphitryon Ov., 1946; The Colors of Youth, 1951; Portrait, vn,

orch, 1952; Dance Scenes, 1953; Variations on a Song by Moussorgsky, 1960; New Japanese Dances, 1961; Apparitions, 1967
Small orch: 5 Norwegian Folk Songs; Rhapsody Nocturne; Soliloquy no.1, fl, str, 1922; Pastorale, 11 insts, 1924; Once upon a Time, 1936; Fantasy, fl, va, str, 1937; Soliloquy no.2, bn, str, 1938; The Plains, 1940; Characters from Hans Christian Andersen, 1946; Elegy, 1947; The Silver World, 1949; Fantasy, hn, timp, str, 1952; Allegory, 1961; Pastorale mistico [prelude to The Passion], 1966

OTHER WORKS
Vocal orch: Buona notte, T, orch; Aladdin, dramatic scene, T, B, orch; Arab Love Songs, S, orch, 1927; Horse Opera (M. Keller), narrator, orch, 1948; Leaves from the Tale of Pinocchio, narrator, orch, 1951; Psalm lxviii, Bar, orch, 1951; The Musicians of Bremen, narrator, 13 insts, 1958; Aladdin, narrator, wind ens, 1965
Chamber: Elegy, vc, pf, 1913; Mood, pf trio, 1918; Str Qt no.1, 1918; Free Variations and Fugue, str qt, 1918; Str Qt no.2, d, 1925; Untitled, perc, 2 pf, 1937; The Silver World, fl, ob, str, 1950; Str Trio, 1953; Ballade, bn, va, pf, 1959; Sonata, vn, pf, 1962
12 songs, 4 solo inst pieces, 8 transcriptions

Principal publishers: Elkan-Vogel, MCA, Southern
MSS in *US-R*

WRITINGS
The Art of Orchestration (New York, 1951)
'The Passion', *The Composer's Point of View*, ed. R. Hines (Norman, Oklahoma, 1963), 56
'Teaching to Compose, an Inflamed Art', *Music Journal Anthology*, xxv (1963), 116

BIBLIOGRAPHY
A. Cohn: 'Rochester's 11th U.S.A. Festival', *MM*, xviii (1941), 259
H. Hanson: 'Bernard Rogers', *MM*, xxii (1945), 170
D. Diamond: 'Bernard Rogers', *MQ*, xxxiii (1947), 207
——: 'Bernard Rogers', *Proceedings of the National Institute of Arts and Letters*, 2nd ser. (1968), no.19, p.119
RUTH T. WATANABE

Rogers, John (*b* ?1605–10; *d* ?London, 1676). English lutenist. One of Cromwell's musicians in 1658, he succeeded to the illustrious place of Jacques Gaultier in the King's Musick at the Restoration in 1660. He belonged to John Playford's Old-Jewry Musick Society and was described in John Batchiler's life of Susannah Perwich (*The Virgin's Pattern*, 1661) as 'the rare Lutenist of our Nation'. Rogers lived in the City of London, near Aldersgate, and was referred to by Mace in 1676 as the lute's greatest friend, although 'he grows old now; he has not long to stay'. He was dead by Michaelmas the same year.

IAN SPINK

Rogers, Nigel (David) (*b* Wellington, Shropshire, 21 March 1935). English tenor. He studied at King's College, Cambridge, under Boris Ord (1953–6), then privately in Rome (1957), Milan (1958–9) and at the Städtische Hochschule für Musik in Munich (1959–64), where he was taught by Gerhard Husch. There in 1960 he was concerned in the foundation of the Studio der frühen Musik, a quartet specializing in early music, and it was with that group that he made his professional début in 1961. Since 1964 he has also pursued a career as a soloist, particularly in music of the Baroque period, on the Continent, especially in Germany and the Netherlands; he has also sung in Britain and in North America. He teaches at the Schola Cantorum Basiliensis. Rogers has specialized in Monteverdi's operas, singing principal roles in *Il ritorno d'Ulisse in patria* (Vienna, 1971, under Harnoncourt), *L'incoronazione di Poppea* (Amsterdam, 1972, under Leonhardt), *Il combattimento di Tancredi e Clorinda* (Milan, 1973, under Berio, and under his own direction at Bordeaux Festival, 1976) and *Orfeo* (Amsterdam, 1976, under Harnoncourt). Rogers has been associated with several early music groups, but has not confined

himself to music of the 17th century and earlier; he has sung in several 20th-century works (including Goehr's *Arden must Die* in 1974), and his recordings include Bach's *St Matthew Passion* and Schubert's *Die schöne Müllerin* (with fortepiano accompaniment) as well as music by Monteverdi, Morley, the lute-song repertory and 16th- and 17th-century music. His keen sense of style and natural feeling for the expressive character of Baroque music, coupled with an exceptional control in florid music, made him a leading figure in the early music revival of the 1960s and 1970s. His voice, apt in scale to Baroque music, has a certain incisive quality, clear in line and a little grainy in tone; he has a ready command of the *trillo* and of fast-moving, elaborate lines such as those of Orpheus's 'Possente spirto' from *Orfeo*, an interpretation that has won him special praise.

STANLEY SADIE

Rogers [Rajonski], **Shorty** [Milton M.] (*b* Great Barrington, Mass., 14 April 1924). American jazz composer, arranger, trumpeter and flugelhorn player. He studied the trumpet at the High School for Music and Art, New York, and composition at Los Angeles Conservatory. After US Army service in 1943–5 he was associated with Woody Herman for various periods between 1945 and 1951, arranging such representative scores as *Keen and Peachy* and *That's Right*; he also worked with Charlie Barnet and Stan Kenton, producing for Kenton the noteworthy scores *Round Robin* and *Jolly Rogers*. From 1951 he led his own group, but thereafter became increasingly involved with cinema, composing *The Wild One*, *Private Hell 36* and many other film scores. In the 1950s and 1960s he continued to play and record jazz.

Although Rogers was a mediocre jazz soloist, his themes proved stimulating to other performers, and his forceful, inventive scores for big band like *Infinity Promenade* or *Sweetheart of Sigmund Freud* (from *Big Band Express*, 1953) made him one of the most important figures of 'West Coast' jazz. His *Three on a Row* helped pioneer the use of serial technique in jazz. He also contributed to other musicians' recordings, for instance in his scoring for Serge Chaloff's *Bopscotch*. He is mentioned in Robert Craft's *Conversations with Stravinsky*, where the composer says his flugelhorn playing may have prompted the use of that instrument in *Threni*.

BIBLIOGRAPHY
N. Shapiro and N. Hentoff, eds.: *Hear me Talkin' to ya* (New York, 1955), 350ff
A. Morgan: 'Shorty Rogers', *Modern Jazz: the Essential Records*, ed. M. Harrison (London, 1975), 56ff
MAX HARRISON

Rogers, William. See ROGER, WILLIAM.

Rogers Virginal Book (*GB-Lbm* Add.10337). See SOURCES OF KEYBOARD MUSIC TO 1660, §2(vi).

Rogg, Lionel (*b* Geneva, 21 April 1936). Swiss organist. He studied the organ with Pierre Segond and piano with Nikita Magaloff at the Geneva Conservatory and won *premiers prix* on both instruments. In 1961 he played all Bach's organ works in ten recitals in the Victoria Hall, Geneva, and in the mid-1960s recorded them (18 discs) on the Metzler organ in the Grossmünster, Zurich. This laid the foundation of his international reputation as a Bach specialist. At that time he sounded like an extraordinarily accomplished robot: his playing revealed technical skill of an exceptionally high order; depth of interpretation had yet to come. Rogg himself thought that he was 'too respectful' to Bach; since then he has greatly developed as an artist, his playing has become more lyrical and more fluid. His *Die Kunst der Fuge* (recorded in 1970 in St Peter's Cathedral, Geneva) was a masterpiece which won the Grand Prix du Disque; it was warm as well as lucid and shed a new and searching light on the work. Rogg does not accept that total fidelity to the Baroque style in tempo, articulation and registration is obligatory in performance; his individuality is manifest in every piece he plays. Nor has he confined himself to Bach; he has proved equally resourceful with Buxtehude and his contemporaries, François Couperin's organ masses and works by Liszt and Brahms. He has visited Europe, the USA, Canada and Australia for concert tours and master classes. He became professor of counterpoint (1960), the organ (1964) and of form and style (1971) at the Geneva Conservatory; he has composed piano, choral and organ music (12 chorale preludes have been published) and has written a booklet *Eléments de contrepoint* for use at the conservatory.

WRITINGS
'De la registration', *SMz*, cvii (1967), 279
'Interpreting Bach', *MT*, cxi (1970), 310
Many articles in *Tribune de l'orgue* (Lausanne, 1963–)

BIBLIOGRAPHY
P. Pernoud: 'Enregistrement intégral de l'oeuvre d'orgue de Bach par Lionel Rogg (Ripieno)', *Tribune de l'orgue*, xvi (Lausanne, 1964)
STANLEY WEBB

Roggenkamp, Peter (*b* Hamburg, 18 Feb 1935). German pianist. He studied musicology and English at Hamburg University as well as the piano under Schröter and Henry at the Musikhochschule in Hamburg, 1954–9; he then continued his piano studies under Stefan Askenase, 1961–5, and found further stimulus by attending several of the Darmstadt summer courses. From 1969 to 1971 he taught the piano at the Hamburg Musikhochschule, and at the Lübeck Musikhochschule he became a piano teacher (1971), director of the schools' music department (1974) and director of the Musica Viva concerts (1975). He was elected a full member of the Freie Akademie der Künste in Hamburg in 1973. Since about 1950 Roggenkamp has toured most European countries, North and South America and the East. He has won particular renown for his interpretation of contemporary music, and has played many times at the ISCM Festival, among others, and has held courses in early and modern music in Germany, Greece, Lebanon, and North and South America. He has given the first performances of works by, among others, Günther Becker, Günter Bialas, Paul Dessau, Hans Ulrich Engelmann, Hans Joachim Hespos, Marek Kopclent, Helmut Lachenmann and Norbert Linke. He gives frequent broadcasts, and has made a number of recordings.

RUDOLF LÜCK

Roggius, Nicolaus (*b* Göttingen, *c*1518; *d* Brunswick, 29 Nov 1567). German Kantor and music theorist. He was a Kantor at St Martin's School in Brunswick from 1551 to 1567. In 1566 he published a treatise entitled *Musicae practicae sive artis canendi elementa* (4/1596) in which he made use of several principles advocated by leading theorists of the time. Following Sebald Heyden (*De arte canendi*, Nuremberg, 1540) Roggius advocated reducing the three hexachords to two, one employing B♮ and the other B♭. He also simplified the rules for mutation. From Glarean (*Dodecachordon*, Basle, 1547) he took the theory of 12 modes. In his section on mensural music he introduced several polyphonic compositions, including Ludwig Senfl's six-voice canon *Laudate Dominum* and Johann Heugel's *Veni Creator* for three voices. Part of the appeal of the treatise was its question-and-answer format, a procedure popular since medieval times.

BIBLIOGRAPHY
R. Eitner: 'Roggius, Nicolaus', *ADB*
M. Ruhnke: 'Roggius, Nicolaus', *MGG*
CLEMENT A. MILLER

Rogier. See PATHIE, ROGIER.

Rogier, Philippe (*b* Arras, *c*1561; *d* Madrid, 29 Feb 1596). Flemish composer active in Spain. When Gérard de Turnhout became *maestro de capilla* to Philip II he brought with him from the Low Countries a number of boy trebles, among them Philippe Rogier, who arrived in Madrid on 15 June 1572. He was subsequently ordained priest, as is shown in the dedication preceding the 1595 collection of his motets, where the initial S, the usual abbreviation for *sacerdos* ('priest'), is placed after his name. Also, in the roster of the royal chapel from 1586 Rogier is listed among the chaplains.

When George de la Hèle became *maestro de capilla* in 1582 the musical establishment of Philip II flourished. In 1584 Rogier was appointed *vicemaestro de capilla*. In 1585 the chapel travelled to Saragossa for the nuptial festivities of Charles Emmanuel, Duke of Savoy, and the Infanta of Castile. For this occasion Rogier wrote a six-part *Missa 'Ave martyr gloriosa'*, and an eight-part motet, *In illo tempore*. Upon the death of de la Hèle in 1586, Rogier took over the direction of music at the court.

On 2 March 1590 Rogier travelled to the Low Countries to recruit four chaplains, three contrabasses and an assistant for himself. The last Flemish choirboys to come to Spain – a dozen of them – were brought there at his request in 1594.

Because he was a priest, Rogier was provided with non-residential benefices by Philip II to augment his income. As early as May 1581 he was granted such a benefice at the church of Notre Dame in Yvoir. In 1592 the king asked that he be appointed to the first prebend vacant at the Cathedral of Tournai, and at the time of his death he was receiving an annual pension of 300 ducats from the Bishop of Léon. In 1590 the Cathedral of Toledo gave Rogier 30 ducats for a volume of his masses, sumptuously bound in calf.

Rogier's last work, mentioned as such in the catalogue of music in the library of John IV of Portugal, was *Toedet anima mea*, written for a Mass for the Dead. In his will Rogier entrusted his student and *vicemaestro de capilla* Géry de Ghersem with the publication of five of his masses, for which support had been promised by Philip II. However, the king also died before the collection was printed in 1598, and it was dedicated to Philip III. To the five masses by Rogier in this collection, de Ghersem added a sixth of his own composition, *Missa 'Ave Virgo sanctissima'*.

Only a small portion of Rogier's work remains. In the library of John IV of Portugal, Rogier was represented by 243 compositions, including 8 masses, 2 *Magnificat* settings, 2 antiphons, 2 responsories, 27 verses, 66 motets, 65 chansons and 71 villancicos.

Rogier was mentioned by his famous contemporary, Lope de Vega, in the fourth *silva* of his poem *Laurel de Apolo*, written in 1630: 'Rogier, honour, glory, and light of Flanders . . . left this life in the flower of [his] genius, depriving us of our sweet Orpheus'.

WORKS

Editions: *P. Rogier: Opera omnia*, ed. L. J. Wagner, CMM, lxi (1974)
    P. Rogier: Eleven Motets, ed. L. J. Wagner (New Haven, 1966)

SACRED

Cantus . . . quas vulgo Motecta apellant . . . Liber primus (Naples, 1595); 16 motets, 4–6, 8vv
5 masses, 4–6vv, in *Missae sex* (Madrid, 1598[1])
2 masses in MS, one for 8vv, the other in 2 versions, 8 and 12vv, *E-E, V*
2 motets in MS, 4, 5, 6, 8, 12vv, *E-E, SE, V, VAc, VAcp, US-NYhs*

SECULAR

4 chansons, 5, 6vv, in *Le rossignol musical des chansons* (Antwerp, 1597[10])

BIBLIOGRAPHY

E. vander Straeten: *La musique aux Pays-Bas avant le XIXe siècle* (Paris, 1867–88/*R*1969), ii, 12; iii, 214; viii, 152–236, 401, 505, 549
L. J. Wagner: 'Flemish Musicians at the Spanish Court of Philip II', *Caecilia*, lxxxvi (1959), 107
P. Becquart: *Musiciens néerlandais à la cour de Madrid: Philippe Rogier et son école* (Brussels, 1967)

LAVERN J. WAGNER

Rogister, Jean (François Toussaint) (*b* Liège, 25 Oct 1879; *d* Liège, 20 March 1964). Belgian composer and violist. Having studied at the Liège Conservatory, he took charge of the viola classes there from 1900 to 1945, when he moved to a similar position at the Brussels Conservatory (1945–8). In 1925 he founded the Liège Quartet, which gained an international reputation and formed the basis for an ensemble playing old instruments. Trained in the Franckian tradition, in 1925 he submitted some scores to d'Indy, who criticized their construction. Rogister's works generally have an emotional basis which is sometimes made explicit by the title, and his music is often cast in variation form, or else it develops through rhythmic alteration.

WORKS
(*selective list*)

Orch: 3 syms., 4 sym. poems, other pieces; concertante works incl. Vn Conc., 1945, Va Conc., Vc Conc., Trbn Conc.
Chamber: 8 str qts, Wind Qnt, Octet, many other pieces; Suite, va da gamba, hpd; Qnt, 2 quintons, va d'amore, va da gamba, hpd
Vocal: The Bells (Poe), S, fl, ob, str qt, harp, pf, 1923; Requiem, solo vv, chorus, orch, 1944; Lorsque minuit sonna (opera, 1), *c*25 melodies

Principal publishers: Breitkopf & Härtel, Schott (Brussels), Senart

BIBLIOGRAPHY

J. Servais: *Jean Rogister: un musicien du coeur* (n.p., 1972)

HENRI VANHULST

Rognoni [Rogniono, Rognone, Rognoni Taeggio, Rognoni Taegio, Taegio]. Italian family of musicians. 'Taeggio', derived from the place of origin of (1) Riccardo Rognoni, was used only by his sons (2) Giovanni Domenico and (3) Francesco below.

(1) **Riccardo Rognoni** (*b* ?Val Taveggia; *d* Milan, 1619 or 1620). Composer, theorist and instrumentalist. After being expelled from the Val Taveggia he lived in Milan, where he is known to have been in the service of the governor in 1592. He appears to have been still alive in 1619 but is referred to as dead in his son Francesco's *Selva de varii passaggi* of 1620. As well as a few compositions he wrote a treatise on diminutions, a

practice common during the transformation of the polyphonic style of the 16th century into the monodic style of the 17th. This work, lost in World War II, survives in a manuscript copy (at *US-SFsc*) made by Friedrich Chrysander in 1890. Compared with other works of the period on the same subject, such as those of Girolamo Dalla Casa (1584) and Giovanni Bassano (1585), Rognoni's treatise has a markedly didactic character, since it contains not entire pieces but rather examples of figurations arranged in progressive order of complexity and difficulty. Furthermore, in the introduction he made a distinction between the techniques of string and wind instruments, and he supplied detailed instructions about the use of the bow, with special reference to legato bowing. Here he could draw on his practical experience as a virtuoso performer on the violin, viol and wind instruments.

WORKS

Canzonette alla napoletana, 3, 4vv (Venice, 1586); lost, cited in Picinelli
Pavane e balli con 2 canzoni e diverse sorti di brandi, a 4, 5 (Milan, 1603); lost, cited in Picinelli
2 works, insts, 1598[13]; 1 work, a 5, in F. Rognoni Taeggio: Canzoni francese per sonar (Milan, 1608); 1 sacred madrigal in F. Rognoni Taeggio: Il primo libro de madrigali, 5vv, bc (hpd/chit) (Venice, 1613)
Domine quando veneris, 1v, *PL-WRu*
Canzon 10 detta La biffa, vn, *WRu*

THEORETICAL WORKS

Passaggi per potersi essercitare nel diminuire terminatamente con ogni sorte di instromenti, et anco diversi passaggi per la semplice voce humana (Venice, 1592); lost, MS copy by F. Chrysander, *US-SFsc*

(2) **Giovanni Domenico Rognoni Taeggio** (*b* Milan; *d* ?Milan, before 1626). Composer and organist, son of (1) Riccardo Rognoni. He was a priest and appears to have spent his entire life in Milan. He was *maestro di cappella* of S Marco in 1605, and according to Picinelli he held a similar post at S Fedele. In 1619 he was musical director at the ducal court; he was connected with Prospero Lombardo's academy. Like other works of the period his canzoni of 1605 were designed for performance by either voices or instruments: although some of them have texts (in Latin) Rognoni Taeggio stated that he had been requested to publish too a version for organ and had agreed, since the music was intended to be 'played in the usual way', and he expressed a preference for this version. The canzoni are often quite complex in structure. In general they consist of alternating contrapuntal and homophonic sections and their harmony and tonality are frequently quite advanced.

WORKS

Canzoni, libro primo, a 4, e 8vv (Milan, 1605[20])
Il primo libro de madrigali, 5vv (Venice, 1605)
Madrigali, 8vv (Milan, 1619[14])
Works in 1596[1], 1598[13], 1600[17], 1605[6], 1608[13], F. Rognoni Taeggio: Canzoni francese per sonar (Milan, 1608), 1612[9], 1615[13], 1619[3], 1623[3], 1624[6], 1626[5]
Pater noster, 5vv, *I-Mcap*

(3) **Francesco Rognoni Taeggio** (*b* ?Milan; *d* ?before 1626). Composer, theorist and instrumentalist, son of (1) Riccardo Rognoni. From the evidence of Francesco Lomazzo (son of the publisher Filippo Lomazzo), who was his pupil, and of Morigia, it is known that he was a virtuoso performer on the violin, viol and flute. As a young man he was in the service of King Sigismund III of Poland. He later lived in Milan, where in 1608 he belonged to the academy of Marco Maria Arese. In 1610 he was director of music to the Prince of Masserano. From 1613 until at least 1624 he was director of instrumental music to the governor of Milan and

from 1620 was also *maestro di cappella* of S Ambrogio. He was a knight and count Palatine. Like his father he made an important contribution to music theory, with his *Selva de varii passaggi*. The work is divided into two clearly defined sections dealing respectively with voices and instruments. The instructions in both are highly detailed. In the one devoted to wind instruments various types of articulation are distinguished. Among other matters in the section on strings the author discussed several kinds of bowing, including the playing of several notes on a single bow, for which he used the terms 'lireggiare' and 'archeggiare'. He described a special affective technique ('il lireggiarc affettuoso o con affetti') by means of which 'the wrist of the bow arm strikes each note with a bouncing motion' (see Horsley).

WORKS

Canzoni francese per sonar con ogni sorte de instromenti, a 4, 5, 8 (Milan, 1608)

Messa, salmi intieri e spezziati, Magnificat, falsibordoni, motetti, 5vv, op.2 (Milan, 1610)

Il primo libro de madrigali, 5vv, bc (hpd/chit) (Venice, 1613)

Aggiunta del scolaro di violino et altri stromenti, vn, other insts, bc (org) (Milan, 1614); lost, cited in Picinelli

Missarum et motectorum, 4, 5vv, org (Venice, 1624)

Correnti e gagliarde a 4, con la quinta parte ad arbitrio per sonar su varii strumenti (Milan, 1624); lost, cited in Picinelli

Works in 1612⁹, 1619³, 1619¹⁴, 1626⁵

THEORETICAL WORKS

Selva di varii passaggi secondo l'uso moderno per cantare e suonare con ogni sorte de stromenti (Milan, 1620/*R*1970)

BIBLIOGRAPHY

EitnerQ

P. Morigia: *Nobiltà di Milano* (Milan, 1619)

F. Picinelli: *Ateneo de' letterati milanesi* (Milan, 1670)

O. Kinkeldey: *Orgel und Klavier in der Musik des 16. Jahrhunderts* (Leipzig, 1910/*R*1968)

A. Moser: *Geschichte des Violinspiels* (Berlin, 1923, rev., enlarged 2/1966–7)

E. T. Ferand: 'Communication', *JAMS*, ix (1956), 250

C. Sartori: *La cappella musicale del duomo di Milano: catalogo delle musiche dell'archivio* (Milan, 1957)

M. Donà: *La stampa musicale a Milano fino all'anno 1700* (Florence, 1961)

E. T. Ferand: 'Die *Motetti, Madrigali, et Canzoni francese . . . diminuiti* . . . des Giovanni Bassano (1591)', *Festschrift Helmuth Osthoff* (Tutzing, 1961), 75

I. Horsley: 'The Solo Ricercar in Diminution Manuals: New Light on Early Wind and String Techniques', *AcM*, xxxiii (1961), 29

G. Barblan: 'I *Rognoni*, musicisti milanesi tra il 1500 e il 1600', *Anthony van Hoboken: Festschrift zum 75. Geburtstag* (Mainz, 1962), 19

——: 'La musica strumentale e cameristica a Milano dalla seconda metà del cinquecento a tutto il seicento', *Storia di Milano* (Milan, 1962)

A. Ponzoni: 'Le canzoni a quattro voci di Gio. Domenico Rognoni', *Annuario 1966–67 del Conservatorio di musica 'G. Verdi' di Milano* (Milan, 1967)

H. M. Brown: *Embellishing Sixteenth-century Music* (London, 1975)

SERGIO LATTES

Rognoni, Luigi (*b* Milan, 27 Aug 1913). Italian musicologist. Having been a music student of Alfredo Casella and a philosophy student of Antonio Banfi at Milan University, Rognoni's interest focussed on contemporary music; in 1935 he founded and edited the avant-garde monthly *Vita e cultura musicale*, which was forced to close because of the political situation; in 1936 he became editor of the revived *Rivista musicale italiana*. With Ferdinando Ballo he formed an orchestra in Milan (1937) to perform contemporary chamber music, and at that time was also connected with the cinema as one of the founders of Cineteca Italiana (1935), dedicated to using contemporary music (e.g. Dallapiccola, Flavio Testi) in its many documentaries. After the war, with Alberti Mantelli, he created the

Third Programme for Italian radio. From 1957 to 1970 he was professor of music history at the University of Palermo, and in 1971 moved to the University of Bologna.

As a promoter of contemporary music Rognoni organized the first radio performances of Schoenberg, Berg, Webern and Mahler in Italy. His writings deal with expressionism and the phenomenology of Husserl as applied by Adorno; after the war he widened his scope and originated the series Estetica Musicale, of which 17 volumes were published (including Banfi's *Vita dell'arte*; a new Italian version of Hanslick's *Il bello musicale*; and a modern edition of Galilei's *Dialogo della musica antica e della moderna*). While at Palermo he began to collect and edit microfilms of 16th- and 17th-century Sicilian music. His musical editions also include *Chansons des mendiants. . .di anonimo francese del sec. XV°* (Milan, 1937) and Leone Sinigaglia's *24 canzoni popolari piemontesi* (Milan, 1956).

WRITINGS

'Il quinto festival internazionale di musica contemporanea', *RMI*, xli (1937), 580

'Le prime rappresentazioni in Italia: *Lucrezia* di Ottorino Respighi', *RMI*, xli (1937), 199

Un opera incompiuta di Mozart: 'L'oca del Cairo' (Milan, 1937)

Ritratto di Louis Cortese (Milan, 1941)

Il 'Mandarino meraviglioso' di Bartók e 'Anfione' di Honegger (Milan, 1942)

Il 'Concerto in re min.' di Mozart (Milan, 1944)

La 'Passione secondo S. Matteo' di J. S. Bach (Milan, 1944)

Espressionismo e dodecafonia (Turin, 1954, enlarged 2/1966 as *La scuola musicale di Vienna*) [with appx of writings by Schoenberg, Berg, Kandinsky]

Rossini (Parma, 1956, rev. 2/1968 as *Gioacchino Rossini*)

'Leone Sinigaglia', *Musicisti piemontesi e liguri*, Chigiana, xvi (1959), 57

'Gli scritti e i dipinti di Arnold Schönberg', *Approdo musicale* (1960), no.12, p.95

'Riscatto e attualità di Gustav Mahler', *Approdo musicale* (1963), nos.16–17, p.59

'Sulla preparazione dell'*Ottava* a Monaco: lettera inedita di Mahler a Emil Gutmann', *Approdo musicale* (1963), nos.16–17, p.156

'Due colloqui con Arthur Honegger', *Approdo musicale* (1965), nos.19–20, p.131

Fenomenologia della musica radicale (Bari, 1966, enlarged 2/1974)

'Italien', *Symposion für Musikkritik: Graz 1967*, 57

'Una singola lettera di Debussy a Leone Sinigaglia', *Spettatore musicale*, vii/5 (1972), 2

'Meditazione su Anton Webern', *Quadrivium*, xiv (1973), 405

'I tre Pinto', *Rassegna musicale Curci*, xxvii (1974), 35

ed.: *Carl Maria von Weber: Die drei Pintos* (Turin, 1975)

CAROLYN M. GIANTURCO

Rogowski, Ludomir Michał (*b* Lublin, 3 Oct 1881; *d* Dubrovnik, 14 March 1954). Polish composer. Coming from a musical family, he had his early training at home, then studied at the Warsaw Conservatory with Noskowski (composition) and Młynarski (conducting), and in 1906 went to Leipzig for further studies with Nikisch and Riemann. In 1909 he returned to Poland as director of the Vilnius Organ School, and in 1910 he became founder-conductor of the Vilnius SO. Further travels took him to Paris (1911), Warsaw (1912–14, working as a theatre conductor), France and Belgium (during World War I) and back to Poland. In 1926 he settled in Dubrovnik; he received the Polish State Music Prize in 1938.

Rogowski's early works show little originality, but his studies of impressionist and oriental (at first Persian) musics led him to a distinctive modal style. He made use of the Slavonic scale (Lydian mode with flattened 7th: C–D–E–F♯–G–A–B♭–C), a Persian scale of alternating semitones and tones beginning on C (one form of the mode later classified by Messiaen as mode 2) and the whole-tone scale. His forms, however, were traditional, filled with broad rhythms, compelling sounds and subjective feelings. Much of his material was taken from the folksong of Poland, France, Belorussia, Bosnia and Dalmatia.

WORKS
(selective list)
STAGE

Operas: Tamara (lyrical legend, F. Hellens), 1918; Serenada (grotesque opera, 1), 1920; Wielkie zmartwienie małej Ondyny [The great trouble of the little Ondyna] (1, Rogowski, L. Orechwa), 1920; Na postoju [On the halt], 1, Warsaw, 1923; Syrena [The mermaid] (3, M. Grif), 1924; Królewicz Marco [Prince Marco] (5, I. Goleniszczew-Kutuzow, after idea by Rogowski), 1930
Operetta: Legionistka (3, B. Hertz), Kraków, 1912
Ballets: Bajka [Fairy tale], 1923; Kupała, 1926; Z ogrodów Harun-al-Raszyda [From the gardens of Harun-al-Rashid]; Korowaj (pantomime)

OTHER WORKS

Orch: 7 syms., 1926, 1936, 1940–41, 1943, 1947, 1949, 1951; sym. poems, suites, other pieces
Vocal: Fantasmagorie, 1v, orch, 1920; cantatas, sacred music, other choral pieces, folksong arrs.
Chamber: 2 str qts; Méditation, 4 vc; Bibelots chinois, fl, cel, pf (1916); Ukrainka, ob, cl, str qt; pieces for vn/va/va, pf
Pf: 6 préludes: Réflexions musicales; 2 miniatury; Propos sérieux et plaisants

Principal publishers: Gebethner & Wolff, Polskie Wydawnictwo Muzyczne, Roudanez
MSS in YU-Dsmb

BIBLIOGRAPHY

S. Kaszyński: 'Ludomir Michał Rogowski: zapomniany polski kompozytor', Ruch muzyczny (1959), no.15, p.14
Z. Stoberski: 'Spotkania z Ludomirem Michałem Rogowskim', Ruch muzyczny (1963), no.6, p.12
M. Bristiger: 'L. M. Rogowskiego skale i idee muzyczne', Studia Hieronymo Feicht septuagenario dedicata (Kraków, 1967), 446
BOGUSŁAW SCHÄFFER

Rohaczewski, Andrzej (fl c1620). Polish composer and organist. He was organist at the court of Albert Radziwiłł at Ołyka and Nieśwież. The Pelplin Organ Tablature, compiled during the 1620s, contains two compositions by him. One is a motet, Crucifixus surrexit, for nine voices in two choirs of four and five respectively (ed. in WDMP, xlvi, 1961; AMP, vi, 1965, pp.230f [facs.]). The other is a four-part canzona (ed. in WDMP, xliii, 1960; AMP, vii, 1965, pp.158f [facs.], and viii, 1970, pp.320ff; MAP, Barok, ii, 1969, pp.23f), which, together with similar works by Adam Jarzębski, is the earliest piece of this type in Poland. Its style indicates that it was originally composed for a string ensemble and not, as has sometimes been suggested, for organ.

BIBLIOGRAPHY

SMP
A. Sutkowski: 'Charakter tematów instrumentalnej canzony na początku XVII wieku' [The types of theme in instrumental canzonas at the beginning of the 17th century], Muzyka, iii/4 (1958), 49
——: 'Nieznane polonika muzyczne z XVI i XVII wieku' [Unknown Polish music of the 16th and 17th centuries], Muzyka, v/1 (1960), 62
A. Sutkowski and A. Osostowicz-Sutkowska, eds.: The Pelplin Tablature: a Thematic Catalogue, AMP, i (1963), 572f, 643
J. Gołos: Polskie organy i muzyka organowa (Warsaw, 1972), 160ff
MIROSŁAW PERZ

Rohloff, Ernst (b Graudenz, West Prussia [now Grudziądz, Poland], 17 April 1899). German musicologist and organist. He was a pupil of Reger in Leipzig and Meiningen (1909–12) and studied the organ with Straube at Leipzig Conservatory and musicology under Abert and Kroyer at Leipzig University (1919–22); he took his doctorate there in 1926 with a dissertation on the musical treatise of Johannes de Grocheo, and passed the state teacher's examination in 1927.

Having taught in schools in Saxony until 1937 he became an organist in Weissenfels, from 1943 at the Marienkirche and from 1955 at the Schlosskirche. His publications include the Singspiel Sternsinger-Kumpanei (Leipzig, 1939) to a text partly based on E. A. Herrmann's Christmas play Das Gottes Kind (1911), Der Schöne Mai ist kommen (Leipzig, 1955), a short survey of four centuries of German song, and studies of the Lochamer Liederbuch.

WRITINGS

Studien zum Musiktraktat des Johannes de Grocheo (diss., U. of Leipzig, 1926; Leipzig, 1930–1943)
Die einstimmigen Weisen des Lochamer Liederbuches (Halle, 1953)
Der schöne Mai ist kommen (Leipzig, 1955)
'Rückerinnerung und Erwiderung', Mf, viii (1955), 471; correction, ix (1956), 256
' "Mit ganzem Willen wünnsch ich dir" ', AMw, xiii (1956), 236
Die Quellenhandschriften zum Musiktraktat des Johannes de Grocheio (Leipzig, 1972) [facs. edn.]
'Anmerkungen zum Lochamer-Liederbuch', Wissenschaftliche Zeitschrift der Martin-Luther-Universität Halle-Wittenberg, xxvi (1977)

EDITIONS

Neidharts Sangweisen, i–ii, Abhandlungen der Sächsischen Akademie der Wissenschaften zu Leipzig: Philologisch-historische Klasse, lii/3–4 (Berlin, 1962)
HORST SEEGER

Rohrblatt (Ger.). REED.

Röhrenglocken (Ger.). TUBULAR BELLS.

Rohrflöte (Ger.). An ORGAN STOP.

Rohrstimmen [Rohrwerk] (Ger.). The REED-WORK of an organ.

Rohwer, Jens (b Neumünster, Holstein, 6 July 1914). German musicologist and composer. He studied school music at the Hochschule für Musikerziehung und Kirchenmusik in Berlin from 1935 to 1938. Invalided out of the army during World War II, he became a lecturer at the music school in Posen (1943–5), then at the regional music school of Schleswig-Holstein in Lübeck (1946–50) and at its successor the Schleswig-Holstein Academy (1950–55). In 1956 he continued his musicological studies under Blume in Kiel, where he took the doctorate in 1958 with a dissertation on harmony. From 1955 to 1971 he was director of the Schleswig-Holstein Academy (since 1970 the Staatliche Fachhochschule), and from 1971 professor.

In his youth he was influenced by the ideals of the Jugendbewegung, then associated with such music educationists as Georg Götsch, Fritz Jöde and Gottfried Wolters. As an adherent of cultural and educational aims similar to those of the Arbeitskreis für Musik in der Jugend, he doubted the expressive and cultural worth of avant-garde music and tried both as a scholar and teacher to counteract it with systematic research into 'Tonsatzstruktur' and a type of music training based on anthropological methods of education and culture-criticism. These views shaped his prolific activity as a composer. His youth songs and choruses (1945–52) and later his church music have been notably successful. He has also written oratorios, cantatas, orchestral and chamber music, and music for the organ and the piano.

WRITINGS

Tonale Instruktionen und Beiträge zur Kompositionslehre (Wolfenbüttel, 1951)
Der Sonanzfaktor im Tonsystem (diss., U. of Kiel, 1958; rev. as Die

harmonischen Grundlagen der Musik, Kassel, 1970)
'Anmerkungen zum "seriellen Denken" ', Mf, xvii (1964), 245
Neueste Musik: ein kritischer Bericht (Stuttgart, 1964)
'Systematische Musiktheorie', Festschrift für Walter Wiora (Kassel, 1967), 131
'Die Grundlagen der Musik: Anmerkungen zu Ernest Ansermets Buch', Mf, xx (1967), 430
Sinn und Unsinn in der Musik: Versuch einer musikalischen Sinnbegriffs-Analyse (Wolfenbüttel and Zurich, 1969)
Die harmonischen Grundlagen der Musik (Kassel, 1970)
'Neue Musik – kirchenfeindlich?', Musik und Kirche, xlii (1972), 64, 112
'Von Tonmusik zu Klangmusik', Zeitschrift für Musiktheorie, iii/2 (1972), 28
'Das "Ablösungsprinzip" in der abendländischen Musik', Zeitschrift für Musiktheorie, vii/1 (1976), 4

HANS HEINRICH EGGEBRECHT

Roi, Bartolomeo. See ROY, BARTOLOMEO.

Roi, Chansonnier [Manuscrit] **du** (F-Pn fr.844). See SOURCES, MS, §III, 4.

Roiha, Eino (Vilho Pietari) (b Wiborg, 12 June 1904; d Helsinki, 20 Oct 1955). Finnish musicologist and composer. He studied at Helsinki Conservatory (until 1929) and Helsinki University, where he took the doctorate in 1943 with a dissertation on Sibelius's symphonies. After teaching music at the teacher-training college (1930–35) and high school (1935–48) in Jyväskylä he held a lectureship at Helsinki University (1948–55) and also taught at the high school in Helsinki (1948–55). His main musicological interests were the psychology of music and contemporary music; he was the first chairman of Nykymusiikki, a society founded in 1949 to promote new music, and of the Finnish section of ISCM from 1951. His structural analyses of Sibelius's symphonies were based on theories of Gestalt psychology. He was also active as a choir conductor, music critic and composer in a mildly modern style; his works include two orchestral suites, a Concertino for piano and orchestra, violin and piano sonatas, piano pieces and songs.

WRITINGS

Die Symphonien von Jean Sibelius: eine formanalytische Studie (diss., U. of Helsinki, 1943; Jyväskylä, 1941)
Johdatus musiikkipsykologiaan [Introduction to the psychology of music] (Jyväskylä, 1949, 2/1965)
'Sibeliuksen Karelia-sarjan historiallista taustaa' [Historical background of Sibelius's Karelia Suite], Kalevalaseuran vuosikirja xxxiii (1953), 161
On the Theory and Technique of Contemporary Music (Helsinki, 1956)

BIBLIOGRAPHY

Autobiography completed by K. Rydman, Suomen säveltäjiä, ii, ed. E. Marvia (Porvoo, 2/1966), 248

ERKKI SALMENHAARA

Roince [Rouince, Roynci, Ruince, Rovince], **Luigi** [Aloisio, Luisio, Aloigi, Aluigi] (d Piacenza, 6 June 1597). French composer active in Italy. He is described as 'francese' in almost all documents referring to him and in the ascription of his one surviving chanson (in RISM 1564[11]), probably composed before he moved to Piacenza. According to documents (in I-PCsa) he had assumed the post of maestro di cappella at Piacenza Cathedral by 30 May 1571 and in a letter of 14 May 1572 Paolo Burali, the Bishop of Piacenza, stated his satisfaction with 'signor Aluigi the Frenchman'. Roince's admiration for his teacher Annibale Zoilo is evident in letters that he wrote to Cardinal Guglielmo Sirleto, an educated man and patron of musicians: in one dated 24 January 1582 Roince claimed 'you will not hear harmony so sweet as that of my most excellent

master Hannibale Zoilo' and he enclosed one of his own motets as a present to the cardinal; in another letter of 9 May 1585 he sent Sirleto a 'spiritual sonnet in music' and a Te Deum to offer to the recently elected Pope Sixtus V. He continued as maestro di cappella at Piacenza until his death and was succeeded by Tiburtio Massaino in 1598. Some of his compositions were published posthumously by his pupil Giulio Cesare de Colli, with prefaces and dedications to civic dignitaries written by Roince's wife.

WORKS

Liber secundus missarum, 6vv (Venice, 1599)
Litaniae BVM, 4–8, 12vv (Venice, 1599)
Cantica per omnes tonos BVM, 5vv (Venice, 1603)
Sacra omnium solemnitatum vespertina duoque beatae virginis cantica, 5vv (Venice, 1604)
Works in 1564[11], 1596[11]

BIBLIOGRAPHY

EitnerQ
R. Casimiri: 'Lettere di musicisti (1579–1585) al Cardinal Sirleto', NA, ix (1932), 97
F. Bussi: Piacenza, Archivio del Duomo: catalogo del fondo musicale (Milan, 1967)
——: Due importanti fondi musicali di Piacenza: la Biblioteca-Archivio capitolare del Duomo e la Biblioteca del Conservatorio statale di musica 'Giuseppe Nicolini' (Piacenza, 1972)

FRANCESCO BUSSI

Rojo Olalla, Casiano (b Hacinas, nr. Burgos, 5 Aug 1877; d Silos, nr. Burgos, 4 Dec 1931). Spanish scholar of plainchant. In 1896 he became a Benedictine monk at Santo Domingo de Silos, where he received his first training; he continued his musical education in Belgium under Pothier. From 1921 to 1931 he was prior at Silos. He systematically explored the music archives of the main cathedrals in Spain, transcribing and publishing many of the pieces he found and giving courses and lectures on Gregorian chant in schools and seminaries throughout Spain and Portugal. His research and its practical application is, with that of G. Prado, of prime importance for the restoration of liturgical chant in Spain.

WRITINGS

Método de canto gregoriano (Silos, 1906)
Manual de canto gregoriano (Silos, 1908)
Cantus Lamentationum (Bilbao, 1917)
'El canto español de las Lamentaciones según el códice de Silos (siglo XIII)', Música sacro-hispana, x (1917), 26, 38
with G. Prado: El canto mozárabe (Barcelona, 1929)
'The Gregorian Antiphonary of Silos and the Spanish Melody of Lamentations', Speculum, v (1930), 306

BIBLIOGRAPHY

Obituary, Tesoro sacro musical, xvi (1932), 4, 18
Obituary, Revista musical catalana, xxix (1932), 87
Obituary, Revue du chant grégorien, xxxvi (1932), 28

FRANCISCO LARA

Rokitansky, Hans Freiherr von (b Vienna, 8 March 1835; d Schloss Laubegg, Styria, 2 Nov 1909). Austrian bass. He studied at Bologna and Milan, making his concert début in 1856 in London and his first stage appearance in 1857 at the Théâtre-Italien, Paris, as Oroveso in Norma. He began an engagement at Prague on 23 October 1862 as Cardinal Brogny in La juive. From 1 July 1864 to his retirement on 31 December 1893, he was engaged at the Vienna Court Opera. He appeared at Her Majesty's Theatre in 1865 and in 1866, when he sang Osmin at a revival of Die Entführung aus dem Serail (given in Italian as Il seraglio) on 30 June; he returned to London in 1876 and 1877. His roles included Leporello, Sarastro, Bertram (Robert le diable), Verdi's Fiesco, Weber's Caspar, the Landgrave (Tannhäuser), Heinrich (Lohengrin) and Sir George (I *puritani*). From 1894 he taught at the Vienna Conservatory. His voice, a deep bass of great resonance, suffered towards the end of his career from faulty production, which affected his intonation. His brother, Victor Freiherr von Rokitansky (*b* Vienna, 9 July 1836; *d* Vienna, 17 July 1896), was a singer and song composer who taught at the Vienna Conservatory between 1871 and 1880.

BIBLIOGRAPHY
V. von Rokitansky: *Über Sänger und Singen* (Vienna, 1891, 2/1896)
B. Marchesi: *The Singer's Catechism and Creed* (London, 1932)
ELIZABETH FORBES

Rokitansky, Victor Freiherr **von.** Singer and composer, brother of HANS VON ROKITANSKY.

Rokseth [née Rihouët], **Yvonne** (*b* Maison-Laffitte, Paris, 17 July 1890; *d* Strasbourg, 23 Aug 1948). French musicologist. She studied the organ with Abel Decaux and composition with d'Indy at the Paris Conservatoire and Schola Cantorum, composition privately with Roussel and music history with Pirro at the Sorbonne (from 1920), where she took the diploma in natural sciences and philosophy (1915) and a doctorat ès lettres (1930) with a dissertation on organ music in the late 15th and early 16th centuries. A qualified librarian (1933), she catalogued autographs at the Conservatoire and organized the music department at the Bibliothèque Nationale (1934–7), where she also arranged concerts of medieval music and formulated plans for a musicological institute at the university. In 1937 she became *maître de conférences* at Strasbourg University; during the university's wartime removal to Clermont-Ferrand, she continued its musical activities by founding a choir, orchestra and musical society. After World War II (during which she was an active member of the Resistance) she became professor of musicology at Strasbourg (1948); she was a visiting lecturer in Germany and Switzerland and gave courses at the American Institute of Musicology, Florence.

Few musicologists have brought to their task such enviable mental and practical qualities as Rokseth possessed. Her literary studies brought a memorable quality to her writing, and a scientific training added the precision with which she marshalled the facts derived from intensive study of unfamiliar subjects; moreover, her experience as a composer engendered sympathy for works which her practical musicianship brought to life on the concert platform. Her doctoral dissertation *La musique d'orgue* found an immediate publisher. The period 1450–1531 covered by the survey (which deals not only with music but with every aspect of the instrument) is represented at one end by the German didactic tablatures of Ileborgh and Paumann, and at the other by France's first contribution to the genre published by Attaingnant (1531). In the absence of any previous French tablature, Rokseth reached her conclusions about French practice by relating it to that shared by the countries of western Europe. By-products of this study included editions of Attaingnant's *Deux livres* and *Treize motets*, which embody instruction in the crafts of diminution, improvisation and free composition.

Rokseth's second important work was a definitive four-volume edition (with facsimile, transcription and commentary) of Montpellier MS H.196, a compendium of the 13th-century French motet which has intrigued musicologists since Coussemaker's time. Other important undertakings included the unfortunately incomplete *Trois chansonniers*, particularly valuable for reconstituting 15th-century poetic forms, and a contribution (*NOHM*, iii) on early instrumental music, which rightly praises the wide growth of keyboard music while underestimating that of consort music. Rokseth died at the height of her powers leaving a lavishly documented body of work which, in Schrade's words, 'is marked by that thoroughness, comprehensiveness, rigid discipline and devotion that are always characteristic of Pirro's school'.

WRITINGS

'Un motet de Moulu et ses diverses transcriptions pour orgue', *Kongressbericht: Basel 1924*, 286
Histoire de la musique (Paris, 1925, rev. 2/1931) [ed. and trans. of K. Nef: *Einführung in die Musikgeschichte*, Basle, 1920]
'Notes sur Josquin des Prés comme pédagogue musical', *RdM*, viii (1927), 202
La musique d'orgue au XVe siècle et au début du XVIe (diss., U. of Paris, 1930; Paris, 1930)
'La musique d'orgue du XIIIe au XVIIe siècle', *Bulletin trimestriel des amis de l'orgue*, nos.6–24 (1931–6) [series of articles]
Review of F. Gennrich: *Rondeaux, Virelais und Balladen aus dem Ende des XII., dem XIII. und ersten Drittel des XIV. Jahrhunderts* (Dresden, 1921–7), *Studi medievali*, new ser., iv (1931), 204
Grieg (Paris, 1933)
'Instruments à l'église au XVe siècle', *RdM*, xiv (1933), 206
'Le contrepoint double vers 1248', *Mélanges de musicologie offerts à M. Lionel de la Laurencie* (Paris, 1933), 5
'Une source peu étudiée d'iconographie musicale', *RdM*, xiv (1933), 74
'Les femmes musiciennes du XIIe au XVe siècle', *Romania*, lxi (1935), 464
Review of M. Schneider: *Geschichte der Mehrstimmigkeit* (Berlin, 1934–5), *RdM*, xvi (1935), 245; xvii (1936), 91
'Antonio Bembo, Composer to Louis XIV', *MQ*, xxiii (1937), 147
'Du rôle de l'orgue dans l'exécution de la musique polyphonique du XIIIe siècle', *Dix années au service de l'orgue français* (Paris, 1937), 45
'Les "Laude" et leur édition par M. Liuzzi', *Romania*, lxv (1939), 383
Preface to J. Marix: *Histoire de la musique et des musiciens de la cour de Bourgogne sous le règne de Ph. le Bon* (Strasbourg, 1939)
'André Pirro', *RdM*, xxiii (1944), 25
'Réaction de la réforme contre certains éléments réalistes du culte', *Revue d'histoire et de philosophie religieuses*, xxvi (1946), 146
'Musical Scholarship in France during the War', *JRBM*, i (1946–7), 81
'Un "Magnificat" de Marc-Antoine Charpentier', *JRBM*, i (1946–7), 192
'Danses cléricales du XIIIe siècle', *Mélanges 1945 des publications de Faculté des lettres de Strasbourg*, no.106 (Paris, 1947), 93–126 [with transcrs. of 60 rondeaux from Antiphonarium Medium in *I-Fl*]
'La polyphonie parisienne du treizième siècle: étude critique à propos d'une publication récente', *Les cahiers techniques de l'art*, i/2 (Strasbourg, 1947), 33 [on H. Husmann, ed.: *Die drei- und vierstimmigen Notre-Dame-Organa*, Publikationen älterer Musik, xi (Leipzig, 1910)]
'Aimer la musique ancienne', *Polyphonie*, iii (1949), 5
'The Instrumental Music of the Middle Ages and the Early Sixteenth Century', *NOHM*, iii (1960), 406–65; It. trans., 1964

EDITIONS

Deux livres d'orgue paru chez Pierre Attaingnant (1531), PSFM, 1st ser., i (1925/R1968)
with E. Droz and G. Thibault: *Trois chansonniers français du XVe siècle* (Paris, 1927/R1977) [inc.]
Treize motets et un prélude réduits en la tablature des orgues: transcription du 3e livre d'orgue édité par Attaingnant (1531) (supplementary diss., U. of Paris, 1930; PSFM, 1st ser., v, 1930)
Polyphonies du XIIIe siècle: le manuscrit H 196 de la Faculté de médecine de Montpellier (Paris, 1935–9)
Lamentation de la Vierge au pied de la Croix (XIIIe siècle) (Paris, 1937)

BIBLIOGRAPHY
G. Thibault:'Yvonne Rokseth', *RdM*, xxvii (1948), 76
F. Lesure: 'Bibliographie de l'oeuvre musicologique d'Yvonne Rokseth', *RdM*, xxvii (1948), 85
L. Schrade: 'Yvonne Rokseth: in memoriam', *JAMS*, ii (1949), 171
V. Fédorov: 'André Pirro and Yvonne Rokseth', *Mf*, iii (1950), 106 [with list of writings, by F. Lesure]
——: 'En souvenir d'Yvonne Rokseth', *Contrepoints*, no.6 (1950), 187
G. B. SHARP

Roland-Manuel [Lévy, Roland Alexis Manuel] (*b* Paris, 22 March 1891; *d* Paris, 2 Nov 1966). French composer and writer on music. After living for three years in Florida and nine years in Liège, he returned to Paris in 1905, following the death of his father. He was a pupil of Roussel at the Schola Cantorum (where he also studied the violin) and later, on Satie's advice, he went to study with Ravel, becoming a devoted follower of that composer. Besides his work as composer, he was active as an administrator and writer. In 1947 he became vice-president of the French section of the ISCM and a professor at the Paris Conservatoire, giving classes in music culture and aesthetics. In 1949 he became associated with the UNESCO Music Council. He achieved wide recognition as an original popularizer of music when he inaugurated a long-running Sunday series on French radio entitled 'Plaisir de la Musique' (subsequently published in book form), which he continued until his death.

Roland-Manuel as a composer was firmly in the tradition of the 18th-century artist whose function it was to be impersonal and specialized, in complete antithesis to 19th-century Romantic self-glorification. 'We make music', he said, 'with material which is neutral and mouldable. The individual is of no interest, and art can certainly be something other than a medium of self-expression. Vanity is the death of an artist'. He was a humanist; and he had no sympathy for 'systems'. From his early songs based on Persian texts, *Farizade au sourire de rose*, his music was essentially French in its fastidiousness, restraint, refinement and sensibility. It was anti-Romantic, as Ravel's music was, avoiding a direct display of emotion.

Within that aesthetic framework many different kinds of work were possible, though Roland-Manuel's output was not very large. A mystic side can be found in the polyphonic choral works *Bénédictions* and *Le cantique de la sagesse*. Earlier, however, after war service, he had fully entered into the very different Parisian world of Les Six, sometimes expressing in his music the frivolous spirit of that time. The restrained nature of his art kept him from any excess, and also prevented a fully dramatic expression in *Isabelle et Pantalon*, bold and imaginative as this *opéra comique* is in conception. His ingenious, precise, basically simple style found personal and most convincing form in instrumental music. For ballet, his clearcut melodic invention and precise rhythmic designs were practical and effective in, for example, *L'écran des jeunes filles*, where an 18th-century spirit finds integrated modern expression. Of his chamber works, the two trios are more contrapuntal than usual, pointed with characteristic harmonic asperities; and classical forms are used very flexibly. The *Suite dans le goût espagnol* is bold and direct, a personal Spanish impression which avoids any obvious clichés.

WORKS
(selective list)

Stage: Isabelle et Pantalon (opéra comique, M. Jacob), 1920; Le tournoi singulier (ballet), 1924; L'écran des jeunes filles (ballet), 1928; Le diable amoureux (opéra comique, R. Allard), 1932; Elvire (ballet) [after Scarlatti], 1936; Échec à Don Juan (opera, C. A. Puget), 1941; La Célestine (opera, M. Achard, after F. de Rojas), 1942; Jeanne d'Arc (opera, Péguy), 1955

Orch: Le harem du vice-roi, sym. poem, 1919; Tempo di ballo, sym. poem, 1924; Peña di Francia, suite, 1938; Pf Conc., D, 1938

Choral: Jeanne d'Arc (E. Fleg), oratorio, 1937; Bénédictions, SSA, 1938; Le cantique de la sagesse (Proverbs), oratorio, 1943–53

Chamber: Pf Trio, 1917; Str Trio, 1922; Suite dans le goût espagnol, ob, bn, tpt, hpd, 1933

Songs: Farizade au sourire de rose (Persian), 1v, pf, 1913; 2 rondels (P. d'Armentière), 1v, pf, 1918; 3 romances (P. J. Toulet), 1v, orch, 1922; Délie, objet de plus haute vertu (M. Scève), 1v, pf, 1923

Principal publisher: Durand

WRITINGS
Maurice Ravel et son oeuvre (Paris, 1914)
Erik Satie (Paris, 1916)
Maurice Ravel et son oeuvre dramatique (Paris, 1929)
Manuel de Falla (Paris, 1930)
Maurice Ravel (Paris, 1938, 2/1948; Eng. trans., 1947)
Plaisir de la musique (Paris, 1947–55)
Sonate, que me veux-tu? (Lausanne, 1957)
ed.: *Histoire de la musique*, Encyclopédie de la Pléiade (Paris, 1960–63)

DAVID COX

Roldán, Amadeo (*b* Paris, 12 July 1900; *d* Havana, 7 March 1939). Cuban composer, violinist, conductor and teacher. He studied the violin with Bordas at the Madrid Conservatory (graduating in 1916), won the Sarasate Prize and began a career as a performer. Then he had composition lessons with del Campo in Madrid and with Pedro Sanjuán. In 1921 he settled in Havana, where he was until his death a most active and influential figure in musical life, stimulating the rather dormant cultural activities of the city during the 1920s and 1930s. He was successively appointed leader (1924), assistant conductor (1925) and conductor and music director (1932) of the Havana PO. In 1927 he founded the Havana String Quartet, which, like the Havana PO, presented many concerts of contemporary music, then almost unknown in Cuba. He was professor of composition at the Havana Conservatory from 1935.

Together with Caturla, Roldán brought to Cuban art music a much-needed imaginativeness, seriousness of purpose and technical accomplishment. His polished compositions use the rhythms of Afro-Cuban music, and he was the first to bring into the concert hall the forceful elements of black Cuban folklore (tango conga, conga, comparsa, son and rumba), which he deployed in a refined, partly impressionist, partly dissonant, Stravinskian style. He became the figurehead and the guiding spirit for a younger generation of Cuban composers, united by common artistic ideals and aspirations. A mulatto himself, he thoroughly assimilated the mestizo features of Cuban music, and his works are often imbued with Afro-Cuban mythology. He was something of an intellectual, and in the late 1920s and early 1930s he associated with young Cuban painters and writers, some of whom established the Grupo de Avance, which led a renovation of Cuban artistic life. A close relationship with Carpentier produced a series of remarkable works, most importantly the ballet *La rebambaramba*. Other major compositions include *Rítmicas V* and *VI* (1930), which, with Varèse's *Ionisation*, were among the first Western works for percussion ensemble.

WORKS
(selective list)

Ballets: La rebambaramba (Carpentier), 1927–8; El milagro de Anaquillé (1, Carpentier), 1928–9, reorchd 1931

Orch: Obertura sobre temas cubanos, 1925; 3 pequeños poemas, 1926; 3 toques, chamber orch, 1931

Vocal: Fiestas galantes (Verlaine), 1v, pf, 1923; Danza negra (F. Palés Matos), 1v, 2 cl, 2 va, perc, 1929; Curujey (N. Guillén), chorus, 2 pf, 2 perc, 1931; Motivos de son (Guillén), S, 7 insts, 1934

Inst: A changó, lute qt, 1928; 2 Cuban Folksongs, vc, pf, 1928; Rítmicas I–IV, wind qnt, pf, 1930; Rítmicas V–VI, perc ens, 1930; Mulato, pf, 1934

Principal publishers: Biblioteca Nacional José Martí, New Music Edition, Southern

MSS in Biblioteca Nacional, Havana

BIBLIOGRAPHY

A. Roldán: 'The Artistic Position of the American Composer', *American Composers on American Music*, ed. H. Cowell (Stanford, Calif., 1933), 175

L. Argeliers: 'Las obras para piano de Amadeo Roldán', *Revista de música*, i/4 (Havana, n.d.), 112

H. Cowell: '*Motivos de son*, a Series of 8 Songs for Soprano with a Small Orchestra', *MQ*, xxxvi (1950), 270

Compositores de América/Composers of the Americas, ed. Pan American Union, i (Washington, DC, 1955), 77

AURELIO DE LA VEGA

Roldán, Juan Pérez. *See* PÉREZ ROLDÁN, JUAN.

Rolfe. English firm of piano makers, publishers and music sellers. It is thought that the business started in 1785 at 112 Cheapside, London. From 1795 to 1797 William Rolfe, Thomas Culliford and a Mr Barrow formed a partnership, and Rolfe managed the business on his own from 1800 until about 1814, when his sons joined him to form W. Rolfe and Co. The firm ceased production in 1888. In 1797, with Samuel Davis, Rolfe patented (no.2160) the earliest specification for 'Turkish music' in pianos, where a hammer strikes the soundboard to produce the sound of a drum. The hammer action, based on the English single action (*see* PIANOFORTE, §I, 4) and operated by a pedal, is illustrated in Harding (p.135). The patent also specifies that instead of using the soundboard, a kind of frame drum, made from skin, cloth or paper fixed on a frame, could be placed inside the piano for the drum mechanism to strike. Surviving Rolf squares are attractive and colourful. An early one (no.4481) is at the Cambridge University Music School; it has five octaves and looks as though it may originally have had hand stops. By the time the serial number 7024 was reached the firm's squares generally had a compass of five and a half octaves. Whereas the early models had French stands (i.e. in the style of Sheraton with a shelf for the music), by 1825 the squares had six turned legs (four in the front and two at the back) and often three drawers, the middle one being curved.

BIBLIOGRAPHY

R. E. M. Harding: *The Piano-forte: its History Traced to the Great Exhibition of 1851* (Cambridge, 1933, rev. 2/1978)

MARGARET CRANMER

Rolla. Italian family of publishers. Two members of the family published music in Milan during the 17th century. Giorgio Rolla (*d* Milan, ?1651) was a printer for Milan Cathedral in 1619, and his press published music until 1651. He appears to have produced only one or two music publications each year, almost all of local minor composers and not running to second editions. Most of the music is sacred. In 1649 he collaborated with Carlo Camagno for one title; he composed a little music, printing it in some of his collections (*RISM* 1619³, 1619⁴, 1623³, 1649¹). He was succeeded by his son, Carlo Francesco Rolla, who had started printing in 1650, and who continued either in his own name or as his father's heir. He printed one title with Camagno in 1651, and fewer than ten on his own; he seems to have stopped printing by the end of the decade.

BIBLIOGRAPHY

C. Sartori: *Dizionario degli editori musicali italiani* (Florence, 1958)

M. Donà: *La stampa musicale a Milano fino all'anno 1700* (Florence, 1961) [incl. nearly complete list of Rolla's music publications]

STANLEY BOORMAN

Rolla, Alessandro (*b* Pavia, 6 April 1757; *d* Milan, 15 Sept 1841). Italian violinist, violist and composer. He was probably trained in Milan; the tradition that he studied with Giacomo Conti, only five years his senior and active in Vienna, is at best doubtful. He then led an exceptionally stable career. From 1782 to 1802 he was at the ducal court in Parma, entering as first violist, then becoming first violinist (1792) and finally director of concerts. In 1803 he was appointed first violinist and director of the orchestra at La Scala in Milan, and in 1808 he became the first professor of violin and viola at the new Milan Conservatory. He retired from La Scala in 1833 and from the conservatory in 1835.

During his years in Milan Rolla was an influential figure, held in the highest regard as a man and as an artist. His wide renown seems to have come largely from his compositions and his ability as a leader. Spohr, writing in 1816, praised the precision with which Rolla controlled the orchestra from his place in the first violins, and admired the care given to the accompaniment of concertos. As a teacher Rolla was an important influence in the continuation of a more conservative Italian tradition in the face of Paganini's flamboyant technical achievements. His most important pupils were Bernardo Ferrara who succeeded him at the conservatory, and his son Giuseppe Antonio Rolla (*b* Parma, 18 April 1798; *d* Dresden, 19 May 1837), who was leader of the Italian Opera orchestra in Dresden (1823–35) and published a violin concerto and other pedagogical and virtuoso works for violin and viola. That he taught Paganini at Parma has been refuted.

Rolla was a prolific composer. A few of his compositions were issued in Paris, Vienna, and by André in Offenbach during his years at Parma, but most of his published works appeared after the establishment of Ricordi in Milan in 1808. A considerable number, including a majority of his concertos, exist only in manuscript. Although conventional in form and without striking originality, Rolla's works are unfailingly idiomatic, with brilliant figuration and sensitive, fluent melodic writing. His concert solos (usually an Adagio followed by a polonaise or theme with variations) are early Romantic virtuoso pieces and reflect most convincingly his fine technique. His published concertos, apparently early works, stand close to the early concertos of Viotti, showing French influence along with a few specifically Italian traits. Of his chamber music, the string trios are notable for their unusually serious expression and rich texture, and the duets still maintain a small but deserved place as student pieces and as amateur chamber music. Rolla also wrote many practical yet pleasing pedagogical works, and several ballets which evidently survive only in miscellaneous dances and possibly in the one-movement overtures called *sinfonie*. The extent and quality of his achievements testify to a continuing instrumental tradition in a country then largely dominated by opera.

WORKS

PUBLISHED

Orch: 3 vn concs.; 3 va concs., Va Concertino; at least 10 other vn works; 2 sinfonie

Chamber: Serenade, 2 vn, 2 va, 2 hn; Str Qnt; 6 str qts; 9 str trios; 3 trios, 2 vn, vc/va; 3 terzettini, 2 fl, va; at least 33 duets, 2 vn; at least 27 duets, vn, va; 3 sonatas, vn, acc. va

Pedagogical: 24 intonazioni, vn; 24 scale, vn, acc. vn; 6 solfeggi, vn, acc. vn; Studi, vn, ad lib vn; Frammenti d'opere di studio, va

MSS

(*all in I-Mc*)

Orch: 7 vn concs.; 12 va concs.; 5 vn solos; 5 va solos; 3 sinfonie, incl. nos.4, 10

Chamber: Sonata, vn, b; Sonata, va, acc. va; 2 sonatas, va, acc. vn; prelude and variations on a theme by Weigl (pf, harp)/(harp, vn)

Pedagogical: many arpeggii, giri, cadenze, vn and va

Minuets, monferrine, trattimenti notturni, waltzes, for various small ensembles

MSS also at *A-Wgm, D-Dlb, F-Pn, GB-Lbm*

BIBLIOGRAPHY

L. Spohr: *Selbstbiographie* (Kassel, 1869/*R*1955; Eng. trans., 1878/*R*1969)

E. de' Guarinoni: *Indice generale dell'Archivio Musicale Noseda* (Milan, 1897), 316ff

A. Moser: *Geschichte des Violinspiels* (Berlin, 1923, rev., enlarged 2/1966–7), 259f

G. Zampieri: *L'epoca e l'arte di Alessandro Rolla* (Pavia, 1941)

A. Bonaccorsi: 'Musiche dimenticate del sette-ottocento', *RaM*, xxvi (1956), 257

CHAPPELL WHITE

Rolland, Romain (*b* Clamecy, 29 Jan 1866; *d* Vézelay, 30 Dec 1944). French man of letters and writer on music. Educated at the Ecole Normale Supérieure (1886–9), he spent the years 1889 to 1891 in Rome where he completed his *mémoire d'étude* in the diplomatic history of the early 16th century. It was also in Rome that he began to expand his musical interests and to lay the foundations for his doctoral dissertation *Les origines du théâtre lyrique moderne* presented at the Sorbonne in 1895. After several years teaching courses in art history at various lycées in Paris (during which time he organized the first music history congress to be held in Paris, in 1900, and the next year was a co-founder of the *Revue d'histoire et de critique musicales*), and then as director of the newly founded music school of the Ecole des Hautes Etudes Sociales (1902–11), he was appointed in 1903 to the first chair of music history at the Sorbonne where he had a profound influence on a whole new generation of scholars including Henry Prunières, Paul-Marie Masson and Louis Laloy. Resigning his post because of ill-health, he spent the years from 1913 until his death in retirement in Switzerland and France.

As historian, critic, biographer, novelist, playwright and polemicist, Rolland ranged inexhaustibly over a wide field of intellectual activity, from music and the fine arts, through literature, to politics, international relations, the peace movement, civil liberties, the emancipation of women and so on. It is significant that in his doctoral dissertation, a solid piece of work now mainly remembered for its rehabilitation of the Neapolitan composer Francesco Provenzale, Rolland subordinated analysis of form and structure to biographical sketches and plot summaries set in a scrupulously documented cultural and political context. For it already clearly elucidates the synthesizing and rigorously moral tone of the personal view of history that he was to elaborate in his inaugural lecture 'De la place de la musique dans l'histoire générale' and which was to give a distinctive flavour to his biographies of Beethoven (of whom he wrote a single-volume life and a seven-volume study) and Handel, and to his articles on a variety of musical subjects contributed to numerous journals and later reprinted in his collections *Musiciens d'aujourd'hui*, *Musiciens d'autrefois* and *Voyage musical au pays du passé*. Stressing the importance of intuition rather than reason, of a kind of intuitive penetration into the innermost nature of the creative individual and the time in which he lived, Rolland saw history primarily in terms of the noble, superior soul, of a Beethoven triumphing over every adversity, or Handel as the heroic embodiment of the popular spirit of his age. Because of its universality, its profundity and spontaneity, music, he believed, was often the first to give expression to fun-

damental changes in society that were then translated into words and only later into actions. It was in this spirit that he composed his vast 'roman fleuve' *Jean-Christophe*, for which in 1916 he was awarded the Nobel Prize, using the life of the fictional composer of its title as a central symbol around which to synthesize his convictions about the nature, history and moral significance of music, its specifically racial characteristics and its function in the modern world.

WRITINGS

Les origines du théâtre lyrique moderne: l'histoire de l'opéra en Europe avant Lully et Scarlatti (diss., U. of Paris, Sorbonne, 1895; Paris, 1895/*R*1971, 4/1936)

Beethoven, Vies des hommes illustres (Paris, 1903, 2/1927 as *La vie de Beethoven*; Eng. trans., 1969)

Jean-Christophe (Paris, 1904–12, and many later edns.; Eng. trans., 1910–*R*1969)

La vie de Haendel (Paris, 1906, 2/1910; Eng. trans., 1916/*R*1975, as *Händel*); rev., enlarged by F. Raugel (Paris, 1974)

Musiciens d'aujourd'hui (Paris, 1908; Eng. trans., 1915/*R*1969)

Musiciens d'autrefois (Paris, 1908; Eng. trans., 1915/*R*1968)

Voyage musical au pays du passé (Paris, 1919; Eng. trans., 1922/*R*1967)

'L'opéra au dix-septième siècle en Italie'; 'Les origines de l'opéra allemand'; 'L'opéra au dix-septième siècle' [in France]; 'L'opéra anglais au dix-septième siècle', *EMDC*, I/ii (1921), 685–749, 911–971; I/iii (1921), 1343, 1881

Beethoven: les grandes époques créatrices (Paris, 1928–45; Eng. trans., 1964)

Introduction to H. Prunières: *Nouvelle histoire de la musique* (Paris, 1934–6; Eng. trans., 1943/*R*1972)

'Souvenirs sur Richard Strauss', *Oeuvres libres*, no.27 (1948), 3

ed. D. Ewen: *Essays on Music* (New York, 1948)

BIBLIOGRAPHY

Alain: 'Sur le Jean Christophe de Romain Rolland,' *Europe*, no.10 (1926), 272

H. Prunières: 'Romain Rolland et l'histoire musicale', *Europe*, no.10 (1926), 300

S. Zweig: *Romain Rolland: sa vie – son oeuvre* (Paris, 1929)

L. Schrade: *Beethoven in France* (New Haven, 1942)

J. W. Klein: 'Romain Rolland', *ML*, xxv (1944), 13

M. Doisy: *Romain Rolland: 1866–1944* (Brussels, 1945)

Choix de lettres à Malwilda von Meysenburg, Cahiers Romain Rolland, i (Paris, 1948)

Correspondance entre Louis Gillet et Romain Rolland, Cahiers Romain Rolland, ii (Paris, 1949)

R. Arcos: *Romain Rolland* (Paris, 1950)

W. T. Starr: *A Critical Bibliography of the Published Writings of Romain Rolland* (Evanston, 1950)

Richard Strauss et Romain Rolland: correspondance, Cahiers Romain Rolland, iii (Paris, 1951; Eng. trans., 1961)

J.-B. Barrère: *Romain Rolland par lui-même* (Paris, 1955)

H. Fähnrich: 'Romain Rolland als Musikwissenschaftler', *Mf*, ix (1956), 34 [with list of writings on music]

F. Raugel: 'Romain Rolland', *Revue de l'enseignement supérieur*, ii (1956), 65

J. Bonnerot: 'Saint-Saëns et Romain Rolland', *RdM*, xl (1957), 196

J. Robichez: *Romain Rolland* (Paris, 1961)

R. Cheval: *Romain Rolland, l'Allemagne et la guerre* (Paris, 1963)

E. Bondeville: *Romain Rolland à la recherche de l'homme dans la création artistique* (Paris, 1966)

Romain Rolland: sa vie, son oeuvre (Paris, 1966) [Rolland exhibition catalogue]

D. Sices: *Music and the Musician in Jean-Christophe* (New Haven, 1968)

ROBERT HENDERSON

Rolle, Johann Heinrich (*b* Quedlinburg, 23 Dec 1716; *d* Magdeburg, 29 Dec 1785). German composer. His father, Christian Friedrich Rolle (*b* Halle, 14 April 1681; *d* Magdeburg, 25 Aug 1751), wrote several Passions and some chamber music; along with Bach and Kuhnau, he judged a new organ in Halle in 1716, and he was among Bach's competitors for the Kantorate at the Leipzig Thomaskirche. He was Kantor at Quedlinburg until 1721, then left for a similar position in Magdeburg, where he later became city music director. J. H. Rolle received his early training from his father. He served as organist in Magdeburg from 1732 to

1736, when he left for Leipzig, where he probably continued his music studies (he was never enrolled as a law student there, as is often stated). In 1741 Rolle, now in Berlin, was engaged as a violinist (later violist) in Frederick the Great's court orchestra. None of his compositions from this period survives, but his later works reveal the importance of his contact with the Grauns, Bendas and C. P. E. Bach, and with the operas of Hasse and C. H. Graun. In 1747 he obtained his dismissal from Frederick's orchestra and returned to Magdeburg to become organist at the Johanniskirche. On his father's death in 1751 he was unanimously appointed to succeed him as city music director, a position he held until his death.

In Magdeburg he participated in a local gathering of intellectuals, the Gelehrte Clubb, started in 1760. On the advice of several members, he founded in 1764 (after the Seven Years War) a series of public concerts, the second of its kind in Germany (the Leipzig Gewandhaus Concerts were established in 1741). He presented his most important works, nearly 20 oratorios or 'musikalische Dramen', at these 'öffentliche Concerte'.

Rolle was virtually alone at this time in writing biblical–historical oratorios. Composed from 1766 to 1785, they become progressively more dramatic, paralleling trends in German letters (but not those in sacred music). Most composers continued setting the popular texts of K. W. Ramler (e.g. *Tod Jesu*), in which plot and characterization are peripheral to a core of meditative, often maudlin verse. After experimenting with the similar but more elevated style of his friend Klopstock (including scenes from *Messias*, 1764), Rolle turned to the librettos of Samuel Patzke and later the even more dramatic texts of A. H. Niemeyer (both Gelehrte Clubb members). The librettos Rolle chose show an obsession with sacrificial, often gory subjects, of a kind to call forth strongly emotional yet religious responses from the main characters. With his setting of Patzke's *Tod Abels* (1769), Rolle's reputation spread quickly throughout Germany and beyond. Each new work brought increased fame, and generated feverish local interest. He arranged 12 of his oratorios in keyboard reductions for publication, by Breitkopf and Schwickert in Leipzig, whose printed lists of subscribers reveal a large, broadly based audience.

Like other German oratorios, Rolle's place great weight on the chorus, and they also provide the chorus with a dramatic role. All his mature scores are continuous; traditional aria–recitative patterns, though unnumbered, are clearly perceptible, but at important moments the music is allowed to respond to a situation with a fluid mixture of arioso and obbligato recitative. In such passages one sees a clear parallel to Benda's melodramas. His music-dramas are virtually concert operas, a lone Protestant equivalent to Jesuit school plays. The Patzke texts still show the oratorio's usual bipartite division, but the Niemeyer dramas are in three parts, each designated an 'act'. Most curious (and revealing) are the stage directions in Rolle's scores, indicating scenery, costuming and gestures. While there is no evidence that these works were ever staged, nothing is left to the imagination of anyone wishing to do so.

Rolle wrote his best, most dramatic oratorios when in his 60s, especially *Abraham auf Moria*, *Lazarus* (the same text Schubert set in part), and *Thirza und ihre Söhne*. Here tonal and dramatic units are organized on a larger scale; Schering noted that in *Thirza* the drama unfolds 'as one great scene'. According to his necrologist, Köpken, Rolle studied his texts intently, then mapped out the key areas of an entire work before beginning composition. Unfortunately, larger effects are sometimes vitiated by a sentimental melodic style, reminiscent of Graun, full of weakly diatonic patterns repeated once too often, square phrases, an abundance of parallel 3rds and 6ths, melodic sighs and cadential appoggiaturas. Stirring and startling in one place, then soft and touching in another, Rolle rarely succeeded in blending these stylistic elements into a convincing union.

Rolle's cousin Christian Carl Rolle (*b* Cöthen, baptized 6 July 1725; *d* Berlin, 8 March 1788), was Kantor at the Berlin Jerusalem-Kirche; he wrote a theoretical-didactic treatise, *Neue Wahrnehmung zur Aufnahme . . . der Musik* (Berlin, 1784), including complaints about the fallen state of church music and biographies of Graun and J. F. Agricola. Gerber found it replete with 'nonsensical chatter'.

WORKS

ORATORIOS
(*all first performed in Magdeburg*)

Concert oratorios, pubd in kbd reduction in Leipzig unless otherwise stated: Befreiung Israels (F. W. Zachariä), 1764, *D-B*, formerly Berlin, Singakademie, rev. (1784); David und Jonathan (Klopstock), 1766, *B-Bc*, *D-B* (1773); Idamant, oder Das Gelübde (S. Patzke), 1766, *D-Mbs* (?1782); Davids Sieg im Eichthale (Patzke), 1766, *B-Bc*, *D-B* (Halle, 1776); Der Tod Abels (Patzke, after S. Gessner), 1769, autograph *A-Wn*, copies *B-Bc*, *D-B*, *SWl* (1771); Saul, oder Die Gewalt der Musik (Patzke, after J. J. Eschenburg's trans. of J. Brown), 1770, autograph *D-B*, copies *B-Bc*, *D-SWl* (1776); Hermanns Tod (Patzke, after Klopstock), 1771, *D-B* (1783); Abraham auf Moria (A. H. Niemeyer), 1776, *B-Bc*, *D-B*, *LÜh*, *SWl* (1777); Lazarus, oder Die Feier der Auferstehung (Niemeyer), 1778, *B-Bc*, *D-B*, *Kl*, *LÜh*, *ROu* (1779); Thirza und ihre Söhne (Niemeyer), 1779, *B-Bc*, *D-B* (1781); Mehala, die Tochter Jephta (Niemeyer), 1781 (1784); Simson (Patzke), 1782 (1785); Gedor, oder Das Erwachen zum bessern Leben (C. F. W. Herrosee), 1785, ed. Zachariä (1787)

Concert oratorios, unpubd: L'aposteoso di Romolo; Die Regungen der Freude, Dankbarkeit und Liebe; Die Opferung Isaacs (Metastasio), *D-B*; Jakobs Ankunft in Aegypten (G. S. Rötger), autograph *D-B*; Messias (Klopstock), 1764; Götter und Musen (Patzke), 1765; Die Schäfer (J. A. Eberhard), 1766; Orest und Pylades, 1768; Die Taten des Herkules (Patzke), 1770

Passion oratorios: Passion, 1753; Das Leiden und der Tod Jesu Christi, 1769; Der leidende Jesu (Klopstock), 1771, *D-B*, *Mbs*; Die Leiden Jesu (Patzke), 1776; Passion (*c*1781); Die Feyer des Todes Jesu (Niemeyer), 1783

Other oratorios for Christmas, Easter, Whitsunday, Advent, *D-B*, *B-Bc*; miscellaneous Passion music, *D-B*, *SWl*

OTHER VOCAL

Stage works: Der Sturm, oder Die bezauberte Insel (Patzke, after Shakespeare), Berlin, 1782; Melida, ein Singspiel (opera, C. J. Sucro), 1784 (Leipzig, 1785)

Kyrie, Gloria, chorus, orch, *GB-Lcm*

*c*60 motets, some arr. from oratorio choruses, *A-Wn*, *D-B*, *Dlb*, *SWl*; 20 ed. in G. Rebling, *Gesammelte Motetten* (Magdeburg, *c*1870); 23 ed. in J. Sanders, *Heilige Cäcilia* (Berlin, 1818–19)

*c*61 cantatas, see C. Ledebur, *Tonkünstler-Lexicon Berlin's* (Berlin, 1861/*R*1965), *B-Bc*, *D-B*

Secular solo cantatas: Der Nachtwächter, *B-Bc*, *D-B*; Quando un cor vive lontano, *B-Bc*

Lieder, incl.: Sechzig auserlesene Gesänge über die Werke Gottes in der Natur (Halle, 1775); Sammlung geistliche Lieder für Liebhaber eines ungekünstelten Gesang (Leipzig, 1775); Lieder nach dem Anakreon (Berlin, 1775); 6 Lieder, addns. to pubd kbd reduction of Hermanns Tod (Leipzig, 1783)

INSTRUMENTAL

Sym., D, 10 insts, ?*D-SWl*

6 syms.: B♭, 4 insts; F, G, A, 6 insts; D, D, 8 insts; all lost, cited in Breitkopf catalogue, 1762

Ov., D, *D-DS*

Partita, B♭, 8 insts, lost, cited in Breitkopf catalogue, 1772

Kbd concs., D, g, d, F, C, a, F; all cited in Breitkopf catalogues, 1763, 1767, 1769, 1778; 3 pubd as Trois concerts, op.1 (Berlin, *c*1782)

4 trios, kbd, vn, b, *D-Bds*; Trio, kbd/vn, fl, b, *Bds*

Vn sonata, F, *?D-SWl*; vn sonatas, F, f♯, C, G, c, G; all lost, cited in Breitkopf catalogue, 1763

Kbd sonatas: E♭, autograph *Bds*, pubd in F. W. Birnstiel, *Musikalisches Allerley*, vii (Berlin, 1762), ed. in L. Köhler, *Maîtres du clavecin* (Brunswick, 1860–73), and in E. Pauer, *Alte Meister* (Leipzig, 1868–85); G, *D-Bds*, pubd in F. W. Birnstiel, *Musikalisches Allerley*, viii (Berlin, 1763); f, pubd in kbd reduction of Idamant (Leipzig, 1782)

Kbd solos, e♭, d, *Bds*; 7 kbd suites, G, B♭, A, E♭, C, F, G, lost, cited in Breitkopf catalogue, 1763

Org fugue, E♭, in G. F. Körner, *Der Orgel-Virtuose*, no.193 (Erfurt, 1845)

BIBLIOGRAPHY

J. F. Reichardt: *Briefe eines aufmerksamen Reisenden*, ii/5 (Frankfurt and Breslau, 1776)

F[riedrich] von K[öpken]: 'Ueber dem verstorbenen Musikdirektor', *Der teutsche Merkur* (Weimar, 1787), ii, 223

A. Schering: *Geschichte des Oratoriums* (Leipzig, 1911/R1966)

H. von Hase: 'Beiträge zur Breitkopfschen Geschäftsgeschichte', *ZMw*, ii (1919–20), 454

R. Kaestner: *J. H. Rolle: Untersuchungen zu Leben und Werk* (Kassel, 1932)

E. Valentin: 'J. H. Rolle: ein mitteldeutscher Musiker', *Sachsen und Anhalt: Jb der Historischen Kommission*, ix (1933), 109–60

W. S. Newman: *The Sonata in the Classic Era* (Chapel Hill, 1963, rev. 2/1972)

K. Hortschansky: 'Pränumerations- und Subskriptionslisten', *AcM*, xl (1968), 154

E. Olleson: 'Church Music and Oratorio', *The Age of Enlightenment*, NOHM, vii (1973), 328

P. Radcliffe: 'Keyboard Works', *The Age of Enlightenment*, NOHM, vii (1973), 594

R. Strohm: 'Hasse, Scarlatti, Rolle', *AnMc*, no.15 (1975), 220–57

THOMAS A. BAUMAN

Roller, Alfred (*b* Brno, 2 Oct 1864; *d* Vienna, 12 June 1935). Austrian stage designer and painter. He studied painting with Griepenkerl and Lichtenfels at the Vienna Academy and in the 1890s helped to found the Vienna Secession, a group of painters and architects with close affinities to Jugendstil. In 1900 he became a professor at the Vienna Kunstegewerbeschule and was its director from 1909 to 1934. Appointed Mahler's designer for the Hofoper (later the Staatsoper) in 1902, he was chief designer there for almost 30 years (1903–9, 1918–34); he held the same post at the Burgtheater (1918–34), and also worked for other major theatres there and at Berlin, Dresden, Salzburg, New York, Philadelphia and Bayreuth.

Under the influence of Mahler, Roller's ambition in the theatre was to create a flexible and functional area on the stage, integrating music, drama and scenery in reviving the idea of Gesamtkunstwerk. He achieved this by a stylization that was in accordance with the anti-historicism theories of the Secession, instigated in Mahler's Wagner productions and fully realized in his Mozart productions (especially *Don Giovanni*, 1906). Simple architectural elements (*Rollertürme*: 'Roller's towers') served to frame and articulate a stage area defined by a horizon of intense colour, and, with responsive lighting, ensured the musical and dramatic continuity of the work being performed. Roller's preference

Stage design by Alfred Roller for Richard Strauss's opera 'Elektra' (Vienna, 1909) (Institut für Theaterwissenschaft, University of Cologne)

for monumental, romanticizing forms was on the whole best suited to anti-realistic interpretations. His designs for contemporary operas, especially the work produced in collaboration with Richard Strauss (*Elektra*, 1909, see illustration; *Der Rosenkavalier*, 1911; *Die Frau ohne Schatten*, 1919), demonstrate that Roller's conceptions of stage design, in conjunction with those of Appia and Craig, were of seminal importance for the dominant tendencies in modern musical theatre. (*See also* OPERA, §VIII, 6.)

WRITINGS

'Bühnenreform?', *Der Merker*, i (1909), 193
Regieskizze 'Der Rosenkavalier' (Berlin, 1910)
Skizzen zu Kostümen und Dekorationen von R. Strauss' 'Die Frau ohne Schatten' (Berlin, 1919)
'Das Theater ist zweiern', *Die Szene*, xviii (1928), 12
'Bühne und Bühnenhandwerk', *Thespis*, ed. R. Roessler (Berlin, 1930)

BIBLIOGRAPHY

L. Hevesi: *Altkunst-Neukunst: Wien 1894–1908* (Vienna, 1909), 259ff, 269ff
M. Mell: *Alfred Roller* (Vienna, 1922)
Gedächtnisausstellung: Alfred Roller (Reichenberg, 1939) [catalogue of designs]
L. Kitzwegerer: *Alfred Roller als Bühnenbildner* (diss., U. of Vienna, 1960)
F. Hadamowsky: 'Alfred Roller', *ES*
W. Schuh, ed.: *Der Rosenkavalier: Fassungen, Filmszenarium, Briefe* (Frankfurt, 1971)

MANFRED BOETZKES

Roller [Rollet], Johannes. *See* ROULLET, JOHANNES.

Rollet, Marie François Louis Gand Leblanc. *See* ROULLET, MARIE FRANÇOIS LOUIS GAND LEBLANC.

Rolli, Paolo Antonio (*b* Rome, 13 June 1687; *d* Todi, 20 March 1765). Italian poet and librettist. The son of an architect, he was a pupil of the dramatist Gian Vincenzo Gravina, one of the founders of the Arcadian Academy, from whom he imbibed the same neo-classical ideals as his fellow student Metastasio. He may have taken minor clerical orders. In 1715 he was invited to England by the Earl of Pembroke or the Earl of Stair (or both). He remained in London for 29 years. His main occupation was teaching Italian language and literature to noble families, including the children of George II; from 1734, if not earlier, he received £73 10s. a year for instructing the Princesses Amelia and Caroline. Rolli had many other patrons, including the Prince of Wales, Lords Burlington and Bathurst and the Duke of Rutland. In London he published several volumes of poems, a treatise on Italian adverbs and prepositions, translations of Anacreon, Virgil and other classical authors and of B. van Overbeke's book on Roman antiquities (1739), and editions of Alessandro Marchetti's translation of Lucretius (1717), several works by Ariosto, and Boccaccio's *Decameron* (1725). His most ambitious literary undertaking was the first complete Italian translation of *Paradise Lost* (1729–35), which he claimed as 'the most exact transposition from one language into another that has ever been read', though he omitted or modified passages offensive to the Catholic Church (that did not prevent it being put on the Index). He dedicated his work to the Prince of Wales, who contributed £100 towards the publication. Rolli also translated Sir Richard Steele's play *The Conscious Lovers* (1724) and, after his return to Italy, Racine's *Athalie* (1754) and Newton's *Chronology* (1757). His posthumous satires, *Marziale in Albion* (1776), attacked some of his London enemies. He wrote a bathetic poem on the death of Pope, who had mentioned him in *The Dunciad* (ii.204) for flattering his patrons. Rolli was elected a Fellow of the Royal Society in 1729. The town of Todi, his mother's birthplace, gave him a patent of nobility in 1735. The following year he tried unsuccessfully to obtain the succession to Zeno's post as court poet in Vienna.

Rolli is remembered by musicians for his activities as a librettist. In 1719 he was appointed Italian secretary to the Royal Academy of Music, but dismissed in 1722 in favour of Haym after quarrelling with the directors. To this period belong ten librettos, including those of Porta's *Numitore*, with which the Academy opened, the composite *Muzio Scevola*, Handel's *Floridante*, and Bononcini's *Astarto*, *Crispo*, *Griselda* and *Erminia*. In 1726–7 Rolli adapted three more librettos for Handel, *Scipione*, *Alessandro* and *Riccardo Primo*. He was one of the prime movers in the establishment of the Opera of the Nobility, to which he became secretary and for which in 1733–7 he supplied nine librettos, six of them (including the oratorio *Davide e Bersabea* and a serenata) for Porpora. His *Sabrina* (1737, a pasticcio opera) was based on Milton's *Comus*. He later wrote texts for Veracini's *Partenio* (1738), Handel's *Deidamia* (1741), three for the New Haymarket Theatre in 1740, and seven for Lord Middlesex's King's Theatre company in 1741–4, including Galuppi's *Penelope*, Lampugnani's *Alfonso* and *Alceste*, and Veracini's *Rosalinda* (based on *As You Like It*). His fee for a libretto at this period was £300. He may have produced others, including that of Handel's *Sosarme*. They were seldom original works, though Rolli, having greater literary pretensions than his rival Haym, was cleverer at concealing his sources – seldom to dramatic advantage. Claims have been made for Rolli as a lyric poet in Metastasio's manner, but his librettos are clumsy in plot and weak in characterization. Of those he wrote for Handel, *Deidamia* is by far the best. Handel also set at least three of his cantata texts.

A friend of Bononcini and Senesino, and the centre of an Italian coterie in London, Rolli was on bad terms with Handel; he told Senesino on 4 February 1729 that he had 'always been and will always be most reserved towards him, nor did I wish him well on his departure', and to Giuseppe Riva (12 June 1730) he expressed contempt for Handel's 'worthless operas ... [which] succeed no better than they deserve'. Rolli's voluminous correspondence with Riva, the Modenese envoy in London and later in Vienna, though full of obscure references, throws much light on London musical life; it reveals Rolli as an inveterate intriguer. He was involved in several literary controversies, including one with Voltaire (1727–8) on epic poetry, and did not abstain from personal malice. A letter to the Tory paper *The Craftsman* (7 April 1733) containing a bitter attack on Handel was signed with his name, though its authenticity has been questioned. An anonymous engraved portrait of Rolli was prefixed to his translation of *Paradise Lost* (1735). One of his brothers, Giovanni, a musician, lived with him for many years in London and published cantatas and harpsichord lessons there in 1733.

BIBLIOGRAPHY

G. B. Tondini, ed.: *Marziale in Albion. . .premesse le memorie della vita dell'autore* (Florence, 1776) [Rolli's memoirs]
S. Fassini: 'Il melodramma italiano a Londra ai tempi del Rolli', *RMI*, xix (1912), 35–74, 575–636

——: *Il melodramma italiano a Londra nella prima metà del settecento* (Turin, 1914)

L. Cellesi: 'Un poeta romano e un sopranista senese', *Bullettino senese di storia patria*, xxxvii (1930), 320

T. Vallese: *Paolo Rolli in Inghilterra* (Milan, 1938)

G. E. Dorris: *Paolo Rolli and the Italian Circle in London* (The Hague, 1967)

WINTON DEAN

Röllig, Johann Georg (*b* Berggiesshübel, nr. Pirna, 1710; *d* Zerbst, 29 Sept 1790). German composer. He received his first musical instruction from J. B. Grellmann, the Rektor of his local school. While he was a pupil at the Dresden Kreuzschule from 1727 to 1735 he studied composition with T. C. Reinhold, Kantor of the Kreuzkirche, and learnt the piano, the cello and the organ. Thanks to his friendship with Zelenka he was able to develop his musical accomplishments further, particularly in instrumentation; he was writing successful church and instrumental pieces by that time. After finishing his studies at Dresden, he studied theology at Leipzig University; Prince Johann August von Anhalt-Zerbst heard him playing the organ and cello there and appointed him court organist and chamber musican at Zerbst. He became vice-Kapellmeister there, and after J. F. Fasch's death in 1758 became acting Kapellmeister and councillor. The 1761 Breitkopf catalogue, which includes 13 cantatas by Röllig, also describes him as Konzertmeister. Gerber called him 'one of the best and most diligent composers' of the 18th century. Most of his output consisted of cantatas and motets, of which few have survived. Fragments (solos and choruses) of his *St Matthew Passion* show him still to have been firmly entrenched in the strict Baroque tradition; according to Schering the work was performed in Leipzig under Bach's direction (as others of his cantatas may have been; the Thomasschule once had a complete set). His later works, however, especially the instrumental ones, show the influence of the stylistic changes of the mid-18th century.

WORKS

4 cantatas, *A-Wgm*, *Wn*; 65 cantatas, formerly *D-LEt*, lost
4 motets, *A-Wn*, *D-Bds*
St Matthew Passion (inc.), *ROu*
Festo Jacobi, *ORB*
Sanctus, 1743, *Dlb*
14 syms.; 25 concs.; 6 trios, fl, vn, b; 9 trios, hn, ob, bn; Parthia, 2 fl, 2 vn, b; Parthia, 2 fl, 2 vn, 2 va, b; 24 minuets, 12 polonaises; all *SWl*
Other, doubtful items cited in *EitnerQ*

BIBLIOGRAPHY

EitnerQ; *GerberL*
H. Wäschke: 'Die Zerbster Hofkapelle', *Zerbster Jb* (1906)
A. Schering: *J. S. Bach und das Musikleben Leipzigs im 18. Jahrhundert* (Leipzig, 1941)

DIETER HÄRTWIG

Röllig, Karl Leopold (*b* Hamburg; *d* Vienna, 4 March 1804). German glass harmonica player and composer. His birthdate is often given as about 1754 (a calculation from the age of 50 given in the Viennese register of deaths) but it is presumably too late, since Röllig was musical director of Ackermann's theatrical company in Hamburg from 1764 to 1769 and in 1771–2. His lost opera *Clarisse* was performed in Hamburg in 1771 and two years later in Hanover. About 1780 he took up the glass harmonica and went on a concert tour; in Dresden he was the guest of J. G. Naumann, and appearances in Hamburg (1781 and 1788) and Berlin (1787). From 1791 to his death he lived in Vienna, where he had a post at the court library and frequently performed on the glass harmonica. Röllig was much concerned with the improvement of

Franklin's glass harmonica. He visited most of the glassworks of Bohemia and Hungary in his search for the best glasses, and about 1785 developed a system of marking the chromatic glasses with gold rims (Franklin had distinguished the diatonic glasses by the seven colours of the spectrum). Since the instrument placed a great strain on the player's nervous system, in 1784 Röllig (like P. J. Frick 15 years earlier but independently of other contemporary developments) attempted to eliminate direct contact with the glasses by means of a keyboard mechanism. The keyboard action, however, compromised the delicacy of touch that was the instrument's hallmark (*see* MUSICAL GLASSES).

Röllig also invented the ORPHICA in about 1795 and the related xänorphica in 1801, and published numerous essays on the subject of instrument building. His compositions show good ideas but little skill in handling his musical material. Naumann praised his 'subtle use of diminished and augmented intervals and harmonies and their resolution', but Rochlitz in the *Allgemeine musikalische Zeitung* reported that he 'plays far better than he writes'; his playing is said to have 'forced the audience to flee on account of the endless diminished 7ths and disconnected progressions'. Reichardt wrote two pieces for Röllig's glass harmonica.

WORKS

Pubd: Kleine Tonstücke, glass harmonica/pf, nebst einigen Liedern, pf (Leipzig, 1789); 6 deutsche Lieder, acc. orphica/kbd (Vienna, 1797); Kleine und leichte Tonstücke, orphica, nebst 3 Solfeggi für eine Hand allein (Vienna, 1797)
A-Wn: 4 concs., glass harmonica, orch; orch interlude to opera Teutomar; ballo, orch; Minnelied, 1v, pf; recit–aria
Clarisse oder Das unbekannte Dienstmädchen (opera), Hamburg, 10 Oct 1771, lost

WRITINGS

Über die Harmonika (Berlin, 1787)
Versuch einer musikalischen Intervallentabelle (Leipzig, 1789)
Orphica, ein musikalisches Instrument erfunden von C. L. Röllig (Vienna, 1795); repr. in *Journal des Luxus und der Moden*, xi (1796), 87
Versuch einer Anleitung zur musikalischen Modulation durch mechanische Vortheile (Vienna, 1799)
Miscellanea, figurierter Kontrapunkt (MS, *A-Wn*)
Articles in *Journal des Luxus und der Moden*, xvi (1801) [incl. description of the xänorphica] and *AMZ*, iv–v (1801–3)

BIBLIOGRAPHY

GerberL; *GerberNL*
A. H. King: 'The Musical Glasses and Glass Harmonica', *PRMA*, lxii (1945–6), 97
R. Federhofer-Königs: 'Röllig, Karl Leopold', *MGG*

BRUNO HOFFMANN

Rolling Stones. English rock group. Its members were Mick (Michael Philip) Jagger (*b* 1944), voice; Keith Richard (*b* 1944), voice and guitar; Brian Jones (1944–69), guitar and harmonica; Charlie (Charles Robert) Watts (*b* 1942), drums; and Bill Wyman (*b* 1941), bass guitar. In 1969 Jones's place was taken by Mick Taylor, and in 1974 by Ron Wood. The group was formed in London by June 1962, in the aftermath of the skiffle craze in England, and soon attracted sufficient following to rival the Beatles in popularity. By autumn 1964 they had made several records and toured Great Britain and the USA, cultivating an image of unconventional dress and behaviour. Their early work derived closely from rhythm and blues artists, particularly Bo Diddley and Muddy Waters (some of whose songs they recorded), but by 1964 Jagger and Richard were composing most of their material, producing in the next few years an outstanding series of popular and influential songs (e.g. *Satisfaction, 19th Nervous Breakdown, Mother's Little*

Helper and *Let's spend the night together*); the functional, riff-like melodies of these pieces and their simple diatonic harmony were foils for inventive accompaniment textures and forceful texts, whose expression of dissatisfaction, tough-minded independence and contempt for acceptable standards represented the prevailing attitudes of their generation. They later widened their instrumentation but largely avoided studio effects and electronic distortion (the only significant piece to use them, *Their Satanic Majesties Request* of 1967, was a failure). The recordings *Sticky Fingers* (1970) and *Exile on Main Street* (1972), both in the group's earlier manner, restored their popularity, and by the mid-1970s they were the longest surviving and most consistent, in style as in popular acclaim, of all rock groups. Latterly Jagger became the group's dominant figure and a leading personality of avant-garde pop culture, his performing style incorporating flamboyant dress and obscene gestures, and influencing the still more exhibitionistic performances of Alice Cooper, David Bowie and other rock singers of the 1970s.

BIBLIOGRAPHY
Rolling Stones and P. Goodman: *Our Own Story* (London, 1964)
T. Hewat, ed.: *Rolling Stones File* (London, 1967)
P. Bas-Rabérin: *Les Rolling Stones* (Paris, 1972)
D. Dalton, ed.: *Rolling Stones* (London and New York, 1972)
M. Dimmick: *The Rolling Stones: an Annotated Bibliography* (Pittsburgh, 1972)

BRADFORD ROBINSON

Rollins, Sonny [Theodore Walter] (*b* New York, 7 Sept 1930). Black American jazz saxophonist. Brought up in the same neighbourhood as Coleman Hawkins, Thelonious Monk and Bud Powell, the young Rollins was a devoted observer of these musicians' efforts when bop was emerging as the dominant jazz style. He made his first professional recording with Babs Gonzales in 1948, and in the following year recorded with Bud Powell and Fats Navarro. In 1950 he travelled to Chicago to study and work with the drummer Ike Day; in 1951 he made both his first recording with Miles Davis and the first with his own group. The years 1951–4 were extremely productive: he recorded with Davis, Parker (on the tenor saxophone), Monk, Horace Silver, Kenny Clarke and the newly founded Modern Jazz Quartet, and composed three of his best-known jazz tunes, *Oleo*, *Doxy* and *Airegin*. In November 1954 he began the first of a series of self-imposed retirements, apparently the result of extreme self-criticism; until November 1955, when he joined the Max Roach–Clifford Brown Quintet, he worked as a day-labourer in Chicago. A second period of isolation, from August 1959 to November 1961, was spent in New York, while the third, from 1963 to 1965, marked his trips to Japan and India and the beginning of his formal study of yoga. Another period of withdrawal, from 1967 to 1972, ended in the release of *Sonny Rollins' Next Album* (1973).

Rollins's most significant contributions to jazz were made between 1955 and 1959, when he was generally regarded as the leading jazz tenor saxophonist. His playing on the record *Worktime* with the Roach–Brown Quintet drew attention to the technical mastery he had acquired during his first retirement, and his composition *Valse Hot* started a series of jazz waltzes and further metric exploration by other jazz musicians. After Brown's death (1956) Rollins's playing became somewhat erratic. However, his *Freedom Suite* (1958) is perhaps the best and most significant work of his career; it is a unified improvisation that successfully organizes 19½ minutes of continuous musical thought. Of clear formal structure (*ABCDBCE*), the work was pivotal for avant-garde jazz development. Another milestone was his improvisation on *Blue 7* from *Saxophone Colossus* (1957), which Gunther Schuller called an example of 'real variation technique', a concept not consciously adopted by jazz musicians of the period. After 1961 Rollins's playing was considered old-fashioned, eclectic and somewhat undirected.

BIBLIOGRAPHY
N. Hentoff: 'Sonny Rollins', *Downbeat* (28 Nov 1956), 15
W. Balliet: 'Jazz Records', *New Yorker* (15 June 1957), 78
D. Cerulli: 'Theodore Walter Rollins', *Downbeat* (10 July 1958), 16
G. Schuller: 'Sonny Rollins and the Challenge of Thematic Improvisation', *Jazz Review* (1958), Nov, 21
R. Hadlock: 'Sonny Rollins' Freedom Suite', *Jazz Review* (1959), May, 10
R. G. Reisner: *The Jazz Titans* (New York, 1960), 117ff
J. Grunnet Jepsen: *Jazz Records*, vi (Holte, 1963), 315ff
J. Goldberg: *Jazz Masters of the Fifties* (New York, 1965), 87
I. Gitler: 'Sonny Rollins: Music is an Open Sky', *Downbeat* (29 May 1969), 18
M. Williams: *The Jazz Tradition* (New York, 1970), 167ff

FRANK TIRRO

Rolltrommel (Ger.). Tenor drum; *see* DRUM, §4.

Rolón, José (*b* Jalisco, 22 June 1883; *d* Mexico City, 3 Feb 1945). Mexican composer. After early theory studies with his father in Jalisco, he went to Paris (1903–7), where he was a pupil of Moszkowski (piano) and Gédalge (fugue). On returning to Mexico he founded a music school that developed into the most important in western Mexico; he directed this until 1927. From then until 1929 he was back in Paris for further studies with Boulanger and Dukas at the Ecole Normale. Subsequently he taught composition at the Mexican National Conservatory (1930–38). His early compositions were in a German Romantic style, but in 1925 he wrote a ballet, *El festin de los enanos*, based on Mexican folk materials, and this initiated the nationalist leanings in his music (combined with the influences of Debussy and Ravel) which culminated in his two outstanding works, the symphonic poem *Cuauhtémoc* and the Piano Concerto.

WORKS
(selective list)
Orch: Zapotlán, sym. suite, 1895, reorchd 1925; Sym., 1918–19; El festin de los enanos (ballet), 1925; Cuauhtémoc, sym. poem, 1929; Pf Conc., 1935
Chamber: Pf Qt, E♭, op.16, 1912; Qt no.3, op.35, str, 1920s
Other works: pf pieces, incl. 3 danzas indigenas, 1930; songs
Principal publishers: Ediciones Mexicanas de Música, Eschig

WRITINGS
'La música autoctona mexicana y la tecnica moderna', *Música* (15 Aug 1930), 16

JUAN A. ORREGO-SALAS

Roma, Giovannino da. *See* COSTANZI, GIOVANNI BATTISTA.

Roman, Johan Helmich (*b* Stockholm, 26 Oct 1694; *d* Haraldsmåla, nr. Kalmar, 20 Nov 1758). Swedish composer. He was master of the royal chapel and a leading figure in Swedish music of the 18th century.

1. LIFE. His father, Johan Roman, was a member of the Swedish royal chapel; his mother came from a family of German descent who had settled in Sweden during the

17th century. His paternal ancestors, of Swedish origin, had lived in Finland; the name Roman may be derived from the Finnish place name Raumo. Roman became a member of the royal chapel as early as 1711, his principal instruments being violin and oboe. King Charles XII's special permission enabled him to pursue his musical studies in England from about 1715 to 1721; there he seems to have studied with Pepusch, had contact with Ariosti, G. B. Bononcini, Geminiani and Handel among others, and (according to an unsubstantiated report) was for a time in the service of the Duke of Newcastle. Although none of Roman's compositions can be dated with certainty from this time, his years in England were of decisive importance for him as a musician and composer. After his return to Sweden he was appointed deputy master of the chapel in 1721 and became chief master in 1727; he held that post until 1745, when he retired because of deafness and ill-health. He was then granted the title of 'hovintendent' (court steward).

During the 1720s Roman composed several cantatas for the court and in 1727 published a collection of 12 sonatas for flute, his only complete work to appear in print. At the same time he was extremely active as an organizer: he considerably improved the standard of the royal chapel and in 1731 introduced the first public concert activity at Stockholm, in the form of benefit concerts with the joint participation of amateurs and members of the royal chapel.

A year after the conclusion of his brief first marriage (1730–34) Roman embarked on his second journey outside Sweden, this time visiting England, France, Italy, Austria and Germany (1735–7); he returned with vivid new impressions and also brought back much music for the royal chapel. In 1738 he married again and in 1744, with five children, was widowed for the second time. In 1740 he was elected a member of the Royal Academy of Science (established in 1739), thanks probably in large part to his strong interest in demonstrating 'the suitability of the Swedish language to church music'.

The death of Queen Ulrika Eleonora in 1741 marked something of a turning-point for Roman; the following year he was beset by ill-health and professional opposition. The new crown princess, Lovisa Ulrika of Prussia (sister of Frederick the Great), brought to Sweden new tastes, and her husband Adolphus Frederik had a competing princely chapel. Roman composed for the royal wedding in 1744 the large orchestral suite *Drottningholmsmusiquen*, one of his finest works; on his retirement half a year later he left Stockholm to settle on the small estate of Haraldsmåla near the town of Kalmar in south-east Sweden. He made a last visit to Stockholm in 1751–2, in part to direct the funeral and coronation music on the accession of Adolphus Frederik. His principal activity in the remaining years of his life seems to have been the translation into Swedish of theoretical works on music, including those of Gasparini and Keller. Several of his sacred vocal works may also date from that last period. In 1767, nine years after his death, the Royal Academy of Science held a commemorative ceremony; the *Äreminne* (memorial) by the royal secretary A. M. Sahlstedt on that occasion is the earliest summary of Roman's career and significance, and portrays the composer sympathetically, stressing his humility and equable temper as well as his skill and industry. No portrait of Roman survives.

2. WORKS. Roman emerges in many respects as the central figure in Swedish musical culture during the 'Era of Freedom' (*c*1720–70). He was symbolic of the new spirit of the rising middle class, and widened contacts with foreign music, particularly Italian and English. Before him, Sweden had had no native composer of real significance. His achievements not only justify the title 'the father of Swedish music' which was later applied to him, but mark him – like Franz Berwald in a later era – as a leading figure in the country's musical history. There is also a grain of truth in the epithet 'the Swedish Handel', for Roman, greatly impressed by Handel's music during his first trip to England (*c*1715–21), later had many of his works sent to Sweden and performed a number of them, including several anthems, using translations of the texts into Swedish.

There is no sharp dividing line between Roman's work as master of the royal chapel, arranger and translator of texts on the one hand and his activity as a composer on the other. In a letter of 1772 his pupil J. Miklin stated that he had 'imitated all the nations of Europe, or sought to express and copy their taste in music'. A typical example of such 'imitation' is his arrangement in 1747 of a *Dixit* by Leo, written five years earlier: Roman replaced the Latin text by a Swedish one and reduced the two choirs to a single four-voice choir; all degrees of reworking are apparent, from straight copying of choral sections (particularly fugal ones) to complete transformation involving changes in melodic line, harmony and key, but the most radical changes are to the orchestral writing, which is considerably enriched and which thereby takes on the characteristics of Roman's personal style.

The extensive collection of sketches and 'musical jottings' which survives as no.97 of the Roman collection (*S-Skma*) includes, besides sketches of Roman's own compositions, copies, reworkings, fragments and themes of works by more than 50 composers from Lassus and Albrici to Lampugnani, Leo and Porpora; they afford a fascinating insight into Roman's manner of practising 'the science of music'. Another volume, no.95 in the same collection, contains scores in Roman's hand of sacred choral works for all major feasts of the liturgical year, supplied with Swedish texts; among the composers are Carissimi, Fux, Handel and Pepusch. Certain works attributed to Roman are labelled 'alla Corelli', 'alla Marcello' and so on, and in some cases are based on instrumental models; there are also vocal movements turned into instrumental, for example a trio by Handel arranged by Roman as an orchestral movement. Roman was a modest man who aimed above all to enrich the repertory with the best possible music; he rarely put his name even to autographs of his own works, which renders yet more difficult the problems of authenticity.

A fresh Handelian choral style marks the Swedish settings of the *Jubilate* (Psalm c), *Te Deum* and the mass among Roman's vocal works. The sacred songs for solo voice or duet also include many fine, heartfelt pieces in which the basically orthodox Protestant attitude at times acquires a Pietistic shading. Most are accompanied by continuo alone, but a few also have a solo obbligato part (in one case of considerable virtuosity), and occasionally the indication 'si suona' suggests that such a part is needed. The texts are largely drawn from the Psalter, but in very many cases take the form of metrical paraphrases, usually in hexameters; many of these are by the poet and customs official Anders

Nicander. An evaluation of Roman's secular songs must await the expulsion of spurious works and parodies from the canon.

Roman's instrumental music exhibits stylistic traits reminiscent of Geminiani, Tartini, Handel and others; the early overtures even have points of contact with the school of Lully. His style clearly represents the transition from late Baroque to the *galant*. This technically solid personal style is characterized by an unmistakable rhythmic individuality and an absence of the slightly mechanical additive technique with immediate repetition of motifs, and of the simple fanfare melodies so popular in the 1740s and 1750s. He employed the 'learned' style only exceptionally, notably in overtures and trio sonata movements. For a composer who worked in so remote a country as Sweden, Roman produced music which in some respects seems modern for its time, including the numerous symphonies (most of them probably from c1735–50), of which several are in four movements. The finest of his large orchestral suites is the famous *Drottningholmsmusiquen*, which has rightly become his best-known and most widely performed work. Of the chamber music the 12 agreeable flute sonatas of 1727 have gained particular popularity. The striking *Assaggi* for unaccompanied violin deserve mention; they constitute one of the most extensive contributions of the time to this specialized repertory. These pieces, all in several movements, show familiarity with contemporary violin technique and contain passages with multiple stopping. About 400 works attributed to Roman survive; most are in manuscript, in the Roman collection of the Royal Swedish Academy of Music in Stockholm. About a quarter are autograph; the rest are copies by perhaps 200 different hands, ranging in period from about 1720 to 1810. This material poses many difficult problems of authenticity, dating and relationship between different versions, as well as those having to do with techniques of reworking and parody. For the instrumental music these questions have essentially been solved by the work of Ingmar Bengtsson. Much research remains to be done on the vocal music; Vretblad's thematic catalogue provides an overview, but is not reliable. The following summary of works is based for the instrumental music on Bengtsson (1955), for the vocal music on preliminary and unpublished documentary research, only partly supplemented by stylistic evaluation.

WORKS

(*principal sources: S-L, Skma, Uu*)

OCCASIONAL VOCAL

Hoggi sul'orizonte [Festa musicale] (A. Papi), S, T, B, chorus, orch, birthday of Frederik I, 17 April 1725
Verdopple Sonne deinen Schein [Freudige Bewillkommung] (J. C. Lohman), S, B, orch; birthday of Ulrika Eleonora, 23 Jan 1726
Süsse Zeiten eilet nicht [Cantata zu einer Taffel Music] (J. von Köppen), S, B, orch, New Year 1727
Statt up du trogna folk (cantata, J. Neresius), S, B, orch, 23 Jan 1727
Förnöijen eder sälla paar [Bröllops music] [wedding music] (U. Rudenschöld), S, B, orch, ? late 1720s
Warelse som utan dagar (ode/cantata, S. E. Brenner), S, chorus, orch, 23 Jan 1730
Välkommen store kung igen [Cantata vid Hans Kongl. Maj:ts . . . återkomst ifrån des tyske arf länder], S, T, B, chorus, orch, Nov 1731
Herren känner de frommas dagar (anthem), S, chorus, orch, funeral of Frederik I, 27 Sept 1751
Prisa Jerusalem Herren, chorus, orch, coronation of Adolphus Frederik, 26 Nov 1751, doubtful authenticity

SACRED VOCAL

Svenska Messan [Ky–Gl with Swed. text], S, chorus, orch, c1752
Frögdens Herranom al verlden [Ps c], S, B, chorus, orch, ?1743, ed. in *Äldre svensk musik*, v (Stockholm, 1938)
O Gud vi lofve Tig [Te Deum], S, T, chorus, orch

c10 other choral pieces, mostly psalms
Dixit Dominus, solo vv, chorus, orch, 1747, partial reworking of Dixit Dominus, 1742, by L. Leo
Beati omnes, attrib. Roman, doubtful authenticity
c100 works for 1/2vv, bc/str. on psalm texts metrically paraphrased by Swed. poets, incl. c75 probably authentic [23 in form of cantatas or verse anthems, incl. Tig vi lofve O Gud (Te Deum), 2vv, bc; c52 in 1 movt]
c70 songs on non-biblical Swed. texts, 1v, bc, incl. c35 probably parodies of the inst. works, c35 on texts by Swed. poets
Numerous reworkings of pieces by other composers, incl. Carissimi, Fux, Handel and Pepusch

SECULAR VOCAL
(*authenticity not yet determined*)

2 cantatas: Pianti amiche, S, orch; Tu parti amato bene, S, bc
c70 solo songs on Swed. texts (several probably parodies); c15 solo songs in c8 other languages

ORCHESTRAL
(*thematic catalogue in Bengtsson, 1955*)

Musique satt til en festin hos Ryska Ministren Gref Gollowin [Golovinmusiken], suite, 1728
Bilägers musiquen [Royal wedding music] [Drottningholmsmusiquen], suite, 1744, ed. C. Genetay (Stockholm, 1958)
7 suites, 1 ed. H. Rosenberg (Stockholm, 1944); 1 suite, doubtful authenticity
17 sinfonias, a 3 and 4, 1 ed. in *Äldre svensk musik*, iv (Stockholm, 1935), 3 ed. in MMS, iv (1965), nos. 16 and 20 ed. C. Genetay (Stockholm, 1951); sketches for 2 sinfonia movts; 1 sinfonia, doubtful authenticity
4 ovs.; 8 pieces and other sketches
4 vn concs., 2 [D, F] ed. in *Äldre svensk musik*, ii, iii (Stockholm, 1935); 1 conc., Bb, ob, str, ed. H. Blomstedt (Berlin, 1959); conc., D, ob d'amore, str; conc., G, fl, previously attrib. F. Zellbell

CHAMBER
(*thematic catalogue in Bengtsson, 1955*)

12 sonate, fl, vle, hpd (Stockholm, 1727), ed. P. Vretblad (Stockholm, 1937)
13 trio sonatas, 2 vn, bc, ed. P. Vretblad (Stockholm, 1947–9), 1 ed. in *Äldre svensk musik*, i (1935); 1 trio sonata, d, vn, vc, bc; 2 trio sonatas, only bc extant
5 sonatas, 1 inst, bc; duet, a, 2 vn; piece, A, 2 vn
15 Assaggi, vn, 6 ed. in MMS, i (1958); 3 assaggi fragments, vn; 23 études, vn, incl. 9 doubtful authenticity
12 sonatas, hpd, ed. P. Vretblad (Stockholm, 1947); 1 sonata, C, hpd, doubtful authenticity
Miscellaneous pieces and minuets
XII Sonate . . . del Signore Romano, libro Io, 2 fl, bc (Amsterdam, n.d.), spurious

BIBLIOGRAPHY

A. M. Sahlstedt: *Äreminne öfwer hofintendenten kongl. capellmästaren . . . Johan Helmich Roman* (Stockholm, 1767)
F. Cronhamn: 'Svenska musikens fader: några anteckningar om Johan Helmich Roman (1694–1758)', *Anmärkningar till Oscars Fredriks högtidstal i Kongl. musikaliska akademien* (Uppsala, 1885)
P. Vretblad: *Johan Helmich Roman 1694–1758: svenska musikens fader* (Stockholm, 1914)
S. Walin: *Beiträge zur Geschichte der schwedischen Sinfonik* (Stockholm, 1941)
C.-A. Moberg: 'Johan Helmich Roman – den svenska musikens fader', *STMf*, xxvi (1944), 5
I. Bengtsson: *J. H. Roman och hans instrumentalmusik: käll- och stilkritiska studier* (Uppsala, 1955)
I. Bengtsson and R. Danielson: *Handstilar och notpikturer i Kungl. musikaliska akademiens Romansamling* (Uppsala, 1955)
I. Bengtsson: 'Johan Helmich Roman – ett tvåhundraårsminne', *STMf*, xl (1958), 5
———: ' "Signor Leos Dixit imiterat af Roman": en inledande studie över J. H. Romans musikaliska bearbetningsteknik', *STMf*, xl (1958), 15–60
G. Weiss: '57 unbekannte Instrumentalstücke (15 Sonaten) von Attilio Ariosti in eine Abschrift von Johan Helmich Roman', *Mf*, xxiii (1970), 127
I. Bengtsson: *Mr Roman's Spuriosity Shop: a Thematic Catalogue of 503 Works . . . from ca.1680–1750* (Stockholm, 1976)

INGMAR BENGTSSON

Roman, Stella (*b* Romania, 1910). Romanian soprano. She studied in Rome with Giuseppina Baldassare-Tedeschi and subsequently made her début in Italy in 1934. She also made successful appearances at the Rome Opera. At Milan, she sang the role of the Empress in the first La Scala performance of *Die Frau ohne*

Schatten in 1940. She made her Metropolitan Opera début as Aida on 1 January 1941. For ten years (1941–50), she alternated with Zinka Milanov in such operas as *Il trovatore*, *Otello*, *Un ballo in maschera*, *Cavalleria rusticana*, *La Gioconda* and *Tosca*. An unorthodox and sometimes hectic technique prevented the singer and her warm, beautiful lirico-dramatic voice from achieving greatness. She was not distinguished, but was a fascinating artist with easy access to high *pianissimos* and vibrant climaxes. On retirement, she took up painting and her work has been exhibited.

MAX DE SCHAUENSEE

Romance (Fr. and Sp.; It. *romanza*; Ger. *Romanze*). From the 15th century, *romance* in Spain and *romanza* in Italy have nearly always signified a ballad; the narrative *romance* was, next to the villancico, the most popular song type in Spanish-speaking countries. In France and Germany the term came to indicate an extravagant, sentimental or 'romantic' tale in either prose or strophic verse. Since the 18th century vocal and instrumental settings entitled 'romance' have continued to express these 'romantic' and lyrical qualities (in this sense, the appropriate Spanish word is 'romanza').

1. Spain. 2. Latin America. 3. The vocal romance in other countries. 4. The instrumental romance.

1. SPAIN. As in other countries, Spanish *romances* (ballads), though probably story-songs at root, often dwell on a single situation taken from a story, the effect being rather more often a heightening of the dramatic tension than of lyricism. There is controversy about their origins. Menéndez Pidal has argued persuasively that *romances* are unique in European balladry in that they began as fragments of longer epic poems, and, though developing variants by transmission through oral tradition, have been preserved longer and more authentically than have ballads in other countries. Some objections to this theory (see Entwistle, Sage) are these: there is no evidence that Spanish epics preceded the *romances* they are presumed to have engendered, nor that epic ballads came earlier than other types of ballad; the earliest surviving texts are related not to any uniquely Spanish epic but rather to Carolingian, Arthurian and other cycles well known in European balladry generally, as well as to Spanish history (notably about border incidents involving the Moors or about King Peter the Cruel); and the earliest surviving tunes do not suggest an affinity with the postulated chant or recitation of epics. There is, however, general agreement that *romances* may be seen as folksongs, not in the sense that they were originally created by or for common people, but rather that they were adopted and continually adapted by common people.

There is strong evidence that, in the 14th century or even the 13th, *romances* were sung by professional musicians (perhaps jongleurs) for the entertainment of courtly, aristocratic and possibly urban customers. By the middle of the 15th century, though still in demand at court, they seem to have been taken up by amateur singers in other walks of life. By the middle of the 16th century, old ballads had been plebeianized enough for cultured poets and musicians, while often imitating them in new ballads of a more artful kind, sometimes to speak disparagingly of them. On the whole, though, ballads clearly met with more favour in Iberian cultured circles

of the 15th and 16th centuries than they did in other countries. Thanks to this patronage, ballads with their music were set down in manuscripts in Spain a century earlier than in most other countries. The poetic form of these early *romances* was based on an octosyllabic quatrain with assonance (vowel-rhyme) in alternate lines, though some of the more cultured *romances* from the later 15th century have full rhyme. Menéndez Pidal maintained that the earliest form was the couplet of 16 or even eight syllables; however, none of the earliest extant ballad tunes has a two-phrase musical structure. With some exceptions, such as some versions for voice and vihuela of the famous ballad on the taking of Alhama which interpolate a recurring lament '¡Ay de mi Alhama!' (ex.1), Spanish ballads up to 1550 or so never had a refrain; by the 17th century they often had one, a change brought about not so much by the re-creative process of oral tradition or poetic fashion but rather by musicians in their search for expressiveness (see Fernández Montesinos).

Ex.1 L. de Narváez: *Los seys libros* (1538)

The Cancionero Musical de Palacio (ed. in MME, v, x, xiv, 1947–51; *see* CANCIONERO), compiled between 1505 and 1520, contains over 40 *romances* set for three or four parts. If one can assume that historical ballads were composed in the year of the event they describe, the earliest, *Alburquerque, Alburquerque*, dates from 1430 (ex.2). Others that can be dated in this way are *Pascua d'espíritu santo* (1435) and *Sobre Baça estaba el Rey* (1489). Most of the ballads in this cancionero and others of about 1500 show every sign of being arrangements by court composers (including Juan del Encina, Juan de Anchieta and Francisco de la Torre

Ex.2 Anon., Cancionero Musical de Palacio, no.106

Al - bur - quer - que, Al - bur - quer - que,____
me - re - çí - a ser on - ra - do; en ti es-
- tán los dos in - fan - tes, fi - jos del rey
Don Fer - nan - - - - - do.

among others both named and anonymous) of pre-existing tunes for performance by musicians in the court's employ. Over 50 of these *romance* tunes have survived in arrangements made during the period from about 1450 to 1550. Francisco de Salinas (*De musica libri septem*, 1577) implied that a single ballad tune served a variety of texts, a contention which conflicts strangely with the musical evidence, for, though there is certainly a remarkable homogeneity about these 50 tunes, every melody – Salinas's examples apart – is distinct in its own right. The homogeneity of these tunes (almost certainly the superius in most cases) derives from several factors: they are all remarkably restrained, moving normally by step and jumping rarely by more than a 3rd; they all consist of four balanced phrases (*ABCD*), exactly matching the octosyllabic quatrain; they hardly ever indulge in any repeated or imitative passages or refrains; each phrase ends with a cadence often marked by a fermata; duple metres are used exclusively whereas other Spanish songs of the period indicate a variety of metres; most syllables are sung to one note, yet there is an equally characteristic fondness for expanded phrases, especially at cadences, of up to 12 notes per syllable. The striking similarity between these melodies and modern chorales (Stevenson, p.206) or hymns lends support to the theory that there were common roots between Iberian popular song and church music in medieval times. Almost as striking is the similarity to early English songs of popular type, such as *Three Ravens* in Ravenscroft's *Melismata* (1611) or *Western Wind* and *Cull to me* in their duple-time forms of the 15th or 16th centuries (see J. Ritson: *Ancient Songs and Ballads*, London, 1829). This resemblance suggests that the lost music for English ballads of the 15th and 16th centuries may have shared at least some of the above characteristics with their Iberian counterparts, especially since there are obvious parallels, in the growing addiction to triple time and refrains, between the balladry of both countries in the 17th century.

The evidence about performance of the early Spanish *romances* indicates that there was no set way of presenting them, but that up to about 1550 they were most often sung in court as three- or four-part homophonic choruses. In most cases one part only is underlaid in the manuscripts, and this has led some students to conclude that such pieces would be performed by a solo voice singing the underlaid part to an instrumental accompaniment. Certainly at times in the 15th century ballads were sung to lute accompaniment apparently played by the singer himself (Menéndez Pidal, 1953, pp.19, 72); it seems reasonable to conclude that the pre-existing tunes were performed also as unaccompanied solos. The qualities most often praised in ballad-singing in this period were sweetness and intense emotion; there is barely a hint of any rough 'folklike' singing.

After 1520 the only known sources for old ballad tunes are the vihuela books from Milán's *El maestro* (Valencia, 1536) to Esteban Daza's *El Parnaso* (Valladolid, 1576), where they are adapted for solo voice and vihuela accompaniment, and two madrigals by Juan Vásquez in his *Recopilación de sonetos y villancicos* (Seville, 1560; ed. H. Anglès, Barcelona, 1946, nos.28, 44). The indisputable similarities between the melodies of particular ballads in these settings and those of the Cancionero Musical de Palacio and other collections of about 1500 (ex.3) may be attributed to common traditional sources or to the desire of 16th-century com-

posers to re-create tunes taken directly from courtly songbooks collected as much as a century earlier. Milán advised singer and instrumentalist alternately to embellish ('glosar') some of these ballads and later vihuelists also recommended judicious ornamentation; this should be seen, perhaps, not as an innovation but as another stage in the traditional re-creation of the cadential flourishes found in the ballads of the Cancionero Musical de Palacio (ex.3b). Possibly the insertion of instrumental interludes at the ends of phrases and between strophes also reflects this re-creative process, though the vihuelists were clearly more concerned with providing opportunities for the exercise of vihuela technique than with preserving authentic traditions. *Romance* tunes of the older type appeared less and less frequently as the century progressed. They may be detected occasionally in the works of 16th-century composers such as Morales (*Missa 'Desilde al cavallero'*) and Gombert (*Decidle al caballero*, a madrigal based on the same tune, as is *Por vida de mis ojos* by Juan Vásquez and Cabezón's organ variations *Diferencias sobre 'El caballero'*). During the latter half of the century the old tunes seem to have been subjected to such a degree of re-elaboration by oral transmission or cultured refinement, or both, that they are barely recognizable as derivatives of the older type. In the Cancionero Musical de Medinaceli, for example, these apparently new types have music in a variety of duple and triple rhythms and forms (*ABCDD, ABCDCC, ABCDEFG* etc). By 1600

Ex.3

(a) Francisco Millán, Cancionero Musical de Palacio, no.445

(b) Luis de Milán: *El maestro* (1536)

published ballads suggest that either the old type of tune had been altered practically out of recognition, or it had been replaced by a categorically 'new' type.

A consistent characteristic of the 'new' *romance* was the addition of a refrain. The ballads in a collection from the early part of the century, *Romances y letras a tres vozes* (ed. M. Querol Gavaldá, Barcelona, 1956), appear with refrains (called 'estribillo', 'buelta' or 'letra'). Musically these are given prominence over the quatrains, which are often set in a new quasi-recitative style with repeated phrases and agitated rhythms. The refrains are more melodic, use more imitation, are often in a different metre and are up to ten times as long as the strophes, even when the refrain texts are short. The refrain was often printed after each strophe, but it seems to have been sung increasingly at the beginning. By 1630, then, in the Cancionero Musical de Sablonara (ed. J. Aroca, Madrid, 1916) for example, the *romance* had become, from a musical point of view, virtually indistinguishable from the villancico. Later in the century different verses were frequently provided with different music, and the refrains were set for eight to 12 parts in contrast to the three or four parts of the strophes. They were accompanied by organ, harp and continuo.

In poetry, however, the *romance* form outshone the refrain song during the 17th century and beyond. Manuscript collections (see Wilson) occasionally contain ballad texts with guitar cyphers (at first numbers, later an 'alphabet') over the words, indicating chords to be strummed to a known tune. Such evidence shows that ballads were sung to guitar accompaniment in at least some households. Most 17th-century composers (e.g. Juan de Blas, Juan Palomares, Juan de la Vado, Carlos Patiño, Manuel Machado, J.-B. Comes, Juan Hidalgo) set the new *romances* with their refrains to music for performance both in aristocratic circles and in the public theatre. Indeed, some of these cultured *romances* became very popular, especially when incorporated into musical interludes (*bailes*) in the theatre.

Thousands of sacred so-called *romances* for three to six voices and accompaniment are extant; they were sometimes interpolated into Matins and sung at the end of a Nocturn in place of the responsory.

There is little evidence to suggest that any kind of *romance* enjoyed a comparable vogue as a song in the 18th century. Works called *romances*, but properly more like villancicos, took on the appearance of cantatas, normally consisting of an instrumental introduction, recitatives, arias and choruses. In the first half of the century the accompaniment was predominantly the organ, basso continuo and two violins; later oboe, horn and other instruments were added. Composers of these cantata-like *romances*, mostly representatives of the Valencian school, include José Pradas Gallen, Pedro Rabassa, Pascual Fuentes and Francisco Morera. Estébanez Calderón, writing in 1847, named 'un romance o corrida' as one of the (presumably traditional) gypsy songs he had heard and seen performed; *romances* sung in 20th-century flamenco style, however, seem to bear no musical relationship to the old type of tune of the Cancionero Musical de Palacio. 20th-century Iberian ballads often have texts which go back as far as the 15th century, though their tunes, with the intervals, rhythms, triplets and cadences characteristic of other 20th-century folksong in the peninsula, are far removed (*see* SPAIN, §II). There are many variants and versions of these 20th-century tunes, which can be grouped into

families with interrelationships rather as they can in English balladry. The verse form is still predominantly the octosyllabic quatrain, though the *romancillo* with shorter lines (six syllables or even seven and five) is more in evidence. They are probably as often performed by choirs as by solo voice with guitar accompaniment. *Romances de ciegos* (sung and/or accompanied by a blind man or woman) sometimes retain something of the balanced shape and restraint of the old ballad.

In recent years many ballads have been collected from communities of Sephardic Jews, a people banished from Spain in 1492. The texts are, again, interesting derivatives of 15th- or 16th-century *romances*, yet the tunes are so far removed from the early melodies and so akin to modern Iberian folksong that they point once more to the conclusion that musical traditions are more volatile than literary traditions.

2. LATIN AMERICA. The *romance* was taken to the New World by the first explorers and colonists, and retained its roots in the Spanish form. Many *romances* such as *Del gadina*, *Estaba Catalina* and *Muérete de Elena* survive, and were performed by travelling fiddlers or *payodores* who accompanied themselves on the *guitarrón* (large guitar). Versions of traditional ballads are still sung by the Spanish population in the south-west USA, as are the *décima* (a type of *romance* that uses the octosyllabic verse in ten-line stanzas preceded by a four-line introductory strophe) and the canción. Variants have been collected in Mexico, Venezuela, Argentina, Chile and Uruguay. Like the old Spanish *romances* Latin American *romances* often celebrated important events. The Mexican type shows both a literary and a musical affinity with the Spanish, especially the Andalusian with which it shares the name 'corrido'. Although there are many metrical variants of the Mexican *corrido*, the octosyllabic quatrain is the most common, often with an added refrain (*estribillo*). The major modes are more in evidence than in Spanish ballads, but the melodic structure retains the same resemblance to older liturgical models. In both the Mexican and Andalusian types ternary rhythms are prevalent. The *corrido* is accompanied usually by the guitar, often the harp and, in Jalisco, an instrumental ensemble (*mariachi*) that includes violins.

3. THE VOCAL ROMANCE IN OTHER COUNTRIES.
(*i*) *France*. The French used the term 'romance' in the first half of the 18th century to denote a strophic poem recounting an ancient story of love and gallantry. The simplicity of expression exemplified in the works of F. A. Paradis de Moncrif and J.-J. Rousseau was easily adapted by French songwriters, and settings of these poems entitled 'romance' began to appear by midcentury. One of the earliest examples of the new genre is Rousseau's 'Dans ma cabane obscure' from *Le devin du village* of 1752 (ex.4). The strophic form, recurring three-bar phrases, thin texture and narrow range reflect the naive, natural state of the young peasant. Rousseau established a sentimental mood through expressive devices such as the sudden expansion of the melodic range in the second half and the fuller texture and chromatic harmonic shifts near the final cadence. The *romance* was ideally suited to exploit the vein of sentimentalism in *opéra comique*; the strophic form, unadorned melody, subordinate accompaniment and simple expression were generally retained by the leading *opéra comique* composers of the next three decades,

including Philidor (*Le sorcier*, 1764), Monsigny (*Le roy et le fermier*, 1762) and Grétry (*L'amitié à l'épreuve*, 1770). Philidor's *Le bûcheron* (1763) contains one of the earliest *romances* with alternation between major and minor sections, a common procedure in the later *romance*.

Ex.4 J.-J. Rousseau, *Le devin du village*, 1752

The *romance* also appeared in collections for drawing-room performance, such as *Recueil de romances historiques, tendres et burlesques tant anciennes que modernes avec les airs notés* by 'M. de Lusse' (1767), *Romances d'Arnaud Berquin mises en music par de Blois et Gramagnac* (1776) and *Consolations des misères de ma vie ou Recueil d'airs, romances et duos de J.-J. Rousseau* (1781). These works are distinguished from opera *romances* by their limited accompaniment (basso continuo only) and by the frequent use of eight or more stanzas (Rousseau's *Pour quoi vompre* has 29). J. P. A. Martini's *Plaisir d'amour* is often cited as a landmark in the development of the *romance*: it has a realized accompaniment and the normal strophic form is replaced by a rondo pattern, which became increasingly popular in the 19th century. By the end of the 1780s the *romance* was very fashionable, especially at the court of Marie Antoinette, who is credited with the composition of the *romance Ah s'il est dans mon village*.

With the advent of the Revolution the *romance* changed rapidly. The charm and sentimentality of Rousseau's conception were replaced by patriotism

(Gossec's *Ode sur l'enfance*), reflection of current events (François Devienne's *Romance patriotique sur la mort du jeune Bara*), tragedy (*Marie Stuart*, by Martini), and terror (*La mort de Werther*, by L. E. J. Jadin). A new and freer lyricism developed, and the accompaniment, generally indicated for 'piano, harp or guitar', became more elaborate. By the turn of the century there was a continuous flow of these songs, affirming their immense popularity. Leading composers of the genre include Gossec, Méhul, Rodolphe Kreutzer, C.-H. Plantade, P. J. Garat and Boieldieu. One indication of the extent of *romance* production is the appearance of ten volumes of *romances* entitled *Collection de morceaux de chant, extraits des meilleurs acteurs avec accompagnement de guitare* published in Paris in the early 19th century. Although the *romance* was well received by the general public, many contemporary critics held the genre in complete contempt.

After 1830 the *romance* began to give way gradually to the more dramatic *mélodie*. Several attempts to dramatize the *romance* (e.g. by Spontini) and the *romance dialoguée*, with a solo instrument (e.g. *Le songe de Tartini* which contains a virtuoso violin part), were unable to revitalize the genre. The most successful composers during this period were A. Romagnési, Pauline Duchambge, Auguste Panseron, Loïsa Puget, and F. Masini. The *romance* continued to appear in *opéra comique*, especially in the works of Méhul (*Joseph*, 1807, contains two excellent examples), Cherubini, Boieldieu and Auber. As the century progressed operatic settings became more elaborate, often including choruses and exploiting orchestral colour. The extensive ornamentation in Rossini's 'Sombre forêt' from *Guillaume Tell* (1829) exemplifies an attempt to dramatize the *romance*. The broadening application of the term during the Second Empire (1851–70) meant its dissolution as an independent genre, and the term 'romance' soon became interchangeable with 'chanson' and 'mélodie'. Of the composers who continued to produce these works in quantity, Lamartine and Monpou were the most outstanding. Other leading 19th-century composers who used the term include Berlioz, Gounod, Bizet, Saint-Saëns, Lalo, Duparc and Fauré. Since 1870 the term has been applied to a variety of works with no common form or expression, but characteristic traits survive (e.g. references to the troubadours, old Spanish or pre-revolutionary French settings, amorous adventures, simplicity and lyricism).

(ii) *Germany*. French influence on the German *Romanze* was considerable; the earliest German examples imitated the strophic form, simple melodies, phrase structure and harmonies of the Parisian models. Elements of folksong were also assimilated, and the *Romanze* attained a distinctive German character. The earliest published collections are *Romanzen mit Melodien, und einem Schreiben an den Verfasser derselben* (1762) and *Romanzen mit Melodien* (1767) by J. A. Hiller. Other 18th-century *Romanze* composers include Johann André, G. W. Gruber, F. W. Weis, C. G. Neefe, and E. J. B. Lang. Many of the leading German poets, such as Herder, Goethe, Schiller and Tieck, provided *Romanze* texts, and settings of their works often appeared in collections, such as *Lieder, Balladen und Romanzen von Göthe* by Peter Grönland (1817) and *Göthe's Lieder, Oden, Balladen und Romanzen* by J. F. Reichardt (1809). The terms 'Romanze' and 'Ballade' were frequently interchanged, and even contemporary theorists had difficulty in differentiating them. The essential distinction was only one of emphasis: the *Ballade* maintains an epic character, as the story is the essential feature; the *Romanze*, though less dramatic and lyric than the lied, places more emphasis on musical elements, especially the vocal line.

Settings of *romances* with French texts and *Romanzen* with both French and German texts were published sporadically throughout the 19th century. Among the works which have appeared with these designations are Beethoven's *Que le temps me dure* (text by Rousseau), Schubert's *Sah' ein Knab* and *Das Wasser rauscht*, Schumann's *Les adieux*, and Wagner's *Mignonne, allons voir* and *Adieux de Marie Stuart*. Like the French *romance*, the term 'Romanze' lost any specific formal meaning in the 19th century: strophic, rondo, *ABA* and through-composed patterns were all common.

The *Romanze* became a standard feature in Singspiel. The folk quality of the melody was ideal for expressing simple sentiments, as in Hiller's popular 'Als ich auf meiner Bleiche' in *Die Jagd* (1770). In addition, the texts often suggested ancient or exotic places. Mozart exploited this element in Pedrillo's *Romanze* in *Die Entführung aus dem Serail* with its modal features and pizzicato accompaniment, suggesting a Spanish guitar. Many 19th-century stage works contain two or three *Romanzen*. A common feature is the alternation of major and minor sections, as exemplified in Schubert's 'Die Vollmond strahlt' from *Rosamunde* (1823). Gruesome texts ('Ein Vampyr nimmt wohl die Gestalt von jedem Menschen auf' in Lindpaintner's *Die Vampyr*, 1828) and effective use of orchestral colour ('Nero, dem Kettenbund' in Weber's *Der Freischütz*, 1821) also became prevalent characteristics of the operatic *Romanze*.

(iii) Other countries. The term appears frequently in Italy and Russia. Settings by Italian composers, notably Rossini and Donizetti, began to appear in the early 19th century. Verdi effectively used the genre in several operas, including *Il trovatore*, *Un ballo in maschera* and *Aida*. At St Petersburg, where Parisian manners were much admired, the *romance* was cultivated in the 18th century, and many later Russian composers, including Tchaikovsky, Rakhmaninov and Shostakovich, continued to use this title. English composers, preferring 'ode' and 'ballad', rarely employed the term.

4. THE INSTRUMENTAL ROMANCE. The simplicity, lyricism and form of the vocal *romance* were easily adapted by instrumental composers. In the 18th century the term was most frequently applied to slow movements with a rondo, *ABA* or variation structure which featured a simple binary theme. Gossec's Symphony in E♭ op.5 no.2, written for Paris in 1761 or 1762, contains the first known appearance of such a movement; Dittersdorf is credited with introducing it to Vienna in his Symphony in E♭ op.7 no.1 (1773). The variation structure, as exemplified in Haydn's Symphony no.85 in B♭, 'La reine', was most popular in French symphonies and in the *quatuor concertant*. In Germany, instrumental *Romanzen* in *ABA* and rondo forms were the most common and appeared in a variety of genres: Hoffmeister's String Quartet op.14 no.2, Mozart's Serenade K525 (*Eine kleine Nachtmusik*) and, in the 19th century, Schumann's Symphony in D minor. Rondo-like structure is an essential feature of the

romance of Mozart's Piano Concerto in D minor K466, with the return of the simple, unadorned tune after a contrasting section of stormy virtuosity. Although Mozart did not use the title in any other piano concerto, the juxtaposition of simplicity and virtuosity in the slow movements of K491 in C minor and K595 in B♭ illustrate the same striking procedure. Other concertos with movements of a similar construction include one of Haydn's for two *lire organizzate* (the movement later reappears in the 'Military' Symphony, no.100), several of Mozart's horn concertos, Chopin's Piano Concerto in E minor and many of the works produced by the French violin school centring on Viotti, Rode and Kreutzer. Beethoven employed this form in three single-movement works – *Romanze cantabile* for piano, flute, bassoon and orchestra and two *Romanzen* for solo violin and orchestra, opp.40 and 50. The latter works are models of the lyric capabilities of the genre.

The earliest *Romanzen* for piano solo are the simple tunes in D. G. Türk's *Sechzig Handstücke für angehende Klavierspieler* (1797–8) and Reichardt's *Kleine Klavier- und Singstücke* (1783). More elaborate settings appeared in southern Germany during the late 18th century, using *ABA* or rondo structures. Variations on a *Romanze* theme, such as Hummel's *Thèmes variés* and Clara Wieck's *Romances variées*, appeared occasionally in the 18th and 19th centuries. The most frequent application of the term in the 19th century was to small character-pieces with no common formal pattern, for example Schumann's *Drei Romanzen* op.28. In such works the *Romanze* bears connotations of love or antiquity and is predominantly lyrical. It is this last feature that has remained constant in the wide variety of instrumental *Romanzen*.

BIBLIOGRAPHY

SPAIN, LATIN AMERICA

J. Vicuna Cifuentes: *Romances populares y vulgares, recogidos de la tradición oral Chilena* (Santiago, 1912)
C. Poncet: *El romance en Cuba* (Havana, 1914)
E. M. Torner: 'Ensayo de clasificación de las melodias de romances', *Homenaje ofrecido a Menéndez Pidal* (Madrid, 1925), ii, 391
J. B. Trend: *The Music of Spanish History to 1600* (New York, 1926), 103f
R. Menéndez Pidal: 'Las primeras noticias de romances tradicionales en América . . . y especialmente en Colombia', *Homenaje a Enrique Jose Varona* (Havana, 1935), 23
J. Bal y Gay: *Romances y villancicos españoles del siglo XVI*, i (Mexico City, 1939)
W. J. Entwistle: *European Balladry* (Oxford, 1939, 2/1951)
V. T. Mendoza: *El romance español y el corrido mexicano* (Mexico City, 1939)
R. Menéndez Pidal: *Los romances de América, y otros ensayos* (Buenos Aires, 1939)
M. Joaquim, ed.: *O cancioneiro musical e poético da Biblioteca Pública Hortênsia* (Coimbra, 1940)
G. Chase: *The Music of Spain* (New York, 1941, rev. 2/1959)
O. Mayer-Serra: 'Silvestre Revueltas and Musical Nationalism in Mexico', *MQ*, xxvii (1941), 123
K. Schindler: *Folk Music and Poetry of Spain and Portugal* (New York, 1941)
Romances tradicionales y canciones narrativas existentes en el folklore español, Instituto Español de Musicología (Barcelona, 1945)
R. Menéndez Pidal: *Romancero hispánico* (Madrid, 1953)
M. Querol Gavaldá: 'Importance historique et nationale du *romance*', *Musique et poésie au XVIe siècle: CNRS Paris 1953*, 299
D. Devoto: 'Sobre el estudio folklórico del romancero español', *Bulletin hispanique*, lvii (1955), 233–91
J. Fernández Montesinos: 'Algunos problemas del romancero nuevo', *Ensayos y estudios de literatura española* (Mexico City, 1959, 2/1970), 75
I. Lévy: *Chants judéo-espagnols* (London, 1959)
R. Stevenson: *Spanish Music in the Age of Columbus* (The Hague, 1960)
E. Gerson-Kiwi: 'On the Musical Sources of the Judaeo-Hispanic Romance', *MQ*, l (1964), 31

J. Romeu Figueras: *La música en la corte de los Reyes Católicos: Cancionero musical de Palacio: introducción y estudio de los textos* (Barcelona, 1965)

P. Bénichou: *Romancero judeo-español de Marruecos* (Madrid, 1968)

R. Goldberg: 'Un modo de subsistencia del romancero nuevo: romances de Góngora y de Lope de Vega en bailes del Siglo de Oro', *Bulletin hispanique*, lxxii (1970), 56–95

M. Querol Gavaldá, ed.: *Cancionero musical de la Colombina* (Barcelona, 1971)

D. Catalán, S. G. Armistead and A. Sánchez Romeralo: *El romancero en la tradición oral moderna* (Madrid, 1972)

S. G. Armistead, J. H. Silverman and P. Montero: *Indice-catálogo de romances y canciones tradicionales judeo-españoles en el Archivo Menéndez Pidal* (Madrid, 1973)

E. M. Wilson: *Poems from the 'Cancionero' of Don Joseph del Corral* (Exeter, 1973)

J. Sage: 'Early Spanish Ballad Music: Tradition or Metamorphosis?', *Medieval Hispanic Studies Presented to Rita Hamilton* (London, 1976)

OTHER COUNTRIES

J.-J. Rousseau: *Dictionnaire de musique* (Paris, 1768)

J. G. Sulzer: *Allgemeine Theorie der schönen Künste* (Leipzig, 1792–4)

H. Engel: *Das Instrumentalkonzert* (Leipzig, 1932)

S. Goslich: *Beiträge zur Geschichte der deutschen romantischen Oper* (Leipzig, 1937)

H. Gougelot: *Catalogue des romances françaises parues sous la Révolution et l'Empire* (Melun, 1937–43)

——: *La romance française sous la Révolution et l'Empire* (Melun, 1938–43)

B. Lupo: 'Romanza, notturni, ariette nel primo Ottocento', *RaM*, xix (1941), 81

F. Noske: *La mélodie française de Berlioz à Duparc: essai de critique historique* (Amsterdam and Paris, 1954; Eng. trans., rev., 1970)

M. Pincherle: Discussion in *Influences étrangères dans l'oeuvre de Mozart*, ed. A. Verchaly (Paris, 1956), 251ff

D. C. Ossenkop: *The Earliest Settings of German Ballads for Voice and Clavier* (diss., Columbia U., 1968)

JACK SAGE (1), ROGER HICKMAN (3, 4)

Romancero (Sp.). A collection of Spanish ballads; *see* CANCIONERO and ROMANCE, §1. *See also* JEWISH MUSIC, §II, 5(iii).

Romancillo. A type of Spanish ROMANCE.

Roman de Fauvel. *See* FAUVEL, ROMAN DE.

Romanelli, Luigi (*b* Rome, 21 July 1751; *d* Milan, 1 March 1839). Italian librettist. For over 30 years, from the end of the 18th century, he was principal librettist of La Scala, producing more than 60 librettos and collaborating with a large number of composers, including most of the important ones of the day, including Farinelli, Federici, Fioravanti, Generali, Mayr, Mercadante, Morlacchi, Mosca, Nicolini, Pacini, Pavesi, Pucitta, Rossini, Vaccaj, Weigl and Zingarelli. From 1816 to 1831 he was also professor of rhetoric and literature at the conservatory. His education was predominantly classical, and it is primarily in his systematization of the lexical and linguistic resources of the language of librettos that his influence lies. From various sources in operatic and literary tradition he made compilations of classical terms which also occurred in the theatrical and linguistic vocabulary of the opera libretto. He devised a formulary of stock passages and a vocabulary of rare terms and conventional locutions that were to be accepted into opera as the established language. Not an innovator, he selected and compiled the most 'classical' examples on the basis of their frequency and importance. But the fact that he was a classicist did not prevent his entering into contemporary developments in the libretto. Thus in theory he sided with the classicists in criticizing the abuse of taking subject matter from novels and foreign dramas, but in practice he did not exclude from his own works those elements of Romanticism that were at this time entering opera. A large number of his librettos were collected in eight volumes under the title *Melodrammi* (Milan, 1832). Salvioli's work presents bibliographical information on librettos not included in this collection.

BIBLIOGRAPHY

L. Lianovosani [G. Salvioli]: *Bibliografia melodrammatica di Luigi Romanelli* (Milan, 1878)

FRANCA CELLA

Romanesca. A musical scheme used particularly in Italy from about 1550 to 1650 for songs and instrumental variations. Such titles as Frescobaldi's *Partite sopra l'aria della romanesca* suggest that the romanesca was basically an *aria per cantare*, a scheme for songs. It was based on the Renaissance chordal scheme III–VII–i–V–III–VII–i–(V)–i (*see* GROUND, ex.2a). These framework chords could be disposed at equal or unequal intervals in duple or triple metre and could be varied harmonically or melodically by adding new chords or notes. Often standard or double *B molle riprese* or ritornellos were attached, to be played in pairs between repetitions of the scheme (*see* RIPRESA, exx.1a and 1f).

Ex.1 shows a romanesca for the five-course Spanish guitar, the notes representing triads and the stems the direction in which the hand strums the chords. Most of the framework chords (indicated by numbers above the staff and circles round the chord numerals) occur at equal intervals, and variation chords have been added relating to each framework chord as V or IV–V to I; a standard ritornello appears at the end. Ex.2 presents the bass line from a vocal piece and illustrates unequal distribution of the framework chords (indicated by numbers above the staff), a repetition of the second half of the scheme, and the melodic filling-in of the leaps occurring in the bass line of the original harmonic progression. During the 17th century the bass line of the harmonic scheme of the romanesca tended to be increasingly used as a melody, as indicated in such titles as d'India's *Musica sopra il basso della romanesca* (1609).

Ex.1 Carlo Milanuzzi: *Secondo scherzo delle ariose vaghezze* (Venice, 2/1625), Romanesca

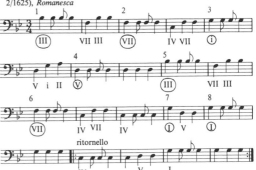

The term 'romanesca' first occurred in 1546 in a Phalèse lute collection and in Mudarra's vihuela book. The chordal scheme itself had appeared earlier in some Attaingnant galliards of 1530, in a pavan of Borrono (1536) and in variations on *Guárdame las vacas*, beginning in 1538 with Narváez's set (see HAM, no.124, for variations by Valderrábano). Mudarra's title, *Romanesca: o Guárdame las vacas*, shows a close connection between the two forms. The main development of the romanesca, however, took place in Italy. 16th-century examples are not numerous; they include lute

Ex.2 Milanuzzi: *Terzo scherzo delle ariose vaghezze* (Venice, 1623), *Romanesca, prima parte*, bass line

pieces by M. A. di Becchi (1568), Bottegari (1574) and Vincenzo Galilei (1584) and keyboard variations by Antonio Valente (1576).

The highpoint of the form occurred in Italian songbooks during the first third of the 17th century, with examples, generally for one and two voices, by Giulio Caccini, Cifra, G. D. Puliaschi, Paolo Quagliati, Nicolò Borboni, Francesca Caccini, Giovanni Stefani, Monteverdi, Stefano Landi, Giovanni Valentini, Raffaello Rontani, Banchieri, Francesco Severi, Giuseppe Cenci, Frescobaldi and Domenico Mazzocchi; P. A. Giramo wrote a version for four voices. Sets of variations were written for chitarrone by J. H. Kapsberger (1604) and Alessandro Piccinini (1623), for ensemble by Salamone Rossi (1613), Giovanni Ghizzolo (1614), Marini (1620; HAM, no.199) and Buonamente (1626), and for keyboard by Ercole Pasquini (CEKM, xii), Mayone (1609), Frescobaldi (several different sets from 1615 to 1637; HAM, no.192), Scipione Stella (CEKM, xxiv), Michelangelo Rossi (CEKM, xv), Bernardo Storace (1664) and Gregorio Strozzi (1687). A number of keyboard sets also appear in the Chigi manuscripts (CEKM, xxxii/3).

From 1619 to 1650 single statements of the romanesca scheme occurred in numerous Italian tablatures for the guitar, some presenting only the framework chords, others with variation chords added as in ex.1. The romanesca was used on rare occasions for dancing, and the chordal scheme occurred also in other forms such as the FAVORITA and the FANTINELLA, as well as in Diego Ortiz's *Tratado de glosas* (Rome, 1553/R1967). Francisco de Salinas gave an example in 1577 of the romanesca melody and of others that fit the chordal scheme; most of these are based on a framework matching the chords III–VII–i–V with the fifth, fourth, third and second degrees of the scale.

BIBLIOGRAPHY
H. Spohr: *Studien zur italienischen Tanzkomposition um 1600* (diss., U. of Freiburg, 1956), 31ff
J. M. Ward: 'Romanesca', *MGG*

RICHARD HUDSON

Romani, Felice (*b* Genoa, 31 Jan 1788; *d* Moneglia, 28 Jan 1865). Italian librettist, poet, critic and editor. After squandering his inheritance, Romani's father abandoned his family, and young Felice – the eldest of 11 children – had to assume responsibility. He managed to continue his studies, taking his degree at the University of Pisa. A period of teaching in Genoa was followed by extensive travel abroad. He then settled in Milan, where he formed several literary friendships, most importantly with the poet and classicist Vincenzo Monti. His friendship with the composer J. S. Mayr led to his first librettos, for

Mayr's *La rosa bianca e la rosa rossa* and *Medea in Corinto* (both performed in 1813). He served as literary critic of the *Gazzetta ufficiale piemontese*, and in 1834, moving to Turin, became its editor. His activity as a librettist, which continued after his move to Turin, was prodigious both in its quality and its quantity (he produced as many as eight librettos in a single year). The elegance of his verse and his dramatic sense made all the composers in Italy eager to work with him. His texts, which were derived, as was the practice, from previously published works (often French plays), were set by more than 100 different composers throughout the 19th century (even Puccini, as a student in Milan, set some Romani verses). His most important collaborations, however, were with Rossini (*Aureliano in Palmira*, *Bianca e Faliero*, *Il turco in Italia*), Donizetti (*L'elisir d'amore*, *Anna Bolena*, *Parisina d'Este*, *Lucrezia Borgia*), and – most importantly – Bellini, all of whose librettos from *Il pirata* to *Beatrice di Tenda* Romani supplied. In Bellini Romani found a composer whose elegiac, noble style was ideally suited to his shapely verses; and in Romani Bellini found not only a gifted poet but also something of an intellectual guide. Romani's notorious laziness (coupled with his habit of accepting too many commissions) caused grave problems during the composition of *Beatrice di Tenda*, and the opera's failure exacerbated the dissension between composer and poet. Bellini's last opera, *I puritani*, was by a different librettist. The breach was eventually healed, but only a short time before Bellini's death.

Romani published numerous poems and critical articles, and supplied stately verse for official occasions. In 1844 he married Emilia Branca (who in 1882 published a lively, unreliable biography of him). In 1855 he wrote his last libretto (*Cristina di Svezia* for Thalberg), then retired to his family home, near Genoa, where he died. Verdi – whose music Romani disliked – set only one Romani text, *Un giorno di regno*; it was originally written for another composer as *Il finto Stanislao*.

In the conflict between Classicists and Romantics that stirred early 19th-century literary circles in Europe, Romani was at heart a Classicist. For professional reasons, however, he found himself adapting works of arch-Romantics like Byron, Hugo and Walter Scott. His work has been defined, over simply, as 'Classic in form and Romantic in content'. His adaptations of Romantic works (e.g. of Hugo's *Lucrèce Borgia*) undeniably prepared the way for later librettists such as Cammarano and Piave.

BIBLIOGRAPHY
L. Lianovosani [G. Salvioli]: *Saggio bibliografico relativo ai melodrammi di F. Romani* (Milan, 1878)
E. Branca: *F. Romani ed i più riputati maestri di musica del suo tempo* (Turin, Florence and Rome, 1882)
C. Paschetto: *Felice Romani* (Turin, 1907)
L. Miragoli: *Il melodramma italiano nell'Ottocento* (Rome, 1924)
B. Tamassia Mazzarotto: 'La riforma del Romani e i primi librettisti di Verdi', *Ateneo veneto*, cxviii (1935)
M. Rinaldi: *Felice Romani* (Rome, 1965)
B. Fischer-Williams: 'Prince of Sluggards', *Opera News*, xxxvii/15 (1973), 24

WILLIAM WEAVER

Romani, Pietro (*b* Rome, 29 May 1791; *d* Florence, 11 Jan 1877). Italian conductor and composer. He was a pupil of Fenaroli and was for many years singing teacher at the Reale Istituto Musicale and conductor at the Teatro della Pergola at Florence. He wrote two operas, *Il qui pro quo* (Rome, 1817) and *Carlo Magno*

(Florence, 1823), and music for several ballets, 1815–22. For the performance at the Pergola of Rossini's *Il barbiere di Siviglia* in November 1816 Romani wrote a new bass aria for Bartolo, 'Manca un foglio', to replace the original 'A un dottor della mia sorte', which seems to have been beyond the capacity of the singer Paolo Rosich. This is still to be found in some modern editions of the vocal score and continues to be sung occasionally. Romani was a friend of Rossini and Meyerbeer. As a teacher he was highly esteemed by his contemporaries.

BIBLIOGRAPHY
L. F. Casamorata: 'L'opera e la mente di Pietro Romani', *Gazzetta musicale di Milano*, xxxii (1877), 237
ALFRED LOEWENBERG/R

Romani, Stefano (*b* Pisa, 2 Feb 1778; *d* after 1850). Italian composer. He studied composition at the Turchini Conservatory, Naples, under Tritto and Sala. In Carnival 1800 his opera *Il fanatico per la musica*, a one-act *dramma giocoso*, was performed at Florence, and later he composed two others, *I tre gobbi* (Pisa, *c*1810) and *L'isola incantata* (Livorno, 1815). From 1812 until his retirement on 31 May 1850 he was *maestro di cappella* at the church of the Cavalieri di S Stefano, Pisa, where some of his sacred music is preserved, including eight masses, a requiem (1824) for four voices and orchestra, seven responsories, three Lamentations, hymns, versets, graduals and motets. Two masses in concerted style for voices and instruments, one dated 1819–23, are divided into numerous sections to facilitate performance in alternation.

BIBLIOGRAPHY
C. Gervasoni: *Nuova teoria di musica* (Parma, 1812)
F. Baggiani: *La cappella musicale della chiesa dei Cavalieri di S. Stefano in Pisa* (in preparation)
FRANCO BAGGIANI

Romania [Roumania, Rumania]. Republic in south-east Europe. Modern Romania corresponds roughly to the Roman province of Dacia (AD 106–271), and its people are of Latin stock. After the withdrawal of the Romans the area was successively overrun by Goths, Huns, Bulgars, Slavs and, in the 15th and 16th centuries, Turks. Romania was formed in 1859 by the unification of Wallachia and Moldavia, to which Transylvania, formerly part of the Austro-Hungarian Empire, was added in 1918. It became a people's republic in 1947 and a socialist republic in 1965.

I. Art music. II. Folk music.

I. Art music. Until the 19th century Romanian art music developed largely within the church. In the 14th century, hymns were composed by Filothei of the Cozia monastery, and in the 15th century Romanian musicians at the Psalm Music School at Putna in Moldavia composed for the Byzantine Church. Transylvania was in closer contact with western European culture than were Wallachia and Moldavia, and there Byzantine and Gregorian chant developed simultaneously. Later important Transylvanian musicians included the organist Hieronimus Ostermayer (1500–61) and the composers Reilich (?1630–77), Croner (1656–1740) and Johann Sartorius (1712–87). At the beginning of the 18th century the use of the Romanian language was introduced into church music and Filothei sîn Agăi Jipei was the most important of a group of composers active in Bucharest who wrote psalm settings in the vernacular, a tradition continued by Naum Rîmniceanu and Macarie

Ieromonahul (?1780–1836). This school reached a peak in the 19th century with Anton Pann and Dimitrie Suceveanu (1816–98).

Secular music was cultivated at the courts of Bucharest, Jassy (now Iaşi), Suceava, Karlsburg (now Alba Iulia), Hermannstadt (now Sibiu), Kronstadt (now Braşov) and Klausenburg (Kolozsvár; now Cluj-Napoca); among their best-known musicians were the Kronstadt lutenist Bakfark (1507–76) and the composers Căianu (1627–98) and Cantemir (1673–1723).

In the mid-19th century Romania, like other east European countries, produced a nationalist school of composers, the nucleus of which comprised Pann, Flechtenmacher, Filimon, Miculi, Ioan Cartu, Dimitrie Florescu, A. T. Zissu and Vorobchievici. These were augmented by a number of foreign musicians who had come to Romania as teachers or as members of touring companies. After the foundation of the state conservatories of Iaşi (1860) and Bucharest (1864) a generation of distinguished composers and performers grew up. In 1868 Eduard Wachmann formed the Societatea Filarmonică Română in Bucharest, and after the foundation there of the Romanian Opera in 1877 native opera companies were established. The late 19th century also saw the growth of a large number of amateur choirs. Romanian conductors, choirmasters and bandleaders of the time included Caudella, Stephănescu, Musicescu, Dima, Constantin Dimitrescu, Porumbescu, Mureşianu, Vidu and Kiriac; singers with international careers included Darclée, Teodorini, D. Popovici-Bayreuth and Alma Gluck.

The years preceding World War I, during which George Enescu became a prominent figure in Romanian music, witnessed a revival of interest in folk music. The influence of traditional psalm settings, and of folk genres and forms (carol, ballad, *doina*), is seen in the modal harmony, free rhythms, characteristic cadences and micro-intervals used in works of this time. During the inter-war period the Romanian folk idiom became even more widely used, encouraged by the Romanian Union of Composers and Musicologists (founded in 1920) and the research of the Institute of Ethnography and Folklore in Bucharest (founded in 1928 as the Arhiva de Folclore). Folk influence was apparent in all forms of music, particularly in the works of Jora (ballet), Drăgoi (opera), Lazăr, Otescu, Negrea and Rogalski (programme music), Andricu (symphony), and above all in the works of Enescu. In their works a 'parlando-rubato' style (see §II, 1 below) is prominent, and harmony, polyphony and instrumental colour all derive from folk sources.

Romanian musicology, pioneered in the 19th century by Burada, was expanded in the 20th century by Petrescu (Byzantinology), Brăiloiu (ethnomusicology), Cuclin (aesthetics) and Breazul (historiography). Performers of renown include Enescu as a violinist, the conductors Georgescu and Perlea, the pianists Lipatti, Haskil and Boskoff, and the singers Cristoforeanu, Ursuleac and Maria Cebotari.

The socialist political system established after World War II resulted in the reorganization of Romanian music. The period 1944–55 saw the restructuring of the educational system, the reorganization of the Union of Composers and Musicologists (1949), the Institute of Ethnography and Folklore (1949) and the Institute of the History of Arts (1950), and the formation of more than 20 state philharmonic societies, 10 opera houses and many dance troupes and popular orchestras. The second generation of composers after the war includes such capable musicians as Jora, Constantinescu, Gheorge and Ion Dumitrescu, Toduță, Vieru and Stroe who have found their musical material in the folk tradition, but have at the same time kept closely in touch with the international avant garde.

See also BRAŞOV, BUCHAREST, CLUJ-NAPOCA.

BIBLIOGRAPHY
I. D. Petrescu: *Arta artelor sau elemente de istoria musicei* (Bucharest, 1872)
T. T. Burada: *Istoria teatrului în Moldova* (Iaşi, 1915–75)
M. G. Posluşnicu: *Istoria muzicii la români* (Bucharest, 1928)
G. Onciul: *Istoria muzicii* (Bucharest, 1929–33)
P. Niţulescu: *Muzica românească de azi* (Bucharest, 1940)
G. Breazul: *Patrium Carmen: contribuţii la studiul muzicii româneşti* (Craiova, 1941)
R. Ghircoiaşiu: *Contribuţii la istoria muzicii româneşti* (Bucharest, 1963)
A. Benkő: 'Date privind prezenţa unor instrumente şi instrumentişti în viaţa oraşului Bistriţa din secului XVI' [Information on the presence of instruments and performers in the life of Bistriţa in the 16th century], *LM*, ii (1966), 233
V. Cosma: 'Archäologische musikalische Funde in Rumänien', *BMw*, viii (1966), 3
——: 'Aspects de la culture musicale sur le territoire de la Roumanie entre le XIVe et le XVIIIe siècle', *Musica antiqua Europae orientalis I: Bydgoszcz 1966*, 403
V. Herman: 'Aspecte şi perspective ale înnoirii limbajului muzical' [Aspects and perspectives of contemporary musical language], *LM*, ii (1966), 133
D. Popovici: *Muzica corală românească* (Bucharest, 1966)
E. Comişel, ed.: *Constantin Brăiloiu: Opere* (Bucharest, 1967–74) [in Rom. and Fr.]
V. Cosma: 'Începuturile teatrului muzical românesc' [The beginnings of Romanian musical theatre], *Muzica*, xvii/3 (1967), 26
R. Ghircoiaşiu: 'Dezvoltarea creaţiei simfonice româneşti în secolul XIX' [The development of Romanian symphonic composition in the 19th century], *LM*, iii (1967), 125
G. Breazul: *Pagini din istoria muzicii româneşti* (Bucharest, 1968–74)
A. Colfescu: 'Opereta ieri, astăzi şi mîine' [Light opera, past, present and future], *Muzica*, xviii/1 (1968), 27
M. Jora: *Momente muzicale* (Bucharest, 1968)
C. Tăranu: 'Etape post enesciene' [Post-Enescu trends], *LM*, iv (1968), 25
Z. Vancea: *Creaţia muzicală românească, sec. XIX–XX* (Bucharest, 1968)
F. Zagiba: 'Musik in Südosteuropa', *NZM*, Jg.129 (1968), 34
P. Brâncuşi: *Istoria muzicii româneşti* (Bucharest, 1969)
G. Ciobanu: *Les manuscrits musicaux en notation byzantine dans la République populaire roumaine* (Kassel, 1969)
V. Cosma: 'Cultura muzicală românească în epoca Renaşterii', *Muzica*, xix/12 (1969), 29
G. Firca: 'Principes et traits de style communs à la littérature, aux arts plastiques et à la musique pendant la Renaissance roumaine', *Musica antiqua Europae orientalis II: Bydgoszcz 1969*, 241
V. Bickerich: 'La musique d'orgue dans notre pays', *Muzica*, xx/2 (1970), 40 [A history of organ music in Transylvania]
V. Cosma: *Muzicieni români: compozitori şi muzicologi* (Bucharest, 1970)
C. Ghenea: 'Documente cu privire la viaţa muzicală de pe teritoriul României în Renaştere' [Documents concerning musical life in Romanian territory during the Renaissance], *Muzica*, xx/1 (1970), 14
D. Popovici: *Muzica românească contemporeană* (Bucharest, 1970)
G. Bărgăuanu: 'Educaţia muzicală', *Studii de muzicologie*, vii (1971), 175
T. Moisescu, ed.: *Valori şi tendinţe ale muzicii româneşti, 1921–1971* (Bucharest, 1971)
P. Brâncuşi and N. Călinoiu: *Muzica în România socialistă* (Bucharest, 1973)
O. L. Cosma: *Hronicul muzicii româneşti* (Bucharest, 1973–5)
V. Tomescu: *Histoire des relations musicales entre la France et la Roumanie* (Bucharest, 1973–)
G. Ciobanu: *Izvoare ale muzicii româneşti* (Bucharest, 1976)
V. Cosma: *Două milenii de muzică pe pămîntul României* (Bucharest, 1977)

II. Folk music. Romanian folk music is closely linked with the events of the life cycle, and is an expression of national feeling and aspiration. It is an integral part of social life and has crystallized into a number of types and repertories with definite aims, appropriate to specific circumstances.

1. Structure. 2. The music of folk customs. 3. Pastoral music. 4. The 'doina'. 5. Ballads. 6. Songs. 7. Dances. 8. The 'lăutari'. 9. Folk instruments and research.

1. STRUCTURE. Romanian songs are in octosyllabic or hexasyllabic lines. The latter form is rarer and is apparently the earlier; it occurs particularly in ritual songs and in some ballads and non-occasional songs that are thought to be ancient. Romanian folk verse is nonstrophic, and the lines rhyme in succession; rhyme is often replaced by assonance. The invariably regular stress on alternate syllables divides them into pairs, the first of each bearing the metrical stress.

The metrical accent overrules normal syllable stress, except in the last pair of syllables, where the metrical accent usually coincides with that of ordinary speech. Both octosyllabic and hexasyllabic lines admit catalectic variations (hepta- or pentasyllabic). The same text often combines complete and catalectic lines (octosyllabic with heptasyllabic and hexasyllabic with pentasyllabic, and sometimes, through contamination, octosyllabic with hexasyllabic).

When a catalectic line is to be sung to a section of melody designed for a full line the singer completes it in a manner characteristic of Romanian folksong, by transforming the final semi-vowel of the catalectic line into a full vowel or by adding a syllable such as u, o, î, le, re, mă, măi etc. On the other hand, when a complete line is to be sung to a melodic phrase designed for a catalectic line (i.e. one with a masculine ending), apocope occurs, the last unstressed syllable of the line being omitted. The singer sometimes anticipates the beginning of the melodic line with a softly enunciated 'anacrustic syllable' (i, e, ai, ei, şi, păi etc), or a nasal consonant (n, m). The completive syllables at the end of the line, as well as in the anacrusis, are artifices determined by the singing style. The style also determines the repetition of some lines or the replacement of others by a corresponding number of syllables from the refrain.

Refrains, which appear in certain categories of Romanian folksong, sometimes have individual rules of versification, with more or fewer syllables to the line than the preceding text lines; when the syllables are arranged in groups of three, the stress-accents are identical with those of speech.

Within certain genres (according to the number of syllables in the line) different texts can be sung to the same melody, and a given text can be sung to various melodies. The process of fitting a given text to a given melody, or the choice of a tune for a given text usually occurs at the moment of singing. The apparently arbitrary association of the text and melody is based on a similarity of content: the singer chooses a melody appropriate to the text he wishes to sing, or vice versa.

Bartók was the first to describe and analyse the characteristics of Romanian folk verse in songs; his research was continued and completed by Constantin Brăiloiu, who made it the subject of a special study (in Comişel, 1967).

There is often a causal interdependence between metre and rhythm. An important rhythmic system of Romanian folksong, which undoubtedly originated in metrics, was called by Brăiloiu 'giusto syllabic': it is based on the combination of two units of duration, one short and one long, in the ratio 1 : 2 or 2 : 1, conventionally represented in notation by a crotchet and a quaver. The possible combinations of these durations give the pairs of syllables a striking resemblance to the ancient simple measures: pyrrhic, iambic, trochaic and spondaic. The various combinations of these, applied to the syllables of the text lines (hexasyllabic verse affords 64 possible combinations, octosyllabic 256), are further extended by the ternary groups of the refrains (see ex.1). Paeonic types occur more rarely.

Ex.1 Ternary syllabic groups

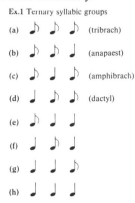

Bartók discovered a variant of the giusto syllabic rhythm in Romanian folk music, in which the ratio of the two durations (short and long) is 2:3 or 3:2, conventionally represented by a quaver and a dotted quaver. This rhythm, which Brăiloiu called *aksak* – a term borrowed from Oriental theory – is rare in vocal music and more often found in dance music. The commonest formulae are shown in ex.2.

Ex.2 Common *aksak* formulae in Romanian folk music

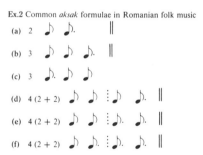

An important type of melody, appearing in several genres of Romanian folksong, has a free varied declamatory rhythm which Bartók called 'parlando' or 'parlando-rubato'. In several melodies based on this kind of rhythm, various amplifications and compressions of the rhythmic groups peculiar to giusto syllabic rhythm appear, probably because of the rubato performance. This suggests a possible derivation of parlando-rubato rhythm from a very ancient giusto, unless it is merely the result of simple contamination between different rhythmic systems. The newest rhythmic system of Romanian folk music seems to be that of the modern division into bars found particularly in instrumental dance music and in songs influenced by dance melodies.

Romanian folk music uses a great number of scales: pre-pentatonic and pentatonic (pure or with occasional *pien*, or exchange notes), tetrachordal, pentachordal, hexachordal, and a variety of diatonic and chromatic modes. Ex.3 shows a highly characteristic scale, thought to be of pentatonic origin. Its principal degrees are 6_1 (final) and 5_1 (cadence of the principal or secondary

Ex.3 A characteristic Romanian scale

caesuras); degrees of secondary importance are 1 and 3 (sometimes cadential notes) and 2 (more rarely cadential). The secondary notes 7_1 and 4 have a fluctuating character: they are sometimes altered and sometimes not, and their intonation is often neutral (between F and F♯, or between C and C♯). The skeleton of the melody usually consists of 5_1–1–3 (occasionally extended to 5), which results in a fundamental triadic effect. The relation of this with the final 6_1, a note which often appears only in the last part of the melody, produces the major–minor parallelism characteristic of Romanian folk music. Many tunes are limited to a pentachord or hexachord. The commonest modes are the D mode, the A mode, the E mode and, among the 'major' modes, those of C and F, the latter often with a flattened 7th and sometimes with the final cadence on the second degree. Similar 'semi-cadences' are also found in other scales, diatonic or chromatic, especially in songs from the western part of the country (Banat). The chromatic modes (usually with an augmented 2nd) include a D mode with a sharpened 4th (an augmented 2nd between degrees 3 and 4), which is the most frequent and most ancient, an F mode with a sharpened 2nd and a flattened 7th (an augmented 2nd between degrees 1 and 2), a G mode with a sharpened 2nd (an augmented 2nd between degrees 1 and 2) and a G mode with a flattened 2nd and 6th (an augmented 2nd between degrees 2 and 3); the last three chromatic modes, probably of Oriental origin, occur particularly on the Danubian plain. There are also instances of interpenetration and contamination between different scales, hybrid scales and 'modulations' (including those in which the melody is displaced to the lower 5th or to the relative). Most Romanian folk melodies have a descending melodic profile.

The forms of Romanian folksongs also vary. Some melodies are in a free form, in which improvisation plays an important part; others have a fixed structure, with a constant number of melodic lines (one or more), always arranged in the same way. There are a few melodies of a single line: children's songs or very ancient ritual genres. Most Romanian folksongs with a fixed form have three or four melodic lines, the principal caesura generally falling after the second line, often on a subtone. In three-line songs with refrain, the refrain is usually the middle line, while in four-line songs, the refrain constitutes the final line, the last two lines, or the second and fourth lines. The musical content most commonly takes the forms *ABA*, *AAB*, *ABB* or *ABC* in three-line songs, and *AABB*, *ABAB*, *ABBA*, *ABBB*, *AABC*, *ABBC*, *ABCB* or *ABCD* in four-line songs.

2. THE MUSIC OF FOLK CUSTOMS. As folk genres are closely linked to social life, their function, content and manner of performance constantly change with the changing social order or pattern of existence. Several ritual genres whose original magical function has lapsed have been transformed or are changing into festive, ceremonial or independent forms of which spectacle is the main ingredient.

The winter festivals contain numerous ceremonies accompanied by music, beginning on Christmas Eve or the day before, and lasting until Epiphany. The most important is *colindat* (carolling), a ritual formerly marking the start of the new solar year. Groups of *colindători* (carollers) go from house to house and sing, at the windows or inside, ancient songs of felicitation called *colinde* (carols). The carollers are boys, youths, girls, adults or mixed groups, usually with eight to twelve members, depending on the region. The content of the texts is sacred or secular. The secular texts describe, for example, the contest between the horse and the hawk; the incredibly large dowry demanded of a marriageable maiden, a dowry which the suitors renounce on seeing her beauty and being convinced of her industry; or a hunter's nine sons who are turned into stags while hunting a giant deer. The religious *colinde* contain popular legends of God and the saints: God as an old shepherd with a white beard, playing the flute as he watches a flock of sheep; God and St Peter dressed as beggars, driven out of the rich man's house, and welcomed and fed on what little the poor have, etc. The worldly character of the *colinde*, the pagan content of the secular kind and the apocryphal content of the religious kind, prompted churchmen to try to suppress them, and the *cîntece de stea* ('star songs'), with texts inspired by the Scriptures, were created in an attempt to replace them. The melodies and rhythms of the star songs connect them more closely with the pious Christmas hymns of the West. In places (e.g. western Oltenia) star song texts are apparently set to ancient *colinde* melodies. They are usually sung by children carrying a painted paper star.

The purpose of the *colinde* is to bestow good luck, health and good crops, and to praise allegorically those to whom they are sung, hence their specialization in some areas (carols addressed to a young man, a young girl, a newly-wed couple, a shepherd, a hunter, a fisherman, etc).

The carols' vigorous rhythm and dynamic delivery, invariably powerful, produce (as Bartók observed) a 'wild warlike' impression rather than a 'humble religious' one. This character is enhanced in Hunedoara and neighbouring regions of Transylvania and Banat by the beating of the *dube*, small double-headed drums carried by the group of carollers.

Although there is no single style of *colinde*, the most typical structure consists of three melody-lines with the main caesura at the end of the second line. In the familiar *ABA* form, the refrain – an important feature of the *colinde* – is the *B* line. The *colinde* are often restricted in range to a tetra- or pentachord, and in some districts neutral intonations are common, with the third degree slightly raised and the fourth lowered. The most important rhythm of the Romanian *colinde* is giusto syllabic. The melodies are isorhythmic or, more frequently, heterorhythmic (consisting of various combinations of different binary and ternary groups: ex.4).

The luck-wish ceremony of the *plug* (plough), the *plugușor* (little plough) or the *buhai* (bull) is an ancient agrarian fertility rite performed in Wallachia (southern Romania) and Moldavia on New Year's Eve and New Year's Day. A long recitation in verse allegorically representing the whole round of farm work, from ploughing to the kneading and baking of rolls of pure wheat flour, is intoned to the accompaniment of a friction drum called *buhai*, and sometimes a flute or other instrument as well: the well-wisher punctuates his recital, interspersed with jokes, with the clanging of a cattle-bell. From time to time the wishes are interrupted by shouts and whip-cracks from the luck-wish party who go through the village with a beautifully decorated plough, pulled by one or two pairs of oxen, also adorned.

Among the masked dances performed during the winter feasts, the most remarkable is the *capra* (goat, symbolizing fecundity). This custom, its magical significance now forgotten, consists of a dance by a masked man generally representing a goat or stag. The muzzle of the mask – sometimes the beak of a duck or stork – is made of two pieces of wood covered with hareskin. The lower jaw is articulated and the dancer snaps it against the upper one in time to the dance rhythm by means of a simple device. The details of the ritual and the melodies used for the dance vary from one region to another, and even from one place to another. In northern Moldavia and in Bukovina, a number of 'goats' and a 'he-goat' are led by a 'shepherd' who calls them with a *bucium* (alphorn).

Other rituals with music take place in spring and summer. On the Thursday before Easter the children of some villages in Oltenia climb the church bell-tower and sing a song expressing their joy at the end of the fast while rhythmically beating a suspended wooden board (*toaca*).

The *paparuda* ('rain-caller') ritual dance is performed in spring (the exact date varies from place to place); it has survived in many villages of Wallachia, Oltenia and the Banat. The rain-callers, dressed in green leaves, go from house to house, singing and dancing, and the peasants splash them with water. In northern Oltenia and neighbouring Transylvania the rite is performed by children, especially boys; in other regions by women, usually gypsies. The dance is largely forgotten (the *paparude* sketch a few grotesque steps and pirouettes when they are splashed with water), but the rainmaking ritual songs survive intact.

Another agrarian rite meant to bring rain and ensure the fertility of the fields is the *scaloianul*, also celebrated in spring. Children make a clay doll called *scaloian*, *caloian*, *ududoi* or *mumulița ploii* ('little mother of rain') which they decorate with flowers and lighted candles, submitting it to a sham burial with funeral songs, and finally throwing it in the water; it is sent to get the keys that lock the gates of Heaven and keep back the rain. By extension, both the *paparuda* and the *scaloian* (musical customs which are gradually disappearing) are performed on any day during periods of drought.

The *drăgaica* is celebrated on 24 June, St John's Day. This very ancient agrarian custom connected with the harvest still survives sporadically in certain villages in southern Wallachia. The *drăgăici* are 11- to 12-year-old girls adorned with ears of corn. They sing and dance in a circle without holding hands, whirling round and yelling at intervals.

In Transylvania another custom linked with harvest survives more vigorously. At the end of the harvest a

Ex.4 A *colindă* (carol) from Wallachia, Ilfov district

Le-roi-leo! Ici in ces-te cur-ți Și-n ces-te dom-

-nii le, *Le-roi-leo,* Năs-cut, au cres-cut.

bunch called *buzdugan* ('club') or *cunună* ('wreath') is plaited from the best ears of grain in the field and is carried by a young girl to the house of the peasant whose corn has been harvested, accompanied by a procession of harvesters singing a ceremonial song; as she goes through the village streets the girl is splashed with water. The wreath is kept hanging from a rafter of the house till sowing-time, when its grains are mixed with those to be sown. The melody associated with this rite has a solemn processional character (ex.5).

Ex.5 *Cîntecul cununii* (harvest song) from the Bistriţa-Năsăud district of Transylvania

The text of harvest songs from the north of the country describes the young girls who reaped the field, one of whom wounded herself with the sickle, bewitched by the handsome appearance of her beloved; at the same time the master is assured that the crop has been rich, and presents are demanded for the reapers. In southern Transylvania the harvest song retains ancient mythological elements, and consists of a dispute between the Sun's sister and the Wind's sister over their brothers' qualities.

This agrarian custom has undergone numerous changes in the course of time. Some surviving texts mention the exhausting labour of farmworkers (*robii cîmpilor*, 'the slaves of the field'; *iobagii domnilor*, 'the serfs of the lords') who ask the sun to set sooner, that the day's torture on alien soil may end. With the socialist transformation of agriculture the custom has begun to acquire a new aspect, changing into a festive ceremony for the end of the cooperative farm harvest.

Căluşul or *jocul călusarilor* (the dance of the *că-luşari*) is danced at Whitsuntide to invoke fertility, but is also intended as a prophylactic and as a cure for certain diseases. It was formerly known throughout Romania. It has completely disappeared from Moldavia but has left some traces in certain men's dances of the region, while in Transylvania and the Banat it was abandoned in favour of a drawing-room dance, created towards the mid-19th century from elements of the old ritual dance by a group of intellectuals in Braşov. But in Oltenia, Wallachia and certain parts of Dobruja the original dance of the *călusari* survived in fairly coherent forms. Generally the custom takes the following form. After binding themselves by oath to dance together for a certain number of years and to respect the discipline imposed by tradition, the dancers begin rehearsals. The team, led by a captain, generally consists of an odd number of dancers. One, *mutul* ('the dumb man'), is masked. Nowadays he is the buffoon of the troupe, but apparently his role used to be much more important. The *călusari* wear a special festive costume and carry sticks, while the *mut* holds a sword. The team also carries a pole garlanded with coloured ribbons and topped with a bunch of wormwood and garlic, healing herbs sought by the onlookers. The dance is performed during the whole of Whitweek (sometimes called *Căluş-*week), when the team also visits some neighbouring localities. The dance, a circular promenade alternating

with increasing intricate figures, has a special dynamism and is extremely spectacular (fig.1). Apparently it has gradually assimilated several other ritual dances – war, fertility, prophylactic and healing dances – hence its complex character. Since it lost its magic significance, it has been turned to account by a number of amateur and professional artistic teams, sometimes with resounding success in performances abroad and in international competitions.

The most strongly maintained ritual is possibly that of burial. The *bocete* (laments), sung by the kinswomen and female friends of the deceased, are known everywhere. Three different types of *bocet* are known. The type widespread in Wallachia and Moldavia is mainly improvised, with texts in prose sung to a kind of melopoeia of recitative character. A type proper to Oltenia has texts that are improvised, usually in hexasyllabic lines, at the very moment of singing. A type known in Transylvania, the Banat, Bukovina and northern Moldavia has known texts in verse and seems to be the most highly developed: improvisation is limited to adapting the poetic formula to the specific context in which the lament is sung. The melodies are numerous and diverse; they often differ from one place to the next. Frequently several lament melodies are known in one village, sometimes differentiated according to the age of the dead person (one melody for young people, another for the aged, etc).

An extensive area in the west comprising northern Oltenia, the Banat and the neighbouring part of Transylvania has a series of ritual funeral songs (not laments) sung *pe glas fără durere* ('in a voice without distress') by experienced women specially employed, who must not be close relations of the dead person. The songs are sung at certain moments of the burial, in strict accordance with the unwritten laws of tradition. The most important is the *cîntecul zorilor* ('dawn song') which announces the death to the village at early dawn. The women, sometimes holding lighted candles, their faces turned eastwards, implore the dawn to delay its coming until 'the sweet white-faced wanderer' has prepared everything he needs for the long journey 'from the land of longing to the land without longing; from the land of pity to the land of no pity'. Another important ceremonial funeral song, *cîntecul bradului* ('the song of the fir-tree', ex.6), is sung for those who die young and

Ex.6 *Cîntecul bradului* (song of the fir-tree) from Transylvania, Alba district

unmarried; the fir-tree brought from the forest and decorated represents the wedding fir-tree. The text includes the complaint of the fir-tree that it was made to believe it would be used in the building of a house when in fact it will be left to wither at the head of a grave. This repertory contains other songs – *la fereastră* ('at the window'), *al drumului* ('on the road'), *de petrecut* ('for accompanying'), *al gropii* ('at the grave') and others – comprising instructions for the dead person about his route; he is advised to make friends with the otter who knows about the rivers and fords, and with the wolf who knows the secret pathways of the forests. These songs also mention Samodiva, who notes down the names of the living in red ink and the dead in black ink, or tell of the cuckoo's quarrel with Death; their texts are often highly impressive.

Weddings also have various traditional melodies; in Wallachia, Oltenia, the Banat and Moldavia they are played by *lăutari* (professional folk musicians), while in Transylvania they are performed by the guests themselves. The most important wedding song, known everywhere, but with a varying melody (and sometimes text), is the *al miresei* ('to the bride'), sung either at the solemn moment when she takes leave of her parents and home, or when she changes her maiden's head-dress for that of a married woman. Its commonest themes are the bride's leave-taking of her former life, a description of her life in her parents' house contrasted with that in her parents-in-law's, the change of dress from the style of a girl to that of a wife, the mother's appeal to the sun to lengthen the day of separation, the sorrow of the mother losing her daughter and the joy of the mother-in-law who acquires her, and the comparison of girls with apples on a branch – as they ripen their number lessens. In Wallachia and Oltenia a similar song is sung for the bridegroom. As he is ceremonially shaved, the song describes in glowing terms the bachelor life he is leaving. The complex ritual of Romanian marriage is heightened by songs for the parents-in-law and godparents and by dances (some originally with a magical purpose).

3. PASTORAL MUSIC. An important repertory of occupational melodies, that of shepherds, belongs to the ancient Romanian pastoral tradition, which began to decline only during the first quarter of the 19th century. The shepherds developed an independent form of

Ex.7 *A oilor* ('of the sheep'), a *bucium* melody from Ţara Oaşului, Satu Mare district

instrumental music, sometimes determined by the construction of the instruments used; the alphorn, for instance, can produce only a single harmonic series (ex.7).

The pastoral repertory, a direct result of the shepherds' everyday life, contains certain melodies whose ancient magical meaning has been lost in the course of time. Their titles refer to tasks in the shepherd's daily routine, such as milking the sheep and making sheep's-milk cheese. Other tunes are used when moving or grazing the flocks. A further group comprises signals, such as those for mustering the sheep to the fold and rounding them up on the mountains.

The ancient musical legend of the shepherd who lost his flock, a virtual folk tone-poem which originated in pastoral society, is known in many parts of the country. Its simple subject-matter is common knowledge, and the

1. Căluşari (Whitsun fertility dance), Wallachia

performance – usually on shepherd's flute or bagpipe – consists of developing a sequence of contrasted melodies, a song of sorrow alternating with a lively (dance) tune etc. The 'programme' (there is no text) concerns a shepherd sadly looking for his lost flock; suddenly he seems to see his sheep in the distance, and the sorrowful tune turns into a lively one, usually a dance. But the shepherd was mistaken: he was deluded by some white rocks, and the sad melody returns. Eventually he finds his sheep and the story ends with a dance of joy. Sometimes the 'programme' is considerably amplified by interpolated episodes illustrated by music, requiring a recited explanatory text.

4. THE 'DOINA'. Certain melodies are not connected with a specific occasion but are sung in response to a particular state of mind. These include the *doina* proper, a term which Brăiloiu and succeeding Romanian folklorists used to describe a specific style of melody, a particularly lyrical melopoeia in free form, based on improvisation with some more or less invariable melodic elements (*see* HORA LUNGA). This sort of song is popularly called *lung* ('long') or *prelung* ('prolonged'), *de coastă* ('of the slopes'), *de codru* ('of the forest'), *de ducă* ('of departure') etc; it occurs in Oltenia, Wallachia, Dobruja, Moldavia, Bukovina, Maramureş, Oaş, Sălaj, Năsăud, on the Someş and Mureş and on the two Tîrnava rivers, in the Ţara Bîrsei, the Ţara Oltului and in Sibiu; vestiges of the *doina*, particularly instrumental forms, have been found in the Banat and the neighbouring Transylvanian regions. Because of their similar constituent elements, the *doine* found throughout the country have a unified and homogeneous style; there are only a few, relatively similar types which in places have acquired local colour. Specific introductory and concluding formulae frame passages of a recitative character, cadences and ample ornamental melodic variations.

Doine are usually in the D mode with a fluctuating 4th, sometimes natural and sometimes sharpened (ex.8). While the form is initially freely improvised it oc-

Ex.8 The most common scale of the *doina*

Ex.9 A *doina* from the Suceava district

casionally becomes fixed with a constant number and succession of melodic lines, irrespective of the amount of repetition involved. This crystallization is increasingly common in the regions where the *doina* is in decline. The *doina* has an introductory formula consisting of: an interjection sung on 5 or 4, held for a prolonged time and sometimes with an upward attack from 5_1 or from 1, with an appoggiatura, portamento or a roulade; a *recto-tono* recitative of eight syllables at the most on one of these two degrees (5 or 4); the alternation of

2. *Bucium (alphorn) players, Wallachia*

degrees 6 and 5, 6 acting as an appoggiatura to 5; sometimes the alternation of degrees 5 and 4, 5 acting as an appoggiatura to 4. This alternation of degrees may begin the melody or may follow one of the two introductory formulae mentioned above. The introductory formula is followed by an improvised passage characterized by ornamentation on degrees 5, 4, 3 and 2 (often with an augmented 2nd between 3 and 4, produced by sharpening the 4th), alternating with recitative on degrees 4, 2 and 1. The concluding formula is usually a recitative on 1, but occasionally the final cadence is reached by a recitative on 2 or by sliding from 1 to 5_1, usually in a parlando manner (which changes the authentic final into a plagal one). Most of these features can be seen in ex.9. Instrumental *doine* are usually performed more freely and have more ornamentation than vocal ones.

The texts of the *doine* are particularly varied and include poems of grief, regret, trouble and alienation, derived from the former hard life of the working people. They are not essentially pessimistic but are invigorated by a strong sense of social injustice, expressed in accents of revolt and sometimes of blind fury, particularly in texts concerning outlaws. Gentle poems of love, praise of natural beauty, wedding poems, epic ballads, and even certain modern poems, echoes of the new social conscience, are also set to *doina* melodies. In each case the performer tries to interpret as fully as possible the content of the poem he is bringing to life; an active process of creation, facilitated by the improvisatory character of the *doina*, occurs at the very moment of performance.

In the plain of Wallachia and neighbouring areas, there is a local type of *doina*, possibly of professional minstrel origin, now called *de dragoste* ('of love'); it appears to have evolved from typical *doina* formulae interspersed with certain Oriental elements. Its scales are chromatic, sometimes richly so and with a great mobility of steps; its range exceeds an octave and its rhythm is fairly regular; its texts deal exclusively with love and are usually highly erotic.

5. BALLADS. The *cîntece bătrîneşti* ('old time songs') as they are popularly called, or 'ballads' as they have been known since the days of the poet Vasile Alecsandri (1811–90), are songs with lengthy texts describing fantastic, heroic and romantic events, and form the most important part of the epic genre of Romanian folk music. Their origin is too early to be traced, and they contain the modifications of successive generations. Dragons and monsters are successively replaced by the invaders of the ancestral land, by the tyrant prince and his nobles, and finally by grasping landlords. The events and heroes of the older ballads represent typical circumstances and widely known facts in which historical reality is transformed and interpreted through words and sounds. The more recent epic creations, however, have a more authentic and defined socio-historical character. They are often simple rhymed chronicles of certain facts or happenings that particularly impressed the creator. As a rule, their viability is limited to a small area.

Ballads are now gradually disappearing. This does not imply a weakening of popular creativity, but is symptomatic of the natural evolution of folklore. During socio-historical evolution the function of the ballad is taken over by other genres. In Transylvania and nor-

Ex.10 A *miorița* (ballad) from the Vrancea district of Moldavia
(a) Rubato ♪ = 176

VIOLIN

(b) Parlando

i Foa-e d-un su – sa-iu, Foa-e d-un su – sa-iu,____

Pe gu – ră de ra-iu,____ Pe gu – ră de rai,

Pe pi –cior de pla-iu,____ Pe pi – cior de pla-i. i

Tot mi să co – boa-ră, Tot mi să co – boa-ră,____

De trei cio-bă – ne-i,____ Cu trei tur –me de o – i,____

Cu trei tur – me de o – i. etc

thern Moldavia, where ballads have become notably scarcer, epic texts are sung to *doina* melodies or to those of songs proper, whereas in southern Moldavia, Dobruja, Wallachia, Oltenia and the Banat specific melodies are exclusively assigned to the narrative ballad type. Epic ballads have almost completely disappeared in the Banat but are still vigorously alive in the other provinces just named, notably in Wallachia and southern Oltenia, where they occur mainly in the repertory of the *lăutari*, the professional folk musicians.

The ballads are performed mainly at the peasant wedding festive dinner, and are sometimes preceded by a *taxîm*, an instrumental prelude designed to create a suitable atmosphere for narration (ex.10a). Imperceptibly the musician passes to the actual instrumental introduction, borrowed from the musical content of the ballad he is performing. There are several formulae which the performer uses to arouse the audience's interest and ensure attentive listening to the ensuing narrative. Instrumental interludes allow the singer to rest his voice and marshal his thoughts. He tries to involve the emotions of the audience, stressing certain moments of the action and dialogue with mimicry and other dramatic devices. After a ceremonious 'dedication' addressed to the audience, the song ends with a *vivart*, a lively instrumental piece, usually any dance from the local repertory.

Narrative, more or less dramatic recitative, is a central element of Romanian ballads. In their use of recited melopoeia, and sometimes in the musical scales employed, the ballads partly resemble the *doina* (ex.10*b*). Their form is sometimes flexible: the same song interpreted by the same performer may be condensed or amplified, according to the degree of interest of the audience and the performer's mood. Epic works of the 19th and 20th centuries have tended to dispense with the epic recitative; they are increasingly sung to *doina* or song-proper melodies.

6. SONGS. The songs proper form the richest and most vital part of the Romanian folk music repertory. Unlike the *doine* and the ballads, they have a regular, strophic form: the melodic lines which make up the song succeed one another in the same order, in invariable 'melodic strophes', however often the melody is repeated. The small differences of rhythm or melody, or both, between melodic strophes reflect the prevalence of variation as a shaping factor of Romanian folksongs, particularly those not tied to specific occasions. Sometimes the structure itself is modified from one melodic strophe to another: a melodic line or two may be repeated or even omitted. But the order of the lines is never altered, nor are new melodic lines inserted (as they are in the *doine*). The songs differ substantially from one region to another, constituting actual regional musical idioms, which Bartók called 'musical dialects'. They are differentiated by the number of the melodic lines, the note on which the principal cadence (caesura) is sung and its place within the song, the notes on which the secondary cadences are sung and the relationship of the cadences to the final, the musical scale, the kind of melody (syllabic or melismatic) and the character of the ornamentation, the specific melodic formulae, the rhythm, the movement and the characteristic vocal production.

The pre-eminently lyrical and nostalgic texts cover the whole range of human feeling. As mentioned above, in Transylvania and northern Moldavia texts of ballads are sung to melodies of songs proper. In the other regions of the country, where the early ballads have their own melodies of specifically recitative character, new epic songs also employ the melodies of songs proper.

The regional musical idioms, which probably evolved during feudal times, formerly had distinct characters but with increasing interpenetration are gradually coalescing into a new more homogeneous style first noticed by Brăiloiu. It began its development in Wallachia, and is spreading rapidly there and into other regions. The characteristic exuberance of songs in this style derives largely from their regular movement (giusto) in place of the free movement (rubato) of the older musical idioms, the exchange of free rhythm (parlando) for regular rhythm corresponding in most cases to modern measures, the almost complete absence of melodic ornamentation and a preference for the modern major and minor, rather than the earlier modal variety. Refrains are common, as are amplifications of the old form of the melodic line through the addition of interjections or of syllables from the refrain. Songs in this new style are frequently sung in groups during work, though they are not work songs in the true sense of the word. They are mostly about love.

In south-western Romania (Oltenia), 20th-century folk music has adopted the style of dance-songs. New songs are the vocal *hora* and, especially, *sîrbă*, and exist in a condition of continual change and creation; they are

songs for dancing to, as well as simply for singing. The repertory of the songs proper is constantly being enriched with melodies of regular rhythm, such as dance-tunes and songs originally intended for dancing to, or songs influenced by them.

7. DANCES. Like the songs, the dances differ according to region. In some areas over 30 different dances are known in a single village. They are performed in a closed or open circle, in single file or a semi-circle, or they are danced in couples. Solo dances or dances for small independent groups are rare.

The predominant rhythm of Romanian folkdances is duple. Strictly speaking, examples in the Western triple rhythm are not known. However, throughout the country, dances in *aksak* rhythm, based particularly on the formulae described in §1 above, are fairly common. Occasionally a 'blunting' of the *aksak* rhythm transforms its formulae into commonplace duple or triple rhythmic formulae, as shown in ex.11. In Moldavia especially, dances in ternary rhythm are derived from the *aksak* formulas in ex.11*a*.

Ex.11 *Aksak* rhythmic formulae and their regularized versions.

While some Romanian folkdances have a fixed formal structure, there are many dances with free improvisation based on the varied repetition of a single motif, or on the combination and variation of two or more motifs. Dances without instrumental accompaniment, which the dancers perform to their own singing, are rare and apparently very ancient. In Transylvania instrumental dance melodies are accompanied by the declamation of short poems, usually jocular and often improvised on the spot. In the north and west of the province (Maramureş, Oaşului region and Crişana), such poems are recited to a simplified form of the instrumental melody, with which the voices of the dancers blend in an interesting heterophony. Numerous interjections, cries, whistling and sometimes hand-clapping are added, giving the dances of this region (especially those of the north) a distinctive dynamism. In the other regions of Transylvania and in Bukovina, the poems (called *strigături*) which accompany the dance are rhythmically shouted by the dancers (sometimes also by the spectators), usually by men, but sometimes as loudly by girls and women. Often a vigorous duel of *strigături* occurs between girls and youths during the dance, in a rapid exchange of taunts.

8. THE 'LĂUTARI'. The performance of dance-tunes is the province of the *lăutari* (professional or semi-professional popular musicians, frequently gypsies), who have an important part in popular musical life; they play at weddings, dances and parties, at Christmas carolling and in some places at funerals. Through them, a number of important instruments used in towns (violin, viola, cello, double bass, clarinet, various brass instruments etc) were brought into folk use. They are also responsible for enriching the Romanian folk music repertory with a special category of tunes (called 'for listening'), folk concert pieces, of which one of the most

3. Tilinca (flute without finger-holes), Bukovina

4. Nai (panpipes) played by Fănică Luca

famous, *Ciocîrlia* ('the skylark'), imitates the soaring flight of the bird and is believed to be derived from a very ancient dance.

9. FOLK INSTRUMENTS AND RESEARCH. There is a remarkably rich variety of Romanian folk instruments, the most numerous of which are aerophones. Five differ-

ent types of *bucium* (alphorn, fig.2) have been identified, with a straight or curved, cylindrical or conical tube, which can be from 1·5 to more than 3 metres long; and six different types of *cimpoi* (bagpipe), four with a single chanter, two with a double chanter, and with a variable number of finger-holes. There are some 17 varieties of *fluier* (flute): transverse or lateral; with the tube

5. Cobza (lute), Wallachia

6. Ţambal (cimbalom), Wallachia

either fully open at both ends or with a small air duct device at the upper end called *dop* (cork); simple or double; without finger-holes or with five, six, seven or eight finger-holes. Fig.3 shows a *tilinca*, a flute without finger-holes. The ancient *nai* (panpipe, fig.4) is used solely by the *lăutari*. Other instruments used professionally are the *cobza* (lute, fig.5), which has existed in Romania since the 16th century, and the *ţambal* (cimbalom, fig.6), used at least since the 18th century. A leaf, a blade of grass, a piece of birch-bark or a fish-scale are also used as musical instruments, being placed in the mouth and blown, on the same principle as reed instruments.

The collection and study of Romanian folk music is entrusted to the Institutul de etnografie şi folclor (Institute of Ethnography and Folklore) in Bucharest, where by the end of 1973 the collections comprised approximately 100,000 items of musical folklore, recorded on cylinder, disc or magnetic tape.

BIBLIOGRAPHY
COLLECTIONS

P. Pirvescu: *Hora din Cartal: cu arii notate de C. M. Cordoneanu* (Bucharest, 1908)

B. Bartók: *Cîntece poporale româneşti din Comitatul Bihor (Ungaria)* [Romanian folksongs from the Bihor district] (Bucharest, 1913) [incl. Fr. summary]; repr. in *Béla Bartók: Ethnomusikologische Schriften; Faksimile Nachdrucke*, iii, ed. D. Dille (Budapest, 1967)

G. Fira: *Cîntece şi hore* (Bucharest, 1916)

B. Bartók: *Volkmusik der Rumänen von Maramureş* (Munich, 1923); repr. in *Bela Bartók: Ethnomusikologische Schriften; Faksimile Nachdrucke*, ii, ed. D. Dille (Budapest, 1966), and in *Béla Bartók: Rumanian Folk Music*, v, ed. B. Suchoff (The Hague, 1975)

S. V. Drăgoi: *303 colinde* (Craiova, 1930)

C. Brăiloiu: *Colinde şi cîntece de stea* [Colinde and star songs] (Bucharest, 1931)

——: *Cîntece bătrîneşti din Oltenia, Muntenia, Moldova şi Bucovina* [Ballads from Oltenia, Wallachia, Moldavia and Bukovina] (Bucharest, 1932)

B. Bartók: *Melodien der rumänischen Colinde (Weihnachtslieder)* (Vienna, 1935); repr. in *Béla Bartók: Ethnomusikologische Schriften; Faksimile Nachdrucke*, iv, ed. D. Dille (Budapest, 1968) [incl. texts] and in *Béla Bartók: Rumanian Folk Music*, iv, ed. B. Suchoff (The Hague, 1975)

C. Brăiloiu: *'Ale mortului' din Gorj* ['The songs of the dead' from Gorj district] (Bucharest, 1936); also in *Mesures*, v/4 (1939), 85

C. Brăiloiu, ed.: *G. Cucu: 200 colinde populare* (Bucharest, 1936)

I. Caranica: *130 de melodii populare aromâneşti* [130 Aromanian folk melodies] (Bucharest, 1937)

S. V. Drăgoi: *122 melodii populare din judeţul Caraş* [122 folktunes from the Caraş district] (Bucharest, 1937)

C. Brăiloiu: *Bocete din Oaş* [Laments from Oaş] (Bucharest, 1938)

M. Friedwagner: *Rumänische Volkslieder aus der Bukowina*, i (Würzburg, 1940)

G. Ciobanu and V. D. Nicolescu: *200 cîntece şi doine* [200 songs and doine] (Bucharest, 1955, 2/1962)

G. Ciobanu, ed.: *A. Pann: cîntece de lume: transcrise din psaltică în notaţie modernă* [Secular songs: transcribed into modern notation from oriental church notation] (Bucharest, 1955)

C. G. Prichici: *125 melodii de jocuri din Moldova* [125 dance-tunes from Moldavia] (Bucharest, 1955)

A. Amzulescu and G. Ciobanu: *Vechi cîntece de viteji* [Old heroic songs] (Bucharest, 1956)

T. Brediceanu: *170 melodii populare româneşti din Maramures* (Bucharest, 1957)

N. Ursu: *Cîntece şi jocuri populare din Valea Almăjului (Banat)* [Folksongs and dances from the Almăj valley, Banat] (Bucharest, 1958)

T. Alexandru, ed.: *N. Lighezan: Folclor muzical bănăţean* (Bucharest, 1959)

E. Comişel: *Antologie folclorică din ţinutul Pădurenilor (Hunedoara)* [Anthology of folklore from the Pădureni region, Hunedoara] (Bucharest, 1959, rev. 2/1964)

A. Sachelarie: *Cîntece populare româneşti – rumunské lidové pisně* (Prague, 1959)

T. Alexandru: *I. Cocişiu: Cîntece populare româneşti* [Romanian folksongs] (Bucharest, 1960, 3/1966)

V. Popovici, ed.: *D. G. Kiriac: cîntece populare româneşti* (Bucharest, 1960)

V. Nicolescu and C. G. Prichici: *Cîntece şi jocuri populare din Moldova* (Bucharest, 1963)

P. Carp and A. Amzulescu: *Cîntece şi jocuri din Muscel* (Bucharest, 1964)

E. Cernea, M. Brătulescu, V. D. Nicolescu and N. Rădulescu: *Cîntece şi strigături populare noi* [New folksongs and *strigături*] (Bucharest, 1966)

B. Suchoff, ed.: *Béla Bartók: Rumanian Folk Music* (The Hague, 1967–75)

C. Georgescu: *Melodii de joc din Oltenia* [Dance-tunes from Oltenia] (Bucharest, 1968)

V. Medan: *160 melodii populare instrumentale* (Cluj, 1968) [incl. Fr. summary]

T. Mîrza: *101 cîntece şi melodii de joc de pe Crişuri* [101 songs and dance-tunes from the Crişana region] (Oradea, 1968)

N. Ursu: *Cîntece şi jocuri populare bănăţene din comuna Naidăş (Caraş), Banat* [Folksongs and dances from the village of Naidăş (Caraş), Banat] (Reşiţa, 1969)

C. G. Prichici: *Melodii de jocuri populare din judeţele Ilfov, Ialomiţa, Teleorman* [Folkdance-tunes from the districts of Ilfov, Ialomiţa and Teleorman] (Bucharest, 1970)

E. Cernea: *Folclor muzical din Sălaj* (Zalău, 1972)

E. Moldoveanu-Nestor: *Folclor muzical din Buzău* (Bucharest, 1972)

C. Zamfir, ed.: *T. Brediceanu: melodii populare româneşti din Banat: din colecţia '810 melodii populare româneşti din Banat'* (Bucharest, 1972)

I. R. Nicola: *Folclor muzical din Ţara Moţilor* (Alba Iulia, 1973)

T. Mîrza: *Folclor muzical din Bihor* (Bucharest, 1974)

G. Suliţeanu: *Muzica dansurilor populare din Muscel-Argeş* [Dance-tunes from Muscel-Argeş] (Bucharest, 1976)

BOOKS AND ARTICLES

G. Fira: *Nunta în judeţul Vîlcea* [The wedding in the Vîlcea district] (Bucharest, 1928)

C. Brăiloiu: *Despre bocetul de la Drăguş (Jud. Făgăraş)* [On the lament in the village of Drăguş (Făgăraş district)] (Bucharest, 1932) [incl. Fr. summary]

C. Brăiloiu and H. H. Stahl: 'Vicleiul din Tîrgu-Jiu' [The nativity play from the town of Tîrgu Jiu], *Sociologie românească* (1936), no.12, p.15

C. Brăiloiu: 'La musique populaire roumaine', *ReM* (1940), no.196, p.146

E. Riegler-Dinu: *Das rumänische Volkslied: eine musikwissenschaftliche Studie mit 162 Liederbeispielen und 2 Tabellen* (Berlin, 1940)

G. Breazul: *Patrium Carmen: contribuţii la studiul muzicii româneşti* (Craiova, 1941)

I. Cocişiu: 'Folclor muzical din judeţul Tîrnava Mare: schiţă monografică', *Monografia judeţului Tîrnava Mare* (Sighişoara, 1944), 393–492

T. Alexandru: *Instrumentele muzicale ale poporului român* (Bucharest, 1956) [incl. Fr. and Russ. summary]

Revista de folclor (Bucharest, 1956–63); continued as *Revista de etnografie şi folclor* (1964–)

T. Alexandru: *Béla Bartók despre folclorul românesc* [Bartók on Romanian folklore] (Bucharest, 1958)

——: 'Anthology of Romanian Folk Music', EPD 78, EPD 81, EPD 86, EPD 1015–17, EPE 01220–25 [disc notes in Rom., Eng., Fr. and Russ.]

C. Brăiloiu: *Vie musicale d'un village: recherches sur le répertoire de Drăguş (Roumanie) 1929–1932* (Paris, 1960)

T. Alexandru and A. L. Lloyd: 'Folk music of Rumania', AKL 5799 [disc notes]

T. Alexandru and A. Amzulescu: 'Cîntece bătrîneşti (balade)' [Songs of olden times (ballads)], EPD 1065–6 [disc notes in Rom. and Fr.]

E. Comişel: *Folclor muzical* (Bucharest, 1967)

E. Comişel, ed.: *Constantin Brăiloiu: Opere* (Bucharest, 1967–74) [in Rom. and Fr.]

N. Jula and V. Mănăstireanu: *Tradiţii şi obiceiuri româneşti: anul nou în Moldova şi Bucovina* [Romanian traditions and customs: the New Year in Moldavia and Bukovina], Antologie muzicală, ed. I. Herţea (Bucharest, 1968) [incl. Fr. summary]

M. Kahane and L. Georgescu: 'Repertoriul de şezătoare – specie ceremonială distinctă' [The repertory of the working bees, a distinct ceremonial genre], *Revista de etnografie şi folclor*, xiii (1968), 317 [incl. Fr. summary]

G. Ciobanu: *Lăutarii din Clejani* [Lăutari from the village of Clejani] (Bucharest, 1969)

A. Bucşan: *Specificul dansului popular românesc* [The specific character of the Romanian folkdance] (Bucharest, 1971) [incl. Fr. summary]

E. Comişel and O. Bîrlea: 'Carol Singing Customs and Carols (Colindatul)', EPD 1257–8 [disc notes in Rom., Eng., and Russ.]

G. Rouget, ed.: *Constantin Brăiloiu: problèmes d'ethnomusicologie* (Geneva, 1973)

G. Ciobanu: *Studii de etnomuzicologie şi bizantinologie* (Bucharest, 1974)

G. Habenicht: 'Die rumänischen Sackpfeifen', *Jb für Volkslied Forschung*, xix (1974), 117–50

T. Alexandru: *Muzica populară românească* (Bucharest, 1975)

E. Cernea: *Melodii de joc din Dobrogea* [Dance-tunes from Dobrudja] (Bucharest, 1977) [incl. Fr. and Eng. summary]

G. Marcu: *Folclor muzical arômân* [Aromanian folk-melodies] (Bucharest, 1977) [preface and introductory study in Rom. and Eng.]

VIOREL COSMA (I), TIBERIU ALEXANDRU (II)

Romanian letters. *See* SIGNIFICATIVE LETTERS.

Romanina, La. *See* ARCHILEI, VITTORIA.

Romano, Alessandro [Alexander]. *See* MERLO, ALESSANDRO.

Romano, Eustachio. *See* EUSTACHIO ROMANO.

Romano, Filippo. *See* RUGE, FILIPPO.

Romano, Giulio (i). *See* CACCINI family.

Romano, Giulio (ii) (*fl* early 17th century). Italian composer. He has sometimes been confused with Alessandro Merlo (also known as Alessandro Romano), Romano da Siena and Giulio Caccini (also known as Giulio Romano). He is known to have composed a set of seven *Concenti spiriti*, 1–6vv (Venice, 1612), now lost. He was also probably the composer of *Fuggilotio musicale* (Venice, ?2/1613), Fétis's misattribution of which to Caccini in his *Biographie universelle des musiciens* (Paris, 2/1860–65) was generally accepted until 1972. The *Fuggilotio*, dedicated to a Venetian nobleman by its composer, whose name is given on the title-page as 'D[on] Giulio Romano', is a collection of 18 monodies and 14 duets; the monodies (madrigals, arias and two pieces based on the romanesca), at least, are modelled on Caccini's *Le nuove musiche*.

BIBLIOGRAPHY

H. W. Hitchcock: 'Depriving Caccini of a Musical Pastime', *JAMS*, xxv (1972), 58

H. WILEY HITCHCOCK

Romano, Il. *See* DE GRANDIS, VINCENZO (i).

Romano, Marcantonio (*b* Salerno, *c*1552; *d* Split, 1636). Italian composer and organist. He was composer and organist of Split Cathedral from 1609 to 1636. He probably went to Split with the help of the cathedral's composer and *maestro di cappella*, Tomaso Cecchini, who worked in Split under the immediate influence of the Archbishop, Marcantonio de Dominis. In the dedication of the work *Amorosi concetti il terzo libro de madrigali a una et due voci di Tomaso Cecchino Veronese* (Venice, 1616), Romano is mentioned as 'industriosissimo conciliatore dell'Arte dell'Imitazione'. In the same collection Romano's madrigal for solo voice, *Mori mi dite*, was printed. Two further works of Romano, *Donne noi siamo* and *Haggio fin qui patito*, appear in *Di Filippo Azzaiolo Bolognese Il terzo libro delle villotte* (Venice, 1569²⁴) and *Il primo libro della raccolta de napolitane* (Venice, 1570¹⁹).

BIBLIOGRAPHY

N. Kalogjera: 'Povjesne crtice o glazbenim prilikama Splitske stolne crkve' [A critical history of musical conditions at Split Cathedral], *Sv Cecilija*, xviii (1924)

D. Plamenac: 'Toma Cecchini, kapelnik stolnih crkava u Splitu i Hvaru u prvoj polovini 17 stoleća' [Tomaso Cecchini, choirmaster of Split and Hvar Cathedrals in the first half of the 17th century], *Rad JAZU*, cclxii (1938), 77

M. Asić: 'Marc'Antonie de Dominis promicatelj muzike ranog baroka u Splitu' [Marcantonio de Dominis, promoter of early Baroque music at Split], *Zvuk*, cxxi–cxxiii (1972)

MILO ASIĆ

Romanos the Melode (*b* ?Emesa, Syria, late 5th century; *d* Constantinople, after 555). Byzantine hymn writer and composer, perhaps of Jewish descent. He was a deacon in the Church of the Resurrection in Beirut and came to Constantinople around the end of the century. Here he served at the Church of the Virgin in the quarter of the city called Kyrou. A hymn in his honour mentions his acquaintance with the imperial court, and it is probable that he was famous in his lifetime, since a papyrus fragment almost contemporary with him, containing part of a well-known hymn of his, has been found in Egypt; it is, however, uncertain whether he was the 'presbyteros' and 'ekklēsiekdikos' mentioned in the acts of the Synod of 536. He was canonized and is still commemorated by the Greek Orthodox Church.

According to his *vita*, the Virgin inspired Romanos to write kontakia, but this designation was never used by Romanos himself, who described his hymns in more general terms such as 'ainos' (praise), 'ōdē' (song) or 'deēsis' (prayer). The KONTAKION is a 'metrical sermon' that was recited after the reading of the Gospel (Maas and Trypanis, *Canticum* 11). It is a poem which normally contains between 18 and 30 metrically identical stanzas (oikoi) and a shorter preface (koukoulion) in a different metre; all the strophes are bound together by a refrain, and the initial letters of the oikoi form an acrostic. The genre may have originated in Syriac ecclesiastical poetry, and was certainly influenced by it. According to the *vita*, Romanos wrote 1000 kontakia, and is the greatest representative of the kontakion, though only 85 attributed to him have survived and of these only about 60 (those which have his name as part of the acrostic) are considered genuine: the hagiological kontakia are rejected by most scholars. The kontakia treat theological matters, and often in a theoretical or polemical way; but they are vivid and passionate, owing to Romanos's comparatively simple and direct language, and his use of dialogue embellished by rhetorical devices such as parallelism, oxymoron and word play. The famous akathistos hymn may have been the work of Romanos, but this question is still not settled and the hymn has also been ascribed to Sergios, Germanos and even Photios.

None of Romanos's own music has survived. The earliest melodies associated with his texts are found in 13th-century MSS and are melismatic; but the melismatic style may have arisen only after the singing of the kontakion was restricted to the singing of the koukoulion and the first oikos in the 8th or 9th century. Originally the poems were recited in full during the services; since they are very long, the music was probably syllabic. This theory rests partly on the further assumption that Romanos's metrical system is stable and conforms to the principles of homotonia (identical stress pattern in corresponding verses) and isosyllabia (identical number of syllables in corresponding verses). The text as we have it, however, does not always fit into the rhythmical pattern required by the theory; thus the champions of this theory (put forward by Pitra and elaborated by Krumbacher, Maas and Trypanis) are forced to make a number of textual alterations. The opposite view holds that only the number of main stresses in the verse is constant, and that the position of the stress and the number of unstressed syllables can vary. In this case the music (which may have been simply cantillation) could have been adapted to varying metrical patterns, and it is unnecessary for a modern editor to 'correct' the text for the sake of the rhythm. This position was maintained implicitly by Tomadakis and to some degree also by Zuntz.

WRITINGS

N. B. Tomadakis, ed.: *Romanou tou Melodou hymnoi* (Athens, 1952–61)

P. Maas and C. A. Trypanis, eds.: *S. Romani Melodi cantica*, i (Oxford, 1963); ii (Berlin, 1970)

J. Grosdidier de Matons, ed. and trans.: *Romanos le Mélode: hymnes* (Paris, 1964–7)

M. Carpenter, ed. and trans.: *Kontakia of Romanos, Byzantine Melodist* (Columbia, 1970)

BIBLIOGRAPHY

T. M. Wehofer: 'Untersuchungen zum Lied des Romanos auf die Wiederkunft des Herrn', *Sitzungsberichte der Kaiserlichen Akademie der Wissenschaften: Philosophisch-historische Klasse*, cliv/5 (Vienna, 1907)

E. Wellesz: 'The Akathistos Hymn', MMB, *Transcripta*, ix (Copenhagen, 1957)

K. Levy: 'An Early Chant for Romanus' Contacium trium puerorum?', *Classica et mediaevalia*, xxii (1961), 172

C. Floros: 'Fragen zum musikalischen und metrischen Aufbau der Kontakien', *XIIᵉ congrès international d'etudes byzantines: Ohrid 1961*, ii, 563

G. Zuntz: 'Probleme des Romanos-Textes', *Byzantion*, xxxiv (1964), 469–534

C. A. Trypanis: 'The Metres of Romanos', *Byzantion*, xxxvi (1966), 560–623

GUDRUN ENGBERG

Romanov. The Russian imperial family. As patrons of the arts they exercised a decisive influence from about 1730 to 1800, effectively laying the foundations for the development of Russian secular music. Until the 18th century, Russian music had remained isolated from the evolutionary processes that had occurred in Western music: sacred music had developed (and to a large extent continued to develop) only within the strict confines of the Orthodox tradition, while secular music, other than folksong, was almost non-existent. During the reign of Tsar Alexey (1645–76), attempts to stage theatrical entertainments with incidental music had come to little, but with the more Westward-looking policies of Peter the Great (1682–1725) music played a more prominent, if purely utilitarian, role. Peter was no lover of the arts, but he revelled in ceremonial: the spectacular celebrations of his military victories were supplemented by vocal *kantï*, and from 1711 each of his regiments maintained a wind band, trained initially by musicians imported from Germany. The court musicians (who were 'taught musick . . . by the help of the batogs – cudgels –, without which discipline nothing goes down with them', wrote one contemporary observer) were responsible for fanfares at state occasions, music for banquets and, above all, dance music for the tsar's newly established *assemblées* – gatherings (deliberately copied from France) which were intended to acquaint the boyars with the principles of etiquette, but, more often, were mere excuses for wild debauchery. Peter also formed at St Petersburg the choir that in 1763 was named the Pridvornaya Pevcheskaya Kapella (Court Chapel Choir) and that exists to this day as the Leningradskaya Gosudarstvennaya Akademicheskaya Kapella imeni M. I. Glinki (Leningrad State Academic Glinka Choir).

Not until the reign of the Empress Anna (1730–40) did music in Russia take a more professional turn. Before her accession she had lived at Mitau (now Jelgava, Latvia) and was therefore more fully aware of cultural developments abroad. She invited to St Petersburg a number of foreign opera companies, the most important of which was the Italian troupe headed by Francesco Araia, whom Anna appointed *maestro di cappella* in 1735. He remained at St Petersburg until 1759, thriving on the court's taste for Italian opera and also composing (in 1755) the first opera to a Russian text, Sumarokov's *Tsefal i Prokris*; and he paved the way for a vast number of other foreign musicians who worked at the Russian court and educated the native Russian composers who began to appear towards the end of the century. After Anna's death and the subsequent deposition of the infant Tsar Ivan VI, the crown passed to Elizabeth (1741–62), a daughter of Peter the Great and one of the most artistically enterprising of Russia's 18th-century rulers. Music – particularly Italian music – played an important part in the sumptuous court functions, and it was through Elizabeth's influence that new theatres were opened in St Petersburg and Moscow.

Catherine II (1762–96), widow of the murdered Tsar Peter III, contributed most to the early development of Russian art, though she herself was no connoisseur: she bought paintings indiscriminately from England, France and Germany (forming, incidentally, a priceless collection which is still at the Winter Palace, Leningrad), and she furnished her palaces with the finest tapestries, silks, furniture and porcelain. She knew little about music and commented to her confidant, Baron Grimm, 'I want to listen to and love music; but I have to confess that it is a noise, and that's all'. Nevertheless, she employed a large number of musicians, who not only performed duties at court but also played for the operas which were rapidly increasing in popularity: in addition to the Kamennïy Teatr (Stone Theatre, founded in 1783) she established her own theatre in the Hermitage (the cultural centre that she built on to the Winter Palace), and the direction of the several different opera companies in the capital (French, German, Italian, Russian) became the responsibility of the government. Catherine also wrote competent librettos (some in collaboration with A. V. Khrapovitsky): her *Fevey* was set by Pashkevich (1786), *Novgorodskiy bogatïr' Boyeslayevich* ('The Novgorod bogatïr Boyeslayevich') by Fomin (1786), *Khrabrïy i smelïy vityaz' Akhrideich* ('The brave and bold knight Akhrideich') by Vančura (1787), *Gore-bogatïr' Kosometovich* ('The woeful bogatïr Kosometovich') by Martín y Soler (1789), her 'historical spectacle' *Nachal'noye upravleniye Olega* ('The early reign of Oleg') by Canobbio, Pashkevich and Sarti (1790) and *Fedul s det'mi* ('Fedul and the children') by Pashkevich and Martín y Soler (1791). Catherine's influence on her countrymen was far-reaching, and with the spread of musical activity and patronage among other leading members of the aristocracy and with the increase of public concert-giving during the 19th century the crucial importance of the Romanov family declined. Although artistic institutions continued to enjoy imperial patronage until the Revolution of 1917, the family's valuable pioneering work of the 18th century remained their major contribution to Russian music.

BIBLIOGRAPHY

N. F. Findeyzen: *Ocherki po istorii muzïki v Rossii s drevneyshikh vremyon do kontsa XVIII veka* [Essays on the history of music in Russia from ancient times to the end of the 18th century], ii (Moscow and Leningrad, 1929)

R. A. Mooser: *Annales de la musique et des musiciens en Russie au XVIIIme siècle* (Geneva, 1948–51)

T. Livanova: *Russkaya muzïkal'naya kul'tura XVIII veka* [18th-century Russian musical culture] (Moscow, 1952–3)

Yu. V. Keldïsh: *Russkaya muzïka XVIII veka* [18th-century Russian music] (Moscow, 1965)

For further bibliography *see* UNION OF SOVIET SOCIALIST REPUBLICS, §IX.

GEOFFREY NORRIS

Romanowicz, Alina. *See* NOWAK-ROMANOWICZ, ALINA.

Romantic. A term generally used, in music, to designate the apparent domination of feeling over order, whether applied to a single gesture within a Classical or Baroque structure, to an entire work emphasizing these tendencies or to the period of European music between approximately 1790 and 1910 (hence sometimes known as the Age of Romanticism).

1. Etymology and usage. 2. Background and general considerations. 3. Application to opera and instrumental music. 4. Technical considerations.

1. ETYMOLOGY AND USAGE. In its first, literal meaning, Romantic is derived from Romance, the *lingua romana* that was the ancient vernacular of France. From this derived the nouns *romance* or *romant* in French, *Roman* in German, romaunt in English, to describe the poem or tale that was the most important product of Romance literature; and in turn, since the most characteristic feature of that literature was adventure and the free play of imagination, Romantic came to mean adventurous both in subject matter and in the invention and manner of description. There was thus from the start a contrast with the discipline and restraint of the literature based on classical precept. The adjective Romantic first appeared in England as early as 1659 (in France and Germany by the end of the 17th century) and was common in the 18th century as generally synonymous with 'wild' or 'fanciful' (Dr Johnson). It is, significantly, not until the 19th century that the derivative 'Romanticism' was needed to describe a movement of art and thought. Its first application to music cannot now be precisely determined, though the word 'romanesque' (associated with 'étrange') occurs in Cherubini's *Eliza* (1794). However, the term *Romantik* (Ger.: 'romanticism') gained universal currency in Germany after the work of E. T. A. Hoffmann, who in his essay on Beethoven's instrumental music (1813) discussed Beethoven's Romanticism.

2. BACKGROUND AND GENERAL CONSIDERATIONS. It is essential, if the term Romantic is to have any useful historical meaning, to set limits to its application. There are elements that might reasonably be called Romantic in Bach's Passions and in Stravinsky. But the only effective application of the term in such contexts is as representing a gesture divergent from a more ordered and contained norm. The Romantic movement may have cultivated certain qualities always present in art and in turn have bequeathed them to a succeeding age; but any valid discussion of it must concern the period in which such qualities were dominant and guided a majority of artists. This may generally be taken to be from the closing years of the 18th century to the first years of the 20th, with the essential provisos that artistic forms gather and disperse gradually, and that co-existing with them are reactionary forces.

In general application, it may be said that Romanticism represents the period of an apparent domination of instinct over reason, of imagination over form, of heart over head, of Dionysos over Apollo. It sprang from the desire to assert instinctual needs which had been too far suppressed in the Enlightenment and which developed when the claim of rationalism that Man was capable of solving his problems by the exercise of reason was shown to have left too much out of account. Some deplored the cracks in the artistic conventions constructed in the period which idealized the order of classical antiquity. Goethe, in a famous moment of irritation, declared Classicism to be health, Romanticism sickness. For others, the cracks admitted some much-needed light.

Certain distinctive traits were quick to emerge with Romanticism, providing musicians as well as other artists with characteristic subjects. One, perhaps the most important of many deriving from the key figure of Rousseau, was a new preoccupation with Nature. Previously the town, with its ordered society and its opportunity for the rational association of minds and exchange of opinions, had been regarded as the most civilized human condition. The concept of Nature, for Dr Johnson meaning native state or a piece of obsolete mythology, acquired a force in its own right, by turns benign in its liberating qualities and destructive in the irrational elements released. Connected to this was a turn from the rational and explicable towards the mystic and supernatural, both religious (expressed partly in the new enthusiasm for Roman Catholicism in Protestant countries) and merely spooky. Another trait was a fascination with the past, especially with the previous age of Romanticism and the legends of medieval chivalry. Still more important was the new attention given to national identity; and the search for it rent Europe with revolution and war for many decades after the reverberant example of the French Revolution was succeeded by the powerful impact of Napoleon; this reflected each man's search for individual identity. The more intense, powerful and fully expressed this was the better, even if it brought violence and destruction in its wake. This was the age of the Hero.

However, Romanticism is not to be summarized by the isolation of some of its principal characteristics, not least since one overriding trait is its apparent contradic-

Caspar David Friedrich's painting 'Wanderer above a Sea of Mist' (c1818) in the Kunsthalle, Hamburg

toriness – ambitions for the future mingling with dreams of the past; a determination to overthrow coupled with nostalgia for the rejected world of order and balance; fervent brotherhood yet the exaltation of the individual; proud selfconsciousness yet the sense of acute isolation; the assertion of Man yet an ache for the lost God. One source of misunderstanding has been failure to realize that such manifestations are not causes but effects. The collapse of the old certainties, political, social and religious, had cast Man upon his own resources. Before long the new freedom, however heady, was to prove burdensome; for Man, having called into question an entire system of ideas, was now required to formulate answers out of his own individuality, to attempt complete self-sufficiency. But the early days seemed a dawn of new feeling in which, as Wordsworth found, it was bliss to be alive – apparently alive as Man had never so fully been before. Goethe urged that Man must keep within the limitations of his nature; the Romantic ideal was to overcome them, and thereby to open up a range of new impulses and connections. Not only were distinctions between different styles and periods swept away, but the careful barriers between the different arts erected by Lessing's *Laokoon* were trampled underfoot in the new exuberance. Closer links were formed not only between the arts but between them and politics, philosophy and religion, with the artist taking the initiative from priest and ruler in voicing popular aspiration, and being revered as the highest manifestation of the active spirit of Man. And of all the arts, it was to music that, especially in Germany, most painters, poets and philosophers looked as the ideal. This was the art that seemed to express the most with the least definition, and that by existing in time embodied the condition of flux, of change and progress, of movement between emotional states.

The aspect which the new movement of ideas took naturally varied from country to country, with common features differently stressed and with music differently involved. In Italy, Romanticism was closely connected with politics and the unification of the peninsula: it is not surprising that a nation, or would-be nation, of singers should find the laureate of the Risorgimento in Verdi. In Germany, where Romanticism was also bound up with the struggle for national unity, it was Weber who first vividly voiced the mood of Romanticism in music and who set an example, in his mastery of the theatrical crafts, of the unification of the arts that was to open the way to Romanticism's culminating artist, Wagner. England, with a largely cosmopolitan musical tradition, made its greatest contribution in poetry, criticism and painting, producing in Byron a figure for European Romantic mythology and in Scott a master of the kind of romance now cultivated. Among France's contributions was an emphasis, in music, painting and the theatre, on the claims of the Hero.

3. APPLICATION TO OPERA AND INSTRUMENTAL MUSIC. Through all Romantic thought runs the assumption that the answer to the greatest questions were no longer to be accepted as an act of faith or discovered by rational inquiry but actually fashioned by the efforts of the imagination. In his centenary tribute to Beethoven (1870), Wagner declared that 'Music which does not represent the ideas contained in the phenomena of the world, but is itself an Idea, indeed, a comprehensive Idea of the world, embraces the drama as a matter of course,

seeing that the drama, again, represents the only Idea of the world adequate to music'. From sonata, the dominant principle of classical proportion and reasoned progress, the emphasis passed to more dramatic, empirical forms. Opera entered on a period of rapid development and propagation before a new range of audiences, especially the newly emergent middle class, proving as it did the most vivid and adaptable receptacle for the new ideas that were proliferating. The subjects included 'rescue opera' (a popular genre in the wake of the perilous times of the French Revolution), of which Cherubini's *Les deux journées* (1800) is a famous example and Beethoven's *Fidelio* (1805) the greatest; operas in which Nature played an increased role, such as Cherubini's *Eliza* (1794); operas dealing in the sinister supernatural, such as Weber's *Der Freischütz* (1821) and Marschner's *Der Vampyr* (1828); magic operas, such as Weber's *Oberon* (1826); operas dealing in the contact between the human and spirit worlds (a genre influenced by the Viennese magic theatre), such as Hoffmann's *Undine* (1816); operas celebrating national identity such as Glinka's *A Life for the Tsar* (1836), Erkel's *Bánk Bán* (composed 1844–52), Moniuszko's *Halka* (1848) and Smetana's *The Bartered Bride* (1866); operas with remote or exotic settings, such as Spohr's *Jessonda* (1823) and Schubert's *Fierrabras* (composed 1823); and operas also set in remote (though seldom classical) times, such as Méhul's *Uthal* (1806) and Boieldieu's *La dame blanche* (1825).

In opera, too, the tendency was to give greatly increased prominence to the orchestra as capable of depicting scenic backgrounds, emphasizing emotional or sensational states, commenting and developing (in the new importance given to reminiscence motif and then leitmotif) and exploring psychological states. With the decline of the castrato, the role of the hero generally passed to the tenor; and new importance was given to the chorus, who increasingly played a functional role in the drama. There was a greater tendency to mingle popular songs and dances in the action, and for forms to loosen and to grow towards full continuity. In all these matters, and many others, German Romantic opera took its example from the new paths explored by French *opéra comique* of the years during and after the Revolution and Empire. In all its variety, Romantic opera addressed itself more fully than ever before to the feelings of audiences that represented a new cross-section of society, and in doing so it assumed a role increasingly political and moral. French grand opera could reflect the interests and tastes of a new, prosperous bourgeoisie, Verdi's operas could be seized on for a real or imagined political message by the men of the Risorgimento, while Wagner, in whom the forces of Romanticism reached their climax, could conceive of his ideal theatre as a vast public rite.

It was also inevitable that instrumental music should develop new and more flexible forms. Sonata form itself, though frequently used automatically as a receptacle for ideas that little suited it, was to prove more adaptable than might have been expected, though it needed genius of Beethoven's scale to lead a way in extending the harmonic range successfully without destroying the fundamental balance. Hoffmann claimed Beethoven as a Romantic: Beethoven is Romantic in his determination to use music as a moral force, and though the Sixth Symphony is obviously Romantic in its response to scenery with feeling rather than mere imitation, the

Third and Fifth are more centrally Romantic in their account of Man struggling to assert his domination over his world, while in the Ninth, as Wagner observed, 'Beethoven's wish to construct the Idea of the Good Man guided him in his quest for the *melody* proper to this Good Man'. However, the Ninth Symphony originally struck Wagner as symphonic music crying out for redemption by poetry; and, for all the volume of 19th-century symphonies and sonatas, it is in other instrumental forms that the Romantic spirit most fully manifested itself. Significantly, Romantic symphonies and sonatas tended to acquire titles, not only to suggest a declared or concealed programme but to emphasize connections with other arts and with emotional states, in general terms as with Tchaikovsky's 'Pathetic' or Bruckner's 'Romantic' symphonies, or in specific terms as with Rubinstein's 'Ocean' or Liszt's 'Faust' symphonies.

Concerto was an obvious medium to be given new emphases for its embodiment of the Artist as Hero; and from Weber's *Konzertstück* to Liszt's *Totentanz* and beyond, the Romantic concerto developed, alongside conventionally shaped works in which the display element was sensationally increased, other forms guided by literary or dramatic ideas. It was Liszt, too, himself embodying a Romantic dichotomy of untrammelled personal flamboyance and longing for the stability of faith, who developed the orchestral work based not on pure form but on a dramatic programme, using for it a title that typically embraced two arts, 'symphonic poem'. Among much else in his achievement, Berlioz, an artist Romantically conscious of his role as Artist, attempted for large works constructive methods based on literary and dramatic analogy: his developments include use of a programme related to symphonic form in the *Symphonie fantastique*, and quasi-literary methods, consciously derived from Shakespearean free form, used to embody a drama for *Roméo et Juliette*. Smaller forms, especially when cultivated by composers with the extreme sensibility of Schumann and Chopin, were more easily able to take their shape from little more than a mood, as expressions of a nervous sensation responding to an impulse either poetic, or pictorial, or even connected to instrumental technique. Again, titles emphasizing the connection with emotions aroused by other arts became common, as with Nocturne, Ballade or Eclogue. From Schubert to Wolf and beyond, poetry and music were fused together with a new expressive potency in the great age of art song, above all the German lied. It is significant that composers now gave poetry a new importance in the shaping of the imagery and form of a song, and that songs were linked narratively to create a new form, song cycle.

4. TECHNICAL CONSIDERATIONS. In all its manifestations, the Romantic spirit laid its greatest stress on the individual's nervous sensations and emotional impulses acting as his guide. Composers were hence committed to music that would fashion its own forms more freely than in past ages and according to the emotional demands placed on it, while the new importance of sensation as a structural guide naturally meant not only a greater reliance on instrumental colour but also, more crucially, on a subtly extending harmonic language. Though tonal harmony remained the supreme harmonic principle of the 19th century, it was of the essence of Romanticism to extend this as far as possible without causing it to break down. Thus, remoter key relationships were explored from Beethoven onwards, as a matter of course; greater fluency of modulation, including enharmonic, was cultivated, and with it an increased rate of harmonic rhythm. Further, tonal harmony was extended by the use of altered and added notes, by a greatly increased use of unprepared and unresolved discords, and of chords of the 7th, 9th, 11th and 13th. Formerly exceptional or incidental chords, such as that of the added 6th, now acquired a new prominence; and a particular role was found for the diminished 7th, both for its purely sensational qualities (associated with the supernatural by Weber with Samiel's chord in *Der Freischütz*) and for its capacity as a pivot chord permitting modulation to virtually any key. In all its varied aspects, Romantic harmony gave greater importance to emotional than to formal demands. There was, of course, a limit to which the increasing chromaticization of tonal harmony could go without changing its fundamental structure. Liszt, Chopin and Wagner all by different paths found themselves at the end of their lives in a region on the further fringes of tonality to which a new structural principle would one day have to be applied.

If the emphasis passed increasingly to harmonic exploration, melody also acquired a new significance. The increased importance of opera and song stimulated singers and in turn encouraged melody in which the display elements of the 18th century and before were subjugated to greater expressive demands, whether in Italian Romantic opera, as with the long, sensitively inflected melodies of Bellini, or in the greater melodic span introduced to symphonic music especially by Schubert. Though the instrumental 'song-melody' was no 19th-century invention, its development and its prominence as central in symphonic music was a characteristic of Romanticism. The supremacy of melody was a distinctive element in the Romantic symphony as, in various applications, with Brahms and Dvořák, while Tchaikovsky gave such importance to melody as the 'lyrical moment' as to threaten the capacity for development in his sonata structures. The 'vocal' element in melody was emphasized especially in the Romantic concerto (as with Weber's aria-like slow movements and Spohr's construction of a violin concerto as a *Gesangszene*), with the increased personalization of art showing in the interest in instruments' singing qualities. Further, the same personalization may be traced as the impetus towards ever greater virtuosity, with the artist presented as in superhuman mastery over his instrument. The cult of Paganini was partly based on personal magnetism, but his introduction of virtuosity as a functional element in compositional forms with his Caprices had a profound influence on Liszt and thence on other composer–virtuosos.

Rhythm, the weakened element in the new proportions given to music, remained basically connected to the traditional eight-bar period. However, it was typical of Romanticism to strain at this pattern, without seeking to break it and thereby to bring about a situation in which a fundamentally new approach would be required. This was achieved in various ways. From earlier practice was inherited the normal variation of expected patterns with unexpected extensions or diminutions, now given greater attention; the interest in indigenous folk music, arising from heightened awareness of nationality, encouraged irregular phrase lengths and rhythms, even bar lengths, for particular effect; and, especially with Wagner's late work, there grew a tendency to blur rhythm and even virtually to annihilate it.

The orchestra, similarly, was retained in its basic 18th-century proportions but greatly expanded in scope and content. It was characteristic of Romanticism to give increased attention to the individual qualities of instruments: this subtle understanding of instrumental personality was a trait of Weber's which was inherited and developed with distinction by Berlioz and Mahler. It was equally characteristic to seek a smooth, sensuous blend of tone such as is above all identified with Wagner. The enlarging of the orchestra was a natural outcome of both tendencies: the growth from the normal orchestra of Mozart's day, with double woodwind, trumpets, horns, drums and a relatively small string complement, to the 120-strong or even larger orchestra of Mahler, Strauss and others, was accompanied by the regular addition of extra instruments. Some were the obsolete members of an established instrumental family, such as the english horn or piccolo; some were new inventions, occasionally imported, such as the saxophone, products of an age of mechanical experiment and industrial expansion. All instruments capable of it were given substantial technical improvements, both answering and stimulating the virtuosity characteristic of the age. Most notable, perhaps, was the development of the piano from a light, wooden-framed instrument with leather-covered hammers to the metal-framed, overstrung, felt-hammered instrument appropriate to the power, warmth and range demanded of it by the great age of keyboard virtuosos. The new orchestra, enlarged beyond any connection with chamber groupings, brought about the appearance of the virtuoso conductor. In opera, the turn from technical display towards emotional display demanding different techniques hastened the end of the castrato and led to a tradition of singers whose dramatic grasp would ideally, though often not actually, match their musical and vocal powers: it was the example of Wilhelmine Schröder-Devrient, dramatically gifted but vocally less distinguished, that by his own testimony set the young Wagner on his career as a composer.

It is in Wagner that most of the traits of Romanticism meet in some form; and an essential part of his genius rests in his ability to confer on the disparate tendencies of the movement his own renewal of order based not on a return to Classical practice but on the achievements of Romanticism. The extended harmonic range, the enriched orchestral palette, the commitment to 'endless melody', the motivic method flexible to the articulation of ideas and images and able to probe deep into emotion and psychology, the many technical and imaginative features observed in the earlier Romantics, are all at the service of a consistent and developing Romantic view of the world. After so powerful and systematic an artist, reaction was inevitable. Despite the work of major late Romantic composers, notably Mahler, within two decades of Wagner's death in 1883 the movement was significantly weakened, and within three had substantially spent its force.

BIBLIOGRAPHY
J. Tiersot: *La musique aux temps romantiques* (Paris, 1930)
W. Reich: *Musik in romantischer Schau* (Basle, 1946)
A. Einstein: *Music in the Romantic Era* (New York, 1947)
W. L. Crosten: *French Grand Opera* (New York, 1948)
J. Barzun: *Berlioz and the Romantic Century* (New York, 1950, rev. 2/1956 as *Berlioz and his Century*, 3/1969)
R. Huch: *Die Romantik – Ausbreitung, Blütezeit und Verfall* (Tübingen, 1951)
R. Benz: *Die deutsche Romantik: Geschichte einer Bewegung* (Stuttgart, 1956)
G. Knepler: *Musikgeschichte des XIX. Jahrhunderts* (Berlin, 1961)
I. Babbitt: *Rousseau and Romanticism* (Chicago, 1962)
N. Frye, ed.: *Romanticism Reconsidered* (Cambridge, 1963)
H. Schenk: *The Mind of the European Romantics* (London, 1966)
A. Thorlby, ed.: *The Romantic Movement* (London, 1966) [selection of documents and critical comments, incl. A. Lovejoy: 'On the Discriminations of Romanticism']
G. Abraham: *Slavonic and Romantic Music* (London, 1968)
L. Furst: *Romanticism in Perspective* (London, 1969)
R. M. Longyear: *Nineteenth-century Romanticism in Music* (Englewood Cliffs, 1969, 2/1973)
S. Prawer, ed.: *The Romantic Period in Germany* (London, 1970)
R. Taylor, ed.: *The Romantic Tradition in Germany* (London, 1970)
R. Cardinal: *German Romantics in Context* (London, 1975)
E. J. Dent: *The Rise of Romantic Opera*, ed. W. Dean (Cambridge, 1976) [lectures, 1937–8]

JOHN WARRACK

Romanus, Christiane Mariane von. *See* ZIEGLER, CHRISTIANE MARIANE VON.

Romanza (It.; Ger. *Romanze*). ROMANCE.

Romanzini, Maria Theresa. *See* BLAND family.

Romberg. German family of musicians. Bernhard Anton Romberg (*b* Münster, 6 March 1742; *d* Münster, 14 Dec 1814), a bassoonist and cellist, played in the orchestra of the Prince-Bishop of Münster from 1776 to 1803. His children were (2) Bernhard Heinrich Romberg; Anton Romberg (*b* Münster, 6 March 1771; *d* Munich, 1842), a bassoonist and cellist in the Münster orchestra from 1793 to 1802, active in Vienna 1808–19 under Prince Kinsky and Prince Lobkowitz and in the court opera; and Angelica Romberg (*b* Münster, 21 July 1775; *d* after 1803), a soprano soloist in the Münster Kapelle 1794–1803 and a pianist. His brother Gerhard Heinrich Romberg (*b* 8 Aug 1745; *d* 14 Nov 1819) was a clarinettist and violinist who also played in the orchestra of the Prince-Bishop of Münster in the last quarter of the 18th century. The descendants of (1) Andreas Jakob Romberg and (2) Bernhard Heinrich Romberg are listed below.

(1) Andreas Jakob Romberg (*b* Vechta, nr. Münster, 27 April 1767; *d* Gotha, 10 Nov 1821). Violinist and composer, son of Gerhard Heinrich Romberg. He learnt the violin with his father and made his début in Münster at the age of seven with his cousin (2) Bernhard Heinrich Romberg. They then accompanied their fathers on concert tours, to Frankfurt am Main (1782) and Paris (1784 and 1785), where their performances at the Concert Spirituel were applauded. In 1790 the cousins (who sometimes made themselves out to be brothers) joined the electoral orchestra in Bonn, which was then at its peak and included the young Beethoven among its members. When the French army invaded the Rhineland in 1793 they escaped to Hamburg, where they found employment in the opera orchestra of the Ackermann Theatre, then under the direction of the actor F. L. Schröder. They also earned a high reputation as soloists and composers, but left the city in 1795 for a two-year concert tour of Italy. A visit to Vienna in 1796 led to friendly relations with Haydn and a concert with Beethoven. They returned to Hamburg and remained there until about 1800.

After another trip to Paris in 1801, Andreas made Hamburg his permanent home; his circumspect temperament made him less enterprising than Bernhard, and he turned his intentions increasingly towards composition.

In 1809, the year his *Lied von der Glocke* op.25 was published, he received an honorary doctorate from the University of Kiel. The catastrophic plight of Hamburg under the French occupation put his family into financial difficulties; in the hope of obtaining a regular income he took up the post of Hofkapellmeister in Gotha. But his health soon began to fail and he died in poverty. Romberg's reputation as a violinist faded early; Rochlitz described his playing as 'robust, rather than fiery, vigorous and grainy, rather than emotionally overwhelming'; Spohr, on the other hand, found his playing 'inexpressibly cold and dry' in Berlin about 1815, but acknowledged him as a 'cultured and thoughtful artist'. He won European recognition as a composer, modelling his technique on Haydn and Mozart and setting himself the task of writing works musically more substantial than the usual run of virtuoso pieces. The success of his setting of Schiller's *Lied von der Glocke* reached as far as New York; the work was still being performed after 1900, sometimes in its individual sections, and ran to a number of editions. A large number of his songs with piano accompaniment and *a cappella* choral works were popular among amateurs. He had little success as an opera composer; only five of his eight operas were performed. He had two sons: Heinrich Maria (*b* Paris, 4 April 1802; *d* Hamburg, 2 May 1859), who became the leader of the imperial opera in St Petersburg in 1827 and later its music director, and Ciprian Friedrich (*b* Hamburg, 28 Oct 1807; *d* Hamburg, 14 Oct 1865), the leading cellist in the orchestra of the German Opera at St Petersburg from 1835 to 1845.

Bernhard Heinrich Romberg: lithograph by Kräger after Gentili

WORKS

OPERAS

Das blaue Ungeheuer (3, A. W. Schwick, after Gozzi), 1790–93, unperf.
Die Macht der Musik (3), 1791, unperf.
Die Nebelkappen (3), 1793, inc.
Der Rabe (Schwick, after Gozzi), Hamburg, 1794
Don Mendoza, Paris, 1802, collab. B. H. Romberg
Point de bruit (opéra comique), Paris, 1810
Die Ruinen von Paluzzi (romantic opera, 3, J. F. Schink), Hamburg, 27 Dec 1811
Die Grossmut des Scipio (heroic opera), Gotha, 1816

VOCAL

Sacred choral: Der Messias (Klopstock); Mass, B♭; Te Deum; Der Erbarmer (Klopstock); Pater noster; several psalm settings
Secular vocal: numerous choral settings of texts by Klopstock, Schiller and L. Kosegarten, incl. Das Lied von der Glocke (Schiller), op.25; 18 partsongs on texts by J. W. L. Gleim, C. Westphalen and Lessing; many lieder to texts by Klopstock, Herder, Goethe, Kosegarten, others

INSTRUMENTAL

Orch: 10 syms., 4 pubd; 20 vn concs., 4 pubd; 5 double concs., 2 for vn, vc, 2 for 2 vn (1 pubd), 1 for cl, vn; various other works, vn, orch, c5 pubd
For str qt: 19 str qts, 4 fantasias, 3 rondos 'alla polacca', 3 variation sets, capriccio
Other chamber: Octet, str; Cl Qnt; 8 fl qnts; Str Qnt; Pf Qt; 3 vn sonatas; 8 duos, vn, vc, collab. B. H. Romberg; 9 duos, 2 vn; 3 sonatas, vn solo

(2) Bernhard Heinrich Romberg (*b* Dinklage, Oldenburg, ?11 Nov 1767; *d* Hamburg, 13 Aug 1841). Cellist and composer, son of Bernhard Anton Romberg. He learnt the cello from his father and followed a career identical to that of his cousin (1) Andreas Jakob Romberg until 1801, when he toured Spain on his own. He then took a teaching post at the Paris Conservatoire, but moved the next year to Berlin, where he joined the royal court orchestra in 1805. He fled from the disturbances of the war over the next few years by making lengthy concert tours, including one to Russia. He played in England in 1814. In 1816 he was promoted to Hofkapellmeister in Berlin, but failed in his ambition to become the director of the opera there. After Spontini's appointment as general music director in Berlin (1819), Romberg resigned his post and used his regained freedom to extend his international reputation as a solo cellist. From 1820 he lived in Hamburg (apart from returning to Berlin 1826–31); he died a wealthy man.

Contemporaries particularly praised the lightness and grace of Romberg's playing. His early training in the German tradition meant that he always strove for an even, clear tone. To this he added some aspects of French and Italian technique, but was unreceptive towards new developments, especially in bowing. His *Méthode de violoncelle* (Berlin, 1840) is informative about his individual, at times wilful, manner of playing. His numerous cello compositions could be described in the same terms as his playing; they have no enduring musical value, but for a long time proved good practice material. Among his orchestral works, the *Trauer-Symphonie* op.23, written in memory of Queen Louise of Prussia, and the children's symphony op.62 were especially popular. Like his cousin, he had little success as an opera composer; three of his five operas were produced, none of which enjoyed lasting success.

Romberg had two children who became musicians: Bernhardine (*b* Hamburg, 14 Dec 1803; *d* Hamburg, 26 April 1878), a concert singer, and Karl (*b* Moscow, 16 Jan 1811; *d* Hamburg, 6 Feb 1897), who played the cello in the orchestra of the German Opera in St Petersburg from 1830 to 1842.

WORKS

THEATRICAL

Der Schiffbruch (operetta, Pfeiffer), 1791, unperf.
Die wiedergefundene Statue (opera, A. W. Schwick, after Gozzi), c1792, unperf.
Ulisse und Circe (opera, after Calderón), Berlin, 1807
Rittertreue (opera, F. W. Trautvetter), Berlin, 1817
Daphne und Agathokles (ballet), Berlin, 1818
Alma (opera), Copenhagen, 1824
Incidental music: Heinrich IV. (Francke); Phèdre (Racine)

ORCHESTRAL

5 syms., op.23 ('Trauer-Symphonie'), op.28, op.53, 2 without op. no.; Symphonie burlesque, children's insts, orch, op.62; 2 ovs., op.11, op.34

10 vc concs., op.2, op.3, op.6, op.7, op.30, op.31 ('Military'), op.44 ('Swiss'), op.48 ('Brillante'), op.56 ('Grand'), op.75 ('Brillante'); Fl Conc., op.30; Concertino, 2 hn, orch, op.41; Double conc., vn, vc, orch

c50 rondos, variations, fantasias, capriccios, divertimentos, potpourris, vc, orch and vc, str orch/str qt; other concert works with solo fl, vn, pf and harp

OTHER WORKS

Chamber: 11 str qts, 3 as op.1, op.12, 3 as op.25, op.37, op.39, op.59, op.60; Pf Qt, op.22; Divertissement, pf trio, op.71; Str Trio, op.8; 3 Trios, 2 vc, va, op.38; 3 sonatas, vn/vc, pf/harp, op.5, op.6, 1 without op. no.; 9 duos, vn, vc, 3 as op.4, 3 as op.9, 3 as op.33

Vc studies, 3 bks

Variations, dance pieces, pf solo

Vocal: Laudate Jehova, motet (Russ. text); Ich weiss, das mein Erlöser lebt (P. Gerhardt); 3 passion songs; several solo songs

BIBLIOGRAPHY

F. Rochlitz: 'Andreas Romberg', Für Freude der Tonkunst, i (Leipzig, 1824, 3/1868)

H. Schäfer: Bernhard Romberg: sein Leben und Wirken (diss., U. of Bonn, 1931)

K. Stephenson: Andreas Romberg: ein Beitrag zur Hamburger Musikgeschichte (Hamburg, 1938)

E. Wulf: 'Romberg, Andreas Jakob', 'Romberg, Bernhard Heinrich', Rheinische Musiker, i, ed. K. G. Fellerer (Cologne, 1960) [with complete lists of works]

KURT STEPHENSON

Romberg, Sigmund (*b* Nagykanizsa, 29 July 1887; *d* New York, 9 Nov 1951). American composer of Hungarian birth. He learnt the violin, and studied composition with Heuberger in Vienna, but became an engineer. In 1909 he went to the USA, worked as a pianist and as a restaurant dance-band leader, and in 1912 had his first dances published. In 1914 he became the staff composer for revues produced by the Shubert brothers, notably the *Passing Show* series. He began writing romantic operettas, drawing on the European style he had known as a student; those of the 1920s were among the last widely popular works in that genre in the USA. *Blossom Time* was based on the life of Schubert, whose melodies Romberg adapted for the score. With *Up in Central Park* he made a successful transition to the style of American musical comedy. Many of his other stage shows, though undistinguished, included other composers' first stage songs (e.g. Gershwin's 'Making of a Girl' in *The Passing Show*, 1916; Rodgers's songs in *Poor Little Ritz Girl*, 1920) or popular hits (e.g. Al Jolson's interpolations in *Sinbad*, *Bombo* etc). In the early 1930s Romberg moved to Hollywood to write scores and adapt his works for films. From 1942 until his death he toured the USA with his own orchestra. A film biography, *Deep in my Heart*, was made in 1954.

WORKS

(*selective list*)

The Passing Show (revue, lyrics mostly H. Atteridge), collab. H. Carroll, 1914, collab. O. Motzan, 1916–17, collab. J. Schwartz, 1918–19, 1923–4; The Blue Paradise (operetta, book E. Smith, lyrics H. Reynolds), 5 Aug 1915; Robinson Crusoe jr (revue, Atteridge and Smith), 17 Feb 1916; Follow Me (musical comedy), 1916; Maytime (operetta, R. J. Young and C. Wood), 16 Aug 1917; Over the Top (revue), 1 Dec 1917

Sinbad (revue, Atteridge), 14 Feb 1918; The Poor Little Ritz Girl (musical, G. Campbell and L. Fields), collab. R. Rodgers, 28 July 1920; Blossom Time (operetta, D. Donnelly), 29 Sept 1921; Bombo (revue, Atteridge and G. B. De Sylva), 6 Oct 1921; The Rose of Stamboul (operetta), 1922; The Student Prince (operetta, Donnelly), 2 Dec 1924; The Desert Song (operetta, O. Harbach, O. Hammerstein II and F. Mandel), 30 Nov 1926

Rosalie (operetta, book G. Bolton and W. A. McGuire; lyrics I. Gershwin and P. G. Wodehouse), collab. G. Gershwin, 10 Jan 1928; The New Moon (musical comedy, Hammerstein, Mandel and L. Schwab), 11 Sept 1928; May Wine (musical play, book Mandel;

lyrics Hammerstein), 5 Dec 1935; Up in Central Park (musical comedy, H. and D. Fields), 27 Jan 1945; The Girl in Pink Tights (musical comedy, book J. Chodorov and J. Fields; lyrics L. Robin), 5 March 1954

Other songs: for The Whirl of the World (revue), 1914; When Hearts are Young, for Lady in Ermine (musical), 1922; for Artists and Models (revue), music J. F. Coots, 1924

BIBLIOGRAPHY

S. Green: *The World of Musical Comedy* (New York, 1960, rev. 3/1968)

DEANE L. ROOT

Rombouts, Pieter. Netherlands violin maker, stepson of HENDRIK JACOBS.

Rome. I. Ancient. II. The Christian era.

I. Ancient

1. Introduction. 2. Music in religion and ritual. 3. Secular music. 4. Instruments and theory.

1. INTRODUCTION. Historians of Roman music once devoted themselves almost entirely to two limited areas of investigation, late classical music theory and organology, drawing their evidence from Greek and Roman authors. Consequently, writers of general music histories did not dispute the widely held views – still common – of the 'unmusicality' of the Romans and the 'decline' and 'decadence' of music after the Hellenistic period. These views, maintained even after the discovery of compositions from the Hellenistic and Roman period, unmistakably arise from an uncritical bias towards classical Hellenism and Roman culture.

Since the 1930s, through the systematic evaluation of literary and epigraphical references and archaeological discoveries, scholars (Machabey, Scott, Wille, Fleischhauer, Baudot, etc) have increasingly begun to appreciate the importance of music in Roman life. From the era of the Kings (*c*750–510 BC) and in the early republic (509–265 BC), the Romans had liturgical and other public music, military music and work songs.

Moreover, Roman music was subject to foreign influences: at an early date that of the Etruscans, later that of the Greeks, and, during the late republican and the imperial periods, that of the orient. The Romans assimilated, modified and extended the music of the nations they conquered. From the 2nd century BC, after the subjugation of the Hellenistic kingdoms in Macedonia, Syria and Egypt, new musical genres developed under sustained Hellenistic and oriental influence.

The greatest efflorescence of Greco-Roman music occurred (so far as can be judged from literary, epigraphical and iconographical sources) during the Augustan principate (27 BC–AD 14) and under the imperial dynasties of the Julio-Claudians (AD 14–68), the Flavians (AD 69–96) and the Antonines (AD 96–192). Professional virtuosos, mainly of Greek origin, sang and played instruments; outstanding Egyptian and Syrian *pantomimi* performed in public; Greek and Roman musicians and actors were active in organized bodies at Rome and elsewhere; dancers and musicians were imported as slaves from all parts of the empire; musical instruments and musical scholarship were developed; and the participation of music lovers in public events increased.

At the same time writers, philosophers and historians, including Seneca, Quintilian, Plutarch, Juvenal and Tacitus, attacked the demoralizing and effeminate effects of theatrical music, and the 'decline' of music in the service of luxury, on national, social, musical and moral grounds. Many actors, dancers and musicians continued, nevertheless, to enjoy public favour, despite their low legal and social position. Even after the fall of the western Roman Empire in AD 476 they became the means by which the instruments and musical practice of antiquity were transmitted to the itinerant musicians (*joculatores*) of the Middle Ages.

2. MUSIC IN RELIGION AND RITUAL.

(*i*) *The Roman religion.* The Romans imputed an extraordinary importance to the magical functions of music in ritual. The companies (*sodalitates*) of priests known as the *Salii* were founded as early as the legendary era of the Kings (*c*750–510 BC) and survived into imperial times, when the group consisted of 12 members of the nobility; under a leading singer (*vates*) and a leading dancer (*praesul*) they performed archaic armed dances and responsorial *carmina* (songs), in honour of Mars and Quirinus, according to a strict ritual (Livy, i, chap.20, §4). Another ancient priestly company, the Arval Brethren (*fratres Arvales*), even as late as the early 3rd century AD, still performed their traditional ritual song, the *carmen Arvale*, intended to banish malevolent influences during a procession around the sacred grove.

Tibia players (*tibicines*), probably originally from Etruria, constituted one of the oldest professional organizations at Rome (Plutarch, *Numa*, chap.17) and their participation in the ritual also had a magical function; their playing was intended to render inaudible any maleficent noises during the rigidly prescribed Roman sacrificial rites (Pliny, *Naturalis historia*, xxviii, chap.2, §11), to banish evil spirits and to summon up benevolent deities. For similar reasons during the empire, tibia players invariably accompanied funeral processions and ceremonies and sacrifices, whether made by peasants or on the highest state occasions; they were frequently depicted in reliefs on altars, triumphal arches, sarcophagi (see fig.1) and on coins. The *tibicines* were sometimes supported by lyre players (*fidicines*); however, the tibia (originally a bone pipe with three or four finger-holes, and later, like the Greek aulos, a double-pipe reed instrument with two pipes made from ivory, silver or boxwood) remained the national ritual instrument of the Romans.

The *tibicines* owed their esteemed position to the part they played in the sacred rite (Ovid, *Fasti*, vi, ll.657f); they enjoyed state privileges, and commemorated their legendary strike of 311 BC (Livy, ix, chap.30, 5ff) every year in Rome with a guild festival, processions and a public feast in the temple of Jupiter on the Capitol. During the later days of the republic and in the early empire the members of the municipal Roman *collegium tibicinum* were freedmen (*liberti*), whereas the trumpeters of the state religion (*tubicines sacrorum populi Romani*) held the rank of priest. From the 2nd century BC choirs of boys and girls sang, after the Greek fashion, in processions of atonement or supplication; during the secular games of Augustus in 17 BC these choirs sang alternate strophes of the *carmen saeculare* composed and directed by Horace. Similar choirs sang

1. Tibia player at the sacrificial offering of a bull: detail of a relief on a sarcophagus (mid-2nd century AD) in the Museo del Palazzo Ducale, Mantua; for a further illustration see TIBIA (i)

2. *Musicians in a Dionysiac celebration; marble relief (late 1st or early 2nd century* AD*) in the Museo Nazionale, Naples; Dionysus (centre) in a drunken daze is supported by a satyr, the two maenads play the cymbala (left, with her arms raised above her head) and the Phrygian auloi (or Berecyntian tibiae, right)*

hymns of mourning at the funeral of the Emperor Pertinax in AD 193.

(*ii*) *Music in the cults of Cybele, Dionysus and Isis.* The ritual music of the Romans was influenced by the mystery religions of Cybele (the *magna mater*), Dionysus (Bacchus) and Isis, which originated in Phrygia, Greece and Egypt respectively.

The cult of Cybele was officially introduced at Rome as early as 204 BC; festivals, lasting for several days and accompanied by scenic games (*ludi Megalenses*), were held annually to commemorate the dedication of her temple on the Aventine. The priests carried the cult-idol of the goddess in triumphal procession to the music of bronze cymbala, frame drums or tambours (tympana), cornua (horns) and 'Phrygian auloi' or 'Berecyntian tibiae' (i.e. tibiae pertaining to Cybele) whose deeper-sounding left pipe had an upturned horn-shaped bell (see fig.2; AULOS, fig.3, and TYMPANUM). These instruments were also played during the orgiastic dances of the priests in the temples (Catullus, lxiii, ll.19ff).

Livy gave an account (xxxix, chap.8, §8) of the ecstatic nature of the music in the cult of Dionysus: the loud beating (by hand) of the tympana and cymbala drowned the cries of those being violated. Despite the proscription of Dionysiac festivals by senate decree in 186 BC, they were repeatedly held during the last century of the republic and during the early empire. Pompeiian wall paintings and a few sarcophagal reliefs of the 2nd and 3rd centuries clearly show the orgiastic and cathartic nature of this music in many depictions of different kinds of wind and percussion instruments

(tibiae, transverse flutes, cymbala, tympana, foot-clappers, small bells etc; see fig.2).

After the conquest of Egypt in 30 BC, the cult of Isis also spread through the Roman Empire; this process continued during the reigns of the Flavians, the Antonines and the Severans, in the 1st, 2nd and 3rd centuries AD. The characteristic and traditional instrument of the Isis cult was the sistrum, a bright-sounding metal rattle, which was used to banish the influence of malevolent spirits (for illustration, *see* ISIS); Old Egyptian vertical long flutes and angle harps were also played during processions, sacrificial ceremonies and mystery rites of the cult. As in the cults of Cybele and Dionysus, instrumentalists and hymn singers were attached to the temple.

3. SECULAR MUSIC.
(*i*) *Military music.* There was an ancient tradition of military music in Rome. Trumpeters (*tubicines*) and horn players (*cornicines*) are mentioned as early as the constitutional reforms (attributed to Servius Tullius) of the 5th century BC. The Romans inherited their instruments from the Etruscans: the straight tuba, a conical bronze or iron tube with a small bell (see fig.3); the long-stemmed lituus with a hook-shaped bell which was bent back (for illustration, *see* TIBIA (i)); and the cornu, which was circular with a handle attached diagonally (for illustration, *see* CORNU). There are originals and modern reproductions of these instruments in museums in Rome, Naples, Mainz, etc.

The duties of the Roman military musicians were still

described in the late 4th century AD by the late classical author Vegetius (*De re militari*, ii, chap.22), whose evidence is corroborated and supplemented by literary and iconographic evidence of earlier centuries, such as the reliefs on Trajan's Column at Rome (for illustration, *see* TUBA (i)). The trumpeters gave fixed signals to sound the alarm, break camp, attack or retreat. They signalled changes of the watch and also played on the march, at funerals and in triumphal and sacrificial processions. The lituus players generally belonged to the cavalry and auxiliary cohorts, whereas horn players gave special signals to standard-bearers during the legion's tactical manoeuvres and are therefore frequently depicted standing near them.

In battle the sharp ringing sounds of the trumpets would have mingled with the dark coarse noise of the horns, the combined sound (*concentus*) of the instruments being designed to encourage the Roman ranks and to confuse the enemy (Livy, xxx, chap.33, §12; Tacitus, *Annals*, i, chap.68, §3). In the army hierarchy, the military musicians ranked among the 'non-commissioned officers' (*principales*); under Septimius Severus (AD 193–211), in order to improve their position, they formed themselves into bodies with common funds. This is attested by inscribed statutes (*leges*) and by membership lists of trumpeters and horn players of the 3rd Augustan Legion in Lambaesis (Numidia) (G. Wilmanns, ed.: *Inscriptiones Africae latinae*, Corpus inscriptionum latinarum, viii, Berlin, 1881, no.2557, p.295).

(*ii*) *Folksongs and work songs.* Literary references from several centuries show that the Romans had many folk- and work songs in everyday use (Varro, *Saturae Menippeae*, 363): singing and instrumental music provided a rhythmical accompaniment for rowing, reaping, treading grapes, weaving etc. Traditional folksongs of the following types are attested: table songs, songs of mourning (e.g. the *nenia*), lullabies, nursery rhymes, soldiers' victory songs, birthday and wedding songs (e.g. the *fescennini*), songs of love, joy, invective and satire. Satirical songs were popular in pre-literary times, as is shown by their prohibition in the Twelve Tables (the earliest Roman code of laws, drawn up in 451–450 BC); and they repeatedly served as mass political songs in the last days of the republic (e.g. Cicero, *Pro Sestio*, chap.55, §118).

(*iii*) *Entertainment and theatre.* After the expansion of the Roman Empire during the Punic Wars (3rd and 2nd centuries BC) and the annexation of kingdoms in the eastern Mediterranean (Macedonia, Syria and Egypt), the Hellenistic and oriental features in Roman music became more firmly established and widespread, and the following centuries saw the development of various genres of Roman theatrical, dance and entertainment music. In Rome, as early as 364 BC, Etruscan *histriones* or *ludiones* (actor dancers) performed pantomimic dances to the accompaniment of tibiae at a sacred festival; the young people of Rome were stimulated to emulate this (Livy, vii, chap.2, §3ff).

However, from the middle of the 3rd century BC, Roman theatrical music was decisively and increasingly influenced by the Greek theatre. Latin adaptations of Greek dramas were produced in Rome for the first time in 240 BC by Livius Andronicus, a Greek from Tarentum. Then Plautus (*c*254–184 BC) incorporated features of Hellenistic song and Euripidean monody,

together with the literary style of Greek comedies, in his Roman comedies, which included sung portions (*cantica*), monodies, duets and trios. *Tibicines* performed a prelude at the beginning, accompanied the *cantica* and various (spoken) verse passages of the actors and singers, and provided music between the acts as well as an accompaniment for dance interludes (*see* HELLENISTIC STATES, fig.1). *Tibicines* from the slave classes were commissioned to compose the accompanying music for Plautus's *Stichus* and for the five surviving comedies of Terence (*c*190–159 BC).

After the conquest of Macedonia in 167 BC and the destruction of Corinth in 146 BC, Greek actors and musicians came to Italy in vast numbers; initially they appeared in the triumphal games of Roman generals such as L. Anicius Gallus (167 BC) and L. Mummius (146 BC). Their organized guilds of 'Dionysiac artists' (*Dionysiaci artifices*, or in Greek *Synodoi tōn peri Dionyson technitōn*) included all the types of artist necessary for staging public festivals: tragic and comic poets and actors, musicians, players of the kithara and tibia, trumpeters and stage personnel. The existence of these organized bodies meant that Roman organizers of games (Sulla, Antonius etc, and later the emperors) could easily present musical and theatrical festivals; the latter increased in numbers and became more widely diffused in the early days of the empire and caused the founding of local theatrical organizations. The majority of the Dionysiac artists, predominantly Greeks, formed a guild, centred on Rome at least from the time of

3. *Trumpeter playing a straight tuba in the triumphal procession of Marcus Aurelius: relief from a ruined triumphal arch (2nd half of the 2nd century AD) now in the Palazzo dei Conservatori, Rome*

4. *Preparations for the performance of a satyr play: mosaic* (AD 62–79) *from Pompeii, now in the Museo Nazionale, Naples; the woman is playing the tibia*

Claudius (AD 41–54); they cultivated and disseminated theatrical and musical works in festivals, and also in the imperial cult, in all the larger cities of the empire. Augustus, Claudius, Hadrian, Septimius Severus, Caracalla and Diocletian (*d* AD 305) granted and confirmed their old privileges of immunity, freedom from taxation etc.

Following the example of the Greek musicians, Roman actors joined together as an organized body, the *parasiti Apollinis*, probably as early as the middle of the 2nd century BC, to improve their position in society. The growing number of theatrical and musical performances during state-sponsored games (such as the *ludi Romani*, *ludi Plebei* or *ludi Apollinares*) also helped to unite these artists. Despite their legally dishonourable status (*infamia*), some outstanding actors, such as Q. Roscius, and some foreign *pantomimi* enjoyed the favour of all classes in the early empire and were honoured by cities and communities issuing decrees and erecting statues in their honour (H. Dessau, ed., *Inscriptiones Latii veteris latinae*, Corpus inscriptionum latinarum, xiv, Berlin, 1887, no.2113, p.199; no.2977, p.319).

(*iv*) *Hellenistic song*. During the later days of the republic, Hellenistic art song was introduced to Rome with immediate success. Women playing string instruments of all kinds, among them harpists (*psaltriae sambucistriaeque*), and singers (*cantores*, both male and female) from Greece and Asia Minor performed lyric poems to instrumental accompaniment.

Vocal settings were made first of the elegies of Valerius Aedituus, Porcius Licinus and Q. Lutatius Catulus (late 2nd and early 1st century BC), and soon after of other genres of poetry. Virgil's *Eclogues* came to be interpreted by singers in the theatre; the hendecasyllables of Pliny the Younger (AD 62–113) were sung to the lyre or kithara (Pliny, *Epistulae*, vii, letter 4, §8) and similar performance may be assumed for some of the

lyric poems of Catullus (*c*87–54 BC) and the odes of Horace (65–8 BC).

Actor–singers and itinerant kitharodes appeared increasingly as performers of Greek music at public events, such as the musical competitions (*agones*) established at Rome by Nero in AD 60 and Domitian in AD 86. For their performances of Greek hymns, and of dramatic and pathetic solos from tragedies in concert performance, they received enormous fees (Suetonius, *Vespasian*, §19) and the privileges of honorary citizens. Their audiences praised virtuoso performances with enthusiastic applause and criticized mistakes (e.g. rhythmic inaccuracy). Emulating them, many amateurs (among them senators and emperors such as Caligula, Nero, Hadrian, Commodus, Elagabalus and Severus Alexander) cultivated singing and playing solo instruments (kithara, trumpet, tibiae, hydraulis, bagpipes, etc); they took instruction with famous virtuosos (e.g. Terpnus, Diodorus) and even competed, as did Nero, with professional artists in public (Suetonius, *Nero*, §§21ff). Some performers were also celebrated composers, like the Cretan kitharode Mesomedes, who served at the court of Hadrian.

(*v*) *Mime and pantomime*. From the beginning of the Augustan principate the pantomime enjoyed great popularity in Rome and Italy. Vocal and instrumental music was accompanied by foreign solo dancers representing mythological figures or individual characters, or miming well-known scenes from Greek tragedy. The instrumentation for these dancers ranged from a single pair of tibiae, preferred by the famous Alexandrian *pantomimus* Bathyllus, to an ensemble with chorus, which is supposed to have been introduced by his rival, Pylades of Cilicia, in 22 BC (Macrobius, *Saturnalia*, ii, chap. 7, §18).

The pantomime was further developed by dancers from Egypt, Syria and other provinces and during the empire acquired a stylized repertory of gestures and dance figures for the interpretation of mythological and dramatic material. Even in late classical times *pantomimi* were accompanied by the tibiae, syrinx, kithara and other instruments; the dancers, singers and instrumentalists were directed rhythmically by tibia players with foot-clappers (*scabillarii*; see fig. 5).

From the late republican period the mime was the most popular form of Roman theatre not only with slaves and freedmen, but also with citizens. Male and female *mimi* without masks realistically acted scenes from everyday life and also depicted events and characters borrowed in part from Greek comedy. That their acting was sometimes supplemented by interludes of dance and song is confirmed by stage instructions of the 2nd century AD which indicate the use of hand-clappers (crotala) and tambours (tympana) in the *Chariton* mime (B. P. Grenfell and A. S. Hunt, eds., *The Oxyrhynchus Papyri*, iii, London, 1903, no.413, pp.41ff).

(*vi*) *Other foreign influences.* After Roman campaigns and conquests in Greece and Asia Minor, the influx of foreign musical entertainers and street musicians increased in the 1st century BC. Chrysogonus, a wealthy favourite of Sulla, surrounded himself with singers and *tibicines* by day and night; at the health resort of Baiae the guests took pleasure in vocal and instrumental performances (*acroamata*), and Caesar also enjoyed music at table (Macrobius, *Saturnalia*, ii, chap.4, §28). It was mainly the hired slaves who sang and played string instruments at the domestic concerts of Roman music lovers.

The increasing luxury of the ruling classes attracted even larger numbers of foreign artists during the early days of the empire. Famous (and notorious) female dancers (*saltatrices*) from Egypt, Syria and Spain performed their exotic dances in taverns, on the street and in the squares to the varied accompaniment of crotala, cymbala, tympana and foreign wind instruments, like the Syrian *ambubaiae* (Horace, *Satirae* [= *Sermones*], i, 2, l.1). Their example, and the impetus which came from the theatrical dancing of the *pantomimi*, furthered dancing in all levels of society, despite the constant criticism of conservative Romans (Cicero, Seneca, Juvenal, Tacitus and others); dancing schools flourished, and the nobility employed dancing and music teachers.

The extent of the passion for dancing and music even in late Roman times can be seen from the frequent condemnation by early Christian ecclesiastical authors of popular music, and of the music of the theatre and the pagan cults, and also from the telling piece of information that, during the famine of AD 353, foreign tutors of general subjects had to leave Rome, whereas 3000 female dancers were allowed to remain in the city with their choirs and instructors (Ammianus Marcellinus, xiv, chap.6, §19).

4. INSTRUMENTS AND THEORY. The multifarious character of Roman musical life is reflected in the musical instruments, as pictorial representations, literary references and some surviving instruments show. The international musical culture of Rome, from the last days of the republic to the fall of the Western Roman Empire in AD 476, was stimulated by foreign influences fostered by trade and traffic, wars, and by the immigration of musicians, virtuosos and slaves who came to Italy and Rome from all the countries of the empire, importing their own instruments and music. The Romans adopted Etruscan, Greek and oriental instruments, and perfected and developed them. The number of strings on the lyre and kithara was increased and their bodies were enlarged (see fig.6); this was important for the art music of the virtuosos. The angle harp with a vertical soundbox, and the long-necked lute, originating in the orient and popular in late Roman times, were further developed by the Romans for use on public and domestic occasions. Frame drums or tambours (tympana), bronze cymbala and other percussion instruments were introduced to Rome with the Hellenistic mystery cults, and were used in the popular music of the theatre, the dance and entertainment in general. Small bells, foot-clappers and transverse flutes were used in the cult of Dionysus, and the sistrum and the Old Egyptian long flute were still used in the Isis cult. The combination of crotala and cymbals produced forked cymbals, whereas foot-clappers (scabella) were favoured for marking dance rhythms in the accompaniment of *pantomimi* (see fig.5 above). Military brass instruments of Etruscan origin (the tuba, lituus and cornu) were played by the Romans in processions, at funerals and public games (e.g. gladiatorial combats).

To increase its technical and acoustic possibilities,

5. *Musicians and dancers, probably entertaining guests at an inn: detail of a floor mosaic (end of the 3rd century* AD) *from the temple of Diana on the Aventine, now in the Museo Pio Clementino, Vatican City: the group includes a man playing the tibia and scabellum (left), two male dancers with cymbala, and a female dancer with two pairs of crotala in her raised hands*

6. Music lesson on a kithara: wall painting (1st century AD) from Herculaneum, now in the British Museum, London

the Phrygian or 'Berecyntian tibia', used mainly in the cults of Cybele and Dionysus and in the theatre, was given an attachment of movable metal rings (Horace, *De arte poetica*, l.203) by means of which the increased number of finger-holes of both pipes could be opened or closed for transposition (*see* METABOLĒ) when necessary (*see* AULOS, fig.3); this meant that the desired scale could be engaged more easily. Originals from Pompeii and Herculaneum and pictorial representations (reliefs and mosaics) demonstrate the technical refinement of this widely used wind instrument.

The organ (hydraulis), an invention attributed to Ctesibius, an Alexandrian engineer (3rd century BC), later came into favour as an instrument for domestic music at Rome and in the provinces, and because of its loud volume it was also used in amphitheatres (*see* HYDRAULIS, fig.1, and ORGAN, §IV, 1). It was supplemented with a register-like series of open and stopped pipes in various scales (as in the organ of Aquincum near Budapest, dating from AD 228; *see* ORGAN, §IV, fig.23); in the 4th century AD, portable pneumatic (bellows) organs were also developed.

Solo instrumental music was practised in public and private by famous virtuosos and by Roman amateurs with the aim of achieving artistic perfection. Groups of instrumentalists formed small ensembles to accompany singers or dancers, or larger ensembles (after the fashion of Alexandria and the orient) to perform in theatres (Seneca, *Epistulae morales*, 84, 10) and at popular spectacles (Vopiscus Carinus, 19, 2).

Some Romans tried to make the heritage of Greek music theory their own, to propagate it in their writings and to make it available for other disciplines (rhetoric, architecture and medicine). Music was accorded its distinguished position in the educational system of the liberal arts as early as the 1st century BC by Varro (116–27 BC), in more detail by St Augustine (late 4th century AD) and, in allegorical guise, by Martianus

Capella (early 5th century AD).

The poet–philosopher Lucretius (*c*98–55 BC) devoted himself to the history and psychology of music. Cicero (106–43 BC) frequently recommended that orators should receive musical training, and expounded Stoic and Epicurean musical aesthetics. The architect Vitruvius (*c*84–14 BC) described the acoustic problems of theatre construction (*see* ACOUSTICS, §I, 7) and organ building, and Quintilian (AD *c*35–96) dealt with voice training and musical delivery by orators.

In some later Latin writers on music, such as Censorinus (3rd century AD) and Macrobius, there is a widening gulf between theory and contemporary practice, for neo-Platonic and neo-Pythagorean influence prompted a tendency towards a mathematical, speculative and mystical attitude. Boethius (*c*480–524) and Isidore of Seville (*c*560–636), however, applied an encyclopedic method to traditional classical theories of music and harmonics; thus they transmitted some of the definitions, classifications and harmonic knowledge of Greek and Roman antiquity to the Middle Ages.

See also ETRURIA; GREECE, §I; HELLENISTIC STATES.

BIBLIOGRAPHY

GENERAL

H. Abert: 'Musik', *Darstellungen aus der Sittengeschichte Roms in der Zeit von Augustus bis zum Ausgang der Antonine*, ed. L. Friedlaender, ii (Leipzig, 1863, 10/1922/*R*1964), 163

O. Tiby: *La musica in Grecia e a Roma* (Florence, 1942), 149ff

A. Machabey: 'Musique latine', *La musique des origines à nos jours*, ed. N. Dufourcq (Paris, 1946, rev., enlarged, 3/1959)

F. Behn: *Musikleben im Altertum und frühen Mittelalter* (Stuttgart, 1954), 79–142

M. Wegner: 'Etrurien', *MGG*

J. E. Scott: 'Roman Music', *NOHM*, i (1957), 404

G. Fleischhauer: *Etrurien und Rom*, Musikgeschichte in Bildern, ii/5 (Leipzig, 1964)

G. Wille: *Musica romana* (Amsterdam, 1967) [with detailed documentation of sources and extensive bibliography]

SPECIFIC SUBJECTS

F. Behn: 'Die Musik im römischen Heere', *Mainzer Zeitschrift*, vii (1912), 36

F. Celentano: 'La musica presso i romani', *RMI*, xx (1913), 243, 494

H. Bier: *De saltatione pantomimorum* (diss., U. of Bonn, 1917; Brühl, 1921)

G. Kenneth and G. Henry: 'Roman Actors', *Studies in Philology*, xvi (1919), 334–82

H. Wagenvoort: 'Pantomimus und Tragödie im augusteischen Zeitalter', *Neue Jahrbücher für das klassische Altertum*, xxiii (1920), 101

A. Krumbacher: *Die Stimmbildung der Redner im Altertum bis auf die Zeit Quintilians* (diss., U. of Würzburg, 1920)

M. Rostovtzeff: *The Social and Economic History of the Roman Empire* (Oxford, 1926, 2/1957)

F. Weege: *Der Tanz in der Antike* (Halle, 1926)

F. Marx: 'Römische Volkslieder', *Rheinisches Museum*, lxxviii (1929), 398

J. Quasten: *Musik und Gesang in den Kulten der heidnischen Antike und christlichen Frühzeit*, Liturgiegeschichtliche Quellen und Forschungen, xxv (1930), 78–157

E. Wüst: 'Mimos', *Paulys Real-Encyclopädie der classischen Altertumswissenschaft*, 1st ser., xv (Stuttgart, 1931–2), 1727

A. Machabey: 'Etudes de musicologie pré-médiévale', *RdM*, xvi (1935), 64, 129, 213; xvii (1936), 1

W. Gordziejew: *Ludi scaenici et circenses quid in rebus publicis antiquorum valuerint* (diss., U. of Warsaw, 1936)

M. Pallottino: 'La musica', *Mostra Augustea della Romanità*, ed. O. Giglioli (Rome, 3/1937–8), 792

M. Bieber: *The History of the Greek and Roman Theater* (Princeton, 1939, 2/1961)

B. Varneke: *Istoriya antichnovo teatra* (Moscow, 1940)

U. Kahrstedt: *Kulturgeschichte der römischen Kaiserzeit* (Munich, 1944, 2/1958)

O. Weinreich: *Epigrammstudien, i: Epigramm und Pantomimus* (Heidelberg, 1948)

M. Lenchantin de Gubernatis: 'Lirica e musica nel dramma latino', *Università degli studi di Pavia* (1948–9), 15

E. Wüst: 'Pantomimus', *Paulys Real-Encyclopädie der classischen Altertumswissenschaft*, 1st ser., xviii (Stuttgart, 1939–49), 843

W. M. A. Beare: *The Roman Stage: a Short History of Latin Drama in* the Time of the Republic (London, 1950, 2/1955)

H. Wiemken: Der griechische Mimus: Aufführungspraxis der griechischen Mimen in der Kaiserzeit (diss., U. of Göttingen, 1951)

G. E. Duckworth: The Nature of Roman Comedy: a Study in Popular Entertainment (Princeton, 1952)

I. S. Ryberg: Rites of the State Religion in Roman Art, Memoirs of the American Academy in Rome, xxii (Rome, 1955)

H. G. Marek: Der Schauspieler in seiner gesellschaftlichen und rechtlichen Stellung im alten Rom (Vienna, 1956)

W. M. A. Beare: Latin Verse and European Song (London, 1957)

K. Büchner: Römische Literaturgeschichte (Stuttgart, 1957)

M. P. Nilsson: The Dionysiac Mysteries of the Hellenistic and Roman Age (Lund, 1957)

V. Rotolo: Il pantomimus: studi e testi (Palermo, 1957)

M. Kokolakis: 'Pantomimus and the Treatise Peri orchēseōs', Platōn, x (1959), 3–56

G. Fleischhauer: Die Musikergenossenschaften im hellenistisch-römischen Altertum: Beiträge zum Musikleben der Römer (diss., U. of Halle, 1959)

R. Benz: Unfreie Menschen als Musiker und Schauspieler in der römischen Welt (diss., U. of Tübingen, 1961)

E. Paratore: 'Plaute et la musique', Maske und Kothurn: Vierteljahrsschrift für Theaterwissenschaft, xv (1969), 131

D. P. Kallistov: Antichny teatr (Leningrad, 1970; Ger. trans., 1974), 187–206

A. Baudot: Musiciens romains de l'antiquité (Montreal, 1973)

G. Wille: 'Aufstieg und Niedergang der römischen Musik', Aufstieg und Niedergang der römischen Welt, ed. H. Temporini, i/4 (Berlin and New York, 1973), 971

A. Baudot: 'La tradition musicale à Rome', Cahiers des études anciennes, iii (1974), 5

G. Wille: Einführung in das römische Musikleben (Darmstadt, 1977)

ORGANOLOGY

A. Howard: 'The Aulos or Tibia', Harvard Studies in Classical Philology, iv (1893), 1–60

H. Degering: Die Orgel: ihre Erfindung und ihre Geschichte bis zur Karolingerzeit (Münster, 1905)

H. J. W. Tillyard: 'Instrumental Music in the Roman Age', Journal of Hellenic Studies, xxvii (1907), 160

F. Behn: 'Die Laute im Altertum und frühen Mittelalter', ZMw, i (1918–19), 89

A. Voigt: 'Die Signalinstrumente des römischen Heeres und der Lituus', Deutsche Instrumentenbauzeitung, xxxiv (1933), 347

T. Norlind: 'Lyra und Kithara in der Antike', STMf, xvi (1934), 76

W. Vetter: 'Tibia', Paulys Real-Encyclopädie der classischen Altertumswissenschaft, 2nd ser., vi/1 (Stuttgart, 1936), 808

C. Sachs: The History of Musical Instruments (New York, 1940), 128

U. Schweitzer: 'Eine selten grosse Glocke', Ur-Schweiz, x (1946), 18

W. Apel: 'Early History of the Organ', Speculum, xxiii (1948), 191

H. Hickmann: 'Cymbales et crotales dans l'Égypte ancienne', Annales du service des antiquités de l'Egypte, xlix (1949), 451

H. G. Farmer: 'An Early Greek Pandore', Journal of the Royal Asiatic Society (1949), 177

H. Hickmann: 'The Antique Cross-flute', AcM, xxiv (1952), 108

T. Schneider: 'Organum hydraulicum', Mf, vii (1954), 24

A. Buchner: Hudební nástroje od pravěku k dnešku [Musical instruments through the ages] (Prague, 1956; Eng. trans., 1956, 4/1962)

R. P. Winnington-Ingram: 'The Pentatonic Tuning of the Greek Lyre', Classical Quarterly, l (1956), 169

Z. Raheva-Morfova: 'Instruments de musique de l'antiquité dans les trouvailles archéologiques de Bulgarie', Bulletin de l'Institut de musique Sofia, v (1959), 77–122

G. Fleischhauer: 'Bucina und Cornu', Wissenschaftliche Zeitschrift der Martin-Luther-Universität Halle, ix/4 (1960), 501

F. Harrison and J. Rimmer: European Musical Instruments (London, 1964)

J. Perrot: L'orgue d ses origines hellénistiques à la fin du XIIIᵉ siècle (Paris, 1965; Eng. trans., 1971)

H. Becker: Zur Entwicklungsgeschichte der antiken und mittelalterlichen Rohrblattinstrumente (Hamburg, 1966)

V. Cosma: 'Archäologische musikalische Funde in Rumänien', BMw, viii (1966), 3

W. Walcker-Mayer: Die römische Orgel von Aquincum (Stuttgart, 1970)

M. Klar: 'Musikinstrumente der Römerzeit in Bonn', Bonner Jb, clxxi (1971), 301

G. Tintori: Gli strumenti musicali (Turin, 1971), 561f

B. Janda: 'Blechblasinstrumente des römischen Heeres', Listy filologicke, xcvi (1973), 217

W. Stauder: Alte Musikinstrumente (Brunswick, 1973)

M. Kaba: Die römische Orgel von Aquincum (Budapest, 1976)

MUSIC THEORY

C. Schmidt: Quaestiones de musicis scriptoribus romanis (diss., U. of Giessen, 1899; Darmstadt, 1899)

H. Abert: Die Musikanschauung des Mittelalters und ihre Grundlagen (Halle, 1905/R1964)

H. Edelstein: Die Musikanschauung Augustins nach seiner Schrift De musica (diss., U. of Freiburg, 1929)

T. Gérold: Les pères de l'église et la musique (Paris and Strasbourg, 1931)

G. Pietzsch: Die Musik im Erziehungs- und Bildungsideal des ausgehenden Altertums und frühen Mittelalters (Halle, 1932/R1968)

C. Bouvet: 'Censorinus et la musique', RdM, xiv (1933), 65

R. Schäfke: Geschichte der Musikästhetik in Umrissen (Berlin, 1934/R1964)

H. I. Marrou: Mousikos anēr: étude sur les scènes de la vie intellectuelle figurant sur les monuments funéraires romains (Grenoble, 1938/R1964)

O. Gombosi: Tonarten und Stimmungen der antiken Musik (Copenhagen, 1939, 2/1951)

L. Schrade: 'Music in the Philosophy of Boethius', MQ, xxxiii (1947), 188

P. R. Coleman-Norton: 'Cicero musicus', JAMS, i (1948), 3

H. Antcliffe: 'What Music meant to the Romans', ML, xxx (1949), 337

H. I. Marrou: Histoire de l'éducation dans l'antiquité (Paris, 1950, 6/1965)

G. Wille: 'Zur Musikalität der alten Römer', AMw, xi (1954), 71

H. Hüschen: Untersuchungen zu den Textkonkordanzen im Musikschrifttum des Mittelalters (Habilitationsschrift, U. of Cologne, 1955)

A. Neubecker: Die Bewertung der Musik bei Stoikern und Epikureern (Berlin, 1956)

H. Potiron: Boethius, théoricien de la musique grecque (Paris, 1961)

G. Wille: 'Quintilian', MGG

J. Mountford: 'Music and the Romans', Bulletin of the John Rylands Library, xlvii (1965), 198

L. Richter: 'Griechische Traditionen im Musikschrifttum der Römer', AMw, xxii (1965), 69

G. Wille: 'Vitruv', MGG

U. Mueller: 'Zur musikalischen Terminologie der antiken Rhetorik', AMw, xxvi (1969), 29, 105

E. Pöhlmann: Denkmäler altgriechischer Musik: Sammlung, Übertragung und Erläuterung aller Fragmente (Nuremberg, 1970)

II. The Christian era

1. The Middle Ages. 2. The Renaissance and Baroque. 3. Secular music and early opera. 4. Publishing. 5. The Accademia di S Cecilia. 6. Other concerts. 7. Opera. 8. Other institutions.

1. THE MIDDLE AGES. The earliest history of music in Rome after the official establishment of Christianity is intimately bound up with the growing influence of the papacy and its institutions. Constantine's edict of 313 need not have directly affected the practice of secular music still continuing in Rome; that practice, however, strongly opposed by Christian writers, soon dwindled because of the opposition and because the city, no longer seat of the imperial court, was undergoing a rapid deterioration of its social structures and economic conditions.

From the second half of the 4th century various popes laid down rules about texts and melodies to be sung during the liturgical year and ways to perform them. The terms in which the repetitive reports are cast ('similarly he [the pope] issued an annual edict on singing' is a typical phrase) suggest a flexible tradition, adjusted to changing conditions and needs, or to each pope's view of those needs. Parallel to this, the popes' concern for the availability and quality of their singers slowly shaped what was later known as the Schola Cantorum, whose final organization is traditionally credited to Gregory the Great (590–604). The Schola, near the residence of the pope in the Lateran Palace and the adjacent basilica of St John, comprised adult singers (paraphonistae) and boys (pueri paraphonistae). It thus provided for the training of new singers besides being at hand for the functions attended or organized by the pope. Boys who were taught there, chosen from those who showed outstanding musical gifts, received a com-

7. *Bernini's apse in the church of S Lorenzo in Damaso: painting attributed to G. P. Pannini in the Museo di Roma; the apse was commissioned by Cardinal Francesco Barberini to serve as an auditorium for ecclesiastical music and was inaugurated in 1640; music by Corelli and his contemporaries was performed there under the patronage of Cardinal Ottoboni (the apse was destroyed by fire in the 19th century)*

plete education in all the principal scholastic subjects; several of the 7th-century popes who were remembered for their fine musicianship had started their ecclesiastical career as pupils in the Schola. The youngest members are also known to have taken a prominent part as early as the end of the papacy of John VIII (872–82) in some secular events, singing joyous or burlesque songs at the popular feasts of the Carnival, mid-Lent and Whit Sunday.

The Lateran Schola became the model for other similar institutions; in Rome it was soon followed by a Vatican school at St Peter's. Its singing came also to be regarded as the model on which the unification of liturgical singing, fervently advocated by the Carolingian emperors after the restoration of the empire in the West (800), should be based. There is considerable debate, however, as to whether the liturgical repertory commonly known as Gregorian chant (after Gregory the Great) actually originated in Rome or was of Frankish origin. To this problem another is related: the historical assessment of the so-called Old Roman chant, a liturgical repertory apparently earlier than the Gregorian, yet recorded in Roman sources of the 11th century to the 13th (*see* GREGORIAN AND OLD ROMAN CHANT).

It has also been debated whether liturgical singing in Rome was purely monophonic or admitted polyphonic procedures of some sort. The latter opinion, formerly bearing almost exclusively on the use of the term 'paraphonista' (which may or may not have been related to the singing in 4ths or 5ths), is now strengthened by various documents referring to a practice of evidently improvised organum, the earliest of which dates from the 11th century, about the time when Guido of Arezzo described organum in parallel 4ths and 5ths as a current practice. There can be no truth in the assertion that Guido of Arezzo settled in Rome in 1027 and intended to establish a specific singing school there; in his *Epistola de ignoto cantu* he stated that, having been invited to Rome by Pope John XIX (probably after 1027), he agreed to come back for a second visit (of which there is no record) to further expound his teaching methods to the pope and clergy.

The gradual decline of the Schola Cantorum led to its complete cessation during the period when the papal seat was transferred to Avignon (1309–77), and it was altogether suppressed by Urban V in 1370. Only a small part of its functions and its importance was inherited by the chapel at Avignon, which cultivated French polyphony almost exclusively. Only adult singers were employed, many of whom also had a reputation as composers; even after the return of the popes to Italy the singers were mostly non-Italians. A stormy period in ecclesiastical history followed (until almost the mid-15th century), during which the *cappella*, part of the pope's personal retinue, rarely had its centre permanently in Rome; it was thus unable to exercise any real artistic influence locally, although it had sometimes among its members artists of international renown such as Dufay (1428–33 and 1435–7).

The *cappella* was definitively brought back to Rome in 1443 by Pope Eugene IV, whose relatively long papacy (1431–47) contributed to give it a more stable basis. The principle was established that its personnel should not have to be completely renewed each time a new pope was elected (the first of a series of privileges granted by the popes or set by custom). At the same time demands for ecclesiastical reform repeatedly advocated by various councils must have influenced the *cappella* repertory, favouring simple polyphonic elaborations of liturgical melodies, either composed or improvised. These restrictions, which did not completely exclude more artistic kinds of polyphony, may have been the starting-point of later special traditions of the *cappella*, such as unaccompanied singing and *falsobordone*.

Outside the *cappella papale* the most noteworthy musical events in Rome about which there is information are those of a popular religious character connected with the activities of the numerous religious fraternities which had arisen during the second half of the 13th century on the model of those of Umbria and Tuscany. In Rome, too, the singing of religious *laude* practised by the fraternities soon gave rise to the so-called *devozioni* (sung and acted dramatic scenes). The words of a few of these popular religious dramas performed in the 14th and 15th centuries have survived, though without music; the most extensive is a *Lauda in decollatio Sancti Johannis Baptistae*. The custom prevailed for a long time; as late as 1490 the Arciconfraternità del Gonfalone, in which all the most ancient fraternities had become united, was granted permission to use the Colosseum for the staging of the grandiose *rappresentazioni* of the Passion, held most years on Good Friday before a great crowd. Other sacred dramas were enacted near the basilicas of St John Lateran and St Peter until Paul III put an end to them in 1539 by an interdict. The *rappresentazione* which the Florentines were allowed to organize every year on 24 June, the day of their patron saint, was mounted on floats.

On special occasions, such as the translation to St Peter's of St Andrew's head (1462) or the state visit of Ercole I d'Este, Duke of Ferrara (1471), wealthy people whose houses stood along the route of the procession or parade displayed special decorations and had classical allegories enacted with singing (particularly by boys) and instrumental music. Cardinals who distinguished themselves for the secular splendour of their way of life (e.g. Rodrigo Borgia, Pietro Riario, Francesco Gonzaga) must have had musicians in their retinue; about 1490 Cardinal Ascanio Sforza had in his service Josquin and Serafino Aquilano, respectively the most famous representatives of that time of the elaborate polyphony in the Franco-Flemish style and of the humanistic tradition of monodic singing with lyre or lute accompaniment.

2. THE RENAISSANCE AND BAROQUE. The humanistic taste for artistic refinement induced Pope Sixtus IV (1471–84) to give the *cappella papale* a new impetus, strengthening its organization and increasing the number of its singers first to 20 and later to 24; above all he increased its status by having a new *cappella grande* (later the Cappella Sistina) built in the Vatican palace, and by having official daily functions performed there by the chapel independently from those held in private for the pope. An international, select body of musicians in a position of privilege and authority, the *cappella* was to set exacting standards which deeply affected the development of the Roman polyphony in the 16th century, leading to the exquisite contrapuntal refinement and spiritualized expressive restraint of Palestrina's music, in turn the model for the Baroque ideal of a *stile antico* (*stylus gravis*, *prima prattica*) as opposed to the expressive freedom of the *stile moderno* (*stylus luxurians*, *seconda prattica*).

Sixtus IV planned to improve the music of St Peter's, which during the entire 15th century had consisted of organ playing and singing by no more than four singers. His idea, the establishment of a musical *cappella* separate from the papal one, was not carried out until 1513, when Julius II assigned to the new *cappella*, which took its name (Cappella Giulia) from him, the revenues required to maintain 12 singers and 12 scholars, with two masters of music and grammar. This pope was particularly anxious that the school thus constituted should help to prepare singers, who until then had been recruited from abroad, for the *cappella papale*. Nevertheless, it was not until 1539 that Arcadelt was appointed as its first *maestro de' putti*, and in 1551 Palestrina was the first to bear the title of *maestro di cappella della basilica Vaticana*. The most famous *maestri* to follow him were Virgilio Mazzocchi (1629–46), Orazio Benevoli (1646–72), Domenico Scarlatti (1715–19) and Niccolò Jommelli (1749–53). Famous organists in St Peter's included Ercole Pasquini (1597–1608) and Girolamo Frescobaldi (1608–28 and 1633–43).

Following the example of the Vatican, other *cappelle* arose in various Roman churches during the most glorious era of Italian sacred polyphony. The *cappella* of St John Lateran was founded in 1535 by Cardinal de Cupis; Palestrina became *maestro di cappella* there (1555–61) after his dismissal from the Vatican. The *cappella* at the Basilica Liberiana (S Maria Maggiore) was founded about the same time as that of St John Lateran; among its children listed from 1537 (earlier records are lost) was Palestrina, whose masters there were Robin Mallapert and possibly Firmin Lebel. It counted among its most famous *maestri* Palestrina (1561–7), G. M. Nanino (1567–75), Domenico Allegri (1610–29), A. M. Abbatini (1640–45 and 1649–57) and Alessandro Scarlatti (1707–9).

The churches of S Lorenzo in Damaso, SS Apostoli, S Luigi dei Francesi and S Giovanni dei Fiorentini also had musical *cappelle* before long; and other religious establishments practised and taught music, such as the Seminario Romano and the Ospedale di S Spirito in Saxia, where, following an old custom, the infirm were entertained with musical performances. The teaching of music had particular importance at the Collegio Germanico, whose students were to exert their ministry in face of a Protestant opposition and were expected to learn to perform the Catholic rites with maximum liturgical precision and artistic decorum. The college was

8. *Interior of the 16th-century Oratorio del Gonfalone*

also attended by Italian pupils, many of whom became distinguished performers and composers; its most important teachers were Victoria (1573–7), Annibale Stabile (1578–90) and Carissimi (1629–74). For recreation as well as religious edification music was cultivated at the oratories of S Girolamo della Carità and of S Maria in Vallicella, both founded by S Filippo Neri, and at the Oratorio del Crocifisso; from their practices a new genre of religious dramatic music, the oratorio, arose, soon imitated by other institutions, among them the old Arciconfraternità del Gonfalone with its newly built and beautifully decorated oratory (fig.8). The composition of oratorios, of which there are examples both in Latin (at the Crocifisso) and in the vernacular (at the Neri oratories), reached a peak in those of Carissimi, while with Stradella the genre developed towards a more dramatic and therefore more operatic style. While Carissimi represents the culmination of the Latin oratorio in the musical practice of the Oratorio del Crocifisso, Stradella's oratorios continued and developed a stylistic trend which had its antecedents in the Phillipine *laude*, in Cavalieri's *Rappresentatione di Anima, et di Corpo* (1600) and in the *dialoghi* of Anerio's *Teatro armonico spirituale* (1619). At the time of Stradella, however, the vernacular oratorio blending operatic and instrumental stylistic features was prevalent, for example in those of G. O. Pitoni and Ercole Bernabei. At the beginning of the 18th century Alessandro Scarlatti's oratorios represented a perfect blend of these stylistic features.

Churches and oratories were the schools which trained not only the masters of sacred music but also the composers and performers of madrigals and of many of the early operas. Details of schools run privately, apart from those attached to the churches, mostly come from later records or interpretations of documents. Nicola Vicentino kept a small private school about 1549; but his teaching, which originated in an acrimonious dispute on the part of this would-be restorer of the ancient Greek scales, had no appreciable direct results. Information about the methods of teaching is given by G. A. Bontempi, a pupil of Mazzocchi:

The Roman schools asked the pupils to spend an hour every day singing difficult, arduous pieces, . . . a second practising the shake and a third practising passages; another studying literature and still another singing exercises before a mirror with the master listening [to them]. . . . In the afternoon half an hour was given to music theory; another half to counterpoint [?improvised] on a cantus firmus; an hour . . . to written counterpoint [contrapunto sopra la cartella]; and the remainder of the day to practising the harpsichord and composition.

The study of music was often begun at a very tender age: Pitoni, afterwards the master of Durante and Leo, was sent at the age of five to learn music from Pompeo Natali at S Maria Maggiore. Those who chiefly devoted themselves to vocal teaching in the second half of the 17th century included Giuseppe and F. M. Fede and Giuseppe Amadori, a pupil of Agostini.

3. SECULAR MUSIC AND EARLY OPERA. The brilliance of social life in Rome was accompanied by intense activity in secular music. Ballet, dance and dance music are reflected in one of the most famous treatises of the Renaissance, *Il ballarino* (Venice, 1581, 1605 ed. as *La nobiltà di dame*) by the Roman master Fabritio Caroso. The most famous representatives of Roman sacred polyphony, including Palestrina, wrote madrigals and canzonettas, in spite of restraints put on such activities by their being employed as papal or church musicians. Marenzio's output, unrestricted by his connection with Cardinal Luigi d'Este, was almost exclusively madrigalistic. Female singers often took part in the

singing of secular polyphony, and seem also to have developed highly sophisticated styles of solo performance, in which Vittoria Archilei, who later followed Cardinal Ferdinando de' Medici to Florence and had an active part in the transition from polyphony to accompanied monody, was not alone. Even during the 17th century a number of female singers well known throughout Italy were given the surname 'Romana' or 'Romanina' because of their provenance.

The first operatic performances in Rome were, as before at Florence, sumptuous private entertainments enacted in the palaces of the most powerful Roman families. The Barberini family was particularly lavish and gave a long series of spectacles (1631–43 and again 1653–6) either in the family's splendid new palace at the Quattro Fontane or in the Palazzo della Cancelleria, residence of Cardinal Barberini, secretary of state to his uncle, Urban VIII; these included operas by Virgilio Mazzocchi, Marco Marazzoli and Luigi Rossi, elaborately staged by Lorenzo Bernini. There is a complaint in a satire by Salvator Rosa that the singers who had impersonated Phyllis or Chloris in the evening would the next morning take part in a church service. The fact is that even before Innocent XI decided to enforce Sixtus V's decree against women acting on stage, female roles had often been interpreted by castratos, quite numerous in Rome from the end of the 16th century; thus, for instance, the parts of Angelica and Bradamante in Rossi's *Il palazzo incantato* were entrusted in 1642 to the two most famous male sopranos of the time, Loreto Vittori (himself an opera composer) and

Marc'Antonio Pasqualini, both singers in the Cappella Sistina.

Other private or semi-private theatres (privacy, real or nominal, helped to circumvent papal opposition to female singers) were inaugurated in the late 1660s by Prince Lorenzo Onofrio Colonna and Marquis Pompeo Capranica. In 1669 Clement IX, who as Monsignor Giulio Rospigliosi had been the librettist of almost all the Barberini operas, authorized Count Giacomo d'Alibert, gentleman of the exiled Queen Christina of Sweden, to erect a theatre intended for the public performance of operas. The Teatro Tordinona was opened in 1670 with Cavalli's *Scipione Africano* (which had already been given in Venice in 1664), with a prologue and additional numbers by Stradella. The theatre, opposed by Clement IX's successors, was closed in 1674 but reopened from 1690 to 1697 when it was pulled down; its rebuilding in 1733 reflected the changing attitude of the papacy. The gaps in its activity encouraged further private performances and the building of two more private theatres, one built by Carlo Fontana in 1684 in the palace of Cardinal Benedetto Pamphili, and the other about 1708 in the Palazzo della Cancelleria by Filippo Juvarra for Cardinal Pietro Ottoboni. Both cardinals wrote opera librettos, and Ottoboni's academies at the Cancelleria were highpoints of Roman musical life at the end of the century.

Queen Christina, who lived in Rome from 1654 until her death in 1689, initiated frequent musical performances in her palace (now Corsini) with such musicians resident in Rome as Corelli, Pasquini and

9. Design by Filippo Juvarra for a staged performance of an oratorio in the grand salon, Sala Riaria, of Cardinal Pietro Ottoboni's Palazzo della Cancelleria (Biblioteca Nazionale, Turin)

10. Ballet of nymphs and shepherds at the House of the Falconieris during Carnival 1634: engraving by Andrea Sacchi in Vitale Mascardi's 'Festa fatta in Roma' (1635)

11. Set (showing the banks of the Tiber, St Peter's and the Castello S Angelo) for the final scene of Marco Marazzoli's opera 'La vita humana', performed in 1656 in the Barberini palace at the Quattro Fontane, in honour of Queen Christina of Sweden: etching by G. B. Galestruzzi after G. F. Grimaldi

Alessandro Scarlatti. Most of the musical performances around the turn of the century are bound to the name Francesco Maria Ruspoli; among those in his service were Margherita Durastanti and Antonio Caldara (*maestro di cappella* 1709–16), who wrote both oratorios and operas to be performed in Ruspoli's palaces on the Corso, the Palazzo S Maria in Aracoeli and the Palazzo Bonelli in Piazza SS Apostoli (because it held a large number of people) and in the gardens of his villa near S Matteo in Merulana all'Equilino. During his stay in Rome, Handel wrote *Il trionfo del Tempo e del Disinganno*, *Il delirio amoroso* and *La Resurrezione* for Ruspoli. Another example of musical patronage in Rome during this period (though much less conspicuous) is that of Maria Casimiri of Poland, in whose palace theatre at Trinità de' Monti operas by Domenico Scarlatti were performed from 1710 to 1714, the young composer being in the service of the often insolvent queen.

In the 18th century the Teatro Tordinona, devoted mainly to serious opera after its reconstruction, was subject to the competition of other theatres. The Teatro Capranica, after serving for private performances, was opened to the public in 1695; from 1711 to 1747 serious operas were given there, but after its reopening in 1754 it served for comic opera. The Teatro delle Dame, built in 1717 by Count d'Alibert's son, for a century divided the honours of *opera seria* production with the Teatro Argentina, built in 1732 by Duke Giuseppe Sforza-Cesarini (see fig.12). The Teatro Pace and the Teatro Valle were musically less important; according to the reports of foreign visitors, these theatres, although among the largest in Europe, were not well kept or decorated. Even so, the managers and the papal government were often troubled over the disputes that arose between Roman families or foreign ambassadors over the appropriation of the best boxes. Performances at first took place only in the Carnival, but later were also allowed in the autumn and spring.

Among the many cantata composers, Luigi Rossi, Carissimi, Stradella and Alessandro Scarlatti are the most famous. Celebratory pieces were performed either indoors or on terraces and in gardens, including those of the splendid summer residences on the hills surrounding the city: groups of singers and instrumentalists were often mounted on floats and brought to perform serenades under the windows of friendly listeners. Instrumental music was extensively practised in the form of solo violin sonatas, trio sonatas and compositions for larger (occasionally very large) groups, where the music was often played with small and large groups in alternation (later the basic principle of the concerto grosso). Distinguished composers and performers were Carlo Caproli and Carlo Mannelli, both called 'del violino', C. A. Lonati, Lelio Colista and above all Arcangelo Corelli, a protégé of cardinals Pamphili and Ottoboni. Corelli spent most of his life in the service of Cardinal Ottoboni as well as in that of Queen Christina, devoting himself mostly to the practice of pure instrumental music, writing compositions which he elaborated and polished before publishing; his compositions became in this way the first example of 'classical' instrumental music, and were imitated throughout Europe during the rest of the century.

4. PUBLISHING. The very active musical life during the 16th and 17th centuries was reflected in a remarkable activity in music printing. After those issued in Venice by Petrucci, the earliest publications of musical works were printed in Rome, from 1510 onwards, by Andrea Antico. In 1518 Antico became associated with the Florentine Jacopo Giunta, who later also financed G. G. Pasotti and the brothers Dorico of Brescia. During the second half of the 16th century and in the 17th century there followed Antonio Barré, Paolo Masotti, L. A. Soldi, G. B. Robletti, Bartolomeo Zannetti, the Mascardi family and G. G. Komarek. Roman printing is also noteworthy for the introduction of copperplate engraving instead of composition with movable type; this was begun in 1586 by Simone Verovio, who was followed by Niccolò Muzio and Nicolò Borboni.

5. THE ACCADEMIA DI S CECILIA. The foundation of one of the most important Roman musical institutions, the Congregazione dei Musici di Roma (later the Accademia di S Cecilia) is traditionally given as 1566. In a decree dated 1 May 1585 Sixtus V converted the canonical sanction granted by Gregory XIII into a public assignment. The names of Felice Anerio as its first director and 19 of its members (among them Palestrina, Marenzio, the brothers Nanino, Annibale Stabile, Annibale Zoilo, Ruggiero Giovannelli, Francesco Soriano and Paolo Quagliati) are in a collection of madrigals published in 1589, entitled *Le gioie: Madrigali a cinque voci di diversi eccellomi musici della Compagnia di Roma* (*RISM* 1589[7]).

Housed at first in the Church of S Maria della Rotonda (the Pantheon), the company had its seat by 1622 at S Paolo Decollato, a church of the Barnabites in the Piazza Colonna, and later in the churches of S Cecilia in Trastevere (1652), S Nicolò dei Cesarini (1661) and S Maria Maddalena. In 1685 it moved to another Barnabite church, S Carlo ai Catinari, where it erected a chapel of its own. Its chief aims were that of mutual assistance, both material and spiritual, and public charity; but evidently its activities were accompanied from the beginning by attempts to establish a monopoly on the musical profession, immediately resented by the papal singers. A decree of 1624 by which Urban VIII had conceded to the Congregazione the supervision of musical education and publications of sacred music was revoked two years later. But in 1684 all musicians except papal singers were bound by papal decree to observe the statutes of the Congregazione, whose licence was necessary for exercising the profession; despite opposition, the decree was renewed in 1716 and 1794. Those qualified for admission were *maestri di cappella*, organists, public singers and instrumentalists. Corelli was head of the instrumental section in 1700.

The Congregazione deteriorated during the early decades of the 19th century because of political events and the general decline of church music. About 1839 it assumed the title of Accademia and gradually transformed into a cultural institution with greater opportunity for national and international contacts; honorary membership was conferred on musicians of various countries representing a broader spectrum of musical activities (including female singers and dancers). After two futile attempts to found a music school (1847 and 1857) two young members, Giovanni Sgambati and Ettore Pinelli, opened free courses for the piano and the violin in the building of the Accademia (then in the via Ripetta); this paved the way for the establishment of a

Liceo Musicale, inaugurated on 3 March 1876 in the Accademia's later home, the ex-convent of the Ursulines between via dei Greci and via Vittoria. The library of the Accademia was opened to the public in 1878; in 1882 it received a government section comprising the Orsini collection (acquired by the state in 1875) and 16th-century and later music from various Roman libraries and suppressed monasteries, thus forming the Biblioteca Musicale Governativa S Cecilia, one of the most important music collections in Italy. The Liceo was transformed in 1919 into a state conservatory, but the Accademia reserved for itself the organization of special finishing courses.

The building of a large concert hall equipped with a concert organ made it possible for the Accademia in 1895 to launch important musical performances. From 1908 onwards the hall was given over almost exclusively to chamber music. Orchestral concerts, strengthened by the establishment of a permanent orchestra and chorus, were given at the Augusteo (until 1936), the Teatro Adriano (1936–46), the Teatro Argentina (1946–58) and later in the Auditorio della Conciliazione. Open-air summer concerts at the Basilica di Massenzio began in 1935.

6. OTHER CONCERTS. The Accademia Filarmonica Romana was founded in 1821 by Marquis Raffaele Muti Papazurri chiefly to give concert performances of operas that for various reasons (mainly for the severity of the papal censorship) were prevented from appearing on the Roman stage. Dissolved in 1861 for its demonstrations in favour of national unity, it was reconstituted in 1868. After the fall of the papal government in 1870 it devoted itself to the performance of important choral works never before given in Rome. In 1920 it organized the first of its annual series of chamber music, furthering especially new compositions or works never before given in Rome. It has for many years had its own permanent string quartet and, according to the purpose for which it was founded, still encourages among its members the formation of instrumental and choral groups of amateurs. Its present home in the Teatro Olimpico has enabled the performance of rare operas, both early and contemporary.

Aimed at disseminating chamber and orchestral music were the Società Musicale Romana and the Società Orchestrale Romana, both founded in 1874. The former, in association with the Quintetto della Regina (founded by Sgambati in 1881), introduced the Roman audience to the chamber music of the most important Romantic composers, until it disbanded in 1889. The latter, conducted by Ettore Pinelli, upheld its activity until 1898, thus anticipating the orchestral concerts of the Accademia di S Cecilia. The Società

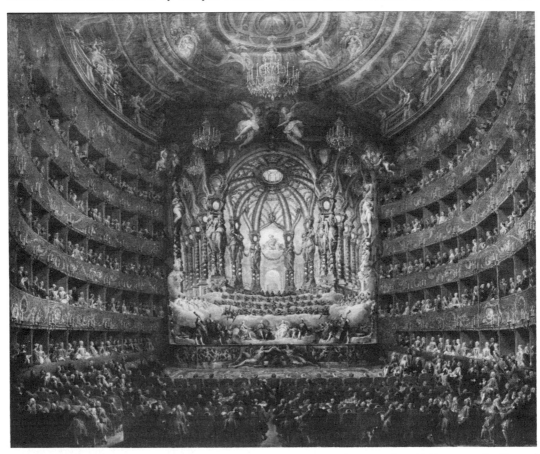

12. Interior of the Teatro Argentina during the performance of a cantata by Jommelli in 1747: painting by Giovanni Paolo Pannini (c1692–1765/8) in the Musée du Louvre, Paris

Bach of via Belsiana had a similar purpose, while the Banda Comunale, conducted from 1885 to 1925 by Alessandro Vessella, aimed at a larger audience with excellent arrangements of opera selections and symphonic masterpieces.

Concerts include the annual seasons offered by the Società del Quartetto in the Sala Borromini and by the Istituzione Universitaria dei Concerti founded in 1946. The Coro Polifonico Romano, founded in 1953 by Gastone Tosato and housed from 1960 in the exquisite historical Oratorio del Gonfalone, dedicates its programmes to seldom-performed vocal and instrumental music of the 16th to 18th centuries. The Radiotelevisione Italiana (RAI) has one of its principal broadcasting stations in Rome with a permanent orchestra and chorus; the public symphonic season has been held annually in the Auditorio del Foro Italico since 1958.

7. OPERA. The public taste for opera by no means diminished in Rome during the 19th century. In the first half of that century the Argentina, Apollo (formerly Tordinona) and Valle theatres vied with those of Milan and Naples. On their stages numerous operas by Rossini (*Demetrio e Polibio*, 1812; *Il barbiere di Siviglia*, 1816; *La Cenerentola*, 1817; *Matilde di Shabran*, 1821), Donizetti (*Zoraide di Granata*, 1822; *L'aio nell'imbarazzo*, 1824; *Il Furioso all'isola di San Domingo*, 1833; *Torquato Tasso*, 1833), Pacini, Mercadante, Petrella and Verdi (*I due Foscari*, 1844; *La battaglia di Legnano*, 1849; *Il trovatore*, 1853; *Un ballo in maschera*, 1859) were first performed. After a period of decline a new opera house, the Teatro Costanzi, was opened in 1880, where various operas had their first performances, including several by Mascagni (*Cavalleria rusticana*, 1890) and Puccini's *Tosca* (1900). The Teatro Apollo was demolished in 1889 after more than two centuries of activity. The Teatro Costanzi, redecorated and modernized, was renamed Teatro dell'Opera in 1928 and is subsidized by the state and local government; in addition to the standard repertory, it mounts productions of Italian and foreign novelties and of early operas of special interest. Since 1938 outdoor operatic performances are also given during the summer in the impressive setting of the ruins of the Terme di Caracalla. An operatic season is offered every autumn by the Teatro Eliseo.

8. OTHER INSTITUTIONS. Among the institutions concerned with church music, the Schola Cantorum of S Salvatore in Lauro, founded in 1869 by Pius IX, helped to further Pius X's reform of sacred music. The Scuola Superiore di Musica Sacra, established in 1911 under Pius X, became in 1931 the Pontificio Istituto di Musica Sacra, for the teaching at university level of Gregorian chant, composition of sacred music and organ, as well as the history and criticism of church music.

The Istituto Italiano per la Storia della Musica, a cultural institution founded in 1938, has published the complete works of Palestrina, works of Gesualdo, Carissimi, Boccherini and Donizetti's 18 quartets. The Collegium Musicum Italicum, founded in 1948 by Renato Fasano, centres its activity on the performance of 18th-century music. Nuova Consonanza, a 'gruppo d'improvvisazione' that performs contemporary music, was founded in 1960 by Franco Evangelisti, Mario Bertoncini and Egisto Macchi who, with Domenico Guaccero, founded an electronic studio, R7, in 1957.

13. Interior of the concert hall of the Accademia di S Cecilia

BIBLIOGRAPHY

P. Alfieri: *Brevi notizie storiche sulla Congregazione ed Accademia de' maestri e professori di musica di Roma* (Rome, 1845)

F. X. Haberl: 'Die römische "Schola Cantorum" und die päpstlichen Kapellsänger', *VMw*, vi (1887), 189–296

A. Ademollo: *I teatri di Roma nel secolo decimosettimo* (Rome, 1888)

A. Parisotti: *I 25 anni della Società orchestrale romana* (Rome, 1899)

G. Radiciotti: *Teatro e musica in Roma nel secondo quarto del secolo XIX* (Rome, 1905)

E. Celani: 'I cantori della cappella pontificia nei secoli XVI–XVIII', *RMI*, xiv (1907), 83–104, 752–90; xvi (1909), 55–112

M. Incagliati: *Il teatro Costanzi (1880–1907)* (Rome, 1907)

D. Alaleona: *Studi sulla storia dell'oratorio musicale in Italia* (Turin, 1908, 2/1945 as *Storia dell'oratorio musicale in Italia*)

E. Celani: 'Musica e musicisti in Roma (1750–1850)', *RMI*, xviii (1911), 1–63; xx (1913), 33–88; xxii (1915), 1–56, 257–300

G. de Dominicis: *I teatri di Roma nell'età di Pio VI* (Rome, 1922)

G. Pavan: 'Saggio di cronistoria del teatro musicale romano: il teatro Capranica', *RMI*, xxix (1922), 425

G. de Dominicis: 'Roma centro musicale nel Settecento', *RMI*, xxx (1923), 511

A. Cametti: *L'Accademia filarmonica romana dal 1821 al 1860* (Rome, 1924)

R. Casimiri: 'L'antica Congregazione di S. Cecilia . . . nel secolo XVII', *NA*, i (1924), 116

——: '"Disciplina musicae" e "mastri di cappella" dopo il Concilio di Trento nei maggiori istituti musicali di Roma', *NA*, xii (1935), 1, 73; xv (1938), 1, 49, 97, 145, 225; xvi (1939), 1; xix (1942), 102, 159; xx (1943), 1

A. Cametti: *Il teatro di Tordinona* (Rome and Tivoli, 1938)

P. Santini: 'Opera – Papal and Regal', *ML*, xx (1939), 292

H.-W. Frey: 'Regesten zur päpstlichen Kapelle unter Leo X und zu seiner Privatkapelle', *Mf*, viii (1955), 58, 178, 412; ix (1956), 46, 139, 411

L. Montalto: *Un mecenate in Roma barocca: il cardinale Benedetto Pamphilj (1653–1730)* (Florence, 1955)

L. Feininger: 'La scuola policorale romana', *CHM*, ii (1957), 198

A. Liess: 'Materialien zur römischen Musikgeschichte des Seicento', *AcM*, xxix (1957), 137–71

J. E. Scott: 'Roman Music', *NOHM*, i (1957), 404

R. Lunelli: *L'arte organaria del rinascimento in Roma* (Florence, 1958)

H. Wessely-Kropik: 'Mitteilungen aus dem Archiv der Arciconfraternità di San Giovanni dei Fiorentini', *SMw*, xxiv (1960), 43

A. Ducrot: 'Histoire de la Cappella Giulia au XVI⁰ siècle depuis sa fondation par Jules II (1513), jusqu'à sa restauration par Grégoire XIII (1578)', *Mélanges d'archéologie et d'histoire*, lxxv (1963), 179–240, 467–559

P. Kast: 'Biographischen Notizen zu römischen Musikern des 17. Jahrhunderts', *AnMc*, no.1 (1963), 38–69

H.-W. Frey: 'Die Kapellmeister an der französischen Nationalkirche San Luigi dei Francesi in Rom im 16. Jahrhundert', *AMw*, xxii (1965), 274

G. Wille: *Musica romana* (Amsterdam, 1967)

H. J. Marx: 'Die Musik am Hofe Pietro Kardinal Ottobonis unter Arcangelo Corelli', *AnMc*, no.5 (1968), 104–77

L. L. Perkins: 'Notes bibliographiques au sujet de l'ancien fond musical de l'Eglise de Saint-Louis des Français à Rome', *FAM*, xvi (1969), 57

T. D. Culley: *A Study of the Musicians connected with the German College in Rome during the 17th Century*, i (Rome, 1970)

R. Giazotto: *Quattro secoli di storia dell'Accademia nazionale di S. Cecilia* (Milan, 1970)

H.-W. Frey: 'Das Diarium der Sixtinischien Sängerkapelle in Rom für Jahr 1594', *AnMc*, no. 14 (1974), 445

C. Gianturco: 'Evidence for a Late Roman School of Opera', *ML*, lvi (1975), 4

H. E. Smither: *A History of the Oratorio*, i: *The Oratorio in the Baroque Era: Italy, Vienna, Paris* (Chapel Hill, 1977)

M. Rinaldi: *Due secoli di musica al Teatro Argentina* (Florence, 1978)

T. D. Culley: 'Musical Activity in Some Sixteenth Century Jesuit Colleges with Special Reference to the Venerable English College in Rome from 1579 to 1589', *AnMc*, no.19 (1979), 1

R. F. Hayburn: *Papal Legislation on Sacred Music 95 a.d. to 1977 a.d.* (Collegeville, Minnesota, 1979)

A. Silbiger: 'The Roman Frescobaldi Tradition', *JAMS*, xxxiii (1980), 42–87

GÜNTER FLEISCHHAUER (I)
NINO PIRROTTA, RAOUL MELONCELLI (II)

Rome, Harold (Jacob) (*b* Hartford, Conn., 27 May 1908). American songwriter and lyricist. At Yale University he read law and took a postgraduate degree in architecture (1934); he also studied the piano under Arthur Lloyd and Loma Roberts, and composition under Joseph Schillinger, Lehman Engel and Meyer Kupferman. *Pins and Needles* (1937), written for and performed by members of the International Ladies' Garment Workers Union, was the first in his series of musicals with social or political commentary (mostly to his own lyrics). One of the most successful Broadway musicals, it ran for over three years, and was frequently revived and taken on tour with current topical songs added. During World War II Rome organized and wrote shows for the US Army. At the end of the war he wrote his last social-political revue, *Call Me Mister* (1946), then turned successfully to musical plays (e.g. *Fanny*, 1954; *Destry Rides Again*, 1959, and *I can get it for you wholesale*, 1962).

BIBLIOGRAPHY

I. Stambler: *Encyclopedia of Popular Music* (New York, 1965)

R. D. Kinkle: *The Complete Encyclopedia of Popular Music and Jazz 1900–1950* (New Rochelle, NY, 1974)

DEANE L. ROOT

Rome Quartet [Quartetto di Roma]. Italian piano quartet founded in 1956; *see* SANTOLIQUIDO, ORNELLA.

Römer [Remer, Remmer, Römmer]. The family name of several Austrian organ builders, active from the second half of the 17th century to after the middle of the 18th.

Johann Ulrich Römer (*b* Vienna, ?after 1650) was married in 1683 and became a citizen of Vienna in 1685. In an organ building contract dated 12 February 1688, made between himself and his brother Ferdinand Josef on the one hand, and the abbey of Heiligenkreuz, near Vienna, on the other, he is described as a 'citizen and organ builder of Vienna'. In 1695 he installed an instrument, which now no longer exists, with seven stops and one manual in the parish church at Hainburg, Lower Austria.

His brother Ferdinand Josef (*b* c1657; *d* probably in Vienna, 1723) married in 1682 and from 1684 was organ builder and organ blower to the court. In the 1688 contract referred to above he is described as 'Imperial organ maker'. He is known to have built the choir organ of St Stephen's, Vienna, in 1701, and the cathedral's great organ (32 stops, ?three manuals) in about 1720. The casework of both was destroyed by fire in 1945. He supplied a new instrument for the abbey church at Heiligenkreuz in 1721. He and his brother Johann Ulrich had already built a smaller organ (12 stops, one manual) for the abbey in 1688, 'to be used as well for figural as for choral music, in accordance with a proposed specification, from which an organ has already been built before this, in a monastery at Ossek in Bohemia'. The imperial Kapellmeister Johann Joseph Fux seconded his petition of 10 December 1723 that 'his position be conferred on his son Johann Römmer, at present his assistant . . .'. In all probability Ferdinand Josef is to be identified with the Josef Remmer who in 1691 built the two choir organs of the abbey of St Florian, Upper Austria. The original casework still exists and is probably the only surviving example of his work. Ferdinand Josef seems to have enjoyed the greater reputation of the two brothers. Their instruments represent the transition from the early to the high Baroque period.

Andreas Römer (*b* Brno, 1704; *d* probably Brno, before 1750) was an organ builder in Brno and the father of Anton Römer (*b* Brno, 1724; *d* Graz, 14 July 1779). The latter left Brno for Graz, and there married the widow of the Graz organ builder Cyriacus Werner, on 19 April 1750. After his death his second wife, whom he married on 24 September 1758, married another local organ builder, C. M. Schwandtner, who apparently took over his business. Anton Römer has been more fortunate than the two Viennese Römers in that the casework of two of his Styrian organs has survived. Unfortunately, what was probably his largest instrument (the organ of Graz cathedral: 22 stops, two manuals, dating from 1770–72) has been totally destroyed. On the other hand, the casework of the organ of the abbey of Rein, near Graz (1772; 17 stops, two manuals) still exists in part. The organ of the pilgrimage church of Maria Rehkogel in Frauenberg, near Bruck an der Mur, Styria, dating from 1774–5, also still survives. This two-manual instrument has 19 stops, 14 of them the original ones. A clavichord dated 1774 from his workshop has also survived, and now belongs to the Graz violin maker R. Schuster.

BIBLIOGRAPHY

L. von Köchel: *J. J. Fux* (Vienna, 1872)

D. Frey: *Die Denkmale des Stiftes Heiligenkreuz*, Österreichische Kunsttopographie, xix (Vienna, 1926)

O. Eberstaller: *Die Haydn-Gedächtnisorgel der Stadtpfarrkirche in Hainburg* (Graz, 1932)

G. Frotscher: *Deutsche Orgel-Dispositionen aus fünf Jahrhunderten* (Wolfenbüttel, 1939)

H. Federhofer: 'Beiträge zur Geschichte des Orgelbaues in der Steiermark', *Aus Archiv und Chronik, Blätter für Seckauer Diözesangeschichte*, iv (Graz, 1951)

O. Eberstaller: *Orgeln und Orgelbauer in Österreich* (Graz, 1955)

RENATE FEDERHOFER-KÖNIGS

Romer, Emma (*b* 1814; *d* Margate, 11 April 1868). English soprano. A pupil of Sir George Smart, she made a successful début at Covent Garden in 1830 in Linley's *The Duenna*. Engaged at the English Opera House (Lyceum Theatre), she appeared in the first performance of Barnett's *The Mountain Sylph* (1834). At Drury Lane she sang in the first performances of many other

English operas, including Barnett's *Fair Rosamond*, Balfe's *Catherine Grey* and *Joan of Arc* (1837); Benedict's *The Gypsy's Warning* and Balfe's *Diadaste* (1838); Hatton's *Queen of the Thames* (1843), Benedict's *Brides of Venice* (1844), Balfe's *The Enchantress* and Wallace's *Maritana* (1845) and Balfe's *The Bondsman* (1846). She also appeared in her brother Frank Romer's *Fridolin* at the short-lived National English Opera (Prince's, later St James's Theatre) in 1840 and sang in the first performance in English of Donizetti's *La favorite* (Drury Lane, 1843). In 1848 she took part in Bunn's autumn season of opera in English at Covent Garden, singing Adina in Donizetti's *L'elisir d'amore* and also Amina in Bellini's *La sonnambula*, a role for which she was particularly admired. For several seasons she was manager of the Surrey Theatre.

BIBLIOGRAPHY
E. Fitzball: *35 Years of a Dramatic Author's Life* (London, 1859)
C. L. Kenney: *A Memoir of Michael William Balfe* (London, 1875)
W. A. Barrett: *Balfe: his Life and Work* (London, 1882)
E. W. White: *The Rise of English Opera* (London, 1951)
B. Carr: 'The First All-sung English 19th-century Opera', *MT*, cxv (1974), 125

ELIZABETH FORBES

Römer von Zwickau. *See* REINMAR VON ZWETER.

Romero. Spanish firm of music publishers, absorbed by the UNIÓN MUSICAL ESPAÑOLA.

Romero, Jesús C(arlos) (*b* Mexico City, 15 April 1893; *d* Mexico City, 1958). Mexican musicologist. While studying medicine (graduated 1924) and history (graduated 1932), he studied harmony under Juan Fuentes and music history on his own. He became professor of music history at the National Conservatory (1929) and at the music department of the National Autonomous University (1945), participated in the National Music Congresses in Mexico of 1926 and 1928 and collaborated in editing several music periodicals, particularly *Música*, directed by Chávez, and *Cultural musical*, directed by Ponce. He was a member of the Mexican Academy of History and a research associate of the Secretariat of Public Education. In his publications he attempted to reconstruct the music history of the various Mexican provinces, and studied carefully several aspects of Mexican folk music traditions.

WRITINGS
La historia crítica de la música en México (Mexico City, 1927)
El estudio de nuestra prehistoria musical (Mexico City, 1928)
José Mariano Elízaga (Mexico City, 1934)
'Estado de la cultura musical de España durante el siglo XVI', *Orientación musical*, no.6 (1941), 5
'Melesio Morales, estudio bibliográfico', *Revista musical mexicana*, iii/11 (1943), 248
'Música precortesiana: estudio histórico-crítico de nuestra protohistoria musical', *Orientación musical*, nos.19–24 (1943), 12
'Reseña histórica de la fundación del Conservatorio Nacional de Música', *Orientación musical*, nos.25–35 (1944), 9
'La folklorología: lugar del folklore en los conocimientos humanos', *Orientación musical*, no.52 (1945), 10
Historia de la música en Yucatán (Mexico City, 1945)
'Historia del conservatorio', *Nuestra música*, i (1946), 153, 251
'El folklore en México', *Boletín de la sociedad mexicana de geografía y estadística*, lxiii (1947), 657
'Galería de maestros mexicanos de música: Rafael J. Tello', *Boletín del departamento de música del Instituto nacional de bellas artes*, no.4 (1947), 38
La ópera en Yucatán (Mexico City, 1947)
Música precortesiana (Mexico City, 1947)
'Rafael J. Tello', *Nuestra música*, ii (1947), 33
'Una ópera cervantina en México', *Nuestra música*, ii (1947), 211
'Manuel M. Ponce, premio nacional', *Nuestra música*, iii (1948), 90
'Durango en la evolución musical de México', *Memorias del Congreso mexicano de historia* (1949), 273
'El francesismo en la evolución musical de México', *Carnet musical*, v/4 (1949), suppl. no.1
'Ricardo Castro: su biografía en más de cien efemérides musicales', *Nuestra música*, iv (1949), 156
'Efemérides de Manuel (María) Ponce', *Nuestra música*, v (1950), 164
'Candelario Huízar', *Nuestra música*, vii (1952), 45
'El periodismo musical mexicano en el siglo XX', *Carnet musical*, ix/3 (1952), 138
'Biografía y bibliografía de Juventino Rosas', *Memoria de la Academia nacional de historia y geografía*, xiv/5 (1958), 31
La música en Zacatecas y los músicos zacatecanos (Mexico City, 1963)
BIBLIOGRAPHY
O. Mayer-Serra: *Música y músicos de Latinoamérica* (Mexico City, 1947), 856
H. de Grial: *Músicos mexicanos* (Mexico City, 1965), 149

GERARD BÉHAGUE

Romero, Juan (*fl* 1675–9). Spanish composer. He was a Mercedarian friar and *maestro de capilla* of the Mercedarian church at Madrid from at least 1675 to 1679. The Madrid city council commissioned him to supply music for the *autos sacramentales* of Calderón given at Corpus Christi in 1676, 1677, 1679 and possibly 1680. Two villancicos by him survive (in *D-Mbs*). *Agan plaza a las luces*, for nine voices, modulates frequently and exploits the contrast between a solo bass and a double choir, which often sings antiphonally. The six-part *Suene el clarin* (1678) includes parts for trumpets and is full of striking effects, such as echo passages and abrupt changes of pace.

BIBLIOGRAPHY
J. J. Maier: *Die musikalischen Handschriften der K. Hof- und Staatsbibliothek* (Munich, 1879), 103f
C. Pérez Pastor: *Documentos para la biografía de D. Pedro Calderón de la Barca* (Madrid, 1905), 349, 351, 363, 368
M. Querol Gavaldá: 'Corresponsales de Miguel Gómez Camargo', *AnM*, xiv (1959), 175
N. D. Shergold and J. E. Varey: *Los autos sacramentales en Madrid en la época le Calderón 1637–1681* (Madrid, 1961), xxvif, 313, 328, 332, 346

ROBERT STEVENSON

Romero, Mateo [Rosmarin, Mathieu; 'El Maestro Capitán'] (*b* Liège, 1575 or 1576; *d* Madrid, 10 May 1647). Spanish composer of Netherlands birth. Romero was born Mathieu Rosmarin into a prominent Liège family. After his father's early death he was taken to Madrid, where he was a royal choirboy under George de la Hèle and Philippe Rogier from 1586 to 1593 and then a member of the Flemish chapel. He was *maestro de capilla* from 19 October 1598 until he retired with full pay in 1634. In 1605 he began to study for the priesthood and was ordained in 1609. He became chaplain to Philip III in 1605, *capellán de Banco* on 8 April 1608, clerk of the Order of the Golden Fleece on 6 May 1621 and *capellán de los Reyes Nuevos de Toledo* on 4 March 1624. On 1 April 1644 John IV of Portugal gave him the lucrative non-residential post of chaplain to his court and when Romero died John was trying to acquire a complete collection of his works.

Romero was one of the last of the international Netherlanders, but he was also influential in introducing the *stile nuovo* into Spain. His Spanish contemporaries had a high regard for his music, which John IV cited in his *Defensa de la música moderna* (Lisbon, 1649) to show the validity of the new style. Cerone thought him one of the most celebrated musicians of his age. It is difficult to assess his music, since at least 15 masses, 4 settings of the *Magnificat*, 15 motets, 53 villancicos, 4 secular works and a treatise, *El porqué de la musica*, have been lost, and some of it is incomplete. Many of the lost works seem to have been in the Netherlands polyphonic style, but his surviving sacred works show that Romero was a master of polychoral homophony. His secular works are of two types: those showing the influence of the Italian madrigal, and those in a popular style directly inspired by the villancico; nearly all call for a continuo.

WORKS

Editions: *Cancionero musical y poético del siglo XVII, recogido por Claudio de la Sablonara*, ed. J. Aroca (Madrid, 1916) [incl. 22 of the secular works]
Música barroca española I: polifonía profana, ed. M. Querol Gavaldá, MME, xxxii (1970) [incl. 6 of the secular works]

Missa 'Bonae voluntatis' (2 versions), 1 for 9vv, org/harp, bc, the other for 5vv, bc; Missa breve, 4vv; Missa 'Dolce fiamella mia', 5vv (on Nanino's madrigal): Missa ferialis (Ky, San, Ag), 4vv; Missa 'Qui habitat', 8vv, bc; Missa 'Turleman' (or 'Inturleman'), 8vv, 2 org, bc (T ii missing)
3 other masses: 1, 4vv; 1, 8vv (T i, ii missing); 1, 8vv, bc, inc. (bc only)
Attolite portas, 8vv, 2 org, bc; Cum invocarem, 8vv, org, harp; Dixit Dominus, 8vv, 2 org, bc; Domine quando veneris, 4vv; Laudate Dominum, omnes gentes, 12vv, 3 org, bc; Libera me, Domine, 8vv, bc; 3 Magnificat (tones 1, 7, 8), 8vv, 2 org, bc; Miserere mei quoniam infirmus, 4vv, bc; Qui habitat, 8vv, 2 org, bc; O beatum apostolum, 8vv, 2 vn, ob, b; O crux, 8vv, 2 vn, ob, b
5 villancicos: 3, 4vv, bc; 1, 4vv; 1, S, bc
31 secular works (canción, décimas, folía, letra, letrilla, novenas, octavas, romance, sequidillas, tono humano): 10, 4vv; 13, 3vv; 8, 2vv

Sources: *D-Mbs*; *E-Bc*, *C*, *E*, *GRc*, *Mn*, *MO*, *PAc*, *SE*, Don Arciñega's Library (?lost), Saragossa, *V*, *VAcp*, *Zp*; *I-Rc*; *P-VV*; Puebla Cathedral Library, Mexico

BIBLIOGRAPHY

E. vander Straeten: *La musique aux Pays-Bas avant le XIXᵉ siècle*, viii (Brussels, 1888/*R*1969)
R. Stevenson: *Spanish Cathedral Music in the Golden Age* (Berkeley and Los Angeles, 1961)
P. Becquart: 'Matheo Romero ou Mathieu Rosmarin (1575–1647), maître de chapelle et compositeur de Philippe III et Philippe IV, greffier de l'Ordre de la Toison d'Or', *Archives et Bibliothèques de Belgique*, xxiv (1963), 11–47
——: *Musiciens néerlandais à la cour de Madrid: Philippe Rogier et son école (1560–1647)* (Brussels, 1967)
M. Querol Gavaldá: 'La producción musical del compositor Mateo Romero (1575–1647)', *Renaissance-muziek, 1400–1600: donum natalicium René Bernard Lenaerts* (Louvain, 1969), 215
R. A. Pelinski: *Die weltliche Vokalmusik Spaniens am Anfang des 17. Jahrhunderts: der Cancionero Claudio de la Sablonara* (Tutzing, 1971)

BARTON HUDSON

Romero de Ávila, Manuel Jerónimo (*b* Herencia, nr. Toledo, 26 March 1717; *d* ?Toledo, 15 Dec 1779). Spanish theorist and composer. It is believed that he was a choirboy in Toledo. He competed unsuccessfully for the post of *maestro de capilla* at Toledo Cathedral, but did serve there from 1749 until his death as *maestro de melodía* (director of plainsong). Romero assisted in one of the 18th-century attempts to reconstruct Mozarabic chant for use in Toledo Cathedral, the 1775 *Breviarium gothicum* of Cardinal Lorenzana. To this volume he contributed an explanation of the notation, with specimen transcriptions; neither the introduction nor the contents of the *Breviarium* has much relationship to the still undecipherable ancient notation, but are based on the versions prepared about 1500 under Cardinal Cisneros. In 1761 Romero published an elementary *Arte de canto llano y órgano* which enjoyed great popularity and numerous reprintings, the last in 1830. Based on the ancient musical tradition still used in Spain, which included the hexachord system and the eight modes, its four books cover the theory and practice of plainchant, mensural chant and polyphony. Romero also edited manuscripts of the Gregorian masses as used in Spain, arranged two supposedly Mozarabic masses in metrical plainsong and composed original monodic masses (some with figured bass accompaniment) and a number of textless duos.

WORKS

[Graduale], Parte segunda: contiene [10] missas de tonos todos, con sus acompañamientos, 1v, bc, 1774, *E-Mn*
Gloria–Credo, 1v; duos, 1v, bc: in Arte de canto llano y órgano (Madrid, 1761)

EDITIONS

[Graduale], Libro segundo, primera parte: el qual contiene todas las misas que ocurren desde la Dominica de Resurrección hasta la última de Pentecostes (MS, *Mn*, 1774)
Missa de canto gothico, ò mozarabe, para el día de la Exaltación de la Cruz, y los hymnos propios de Sn Lucas y Sn Torquato (MS, *Tp*, 1775)
Missa gothica, ò mozárabe, al Sacratísimo Cuerpo de Nro Señor Jesuchristo . . . reducida de lo góthico, à figuras del presente tiempo (MS, *Tp*, 1776)

WRITINGS

Arte de canto llano y órgano, o Promptuario musical, dividido en quatro partes (Madrid, 1761, 5/1830)
Sobre el canto góthico, y Eugeniano, vulgo melodía (MS, *Tp*, 1774); apparently 1st draft of 'Cantu Eugeniani seu melodici explanatio', *Breviarium gothicum secundum regulam Beatissimi Isidori . . . nunc operá Exc.mi Francisci Antonii Lorenzana* (Madrid, 1775)

BIBLIOGRAPHY

LaborD ('Gerónimo Romero de Ávila')
R. Mitjana y Gordón: 'La musique en Espagne', *EMDC*, I/iv (1920), 1917, 2119
F. Rubio Piqueras: *Música y músicos toledanos* (Toledo, 1923)
H. Anglès and J. Subirá: *Catálogo musical de la Biblioteca nacional de Madrid*, i, ii (Barcelona, 1946–9)
W. Thoene: 'Romero de Ávila', *MGG*
F. J. León Tello: *La teoría española de la música en los siglos XVII y XVIII* (Madrid, 1974)

ALMONTE HOWELL

Römhild [Römhildt; 'Mielorth'], **Johann Theodor** (*b* Salzungen, nr. Eisenach, 23 Sept 1684; *d* Merseburg, 26 Oct 1756). German organist and composer. His earliest musical education was probably received from his father, Johann Elias, a substitute minister who moved his family to nearby Steinbach three years after his son's birth. According to Gerber, he also studied with Johann Jacob Bach in the neighbouring town of Ruhla when the latter arrived there in 1694. In 1697 he became a student at the Leipzig Thomasschule, where his distinguished teachers were Schelle and Kuhnau, and his fellow students included Graupner, Fasch and Heinichen. Römhild became a university student in Leipzig in 1705, remaining six terms before accepting in 1708 his first musical position as Kantor of the school in Spremberg (Lusatia); in 1714 he was also named rector and Kapelldirector. In 1715 he went to Freystadt (Lusatia) as music director and Kantor of the newly constructed parish church, but returned to Spremberg in 1726 as court Kapellmeister to Duke Heinrich. When the latter became Duke of Saxony-Merseburg he took Römhild to Merseburg as his court Kapellmeister. In 1735 Römhild became organist of Merseburg Cathedral, and began a period of great compositional activity, including more than 200 sacred cantatas and a *St Matthew Passion*.

Römhild was a major composer of sacred music in the north German Baroque; but uncertainty as to the survival of many of his manuscripts, found before World War II in libraries and church archives in northeast Europe, makes impossible even an accurate survey of his surviving compositions. As Paulke showed in his description of a portion of Römhild's manuscripts discovered early in this century, the more than 250 church cantatas, including some 50 solo cantatas, were written in a variety of forms and instrumental combinations characteristic of the late Baroque and illustrating almost every formal and stylistic type. Römhild's *St Matthew Passion* (described in some detail by H. Römhild) remains an important example of a late Baroque setting of the Passion text, without free poetic insertions for arias or ariosos, but with chorales common to a tradition found in and around Danzig.

Johann Casper Römhild, possibly related to Johann Theodor, was a student at Brunswick and Helmstedt University. He was choir prefect at St Michael's school in Lüneburg, Kantor in Lauenburg, and held posts at the cathedral gymnasium in Güstrow, 1776–95, and afterwards until 1804 in Parchim. Five cantatas by him are extant (three in *B-Bc*, two in *D-GÜ*).

WORKS

St Matthew Passion, ? formerly *PL-GD*, ed. K. Paulke (Leipzig, 1921); 2 masses, *D-MÜG*; Kyrie, *BIT*; Kyrie, Żary, Poland
Magnificat, *D-MÜG*
Cantatas: 3 in *D-Bds*, 1 in *BIT*, 1 in Bückeburg, 2 in *CR*, 7 in *GMl*, 1 in Guben, 22 in *LUC*, 4 in *MEIk*, 42 in Mücheln, 38 in *MÜG*, 1 in *F-Sc*, 112 in *PL-GD*, 1 in Żary
Motet, *D-BIT*; partita, hpd, vn, vc, *SWl*: both according to *MGG*
22 org preludes, ?lost

For inventory and fuller list of works, see Paulke

BIBLIOGRAPHY

GerberL
K. Paulke: 'Johann Theodorich Roemhildt (1684–1756)', *AMw*, i (1918–19), 372–401
W. Lott: 'Zur Geschichte der Passionsmusiken auf Danziger Boden mit Bevorzugung der oratorischen Passionen', *AMw*, vii (1925), 297–329
H. Römhild: 'Die Matthäus-Passion von Johann Theodor Römhild', *Mf*, ix (1956), 26

GEORGE J. BUELOW

Romieu, Jean-Baptiste (*b* Montpellier, 14 Sept 1723; *d* Montpellier, 8 Nov 1766). French dilettante and scientist. In December 1751 he announced his discovery of difference tones, which he had made by experiments with wind instruments. (Nearly three years later Tartini, evidently unaware of Romieu's work, published his discovery of the same phenomenon observed in double stops on the violin.) Romieu's 'Mémoire théorique & practique sur les systèmes temperés de musique', published in the 1758 *Mémoires* of the Académie Royale des Sciences, surveyed various regular tuning systems and expressed preference for $\frac{1}{4}$-comma meantone temperament and its theoretical equivalent, the division of the octave into 55 equal parts.

BIBLIOGRAPHY

E. Roche: 'Notice sur les travaux de J.-B. Romieu', *Mémoires de l'Académie des sciences et lettres de Montpellier*, ix (1879)
J. M. Barbour: *Tuning and Temperament: a Historical Survey* (East Lansing, Mich., 1951, 2/1953)

MARK LINDLEY

Rommelpot. *See* FRICTION DRUM.

Römmer. *See* RÖMER family.

Ron, (Jean) Martin de (*b* Stockholm, 13 Nov 1789; *d* Lisbon, 20 Feb 1817). Swedish merchant, composer and chamber musician. He presumably worked for his father's banking and shipping firm in Stockholm, and even on business trips to Amsterdam, Viborg (in Finland; now Vyborg, USSR), Dublin and Lisbon he pursued his interest in chamber music. He was a capable bassoonist and violinist and is reported to have studied with the clarinettist and composer Bernard Crusell. According to an obituary he introduced some of the string quartets of Haydn, Mozart and Beethoven to Lisbon. He was also a contributor to the *Allgemeine musikalische Zeitung*, and among his articles is one on music in Portugal (xviii/26, 1816). De Ron's compositions were influenced by Mozart, Grétry, Dalayrac, Méhul and Cherubini, whose works were popular in Sweden during

his youth; his harmonic style is similar to that of his contemporaries Spohr and Weber. Many of his works display an independence and artistic maturity that is remarkable in view of his amateur status and early death. In his chamber music and certain songs he experimented with new means of harmonic, melodic and rhythmic expression.

WORKS
(all MSS in S-Skma)

Inst: Qnt, pf, fl, cl, hn, bn, op.1 (Leipzig, n.d.); Andante and Polonaise, bn, orch, op.2 (Leipzig, n.d.); Thème finois avec variations, cl, orch (Leipzig, n.d.); Str Qt, C; Str Qt, f, ed. (Stockholm, 1940); Str Qt, c, 1816; 2 str qt frags.; Trio, pf, cl, bn, 1816; Lundum da Bahia, pf
Vocal: Scena, T, orch; Willst du wohl ein Gläschen, A, T, B, 1811; 30 songs, 1v, pf; 8 Canzonette, 1v, pf; 8 cancions espanholas, 1v, pf, gui

BIBLIOGRAPHY

FétisB
Obituary, *AMZ*, xix/24 (1817), col.410
S. E. Svensson: 'Martin de Ron: en svensk förromantiker', *STMf*, xxii (1940), 5

BIRGIT KJELLSTRÖM

Ronald [Russell], Sir Landon (*b* London, 7 June 1873; *d* London, 14 Aug 1938). English conductor, pianist and composer, son of Henry Russell. He entered the RCM in 1884 and in 1891 became accompanist and coach under Mancinelli at Covent Garden, where he first appeared as conductor in 1896 with *Faust*. He had already toured as conductor of Augustus Harris's Italian Opera Company in 1892, conducted opera at Drury Lane, and toured the USA in 1894 as accompanist to Melba. From 1898 to 1902 he conducted musical comedy in London and summer concerts at Blackpool, a reflection of how little opportunity England then offered to a very experienced conductor. From 1904 to 1907 he was a guest conductor of the newly formed London SO; this led in 1908 to engagements in Berlin, Vienna, Leipzig and Amsterdam. He was conductor of the New SO, 1909–14 and of the Scottish Orchestra, 1916–20. Thereafter he was a regular guest conductor of the leading British orchestras and an expressive exponent of the music of his friend Elgar, who dedicated *Falstaff* to him; Ronald had conducted the first Rome performance of Elgar's Symphony no.1 in 1909. He also played an important educative role in English musical life as principal of the Guildhall School of Music, 1910–38, and wrote a large amount of criticism. He was a close friend of Kreisler, who liked to have Ronald as conductor for his concerto recordings. Ronald was knighted in 1922. His compositions include a symphonic poem, an overture and incidental music to Robert Hichens's *The Garden of Allah* (Drury Lane, 1921), but it is his song *Down in the Forest* that has survived. He also published two books of reminiscences, *Variations on a Personal Theme* (London, 1922) and *Myself and Others* (London, 1931).

MICHAEL KENNEDY

Roncaglia, Gino (*b* Modena, 7 May 1883; *d* Modena, 27 Nov 1968). Italian musicologist and composer. He studied the piano with his father, the musician and writer Alessandro Roncaglia, the violin with Giuseppe Ferrari and Zelmira Barbi, and composition with L. Sinigaglia. He graduated in natural sciences at Modena (1907). In 1926 he became a member of the Deputazione di Storia Patria, and in 1932 of the Accademia di Scienze, Lettere e Arti at Modena, of which he was also president (1950–52). In 1919 he helped to found the Società Amici della Musica at Modena. His writings deal almost exclusively with

Italian music, particularly operatic music and music from Modena; in addition to studies of Verdi, Puccini, Rossini and Stradella he has written several popular guides. His compositions include orchestral, chamber and vocal works.

WRITINGS

Appunti musicali: saggi critici (Milan, 1905)
E. Panzacchi e la musica (Modena, 1907)
Giuseppe Verdi (Naples, 1914, rev. 2/1940 as *L'ascensione creatrice di Giuseppe Verdi*, 3/1951)
'I "Maggi" modenesi', *Cultura musicale*, ii–iii (Bologna, 1923), 55; also in *RaM*, viii (1935), 263
La rivoluzione musicale italiana (Milan, 1928)
Di insigni musicisti modenesi: documenti inediti (Modena, 1929)
'Di G. G. Cambini quartettista padre', *RaM*, vi (1933), 267; vii (1934), 131; 'G. G. Cambini quartettista romantico', *RaM*, vii (1934), 423
Il melodioso Settecento italiano (Milan, 1935)
La musica e il Tassoni (Modena, 1936)
Sommario di storia della musica (Bologna, 1937)
'Le composizioni di A. Stradella', *RMI*, xliv (1940), 81, 337; xlv (1941), 1, 133; xlvi (1942), 1
Invito alla musica (Milan, 1946, 4/1958)
Rossini l'olimpico: vita e opere (Milan, 1946, 2/1953)
Invito all'opera (Milan, 1949, 4/1958)
'G. Colombi e la vita musicale modenese durante il regno di Francesco II', *Accademia di scienze, lettere e arti di Modena*, v/10 (1952), 31
'La scuola musicale modenese', *Musicisti della scuola emiliana*, Chigiana, xiii (1956), 69
La cappella musicale del Duomo di Modena (Florence, 1957)
'Il sentimento bucolico nell'opera di I. Pizzetti', *La città dannunziana a Ildebrando Pizzetti* (Milan, 1958), 105
'La poetica di Giacomo Puccini', *Giacomo Puccini nel centenario della nascita* (Lucca, 1958), 31
Galleria verdiana (Milan, 1959)
Further articles in *Chigiana, Accademia di scienze, lettere e arti, Bergomum, Deputazione di storia patria, RMI*

FERRUCCIO TAMMARO

Roncal, Simeón (*b* Sucre, 20 April 1870; *d* La Paz, 12 Jan 1953). Bolivian composer and pianist. He was a choirboy at Sucre Cathedral. About 1910 he went to Potosí to teach at the Colegio Pichincha, and in 1917 he founded the Círculo de Bellas Artes de Potosí, at whose meetings he performed his piano compositions. These are sophisticated stylizations of Bolivian popular dances: *cuecas, bailecitos, tonadas* and *burro katinas*. He was the outstanding composer in these genres, and his pieces were published by various houses in Germany and in Buenos Aires. His early works include two funeral marches: *Tres de febrero* and *Las campanas de la catedral*.

BIBLIOGRAPHY
A. Alba: *Don Simeón Roncal* (Potosí, 1970)

CARLOS SEOANE

Roncalli, Conte Ludovico (*fl* late 17th century). Italian guitarist and composer. The often-encountered spellings 'Roncelli' and 'Rancalli' are erroneous. Roncalli is known only through his *Capricci armonici sopra la chitarra spagnola* (Bergamo, 1692). This collection contains nine 'sonatas' or suites for five-course Baroque guitar notated in Italian guitar tablature; each one comprises from five to seven movements. Each suite begins with a preludio and alemanda, which are followed by other typical late 17th-century Italian dance forms such as the corrente, giga, sarabanda and gavotta. Despite their Italian titles the movements show some French influence. Roncalli gave no indication of the tuning for his pieces, but their style and textures seem to indicate the 'French' tuning *A/a–d/d′–g/g–b/b–e′* used by his contemporaries Corbetta, Derosier and Visée.

BIBLIOGRAPHY
R. Strizich: 'Ornamentation in Spanish Baroque Guitar Music', *Journal of the Lute Society of America*, v (1972), 37

ROBERT STRIZICH

Ronconi, Giorgio (*b* Milan, 6 Aug 1810; *d* Madrid, 8 Jan 1890). Italian baritone. Son of Domenico Ronconi (*b* Lendinara, Rovigo, 11 July 1772; *d* Milan, 13 April 1839), a tenor who sang at La Scala in 1808 and later became a famous singing teacher, he studied with his father and made his début in 1831 at Pavia as Valdeburgo in Bellini's *La straniera*. The following year he appeared in Donizetti's *L'esule di Roma* at the Teatro Valle, Rome, where in 1833 he sang Cardenio in *Il furiosa all'isola di San Domingo* and the title role of *Torquato Tasso*, both first performances. He also took part in five other Donizetti premières, *Il campanello* (Naples, 1836), *Pia de' Tolomei* (Venice, 1837), *Maria di Rudenz* (Venice, 1838), *Maria Padilla* (Milan, 1841) and *Maria di Rohan* (Vienna, 1843), which he repeated at the Théâtre-Italien, Paris. Having first sung at La Scala in 1839 as Henry Ashton in *Lucia di Lammermoor*, he created the title role of Verdi's *Nabucco* there on 9 March 1842. The same year he made his London début at Her Majesty's Theatre, and from 1847 to 1866 he sang nearly every season at Covent Garden. His large repertory also included roles by Mozart and Rossini; and in 1853 he became the first London Rigoletto. Although his voice, according to Chorley, was 'limited in compass (hardly exceeding an octave) . . . inferior in quality . . . weak . . . habitually out of tune' and his appearance was unremarkable, Ronconi became one of the finest singing actors of the mid-19th century, equally gifted for tragedy or comedy; his ability to project a role or to bring a character to life was unrivalled among his contemporaries.

Ronconi was married to the soprano Elguerra Giannoni; his brother Felice (*b* Venice, 1811; *d* St Petersburg, 10 Sept 1875) was a noted singing teacher, and another brother, Sebastiano (*b* Venice, May 1814; *d* Milan, 6 Feb 1900), was a baritone who made his début at Lucca in 1836 and had a successful career in Europe and the USA.

BIBLIOGRAPHY
H. F. Chorley: *Thirty Years' Musical Recollections* (London, 1862, 2/1926)
H. Rosenthal: *Two Centuries of Opera at Covent Garden* (London, 1958)
H. Weinstock: *Donizetti and the World of Opera in Italy, Paris and Vienna in the First Half of the Nineteenth Century* (New York, 1963)

ELIZABETH FORBES

Ronde (Fr.). (1) SEMIBREVE (whole note); *semibrève* and *entière* are also used. *See also* NOTE VALUES.
(2) A round, or a round dance.

Rondeau (i). One of the three fixed forms, together with the ballade and the virelai, which dominated French song and poetry in the 14th and 15th centuries. Unlike the ballade and the virelai, the rondeau had taken on its definitive structure by the early 13th century, when it was already a dance-song form of importance. At that stage it was known as *ronde, rondet, rondel* and *rondelet* (English 'roundelay') derived from the Latin forms *rotundettum* or *rotundellum*, diminutives meaning 'circular'; this is generally taken to imply circular motion in the dances for which such pieces were originally sung.

The earliest known Old French rondeaux are found among the courtly and popular songs interpolated into the romance of *Guillaume de Dôle* by its author, Jean Renart, in 1228. There are 16 in all with varied metres and rhyme schemes and frequent 'irregularities' not to be found later in the rondeau's history. Fundamentally,

1. Machaut's three-part rondeau 'Ma fin est mon commencement/Et mon commencement ma fin' from MS 'G' (F-Pn fr.22546, f.153r)

however, they all come to a six-line type with music on the pattern I–I–II–I–II. To take a typical example, no.6 reads:

> Aaliz main se leva,
> *Bon jor ait qui mon cuer a!*
> Biau se vesti et para,
> Desoz l'aunoi.
> *Bon jor ait qui mon cuer a!*
> *N'est pas o moi.*

Structurally this comes to: $I(a_7)$ $I(A_7)$ $I(a_7)$ $II(b_4)$ $I(A_7)$ $II(B_4)$. The essential features here are the presence of a final refrain which occupies the entire two-section melody, and the anticipation of the first part of this refrain in line two. At the earliest stage variations often existed between the exact phraseology of the refrain and its anticipation, but later the anticipation became exact. Rondeaux of the six-line type are also to be found within the *Lai d'Aristote* by Henri d'Andeli. The next stage was to introduce the refrain at the opening of the composition as well, giving the overall musical form which was to remain the basis of the rondeau thereafter: I–II–I–I–I–II–I–II. The resultant eight-line type is the most common in the late 13th and 14th centuries. Numerous examples of it, together with subsequent extensions, are to be found again interpolated into narrative works such as *Cleomadès* by Adenet le Roi, *Le roman du Chastelain de Couci* by Jakemes, *Meliacin* by Girart d'Amiens, *Le roman de Fauvel* by Gervais de Bus, and other scattered sources, quite apart from rondeaux forming part of the lyric output of known poet-musicians such as Adam de la Halle (whose 14 three-part settings in conductus style are the first polyphonic examples), Guillaume d'Amiens and Jehannot de l'Escurel, at the turn of the 13th and 14th centuries.

The emergence of the refrain at the opening of the composition invites a comparison with virelai form and, indeed, has led some distinguished musicologists, especially Gennrich, to contrive complicated interconnections between the histories of the two. Others doubt the necessity for this and see the two forms as entirely distinct from one another. A vital differentiating factor is the particular importance acquired by the rondeau refrain, since its performance, though it may only be two lines long, entails the use of the whole melody and not simply part of it. This may well be the reason why rondeau refrains took on a life of their own and are often to be found inserted into other songs, motets, romances and many miscellaneous literary works. Some 13th-century motets use an entire rondeau as one of the voice parts or as the fundamental tenor, a fact which occasionally makes possible the reconstruction of a piece found elsewhere without music. Others, known as *motets entés* ('grafted' motets), use simply a rondeau refrain in one voice, but with considerable new textual and musical material interpolated between its original opening and closing lines. An excellent example of this is the treatment accorded to Adam de la Halle's rondeau *A Dieu commant amouretes* (ex.1) in his motet *A Dieu commant amouretes/Aucun se sont loé d'amours/Super te.* Rondeau refrains, particularly in the 13th century, often seem to have been common property, and likewise certain phrases such as 'Main se leva bele Aaliz', 'C'est tot la gieus', 'La jus, desouz l'olive' recur in sources apparently otherwise unconnected with each other. The example by Adam de la Halle quoted is a 13-line type and this is merely one of a number of possible extensions made simply by setting varying numbers of lines

of text to the two underlying music sections, the pattern of which never changes. Table 1 shows typical possibilities.

The rhyme and metre may vary. In the 13th and early 14th centuries the eight-, 11- and 13-line types are frequent and often use mixed metres. From Machaut onwards the eight- and 16-line types dominate, with the 21-line type becoming popular in the 15th century, and mixed metres are rare in musical rondeau settings, though they may be encountered more often in unset verse (as, for example, in Christine de Pisan, who also promoted the use of shortened refrains).

Machaut's 22 rondeaux are all polyphonic, for solo voice and one, two or three accompanying instruments. Some, such as *Doulz viaire gracieus*, 12 bars long, are very brief musically and comparable in this respect with the earlier type; others, such as *Tant doucement*, 52

TABLE 1

Type	I	II	I	I	I	II	I	II
8-line	A	B	a	A	a	b	A	B
11-line	A	AB	a	A	a	ab	A	B
13-line	AB	B	ab	AB	ab	b	AB	B
16-line	AB	BA	ab	AB	ab	ba	AB	BA
21-line	ABB	BA	abb	ABB	abb	ba	ABB	BA

Ex. 1

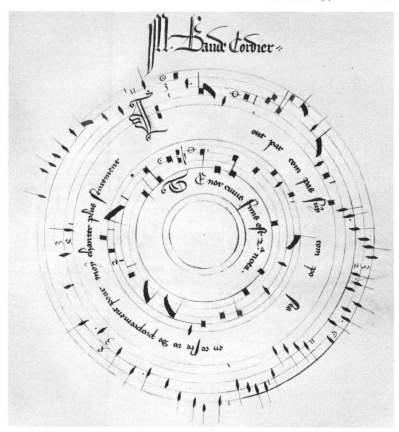

2. Canonic rondeau 'Tout par compas suy composés' by Baude Cordier (F-CH 1047, f.12r)

bars long, are more extended and make much use of long melismatic decoration on single syllables, a common feature of contemporary ballades. The idea of circular motion implied in the word 'rondeau', long after it had become dissociated from the dance, appealed to the medieval mind in more ways than one and Machaut gives a particularly fine example of ingenuity in this respect in his three-part rondeau *Ma fin est mon commencement/Et mon commencement ma fin* (fig.1). In this the music literally illustrates the text, for at its close it has indeed returned to its beginning: section II of the instrumental tenor is the exact retrograde of its section I; the cantus section II is the retrograde of the instrumental triplum section I; the triplum section II is the retrograde of the cantus section I. Ex.2 demonstrates this by giving the first four and the last four bars of the whole composition. A further, graphic example of the 'circular' rondeau idea is given by Baude Cordier in the early 15th century, whose canonic rondeau *Tout par compas suy composés* (see fig.2) is notated in circular form on a preliminary page of *F-CH* 1047 along with an equally imaginative notation in heart shape of his rondeau *Belle, bonne, sage.*

The rondeau text, like that of most ballades and virelais, was uually concerned with courtly love, though the treatment of this theme was generally rather lighter than in the ballade, given the rondeau's relative brevity. In one special area, however, the rondeau became widely used for a different purpose, namely in religious drama. Few religious rondeaux have survived with musical settings, but two or more texts are contained in each of the 40 14th century *Miracles de Nostre Dame*, written and performed by the Goldsmiths' Guild in Paris, and are normally sung by two or three voices as angels escort Our Lady to and

Ex. 2(a)

from Paradise. It seems likely that these texts, which structurally seem to belong more to the early 14th century, were contrafacta of already existing secular rondeaux and thus used the already existing music with a simple substitution of religious for amorous sentiments. In this way the religious rondeau continued the 13th-century tradition of the *chanson pieuse*. In the great 15th-century French Passion cycles, for example by Arnoul Greban and Jean Michel, the rondeau, with much other incidental music, continued to be most important, even extending to cacophonous devils' songs, and it also became a characteristic feature, in secular guise once more, of the 15th-century farce.

The 15th century was the true heyday of the rondeau, when it completely dominated all rival lyric forms. (For a detailed discussion of the relative popularity of rondeau, ballade and virelai in the 14th and 15th centuries *see* VIRELAI.) Hundreds were composed with music and hundreds more without. Of the most famous early 15th-century musicians Dufay left 59 and Binchois 47; many more remain by lesser figures such as Baude Cordier, Césaris, Haucourt, Lebertoul, Johannes Le Grant and Malbecque. Of the rondeaux written by non-musician poets the most important are by Christine de Pisan, Alain Chartier and Charles d'Orléans. Following the divorce between poets and musicians largely brought about by the great intricacy of late 14th-century musical style, it became more common than previously for musicians to set texts written by some poet other than themselves. A good and characteristic example is Binchois' setting of Chartier's rondeau *Triste plaisir et douleureuse joye*. Ex.3 gives the opening of this and demonstrates the characteristic instrumental prelude before the entry of the voice in bar five. The style is mellifluous, simple but extremely touching and perfectly suited to the sentiments of the text.

The increasing appearance in this repertory of vocal

writing with texts provided for all parts, reminiscent of Adam de la Halle, but probably under Italian influence, together with ever more use of imitation, point forward to important stylistic features of the late 15th- and 16th-century chanson.

For bibliography *see* CHANSON and FRANCE, BIBLIOGRAPHY OF MUSIC TO 1600.

NIGEL WILKINS

Rondeau (ii). French term for a composition, instrumental or vocal, based on the alternation of a main section (refrain, reprise, *grand couplet* or 'rondeau') with subsidiary sections (couplets, episodes). The term was also used by German and English composers for pieces in the form, particularly if they were written in the French style. In England the corruption 'Round O' was equally common. *See* RONDO, §§2, 3; ROUND O.

MALCOLM S. COLE

Rondelli, Jo. (*fl* 1420–25). Italian composer. He is known solely for a three-voice motet *Verbum tuum, verbum sane bonum/In te cruce* which survives only in *I-Bc* Q15. The work is for two high, equal voices and a textless tenor.

BIBLIOGRAPHY
G. de Van: 'An Inventory of the Manuscript Bologna, Liceo Musicale, Q 15 (olim 37)', *MD*, ii (1948), 231

For further bibliography *see* ITALY: BIBLIOGRAPHY OF MUSIC TO 1600.

TOM R. WARD

Rondellus. A technique of composition for three voices cultivated in 13th-century England; also, a piece completely composed in this manner.

The technique is rooted in the compositional device known as VOICE-EXCHANGE (more accurately, phrase-exchange). There were two ways in which 13th-century English composers applied voice-exchange technique to the three-part texture preferred by them. They either restricted it to the two upper voices supporting it with a repetitive tenor or *pes*, or they wrote triple voice-exchange, i.e. a melody consisting not of two, but of three fairly concise elements (ex.1), all of which are combined simultaneously.

Ex. 1 *English Polyphony*, no. 29

beginning of final cauda (tenor)

This procedure, which as horizontal projection of a simple harmonic scheme depends on 3rds, 5ths and octaves as constitutive intervals, was known by the medieval Latin term 'rondellus'. The only medieval writer to describe it was an Englishman, Walter Odington (*c*1300):

And when what is sung by one may be sung by everybody in turn, such a tune is called rondellus, i.e. a rotational or rounded melody. . . . Rondelli are to be composed as follows: contrive a melody, as beautiful as possible. . . . To this melody, with or without text, and sung by each, should be fitted one or two others consonant with it. Each thus sings the other's part [that is, in alternation].

Odington's musical example consists of twice three melodic elements; the first half is melismatic (in effect demonstrating the rondellus technique that occurs in many caudas of English conductus), while only one of the remaining three elements has text, which is therefore sung successively by each of the three voices. This latter procedure is the one that occurs most commonly, though some pieces composed near the end of the

Ex. 3

Tris-te plai - sir___ et dou-leu-reu-se joi - -

- e.

century exhibit more complex arrangements, such as that shown in ex.2.

Ex. 2 *English Polyphony*, no. 38

In conductus, voice-exchange and rondellus technique could enliven the melismatic caudas; in one case the evidence seems to indicate that poetry came to be applied to some of these 'rondellus caudas'. In any event, several English conductus prove that rondellus technique could be employed in texted sections as well as in caudas. The close relationship between rondellus and conductus was recognized by Odington, who pointed out that any polyphonic composition exhibiting all the features of a rondellus except its imitative technique would be a conductus. Voice-exchange over a *pes* and rondellus technique were also applied in the introductory tropes to the polyphonic settings of the verses and, especially, of the responds (solo portions) of alleluias.

About 100 years before Odington wrote his treatise, Giraldus Cambrensis gave the following report on Welsh music in his *Descriptio Cambriae* (1198):

When they make music together, they sing their songs not in unison, as is done elsewhere, but in parts, with many [simultaneous] modes [*modis*] and phrases [*modulis*], so that in a crowd of singers . . . you would hear as many songs and different intervals [*discrimina vocum varia*] as you could see heads; yet, they all accord in one consonant [*consonantiam;*

recte ? *consonantem*] polyphonic song [*organicam melodiam*], marked by the enchanting delight of B♭ [?F major].

The assumption that Giraldus here described the rondellus is strengthened by the probable provenance of those English sources that for the first time transmit pieces exhibiting rondellus technique. While they postdate the *Descriptio* by five or more decades, some of them seem to have originated in localities 30 to 60 km east of Wales. That rondellus and related techniques were particularly prominent in these areas, from which they spread, and seem to go back at least to the turn of the century is indicated not only by SUMER IS ICUMEN IN and its presumptive antecedents, but also by a French double motet which pokes fun at English and Scottish *godaliers* (guzzlers of good ale). This composition, dating from the second quarter of the 13th century, is the only continental cantus firmus motet of the time whose upper voices engage in voice-exchange, a procedure made possible by the unusual selection of a sequence as tenor. This motet is therefore a strong argument for the assumption that the parodied musical practice, abandoned by French composers as a result of their waning interest in conductus and organum, was known as typically and perhaps rather quaintly English at least as early as c1225.

Apart from the Summer Canon, which can be regarded as a potential multipart rondellus, there are no rondelli in existence for more than three voices. After 1300 the expansion of the two-voice framework beyond one octave (i.e. the regular acceptance of the 10th or 12th as the largest contrapuntal interval between the outer voices) caused voice-exchange and especially rondellus to become moribund practices. With their individual voice-exchange passages growing ever more lengthy, a number of compositions exhibit a hypertrophy characteristic of many species of art in their late stage. The most expansive complexity is reached by two long compositions in *GB-Cgc* 543/512, ff.248v 249 and ff.252v–253 (*Virgo Maria patrem parit/Virgo Maria flos divina* and *Tu civium primas/ Tu celestium primas*). In both pieces *signa congruentiae* indicate that the second halves of the two voices are to sound together with the first.

Continental rondellus compositions are relatively rare and, apart from involving three voices, their counterpoint as a rule hardly exceeds the level of complexity represented by ex.1 of VOICE-EXCHANGE. (The identification by Falck of two monophonic compositions in fasc.11 of *I-Fl* Plut.29.1 as rondelli is untenable.)

In continental medieval treatises 'rondellus' was generally used as the Latin term for rondeau.

BIBLIOGRAPHY

W. Wiora: 'Der mittelalterliche Liedkanon', *GfMKB Lüneburg 1950*, 71

L. A. Dittmer: 'An English "Discantuum Volumen"', *MD*, viii (1954), 19–58

——: 'Beiträge zum Studium der Worcester-Fragmente', *Mf*, x (1957), 29

——, ed.: *The Worcester Fragments*, MSD, ii (1957)

F. Ll. Harrison: *Music in Medieval Britain* (London, 1958, 2/1963)

E. Apfel: *Studien zur Satztechnik der mittelalterlichen englischen Musik* (Heidelberg, 1959), chap.1

E. H. Sanders: 'Tonal Aspects of 13th-century English Polyphony', *AcM*, xxxvii (1965), 19

H. H. Eggebrecht and F. Reckow: 'Das Handwörterbuch der musikalischen Terminologie', *AMw*, xxv (1968), 257

R. Falck: '"Rondellus", Canon, and Related Types before 1300', *JAMS*, xxv (1972), 38

E. H. Sanders, ed.: *English Music of the Thirteenth and Early Fourteenth Centuries*, PMFC, xiv (1979)

For further bibliography *see* ENGLAND: BIBLIOGRAPHY OF MUSIC TO 1600.

ERNEST H. SANDERS

Rondeña. Song and group dance of Andalusian origin and flamenco type; *see* FLAMENCO, Table 1, and SPAIN, §II, 6.

Rondo (It., also Eng. and Ger. by usage; Fr. *rondeau*). One of the most fundamental designs in music, the rondo is a structure consisting of a series of sections, the first of which (the main section or refrain) recurs, normally in the home key, between subsidiary sections (*couplets*, episodes) before returning finally to conclude, or round off, the composition (*ABAC . . . A*).

1. Origins and development of the formal concept. 2. The rondeau in France in the 17th and early 18th centuries. 3. The spread of the rondo. 4. The rondos of C. P. E. Bach. 5. The rondo as a movement in a larger work. 6. The sonata-rondo. 7. The independent rondo. 8. The rondo in the 19th and 20th centuries.

1. ORIGINS AND DEVELOPMENT OF THE FORMAL CONCEPT. The very simplicity of the rondo concept, and its consequent wide usage, makes it difficult to give any precise account of its origins. Any connection between the medieval or Renaissance rondeau and that of the 17th and 18th centuries is at best tenuous; and parallels between the later rondo and (for example) the ritornello principle and the rondo cantata need to be more thoroughly investigated. Those few 18th-century theorists who mentioned influences on the rondo confined themselves to such popular examples as the *Frantzösischer Ringel-Tantz* (Walther), the *Kreiz* or *Circul-Tantz* (Niedt), the *Zirkelstück* (Marpurg, Türk), and the *Rundgesang* (Türk). Mattheson, however, indignantly noted that although 'rondeau' does indeed derive from 'rond' or 'rund' (circle), the music to which this term is properly applied originates neither in the circle-dance nor in the *Runda* (a relative of the French *ronde de table*), a type of drinking-song in which a rousing refrain sung by all the merrymakers followed each participant's verse.

Later writers have suggested two principal influences from art music. Lully is alleged to have devised the rondeau of two *couplets*, sometimes called 'French rondeau'. The multi-*couplet* rondo (or chain rondo, *ABACAD...A*), sometimes called 'Italian rondo', presumably developed from early Italian opera. Peri's *Euridice* (1600), for example, contains two choral refrain–recitative complexes arranged in rondo fashion ('Al canto al ballo' and 'Sospirate aure celesti'). In the former, the sequence is: choral refrain–solo for nymph–refrain–solo for shepherd–refrain–solo for another nymph–refrain (*ABACADA*). The prologue of Monteverdi's *Orfeo* (1608) is a parallel example, with instrumental ritornellos instead of choral refrains. Similar structures were used throughout the century.

2. THE RONDEAU IN FRANCE IN THE 17TH AND EARLY 18TH CENTURIES. The rondeau in France enjoyed considerable popularity throughout the later 17th and early 18th centuries. It appeared in a wide range of media: ballet, opera and related genres (as instrumental piece, chorus and ultimately air or duo *en rondeau*), orchestral music, pieces for harpsichord and sonatas for violin. Composers appended the qualification 'en rondeau' to any dance title: gigue, minuet, gavotte, loure.

Of the early generation of rondeau composers, Lully was most important in the fields of opera and ballet, Chambonnières and Louis Couperin in keyboard music. The 'Rondeau pour les basques' from the *Ballet de Xerxes* furnishes an elementary example of the two-couplet design favoured by Lully. Each section, refrain and *couplets* alike, is in the tonic key and is eight bars long; in the first *couplet* the refrain idea is transposed, in the second it is inverted. A more complicated example is the 'Rondeau pour la gloire' from the prologue to *Alceste*. Refrain and *couplets* are of different lengths, *couplets* being further distinguished by contrasts in scoring and changes of key. A portion of Act 1 scene vii of *Alceste* may be viewed as a large rondo, the introductory rondeau itself serving as refrain for *couplets* allotted to various characters and the chorus. 'Suivons Armide' from *Armide* exemplifies the choral rondeau (Act 1 scene iii). Chambonnières, who favoured the two-*couplet* design, composed one work specifically entitled 'Rondeau' and several chaconnes-rondeaux, one of which has five *couplets*. Louis Couperin preferred the multi-*couplet* disposition, his chaconnes-rondeaux containing three and four *couplets*, his Passacaille eight.

In the following generation, François Couperin was the unrivalled master of the harpsichord rondeau, of which there are many examples in his Ordres; like most of his movements, they often bear fanciful titles (such as *Les baricades mistérieuses*, Ordre 6). He offered the richest structural variety of his day, the rondeaux containing one (*Les abeilles*, Ordre 1) to eight *couplets* (*Passacaille*, 8), but more often two (*Les silvains*, 1), three (*Soeur Monique*, 18) or four (*L'enchanteresse*, 1). Couperin's refrain is a discrete cell, often of eight or 16 bars and frequently framed with repeat signs (*La badine*, 5). In *Les bergeries* (6), an internal repeat is specified as well. Subsequent returns of the refrain are usually complete and literal, but in *Les bergeries* Couperin abbreviated the first return – his first use of this effective device for alleviating the monotony that can result from too many complete restatements of a refrain. In his earlier music Couperin's *couplets* are usually about the same length as the refrain; in later works they are often expanded (for example the final *couplets* of *La triomphante*, 10, and *L'ingénuë*, 19). Although it is not unknown for all *couplets* to remain in the main key (*La badine*), Couperin usually set them in related keys. To heighten the contrast between refrain and *couplet*, he sometimes changed the register of the *couplet* or altered its texture; more animated figuration is common in a final *couplet* (*Soeur Monique*). While *couplet* material may contrast sharply with the refrain (*Les gondoles de Délos*, 23, third part), it is often derived in some way: common techniques include such unifying devices as transposition of the refrain (*Le gazoüillement*, 6, second couplet), free continuation and expansion of a refrain motif (*Soeur Monique*, second *couplet*) and inversion (*L'ingénuë*, third *couplet*) or tonal answer of refrain motifs (*Le petit-rien*, 14, first *couplet*). Couperin's output also shows the evolution of the 'second rondeau' from an entity bound to the preceding rondeau only by a common tonic (*L'angélique*, 5) to one that functions as an organic component of the primary work (*Les gondoles de Délos*, third part in separate rondeau; *L'épineuse*, 26, fourth *couplet* in separate rondeau).

Following Couperin, Rameau further refined some of his predecessor's techniques but on the whole he standardized the rondeau, settling almost exclusively upon the two-*couplet* design in his harpsichord works. Jean Dubreuil, a theorist of the time, codified Rameau's practice. The refrain is always in the main key. With a rondeau in the major, the first *couplet* is in the dominant, the second in the submediant minor; with a rondeau in the minor, the first *couplet* is in the relative major, the second in the dominant minor. The singular and extensive *Les cyclopes* provides a striking exception to this remarkably consistent approach. In his dramatic works, Rameau not only produced several rondeaux with a single *couplet*; he also combined two such designs, with a modal shift of the second and a da capo of the first, to produce an expanded ternary configuration (*ABA C ABA*), as in the first and second 'Gavottes en rondeau' (C major, C minor) from *Les fêtes d'Hébé* (third entrée).

Leclair contributed to later 18th-century rondeau techniques, especially in his Aria movements for violin. His designs were fairly consistent, but he was among the first to use a linking passage to connect a *couplet* with an ensuing return of the refrain (op.2 no.4, Aria), to change metre and tempo within a couplet (op.1 no.9, Allegro ma non presto), and to incorporate a rondeau within a rondeau in the final couplet (op.1 no.1, Aria).

3. THE SPREAD OF THE RONDO. The rondeau cultivated by French composers quickly spread to other countries. Englishmen like Purcell and Germans like Georg Muffat and J. C. F. Fischer adopted French forms and techniques. J. S. Bach demonstrated his mastery in such compositions as the Passepied I from English Suite no.5 (BWV810) and the Rondeaux of the Partita no.2 for keyboard (BWV826), Partita no.3 for solo violin (BWV1006) and the B minor Ouverture (BWV1067). In Italy, E. F. Dall'Abaco and others used the form.

By the middle of the 18th century, the rondeau of French stamp was solidly established throughout Europe. Its assimilation into the music of other nations and its transformation into the rondo of the Classical period have not been adequately investigated. Theorists active at the middle of the 18th century described only the French rondeau, and it seems that German composers used the rondo rarely. However, from essays by music critics of the following generation, from correspondence by C. P. E. Bach and Mozart, and from the marked increase in the number of rondos composed, it appears that in the early 1770s there began a vogue for simple, tuneful rondos of a quite different stamp from the French products. German critics scolded Eichner and Dittersdorf for writing too many rondos. One theorist suggested that most fashionable pieces of this type have little true inner value (Forkel), another that the species was appearing ad nauseam in keyboard music (Cramer); one critic pointed to a flood of Italian imports, another to a popular rondo from an oboe concerto by J. C. Fischer. C. P. E. Bach admitted frankly that he included rondos to further the sale of his collections. In several letters, Mozart reported that audiences forced him to repeat the very rondos which he had composed specifically to replace movements in other forms (for example the finale K382 for the Piano Concerto K175, which however is not a true rondo by any accepted criteria for the form; as we shall see, the term was sometimes applied to movements of a popular type in which the main features of rondo structure are absent). In England a type of finale, characterized by simple tunefulness and light texture, became known as the 'Vauxhall rondo' by association with the pleasure gardens of that name; its exponents included Samuel Arnold and James Hook.

It is difficult to formulate a historical explanation of the vogue, because no single nation, musical type, composer or work appears to have been solely or primarily responsible. *Opera buffa*, however, provided much of the impetus. *Buffo* composers like Sarti, Paisiello and Piccinni sometimes ended their overtures with rondos, and interspersed vocal rondos throughout their scores. Imbued with lightness and simplicity, these compositions established the stereotype of a 'pleasing', 'charming', 'cheerful', 'clear', 'comprehensible' rondo theme, an idea that must be new and worth hearing six to eight times. German theorists, some of whom recognized the interaction of the vocal and instrumental spheres, frequently cited and even printed examples either from *opera buffa* or from German imitations in their essays on rondo (Reichardt, Koch). The content and form of texts appropriate for rondo setting particularly occupied French theorists, the consensus being that although texts should as a rule be light, Gluck's famous 'J'ai perdu mon Eurydice' (originally 'Che farò senza Euridice'; *Orfeo*, 1762) proves that a serious text may be effectively set in rondo form.

German composers, notably J. C. Bach, who absorbed the spirit and technique of the *opera buffa*, appear to have been the prime agents in the transformation and diffusion of this newer kind of rondo. J. C. Bach was also fond of the *menuet en rondeau* finale (for example in his Symphony op.9 no.2), and Mozart's frequent use of it, as in his Bassoon Concerto K191/186e, is clearly indebted to him. Within the older structural designs, primarily the two-*couplet* and the multi-*couplet* arrangements, such composers used in rapid tempos the gesture-like thematic style of the *buffo* overture, in slower tempos the lyrical manner of the *buffo* air. Rondos in all tempos show a more marked periodic arrangement, sharper contrast between refrain and episodes, and they often have a coda.

4. THE RONDOS OF C. P. E. BACH. One by-product of the rondo vogue was a series of critical essays whose authors, reluctantly acknowledging popular taste, advocated as models the singular examples by C. P. E. Bach. From the finale of the G major Trio (WQ90 no.2, 1776), which includes varied and transposed statements of the refrain, Forkel derived rules for the construction of a good rondo. Cramer, inventing fanciful characters and programmes, chose the fourth collection 'for Connoisseurs and Amateurs' (WQ58). That Bach himself was aware of the general trend in favour of light, cheerful rondos is shown in the dedication of his *Abschied von meinem Silbermannischen Claviere* (WQ66), in which he notes that one can – as this example proves – compose lamenting rondos.

C. P. E. Bach's rondos stand outside the mainstream of the genre's evolution. Indeed, a gulf separates Bach's own early, French-inspired rondos (*La Xénophon, La complaisante, Les langueurs tendres* WQ117, 1761) from the 13 refined, independent rondos of the series for 'Connoisseurs and Amateurs' (WQ56–9, 61, 1778–86). These are extended, leisurely compositions built sometimes on a lyrical theme, sometimes on a characteristic motif. On occasion Bach explored an idea rather than a theme, for example the harmonic progression from the tonic to the diminished 7th in the A minor Rondo of the second collection. Avoiding extremes of tension, he elaborated, embroidered and spun out his themes in conjunction with imaginative harmonic shifts and modulations. Episode material is often non-thematic, consisting of arpeggiated figuration, sequential passages and chains of chords that serve to prepare refrain statements in related keys. Bach often developed aspects of a refrain theme. Episodes tend to be lengthy and of open design rather than in the closed binary and ternary substructures used by his contemporaries (like J. C. Bach). Fused with the rondo principle of return are the technique of variation, the ritornello practice of transposition and improvisatory elements of the fantasy, such as figuration, dynamic juxtapositions, abrupt alternation of the lyric and the rhapsodic, and changes of metre and tempo within a composition (E major Rondo, third collection). At times, in fact, Bach dispensed with bar-lines altogether, as in the cadenza concluding the B♭ Rondo of the fourth collection, which one contemporary reviewer likened to a flight of the gods. Structural freedom, refrain transposition, fantasia figurations, harmonic sophistication and dynamic contrasts combine to make Bach's rondos personal and ingenious treatments of the form.

5. THE RONDO AS A MOVEMENT IN A LARGER WORK. In the mainstream of music in the Classical period, the rondo functioned most commonly as one movement within a large composition, appearing rarely as the first movement (Haydn, Piano Sonata HXVI:48), more frequently as the second (Beethoven, Piano Sonata op.13) or other interior movement (Mozart, Serenade K250/248b) and relatively often as the finale. It had limited use in chamber music and the symphony; it was more freely employed in sonatas and serenades, but only in the concerto was it the almost invariable choice for finales.

The substantial outputs of Haydn, Mozart and Beethoven elegantly summarize the rondo techniques of the late 18th and early 19th centuries. Haydn began composing rondos in the early 1770s; his best examples are found in his symphonies, string quartets and piano trios. Mozart used rondo form, in a variety of media, throughout his career. Beethoven, who used rondo form in his early chamber works, sonatas and concertos, abandoned it almost completely in his last years. Of particular interest is the apparent interaction between Haydn and Mozart, the former responding to Mozart's thematic complexes and preference for sonata-rondo design, the latter incorporating Haydn's thematic economy, thematic motivation and contrapuntal textures in all sections of a rondo. Each composer moved from a simple, sectional structure to a complex, integrated form into which he built surprise and variety, and within which he attempted to offset and even exploit the regularity inherent in the traditional layout.

Mozart wrote only four rondos, as finales or independent works, completely in the minor mode; Beethoven wrote five (including the finale of op.13, which is commonly cited as a model sonata-rondo). Because the typical rondo was supposed to be bright and cheerful, composers customarily chose other forms for finales in minor-key works (sonata-allegro, variation, fugue), but when they did conclude with a rondo, they sometimes placed the entire movement (Mozart, String Quintet K516) or at least the coda (Mozart, Piano Concerto K466) in the major. Duple (2/4, ¢, 6/8, rarely C) replaced the buffo and minuet-based variants of triple as the normal metre in rondo movements. Although each composer approached the problem of design differently, the formal arrangements of the earlier 18th century

remained in use. The two-episode structure (on occasion ABABA; more commonly ABACA, as in Beethoven's Piano Sonata op.53) was often used, Mozart and Beethoven employing it more than any other except the sonata-rondo and Haydn particularly favouring it. In his hands the design evolved from a sectional, variation type, in which the dominant is rarely the goal of the first episode (for example Symphony no.42), to one that in tonal scheme, disposition of the first episode and developmental second episode rivalled the opening movement and the mature sonata-rondo in integration and complexity (as in Symphony no.96). All three composers cultivated the multi-couplet rondo, Haydn and Beethoven at times incorporating fantasy or improvisatory elements (Haydn, Piano Concerto HXVIII:11; Beethoven, Piano Concerto WoO4). Haydn, notably in his piano trios, used the rondo of ternary design (ABACABA).

The Classical composers often used in rondo refrains the rhythms, the thematic character and the phrase regularity of the dance (for example the minuet and especially the contredanse). Folk- and popular song provided another stimulus, composers borrowing authentic folktunes on occasion (Haydn, Symphony no.103) and, more important, distilling their essence to produce a folklore imaginé that finds its most obvious expression in certain Hungarian, gypsy, Turkish or otherwise exotic works (Mozart, Piano Sonata K331/300i, 'alla turca'; Haydn, Piano Trio HXV:25, 'Rondo all'ongarese'). Often other formal principles (fantasy, variation, sonata) interacted, with results defying categorization.

The refrain, because of its fundamental importance, invites particular scrutiny. Composers occasionally connected the rondo with a preceding slow movement; Beethoven used this link in the Piano Concerto op.73 to anticipate the refrain theme. Mozart and Beethoven prefaced some refrains with a slow introduction (Beethoven, String Quartet op.132), while Haydn and Beethoven sometimes preceded the main theme with an introduction in tempo. In the early 1770s, Haydn and Mozart abandoned the rushing, buffo-inspired tutti refrain, preferring a moderate dance-like theme scored for reduced orchestra. Phrase structure is usually regular, harmonic rhythm slow. Beethoven, who extended the limits of admissible refrain material (for example in his Second Symphony), sometimes used non-tonic beginnings and allowed tonal ambivalence within the refrain. While Haydn consistently preferred ternary design, Mozart used a wide range of structures (often, mainly in the concertos, appending long closing groups); Beethoven added the threefold announcement of a single idea (Violin Concerto) and the open refrain (Second Symphony). A refrain is commonly a discrete cell, articulated from the following episode by changes of scoring, dynamics, register and texture. Haydn, in his use of first and second endings, showed some concern for relating the refrain functionally with the remainder of the work, and Beethoven sometimes blurred the structural joint between refrain and episode (Quartet op.132).

With the growing sense of tonic–dominant polarity in the Classical period, it is natural that we find most first episodes (except in Haydn's earlier works) in the dominant. As in sonata-allegros, the transitions developed from perfunctory bridges to passages of melodic, harmonic, rhythmic or textural interest; sometimes transition material (which is often merely figural) is derived from the main theme, or it may even anticipate the episode theme. The episode itself may contain a thematic complex, a single new theme, no distinct theme at all, a transposed statement of a refrain idea or one derived from it (again parallel to the contemporary development of the sonata-allegro). There may be a separate closing unit confirming the new tonality.

In rondos of the early Classical period, returns of the refrain were usually literal. Later, altered versions were common, in which variation, rescoring, extension and even transposition (partial or complete) may appear. Mozart often used long refrains of an *ABA* pattern, with only the *A* section reappearing in intermediate statements. Beethoven, for example in his Violin Concerto, sometimes placed final statements of the refrain in remote keys.

Second and later episodes usually enter without preparation (like the trios of minuets) in the earlier rondos of Haydn, Mozart and Beethoven. Later, the refrain statement is often reshaped to connect with the ensuing episode. All three composers began by placing the episode in the closest related keys (apart from the dominant) – the submediant, tonic minor and subdominant; later they expanded the range, and the number of keys touched upon increased parallel with the use of development. Changes of metre and tempo are rare in Haydn or Beethoven, but appear in several Mozart works (Violin Concertos K216, 218, 219; *Serenata notturna* K239; Piano Concertos K271, 415, 482), emphasizing the form's essentially sectional nature. Central episodes of closed design (binary or ternary) are common, and within them there may appear contrasting material, a derived theme, or virtuoso passage-work. Particularly important is the tendency to use developmental techniques, including eventually fugato, canon, inversion and double counterpoint (sometimes alongside new material); Haydn preceded Mozart in the use of such techniques.

The coda, at first merely a cadential tag, later became almost an additional development section, and was sometimes long and intricate. Haydn, Mozart and Beethoven all on occasion digressed to the minor mode and to other keys (the subdominant being particularly favoured), and they often used development of a humorous character, with unexpected rests, tempo fluctuations, scoring and dynamic contrasts, tremolos and similar devices (for example Haydn, Symphony no.102). Beethoven in particular sometimes changed the metre and accelerated the tempo at this point and, primarily in codas of concerto rondos, even introduced new themes.

6. THE SONATA-RONDO. One of the most significant innovations of the Classical period is the sonata-rondo, a design confined almost exclusively to finales. The specific components of a sonata-rondo have been, and remain, the subject of disagreement. In this fusion of rondo design with a sonata-allegro tonal plan – which entails the recapitulation in the tonic of the first episode and, possibly, the replacement of the contrasting central episode with a development of earlier material – Mozart, Haydn and Beethoven created some of the most complex finales of the period. Mozart, in the String Quartet K157 (1772–3), composed the first known sonata-rondo; during the remainder of his career he refined the form, experimenting with a wide range of structural possibilities. Haydn, on the other hand, adopted it relatively late (Symphony no.77, 1782) and used it

sparingly. In fact, he wrote sonata-rondos in significant numbers only in the 1790s. In ten of the 12 London symphonies he created some of the most unusual, complex, yet immediately appealing rondos and sonata-rondos of the period. Like Mozart, Beethoven wrote many sonata-rondos, using techniques of surprise to enliven a relatively standardized design. The general plan of a sonata-rondo is as follows:

A: the main theme (refrain); in spite of increasing length and complexity, it was normally treated as a self-contained unit with a cadence in the tonic.

B: the first episode, usually in the dominant (or relative major in a minor-key movement); analogous in function to the second group in a sonata exposition.

A: the first return, literal, varied, abbreviated, rescored, extended or even transposed.

C: the second episode, usually starting in the tonic minor, submediant or subdominant; it may range from a closed, contrasting substructure to a complex contrapuntal development.

(*A*): this and subsequent returns may be omitted (Mozart ultimately favoured this abbreviation: *ABACB¹A*, coda).

B¹: recapitulation in the tonic of material from the first episode; it may be an exact recapitulation, or the material may be rearranged, compressed or extended, and in the mature music of Haydn, Mozart and Beethoven it is normally rescored.

(*A*): the final return; usually omitted, or telescoped with the coda, by Haydn and Beethoven.

Coda: it may range from a cadential flourish to an additional development.

In early sonata-rondos, Mozart often included a fourth episode, so that the structure was *ABACADAB¹A*. A fascinating aspect of his personal evolution is his move from these multi-*couplet*, sectional sonata-rondos to a concise, complex and integrated form of the pattern *ABACB¹A*.

The sonata-rondo in the concerto created further complications and offered the composer special challenges and opportunities. Mozart's piano concertos provide a particularly fertile field for study, their composer facing such problems as the feasibility of a double exposition, the presentation and subsequent role of a solo entry theme, the rearrangement and consolidation of the recapitulation, the placing of one or more cadenzas, and the transformation of the coda from a closing ritornello to an additional development.

In addition to rondos and sonata-rondos, each composer produced several examples of finales that cannot firmly be assigned to any one formal category. Some are clearly experimental (Beethoven, Symphony no.1); others are consummate fusions of the composer's most mature techniques (Beethoven, String Quartets opp.130, 135). Some fall in the rondo sphere, but whether or not they are strictly sonata-rondos is open to argument (Haydn, Symphony nos.88, 101); Haydn in particular often incorporated sonata procedures in rondos which lack the sonata-rondo recapitulation. Of special interest are Mozart's Rondo K485 and the finales of Haydn's Piano Trio HXV:14 and Mozart's Serenade K525, which by generally accepted criteria are in sonata form. The composers themselves, however, specifically marked the movements 'Rondo'. In conjunction with essays by Kollmann and Momigny, the impression emerges that to the later 18th century the term 'rondo', for more recent theorists purely a formal pattern, implied something less definite – a theme type, a character designation specially appropriate for the finale of a work in several movements.

7. THE INDEPENDENT RONDO. C. P. E. Bach was not the only composer of the Classical period to write independent rondos. Mozart, in addition to his substitute works (K382, Rondo K269/261*a*), created memorable examples in the F major Rondo K494 and the great A minor Rondo K511, a rich, chromatic outpouring that foreshadows the piano genre pieces of the 19th century. The Adagio and Rondeau for glass harmonica and four other instruments (K617), Mozart's only independent instrumental rondo with slow introduction, seems to be related in form to his vocal scenas, which consist of a recitative and aria *en rondeau* (such as K255, 374, 416). His arias marked 'Rondò', however, belong to a different category (*see* RONDÒ). In his early years, Beethoven composed several independent rondos for piano including the lyrical op.51 no.1 and the wild, brilliant, Hungarian *Rondo a capriccio* (op.129), a rondo in the improvisatory style of the fantasia.

Noted by Czerny as one of the few forms that can stand independently, the rondo flourished as a separate composition in the 19th century, particularly as a virtuoso, bravura piece. Dussek, Hummel, Weber, Kalkbrenner, Moscheles, Herz, Thalberg and others left many examples, of which the titles alone indicate their primary purpose: 'Rondeau brillant' is typical. Further qualifying terms alert the listener to the composers' intentions to simulate national flavour (Spanish, Polish, Russian), exploit a popular tune, or capture a mood (pastoral, sentimental, military). Primarily but by no means exclusively for piano, these freely, often loosely constructed display vehicles were commonly framed by an arresting introduction and a breathlessly rushing coda.

The great composers too were receptive to this aspect of the continuing vogue for rondos. Schubert wrote an Adagio and Rondo concertante for piano, violin, viola and cello (D487) as well as examples for solo piano (D506), piano duet (D608) and piano and violin (D895). Chopin's first published composition was a rondo (op.1) which he followed with a *Rondo à la Mazur* (op.5) and two other rondos (opp.16, 73). Liszt based a virtuoso *Rondeau fantastique* on an allegedly Spanish tune, 'El contrabandista', and Mendelssohn wrote the famous *Rondo capriccioso* for piano (op.14, with introduction) and the *Rondo brillant* for piano and orchestra (op.29).

8. THE RONDO IN THE 19TH AND 20TH CENTURIES. Rondos were composed in smaller numbers in the 19th century than at the end of the 18th, but the form remained current throughout the 19th century, especially in the concerto. Most composers retained the scheme perfected by Haydn, Mozart and Beethoven. Schubert was a notable exception. In his early years he favoured an *ABABA* design, rarely using the more common *ABACA* pattern or the sonata-rondo. Like his Viennese predecessors, he occasionally placed returns of the refrain in keys other than the tonic: in the second movement of the Piano Sonata D537, for example, the first return is in the flat supertonic. He also favoured lengthy, tonally complex episodes. In his later sonatas he retained the *ABABA* form for slow movements, but for finales he preferred the *ABACA* design (D850, 894) and the sonata-rondo (D845, 958, 959, 960). Some of these are extremely long: the sonata-rondo of D958

takes 717 bars. Initial refrain statements became extended complexes, which Schubert altered on their return. Unlike Haydn and Beethoven, who usually wrote lengthy second (central) episodes, Schubert laid more weight on the first episode. In the finale of the celebrated Sonata in B♭ (D960), the central episode is of 58 bars, the refrain 73 and the first episode 152; the episode material is organized into two distinct and harmonically dazzling groups, the first basically in the major mode, the second in the minor. Having devised such magical relationships, Schubert was content to restate them almost literally in the recapitulation.

Of composers closer to Beethoven's legacy, Schumann extended the range of tonal possibilities for episodes; the sonata-rondo of 'Aufschwung' of the *Fantasiestücke* (op.12), for example, has a singular tonal plan. The *moto perpetuo* finale of the G minor Sonata (op.22) contains notable instances of the false reprise and the first episode, in B♭, is recapitulated in E♭. Brahms made much use of the rondo and the sonata-rondo finale; there are elegantly proportioned examples in many of his works from the Serenade op.11 to the String Quintet op.111. All his rondo finales are in duple metre, and all are in major keys except the 'Rondo alla zingarese' from the Piano Quartet op.25 and the finale of the D minor Piano Concerto. Brahms's rondo practices often recall Beethoven's, for example the non-tonic beginning in Piano Concerto no.2 and the change of metre in the central episode of the Violin Concerto as well as its accelerated coda. Mendelssohn employed the sonata-rondo as finale in his two piano concertos (opp.25, 40) and the Violin Concerto, all of which open with movements in the minor mode. Each finale, however, is in the major. There are introductions before the refrains in Piano Concerto no.1 and the Violin Concerto, while the abbreviated first return of the latter is in the mediant. Tchaikovsky's Violin Concerto and Grieg's Piano Concerto in A minor are other celebrated concertos with rondo finales, the latter a sonata-rondo with a contrasting central episode and an accelerated, strikingly transformed coda in A major.

Standing somewhat apart are those late 19th- and early 20th-century compositions in which the rondo principle is operative in a broad sense. Perhaps the most famous example is Richard Strauss's *Till Eulenspiegels lustige Streiche nach alter Schelmenweise, in Rondeauform*. In fact rondo, symphonic development and variation unite in as free an adaptation of the Classical rondo as Strauss's adaptation of sonata-allegro had been in earlier tone poems. Mahler's Fifth Symphony concludes with a Rondo-Finale, a gigantic structure with an introduction in tempo and accelerated close. The third movement of the Ninth Symphony, Rondo-Burleske, is another free and expansive treatment of the Classical rondo.

The rondo and sonata-rondo have survived in the 20th century in the works of composers influenced by the traditions of the Classical period. In the sonata-rondo finale of Prokofiev's Piano Sonata no.4 (C minor, finale in C major), the refrain is a discrete cell with an anacrusis recalling Beethoven's Piano Sonata op.2 no.2; the rushing tempo slackens in the central episode, and there is a brief codetta. In his Piano Sonata no.9, the refrain is open, tempo fluctuations reinforce the articulation of each episode, and the coda is a further development. Bartók superbly realized the independent rondo in 20th-century terms in his Three Rondos on

Folktunes (1916–27). In the Piano Sonata (1926), he achieved an effective fusion of monothematic sonata-rondo and variation in a folklike finale that recalls Haydn, while in Piano Concerto no.3 he created a rondo with brilliant fugal episodes. Further examples of the wide range of techniques employed in 20th-century rondos are furnished by Hindemith in Sinfonietta in E (1949), Stravinsky in the Concerto in D for strings (1946), and Piston in the String Quartet no.3 (1947), a model sonata-rondo in contemporary terms.

BIBLIOGRAPHY
GENERAL
WaltherML

F. E. Niedt: *Friederich Erhard Niedtens Musicalischer Handleitung . . . von der Variation des General-Basses* (Hamburg, rev. 2/1721 by J. Mattheson), 104f

J. Mattheson: *Der Vollkommene Capellmeister* (Hamburg, 1739/R1954), 230

J. Grassineau: *A Musical Dictionary* (London, 1740/R1966), 205

F. W. Marpurg: *Des Critischen Musicus an der Spree* (Berlin, 1750/R1970), no.6, pp.46f

J. Dubreuil: *Manuel Harmonique, ou Tableau des accords pratiques . . . & deux nouveaux menuets en rondeau* (Paris, 1767)

J. J. Rousseau: *Dictionnaire de musique* (Paris, 1768/R1969; Eng. trans., 1779), 421

J. N. Forkel: *Musikalisch-kritische Bibliothek*, ii (Gotha, 1778–9/R1970), 181ff

J. F. Reichardt, ed.: *Musikalisches Kunstmagazin*, i (Berlin, 1782), 168ff

C. F. Cramer, ed.: *Magazin der Musik*, i (Hamburg, 1783/R1971), 1241ff

D. G. Türk: *Klavierschule, oder Anweisung zum Klavierspielen für Lehrer und Lernende* (Leipzig and Halle, 1789/R1963), 398

H. C. Koch: *Versuch einer Anleitung zur Composition*, iii (Leipzig, 1793/R1969), 248ff

A. F. C. Kollmann: *An Essay on Practical Musical Composition* (London, 1799), 4, 6

H. C. Koch: *Musikalisches Lexicon* (Frankfurt am Main, 1802), cols.1271–4

J. J. de Momigny: 'Rondeau/rondo', *Encyclopédie méthodique*, ii (Paris, 1818), 408ff

A. Reicha: *Traité de haute composition musicale*, ii (Paris, 1824–5), 301ff

A. B. Marx: *Die Lehre von der musikalischen Komposition*, iii (Leipzig, 1845, 2/1848), 94–200, 307–13

C. Czerny: *School of Practical Composition*, i (London, 1849), 67ff

B. Widmann: *Formenlehre der Instrumentalmusik* (Leipzig, 1862), 87–118

A. von Dommer, ed.: *Koch's Musikalisches Lexicon* (Heidelberg, 2/1865), 736f, 787f

H. Mendel: *Musikalisches Conversations-Lexicon*, viii (Berlin, 1877), 408ff

E. Prout: *Applied Forms* (London, 1895), 107ff, 212ff

V. d'Indy: *Cours de composition musicale*, ii (Paris, 1909), 312ff

F. Piersig: 'Das Rondo', *Musikalische Formen in historischen Reihen*, iv (1909)

W. Chrzanowski: *Das instrumentale Rondeau und die Rondoformen im xviii. Jahrhundert* (Leipzig, 1911)

H. Leichtentritt: *Musikalische Formenlehre* (Leipzig, 1911, 3/1948; Eng. trans., 1935, 1951)

R. von Tobel: *Die Formenwelt der klassischen Instrumentalmusik* (Leipzig, 1935), 180ff

L. J. Beer, ed.: *Das Rondo, neun Klavierstücke aus dem 17. und 18. Jahrhundert* (Leipzig, 1941)

H. Engel: 'Rondeau–Rondo', §C, *MGG*

M. S. Cole: *The Development of the Instrumental Rondo Finale from 1750–1800* (diss., Princeton U., 1964)

——: 'Sonata-Rondo, the Formulation of a Theoretical Concept in the 18th and 19th Centuries', *MQ*, lv (1969), 180

——: 'The Vogue of the Instrumental Rondo in the Late 18th Century', *JAMS*, xxii (1969), 425–55

——: 'Rondos, Proper and Improper', *ML*, li (1970), 388

C. Rosen: *The Classical Style* (New York, 1972)

INDIVIDUAL COMPOSERS
C. F. Abdy Williams: 'The Rondo Form, as it is Found in the Works of Mozart and Beethoven', *PMA*, xvii (1890–91), 95

M. Friedlaender: 'Ein unbekanntes Jugendwerk Beethovens', *JbMP 1898*, 68

E. Mandyczewski: 'Beethoven's Rondo in B für Pianoforte und Orchester', *SIMG*, i (1899–1900), 295

S. Clercx: 'La forme du rondo chez Carl Philipp Emanuel Bach', *RdM*, xvi (1935), 148

W. McNaught: 'Is "Till Eulenspiegel" a Rondo?', *MT*, lxxviii (1937), 789

R. Tenschert: 'Rondo- oder Sonatenform?', *ZfM*, Jg.108 (1941), 775

H. J. Therstappen: *Joseph Haydns sinfonisches Vermächtnis* (Wolfenbüttel, 1941)

J. Gehring: 'Mozarts Rondo in D, K.-V. Nr.485', *SMz*, lxxxv (1945), 73

E. Hertzmann: 'The Newly Discovered Autograph of Beethoven's *Rondo à Capriccio*, Op.129', *MQ*, xxxii (1946), 171

M. Bedbur: *Die Entwicklung des Finale im Symphonien von Haydn, Mozart und Beethoven* (diss., U. of Cologne, 1953)

M. Chusid: *The Sonata-rondo in Mozart's Instrumental Works* (diss., U. of California, Berkeley, 1955)

R. Tenschert: 'Zwischen den Formen: . . . (Mozarts Klavierrondo K.V.485)', *Festschrift Wilhelm Fischer* (Innsbruck, 1956), 33

T. D. Hibbard: 'John Field's Rondeaux on *Speed the Plough* ', *MR*, xxiv (1963), 139

R. Dumm: 'An Analytic-interpretive Lesson on Mozart's Rondo in A Minor', *Clavier*, iii (1964), 28

P. Barford: *The Keyboard Music of C. P. E. Bach* (London, 1965), 122ff

H. Neumann and C. Schachter: 'The Two Versions of Mozart's Rondo K.494', *Music Forum*, i (1967), 1–34

M. S. Cole: 'The Rondo Finale: Evidence for the Mozart-Haydn Exchange?', *MJb 1968–70*, 242

——: 'Techniques of Surprise in the Sonata-rondos of Beethoven', *SM*, xii (1970), 233–62

——: 'Mozart Rondo Finales with Changes of Meter and Tempo', *SM*, xvi (1974), 25

——: 'Czerny's Illustrated Description of the Rondo or Finale', *MR*, xxxvi (1975), 5

E. W. Murphy: 'Sonata-rondo Form in the Symphonies of Gustav Mahler', *MR*, xxxvi (1975), 54

MALCOLM S. COLE

Rondò. A term used for a type of aria popular in the late 18th century, marginally related to rondo form. Arteaga, after mentioning that the term was loosely used, described the rondò as an extended and sublime aria, containing two sections, one slow and one fast, each repeated just twice; he claimed that such arias were 'certainly better than the so-called old-fashioned aria cantabile, because more natural, more truthful and more expressive'. As Framery stated, the form originated in the 1760s in the arias of Piccinni, and most examples, following Piccinni's practice, are in gavotte rhythm. Sarti was another notable user of the form. The best-known examples are by Mozart, who did not always observe the rule about repeating each section; they include 'Non temer, amato bene' (K490, written for *Idomeneo* in 1786), 'Non mi dir' (*Don Giovanni*, K527) and 'Per pietà' (*Così fan tutte*, K588). The rondò is an important precursor of the cantabile–cabaletta scheme of the early 19th century.

The spelling 'rondò' was commonly used for this form; but as other spellings (rondo, rondeau) are also found, and as 'rondò' was sometimes used in other contexts, it would be mistaken to regard it as prescriptive.

BIBLIOGRAPHY
E. Arteaga: *Le rivoluzioni del teatro musicale italiano* (Bologna and Venice, 1783–8), iii, 194ff

N. E. Framery: *Encyclopédie methodique*, i (Paris, 1791)

D. Heartz: 'Mozart and his Italian Contemporaries: "La clemenza di Tito" ', *MJb 1978–9*, 275

Ronga, Luigi (*b* Turin, 19 June 1901). Italian musicologist. After taking an arts degree at the University of Turin, he studied musicology at Dresden. On his return to Italy he taught music history at Palermo Conservatory (1926) and in Rome at the Accademia di S Cecilia and the Pontificio Istituto di Musica Sacra (1930), before being appointed lecturer (1938) and professor (1958–71) at the university. He received his *libera docenza* in 1930. He was editor of *Rassegna musicale* (1928–9) and *Rivista musicale* *italiana* (1954–5), and has also served as president of the Istituto Italiano per la Storia della Musica, and as a member of the Accademia di S Cecilia and the Lincei. Ronga's early period abroad afforded him contact with German musicology and he acquired a grounding unusual for Italian musicologists of his generation. He has been highly thought of by Italian scholars of other disciplines, an asset which has furthered his efforts to reconcile their attitudes towards music (based, as were his own, on the aesthetic teaching of Benedetto Croce) with the more intellectual German approach, but which he attempted to accomplish by employing a language that is non-technical.

WRITINGS

Scritti sulla musica e sui musicisti (Milan, 1925; repr. 1942 as *La musica romantica*, 4/1958) [trans. of R. Schumann: *Gesammelte Schriften über Musik und Musiker*, Leipzig, 1854]
Per la critica wagneriana (Turin, 1928)
Gerolamo Frescobaldi, organista vaticano, nella storia della musica strumentale (Turin, 1930)
Lezioni di storia della musica (Rome, 1933–5)
'Nuove tendenze nella critica musicale europea', *1° congresso internazionale di musica: Firenze 1933*, 31
Rossini (Florence, 1939)
Lineamenti del romanticismo musicale (Rome, 1943)
La musica nell'antichità (Rome, 1945)
Claude Debussy e l'impressionismo musicale (Rome, 1946)
Il dramma musicale di Richard Wagner (Rome, 1947)
'Aspetti del costume musicale contemporaneo', *5° congresso internazionale di musica: Firenze 1948*, 66
'Soggettivismo e oggettivismo nell'espressione musicale', *6° congresso internazionale di musica: Firenze 1949*, 27
'Tasso e la musica', *Torquato Tasso: Ferrara 1954*, 187
Arte e gusto nella musica: dall'ars nova a Debussy (Milan and Naples, 1956)
Bach, Mozart, Beethoven (Venice, 1956)
'I generi nella critica musicale', *Critica e poesia*, ed. M. Fubini (Bari, 1956), 275
The Meeting of Poetry and Music (New York, 1956)
'La musica', *La civiltà veneziana nell'età barocca* (Florence, 1959), 123
Il linguaggio musicale romantico (Rome, 1960)
L'esperienza storica della musica (Bari, 1960)
Introduzione a 'La Diana schernita' di Cornacchioli (Rome, 1961)
La musica europea nella seconda metà dell'ottocento (Rome, 1961)
Storia della musica (Rome, 1962–3)
'L'opera metastasiana', *P. Metastasio: Opere*, ed. M. Fubini (Milan and Naples, 1968), p.vii

BIBLIOGRAPHY

Scritti in onore di Luigi Ronga (Milan and Naples, 1973) [incl. V. Gui: 'Luigi Ronga', 19]

CAROLYN M. GIANTURCO

Ronger, Florimond. *See* HERVÉ.

Ronghe, Albericus de. Flemish musician; a volume of five-part pieces for voices and instruments, now thought to be by MICHAËL DE RONGHE, has been attributed to him.

Ronghe, Michaël de (*b* 30 Oct 1620; *d* ?Hemiksem, nr. Antwerp, 8 Jan 1696). Flemish composer. He entered the Cistercian abbey of St Bernard at Hemiksem on 5 August 1640 and was ordained on 17 March 1646. For much of his life he was 'cantor perpetuus' of the abbey and in this capacity compiled several volumes of liturgical music. He was almost certainly the composer of a lost volume of five-part pieces for voices and instruments, *Nardus odorifera, harmonica, dorica, fugata, opus integrum musicum* (Antwerp, 1663), which has traditionally been attributed to Albericus de Ronghe (1615–66), a sometime colleague at St Bernard who published two devotional works; in one of them he is referred to as an able organist.

NIGEL FORTUNE, GODELIEVE SPIESSENS

Ronly-Riklis, Shalom (*b* Tel-Aviv, 24 Jan 1922). Israeli conductor. He studied at the music academy in Jerusalem (1940–42), was a horn player (1942–6) in the British Army Orchestra (later the orchestra of the Jewish Brigade) and, in 1946, conducted it. He then studied (1946–8) at the music academy in Tel-Aviv and, on the foundation of the Israel Defence Forces Band, was appointed its chief conductor (1949–60). With the founding of the Israel Defence Forces SO (1951) and its amalgamation with the Gadna National Youth Orchestra (1957), Ronly-Riklis came to hold an important position in Israeli musical life. Between 1957 and 1970 the Gadna Youth Orchestra under him toured Europe, Canada, the USA and Latin America, and won the Queen Juliana of Holland Prize for amateur orchestras. Ronly-Riklis was director of the Israel Broadcasting SO (1961–70) and in 1969 was invited to assist in founding the National SO of Singapore, visiting it as conductor and musical adviser. In 1971 he was appointed artistic coordinator of the Israel PO, and founded the Junior PO in conjunction with the Rubin Academy of Music, Tel-Aviv; in 1969 he began teaching conducting. He also founded a chamber orchestra at the Academy of Tel-Aviv. As a guest he has conducted other orchestras in Israel as well as in Europe, Iceland, the USA and South Africa. He was a professor at Tel-Aviv University from 1977.

WILLIAM Y. ELIAS

Rönnagel [Rennagel], Johann Wilhelm (*b* Nuremberg, 29 Oct 1690; *d* Ansbach, 30 March 1759). German music publisher. In 1716 he settled in Ansbach as the court book dealer with the margrave's special permission. From 1716 to 1738 he also worked in Nuremberg as a book dealer and publisher and produced approximately 20 music prints, including a work by Pachelbel. However, he had insufficient musical knowledge to compete with other Nuremberg music publishers. He became bankrupt, his premises were sold by auction in 1739–40 and he retired to Ansbach.

BIBLIOGRAPHY

R. Eitner: *Buch- und Musikalien-Händler* (Leipzig, 1904)
A. Bayer: *Ansbacher Buchdruck in 350 Jahren* (Ansbach, 1952)
R. Merkel: *Buchdruck und Buchhandel in Ansbach* (Erlangen, 1965), 307ff

WOLFGANG SPINDLER

Ronnefeld, Peter (*b* Dresden, 26 Jan 1935; *d* Kiel, 6 Aug 1965). German composer and conductor. He studied the piano with Riebensahm and composition with Blacher at the Berlin Musikhochschule (1950–54) and continued his composition studies with Messiaen at the Paris Conservatoire (1954–5). In 1955 he won first prize in the Hilversum Conducting Competition and became a teacher of the piano, aural training and theory in Salzburg, where he also worked as assistant to Dorati and Wallberg at the Salzburg festivals. Between 1958 and 1961 he was Karajan's assistant at the Vienna Staatsoper and harpsichordist with the Vienna Concentus Musicus. He was then chief conductor at the Theater der Stadt, Bonn (1961–3), and finally Generalmusikdirektor in Kiel. As a conductor he appeared in several German cities and in Copenhagen as well as on radio and record; he was particularly interested in performing contemporary music. His most notable compositions are for the theatre, displaying a forceful character through advanced compositional technique, ironical disdain and a brilliant use of stylistic parody.

WORKS

Stage: Peter Schlemihl (ballet), 1955–6; Nachtausgabe (chamber opera), 1956, Salzburg, 1956; Die Ameise (opera, 4, R. Bletschacher, Ronnefeld), 1959–61, Düsseldorf, 1961; Die Spirale (ballet), 1961

Orch: Little Suite, 1949; Concertino, chamber orch, 1950; Non scholae, ov., 1951; Sinfonie 52, 1952; Rondo, 1954; Improvisation, 1954; 2 Episoden, chamber orch, 1956; Ameisen-Suite [from opera], 1961

Vocal: Jahrmarkt, 5 songs, 1953–4; 5 Lieder im Herbst, S/T, pf, 1954; 4 Wiegenlieder (textless), S, fl, 1955; 2 Lieder zur Pauke, A, fl, 4 timp, 1955; Quartär, cantata, S, chorus, speaking chorus, orch, 1958–9

Inst: Sonata, vn, pf, 1951; Str Trio, 1952; Sonata, vn, pf, 1953; 2 nocturnes, vc, pf, 1954; 6 Skizzen, pf, 1955

Principal publisher: Modern

MONIKA LICHTENFELD

Ronsard, Pierre de (*b* La Poissonnière, nr. Vendôme, 11 Sept 1524; *d* Abbey of St Cosme, Touraine, 27 Dec 1585). French poet. He was the leader of the literary group known as the Pléiade. He entered court life at the age of 12 when his father secured for him the position of page to the dauphin; when the dauphin died soon afterwards, he entered the service of the Duke of Orleans and was later sent to Scotland as a member of the retinue of Madeleine, the duke's sister, when she married James V. Madeleine too died young and Ronsard remained in Scotland until James's marriage to Marie de Guise. In 1539 he returned to France and, because he was becoming deaf, withdrew from court to study with Jean Dorat at the Collège de Coqueret. His fellow pupils included Belleau, Baïf and du Bellay whose *Défense et illustration de la langue française* (Paris, 1549) was the first published statement of the ideals of the Pléiade. The first important creative fruits of the group were Ronsard's five books of *Odes* (1550–52), modelled on Horace and Pindar, and the Petrarchan sonnets *Les Amours de Cassandre* (1552–3) which were all immediately successful; as a result of these and subsequent successes he was drawn back into court circles and enjoyed the protection of Charles IX and his sister, and the patronage of Mary Stuart. He received an annual stipend and the benefices of two priories.

At court Ronsard collaborated with musicians in devising entertainments for Charles IX and later Henri III. Nicolas de La Grotte published settings of his *Chant triomphal*, celebrating the victory at Jarnac in 1569, and *Stances promptement* and *Pour le trophée d'amour* which were sung as an *intermède* between the acts of *La belle Genvièvre*, a comedy translated from Ariosto and performed at Fontainebleau in February 1564. After Charles's death in 1574 Ronsard became less involved with court life but he continued to write and published a new collection of love poems, *Sonnets pour Hélène*, in 1578. When he died in 1585 a requiem mass was composed by Jacques Mauduit.

Like most of his humanist contemporaries Ronsard's works frequently refer to music; but although his poetry is permeated by the idea of music as a metaphor for poetic composition it reveals no evidence of practical skill or knowledge. His musical references are generally neo-Platonic, using, for example, the imagery of musical instruments to symbolize the subject and tone of the poem (the lyre, lute, guitar or harp for the lyrical, the flute, flageolet, chalumeau, cornemuse, musette for the pastoral) and figures from ancient mythology to lend authority to the ideas expressed. In 1560 he wrote the dedication to François II of an important

anthology of chansons and revised it for a second edition addressed to Charles IX (*RISM* 1572[2]); the philosophic arguments used to convince the king of the benefits of music – notably its moral virtues and its modal 'effects' – are substantially those of Plutarch and Boethius, but Ronsard claimed that the compositions of Lassus had surpassed all those of the ancients, including even Josquin and his disciples. Elsewhere in his poetry Ronsard extolled virtuoso performers such as Alberto de Ripa, Alfonso Ferrabosco (ii) and the castrato Estienne le Roy.

Between 1552 and 1600 more than 200 of Ronsard's poems were set, some of them many times, by more than 30 composers. His works were all published in Paris; collections particularly favoured by composers include the *Odes* (1550–52) which abound in lyrical metaphors, the *Amours* (1552–3) addressed to Cassandre de Salviati, the *Amours* (1555–6) addressed to Marie, which are less Italianate and more sensual in expression, the humorous *Folastries* (1553), the pastoral *Bocage* (1554) and the lyrical pieces for court entertainment *Elégies, mascarades et bergeries* (1565) (all ed. P. Laumonier, *Oeuvres complètes*, Paris, 1914–75). In the preface to his first book of odes he explained that he had taken great care to give the poems a metrical regularity so that they could be set to music. This mystique of the union of poetry and music stemmed from the attempt to re-create classical lyricism in which Ronsard was encouraged by his friend M. A. Muret, whose setting of the ode to Cassandre, *Ma petite colombelle*, was published in July 1552. The first book of *Amours*, which appeared two months later, contained an appendix of nine four-voice settings by Muret, Janequin, Certon and Goudimel. Four of the pieces were presented as polyphonic *timbres* suitable for other sonnets of similar structure; thus Janequin's setting of *Qui voudra voir* provides a model for 92 other poems with the same rhyme-scheme and his *Nature ornant* for another 60. In the preface Ambroise de la Porte explained that Ronsard had taken care to measure his verse 'à la lyre', while the poet himself, in his *Abbregé de l'art poétique françois* (1565), stressed the musical advantages of alternating masculine and feminine rhymes.

The chanson anthologies published at Paris in the 1550s and 1560s included polyphonic settings by Lassus, Arcadelt, M. Blancher, P. Durand, Estienne du Tertre, Entraigues, Nicolas Millot, François Roussel and Guillaume Costeley. In 1559 Pierre Clereau set five Ronsard texts for four voices and seven for three; the latter were reprinted in 1566 in a collection entitled *Premier livre d'odes de Ronsard*. Clereau published a second book of three-voice settings of the odes in 1566 and both books were incorporated into a new edition in 1575. Ronsard's name figures again (alongside that of Desportes) on the title-page of Nicolas de La Grotte's four-voice chansons of 1569. During the 1570s Flemish composers (notably Lassus, Monte, Jean de Castro and François Regnard), became increasingly interested in Ronsard's work, as did provincial French composers such as Guillaume Boni, Jean Maletty, Antoine de Bertrand and Blockland; a number of these published collections consisting entirely of settings of Ronsard's poems. Although monophonic settings by Jehan Chardavoine and homophonic *airs* by Didier Le Blanc, F. M. Caietain, Le Jeune and Bonnet appeared during the last quarter of the century, Desportes supplanted Ronsard in popularity.

Clereau's settings of the odes and Boni's settings of the sonnets were reprinted in the early 17th century by Ballard, but Ronsard's poetry, condemned by Malherbe, soon fell into oblivion. Its revival in the 19th century gave rise to settings by many composers including Wagner (1840), Victor Massé (1849), Bizet (1866) and Gounod (1872); 20th-century settings of his verse include works by Casella (1910), Honegger (1924, 1945), Frank Martin (1930), Roussel (1924), Poulenc (1925, 1935), Milhaud (1934, 1941), Dukas (1935), Florent Schmitt (1940) and Lennox Berkeley (1947).

BIBLIOGRAPHY
J. Tiersot: *Ronsard et la musique de son temps* (Paris, 1902)
ReM, xxiv (1924) [special Ronsard no.; contributions by F. Laloy, H. Prunières, H. Quittard, A. Schaeffner, A. Suarès and C. van den Borren]
G. Thibault and L. Perceau: *Bibliographie des poésies de Ronsard mises en musique au XVIe siècle* (Paris, 1941)
F. A. Yates: *The French Academies of the Sixteenth Century* (London, 1947)
R. Lebègue: 'Ronsard et la musique', *Musique et poésie au XVIe siècle: CNRS Paris 1953*, 105
——: 'Ronsard corrigé par un de ses musiciens', *RdM*, xxxix (1957), 71
B. Jeffery: 'The Idea of Music in Ronsard's Poetry', *Ronsard the Poet*, ed. T. Cave (London, 1973), 209–39
FRANK DOBBINS

Rontani, Raffaello [Rafaello] (*b* ?Florence; *d* Rome, 1622). Italian composer. He is called 'Florentine' by the editor of *RISM* 1629⁹. From 1610 he was a musician in the service of Antonio de' Medici in Florence. From 1616 until his death he was *maestro di cappella* of S Giovanni dei Florentini, Rome, and while in Rome seems also to have served at least two noblemen as a musician, e.g. he mentions in the dedication of his op.6 that he is 'capo del . . . concerto' of Duke Sforza. He appears to have been one of the most popular Italian composers of his time of secular vocal chamber music, particularly solo songs: half of his books of *Varie musiche* were reprinted (the first one twice), and nearly a third of their contents also survive in MS. The six books contain a total of 97 pieces, some 60 of which are monodies. Most of them are strophic songs, and it is these in particular that seem to have been found attractive. Although Rontani is not a very appealing melodist it is easy to see that his long curving lines, lively rhythms and subtle phrasing (ex. in *NOHM*, iv, 168) could excite admiration. He published all but the first of his books after he had moved to Rome, and indeed in style and content they are more Roman than Florentine: for example, several of his other songs are strophic variations, which were popular in Rome, and the vocal ornamentation in them is less subtle and more instrumental in nature than that of Caccini and other Florentine composers. For all his contemporary success and his more interesting qualities he appears now as a much less rewarding composer of strophic songs than other Italian songwriters of the time such as Calestani and Berti.

WORKS
Gl'Affettuosi: il primo libro di madrigali a 3vv, bc (chit) (Florence, 1610)
Le varie musiche, 1–3vv, bc, libro primo (Florence, 1614); 3 ed. K. Jeppesen, *La Flora*, iii–iii (Copenhagen, 1949) [1 piece incorrectly stated to be anon.]
Le varie musiche, 1–3vv, bc (theorbo), libro secondo, op.6 (Rome, 1618)
Le varie musiche, 1–2vv, bc, libro terzo, op.7 (Rome, 1619)
Varie musiche, 1–2vv, bc, libro quarto, op.8 (Rome, 1620); 1 piece ed. in Wolf, 192f
Varie musiche, 1–2vv [1 piece for 3vv], bc, libro quinto, op.9 (Rome, 1620)

Le varie musiche, 1–2vv, bc, libro sesto, op.11 (Rome, 1622)
Song, 1v, song, 2vv, bc, in 1621¹⁵; 2 pieces in 1621¹⁶; litany in 1622¹; song, 1v, bc, in 1629⁹
29 songs, 1–2vv, bc from vols. of Varie musiche, *GB-Lbm, I-Fc* and *I-Fn*
Sacred contrafactum of piece from op.9, *I-Rc*

BIBLIOGRAPHY
J. Wolf: *Handbuch der Notationskunde*, ii (Leipzig, 1919), 192f, 215
F. Ghisi: *Alle fonti della monodia* (Milan, 1940), 25ff
——: 'An Early Seventeenth Century MS. with Unpublished Italian Monodic Music by Peri, Giulio Romano and Marco da Gagliano', *AcM*, xx (1948), 46
N. Fortune: 'A Florentine Manuscript and its Place in Italian Song', *AcM*, xxiii (1951), 134f
——: *Italian Secular Song from 1600 to 1635: the Origins and Development of Accompanied Monody* (diss., U. of Cambridge, 1954)
P. J. Willetts: 'A Neglected Source of Monody and Madrigal', *ML*, xliii (1962), 329
J. Racek: *Stilprobleme der italienischen Monodie* (Prague, 1965), 15f, 98, 100, 137, 149, 205, 285
N. Fortune: 'Solo Song and Cantata', *NOHM*, iv (1968), 167
NIGEL FORTUNE

Röntgen. Dutch family of musicians.

(1) Engelbert Röntgen (i) (*b* Deventer, 30 Sept 1829; *d* Leipzig, 12 Dec 1897). Violinist. He studied with Moritz Hauptmann and Ferdinand David at the Leipzig Conservatory (1848–53). From 1853 until his death he was a violinist in the Gewandhaus orchestra; he succeeded David as its leader in 1873. He also taught at the conservatory from 1869, and published 'Einiges zur Theorie und Praxis in musikalischen Dingen' in the *Vierteljahrsschrift für Musikwissenschaft*, x (1893).

(2) Julius Röntgen (i) (*b* Leipzig, 9 May 1855; *d* Bilthoven, nr. Utrecht, 13 Sept 1932). Composer, conductor and pianist, son of (1) Engelbert Röntgen (i) and the most celebrated member of the family. He studied composition with Friedrich Lachner, harmony and counterpoint with Hauptmann and E. F. Richter, and the piano with Louis Plaidy and Carl Reinecke. He began composing at the age of nine, and in 1869 he made his début as a composer at the Niederrheinisches Musikfest in Düsseldorf with a duo for two violins, performed by his father and Joseph Joachim. After giving concerts in Düsseldorf, Hamburg and Baden-Baden he settled in Cannstatt (1873–4) as accompanist to the baritone Julius Stockhausen. He visited Liszt in Weimar in 1870.

From 1877 to 1925 Röntgen lived in Amsterdam, where he became a piano teacher at the music school in 1878 (the school acquired conservatory status in 1884). From 1912 to 1924 he was director of the Amsterdam Conservatory, succeeding Frans Coenen and Daniël de Lange, and he remained there as a piano teacher until 1926. He succeeded G. A. Heinze as conductor of the choral society Excelsior (1884–6) and Johannes Verhulst as conductor of the Amsterdam Toonkunstkoor (1886–98); he also directed the Felix Meritis concerts for some time. As a pianist, he gave many recitals, was accompanist to the Dutch baritone Johannes Messchaert and Pablo Casals and, with his sons (3) Julius Röntgen (ii) and (4) Engelbert Röntgen (ii), formed the Röntgen Trio before World War I. During his stay in Amsterdam he became friendly with Brahms, who visited the Netherlands in 1884 and 1885; he was also friendly with Grieg, who dedicated his *Lyrische Stücke* op.54 to him (1891). In 1925 he retired to a villa in Bilthoven to spend the remaining years of his life composing and writing; after World War II the Gaudeamus Foundation was established in his house.

A prolific composer, Röntgen belongs to the late Romantic school. His early works show the influence of

Schumann (in the Serenade for Wind op.14) and Brahms (in the *Toskanische Rispetti* op.9); in other works a Scandinavian influence can be detected, even in some written before his acquaintance with Grieg. He was also attracted by the folk music of many countries, especially evident in his *Boerenliedjes en contradansen*. In later years the influence of Reger is apparent in his polyphonic works, and the bitonal Symphony of 1930 looks back to Debussy.

His first wife, Amanda Maier (*b* Landskrona, 19 Feb 1853; *d* Amsterdam, 15 July 1894), a violinist, studied at the Stockholm Conservatory and with (1) Engelbert Röntgen (i) in Leipzig.

WORKS
(*MSS in NL-DHgm*)

Orch: numerous works, incl. 21 syms.; 7 pf concs., 2 vn concs., 2 vc concs., other concerted works; Toskanische Rispetti
Chamber: Serenade, other works, wind; Str Sextet; 3 pf qnts; 2 qnts, 2 vn, 2 va, vc; 2 pf qts; 19 str qts; 11 pf trios; Trio, cl, vc, pf; 16 str trios; Duo, 2 vn
Acc. inst and kbd: 5 vn sonatas; 2 va sonatas; 14 vc sonatas; Ob Sonata; other works, vn, pf and vc, pf; works for pf solo, pf 4 hands, org
Vocal: operas, incl. De lachende cavalier, Agnete; choral works; duets and solo songs
Arr.: Boerenliedjes en contradansen; works by Locatelli, P. Hellendaal

WRITINGS
ed.: *Brahms im Briefwechsel mit Th. W. Engelmann*, Deutsche Brahms Gesellschaft, xiii (Berlin, 1918)
Grieg, Beroemde musici, xxx (The Hague, 1930)

(3) Julius Röntgen (ii) (*b* Amsterdam, 20 May 1881; *d* Bilthoven, 23 Jan 1951). Violinist, eldest son of (2) Julius Röntgen (i). A pupil of his mother and later of Cramer and Joachim, he played in various orchestras before settling in New York as a teacher at the Musical Art Institute. He was a member of the Kneisel Quartet. On his return to the Netherlands he became a member of various chamber music societies and chief professor at the Amsterdam Conservatory.

(4) Engelbert Röntgen (ii) (*b* Amsterdam, 12 Aug 1886; *d* 's-Hertogenbosch, 7 Sept 1958). Cellist, son of (2) Julius Röntgen (i). He studied with Mossel in Amsterdam, Klengel in Leipzig and finally with Casals. He became solo cellist of the opera in Rostock, later in Zurich and from 1912 to 1914 in Vienna (Court Opera). As a cellist with the Damrosch orchestra he visited the USA, where he became chief professor at the Mannes School of Music. Finally he was appointed solo cellist of the Metropolitan Opera in New York.

(5) Johannes Röntgen (*b* Amsterdam, 30 Sept 1898; *d* Amsterdam, 28 April 1969). Pianist, conductor and composer, son of (2) Julius Röntgen (i). He was taught the piano by his father and then studied composition and orchestration with Johan Wagenaar at the Amsterdam Conservatory and conducting with Tovey at Edinburgh University. From 1922 to 1924 he was Kapellmeister of the opera in Vyhedly (now Ústí nad Labem). He also appeared many times as a concert pianist and as an accompanist of such famous musicians as Casals, Manén and Marteau. In 1928 he settled in Amsterdam as a pianist, conductor and teacher. He taught the piano at the conservatory (1943–63) and for a long time directed the Amsterdam Vocal Quartet and various choirs. He formed a trio with his younger brothers Edvard Frants (*b* Amsterdam, 12 June 1902; *d* Meran, 14 Sept 1969) and (6) Joachim Röntgen. He composed chamber music (including a string trio, a piano trio and cello sonatas), a piano sonatina (1952) and a quantity of vocal music.

(6) Joachim Röntgen (*b* Amsterdam, 27 Oct 1906). Violinist, youngest son of (2) Julius Röntgen (i). He studied with Felix Togni in Amsterdam, Bram Eldering in Cologne and Flesch in Leipzig. From 1928 he was the leader of the city theatre orchestra in Winterthur, a teacher at the conservatory there and the leader of the Winterthur Quartet. He was a violinist in the festival orchestra in Lucerne under Toscanini (1938–9). In 1939 he became a violin teacher at the Royal Conservatory in The Hague, and the following year he founded the Röntgen Quartet. He retired in 1972.

BIBLIOGRAPHY

H. Viotta: *Onze hedendaagse toonkunstenaars* (Amsterdam, 1892)
S. Dresden: *Het muziekleven in Nederland sinds 1880*, i (Amsterdam, 1923)
J. D. C. van Dokkum: *Honderd jaar muziekleven in Nederland* (Amsterdam, 1929)
A. Röntgen-Des Amorie van der Hoeven: *Brieven van Julius Röntgen* (Amsterdam, 1934)
D. Tovey: *Essays in Musical Analysis* (London, 1935–9/R1972)
C. Backers: *Nederlandse componisten van 1400 tot op onzen tijd* (The Hague, 1942)
W. Pijper: 'Alphons Diepenbrock en de anderen', *Mens en melodie*, i (1946), 137
W. Paap: 'Herdenking van Julius Röntgen', *Mens en melodie*, ii (1947), 293
W. H. Thijsse: *Zeven eeuwen Nederlandsche muziek* (Rijswijk, 1949)
E. H. Reeser: *Een eeuw Nederlandse muziek* (Amsterdam, 1950)
W. J. Schmidt: 'Een vergeten Nederlands pianowerk', *Mens en melodie*, vii (1952), 10
W. Paap: 'Marionettentheater Joffer Marianne' *Mens en melodie*, viii (1953), 329
J. H. van der Meer: 'Julius Röntgen 1855–1932', *Mededelingen Gemeentemuseum Den Haag*, x (1955), 21
W. Paap: 'Het Amsterdams vocaal kwartet', *Mens en melodie*, xi (1956), 61
F. Wertwijn: 'Johannes Röntgen 70 jaar', *Mens en melodie*, xxiii (1968), 348

ROGIER STARREVELD

Ronzi de Begnis, Giuseppina (*b* Milan, 11 Jan 1800; *d* Florence, 7 June 1853). Italian soprano. Born Ronzi, she married the bass Giuseppe de Begnis in 1816, the year of her début at Bologna. The following season she appeared at Genoa, Florence and Bergamo. In 1818 she sang Ninetta in *La gazza ladra* at Pesaro in a performance prepared and conducted by Rossini. From 1819 to 1822 she appeared with her husband at the Théâtre-Italien, where she sang Rosina in the first Paris performance of *Il barbiere di Siviglia* (26 October 1819). She made her London début with De Begnis at the King's Theatre on 19 May 1821 in *Il turco in Italia*. Having sung in a concert performance of *Mosè in Egitto* at Covent Garden on 30 January 1822, she took part in a staged version of the work (given as *Pietro l'eremita*) at the King's on 23 April that year. During Rossini's visit to London in 1823 she sang in *La donna del lago* and *Matilde di Shabran*.

After the 1825 season Ronzi de Begnis separated from her husband and returned to Italy, where she was engaged at Naples for several years. There she sang in the premières of Mercadante's *Zaira* (1831) and of four Donizetti operas: *Fausta* and *Sancia di Castiglia* (1832), *Maria Stuarda* (under the title of *Buondelmonte*, 1834) and *Roberto Devereux* (1837). She also created the title role in *Gemma di Vergy* at La Scala (1834), and sang in Donizetti's *Anna Bolena*, *Parisina*, *Belisario* and *Pia de' Tolomei*. Having appeared as Juliet in Zingarelli's *Giulietta e Romeo*, she took the role of Romeo in Bellini's *I Capuleti ed i Montecchi*, singing the composer's own last act after Malibran had initiated the practice of substituting Vaccai's. Her repertory also included *Beatrice di Tenda* and *Norma*, and she sang Norma in English at Covent Garden in 1843, when her voice was no longer in prime condition. Described in her youth by John Ebers, manager of the King's Theatre, as 'the model of voluptuous beauty', she had such facility of execution that, according to T. C. Cox, 'she positively revelled in the superabundantly luxuriant roulades which are met with in Rossini's operatic music'. A spirited actress in both comic and serious opera, she was a fine Mozart singer and excelled as Donna Anna.

BIBLIOGRAPHY

J. Ebers: *Seven Years of the King's Theatre* (London, 1828)

T. C. Cox: *Musical Recollections of the Last Half Century* (London, 1872)

ELIZABETH FORBES

Rooke [O'Rourke, Rourke], **William Michael** (*b* Dublin, 29 Sept 1794; *d* London, 14 Oct 1847). Irish violinist and composer. He was the son of John Rourke, or O'Rourke, a Dublin tradesman, and almost completely self-taught in music. In 1813 he took to music as a profession (having altered the form of his name), learned counterpoint under P. Cogan, and became a teacher of the violin and piano. Among his pupils on the violin was Balfe, then a boy. In 1817 he was appointed chorus master and deputy leader at the theatre in Crow Street, Dublin, and soon afterwards composed a polacca, *Oh Glory, in thy brightest hour*, which was sung by Braham and met with great approbation.

In 1818 Rooke composed his first opera, *Amilie, or The Love Test*, and in 1821 he moved to England. In 1826 he was leading oratorios at Birmingham, and in the same year he went to London and sought the appointment of chorus master at Drury Lane Theatre under Tom Cooke. He was leader at Vauxhall Gardens (1830–33) under Bishop. He also established himself as a teacher of singing. *Amilie* was at last brought out at Covent Garden Theatre on 2 December 1837, with decided success. He immediately began the composition of a second opera, and on 2 May 1839 Covent Garden produced *Henrique, or The Love Pilgrim*, which, although favourably received, was withdrawn after five performances because of an argument with Macready, the theatre manager, who had little patience with or respect for musicians.

WORKS

The Pirate (musical play, W. Dimond, after Scott), London, Drury Lane, 15 Jan 1822

Amilie, or The Love Test (opera, 3, J. T. Haines), 1818, London, Covent Garden, 2 Dec 1837 (1837), lib pubd

Henrique, or The Love Pilgrim (opera, 3, Haines), London, Covent Garden, 2 May 1839, lib pubd

Cagliostro (opera), not performed

The Valkyrie (opera), not published

BIBLIOGRAPHY

W. C. Macready: *Reminiscences*, ed. F. Pollock (London, 1875), i, 426f [5 and 7 Aug 1837]

L. M. Middleton: 'Rooke, William Michael', *DNB*

W. C. Macready: *Diaries*, ed. W. Toynbee (London, 1912), i, 418ff [21–7 Dec 1837], 491 [18 Jan 1839]

W. H. HUSK/W. H. GRATTAN FLOOD/R

Rooley, Anthony (*b* Leeds, 10 June 1944). English lutenist. He studied the guitar at the RAM with Hector Quine from 1965 to 1968, and from 1969 to 1971 was on the staff there, teaching the guitar, and later the lute, in which he was self-taught. In 1969, with James Tyler, he founded the Consort of Musicke, a group of variable size, based on the instruments played by Rooley and Tyler (plucked instruments and viols), and incorporating other lute and string players, usually with a singer:

Martyn Hill was the first to sing regularly with the consort. The group's London début was in 1969, and it has since given many recitals in Britain, generally with a unifying Renaissance theme. In 1972 Rooley became the sole director of the consort. He has also given many solo recitals and the many recordings he has directed include the complete works of Dowland.

Rooley was one of the first of the younger generation of lutenists in England to specialize in Renaissance music in general and not just its English aspect. His scholarship is fired with enthusiasm, having the practical needs of performance well to the fore, and his playing is both technically fluent and idiomatic.

WRITINGS

'The Lute Solos and Duets of John Danyel', *LSJ*, xiii (1971), 18

with J. Tyler: 'The Lute Consort', *LSJ*, xiv (1972), 13

The Penguin Book of Early Music (Harmondsworth, 1980)

DAVID SCOTT

Roos, Robert de (*b* The Hague, 10 March 1907; *d* The Hague, 18 March 1976). Dutch composer. At the Conservatory of The Hague he studied the piano, the violin, the viola and, with Wagenaar, composition. Thereafter he studied privately in Paris with Philipp (piano), Koechlin and Manuel (counterpoint), and Monteux (conducting); he had further lessons from Scherchen (conducting) and Dresden (orchestration). In 1946 he was appointed cultural attaché in Paris, later holding similar posts in Caracas, London and Buenos Aires.

WORKS

(*selective list*)

Orch: Pf Conc., 1944; Variations sérieuses, 1947; Vn Conc., 1950; Suggestioni, 1961; Rapsodia e danza, 2 fl, orch, 1972–3

Chamber: Sextet, 1935; Pf Trio, 1968; 2 moti lenti, 2 vn, vc, 1970; 4 pezzi, wind trio, 1970–71; Musica, vn, vc, db, 1971; 7 str qts

Opera, ballets, incidental music, songs, pf pieces

Principal publisher: Donemus

BIBLIOGRAPHY

W. Paap: 'Nederlandsche componisten van onzen tijd, v: Robert de Roos', *Mens en melodie*, i (1946), 198

——: 'Drie Nederlandse compositieprijzen', *Mens en melodie*, xvi (1961), 108

ROGIER STARREVELD

Roosevelt, Hilborne Lewis (*b* New York City, 21 Dec 1849; *d* New York City, 30 Dec 1886). American organ builder. He was a member of the prominent New York family which included President Theodore Roosevelt (a second cousin). Roosevelt apprenticed himself to the organ building firm of Hall & Labagh, much against the will of his well-to-do parents, and his first organ was built in their shop in 1869. This was unique in that it was the first in America to be built with electric action. Shortly afterwards he opened his own factory with his brother Frank (1862–95) and quickly established a reputation for high quality and avant-garde ideas. It is doubtful whether the Roosevelts ever had to worry about financial solvency, and were thus able not only to experiment freely but also to use the costliest materials and most skilled craftsmen. Hilborne had an undeniable mechanical gift, making many improvements in mechanical, pneumatic and electrical actions, including the development of a practical combination mechanism. Tonally, Roosevelt organs were influenced by the European Romantic tradition, to the point where some even contained reed stops imported from Cavaillé-Coll, and were among the best American examples of this genre. After Hilborne's death, the business was continued until 1892 by Frank Roosevelt, who then sold his patents to Farrand & Votey. Among his notable instruments were those built for Grace Church (1878) and Carnegie Hall (1891) in New York, Incarnation Cathedral, Garden City, New York (1885), and the Auditorium, Chicago (1890).

BARBARA OWEN

Root. In tertiary harmony, such as that used in the major–minor tonal system, the lowest note of a vertical sonority or chord, when the notes of the chord are rearranged as a sequence of 3rds (ex.1*a*). If no rearrangement is necessary the chord is said to be in root position; if the root is not the lowest note it is said to be in INVERSION. Some chords are built in 3rds but lack one or more notes; these can often be interpolated, and the roots can be determined from the completed structure; occasionally this method produces ambiguities (ex.1*b*). If a chord is based on the superposition of some other interval, for example a 4th, then its root cannot be determined (ex.1*c*).

Ex.1

Root, George Frederick (*b* Sheffield, Mass., 30 Aug 1820; *d* Bailey's Island, Maine, 6 Aug 1895). American composer and music educator. He spent his early years on a farm, and decided to become a musician when he first visited Boston at the age of 18. After two years of study he was hired as assistant in Lowell Mason's children's singing classes. So appealing were Mason's methods that in 1844 Root introduced them in New York, where he also led choirs. Always a pragmatic man, he compiled his first book to meet the needs of his pupils. In 1850 he went to Paris to study singing and the piano. His first cantata, *The Flower Queen*, was written in 1851, again for his pupils, while his first 'people's' song, *Hazel Dell*, using the pseudonym G. Friedrich Wurzel, was written for the public market. In 1853 he was instrumental in founding the first Normal Musical Institute for training teachers in the methods of Lowell Mason.

With his publications and his teachers' classes well established, he abandoned classroom teaching. When his brother, together with C. M. Cady, founded the firm of Root & Cady in Chicago in 1858, Root invested funds; in 1860 he became a partner in charge of publications. In selecting works for publication he urged composers to conform to the severe limitations of range and difficulty he imposed on his own music to make it accessible to the widest public. During the Civil War he wrote a number of universally popular war songs. Throughout his career, he remained a layman's musician, thinking of music primarily in terms of classroom singing, the church and the home.

WORKS

Cantatas: The Flower Queen (New York, 1852), The Pilgrim Fathers (New York, 1854), The Haymakers (New York, 1857), others
Many teaching methods, song collections, for church and school
Numerous songs, notably Hazel Dell (New York, 1852), There's Music in the Air (New York, 1854), Rosalie, the Prairie Flower (Boston, 1858), The Vacant Chair (Chicago, 1861), The Battle Cry of Freedom (Chicago, 1862), Just Before the Battle, Mother (Chicago, 1863), Tramp! Tramp! Tramp! (Chicago, 1865)

BIBLIOGRAPHY
G. F. Root: The Story of a Musical Life (Cincinnati, 1891/R1970)

D. J. Epstein: *Music Publishing in Chicago before 1871: the Firm of Root & Cady, 1858–1871* (Detroit, 1969)

DENA J. EPSTEIN

Root & Cady. American music publishers and dealers. Founded by Ebenezer Towner Root and Chauncey Marvin Cady in December 1858, the firm soon became Chicago's leading music dealer and publisher; in 1860 George Frederick Root joined it as chief of publications. It initially conducted a general music trade, publishing simple sheet music for a local market. With the outbreak of the Civil War, trade in instruments for regimental bands soared, while the firm found a national market for its succession of patriotic songs by G. F. Root, Henry Clay Work and others, including *The Vacant Chair* (1861), *Kingdom Coming*, *The Battle Cry of Freedom* (both 1862), *Marching Through Georgia* and *Tramp! Tramp! Tramp!* (both 1865).

Beginning with *The Silver Lute* (1862) the firm issued a succession of popular instruction books for schools, musical conventions and choirs, again reaching a national market. After the Civil War, while American public taste grew more diversified, the policies of the firm remained almost unchanged. Crippling losses followed the Chicago fire of October 1871 and the firm did not recover. On 24 October 1871 G. F. Root and his sons withdrew, leaving the original partners, who (with William Lewis) retained the name Root & Cady. The new firm sold the sheet music catalogue on 17 November 1871 to S. Brainard's Sons of Cleveland and the book catalogue to John Church & Co., Cincinnati, on 23 February 1872. In October 1872 Root & Cady were bankrupt. Cady withdrew, and a new firm, Root & Lewis, was formed, continuing until 1 January 1875, when it merged with Geo. F. Root & Sons and Chandler & Curtiss to form the Root & Sons Music Co.

BIBLIOGRAPHY
G. F. Root: The Story of a Musical Life (Cincinnati, 1891/R1970)
D. J. Epstein: Music Publishing in Chicago before 1871: the Firm of Root & Cady, 1858–1871 (Detroit, 1969)

DENA J. EPSTEIN

Rootham, Cyril (Bradley) (*b* Bristol, 5 Oct 1875; *d* Cambridge, 18 March 1938). English organist, teacher, conductor and composer. He read classics and music at St John's College, Cambridge (BA 1897, MusB 1900, MA 1901) and then studied under Stanford, Parratt and Barton at the RCM while serving as organist of Christ Church, Hampstead. In 1901 he was made organist of St Asaph Cathedral, but within the year he returned to St John's as organist and musical director, remaining there until his death. He contributed much to the musical life of the university and became conductor of its musical society (1912), a lecturer in music (1913) and a Fellow of St John's (1914). As a composer he made his mark with a series of large-scale choral works, which brought out the more delicate qualities of his music. Chief among these is the *Ode on the Morning of Christ's Nativity*, a work that won him a Carnegie Award. He had devoted the closest thought to devising a musical form worthy of the massive proportions of Milton's text: the result was a noble piece culminating in a set of free variations. Rootham then turned to symphonic composition. The First Symphony is vigorous and genial; the Second, sketched with the aid of friends and pupils and completed by Hadley at Rootham's wish, bears the signs of physical and spiritual struggle, reaching a climax with a choral finale setting the text 'There shall be no more death' from the *Revelation* of St John.

WORKS
(selective list)

Opera: The Two Sisters (3, M. Fausset), 1920; Cambridge, 1922

Choral orch: Andromeda, solo vv, chorus, orch, Bristol, 1908; Coronach, Bar, chorus, orch, 1910; 3 Songs, chorus, pf/orch, 1910; the Quest, chorus, str, pf, 1911; For the Fallen (Binyon), 1915; Brown Earth (T. Moult), 1921, London, 1923; Ode on the Morning of Christ's Nativity (Milton), solo vv, chorus, orch, 1928, Cambridge, 1930; Psalm ciii, 1934; City in the West, 1936; Sym. no.2 (Revelation), female vv, orch, 1938, cond. Boult, BBC, 1939

Orch: Pan, 1912; Processional for the Chancellor's Music, 1920; Miniature Suite, orch/str, pf, 1921; Rhapsody on the Tune 'Lazarus', double str, 1922; St John's Suite, small orch, 1921; Psalm of Adonis, 1930; Sym. no.1, c, 1932

Unaccompanied choral: Lullaby, female vv, 1910; Oh, may I join the Choir Invisible, female vv, 1910; The Stolen Child, 1911; Sweet Content, 1911; Achilles in Scyros, female vv, 1912; Twa Sisters of Binnorie, 1922; The Golden Time, female vv/SATB, 1925; Daybreak at Sea, 6vv, 1933; Guy's Cliffe at Night, female vv, 1935; In London Town, female vv, 1935; Full Fathom Five, female vv, 1937; Sigh no more, Ladies, 1937; Hark, where Poseidon's White Horses, SSATB

Chamber: Str Qnt, D, 1909; Str Qt, C, 1914; Suite, fl, pf, 1921; Sonata, g, vn, pf, 1925; Septet, va, wind qnt, harp, 1930; Pf Trio, 1931

Principal publishers: Curwen, Oxford University Press, Stainer & Bell

H. C. COLLES/R

Root position. An arrangement of the notes of a chord in which the ROOT of the chord is the lowest-sounding note. *See also* INVERSION.

Rooy, Anton van. *See* VAN ROOY, ANTON.

Ropartz, Joseph Guy (Marie) [Guy-Ropartz, Joseph] (*b* Guingamp, Côtes du Nord, 15 June 1864; *d* Lanloup, Côtes du Nord, 22 Nov 1955). French composer and conductor. He showed a lively interest in music from an early age; while at school at the Jesuit College in Vannes, he played the bugle, the horn and the double bass in amateur orchestras. In deference to his father's wishes he studied law at Rennes, and graduated in 1885, but he decided on a musical career, entering the Paris Conservatoire to study composition with Dubois and later Massenet. In 1886 he was deeply impressed by d'Indy's *Le chant de la cloche* and left the Conservatoire to study with Franck. He remained faithful to Franck and his teaching, but despite this unquestionable influence, there is an individual character in Ropartz's large output of almost 200 works. In 1894 he was appointed director of the conservatory in Nancy, where he conducted orchestral concerts in a manner that was always sober and profound. Having brought about a musical renaissance in Nancy, he left in 1919 to undertake the same task in Strasbourg, and there he applied himself to the promotion of French music, which had been neglected during the years of German rule. He retired to his native Brittany in 1929, and continued to compose prolifically; in 1949 he was made a member of the Institut in succession to Hahn.

His music skilfully draws on the Celtic folklore of Brittany, and on its landscape. A Breton tale formed the basis for one of his greatest achievements, the opera *Le pays*, which was first performed at the Opéra-Comique in 1913 and which displays Ropartz's nobility and sincerity. His orchestral output includes several symphonic poems of which the best known are *La cloche des morts* and *La chasse du Prince Arthur*, pieces highly characteristic of his style and orchestration (which was quite different from that of Franck) that Honegger took as models for their structural clarity. Ropartz published

three volumes of verse in his youth: *Adagiettos, Modes mineurs* and *Les nuances* (Paris, 1888–92).

WORKS
(selective list)

STAGE AND ORCHESTRAL

Stage: Pêcheur d'Islande, incidental music, 1891; Le pays (opera, 3, after C. Le Goffic: L'islandaise), 1910; Oedipe à Colonne (incidental music, Sophocles) (1914); Prélude dominical et 6 pièces à donner pour chaque jour de la semaine, ballet, 1929; L'indiscret (ballet, 1), 1931

Orch: La cloche des morts, 1887; Les landes, 1888; Dimanche breton, 1893; Sym. no.1, 1894; Sym. no.2, 1900; Sym. no.3, E, chorus, orch, 1905; Sym. no.4, 1910; A Marie endormie, 1911; La chasse du Prince Arthur, 1912; Soir sur les chaumes, 1913; Divertissement, 1915; Rapsodie, vc, orch, 1928; Conc., D, 1930; Sérénade champêtre, 1932; Bourrées bourbonnaises, 1939; Petite symphonie, chamber orch, 1943; Sym. no.5, G, 1944; Divertimento, 1947

CHAMBER AND INSTRUMENTAL

Str Qt no.1, g, 1893; Sonata no.1, g, vc, pf, 1904; Sonata no.1, d, vn, pf, 1907; Str Qt no.2, d, 1911; Musiques au jardin, pf, 1916; Sonata no.2, vn, pf, 1917; Pf Trio, 1918; Sonata no.2, a, vc, pf, 1918; Str Qt no.3, G, 1924; Sonata no.3, A, vn, pf, 1927; Jeunes filles, pf, 1929; Sonatine, fl, pf, 1930; Str Qt no.4, E, 1933; Str Trio, A (1938); Str Qt no.5, D, 1940; Str Qt no.6, F (1951); other pieces for pf, org, wind ens

VOCAL

Psalm cxxxvi, solo vv, chorus, orch, 1897; Messe en l'honneur de Ste Anne, chorus, org, 1921; Messe en l'honneur de Ste Odile, chorus, org, 1923; 6 chansons populaires du Bourbonnais, chorus, 1936; Nocturne, chorus, orch, 1938; Requiem, solo vv, chorus, orch, 1938; Psalm cxxix, B, chorus, orch, 1941; several other pieces

Songs: 4 poèmes de l'intermezzo (Heine), 1v, pf, 1899; Odelettes (Régnier), 1v, pf, 1914; Les heures propices (L. Mercier), 1v, pf, 1927; many others

Principal publishers: Baudoux, Durand, Lerolle, Schola Cantorum

WRITINGS

with L. Tiercelin: *Le Parnasse breton contemporain* (Paris, 1889)
Notations artistiques (Paris, 1891)
Les concerts et le conservatoire de Nancy 1881–97 (Nancy, 1897)
Leçons d'harmonie données aux concours du conservatoire de Nancy (Nancy, 1902, 2/1925)
Leçons de solfège à changements de clés (Paris, 1903)
Vocalise-étude (Paris, 1907)
Ecole de style: soixante leçons de solfège à changements de clés (Paris, 1909–12)
Enseignement du solfège (Paris, 1926)
Ecole de style: petits exercices d'harmonie (Paris, 1930)

BIBLIOGRAPHY

F. Lamy: *Joseph Guy-Ropartz: l'homme et l'oeuvre* (Paris, 1948)
L. Kornprobst: *Joseph Guy-Ropartz* (Strasbourg, 1949)

ARTHUR HOÉRÉE

Ropek, Jiří (*b* Prague, 1 June 1922). Czech organist. He studied the organ under Bedřich Wiedermann at the Prague Conservatory (1941–6) and at the Academy of Musical Arts (1946–50), simultaneously studying music at Prague University. He then worked as a postgraduate student at the academy and as professor of organ playing at the Prague Conservatory. In addition to his concert appearances he is organist at the Prague Cathedral of St James, where he frequently performs at his 'organ lessons'. As well as playing the works of early Czech composers (Černohorský, Seger, Brixi) and the standard organ repertory, he specializes in the performance of works by French composers of the 19th and 20th centuries. His playing is remarkable for its plasticity of expression and inner tension; it is rich in timbre and highly musical. Ropek has performed several times in Great Britain, where he has made recordings, and has visited the USSR and other European countries. In 1968 he gave two concerts in Mexico City during the Olympic Games.

ALENA NĚMCOVÁ

Roqueta, Jaime Moll. *See* MOLL, JAIME.

Rorantists. Name given to members of the Capella Rorantistarum founded in Kraków in 1540; *see* KRAKÓW, §2.

Rorate chants. Czech chants and songs named after the introit for the fourth Sunday in Advent (*Rorate coeli*). In Czech 'Rorate' designates the votive masses sung in honour of the Blessed Virgin Mary during the early hours of the morning. In the second half of the 14th century sacred Latin songs (*cantiones*) were sung in Bohemia in celebration of the coming of Christ and were incorporated into the votive masses. A manuscript of 1410 (*CS-Pnm* V B42) has the rubrics 'In adventu ad missam Rorate' before the song *Ave hierarchia coelestis*, and 'cancio in nativitate Christi ad primam missam ante introitum cantetur' preceding the Christmas song *Hodie Christus nasci voluit*. Early in the 15th century Jan Hus advocated the interpolation into the Mass of vernacular sacred songs (now in Jistebnický Kancionál, *CS-Pnm* II C7) and by the 16th century the Rorate were sung each day to Czech texts, as in the Utraquist graduals (such as *CS-Pnm* V B5, I A17; *HK* II A44). A special manuscript, the Rorátník, was compiled by the literary societies, male cathedral choirs of the Utraquist congregations, containing the chants for the entire week (*CS-Pu* XVII F45; *HK* II A11). The Rorate mass, derived from Gregorian chant with free melodic and textual troping and song interpolations, usually has the order: opening song, introductory antiphon and oratio, introit, Kyrie, gradual, alleluia, *prosa* (sequence), Patrem (Credo), Sanctus (optional) and the hymn to the Blessed Virgin Mary (optional) (Státní archiv, Brno, G10/117). The dissemination of the Rorate chants and the influence of the literary societies led to the establishment in 1543 by Sigismund I of the Collegium Rorantistarum, a chapel choir at Kraków that existed until 1872. The Rorate were sung in Bohemia and Czechoslovakia until the beginning of World War II (*see* KRAKÓW).

BIBLIOGRAPHY

K. Konrád: *Dějiny posvátného zpěvu staročeského* [The history of old Bohemian sacred song] (Prague, 1881–93)

Z. Nejedlý: *Dějiny předhusitského zpěvu v Čechách* [The history of pre-Hussite song in Bohemia] (Prague, 1904, repr. 1954 as *Dějiny husitského zpěvu*, i)

——: *Dějiny husitského zpěvu za válek husitských* [The history of Hussite song during the Hussite wars] (Prague, 1913, repr. 1954–6)

J. Kouba: 'Období reformace a humanismus (1434–1620)' [The period of the Reformation and humanism, 1434–1620], *Československá vlastivěda* [Czechoslovak encyclopedia], pt.ix, iii (Prague, 1971), 53–86

J. Mráček: 'Sources of Rorate Chants in Bohemia', *HV*, xiv (1977), 230

JAROSLAV MRÁČEK

Rore, Cipriano de (*b* Machelen, nr. Ghent, or Mechelen, 1515 or 1516; *d* Parma, Sept 1565). Flemish composer active mainly in Italy. His early music shows a mastery and fusion of northern polyphony and Italian lyricism, while his later compositions demonstrate a gradual refinement of *seconda prattica* elements. He was admired both by contemporary composers and by those of later generations, including Monteverdi, particularly for the progressive aspects of his later works.

1. LIFE. His birthplace has not been established precisely by archival documents. Since Sweertius (*Athenae belgicae*, Antwerp, 1628) referred to him as 'Ciprianus Rorus Machliniensis', it has been assumed that he was born in Mechelen. Eitner suggested, on

1. Cipriano de Rore: anonymous portrait in the Kunsthistorisches Museum, Vienna

the basis of a letter in which Rore indicated that he was born in Flanders, that Antwerp may have been his birthplace; if this letter refers to the specific province rather than to the Netherlands in general, then Sweertius's citation may refer to Machelen, a suggestion strengthened by Vander Straeten's circumstantial evidence. The date of birth can be determined from the memorial plaque in Parma Cathedral which states that Rore was 49 years old when he died.

It is not known when Rore first went to Italy or where he received his early training. On the evidence of the text of *Alma real, se come fida stella*, written for Margaret of Parma at the end of 1559, Meier suggested that Rore was in Margaret's service before her marriage to Alessandro de' Medici in 1536, and that he stayed at Machelen in his youth (*Opera omnia*, CMM, xiv/5, p.xiv). The only other indication of his activity before his departure to Italy is in a letter accompanying a manuscript of his compositions, presented to Cardinal Borromeo in Milan in 1606 by Rore's pupil Luzzaschi. Luzzaschi described a *Miserere* in the compilation as written by Rore in 'Fiandra quando ero giovane'; this piece is of such competence that if Luzzaschi's account is true Rore must already have been well versed in polyphonic techniques before he reached Italy. Luzzaschi's claim seems doubtful, however, since this motet, together with a number of other works in the manuscript, was never published. Caffi stated, without supporting documentation, that when Rore was a youth he was a singer at St Mark's, Venice, and he was undoubtedly associated with Willaert and other musicians in Venice during the 1540s. His 1542 publication of madrigals indicates that he was already an accomplished composer, presenting him to the public in a manner usually reserved for established composers. His association with musicians in Venice is further at-

2. *The first stanza of 'Alla dolce ombra', in score, from 'Tutti i madrigali di Cipriano di Rore a quattro voci'* (*Venice: Angelo Gardano, 1577*)

tested by the appearance in 1546 of an acrostic sonnet directed to him by Hieronimo Fenaruolo (printed in Giazotto).

By 1547 Rore was already *maestro di cappella* at Ferrara. He may have been employed there from 1545 or 1546, as the records for those years are missing, and he worked there uninterruptedly for more than ten years. Early in 1558 he visited his parents in Flanders but had returned to Ferrara by December. In July 1559 he again travelled to the north, determined to remain with his parents, but when he received news of Duke Ercole II's death on 3 October 1559 he immediately offered his services to Alfonso II, his successor. This proposal was refused, however, and he was forced to look elsewhere for employment. He accepted an offer from Margaret of Parma, governor of the Netherlands, but remained with her in Brussels only until he moved to Parma to enter the service of Ottavio Farnese, her husband. He travelled via Paris and arrived in Parma early in 1561. After two years there he was elected to succeed Willaert as *maestro di cappella* in Venice, but the prestige of the appointment was clouded by difficult conditions in the *cappella*, and he returned to Parma on 1 September 1564 and died there a little more than a year later. Two portraits of Rore are extant: one, in a sumptuous manuscript illuminated by Hans Mielich containing 26 motets by Rore, completed in 1559, may have been painted in Munich during Rore's journeys to and from the Netherlands in 1558 and 1559; the other, in the 16th-century portrait collection of Archduke Ferdinand of Tyrol (now in *A-Wkm*; see fig.1), was possibly painted in Venice or Parma towards the end of Rore's life.

2. WORKS. Rore's fame rests so securely on his Italian madrigals that his sacred music is often overlooked. It is in these works, however, that he displayed the origins of his style and technique, and his relationship to musicians of the previous generation is shown particularly in his masses. His first mass, '*Vous ne l'aurez pas*', is based on the same chanson melody used by Josquin and Willaert, and the *Missa Vivat felix Hercules*, judged on stylistic grounds to be his second mass, is modelled on the same techniques as Josquin's *Missa Hercules dux Ferrariae*. It was presumably towards the end of Rore's service in Ferrara that he apostrophized Ercole II in another parody mass, based on Josquin's motet *Praeter rerum seriem*, that reveals

the esteem in which Josquin's work was still held. These first three masses are thus a response to the challenge of his heritage and more specifically to the music of one of his most illustrious predecessors at Ferrara. Two further masses, undoubtedly late works, are parodies of chansons: one, based on his own chanson *Tout ce qu'on peut*, bears the designation 'a note negre' in keeping with the madrigal style of the model and its notation; the other, based on Sandrin's *Doulce mémoire*, is similar in style to Willaert's *Missa super 'Mittit ad virginem'*. The vesper psalms and the *Passio . . . secundum Joannem* are stylistically within the established tradition for works in these genres. The style of the motets, on the other hand, lies between that of the strictly liturgical compositions and the madrigals. Although most of the texts are liturgical or biblical, a significant number are from classical or contemporary Latin verse.

In addition to the madrigals for which Rore is chiefly remembered he composed seven chansons. Although Duchess Renée, wife of Ercole II and daughter of Louis XII of France, maintained a circle of attendants cultivating the French style of manners and dress at Ferrara, only one of Rore's chansons, *En voz adieux* (and its response *Hellas, comment*) can be linked with the French coterie at court (see Meier). Rore's first book of five-voice madrigals was published in Venice by Scotto in 1542. Although he was only 26 and his works had not appeared in print, this first book presented him with all the dignity of an established composer. Moreover, it was evidently successful, since both Gardane and Scotto reprinted the madrigals two years later, Gardane advertising a novel attribute of the collection by describing the works as 'madrigali cromatici', a term referring only to the notation. Whatever the significance of this change in notation in other madrigalists' work it was of no revolutionary consequence for Rore, and after the first book of madrigals he used it only sparingly. The importance of these early madrigals lies rather in the seriousness of their style, form and choice of texts, features they share with Willaert's late works. Rore favoured the sonnet and particularly Petrarch's verse: each madrigal is normally laid out in two parts, the first containing the quatrains and the second the tercets, a formal disposition analogous to the responsory motet, as is the polyphonic texture. The form of Rore's madrigals, in contrast with those of earlier composers, is sometimes dictated by the sense of the words rather than by the structure of the verse. It is these motet characteristics that lend a serious tone to the madrigal. *Il secondo libro de madregali a cinque voci* (1544) contains only a few new compositions, together with pieces by Willaert and others. Einstein (1942) suggested that these new works were not newly composed but remainders from a portfolio of compositions prepared by Rore for the 1542 collection.

After the first two motet books (1544 and 1545) Rore was apparently occupied with official duties at Ferrara and published nothing until *Il terzo libro di madrigali a cinque voci* (1548). His experiences at Ferrara seem barely to have affected his creative career but he now took a bold step in setting the whole of Petrarch's *Vergine* cycle as the opening item of the *Terzo libro*. The cycle comprises ten stanzas of 13 lines and the closing *commiato* of seven lines – a total of 137 verses set in 11 sections. Different dedications are provided in the Scotto and Gardane editions, neither, surprisingly, addressed to Duke Ercole II of Ferrara. Scotto's is dedicated to Gottardo Occagna by Paolo Vergelli, 'musico padoano', and Gardane's (of the same year) to 'Iovanni della Casa', as written by Perissone Cambio; this suggests that Vergelli and Cambio obtained some of the *Vergine* madrigals before the cycle had been completed, and published them hastily. In fact Scotto's edition contains only the first six stanzas, the only ones listed in the table of contents. Some copies of Gardane's edition also contain only these stanzas, but in others an extra gathering has been inserted containing the rest of the cycle and three unsigned madrigals, the third of which is identified in later editions as the work of Nicolo Dorati. The other two, *Quando lieta sperai* and *A che con nuovo laccio*, have been assumed to be by Rore in later editions but their authenticity is doubtful. In addition to the *Vergine* cycle and these three madrigals, the remaining pieces are by Rore (eight sonnets on texts of Petrarch and five by unknown poets) and Willaert.

During his first years in Ferrara Rore also turned his attention to four-voice madrigals. Although *Il primo libro de madrigali a quattro voci* was not published until 1550, three of the madrigals, including the popular setting of Alfonso d'Avalos's *Ancor che col partire*, were printed in Cambio's *Primo libro de madrigali* (*RISM* 1547¹⁴), which, together with four more, also appeared in a collection of 1548. Rore's four-voice madrigals with their more transparent texture are less austere and pervasively contrapuntal than the five-voice settings; they must have remained for many years in undiminished favour, for reprints continued to appear until 1590. Except for three Petrarch settings published in 1557, a posthumously printed fragment of a canzone stanza, and the three settings at the head of the collection (*Alla dolce ombra, Signor mio coro* and *Io canterei d'amor*) Rore seems to have abandoned Petrarch after 1550; the remaining four-voice pieces in this first book set contemporary verse. Two use texts from *Selene* by Cinzio: *La giustitia immortale*, the final chorus, and *L'inconstantia che seco han*, the chorus from the end of Act 1. This volume marks a turning-point in Rore's attitude to the madrigal: he subsequently moved away from the sonnet and Petrarch's verse, preferring other verse forms and contemporary poetry.

Rore's new approach to the madrigal was slow to show itself, and it was not until 1557 that he was ready to publish further madrigals. *Il secondo libro de madregali a quattro voci* (*RISM* 1557²⁴), shared with Palestrina, and *Il quarto libro de'i madrigali a cinque voci* (*RISM* 1557²³), shared with several other composers, were both published in the same year. The four-voice book contains sonnets by Bartholommeo Ferrino and Giovanni della Casa, two by Petrarch and the first two stanzas of a Petrarch sestina. However, except for the Della Casa sonnet, Rore set the quatrains and tercets in one extended composition, departing from the two-part disposition as he had only exceptionally done before. The five-voice book includes four settings of *ottava rima*, three from Ariosto's *Orlando furioso* and one by Brevio. Two of the Ariosto stanzas are set canonically, a procedure to which he returned for the Ariosto piece in the fifth madrigal book. These three works are the only examples of canonic writing in the madrigals, and in each case the canonic melody has a regular phrase structure strikingly unusual for a madrigal. Two sonnets in the fourth book celebrate the return of Prince Alfonso of Ferrara from France on 26 September 1554 and two others, a six-voice setting and an eight-voice dialogue, are by unknown authors; all but one follow the normal two-part disposition demanded, perhaps, by the heavier five-voice texture.

Except for a few in large anthologies, the rest of Rore's madrigals were published posthumously in two volumes: Scotto's *Le vive fiamme* (*RISM* 1565¹⁸) with a dedication signed by Giulio Bonagionta on 8 November 1565, and *Il quinto libro de madrigali* (*RISM* 1566¹⁷) with a dedication to Ottavio Farnese, Duke of Parma, signed by Gardane. In this dedication Gardane praised Rore's work as a distillation of the achievement of Josquin, Mouton and Willaert, an evaluation couched in terms entirely appropriate to the Franco-Flemish tradition, focussing on Rore's excellence in counterpoint, melody and harmony. Vincenzo Galilei in an unpublished treatise also expressed admiration for Rore's contrapuntal skills (see Palisca, 1956), and when Rore's four-voice madrigals were published in score in 1577 they were advertised on the title-page 'per sonar d'ogni sorte d'Istrumento perfetto, & per Qualunque studioso di Contrapunti'. Later generations of composers appreciated not only his skill as a contrapuntist, but also his effective portrayal of the sense of the text. Bardi remarked that 'straining every fibre of his genius, he devoted himself to making the verse and the sound of the words intelligible in his madrigals' and 'this great man told me himself, in Venice, that this was the true manner of composing and a different one' (printed in G. B. Doni, *Lyra Barberina*, ii, ed. A. F. Gori and G. B. Passeri, Florence, 1763). Monteverdi well understood Rore's relationship to the Franco-Flemish tradition, perceiving at the same time the emergence of the *seconda prattica* in his music.

Rore embellished Italian lyric poetry with sophisticated polyphony in the Franco-Flemish tradition. The passionate, evocative imagery of the poetry was an open invitation to affective musical expression, with its temptation towards slavish imitation of poetic flights, and thence to disintegration of any coherent, independent musical structure. Rore seems to have taken great care to avoid this danger by incorporating into traditional polyphony only those contemporary means of textual expression consistent with its fundamental tenets. Although he sought to expand his musical language in the service of poetic expression, naive madrigalisms and disruptive chromatic progressions play a limited role in his music; his innovations were the result of artistic impulses rather than of theoretical experimentation. Einstein (1949) wrote that all madrigal music of the 16th century that lays claim to serious dignity is dependent upon Rore. Lasso and Monte are inconceivable without him. Palestrina, who began as an imitator of Arcadelt, changed his style after his acquaintance with Rore. But Rore's true spiritual successor was Monteverdi. Rore holds the key to the whole development of the Italian madrigal after 1550.

WORKS
Printed works except anthologies published in Venice unless otherwise stated

Edition: *C. de Rore: Opera omnia*, ed. B. Meier, CMM, xiv (1959–) [M]

SACRED
Motectorum liber primus, 5vv (1544[6]) [1544[9]]
Motetta, 5vv (1545) [1545]
Il terzo libro di motetti, 5vv (1549[8]) [1549[8]]
Passio . . . secundum Joannem, 2–6vv (Paris, 1557) [1557]
Motetta, 4vv (1563[4]) [1563[4]]
Sacrae cantiones, 5–7vv (1595) [1595]
Works in 1549[7], 1551[16], 1554[17], 1555[1], 1566[1], 1567[3], 1569[7]

Missa a note negre, 5vv (on Rore's Tout ce qu'on peut); M vii, 91
Missa 'Doulce mémoire', 5vv, 1566[1] (on Sandrin's chanson); M vii, 122
Missa 'Praeter rerum seriem', 7vv (on Josquin's motet); M vii, 55
Missa Vivat felix Hercules, 5vv (c.f. on soggetto cavato); M vii, 32
Missa 'Vous ne l'aurez pas', 5vv, 1555[1] (on Josquin's chanson); M vii, 1
Ad te levavi, 5vv, 1567[3]; M vi, 135
Agimus tibi gratias, 5vv, M vi, 47
Angustiae mihi sunt, 5vv, 1549[7]; M i, 147
Ave regina, 7vv, M vi, 95
Beatam me dicent [= Pulchrior italicis], 5vv, 1595
Beati omnes, 4vv, M vi, 23
Beatus homo, 5vv, 1545; M i, 34
Beatus vir, vesper psalm, 4vv, 1554[17]
Benedictum est nomen, 5vv, M vi, 57
Benedictus Deus, 5vv, 1544[6]; M i, 26
Cantantibus organis, 5vv, 1545; M i, 79
Caro mea, 4vv, M vi, 34
Clamabat autem, 5vv, 1549[8] (actually by Morales); M i, 143
Confitebor, vesper psalm, 4vv, 1554[17]
Confitebor tibi, 5vv, M vi, 43
Cum sublevassit oculos, 4vv, E-*Mmc* (authenticity doubtful)
Da pacem, 5vv, M vi, 67
De profundis, vesper psalm, 4vv, 1554[17]
Descendi in ortum meum, 7vv, M vi, 1
Dinumerabo eos, 5vv, E-*Mmc* (authenticity doubtful)
Dixit Dominus, vesper psalm, 4vv, 1554[17]
Domine Deus, 5vv, 1549[8]; M i, 133
Domine quis habitabit, 5vv, 1545; M i, 104
Ecce odor filii mei, 5vv, M vi, 78
Exaudiat me Dominus, 5vv, 1545; M i, 56
Expectans expectavi, 5vv, 1595; M vi, 158
Fratres scitote, 5vv, M vi, 164
Fulgebant justi, 4vv, 1569[7]; M vi, 169
Gaude Maria virgo, 5vv, 1544[6]; M i, 12
Gratia vobis et pax, 4vv, M vi, 38
Hic est panis, 5vv, 1595; M vi, 149
Hic vir despiciens, 5vv, formerly I-*TVca*, destroyed World War II
Hodie Christus natus est, 6vv, M vi, 83
Hodie scietis, 5vv, formerly I-*TVca*, destroyed World War II
Illuxit nunc sacra dies, 5vv, 1549[7]; M i, 152
In convertendo, 5vv, 1545; M i, 40
In die tribulationis, 5vv, 1544[6]; M i, 18
In Domino confido, 5vv, 1545; M i, 51
Infelix ego, 6vv, 1595; M vi, 184
Iubilate Deo, 5vv, 1595; M vi, 118
Iustus es Domine, 5vv, M vi, 61
Laudem dicite Deo, 5vv, M vi, 64
Levate in coelum, 5vv, 1595; M vi, 141
Levavi oculos, 5vv, 1545; M i, 98
Magnificat, 4vv, 1554[17]
Magnificat, 4vv, I-*TVca*
Memento domine David, vesper psalm, 4vv, 1554[17]
Miserere mei Deus, 5vv, M vi, 198
Miserere nostri Deus, 4vv, M vi, 26
Mulier quae erat, 5vv, formerly I-*TVca*, destroyed World War II
Nulla scientis melior, 5vv, 1544[6]; M i, 1
Nunc cognovi, 6vv, 1545; M i, 44
O altitudo divitiarum, 5vv, 1549[7]; M i, 122
O crux benedicta, 4vv, M vi, 32
O Gregori, 5vv, formerly I-*TVca*, destroyed World War II
O salutaris hostia, 5vv, 1595; M vi, 124
Parce mihi (2p. Peccavi quid faciam), 5vv, 1595
Passio . . . secundum Joannem, 2–6vv, 1557; ed. A. Schmitz, *Oberitalienische Figuralpassion* (Mainz, 1955), 57
Pater noster, 5vv, M vi, 49
Peccavi quid faciam (2p. of Parce mihi), 5vv, 1595

Petre amas me, 5vv, formerly I-*TVca*, destroyed World War II
Plange quasi, 5vv, 1545; M i, 63
Prudentes virgines, 5vv, formerly I-*TVca*, destroyed World War II
Quae est ista, 4vv, M vi, 116
Quanti mercenarii, 5vv, 1545; M i, 86
Quem vidistis pastores, 7vv, M vi, 100
Quid gloriaris, 5vv, 1545; M i, 90
Regina coeli, 3vv, 1551[16]
Regnum mundi, 5vv, formerly I-*TVca*, destroyed World War II
Repleatur os meum, 5vv, M vi, 169
Sacerdos et pontifex, 4vv, E-*Mmc* (authenticity doubtful)
Salve crux pretiosa, 5vv, 1595; M vi, 147
Sicut cervus desiderat, 4vv, E-*Mmc* (authenticity doubtful)
Si ignoras te, 5vv, 1545; M i, 74
Si resurrexistis, 5vv, formerly I-*TVca*, destroyed World War II
Stetit Jesus in medio, 4vv, 1563[4]; M vi, 111
Sub tuum praesidium, 4vv, M vi, 209
Sub tuum praesidium, 4vv, M vi, 30
Sumens illud, 4vv, E-*Mmc* (authenticity doubtful)
Tribularer si nescirem, 5vv, 1544[6]; M i, 28
Tu es Pastor ovium, 4vv, E-*Mmc* (authenticity doubtful)
Usquequo Domine, 5vv, 1545; M i, 68
Vado ad eum, 5vv, 1544[6]; M i, 22
Vias tuas, 5vv, 1545; M i, 109
Virtute magna, 5vv, 1595; M vi, 153
Voce me ad Dominum, 5vv, 1595; M vi, 126

MADRIGALS
I madrigali, 5vv (1542, enlarged 2/1544 as Il primo libro de madregali cromatici) [1542; 2/1544]
Il secondo libro de madregali, 5vv (1544[17]) [1544[17]]
Il terzo libro di madrigali, 5vv (1548[9]) [1548[9]]
Musica . . . sopra le stanze del Petrarcha . . . libro terzo, 5vv (1548[10]) [1548[10]]
Il primo libro de madrigali, 4vv (Ferrara, 1550) [1550]
Il quarto libro de'i madrigali, 5vv (1557[23]) [1557[23]]
Il secondo libro de madregali, 4vv (1557[24]) [1557[24]]
Li madrigali libro quarto, 5vv (1562[21]) [1562[21]]
Le vive fiamme de' vaghi e dilettevoli madrigali, 4, 5vv (1565[18]) [1565[18]]
Il quinto libro de madrigali, 5vv (1566[17]) [1566[17]]
Works in 1547[14], 1548[7], 1549[34], 1560[23], 1561[15], 1564[16], 1565[8], 1566[2], 1568[13], 1570[5], 1575[4], 1575[15], 1576[5], 1591[23]

A che con nuovo laccio, 5vv, 1548[10] (authenticity doubtful); M iii, 37
A che piu stral amor (Ariosto), 4vv, 1575[4]; M v, 29
Alcun non puo saper (Ariosto), 5vv, 1557[23]; M iv, 87
Alla dolce ombra (Petrarch), 4vv, 1550; M iv, 7
Alma real, se come fida stella, 5vv, 1565[18]; M v, 83
Alma Susanna, 5vv, 1565[18]; M v, 49
Alme gentili, 5vv, 1576[5]; M v, 131
Altiero sasso (F. M. Molza), 5vv, 1542; M ii, 25
Amor ben mi credevo, 4vv, 1550; M iv, 28
Amor che t'ho fatt'io, 5vv, 1565[18]; M v, 71
Amor che vedi (Petrarch), 5vv, 1542; M ii, 87
Amor se cosi dolce, 8vv, 1557[23]; M iv, 120
Anchor che col partire (A. d'Avalos), 4vv, 1547[14]; M iv, 31
Beato mi direi, 4vv, 1557[24]; M iv, 64
Ben qui si mostra, 4vv, 1561[15]; M v, 1
Ben si conviene, 5vv, 1542; M ii, 93
Candido e vago fiore, 5vv, 1565[18]; M v, 74
Cantai mentre ch'i arsi (G. Brevio), 5vv, 1542; M ii, 1
Cantiamo lieti, 5vv, 1544[17]; M ii, 108
Che giova dunque (Petrarch), 5vv, 1576[5]; M v, 127
Chi con eterna legge, 4vv, 1548[7]; M iv, 51
Chi non sa, 4vv, 1557[24]; M iv, 58
Chi vol veder tutta (G. Parabosco), 4vv, 1565[18] (also attrib. Ingegneri); M v, 15
Chi vuol veder quantunque (Petrarch), 5vv, 1542; M ii, 69
Come la notte (Ariosto), 5vv, 1557[23]; M iv, 93
Com'havran fin, 4vv, 1547[14]; M iv, 34
Convien ch'ovunque (Ariosto), 5vv, 1566[17]; M v, 108
Da le belle contrade, 5vv, 1566[17]; M v, 96
Da l'estrem'orizonte, 5vv, 1565[18]; M v, 53
Da quei bei lumi (G. Brevio), 5vv, 1542; M ii, 100
Datemi pace (Petrarch), 4vv, 1557[24]; M iv, 73
Deh hor fuss'io (Petrarch), 5vv, 1562[21]; M v, 41
Deh se ti strinse amore, 5vv, 1544[17]; M iv, 143
Di tempo in tempo (Petrarch), 4vv, 1550; M iv, 36
Di virtu di costumi, 5vv, 1557[23]; M iv, 100
Donna ch'ornata sete, 4vv, 1550; M iv, 39
Era il bel viso (Ariosto), 4vv, 1561[15]; M v, 3
Far potess'io vendetta (Petrarch), 5vv, 1542; M ii, 81
Felice sei Trevigi, 4vv, 1565[18]; M v, 12
Fera gentil, 5vv, 1565[18]; M v, 43
Fontana di dolore (Petrarch), 4vv, 1557[24]; M iv, 70
Fu forse un tempo (Petrarch), 5vv, 1544[17]; M ii, 137

Grave pen'in amor (Ariosto), 3vv, 1549[34]; M iv, 1
Hor che l'aria, 5vv, 1542; M ii, 96
Hor che'l ciel (Petrarch), 5vv, 1542; M ii, 4
Il desiderio, 4vv, 1566[2]; M v, 23
Il mal mi preme (Petrarch), 5vv, 1542; M ii, 44
I mi vivea (Petrarch), 5vv, 1544[17]; M ii, 126
Io canterei d'amor (Petrarch), 4vv, 1550; M iv, 19
Io credea che'l morire, 4vv, 1550; M iv, 33
Ite rime dolenti, 5vv, 1548[10]; M iii, 80
La bella Greca, 5vv, 1557[23]; M iv, 82
La bella netta ignuda, 4vv, 1548[7]; M iv, 21
La giustitia immortale (G. Cinzio), 4vv, 1548[7]; M iv, 26
L'alto signor (Petrarch), 6vv, 1557[23]; M iv, 113
Lasso che mal accorto (Petrarch), 5vv, 1548[9]; M iii, 41
L'augel sacro, 5vv, 1548[10]; M iii, 76
La vita fuge (Petrarch), 5vv, 1542; M ii, 34
Lieta vivo e contente, 6vv, 1591[23] (cf I-MOe C.311); M v, 136
L'inconstantia che seco han (G. Cinzio), 4vv, 1548[7]; M iv, 46
L'ineffabil bonta (Ariosto), 5vv, 1557[23]; M iv, 105
Madonn'hormai (A. Molino), 4vv, 1564[16]; ed. S. Cisilino, Celebri raccolte musicali venete del Cinquecento, i (Padua, 1974); M v, 7
Mentre la prima, 4vv, 1557[24]; M iv, 76
Mentre lumi maggior, 5vv, 1566[17]; M v, 92
Mia benigna fortuna (Petrarch), 4vv, 1557[24]; M iv, 79
Ne l'aria in questi di, 4vv, 1568[13]; M v, 26
Non è ch'il duol, 4vv, 1550; M iv, 23
Non è lasso martire (F. Spiro), 5vv, 1566[17]; M v, 105
Non gemme non fin oro, 4vv, 1550; M iv, 44
Non mi toglia, 4vv, 1565[8] (also attrib. Ingegneri); M v, 18
O dolci sguardi (Petrarch), 5vv, 1544[17]; M ii, 121
O morte eterno fin (G. Brevio), 5vv, 1557[23]; M iv, 84
O santo fior felice, 5vv, 1566[17]; M v, 115
O sonno (G. della Casa), 4vv, 1557[24]; M iv, 66
O voi che sotto, 5vv, 1560[23]; M v, 34
Padre del ciel (Petrarch), 5vv, 1544[17]; M ii, 132
Per mezz'i boschi (Petrarch), 5vv, 1542; M ii, 51
Perseguendomi amor (Petrarch), 5vv, 1542; M ii, 62
Poggiand'al ciel, 5vv, 1542; M ii, 9
Poi che m'invita amore, 5vv, 1565[18]; M v, 78
Pommi ov'il sol (Petrarch), 5vv, 1548[10]; M iii, 68
Qual donn'attende (Petrarch), 5vv, 1548[9]; M iii, 52
Qual'è più grand'o amore, 4vv, 1550; M iv, 49
Qualhor rivolgo il basso, 5vv, 1566[17]; M v, 99
Quand'io son tutto (Petrarch), 5vv, 1542; M ii, 14
Quand'io veggio, 5vv, 1548[10]; M iii, 72
Quando fra l'altre (Petrarch), 5vv, 1548[9]; M iii, 64
Quando lieta sperai (E. Anguisciola), 5vv, 1548[10]; M iii, 34 (? by Morales)
Quando signor lasciaste, 5vv, 1557[23]; M iv, 96
Quanto più m'avicino (Petrarch), 5vv, 1542; M ii, 56
Quel foco che tanti anni, 4vv, 1547[14]; M iv, 52
Quel sempre acerbo (Petrarch), 5vv, 1542; M ii, 72
Quel vago impallidir (Petrarch), 5vv, 1548[9]; M iii, 48
Quest'affanato, 5vv, 1565[18]; M v, 61
S'amor la viva, 5vv, 1548[10]; M iii, 84
Scarco di doglia, 5vv, 1548[10]; M iii, 88
Schiet'arbuscel (B. Ferrino), 4vv, 1557[24]; M iv, 60
Scielgan l'alme sorella, 5vv, 1544[17]; M ii, 116
Se com'il biondo crin (Petrarch), 5vv, 1566[17]; M v, 121
Se ben il duol, 5vv, 1557[23]; M iv, 107
S'eguale a la mia voglia, 6vv, 1591[23]; M v, 138
Se 'l mio sempre, 4vv, 1550; M iv, 41
Se qual è 'l mio dolore, 4vv, 1575[15]; M v, 32
Se voi poteste (Petrarch), 5vv, 1548[9]; M iii, 60
Sfrondate o sacre dive, 5vv, 1544[17]; M ii, 113
S'honest'amor (Petrarch), 5vv, 1548[9]; M iii, 43
Signor mio caro (Petrarch), 4vv, 1550; M iv, 15
S'io'l dissi mai, 5vv, 2/1544; M ii, 103
Si traviato e 'l folle (Petrarch), 5vv, 1548[9]; M iii, 56
Solea lontana (Petrarch), 5vv, 1542; M ii, 20
Spesso in parte (L. Gonzaga), 4vv, 1565[18]; M v, 10 (also attrib. Ingegneri)
Strane ruppi (L. Tansillo), 5vv, 1542; M ii, 29
Tra più beati, 5vv, 1565[18]; M v, 56
Tu piangi, 5vv, 1542; M ii, 40
Tutt'il di piango (Petrarch), 3vv, 1549[34]; M iv, 4
Un'altra volta, 4vv, 1557[24]; M iv, 54
Vaghi pensieri, 5vv, 1565[18]; M v, 66
Vieni dolce Himineo, 5vv, 1570[5]; M v, 123
Vergine bella (Petrarch), 5vv, 1548[9] (strophes 1–6 only), 1548[10] (complete); M iii, 1
Volgend'al ciel, 5vv, 1562[21]; M v, 38
Volgi'l tuo corso, 5vv, 1557[23]; M iv, 90

CHANSONS

Il primo libro de madrigali, 4vv (Ferrara, 1550) [1550]

Amour ne fais, 5vv, 1570[5]
En voz adieux, 4vv, 1550
Mon petit cueur, 8vv, 1550[14]
Reiouyssons nous, 4vv, 1545[16]
Susann'ung iour, 5vv, 1570[5]
Tout ce qu'on peut, 4vv, 1557[11]
Vous scavez bien, 4vv, 1552[13], F-CA 125–8 (anon., dated 1542)

SECULAR LATIN MOTETS

Motetta, 5vv (1545) [1545]
Le vive fiamme de' vaghi e dilettevoli madrigali, 4, 5vv (1565[18]) [1565[18]]
Il quinto libro de madrigali, 5vv (1566[17]) [1566[17]]
Works in 1544[6], 1544[22], 1549[7], 1549[8], 1555[19]

Calami sonum, 4vv, 1555[19]; M vi, 108
Concordes adhibete, 5vv, 1566[17]; M v, 118
Dispeream nisi sit dea, 5vv, 1549[8]; M i, 140
Dissimulare etiam (Virgil), 5–7vv, M vi, 6
Donec gratus eram tibi (Horace), 8vv, M vi, 16
Hesperiae cum laeta, 5vv, 1549[7]; M i, 127
Itala quae cecidit, 5vv, 1544[6]; M i, 7
Labore primus Hercules, 5vv, M vi, 53
Mirabar solito laetas (N. Stoppius), 6vv, M vi, 87
Musica dulci sono, 4vv, 1565[18]
O fortuna potens, 5vv, M vi, 73
O qui populos suscipis, 5vv, M vi, 70
O socii neque enim (Virgil), 5vv, 1566[17]
Pulchrior italicis [= Beatam me dicent], 5vv, 1545; M i, 48
Quis tuos praesul, 6vv, 1544[22]; M vi, 176
Rex Asiae et Ponti, 5vv, 1565[18]; M v, 88

BIBLIOGRAPHY

F. Caffi: Storia della musica sacra nella già cappella ducale di San Marco in Venezia dal 1318 al 1797 (Venice, 1854–5, repr. 1931), 124
E. vander Straeten: La musique aux Pays-Bas avant le XIXe siècle, vi (Brussels, 1882/R1969)
R. Eitner: 'Ciprian de Rore', MMg, xvii (1885), 37; xxi (1889), 41, 57, 73
U. Rossi: Sei lettere di Cipriano de Rore, con cenni biografici (Reggio Emilia, 1888)
A. So’lerti: Ferrara e la corte Estense nella seconda metà del secolo decimosesto: i discorsi di Annibale Romei, gentilhuomo ferrarese (Città di Castello, 1891, 2/1900 with suppl.)
F. Kenner: 'Die Porträtsammlung des Erzherzogs Ferdinand von Tirol', Jb der kunsthistorischen Sammlungen des Allerhöchsten Kaiserhauses, xv (1894), 147
E. vander Straeten: 'A la recherche du berceau de Cyprien de Rore', Guide musical, xl (1894), 669
G. P. Clerici: 'Una copiosa raccolta manoscritta di musica e poesia del Cinquecento', La bibliofilia, xviii (1916–17), 305
J. Reiss: 'Jo. Bapt. Benedictus, De intervallis musicis', ZMw, vii (1924–5), 13
J. C. Hol: 'Cipriano de Rore', Festschrift Karl Nef zum 60. Geburtstag (Zurich and Leipzig, 1933), 134
J. Musiol: Cyprian de Rore, ein Meister der venezianischen Schule (Breslau, 1933)
W. Weyler: 'Documenten betreffende de muziekkapel aan het hof van Ferrara', Vlaamsch Jb voor muziekgeschiedenis, i (1939), 81; also pubd in Bulletin de l'Institut historique belge de Rome, xx (1939), 187
A. Einstein: 'Cipriano de Rore and the Madrigal', BAMS, vi (1942), 17
W. Weyler: 'De teksten von de Rore's madrigalen', Vlaamsch Jb voor muziekgeschiedenis, iv (1942), 165
A. Einstein: The Italian Madrigal (Princeton, 1949/R1971)
A. H. Johnson: 'The Masses of Cipriano de Rore', JAMS, vi (1953), 227
R. Giazotto: Harmonici concenti in aere Veneto (Rome, 1954)
A. H. Johnson: The Liturgical Music of Cipriano de Rore (diss., Yale U., 1954)
W. Senn: Musik und Theater am Hof zu Innsbruck (Innsbruck, 1954)
C. V. Palisca: 'Vincenzo Galilei's Counterpoint Treatise: a Code for the Seconda pratica', JAMS, ix (1956), 86
N. Bridgman and F. Lesure: 'Une anthologie "historique" de la fin du XVIe-siècle: le Manuscrit Bourdeney', Miscelánea en homenaje a Monseñor Higinio Anglés, i (Barcelona, 1958), 151
C. V. Palisca: 'Scientific Empiricism in Musical Thought', Seventeenth Century Science and the Arts, ed. H. H. Rhys (Princeton, 1961)
E. T. Ferand: 'Anchor che col partire: die Schicksale eine berühmten Madrigals', Festschrift Karl Gustav Fellerer (Regensburg, 1962), 137
L. D. Nuernberger: The Five-voice Madrigals of Cipriano de Rore (diss., U. of Michigan, 1963)
B. Meier: 'Melodiezitate in der Musik des 16. Jahrhunderts', TVNM, xx/1–2 (1964), 7, 12
J. Haar: 'The note nere Madrigal', JAMS, xviii (1965), 22
O. Mischiati: 'Nota bibliografica su Cipriano de Rore', Chigiana, xxii

(1965), 35
H. Beck: 'Grundlagen des Venezianischen Stils bei Adrian Willaert und Cyprian de Rore', *Renaissance-muziek 1400–1600: donum natalicium René Bernard Lenaerts* (Louvain, 1969), 39
D. Harran: 'Verse Types in the Early Madrigal', *JAMS*, xxii (1969), 27
W. Osthoff: *Theatergesang und darstellende Musik in der italienischen Renaissance (15. und 16. Jahrhundert)* (Tutzing, 1969), i, 319ff
B. Meier: 'Staatskompositionen von Cyprian de Rore', *TVNM*, xxi/2 (1970), 81–118
L. F. Bernstein: 'La courone et fleur des chansons a troys: a Mirror of the French Chanson in Italy in the Years between Ottaviano Petrucci and Antonio Gardane', *JAMS*, xxvi (1973), 1–68
D. Harran: 'Rore and the *Madrigale cromatico*', *MR*, xxxiv (1973), 66
G. Barblan and A. Z. Laterza: 'The Tarasconi Codex in the Library of the Milan Conservatory', *MQ*, lx (1974), 195
J. A. Owens: 'Cipriano de Rore a Parma (1560–1565): nuovi documenti', *RIM*, xi (1976), 5
A. H. Johnson: 'The 1548 Editions of Cipriano de Rore's Third Book of Madrigals', *Studies in Musicology in Honor of Otto E. Albrecht* (Kassel, 1977)
R. G. Luoma: 'Relationship between Music and Poetry (Cipriano de Rore's *Quandro signor lasciaste*)', *MD*, xxxi (1977), 135

ALVIN H. JOHNSON

Rorem, Ned (*b* Richmond, Ind., 23 Oct 1923). American composer, diarist and essayist. Brought up in Chicago, his early training in piano and composition (the latter with Leo Sowerby in 1938 and 1939) was augmented by studying recordings of the music of Debussy, Ravel, Varèse and the blues singer Billie Holiday. Later he studied at the Curtis Institute (1943) and the Juilliard School of Music (BSc 1945–6, MSc 1947–8) and privately in New York with Virgil Thomson (1944) and David Diamond.

In 1948 *The Lordly Hudson* won recognition as 'the best published song of the year', and Rorem received the Gershwin Prize for an orchestral work from his student days. He left America in 1949 after winning a Fulbright scholarship to study with Honegger in Paris. After several months in Paris, he moved to Morocco for two years and seriously committed himself to musical composition. His literary preoccupations found release in song settings, upon which his recognition largely rests, and in the writing of journals whose candid revelations and presumptive observations both shocked the music world and delighted the literary intelligentsia.

In 1952 he returned to Paris where his personal charm and sometimes outrageous behaviour won him acceptance in the cultural milieu headed by Poulenc, Auric and Cocteau. While his social reputation flourished under the patronage of the Viscountess Marie Laure de Noailles, his music was less well received, although in America his songs and orchestral works were being performed more frequently. In 1958 Rorem returned to New York.

Rorem's early concentration on writing solo songs has, since 1958, yielded to an interest in combining varied instrumental and vocal forces, and to greater stress on rhythmic variety and form. His experiments with the song cycle have resulted in *Poems of Love and the Rain* (1963) in which the second half of the cycle consists of a contrasting setting of each poem of the first half, in reverse order, and *Sun* (1967), which presents eight poems in one continuous movement for soprano and orchestra. His later instrumental writing shows him to be absorbed by colouristic possibilities and by expanding the uses of tonality through altered chords, tone clusters, modality and polymodality. Beginning in the late 1960s, his compositions are sometimes based on various modified serial techniques while maintaining tonal harmonic references. Although his instrumental

and orchestral works since 1958 avoid large-scale development, being instead semi-programmatic tone poems, variation forms, or multi-movement pieces, his later vocal writing is almost entirely in extended cyclic forms. In 1976 he was awarded the Pulitzer Prize for his *Air Music* (1974).

WORKS

SONGS

A Psalm of Praise (Psalm c), 1945; A Song of David (Psalm cxx), 1945; Reconciliation (Whitman), 1946; On a Singing Girl (E. Wylie), 1946; Alleluia, 1946; Absalom (P. Goodman), ?1946; Spring and Fall (G. M. Hopkins), 1946; The Lordly Hudson (Goodman), 1947; Spring (Hopkins), 1947; Catullus: On the Burial of His Brother (trans. Beardsley), 1947; Echo's Song (B. Jonson), 1948; Three Incantations from a Marionette Tale (C. Boultenhouse), cycle, 1948; Requiem (R. L. Stevenson), 1948; The Silver Swan (O. Gibbons), 1949; Little Elegy (Wylie), 1949; Rain in Spring (Goodman), 1949; The Sleeping Palace (Tennyson), 1949; What if Some Little Pain (Spenser), 1949

Six Irish Poems (G. Darley), cycle, 1950; Flight for Heaven (10 poems, R. Herrick), cycle, 1950; Philomel (R. Barnefield), 1950; Lullaby of the Woman of the Mountain (P. Pearse), 1950; To a Young Girl (Yeats), 1951; From an Unknown Past (7 anon. poems, 15th–16th century), cycle, 1951; The Nightingale (anon., 16th century), 1951; Cycle of Holy Songs (Psalms cxxxiv, cxlii, cxlviii, cl), 1951; A Christmas Carol (anon., 16th century), 1952; The Resurrection (St Matthew), 1952; An Angel Speaks to the Shepherds (St Luke), 1952; The Mild Mother (15th century), 1952; Epitaph on Eleanor Freeman (anon., 1650), 1953; Poèmes pour la paix (Regnier, Ronsard, de Magny, Daurat, de Baïf), cycle, 1953; Love (T. Lodge), 1953; Jack l'Eventreur (M. Laure), 1953; The Tulip Tree, The Midnight Sun, Sally's Smile, For Susan, Clouds (Goodman), 1953; Six Songs for High Voice (Dryden, Browning), 1953; Three Songs by Demetrios Capetanakis, 1954; Youth, Day, Old Age and Night (Whitman), 1954; I Am Rose (G. Stein), 1955; Early in the Morning (R. Hillyer), 1955; See How They Love Me (H. Moss), 1956; What Sparks and Wiry Cries (Goodman), 1956; Conversation (E. Bishop), 1957; Such Beauty as Hurts to Behold (Goodman), 1957; Look Down, Fair Moon (Whitman), 1957; Sometimes with One I Love, O You Whom I Often and Silently Come, To You (Whitman), 1957; The Lord's Prayer, 1957; As Adam Early in the Morning, Gods, Gliding O'er All (Whitman), 1957; Visits to St Elizabeths (E. Bishop), 1957; Orchids, Memory, The Waking, Root Cellar, Snake, Night Crow, My Papa's Waltz, I Strolled Across an Empty Field (T. Roethke), 1959

King Midas, A Cantata in Ten Scenes (Moss), 1961; Poems of Love and the Rain (Windham, Auden, Moss, Dickinson, Roethke, Larson, Cummings, Pitchford), cycle of 17 songs, 1963; Ask Me No More, Now Sleeps the Crimson Petal, Far-Far-Away (Tennyson), 1963; For Poulenc (F. O'Hara), 1963; Hearing (K. Koch), cycle of 6 songs, 1966; War Scenes (Whitman), cycle of 5 songs, 1969

The Serpent (Roethke), 1971; To Jane (Shelley), 1974; Where we came (J. Garrigue), 1974; Women's Voices (various women poets), 11 nos., 1975–6; A Journey (A. Glaze), 1976
125 unpubd songs

VOICE AND INSTRUMENTS

Absalom (P. Goodman), version for medium v, orch, 1947
Mourning Scene from 'Samuel', medium v, str qt, 1947
Six Songs for High Voice and Orchestra (Dryden, Browning), 1953
Four Dialogues for Two Voices and Two Pianos (F. O'Hara), S, T, 2 pf, 1954
Poèmes pour la paix (Regnier, Ronsard, de Magny, Daurat, de Baïf), version for medium v, orch, 1956
Sun (Ikhnaton, Byron, Goodman, Blake, Morgan, Shakespeare, Whitman, Roethke), S, orch, 1967
Some Trees (J. Ashbery), S, Mez, B-Bar, pf, 1968
Gloria, S, Mez, pf, 1970
Ariel (Plath), S, cl, pf, 1971
Last Poems of Wallace Stevens, S, vc, pf, 1972
Serenade on Five English Poems, 1v, vn, va, pf, 1976

OPERA

A Childhood Miracle (1, E. Stein), 6vv, chamber orch, 1952
Miss Julie (2, K. Elmslie), 1965
Bertha (1, K. Koch), 6 or more vv, chorus, pf, 1968
Three Sisters Who Are Not Sisters (1, G. Stein), 5vv, pf, 1969
Fables – Five Very Short Operas (1, La Fontaine, trans. M. Moore), 4 or more vv, optional chorus, pf, 1970
Hearing (5 scenes, K. Koch, J. Holmes), S, Mez, T, Bar, 7 insts, 1976

CHORAL

The Seventieth Psalm, SATB, fl, ob, cl, bn, 2 hn, tuba, 1943; Four Madrigals, SATB, 1947; A Sermon on Miracles (P. Goodman), 1v, unison vv, str, 1947; Three Incantations from a Marionette Tale (C. Boultenhouse), unison, pf, 1948; From an Unknown Past, 7 choruses, SATB, 1951; The Mild Mother, unison vv, pf, 1952; The

Corinthians, SATB, org, 1953; A Far Island, SSA, 1953; Five Prayers for the Young, SSA, 1953; Gentle Visitations, SSA, 1953; I Feel Death, TTB, 1953; All Glorious God, SATB, 1955; Sing My Soul, SATB, 1955; Christ the Lord is ris'n today, SATB, 1955; Miracles of Christmas (R. Jacob), 7 choruses, SATB, org, 1959; Prayers and Responses, 5 choruses, SATB, 1960; Virelai, SATB, 1961; Two Psalms and a Proverb, SATB, str qnt, 1963; Lift Up Your Heads (The Ascension), SATB, ww/brass qt/org, 1963; Laudemus tempus actum, SATB, orch, 1964; Love Divine, All Loves Excelling, SATB, 1966; Letters from Paris (J. Flanner), 9 choruses, SATB, orch, 1966; Proper for the Votive Mass of the Holy Spirit, 4 choruses, unison vv, org, 1966; Truth in the Night Season, SATB, org, 1966; He Shall Rule from Sea to Sea, SATB, org, 1967; Praises for the Nativity, SSAATTBB, org, 1970; Seven Canticles, SATB, 1971; Three Motets, SATB, org, 1973; Four Hymn Tunes, 2 for chorus, 2 for 1v, pf, 1973; In Time of Pestilence (T. Nash), unacc., 1973; Little Prayers (P. Goodman), S, Bar, chorus, orch, 1973; 3 Motets (Hopkins), chorus, org, 1973; Missa brevis, S, T, chorus, 1974; Arise, shine, for your light has come, chorus, org, 1977; Three Christmas Choruses, SATB, 1978

CHAMBER AND INSTRUMENTAL

Str Quartet no.1, 1947, withdrawn; Pf Sonata no.1, 1948; A Quiet Afternoon, 9 pieces, pf, 1948; Conc. no.1, pf, orch, 1948, withdrawn; Three Barcarolles, pf, 1949; Pastorale for organ, 1949; Sonata, vn, pf, 1949; Mountain Song, fl/ob/vn/vc, pf, 1949; Pf Sonata no. 2, 1950; Conc. no.2, pf, orch, 1950; Lento for Strings, 1950; Sicilienne, 2 pf, 4 hands, 1950; Pf Sonata no.3, 1954; Sinfonia for Winds (optional perc), 1957; Pilgrims for Strings, 1958; Eleven Studies for Eleven Players, fl, ob, cl, tpt, 2 perc, harp, pf, vn, va, vc, 1960; Trio for Flute, Cello and Piano, 1960; Lovers – a Narrative in Ten Scenes, solo hpd, ob, vc, perc, 1964; Spiders for Harpsichord, 1968; Concerto in Six Movements for Piano and Orchestra, 1969; Day Music for Piano and Violin, 8 pieces, 1971; Night Music for Violin and Piano, 8 Pieces, 1972; 8 Etudes, pf, 1975; Book of Hours, fl, harp, 1975; Sky Music, harp, 1976; A Quaker Reader, org, 1976; Romeo and Juliet, fl, gui, 1977

ORCHESTRAL

Sym. no.1, 1950; Design for Orchestra, 1953; Sym. no.2, 1955; Sym. no.3, 1958; Eagles, 1958; Ideas for Easy Orchestra, 1961; Lions, 1963; Water Music for Violin, Clarinet and Orchestra, 1966; Solemn Prelude, 1973; Air Music, 1974; Assembly and Fall, 1975; Sunday Morning, 1977

Principal publishers: Boosey & Hawkes, Southern, Peters

WRITINGS

The Paris Diary of Ned Rorem (New York, 1966)
The New York Diary (New York, 1967)
Music from Inside Out (New York, 1967)
Music and People (New York, 1969)
Critical Affairs: a Composer's Journal (New York, 1970)
Pure Contraption (New York, 1973)
The Final Diary (New York, 1974)
An Absolute Gift (New York, 1978)

BIBLIOGRAPHY

G. Anderson: 'The Music of Ned Rorem', Music Journal, xxi (1963), April, 34, 71
W. S. W. North: Ned Rorem as a Twentieth Century Song Composer (diss., U. of Illinois, 1965)
L. G. Rickert: 'Song Cycles for Baritone', NATS Bulletin, xxiii (1967), Nov, 13
B. Middaugh: 'The Songs of Ned Rorem: Aspects of Musical Style', NATS Bulletin, xxiv (1968), May, 36
S. A. Atack: Ned Rorem and his Songs (diss., U. of Nebraska, 1969)
M. R. Bloomquist: Songs of Ned Rorem: Aspects of the Musical Setting of Songs in English for Solo Voice and Piano (diss., U. of Missouri, Kansas City, 1970)
V. Thomson: American Music since 1910 (New York, 1971), 87, 169f
J. Gruen: The Party's Over Now (New York, 1972)
P. L. Miller: 'The Songs of Ned Rorem', Tempo (1978), no.127, p.25

JAMES HOLMES

Ros, Edmundo (b Caracas, 7 Dec 1910). Venezuelan band-leader active in Britain. He was a bass drummer in the Venezuelan Military Academy Band and a tympanist in the Venezuelan SO; he also learnt the saxophone and American 'hot' music and formed his own dance band. At the RAM, London, he studied harmony, composition and orchestration, financed by a Venezuelan government grant (1937–42); concurrently he performed with Latin-American bands in London and was the vocalist and drummer of Don Marino Baretto's band

at the Embassy Club. In 1940 he formed his first London band and by 1942 he was broadcasting, recording and playing for films and private engagements. The staple of Ros's repertory in his heyday around 1950 was samba and rumba music, which he helped to popularize in Britain.

Rosa [Rose], Carl (August Nikolaus) (b Hamburg, 22 March 1842; d Paris, 30 April 1889). German impresario, violinist and conductor. At the age of 12 he toured England, Denmark and Germany as a violinist. After studies (from 1859) at the conservatories of Leipzig and Paris, he was appointed Konzertmeister in Hamburg (1863–5). In 1886 he went to London and on 10 March appeared as a soloist at the Crystal Palace. After a short stay in England he joined Bateman in a concert tour of the USA, where he met the soprano Euphrosyne Parepa; they were married in New York in February 1867. His wife's success in opera led to the formation of a company under Rosa's management and conductorship, which in its early seasons also included Wachtel, Santley, Ronconi and Formes. Early in 1871 he returned with his wife to England, and then they made an extended visit to Egypt for reasons of health; after this they returned again to London, but Parepa-Rosa died almost immediately, on 21 January 1874. Rosa, however, was resolved to test the fortunes of opera in English in London, and on 11 September 1875 the CARL ROSA OPERA COMPANY opened its first season at the Princess's Theatre with The Marriage of Figaro and a cast including Rose Hersee and Santley, and Rosa himself conducting. Between 1876 and 1882 his opera seasons in London and the provinces were noteworthy for the careful manner in which repertory was chosen, rehearsed and mounted. In addition to the premières of British works such as Goring Thomas's Esmeralda (1883) and Nadeshda (1885), Stanford's Canterbury Pilgrims (1884) and Corder's Nordisa (1887), the company staged the first performances in English of Der fliegende Holländer (1876), Mignon (1880), Lohengrin (1880) and Aida (1880), among other works. In 1883 Rosa became associated with Augustus Harris, manager of the Theatre Royal, Drury Lane, and a prosperous five years for the company followed.

BIBLIOGRAPHY

H. Klein: Thirty Years of Musical Life in London (London, 1903)
E. W. White: The Rise of English Opera (London, 1951)
R. Smith Brindle: 'Rosa, Carl', ES

FRANK WALKER/HAROLD ROSENTHAL

Rosa, Carlantonio de, Marquis of Villarosa (b Naples, 1 Jan 1762; d Naples, 30 Jan 1847). Italian historian and writer on music. He was trained in the arts, law and philosophy and in 1823 was made royal historian. He published a number of biographies and biographical dictionaries of Neapolitan figures. Of musical interest among them are the Lettera biografica intorno alla patria ed alla vita di G. B. Pergolesi (Naples, 1831; 2/1843 as Biografia di G. B. Pergolesi), in which he introduced archival proof of the date and place of Pergolesi's birth, and Memorie dei compositori di musica del regno di Napoli (Naples, 1840). As Villarosa explained in the preface, Memorie was based on a manuscript entitled Apoteosi della musica, left by Giuseppe Sigismondo, a librarian of the Naples Conservatory; it was not fit to be published as it stood but contained valuable notices of some earlier musicians to which Villarosa added material gathered from living persons and archival sources. The result is highly uneven in the amount of space devoted to composers of importance and in the accuracy of its information. This book was the source for many errors carried on by Fétis, Florimo and others and, though occasionally useful, is mainly of historical interest.

Rosa, Salvator [Salvatore] (b Arenella, Naples, ?21 July 1615; d Rome, 15 March 1673). Italian painter and poet. He left his place of birth in 1635. After a brief sojourn in Rome he lived in Florence from 1640 to 1649. There he gained many artistic friends, notably the composer Antonio Cesti (for whom Rosa's letters are an important source of biographical information), the poet and librettist Giovanni Apolloni and the playwright Giovanni Battista Ricciardi. He returned in 1649 to Rome, where he remained for the rest of his life. Although he may have been an amateur musician, the traditional assertion that he composed music has been proved false (see Walker). Cesti set to music at least four of Rosa's smaller poems; he solicited from him an opera libretto as well, but without success. Rosa's principal significance for music derives from his satire *La musica*, in which his keen vision of the follies of the musical world receives trenchant expression. The satire, one of six, was printed repeatedly throughout the 18th century and was the object of a lengthy and curious attack in 1749 by Mattheson, who renamed the author 'Perditor Spina'. Rosa's life, suitably transformed, furnished material for several opera librettos in the 19th century.

BIBLIOGRAPHY

J. Mattheson: *Mithridat wider den Gift einen welchen Satyre* (Hamburg, 1749)

G. B. Passeri: *Vite de' pittori, scultori ed architetti che anno lavorato in Roma morti dal 1641 fino al 1673* (Rome, 1772)

G. Carducci, ed.: *Satire, odi e lettere di Salvator Rosa* (Florence, 1860/R1916)

G. A. Cesareo, ed.: *Poesie e lettere edite e inedite di Salvator Rosa* (Naples, 1892)

L. Ozzola: *Vita e opere di Salvator Rosa pittore, poeta, incisore con poesie e documenti inediti* (Strasbourg, 1908)

A. de Rinaldis, ed.: *Lettere inedite di Salvator Rosa a G. B. Ricciardi* (Rome, 1939)

F. Walker: 'Salvator Rosa and Music', *MMR*, lxxix (1949), 199; lxxx (1950), 13, 32

U. Limentani, ed.: *Poesie e lettere inedite di Salvator Rosa* (Florence, 1950)

N. Pirrotta: 'Cesti nell'epistolario di S. Rosa', *La scuola romana: G. Carissimi–A. Cesti–M. Marazzoli*, Chigiana, x (1953), 56

F. Schlitzer: 'Una lettera inedita di A. Cesti e un frammento di lettera di Salvator Rosa', ibid, 93

——: 'A Letter from Cesti to S. Rosa', *MMR*, lxxxiv (1954), 150

THOMAS WALKER

Rosales, Antonio (b Madrid, c1740; d Madrid, 1801). Spanish composer. He was chiefly a composer of tonadillas, of which he wrote at least 150, the first dating from 1762. His first success as a zarzuela composer came on 28 November 1767, when the one-act burlesca *El tio y la tia* (libretto by Ramon de la Cruz, score in *E-Mm*), was staged in Madrid at the Teatro de la Cruz. In 1769 he was made *músico secundario* by the Madrid theatre company manager Manuel Martínez, and on 1 July 1776 his one-act zarzuela *El licenciado Farfulla*, also to a libretto by Cruz, had its première at the Teatro del Principe. This popular work, which was sung everywhere in Spain until 1813, mixed Spanish folk airs with dances such as the *jácara*, *folia*, *seguidillas* and *coplas*

de caballo. About 1787 he succeeded Rodriguez de Hita as *maestro de capilla* of the royal Encarnación convent at Madrid. 149 *tonadillas* by him are at the Biblioteca Municipal in Madrid; one, *El recitado*, has been edited by Subirá (Madrid, 1930). Rosales also composed *entremeses* and *sainetes*; 14 of the latter survive (in *E-Mm*), the earliest dated 1763.

BIBLIOGRAPHY

J. Subirá: *La tonadilla escénica*, iii (Madrid, 1930), 54ff

E. Cotarelo y Mori: *Historia de la zarzuela* (Madrid, 1934), 140, 148f, 152

J. Subirá: 'Rosales, Antonio', *MGG*

ROBERT STEVENSON

Rosalia (It.; Ger. *Schusterfleck*: 'cobbler's patch'). The pejorative name, taken from an old Italian popular song *Rosalia, mia cara*, for the identical repetition of a melody a step higher. It may often involve transposition, and by giving the effects both of rapid modulation and of melodic sequence it can provide great dramatic power and climax, as in the Hallelujah Chorus from Handel's *Messiah* ('King of kings' etc). Whenever it is used polyphonically, however, the part-writing is threatened with consecutive 5ths or octaves, and for this reason it has been regarded disparagingly as a compositional device. But in the hands of a skilled contrapuntist it can create the impression of a delicately elusive tonality without hinting at questionable part-writing; Mozart used it with great skill in the first movement of his String Quartet K575.

WILLIAM DRABKIN

Rosas, John (Anders) (b Lappträsk, 30 Nov 1908). Finnish musicologist. He studied at Helsinki Conservatory and University and the Turku Academy (MA 1934), where he took the doctorate in 1950 with a dissertation on Fredrik Pacius and where he became a music teacher (1937–55), lecturer (1953–62) and professor of musicology and folk literature (appointed 1962). His work in these positions and as a music critic, a choral and orchestral conductor, a board member of numerous music organizations and curator of the Sibelius Museum (from 1959) has made him a leading personality of musical life in Turku. In his research he has continued the tradition founded by Otto Andersson, focussing his interest on early Finnish music history. His compositions include cantatas, partsongs and solo songs.

WRITINGS

Fredrik Pacius som tonsättare (diss., Turku Academy, 1950; Turku, 1949)

Musikaliska sällskapet och symfoniföreningen i Helsingfors 1827–1853 (Helsinki, 1952)

Ernst Mielck (1877–1899) (Turku, 1955)

'Turun musiikkielämää 1856–1917' [Musical life in Turku 1856–1917], *Turun kaupungin historia 1856–1917* (Turku, 1957), 909–51

Otryckta kammarmusikverk av Jean Sibelius (Turku, 1961)

'Sibelius' musik till skådespelet Ödlan', *Suomen musiikin vuosikirja 1960–61* (Helsinki, 1961), 49

'Bidrag till kännedom om tre Sibelius-verk', *Suomen musiikin vuosikirja 1964–65* (Helsinki, 1965), 71 [with Eng. summary]

'Tondikten Aallottaret (Okeaniderna) opus 73 av Jean Sibelius', *Festskrift till Erik Tawaststjerna* (Helsinki, 1976), 37–78

ERKKI SALMENHAARA

Rosas, Juventino (b Santa Cruz de Galeana, 23 or 25 Jan 1868; d Batabanó, Cuba, 13 July 1894). Mexican violinist and composer. He was a pure-blooded Otomí Indian. His father, a harpist, took him to Mexico City at the age of six to play in a family quartet with his brothers Manuel (guitarist) and Patrocinio (singer).

Shortly afterwards he joined the S Sebastian church orchestra and at 15 was a member of the first violin section of Angela Peralta's touring opera orchestra. He then settled in Mexico City and began to compose salon music, publishing an enormous number of waltzes, polkas, mazurkas and schottisches. Many of them are in the library of the national conservatory. They have no recognizable Indian flavour. The set of five waltzes titled *Sobre los olas* (1891) gained such wide international popularity that it was even attributed to Johann Strauss. Rosas died of a fever after joining a travelling zarzuela company.

BIBLIOGRAPHY
R. Stevenson: *Music in Mexico* (New York, 1952, 2/1971), 206ff
JUAN A. ORREGO-SALAS

Rosbaud, Hans (*b* Graz, 22 July 1895; *d* Lugano, 29 Dec 1962). Austrian conductor. He studied the piano with Alfred Hoehn and composition with Bernhard Sekles at the Hoch Conservatory, Frankfurt, and in 1921 was appointed director of the Städtische Musikschule at Mainz, where he also conducted the symphony concerts. From the outset he showed enthusiasm for contemporary music, which he championed throughout his career. His first season's programmes included new music by Hindemith, with whom he had studied for three years. As musical director of Frankfurt radio (1928–37) he became closely associated with Schoenberg, Berg, Webern, Bartók, Stravinsky and others, whose works he performed with considerable feeling and penetrating insight; he gave the premières of Schoenberg's Four Songs with orchestra op.22 (1932) and Bartók's Piano Concerto no.2 with the composer as soloist (1933). Rosbaud then became Generalmusikdirektor successively at Münster (1937–41), Strasbourg (1941–4)

Hans Rosbaud, 1961

and of the Munich PO (1945–8). From 1948 until his death he was principal conductor of the South-west German RO at Baden-Baden, which became recognized as one of the best in Germany, and was internationally known through its broadcasts and gramophone records. He also became closely concerned with annual festivals: from its foundation in 1948 the Aix-en-Provence Festival, where his conducting of Mozart operas was sometimes thought to lack warmth and sentiment; at Donaueschingen, where he supported contemporary music, notably the early works of Boulez and Stockhausen; and at the festivals of the ISCM, whose Schoenberg Medal he received in 1952. In 1954, replacing Schmidt-Isserstedt, he conducted the première of Schoenberg's *Moses und Aron* for Hamburg radio (a performance later issued as the opera's first gramophone recording), and he also conducted its first stage production at Zurich in 1957. At the 1958 Holland Festival he conducted a highly praised double bill of Schoenberg's *Erwartung* and *Von heute auf morgen*.

Rosbaud toured widely as a guest conductor in Europe, North and South America and Africa, and from 1950 he appeared regularly with the Zurich Tonhalle Orchestra, whose chief conductor he became in 1957 in addition to his Baden-Baden appointment. His performances were distinguished by intellectual strength and severe functional style, matched by a fine musicality, and he invariably sought to avoid self-projection in his concern for the work itself. His clear, precise and objective approach influenced many younger conductors, particularly Boulez and others of his school.

BIBLIOGRAPHY
L. Gerber: 'Hans Rosbaud Discography', *Journal of the Association for Recorded Sound Collectors*, iv/1–3 (1972), 47
GERHARD BRUNNER

Roscelli, Francesco. *See* ROUSSEL, FRANÇOIS.

Rosé, Arnold (Josef) (*b* Iaşi, Romania, 24 Oct 1863; *d* London, 25 Aug 1946). Austrian violinist. He studied at the Vienna Conservatory with Heissler and made his first appearance at a Leipzig Gewandhaus concert in 1879. In 1881 he became leader of the Vienna Court Opera (later Staatsoper) orchestra and of the Vienna PO, positions that he held until 1938. He taught at the Vienna Academy of Music from 1893 to 1924 with some breaks. From 1888 he frequently led the orchestra at the Bayreuth Festival. In 1882 he founded the Rosé Quartet, which first appeared in Vienna in 1883. At that time the members were Rosé, Egghard, Loh and Eduard Rosé (Arnold's brother). The personnel changed more than once but between 1905 and 1920, the period of the quartet's greatest success, it remained constant with Rosé, Fischer, Ruzitska and Buxbaum. They established themselves above all in central Europe as the successors to the Joachim and Hellmesberger quartets, toured widely, and were regarded everywhere as one of the finest quartets of their time. In their earlier days they gave the first performances of some of Brahms's later works and, in succeeding years, of works by Pfitzner, Reger, Schoenberg and other notable composers. Rosé, whose wife Justine was Mahler's sister, collaborated closely with Mahler during his years as director of the Vienna Court Opera. In 1938, after the Anschluss, Rosé became an exile in England where, with Buxbaum and other colleagues, he continued to play chamber music. His last appearances were in 1945, making his career one of the longest in the history of violin playing.

He laid little emphasis on display but his technique was extraordinarily reliable, the certainty of his left hand and the purity of his intonation being especially notable. Although Rosé did not make an international reputation as a soloist, he was regarded as a great chamber player and an ideal orchestral leader who carried his colleagues with him and supported the conductor to the utmost. He published editions of Bach's and Beethoven's violin sonatas and of Beethoven's Quartets op.18.

BIBLIOGRAPHY
A. Boult: 'Rosé and the Vienna Philharmonic', *ML*, xxxii (1951), 256
C. Flesch: *Memoirs* (London, 1957, 2/1958; Ger. orig., Freiburg, 1960, 2/1961), 49ff
J. Hartnack: *Grosse Geiger unserer Zeit* (Munich, 1967), 124f
J. Creighton: *Discopaedia of the Violin, 1889–1971* (Toronto, 1974)
RONALD KINLOCH ANDERSON

Rose, Barry (Michael) (*b* Chingford, Essex, 24 May 1934). English organist. He held posts at St Anne's, Chingford, as a boy of 11, and at St Andrew's, Kingsway, London, while studying with C. H. Trevor at the RAM (1958–60). An able all-round musician, he was appointed organist and master of the choristers when the new Guildford Cathedral was consecrated in 1960. It is the only cathedral in the world to maintain full daily services without a choir school, but under Rose's direction the choir has won a high reputation and made many recordings. A regular broadcaster as an organist and a choral conductor, Rose succeeded Thalben-Ball in 1970 as music adviser on religious broadcasting to the BBC, where he is responsible for the music for the daily radio service. In 1974 he was appointed assistant organist of St Paul's Cathedral, London.

STANLEY WEBB

Rose, Bernard (William George) (*b* Little Hallingbury, Herts., 9 May 1916). English organist, musicologist and composer. He was educated at Salisbury Cathedral School (1925–31) and studied under Sir Walter Alcock at the RCM (1933–5) before going as organ scholar to St Catharine's College, Cambridge, where he was a pupil of Hubert Middleton and Edward Dent (BA 1938, MusB 1939). In 1939 he became organist at Queen's College, Oxford, and conductor of the Eglesfield Musical Society; he was appointed supernumerary Fellow of Queen's College in 1949 and university lecturer in 1955 (having lectured in the faculty since 1946). He was made official Fellow of Queen's College in 1954, took the DMus in 1955, and became Fellow, organist and *Informator choristarum* at Magdalen College in 1957. He was appointed conductor of the Oxford Orchestral Society in 1971 and in 1973–5 was vice-president of Magdalen College. He was president of the RCO in 1974–6.

Rose has made a special study of the choral music of Tomkins (see *PRMA*, lxxxii, 1965–6, p.89), and has prepared many editions of English music from the 16th to 18th centuries. His chief work as organist and conductor has been with Magdalen College choir; under his direction the choir has made a number of recordings and ranks as one of the finest English college choirs. His published compositions are all liturgical, and many are in the standard cathedral repertory.

EDITIONS
T. Tomkins: *Musica Deo sacra* [verse anthems only], EECM, v, ix, xiv (1965, 1968, 1974)
G. F. Handel: *Susanna*, Hallische Händel-Ausgabe, i/28 (Kassel, 1967)
ERIC BLOM/DAVID SCOTT

Rose, Carl. *See* ROSA, CARL.

Rose [Donington], Gloria (*b* New York, 20 May 1933; *d* Buffalo, 25 April 1974). American musicologist. She was educated at Hunter College, New York (BA 1953), and at Yale (PhD 1960). She was greatly influenced by Leo Schrade, with whom she studied at Yale, and for whom she worked as a research assistant (1957–8). After two years (1958–60) as music librarian at Wellesley College, she taught at the University of Pittsburgh (1960–62). She also held visiting lectureships at Rutgers University (1968) and the State University of New York at Buffalo (1972). She was married to the English musicologist Robert Donington. Her published works deal with 17th-century Italian music, particularly Carissimi's chamber cantatas, of which she published an edition in 1969, and with problems relating to thoroughbass. In 1976 her research materials were acquired by the Music Library of the University of Birmingham.

WRITINGS
The Cantatas of Carissimi (diss., Yale U., 1960)
'The Cantatas of Giacomo Carissimi', *MQ*, xlviii (1962), 204
'Agazzari and the Improvising Orchestra', *JAMS*, xviii (1965), 382
'Polyphonic Italian Madrigals of the Seventeenth Century', *ML*, xlvii (1966), 153
Giacomo Carissimi (1605–1674), WECIS, v (1966)
'Purcell, Michelangelo Rossi and J. S. Bach: Problems of Authorship', *AcM*, xl (1968), 203
'A Portrait Called Carissimi', *ML*, li (1970), 400
'Two Operas by Scarlatti Recovered', *MQ*, lxviii (1972), 420
'Cantata, La', *RicordiE*
'The Italian Cantata of the Baroque Period', *Gattungen der Musik in Einzeldarstellungen: Gedenkschrift für Leo Schrade*, i (Berne and Munich, 1973), 655
'Pasqualini as Copyist', *AnMc*, no.14 (1974), 170
HOWARD MAYER BROWN

Rose [Ross], John (*fl* second half of 16th century). The name of two English instrument makers, father and son. Their identities and activities are now largely inseparable; they worked in Bridewell, London, making mainly lutes and viols. The younger Rose died in 1611 (buried 29 July) and his father may have died about 1562. If so, then the only extant instrument that might be attributed to the elder Rose is a large consort bass in the Victoria and Albert Museum, London. A particularly fine bass viol (*c*1600) attributed to Rose is in the Hill collection at the Ashmolean Museum, Oxford. Rose's most famous instrument is the so-called Queen Elizabeth lute, an ORPHARION reputedly given to an ancestor of Lord Tollemache by Queen Elizabeth I. Its label reads: 'IOANNES ROSA/LONDINI/FECIT/In Bridwell the 27 of July/1580'. A gamba by 'John. Rose in Brattwell 1599' is mentioned in an auction catalogue published at The Hague in 1759. John Stow (*Annales*, 1631, p.869) credited the elder Rose with the invention of the BANDORA in 1562, and Thomas Mace (*Musick's Monument*, 1676, p.245) regarded the younger Rose, along with Bolles, as the finest of all viol makers.

BIBLIOGRAPHY
W. L. von Lütgendorff: *Die Geigen- und Lautenmacher vom Mittelalter bis zur Gegenwart* (Frankfurt am Main, 1904, 3/1922/R1969)
R. Vannes: *Essai d'un dictionnaire universel des luthiers* (Paris, 1932, 2/1951/R1972 as *Dictionnaire universel des luthiers*, suppl. 1959)
D. Gill: 'An Orpharion by John Rose', *LSJ*, ii (1960), 33
D. Abbott and E. Segerman: 'The Cittern in England before 1700', *LSJ*, xvii (1975), 24
R. Hadaway: 'An Instrument-maker's Report on the Repair and Restoration of an Orpharion', *GSJ*, xxviii (1975), 37
J. Pringle: 'John Rose, the Founder of English Viol-making', *Early Music*, vi (1978), 501

Rose, Jürgen. German stage designer who has worked on several productions with OTTO SCHENK.

Rose, Leonard (Joseph) (*b* Washington, DC, 27 July 1918). American cellist. He began lessons at the age of ten with Walter Grossman at the Miami Conservatory, and later in New York with his cousin Frank Miller, principal cellist with the NBC SO. He won a scholarship to the Curtis Institute, Philadelphia, where he studied with Felix Salmond, 1934–8; he then left to become assistant principal cellist with the NBC SO under Toscanini. After one season he became principal cellist of the Cleveland Orchestra under Rodzinski, 1939–43, and directed the cello department of the Cleveland Institute. He next joined the New York PO, 1943–51, with which he made his concerto début at Carnegie Hall in 1944. His last solo appearance as a member of the New York PO was also his first in Britain, at the 1951 Edinburgh Festival; he then began touring widely as a soloist, and first appeared in London at the Festival Hall in 1958, playing Brahms's Double Concerto with Stern. He taught at the Juilliard School from 1947 and at the Curtis Institute until 1962; his pupils included Lynn Harrell, Ronald Leonard and the principal cellists of many leading American orchestras. Salmond presented him with his own music library, and Rose has edited performing editions of a number of cello works. His large-toned but firmly controlled playing is heard to advantage in the Romantic repertory, most of which he has also recorded, and he is much admired as a chamber player, especially in trios with Stern and Istomin, and in sonatas with various pianists, notably Graffman. He plays a cello by Nicolo Amati dated 1662.

RICHARD BERNAS

Roseingrave. English family of organists and composers, possibly of Irish origin.

(1) Daniel Roseingrave (*d* Dublin, May 1727). There is no support for Hawkins's testimony that he was 'educated in the Chapel Royal' but, from his knowledge of the dispute between Renatus Harris and Bernard Smith about the building of an organ for the Temple Church which (2) Thomas Roseingrave communicated to Burney, it is apparent that he was in London as a youth and was in some way associated with Blow and Purcell. Leases granted by Christ Church Cathedral, Dublin, in the 17th century mention the name Roseingrave and it is therefore possible that he came from Ireland. Nevertheless, he spent the early part of his career in England, as organist successively of Gloucester Cathedral (1679–81), Winchester Cathedral (1682–92) and Salisbury Cathedral (1692–8). He then moved to Dublin, taking up the appointments of organist (and 'stipendiary') of Christ Church Cathedral, and organist (and lay vicar) of St Patrick's Cathedral together in 1698. In February 1719 he resigned his posts at St Patrick's on account of poor health and was succeeded at his own request by his son (3) Ralph Roseingrave; thus father and son between them covered the period when Jonathan Swift was dean of St Patrick's. He retained his posts at Christ Church Cathedral until his death, when Ralph again succeeded him.

Among his colleagues at Dublin was Robert Hodge, Master of the Choristers of Christ Church from 1697 and of St Patrick's from 1698; he had been Roseingrave's predecessor as organist of St Patrick's.

Hodge had likewise come from England, having been organist of Wells Cathedral (1688–90) and formerly a private pupil of Henry Purcell. There is evidence in the Cathedral Act Books that both made some effort to improve the repertory of the Dublin cathedrals by transcribing music introduced from England. Nevertheless, the two men quarrelled and fought, thereby incurring the censure of the Christ Church chapter in December 1699.

Roseingrave appears to have composed some church music, but it never formed part of the general repertory. Burney and Hawkins wrote appreciatively of him as a composer; his verse anthem *Lord, thou art become gracious* is an extended work of some elaboration and expressive power. The payment to him for 'writing three services and two Creeds' recorded in the Christ Church Chapter Acts in 1699 probably refers to transcribing rather than composing.

Of his three sons, Thomas and Ralph are noted separately below. Daniel (*b* 1685; BA Dublin, 1707) became organist of Trinity College, Dublin, in 1705.

WORKS

Jerusalem, canon, 3vv, in T. Warren, *A Collection of Catches, Canons and Glees*, i (London, 1763), perhaps by Thomas Roseingrave
Anthems: Haste Thee, O God, to deliver me, *GB-Lbm*; Lord, thou art become gracious, *Lbm, Och, US-BE*; Bow down thine ears, O Lord, *BE*; The voice of my beloved, *BE*; O clap your hands, *BE*
Service, F, cited in Duckles

(2) Thomas Roseingrave (*b* Winchester, 1688; *d* Dunleary, 23 June 1766). Son of (1) Daniel Roseingrave. As a boy he went to Dublin with his father, under whom he first studied music, and in 1707 entered Trinity College but did not stay to complete his degree. The 'young Roseingrave' who, according to the college register, was appointed organist of Trinity College Chapel in 1705 was probably Daniel junior rather than Thomas, who was then 17. He was sent to Italy in 1709 with the financial assistance of the dean and chapter of St Patrick's Cathedral 'to improve himself in the art of music . . . that hereafter he may be useful and serviceable to the said Cathedral' (Chapter Acts, 14 December 1709). In Venice he attended a concert at a nobleman's house; Roseingrave was invited to play, and later told Burney: 'finding myself rather better in courage and finger than usual, I exerted myself . . . and fancied, by the applause I received, that my performance had made some impression on the company'. Burney continued:

a grave young man dressed in black and in a black wig, who had stood in one corner of the room, very quiet and attentive while Roseingrave played, being asked to sit down to the harpsichord, when he began to play, Rosy said, he thought ten hundred d----ls had been at the instrument; he never had heard such passages of execution and effect before. . . Upon enquiring the name of this extraordinary performer, he was told it was Domenico Scarlatti, son of the celebrated Cavalier Alessandro Scarlatti. Roseingrave declared he did not touch an instrument himself for a month; after this rencontre, however, he became very intimate with the young Scarlatti, followed him to Rome and Naples, and hardly ever quitted him while he remained in Italy. . .

Roseingrave composed the anthem *Arise, shine, for thy light is come* in Venice in 1713, for the Peace of Utrecht. The only surviving copy is in the Tudway Collection; Tudway referred to the work in a letter to Humfrey Wanley:

The Artful part is very fine, and he [Roseingrave] has show'd himself a great Master, but for want I believe to being us'd to set Church Music, he keeps too theatrical a style, and introduces in most places his words, with very great Levetees; . . . This is also Mr Hendale's fault.

Burney commented that there was 'much fire in the

introductory symphony, which is of a very modern cast'.

Roseingrave probably returned to England in 1714 or 1715. In 1718 he was mentioned in an advertisement in the *Daily Courant* as composer of an Italian cantata, and he was active in London's musical life during the next few years, particularly as a champion of Domenico Scarlatti. In 1720 he produced Scarlatti's opera *Amor d'un'ombra e Gelosea d'un'aura* under the title *Narciso* at the Haymarket Theatre, adding two arias and two duets of his own. His famous edition of 42 sonatas by Scarlatti appeared in 1739, including sonatas from the *Essercizi* of the previous year and others of which he evidently had manuscript copies.

In 1725 Roseingrave became organist of Handel's parish church, St George's, Hanover Square, where a new three-manual organ had been completed in the same year by Gerard Smith. The vestry, refusing to be 'teazed by the solicitations of candidates of mean abilities', appointed a panel of advisers. There are widely differing accounts regarding the numbers of candidates and judges (quoted by Butcher). Burney wrote that Roseingrave's style:

though too crude and learned for the generality of hearers when left to himself, treated the subjects given with such science and dexterity, inverting the order of notes, augmenting and diminishing their value, introducing counter-subjects, and turning the themes to so many ingenious purposes that the judges were unanimous in declaring him the victorious candidate.

Roseingrave's accomplished fugal extemporizations were no doubt the result of his enthusiasm for contrapuntal textures; he had a deep admiration for Palestrina's style, examples of which were seen by John Hawkins on scraps of paper on the walls of Roseingrave's bedroom. He received a modest salary at St George's, and was allowed sufficient time for composition, 'a science too greatly my delight not to be continually my study', as he later wrote. Roseingrave was now at the height of his powers; he had acquired an outstanding reputation as organist and teacher: Handel's amanuensis John Christopher Smith, Henry Carey and John Worgan were among his pupils. Although Roseingrave's manner of composing was commonly censured as being both 'harsh and disgusting, manifesting great learning, but void of eloquence and variety' (Hawkins), his virtuosity as executant and improviser was beyond question. Burney wrote that he 'had a power of seizing the parts and spirits of a score and executing the most difficult music at sight beyond any musician in Europe'. A promising career was brought to a premature end by a broken heart, or 'creation' (as Roseingrave himself called it). Coxe described its cause:

His reputation was . . . so high that on commencing teaching he might have gained one thousand pounds a year, but an unfortunate event reduced him to extreme distress. Among Roseingrave's scholars was a young lady to whom he was greatly attracted, and whose affections he had gained, but her father, who intended to give her a large fortune, did not approve of her marrying a musician, and forbade Roseingrave his house. This disappointment affected his brain, and he never entirely recovered the shock. He neglected his scholars and lost his business. He lived upon fifty pounds per annum, which his place produced, and was often in indigence. He was perfectly rational upon every subject but the one nearest his heart: whenever that was mentioned he was quite insane.

At a vestry meeting at St George's on 20 February 1738 a suggestion that the organist's salary be reduced was rejected; it was resolved 'That the Salary to Mr Thos. Roseingrave . . . be continued at Forty Five Pounds a year'. There is no mention of any inadequacy on Roseingrave's part until the vestry meeting of 22 March 1744 when a complaint was made that Roseingrave's deputies had not 'behaved in so decent a manner as they ought, with respect to the Airs and Voluntary's played in the church, which has given offence to several of the Parishioners'. In his reply Roseingrave 'signified that by Infirmity he was render'd incapable of playing the organ'; the vestry then resolved to 'appoint an assistant to the said Mr Roseingrave to officiate at the church, the allowance for his trouble out of Mr Roseingrave's salary'. On 23 April 1744 John Keeble was appointed assistant organist; Roseingrave, 'on account of his infirmitys', was allowed half of the salary for the remainder of his life. He stayed for some time at Hampstead where, although he would occasionally alarm his hosts by leaving his bed in the middle of the night to go to the harpsichord, he seems to have recovered to some extent, for Burney was often tempted to visit him 'on account of his sweetness of temper, his willingness to instruct young pupils, and his entertaining conversation'.

Roseingrave eventually retired to Dublin, where his brother Ralph was organist. He stayed in the house of his nephew William Roseingrave (*b* 1725), a son of Ralph, then (1753) chief chamberlain of the exchequer court. Mrs Delany wrote in her autobiography on 12 January 1753 that 'Mr Roseingrave, who was sent away from St George's Church on account of his mad fits, is now in Ireland, and at times can play very well on the harpsichord'. It was announced in the *Dublin Journal* (3 February 1753) that the opera *Phaedra and Hippolitus*, 'by Mr Roseingrave lately arrived from London', would be performed, and that Roseingrave would play 'Scarlatti's "Lessons on the Harpsichord", with his own additions, and . . . his celebrated "Almand" '. The same journal reported on 27 February:

Yesterday there was a public rehearsal of Mr Roseingrave's Opera of 'Phaedra and Hippolytus' at the great Music Hall in Fishamble Street, to a numerous audience, which met the highest applause, the connoisseurs allowing it to exceed any musical performance ever exhibited here, in variety, taste, and number of good songs.

Roseingrave was buried in the family grave in the churchyard of St Patrick's Cathedral. The inscription adds that he died in his 78th year, 'a most celebrated musician and accomplished man'.

Roseingrave's relationship with Scarlatti was of considerable importance and was directly responsible for the beginning of the 'Scarlatti cult' in England. Arne, Avison, Boyce, Greene, Loeillet, Pepusch and Stanley were among the 95 subscribers to Roseingrave's edition of Scarlatti. Roseingrave's own harpsichord music, while occasionally indebted to Scarlatti, on the whole shows surprisingly little of any such influence. Roseingrave's organ music is closer to the earlier English tradition of John Blow and Purcell than to his continental contemporaries. There is nothing of the clear part-writing and simple textures of most keyboard composers of the period: the printed page is often confusing, with isolated notes on the staff belonging to none of the contrapuntal lines. Roseingrave's fondness for chromatic intricacies, irregular phrases and flexibility of form suggests a compositional approach motivated by his brilliant powers of improvisation. The solos for flute and the Italian cantatas are pleasing works, but lack character: it is only in his keyboard works that Roseingrave's true originality appears.

WORKS

WORKS

(all printed works published in London)

VOCAL

2 songs and 2 duets in D. Scarlatti's Narciso (opera), London, King's, 30 May 1720, pubd (1720)

Phaedra and Hippolitus (opera), Dublin, Fishamble Street Music Hall, 6 March 1753, recits and arias, *GB-Lbm*

[12] Italian cantatas (1735)

Anthems: Great is the Lord and marvelous, *GB-Lbm*; Arise, shine, for thy light is come, thanksgiving for the peace, Venice, 1713, *Lbm*, ed. P. M. Young (London, 1968); O Lord our Governor, *Lcm*; Great is the Lord, *Lcm*; Blessed is he; O come hither; Bow down thine ear; Sing unto God; I will cry unto God; Praise the Lord; I will magnify Thee: all *T*

Songs, pubd singly (*c*1720): Celia conscious of her beauty; Fairest charmer, lovely dear; This mercenary age despise

Other songs etc pubd in 18th-century anthologies

INSTRUMENTAL

8 Suits of Lessons, hpd/spinet (1725)

Voluntaries and Fugues (1728)

XII Solos, fl, hpd (1730)

6 Double Fugues, org/hpd ... to which is added, Sig. Domenico Scarlatti's Celebrated Lesson, hpd, with addns by Roseingrave (1750)

A Celebrated Concerto, hpd (*c*1770)

Other works pubd in 18th-century anthologies

Conc., D, hpd; Allemande, B♭, *c*1740; Menuette, vn, *c*1730: all *GB-Cfm*

2 fugues, f, e, org, *Lcm*

EDITIONS

XVII suites de pièces, hpd ... composées par Domenico Scarlatti (1739), with add. movt by Roseingrave

(3) Ralph Roseingrave (*b* Salisbury, *c*1695; *d* Dublin, 1747). Son of (1) Daniel Roseingrave. He received his musical education from his father, whom he succeeded as organist of St Patrick's Cathedral, Dublin, in effect from 1719 but formally only in 1726. On his father's death, in 1727, he also became organist of Christ Church Cathedral. He was buried in the churchyard of St Patrick's Cathedral; the headstone mentions that his wife Sarah, who died in 1746, and four of their children, were buried with him, as were his mother Ann Roseingrave and his brother Thomas.

Roseingrave composed mainly for the church: eight of his anthems and two services, in C and F, are in the library of Christ Church, Dublin. He contributed to *The Second Book of the Divine Companion* (London, 1731), and an anthem *O God of Truth* is in J. P. Hullah's *Part Music* (London, 1842). Swanton noted that some organ music by Roseingrave had been discovered. A copy of Purcell's Evening Service in G minor, in the Song School, York, contains an added Gloria by 'Mr Rosengrave, junior', which has been attributed to Ralph (modern edition by M. Bevan, 1968).

BIBLIOGRAPHY

BurneyH; *HawkinsH*

[W. Coxe]: *Anecdotes of George Frederick Handel and John Christopher Smith* (London, 1799)

C. Burney: 'Roseingrave', *Rees's Cyclopaedia* (London, 1819)

C. Lambert: 'Thomas Roseingrave', *PMA*, lviii (1932–3), 67

V. Butcher: 'Thomas Roseingrave', *ML*, xix (1938), 280

R. Newton: 'The English Cult of Domenico Scarlatti', *ML*, xx (1939), 138

F. C. J. Swanton: 'The Training of the Organist and Choirmaster', *Music in Ireland: a Symposium*, ed. A. Fleischmann (Cork, 1952)

R. Kirkpatrick: *Domenico Scarlatti* (Princeton, 1953, 3/1968)

A. McCredie: 'Domenico Scarlatti and his Opera "Narciso" ', *AcM*, xxxiii (1961), 19

V. Duckles: 'Roseingrave', *MGG*

F. Dawes: 'The Secret of Thomas Roseingrave', *The Times* (2 Dec 1966)

WATKINS SHAW (1), GERALD GIFFORD (2–3)

Rosen, Charles (Welles) (*b* New York, 5 May 1927). American pianist and writer on music. He started piano lessons at the age of four and studied at the Juilliard School of Music between the ages of seven and 11. Then, until he was 17, he was a pupil of Moriz Rosenthal and Hedwig Kanner-Rosenthal, continuing under Kanner-Rosenthal for a further eight years. He also took theory and composition lessons with Karl Weigl. He studied at Princeton University, taking the BA (1947), MA (1949) and PhD (1951), in Romance languages. Some of his time there was spent in the study of mathematics; his wide interests also embrace philosophy, art and literature generally. After Princeton he had a spell in Paris, and a brief period of teaching modern languages at the Massachusetts Institute of Technology. But in the year of his doctorate he was launched on a pianist's career, when he made his New York début and the first complete recording of Debussy's Etudes. Since then he has played widely in the USA and Europe. He joined the music faculty of the State University of New York at Stony Brook in 1971.

As a pianist, Rosen is severe and intellectual. His playing of Brahms and Schumann has been criticized for lack of expressive warmth; in music earlier and later he has won consistent praise. His performance of Bach's Goldberg Variations is remarkable for its clarity, its vitality and its structural grasp; he has also recorded *The Art of Fugue* in performances of exceptional lucidity of texture. His Beethoven playing (he specializes in the late sonatas, particularly the Hammerklavier) is notable for its powerful rhythms and its unremitting intellectual force. In Debussy his attention is focussed rather on structural detail than on sensuous beauty. He is a distinguished interpreter of Schoenberg and Webern; he gave the première of (1961) and has recorded Elliott Carter's Concerto for piano and harpsichord (with Ralph Kirkpatrick); and he has played and recorded sonatas by Boulez, with whom he has worked closely.

Rosen's chief contribution to the literature of music is *The Classical Style*. His discussion, while taking account of recent analytical approaches, is devoted not merely to the analysis of individual works but to the understanding of the style of an entire era. Rosen is relatively unconcerned with the music of lesser composers as he holds 'to the old-fashioned position that it is in terms of their [Haydn, Mozart and Beethoven's] achievements that the musical vernacular can best be defined'. Rosen then establishes a context for the music of the Classical masters; he examines the music of each in the genres in which he excelled, in terms of compositional approach and particularly the relationship of form, language and style: this is informed by a good knowledge of contemporary theoretical literature, the styles surrounding that of the Classical era, many penetrating insights into the music itself, and a deep understanding of the process of composition. Rosen's volume won the National Book Award for Arts and Letters in 1972. His smaller monograph on Schoenberg concentrates on establishing the composer's place in musical and intellectual history and on his music of the period around World War I. He has also written many shorter articles, and contributes on a wide range of topics to the *New York Review of Books*.

WRITINGS

The Classical Style: Haydn, Mozart, Beethoven (New York, 1971, 2/1972)

Arnold Schoenberg (New York, 1975)

Sonata Forms (New York, 1980)

STANLEY SADIE

Rosen, Jerome (*b* Boston, Mass., 23 July 1921). American composer, clarinettist and teacher. He was educated at New Mexico State College, the University of California at Los Angeles and the University of California at Berkeley, where he studied composition with Denny and Sessions; he also took lessons with Milhaud in Paris (1949–51). In 1952 he was appointed to teach at the University of California at Davis, where he became professor of music and director of the electronic studio. He has received Fromm Awards (1953, 1954, 1960), a Guggenheim Fellowship (1958–9) and awards from the Institute for Creative Arts (1965, 1972). The highly chromatic, tonal, neo-classical language of his early music has developed into a free chromaticism in which successive tonal centres define the structure.

WORKS
(*selective list*)
Sonata, cl, vc (*c*1954); Str Qt no.1 (1955); Sax Conc., 1947–57; Conc., cl, trbn, band, 1964; Synket Conc., 1968; 3 Pieces, 2 rec, orch, 1971
Opera, 3 song cycles, other chamber pieces

Principal publisher: Boosey & Hawkes
MSS in *US-Wc* [Str Qt no.1, Sax Conc.]

RICHARD SWIFT

Rosenbaum, Maria Therese. Austrian singer, daughter of FLORIAN LEOPOLD GASSMANN.

Rosenberg, Herbert (*b* Frankfurt am Main, 13 Oct 1904). Danish musicologist of German birth. He studied musicology with Abert, Blume, Hornbostel, Sachs and Wolf at the University of Berlin, where he took the doctorate in 1931 with a dissertation on 15th-century German song. He was a lecturer at the Klindworth-Scharwenka Conservatory, Berlin (1932–5), before working in Copenhagen (1935–43) and Stockholm (1943–6); on his return to Copenhagen (1946) he became recording manager for the Danish branch of EMI (1946–64) and subsequently head of the recorded sound department (Nationaldiskoteket) of the Danish National Museum (1964–73). In 1966 he was appointed lecturer at the Malmö Conservatory, and in 1967 he also became a lecturer in musicology at Lund University. His publications include articles on the frottola, the Lochheimer Liederbuch and Scandinavian musicology, a book on understanding music and several discographies.

WRITINGS
'Übertragungen einiger bisher nicht aufgelöster Melodienotierungen des Locheimer Liederbuches', *ZMw*, xiv (1930–31), 67
Untersuchungen über die deutsche Liedweise im 15.Jahrhundert (diss., U. of Berlin; Wolfenbüttel and Berlin, 1931)
Musikforståelse (Copenhagen, 1941–2, rev. and enlarged, 1969–71; Swed. trans., 1945–6 as *Konsten att förstå musik*)
'Frottola und Deutsches Lied um 1500: ein Stilvergleich', *AcM*, xviii–xix (1946–7), 30–78
'La frottola e il lied tedesco nel '500', *RMI*, xlviii (1946), 30–66
'Musikwissenschaftliche Bestrebungen in Dänemark, Norwegen und Schweden', *AcM*, xxx (1958), 118
Discographies: with C. Fabricius-Bjerre: *Carl Nielsen* (Copenhagen, 1965, 2/1968)); *Aksel Schiøtz* (Copenhagen, 1966); *Edition Balzer: a History of Music in Sound in Denmark* (Copenhagen, 1966); with D. Yde-Andersen: *The Danish HMV M-series 1920–33* (Copenhagen, 1966); with E. Skandrup Lund: *Jussi Björling* (Copenhagen, 1969); with H. Smidth Olsen: *Wilhelm Furtwängler* (Copenhagen, 1970); *The Scandinavian HMV V-series 1920–32* (Copenhagen, 1973)
JOHN BERGSAGEL

Rosenberg, Hilding (Constantin) (*b* Bosjökloster, Ringsjön, Skåne, 21 June 1892). Swedish composer and conductor. In boyhood he studied the organ and the piano, and, after taking the organ examination, he held a

post as organist for several years. He travelled in 1914 to Stockholm, where he studied the piano with Andersson and where in 1915 he entered the Royal Academy of Music. There he studied composition with Ellberg for a year and took a longer course in conducting. In 1916 he was introduced to Stenhammar, who gave him much encouragement. He made his first journey abroad in 1920, travelling to Berlin and Dresden and coming into contact with the music of Hauer and Schoenberg; he went on to Vienna and Paris, where he heard works by Stravinsky and Les Six. In the mid-1920s Rosenberg studied counterpoint with Stenhammar, took a leading part in the Swedish section of the ISCM and became known as an excellent chamber musician. He began in 1926 a long and fruitful association with the theatre director Per Lindberg. At the beginning of the 1930s he studied conducting with Scherchen, and in 1932 he was appointed coach and assistant conductor at the Royal Opera of Stockholm, where he was made chief conductor in 1934. Subsequently, as a result of an increasing volume of commissions from Swedish radio, he concentrated more and more on composition, though he continued to make guest appearances conducting his own works in Scandinavia and the USA (1948). He has also exerted a great influence on Swedish musical life as a teacher, his pupils including Blomdahl, Lidholm and Bäck.

Rosenberg is held by many to be the leading figure in 20th-century Swedish music. During the 1920s he was a pioneer, together with Broman and Jeanson, in the effort to free Swedish composition from the national Romantic tradition. His very first works reveal the influence of Sibelius, but he was soon experimenting with various styles displaying diverse models; in Sweden he was regarded as an extreme radical. The European tour of 1920 brought him into contact with the music of Schoenberg, Stravinsky and Hindemith. From early childhood he had been familiar with Lutheran chorales and Gregorian chant, and this, combined with his eager acceptance of Hindemith's principles and his studies of Bach, formed a foundation for his fine contrapuntal technique. He shares Schoenberg's feeling for melody, and lyricism is an integral part of his art; the First String Quartet (1920), a work that has much in common with early Schoenberg, is a good example. The creative culmination of his Bach studies came in the Piano Sonata no.4 (1927), while the *8 plastiska scener* (1921) are close to Bartók, a composer then unknown to Rosenberg. Again like Bartók he took an interest in his country's folk music, composing the Suite on Swedish Folktunes for strings (1927), which combines contrapuntal, lyrical and newer elements.

In 1926 Rosenberg began working in the theatre, where he was active for more than 25 years, producing incidental music to over 40 plays. His work for the stage gave him the opportunity to experiment, and to develop his innate dramatic sense. Several incidental scores gave rise to large-scale works, including the three major operas, *Marionetter*, *Lycksalighetens ö* ('The isle of felicity') and *Hus med dubbel ingång* ('The house with two doors'). His first opera, *Resa till Amerika* ('Journey to America', 1932) was the source of an orchestral suite which incorporates the celebrated 'Railway Fugue'. This was also the period of an important work in Rosenberg's development, the Second Symphony (1928–35), where there began to emerge a more individual style marked by melodic cantilenas, long pedal points and well-worked, often two-part contrapuntal sections. Bach's influence is again evident in the trio sonata texture at the beginning of the second movement and the presence of a chorale and passacaglia in the finale. The influences of Nielsen and Sibelius are still apparent, though in many respects the style is similar to that of Vaughan Williams.

During the 1930s Rosenberg made a rapprochement with the public, simplifying his style and using clearer, essentially diatonic harmonies, chromaticism becoming more a melodic embellishment. Among the many successful works which appeared during the later 1930s are the Christmas oratorio *Den heliga natten* ('The holy night') and its Passion counterpart *Huvudskalleplats* ('Calvary'), the opera *Marionetter* and the ballet *Orfeus i sta'n* ('Orpheus in town'). A more lyrical, meditative mood is notable in the Third Symphony and the Fourth Quartet. In 1940 Rosenberg produced one of his greatest works, the Symphony no.4 'Johannes uppenbarelse' ('The revelation of St John'), a vast composition in eight movements for baritone, chorus and orchestra. The piece is dramatically conceived, with sharp contrasts both in mood and style between the choral-orchestral movements (at times recalling Mahler) and the baritone recitatives, whose tonality is more advanced. The linking *a cappella* chorales draw on Palestrina and Schütz, but they also continue, from Stenhammar, the development of the Swedish choral tradition.

The 1940s was a decade of further large-scale choral works, reaching a climax in the massive opera-oratorio after Mann *Josef och hans bröder* ('Joseph and his brothers'), commissioned by Swedish radio. The same period saw the composition of the opera *The Isle of Felicity* and the Fifth Symphony, a work in a pure classical spirit, forming a pastoral equivalent and complement to the *Revelation* symphony. After 1949 there was a return to purely instrumental works. Rosenberg's style became more homogeneous and his part-writing further refined, as in the excellent Fifth Quartet. Other outstanding works written at this time include the Sixth Symphony (1951) and several concertos, among them the Piano Concerto (1950) and the Violin Concerto no.2 (1951). The Sixth Quartet followed in 1954, and two years later Swedish radio commissioned a further six. In the Twelfth (1956) Rosenberg returned to material from the First Quartet (1920), a retrospective glance that brought about a renewed interest in atonality and 12-note technique. Two important works that display the lyrical expressionism of Rosenberg's late style are *Åt jordgudinnan* ('To the earth goddess', 1960) for voice and six instruments and *Dagdrivaren* ('The sluggard', 1962) for baritone and orchestra.

WORKS

OPERAS

Resa till Amerika [Journey to America] (A. Henriksson), 1932; Stockholm, 24 Nov 1932
Spelet om St Örjan (children's opera), 1937, rev. 1941
Marionetter (J. Benavente), 1938; Stockholm, 14 Feb 1939
De två konungadöttrarna [The two princesses] (children's opera, Rosenberg), 1940; Stockholm, 19 Sept 1940
Lycksalighetens ö [The isle of felicity] (P. D. A. Atterbom), 1943; Stockholm, 1 Feb 1945
Josef och hans bröder [Joseph and his brothers] (opera-oratorio, after Mann), 1946–8; Swedish radio, pt.1 30 May 1946, pt.2 19 Dec 1946, pt.3 9 Sept 1947, pt.4 23 Jan 1948
Kaspers fettisdag [Punch's Shrove Tuesday] (Strindberg), 1953; Swedish radio, 28 Feb 1954
Porträttet (after Gogol), 1955; Swedish radio, 22 March 1956; rev. 1963
Hus med dubbel ingång [The house with two doors] (after Calderón), 1969; Stockholm, 24 May 1970

BALLETS AND PANTOMIME

Yttersta domen [The last judgment] (pantomime, Karlfeldt), 1929; unperf.
Orfeus i sta'n [Orpheus in town] (ballet), 1938; Stockholm, 19 Nov 1938
Eden (Adam and Eve) (ballet) [after Concerto no.1], 1946; New York, 1961
Salome (ballet) [after Metamorfosi sinfoniche nos.1–2], 1963; Stockholm, 28 Feb 1964
Sönerna (Cain and Abel) (ballet) [after Metamorfosi sinfoniche no.3], 1964; Swedish television, 6 Dec 1964
Babels torn [The tower of Babel] (ballet) [after Symphony for Wind and Perc], 1966; Swedish television, 8 Jan 1968

ORATORIOS, CANTATAS, ETC

Den heliga natten [The holy night] (H. Gullberg), oratorio, 1936; Swedish radio, 27 Dec 1936
Perserna [The Persians] (after Aeschylus), oratorio, 1937; unperf.
Huvudskalleplats [Calvary] (Gullberg), oratorio, 1938; Swedish radio, 15 April 1938; rev. 1964–5
Prometheus och Ahasverus (V. Rydberg), melodrama, 1941; Swedish radio, 27 April 1941
Julhymn av Romanus (Gullberg), cantata, 1941; Swedish radio, 25 Dec 1941
Svensk lagsaga (old Swed. verse), oratorio, 1942; Swedish radio, 24 Feb 1942
Djufars visa [Djufar's song] (V. von Heidenstam), melodrama, 1942; Swedish radio, 18 Dec 1942
Cantata to the National Museum (Gullberg), 1942; Swedish radio, 1 June 1943
Lyrisk svit (H. Martinson), cantata, 1954; Göteborg, 2 Oct 1954
Hymnus (Gullberg), oratorio, 1965; Swedish radio, 24 July 1966
Hymn to a University (Gullberg, E. Tegnér), cantata, 1967; Lund, 13 June 1968

ORCHESTRAL

Adagio, 1915
Symphony no.1, 1917, rev. 1919; Göteborg, 1921; rev. 1971
3 fantasistycken, 1918; Göteborg, 1919
Sinfonia da chiesa no.1, 1923; Stockholm, 16 Jan 1925; rev. 1950
Sinfonia da chiesa no.2, 1924; Stockholm, 20 Jan 1926
Violin Concerto no.1, 1924; Stockholm, 8 May 1927
2 suites from opera Marionetter, small orch, 1926
Suite on Swedish Folktunes, str, 1927; Swedish radio, 13 Sept 1927
Suite [from incidental music Livet en dröm], small orch, 1927
Threnody for Stenhammar (Sorgemusik), 1927
Trumpet Concerto, 1928; Stockholm, 16 Jan 1929
2 preludes and 2 Suites [from pantomime Yttersta domen], 1929
Suite [from incidental music Moralitet], 1930
Suite [from opera Resa till Amerika], 1932; Stockholm, 29 Sept 1935
Overtura piccola, 1934
Symphony no.2 (Sinfonia grave), 1928–35; Göteborg, 27 March 1935
Symphonie concertante, vn, va, ob, bn, orch, 1935; Göteborg, Jan 1936
Suite [from film score Bergslagsbilder], 1937; Swedish radio, 16 Nov 1937
Overture and Dance Suite [from opera Marionetter], 1938
Dance Suite [from ballet Orfeus i sta'n], 1938
Cello Concerto no.1, 1939
Symphony no.3 'De fyra tidsåldrarna' [The four ages of man], 1939; Swedish radio, 11 Dec 1939; rev. 1952
Adagio funèbre, 1940
Suite (I bergakungens sal [In the hall of the mountain king]), 1940
Symphony no.4 'Johannes uppenbarelse' [The revelation of St John], Bar, chorus, orch, 1940; Swedish radio, 6 Dec 1940
Suite [from melodrama Djufars visa], 1942
Viola Concerto, 1942; Swedish radio, 11 Feb 1943
Vindarnas musik [from opera Lycksalighetens ö], 1943
Symphony no.5 'Hortulanus' (Örtagårdsmästaren [The keeper of the garden]), A, chorus, orch, 1944; Swedish radio, 17 Oct 1944
Concerto no.1, str, 1946; Swedish radio, 6 July 1947
Overtura bianca-nera, 1946
Partita [from opera-oratorio Josef och hans bröder], 1948
Concerto no.2, 1949; Malmö, 12 Jan 1950
Piano Concerto, 1950; Göteborg, 14 March 1951
Symphony no.6 (Sinfonia semplice), 1951; Gävle, 24 Jan 1952
Violin Concerto no.2, 1951; Stockholm, 25 March 1952
Ingresso solenne del premio Nobel, 1952
Cello Concerto no.2, 1953; Swedish radio, 25 April 1954
Variations on a Sarabande, 1953
Concerto no.3 'Louisville', 1954; Louisville, Ken., 1954; rev. 1968
Riflessioni no.1, str, 1959; Swedish radio, 24 April 1965
Riflessioni no.2, str, 1960; Swedish radio, 2 March 1962
Riflessioni no.3, str, 1960; Lucerne, 1961
Dagdrivaren [The sluggard] (S. Alfons), Bar, orch, 1962; Stockholm, 28 Oct 1964
Metamorfosi sinfoniche nos.1–3, 1963–4
Symphony for Wind and Perc, 1966
Concerto no.4, str, 1966; Stockholm, 14 Sept 1968

Symphony no.7, 1968; Swedish radio, 29 Sept 1968
Symphony no.8 'In candidum', chorus, orch, 1974

CHAMBER AND INSTRUMENTAL

Str qts: no.1, 1920, Stockholm, 6 March 1923; no.2, 1924, Stockholm, 6 March 1925; no.3 (Quartetto pastorale), 1926, Göteborg, 3 April 1932; no.4, 1939, Stockholm, 2 Nov 1942; no.5, 1949, Stockholm, 23 May 1950; no.6, 1954, Stockholm, 25 May 1954; no.7, 1956, Swedish radio, 13 Nov 1958; no.8, 1956, Swedish radio, 20 Dec 1958; no.9, 1956, Swedish radio, 17 March 1959; no.10, 1956, Swedish radio, 12 May 1959; no.11, 1956, Swedish radio, 23 Oct 1959; no.12 (Quartetto riepilogo), 1956, Swedish radio, 11 Dec 1959

Other works for 2–5 insts: Trio, fl, vn, va, 1921; Suite, D, vn, pf, 1922; Sonatina, fl, pf, 1923; Sonata no.1, vn, pf, 1926; Trio, ob, cl, bn, 1927; Divertimento, str trio, 1936; Taffelmusik, pf trio/chamber orch, 1939; Serenade, fl, vn, va, 1940; Sonata no.2, vn, pf, 1940; Wind Qnt, 1959; Moments musicaux, str qt, 1972

Pf: 3 intermezzi, 1916; 8 plastiska scener, 1921; 4 sonatas, 1923, 1925, 1926, 1927; Suite, 1924; 11 små föredragsstudier, 1924; 2 Pieces (Musik för nordens barn), 1927; Improvisations, 1939; Tema con variazioni, 1941; 6 Polyphonic Studies, 1945; 11 nya små föredragsstudier, 1949; Sonatina, 1949; Le dilette secunde, 1962

Other solo inst: 3 sonatas, vn, 1921, 1953, 1963, no.3 rev. 1967; Fantasia e fuga, org, 1941; Prelude and Fugue, org, 1948; Toccata, Aria pastorale, Ciacona, org, 1952; Sonata, fl, 1959; Sonata, cl, 1960; Sekvens 40, org 1961

SMALL-SCALE VOCAL

Choral: Song of Mourning and Pastoral [from incidental music Medea], female vv, pf, 1931; 2 Female Choruses (Fröding), 1931; 5 Motets, 1949; 3 Swedish Folksongs, 1953; Indianlyrik från Nordamerika (Fredenholm), female vv, 2 fl, gui, perc, 1969

Songs for 1v, pf: 3 Songs (Heidenstam), 1918; 2 Songs (Hebbel), 1920; 3 Songs (Blomberg), 1926, orchd; Glaukes sånger [from incidental music Kvinnan i Hyllos hus], 1940, rev. 1959; 4 Jewish Songs (Josephson), 1941, orchd; 14 Chinese Songs, 1945–51; 4 Songs (Edfelt), 1959

Other works: Grekiska strövtåg [Greek excursion], 1v, reciter, fl, pf, 1940; 2 Songs (Edfelt), 1v, fl, 2 cl, vc, 1960; Åt jordgudinnan [To the earth goddess] (Edfelt), Mez/Bar, fl, cl, lute, str trio, 1960; Ensam i tysta natten (G. Ekelöf), T, str qnt, 1976

INCIDENTAL MUSIC

De skapade intressena [The created interests] (Benavente), 1926; Kung Oidipus (Sophocles), 1926; Livet en dröm [Life in a dream] (Calderón), 1927; Lek ej med kärleken [Don't play with love] (Musset), 1927; Tusen och en natt [Thousand and one nights] (Hallström), 1927; Molnen [The clouds] (Aristophanes), 1927; Porten [The door] (H. Bergman), 1927; Längtans land [The land of heart's desire] (Yeats), 1927; Agamemnon (Aeschylus), 1928; Hans nåds testamente [His Grace's will] (Bergman), 1929; Dåren och döden [Death and the fool] (Hofmannsthal), 1929; Markurells i Wadköping (Bergman), 1930; De trogna [The faithful] (Masefield), 1930; Moralitet or Spelet om flickan och frestaren [Morality or The play of the girl and the tempter] (Bergman), 1930; Lycksalighetens ö [The isle of felicity] (Atterbom), 1930

Gravoffret (Aeschylus), 1930; Betongen och skogen [The concrete and the forest] (Henrikson), 1930; Medea (Euripides), 1931; Trettondagsafton [Twelfth night] (Shakespeare), 1932; Alcestis (Euripides), 1933; Stora landsvägen [The great highway] (Strindberg), 1933; Hus med dubbel ingång [House with two doors] (Calderón), 1934, 1950; Lysistratus (Aristophanes), 1934; Antigone (Sophocles), 1934; Circus Juris (Borberg), 1935; Noak (Obey), 1935; Kvinnan av börd och mannen av folket [The woman of birth and the man of the people] (Lope de Vega), 1935; Köpmannen av Venedig (Shakespeare), 1935; Den store guden Brown (O'Neill), 1936; Fåglarna [The birds] (Aristophanes), 1936

Spökdamen [The phantom lady] (Calderón), 1936; Perserna (Aeschylus), 1937; Ifigenia på Tauris (Goethe), 1940; Långfredag (Masefield), 1940; Kvinnan i Hyllos hus (Byström-Baeckström), 1940; Fårakällan [The sheep spring] (Lope de Vega), 1944; Blodsbröllop (Lorca), 1944; Djami och vattenandarna [Djami and the water spirits] (Siwertz), 1945; Oidipus på Kolonos (Sophocles), 1945; Flygorna (Sartre), 1945; Bron vid Arta [The bridge at Arta] (Theotokas), 1945; Philoktetes (Sophocles), 1947; Richard III (Shakespeare), 1947; Yerma (Lorca), 1948; Egmont (Goethe), 1949; Hippolytos (Euripides), 1950; Ajax (Sophocles), 1950; Oidipus (Sophocles), 1951; Wadköping runt (Henriques), 1952

FILM SCORES

Bergslagsbilder [Scenes from Bergslagen], 1937; Stål [Steel], 1940; I paradis, 1941; Det sägs på sta'n [There's a rumour in town], 1941; Trut [Gull]; Hets [Bustle]; Ödemaktsprästen [The priest of fate]; The Missionary and the Medicine Man; The World of Beauty, 1960; Pan, 1962

Principal publisher: Nordiska Musikförlaget
MSS in S-Sic

WRITINGS

En bok om Per Lindberg (Stockholm, 1944)
'Lycksalighetens ö', Musikvärlden, i/1 (1945), 3
'Min skånska barndom' [My childhood in Skåne], Sydsvenska dagbladet (19 Nov 1950)
'Tankar-minnen' [Recollected thoughts], Nutida musik, v/4 (1961–2), 1

BIBLIOGRAPHY

R. Hove: 'Tre nordiske symphonikere', Nordisk tidskrift (1936), 571
——: 'Hilding Rosenberg', Levande musik (1942), 87
M. Pergament: 'Hilding Rosenberg', Svenska tonsättare (Stockholm, 1943), 102
E. Kallstenius: 'Hilding Rosenberg', Svenska orkesterverk (Stockholm, 1947)
M. Pergament: 'A Journey in Modern Swedish Music', ML, xxviii (1947), 249
G. Stern: 'Örtagårdsmästaren' [The gardener], Musikvärlden, v/4 (1949), 111
N. L. Wallin: 'Hilding Rosenberg's "The Revelation of St. John"', Musikrevy, vi/1 (1951), 17
B. Wallner: 'Melodiken i Hilding Rosenbergs senaste instrumentalverk', Ord och bild (1952), no.61
M. Pergament: Hilding Rosenberg, a Giant of Modern Swedish Music (Stockholm, 1956)
B. Wallner: 'Hilding Rosenberg och teatern', Operan (26 Oct 1956)
——: 'Kammermusikalisk sammanfattning', Nutida musik, ii/1–2 (1958–9), 3
——: 'Hilding Rosenbergs sjätte stråkkvartett', Nutida musik, v/4 (1961–2), 35
——: 'Kring Rosenbergs Riflessioni 1–3', Nutida musik, v/4 (1961–2), 3
——: 'En oceanisk musik i orons öppna hus', Nutida musik, viii/2 (1964–5), 19
——: 'Om Rosenbergs uppenbarelsesymfoni', Nutida musik, ix/8 (1965–6), 2
H. Åstrand: 'Fallet Rosenberg', Konsertnytt, iii/1 (1967), 3
S.-D. Sandström: Hilding Rosenberg som kompositör i 1920-talets Stockholm (diss., U. of Stockholm, 1967)
B. Wallner: 'Hilding Rosenbergs symfoni nr.7 och blåsarsymfoni', Nutida musik, xii/1 (1968–9), 70
P. H. Lyne: Hilding Rosenberg: Catalogue of Works (Stockholm, 1970)
B. Wallner: 'Rosenberg och 20-talet', Nutida musik, xv/4 (1971–2), 3; xvi/1 (1972–3), 20
H. Connor: 'Hilding Rosenberg', Samtal med tonsättare (Borås, 1971), 117
B. Wallner: 'Komik, romantik, epik, etik, politik', Operan 200 år (Lund, 1973), 140

PETER H. LYNE

Rosenfeld, Gerhard (b Königsberg, 10 Feb 1931). German composer. He studied musicology at Berlin University (1952–4) and composition under Wagner-Régeny at the Berlin Hochschule für Musik (1954–7), completing his studies in the master classes of Eisler and Spies at the German Academy of Arts (1958–61). After working in film music and as a lecturer in music theory, he gave his time to composition from 1964. He first came to public attention when Gustav Schmahl gave an impressive first performance of the First Violin Concerto in Dresden in 1963, and his characterful, concise and pleasing music has established him in popular esteem in East Germany.

WORKS
(selective list)

Orch: 2 vn concs., 1963, 1972; Vc Conc., 1967; Fresken, 1968; Pf Conc., 1969; Conc., A, orch, 1971; Conc., harp, db, orch, 1971; Chamber Conc., fl, str, perc, 1972; Reger-Variationen, 1973

Other works: Die Fabeln von Aesop, chorus, 1958; 2 quartettinos, str qt, 1968, 1972; Das alltägliche Wunder (opera, after J. Schwarz), 1972; 5 Nocturnos, ob, vc, hpd, 1973; music for theatre, cinema, radio

Principal publishers: Henschel, Hofmeister, Internationale Musikbibliothek, Peters (Leipzig)

BIBLIOGRAPHY

H.-P. Müller: 'Werkstattgespräch mit Gerhard Rosenfeld', Musik und Gesellschaft, xx (1970), 365

Rosenfeld, Paul (b New York, 4 May 1890; d New York, 21 July 1946). American writer on the arts. He studied at Yale (BA 1912) and with Talcott Williams at the Columbia School of Journalism (LittB 1913). In 1916 he began to contribute essays and reviews to the *Seven Arts*, the *New Republic*, *The Dial* (of which he was music critic from 1920 to 1927), *Vanity Fair* and others. Almost all his music criticism appeared in the 'little magazines' with his essays on the plastic arts and literature: the only music journal to publish a substantial number of his articles was *Modern Music*.

Rosenfeld was an unflinching and intelligent champion of new music. He was primarily an essayist: of his five books concerned mainly with music the two which are least successful represent contributions to publishers' series rather than collections of essays. His approach is impressionistic rather than analytical (with particular success in *Modern Tendencies in Music*); his interest in the way music reflects reality as perceived by both composer and listener has produced valuable critical assessments notable for their taste and intelligence.

At his succession of modest New York homes Rosenfeld brought together those interested in new literature, art and music; his help to individual artists included finding a patron for Copland on his return from Europe.

WRITINGS
Musical Portraits (London, 1922) [20 modern composers]
Musical Chronicle (New York, 1923/R1972) [New York seasons 1917–23]
Modern Tendencies in Music (New York, 1927)
By Way of Art (New York, 1928)
An Hour with American Music (Philadelphia and London, 1929)
Discoveries of a Music Critic (New York, 1936)
On Music and Musicians (New York, 1946) [trans. of R. Schumann: *Gesammelte Schriften über Musik und Musiker*, Leipzig, 1875]
ed. H. A. Leibowitz: *Musical Impressions: Selections from Paul Rosenfeld's Criticism* (New York, 1969)

BIBLIOGRAPHY
J. Mellquist and L. Wiese, eds.: *Paul Rosenfeld, Voyager in the Arts* (New York, 1948)

WAYNE D. SHIRLEY

Rosenhain, Jacob [Jakob, Jacques] (*b* Mannheim, 2 Dec 1813; *d* Baden-Baden, 21 March 1894). German pianist and composer. He studied with Jakob Schmitt, Kalliwoda and Schnyder von Wartensee; he made a successful début in 1832 in Frankfurt am Main, after which he took up residence there. His one-act opera *Der Besuch im Irrenhause* was performed there in 1834. In 1837 he went to London, where he played in numerous concerts, and then to Paris, where he settled and became a prominent figure, particularly through his chamber music evenings given with Alard, Ernst and other eminent players and frequented by Cherubini, Rossini and Berlioz. In 1841 his second one-act opera, *Liswenna* (1836), was performed. In 1843 he founded a piano school in collaboration with J. B. Cramer, and in 1851 *Liswenna*, provided with a new libretto and renamed *Le démon de la nuit*, was produced at the Opéra, although with limited success. His final opera, *Volage et jaloux*, was produced in 1863 at Baden-Baden, where he settled in 1870 and again became the centre of a distinguished artistic circle. Rosenhain also wrote three symphonies (the first of which, in G minor, was played by the Gewandhaus orchestra under Mendelssohn in 1846), a piano concerto, four piano trios, three string quartets, two cello sonatas and songs, as well as many piano works.

BIBLIOGRAPHY
FétisB
H. R. Schäfer: article in *Neue Musik-Zeitung*, xi (1890), 234

E. Kratt-Harveng: *Jacques Rosenhain, Komponist und Pianist: ein Lebensbild* (Baden-Baden, 1891)
R. Sietz: 'Rosenhain, Jakob', *MGG*

GEORGE GROVE/R

Rosenman, Leonard (*b* Brooklyn, NY, 7 Sept 1924). American composer. He was originally trained as a painter. He began musical studies at 15 and after war service worked with Schoenberg, Sessions and Dallapiccola (composition) and Bernard Abramowitsch (piano). In 1953 he was composer-in-residence at the Berkshire Music Center and received a Koussevitzky Foundation commission for an opera. From 1962–6 he lived in Rome where he gained experience as a conductor. He has taught at the University of Southern California, is a member of the board of directors of the ISCM in California, and is musical director of the New Muse, a chamber orchestra specializing in performances of avant-garde music.

Rosenman is an important figure in the history of American film music; his scores for the James Dean films *East of Eden* and *Rebel Without a Cause* struck a note of unprecedented modernity. He has effected in his film music a successful synthesis between traditional and modern, albeit one which has founded no real school.

WORKS
INSTRUMENTAL AND CHAMBER
Concertino, pf, wind, 1948
Piano Sonata, 1949
Violin Concerto, 1951
Theme and Elaborations, pf, 1951
6 Songs (Lorca), Mez, pf, 1952–4
Duo, cl, pf, 1960
Chamber Music 1, 16 players, 1961
Chamber Music 2, 10 players, S, tape, 1968
Fanfare, 8 tpt, 1970
Threnody on a Song of K.R., orch, jazz group, 1971
Foci, orch, tape, 1972
A Short History of Civilisation, theatre work with film, 1972

FILM MUSIC
(*selective list*)
East of Eden, 1954; Rebel Without a Cause, 1955; The Chapman Report, 1959; Pork Chop Hill, 1959; A Covenant with Death, 1966; The Fantastic Voyage, 1966; A Man Called Horse, 1969; Beneath the Planet of the Apes, 1969; Battle for the Planet of the Apes, 1973

WRITINGS
'Notes from a Sub-culture', *PNM*, vii/1 (1968), 122

CHRISTOPHER PALMER

Rosenmüller, Johann [Rosenmiller, Giovanni] (*b* Oelsnitz, nr. Zwickau, *c*1619; *d* Wolfenbüttel, buried 12 Sept 1684). German composer, organist and teacher. Although he spent the major part of his creative life in Italy, his music was held in high esteem in Germany, making him an important figure in the transmission of Italian styles to the north.

1. LIFE. Rosenmüller received his early musical training at the Lateinschule at Oelsnitz and matriculated in the theological faculty of the University of Leipzig in 1640. There he most likely continued his musical studies with Tobias Michael, Kantor of the Thomaskirche, and he is listed as an assistant at the Thomasschule in 1642, teaching music in the lower classes. By 1650 he had become the first assistant; in 1651 he was also appointed organist of the Nicolaikirche, and in 1653 the Leipzig city council promised him the succession to the Thomaskirche cantorate. The following year he also became director of music *in absentia* to the Altenburg court. This promising career came to an abrupt halt in spring 1655, when he and several of the schoolboys

were arrested and imprisoned on suspicion of homosexuality. He escaped from gaol and is thought to have gone to Hamburg, though there is no documentary evidence for his presence there.

Rosenmüller was employed as a trombonist at St Mark's, Venice, in early 1658 and by 1660 had established himself as a composer there; an emissary from the court at Weimar obtained some compositions from him there that year. Johann Philipp Krieger studied composition with him in Venice about 1673–4; Rosenmüller also held the post of composer at the Ospedale della Pietà from 1678 until July 1682. Towards the end of his life he returned to Germany as Kapellmeister of the court at Wolfenbüttel. His connections with the house of Brunswick-Lüneburg had probably been established in 1667, when Duke Johann Friedrich visited Venice and Rosenmüller dedicated his first sonata collection to him. The duke's cousin, Anton Ulrich, to whom the 1682 sonatas are dedicated, returned to Wolfenbüttel in 1682 from a visit to Italy, perhaps taking Rosenmüller with him. Rosenmüller's epitaph in Wolffenbüttel declared him to be 'the Amphion of his age'.

2. WORKS. Rosenmüller's publications of instrumental music span his creative career, from 1645 to 1682, and a clear line of stylistic development can be traced through them. The first three have in common the organization into suites of quite short, functional dance pieces, usually in duple–triple pairs in the order allemande, courante (correnta), ballet (ballo) and sara-

First page of the 'prima vox' part of Rosenmüller's 'Kern-Sprüche' (Leipzig: Author, 1648)

bande, introduced by a longer, more stylized movement. In the case of the *Paduanen* (1645) and *Studenten-Music* (1654) this opening movement is also a dance, a pavan. Lehmann claimed that the 1645 collection is the first to use a pavan in this way, without a galliard; however, it contains only four such suites, the other 30 pieces being single dances, mostly allemandes. In the *Studenten-Music* there are ten suites, systematically arranged in ascending order of key. The greatest growth is seen in the introductory pavans, where all five parts engage in motivic interplay. The other dances, like the 1667 sonatas, may also be played *a* 3: the middle parts are only harmonic filling.

Italian influence, particularly that of Legrenzi, is clear in Rosenmüller's last two collections. In the 1667 *Sonate da camera* the opening pavan has given way to a much longer sinfonia made up of sections contrasting strongly in tempo, metre and texture. The main sections always fall into the form *ABCB*, *B* being in a cantabile 3/2; this produces a rich, nicely balanced movement. There is no corresponding growth in the dances, however, and they disappear completely from the 1682 sonata collection. These sonatas clearly represent an expansion of the 1667 sinfonias, but they show a much greater variety in both scoring and overall structure. There are three to five main movements, one of which is often repeated at the end; many are fugal, and there is a marked increase in the number of chromatic themes. The slow, chordal transition sections are longer, more dramatic and often startling in their harmonic boldness. While these sonatas are neither as 'classical' in structure nor as secure in tonality as those of Corelli's op.1 (1681), this collection is rightly regarded as Rosenmüller's instrumental masterpiece.

With only minor exceptions, all of Rosenmüller's vocal music is sacred. Prints are confined to the Leipzig period; after 1654 he followed the practice of all the better German composers of the time and preferred to have his sacred music disseminated in manuscript. Much of it must have been composed in Italy, but it seems to have survived only in German sources, of which the Bokemeyer Collection, copied mainly in the 1690s by Georg Österreich, is the most important. Approximately 150 surviving manuscript works and inventories of lost collections in Lüneburg, Rudolstadt, Weissenfels and Ansbach attest the fact that he was one of the most popular composers of his day.

The funeral songs, each published separately on the occasion, are strophic, homophonic *a cappella* hymns. The most famous of them, *Welt ade, ich bin dein müde*, was taken over intact by J. S. Bach into his Cantata no.27. The *Kern-Sprüche* and *Andere Kern-Sprüche* are collections of small sacred concertos, careful settings of short German and Latin texts in the style of Schütz's *Symphoniae sacrae*. Rosenmüller was in fact Schütz's Leipzig agent for the distribution of the second set of *Symphoniae sacrae* (1647), and Schütz had contributed a congratulatory poem to Rosenmüller's first publication (the *Paduanen* of 1645). Although the contents of the *Kern-Sprüche* are the best represented in modern editions of Rosenmüller's vocal music, they give a little hint of the expressiveness, clarity of form and idiomatic vocal writing of his later works.

Of the extant manuscript works, most of the 32 with German texts were probably composed before he settled in Italy. These include a few small concertos similar to those in the *Kern-Sprüche*, large concertos contrasting vocal soloists with a choral tutti, dialogues of both the dramatic and allegorical type, sometimes with a concluding chorale, and his first two settings of complete psalms. Most of the manuscript works, however, have Latin texts and were probably composed in Italy. There is little music for the Mass, but Italian liturgical practice is reflected in the large number of pieces proper to Vespers or Compline; there are 53 settings of complete Latin psalms, including multiple settings of the Sunday and Marian vesper psalms. These range from works for solo voice with two violins and continuo to large concertos with double chorus, soloists and instruments (e.g. NM, lix and lxxxi). Most of them share a clear overall structure articulated by instrumental ritornellos. The vocal writing consists mainly of arioso, with some concertato sections and often a virtuoso setting of the 'Gloria Patri'. The very expressive setting of words from the Lamentations (NM, xxvii–xxviii), Rosenmüller's only purely monodic work, is also liturgical. His cantatas for solo voice, on the other hand, are modelled on the secular cantatas of Carissimi and Cesti. Based on Latin devotional texts of mixed prose and poetry, they are set as recitative, arioso and arias and include closed forms (examples are *Homo Dei creatura* and *Ad pugnas ad bella*, both in Snyder). Rosenmüller's incorporation of elements of the solo cantata and Italian operatic and instrumental styles into sacred music that was widely performed in Germany clearly helped prepare the way for the emerging German sacred cantata.

WORKS

(complete catalogue in Snyder)

Edition: *J. Rosenmüller: Concertos and Cantatas*, ed. K. J. Snyder, WE, xiii (in preparation)

SACRED VOCAL

Kern-Sprüche mehrentheils aus heiliger Schrifft Altes und Neues Testaments (Leipzig, 1648); some ed. D. Krüger (Hohenheim, nr. Stuttgart, 1960–68):
Aeterne Deus, clementissime Pater, 1v, 2 str, bc; Christum lieb haben, 3vv, 2 str, bc; Coeli enarrant gloriam Dei, 3vv, 2 str, bc; Danket dem Herren und prediget, 2vv, 2 str, bc; Danksaget dem Vater, 5vv, 2 str, bc; Daran ist erschienen die Liebe Gottes, 5vv, 2 str, bc; Das ist das ewige Leben, 3vv, 2 str, bc; Das ist ein köstlich Ding, 2vv, 5 str, bc; Die Augen des Herren, 4vv, 2 str, bc; Ein Tag in deinen Vorhöfen, 3vv, 2 str, bc; Habe deine Lust an dem Herren, 1v, 5 str, bc; Hebet eure Augen auf gen Himmel, 2vv, 2 str, bc; In te Domine speravi, 4vv, 2 str, bc; Lieber Herr Gott, 1v, 3 str, bc; Mater Jerusalem, civitas sancta Dei, 2vv, 2 str, bc; Meine Seele harret nur auf Gott, 3vv, 2 str, bc; O admirabile commercium, 2vv, 4 str/brass, bc; O Domine Jesu Christe, adoro te, 3vv, bc; O nomen Jesu, nomen dulce, 4vv, bc; Treiffet ihr Himmel von oben, 1v, 2 str, bc
Andere Kern-Sprüche (Leipzig, 1652–3); some ed. A. Tunger (Hohenheim, nr. Stuttgart, 1960–63):
Also hat Gott die Welt geliebet, 5vv, 5 str/brass, bc; Amo te Deus meus amore magno, 2vv, 4 str/brass, bc; Christum ducem, qui per crucem, 1v, 2 str, bc; Das ist meine Freude, 1v, 2 str, bc; Der Name des Herren, 5vv, 2 str, bc; Die Gnade unseres Herren Jesu Christi, 4vv, bc; Domine Deus meus, 2vv, 2 str, bc; Herr mein Gott, ich danke dir, 3vv, 2 str, bc; Herr, wenn ich nur dich habe, 1v, 5 str, bc; Ich bin das Brod des Lebens, 3vv, 2 str, bc; Ich hielte mich nicht dafür, 4vv, bc; Ist Gott für uns, 1v, 5 str, bc; Kündlich gross ist das gottselige Geheimnis, 3vv, bc; O dives omnium bonarum dapum, 1v, 3 str/brass, bc; O dulcis Christe, bone Jesu charitas, 2vv, 3 str/brass, bc; Siehe an die Wercke Gottes, 5vv, 5 str/brass, bc; Siehe des Herren Auge, 3vv, 2 str, bc; Vulnera Jesu Christi, 1v, 5 str, bc; Wahrlich, wahrlich ich sage euch, 4vv, 2 str, bc; Weil wir wissen, dass der Mensch, 3vv, 2 str, bc
Funeral songs, 5vv; ed. F. Hamel, Acht Begräbnisgesänge zu fünf Stimmen (Wolfenbüttel, 1930) [H]:
Alle Menschen müssen sterben, in Letzte Ehre (Leipzig, 1652), H 4; Meines Lebens letzte Zeit, in Melodia . . . Heinrich Beckers (n.p., 1654), H 8; Nun Gott lob, es ist vollbracht, in Valet- und Trost-Lied (Leipzig, 1652), H 3; Nur Kreuz und Not, in Letzte Ehre (Leipzig, 1654), H 7; Tret her, die ihr voll Jammer seid, in Melodia . . . J. E. Bosen (Leipzig, 1654), H 5; Was hat der Mensch auf dieser Erden, in Letzter Abschied (Leipzig, 1650), H 2; Was ist es doch, in Melodia . . . Wirthens (Leipzig, 1654), H 6; Welt ade, ich bin dein müde, in Valet- und Trost-Lied (Leipzig, 1649), H 1

Credo, 8vv, 2 str, bc, *GB-Lbm*
Dies irae, 4vv, 6 str, bc, *D-B*
Gloria in excelsis Deo, 4vv, 4 str, brass, bc, *B* 18880/4
Gloria in excelsis Deo, 8vv, 3 str, brass, bc, *B* 18880/5
Lamentationes Jeremiae, 1v, bc, *B*; ed. F. Hamel, NM, xxvii–xxviii (1929)
Magnificat, 8vv, 5 str, brass, bc, *B*
Magnificat, 5vv, 5 str, bc, *GB-Lbm*
Missa (Ky, Gl, Cr), 4vv, bc, *D-B*
Missa, 4vv; lost, ed. F. Commer, Musica sacra, xxiv (Regensburg, 1863)
Missa brevis (Ky, Gl), 5vv, 5 str, brass, bc, *B*
Nunc dimittis, 1v, 3 str, bc, *B* 18883 ff.111r–113v
Nunc dimittis, 4vv, 5 str, bc, *B* 18882 pp.281–92
[Te Deum], 4vv, 5 str, brass, bc, *B*

Ach dass Gott erbarm, 1v, 5vv, 2 str, brass, bc, *D-B*; Ach Herr, es ist nichts gesundes, 4vv, str, bc, *Dlb*; Ach Herr, strafe mich nicht (Ps vi), 1v, 5 str, bc, ed. in Snyder, 1; Ach mein herzliebes Jesulein, 5vv, fl, 5 str, bc, inc., *Dlb*; Ach was erhebt sich doch, 3vv, 2 str, bc, *Dlb* (inc.); Ad Dominum cum tribularer, 4vv, 5 str, bc, *B*; Ad proelium mortales, 1v, 5 str, bc, *B*; Ad pugnas ad bella, 1v, 5 str, brass, bc, ed. in Snyder, 19; Afferte Domino, 4vv, 2 str, bc, *B*; Als der Tag der Pfingsten, 7vv, 4 str, brass, bc, *B*; Ascendit Christus in altum, 1v, 5 str, bc, ed. in Snyder, 54; Ascendit invictissimus Salvator, 1v, 5 str, bc, *B*
Aude quid times, 1v, 5 str, bc, *B*; Aurora rosea sit semper rutilans, 1v, 2 str, bc, *B*; Beati omnes qui timent, 4vv, 5 str, bc, *B*; Beatus vir qui timet Dominum, 3vv, bc, *B* 18887/1, *Dlb*; Beatus vir qui timet Dominum, 4vv, 5 str, brass, bc, *B* 18887/2, *GB-Lbm*; Beatus vir qui timet Dominum, 4vv, 4 str/brass, bc, *B* 18887/3; Beatus vir qui timet Dominum, 4vv, 5 str, bc, *B* 18887/4 [2 settings], *Dlb, GB-Cfm, Lbm*; Beatus vir qui timet Dominum, 4vv, 5 str, bc, *D-B* 18887/5; Beatus vir qui timet Dominum, 5vv, 5 str, bc, *Dlb*; Beatus vir qui timet Dominum, 8vv, 9 str, bc, *B* 18887/6; Benedicam Dominum, 3vv, bc, *B*; Bleibe bei uns, Herr Jesu Christ, 5vv, 5 str, brass, bc, *B*; Caelestes spiritus, surgite, 1v, 2 str, bc, ed. in Snyder, 81
Christus ist mein Leben, 5vv, 5 str, bc, *B*; Classica tympana, tubae per auras, 10vv, 10 str, bc, *B*; Confitebor tibi Domine (Ps cx), 1v, 2 str, bc, *Dlb, W*; Confitebor tibi Domine (Ps cx), 1v, 5 str, bc, *B* 18886/1; Confitebor tibi Domine (Ps cx), 2vv, 5 str, bc, *B* 18886/2; Confitebor tibi Domine (Ps cx), 3vv, 5 str, bc, *B* 18886/3; Confitebor tibi Domine (Ps cx), 4vv, 5 str, bc, *B* 18886/4; Confitebor tibi Domine (Ps cx), 4vv, 5 str, bc, *B* 18886/6; Confitebor tibi Domine (Ps cx), 4vv, 5 str, bc, *B* 18886/7; Confitebor tibi Domine (Ps cx), 4vv, 7 str, bc, *B* 18886/8; Confitebor tibi Domine (Ps cx), 8vv, brass, bc, *B* 18886/9; Confitebor tibi . . . quoniam (Ps cxxxvii), 4vv, 3 str, bc, *B*, ed. F. Hamel, NM, lix (1930)
Congregati sunt inimici, 2vv, 2 str, bc, *B, S-Uu*; Cor meum eja laetare, 2vv, 2 str, bc, *D-B*; Das Blut Jesu Christi, 4vv, bc, *SWl*; Delectare in Dominum, 4vv, 2 str, bc, *GB-Cfm* (doubtful); De profundis clamavi, 4vv, 5 str, bc, *D-B*; Der Herr ist mein Hirte (Ps xxiii), 3vv, 5 str, bc, *B*; Dilexi quoniam exaudiet Dominus (Ps cxiv), 8vv, 5 str, brass, bc, *B*; Dixit Dominus Domino meo (Ps cix), 4vv, 5 str, bc, *B* 18888/1; Dixit Dominus Domino meo (Ps cix), 4vv, 6 str, brass, bc, *B* 18888/2; Dixit Dominus Domino meo (Ps cix), 4vv, 5 str, bc, *B* 18888/3; Dixit Dominus Domino meo (Ps cix), 8vv, 5 str, brass, bc, *B* 18888/4; Domine cor meum jam ardet, 1v, 5 str, bc, *B, Dlb*
Domine ne in furore tuo (Ps vi), 1v, 5 str, bc, *B*, ed. F. Commer, Cantica sacra, ii (Berlin, n.d.); Domine probasti me et cognovisti (Ps cxxxviii), 8vv, 5 str, brass, bc, *B, GB-Lbm*; Ecce nunc benedicite (Ps cxxxiii), 1v, 3 str, bc, *D-B* 18883 ff.8r–11v, ed. F. Hamel, NM, lxxxi (1930); Ecce nunc benedicite (Ps cxxxiii), 1v, 2 str, bc, *B* 18883 ff.42r–45r; Ego te laudo et saluto, 3vv, bc, *B* 18900; Eja torpentes animae surgite, 1v, 5 str, bc, *B*; Entsetze dich Natur, 6vv, 2 str, brass, bc, *B*; Es gingen zwei Menschen, 3vv, 5vv, 4 str, bc, *B*; Estote fortes in bello, 2vv, 5 str/brass, bc, *B*; Exsultate Deo adjutori nostro, 1v, 5 str, bc, *B*; Fürchte dich nicht, 5vv, 5 str, bc, *B, S-Uu*; Gelobet sei der Herr, 5vv, 5 str, bc, *D-B*
Gloria/Das Wort ward Fleisch, 5vv, 2 str, brass, bc, *D-B* 18880/3, 18901; Herr mein Gott, wende dich, 4vv, 2 str, bc, *Dlb*; Homo Dei creatura, 1v, 3 str, bc, ed. in Snyder, 113 and Hamel (Kassel, 1950); Ich weiss dass mein Erlöser lebet, 1v, 4 str, bc, *Dlb*; Ich will den Herrn loben allezeit, 2vv, 5 str, bc, *B*; In hac misera valle, 3vv, bc, lost, ed. M. Seiffert, Organum, i/24 (Leipzig, 1933); In te Domine speravi, 1v, 3 str, bc, ed. in Snyder, 125; In te Domine speravi, 1v, 5 str, bc, *B* 18889/2, 18891/4; In te Domine speravi, 1v, 2 str, bc, ed. in Snyder, 144; In te Domine speravi, 2vv, 3 str, bc, *B* 18889/5, *Dlb*; In te Domine speravi, 2vv, 2 str, bc, *B* 18889/6; In te Domine speravi, 8vv, 5 str, brass, bc, *B* 18889/7
Jauchzet dem Herrn alle Welt, 3vv, 3 str, bc, *B* 18903; Jauchzet dem Herrn alle Welt, 5vv, 2 str, bc, *B* 18900; Jesu mi amor, spes dulcedo, 3vv, bc, *B*; Jube domne benedicere, 8vv, 5 str, brass, bc, *B, GB-Lbm, US-Bp*; Jubilate Deo, omnis terra (Ps xcix), 1v, 2 str, bc, *D-B*; Jubilent aethera, 1v, 5 str, bc, ed. in Snyder, 168; Laetatus sum (Ps cxxi), 3vv, 3 str, bc, *B* 18882 pp.1–11; Laetatus sum (Ps cxxi), 8vv, 5 str, brass, bc, *B* 18882 pp.15–58

Lauda Jerusalem (Ps cxlvii), 4vv, 5 str, bc, *Lbm* R.M.24.a.3 (2), *S-Uu* 66/2, 86/47 (tablature); Lauda Jerusalem (Ps cxlvii), 8vv, 5 str, brass, bc, *D-Dlb*, *GB-Lbm*; Lauda Sion Salvatorem, 3vv, 2 str, bc, *B*; Laudate Dominum omnes gentes (Ps cxvi), 6vv, 5 str, brass, bc, *B* 18882 pp.99–107; Laudate Dominum omnes gentes (Ps cxvi), 8vv, 5 str, brass, bc, *B* 18882 pp.69–97; Laudate pueri Dominum (Ps cxii), 3vv, 5 str, brass, bc, *B* 18890/1; Laudate pueri Dominum (Ps cxii), 3vv, 4 str, brass, bc, *B* 18890/2; Laudate pueri Dominum (Ps cxii), 4vv, 5 str, bc, *B* 18890/3; Laudate pueri Dominum (Ps cxii), 4vv, 5 str, bc, *B* 18890/4, *GB-Lbm* R.M.24.a.1(3)
Laudate pueri Dominum (Ps cxii), 5vv, 5 str, bc, *D-B* 18890/5; Laudate pueri Dominum (Ps cxii), 5vv, 5 str, bc, *B* 18890/6; Laudate pueri Dominum (Ps cxii), 6, 7vv, 5 str, bc, *B* 18890/7, 18890/8 [2 versions], *GB-Lbm* R.M.24.a.5(2) (version 7vv only); Laudate pueri Dominum (Ps cxii), 8vv, 5 str, brass, bc, *D-B* 18890/9; Laudate pueri Dominum (Ps cxii), 10vv, 5 str, brass, bc, *B* 18890/10, *GB-Lbm* R.M.24.a.3(3); Levavi oculos meos (Ps cxx), 8vv, 5 str, brass, bc, *D-B*; Lobt Gott, lobt alle Gott, 4vv, 2 str, brass, bc, *B* 18892 (doubtful); Lumina verte in me, 1v, 5 str, bc, *B*, *W*; Mater Jerusalem, 3vv, bc, *B*; Meine Sünden betrüben mich, 6vv, 5 str, bc, *B* (doubtful)
Mein Gott, ich danke dir, 2vv, 5vv, 3 str, bc, *B*; Miserere mei Deus, 3vv, 2 str, bc, *Dlb*, *GB-Och*; Misericordias Domini, 1v, 5 str, bc, *D-B*; Nihil novum sub sole, 5vv, 5 str/brass, bc, *B*, *Dlb*; Nisi Dominus aedificaverit domum (Ps cxxvi), 1v, 2 str, bc, *B* 18889/8; Nisi Dominus aedificaverit domum (Ps cxxvi), 3vv, 2 str, bc, *B* 18889/9, *Dlb* 1739/E1512; Nisi Dominus aedificaverit domum (Ps cxxvi), 4vv, 5 str, bc, *B* 18889/10, *Dlb* 1739/E1513; Nisi Dominus aedificaverit domum (Ps cxxvi), 8vv, 4 str, bc, *B* 18889/11; Nun gibst du Gott, 7vv, 5 str, brass, bc, *B*; O anima mea, suspira ardenter, 1v, 2 str, bc, *Dlb*, *S-Uu*; O Deus meus et omnia absorbeat, 2vv, bc, *D-B*
O felicissimus paradysi aspectus, 1v, 5 str, brass, bc, *B*; O Jesu süss, 1v, 2 str, bc, ed. in Snyder, 203; O lux beata trinitas, 4vv, 6 str, bc, *B*; O quam felix, quam serena, 1v, 2 str, bc, *B*; O sacrum convivium, 2vv, bc, *B*; O Salvator dilectissime, 1v, 5 str, bc, *B*; O welch eine Tiefe des Reichtums, 4vv, 5 str, bc, *B*; Puer natus est nobis, 4vv, 4 str, brass, bc, *Dlb*; Qui habitat in adjutorio altissimi (Ps xc), 8vv, 4 str/brass, bc, *B*; Resonent organa, 5vv, 5 str, bc, *B* (doubtful); Salve dulcis Salvator, 1v, 5 str, bc, ed. in Snyder, 203; Salve mi Jesu, adoro te, 2vv, 3 str, bc, *B*; Salve mi Jesu, Pater misericordiae, 1v, 5 str, bc, ed. in Snyder, 238; Salve mi Jesu, Pater misericordiae, 3vv, 4 str, bc, *B* 18882 pp.203–8
Seine Jünger kamen, 5vv, 5 str, brass, bc, *Dlb*; Selig sind die Augen, 2vv, 3 str, bc, *B*; Si Deus pro nobis, 1v, 2 str, bc, ed. in Snyder, 256; Siehe eine Jungfrau, 6vv, 4 str, brass, bc, *Dlb*; Sit gloria Domini in seculum, 1v, 4 str, bc, *B*; So spricht der Herr, 4vv, 15 str, bc, *B*; Surgamus ad laudes, 2vv, bc, *B*; Tanquam sponsus de thalamo, 1v, 2 fl, 2 str, bc, *B*; Turris fortissime nomen Domini, 3vv, 2 bn, bc, *GB-Och* (doubtful; text missing)
Unser Trübsal, die zeitlich, 4vv, 5 str, bc, *D-B*; Vater, ich habe gesündigt, 4vv, 3 str, bc, *Dlb*; Vox dilecti mei, 1v, 2 str, bc, *B*; Was steht ihr hier müssig, 4vv, 5 str, bc, *B*; Wenn ich zu dir rufe, 4vv, 4 str/brass, bc, *B*; Wie der Hirsch schreiet (Ps xlii), 1v, 5 str, bc, *S-Uu*; Wie lieblich sind deine Wohnungen, 5vv, 4 str, brass, bc, *D-Dlb*

SECULAR VOCAL

Works in *D-GOL*, *Ju*, *Z*

INSTRUMENTAL

Paduanen, Alemanden, Couranten, Balletten, Sarabanden, a 3, bc (org) (Leipzig, 1645)
Studenten-Music, 3, 5 str, bc (Leipzig, 1654); 2, ed. F. Hamel, NM, lxi (1929)
[11] Sonate da camera, 5 str, other insts (Venice, 1667/*R*1670); ed. K. Nef, DDT, xviii (1904/*R*)
[12] Sonate, 2–5 str, other insts, bc (Nuremberg, 1682); ed. E. Pätzold (Berlin, 1954–6)
Other sonatas, dances, canons, etc, *A-Wn*, *D-Bds*, *F-Pn*

BIBLIOGRAPHY

C. von Winterfeld: *Der evangelische Kirchengesang* (Leipzig, 1843–7/*R*1966)
A. Horneffer: *Johann Rosenmüller (ca.1619–1684)* (Charlottenburg, 1898); summarized in *MMg*, xxx (1898), 102
A. Schering: *Musikgeschichte Leipzigs*, ii: *Von 1650 bis 1723* (Leipzig, 1926)
F. Hamel: *Die Psalmkompositionen Johann Rosenmüllers* (Strasbourg, 1933)
E. H. Meyer: *Die mehrstimmige Spielmusik des 17. Jahrhunderts in Nord- und Mitteleuropa* (Kassel, 1934)
W. S. Newman: *The Sonata in the Baroque Era* (Chapel Hill, 1959, rev. 2/1966/*R*1972)
A. Lehmann: *Die Instrumentalwerke von Johann Rosenmüller* (diss., U. of Leipzig, 1965)
F. Krummacher: *Die Überlieferung der Choralbearbeitungen in der frühen evangelischen Kantate* (Berlin, 1965)
W. Reich: *Threnodiae sacrae* (Dresden, 1967)
T. Antonicek: 'Johann Rosenmüller und das Ospedale della Pietà in
Venedig', *Mf*, xxii (1969), 460
H. Kümmerling: *Katalog der Sammlung Bokemeyer* (Kassel, 1970)
K. J. Snyder: *Johann Rosenmüller's Music for Solo Voice* (diss., Yale U., 1970)
E. Selfridge-Field: 'Addenda to some Baroque Biographies', *JAMS*, xxv (1972), 236

KERALA JOHNSON SNYDER

Rosenroth, Christian Knorr von. *See* KNORR VON ROSENROTH, CHRISTIAN.

Rosenthal, Albi (*b* Munich, 5 Oct 1914). English antiquarian music dealer of German birth. He was educated at the Wilhelmsgymnasium in Munich and continued his studies at the Warburg Institute in London, where he worked on palaeography, medieval book illustration and iconography as assistant to Wittkower and Saxl. Rosenthal studied musicology privately with Wellesz and palaeography with Robin Flower. In 1955 Rosenthal and his wife Maude bought the London business of Otto Haas, which they continued under Haas's name, extending its tradition of scholarly expertise. Rosenthal's fine judgment, based on his specialized academic training, has contributed to the firm's leading position among antiquarian dealers. It has handled the sale of many famous collections, including those of Cortot, Scholes and Prunières, as well as many notable single items. He became Hon. MA (Oxon) in 1979.

WRITINGS

'Le manuscrit de la Clayette retrouvé', *AnnM*, i (1953), 105
with J. A. Westrup and F. Ll. Harrison: *English Music* (Oxford, 1955) [valuable catalogue of exhibition held at the Bodleian Library]
'A Bibliography of Egon Wellesz', *MQ*, xlii (1956), 6
'Two Unknown 17th Century Music Editions', *CHM*, ii (1956), 373
'The "Music Antiquarian" ', *FAM*, v (1958), 80
'A Hitherto Unpublished Letter of Claudio Monteverdi', *Essays Presented to Egon Wellesz* (Oxford, 1966), 103
'Otto Haas, Antiquarian Bookseller (1874–1955)', *Brio*, iii (1966), 3

ALEC HYATT KING

Rosenthal, Harold D(avid) (*b* London, 30 Sept 1917). English writer on music. He studied at University College, London (BA 1940), and embarked on a teaching career, but became increasingly involved in music activities, principally as critic and lecturer. In 1948–9 he worked with the Earl of Harewood on the journal *Ballet and Opera*, and he was Harewood's assistant editor when *Opera* was founded in 1950. The same year, he was appointed archivist of the Royal Opera House, Covent Garden, a post he held until 1956. In 1953 he became editor of *Opera*; under his guidance the journal has come to provide an extensive coverage of operatic events throughout the world and has exercised considerable influence on operatic life in Britain.

Besides his work for *Opera*, Rosenthal has written extensively for other periodicals, notably in the USA: he has been a correspondent of *Opera News* (1947–52) and *Musical America* (1955–60). He has been much engaged in broadcasting and in lecturing (in the USA as well as Britain) on operatic topics. His work is highly regarded for its judiciousness, based on a thorough knowledge of the human voice and the standard operatic repertory.

WRITINGS

Sopranos of Today (London, 1956)
Two Centuries of Opera at Covent Garden (London, 1958)
with J. Warrack: *Concise Oxford Dictionary of Opera* (London, 1964, rev. 2/1979)
ed.: *The Opera Bedside Book* (London, 1965)
ed.: *The Mapleson Memoirs* (London, 1966)
Covent Garden: a Short History (London, 1967)

STANLEY SADIE

Rosenthal, Manuel (*b* Paris, 18 June 1904). French conductor and composer. At the Paris Conservatoire (1918–23) he studied violin with Jules Bouchit, fugue and counterpoint with Jean Huré and composition with Ravel. In 1934 he was appointed co-conductor of the Orchestre National of French radio, assuming full responsibilities between 1944 and 1947. He was conductor of the Seattle SO (1948–51) and then pursued an international career, specializing in the 20th-century French repertory. In 1962 he was made professor of the orchestral class at the Paris Conservatoire, and from 1964 to 1967 he was conductor of the Liège Orchestra. His own music is cast in a noble neo-classical style.

WORKS
(*selective list*)

STAGE
Rayon des soieries (opéra-bouffe, 1, Nino), 1926–8
Un baiser pour rien [La folle du logis] (ballet, 1, Nino), 1928–9
La poule noire (comédie musicale, 1, Nino), 1934–7
Que le diable l'emporte (ballet, 1, Derain), 1948
Les femmes au tombeau (opera, 1, de Ghelderode) (1956)
Hop, signor! (opera, 3, de Ghelderode), 1957–61

ORCHESTRAL
Serenade, 1936; Les petits métiers, 1936; Jeanne d'Arc, 1936; La fête du vin, 1937; Musique de table, 1941; Noce villageoise [from Lully], 1941; Symphonies de noël, 1947; Aesopi convivium, vn, pf, orch, 1948; Magic Manhattan, 1948; Sym., C, 1949; Offenbachiana, 1953; 2 études en camaïeu, 1969; Aeolus, wind qnt, orch, 1970

CHORAL
Saint François d'Assise, speaker, chorus, orch, 1936–9; 3 burlesques, chorus, orch, 1941; La pietà d'Avignon, SATB, tpt, str orch, 1943; Cantate pour le temps de la Nativité, S, chorus, orch, 1943–4; A choeur vaillant, chorus, 1952–3; Mass 'Deo Gratias', S, Mez, T, Bar, chorus, orch, 1953; 3 pièces liturgiques, chorus, orch, 1958

CHAMBER AND INSTRUMENTAL
Sonatine, 2 vn, pf, 1923; 8 Bagatelles, pf, 1924; 6 Pieces, pf, 1926; Serenade, pf, 1927; Saxophone-Marmelade, a sax, pf, 1929; Les petits métiers, pf, 1933; Les soirées du petit Juas, str qt, 1942; La belle Zélie, 2 pf, 1948

SONGS
5 chansons juives, 1925; 5 ronsardises, 1928; 3 poèmes de Marie Roustan, 1933; Chansons du monsieur Bleu (Nino), 1934; 3 chansons d'amour (J. de Lescurel), 1941; 3 précieuses (V. Voiture, G. de Scudery, I. de Benserade), 1941; 2 prières pour les temps malheureux (Jeremiah), 1942; 6 chansons coloniales (Nino), 1942; 3 chansons berbères, 1942; 2 sonnets de Jean Cassou, 1944

Principal publishers: Jobert, Heugel, Eschig, Sofirad
ANNE GIRARDOT

Rosenthal, Mark. *See* RÓZSAVÖLGYI, MÁRK.

Rosenthal, Moriz (*b* Lemberg [now L'vov], 18 Dec 1862; *d* New York, 3 Sept 1946). Ukrainian pianist. The son of a professor at the Lemberg Academy, he began learning the piano at the age of eight under Galloth, and from 1872 studied with Karol Mikuli at the Lemberg Conservatory. In 1875, primarily to further the boy's education, his family moved to Vienna, where his piano teacher was Joseffy. A recital début in 1876 was followed by a tour; but in 1877 he met Liszt, and this proved to be a turning-point in Rosenthal's career. Musically he remained under Liszt's supervision during the remaining nine years of the old man's life. Nevertheless Rosenthal retired from the concert platform for six years to study philosophy at Vienna University. When he started playing again, he was immediately recognized as a player of the most extraordinary technical and artistic resources. Brahms, Johann Strauss (ii) and Tchaikovsky were among the musicians who were interested in his early career. In 1888–9 he toured the USA, partly with the young Kreisler, and in 1895 he

Moriz Rosenthal

appeared in London. He married one of his pupils, Hedwig Kanner, and after 1938 they lived in New York.

Although Rosenthal's early reputation was principally as a virtuoso technician, in later years he became known more for sensitive tonal balance and sustained phrasing, which may be heard in his gramophone recordings. His long phrases were supported and illuminated by a tone superbly varied, full and delicate even in the highest registers of the piano, and which he created by means of a prodigiously quick finger action. These qualities made him one of the finest players of Chopin's music. Rosenthal wrote some piano salon pieces of high technical difficulty, and he collaborated with Schytte in an advanced piano method, *Schule des höheren Klavierspiels.*

BIBLIOGRAPHY
E. Sackville-West: 'Rosenthal', *Recorded Sound*, vii (1962), 214 [with discography by H. L. Anderson and P. Saul]
JERROLD NORTHROP MOORE

Rosé Quartet. Austrian string quartet founded by ARNOLD ROSÉ.

Roser [von Reiter], **Franz de Paula** (*b* Naarn, Upper Austria, 17 Aug 1779; *d* Budapest, 12 Aug 1830). Austrian composer, Kapellmeister and tenor, son of Johann Georg Roser. He studied singing, the playing of instruments and music theory under his father, and is said to have been a pupil of Mozart in Vienna for a short time in 1789. He studied further with Georg Pasterwiz in Kremsmünster and J. G. Albrechtsberger in 1795. In 1796 he became a novice in the Cistercian monastery of Wilhering, Upper Austria, but did not take his vows; instead he became a soldier, then decided to make a career in music, probably from 1799 when he became musical director in Freiburg. Later he was a Kapellmeister of travelling opera troupes in Paris (1800) and Verona (1802), a tenor in theatres at Klagenfurt (1803) and Pest (1804), and from 1806 a composer in the service of Ignaz von Vegh at Vereb (now Székesfehérvár). After a year as a theatre

Kapellmeister in Linz (1811–12) Roser settled in Vienna, where from 1812 to 1819 he was Kapellmeister at the Theater in der Josefstadt. In 1817 he founded a music lending and copying concern, in 1819 became assistant Kapellmeister at the Kärntnertortheater, from 1820 was Kapellmeister at the Theater an der Wien and from 1824 at the German theatre at Pest. From 1826 he worked in Vienna as a successful freelance composer for a number of farce theatres.

Roser was one of the most prolific composers for the Vienna stage in the early 19th century. His operas, operettas, farces, ballets and other comic works written between 1800 and 1830 number at least 63; almost a third were to texts by J. A. Gleich, and most are lost. Roser also wrote 19 masses and numerous shorter sacred works, some possibly attributable to his father, as well as several orchestral works and dances for military band, chamber ensembles or piano.

BIBLIOGRAPHY

O. Wessely: 'Roser', MGG [with full bibliography and list of works]

OTHMAR WESSELY

Roser, Johann Georg (*b* Naarn, Upper Austria, baptized 19 March 1740; *d* Linz, Upper Austria, 23 Sept 1797). Austrian composer, father of FRANZ DE PAULA ROSER. He became a schoolmaster at Naarn and in 1786, through the intervention of Leopold Mozart, was appointed Kapellmeister of the cathedral and the parish church at Linz, succeeding Georg Haller. Roser is said to have invented the *harmonie parfaite*, a just-intonation instrument with an enharmonic keyboard; the assertion that W. A. Mozart composed a rondo for the instrument cannot be substantiated. Roser's compositions, some possibly attributable to his son, are apparently all lost; they included two requiems, six graduals, a mass and shorter sacred works, and were formerly at Linz Cathedral and other churches in Upper Austria.

OTHMAR WESSELY

Rosetti [Rösler, Rosety, Rossetti, Rössler], **(Francesco) Antonio** [Franz Anton, František Antonín] (*b* Leitmeritz [now Litoměřice], *c*1750; *d* Ludwigslust, 30 June 1792). Bohemian composer and double bass player. The Ludwigslust parish records give his death as 'at the age of 42 years', yet many reference books give the date of his birth as 1746. The confusion no doubt arises from the original form of his name, Rösler, and from an entry in the baptismal register for the parish church of Niemes (now Mimoň), a village in the Leitmeritz district, that records the birth in 1746 of one Franz Anton Rössler, later a cobbler. The composer's arms – a single gules rose on a sable field – rules out his identity with the Niemes cobbler and points to the Italianized form of his name, Rosetti ('little roses'), which he used professionally. Adding further to the confusion, there were no fewer than five Antonio Rosettis active during his lifetime. Among the musicians who have been confused with him are the composer Antonio Rosetti (*b* Milan, 1744), whose *Olimpiade* and *Il gran Cid* were performed in Milan in 1777 and 1780 respectively (*FétisB*, *GerberL* and *EitnerQ* wrongly ascribe his date of birth to F. A. Rosetti); the violinist Antonio Rosetti, who in 1766 became Konzertmeister to Count Althann, led Prince Esterházy's orchestra from 1776 to 1781 (he performed a violin concerto at Eszterháza in February 1778), and was referred to by Haydn on an orchestral violin part as 'illustrissimo Sig. Rosetti'; and the composer Jan Josef Rösler, who is called 'Rosetti' by Arbes and Teuber.

Rosetti began his earliest formal education in Prague at the age of seven. In 1763–9 he was a novice at the Jesuit College at Kuttenberg, then continued his studies in music and theology while practising as a lay teacher in the seminaries at Znaim (Znojmo) and later Olmütz (Olomouc). In 1773 he completed his training as a theologian; rather than be ordained, he received dispensation from his monastic vows (he later married) and turned to a career in music, entering the service of Kraft Ernst, Prince of Oettingen-Wallerstein, as a double bass player. His name first appears in court treasury accounts in November 1773; in a petition to the prince (23 December 1775) Rosetti mentioned his two and a quarter years in service, indicating that he began his duties there in September 1773. As early as 1780 he was deputy to the Kapellmeister, Josef Reicha, and succeeded him after Reicha left Wallerstein in 1785.

Rosetti's years at Wallerstein were formative in his development as a conductor and composer. He owed much of his mastery in writing for wind instruments to the stimulus afforded by the ensemble (*Harmonie*) at Wallerstein, the best in Europe (*see* HARMONIEMUSIK). He committed to memory instrumental works of Haydn (whom he adopted as his model), Stamitz and Mozart, and wrote countless occasional pieces for weekly concerts at court. When he went to Paris in 1781, his works were acclaimed and he was a frequent guest of Gluck and Piccinni. In 1783 he undertook a concert tour, and was particularly applauded at Ansbach and Mainz. Faced with mounting debts, he became Kapellmeister for the Duke of Mecklenburg-Schwerin in 1789 at treble his Wallerstein salary. The Elector of Trier commissioned a series of symphonies from him, and in 1791 Rosetti was asked to write a Requiem which he conducted at the memorial service for Mozart in Prague with '120 of the best artists'. Rosetti was called to the Berlin court by the future Friedrich Wilhelm III in autumn 1791; there he wrote a serenade (now lost) for the marriage of Princess Frederika to the Duke of York, and his oratorio *Jesus in Gethsemane* was performed before the entire court and clergy. He returned to Ludwigslust three months before his death.

Rosetti was a prolific composer, mostly of orchestral and chamber music. In his earliest works he combined both Baroque and Classical elements; his transitional style resembles that of the young Haydn. The ritornello is a frequent device in his sonatas and concertos. There is rarely a contrasting second subject; rather, the first subject is restated in the dominant and linked to a closing episode. His lyrical slow movements foreshadow the character-pieces of the 19th century in their use of ternary form and Austrian or Bohemian folk melodies. In the final movements of the concertos he retained the Baroque French rondeau. Rosetti's highly idiomatic writing for the horn contributed much to the development of a melodic style for the instrument. He was most original in his wind concertos and partitas, and Riehl praised his symphonies. Rosetti's contemporaries ranked him with Haydn and Mozart.

WORKS

Editions: *A. Rosetti: Ausgewählte Werke, i: Sinfonien*, ed. O. Kaul, DTB, xxii, Jg.xii/1 (Leipzig, 1912) [K i]
　　A. Rosetti: Ausgewählte Werke, ii: Orchester- und Kammermusik, ed. O. Kaul, DTB, xxxiii, Jg.xxv (Leipzig, 1925) [K ii]

ORCHESTRAL
(thematic catalogue in K i)
Syms.: 3 as op.1 (Paris, 1779); Sinfonia concertante (Paris, ?1782); 6 as op.3 (Paris, ?1786), 2 ed. in K i; 2 as op.4 (Paris, ?1786); 3 as op.5 (Berlin, ?1786), 2 incl. in 3 syms., op.5 (Vienna, 1786), with 1 new sym., 2 ed. in K i; 2 as op.6 (Paris, c1786); 2 as op.13 (Offenbach, 1794); Sinfonie à grand orchestre (Amsterdam, 1796); Grande symphonie, D (Berlin, c1797); Simphonie de chasse, D (Paris, c1801); Telemaque, perf. 1791 (Paris, n.d.) [cited in *GerberNL*]; 3 pubd in anthologies (Paris, 1783; Mainz, c1785); c13 others, *A-Wgm, B-Bc, D-DO, HR* (some autograph; 1 ed. in K i), *SWl*
Concs.: 5 for pf: G, op.2 (Amsterdam, c1783), G, op.3 (Frankfurt, n.d.), 1 pubd (Paris, ?1788), no.3 (Offenbach, 1796), 1 in *Mbs*; 7 for vn: *HR*, 6 listed in Hummel catalogue (1783); ?10 for fl: nos.1–4 (Paris, n.d.), nos.1–6 (Amsterdam, 1781), no.14 (Offenbach, 1796), 3 in *Rtt*; 5 for ob, *A-Wgm, D-HR, Rtt*; 4 for cl: no.4 (Paris, 1782), 1 in *Rtt*, 2 lost; 15 for hn: nos.1, 3, 4 (Paris, ?1782), 1 in E (Paris, c1786), no.20 (Brunswick, n.d.), 10 in *A-Sm, D-HR* (1 ed. in K ii), *Rtt*; 6 for 2 hn, *A-Sm, D-HR*, 2 lost; 8 for bn: 6 in *SWl*, 2 listed in Breitkopf catalogues (1782, 1785); 3 sinfonies concertantes, 1 for 2 vn, 2 for 2 hn (Paris, n.d.), lost; Concertino, *Rtt*
Other orch: Serenade, *HR*; Notturno, *Rtt*; 12 minuets, *SWl*

CHAMBER
(thematic catalogue in K i)
Wind insts: Harmonie, 2 ob, 2 cl, 2 bn, 2 hn (Paris, 1800); 2 Harmonie, a 7, 8, *A-Wgm*; 13 parthias, a 7–11, *Wgm, D-DO, HR* (3 ed. in K ii); qnt, *HR*; divertimento a 9, *Mbs*
2–6 insts: Sextet, vn, 2 va, fl, hn, b, op.1 (Speyer, n.d.); str qts: 3 as op.2 (Paris, n.d.), 3 as op.4 (Offenbach, c1783), 6 as op.6 (Vienna, 1787) (also as op.7; ed. in K ii), no.2, E♭ (Amsterdam, c1790); pf trios: 3 divertissements, op.1 (Amsterdam, 1785), 6 as op.2 (Offenbach, n.d.), 3 as op.3 (Mannheim, ?1784) (also as opp.4, 5; identical to 3 of vn sonatas, op.6), 3 as op.6 (Offenbach, n.d.), 4 as op.7 (Mainz, 1790) (1 ed. in K ii), 3 as op.9 (Speyer, ?1790), 3 as op.13 (Paris, n.d.), 2 divertimentos, *W, WD*; vn sonatas: 6 as op.1 (Mainz, c1784) (also as opp.2, 3), 3 as op.5 (Offenbach, 1794), 6 as op.6 (Mainz, c1786), 2 pubd (Venice, n.d.); 6 duos faciles, 2 vn (Paris, n.d.); 6 duetti, 2 vn (Vienna, 1787)
Pf: 4 Sonatas (London, c1795); 44 works in Blumenlese für Klavierliebhaber, ed. H. Bossler, i–v (Speyer, 1782–7); 13 works in Recueil de pièces de galanterie (Speyer, c1793); other works in 18th-century anthologies, incl. Sammlung vermischter Clavierstücke, i–iii (Nuremberg, 1782–4); smaller works pubd Leipzig, Speyer

VOCAL
Sacred: Der sterbende Jesus (C. Zinkernagel), oratorio, 4vv, chorus, orch (Vienna, 1786); Jesus in Gethsemane (H. J. Tode), oratorio, solo vv, orch, 1790, *SWl*; Der Tod Jesu (K. W. Ramler), oratorio, *Rp* [shortened version of Jesus in Gethsemane]; Requiem, E♭, 26 March 1776, *A-Wgm, D-IIR, Mbs, Rtt*; Requiem, d, *Mbs*; Requiem (for Mozart), 1791, lost, title-page *SWl*; Hallelujah (Tode), cantata, 4vv, orch, 1791, *SWl*; 8 Salve regina, Miserere, solo vv, orch, ?*Bds*; 7 single works with orch, *HR, SWl*
Secular: Das Winterfest der Hirten, drama with orch, Ludwigslust, 10 Dec 1789, *SWl*; La matinée des artistes, vaudeville with orch, *SWl*; Liedersammlung (Speyer, ?c1800); numerous lieder in Bibliothek der Grazien, i–ii, ed. H. Bossler (Speyer, 1789–90); arias in anthologies (Paris, 1782; Mainz, 1812)

BIBLIOGRAPHY
Catalogus personarum et officiorum Societatis Jesu Bohemiae (1763–73)
J. A. Riegger, ed.: *Materialien zur alten und neuen Statistik von Böhmen*, vii (Prague, 1798)
A. Choron and F. Fayolle: *Dictionnaire historique des musiciens* (Paris, 1810–11/R1971)
G. J. Dlabacž: *Allgemeines historisches Künstler-Lexikon* (Prague, 1815/R1973)
J. W. Ridler, ed.: *Oesterreichisches Archiv für Geschichte*, ii (Vienna, 1832), 396
'Rösler', *Oesterreichische National-Encyklopädie*, iv (Vienna, 1836)
W. H. Riehl: *Musikalische Charakterköpfe*, i (Stuttgart, 1853, 8/1899), 180ff
J. J. Arbes: *Gesammelte Schriften* (Pilsen, 1880–83)
O. Teuber: *Geschichte des Prager Theaters* (Prague, 1883–5)
L. Schiedermair: 'Die Blütezeit der Öttingen-Wallerstein'schen Hofkapelle', *SIMG*, ix (1907–8), 83–130
H. F. O. Kaul: *Anton Rosetti: sein Leben und seine Werke* (diss., U. of Munich, 1911); chap. pubd as *Die Vokalwerke Anton Rosettis* (Cologne, 1911)
A. Diemand: 'Josef Haydn und der Wallersteiner Hof', *Zeitschrift des Historischen Vereins für Schwaben und Neuburg*, xlv (1920–21), 1–40
C. Meyer: 'Kleine Beiträge: Anton Rosettis Geburtsdatum', *ZMw*, xvi (1934), 176 [see also O. Kaul, ibid, 248]
J. Racek: *Česká hudba* (Prague, 1949, enlarged 2/1958)
H. Fitzpatrick: 'Antonio Rosetti', *ML*, xliii (1962), 234
S. E. Murray: 'The Rösler–Rosetti Problem: a Confusion of Pseudonym and Mistaken Identity', *ML*, lvii (1976), 130
HORACE FITZPATRICK

Rosier [Rosiers, de Rosier], **Carl** [Charles] (*b* Liège, 26 Dec 1640; *d* Cologne, 1725, before Dec 12). Flemish composer and violinist, resident mainly in Germany. From about 1664 he was a violinist at the court of the Elector Maximilian Heinrich in Bonn and later became vice-Kapellmeister there. From 1675 he lived principally in Cologne, but from about 1683 to 1699 he also worked in Holland, where he was highly regarded as a violinist and numbered Carolus Hacquart among his colleagues. On a title-page of 1691 he is described as vice-Kapellmeister at the court at Cologne. In 1699 he was Kapellmeister of Cologne Cathedral and in 1701 was appointed to a similar post by the city council: he thus held simultaneously the two most important positions in the musical life of Cologne. His daughter Maria Anna married Willem de Fesch. His first two publications were of sacred music, but his only other church music, in MS, dates from much later in his life. He is most notable as a composer of instrumental music, which includes 57 attractive dance pieces for three violins without continuo (1679) and, in his other publications, works ranging from Italianate trio sonatas to those showing the influence of the French overture.

WORKS
Edition: *Ausgewählte Instrumentalwerke*, ed. U. Niemöller, Denkmäler rheinischer Musik, vii (Düsseldorf, 1957)
In fletu solatium, sive cantiones sacrae, 3, 4 solo vv, 2 vn, bc (Cologne, 1667)
Motetta, sive cantiones sacrae, 3, 4 solo vv, 2 vn, bc (Cologne, 1668)
Antwerpsche vrede vreught, 3 vn/2 vn, va (Amsterdam, 1679⁸)
Pièces choisies à la manière italienne, 2 fl/vn, bc (Amsterdam, 1691) [referred to as Les symphonies by Eitner and vander Straeten]
14 sonate, ob/tpt, 2 vn, va, bc (Amsterdam, c1700)
Französische Partien, a 3 (Augsburg, 1710), lost
12 masses, 18 motets, 1705–13, *D-KNmi, Bds, F-Pn*

BIBLIOGRAPHY
EitnerQ
E. vander Straeten: *La musique aux Pays-Bas avant le XIXe siècle*, v (Brussels, 1880/R1969)
U. Niemöller: *Carl Rosier (1640–1725), Kölner Dom- und Ratskapellmeister*, Beiträge zur rheinischen Musikgeschichte, xxiii (Cologne, 1957)
K. W. Niemöller: *Kirchenmusik und reichsstädtische Musikpflege im Köln des 18. Jahrhunderts*, Beiträge zur rheinischen Musikgeschichte, xxxix (Cologne, 1960)
URSEL NIEMÖLLER

Rosiers [Roziers], **André**, Sieur de Beaulieu (*fl* Paris, 1634–72). French composer. He may have been a descendant of the Sieur de Beaulieu who composed part of the *Balet comique de la Royne* (1581), but it is unlikely that he belonged to the Rosier family of Parisian musicians of the 17th century, who were illiterate.

Rosiers was the most prolific and important composer of drinking- and dance-songs in mid-17th-century Paris. In addition to his own numerous publications he was the only contributor acknowledged by the publisher Robert Ballard in his many collections of *chansons pour dancer et pour boire*. After two books of four-part drinking-songs, *Les libertez*, Rosiers concentrated on solo songs, either accompanied by lute or unaccompanied, and on duets. According to the composer these lighter songs were sung by members of the court at the dinner table, not for any aesthetic purpose but to increase the general mood of gaiety.

Despite a common simple style there are several basic differences between the drinking- and dance-songs. The former are always for two voices (soprano and bass), and include a few dialogues; the latter are always monophonic. The dance-songs are always built of symmetrical motivic units; for example *Cardez vous bien* and *J'ayme le sexe des filles* each consists of the following pattern of bars (mostly crotchets, always four beats to a bar): $(2+2)-4-(4+4)$. On the other hand, the drinking-songs are often asymmetrical; *Le premier mot quand on s'esveille*, for instance, has the pattern $(3+3)-3\frac{1}{2}-(4+4)$. All the chansons are strophic, in a variety of popular simple forms.

WORKS
(all pubd in Paris)
Les libertez, 4vv, 2 vols. (1634–8)
L'eslite des libertez, 2vv, 16 vols. (1644–72)
Alphabet de chansons pour danser et pour boire, 1, 2vv (1646)
12 songs in vol.x, 12 in vol.xi and 12 in vol.xii of Chansons pour dancer et pour boire (1637⁴, 1638⁶, 1639³)
2 sacred contrafacta in La philomèle séraphique (1640⁵)

JOHN H. BARON

Rosin [resin, colophony, colophonium, colophane] (Fr. *colophane*; Ger. *Kolophonium*, *Geigenharz*; It. *colofonia*). A substance rubbed on the hair of the bow of a string instrument to give the bow hair the necessary 'bite' on the strings. Rosin is obtained by distilling oil of turpentine. The resulting solid residue is refined further when intended for musical use, the rosin then being cast into conveniently rounded or rectangular shapes. Rosin is a hard, brittle solid whose colour varies from a light, clear amber to dark brown. For a newly haired bow, powdered rosin, which looks like a fine white dust, is normally used. Pure rosin is best for violin, viola and cello bows, but the double bass bow requires a stiffer preparation made of pure rosin and white pitch in equal proportions.

Strictly speaking, there is a distinction between rosin and resin although the word 'rosin' is doubtless derived from 'resin' and the two terms are often used interchangeably. Resin is the natural gummy exudation from the trunks of trees, especially coniferous trees, while rosin is the end-product of the distillation described above which starts with a turpentine resin (there are also chemical resins). Another term for rosin, 'colophony', may derive from Colophon, an ancient city in Asia Minor, where the best rosin presumably came from.

References to the musical uses of rosin occur at least as early as the 16th century. In his *Musica teusch* (1532), Hans Gerle tells the string player to rub the bow 'with colfanium or with English rosin which one finds at the apothecary' ('Mit Colfanium oder mit Englischem hartz das findt man in der appotekgen').

DAVID D. BOYDEN

Rosin, Armin O(tto) (*b* Karlsbad [now Karlovy Vary, Czechoslovakia], 21 Feb 1939). German trombonist. He studied the trombone at the Munich Hochschule für Musik (1960–63), musicology at the University of Erlangen-Nuremberg (1963–8), and conducting with Keilberth and Celibidache (1972–3). He played first trombone with the Bamberg SO from 1961 to 1966 and, from 1968, with the South German RO at Stuttgart. He was a founder-member of the Ars Nova Ensemble of Bavarian radio (1967–70), and in 1970 joined the Edward Tarr Brass Ensemble. As Globokar's successor in Kagel's Cologne Ensemble for New Music (1970), Rosin gained useful experience in the interpretation of contemporary music, for which he is best known. In 1972 he was the first trombonist to receive a prize

in the International Gaudeamus Competition in Rotterdam. He has taught at the Darmstadt (from 1973) and Weikersheim (1975–6) summer courses. In 1975 he was appointed to the Staatliche Musikhochschule in Stuttgart to teach the trombone and wind ensemble music. His recordings include Martin's *Ballade* and Werner Heider's *Einander* (1971), each conducted by the composer.

EDWARD H. TARR

Rositsky, Jacek. *See* RÓŻYCKI, JACEK.

Roslavets, Nikolay Andreyevich (*b* Dushatino, Chernigov region, Ukraine, 5 Jan 1881; *d* Moscow, 23 Aug 1944). Russian composer. Coming from a rural background, he was initially musically self-taught, and then had violin lessons from his uncle and theoretical instruction from A. M. Abaza in Kursk. He studied under Hřimalý (violin), Il'insky (counterpoint) and Vasilenko (composition and orchestration) at the Moscow Conservatory (1902–12), graduating with a silver medal for the Byron cantata *Heaven and Earth*. Models for his work at this time came from French impressionism. In the songs *Volkovo kladbishche* (Burlyuk) and *V i nosite lyubov* (Bolshakov), both from the end of 1913, he achieved a new harmonic ordering which was not diatonic and which he referred to as the 'synthetic chord' technique; there are certain parallels with Skryabin's harmony, but Roslavets's system is independent. He developed the technique in piano miniatures, so that by 1915 it had become a 12-note system, embracing concepts of 12-note serialism and mirror symmetry. In the Violin Concerto (1925) he added the principle of complementary pitch-class groups which together form 12-note sets. His sensitive, consistent 12-note writing has many similarities with that of Schoenberg, whose work, however, Roslavets did not encounter until 1923.

In the 1920s Roslavets was one of the leaders of Russian musical life: he was temporary director of the Khar'kov Conservatory (1922); then he worked on the editorial staff of the Moscow State Music Publishing House, notably as editor of the periodical *Muzïkal'naya kul'tura*, and until 1929 he was a member of the board of the Association for Contemporary Music (ASM), at that time reorganized as the All-Russian Society for Contemporary Music. But as a journalistic spokesman for new music (he wrote the first Russian introduction to *Pierrot lunaire*), he came into increasing conflict with the more conventionally orientated Association of Proletarian Musicians, which reproached him for his 'bourgeois ideology'. He gave a Marxist defence of an aesthetic of 'musical positivism', which opposed the idea of an objectively definable emotional quality and which saw the creative act as 'a moment of the human intellect's highest exertion', looking forward to 'the subconscious being realized in the form of the conscious' and to music based on a 'new fixed system of tone organization'. For a while during the 1930s he worked in Tashkent, but after 1930 his name was absent from Soviet dictionaries and concert programmes.

WORKS
INSTRUMENTAL
Orch: Sym., 1922, unpubd; Man and Sea, sym. poem, after Baudelaire, unpubd; World's End, sym. poem, after Laforgue, unpubd; Vn Conc., 1925
Str qts: no.1, 1913; no.2, unpubd; no.3, 1920; no.4, unpubd; no.5, 1941, unpubd
Pf trios: nos.1–2, unpubd; no.3, 1921

Sonatas for vn, pf: no.1, c1913–14; nos.2–3, unpubd; no.4 (1924); no.5, unpubd
Pf: 3 compositions, 1914; 3 etyuda (3 études), 1914; 2 sochineniya (2 compositions): Quasi prélude, Quasi poème, 1915; Prélude, 1915; 5 Preludes, 1919–22; 2 poemï (2 poèmes), 1920; Sonata no.5, 1923
Other works: Noktyurn (Nocturne), ob, harp, 2 vn, vc, 1913; Poema, vn, pf (1915); Razdum'ye (Méditation), vc, pf, 1921; Sonata, vc, pf, 1921; 3 danses, vn, pf, 1921; Legenda, vn, pf, 1940–41, unpubd; 24 Preludes in all the keys, 1942, unpubd

VOCAL
Choral: Heaven and Earth (cantata, after Byron), 1912, unpubd; Oktyabr' (S. Rodov) (1926); Gimn sovetskoy raboche-kres'yanskoy militsii [Hymn of the Soviet workers' and peasants' militia] (Vyatich-Beryoznïch), wind band/chorus, orch ad lib (1926); Tokarya (A. Tver'diy) (1926)
Songs for 1v, pf: 3 sochineniya [3 compositions] (V. Bryusov, Blok), 1913; Grustnïye peyzazhi [Paysages tristes] (Verlaine), 1913; 4 sochineniya [4 compositions] (I. Severyanin, K. Bol'shakov, D. Burlyuk, V. Gnedov), 1913–14; Pesenka Arlekina [Harlequin's little song] (E. Guro), 1915; 7 others (1925–42)
Agit-prop songs: contributions to the cycles Pesni o 1905 gode [Songs of the year 1905], Pesni revolyutsii, Dekabristi, Poeziya rabochikh professiy [Poetry of the workers' calling] (P. Oreshin, Litkovsky, E. Tarasov, A. Andreyev, Pushkin, F. Odoyevsky, G. Galinaya, G. Korenev, A. Tverdïy, P. Druzhinin)

Principal publishers: Muzgiz, Muzsektor

WRITINGS
'Lunnïy P'yero Arnol'da Shyonberga', K novïm beregam (1923), no.3, p.28
'Nik. A. Roslavets o sebe i o svoyom tvorchestve' [Roslavets on himself and his work], Sovremennaya muzïka, i (1924), 132
'O reaktsionnom i progressivnom v muzïke', Muzïkal'naya kul'tura (1924), no.1 [probable writer of article signed 'Dialektik']
'Po povodu . . . (Proletariat i utonchyonnost')' [Apropos . . . (Proletariat and refinement)], Muzïkal'naya kul'tura (1924), no.2 [probably writer of article signed 'Dialektik']
Ed. or co-ed. of: A. Abaza-Grigoryev: Muzïka i tekhnika (Moscow, 1925); A. F. Grebnyov: Kak vesti khorovuyu rabotu v klubakh (Moscow, 1925); M. Ivanov-Boretsky: Pervobïtnoye muzïkal'noye iskusstvo (Moscow, 1925); L. L. Sabaneyev: Chto takoye muzïka (Moscow, 1925, 2/1928); P. N. Zimin: Kakiye bïvayut muzïkal'nïye instrumentï i kakimi sposobami poluchayutsya iz nikh muzïkal'nïye zvuki (Moscow, 1925)

BIBLIOGRAPHY
L.: 'N. A. Roslavets', Sovremennaya muzïka, i (1924), 33; Ger. trans. in Musikblätter des Anbruch, vii (1925), 179
L. Kaltat: 'O podlinno-burzhuaznoy ideologii gr. Roslavtsa' [On the truly bourgeois ideology of citizen Roslavets], Muzïkal'noye obrazovaniye (1927), nos 3–4, p.32
V. Belïy: ' "Levaya" fraza o "muzïkal'noy reaktsii" ', Muzïkal'noye obrazovaniye (1928), no.1, p.43
L. Lebedinsky: 8 let borbï za proletarskuyu muziku (Moscow, 1931), 18
D. Gojowy: 'Nikolaj Andreevič Roslavec', Mf, xxii (1969), 22
— : Neue sowjetische Musik der 20er Jahre (Laaber, 1980)
DETLEF GOJOWY

Rösler, Anton [Franz Anton; František Antonín]. See ROSETTI, ANTONIO.

Rösler, Endre (b Budapest, 27 Nov 1904; d Budapest, 13 Dec 1963). Hungarian tenor. He made his Budapest Opera House début in 1927 as Alfredo, having studied first privately, and then in Italy with De Lucia and Garbin. From the outset he undertook a wide range of roles, both lyric and dramatic – more than 80 in 35 years – favouring the Mozart repertory above all. His performances were notable not so much for beauty of voice (as a young singer he had contracted an inflammation of the vocal cords that affected his higher register) as for expressive power, great musicality, a keen sense of style, excellent acting ability and versatility in character parts such as Shuisky (Boris Godunov), Malatestino (Zandonai's Francesca da Rimini) and Loge, perhaps his greatest part. He played Florestan under Toscanini at Salzburg (1935), sang in concert at La Scala (1940), and appeared several times at the Florence Maggio Musicale and elsewhere. At the end of the 1950s he resigned his leading roles (and his high salary), playing only comprimario and character parts. He was also a leading Hungarian recitalist and concert singer, appearing in the recording of Kodály's Psalmus hungaricus under the composer. From 1953 until his death he taught at the Liszt Academy of Music, Budapest. He held the title Life Member of the Opera House.

BIBLIOGRAPHY
P. P. Várnai: Rösler Endre (Budapest, 1969)
PÉTER P. VÁRNAI

Rösler, Gregorius (fl 1748–9). German composer. A member of an Augustinian community at Regensburg, he published in Augsburg three volumes of church music (Melodrama ecclesiasticum . . . offertoria, op.1, 1748; Vineae florentes . . . litaniis lauretanis, op.3, 1749; Botrus Cypri . . . missae solemniores, op.4, 1749) and a set of symphonies (Oves octo harmonicae . . . synphoniae, op.2, 1748). The solo vocal writing in Rösler's sacred music, especially in the Offertories, is among the most heavily ornamented to be found in contemporary published church music; but his choral writing shows a severe lack of melodic and harmonic invention.
ELIZABETH ROCHE

Rösler, Jan Josef [Jozef] [Rössler, Johann Joseph] (b Banská Štiavnica, 22 Aug 1771; d Prague, 28 Jan 1813). Bohemian composer. He studied music formally with his father but was mainly self-taught in composition. His earliest successes, the pantomimes Das Zauberhörnchen and Die Geburt des Schneiders Wetz Wetz Wetz, date from 1796. He wrote both Singspiels and Italian operas, most of which were given at the Nostitz Theatre in Prague; they include L'assassino per vendetta, given later in German and also Czech, and Elisene, Prinzessin von Bulgarien, his most famous opera, which was first performed in 1807 and later presented successfully at the Vienna court theatre (1809). Rösler went to Vienna in 1805 and worked for a while at the court theatre; he also spent some time in the service of the Countess Lobkowitz.
Although renowned as a theatre musician, Rösler also won a reputation as a keyboard virtuoso and composer. His Piano Concerto in D op.15 is one of his most important works, and his keyboard sonatas and smaller piano pieces were popular in his day. Stylistically, Rösler, like so many of his contemporaries, falls between Mozart and Beethoven; his Cantate auf Mozart's Tod (1798) shows his indebtedness to the former but his Piano Concerto leans towards the latter.
BIBLIOGRAPHY
ČSHS
'Nachrichten vom Leben und den Werken des Tonsetzers Joseph Rösler', Monatsbericht der Gesellschaft der Musikfreunde (Vienna, 1829), 61
T. Volek: 'Repertoir nosticovského divadla v Praze z let 1794, 1796–98' [The repertory of the Nostitz Theatre in Prague from the years 1794 and 1796–8], MMC, xvi (1961), 5–190
ADRIENNE SIMPSON

Rosmarin, Mathieu. See ROMERO, MATEO.

Rosowsky, Solomon (b Riga, ?1878; d New York, 31 July 1962). Russian-Lithuanian musician, scholar of Hebrew Bible cantillation. His father was the noted Jewish cantor Baruch Leib Rosowsky (1841–1919). He studied composition under Rimsky-Korsakov, Glazunov and Lyadov at the St Petersburg Imperial Conservatory and conducting under Nikisch at the Leipzig Conservatory. After studying law he returned to music; he was a co-founder of the Society of Jewish

Folk Music (1908) and started collecting and editing Jewish folksong and liturgies. For a while he directed music at a Riga theatre, was active as a music critic, and founded the Riga Jewish Conservatory of Music (1920). From 1925 to 1947 he lived in Palestine. He wrote incidental music for the Hebrew theatre, some chamber music, and popular songs, and emerged as a leading authority on the chanting of the Hebrew Bible. He initiated courses on Bible cantillation at the Palestine Conservatory of Music, Jerusalem (now the Rubin Academy of Music). In 1946 he was awarded the J. Engel Music Prize (Tel-Aviv) and elected chairman of the Musicians' Association of Israel. In 1947 he settled in the USA where he lectured first at the New School for Social Research and later at the Jewish Theological Seminary of America, New York.

His lasting contribution to musicology is *The Cantillation of the Bible: the Five Books of Moses* (1957). In this comprehensive study, a branch of the research initiated by A. Z. Idelsohn and Robert Lachmann, an attempt is made to find a key for the reading and musical rendering of the Hebrew neumes system (tě'amey-hamiqra), which survives in many local versions. The principal aim was to establish the relation between the written symbols and their actual performance, using the Lithuanian congregational tradition as a model. A major result is the melodization of whole phrases, chapters and even books of the Bible through the continuous concatenation of the single neumatic motifs.

BIBLIOGRAPHY
Reviews of *The Cantillation of the Bible*: A. Sendrey, *JAMS*, xi (1958), 68; J. Yasser, *Judaism*, vii (1958), 188; J. Yasser, *MQ*, xliv (1958), 393; E. Werner, *Jewish Quarterly Review*, xlix (1958–9), 287
EDITH GERSON-KIWI

Rospigliosi, Giulio, Pope Clement IX (*b* Pistoia, 28 Jan 1600; *d* Rome, 9 Dec 1669). Italian librettist. After studying philosophy, theology and law at Pisa, he went to Rome and entered the service of the Barberini family, in whose theatre most of the settings of his librettos were performed. In 1644 he became the papal nuncio in Spain, returning to Rome in 1655. Under the pontificate of Alexander VII he was appointed apostolic secretary of state and became a cardinal in 1657. In 1667 he was elected to the papacy. During his brief reign, opera in Rome enjoyed such a revival that it was afterwards able to sustain the indifference or hostility of his successors.

Rospigliosi was the most important librettist of his day for Roman opera; he created the genre of sacred opera and wrote the librettos of the earliest significant comic operas. His most important librettos are *Il Sant'Alessio* (1632, sacred opera for the inauguration of the Teatro Barberini, music by Landi), *Erminia sul Giordano* (1633, pastoral opera, music by Michelangelo Rossi), *Chi soffre speri* (1639, comic opera, music by Virgilio Mazzocchi with additions by Marazzoli), *Il palazzo incantante* (1642, machine opera, music by Luigi Rossi), *Dal male il bene* (1653, comic opera, music by Abbatini and Marazzoli), *La vita humana* (1656, sacred opera, music by Marazzoli) and *La comica del cielo, ovvero La Baltasara* (1668, religious or moral opera, music by Abbatini). His librettos are celebrated for the quality of their poetry, skilful adjustment to the demands of the staging and music, the introduction of comic roles, and a human realism derived from late medieval literature (the plot of *Dal male il bene* is taken from Boccaccio) and from Spanish drama (especially in *Chi soffre speri*).

BIBLIOGRAPHY
G. Canevazzi: *Papa Clemente IX poeta* (Modena, 1900)
A. Salsa: 'Drammi inediti di Giulio Rospigliosi poi Clemente IX', *RMI*, xiv (1907), 473
P. M. Capponi: 'Rospigliosi, Giulio', *ES*
M. K. Murata: *Operas for the Papal Court with Texts by Giulio Rospigliosi* (diss., U. of Chicago, 1975)
ROBERT LAMAR WEAVER

Ross, Jerry. Songwriter, collaborator with RICHARD ADLER.

Ross, John (i). See ROSE, JOHN.

Ross, John (ii) (*b* Newcastle upon Tyne, 12 Oct 1763; *d* Aberdeen, 28 July 1837). Scottish composer and organist. He studied the organ and composition with Matthias Hawdon. In 1783 he was invited to Aberdeen to take up the post of organist at St Paul's Episcopal Chapel; the retiring organist, Robert Barber, was also a native of Newcastle. Ross held the post for 53 years, retiring in 1836. In 1787 he married Jean Tait, a relation, possibly niece, of Andrew Tait (*d* 1778), who was Barber's predecessor in the same post.

During the winters of 1812 and 1813 Ross organized charity concerts at St Paul's Chapel at which oratorios were performed, raising £314 for relief of the poor, following a crop failure; this was perhaps the most notable event in his career as a practical musician. He was also resident continuo player at the Aberdeen Musical Society concerts until they ceased around 1800.

As a composer Ross was energetic and successful; from Aberdeen he remained in contact with many London publishers and had a shrewd idea of the religious, educational and domestic markets for his work. His most imaginative compositions are the six piano concertos op.1 and the ten songs op.2, both published around 1790 at his expense; but his work after about 1795 is repetitive and pitted with safety-first devices, while certain technical weaknesses of opp.1 and 2, such as an inability to control long-range modulation, became marked. Ross's compositions fall into two main genres: solo piano works, some with optional additional parts, and drawing-room songs. He also wrote a keyboard tutor, *A Complete Book of Instruction for beginners* (London, c1795, enlarged 2/1815), and edited two collections of church music (1818, c1830). Sainsbury's *Dictionary of Music* (2/1827) mentions an *Ode to Charity*, now lost, 'consisting of Airs, Recitatives, and Choruses, with an Acc. for the Organ', which may have been written for his 1812–13 charity concerts.

WORKS
KEYBOARD
6 pf concs., op.1; 14 sonatas with vn/fl, opp.5, 6, 15, 16, 17, 23; sonatas and duets, opp.43, 46, etc; many waltzes, marches, variations, including opp.3, 8, 9, 45

VOCAL
Songs and canzonets, opp.2, 4, 7, 11, 12, 18, 28; many single songs; Collection of Ancient and Modern Scots Airs
Ode to Charity, lost

BIBLIOGRAPHY
D. Laing: Preface to *The Scots Musical Museum* (Edinburgh, 1839), p.lxxix
D. Johnson: *Music and Society in Lowland Scotland in the 18th Century* (London, 1972)
DAVID JOHNSON

Rosse, Frederick (*b* Jersey, 1867; *d* Brighton, 20 June 1940). English composer, conductor and baritone. He was educated at Harrow and from the age of 19 studied singing in Leipzig, Dresden, Brussels and Vienna. On his return to England he sang at concerts and in comic opera, appearing in 1896 in Jones's *The Geisha* at Daly's Theatre, London, where he was also chorus master for George Edwardes. He composed songs and a comic opera *All Abroad*, and was later musical director of various London theatres. He wrote incidental music for several plays, notably *Monsieur Beaucaire* (Booth Tarkington; Comedy, 1902) and Arthur Bourchier's production of *The Merchant of Venice* (Garrick, 1905). He later composed a number of popular orchestral suites, including *Suite Gabrielle* (1916), *Petite suite moderne* (1918), *Intermezzi: suite dansante* (1920) and *Cyrano de Bergerac* (1923).

ANDREW LAMB

Rosseau, Norbert (Oscar Claude) (*b* Ghent, 11 Dec 1907; *d* Ghent, 1 Nov 1975). Belgian composer and violinist. He spent his youth in Italy, and from the age of seven gave evidence of considerable gifts as a violinist. He studied at the Accademia di S Cecilia, Rome, 1925–8, with Mulé (composition), Silvestri (piano) and Dobici (fugue), completing his studies with Respighi. Concurrently he followed courses at Rome University. An injury to his right hand forced him to abandon a career as a performer and devote himself to composition. In 1964 he took part in electronic music research at Ghent University, and he directed a seminar at the conservatory there between 1967 and 1969. His earliest works show evidence of diverse influences; it is scarcely possible to detect any consistent development in his work, since he was always subject to varied tendencies, and produced quite different pieces at the same time. In his serial writing he used his 'harmonic dodecaphonic system'; that is, the series is divided to form four perfect triads, as in *Maria van den Kerselaar*. From 1957 he became increasingly interested in electronic music (*Impromptu: ode aan Gent*, 1969), but he continued to be involved with the past, as is evident in the orchestral *Sinfonia liturgica* (1963), which is – except for octave doublings – entirely monodic.

WORKS
(*selective list*)

Orch: Suite agreste, op.20, 1936; H₂O, op.22, 1939; Prelude and Fugue, org, str, 1947; Conc. for Orch, op.37, 1948; Pièces symphoniques, op.38, 1949; Sym., op.48, 1953; Sinfonia liturgica, 1963; Variations, 1964; Sonata a 4, 4 vn, str, 1965; Va Conc., 1965; Hn Conc., 1967
Choral: Inferno, oratorio, 1940–44; L'an mille, op.32 (oratorio, Weterings), 1946; Mass, op.40, 2vv, 1948; Incantations, op.42 (cantata, Weterings), 1951; Maria van den Kerselaar, op.44 (oratorio, G. Helderenberg), 1952; Missa solemnis, op.46, 8vv, db, 1953; 3 sonetti di Michelangelo, op.52, 1955; Il paradiso terrestre (Dante), Mez, vv, orch, 1968; Incoronazione di Maria (Dante), 16 solo vv, boys' vv, 1969; Stenen en brood (cantata, Boone), 1972; many other works
Stage: Le dernier rendez-vous (ballet, Weterings), 1946; Sicilienne (opera, Weterings), 1947; Les violons du prince (concert opera, Weterings), 1954
Songs, chamber music, kbd pieces

Principal publishers: CeBeDeM, De Monte
MSS in *B-Bcdm*

BIBLIOGRAPHY
R. Wangermée: *La musique belge contemporaine* (Brussels, 1959)
Music in Belgium (Brussels, 1964)

HENRI VANHULST

Rosselli [Rossello], **Francesco.** *See* ROUSSEL, FRANÇOIS.

Rossellini, Renzo (*b* Rome, 2 Feb 1908). Italian composer and critic. A pupil of Sallustio, Setaccioli and Molinari, he has followed the Italian 19th-century tradition in his compositions (as music critic for the Rome *Messaggero* he has vigorously opposed innovation). He has written scores for films directed by his brother, Roberto Rossellini, and others. He has taught in Pesaro and Rome, and in 1973 became artistic director of the Monte Carlo Opera.

WORKS
(*selective list*)

Operas: La guerra (Rossellini), Naples, 1956; Uno sguardo dal ponte (Rossellini, after Miller), Rome, 1961; Il linguaggio dei fiori (Rossellini, after Lorca), Milan, 1963; La leggenda del ritorno (D. Fabbri, after Dostoyevsky), Milan, 1966; L'annonce faite à Marie (P. Claudel), Paris, 1970; La reine morte, Monte Carlo, 1973
Other works: orch and chamber pieces

ALBERTO PIRONTI

Rosseter, Philip (*b* 1567 or 1568; *d* London, 5 May 1623). English court musician, composer and theatrical manager. In testimony given on 22 June 1601 during the hearing of a lawsuit in connection with the printing of Dowland's *Second Booke of Songs* he gave his age as 33. His first works to be printed were three galliards in William Barley's *A New Booke of Tabliture* (1596), and in 1601 his *Booke of Ayres* was published, the first half of which is devoted to songs by Thomas Campion and the second to his own songs. From the dedication and the address 'To the Reader' it is likely that he was by then under the patronage of Sir Thomas Monson (as was Campion); he had certainly by then formed the friendship with Campion that lasted until Campion's death. Rosseter was living at this time in Fleet Street. At midsummer 1603 he was appointed a lutenist at the court of James I, at a salary of £20 a year with £16 2s. 6d. for livery.

In 1609 Rosseter's *Lessons for Consort* appeared. It seems possible from the wording of the dedication to Sir William Gascoigne that he may, at some time, have been under the patronage of that Yorkshire gentleman. In the *Lessons* are Rosseter's arrangements for broken consort of his own music and that of other composers. Like Morley's set of consort lessons, some partbooks are now missing; unlike Morley's work, unfortunately, Rosseter's arrangements cannot be reconstructed in their entirety. In 1609 Rosseter became associated with Robert Keysar, a London goldsmith, in the management of the company of boy actors known at that time as the Children of Whitefriars. Together they presented the company at court in five plays during winter 1609–10. Rosseter, mainly through the influence of Sir Thomas Monson, secured a new patent (dated 4 January 1610) which once more permitted the company to call itself the Children of the Queen's Revels, a name which it had (some time before Rosseter's management) been forbidden to use; this injunction followed the presentation of certain plays considered offensive to the royal family.

In the next few years the history of the company was somewhat chequered, and partial amalgamation took place with two other groups. On 3 June 1615, however, a patent was issued to Rosseter, Reeves, Robert Jones and Philip Kingham to build a new Blackfriars theatre in a house known as Porter's Hall, in which the Children of the Queen's Revels could present their plays, Rosseter's lease of the Whitefriars having expired in 1614. A protest from the Lord Mayor and the aldermen of the City almost succeeded in bringing the project to a halt, but Rosseter continued with his plan, and two plays were presented, before the king (in spite of his previous licence) finally put an end to the Porter's Hall playhouse early in 1617. When this blow fell the Children of the Revels were disbanded and Rosseter's connection with the theatre was severed.

Rosseter continued in the service of the king until he died; he was buried at St Dunstan-in-the-West from his house in Fetter Lane. In his will (PCC, 41 Swann) his wife (Elizabeth) and two sons (Dudley and Thomas – see Vlam and Dart) are mentioned.

His early lute music is in the traditional, contrapuntal style, but in his songs he seems consciously to have abandoned this form. The songs are mainly light in character, and many have charming and memorable tunes. It is in the accompaniment, however, that his new outlook is apparent, since he avoided the style he termed 'intricate, bated with fuge' (in his address 'To the Reader', *A Booke of Ayres*) in favour of a purely chordal structure for the lute.

WORKS

A Booke of Ayres, set foorth to be song to the Lute, Orpharian, and Base Violl (London, 1601/R1970); ed. E. H. Fellowes, rev. T. Dart, EL, ser.1, viii, ix (London, 2/1966) [21 songs each by Rosseter and Campion]
Lessons for Consort (London, 1609) [inc., see Harwood]
Lute: Prelude, *GB-Cfm* Mus.689; 2 pavan and galliard pairs: *Cfm* Mus.689, 1596[20] [Another galliard of the Countess of Sussex (i)]; *Lbm* Eg.2046, *Cu* Dd.ix.33; 2 pavans: *Cfm* 689, *Lbm* Add.2046; 3 galliards: *D-Kl* Mus.108, *GB-Cfm* Mus.32.G.29 [set by Farnaby for kbd]; The Countesse of Sussex galliard, 1596[20]; Another galliard of the Countesse of Sussex (ii), 1596[20]

BIBLIOGRAPHY

E. Stokes: 'Lists of the King's Musicians from the Audit Office Declared Accounts', *MA*, ii (1910–11), 177; iii (1911–12), 54, 110
E. K. Chambers: *The Elizabethan Stage* (Oxford, 1923)
E. H. Fellowes: *English Madrigal Verse* (Oxford, 1929, rev. 3/1967)
M. Dowling: 'The Printing of John Dowland's *Second Booke of Songs or Ayres*', *The Library*, 4th ser., xii (1932–3), 365
I. Smith: *Shakespeare's Blackfriars Playhouse* (New York, 1946)
C. Vlam and T. Dart: 'Rosseters in Holland', *GSJ*, xi (1958), 63
N. Fortune: 'Philip Rosseter and his Songs', *LSJ*, vii (1965), 7
I. Harwood: 'Rosseter's *Lessons for Consort*, 1609', *LSJ*, vii (1965), 15
E. Doughtie, ed.: *Lyrics from English Airs, 1596–1622* (Cambridge, Mass., 1970)

DIANA POULTON

Rossetti, Antonio. *See* ROSETTI, ANTONIO.

Rossetti, Biagio (*b* Verona, 2nd half of the 15th century; *d* Verona, after 1547). Italian theorist and organist. As a boy he studied in the Scuola degli Accoliti of Verona Cathedral, and after becoming a priest entered the cathedral chapter in 1495 as chaplain and cantor. Soon afterwards he became cathedral organist and held the post at least until 1547 and probably until his death. His single published treatise, *Libellus de rudimentis musices* (Verona, 1529/R1973), is a manual for the training of choirboys and cantors, concentrating on plainsong. The conventional divisions of the subject, such as the gamut, solmization, intervals and the church tones, are discussed in a manner traditional with Italian theorists as early as Marchetto da Padova. The treatise zealously condemns such abuses as singing only for money, garbling texts by bad accentuation and syllabification, and poor vocal technique and tone quality, thus giving a clear idea of what average or poor choir singing must have been like in his day. In an attempt to inspire more reverent performance, Rossetti gave considerable space to liturgical and theological explanations of the musical portions of the Mass and Office. The treatise is of special interest for its numerous observations about practical subjects like vocal technique, physical culture of singers, and training and leadership of choirboys.

PETER BERGQUIST

Rossetti, Pietro (*b* Trieste, 1659; *d* Trieste, 1709). Italian writer, composer and teacher. As a priest and public teacher he received a salary from the municipality of Trieste from 1680 to 1692, when the struggle between Jesuits and local authorities for the creation of public teachers was won by the latter. He wrote sonnets and songs and also gave instruction in how to write them. He wrote a play with music, *La fidutia in Dio, ovvero Vienna liberata dalle armi turchesche* (now in the Trieste State Archives), which was performed for the first time on 12 February 1684 in the city hall, Trieste. It is in three acts and 35 scenes, with a prologue and epilogue, and required 33 performers. At the end of each act the actors performed a chorus and a dance in which words and movements were closely allied to the events portrayed.

BIBLIOGRAPHY

A. Hortis: 'Delle rappresentazioni sceniche in Trieste prima del Teatro di S. Pietro', *Archeografo triestino*, new ser., viii (1881–2), 144
See also TRIESTE.

SERGIO CHIEREGHIN

Rossetto, Il. *See* BIANCHINI, DOMENICO.

Rossetto [Rossetti], **Stefano** (*b* Nice; *fl* 1560–80). Italian composer. He took part in the wedding festivities of Emmanuel Philibert of Savoy and Marguerite of Valois at Nice in 1560. Shortly before this he was in the service of the Giustiniani on the Genoese-held Aegean island of Chios; his volume of four-part madrigals (1560) is dedicated to one member of this commercial clan, and individual pieces in this book and in his book for five voices of the same year are inscribed to others. After a brief period at Novara he went in 1564 to Florence. In 1566–7 he was in the service of Cardinal Ferdinando de' Medici and his sister, the unhappy Isabella Medici Orsina, Duchess of Bracciano; for the latter he wrote one of his most ambitious works, the 17-part cyclic *Lamento d'Olimpia* (a setting of parts of Canto X of *Orlando furioso*). He also composed some of the music for the 1567 Carnival in Florence. A volume of motets (1573) dedicated to Ferdinand of Austria suggests that he had some connection with the Habsburgs, and in 1579–80 he seems to have been at the court in Munich as organist. He may also have been responsible for the music of one of the *intermedi* for the Florence performance (1583) of Fedini's *Le due Persilie* (see Pirrotta and Povoledo).

Rossetto's motets, apparently designed for instrumental accompaniment, are modest works using plainchant paraphrase in workaday fashion. His madrigals are more varied in character, with flexible rhythmic declamation and some touches of chromaticism, as in the opening of the six-part *I dolci basci* (1566) and the five-part *Il canto novo* (1560). He (or perhaps his publishers) noted cadential accidentals with great, almost unnecessary, precision. He was particularly fond of cycles and set cyclic texts with some eye for effect, even tampering a little with the text (in the *Lamento d'Olimpia*) for dramatic purposes.

WORKS

Il primo libro de madregali, 4vv (Venice, 1560); ed. in RRMR, xxvi (1977)
Il primo libro de madregali, 5vv (Venice, 1560)
Musica nova del Rossetto, 5vv (Rome, 1566)
Il primo libro de' madrigali, 6vv (Venice, 1566)
Il lamento di Olimpia con 1 canzone, 4–10vv (Venice, 1567)

Novaequaedam sacrae cantiones, quas vulgo motetas vocant, 5–6vv, ita compositae, ut ad omnis generis instrumenta attemperari possint (Nuremberg, 1573); ed. in RRMR, xv (1973)
Madrigals in 1561[16], 1567[3], 1567[16], 1568[13], 1586[12]
Works in D-Bds, Mbs, GB-Lbm, I-Tn, PL-WRu

BIBLIOGRAPHY
W. Boetticher: Orlando di Lasso und seine Zeit, 1532–1594 (Kassel, 1958), 433, 536
A. Skei: Preface to RRMR, xv (1973)
N. Pirrotta and E. Povoledo: Li due Orfei: da Poliziano a Monteverdi (Turin, rev. 2/1975), 219f, 265, 267
A. Skei: 'Stefano Rossetti, Madrigalist', MR, xxxix (1978), 81
D. S. Butchart: The Madrigal in Florence, 1560–1630 (diss., U. of Oxford, 1979)

JAMES HAAR

Rossi [de Rossi], Francesco. Several Italian composers of this name were active c1650–c1725. Since Rossi is such a common Italian surname and because of a scarcity of documentary and musical evidence, it is difficult to disentangle the biographies of these composers or even to determine their number.

The most clearcut identity is that of an opera composer active in Milan, organist at S Maria presso S Celso about 1670 and maestro di cappella there and at S Giovanni in Conca in 1689 and 1692. His contribution typifies the evolution of Milanese opera, which tended to be independent of the Venetian repertory. He set to music two librettos by Carlo Torre, La ricchezza schernita ('dramma scenico-morale', 1658; with three other composers) and L'Arianna (Pavia, summer 1660); furnished new music for a strongly opposed performance of Cavalli's Artemisia (June 1663); and set to music two dramas by the impresario and comic singer Carlo Righenzi, Il Crispo (December 1663) and La farsa musicale (Carnival 1664), the latter a comic opera in the Florentine manner, with prologue and comic scenes in Milanese dialect. As frequently happened with stage works at Milan, La Regina Floridea, whose subject matter is drawn from Spanish comedy, was composed in collaboration with other composers, in this case Lodovico Busca and P. S. Agostini (?1669; it is impossible to determine whether the music of Floridea, privately performed in Venice late in 1687 and attributed by Bonlini to 'diversi', was by Rossi). Bianca di Castiglia (C. M. Maggi) was performed in October 1669 in the little theatre of Count Vitaliano Borromeo on Isola Bella, Lake Maggiore, and in 1674 and 1676 at the Teatro Regio Ducal, Milan. Rossi may have set to music other dramas by the principal playwright of 17th-century Milan (see MAGGI, CARLO MARIA). In February 1689 his Cantate a gloria del SS.mo Sacramento was performed at Milan; there is a motet by him in RISM 1692[1].

From November 1669 to February 1672 a 'Don Francesco Rossi' was maestro di cappella of the Neapolitan conservatory S Onofrio; his only almost certainly authentic surviving works are an oratorio, La caduta de gl'angeli (G. Scaglione; I-Nf), two psalm settings for four voices with violins (copies, dated 1797, in Nf), and a cantata Vanne, foglio volante (in Nc). He is probably not identifiable with the Milanese Francesco Rossi, who is never named with ecclesiastical titles.

'D. Francesco de Rossi, canon of Bari Cathedral', perhaps identifiable with the preceding, dedicated his Salmi et messa a cinque voci op.1 (Venice, 1688) to Ferdinand III, Grand Duke of Tuscany. In 1697 an 'abbate Rossi' was maestro di cappella at the Conservatorio dei Mendicanti in Venice. This title is

also applied to the 'D. Francesco Rossi' who composed an oratorio for five voices and instruments S Filippo Neri (A-Wn) and to the 'Russi' whose cantata Lunga stagione dolente survives among arias by Scarlatti and Bononcini (E-Mn). Venetian theatre chronicles describe as 'abate Pugliese' the Francesco Rossi who is credited with the music for three dramas given at the Teatro S Moisè: Il Sejano moderno della Tracia (A. Girapoli, 1686; it 'had the misfortune not to be listened to all the way through on its first night', according to Allacci), La Corilda and La pena degl'occhi (both 1688). Bonlini attributed to 'D. Francesco Rossi' La ninfa Apollo (performed by the Accademici Liberali at the Teatro S Michiel, Murano, in 1726), a greatly altered version of a pastorale by the classicist poet Francesco de Lemene, originally published in 1692 and set to music several times. If all these Venetian operas are supposed to be by the same composer, then the birth date given by Bellucci (Bari, 17 June 1627) would seem to refer to a different Francesco Rossi.

Theatre chronicles do not mention a Mitrane of 1689, from which Fétis claimed to have taken the contralto aria 'Ah, rendimi quel core', which was performed in March 1833 at one of his historical concerts in Paris and won some popularity in the 19th century. This opera never existed. The piece is from the second half of the 18th century and doubtless came from an opera including a character named Mitrane, such as Demetrio (Metastasio) or La vendetta di Nino (Moretti), both with music by Francesco Bianchi (Venice, 1780, and Naples, 1790, respectively); perhaps the character was sung by a Francesco Rossi, such as the one active at Venice in 1794–7.

A Francesco Rossi 'Dottore Veneziano' was the author of several drammi per musica for Venice between 1699 and 1719. A 'Don Francesco Rossi' played the violone at St Mark's, Venice, from 1665 to at least 1691; and a Francesco Rossi was a member of the Venetian instrumentalists' guild in 1727 (see Selfridge-Field, 1971). During the same period at least two musicians of this name are traceable in Rome (see Celani, Casimiri, Kast).

BIBLIOGRAPHY
EitnerQ; FétisB; SchmidlD; SchmidlDS
C. M. Maggi: Rime varie (Milan, 1700), iv, 193, 239; v, 31ff
G. C. Bonlini: Le glorie della poesia e della musica (Venice, 1730)
L. Allacci: Drammaturgia (Venice, rev. 2/1755)
L. N. Galvani [pseud. of G. Salvioli]: I teatri musicali di Venezia nel secolo XVII (1637–1700): memorie storiche e bibliografiche (Milan, 1879), 63f, 74, 134, 149
M. A. Bellucci: 'I musicisti baresi', Rassegna pugliese di scienze, lettere ed arti, ii (1885), 197
T. Wiel: I teatri musicali veneziani del Settecento (Venice, 1897/R1975)
A. Cipollini: Per Carlo Maria Maggi (Milan, 1900), 7
E. Celani: 'I cantori della Cappella Pontificia nei secoli XVI–XVIII', RMI, xvi (1909), 68
R. Casimiri: 'L'antica congregazione di S. Cecilia fra i musici di Roma nel sec. XVII', NA, i (1924), 128
S. di Giacomo: I quattro antichi conservatorii musicali di Napoli (Milan and Naples, 1924–8), i, 50, 131, 133, 141f; ii, 270
E. Dagnino: 'Ancora degli oratori di Bernardo Pasquini', NA, xi (1934), 69
G. Barblan: 'Il teatro musicale in Milano nei secoli XVII e XVIII', Storia di Milano, xii (Milan, 1959), 961
P. Kast: 'Biographische Notizen zu römischen Musikern des 17. Jahrhunderts', AnMc, i (1963), 61f
L. G. Clubb: Italian Plays, 1500–1700, in the Folger Library (Florence, 1968), 225f
T. Antonicek: 'Johann Rosenmüller und das Ospedale della Pietà in Venedig', Mf, xxii (1969), 460
E. Selfridge-Field: 'Annotated Membership Lists of the Venetian Instrumentalists' Guild, 1672–1727', RMARC, ix (1971), 39; see

also correction, xii (1974), 154
——: *Venetian Instrumental Music from Gabrieli to Vivaldi* (Oxford, 1975), 302

LORENZO BIANCONI

Rossi, Gaetano (*b* Verona, 18 May 1774; *d* Verona, 25 Jan 1855). Italian librettist. He was long a dramatist at La Fenice in Venice and later stage manager to the Teatro Filarmonico in Verona. During his long career, which began in the early 1790s and continued until his death, he wrote more than 120 librettos, including those of some of the most important and successful operas by several generations of composers, among them Mayr (*Adelaide di Gueselino*, Venice, 1799; *Ginevra di Scozia*, Trieste, 1801), Rossini (*Tancredi*, Venice, 1813; *Semiramide*, Venice, 1823), Meyerbeer (*Emma di Resburgo*, Venice, 1819; *Il crociato in Egitto*, Venice, 1824), Mercadante (*Il giuramento*, Milan, 1837) and Donizetti (*Linda di Chamounix*, Vienna, 1842). Some of his other collaborators were Carafa, Celli, Coccia, Farinelli, Gabussi, Generali, Hiller, Morlacchi, Nasolini, Nicolai, Nicolini, Pacini, Pavesi, Pedrotti, F. Ricci, L. Ricci, Vaccai and Zingarelli. Rossi worked with them in the renovation of the repertory and of musical forms that was accomplished in this period. At the beginning of his career he saw that public taste was ready to bridge the gaps in contemporary culture, and that it was his task to act as a link between the new cultural values and the undiscerning but curious public. Without having pretensions about the verses he used, he tried to infuse a broad spectrum of new material into opera. With the development of musical form at that time, his librettos displayed a more modern dramatic breadth and a freer style. His subject matter embraced a wide variety of sentiment, and his dramatic situations became more varied and intense, making use of typical Romantic themes. The *opera buffa*, which he saw was at a point of crisis, began to turn from traditional parodistic themes to the Romantic and dramatic, totally changing its nature.

BIBLIOGRAPHY
A. Pighi: 'Pagina autobiografica di un librettista veronese', *Nozze Biadego-Bernardinelli* (Verona, 1896)
L. Miragoli: *Il melodramma italiano nell'ottocento* (Rome, 1924)
H. Becker, ed.: *Giacomo Meyerbeer: Briefwechsel und Tagebücher* (Berlin, 1960–70) [with many letters to and from Rossi]
FRANCA CELLA

Rossi, Giacomo (*fl* 1710–31). Italian librettist. He was one of many Italians who settled in London early in the 18th century, perhaps as a language teacher. Late in 1710 he was employed by Aaron Hill to versify the scenario he had prepared from Tasso's *Gerusalemme liberata* for Handel's first London opera, *Rinaldo*. In an apologetic address to the reader of the libretto (February 1711) Rossi called it 'the delivery of but a few evenings' and complained that Handel composed the music in a fortnight and 'scarcely gave me the time to write'. Handel must have collaborated in the work, for the libretto as well as the score contains material from works composed in Italy. The same is true of Rossi's second libretto for Handel, *Il pastor fido* (November 1712), ruthlessly altered from Guarini's famous play. Rossi also supplied the librettos of the unsuccessful pasticcio *Ercole* (May 1712) and Handel's *Silla* (Burlington House, June 1713), and no doubt other operas of this period, including perhaps *Amadigi*. He showed little literary or dramatic skill. His rival Rolli satirized him in one of his epigrams after Martial. On Haym's death in August 1729 Rossi became, according to Rolli, 'Handel's accredited bard', and may have provided the librettos of *Lotario* and other operas, all adapted from earlier originals. He made revisions and additions for the revival of *Rinaldo* in April 1731. He was not the Jacopo Rossi who wrote a libretto for Lucca in 1685.

WINTON DEAN

Rossi, Giovan Carlo (*b* Torremaggiore, *c*1617; *d* Rome, 13 June 1692). Italian harpist, organist and composer, youngest brother of LUIGI ROSSI. He joined his brother in Rome about 1630 and deputized for him during his absences from his post as organist of S Luigi dei Francesi in 1635, 1643 and 1647–9. In 1653 he wrote the epitaph for his brother's tombstone. In 1659 he was among the composers whom Francesco Buti and Cardinal Mazarin considered might set to music a libretto, *Ercole amante*, written by Buti for the French court; however, their first choice, Cavalli, finally accepted the commission, but Rossi played the harp in its eventual performance in 1662. He served the French court from 1661 to 1666, and the title and privileges of *maître de la musique du cabinet du Roy* were bestowed on him during this period. His wife, Francesca Campana, was probably the musician of that name (*see* CAMPANA, FRANCESCA). The notary papers regarding her death in 1665 indicate that they possessed paintings by Leonardo da Vinci, Raphael and Salvator Rosa, a good library and an excellent collection of musical instruments (which probably included those that had belonged to Luigi Rossi). From 1666 Rossi lived in Rome. A few chamber cantatas by him are extant: *Chi mi soccorre, ohimè* (*F-Psg* 3372), *Core, a te è tardo* (*I-Rdp* 51), *Deh, come devo fare* (*Vbn* It.IV 466), *Dove vai, pensiero audace* (*Rc* 2478), *E così dolce la pena* (*Rvat* Chigi Q IV 18), *In amor ciascun* (*Vbn* It.IV 466) and *Vanne, mio core, alle stelle* (*Rdp* 51), all for soprano and continuo; and *Non ho che perder più* (*Rvat* Chigi Q IV 16), for soprano, baritone and continuo.

BIBLIOGRAPHY
A. Cametti: 'Alcuni documenti inediti su la vita di Luigi Rossi compositore di musica (1597–1653)', *SIMG*, xiv (1912–13), 1
H. Prunières: *L'opéra italien en France avant Lulli* (Paris, 1913)
A. Cametti: 'Luigi Rossi, organista a San Luigi de' Francesi', *Critica musicale* (Florence, 1919)
A. Ghislanzoni: *Luigi Rossi: biografia e analisi delle composizioni* (Milan, 1954)
ELEANOR CALUORI

Rossi, Giovanni (i) (*fl* Bologna, 1558–95). Italian music publisher. He opened his first printing house in Venice in 1557 and transferred it to Bologna in 1558 or 1559, at first in partnership with the brothers Benacci. From 1561, however, his publications were signed with his name alone. In 1563 his printing press was on the street of S Mamolo, bearing the title 'Episcopal printer' (i.e. official printer to the church). In 1572 he was elected the official typographer of a Bolognese society of men of letters, historians etc. A Senate decree (renewed in 1593) declared that Rossi was obliged to provide good type characters, in particular musical ones, to be replaced whenever necessary. He was the first to print music in Bologna using movable metal type, producing an elegant edition of Camillo Cortellini's *Il secondo libro di madrigali a cinque voci* (11 May 1584); his typographical mark was a winged Mercury with the motto 'Coelo demissus ab alto'. His only other musical work that survives is a small publication by Ascanio Trombetti, *Musica sopra le conclusioni di legge* (1587).

Giovanni died in 1595 and his son Perseo succeeded to the printing business, using the title 'Heredi di G. Rossi'. The firm published some works by Adriano Banchieri – *Conclusioni nel suono dell'organo* (1609), *Terzo libro di pensieri ecclesiastici* (1613), *Cartellina del canto fermo gregoriano* (1614), *Due ripieni in applauso musicale* (1614) and *Prima parte del primo libro al direttorio monastico di canto fermo* (1615) – as well as Ercole Porta's *Vaga ghirlanda di ... fiori musicali* (1613) and Coma's *Sacrae cantiones* (1614). Giovanni Rossi's publications are characterized by a finesse and elegance which the firm did not retain after his death.

BIBLIOGRAPHY
L. Sighinolfi: 'La prima stampa della musica in Bologna', *L'archiginnasio*, xvii (1922), 192
F. Vatielli: 'Editori musicali dei secoli XVII e XVIII', *Arte e vita musicale a Bologna* (Bologna, 1927/R1969), 239
A. Sorbelli: *Storia della stampa a Bologna* (Bologna, 1929)
L. Gottardi: *La stampa musicale in Bologna dagli inizi fino al 1700* (diss., U. of Bologna, 1951)
C. Sartori: *Dizionario degli editori musicali italiani* (Florence, 1958)
ANNE SCHNOEBELEN

Rossi, Giovanni (Gaetano) (ii) (*b* Borgo S Donnino, Parma, 5 Aug 1828; *d* Genoa, 31 March 1886). Italian composer. He studied music with his father Marco Rossi, the town organist, and at the Milan Conservatory (1846–8) under Antonio Angeleri, Felice Frasi and Pietro Ray. In 1851 he became deputy *maestro concertatore* at the Teatro Regio, Parma, and in 1852 was promoted to *maestro concertatore*, also becoming organist at the court chapel and deputy singing master at the conservatory. He was subsequently appointed deputy composition master (1853), composition master and vice-director (both 1856) and director of the conservatory (1864), a post he held for ten years. In 1873 he was assistant conductor at the Teatro Carlo Felice, Genoa, and, from 1874 until his death, director of the Liceo Musicale there. Rossi composed four operas, *Elena di Taranto* (Parma, 1852), *Giovanni Giscala* (Parma, 1855), *Nicolò de Lapi* (Parma, 1865) and *La contessa d'Altenberg* (Borgo S Donnino, 1871); they were written in an up-to-date Verdian style but were not particularly successful. He also composed a few sacred works, including an oratorio *Le sette parole*, three *messe di gloria* and a requiem.

BIBLIOGRAPHY
N. Pelicelli: 'Musicisti in Parma dal 1800 al 1860', *NA*, xii (1935), 341
MARVIN TARTAK

Rossi, Giovanni Battista (*b* ?Genoa; *fl* 1618). Italian composer and theorist. That he was from Genoa and belonged to a religious order, the Chierici Regolari di Somasca, is stated on the title-page of his *Organo de cantori per intendere da se stesso ogni passo difficile che si trova nella musica, et anco per imparare contrapunto* (Venice, 1618). This is a theoretical work displaying a conservative mind, for much of the discourse is on mensural notation, which was hardly relevant to current or even recent practice. Some cantilenas for two to five voices printed in the second part are either for voices without continuo in a late 16th-century motet or canzonet idiom (the latter with Italian texts) or for instruments with continuo; they are dull and lacking in invention. Rossi also published a volume of four-part masses, one with a *Magnificat* (Venice, 1618).

JEROME ROCHE

Rossi [Rosso], Giovanni Maria de [del] [Il Rosso] (*b* Brescia, *c*1522; *d* Mantua, 30 April 1590). Italian organist, composer and singer. He was active at the Mantuan court during the second half of the 16th century; between 1553 and 1559 he is mentioned as curator of the duke's instrument collection, under the supervision of Regent Cardinal Ercole Gonzaga. In 1563 he became *maestro di cappella* at Mantua Cathedral, a post he held until 1576. During this period he also became a priest. In 1567 he was one of three singers who, with the court *maestro di cappella* Giaches de Wert, participated in a concert trip to Venice. From 1582 to 1585 he was organist at the cathedral and as late as 1587 was once again listed as a court singer. During his last years he suffered from gout, which eventually caused his death. Like his younger colleague Francesco Rovigo, Rossi was closely connected with Claudio Merulo who published the composer's main works.

WORKS
Motetti, 5vv, libro I (Venice, 1567)
Madrigali, 4vv, libro I (Venice, 1567)
Missa 'Ultimi miei sospiri', 6vv, D-Mbs, I-Rvat
2 madrigals, 4vv, in 1558[13]

BIBLIOGRAPHY
P. Canal: *Della musica in Mantova* (Venice, 1881)
P. M. Tagmann: *Archivalische Studien zur Musikpflege am Dom von Mantua (1500–1627)* (Berne, 1967)
PIERRE M. TAGMANN

Rossi, Giuseppe de (*b* Rome, mid-17th century; *d* Rome, *c*1719–20). Italian composer. He may have been a pupil of Orazio Benevoli. He was for a time *maestro di cappella* at the Castel S Angelo, Rome. He held a similar position, at the Santa Casa, Loreto, from 16 March 1701 until July 1711, whereupon he took over the position, vacated by G. P. Franchi, of *maestro di cappella* at Ss Madonna dei Monti, Rome, while Franchi succeeded him at Loreto. His extant music is exclusively sacred, and much of it, the masses in particular, is written in the massive polychoral style cultivated by Benevoli and several other Roman composers. A characteristic device in his works is to present the augmented theme in the same voice in each choir, in the manner of a cantus firmus. Some of his 16-part masses have titles (e.g. *Missa 'Maria meliorem partem elegit'* and *Missa 'Maria jam jucundabatur'*) taken from St Augustine's sermon for the Feast of the Assumption.

WORKS
13 masses, 5, 8, 12, 16vv, some with insts, 1676–1717; 2 graduals, 2, 3vv, insts, bc, 1713–17; Magnificat, 8vv; Miserere, 4vv; Benedictus, 4vv; 13 antiphons, 1–4, 8vv, 1710–15; 27 responsories, 4vv; 12 psalms, 4, 6, 8, 12, 16vv; 4 motets, 2, 3vv; 3 hymns, 4vv: *D-Bds* (autograph; 1 mass wrongly attrib. Benevoli), *MÜp*, *I-Bc* (1 mass wrongly attrib. Benevoli, probably by Rossi; 1 mass, inc., anon. probably by Rossi), *Rc*, *Rli*, *Rsg*, *Rvat* (1 mass inc., anon., probably by Rossi); graduals ed. in Documenta maiora liturgiae polychoralis, x (Rome, 1964)

BIBLIOGRAPHY
F. Parisini, ed.: *Carteggio inedito del Padre Giovanni Battista Martini* (Bologna, 1888), 151, 253
G. Gaspari: *Catalogo della biblioteca del Liceo musicale di Bologna*, ii (Bologna, 1892/R1961), 134, 302
G. Tebaldini: *L'archivio musicale della Cappella Lauretana* (Loreto, 1921), 67, 81, 118f
O. Mischiati: 'Rossi, Giuseppe De', *MGG*

Rossi, Lauro (*b* Macerata, 19 Feb 1812; *d* Cremona, 5 May 1885). Italian composer, teacher and musical director. He studied at the Naples Conservatory under Zingarelli, Furno and Crescentini, obtaining his diploma in 1829. That year he made a successful opera début at the Teatro La Fenice, Naples, with the comedy *Le contesse villane*. In 1830 *Costanza e Oringaldo*, written in collaboration with Pietro Raimondi, musical director of all the royal theatres in Naples, gave him entrée to the Teatro S Carlo. Three more comedies, given at the Teatro Nuovo in 1831 and all well received, brought him to the attention of Donizetti, who recommended him as assistant director of the Teatro Valle, Rome, a post he held until 1833. In 1834 his *La casa disabitata*, given at La Scala, Milan, so impressed Maria Malibran that she persuaded the impresario Barbaia to commission him to write an opera for her. Unfortunately, Malibran had insisted that this work, *Amelia, ovvero Otto anni di costanza* (Naples, 1834), include a pas de deux for herself and the ballerina Mathis, but as the many accomplishments for which she was famous did not extend to ballet dancing, the opera was hissed off the stage.

Embittered by this, it is said, and in spite of the fair success of his *Leocadia* (Milan, 1835), Rossi accepted an appointment as director of an opera company touring Mexico, where his next opera *Giovanna Shore* had its première in 1836. When in 1837 the company broke up because of political unrest and the hazards of travel, Rossi set up as an impresario in his own right. In June 1840 he was in Milan to engage a company for Havana under a Spanish impresario and with himself as musical director. Those engaged included a young Bohemian soprano, Isabella Obermeyer, who had that year made a highly successful Italian début as a prima donna under the name Ober. The company appeared briefly in New York in September on the way to Havana, where they opened on 27 October. In 1841 Rossi married Obermeyer, who sang thereafter as Ober-Rossi. In spring 1842 the company performed in New Orleans, returning then to Havana. In 1843 Rossi and his wife were back in Europe to convalesce from yellow fever, after which he settled in Milan and began a second phase of his operatic career with a triumphant revival of *La casa disabitata*, revised as *I falsi monetari* and in that form a part of the standard repertory for many years. Ober-Rossi sang successfully at La Fenice, Venice, in Carnival 1844, and in 1846–8 at the Teatro del Circo, Madrid.

In 1846 Rossi's *La figlia di Figaro* was given at the Kärntnertor-Theater in Vienna, while in Milan *Il domino nero* was warmly received in 1849. Being now a figure of some consequence, Rossi was appointed director of the Milan Conservatory. During his 20 years in this post, his operatic output diminished considerably as he devoted himself more and more to academic pursuits. To this period belongs a *Guida ad un corso d'armonia practica orale* (Milan, 1858), which was to become a standard textbook. Though in no sense a modernist himself, he pursued a liberal policy and his regime saw the emergence with high honours of Faccio and Boito and the founding of a chair of dramatic poetry, with Emilio Praga as its first incumbent. Rossi was among the founders of the Milan Società del Quartetto in 1862 and also of the society's journal, which carried some of Boito's fieriest attacks on the state of music and literature in Italy. In 1868 he formed part of the commission appointed to select 13 of Italy's leading composers who would contribute to a composite mass in honour of Rossini – the plan which, though abortive, resulted eventually in the composition of Verdi's Requiem. In 1870 the death of Mercadante led to Rossi's nomination

as head of the Naples Conservatory. Popular in Milan, he was little liked in Naples and in 1878 he resigned his supreme position to form part of a triumvirate, appointed to carry out the government's plans for reforming the institution. In 1880 he retired to Cremona.

During his years at Naples, Rossi produced a number of instrumental and sacred vocal works and composed two operas for Turin, *La contessa di Mons* (1874) and *Cleopatra* (1876), the first of which enjoyed a *succès d'estime*. His last opera, *Biorn*, was written to an English libretto and performed in the Queen's Theatre, London, in January 1877. A version of *Macbeth* with the action transferred to Norway and the witches turned into Norns, it failed disastrously; none of the music, described by the critic Joseph Bennett as written at so much per yard, survives in print.

As a creative artist Rossi belonged to that generation of minor composers who achieved a certain individuality within the post-Rossinian tradition, but whose talent was unable to survive the tradition's collapse. Works like *I falsi monetari* (known at the time as Rossi's *Barbiere*) and *Il domino nero* show a real invention, combined with a flair for comedy that caused Felice Romani to consider Rossi Donizetti's successor in *opera buffa*. Indeed *I falsi monetari* (in its original form), with its blunt rhythms and classical tonal schemes, would seem to have been the nearest single model for the style of Verdi's youthful *Un giorno di regno*. *Cleopatra* and *La contessa di Mons*, on the other hand, while showing an attempt to keep up with the times, offer little more than the old operatic framework shorn of *fioriture* and cabalettas and garnished with recherché harmonies, calculated irregularities of phrasing and an occasional excursion into local idioms (*La contessa di Mons* quotes from the famous *Jota aragonesa*). Among the later stage works exception should be made of the one-act *Il maestro e la cantante*, in which Rossi shows a Sullivanesque talent for musical foolery, at one point combining a cabaletta by Bellini in the voice part with one by Donizetti in the orchestra. But Rossi was famous chiefly as an academic, and one of the first in Italy to show a genuine interest in the revival of old music. He transcribed Frescobaldi's *partite*, and a performance by the students of the Milan Conservatory of Janequin's *La bataille de Marignan* under his direction was remembered as an important cultural event. His harmony course is lucidly written and eminently practical for its time.

WORKS

OPERAS

Le contesse villane (opera buffa, A. Passaro), Naples, La Fenice, carn. 1829; rev., Naples, 1831, Turin, 1846; *I-Nc* (as Le principesse villane); vocal score (Milan, n.d.)

Costanza e Oringaldo (melodramma, R. Fortini), Naples, S Carlo, 30 May 1830, collab. P. Raimondi; autograph *Nc*

La sposa al lotto (V. Torelli), Naples, Nuovo, June 1831

La casa in vendita, ovvero Il casino in campagna (Torelli), Naples, Nuovo, sum. 1831

La scommessa di matrimonio, Naples, Nuovo, 30 Nov 1831; autograph *Nc*

Baldovino, tiranno di Spoleto (Servi), Rome, Casa Contini, carn. 1832

Il maestro di scuola (Servi), Rome, Casa Contini, spr. 1832

Il disertore svizzero, ovvero La nostalgia (opera seria, 2, F. Romani), Rome, Valle, 9 Sept 1832; *Mr*; excerpts (Milan, n.d.)

Le fucine di Bergen (opera semiseria, 2, J. Ferretti, after B. Merelli), Rome, Valle, 16 Nov 1833

La casa disabitata, ovvero Don Eustachio di Campagna (melodramma giocoso, 2, Ferretti), Milan, La Scala, 11 Aug 1834; autograph *Mr*; rev. as I falsi monetari, Turin, 1844; *Mr*, *Nc*; vocal score (Milan, 1852)

Amelia, ovvero Otto anni di costanza (melodramma, C. Bassi), Naples,

S Carlo, 31 Dec 1834; autograph *Nc*, copy *Mr*; excerpts (Milan, 1835; London, 1835)

Leocadia (melodramma serio, 3, Cavallini), Milan, Canobbiana, 30 April 1835; autograph *Mr*

Giovanna Shore (melodramma serio, 3, Romani), Mexico City, Municipale, sum. 1836; autograph *Nc*

Il borgomastro di Schiedam (G. Peruzzini, after Mélésville), Milan, Re, 1 June 1844; *OS*; vocal score (Milan, n.d.)

Dottor Bobolo, ovvero La fiera (melodramma buffo, 3, F. Rubino), Naples, Nuovo, 2 March 1845; scena e duetto (Milan, n.d.)

Cellini a Parigi (G. Peruzzini), Turin, d'Angennes, 2 June 1845; autograph *Mr*; vocal score (Milan, n.d.)

Azema di Granata, ovvero Gli abencerragi ed i zegrini (melodramma tragico, 2, Bassi), Milan, La Scala, 21 March 1846; autograph *Mr*; excerpts (Milan, 1846)

La figlia di Figaro (melodramma giocoso, 3, Ferretti), Vienna, Kärntnertor, 17 April 1846; autograph *Mr*, copy *GB-Lbm*; vocal score (Milan, 1846)

Bianca Contarini (dramma tragico, prol, 3, F. Jannetti), Milan, La Scala, 24 Feb 1847; *I-Mr*, *Nc*; excerpts (Milan, 1846)

Il domino nero (opera comica, 3, F. Rubino), Milan, Canobbiana, 1 Sept 1849; autograph *Mr*, copy *GB-Lbm*; vocal score (Milan, 1849)

Le sabine (melodramma, prol, 2, Peruzzini), Milan, La Scala, 21 Feb 1852; autograph *I-Nc*

L'alchimista (M. d'Arienzo), Naples, Fondo, 23 Aug 1853; autograph *Nc*; excerpts (Milan, n.d.)

La sirena (Peruzzini), Milan, Canobbiana, 11 Oct 1855

La zingara rivale (farsa, 1, ? S. Cammarano), Milan, Canobbiana, spr. 1867; rev., Turin, 1867; excerpts (Turin, n.d.)

Il maestro e la cantante (scherzo comico, 1, possibly Rossi), Turin, Nota, Sept 1867; *Nn*, *GB-Lbm*; vocal score (Turin, 1868)

Gli artisti alla fiera (melodramma buffo, 3), Turin, Carignano, 7 Nov 1868; *I-Nc*; vocal score (Milan, n.d.)

La contessa di Mons (melodramma, 4, D'Arienzo, after Sardou: Patrie), Turin, Regio, 31 Jan 1874; autograph *Nc*, copy *GB-Lbm*; vocal score (Turin, 1874)

Cleopatra (tragedia lirica, 4, D'Arienzo), Turin, Regio, 5 March 1876; *Lbm*, *I-Nn*; vocal score (Turin, 1876)

Biorn (tragic opera, 5, F. Marshall, after Shakespeare: Macbeth), London, Queen's, 17 Jan 1877; autograph *Nc* (as Macbeth)

OTHER WORKS

Vocal: Saul, oratorio, Rome, 1833; choruses for Plautus: The Prisoners; Cantata for the 400th anniversary of Raphael's birth, Urbino, 28 March 1883; Mass; Kyrie, 3vv, d; songs, incl. In morte di Vincenzo Bellini, S, pf (Milan, 1835); Mille nuvole d'argento, serenata, solo vv (Milan, 1850); Tremi, tremi pel figlio', aria, S, orch, *I-BGc*; single chamber works, 1–4vv, pf, *BGc*, *Gl*, *Mc*, *OS*, *Pci*

Inst: March for the Emperor of Brazil, arr. pf 4 hands (Milan, n.d.), Marcia trionfale, for marriage of Umberto and Margherita, arr. pf (Milan, 1868); chamber works, incl. Divertimento, pf, harp (Milan, 1835)

Pedagogical: Guida ad un corso di armonia pratica orale per gli allievi del R. Conservatorio di musica in Milano (Milan, 1858); 12 esercizi a complemento dello studio dei solfeggi e dei vocalizzi, S (Milan, ?1863); 8 vocalizzi, S (Milan, 1866); 6 solfeggi, 3vv, *Mr*

BIBLIOGRAPHY

F. Florimo: *La scuola musicale di Napoli e i suoi conservatorii* (Naples, 1880–83/*R*1969)

A. Colombani: *L'opera italiana nel secolo XIX* (Milan, 1900)

G. Radiciotti: *Elenco delle opere di Lauro Rossi* (Macerata, 1910)

G. Pannain: *Ottocento musicale italiano* (Milan, 1952)

JULIAN BUDDEN

Rossi, Lemme (*b* Perugia, *c*1602; *d* Perugia, 2 May 1673). Italian philosopher, mathematician, astronomer, authority on the Greek language and music theorist. He was professor of philosophy and mathematics at the University of Perugia but had retired by the time he published a brief method on astronomy there in 1664. He is known to musicians for his *Sistema musico, overo Musica speculativa* (Perugia, 1666); 23 copies are known to survive, and a second edition (which had appeared by 1669) is lost. Burney described this work as 'one of the clearest and best digested treatises of harmonics [systems of tuning] that was produced in Italy, during the last century'. In it Rossi discussed the work of many earlier theorists, from Pythagoras to Kircher, and described the equal-tempered system. It appears to have stimulated Bontempi to write his *Historia musica*, which contains 'many copious extracts' (Hawkins) from

it, and tables based on Rossi's work are included in the *Storia della musica* of Padre Martini.

BIBLIOGRAPHY

BurneyH; EitnerQ; GerberNL; HawkinsH; WaltherML

Anon.: review of *Sistema musico*, *Giornale de' letterati*, ii (Rome, 1669), 39ff

A. Oldoini: *Athenaeum Augustum in quo Perusinorum scripta publice exponuntur* (Perugia, 1678), 205

G. A. Bontempi: *Historia musica* (Perugia, 1695/*R*1976)

G. B. Martini: *Storia della musica* (Bologna, 1757–81/*R*1967), esp. i, 316ff

J. N. Forkel: *Allgemeine Litteratur der Musik* (Leipzig, 1792/*R*1962), 245f

G. Gaspari: *Catalogo della biblioteca del Liceo musicale di Bologna*, i (Bologna, 1890/*R*1961), 251

COLIN TIMMS

Rossi, Luigi (*b* Torremaggiore, *c*1597; *d* Rome, 20 Feb 1653). Italian composer, singing teacher, lutenist and keyboard player. He was a conspicuous figure on the musical scene both in Italy and, for a time, in France: he was one of the finest composers of chamber cantatas in the Baroque period and the leading composer of vocal music in the Rome of his day.

1. LIFE. The documents that would have given precise information about Rossi's birth and other particulars about his family were lost in the earthquakes of 1627 and 1638 which destroyed the archives of the two parish churches of Torremaggiore. An autograph manuscript (*GB-Lbm* Add.30491) indicates that Rossi was a pupil of Giovanni de Macque in Naples and that he spent 14 years at the Neopolitan court; perhaps, as Ghislanzoni suggested, he went there as a page in the household of Prince Paolo de Sangro, whose family governed Torremaggiore. It was probably about 1608–14 that he studied with Macque, who was then *maestro di cappella* at the court and who taught him the organ, the lute, singing and composition (in the above-mentioned manuscript Rossi included, among other items, instrumental pieces by his master and, at a later stage, Peri's *Tu dormi* and Monteverdi's *Lamento d'Arianna*: see illustration).

Rossi eventually moved to Rome. Ghislanzoni suggested that he entered the service of the Borghese family after the death of Philip III of Spain on 31 March 1621; Marc'Antonio Borghese possibly invited him to become part of his large household when he was in Naples for the assembly at which the Italian Grandi di Spagna pledged allegiance to the new king. On 3 July 1627 Rossi married the celebrated harpist Costanza de Ponte. On 1 April 1633 he became organist of S Luigi dei Francesi, Rome, a position once held by Macque and one that Rossi retained until his death. Three documents testify to their association with the Borghese family: one (in *I-Bc* Q49) was copied about 1630 and contains an early *arietta corta* attributed to 'Luigi de Rossi di Borghese', and two letters dated May 1635. The first of these letters, written by Camilla Borghese, presents 'Luigi Rossi Musico' and his wife to the dowager Grand Duchess of Tuscany, and in the second Costanza Rossi told Camilla Borghese of her performances for the Florentine nobility – Rossi was given leave of absence from S Luigi dei Francesi so that he and Costanza could accept an invitation to stay from May to November 1635 at the court of Ferdinando II de' Medici. By about 1640 Rossi had become recognized as one of the leading Italian musicians of his time. In his letter *Della musica dell'età nostra* (1640) Pietro Della Valle offered his cantata *Horche la notte* as an

Rossi's autograph copy of the opening of Monteverdi's 'Lamento d'Arianna' (GB-Lbm Add.30491, f.39r)

example of the serious type of canzonetta then in vogue, and in the same year he was represented among the leading Roman composers by the inclusion of six pieces in the *Raccolta d'arie spirituali* edited by Vincenzo Bianchi. In 1641 Ottavio Castelli considered Rossi's cantata on the death of the Swedish king Gustavus Adolphus, *Un ferito cavaliero*, a worthy gift to present to Cardinal Richelieu. Towards the end of the 1640s Severo Bonini, in his *Prima parte de' discorsi e regole sovra la musica*, named him head of the Roman school of musicians.

In 1641 Rossi left the Borghese household to become a musician in the service of Cardinal Antonio BARBER-INI, an ardent and influential patron of the arts, who employed the most active and famous musicians and artists in Rome. In the will that he drew up during a serious illness in November 1641, Rossi demonstrated his gratitude and appreciation by leaving the cardinal all his music and by recommending his wife and youngest brother, GIOVAN CARLO ROSSI, to his care. There are also several indications of the high regard and affection that Cardinal Antonio felt for Rossi, among them the fact that in 1642 he appointed him to compose the chief work to be produced in his theatre during Carnival, he himself devoting careful and constant attention to the preparations and spending great sums of money. This opera, Rossi's first, was *Il palazzo incantato*, the performance of which, on 22 February 1642, caused much excitement among Roman noblemen, churchmen, artists, poets, musicians and visiting statesmen. Leading singers such as Marc'Antonio Pasqualini, Mario Savioni and Loreto Vittori took part in it, and machines and costumes were prepared by hundreds of skilled craftsmen. Despite some minor mishaps, the opera, which

lasted seven hours, is said to have delighted the vast majority of the audience.

At the end of 1642 Rossi was again released from his duties at S Luigi dei Francesi, this time for a year's sojourn at Bologna in the service of Cardinal Antonio Barberini; at the end of April 1644 he was once more requested to serve the cardinal there, for a few weeks. A letter from Atto Melani to his patron, Prince Mattia de' Medici, dated 4 June 1644, tells of an academy to be held at Rossi's home during the summer months at which all the best virtuosos in Rome would gather. Melani had been invited to join this academy, and others present probably included Pasqualini, Savioni, Vittori, Filippo Vitali, Antonio Francesco Tenaglia and Carlo Caproli, most of whom were in the employ of Cardinal Antonio Barberini; the influence that these composers exerted on one another is evident in the stylistic similarities found in their cantatas. Another famous singer who enjoyed Rossi's friendship and appreciated his music was Leonora Baroni, who in a letter of 25 September 1645 promised her French patron the gift of 'two new and truly beautiful songs of Luigi de Rossi'. The following year, when he was in Paris, the admiration that Rossi inspired in his colleagues is found too in the correspondence of Thomas Gobert and Constantijn Huygens: Gobert sent Huygens some of Rossi's cantatas (among them *Anime, voi che sete*), which he had received from the composer. It was probably because of repeated instances of such enthusiasm that Rossi's cantatas were so widely disseminated.

Rossi's specially close association with Antonio Barberini ended in 1645, when the Barberini family departed for France, where they remained in exile until 1653 (the year of Rossi's death). Since no more operas were staged in their theatre until their return, Rossi might well have had no opportunity to compose another opera had it not been for the desire of the French court to produce a work similar to those that had been staged by Antonio Barberini. Invited personally by JULES MAZARIN, Rossi arrived in Paris in June 1646. During his year at the French court he not only composed his second opera, *Orfeo*, and helped to recruit distinguished singers for its performance but also served Anne of Austria by composing cantatas for the private concerts in her salon. He was often the keyboard accompanist in the concerts given by the Italian singers who had come to Paris to take part in his opera. He also collaborated with French musicians in the entertainments presented during the court's summer sojourn at Fontainebleau between July and September 1646, and he renewed his friendship with the singer Pierre de Nyert, whose interpretations of his cantatas, it was said, he greatly admired. At the end of 1646 the unexpected news of his wife's death reached him, and his grief may have delayed the completion of *Orfeo*, for there were complaints that a few singers had still not received their parts nine days before the first performance on 2 March 1647. Mazarin himself had been involved in the preparations, which included the enlargement of a hall within the palace and the employment of some 200 workers to realize the scenery. The six-hour performance, which was attended by the entire court, was a resounding success, a sensational event spoken of in numerous contemporary letters and journals. A second performance followed before Lent and six others after it. Invited by Queen Anne and Mazarin to name a favour they could bestow on him, Rossi asked only that his brother-in-law receive the benefice of the chapel of S Petronilla in the Vatican, which was in the gift of the French monarch; in a letter to Rome of 15 March 1647 Mazarin requested that the matter be attended to at once.

After the performances of *Orfeo* in April and May – two of them in honour of the Queen of England, who was a guest of the French court – Rossi returned to his post at S Luigi dei Francesi. He resumed it at the beginning of July, only to leave it again at the end of the year. Recalled to Paris by Mazarin at the request of the queen, he did not hesitate to accept what must have seemed an opportunity to compose another opera. However, no theatrical spectacles were produced by Italian artists at the French court during his second sojourn there, which lasted from January 1648 to September 1649. The queen had been advised against them by her spiritual counsellor, and Mazarin had renounced them in the hope of putting an end to the calumnies spread against him since the production of *Orfeo*. Because of the miserable conditions in which they lived while the court lavished large sums of money on entertainments, the French people were incensed by the queen and her ministers. By the end of 1648 the situation in Paris had become so bad that the queen, Mazarin and the court took refuge at St Germain-en-Laye, and Rossi and other Italian musicians were probably among the refugees. Whether he moved to Amiens with the queen and her court in March 1649 is not known, but on 17 September he left Paris and joined Antonio Barberini at a castle near Lyons. It is not known when he returned to Italy, but he was probably there by the beginning of 1650. He was buried at S Maria in via Lata, where his tombstone can still be seen.

Rossi was not soon forgotten. Cesti paid tribute to him in his cantata *Aspettate*, dating from not long after his death. A few of his pieces were published in Rotterdam and Paris as well as in Italy. He was remembered as one of the great musicians of his time by such well-known writers as Bacilly, Berardi, Raguenet, Le Cerf de la Viéville, Saint-Evremond and Brossard.

2. WORKS. The great esteem in which Rossi was held by his contemporaries was in large part due to his chamber cantatas, which were his major achievement and which exist in more copies than those of any other Italian cantata composer. About 300 authenticated cantatas survive. They include *ariette corte*, short pieces in clear, well-defined forms; *arie di più parti*, the form of each of which is unique; and laments that recall the earlier dramatic recitatives but are now characterized by a particular order of textual and musical events. The *ariette corte*, which account for more than half of the cantatas, display Rossi's bel canto style of melody at its best and are the most notable examples of the exquisitely organized vocal forms developed by him and his contemporaries: simple binary, strophic binary with closing refrain, rounded binary, ternary and rondo. The *arie di più parti* are settings of longer, more complex texts with verses differing in length and mood, and they consequently embrace diverse and multiple musical sections. They include fine examples of the fluid mingling of aria, recitative and arioso characteristic of Rossi's music in general. *Arie di più parti* account for only a fifth of his cantatas, but, perhaps to some extent because of his example, they became the commonest type of cantata in the 1660s and 1670s. Like his contemporaries Carissimi, Caproli, Tenaglia and Marazzoli, Rossi composed few laments. His 17 examples consist primarily of recitative, usually with an arioso refrain articulating the long middle section and with a short aria forming the final section.

Rossi played a not insignificant part in the development of opera. His two examples represent the culmination of the early 17th-century Roman opera. Like other such works they were grand, festive and extravagant spectacles and have choruses, ballets, many characters and scenes, much intrigue and comic episodes. In them, however, one finds a new, warm lyricism manifested in the many arias, which resemble the *ariette corte* among Rossi's cantatas. Emotive, well-shaped and beautiful melodies prevail, especially in *Orfeo*. There is more recitative in *Il palazzo incantato*, but it tends to be lyrically expressive rather than just dry declamation, and many who witnessed this opera found it very moving.

Rossi's music represents a new ideal of vocal music formulated in Rome and diffused from there throughout Europe. The development of his bel canto style was no doubt influenced by many factors: his memory of the spontaneity of Neapolitan popular song; his appreciation of Florentine recitative and of the eloquent music of Monteverdi; his desire to find means of expressing varied and passionate sentiments; his fine architectural sense, through which he discriminatingly chose simple, elegant forms; and the receptive quality of his mind and imagination, which were alert and responsive to the intellectual and humanist movements of his time.

WORKS

OPERAS

Il palazzo incantato, overo La guerriera amante (G. Rospigliosi), Rome, Palazzo Barberini, Quattro Fontane, 22 Feb 1642, *I-Bc*, *Rvat*; facs. (New York, 1977)

Orfeo (F. Buti), Paris, Palais Royal, 2 March 1647, *Rvat*; extracts ed. in Goldschmidt, 295, in Abert, 194, and in Ghislanzoni (1954)

ORATORIOS, ORATORIO CANTATAS
(*all anon. in sources*)

Giuseppe, figlio di Giacobbe (Buti), 4vv, chorus, 2 vn, vle, bc, *I-Fn* [lost], *Rvat*; ed. C. V. Palisca, Italian Oratorios of the Baroque Era (in preparation)
Oratorio per la Settimana Santa (G. C. Raggioli), 3vv, chorus, 2 vn, lute, bc, *Rvat*; ed. H. Smither, Italian Oratorios of the Baroque Era (in preparation)
La cecità (Lotti), cantata morale, 5vv, 2 vn, bc, *Rvat*
La predica del sole (Lotti), 5vv chorus, 2 vn, lute, bc, *Rvat*
Un peccator pentito (Lotti), 5vv, 2 vn, lute, bc, *Rvat*
S Caterina alla rota; listed in 1682 inventory of *I-Bof* (possibly by Marazzoli)

CANTATAS

A chi, lasso crederò, 1v, bc, *F-Pn*; Acuto gelo, tu che mordace, 1v, bc, 1640²; Adagio, speranze, al suono pietoso, 1v, bc, *F-Pn*; Addio, addio, perfida, 1v, bc, *D-SWl*; Adorate mie catene, 1v, bc, *GB-Ckc*; Ahi, dunque è pur vero, 2vv, bc, *I-Fc*; Ahi, quante volte io moro, 2vv, bc, *Fc*; A i sospiri, al dolore, 2vv, bc, *F-Pthibault*; A la rota, a la benda, 1v, bc, *I-Rc*; Al cenno d'una speranza, 1v, bc, *B-Br*; All'hor ch'il ben dal male, 1v, bc, *I-Bc*; All'hor ch'il forte Alcide, 1v, bc, *F-Pn*; All'ombra d'una speranza, 1v, bc, *GB-Lbm*; Al soave spirar d'aure serene, 1v, bc, *I-Rvat*
Amanti, piangete a miei pianti, 1v, bc, *Nc*; A me stesso il pensier mio, 1v, bc, *B-Br*; Amor, con dolci vezzi, 2vv, bc, *I-Fc*; Amor così si fà, 1v, bc, *Rvat*; Amor, e perche con pianti, 1v, bc, *F-Pn*; Amor giura che m'aiuta, 1v, bc, *Pn*; Amor, se devo piangere, 2vv, bc, *GB-Och*; Amor s'io mi querelo, 1v, bc, *I-Rc*; Anime, voi che sete, 1v, bc, *B-Br*; Apritevi, o begl'occhi, 2vv, bc, *I-Fc*; A qual dardo il cor si deve, 1v, bc, *Bc*; Ardo, sospiro e piango, 2vv, bc, *Nc*; Armatevi di sdegno, offesi amanti, 1v, bc, 1644, *Rvat*; Armatevi d'orgoglio, luci belle, 1v, bc, *F-Pn*; A tanti sospiri, a lagrime tante, 1v, bc, *I-Rc*
A te, mio core, 2vv, bc, *GB-Och*, ed. in Alte Meister des Bel Canto, ii (Leipzig, 1912); Atra notte il velo ombroso, 1v, bc, *F-Pn*; Augellin di sete acceso, 2vv, bc, *I-Fc*; Begl'occhi, che dite, 1v, bc, *F-Pn*; Begl'occhi, pietà, son vinto, 1v, bc, *Pn*; Bella bocca tutta fiori, 2vv, bc, *I-Rc*; Benche roca pur impetra, 1v, bc, *Gil*; Che cosa mi dite, 1v, bc, *F-Pn*; Che dici, mio core, 1v, bc, *Pn*; Che farò, m'innamoro, 1v, bc, *I-Bc;* Che non puote sereno sguardo, 2vv, bc, *Rc*; Che pretendete, begl'occhi da me, 3vv, bc, *Bc*; Che sospiri, martiri, che dolori, 2vv, bc, *Fc*; Che sventura, son tant'anni, 1v, bc, *Nc*; Che tardi più, 1v, bc, *F-Pc*; Che vuoi più da me, 1v, bc, *Pn*; Chi batte il core, 1v, bc, *I-Rc*; Chi cercando và le pene, 1v, bc, *F-Pn*
Chi consiglia un dubbio core, 1v, bc, *US-SFsc*; Chi d'amor sin'a i capelli, 2vv, bc, *I-Bc, Fc* [2 settings]; Chi desia di salire al monte, 1v, bc, 1640²; Chi di voi nova mi da, 1v, bc, *F-Pn*; Chi mi credeva instabile, 1v, bc, *GB-Lbm*; Chi non ha speranza alcuna, 1v, bc, *I-Rc*; Chi non sà com'un sol sguardo, 2vv, bc, *Fc*; Chi non sa fingere, goder non sa, 1v, bc, 1679⁶; Ch'io sospiri al vostro foco, 1v, bc, *F-Pn*; Ch'io speri o disperi, 1v, bc, *I-Gil*; Chi può resister, 2vv, bc, *Bc*; Chi trovasse una speranza, 1v, bc, *F-Pn*
Chiuda quest'occhi il sonno, 1v, bc, *I-Rc, Rvat* [2 settings]; Come è breve il gioir, 1v, bc, *F-Pn*; Come penare, non l'intendo, 1v, bc, *I-Rc*; Come sete importuni, 2vv, bc, *Fc*; Come tosto sparisce beltà, 1v, bc, *Rc*; Compatite un cor di foco, 2vv, bc, *Fc*; Con amor e senza spene, 1v, bc, *Gil*; Con amor si pugna invano, 1v, bc, *Rc*; Con occhi belli e fieri, 1v, bc, *Rc*; Con voi parlo, amanti, 1v, bc, *Fc*; Corilla danzando sul prato, 2vv, bc, *Fc*; Così và, dice il mio core, *Nc*; Da perfida speranza un alma lusingata, 1v, bc, *GB-Lbm*; Datemi pace una brev'hora, 2vv, bc, 1646⁷; Degg'io dunque in amore essere sempre tradito, 1v, bc, *F-Pn*; Deh, soccorri ad un che more, 1v, bc, *Pn*
Deh, soffri, mio core, 1v, bc, *D-SWl*; De la vita in su l'aurora, 1v, bc, *I-Rsc*; Di capo ad Amarilli, 2vv, bc, *Fc*; Difendi, mio core, l'entrata, 1v, bc, *Rc*; Difenditi, amore, per foco di sdegno, 1v, bc, *Bc*; Difenditi, o core, per lampo fugace, 1v, bc, *GB-Lbm*; Disperati, che aspetti più, 1v, bc, *F-Pn*; Dissi un giorno ad amore, 1v, bc, *Pn*; Dite, o cieli, se crudeli, 2vv, bc, *I-Rvat*; Diva, tu che in trono assisa, 1v, bc, 1640²; Dopo lungo penare, 1v, bc, *F-Pn*; Dove, dove più giro fra queste piante, 1v, bc, *I-Rvat*; Due feroci guerrieri, 2vv, bc, *Fc*; Due labbra di rose fan guerra, 2vv, bc, *Nc*, ed. in AMI, v (1897); D'una bella infedele, 1v, bc, *GB-Lbm* Harl.1273, arr. 3vv, bc, *Lbm* Add.14336; E che cantar poss'io, 1v, bc, *Och*; E che pensi, mio core, 1v, bc, *I-Nc*; E chi non v'ameria, 1v, bc, *GB-Lbm*; E d'amore foll'inganno, 1v, bc, *I-Rsc*; E può soffrirsi amore, 1v, bc, *GB-Lbm*; Erminia sventurata, 1v, bc, *Lbm*; E si crede ch'io no 'l sò, 1v, bc, *I-Rc*
Fanciulla son io ch'amare non so, 1v, bc, *F-Pn*, ed. in Les gloires de l'Italie, ii (Paris, 1868); Fanciulle, tenete il guard'a voi, 1v, bc, *Psg*; Fate quel che volete, begl'occhi, 1v, bc, *Pn*; Ferma, Giove, ferma, non piover più, 1v, bc, *I-Rdp*; Fillide mia, deh, come tu mi comparti, 1v, bc, *F-Psg*; Filli, non penso più a destarti, 2vv, bc, *I-Fc*; Fingi ch'io t'ho tradito, 1v, bc, *Rn*; Frena il pianto, ahi, 2vv, bc, *Fc*; Gelosia che a poco a poco, 1v, bc, 1646⁷, ed. in Les gloires de l'Italie, i (Paris,

1868); Già finita è per me, 1v, bc, *F-Pn*; Già nell'oblio profondo, 1v, bc, *GB-Lbm*
Giusto così va detto, 1v, bc, *Lbm*; Guardate dove và la mia vana speranza, 2vv, bc, *I-Fc*; Guardatevi, olà, nemica io sono, 1v, bc, *B-Br*; Ha cent'occhi il crudo amore, 2vv, bc, *I-Fc*; Ho perduto la fortuna che fuggendo, 1v, bc, *F-Pn*; Ho perso il mio core e chi con frode, 2vv, bc, *I-Fc*; Hora ch'ad ecclissar la luna, 1v, bc, *Rdp*; Horch'avvolte in fosco velo, 1v, bc, *Rsc*; Horche di marte il grido, 1v, bc, *Rc*; Horche la notte del silentio amica, 1v, bc, *Rn*, anon. in source, attrib. Rossi by P. Della Valle, Della musica dell'età nostra, ed. A. Solerti, *Le origini del melodramma* (Turin, 1903/*R*1969); Horche l'oscuro manto, 1v, bc, *GB-Och*; Horch'io vivo lontano dal mio ben, 1v, bc, *F-Pn*
Hor guardate come và la fortuna, 1v, bc, *Pthibault*; Hor si, versate, o lumi, 1v, bc, *Pthibault*; Ho vinto gridava amore, 1v, bc, 1640²; Ho voto di non amare, 1v, bc, *GB-Ckc*; Il contento che mi deste, 2vv, bc, *I-Nc*; Il cor mi dice che vicino, 1v, bc, 1640²; Infelice pensier, che mi conforta, 2vv, bc, *I-Fc*, extract ed. in Alte Meister del Bel Canto, ii (Leipzig, 1912); Ingordo human desio, che con avide, 1v, bc, *GB-Och*; In solitario speco, 1v, bc, *Och*; Invan mi tendete il visco e la rete, 2vv, bc, *I-Fc*; Io che sin hor le piante, 1v, bc, *F-Pthibault*, ed. in Les maîtres du chant, v (Paris, 1924–7); Io ero pargoletta quant'altri, 1v, bc, *CS-Pnm, I-Bc*; Io lo vedo, 1v, bc, *B-Br*, ed. in HAM, ii; Io non amo, si, ma cerco, 1v, bc, *I-Rc*; Io piangea presso d'un rio, 1v, bc, *GB-Och*
La bella che mi contenta, 1v, bc, *I-Rsc*; La bella per cui son cieco, 1v, bc, *Rvat*; La bella più bella che il cor mi feri, 1v, bc, *F-Pn*; Lascia, speranza, ohimè, 1v, bc, *B-Br*; Lasciate ch'io ritorni a miei lamenti, 1v, bc, *GB-Lbm*; Lasciatemi qui solo, speranze, 1v, bc, *I-Rc; *Libertà, ragion mi sgrida, 2vv, bc, *Bc*; Lo splendor di due begl'occhi, 2vv, bc, *Bc*, ed. in Antiche cantate d'amore, i/1 (Bologna, 1916–20); Luci belle, dite, ohimè, 1v, bc, *GB-Lbm*; Luci mie, da me sparite, 1v, bc, *I-MOe*; Lungi da me, speranze, 1v, bc, *B-Br*; Mai finirò d'amare, 1v, bc, *F-Pthibault*; Mai no 'l dirò chi sia, 1v, bc, *Rc*; Mani altere e divine, 1v, bc, *GB-Och*; Mentre sorge dal mare la bella aurora, 1v, bc, *I-Rc*
Mi contento così, se sciolse, 1v, bc, *Rdp*; Mi danno la morte due luci, 1v, bc, *Nc*; Mio core languisce e mai non si more, 1v, bc, *F-Pn*; Misero cor, perche pensando vai, 1v, bc, *I-Nc*; Mostro con l'ali nere, 1v, bc, *F-Pn*; M'uccidete, begl'occhi, 1v, bc, *I-Rc*; Nel dì che al Padre eterno, 1v, bc, *GB-Och*; Ne notte ne dì riposa, 1v, bc, *D-SWl*; Nessun sene vanti di viver, 1v, bc, *Nc*; No, mio bene, non lo dite, 1v, bc, *F-Pn*; Non cantar libertà, misero core, 2vv, bc, *GB-Och*; Non c'è che dire, 1v, bc, *Och*; Non la volete, intendere, 1v, bc, *I-Rc*; Non m'affligete più, 1v, bc, 1679⁶; Non mi fate mentire, 1v, bc, *D-SWl*
Non mi lusingar più, 2vv, bc, *I-Bc*; No, no, non ci pensa, 1v, bc, *Rc*; Non più strali, o crudo amore, 2vv, bc, *Fc*; Non più viltà, 1v, bc, *GB-Lbm*; Non sarà, non fù, 2vv, bc, *Fc*; Non ti doler, mio core, 1v, bc, *I-MAC*; O biondi tesori inanellati, 2vv, bc, *Fc*; Occhi ardenti, pupille belle, 1v, bc, *GB-Och*; Occhi belli, occhi miei cari, 2vv, bc, *F-Pn*; Occhi belli, occhi vezzosi, 1v, bc, *GB-Och*; Occhi, quei vaghi azuri, 2vv, bc, *Cfm*; Occhi soavi ogn'aspro cor, 2vv, bc, *I-Fc*; O cieli, pietà, e l'alma, 2vv, bc, *GB-Och*; O dura più d'un sasso, 1v, bc, *Och*; O gradita libertà, 2vv, bc, *I-Nc*; O grotta, o speco, o sasso, 1v, bc, *Rvat*
Ohimè, madre, aita, 1v, bc, *F-Psg*; Olà, pensieri, olà, 1v, bc, *I-Nc*; Ombre, fuggite, e voi, 1v, bc, *GB-Och*; Orrida e solitaria era una selva, 1v, bc, *D-SWl*; Partii dal gioire, già venni alle pene, 1v, bc, *F-Pn*; Patienza, tocca a me di languir, 1v, bc, *I-Rc*; Pender non prima vide sopra vil tronco, 1v, bc, *GB-Och*; Pene, pianti e sospiri, 2vv, bc, *Och*; Pensoso, afflitto, irresoluto, 1v, bc, *Cfm*; Perche chieder com'io stò, 1v, bc, *B-Br*; Perche ratto così, 1v, bc, *I-Rc*; Perche speranze, ohimè, perche tornate, 1v, bc, *F-Pn*; Pietà, spietati lumi, non ti chieggio, 2vv, bc, *P-La*; Poiche mancò speranza che mi nutriva, 2vv, bc, *GB-Och*, ed. in Alte Meister des Bel Canto, ii (Leipzig, 1912); Precorrea del sol l'uscita, 1v, bc, *I-Rvat*; Presso un ruscel sedea, 1v, bc, *Rvat*; Pria ch'al sdegno tu mi desti, 1v, bc, *Rdp*; Provai d'amor le pene, 2vv, bc, *Fc*
Quando Florinda bella s'avvide, 1v, bc, *Nc*; Quando meco tornerai, 1v, bc, *Rn*; Quando mi chiede amore s'io sarò sempre amante, 2vv, bc, *F-Pthibault*; Quando più mia libertà si vantava, 1v, bc, *I-Gil*; Quando spiega la notte, 1v, bc, *F-Pn*; Quante volte l'ho detto, cor mio, 1v, bc, *GB-Lbm*; Quanto è crudelo il mio core, 1v, bc, *I-Gil*; Querelatevi di me se vi miro, 1v, bc, *I-Gil*; Queste dure catene che strascinar, 2vv, bc, *GB-Och*; Questi caldi sospiri, 1v, bc, *CS-Pnm, I-Bc* (anon.); Questo picciolo rio che con lingua, 1v, bc, *F-Pn*
Ragion mi dice lascia d'amare, 1v, bc, *Pn*; Ravvolse il volo e si librò, 1v, bc, *Pn*; Rendetevi, pensieri, non contrastate più, 1v, bc, *Pn*; Respira, core, forze raduna, 1v, bc, *I-Rc*; Risolvetevi o martiri, 2vv, bc, *Rvat*; Satiatevi, o cieli, e con man di dolore, 1v, bc, *Bc*; Se dolente e flebil cetra, 1v, bc, *Nc*; Sei pur dolce, o libertà, 1v, bc, *F-Pthibault*; Se mai ti punge il seno, 1v, bc, *I-Rc*; Se mi volete morto, occhi tiranni, 1v, bc, *Nc*; Sempre, dunque, negarete, belle ninfe, 2vv, bc, *Rc*; Se nell'arsura ch'amor ti diede, 1v, bc, *Bc*; Se non corre una speranza a dar vita, 1v, bc, *MOe*; Sento al cor un non so che, 1v, bc, *Rsc*; S'era alquanto addormentato per dar tregua, 1v, bc, *GB-Cfm*

Si o no, dissi al mio core, 2vv, bc, *I-Bc*, ed. in Alte Meister des Bel Canto, ii (Leipzig, 1912); S'io son vinto, occhi belli, 1v, bc, *F-Psg*; Si, v'ingannate, si, 1v, bc, *I-Nc*; Soffrirei con lieto core, 2vv, bc, *P-La*; Sognai, lasso, sognai che la crudele, 1v, bc, *I-Rc*; Son divenuto amante, 1v, bc, *Bc*; Sopra conca d'argento la bella Citherea, 1v, bc, *Bc*; Sospiri miei di foco, 1v, bc, *GB-Lbm*; Sospiri, olà, che fate, 1v, bc, *Cfm*; Sospiri, su, su, 1v, bc, *I-Rc*; Sotto l'ombra d'un pino, 1v, bc, *GB-Och*; Sparite dal core, 1v, bc, *I-Rsc*; Sparite dal volto, loquaci pallori, 1v, bc, *Rvat*; Sparsa il crine e lagrimosa, 1v, bc, *F-Pn, I-Rvat* [2 versions]; Spenti gl' affanni ond'io perdei servendo, 1v, bc, *Rc*; Speranza, al tuo pallore, 2vv, bc, *Rc*, ed. in Alte Meister des Bel Canto, ii (Leipzig, 1912); Speranze, che dite, 1v, bc, *Rsc*; Speranze, sentite, vi chiama, 2vv, bc, *Nc*; Spiega un volo così altero, 2vv, bc, *P-La*; Su, consiglio, o miei pensieri, 1v, bc, *I-Rsc*; Su la veglia d'una speme, 1v, bc, *GB-Ouf*; Su, su, su, mio core, la guerra, 1v, bc, *I-Rn* Taci, ohimè, non pianger più, 1v, bc, *F-Pn*; Tenti e ardisca in amore, 1v, bc, *I-Rc*; Torna indietro, pensier, dove si và, 1v, bc, *GB-Och*; Tra montagne di foco romito vive, 1v, bc, *B-Br*; Tra romite contrade, mesta il cor, 1v, bc, *F-Pn*; Tu giuri ch'è mio quel seno che vedo, 2vv, bc, *GB-Lbm*; Tu sarai sempre il mio bene, 2vv, bc, *I-MOe*; Tutto cinto di ferro, 1v, bc, *GB-Och*; Un amante sen' viene, 2vv, bc, *I-Rvat*; Un cor che non chiede aita, 1v, bc, *GB-Ouf*; Un ferito cavaliero di polve, 1v, bc, *I-Rc*; Un pensier nobile si mi ragiona, 1v, bc, *Rvat*; Un tiranno di foco, 2vv, bc, *Fc*; Uscite di porto, pensieri volanti, 1v, bc, *Rc*; V'è, v'è, che miro, 1v, bc, *Rc*; Viemmi, o sdegno, a difendere, 2vv, bc, *Fc*; Voi siete troppo belle, 1v, bc, *US-LAu*; Vorrei scoprirti un di, 2vv, bc, *GB-Lbm*

For complete list of sources and concordances see Caluori (1965 and 1972)

OTHER VOCAL

Stabat mater; lost, cited in *I-Fn* Magl.XIX.22
Domine, quinque talenta tradidisti mihi, 4vv, bc, *GB-Och*
Exulta jubila mater ecclesia, 2vv, bc, *Och*
O amantissime Jesu dilecte mi, 1v, bc, *I-Rc*
O si quis daret concentum, 3vv, vn, harp, org, *GB-Och*
Peccantem me quotidie, 3vv, bc, *Och*
Summi regis, 2vv, bc, *Och*
2 ariette caudate, 1v, bc; Floret ager, ridet humus; Mundi mentes scena volubilis: *I-Bc*
6 pieces in Canzonette amorosi (Rotterdam, 1656)

INSTRUMENTAL

Passacaille del seigneur Luigi, *F-Pn*
Sarabande en tablature de guitare, gavotte, *Pn*
Sarabanda, balletto, *I-Rvat* (anon., attrib. Rossi in Ghislanzoni, 1954)

BIBLIOGRAPHY

R. Rolland: *Histoire de l'opéra en Europe avant Lully* (Paris, 1895)
——: 'Notes sur l'Orfeo de Luigi Rossi et sur les musiciens italiens à Paris sous Mazarin', *RHCM*, i (1901), 191
H Goldschmidt: *Studien zur Geschichte der italienischen Oper im 17. Jahrhundert* (Leipzig, 1901-4/R1967)
R. Rolland: *Musiciens d'autrefois* (Paris, 1908)
A. Wotquenne: *Etude bibliographique sur le compositeur napolitain Luigi Rossi* (Brussels, 1909)
H. Prunières: 'Notes sur la vie de Luigi Rossi', *SIMG*, xii (1910-11), 12
A. Cametti: 'Alcuni documenti inediti su la vita di Luigi Rossi compositore di musica (1597-1653)', *SIMG*, xiv (1912-13), 1
H. Prunières: 'Les représentations du Palazzo d'Atalanta a Rome', *SIMG*, xiv (1912-13), 218
——: *L'opéra italien en France avant Lulli* (Paris, 1913)
——: 'Notes bibliographiques sur les cantates de Luigi Rossi au Conservatoire de Naples', *ZIMG*, xiv (1912-13), 109
A. Cametti: 'Luigi Rossi, organista a San Luigi de Francesi', *Critica musicale* (Florence, 1919)
P. Nettl: 'Über ein handschriftliches Sammelwerk von Gesängen italienischer Frühmonodie', *ZMw*, ii (1919-20), 83
H. Prunières: 'Les musiciens du Cardinal Antonio Barberini', *Mélanges de musicologie offerts à M. Lionel de la Laurencie* (Paris, 1933), 119
F. Liuzzi: *I musicisti italiani in Francia* (Rome, 1946)
A. Abert: *Claudio Monteverdi und das musikalische Drama* (Lippstadt, 1954)
A. Ghislanzoni: *Luigi Rossi: biografia e analisi delle composizioni* (Milan, 1954)
——: 'Tre oratori e tre cantate morali di Luigi Rossi', *RBM*, ix (1955), 3
E. Caluori: *Luigi Rossi*, WECIS, iii/a-b (1965) [thematic index of Rossi's cantatas]
——: *The Cantatas of Luigi Rossi* (diss., Brandeis U., 1972)
H. E. Smither: *A History of the Oratorio*, i (Chapel Hill, 1977)

ELEANOR CALUORI

Rossi, Mario (*b* Rome, 29 March 1902). Italian conductor. He studied composition with Respighi and conducting with Setaccioli at the Rome Conservatory, graduat-ing in 1925. He first directed a workers' amateur choir in Rome (1923-6), which led to his appointment as deputy conductor, under Bernardino Molinari, of the Augusteo Orchestra, with which he made his début in 1926. He also began to conduct in other Italian cities. In 1936 he left the Augusteo and went to Florence, where he was appointed resident conductor of the Maggio Musicale Orchestra, and conducted his first opera, Mascagni's *Iris*, at the Teatro Comunale in 1937. He remained in Florence until 1944, meanwhile conducting at other theatres, including La Scala. Toscanini, on his return to Italy from the USA in 1945, proposed Rossi as artistic adviser at La Scala, but he preferred to accept a post as resident conductor of the Turin RSO. Under his direction from 1946 to 1969, this became one of the finest Italian symphonic organizations, and was also admired outside Italy. In 1953 he was awarded the Schoenberg Prize for the dissemination of contempor-ary music, and in 1960 he was given the Viotti Gold Medal. A member of the Accademia di S Cecilia and of the Philharmonic Societies of Rome and Bologna, he has also held a course in conducting at the Turin Conservatory. His repertory, mainly symphonic, is ex-tensive, especially in contemporary music, and he has conducted many first performances, including those of several works by Petrassi.

LEONARDO PINZAUTI

Rossi, Michelangelo [Michel Angelo del Violino] (*b* Genoa, 1601-2; *d* Rome, buried 7 July 1656). Italian composer, violinist and organist. He was one of the lead-ing 17th-century Italian composers of keyboard music.

1. LIFE. The recently discovered record of Rossi's burial has dispelled uncertainties regarding his dates, origins and later career. In the register of S Andrea delle Fratte, Rome, the entry for 7 July 1656 records that

Michel Angelo Rossi of Genoa, son of Carlo Rossi, an excellent musician and particularly fine violinist aged 54, who lived in the house of Signor Thimoteo Ximenes in the Via Gregoriana . . . and died after a long illness, was buried in our church near the chapel of S Elena.

His uncle, Lelio Rossi, who was a Servite friar, was principal organist at the cathedral of S Lorenzo, Genoa, from 1601 to 1638. From a payment made on 26 June 1620, it is apparent that he was his uncle's assistant for a time. By 1624 he had moved to Rome and become a musician in the service of Cardinal Maurizio of Savoy, son of Duke Carlo Emanuele I of Savoy and patron of Sigismondo d'India. Not only must he have made con-tact with d'India, but it must have been at this time that he first came under the influence of Frescobaldi, who became his teacher and friend. In 1629 he travelled with the cardinal to the Savoy court at Turin and took part in a performance there of the opera *Arione* by the lutenist Paolo Bisogni.

Returning to Rome in 1630, Rossi moved into the circles of the Barberini family, the most powerful patrons in the city during the papacy of Urban VIII (Maffeo Barberini). It was to the wife of Don Taddeo Barberini, the Prefect of Rome and nephew of the pope, that he dedicated his opera *Erminia sul Giordano*. The first performance took place in the theatre of the Palazzo Barberini on 2 February 1633, and the work was revived and published in 1637. The description of the performance in the introduction to the published score and the accompanying illustrations of the designs leave no doubt as to the spectacular nature of Bernini's sets and Guitti's production. Rossi himself took part as

Engraving showing the walls of Jerusalem from the first edition of the score of Rossi's 'Erminia sul Giordano' (Rome: Paolo Masotti, 1637)

Apollo, playing the violin 'on the loftiest part of the chariot' borne by the Muses.

In 1638 he travelled north. His activities included service for the Este family at Modena and composition of the opera *Andromeda* for the wedding of Cornelio Bentivoglio and Costanza Sforza at Ferrara. He therefore enjoyed the patronage of three of the most influential families in northern Italy. An eye injury prevented a projected visit to Venice in the spring of 1639, but in May of that year he was involved in celebrations at Bologna for Cardinal Antonio Barberini, another of the pope's nephews. References to his appointment as *maestro di cappella* at Forlì in the same year have recently been questioned: such a move would indeed seem out of character with the pattern of his career. Moreover there is a reference in a Florentine document of 1641 to 'Angelo de Rossi' as 'musico del duca Sforza'. In due course he returned to Rome, and there is evidence of his association with Lelio Colista, Athanasius Kircher and Caspar Schott in 1652. The suggestion that he was working at Faenza in 1670 can now be dismissed.

2. WORKS. Rossi's contemporary fame in the sphere of instrumental music was as a virtuoso violinist; it earned him the nickname 'Michel Angelo del Violino', and his outstanding playing is mentioned in the descriptions of his two known operas. But it is his keyboard music that has survived. The first edition of his ten toccatas and ten correntes bears the Barberini arms but no date or dedication. The addition by a later hand of the date 1640 on the sole surviving copy (in *I-Bc*) may not be far wrong; certainly the implied patronage of the Barberini family suggests that it was published before their voluntary exile from Rome in 1644, after the death of Pope Urban VIII. The second edition (1657) bears the arms of the Aldobrandini family. Stylistically, Rossi's music may be compared with that of his teacher, Frescobaldi, especially the second volume of toccatas (1627), and also with that of Froberger. He continued to write in the tradition of the quasi-improvised Neapolitan toccata, and like Frescobaldi he used slow opening chords, short

impetuous figures often in Lombard rhythm, unusual harmonic juxtapositions and sections of brilliant passage-work. What his pieces lack is the emotive tension of Frescobaldi's harmonic style, which persistently delays or interrupts cadences, and the rhetoric and drama of Frescobaldi's total concept of the toccata. His own harmonic style is more regular in both pace and progressions, and his figuration has more consistent patterns. These features are also found in Froberger's toccatas, and they point towards the breakdown of this type of toccata. Rossi also included imitative sections in the toccatas; this practice recalls the north Italian toccatas of Merulo, but the style and texture recall Frescobaldi's canzonas of 1627. In some cases he also used the technique of thematic variation found throughout Frescobaldi's canzona output. Only in the seventh toccata is there any extensive chromatic writing. The correntes are not far removed from the style of Frescobaldi's short dance movements, and they display the same economy of texture; some, however, are longer and include imitative writing. Keyboard sonatas by the 18th-century composer Lorenzo de Rossi have in the past been wrongly attributed to Michelangelo Rossi, and a toccata in A, added to a manuscript copy of five of Rossi's toccatas (in *GB-Lbm* Add.24313), and in other sources and editions ascribed to Purcell and Bach, appears to belong to a later period, probably about 1700 or shortly after (see Rose).

Erminia sul Giordano, the libretto of which is based on the sixth and seventh cantos of Tasso's *Gerusalemme liberata*, indicates contemporary trends in Roman opera. Moving away from the extended declamatory passages of the early Florentine operas, the recitatives are in general functional, if more melodious. Far more emphasis is placed on the ensembles and choruses, where much of the most interesting music is to be found.

WORKS

Erminia sul Giordano (G. Rospigliosi), opera (Rome, 1637), Rome, Palazzo Barberini, 2 Feb 1633; extracts ed. in Goldschmidt, 258ff
Andromeda (A. Pio), Ferrara, Palazzo Ducale, 1638, music lost
2 It. arias, 1v, bc, *I-Vc*

Toccate e correnti, org/hpd (Rome, n.d., [?1640], 2/1657); ed. in AMI,

iii (*c*1900); ed. in CEKM, xv (1966)
4 toccatas, 2 versetti, 4 Partite sopra la Romanesca, kbd, *Bc* (added in MS to 1657 edn. of Toccate e correnti); ed. in CEKM, xv (1966)

BIBLIOGRAPHY

Archivio segreto vaticano, sezione Vicariato di Roma, S Andrea delle Fratte, morti, iii (1647–85), f.104*v*

E. von Werra: 'M. A. Rossi, ein Komponist des 17. Jahrhunderts', *MMg*, xxviii (1896), 122, 141

L. Torchi: 'La musica strumentale in Italia nei secoli XVI, XVII, XVIII', *RMI*, v (1898), 485; repr. in book form (Turin, 1901)

H. Goldschmidt: *Studien zur Geschichte der italienischen Oper im 17. Jahrhundert,* i (Leipzig, 1901/*R*1967), 62ff, 258ff

G. Gaspari: *Catalogo della Biblioteca del Liceo musicale di Bologna,* iv (Bologna, 1905/*R*1961), 62

H. Prunières: *L'opéra italien en France avant Lulli* (Paris, 1913), 12f

A. Toni: 'M. A. Rossi: cenni biografici', *Bollettino bibliografico musicale,* ii/6 (1927), 1

S. Cordero di Pamparato: 'I musici alla corte di Carlo Emanuele I di Savoia', *Biblioteca della Società storico subalpina,* new ser., cxxi (1930), 31–142

U. Rolandi: 'L'Andromeda musicata da M. A. Rossi (1638)', *Rassegna dorica,* iii (1931–2), 48

G. Frotscher: *Geschichte des Orgel-Spiels und der Orgel-Komposition,* i (Berlin, 1935, enlarged 3/1966)

R. Giazotto: *La musica a Genova nella vita pubblica e privata dal XIII al XVII secolo* (Genoa, 1951), 171f, 268

F. W. Riedel: *Quellenkundliche Beiträge zur Geschichte der Musik für Tasteninstrumente in der zweiten Hälfte des 17. Jahrhunderts* (Kassel, 1960), 71f

H. Wessely-Kropik: *Lelio Colista* (Vienna, 1961), 37ff

W. Apel: *Geschichte des Orgel- und Klaviermusik bis 1700* (Kassel, 1967); Eng. trans., rev. (1972), 486ff

G. Rose: 'Purcell, Michelangelo Rossi and J. S. Bach: Problems of Authorship', *AcM,* xl (1968), 203

S. Towneley: 'Early Italian Opera', *NOHM,* iv (1968), 838ff

O. Wessely: 'Aus römischen Bibliotheken und Archiven', *Symbolae historiae musicae: Hellmut Federhofer zum 60. Geburtstag* (Mainz, 1971), 81f

E. Darbellay: 'Peut-on découvrir des indications d'articulation dans la graphie des tablatures de clavier de Claudio Merulo, Girolamo Frescobaldi et Michel-Angelo Rossi?', *IMSCR, xi Copenhagen 1972,* 342

L. Bianconi and T. Walker: 'Dalla *Finta pazza* alla *Veremonda*: storie di Febiarmonici', *RIM,* x (1975), 440

M. K. Murata: *Operas for the Papal Court with Texts by Giulio Rospigliosi* (diss., U. of Chicago, 1975)

J. H. Peterson: *The Keyboard Works of Michelangelo Rossi* (diss., U. of Illinois, 1975)

A. Silbiger: 'The Roman Frescobaldi Tradition, c. 1640–1670', *JAMS,* xxxiii (1980), 42–87

JOHN HARPER

Rossi, Salamone [Salomone, Salamon de', Shlomo] (*b* ?Mantua, probably 19 Aug 1570; *d* ?Mantua, *c*1630). Italian composer and instrumentalist. He is specially important for his contribution to the development of the trio sonata and chamber duet.

1. LIFE. Since his first published work, the *Canzonette* of 1589, contains 19 pieces, was dedicated on 19 August 1589 and includes a table of contents whose initial letters include the acrostic VIVAT S R, it is probable that Rossi was born on 19 August 1570. Zunz and Werner (1959) claimed that he was the son of the distinguished historian Azariah de' Rossi, but the latter himself noted in his *Meor enayim* (Mantua, 1573) that he had no surviving son. The theory, advanced by Einstein (1950–51), that there were two composers of this name is now generally discredited (it was based mainly on the fact that in their dedications Rossi described both the *Canzonette* and *Il primo libro de madrigali a 5 voci* as his first works). It seems likely that Rossi was born in Mantua. He spent his entire professional career there and had strong connections with the Gonzaga court. He was presumably too young to contribute to *L'amorosa caccia* (Venice, 1588), an anthology of pieces by Mantuan-born composers, but his first three publications suggest contact with the court. The book of canzonettas is dedicated to Duke Vincenzo Gonzaga and opens with a piece in honour of the duke and duchess; the first book of five-part madrigals is again dedicated to Vincenzo, with the acknowledgment that 'under the happy shade of your service I have learnt everything'; and the second book is dedicated to the Marquis of Pallazuolo, a prominent member of the Mantuan court. Rossi was evidently well regarded by Vincenzo, since the compulsory wearing of the yellow badge, introduced as part of the restrictions imposed on the Jewish community in response to popular agitation during the early part of Vincenzo's rule, was relaxed in his case by ducal decree in 1606; this privilege was renewed by the new duke, Francesco II, only six days after his accession in 1612. Later, however, Rossi's relations with the court seem to have become less close, and that he dedicated none of his later works either to Gonzagas or to members of the court is consistent with the general impression of a decline in the musical life of the court in the years following Vincenzo's death.

Despite the implications of his above-quoted remark in the dedication of his first book of five-part madrigals – which are probably no more than a piece of extravagant lip-service – it should not be assumed that Rossi was a permanent or official member of the Gonzaga musical establishment, though he was salaried there for some isolated years. Leo da Modena's comment in the preface to *Hashirim asher lish'lomo* that he 'succeeded by his abilities in rising to the position of the singers in the Duke of Mantua's choir' can only refer to his comparative stature and talent since he is recorded in the Mantuan archives only as an occasional instrumentalist, does not appear in the salary rolls of S Barbara and in any case would presumably have been debarred from such a position because of his Jewish faith. So although he was not one of the seven court violists recorded in a Mantuan salary list of 1599, he did appear in the *Registrati de' musici straordinarii* (in *I-MAc*) between 1587 and 1600, and Bertolotti noted a further payment for viol playing in 1622. It seems likely for a variety of reasons that his principal professional connections were with one of the Jewish theatrical troupes that played such a significant role in Mantuan theatrical life, not only in the ghetto but also in the Christian community and at court. This assumption is reinforced by a memorandum from Carlo Rossi to the duke on 27 February 1608 reporting Salamone's selection as the composer of the first of the five *intermedi*, to texts by Chiabrera, that were to accompany the performance of Guarini's comedy *L'idropica*, planned for presentation at Mantua on 2 June 1608 as part of the festivities celebrating the marriage of Francesco Gonzaga to Marguerite of Savoy. He also contributed a balletto to the incidental music for G. B. Andreini's *La Maddalena*, given in 1617. Moreover, in 1612 Alessandro Pico, Prince of Mirandola, to whom he dedicated his third book of five-part madrigals, requested that he and 'his group of musicians' be sent to Mirandola to entertain the Duke of Modena and other guests.

With the exception of the virtuoso singer known as Madama Europa who was his sister, Rossi was probably not related to any of the other Mantuan musicians with the same surname. Both Carlo and Mattheo Rossi must have been Christians (or converts) since they appear in the salary rolls of the ducal chapel of S Barbara, and the same is true of Anselmo Rossi, who contributed one piece to a motet collection (*RISM* 1618[4]). The dedication of Rossi's last published work is dated 3 January 1628. He may well have perished during the destruction of the ghetto and the severe plague that followed the sack of Mantua at the hands of the imperial troops in July 1630.

2. WORKS. Rossi's music has often been misrepresented as a result of the blanket application of preconceived concepts of periodization and the consequent highlighting of what are believed to be 'proto-Baroque' elements in it. Most of the pieces in the five books of five-part madrigals, however, are cast in a light, sonorous style that breathes the freshness and spirit of the pastoral Marenzio and the early Monteverdi. Much has been made of his inclusion of a basso continuo part in the second book (1602), following hard upon his experiment with an accompanying chitarrone tablature in the first (1600). These are indeed the first published examples of continuo madrigals, but they are rather tame. Moreover, current knowledge of the way in which vocal music was accompanied by instruments, supported by the evidence of sources as early and disparate as the explicit reference to a type of continuo part in Diego Ortiz's *Tratado de glosas* (1553) and the surviving organ bass part to a 40-part motet *Ecce beatam lucem* (1568) by Alessandro Striggio (i), suggests that this may be no more than printed confirmation of a well-established performing practice. Significantly, the basso continuo part for the second book was not issued separately but was printed opposite the cantus part after the traditional arrangement of lute tablatures. Again, no figures appear in this book, and few occur in the third (1603); only the last two books (1610, 1622) are provided with genuine, figured continuo parts. The overwhelming conservatism of the music in all five books also characterizes the four-part volume, the very appearance of which as late as 1614 must be regarded as archaic: only a handful of books of four-part pieces were published after 1600, mostly by Neapolitan and Sicilian composers. Ten of the texts are by Guarini, and seven of these are from *Il pastor fido*. On grounds of poetic taste and musical style, Newman has suggested that the pieces in the book date from 1600–03, a hypothesis supported by the enthusiasm for the play at Mantua during this period and by the keen interest generally aroused by the publication of the Ciotti edition at Venice in 1602. Yet the impression of comfortable stylistic uniformity throughout the madrigal books may be misplaced, since of the fifth five-part book, which contains a number of pieces described as *madrigali concertati*, only the continuo part survives, and other exceptions are the six similarly labelled pieces in the first book, which can be performed either by five voices or as solo songs.

Traditional approaches certainly characterize *Hashirim asher lish'lomo* ('The Songs of Solomon'), a collection of 33 polyphonic settings of Hebrew psalms, hymns and synagogal songs whose importance has perhaps been overemphasized by Jewish liturgists. Moreover, Adler's studies strongly suggest that even within the traditions of synagogal music Rossi's collection is not the isolated example of concerted music before the 19th-century liturgical reforms that it was once thought to be. The existence of *cori spezzati* fragments written out around 1630–50 (see Werner, 1943–4) and thought to

Title-page of Salamone Rossi's 'Hashirim asher lish'lomo' (*Venice: Pietro & Lorenzo Bragadino, 1622–3*)

have emanated from Leo da Modena's Jewish musical academy in Venice may suggest that *The Songs of Solomon* formed part of the repertory of some other such body. The title of the collection is probably a pun on Rossi's name, since none of the texts, though largely taken from the Old Testament, actually comes from *The Song of Solomon*. The style of the music reflects not only the expected influences of Mantuan colleagues, particularly Monteverdi, and, in the three-part pieces, the ballettos and canzonettas of Gastoldi, but also, in the works for larger forces, the music of the Venetian school. *L'mi ehpots*, a setting of a text in the popular Jewish verse form of the wedding ode, is an echo dialogue whose ornamented final cadence borrows the gestures of secular monody.

It is in his lighter vocal pieces and in his instrumental music that Rossi appears at his most novel and prophetic. The three-part canzonettas comprise a variety of musical and poetic types, though most of them are genuine canzonettas for two high voices and a tenor or baritone. *Voi che seguit'il ciec'ardor* is unusual in its use of *terza rima* with sdrucciola rhythms, and *Mirate che mi fa* is almost a madrigal in three sections, with an extended last line. Rossi's most important achievement is his contribution to the transformation of the instrumental canzona, with its homogeneous texture, into the trio sonata, with its prominent equal upper parts and supporting bass. This development, which was influenced by the characteristic textures exhibited by the virtuoso singers at the Ferrarese and Mantuan courts in the late 1580s and 1590s, occurs mostly in the sinfonias of his instrumental collections rather than in the dance movements. Some of the dances, which are characterized by a polarization of upper and lower parts, are named after members of the nobility or after other composers, such as 'La Cecchina' (Francesca Caccini), or are based on popular bass melodic patterns. Although the chitarrone part is unfigured, it functions as a true continuo part, and the presence of dynamic markings is a typical feature of the emergence of instrumental music as a separate genre. The sinfonias, which may have been meant as instrumental preludes in the manner of the lutenists' ricercares or *tastar da corde* or the instrumental ritornellos which occur in some of Ludovico Agostini's madrigals, are so clearly related in texture and structure to the *Canzonette* of 1589 that the influence of the one style upon the other seems indisputable. While the sinfonias are essentially textless canzonettas, the *Madrigaletti* of 1628, which include two strophic arias with short instrumental ritornellos between the strophes, are finely wrought early examples of the short duet so successfully cultivated by Monteverdi and later by Carissimi and Luigi Rossi. Yet despite the intriguing transitional features here and in the instrumental music, Rossi's contemporaries, inasmuch as they admired his music at all, preferred the comparatively bland style of the concerted pieces from the first set of five-part madrigals, though Francis Tregian did copy madrigals from the third book into his manuscript score (in *GB-Lbm*). Weelkes was also evidently acquainted with Rossi's music: his settings of *I bei ligustri e rose* and *Donna, il vostro bel viso* in the *Ayeres or Phantasticke Spirites* (1608), which are clearly related to his five-voice settings of English versions of the same texts in the *Madrigals to 3, 4, 5 and 6 Voices* (1597), are so close to Rossi's settings of the same texts in his *Canzonette a tre voci* that it is difficult to believe that Weelkes had not actually seen Rossi's versions.

WORKS

Editions: *S. Rossi: Cantiques,* ed. S. Naumbourg and V. d'Indy (Paris, 1877) [N]

Sinfonie, Gagliarde, Canzone, i, ii, ed. J. Newman and F. Rikko (New York, 1965) [R]

(all published in Venice)

SECULAR VOCAL

Il primo libro delle canzonette, 3vv (1589); ed. H. Avenary (Tel-Aviv, 1976)

Il primo libro de madrigali . . . con alcuni di detti madrigali nel chittarrone, 5vv, chit (1600); 11 in N

Il secondo libro de madrigali, 5vv, bc . . . ed un dialogo, 8vv, nel fine (1602)

Il terzo libro de madrigali, con una canzona de baci nel fine, 5vv, bc (1603)

Il quarto libro de madrigali, 5vv, bc (1610); 11 in N

Il primo libro de madrigali, 4vv, bc (1614)

Il quinto libro de madrigali, 5vv, bc (1622)

Madrigaletti per cantar a due soprani o tenori, 2vv, op.13 (1628); 6 ed. L. Landshoff, *Alte Meister des Bel Canto,* iv–v (Leipzig, 1927)

Balletto, 3vv, 1617[3]

SACRED VOCAL

Hashirim asher lish'lomo, 3–8vv, ed. Leo da Modena (1622–3); ed. F. Rikko (New York, 1967–73); 30 in N

INSTRUMENTAL

Il primo libro delle sinfonie e gagliarde . . . per sonar, 2 va/cornetts, chit/other inst (1607); 5 in R i, 6 in R ii, 1 in appx

Il secondo libro delle sinfonie e gagliarde, a 3, per sonar . . . con alcune delle dette a 4, 5, ed alcune canzoni per sonar, a 4, nel fine, vas, chit (1608); 8 in R i, 6 in R ii

Il terzo libro di varie sonate, sinfonie, gagliarde, brandi e corrente, 2 va da braccio, chit/other inst, op.12 (1623)

Il quarto libro di varie sonate, sinfonie, gagliarde, brandi e corrente, 2 vn, chit (1622); 1 in R, appx

BIBLIOGRAPHY

L. Zunz: *Kerem chemed,* v (1841), 132

F. I. Papotti: 'Annali o memorie storiche della Mirandola, i: 1500–1673', *Memorie storiche della città e dell'antico ducato della Mirandola,* iii (1876), 99 n.2

S. Naumbourg: *Essai sur la vie et les oeuvres de Salamon Rossi* (Paris, 1877; It. trans., 1974)

P. Canal: *Della musica in Mantova* (Venice, 1881)

A. Ademollo: *La bell'Adriana ed altre virtuose del suo tempo* (Città da Castello, 1888), 29ff

A. Bertolotti: *Musici alla corte dei Gonzaga in Mantova dal secolo XV al secolo XVIII* (Milan, 1890/R1969), 68

A. d'Ancona: *Origini del teatro italiano,* ii (Turin, 1891), appx ii, chap.5: 'Gli ebrei di Mantova e il teatro'

E. Birnbaum: *Jüdische Musiker am Hofe zu Mantua von 1542–1628* (Vienna, 1893; Eng. trans., rev., enlarged 1978)

A. Solerti: *Gli albori del melodramma* (Milan, 1904/R1969), i, 92

P. Nettl: 'Musicisti ebrei del rinascimento italiano', *Rassegna mensile di Israel,* ii (1926), 69ff

——: 'Some Early Jewish Musicians', *MQ,* xvii (1931), 40

E. Werner: 'The Edward Birnbaum Collection of Jewish Music', *Hebrew Union College Annual,* xviii (1943–4), 407

P. Gradenwitz: 'An Early Instance of Copyright, Venice 1622', *ML,* xxvii (1946), 185

A. Einstein: *The Italian Madrigal* (Princeton, 1949/R1971)

——: 'Salamone Rossi as Madrigal Composer', *Hebrew Union College Annual,* xxiii (1950–51), 383

W. S. Newman: *The Sonata in the Baroque Era* (Chapel Hill, 1959, rev. 2/1966/R1972)

C. Roth: *The Jews in the Renaissance* (Philadelphia, 1959), 285ff

E. Werner: *The Sacred Bridge* (London, 1959), 404

J. Newman: *The Madrigals of Salamon de' Rossi* (diss., Columbia U., 1962)

S. Simonsohn: *Toldoth ha-jehudim he-duchsuth Mantova* [History of the Jews in the duchy of Mantua] (Jerusalem, 1962–4)

I. Adler: *La pratique musicale savante dans quelques communautés juives en Europe aux XVIIe et XVIIIe siècles* (Paris, 1966)

——: 'The Rise of Art Music in the Italian Ghetto: the Influence of Segregation on Jewish Musical Praxis', *Jewish Medieval and Renaissance Studies,* ed. A. Altmann (Cambridge, Mass., 1967), 321–64

P. M. Tagmann: 'La cappella dei maestri cantori della basilica palatina di Santa Barbara a Mantova (1565–1630): nuovo materiale scoperto negli archivi mantovani', *Civiltà mantovana,* iv/24 (1970), 386

J. Newman and F. Rikko: *A Thematic Index to the Works of Salamon Rossi* (Hackensack, NJ, 1972)

W. Apel: 'Studien über die frühe Violinmusik', *AMw,* xxx (1973), 153–74; xxxi (1974), 185–213

IAIN FENLON

Rossi Codex (*I-Rvat* Rossi 215). *See* SOURCES, MS, §VIII, 2.

Rossignol (Fr.). A bird-imitating ORGAN STOP (*Vogelgesang*).

Rossignol, Félix Ludger. *See* JONCIÈRES, VICTORIN DE.

Rossi-Lemeni, Nicola (*b* Istanbul, 6 Nov 1920). Italian bass. A pupil of his mother, Xenia Macadon, a singing teacher of Russian origin, and of Carnevali-Cusinati, he made his début at La Fenice, Venice, in 1946 as Varlaam in *Boris Godunov,* a role he repeated in 1947 at La Scala, where he continued to appear until 1960. He has sung in all the major Italian theatres and also at Buenos Aires (1949 and several later seasons), San Francisco (1951–3), Covent Garden (1952, as Boris), the Metropolitan (1953–4), Chicago and other houses. An interpreter of marked intelligence and sensitivity both musical and dramatic, and originally endowed with a smooth, mellow and well-focussed voice, at first he was heard as Boris, Philip II, and Mephistopheles (Gounod and Boito). Later in his career he compensated for his premature vocal decline with eloquent phrasing, vigorous declamation and the versatility of his temperament, and specialized in modern operas such as Pizzetti's *L'assassinio nella cattedrale* (première at La Scala, 1958, and elsewhere), *Wozzeck,* Bloch's *Macbeth* and Britten's *Billy Budd* (first Italian performance,

Florence, 1965). He has a degree in law and the title of Grand Officer of the Order of Merit of the Italian Republic. His second wife is the soprano Virginia Zeani.

BIBLIOGRAPHY

R. Celletti: 'Rossi-Lemeni, Nicola', *Le grandi voci* (Rome, 1964) [with opera discography]

RODOLFO CELLETTI

Rossini, Gioachino (Antonio) (*b* Pesaro, 29 Feb 1792; *d* Passy, 13 Nov 1868). Italian composer. No composer in the first half of the 19th century enjoyed the measure of prestige, wealth, popular acclaim or artistic influence that belonged to Rossini. His contemporaries recognized him as the greatest Italian composer of his time. His achievements cast into oblivion the operatic world of Cimarosa and Paisiello, creating new standards against which other composers were to be judged. That both Bellini and Donizetti carved out personal styles is undeniable; but they worked under Rossini's shadow, and their artistic personalities emerged in confrontation with his operas. Not until the advent of Verdi was Rossini replaced at the centre of Italian operatic life.

Yet the image of Rossini as man and artist remains distorted. As a man he most often appears the indolent raconteur, the gourmet, the spirit of an elegant Second Empire salon. This image results largely from the nature of extant biographical sources. Almost all surviving documentation concerning Rossini's life derives from the period after he withdrew from operatic composition in 1829. Of his active career little is known but what Stendhal related in his brilliant but unreliable *Vie de Rossini*, what Rossini recounted to visitors in Paris some 40 years later, and what can be pieced together from the bald facts of his performed works and a few surviving early letters. The fascinating insights into a composer's growth that can be gleaned from the correspondence of Bellini or Verdi, the interrelations of the composer and his librettists, the aesthetic creeds formulated in moments of artistic inspiration, all these are totally lacking.

The general view of Rossini the composer is equally mistaken. Until recently Rossini's historical position was distorted by the prominence of his great comic operas, which are among the last and finest representatives of *buffo* style. His ties with the 18th century were consequently emphasized, while his position in the 19th was misunderstood. Superb as the *buffo* operas are, Rossini is historically more important as a composer of *opera seria*. He threw off 18th-century formulae and codified new conventions that dominated Italian opera for half a century. Between 1810 and 1850 Italian opera was reformed in many ways: techniques of singing and melodic style altered drastically; the Romantic theatre routed dramatic conventions that had tyrannized both theatre and opera, thus offering a new wellspring of operatic subjects and techniques; the self-image of the composer changed, that of the craftsman giving way to that of the creative artist, while each individual work of art consequently gained new significance. But throughout, Italian opera depended upon the musical forms, the style of orchestration, the rhythmic vitality and the role of music in defining and shaping the drama first developed fully in the operas of Rossini.

1. Early years. 2. First period, 1810–13. 3. From 'Tancredi' to 'La gazza ladra'. 4. Naples and the opera seria, 1815–23. 5. Europe and Paris, 1822–9. 6. Retirement. 7. A new life.

1. EARLY YEARS. Rossini was born in Pesaro, a small city on the Adriatic in the region known as the Marches, on 29 February 1792. His immediate paternal ancestors can be traced in Lugo, while his mother's family came from Urbino. Both his parents were musicians. Giuseppe Antonio Rossini was a horn player of some ability, having preceded his son into membership in the Bologna Accademia Filarmonica in 1801. During his early career he performed in military bands and served the ceremonial function of public *trombetta*, the position he obtained in Pesaro when he took up residence there in 1790. The building into which he moved also housed the Guidarini family, whose daughter Anna he married on 26 September 1791.

Rossini's earliest years, spent in Pesaro, were not peaceful. The Napoleonic wars, bringing with them French and papal soldiers in confusing alternation, were particularly hard on Giuseppe, whose enthusiasm for the cause of liberty displeased the papal authorities and resulted in his brief imprisonment in 1800. Memories of his father's misadventures may have dampened Gioachino's enthusiasm for Italian nationalism later in his life. The child was frequently left with his maternal grandmother while his parents toured opera houses in the region, his father playing in the orchestra, his mother singing small roles.

By the time the family moved to Lugo in 1802, Rossini's father was teaching him to play the horn, while a local canon, Giuseppe Malerbi, whose musical knowledge and fine collection of scores seem to have exercised a generally beneficent influence on the child's musical taste, instructed him in singing. After a throat ailment forced Anna to retire from her theatrical career, the family established permanent residence in Bologna. That Gioachino was immensely gifted as a singer must have been soon apparent, for in June 1806 he followed his father into the Accademia Filarmonica, a singular honour for so young a man. His early musical activities are poorly documented, but they certainly included singing (his performance as the boy, Adolfo, in Paer's *Camilla* at the Teatro del Corso in Bologna during the autumn season of 1805 is attested to by a libretto printed for the occasion), composition (several works appear to predate his formal instruction, in particular the six *sonate a quattro* probably written in 1804) and instrumental performance (he often served as *maestro al cembalo* in theatres during this period).

In Bologna, Rossini studied music privately with Padre Angelo Tesei. His progress was rapid and by April 1806 he was able to enter the Liceo Musicale. There he followed courses in singing, the cello, piano and, most important, counterpoint under Padre Stanislao Mattei, the director of the Liceo and successor to Padre Martini. Rossini, always an eminently practical man, did not react well to the more esoteric processes of counterpoint. He later reported to his friend Edmond Michotte that Mattei considered him the 'dishonour of his school'. Nonetheless, Rossini profited enormously from prolonged exposure to more 'serious' musical styles than those prevailing in Italian theatres. He devoured the music of Haydn and Mozart, later referring to Mozart as 'the admiration of my youth, the desperation of my mature years, the consolation of my old age', and was forced to submit to exercises in strict composition. Though he culled only what could be of direct use to him in a practical career, the sureness of his harmony, clarity of his part-writing (hardly marred by occasional 'forbidden' progressions) and precision of his orchestration derive ultimately from this traditional training.

During his student years Rossini wrote little: a few instrumental pieces, some sacred music (including a mass) and a rather poor cantata, *Il pianto d'Armonia sulla morte d'Orfeo*, which nonetheless won a prize at the Liceo and was performed there for an academic convocation on 11 August 1808. It is often said that he supplied many arias for insertion into operas performed in Bologna, but this claim has never been systematically investigated. His first opera was commissioned, perhaps as early as 1807, by the tenor Domenico Mombelli, who together with his two daughters formed the nucleus of an operatic troupe. As Rossini later told Ferdinand Hiller, Mombelli asked him to set some numbers from a libretto entitled *Demetrio e Polibio*. Not even knowing the entire plot, he proceeded one number at a time until the entire score was finished. Though this was Rossini's first opera, it was not performed until 1812, after four other works had brought the young composer advance publicity. It is not clear how much of the opera is Rossini's and how much may have been supplied or tampered with by Mombelli; but with it Rossini was initiated into the realities of Italian operatic life.

2. FIRST PERIOD, 1810–13. The first decade of the 19th century was a period of transition in Italian opera. The deposited mantles of Cimarosa and Paisiello were unfilled. The Neapolitan *buffo* tradition was in decline, and the operas of Farinelli or Fioravanti merely repeated its gestures without its substance. Though the conventional world of Metastasian *opera seria* had dissolved, the future was murky. Composers set heavily revised Metastasian texts, or imitations of them, to music in which typical 18th-century devices were precariously balanced with more progressive features. The simple tonal procedures of older *opera seria* were inadequate for longer ensembles and elaborate scenas, yet no Italian composer could or would adopt the more sophisticated tonal schemes of Mozart. As librettos turned from classical history to semi-serious subjects, medieval epic, and ultimately Romantic drama, the orchestral forces of the 18th century proved increasingly inadequate. As characters emerged from the cardboard figures of earlier days, melodic lines required more careful delineation, while the indiscriminate improvisation of vocal ornaments became less palatable. As Italian composers such as Paisiello, Cherubini and Spontini travelled to other European capitals, particularly Paris, Italian opera felt the influence of other national schools.

These challenges to a dying tradition drew little response from even the best composers of the decade, Giovanni Simone Mayr or Ferdinand Paer. Though they brought new orchestral richness to Italian opera and began to construct larger scenic complexes than were found in the post-Metastasian period, they seemed incapable of fusing a new style from the disparate elements demanding their attention. Stendhal, in his forthright manner, found these composers essentially wanting. Mayr was learned, able, 'the most correct composer', but only with Rossini did a composer of genius appear. Indeed, for Stendhal, Rossini's very earliest works are his best, with *Tancredi* an apotheosis of the freshness that illuminates them. One need not follow Stendhal in denigrating Rossini's mature operas in order to recognize the charm of his first operas. Amid the

resplendent glories of *Guillaume Tell* one can still yearn with Stendhal for 'the freshness of the morning of life', the spontaneity and sheer melodic beauty of a piece such as the duet 'Questo cor ti giura amore' from *Demetrio e Polibio*.

Rossini's operatic career began in earnest in 1810, with a commission from the Teatro S Moisè of Venice to compose the music for Gaetano Rossi's one-act *farsa*, *La cambiale di matrimonio*. According to a student of Giovanni Morandi, cited by Radiciotti, a German composer scheduled to write the opera reneged on his contract. Through the good offices of Morandi and his wife, the singer Rosa Morandi, friends of the Rossinis, the inexperienced Gioachino was approached instead. It was a fortunate opportunity, as he later recalled:

That theatre also made possible a simple début for young composers, as it was for Mayr, Generali, Pavesi, Farinelli, Coccia, etc, and for me too in 1810. . . . The expenses of the impresario were minimal since, except for a good company of singers (without chorus), they were limited to the expenses for a single set for each *farsa*, a modest staging, and a few days of rehearsals. From this it is evident that everything tended to facilitate the début of a novice composer, who could, better than in a four- or five-act opera, sufficiently expose his innate fantasy (if Heaven had granted it to him) and his technical skill (if he had mastered it).

Five of Rossini's first nine operas were written for the S Moisè.

It was a full year before Rossini's next opera, *L'equivoco stravagante*, was performed in Bologna on 26 October 1811. The libretto, in which the heroine's poor lover convinces the rich imbecile preferred by her father that the girl is really a eunuch disguised as a woman, was considered in such bad taste that the Bolognese authorities closed the show after three performances. But Rossini had no time to be upset by this fiasco, since the Teatro S Moisè was already awaiting his next *farsa*. *L'inganno felice*, which had its Venetian première in January 1812, was Rossini's first truly successful work, remaining popular throughout Italy during the next decade.

Commissions from other theatres followed rapidly. Despite statements from writers north of the Alps about the decadence of Italian music in this period, operatic life was in one sense remarkably healthy. Many important centres existed, and theatres and impresarios sought to outdo one another in obtaining new works, exploring new talent, training new musicians. That there was much bad music composed and performed is undeniable, but a flourishing, lively culture could give a composer the opportunity to come to maturity, and Rossini did not lack for opportunity. His sacred opera *Ciro in Babilonia* was presented in Ferrara during Lent, followed by yet another work for S Moisè, *La scala di seta*. The pinnacle of Rossini's first period, though, was the première of his two-act *La pietra del paragone*, at the Teatro alla Scala, Milan, on 26 September 1812. Just as Verdi, 30 years later, was assisted by Giuseppina Strepponi in obtaining his entrée to La Scala, so Rossini benefited from the recommendations of two singers who had taken part in his earlier operas, Maria Marcolini and Filippo Galli, both of whom were to sing in the cast of *La pietra del paragone*. The work was an unquestionable triumph. Rossini told Hiller that it earned him exemption from military service. He hurried back to Venice, where he composed two more *farse* for the Teatro S Moisè, *L'occasione fa il ladro* and *Il Signor Bruschino*. It is distressing that, 50 years after Radiciotti destroyed the myth of the latter opera's being a jest at the impresario's expense, the story continues to circulate. *Il Signor Bruschino* is perhaps the best of Rossini's early *farse*, comic, witty and sentimental by turns. The famous sinfonia, in which the violins occasionally beat out rhythms with their bows against the metal shades of their candle holders or, in modern times, against their music stands, is delightful both for its absurdity and for the totally natural and logical way in which the effect is woven into the composition.

In the 16 months from *L'equivoco stravagante* to *Il Signor Bruschino*, Rossini composed seven operas. With the sheer press of commitments on him, he often used individual pieces in more than one opera. Though famous examples of self-borrowing are found later in his life, no compositions ever saw such service as two from *Demetrio e Polibio*, the duet 'Questo cor ti giura amore' mentioned above (which reappeared in five later operas) and the quartet 'Donami omai Siveno' (about which Stendhal wrote, 'had Rossini written this quartet alone, Mozart and Cimarosa would have recognized him as their equal'). One can understand, if not wholly respect, the insouciance with which Rossini simplified his task of grinding out so many operas. What is remarkable is how much fine music they contain.

Rossini's *farse* and *La pietra del paragone* are superior to his early *opere serie*. Despite some beautiful moments, *Demetrio e Polibio* remains colourless, while *Ciro in Babilonia*, if not the fiasco that Rossini later labelled it, is scarcely distinguishable from the host of pseudo-religious operas prepared yearly for Lent. In the *farse* and comic operas, however, Rossini's musical personality began to take shape. Formal and melodic characteristics of his mature operas appear only occasionally, but many elements emerge that remain throughout his career. A love of sheer sound, of sharp and effective rhythms, is one of them. Pacuvio's aria 'Ombretta sdegnosa' in *La pietra del paragone*, with its babbling 'Misipípí, pípí, pípí' that rapidly acquired the

status of a folksong, or the younger Bruschino's funereal 'son pentito, tito, tito', proclaim a love for words and their sounds that blossomed in the first finale of *L'italiana in Algeri*. Orchestral melodies give the singer scope for *buffo* declamation. Built almost exclusively in this way is 'Chi è colei che s'avvicina?', the aria of the parodied journalist, Macrobio, in *La pietra del paragone*. But sometimes, especially in these earlier works, the orchestral bustle seems rather faceless. Thus much of the introduction in *La cambiale di matrimonio* revolves around an orchestral figure (ex.1), over which

Ex.1

the pompous Mill attempts unsuccessfully to calculate from a world map the distance from Canada to Europe and then engages in a spirited dialogue with his servants. The same figure recurs in *L'inganno felice*, during the aria 'Una voce m'ha colpito', in which Batone realizes that the woman he thought to have murdered is alive. Rather than being particularly jarring in these diverse situations, the orchestral motif is simply appropriate to neither: its very limitations make it extremely adaptable.

Alongside the comic elements is the sentimental vein that pervades much of Rossini's *opera buffa*. Florville's opening solo in the introduction of *Il Signor Bruschino*, 'Deh! tu m'assisti, amore!', Isabella's 'Perchè del tuo seno' in *L'inganno felice*, or the cavatina of Berenice in *L'occasione fa il ladro*, 'Vicino è il momento che sposa sarò' (ex.2) are all lovely examples. Rossini's vocal lines here are less florid than in his later operas. Although some ornamentation would have been applied by singers, particularly in repeated passages, the style imposes limitations. Isabella in *L'inganno felice* could hardly sing in the vein of the heroines of *Semiramide* or *Elisabetta, regina d'Inghilterra*. The simplicity and balance of these melodic periods, which avoid the deformations that give Rossini's later melodies such variety, help explain their freshness and appeal. When a singer does break into coloratura, as Berenice in her expansive aria 'Voi la sposa pretendete', it normally forms a quasi-independent section before the final cadences, a procedure Rossini abandoned after his earliest operas.

Whereas Rossini grew in stature as a dramatist during his career, he was from the outset a consummate composer of overtures. Though early specimens do not exhibit all the typical characteristics of the more mature works, their appeal is immediate and genuine. Formally they are sonata movements without development sections, usually preceded by a slow introduction with a cantabile melody for oboe, english horn or french horn. The first group is played by the strings; the second group features the wind. The crescendo is part of the second group, though in these early works it is not fully standardized. Within this schema, clear melodies, exuberant rhythms, simple harmonic structure and a superb feeling for sound and balance, together with such splendid details as the wind writing in *La scala di seta* or the beating bows in *Il Signor Bruschino*, give the overtures their unique character. The qualities that make them unique as a group, though, are also the qualities which

1. Gioachino Rossini: drawing by Thomas Lawrence (1769–1830) in a private collection

Ex.2

make them generic among themselves. Almost all these overtures served for more than one opera. Some of the transferences, as from *La pietra del paragone* to *Tancredi*, seem no less incongruous than the infamous vicissitudes of the overture to *Il barbiere di Siviglia*.

In a famous letter to Tito Ricordi, written in 1868, Rossini chided Boito for attempting innovations too rapidly. 'Don't think I am declaring war on innovators', he continued; 'I am opposed only to doing in one day what can only be achieved in several years . . . look, with *compassion*, at *Demetrio e Polibio*, my first work, and then at *Guglielmo Tell*: you will see that I was no snail!!!'. Still, Rossini's early works have their own charms, and to anyone who has a touch of Stendhal in his blood they remain delightful.

3. FROM 'TANCREDI' TO 'LA GAZZA LADRA'. With no effective copyright legislation existing in an Italy of separate states, Rossini's earnings from an opera were limited to performances in which he participated, and payments to a composer did not match those to a prima donna. Obliged to support both himself and, increasingly, his parents, Rossini plunged into one opera after another. The period from *Tancredi* to *La gazza ladra*, which intersects with his Neapolitan years, was one of constant travelling and frenetic compositional activity. Entire operas were prepared in a month, and Rossini's masterpiece, *Il barbiere di Siviglia*, occupied him for about three weeks. During this period he produced his great comic operas, works ranging from pure *buffo* to sentimental comedy, his more 'classical' serious operas, and his finest opera in the *semiseria* genre.

Unfortunately almost nothing is known of Rossini's life during these years. Anecdotes pertaining to his amorous pursuits and filial devotion abound, but documents do not. Nor can reports from later in the century be trusted, even those originating with close friends such as Hiller, Alexis Azevedo or Edmond Michotte: so many of the statements they attribute to Rossini are palpably false that one must suspect that either they embroidered his remarks or that he saw his early life and attitudes through the tinted glasses of his old age. One can be certain only that Rossini now became the leading Italian composer. His music was played and enthusiastically received almost everywhere.

Rossini's first two operas to win international acclaim were written consecutively for Venetian theatres: *Tancredi*, the idyllic *opera seria*, given at the Teatro La Fenice on 6 February 1813, and the zaniest of all *buffo* operas, *L'italiana in Algeri*, produced at the Teatro S Benedetto on 22 May 1813. For later generations the fame of *Tancredi* appeared to rest on the cavatina 'Tu che accendi', with its cabaletta 'Di tanti palpiti'. One need not invoke the old images of gondoliers singing and juries humming the tune to gauge its appeal. Thanking Tito Ricordi for a New Year's *panettone* in 1865,

Rossini assured him it was worthy of 'the greatest Publisher (donor) and the author of the too famous cavatina "Di tanti palpiti" (receiver)'. Wagner's parody, the Tailors' Song in Act 3 of *Die Meistersinger*, is further evidence of its longevity. Rossini's melody seems to capture the melodic beauty and innocence characteristic of Italian opera, while escaping naivety by its enchanting cadential phrase, which instead of resting on the tonic F jumps to the major chord on the flattened third degree Ab (ex.3). Rossini delighted in such harmonic games, even within the simplest phrase, and their piquancy gives his melodies their special charm.

Ex.3

But *Tancredi* is more than 'Di tanti palpiti'. It is Rossini's first great *opera seria*, and it exhibits the freshness of first maturity, of first formulated principles. There is little in *Semiramide* whose roots cannot be traced here. Formal procedures in particular, uncertain and tentative in earlier operas, assume the characteristics that were now to dominate Italian opera. It is impossible to prove that Rossini was an innovator here, since so little is known of the music of his contemporaries, but the force of his example was felt strongly by the legions of opera composers after him.

Rossini's formal procedures were compelling because they fused in a simple yet satisfactory manner the urge for lyrical expression and the needs of the drama. Although in *Tancredi* secco recitative still separates formal musical numbers, many important dramatic events occur within these numbers. There are occasional isolated lyrical moments, such as Amenaide's exquisite 'No, che il morir non è' of Act 2, but these play a decreasing role in Rossini's operas as they matured. Instead they are incorporated into larger musical units in alternation with dramatic events which motivate lyrical expression. The formal structure of standard arias, duets and first-act finales demonstrates this in various ways.

The problem of the aria is to permit lyrical expression to predominate without freezing the action. Often, especially in his cavatinas (entrance arias), Rossini composed two successive, separate lyrical sections, an opening cantabile and concluding cabaletta, thus giving the impression of dramatic change even when actual change is slight or non-existent. More normal is the approach taken in Amenaide's 'Giusto Dio che umile adoro' of Act 2 of *Tancredi*. Amenaide is alone on the stage; after a short scena her aria begins with a lyrical solo, a prayer for the victory of her champion. In a section of contrasting tempo and tonality, the chorus enters and describes his victory. Emphatically not lyrical, the music depends instead on orchestral figures, declamatory non-periodic solos and choral interjections. The cabaletta now concludes the aria in its original key. Amenaide contemplates her joy in a lyrical period, first expressively, then in exuberant coloratura. 'The chorus and other characters immediately applaud', in the words of Pietro Lichtenthal, a contemporary detractor, 'and She [Queen Cabaletta], all kindness, returns to content her faithful audience by repeating with the same instrumental plucking the celestial melody.' Rossini's multi-sectional aria with cabaletta may not be the ideal solution to the problem of the aria, but it permits lyrical sections to coexist with dramatic action and gives the singer, during the repetition of the cabaletta theme, the flattering option of ornamenting the melody. That the cabaletta was both useful and aesthetically satisfying was perceived by Verdi as late as *Aida*, when he wrote to Opprandino Arrivabene in reaction to criticism about his use there of a quasi-cabaletta: 'it has become fashionable to rail against and to refuse to hear cabalettas. This is an error equal to that of the time when only cabalettas were wanted. They scream so against convention, and then abandon one to embrace another! Like flocks of sheep!!'.

The duet poses a different problem. 18th-century *opera seria* tended to minimize ensembles. Under the influence of *opera buffa*, ensembles gradually infiltrated the grand Metastasian design, until by 1800 ensembles within the act and lengthy finales were the norm. As Rossini matured, the number of his solo arias (with or without assisting chorus) decreased until, in an opera such as *Maometto II*, they play a small role. There are of course purely lyrical duets, like the already-cited 'Questo cor ti giura amore' from *Demetrio e Polibio*. But Rossini's problem was to perfect a duet form that offered the characters opportunity for lyrical expression while centring on their dramatic confrontation. The duet 'Lasciami, non t'ascolto!' for Tancredi and Amenaide exemplifies his solution. Essentially in four parts, the duet begins with a confrontation that dramatically motivates the whole composition, Tancredi's belief in Amenaide's guilt and her protestations of innocence. The initial clash is presented in parallel poetic stanzas, normally set to the same or similar music. Here the settings differ only in details of ornamentation and in tonality: Tancredi's is in the tonic, Amenaide's modulates to and remains in the dominant. Once positions have been stated, the characters often continue in dialogue, though in this example an orchestral modulation (typically to the mediant major) leads directly to the second section. The latter is a lyrical contemplation of the dramatic situation. Though the characters basically have quite different views, they express them in 'pseudo-canon' to the same or parallel texts, one character singing a lyrical phrase alone, the other repeating it while the first supplies brief counterpoints. Overlapping lyrical phrases and cadences, often in 3rds and 6ths, bring the section to a close. The third section can recall the first, but is freer in design. Action is taken, new positions defined, a motivating force established, while the music follows the events, preparing the final section, a cabaletta *a due*. Using the form outlined above, the characters reflect on their new positions, shout out new challenges, and so on. (In the *Tancredi* duet, printed editions do not show the repetition of the cabaletta theme, but it is in the autograph.)

The first-act finale is quite similar to the duet, with the standard addition of a short opening ensemble or chorus. Since more action is to be incorporated into the music, the kinetic sections are longer and more flexible. Action is advanced through passages of arioso and simple declamation over orchestral periods, often identical in both kinetic sections. The latter are followed, respectively, by a slow ensemble, called a 'Largo', and a concluding cabaletta, referred to in the finale as a 'stretta' but indistinguishable in shape and function from the normal cabaletta. The *Tancredi* finale is a pure example, but with the addition of extra internal movements the model holds for most contemporary *opera seria*. Indeed, except for a less rigid stretta, the act 'Il contratto nuziale' from Donizetti's *Lucia di Lammermoor* concludes with a textbook example of the Rossini finale, the famous sextet forming the Largo. The same holds for the first-act finale of Verdi's *Nabucco*. Once again, Rossini's underlying plan balances various forces, musical, dramatic and vocal.

The difficulty with these formal conventions is that form too easily degenerates into formula. But the procedures do permit diverse handling and effective modifications. *Tancredi* manifests them in their pristine state. The lines are clear, the melodies crystalline, the rhythms vital without being exaggerated, the harmonies simple but with enough chromatic inflections to keep the attention. Orchestral writing is kept in perfect control, with the wind offering numerous colouristic solos. Heroic and idyllic moods dominate, and Rossini captured well the pseudo-Arcadian spirit. Though the world of *Semiramide* is implicit here, its realization seems far off.

L'italiana in Algeri, to a libretto by Angelo Anelli first set by Luigi Mosca (1808), fully shared the success of *Tancredi*. It is an *opera buffa* that moves easily among the sentimental (Lindoro's 'Languir per una bella'), the grossly farcical (the 'Pappataci' trio), the patriotic (Isabella's 'Pensa alla patria'), and the sheer lunatic (the 'cra cra, bum bum, din din, tac tac' of the first finale). Too often, critics stress the extent to which Rossini's *opera seria* is enriched through elements of the *opera buffa* without looking at the reverse: how *opera buffa* adopted elements from the *seria*. The aria 'Pensa alla patria' would have no place in a classical *opera buffa*, and this tendency develops further in *La Cenerentola*. Similarities between the genres are as important as their divergences. Of course there are no buffo arias *per se* in Rossini's serious operas, and devices such as mechanical repetition, rapid declamation to the limits of the possible, the use of large intervals in a grotesque manner ('Pappataci Mustafà') or exaggerated contrasts of tempo are part of *buffo* technique. Similarly, elaborate, orchestrally introduced scenas, often preceding major arias in Rossini's serious operas, rarely appear in the *buffo* world. The heroic *coro e cavatina* is reserved for the *opera seria*, though Rossini satirized the procedure in Dandini's mock-heroic entrance in *La Cenerentola*, 'Come un'ape ne' giorni d'aprile', or even in Isabella's 'Cruda sorte! amor tiranno!' from *L'italiana*.

But so many elements are similar. All the formal designs of the *opera seria* recur in the *opera buffa*, though treated with the greater internal freedom characteristic of the *buffo* heritage. The rhythmic verve of *opera buffa*, which depends on rapid orchestral melodies as a background for quasi-declamatory vocal lines, easily passes to the serious style and helps expand enormously the amount of action incorporated into musical numbers. Though the stretta of an *opera seria* finale would never adopt the 'bum bum' fracas of *L'italiana*, there is really scant difference in character between the close of the first-act finale in the serious *Aureliano in Palmira* and the comic *Il turco in Italia*. Nor does the orchestration differ greatly between the genres. The ease with which a single overture could introduce a serious or a comic opera is well known. This confounding of types, particularly the rhythmic vitality injected from the *opera buffa* into the *seria* and the introduction of more noble sentiments into stock *buffo* figures, is central to an understanding of Rossini's music and its effect on his contemporaries. Though the traditional *buffa* prevails gloriously in *L'italiana*, *La Cenerentola* is only four years away.

After *Tancredi* and *L'italiana*, Rossini's fame was assured. From the end of 1813 until the summer of 1814 he was largely in Milan, mounting and revising for the Teatro Re his two Venetian successes, and composing for La Scala two new operas, *Aureliano in Palmira* (26 December 1813) and *Il turco in Italia* (14 August 1814). The role of Arsace in the former was sung by the last great castrato, Giambattista Velluti. Although the castrato hero had been superseded by the contralto (Rossini's Tancredi, Malcolm in *La donna del lago*, Calbo in *Maometto II*, and Arsace in *Semiramide* are all breeches roles) and by the tenor (Othello, Rinaldo in *Armida*, Osiride in *Mosè in Egitto* and Ilo in *Zelmira*), Velluti remained a powerful figure. Rossini again wrote a part for him in his 1822 cantata *Il vero omaggio*, prepared for the Congress of Verona, but Velluti's greatest triumph was as Armando in Meyerbeer's last Italian opera, *Il crociato in Egitto* of 1824, one of the last significant castrato roles.

Velluti's importance for Rossini centres on an anecdote too widely accepted, according to which Velluti so ornamented Rossini's music that it was unrecognizable. Enraged, the composer vowed thenceforth to write out all ornamentation in full. It is an amusing story; but Rodolfo Celletti has conclusively demonstrated its fatuousness. While Rossini's melodies do tend more and more towards the decorative and florid, it is a gradual process. Rather than a matter of disciplining singers, Rossini's florid style is a mode of musical thought whose development can be traced from *Demetrio e Polibio* to *Semiramide*. At least one piece from *Aureliano* was published with Velluti's ornaments, the duet 'Mille sospiri e lagrime'. It is not certain that these are the variants he sang in Milan, but they are no more objectionable than ornamented versions of Rossini arias by other singers published in Paris in the 1820s. There is no hard evidence that Velluti had any effect on Rossini's vocal style, and there is no quantum jump between *Aureliano* and *Elisabetta, regina d'Inghilterra*, Rossini's first Neapolitan opera and, according to legend, the first opera for which he wrote out the entire vocal part.

Aureliano was only moderately successful with the Milanese; *Il turco in Italia*, to a libretto by Felice Romani, fell flat. The fault did not lie with the opera, which is as masterful as *L'italiana* and, particularly in its Pirandellian Poet, even more sophisticated. The Milanese believed *Il turco* to be a mere inversion of *L'italiana* and claimed to hear extensive self-borrowing. But *Il turco* is actually one of Rossini's most carefully constructed comic operas, and except for a few short motifs (e.g. the opening motif of the duet 'Io danari vi darò' from *Il Signor Bruschino* is the basis for the first

section of the magnificent Geronio–Fiorilla duet 'Per piacere alla signora'), the opera is newly composed. In the ensembles Rossini shines, and the quintet 'Oh guardate che accidente!' is one of the funniest he ever wrote. The trio 'Un marito scimunito!' presents the Poet projecting a plot around the misfortunes of his friends, until in fury they turn on him singing:

Rossini's setting is unique among his ensembles. The entire piece grows from a figure in semibreves, played alone and then accompanying the orchestral motif round which the *buffo* declamation revolves (ex.4).

Ex.4
(a)

(b)

By the end of the year Rossini was again in Venice, writing *Sigismondo* for the Carnival season at La Fenice. Although its failure was deserved, some of the numbers that critics praise in *Elisabetta, regina d'Inghilterra* were originally written for *Sigismondo*. Azevedo quoted Rossini concerning the publication of his complete works by Ricordi in the 1850s:

I remain furious ... about the publication, which will bring all my operas together before the eyes of the public. The same pieces will be found several times, for I thought I had the right to remove from my fiascos those pieces which seemed best, to rescue them from shipwreck by placing them in new works. A fiasco seemed to be good and dead, and now look they've resuscitated them all!

The extent and character of Rossini's self-borrowing remains to be investigated.

Rossini's next opera, *Elisabetta, regina d'Inghilterra* (4 October 1815), opens his Neapolitan period and almost exclusive involvement with *opera seria*. During the first years (1815–17) of his association with Naples, however, Rossini produced several major works for other cities, including two comic operas, *Il barbiere di Siviglia* and *La Cenerentola*, and two in the *semiseria* genre, *Torvaldo e Dorliska* and *La gazza ladra*. These works, so different as a group from his Neapolitan operas, may be examined first.

Soon after the première of *Elisabetta* Rossini went to Rome, where he wrote two operas during the Carnival season. The first, *Torvaldo e Dorliska*, opened the season at the Teatro Valle (26 December 1815). There are attractive elements in this 'rescue opera', but its reception was mediocre. 11 days before the première, Rossini signed a contract with the rival Teatro Argentina to compose an opera, to a libretto chosen by the management, for the close of carnival. After a subject offered by Jacopo Ferretti had been rejected, Cesare Sterbini, author of *Torvaldo*, was summoned. The resulting opera was *Almaviva, ossia L'inutile precauzione*, a title adopted to distinguish it from Paisiello's well-known *Il barbiere di Siviglia*, although

2. Autograph MS from Rossini's 'La Cenerentola', first performed in Rome, 25 January 1817 (I-Baf)

the more common title appeared when the work was revived in Bologna during the summer of 1816. The dreadful failure of *Almaviva* on opening night is hardly surprising, if one considers the speed with which it was mounted. But stories, even by the original Rosina, Geltrude Righetti-Giorgi, which claim that Rossini extensively altered the opera are constructed on air. The overture may have been different at the première, but the standard one was unquestionably performed during the season. Since Rossini often prepared overtures last, he more probably turned to the overture of *Aureliano in Palmira* for lack of time or lack of will to compose another. (He turned to *Aureliano* and not to *Elisabetta*: the latter overture, though largely the same, differs in detail and has a heavier orchestration.) Manuel García, the original Lindoro, cannot be shown ever to have inserted a serenade of his own, though Rossini may have permitted him to improvise an accompaniment to 'Se il mio nome saper voi bramate'. The autograph contains the melody in Rossini's hand and guitar chords in another, except for an important modulation that Rossini obviously feared might be misinterpreted by his singer–guitarist. The libretto printed for the première gives essentially the same text as modern editions; the opera played on 20 February 1816 was the opera known today.

Il barbiere di Siviglia is perhaps the greatest of all comic operas. Beethoven thought well of it; Verdi wrote to Camille Bellaigue in 1898: 'I cannot help thinking that *Il barbiere di Siviglia*, for the abundance of true musical ideas, for its comic verve and the accuracy of its declamation, is the most beautiful *opera buffa* there is'. Faced with one of the best librettos he ever set, one in which the characters are keenly sketched and the dramatic situations are planned for a maximum of effective interaction among them, one which is itself based on an excellent play by Beaumarchais, featuring the incomparable Figaro, Rossini took fire. The opera soon gained an enormous success that has never diminished. From Lindoro's miniature canzona 'Se il mio nome saper' to Rosina's delicious cavatina 'Una voce poco fa', which so perfectly captures the wily heroine, to the uproarious first-act finale, the compositions achieve in turn melodic elegance, rhythmic exhilaration, superb ensemble writing, original and delightful orchestration – particularly when heard in Alberto Zedda's critical edition (Milan, 1969), stripped of the extraneous accretions of 'tradition'. The formal models of earlier operas are adapted to specific dramatic situations with such cleverness and irony that they seem eternally fresh. Basilio's 'La calunnia' is an apotheosis of the Rossini crescendo. The orchestral phrase that is to serve for the crescendo first appears in the strings alone, *sul ponticello* and *pianissimo*, as an orchestral background for Basilio's narration. Then a gradual increase in orchestral forces, with a movement upwards in register, a change to the regular position in the strings, and the introduction of staccato articulation, all produce the enormous crescendo as rumour spreads from mouth to mouth. Bartolo's 'A un dottor della mia sorte', on the other hand, is one of the most rapid patter songs ever written. Its concluding section is amusingly worked out, contrary to Rossini's normal procedures in vocal compositions, in strict sonata form, a wonderfully ironic comment on the pedantic character of the tutor. There is the delightful incongruity of form and content in the trio 'Ah! qual dolce inaspettato!', where the Count and Rosina go through 'obligatory' formal conventions, including a strict cabaletta repeat of 'Zitti zitti, piano piano', while their escape ladder disappears and Figaro hopelessly mimics and prods them along, only to be forced to wait out the exigencies of form. Every piece is filled with such riches. *Il barbiere di Siviglia* is an opera that can be appreciated on many levels, and what it may lack in the humanity of Mozart's *Le nozze di Figaro* it retrieves in glorious musical spirit and wit.

After two more Neapolitan operas, *La gazzetta* and *Otello*, Rossini returned to Rome, where on 25 January 1817 he produced *La Cenerentola*, with the contralto Righetti-Giorgi again in the title role. *La Cenerentola* markedly turns away from the delirious style of *L'italiana* and *Il turco*. There are, of course, the normal *buffo* roles. Don Magnifico is rather conventional, but Dandini, the servant dressed as the prince and trying to sound like him, is more subtle and more amusing. The duet 'Un segreto d'importanza', in which Dandini reveals his true identity to Magnifico, is brilliantly witty, and Rossini's setting is superb. Once the secret is out, the tentative opening phrase (ex.5a) is transformed into the spirited tune of the final Allegro (ex.5b). In the fashion of *L'italiana* the confused Magnifico babbles:

> Tengo nel cerebro un contrabbasso
> Che basso basso frullando va,

with the requisite leaps and quick patter. What sets *La Cenerentola* apart, though, is the nature of the Cenerentola–Don Ramiro story, the sentimental tale, the transformation of the scullery maid who sings 'Una volta c'era un re' in the introduction of Act 1 into the royal maiden who, with full coloratura regalia, ends the opera with 'Nacqui all'affanno e al pianto'. The shy mouse of the duet 'Un soave non so che', with her charmingly incoherent 'Quel ch'è padre non è padre',

Ex.5

grows into the mature woman who, in the sextet 'Siete voi? Voi Prence siete?', can, to the beautiful melody 'Ah signor, s'è ver che in petto', forgive those who have wronged her. Far removed from the tone of an Isabella or Rosina, Cenerentola is a character who anticipates the heroines of sentimental dramas, such as Bellini's *La sonnambula*.

La gazza ladra, produced in Milan on 31 May 1817, takes the process further. The rustic setting, as later in *La sonnambula*, heralds a tragi-comedy, the *opera semiseria* genre so popular in this period. Not until Verdi's *Luisa Miller* was a rustic scene permitted to serve as background to real tragedy. Some critics have deplored a lack of profundity in Rossini's characterization of the evil forces in the opera, particularly the Podestà, but this objection loses sight of the genre. The Podestà must function as a semi-*buffo* figure to sustain disbelief in the reality of the forces that appear to be bent on Ninetta's inevitable destruction. Indeed Rossini develops the characters quite carefully, avoiding both the exaggerations of *buffo* style and the postures of *opera seria*. Ninetta's simplicity, even when overwhelmed by events, differentiates her entirely from his earlier, more sophisticated heroines. In both the sweetness of the opening of her duet with Pippo, 'Ebben, per mia memoria', and the almost monotone declamation at 'A mio nome deh consegna questo anello', set over a theme used earlier in the sinfonia, Ninetta is the image of persecuted innocence. Her prayer at the start of the second-act finale, framed by a funeral march, is extremely touching, the more so for Rossini's restraint in the use of ornament. Fernando, her father, is one of the composer's finest bass roles, and his agony is vividly expressed musically. The pedlar, Isacco, is sketched with just a few touches but they are witty and telling, especially in his street song, 'Stringhe e ferri'. Though Giannetto makes a bland lover, his parents are well characterized. To begin the opera, Rossini wrote one of his finest overtures, filled with novel and striking ideas from the opening antiphonal snare drum rolls and military march, to the first group in the minor (later employed in Ninetta's prison scene), and the superb crescendo.

Rossini began his maturity close to 18th-century models, but gradually established his own approaches to musical form, melodic writing, and dramatic characterization. Since this period of his first maturity includes his better-known music, one tends to characterize his total operatic output by it and to see him as essentially Classical rather than Romantic. But if the Romantic tradition in Italian opera is defined through the works of Bellini and Donizetti, this tradition is unthinkable without the developments that Rossini's style underwent both in his first maturity and in the years immediately following, years in which the composer's base of operations was established in Naples.

4. NAPLES AND THE OPERA SERIA, 1815–23. By 1815 Rossini's operas were played almost everywhere, but in Naples they were ignored. That the Neapolitans, with their long, flourishing native traditions, were loath to welcome a brash northener into the temple of Cimarosa and the still-living Paisiello is understandable. Indeed, the advent of Rossini marked the end of Neapolitan dominance in Italian opera. But the powerful and shrewd impresario of the Neapolitan theatres, Domenico Barbaia, seeking to revitalize operatic life in

3. Stage design by Alessandro Sanquirico for the 1824 Milan performance of 'Semiramide' (Museo Teatrale alla Scala, Milan)

Naples, invited Rossini both to compose for his theatres and to serve as their musical and artistic director. From 1815 until 1822 Rossini was to reign over this domain, and the initial resistance he encountered from the fiercely nationalistic Neapolitans gradually dissolved as he became their adopted favourite son.

Although Rossini was granted the right to travel and compose for other theatres, after *La gazza ladra* the fruits of these travels paled in comparison with the Neapolitan operas. Indeed Rossini's Neapolitan period was important precisely because he wrote for a specific theatre, the Teatro S Carlo, with a fine orchestra and superb singers. He could write more deliberately and be assured of adequate rehearsals. He could come to know the strengths of his company and they could develop together. The growth of Rossini's style from *Elisabetta, regina d'Inghilterra* to *Zelmira* and, ultimately, *Semiramide*, is a direct consequence of this continuity. Not only did Rossini compose some of his finest operas for Naples, but these operas profoundly affected operatic composition in Italy and made possible the developments that were to lead to Verdi.

It is usually asserted that Rossini's first Neapolitan opera, *Elisabetta*, opened a new stylistic era, but in fact the chronologically significant point is not equally important musically. *Elisabetta* belongs to the world of *Aureliano in Palmira* and *Sigismondo*, not to the world of *Mosè in Egitto* or *La donna del lago*. To call it the first opera in which Rossini wrote out the coloratura is a great exaggeration (see above). Although it is the first of his operas in which all recitative is accompanied by strings, Mayr had done this two years earlier in *Medea in Corinto*, written for the same Neapolitans who,

largely under French influence, were demanding the rejection of secco recitative in *opera seria*. Much of the music of *Elisabetta* is salvaged from earlier operas, and the new pieces offer little novelty. As Rossini's first opera for Isabella Colbran, whose highly ornamental style of singing was to affect Rossini's musical thought, *Elisabetta* is important, but it marks no significant reform or progress in the character of the *opera seria*.

The same cannot be said of *Otello*, composed a year later. After the première of *Elisabetta*, Rossini returned to Rome for *Torvaldo e Dorliska* and *Il barbiere di Siviglia*. During his absence fire destroyed the old Teatro S Carlo. While Barbaia rapidly rebuilt it, Rossini composed two operas for other Neapolitan theatres, *La gazzetta* and *Otello*. The former was given at the Teatro dei Fiorentini on 26 September 1816. This theatre was the home of traditional Neapolitan *opera buffa*, and Rossini used Neapolitan dialect for the main *buffo* role, Don Pomponio, sung by Carlo Casaccia, who made a speciality of such parts. Indeed, when *La Cenerentola* was revived for the Teatro del Fondo in the spring of 1818, Casaccia played Don Magnifico in dialect, perhaps with Rossini's approval. *La gazzetta* was even more derivative than *Elisabetta*. It is as if Rossini were gauging his new audience by drawing together successful numbers from lesser-known operas before attempting an original work. Several numbers are lifted whole from *Il turco in Italia*, including the entire masked scene in Act 2, with the chorus 'Amor la danza mova' and the quintet, 'Oh! vedete che accidente'; a trio is taken without change from *La pietra del paragone*; and several pieces are largely derived from *Torvaldo e Dorliska*. These operas were unknown in Naples, Rossini had no desire to revive them (unlike *L'italiana in Algeri*, which he offered in 1815 contemporaneously with the production of *Elisabetta*), and thus they could be freely pillaged. After *La gazzetta* he rarely resorted to borrowing for his Neapolitan operas.

Even *Otello*, given at the Teatro del Fondo on 4 December 1816, stands out from the more limited world of Rossini's earlier *opere serie* only in its masterful third act. The act is conceived as a musical entity, and although one can identify the Gondolier's canzona, the Willow Song and prayer, the duet, and the final catastrophe, none is truly independent. Desdemona's Willow Song is ostensibly strophic, but Rossini's handling of vocal ornamentation gives it a more sophisticated structure. The first strophe is simple, a beautiful harp-accompanied melody. The second is more ornamented, and the third is quite florid. But the storm brews without and within, and when, after a short section of arioso from the frightened Desdemona, she begins the final strophe, it is utterly barren of ornament. Finally, unable to finish, she trails off into arioso. Although the first section of the Othello–Desdemona 'duet' is traditional, its ending, which builds in intensity until Othello kills Desdemona, is not. There is no room for a cabaletta, and Rossini offers none, though the text had been fashioned to suggest the typical cabaletta structure. Throughout this act, the drama is the controlling element, and the music, while never abdicating its own rights, reinforces it. In Act 3 of *Otello* Rossini came of age as a musical dramatist.

After trips to Rome and Milan for *La Cenerentola* and *La gazza ladra*, Rossini returned to Naples, where from 1817 until 1822 all his significant operas were written. These include *Armida* (11 November 1817), *Mosè in Egitto* (5 March 1818), *Ricciardo e Zoraide* (3 December 1818), *Ermione* (27 March 1819), *La donna del lago* (24 September 1819), *Maometto II* (3 December 1820), and *Zelmira* (16 February 1822). Though written for Venice, *Semiramide* (3 February 1823) is a fitting climax to this period and brings to a close Rossini's Italian career. None of the works written for other cities approaches the Neapolitan ones. *Adelaide di Borgogna* (Rome, 27 December 1817), *Adina* (a one-act *farsa* written in 1818, though not performed until 22 June 1826 in Lisbon), *Eduardo e Cristina* (Venice, 24 April 1819, but a pasticcio), and *Bianca e Falliero* (Milan, 26 December 1819) are clearly inferior in quality. The only work that escapes mediocrity is *Matilde di Shabran* (Rome, 24 February 1821), a rather serious *opera semiseria*, and the only one of these operas that Rossini produced in Naples (in an extensively revised version at the end of 1821).

Criticism of Rossini's Neapolitan operas, beginning with Stendhal, has concentrated too heavily on the singers Isabella Colbran, Andrea Nozzari, Giovanni David and Rosmunda Pesaroni, whose vocal talents left an indelible and not wholly positive mark on Rossini's style. They all specialized in florid singing that could be dazzling in its splendour but monotonous in its ubiquity. In his Neapolitan works Rossini rarely failed to exploit the characteristic strengths of these voices. Attention given to this aspect of Rossini's art was intensified by his personal relations with Isabella Colbran. When Rossini arrived in Naples, she appears to have been Barbaia's mistress. Her unusual vocal abilities, as a dramatic soprano capable of elaborate fioritura, and her Spanish beauty combined to entrance the composer.

Sometime between 1815 and 1822 he replaced Barbaia as Colbran's favourite, and in 1822, in Bologna, married her. The marriage was never very fortunate, but a false image of Rossini led by the whims of his prima donna has persisted. Though she clearly exerted some influence on his musical style, the exaggeration of its importance is based on a misreading of the Neapolitan operas.

Solo singing is of course important in these works. Malcolm's cavatina 'Elena! oh tu che chiamo' from *La donna del lago*, Orestes' cavatina 'Che sorda al mesto pianto' from *Ermione*, and Arsace's cavatina 'Ah! quel giorno ognor rammento' from *Semiramide*, each a standard entrance aria with an introductory scena, a slow and florid *primo tempo* and a rousing cabaletta, are all beautiful pieces, but they define their characters so generically that they were used almost interchangeably during the 19th century. Rossini himself put 'Che sorda al mesto pianto' into *La donna del lago* (Naples, 1819) and its *primo tempo* (together with a cabaletta from *Otello*) into *Matilde di Shabran* (Paris, 1829). Since he had neglected to compose a cavatina for Desdemona in *Otello*, the great singer Giuditta Pasta supplied her own, adopting 'Elena! oh tu che chiamo' for the purpose. This same interchangeability affects the final rondos Rossini composed for many operas. Elena's 'Tanti affetti in tal momento', which brings down the curtain in *La donna del lago*, found a home in many Rossini operas, at least twice through the composer's actions (in *Bianca e Falliero* and in the 1823 Venetian revision of *Maometto II*). These arias, all virtuoso pieces, offer enormous technical difficulties, but also contain simpler vocal periods and delicate orchestral shading to raise them above the level of pure technique. What they may lack in delineation of character they recover in the glorious sound that wells inexhaustibly from Rossini.

Focussing undue attention on the soloists can mask the far-reaching advances in musical thought in these Neapolitan operas. Though *Guillaume Tell* is Rossini's most ambitious opera, its basis is laid in Naples. And Rossini was not first exposed to French opera in Paris: he directed the revival of Spontini's *Fernand Cortez* at the Teatro S Carlo in 1820, shortly before he composed *Maometto II*. The importance Rossini attached to the latter is apparent. After its indifferent reception in Naples, he revised it for Venice in 1823, immediately before the *Semiramide* première, and in 1826 used it to initiate his Parisian career, as *Le siège de Corinthe*. Similarly, the finest numbers in *Moïse*, Rossini's second Parisian opera, are already found in its Italian model, *Mosè in Egitto*.

The Neapolitan operas show an enormous expansion in musical means, particularly an increase in the number and length of ensembles, with a corresponding decrease in the prominence of solo arias, and a profound shift in the role of the chorus, which now acts not as a passive observer but as an active participant. For the musical and dramatic requirements these changes imply, Rossini created a more dramatic accompanied recitative (Ermione's soliloquy before the final duet of that opera exemplifies this), and generally made his orchestra more prominent (earning himself the criticism of being Germanic). He attacked the tyranny of the 'number' from within, and it is arguable that the Neapolitan version of *Maometto II* is more audacious in this respect than its French revision.

Most operatic reformers are credited with expanding

musical means, achieving a more continuous dramatic structure, and turning from a style dependent on the solo aria. A traditional way of achieving this is seen in the second act of *Armida*. This act reveals a continuous, additive musical and dramatic structure (short choruses alternating with recitative, duets, dances, even a *tema con variazioni* for soprano), deriving from earlier French tradition and characteristic of the Gluckian reform. Such a musically shapeless but dramatically responsive series of elements is scarcely original with Rossini. Paer and Mayr both featured this technique prominently, and it occurs in Rossini's earliest operas. The finale of Act 2 of *Semiramide* is a later example of such scenic construction.

Central to Rossini's reform, though, is the internal expansion of the musical unit. The simpler forms of *Tancredi* are pressed far beyond their original confines to incorporate extended dramatic action and diverse musical elements. The introductions of *Tancredi* and *Semiramide* are recognizably in the same tradition, but the latter is enormously expanded, presenting most of the characters, establishing the main lines of the plot, and comprising an introductory solo scena, a chorus, a trio for Idreno, Oroe, and Assur, another chorus followed by a quartet in pseudo-canon, a dramatic scena for soloists and chorus, and a final cabaletta led by Semiramis but incorporating all four soloists and chorus. The music is largely continuous, themes recur from one section to another, and the entire composition forms a dramatic, musical, and tonal entity. Perhaps the most remarkable number in these operas is the first-act 'terzettone' (as Rossini called it) in *Maometto II*, 'Ohimè! qual fulmine'. Practically the longest unit in the opera, this number shows in the extreme how Rossini expanded internally standard forms. The ensemble begins as if it were to be a simple trio, with a static section followed by a kinetic one. Though normally this would address a concluding cabaletta, here a cannon shot announces Maometto's impending siege, and Anna, Erisso and Calbo leave the stage. As the scene changes, the 'trio' is left incomplete, but the music continues into a chorus and solo prayer for Anna. Erisso and Calbo return, and with the members of the initial trio reassembled, they launch a typical four-part design that concludes with a cabaletta to bring the entire scene to completion. The whole composition is tonally closed, with the initial 'Ohimè! qual fulmine' and concluding cabaletta 'Dicesti assai! t'intendo' both in E major. Tonal closure is essential to Rossini's technique, and helps unify his expanded ensembles. Though this terzettone, which fills more than a third of Act 1, incorporates many different dramatic events and musical sections, it clearly represented a unit for Rossini and must be heard as such to make formal sense. To break it up into a 'Scena e Terzetto', 'Scena', 'Coro', 'Preghiera', and 'Scena e Terzetto', as in standard vocal scores of the opera, is to substitute chaos for an effective and coherent plan. This is an extreme but characteristic example of Rossini's efforts to incorporate more musical material and dramatic action into the individual number. Though the number remains sectional, these sections define a larger design, as the composer expands, almost to the limits of intelligibility, the possibilities of those formal patterns he had established earlier as basic elements in Italian operatic structure.

Equally important is the new emphasis Rossini placed on the chorus. From an inert mass in *Tancredi*, the chorus becomes in *Mosè in Egitto* or *La donna del lago* a central character in the drama, a role further developed in Rossini's French operas. Whereas in earlier operas the chorus merely comments on the actions of the principal characters, in the first-act finale of *La donna del lago*, with its famous 'Coro dei Bardi', the chorus dominates as the various melodic strands of the finale are brought together into a powerful ensemble. The opening chorus from *Mosè in Egitto*, 'Ah! che ne aita!', draws its source from the tradition of the Bach prelude rather than from simple song forms, with the melody of ex.6 winding from key to key as the chorus intones its pleas for mercy, interspersed with cries from the soloists. The simplicity and strength of these choruses, the most famous of which is the prayer for soloists and chorus from *Mosè*, 'Dal tuo stellato soglio', further balance the florid solo writing.

Ex.6

Even Rossini's approach to the overture changed drastically in Naples. After *Elisabetta* and *Otello*, both of whose overtures were composed for other operas, the former for *Aureliano in Palmira*, the latter for *Sigismondo*, Rossini firmly avoided prefacing his Neapolitan operas with standard overtures. Indeed *Mosè*, *Ricciardo e Zoraide*, *La donna del lago*, *Maometto II*, and *Zelmira* have no overtures at all, but at most introductory orchestral material melodically related to the ensuing introductions. *Armida* has an overture, but it is not in Rossini's traditional mould. The overture to *Ermione* is the most fascinating, for although its structure largely parallels the norm, at several points during this overture the chorus is heard, from behind the curtain, lamenting the fate of Troy; in the introduction, these choral interjections are developed into a full chorus. In his operas for other cities, however, Rossini continued to supply overtures, though many are derivative and only the overture to *Semiramide* is worthy of the composer. Impresarios elsewhere were presumably in a position to demand overtures, whether the composer wanted to write one or not, but in Naples Rossini could exercise his will. The absence of traditional overtures there evidently reflects an artistic decision, and it seems likely that Rossini sought to involve his audience with the drama from the opening chord. A formal overture was extraneous, and hence was sacrificed. The significance of this approach for later Italian composers needs hardly be stressed. Indeed it is to Rossini's Neapolitan operas that a generation of composers, including Bellini and Donizetti, looked for inspiration and guidance.

Rossini also composed in these years a number of cantatas for state occasions and royal visits, as well as a *Messa di gloria*. The mass is a remarkable work; it draws on both Rossini's operatic style and techniques characteristic of sacred music generally absent from the operas, such as the extensive participation of obbligato orchestral instruments in complete ritornello arias and

4. Gioachino Rossini: photograph

the employment of more contrapuntal textures. Far from being pieced together from fragments of his operas, as earlier writers ignorant of the score claimed, the *Messa di gloria* is an entirely original and excellent work, as worthy of modern performance as the great sacred works of Rossini's post-operatic career.

5. EUROPE AND PARIS, 1822–9. Rossini's operas had gained international acclaim. Both France and England were bidding for his services, but Barbaia provided the impetus for Rossini's first foreign voyages just as he had initiated the composer's stay in Naples. The men were tied professionally, personally (through Colbran) and financially. Indeed, Rossini's wealth grew from his association with Barbaia in a company running the profitable gambling tables in the foyer of the Teatro S Carlo. Assuming directorship of the Kärntnertor-Theater in Vienna at the end of 1821, Barbaia imported his Neapolitan company, together with its composer, for a Rossini festival. It began on 13 April 1822 with *Zelmira*, which had had its Neapolitan première in February, and lasted until July. Six operas were given

with extraordinary success. The city of Beethoven and Schubert welcomed Rossini as a hero. He may have been introduced to Beethoven, who according to Michotte told him to write only comic operas, faintly malicious advice to a composer who had written little but *opera seria* since 1817.

After his Viennese stay, Rossini parted company with Barbaia and Naples. He returned to Italy during the summer of 1822 and remained until the autumn of 1823. At the invitation of Prince Metternich, he composed two cantatas for the Congress of Verona at the end of 1822 (both patched together from earlier works). The Carnival season of 1823 found him at the Teatro La Fenice in Venice, revising *Maometto II* to open the season and composing his last opera for Italy, *Semiramide*. It is one of the few Rossini operas whose genesis can be partly followed. Gaetano Rossi, the librettist, was a guest of the Rossinis in Bologna during the autumn of 1822, and his letters to Meyerbeer frequently refer to the opera being composed.

The Rossinis spent the summer of 1823 in Bologna. On 20 October they departed for Paris and England.

That they were to abandon Italian theatres for ever probably occurred to neither of them. Rossini left Italy as the most important and popular composer of his time. He had written 34 operas, the best of which formed a large proportion of the repertory in opera houses throughout the peninsula. He was 31 years old.

They stopped briefly in Paris, where many of Rossini's operas were known, even if productions at the Théâtre-Italien were often so radically altered in content that Stendhal accused its directors of attempting to sabotage Rossini's reputation in France. Royally fêted, he began negotiations concerning future activities in Paris. The Rossinis then continued to London, arriving late in 1823. A Rossini season was organized at the King's Theatre, but many of the operas were unsuccessful. *Zelmira* made a particularly poor impression because of the inadequacy of Colbran in the title role. Her voice was gone, her career effectively over. Rossini was supposed to write a new opera, *Ugo, re d'Italia*. Although he may have composed at least part of it, nothing survives. In the autograph score of *Ermione*, however, several pieces are underlaid with alternative texts, in which the character Ugo appears. Rossini, who had kept the *Ermione* autograph as he had those for all his Neapolitan operas, apparently intended to use at least part of this score, performed only in Naples, as the

basis for his English opera. Again Rossini's first reaction to a new artistic environment was to adapt an older work rather than to compose a new one. Most of his time, though, was spent growing wealthy on the foibles of English aristocrats, who were willing to spend outrageous sums to have the composer and his wife participate in household musical gatherings or to give lessons to their spoilt daughters.

By 1 August 1824 Rossini was in Paris, where he agreed to become director of the Théâtre-Italien. He also contracted to produce his older operas there, introduce other Italian operas and compose new operas for both the Théâtre-Italien and the Opéra. By the end of 1824, after a Bolognese vacation, the Rossinis established residence in Paris, where they were to live together for almost five years. Rossini first concentrated on the Théâtre-Italien. For the coronation of Charles X he composed *Il viaggio a Reims*, performed on 19 June 1825. Much of the music of this occasional opera was re-used in *Le Comte Ory*. As director of the theatre, Rossini introduced to Paris the finest Italian singers in first-rate performances of his most advanced Neapolitan operas, including *La donna del lago*, *Zelmira* and *Semiramide*, supervising the productions and often making significant revisions. The operas he produced by other composers included *Il crociato in Egitto*, which launched Meyerbeer's phenomenal Parisian career. The two men remained close throughout their lives. With Rossini at its helm, the Théâtre-Italien enjoyed its moment of greatest glory, and until his seemingly definitive departure from Paris in 1836, Rossini continued to assist in running the theatre.

His goal, however, was to compose operas in French for the Académie Royale de Musique. By October 1826 he signed a new contract, relieving him of most formal duties at the Théâtre-Italien and permitting him to devote his energy to composition for the Opéra. An honorary post was created for him as *premier compositeur du roi* and *inspecteur général du chant en France*. Having to learn French and master the intricacies of its declamation, Rossini approached his new task gingerly. He reserved two Neapolitan works for adaptation to the French stage, withholding them from production at the Théâtre-Italien during his tenure. Thus *Maometto II* became *Le siège de Corinthe* on 9 October 1826 and *Mosè in Egitto*, on 26 March 1827, became *Moïse*.

The differences between the Neapolitan originals and Parisian revisions result from a dialectical process internal to the Neapolitan works. In the latter, extremely florid solo vocal lines, emphasizing the virtuoso and generic, co-exist with far-reaching experiments in musical structure, which seek to give musical expression to particular dramatic situations. In the Paris revisions both extremes are planed down, resulting in a more consistent, if less audacious, dramatic continuum, and a reduced gulf between declamatory lines and florid passages. Ex.7 shows the purification of a melody from the introduction of *Maometto II* (7a) in its French revision (7b). Similarly modifying his structural experiments, Rossini eliminated many internal sections from the terzettone analysed above, leaving a truncated and more conventional residue in *Le siège de Corinthe*. Arias further decline in importance. Instead Rossini tended to compose larger units in which solo voices and chorus combine more dramatically. The scene in which Hiéros blesses the soon-to-be-martyred Greek warriors and

SIGNOR ROSSINI'S FIRST CONCERT,
ALMACK'S.
FRIDAY, MAY the 14th.

Her Excellency COUNTESS LIEVEN,	LADY GRANTHAM,
MARCHIONESS OF LANSDOWNE,	COUNTESS COWPER,
COUNTESS OF JERSEY,	LADY GWYDYR,
MARCHIONESS OF WATERFORD,	COUNTESS OF SEPTON,
MARCHIONESS OF CHOLMONDELEY,	COUNTESS OF MORLEY,
COUNTESS BATHURST,	and
MARCHIONESS OF CONYNGHAM,	The Hon. MRS. HOPE.

The Second Concert will be on *Friday* the 11th of June.

Subscriptions to both, *Two Guineas.*

Part the First.

SINFONIA—(Gazza Ladra) . . . . *Rossini.*
DUETTO—"Della casa,"—M. and Madame Ronzi De Begnis *Generali.*
QUARTETTO—"Vedi come esulta,"—Madame C. Rossini, Madame Caradori, Signor Garcia, and Signor Curioni . *Rossini.*
SESTETTO—"E palese,"—Madame Caradori, Madame C. Rossini, Signor Curioni, Signor Placci, Signor Remorini, and Signor Benetti . . . . *Rossini.*
CAVATINA—"Quell' istante,"—Madame Catalani . . . *Rossini.*
DUETTO—"Un se puoi,"—Madame Pasta and Signor Curioni *Rossini.*
CAVATINA—"Di piacer,"—Madame Caradori . . . . . *Cimarosa.*
DUETTO—"Se fiate in corpo avete,"—Madame Catalani and Signor Rossini . . . . *Cimarosa.*

Part the Second.

SINFONIA—(Tancredi) . . . . *Rossini.*
TERZETTO—"Cruda sorte,"—Madame Catalani, Madame Vestris, and Signor Garcia . . . . *Rossini.*
ARIA—Madame Pasta . . . . *Zingarelli.*
TERZETTO—"In questo estremo,"—Madame C. Rossini, Madame Pasta, and Signor Garcia . . . . . . *Rossini.*
ARIA—"Pensa a la patria,"—Madame Catalani, with chorus *Rossini.*
DUETTO—"Ebben per mia memoria,"—Madame Caradori and Madame Vestris . . . . *Rossini.*
CAVATINA—(Figaro)—Signor Rossini. . . . . . . *Rossini.*
TERZETTO—"Giuro alla terra,"—Signor Garcia, Signor Remorini, and Signor Benetti . . . . *Guglielmi.*
FINALE—God save the King.

✱⁎✱ To begin at *Nine* o'Clock.

Vouchers issued by the Ladies Patronesses, to be exchanged for Tickets, at the *Opera Office*, 105, Quadrant.

☞ Signor Rossini respectfully begs leave to state, that having unexpectedly been deprived of the assistance of M. and Madame Ronzi De Begnis, for the latter part of the Concert, Madame Caradori, although unwell, and Signor Benetti, both at a very short notice, most obligingly granted their services on the occasion.

5. Programme for Rossini's first concert at Almack's, London, on 14 May 1824

prophesies future greatness for Greece is impressive and anticipates the patriotic scenes of Auber's *La muette de Portici* and, of course, Rossini's own *Guillaume Tell*. Three of the four original arias in *Mosè in Egitto* were omitted for Paris. The one added aria, Anaï's 'Quelle horrible destinée', is in its force of utterance and starkness of melodic line far removed from the Neapolitan florid aria.

These two revisions prepared for Rossini's great French operas, the *opéra comique Le Comte Ory* (20 August 1828) and *Guillaume Tell* (3 August 1829). Both works effectively unite elements of Italian and French operatic style; by fusing Italian lyricism with French declamation and spectacle, they add another link to the chain that will lead to grand opera. *Le Comte Ory* is a problematical work, episodic in structure, but given its sources, it is surprising the opera hangs together at all. The librettists, Eugène Scribe and Charles Gaspard Delestre-Poirson, derived the second act from their own earlier vaudeville, adding to it a first act incorporating music from Rossini's *Il viaggio a Reims* of 1825. The plot has its origins in a medieval ballad that recounts deeds of the notorious Count Ory, and Rossini used the ballad's tune both in the orchestral prelude and the second-act drinking chorus. Only the Countess's aria, 'En proie à la tristesse', borrowed from *Il viaggio a Reims*, features virtuoso solo writing. More characteristic of the opera are its ensembles: the trio 'A la faveur de cette nuit obscure' reveals a wealth of musical detail that belies common views of Rossini's style. By this time he could encompass and yet unify a wide variety of musical techniques, ranging from the delicacy of this trio to a boisterous drinking-chorus, 'Buvons, buvons soudain', with its parody of an unaccompanied prayer, 'Toi que je révère', and from the Italianate aria of the Countess to Raimbaud's humorous tale of pillaging the wine cellars. In his orchestra Rossini could create the most miraculous turns with a few instruments, but when necessary he could pound on the bass drum too. His genius held these contrasting forces in equilibrium, and despite some illogical turns in the plot, *Le Comte Ory* is a fine opera.

Rossini's last opera, *Guillaume Tell*, based on Schiller's play, is more honoured than understood. Its

6. *Title-page of the first edition of the vocal score of Rossini's 'Guillaume Tell' (Paris: Troupenas, 1829)*

occasional revivals have suffered from excessive editing, as if the music and drama would be completely indifferent to mutilation, as if music whose grandeur is built architecturally could sustain itself when the repeat of a phrase almost inevitably attracts the ignorant conductor's scissors, as if depleting the work of its personal approach to music drama would somehow render it more 'dramatic' in a Verdian or Wagnerian sense. The bitter anecdote in which the head of the Opéra met Rossini on the street and proudly reported: 'Tonight we are performing the second act of your *Tell*', only to have the composer respond: 'Indeed! All of it?', rings true; the opera must be heard as the towering entity it is to be properly appreciated. Carefully written, harmonically daring, melodically purged of excessive ornamentation (though the extremely high range of the tenor part poses problems for modern singers), orchestrally opulent, *Guillaume Tell* represents a final purification of Rossini's style.

Rossini wove into this historical panorama elements of the pastoral (with actual quotations from Swiss 'ranz des vaches'), patriotic deeds (very much in vogue on the eve of the 1830 revolutions) and superbly drawn characters. The whole is a rich tapestry of his most inspired music. Ensembles dominate and the interests of the drama are well served. Tell's declamatory solo within the finale of Act 3, 'Sois immobile', won the approval even of the mature Wagner. The great overture is unabashedly programmatic. The extensive spectacular elements, ballets and processions derive from French operatic tradition, but are effectively integrated into the opera. The chorus is central both musically and dramatically, and much of the opera revolves about magnificent choral ensembles such as 'Vierge que les

Ex.7

chrétiens adorent' in the first-act finale, or the final ensemble, 'Tout change et grandit en ces lieux'. Act 2, in particular, is music-theatre at its finest; its finale, in which the three Swiss cantons, each characterized musically, are called together to plan the revolt, is perhaps the greatest single scene Rossini ever wrote.

6. RETIREMENT. And then, silence. For almost 40 years Rossini lived on, lauded by many, execrated by some, begged to compose; but no more operas issued from his pen. There are no simple reasons for such a personal decision, if indeed it was consciously made. That Rossini was tired in body and mind, indeed was a semi-invalid for much of the rest of his life, was partly responsible. His rate of composition of operas diminished significantly during his active career, from an average of three new operas a year from 1811 to 1819 to only one a year from 1820 to 1823, and even fewer in Paris. *Tell* absorbed more of his energy than any other work, and letters and contemporary reports show that while Rossini composed it he considered terminating his operatic career. The financial security he had now gained may also have been a contributory cause.

Political and artistic events of the next years probably solidified his resolve to abandon his career at its height. Before the première of *Tell* he had negotiated a contract with the government of Charles X, in which he was assured a lifetime annuity, independent of his activities, although he did declare his readiness to write at least four new operas, one every other year, for the Opéra. During negotiations he had threatened to withdraw *Guillaume Tell* before its performance if the annuity was not guaranteed. With the agreements signed and *Tell* launched, Rossini and his wife returned to Bologna for a vacation, his next Parisian opera scheduled for 1831. He contemplated composing a *Faust* based on Goethe, but never received a completed libretto. Instead, his vacation was abruptly shattered by news of the 1830 Revolution, in which Charles X was dethroned and contracts under the old regime were suspended. In early September 1830, Rossini left for Paris alone, relations with his wife having grown strained. He hoped quickly to regulate his financial affairs, but the courts did not decide the future of his annuity until six years later.

The administration of the Opéra had changed hands. Rossini had been so closely associated with the old regime that his influence there was gone, but he maintained ties with the Théâtre-Italien, actively supporting the production of works by his younger contemporaries, particularly Donizetti and Bellini. Mostly he was kept in Paris by a protracted legal battle to maintain his right to the annuity provided by Charles X. He composed little; two works, the *Stabat mater* and the *Soirées musicales*, were important. During a trip to Spain in 1831 with his banker friend Alexandre Aguado, Rossini was commissioned by Fernandez Varela, a state counsellor, to set the *Stabat mater*. He wrote only half the score (nos.1 and 5–9) before asking his friend Giovanni Tadolini to complete six additional movements. It was almost ten years before Rossini replaced Tadolini's handiwork, and then only under pressure from his Parisian publisher, Eugène Troupenas. Rossini's conduct was not motivated by pure laziness: by 1832 he was not well, and, whether psychological or not, his ills augured a period of morbid sickness that lasted for 25 years. In this sickness he was nursed and comforted by Olympe Pélissier. Their long affair, which began in Paris early in the 1830s, cul-

minated in marriage in 1846, after the death of Isabella Colbran.

In Paris Rossini did complete the set of eight chamber arias and four duets known as the *Soirées musicales*, pieces which prove that Rossini's departure from the operatic stage had nothing to do with any decline in his inspiration. They embrace a wide range of moods: the dramatic *Li murinari*, the Tyrolean *La pastorella dell'Alpi*, the Neapolitan abandon of the ever-popular *La danza*. Melodically attractive, they are filled with beautiful details manifesting Rossini's skill; note, for example, the unanticipated G and D harmonies near the end of the B♭ major *La serenata*. These pieces were probably composed individually for various society figures during the early 1830s and then collected into a volume for publication by Troupenas in 1835.

All these factors – illness, changes in the artistic and political climate, financial security, general exhaustion – together with the enormous success of Meyerbeer's first French operas, *Robert le diable* (1831) and *Les Huguenots* (1836), which took to an extreme many techniques of *Tell* while abandoning the 'classical' tendencies of that opera, created a physical and artistic climate in which the composition of new operas had little savour for Rossini. But the reports of rivalry between Rossini and Meyerbeer seem fundamentally false. Whatever he thought about Meyerbeer's 'grand operas', Rossini remained on good personal terms with Meyerbeer from 1825, when he introduced him to the Parisian public, until his death in 1864, for which Rossini composed a *Chant funèbre*.

With the pension affair settled in his favour, Rossini took a short trip to Germany with another banker, Lionel de Rothschild, meeting both Mendelssohn and Hiller. Mendelssohn, despite himself, came away enormously impressed, writing to his mother and sister: 'intelligence, vivacity and polish at all times and in every word; and whoever doesn't think him a genius must hear him hold forth only once, and he'll change his mind immediately'. Hiller became a friend for life. By the end of the summer of 1836 Rossini returned to Paris to tidy up his affairs, departing again on 24 October for Italy. He did not take Olympe, but soon afterwards, in February 1837, she followed him to Bologna.

An account of the events of Rossini's life between the time he left Paris and his return in 1855 makes depressing reading. He was continually ill, did almost nothing, seemed indeed to be living on the brink of spiritual, if not physical, death. He and Olympe established a salon in Milan during the winter of 1837–8 and gave a number of musical soirées similar in style to the more famous Parisian ones of the 1860s. But the death of his father in 1839 further weakened Rossini (his mother had died in 1827 during rehearsals for *Moïse*). His only activity was as honorary consultant to the Bologna Liceo Musicale. There, starting in 1840, he attempted to regenerate the conservatory and improve its curriculum. It is known that he played at least a small role in the performance of his works there, since in the library of the conservatory is a set of orchestral parts for the quartet from *Bianca e Falliero*, 'Cielo, il mio labbro inspira', in which the part for second horn is in Rossini's hand. A note on the manuscript reads: 'Original writing of Rossini. May 1844'. But his health was poor, urethral disorders in particular requiring prolonged and painful treatment, and so Rossini could do little for the conservatory.

When, after the death of Varela, the original version of the *Stabat mater* fell into the hands of the Parisian publisher Aulagnier, who printed it and arranged a performance, Rossini, partly at the prompting of Troupenas and partly because the work published by Aulagnier was a composite, disowned this version and decided to complete the work himself. The revised *Stabat mater* was ready by the end of 1841. The first performance, arranged by the brothers Léon and Marie Escudier, was in Paris at the Théâtre-Italien on 7 January 1842. It was received with enormous enthusiasm. The first Italian performance, at Bologna, followed in March under the direction of Donizetti. Among the soloists were Clara Novello and Nikolay Ivanov, who became a close friend of Rossini and for whom, at Rossini's request, Verdi expressly composed some substitute arias. Donizetti, reporting the reception of the *Stabat mater* in Bologna, wrote:

The enthusiasm is impossible to describe. Even at the final rehearsal, which Rossini attended, in the middle of the day, he was accompanied to his home to the shouting of more then 500 persons. The same thing the first night, under his window, since he did not appear in the hall . . .

The *Stabat mater* is often said to be operatic. If by this is meant that the work is lyrical rather than symphonic in conception, it seems a harmless statement. But it is important to recognize that the statement is really a disguised attack on its style, affirming by implication

that the piece is neither specifically religious in quality nor deeply felt. Leaving aside the thorny problem of what is theoretically appropriate for religious music, Rossini's setting of the *Stabat mater* contains almost no music that would normally enter into his operas, whether for reasons of structure, orchestration, melody, use of chorus or a host of other considerations. No doubt the tenor aria 'Cujus animam' is melodically rich, but no similar Andantino maestoso movement exists in any Rossini opera, especially with the wealth of orchestral detail present here. One need not point to the specifically 'sacred' conceptions, the magnificent unaccompanied quartet, 'Quando corpus morietur', with its sinking chromatic lines, the final choral fugue on 'In sempiterna saecula amen', or the dramatic interaction between soprano and chorus in 'Inflammatus', in order to recognize that Rossini was striving to apply his artistic talents to the service of sacred music. From beginning to end there is a spirit quite unlike that of the operatic world that Rossini had abandoned a decade before completing his hymn to the Virgin. The opening movement, beginning with the dark sonority of cellos doubled by bassoons leading to the tutti at 'juxta crucem lacrimosa', is a stunning testimony to the vitality and success of his efforts.

Though it did not stir Rossini to further composition, he seems to have been genuinely moved by its triumph. He was particularly grateful to Donizetti for directing

7. *Autograph MS from the 2nd version of Rossini's 'Stabat mater', composed 1841 (GB-Lbm Add.43970, f.95r)*

the Bolognese performance, but was unsuccessful in convincing the younger *maestro* to assume the directorship of the Bologna Conservatory. Physically Rossini remained weak, and in search of medical help he travelled with Olympe to Paris in 1843. They soon returned to Italy, where Rossini remained indolent. In 1845 Isabella Colbran died, and on 16 August 1846 Rossini married Olympe Pélissier, with whom he had now lived for almost 15 years. He composed some trifles, mostly drawn from earlier works, adapting the famous 'Coro dei Bardi' from *La donna del lago* to unveil a monument to Tasso in 1844 and to praise Pope Pius IX in 1846. He also prepared a short cantata, derived in part from pieces in *Le siège de Corinthe*, in honour of the new pope.

The revolutionary movements that swept Italy in 1848 marked a significant turning-point in Rossini's life. He found himself out of favour with many Bolognese townsmen for what they considered his lack of enthusiasm towards the movement for national unity. Prompted by demonstrations directed against them, the Rossinis left Bologna for Florence. He always recalled this period in extremely morbid terms, claiming that his life and that of his wife had been in danger, and speaking of the Bolognese as assassins. The incident, together with his physical ills, further demoralized him. He stayed with Olympe in Florence or took cures at Montecatini or Lucca. Contemporary reports about him (from Emilia Branca Romani, Giuseppina Strepponi, and many others) give uniformly depressing and pessimistic accounts. In a letter of 1854 Rossini wrote of 'the deplorable state of health in which I find myself for five long months, a most obstinate nervous malady that robs me of my sleep and I might say almost renders my life useless'. In the hope that French doctors might be able to help him where the Italians failed, the Rossinis decided to return to Paris in the spring of 1855.

7. A NEW LIFE. The last years of Rossini's life must be understood against the background of his physical illness and mental exhaustion during the previous 20 years; for it is no exaggeration to say that, in Paris, Rossini returned to life. His health improved dramatically; his famous sense of humour returned; he bought a parcel of land in the suburb of Passy and built a villa; he rented city quarters on the rue de la Chaussée d'Antin, where before long he reigned over one of the most interesting and elegant salons in Paris. Even more remarkably, he began to compose again. The first new work was the *Musique anodine*, six settings of Rossini's favourite text for albumleaves, 'Mi lagnerò tacendo'. But these pieces, which are dedicated (14 April 1857) to 'my dear wife Olimpia as a simple testimony of gratitude for the affectionate and intelligent care she offered me during my too long and terrible sickness', have far more scope than the albumleaves he continued to dash off during his retirement. They were to begin a surge of composition that ultimately included over 150 piano pieces, songs, small ensembles and the *Petite messe solennelle*. Most of the shorter pieces were first performed at the Rossinis' 'Samedi soirs', whose participants included most of the great artists and public figures living in or passing through Paris.

Rossini referred to these pieces as his *Péchés de vieillesse*, the 'Sins of Old Age', and in them he turned his wit into musical terms, incorporating in various measure grace and charm, sharp parody, a dash of sentiment, and throughout a unique combination of sophistication and naivety. He refused to permit their publication, and although some did appear in the 19th century, they remained barely known until the Fondazione Rossini began editing them in the 1950s. Since then they have received increasingly sympathetic attention. Their historical position remains to be assessed, but it seems likely that their effect, direct or indirect, on composers like Camille Saint-Saëns and Erik Satie was significant.

Many of the piano pieces are parodies, but parodies so appealing and plausible that they could sometimes be mistaken for the things they parody, were it not that blatant excesses and Rossini's superb titles reveal his intention. One of the best is the *Petit caprice (style Offenbach)*, allegedly a *quid pro quo* after Offenbach's outrageous 'Trio patriotique' in *La belle Hélène*, 'Lorsque la Grèce est un champ de carnage' (with its wonderful line 'Tu t' fich' pas mal de ton pays!') brought Rossini's *Guillaume Tell* trio, 'Quand l'Helvétie est un champ de supplices' to the stage of the Théâtre des Variétés. The tempo indication 'Allegretto grotesco' leads the way, as does the bizarre fingering, but once the music begins one feels surrounded by a slightly tipsy Offenbach cancan. The chromatic inflection of the main theme (ex.8) is suggestive. Then, within an apparently innocent F major context, Rossini first deploys a curious melodic D♭, and finally rings out a truly bizarre F♯; the piece continues as if nothing has happened, and modulates naively back to the tonic and the main theme.

Ex.8

Although Rossini referred to himself as a 'pianist of the fourth class', these pieces are often technically challenging, but they are also constantly delightful. The *Prélude prétentieux* is just that, with a fugal subject and development that parody one contrapuntal cliché after another. *Mon prélude hygiénique du matin*, with its opening C major and A minor arpeggios, is sure to bring a wistful smile to those whose piano practice has started each day with appropriate exercises. The absurd dance rhythms of the *Fausse couche de polka-mazurka* and the asthmatic theme of the *Valse torturée*, in which the tonic is defined by the chord progression D major – D augmented – D diminished – D major, take salon music as their target. Bach and Chopin are never far from the surface, but they are viewed through a level of ironic respect that renders Rossini's homages a pleasure.

The songs and choruses are less inventive but no less enjoyable. *La chanson du bébé*, with its refrain, 'Pipi . . . maman . . . papa . . . caca', is a charming spoof on the nursery. *L'amour à Pékin*, Rossini's nod at the whole-tone scale, is preceded by several piano vignettes, harmonizations first of the chromatic scale, then of the whole-tone scale, but the song itself is a disappointment. It is a straightforward *romance*, with the whole-tone scale appearing only briefly in a cadential context (using the harmonization worked out previously in the piano vignette). The descriptive *Choeur de chasseurs démo-*

crates, written by Rossini at the request of the Baroness de Rothschild for the visit of Napoleon III in December 1862 to the Château de Ferrières, is a fine hunting chorus. The D major tonality of the main section is nicely balanced in the centre by Rossini's use of chromatic sequences, a frequent device in these late works. Among the songs there are more traditional, sentimental, even maudlin compositions, such as *L'orphéline du Tyrol*, or the *Chanson de Zora*. But even without a layer of ironic distance these pieces have more appeal than one might expect, for Rossini at his most conventional remains a remarkable composer.

The finest work of Rossini's late years, and indeed one of his greatest achievements, is the *Petite messe solennelle* for 12 voices, two pianos and harmonium, written for the Countess Louise Pillet-Will and first performed at the consecration of her private chapel in March 1864. Rossini later orchestrated the work, for fear that someone else would do it if he did not, but the mass is most effective in its original form. In an introductory note to 'le bon Dieu', Rossini referred to the mass as 'the last mortal Sin of my Old Age', and in an envoi at the end of the autograph score he addressed God as follows: 'Dear God. Here it is, finished, this poor little Mass. Have I written sacred music [*musique sacrée*] or damned music [*sacrée musique*]? I was born for *opera buffa*, you know it well! Little science, some heart, that's all. Be blessed, then, and grant me a place in Paradise'. There is something enormously appealing about this ironic naivety. Whatever Rossini's public defences that caused him to gain a reputation for coldness and aloofness, in his greatest music they fall and here he sang the praises of God *con amore*.

From 1857 until his death, Rossini was among subscribers to the critical edition of the works of Bach. Many of his piano compositions reveal his knowledge of Bach, and this is true also of the *Petite messe*. There is no mere imitation, but an attempt to return to historical traditions while holding fast to a modern compositional vocabulary. And through all the contrapuntal writing, elaborate chromaticism and harmonic audacity, beautiful melodies abound. Some pieces, such as the tenor aria 'Domine Deus rex coelestis,' reminiscent of 'Cujus animam' from the *Stabat mater*, are frankly operatic in the prominence they give to good tunes. But even knowing the contrapuntal movements of his earlier sacred works, one is unprepared for the richness of the double fugues on 'Cum Sancto Spiritu' and 'Et vitam venturi saeculi Amen'. The entire Credo (with its tempo indication 'Allegro cristiano') is a masterpiece of economy. A few musical ideas are basic to the entire composition, with the text and music 'Credo' acting as a refrain. The 'Crucifixus' is set apart from its surroundings, a soprano aria with the simplest possible accompaniment, the melody studded with chromatic alterations, the middle section modulating rapidly through the octave by minor 3rds. Here, as elsewhere in the mass, Rossini tended to be somewhat literal about his chromatic techniques, but within the context they seem entirely appropriate. The *Petite messe solennelle* has continued to impress later generations as a deep revelation of the man whose outward character often seemed a mere witticism.

In his last years Rossini lived in honoured retirement, a composer whose fame rested on work done 40 years before, and yet a composer who after a long silence had recovered his voice. Neither an anachronism, then, nor

part of current musical trends, he was content to write for himself and his circle, while expounding to those who would listen his attitudes towards art and stories of his youth. Accounts of these years were published by many, including Hiller, Saint-Saëns and Hanslick. The most significant (even if perhaps in part invented) is the alleged transcription made by Edmond Michotte of the meeting between Rossini and Wagner in 1860. Rossini's last letters too are filled with aesthetic judgments and precepts to Italian composers. He wrote in 1868 to Lauro Rossi, head of the Milan Conservatory: 'Let us not forget, *Italians*, that Musical Art is all ideal and expressive . . . that Delight must be the basis and aim of this Art: Simple Melody – clear Rhythm'. And in an aside, referring to modern tendencies in Italian music, he added: 'these new gross philosophers . . . are simply supporters and advocates of those poor musical composers who lack *ideas, inspiration*!!!'. He expressed similar thoughts later that year in a letter to the Milanese critic Filippo Filippi, a champion of Wagnerian ideals in Italy. Here Rossini also entered into other favourite themes, the decline in vocal art and the need to seek 'expressive' rather than 'imitative' music. Though aware of his own compositional growth in 20 years of writing opera, he objected to instant progress, the search for extreme novelty that he observed in composers who fell under Wagner's influence. He railed against those who spiced their writings with 'certain dirty words, such as Progress, or Decadence, Future, Past, Present, Convention, etc', adding:

Do not think, my dear doctor Filippi, that I favour an anti-dramatic system, no indeed; and though I was a virtuoso of Italian bel canto before becoming a composer, I share the philosophic maxim of the great poet who said:

> All genres are good,
> Except the boring one.

It might be said that Rossini's ideals never changed. When he abandoned composition in 1829 the world was changing, but when he took up his pen again he foreshadowed a movement of neo-classicism one of whose earliest proponents was his young admirer Saint-Saëns, and whose effects can be felt still in the music of Stravinsky. Just as his operas had defined the nature of opera for the first half of the 19th century, the *Péchés de vieillesse*, the music that cultivated Paris flocked to hear at the 'Samedi soirs', cast their spell on a younger generation of French composers.

Rossini fell seriously ill in the autumn of 1868. Soon afterwards, on 13 November, he died in his villa in Passy. His funeral was attended by thousands, and memorial services were held throughout France and Italy. He was buried in Père Lachaise cemetery in Paris. Olympe, who had hoped to be buried with him, was persuaded to permit Rossini's remains to be transported to Italy after her death. This occurred in 1887, and at a solemn ceremony on 2 May 1887 Rossini found his final resting-place at Santa Croce in Florence.

In his will, Rossini left a large endowment to found a conservatory in his birthplace, Pesaro. He also left to Pesaro his remaining autographs, including those of the *Péchés de vieillesse*. The Fondazione Rossini, through its *Bollettino* and its *Quaderni rossiniani*, has been instrumental in the revival of interest in Rossini since the early 1950s, and has issued editions of many of Rossini's unpublished compositions. Work began during the 1970s on a critical edition of Rossini's music.

WORKS

Edition: *Quaderni rossiniani, a cura della Fondazione Rossini* (Pesaro, 1954–) [QR]

BC — *Teatro del Corso, Bologna*
FC — *Teatro Comunale, Ferrara*
LC — *Teatro de S Carlos, Lisbon*
MS — *Teatro alla Scala, Milan*
NC — *Teatro S Carlo, Naples*

NFi — *Teatro dei Fiorentini, Naples*
NFo — *Teatro del Fondo, Naples*
PI — *Théâtre-Italien, Paris*
PO — *Opéra, Paris*
RAp — *Teatro Apollo, Rome*

RAr — *Teatro Argentina, Rome*
RV — *Teatro Valle, Rome*
VB — *Teatro S Benedetto, Venice*
VF — *Teatro La Fenice, Venice*
VM — *Teatro S Moisè, Venice*

* – *autograph*   † – *authenticated MS copy*

OPERAS

(*composed shortly before first performance unless otherwise stated*)

Title and genre	Libretto	First performance	MS, publication
Demetrio e Polibio (dramma serio, 2)	V. Viganò-Mombelli	RV, 18 May 1812, composed before 1809	Milan, 1825–6
La cambiale di matrimonio (farsa comica, 1)	G. Rossi, after Camillo Federici's play (1790)	VM, 3 Nov 1810	Milan, 1847
L'equivoco stravagante (dramma giocoso, 2)	G. Gasparri	BC, 26 Oct 1811	Milan, 1851
L'inganno felice (farsa, 1)	G. Foppa, after G. Palomba's lib for Paisiello (1798)	VM, 8 Jan 1812	Leipzig, 1819; full score, Rome, 1827
Ciro in Babilonia, ossia La caduta di Baldassare (dramma con cori, 2)	F. Aventi	FC, ?14 March 1812	Milan, 1852
La scala di seta (farsa comica, 1)	Foppa, after Planard: L'échelle de soie, lib for P. Gaveaux (1808)	VM, 9 May 1812	Milan, 1852
La pietra del paragone (melodramma giocoso, 2)	L. Romanelli	MS, 26 Sept 1812	* I-Mr; Milan, 1846
L'occasione fa il ladro (burletta, 1)	L. Prividali	VM, 24 Nov 1812	* F-Pc; Milan, 1853
Il Signor Bruschino, ossia Il figlio per azzardo (farsa giocosa, 1)	Foppa, after A. de Chazet and E.-T. Maurice Ourry: Le fils par hazard (1809)	VM, Jan 1813	* Pc; Milan, 1854
Tancredi (melodramma eroico, 2)	G. Rossi, after Voltaire (1760)	VF, 6 Feb 1813	* I-Ms; Mainz, ?1816–19
L'italiana in Algeri (dramma giocoso, 2)	A. Anelli, after own lib for L. Mosca (1808)	VB, 22 May 1813	* Mr, Ms; Mainz, 1818–20
Aureliano in Palmira (dramma serio, 2)	G.-F. Romanelli	MS, 26 Dec 1813	* frag. in Fonds Michotte, Brussels; Milan, 1855
Il turco in Italia (dramma buffo, 2)	F. Romani	MS, 14 Aug 1814	* I-Mr; Leipzig, 1821
Sigismondo (dramma, 2)	Foppa	VF, 26 Dec 1814	* Mr; Milan, 1826
Elisabetta, regina d'Inghilterra (dramma, 2)	G. Schmidt, after Carlo Federici's play (1814) based on S. Lee: The Recess (novel, 1783–5)	NC, 4 Oct 1815	* Fondazione Rossini, Pesaro; Bonn and Cologne, 1819–20
Torvaldo e Dorliska (dramma semiserio, 2)	C. Sterbini	RV, 26 Dec 1815	* F-Pc; Milan, 1855
Almaviva, ossia L'inutile precauzione, later called Il barbiere di Siviglia (commedia, 2)	Sterbini, after the play by Beaumarchais (1775) and G. Petrosellini's lib for Paisiello: Il barbiere di Siviglia (1782)	RAr, 20 Feb 1816	* I-Bc; Paris, 1820–21; full score, Rome, 1827
La gazzetta (dramma [opera buffa], 2)	Palomba, after Goldoni: Il matrimonio per concorso (1763)	NFi, 26 Sept 1816	* Nc; Paris, 1855
Otello, ossia Il moro di Venezia (dramma, 3)	F. Berio di Salsa, after Shakespeare	NFo, 4 Dec 1816	* Fondazione Rossini; Leipzig, 1819–20
La Cenerentola, ossia La bontà in trionfo (dramma giocoso, 2)	G. Ferretti, after Perrault: Cendrillon (1697), ? C.-G. Etienne's lib for N. Isouard (1810) and ? F. Romani's lib for S. Pavesi: Agatina, o La virtù premiata (1814)	RV, 25 Jan 1817	* Baf, Fondazione Rossini; Paris, 1822–3
La gazza ladra (melodramma, 2)	G. Gherardini, after d'Aubigny and Caigniez: La pie voleuse (1815)	MS, 31 May 1817	* Mr; Bonn and Cologne, 1819–20
Armida (dramma, 3)	Schmidt, after Tasso: Gerusalemme liberata	NC, 11 Nov 1817	* Fondazione Rossini; Paris, 1823–4
Adelaide di Borgogna (dramma, 2)	Schmidt	RAr, 27 Dec 1817	Milan, 1858
Mosè in Egitto (azione tragico-sacra, 3)	A. L. Tottola, after F. Ringhieri: L'Osiride (1760)	NC, 5 March 1818	* F-Pc; Paris, 1822; full score, Rome, 1825
Adina (farsa, 1)	G. Bevilacqua-Aldobrandini	LC, 22 June 1826; composed 1818	* Fondazione Rossini; Milan, 1859
Ricciardo e Zoraide (dramma, 2)	Berio di Salsa	NC, 3 Dec 1818	* I-Nc; Mainz, 1821–2; full score, Rome, 1828
Ermione (azione tragica, 2)	Tottola, after Racine: Andromaque	NC, 27 March 1819	* F-Po, excerpt in Fondazione Rossini; Milan, 1858
Eduardo e Cristina (dramma, 2)	Schmidt, rev. Bevilacqua-Aldobrandini and Tottola from original lib for Pavesi: Odoardo e Cristina (1810)	VB, 24 April 1819	Paris, 1826–7
La donna del lago (melodramma, 2)	Tottola, after Scott: The Lady of the Lake	NC, 24 Sept 1819	* Fondazione Rossini; Paris, 1822–3
Bianca e Falliero, ossia Il consiglio dei tre (melodramma, 2)	Romani, after A. van Arnhault: Blanche et Montcassin (1798)	MS, 26 Dec 1819	* I-Mr; Milan, 1828
Maometto II (dramma, 2)	C. della Valle, after own play Anna Erizo (1820)	NC, 3 Dec 1820	* Fondazione Rossini, *excerpt in US-NYp; Vienna, 1823
Matilde (di) Shabran ossia Bellezza, e cuor di ferro (melodramma giocoso, 2)	Ferretti, after F.-B. Hoffmann's lib for Méhul: Euphrosine (1790) and J. M. Boutet de Monvel: Mathilde (play, 1799)	RAp, 24 Feb 1821	* Fonds Michotte, Brussels; Vienna, 1822; full score, Rome, 1832
Zelmira (dramma, 2)	Tottola, after Dormont de Belloy (1762)	NC, 16 Feb 1822	* F-Pc, excerpt in Fonds Michotte, Brussels; Vienna, 1822

Title and genre	Libretto	First performance	MS, publication
Semiramide (melodramma tragico, 2)	Rossi, after Voltaire (1748)	VF, 3 Feb 1823	*I-Vt; Vienna, 1823; full score, Rome, 1826
Il viaggio a Reims, ossia L'albergo del giglio d'oro (dramma giocoso, 1)	L. Balocchi	PI, 19 June 1825	orig. material F-Pc, *excerpts in I-Rc
Le siège de Corinthe [rev. of Maometto II] (tragédie lyrique, 3)	Balocchi and A. Soumet, after lib for Maometto II	PO, 9 Oct 1826	*excerpts in F-Pc, Po, I-FOc and elsewhere; Paris, 1826; full score, Paris, 1827
Moïse et Pharaon, ou Le passage de la Mer Rouge [rev. of Mosè in Egitto] (opéra, 4)	Balocchi and E. de Jouy, after lib for Mosè in Egitto	PO, 26 March 1827	*excerpts in F-Pc, US-NYp, STu, private collection of H. Moldenhauer (Chicago) and elsewhere; full and vocal scores, Paris, 1827
Le Comte Ory (opéra [opéra comique], 2)	E. Scribe and C. G. Delestre-Poirson, after their own play (1817)	PO, 20 Aug 1828	*excerpts in Fonds Michotte, Brussels, and F-Po; full and vocal scores, Paris, 1828
Guillaume Tell (opéra, 4)	Jouy, H.-L.-F. Bis and others, after Schiller (1804)	PO, 3 Aug 1829	*Pc; full and vocal scores, Paris, 1829

Note: 11 operas pubd in Early Romantic Opera, vii–xvii (New York, 1976–) [facs.: 5 autographs, 1 contemporary copy, 5 printed scores]

SACRED

Title, performing forces	Composition, first performance	MS, publication	

Messa (Bologna), 3 sections
  Christe eleison, 2 T, B, orch
  Benedicta et venerabilis, grad, 2 T, B, orch
  Qui tollis; Qui sedes, S, hn, orch
	Bologna, Chiesa della Madonna di S Luca, 2 June 1808	I-Bc (3 MSS, incl.2*)	composite mass by students at the Liceo Musicale

Messa (Ravenna), solo male vv, male chorus, orch	Ravenna, 1808	*Mc	only Kyrie, Gloria and Credo
Messa (Rimini), S, A, T, B, orch	Rimini Cathedral, 1809	F-Pc; Paris, 1881	
Laudamus, ? S, orch			lost, mentioned in Radiciotti (1927–9), iii, 253
Quoniam, B, orch	Sept 1813	full and vocal scores, Milan, 1851	
Messa di gloria, solo vv, chorus, orch	Naples, S Ferdinando, 24 March 1820	†Nc, *frag. in Fonds Michotte, Brussels; Paris, 1860	
Preghiera 'Deh tu pietoso cielo', S, pf	c1820	Naples, 1828	
Tantum ergo, S, T, B, orch	1824	Biblioteca Comunale, Rieti	
Stabat mater, 2 S, T, B, chorus, orch 1st version	1832, Madrid, Cappella di S Filippo El Real, Good Friday, 1833	*GB-Lbm; Paris, 1841	12 nos., 6 by Rossini, others by G. Tadolini
2nd version	1841, PI, 7 Jan 1842	*Lbm; full and vocal scores, Paris, 1841–2	10 nos., all by Rossini

3 choeurs religieux, female vv, pf
  1 La foi (P. Goubaux)
  2 L'espérance (H. Lucas)
  3 La charité (L. Colet)
	Paris, Salle Troupenas, 20 Nov 1844	Paris, 1844	

Tantum ergo, 2 T, B, orch	Bologna, Chiesa di S Francesco dei Minori, 28 Nov 1847	*I-Mr; full and vocal scores, Milan, 1851	
O salutaris hostia, S, A, T, B	29 Nov 1857	pubd in La maîtrise (15 Dec 1857)	facs. in Azevedo
Laus Deo, Mez, pf	1861	pubd in Il Piovano Arlotto (Florence, 1861)	
Petite messe solennelle 1st version, 12 (solo) vv, 2 pf, harmonium	1863, Paris, home of Countess Louise Pillet-Will, 14 March 1864	*Fondazione Rossini; Paris, 1869	for 4 solo vv, chorus of 8vv
2nd version, 12 (solo) vv, orch acc.	1867, PI, 24 Feb 1869	*Fondazione Rossini; full score, Paris, 1869	

CANTATAS, INCIDENTAL MUSIC, HYMNS AND CHORUSES

Title, genre, performing forces	Composition, first performance	MS, publication
Il pianto d'Armonia sulla morte di Orfeo (G. Ruggia), cantata, T, chorus, orch	Bologna, Liceo Musicale, 11 Aug 1808	*I-Bc
La morte di Didone, cantata, S, chorus, orch	1811, VB, 2 May 1818	F-Pn; excerpts, Milan, 1820–21
Dalle quete e pallid'ombre, cantata (P. Venanzio), S, B, pf	Venice, 1812	*I-Ms
Egle ed Irene, cantata, S, A, pf	Milan, 1814	*Vnm; Milan, 1820

Title, genre, performing forces	Composition, first performance	MS, publication
Inno dell'Indipendenza ('Sorgi, Italia, venuta è già l'ora') (G. Giusti), hymn	Bologna, Teatro Contavalli, 15 April 1815	lost
L'Aurora, cantata, A, T, B, pf	Rome, Nov 1815	*USSR-Mcm*; ed. in *SovM* (1955), no.8, p.60
Le nozze di Teti, e di Peleo (A. M. Ricci), cantata, 3 S, 2 T, chorus, orch	NF, 24 April 1816	**I-Nc*
Edipo a Colono (Giusti, after Sophocles), incidental music, B, chorus, orch	before 1817	**US-NYpm*; 1 aria, Paris, c1850
Omaggio umiliato (A. Niccolini), cantata, S, chorus, orch	NC, 20 Feb 1819	**I-Nc*; version for pf solo, Paris, 1864
Cantata . . . 9 maggio 1819 (G. Genoino), for Francis I's visit, S, 2 T, chorus, orch	NC, 9 May 1819	microfilm in *US-NYp*
La riconoscenza (Genoino), cantata, S, A, T, B, chorus, orch	NC, 27 Dec 1821	*Fondazione Rossini; Milan, 1826
La Santa Alleanza (G. Rossi), cantata, 2 B, chorus, orch	Verona, Arena, 24 Nov 1822	lost
Il vero omaggio (Rossi), cantata, Sopranista, S, 2 T, B, chorus, orch	Verona, Teatro Filarmonico, 3 Dec 1822	lost, largely based on La riconoscenza
Omaggio pastorale, cantata, 3 female vv, orch	Treviso, ?1 April 1823 (MS dated 17 May 1823)	**I-TVco*
Il pianto delle muse in morte di Lord Byron, canzone, T, chorus, orch	London, Almack's Assembly Rooms, 9 June 1824	**GB-Lbm*; London, 1824
De l'Italie et de la France, hymn, ?for Charles X's coronation, S, B, chorus, orch	PI, ?19 June 1825	*Fondazione Rossini; full score, QR ix, 62
Cantata per il battesimo del figlio del banchiere Aguado, 6 solo vv, pf	Paris, home of A.-M. Aguado, 16 July 1827	**Lbm*; Paris, 1827, as 3ème quartetto da camera
L'armonica cetra del nume, in honour of Marchese Sampieri, solo vv, chorus, pf	Bologna, home of Sampieri, 2 April 1830	mentioned in Radiciotti (1927–9), iii
Giovanna d'Arco, cantata, S, pf, rev. with str for recit	Paris, 1832, rev. 1852	*Fondazione Rossini; QR xi, 1
Santo Genio dell'Italia terra (G. Marchetti), for tercentenary of Tasso's birth, chorus, orch	Turin, Palazzo Carignano, 11 March 1844	* Fonds Michotte, Brussels
Su fratelli, letizia si canti (Canonico Golfieri), for Pope Pius IX, chorus, orch	Bologna, Piazza Maggiore, 23 July 1846	*I-Bc*; Milan, 1847
Cantata in onore del Sommo Pontefice Pio Nono (Marchetti), 4 solo vv, chorus, orch	Rome, Senate (Campidoglio), 1 Jan 1847	* frags. in Fondazione Rossini
Segna Iddio ne'suoi confini (F. Martinelli), chorus of the Guardia Civica of Bologna, acc. arr. D. Liverani for band	Bologna, Piazza Maggiore, 21 June 1848	**Bc*
È foriera la Pace ai mortale (G. Arcangeli, after Bacchilde), hymn, Bar, male vv, pf	26 June 1850	in private collection of Baroness F. De Renzis Sonnino (Florence); QR xii, 1
Dieu tout puissant (E. Pacini), hymn, Bar, chorus, orch, military band	Paris, Palais de l'Industrie, 1 July 1867	* Fondazione Rossini; London, 1873 as National Hymn; QR xii, 21

MISCELLANEOUS VOCAL

Title, genre, performing forces	Composition	MS, publication	Remarks
Se il vuol la molinara, S, pf	?1801	**US-NYpm*; Milan, 1821	
Dolce aurette che spirate, T, orch	1810	*I-Bc*	
La mia pace io già perdei, T, orch	1812	*Bc*	
Qual voce, quai note, S, pf	1813	MS in private collection (Brescia)	
Alla voce della gloria, B, orch	1813	**Ms*; Milan, 1851	
Amore mi assisti, S, T, pf	c1814	**US-NYpm*	
3 compositions for G. Nicolini: Quinto Fabio	1817		
1 Coro e cavatina 'Cara Patria, invitta Roma', S, chorus, orch		*F-Pc*; Rome, 1822	first pubd as Alme fide a questi accenti
2 Aria 'Guida Marte i nostri passi', T, chorus, orch		*I-PAc*	
3 Duet 'Ah! per pietà t'arresta', 2 S, orch		MS in collection of Opera Rara (London)	possibly not by Rossini
Il trovatore ('Chi m'ascolta il canto usato'), T, pf	1818	**US-Wc*; Naples, 1818	
Il Carnevale di Venezia ('Siamo ciechi, siamo nati') (Rossini, Paganini, M. d'Azeglio, Lipparini), 2 T, 2 B, pf	carn. 1821	Milan, 1847	*facs. in G. Monaldi: 'Una canzone inedita di Rossini', Noi e il mondo (1925), Aug
Beltà crudele ('Amori scendete') (N. di Santo-Magno), S, pf	1821	**F-Pc* and *I-FOc*; Naples, 1847	3rd *facs. in J. Subirá: La música en la Casa de Alba (Madrid, 1927)
La pastorella ('Odia la pastorella') (Santo-Magno), S, pf	c1821	Naples, 1847	copy of 1st edn. not located; 2nd edn. Milan, c1850
Canzonetta spagnuola 'En medio a mis colores' ('Piangea un dì pensando'), S, pf	1821	*F-Pc*; Naples, 1825	
Infelice ch'io son, S, pf	1821	**A-Wgm*	2nd *facs. ed. L. Schmidt, Emil Naumanns illustrierte Musikgeschichte (Dresden, 9/1928)
Addio ai viennesi ('Da voi parto, amate sponde'), T, pf	1822	*I-Nc*; Vienna, 1822	also known as Addio di Rossini
Dall'Oriente l'astro del giorno, S, 2 T, B, pf	1824	**GB-Lbm*; London and Paris, 1824	London 1st edn. not located
Ridiamo, cantiamo, che tutto sen va, S, 2 T, B, pf	1824	*I-Nc*; London, 1824	
In giorno sì bello, 2 S, T, pf	1824	*GB-Lbm*; London, 1824	

Title, genre, performing forces	Composition	MS, publication	Remarks
3 quartetti da camera			
1 (unidentified)		Paris, 1827	copy of 1st edn. not located
2 In giorno sì bello, 2 S, T, B, pf	1827	Paris, 1827	
3 Oh giorno sereno, S, A, T, B, pf	1827	Paris, 1827	
Les adieux à Rome ('Rome pour la dernière fois') (C. Delavigne), T, pf/harp	1827	pubd in C. Delavigne: 7 messéniennes nouvelles (Paris, 1827)	
Orage et beau temps ('Sur les flots inconstans') (A. Betourne), T, B, pf	c1830	*in private collection of R. Macnutt (Tunbridge Wells, Kent); Leipzig, n.d.	
La passeggiata ('Or che di fiori adorno'), S, pf	1831	pubd in Cartas españolas (Madrid, 11 April 1831)	also known as Anacreontica
La dichiarazione ('Ch'io mai vi possa lasciar d'amare') (Metastasio), S, pf	c1834	Milan, 1834–5	
Les soirées musicales	c1830–35	Paris, 1835; *of no.2 only, US-Wc	
1 La promessa ('Ch'io mai vi possa lasciar amare') (Metastasio), S, pf			
2 Il rimprovero ('Mi lagnerò tacendo') (Metastasio), S, pf			
3 La partenza ('Ecco quel fiero istante') (Metastasio), S, pf			
4 L'orgia ('Amiamo, cantiamo') (C. Pepoli), S, pf			
5 L'invito ('Vieni o Ruggiero') (Pepoli), S, pf			
6 La pastorella dell'Alpi ('Son bella pastorella') (Pepoli), S, pf			
7 La gita in gondola ('Voli l'agile barchetta') (Pepoli), S, pf			
8 La danza ('Già la luna è in mezzo al mare') (Pepoli), T, pf			
9 La regata veneziana ('Voga o Tonio benedetto') (Pepoli), 2 S, pf			
10 La pesca ('Già la notte s'avvicina') (Metastasio), 2 S, pf			
11 La serenata ('Mira, la bianca luna') (Pepoli), S, T, pf			
12 Li marinari ('Marinaro in guardia stà') (Pepoli), T, B, pf			
2 nocturnes (Crével de Charlemagne), S, T, pf	c1836	Paris, 1836	
1 Adieu à l'Italie ('Je te quitte, belle Italie')			
2 Le départ ('Il faut partir')			
Nizza ('Nizza, je puis sans peine', 'Mi lagnerò tacendo') (E. Deschamps and Metastasio), S, pf	c1836	Paris, c1837	
L'âme délaissée ('Mon bien aimé') (Delavigne), S, pf	c1844	Paris, 1844	*facs. in La France musicale (Paris, 1844); also pubd as L'âme du Purgatoire
Recitativo ritmato ('Farò come colui che piange e dice') (Dante), S, pf	1848	*Fondazione Rossini (2 copies), Florence, 1800	
La separazione ('Muto rimase il labbro') (F. Ucceili), S, pf	c1858	Paris, c1858	originally composed as Mi lagnerò tacendo
2 nouvelles compositions (Pacini), S, pf	c1860	*Fondazione Rossini; Paris, c1863; QR v, 90 (no.1)	
1 A Grenade ('La nuit règne à Grenade')			
2 La veuve andalouse ('Toi pour jamais')			
Mi lagnerò tacendo (Metastasio), numerous versions composed as albumleaves, of which the following are representative:			
L'amante discreto, S, pf	1835	*F-Pc (2 copies), Pn, I-FOc; Milan, 1839	
Mi lagnerò tacendo, S, pf	before 1847	*F-Pn, I-Baf, private collection of R. O. Lehman (New York)	
Mi lagnerò tacendo, S, pf	?1833–9	*F-Pc (3 copies); pubd in Gazette musicale (Paris, 1840)	also pubd Paris, c1840, as Beppa la napolitaine
Mi lagnerò tacendo, S, pf	1850	*GB-Lbm, I-Sc; ed., London, 1959	
Mi lagnerò tacendo, S, pf		*in private collection of M. and R. Floersheim (Switzerland)	*facs. in E. Winternitz: Musical Autographs from Monteverdi to Hindemith (Princeton, 1955), plate 103

INSTRUMENTAL

Title, key, performing forces	Composition	MS, publication	Remarks
6 sonate a quattro, G, A, C, Bb, Eb, D, 2 vn, vc, db	c1804	*US-Wc; Milan 1825–6, for str qt (nos.1, 2, 4–6), QR i, 1 (no.3)	
5 duets, Eb, Eb, Bb, Eb, Eb, 2 hn	c1806	ed., Hamburg, 1861	source for 1st edn. not known
Sinfonia, D, orch	1808	I-Bc; QR viii, 1	
Sinfonia, Eb, orch	1809	Bc	rev. as ov. to La cambiale di matrimonio

Title, key, performing forces	Composition	MS, publication	Remarks
Variazioni a più istrumenti obbligati, F, 2 vn, va, vc, cl, orch	1809	Bc; QR ix, 1	
Variazioni di clarinetto, C, cl, orch	1809	Bc; parts, Leipzig, 1824; QR vi, 57	
Andante e Tema con variazioni, F, fl, cl, hn, bn	1812	*F-Pc; Paris and Mainz, 1827–8; QR vi, 18	
Andante con variazioni, F, harp, va	c1820	Naples, 1820–24; QR vi, 1	
Passo doppio, military band	1822	lost	mentioned in Radiciotti (1927–9)
Waltz, E♭, pf	?1823	*Pc, I-FOc	3rd *facs. in Revue et gazette musicale (Paris, 1841)
Serenata, E♭, 2 vn, va, vc, fl, ob, eng hn	1823	US-NYp; parts, Leipzig, 1829; QR vi, 31	
Duetto, D, vc, db	1824	ed., London, 1969	*sold at Sotheby's, London (1968)
Rendez-vous de chasse, D, 4 corni da caccia, orch	1828	*F-Pc; Paris, 1828; QR ix, 45	
Fantasie, E♭, cl, pf	1829	Paris, 1829	
Mariage du Duc d'Orléans, 3 military marches, G, E♭, E♭, military band	1837	parts, Leipzig, 1837	
Scherzo, a, pf	1843, rev. 1850	*Pc, rev. version in I-MOe; ed., Milan, n.d.	
Tema originale di Rossini variato per violino da Giovacchino Giovacchini, A, vn, pf	1845	*Fonds Michotte, Brussels; I-Fc (theme only)	
March ('Pas-redoublé'), C, military band	1852	Milan, 1853	
Thème de Rossini suivi de deux variations et coda par Moscheles Père, E, hn, pf	1860	Leipzig, n.d.	
La corona d'Italia, E♭, military band	1868	*frag., Fondazione Rossini; Rome, 1878	

PÉCHÉS DE VIEILLESSE (1857–68)

Complete set of autograph MSS in Fondazione Rossini; for a somewhat different ordering, see autograph catalogue of these pieces in Fonds Michotte, Brussels

Vol.i: Album italiano
1   Quartettino 'I gondolieri', S, A, T, B, pf; QR vii, 1
2   Arietta 'La lontananza' (G. Torre), T, pf (London, c1880); QR iv, 12
3   Bolero 'Tirana alla spagnola' (Rossinizzata) (Metastasio), S, pf; QR iv, 30; music identical with vol.xi, no.3
4   Elegia 'L'ultimo ricordo' (G. Redaelli), Bar, pf; QR iv, 19
5   Arietta 'La fioraja fiorentina', S, pf; QR iv, 5
6   Duetto 'Le gittane' (Torre), S, A, pf (London, c1880)
7   Ave Maria su due sole note, A, pf; QR iv, 51
8–10   La regata veneziana, 3 canzonettas, Mez, pf (Milan, 1878)
8   Anzoleta avanti la regata (Barcarolle 'Plus de vent perfide')
9   Anzoleta co passa la regata
10   Anzoleta dopo la regata
11   Arietta (Sonetto) 'Il fanciullo smarrito' (A. Castellani), T, pf, pubd in Strenna del giornale la lega della democrazia (Rome, 1881)
12   Quartettino 'La passeggiata', S, A, T, B, pf; QR vii, 16

Vol.ii: Album français (E. Pacini)
1   Ottettino 'Toast pour le nouvel an', 2 S, 2 A, 2 T, 2 B; QR vii, 50
2   Roméo, T, pf
3   Ariette 'Pompadour, la grande coquette', S, pf
4   Complainte à deux voix ('Un sou'), T, Bar, pf; QR v, 58
5   Chanson de Zora ('La petite bohémienne') (E. Deschamps), Mez, pf; QR v, 49
6   La nuit de Noël, B solo, 2 S, 2 A, 2 T, 2 Bar, pf, harmonium; QR vii, 62
7   Ariette 'Le dodo des enfants', Mez, pf; QR v, 9
8   Chansonette de cabaret ('Le lazzarone'), Bar, pf
9   Elégie ('Adieux à la vie'), sur une seule note, Mez, pf, †Fondazione Rossini; QR v, 75
10   Nocturne ('Soupirs et sourires'), S, T, pf, also with It. text as Il cipresso, e la rosa (G. Torre)
11   Ballade élégie ('L'orphéline du Tyrol'), Mez, pf; QR v, 31
12   Choeur de chasseurs démocrates, male vv, tam-tam, 2 tamburi; QR vii, 35

Vol.iii: Morceaux réservés
1   Quelques mesures de chant funèbre: à mon pauvre ami Meyerbeer (Pacini), male vv, tamburo; QR vii, 84
2   Arietta 'L'Esule' (Torre), T, pf; QR iv, 25
3   Tirana pour deux voix ('Les amants de Séville') (Pacini), A, T, pf; QR v, 37
4   Ave Maria, chorus, org (London, 1873); QR xi, 43
5   L'amour à Pékin: petite mélodie sur la gamme chinoise (Pacini), A, pf; QR v, 81
6   Le chant des titans (Pacini), 4 B, pf, harmonium, arr. 4 B, orch,

vocal score (London, 1873); QR viii, 66 (orch version) [originally written to text Mi lagnerò tacendo]
7   Preghiera, 4 T, 2 Bar, 2 B; QR vii, 89 [also exists with Fr. text]
8   Elégie ('Au chevet d'un mourant') (Pacini), S, pf; QR v, 17
9   Romance 'Le sylvain' (Pacini), T, pf; QR v, 1
10   Cantemus: imitazione ad otto voci reali, 2 S, 2 A, 2 T, 2 B (London, 1873); QR xi, 53
11   Ariette à l'Ancienne (J.-J. Rousseau), Mez, pf (London, c1880); QR v, 69
12   Tyrolienne sentimentale ('Le départ des promis') (Pacini), 2 S, 2 A, pf

Vols.iv–viii: Un peut de tout: recueil de 56 morceaux semi-comiques pour le piano
Vol.iv: Quatre mendiants et quatre hors d'oeuvres
Quatre mendiants
1   Les figues sèches, D; QR xix, 1
2   Les amandes, G (Paris, c1880–85); QR xix, 13
3   Les raisins, C; QR xix, 23
4   Les noisettes, b–B; QR xix, 36

Quatre hors d'oeuvres
1   Les radis, a; QR xix, 47
2   Les anchois, D; QR xix, 63
3   Les cornichons, E; QR xix, 73
4   Le beurre, B♭; QR xix, 79

Vol.v: Album pour les enfants adolescents
1   Première Communion, E♭; QR xv, 1
2   Thème naïf et variations idem, G; QR xv, 11
3   Saltarello à l'italienne, A♭; QR xv, 21
4   Prélude moresque, e; QR xv, 30
5   Valse lugubre, C (Paris, c1880–85); QR xv, 41
6   Impromptu anodin, E♭; QR xv, 48
7   L'innocence italienne; La candeur française, a, A; QR ii, 19
8   Prélude convulsif, C (Milan, c1879); QR xv, 59
9   La lagune de Venise à l'expiration de l'année 1861!!!, G♭; QR xv, 72
10   Ouf! les petits pois, B; QR ii, 30
11   Un sauté, D; QR xv, 83
12   Hachis romantique, a; QR xv, 93

Vol.vi: Album pour les enfants dégourdis
1   Mon prélude hygiénique du matin, C; QR x, 28
2   Prélude baroque, a; QR xvi, 1
3   Memento homo, c (Paris, c1880–85); QR x, 87
4   Assez de memento: dansons, F; QR x, 94
5   La pesarese, B♭ (Paris, c1880–85); QR x, 60
6   Valse torturée, D; QR xvi, 16
7   Une caresse à ma femme, G (Paris, c1880–85); QR ii, 37
8   Barcarole, E♭; QR xvi, 29
9   Un petit train de plaisir comico-imitatif, C; QR ii, 42
10   Fausse couche de polka mazurka, A♭; QR xvi, 38
11   Etude asthmatique, E; QR xvi, 46

12   Un enterrement en Carnaval, D; QR x, 68

Vol.vii: Album de chaumière
1   Gymnastique d'écartement, A♭ (Paris, c1880–85); QR xiv, 1
2   Prélude fugassé, E; QR xiv, 18
3   Petite polka chinoise, b (Milan, c1878); QR xiv, 25
4   Petite valse de boudoir, A♭; QR xiv, 35
5   Prélude inoffensif, C; QR ii, 8
6   Petite valse ('L'huile de Ricin'), E; QR xiv, 43
7   Un profond sommeil; Un reveil en sursaut, b, D, 1st part ed. G.
      Puccio, *Alfonso Rendano* (Rome, 1937); QR xiv, 62 (both
      parts)
8   Plein-chant chinois, scherzo, a; QR xiv, 91
9   Un cauchemar, E; QR xiv, 104
10   Valse boiteuse, D♭ (Milan, c1879); QR xiv, 126
11   Une pensée à Florence, a; QR xiv, 137
12   Marche, C; QR xiv, 150

Vol.viii: Album de château
1   Spécimen de l'ancien régime, E♭; QR ii, 59
2   Prélude pétulant-roccoco, G; QR xvii, 1
3   Un regret; Un espoir, E (Paris, c1880–85); QR xvii, 17
4   Boléro tartare, a; QR xvii, 33
5   Prélude prétentieux, c–C; QR x, 1
6   Spécimen de mon temps, A♭; QR x, 38
7   Valse anti-dansante, F; QR xvii, 60
8   Prélude semipastorale, A; QR xvii, 78
9   Tarantelle pur sang (avec Traversée de la procession), b, chorus,
      harmonium and clochette ad lib, full scoring (Milan, c1879);
      QR ii, 83 (as pf solo)
10   Un rêve, b; QR x, 11
11   Prélude soi-disant dramatique, F♯; QR xvii, 109
12   Spécimen de l'avenir, E♭; QR x, 104

Vol.ix: [Album pour piano, violin, violoncelle, harmonium et cor]
1   Mélodie candide, A, pf; QR xvi, 67
2   Chansonette, E♭, pf; QR xvi, 87
3   La savoie aimante, a, pf; QR xvi, 74
4   Un mot à Paganini, élégie, D, vn, pf
5   Impromptu tarantulisé, F, pf; QR xvi, 95
6   Echantillon du chant de Noël à l'italienne, E♭, pf; QR ii, 102
7   Marche et reminiscences pour mon dernier voyage, A♭, pf; QR ii,
      108
8   Prélude, thème et variations, E, hn, pf; QR iii, 1
9   Prélude italien, A♭, pf; QR xvi, 107
10   Une larme: thème et variations, a, vc, pf
11   Echantillon de blague mélodique sur les noires de la main droite,
      G♭, pf (Milan, c1879)
12   Petite fanfare à quatre mains, E♭, pf 2 or 4 hands

Vol.x: Miscellanée pour piano
1   Prélude blagueur, a; QR xviii, 1
2   Des tritons s'il vous plaît (montée–descente), C; QR xviii, 21
3   Petite pensée, E♭; QR xviii, 25
4   Une bagatelle, E♭ (Paris, c1880–85); QR xviii, 29
5   Mélodie italienne: une bagatelle ('In nomine Patris'), A♭ (Paris,
      c1880–85), QR xviii, 1
6   Petite caprice (style Offenbach), C (Paris, c1880–85); QR ii, 1

Vol.xi: Miscellanée de musique vocale
1   Ariette villageoise (J.-J. Rousseau), S, pf; QR v, 72
2   La chanson de bébé (Pacini), Mez, pf; QR v, 25
3   Amour sans espoir ('Tirana all'espagnole rossinizé') (Pacini), S, pf,
      music identical with vol.i, no.3
4   A ma belle mère ('Requiem eternam'), A, pf; QR xi, 58
5   O salutaris, de campagne, A
6   Aragonese (Metastasio), S, pf; QR iv, 44
7   Arietta all'antica, dedotta da O salutaris ostia (Metastasio), S, pf,
      based on O salutaris hostia (29 Nov 1857); QR iv, 60
8   Il candore in fuga, 2 S, A, T, B
9   Salve amabilis Maria ('Hymne à la musique'), motet, S, A, T, B;
      QR vii, 77
10   Giovanna d'Arco, cantata, S, pf, str; QR xi, 1
Vol.xii: Quelques riens pour album, 24 pieces, pf (Paris, c1880–85);
      nos.1, 2, 10, 11, 19, 20, 21 and 24 ed. L. Rognoni (Milan, 1951),
      nos.11, 12, 14 and 16 ed. Stravinsky (New York, Frankfurt and
      London, 1962)
Vol. xiii: Musique anodine (Metastasio), 15 April 1857; QR iv, 62
      Prélude, pf
6 petites mélodies: 1 Alto, pf; 2 Bar, pf; 3–4 S, pf; 5 Mez, pf; 6 Bar, pf

OTHER LATE WORKS
(*MS in Fondazione Rossini unless otherwise stated*)
Canone scherzosa a quattro soprani democratici, 4 S, pf
Canone antisavant (Rossini), 3 vv
Canzonetta 'La vénitienne', C, pf; QR xviii, 33
Petite promenade de Passy à Courbevoie, C, pf

Une réjouissance, a, pf; QR xviii, 46
Encore un peu de blague, C, pf; QR xviii, 52
Tourniquet sur la gamme chromatique, ascendante et déscendante, C,
      pf; QR xviii, 55
Ritournelle gothique, C, pf; QR xviii, 63
Un rien (pour album): Ave Maria, S, pf; QR xi, 60
Pour album: Sogna il guerrier (Metastasio), Bar, pf
Brindisi 'Del fanciullo il primo canto', B, chorus
Solo per violoncello, a; QR vi, 9 [with added pf acc.]
Questo palpito soave, S, pf
L'ultimo pensiero ('Patria, consorti, figli') (L. F. Cerutti), Bar, (?) pf,
      Fonds Michotte, Brussels
Thème, E♭, pf, *I-Trt*, partial facs. in *La Musica E*

MISCELLANEOUS
Teodora e Ricciardino, introduction to opera, sketched c1815,
      Fondazione Rossini
Gorghcggi e solfeggi, studies, 1v, pf, c1827 (Paris, 1827)
15 petits exercices, 1v, 1858 (Paris, c1880)
Petit gargouillement, exercice, 1v, 1867, *F-Po*
Giovinetta pellegrina, variations on a romance by N. Vaccai, ed. in *La
      cronaca musicale* (Pesaro, 1912)
Vocal variants, cadenzas, etc for Rossini's operas, autographs in Fonds
      Michotte, Brussels, *F-Po*, *I-Mc*, *US-Cu*, *NYpm*, and elsewhere

ADAPTATIONS INVOLVING ROSSINI'S PARTICIPATION
Ivanhoé (opera, E. Deschamps and G.-G. de Wailly), Paris, Théâtre de
      l'Odéon, 15 Sept 1826, MS excerpts in *GB-Lbm*, full score (Paris,
      1826) [adapted by A. Pacini, from several of Rossini's operas]
Robert Bruce (opera, A. Reyer and G. Vaëz), PO, 30 Dec 1846, full
      score (Paris, 1847) [adapted by A.-L. Niedermeyer from several of
      Rossini's operas, especially La donna del lago]

WORKS NOT TRACED OR OF UNCERTAIN AUTHENTICITY
(*sacred*)
Miserere, solo vv, chorus, orch, full score (Leipzig, 1831) as Trost und
      Erhebung
Dixit Domino, solo vv, chorus, orch, *I-Mc*

(*other vocal*)
Aria di Filippuccio ('Il secreto se si perde'), buffo v, orch, ed. (Trieste,
      1892)
La calabrese ('Colla lanterna magica'), S, A, pf, *Vc*
Cara, voi siete quella, ? T, orch, ed. (Florence, 1902)
Duetto buffo di due gatti, 2vv, pf, Fondazione Rossini; QR iv, 1
Quando giunse qua Belfior, S, orch, ?1824–35, *FOc*, ed. A. Garbelotto,
      6 arie inedite (Padua, 1968)
Il rimprovero ('Se fra le trecce d'Ebano'), S, pf, ed. (Florence, 1944)
Vieni sull'onde, S, T, pf, Fonds Michotte, Brussels
L'absence, ? pubd Paris, n.d., mentioned in Radiciotti (1927–9), iii,
      250; not traced
Il baco da seta, ?1862, ? pubd Paris, 1862, mentioned in Montazio,
      125; not traced

(*instrumental*)
12 valzer per due flauti, on themes from Rossini's operas (Milan, c1827)
Sinfonia di Odense, A, orch, MS parts in Odense; QR viii, 17

BIBLIOGRAPHY
SOURCE MATERIALS
G. Mazzatinti: *Lettere inedite di Gioacchino Rossini* (Imola, 1890, rev.
      2/1892 as *Lettere inedite e rare di G. Rossini*, rev. 3/1902 as *Lettere
      di G. Rossini*, with F. and G. Manis)
A. Allmayer: *Undici lettere di Gioachino Rossini pubblicate per la
      prima volta* (Siena, 1892)
G. Biagi: 'Undici lettere inedite di G. Rossini', *Onoranze fiorentine a
      Gioachino Rossini* (Florence, 1902), 101
R. De Rensis: 'Rossini intimo: lettere all'amico Santocanale', *Musica
      d'oggi*, xiii (1931), 343
F. Schlitzer: *Rossiniana: contributo all'epistolario di G. Rossini*,
      Quaderni dell'Accademia chigiana, xxxv (Siena, 1956)
——: *Un piccolo carteggio inedito di Rossini con un impresario italiano
      a Vienna* (Florence, 1959)
F. Walker: 'Rossiniana in the Piancastelli Collection', *MMR*, xc (1960),
      138, 203
V. Viviani, ed.: *I libretti di Rossini* (Milan, 1965)
P. Gossett: 'Le fonti autografe delle opere teatrali di Rossini', *NRMI*, ii
      (1968), 936
——, ed.: *La Cenerentola: riproduzione dell'autografo esistente presso
      l'Accademia filarmonica di Bologna* (Bologna, 1969)
——: *The Operas of Rossini: Problems of Textual Criticism in
      Nineteenth-century Opera* (diss., Princeton U., 1970)
B. Cagli, P. Gossett and A. Zedda: 'Criteri per l'edizione critica delle
      opere di Gioachino Rossini', *Bollettino del Centro rossiniano di studi*
      (1974), no.1
F. Lippmann: 'Autographe Briefe Rossinis und Donizettis in der
      Bibliothek Massino, Rom', *AnMc*, no. 19 (1979), 330

MEMOIRS BY CONTEMPORARIES

Stendhal: *Rome, Naples, et Florence en 1817* (Paris, 1817; Eng. trans., 1959)

G. Righetti-Giorgi: *Cenni di una donna già cantante sopra il maestro Rossini* (Bologna, 1823; repr. in Rognoni, 2/1968)

G. Carpani: *Le rossiniane ossia Lettere musico-teatrali* (Padua, 1824)

J. Ebers: *Seven Years of the King's Theatre* (London, 1828)

L. Escudier: *Mes souvenirs* (Paris, 1863–8)

G. Pacini: *Le mie memorie artistiche* (Florence, 1865, rev. 2/1872)

F. Hiller: 'Plaudereien mit Rossini (1856)', *Aus dem Tonleben unserer Zeit*, ii (Leipzig, 1868, 2/1871), 1–84

R. Wagner: 'Eine Erinnerung an Rossini', *Allgemeine Zeitung* (Augsburg, 17 Dec 1868; repr. in *Gesammelte Schriften und Dichtungen*, viii, Leipzig, 1883, 2/1888; Eng. trans., 1895/R1966)

F. Mordani: *Della vita privata di G. Rossini: memorie inedite* (Imola, 1871)

G. De Sanctis: *Gioacchino Rossini: appunti di viaggio* (Rome, 1878)

G. L. Duprez: *Souvenirs d'un chanteur* (Paris, 1880)

E. Branca: *Felice Romani ed i più riputati maestri di musica del suo tempo* (Turin, Florence and Rome, 1882)

G. Dupré: *Ricordi autobiografici* (Florence, 1895, 2/1896 as *Pensieri sull'arte e ricordi autobiografici*)

A. Cametti: *Un poeta melodrammatico romano: appunti e notizie in gran parte inedite sopra Jacopo Ferretti e i musicisti del suo tempo* (Milan, 1898)

E. Michotte: *Souvenirs personnels: la visite de R. Wagner à Rossini (Paris, 1860)* (Paris, 1906, repr. in Rognoni, 2/1968; Eng. trans., 1968, ed. H. Weinstock)

——: *Souvenirs: une soirée chez Rossini à Beau-Séjour (Passy) 1858* (Brussels, c1910; Eng. trans., 1968, ed. H. Weinstock)

C. Saint-Saëns: *Ecole buissonnière* (Paris, 1913; Eng. trans., 1919, as *Musical Memories*)

GENERAL LITERATURE

Guerre aux Rossinistes (Paris, 1821)

Stendhal: *Vie de Rossini* (Paris, 1824, rev. 2/1922 by H. Prunières; Eng. trans., 1956, 2/1970 with introduction by R. N. Coe)

A. Wendt: *Rossinis Leben und Treiben* (Leipzig, 1824)

H. Berton: *De la musique mécanique et de la musique philosophique* (Paris, 1826)

J.-L. d'Ortigue: *De la guerre des dilettanti* (Paris, 1829)

P. Brighenti: *Della musica rossiniana e del suo autore* (Bologna, 1830, 2/1833)

A. Zanolini: *Biografia di Gioachino Rossini* (Paris, 1836, rev. Bologna, 1875)

M. and L. Escudier: *Rossini: sa vie et ses oeuvres* (Paris, 1854)

Castil-Blaze: *L'Opéra-Italien de 1548 à 1856* (Paris, 1856)

E. Montazio: *Giovacchino Rossini* (Turin, 1862)

A. Aulagnier: *G. Rossini: sa vie et ses oeuvres* (Paris, 1864)

A. Azevedo: *G. Rossini: sa vie et ses oeuvres* (Paris, 1864)

H. S. Edwards: *The Life of Rossini* (London, 1869, rev. 2/1881 as *Rossini and his School*)

A. Pougin: *Rossini: notes, impressions, souvenirs, commentaires* (Paris, 1871)

L. S. Silvestri: *Della vita e delle opere di Gioachino Rossini: notizie biografico-artistico-aneddotico-critiche* (Milan, 1874)

E. vander Straeten: *La mélodie populaire dans l'opéra 'Guillaume Tell' de Rossini* (Paris, 1879)

Bollettino del primo centenario rossiniano (Pesaro, 1892)

L. Dauriac: *La psychologie dans l'opéra français: Auber, Rossini, Meyerbeer* (Paris, 1897)

——: *Rossini: biographie critique* (Paris, 1906)

A. Sandberger: 'Rossiniana', *ZIMG*, ix (1907–8), 336; repr. in *Ausgewählte Aufsätze* (Munich, 1921)

E. Istel: 'Rossiniana', *Die Musik*, x/19 (1910–11), 1

A. Soubies: *Le Théâtre-Italien de 1801 à 1913* (Paris, 1913)

E. Celani: 'Musica e musicisti in Roma (1750–1850)', *RMI*, xxii (1915), 257–300

G. Fara: *Genio e ingegno musicale: Gioachino Rossini* (Turin, 1915)

A. Cametti: 'La musica teatrale a Roma cento anni fa', *Regia Accademia di Santa Cecilia: annuario* (Rome, 1915–30)

F. Vatielli: *Rossini a Bologna* (Bologna, 1918)

A. Casella: 'Some Reasons why a Futurist may Admire Rossini', *The Chesterian*, ii (London, 1920), 321

H. de Curzon: *Rossini* (Paris, 1920)

V. Cavazzocca Mazzanti: 'Rossini a Verona durante il Congresso del 1822', *Atti e memorie dell'Accademia di agricoltura, scienze e lettere di Verona*, 4th ser., xxiv (Verona, 1922), 53–112

G. Radiciotti: *Gioacchino Rossini: vita documentata, opere ed influenza su l'arte* (Tivoli, 1927–9)

——: *Aneddoti rossiniani autentici* (Rome, 1929)

J.-G. Prod'homme: 'Rossini and his Works in France', *MQ*, xvii (1931), 119

G. H. J. Derwent: *Rossini and some Forgotten Nightingales* (London, 1934)

F. Toye: *Rossini: a Study in Tragi-comedy* (London, 1934, 2/1954/R1963)

H. Faller: *Die Gesangskoloratur in Rossinis Opern und ihre Ausführung* (Berlin, 1935)

Rossiniana (Bologna, 1942)

A. Capri: 'Rossini e l'estetica teatrale della vocalità', *RMI*, xlvi (1942), 353

A. Della Corte: 'Fra gorgheggi e melodie di Rossini', *Musica*, i (1942), 23

U. Rolandi: 'Librettistica rossiniana', *Musica*, i (1942), 40

L. Ronga: 'Vicende del gusto rossiniano nell'ottocento', *Musica*, i (1942), 6

——: 'Svolgimento del gusto rossiniano al novecento', *Musica*, ii (1943), 184

G. Roncaglia: *Rossini l'olimpico* (Milan, 1946, 2/1953)

F. Barberio: 'La regina d'Etruria e Rossini', *RMI*, lv (1953), 64

Rassegna musicale, xxiv/3 (1954), 209–303 [special issue]

Bollettino del Centro rossiniano di studi (1955–60, 1967–)

L. Rognoni: *Rossini* (Parma, 1956, 2/1968, rev. 3/1977)

F. Schlitzer: *Rossini e Siena*, Quaderni dell'Accademia chigiana, xxxix (Siena, 1958)

A. Toni and T. Serafin: *Stile, tradizioni e convenzioni del melodramma italiano del settecento e dell'ottocento* (Milan, 1958)

R. Bacchelli: *Rossini e Esperienze rossiniane* (Milan, 1959)

E. N. McKay: 'Rossinis Einfluss auf Schubert', *ÖMz*, xviii (1963), 17

D. W. Schwartz: 'Rossini: a Psychoanalytic Approach to the Great Renunciation', *Journal of the American Psychoanalytic Society*, xiii (1965), 551

R. Celletti: 'Vocalità rossiniana', *L'opera*, ii (Milan, 1966), 3

F. d'Amico: *L'opera teatrale di Gioacchino Rossini* (Rome, 1968)

G. Barblan: 'Rossini e il suo tempo', *Chigiana*, xxv (1968), 143–79

F. Bisogni: 'Rossini e Schubert', *NRMI*, ii (1968), 920

A. Bonaccorsi, ed.: *Gioacchino Rossini* (Florence, 1968)

R. Celletti: 'Origini e sviluppi della coloratura rossiniana', *NRMI*, ii (1968), 872–919

——: 'Il vocalismo italiano da Rossini a Donizetti: Parte I: Rossini', *AnMc*, v (1968), 267

M. Fabbri: 'Ignoti momenti rossiniani', *Chigiana*, xxv (1968), 265

P. Gossett: 'Rossini and Authenticity', *MT*, cix (1968), 1006

F. Lippmann: 'Per un'esegesi dello stile rossiniano', *NRMI*, ii (1968), 813–56

H. Weinstock: *Rossini: a Biography* (New York, 1968)

P. Gossett: 'Gioachino Rossini and the Conventions of Composition', *AcM*, xlii (1970), 48

J. Loschelder: 'L'infanzia di Gioacchino Rossini', *Bollettino del Centro rossiniano di studi* (1972), no.1, p.45; no.2, p.33

——: 'Rossinis Bild und Zerbild in der Allgemeinen musikalischen Zeitung Leipzig', *Bollettino del Centro rossiniano di studi* (1973), no.1, p.23; no.2, p.33

STUDIES OF INDIVIDUAL WORKS

H. Berlioz: 'Guillaume Tell', *Gazette musicale*, i (1834), Oct–Nov, 326, 336, 341, 349; Eng. trans. in *Source Readings in Music History*, ed. O. Strunk (New York, 1950)

J. L. d'Ortigue: Le *'Stabat' de Rossini* (Paris, 1841)

A. Aulagnier: *Quelques observations sur la publication du 'Stabat Mater' de Rossini* (Paris, 1842)

J. A. Delaire: *Observations d'un amateur non dilettante au sujet du 'Stabat' de M. Rossini* (Paris, 1842)

A. W. Ambros: 'Die "Messe solennelle" von Rossini', *Bunte Blätter*, i (Leipzig, 1872), 81

G. C. Hirt [pseud. of L. Torchi]: 'Di alcuni autografi di G. Rossini', *RMI*, ii (1895), 23 [on *Péchés de vieillesse*]

G. Romagnoli: 'Gioacchino Rossini, Giulio Perticari e la "Gazza ladra"', *Vita italiana*, iii (1897), 106

A. Cametti: 'Il "Guglielmo Tell" e le sue prime rappresentazioni in Italia', *RMI*, vi (1899), 580

G. M. Gatti: *Le 'Barbier de Séville' de Rossini* (Paris, 1925)

H. Prunières: 'L' "Edipo a Colono" de Rossini', *RdM*, xiv (1933), 32

P. Ingerslev-Jensen: 'An Unknown Rossini Overture: Report of a Discovery in Odense', *MR*, xi (1950), 19 [on so-called *Sinfonia di Odense*]

P. R. Kirby: 'Rossini's Overture to "William Tell"', *ML*, xxxiii (1952), 132

A. Melica: 'Due operine di Rossini', *Musicisti della scuola emiliana*, Chigiana, xiii (1956), 59 [on *L'inganno felice* and *L'occasione fa il ladro*]

G. Confalonieri: 'Avventure di una partitura rossiniana: l' "Adina ovvero Il califfo di Bagdad"', *Le celebrazioni del 1963 e alcune nuove indagine sulla musica italiana del XVIII e XIX secolo*, Chigiana, xx (1963), 206

J. W. Klein: 'Verdi's "Otello" and Rossini's', *ML*, xlv (1964), 130

A. Porter: 'A Lost Opera by Rossini', *ML*, xlv (1964), 39 [on *Ugo, re d'Italia*]

A. Damerini: 'La prima ripresa moderna di un'opera giovanile di Rossini: "L'equivoco stravagante" (1811)', *Chigiana*, xxii (1965), 229

A. Zedda: 'Appunti per una lettura fiologica del "Barbiere" ', *L'opera*, ii (Milan, 1966), 13

P. Gossett: 'Rossini in Naples: some Major Works Recovered', *MQ*, liv (1968), 316 [on *Le nozze di Teti, e di Peleo, Messa di gloria*, etc]

M. Tartak: 'The Two "Barbieri" ', *ML*, 1 (1969), 453

G. Carli Ballola: 'Una *pièce à sauvetage* da Salvare', *Bollettino del Centro rossiniano di studi* (1971), 11 [on *Torvaldo e Dorliska*]

P. Petrobelli: 'Balzac, Stendhal e il *Mosè* di Rossini', *Conservatorio di musica 'G. B. Martini' di Bologna: Annuario 1965–1970* (1971), 205

B. Cagli: 'Le fonti letterarie dei libretti di Rossini', *Bollettino del Centro rossiniano di studi* (1972), no.2, p.10 [on *Maometto II*]; (1973), no.1, p.8 [on *Bianca e Falliero*]

G. Carli Ballola: 'Lettura dell'*Ermione*', *Bollettino del Centro rossiniano di studi* (1972), no.3, p.13

S. Martinotti: 'I "peccati" del giovane e del vecchio Rossini', *Quadrivium*, xiv (1973), 249–72

M. Tartak: 'Matilde and her Cousins', *Bollettino del Centro rossiniano di studi* (1973), no.3, p.13

P. Isotta: 'I diamanti della corona: grammatica del Rossini napoletano', *Mosè in Egitto*, Opera: collana di guide musicali, iv (Turin, 1974)

P. Gallarati: 'Dramma e ludus dall'*Italiana* al *Barbiere*', *Il melodramma italiano dell'ottocento: studi e ricerche per Massimo Mila* (Turin, 1977)

P. Gossett: *The Tragic Finale of 'Tancredi'* (Pesaro, 1977)

F. Tammaro: 'Ambivalenza dell'*Otello* rossiniano', *Il melodramma italiano dell'ottocento: studi e ricerche per Massimo Mila* (Turin, 1977)

PHILIP GOSSETT

Rossino Mantovano (*fl* 1505–11). Italian composer. He was an alto at Mantua Cathedral in 1509 and *maestro di cappella* there in 1510–11. Five frottolas by him survive (*RISM* 1505³, 1505⁴, 1507⁴; 4 ed. G. Cesari and others, *Le frottole nell'edizione principe di Ottaviano Petrucci*, i, Cremona, 1954); they are compactly written in the forms of the *barzelletta* and *oda*.

BIBLIOGRAPHY

P. M. Tagmann: *Archivalische Studien zur Musikpflege am Dom von Mantua* (Berne, 1967)

K. Jeppesen: *La frottola* (Copenhagen, 1968–70), i, 82ff, 106, 118, 128ff; ii, 265ff

W. Prizer: *Marchetto Cara and the North Italian Frottola* (diss., U. of North Carolina, 1974)

JOAN WESS

Rössler, Anton [Franz Anton; František Antonín]. *See* ROSETTI, ANTONIO.

Rössler, Ernestine. *See* SCHUMANN-HEINK, ERNESTINE.

Rössler, Johann Joseph. *See* RÖSLER, JAN JOSEF.

Rosso, Giovanni Maria del. *See* ROSSI, GIOVANNI MARIA DE.

Rosso [Roth], **Hieronymus** [Girolamo] (*b* Ancona; *fl* 1614). German composer and organist of Italian birth. In his only known work, *Missae quatuor octonis vocibus, quae variis instrumentis chorisque coniunctis ac separatis concini possunt* (Frankfurt am Main, 1614), he is described as 'Anconitanus' and organist of Worms Cathedral. The wording of the title defines him as an adherent of the concertato mass, which was being developed in Germany and Italy in the early 17th century. All four works are parody masses, and the material on which they are based is named.

AUGUST SCHARNAGL

Rosso, Il. *See* BIANCHINI, DOMENICO.

Rosso de Chollegrana. Italian composer. His only known composition is a two-voice madrigal, *Tremando più che foglia*, in *GB-Lbm* 29987 (no.101). Stylistically the piece belongs to the Tuscan circle of *c*1350–60. Any

identification with the composer P. Rosso (Petrus Rubeus) of *I-Bc* Q15 and *GB-Ob* 213 is thus out of the question.

BIBLIOGRAPHY

J. Wolf: *Geschichte der Mensuralnotation von 1250–1460* (Leipzig, 1904/*R*1965), ii, iii, no.60

N. Pirrotta, ed.: *The Music of Fourteenth-century Italy*, CMM, viii/3 (1962), 43 and p.ii

W. T. Marrocco, ed.: *Italian Secular Music*, PMFC, vii (1971), 27

For further bibliography *see* SOURCES, MS.

KURT VON FISCHER

Rossoni, Giulio (*fl* 1665–81). Italian singer and composer. He was a tenor and was employed as a chamber musician at the Bavarian court at Munich from at least the beginning of 1665 to 1681. In 1667 he sang in J. K. Kerll's opera *Le pretensioni del sole* (text by the court poet D. Gisberti). He composed the opera *L'Adelaide Regia Principessa di Susa* (to a libretto by G. B. Rodoteo), performed at Munich on 31 October 1669 in celebration of the birthday of Duke Ferdinand of Bavaria and formerly attributed to GIULIO RIVA. He sang in operas at Milan in 1678 and at Parma in 1681.

BIBLIOGRAPHY

EitnerQ

F. M. Rudhart: *Geschichte der Oper am Hofe zu München* (Freising, 1865)

J. J. Maier: 'Archivalische Excerpte über die herzogliche Hof-Kapelle in München', *KJb*, ix (1894), 67

L. Schiedermair: 'Die Anfänge der Münchener Oper', *SIMG*, v (1903–4), 454

THOMAS WALKER

Rossum, Frederik (Leon Hendrik) van (*b* Elsene, Brussels, 5 Dec 1939). Belgian composer of Dutch origin. He took Belgian nationality at the age of 18 and studied composition under Souris and Marcel Quinet at the Brussels Conservatory. Thereafter he was appointed piano teacher at the Brussels Conservatory (1965), professor of counterpoint at the Liège Conservatory (1968), professor of analysis at the Brussels Conservatory (1971) and director of the Watermael-Bosvoorde Music Academy. In 1965 he won the Belgian Prix de Rome and in 1973 the Paul Gilson Prize for *Rétrospection*.

WORKS
(selective list)

Orch: Sinfonietta, op.7, 1964; Symphonie concertante, op.11, hn, pf, perc, orch, 1967; 12 miniatures, op.15, 1967; Der blaue Reiter, op.23, 1971; Epitaphi, op.25, str, 1972; Réquisitoire, op.28, brass, perc, 1973; Pf Conc., op.30, 1975; Petite suite réactionnaire, op.32, 1975

Vocal: Threni, op.22, Mez, orch, 1969; Rétrospection, op.27, S, A, chorus, 5 perc, 2 pf, 1973; De soldaat Johan, op.33 (television opera), 1975–6; songs (Rilke, Apollinaire)

Incidental music, chamber and pf pieces incl. Hommage à Kafka, op.35, pf, perc, 1979

Principal publishers: CeBeDeM, Schmitt, Hall and McCreary, Schott

CORNEEL MERTENS

Rost, Franz (*b* Mahlberg, nr. Lahr, Baden, probably shortly before 1640; *d* Strasbourg, 1688). German church musician, copyist and ?composer. He appears to have attended the Jesuit college at Baden-Baden and he sang at the collegiate church there. He started to learn the organ in 1653, and he may have learnt the violin as well. He may have been taught both instruments by the Kantor of the collegiate church, whom he later (at an uncertain date) succeeded in that office. He also entered holy orders. From about 1660, Rost seems to have been entrusted – possibly by the Margrave of Baden-Baden for use at court – with the copying of trio sonatas by prominent composers of the time. He was able to take his MS, the so-called Rost MS, with him when he moved to take up an ecclesiastical post at St Peter's, Strasbourg, some time in the 1680s; it was thus saved from the destruction of the margrave's residence in 1689. Brossard bought it from Rost's heirs. From him it passed in 1726 to the Bibliothèque Royale, Paris, now the Bibliothèque Nationale, where it is MS Rés.Vm⁷653.

The Rost MS consists of 157 works, the vast majority sonatas or sonata-like pieces; 27 composers are named and 28 works are known to be Italian. There are 81 anonymous pieces, some of which may be by Rost himself. Since the margraves were buried in the collegiate church it is understandable that the collection contains many *tombeaux* and funeral pieces and others marked 'grave', as well as several church sonatas. But it also contains chamber sonatas mostly for two violins and continuo, and comic and entertainment music, such as 'Polish bagpipe' and pieces by J. H. Schmelzer, numerous capriccios by Rosenmüller and Giuseppe Zamponi among others, and an even larger number of battaglias, including four each by J. M. Nicolai and the younger Stoss of the Düsseldorf Kapelle and one by Schmelzer.

Carl Rosier is the best-represented composer in the MS, with 22 works. Then come Schmelzer (18 works), Cazzati (14) and one Toleta (12). Of other well-known composers, G. B. Vitali and Bertali are represented by four works and Rosenmüller by three. There are also single pieces by more than a dozen composers, among them such well-known names as Fux, Kerll, J. P. Krieger and Carissimi, who is represented by the only motet, the solo Christmas piece *Salve, puellulae regalis animi*. Others include Zamponi and Balthazar Richard, both from Brussels, and the Pole, Marcia Mielczewski. Such names as these highlight the wide area upon which Rost drew in his compilation. This is possibly accounted for by the number of courts that had friendly relations with the young margrave (who was known as 'Türkenlouis' for his part in repulsing the Turkish threat to eastern Europe) and thus lent him MSS for copying. The Habsburgs seem to have been particularly generous, since the MS contains works by 13 German and two Italian composers working at the Viennese court.

BIBLIOGRAPHY
H. J. Moser: 'Eine pariser Quelle zur wiener Triosonate des ausgehenden 17. Jahrhunderts: der Codex Rost', *Festschrift Wilhelm Fischer* (Innsbruck, 1956), 75
F. Baser: *Musikheimat Baden-Württemberg* (Freiburg, 1963)
——: 'Der "Codex Rost": aus der Heimat des Grossvaters Leopold Mozarts', *Acta Mozartiana*, xviii (1971), 14
——: *Grosse Musiker in Baden-Baden* (Tutzing, 1974)
FRIEDRICH BASER

Rost, Nicolaus. See ROSTHIUS, NICOLAUS.

Rostal, Max (*b* Teschen, Silesia, 7 Aug 1905). British violinist of Austrian birth. He studied with Arnold Rosé in Vienna and Carl Flesch in Berlin, and gave public performances from the age of six. He also took composition lessons at the Berlin Hochschule für Musik with Emil Bohnke and Matyás Seiber. In 1928 he was appointed assistant to Flesch, and later became the youngest professor at the Berlin Hochschule (1930–33). He left Germany to settle in London, where he was a professor at the GSM (1944–58) and profoundly influenced a generation of violinists whom he taught and encouraged. Among his pupils were Yfrah Neaman and members of the Amadeus Quartet. In 1957 he was appointed a professor at the Cologne Academy, and in 1958 at the

conservatory at Berne, where he settled.

During his years in Britain Rostal toured frequently as a soloist, winning consistent acclaim for a sweet and transparent tone underlaid by rhythmic drive and incisive attack. He introduced to Britain Khachaturian's Violin Concerto and Bartók's Second Concerto (for which he was specially distinguished), and gave first performances of concertos dedicated to him by Alan Bush, Benjamin Frankel, Franz Reizenstein and Bernard Stevens, and the *Fantasia* by Mátyás Seiber. A number of his teaching compositions have been published, as well as editions and transcriptions, including a transcription for violin of the cadenzas Beethoven wrote when he transcribed his Violin Concerto for piano. Rostal has made numerous recordings, and from time to time has led and conducted chamber ensembles. He has also formed excellent duo partnerships with Franz Osborne and (from 1954) Colin Horsley, and played in a piano trio with his Cologne colleagues Heinz Schröter and Siegfried Palm. He owned a 1698 violin by Antonio Stradivari, now known as the 'Max Rostal', and also possesses the 'Charles Reade' Guarneri 'del Gesù' (1733) and a viola by Giuseppe Guadagnini. In association with Menuhin, Palm and others, he established in 1974 the European String Teachers' Association for the exchange of information on the technique and teaching of string playing, and described its purpose in *The Listener*, xcii (1974), 20. He was made a CBE in 1977.

BIBLIOGRAPHY
D. Brook: *Violinists of Today* (London, 1948)
NOËL GOODWIN

Rostand, Claude (*b* Paris, 3 Dec 1912; *d* Villejuif, Val de Marne, 9 Oct 1970). French music critic. He read literature and law at the Sorbonne and studied the piano, harmony, counterpoint, composition and music history privately with Edouard Mignan, Marc Vaubourgoin, Jacques Février and Norbert Dufourcq. For many years he was music critic of *Carrefour*, *Le Figaro littéraire* and *Le monde*, and French correspondent of *Melos*, the *New York Times* and *Musical America*; he was a humanist scholar of great erudition, but his articles and his popular lectures to the Jeunesses Musicales were lucid and direct. He also worked as a producer for ORTF (French television) and for various German radio stations. He was a constant student and supporter of contemporary music, becoming vice-president of the ISCM in 1961; he gave a weekly series of radio lectures called 'Ephémérides de la musique contemporaine' and from 1958 organized concerts of contemporary music called 'Musique d'aujourd'hui' in the Théâtre National Populaire. Rostand's *Dictionnaire de la musique contemporaine*, his last book, is a further product of his deeply felt desire to bring 20th-century music to a wider audience.

WRITINGS
L'oeuvre de Gabriel Fauré (Paris, 1945)
Les chefs-d'oeuvre du piano (Paris, 1950)
Les chefs-d'oeuvre de la musique de chambre (Paris, 1952)
Entretiens avec Darius Milhaud (Paris, 1952)
Brahms (Paris, 1954–5)
Entretiens avec Francis Poulenc (Paris, 1954)
Olivier Messiaen (Paris, 1957)
Entretiens avec Igor Markevitch (Paris, 1959)
La musique allemande (Paris, 1960)
Liszt (Paris, 1960; Eng. trans., 1970)
Richard Strauss: l'homme et son oeuvre (Paris, 1964)
Hugo Wolf (Paris, 1967)
Anton Webern (Paris, 1969)
Dictionnaire de la musique contemporaine (Paris, 1970)
YVONNE TIÉNOT

Rosthius [Rost], **Nicolaus** (*b* Weimar, *c*1542; *d* Kosma, nr. Altenburg, Thuringia, 22 Nov 1622). German composer. He may have been a pupil at the choir school in Torgau, but by 1560 was attending school in Altenburg where he was also a member of the municipal choir, at that time directed by Köler. Rosthius followed Köler to the court at Schwerin in 1563, but returned to Altenburg in 1564. In 1568 he is known to have been a member of the court chapel in Weimar, being promoted to Kapellmeister in 1569; the choir was disbanded in 1571.

After 1571 Rosthius became a citizen of Weimar and probably held a municipal appointment. From 1578 to 1579 he taught music at the Protestant state school in Linz (on the Danube). Late in 1579 he matriculated at Heidelberg, where, shortly afterwards, he was appointed a master and singer at the academy. He was in the service of Count von Erbach (Odenwald) in about 1590, but returned to Altenburg probably in 1593 to serve in the court chapel of the Ernestine Duchy of Saxe-Altenburg: there in 1594 he described himself as 'Cappelneltester'. He held the post of court Kapellmeister until 1601, then moving to nearby Kosma where, until his death, he was a minister.

Rosthius's song motets and occasional *Spruchmotette* show him to have been a master of the smaller forms. The texted galliards are curious, for usually galliards appear only as purely instrumental music. Of greater significance, however, is his *Die trostreiche Historie von der fröhlichen Auferstehung . . . Jesu Christi*, which forms a link between, on the one hand, the corresponding anonymous work of around 1550 and that of A. Scandello, and on the other hand, that by Schütz. It belongs to the so-called mixed type, involving elements of both the motet-Passion and the dramatic Passion. A poem about the abduction of the two Saxon princes in 1455 does not survive.

WORKS

Fröliche newe teutsche Gesäng, 4–6vv (Frankfurt am Main, 1583)
XXX newer lieblicher Galliardt, mit schönen lustigen Texten, 4vv (Erfurt, 1593), 2 vols; 1 ed. Antiqua Chorbuch, ii/4 (Mainz, 1951–2), 193
Die trostreiche Historie von der fröhlichen Auferstehung . . . Jesu Christi, D-Bds, 1598; ed. in Handbuch der deutschen evangelischen Kirchenmusik, i/3–4 (in preparation)
Psalmus 127, 8vv (Jena, 1603)
Klagelied aus Esaia 56, 8vv (Jena, 1603)
Cantiones selectissimae, 6, 8vv (Gera, 1613/14)
1 motet in D-Z: Congratulamini nunc, 6vv
3 German works in PL-WRu: Es erhub sich ein Streit, 5vv; Hört zu und seid fein still, 5vv; Nun lobt den Herrn mit Andacht, 5vv
3 works in 1606¹⁴, 1609²⁸, 1622¹⁵

BIBLIOGRAPHY

J. Löbe: Geschichte der Kirchen und Schulen des Herzogtums Sachsen-Altenburg (Altenburg, 1886)
A. Aber: Die Pflege der Musik unter den Wettinern und wettinischen Ernestinern (Bückeburg and Leipzig, 1921)
H. J. Moser: Die Musik im frühevangelischen Österreich (Kassel, 1954)
G. Eismann: David Köler: ein protestantische Komponist des 16. Jahrhunderts (Berlin, 1956)
G. Pietzsch: Quellen und Forschungen zur Geschichte der Musik am kurpfälzischen Hof zu Heidelberg bis 1622 (Wiesbaden, 1963)
WALTER BLANKENBURG

Rostock. City in the German Democratic Republic, at the estuary of the Warnow. The earliest records of musical activity date from the late 13th century; names such as Herbordus 'timponator' (1287), Stacius 'basunre' and Johannes 'lireman' (1288) probably refer to civic musicians. Records have survived from before the Reformation listing town musicians, minstrels and organists. Rostock was an important Hanseatic centre until the Thirty Years War (1618–48), and the first university in northern Europe was founded there in 1419. During 1465–87 the Rostocker Liederbuch was compiled at the university. The first hymnbooks in Low German were published in Rostock in 1525 and 1531 by the reformer Joachim Slüter. The number of town musicians (*fistulatores, piper, bassuner*, and in the 16th century *stadt spellude* or *Kunstspielleute*) was increased to three in 1453 and four in 1574.

In 1623 the council appointed Balthasar Kirchhof as the first director of instrumental music. Joachim Burmeister was Marienkantor until 1593 and Magister of the Nikolaischule until 1629, Daniel Friderici was Marienkantor in 1618–38 and 'Kapellmeister in allen Kirchen' from 1623, and Nikolaus Hasse was organist of the Marienkirche from 1642 to 1670. Other notable Kantors and organists were Antonius Mors, Nikolaus Gottschovius and Georg Patermann. The collection of songs of Petrus Fabricius, a student there from 1603 to 1608, and the two-volume *Delitiae musicae* (1656–8) by Hasse, dedicated to members of the university, attests to the musical activities of students.

The Thirty Years War and a disastrous fire in 1677 impaired the development of Rostock's musical life. After 1697 only one Stadtmusikant was employed. However, in the 18th century middle-class concert life developed. After 1726 public amateur concerts were given, known from 1757 as 'Wochenkonzerte', which achieved particular importance under the composer, author and organist Eucharius Florschütz (1756–1831) and F. W. Pannenberg. The first concerts by travelling virtuosos were given in 1769 and in 1781 Florschütz founded monthly public concerts, given by the Stadtkapelle. German and Italian troupes performed opera and operetta in the Hoftheater (opened 1751), 'Ballhaus', and, after 1786, the new Schauspielhaus. However, a permanent opera company was not formed until the second half of the 19th century.

In 1819 the first Rostocker Musikfest was held under the direction of J. A. Göpel, organist of the Jakobikirche, with the choral society that he had founded in the same year, later the Singakademie. In 1843 the fourth Norddeutsche Musikfest, directed by Heinrich Marschner, was held in Rostock and three of the 15 Mecklenburg festivals, of which the most important was the ninth (1885, directed by Hermann Kretzschmar) were subsequently held there. As a teacher of music, director of music and lecturer on music history Kretzschmar was the most important musical figure in Rostock in the decade 1877–87. He founded the Rostocker Konzertverein (1877), which organized four concerts annually with the orchestra of the Verein Rostocker Musiker, formed from the 'Bürgerkapelle' and the Hautboisten-Corps.

Gustav Eggers (1835–60), a lieder composer admired by Liszt, and Carl Grädener were the leading composers of 19th-century Rostock. The new Stadttheater was opened in 1895 and in 1897 the Stadt- und Theaterorchester was founded, which gave a new impetus to Rostock's musical life. Willibald Kähler was conductor there from 1897 to 1899, establishing a tradition of Wagner opera that drew many famous singers and such conductors as Nikisch and Richard Strauss. E. W. Mörike and Schmidt-Isserstedt also conducted in Rostock.

Since World War II Rostock has been a regional capital and the DDR's largest port. The main musical activities are the operas produced by the Volkstheater and the concerts given by the Philharmonic Orchestra. Other ensembles connected with the Volkstheater are the Rostock Nonet and the Rostock Chamber Orchestra. Among choirs the University Choir, directed by Hans-Jürgen Plog, is outstanding. Educational institutions include the Musikhochschule, founded in 1947 and directed by Wagner-Régeny until 1950, when it became a conservatory; and the Institute of Musicology, founded by Erich Schenk in 1929, and directed from 1970 by Rudolf Eller.

BIBLIOGRAPHY

H. Ebert: *Versuch einer Geschichte des Theaters in Rostock* (Güstrow, 1872)
K. Koppmann: *Geschichte der Stadt Rostock* (Rostock, 1887)
M. Seidel: *Geschichte des Rostocker Städtischer Orchesters* (Rostock, 1922)
R. Bauer: *Rostocks Musikleben im 18. Jahrhundert* (diss., U. of Rostock, 1938)
H. Erdmann: *Schulmusik im Mecklenburg-Schwerin von Pestalozzi bis zum Ende des 19. Jahrhunderts* (diss., U. of Rostock, 1940)
H. J. Daebeler: *Musiker und Musikpflege in Rostock von der Stadtgründung bis 1700* (diss., U. of Rostock, 1967)
A. Hingst: *Musiklehre und Musikleben an der Universität Rostock von ihrer Gründung 1419 bis zum Ende des 18. Jahrhunderts* (diss., U. of Rostock, 1970)
H. Tantzier: *75 Jahre Philharmonisches Orchester Rostock* (Rostock, 1972)

DIETER HÄRTWIG

Rostropovich, Mstislav (Leopoldovich) (*b* Baku, 27 March 1927). Soviet cellist, pianist and conductor. He began musical studies in early childhood with his parents, his mother being an accomplished pianist and his father a former student of Casals and a distinguished cellist who taught at the Gnesin Institute, Moscow, where Mstislav first studied. In 1943 he entered the Moscow Conservatory, studying the cello with Semyon Kozolupov and composition with Shostakovich and Vissaryon Shebalin. Rostropovich graduated with the highest distinction, and in the late 1940s won competitions in Moscow, Prague and Budapest. He received a Stalin Prize in 1951, and in 1956 he was appointed cello professor at the Moscow Conservatory. In 1970 he was awarded the Royal Philharmonic Society's gold medal, and in 1975 the honorary degree of MusD from Cambridge University.

After the improvement in cultural relations between the USSR and the West in the 1950s Rostropovich travelled widely on concert tours, making his British début at the Festival Hall in March 1956, and his American début at Carnegie Hall, New York, in April the same year. Musicians and audiences alike were quick to appreciate his exceptional mastery of style and technique. His playing combines unusual accuracy of intonation and fullness of tone in all registers, and his range of tone extends from eerie *sul ponticello* to a threatening rasp, from a lute-like plangency in pizzicato to a sonorous bell-like thrum. He effortlessly employs a variety of special techniques, such as *style brisé*, left-hand pizzicato, gradations of pizzicato dynamics and cross-rhythms, and sustains a powerful initial attack with continued intensity of character throughout the work. His instinctive feeling for the composer's intentions is as apparent in contemporary works as in the repertory of established classics, although on occasion his enthusiasm has been known to get the better of his judgment.

Several composers have written works for Rostropovich, beginning in the USSR with Glier, Khachaturian, Myaskovsky and Prokofiev, whose Sinfonia concertante op.125 was revised in 1952 with the cellist's collaboration, and whose unfinished Concertino op.132 was completed by Rostropovich and Kabalevsky after the composer's death in 1953. Shostakovich wrote his Cello Concerto no.1 op.107 for him, and it was when he introduced this to London in 1960 that he met and formed a lasting friendship with Britten, reawakening the latter's interest in instrumental music after a long period of mostly vocal composition. It brought about Britten's Sonata for cello and piano op.65, the Symphony for cello and orchestra op.68, and the three suites for unaccompanied cello opp.72, 80 and 87. They were all written for Rostropovich and first performed by him, mostly during the 1960s, with the Suite no.3 in 1974.

Rostropovich's skill and musical perception as a pianist has been readily apparent in song recitals with the soprano Galina Vishnevskaya, whom he married in 1955; and he made his conducting début in 1968 with *Eugene Onegin* at the Bol'shoy Theatre, Moscow, in which his wife sang Tatyana. He conducted this again during a visit by the Bol'shoy company to Paris in December 1969 to January 1970, when a performance was also recorded for the gramophone. His conducting at this time was widely felt to be over-indulgent towards the music's sentiment, and in his British début as a conductor with the New Philharmonia Orchestra at the Festival Hall in September 1974, his freedom and flexibility of phrasing made the most of emotional character at the cost of some precision of orchestral ensemble. A recording of *Tosca* made in Paris with the Bol'shoy company was vetoed by the Soviet authorities, but he conducted *The Queen of Spades* at San Francisco in 1975. He was appointed music director of the National SO of Washington, DC, in 1977 and became a regular guest conductor with the LPO, with whom he performed and recorded the cycle of Tchaikovsky symphonies and also made the first recording of Shostakovich's *Lady Macbeth of Mtsenk*. He conducted *Eugene Onegin* at the Aldeburgh Festival in 1979 and at the Florence Maggio Musicale in 1980.

In 1970 Rostropovich wrote an open letter (which remained unpublished) to leading Soviet newspapers and magazines in support of the proscribed Russian author and Nobel prizewinner Alexander Solzhenitsyn, and in protest at new Soviet restrictions on cultural freedom. His travels in the West were thereupon much curtailed until, in 1974, he was allowed to leave the USSR with his wife and family for a two-year stay abroad, based in Britain. He gave his reasons in a letter that appeared in *La pensée russe*, a Russian-language weekly published in Paris, and in a signed article in the *New York Times* (6 March 1975). In July the same year at Monte Carlo he gave the first performance of a Cello Concerto by Khachaturian with the composer conducting, and in September he made his British conducting début as mentioned above. Some weeks later he bought from the estate of Gerald Warburg the 'Duport' cello of 1711 by Antonio Stradivari; it was in perfect condition except for a scar on the lower part of its body, reputedly inflicted accidentally by Napoleon's spur after Duport had played to him and the emperor had asked to examine it. Rostropovich's compositions include two piano concertos, several piano pieces and a string quartet. He contributed to *Tribute to Benjamin Britten on his Fiftieth Birthday* (London, 1963).

For photograph *see* VIOLONCELLO, fig.6.

BIBLIOGRAPHY
T. Gaidamovich: *Mstislav Rostropovich* (Moscow, 1969)
A. Blyth: 'Rostropovich: Always a Fresh View', *The Times* (6 Dec 1974)
R. Wigg: 'Rostropovich on Music-making in the West', *The Times* (29 Jan 1976)
A. Blyth: 'Mstislav Rostropovich Talks', *Gramophone*, liv (1976–7), 1379
NOËL GOODWIN

Rosvaenge [Roswaenge], **Helge** (*b* Copenhagen, 29 Aug 1897; *d* Munich, 19 June 1972). Danish tenor. He turned to singing after a scientific education. His wife was a singer, and together they gave a concert at Schwerin; this was so successful that he was engaged at Neustrelitz, where he made his début as Don José in 1921. Engagements followed at Altenburg, Basle, Cologne (1927–30) and the Berlin Staatsoper, where he was leading tenor (1930–44), being especially distinguished in the Italian repertory; he also sang regularly in Vienna and Munich. He appeared at Salzburg in 1933, as Tamino, Huon in *Oberon* and in Verdi's Requiem; in 1937, also at Salzburg, he sang Tamino, the Requiem and Florestan under Toscanini, and appeared as Florestan at Covent Garden the following year. He sang Parsifal at Bayreuth in 1934 and 1936, but otherwise avoided the Wagnerian repertory. His only American appearance was as a concert singer in 1962. After World War II Rosvaenge divided his time between Berlin and Vienna. His voice showed no sign of age; it was warm and sonorous, even throughout its scale, and brilliant and lustrous in its top register.

WRITINGS
Skratta Pajazzo (Copenhagen, 1945; Ger. trans., 1953 as *Lache Bajazzo*)
Mach es besser, mein Sohn (Leipzig, 1963)

BIBLIOGRAPHY
A. Natan: 'Roswaenge, Helge', *Primo uomo* (Basle, 1963) [with LP discography]
G. Gualerzi: 'Roswaenge, Helge', *Le grandi voci* (Rome, 1964) [with opera discography by R. Vegeto]
J. Dennis: 'Helge Rosvaenge', *Record Collector*, xxiii (1976), 101 [with discography]
F. Tassie: *Helge Rosvaenge* (Augsburg, 1975)
HAROLD ROSENTHAL

Roswitha. *See* HROTSWITHA.

Rota (Lat.: 'wheel'). A term used to designate a round in the 13th (? and 14th) centuries. The only differences between rota and rondellus are the successive entries of the voices in the former, as against the simultaneous entries in the latter and the necessity for ending it arbitrarily. The difference between rota and canon (the medieval *fuga*) is more fundamental. The former achieves tonal equipoise through static circularity, while the latter is characterized by dynamic pursuit of an end. It is the difference between chordal homogeneity achieved with a melody whose built-in harmonic potential must be realized through imitative projection and counterpoint, whose rigidly canonic procedure is not restricted to imitation at the prime.

The singing of rotas in medieval England was doubtless based on a pre-13th-century tradition and must have been practised to a much greater extent than the preserved sources show. These assumptions are justified not only by the fragmentary preservation of the sources, particularly the almost complete absence of manuscripts containing polyphony with vernacular texts, but also the fact that rounds are rather easily improvised and therefore, unlike motets, were probably not regarded as *ars musica* requiring notation, unless they were unusually artful. One such composition, the only known piece specifically labelled rota in the manuscript, is the famous setting *Sumer is icumen in* (for further information and facsimile *see* SUMER IS ICUMEN IN). Another, with strophically continuous text, though lacking any designation as rota, is identifiable as such, because the three successive voice entries are indicated in the manuscript (*English Music*, no.35). BAUDE CORDIER's 'rode' (?ronde) *Tout par compas* (early 15th century) is not so much a round as a French caccia in the quasi-strophic rondeau form; it is therefore sung three times fully as the text indicates, and twice in part. On the other hand, ROBERT WILKINSON's setting of *Jesus autem transiens – Credo in Deum* (*c*1500) is a true 13-part rota, though not specifically designated as such in the Eton Choirbook, which preserves it. No medieval writer on music reported on the use and meaning of 'rota' (JOHANNES DE GROCHEO's discussion of 'rotunda vel rotundellus' refers to the rondeau).

BIBLIOGRAPHY
W. Wiora: 'Der mittelalterliche Liedkanon', *GfMKB, Lüneburg 1950*, 71
F. Ll. Harrison: *Music in Medieval Britain* (London, 1958, 2/1963), 141f, 413f
E. H. Sanders: 'Tonal Aspects of 13th-century English Polyphony', *AcM*, xxxvii (1965), 19
——, ed.: *English Music of the Thirteenth and Early Fourteenth Centuries*, PMFC, xiv (1979)
ERNEST H. SANDERS

Rota, Andrea (*b* Bologna, *c*1553; *d* Bologna, June 1597). Italian composer. He began his career in Rome, where his first printed work was published in 1579. In May 1583 he was proposed for the position of *maestro di cappella* at S Petronio, Bologna, by Cardinal Giacomo Boncompagni who claimed that Rota was 'already known to be as good a musician and composer as anyone today, and a skilled teacher, having had many years' experience and a great many pupils'. Rota was duly appointed and in June took charge of the exceptionally large choir which comprised 34 *cantori* (not including the choirboys), 12 *chierici* and three instrumentalists. His career at S Petronio appears to have been extremely successful. In 1584 he published his *Motectorum liber primus* and this work was reprinted as an act of homage three years later by one of his pupils, Damiano Scarabelli. In 1595 Rota was given 80 lire by the church authorities to assist with the publication of his *Missarum liber primus*. In December of that year a *maestro del canto* was appointed to free Rota from his teaching duties, presumably to allow him more time for composition, but Rota died without publishing further works.

Rota's madrigals are in the Roman tradition. Although they appear conservative, with sparing use of word-painting, chromaticism and dissonance, they are attractive, finely balanced works. His sacred works are more modern, particularly the second book of motets and the unpublished psalms and motets, which follow the Venetian tradition of *cori spezzati*. One of his unpublished masses, the *Missa 'En voz à Dieux'*, and the two printed masses *'Qual è più grand'amore'* and *'Non mi toglia il ben mio'* are parodies on madrigals by Rore. Burney mentioned a *Da pacem, Domine* in six parts which he said demonstrates Rota's skill in writing *a cappella*, 'in which style he seems to have been equal to any of the masters of this learned period'.

WORKS
(all printed works except anthologies published in Venice)

SACRED
Motectorum liber primus, 5–8vv (1584); ed. in AntMI, *Monumenta bononiensia*, iv/1 (in preparation)

Motectorum liber secundus, 5–8, 10vv (1595); ed. in AntMI, *Monumenta bononiensia*, iv/2 (in preparation)
Missarum liber primus, 4–6vv (1595); 1 ed. in AntMI, *Monumenta bononiensia*, iv/3 (1962)
Works in 1598², 1600²
Da pacem, Domine, 6vv, in G. B. Martini: *Esemplare ossia saggio fondamentale pratico di contrappunto sopra il canto fermo* (Bologna, 1774–5)
4 masses: Missa brevis, 4vv; Missa de bello; Missa 'En voz à Dieux'; Missa primi toni: *I-Bsp*
3 psalms: Dixit Dominus, 8vv (2 settings), *Bc*, 1 ed. in AMI, i (1897/*R*); Hodie Christus natus est, 9vv, *Bc*
2 Magnificat, 5vv, 12vv, *Bc*, *Bsp*

SECULAR

Il primo libro de madrigali, 5vv (1579); ed. in Le opere dei musicisti bolognesi, ii (Bologna, 1964); 1 ed. in AMI, i (1897/*R*)
Il secondo libro de madrigali, 5vv (1589)
Il primo libro de madrigali, 4vv (1592)
Works in 1583¹⁰, 1586¹⁰, 1590¹³, 1591⁸, 1594⁶, 1597¹⁵

BIBLIOGRAPHY
BurneyH
G. Gaspari: *Musica e musicisti a Bologna* (Bologna, 1868–80/*R*1970)
O. Mischiati: 'Rota, Andrea', *MGG*

K. BOSI MONTEATH

Rota, Antonio. See ROTTA, ANTONIO.

Rota [Rinaldi], Nino (*b* Milan, 3 Dec 1911; *d* Rome, 10 April 1979). Italian composer, grandson of the pianist–composer Giovanni Rinaldi (1840–95). In 1919 he began studying the piano with his mother and solfège with A. Perlasco, and at the age of eight he started to compose (an oratorio for soloists, chorus and orchestra was performed in Milan and Lille in 1923). He entered the Milan Conservatory in 1923, and there he was a pupil of Delachi, Orefice and Bas. Later he studied privately with Pizzetti (1925–6) and then with Casella in Rome, where he received a diploma in composition at the Accademia di S Cecilia in 1930. He attended courses given by Scalero (composition), Reiner (conducting) and Beck (history) at the Curtis Institute, Philadelphia (1931–2), and in 1937 he took an arts degree at Milan University with a thesis on Zarlino. In 1937–8 he taught theory and solfège at the Taranto music school; in 1939 he joined the Bari Conservatory as a teacher of harmony, later teaching composition there and becoming director (1950).

Well acquainted with new musical developments from his youth (during which he enjoyed a long personal friendship with Stravinsky), Rota followed a quite different path in his own music, retaining the supremacy of melody, a tonality free of harmonic complexity, established patterns of rhythm and form, and a concept of music as spontaneous, direct expression. His humour, too, is ingenuous and never satirical. Avoiding sentimentality, he worked in all genres with a discernment and technical mastery that gained him the respect even of those who regarded his attitude as outdated. He had particular success with two operas – the exhilarating *Il cappello di paglia di Firenze*, which had many productions, notably Strehler's at the Piccola Scala, and *La visita meravigliosa*, which may be regarded as an allegory of his philosophy – and with the *Mysterium*, *La vita di Maria*, the sonatas, of a delicate and penetrating grace, and the Harp Concerto. But he owed his international renown largely to his scores for the cinema, many of them composed for important films (including those of Fellini, who then used no other composer); these show his adaptability to the most diverse tasks. In this field his extreme facility in piano improvisation enabled him to collaborate closely with directors.

WORKS
(*selective list*)

STAGE

Operas: Il principe porcaro (3, Rota, after Andersen), 1925, unperf.; Ariodante (3, E. Trucchi, after Orlando furioso), Parma, 1942; Torquemada (4, Trucchi, after Hugo), 1943, Naples, S Carlo, 1976; I due timidi (radio opera, 1, S. Cecchi d'Amico), Italian radio, 1950, arr. stage, London, 1952; Il cappello di paglia di Firenze (4, N. Rota, E. Rota, after Labiche), 1946, Palermo, 1955; Lo scoiattolo in gamba (1, E. De Filippo), Venice, 1959; La notte d'un nevrastenico (radio opera, 1, R. Bacchelli), Italian radio, 1959, arr. stage, Milan, 1960; Aladino e la lampada magica (3, V. Verginelli), Naples, 1968; La visita meravigliosa (3, Rota, after H. G. Wells), Palermo, 1970; Napoli milionaria (3, E. De Filippo), Spoleto, 1978
Ballets: Rappresentazione di Adamo ed Eva, A. M. Milloss, Perugia, 1957; La Strada, Fellini, Milan, 1966, rev. 1978; Le Molière imaginaire, Béjart, Paris, 1976

CHORAL AND ORCHESTRAL

Oratorios and cantatas: L'infanzia di S Giovanni Battista (S. Pagari), Milan, 1923, rev. Lille, 1923; Mysterium (Verginelli), Assisi, 1962; La vita di Maria (Verginelli), Perugia, 1970; Roma capomunni (Verginelli), Rome, 1972; Rabelaisiana (Rabelais), 1978
Orch: Balli, 1932; Serenata, 1932; 3 syms., G, 1936–9, F, 1938–43, C, 1957; Sinfonia sopra una canzone d'amore, 1947–72; Harp Conc., 1948; Variazioni sopra un tema gioviale, 1954; Conc. festivo, 1958; Conc.-soirée, pf, orch, 1961; Trbn Conc., 1968; Divertimento concertante, db, orch, 1968–9; Vc Conc., 1973; Castel del Monte, hn, orch, 1975–6; Conc., bn, orch, 1974–7; Conc. ('Piccolo mondo antico'), pf, orch, 1979

FILM SCORES

Zazà, dir. R. Castellani, 1944; Le miserie del signor Travat, dir. M. Soldati, 1946; Come persi la guerra, dir. C. Borghesio, 1948; Sotto il sole di Roma, dir. Castellani, 1948; The Glass Mountain, dir. H. Cass, 1950; Napoli milionaria, dir. E. De Filippo, 1950; È primavera, dir. Castellani, 1950; Anni facili, dir. L. Zampa, 1953; War and Peace, dir. K. Vidor, 1956; La diga sul Pacifico, dir. R. Clément, 1957; Le notti bianche, dir. Visconti, 1957; La grande guerra, dir. M. Monicelli, 1959; Plein soleil, dir. Clément, 1960; Rocco e i suoi fratelli, dir. Visconti, 1960; Il gattopardo, dir. Visconti, 1963; The Taming of the Shrew, dir. Zeffirelli, 1966; Romeo and Juliet, dir. Zeffirelli, 1968; Waterloo, dir. S. F. Bondarchuk, 1969; The Godfather, dir. Coppola, 1972
Films dir. Fellini; total of c80 scores

OTHER WORKS

Chamber: Invenzioni, str qt, 1933; Sonata, va, pf, 1934; Canzona, 11 insts, 1935; Qnt, fl, ob, va, vc, harp, 1935; Sonata, vn, pf, 1937; Sonata, fl, harp, 1937; Piccola offerta musicale, wind qnt, 1943; Sarabanda e toccata, harp, 1945; Sonata, qt, 1947; Trio, fl, vn, pf, 1958; Sonata, org, 4 brass, 1968; Nonet, 1976
Pf: Variazioni e fuga sul nome B–A–C–H, 1950; 15 preludi, 1966
Vocal: songs, 3 masses, other sacred works
Incidental music

Principal publisher: Ricordi

BIBLIOGRAPHY
S. M.: 'Un compositore quattordicenne: Nino Rota Rinaldi', *Cronache musicali*, ii (1926), no.6, p.2
G. Gavazzeni: *Musicisti d'Europa* (Milan, 1954)
M. Mila: *Cronache musicali 1954–59* (Turin, 1959)
F. d'Amico: 'Passaporto per un angelo', *L'espresso* (Rome, 1970), no.7
L. Pinzauti: 'Intervista con Nino Rota', *NRMI*, v/1 (1971)
G. Vigolo: *Mille e una sera* (Florence, 1971)
F. Fellini: 'L'amico magico', *Il messaggero* (13 April 1979)

FEDELE D'AMICO

Rotata (It.). HURDY-GURDY.

Rotenbucher [Rothenpucher, Rottenbücher, Haunreuter, Hannreither, Haureuther], **Erasmus** (*b* Braunau, Upper Austria, *c*1525; *d* Nuremberg, buried 15 July 1586). German music editor, ?composer and schoolmaster. He was originally called Haunreuter; it is not known how he came to be called Rotenbucher. He probably attended the school of the monastery of St Nikola, just outside Passau, where Leonhardt Päminger was headmaster; he enjoyed a lifelong friendship with Päminger's son Sophonias and wrote an elegy on Päminger's death in 1567. In 1542 he began his studies at the University of Ingolstadt, moving to Wittenberg University in 1543. It was there, encouraged by Georg

Rhau, that he decided to edit collections of music. Soon after Rhau's death, probably in 1548, he joined the staff of the St Egidien school at Nuremberg, where he eventually became *supremus* (i.e. ranking third, after the Rektor and Kantor). He may have taught Hans Leo Hassler. With the arrival of Friedrich Lindner as Kantor in the late autumn of 1574 he retired from teaching and became sacristan and almoner at the church of St Sebald. His two anthologies of bicinia are extremely important both in their size and in the nature and quality of their contents: several pieces, including some by leading composers of the early 16th century, are known only through them. The first, *Diphona amoena et florida* (Nuremberg, 1549[16]; 22 ed. in HM, lxxiv, 1951), contains 99 pieces all to Latin texts, most of them very short and written in the florid contrapuntal style of the time; the composers are mainly Franco-Flemings, and include Isaac and Josquin. In this varied and colourful collection, a cycle of six songs in praise of music (nos.1–5 and 98) and two complete groups of mass and *Magnificat* movements (nos.40–64 and 66–72 respectively) are particularly notable. The anonymous five-part circular canon on the title-page of both part-books and the first piece, *Encomium musices*, which is also anonymous, may be by Rotenbucher himself. His second anthology, *Bergkreyen* (Nuremberg, 1551[20]; three ed. F. Piersig, Kassel, 1930), comprises 28 German sacred and secular songs by German composers of a younger generation, including Heller and Stoltzer, and ten anonymous pieces all with French texts. As the title of the collection would lead one to expect (*see* BERGREIHEN), the pieces are in strict note-against-note style in the manner of improvised discant.

BIBLIOGRAPHY
F. Krautwurst: 'Rotenbucher, Erasmus', *MGG* [incl. full bibliography]

FRANZ KRAUTWURST

Roth, Christian (*b* c1585; *d* c1640). German composer and organist. In the early 17th century he worked as a church organist at Leitmeritz, Bohemia (now Litoměřice). He published *Couranten Lustgärtlein, in welchem 74 Couranten, so zuvor nie in Druck ausgangen, zu finden, welche auff allerhand musicalischen Instrumenten gantz lieblich und lustig können gebraucht werden*, in four and five parts (Dresden, 1624[18]). The courantes have attractive melodies and rhythms; two of them are by Albert Crantz. Another collection by Roth, *Opusculum sacrarum cantionum*, for four to eight voices, is recorded in an inventory at Pirna of 1654 but is lost. Two works, copied by Johann Cadner of Pirna in 1615 – *Gloria in excelsis Deo*, for two voices, and *Nun lob mein Seel den Herren*, for eight – are extant (in D-Dlb).

BIBLIOGRAPHY
EitnerQ; FétisB; GerberL
W. Nagel: 'Die Kantorei-Gesellschaft zu Pirna', *MMg*, xxviii (1896), 148 [incl. inventory]
R. Vollhardt: *Geschichte der Cantoren und Organisten von den Städten im Königreich Sachsen* (Berlin, 1899), 257, 259
E. H. Meyer: *Die mehrstimmige Spielmusik des 17. Jahrhunderts in Nord- und Mitteleuropa* (Kassel, 1934/R), 239
D. Härtwig: 'Roth, Christian', *MGG*

BERND BASELT

Roth, Ernst (*b* Prague, 1 June 1896; *d* Twickenham, Middlesex, 17 July 1971). English music publisher and writer of Czech birth. He studied law, music and philosophy at Prague University, both before and after military service on the Eastern Front in World War I.

In 1921, after gaining his doctorate in law, he settled in Vienna, studying music at the university there under Adler. In the following year he began his career as a music publisher, at first with Universal Edition, of which he became head of publications in 1928. After the German annexation of Austria, Roth moved to London in 1938 and joined the firm of Boosey & Hawkes: he became chairman of the music publishing company in 1963. In the development of this catalogue Roth was closely associated, as publisher, friend and adviser, with both Strauss (the final setting of whose *Vier letzte Lieder* is dedicated to him) and Stravinsky; in his book *The Business of Music* he has left absorbing reminiscences about each. Apart from an early novel, *Magalhaes* (Berlin, 1919), Roth also wrote *A Tale of Three Cities*, an evocative account of Vienna, Budapest and Prague in the early part of the 20th century, and numerous articles on literature, history, art, philosophy and music. His fluency in most European languages was put to use in his many translations of operatic and vocal music. His professional expertise in both music and law enabled him to play a leading part in formulating the complex legislative control of international rights in music (he became in 1959 vice-president of the Music Section of the International Publishers' Association). His widely varied knowledge ensured his reputation as one of the leading music publishers of the 20th century.

WRITINGS
Die Grenzen der Künste (Stuttgart, 1925)
Vom Vergänglichen in der Musik (Zurich, 1949)
European Music: a Short History (London, 1961)
Musik als Kunst und Ware (Zurich, 1966; Eng. trans., 1969 as *The Business of Music: Reflections of a Music Publisher*)

BIBLIOGRAPHY
E. Roth: *A Tale of Three Cities* (London, 1971)
W. Schuh: 'Ernst Roth 1896–1917', *Tempo* (1972), no.98, p.1
E. Roth: *Von Prag bis London: Erfahrungen autobiographische Fragmente* (Zurich and Freiburg, 1974) [incl. W. Schuh: 'Ernst Roth zum Gedächtnis']

ALAN FRANK

Roth, Hieronymus. *See* ROSSO, HIERONYMUS.

Roth [Rothe], Martin (*b* ?Naumburg, c1580; *d* 1610). German composer. From 1606 to 1608 he was Kantor at Schulpforta, where his pupils will have included the young Schein. His only known printed works are 16 motets for seven and eight voices which appear in the two-volume anthology edited by Erhard Bodenschatz, one of his predecessors at Schulpforta: *Florilegium Portense* (*RISM* 1618[1]) and *Florilegium musici Portensis* (1621[2]). In the latter he is represented by no fewer than 15 pieces, giving him by far the largest share of any composer. These motets are settings of both Latin and German texts, and nearly all are written for the eight-part, double-choir arrangement which was so popular in Germany at the turn of the century and which predominates throughout the *Florilegium*. Their style resembles most closely that of Jacob Handl, particularly in their use of choirs of the same pitch and in the resultant unison antiphony which, when applied to very short phrases, becomes almost like an echo. Also common to both composers is a fundamentally diatonic harmony and a syllabic style of contrapuntal writing in which the interest is not so much in the movement of lines as in the juxtaposition of blocks of chords. The harmonic rather than melodic nature of the bass lines is another indication of this tendency towards vertical thinking. An interesting feature of Roth's eight-part writing is his grouping of the voices across the original division into identical choirs, so that high and low vocal groups are sometimes contrasted with each other. Although all the pieces are provided with a continuo part, it is virtually certain that this was added by Bodenschatz; it is in every case no more than a *basso seguente*. While he showed little originality in either melody or rhythm, Roth's attempts at formal organization and his vertical concept of composition are indications of progressive thought.

BIBLIOGRAPHY

A. Prüfer: *Johan Herman Schein* (Leipzig, 1895), 8

H. J. Moser: *Die mehrstimmige Vertonung des Evangeliums*, i (Leipzig, 1931/R1968), 8

F. Blume: *Geschichte der evangelischen Kirchenmusik* (Kassel, 2/1965; Eng. trans., enlarged, as *Protestant Church Music: a History*, 1974), 128

O. Riemer: 'Florilegium Portense', *MGG*

A. LINDSEY KIRWAN

Röth, Philipp (*b* Munich, 6 March 1779; *d* Munich, 27 Jan 1850). German composer. He studied the cello and other instruments with Anton Schwarz, a Bavarian court musician, and composition with Peter von Winter. He was appointed a Bavarian court musician in 1796. His early works include songs, variations for flute, and a number of concertos. In 1809 an opera, *Holnara*, was performed with success at the Munich court theatre, and a second, *Pachter Robert*, followed two years later. He also wrote a number of Singspiels in the Vienna pattern for Munich (e.g. *Zemire und Azor*, a version of Bäuerle's *Der verwunschene Prinz*, given at the Isartor Theatre on 22 March 1823). Perhaps his most successful score was the *Freischütz* parody music that he and Riotte provided for Heigel's *Staberl in der Löwengrube* (also known as *Alles à la Freischütz* and *Staberl als Freischütz*), mounted at the Isartor Theatre on 4 December 1822 by Karl Carl and performed frequently before the company (including Röth himself) brought it to the Theater an der Wien during their guest season in 1826. It continued to be performed in Vienna until 1850. Röth's other successes in Vienna include *Der hölzerne Säbel* (staged successfully in all three Viennese suburban theatres between 1820 and 1822), *Der Kampf mit dem Drachen* and *Das Abenteuer im Guadarama-Gebirge* (both performed in 1825). Röth returned to Munich in 1828. His published works include a flute concerto, dances and chamber music.

BIBLIOGRAPHY

FétisB

F. J. Lipowsky: *Baierisches Musik-Lexicon* (Munich, 1811), 284f

E. Bernsdorf: *Neues Universal-Lexikon der Tonkunst*, suppl.1 (Offenbach, 1865), 307f

H. Mendel and A. Reissmann: *Musikalisches Conversations-Lexikon*, viii (Berlin, 1877), 386

PETER BRANSCOMBE

Roth, Wilhelm August Traugott (*b* nr. Erfurt, *c*1720; *d* Halle, 20 April 1765). German organist and composer. He studied the organ with Jacob Adlung in Erfurt and composition and the harpsichord with J. G. Walther in Weimar. At Halle University he studied philosophy and theology, after which he went to Berlin as a music teacher (1754). There he contributed a number of compositions to the weekly journal *Der Freund*, whose music editor he became in 1757. In the same year ten of his lieder for the journal were published separately. This collection was followed by his *Neueste Sammlung teutscher Lieder* (1759), with a treatise on the German lied, and, in the next year, by its sequel, *Erste Nachlese*

zu den neuesten Sammlungen von teutschen Liedern. During these years he continued his music studies in Berlin with J. G. and C. H. Graun, C. P. E. Bach, J. F. Agricola and F. W. Marpurg, and served as organist at St Peter's Church (from 1758). From summer 1764 he briefly succeeded W. F. Bach as organist at the Church of Our Lady in Halle. His only other known works are a few lieder and a harpsichord sonata in contemporary collections. Most of his lieder are in the *galant* style, often with highly embellished melodies in an instrumental idiom and with figured basses.

BIBLIOGRAPHY

EitnerQ; *GerberL*

M. Friedlaender: *Das deutsche Lied im 18. Jahrhundert* (Stuttgart and Berlin, 1902/R1970)

W. Serauky: *Musikgeschichte der Stadt Halle*, ii/2 (Halle and Berlin, 1942/R1971)

RAYMOND A. BARR

Rothenberger, Anneliese (*b* Mannheim, 19 June 1924). German soprano. She studied in Mannheim with Erika Müller and made her début at Koblenz in 1943 in small roles, soon singing such parts as Gilda and the title role in Pfitzner's *Das Christelflein*. From 1946 to 1956 she was a member of the Hamburg Staatsoper, where her roles included Cherubino, Blonde, Oscar, Musetta, Olympia and the three soprano roles of Einem's *Der Prozess* in its first performance in Germany. At the 1952 Edinburgh Festival she was Regina in the Hamburg company's performance of *Mathis der Maler*, its British première. She first appeared at Salzburg in 1954, creating Telemachus in Liebermann's *Penelope*; she returned to create Agnes in the German version of his *Die Schule der Frauen* (1957), and also as Zdenka (*Arabella*), Flaminia (*Il mondo della luna*), Sophie and Constanze. Her many appearances as Sophie included those at Glyndebourne (1959–60) and in the 1960 Salzburg film; in 1960 she made her Metropolitan Opera début as Zdenka. She sang regularly at Munich from 1955 and Vienna from 1957. Her large repertory included Mozart's Ilia, Susanna and Pamina, Berg's Lulu, Adele (*Die Fledermaus*), and the title role of Sutermeister's *Madame Bovary* at its première (Zurich, 1967). Rothenberger's unusual acting ability, lithe figure and well-schooled, if light, voice, made her one of the most sought-after performers of the 1950s and 1960s.

HAROLD ROSENTHAL

Rothenpucher, Erasmus. *See* ROTENBUCHER, ERASMUS.

Rother, Artur (Martin) (*b* Stettin [now Szczecin], 12 Oct 1885; *d* Aschau, 22 Sept 1972). German conductor. He was taught by his father, and then studied composition under Hugo Kaun in Berlin, and musicology and philosophy in Tübingen and Berlin. In 1905, as a pianist, he gave concerts with the violinist Willy Burmester. From 1907 to 1914 he was an assistant at the Bayreuth Festival, and from 1927 to 1934 general director of music in Dessau. From 1938 to 1958 he was principal Kapellmeister at the Städtische Oper in Berlin, and after World War II he was also principal conductor of Berlin radio. Rother was an accomplished musician of wide interests. He prepared new editions of Gluck's *La rencontre imprévue* and Mozart's *Idomeneo*, and composed chamber music, lieder and dramatic music. In 1952 he was awarded the Kunstpreis der Stadt Berlin.

HANS CHRISTOPH WORBS

Rothmüller, (Aron) Marko (*b* Trnjani, nr. Brod, Croatia, 31 Dec 1908). Yugoslav baritone and composer. He studied in Zagreb and then in Vienna with Berg, Regina Weiss and Franz Steiner. He made his début at Hamburg-Altona at the Schiller Theatre in 1932, as Ottokar (*Der Freischütz*), and soon established himself as one of the most promising baritones of the day. Being of Jewish birth, he had to leave Germany in the early 1930s; he returned to Zagreb for two years and in 1935 was engaged by the Zurich Opera, where he sang regularly until 1947, scoring particular successes in Verdi and Wagner, and as Truchsess in the première of Hindemith's *Mathis der Maler* (1938). In 1946 he joined the Vienna Staatsoper, singing there until 1949. Rothmüller had made his London début in 1939 as Krushina (*The Bartered Bride*) under Beecham at Covent Garden; in 1947 when he sang the title role in *Rigoletto* with the New London Opera Company at the Cambridge Theatre, he was immediately recognized as one of the finest singing actors of his generation. At Covent Garden later that year he played John the Baptist (*Salome*) during the Vienna Staatsoper's season there, and from 1948 to 1952 was a member of the Covent Garden company, with which he sang a wide variety of roles, including Tomsky in *The Queen of Spades* (1950, in English), and the title role in *Wozzeck* in its first London performances (1952). He appeared with the Glyndebourne Opera (1949–55) as Guglielmo, Count Almaviva, Don Carlo (*La forza del destino*), Macbeth and Nick Shadow. His New York début was with the New York City Opera (1948) and he later joined the Metropolitan Opera (1959–61, 1964–5). In 1962 he began teaching at Indiana University, Bloomington.

Interested in Hebrew music, Rothmüller founded Omanut, a society for the advancement of Jewish music, in Zagreb (1932) and in Zurich (1942). He published *Die Musik der Juden: Versuch einer geschichtlichen Darstellung ihrer Entwicklung und ihres Wesens* (Zurich, 1951; Eng. trans., 1953, rev. 2/1967) and his compositions include Sephardic religious songs and a setting of Psalm xv, as well as a Symphony for strings and two string quartets.

BIBLIOGRAPHY
D. Shawe-Taylor: 'Marko Rothmüller', *Opera*, ii (1951), 169
HAROLD ROSENTHAL

Rothwell [Barbirolli], Evelyn (*b* Wallingford, 24 Jan 1911). English oboist. She studied under Leon Goossens at the RCM, London. In 1931 she joined the Covent Garden Opera touring orchestra (where she met the conductor John Barbirolli, whom she was to marry in 1939). Engagements followed with the Scottish Orchestra (1933–6), the LSO (1935–9) and the Glyndebourne Festival Orchestra (1934–9). After her marriage she began her career as a soloist. Gordon Jacob, Arnold Cooke, Stephen Dodgson, Arthur Benjamin, Edmund Rubbra and Elizabeth Maconchy, as well as her husband, have dedicated works to her. In 1934 at Salzburg she gave the first performance of the rediscovered Mozart Oboe Concerto K314/271*k*. She has formed duos with Iris Loveridge (piano) and Valda Aveling (harpsichord and piano).

WRITINGS
Difficult Passages from Orchestral Repertoire (London, 1953)
Oboe Technique (London, 1953) [with list of repertory]
Difficult Passages from Bach (London, 1955)
The Oboist's Companion (London, 1974–)
PHILIP BATE

Roto-toms. Small, single-headed drums with a shallow shell, having a compass of several notes. They are fixed at their open end to a rigid stand and tuned by rotating (clockwise for raising the pitch). They can be used purely as rhythm instruments, or – in schools, for example – in lieu of timpani.

Rotrouenge [rotruenge, retroncha]. A medieval term applied to certain troubadour and trouvère poems, usually denoting the presence of a refrain and of distinguishing features of rhyme scheme. The term in its various forms occurs fairly seldom in the surviving troubadour and trouvère repertory; nevertheless, it has attracted considerable attention among modern scholars.

From Provençal treatises about poetry we can conclude that the *retroncha* had a refrain, but it is not clear what other distinguishing elements it had, if any. Songs with refrain are relatively rare in the surviving troubadour repertory, but neither in treatises nor in song collections does there appear to be any reason for using the term 'retroncha' for all troubadour songs with refrain. According to Jeanroy, only four Provençal poems bear the term as a label in the manuscripts; all four have a refrain which in Jeanroy's estimation is the only detail in the text that distinguishes them from the ordinary chanson. Of these four songs, three survive with music – all three are by Guiraut Riquier and occur in *F-Pn* f.fr.22543, f.111*v*. An evaluation of the style and form of these melodies in comparison with troubadour melodies in general is hazardous because of the small number of troubadour melodies that survive, and because those by Guiraut amount to almost a fifth of the total repertory. Nevertheless, it can safely be said that the three melodies under consideration differ from one another approximately as much as all of Guiraut's 48 melodies differ from one another.

Among the trouvère chansons there are six that are called 'rotrouenge' in the texts of the poems. Four of these are attributed to Gontier de Soignies (R.354, 636, 1505*a* and 1914; R.2082 has sometimes erroneously been included among these). One more song called 'rotruenge' by its author may have been composed by Gontier, because the name 'Gontier' is mentioned in the song in a manner similar to that in which it occurs in some of the songs that are ascribed to him. The remaining song is *Retrowange novelle Dirai et bonè et belle* (R.602), attributed to Jaque de Cambrai. Gontier de Soignies lived around 1200 or before, and Jaque de Cambrai lived in the second half of the 13th century. Both are rather unusual trouvères, Gontier because he used exclusively certain rhyme patterns that were infrequently used by other trouvères and Jaque because he wrote almost exclusively contrafacta. The music for only one of the six songs (R.636) has been preserved along with the text, and there is nothing unusual about the melody except for its form, which corresponds to the form of the poem. Ex.1 shows the first and last strophes. In content the poems do not reveal any significant aspects which set them apart as a group from the trouvère repertory in general. Thus only form or rhyme scheme can give any indication of what, if anything, may have been the distinct properties of a medieval song genre called 'rotrouenge'. Table 1 shows the metrical

TABLE 1

	a₁₁	a₁₁	a₁₁	a₁₁	B⁻₄	B⁻₁₁		(?Gontier, R.1411)
	a₈	a₈	a₈	a₈	a₈	B₈	B₈	(Gontier, R.354, R.1914)
a₁₁	a₁₁	a₁₁	a₁₁	a₁₁	a₁₁	B₁₁	B₉	(Gontier, R.1505a)
	a₈	a₈	a₈	B₄	a₈	b₉		(Gontier, R.636: ex.1)
a⁻₆	a⁻₆	a⁻₆	a⁻₆	a⁻₇	b₅	a⁻₇	b₅	(Jaque de Cambrai, R.602)

scheme and rhyme patterns of the songs (letters denote rhyming sounds; the sign ⁻ denotes a feminine rhyme; capital letters signify refrains; subscript numerals indicate the number of syllables in the line). It indicates clearly that in rhyme scheme these songs differ from the vast majority of the trouvère poems. Four of the rotrouenges have a refrain at the end of the strophe, another has its refrain approximately in the middle of the stanza, and one has no refrain at all. Refrains are not unusual in the trouvère repertory, although songs with a refrain form only a fairly small minority. The monorhyme opening found in all six songs is decidedly an infrequent phenomenon, but it is certainly not unique to the songs called 'rotruenge'; in fact, there are several dozen songs with similar rhyme patterns, including seven others by Gontier de Soignies. Some of them (none by Gontier however) are called 'chanson' in their text. There is one song (R.1312) with exactly the same metrical scheme and rhyme pattern as the two 'rotruenges', R.354 and R.1914, except that their refrains have a feminine ending instead of a masculine one.

Ex.1 First and last strophes of R.636 by Gontier de Soignies, *F-Pn* fonds fr. f. 115

Chan-ter   m'es - tuet   de   re - co — mens

Quant l'ore   est   doche   et   clers   li   vens,

Et   non   pour   quant   si   sui   do — lens,

O - ies   pour quoi,

Quant cele a   qui   sui   a — ten - dens

Ne velt   a — voir mer - chi   de moi.

Despite the absence of unambiguous medieval information about the specific characteristics of the rotrouenge, both Gennrich and Spanke developed extensive theories about its textual and melodic form. Even though the two scholars disagreed on certain details, by implication both excluded from the genre 'rotrouenge' certain songs that were explicitly given that name in the Middle Ages. Frappier, in his survey of medieval lyric poetry, remarked: 'we are not absolutely sure that we have any authentic specimens of the rotrouenge'. Thus the best conclusion may well be that by the late 12th and the 13th centuries 'rotrouenge' was no more than an attractive old term and that, as far as form and content are concerned, the rotrouenge had lost its identity if it ever had one.

BIBLIOGRAPHY

F. Gennrich: *Die altfranzösiche Rotrouenge* (Halle, 1925)

H. Spanke: *Eine altfranzösische Liedersammlung* (Halle, 1925), 294ff

F. Gennrich: *Grundriss einer Formenlehre des mittelalterlichen Liedes* (Halle, 1932), 52ff

J. Frappier: *La poésie lyrique en France aux XIIe et XIIIe siècles: les auteurs et les genres* (Paris, 1960)

For further bibliography *see* TROUBADOURS, TROUVÈRES.

HENDRIK VANDERWERF

Rott, Hans (*b* Vienna, 1 Aug 1858; *d* Vienna, 25 June 1884). Austrian composer. He studied at the Vienna Conservatory under Bruckner (organ), L. Landskron (piano), H. Graedener (harmony) and F. Krenn (counterpoint and composition). For some years up to 1878 he was organist at the Piarist church in Vienna but thereafter remained without a post. On 17 September 1880 he visited Brahms to seek his advice, but, like Wolf, he was rebuffed; within a month he had become insane. His importance as a composer lies in his influence on his close friend Mahler. In particular, his Symphony in E (1878–80) anticipates those of Mahler in its thematic material and compositional techniques. Rott's many other works (in *A-Wn*) include songs, several orchestral pieces, a string quartet and a string quintet.

BIBLIOGRAPHY

M. Löhr: 'Hans Rott: der lieblings Schüler Anton Bruckners', *Lebendige Stadt* (Vienna, 1958)

H.-L. de La Grange: *Mahler: a Biography* (New York, 1973)

L. Nowak: 'Die Kompositionen und Skizzen von Hans Rott in der Musiksammlung der Österreichischen Nationalbibliothek', *Beiträge zur Musikdokumentation: Festschrift für Franz Grasberger* (Tutzing, 1975), 273–340

PAUL BANKS

Rotta [Rota], **Antonio** (*b* ?Padua, *c*1495; *d* Padua, 1549). Italian lutenist. Canon Scardeonius of Padua wrote in 1560 that Rotta was not only virtually unrivalled in Italy as a lutenist, but was also an excellent teacher and had grown quite rich by giving lessons on the lute. Scardeonius also mentioned that Rotta had published 'praecepta notabilia' for playing the lute, presumably meaning the appendix to Rotta's *Intabolatura* (Venice, 1546), 'Regula alli lettori', an introduction to the lute based on Italian tablature. The *Intabolatura* contains intabulations of six French chansons, six madrigals, four motets by Jaquet of Mantua, Mouton, Willaert and Gombert, 26 dances and dance-songs and six ricercares. The composers of the vocal models are Arcadelt, de Porta, Costanzo Festa, Maille, Robert Meigret, Rogier Pathie and Nicolas Payen. Rotta's own dance suites comprise passamezzo, galliard and paduana in triple time. The galliard and paduana are developed from the passamezzo, using different rhythms. The writing is chordal but enlivened by diminutions. Some of his ricercares are in an imitative polyphonic style, others are more impromptu in character.

WORKS

Intabolatura de lauto . . . libro primo (Venice, 1546³²)

13 ricercares, 1552²⁹, 1552³¹, Theatrum musicum (Louvain, 1563), 1568²³

Des chansons, gaillardes, paduanes & motetz, reduitz en tabulature de luc, livre v (Louvain, 1547) [20 dances], 1552³¹

Des chansons . . . in tabulature de luc, livre v (Louvain, 1547) [5 song intabulations]; intabulation of motet by La Fage, *D-Mbs* Mus.267

BIBLIOGRAPHY

B. Scardeonius: *De antiquitate urbis Patavii, & claris civibus Patavinis* (Basle, 1560), 263

T. Norlind: 'Zur Geschichte der Suite', *SIMG*, vii (1905–6), 172, esp. 176

A. R. Malecek: 'Anton Rotta: eine biographische Skizze', *Festschrift Adolph Koczirz* (Vienna, 1930)
——: *Der Paduaner Lautenmeister Antonio Rotta* (diss., U. of Vienna, 1930)
J. Dieckmann: *Die in deutscher Lautentabulatur überlieferten Tänze des 16. Jahrhunderts* (Kassel, 1931), 40

HANS RADKE

Rotte (i). Another name for the triangular psaltery (see illustration). An epigram in an 11th-century German manuscript refers to 'psalterium triangulum ie. rottam', and in the 12th century a copyist of Notker Balbulus complained that the ancient ten-string psaltery had been adopted by musicians and actors, who had altered its mystic triangular shape to suit their convenience, increased the number of strings, and given it the barbarian name 'rotta'. Sachs (1920) took this 'improved' version of the psaltery to be a larger but still basically triangular instrument – a 'Spitzharfe'. This is a credible enough interpretation which leaves open the possibility that the musicians applied to the new instrument, whatever its shape, the name of one already familiar to them though perhaps different in appearance – the Germanic lyre. The name 'rotte' seems to have been loosely applied to various kinds of string instruments at one time or another. A 15th-century dictionary gives the definition 'Rott, rubeba est parva figella' ('A rotte, or rybebe, is a small fiddle').

BIBLIOGRAPHY
C. Sachs: *Handbuch der Musikinstrumentenkunde* (Leipzig, 1920), 158ff
H. Steger: 'Die Rotte', *Deutsche Vierteljahrsschrift für Literatur und Geistesgeschichte*, xxxv (1961), 96

MYRTLE BRUCE-MITFORD

King David playing a rotte or triangular psaltery: miniature from an 11th- or 12th-century MS (D-Mbs Clm 13067, f.18r)

Rotte (ii). The name given in Middle German to one of the most widely used plucked string instruments in north-western Europe from pre-Christian to medieval times. (For some related meanings of the term, *see* ROTTE (i).)

This instrument was a descendant of the ancient LYRE which originated in western Asia and Egypt and was adopted and developed by the Greeks. Representations of lyre-playing figures incised on pottery urns of the 6th century BC from Sopron, Hungary, and on a bucket from Kleinglein in Styria, Austria, both of the Hallstatt 'C' culture, show that the early Celtic peoples of Europe possessed a similar instrument; of the later pre-Christian Celts the historian Diodorus Siculus, writing in the 1st century BC, records that they played on instruments 'resembling lyres'. Concrete evidence in the form of a curved antler plaque with circular perforations, very possibly part of the yoke of a lyre, was excavated in 1957 from a Celtic hill-fort of the 3rd century BC at Dinorben, Denbighshire.

The Celtic 'crwth', 'cruit' and 'crot', English 'rote' and 'crowd', French 'rote' and German 'rotte' are obviously closely related etymologically, but whether the use of the instrument spread to Germany eastwards from Ireland or north-westwards from central Europe, or whether it developed in several countries simultaneously, is uncertain. The generic Latin term for plucked instruments, 'cithara', comes from a verb meaning 'to pluck', as does the Anglo-Saxon word 'hearpe'. Recent archaeological discoveries combined with the evidence of manuscript illustrations and the writings of early theorists suggest that, in Anglo-Saxon and early medieval times at least, the words 'hearpe', 'rotte' and 'cithara' were all used to describe the same instrument, or type of instrument. It seems probable that the 6th-century poet Venantius Fortunatus was referring to varieties of the same class of instrument in his much quoted couplet:

Romanusque lyra, plaudat tibi barbarus harpa,
Graecus Achilliaca, chrotta Britanna canat.

('Let the Roman praise you with the lyre, the barbarian with the harp, the Greek with the Achilliaca; let the British [or Breton] rotte sing.')

Instruments of the lyre class consist of a soundbox with two symmetrical arms rising from it and a yoke or cross-bar joining them at the top. The strings run across the soundbox and are usually connected to it by a bridge. The rotte, or Germanic lyre, had more in common with the ancient Greek kithara than with the other important Greek string instrument, the lyra. In both kithara and rotte the upright arms formed a continuation of the soundbox and were hollowed out for part of their length to provide an extension of the resonating space. In the kithara, however, the strings were secured to a straight cross-bar which projected beyond the arms at either end, whereas in the rotte this yoke section was curved and in almost all cases merged with the arms so that the rounded shape of the upper part resembled, or sometimes exactly mirrored, that of the lower.

Remains of several 'round' lyres have been excavated since the mid-19th century, and from the combined evidence of these sets of fragments a clear and precise idea of the shape, size and construction of the rotte during the 5th to 8th centuries can be formed. The most important are three found in England (at Abingdon, Berkshire, Taplow, Buckinghamshire, and Sutton

1. King David playing a round lyre, or rotte, with horns and trumpets: miniature from an Anglo-Saxon MS, 8th century (GB-Lbm Cotton Vespasian A 1, f.30v)

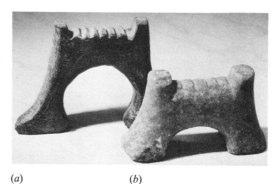

(a)   (b)

3. Lyre bridges found at: (a) Broa i Halle, Gotland, 8th century; (b) Birka, Sweden, 9th century (Riksantikvarie-ämbetet och Statens Historiska Museum, Stockholm)

(a)   (b)   (c)

2. Reconstructions of Germanic lyres from: (a) Sutton Hoo, Suffolk, early 7th century (British Museum, London); (b) Oberflacht, Württemberg, ?6th century (Museum für Vor- und Frühgeschichte, Berlin); (c) Cologne, AD c700 (Römisch-Germanisches Museum, Cologne)

4. Remains of a 14th-century lyre found at Kravik in Numedal, Norway (Norsk Folkemuseum, Oslo)

Hoo, Suffolk), and three in Germany (two at Oberflacht, Württemberg, and one in Cologne). At Abingdon, bone facings from the yoke of a 5th-century round lyre were excavated by E. T. Leeds and D. B. Harden in 1936 and are now in the Abingdon Museum; there appear to have been six peg-holes. The Taplow remains, excavated by Joseph Stevens in 1883 and now in the British Museum, date from about 600 AD and consist of the yoke section, fragments of the arms at their junction with the yoke, and two bird-headed escutcheons of gilt-bronze which covered the joints; materials as maple wood inlaid with horn and decorated with a bronze strip; apparently there were six peg-holes. Lyre remains from Sutton Hoo (fig.2a) consist of the yoke and most of the two parallel arms, fragments of pegs, and two bird-headed gilt-bronze escutcheons covering the joints between arms and yoke. The arms are hollow for part of their length and there are six peg-holes; yoke and arms are of maple wood, with pegs of poplar or willow. These remains, dating from the 7th century, before AD 625, were excavated in 1939 and are now in the British Museum.

Of the two Alemannic lyres found at Oberflacht, one was excavated in 1846 by F. Dürrich and W. Menzel and the other is recorded as having been acquired in 1896 by the Berliner Museum für Völkerkunde but was probably excavated at the same time. Just under half of the first instrument, which was of oak, has survived, including the whole length of one side and a considerable portion of the soundbox. The remaining arm is hollow for most of its length. Almost all of the yoke is missing and the number of peg-holes cannot be estimated. The lyre is 7th century, and is now in the collection of the Württembergisches Landesmuseum, Stuttgart. The second instrument (fig.2b), probably from the 6th century, had six peg-holes and was also of oak. It was complete apart from strings, pegs and tailpiece, but was destroyed during World War II. The Cologne lyre (fig.2c), from about AD 700, was discovered in a Frankish grave beneath the floor of St Severin's Church in 1938 by F. Fremersdorf. The pegs disintegrated on exposure to the air but the greater part of the instrument survived until its destruction by bombing during World War II. The arms were partially hollowed out, and there were six peg-holes in the yoke. Remains of a substantial iron tailpiece were also recovered. The lyre itself was of oak, with a maple soundboard.

In addition to instruments, no fewer than nine lyre bridges have been found. The earliest, dating from the 8th century, was unearthed at Broa i Halle, Gotland, (fig.3a), and others were found at Birka, Sweden (fig.3b), and Concevreux, northern France. These three were of amber, bone and bronze respectively; two bridges now in the Zentralmuseum, Utrecht, two excavated at Elisenhof, Schleswig, in 1969, and another found at Dorestad in Holland in 1974, were also of amber. In no case has a bridge been found together with lyre remains, but notches cut for the strings show that with one exception (the Birka bridge, apparently intended for a seven-string instrument) all the bridges were designed to take six strings.

To the catalogue of 'accessories' can be added four bone pegs (now in the British Museum) which were almost certainly tuning-pins for a rotte. They were excavated in 1925 from the site of the Saxon monastery at Whitby, Yorkshire (see *Archaeologia*, lxxxix, 1943, p.71), but remained unidentified until 1974 when Donald K. Fry of the State University of New York

recognized their true function. The particular interest of these pegs lies in the fact that they were found in the place where the Anglo-Saxon poet Caedmon lived and worked, and may have belonged to his period – the 7th century. Bede recounted how the poet, who until his divine visitation was unable to sing to the cithara as custom demanded, would leave the room in shame as the instrument, passed from hand to hand, approached his place at the table.

On the question of size, Schlesinger argued convincingly that there must have been at least three different sizes of rotte, basing her theory on an illustration in an 11th-century manuscript at Klosterneuburg, near Vienna, in which three rottes of treble, tenor and bass size are depicted, each held in a different position. However, all these rottes are bowed, not plucked. The bow appears to have been introduced some time during the 9th or 10th century, and the evidence of both archaeological material and manuscript illustrations suggests that during the centuries before the bowed version was adopted only one size of rotte was used. The small lyre-playing figure in the 9th-century Utrecht Psalter, also mentioned by Schlesinger, is too ambiguous to allow a firm conclusion as to the size of the instrument in relation to the player.

The surviving remains, though incomplete, tend to complement each other so that when studied together they yield positive information about almost every detail of the instrument. Thus it appears that (with some variations) an average rotte of the 5th to 8th centuries was a six-string instrument measuring about 76 cm in length, 20 cm in breadth and 2·5 cm in depth. The strings were secured to a tailpiece which was either clamped round the bottom of the instrument and fastened at the back or secured by a cord tied round a button or peg as on a violin; they then passed over a bridge and up to the pegs in the yoke. The body and arms, and in German instruments the yoke section as well, were cut from a single piece of wood, and the resonating space was hollowed out of the solid, extending part of the way up the arms. The hollowed area was covered by a soundboard about 2 mm thick; sometimes bronze pins were used to secure the soundboard to the body. There is positive evidence that rottes of this period had no soundholes. The shape of the instrument varied, some versions being gently waisted or tapered from top to bottom and from front to back, while others were straight-sided.

The scanty remains of the rotte from Taplow are of maple wood, as is the whole of the Sutton Hoo instrument, the best-preserved English specimen. In the German rottes, however, maple or some other equally fine-grained wood was used for the soundboard only, and the rest of the instrument was made of oak.

With one exception (see fig.4) there is as yet no archaeological material to show how the rotte developed during the centuries between the Cologne instrument and the Welsh CRWTH (a folk instrument, directly descended from the rotte). Representations in illuminated manuscripts and sculpture reflect the evolution of the instrument during this period. The earliest illustrations of the rotte, in Anglo-Saxon manuscripts of the 8th century, show an instrument closely similar to the excavated specimens of the same period (fig.1), but within two centuries several important changes can be observed. Two French manuscripts of the 9th century depict a plucked instrument of rotte-like shape (though

5. King David playing a waisted lyre: miniature from the Codex Gertrudianus, 10th century, from Reichenau (Museo Archeologico Nazionale, Cividale del Friuli, Codex CXXXVI, f.20v)

6. King David playing a lyre in the shape of a figure 8: miniature from a 12th-century MS from St Gall (CH-SGs Codex 21, p.5)

executed in late antique style) with a fingerboard running down the centre parallel with the upright arms. In south German manuscripts the waisted shape persists, with the curves becoming increasingly pronounced (see fig.5); but from the 10th-11th centuries it frequently resembles a figure 8 (fig.6). Round-topped lyres on Irish stone crosses of the same period, on the other hand, are straight-sided with a squared-off bottom edge. Soundholes are occasionally depicted from the 10th century onwards, and in the Klosterneuburg manuscript bow and soundholes appear together. A particularly interesting example in an 11th- to 12th-century French manuscript shows a bowed rotte with fingerboard and bridge, but without soundholes – an early version of the crwth (see CRWTH, fig.2). In all these representations the instrument is shown being played by King David.

The plucked rotte was usually held on the knee either upright or inclined slightly away from the player. One hand gripped the frame – very often at the top with the index and middle fingers clamped round the yoke – while the other plucked the strings in the open area. Left- and right-handed players are shown with equal frequency. There is a possibility that the instrument was held with the front facing the player; manuscript evidence is conflicting on this as on almost every other point, but several illustrations clearly show it in this position, and the minstrel in the Cologne grave was buried with the bridge side of his rotte clasped against his chest.

There is no record of how the rotte was tuned, though from the prevalence of the six-string version a pentatonic scale seems likely. Tuning-keys in use are often depicted, possibly suggesting the need for frequent retuning to different modes, or perhaps merely indicating that ill-fitting pegs were common in early times.

The triangular harp, which first appears in manuscripts and sculpture about 900, gradually supplanted the round lyre in representations of King David the musician, and from the 13th century the lyre occurs less and less frequently, its disappearance from manuscripts reflecting its loss of status as an instrument associated with royalty and the nobility. A 14th-century lyre found at Kravik, Numedal (now in the Norsk Folkemuseum in Oslo; fig.4), which probably belonged to a prosperous farmer, is crudely designed and finished in comparison with the clean lines and superior craftsmanship of earlier instruments.

A bowed instrument of lyre type continued to flourish in rural cultures for several centuries. The Finnish *kantele*, Swedish *stråkharpa*, Norwegian *giga*, Shetland *gue* and Welsh crwth, all varieties of bowed rotte, were still being played until well into the 19th century and even later (see Andersson). A similar instrument also existed among the east European peoples. 13 *guslis*, dating from the 12th to 15th centuries, were recently found at Novgorod, USSR, and in Poland others of the 11th and 13th century have been excavated in Opole and Gdansk respectively. The medieval *gusli*, or *gęśl*, was a plucked instrument with strings varying in number from three to eight according to size. It was held flat across the knees like a zither and in appearance resembled a kind of primitive crwth without fingerboard and with an asymmetrical yoke. This instrument, too, persisted until well into the 19th century.

BIBLIOGRAPHY

F. W. Galpin: *Old English Instruments of Music* (London, 1910), rev. 4/1965 by T. Dart)

K. Schlesinger: *The Instruments of the Modern Orchestra and Early Records of the Precursors of the Violin Family*, ii (London, 1910)

O. Andersson: *The Bowed-harp* (London, 1930)

H. Panum: *The Stringed Instruments of the Middle Ages*, rev. and ed. J. Pulver (London, 1940/R1971)

J. Werner: 'Leier und Harfe im germanischen Frühmittelalter', *Aus Verfassungs- und Landesgeschichte: Festschrift zum 70. Geburtstag von Theodor Mayer* (Lindau and Konstanz, 1955), i, 9

A. Simon: 'An Early Medieval Slav *Gesle*', *GSJ*, x (1957), 63

H. Steger: *David rex et propheta* (Nuremberg, 1961), 41–75

R. and M. Bruce-Mitford: 'The Sutton Hoo Lyre, *Beowulf* and the Origins of the Frame-harp', *Antiquity*, xliv (1970), 7; rev., enlarged in *Aspects of Anglo-Saxon Archaeology* (London, 1974), 188

F. Crane: *Extant Medieval Musical Instruments: a Provisional Catalogue by Types* (Iowa City, 1972)

P. Paulsen and H. Schach-Dörgas: *Holzhandwerk der Alemannen* (Stuttgart, 1972), 99ff

MYRTLE BRUCE-MITFORD

Rottenbücher, Erasmus. See ROTENBUCHER, ERASMUS.

Rottenburgh. Flemish family of instrument makers working in Brussels in the 17th and 18th centuries. Godefroid-Adrien-Joseph Rottenburgh (i) (*b* Brussels, 1642; *d* Brussels 1720) was the first of three generations of instrument makers. None of his instruments seems to have survived, but his son, Jean-Hyacinth-Joseph (*b* Brussels, 1672; *d* Brussels, 1765), working near the Hôpital St Jean, made many recorders, flutes and oboes which are in museums in Berlin, Brussels, The Hague, Hälsingborg, Stockholm and in private collections. His instruments show excellent tonal characteristics and a perfection in scaling seldom found in surviving instruments by his French contemporaries.

Jean-Hyacinth-Joseph Rottenburgh was buried in the Eglise des Récollets in Brussels. His three sons are all said to have made instruments, but the only one whose work survives today was Godefried-Adrien-Joseph Rottenburgh (ii), whose shop was in rue de l'Hôpital. Surviving instruments by him include flutes, oboes and clarinets, all unmistakably in late 18th-century style and clearly not the work of his grandfather.

BIBLIOGRAPHY

V. C. Mahillon: *Catalogue descriptif et analytique du Musée instrumental du Conservatoire royal de musique de Bruxelles* (Ghent, 1909)

E. Closson: *La facture des instruments de musique* (Brussels, 1935)

L. Langwill: *An Index of Musical Wind-instrument Makers* (Edinburgh, 1960, rev. 5/1977)

FRIEDRICH VON HUENE

Rottenstein-Pock. See RODENSTEEN family.

Rotterdam. Dutch city. As a musical centre it was overshadowed by Amsterdam and The Hague, music being a privilege of the wealthy, until the 19th century when Rotterdam developed into one of the great musical centres of Holland. Wouter Hutschenruyter, a conductor and director of the school of music, contributed significantly to the popularization of music. Important work was done by the Maatschappij tot Bevordering der Toonkunst (Association for the Promotion of the Art of Music), founded in 1829: it encouraged and supported composers, founded choirs and schools of music and organized music festivals. Under the direction of Johannes Verhulst the Toonkunst branch in Rotterdam flourished; after he left for Amsterdam in 1863 and was succeeded by Woldemar Bargiel, a German, Rotterdam musical life came under strong German influence. The Duitse Opera, established in Rotterdam in 1860, greatly affected musical life in Holland. The best German singers went to Rotterdam, as guests or on long-term engagements, and many excellent German instrumentalists were engaged in the opera orchestra and contributed to the development of instrumental education as teachers at the school of music. The society was abolished in 1890 because of financial deficits.

In the 20th century Rotterdam again became an important musical centre, with several flourishing choirs and an important orchestra. The Rotterdam PO was founded in 1918 through the initiative of a number of local musicians; Eduard Flipse, a pioneer of the interpretation of modern music, became its conductor in 1930. During the bombing of Rotterdam in 1940 all the instruments and scores were lost, and the old Doele, the orchestra's concert hall, was destroyed. Various buildings were used until De Doelen was opened in 1966. This hall has a capacity of 2230; its organ, made by D. A. Flentrop, has a predominantly horizontal formation. Eduard Flipse was succeeded by Franz Paul Decker, Jean Fournet and Edo de Waart. The orchestra has made several world tours.

The most important church is the St Laurenskerk (begun in 1409), which has a long history of organ playing. From the 17th century recitals were given daily on the organ, built by H. Goldfuss in 1644. A new instrument was begun by A. Wolferts in 1791 and completed in 1844 by C. G. Witte. During World War II the church was badly damaged and the organ was totally destroyed; a new organ was commissioned from the Danish organ builders Marcussen & Son.

BIBLIOGRAPHY

H. W. de Ronde: 'Muziekleven in Rotterdam', *Gedenkboek Rotterdam 1328/1928* (Rotterdam, 1928), 465

W. A. Wagener: *Muziek aan de Maas* (Rotterdam, 1968)

HANS VAN NIEUWKOOP

Röttger, Heinz (*b* Herford, Westphalia, 6 Nov 1909; *d* Dessau, 26 Aug 1977). German conductor and composer. He studied at the Munich Academy of Music (1928–31), and from 1930 to 1934 he studied musicology, graduating from Munich University in 1937 with a dissertation *Das Formproblem bei Richard Strauss* (Berlin, 1937). His conducting career began in Augsburg; he was then appointed successively music director at the Stralsund Stadttheater (1948), general music director at the Rostock People's Theatre (1951), and chief music director at the Dessau Landestheater (1954). He made a reputation in the performance of Wagner, and his success as a composer was also in the field of opera, *Der Heiratsantrag* proving particularly popular. All of his work is characterized by strong rhythm and clear construction.

WORKS
(selective list)

Stage: Bellmann, opera, 1, 1946; Phaëton, opera, 1, 1957; Der Heiratsantrag (comic opera, 1, after Chekhov), 1959; Die Frauen von Troja, opera, 1961; . . . und heller wurde jeder Tag, ballet, 1964; Der Kreis, ballet, 1964; Der Weg nach Palermo (opera, E. Weeber-Fried), 1965

Other works: Sym. Prelude, 1937; Sym., g♯, 1939; Concs., vn, 1942, 1970, pf, 1950, vc, 1962, db, va, 1966, db, 1969; Sonata, vc, pf, 1947; Vn Sonata, 1948; 2 str qts, 1952, 1959; 4 Pieces, pf, 1957; Mahomed-Kantate, 1958; Borchert-Kantate, 1958; Concertino, db, pf (1962); Sinfonische Meditationen, 1964; Dessauer Sinfonie, 1966–7; Sinfonietta, str (1969); Constellation, str qt (1974)

Principal publishers: Breitkopf & Härtel, Deutscher Verlag für Musik

Rouart–Lerolle. French firm of music publishers. It was founded in 1905 by Alexis Rouart (1869–1921) through the acquisition of the publishing companies Meuriot and Badoux. Badoux had published several works of Jaques-Dalcroze and Lefebvre, as well as Satie's *Le fils des étoiles*. Satie's cabaret works, which had been published in 1903–4 by Bellon, Ponscarme & Cie, were also acquired. In 1908 Jacques Lerolle, a nephew of Chausson, joined the company and directed it after Rouart died. With Jacques Durand, Rouart had the idea of creating a collected French classical edition, and he began issuing new editions by d'Indy, Bordes and others. The company maintained a progressive programme, publishing works by notable French and Spanish composers including Albéniz, Chausson, Duparc, d'Indy, Koechlin, Hüe, Ladmirault, Poulenc, Ropartz, Satie, Séverac and Turina. In October 1941 the company was bought by Francis Salabert, and its publications were incorporated into the Salabert catalogue.

BIBLIOGRAPHY
P. Bordes: *L'édition musicale* (Paris, 1947)

ALAN POPE

Roucourt, Pierre de. *See* ROCOURT, PIERRE DE.

Rouen. City in north-west France. In 912 it became capital of Normandy. Important among early archbishops were St Ouen (640–83), during whose episcopate the monasteries of Fontenelle, Jumièges and Fécamp were founded; St Remi (Remigius, 754–72), who persuaded his brother King Pepin to ask Pope Paul I to send a cantor from Rome to instruct the diocese, and who sent two monks to Rome to learn chant; and Jean de Bayeux (1069–79), whose book on liturgical use became a model for the diocese. The Cathedral of Notre Dame had a strong musical tradition and its choir was noted always for singing from memory from the Middle Ages right up to the Revolution. In 1517 François I heard the choir and expressed his desire to have some of the boys for his own chapel, whereupon a band of his courtiers abducted two of the choristers by night. The 1546 registers record possession of masses by Certon and Morales. Pierre Caron (master of the song school, 1565–79) performed masses by Certon, motets by Guerrero and chansons by Arcadelt and Lassus. Masters of the choristers whose compositions were published were Dulot (1522–30), Guillaume Leroy (1530–36), Frémart (1611–25) and Lallouette (1693–5). The choir school was known as the Maîtrise St Evode from 1898 and the Institut Jehan Titelouze from 1956. Among its more distinguished pupils were Adrien Boieldieu, Paray and Duruflé.

Rouen's most celebrated organist was Titelouze, who was at St Jean from 1585 and at the cathedral from 1588, where the instrument was rebuilt by Crespin Carlier in 1606. Jacques Boyvin worked in Rouen from 1674; two books of his organ music were published in 1689 and 1700. Robert Clicquot restored the organ between 1685 and 1692; it then had four manuals and pedals, and 48 stops. Charles Broche published keyboard sonatas (1782–7), and from 1786 to 1792 taught the young Boieldieu, whose first two lyric dramas appeared at Rouen's Théâtre des Arts, *La fille coupable* (1793) and *Rosalie et Myrza* (1795, the year he left for Paris). The Dupré family of organists are from Rouen: Albert Dupré was organist at the old abbey church of St ⌐n (1911–39), and Marcel Dupré's first post, which

he held at the age of 12, was at the church of St Vivien. St Ouen has a Cavaillé-Coll organ of 1890. New organs were built in the cathedral by Merklin & Schutze (1858–60) and, after World War II, by Jacquot-Lavergne.

The Théâtre de Rouen was opened in 1776 with a repertory of *tragédie lyrique* and *opéra comique*. Renamed the Théâtre de la Montagne in 1793 and the Théâtre des Arts in 1794, it was burnt down in 1876. It opened again in 1882, and in 1890 staged the first French production of Saint-Saëns's *Samson et Dalila*. This house was destroyed in 1940, and a new theatre was built after the war. Its season usually lasts from October to May, with about 10 opera or ballet performances each month.

In 1945 a Conservatoire Municipal de Musique was opened in Rouen; it became the Ecole Nationale de Musique in 1947, and in 1949 the Conservatoire National de Musique de Rouen.

BIBLIOGRAPHY
J. E. Bouteiller: *Histoire complète et méthodique des théâtres de Rouen* (Rouen, 1860–90)
A. Collette and A. Bourdon: *Histoire de la maîtrise de Rouen* (Rouen, 1892)
——: *Notice historique sur les orgues et les organistes de la cathédrale de Rouen* (Rouen, 1894)
J. Pothier, A. Collette and A. Bourdon: *Mémoires sur la musique sacrée en Normandie* (Rouen, 1896)
J. Pothier, A. Collette and H. Loriquet: *Le graduel de l'église cathédrale de Rouen au XIIIe siècle* (Rouen, 1907)
H. Geispitz: *Histoire du Théâtre-des-arts de Rouen, 1882–1913* (Rouen, 1913)
N. Dufourcq: *Le livre de l'orgue français, 1589–1789*, i (Paris, 1971), 23ff, 105ff, 207ff, 345ff

DAVID HILEY

Rouge, Filippo. *See* RUGE, FILIPPO.

Rouge [Le Rouge, Ruby], **Guillaume** (*b* c1385; *d* c1456). French composer. Guillaume Rouge was named by the poet Eloy d'Amerval along with Dunstable, Dufay, Binchois and others as one of the 'great musicians' of the 15th century. Rouge apparently received his musical training at the Cathedral of Rouen and is recorded as having played the organ there in 1399. However, he was not a member of the chapel of King Charles VI of France in the early years of the 15th century, as has often been stated. In the summer of 1415 Rouge joined the chapel of the Duke of Burgundy and during the 1420s he evidently served at the collegiate church of the Sainte-Chapelle in Dijon. By 1431 he had returned to the domestic chapel of the court of Burgundy under Duke Philip the Good and was a singer, scribe and composer there for 20 years. In 1451 Rouge left the court of Burgundy and entered the chapel of the poet-prince, Duke Charles of Orleans. He last appears in the documents of the court of Orleans for 1456. Only two pieces by Rouge survive: a complete three-voice mass cycle *Soyez aprantiz* (DTÖ, cxx) preserved in *I-Rvat*, S Pietro B 80 and *TRc* 90; and a three-voice bergerette *Se je fayz dueil* is in the Mellon Chansonnier (*US-NH*) and the Schedelsches Liederbuch (*D-Mbs* Cim.315a). The mass *Soyez aprantiz* is based on Walter Frye's ballade *So ys emprintid in my remembrance* and is one of the earliest masses to incorporate a secular chanson. According to Johannes Tinctoris (*CS*, iv, 171), Rouge also composed a mass *Mon cuer pleure*, but this work now appears to be lost.

BIBLIOGRAPHY
J. Marix: *Histoire de la musique et des musiciens de la cour de Bourgogne sous le règne de Philippe le Bon* (Strasbourg, 1939)

E. Reeser: 'Een "iso-melische mis" uit den tijd van Dufay', *TVNM*, xvi/3 (1942), 151, 312
J. Daniskas: 'Een bijdrage tot de geschiedenis der parodie-techniek', *TVNM*, xvii/1 (1948), 21
C. Wright: *Music at the Court of Burgundy, 1364–1419* (diss., Harvard U., 1972), 318ff

CRAIG WRIGHT

Rouget, Gilbert (*b* Paris, 9 July 1916). French ethnomusicologist. He studied at the Sorbonne (1935–42) and was particularly influenced by the teaching of André Schaeffner and (later) Constantin Brăiloiu. He joined the ethnomusicology department at the Musée de l'Homme in 1941 and succeeded Schaeffner as its director in 1965; he also became director of research at the CNRS in 1972. His special field is the music of black Africa, particularly of southern Benin. In the course of several expeditions to equatorial and west Africa between 1946 and 1970 he made three films in collaboration with Jean Rouch (*Sortie des novices de Sakpata, Batteries dogon: éléments pour une étude des rythmes* and *Danses des reines à Porto-Novo*). He has also made recordings of pygmy and Bantu music of the middle Congo and Gabon, Moorish music, the music of the Maninka (Guinea) and of the Baule (Ivory Coast) and particularly the music of the Fon, Gun and Yoruba of Benin. His most important articles deal with African music itself, its relationship with the spoken language and its methodological problems. The originality and rigorous scholarship of Rouget's work make it an extremely valuable contribution to African ethnomusicology.

WRITINGS
'Un chromatisme africain', *L'homme: revue française d'anthropologie*, i/3 (1961), 32
'Tons de la langue en Gun (Dahomey) et tons du tambour', *RdM*, l (1964), 3
'Notes et documents pour servir d'étude à la musique yoruba', *Journal de la Société des africanistes*, xxxv/1 (1965), 67–107
'Sur les xylophones équiheptaphoniques des Malinké', *RdM*, lv (1969), 47 77
'Transcrire ou décrire?: chant soudanais et chant fuégien', *Echanges et communications: mélanges offerts à Claude Lévi-Strauss* (Paris and The Hague, 1970), i, 677
'Court Songs and Traditional History in the Ancient Kingdoms of Porto-Novo and Abomey', *Essays on Music and History in Africa*, ed. K. P. Wachsmann (Evanston, 1971), 27–64
with J. Schwarz: 'Chant fuégien, consonance, mélodie de voyelles', *RdM*, lxii (1976), 7
La musique, l'extase et la transe: éléments pour une théorie générale des relations de la musique et la possession (in preparation)

CHRISTIANE SPIETH-WEISSENBACHER

Rouget de Lisle [l'Isle]**, Claude-Joseph** (*b* Lons-le-Saunier, 10 May 1760; *d* Choisy-le-Roi, 26 or 27 [about midnight] June 1836). French poet and composer. He entered the Ecole Royale du Génie at Mézières in 1782, became a cadet officer in 1784 and was promoted to second lieutenant in 1788 and lieutenant in 1790. On 1 May 1791 he was posted to Strasbourg, where he soon became popular owing to his talent as a poet, violinist and singer. His *Hymne à la liberté*, set to music by Ignace Pleyel, was performed on 25 September, and of his several plays *Bayard dans Bresse* was set to music by Stanislas Champein and performed in Paris on 21 February. In Strasbourg, during the night of 25 April 1792, he wrote the words and music of the *Chant de guerre pour l'armée du Rhin*, which, because of its frequent performance by the Marseilles Volunteer Battalion, became known as the *Marseillais' Hymn* and, finally, the *Marseillaise*.

The son of royalist parents and a member of the Constitutional party, Rouget de Lisle opposed the abolition of the monarchy and was cashiered and imprisoned until the fall of Robespierre (an event which he celebrated by writing a *Dithyrambic Hymn*). He was then reinstated in the army and fought in the wars of the Vendée, under the command of Hoche. The *Marseillaise* was sanctioned as a national song in 1795 but fell out of favour during the Empire and the Restoration. Rouget de Lisle lived deserted and in poverty, and was harassed by the authorities, who even imprisoned him for debt. Béranger and David d'Angers defended him, and towards the end of his life he was befriended by the Voïart family in Choisy-le-Roi, who provided him with aid and shelter. With the July Revolution in 1830, the *Marseillaise* regained acceptability and Rouget de Lisle was granted a pension by Louis-Philippe.

Rouget de Lisle died unmarried, without descendants, but his nephew Amédée Rouget de Lisle later became involved in lengthy disputes with historians who sought to cast doubt on the authorship of the *Marseillaise* because of its success, in stark contrast to the mediocrity of Rouget de Lisle's other compositions; his authorship is now, however, commonly accepted. Once definitive official recognition of the *Marseillaise* as the French national anthem was confirmed in 1879, various marks of honour were granted to its author; statues were erected to his memory in Lons-le-Saunier and Choisy-le-Roi. On Bastille Day (14 July) 1915 his ashes were transferred to the Invalides, an event which marked the culmination of the glorification of the *Marseillaise* as the song symbolizing the 'Sacred Union' (Poincaré's words when speaking of the union of all French people against the enemy). In 1936, the centenary of Rouget de Lisle's death, solemn and impressive tributes were paid to his memory, but for a different purpose. Maurice Thorez made a speech at Choisy-le-Roi, reminding the public of the origin and Revolutionary inspiration of the song, contrasting it with the *Internationale*. In 1960 official celebrations took place at a local level in Lons-le-Saunier, and in the town's library musical works were discovered which were previously unknown or which had been thought lost.

The *Marseillaise* has been quoted by Schumann (*Die beiden Grenadiere*) and Tchaikovsky (*1812 Overture*) among others. Besides other Revolutionary works Rouget de Lisle also composed *romances* and wrote librettos for operas by Chelard, Della-Maria and Grétry.

WORKS
Chant de guerre pour l'armée du Rhin [La Marseillaise], 1v, hpd (Paris, *c*1792); numerous edns. and arrs.
Premier recueil de 24 hymnes, chansons ou romances, acc. pf, vn obbl (Paris, 1796); bk 2 (Paris, n.d.)
50 chants français, acc. pf (Paris, 1825)
Other romances and Revolutionary songs, hymns

WRITINGS
Essais en vers et en prose (Paris, 1796)
Historique et souvenirs de Quiberon (Paris, 1834)
Librettos for S. Champein: *Bayard dans Bresse* (1791); Grétry: *Cécile et Ermancé* (1792), collab. J. B. D. Desprez; D. Della-Maria: *Jacquot, ou L'école des mères* (1798), collab. Desprez; H. Chelard: *Macbeth* (1827)

BIBLIOGRAPHY
A. Leconte: *La vérité sur la paternité de La Marseillaise* (Paris, 1865)
A. Leconte: *Rouget de Lisle: sa vie, ses oeuvres* (Paris, 1892)
J. Tiersot: *Rouget de Lisle: son oeuvre, sa vie* (Paris, 1892)
C. Pierre: *Les hymnes et chansons de la Révolution* (Paris, 1904)
M. La Fuye and E. Guéret: *Rouget de Lisle, inconnu* (Paris, 1943)
G. de Froidcourt: *Grétry, Rouget de Lisle et La Marseillaise* (Liège, 1945)

F. Chailley: 'La Marseillaise: étude critique sur ses origines', *Annales historiques de la Révolution française*, xxxii (1960), 266

FRÉDÉRIC ROBERT

Rouince, Luigi. *See* ROINCE, LUIGI.

Rouleau, Joseph (Alfred) (*b* Matane, Quebec, 28 Feb 1929). Canadian bass. After studying in Montreal and later in Italy, he made his début at New Orleans in 1955. He first appeared at Covent Garden in 1957 as Colline, and at the Paris Opéra in 1960 as Bide-the-Bent in *Lucia di Lammermoor*. Since then he has sung throughout western Europe, in the USSR, North and South America and Australia. He is a reliable, versatile artist, whose large repertory includes Basilio, Rodolfo (*La sonnambula*), Oroveso (*Norma*), Sir George Walton (*I puritani*) and Sparafucile; particularly at home in French, he is a fine Philip II, Pope Clement (*Benvenuto Cellini*), Narbal (*Les troyens*), Mephistopheles, Arkel and Don Quichotte, while he also sings Boris Godunov, Pimen and Dosifey (*Khovanshchina*) with success. In 1967 he created the role of Bishop Tâché in Harry Somers's *Louis Riel* at Toronto.

ELIZABETH FORBES

Roullet [Rollet, Roller], **Johannes** (*fl* c1435–45). Composer of the Dufay era, probably French. The majority of his compositions are very modest functional settings of liturgical texts with unelaborate chant paraphrase in the discantus and fauxbourdon or fauxbourdon-like accompaniments. His music is found mainly in *D-Mbs* Clm 14274 and *I-TRmn* 87; and the prominence of his name in the first of these indicates that he may have had some close connection with the compiler of that manuscript.

The greatest interest lies in the four sequence settings in which Roullet offers a variety of formal solutions to accommodate the lengthy texts. The largest is *Laus tibi Christe*, in which the first half of each binary verse is presented as chant and then repeated with the melody paraphrased in the discantus; second halves of verses are omitted entirely. Variety in the polyphonic sections is achieved through the use of four different mensurations (O, Φ, C and Ȼ) and the use of fauxbourdon in some internal verses. The polyphonic segments are equally varied in *Omnes sancti seraphim*, in which the entire text is laid out *ad alternatim* with chant. No plainsong is sung in *O beata beatorum*, where the two halves of each verse are given as double text underlay and the variety among the verses is less pronounced. *Sacerdotem Christi* is the most straightforward and least interesting of the settings. Charles Hamm has remarked that the sequences of Roullet may have had a common origin with the three sequences of Dufay which immediately precede them and are the only other music in the sixth gathering of *I-TRmn* 87.

The songs survive only as sacred contrafacta with the titles added in the margin; but their form leaves little doubt as to their origin.

WORKS

MASS MOVEMENTS

Kyrie paschale, 2vv + fauxbourdon (discantus paraphrases Kyrie paschale or 'Lux et origo'), *D-Mbs* 14274, f.95v, *I-TRmn* 87, f.99
Et in terra, 3vv, *A-Z*, frag. MS without shelf-mark, f.80v (orig. paired with Patrem, f.175r, lost)
Sanctus paschale, 3vv with tropes 2vv (marked 'Gemell': 'Crux columpna'), *D-Mbs* 14274, f.143v
Benedicamus Domino, 3vv, *I-TRmn* 87, f.92

HYMN

Rex gloriose martyrum, 2vv + fauxbourdon (discantus paraphrases chant, *Liber usualis* 1144), *D-Mbs* 14274, f.85, *I-TRmn* 87, f.16

SEQUENCES

Laus tibi Christe (St Mary Magdalen; Analecta hymnica, l, 346), 3vv alternating with 2vv + fauxbourdon, *TRmn* 87, f.67v
O beata beatorum (Martyrs; Analecta hymnica, 1v, 20), 2vv + fauxbourdon alternating with 2vv, *TRmn* 87, f.72v
Omnes sancti seraphim (All Saints, Analecta hymnica, liii, 196), 3vv alternating with 2vv + fauxbourdon, *TRmn* 87, f.71v
Sacerdotem Christi (St Martin; Analecta hymnica, liii, 294), 3vv alternating with 2vv + fauxbourdon, *TRmn* 87, f.70

SECULAR WORKS

Amours helas (rondeau), 3vv [texted: Vexillum victoris], *D-Mbs* 14274, f.142v
Hardament (ballade), 3vv, *Mbs* 14274, f.98v [texted: Christus natus est hodie], f.93
Joye et confort (rondeau), 3vv [texted: Post biduum victor], *Mbs* 14274, f.143
Umb inj pad, 3vv [texted: Ecce panis angelorum], *Mbs* 14274, f.120
Wo ich in aller werld hin, 3vv, *Mbs* 14274, f.97

BIBLIOGRAPHY

K. Dèzes: 'Der Mensuralcodex des Benediktinerklosters "Sancti Emmerami" zu Regensburg', *ZMw*, x (1927–8), 65
P. Gülke: 'Roullet', *MGG*
K. von Fischer: 'Neue Quellen zur Musik des 13., 14. und 15. Jahrhunderts', *AcM*, xxxvi (1964), 79
C. Hamm: *A Chronology of the Works of Guillaume Dufay* (Princeton, 1964), 81

RICHARD LOYAN

Roullet [Rollet, Durollet, Du Rollet], **Marie François Louis Gand Leblanc,** Bailli du (*b* Normanville, Eure, 10 April 1716; *d* Paris, 2 Aug 1786). French writer. A nobleman, who served as an officer of the Gardes Françaises and as a *commandeur* in the Ordre de Malte, he also had a literary career. His first stage work, a comedy entitled *Les effets du caractère* (1752), was a failure. As an attaché to the French embassy in Vienna, he met Gluck and became his first and principal propagandist in Paris. Supported by Marie-Antoinette, he made imperious demands on the Opéra in 1774; later, he may have acted discreditably in Gluck's interest by endeavouring to prevent improvements in the libretto of Sacchini's *Renaud*. He started the fashion for adapting 17th-century tragedies for the Opéra with *Iphigénie en Aulide* (for Gluck) in 1774, apparently the only libretto for which he was wholly responsible. He also translated the prefaces to Gluck's *Alceste* and *Paride ed Elena* for the *Gazette de littérature* (1774), wrote a *Lettre sur les drames-opéras* (1776) and probably 'ghosted' French articles signed by Gluck. He undertook the extensive alteration and translation for the French *Alceste* (1776) and collaborated with Baron Tschudi on *Les Danaïdes* (1784), taken without permission from Calzabigi and staged with Salieri's music, although advertised as being partly by Gluck. Articles by Roullet are included in a compilation entitled *Mémoires pour servir à l'histoire de la révolution opérée dans la musique par. . .Gluck* (Paris and Naples, 1781). He is generally regarded as an *homme d'esprit* rather than a major literary figure.

BIBLIOGRAPHY

A. Beuchot: 'Durollet', *Biographie universelle*, ed. L. G. Michaud (Paris, 1843–65)
J. C. F. Hoefer, ed.: 'Rollet (Marie-François-Louis-Gand-Leblanc)', *Nouvelle biographie générale* (Paris, 1852–66)
G. Le Brisoys Desnoiresterres: *Gluck et Piccinni* (Paris, 1872, 2/1875)
A. Jullien: *La cour et l'Opéra sous Louis XVI* (Paris, 1878)
J. Tiersot: *Gluck* (Paris, 1910, 4/1919)
P. Howard: *Gluck and the Birth of Modern Opera* (London, 1963)
P. Smith: *The Tenth Muse: a Historical Study of the Opera Libretto* (London, 1971)

R. Angermüller: 'Reformideen von Du Roullet und Beaumarchais als Opernlibrettisten', *AcM*, xlviii (1976), 227

JULIAN RUSHTON

Round. (1) A perpetual canon at the unison for three or more voices; the words may equally well be sacred or secular. The medieval Latin term was 'rota' (wheel) – the word used in the rubric of *Sumer is icumen in*, which also has a Latin text: 'Perspice, Christicola'. In this 13th-century example the round is sung over a two-part vocal ostinato (called *pes* in the MS) which is actually a miniature RONDELLUS, i.e. a canon in which the voices begin together. A particularly elaborate round from the end of the 15th century is Robert Wilkinson's *Jesus autem transiens: Credo in Deum* in the Eton Choirbook (MB, xii, no.50), which is for 13 voices: the opening phrase, which serves as a cantus firmus, is the first part of the *Magnificat* antiphon for the third Sunday in Lent.

The English term appears, apparently for the first time, in *Pray we to God* (*GB-Lbm* Add.31922, f.103; MB, xviii, no.97), where the last two lines are:

> Now let us sing this round all three;
> Saint George grant him the victory.

(It is possible, however, that 'round' is here an adverb.) The same MS, dating from the early years of the 16th century, includes a number of other rounds, one of which has a free part, apparently designed for an instrument. A particular form of round which was popular in the 16th, 17th and 18th centuries was the CATCH. The only difference between the two was that the round could be serious, whereas the catch was always frivolous.

On the Continent the equivalent of the round was known by the generic term 'canon'. Most of Haydn's canons are in effect rounds. Beethoven amused himself from time to time by writing pieces of this kind. For obvious reasons rounds were rarely incorporated into larger works, though the principle might be observed: for instance the quartet 'Mir ist so wunderbar' in Beethoven's *Fidelio* has the character of an accompanied round with a coda, though there is no repetition after the fourth voice has completed the melody. Though the singing of rounds as a form of social recreation had declined by the 20th century they found a permanent home in school songbooks, where they proved to be an effective way of teaching children to sing independent parts. Rounds in foreign languages, e.g. *Frère Jacques*, served a double purpose in the classroom.

(2) In general, a country dance. In particular, a 'round dance', i.e. one in which the dancers, men and women alternately, are grouped in a circle; there are several examples in John Playford's *The English Dancing Master* (1651), e.g. *If all the world were paper*. One of the oldest dances of this type of which the tunes survive is 'Sellenger's Round', on which Byrd wrote keyboard variations (MB, xxviii, no.84); another is *Gypsies*.

BIBLIOGRAPHY
J. Stevens: 'Rounds and Canons from an Early Tudor Song-Book', *ML*, xxxii (1951), 29
J. Vlasto: 'An Elizabethan Anthology of Rounds', *MQ*, xl (1954), 222
M. Dean-Smith: *Playford's 'English Dancing Master'* (London, 1957)
F. Ll. Harrison: *Music in Medieval Britain* (London, 1958, 2/1963)
——: 'Rota and Rondellus in English Medieval Music', *PRMA*, lxxxvi (1959–60), 98

JACK WESTRUP

Round, Catch and Canon Club. London club founded in 1843; see LONDON, §VI, 3(i).

Round O. English corruption of the French 'rondeau'. The term occurs in Jeremiah Clarke's *Choice Lessons for the Harpsichord or Spinett* (London, 1711) and similar publications of the time, in conjunction customarily with compositions of a five-section rondeau design, *ABACA*. A keyboard piece by Matthew Locke provides an early instance of its use applied to an even simpler structure. From the realm of practice, this terminological variant found its way into some music dictionaries of the later 18th century, such as John Hoyle's *A Complete Dictionary of Music* (London, 1770), where it appears as an alternative spelling in a rondeau definition that is little more than a reprint of James Grassineau's translation and codification (1740) of Brossard. *See* RONDO, §2.

MALCOLM S. COLE

Rounds. Almost the oldest of Western dance forms, and probably second only to the ancient chain-dance in a file known as the farandole. Rounds were depicted on the shield of Achilles (*Iliad* xviii.593–601). They are basically of two kinds, 'essential' and 'accidental'. 'Essential' rounds are true ring dances. The dancers must form a complete, though not necessarily a linked, circle. 'Accidental' rounds may be danced in an arc of a circle, but the dancers must be linked in some way, usually by their hands.

'Essential' rounds can be subdivided into central and peripheral types. The former have an imaginary central focus. This must originally have been a cult object, often a tree, which persisted in the maypole until the 17th century. The dancers go in and out, to and from this centre, though there are some subsidiary lateral movements. 'Sellenger's Round' is our clearest example, with 'Gathering Peascods' a fancier version. In a peripheral round the dancers progress in a pattern round the circumference, e.g. 'Millfield'. Here the arches made by the dancers' arms give a clue to its origins, showing that probably both these forms were the culminating figure in the farandole, with the head and tail of the file joining up to form a ring.

'Accidental' rounds are not a final figure of farandole but an alternative version of the dance. Their contribution to dance form consists of their rhythms, in contrast to the figures, i.e. spatial patterns, made by the farandole. The French medieval and Renaissance version of the carole called a branle (the English braule or brawl) is the form in which we meet the 'accidental' round. The linked dancers in the old farandole file have each made a quarter-turn to the right and now face inwards to the centre of an arc, or a full circle, moving sideways to the left and the right, instead of facing and moving forwards.

BELINDA QUIREY

Rourke, William Michael. *See* ROOKE, WILLIAM MICHAEL.

Rousée, Jean (*fl* Paris, 1534–60). French composer. According to Fétis he was a singer in Henri II's chapel between 1547 and 1559. Six motets and three chansons were published in anthologies by Attaingnant and Le Roy & Ballard. Four of the motets form a group for the feasts of Christmas, St Stephen, All Saints and St Nicholas. The anonymous three- and four- voice models of the late chansons were printed by Attaingnant (*RISM* 1529⁴, 1530⁴) and may also have been by Rousée.

WORKS

Edition: *Treize livres de motets parus chez Pierre Attaingnant en 1534 et 1535*, ed. A. Smijers and A. T. Merritt (Paris and Monaco, 1934–63) [S]

Congratulamini michi omnes, 4vv, 1534⁹, S vii; Exurge, quare obdormis, Domine, 6vv, 1534¹⁰, S viii; Lapidaverunt Stephanum, 4vv, 1534⁹, S vii; Laudem dicite Deo nostro, 4vv, 1534⁹, S vii; Regina caeli, 8vv, 1535⁴, S xii; Sospitati dedit aegros, 4vv, 1534⁹, S vii

Fortune laisse-moy la vie, 5vv, 1572²; J'ay veu soubz l'ombre d'ung buisson, 4vv, 1534¹⁴; La rousée du moys de may, 6vv, 1572²

FRANK DOBBINS

Rousseau, Jean (*b* Moulins, 1 Oct 1644; d ?c1700). French bass violist, composer, theorist and teacher. He lived in Paris from 1676; he was a pupil of Sainte-Colombe and became widely known as a teacher and a prominent member of the French bass viol school of the later 17th century. He is best known for his *Traité de la viole* (Paris, 1687/*R*1975; Eng. trans. in *The Consort*, xxxiii–, 1977–), which provides much more than instrumental instruction. Separate sections explore the history of the viol, ornamentation, transposition and the different ways of playing the instrument. These include 'le jeu de melodie' (the melodic style) and 'le jeu d'harmonie' (the harmonic style). Each manner had its proponents, and part of the argument survives in print (see Lesure). In the preface to his *Pièces de violle* (1685) Machy ridiculed those who preferred unharmonized compositions. Rousseau responded acidly in his *Traité* and in a *Réponse à la lettre d'un de ses amis qui l'avertit d'un libelle diffamatoire que l'on a écrit contre luy* (dated 30 October 1688), supporting the melodic style as more natural and more nearly approaching the human voice. He in fact also published a didactic work on singing, *Méthode claire, certaine et facile pour apprendre à chanter la musique* (Paris, 1678), which was popular enough to go into a sixth edition by 1707 (*R*1976). He composed *Premier et deuxième livre de pièces de viole, avec des exercises sur plusieurs nouvelles manières de l'accorder* (Paris, n.d.; now lost) and possibly a few bass viol pieces marked 'J. R.' in a MS (*F-Pn*).

BIBLIOGRAPHY

E. Titon du Tillet: *Le Parnasse françois* (Paris, 1732/*R*1971)
J.-B. de La Borde: *Essai sur la musique* (Paris, 1780/*R*1972)
F. Lesure: 'Une querelle sur le jeu de la viole en 1688: Jean Rousseau contre Demachy', *RdM*, xlvi (1960), 181
R. A. Green: 'Jean Rousseau and Ornamentation in French Viol Music', *Journal of the Viola da Gamba Society of America*, xiv (1977), 4–41
G. J. Kinney: 'A "Tempest in a Glass of Water", or a Conflict of Esthetic Attitudes', *Journal of the Viola da Gamba Society of America*, xiv (1977), 42
J. A. Sadie: *The Bass Viol in French Baroque Chamber Music* (Ann Arbor, 1981)

CLYDE H. THOMPSON

Rousseau, Jean-Baptiste (*b* Paris, 6 April 1671; *d* Brussels, 16 March 1741). French poet. He wrote the librettos of *Jason; ou la toison d'or* (music by Collasse, 1696) and *Vénus et Adonis* (music by Desmarets, 1697). Soon afterwards he turned to the writing of cantata texts, which was his most important contribution to French music. Rousseau's own knowledge of music gave him unusual insight into the problems of writing words for music and his 26 published cantata texts were regarded as models of their kind. As well as providing material for the rising school of cantata composers in France Rousseau's texts also initiated a minor poetic form there.

BIBLIOGRAPHY

H. A. Grubbs: *Jean-Baptiste Rousseau: his Life and Works* (Princeton, 1941)
D. E. Tunley: *The 18th Century French Cantata* (London, 1974)

DAVID TUNLEY

Rousseau, Jean-Jacques (*b* Geneva, 28 June 1712; *d* Ermenonville, 2 July 1778). Swiss philosopher, author and composer, of French Protestant descent. His views on music had a strong impact throughout Western civilization. Two of his poetic-musical creations proved epochal: *Le devin du village* of 1752 showed the way to French *opéra comique*, as it was definitively coined during the third quarter of the 18th century; *Pygmalion* of 1770 inaugurated the genre of spoken drama with instrumental interjections later known as melodrama.

Rousseau's early training in music was poor. It consisted mainly of vocal instruction, but this did not prevent him from posing as a teacher of composition as well as singing from the age of 18. He tried to educate himself by reading Rameau's treatise on harmony, and by copying music, which he also did as a profession, even late in life. By 1739–40, in Chambéry, he was already attempting to write both words and music for a serious opera. At Lyons in 1742 he composed the music for part of another opera. He moved to Paris in 1742, at which time he presented to the Académie des Sciences a scheme for simplifying musical writing by substituting ciphers for notes. The system was ill-adapted to anything more complex than melodies with simple accompaniments – precisely the ideal of music Rousseau propounded all his life – and it was rejected. He then sought the support of Rameau, who pointed out the inadequacies of the system at once. His *Dissertation sur la musique moderne* of 1743 is an embittered defence of his invention; it won no converts. During the same year he began composition of the text and music of an *opéra-ballet*, *Les muses galantes*, modelled on Rameau's *Les Indes galantes*. The work was interrupted by his departure for Venice in May 1743 as secretary to the French ambassador there.

Rousseau had copied Italian scores and heard individual arias in concert prior to this time, but his first experience of Italian opera on the stage was in Venice. His enthralled reactions are described in the *Confessions*. He was enchanted even more by the concerts given at the various conservatories for orphaned girls, although his description of them leaves no doubt that the stimulation afforded was largely sexual. He singled out for special praise the music at the Mendicanti, then directed by Galuppi. He also took interest in Venetian popular songs, such as the verses by Tasso declaimed by gondoliers, examples of which he copied into his own collection of favourites, published posthumously as *Les consolations des misères de ma vie*. The sojourn at Venice in 1743–4 marked the end point of Rousseau's knowledge of Italian opera; he took no interest in its many advances during the following decades.

Returning to Paris in October 1744 he continued work on *Les muses galantes*, which was finished by mid-1745. He again sought out Rameau and tried to have him examine the score. Rameau refused but later consented, reluctantly, to listen to selections from the work performed at the house of his friend and patron La Pouplinière. He pronounced directly to the point, as always, calling what he heard partly the work of an inspired melodist, and partly that of a musical ignoramus. The implication was that Rousseau was responsible only for the latter part. Ten years later, after the final rupture between the two men, Rameau elaborated his judgment, saying that the good part, the violin accompaniments in the Italian style, could not have been by

Rousseau. Charges of plagiarism plagued Rousseau throughout his life. They were perhaps inevitable if only because, though lacking professional training as a composer, he nevertheless posed as one, and even imagined himself a rival of Rameau. Rivalry with the other great minds of Paris, particularly that of Diderot, played a part in his ambitions also. He admitted in the *Confessions* that he wished to be regarded as a composer in order to show his superiority to the other *philosophes*.

Another task involving Rousseau's talents as a poet-musician was the hasty revision of *La princesse de Navarre* by Voltaire and Rameau as *Les fêtes de Ramire*, an occasional piece commissioned by the court to celebrate a victorious battle. The work was staged at Versailles at the end of 1745, and as a result put Rousseau on good terms with the forces of the Opéra at Paris. Revisions of *Les muses galantes* occupied another two years, when the Paris troupe put it into rehearsal. It was even brought to a general rehearsal, witnessed by a large audience, but at this point the composer withdrew the work (it was not rejected, as claimed by his enemies).

Not until *Le devin du village* was given before the court at Fontainebleau in October 1752 did Rousseau realize his dearest wish. The success of the little *intermède* was instantaneous and so thoroughgoing that it held the stage for some 60 years in France, and was also given widely outside the country. Burney made a successful English adaptation under the title *The Cunning-*

Title-page of Rousseau's 'Les consolations des misères de ma vie' (Paris: De Roullède etc, 1781)

Man (1766). However slight the work, its message was deeply felt and pertinent to those social stirrings that made Rousseau such a prophet to his own and later times: the triumph of rustic simplicity and virtue over higher-class corruption and venality. After being carried out in the main plot, this theme is re-enacted in pantomime during the final ballet. Rousseau's verve and style as a librettist accounted for no small part of the work's renown. But it was as a poet-musican that he wanted to be hailed, and indeed was. His model for the form of the whole was the Italian intermezzo. The dimensions of the work are small (it lasts about an hour and has only three characters) and there is no spoken dialogue, a departure from similar French works before this time. The brilliant Italian style of violin accompaniment distinguishes a few of the airs. Many have only a continuo accompaniment and are in a style so plain and unornamented as to suggest the music of 50 years earlier. A folklike simplicity of tone pervades the whole. Dance rhythms are prominent, especially the gavotte pattern. It is an irony of history that Rousseau should have learnt so much from Rameau's dances, and that both men, though they had become arch-enemies, should have drawn inspiration so successfully from traditional French dance and song.

Rousseau collected French as well as Italian folk music, as is evident from the branles in his *Consolations*. The weaker elements in *Le devin* are the recitatives and the part-writing in some of the set pieces. Thin-sounding chords, bad spacing, parallel 5ths in the outer voices, doubled leading notes and other insensitivities abound; but neither were they infrequent in the operas, particularly the comic ones, of Rousseau's proclaimed heroes, Vinci and Pergolesi. In one sense, shoddy part-writing was only an aspect of being 'modern'. Sometimes Rousseau's harmonies are so audacious as to be prophetic. In the final *romance* 'Dans ma cabane obscure', for example, the treatment of the diminished 7th chord before the cadence predicts a cliché of 19th-century harmony. It is needless to ask whether a work of genius such as this opera is 'good' – it held the attention of several generations and continued to form musical tastes to the time of Berlioz.

A culmination of another kind was reached with Rousseau's *Lettre sur la musique française* of the following year (1753), at once the most eloquent and most extreme statement of hostility to French opera, and all the more paradoxical, following upon the success of *Le devin*. It was his major contribution to the Querelle des Bouffons. The philosophy of music propounded in it, and in the various articles on music for the *Encyclopédie* (later incorporated into the *Dictionnaire* of 1768), led Rousseau to conclude that opera was not possible in the French language. A direct consequence of this conclusion was the radical experiment represented by *Pygmalion*, a spoken monodrama sketched in the 1760s and performed at Lyons in 1770 with introductory symphony and instrumental interludes by Horace Coignet (except for two Andantes in the hand of the author). When the work was performed subsequently in Paris, Rousseau did not take the trouble to indicate the role of Coignet, who promptly claimed it in public. The incident provided further cause for calumny and for doubts about the musical abilities of the philosopher. Rousseau took little interest in the advances being made by German music during his lifetime, and he seems to have been unaware that the example of *Pygmalion* set off a wave of German imitations during the 1770s. As late as 1777, the date of his essay on Gluck's *Alceste*, he believed that his example had been unheeded. Rousseau's final reconciliation with Gluck and his admiration for the operas that Gluck directed at Paris gave the lie to his earlier insults about the impossibility of opera in French. His critical gibes should not have been taken as seriously as they were and continued to be. It is characteristic of Rousseau that he never retracted, never forgave and admitted no mistakes. At the time of his death he was working on another pastoral opera, *Daphnis et Chloé*, the completed part of which was printed after his death. In style it is very close to *Le devin*.

Rousseau's views on the art depart from the humanist notion that music arises in response to text, a position strongly maintained in French letters since Ronsard. Dubos elaborated the same view in the early years of the 18th century with his doctrine of imitation: music, like painting and poetry, is an imitation of nature; if it paints nothing, it expresses nothing. Rousseau went beyond this and claimed that the origins of music were neither word nor tone but song, by which he meant accented declamation, the original cry of passion of primitive man. His anathema hurled at French music in 1753 represents the extreme consequence of this line of thinking: the French language (he maintained) was expressive only of ideas, not sentiments; it had no marked accent and therefore could not not give rise to song. Song in this special sense appealed to the emotions, whereas music in general had degenerated, with increasing civilization, into a language that appealed only to the intellect – with the sole exception of Italian music. Mystical views such as these about the superiority of feeling over reason enchanted ensuing generations of Romantics and started a line of thought that led, by way of Herder, Haman and Goethe, to the Wagnerian theory of music drama.

There were obvious drawbacks to the theory that music could be expressive only through language. It allowed for national musics only, not for a supranational art. It excluded the possibility of the kind of classical universality expressed in Haydn's famous remark that all the world understood his language. Rousseau could not and did not, in his theoretical writings, acknowledge the growing independence and power of 'pure' instrumental music. The omission led him into many contradictions. He knew by experience how powerful and independent the orchestra had become in certain parts of Italian opera. His enthusiasm for obbligato recitative led him to say that the orchestra expresses what the words cannot. His controversy with Rameau in 1753–4 about Lully's setting of Armide's monologue turned partly on the same issue. He wanted the orchestra to paint Armide's change of heart before she gave utterance to it in words. The genre of melodrama was a consequence of such intuitive views. But even earlier, in *Le devin*, Rousseau showed that he knew well how to portray character through instrumental music, independently of the text.

WORKS
(all printed works published in Paris)

STAGE
(all texts by Rousseau unless otherwise stated)
Iphis et Anaxorète (tragédie lyrique), Chambéry, c1740; music lost
La découverte du nouveau monde (tragédie lyrique, 3), Lyons, 1741; music lost
Les muses galantes (opéra-ballet, 3), Paris, residence of La Pouplinière, ?1745; music lost; music to later entrée Hésiode (orig. La tasse) in

Musée Chalis, nr. Senlis; Musette en rondo, ed. in *BSIM*, viii/6 (1912), 49, see also Brook
Les fêtes de Ramire, Versailles, late 1745; rev. of Rameau's La Princesse de Navarre (comédie-ballet, 3, Voltaire), music lost
Le devin du village (intermède, 1), Fontainebleau, 18 Oct 1752; score (1753), 6 nouveaux airs (1778)
Pygmalion (scène lyrique), Lyons, Hôtel de Ville, 1770, collab. H. Coignet; score, *F-Pcf*; parts, *Pn*
Daphnis et Chloé (pastorale, prol, 4, P. Laujon), unperf.; Act 1, with sketches of prol, Act 2, divertissement (1779); ov. (n.d.)

OTHER VOCAL
Motets, *F-Pn*: Salve regina, 1v, insts, 1752; Ecce sedes hic tonantes, 1v, insts, ed. in *BSIM*, viii/6 (1912), 50; Quam dilecta tabernacula, 1v, bc, 1769; Quomodo sedet sola civitas, 1v, bc, 1772; Principes persecuti sunt
Canzoni da batello: Chansons italiennes ou Leçons de musique pour les commençants (1753)
Les consolations des misères de ma vie ou Recueil d'airs, romances et duos (1781)
Recueil de [6] chansons, 1v, 2 vn, bn/va, bc; Airs, 1v, 2 vn, va, b, ded. Countess of Egmont: *GB-Lbm*
Other pieces pubd separately, in *Mercure de France* and in contemporary anthologies

INSTRUMENTAL
Symphonie, Lausanne, 1730, lost
Symphonie à cors de chasse, Concert Spirituel, 23 May 1751, lost, ? extracted from Les muses galantes
Le printemps di Vivaldi, arr. fl solo (n.d.)
Carillon, appx to *Dictionnaire de musique* (Geneva, 1768)
Air de cloches, *F-Pn*, ed. in various edns. of Oeuvres; Airs pour être joués, la troupe marchant, *Pn*; airs, 2 cl, *Pn*, Rousseau Society, Geneva
Sonate, 2 vn, b, formerly in collection of J. Ecorcheville
Pieces in contemporary anthologies

WRITINGS
Only those relating to music are included; most were reprinted in *Ecrits sur la musique*, Oeuvres complètes . . . nouvelle édition, classée par ordre de matières, xix–xxii (Paris, 1788–93) and in numerous subsequent editions of the complete works.

P – published collectively with 'Projet . . . 1742' (Geneva, 1781)

Projet concernant de nouveaux signes pour la musique . . . à l'Académie des sciences, le 22 août 1742 (Geneva, 1781)
Dissertation sur la musique moderne (Paris, 1743), P
Lettre à M. Grimm au sujet des remarques ajoutées à sa lettre sur Omphale (Paris, 1752)
Lettre d'un symphoniste de l'Académie royale de musique à ses camarades de l'orchestre, 1753, Théâtre et poésies (Geneva, 1781)
Lettre sur la musique française (Paris, 1753, 2/1753) [abridged Eng. trans. in O. Strunk, ed.: *Source Readings in Music History* (New York, 1950)]
Lettre à Monsieur l'Abbé Raynal au sujet d'un nouveau mode de musique, inventé par M. Blainville, 1754, Oeuvres . . . nouvelle édition, v (Neuchâtel, 1764), P
Examen de deux principes avancés par M. Rameau, dans sa brochure intitulée: 'Erreurs sur la musique dans l'Encyclopédie', 1755, P
J. J. Rousseau . . . à Mr. d'Alembert . . . sur son article 'Genève' dans . . . l'Encyclopédie et particulièrement sur le projet d'établir un théâtre de comédie en cette ville (Amsterdam, 1758)
Lettre à Monsieur Le Nieps . . . le 5 avril 1759, Théâtre et poésies (Geneva, 1781)
Essai sur l'origine des langues, où il est parlé de la mélodie et de l'imitation musicale, c1760, P
*Extrait d'une lettre . . . à M.*** sur les ouvrages de M. Rameau*, Oeuvres, ii (Neuchâtel, 1764)
Dictionnaire de musique (Paris, 1768/R1969; Eng. trans., 1771)
Lettre à M. Burney sur la musique, avec fragments d'observations sur l'Alceste italien de M. le chevalier Gluck, c1777, P
Extrait d'une réponse du petit faiseur à son prête-nom, sur un morceau de l'Orphée de M. le chevalier Gluck, ?1774, P
Letters to Lesage *père*, 1754; Perdriau, 1756; Ballière, 1765; Lalande, 1768; various minor writings in Jansen (1884), appx

BIBLIOGRAPHY
A. Jansen: *Jean-Jacques Rousseau als Musiker* (Berlin, 1884/R1971)
E. Istel: *J.-J. Rousseau als Komponist seiner lyrischen Scene Pygmalion* (Leipzig, 1901) [see also *Annales de la Société Jean-Jacques Rousseau 1905*, 141–72; rejoinders, ibid *1907*, 119–55]
A. Pougin: *Jean-Jacques Rousseau musicien* (Paris, 1901)
A. Arnheim: 'Le devin du village von J. J. Rousseau und die Parodie "Les amours de Bastien et Bastienne" ', *SIMG*, iv (1902–3), 686–727
P. M. Masson: *Les idées de J.-J. Rousseau sur la musique* (Paris, 1912)
P. P. Plan: 'Jean-Jacques Rousseau et Malesherbes: documents inédits', *Mercure de France*, xcvii (1912), 5–38

J. Tiersot: *Jean-Jacques Rousseau* (Paris, 1912, 2/1920/*R*1977)

A. Pochon: *J.-J. Rousseau musicien et la critique* (Montreux, 1940)

A. Mooser: *Pygmalion et Le devin du village en Russie au XVIIIe siècle* (Geneva, 1946)

A. R. Oliver: *The Encyclopaedists as Critics of Music* (New York, 1947)

J. Sénelier: *Bibliographie générale des oeuvres de Jean-Jacques Rousseau* (Paris, 1949)

A. Bruyère: 'Les muses galantes, musique de Jean-Jacques Rousseau', *ReM* (1952), no.218, p.5

J. van der Veen: *Le mélodrame musical de Rousseau au Romantisme* (The Hague, 1955)

B. S. Brook: *La symphonie française dans la seconde moitié du XVIIIe siècle* (Paris, 1962), esp. i, 95ff

R. Cotte: 'Bemerkungen über das Verhältnis Jean-Jacques Rousseaus zur Musik', *BMw*, v (1963), 81

A. Whittall: 'Rousseau and the Scope of Opera', *ML*, xlv (1964), 369

E. Fubini: 'Il concetto di natura e il mito della musica italiana nel pensiero di Jean-Jacques Rousseau', *Rivista di estetica*, x (Turin, 1965), 55

B. Ebisawa: 'Ruso to Bani' [Rousseau and Burney], *Nomura Festschrift* (Tokyo, 1969), 50 [with Fr. summary]

E. Fubini, ed.: *Gli illuministi e la musica* (Milan, 1969)

M.-E. Duchez: '*Principe de la mélodie* et *Origine des langues*: un brouillon inédit de Jean-Jacques Rousseau sur l'origine de la mélodie', *RdM*, lx (1974), 33

G. Morelli: ' "Eloges rendus à un singulier mélange de philosophie, d'orgueil, de chimie, d'opéra, etc": sulle ascendenze melodrammatiche della antropologia di Jean-Jacques Rousseau', *RIM*, ix (1974), 175

R. Cotte: *Jean-Jacques Rousseau, le philosophe musicien* (Braine-le-Comte, 1976)

J. F. Strauss: 'Jean Jacques Rousseau: Musician', *MQ*, lxiv (1978), 474

DANIEL HEARTZ

Rousseau, Jean-Marie (*b* Dijon, early 18th century; *d* Lille, 17 Feb 1784). French composer. He was a chorister at Dijon and later choirmaster at Arras, Beauvais and, from 1762 until his death, at Tournai Cathedral. In September 1762 he visited Dijon briefly to enter the priesthood; on his return he was named a beneficed clergyman and chaplain of Ste Catherine's Chapel at Tournai Cathedral. In 1781, probably because of poor health, he was relieved of some of his duties. He died while travelling to Lille to direct a performance of his last composition, a Requiem for a recently deceased friend; the work was used for his own funeral and enjoyed subsequent success in Douai and Paris.

Rousseau's compositions are almost exclusively sacred, and include 16 masses (of which three are Requiem settings; six were published in Brussels, n.d.), three settings of the *Te Deum* and 41 motets, all in the Tournai Cathedral archives; and three cantatas (1776–81), of which only the texts are extant (*B-Gu*). His works have a solid but conservative style of little originality, not far removed from Charpentier or Lalande, and maintain the traditional alternation of plainsong and polyphony.

BIBLIOGRAPHY

EitnerQ; *FétisB*

P. Bergmans: 'Rousseau, Jean-Marie', *BNB*

R. Vannes: *Dictionnaire des musiciens (compositeurs)* (Brussels, 1947)

J. Remacle: *Jean-Marie Rousseau et la maîtrise de la cathédrale de Tournai au XVIIIe siècle* (diss., U. of Louvain, 1974)

PHILIPPE MERCIER

Rousseau, Marcel. *See* SAMUEL-ROUSSEAU, MARCEL.

Roussel, Albert (Charles Paul Marie) (*b* Tourcoing, 5 April 1869; *d* Royan, 23 Aug 1937). French composer.

1. LIFE. He was born into a family of wealthy industrialists; his parents died during his early childhood, and at the age of seven he went to live with his grandfather, Charles Roussel-Defontaine, mayor of Tourcoing. On the latter's death in 1880 he was taken into the care of his maternal aunt, Mme Félix Requillard, and her husband. He showed musical promise, but decided upon a naval career. After two preparatory years at the Collège Stanislas in Paris, during which time he took music lessons with Jules Stoltz, organist of St Ambroise, he was admitted to the Ecole Navale as a cadet in 1887. He passed out as a midshipman in 1889 and was later commissioned. He saw service at home and overseas, including the Far East, but a continuing interest in music led to some attempts at composition. He showed his work to the director of the Roubaix Conservatory, who encouraged him to devote himself to music, and in June 1894 he resigned his commission and went to Paris to study with Gigout. His first success came in 1897 when two *a cappella* madrigals submitted under different pseudonyms won joint first prizes in a competition organized by the Society of Composers.

In 1898 he was introduced to d'Indy, and he enrolled as a student at the newly created Schola Cantorum. He completed the lengthy course ten years later. In the meantime he had been appointed professor of counterpoint in 1902, a position he held until 1914 (among his Schola pupils were Satie and Varèse). By 1908 he had written several major works, including the Piano Trio and his First Symphony, the programmatic *Poème de la forêt*. In the same year he married Blanche Preisach, and in 1909 the Roussels went on an extended tour of India and south-east Asia. This experience had important consequences for the composer's work, and led directly to the composition of the orchestral suite *Evocations*, based on impressions of India, and the *opéra-ballet* *Padmâvatî*, on a Hindu legend. Roussel was working on the latter score when war broke out in 1914. He had been removed from the naval reserve list for health reasons in 1902 but, after a period with the Red Cross, he obtained a commission in the artillery in 1915, and served as a transport officer until he was invalided out in January 1918. He retired to Perros-Guirec on the Brittany coast to convalesce, and there completed *Padmâvatî*. From 1919 to 1921 he worked on his second symphony and the symphonic poem *Pour une fête de printemps*.

In 1922 Roussel acquired a property at Vasterival, near Varengeville on the Normandy coast, which became his permanent home. Despite his indifferent health there was no diminution in his creative energy in the following years, and he produced a succession of major orchestral and chamber works. His status as a leading French composer was confirmed by the Roussel Festival held in Paris in 1929 to commemorate his 60th birthday. His reputation extended abroad: in 1930 he visited America for the first performance of his Third Symphony, commissioned for the 50th anniversary of the Boston SO, and in 1931 he attended a London performance of his setting of the English text of Psalm lxxx.

Roussel said that he 'remained somewhat apart in order to have the freedom of personal vision', and so he did not associate himself with any groupings or movements; but he was always ready to help other musicians, especially younger ones, and he had a strong sense of social responsibility. In 1936, failing in health, he undertook the organization of the music section of the Paris Exhibition, and he read all of the French scores submitted for the ISCM Festival. He had a deep interest in music education, and he was working on a large-scale theatrical composition which would involve workers' choral groups. All these efforts exhausted him and, suffering from angina pectoris, he was advised to move to a warmer climate. He went to Royan in the summer of 1937, and there he died after a heart attack. He was buried, in accordance with his own wishes, in the little cemetery of Varengeville, overlooking the sea.

Albert Roussel

2. WORKS. The nature and scope of Roussel's oeuvre was influenced by his comparatively late start. He came to composition after reaching maturity, when he was capable by temperament and training of detachment and self-evaluation. So he saw each composition as a step in the evolution of a personal style, achieved by the solution of some specific problem of expression. This outlook accounts for the relatively high proportion of single compositions for any one medium, and for the steady progression of style from the apprentice work to the final period. This progression is not, however, unrelated to trends in French music at the time. Roussel has been called an isolated figure, but his isolation is that of an individual viewpoint, not of an artist indifferent to the work and ideas of his contemporaries.

The early works inevitably reflect the dogmatic instruction of d'Indy. The Piano Trio (1902), the First Symphony (1904–6) and the First Violin Sonata (1907–8) employ the cyclic forms typical of the Schola. There are signs of individuality in the melodic and harmonic ideas, but the inflated compositional apparatus inhibits the composer's self-expression. It is in the shorter pieces and the songs that Roussel's personality began to emerge most clearly. The Divertissement for piano and wind (1906), although indebted to the example of d'Indy's *Chansons et danses: divertissement*, reveals Roussel's increasing independence in its succinct melodic phrases, its sprightly rhythms and its greater

dissonance content. The eight songs of opp.3 and 8 are handicapped by the banality of Henri de Régnier's texts, but in the *Deux poèmes chinois* (op.12) Roussel found a literary tradition much more in accordance with his own fastidious tastes, and one that he translated into subtle and expressive music.

Impressionist influence, already discernible in the orchestration of the First Symphony and in the delicate incidental music to *Le marchand de sable qui passe* (1908), becomes strongly evident in the opulent scoring of *Evocations* for soloists, chorus and orchestra (1910–11). Roussel was closer to Ravel than to Debussy at this stage, preferring clearly drawn lines and continuous rhythms to melodic and rhythmic flux. His personal adaptation of impressionist techniques culminated in his score for the ballet *Le festin de l'araignée* (1912). This fable of life and death in the insect world was ideally suited to his temperament, and the drama and emotions of the Lilliputian universe are exactly matched by the vivid melodies, wry harmonies and the fine, yet strongly woven, threads of instrumental colour. Despite the ballet's success, however, Roussel was moving away from impressionism, under the influence of his Indian experience. In *Padmâvatî* he made a direct attempt to communicate the savage power of this medieval Hindu legend of violence and sacrifice. There was a corresponding change of technique, one that was foreshadowed in the Suite in F♯ minor for piano (1909–10). Melody and harmony are based on Hindu scale forms (for example, C–D♭–E–F♯–G–A♭–B; or D–E–F–G♯–A–B♯–C♯) resulting in a tonal but strongly dissonant idiom. Irregular metres, angular ostinato figures and stark orchestral textures add to the impact of the score. The use of chromatic alteration and addition within a basically tonal chord structure, with a consequent increase of dissonance, became henceforth a feature of Roussel's language; although, with the exception of *Krishna* in *Joueurs de flûte* (1924), he never again applied a particular altered scale form in a strict manner.

With the Second Symphony (1919–21) and the symphonic poem *Pour une fête de printemps* (originally intended as the Scherzo of the symphony) Roussel returned to orchestral composition and applied the harmonic and rhythmic techniques of *Padmâvatî* to large-scale symphonic form. The formal procedures inherited from the Schola are handled in a totally individual manner, the finale being treated as a resumed development of the first movement. The harmonic idiom is based on a carefully controlled dissonance, polytonal in implication. The result is Roussel's most uncompromising and complex work. Perhaps influence by a lukewarm public reaction, Roussel later described the Second Symphony as 'too hermetic', and envisaged a style 'more pruned, more distilled, more schematized'. He reacted against programmatic music (the Second Symphony was originally provided with a programme): 'What I should like to achieve is music ... divorced from any illustrative or descriptive elements'. This intention accorded well with the trend in the 1920s towards neo-classicism. Roussel's interpretation of neo-classicism was a distinctly personal one. Unlike Stravinsky, he did not reject emotion; on the contrary, he increased the emotional tension of his music, especially of the slow movements. He 'schematized' his forms, not always avoiding the danger of sectionalism. But he did not simplify his harmonic idiom, nor his textures – indeed, he used contrapuntal elaboration as an expressive component.

The series of neo-classical orchestral works began with the Suite in F (1926), the Concerto for small orchestra (1926–7) and the Piano Concerto (1927), and included the Little Suite (1929), and the Third and Fourth Symphonies (1929–30 and 1934). These compositions mark the final stage in the evolution of Roussel's musical language. Although the cyclic relationship between movements has almost disappeared, it is still traceable in the Third Symphony. The forms are clearly defined: the outer movements are in sonata and rondo forms, while the inner movements are generally ternary in design, with a central climax (Suite in F, Third and Fourth Symphonies). The predominating texture consists of a principal melodic line, with subsidiary counterpoints, combined with ostinato figures or ornamented pedals in the inner parts or the bass. A purely contrapuntal texture is rare (Third Symphony: Adagio) and a harmonic texture generally occurs only at the climaxes. The harmonic structure is basically tonal with complete freedom of chromatic inflection and addition in the chord structure, producing chords of high dissonance content, often involving flattened 2nds, raised 4ths and major 7ths. Polytonality is used as a temporary suspension of monotonality: 'polytonality which, under the governing influence of a firmly established key, sets in motion designs which are foreign to this key, weaving them together in flowing counterpoint, must necessarily enrich the language of music' (Roussel). The elastic, irregular metric patterns of the earlier works are replaced by strongly marked motor rhythms, set up in the opening bars of a movement or section (Suite in F: Prélude; Piano Concerto: Allegro molto). The temporary withdrawal of the motor rhythm in sonata form movements emphasizes the difference between sections (Third Symphony: Allegro vivo).

Certain rhythmic figures recur in Roussel's work, especially the anapest (Sinfonietta, Third Symphony). The melodic idiom embraces wide-ranging angular themes in the opening movements, short epigrammatic (and often diatonic) motifs in the scherzos and long-breathed, oscillatory, chromatic themes in the slow movements. Instrumentation is full and highly coloured, but calculated to underline the relative importance of the simultaneously heard strands in the texture.

The same techniques are applied *mutatis mutandis* in the late chamber music. Two trends are discernible in Roussel's early chamber music, represented respectively by the large-scale Piano Trio and the Divertissement. The String Quartet (1931–2) belongs to the weightier tradition. Roussel referred to 'this severe form, the quartet', and he ends the work with an extended and uncharacteristically academic fugue. The Serenade for flute, harp and string trio (1925) is the mature successor to the Divertissement. The two tendencies are combined in the Flute Trio (1929) and the String Trio (1937, Roussel's last completed work), which are both dense and colourful.

Fortunately, Roussel did not take his abnegation of illustrative music too literally. His comic opera *Le testament de la tante Caroline* (1932–3) was a failure, but in the ballets *Bacchus et Ariane* and *Aenéas* he showed that he could adapt his mature technique to descriptive ends. *Bacchus* in particular is a score of outstanding quality. Stimulated by the classical legend and unhampered by large-scale formal considerations,

Roussel provided the dancers with music of great plastic expressiveness which has at once a precise application and a general validity. His setting of Psalm lxxx (1928) shows his responsiveness to a pictorial and dramatic biblical text, as well as his understanding of choral writing. The same evocative qualities are apparent in the later songs, especially the later *Poèmes chinois* (opp.35 and 47), and in the settings of René Chalupt (opp.20 and 50).

Roussel's position in French music is not easy to summarize. On the one hand he upheld and developed the tradition of French symphonic writing, passed from Franck to d'Indy, although his abrasive final style is far removed in its attitudes from the works of the Schola. On the other hand he belonged to the succession of French pictorial composers stretching back to the 17th-century harpsichordists, with his ability to translate visual and verbal imagery into precise musical terms. He shared some of the assumptions of composers of the interwar period in his move towards more concise, more abstract forms. Yet he did not follow the Gallic trend towards a lighter, more popular idiom. He was admired by such diverse composers as Satie, Poulenc, Prokofiev and Martinů, yet his direct influence has been slight. As his style was essentially an eclectic one, based on a personal manipulation of traditional elements, it did not lend itself to further development. His historical importance lies in the fact that he was one of the handful of 20th-century composers who have been able to create a modern and personal symphonic idiom on essentially traditional foundations.

WORKS
STAGE

op.

13 Le marchand de sable qui passe (incidental music, 1, G. Jean-Aubry), 1908; cond. Roussel, Le Havre, 16 Dec 1908

17 Le festin de l'araignée (ballet-pantomime, 1, G. de Voisins after H. Fabre: Souvenirs entomologiques), 1912; cond. G. Grovlez, Paris, Arts, 3 April 1913; extracts arr as Fragments symphoniques, 1912

18 Padmâvatî (opéra-ballet, 2, L. Laloy), 1914–18; cond. P. Gaubert, Paris, Opéra, 1 June 1923

24 La naissance de la lyre (incidental music, 1, T. Reinach, after Sophocles), 1923–4; cond. P. Gaubert, Paris, Opéra, 1 July 1925

— Sarabande [for L'éventail de Jeanne], ballet, 1927; cond. Désormière, Paris, 16 June 1927

43 Bacchus et Ariane (ballet, 2, A. Hermant), 1930; cond. P. Gaubert, Paris, Opéra, 22 May 1931; extracts arr. as 2 orch suites: no.1, Paris SO, cond. Munch, Paris, Salle Pleyel, 2 April 1933; no.2, Paris SO, cond. Monteux, Paris, Salle Pleyel, 2 Feb 1934

— Le testament de la tante Caroline (opéra-bouffe, 3, Nino), 1932–3; cond. A. Heller, Olomouc, 14 Nov 1936

54 Aenéas (ballet, 1, J. Weterings), chorus, orch, 1935; cond. Scherchen, Brussels, Palais des Beaux Arts, 11 July 1935

— Prelude to Act 2 of Le quatorze juillet (incidental music, Rolland), 1936; cond. Désormière, Paris, Alhambra, 14 July 1936

59 Elpénor (radio score, Weterings), fl, str qt (1947)

ORCHESTRAL

— Marche nuptiale, 1893

4 Résurrection, symphonic prelude after Tolstoy, 1903; cond. A. Cortot, Paris, Nouveau-Théâtre, 17 May 1904

— Vendanges, symphonic sketch, c1905; cond. Cortot, Paris, Nouveau-Théâtre, 18 April 1905; destroyed

7 Le poème de la forêt (Symphony no.1). Forêt d'hiver, Renouveau, Soir d'été, Faunes et dryades, 1904–6; complete, cond. S. Dupuis, Brussels, Monnaie, 22 March 1908

15 Evocations (M. D. Calvocoressi): Les dieux dans l'ombre des cavernes, La ville rose, Aux bords du fleuve sacré, A, T, Bar, chorus, orch, 1910–11; cond. R. Baton, Paris, Salle Gaveau, 18 May 1912

22 Pour une fête de printemps, symphonic poem, 1920; cond. Pierné, Paris, Chatelet, 29 Oct 1921

23 Symphony no.2, B♭, 1919–21; cond. Baton, Paris, Champs-Elysées, 4 March 1922

33 Suite, F, Prélude, Sarabande, Gigue, 1926; cond. Koussevitzky, Boston, Mass., 21 Jan 1927

34 Concerto, small orch, 1926–7; cond. W. Straram, Paris, 5 May 1927
36 Piano Concerto, G, 1927; A. Borovsky, cond. Koussevitzky, Paris, 7 June 1928
39 Little Suite: Aubade, Pastorale, Mascarade, 1929; cond. Straram, Paris, Champs-Elysées, 11 April 1929
42 Symphony no.3, g, 1929–30; Boston SO, cond. Koussevitzky, Boston, Mass., 24 Oct 1930
48 A Glorious Day, military band, 1932; Garde Républicaine, Paris, July 1933
52 Sinfonietta, str, 1934; cond. J. Evrard, Paris, Salle Gaveau, 19 Nov 1934
53 Symphony no.4, A, 1934; cond. A. Wolff, Paris, Opéra-Comique, 19 Oct 1935
56 Rapsodie flamande, 1936; cond. Kleiber, Brussels, 12 Dec 1936
57 Concertino, vc, orch, 1936; Fournier, cond. Siohan, Paris, Salle Pleyel, 6 Feb 1937

CHAMBER

— Fantaisie, vn, pf, 1892, destroyed
— Andante (Ave Maria), vn, va, vc, org, 1892, destroyed
— Horn Quintet, c1901; Paris, 2 Feb 1901; ?destroyed
— Violin Sonata, c1902; Paris, 5 May 1902; ?destroyed
2 Piano Trio, 1902; Paris, 14 April 1904; rev. 1927
6 Divertissement, wind qnt, pf, 1906; Société Moderne des Instruments à Vent, E. Wagner, Paris, Salle des Agriculteurs, 10 April 1906
11 Violin Sonata no.1, d, 1907–8; A. Parent, M. Dron, Paris, Salon d'Automne, 9 Oct 1908; rev. 1931
21 Impromptu, harp, 1919; L. Laskine, Paris, 6 April 1919
— Fanfare pour un sacre païen, brass, drums, 1921; Lamoureux Orch, cond. Wolff, Paris, Opéra, 25 April 1919
27 Joueurs de flûte: Pan, Tityre, Krishna, Monsieur de la Péjaudie, fl, pf, 1924; L. Fleury, J. Weill, Paris, Vieux-Colombier, 17 Jan 1925
28 Violin Sonata no.2, A, 1924; Asselin, L. Caffaret, Paris, Salle Gaveau, 15 Oct 1925
29 Ségovia, gui, 1925; ?Segovia, Madrid, 25 April 1925
30 Sérénade, fl, vn, va, vc, harp, 1925; Paris Instrumental Quintet, Paris, Salle Gaveau, 15 Oct 1925
— Duo, bn, vc/db, 1925; F. Oubradous, G. Marchésini, Paris, Salle Chopin, 23 Dec 1940
40 Trio, fl, va, vc, 1929; ?première, Barrère, Tertis, H. Kindler, Paris, 29 Oct 1929
41 Prelude and Fughetta, org, 1929; Pédelièvre, Paris, 18 May 1930
45 String Quartet, D, 1931–2; Pro Arte Qt, Brussels, 9 Dec 1932
51 Andante and Scherzo, fl, pf, 1934; Milan, 17 Dec 1934
— Pipe, D, flageolet, pf, 1934
58 String Trio, 1937
— Andante [for inc. Trio], ob, cl, bn, 1937; Paris Wind Trio, 30 Nov 1937

VOCAL

— Two Madrigals, chorus 4vv, 1897; cond. Roussel, Paris, Salle Pleyel, 3 May 1898; unpubd, ?destroyed
— Les rêves (A. Silvestre), Pendant l'attente (Mendès), Tristesse au jardin (L. Tailhade), 1v, pf, c1900
3 Quatre poèmes (H. de Régnier): Le départ, Voeu, Le jardin mouillé, Madrigal lyrique, 1v, pf, 1903; J. Bathori, Cortot, Paris, Salle Pleyel, 21 April 1906
8 Quatre poèmes (Régnier): Adieux, Invocation, Nuit d'automne, Odelette, 1v, pf, 1907; Bathori, Roussel, Paris, Salle Erard, 11 Jan 1908; no.1 orchd, 1907
9 La ménace (Régnier), 1v, pf/orch, 1908; E. Engel, cond. L. Hasselmans, Paris, 11 March 1911
10 Flammes (Jean-Aubry), 1v, pf, 1908; S. Berchut, Le Havre, 14 Feb 1909
12 Deux poèmes chinois (H. P. Roché, after Giles): Ode à un jeune gentilhomme, Amoureux séparés, 1v, pf, 1907–8; no.1, Le Havre, 28 June 1907; no.2, Le Havre, 14 Feb 1909
19 Deux mélodies: Light (Jean-Aubry), A Farewell (E. Oliphant), 1v, pf, 1918; Lucy Vuillemin, Louis Vuillemin, Paris, Salle des Agriculteurs, 27 Dec 1919
20 Deux mélodies (R. Chalupt): Le bachelier de Salamanque, Sarabande, 1v, pf/orch, 1919; orch, Croiza, Paris SO, cond. L. Fourestier, Paris, 9 Dec 1928
25 Madrigal aux muses (G. Bernard), SSA, 1923; Groupe Nivard, Paris, Salle Pleyel, 6 Feb 1924
26 Deux poèmes de Ronsard: Rossignol, mon mignon, Ciel, aer et vens, 1v, fl, 1924; no.1, N. Vallin, Paris, Vieux-Colombier, 15 May 1924; no.2, Croiza, Paris, 28 May 1924
31 Odes anacréontiques (trans. de Lisle): Ode XVI: Sur lui-même, Ode XIX: Qu'il faut boire, Ode XX: Sur une jeune fille, 1v, pf, 1926; no.3, Bathori, 17 May 1926; complete, E. Warnery, 30 May 1927; no.1 orchd, n.d.
32 Odes anacréontiques (trans. de Lisle): Ode XXVI: Sur lui-même, Ode XXXIV: Sur une jeune fille, Ode XLIV: Sur un songe, 1v,

pf, 1926; no.3, Bathori, 17 May 1926; complete, E. Warnery, 30 May 1927; nos.1, 2 orchd, n.d.
— Le bardit des francs (Chateaubriand), male chorus 4vv, brass and perc ad lib, 1926; Chorale Strasbourgeoise, cond. E. G. Münch, Strasbourg, 21 April 1928
35 Deux poèmes chinois (H. P. Roché, after Giles): Des fleurs font une broderie, Réponse d'une épouse sage, 1v, pf, 1927; no.1, Bernac, Fontainebleau, 5 July 1928; no.2, M. Gerar, Paris, 23 May 1927; no.2 orchd, c1927; Croiza, Paris SO, cond. Fourestier, Paris, 9 Dec 1928
— Vocalise no.1, 1v, pf, 1927; J. Darnay, 20 Dec 1928
— Vocalise no.2, 1v, pf, 1928; R. de Lormoy, P. Maire, Paris, 13 April 1929; orchd A. Hoérée, c1930; arr. A. Hoérée as Aria, fl/ob/cl/va/vc, pf/orch, n.d.
37 Psalm lxxx, T, chorus, orch, 1928; Jouatte, Nantes Schola Chorus, Lamoureux Orch, cond. Wolff, Paris, Opéra, 25 April 1929
— O bon vin, où as-tu crû? (Champagne trad.), 1v, pf, 1928; Lormoy, Roussel, 13 April 1929
38 Jazz dans la nuit (R. Dommange), 1v, pf, 1928; Croiza, Paris, Salle Gaveau, 18 April 1929
44 Deux idylles: Le kérioklèpte (Theocritus, trans. de Lisle), Pan aimait Ekho (Moskhos, trans. de Lisle), 1v, pf, 1931; Lormoy, Hoérée, Paris, 5 March 1932
— A Flower Given to my Daughter (Joyce), 1v, pf, 1931; D. Moulton, London, 16 March 1932
47 Deux poèmes chinois (H. P. Roché, after Giles): Favorite abandonnée, Vois, de belles filles, 1v, pf, 1932; Bourdette-Vial, Paris, 4 May 1934
50 Deux mélodies (Chalupt): Coeur en péril, L'heure de retour, 1v, pf, 1933–4; no.1, M. Bunlet, Jan 1935; no.2, Bunlet, Dec 1934
55 Deux mélodies (G. Ville): Vieilles cartes, vieilles mains, Si quelquefois tu pleurs . . ., 1v, pf, 1935; Blanc-Audra, Paris, 24 Jan 1936

PIANO

1 Des heures passent: Graves, légères . . ., Joyeuses . . ., Tragiques . . ., Champêtres . . ., 1898
— Conte à la poupée, 1904
5 Rustiques: Danse au bord de l'eau, Promenade sentimentale en forêt, Retour de fête, 1904–6; B. Selva, Paris, Salle Pleyel, 17 Feb 1906
14 Suite, f♯: Prélude, Sicilienne, Bourrée, Ronde, 1909–10; Selva, Paris, Salle Pleyel, 28 Jan 1911
16 Sonatine, 1912; Dron, Paris, Salle Erard, 18 Jan 1913
— Petit canon perpetuel, 1913
— Doute, 1919; Mme Grovlez, Paris, 15 May 1920
— L'accueil des muses [in memoriam Debussy], 1920; E. Lévy, Paris, Salle des Agriculteurs, 24 Jan 1921
46 Prelude and Fugue, 1932–4; H. Gil-Marchez, Paris, 23 Feb 1935
49 Three Pieces, 1933; R. Casadesus, Paris, 14 April 1934

Principal publisher: Durand

BIBLIOGRAPHY

L. Vuillemin: *Albert Roussel et son oeuvre* (Paris, 1924)
Courrier musical (15 April 1929) [Roussel issue]
ReM, x/3 (1929) [Roussel issue]
ReM (1937), no.178 [Roussel issue]
A. Hoérée: *Albert Roussel* (Paris, 1938)
Catalogue de l'oeuvre d'Albert Roussel (Paris, 1947)
N. Demuth: *Albert Roussel: a Study* (London, 1947)
R. Bernard: *Albert Roussel* (Paris, 1948)
W. Mellers: 'Albert Roussel and "la musique française" ', *Studies in Contemporary Music* (London, 1948)
M. Pincherle: *Albert Roussel* (Geneva, 1957)
B. Deane: *Albert Roussel* (London, 1961)
J. M. Eddins: *The Symphonic Music of Albert Roussel* (diss., Florida State U., 1967)
A. Surchamp: *Albert Roussel* (Paris, 1967)
Zodiaque, lxxx (1969) [Roussel issue]
R. Crichton: 'Roussel's Stage Works', *MT*, cx (1969), 729
F. Lesure: *Albert Roussel, 1869–1937* (Paris, 1969) [exhibition catalogue]
E. D. R. Neill: 'Albert Roussel', *Musicalia*, i/1 (1970), 5 [with work-list and discography]
R. Myers: *Modern French Music* (Oxford, 1971)
Cahiers Albert Roussel, i– (1978–) [pubd by Amis Belges d'Albert Roussel, Brussels]

BASIL DEANE

Roussel, François [Rosselli, Francesco] (*b* c1510; *d* after 1577). ?French composer. As his madrigals were published under various italianized forms of his name (Rosselli, Rossello, Roscelli, etc) historians have generally concluded that he was Italian, but in a document cited in *I-Rslf* he is referred to as 'Franciscus Roussel gallus'. All we know of his activities outside

Italy is that before 1568 he was a protégé of the seneschal Guillaume de Gadagne in Lyons. Over a period of 27 years he served as *maestro di cappella* in Rome: from 12 February 1548 to 26 February 1550 at the Cappella Giulia of St Peter's Basilica; from about 1562 to 30 November 1566 at S Lorenzo in Damaso; from 1 December 1566 to 26 March 1571 at S Luigi dei Francesi; and from 11 October 1572 to 10 May 1575 at St John Lateran.

Roussel's secular music, although not especially individual, is very varied. He was an early master of *note nere* writing in madrigals in the 1540s; complex rhythms characterize his works in this style, which he also adopted in many chansons. Other pieces bear the mark of his Roman sojourn in their calm flow and abstract treatment of the text. On the other hand certain mature works show the influence of Rore, judging by their greater use of dissonance and chromatic colour for expressive purposes. Roussel's sacred output is relatively small. Occasionally he used obsolete contrapuntal devices but the style of his motets and masses is that common to Arcadelt and his generation. Loys Bourgeois and Palestrina were among those who expressed admiration for his music. His best-known motet is *Adoramus te Christe*, which in a version with different lower vocal lines was incorrectly attributed to Palestrina by some 19th-century scholars (e.g. J. F. Rochlitz) – this version was probably composed later than the 16th century.

WORKS

Edition: *F. Roussel: Opera omnia*, ed. G. Garden, CMM, lxxxiii (in preparation)

SACRED

8 masses: *I-Ls* A8: De fantasia, 'De mes ennuitz' (on Arcadelt's chanson), 'Emendemus in melius' (on Gombert's motet), 'La sol fa me re ut', 'Souspirs ardans' (on Arcadelt's chanson), 'Virtute magna' (on ?M. Lasson's motet); *PS* sec.XVI.B.42.2: a 6; *MOd* Mus.ms.VI: Rossella (cantus only)

14 motets (1 also attrib. Maillard): 1564⁴ (1 motet); *D-Mϋs* Sant.Ms. 1244 (4 motets); Sant.Ms.3431 (2 motets); *GB-T* 630 (1 motet and 1 earlier piece); *I-Rvat* 484 (6 motets, canto only)

SECULAR

Il primo libro delli [39] madrigali, 5vv (Rome, 1563)
Il primo libro delli [33] madrigali, 4vv (Rome, 1565)
[43] Chansons nouvelles mises en musique, 4–6vv (Paris, 1577)
Madrigals in 1546¹⁵, 1554²⁹ (2 attrib. Ruffo in 1555³¹), 1558¹³, 1559¹⁶, 1560¹⁸, 1561¹⁰, 1562⁷, 1562⁸, 1562²² (2 ? by Waelrant), 1566¹³, 1566²³, 1574⁴
Chansons in 1559¹³, 1559¹⁵, 1572², 1587⁷, *I-Fn* Magl.XIX.57 (inc.)

BIBLIOGRAPHY

H. W. Frey: 'Die Kapellmeister an der französischen Nationalkirche San Luigi dei Francesi in Rom im 16. Jahrhundert', *AMw*, xxii (1965), 287
G. Garden: 'François Roussel: a Northern Musician in Sixteenth-century Rome', *MD*, xxxi (1977)

GREER GARDEN

Roussier, Pierre-Joseph (*b* Marseilles, 1716 or 1717; *d* Ecouis, Normandy, 18 Aug 1792). French theorist. He trained as an ecclesiastic in Marseilles, where he later served as a parish priest. According to La Borde he came late to music, yet he apparently spent many years as a teacher of composition and vocal music in Lyons (1737–63). Little of his music survives. He later made his home in Ecouis, where he had received an appointment as canon in 1754. During his lifetime, Roussier became known as a proponent of Rameau's works, which form the basis for his principal contributions to music theory. He proposed expansions of Rameau's ideas, particularly in the construction of added 6th and augmented 6th chords and their inversions. He also dealt with problems of musical temperament, particularly in the *Mémoire sur la musique des anciens*, which rejected contemporary systems in favour of a Pythagorean tuning, and in his annotated edition of Amiot's Chinese notebooks.

WORKS

Les Klas, ou Carillon de Marseille pour les morts, motet, 1v, insts, avec un Requiem à grand-choeur (Paris, 1765)
Pseaume CL, petit motet (Paris, 1766)

THEORETICAL WORKS

Traité des accords et de leur succession (Paris, 1764/*R*)
Observations sur différens points d'harmonie (Geneva and Paris, 1765, 2/?1775/*R*)
Mémoire sur la musique des anciens (Paris, 1770/*R*)
'Lettre[s] de M. l'Abbé Roussier . . . touchant la division du zodiaque, et l'institution de la semaine planétaire, relativement à une progression géométrique, d'où dépendent les proportions musicales', *Journal des beaux-arts et des sciences* (1770–71) [reissued separately, Paris, 1771]
L'harmonie pratique, ou exemples pour le Traité des accords (Paris, 1775)
ed.: J. Amiot: *Mémoire sur la musique des chinois* (Paris, 1779) [with annotations and index by Roussier]
'Remarques de M. l'Abbé Roussier sur les Observations de M. Vandermonde', in J.-B. de La Borde: *Mémoires sur les proportions musicales . . . Supplément à l'Essai sur la musique* (Paris, 1781), 42ff
Mémoire sur le nouveau clavecin chromatique de M. de Laborde . . . suite du Supplément à l'Essai sur la musique (Paris, 1782/*R*)
Mémoire sur la nouvelle harpe de M. Cousineau (Paris, 1782/*R*)
'Lettre . . . sur l'acception des mots Basse fondamentale, dans le sens des Italiens et dans le sens de Rameau', *Journal encyclopédique* (Sept 1783), 330

BIBLIOGRAPHY

FétisB
L. Vallas: *Un siècle de musique et de théâtre à Lyon 1688–1789* (Lyons, 1932)
R. D. Osborne: *The Theoretical Writings of Abbé Pierre-Joseph Roussier* (diss., Ohio State U., 1966)
E. R. Jacobi: Introductions to *J.-P. Rameau: Complete Theoretical Writings*, Miscellanea, iii/5–6 (1969–72)

ALBERT COHEN

Routh, Francis (John) (*b* Kidderminster, 15 Jan 1927). English composer and writer on music. He studied at King's College, Cambridge (1948–51), where he was specially influenced by Boris Ord, and at the Royal Academy of Music (1951–3) with Wesley Roberts and others. In 1954 he began a period of private study with Matyás Seiber. The following year he produced his first acknowledged work, but he composed little until the mid-1960s, by which time he had established a style which, unusually, combines orderly Stravinskian neo-classicism with certain English traits. His music is neatly made and even in tone. In 1964 he founded the Redcliffe Concerts of British Music, which have offered a valuable platform for works by lesser-known living composers and for revivals of earlier English music.

WORKS

Orch: Vn Conc., op.7, 1965; Dance Suite, str [arr. of str qt work, op.13], 1974; Dialogue, op.16, vn, orch, 1968; Double Conc., op.19, vn, vc, orch, 1970; Sym., op.26, 1972–3; Vc Conc., op.27, 1973; Pf Conc., op.32, 1976
Choral: Balulalow, op.1 (Wedderburn), SATB, 1955; Ode to the Evening Star (Blake), op.11, SSAATTBB, 1967; On a Deserted Shore (K. Raine), op.30, S, Mez, T, B, SSAATTBB, 2 pf, perc, 1975
Solo vocal with orch/insts: Elegy, op.6 (St John of the Cross, trans. Campbell), Mez/Bar, pf, vn obbl, 1964; Circles, op.18 (S. Tunnicliffe), S, cl, va, pf, 1969; Spring Night, op.23, concert aria, Mez, orch, 1971
Chamber and inst: Duo, op.12, vn, pf, 1967; Dance Suite, op.13, str qt, 1967; Sonata, op.21, vc, 1971; Pf Qt, op.22, 1971; Serenade, op.24, str trio, 1972; Sonata, op.31, vc, pf, 1975; Mosaics, op.33, 2 vn, 1976
Org: Fantasia no.1, op.2, 1960; The Manger Throne, op.3, 1959; Sonatina, op.9, 1965; Fantasia no.2, op.14, 1967; Lumen Christi, op.15, 1968; Aeterne rex altissime, op.20, 1970; Gloria tibi Trinitas, op.29, 1974, pubd with opp.3, 15 and 20 as Sacred Tetralogy
Pf: Little Suite, op.28, 1974
Songs: A Woman Young and Old, op.4 (Yeats), 7 nos., S/T, pf, 1962; 4

Shakespeare Songs, op.5, S/T, pf, 1963; Songs of Farewell, op.8 (Raine, Coleridge, Herrick, Swinburne, Gascoigne), S/T, pf, 1965; Songs of Lawrence Durrell, op.10, S/T, pf, 1966; The Death of Iphigenia, op.25 (Aeschylus, trans. Murray), Mez, pf, 1972; 3 Short Songs (Auden), Mez/Bar, pf, 1973

Principal publishers: Boosey & Hawkes, Hinrichsen (Peters), Lengnick, Redcliffe

WRITINGS
Contemporary British Music: the Twenty-five Years from 1945–1970 (London, 1972)
Early English Organ Music from the Middle Ages to 1837 (London, 1973)
Stravinsky (London, 1975)

Routley, Erik (Reginald) (*b* Brighton, 31 Oct 1917). English writer on church music. He read classics at Magdalen College, Oxford (1936–40, BA 1940), and theology at Mansfield College, Oxford (1940–43), and in 1943 became a minister in the Congregational Church of England and Wales. He took the Oxford BD in 1946 with a thesis on church music and theology (published as *The Church and Music*) and in 1948 joined the staff of Mansfield College as director of music; he took the Oxford DPhil in 1952 with a dissertation on the music of Christian hymnody. He served as a minister in Edinburgh (1959) and Newcastle upon Tyne (1967) before becoming professor of church music at Westminster Choir College, Princeton, New Jersey (1975).

In addition to his pastoral work and writing Routley has been active as an organist. He was the first president of the Guild of Congregational Organists (1951–9, re-elected 1970) and in 1965 was made a Fellow of the Royal School of Church Music. His work on the history of church music, particularly the music of nonconformist movements, broke much new ground, and as secretary to the editorial committee of *Congregational Praise* (1944–51) he contributed greatly to the value of that hymnbook. In 1961 he edited the *University Carol Book*, and in 1964 became editor of the series Studies in Church Music, in which his book on the Wesleys appeared. His compositions have been chiefly for the church.

WRITINGS
The Church and Music: an Enquiry into the History, the Nature and the Scope of Christian Judgment of Music (London, 1950, enlarged 2/1967)
An Historical Study of Christian Hymnology: its Development and Discipline (diss., U. of Oxford, 1952; London, 1957, as *The Music of Christian Hymnody*)
with K. L. Parry: *Companion to Congregational Praise* (London, 1953)
The English Carol (London, 1958)
Ecumenical Hymnody (London, 1959)
Hymns Today and Tomorrow (New York, 1964)
Twentieth Century Church Music (London, 1964)
Words, Music and the Church (Nashville, 1968)
The Musical Wesleys (London, 1969)

DAVID SCOTT

Rouwyzer [Rouwizer], François Léonard (*b* Maastricht, 2 July 1737; *d* Maastricht, 9 Dec 1827). Netherlands composer and violinist. He played first violin at the Maastricht theatre and, according to the archives of St Servatius, Maastricht, was a violinist at that church from 1758. Apart from an opera, *Laure et Pétrarque* (1780), his compositions comprise sacred works (requiems, motets, hymns and psalms) in an 18th-century Italian style, most of which were performed at St Servatius. Most require four voices with a subordinate accompaniment of strings and continuo, rather archaic for the period. Because of the close episcopal and cultural relationship between Maastricht and Liège,

Rouwyzer's works also reflect the Franco-Italian style evident in Liège among such composers as Grétry.

WORKS
(all MS; most in B-Lc, Fonds L. Terry)
Stage: Laure et Pétrarque (opera, F. d'Eglantine), Maastricht, 17 Feb 1780
Sacred (most for 4vv, str, bc, some with wind, perc): 2 requeims (1 inc.); 1 Te Deum; 4 Tantum ergo; 2 Alma redemptoris mater; Salve regina; Regina coeli laetare; Litaniae lauretanae; other works

BIBLIOGRAPHY
A. Auda: *La musique et les musiciens de l'ancien pays de Liège* (Brussels, Paris and Liège, 1930)
R. Vannes: *Dictionnaire des musiciens (compositeurs)* (Brussels, 1947)
M. de Smet: 'Rouwyzer, François Léonard', *MGG*

JAN TEN BOKUM

Rovelli, Pietro (*b* Parma, 6 Feb 1793; *d* Bergamo, 8 Sept 1838). Italian violinist and composer. His father, Alessandro Rovelli, was a conductor at the court of Weimar, and his uncle, the violinist Giuseppe Rovelli (*b* Bergamo, 1753; *d* Parma, 12 Nov 1806), was from 1782 a *virtuoso da camera* at the court of Parma. He studied the violin first with his grandfather, Giovanni Battista Rovelli (*b* Bergamo, 1740; *d* Bergamo), first violin at S Maria Maggiore in Bergamo, then in Paris with Kreutzer. He led an intensely active life as a virtuoso. He went with his father to Weimar in 1810, but later resumed his studies with Kreutzer. From 1815 he was first violin at the Munich court, with the titles *musicista della reale camera bavarese* and *primo virtuoso*. In 1819 he moved to Bergamo, where he taught at the Istituto Musicale, conducted at the Teatro Riccardi and was *maestro di cappella* at S Maria Maggiore, occupying the post which had been held by his grandfather. Among his numerous pupils were Bernard Molique and Thomas Täglichsbeck. About 1820 he married the pianist Micheline Förster, daughter of Emanuel Alois Förster.

Rovelli's playing was described in the *Allgemeine musikalische Zeitung* as 'simple, expressive, graceful, noble, in a word, classic'. The formal conception of his compositions derives directly from virtuoso intentions: sectional structure, with each section displaying a different violin technique and a different expressive character. This is especially true of his works in the popular form of the variation and potpourri. In his quartets the first violin parts are pre-eminent. His 12 caprices for solo violin op.3 were widely used as teaching pieces and were followed by another set of six, op.5.

BIBLIOGRAPHY
FétisB
Obituary, *AMZ*, xl (1838), col.871
A. Geddo: *Bergamo e la musica* (Bergamo, 1958)

GUIDO SALVETTI

Rovenský, Václav Karel Holan. See HOLAN ROVENSKÝ, VÁCLAV KAREL.

Rovescio, al. See AL ROVESCIO.

Rovetta, Giovanni (*b* Venice, *c*1595; *d* Venice, 23 Oct 1668). Italian composer and singer. He spent his life at St Mark's, Venice, where his father was an instrumentalist. He was first a boy treble, played in the orchestra from 1615 to 1617 and was appointed a bass singer in 1623, about which time he was ordained priest. On 22 November 1627 he succeeded Alessandro Grandi (i) as assistant *maestro di cappella* to Monteverdi, after whose death he became full *maestro* on 21 February 1644, remaining in this post until his own death.

Along with Grandi and Ignazio Donati, Rovetta was one of the most talented composers of the second rank to exploit the concertato style of northern Italy. Like Grandi he added to his large sacred output some volumes of continuo madrigals, but he wrote only a few monodies. His motets, of which there are four volumes as well as a number in his op.1 and in anthologies, are nearly all for the small-scale concertato textures of two to four voices and organ frequently found in the 1630s and 1640s. He normally reserved larger forces, and parts for violins and occasionally lower strings, for masses and psalms, which are either ceremonial in nature (e.g. op.4) or somewhat more intimate (op.7), no doubt to be chosen in accordance with the liturgical occasion; his op.1 combines the two types, some pieces having violins, others not. While several of his motets were republished in Antwerp and two concertato psalms (one each from op.4 and op.7) were reprinted in anthologies, his psalms for double choir, opp.8 and 12, were confined to local use – the latter is marked 'all'uso di Venetia' – and are written in what is in effect the *stile antico*; this style is found too in a number of MS works (in *I-Vnm* and *D-Mbs*), including a Passion setting with the turba part in simple homophony.

Rovetta worked in the shadow of his superior Monteverdi, and this inevitably shows in his style, but sometimes a more distinctive voice appears. The *Salve regina* of op.1 is as fine a tenor duet as any written in the mid-1620s, with its wayward modulations, declamatory dialogue, brilliant counterpoint and striking changes of mood; 21 years later, in op.10, he published an equally fine setting of this text in which a solo alto is richly accompanied by five-part strings. Solo melody plays a larger part in Rovetta's small-scale motets than in earlier ones by other composers, as also does triple time, in which his music tended to become like the arioso of contemporary opera and sometimes includes quite brilliant melismas. He was also interested in structural coherence, even in small motets, as can be seen in his refrain forms with carefully defined sections, e.g. *ABACD, ABCBD* or *ABACAD*.

Of Rovetta's three masses, the ceremonial one of op.4 is the most impressive. It lacks Sanctus and Agnus Dei (a Venetian practice inspired by liturgical propriety); the Kyrie, Gloria and Credo are scored for five, six and seven voices respectively, with violins, the longer movements being tightly knit yet varied, with sections for soloists in triple time or in *stile antico* and with dramatic tuttis. Like Monteverdi, Rovetta in his psalm settings gradually introduced formal designs to give overall unity. Those of 1626 have no organization, consisting rather of a succession of distinct ideas, adroitly worked out in counterpoint, with some dramatic word-painting. By 1639 (op.4) various subtle rondo, ternary and chaconne forms had appeared (cf Monteverdi's *Selva morale*, 1640). The same devices are present in op.7, which contains a psalm in the then unusual key of A major. It is particularly in such smaller pieces that Rovetta demonstrates a charm, in both vocal melodies and violin writing, independent of Monteverdi's influence.

Rovetta's madrigal books are similar in content to Monteverdi's seventh and eighth books, with a mixture of chamber duets, dialogues, strophic canzonettas with violin ritornellos, and large concertato pieces, of which

A che bramar (1640) is outstanding, if very Monteverdian. The two operas he is known to have written are both lost, but there is an account of *Ercole in Lidia* by John Evelyn. He also included some lively instrumental pieces in his op.1.

WORKS
(all published in Venice except some anthologies)

SACRED

Salmi concertati, 5–6vv, et altri con violini, con motetti, 2–3vv, et alcune canzoni per sonar, 3–4vv, bc, op.1 (1626)

Motetti concertati, 2–5vv, con le Litanie della madonna, et una messa concertata a voci pari, op.3 (1635, 2/1648 as Bicinia sacra [duets only]; Gemma musicalis, 1649 [remainder])

Messa, e salmi concertati, 5–8vv, 2 vn, op.4 (1639)

Motetti concertati, 2–3vv, con le Litanie della madonna, 4vv, op.5 (1639)

Salmi, 3–4vv, aggiontovi un Laudate pueri, 2vv, et Laudate Dominum, 1v, et un Kirie, Gloria et Credo pur, 3vv; tutto concertato con 2 vn, op.7 (1642)

Salmi, 8vv, op.8 (1644)

Motetti concertati, 2–3vv, libro terzo, op.10 [incl. Salve Regina, 1v, 5 viols, bc] (1647, 2/1648 as Manipule e messe musicus)

Motetti, 2–4vv, libro quarto, op.11 (1650)

Delli salmi, 8vv . . . alla breve secondo l'uso della Serenissima capella ducale di S Marco, op.12 (1662)

Sacred works, some reprinted from earlier collections, in 1620[2], 1624[2], 1625[2], 1641[2], 1641[3], 1642[4], 1646[3], 1646[4], 1649[1], 1649[6], 1653[1], 1656[1], 1659[3], 1668[2], 1669[1]

Various sacred works including a Passion in *D-DS, Dl, Kl, LEst, Mbs, I-Vnm, PL-WRu, S-Uu*

SECULAR

Madrigali concertati, 2–6vv, 2 vn, con un dialogo . . . et una cantata, 1v, libro primo, op.2 (1629)

Madrigali concertati, 2–3, 5–6, 8vv, 2 vn, et . . . una cantata, 4vv, libro secondo (1640)

Madrigali concertati, 2–4vv, libro terzo (1645)

Madrigals, 4vv, bc, in *GB-T*

2 operas: Ercole in Lidia, 1645, Argiope, 1649, both lost

BIBLIOGRAPHY

J. Evelyn: *Memoirs*, ed. W. Bray (London, 1819), i, 191

F. Caffi: *Storia della musica sacra nella gia cappella ducale di San Marco in Venezia dal 1318 al 1797* (Venice, 1854–5/R1972)

S. Worsthorne: *Venetian Opera in the Seventeenth Century* (Oxford, 1954/R1968), 31f

D. Arnold and N. Fortune, eds.: *The Monteverdi Companion* (London, 1968), 124, 127, 188, 190, 204

J. L. A. Roche: *North Italian Liturgical Music in the Early 17th Century* (diss., U. of Cambridge, 1968)

——: 'Rovetta and Tunder – Misattribution or Plagiarism?', *Early Music*, iii (1975), 58

E. Selfridge-Field: *Venetian Instrumental Music from Gabrieli to Vivaldi* (Oxford, 1975)

J. Roche: 'Giovanni Antonio Rigatti and the Development of Venetian Church Music in the 1640s', *ML*, lvii (1976), 256

JEROME ROCHE

Rovetta [Rovettino], Giovanni Battista. *See* VOLPE, GIOVANNI BATTISTA.

Rovigo, Francesco [Franceschino] (*b* 1541 or 1542; *d* Mantua, 7 Oct 1597). Italian organist and composer. He was sent to Venice in 1570 to study with Merulo and others. In 1573, his hymns, now lost, were sung in the ducal chapel of S Barbara in Mantua; this is the first record of him as a composer. His name first appears on the salary lists of the Mantuan court in 1577, and on 1 May 1582 he was appointed court chapel organist to Archduke Carl II in Graz, where his duties included the musical education of the archduke's children. His monthly salary of 25 florins was a primary reason why he decided to remain at Graz, in spite of efforts to recall him to Mantua. He was evidently appreciated, since Wilhelm V of Bavaria attempted unsuccessfully to obtain his transfer to his own court. After the archduke's death in 1590, Rovigo returned to Mantua to serve as organist in S Barbara, and in 1591 he was commissioned together with Wert to compose music for a projected performance of Guarini's *Il pastor fido*.

Most of Rovigo's music is liturgical. His secular vocal music was evidently popular, for his madrigals were included in several famous anthologies. His *Missa dominicalis* was published together with other masses on the same Mantuan chants by Palestrina, Wert, Gastoldi, Contino and Alessandro Striggio (i). Zacconi praised him as a composer and organist, and Monteverdi referred to him twice in his letters, once indicating Rovigo's favoured position at court (28 November 1601), and later (2 December 1608) naming him as a highly paid musician.

WORKS

SACRED VOCAL

Missa dominicalis, 5vv, 1592¹, ed. in DTÖ, xc (1954)
3 masses, 5vv; mass, 12vv (inc., 2 partbooks only); 2 litanies, 4, 6vv; 3 Magnificat, 4, 6vv; St Luke Passion, 5vv; psalm, 4vv; motet, 8vv: *A-Gu, KR, Wn, D-Kl, I-MAad, Mc, YU-Lu*

SECULAR VOCAL

Madrigali . . . libro primo, 5vv (Venice, 1581)
Madrigals, 5, 6vv, in 1583¹⁰, 1585¹⁷, 1588¹⁴, 1600⁵ᵃ (transcr. lute); canzone, 3vv, 1584¹⁰; 1 madrigal ed. in DTÖ, lxxvii, Jg.xli (1934/*R*)

INSTRUMENTAL

Partitura delle canzoni da suonare, a 4, 8 (Milan, 2/1613¹⁶; 1st edn., ?1583, lost) [7 works by Rovigo; all canzonas a 4 transcr. org, *I-Tn* (tablature)]
Canzona, a 4, in F. Rognoni Taeggio: Canzoni francese (Milan, 1608)
Toccata, *A-Wn*

LOST WORKS

Canzonette, 4vv [also incl. works by Trofeo], cited in Giunta catalogue, see Kast
Canzonette per sonar, a 4 (printed) [? transcrs. of Canzonette, 4vv], cited in Giunta catalogue, see Kast
Hymns, performed in 1573

BIBLIOGRAPHY

L. Zacconi: *Vita con le cose avvenute al P. Bacc. Lodovico Zacconi da Pessa* (MS, *I-PESo* 563)
P. Canal: *Della musica in Mantova* (Venice, 1881)
A. Bertolotti: *Musica alla corte dei Gonzaga in Mantova dal secolo XV al XVIII* (Milan, 1890/*R*1969)
B. A. Wallner: *Musikalische Denkmäler der Steinätzkunst des 16. und 17. Jahrhunderts* (Munich, 1912)
A. Einstein: 'Italienische Musik und italienische Musiker am Kaiserhof und an den erzherzoglichen Höfen in Innsbruck und Graz', *SMw*, xxi (1934), 10
H. Federhofer: 'Matthia Ferrabosco', *MD*, vii (1953), 205
K. Jeppesen: 'Pierluigi da Palestrina, Herzog Guglielmo Gonzaga und die neugefundenen Mantovaner-Messen Palestrinas', *AcM*, xxv (1953), 132–79
P. Kast: 'Die Musikdrucke des Kataloges Giunta von 1604', *AnMc*, no.2 (1965), 41
H. Federhofer: *Musikpflege und Musiker am Grazer Habsburgerhof der Erzherzöge Karl und Ferdinand von Innerösterreich (1564–1619)* (Mainz, 1969), 125ff
D. de' Paoli: *Claudio Monteverdi: lettere, dediche e prefazione* (Rome, 1973), 17, 35; Eng. trans. in D. Arnold and N. Fortune, eds.: *The Monteverdi Companion* (London, 1968), 23, 28
PIERRE M. TAGMANN, MICHAEL FINK

Rovince, Luigi. *See* ROINCE, LUIGI.

Rovitti, Olerto. *See* VITTORI, LORETO.

Rovsing Olsen, Poul. *See* OLSEN, POUL ROVSING.

Row. *See* SERIES.

Rowaldt, Johann Jacob (*b* 25 Aug 1718; *d* Marienburg [now Malbork, Poland], 14 Oct 1775). German composer and organist. He was active at Marienburg from 1738 as an instrumentalist and organist; at his death he was organist at St George's there. He composed a com-

plete cycle of cantatas for the ecclesiastical year, 44 of which were formerly in the library of St George's but are now lost; Riemann praised the arias with obbligato instruments. The texts of the entire cycle were published as *Geistliche Cantaten auf die Evangelia aller Sonntage und der vornehmsten Feste des ganzen Jahres gerichtet* (Danzig, 1743). The librettist was S. E. Fromm, the minister of St George's; he wrote the recitative texts in unrhymed verse, thereby anticipating the style later advocated by J. A. Hiller in his *Beyträge zu wahrer Kirchenmusik* (Leipzig, 2/1791). An aria by Rowaldt to be sung at Communion on Good Friday was formerly extant in a manuscript copy of 1745 in St George's church library.

BIBLIOGRAPHY

RiemannL 8
H. Springer, M. Schneider and W. Wolffheim, eds.: *Miscellanea musicae bio-bibliographica: Nachträge und Verbesserungen zu Eitners Quellenlexikon*, ii/3 (Leipzig, 1913, enlarged 2/1947), 72
based on *MGG* (xi, 1022) by permission of Bärenreiter
GEORG FEDER

Rowe, Walter (*d* probably at Berlin, ?1647). English composer and viol player active in Germany. According to Moser, he was a pupil of Alfonso Ferrabosco (ii). On 24 June 1614 he was appointed as a viol player to the Hofkapelle of the Elector of Brandenburg at Berlin, but he seems to have delayed some time before taking up the position. During August he stayed at Hamburg, where his fellow expatriate William Brade was leader of the town musicians, and on 4 August he entered a courante in the album of the nobleman David von Mandelsloh, who was visiting the town; the dance (formerly in *D-LÜh*, surviving in edn. of album by W. L. von Lütgendorff, Hamburg, 1893, also transcr. in Stiehl) is for viola bastarda or viola da gamba and is notated in lute tablature. Rowe's considerable reputation as a viol player is reflected in his salary at Berlin; in the year of his appointment he received 400 thalers, in 1621 900 thalers, and in 1647, when his name last appears in the records, his salary was 300 thalers. Among his many pupils were S. T. Staden and the talented Michael Rode, whose tuition and expenses were paid by the Duke of Mecklenburg-Güstrow after hearing Rowe play in 1626. Rowe also taught the Brandenburg princesses Louise Charlotte and Hedwig Sophia; it was probably for the former that, in 1632, he began to compile a songbook (now in *D-Kl*) which contains four of his own melodies as well as pieces by German composers such as Heinrich Albert, Hammerschmidt and Schein and a number of English and French songs.

The coincidence of their names and the similarity of their careers has led to confusion between Walter Rowe and his son, also called Walter Rowe (*d* April 1671). The younger Rowe was taught by Mathias Strebelow, a viola da gamba player at the electoral court, and became a viol player in the Hofkapelle, where he presumably worked with his father. He probably remained at Berlin until his death.

BIBLIOGRAPHY

J. Mattheson: *Grundlage einer Ehren-Pforte* (Hamburg, 1740); ed. M. Schneider (Berlin, 1910/*R*1969)
F. Chrysander: 'Englische, deutsche und französische Musiker des 17. Jahrhunderts', *Niederrheinische Musikzeitung*, xlv (1855), 355
J. Bolte: 'Lieder-Handschriften des 16. und 17. Jahrhunderts, iii: Das Liederbuch der Prinzessin Luise Charlotte von Brandenburg', *Zeitschrift für deutsche Philologie*, xxv (1893), 33

C. Stiehl: 'Stammbuchblätter von Jakob Praetorius und Walter Rowe', *MMg*, xxvi (1894), 157; xxvii (1895), 43

C. Sachs: *Musik und Oper am kurbrandenburgischen Hofe* (Berlin, 1910)

H. Kretzschmar: *Geschichte des neuen deutschen Liedes* (Leipzig, 1911/R1966), 148

C. Meyer: *Geschichte der Güstrower Hofkapelle* (Schwerin, 1919), 18

H. J. Moser: *Geschichte der deutschen Musik*, ii (Stuttgart and Berlin, 1922, 5/1930)

R. Haas: *Musik des Barocks*, HMw (1928), 114

E. H. Meyer: *English Chamber Music: the History of a Great Art from the Middle Ages to Purcell* (London, 1946, rev. 2/1951)

T. Dart: 'English Musicians Abroad', *Grove 5*

based on *MGG* (xi, 1023–4) by permission of Bärenreiter

DIETER HÄRTWIG

Rowicki, Witold (*b* Taganrog, 26 Feb 1914). Polish conductor, violinist and composer. He studied the violin under Malawski and composition under Piotrowski and Wallek-Walewski at the Kraków Conservatory, graduating in 1938 with a diploma in violin playing. He continued further private training in composition and conducting, having made his conducting début in 1933 while still a student; but the early part of his career was as a violinist and violin teacher at Kraków. After the war he became a conductor and music organizer, and was a key figure in rebuilding Polish musical life by forming the Polish Radio SO in Katowice in 1945, and re-forming the National PO in Warsaw in 1950. He trained both orchestras to a high level of proficiency, and established the high reputation of the National PO, which he has conducted on international tours and of which he became artistic director and chief conductor. He did much to bring about the rebuilding of Warsaw's Philharmonic concert hall, and inaugurated the new hall in 1955. He tours widely as a guest conductor (including appearances in Britain from the late 1950s), and enjoys a reputation for musicianly elegance and polished style in performance; his experience as a player has given him a spontaneous rapport with orchestras. As well as a wide standard repertory, he champions the music of Szymanowski and has encouraged the new school of Polish composers. His own works include symphonies, chamber music and songs. Numerous gramophone records, with his own and other orchestras, testify to his skill and individuality. He has three times received his country's state prize for his services to Polish musical life.

Rowlard (*fl c*1400). English composer. No convincing biographical identifications have been proposed. His name is attached to a three-part Gloria in the Old Hall MS (no.29) which also appears in the Fountains MS (*GB-Lbm* Add.40011B). It has a fast-moving texted upper part and two textless supporting parts. It may have formed a pair with a setting of which the tenor and contratenor survive in a fragment in *STb* (Willoughby de Broke 1744, larger leaf) whose verso contains a Credo by Picart (*see* PICARD). The Stratford and Old Hall compositions share the same sequence of time signatures, nearly identical ranges and general stylistic affinity.

For bibliography *see* OLD HALL MS.

MARGARET BENT

Rowley, Alec (*b* London, 13 March 1892; *d* London, 11 Jan 1958). English teacher, composer and pianist. He studied under Corder at the RAM, where he won the Smart and Gooch scholarships and the Mortimer and Prescott prizes. In 1920 he was appointed to the staff of Trinity College of Music, and in 1934 he was elected a Fellow of the RAM. As a performer he was best known for his broadcasts of piano duet music with Edgar Moy. He published, 1940–55, several books on musicianship, repertory, performance and teaching.

WORKS
(*selective list*)

Orch: Rhapsody, va, orch, perf. 1936; Pf Conc. no.1, pf, band, perf. 1938; Pf Conc. no.2, perf. 1938; Ob Conc.

Chamber: 2 trios, fl, ob, pf, 1930; Str Qt, 1932

Many pf works, incl. educational pieces; vocal music

Principal publishers: Boosey & Hawkes, Curwen, Elkin, Oxford University Press, Paxton, Stainer & Bell, Williams

H. C. COLLES/R

Roxburgh, Edwin (*b* Liverpool, 6 Nov 1937). English composer, teacher, oboist and conductor. He studied at the Royal College of Music, London, and St John's College, Cambridge, and had instruction in composition from Nono, Dallapiccola and Boulanger. In 1967, after three years as principal oboist with Sadler's Wells Opera, he joined the staff of the RCM as professor of composition and director of the 20th-century department. He has continued his career as an oboist, specializing in contemporary music, and is conductor of the 20th Century Ensemble of London.

In spite of the several prizes and distinctions his early compositions gained him, Roxburgh withdrew his works written before 1961. That date marks a development in his music from a conscientious form of serialism to a less formal, more experimental style which allows him to pursue his interest in instrumental sonorities and textures. The later music is, however, no less well disciplined, even in an entertainment piece like *How Pleasant to Know Mr Lear*. He collaborated with Leon Goossens on *The Oboe* (London, 1976).

WORKS

Orch: Variations, 1963; The Tower (ballet), 1964; Montage, 1977

Choral: Westron Wynde, motet, 1961; The Rock (1979)

Solo vocal: Recitative after Blake, A, str, 1961; Chamber Music (Joyce), T, perc, harp, 1962; And Sun and Silence (Cummings), T, pf, perc, 1965; Night Music, S, perc, orch, 1969; How Pleasant to Know Mr Lear, narrator, orch, 1971; A Mosaic for Cummings, 2 narrators, orch, 1973; Convolutions, S, T, hpd ens, 1974

Chamber and inst: Movts, str qt, 1961; Introduction and Arabesques, pf, 1963; Foreign Scenes, children's perc ens, 1963; Qt, fl, cl, vn, vc, 1964; Music for 3, str trio, 1966; Images, ob, pf, 1967; Labyrinth, pf, 1970; Partita, vc, 1970; Eclisse, ob, str, 1971; Dithyramb I, cl, perc, 1972; Dithyramb II, 3 perc, pf, 1972; Nebula I, cl choir, 1974; Nebula II, wind qnt, 1974

Principal publisher: United

GERALD LARNER

Roy [Le Roy, Le Roi, Roi, Lo Roi, Lo Roy], **Bartolomeo** (*b* Burgundy, *c*1530; *d* Naples, 2 Feb 1599). French composer and violinist active in Italy. In 1570 he succeeded Annibale Zoilo as *maestro di cappella* of St John Lateran, Rome, a position he held until 1572. His name appears again in the Roman archives of 1574, but his post is not specified. In September 1579 he succeeded Monte as *maestro di cappella* of the Collegio Inglese, Rome, a post he apparently left in July 1581 to enter the service of Don Fabrizio Gesualdo as a member of the Camerata at Gesualdo. He was appointed *maestro di cappella* to the viceroy of Naples in 1583 and presumably remained there until his death; he introduced the use of woodwind and string instruments into the liturgy there. Roy seems to have enjoyed considerable esteem as a musician and composer in his later years; his music appeared in numerous anthologies and the *Missa 'Panis quem ego dabo'* was published with Palestrina's *Missa 'Confitebor tibi'* in 1585. Like Palestrina and other Roman composers, he was a member of the Compagnia de Musica of Rome. He taught Francesco Soriano, and his recommendation secured for Giovanni de Macque the position of first organist at the Annunziata, Naples.

WORKS

SACRED VOCAL

Missa 'Panis quem ego dabo', 4vv; 3 motets, 4, 8vv; 2 laude, 3vv: 1585[5], 1599[6], 1600[11], 1604[11], 1614[3]; 1 ed. F. Commer, *Musica sacra*, xxv (1884), 35

5 masses, 5, 6vv, *E-V* (inc.); Invitatorium, 4vv, *I-Bc*; 5 motets, 6vv, *E-V* (inc.); 2 hymns, 4vv, *I-Bc, Rsg*

SECULAR VOCAL

[20] Madrigali libro primo, 5vv (Rome, 1591); ed. in Watanabe
12 madrigals, 4–6vv; 2 canzone, 3vv: 1566[9], 1566[10], 1573[16], 1574[4], 1582[4], 1583[10], 1585[29], 1589[7], 1590[15], 1593[5], 1600[13]

BIBLIOGRAPHY

S. Cerreto: *Della prattica musica vocale et strumentale* (Naples, 1601)
R. Micheli: *Musica vaga et artificiosa* (Venice, 1615)
G. Pitoni: *Notitia de contrapuntisti e de compositori di musica* (MS, *I-Rvat* C.G., I/1–2, c1725)
F. Florimo: *La scuola musicale di Napoli e i suoi conservatorii* (Naples, 1880–83/*R*1969)
F. Parisini, ed.: *Carteggio inedito del Padre Giambattista Martini* (Bologna, 1888)
J. Schmidt-Görg: 'Vier Messen aus dem XVI. Jahrhundert über die Motette "Panis quem ego dabo" des Lupus Hellinck', *KJb*, xxv (1930), 77
U. Prota-Giurleo: 'Notizie sul musicista belga Jean Macque', *IMSCR, i Liège 1930*, 191
G. Pannain: 'L'oratorio dei Filippini e la scuola musicale de Napoli', introduction to IMi, v (1934), p.xvi
R. Casimiri: '"Disciplina musicae" e "mastri di capella" dopo il Concilio di Trento nei maggiori istituti ecclesiastici di Roma: Seminario romano – Collegio germanico – Collegio inglese (sec. XVI–XVII)', *NA*, xx (1943), 17
R. Watanabe: *Five Italian Madrigal Books of the Late Sixteenth Century* (diss., U. of Rochester, 1951)
U. Prota-Giurleo: 'Giovanni Maria Trabaci e gli organisti della Real cappella di Palazzo di Napoli', *L'organo*, i (1960), 185
W. Summers: *An Analytic Study of Three Parody Masses after the Motet 'Panis quem ego dabo'* (diss., California State U., Hayward, 1973)

WILLIAM JOHN SUMMERS

Royal Academy of Music. (1) London association of noblemen, supported by the king, founded in 1718–19 for the promotion of Italian opera; *see* HANDEL, GEORGE FRIDERIC, §7, and LONDON, §VI, 1.

(2) (RAM) London conservatory founded in 1822; *see* LONDON, §VII, 3(i).

Royal Albert Hall. London concert hall built in 1871; *see* LONDON, §VI, 5(iii). The Royal Albert Hall Choral Society was founded in the same year and renamed the Royal Choral Society in 1888; *see* LONDON, §VI, 3(i). The Royal Albert Hall Orchestra was formed on the model of the Queen's Hall Orchestra in 1905; *see* LONDON, §VI, 2(ii).

Royal Amateur Orchestral Society. London orchestra founded in 1872, known until 1880 as the Amateur Orchestral Society; *see* LONDON, §VI, 2(iii).

Royal Choral Society. The oldest surviving London choral society, founded in 1871 and known as the Royal Albert Hall Choral Society until 1888; *see* LONDON, §VI, 3(i).

Royal Coburg Theatre. London theatre, built in 1817–18; it was renamed the Royal Victoria Theatre in 1833 and the Royal Victoria Hall in 1880, and is generally known as the Old Vic. *See* LONDON, §IV, 3.

Royal College of Music (RCM). London conservatory founded in 1883 to succeed the National Training School for Music; *see* LONDON, §VII, 3(v).

Royal College of Organists (RCO). London college founded in 1864 and known as the College of Organists until 1893; *see* LONDON, §VII, 4.

Royal English Opera House. London theatre built in 1891 and renamed the Palace Theatre in 1911; *see* LONDON, §IV, 3.

Royal Festival Hall. London concert hall on the South Bank, opened in 1951; *see* LONDON, §VI, 5(iv).

Royal Holloway College. Part of the University of London; *see* LONDON, §VII, 2.

Royal Irish Academy of Music. Dublin conservatory founded in 1848; *see* DUBLIN, §10.

Royal Italian Opera. The name given to various London theatres, and the companies using them, when Italian opera was being sung there during the 19th century; *see* LONDON, §IV, 3.

Royal Kent bugle. *See* KEYED BUGLE.

Royal Military School of Music. London conservatory founded in 1857 and known as the Military School of Music until 1865; *see* LONDON, §VII, 3(ii).

Royal Musical Association. A society founded, as the Musical Association, in 1874 in London 'for the investigation and discussion of subjects connected with the art, science and history of music'. After some private canvassing of opinion by John Stainer who had discussed the idea with William Pole, William Spottiswoode invited 22 leading musicians to a preliminary meeting. Those who attended (besides the above) were Tyndall, Sedley Taylor, Grove, Macfarren, Hullah and William Chappell. An inaugural general meeting took place on 29 May in the board room of the South Kensington Museum. In July C. K. Salaman became secretary and in August Frederick Gore Ouseley was elected president. (It is noteworthy that of the 70 or more members enrolled by mid-1874, 17 had been involved 22 years earlier with the MUSICAL INSTITUTE OF LONDON, whose activities were similar to those of the association.) The first session began on 2 November 1874 with a paper read at the Beethoven Rooms in Harley Street, where the association continued to meet until 1891. Since then it has generally met at one of the London schools or colleges of music.

Since the association's inception its *Proceedings* have appeared annually; until the 83rd session (1956–7) they included, besides the text of the papers, a transcript or summary of the subsequent discussions, which sometimes contained much of additional value.

The papers read to the association in its early years tended towards the acoustical and theoretical aspects of music, but by the 1890s more attention was paid to history and criticism. (The change can be seen clearly in the *Classified List of Contents* to vols.i–xc of the *Proceedings*, compiled by Alan Smith, and published in 1966: it supersedes the *Index to Papers 1874 to 1941* published in 1948.) As early as 1886 the association resolved to invite distinguished foreign scholars to become honorary members. From 1899 to 1914 it represented the International Musical Society in Britain.

In 1904 the association was incorporated under the Companies' Acts, but this, while defining the legal position and responsibilities of the council, did nothing to increase the number of members, which then stood at about 220, a figure that remained static for the next 40 years or so. In 1944 the status of the association was enhanced when the president, E. H. Fellowes, received a command from the king that it should 'henceforth be known as the Royal Musical Association'. Fellowes also initiated an effective drive for increased membership, so that by the mid-1950s it reached over 300. Several factors led to further growth: the expansion of music facilities in British universities, the creation of a new category, of student members, and the increase in institutional membership. By the mid-1970s the total had risen to nearly 800.

One of the most notable events of the RMA's history occurred in 1951, when, with the financial support of the Arts Council, it published the first volume of Musica Britannica, 'an authoritative national collection of the classics of British music', whose volumes have added greatly to the RMA's prestige. A small but significant change took place in 1953 when the council decided to establish a *Proceedings* committee to invite, or consider offers of, papers to be read, in place of the rather haphazard arrangement of earlier years.

Another important publication, the *RMA Research Chronicle*, appeared in 1961; it contains (in the words of Thurston Dart, its first editor) 'musicological raw material – lists, indexes, catalogues, calendars, extracts from newspapers, new fragments of biographical information, and so on'. Originally issued with the support of the Fellowes Memorial Fund and the Vaughan Williams Trust, from the mid-1960s it received the support of the British Academy. In 1961, to commemorate one of its most distinguished presidents, the RMA established the Dent Medal which is awarded annually to a musicologist of international repute in association with the International Musicological Society. To mark the Beethoven bicentenary in 1970 the RMA cooperated with the trustees of the British Museum in publishing a facsimile of the 'Kafka' sketchbook (*GB-Lbm* Add.29801, ff.39–162).

The widening aims of the RMA have been matched by a new emphasis in its meetings. In 1965, on the initiative of its president Anthony Lewis, the first weekend conference was held in London. The conference is now an annual event, and one that has proved increasingly attractive to members living too far away from London to attend the other sessional meetings. In 1972 the Northern Chapter of the association – the first of its kind – was established to serve as a focus for the interests principally of the academic members. A Midlands Chapter was set up in 1973.

The RMA's centenary was marked by a special conference held on 8 and 9 November 1974, to which distinguished scholars from abroad were invited, and a concert included a new work specially commissioned from John Joubert. To commemorate the occasion, besides a special issue of the *Proceedings*, the association published, in cooperation with the Scolar Press, a facsimile of the 'Tenbury' score of Handel's *Messiah*, a manuscript in the hand of J. C. Smith the elder contain-

ing numerous markings and several recomposed versions by the composer.

BIBLIOGRAPHY
J. P. Baker: 'The Musical Association: a Fifty Years Retrospect', *PMA*, 1 (1923–4), 129
G. Abraham: 'Our First Hundred Years', *PRMA*, c (1973–4), v
ALEC HYATT KING

Royal Opera House. London theatre, also known as Covent Garden; see LONDON, §IV, 3.

Royal Philharmonic Orchestra (RPO). London orchestra founded in 1946 by Thomas Beecham; see LONDON, §VI, 2(ii).

Royal Philharmonic Society. London concert organization founded in 1813 and known as the Philharmonic Society until 1911; see LONDON, §VI, 4(ii).

Royal School of Church Music (RSCM). London college founded in 1927 and known as the School of English Church Music until 1945; see LONDON, §VII, 4.

Royal Scottish Academy of Music and Drama. GLASGOW conservatory founded in 1890.

Royal Society of Musicians of Great Britain. Society for the maintenance of aged and infirm musicians, their widows and orphans. It was founded in 1738, as the Society of Musicians, by three celebrated musicians: the violinist Festing, the flautist Weidemann and the bassoonist Vincent. Members included Arne, Boyce, Carey, Greene, Handel and Pepusch. In 1739, with 226 members, the society drew up a Deed of Trust enrolled in the Chancery Court, which laid down rules for membership and for the distribution of funds. Money was raised by concerts, notably of Handel's works: *Alexander's Feast* (1739) was followed by *Acis and Galatea* (1740), *Parnasso in festa* (1741) and the first London performance of *Messiah* (23 March 1743). Handel left £1000 to the society, and the Handel Commemoration of 1784 (see LONDON, §VI, 6) raised £6000. In 1790 a royal charter was granted by George III, giving the society its present title, and its management was entrusted to elected governors and a 'court of assistants' (which included Burney). In 1792 Haydn wrote a march for the society's festival, as did Weber for the 1826 dinner. In 1824 the young Liszt played to the society, and Mendelssohn did so in 1829. Notable members in the 19th century included Cipriani Potter, Vincent Novello, Ebenezer Prout, Henry Bishop and William Sterndale Bennett. Women members were admitted from 1866, when the society united with the Royal Society of Female Musicians (founded 1839). In 1909 a Samaritan Fund was set up to aid non-members. The society was still active in the 1970s.

BIBLIOGRAPHY
P. Drummond: 'The Royal Society of Musicians in the Eighteenth Century', *ML*, lix (1978), 268

Royal Victoria Hall. London theatre generally known as the Old Vic; see LONDON, §IV, 3.

Royan Festival. An annual festival, formally called Festival International d'Art Contemporain, held in Royan, a French town in the Charente-Maritime département. The festival was founded in 1964 and is held during the week before Easter. It is devoted chiefly to contemporary music, but other arts are also represented, e.g. theatre, dance, cinema and the visual arts; non-European music is also performed. From 1967 to 1972 a piano competition (in 1972 a flute competition) for contemporary music called the Concours Olivier Messiaen was part of the festival.

Among the works which have received their first performances at Royan are Barraqué's *Le temps restitué* (1968), Xenakis's *Terretektôrh* (1966), *Nuits* (1968), *Nomos gamma* (1969) and *Synaphaï* (1971), and works by Amy, Boucourechliev, Denisov, Jolas, Maderna, Pablo and Penderecki, among many others. The festivals have also included the French premières of pieces by Berio, Kagel, Ligeti, Stockhausen and others.

The Royan Festival was initiated by Bernard Gachet and from 1965 Claude Samuel was the artistic director, but Samuel, supported by the four members of the Comité d'honneur (Messiaen, Auric, Maurice le Roux and Michel Philippot), moved 70 km from Royan to La Rochelle to establish, in 1973, the Rencontres Internationales d'Art Contemporain with the continuing Concours Messiaen, while the local committee of the Royan Festival engaged the Belgian musicologist Harry Halbreich as artistic adviser for the tenth festival (April 1973).

CLAUDE SAMUEL

Royer, Joseph-Nicolas-Pancrace (*b* Turin, *c*1705; *d* Paris, 11 Jan 1755). French composer and concert organizer. A son of a Burgundian gentleman, captain in the artillery, commandant and intendant of fountains and gardens at the court of Savoy, Royer first took up music for amusement, but when his father died leaving nothing he turned to it as a profession, gaining a reputation as harpsichordist and organist. It is not unlikely that he studied with Marc Roger Normand, first cousin of François Couperin *le grand*, who was court organist and *controllore della cappella* at the time. In 1725 he moved to Paris, became naturalized and evidently supported himself by teaching singing and harpsichord, perhaps also by involvement with *opéra comique*. According to Laborde, he was *maître de musique* at the Opéra (the Académie Royale de Musique) from 1730 to 1733; his first major work, *Pyrrhus*, was given there in 1730. On 15 November 1734 he received an appointment as *maître de musique des enfans de France*, to be exercised jointly with Jean-Baptiste Matho; and on 20 March of the following year he obtained the reversion of Matho's post as *chantre de la musique de la chambre du roi*. Matho died in spring 1746, leaving Royer in charge of the musical training of the royal children. The Duke of Luynes recounted the circumstances surrounding the composition of the ode *La fortune*. The dauphin, just turned 17 but already possessing a good baritone voice as well as considerable talent, suggested to Royer that he should set the text of J.-B. Rousseau. Although the job was difficult, the verses 'not being made to be sung', Royer succeeded in turning out a 45-minute divertissement, which the young prince sang in his sisters' apartments, surprising the courtiers, since he had only just begun music lessons. The work was repeated at court and at the Concert Spirituel with a professional singer.

In 1748 Royer, in association with the violinist Caperan, signed a 14-year lease (at 6000 to 9000 livres a year) with the Académie Royale de Musique for the direction of the Concert Spirituel, which had been suffering a financial decline. He had the hall (in the palace of the Tuileries) remodelled and an organ installed, and the results at the opening (1 November 1748) were more than satisfying. Although the principal works continued to be the *grands motets* of Mondonville, who was continued on a retainer, Royer introduced symphonies by such composers as C. H. Graun, J. J. Rousseau, Hasse, Jommelli and J. W. A. Stamitz; he took advantage of the publicity surrounding the Querelle des Bouffons to introduce Pergolesi's *Stabat mater* (1753), and himself revised older works to bring them up to date, including Carissimi's *Sunt breves mundi rosae* and Gilles' *Requiem*. During this time he continued to have works performed elsewhere: *Almasis* (1748) and *Myrtil et Zélie* (1750) were given at Versailles and *Prométhée et Pandore* was rehearsed in the house of the Marchioness of Villeroy (1752).

On 22 September 1753, he bought from Rebel and Bury the reversion of the post of *maître de musique de la chambre du roi*. At a ceremony on 13 December of that year (attended by the famous Neveu de Rameau), the City of Paris, which had taken over the Académie Royale de Musique in 1749 as an economy measure, appointed Royer composer and leader of the orchestra of the Opéra.

Royer's music is thoroughly professional and shows a marked predilection for fiery dotted rhythms, *tirades* (ornamental sweeps up the scale) and brilliant vocal writing. His command of functional harmony is more secure than that of many of his colleagues, perhaps owing to a youth spent among Italians; he knew how to modulate, how to balance one harmonic area against another, and how to delay cadences. His most celebrated work, *Zaïde*, enjoyed revivals over a period of 30 years.

WORKS

STAGE

(all performed in Paris)

Le fâcheux veuvage (opéra comique, 3, A. Piron), Foire St Laurent, Aug 1725, *F-Pc*

Crédit est mort (opéra comique, 1, Piron), Foire St Germain, 19 Feb 1726, *Pc*

Pyrrhus (tragédie lyrique, prol, 5, J. Fermelhuis), Opéra, 26 Oct 1730 (Paris, 1730)

Zaïde, reine de Granade (opéra-ballet, prol, 3, Abbé de la Marre), Opéra, 3 Sept 1739 (Paris, 1739)

Le pouvoir de l'amour (opéra-ballet, prol, 3, C.-H. Le Fèvre de Saint-Marc), Opéra, 23 April 1743 (Paris, 1743)

Almasis (opéra-ballet, 1, F.-A. P. de Montcrif), Versailles, 26 Feb 1748 (Paris, *c*1750)

Myrtil et Zélie (pastorale héroïque with prol), Versailles, 20 June 1750, ?lost, cited in *MGG*

Prométhée et Pandore (opera, F. M. Voltaire), rehearsed 5 Oct 1752 at house of Marchioness of Villeroy, not perf., ?lost

OTHER WORKS

Pièces de clavecin, 1er livre (Paris, 1746)

La fortune (ode, J.-B. Rousseau), Bar, insts, Paris, Concert Spirituel, 1746, *F-Pc*

Venite exultemus (motet), Bar, orch, Paris, Concert Spirituel, 8 Dec 1751, *Pn*

Air, 1v, in Recueil d'airs pour voix seul, *Pn*

Numerous hpd pieces, cited by Labbet and Léris, ?lost

BIBLIOGRAPHY

P.-L. Daquin: *Siècle littéraire de Louis XV* (Amsterdam, 1753)

J.-B. de La Borde: *Essai sur la musique ancienne et moderne* (Paris, 1780/*R*1972)

A. J. Labbet and A. Léris, eds.: *Sentiment d'un harmoniphile* (Paris, 1782/*R*1972)

M. Brenet: *Les concerts en France sous l'ancien régime* (Paris, 1900/*R*1969)

J.-G. Prod'homme: 'Une "prise de possession" de l'opéra en 1753', *RdM*, ii (1920–21), 102

N. Dufourcq, ed.: *La musique à la cour de Louis XIV et de Louis XV d'après les Mémoires de Sourches et Luynes* (Paris, 1970)

R. Machard: 'Les musiciens en France au temps de Jean-Philippe Rameau', *RMFC*, xi (1971), 5–77
C. Pierre: *Histoire du Concert spirituel 1725–1790* (Paris, 1975)

DAVID FULLER

Roy Henry (*fl c*1410). English composer of two works in the Old Hall MS. Identifications with various English monarchs of this name have been suggested since the rediscovery of the MS. Barclay Squire, rejecting Henry VIII and Henry VII, settled for Henry VI (reigned 1422–61, 1470–71), using the dates of Damett's and Sturgeon's Windsor canonries during this reign as supporting evidence. He did not consider Henry V (reigned 1413–22), for whom Lederer first put up a case, though mainly for misguided reasons. When John Harvey's researches linked the same composers with the Royal Household Chapel of Henry V, Bukofzer argued in favour of Roy Henry being this monarch. His reasons, too, were unsound, as they failed to separate the original compilation from the later additions to Old Hall. The composers with royal associations occur only among the latter and could not, as Bukofzer supposed, following Barclay Squire, have 'directly participated in or supervised the compilation of the MS'. Harrison superimposed a correct separation of the layers on to Bukofzer's framework, arguing that, since the second-layer composers can be associated with Henry V's chapel from the beginning of his reign, and that since the second layer is later than the first, the latter must belong to the previous reign. Roy Henry, he claimed, was Henry IV (reigned 1399–1413), an identification more consistent with the date of the musical style as we now understand it. This is undoubtedly true of the music itself, but Harrison reverted to a confusion which Bukofzer avoided, between the date of composition and the date of compilation.

The evidence of literary and archival sources is inconclusive. There is some testimony to youthful activity on musical instruments for both kings. Early biographies of Henry V tell us that he 'delighted in songs and metres', and 'was in his youth a diligent follower of idle practices, much given to instruments of music, and fired with the torches of Venus herself'. The Old Hall composer need not have been 'roy' (king) when he wrote the music, but only when the scribe made his attribution. A date during the latter part of Henry IV's reign is consistent with the musical style, years during which the king was declining. One reference to Henry IV does seem to imply specific musical aptitude ('in musica micans'), though taken in the context of a long laudatory catalogue it may be no more than conventional praise. The possibility can still not be discounted that Roy Henry might after all not have been a king.

His Gloria (Old Hall, no.16) and Sanctus (no.94) stand at the heads of their respective sections in the MS, and were not later additions, as has sometimes been suggested. The Sanctus, written in score, is severely archaic, but its mensuration changes betray an origin later than that of the most old-fashioned descant pieces. The Gloria, likewise in three parts but written out in choirbook format, is characterized by a well-poised and moderately florid melodic line with two slower-moving lower parts which frequently cross. It opens in major prolation with seminims, later changing to duple time. The tessitura is low, as is often the case with pieces having partial signatures of one, two and two flats respectively. No certain plainsong identification has been made for either piece, and Dom Anselm Hughes's ingenious claim that both movements are based on the relevant chants from Vatican Mass IX has not won general acceptance.

Possible confirmation of an identity between Roy Henry and Henry V is provided by Brian Trowell's discovery of an *Alleluia virga Jesse* in the Worcestershire Record Office (b705:4 BA 54) ascribed to 'henrici quinti'. This four-part piece is no more similar in style to the two Old Hall items than these are to each other.

BIBLIOGRAPHY
A. Hughes: 'Background to the Roy Henry Music', *MQ*, xxvii (1941), 205
B. Trowell: 'Heinrich IV', 'Heinrich V', 'Heinrich VI', *MGG*
For further bibliography and illustration *see* OLD HALL MS.

MARGARET BENT

Royllart, Philippus (*fl* late 14th century.) French composer to whom is attributed only one work: the isorhythmic motet *Rex Karole/Letitie pacis* in honour of King Charles V (1364–80). However, the ascription appears only in the lost MS *F-Sm* 222 C 22, which has many doubtful ascriptions. The work has only three voices in this MS, whereas in the main source, *F-CH* 564 (ed. in CMM, xxix, 1962), it has four, though even so only with a solus tenor rather than the original tenor. The possibility has also been suggested that ROWLAND, the composer of a three-voice Gloria in the Old Hall MS which also appears in *GB-Lbm* Add.40011B, is identical with Royllart. This seems doubtful, as does the ascription to one John Rowland mentioned in the Windsor archives in 1454.

GILBERT REANEY

Roynci, Luigi. *See* ROINCE, LUIGI.

Royzman, Leonid (Isaakovich) (*b* Kiev, 4 Jan 1916). Soviet organist, pianist, teacher and musicologist. At the Moscow Conservatory he graduated from Goldenweiser's piano class in 1938 and from Alexander Gedike's organ class in 1941, then took a postgraduate course under their supervision, 1941–6. He joined the staff of the conservatory in 1942 and was made a professor in 1963. He has given recitals in the USSR and in Czechoslovakia, Hungary, Yugoslavia and East Germany. He combines a commanding technique, a sense of proportion and an expressive style with clarity of interpretation. His repertory ranges from Bach and Mendelssohn to Hindemith, Britten, Dupré, Gedike and Shostakovich. From 1958 to 1969 he was president of the standing committee on organ construction for the ministry of culture of the USSR. Under his supervision large organs were built and others restored in many Soviet towns. Royzman has published editions of keyboard music by J. S. Bach, Handel and Haydn and of over 500 piano pieces for children by Soviet composers, and the anthology *Sovetskaya organnaya muzika* (Moscow, 1972). He was made Honoured Art Worker of the RSFSR in 1966.

WRITINGS
'M. I. Glinka i organnaya kul'tura v Rossii v pervoy polovine XIX stoletiy' [Glinka and the art of the organ in Russia in the first half of the 19th century], *Pamyati Glinki*, ed. V. A. Kiselyov and others (Moscow, 1958), 296–325
'Gedike-organist', *A. F. Gedike: sbornik statey*, ed. K. Adyemov (Moscow, 1960), 156
'Iz istorii organnoy kul'turï v Rossii: vtoraya polovina XVII veka' [From the history of organ culture in Russia: second half of the 17th

century], *Voprosï muzïkoznaniya*, iii, ed. Yu. V. Keldïsh (Moscow, 1960), 565–97

Organnaya kul'tura Estonii [The art of the organ in Estonia] (Moscow, 1960)

'Iz istorii organnovo iskusstva v Rossii vo vtoroy polovine XVIII stoletiya' [From the history of the art of the organ in the second half of the 18th century], *Voprosï muzïkal'no-ispolnitel'skovo iskusstva*, iii, ed. A. A. Nikolayev and others (Moscow, 1962), 298–347

with M. Jouvencel: 'L'orgue à la cour moscovite au cours de la deuxième moitié du XVIIe siècle', *L'orgue* (1965), no.118, p.65

'A. B. Gol'denveyzer: chelovek, muzïkant, pedagog' [The man, musician and teacher], *A. B. Gol'denveyzer: sbornik statey*, ed. D. Blagoy (Moscow, 1968), 323

'Sovetskaya organnaya kul'tura i eyo svoyeobrasiye' [Soviet organ culture and its distinctive characteristics], *Voprosï muzïkal'no-ispolnitel'skovo iskusstva*, v, ed. A. Nikolayev and others (Moscow, 1969), 297

BIBLIOGRAPHY
D. Blagoy: 'Vïdayushchiysya organist' [An eminent organist], *SovM* (1969), no.12, p.60

I. M. YAMPOL'SKY

Rozanov, Sergey (Vasil'yevich) (*b* Ryazan, 5 July 1870; *d* Moscow, 31 Aug 1937). Russian clarinettist and teacher. He studied in F. K. Zimmermann's class at the Moscow Conservatory (1886–90), played in various Moscow opera house orchestras (1891–4) and then with the Bol'shoy (1894–1929, first clarinet from 1897). He also performed as a soloist in symphony and chamber concerts. He was an active organizer of the Persimfans Orchestra, the first orchestra without a conductor, and taught at the Moscow Conservatory, 1916–37. An outstanding virtuoso, he had a tone of rare beauty and warmth. In 1905 he modified the construction of the clarinet to facilitate trilling from *b* to *c♯'* and to improve intonation on certain notes. He published *Osnovï metodiki prepodavaniya na dukhovïkh instrumentakh* ('The principles of teaching wind instruments', Moscow, 1955); *Shkolï igrï na klarnete* ('Schools of clarinet playing', Moscow, 1947, 7/1968); *Uprazhneniy dlya razvitiya tekhniki na klarnete* ('Exercises for the development of clarinet technique', Moscow, 1928, 2/1951). He also transcribed for the clarinet many works by Soviet and west European composers. He was made Honoured Art Worker of the RSFSR in 1934.

I. M. YAMPOL'SKY

Roze, Abbé (L.) Nicolas (*b* Bourg-Neuf, 17 Jan 1745; *d* Saint Mandé, nr. Paris, 30 Sept 1819). French composer. At the age of seven he was admitted as a chorister to the collegiate church at Beaune. Shortly thereafter he began composition lessons with Jean-Marie Rousseau in Dijon and by the age of ten had made sufficient progress for a motet of his to be performed with full orchestra in the Beaune church. A year later he was appointed successor to a certain Richer in the Pages of the King's Music, but he chose to complete his studies at the Collège de Beaune and the seminary of Autun; he composed several pieces for the seminary diocese.

After leaving the seminary Roze became music master at the Beaune church, on 5 February 1768; in 1769 he composed a mass with full orchestra, which he took to Paris to show Dauvergne, superintendent of the King's Music. Dauvergne then engaged him to compose a motet for the Concert Spirituel. From 1770 to 1775 he was music master to the cathedral of St Maurice in Angers, and then returned to Paris as music master at the church of the Holy Innocents, where the *sous-maître* Le Sueur was one of his pupils. He held that position until 1 November 1779, after which he devoted himself to teaching harmony and accompaniment. Laborde published a summary of Roze's unpublished *Système d'har-*

monie in his *Essai sur la musique*.

Roze wrote several motets for the Concert Spirituel between 1775 and 1779, but apparently wrote no more important compositions until 1802 when a mass with full orchestra was performed at the church of St Gervais. He also wrote in 1802 a *Te Deum* and a motet for the coronation of Napoleon. The motet finale, *Vivat Rex*, was a popular ceremonial piece in the early years of the 19th century. On Langlé's death in 1807 Roze was appointed librarian to the Paris Conservatoire, a position he held until his death. He was responsible for the reorganization of the cataloguing system, and for many acquisitions, including all his own manuscripts.

WORKS
(*MSS in F-Pc*)

Sacred: many motets, incl. Confitebor, 1775, Benedicam Dominum, 1776, De profundis, 1778, Magnus Dominus, 1779, Laudate pueri, ?1775–9 (Paris, n.d.); Messe [for St Gervais], 1802; Te Deum, 1802; 3 litanies; several masses and mass fragments, 1775–1817

Other vocal: Hymne à Apollon, 1784; Hymne aux martyrs de la liberté, 1793; Vivat in aeternum–Vivat Rex, motet (Paris, 1802); many ariettas and romances, some pubd

Inst: [2] Symphonie[s] à 4, 1770; Symphonie à 8, op.2 (Paris, 1770s), lost; Quartetto (?1769)

Pedagogical: Méthode de plain-chant (Paris, n.d.)

BIBLIOGRAPHY
EitnerQ; *FétisB*

J.-B. de La Borde: *Essai sur la musique ancienne et moderne* (Paris, 1780/*R*1972)

A. Choron and F. Fayolle: *Dictionnaire historique des musiciens* (Paris, 1810–11/*R*1971)

C. E. Poisot: *Essai sur les musiciens bourguignons* (Dijon, 1854)

J.-B. Weckerlin: *Bibliothèque du Conservatoire national de musique et de déclamation: catalogue bibliographique* (Paris, 1885)

J. Tiersot: *Lettres de musiciens écrites en français du XVe au XXe siècle*, i (Turin, 1924), 475ff

B. S. Brook: *La symphonie française dans la seconde moitié du XVIIIe siècle* (Paris, 1962)

V. Fédorov: 'Roze, Abbé Nicolas', *MGG*

C. Pierre: *Histoire du Concert spirituel 1725–1790* (Paris, 1975)

LAURIE SHULMAN

Rozhdestvensky, Gennady (Nikolayevich) (*b* Moscow, 4 May 1931). Soviet conductor. Son of Nikolay Anosov (conductor and professor at the Moscow Conservatory) and the singer Natal'ya Rozhdestvenskaya, he received his musical education at the Moscow Conservatory, where he studied conducting with his father and took piano lessons with Lev Oborin. While still a student at the conservatory he made his début at the age of 20 in a performance of Tchaikovsky's *Nutcracker* at the Bol'shoy Theatre. When he graduated he was already well known as a conductor both in the USSR and abroad, having twice conducted the student orchestra in prize-winning performances at international music competitions in Berlin and Bucharest. From 1951 to 1961 he was conductor and from 1964 to 1970 principal conductor at the Bol'shoy, where he conducted the Russian premières of Britten's *A Midsummer Night's Dream* (1965) and Khachaturian's *Spartacus* (1956) and the Bol'shoy première of Prokofiev's *War and Peace* (1959). From 1961 he was permanent principal conductor and artistic director of the Symphony Orchestra of All-Union Radio and Television; in 1974 he was appointed artistic director of the Stockholm Philharmonic Orchestra. He tours extensively, and made his London début in 1956. In 1978 he became chief conductor of the BBC SO. He was made People's Artist of the RSFSR in 1966, and was awarded the Lenin Prize in 1970.

Rozhdestvensky is a versatile conductor, a highly cultured musician with a supple stick technique and

Gennady Rozhdestvensky in 1966

brilliant executant skill. He moulds his interpretations to give a clear idea of the structural outlines and emotional content of a piece, revealing to an audience new and unexpected aspects. His performing style combines logic, intuition and spontaneity. A fine performer of the classics, Rozhdestvensky is also one of the most interesting interpreters of contemporary Soviet and foreign music. He renewed interest in such forgotten works as the Second, Third and Fourth Symphonies of Prokofiev, as well as a number of works by Hindemith, Berg, Schoenberg and Martinů, Stravinsky's opera *Mavra*, Prokofiev's *The Gambler* and Poulenc's *La voix humaine*. He is a tireless champion of works by the younger generation of Soviet composers, including nearly all the orchestral compositions of Shchedrin, and works by Mirzoyan, Kancheli, Organesian, Skorik and Slonimsky. In 1969 he married the pianist Victoria Postnikova.

BIBLIOGRAPHY
R. Kosachova: 'Iskusstvo "videt" v zvukhakh' [The art of 'seeing' in sounds], *SovM* (1972), no.9, p.53

I. M. YAMPOL'SKY

Roziers, André. *See* ROSIERS, ANDRÉ.

Rozkošný, Josef Richard (*b* Prague, 21 Sept 1833; *d* Prague, 3 June 1913). Czech composer and pianist. In Prague he studied the piano with Josef Jiránek and composition with J. B. Kittl, the director of the conservatory. After his début at the age of 17, he made a concert tour of Bohemia and Moravia and in 1855 gave recitals in a number of European cities, but he eventually chose a career in banking. A cultivated intellectual who had studied philosophy and painting, he became an important figure in the cultural and social life of Prague, as choirmaster of the Lukes Choral Society in Prague-Smíchov (1869–75) and as chairman (1871–3, 1881–9) of the musical section of the Umělecká Beseda (Artists' Society), one of the leading Czech cultural institutions. In recognition of his services to music he was appointed a member of the Czech Academy of Sciences and Arts in 1897, despite his role as head of the conservative magazine *Hudební listy* in a campaign of attacks against Smetana in 1873. Rozkošný maintained a neutral position even though Smetana favoured his operas at the Provisional Theatre and, as conductor, contributed to the remarkable success of his *Svatojanské proudy* ('The Rapids of St John').

In his musical style, too, Rozkošný was greatly indebted to Smetana, whose influence was already apparent in his comic opera *Mikuláš* (1869), to a Czech text by Karel Sabina, Smetana's librettist, though he could not match the older composer's sense of dramatic effect nor his originality. A similar lack of artistic independence is found in Rozkošný's other operas, most of which were staged at the Provisional Theatre or at the National Theatre without notable success. An exception was *The Rapids of St John* (1871) which was given 34 repeat performances at the two Prague theatres, largely owing to its inclusion of fairytale motifs and scenes of hunting and nature, much favoured at the time; however, it was soon overshadowed by Dvořák's *The Devil and Kate* and *Rusalka*. The one-act *Stoja* (1894), which held the stage of the National Theatre for nine performances, was the first Czech opera in the style of *verismo*, but Rozkošný's inability to free himself from foreign influence (in this case Mascagni) caused his works to fall into obscurity after the appearance of such Czech realistic operas as Kovařovic's *Psohlavci* ('The Dogheads', 1898) and Foerster's *Eva* (1899). A number of Rozkošný's songs and choruses on Czech texts, poetic piano pieces and chamber works were published during his lifetime, but these too have fallen into oblivion. His only work still occasionally performed is the overture to *The Rapids of St John*, which recalls Smetana's *Vltava* in its vividly descriptive tone-painting.

WORKS
(all printed works published in Prague unless otherwise stated)

STAGE
(unless otherwise stated, all operas and all first performed in Prague)
Ave Maria (1), private perf., 1856
Mikuláš [Nicholas] (comic opera, 2, K. Sabina), 1869, Provisional Theatre, 5 Dec 1870; ov., arr. by B. Simák and E. Wetzler for pf 4 hands (n.d.)
Svatojanské proudy (Vltavská víla) [The rapids of St John (The Vltava nymph)] (romantic opera, 4, E. Rüffer), 1869, Provisional Theatre, 3 Oct 1871, vocal score (1882)
Záviš z Falkenštejna [Záviš of Falkenstein] (4, J. Böhm), 1871–7, Provisional Theatre, 14 Oct 1877
Mladí pytláci [The young poachers] (Böhm), Měšťanská Beseda, May 1877
Alchymista [The alchemist] (Böhm), unperf.
Popelka [Cinderella] (3, O. Hostinský), 1880–82, National Theatre, 31 May 1885; excerpts (n.d.)
Krakonoš (3, J. Borecký), National Theatre, 18 Oct 1889; excerpts, arr. pf (n.d.)
Stoja (1, O. Kučera, after J. O. Konrád), National Theatre, 6 June 1894; excerpts, arr. pf (n.d.)
Satanella (3, K. Kádner, after J. Vrchlický), National Theatre, 5 Oct 1898; excerpts, arr. pf (n.d.)
Černé jezero [The black lake], orig. title, Šumavská víla [The Šumava nymph] (romantic-comic opera, 3, Kádner, after A. Heyduk), National Theatre, 6 Jan 1906

OTHER WORKS
Vocal: sacred works, incl. Mass, Bb, 1856; Lumír, sym. cantata, 1881; Lásky maj [May love] (K. Kádner), pastoral intermezzo (n.d.); Růže [Rose] (Kádner), melodrama (n.d.); works for unacc. chorus, incl. Večerní písně [Evening songs], mixed vv (1896); songs
Orch: Odysseus, sym. poem, 1884; Sen lásky [Dream of love], sym. poem, 1886; Scherzo (Fantastické scherzo), 1886; dances
Chamber: Rêverie, 9 str, vc solo (n.d.); 2 novellettes, str qnt (1905); Trio, ob, cl, bn (1905); Romance, vn, pf (1909); Feuillet d'album, vn, pf (1911); [2] Nálady [Caprices], vn, pf (n.d.); Nocturno, vn/ob, pf

(n.d.); Solitude, vn/ob, pf, also arrs. for cl, pf and for vc, pf (Hanover, n.d.); Vn Sonata; Tarantella, vc, pf
Pf: Colibri, op.4; La chasse, op.6; Un soir à la mer, op.7; La gondolière, op.10; Waldlieder, op.11; Chant du soir, op.23 (n.d.); La cascade, op.24 (n.d.); Impromptu, in *SH* (Jan 1888); Jarní píseň [Spring song], in *Zlatá Praha* (Jan 1897), no.6, suppl.; Rêverie, in *Zlatá Praha* (Feb 1898), no.12, suppl.

BIBLIOGRAPHY
ČSHS [gives fuller bibliography and lists contemporary reviews]
L. Janáček: 'Svatojanské proudy' [*The Rapids of St John*], *Hudebni-listy*, iii (1886–7), 65
Z. Nejedlý: 'J. R. Rozkošný', *Smetana*, iii (1913), 253
J. Pihert: 'Josef Richard Rozkošný', *HR*, vi (1912–13), 575
A. Hostomská: *Opera* (Prague, 1955, 5/1962)
V. Lébl: '125 let od narození Josefa Richarda Rozkošného' [125 years since Rozkošný's birth], *HRo*, xi (1958), 688
JIŘÍ VYSLOUŽIL

Rozo Contreras, José (*b* Bochalema, Norte de Santander, 7 Jan 1894). Colombian band director and composer. He began musical studies in Pamplona and learnt to play the flute, clarinet and saxophone in the Fifth Santander Regiment Band, which he directed after 1920. During these early years he also taught music in nearby Bucaramanga. In 1924 he left for Rome, having received a scholarship from the assembly of Norte de Santander to study in Europe; he took composition lessons with Dobici and from 1925 to 1928 concentrated on band orchestration with Vassella, then director of the Municipal Band of Rome. He also studied composition with Zádor and orchestral conducting with Nilius at the New Vienna Conservatory (1929–31). Returning to Colombia in 1931 he resumed his position as conductor of the Fifth Santander Regiment Band and taught music and singing at several schools in Bucaramanga. Appointed director of the National Band of Bogotá in 1933, he completely reorganized that body to conform more to the Italian type; he then took the band on tour through Colombia and Venezuela (1935–7). Later he became inspector general of the symphony orchestra and military bands of Colombia, and taught at the National Conservatory, Bogotá, from 1946 to 1971.

WORKS
(*selective list*)
Orch: Tierra colombiana, suite, 1930; Ov. no.2, 1936; Burlesca, 1940
Vocal: Ave María, 4vv, 1927; A tí, romanza, 1v, pf, 1928; María, romanza, 1v, pf, 1928; En el Brocal, romanza, 1v, pf, 1932; Himno de la Cabellería Mecanizada, 1962; Himno a la Comunión, 1968

WRITINGS
La banda: su disarrolo y su importancia para el arte y la cultura musical (Bogotá, 1938)
Memorias de un músico de Bochalema (Bogotá, 1960)
JOHN M. SCHECHTER

Rózsa, Miklós (*b* Budapest, 18 April 1907). American composer of Hungarian birth. He received his first violin lessons from Lajos Berkovits at about five years of age and soon developed a love of folk music from hearing the peasants singing in the fields on his father's country estate; at seven he was composing, and performing in public. He was educated in Budapest before enrolling at the Leipzig Conservatory (1926), where Hermann Grabner expressed a high opinion of his talents; during the last years of his studies Rózsa often deputized for Grabner in his classes.

In 1929 his First Violin Concerto was successfully performed in Leipzig; in the same year his op.1 (a string trio) was published. From 1931 Rózsa lived in Paris and his works began to figure on the programmes of European and American orchestras. He came to London in 1935, composed the ballet *Hungaria* for the Markova–Dolin company and began his long, successful career as a film composer by writing music for a number of Sir Alexander Korda's London Film Productions. He accompanied Korda to America in 1940 and settled in Hollywood, where he continued to compose for films. From 1945 to 1965 he was a faculty member of the University of Southern California; he now divides his time between Italy and America. He has been honoured by degrees and awards, particularly by the Budapest Municipality which awarded him two Franz Josef Prizes, and by the Academy of Motion Picture Arts and Sciences in Hollywood, which awarded him three 'Oscars' for film scores.

Although Rózsa's style is firmly rooted in Magyar peasant music he has managed to achieve a synthesis between folksong and symphonic form. The most distinctive feature of his music is its lyricism, which is either pentatonic or modal and, like its harmony, full of the characteristic intervals of Hungarian folk music. However, Rózsa never borrows folk material but gives his own themes the imprint of folksong. His mature style crystallized in the *Theme, Variations and Finale* (op.13). Among his best works are the Concerto for Strings, the Piano Sonata, the Violin Concerto and the Overture to a Symphony Concert. His film music is fuller and expressive in a more conventional way (especially the scores for *The Thief of Bagdad* and *Jungle Book*). The rhythmic and harmonic elements of his nationalist style accorded well with the genre known as *film noir* which flourished in the 1940s, and his modal melody and harmony produced the stylized archaic effect required by 'epics' such as *Quo vadis?* and *Ben-Hur*. He has won Academy Awards for his scores to *Spellbound*, *A Double Life* and *Ben-Hur*.

See also FILM MUSIC.

WORKS
Many unpublished MSS in the George Arents Research Library, Syracuse U., Syracuse, NY; MSS of film music since 1940 in composer's possession.

ORCHESTRAL
op.
3   Rhapsody, vc, orch, 1929
4   Variations on a Hungarian Peasant Song, vn, orch/pf, 1929
5   North Hungarian Peasant Songs and Dances, vn, orch/pf, 1929
6   Symphony, 1930
10 Serenade, small orch, 1932
11 Scherzo, 1930
13 Theme, Variations and Finale, 1933, Finale rev. 1943
14 3 Hungarian Sketches, 1938
17 Concerto for strings, 1943, rev. 1957
23 The Vintner's Daughter: 12 Variations on a French Folksong, orch/pf, 1952
24 Vn Concerto, 1956
25 Hungarian Serenade, small orch, 1946
26 Overture to a Symphony Concert, 1957
28 Notturno ungherese, 1964
29 Sinfonia concertante, vn, vc, orch, 1968
31 Pf Concerto, 1966
32 Vc Concerto, 1971
33 Tripartita, 1972

CHAMBER
1   Trio-Serenade, vn, va, vc, 1927
2   Pf Quintet, 1928
7   Duo, vn, pf, 1931
8   Duo, vc, pf, 1931
9   Variations, pf, 1932
12 Bagatellen, pf, 1932
15 Sonata, 2 vn, 1933, rev. 1973
19 Kaleidoscope, pf, c1948
20 Sonata, pf, c1949
22 Str Quartet, 1950
27 Sonatina, cl solo, 1951

VOCAL
16 2 Songs (Lord Vansittart), A, pf, 1940
18 Two Choruses: Lullaby and Madrigal of Spring, women's vv, 1944

21 To everything there is a season (Ecclesiastes iii.1–8), motet, 8vv, org ad lib, 1945
30 The Vanities of Life (Ecclesiastes i.1–18), motet, 4vv, org ad lib, 1967
34 Psalm xxiii, 4vv, 1972

FILM MUSIC

Knight without Armour, 1937; The Four Feathers, 1939
The Thief of Bagdad, 1940; Jungle Book, 1942 (reworked for concert perf. as Jungle Book Suite); Jacare, 1942; Double Indemnity, 1944; The Lost Weekend, 1945; Spellbound, 1945 (reworked as Spellbound Concerto, pf, orch); The Strange Love of Martha Ivers, 1946; The Red House, 1947; A Double Life, 1948; Madame Bovary, 1949
Quo vadis?, 1951; Ivanhoe, 1952; Plymouth Adventure, 1952; Julius Caesar, 1953; Knights of the Round Table, 1954; Lust for Life, 1956; Ben Hur, 1959; King of Kings, 1961; El Cid, 1962; The Private Life of Sherlock Holmes (based on material from Vn Concerto op.24), 1969; The Golden Voyage of Sinbad, 1973

Principal publishers: Breitkopf & Härtel, Broude Brothers, Eulenburg

BIBLIOGRAPHY

C. Palmer: *Miklós Rózsa: a Sketch of his Life and Work* (London, 1974)

JOHN S. WEISSMANN/CHRISTOPHER PALMER

Rózsavölgyi [Rosenthal], **Márk** (*b* Balassagyarmat, 1789; *d* Pest, 23 Jan 1848). Hungarian composer and violinist. The son of a poor Jewish tradesman, he began studying the violin at the age of eight. After a time in Nyitra and Pozsony he went to Prague, where he studied both music and calligraphy. In 1808 he moved to Pest, first working as a bookkeeper for a wholesaler. In the same year he gave a violin recital there, playing works by Kreutzer and compositions of his own in the Hungarian style; after this concert he decided to devote himself exclusively to music. In 1809 he joined the second Hungarian Theatrical Company in Pest as a violinist, later becoming its musical director; on 12 April 1812 this company performed the play *Angyal Bandi* with his music. He lived in Baja from 1813 to 1819, when a fire destroyed all his possessions, including his manuscripts. From 1819 to 1821 he worked as a violinist in the theatre of Temesvár (now Timişoara, Romania). Between 1821 and 1833 he once again lived in Baja, where he led his own orchestra during Carnival. On 13 May 1824 he took part in a meeting of the Music Society of the County of Veszprém in Balatonalmádi; the society's notary, Gábor Sebestyén, gave him the artistic name Rózsavölgyi (officially approved in 1846). Between 1824 and 1831, 18 *verbunkos* by Rózsavölgyi appeared in the society's publication *Magyar nóták Veszprém vármegyéből* ('Hungarian tunes from County Veszprém'). In 1827 he composed the music to the play *Illés sapkája* ('Elijah's cap') in Baja. In 1830 he played before Prince Ferdinand d'Este in Baja. From 1833 until his death he lived in Pest, where he was appointed principal violin at the newly opened Hungarian National Theatre in 1837; for its opening performance on 22 August 1837 he composed the orchestral work *Nemzeti örömhangok* ('National sounds of jubilation'). Ferenc Erkel released him from the service of the theatre on 15 February 1838. On 16 April 1839 his three-act comic opera, *Visegrádi kincskeresök* ('The treasure hunters of Visegrád'), was given its first performance in the National Theatre in Pest, though without success. In the 1840s Rózsavölgyi founded his own gypsy band, with which he played before Liszt in the Pest National Circle on 6 May 1846 (Liszt used themes by Rózsavölgyi in his Hungarian Rhapsodies nos.8, 12 and 13). His playing deteriorated in the mid-1840s; a concert tour in October 1846 was discontinued because of ill-health. Rózsavölgyi was celebrated as the last important

master of the *verbunkos* and the first of the more modern Hungarian dance, the *csárdás*, which became the most popular genre of 19th-century Hungarian music. From the second half of the 1830s he dedicated a *csárdás* to every great political or private occasion. His name is also associated with the creation of the Hungarian drawing-room and social dance as well as the cyclical, repetitive dance form. Sándor Petőfi, the most important contemporary poet in Hungary, defended him publicly against attacks in the press. Similarly, Ferenc Erkel thanked him publicly for the dedication of his *csárdás*, *Halljuk* ('Hear, hear!'). In the poem which Petőfi wrote on the occasion of his death Rózsavölgyi was referred to as a 'rouser of national consciousness'.

In 1844 the Pest National Circle decided to publish the collected works of Rózsavölgyi, but the undertaking was never completed. Over 40 volumes of his works were published in Pest during his life; these include *Hat eredeti magyar nóták* ('Six original Hungarian tunes', 1828), *Nemzeti nóták* ('National tunes', 1833–4) and a six-volume collection of 35 dances (1844–6). A collection of 24 Hungarian dances appeared posthumously, in 1860. His autobiography (in *H-Br*) and many of his works (*Bn*) survive in manuscript.

Rózsavölgyi's son Gyula (1822–61) founded the publishing firm RÓZSAVÖLGYI ÉS TÁRSA.

BIBLIOGRAPHY

E. Major: 'Rózsavölgyi Márk önéletrajza' [Autobiography of Rózsavölgyi], *Zenei szemle*, xii (1928), 48
K. Isoz: 'Rózsavölgyi Márk pesti letelepedése és névmagyarosítása' [Rózsavölgyi's settling in Pest and the Magyarization of his surname], *A zene*, xiii (1931), 92
B. Szabolcsi: *A magyar zenetörténet kézikönyve* [Handbook of Hungarian music history] (Budapest, 1947, 3/1978; Eng. trans., 1964, as *A Concise History of Hungarian Music*)
B. Szabolcsi: *A XIX. század magyar romantikus zenéje* [Hungarian Romantic music of the 19th century] (Budapest, 1951)
E. Major and I. Szelényi: *A magyar zongoramuzsika 100 éve* [100 years of Hungarian piano music] (Budapest, 1956)
F. Bónis: 'Rózsavölgyi Márk, a "csárdás atyja"' [Rózsavölgyi, father of the csárdás], *Népszabadság*, xxxi (1973)
Z. Réti: *Rózsavölgyi Márk* (Budapest, 1975) [with complete catalogue of MSS in *H-Bn*]

FERENC BÓNIS

Rózsavölgyi és Társa. Hungarian firm of music publishers. It was founded in Pest in 1850 by Gyula Rózsavölgyi (1822–61, son of Márk Rózsavölgyi) and Norbert Grinzweil (1823–90), and immediately established links with music publishers in Austria, France, Germany and England. Through the founders' excellent work the firm prospered and by the end of the century had become the largest music publisher in Hungary, having taken over smaller firms including Wagner (1858) and Treichlinger (1864), and later incorporating Rozsnyai (1936). After Rózsavölgyi's death, Grinzweil went into partnership with his brother-in-law János Nepomuk Dunkl; from 1908 the owners were Gusztáv Bárczi, Victor Alberti and Béla Ángyán, although the original name was retained. They issued works by leading contemporary composers including Erkel, Liszt, Mosonyi and Volkmann, and at the turn of the century works by Bartók, Kodály, Dohnányi, Weiner, Lajtha and others. From 1873 they also promoted concerts ('Evenings of new music', 'Concerts populaires'), and their music lending library contained some 100,000 items. From 1880 the firm held a royal appointment and from 1894 it published the periodicals *Zeneirodalmi szemle* ('Review of music literature') and *Művészeti lapok* ('Arts news'). Its publishing activities expanded in the 1930s to include books on music. The firm always gave plate numbers to its publications; until Rózsavölgyi's death the number was preceded by a combination containing his initial (R. et C., R. et Co., R. és T.Sz. etc), thereafter Grinzweil's initials were used (G.N., N.G., G.No.N., N.G.Sz. etc). Unfortunately the numerical sequence does not indicate the chronological order of publication; Grinzweil in particular often reissued works and several have the same plate number. The plate numbers of incorporated firms were retained, although on the cover the former publisher's name was replaced. At one time agency publications were separately indicated (C.1. etc). Rózsavölgyi is now the name of the biggest Hungarian music retailer; since nationalization (1949) the publishing activities of the firm have been continued by its legal successor EDITIO MUSICA BUDAPEST.

BIBLIOGRAPHY

K. Abrányi: *A magyar zene a 19-k században* [Hungarian music in the 19th century] (Budapest, 1900)
K. Isoz and R. Alberti: *A Rózsavölgyi és Társa cég története 1908–1949* [History of Rózsavölgyi & Co.] (Budapest, 1973)

ILONA MONA

Rozsnyai. Hungarian firm of music and book publishers. It was founded in Budapest by Károly Rozsnyai in 1889 and later run by Róbert Rozsnyai. Its publications were primarily pedagogical and are still of value, having been written by teachers at the then National Academy of Music including József Bloch (violin), Kálmán Chován and Árpád Szendy (piano) and Albert Siklós (singing and composition). Bartók's editions of *Das wohltemperirte Clavier* and the works of Mozart, Scarlatti and Couperin were also published by Rozsnyai, as well as Bartók's own works including the 14 Bagatelles, the two Elegies for piano and the *Gyermekeknek* ('For children') cycle for violin and piano (with Tivadar Országh). In 1936 the firm was taken over by Rózsavölgyi és Társa.

ILONA MONA

Różycki, Aleksander (*b* Zhitomir, 26 Feb 1845; *d* Warsaw, 15 Oct 1914). Polish teacher, pianist and composer. He studied with Karol Studziński and Rudolf Strobl at the Warsaw Institute of Music. Active mainly as a teacher, he was professor of piano at the institute from 1884 and also at the Aleksandryjsko-Maryjski Ladies' College in Warsaw; his pupils included Artur Rubinstein. He wrote numerous teaching manuals, among them two for the piano: *ABC Nowa szkoła na fortepian* (Warsaw, 1897) and *Szkoła techniki fortepianowej w dwóch częściach* ('Manual of piano technique, in two parts', Warsaw, n.d.). He also composed studies and exercises, which for some decades were basic material for piano teachers, solo and choral songs and several piano miniatures which achieved some popularity.

BIBLIOGRAPHY

SMP
W. Okręt: *Rocznik naukowo-literacko-artystyczny na rok 1905* [Scientific, literary and artistic yearbook for 1905] (Warsaw, 1905)
Tygodnik ilustrowany, xlvii (1914), 744
A. Rubinstein: *My Young Years* (London, 1973)

ZOFIA CHECHLIŃSKA

Różycki [Rozycki, Rożycki, Rositsky, Ruziski], **Jacek** [Hyacinthus, ?Sebastian] (*b* ? at or near Łęczyca; *d* in or after 1697). Polish composer. He was probably the son of Stanisław Różycki, an impoverished nobleman of Doliwa ancestry from the Łęczyca district. He appears to have entered the royal chapel at Warsaw in the mid-1640s (a council resolution of 1676 stated that he had given 'some thirty years' service' there). He probably entered as chorister, but he may well not have been a pupil of the choirmasters Marco Scacchi and Bartłomiej Pękiel, as has been suggested, since the payroll reveals that the boys of the chapel were under the care of other musicians (e.g. Piotr Elert). He may, however, have studied with Pękiel when he was older. In time he himself became choirmaster and indeed may have succeeded Pękiel. The exact date of his appointment is not known, and it should be added that sources of 1670, during his period of office, mention another choirmaster, Fabian Redzius [?Reggius]. There is also a reference, however, to Różycki's being choirmaster to four successive rulers; the first of these, Jan Casimir, ceased to rule in 1668, and the last, August II, succeeded in 1697. August, who was the Elector of Saxony, reformed the Warsaw chapel in 1697, amalgamating it with the Kapelle at Dresden; Różycki was named Kapellmeister jointly with J. C. Schmidt.

Różycki composed some masterly motets and concertos using the Italianate concertato technique conspicuous in Polish Baroque music; he also followed traditional models of sacred vocal polyphony. In a number of these works he included quotations from Polish folksongs and can thus be seen as a successor to Marcin Mielczewski. His other music comprises simple hymns for four voices, in which he renounced imitative polyphony in favour of homophonic writing in clearcut phrases and emphasizing the melody of the highest voice; these pieces are thus similar to Protestant chorales and exceptional in Polish music of the period. Although none of Różycki's music was published, it seems to have become popular; for example, Nikolay Diletsky referred to him and quoted from his works in his treatise *Musikīskaya grammatika*, and about 1700 Charśnicki based his *Aeterna Christi munera* on Różycki's hymn of that name.

WORKS

Magnificat, 4vv, chorus 4vv/cornetto and 3 trbn, 2 vn, violetta, va, va da gamba (ad lib), 2 cornettini (ad lib), bombard/bn (ad lib), db (ad lib), bc (org), *PL-GD*; ed. in WDMP, liv (1964)
Confitebor, 4vv, 2 vn, bc (org); ed. in WDMP, lx (1966)
Dixit Dominus, 4vv, chorus 4vv, 2 vn, 2 va, cornetto, 2 cornettini (ad lib), b viol (ad lib), bombard/bn (ad lib), bc (org), *GD*
Exsultemus omnes, 3vv, bc (org), *Kj*; ed. in WDMP, xliv (1961, 2/1966)
Fidelis servus, 5vv, 2 vn, vn II 'di capella' (ad lib) (vn I 'di capella' lost), bc (org), *Kj* (inc.)
Iste sanctus, 3vv, 2 vn, va da gamba, bc (org), *Kj*; ed. H. Feicht, *Muzyka staropolska* (Kraków, 1966)
Magnificemus in cantico, 2vv, bc (org), *Kj*; ed. in WDMP, xvi (1937, 2/1964)
13 Lat. hymns (1 inc.), 4vv, some *Kk*; 9 ed. in WDMP, iii (1929, 2/1947); 1 also ed. in MAP, *Baroque*, i (1969)

LOST WORKS

Missa a 9, 4vv, 4 insts, ?bc, cited in Przemyśl inventory, see Perz
Missa a 10, 5vv, 5 insts, ?bc, cited in Przemyśl inventory, see Perz
Missa concertata, 4vv, 2 vn, bc (org), formerly *Wn*, see Chybiński, 1949
Litaniae de BVM, 3vv, 2 vn, bc (org), formerly *Wn*, see Chybiński, 1949
Ave sanctissima Maria, 1v, 2 vn, bc (org), formerly *Wn*, see Chybiński, 1949
Catharinae virginis, 4vv, 2 tpt, 2 vn, bc (org), formerly *Wn*, see Chybiński, 1949
O sydus Hispaniae, 2vv, 2 vn, bc (org), formerly *Wn*, see Chybiński, 1949

BIBLIOGRAPHY

SMP
M. Fürstenau: *Zur Geschichte der Musik und des Theaters am Hofe zu*

Dresden, ii (Dresden, 1862/*R*1971), 18f

A. Chybiński: 'Jacek Różycki, nadworny kapelmistrz i kompozytor Jana III' [Jacek Różycki, court choirmaster and composer to Jan III], *Przegląd muzyczny* (1911), nos.4–5

——: 'Przyczynki bio- i bibliograficzne do dawnej muzyki polskiej [Biographical and bibliographical notes on early Polish music], iii: Jacek (Hyacinthus) Różcki', *Przegląd muzyczny* (1929), no.4

——: 'Nowe szczegóły do biografii Jacka Różyckiego' [New details towards a biography of Jacek Różycki], *Przegląd muzyczny* (1929), no.11

——: 'Jacek Różycki, kapelmistrz Jana Sobieskiego' [Jacek Różycki, choirmaster to Jan Sobieski], *Kurier literacko-naukowy* (1933), no.20

——: *Słownik muzyków dawnej Polski* [Dictionary of early Polish musicians] (Kraków, 1949), 108

W. Dworzyńska: 'Kapelmistrze prywatnej kapeli królewskiej w latach 1657–97' [Choirmasters of the royal private chapel, 1657–97], *Muzyka*, ii/3 (1957), 61

A. Pellowski: 'Jacek Różycki', *Poradnik muzyczny* (1960), nos.7–8

Z. M. Szweykowski: *Miejsce Jacka Różyckiego w polskim stylu muzycznym drugiej połowy XVII w.* [The place of Jacek Różycki in the style of Polish music in the second half of the 17th century] (MS in author's possession, 1960)

——: 'Z zagadnień melodyki w polskiej muzyce wokalno-instrumentalnej późnego baroku' [Questions of melody in Polish vocal-instrumental music of the late Baroque period], *Muzyka*, vi/2 (1961), 53

D. Lehmann: 'Mikołaj Dylecki a muzyka polska w XVII wieku' [Nikolay Diletsky and Polish music in the 17th century], *Muzyka*, x/3 (1965), 38

Z. M. Szweykowski: 'Kapelmistrz herbu Doliwa' [A choirmaster of Doliwa ancestry], *Ruch muzyczny* (1966), no.3

——: 'Some Problems of Baroque Music in Poland', *Musica antiqua Europae orientalis I: Bydgoszcz 1966*, 294

A. Szweykowska: 'Kapela królewska Jana Kazimierza w latach 1649–1652' [The royal chapel of Jan Casimir, 1649–52], *Muzyka*, xiii/4 (1968), 40

Z. M. Szweykowski: 'Styl koncertujący w polskiej muzyce wokalno-instrumentalnej' [The concertato style in Polish vocal-instrumental music], *Muzyka*, xv/1 (1970), 3

A. Szweykowska: 'Notatki dotyczące kapeli królewskiej w XVII wieku' [Notes about the royal chapel in the 17th century], *Muzyka*, xvi/3 (1971), 91

M. Perz: 'Inwentarz przemyski (1677)' [A Przemyśl catalogue of 1677], *Muzyka*, xix/4 (1974)

MIROSŁAW PERZ

Różycki, Ludomir (*b* Warsaw, 6 Nov 1884; *d* Katowice, 1 Jan 1953). Polish composer. He studied with Zawirski (piano) and Noskowski (composition) at the Warsaw Conservatory and then with Humperdinck at the Berlin Academy (1905–8). Back in his native country he joined the Young Poland group of composers and in 1907 was appointed opera conductor and piano teacher at the Lwów Conservatory. He spent the years 1914–20 in Berlin and again returned to Poland, where he became conductor of the Warsaw Opera. In 1926 he initiated the foundation of the Polish Composers' Union, of which he was first president, and in 1930 he was appointed professor at the Warsaw Conservatory. He moved to Katowice in 1945 and there gave composition classes at the conservatory while writing widely on music. The honours he received included the State Prize (1930, for the opera *Eros i Psyche*) and the State Prize, first class (1952).

Różycki was a composer of, predominantly, dramatic works and programmatic orchestral music; he possessed a great facility, which was the cause of both his early successes and his later failures. His youthful symphonic poems on subjects from Polish history – composed in an individual and spontaneous style not lacking in fantasy – gained him many followers. Less gifted and more eclectic than Szymanowski, he found an easier path to opera. His first such work, *Bolesław Śmiały*, derived its creative impulses and thematic ideas almost directly from a contemporary symphonic poem of the same name. Różycki achieved a more complete success with

Eros i Psyche, first presented at Wrocław on 10 March 1917 and later heard in Warsaw and several German towns; but the time was far from auspicious for opera. The comic opera *Casanova*, which contains some felicitous operetta-like arias, won notable popularity. In subsequent works for the theatre Różycki remained a fairly faithful imitator of 19th-century styles; only when he hinted at Polish themes, original or taken from folk music, did he become more individual, as in the ballet *Pan Twardowski*, a work crowded with activity. Together with Szymanowski he held a leading position in Polish music for many years, but by the beginning of the 1930s he had renounced the greater part of his creative ambitions to become almost a commercial purveyor. His works of the war and postwar years are devoid of both the dramatic acuity and instrumental colour for which he had been famed in his youth, and they played no part in the development of Polish music. Indeed, his stylistic evolution was the inverse of that of Szymanowski: original in expression and innovatory in technique in his early years, he became increasingly conventional.

WORKS
(selective list)
STAGE

Operas: Bolesław Śmiały (3, A. Bandrowski, after Wyspiański), 1908; Meduza (C. Jellenta), 1911; Eros i Psyche (5, J. Żuławski, 1916), Casanova (3, J. Krzewiński), 1922, reorchd 1948; Beatrix Cenci (4, S. Różycka, after J. Słowacki), 1926; Młyn diabelski [The devil's mill] (6, J. Maszyński), 1930; Pani Walewska (3, Krzewiński, Różycki, after W. Gąsiorowski), 1935, inc.

Operetta: Lili chce śpiewać [Lili wants to sing] (Krzewiński), 1932

Ballets: Pan Twardowski (10 scenes, Różycka, after J. I. Kraszewski), 1920; Apollo i dziewczyna [Apollo and the maiden] (S. Karpiński), 1937

Incidental music

ORCHESTRAL

Stańczyk, sym. scherzo, 1903; Ballada, pf, orch, 1904; Bolesław Śmiały, sym. poem, 1906; Pan Twardowski, sym. poem, 1906, destroyed; Anhelli, sym. poem, 1909; Król Kofetua, sym. poem, 1910; Mona Lisa Gioconda, sym. poem, 1911; 2 pf concs., 1918, 1942; Suite of 3 Dances, 1935; Pietà: na zgliszczach Warszawy [Pietà: on the ruins of Warsaw], dramatic fragment, 1942; Vn Conc., 1944; Polonez uroczysty [Solemn polonaise], 1946; Warszawa wyzwolona [Warsaw liberated], sym. poem, 1950

VOCAL

Choral: Cantata, chorus, orch, 1912; 3 Songs, unacc., 1924

Solo vocal orch: Narzeczona z Koryntu [The fiancée from Corinth] (Goethe), speaker, orch, 1918; Dzwony [Bells] (Różycka), Mez/Bar, orch, 1944

Songs: Songs (Ibsen, Jellenta, T. Miciński, Nietzsche), 1906; 6 Songs (Miciński), 1906; Z erotyków, 1925; many others, vocalises

CHAMBER AND INSTRUMENTAL

Chamber: Sonata, vn, pf, 1904, lost; Sonata, vc, pf, 1906; 2 melodie, vn, pf, 1909; 2 nokturny, vn, pf, 1913; Rapsodia, pf trio, 1913; Pf Qnt, 1913; Str Qt, 1916

Pf: 2 sonatas, 1903, lost; Variations, 1903, lost; Variations, 1904; Serenada, 1904; Nokturn, 1904; 5 préludes et 2 nocturnes, 1904; Im Spiel der Wellen, after Böcklin, 1904; 4 Impromptus, 1904; Fantazja, 1905; 3 morceaux, 1905; Legenda, 1905; Mélancolie, Poème, Conte d'une horloge, 1905; Menuet, 1905; Berceuse, 1905; Balladyna, 1909; Tańce polskie, 3 vols., 1915; Air, 1915; Laguna, 1915; 9 esquisses, 1915; 4 Intermezzos, 1915; Fantasiestücke, 1915; Italia, 1923; 4 Pieces, 1923; 6 morceaux caractéristiques, 1923

Principal publishers: Hansen, Piwarski, Stahl, Polskie Wydawnictwo Muzyczne

BIBLIOGRAPHY

A. Chybiński: 'Z najnowszej polskiej fortepianowej twórczości' [From the newest Polish piano works], *Nowości muzyczne* (1906), nos.3–5

J. Leszczyński: *Objaśnienia do dramatu Ludomira Różyckiego 'Bolesław Śmiały'* [Interpretation of Różycki's drama 'Bolesław Śmiały'], ed. H. Altenberg (Lwów, 1909)

A. Wieniawski: *Ludomir Różycki* (Warsaw, 1928)

J. Prosnak: 'Ludomir Różycki w 50-lecie pracy twórczej', *Życie śpiewacze* (1951), nos.3–4

J. Kański: *Ludomir Różycki* (Kraków, 1955)

Z. Folga: '"Bolesław Śmiały" Ludomira Różyckiego jako dramat muzyczny', *Ryszard Wagner a polska kultura muzyczna* (Katowice, 1964), 105ff

BOGUSŁAW SCHÄFFER

Ruano, Cándido José (*b* El Viso, baptized 14 June 1760; *d* Toledo, 17 March 1803). Spanish composer. His earliest musical training was as a choirboy at Toledo Cathedral. He was *maestro de capilla* at Avila Cathedral from 1782 until 14 December 1792, when he was appointed to the same post at Toledo Cathedral, where he remained until his death. His music, extant in Montserrat and the cathedrals of Toledo, Astorga and espicially Avila, exemplifies the change which occurred in Spanish sacred music during the latter decades of the 18th century: it displays an austerity reminiscent of 16th-century Spanish polyphonists, but uses a far wider harmonic vocabulary and a large number of instruments. Like other composers of his time, Ruano gradually abandoned the setting of Spanish texts in favour of Latin liturgical ones.

BIBLIOGRAPHY

LaborD
B. Saldoni: *Diccionario biográfico-bibliográfico de efemérides de músicos españoles*, ii (Madrid, 1880), 119
F. Rubio Piqueras: *Música y músicos toledanos* (Toledo, 1923), 55
J. López-Calo: *Catálogo del archivo de música de la catedral de Ávila* (Santiago de Compostela, 1978), nos.291–456

JOSÉ LÓPEZ-CALO

Rub' (Arabic). QUARTER-TONE.

Rubāb. Sassanid lute with double resonator; *see* PERSIA, §3(ii). *See also* RABĀB.

Rubato (It.: 'stolen'). Of tempo, extended beyond the time mathematically available; thus slowed down, stretched or broadened. *Tempo rubato* ('stolen time') signifies the time thus 'stolen' (i.e. added). In some late Baroque authorities, the meaning is rhythmic alteration of notes within the bar, regarded as a species of ornament. Since the time here 'stolen' is restored with the bar, 'borrowed time' would be a more accurate description. In current usage rubato implies some distortion of the strict mathematical tempo applied to one or more notes, or entire phrases, without restoration; and also to time added as pauses or breaks in the continuity of the tempo, to mark the separation of phrases more conspicuously than merely by a silence of articulation within the tempo.

ROBERT DONINGTON

Rubbert, Johann Martin. See RUBERT, JOHANN MARTIN.

Rubbra, (Charles) Edmund (*b* Northampton, 23 May 1901). English composer, pianist, teacher and writer, a leading English exponent of the symphony in the mid-20th century, and an accomplished composer of chamber and vocal music.

1. LIFE. Born into a poor working-class family, Rubbra took piano lessons, at first from his mother, who was a good amateur singer, from the age of eight. He later discovered the music of Debussy and Cyril Scott, two of his earliest enthusiasms, in his uncle's music shop. He left school at 14 to become a railway clerk, and at 16 he gave a concert in Northampton devoted entirely to Scott's works. This led directly to his becoming a pupil of Scott, for both piano and composition. At 19 he won a composition scholarship to Reading University and in the following year an open scholarship to the Royal College of Music, where his teachers were Holst (composition), R. O. Morris (harmony and counterpoint) and Evlyn Howard-Jones (piano) – not Vaughan Williams, except occasionally when Holst was abroad. His first published compositions – songs and partsongs – date from this period.

On leaving the RCM in 1925, Rubbra took whatever work came his way. This included schoolteaching, playing for ballet and for a travelling theatre group, and music journalism. For many years he reviewed new music for the *Monthly Musical Record* and found the experience valuable: 'it was there that I learnt my trade as a writer'. His own music drew increasing attention, and the appearance of his First Symphony (1937), quickly followed by the Second and Third, brought him wide recognition as one of the major English composers of his generation. During the war he played in a trio, which later became the Rubbra–Gruenberg–Pleeth Trio.

A more settled pattern emerged after the war. From 1947 to 1968 he lectured in music at Oxford University – he began by making an exhaustive analysis of the '48' – and since 1961 he has taught composition at the Guildhall School of Music. Throughout this period he has composed intensively, with outstanding achievements in almost every field except opera and ballet. Rubbra has received honorary doctorates from two universities, those of Durham (1949) and Leicester (1959). Other honours include a Collard Fellowship (Worshipful Company of Musicians, 1938), the Cobbett Medal for services to chamber music (1955) and the CBE (1960). In 1963 he was made a Fellow of Worcester College, Oxford. He is also a Fellow of the Guildhall School of Music and a Member of the Royal Academy of Music. His musical thought has long been influenced by religious and philosophical interests: in 1948 he became a Roman Catholic, his Eighth Symphony bears the inscription 'Hommage à Teilhard de Chardin' and he has involved himself deeply in Buddhism and Tâoism.

2. WORKS. Musically, Rubbra developed slowly, at first reflecting one or other of the senior English composers most congenial to him. As late as the Violin Sonata no.2 (1931) there is certain affinity with Ireland and Bax: one is struck by the lyrical impulse and the firm control rather than by any stylistic pointers to the mature Rubbra. Holst's influence went deeper and took longer to reveal itself. When it did so, it was not at the level of 'reminiscences' but in an attitude of mind, contrapuntal, ascetic, intellectually and spiritually absorbed. To a large extent this development depended on the solving of a problem: that of harnessing lyricism to an organic process capable of sustaining an extended structure. The First Symphony not only shows the problem decisively grasped, but in the scherzo and finale contains the prototypes of two of Rubbra's most characteristic solutions, the one revolving round a fully-formed tune, the other evolving from a melodic germ. Both are in essence monothematic, and both are contrapuntal. Some movements in his symphonies are more or less related to traditional forms, but the main emphasis is on a spontaneous and diversified growth from simple beginnings: Rubbra's symphonism is in his thematic texture.

He through-composes, without making plans or preliminary sketches. 'I never know where a piece is going to go next. . . . When I begin, my only concern is

Edmund Rubbra

with finding a starting point that I can be sure of'. Spontaneity is counterbalanced by an intervallic 'logic' which ensures coherence and unity and is itself rooted in the starting-point. Thus the first movement of the Fourth Symphony grows from its initial phrase – a falling 5th and a rising 3rd – that of the Fifth from a four-note figure embodying a rising augmented 4th and a falling perfect 4th. In speaking of his music, Rubbra seldom mentions key; his emphasis is on the drawing-out of the main thematic thread. His treatment of key, though often subtle, is more a matter of local inflection and emphasis than of long-term planning.

The first four symphonies are described by the composer as 'different facets of one thought'. They are distinct entities, and there is evidence of development from one to another by reaction as well as by continuity, but through them all runs the same concern with finding an alternative to the traditional concept of symphonic architecture. Their scoring has sometimes been criticized as 'drab' and 'unimaginative', but where the thought is convincing, so invariably is its presentation. Severity in the matter of colour must not be confused with ineptness. The Fifth came after the interruption of the war years and is the one that reflects most clearly the composer's interest in chamber music and music for voices. Nos.6 and 7 are more solidly orchestral, but with the warmth and sensuous appeal of no.5 and a more fundamental use of key. In no.8, the first to be written directly in full score, there is a striking renewal of Rubbra's most valuable qualities: the lyricism, the linear textures, the improvisatory feeling for form, the capacity for growth – these are immediately recognizable, and yet different. Especially noticeable is the heightened feeling for colour.

That Rubbra thinks of the *Sinfonia sacra*, a Passion-like work for soloists, chorus and orchestra, as his ninth symphony shows how successfully he has evolved a symphonic method that is flexible and apt for many purposes. From about 1950, if not earlier, even his smallest pieces have usually been rooted in some basic idea that conditions the whole expression. Moreover, his music is invariably vocal in feeling, whatever its physical resources. This is both an inheritance from Holst and Vaughan Williams and a reflection of his interest in 16th-century polyphony. His interests are uncommonly wide and varied – they include Monteverdi, Indian music, Janáček, Orff and Shostakovich – and he has a keen historical sense; one should beware of the notion that he is a narrowly English or 'English pastoral' composer. He is himself wary of being influenced by the surfaces of other men's music – such influences lead to a conflict of styles – and he scorns the tyranny of fashion.

The best of the chamber and vocal music exemplifies the unity and consistency of Rubbra's mature work. The Second and Third String Quartets and the First Piano Trio are among the finest written by English composers; likewise the Cello Sonata and a number of the smaller things. Chamber music textures are ideally suited to his often polyphonic mode of thought. Choral music, too, is a natural medium for a composer whose polyphonic sense is closely allied to a feeling for subtly inflected conjunct melody. Representative achievements include *The Morning Watch* (Vaughan), the St Dominic Mass, *Song of the Soul* (St John of the Cross), *Lauda Sion* (Aquinas), the choral suite *Inscape* (Hopkins) and *Veni, Creator Spiritus* for SATB and brass. These employ various combinations of voices, with and without soloists; some are unaccompanied, others selectively or fully accompanied. While the range of resources is wide, the choice of texts shows a marked preference for the mystical. The liturgical (*a cappella*) St Dominic Mass is masterly in its fitness and concision and a particularly beautiful example of Rubbra's treatment of choral texture. His songs are less important, but the two sets of Spenser sonnets, both with string accompaniments, and *The Jade Mountain*, a Chinese cycle for voice and harp, are notable. Few composers have been more articulate about their own music – or, indeed, the music of others. A gift for precise and direct expression is at the service of a clear analytical mind.

WORKS
(*selective list*)

ORCHESTRAL

op.
38 Sinfonia concertante, pf, orch, 1934
39 Rhapsody, vn, orch, 1934
44 Symphony no.1, 1935–7
45 Symphony no.2, 1937
49 Symphony no.3, 1939
50 Improvisations on Virginal Pieces by Giles Farnaby, 1939
53 Symphony no.4, 1941
57 Soliloquy, vc, orch, 1943–4
62 Festival Overture, 1947
63 Symphony no.5, B♭, 1947–8
75 Viola Concerto, A, 1952
80 Symphony no.6, 1954
85 Piano Concerto, G, 1956
88 Symphony no.7, C, 1957
103 Violin Concerto, 1959
132 Symphony no.8, 1966–8
140 Symphony no.9 (Sinfonia sacra), see 'Choral'
145 Symphony no.10 (Sinfonia da camera), 1974
149 Resurgam, ov., 1975
153 Symphony no.11, 1978–9

CHORAL

37 5 Motets (Herrick, Vaughan, Donne, Crashaw), chorus, 1934

41/1 The Dark Night of the Soul (St John of the Cross, trans. Peers), A, SATB, small orch, 1935
41/2 O Unwithered Eagle Void (C. Collins), SATB, small orch, 1935
51   5 Madrigals (Campion), SATB, 1940
52   2 Madrigals (Campion), SATB, 1941
55   The Morning Watch (Vaughan), SATB, orch, 1941
59   Missa cantuariensis, SSAATTBB, 1945
66   Missa in honorem Sancti Dominici, SATB, 1948
71   Festival Te Deum, S, SATB, orch, 1951
72   9 Tenebrae Motets, SATB, 1951
78   Song of the Soul (St John of the Cross, trans. Campbell), SSATBB, harp, timp, str, 1953
94   Festival Gloria, S, Bar, SSAATTBB, 1957
97   In honorem Mariae matris Dei, S, A, children's chorus, SATB, org/orch, 1957
98   Missa à 3, SA(or T)B, 1958
110   Lauda Sion, S, Bar, SSAATTBB, 1960
111   Cantata di camera (Carey, Spenser), T, SATB, fl, vn, vc, harp, org, 1961
115   Te Deum, SSAATTBB, 1962
122   Inscape (Hopkins), SATB, str, harp, 1964–5
123   Nocte surgentes (Alcuin), SAATBB, 1964
129   In die et nocte canticum (various), SATB, orch, 1965
130   Veni, Creator Spiritus, SATB, brass, 1966
136   Advent Cantata, Bar, SATB, small orch, 1968
140   Sinfonia sacra (Sym. no.9) (various), S, A, Bar, SATB, orch, 1971–2
Several partsongs, motets, anthems, etc, for chorus a cappella

CHAMBER AND INSTRUMENTAL
24   Lyric Movement, str qt, pf, 1929
31   Violin Sonata no.2, 1931
35   String Quartet no.1, f, 1933
60   Cello Sonata, g, 1946
64   Suite: The Buddha, fl, ob, vn, va, vc, 1947
68   Piano Trio [1 movt], 1950
69   Prelude and Fugue [on a theme of Cyril Scott], pf, 1950
73   String Quartet no.2, E♭, 1952
100   Oboe Sonata, C, 1958
104   Introduction, Aria and Fugue, hpd, 1960
112   String Quartet no.3, 1962–3
128   Sonatina, rec, hpd, 1964
131   8 Preludes, pf, 1966
133   Violin Sonata no.3, 1967
138   Piano Trio no.2, 1970
139   4 Studies, pf, 1971
141   Transformations, harp, 1972
150   String Quartet no.4, 1976–7
Several smaller instrumental works [particularly for rec]

VOCAL
32   4 Medieval Latin Lyrics (various), Bar, str, 1932
42   5 Spenser Sonnets, T, str, 1935
43   Amoretti (Spenser), T, str qt, 1935
61   3 Psalms, low v, pf, 1946
87   2 Sonnets (Alabaster), medium v, va, pf, 1955
92   Cantata pastorale (various), high v, rec, vc, hpd, 1956
116   The Jade Mountain (T'ang, trans. Bynner), high v, harp, 1962
—   Fly Envious Time, 1v, pf, 1975
—   Four Short Songs, Mez/Bar, pf, 1976
151   Three Greek Folksongs, SATB, 1977
About 35 songs, most of them early

Principal publisher: Lengnick

WRITINGS
Holst: a Monograph (Monaco, 1947)
'Symphony No.5, in B flat, Op.63', MR, x (1949), 27
'String Quartet No.2, in E flat, Op.73', MR, xiv (1953), 36
'Letter to a Young Composer', The Listener, lvi (1956), 379
Counterpoint: a Survey (London, 1960)
Casella (London, 1964)
'Eighth Symphony', The Listener, lxxxiii (1970), 925
'Sinfonia sacra', The Listener, lxxxix (1973), 220

BIBLIOGRAPHY
A. Hutchings: 'Edmund Rubbra's Second Symphony', ML, xx (1939), 374
W. H. Mellers: 'Rubbra's Symphony no.3', Scrutiny, ix (1940), 120
A. Hutchings: 'Rubbra's Third Symphony', MR, ii (1941), 14
J. A. Westrup: 'Edmund Rubbra's Fourth Symphony', MT, lxxxiii (1942), 204
W. H. Mellers: 'Rubbra and the Dominant Seventh', MR, iv (1943), 145
E. Evans: 'Edmund Rubbra', MT, lxxxvi (1945), 41, 75
C. Mason: 'Rubbra's Four Symphonies', MR, viii (1947), 131
E. Payne: 'Edmund Rubbra', ML, xxxvi (1955), 341
H. Ottaway: 'A Note on Rubbra's Sixth Symphony', MO, lxxix (1956), 653
M. Schafer: British Composers in Interview (London, 1963), 64ff
H. Ottaway: 'Edmund Rubbra and his Recent Works', MT, cvii (1966), 765
M. Dawney: 'Edmund Rubbra and the Piano', MR, xxxi (1970), 241
H. Ottaway: 'Rubbra's Symphonies', MT, cxii (1971), 430, 549
A Complete Catalogue of Compositions by Edmund Rubbra to June 1971 (London, 1971) [Lengnick pubn]

HUGH OTTAWAY

Rubeba. See REBEC.

Rubens, Paul A(lfred) (b Bayswater, London, 29 April 1875; d Falmouth, 5 Feb 1917). English composer. By the age of ten he had written the music to a comic opera with text by Nigel Playfair, whom he then helped to form a dramatic society at Oxford and for whose production of Alice in Wonderland he wrote the score; he was also a member of the University Dramatic Society. At Oxford too he organized an orchestra to give smoking concerts, at which he conducted his own pieces and sang his own comic songs, and it was while he was still at Oxford that a song 'The Little Chinchilla' was accepted by George Edwardes in 1895 for interpolation into The Shop Girl. Rubens entered the Inner Temple as a student, but he soon abandoned law for the theatre. He contributed some songs to Leslie Stuart's musical comedy Floradora (1899) and others, and he composed part of the incidental music for Tree's production of Twelfth Night (1901). Rubens eventually moved on to composing complete musical comedy scores, of which Miss Hook of Holland (1907) was particularly successful and achieved performance in Vienna. Rubens wrote many fine melodies, rivalling Monckton as the most talented of British musical comedy composers. His most successful detached song, I Love the Moon (1912), was dedicated to Phyllis Dare, the leading lady in many of his shows and to whom he was engaged.

WORKS
(selective list)

MUSICAL COMEDIES
Three Little Maids (3, Rubens, P. Greenbank), 1902, collab. H. Talbot; Lady Madcap (2, Rubens, N. Newnham Davies, Greenbank), 1904; The Blue Moon (2, H. Ellis, Greenbank, Rubens), 1905, collab. Talbot; Mr Popple (of Ippleton), 1905; The Dairymaids (2, A. M. Thompson, R. Courtneidge, Rubens, A. Wimperis), 1906, collab. F. E. Tours; Miss Hook of Holland (2, Rubens, A. Hurgon), 1907; My Mimosa Maid (2, Rubens, Hurgon), 1908; Dear Little Denmark (2, Rubens), 1909
The Balkan Princess (3, F. Lonsdale, F. Curzon, Rubens, Wimperis), 1910; The Sunshine Girl (2, Rubens, C. Raleigh, Wimperis), 1912; The Girl from Utah (2, J. T. Tanner, Rubens, A. Ross, Greenbank), 1913, collab. S. Jones; After the Girl (2, Greenbank, Rubens), 1914; To-Night's the Night (2, F. Thompson, Rubens, Greenbank), 1915; Betty (3, Lonsdale, G. Unger, Ross, Rubens), 1915; Tina (3, Rubens, H. Graham, Greenbank), 1915, collab. H. Wood; The Happy Day (2, S. Hicks, Ross, Rubens), 1916, collab. Jones

OTHER WORKS
Stage: Music for Great Caesar (1899), Half-past Eight, revue (1916)
Numbers for many comic operas and musical comedies incl. The Shop Girl (1895), Little Miss Nobody (1898), Floradora (1899), A Country Girl (1902)
Songs incl. I Love the Moon (1912), Your King and Country want you

BIBLIOGRAPHY
N. Playfair: Hammersmith Hoy: a Book of Minor Revelations (London, 1930)

ANDREW LAMB

Rubental, Neidhart von. See NEIDHART VON REUENTAL.

Rubert [Rubbert], Johann Martin (b Nuremberg, 1614; d Stralsund, 1680). German composer and organist. He was educated at Nuremberg and went on to study singing, the organ and composition in Leipzig and Hamburg, where he remained for a considerable time, officiating at the positive organ at the orphanage and belonging to the circle around the poet Johann Rist. His *Friedens-Freude* (1645) includes a reference to his having been court organist at Passenberg, Vogtland. In February 1646 he was invited to Stralsund to compete for the post of organist of St Nicolai, and he was duly appointed on 14 March. He remained in Stralsund until his death and became the focus of informal music-making; the title-page of his *Arien* shows nine musicians (both singers and players) round a table, with the super-scription 'Musica noster amor' – surely a reference to a local collegium musicum. He was highly esteemed in his time both as a composer and as a performer.

The influence of Rist can be seen in Rubert's first two publications, the *Friedens-Freude* and the *Arien*. The latter contains 20 secular arias for two and three voices with instruments – usually two violins – and continuo. The instrumental duets play an important part, providing introductory sinfonias that are repeated as interludes between the verses, resulting in a kind of extended rondo form; in general Rubert shows a strong sense of form. Dynamic and tempo indications are frequent, and there are some dance sections, e.g. courante and 'sorobont'. The *Musicalische Seelen Erquickung* (which includes a tribute from Rist) contains 12 sacred concertos in six to ten parts, including instruments. Planned on a more extensive scale than his earlier music, these settings of basically biblical texts again show formal unity in the treatment of the motivic material, and the vocal and instrumental textures are very varied, those for two or three voices being the commonest; however, neither the instrumental nor the vocal writing is in a consistently distinctive style. There are some comparatively audacious harmonic progressions and modulations.

WORKS

Friedens-Freude, 4vv (Hamburg, 1645)
Musicalischer Arien erster theil, 2–3vv, 3 insts, bc (Stralsund, 1647); aria, 3vv, in H. J. Moser: *Corydon, das ist: Geschichte des mehrstimmigen Generalbassliedes* (Brunswick, 1933), ii, 12
Sinfonien, Scherzi, Balletti, etc, 2vv, bc (Greifswald, 1650)
Glückwünschender Zuruf, T, 5 viols (Stralsund, 1663)
Musicalische Seelen Erquickung, 1–4vv, 2–6 insts, bc (Stralsund, 1664)
Song, 1v, bc, in 1651⁵; song, in 1660³; 2 sacred songs in Suscitabulum musicum (Greifswald, 1661), ed. C. von Winterfeld, *Der evangelische Kirchengesang*, ii (Leipzig, 1847/R1966), and J. Zahn, *Die Melodien der deutschen evangelischen Kirchenlieder* (Gütersloh, 1889/R1963)

BIBLIOGRAPHY

WaltherML
E. Praetorius: 'Mitteilungen aus nord-deutschen Archiven', *SIMG*, vii (1905–6), 242
W. Vetter: *Das frühdeutsche Lied* (Münster, 1928), i, 264f
H. J. Moser: Introduction to *Corydon, das ist: Geschichte des mehrstimmigen Generalbassliedes* (Brunswick, 1933), i, 14ff
A. LINDSEY KIRWAN

Ruberti, Costantino. *See* ROBERTO, COSTANTINO.

Rubeus, Petrus [Pietro dei Rossi, Rosso, Russo] (*b* Parma, 1374; *d* Parma, 1438). Italian composer and theorist. The Petrus Rubeus to whom two motets are ascribed in *I-Bc* Q15 is generally considered the same man as the P. Rosso to whom two ballate are attributed in *GB-Ob* 213, and the Petrus Rubeus to whom the theoretical treatise of Georgius Anselmi of Parma is dedicated. The treatise purports to be Anselmi's tran-scription of three days of conversations with Petrus Rubeus in the Baths of Corsena in September 1433. In it Rubeus is the omniscient teacher and Anselmi the questioning student. There is little connection between the treatise, especially in its notational system, and the works attributed to Rubeus, perhaps because the treatise

was written later than the music. This treatise was known to Gaffurius.

WORKS

Edition: *Early Fifteenth-century Music*, ed. G. Reaney, CMM, xi/5 (1975) [incl. all works]
Caro mea, 3vv
El non mi val penser (ballata), 2vv
Missus est Gabriel, 3vv
O stella (ballata), 3vv

BIBLIOGRAPHY

J. Handschin: 'Anselmi's Treatise on Music Annotated by Gafori', *MD*, ii (1948), 123
G. Massera, ed.: *G. Anselmi: De musica* (Florence, 1961)
G. Reaney: 'The Italian Contribution to the Manuscript Oxford Bodleian Library canonici misc. 213', *L'ars nova italiana del trecento II: Certaldo 1969*, 443
TOM R. WARD

Rubiconi, Grisostomo (*b* ?Rimini, 1576, *fl* 1599–1611). Italian composer and organist. He was a monk of the Olivetan order. In 1599 he was organist at S Pietro, Gubbio, where he remained until 1609 when he was replaced by Girolamo Diruta. Banchieri mentioned Rubiconi in connection with an organ at Gubbio built by Vincenzo Fiamengo. In 1611 Rubiconi was ap-pointed organist at S Benedetto Novello, Padua. His *Il primo libro de madrigali a cinque voci* (Venice, 1599) shuns chromatic passages, harmonic experiments and representational devices, but this economy of means does not preclude effective expression. The *Concerti ecclesiastici alla moderna dove si contengono messa, salmi per vespere e compieta e Magnificat a 3–8 voci con il basso continuo* op.2 (Venice, 1611) show a greater tendency towards homophony; the term 'alla moderna', as Dürr remarked, refers to the homophonic nature of the work, the use of basso continuo and the notation.

BIBLIOGRAPHY

A. Banchieri: *Conclusioni nel suono dell'organo* (Bologna, 1609), 14
G. Gaspari: *Catalogo della Biblioteca del Liceo musicale di Bologna*, ii (Bologna, 1892/R1961), 135; iii (Bologna, 1893/R1961), 165
——: *Miscellanea musicale* (MS, *I-Bc* UU. 12), iii, 4
W. Dürr: 'Rubiconi, Grisostomo', *MGG*
P. Kast: 'Die Musikdrucke des Kataloges Giunta', *AnMc*, no.2 (1965), 41
PIER PAOLO SCATTOLIN

Rubinet. *See* ROBINET DE LA MAGDALAINE.

Rubini, Giacomo. *See* LAURI-VOLPI, GIACOMO.

Rubini, Giovanni Battista (*b* Romano, nr. Bergamo, 7 April 1794; *d* Romano, 3 March 1854). Italian tenor. The son of a horn player, at the age of eight he sang a *Salve regina* in a local monastery so beautifully that his father decided to give him a musical education. After four years' training he was able to sing a female role in an opera in Romano. Thereafter he was engaged at the Riccardi Theatre in Bergamo as violinist and chorister. Wishing to devote himself entirely to singing, he left Bergamo in 1813 and spent the next year in Piedmont as chorister in a touring company, also giving concerts with the violinist Madi. His first professional engagement as a tenor was in Generali's *Le lagrime di una vedova* at Pavia in 1814. The same year his per-formance at the Teatro S Moisè in Venice attracted the attention of Domenico Barbaia, impresario of the S Carlo, who offered him a long-term contract. Rubini's Neapolitan début was in 1815 at the Teatro dei Fiorentini, where he sang Lindoro in Rossini's *L'italiana in Algeri*. During his ten years in Naples, he performed mostly at the smaller houses where comedy prevailed.

Although Rubini created no role of major importance before he was 30, he did benefit from the tuition of Nozzari, one of the leading tenors at the S Carlo. By 1825 world fame was in sight, with engagements at principal theatres in Italy and abroad. In Paris, which he visited that year for the first time, he starred as a Rossini tenor in *La Cenerentola*, *Otello* and *La donna del lago*, earning the title 'roi des ténors', but it was in the new Romantic style of Bellini and Donizetti that he eventually came into his own. Indeed, he proved a vital influence in Bellini's art, creating the tenor leads in *Bianca e Gernando* (Naples, 1826), *Il pirata* (Milan, 1827), *La sonnambula* (Milan, 1831) and *I puritani* (Paris, 1835). During the composition of *Il pirata* he lodged with the composer, trying out each piece as it was written. Likewise, Bellini refused to commit to paper a note of Arturo's music in *I puritani* until Rubini had arrived in Paris and could be consulted. The Donizetti premières in which Rubini was involved include, in Naples, *La lettera anonima* (1822), *Elvida* (1826), *Il giovedì grasso* (1827), *Gianni di Calais* (1828), *Il paria* (1829) and, more importantly, *Anna Bolena* (Milan, 1830), an opera as crucial to Donizetti's evolution as was *Il pirata* to Bellini's, and *Marin Faliero* (Paris, 1835).

Rubini first appeared in London in 1831. From then until 1843 he divided his stage activity between His Majesty's Theatre in the Haymarket, where his parts included the title role of *Don Giovanni* as well as, on occasion, Don Ottavio, and the Théâtre-Italien in Paris. There he formed part of the so-called 'Puritani Quartet', whose name derived from the stellar cast of Bellini's last

Giovanni Battista Rubini as Arturo in Bellini's 'I puritani': lithograph by R. J. Lane after A. E. Chalon

opera, the other members being Giulia Grisi, Antonio Tamburini and Luigi Lablache. In Mercadante's *I briganti* (1836) Grisi was replaced by Giuditta Pasta, and from 1839 onwards Rubini himself yielded his place to the young Mario. He remained no less in demand in concert halls and at provincial festivals (he had sung the tenor of Haydn's *Creation* as early as 1821 in Naples). In 1843 he toured with Liszt in Germany and Holland, then proceeded alone to St Petersburg, where the tsar made him director of singing. After a few sporadic appearances in Vienna and Italy he returned to Russia in 1844 and the following year retired permanently to his villa in Romano, now a Rubini museum, where he died a very rich man. In the course of his career he published a set of six ariettas under the title *L'addio* and a singing manual, *12 lezioni di canto per tenore o soprano*.

Rubini's career coincided with that period in which the tenor, traditionally the young hero of *opera buffa*, was assuming the same role in the serious genre. As male protagonist of the new Romantic opera of the 1830s Rubini disposed of a force and intensity of expression which far outshone the cool heroics of the castratos and their female successors. Yet in a sense, his art was transitional. The phenomenally high range for which he was famed, and which induced Bellini to include high F's for him in the third act of *I puritani*, must be understood in the context of a convention which is unacceptable today. No tenor of those times was expected to sing any note higher than *a'* with full chest resonance (the *ut di petto* of Duprez was regarded as a startling innovation). The upper fifth of Rubini's range was in the less expressive falsetto register. In order both to avoid ugly changes of timbre and to gather strength for high notes, Rubini found it necessary not only to exaggerate differences between loud and soft, but to sing whole numbers in a whispering *pianissimo*, as Wagner noted to his disappointment, instead of allowing his voice to expand naturally and easily. Hence, no doubt, the comparative shortness of his career. He is also credited with introducing Romantic mannerisms such as the 'sob'. He was neither good-looking nor a good actor (Romani and Bellini had much to say about his awkward stage manner). His strength lay in the beauty of his tone and the natural artistry of his phrasing. The English critic Chorley wrote, 'As a singer and nothing but a singer he is the only man of his class who deserves to be named in these pages as an artist of genius'. Nowadays his most famous roles, such as Elvino (*La sonnambula*), are usually adapted and transposed downwards.

BIBLIOGRAPHY

A. Locatelli: *Cenni biografici sulla straordinaria carriera teatrale percossa da Giovanni Battista Rubini* (Milan, 1844)

H. F. Chorley: *Thirty Years' Musical Recollections*, i (London, 1862), 29

G. Donati-Petteni: *L'arte della musica in Bergamo* (Bergamo, 1930)

E. Gara: *Giovanni Battista Rubini nel centenario della morte* (Bergamo, 1954)

C. Traini: *Il cigno di Romano: Giovanni Battista Rubini* (Bergamo, 1954)

JULIAN BUDDEN

Rubini, Nicolò (*b* Crevalcore, nr. Bologna, 21 Oct 1584; *d* Modena, 17 Jan 1625). Italian composer and cornettist. As a boy he moved with his parents to Modena, where he became a pupil of Orazio Vecchi. From 1607 he was a cornettist at S Agostino. In 1616 he moved to the Este court chapel as a chaplain and *maestro di musica*. He died at the hands of a murderer. He was admired in his day as a cornettist – he was known as 'Il Cavaliere del Cornetto' and 'Rubini del Cornetto' – and as a composer, especially for his secular music, which accounts for most of his output and is predominantly lighthearted and simple, with lively, varied rhythms.

WORKS

(all published in Venice)
Primo libro de motetti, 4–10vv, insts (1606)
Madrigali e pazzarelle, libro primo, 2vv, hpd/theorbo (1610)
Coppia de baci allettatrice al bacio: canzone, 3vv (1613)
Madrigali, 5vv, bc (theorbo/hpd/other insts) (1615)

WRITINGS

Regole per imparar di far contraponto sopra il canto fermo: modo breve, e facile per giungere alla vera intelligenza della musica osservata (MS, *I-Bc*)

BIBLIOGRAPHY

A. G. Spinelli: 'Nicolò Rubini contrappuntista modenese del secolo XVII', *La nuova musica* (Florence, 1899), no.xl
G. Roncaglia: *La cappella musicale del duomo di Modena* (Florence, 1957), 289f

NIGEL FORTUNE

Rubinstein [Rubinshteyn], **Anton (Grigor'yevich)** (*b* Vikhvatinets, Podolsk district, 28 Nov 1829; *d* Peterhof, 20 Nov 1894). Russian pianist, composer and teacher, brother of Nikolay Rubinstein. He was one of the greatest pianists of the 19th century; his playing was compared with Liszt's, to the disadvantage of neither. He was also an influential, if controversial, figure in Russian musical circles, and an exceptionally prolific composer.

After early piano lessons from his mother, at the age of seven Rubinstein went to a piano teacher named Villoing. He gave his first public concert in 1839 and between 1840 and 1843 Villoing took him on an extended tour of Europe. Child virtuosos were at that time fashionable; he gave concerts in Paris, where he met Chopin and Liszt, the Netherlands, where he had what was to prove a fruitful meeting with members of the Russian imperial family, and London, where he was received by Queen Victoria. They then travelled by way of Norway and Sweden to Germany, visiting Prussia, Saxony and Austria as well as many of the smaller German sovereignties. After a short stay in Russia, the Rubinsteins settled in Berlin and remained there between 1844 and 1846. Anton received counterpoint and harmony lessons from Siegfried Dehn, whose teaching had been valuable for Glinka some years earlier, and also saw much of Mendelssohn and Meyerbeer. His father died in 1846, and the family returned to Russia, but Anton spent the next two years in Vienna in great poverty, eking out a living by giving piano lessons. On his return to Russia in winter 1848–9, the Grand Duchess Elena Pavlovna, sister-in-law of the tsar and formerly the Princess of Saxe-Altenburg, took the urbane and amusing young man under her wing. He not only had an apartment in one of her palaces, but soon became what he jestingly called her 'musical stoker' and played at her soirées, often in the presence of the tsar and his immediate family.

Rubinstein's professional concert career began in 1854, when he toured Europe with enormous success. In winter 1856–7 he stayed with the grand duchess in Nice, and it was during that time that they made sweeping plans for the improvement of musical education in Russia. In 1859 they founded the Russian Musical

Anton Rubinstein

Society, whose concerts were conducted by Rubinstein, and in 1862 the St Petersburg Conservatory; Rubinstein was its director until 1867, when he resigned from both posts and made another triumphant tour through most of Europe. From 1871 to 1872 he was conductor of the Philharmonic Concerts in Vienna. In 1872 he toured the USA with Wieniawski, and for the next 15 years he was one of the most sought-after pianists in the world. He also built up a considerable reputation as a conductor. In 1887 he again undertook the direction of the St Petersburg Conservatory and in 1889 his jubilee was lavishly celebrated. At his death he was an almost legendary figure as a pianist, and the Rubinstein legend continued well into the 20th century.

Rubinstein composed assiduously during all periods of his life. He was able, and willing, to dash off for publication half a dozen songs or an album of piano pieces with all too fluent ease in the knowledge that his reputation would ensure a gratifying financial reward for the effort involved. But only the Melody in F op.3 no.1 for solo piano achieved lasting popularity (testified to by the 12 pages of arrangements of this piece, for various instrumental and vocal combinations, in the catalogue of the British Library). Some of the songs achieve a certain distinction, and in his chamber music a movement here or there (such as the Scherzo from the String Quartet no.3) sometimes rises above the commonplace. But both here and in his numerous attempts at large-scale works such as operas, symphonies and concertos, there are always, even in the best of them, signs of haste. As Paderewski was later to remark, 'He had not the necessary concentration of patience for a composer'. For example, good ideas in the Symphony no.2 ('Ocean') are developed in a trivial manner and this and other similar works reveal his fatal facility as a note-spinner.

In his earliest operas Rubinstein tried his hand at Russian nationalist subjects, but both *Dmitry Donskoy* and *Fomka-durachok* ('Tom the fool') failed to make any impression on the Russian public. As a result of this failure he wrote a foolish article in the German periodical *Blätter für Theater, Musik und Kunst* (xxix, 1855), in which he stated that it was not possible to create nationalist operas, and that even the greatest of Russian composers (Glinka) in his operas 'suffered disaster'. In the same article other Russian composers were accused of 'ignorant dilettantism'. In the Russian periodical *Vek* (1861, no.1) he returned to the attack with even more virulence. In 1862 the conservatory was founded to combat and eradicate this 'mischievous amateurishness'. Balakirev's group of Russian nationalist composers, none of whom had received a conventional musical education, were irrevocably alienated by the dogmatism with which Rubinstein stated his views. They, together with the influential critic Vladimir Stasov, were equally adamant in their opposition to what they called the 'Teutonic' Petersburg musical circles. Yet the increasing importance in Russian musical life of these amateurs, and the feeling of nationalism and interest in the peasants and folk music which swept Russia in the 1860s after the liberation of the serfs, were to have their effect even on Rubinstein. By the 1870s, like every other notable Russian composer, he had jumped on the folk bandwagon. A nationalist flavour is to be found in a number of his compositions at this time. Parts of the only successful opera he ever wrote, *Demon* ('The demon'), which is mainly in the French lyrical tradition of Gounod's *Faust*, may be cited; but even more important are the opera *Kupets Kalashnikov* ('Kalashnikov the merchant') and the Symphony no.5 in G minor, the latter influenced to some extent by Tchaikovsky's rather Mendelssohnian First Symphony, also in G minor, written some 13 years earlier. Tchaikovsky had been a pupil of Rubinstein at the St Petersburg Conservatory and a number of his compositions, especially the weaker ones, show the influence of his former master: his attitude to songs and piano music, for instance, was very similar to Rubinstein's. But, in addition, certain passages of Tatyana's music in Tchaikovsky's *Eugene Onegin* are derived from similar passages in Rubinstein's *The Demon* allotted to Tamara, who is, however, a puppet-like figure beside Tchaikovsky's incomparable heroine.

Rubinstein's inability to absorb the nationalist idiom in anything but a superficial manner may have been a result of his extremely cosmopolitan childhood and adolescence, and even of his German-Jewish extraction; it is perhaps not surprising that the composers who influenced him most were Mendelssohn and Meyerbeer. It is significant that he once wrote that he was considered a Russian in Germany and a German in Russia. The Rubinstein family had only fairly recently been converted to Christianity and this may be why he felt it incumbent upon himself to write a number of 'sacred operas' to German texts: these were sometimes favourably received in the German press, in spite of their mostly execrable librettos, but they had little success with the public, unlike the Mendelssohn oratorios on which they are modelled. Rubinstein felt the psychological need to succeed as a composer as he had succeeded as an executant, and this resulted in his wooing popularity with sometimes tasteless features in his music which

contrast strangely with his dogmatic idealism as a teacher. He was deeply antipathetic to Wagner and his music.

Stasov's protest that nothing but 'mounting piles of worthless compositions' would be the result of the establishment of the St Petersburg Conservatory was beside the point; and he was certainly quite wrong when he stated that it would be a 'breeding ground for mediocre musicians' as far as instrumentalists were concerned. The standard of playing in Russia greatly improved as a result of Rubinstein's work, as did the social status of musicians generally. Moreover, he had totally abandoned his condescending attitude to Russian composers by the time he again became director of the conservatory in 1887. His far-reaching ideas about state conservatories and state opera in every important city, and music in schools, were to be the basis of music as it is now taught and disseminated in the USSR.

WORKS
(places of publication and MS sources unknown)

STAGE

Dmitry Donskoy (opera, 3, V. A. Sollogub, V. R. Zotov, after Ozerov), 1849–50, St Petersburg, 1852 (c1852)

Sibirskiye okhotniki [The Siberian huntsmen] (opera, 1, A. Zherebtsov), 1852, Weimar, 1854 (1893)

Stenka Razin (opera, 3, M. Voskresensky), 1852, inc.

Hadji-Abrek (opera, 1, A. Zhemchuzhnikov, after Lermontov), 1852–3, St Petersburg, 1858, as Mest' [Revenge]

Fomka-durachok [Tom the fool] (opera, 1, M. L. Mikhaylov), 1853, St Petersburg, 1853

Das verlorene Paradies (sacred opera, 3, A. Schlönbach, after Milton), op.54, 1856, Düsseldorf, 1875 (1860)

Die Kinder der Heide (opera, 4, S. H. Mosenthal, after Beck), 1860, Vienna, 1861 (1861)

Feramors (opera, 3, J. Rodenberg, after T. Moore), 1862, Dresden, 1863, vocal score (1864)

Der Thurm zu Babel (sacred opera, 1, Rodenberg), op.80, 1869, Königsberg, 1870 (1870)

Demon [The demon] (fantastic opera, 3, P. A. Viskovatov, after Lermontov), 1871, St Petersburg, 1875, vocal score (1874), full score (1876)

Die Makkabäer (opera, 3, Mosenthal, after O. Ludwig), 1874, Berlin, 1875, vocal score (1876)

Nero (opera, 4, J. Barbier), 1875–6, Hamburg, 1879 (?1884)

Kupets Kalashnikov [Kalashnikov the merchant] (opera, 3, N. Kulikov, after Lermontov), 1877–9, St Petersburg, 1880 (1879)

Vinogradnaya loza [The vine] (ballet, 3), 1882, perf. 1893

Sulamith (opera-oratorio, 5 scenes, Rodenberg, after the Song of Songs), 1882–3, Hamburg, 1883 (1884)

Unter Räubern (comic opera, 1, E. Wichert), 1883, Hamburg, 1883 (1884)

Der Papagei (comic opera, 1, H. Wittmann, after Persian tale), 1884, Hamburg, 1884 (1884)

Goryusha [The careworn one] (opera, 4, D. Averkiyev), 1888, St Petersburg, 1889 (1889)

Moses (sacred opera, 8 scenes, Mosenthal), op.112, 1885–91, Prague, 1892 (1887–92)

Christus (sacred opera, 7 scenes, prol, epilogue, H. Bulthaupt), op.117, 1887–93, Bremen, 1895 (1894)

VOCAL

op.
—   Russian church chorus, c1851
48 Twelve Songs (Russ. texts), 2vv, pf, 1852 (1852)
31 Six Songs (Ger. texts), 4 male vv, 1854 (1856)
—   Molitva pered bitvoy [Prayer before battle] (A. Maykov), 1v, chorus, 1854
—   Solemn Overture, chorus, org, orch, 1854
58 E dunque vero? (M. Pinto), scene and aria, S, orch, 1861
61 Three Partsongs (Ger. texts), male vv, 1861 (1861)
62 Six Partsongs (Ger. texts), mixed vv, 1861 (1861)
63 Rusalka [The water sprite] (Lermontov), A, female chorus, orch/pf, 1861 (1861)
67 Six Songs (Ger. texts), 2vv, pf, 1864 (1864)
74 Utro [Morning] (Polonsky), cantata, male vv, orch, 1866 (1867)
91 Songs and Requiem for Mignon (from Goethe: Wilhelm Meister), solo vv, chorus, pf, 1872 (1872)
92/1 Hecuba (L. Goldman), aria, A, orch (1872)
92/2 Haga in the Desert (F. von Saar), dramatic scene, S, A, T, orch, 1872

—   Bacchanal (Pushkin), B, male chorus, pf, 1879 (1879)

ORCHESTRAL
—   Piano Concerto, 1847 [1 movt only]
—   Piano Concerto, C, 1849, rev. as Octet, D, 1856
25   Piano Concerto no.1, e, 1850 (1858)
40   Symphony no.1, F, 1850 (1858)
35   Piano Concerto no.2, F, 1851 (1858)
42   Symphony no.2 'Ocean', C: 1st version, 4 movts, 1851 (1857); 2nd version, 6 movts, 1863 (1864); 3rd version, 7 movts, 1880 (1882)
60   Concert Overture, B♭, 1853 (1861) [1st movt of orig. unpubd Sym. no.3, 1853, of which 2nd and 3rd movts added to 2nd version of Sym. no.2]
45   Piano Concerto no.3, G, 1853–4 (1858)
56   Symphony no.3, A, 1854–5 (1861) [orig. no.4]
43   Triumphal Overture, 1855, arr. pf 4 hands (1858), score (1860)
46   Violin Concerto, G, 1857 (1859)
68   Faust, musical picture after Goethe, 1864 (1864) [movt from discarded 'Faust' sym.]
65   Cello Concerto no.1, a, 1864 (1864)
70   Piano Concerto no.4, d, 1864, arr. 2 pf (1866), score (1872)
79   Ivan Groznïy [Ivan the Terrible], musical picture after L. A. Mey, 1869 (1869); arr. pf 4 hands Tchaikovsky, 1869
84   Piano Fantasia, C, 1869, arr. 2 pf (1870), score (1880)
86   Romance and Caprice, vn, 1870 (1871)
87   Don Quixote, musical picture after Cervantes, 1870 (1871); arr. pf 4 hands Tchaikovsky, 1870
94   Piano Concerto no.5, E♭, 1874 (1875)
95   Symphony no.4 'Dramatic', d, 1874 (1875)
96   Cello Concerto no.2, d, 1874, arr. pf (1875), score (1895)
102   Russian Capriccio, pf, orch, 1878 (1879)
107   Symphony no.5, g, 1880 (1881)
—   Rossiya [Russia], sym. piece, 1882 (1882)
110   Fantasia eroica, 1884 (1885)
111   Symphony no.6, a, 1886 (1886)
113   Concertstück, A♭, pf, orch, 1889
116   Antony and Cleopatra, ov., 1890 (1890)
119   Suite, E♭, 1894 (1894)
—   Overture for opening of new building at St Petersburg Conservatory, 1894

CHAMBER
—   Grand Duo, vn, pf, on motifs from Meyerbeer: Le prophète, collab. Vieuxtemps, 1849 (by 1852)
9   Octet, D, fl, cl, hn, vn, va, vc, db, pf, 1856 (1856) [orig. as Pf Conc., 1849]
13   Violin Sonata, G, 1851 (1856)
15   Two Piano Trios: no.1, F, 1851 (1855), no.2, g, c1851 (1857)
17   Three String Quartets (1855): no.1, G, 1852, no.2, c, 1852, no.3, F, 1853
18   Cello Sonata no.1, D, 1852 (1855)
11/1   Three pieces, vn, pf, 1854 (1856)
11/2   Three pieces, vc, pf, 1854 (1856)
11/3   Three pieces, va, pf, 1854 (1856)
19   Violin Sonata no.2, a, 1853 (1858)
49   Viola Sonata, f, 1855 (1857)
55   Quintet, wind, pf, F, c1855, rev. 1860 (1860)
47   Three String Quartets, 1856 (1857): no.1, e, no.2, B♭, no.3, d
39   Cello Sonata no.2, G, 1857 (1857)
52   Piano Trio, B♭, 1857 (1857)
59   String Quintet, F, 1859 (1861)
66   Piano Quartet, C, 1864 (1864)
85   Piano Trio, A, 1870 (1871)
90   Two String Quartets: no.1, g, 1871 (1871), no.2, e, 1871, rev. 1892 (1892)
97   String Sextet, D, 1876 (1877)
98   Violin Sonata no.3, b, 1876 (1877)
99   Piano Quintet, g, 1876 (1876)
106   Two String Quartets: no.1, A♭, 1880 (1881), no.2, f, 1880 (1881), rev. (1892)
108   Piano Trio, c, 1883 (1883)

PIANO
(for pf 2 hands unless otherwise stated)
—   Ondine, study, 1842 [orig. op.1]
—   Four Polkas, 1843–4
—   Sailor's Song, 1847
—   Three Pieces, 1847: Folksong, Rêverie, Impromptu [orig. op.8]
—   Three Characteristic Pieces, pf 4 hands, 1847–8: Russian Song, Nocturne on the Water, The Waterfall [orig. op.9]
6   Tarantella, b, 1848 (c1848–54)
—   Two Nocturnes, F, G, 1848 [orig. op.10]
7   Impromptu-caprice, a, c1848–54 (by 1858)
12   Sonata no.1, E, c1848–54 (by 1858)
20   Sonata no.2, c, c1848–54 (1855)
—   Variation on a romance by A. Varlamov, 1849 [no.3 of set by

various composers]
—   Euphémie-polka, 1849
—   Vnutrenniye golosa [Inner voices], album, 1849–50
23   Six Studies, F, C, c♯, E♭, F, G, 1849–50 (by 1861)
—   Cavalry Trot, 1850
2   Two fantasias on Russian folksongs, 1850 (c1850–54)
29   Two Funeral Marches: K pokhoroman artista [For an artist], f, 1851, K pokhoroman garoya [For a hero], c, 1856
3   Two Melodies, F, B, 1852
5   Three Pieces, 1852: Polonaise, c, Krakowiak, E♭, Mazurka, E
30   Two Pieces (1855–6): Barcarolle, f, 1852, Allegro appassionata, d, 1856
—   Marie-polka, 1853
10   Kamennïy-ostrov [Rocky island], 24 portraits, 1853–4 (1855)
4   Mazurka-fantasia, G, 1854
14   The Ball, fantasia in 10 nos., 1854 (by 1858)
24   Six Preludes, A♭, f, E, b, G, c, 1854
26   Two Pieces, 1854–8: Romance, F, Impromptu, a
50   Six Characteristic Pictures, pf 4 hands, 1854–8: Nocturne, E, Scherzo, F, Barcarolle, g [also arr. pf 2 hands], Capriccio, A, Berceuse, b, March, C
16   Three Pieces, 1855: Impromptu, F, Berceuse, D, Serenade, g
21   Three Caprices, F♯, D, E♭, 1855
22   Three Serenades, F, g, E♭, 1855
38   Suite, 10 movts, 1855 (1856)
41   Sonata no.3, F, 1855
28   Two Pieces, 1856: Nocturne, G♭, Caprice, E♭
37   Laura, acrostic, 1856
—   Barcarolle no.2, a, 1857 [orig. op.45; also orchd]
51   Six Pieces, 1857: Mélancholie, g, Enjouement, B♭, Rêverie, a, Caprice, D♭, Passion, F, Coquetterie, B♭
53   Six Preludes and Fugues in Free Style, A♭, f, E, b, G, c, 1857
—   Hungarian Fantasia, 1858
44   Soirées à Saint-Pétersbourg, 6 pieces, 1860: Romance, E♭ [also arr. as song Noch [Night] (Pushkin)], Scherzo, a, Preghiera, B♭, Impromptu, G, Nocturne, F, Appassionato, b
—   cadenzas to Mozart: Pf Conc. к466; Beethoven: Pf Concs.1–4, 1861
73   Fantasia, f, 2 pf, 1864
75   Album de Peterhof, 12 pieces, 1866: Souvenir, C, Aubade, E♭, Funeral March, g, Impromptu, E♭, Rêverie, d, Russian Capriccio, F, Pensées, f♯, Nocturne, G, Prelude, D, Mazurka, d, Romance, B♭, Scherzo, F
77   Fantasia, e, 1866
69   Five Pieces, 1867: Caprice, A♭, Nocturne, G, Scherzo, a, Romance, b, Toccata, d
71   Three Pieces, 1867: Nocturne, A♭, Mazurka, f, Scherzo, D♭
—   Two Studies, C, 1867, C, 1868
82   Album of Popular Dances of the Different Nations, 1868: Russian Dance and Trepak, Lezghinka, Mazurka, Csárdás, Tarantella, Waltz, Polka
—   Valse caprice, E♭, 1870
81   Six Studies, f, A, g, E, d, E♭, 1870
89   Sonata, D, pf 4 hands, 1870
—   Barcarolle no.4, G [also orchd]
88   Theme and Variations, G, 1871
93   Miscellaneous Pieces, 9 bks, 1872–3 [incl. Barcarolle no.5, a]
100   Sonata no.4, a, 1877
103   Bal costumé, 20 nos., 2 pf, 1879 [also orchd for ballet]
—   Russian Serenade, b, 1879 [pubd in album in memory of Bellini]
104   Six Pieces, 1882–5: Elegy, d, Variations, A♭, Study, C, Barcarolle no.6, c [also orchd], Impromptu, G, Ballade, a
109   Soirées musicales, 9 pieces, 1884: Prelude, a, Valse, e, Nocturne, F, Scherzo, D, Impromptu, G, Rêverie-caprice, g, [8] Badinages, Theme and Variations, D, Study, E♭
—   Bluette, 1885
114   Acrostic no.2, 1890
—   Valse, A♭, 1891
118   Souvenir de Dresde, 6 pieces, 1894: Simplicitas, F, Appassionata, c, Novellette, A, Caprice, C, Nocturne, A♭, Polonaise, E♭
—   transcrs. of Beethoven: Turkish March from Die Ruinen von Athen, 1848, Egmont Ov., 1868; Meyerbeer: ov. to Das Feldlager in Schlesien, 1849; Rubinstein: ov. to Demon, 1875

SONGS
(for 1v, pf unless otherwise stated)
—   Zuruf aus der Ferne (E. Weiden), 1841–2 [orig. op.2]
—   Comment disaient-ils (V. Hugo), 1843–4 [orig. op.3]
—   Prayer (Lermontov), 1843–4 [orig. op.4]
—   The Nightingale, 1843–4 [orig. op.5]
—   The Lark, 1843–4 [orig. op.6]
—   The Siskin (Grot), 1843–4
—   Swedish Song ('Hommage à Jenny Lind'), 1845–6 [orig. op.7; also arr. pf]
1   Six Little Songs in Low German, 1848
—   The Swallow (M. Sukhanov), 1849

WRITINGS

'Istoriya literaturï fortepiannoy muzïki', *Muzïkal'-noye obozreniye* (St Petersburg, 1888; Ger. trans., 1899, as *Die Meister des Klaviers*)

Avtobiograficheskiye vospominaniya (1829–1889) (St Petersburg, 1889; Eng. trans., 1890/R1969, as *Autobiography of Anton Rubinstein, 1829–1889*)

Muzïka i eyo predstaviteli (Moscow, 1891; Eng. trans., 1891, as *Music and its Masters: a Conversation on Music*)

BIBLIOGRAPHY

S. Droucker: *Erinnerungen an Anton Rubinstein* (Leipzig, 1904)

N. T. Findeyzen: *A. G. Rubinshteyn: ocherk evo zhizni i muzïkal'noy deyatel'nosti* [A study of his life and musical activities] (Moscow, 1907)

C. Maclean: 'Rubinstein as Composer for the Pianoforte', *PMA*, xxxix (1912–13), 129

A. Hervey: *Rubinstein* (London, 1913, 2/1922)

I. Glebov [B. Asaf'yev]: *Anton Grigor'yevich Rubinshteyn v evo muzïkal'noy deyatel'nosti i otzïvakh sovremennikov* [A. G. Rubinstein, his musical activities and the opinions of his contemporaries] (Moscow, 1929)

O. Bennigsen: 'The Brothers Rubinstein and their Circle', *MQ*, xxv (1939), 407

C. Drinker Bowen: *Free Artist: the Story of Anton and Nicholas Rubinstein* (New York, 1939)

G. Abraham: 'Anton Rubinstein: Russian Composer', *MT*, lxxxvi (1945), 361

A. Alexeyev: *Anton Rubinshteyn* (Moscow and Leningrad, 1945)

L. Barenboym, ed.: *Izbrannïye pis'ma* [Selected letters] (Leningrad, 1954)

L. Barenboym: *Anton Grigor'yevich Rubinshteyn* (Leningrad, 1957–62)

Numerous recollections, memoirs, sketches and short biographies, notably those by Baskin (1886), Vogel (1888), Lisovsky (1889), MacArthur (1889), Zverev (1889), Zabel (1892), Kashkin (1894), Koreshchenko (1894), Soubies (1894), Bernhard (1895), Martinov (1895), Rodenberg (1895), Wolff (1897), Bessel (1898), Davidova (1899), Weinberg (1905), La Mara (1911), Bernstein (1911)

EDWARD GARDEN

Rubinstein, Artur [Arthur] (*b* Łódź, 28 Jan 1887). Polish pianist, later naturalized American. At the age of three he was taken to Berlin to play for Joachim, who confirmed his immense promise. After lessons in Łódź and Warsaw and a first concert appearance at Łódź at the age of seven, he returned in 1897 to Berlin, where his musical education was supervised by Joachim, Heinrich Barth taking charge of his piano studies and Max Bruch and Robert Kahn his theoretical instruction. In 1899 he played Mozart's A major Concerto K488 in

Artur Rubinstein and Daniel Barenboim

Potsdam, a prelude to his Berlin début in the same work (under Joachim) in December 1900; this concert also included solos by Schumann and Chopin, and Saint-Saëns's G minor Concerto, a vehicle for Rubinstein's virtuosity throughout his career. His success led to further appearances in Germany and Poland, and to his Paris début in 1904.

By this time, Rubinstein had dispensed with regular piano instruction, although he was to spend periods of time with Paderewski in Switzerland; natural facility aided him in greatly enlarging his repertory, and a gift for sight-reading, orchestral transcription and accompanying singers and chamber musicians won him popularity in social as well as concert-hall music-making. In later years he was to recognize that his youthful exuberance, untempered by disciplined study or the prolonged influence of a mature piano master, had allowed him to give many under-prepared performances. Such immaturity was remarked, among expressions of admiration for the evidence of natural flair and vivacity in his playing, by critics at the time of his first American tour in 1906. Appearances in Austria, Italy and Russia preceded his London débuts in 1912, at the Queen's Hall accompanying Casals, and at the Bechstein Hall as soloist. Domiciled mainly in London during World War I, he was active as accompanist to Ysaÿe. He visited Spain and South America in 1916–17, conceiving what was to be a lifelong enthusiasm for the music of Granados, Albéniz, Villa-Lobos and especially Falla.

Thereafter, Rubinstein pursued a similarly active career until his marriage in 1932, after which he withdrew for a long period of contemplation, technical consolidation and re-study of his repertory. A new discipline balancing brilliant temperament was remarked in his playing, especially during his American tour of 1937, when previously grudging critics recognized his place among the great players of the century. After spending World War II in the USA, he became an American citizen in 1946. Rubinstein continued his international concert tours with an energy that seemed increasingly phenomenal. It was not uncommon, in his 70s and 80s, for him to play in a single evening both Brahms concertos or three by Beethoven; in chamber music, he partnered Heifetz and Feuermann (later Piatigorsky), Kochański, Szeryng and the Guarneri Quartet in the 1960s and 1970s. With all he made recordings, adding to a prodigious tally that was also to include the complete piano works of Chopin and three LP versions of the complete Beethoven concertos. On 30 April 1976 he returned to the Wigmore Hall for a recital announced as his last.

Bach, Mozart, Beethoven and the principal 19th-century Romantics, played with a directness owing nothing to the Romantic rhythmic distortions still fashionable in Rubinstein's youth, have all enjoyed a place in his huge repertory. As a young man he was renowned for his ardent championship of such composers as Szymanowski, Stravinsky, Debussy, Ravel, Poulenc, Prokofiev and the Spanish and South American composers already mentioned. Chopin only gradually replaced Brahms as the composer arousing the pianist's strongest and deepest artistic instincts – yet it is above all as a Chopin interpreter that Rubinstein's place among the greatest players of the century is assured. In all the piano works, from the concertos to the F♯ Nocturne op.15 no.2, which has served as a favourite encore, the warmly outgoing and beneficent lyricism of his phrasing, expressed in tones of richest and most gorgeous hue, has provided an ideal standard of Chopin interpretation – not necessarily flawless in virtuosity but imbued with an inimitable spirit of civilized yet passionate eloquence and aristocratic poetry.

Among the numerous honours bestowed on Rubinstein is the United States Medal of Freedom (1976).

BIBLIOGRAPHY

H. C. Schonberg: *The Great Pianists* (London, 1964), 413ff
A. Rubinstein: *My Young Years* (London, 1973)
——: *My Many Years* (London, 1980)

MAX LOPPERT

Nikolay Rubinstein

Rubinstein [Rubinshteyn], **Nikolay (Grigor'yevich)** (*b* Moscow, 14 June 1835; *d* Paris, 23 March 1881). Russian pianist, conductor, teacher and composer, brother of Anton Rubinstein. His talents as a pianist became apparent early on. While the family was in Berlin (1844–6) he studied the piano with Kullak and harmony and counterpoint with Dehn. When they returned to Moscow in 1846 he had piano lessons with Villoing, who toured Russia with the child virtuoso. To avoid army conscription he studied medicine at Moscow University, graduating in 1855.

In spite of his obscure social origins, this gregarious, extrovert, generous, charming *bon vivant* was welcome in all the fashionable aristocratic houses in Moscow, a city for which he had a special affection. He founded the Moscow branch of the Russian Musical Society in the 1859–60 season. In 1864 he moved to a larger house in which he and several colleagues taught various musical subjects. This establishment was granted an imperial charter as a conservatory, but initially it was humbler than that at St Petersburg. Rubinstein engaged the young Tchaikovsky as a teacher of harmony in 1866. It was he, not his brother Anton (who had been Tchaikovsky's teacher), who encouraged Tchaikovsky and performed his compositions, but in a notorious incident he attacked Tchaikovsky's First Piano Concerto at its first, private performance; later he recanted and became a celebrated interpreter of the work. In 1869 when Balakirev, who two years earlier had succeeded Anton Rubinstein as conductor of the St Petersburg branch of the Russian Musical Society, was forced to resign by the Grand Duchess Elena Pavlovna, Nikolay generously gave Balakirev his support while Anton remained aloof. It was indicative of this support and of Nikolay's extraordinary powers as a pianist that he should have given a brilliant first performance of Balakirev's enormously difficult piano piece *Islamey* only two months after its completion, despite a heavy programme of teaching, conducting and administration and his very full social life. He conducted and performed the music of the nationalist 'New Russian School' in the 1860s and 1870s to a much greater extent than his brother.

Anton would not acknowledge that Nikolay was his inferior as a pianist, though the latter was not so well known outside Russia. The technique of both was excellent, but whereas Anton rarely played the same piece twice in the same way (preferring to allow himself to be inspired and to carry away his enraptured audience on the spur of the moment), Nikolay's playing was much more detached and analytical. His performances emphasized salient features of the structure of a piece and revealed great clarity of detail. Nikolay was aware of his own and Anton's limitations as composers, and, when asked why he did not compose more, replied that his brother 'composed enough for three'; his compositions are indeed unimportant. Both brothers were vigorous, uninhibited teachers and frequently screamed at their pupils, who nevertheless adored them. Nikolay's best-known pupils were Taneyev, Ziloti and Emil Sauer. He died of consumption in a Paris hotel on his way to Nice for health reasons. It was typical of him that he ate a dozen oysters on his deathbed. A scholarship in his name was founded by his numerous friends and admirers, and Tchaikovsky composed the Piano Trio in A minor in his memory, basing the variations on (undisclosed) events in Rubinstein's life.

BIBLIOGRAPHY
N. Kashkin: 'Nikolay Grigor'yevich Rubinshteyn i evo rol' v muzïkal'-nom razvitii Moskvï' [Rubinstein and his role in the development of music in Moscow], *Moskovskiye vedomosti* (15/27 Nov, 9/21 Dec 1898)

——: 'Vospominaniya o N. G. Rubinshteyne' [Reminiscences of Rubinstein], *Moskovskiye vedomosti* (22 Jan/3 Feb, 12/24 Feb, 18/30 June, 23 June/5 July, 20 July/1 Aug, 6/18 Aug, 18/30 Aug, 25 Aug/6 Sept, 1/13 Oct 1899; 6/19 June, 26 July/8 Aug, 16/29 Aug 1900) [continuation of series begun in 1898]

O. Bennigsen: 'The Brothers Rubinstein and their Circle', *MQ*, xxv (1939), 407

C. Drinker Bowen: *Free Artist: the Story of Anton and Nicholas Rubinstein* (New York, 1939)

EDWARD GARDEN

Rubinus. See ROBINET DE LA MAGDALAINE.

Rubio, David (Joseph) (*b* London, 17 Dec 1934). English maker of violins, viols, lutes, guitars and harpsichords. He began to learn the guitar while at school and, after taking medical degrees at Trinity College, Dublin (1957), spent four years in Spain perfecting his guitar playing. While studying there with various teachers, principally Pepe Martínez in Seville, he also gathered information about the craft of guitar making. He went to the USA in 1961 as solo guitarist of a Spanish ballet company and remained there, working first as a performer, then gradually becoming more concerned with research and instrument making. He opened his guitar workshop in New York in 1964 and began to build lutes the following year. In 1967 he returned to England, establishing his workshop in Duns Tew, near Oxford, in 1968; in 1979 he moved to Cambridge.

Rubio has gradually expanded his range of instrument production. In 1969 he began to construct harpsichords, mainly large double instruments in the 18th-century French style, but also occasional late Flemish harpsichords after Dulcken. In 1972 he produced his first viols and violins of pre-19th-century design, and later added cellos of an earlier type to his output. Rubio's approach to his craft is essentially historical. His instruments are admired for the perfection of their finish as well as their exceptional tonal qualities.

BIBLIOGRAPHY
'Luthiers: Howard Schott Visits the Workshops of David Rubio and Michael Lowe', *Early Music*, iii (1975), 355

HOWARD SCHOTT

Rubio, Hilarion (Francisco) (*b* Bacoor, Cavite, 21 Oct 1902). Filipino composer and writer on music. At an early age he learnt to play the violin, the piano and the clarinet under an Aglipayan priest. He took preparatory law courses at the Far Eastern Institute (Associate in Arts 1927) and then entered the University of the Philippines Conservatory, where he received a teacher's diploma in theory and composition in 1933. Later he taught at the university and was assistant secretary of its conservatory (1939–41). He also taught in other institutions, becoming director of the Conservatory of Centro Escolar University (1944–5). Founder-president of the Philippine Bandmasters' Association, he has conducted concerts and stage performances in the Philippines and elsewhere in Asia. He has also published articles on Philippine music, into which he has made dedicated research. A grant from the University of the Philippines and the Music Promotion Foundation enabled him to make a study tour of the USA and Japan in 1967, and he made four goodwill trips to Taiwan (1956–60), for which he received the Friend of China Award. Among his prizes and honours is a diploma of merit from the University of the Philippines on his retirement (1967).

WORKS
(*selective list*)

Orch: Florante at Laura, ov., 1933; The Elements, suite, ballet, 1940; Filipinas Kong Mahal [My beloved Philippines], sym. ov., 1960; Sym. for Greatness, 1966; Panamin Vc Conc., 1970; band works, film scores

Choral: National Heroes Day Hymn, 1934; Philippines Triumphant, 1936; To the Filipino Youth, cantata, 1951; Prelude and Fugue, chorus, orch, 1960; Second Decalogue, sym. ode, chorus, orch, 1963; folksong arrs.

Other works: Concertino, C, mar, pf, 1957; Silahis '67 [Rays], ens, 1970; Pf Sonata, 1970; Kundiman [Love-song], 1v, pf

LUCRECIA R. KASILAG

Rubio (Calzón), Samuel (*b* Posada de Omaña, 20 Aug 1912). Spanish musicologist. In his early youth he joined the Augustinian order and studied philosophy and theology. He spent long periods in Benedictine monasteries, including Montserrat and Silos, studying Gregorian chant, and in Solesmes studying Gregorian palaeography. From 1952 to 1955 he studied sacred music and musicology at the Pontificio Istituto di Musica Sacra, Rome, where in 1967 he took the doctorate in musicology under Anglès with a dissertation on Morales. He was choirmaster and organist at the Escorial (1939–59, 1971–2) and in 1972 became professor of musicology at the Madrid Conservatory.

Rubio is the most important Spanish musicologist outside Anglès's group at the Barcelona Spanish Institute of Musicology. His work is more distinctive for its quality than its quantity; it deals with central moments in the history of Spanish music, including a stylistic analysis of Morales, an account of essential facets of Victoria's work and a study and publication of Soler's sonatas. All his work is characterized by thorough and elegant scholarship. In the 1970s he was working on complete editions of the music of Juan de Anchieta and Juan Navarro.

WRITINGS
'Estudios sobre polifonía española del siglo XVI y principios del XVII', *Tesoro sacro musical* (1947–9)

'Un obra inédita y desconocida de Tomás Luis de Victoria, el motete "O doctor optime . . . beate Augustine", a cuatro voces mixtas', *La ciudad de Dios*, no.161 (1949), 525–59

'El archivo de música de la catedral de Plasencia', *AnM*, v (1950), 147

'Historia de las reediciones de los motetes de T. L. de Victoria y significado de las variantes introducidas en ellas', *La ciudad de Dios*, no.162 (1950), 313–51

'La capilla de música del monasterio de El Escorial', *La ciudad de Dios*, no.163 (1951), 59–118

In XVI centenario nativitatis Sancti Patris Augustini: XXIV cantica sacra in honorem S. P. Augustini ex auctoribus antiquis et hodiernis (Bilbao, 1954)

La polifonía clásica (El Escorial, 1956; Eng. trans., 1972)

'A los trescientos cincuenta años de la muerte de Tomás Luis de Victoria', *La ciudad de Dios*, no.174 (1961), 693–727

'Los órganos del monasterio de El Escorial', *La ciudad de Dios*, no.178 (1965), 464

'Las glosas de Antonio de Cabezón y de otros autores sobre el "Pange lingua" de Juan de Urreda', *AnM*, xxi (1966), 45

Cristóbal de Morales (diss., Pontificio Istituto di Musica Sacra, Rome, 1967; El Escorial, 1969)

'Los jerónimos de El Escorial, el canto gregoriano y la liturgia', *Tesoro sacro musical*, lii (1969), 225

'Las melodías de los "libros corales" del Monasterio del Escorial', *Tesoro sacro musical*, liii (1970), 35

'La música de tecla en el Renacimiento', in E. Casares: *La música en el Renacimiento* (Oviedo, 1975), 73

Catálogo del archivo de música del monasterio de San Lorenzo el Real de El Escorial (Cuenca, 1976)

EDITIONS
A. Soler: *Sonatas para instrumentos de tecla* (Madrid, 1952–72); *Seis conciertos para dos órganos* (Madrid, 1968)

Antología polifónica sacra (Madrid, 1954–6)

Canciones espirituales polifónicas, Polifonía española (Madrid, 1955–6)
Organistas de la Real Capilla (siglo XVIII), i: Obras de J. Lidón, Félix Máximo López, Joaquín Oxinaga y Juan de Sessé (Madrid, 1973)
Agenda defunctorum de Juan Vázquez (Madrid, 1975)
J. Navarro (i): Psalmi, hymni, Magnificat ... ac antiphonae B. Virginis (Madrid, 1978)
F. Tovar: Libro de música practica (Madrid, 1978)

JOSÉ LÓPEZ-CALO

Rubsamen, Walter H(oward) (b New York, 21 July 1911; d Los Angeles, 19 June 1973). American musicologist. He studied the flute in New York with George Barrère and Meredith Willson. At Columbia University, where he took the BA in 1933, his professors included Lang, Moore and Mason. He did graduate work at the University of Munich under von Ficker and Ursprung and took the PhD in 1937 with a dissertation on Pierre de La Rue. He taught at the University of California, Los Angeles, from 1938 until his death; from 1966 to 1973 he served as chairman of the department of music. He was also a visiting professor at the University of Chicago, Columbia University and the University of Berne. Rubsamen's interests included music of the Renaissance, ballad opera, music and politics and descriptive music. He studied the secular music of late 15th- and early 16th-century Italy, and his investigations of the verse forms used by the frottola composers resulted in an important monograph on the literary–musical relationships of the period. His research in European and American libraries also produced a number of manuscript studies and articles about his archival discoveries.

WRITINGS

Pierre de La Rue als Messen-Komponist (diss., U. of Munich, 1937)
'Political and Ideological Censorship of Opera', PAMS 1941, 30
Literary Sources of Secular Music in Italy (ca. 1500) (Berkeley, 1943)
'Kurt Huber of Munich', MQ, xxx (1944), 226
'La musica nella vita sociale degli Stati Uniti', RMI, 1 (1948), 259
'Music Research in Italian Libraries: an Anecdotal Account of Obstacles and Discoveries', Notes, vi (1948–9), 220, 543; viii (1950–51), 70
with R. U. Nelson: 'Bibliography of Books and Articles on Music in Film and Radio', HMYB, vi (1949–50), 318
'The Ballad Burlesques and Extravaganzas', MQ, xxxvi (1950), 551
'Schoenberg in America', MQ, xxxvii (1951), 469
'Descriptive Music for Stage and Screen', HMYB, vii (1952), 559
'Unusual Music Holdings of Libraries on the West Coast', Notes, x (1952–3), 546
'Ballad Opera', ES
'Frottola', MGG
'The International "Catholic" Repertoire of a Lutheran Church in Nürnberg (1574–1597)', AnnM, v (1957), 229–327
'The Justiniane or Viniziane of the 15th Century', AcM, xxix (1957), 172
'Mr Seedo, Ballad Opera and the Singspiel', Miscelánea en homenaje a Monseñor Higinio Anglés (Barcelona, 1958–61), 773–809
'The Jovial Crew: History of a Ballad Opera', IMSCR, vii Cologne 1958, 240
'From Frottola to Madrigal: the Changing Pattern of Secular Italian Vocal Music', Chanson and Madrigal 1480–1530: Isham Memorial Library 1961, 51–87
'Scottish and English Music of the Renaissance in a Newly-discovered Manuscript', Festschrift Heinrich Besseler (Leipzig, 1961), 259
'Sebastian Festa and the Early Madrigal', GfMKB, Kassel 1962, 122
'La Rue, Pierre de', MGG
'The Earliest French Lute Tablature', JAMS, xxi (1968), 286
'The Music for "Quant'è bella giovinezza" and other Carnival Songs by Lorenzo de' Medici', Art, Science and History in the Renaissance, ed. C. Singleton (Baltimore, 1968), 163
'Cino da Pistoia in Music of the Renaissance', GfMKB, Bonn 1970, 553
'Unifying Techniques in Selected Masses of Josquin and La Rue: a Stylistic Comparison', Josquin des Prez: New York 1971, 369–400
'Irish Folk Music in Midas, a Ballad Burlesque of the 18th Century', IMSCR, xi Copenhagen 1972, 623
ed.: The Ballad Opera: a Collection of 171 Original Texts of Musical Plays Printed in Photo-facsimile (New York, 1974)
'Ballad opera', Grove 6

PAULA MORGAN

Ruby, Guillaume. See ROUGE, GUILLAUME.

Ruckers [Ruckaert, Ruckaerts, Rucqueer, Rueckers, Ruekaerts, Ruijkers, Rukkers, Rycardt]. Flemish family of harpsichord and virginal makers. In the 16th, 17th and 18th centuries their instruments influenced the manufacture of stringed keyboard instruments throughout western Europe, and during the 20th-century revival of harpsichord making their sound has been highly regarded and emulated.

1. The family. 2. The instruments.

1. THE FAMILY. It seems likely that the family originated in Germany: a merchant named Hans Ruckers whose name appears in documents dating from 1530 is described as from 'Weyssenburg', and a German organ builder named Arnold Rucker was depicted by Dürer when he visited Antwerp in 1520.

(1) **Hans Ruckers** (b Mechelen, between c1540 and c1550; d Antwerp, 1598). He was married in 1575; two of his sons later followed him as harpsichord makers, and his daughter Catharina married into the COUCHET family of instrument makers. In 1579 Hans Ruckers became a member of the Guild of St Luke, the Antwerp arts guild; Antwerp citizenship was usually a condition of membership of the guild and since Ruckers did not become a full citizen until 1594 he may previously have lived outside Antwerp as an 'outside citizen'. In 1584 he rented a house in the Jodestraat of Antwerp, a few metres from where Rubens lived; in 1597 he bought the property. From the marriages that his children and grandchildren made into Catholic families it may be inferred that Ruckers himself was Catholic; one of his children was baptized secretly during the short period of Protestant rule in Antwerp, and his business continued during the religious persecution which affected other builders, some of whom had to leave the city.

The work of Hans Ruckers resembles that of older builders such as Hans Bos and Marten van der Biest, and even in some respects that of Hans Grauwels, but it is not known whether he learnt his craft with any of these makers. Links between Ruckers and Van der Biest are known: Van der Biest (although he seems to have been a Protestant) was a witness at Ruckers's wedding, and a man from the Ruckers workshop joined Van der Biest in Ammsterdam (where he began building after losing his property in Antwerp) after 1585; no link between Ruckers and any other maker is known.

Hans Ruckers built the various parts of his instruments separately and numbered them for later identification and assembly (where an instrument has parts with discrepant numbering it is likely that it was made after his time from parts of different instruments). After assembly he would finish the instrument (according to the report of a lawsuit in 1594 relating to events in 1585) by means of 'the "secret" and his craft' and by stringing, voicing and 'signing it with the usual mark' (his initials worked into the rose of the instrument). The few surviving instruments by Hans Ruckers are mostly virginals from the 1580s and 1590s (see VIRGINAL, figs.4 and 5), now in Berlin, Bruges, New York, Paris and New Haven (Yale University). Although he is known to have been an organ builder (he was paid for work on the organ of the St Jacobskerck and of Antwerp Cathedral from 1591 onwards), no example built by him is known.

(2) Joannes [Hans, Jan] **Ruckers** (*b* Antwerp, baptized 15 Jan 1578; *d* Antwerp, 24 April 1643). The eldest son of (1) Hans Ruckers, he married a granddaughter of the composer Hubert Waelrant. On his father's death he became a partner in the business with his brother, (3) Andreas Ruckers (i), but in 1608 Joannes bought out his brother to become sole owner. The ledgers of the Guild of St Luke record the entry in 1611 of 'Hans Rukers, sone, claversigmaker', evidently Joannes Ruckers; from 1616 he served the archdukes of the Netherlands in Brussels as a builder of organs and harpsichords (in 1623 he shared with Jan Breughel, Rubens and two others the privilege of being excused service in the civic guard). About 1627 his nephew Joannes Couchet joined the Ruckers workshop. In 1656 the house was owned by Joannes Ruckers's grandson, a cloth merchant, and it seems likely that no instruments were made there after Joannes Ruckers died in 1643. His more than 35 extant instruments are now in Berlin, Brussels, Edinburgh, London, Paris and elsewhere.

(3) Andreas [Andries] **Ruckers** (i) (*b* Antwerp, baptized 15 Aug 1579; *d* Antwerp, after 1645). Second son of (1) Hans Ruckers. He and his brother learnt their craft from their father. In 1605 he married. It is not known where he moved after he sold his share in the workshop to his brother in 1608, but in 1616 he seems to have lived 'bij Kerckhof, bij den scoenkramen' (now the Groenplaats en Schoenmarkt; the house has not been identified). In 1644 he lived in Huidevettersstrate, probably as a tenant. He was still alive in September 1645, and references to an Andreas Ruckers as godfather to his daughter Anna's children in 1651 and 1654 may be to him. He does not appear in the records of the Guild of St Luke, but Jan Moretus, dean of the guild, mentioned him as a member in 1616–17, and in 1619 the guild ordered a harpsichord from him. Instruments made or signed by him, dated between 1608 and 1644, are now in Antwerp, Berlin, Boston, Bruges, Brussels, Cincinnati, Edinburgh, The Hague, Leipzig, London, Munich, Nuremberg, Paris, Washington, New Haven (Yale University; *see* HARPSICHORD, fig.5) and elsewhere.

(4) Andreas [Andries] **Ruckers** (ii) (*b* Antwerp, baptized 31 March 1607; *d* Antwerp, before 1667). Only son of (3) Andreas Ruckers (i). He married about 1637, and the mention in 1638 (in the records of the Guild of St Luke) of 'Rickart, claversingelmaker, wijnmeester' may refer to him. He probably learnt his craft in his father's workshop: an inscription dated 1644 refers to his father as 'Andreas, den Ouden', an indication that they were both active in that year. At least seven instruments by Andreas Ruckers (ii) survive from the 1640s and early 1650s. They are in Boston, Copenhagen, Leipzig, London, Nuremberg, Paris and Peeblesshire, and are the last instruments made by this branch of the family.

1. Muselar virginal, probably by Andreas Ruckers (i), in the painting 'The Music Lesson' (1665–70) by Jan Vermeer in the Royal Collection, Windsor Castle

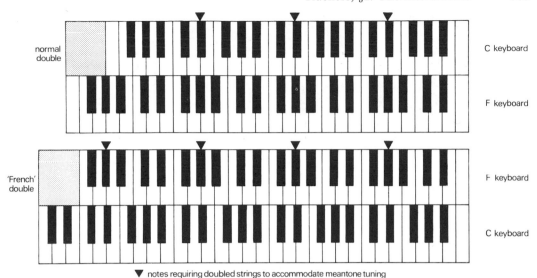

▼ notes requiring doubled strings to accommodate meantone tuning

2. Comparison of the keyboards of the normal and the extended 'French' double-manual harpsichords by Ruckers

Two virginals (in Namur and New York) have roses, with the initials 'CR', that are somewhat like other Ruckers roses. They are built in the Ruckers tradition, are decorated with 17th-century features, and incorporate subsequent alterations. They may have been originally the work of Christoffel Ruckers, an organ player living around the middle of the 16th century, who, however, has not been identified as a member of the main Ruckers family.

2. THE INSTRUMENTS. The extant Ruckers virginals are, with the exception of one six-sided virginal made by (1) Hans Ruckers in 1591, all rectangular in shape with the keyboard on one of the long sides and the strings running almost parallel to the long direction of the instrument. These virginals were made in at least five different sizes depending on their pitch, the larger instruments being 6 Flemish feet (170 cm) long and the smallest slightly less than 3 Flemish feet (79·5 cm). Most of these different sizes of virginal were made in two different types called spinetten and muselars. The spinetten had their keyboard placed towards the left-hand side of the instrument and were rather bright in sound since the strings were plucked near their ends. But the muselars, with their keyboard placed to the right (see fig.1), had a round, 'plummy' sound since the strings were plucked nearer to their middle. The most elaborate virginals combined two instruments, one at octave and one at unison pitch; when the octave instrument was positioned on top of the larger, the actions would couple and play together from the keyboard of the large virginal. The octave instrument was, however, normally stored in an empty space beside the keyboard of the unison virginal from which it was slid for playing; for this reason it was called 'the mother with the child'.

Unlike the virginals, which had only one set of strings each, Ruckers harpsichords had two sets, one an octave above the other. The single-manual harpsichord had a register of jacks for each set of strings. The double-manual harpsichords were unlike such instruments found today in that the two keyboards were not aligned but were positioned to sound a 4th apart. The manuals were completely uncoupled and each activated its own two rows of jacks, thus giving four rows of jacks altogether. When one manual was being used the jacks of the other manual were disengaged. Thus a Ruckers double-manual harpsichord served as two instruments in one, playable at either of two pitches a 4th apart. The Ruckers family also built compound instruments, combining a single- or double-manual harpsichord with a small virginal filling the space normally left outside the bentside of the harpsichord (for illustrations of these instrument types *see* HARPSICHORD and VIRGINAL).

The largest, 6', virginals, most of the single-manual harpsichords, and the upper manual of the normal double-manual harpsichords must all have sounded within about a semitone of modern pitch. This pitch will subsequently be referred to as 'reference pitch'. The smaller sizes of virginal were made at pitches which sounded a tone, a 4th, a 5th and an octave above reference. The lower manual of a normal double-manual harpsichord sounded at a pitch a 4th below reference, and at least one surviving single-manual harpsichord (see catalogue below, (*a*)1612 HR) was made sounding a 5th below reference pitch. The normal compass of the Ruckers keyboard is from C/E (short octave) to *c'''*, except that the quart virginal and the special single-manual harpsichord sounding a quint below reference both had C/E to *d'''* compasses. In addition special extended-compass instruments were made, apparently for export outside Flanders. Single-manual instruments ((*a*)1637 IR and 1639 IR) with chromatic basses to C were probably made for export to England. Extended-compass double harpsichords with a chromatic lower-manual keyboard *G'* to *c'''* and an *F* to *f'''* chromatic upper manual were also made, and the pitch relation between the keyboards of these instruments is the reverse of that of the normal Ruckers double (i.e. with the lower manual at reference pitch and the upper manual pitched a 4th below). This type of instrument seems to have been made specially for customers in France (1616 HR, (*d*)1627 IR and (*b*)1628 IR); the lower-manual compass fits the music of Chambonnières and Louis Couperin, and the upper manual duplicates early French organ pitch and compass; see fig.2.

Ruckers practice was to write a number on many of

3. *Soundboard roses used by members of the Ruckers family.* (*a*) *Hans Ruckers: angel's right wing present, initials have rather flattened surface, diameter 65 mm;* (*b*)–(*e*) *Joannes Ruckers:* (*b*) *angel's right wing missing, initials have rounded upper surface, used in all types of instruments, c1596–1616;* (*c*) *virginal,* (*d*) *single-manual harpsichord and* (*e*) *double-manual harpsichord roses used by Joannes Ruckers after c1611;* (*f*), (*g*) *Andreas Ruckers* (*i*): *used in all types of instruments*

the action parts and on the case of each instrument as it was being made. The single virginals were marked with the length of the instrument in Flemish feet (6, 5, 4½, 4), the 'mother' and 'child' virginals were marked 'M' and 'k' ('Moeder' and 'kind'), and single- and double-manual harpsichords were marked 'St' ('Staartstuk': 'tailpiece'). Underneath these marks the serial number was written, a separate serial being used for each type of instrument. The existence of these numbers has made it possible for some undated instruments to be assigned an approximate date and for the rate of production to be estimated. (3) Andreas Ruckers (i), for example, made about 12 to 14 instruments a year.

The importance of Ruckers instruments lies in their remarkable sound, which is the result of their extremely sophisticated design. The lengths, gauges and materials of the strings were chosen with great care. Both soundboard and bridges were made of good materials and were carefully and accurately tapered to give the right thickness and stiffness in each part of the range. Also, the area of radiating soundboard was contrived to give an even balance between the bass, tenor and treble parts of the compass. The resulting sound is rich and resonant without any part of the register dominating another.

The original decoration of Ruckers instruments was rather elaborate. Block-printed paper patterns (with motifs taken from Renaissance pattern books) were placed inside the key-well (above the keys) and above the soundboard around the inside of the case. These patterned papers were also sometimes used inside the lid in conjunction with a repeating wood-grained paper on which Latin mottoes were printed (see fig.1); or

sometimes the insides of the lids were beautifully painted by contemporary artists such as Rubens, Jan Breughel and Van Balen. The outsides of the instruments were painted with an imitation of marble or sometimes of huge jewels held in place by an iron strapwork. The soundboards were embellished with tempera paintings of flowers, birds, scampi, insects, snails, fruit and the like. The date was also painted somewhere on the soundboard or wrest plank.

Decorative gilded roses placed in the soundboards incorporate the initials and trade mark of the builder, and are surrounded by a wreath or spray of flowers painted on the soundboard. All the roses of the Ruckers family represent an angel playing a harp, with the initials of the builder on either side of the angel. The exact posture of the angel and the layout and modelling of the rose varies from one member of the family to the other (see fig.3) and serves as one of the methods of determining the authorship of the instrument. The roses of (1) Hans Ruckers and the early type of rose used by (2) Joannes Ruckers are virtually identical, both having the initials HR; but the right wing of the angel of the former's rose is clearly visible, whereas it is missed in the rose of the latter. After joining the Guild of St Luke (1611) (2) Joannes Ruckers gradually stopped using the HR rose and began to use an array of IR roses, different designs and sizes being used for virginals, single-manual and double-manual harpsichords. The roses of (3) Andreas Ruckers (i) and (4) Andreas Ruckers (ii) are very similar to each other, but differ in numerous subtle details. A number of instruments, signed simply 'ANDREAS RVCKERS ME FECIT' and made after the year 1636, bear the Andreas (ii) type of rose and may therefore have been made by the younger Andreas.

Ruckers instruments were justly famous in their own day, and their sound became an ideal during the 17th and 18th centuries in almost all of northern Europe. They were often altered and extended to suit later keyboard literature, sometimes by simple, even makeshift alterations and sometimes by an elaborate rebuilding process involving the replacement of all the action parts and the extension and redecoration of the case. This process was commonly applied to double-manual harpsichords, the new keyboards being aligned to allow simultaneous use of contrasting registers. In France the process was known as *ravalement*. By leaving the original soundboard almost unaltered, the beauty of the sound could be preserved. In late 17th- and in 18th-century Europe, Ruckers instruments were more highly valued than those of any other makers. Counterfeits were made with the decoration and appearance of genuine rebuilt instruments, and existing instruments of suitable kinds were modified, given a fake label and rose, and sold at an inflated price.

Ruckers instruments are important not only for their own beauty but also because of their historical position as models for the later schools of harpsichord building. By the middle of the 18th century, the constructional methods of the indigenous schools of England, France, Germany, Flanders and the Scandinavian countries were securely based on the principles perfected by the Ruckers family. Soundboard design, action and stringing all reflect Ruckers practice, and the timbre is clearly reminiscent of Ruckers, even though characteristic also of the musical taste of the period and region.

There are now a number of well-restored Ruckers instruments, some in almost original condition, which can be heard in public concerts and on recordings. These instruments are extremely valuable as examples showing how they may once have sounded. However, restoration is not synonymous with preservation, as it nearly always involves loss as well as gain. The realization is thus growing that certain instruments should be left unrestored, in order that their extant original features may remain intact.

CATALOGUE OF EXTANT INSTRUMENTS

Introduction

Instruments are authenticated by comparing the dimensions, materials, decorations and construction marks with those of undoubted examples. Harpsichords with soundboards made from wood taken from what were probably Ruckers virginals are not included since the tapering of the resulting composite soundboard differs markedly from that of the Ruckers. Instruments dishonestly attributed to Ruckers by their makers, instruments altered and given fake inscriptions, roses, etc, and instruments referred to in the literature but otherwise lost, have not been included.

The virginals and single-manual harpsichords may be assumed originally to have had the compass C/F (short octave) to c''', four octaves, unless otherwise specified. If no alteration is noted this is also the present compass. The double-manual harpsichords originally had their keyboards pitched a 4th apart. Unless otherwise specified these instruments had an upper-manual compass of C/E to c''' (with a block of wood filling up the space of three naturals in the bass) (see fig.2) and a lower-manual compass of C/E to f'''. These compasses refer in all cases to the apparent note played and not to the note sounded. Unless otherwise noted, all double-manual instruments have been altered to align the pitch levels of their keyboards.

The pitch at which the instruments sounded is determined by comparison of the length of their treble strings. The large virginals, 6 Flemish feet in length, most of the single-manual harpsichords, and the upper manual of the normal double-manual harpsichords all have, note for note, treble strings of the same length. The pitch of these instruments is here called 'reference pitch', the pitches of the other instruments being referred to it. The 'mother' and 'child' instruments are all at reference pitch and an octave above respectively.

The virginals are referred to according to their length in Flemish feet. The Flemish *voet* or foot had 11 *duimen* or inches, and each *duim* was about 2·6 cm long. The Flemish foot is thus about 28·4 cm instead of the 30·5 of the English foot. The mother virginals are 6' instruments and the child virginals are of the spinett type. Rose types are shown in fig.3.

Date, rose and instrument type			Compass	Remarks	Location
(1) HANS RUCKERS (*b* c1540–50; *d* 1598) Rose type *a*					
	1581	HR	Muselar mother and child virginals		Beautifully decorated with hand-painted Renaissance motifs; lid painting	Metropolitan Museum of Art, New York
	1583	HR	4' spinett virginal a 5th above reference pitch	Present compass of C/E–g''/a'' is original	Unsigned except for rose; hand-painted Renaissance decoration	F. Meyer, Paris
(*a*)	1591	HR	Polygonal 6' spinett virginal		Ruckers no.30; only extant 6-sided Ruckers virginal; bridge and jack-rail not original	Gruuthuuse Museum, Bruges
(*b*)	[1591]	HR	Muselar mother and child virginals	Present compass of both is C–c''' chromatic	Kbds and nameboard of mother are modern; only lid painting dated	Skinner Collection, Yale U.
	1594	HR	1-manual hpd with octave virginal in bentside	Present hpd C–c''' chromatic; virginal C/E–g''/a'' is original	Virginal has geometric rose	Kunstgewerbmuseum, Schloss Köpenick, Berlin
(2) JOANNES RUCKERS (*b* 1578; *d* 1643) Rose type *b*					
	1595	HR	Child virginal	Present compass C–d''' chromatic	Case and keys much altered; soundboard painting not original	Cincinnati Museum of Art

Date, rose and instrument type	Compass	Remarks	Location
1598 HR 6' spinett virginal	Present compass G'/B'–c'''	Ruckers no.6/61; papier-mâché rose; early example of paper decorations	formerly Countess de Chambure, Paris
(a) [1599] HR Spinett mother and child virginal		Ruckers nos.M/15 and k/15; date estimated from these; only extant spinett double virginal; paper decorations in excellent condition	Castello Sforzesco, Milan
(b) 1599 HR 2-manual hpd	Present compass F'–f'''	Much altered; earliest Ruckers 2-manual hpd	Händelhaus, Halle
1604 HR 5' muselar virginal a tone above reference pitch		Signed 'IOANNES ET ANDREAS RVCKERS ME FECERVNT'; papier-mâché rose	Brussels Museum no.2927
1610 HR Muselar mother and child virginals	Both instruments now C–f''' chromatic	Numbered M/23 and k/23; case much altered and redecorated	Brussels Museum no.275
(a) 1612 HR 2-manual hpd	Originally C/E–d'''; now G'/A'–f'''	Originally 1-manual hpd a 5th below reference pitch	Fenton House, London
(b) 1612 HR 2-manual hpd	G'/B'–d''' with split B'/E♭ key	Ruckers no.St/34; originally normal Ruckers double; soundboard painting in fine condition	Musée d'Histoire Locale, Amiens
[1614] HR 6' muselar virginal		Ruckers no.6/20; soundboard repainted and date obscured	Brussels Museum no.2930
1616 HR Extended-compass 2-manual hpd	Originally F–f''' and G'–c'''; now F'–a''/b''	Ruckers no.St/17; aligned extended 2-manual hpd; still only 2 choirs (1 × 8', 1 × 4')	M. Nirouet, Paris

Rose types: c virginal rose; d 1-manual hpd rose; e 2-manual hpd rose

Date, rose and instrument type	Compass	Remarks	Location
n.d. IR 1-manual hpd with octave virginal in bentside		Kbds and bridges not original; rose c in virginal; rose d in hpd	Berlin Museum no.2232
1612 IR 2-manual hpd	Present compass F'–f'''	18th-century *ravalement* has left much of Ruckers's work intact	Paris Conservatoire
1617 IR 2-manual hpd with ?virginal rose	Present compass G'–f'''	English *ravalement*, painted case and lid	R. Johnson, Los Angeles
(a) 1618 IR Child virginal		Ruckers no.k/5; block-printed papers in excellent condition	Paris Conservatoire
(b) 1618 IR 2-manual hpd	Present compass G'/B'–d'''	Ruckers no.St/12; added keys taken from an Andreas Ruckers hpd; nut position not original	Schloss Cappenberg, Westphalia
(c) 1618 IR 2-manual hpd	Present compass C–d''' chromatic	Soundboard, bridges, keys, decoration etc by J. C. Fleischer, 1724	Kulturhistoriska Museet, Lund
1619 IR 2-manual hpd with quint virginal in bentside	Hpd G'/B' to c'''; virginal C/E–c'''	Most of hpd, incl. soundboard, not original	Brussels Museum no.2935
1620 IR 6' muselar virginal	Present compass C–f''' chromatic	Heavily restored	New England Conservatory of Music, Boston, Mass.
1622 IR 6' muselar virginal	Present compass C–f''' chromatic		Metropolitan Museum of Art New York
1624 IR 2-manual hpd	Present compass G'/A'–d'''	GS rose not original; soundboard painting in exceptional condition; French keys and action	Count Xavier de Sade, Condé en Brie
(a) [1627] IR Muselar mother and child virginals		Ruckers nos.M/33 and k/33; date estimated from these	Harding Museum, Chicago
(b) 1627 IR 1-manual hpd	Present compass C–e''' chromatic	Widened case and key-frame; now 2 × 8'	Berlin Museum no.2227
(c) 1627 IR 2-manual hpd	Present compass G'–c'''	Alignment dated 1701; some original papers	P. de la Raudière, Château de Villebon, Eure-et-Loir
(d) 1627 IR 2-manual hpd, originally of extended compass	Present compass F'–f'''	*Petit ravalement* had G'–d''' aligned kbds by builder who altered 1632 IR	C. Mercier-Ythier, Paris
(a) 1628 IR Mother muselar virginal	Present compass C/D–f'''	Numbered M/34; marquetry veneer on case a later addition	Brussels Museum no.2926
(b) 1628 IR 2-manual hpd, originally of extended compass	Present compass G'–d'''	Important hpd with decoration and compass contemporary with F. Couperin	Versailles Palace
1629 IR 4½' spinett virginal a 4th above reference pitch	C/E–d''' compass is original	Ruckers no.4½/11; has its original jacks	Brussels Museum no.2511
1632 IR 2-manual hpd, originally a normal 1-manual hpd	Present compass F'–e'''	Elaborate Louis XV decoration; *ravalement* by same builder as (b) 1628 IR	Musée d'Histoire et d'Archéologie, Neuchâtel
1636 IR 6' muselar virginal	Present compass C–f''' chromatic	Ruckers no.6/70; papers not original; bridges moved and repinned	Harvard U., Cambridge, Mass.
(a) 1637 IR 1-manual hpd	Present compass A'–f''' (originally C–c''' chromatic)	English *ravalement* and decoration; restored to playing condition	Russell Collection, U. of Edinburgh
(b) 1637 IR 2-manual hpd	Original (unaligned kbds)	Ruckers no.St/14; kbds aligned 18th century; restored to original state 1972; the only playable non-aligned 2-manual hpd	Museo dei Strumenti Musicali, Rome
(a) 1638 IR 6' muselar virginal	Present compass C–d''' chromatic	Ruckers no.6/68; has its original lid papers	Brussels Museum no.2933
(b) 1638 IR 2-manual hpd	Original (unaligned kbds)	Ruckers no.St/41; fine lid painting and paper decorations in good condition	Russell Collection, U. of Edinburgh

Date, rose and instrument type			Compass	Remarks	Location
1639	IR	1-manual hpd	Original compass C–d''' chromatic; kbd missing	The only extant example of this unusual chromatic compass	Victoria and Albert Museum, London
1640	IR	2-manual hpd	Present compass G'/B'–c'''	Ruckers no.St/14; fine lid painting; restored to playing condition	Erbdrostenhof, Münster
(a) 1642	IR	5' muselar virginal a tone above reference pitch		Has IR rose of design similar to Joannes Couchet virginal rose	Musikhistoriska Museet, Stockholm
(b) 1642	IR	2-manual hpd	Present compass G'/B'–d'''	Fine lid painting	H. Gough, New York

(3) ANDREAS RUCKERS (i) (b 1579; d after 1645)
Rose type f unless otherwise noted

Date, rose and instrument type			Compass	Remarks	Location
n.d.	AR	Child virginal	Present compass C/E–d'''	Kbds not original; decoration in style of an early work of (3) Andreas Ruckers (i)	Cincinnati Museum of Art
[1604]	AR	1-manual hpd	Kbd missing	Ruckers no.St/2; date estimated from this	Vleeshuis Museum, Antwerp
1608	AR	2-manual hpd	Present compass G'/B'–d''	Ruckers no.St/19; converted to pf in 18th century; nut positions altered	Russell Collection, U. of Edinburgh
1609	AR	1-manual hpd	Present compass C–d''' chromatic	Soundboard painting in fine condition; English action and veneered case	P. Williams, Edinburgh
1610	AR	4½' muselar virginal a 4th above reference pitch		Ruckers no.4x/35; rose not original	Museum of Fine Arts no.295, Boston, Mass.
1611	AR	6' muselar virginal		Ruckers no.6/16; has its original stand	Vleeshuis Museum, Antwerp
(a) 1613	AR	4' spinett virginal a 5th above reference pitch		Ruckers no.4/11	Brussels Museum no.274
(b) 1613	AR	4' spinett virginal a 5th above reference pitch		Ruckers no.4/40	Brussels Museum no.2928
1614	AR	2-manual hpd	Present compass A'–e'''	English ravalement, action and veneered case	L. Elmhirst, Dartington Hall, Devon
1615	AR	2-manual hpd	Keys missing; originally normal 2-manual hpd	Ruckers no.?4(0); has its original paper decorations and unusual marbled exterior	Vleeshuis Museum, Antwerp
1617	AR	6' spinett virginal	Present compass C–f''' chromatic	Ruckers no.6/23	Deutsches Museum, Munich
1618	AR	1-manual hpd		Ruckers no.St/1; has original kbds, scalings; 1 × 8', 1 × 4'	Berlin Museum no.2224
(a) 1620	AR	4' spinett virginal a 5th above reference pitch		Ruckers no.4/69; has its original printed papers and key arcades	Smithsonian Institution, Washington, DC
(b) 1620	AR	6' muselar virginal	Present compass C–c''' chromatic	Ruckers no.6/27	Brussels Museum no.1597
(c) 1620	AR	2-manual hpd	Present compass G'/B'–f'''	Ruckers no.St/68; has its original stand	Berlin Museum no.2230
(d) 1620	AR	6' muselar virginal	Present compass C–g''' chromatic	Much altered; bridges not original; many original papers	Mme Labeyrie, Gif-sur Yvette
1624	AR	1-manual hpd	Present compass F'–f'''	Originally a normal 2-manual hpd of normal specification	Gruuthuuse Museum, Bruges
[1626]	AR	Child virginal	Present compass C/D–c'''	Ruckers no.k/36; date estimated from this	Sterckshof Museum, Deurne, Belgium
1627	AR	1-manual hpd a 5th above reference pitch		Ruckers no.4/St; decorations in excellent condition; original stand	Gemeentemuseum, The Hague
1628	AR	2-manual hpd	Present compass A'–d'''	Formerly attrib. (2) Joannes Ruckers but in style of (3) Andreas Ruckers (i)	V. Pilkington, Colares, Portugal
1632	AR	4' spinett virginal a 5th above reference pitch	Present compass C–f''' chromatic	Ruckers no.4/38; bridge position and much else altered	Brussels Museum no.1593
(a) 1633	AR	6' muselar virginal	Present compass C–f''' chromatic	Ruckers no.6/70; added keys from another 6' virginal	Brussels Museum no.4600
(b) 1633	AR	1-manual hpd	Present compass C/D–d'''	Ruckers no.St/41; originally 2-manual hpd	Karl-Marx-Universität, Leipzig
1634	AR	Child virginal	Present compass C–a'' chromatic		formerly Countess de Chambure, Paris
1635	AR	1-manual hpd	Present compass C/D–c'''	Much of soundboard missing; lid papers and some case papers extant	M. Thomas, London
1636	AR	2-manual hpd	Present compass F'–f'''	Originally 1-manual hpd C/E–c'''; much altered; ravalement probably by Hemsch	M. Thomas, London
1637	AR	1-manual hpd		Numbered with both St/23 and St/24; original disposition and decoration; rose not original	Germanisches National-museum, Nuremberg
(a) 1639	AR	Child virginal		Ruckers no.k/59; rose type g	Gemeentemuseum, The Hague
(b) 1639	AR	1-manual hpd		Converted to a double, 18th-century, now back to a single; rose type g	Gemeentemuseum, The Hague
(a) 1640	AR	1-manual hpd	Present compass C–c'' chromatic	English kbd and action; original decorations; rose type g	Skinner Collection, Yale U.
(b) 1640	AR	2-manual hpd	Keys missing	Ruckers no.St/2; heavy gessoed decoration not original	Musée de Croix, Namur, Belgium

Date, rose and instrument type			Compass	Remarks	Location
1634	AR	5' muselar virginal a tone above reference pitch	Present compass C–c''' chromatic	Ruckers no.5/37; rose missing, but decorations in the style of (3) Andreas Ruckers (i)	Gemeentemuseum, The Hague
1644	AR	1-manual hpd	Present compass C–c''' chromatic	Ruckers no.St/16; original decorations; signed 'ANDREAS RVCKERS DEN OVDEN ME FECIT'	Vleeshuis Museum, Antwerp

(4) ANDREAS RUCKERS (ii) (b 1607; d before 1667)
Rose type g. The distinction between the instruments of (3) Andreas Ruckers (i) and (4) Andreas Ruckers (ii) is not clear. Instruments dated after 1637, when (4) Andreas Ruckers (ii) entered the Guild of St Luke, have rose type g and many show positive signs of being by the younger Andreas.

1644	AR	Muselar mother and child virginals	Both instruments now C/D–c'''	Child a modern replacement	Karl-Marx-Universität, Leipzig
(a) 1646	AR	1-manual hpd	Present compass C–f''' chromatic		W. P. Ross, Boston, Mass.
(b) 1646	AR	2-manual hpd	Present compass F'–f'''	French ravalement signed 'Refait par Pascal Taskin, Paris 1780' of normal 2-manual hpd	formerly Countess de Chambure, Paris
1648	AR	1-manual hpd	Present compass C–d''' chromatic	Ruckers no.St/69; original decorations; English kbds	Musikhistorisk Museum, Copenhagen
(a) [1651]	AR	1-manual hpd	Present compass C–d''' chromatic	Ruckers no.St/2; original decorations; date ?1641	P. Maxwell-Stuart, Traquair House, Peebles-shire
(b) 1651	AR	2-manual hpd	Present compass G'/A'–f'''	Originally 1-manual hpd; English ravalement	Victoria and Albert Museum, London
1654	AR	2-manual hpd	Present compass G'/B'–f'''	Originally 1-manual hpd	Germanisches National-museum, Nuremberg

BIBLIOGRAPHY

FétisB
K. Douwes: *Grondig ondersoek van de toonen der musijk* (Franeker, 1699/R1970)
Q. van Blankenburg: *Elementa musica* (The Hague, 1739)
J. Verschuere Reynvaan: *Muzykaal kunstwoordenboek* (Amsterdam, 1795)
P. Génard: 'Les grandes familles artistiques d'Anvers', *Revue d'histoire et d'archéologie*, i (1859), 458
L. de Burbure: *Recherches sur les facteurs de clavecins et les luthiers d'Anvers, depuis le seizième jusqu'au dix-neuvième siècle* (Brussels, 1863)
——: Notes on Antwerp keyboard instrument makers (MS, *B-Aa*)
P. Rombouts and T. van Lerius: *De liggeren en andere historische archieven der Antwerpsche Sint Lucasgilde* (Antwerp, 1872–6/R1961)
E. vander Straeten: *La musique aux Pays-Bas avant le XIXᵉ siècle*, iii (Brussels, 1875/R1969), 325ff; v (Brussels, 1880/R1969), 392ff
M. Rooses and P. Rombouts: *Boek gehouden door Jan Moretus II, als deken der St Lucasgilde (1616–1617)* (Antwerp, 1878)
E. Closson: 'L'ornementation en papier imprimé des clavecins anversois', *Revue belge d'archéologie et d'histoire de l'art*, ii (1932), 105
D. F. L. Scheurleer: 'Over het ornament en de authenticiteit van bedrukte papierstrooken in twee clavierinstrumenten', *Mededeelingen van den dienst voor kunsten en wetenschappen der gemeente 's Gravenhage*, vi (1939), 411
J.-A. Stellfeld: *Bronnen tot de geschiedenis der Antwerpsche clavecimbel-en orgelbouwers in de XVIde en XVIIde eeuwen* (Antwerp, 1942)
——: 'Johannes Ruckers de jongere en de koninklijke kapel te Brussel', *Hommage à Charles van den Borren: mélanges* (Antwerp, 1945), 283
S. Marcuse: 'Transposing Keyboards in Extant Flemish Harpsichords', *MQ*, xxxviii (1952), 414
D. Boalch: *Makers of the Harpsichord and Clavichord, 1440 to 1840* (London, 1956, 2/1973)
R. Russell: *The Harpsichord and Clavichord* (London, 1959, rev. 2/1973 by H. Schott)
E. Ripin: 'The Two-manual Harpsichord in Flanders before 1650', *GSJ*, xxi (1968), 33
J. Lambrechts-Douillez: 'Biographical Notes on the Ruckers–Couchet Family', *GSJ*, xxii (1969), 98
J. Barnes: 'The Flemish Instruments of the Russell Collection, Edinburgh', *Restauratieproblemen van Antwerpse klavecimbels: Museum Vleeshuis 1970*, 35
H. Bédard: 'Report on the Restoration of the Virginal by J. Couchet, 1650', ibid, 35
A. Berner: 'Der Ruckers-Bestand des Berliner Musikinstrumenten-Museums: Bemerkungen zu den Konstruktionen', ibid, 53
J. Lambrechts-Douillez: 'The Ruckers–Couchet Instrument in the Museum Vleeshuis: Restoration or Copy?', ibid, 44
J. H. van der Meer: 'Flämische Kielklaviere im Germanischen National-museum, Nürnberg', ibid, 63
E. Ripin: 'Antwerp Harpsichord-building: the Current State of Research', ibid, 71
R. Schütze: 'Die akustischen und klanglichen Veränderungen von Ruckers' Cembali durch die späteren Erweiterungen im Tonumfang (ravalement)', ibid, 23

M. Skowroneck: 'Zu welchem Zweck und Ziel, mit welcher Absicht werden historische Musikinstrumente restauriert?', ibid, 28
G. Thibault de Chambure: 'Les clavecins et épinettes des Ruckers au Musée instrumental du Conservatoire national supérieur de musique', ibid, 77
J. Lambrechts-Douillez: *Sic transit gloria mundi: Antwerpse klavecimbels in het Museum Vleeshuis* (Antwerp, 1970)
——: 'Documents dealing with the Ruckers Family and Antwerp Harpsichord Building', *Keyboard Instruments: Studies in Keyboard Organology*, ed. E. Ripin (Edinburgh, 1971), 36
——: 'Hans Ruckers and his Workshop', *Der klangliche Aspekt beim Restaurieren von Saitenklavieren: Graz 1971*, 41
J. H. van der Meer: 'Beiträge zum Cembalo-Bau der Familie Ruckers', *Jb des Staatlichen Instituts für Musikforschung preussischen Kulturbesitz* (Berlin, 1971), 100–53
——: 'More about Flemish Two-manual Harpsichords', *Keyboard Instruments: Studies in Keyboard Organology*, ed. E. Ripin (Edinburgh, 1971), 47
W. R. Thomas and J. J. K. Rhodes: 'Harpsichord Strings, Organ Pipes and the Dutch Foot', *Organ Yearbook*, iv (1973), 112
G. G. O'Brien: 'The Numbering System of Ruckers Instruments', *Bulletin of the Brussels Instrument Museum*, iv (1974), 75
——: 'Ioannes and Andreas Ruckers', *Early Music*, vii (1979), 453
JEANNINE LAMBRECHTS-DOUILLEZ (1)
G. GRANT O'BRIEN (2)

Rückert, (Johann Michael) Friedrich (*b* Schweinfurt, 16 May 1788; *d* Neusess, nr. Coburg, 31 Jan 1866). German poet. After studying law and philosophy at Würzburg, Heidelberg and Göttingen he embarked on an academic career before undertaking various journeys and temporary jobs as schoolmaster and editor. He took up oriental languages and, with the help of King Ludwig I of Bavaria, was appointed professor at Erlangen. He moved to Berlin in 1841 and retired in 1848.

Rückert published a grammar and a study of Persian poetry, as well as a number of translations from oriental languages that were much read and exerted a lasting influence. He also wrote a number of imitations of Eastern poetry, and translated into German from several European languages. His biblical and historical plays were too undramatic to meet with much success. During the wars of liberation he wrote collections of patriotic songs, but it is in his love lyrics (*Liebesfrühling*, 1823) that he found his most personal note – poems set by, among others, Schubert (4 lieder) and the Schumanns (21 lieder, 5 duets and partsongs by Robert; 5 lieder by Clara). Mahler's *Kindertotenlieder* and five further songs from 1902 are the best-known 20th-century Rückert settings; other lieder to his texts are by Richard Strauss (6, and choral works), Pfitzner (2), Reger (3) and Berg (2).

BIBLIOGRAPHY

K. Goedeke: *Grundriss zur Geschichte der deutschen Dichtung*, viii (Dresden, 2/1905), 142–77
F. Golfing: *Rückert als Lyriker* (diss., U. of Basle, 1935)
M. Duttle: *Rückerts Verskunst* (diss., U. of Würzburg, 1937)
E. Witzig: *F. Rückert: die Eigenart seines lyrischen Schaffens* (diss., U. of Zurich, 1948)
H. Prang: *Friedrich Rückert* (Schweinfurt, 1963)

PETER BRANSCOMBE

Rückführung (Ger.). RETRANSITION; *see also* SONATA FORM.

Rückpositiv (Ger.: 'back positive'). The little organ placed at the organist's back, in the front of the gallery; the second main manual of all major organs from 1400 to 1700. In the smaller organs of most countries it was replaced by the *Brustwerk*, the Choir organ or the Swell, while in Italy there was only ever a handful of examples. The name has varied widely: CHAIR ORGAN, le Positif, Cadireta, Rugwerk since *c*1600, and many others before, such as *organum parvum* (Rouen, 1387), *positivum tergale* (Arnaut de Zwolle, *c*1450), *clavier met positieff* (Delft, 1461), *orgue a la cadira* (Perpignan, 1516), *positiff zu rück* (Schlick, 1511) and *achter den rug* (Amsterdam, 1539). It is by no means certain when any so-called 'little organ' was a *Rückpositiv* and when it was simply a small organ in another part of the church concerned. *Den stoel* or *im Stuhl* was very common, though this too may not always have denoted *Rückpositiv*, since *im Stuhl* could mean 'in the foot of the main case'. Praetorius, Schnitger, etc, wrote *Rückpositiff*, but in areas where it was unfamiliar authors invented more prolix phrases: 'unum parvum organum retro magistri ipsorum tangentis' (Aix, 1489, and Barcelona, 1459) or 'un organetto da concerti dietro le spalle dell'Organista' (Banchieri, 1608). Tonally, the department was always a contrast to the *Hauptwerk*, firstly by having the Mixture of its *Blockwerk* the sooner separated off (Delft, 1458), then by having more single ranks on a slider chest, later still by having more delicate voicing and scaling (Werckmeister, 1698); but the last characteristic had long been known, judging by Arnaut's reference to its 'sweetness' (*dulcedo*). In some areas of Holland, Denmark, etc, it continued to be built until the 1870s, but early in the 18th century central German builders dispensed with it, giving its solo, accompanimental, continuo, colouristic and contrasting functions to the *Oberwerk*. Despite the dangers of heavy mechanism, it is still the most important secondary manual for all classical organ repertories.

PETER WILLIAMS

Rucqueer. *See* RUCKERS family.

Ructis, Ar. de. *See* RUTTIS, AR. DE.

Rudall, Carte. English firm of wind instrument makers and flute specialists, successors to an unbroken line of makers and dealers since the 18th century. The firm was absorbed by Boosey & Hawkes in 1955, but the name has been preserved and is still renowned.

Many of the significant earlier dates can be deduced only from London parish rate books and addresses stamped on surviving instruments. The sequence is claimed to have begun in 1747 with George II's Hanoverian bandmaster, Kramer. He is said to have taken into partnership one Thomas Key, of whom nothing is recorded except for his working dates (1799–1853) and a large number of instruments. Key's (?only) partner was from 1804 to 1808 J. B. Cramer (*see* CRAMER); thereafter he traded only as T. Key. His son Frederick was proprietor of the business from 1854 to 1858, in which year he became associated with George Rudall (1781–1871) as Key, Rudall & Co. At that time Rudall had been in partnership with the Edinburgh flute maker J. M. Rose since *c*1820, first as Rudall & Rose, and then until 1857 as Rudall, Rose & Co. In 1850 Rudall's former pupil Richard Carte (?1808–1891) joined the firm, and in 1857 his name was added to the title. Thus the partnerships of F. Key and of Carte with Rudall overlapped by one year, and a few instruments exist marked Key, Rudall, Rose, Carte & Co. Since 1871, when Rose's name dropped out, the firm has remained Rudall, Carte & Co. Besides making several esteemed models of its own design, this company has built flutes to commission; it held the British manufacturing rights in both of Boehm's flutes, and after Sax's quarrel with the Distins, it was for a time agent for the original saxophones.

For a flute by Rudall & Rose *see* FLUTE, fig.14c.

BIBLIOGRAPHY

R. S. Rockstro: *A Treatise on . . . The Flute* (London, 1890)
A. S. Rose: *Talks with Bandsmen* (London, 1895), 103f
L. G. Langwill: *An Index of Musical Wind-instrument Makers* (Edinburgh, 1960, rev. 4/1977)

PHILIP BATE

Rudbeck [Rudbeckius], **Olof** [Olaus] (the elder) (*b* Västerås, baptized 12 Dec 1630; *d* Uppsala, 17 Sept 1702). Swedish polymath, musician and composer. He became a medical student at Uppsala University in 1648 and defended his thesis there in 1652 shortly after giving a masterly demonstration, in the presence of Queen Christina, of his discovery of the lymph glands. With royal support he continued his studies at Leiden, reached the position of professor at Uppsala as early as 1658 and had his first term as rector of the university in 1661–2. His scientific activities included the laying out of a botanical garden, the editing of a gigantic but unfinished botanical work, *Campi Elysii*, and also antiquarian research. In *Atland* ('Atlantica', Uppsala, 1672–1702) he expounded his fantastic theory that Sweden was the original cradle of Western culture. His wide-ranging talents, both practical and artistic, made him an authority in a number of other fields too: he worked as an architect, engineer, builder, land surveyor, inventor and manufacturer, was also skilled in sketching and painting, had a fine bass voice and performed on several musical instruments.

Music seems to have played an important part in Rudbeck's life. He was an active musician both as a schoolboy in Västerås and at Uppsala, where he was a successful musical entertainer during royal visits. He started teaching music at an early stage in his career as professor and adopted the then new principles of the collegium musicum. Very soon he became a semi-official supervisor of musical life at the university and in the 1660s took a number of important basic steps. The university bought instruments and up-to-date printed music by e.g. Ahle, Briegel, Capricornus, Werner Fabricius, Hammerschmidt, Pfleger, Rosenmüller, Schmeltzer and Scheidt (the collection is mostly in *S-Uu*). He had eight public scholarships reserved for student musicians, thus constituting and ensuring a permanent ensemble. He also wanted to build a monumental organ in the cathedral. However, this enterprise became greatly delayed owing to practical and financial obstacles. The first organ builder engaged was incapable of putting into practice some notable inventions by Rudbeck connected with the layout of the organ, and it was not until 1698 that he saw the magnificent instrument completed by Hans Heinrich CAHMAN. In this connection Rudbeck's role was that of general manager and also master builder of the organ casework. Contemporary accounts of performances conducted or inspired by him show that he favoured a simplified version of the rather old-fashioned polychoral style, often with the alternating vocal and instrumental groups spatially deployed. Only one composition by him has been preserved, a lament for two voices and continuo in the style of Hammerschmidt, written for the funeral of Chancellor Axel Oxenstierna in 1654 (edn. in MMS, v, 1968). Rudbeck and his principal pupil, HARALD VALLERIUS, were commissioned to collect and edit the tunes of the new official Swedish hymnbook, but Vallerius seems to have done the main part of the work (the edition with music was published in 1697).

BIBLIOGRAPHY

(concerning Rudbeck's musical activities only)

C. A. Moberg: 'Musik und Musikwissenschaft an den schwedischen Universitäten', Mitteilungen der Internationalen Gesellschaft für Musikwissenschaft, i (1929), 54

——: 'Olof Rudbeck d.ä. och musiken', Rudbeck studier (Uppsala, 1930), 176–210

B. Kyhlberg: Det stora orgelbygget i Uppsala domkyrka 1664–1698 (diss., U. of Uppsala, 1953)

Å. Davidsson: 'Kring Uppsalaakademiens förvärv av musikalier på 1600-talet' [Concerning the Uppsala Academy's acquisition of 17th-century music], Nordisk tidskrift för bok- och biblioteksväsen, lvi (1969), 66–107

BENGT KYHLBERG

Rude [Rudenius, Rudenus], **Johann** (b after 1555; d ?after 1615). German lutenist and composer. He compiled an extensive collection in two books of music for eight-course solo lute, Flores musicae (Heidelberg, 1600). Son of a Leipzig Stadtpfeifer, he described himself as a student of law in his lutebook, although there is at present little else known of his activities other than that he deputized for an organist at St Thomas, Leipzig, in 1595. The lengthy dedication of the Flores musicae refers, among others, to the Elector Friedrich Wilhelm, and to Johann Ernst and August, dukes of Brunswick-Lüneburg, who may have been his patrons.

Flores musicae, which is in simple French tablature, was intended as a companion publication to Matthias Reymann's Noctes musicae (Heidelberg, 1598), and the majority of works are therefore intabulations of vocal compositions (a total of 171 secular works, mostly canzonettas and madrigals). Some 40 composers are represented, including Ferretti (13 pieces), Hassler and Vecchi (ten each), Marenzio (nine) and Gabrieli (six). 12 pieces are English. Although some of the intabulations are florid, Rude for the most part made exact transcriptions, introducing here and there interesting melodic and harmonic modifications. Flores musicae includes seven intradas, one fantasia, 30 pavan-type pieces, 21 galliards and one chorea.

If Rude composed the 29 unidentified pieces in this collection, he cannot be regarded as of great significance, though the suite-like structure of some of the pavan types is of interest.

BIBLIOGRAPHY

R. Wustmann: Musikgeschichte Leipzigs, i (Berlin, 1909)

H. B. Lobaugh: Three German Lute Books (diss., U. of Rochester, NY, 1968)

——: 'Johann Rude's Flores musicae (1600)', LSJ, xiv (1972), 1

H. B. LOBAUGH

Rudel [Rudelh, Rudel de Blaja], **Jaufre** [Jofre] (fl mid-12th century). Troubadour poet and composer. From medieval times he has been recognized particularly for the poems that he addressed to his amor de lonh ('distant love'). A single reference to him in a poem by Marcabru composed in 1147 allows at least an approximate dating of his activities, and confirms that Rudel took part in the second crusade (1147). His name appears in the sources with or without 'de Blaja' (alternative spellings Blaia, Bleja), and in his vida (for sources, see Pillet and Carstens, p.240) this becomes 'prince de Blaja'. It may be, therefore, that he was a member of the family of that name which maintained a castle on the banks of the Gironde north of Bordeaux. Persons named in his poems also confirm that he was active in the mid-12th century: the 'count of Toulouse' and 'Bertran' referred to in Non sap chantar were probably Alphonse Jourdain and his natural son who took part in the second crusade. The vida states that the object of his distant love was the Countess of Tripoli, although no such person is mentioned in any of his poems. The mystery has itself given rise to an extensive literature; perhaps the most ingenious suggestion is that the reference is not to a lady but to Jerusalem, the 'terra lonhdana' of Quan li rius (see Frank; for illustration see TROUBADOURS, TROUVÈRES, fig.1).

Of the seven poems ascribed to Rudel, four have survived with music. Lanquan li jorn is of particular interest as it was the model for Walther von der Vogelweide's celebrated 'Palästinalied' – Allerest lebe ich mir werde (see Husmann, Brunner, Van der Werf). This is the only known instance of a direct and demonstrable borrowing by a German Minnesinger of a troubadour melody. Walther's song became the model for two subsequent contrafacta, one in Latin and one in German, so that Rudel's melody directly or indirectly spawned three imitations over a period of about 300 years. All four of Rudel's surviving melodies are in bar form, contrary to normal practice in the troubadour tradition; Lanquan li jorn even includes an incipient musical refrain.

WORKS

Editions: Les chansons de Jaufré Rudel, ed. A Jeanroy, Les classiques français du moyen âge, xv (Paris, 1915, 2/1924) [J]

Der musikalische Nachlass der Troubadours, i, ed. F. Gennrich, SMM, iii, iv, xv (1958–65) [G]

Lanquan li jorn son lonc en may, PC 262.2 [contrafactum: Walther von der Vogelweide, 'Allerest lebe ich mir werde'], G 12, J 5, VanderWerf, 85

No sap chantar qui so non di, PC 262.3, G 13, J 6

Quan li rius de la fontana, PC 262.5, G 14, J 2

Quan lo rossinhols el folhos, PC 262.6, G 15, J 1

BIBLIOGRAPHY

A. Stimming: Der Troubadour Jaufré Rudel: sein Leben und seine Werke (Kiel, 1873) [edn. of texts]

E. Monaci: Poesie e vita di Jaufre Rudel (Rome, 1903) [edn. of texts]

G. Frank: 'The Distant Love of Jaufre Rudel', Modern Language Notes, lvii (1942), 528

H. Husmann: 'Das Prinzip der Silbenzählung im Lied des zentralen Mittelalters', Mf, vi (1953), 8

F. Gennrich: 'Jaufre Rudel de Blaia', MGG [edn. of Lanquan li jorn]

H. Brunner: 'Walthers von der Vogelweide Palästinalied als Kontrafaktur', Zeitschrift für deutsches Altertum und Literatur, xcii (1963), 195

J. Boutiere and A.-H. Schutz: Biographies des Troubadours (Paris, 1964), 16

H. van der Werf: *The Chansons of the Troubadours and Trouvères: a Study of the Melodies and their Relation to the Poem* (Utrecht, 1972), 85 [edn. and comparative analysis of *Lanquan li jorn*]

For further bibliography *see* TROUBADOURS, TROUVÈRES.

ROBERT FALCK

Rudel, Julius (*b* Vienna, 6 March 1921). American conductor of Austrian birth. He began his studies at the Vienna Academy of Music, but emigrated to the USA at the age of 17 and became a student at the Mannes School of Music, New York. His long association with the New York City Opera began when he joined the company as a rehearsal pianist in 1943. He made his conducting début with *Der Zigeunerbaron* in 1944, and was appointed the company's director in 1957. Meanwhile, in 1944, he had become an American citizen. Rudel has developed the City Opera into one of the best and most enterprising companies in the USA. Working with a strong commitment to the principle of true ensemble opera, he has placed an emphasis unfamiliar in New York on production values, occasionally drawing criticism for extravagance of ideas but never for dullness. The company's repertory has benefited from Rudel's ability to conduct the work of composers as diverse as Mozart, Monteverdi, Janáček and Ginastera with equal skill and sensitivity. Outside the opera house, where his gifts as an administrator have been of special value, results have been more uneven. But Rudel has enjoyed great success as musical director of the Caramoor Festival in New York state, as music adviser of Wolf Trap Farm Park for the Performing Arts near Washington, DC, and as musical director for the first four seasons of the Kennedy Center in Washington from 1971. He has conducted most of the leading American symphony orchestras and has made guest appearances in many European musical centres and in Israel. In 1961 the Austrian government awarded him its honorary insignia for Arts and Sciences, and he also holds the Grosser Verdienstkreuz der Bundesrepublik Deutschland. His records include Handel's *Giulio Cesare* with the New York City Opera, and much-praised versions of Boito's *Mefistofele* and Massenet's *Thaïs*.

BIBLIOGRAPHY

B. Fischer-Williams: 'Julius Rudel', *Music and Musicians*, xxi/7 (1973), 16

BERNARD JACOBSON

Rudén, Jan Olof (*b* Helsinki, 28 Aug 1937). Swedish musicologist of Finnish birth. He studied at Uppsala University under Ingmar Bengtsson from 1957 (fil kand 1961, fil lic 1969). Subsequently he was assistant librarian of Uppsala University library (1970–74) and in 1974 became librarian and bibliographer of the Swedish Music Information Centre, Stockholm. His work has been chiefly concerned with music bibliography, music for plucked instruments and 17th-century Swedish musical life; and he has worked on watermarks as an aid to dating. He has also prepared editions of 18th-century and earlier Swedish music for Monumenta Musicae Svecicae.

WRITINGS

'Svensk musikhistorisk bibliografi 1962–68', *STMf*, xlv (1963), 251; xlvi (1964), 237; xlvii (1965), 141; xlviii (1966), 283; xlix (1967), 259; l (1968), 181; li (1969), 209

'Käll- och litteraturförteckning i musikvetenskapliga arbeten', *STMf*, xlvi (1964), 119

'Ett nyfunnet komplement till Dübensamlingen', *STMf*, xlvii (1965), 51

Tablaturer för luta och gitarr i svenska bibliotek och samlingar: en översikt (MS, 1967)

Vattenmärken och musikforskning: presentation och tillämpning av en dateringsmetod på musikalier i handskrift i Uppsala Universitetsbiblioteks Dübensamling (n.p., 1968)

Hugo Alfvén: Musical Works: Thematic Index (Stockholm, 1972)

'Stormaktstidens 10 i topp', *STMf*, lviii/2 (1976), 25

'Per Brahe's Lute Book', *STMf*, lix (1977)

Musica intabulata svecana (in preparation) [thematic index with source descriptions of music in tablature in Sweden]

EDITIONS

with C.-A. Moberg: *Three Vocal Compositions from the Swedish Great Power Period*, MMS, v (1969)

J. M. Kraus: *Obsequial Music and Funeral Cantata for Gustav III*, MMS (in preparation)

Rudenius, Johann. *See* RUDE, JOHANN.

Rudenko, Bela (Andreyevna) (*b* Bokovo-Antratsit [now Lugansk province], 18 Aug 1933). Soviet soprano. She studied at the Odessa Conservatory under O. Blagovidova, graduating in 1956. Her operatic début was in Odessa during the 1955–6 season; from 1956 she was a soloist at the Kiev Opera. She appeared at a New York Philharmonic concert in January 1968. One of the leading opera singers of the Ukraine, she possesses a beautiful light soprano, with a virtuoso command of coloratura technique; on stage her performances are marked by their winning simplicity and sincerity. She is a notable Lyudmila (in Glinka's opera), Rosina, Gilda, Lakmé and Natasha (in Prokofiev's *War and Peace*), and has also given fine performances in operas by Ukrainian composers: Yolan in Mayboroda's *Milana*, Yarana in his *Arsenal*. She is a distinguished concert singer and recitalist, and was made a People's Artist of the USSR in 1960.

BIBLIOGRAPHY

V. Timofeyev: *Bela Andreyevna Rudenko* (Kiev, 1964)

I. M. YAMPOL'SKY

Rudenus, Johann. *See* RUDE, JOHANN.

Rudhyar, Dane [Chennevière, Daniel] (*b* Paris, 23 March 1895). American composer and writer of French origin. He studied at the Sorbonne and in 1912–13 at the Paris Conservatoire but was musically mostly self-taught. At the age of 18 he was commissioned by Durand to write a short book on Debussy. He emigrated to the USA in 1916 and moved to Southern California in 1919. While living in Hollywood he became an American citizen in 1926 under the Hindu name that heralded his future devotion to theosophy. He was a leading contributor to Cowell's *New Music Quarterly*, founded in 1927, but after 1930 dispersed his creative talents in many fields. By the mid-1970s, he was best known as an astrologer, with 15 books in print on the subject.

Musically, he was hailed in 1929 as a Skryabin disciple. Throughout his career he was an important pioneer in advocating Asian musical concepts. Despite the voluptuousness of its chords, Rudhyar's music is dominated by melodic line. He used sequences to build towards climaxes and avoided *martellato* or percussive rhythms. Rubato, poignancy and restless yearning inform nearly all his stop-and-go music. Because of his willingness to repeat himself, the titled movements of his four-movement ('tetragram') and five-movement ('pentagram') piano works sometimes sound very similar ('Salutation' and 'Pomp', for instance).

WORKS

(*selective list*)

Orch: Poèmes ironiques, 1917; Vision végétale, 1917; Dithyramb, 1919; Soul Fire, sym. poem, 1920; The Surge of Fire, sym. trilogy,

1921; Syntony no.1, 1920–22; Syntony no.2, 1921; Sinfonietta, 1928; Threnody, 1929; Hero Chants, 1930; Threshold of Light, 1934; Epithalamium, 1934; Eclogue, 1934; 5 Stanzas, str (1938); Emergence, pentagram, str, 1953; Syntony no.5, 1954; Syntony no.6, 1959

Chamber: Pf Qnt, 1919; 3 Songs without Words, fl, vn, pf/harp, 1919; Sonata, vn, pf, 1920; Solitude, str qt, 1955

Pf: Mosaics, 1918; Moments, 15 tone poems, 1924–6; Paeans, 1927; Granites, 1929; Tetragram no.1 'The Quest', 1921; Tetragram no.7 'Tendrils', 1924; Pentagram no.1 'The Summons', 1924; Pentagram no.2 'Enfoldment', 1924; Tetragram no.4 'Adolescence', 1925; Tetragram no.2 'Crucifixion', 1926; Pentagram no.3 'Release', 1926; Pentagram no.4 'The Human Way', 1926; Tetragram no.3 'Rebirth', 1927; Tetragram no.5 'Solitude', 1927; Tetragram no.8 'Primavera', 1928; Tetragram no.6 'Emergence', 1929; Syntony, 1929; Prophetic Rite (1950); Tetragram no.9 'Summer Nights', 1967; Transmutation, 1976

Songs: 3 chansons de Bilitis (Louÿs), 1918; 3 poèmes tragiques (Rudhyar), 1918; Poem (S. Yarrow), 1918; Commune (Abdul Baba), 1920; 2 Affirmations (W. de Voe), 1931; 3 Invocations (A. Bailey), 1939–40

Incidental music: The Pilgrimage Play (C. Wetherill Stevenson), 1920

Principal publishers: Birchard, Composers Facsimile Edition, New Music, Presser

WRITINGS

Claude Debussy et son oeuvre (Paris, 1913)
The Rebirth of Hindu Music (Madras, 1928)
Art as a Release of Power (New York, 1930)

BIBLIOGRAPHY

P. Rosenfeld: *An Hour with American Music* (Philadelphia, 1929), 70
A. Morang: *Dane Rudhyar: Pioneer in Creative Synthesis* (New York, 1939)
J. Shere: *Dane Rudhyar, 1895–: a Brief Biography with a Listing of Works* (San Jacinto, Calif., 1972) [pubd privately]

ROBERT STEVENSON

Rüdinger, Gottfried (*b* Lindau, Bavaria, 23 Aug 1886; *d* Gauting, nr. Munich, 17 Jan 1946). German composer and teacher. After attending the Gymnasium in Neuberg he began to study theology but from 1907 turned his interest entirely to music. He studied composition with Reger in Leipzig and church music under Wilhelm Widmann at Eichstätt Cathedral. From 1910 Rüdinger taught in Munich, first privately and then from 1920 as a member of the theory staff at the Academy of Music. He received the professorship in 1938 and continued to teach until his death. From 1916 he was also a conductor of church choirs in Berg am Laim. Much of Rüdinger's music, such as the *Romantische Serenade* op.9, shows the influence of Brahms and Reger; his vocal works make use of folksongs. Of his approximately 150 compositions, the last third (from the war years) remain unpublished.

WORKS
(selective list)

VOCAL

Stage: Ein Hirtenspiel in Liedern, op.61; Die Tegernsee im Himmel, op.100 (peasant play-opera), 1933; Berchtesgadener Sagenspiel, op.102 (children's opera); König Folkwart (fairy-tale opera); Musikantenkomödie (Singspiel)

Masses: G, op.23, chorus, org; Kleine Vokalmesse, op.26, S, A, Bar; D, op.32, S, A, Bar, org; c, op.76, chorus; C, op.115, chorus, org; F, op.143, chorus, org

Sacred cantatas: Mit Ernst, o Menschenkinder, op.43; Dich grüss ich, Fürstinnin, op.44; Maria, du betrübtes Herz, op.70

Other works: Psalm xcii, op.82, chorus, brass, perc/org; Waldkantate, op.84, solo vv, fl/vn, str trio; Sancta Maria, op.93, 1v, chamber orch; Tannenburg, oratorio, 1939; over 20 motets; over 60 lieder, some with orch, and folksong arrs.; choruses and choral folksong arrs., music for the theatre and cinema

INSTRUMENTAL

Orch: Romantische Serenade, op.9, chamber orch; Sym., op.11, vc, orch; 2 vn concs., op.33, a, op.138; Truderinger Kirchweih, op.39, pf/chamber orch; Schwäbische Musik, op.73, orch; Elegie, op.77, vn, org/orch; Sinfonietta bajuvarica, op.83; Suite, op.117, str; Gautinger Tänze, op.128; Sym., C, op.136

Chamber: Aus der Dachstude, op.3, 2 vn; 6 Skizzen, op.8, vc, pf; 2 str qts, D, op.41, G, op.126; Divertimento, op.45, wind qnt; 2 pf trios, C, op.50, G (Ein Gruss an Papa Haydn), op.51; Sonata, A, op.71, vn,

pf; Partita, op.74, 3 vn; Divertimento, g, op.75, va/cl, t sax/b cl/vc, pf

Solo inst: 4 org sonatas, g, op.4, F, op.54, b, op.68, op.136bis; 2 pf sonatas, e, op.12, G, op.28; 2 sonatinas, a, op.57, G, op.65, zither/pf; other pieces for org, pf, zither

Principal publishers: Volksverein (Munich), Wunderhorn

BIBLIOGRAPHY

L. Gerheuser: 'Gottfried Rüdinger', *ZfM*, Jg.101 (1934), 9
A. Berrsche: *Trösterin Musika* (Munich, 1949), 434ff
A. Würz: 'Rüdinger, Gottfried', *MGG*

WILLIAM D. GUDGER

Rudolf, Max (*b* Frankfurt am Main, 15 June 1902). American conductor of German birth. He began his musical studies at the age of seven, and in addition to learning the piano, organ, cello and trumpet, went on between 1914 and 1922 to study composition with Bernhard Sekles. In 1921 and 1922 he was a student at Frankfurt University and the conservatory. He had several of his chamber works performed, and he made his conducting début in March 1923 in Freiburg. Posts at the Städtisches Theater there and at Darmstadt were followed by a six-year spell as principal conductor of the German theatre in Prague. In 1929 and 1930 Rudolf appeared as guest conductor with the Berlin PO. In 1940, after a five-year residence in Göteborg, Sweden, he left Europe for the USA, first teaching in Chicago, then moving to New York, where he conducted the New Opera Company. In 1945, the year before he took American citizenship, he joined the Metropolitan Opera as conductor, remaining for 14 seasons, and distinguishing himself in the Mozart repertory; he also served as its assistant manager (1950–58). From 1958 to 1970 he was musical director of the Cincinnati SO, leavening his sensitive advocacy of the standard repertory with a number of important premières. He resigned this post to head the opera and conducting departments of the Curtis Institute in Philadelphia (1970–73), after which he resumed appearances at the Metropolitan Opera. His widely used textbook *The Grammar of Conducting* (New York, 1950) testifies to a rare grasp of the mechanics of the art: Rudolf's technique is notable in particular for his ability to subdivide the beat without damaging the pulse.

BERNARD JACOBSON

Rudolf of St Trond [Rodulfus van St Truiden; Rodulfus Sancti Trudonis] (*b* Moustiers-sur-Sambre, nr. Namur, *c*1070; *d* St Truiden, 1138). Flemish ecclesiastic. He was abbot of St Truiden (north-east of Liège) from 1125 until his death. He began the Chronicles of the Abbots of St Truiden (ed. in *PL*, clxxiii, 33–434; and *Monumenta Germaniae historica, Scriptores*, x, Hanover, 1852/*R*1963), in which he described musical practice there, including the teaching of boy scholars according to the methods of Guido of Arezzo. An anonymous tract *Quaestiones in musica* sometimes ascribed to him is probably misattributed.

BIBLIOGRAPHY

R. Steglich: *Die Quaestiones in musica* (Leipzig, 1911)
J. Smits van Waesberghe: *Musikgeschiedenis der Middeleeuwen*, i (Tilburg, 1936–9), 253
P. Fischer: 'Rodulfus von Sint Truiden', *MGG*

See also THEORY, THEORISTS.

GORDON A. ANDERSON

Rudolf [Ruodolf] **von Fenis-Neuenburg** [von Fenis, von Neuenburg, de Neuchâtel] (*b c*1150; *d* before 30 Aug 1196). German Minnesinger. He was of the aristocratic family of Neuenburg, which had ancestors in the royal house of Burgundy. He lived at Burg Fenis, between the lakes of Biel and Neuchâtel (Neuenburg) in western Switzerland, and is mentioned several times in documents as 'Rudolf II von Fenis-Neuenburg'. Together with FRIEDRICH VON HÚSEN and HENDRIK VAN VELDEKE he belonged to an important group of Minnesinger who provided a link with trouvère song, absorbing and adopting elements of form and subject matter from Romance verse. This group laid the foundation for the period of high MINNESANG in Germany, a period that reached its zenith with Walther von der Vogelweide. The derivativeness of his technique shows most in the style of certain images and metaphors and in his adoption of certain verse forms. Rudolf's kinship with French culture comes through in the strongly intellectual tone of his songs, and particularly in his way of thinking in antitheses. Significantly, his mother and probably also his wife were of French origin, and his lands lay across border territory embracing both German and Romance languages. Seven or eight of his poems survive, but without melodies. However three, possibly five, of the Old French and Provençal models on which he based songs provide melodies for his verse.

WORKS

Text edition: *Des Minnesangs Frühling*, ed. K. Lachmann (Leipzig, 1857, rev. 30/1950 by C. von Kraus, 35/1970 without annotations), 102ff [MF]

Music editions: *Singweisen zur Liebeslyrik der deutschen Frühe*, ed. U. Aarburg (Düsseldorf, 1956) [A]
          Ausgewählte Melodien des Minnesangs, ed. E. Jammers (Tübingen, 1963) [J]
          The Art of the Minnesinger, ed. R. J. Taylor, i (Cardiff, 1968) [T]

CERTAIN CONTRAFACTA

Gewan ich ze minnen ie guoten wân, MF 80.1: from Folquet de Marseille 'Sitot me soi a tart aperceubutz', PC 155.21; A

Minne gebiutet mir daz ich singe, MF 80.25: from Gace Brulé 'De bone amour et de leaul amie', R.1102; A, J

Nun ist hât mêre mîn gedinge, MF 84.10: from Peire Vidal 'Pos tornatz sui en Procnsa', PC 364.37; A, T

POSSIBLE CONTRAFACTA

Ich hân mir selben gemachet die swaere, MF 83.11: ?from Gace Brulé 'Tant m'a mené force de seignorage', R 42; A

Mit sange wânde ich mîne sorge krenken, MF 81.30: ?also from Gace Brulé 'Tant m'a mené force de seignorage', R.42; A

BIBLIOGRAPHY

C. von Kraus: *Des Minnesangs Frühling: Untersuchungen* (Leipzig, 1939), 203ff

H. de Boor: *Geschichte der deutschen Literatur*, ii (Munich, 1953, rev. 5/1962, 9/1974), 261

R.-H. Blaser: *Le Minnesinger Rodolphe de Neuchâtel et son oeuvre dans l'histoire du lyrisme allemand du moyen âge* (Neuchâtel, 1955)

U. Aarburg: 'Melodien zum frühen deutschen Minnesang', *Der deutsche Minnesang: Aufsätze zu seiner Erforschung* (Darmstadt, 1961, 5/1972), 378–421

For further bibliography see MINNESANG.

BURKHARD KIPPENBERG

Rudolph (Johann Joseph Rainer), Archduke of Austria (*b* Florence, 8 Jan 1788; *d* Baden, nr. Vienna, 24 July 1831). Austrian patron of music and amateur composer. The youngest son of the Grand Duke of Tuscany and Maria Ludovika, he went to Vienna in 1790 when his father became Emperor Leopold II. His delicate health prevented him from undertaking a military career; instead he became closely associated with art and the Church. In the winter of 1803–4 Beethoven succeeded Anton Tayber as Rudolph's teacher: these lessons in composition, piano and theory continued on an irregular basis for 20 years, during which time Rudolph became Beethoven's greatest patron. They established a true friendship, which survived even Beethoven's aversion to prescribed teaching duties and to the observance

of court regulations. To avoid the first he often pleaded poor health or personal worries, with the second he angrily refused to comply, and it was left to the gentle archduke to concede the point. Rudolph used his influence frequently to help Beethoven in his affairs; but his greatest contribution began on 1 March 1809, when he signed an agreement with Prince Kinsky and Prince Lobkowitz to make annual payments to the composer provided he continued to live in Vienna. Beethoven dedicated opp.58, 73, 81*a*, 96, 97, 106, 111 (except for the London edition), 133 and 134 to his royal pupil. The greatest work bearing a dedication to him was the Mass in D, op.123. In 1805 Rudolph was named co-adjutor of Olmütz (Olomouc); in 1819 he was created Archbishop of Olmütz and cardinal. That June, Beethoven wrote: 'The day on which a High Mass composed by me will be performed during the ceremonies solemnized for Your Imperial Highness will be the most glorious day of my life'. The ceremony took place in 1820 but the mass was not completed until three years later. Rudolph was the first protector of the Gesellschaft der Musikfreunde, to which he bequeathed most of his music library. He was also an enthusiastic art collector and took a keen interest in the theatre. In his own right he was talented as a copperplate engraver and as a musician. His compositions include a clarinet sonata and a set of 40 piano variations on a theme by Beethoven, WoO200; he also contributed an excellent variation, somewhat in Beethoven's manner, to Diabelli's famous collection.

BIBLIOGRAPHY

P. Nettl: 'Erinnerungen an Erzherzog Rudolph', *ZMw*, iv (1921–2), 95
T. Frimmel: *Beethoven-Handbuch*, ii (Leipzig, 1926), 85
K. Kobald: 'Erzherzog Rudolph 1788–1832', *Grosse Österreicher*, ii (Zurich, 1957), 60
D. W. MacArdle: 'Beethoven and the Archduke Rudolph', *BeJb 1959– 60*, 36
E. Forbes, ed.: *Thayer's Life of Beethoven* (Princeton, 1964)

ELLIOT FORBES

Rudolph, Johanna (*b* Crimmitschau, 20 Aug 1902; *d* Berlin, 29 May 1974). German journalist and musicologist. From 1919 she worked in the editorial office of the weekly *Die Weltbühne*; she wrote numerous literary and musical reviews and essays for the Communist daily press, including the *Rote Fahne* and *Der Klassenkampf*. Having emigrated in 1933 she was arrested for illegal work in 1943 and deported to the concentration camps of Auschwitz and Ravensbrück. After 1945 she worked for the State Broadcasting Committee, joined the editorial staff of the newspaper *Neues Deutschland* and was a counsellor and scientific assistant at the Ministry of Culture from 1956. In 1966 she obtained her doctorate at the Humboldt University of Berlin with a dissertation on Handel and the Enlightenment. She specialized particularly in Handel research, though she also wrote on literary theory and criticism.

WRITINGS

'Romain Rolland und sein Händelbild', *HJb 1955*, 29
'Übersetzungsprobleme des "Messias" ', *HJb 1957*, 89
'Händel als ein Vorläufer des "Sturm und Drang" ', *HJb 1958*, 71
'Über die biblische Gewandung von Händels Oratorien', *Händel-Ehrung der Deutschen Demokratischen Republik: Halle 1959*, 181
Händelrenaissance (Berlin, 1960–69)
' "Meine Seele hört im Sehen" (über das Verhältnis von Händel und Brockes)', *HJb 1961–2*, 35–67
Die Rolle des Chors in Händels Oratorien (Leipzig, 1964)
Händels Rolle als Aufklärer (diss., Humboldt U. of Berlin, 1966)
'Reinhard Keiser und "Masaniello": zur Erstaufführung in der Deutschen Staatsoper', *Musik und Gesellschaft*, xvii (1967), 656

with E. H. Meyer: 'Zur Musik der Reformationszeit', *450 Jahre Reformation*, ed. L. Stern and M. Steinmetz (Berlin, 1967), 237
'Die historischen Bezüge des *Messias*', *HJb 1967–8*, 43
'Musikalisches Arkadien', *Sinn und Form*, xxi (1969), 704
'Probleme der Hamburger deutschen Frühoper', *HJb 1969–70*, 7
'Realismus und Antizipation in Werken Beethovens: zur Wechselwirkung der Künste am Beispiel der *Egmont*-Musik und des *Fidelio*-Problems in Shakespeare's *Cymbeline*', *Internationaler Beethoven-Kongress: Berlin 1970*, 249; see also *Shakespeare-Jb*, cviii (1972), 64
'Über das Verhältnis von Aufklärung und Klassik bei Händel des 18. Jahrhunderts', *HJb 1971*, 35
Lebendiges Erbe: Reden und Aufsätze zu Kunst und Literatur (Leipzig, 1972)
'Zu Fragen des musikalischen Erbes', *Forum: Musik in der DDR*, ed. D. Brennecke and M. Hansen (Berlin, 1972), 123
'Das Bild des Volkshelden bei Händel', *HJb 1972–3*, 77
'Bemerkungen zum Thema Heinrich Heine und die Musik', *Festschrift für Ernst Hermann Meyer* (Leipzig, 1973), 237
Further articles in *Festschrift der Händel-Festspiele* (1955, 1957, 1958, 1960, 1962, 1966, 1968, 1973)

BIBLIOGRAPHY
H. Schaefer: 'Zum Tode Johanna Rudolphs', *Musik und Gesellschaft*, xxiv (1974), 430

HORST SEEGER

Rudolph, Johann Joseph. *See* RODOLPHE, JEAN JOSEPH.

Rudolstadt. Thuringian town in the German Democratic Republic. The Heidecksburg on the banks of the Saale was the residence of the princes of Schwarzburg-Rudolstadt from 1599. Rudolstadt is rich in tradition with its collection of instruments, its concert hall, and its library and civic archives which possess valuable documents and musical manuscripts (including the catalogue of Erlebach's works and the manuscript of Bernhardt Müller's study of the Rudolstadt Hofkapelle between 1683 and 1854). From the 18th century the town was held in high repute throughout Europe, and many prominent composers were associated with it: the lutenist E. G. Baron (1720–21); J. A. Bodinus, chamber musician (*b* Rudolstadt, 1725); Adam Drese; Moritz Edelmann; P. H. Erlebach, Hofkapellmeister to 1714; F. W. Graf, virtuoso, composer and Hofkapellmeister from 1756; Traugott Eberwein, Hofkapellmeister (1797–1831); Johann Rosenmüller; C. G. Scheinpflug, court and chamber musician (*b* Rudolstadt, 1772); and Nicolaus Vetter, organist after 1730. Grieg (1884) and Wagner visited the town, as did numerous virtuosos such as Spohr, Liszt and Paganini. Rudolstadt was an influential centre of hymn writing at the time of the Pietists. A series of music festivals, started by M. D. Wollong in 1926, has presented music from the town's past. The town has its own symphony orchestra specializing in contemporary music, and a civic music school. The annual East German Folk Dance Festival, an event of international importance, is held in Rudolstadt.

BIBLIOGRAPHY
B. Engelke: 'Die Rudolstädter Hofkapelle unter Lyra und Joh. Graf', *AMw*, i (1918–19), 594
E. W. Boehme: *Die frühdeutsche Oper in Thüringen* (Stadtroda, 1931)
G. Kraft: *Die thüringische Musikkultur um 1600*, i (Würzburg, 1941)
P. Gülke: *Musik und Musiker in Rudolstadt* (Rudolstadt, 1963)

G. KRAFT

Rudorff, Ernst (Friedrich Karl) (*b* Berlin, 18 Jan 1840; *d* Berlin, 31 Dec 1916). German pianist, teacher and composer. He received his first musical instruction from Marie Lichtenstein, studied the piano and composition with Woldemar Bargiel (1852–7), the violin with Louis Ries (1852–4) and the piano for a short time with Clara Schumann in 1858. From 1859 he studied philosophy and philology at the universities of Berlin and Leipzig,

later turning to music. He studied at the Leipzig Conservatory with Moscheles, Plaidy, Reinecke, Hauptmann, Richter and Rietz, then conducted in Hamburg (1864) and taught and conducted at the Cologne Conservatory (1865–9), where he founded a Bach society in 1867. On the invitation of Joachim (who had noticed Rudorff's musical talents in his youth) he was made professor at the Berlin Hochschule für Musik from 1869 to 1910 and succeeded Bruch as conductor of the Stern Choral Society from 1880 to 1890. He was invited to conduct a series of orchestral concerts in Lisbon in 1887 and was a member of the editorial committee of Denkmäler Deutscher Tonkunst and of the senate of the Royal Academy of the Arts. The University of Tübingen awarded him an honorary doctorate in 1910.

Rudorff's style as a composer was founded on that of Mendelssohn, Schumann and Weber. His earlier compositions (e.g. the op.3 songs) show a lyrical inspiration, but in the later works he became increasingly concerned with abstract construction, often resulting in strange harmonies and complicated rhythmic patterns. His piano works are thus technically difficult, sometimes needlessly so. Among his best works are the Variations on an Original Theme for orchestra op.24, and the three symphonies opp.31, 40 and 50. In the Symphony no.2 in G minor op.40, the melodic lines are rather angular or ascend in odd intervals, and there is much use of cross-rhythms. The String Sextet op.5, published in 1865, shows the influence of Schumann; it is scored for the unusual combination of three violins, one viola and two cellos, after the model of the Sextet op.38 by Ferdinand David (1861). Rudorff also edited the score of Weber's *Euryanthe* (1866), and part of the Breitkopf & Härtel collected editions of Mozart and Chopin.

WORKS
Orch and chamber: 3 syms., opp.31, 40, 50; 3 ovs., Der blonde Ekbert, op.8, Otto der Schütz, op.12, Romantische Ouvertüre, op.45; 2 serenades, opp.20, 21; Variations on an Original Theme, op.24; Ballade, Introduction, Scherzo and Finale, op.15; Romance, vn, orch, op.41; Romance, vc, orch, op.7; Sextet, 3 vn, va, 2 vc, op.5
Pf: Fantasia, op.14; Capriccio appassionato, op.49; Variazioni capricciose, op.54; Fantasiestücke, concert studies, romances; Variations, 2 pf, op.1; works for pf 4 hands
Vocal: songs, duets and choral works, incl. Aufzug der Romanze (Tieck), solo vv, chorus, orch, op.18; 2 Gesänge, S, female vv, orch, op.19; Gesang an die Sterne (Rückert), 6vv, orch, op.26; Herbstlied, 6vv, orch, op.43

BIBLIOGRAPHY
W. Altmann, ed.: *Johannes Brahms: Briefwechsel*, iii (Berlin, 1907, 2/1913) [Deutsche Brahms Gesellschaft edn.]
A. Moser: *Joseph Joachim: ein Lebensbild* (Berlin, 2/1910)
J. Joachim and A. Moser, eds.: *Briefe von und an Joseph Joachim*, iii (Berlin, 1913; Eng. trans., 1914/*R*1972)
W. Nagel: Obituary, *Neue Musik-Zeitung*, xxxviii (1917), 124
E. Rudorff: *Aus den Tagen der Romantik* (Leipzig, 1938) [with complete list of works]
——: 'Johannes Brahms: Erinnerungen und Betrachtungen', *SMz*, xcvii (1957), 81, 139, 182
N. B. Reich: 'The Rudorff Collection', *Notes*, xxxi (1974–5), 247

GAYNOR G. JONES

Rudziński, Witold (*b* Siebież, 14 March 1913). Polish composer, musicologist and teacher. He studied in Vilnius at the university (1931–6) and at the conservatory (1928–36) with Szeligowski (composition), also taking piano lessons with Kaduszkiewiczowa and Szpinalski. In 1938–9 he was a pupil of Boulanger and Koechlin at the Institut Grégorien, Paris. He taught at the conservatories of Vilnius (1939–42) and Łódź (1945–7), headed the music department of the Polish Ministry of Culture (1947–8) and directed the Warsaw

Opera and PO (1948–9). In 1957 he was appointed professor at the Warsaw Conservatory. He won a special mention in the 1963 Prince Rainier III Competition for *Odprawa posłów greckich* ('The dismissal of the Greek envoys') and first prize in the 1966 Hommage à Grieg Competition at Bergen for *Obrazy Świętokrzyskie* ('Pictures from the Holy Cross Mountains'). This, one of his finest works, is distinguished by tender lyricism and colourfulness; in general, his music has a rhapsodic expansiveness and rich romantic harmony.

WORKS
(selective list)

OPERAS

Janko muzykant [Janko the fiddler] (3, T. Borowski, S. Wygodzki, after H. Sienkiewicz), 1948–51
Komendant Paryża [The commandant of Paris] (3, T. Marek), 1955–8
Odprawa posłów greckich [The dismissal of the Greek envoys] (1, B. Ostromęcki, after J. Kochanowski), 1962
Sulamita (1. Ostromęcki), 1964
Żółta szlafmyca [The yellow nightcap] (comic opera, 3, E. Bonacka, after F. Zabłocki), 1969
Chłopi [The peasants] (4, K. Berwińska, W. Wróblewska, after S. Reymont), 1973

VOCAL ORCHESTRAL

Oratorios: Gaude mater Polonia (compiled B. Ostromęcki), speaker, S, A, T, chorus, orch, 1966; Lipce (Berwińska, Wróblewska, after Reymont: Chłopi), chorus, chamber orch, 1968
Cantata: Chłopska droga [Peasants' road] (I. Krasicki, M. Konopnicka, T. Lenartowicz, W. Wolski), S, T, B, chorus, orch, 1952
Choral orch: Na serdeczną nutę [Tunes from the heart], chorus, small orch, 1945; Pieśni kurpiowskie, 1947; Ballada o Janosiku, chorus, small orch, 1955; Od Olsztyna do Mrągowa (trad.), 1960
Melodrama: Dach świata [The roof of the world] (Ostromęcki), speaker, orch, 1960

ORCHESTRAL

Sym. Suite; Pf Conc., 1936; 2 syms., 1938, 1944; Divertimento, str, 1940; Uwertura bałtycka, 1948; Parady, 1958; Musique concertante, pf, chamber orch, 1959; Musica profana, 1960; Obrazy Świętokrzyskie [Pictures from the Holy Cross Mountains], after S. Żeromski, 1965; Uwertura góralska [Highlander ov.], 1970; Conc. grosso, perc, 2 str orchs, 1970

OTHER WORKS

Chamber: Sonatina, fl, pf, 1934; Trio, fl, ob, pf, 1934; Sonatina, cl, pf, 1935; 2 str qts, 1935, 1943; Sonata no.1, vn, pf, 1937; Canzonetta, fl, ob, pf, 1940; Partita, vc, pf, 1940; Sonata, va, pf, 1946; Nonet, wind qnt, str trio, db, 1947; Qnt, fl, str qt, 1954; Variations and Fugue, perc, 1966; Preludes, cl, harp, mar, vib, perc, vn, 1967; Polonaise, vc, pf, 1970; Duo concertante, perc, 1976; Hpd Sonata, 1977
Pf: Preludia, 1940; Ballada, 1942; Suita polska, 1948
Vocal: Cantate ecclésiastique, chorus, org, 1938; 2 portraits de femmes (Ronsard, Rimbaud), 1v, str qt, 1960; songs, mass songs, choral pieces
Dances, incidental music

Principal publisher: Polskie Wydawnictwo Muzyczne

WRITINGS

Lekcje słuchjania muzyki [Lessons on listening to music] (Kraków, 1948)
Muzyka dla wszystkich [Music for everybody] (Kraków, 1948, 2/1967)
Warsztat kompozytorski Béli Bartóka [Bartók's musical technique] (Kraków, 1964)
ed.: *Stanisław Moniuszko: listy zebrane* [Collected letters] (Kraków, 1954–70)

BIBLIOGRAPHY

T. Marek: ' "Janko muzykant" – nowa opera polska', *Przegląd kulturalny* (1953), no.27
J. Olkuśnik: 'Nowe utwory Witolda Rudzińskiego: "Deux portraits de femmes" i "Dach świata"', *Ruch muzyczny* (1961), no.14
Z. Mycielski: 'Nad "Odprawą" Witolda Rudzińskiego', *Ruch muzyczny* (1967), no.2, p.3

BOGUSŁAW SCHÄFFER

Rudziński, Zbigniew (*b* Czechowice, 23 Oct 1935). Polish composer. He studied composition with Perkowski at the Warsaw Conservatory (1956–62), winning a prize in the competition held to celebrate the institution's sesquicentenary in 1960 with the Sonata for two string quartets, piano and timpani; his studies were continued in Paris. In 1962 he was again a prizewinner in the Polish Composers' Union Competition for Young Composers. Works of his were heard at the ISCM Festivals of 1967 (*Contra fidem*) and 1971 (Quartet for two pianos and percussion). His music retains a tonal polarity in an expressionist style; the best works achieve a perceptible unity of the aspects of texture, accent and dynamic.

WORKS
(selective list)

Sonata, 2 str qt, pf, timp, 1960; 4 Songs (J. Tuwim), Bar, ens, 1961; Epigramy, fl, 2 female choruses, pf, perc, 1962; Contra fidem, orch, 1964; Str Trio, 1964; Study for C, variable ens, 1964; Impromptu, 3 vc, 2 pf, 3 perc, 1966; Moments musicaux, orch, 1965–8; Allegro giocoso, orch, 1969; Qt, 2 pf, 2 perc, 1969; Sym. (textless), male chorus, orch, 1969; 3 songs (Pound, Joyce, Bennett), T, 2 pf, 1969; Muzyka nocą [Night music], orch, 1970; Requiem, speaker, chorus, orch, 1971; Tutti e solo, S, fl, hn, pf, 1973; Pf Sonata, 1975; Campanella, perc, 1977

Principal publishers: Polskie Wydawnictwo Muzyczne, Schott

BIBLIOGRAPHY

T. Kaczyński: ' "Moments musicaux" Zbigniewa Rudzińskiego', *Ruch muzyczny* (1966), no.12, p.4

MIECZYSŁAWA HANUSZEWSKA

Rue, Pierre de la. *See* LA RUE, PIERRE DE.

Rueckers [Ruekaerts]. *See* RUCKERS family.

Ruette, Jean-Louis la. *See* LARUETTE, JEAN-LOUIS.

Ruettino, Giovanni Battista. *See* VOLPE, GIOVANNI BATTISTA.

Ruetz, Caspar (*b* Wismar, 21 March 1708; *d* Lübeck, 21 Dec 1755). German composer and writer on church music. He was a son of Joachim Ruetz, a native of Lübeck, a pupil of Buxtehude and tutor in an orphanage at Wismar. Caspar Ruetz received his early education from his father; he also studied the organ with the Wismar organist Hoelken and the flute, oboe and violin with a city musician, Wilken. He attended the University of Jena in 1728, studying law and theology; before completing his education at the University of Rostock in 1732, he went to Hamburg in 1730 as a private tutor. He was also a tutor, in eastern Holstein and in Azbüll near Flensburg, from 1733 to 1736. On 25 April 1737 he became the ninth Kantor and music director of St Katherine's School in Lübeck, succeeding Hinrich Sivers, whose daughter he married the same year.

Almost all the sacred music composed by Ruetz in Lübeck is lost (one exception is a cantata, *Fürchte dich nicht*, in *B-Bc*). However, his three-part work defending and examining church music is an important document in the history of German Protestant church music at the end of the Baroque period. Each of the *Widerlegte Vorurtheile* argues persuasively for retaining music in the Protestant service and denies the validity of charges by conservative purists and especially Pietists that contrapuntal music was inappropriate for the church. The first part (1750) attempts to prove, using evidence from the Bible and writings of the church fathers, that church music is to be justified not only on a historical basis but that it must have been contrapuntal from biblical times. In part ii (1752) Ruetz challenged the Pietists' specific criticisms of church music. Here and in the final part (1753) he expanded on the doctrines of Baroque musical aesthetics, the concept of the Affections as they apply to good church music, which he believed differs from secular music only in its ultimate purpose but not in the means by which it obtains its musical goals. Among the many contemporary German writers influencing Ruetz were Georg Motz, whose *Die vertheidigte Kirchenmusic* (1703) took an early stand against the Pietists in favour of music, and especially Johann Mattheson. Ruetz's final volume gives considerable information about the declining state of musical life in Lübeck churches. Ruetz also wrote a valuable criticism of French aesthetic doctrines of nature imitation as proposed by Charles Batteux: this long essay, a *Sendschreiben* in Marpurg's *Historisch-kritische Beyträge*, i (1754–5), refutes the idea that music is merely a copy of nature, insisting instead that music is the original condition.

On Ruetz's death the *Lübeckischer Anzeiger* (27 December 1755) commented that he was Lübeck's most learned Kantor. Mattheson (*Plus Ultra, dritter Vorrath*, 1755) lamented Ruetz's untimely death and published an elaborate poem of praise in which he pictured him in heaven surrounded by the sounds of sacred music that he had so ably defended while he lived.

WRITINGS
Widerlegte Vorurtheile vom Ursprunge der Kirchenmusic, und klarer Beweis dass die Gottesdienstliche Music sich auf Gottes Worte gründe, und also göttliches Ursprungs sey (Lübeck, 1750)
Widerlegte Vorurtheile von der Beschaffenheit der heutigen Kirchenmusic und von der Lebens-Art einiger Musicorum (Lübeck, 1752)
Widerlegte Vorurtheile von der Wirkung der Kirchenmusik und von den darzu erforderten Unkosten (Rostock, 1753)
'Sendschreiben eines Freundes an den andern über einige Ausdrücke des Herrn Batteux von der Musik', *Historisch-kritische Beyträge zur Aufnahme der Musik*, ed. F. W. Marpurg, i (Berlin, 1754–5), 273–311

BIBLIOGRAPHY
J. Mattheson: *Plus Ultra, ein Stückwerk von neuer und mancherley Art* (Hamburg, 1754–6)
'Lebenslauff Herrn Casparis Ruetz Cantoris und Musikdirectoris zu Lübeck', *Historisch-kritische Beyträge zur Aufnahme der Musik*, ed. F. W. Marpurg, i (Berlin, 1754–5), 357
J. D. Overbeck: *Leben des Hochedlen und Hochgelahrten Herrn Caspar Ruetz* (Lübeck, 1755)
J. H. von Seelen: *Cenotaphium viro praecellentissimo, doctissimoque, Domino Caspari Ruetz* (Lübeck, 1755)
C. Stiehl: *Lübeckisches Tonkünstlerlexicon* (Leipzig, 1887)
——: *Musikgeschichte der Stadt Lübeck* (Lübeck, 1891)
W. Stahl: 'Kaspar Ruetz: ein Lübeckischer Zeit- und Amtsgenosse J. S. Bachs', *Gedenkboek aangeboden aan Dr. D. F. Scheurleer op zijn 70sten Verjaardag* (The Hague, 1925)
GEORGE J. BUELOW

Ruf (Ger.: 'cry', 'shout'). A medieval sacred acclamation in a Germanic language. Friedrich (1936) showed that it was often of one or two lines and could have been used for congregational singing at the end of the sermon, at the end of Mass or on some secular occasion. The LEISE is normally considered a more developed sub-category of the *Ruf* and comprises four lines. *Rufe* are found in German, Dutch and Czech; some can be traced to the 9th century, and many served as bases for German Reformation hymns which have been used ever since.

BIBLIOGRAPHY
A. Hübner: *Die deutschen Geisslerlieder: Studien zum geistlichen Volkslied des Mittelalters* (Berlin and Leipzig, 1931)
E. Friedrich: *Der Ruf: eine Gattung des geistlichen Volksliedes*, Germanistische Studien, clxxiv (Berlin, 1936) [incl. further bibliography]
V. Mertens: 'Der Ruf – eine Gattung des deutschen geistlichen Liedes im Mittelalter?', *Zeitschrift für deutsches Altertum und deutsche Literatur*, civ (1975), 68
DAVID FALLOWS

Rufer, Josef (Leopold) (*b* Vienna, 18 Dec 1893). Austrian musicologist. He took an engineering degree in

Prague, concurrently studying theory with Wilhelm Zemanek and composition with Zemlinsky, the teacher of Schoenberg; after war service in the Austrian army, he studied with Schoenberg in Vienna (1919–22). From 1925 to 1933, when Schoenberg was forced to leave Germany, Rufer was his assistant at the Berlin Academy teaching the younger students according to Schoenberg's theories of harmony, counterpoint and form. He was music critic for the Berlin *Morgenpost* (1928–40) and later also for *Die Welt*. He directed the Neue Musik concert series in Hamburg with Stuckenschmidt (1923–4), and after service in the German Air Force during World War II, published the monthly journal *Stimmen* with him (1947–50); with Paul Höffer he founded and directed the International Music Institute in Berlin (1946–9). He has taught theory at the Free University in Berlin (from 1950), the Berlin Hochschule für Musik (from 1956), the Darmstadt summer course (1956) and in Vienna (from 1959).

Rufer is a leading Schoenberg scholar; his bibliographies, critical editions and analyses are of lasting importance and usefulness. His treatise on the 12-note system (1952), the first major work to appear on the subject, is an authentic exposition of Schoenberg's own concept of his system. Rufer drew on written and oral communication with Schoenberg, who apparently helped him with the book from 1949 until his death in 1951. In the appendix to the German edition 13 composers discuss their own use of the 12-note system; the most illuminating part of the book is Rufer's explanation of Schoenberg's concept of *Grundgestalt* ('basic shape'), which had not previously been clearly defined. In 1957 Rufer undertook the cataloguing of Schoenberg's huge musical, literary and artistic legacy in Los Angeles, which resulted in his invaluable book *The Work of Arnold Schoenberg*. In 1961 the composer's widow invited Rufer to become editor-in-chief of a complete edition, of which the initial volumes show exhaustive attention to details of commentary, documentation and layout.

WRITINGS
Die Komposition mit zwölf Tönen (Berlin, 1952; Eng. trans., 1969)
'Alban Berg: der Mensch und der Künstler', *Das Musikleben*, viii (1955), 205, 251
'Boris Blacher: der Komponist und sein Werk', *ÖMz*, x (1955), 368
'Dokumente einer Freundschaft' [Berg–Schoenberg], *Melos*, xxii (1955), 42
Musiker über Musik (Darmstadt, 1956)
'Arnold Schönbergs Nachlass', *ÖMz*, xiii (1958), 96
'A Talk on Arnold Schoenberg', *Score* (1958), no.22, p.7
Das Werk Arnold Schönbergs (Kassel, 1959; Eng. trans., 1962)
'Kann man Musik "denken": Betrachungen zur Situation der Musik von heute', *ÖMz*, xiv (1959), 355
'Schönberg: gestern, heute und morgen', *SMz*, cv (1965), 190; also in *Beiträge 1967: Österreichische Gesellschaft für Musik* (Kassel, 1967), 19; Eng. trans., *PNM*, xiv/2 (1976)
'Spiegelungen des Eros: zu den drei Operneinaktern von Schönberg', *ÖMz*, xx (1965), 302
'Schönberg als Maler: Grenzen und Konvergenzen der Künste', *Aspekte der neuen Musik: Professor Hans Heinz Stuckenschmidt zum 65. Geburtstag* (Kassel, 1968), 50
'Noch einmal Schönbergs opus 16', *Melos*, xxxvi (1969), 366
Technische Aspekte der Polyphonie in der 1. Hälfte des 20. Jahrhunderts (Ghent, 1969)
'Von der Musik zur Theorie: der Weg Arnold Schönbergs', *Zeitschrift für Musiktheorie*, ii/1 (1971), 1
'Die Grundgestalt in Schönbergs Musik', *1. Kongress der Internationalen Schönberg-Gesellschaft: Wien 1974*

EDITIONS
A. Schoenberg: *Lieder und Kanons*, Gesamtausgabe, ser. A, i/1 (Vienna, 1966)

BRUCE SAYLOR

Ruff. An embellishment used in side-drumming; *see* DRUM, §3.

Ruffa, Girolamo (*b* Tropea, Calabria, *fl c*1700). Italian composer. From the titles and dedications of his published works we know that he was born in Tropea, belonged to the order of the Minor Conventuals and, in about 1700, was *maestro di cappella* of Mileto Cathedral. Gaspari, referring to a passage in the introduction to Domenico Scorpione's *Istituzioni corali*, in which the author said that in 1702 he had delivered to the press an *Introduttorio musicale* 'under a different name', suggested that this was the work of the same title published as by Ruffa. Whoever its author, the *Introduttorio* is a work of considerable interest for its information on mensural and proportional notation.

WORKS

Graduali per tutte le domeniche minori dell'anno, op.1 (Naples, 1700)
Salve, 1–2vv, some with vns, and Litanie, concertate, 3vv (Naples, 1701)
Introduttorio musicale per ben approffittarsi nel canto figurato, op.4 (Naples, 1701)

BIBLIOGRAPHY

EitnerQ
G. Gaspari: *Catalogo della biblioteca del Liceo musicale di Bologna*, i (Bologna, 1890/*R*1961), 258
W. Dürr: 'Ruffa, Girolamo', *MGG*

RENATO BOSSA

Ruffino d'Assisi [Bartolucci, Ruffino] (*b* Assisi, ?*c*1490; *d* in or after 1532). Italian composer. A Franciscan friar, he was probably attached to the Convento dei Frari, Venice. From 2 May 1510 to 2 May 1520 he was *maestro di cappella* at Padua Cathedral. He then moved to the Basilica del Santo and remained there until 1525, when he left Padua for a post at Vicenza Cathedral. He returned to the Santo in 1531 for at least a year.

One mass, two motets, nine psalms (seven incomplete) and three secular pieces by Ruffino survive. His sacred works reveal an adventurous, forward-looking, if sometimes clumsy composer. The motets both have solemn texts and are scored for low voices: *O inexstimabile sacramentum* uses flexible homophony of the kind found increasingly in the more expressive motets of the period; *Miserere mei Domine* is more contrapuntal, with a cantus firmus in long notes in the bass part. The eight-voice psalms are all for two choirs, and predate the publication (and probably the composition) of Willaert's psalms printed in 1550. Ruffino's have tuttis and animated dialogue throughout, unlike most of the early north Italian double-choir psalm repertory, in which such devices are usually reserved for the doxology; he also treated the verse divisions with considerable freedom. The mass, based on a sequence melody, proceeds mainly by antiphonal repetition which is sometimes so overlapping as to produce a quasi-canonic texture. As in the *Miserere*, the contrapuntal sections are the weakest. Particularly in the mass, an audacious (or perhaps incompetent) harmonic style is apparent in simultaneous false relations, sounding of suspensions against their notes of resolution, and, on occasions, an extraordinary suspension and resolution of a whole chord in one choir against a different chord in the other. Two of Ruffino's secular works are in the same volume as the two motets. *Hayme Amor, hayme Fortuna* is a mascherata in frottola form, with text in all voices and a dialogue opening. Jeppesen suggested that *Venite donne belle*, with its clearcut imitative style, may represent the type of Italian piece that influenced such Netherlanders as Josquin. The other piece, *Non finsi mai d'amarte*, is a canzone.

WORKS

Missa super 'Verbum bonum et suave', 8vv, *I-VEaf* 218 (on chant)
Miserere mei Domine, 4vv, 1521[6] (c.f. Tristis est anima mea); O inexstimabile sacramentum, 4vv, 1521[6]: ed. K. Jeppesen, *Italia sacra musica*, ii (Copenhagen, 1962)
2 psalms, 8vv, *TVca*(*d*); 7 psalms, *BGc* 1209D (inc., second choir only)
Hayme Amor, hayme Fortuna, 4vv, 1521[6]; Non finsi mai d'amarte, 4vv, 1526[6]; Venite donne belle, 4vv, 1521[6]

BIBLIOGRAPHY

A. Einstein: 'An Old Music Print at the J. P. Morgan Library in New York', *MQ*, xxv (1939), 507
R. Casimiri: 'Musica e musicisti nella Cattedrale di Padova nei sec. XIV, XV, XVI', *NA*, xviii (1941), 1, esp. 29f; repr. in book form (Rome, 1942), 30ff
A. Einstein: *The Italian Madrigal* (Princeton, 1949/*R*1971)
G. d'Alessi: 'Precursors of Adriano Willaert in the Practice of *Coro Spezzato*', *JAMS*, v (1952), 187
——: *La cappella musicale del Duomo di Treviso* (Treviso, 1954)
K. Jeppesen: 'Über italienische Kirchenmusik in der ersten Hälfte des 16. Jahrhunderts', *SM*, iii (1962), 149
G. d'Alessi: 'Ruffino d'Assisi', *MGG*
A. F. Carver: 'The Psalms of Willaert and his North Italian Contemporaries', *AcM*, xlvii (1975), 270

ANTHONY F. CARVER

Ruffo, Titta [Titta, Ruffo Cafiero] (*b* Pisa, 9 June 1877; *d* Florence, 6 July 1953). Italian baritone. He studied for a short time, and intermittently, with Persichini, Sparapane and Casini. In 1898 he made his début at the Teatro Costanzi, Rome, as the Herald in *Lohengrin*, and then sang at Santiago, Chile (1900), and Buenos Aires (1902). He appeared at Covent Garden in 1903 (Enrico and Rossini's Figaro), but did not return to London, reputedly because of a disagreement with Melba. He made his La Scala début during the 1903–4 season as Rigoletto, and was then in demand at all the major European opera houses. In 1908 he sang for the first time at the Colón, Buenos Aires, where he remained a great favourite until the year of his retirement (1931).

Titta Ruffo as Hamlet in Thomas' opera

He was also very popular in the USA, where he first sang in 1912 at Philadelphia; he then appeared frequently at Chicago (until 1926) and at the Metropolitan (1922–9).

Ruffo's voice was outstanding for its resonance, power, range and the almost tenor-like ring of its top register, for purity and warmth of tone, and for amplitude of breath control. It also had a characteristically dark, sometimes sombre, colour, particularly noticeable in Thomas' Hamlet and in Verdi roles (especially Rigoletto, Di Luna and Renato). He was a vigorous and exuberant actor and his singing was correspondingly dramatic and forceful, if occasionally coarse and loud. His enormous success, in operas such as *L'africaine*, *La gioconda*, *Pagliacci* and *Il barbiere di Siviglia*, finally brought about a complete change in Italian vocal taste for baritone singing, towards an unpolished, aggressive style, and away from the refined, classical 19th-century tradition.

BIBLIOGRAPHY

G. Monaldi: *Cantanti celebri* (Rome, 1929), 290f
T. Ruffo: *La mia parabola* (Milan, 1937/*R*1977 with discography by W. R. Moran)
F. W. Gaisberg: *The Music Goes Round* (New York, 1943, repr. 1946 as *Music on Record*)
A. Wolf: 'Titta Ruffo', *Record Collector*, ii/5 (1947), 11 [with discography]
G. Lauri-Volpi: *Voci parallele* (Milan, 1955), 167ff
R. Celletti: 'Ruffo, Titta', *Le grandi voci* (Rome, 1964) [with opera discography by C. Williams]

RODOLFO CELLETTI

Ruffo, Vincenzo (*b* Verona, *c*1508; *d* Sacile, nr. Pordenone, 9 Feb 1587). Italian composer and *maestro di cappella*. Between 1520 and 1534 he was trained in the Scuola degli Accoliti of Verona Cathedral, where from 1531 he was one of 12 *cappellani accoliti*. He was presumably taught there by Biagio Rossetti, organist at the cathedral and master of the school. A period of residence in Savona in 1528 has been suggested but not yet documented; already substantiated, however, is his departure from Verona in 1534 and again in 1541, although his whereabouts during the intervening years are unknown. In about 1542 he was *musico* to Alfonso d'Alvalos, Marquis of Vasto and governor-general of Milan under Charles V; it may be assumed that Ruffo remained in his service until his death in 1546. Documents discovered by Paganuzzi (1973) show that in 1555 Ruffo was married and the father of two sons aged 16 and 19; combining this with his having become an acolyte in 1520, the date of his birth can be estimated at about 1508.

Between 1547 and 1563 Ruffo was again in Verona, where in 1547 he was an unsuccessful candidate for the post of *maestro di musica* at the Accademia Filarmonica. In 1551–2 he took over this post from Jan Nasco, and by 1544 he had also assumed the position of *maestro di cappella* at Verona Cathedral. Among his students there were Gian Matteo Asola, probably Marc'Antonio Ingegneri, who later taught Monteverdi, and perhaps Andrea Gabrieli. The numerous secular compositions that Ruffo wrote during this period arise from the patronage of the Accademia Filarmonica, then one of the most ambitious amateur musical organizations in Italy, and also demonstrate his connections with patrons in Mantua, Genoa and Brescia.

Between 1563 and 1572 Ruffo was again in Milan, as *maestro di cappella* at the cathedral. During this period he was directly influenced by Cardinal Carlo Borromeo, Archbishop of Milan, whose active efforts on behalf of the Counter-Reformation are directly reflected in Ruffo's sacred compositions written after this time. In 1565, Cardinals Borromeo and Vitellozzo Vitelli held in Rome a famous trial of sacred compositions by several composers, to see if texts could be set to music in a way that would render the words intelligible, a trial for which Palestrina's later biographer, Baini, supposed that the *Missa Papae Marcelli* had been written. Although there is no documentary proof regarding the performance of Palestrina's work on this occasion, letters during the weeks preceding the trial from Borromeo to Nicolo Ormaneto, his vicar in Milan, show that Borromeo had commissioned Ruffo to write a mass 'which should be as clear as possible'. Shortly afterwards he also suggested that a mass of this type should be written by 'don Nicola [Vicentino] who favours chromatic music'. Although it is not known whether Vicentino implemented Borromeo's suggestion, in Ruffo's case it is clear that his published masses of 1570 and many subsequent masses were written expressly to render the texts as intelligible as possible, and, as he explicitly stated, in accordance with the wishes of Cardinal Borromeo, who was permanently resident in Milan after 1565.

After 1572 Ruffo held less important posts. Between 1573 and 1577 he was in charge of music at Pistoia Cathedral. He was again in Verona between 1578 and 1580, although his post there is not known, and his last appointment was in the small Friulian town of Sacile, where he died, according to his memorial stone, 'in extremum usque senium'.

In both sacred and secular music Ruffo can be considered one of the most prolific and adaptable composers of the period 1540–80. Before 1563, the turning-point of his career, he wrote more madrigals than sacred works, and in 1564 published his only collection of instrumental compositions. After 1563 he abandoned secular music entirely in favour of religious compositions on Latin texts, a sign of his explicit conversion to Counter-Reformation ideals. Ruffo wrote at least 260 madrigals (according to Wtorczyk, this is more than any earlier madrigalist). In these madrigals the new *note nere* notation of the 1540s is extensively used, giving these works considerable rhythmic flexibility and liveliness. They remain harmonically conservative, however, showing little use of chromatic degree-inflection. Wtorczyk considered Ruffo's work to be an important link in the development of the madrigal between the generation of Festa and Willaert and that of Andrea Gabrieli. His *Capricci in musica a tre voci* (1564), textless compositions apparently intended for instrumental performance, are studded with technical and notational difficulties, and are the earliest known instrumental pieces to be described as 'capricci'.

Ruffo's sacred music shows a long and complex development from the early to the later works. His motets of 1542 and a single mass of that year show him to have mastered the complexities of imitative polyphony as practised by the generation of Gombert and Clemens, and the 1555 motet collection continues this traditional approach, with the six-part pieces in the collection making extensive use of cantus firmus techniques. The masses of 1557 include three imitation-masses based on well-known motets by Jacquet of Mantua and Richafort. After 1563 Ruffo's style changed drastically under the influence of Cardinal Borromeo and the post-Tridentine ideals that he pursued, and the masses of 1570, experimental works for four voices, are almost entirely written in a homophonic style to make the text as clear as possible. In his later masses and psalms he attempted to leaven this strict style with touches of contrapuntal writing, to achieve musical interest while maintaining a high degree of clarity. In his motets, however, he remained relatively unconcerned with intelligibility of text, though these pieces are less intensely contrapuntal in style than the earlier motets had been; the same is true of his later works in lesser liturgical forms such as the responsories and *falsibordoni*.

WORKS
SACRED
Il primo libro de motetti, 5vv (Milan, 1542)
Motetti, 6vv (Venice, 1555)
Messe, 5vv (Venice, 1557); 2 ed. in RRMR, xxxii (1978)
Magnificat, 5vv (Venice, 1559) (the Magnificat mentioned in *EitnerQ* is dated 1539, probably wrongly)
I sacri et santi salmi che si cantano a compieta, 4vv (Venice, 1568)
Missae quatuor concinate ad ritum concilii mediolani, 4vv (Milan, 1570)
Messe . . . nuovamente composte, secondo la forma del concilio tridentino (?1572, lost; Brescia, 1580); 2 extracts ed. in AMI, i (1897); 1 mass ed. in Musica liturgica, i/1 (Cincinnati, 1958)
Il quarto libro di messe, conforme al decreto del Sacrosancto Concilio di Trento (Venice, 1574)
Salmi suavissimi et devotissimi conformi al decreto del Sacro Concilio di Trento, 5vv (Venice, 1574); 1 ed. in AMI, i (1897)
Li Magnificat brevi et aierosi . . . con tutti li falsi bordoni, 5vv (Venice, 1578)
Sacrae modulationes vulgo motecta liber primus, 6vv (Brescia, 1583)
Sacrae modulationes vulgo motecta, liber secundus, 6vv (Brescia, 1583)
Li soavissimi responsorii della Settimana Santa, 5vv (Milan, 1586[5])
Missae Boromeae, 5vv (Venice, 1592)
Missa 'Alma Redemptoris mater', 1542[3]; ed. in RRMR, xxxii (1978)
Works in 1544[3]; 1547[25]; 1553[16]; 1559[1]; 1564[4]; G. M. Asola: Secondo libro delle messe (Venice, 1586), ed. in Antologia polifonica, i (Rome, 1924); 1588[2]; 1591[1]

For full list of motets and other sacred works see Lockwood (1970)

SECULAR
Li madrigali a notte negre . . . libro primo, 4vv (Venice, 1545)
Il primo libro de madrigali cromatici con la gionta di alquanti madrigali del medesimo autore, 4vv (Venice, 1552)
Il primo libro de madrigali, 5vv (Venice, 1553)
Madrigali scielta seconda, 5vv (Venice, 1554[?9])
Madrigali, 6–8vv, con la gionta de 5 canzone a diverse voci (Venice, 1554)
Il secondo libro de madrigali, 5vv (Venice, 1553[28])
Il terzo libro de madrigali, 5vv (Pesaro, 1555[31])
Il secondo libro de madrigali, 4vv (Venice, 1555)
Opera nova di musica . . . nella quale si contengono 25 madrigali . . . composti con dotta arte et reservato ordine . . . libro quarto, 5vv (Venice, 1556)
Capricci in musica, a 3, a commodo di virtuosi (Milan, 1564)
Works in 1544[22], 1549[30], 1549[31], 1551[10], 1552[20], 1555[25], 1555[27], 1557[17], 1557[18], 1559[16], 1560[10], 1562[6], 1562[7], 1562[22], 1563[7], 1584[15], 1585[19], 1588[19], 1588[20], 1589[12], 1593[5]

BIBLIOGRAPHY
L. Torri: 'Vincenzo Ruffo madrigalista e compositore di musica sacra nel secolo XVI', *RMI*, iii (1896), 635; iv (1897), 233
A. Chiappelli: 'Il Maestro Vincenzo Ruffo a Pistoia', *Bollettino storico pistoiese*, i (1899), 3
G. Vale: 'Gli ultimi anni di Vincenzo Ruffo', *NA*, i (1924), 78
G. Turrini: *La tradizione musicale a Verona* (Verona, 1953)
W. Wtorczyk: *Die Madrigale Vincenzo Ruffos* (diss., Free U. of Berlin, 1955)
L. Lockwood: 'Vincenzo Ruffo and Musical Reform after the Council of Trent', *MQ*, xlii (1957), 342
A. Schmitz: 'Bermerkungen zur Vincenzo Ruffo's Passions-komposition', *Miscelánea en homenaje a Monseñor Higinio Anglés*, ii (Barcelona, 1961)
J. Haar: 'A Gift of Madrigals to Cosimo I: the MS Bibl. Naz. Centrale Magl. XIX, 130', *RIM*, i (1966), 168
L. Lockwood: *The Counter-Reformation and the Masses of Vincenzo Ruffo* (Venice, 1970)
E. Paganuzzi: 'Documenti Veronesi su musicisti del XVI e XVII secolo', *Scritti in onore di Mons. Giuseppe Turrini* (Verona, 1973)

LEWIS LOCKWOOD

Ruffolo [**Ruffulo**], **Lucretio** (*b* Guastalla, probably after 1550; *d* after 1612). Italian composer. His *Il primo libro de madrigali* (Venice, 1598) for five voices is dedicated to Ferrante II, Duke of Guastalla from 1579 to 1630 and Seigneur (later Duke) of Molfetta; Eitner deduced erroneously that this referred to Prince Fernando Gonzaga (see *EitnerQ*). Ruffolo's *Il terzo libro de madrigali . . . con un dialogo* (Venice, 1612) for five and seven voices is dedicated to Cesare Gonzaga. His other known surviving works are two motets (in *RISM* 1606[6] and 1609[15]) and two manuscript works (in *D-Mbs*).

BIBLIOGRAPHY
G. O. Pitoni: *Notitia de contrapuntisti e de compositori di musica* (MS, *I-Rvat* C.G.I/1–2, c1725)

PIER PAOLO SCATTOLIN

Rufilo [**Rufolo**], **Matteo** (*fl* 1561–3). Italian composer. His first extant work, *Il primo libro de madrigali a cinque voci* (Venice, 1561), is dated from Naples, and dedicated to Cesare Gonzaga, founder of the Mantuan Accademia degli Invaghiti and Prince of Molfetta from 1557 until 1575. Rufilo's *Primo libro de madrigali a quattro voci* (Venice, 1563) is dated from Ariano, near Salerno. This latter volume demonstrates his ability to handle current musical styles. Some pieces, such as *Perche Philli*, are written in a simple chordal style with lively rhythms; others show a proficiency in counterpoint. A small group of compositions from this book reveals that Rufilo was sympathetic to the progressive tendencies in contemporary madrigal writing. The setting of Petrarch's *Solo e pensoso*, with its strikingly angular opening motif, is most advanced for its date, particularly in the use of unusual melodic intervals and unfamiliar changes of harmony. It is tempting to speculate that Rufilo may have known and admired the later work of Rore.

IAIN FENLON

Ruge [**Rugge, Rugi, Ruggi, Rouge, Romano**], **Filippo** (*b* Rome, c1725; *d* ?Paris, after 1767). Italian composer and flautist. He may possibly have sojourned in London when Walsh began publishing five sets of his chamber pieces for flute (1751–4). By 1753 he and his wife, a singer, had settled in Paris. His name appears in the Paris press for the first time in March of that year when he performed one of his own flute concertos as a soloist in the Concert Spirituel. The programme included a symphony by 'Romano', undoubtedly of Ruge's composition as well. At this time he and his wife performed in the famous musical salon of La Pouplinière. After 1755 Ruge organized a series of concerts at his home in the rue Plâtrière, where he also taught music. In July 1755 he published *Au dessert*, a set of six vocal duos, and in August of the same year he took out a *privilège général* of ten years for instrumental compositions. The following year saw the publication of *Sei sinfonie* op.1, the fourth of which contained a programmatic movement called 'La tempesta'. This symphony and a later one entitled 'La nova tempesta', or 'La tempête suivie du calme', published separately by Venier in 1761, were performed with considerable success at the Concert Spirituel. It is possible that between 1757 and 1761 Ruge entered the service of the Marquis of Seignelay; a manuscript collection discovered near the ruins of the Seignelay château contains some 40 flute compositions by Ruge, as well as a thematic catalogue in his hand giving the incipits of 111 symphonies and overtures, including five of his own and one by his son.

Evidently Ruge brought a considerable repertory of Italian music with him from Rome; this music was the repertory of most of his concert appearances, and was further disseminated with the publication, in collaboration with Venier in 1757, of *Sei sinfonie nuove de vari autori italiani* (by Conforti, Crespi, Galuppi, Jommelli, Latilla and Mazzoni). After his last known composition, *Duetti a due flauti traversi o due mandolini o due violini*, published by Grangé in 1767, historical notices of him cease.

Ruge was an important agent in the the diffusion and popularization of Italian music and musical style in 18th-century France. His symphonies are typical of the Italian pre-Classical tradition evident in the works of G. B. Sammartini; the Mannheim school mannerisms then coming into vogue are largely absent. The usual fast–slow–fast order of movements is maintained, with slow movements often attractively lyrical. In the flute works, lyricism again prevails over technical display. Although there are few contemporary references to Ruge as a flautist, his appearance as soloist at the Concert Spirituel implies technical prowess of a high order.

WORKS
(printed works published in Paris unless otherwise stated)

Orch: 6 Concertos in 6 Parts, fl, str, bc, op.3 (London, 1753); 6 sinfonie a 4, hn ad lib, op.1 (1756); Sinfonia 'La nova tempesta', D, no.2 in 6 sinfonie di vari autori, op.12 (1761); Sinfonia, D; Minuetto amoroso, G, op.5, *F-Pc*; incipits to 4 other sinfonie, *c*1757, see La Rue, Brook (1962)

Chamber: 6 Solos, fl/vn, bc (hpd/vc) (London, 1751); 6 Sonatas in 3 Parts, 4 for 2 fl/vn, b, 2 for 3 fl, op.2 (London, 1752); [12] Sonatas or Duets, 2 fl/vn, op.4, 2 sets (London, 1753–4); 2 sonate, 2 fl, b, cited in Breitkopf catalogue, 1763; Duetti, 2 fl/mand/vn (1767); Sonata, fl, b, *B-Bc*; Sonata da camera, vn, b, *A-Wgm*; 2 suonate, fl, b, *D-KA*; Trio, 2 fl, b, *KA*; *c*30 sonatas, fl, b, several trios, 2 fl, several fl duets, many minuets etc, fl, b, *c*1750–67, all in *US-SFsc*

Vocal: Au dessert, duetti, 2 S, 2 fl/vn ad lib (1755); L'après souper, duetti, 2 S, 2 fl/vn ad lib (*c*1762), incl. 6 canzonette, 1v, b/gui; Questa è la prima volta, arietta *US-SFsc*; Canzona, 2vv, *F-Pn*; It. airs, 1753, *Pc*

BIBLIOGRAPHY
M. Brenet: *Les concerts en France sous l'ancien régime* (Paris, 1900/R1969)

——: 'La librairie musicale en France', *SIMG*, viii (1906–7), 401–66

G. Cucuel: *La vie parisienne des princes de Wurtemberg-Montbéliard* (Paris, 1912)

——: *Etudes sur un orchestre au XVIIIe siècle* (Paris, 1913)

——: *La Pouplinière et la musique de chambre au XVIIIe siècle* (Paris, 1913)

L. de La Laurencie: *Inventaire critique du Fonds Blancheton* (Paris, 1930–31)

B. S. Brook: *La symphonie française dans la seconde moitié du XVIIIe siècle* (Paris, 1962)

——, ed.: *The Breitkopf Thematic Catalogue, 1762–1787* (New York, 1966)

J. La Rue and M. W. Cobin: 'The Ruge–Seignelay Catalogue: an Exercise in Automated Entries', *Elektronische Datenverarbeitung in der Musikwissenschaft*, ed. H. Heckmann (Regensburg, 1967)

BARRY S. BROOK, SUSAN KAGAN

Rugeri [Ruggeri, Rugieri], **Francesco** ['Il Per'] (*b* 1620; *d c*1695). Italian violin maker. He worked in Cremona, and is thought to have been the first pupil of Nicolo Amati. Although his working life was spent in the shadow of his teacher, he is now regarded as a great maker in his own right, his best instruments almost equal in value to the Amatis'. He had probably left the Amati household by 1641, as census returns survive from that year onwards and his name is not recorded on them. From his workmanship it is assumed that he received instruction in the Amati shop, though his labels do not specify the fact. He copied the Amati style with care and elegance and often even inserted copies of

Nicolo Amati's label, so that he may at times have exported his own work as that of his teacher. As early as 1685 a citizen of Modena laid complaint that the violin he had purchased for 12 pistoles as an Amati was in fact a Rugeri, worth three pistoles at the most: on the removal of the Amati label another of Rugeri had been found underneath.

After about 1670 it was more normal than not for Rugeri to sign his instruments with his own name, 'detto Il Per'. He was helped increasingly by his sons, Vincenzo and Giacinto, both active from about 1675 to about 1730. Giacinto is to some extent shrouded in mystery, and instruments signed by him are very rare. Vincenzo Rugeri, however, was an excellent craftsman whose work bears much the same relationship to Francesco's as the first Giuseppe Guarneri's does to his father Andrea's. Whereas Francesco Rugeri and Andrea Guarneri worked in quite a robust manner, at least to the same extent as Nicolo Amati, the sons of each showed more delicacy, particularly with deeper fluting near the edges, and narrower purfling set closer to the border of their instruments. After 1700 and their fathers' deaths, Giuseppe Guarneri developed into an outstanding maker, but Vincenzo Rugeri showed fewer and fewer signs of activity. He worked as late as 1730, but the delicacy in his instruments turned to weakness, and the splendid golden and orange-red varnishes were replaced by a dull brown.

In addition to their violins, the patterns of which varied like those of the Amati family, the Rugeris made a large number of cellos, but their violas are very rare. At first the cellos were of the large dimensions standard in the 17th century; their effectiveness depends largely on how well their size has been reduced. Francesco later experimented with the form of his cellos, and seems to have been the first Cremonese to produce the smaller, more manageable instrument, shortly before Andrea Guarneri and about 20 years before Stradivari. To that extent he may have been an innovator.

BIBLIOGRAPHY
W. L. von Lütgendorff: *Die Geigen- und Lautenmacher vom Mittelalter bis zur Gegenwart* (Frankfurt am Main, 1904, 6/1922/R1968)

R. Vannes: *Essai d'un dictionnaire universel des luthiers* (Paris, 1932, 2/1951/R1972 as *Dictionnaire universel des luthiers*, suppl. 1959)

F. Hamma: *Meisterwerke italienischer Geigenbaukunst* (Stuttgart, 1933)

W. Henley: *Dictionary of Violin and Bow Makers* (Brighton, 1959–60)

CHARLES BEARE

Rugge, Filippo. See RUGE, FILIPPO.

Ruggeri, Giovanni Maria. See RUGGIERI, GIOVANNI MARIA.

Rugghio di leone (It.). STRING DRUM.

Ruggi, Filippo. See RUGE, FILIPPO.

Ruggi, Francesco (*b* Naples, 21 Oct 1767; *d* Naples, 23 Jan 1845). Italian composer and teacher. He was a pupil of Fenaroli at the conservatory of S Maria di Loreto, Naples. In 1795 he was appointed honorary *maestro di cappella straordinario* of the city of Naples. He composed three operas for Naples in 1794–6 and another for Milan in 1804. This work, *Sofi Trippone* (autograph score in the Ricordi archives, Milan), was successful, but the libretto is said to have contained political allusions of which Ruggi had been unaware, a deception that caused him to give up the stage. He thereafter devoted himself exclusively to teaching and to church music (many of his works are in the Naples Conservatory library). In 1805 he became *maestro di cappella* in the Regina Coeli convent, Naples; later he taught singing to the daughters of Joachim Murat, King of Naples from 1808 to 1815.

Ruggi became one of the best-known contrapuntists of his time, and in 1825 he and Pietro Raimondi succeeded Tritto as counterpoint teachers at the Naples Conservatory. On the retirement of Furno in 1835, Ruggi became teacher of *partimento*, continuing to teach counterpoint during the absences of Donizetti and Raimondi. On Donizetti's resignation in 1838, Ruggi was left as sole master of counterpoint and *partimento*. Among his pupils were Carafa and Petrella (but not Bellini, as is sometimes asserted).

BIBLIOGRAPHY

E. Rocco: 'Francesco Ruggi', *Poliorama pittoresco*, x (1845–6), 289
F. Florimo: *La scuola musicale di Napoli e i suoi conservatorii*, ii (Naples, 1882/R1969), 442   GIOVANNI CARLI BALLOLA

Ruggieri [Ruggeri], **Giovanni Maria** (*fl* c1690–1720). Italian composer. His activity as a composer was apparently centred in Venice. In the preface to his op.1 he called himself a 'dilettante'. The early phase of his career is represented by four published collections of sonatas, both *da camera* and *da chiesa*, in which he shows himself a competent practitioner of the Venetian school of the generation between Legrenzi and Vivaldi. Towards the end of this period he embarked on a successful, or at least fertile, career as an opera composer. Some attention was devoted by writers of about 1750 and later to his *Elisa* (1711), regarded by them as the earliest comic opera produced in the Venetian territory (see Allacci and Scherillo). In 1715 he was *maestro di cuppella* at Pesaro. The Vivaldi literature mentions him as the reviser of a libretto for that composer (*L'inganno trionfante in amore*, 1725), which is not impossible yet appears to be undocumented.

WORKS

OPERAS

(all in 3 acts and produced in Venice, ? all lost)

La Clotilde (G. B. Neri), S Cassiano, wint. 1696; as Amar per vendetta, S Moisè, aut. 1702
La Mariamme (L. Burlini), SS Giovanni e Paolo, aut. 1696
La saggia pazzia di Giunio Bruto (L. Lotti), SS Giovanni e Paolo, aut. 1698
Milciade (Lotti), SS Giovanni e Paolo, carn. 1699
Armida abbandonata (F. Silvani), S Angelo, aut. 1707
Arremone (Silvani), S Angelo, 1708, collab. others
Arato in Sparta (? N. Minato), S Angelo, carn. 1709
Non son quella, è la diffesa (G. A. Falier), S Angelo, aut. 1710
L'ingannator ingannato (A. Marchi), S Samuele, aut. 1710
Elisa (D. Lalli), S Angelo, aut. 1711
Le gare di politica e d'amore (A. Salvi), S Samuele, aut. 1711
Arsinoe vendicata (G. Braccioli), S Angelo, carn. 1712

SACRED VOCAL
(complete list in Gentili, 1927)

XII cantate, some with insts, op.5 (1706)
Gloria, 2 choirs, Venice, 9 Sept 1708, *I-Tn*; Laudate Dominum, motet, 8vv, *D-Z*; Jesu dulcis memoria, Rome, 1689, *A-Wn*
Doubtful attributions: Laetatus, 1v, insts, 10 Sept 1691; Laudate, 1v, 5 insts; Nisi Dominus, 1v, 5 insts: all *I-Tn*

INSTRUMENTAL
(all published in Venice)

Bizzarie armoniche esposte in dieci suonate da camera a due, vn, lute/theorbo, vle/hpd, op.1 (1689)
Scherzi geniali ridotti a regola armonica in dieci suonate da camera a 3, op.2 (1690)
Suonate da chiesa, 2 vn, vle/theorbo, org, op.3 (1693), ed. in Hausmusik, lxiv–lxvii, cxxii–cxxiii, cxxix, cxxxv, cxli–cxlii (1947–)
Suonate da chiesa, 2 vn, vc, org, op.4 (1697)

BIBLIOGRAPHY

SartoriB

L. Allacci: *Drammaturgia* (Venice, rev. 2/1755/R1961)
G. Salvioli [L. N. Galvani]: *I teatri musicali di Venezia nel secolo XVII* (Milan, 1879)
T. Wiel: *I teatri musicali veneziani del settecento* (Venice, 1897)
M. Scherillo: *L'opera buffa napoletana durante il settecento: storia letteraria* (Palermo, 2/1916/R1969)
A. Gentili: 'La raccolta Mauro Foà nella Bibliotecanazionale di Torino', *RMI*, xxxiv (1927), 362
W. S. Newman: *The Sonata in the Baroque Era* (Chapel Hill, 1959, rev. 2/1966/R1972)
M. Chiesa: 'Ruggieri, Giovanni Maria', *MGG*

PIERO WEISS

Ruggiero (It.). A musical scheme for songs, dances and instrumental variations, popular particularly in Italy during the first half of the 17th century. The scheme involves mainly a particular bass melody (ex.1a), which can support a variety of harmonic progressions or discant melodies. It is disposed in four phrases, always in the major mode and ordinarily in duple metre. The Ruggiero in ex.2, from an Italian keyboard manuscript of the early 17th century, shows the extent to which the bass may vary. Ex.3, from the same manuscript, though not entitled Ruggiero has a bass much like ex.1a and, together with ex.2, illustrates the great variety of discant melodies that may accompany the bass. The two chordal settings for the five-course guitar in exx.1b and c (accompaniments, presumably, for the singing of the melody in ex.1a) show the diversity of harmonies possible, especially in the second and third phrases (the stems show the direction the hand moves in strumming the chords).

The music first occurred unnamed in Diego Ortiz's *Tratado de glosas* (Rome, 1553/R1967), where it was included in the table of contents among the 'Italian tenors' used for viol *recercadas* on harmonic grounds. Unlike Ortiz's other 'tenors' (*see* GROUND, ex.2), this one is not confined exclusively to root-position triads; hence the bass line seems, even at this early stage, to be more melodically conceived. The musical scheme was first entitled 'Ruggiero' late in the century, in works

Ex.1 Guitar harmonizations of the Ruggiero

(a) The Ruggiero bass melody

(b) Colonna 1620: *Aria di Ruggiero*

(c) *Roggiero, I-Fr 2793*

Ex.2 Ruggiero, *US-LAu* 51/1

for keyboard by Macque and for lute by Vincenzo Galilei (in a manuscript dated 1584). Probably from the same period come a number of 'Rogero' settings in English manuscripts. The period of greatest popularity occurred during the first half of the 17th century, with sets of variations for chitarrone by J. H. Kapsberger (1604); for instrumental ensemble by Bargnani (1611), Salamone Rossi (1613), Brunelli (1614), Buonamente (1626), Frescobaldi (1634) and Tarquinio Merula (1637); and for keyboard by Ercole Pasquini (CEKM, xii), Mayone (1603), Trabaci (1603) and Frescobaldi (four different sets from 1615, 1624 and 1637), as well as several in the Chigi manuscripts (CEKM, xxxii/3).

Beginning in 1608 the Ruggiero appeared, sometimes designated 'aria di Ruggiero', in monodic or ensemble vocal music by Francesco Rasi, Cifra, Dognazzi, Caspar Kittel, Giovanni Valentini, Raffaello Rontani and P. A. Giramo. The melody appears as a ground in Merula's incorrectly titled *Missa sopra L'Aria del Gran Duca* (1640). The special significance of the bass part is emphasized by d'India's title *Musica sopra il basso dell'aria di Ruggiero di Napoli* (1609). Frescobaldi

Ex.3 *O destin' perverso, US-LAu* 51/1

included the word 'aria' also in the title of his *Partite 12 sopra l'aria di Ruggiero*, suggesting that the scheme was originally for singing poetry (each statement of the music accommodates two 11-syllable lines). Cifra (1617) used the Ruggiero music for a stanza from Ariosto's *Orlando furioso* (xliv.61) beginning 'Ruggier, qual sempre fui'. This text, set by Valderrábano in 1547 to different music, may have been the source of the name Ruggiero.

Numerous Italian guitar books from the first half of the 17th century contain many single statements of the Ruggiero music, with the duple version sometimes followed by a *rotta di ruggiero* in triple metre. Dance use was also indicated by Corbetta (1639), whose Ruggiero was followed by 'sua corrente'. In addition Crivellati gave verbal directions in 1628 to make 'doi volte le represe di Ruggiero' (*see* RIPRESA). A few Ruggiero pieces were written after 1650: for example a keyboard work by Bernardo Storace, chamber pieces by Agostino Guerrieri and G. B. Vitali and guitar examples by Ruiz de Ribayaz, Sanz and an unknown composer in *I-MOe* F1528. Matteo Coferati, in *Corona di sacre canzoni . . . seconda impressione* (1689), gave a discant melody entitled *Ruggieri, o Aria dell'Ortolano, ovvero Donne, mi chiamo il maturo*, which fits the bass melody of ex.1a.

BIBLIOGRAPHY
A. Einstein: 'Die Aria di Ruggiero', *SIMG*, xiii (1911–12), 444
R. Casimiri: 'Girolamo Frescobaldi, autore di opere vocali sconosciute, ad otto voci', *NA*, x (1933), 16
A. Einstein: 'Ancora sull'*aria di Ruggiero*', *RMI*, xli (1937), 163
D. Plamenac: 'An Unknown Violin Tablature of the Early 17th Century', *PAMS 1941*, 144
H. Spohr: *Studien zur italienischen Tanzkomposition um 1600* (diss., U. of Freiburg, 1956), 100ff
J. M. Ward: 'Music for *A Handefull of Pleasant Delites*', *JAMS*, x (1957), 170ff
——: 'Ruggiero', *MGG*
C. M. Simpson: *The British Broadside Ballad and its Music* (New Brunswick, 1966), 612ff

RICHARD HUDSON

Ruggles, Carl [Charles] **(Sprague)** (*b* East Marion, Mass., 11 March 1876; *d* Bennington, Vermont, 24 Oct 1971). American composer. He was an associate in the 1920s and 1930s of Ives, Varèse and Cowell, and with them he strove for a new, radical spirit in music. His non-tonal, polyphonic works have, however, little in common with anything composed by his colleagues.

1. LIFE. Born into a long-established New England family, Ruggles began at the age of six to play a 'violin' he had made from a cigar box. Later he was given a proper instrument and took lessons with George Hill, a New Bedford bandmaster. In his late teens, while working in theatre orchestras, he began to attend Boston SO concerts and to play in chamber groups with members of the orchestra. He continued violin lessons with Felix Winternitz, who had him perform before Kreisler. The outcome was a plan that Ruggles should study in Prague, taking composition with Dvořák, but the project fell through on the death of the financial sponsor. Ruggles then had private lessons in theory with Josef Claus and in composition with Paine at Harvard. He struck up a friendship with Alfred de Voto, pianist of the Boston SO, who accompanied him in performances of some early songs (these were destroyed by Ruggles not long afterwards, but two survive in copies at the Library of Congress). About the turn of the century Ruggles was working as an engraver for the Boston music publisher F. H. Gilson and writing music

Carl Ruggles

criticism for a Cambridge paper. He enrolled in Barrett Wendell's English literature course at Harvard in 1903, and in 1906 he gave some music-club lectures on modern music, praising Wagner, Franck, d'Indy and, above all, Debussy.

In 1907 Ruggles moved to Winona, Minnesota, where he taught at the Mar d'Mar School of Music and founded the Winona SO, conducting several operas in concert form. Before long he was working on an opera of his own, *The Sunken Bell*. Hoping to interest the Metropolitan in the work, he settled in New York in 1917, and there he received support from private patronage, gave composition lessons and started an orchestra at the Rand School. The song *Toys* was written in 1919 for the fourth birthday of his son Micah; printed in 1920, it was his first published composition. Also in New York Ruggles met Varèse, whose International Composers' Guild provided a platform for the works that he now produced more rapidly than at any other period: *Angels* for muted brass was presented by the guild in 1922, *Toys* in 1923, *Vox clamans in deserto* for soprano and small orchestra in 1924, the orchestral suite *Men and Mountains* also in 1924, and *Portals* for string orchestra in 1926. The last two were published in Cowell's New Music Edition (NME), *Men and Mountains* as the first issue (1927). Ives, a subscriber to the NME, was impressed by the strength of Ruggles's piece, and after their meeting (probably in 1929) the two composers developed a deep mutual friendship and respect. When Ives's *Lincoln the Great Commoner* was published in the NME in 1932, Ruggles designed the cover (he had begun to paint some years earlier). In 1932 Ruggles's biggest composition, *Sun-treader* for orchestra, was given its first performances under Slonimsky in Paris and Berlin. It was published in the NME (1934) and played again at the 1936 ISCM Festival (*Angels* had been given at the festival of 1925). Ruggles first heard the piece only in 1965, and then from a recording; the American première did not take place until 1966.

From the 1920s onwards Ruggles spent most summers

in Vermont, where he eventually settled permanently. His last teaching post was as director of a composition class at the University of Miami (1938–43). These were the years of his last important compositions, the *Evocations* for piano and *Organum* for orchestra. Thereafter he continued, as always, to revise his scores and he embarked on some new compositions – during the 1950s he mentioned a work for piano and large orchestra as well as several piano pieces with flower titles – but he completed only a textless hymn tune, *Exaltation* (1958), composed as a memorial to his wife. Most of his creative energy was now going into painting. Yet these late years saw his work as a composer officially honoured: he was elected to the National Institute of Arts and Letters through Ives's insistence (1954), made an honorary DMus of the University of Vermont (1960) and given a Brandeis University Creative Arts Award (1964); his 85th birthday was declared 'Carl Ruggles Day' in Vermont; and in 1966 there was a Ruggles festival at Bowdoin College, Maine.

2. WORKS. As it appears in his eight published compositions, the Ruggles style is both well defined and highly distinctive. Though *Angels* has many chords that can feasibly be related to diatonic triads (in the final version it begins and ends 'in' A♭ major), Ruggles's structures are not tonal; indeed, his harmonies and melodies are usually intensely chromatic. He was aware of the work of the Second Viennese School and had a particular regard for Berg, but his handling of atonality owes little to any example and had been developed before he could have known any serial music. Similarly, his hardy independence made him resistant to influences from his friends Varèse and Ives.

Writers close to Ruggles (Seeger and Cowell) stressed his way of writing melodies so that no note was repeated until a large number (seven to ten) of others had been sounded, for which purpose he regarded octave transpositions as equivalent. Occasionally this results in a full 12-pitch-class succession (at the opening of *Evocation no.2*, for example), but Ruggles's method is not serial. Gilbert has drawn attention to the importance of three-note sets in generating both melody and harmony in the *Evocations*, *Sun-treader* and *Organum*. As an instance of this, ex.1 shows the predominance of the

Ex.1 *Sun-treader*

set of a tritone plus a semitone (octave displacements treated as equivalent) in the top part of the two opening phrases of *Sun-treader*; note that only the last two set forms are disposed so that the melodic expression of a tritone is avoided. The same set occurs prominently in *Evocation no.2*, *Organum* and other pieces.

The first phrase of *Sun-treader*, heard over a regular pounding in the timpani, is typical of the mounting declamations of heroic striving that are common in Ruggles's music. Here it recurs, sometimes in altered form, as an initiator of fresh departure throughout the single-movement work, which bounds to its conclusion through several such reopenings. The other principal material of *Sun-treader* is, again characteristically, more involuted, narrower in melodic interval, quieter and more richly polyphonic. These two types of music are developed, generally in alternation, as the work presses forward. Of its two main sections, the second may be viewed as a shortened and varied recapitulation.

Other works of Ruggles have forms similar to that of *Sun-treader*: both *Lilacs* and *Organum* come to a definite halt before starting on a recapitulatory section, and *Portals* is comparable in its separate development of powerful rising phrases and tendrillous descents. All of these are much shorter than *Sun-treader*, which, at about 17 minutes, is by far the longest of Ruggles's compositions. *Lilacs*, the middle movement of *Men and Mountains*, provides a moment of relative stillness between *Men*, a declamatory invocation with horns forward, and *Marching Mountains*, which is as rugged as its title. When Ruggles revised *Men and Mountains* in 1941 he added a new ending to *Marching Mountains*, scaling it down by retrograde from the peak at which it had originally finished (there is a retrogradation on a larger scale in *Sun-treader*).

Despite his admiration for Debussy, Ruggles did not use the orchestra primarily as a resource for colour; rather his aim was the clearest and boldest presentation of the features that were most important to him: line and polyphony. Of his two major non-orchestral works, the *Evocations* are texturally simpler than, for example, *Sun-treader*, but their style is not specifically 'pianistic'; indeed, they were all orchestrated by Ruggles. The slow harmonies of *Angels* have an apt distant glow when heard on muted brass, yet the piece was originally made available for any other group of like instruments – strings and clarinets were alternatives suggested (the third published version (1960), however, withdraws those options). Instrumentation was thus a secondary matter: in Ivesian terms, Ruggles was less concerned with 'manner' than with 'substance', and it was to strengthen and intensify that substance that he laboured so hard and long in composition and revision.

Ruggles also shared Ives's reverence for the great English and American poets of the Romantic period. His beautiful settings of Browning and Whitman in *Vox clamans in deserto* show this, as do his titles and epigraphs. 'Sun-treader' was Browning's epithet for Shelley, and *Men and Mountains* carries an inscription from Blake: 'Great things are done when men and mountains meet', while the words of Whitman written above *Portals* have a wider reference in the work of one who persistently strove for the sublime and the ecstatic: 'What are those of the known but to ascend and enter the Unknown?'

WORKS

The Sunken Bell (opera, C. H. Meltzer, after Hauptmann: Die versunkene Glocke), c1912–1923, inc., destroyed except for many sketches
Mood, vn, pf, c1918
Toys (Ruggles), 1v, pf, 1919
Men and Angels, 1920: Men, orch, destroyed; Angels, 6 tpt, rev. 4 tpt, 3 trbn, 1938; Sun-treader, orch, rev. as Men of Men and Mountains
Vox clamans in deserto, S, small orch, 1923: Parting at Morning (Browning), Son of Mine (Meltzer), A Clear Midnight (Whitman)
Men and Mountains, small orch, 1924, rev. large orch, 1936, rev. 1941: Men; Lilacs, str; Marching Mountains
Portals, 13 str, 1925; rev. str orch, 1929, rev. 1941, rev. 1952–3
Sun-treader, orch, 1926–31
Evocations, 4 chants, pf, 1935–43, rev. 1954; no.2 orchd 1942, others later, unpubd

Organum, orch, 1944–7; arr. 2 pf, 1946–7, unpubd
Exaltation, hymn tune, unison vv, 1958, unpubd

Principal publishers: American Music Edition, New Music Edition
MSS in *US-NH*, *Wc*
For details of some unfinished works see Kirkpatrick

BIBLIOGRAPHY
H. Cowell: *New Musical Resources* (New York, 1930, 2/1969)
C. Seeger: 'Carl Ruggles', *MQ*, xviii (1932), 578; repr. in *American Composers on American Music*, ed. H. Cowell (Stanford, Calif., 1933), 14ff
L. Harrison: *About Carl Ruggles* (Yonkers, NY, 1946); most repr. in *The Score* (1955), no.12, p.15
T. E. Peterson: *The Music of Carl Ruggles* (diss., U. of Washington, 1967)
J. Saecker: *Carl Ruggles in Winona* (diss., Winona State College, 1967)
J. Kirkpatrick: 'The Evolution of Carl Ruggles: a Chronicle Largely in his Own Words', *PNM*, vi/2 (1968), 146
M. J. Ziffrin: 'Angels – Two Views', *MR*, xxix (1968), 184
S. E. Gilbert: 'The "Twelve-tone System" of Carl Ruggles: a Study of the Evocations for Piano', *JMT*, xiv (1970), 68
——: 'Carl Ruggles and Total Chromaticism', *Yearbook for Inter-American Musical Research*, vii (1971), 43
V. Thomson: 'Ruggles', *American Music Since 1910* (New York, 1971), 31
S. E. Gilbert: 'Carl Ruggles (1876–1971): an Appreciation', *PNM*, xi/1 (1972), 224
C. Seeger: 'In memoriam: Carl Ruggles (1876–1971)', *PNM*, x/2 (1972), 171
S. Faulkner: *Carl Ruggles and his Evocations for Piano* (diss., American U., Washington, DC, 1973)
N. M. Archabal: *Carl Ruggles, Composer and Painter* (diss., U. of Minnesota, 1975)
                    PAUL GRIFFITHS, MARILYN J. ZIFFRIN

Rugi, Filippo. *See* RUGE, FILIPPO.

Rugieri, Francesco. *See* RUGERI, FRANCESCO.

Rühling, Johannes (*b* Borna, baptized 30 Aug 1550; *d* Groitzsch, 2 April 1615). German organist and arranger. He spent his entire life in Saxony, specifically in the Leipzig area. From 1572 to 1575 he held an organ post at Geithain, later at Döbeln, and in 1582 at Groitzsch, where he also served as town clerk. He published *Tabulaturbuch auff Orgeln und Instrument* in Leipzig in 1583. This anthology of 143 folios, printed in 'new' German organ tablature, contains 85 motet arrangements, most of which have Latin titles, though five are in German. It includes pieces by Lassus (15), Clemens non Papa (13), Crecquillon (5), Wert (4), Senfl (2), and one each by Arcadelt, Josquin, Gombert, J. Regnart, Richafort, Verdelot, J. Walter and a number of regional figures (see *MGG*), as well as anonymous pieces. The pieces are arranged according to the church calendar. Coloration is absent, so that 'each organist can employ and conveniently use his own additions'. The measures are barred; five-part writing prevails. A second book was promised in the foreword, but it never appeared. Rühling's tablature provided a collection of motets frequently performed on church organs in Saxony at the time, but otherwise holds no great historical significance. A transcription of the title-page, and a detailed index of the contents, is in H. M. Brown: *Instrumental Music Printed before 1600* (Cambridge, Mass., 2/1967).

                    CLYDE WILLIAM YOUNG

Ruhnke, Martin (*b* Köslin, Pomerania, 14 June 1921). German musicologist. After army service and subsequent captivity as POW (1939–49), he studied musicology with Blume at Kiel University, taking the doctorate there with a dissertation on Joachim Burmeister in 1954. From 1954 to 1960 he was an assistant lecturer at the musicology institute of the Free

University, Berlin, where he completed his *Habilitation* in musicology in 1961 with a work on the history of the German *Hofmusikkollegien* in the 16th century. He was a university lecturer until 1964, when he was appointed professor of musicology at the University of Erlangen-Nuremberg.

Ruhnke has been a member of the Musikgeschichtliche Kommission since 1955 and a member of the committee of the Gesellschaft für Musikforschung since 1965; he succeeded Blume and Fellerer as president (1968–74). His research has centred on music history, theory and performing practice. He has also studied the life and work of Telemann: he became general editor of the collected works in 1960 and was himself editor with H. Hörner of Telemann's *St Luke Passion* of 1728. He was also editor of the Stäblein Festschrift (1967).

WRITINGS

Joachim Burmeister: ein Beitrag zur Musiklehre um 1600 (diss., U. of Kiel, 1954; Kassel, 1955)
with F. Blume: 'Aus der Musikgeschichte der Stadt Lüneburg', *Aus Lüneburgs tausendjähriger Vergangenheit*, ed. U. Wendland (Lüneburg, 1956), 109–38
Beiträge zu einer Geschichte der deutschen Hofmusikkollegien im 16. Jahrhundert (Habilitationsschrift, Free U. of Berlin, 1961; Berlin, 1963)
'Moritz Hauptmann und die Wiederbelebung der Musik J. S. Bachs', *Festschrift Friedrich Blume* (Kassel, 1963), 305
ed.: *Syntagma musicologicum: gesammelte Reden und Schriften* [of F. Blume] (Kassel, 1963)
'G. Ph. Telemanns Klavierfugen', *Musica: Beiheft Practica* (1964), 103
'Relationships between Life and Work of G. Ph. Telemann', *The Consort*, xxiii (1967), 271
'Michael Praetorius', *Musik und Kirche*, xli (1971), 229
'Die Pariser Telemann-Drucke und die Brüder Le Clerc', *Quellenstudien zur Musik: Wolfgang Schmieder zum 70. Geburtstag* (Frankfurt, 1972), 149
ed., with A. A. Abert: *Syntagma musicologicum II: gesammelte Reden und Schriften 1962–1972* [of F. Blume] (Kassel, 1973)
'Francesco Gasparinis Kanonmesse und der Palestrinastil', *Musicae scientiae collectanea: Festschrift Karl Gustav Fellerer* (Cologne, 1973), 494
'Lassos Chromatik und die Orgelstimmung', *Convivium musicorum: Festschrift Wolfgang Boetticher* (Berlin, 1974), 291
'Die Librettisten des Fidelio', *Opernstudien: Anna Amalie Abert zum 65. Geburtstag* (Tutzing, 1975), 121
'Das Einlage-Lied in der Oper der Zeit von 1800–1840', *Die Couleur locale in der Oper des 19. Jahrhunderts*, ed. H. Becker (Regensburg, 1976), 75
'Das italienische Rezitativ bei den deutschen Komponisten des Spätbarocks', *AnMc*, no.17 (1976), 79–118
'Zur Hochzeit: die Psalmen Davids: ein Brief von Heinrich Schütz an die Stadt Braunschweig', *Beiträge zur Musikgeschichte Nordeuropas: Kurt Gudewill zum 65. Geburtstag* (Wolfenbüttel, 1977)
'Telemann, Georg Philipp', *Grove 6*

Over 60 articles in *MGG*

EDITIONS

J. Burmeister: *Musica poetica*, DM, 1st ser., x (1955)
A. P. Coclico: *Musica reservata*, EDM, 1st ser., xlii (1958)
with H. Hörner: *G. P. Telemann: Lukaspassion 1728*, Musikalische Werke, xv (Kassel, 1964)

HANS HEINRICH EGGEBRECHT

Rührtrommel (Ger.). Tenor drum; *see* DRUM, §4.

Ruidhle [ruidhleadh] (Gael.). REEL.

Ruijkers. *See* RUCKERS family.

Ruimonte, Pedro. *See* RIMONTE, PEDRO.

Ruince, Luigi. *See* ROINCE, LUIGI.

Ruiz, Juan. *See* ARCIPRESTE DE HITA.

Ruiz, Matías (*d* Madrid, before 12 Sept 1708). Spanish composer. He taught in the 1670s at Madrid, where his best pupil was Vaquedano. In 1675 Ortiz de Zárate rated him with Carlos Patiño as the most active composer of Latin sacred music at Madrid. He was a contender for the post of *maestro de capilla* of the royal chapel won by Cristóbal Galán in 1680; from either 1684 or 1691 he was *maestro de capilla* of the Royal Incarnation Convent at Madrid. In 1779 Iriarte classed him with Morales, Guerrero and Victoria in a list of the 12 outstanding religious composers in Spanish history. Mitjana published an extremely affecting excerpt from his *St Matthew Passion*. Except for one winsome solo love-song, *Oyd del amante*, his known works are sacred pieces.

WORKS

Turba de la Pasión de la Dominica in Palmis, 4vv (Madrid, 1702) [excerpt in Mitjana]
3 masses, *E-MO*; 3 sequences, *MO*; other sacred music, *V*
Numerous villancicos and tonos: *CO-B*; *D-Mbs*; *E-Bc*; Guatemala City Cathedral; Colección Jesús Sánchez Garza, Instituto Nacional de Bellas Artes, Mexico City; Sucre
Oyd del amante, song, 1v, bc, *E-Mn*

BIBLIOGRAPHY

T. de Iriarte: *La música* (Madrid, 1779, 3/1789), 64
R. Mitjana: 'La musique en Espagne', *EMDC*, I/iv (1920), 2051
J. López-Calo: 'Corresponsales de Miguel de Irízar', *AnM*, xviii (1965), 200, 203
R. Stevenson: *Renaissance and Baroque Musical Sources in the Americas* (Washington, 1970), 24, 98, 177, 249

ROBERT STEVENSON

Ruiz Azner, Valentín (*b* Borja, 14 Feb 1902; *d* Granada, 30 Nov 1972). Spanish composer. He began his music studies with Miguel Arnaudas (solfège) and Alejo Cuartero (piano) at the choir school of the Seo in Saragossa. In 1917 he entered the Pontifical University of Comillas, Santander, to continue his ecclesiastical and musical training under the direction of Nemesio Otaño; he also studied at this time with Cándido Alegría and Luís Iruarrízaga. After serving as organist and director of the Schola Cantorum at the Pontifical University, he obtained in 1927 by open competition the post of *maestro de capilla* at Granada Cathedral. Among the artists and intellectuals then in Granada were Falla, who became a close friend and gave Ruiz Azner advice on musical matters, and Lorca. While continuing to work as an organist and composer, Ruiz Azner wrote articles and lectured on church music and was a prominent figure in the movement to reform it led by Otaño. Between 1927 and 1962 he composed the works which he later singled out as being of most interest, in that they adapt to religious use a harmonic style influenced by Falla; these works include the psalm *Deus, Deus meus* for voice and organ, the *Tríptico de navidad*, the *Himno a la virgen de las angustias* and Passions according to St John and St Matthew. Among his secular compositions are *Madrigal*, to words by Gutierre de Cetina, and the *Cinco canciones* for soprano and piano, on traditional texts and poems by Gutierrez Padial and Marie Laffranque (published in 1962 by Caja de Ahorros, Granada); most of Ruiz Azner's output remains in manuscript.

ENRIQUE FRANCO

Ruiz de Ribayaz, Lucas (*b* S María de Ribarredonda, nr. Burgos, probably before 1650). Spanish guitarist, harpist, composer and priest. He studied for the priesthood at the collegiate church of Villafranca del Bierzo, where he later became a prebendary. In his *Luz y norte* *musical* he stated that he began his musical studies after his ordination while in the service of the Counts Lemos and Andrade and their patron Don Fadrique of Toledo, Marquis of Villafranca. Other statements in this book imply possible affiliations with the Spanish court. He also mentioned having visited 'remote and overseas provinces' – undoubtedly a reference to a sojourn in the Spanish colonies of the New World.

Ruiz de Ribayaz is known only through his *Luz y norte musical para caminar por las cifras de la guitarra española y arpa, tañer, y cantar a compás por canto de órgano; y breve explicación del arte* (Madrid, 1677) which contains detailed introductory tutors for the Baroque guitar and two-course harp, theoretical chapters on general musicianship and an appendix, 'Ecos del libro', containing compositions in tablature for both instruments. In the guitar tutor he advocated the Spanish tuning for the five-course guitar – *A/a–d/d′–g/g–b/b–e′* – and also quoted extensively from the text of Gaspar Sanz's *Instrucción de música sobre la guitarra española* of 1674. The 'Ecos del libro' includes guitar pieces by Sanz and harp pieces by Andrés Lorente and Juan del Vado as well as a number of unidentifiable pieces presumably composed by Ruiz de Ribayaz himself. The pieces are in dance forms characteristic of the late 17th-century Spanish Baroque style and predominantly of Iberian origin (*folia, jácaras, canario, passacalles*, etc).

BIBLIOGRAPHY

J. Wolf: *Handbuch der Notationskunde*, ii (Leipzig, 1919/*R*1963), 201f
S. Murphy: 'The Tuning of the Five-course Guitar', *GSJ*, xxiii (1970), 55, 68
W. Kirkendale: *L'aria di Fiorenza, id est Il ballo del Gran Duca* (Florence, 1972)
R. Strizich: 'Ornamentation in Spanish Baroque Guitar Music', *Journal of the Lute Society of America*, v (1972), 18
——: 'A Spanish Guitar Tutor: Ruiz de Ribayaz' *Luz y norte musical* (1677)', *Journal of the Lute Society of America*, vii (1974), 51–81
ROBERT STRIZICH

Ruiz de Robledo, Juan (*b* ?Segovia; *d* ?Berlanga, after 1644). Spanish composer. He was a choirboy at Segovia Cathedral and later spent 34 years as *maestro de capilla* at León and Valladolid; he was at Valladolid by 1627 and was also a canon there. In 1644 he became prior of the collegiate church at Berlanga. Under his direction choral music at León and Valladolid reached a high standard. According to his own account in his *Laura de música eclesiástica* (Madrid, 1644) any benefice holder at León who sang off key or with poor enunciation was automatically liable to be punished, while at Valladolid any prebendary who could not pass a singing test after one year of study was denied bread and wine.

Ruiz's surviving music is contained in his *Misas, psalmos, Magníficas, motetes, y otras cosas tocantes al culto divino* (Madrid, 1627), which, though marked 'ex typographia Regia', was never printed (MS copies are located at *E-Bc, Mn, V, VAc* and elsewhere). It includes seven masses, nine settings of the *Magníficat* and 49 other works; all show that Ruiz was a master of eight-part writing for two antiphonal choirs. His *Laura de música eclesiástica* contains on the title-page the word 'impresso', but it also remains only in MS; two 17th-century copies are in the Real Monasterio, El Escorial; a third, dating from the 19th century, is in the Biblioteca Nacional, Madrid. The *Laura* is chiefly a treatise on matters of liturgical practice, but it also contains an extended defence of music against those who claim that it is purely a mechanical art, without decency, gravity or sound rules.

BIBLIOGRAPHY

H. Anglés and J. Subirá: *Catálogo musical de la Biblioteca nacional de Madrid*, i (Barcelona, 1946)
H. Anglés: 'El archivo musical de la catedral de Valladolid', *AnM*, iii (1948), 59–108
J. Subirá: *Historia de la música española e hispanoamericana* (Barcelona, 1953)
J. M. Alvarez Pérez: 'La polifonía sagrada y sus maestros en la catedral de León durante el siglo XVII', *AnM*, xv (1960), 141
BARTON HUDSON

Rukkers. See RUCKERS family.

Ruloffs, Bartholomeus (*b* Amsterdam, ?Oct 1741; *d* Amsterdam, 13 May 1801). Netherlands violinist, organist, composer, conductor and librettist. His father Reynier Ruloffs was a bassoonist and his brother Jan Pieter a timpanist in the Amsterdam theatre orchestra, in which Bartholomeus became a violinist at the age of 16. In 1766 he was appointed organist at the Nieuwe Zijdskapel. The Amsterdam theatre burnt down in 1773, and Ruloffs succeeded Hendrik Chalons as conductor of the rebuilt theatre's orchestra in 1774. In 1783 he also became the organist at the Wester Church, and in 1791 the first conductor of the Felix Meritis symphony concerts; two years later he was appointed organist at the Nieuwe Kerk, the main Protestant church of Amsterdam. In the same year he married the singer Ernestina Louise Anderegg. In his last years he resigned from his conducting duties but continued to supervise the ballets at the theatre.

Though he did not excel in a particular field, probably because of his diverse talents, Ruloffs was important in the development of early musical life in Amsterdam. He translated many opera librettos (now lost) for the theatre there, including Mozart's *Die Entführung aus dem Serail* and *Die Zauberflöte*, Wranitzky's *Oberon*, Dittersdorf's *Doktor und Apotheker* and *Das rote Käppchen*. He also translated, and inserted his own music into, many French *opéras comiques*, including Grétry's *Les deux avares* ('De twee gierigaards', 1787) and *Richard Coeur-de-lion* ('Richard Leeuwenhart', 1791), Lucille Grétry's *Le mariage d'Antoine* ('Het huwelijk van Antonio', 1791), Monsigny's *La belle Arsène* ('De schoone Arsène', 1789) and Gossec's *Le tonnelier* ('De kuiper', 1792). In addition Ruloffs wrote songs, chamber music and other instrumental works, music for the dedication of the new Amsterdam theatre and a Singspiel.

WORKS

Stage: 5 opéras comiques, arr. and with some new music, after Gossec, A. E. M. Grétry, L. Grétry, Monsigny, 1787–92; De bruiloft van Kloris en Roosje (Singspiel), *c*1800; Komst van Willem den Eersten, Prins van Oranje, te Leyden, 1780, lost; Arlequin, herbergier en taartjesbakker (pantomime), 1785, lost; De bruiloft van Kloris en Roosje (Singspiel), *c*1800; De triumph der liefde, of Elk zijn beurt is niet te veel (pantomime), lost
Vocal: Jephta (cantata), 1779, lost; Zangwijzen tot de nagelatenen stichtelijke gezangen (B. Elikink), 1v, vn, fl, hpd (Amsterdam, 1769), collab. J. G. Meder; Muziekstukjes voor de proeve van kleine gedigten voor kinderen (H. van Alphen) (Amsterdam, *c*1790); Muzikaale verlustiging, bestaande in nieuwe Nederduitsche gezangen, 1v, bc, insts (Amsterdam, *c*1790)
Inst: 6 sonates, hpd/pf, vn, vc, op.1 (Amsterdam, *c*1760); Inwijding van den Amsterdamschen Schouwburg, 1774; Marsch, retraite en vaandelmarsch, kbd, vn (Amsterdam, *c*1785); Musique militaire, 2 cl, 2 hn, bn (Amsterdam, *c*1785); Les récréations d'Apollon, 3 syms. (Amsterdam, 1787); De veldslag, orch, lost

BIBLIOGRAPHY
AMZ, ii (1799–1800), cols.191, 396

E. G. J. Gregoir: *Biographie des artistes-musiciens néerlandais des XVIIIe et XIXe siècles* (Antwerp, 1864)
D. F. Scheurleer: *Het muziekleven in Nederland in de tweede helft der 18e eeuw* (The Hague, 1909)
A. N. Verveen: 'Bartholomeus Ruloffs (1741–1801)', *Amstelodamum*, xlix (1962); also in *Mens en melodie*, xvii (1962)
J. H. van der Meer: 'Ruloffs, Bartholomeus', *MGG*

AREND KOOLE

Rumania. *See* ROMANIA.

Rumba [rhumba]. A popular recreational dance of Afro-Cuban origin. It originated in the dances of the Kikonga cult; the *columbia* and *guaguancó* were pantomimic dances, danced with extensive hip and shoulder movements and improvised acrobatics, and the *rumba yambú* and *rumba de tiempó España* were imitations of old people and housewives. In Cuba the rumba is defined by its accompaniment, with claves, *cucharas*, *tambor grave* and *tambor requinto* (or *quinto*) performing in a complex duple-metre pattern using extensive syncopation and *tresillo* (dotted quaver–dotted quaver–semiquaver) rhythms (*see* CUBA, §II, 3(iv)). The rumba became known in a modified form in the USA as early as 1914 but it did not become popular elsewhere until it was reintroduced to the USA in a less suggestive version in 1931, and it soon spread to Europe. As a ballroom dance it is performed by a solo dancer or by a couple in the normal ballroom embrace but held slightly apart. The characteristic movement is a rocking of the hips, to a quick–quick–slow rhythm, often creating cross-rhythms with the accompaniment, at about 40–50 bars per minute. The melody is often repetitive and much of the character of the music derives from the ostinato one-bar rhythmic pattern played on the maracas (known in German as *Rumbakugeln*), claves (or sticks) and other Cuban percussion instruments. In Europe and the USA in the 1930s the rumba absorbed jazz elements; it continued as a popular ballroom dance into the 1970s and has been the model for the mambo, cha cha cha and other Latin American ballroom dances. The rumba has also been used in concert music, notably by Milhaud in *La création du monde* and in the finale of his Second Piano Concerto.

BIBLIOGRAPHY
A. P. and D. Wright: *How to Dance* (New York, 1942, rev. 2/1958)
P. J. S. Richardson: *A History of English Ballroom Dancing (1910–45)* (London, 1946)

WILLIAM GRADANTE, DEANE L. ROOT

Rumford, (Robert) Kennerley. English baritone, husband of CLARA BUTT.

Rummel. German family of musicians.

(1) Christian (Franz Ludwig Friedrich Alexander Rummel (*b* Brichsenstadt, Bavaria, 27 Nov 1787; *d* Wiesbaden, 13 Feb 1849). Composer, pianist and conductor. He was educated in Mannheim, where he studied the violin with Heinrich Ritter and composition with Karl Jakob Wagner; he also received some guidance from the Abbé Vogler. From 1806 he was a military band director and from 1808 to 1813 served in the Peninsular War, during which he was taken prisoner. He married while in Spain. After the Battle of Waterloo, in which he fought, he left the army and settled in Wiesbaden where he taught until Duke Wilhelm of Nassau invited him to form and lead his court orchestra; Rummel directed it from 1815 to 1842, during which time it became renowned. At the ducal court he taught the Princess of Nassau, for whom he wrote a piano instruction book. When the ducal orchestra was disbanded in 1842, it became amalgamated with the theatre orchestra and Rummel succeeded T. Eisfeld as its director. In his last few years in this position, Rummel was often ill and Konradin Kreutzer temporarily replaced him.

Rummel was an excellent pianist and made concert tours to major cities in Germany, Switzerland, Belgium and Holland. An extremely versatile musician, he also played the clarinet and violin, in addition to teaching, composing and conducting. When he took over the direction of the theatre orchestra at the age of 55, he set out to remedy his previous lack of theatrical experience. He was meticulous in his preparation of a repertory which included operas by Halévy, Auber and Meyerbeer, and won the respect of all with whom he worked; he went to Paris to study Meyerbeer's *Les Huguenots* before he conducted it at Wiesbaden. It is doubtful whether Beethoven was as cordially disposed to Rummel as Pougin asserted in the supplement to Fétis's *Biographie universelle des musiciens*, but certainly Rummel was influenced by Beethoven. Schott wrote to Beethoven on 19 April 1824 recommending Rummel, who would soon be visiting Vienna in the company of the Duke of Nassau. On 29 May 1824, Beethoven replied that he had arranged for Rummel to visit him to show some of his compositions and that he would advise him as to which course to follow.

Rummel wrote many works for solo piano including variations and fantasias on operatic themes and, for piano duet, variations, sonatas and polonaises. He also wrote chamber music for various combinations of wind instruments, a violin and piano sonata, a clarinet concerto, and works for piano and orchestra, in addition to military band music. Rummel composed and arranged works for the orchestra at Wiesbaden, including an arrangement of Beethoven's Kreutzer Sonata; he also made piano transcriptions of operatic numbers. In the *Concerto militaire* for piano and orchestra op.68, Rummel quotes a Beethoven theme which the soloist takes up in brilliant figuration. Concentration on technical display is a typical feature of his writing for piano.

(2) Josephine Rummel (*b* Manzanares, Spain, 12 May 1812; *d* Wiesbaden, 19 Dec 1877). Pianist, eldest child of (1) Christian. Having had piano instruction from her father, Josephine earned a reputation as a pianist through her performances in Germany and abroad. She became court pianist at Wiesbaden.

(3) Joseph Rummel (*b* Wiesbaden, 6 Oct 1818; *d* London, 25 March 1880). Composer, pianist and clarinettist, son of (1) Christian. His father gave him a well-rounded musical education with special emphasis on the clarinet and piano. He entered the service of the Duke of Oldenburg at Wiesbaden until in 1842 he moved to Paris where, after a period in London, he lived from 1847 to 1870. He returned to London in 1870 and remained there for the rest of his life. He was well known as a pianist and clarinettist. His large output, estimated at over 2000 works, consists mainly of arrangements of operatic excerpts for piano solo and duet. He also wrote fantasias on operatic themes, waltzes, mazurkas and studies for piano. The majority of his works were published by Escudier in Paris and Schott in Mainz.

(4) Franziska Rummel (*b* Wiesbaden, 4 Feb 1821). Opera singer, daughter of (1) Christian. She was taught first by her father at Wiesbaden; subsequently she studied singing in Paris with Bordogni and then in Milan with Lamperti. The Wiesbaden opera engaged her as principal singer in 1843. She toured successfully in Germany and Belgium before her marriage to the music publisher Peter Schott, in Brussels. Among her roles were Marguerite de Valois in Meyerbeer's *Les Huguenots*, Amina in Carl Blum's *Die Nachtwandlerin* and Constanze in Mozart's *Die Entführung aus dem Serail*. Some of her performances at Frankfurt am Main (1843 and 1845) and Hamburg (1847) were favourably reviewed in the *Allgemeine musikalische Zeitung*; she was most noted for her brilliant coloratura singing.

BIBLIOGRAPHY
O. Dorn: 'Das Wiesbadener Theater-Orchester und seine Dirigenten (1842–1903)', *Die Musik*, ii (1902–3), 179
F. Pazdírek: *Universal-Handbuch der Musikliteratur* (Vienna, 1904–10/*R*1967)
A. W. Thayer: *Ludwig van Beethoven's Leben*, v (Leipzig, 1908); ed. and trans. E. Forbes (Princeton, 1964, 2/1967)
R. Schumann: *Gesammelte Schriften* (Leipzig, 5/1914/*R*1969)
H. Engel: *Die Entwicklung des deutschen Klavierkonzertes* (Leipzig, 1927)
E. Anderson, ed.: *The Letters of Beethoven* (London, 1961)
GAYNOR G. JONES

Rung, Frederik (*b* Copenhagen, 14 June 1854; *d* Copenhagen, 22 Jan 1914). Danish conductor and composer. Rung's father Henrik (1807–71) was a gifted composer, the author of numerous operas, Singspiels and songs to Danish texts. His son grew up in a keenly musical household, and began to compose when still a child; but neither these works nor his later compositions are very remarkable. As a conductor, however, he distinguished himself, beginning his career brilliantly in the Cæciliaforeningen, a choral society founded by his father in 1851 which devoted itself to Italian Renaissance church music. On his father's death, Rung took charge of the choir and extended the repertory to include Handel's oratorios and Bach's church music. In 1887 he founded the Madrigalkoret, a choir selected from the members of the Cæciliaforeningen, and this became internationally famous. From 1884 he was second conductor at the Royal Theatre (under Johan Svendsen) and from 1908 chief conductor. Here he won acclaim for some outstanding performances of Wagner's and Puccini's operas. His compositions include a number of stage works, two symphonies, smaller orchestral pieces and chamber works, among them two string quartets, a piano quartet and a nonet, smaller choral works, songs and piano music.

BIBLIOGRAPHY
C. Thrant: *Cæciliaforeningen og dens stifter* (Copenhagen, 1901)
G. Lynge: *Danske komponister i det 20. aarhundredes begyndelse* (Aarhus, 1916), 422ff [gives selective list of works]
BO MARSCHNER

Runge. German family of printers. From 1611 Georg Runge managed the press belonging to his father Christoph Runge the elder in the Berlin Minorite monastery. After Georg's death (1639) his widow and heirs carried on the business until 1644, when Georg's son Christoph Runge the younger was able to take it over. Half of the 128 musical works from Berlin (listed by Lenz) were printed on the Runge press, which was particularly active in disseminating the works of Zangius, Johannes Crüger, Hentzschel and others.

BIBLIOGRAPHY
H. U. Lenz: *Der Berliner Musikdruck von seinen Anfängen bis zur Mitte des 18. Jahrhunderts* (diss., U. of Rostock, 1932)

J. Benzing: *Die Buchdrucker des 16. und 17. Jahrhunderts im deutschen Sprachgebiet* (Wiesbaden, 1963)
THEODOR WOHNHAAS

Rúnólfsson, Karl Ottó (*b* Reykjavík, 24 Oct 1900; *d* Reykjavík, 1970). Icelandic composer, teacher and trumpeter. He studied in Copenhagen (1926–7) and with Mixa and Urbancic at the Reykjavík College of Music (1934–9). His activities as a trumpet player and teacher included work with brass bands (he was a member, instructor and director of several in Iceland, particularly Svanur, the Reykjavík band, and in later years one of the city's youth bands) and posts as first trumpet of the Iceland SO (1950–55) and as a teacher at the Reykjavík College of Music (1939–64). A prolific composer, he was in the 1940s considered one of the more audacious composers in Iceland, displaying an unusual talent which compensated for his lack of formal education. He freed himself of 'Nordic sentimentality', though he made good use of Icelandic folksongs and dances. Often witty, his work is never dull.

WORKS
(*selective list*)

Orch: Á krossgötum [On crossroads], suite, 1939; Eywind on the Mountains, ov.; Jón Arason, ov.; Esja, op.54, sym., 1968
Inst: Icelandic Rhyme Songs, vn, pf (1964); Sonata, op.23; tpt, pf (1962)
Principal publishers: Lárusson, Musica Islandica

BIBLIOGRAPHY
B. Tobíasson: *Hver er madurinn?* (Reykjavík, 1944), 20
O. Kristjánsson: *Kennaratal á Íslandi*, i (Reykjavík, 1958), 417
J. Guðhason and P. Haraldsson: *Íslenzkir samtídarmenn*, ii (Reykjavík, 1967), 9
A. Burt: *Iceland's Twentieth-century Composers and a Listing of their Works* (Fairfax, Virginia, in preparation)
AMANDA M. BURT

Runonlaulu. The singing of old poems or Kalevalaic runes in Finland; *see* FINLAND, §II, 2.

Ruodolf de Neuchâtel [von Fenis, von Neuenburg]. *See* RUDOLF VON FENIS-NEUENBURG.

Rupert of Deutz [Rupertus Tuitensis] (*b* ?Liège, *c*1070; *d* Deutz, *c*1130). Benedictine theologian, liturgist and hymnodist. Rupert was an oblate of the monastery of St Lawrence in Liège and was educated there under Abbot Berengar (*d* 1115). His teacher in music may have been a certain Heribrand. Ordained priest in 1106, he moved to the monastery of St Michael in Siegburg about 1115 and some five years later was made abbot of St Heribert in Deutz. His most widely distributed work, to judge from the large number of extant MSS, is *De divinis officiis*; it is on the liturgy and contains a number of observations on plainchant. His copious theological writings involved him in disputes with Anselm of Laon and William of Champeaux. One of them, *De Trinitate*, in the section *De operibus Spiritus Sancti* (vol.vii, chap.16), contains a passage on music of a certain originality, finding in Old Testament citations evidence of the musical proportions usually associated with Pythagoras. There are, in addition, a number of exegetical works; a chronicle of the monastery of St Lawrence formerly ascribed to Rupert is no longer considered authentic. He is thought to have written in his youth hymns in honour of SS Mary Magdalen, Goar, Severinus and Heribert, and Rupert himself refers to his hymn to the Holy Spirit, *Deus meus et Dominus*, which may, however, have been sung to the melody of the *Veni Creator Spiritus*. Rupert's credentials as a composer of melodies are thus not clearly established. His significance in the history of music has perhaps been magnified by his reputation as a theologian and his association with that much studied musical centre, Liège. Collected writings are in *PL*, clxvii–clxx.

BIBLIOGRAPHY
A. Auda: *La musique et les musiciens de l'ancien pays de Liège* (Liège, 1930)
J. Smits van Waesberghe: *Muziekgeschiedenis der middeleeuwen*, i (Tilburg, 1936)

LAWRENCE GUSHEE

Rupff, Conrad. See RUPSCH, CONRAD.

Rupin, Ivan Alexeyevich (*b* c1790; *d* ?St Petersburg, 1850). Russian singer and composer. Rupin was born into a family of serfs. As a youth he sang in a local choir, but was later sent to Moscow to study singing with the celebrated Italian castrato Pietro Muschietti. Liberated from his serfdom he moved to St Petersburg. Here he gave singing lessons and became well known as a performer, adopting the professional name Rupini. For a while he took lessons in harmony and musical theory with T. V. Zhuchkovsky (1785–1838), the composer and sometime director of the imperial theatres. In 1832 he published at St Petersburg a *Muzïkal'nïy al'- bom severnovo pevtsa* ('The northern singer's album of music'), which contained works by Alyabyev, and later produced a collection of his own songs. Entitled *Le bouquet* (St Petersburg, 1839), this contained his song *Rïtsar* ('The knight'), to a poem by Pushkin, three settings of works by F. A. Koni, and *Videniye* ('The vision') to a poem by Polezhayev. Rupin was appointed chorus master of the Italian opera in 1843.

Rupin is known particularly for his collection of Russian folksongs, *Narodnïye russkiye pesni*, published in the years 1831 and 1833 in St Petersburg. This collection is remarkable among the others produced during the first half of the 19th century, since it prints each song in two forms. The first version consists of the solo line accompanied by simple harmonies for the keyboard or guitar; the second is an arrangement of the song for three-part choir. A modern edition by T. Popova was published in Moscow in 1955.

GEOFFREY NORRIS

Ruppe, Christian Friedrich [Fredrik] (*b* Salzungen, Saxe-Meiningen, 22 Aug 1753; *d* Leiden, 25 May 1826). Netherlands composer, theorist, performer and university professor of German birth, brother of F. C. Ruppe. His father, a hatter, built instruments and was the organist at Wilprechtsrode. According to Kist he had already moved to Leiden by 1772, but his name does not appear there until 20 June 1787, when he enrolled at the university. In requesting the right to publish his compositions for 15 years from 20 July 1790, he called himself 'organist of the Lutheran church in Leiden'; the petition lists many works that are now lost, including keyboard concertos, French and Italian arias, and quartets. On 18 October 1790 he was appointed *Kapelmeester* of the University of Leiden. He founded a choral society in Leiden in 1800. Although he began to teach courses on music in 1802 and wrote a book on the theory of 'modern' music (1809–10), it was not until 13 May 1816 that King Wilhelm I appointed him 'lector in music', with the stipulation that he continue his activities as music director of the university.

Ruppe was well known in the Netherlands during his lifetime for his theoretical treatise and voluminous compositions, many of which he himself published. Much of his surviving work is chamber music, written in a clear Viennese Classical style that is simple but expressive; the later compositions show a more Romantic attitude. He also wrote keyboard sonatinas (perhaps written for private students), cantatas performed in churches in Leiden and The Hague, children's songs, keyboard character studies inspired by current political events and odes written for university performance, all reflecting his various activities.

WORKS
(published in The Hague, Amsterdam, Rotterdam, Leiden or Haarlem)

VOCAL
Galatée (opéra comique, after J. P. Florian), Leiden, 1804, only lib extant
Cantatas: Gezangen voor het feest van den 19 Dec 1799; Q Horatii Flacci Oda IV et aliae odae (1803), incl. S. Speyert van der Eyk, pubd separately (1802); Vrije navolging der Latijnsche hymnen (H. Hillebrand) (1809–10); Koor voor godsdienstige zanggenootschappen (Ps xxxiii) (1822); 9 others, 1796–1814, lost
Songs: Rhynvis Feith, romances (1787); Oden en gedichten (J. P. and A. Kleyn) (1788); 4 collections of 12 gezangen, 3vv (1802–8); [22] Stukjes uit de gedichtjes voor kinderen (H. van Alphen), opp.33, 36 (c1833)

CHAMBER
Kbd trios: 6 as op.2 (c1779); 3 as op.4 (c1783); 3 as op.14 (c1806); 1 each in opp.18, 25–7 (c1810–19); Ouverture turque, acc. perc, db, op.20 (c1812); Ouverture tartare, op.28 (1820)
Duets (sonatas, sonatines), kbd, vn: 4 as op.1 (1777); 6 as op.3 (c1781); 8 as op.6 (c1787); 9 as op.7 (c1789); 3 as op.8 (1790); 12 as op.9 (1790); 3 as op.11 (c1801), ed. in Oud-Nederlandse speelmuziek, x (The Hague, 1948); La métamorphose, op.32 (1822); 4 sets of variations (c1800)
Kbd solo: 18 pièces, org/pf, op.10 (1799), ed. in Oud-Nederlandse speelmuziek, ix (The Hague, 1948); 12 sonatines, hpd/pf (c1800); De zangwyzen van de psalmen en gezangen, org/hpd/pf (1801); 45 praeludia en 276 interludia nevens 4 fuga's, org (1802); 6 sonatines, pf, op.13 (c1805), no.6 for 4 hands; Zangwijzen der evangelische gezangen, org/hpd/pf (1806); 3 sonates, pf (1811); La grande bataille de Waterloo, pf, op.23 (1815); La paix universelle, pf, op.24 (1815); 6 sérénades, pf, op.31 (c1822); Ouverture grecque, pf, op.34 (c1824); 7 sets of variations; dances and character pieces
Kbd 4 hands: 3 sonates, op.5 (c1785); 3 sonates, op.16 (c1808); Sonates (1809)

THEORETICAL
Theorie der hedendaagsche muziek (Amsterdam, 1809–10, 2/1818)

BIBLIOGRAPHY
EitnerQ; FétisB
F. C. Kist: 'Christian Fredrik Ruppe', *Nederlandsch muzikaal tydschrift* (1841), 94
E. G. J. Gregoir: *Biographie des artistes-musiciens néerlandais des XVIIIe et XIXe siècles* (Antwerp, 1864)
Bouwsteenen: JVNM, i–iii (1869–81)
J. W. Enschedé: 'Christian Friedrich Ruppe', *NNBW*
F. Noske: 'Het Nederlandse kinderlied in de achttiende eeuw', *TVNM*, xix/3–4 (1963), 173
J. H. van der Meer: 'Ruppe, Christian Friedrich', *MGG*

BARRY KERNFELD

Ruppe, Friedrich Christian (*b* Salzungen, Saxe-Meiningen, 18 Feb 1771; *d* Meiningen, 14 Aug 1834). German violinist, keyboard player and composer, brother of C. F. Ruppe. In 1786, when his father died and Salzungen was devastated by fire, he left to study theology at Eisenach and supported himself by giving keyboard lessons. Half a year later he came under the patronage of Duke Georg of Saxe-Meiningen, who provided for his education in music theory and violin playing, as well as in public finance. After further studies in Weimar, Dessau and Wörlitz he was appointed both an administrator and a musician at the court; he gave piano concerts and played the violin in the orchestra. His compositions, which were not well known outside Meiningen, include *Leiden und Tod Jesu* and *Der verlorene Sohn* (oratorios), *Der Sieg der Tugend* (unfinished opera), *Friedenscantate*, a keyboard concerto with choir and various chamber works, of which a trio for keyboard, clarinet and bassoon (Offenbach, c1821) and a sonata for keyboard and strings ad lib (Kassel, n.d.) were published.

BIBLIOGRAPHY
AMZ, xvi (1814), col.589; xxxvii (1835), col.244
For further bibliography see RUPPE, CHRISTIAN FRIEDRICH.

BARRY KERNFELD

Ruppel, Karl Heinrich (*b* Darmstadt, 5 Sept 1900). German critic and writer on music. In his formative years he was strongly influenced by his friendship with the young Erich Kleiber, who taught him music while he attended the Darmstadt Gymnasium. Until 1923 he studied literature, music and art at the Darmstadt Technische Hochschule and at the universities of Frankfurt, Freiburg and Munich. From 1928 to 1944 he worked as editor of the *Kölnische Zeitung* literary supplement, and from 1932 with the paper's editorial staff in Berlin as chief theatre and music critic. He spent five years from 1945 as artistic director of the Württemberg State Theatre in Stuttgart. In 1950 he became chief music critic of the *Süddeutsche Zeitung* in Munich, to which he contributed for more than 25 years. Ruppel's carefully weighed judgments and elegant prose epitomize the best of German music criticism. He is invariably sympathetic, but does not lightly give praise. His writings are thoroughly informed and display sound judgment, based on long experience and enhanced by clear structure and fluent expression. He wrote the libretto for Mihalovici's opera *Die Heimkehr* (1953) and the scenario for Mihalovici's ballet *Thésée* (1964).

WRITINGS

Berliner Schauspiel (Berlin, 1943)
'Verdi und Shakespeare', *Das Musikleben*, iv (1951), 35; repr. in *SMz*, xcv (1955), 137
'Igor Strawinsky und das Ballett', *Musik der Zeit* (1952), no.2, p.47
Musik in Deutschland (Munich, 1952)
with G. R. Sellner and W. Thomas: *Carl Orff: ein Bericht in Wort und Bild* (Mainz, 1955)
'Das dramatische Ensemble: Bemerkungen zu Mozarts Dramaturgie', *Maske und Kothurn*, ii (1956), 134
'Musica viva 1945–1958', *Musica viva* (Munich, 1959), 9–47
Musik in unserer Zeit: ein Bilanz von 10 Jahren (Munich, 1960) [articles and reviews]
Grosses Berliner Theater (Velber, 1962)
'Japanische Impressionen', *Melos*, xxix (1962), 37
with W. Reich: 'Paul Hindemith und sein Werk für die moderne Musik', *Universitas*, xix (1964), 137
'Luigi Dallapiccola', *Melos*, xxxi (1964), 81
'Von der Provokation zum Bekenntnis: über Paul Hindemith's Opern', *Opernwelt*, v/2 (1964), 14
'Die Prinzessin Edmond de Polignac', *Melos*, xxxiv (1967), 188
'Der weltmännische Bauer: Verdis Persönlichkeit', *Musica*, xxii (1968), 31
'Skrjabin heute', *Musica*, xxvi (1972), 13
Grosse Stunden der Musik (Munich, 1975)

HANSPETER KRELLMANN

Ruppich, Conrad. See RUPSCH, CONRAD.

Ruprecht. German family of organ builders. The family relationships have not been established. Hieronymus Ruprecht (*fl* 1626–61) built organs at St Laurentius, Cologne (1626–7; three manuals, 24 stops); Mönchengladbach-Rheindalen (1633; two manuals, 13 stops); Adenau (1639); Halver, Westphalia (1652–5), and Linnich (1661). Johannes Ruprecht worked in Boppard from 1658 to 1675. In 1676 he produced an organ for the Minorite church in Cleves; Conrad Ruprecht (*fl* 1656–1706), who worked both in Anholt and in Boxmeer, Netherlands, built an instrument in 1656 for the Minorite church in Duisburg (Rhine) and another in 1698 for St Maarten's, Doesburg (Netherlands). No instrument by the Ruprecht family has survived.

The specifications used by the family remained fairly close to those of the 16th-century Rhenish–Belgian school, comprising relatively simply distributed diapason choruses, a group of wide-scaled 16′, 8′, 4′, $2\frac{2}{3}$′, 2′ and $1\frac{1}{3}$′ stops, and a small number of reed stops such as Trommet, Crummhorn and Schalmei. Of the stops used by this school, only the five-rank Nachthorn and the pedal stops (2′ Flauto and 8′ Trommet) were evidently never used by the Ruprecht family.

BIBLIOGRAPHY
K. Dreimüller: 'Beiträge zur niederrheinischen Orgelgeschichte', *Beiträge zur Geschichte der Musik am Niederrhein*, ed. K. G. Fellerer (Cologne, 1956), 17–51

HANS KLOTZ

Ruprecht, (Josef) Martin [?Stephan] (*b* ?Vienna, c1758; *d* Vienna, 7 June 1800). Austrian composer and tenor. He was a member of Katherina Schindler's troupe that gave a guest season at the Kärntnertortheater, Vienna, in 1776. He became a founder-member of the German National Singspiel company in 1778, appearing as Fritz in the première of Umlauf's *Die Bergknappen* (which had to be postponed for nearly a month owing to his illness), and later in most of the new productions (including his own *Was erhält die Männer treu?*). He sang with the Italian Opera following the closure of the Singspiel company in 1783 and joined the re-formed German company again in 1785. In 1788 he left the Opera, and shortly afterwards joined the court chapel ensemble, of which he remained a member until his death. He was considered a talented singer, though a rather ordinary actor.

Of his compositions, equal merit and importance attach to his Singspiels and his songs, six of which were published by Artaria in 1785. Evidence for the performance of only four Ruprecht Singspiels can be traced; it seems likely that *Die Wette* was not performed, and that *Der Irrwisch* and *Der Derwisch*, both mentioned by Pollak-Schlaffenberg, are the product of confusion with Umlauf's *Das Irrlicht* and the Schack, Gerl and Henneberg *Der wohltätige Derwisch* respectively. Gerber named *Die natürlichen Wunder* and *Elmire* among Ruprecht's works; the former cannot be traced, and the latter, presumably identical with Goethe's *Erwin und Elmire*, given at the Burgtheater on 20 April 1794, was not (according to Hadamowsky) set to music.

WORKS

Singspiels (first performed in Vienna unless otherwise stated); Die Wette (1), 1777, *A-Wgm*, ?unperf.; Was erhält die Männer treu? (2, L. Zehnmark), Burg, 1 May (? 30 March), 1780, *Wn*; Die Dorfhandel oder Bunt über Eck (2, P. Weidmann), Kärntnertor, 15 Nov 1785, *Wn*; Das wütende Heer oder Das Mädchen im Turme (3, after C. F. Bretzner), Kärntnertor, 1 June 1787; Der blinde Ehemann (J. F. Jünger), Freihaus, 21 Oct 1794; Die natürlichen Wunder, c1795, and Elmire, cited in Gerber

Lieder: 6 Lieder für das Pianoforte (Vienna, 1785), 3 ed. in DTÖ, liv, Jg.xxvii/2 (1920/*R*), 1 ed. in Friedlaender, i/2; 12 Gesänge, pf acc. (Vienna, c1789), 2 ed. in Friedlaender, i/2

BIBLIOGRAPHY
FétisB; *GerberNL*
M. Friedlaender: *Das deutsche Lied im 18. Jahrhundert* (Stuttgart and Berlin, 1902/*R*1970)
O. Teuber and A. von Weilen: *Die Theater Wiens*, ii/2/1 (Vienna, 1903)
I. Pollak-Schlaffenberg: 'Die Wiener Liedmusik von 1778 bis 1789',

SMw, v (1918), 104
O. E. Deutsch: 'Das Freihaus-Theater auf der Wieden', Mitteilungen des Vereines für Geschichte der Stadt Wien, xvi (1937), 30–73
F. Hadamowsky: Die Wiener Hoftheater (Staatstheater), 1776–1966, i (Vienna, 1966)
O. Michtner: Das alte Burgtheater als Opernbühne (Vienna, 1970)
PETER BRANSCOMBE

Rupsch [Ruzsch, Rupff, Ruppich], **Conrad** (b Kahla, Thuringia, c1475; d Torgau, Saxony, 1530 or after). German musician. He was a singer in the Elector of Saxony's court chapel (established in 1491) from 1504 until 1526, when it was disbanded. In 1505 he became a priest and two years later he was given a prebend of the collegiate church of St George in Kahla. It is possible that in 1515 or 1519 he was for a short time director of the court chapel of King Christian II in Copenhagen. In about 1520 he became the last *Sangmeister* (director) of the Saxon court chapel, and surviving documents attest that he devoted much care and attention to it. At about the same time he came into contact with the Reformation movement and with the radical group of *Schwärmer* (enthusiasts) headed by Andreas Bodenstein von Karlstadt, although apparently he was with this latter group for only a short time; according to Johann Walter (i) (reported in Michael Praetorius, *Syntagma musicum*, i), both Rupsch and Walter stayed with Martin Luther at Wittenberg in October 1525 to give advice on musical matters during the completion of Luther's German Mass. After the dissolution of the court chapel in 1526 Rupsch probably continued to live in Torgau in retirement. In 1530 he bequeathed part of his fief to Walter who, like him, came from Kahla.

No extant works can be firmly assigned to Rupsch (some are ascribed to him in *PL-Wu* Mf.2016); it is likely that he wrote for the early Reformed Church and that he had at least some part in the compilation of the last of the Jena choirbooks which were written in Saxony and belonged to the repertory of the court chapel in the last years of its existence.

BIBLIOGRAPHY
N. Müller: Die Wittenberger Bewegung (Leipzig, 1911)
A. Aber: Die Pflege der Musik unter den Wettinern und wettinischen Ernestinern (Bückeburg and Leipzig, 1921)
F. Gebhardt: 'Die musikalischen Grundlagen zu Luthers Deutscher Messe', Luther-Jb, x (1928), 56–169
W. Gurlitt: 'Johannes Walter und die Musik der Reformationszeit', Luther-Jb, xv (1933), 1–112
K. E. Roediger: Die geistlichen Musikhandschriften der Universitätsbibliothek Jena (Jena, 1935)
C. Gerhardt: Die Torgauer Walter-Handschriften: eine Studie zur Quellenkunde der Musikgeschichte der deutschen Reformationszeit (Kassel, 1949)
W. Blankenburg: Johann Walter: Leben und Werk (in preparation)
WALTER BLANKENBURG

Ruremunde, Christophe van. See REMUNDE, CHRISTOPHE VAN.

Rush, George (fl London, c1760–80). English composer, harpsichordist and guitarist. According to Dibdin, he travelled and studied in Italy before emerging as a theatre composer in London. His greatest success came with two English operas performed in 1764. *The Royal Shepherd*, using a libretto revised by R. Rolt from Metastasio's *Il rè pastore*, was staged on 24 February 1764 at the Drury Lane Theatre. It was intended as competition to Arne's *Artaxerxes*, in the Covent Garden repertory. The overture was very popular as a concert piece, in part because of the still exceptional use of timpani. It was published both for orchestra and in harpsichord reduction, the latter

reprinted as late as the end of the century. Rush's second opera, *Capricious Lovers*, was staged on 28 November 1764 at Drury Lane, the libretto devised by R. Lloyd from Favart's *Le caprice amoureux ou Ninette à la cour* (a parody of Goldoni's *Bertoldo*); it was reduced to a two-act farce and performed as an afterpiece from 2 March 1765. In 1768 Rush composed the music (now apparently lost) for *The Statesman Foiled* by R. Dossie, introduced as an afterpiece at the Haymarket Theatre on 8 July 1768. Several numbers of *The Royal Shepherd* were retained and at least one song rewritten by Rush when it was restaged as a pasticcio, *Amintas*, by G. F. Tenducci and T. E. Carter at Covent Garden on 15 December 1769.

Rush was also active in instrumental music. He supplied the overtures to both parts of the programme of Signora Gambarini's benefit concert, advertised 21 January 1760. On 22 March 1770 he conducted and performed his works at a concert for the Lord Mayor, Sir William Beckford. His published series of concertos, of which the first (in F) was especially popular, suggests that he was successful as a harpsichordist. Rush's style in the instrumental works is 'advanced' and pre-Classical, reflecting an uncommon synthesis of various national trends. Although Dibdin and the *ABC Dario* categorized Rush's operas as too Italian for English tastes, these works must be granted a historical niche in a period of transition from the ballad opera to the age of Dibdin.

An extended visit to Holland, perhaps under the patronage of Sir Joseph Yorke (Baron Dover), minister to The Hague, was postulated by Roscoe and is supported by the publication of several works there.

WORKS
(all published in London unless otherwise stated)

STAGE
The Royal Shepherd (R. Rolt, after Metastasio), Drury Lane, 24 Feb 1764, vocal score (1764), ov. (c1764) and in Three Celebrated English Overtures (c1798); adapted as pasticcio Amintas, Covent Garden, 15 Dec 1769, by G. F. Tenducci and T. E. Carter, vocal score (1770)
Capricious Lovers (R. Lloyd, after Favart and Goldoni), Drury Lane, 28 Nov 1764, vocal score (1764), ov. (c1764)
The Statesman Foiled (R. Dossie), Haymarket, 8 July 1768, lost

OTHER VOCAL
An Epithalamium or Nuptial Song (?London, c1775)

INSTRUMENTAL
op.
1   6 Easy Lessons, hpd (c1759)
2   12 Favourite Lessons or Airs, 2 gui (c1760)
[?3] A First Set of Sonatas, gui, gui/vn (c1763)
[?4] A Set of [4] Sonatas, hpd, vn acc. (c1766); also incl. Concerto no.1 and an overture
5   A Second Set of [4] Sonatas, hpd/pf, vn acc. (c1770)
—   A First Concerto, hpd, 2 vn, vc, 2 hn (c1770); also pubd as Concert Liv. 1 [Concerto Choisie], hpd, 2 vn, vc, 2 hn, 2 ob (The Hague, c1768); arr. pf, vn (c1783)
—   Concert, liv 2, hpd, 2 vn, vc, 2 hn, 2 ob (The Hague, c1772); also pubd as A Second Concerto, hpd, 2 vn, vc (c1772)
3   6 sonatas, hpd, vn acc. (The Hague, c1772); from opp.[?4]–5
—   A Third Concerto, hpd/pf, 2 vn, vc (c1773)
—   3 Quartets, 2 vn, va, vc (c1775)
—   A Fourth Concerto, hpd/pf, 2 vn, vc (c1777)
1 piece each in Elegant Extracts for the Guitar (c1800); The New Musical Magazine (1774–5)

BIBLIOGRAPHY
EitnerQ; GerberL; GerberNL
C. Dibdin: A Complete History of the Stage, v (London, 1800), 226
P. C. Roscoe: 'George Rush: a Forgotten English Composer', MT, lxxxvii (1946), 297
The London Stage 1660–1800 (Carbondale, Ill., 1960–68)
R. R. Kidd: The Sonata for Keyboard with Violin Accompaniment in England (1750–90) (diss., Yale U., 1967), 391
——: 'The Emergence of Chamber Music with Obbligato Keyboard in

England', *AcM*, xliv (1972), 137
R. Fiske: *English Theatre Music in The Eighteenth Century* (London, 1973)

RONALD R. KIDD

Rushing, Jimmy [James Andrew] ['Mr Five by Five'] (*b* Oklahoma City, 26 Aug 1903; *d* New York, 8 June 1972). Black American jazz singer. He was born into a musical family and learnt the violin, piano and singing. He appeared in the Midwest, in California, and in a touring show before singing with Walter Page's Blue Devils (1927–9) and Bennie Moten's Kansas City Orchestra (1929–35). With these important bands he developed a mature singing style derived from the blues and completely idiomatic to the rhythms of jazz, an uncommon accomplishment even for experienced black singers in the late 1920s. He first achieved renown with Count Basie's band from 1935, his excellent intonation and robust yet sensitive manner perfectly complementing the group and helping to shape its identity. He remained with Basie until 1950, and thereafter worked with his own group and alone, making foreign tours with several bands, including Basie's and Benny Goodman's; he appeared at jazz festivals from 1967 to 1970.

BIBLIOGRAPHY
J. Grunnet Jepsen: *Jazz Records: 1942–1962*, vi (n.p., 1963)
B. Rust: *Jazz Records: 1897–1942* (London, 1965, rev. 2/1969)
JAMES DAPOGNY

Rushworth & Dreaper. English firm of organ builders. It was founded in Liverpool by William Rushworth in the early 1800s. The firm became Rushworth & Dreaper in the early 1900s when Rushworth absorbed the Dreaper brothers' retail music firm; other retail businesses were absorbed later. The firm has been known for its well-built, conservatively styled organs, but in the 1960s it began to build instruments based on classical principles. This change in direction is due to the extensive travels of Alastair Rushworth, who studied with Dirk Flentrop and with Lawrence Phelps. The firm is noted for its instruments at Ealing Abbey (1976), Guildford Cathedral, the Liverpool Philharmonic Hall and Mold Parish Church, as well as the restoration of the organ at Chester Cathedral.

ANTHONY D. ROLLETT

Ruspoli, Francesco Maria, Marquis of (*b* Rome, 5 March 1672; *d* Rome, 12 or 14 July 1731). Italian patron of music. He was the son of Alessandro, Count Marescotti. He inherited both his father's and his great-uncle Bartolomeo Ruspoli's fortunes and, in the early 18th century, was one of the richest men in Rome. In music he was a rival of Cardinal Pietro Ottoboni and Cardinal Benedetto Pamphili, but he did not share their literary ambitions. Ruspoli was a member of the Accademia dei Arcadi, taking the name of Olinto Arsenio. In 1707 he placed his gardens on the Esquiline Hill at the disposal of the academy for its summer meetings. A number of *virtuosi di canto e suono* belonged to his household, which comprised some 80 people in 1709.

The outstanding musician at his establishment was George Frideric Handel, who had come to Italy at the age of 21 and was in Ruspoli's service for a time. Handel's stay in the Palazzo Bonelli in the Piazza SS Apostoli lasted, apart from brief interruptions, some 11 months (from 16 May to 14 October 1707, from the end of February to the end of April, and from the

middle of July to the end of November 1708). During this period he wrote more than 50 cantatas, mainly with Italian texts, for Ruspoli. For Lent in 1708 he composed the oratorio *La Resurrezione di Nostro Signor Gesù Cristo*; it was first performed on Easter Day that year with a large orchestra directed by Arcangelo Corelli.

Alessandro Scarlatti and Antonio Caldara also wrote several works for Ruspoli. From 1709 to 1716 Caldara was *maestro di cappella* at the marquis's court. In 1715 J. F. A. Uffenbach praised the Sunday academies at Ruspoli's palace as 'die besten allhier' (that is, the best in Rome); money was lavished on them. In his last years Ruspoli lived mainly in Vignanello, near Rome, where he directed the rebuilding of his palace.

BIBLIOGRAPHY
U. Kirkendale: *Antonio Caldara: sein Leben und seine venezianisch-römischen Oratorien* (Graz and Cologne, 1966)
——: 'The Ruspoli Documents on Handel', *JAMS*, xx (1967), 222–73
E. T. Harris: *Handel and the Pastoral Tradition* (London, 1980)
HANS JOACHIM MARX

Russell (*d* London, *c*1745). English countertenor. He is first mentioned in 1729, when he sang in the première of Samuel Johnson's successful burlesque *Hurlothrumbo* at the New Haymarket Theatre (29 March). In the same season he appeared in the pantomime *The Humours of Harlequin*, in which he had a benefit on 28 July, and the ballad opera *Flora*. In June 1730 he was singing at Goodman's Fields. He made his Covent Garden début in a revival of *Flora* in November 1734, and returned to the New Haymarket in *The Beggar's Opera* in June 1736. Handel cast him as David in the first performance of *Saul* at the King's Theatre on 16 January 1739; Lord Wentworth wrote in a letter of 9 January that 'for a chief performer [Handel] has got one Russell an Englishman that sings extreamly well'. Between January and May 1740 Russell sang in eight concerts at Hickford's Room, appearing in J. C. Smith's *Rosalinda* and *David's Lamentation over Saul and Jonathan* and two of Handel's Chandos Anthems. He had benefits at the New Haymarket on 13 March 1741 and 4 April 1744. He was probably the Russell who early in 1745 set up at Hickford's 'a puppet show to ridicule opera . . . with foolish Italian songs burlesqued in Italian' (Horace Walpole); according to Smollett's satire *Advice* (1746) the target was Handel's oratorios, and Russell was encouraged by 'certain Ladies of Quality' who had a grudge against the composer. The actress and singer Charlotte Charke, who assisted Russell, said that the performances were 'carried on by Subscription, in as grand a Manner as possible', with an orchestra of ten. Russell fell rapidly into debt, went out of his mind, and died soon after in the Fleet Prison.

WINTON DEAN

Russell, Charles Ellsworth. *See* RUSSELL, 'PEEWEE'.

Russell, George (Allan) (*b* Cincinnati, 23 June 1923). American jazz composer. He began his career as a drummer and in the early 1940s wrote scores for Earl Hines's band. During a long illness in 1945–6 he formulated the basis of his 'Lydian Chromatic Concept of Tonal Organization', a system of composition based on grading intervals by the distance of their pitches from a central note. After his recovery he wrote scores for Dizzy Gillespie (*Cubana Be and Cubana Bop*, 1947) and Buddy de Franco (*A Bird in Igor's Yard*, 1949), and composed *Ezzthetic* and *Odjenar* for Lee Konitz (1951). The completion and publication of his system in 1953 was followed by works on an increasingly large scale, which established him, with Gil Evans, as a leading postwar jazz composer; he combined advanced jazz idioms with an unusually rigorous concern for structure, harmony and the balance between composition and improvisation. In 1958–9 he taught at the Lenox School of Jazz in Massachusetts, and about that time took up the piano, which he played in his jazz sextet (1960–61). He has lectured on his system in the USA and Europe.

BIBLIOGRAPHY

D. Cerulli: 'George Russell', *Down Beat*, xxv (29 May 1958), 15
L. Gottlieb: 'Brandeis Festival Album', *Jazz*, i (1959), spr., 151
J. Brooks: 'George Russell', *Jazz Review*, iii (1960), Feb, 38
M. Harrison: 'George Russell', *Jazz Review*, iii (1960), Nov, 29
G. Russell: 'Where do we go from here?', *The Jazz Word*, ed. D. Cerulli (New York, 1960), 233
N. Hentoff: *George Russell: a List of Compositions Licenced by B.M.I.* (New York, 1961)
M. Harrison: 'George Russell', *Jazz on Record*, ed. A. McCarthy (London, 1968), 251

JAMES G. ROY JR

Russell, Henry (*b* Sheerness, 24 Dec 1812; *d* London, 8 Dec 1900). English composer, pianist and singer. He first appeared on stage at the age of three and started piano lessons at six. He sang with Robert Elliston's children's opera troupe, receiving personal congratulations from the king; after his voice broke he studied composition with Rossini and Bellini in Italy (some sources claim that he won the Naples Conservatory prize for the best musical composition of 1833). He returned to England and for a short time was chorus master at Her Majesty's Theatre. In 1834 or 1835 he sailed to Canada to begin a career of solo concerts, but the rigours of the Canadian wilderness soon prompted him to settle in Rochester, New York, where he became organist and choirmaster of the First Presbyterian Church and a teacher at the Rochester Academy of Music. His first song, *Wind of the Winter Night*, was published in New York in 1836 and in autumn that year he made his New York début as a singer. He toured the USA as a composer and performer, first with William Vincent Wallace, then in 1837–41 singing and accompanying himself at the piano in programmes consisting almost entirely of his own compositions, and enjoyed tremendous popularity. He was one of the few major singers of the time to present such unassisted entertainments; even Jenny Lind had supporting singers and instrumentalists. He was particularly active in Boston and New York, where his music and performing style created considerable controversy among the culturally élite. In late 1841 or early 1842 he returned to England and made his London début on 8 March 1842, but after about a year he again travelled to the USA; the young Stephen Foster heard him in Pittsburgh in 1843. In 1844 or 1845 Russell returned permanently to England, where he was active as a singer until the early 1860s and continued to compose almost to the end of his life.

Russell claimed to have written the music and some of the words for over 800 songs. A more realistic figure is about 250, including 75 or so written in the USA and 46 reissued with new lyrics and titles by English poets. About half of his works are simple ballads, derivative of Italian opera in harmony and accompaniment; they often have rather static melodies which allowed Russell to perform them in a speech-song manner. He also composed rousing songs about travelling on land or sea,

and several descriptive multi-sectional pieces, similar in style and emotional content to Italian operatic scenes. Some of Russell's songs were written as statements for social reform; these include *The Maniac* concerning the 'barbarous' conditions of private mental institutions, *The Gambler's Wife* on the plight of a deserted mother and child and *The Indian Hunter* on racial intolerance. He later involved himself in the immigration movement through such works as *A Life in the West* and *The Emigrant's Farewell*, while his songs based on Stowe's novel *Uncle Tom's Cabin* were outcries against slavery. *A Life on the Ocean Wave*, chosen in 1889 as the march of the Royal Marines, *I'm Afloat*, *The Old Sexton* and *Cheer Boys Cheer* were popular into the 20th century.

Russell had two sons, Henry Russell (1871–1937), an opera impresario in the USA and England, and the conductor Sir Landon Ronald.

See also POPULAR MUSIC, §II, 4.

BIBLIOGRAPHY

H. Russell: *Cheer Boys Cheer* (London, 1895) [autobiography]
Obituary, *MT*, xlii (1901), 27
G. C. D. Odell: *Annals of the New York Stage* (New York, 1927–49)
J. T. Howard: *Our American Music* (New York, 1954)
M. W. Disher: *Victorian Song, from Dive to Drawing Room* (London, 1955)
J. A. Stephens: *Henry Russell in America: Chutzpah and Huzzah* (diss., U. of Illinois, 1975)

JOHN A. STEPHENS

Russell, Luis (Carl) (*b* Careening Cay, nr. Bocas del Toro, Panama, 6 Aug 1902; *d* New York, 11 Dec 1963). Black American jazz band-leader, arranger and pianist. His first significant engagement was with King Oliver in Chicago (1925–7). On moving to New York he took over George Howard's band, and several long engagements followed. It was during this period, especially 1929–30, that Russell's most representative recordings were made. Having accompanied Louis Armstrong for several months in 1929, the band provided his backing from 1935 to 1943, although by then it had lost most of its character. Russell then formed another band and worked around New York, without distinction, until 1948, when he abandoned music to become a chauffeur and shopkeeper.

Although an unexceptional pianist, Russell was an important jazz band-leader of the 1920s. He attempted to adapt New Orleans ensemble style to make his group more integrated, but the band's freshness and vigour continued to derive from its solo improvisations. Some of Henry Allen's most characteristic early trumpet work is found in recordings with Russell, and Albert Nicholas's clarinet improvisations around the closing ensembles of pieces like *Panama* resemble Barney Bigard's later work in Duke Ellington's band; other important soloists were the trombonist J. C. Higginbotham and the alto saxophonist Charlie Holmes.

BIBLIOGRAPHY

F. Mankslied: 'Luis Russell Revisited', *Jazz Monthly*, iii (1957), April, 11
A. McCarthy: 'Luis Russell', *Jazz Monthly*, vi (1960), Aug, 9
G. Hoefer: 'Luis Russell', *Down Beat*, xxix (8 Nov 1962), 43
H. Grut: 'Luis Russell', *Jazz Journal*, xvii (1964), March, 12
R. Atkins: 'Luis Russell', *Jazz on Record*, ed. A. McCarthy (London, 1968), 252f
A. McCarthy: *Big Band Jazz* (London, 1974), 25ff

MAX HARRISON

Russell, 'PeeWee' [Charles Ellsworth] (*b* St Louis, 27 March 1906; *d* Alexandria, Virginia, 15 Feb 1969).

American jazz clarinettist. After studying several instruments he took up the clarinet and in the early 1920s played in Texas with Jack Teagarden and in Chicago with Bix Beiderbecke. In 1927 he moved permanently to New York, where he played and recorded first with Red Nichols, and later with a wide variety of important jazz musicians and groups, above all with the banjoist Eddie Condon. His unique, complex style involved seemingly effortless variation of intentionally unorthodox timbres, growls alternating with hard attacks, and softly articulated notes held with a slow, almost sour vibrato. He often played lines composed of greatly contrasting rhythmic values (unlike the successions of quavers preferred by contemporary clarinettists) and unusual choices of pitch; by playing imperceptibly behind the beat he often gave a weighty quality to individual notes. His playing encompassed and was conditioned by 1930s popular music, and is heard to best advantage on his highly individual performances of that repertory (e.g. *A Ghost of a Chance*, 1938, with Bobby Hackett).

BIBLIOGRAPHY
J. Grunnet Jepsen: *Jazz Records: 1942–1962*, vi (n.p., 1963)
B. Rust: *Jazz Records: 1897–1942* (London, 1965, rev. 2/1969)
                                        JAMES DAPOGNY

Russell, Raymond Anthony (*b* London, 27 May 1922; *d* nr. Valletta, 17 March 1964). English writer on early keyboard instruments. He was educated at Eton and at Downing College, Cambridge. While still at school he became interested in the organ; from this evolved an interest, during his Cambridge days, in the harpsichord and kindred instruments. After World War II he assembled a superb private collection of harpsichords, spinets, virginals and clavichords (most of which was given to the Faculty of Music, University of Edinburgh, after his death). He wrote a standard work on the subject, *The Harpsichord and Clavichord*.

WRITINGS
'The Harpsichord since 1800', *PRMA*, lxxxii (1955–6), 61
The Harpsichord and Clavichord (London, 1959, rev. 2/1973 by H. Schott)
Catalogue of Musical Instruments, Victoria and Albert Museum, i: *Keyboard Instruments* (London, 1968)
                                DONALD HOWARD BOALCH

Russell, William (*b* London, 6 Oct 1777; *d* London, 21 Nov 1813). English organist and composer. He was the son of Hugh Russell, a London organ builder and organist at St Mary Aldermary, Bow Lane. At the age of eight he had music lessons from William Cope, organist of Southwark Cathedral, and William Shrubsole; later he studied with John Groombridge, organist of Hackney, and from 1797 to 1800 with Samuel Arnold. From 1789 to 1793 he was the organist of the chapel in Great Queen Street, Lincoln's Inn Fields and, after deputizing for some time at St Mary Aldermary, in 1798 he was appointed organist of St Ann's Limehouse, at an annual salary of £45. From 1800 to 1804 he was pianist and composer at Sadler's Wells Theatre, and composed about 20 pantomimes for it and other theatres. From 1801 he acted as accompanist to Braham, Elizabeth Billington and Nancy Storace at Covent Garden. On 1 April 1801 he was appointed organist of the Foundling Hospital; he probably held other posts simultaneously with the help of deputies. In 1808 he matriculated at Magdalen Hall, Oxford, probably receiving his degree as an external student there at about the same time (a copy of his BMus exercise was at

GB-T, now *Ob*). In 1809 he inspected the organ at Covent Garden (which had been restored after its destruction by fire), and soon became much in demand as an organ inspector, even for his father's instruments. After his death at the age of 36, benefit performances of his works, including his oratorio *Job*, were organized for his widow at the Foundling Hospital. His music library was sold in 1814; some of it is now in the British Museum.

Russell was considered by his contemporaries to be an admirable player of keyboard instruments. His obituary in *The Monthly Magazine* (1814) stated 'As a performer of the pianoforte and organ he has few equals', and Samuel Wesley praised him highly in his memoirs (*GB-Lbm*).

WORKS
(*all printed works published in London*)

SACRED VOCAL
The Redemption of Israel [The Deliverance of Israel] (oratorio); Job (oratorio), Foundling Hospital, 1814, ed. S. Wesley (1826)
Anthems: The Redeemer gave the word (*c*1795); Hear thou, O shepherd of Israel (1809); Psalms, Hymns, and Anthems, for the Foundling Hospital (1809); other anthems, *GB-Lbm*, *T*, and London, Library of the Thomas Coram Foundation; 6 anthems cited in Foster
Mass, 4vv; Morning and Evening Service; Jubilate

STAGE
(*all first performed in London; pantomimes, unless otherwise stated*)
The Highland Camp, Sadler's Wells, 1799, ov. (1799)
The Wizard's Wake, Sadler's Wells, 1801
Rugantino, or The Bravo of Venice (melodrama), Covent Garden, 1805
Adrian and Orilla, or A Mother's Vengeance, Covent Garden, 1806, ov. and incidental music (1806)
Wild Islanders, or The Court of Pekin (ballet), Drury Lane, 1807, ov. (1807)
Harlequin and Time, Covent Garden, 1807, ov. (1807)
The False Friend, or Assassin of the Rocks (melodrama), The Circus, 1809

OTHER WORKS
Odes: On Music; To the Genius of Handel; On St Cecilia's Day; To Harmony
Hamlet's Letter to Ophelia, a Canzonet (*c*1800)
Glees etc, *GB-Lbm* Add.31804, 31806
12 [24] Voluntaries, org/pf, i–ii (1804–12)

BIBLIOGRAPHY
Obituary, *Monthly Magazine*, xxxvi (1813–14), 552
J. D. Brown and S. S. Stratton: *British Musical Biography* (Birmingham, 1897)
M. B. Foster: *Anthems and Anthem Composers* (London, 1901/*R*1970)
based on *MGG* (xi, 1128) by permission of Bärenreiter
                                        CHARLES CUDWORTH

Russell & Tolman. American firm of music publishers. It was active in Boston only from 1858 to 1863, but during that time established itself as one of the major American publishers of the century. The firm published a great quantity of American popular music, marches, polkas and comic songs, as well as the works of established American composers such as George F. Root. Russell & Tolman maintained close business ties with the Chicago firm of Root & Cady, and they frequently interchanged printing plates.

A succession of changing partnerships had resulted, in 1858, in the combination of George D. Russell and Henry Tolman. When they were later joined by Joseph M. Russell, the firm became G. D. Russell & Company. The Russell brothers separated after 14 years and control of the firm went to the Oliver Ditson Company but with G. D. Russell remaining at the head until his death in 1888.

BIBLIOGRAPHY
H. Dichter and E. Shapiro: *Early American Sheet Music* (New York, 1941)
                        W. THOMAS MARROCCO, MARK JACOBS

Russia. *See* UNION OF SOVIET SOCIALIST REPUBLICS, §IX.

Russian and Slavonic church music.

1. Introduction. 2. Russian church music: monophonic chant. 3. Russian church music: polyphonic music. 4. Bulgarian church music. 5. Serbian church music.

1. INTRODUCTION. The Slavs as an ethnic group are divided into eastern Slavs (i.e. Russians, 'Little Russians' or Ukrainians, and 'White Russians' or Belorussians), western Slavs (Poles, Czechs, Slovaks and Lusatian Sorbs) and southern Slavs (Bulgarians, Serbs, Croats and Slovenes, to whom should be added the recently identified nationalities of Montenegrins and Macedonian Slavs).

The eastern Slavs and some of the southern Slavs (Bulgarians and Serbs) accepted Christianity in its Eastern Orthodox form. The remaining Slavonic groups were converted to Roman Catholicism, although some of them had contacts at various times with Eastern Orthodoxy through the intermediary role of Greek missionaries. Within this article only the Eastern Orthodox Slavs will be discussed: those who accepted the Christian religion from the Greeks and the accompanying ritual in its Greek form but translated the services into the Old Slavonic language, the root of all Slavonic languages. This language evolved over many centuries. After the 11th century it became Church Slavonic with strong regional variants so that one may speak of various national recensions of Church Slavonic as it is recorded in written documents.

In talking of Russian church music one is open to criticism for neglecting Ukrainian church music. However, since the concept of Ukrainian nationality is of a fairly recent date, and since the present-day territory of Ukraine covers an area in which the first Russian state (i.e. Kievan Russia) did exist, these territorial and nationalistic claims will be disregarded in this article. The term 'Russian' will therefore be used as a synonym for Eastern Slavs. By the same token, the territorial divisions of present-day Yugoslavia (Serbia, Montenegro, Macedonia, Bosnia and Herzegovina) will be disregarded when discussing Serbian church music of the past, since Serbs inhabit all these provinces.

One common trait of all Eastern Orthodox Slavs with regard to church music is that they practise only vocal music. Musical instruments are banned from religious services. The term 'church music' will here designate the music of the Christian rite. The Slavonic ethnic groups received Christianity at different points in history. All Slavs, however, view the Byzantine missionaries Constantine (who as a monk was named Cyril) and Methodius as the first apostles of Christianity among the Slavs. All celebrate their memory and honour them as saints. This mission, which started in the year 863, is also viewed as the starting-point for literature in any Slavonic language, as some of the first translations of liturgical books are attributed to the Holy Brothers.

2. RUSSIAN CHURCH MUSIC: MONOPHONIC CHANT. Christianity penetrated Russia probably as early as the 9th century, although it is customary to refer to the year 988 as the official date for the christianization of Russia: the date at which Prince Vladimir accepted the religion. With the advent of Christianity into Russia came also Greek missionaries and church dignitaries. Such Greeks occupied important positions in the eccle-

siastical hierarchy during the next few centuries. Byzantine missionaries were already involved in the christianization of the Slavs in the 9th century, with the mission of SS Cyril and Methodius to Moravia in 863. From this it is generally assumed that the liturgical books were available in a Slavonic translation considerably before the conversion of Russians. There are records of the active translation and copying of books in Russia during the first half of the 11th century: during the reign of Yaroslav the Wise (1019–54) who founded the Cathedral of Kiev, which was presumably equipped with all necessary service books at its foundation in 1037.

The earliest surviving musical manuscripts, however, date from the late 11th century and more particularly the 12th. In their typology these manuscripts are faithful translations of the liturgical books of the Greek Orthodox Church (heirmologia, sticheraria, triōdia, etc). Among Russian manuscripts that survive are also the earliest collections of the kontakia with neumatic notation.

There is no longer any doubt about the Byzantine origin of the neumatic notation in Russian musical manuscripts of the early centuries. The neumes in most manuscripts are exceedingly close to an early stage of the Coislin system of the Byzantine neumatic notation. The few surviving kondakaria contain a mixed notation, in two superimposed rows, with a distinct predominance of signs which have since been identified as belonging to the Chartres system of Byzantine neumatic notation. Before the modern development of studies in Byzantine music, there was a school of thought which presumed that the neumes in the kondakaria represented an 'original' Russian notation which was therefore named kondakarian notation.

After lengthy investigation by Russian scholars in the 19th century (Razumovsky, Smolensky, Metallov), Preobrazhensky had by 1909 found evidence which proved the Byzantine origin of neumes in Russian musical manuscripts. In so doing he demonstrated, though only on a limited scale, the dependence of the earliest Russian chants on their Byzantine models. Preobrazhensky's findings have in essence now been fully vindicated. By juxtaposition of identical texts it was found that in an overwhelming number of examples identical neumes were to be found in Byzantine musical manuscripts and their Russian translations (*see* NEUMATIC NOTATIONS, fig.27). These similarities occurred particularly at crucial points within the structure of a hymn: at an opening melodic formula or a cadential formula. This suggests that in the earliest stages of the transmission of Christianity into Russia, melodies sung at the religious services were definitely Byzantine in origin even if lengthy passages did not show the same degree of dependence on their Byzantine models – especially if these passages occurred in the middle of a verse or of the hymn as a whole.

The degree of this identity varies, as is only to be expected with translation from one language to another which is so very different in inflection and accent. Nevertheless there is great flexibility and conscious adaptation of Russian Church Slavonic words and composite terms in emulation of their Greek verbal equivalents.

The possibilities for transcription of these earliest examples into modern notation are limited. This is not because of the scarcity of sources. In fact, for the period from the late 11th century to approximately the mid-14th, about 50 manuscripts and fragments are at present known. The problem lies in the earliest stages of Byzantine notation, which have to be understood before the Russian sources can be transcribed. While in specific instances some of the earliest Byzantine musical manuscripts may be tentatively transcribed without assistance from later documentation, the majority of them are ambiguous, and this is reflected in studies of Russian church music and its notations for the period up to the 14th century.

In addition to the translations from Greek of the nearly complete repertory of chants for services in the newly established Russian Orthodox Church, there are some original creations even in the earliest sources. 12th-century manuscripts already contain hymns in honour of the first Russian saints. Some of these hymns attempt to emulate the structure of better-known hymns to traditional saints, while a few are distinct copies of Greek hymns (akin to parody procedure).

During this period the notational system in Byzantium underwent a gradual transformation which contributed to its readability, and rendered it fairly stable and systematic. In Russia, however, neume forms remained unchanged and without modernization, retaining their ambiguity. Because of invasions during the 13th century the contacts between Russian lands and the fragmented Byzantine Empire may have been less frequent; and on the periphery the old traditions may have been preserved more faithfully than in the whirlpool of changing Byzantine musical concepts. Besides, a great part of the Russian lands was also fragmented as a result of the Tatar invasion which brought to an end the further development of Kievan Russia. During the 14th century new centres of religious and cultural activities appeared. Of great significance for the later development were the centres in Moscow and Novgorod, the tradition of the latter going back several centuries.

Whereas the 12th and 13th centuries are fairly rich in musical documentation, that of the 14th century drops to insignificant proportions. Only in the second half of the 15th century does the number of sources start to grow, reaching nearly astronomical figures for the 16th, 17th and 18th centuries.

On the basis of the few sources, it has been customary since the 19th century to refer to a change in the shape of the neumatic notation and its meaning, to be associated with the late 14th century and possibly the early 15th. With no studies of the sources of this period yet available, so momentous a change is accepted uncritically by almost all writers. Yet, while handwriting had indeed evolved and the cursive minuscule hand had affected the writing of neumatic signs, there is at present no proof that this is the period in which a change in the meaning of the notational signs also took place.

By the second half of the 15th century one finds not only an increase in the number of musical manuscripts copied in Russia but also the first so-called *azbuki* (literally 'alphabets') listing neumes and giving Slavonic names for some of them. This may also be the period in which the terms *znamya* and *kryuk* made their appearance as designations for 'signs' in neumatic notation (thus *znamennaya notatsiya* means 'sign notation' and *kryukovoye pis'mo* 'sign writing'). By conflating these terms into composite ones the technical designation *znamennïy raspev* appears, meaning

'chanting by signs', sometimes known in English as 'znamennïy chant'.

Developments in Russia during the second half of the 15th century, in music as in other fields, were almost certainly associated with the downfall of the Byzantine Empire in 1453 and with the new situation in which Russia was to find itself as the only defender of Orthodox Christians in eastern Europe.

The early lists of notational signs copied in the late 15th century led to a proliferation of these *azbuki*. In the 16th century at least 70 such tables of neumes are known. Problematically, they do not always agree among themselves either in terminology used or in meanings ascribed to individual neumes. One distinct trait that does emerge is a new Russian terminology in which few terms still reflect their Greek origin, most signs bearing Russian names. Some of these are descriptive either of the shape of the sign (*pauk*, 'spider'; *dva v chelnu*, 'two in a boat') or, in rare instances, of the melodic turn.

If there is any one period of Russian history at which the change in meaning of neumatic notation took place and the elements of Russian melodies (primarily folksongs) made inroads into the body of religious chant, then this may have been the moment. A possible earlier intermingling should not however be excluded. The fact is that after 1500 neumatic notation in Russian musical manuscripts no longer seems to have any of the meanings associated with Byzantine neumes.

The history of the development of church music in Russia from the 16th century onwards is eventful and richly documented. The period has yet to be thoroughly studied. There are references to a growing number of singers, their names more faithfully preserved than hitherto. In more than one way developments in Russia resemble events in the late Byzantine Empire when numerous *maistores* and virtuoso singers took not only to composing new pieces but also to recomposing the traditional repertory for the religious services. Even the Byzantine practice of TERETISMATA has its counterpart in 16th-century Russian *anenayki* and in the correspondingly increased length of some of the hymns. One can as yet only hypothesize in this field: that, for example, the melismatic embellishment of originally simple melodies may have led to the establishment of *bol'shoy raspev* ('great chant') which made its first appearance in the late 16th century.

By the time of Ivan the Terrible (ruled 1533–84) there are already references to whole schools of singers being transferred from Novgorod to Moscow, and to the establishment of an imperial chapel. Ivan was himself a composer: at least two hymns are known to have been written by him. By 1589, with the establishment of the Russian patriarchate in Moscow, the Patriarchs had added a 'patriarchal choir' to their retinue.

New variants in the types of chanting made their first appearance during the 16th century. Besides the standard, traditional znamennïy chant there are also references to the 'demestvennïy chant'. This type of chanting is now associated with specially trained, skilled singers: precentors, known as *domestiki* (Gk.) or *demestvenniki* (Russ.). One of its main characteristics was apparently its profusion of melismas, and the evolution of a peculiar system of signs most of which originated in the metamorphosed neumatic notation of past centuries. There are also references to the so-called Kazan chant and notation, associated primarily with the singers of Ivan the Terrible. Yet for all practical purposes our understanding of Kazan chant remains uncertain.

A new development in the 16th century appears to be the staging of some aspects of the services in the manner of liturgical drama. The roots of at least one of these dramas (if that term is applicable) seem to lie in Byzantine cathedral practices which never acquired the pomp and elaborate setting that liturgical drama enjoyed in western Europe in the Middle Ages. Besides the best-known example, *Peshchnoye deystvo* ('Play of the furnace', dealing with the story of the three children in the fiery furnace), there are records of other *deystva* (literally 'actions') such as *Shestviye na oslyati* ('Procession on the donkey' for Palm Sunday) and *Deystvo strashnovo suda* ('Play of the Last Judgment'). Neither of these has been investigated and their impact and tradition were apparently of limited duration.

In Slavonic musical manuscripts of the 16th and 17th centuries neumatic signs appear not only above the vowels and individual syllables but also above some mute letters. This phenomenon, already noted by philologists, suggests that the two signs concerned, which are not nowadays pronounced, did at least have sufficient length to be indicated by neumes in the earliest stages of Old Slavonic. It was during these centuries that a practice known as *khomoniya* evidently prevailed. It consisted in transliterating mute letters into the vowels 'e' and 'o'. The new pronunciation caused deformation of words which led to calls for reform of text and music.

The neumatic notation itself did acquire a new meaning. While in the Byzantine usage neumes were intervallic signs designating relative pitch, the new meaning of neumes in Russian practice of the 16th century (if not early in the century, then certainly by the end) was associated with fixed pitch and with specifically pitched melodic figures. The documented beginnings of this new interpretation may be clearly seen in the first of several notational reforms which were to take place during the 17th century. This first reform is associated with Ivan Shaydur, a singer active in Novgorod and possibly Moscow. His reform is usually dated c1600. The Shaydurov reform consisted in adding special signs (stylized letters) to neumes, spelling out as a mnemotechnic device the particular pitch to which the neume referred at that point. The concept of a gamut encompassing the notes of the melodies seems to have emerged with this reform. To Shaydur (or a musician in his circle) may perhaps be attributed the concept of dividing the tonal range into successions of three notes, each separated by a semitone from the next trichord. These trichords are identical in structure, yielding the gamut in ex.1. This system strongly resembles the Western hexachord system, from which it was probably derived. Each trichord received (immediately, or shortly afterwards) a special name such as 'dark', 'light', 'three times light'. For some of the trichords, notes in identical positions received identical additional signs. These signs were written in red ink and therefore received the designation *kinovarnïye pometï* or *priznaki* (i.e. cinnober labels or indications of an additional sign).

Another singer, Fyodor Khristianin, from the late 16th century, composed a set of hymns (gospel stikhira) which were notated in pre-reform notation. At least a partial transcription of some of these melodies has been possible by means of comparative studies (Brazhnikov). Surprisingly, they reveal certain melodic features which are nowadays viewed as a typically Russian melos, with its extended range and melodic leaps (ex.2). Brazhnikov

Ex.2 Fragment of a melody by Fyodor Khristianin, from Brazhnikov

is inclined to attribute to Fyodor Khristianin the 'invention' of the extended melismatic style known as *bol'shoy raspev*. Whoever invented it, it was certainly the result of a trend that must have ripened over several decades of growth in native practices.

The transmission of the reformed notation with red signs presented problems for copyists as it did for the proposed printing of Russian liturgical books. These problems, together with abuses of singing in churches during the first half of the 17th century, led to the second reform, associated with the name of Alexander Mezenets, which took place in the 1660s. The abuses mentioned appear to have resulted from the protraction of services by additions and embellishments to traditional melodies. To remedy this protraction, singers had adopted the practice of starting the next hymn before the preceding one had ended. At its gravest, several hymns supposed to follow one another may have been chanted at more or less the same time. Whether this practice is a genuine distortion or an emulation of the polyphonic practices that were already infiltrating as far back as the 16th century is still a matter for speculation. From the mid-1650s onwards the possibility of a new reform of singing practices came under public discussion several times. Reform was made doubly problematic by the presence on the patriarchal throne from 1652 to 1656 of Nikon, an advocate of polyphony. To the orthodox clergy of Moscow polyphony smacked of Roman Catholicism and the very acknowledgment of it represented a threat to the purity of the faith if not a symbol of Roman supremacy. Reaction against patriarchal preferences led, among other things, to a schism within the Russian Church itself, establishing on the one hand the official Russian Church and on the other the schismatic groups. Among the latter the best known are the 'old believers', this term in fact embracing more than one group. All of them were, however, united in their opposition to the introduction of polyphony and in claiming zealously that they were preserving melodies of the liturgical repertory unspoilt.

The work of the reform commission took place shortly after the lands of the Ukraine were joined to

Ex.1 The trichords constituting the tonal range of Russian church music

Г *gorazdo nizko* ('very deep')

Н *nizko* ('deep')

Ц [Letter sounding 'ts']

С *srednim glasom* ('in the middle tone')
[this symbol may be abbreviated to a dot]

М *mrachno* ('dark')

П *povïshe* ('higher')

П [stylized form of B] *vïsoko* ('high')

x derived from the Gk. *chamile* ('low')

· derived from *chocholok* ('top')

Russia in 1654. This is significant, since the Ukrainian lands were for a long time in contact with Polish lands and were acquainted through them with the western European polyphony, both religious and secular.

The reforms of the 1650s and 1660s dealt with texts as well as music. *Khomoniya* was banned, and orders were issued to correct liturgical books containing vowels instead of mute letters. Simultaneously the melodies were adjusted to fit the new pronunciation. Mezenets and his commission were concerned with preserving and clarifying the neumatic notation. The 'old believers' however were ultimately the ones to transmit this type of notation into the 20th century. In this reform the added signs were changed from red to black to facilitate printing (the earliest printing, however, dates only from 1772), and further refinement with more additional signs was introduced.

In the process of melismatic elaboration – *bol'shoy raspev* – extensive melodic formulae were assigned to certain neumes (a procedure known as *popevki*, belonging probably to the 16th and 17th centuries). In time, these formulae were assembled into collections, some of them known as *fitnik* (from their previous shorthand notation using the Greek letter *theta*, pronounced *fita* in Russian) or *kokiznik* (from *kokiza*, another term for independent extended melismas). Individual formulae received their own names (e.g. *kobïla*, 'a mare'); and the art of musical composition consisted in the euphonious matching and weaving of such melodic figures. There were at this period other parts of the liturgical repertory which contrasted sharply with *bol'shoy raspev*. There was *malïy raspev* ('small chant') which consisted of abbreviated melodies with far fewer melismas and with recitative patterns on a single note. The recitative pattern was much more characteristic of what came to be known as *grecheskiy raspev* ('Greek chant') which emerged in the middle of the 17th century – the outcome, some believe, of an extended stay by some Greek singers in Moscow in the 1650s. Opinions are divided about the origin of the term *bolgarskiy raspev* ('Bulgarian chant') which also makes its appearance in the mid-17th century. Some scholars see it as an import from Bulgarian lands, others deny this. The term *Kiyevskiy raspev* ('Kievan chant') now seems to have come into use late in the 17th century. It has been claimed that these may be the oldest melodies which became adapted to the musical taste of Ukraine. The characteristics of Kievan chant are the use of contrasting sections, alternating between the recitative and melodic segments, reminiscent of Ukrainian folk music patterns.

During the last quarter of the 17th century there appeared several treatises on music, among them the *Musikïskaya grammatika* ('Musical grammar') attributed to Nikolay Diletsky (1630–1680 or 1690). Besides a discussion of notation this treatise describes what must be interpreted as modes and there are indications of a clearly established concept of major and minor scales and also a 'mixed' scale. Theoretical and notational problems are also discussed in a *klyuch* ('key') by Tikhon Makarevsky, also written before 1700.

While monophonic melodies continued to be copied in subsequent centuries, the acceptance of modern staff notation during the reign of Peter the Great (1689–1725) and the favouring of polyphony shown by the official church made the monophonic traditions increasingly obsolescent in Russia from the 18th century on-

wards. Only the 'old believers', now to be found not so much in the Soviet Union as in Canada and in the USA, still adhere to monophonic chanting (though occasionally intermingled with elements of 'folk polyphony'). Attempts at restoring unison singing in the beginning of the 20th century in Russia were short-lived; and so far they have made no impact on the Russian Orthodox celebration of services.

3. RUSSIAN CHURCH MUSIC: POLYPHONIC MUSIC. Some Russian scholars believe that polyphony was practised in Russian church music before the 16th century. Their view rests solely on the practice of polyphonic singing in Russian folk music. The earliest documented references which carry implications of polyphonic singing date from about the middle of the 16th century. Uspensky has suggested that the term *strochnoye peniye* (from *stroka* meaning 'line', therefore 'line-singing') refers to such a practice. These references mention such singing on feasts and holidays when religious processions played an important role. Since the processions would imply the participation of large numbers of people, and folk-singing may have been a part of such celebrations, some scholars suggest that at least one of the idioms of the Russian polyphonic church music may actually have been derived from folk music.

There is no doubt that sophisticated polyphonic practices penetrated into Russia from the West, primarily through Poland and the Ukraine. The much more refined style of this music represents a separate strain which, at a later date, may have merged with indigenous practices, creating the blend which came to be known as Russian polyphonic church music. The existence of some native polyphonic singing may indeed have facilitated the penetration of Western elements, contributing to the official acceptance of part-singing in place of unison chanting. However, a clear distinction between these two styles, folk polyphony and a 'learnt' polyphony, has yet to be firmly established.

There was more than one way in which Western music could reach Russia. An important trading centre, Novgorod, had maintained contacts with central European cities. Novgorod is mentioned as one of the most important musical centres, and Ivan the Terrible had even moved singers from there to Moscow. The amount of polyphony practised there in the 16th century, however, is still unknown. Polyphonic music was certainly composed and performed in Poland during the 16th century; Polish ties with western Russia and involvement in Russian politics were strong in the late 16th and early 17th centuries. Western polyphonic styles, and five-line staff notation, were certainly already well known in Russia by 1654 when the merger of Ukrainian lands and Muscovy took place, and when Nikon sat on the patriarchal throne.

Demestvenniy chant, as was pointed out earlier, was evidently practised by skilled singers who excelled in their knowledge of music. Some of the earliest polyphonic scores in Russia seem to be settings of this type of chant written out in neumatic notation (*see* NEUMATIC NOTATIONS, fig.29). They are problematic in that the voices sometimes create dissonant intervals, particularly parallel 2nds and 4ths. In the absence of clef indications, one school of thought favours experimenting with transpositions of some of the parts in order to obtain more euphonious chords and progressions. The other justifies the dissonances by referring to the raw harmonic progressions found in early organum of the 11th and 12th centuries.

Most of the polyphony believed to date from before the mid-17th century is essentially for two or three voices. Even in the late 16th century there are technical terms for singers which seem to designate the pitch-range of their voices: for example *verkh* or *verkhnik* ('peak' or 'highest') and *niz* and *nizhnik* ('lowland' or 'the one who is below'). These terms alone would suffice for two-part settings. In compositions for three voices the term *put'* ('way' or 'road') is found, and may perhaps designate a sort of cantus firmus, although in practice the melody given to *put'* was often highly embellished. In some instances the term *demestvo* instead of *put'* may be found. If demestvennïy chant indeed refers to the skill of its singers, then *demestvo* may logically imply a skilful leader of singing assigned to lead the 'way' by singing the traditional melody which, as practice permitted it, could be embroidered.

In the second half of the 17th century the use of Western staff notation became much more prominent. From this time there survive useful manuscripts known as *dvoznamenniki* which contain parallel notation of melodies in neumes and on the staff – a sort of 'Rosetta stone'. The knowledge of neumatic notation diminished rapidly after 1700, and although manuscripts were still copied in the 18th century, it was used only by small groups of people, mostly dissenters from the official Russian church.

In the last quarter of the 17th century several composers of polyphonic church music appeared, among them Nikolay Diletsky and Vasily Titov (active between 1680 and 1710). Their works have much in common technically and stylistically with German choral music of this period (e.g. Schütz). Besides settings for one choir in four parts, polychoral compositions began to proliferate. In such polychoral works for two and three choirs (i.e. for 8 and 12 voices, in one extreme case for 48) the typical features are frequent use of imitation and of sequential progressions. The *partesnïye kontsertï* ('concertos for many parts'), of which more than 500 may survive, abound with highly effective exchanges between individual choruses.

Simultaneously, another musical genre made its appearance. This was *kant* (plural *kantï*, obviously related to 'chant'); it comprised settings of chant, usually for three voices, syllabic and in block chords. Some examples suggest a Polish origin for this genre (possibly as a by-product of influence from the Lutheran chorale). A few even have Polish texts transliterated into the Cyrillic alphabet. The earliest *kantï* have religious texts. Shortly thereafter secular texts were being used; the secular *kant* became highly popular, and there emerged a sub-type known as 'panegyric kant' which flourished in the time of Peter the Great. Secular *kantï* remained popular during much of the 18th century.

The period between the activities of Titov and the second half of the 18th century has not yet been investigated sufficiently to provide a clear picture of the developments of church music. Conscious attempts were being made during the reign of Empress Anna (1730–40) to lure Italian composers to Russia. Contrary to the traditional belief that Italians arriving in Russia found a musical wasteland, the Italians evidently found not only a receptive audience at the court, but also an established practice of polyphony in the church.

During her reign (1762–96) Catherine the Great maintained contacts with western European scholars and philosophers, and surrounded herself with Italian musicians. The interchanges which brought Baldassare Galuppi (1706–85) to St Petersburg and took Maxim Berezovsky (1745–77) to study and work in Italy in 1765 brought music of highly Italianate style into the Russian church. The most influential figure in this was Dmitry Bortnyansky (1751–1825), who after ten years in Italy returned to become musician-in-ordinary to Crown Prince Paul and eventually director in the imperial chapel. He wrote well over 100 works for use in religious services, including at least 35 choral concertos with texts derived from the Psalms. Despite publication by the Russian church of four volumes of znamennïy chant in 1772, and of an *Obikhod* (similar to a *Liber usualis*) in 1778, Bortnyansky did not make great use of traditional melodies.

Although Emperor Paul issued in 1797 an edict banning the singing of concertos during services, nevertheless there were many abuses in the next half-century (including a setting of the words of the Cherubic Hymn to one of the choruses from Haydn's *The Creation*). The edict did not stop Bortnyansky writing his own concertos. In 1816 he was appointed a kind of censor of composition submitted for performance in Russian churches. Thus, for the last decade of his life Bortnyansky had supreme control over church music in Russia. He overshadowed a number of other competent composers of religious music, such as Artemy Vedel' (1767–1806), Stepan Degtyaryov (1766–1813) and Stepan Davïdov (1777–1825).

Bortnyansky's successor as director of the chapel was Fyodor L'vov (1766–1836) who is mainly remembered as an administrator, though he did write a booklet on Russian church music in 1834. He was succeeded by his son, Alexey L'vov (1798–1870), who served as director of the chapel from 1836 to 1861. After the period of Italian musical influence there began a period of German influence. Pyotr Turchaninov (1779–1856) was still writing in an Italianate style, and enjoyed great popularity after official approval of his music had been granted in 1831. L'vov, on the other hand, deeply influenced by the Romantic music of his time, fostered a style which closely resembled that of the German chorale. The melodies used by the imperial chapel were in fact abridged versions of traditional tunes, and L'vov harmonized them in his own style. When the text or melody got in the way of his concepts he introduced choral recitatives on a single note. By comparison with the music of Bortnyansky and Turchaninov, that of L'vov is much richer harmonically and carries the cantus firmus in the top voice. He may be viewed as the creator of a specific style which Gardner has designated the 'St Petersburg School' of Russian church music. Closely related in style were the works of Gavriil Lomakin (1812–85), G. F. L'vovsky (1830–94), M. A. Vinogradov (1810–88), E. S. Azeyev (1851–1918) and those of Alexander Arkhangel'sky (1846–1924) who was the first to introduce female voices into the choir in the 1880s.

Furthermore, L'vov, in collaboration with Vorotnikov and Lomakin, organized the work on an edition of the *Obikhod* which was published in 1848 and which became mandatory for all churches in Russia. The settings for four voices provided in this edition rapidly came into use throughout Russia.

On the positive side L'vov raised the standards for

performance of church music which so deeply impressed Berlioz in 1847.

In the late 1830s Glinka was associated for a short time with the imperial chapel. He wrote a few works in Italianate style. However, he soon became convinced that Russian church music must be harmonized in modal harmony, not in the major and minor keys. Glinka had intended to study the modes and 'church scales' with Dehn when he embarked on his last trip, during which he died. N. M. Potulov (1810–73), often described as a follower of Glinka's ideas, harmonized all the melodies published in the Synodal edition of 1772. His harmonizations were very simple, in a strictly chordal style without dissonances and modulations.

The 1860s saw the beginnings of scholarly study in the history of Russian church music and a new awareness of a specifically Russian musical idiom fostered by 'The Five'. L'vov's successor as director of the chapel, N. I. Bakhmet'yev (1807–91), is seen nowadays as a reactionary in the face of these movements. He resigned his post, apparently in protest against the publication of Tchaikovsky's *Liturgy* op.41 in 1878. Tchaikovsky's publisher, Jürgenson, did not seek approval from the imperial chapel but from the Holy Synod of the Russian Church. After publication litigation ensued which led to the downfall of Bakhmet'yev.

Although Bakhmet'yev was succeeded by Balakirev, who served as director of the chapel (1883–95) and in turn brought Rimsky-Korsakov to be an assistant, the importance of the St Petersburg school was waning. The fact that certain composers, including Alexandr Grechaninov (1864–1956) were writing a more modern style of church music in both St Petersburg and Moscow did not arrest the decline.

Already a new school was developing. Its main vehicle of performance was the Synodal choir in Moscow under the leadership of V. S. Orlov (1856–1907) and Stepan Smolensky (1848–1909). The most significant composers of Russian church music during the two decades before the 1917 Revolution were all associated with the Moscow school, among them Alexandr Kastal'sky (1856–1926) and Pavel Chesnokov (1877–1944). Kastal'sky revised Potulov's settings, and established a style which allowed the cantus firmus to migrate through all voices, and used a type of modal harmony which approximated to the style of Russian folksongs. Others associated with this style were A. B. Nikol'sky (1874–1943) and Vasily Kalinnikov (1866–1901). Above them all towered Rakhmaninov whose *Liturgy of St John Chrysostom* and *All-night Vigil* are now ranked as the highest artistic achievements in the realm of Russian church music.

Under the influence of the Moscow school, the Holy Synod prepared a new edition of the *Obikhod* in 1915, yet with the two revolutions of 1917 ending in the establishment of the Soviet Union, church music lost the exalted position which it had enjoyed for centuries. While some composition of church music may have been going on in the Soviet Union, no information about it is at present available. The Russians in the Diaspora, spread all over the world, mostly perpetuate the style of Bortnyansky and L'vov with only an occasional bow towards Kastal'sky and Chesnokov. Several Russian church choirs have achieved renown in western Europe and in the USA (e.g. those conducted by Ossorguine, Kedrov and Afonsky). Their repertory is mostly traditional with a few new arrangements or compositions which seldom enjoy anything more than a local popularity. Among those who have tried to foster a revival of Russian church music in the mid-20th century and whose works are of more than passing value are Alfred J. Swan (1890–1970) and Johann von Gardner, the latter much better known as a scholar.

4. BULGARIAN CHURCH MUSIC. The Bulgarians were apparently the first among the Slavs to accept Christianity as a state religion in 865. Their proximity to Constantinople, capital of the Byzantine Empire, fostered close ties with the Greek Orthodox Church and its ritual. Yet in spite of this and known cultural developments in medieval Bulgaria the existing documents about music and chant are sparse and fragmentary. As study of the 13th-century Bologna Psalter progresses, in which some segments of the Slavonic text contain Byzantine neumes, more may become known. Similarly, the Zographou Trefologion (or 'Draganov Minej', in the monastery library of Zographou, Mount Athos) contains neumatic notation which has not yet been studied critically. There are also records of Bulgarian inscriptions in Byzantine musical manuscripts. The Slavonic manuscript known as the Synodikon of Boril contains musical examples, but in Greek with Byzantine neumes. This is not a direct source of information for church music in Bulgaria.

The Bulgarians claim as their own one of the most outstanding Byzantine musicians of the 14th century, Joannes Koukouzeles, whose mother was evidently of Slavonic (but not necessarily Bulgarian) origin. One composition attributed to him is customarily referred to as 'Polyeleon Bulgara' (presumably 'Bulgarian woman'), a title which some scholars have interpreted as a tribute to his own mother. Its dating and attribution are as yet uncertain, and all the works of Koukouzeles survive in Greek.

From the downfall of the Bulgarian medieval state in 1396 to the liberation from the Turks in 1877–8, the main centres of religious activity under Turkish domination were the monasteries. The absence of any records of musical activity in such circumstances is understandable. It is again in the monasteries that the first signs of cultural revival were to take place, including the writing of hymns in Bulgarian and the notation of their melodies in late Byzantine neumes. One such prominent centre was the monastery of St John of Rila, south of Sofia, where in the late 18th and early 19th centuries a whole school of singers came into existence around a neophyte monk who has recently been called the first Bulgarian musicologist.

Following the Chrysanthine reform of Byzantine neumatic notation in the first quarter of the 19th century (which spread rapidly through its use in printed books) the Bulgarians were the only other group besides the Greeks to accept this reformed notation not only for church music but also for secular melodies.

With the growth of the national liberation movement in the 19th century, the public libraries played a distinctive role in nationalist cultural activities. From the middle of the century a number of libraries sponsored choral groups which participated actively in religious services in their communities, gave concerts of secular music and cultivated folk music. Conductors of these choruses represent at the same time the first modern composers of Bulgarian church music to accept polyphonic settings. At first many such settings were simple arrangements of traditional melodies, hitherto transmitted only orally. Relying on a relatively recent tradition from the late 17th century and the 18th suggesting the existence of a specifically Bulgarian chant, the main body of church music in use in Bulgaria became divided into 'Damascenian melodies' (presumed to have been written by John Damascene (c675–c749) but in fact mostly simply transferred from 18th- and 19th-century Greek manuscripts) and Bulgarian chant.

The first conductor and arranger worthy of mention is Ianko Mustakov (1842–81). Of greater significance were Nikolay Nikolayev (1852–1938) who was active in Sofia, and Atanas Badev (1860–1908) who, with a number of his contemporaries, combined composition of religious music with the study of folk music. In the first half of the 20th century the most talented and probably the best composer of church music in Bulgaria was Dobri Khristov (1875–1941).

5. SERBIAN CHURCH MUSIC. Although the Serbs accepted Christianity perhaps as early as the 10th century, the first references to the practice of church music come from the Serbian medieval state ruled by members of the dynasty of Nemanjides (late 12th century to 1371). Chanting is mentioned specifically in the Lives of rulers and of saints – a literary genre cultivated particularly after 1219, when the Serbian archbishopric was made independent of the Greek church in Byzantium. This latter event, the work of St Sava (d 1235), prompted a wave of religious activity, including the founding of monasteries, the copying of manuscripts and the fostering of church music. In the absence of any Serbian musical manuscripts before the 15th century it is nonetheless possible to infer the existence of religious poetry and services composed for the feasts of Serbian saints. These contain clear indications that hymns were to be sung either in a particular mode or emulating the melodic patterns of well-known traditional hymns.

The earliest mention of musicians of more than local reputation in medieval Serbia dates from the last decades of Serbian independence, just before the total conquest by the Turks in 1459. With the exception of 'domestik Kyr Stefan the Serb' these singers were Greeks who had also been active in Byzantium: Joakeim the monk of the Harsianites Monastery (in Constantinople) had also the title of 'domestik of Serbia'; even Manuel Chrysaphes (fl c1440–63) resided for a while in Serbia. In the second half of the 15th century the names of Isaiah the Serb and Nicolas the Serb were recorded as composers of religious music. The works of all of these composers are notated in Byzantine neumes with Greek or Slavonic texts, or both. They survive in a few Byzantine manuscripts and bilingual fragments. Stylistically there is no difference between these chants and the melodies known from contemporary Byzantine sources. Medieval Serbian church music thus emulated the style of Byzantine models, although specifically Serbian variants of some chants did exist.

As in the case of Bulgaria, the Turkish domination had cut short cultural growth by almost totally eliminating the educated class of people. Religion became intertwined with the idea of nationality, and church music was viewed as one of the manifestations of national spirit, in the latent struggle for survival. Some scattered records concerning chanting are available from the period of Austrian rule in northern Serbia (c1719–39). At that time closer ties were being established between the Serbian population which had settled in Austria (after retreating from the Turks) and Russian religious centres, especially that of Kiev. While the Serbs retained the tradition of monophonic chanting for some time in the Austrian lands, a new blend of church music, presumably incorporating traditional and also perhaps Russian melodies, was gradually formed. This may be the origin of the so-called Karlovac chant (named after the town of Sremski Karlovci, the seat of the Serbian archbishop who was the spiritual leader of Serbs in Austria). The only other cultural and spiritual centre in which a more or less uninterrupted religious life was maintained among the Serbs was Chilandar monastery, Mount Athos (founded by Nemanja and his son Sava in 1198).

A number of musical manuscripts were copied in the late 18th and the 19th centuries. These contained brief theoretical treatises on music (mostly adaptations of the Greek papadikē) and a large collection of hymns and chants in honour of Serbian saints. Among them is an interesting collection of chants by the well-known Greek musician Petros Peloponnesios, which was copied in the early 1770s (now in US-NH); it includes a number of hymns presumably by him but set in the Serbian recension of Church Slavonic. These late 18th-century documents are all notated in late Byzantine neumes. Melodies tend to be melismatic, and their structure still follows the contemporary Greek melodies, which were by then considerably changed from their medieval prototypes. This body of chant thus represents a new stage in the evolution of Serbian chant which has nothing in common with the melodies collected and published at the turn of the 20th century either in melodic outlines or in the structure of the hymns. The latter melodies are now viewed as the third stage in the evolution of Serbian monophonic chant. The disparity of these melodies raises the question of their origin, which as yet remains uncertain.

With the beginning of gradual liberation from the Turks (starting in 1804 with the first Serbian insurrection), other variants came to the fore in addition to the Karlovac chant. Among these Belgrade chant and Zadar chant (named after a city on the Dalmatian coast) enjoyed considerable popularity. After some individual and rather unsystematic attempts at recording these melodies in modern western European notation, the studious labours of Stevan Mokranjac (1856–1914) as collector and editor of a great number of melodies are a milestone. His edition of the Osmoglasnik (i.e. oktōēchos), published in Belgrade in 1908, became a classic in this field. Monophonic traditions of chanting still continue in Serbia at the present time, though mostly restricted to a few monasteries and smaller churches, whereas in the cathedrals and larger churches polyphonic music now prevails.

Polyphonic settings of Serbian church music appear rather late, in the mid-19th century. The first to compose four-part settings of functional church music was Kornelije Stanković (1831–65) who wrote two liturgies (1851–2), besides collecting melodies of Karlovac chant, most of which still remain unpublished. Probably the greatest Serbian composer of church music was Stevan Mokranjac. By the early 20th century Serbian composers were composing music for liturgical purposes. The main followers of Mokranjac, most of whom were eclectics, were Stevan Hristić (1885–1958), Kosta

Manojlović (1890–1949) and Marko Tajčević (b 1900). These three composers wrote effective church music, combining originality and erudition. Since 1945 fewer composers have shown an interest in church music, but avant-garde composers such as Ljubica Marić (b 1909) and Vlastimir Nikolovski (b 1925) have used traditional Serbian chants, though in works unsuitable for religious services.

BIBLIOGRAPHY

This bibliography is designed to give comprehensive coverage for Russian, Bulgarian and Serbian church music. It is intended to serve not only the foregoing article but also a range of other articles in the same field which carry only short selective bibliographies and are cross-referred to this bibliography for further material.

RUSSIAN CHURCH MUSIC

Reference book
A. V. Preobrazhensky: *Slovar' russkovo tserkovnovo peniya* [Dictionary of Russian chant] (Moscow, 1897)

Bibliography and critical surveys of literature
A. V. Preobrazhensky: *Po tserkovnomu peniyu ukazatel' knig, broshyur, zhurnal'nïkh statey i rukopisey* [Index of literature on chant published in Russia between 1793 and 1896] (Ekaterinoslav, 1897, 2/1900)
I. A. Gardner: *Ukazatel' russkoy i inostrannoy literaturï po voprosam russkovo tserkovnovo peniya* [Index to Russian and foreign literature on Russian chant] (Munich, 1958)
M. Velimirović: 'Stand der Forschung über kirchenslavische Musik', *Zeitschrift für slavische Philologie*, xxxi (1963), 145
——: 'Present State of Research in Slavic Chant', *AcM*, xliv (1972), 235

Catalogues of musical MSS
V. M. Metallov: *Russkaya simiografiya* [Russian sign notation] (Moscow, 1912) [partial catalogue with a palaeographical atlas of notations]
I. M. Kudryavtsev, ed.: *Rukopisnïye sobraniya D. V. Razumovskovo i V. F. Odoyevskovo i arkhiv D. V. Razumovskovo* [The MS collections of D. V. Razumovsky and V. F. Odoyevsky and the archive of Razumovsky] (Moscow, 1960)

Facsimile editions of MSS
R. Jakobson, ed.: *Fragmenta chiliandarica palaeoslavica*, MMB, 1st ser., v (1957)
A. Bugge, ed.: *Contacarium palaeoslavicum mosquense*, MMB, 1st ser., vi (1960)
J. von Gardner and E. Koschmieder, eds.: *Ein handschriftliches Lehrbuch der altrussischen Neumenschrift* [pt.i: Text; pt.ii: Kommentar zum Zeichensystem], Abhandlungen der Bayerischen Akademie der Wissenschaften, Phil.-Hist. Klasse, new ser., lvii (Munich, 1963); lxii (1966)

Studies and monographs
E. Bolkhovitinov: *Istoricheskoye rassuzhdeniye voobshche o drevnem khristianskom bogosluzhebnom penii i osobenno o penii rossiyskoy tserkvi, s nuzhnïmi primechaniyami na onoye* [A historical dissertation on the ancient Christian chant in general and on the Russian chant in particular with the necessary comments on the latter] (Voronezh, 1799, 3/1814); *RMG*, iv (1897), columns 1020–36
F. L'vov: *O penii v Rossii* [On the chant in Russia] (St Petersburg, 1834)
V. M. Undol'sky: 'Zamechaniya dlya istorii tserkovnovo peniya v Rossii' [Remarks on the history of the chant in Russia], *Chteniya v Imperatorskom Obshchestve Istorii i Drevnostey Rossiskikh pri Moskovskom Universitete*, iii (1846)
A. L'vov: *O svobodnom ili nesimmetrichnom ritme* [On the free rhythms of the old Russian church-song] (St Petersburg, 1858; Ger. trans., 1859)
D. V. Razumovsky: 'O notnïkh bezlineynïkh rukopisyakh tserkovnovo znamennovo peniya' [On the staffless musical MSS of the znamennïy chant], *Chteniya v Obshchestve Lyubiteley Dukhovnovo Prosveshcheniya*, i (1863), 55–164
P. Bezsonov: 'Sud'ba pevcheskikh knig' [The fate of singers' books], *Pravoslavnoye Obozreniye*, xix/5–6 (1864)
A. Ryazhsky: 'O proiskhozhdenii russkovo tserkovnovo peniya' [On the origin of the Russian chant], *Pravoslavnoye Obozreniye*, xxi (1866), 36, 194, 292
D. V. Razumovsky: *Tserkovnoye peniye v Rossii* [Chant in Russia], i–iii (Moscow, 1867–9)
N. M. Potulov: *Rukovodstvo k prakticheskomu izucheniyu drevnevo bogosluzhebnovo peniya rossiyskoy tserkvi* [Guide to the practical learning of the old ritual chanting of the Russian church] (Moscow, 1872; many edns.)
P. A. Bezsonov: 'Znamenatel'nïye godï i znamenateyshiye predstaviteli

poslednikh dvukh vekov v istorii russkovo pesnopeniya' [Significant years and the most significant representatives of the last two centuries in the history of Russian chant], *Pravoslavnïy Sobesednik* (1872), nos.2–3
I. de Castro: *Methodus cantus ecclesiastici graeco-slavici* (Rome, 1881)
D. V. Razumovsky: *Bogosluzhebnoye peniye pravoslavnoy greko-rossiyskoy tserkvi*, i: *Teoriya i praktika tserkovnovo peniya* [The liturgical chant of the Orthodox Greco-Russian church, i: Theory and practice of the chant] (Moscow, 1886)
S. V. Smolensky: *Kratkoye opisaniye drevnevo (xii–xiii veka) znamennovo irmologa, prinadlezhashchavo Voskresenskomu, Novïy Iyerusalim imenuyemomu monastïryu* [A brief description of the old (12th–13th-century) notated heirmologion belonging to the monastery of the Resurrection, called the New Jerusalem] (Kazan, 1887)
——: *Azbuka znamennovo peniya (Izveshcheniye o soglasneyshikh pometakh) startsa Alexandra Mezentsa (1668-vo goda)* [The alphabet of the znamennïy chant of Alexander Mezenets of 1668] (Kazan, 1888)
I. Voznesensky: *Osmoglasnïye rospevï tryokh poslednikh vekov pravoslavnoy russkoy tserkvi* [Russian Orthodox osmoglasniye chant during the last three centuries], i: *Kiyevskiy rospev*; ii: *Bolgarskiy rospev*; iii: *Grecheskiy rospev v Rossii*; iv: *Obraztsï rospevov* (Kiev, 1888–93)
——: *O tserkovnom penii pravoslavnoy greko-rossiyskoy tserkvi: bol'shoy i malïy rospev* [Greco-Russian Orthodox Church chant], ii (Riga, 1890)
V. M. Metallov: *Ocherk istorii pravoslavnovo tserkovnovo peniya v Rossii* [Essay on the history of the Orthodox chant in Russia] (Saratov, 1893, 4/1915)
——: *Azbuka kryukovovo peniya* [The alphabet of chanting after neumes] (Moscow, 1899)
S. V. Smolensky: 'O drevnerusskikh pevcheskikh notatsiyakh' [Old Russian chant notations], *Pamyatniki drevney pis'mennosti i iskusstva*, cxlv (St Petersburg, 1901)
V. M. Metallov: *Bogosluzhebnoye peniye russkoy tserkvi: period domongol'skiy* [The liturgical chant of the Russian Church before the Mongol invasion] (Moscow, 1906, 2/1912)
K. I. Papadopulo-Keramevs: 'Proiskhozhdeniye notnovo muzïkal'novo pis'ma u severnïkh i yuzhnïkh Slavyan po pamyatnikam drevnosti, preimushchestvenno vizantiyskim' [The origin of the musical notation among the northern and southern Slavs according to old documents, primarily Byzantine], *Vestnik arkheologii i istorii*, xvii (1906), 134
A. V. Preobrazhensky: *Vopros o edinoglasnom penii v russkoy tserkvi XVII veka* [On monophonic chant in the Russian Church in the 17th century], *Pamyatniki drevney pis'mennosti i iskusstva*, clix (St Petersburg, 1907)
A. Kalashnikov: *Azbuka tserkovnovo znamennovo peniya* [The alphabet of the znamennïy chant] (Kiev, 1908)
K. I. Papadopulo-Keramevs: 'Printsip tserkovnovizantiyskovo notnovo pis'ma po dannïm slavyanskikh i grecheskikh muzïkal'no-bogosluzhebnïkh pamyatnikov' [The system of Byzantine musical notation according to the Slavonic and Greek musical and liturgical documents], *Vizantiyskiy Vremennik*, xv (1908), 49
O. von Riesemann: *Die Notationen des altrussischen Kirchengesanges* (Moscow, 1908); Publikationen der Internationalen Musikgesellschaft, suppl.II/viii (Leipzig, 1909)
A. V. Preobrazhensky: 'O skhodstve russkovo muzïkal'novo pis'ma s grecheskim v pevchikh rukopisyakh XI–XIIvv.' [On the similarity of Russian and Greek musical notations in musical MSS of the 11th–12th centuries], *RMG*, xvi/8–10 (1909)
A. A. Ignat'yev: 'Tserkovno-pravitel'stvennïye kommissii po ispravleniyu bogosluzhebnovo peniya russkoy tserkvi' [The ecclesiastical and governmental commissions for correction of the liturgical chant of the Russian Church], *Pravoslavïy Sobesednik* (1910), Oct
A. V. Preobrazhensky: *Ocherk istorii tserkovnovo peniya v Rossii* [An essay on the history of chant in Russia] (St Petersburg, 1910)
S. V. Smolensky: *Musikiyskaya grammatika Nikolaya Diletskovo* [The 'Musical grammar' of Nikolay Diletsky] (St Petersburg, 1910)
N. Findeyzen: *Muzïkal'naya starina*, v (1911), 1–46
A. Kalashnikov: *Azbuka demestvennovo peniya* [The alphabet of the demestvennïy chant] (Kiev, 1911)
A. A. Ignat'yev: *Bogosluzhebnoye peniye pravoslavnoy russkoy tserkvi s kontsa XVI do nachala XVIII veka* [The liturgical chant of the Russian Orthodox Church from the end of the 14th century to the beginning of the 18th] (Kazan, 1916)
A. V. Preobrazhensky: *Kul'tovaya muzïka v Rossii* [Religious music in Russia] (Leningrad, 1924)
——: 'Greko-russkiye pevchiye paralleli XII–XIIIvv' [Greco-Russian parallels in the chant of the 12th and 13th centuries], *De musica, vremennik otdela istorii i teorii muzïki, izdavayemïy Gosudarstvennïm Institutom Istorii Iskusstv v Leningrade*, ii (1926), 60
N. Findeyzen: *Ocherki po istorii muzïki v Rossii* [Essays on history of music in Russia] (Moscow, 1928–9)

C. Bourdeau: 'Le chant religieux de l'église orthodoxe russe', *EMDC*, II/iv (1929), 2355–98

E. Koschmieder: *Przyczynki do zagadnienia chomonji w hirmosach rosyjskich* [The problem of homonija in Russian hirmoi] (Vilnius, 1932)

——: 'Teorja i praktyka rosyjskiego spiewu neumaticznego na tle tradycji staroobrzedowcow wilenskich' [Theory and practice of Russian chant according to the traditions of the Old Believers in Vilnius], *Ateneum Wilenskie*, x (1935), 295

T. Livanova: *Ocherki i materialï po istorii russkoy muzïkal'noy kul'turï* [Essays and documents for the history of Russian musical culture] (Moscow, 1938)

A. J. Swan: 'The Znamenny Chant of the Russian Church', *MQ*, xxvi (1940), 23, 365, 529

M. V. Brazhnikov: *Puti razvitiya i zadachi rasshifrovki znamennovo rospeva XII–XVIII vekov: primeneniye nekotorïkh statisticheskikh metodov k issledovaniyu muzïkal'nïkh yavleniy* [The development of the znamenniy chant from the 12th century to the 18th and the tasks for its deciphering: the application of some statistical methods to the study of musical phenomena] (Leningrad, 1949)

B. Dobrokhotov: *D. S. Bortnyansky* (Moscow, 1950)

J. Handschin: 'Le chant ecclésiastique russe', *AcM*, xxiv (1952), 3

E. Koschmieder: *Die ältesten Novgoroder Hirmologien-Fragmente*, Abhandlung der Bayerischen Akademie der Wissenschaften, Phil.-Hist. Klasse, new ser., xxxv (Munich, 1952); xxxvii (1955); xlv (1958)

C. Hoeg: 'The Oldest Slavonic Tradition of Byzantine Music', *Proceedings of the British Academy*, xxxix (1953), 37

R. Palikarova-Verdeil: *La musique byzantine chez les bulgares et les russes (du IX au XIV siècle)*, MMB, *Subsidia*, iii (1953)

E. Koschmieder: 'Zur Herkunft der slavischen Krjuki-Notation', *Festschrift für Dmytro Čyževśkyj* (Wiesbaden, 1954), 146

A. J. Swan: 'Russian Church Music', *Grove 5*

C. Hoeg: 'Ein Buch altrussischer Kirchengesange', *Zeitschrift für slavische Philologie*, xxv (1956), 261

V. Belyayev: 'Early Russian Polyphony', *Studia memoriae Belae Bartók sacra* (Budapest, 1957), 307

J. von Gardner: 'Drei Typen des russischen Kirchengesanges', *Ostkirchliche Studien*, vi (1957), 251

I. Shabatin: 'Mitropolit Evgeny Bolkhovitinov', *Zhurnal Moskovskoy Patriarkhii* (1957), no.5, p.57

N. Uspensky: 'Vizantiyskoye peniye v Kiyevskoy Rusi' [Byzantine chant in Kievan Russia], *XI. internationaler Byzantinistenkongress: München 1958*, i, 643

J. von Gardner: 'Einiges über die Orthographie der altrussischen Neumen vor der Reform 1668', *Welt der Slaven*, v (1960), 198

G. Seaman: 'D. S. Bortnyansky (1751–1825)', *MR*, xxi (1960), 106

M. Velimirović: *Byzantine Elements in Early Slavic Chant*, MMB, *Subsidia*, iv (1960)

V. Belyayev: *Drevnerusskaya muzïkal'naya pis'mennost'* (Moscow, 1962)

J. von Gardner: 'Zum Problem der Nomenklatur der altrussischen Neumen', *Welt der Slaven*, vii (1962), 300

——: 'Stilistische Richtungen im russischen liturgischen Chorgesang', *Ostkirchliche Studien*, xi (1962), 161

——: 'Das Cento Prinzip der Tropierung und seine Bedeutung für die Entzifferung der altrussischen linienlosen Notation', *Musik des Ostens*, i (1962), 106

——: 'Zum Problem des Tonleiter-Aufbaus im altrussischen Neumengesang', *Musik des Ostens*, ii (1963), 157

M. Velimirović: 'Liturgical Drama in Byzantium and Russia', *Dumbarton Oaks Papers*, xvi (1962), 351–85

Anfänge der slavischen Musik: Symposia I: Bratislava, 1964 [incl. contributions by E. Arro, V. Belyayev, K. Levy, O. Strunk and M. Velimirović]

K. Levy: 'The Slavic Kontakia and their Byzantine Originals', *Queens College Twenty-fifth Anniversary Festschrift* (New York, 1964), 79

S. Lazarević: 'An Unknown Early Slavic Modal Signature', *Byzantinoslavica*, xxv (1964), 93

A. J. Swan: 'Die russische Musik im 17. Jahrhundert', *Jb für Geschichte Osteuropas*, new ser., xii (1964), 161

M. V. Brazhnikov: 'Arkhivnaya obrabotka pevcheskikh rukopisey' [Archival description of musical MSS], *Voprosï arkhivovedeniya* (Moscow, 1965), no.2

C. Floros: 'Die Entzifferung der Kondakarien-Notation', *Musik des Ostens*, iii (1965), 7–71; iv (1967), 12–44

Yu. Keldïsh: *Russkaya muzïka XVIII veka* [Russian music of the 18th century] (Moscow, 1965)

N. Uspensky: *Drevnerusskoye pevcheskoye iskusstvo* [Old Russian art of chanting] (Moscow, 1965, 2/1971)

J. von Gardner: 'Einige Beobachtungen über die Einschubsilben im altrussischen Kirchengesang', *Welt der Slaven*, xi (1966), 241

M. Velimirović: 'Struktura staroslovenskih muzickih irmologa' [The structure of Old Slavonic musical heirmologia], *Hilandarski zbornik*, i (Belgrade, 1966), 139

M. V. Brazhnikov: 'Russkoye tserkovnoye peniye XII–XVIII vekov' [Russian church chant from the 12th century to the 18th], *Musica antiqua Europae orientalis I: Bydgoszcz 1966*, 455

S. Skrebkov: 'Evolyutsiya stilya v russkoy khorovoy muzïke XVII veka' [The evolution of style in Russian choral music of the 17th century], ibid, 470

M. V. Brazhnikov: *Novïye pamyatniki znamennovo raspeva* [New documents on the znamenniy chant: an anthology of musical examples] (Leningrad, 1967)

J. von Gardner: 'Das Problem des altrussischen demestichen Kirchengesanges und seiner linienlosen Notation', *Slavistische Beiträge*, xxv (Munich, 1967)

——: 'Die Musiktheorie der Russen im 17. Jahrhundert', *Congressus historicae slavicae salisburgensis in memoriam SS Cyrilli et Methodi anno 1963 celebrati*, Annales Instituti Slavici, iii (Wiesbaden, 1967), 160

——: 'Einiges über den Singmeister Alexander Mezenets (d 1676)', *Welt der Slaven*, xii (1967), 173

Yu. Keldïsh: 'K voprosu ob istokakh russkovo partesnovo peniya' [On the origins of Russian polyphony], *Studia Hieronymo Feicht septuagenario dedicata* (Kraków, 1967), 269

D. Lehmann: 'Dilezki und die grosse Wandlung der russischen Musik', *SM*, ix (1967), 343

M. V. Brazhnikov: 'Zur Terminologie der altrussischen Vokalmusik', *BMw*, x (1968), 189

N. D. Uspensky: *Obraztsï drevnerusskovo pevcheskovo iskusstva* [Examples of old Russian chant: an anthology] (Leningrad, 1968)

N. Gerasimova-Persidskaya: 'Kharakternïye kompozitsionnïye chertï mnogogolosiya partesnïkh kontsertov XVII–XVIII st.' [Compositional characteristics of polyphony in the partesnïy concertos of the 17th and 18th centuries], *Musica antiqua Europae orientalis II: Bydgoszcz 1969*, 369

Yu. Keldïsh: 'Ob istoricheskikh kornyakh kanta' [Historical roots of the kant], ibid, 437

A. Tsalai-Iakimenko: 'Muzïkal'no-teoreticheskaya mïsl'na Ukrayne v XVII stoletii i trudï Nikolaya Diletskovo' [Musico-theoretical thinking in the Ukraine in the 17th century and the works of Nikolay Diletsky], ibid, 347

N. Uspensky: 'Problema metodologii obucheniya ispolnitel'skomu masterstvu v drevnerusskom pevcheskom iskusstve' [The problem of the methodology of learning the art of performance in ancient Russian singing], ibid, 467

S. Skrebkov: *Russkaya khorovaya muzïka XVII–nachala XVIII veka* [Russian choral music from the 17th century to the beginning of the 18th] (Moscow, 1969)

C. Floros: *Universale Neumenkunde* (Kassel, 1970)

M. V. Brazhnikov: *Drevnerusskaya teoriya muzïki* (Leningrad, 1972)

J. von Gardner: 'Die Gesänge der byzantinisch-slawischen Liturgie', *Geschichte der katholischen Kirchenmusik*, ed. K. G. Fellerer, i (Kassel, 1972), 148

N. A. Gerasimova-Persidskaya: 'Narodnïye istoki partesnovo kontserta' [The folk origins of the partesnïy concerto], *Musica antiqua Europae orientalis III: Bydgoszcz 1972*, 729–90

A. D. McCredie: 'Some Aspects of Current Research into Russian Liturgical Chant', *MMA*, vi (1972), 55

V. Protopopov: 'Tvoreniya Vasiliya Titova: vïdayushchevosiya russkovo kompozitora vtoroy polovinï XVII–nachala XVIII veka' [The works of Vasily Titov, an outstanding Russian composer of the second half of the 17th century and beginning of the 18th], *Musica antiqua Europae orientalis III: Bydgoszcz 1972*, 847

Discography

J. von Gardner: 'Diskographie des russischen Kirchengesanges', *Ostkirchliche Studien*, ix (1960), 262; x (1961), 136; xii (1963), 39; xiii (1964), 282; xv (1966), 154; xvii (1968), 174; xviii (1969), 23; xix (1970), 185

BULGARIAN CHURCH MUSIC

A. Nikolov: *Liturgy of St John Chrysostom* (1905); *Vespers* (1906) [Lithographed edns. of the melodies of Bulgarian chant]

——: 'K vozrozhdeniyu bolgarskovo tserkovnovo peniya' [The renaissance of Bulgarian chant], *RMG*, xiii/7–8 (1906)

——: *Starobalgarsko tsarkovno peniye po ruskite notni rakopisi ot XVII i XVIII v.* [Old Bulgarian chant after Russian musical MSS from the 17th and 18th centuries] (Sofia, 1921)

P. Dinev: *Dukhovni muzikalni tvorbi na Ioan Kukuzel* [Religious music of Joannes Koukouzeles] (Sofia, 1938)

——, ed.: *Tsarkovnopevcheski sinodalen sbornik* [Collection of liturgical music] (Sofia, 1947–58), i: *Kratak osmoglasnik i bozhestvena liturgiya*; ii: *Obshiren vazkresnik*; iii: *Triod i Pentekostar*; iv: *Prostranni papadicheski pesnopeniya ot liturgiyata*; v: *Tsarkovni trebi i slavi ot Trioda i Pentikostara*

R. Palikarova-Verdeil: 'La musique byzantine chez les bulgares et les russes (du IXe au XIVe siècle)', MMB, *Subsidia*, iii (1953)

P. Dinev: *Rilskata tsarkovno-pevcheska shkola v nachaloto na 19 vek i neynite predstaviteli* [The Rila school of church singing at the beginning of the 19th century and its representatives], *IIM*, iv (1957), 5–82

L. Brashovanova-Stancheva: 'Prouchvaniya varkhu zhivota i deynostta na Ioan Kukuzel' [Investigations about the life and activities of Joannes Koukouzeles], *IIM*, vi (1959), 13

P. Dinev: 'Narodnopesenni elementi v balgarskiya tsarkoven napev' [Folk music elements in the Bulgarian church melos], *IIM*, vi (1959), 39

S. Petrov: *Ochertsi po istoriya na balgarskata muzikalna kultura* [Essays on the history of Bulgarian musical culture] (Sofia, 1959)

S. Petrov: 'Sinodikat na tsar Boril kato muzikalno-istoricheski pametnik' [The Synodikon of Tsar Boril as a musico-historical document], *IIM*, vii (1961), 5–69

S. Petrov: 'Tvortsi, pametnitsi i traditsii na starobalgarskata muzikalna kultura' [Creators, documents and traditions of old Bulgarian musical culture], *Kliment Okhridski: sbornik ot statii po sluchai 1050-god od smrtta mu* [St Clement of Ohrid: a collection of essays commemorating the 1050th anniversary of his death] (Sofia, 1966), 393

V. Krastev: 'Puti razvitiya bolgarskoy muzïkal'noy kul'turï v period XII–XVIII stoletiy' [The development of Bulgarian musical culture from the 12th century to the 18th], *Musica antiqua Europae orientalis I: Bydgoszcz 1966*, 45

P. L'ondev: 'Pesni zapisani s khurmuziyevi nevmi v Balgariya prez XIX vek' [Songs written down in Hurmouzios' neumes in Bulgaria in the 19th century], *IIM*, xii (1967), 161–226

E. Toncheva: 'Muzikalnite tekstove v palauzoviya prepis na sinodika na tsar Boril' [Musical texts in the Palauzov copy of the Synodikon of Tsar Boril], *IIM*, xii (1967), 57–152

V. Krastev, ed.: *Entsiklopediya na balgarskata muzikalna kultura* (Sofia, 1968)

P. Dinev: 'Tserkovnoye peniye v Bolgarii vo vremya I i II gosudarstva (865–1396g.)' [Chant in Bulgaria at the time of the first and second kingdom (865–1396)], *Musica antiqua Europae orientalis II: Bydgoszcz 1969*, 9

V. Krastev: *Ochertsi po istoriya na balgarskata muzika* [Essays on the history of Bulgarian music] (Sofia, 1970), 85

E. Toncheva: 'Elenski prostranen vazkresen tropar "Khristos voskrese" ' [The extended Easter troparion 'Christ is Risen' from the Elena township], *IIM*, xv (1970), 213–53

S. Lazarov: 'The Synodikon of Tsar Boril and the Problem of Byzantino-Bulgarian Relations', *Studies in Eastern Chant*, ii, ed. M. Velimirović (London, 1971), 69

E. Toncheva: *Bolgarskiy rospev* [Bulgarian chant] (Sofia, 1971)

E. Borisova-Toncheva: 'Kompositions- und Strukturbesonderheiten des "Bolgarski rosspew" ', *Musica antiqua Europae orientalis III: Bydgoszcz 1972*, 33–65

SERBIAN CHURCH MUSIC

Bibliography

A. Jakovljević: 'Bibliografija srpskog crkvenog narodnog pojanja', *Pravoslavna Misao* (1963), nos.1, 2

——: 'Bibliographie du chant ecclésiastique populaire orthodoxe serbe', *Byzantinoslavica*, xxv (1965), 477

Studies and monographs

D. Stefanović: 'Izgoreli neumski rukopis br.93 Beogradske narodne biblioteke' [On the burnt neumatic MS 93 of the Belgrade National Library], *Bibliotekar*, xiii/5 (1961), 379

——: 'The Earliest Dated and Notated Document of Serbian Chant', *Zbornik radova Vizantološkog Instituta*, vii (1961), 187

J. Milojković-Djurić: 'Some Aspects of the Byzantine Origin of the Serbian Chant', *Byzantinoslavica*, xxiii (1962), 45

M. Velimirović: 'Joakeim Monk of the Harsianites Monastery and Domestikos of Serbia', *Zbornik radova Vizantološkog Instituta*, viii/2 (1964), 451

P. Konjović: 'Musica divina', *Ogledi o muzici* (Belgrade, 1965), 172

D. Stefanović: 'The Beginnings of Serbian Chant', *Anfänge der slavischen Musik* (Bratislava, 1966), 55

M. Velimirović and D. Stefanović: 'Peter Lampadarios and Metropolitan Serafim of Bosnia', *Studies in Eastern Chant*, i, ed. M. Velimirović (London, 1966), 67

D. Stefanović: 'The Serbian Chant from the 15th to the 18th Century', *Musica antiqua Europae orientalis I: Bydgoszcz 1966*, 140

——: 'Crkvena muzika od XV do XVIII veka' [Church music from the 15th century to the 18th], *Srpska Pravoslavna Crkva 1219–1969: spomenica o 750-godišnjici autokefalnosti* (Belgrade, 1969), 209

——: 'Muzika u Srednjovekovnoj Srbiji', ibid, 117

——: 'New Data about the Serbian Chant', *Essays in Musicology in Honor of Dragan Plamenac* (Pittsburgh, 1969), 321

——: 'Some Aspects of the Form and Expression of Serbian Medieval Chant', *Musica antiqua Europae orientalis II: Bydgoszcz 1969*, 61

Karlovačko pojanje: Srbljak, stavio u note Branko Cvejić [Karlovac chant: feast of Serbian saints, as notated by Branko Cvejić] (Belgrade, 1970)

Srbljak (Belgrade, 1970), i–iii [texts of services for feasts of Serbian saints]

D. Stefanović: 'Pojanje stare srpske poezije' [Chanting of old Serbian poetry], *Srbljak* (Belgrade, 1970), iv

D. Crevar-Petrović: 'Pregled glasova u staroj srpskoj pojanoj poeziji' [Survey of modes in old Serbian chanted poetry], *Srbljak* (Belgrade, 1970), iv

Zbornik radova o Stevanu Mokranjcu (Belgrade, 1971) [memorial volume with 20-page bibliography of studies on Mokranjac]

A. Jakovljević: 'Servikon kratima', *Hilandarski zbornik*, ii (Belgrade, 1971), 131

MILOŠ VELIMIROVIĆ

Russian bassoon, 1833 (Schweizerisches Landesmuseum, Zurich)

Russian bassoon (Fr. *basson russe, serpent-basson, serpent droit, ophibariton*). A variety of upright serpent made in three or four sections, two of which, in a more massive form, resemble the butt and wing joint of the bassoon. The bell section is generally made in two parts, a straight wooden joint fitting into the butt, often capped by a brass flared bell or a painted dragon's head as illustrated here (the dragon's head variety was also called ophibariton). Many instruments of the dragon's head type were made at Lyons by such makers as Sautermeister, Jeantet and Tabard during the second quarter of the 19th century. The instrument is completed by a curved swan-neck crook. Six finger-holes and either three or four keys are normal, while in compass and playing technique it in no way differs from the serpent, except that it is much more convenient to hold.

Its origin may be found in Régibo's serpent, which was announced in Framery's *Calendrier universel musical* for 1789 in the following terms:

J. J. Régibo, Musicien à la Collégiale de St. Pierre à Lille, vient d'inventer un serpent nouveau qui est fait de même qu'un basson; il se

Luigi Russolo and his assistant Piati with 'noise intoners' at their studio in Via Stoppani, Milan

démonte en trois parties et est plus fort que le serpent ordinaire, et plus aisé à jouer; il a la même embouchure, est du même diapason et même gamme. Il a été présenté à MM. du Chapître dans une musique à grande symphonie, et a fait l'admiration des auditeurs par son effet; ils l'ont reçu dans leur musique ordinaire. Ceux qui veulent s'en procurer peuvent s'adresser à l'auteur, rue Pétérinck, Paroisse St. Pierre à Lille. Le prix est 3 louis.

Although this is evidently the starting-point of the countless varieties of upright serpent that became so popular and widespread during the first half of the 19th century, nothing further has been discovered about Régibo's instrument. Obviously it can have met with no success in Paris, since the first upright serpent found there is the Piffault serpent (1806), which bears no resemblance whatever to a bassoon; it was not until considerably later that bassoon-like serpents appeared in any quantity.

It is possible that Régibo's serpent was more encouragingly received further east, whence it seems to have reached Paris, after Waterloo, in Prussian military bands. It appears to have been popular in Belgium, though, to judge from surviving specimens, not before the 19th century.

Different countries seem to have favoured certain types of upright serpent. Thus in Germany the russian bassoon and Streitwolf's chromatic bass-horn are found; Belgium preferred the russian bassoon and the Dupré tuba, France favoured the Forveille serpent and the russian bassoon, while England held exclusively to the bass-horn.

See also SERPENT.

REGINALD MORLEY-PEGGE/R

Russian Symphony Orchestra. New York orchestra active from 1904 to 1918; *see* NEW YORK, §5.

Russischer Musikverlag. *See* EDITIONS RUSSES DE MUSIQUE.

Russkoye Muzïkal'noye Izdatel'stvo (Russ.: 'Russian Musical Editions'). *See* EDITIONS RUSSES DE MUSIQUE.

Russkoye Muzïkal'noye Obshchestvo (Russ.: 'Russian Musical Society'). Moscow society founded in 1859; *see* MOSCOW, §3.

Russolo, Luigi (*b* Portogruaro, 30 April 1885; *d* Cerro di Laveno, Varese, 6 Feb 1947). Italian inventor, painter and composer. He was the most spectacular innovator among the futurist musicians. Unlike his elder brothers Giovanni and Antonio (the latter of whom also wrote futurist music), he was not a fully trained musician: his earliest contributions to the movement were paintings, most of them dating from 1911–13. On 11 March 1913, however, he published a futurist music manifesto far more radical than the three by Pratella which had preceded it: *L'arte dei rumori* advocated a music based not on notes but on sounds relatable to, though not simply imitative of, the noises of daily experience ('we wish to "tune" these very varied sounds [of machines etc] and regulate them harmonically and rhythmically'). Later in the same year he demonstrated at Modena the first of a series of specially constructed 'intonarumori' ('noise intoners'), the 'scoppiatore' ('exploder'). The 'ronzatore', 'crepitatore' and 'stropicciatore' soon followed, and in due course also the 'ululatore', 'sibilatore' and others (the names are mostly onomatopoeic). In 1913 and 1914 groups of these instruments were demonstrated in Milan (where they caused a riot), Genoa and London (in June 1914 at the Coliseum). Most of Russolo's small handful of 'noise' compositions (all, it seems, lost) dated from these years.

After the interruption of World War I (during which Russolo's book *L'arte dei rumori* appeared, developing ideas implicit in the manifesto of the same name) further 'noise concerts' took place, notably in Paris, starting with three in June 1921. These proved fiercely controversial, but several major composers – Ravel, Milhaud, Honegger and especially Varèse – seem to have been impressed by the new possibilities opened up by the machines. Stravinsky, too, showed some interest, both before and after the war. In April 1923 and December 1925 Russolo demonstrated two versions of an 'enharmonic bow', designed to obtain unusual sonorities from ordinary string instruments; and between 1920 and 1929 he gradually developed his most elaborate invention, the 'rumorarmonio' or 'russolofono', combining the characteristics of several 'intonarumori' and controlled by means of a rudimentary keyboard. The Paris demonstration of the final form of this instrument (1929, introduced by Varèse) was the last main peak in Russolo's career as an inventor. Subsequent plans, including one to mass-produce the 'rumorarmonio', were frustrated, partly for political reasons, and he apparently lost heart. In 1932 he left Paris (where he had lived since 1927 as a refugee from fascism) and, after a few years in Spain, he eventually returned to Italy. His main interest now was the occult, and in 1941 he resumed painting. Meanwhile his machines, left in storage in Paris, were all destroyed in World War II.

Ear-witness accounts of Russolo's inventions are so contradictory that it is impossible to form a clear idea of how they sounded: the only recording (Voce del Padrone R6919: two pieces by Antonio Russolo) is too primitive in quality to provide a basis for firm judgment. Nevertheless, however much the machines may have fallen short of their aims, they constituted the first thoroughgoing attempt to achieve something whose full realization came only with the electronic music and *musique concrète* of the post-World War II period.

WORKS
(all for intonarumori and all apparently lost)
Combattimento nell'oasi, 1913; Convegno d'automobili e d'aeroplani, 1913–14; Si pranza sulla terrazza dell'Hotel (Si pranza sulla terrazza del Kursaal), 1913–14; Il risveglio di una città (Il risveglio di una grande città), 1913–14, 7 bars pubd in *Lacerba*, ii (Florence, 1914), 72, repr. in *L'arte dei rumori* (1916), 72, and many secondary sources; incidental music (Marinetti, etc)
Works by Antonio Russolo, all adaptations of pieces for conventional insts, incl: Trio, vn, pf, intonarumori, perf. 1921; Corale, Serenata, intonarumori, insts, recorded 1924

WRITINGS
L'arte dei rumori (Milan, 1913); repr. in *I manifesti del futurismo* (Florence, 1914), 123; Eng. trans. in *Music since 1900*, ed. N. Slonimsky (New York, 4/1971), 1298, and in *Futurist Manifestos*, ed. U. Apollonio (London, 1973), 74
'Conquista totale dell'enarmonismo', *Lacerba*, i (1913), 242
L'arte dei rumori (Milan, 1916); Fr. trans., 1975, ed. G. Lista [incl. full list of Russolo's writings]
'L'arco enarmonico', *Fiamma*, ii/1 (Milan, 1926), 9
'Il musicista futurista Franco Casavola', *Teatro*, v/3 (Milan, 1927), 37
'L'enarmonismo', *Fiera letteraria*, 1st ser., iii/12 (Milan, 1927), 3; repr. in *Futurismo 1932*, ed. F. Depero (Rovereto, 1932)
Al di là della materia (Milan, 1938, 2/1961)

BIBLIOGRAPHY
N. M.: 'Futurismo "in querula" ', *La nuova musica*, xix (1914), 74
A. Coeuroy: 'Les futuristes futuristes', *ReM*, ii/9–11 (1921), 165
Montboron: 'Au théâtre des Champs-Elysées: les bruiteurs futuristes', *Comoedia*, xv/3107 (1921), 2
P. Mondrian: 'De bruiteurs futuristes italiens en het nieuwe in de musik', *De Stijl*, iv/8–9 (1921); Fr. trans. as 'Les manifestations du néoplasticisme dans la musique et les bruiteurs futuristes italiens', *La vie des lettres et des arts* (1922); It. trans. in *NRMI*, iv (1970), 1114
L. Folgore: 'La musica futurista – l'arte dei rumori', *Almanacco italiano*, xxviii (Florence, 1923), 225
F. Casavola: 'Luigi Russolo', *Teatro*, v/3 (1927), 39
A. de Angelis: *L'Italia musicale d'oggi: dizionario dei musicisti* (Rome, 3/1928), pt.2, 161
F. B. Pratella: 'L'arte dei rumori and Other Relevant Essays', *Scritti vari di pensiero, di arte, di storia musicale* (Bologna, 1933)
M. Zanovello Russolo: *Russolo: l'uomo, l'artista* (Milan, 1958)
E. Falqui: *Bibliografia e iconografia del futurismo* (Florence, 1959), 81ff
M. Mila: 'Dall'intonarumori all'elettronica', *Cronache musicali 1955–9* (Turin, 1959), 153
F. K. Prieberg: *Musica ex machina* (Berlin, 1960; It. trans., 1963), 21ff
A. Gentilucci: 'Il futurismo e lo sperimentalismo musicale d'oggi', *Il convegno musicale*, i (Turin, 1964), 25
J. C. G. Waterhouse: 'A Futurist Mystery', *Music and Musicians*, xv/8 (1967), 26
Discoteca alta fedeltà, xii/107 (1971) [futurist number]
M. Kirby: 'Russolo and the Art of Noise', *Futurist Performances* (New York, 1971), 33
G. Lista: *Futurisme: manifestes, documents, proclamations* (Lausanne, 1973), 312ff, 425ff
R. J. Payton: *The Futurist Musicians: Francesco Balilla Pratella and Luigi Russolo* (diss., U. of Chicago, 1974)

F. Escal: 'Le futurisme et la musique', *Europe* (Paris, 1975), no.551, p.85
N. Fiorda: 'Musica e futurismo', *Il mondo della musica*, xiii/2 (1975), 29
G. Lista: 'Russolo, peinture et bruitisme', introduction to Fr. edn. of L. Russolo: *L'arte dei rumori* (1916) (Lausanne, 1975), 9
R. J. Payton: 'The Music of Futurism: Concerts and Polemics', *MQ*, lxii (1976), 25
G. F. Maffina: *Luigi Russolo e l'arte dei rumori* (Turin, 1978)
                                    JOHN C. G. WATERHOUSE

Rust. German family of musicians and editors.

(1) Friedrich Wilhelm Rust (*b* Wörlitz, nr. Dessau, 6 July 1739; *d* Dessau, 28 Feb 1796). Composer, violinist and pianist. As a child he showed remarkable musical gifts and was encouraged by his father. In 1758–62 he studied law at Halle, where he was also a pupil of W. F. Bach. He then entered the service of Prince Leopold III of Anhalt-Dessau, continuing his training as a violinist and keyboard player under G. F. Müller, a pupil of J. G. Goldberg, and Karl Höckh, Konzertmeister at Zerbst. In 1763–4 he lived in Potsdam, studying the violin with Franz Benda and composition with C. P. E. Bach. He travelled to Italy in the retinue of Prince Leopold in 1765, and then returned to Dessau to embark upon the task that was to occupy him for the rest of his life: attempting to establish Dessau as a vital centre of German musical life. He was successful, eventually promoting public concerts and in 1774 founding a theatre for opera and spoken drama. In recognition of his achievements, he was made court music director in 1775.

According to most lexicons Rust was a first-rate virtuoso on the violin, and his compositions for this instrument show something of his remarkable technique. Although he modestly played only a few of his own works in public, they were received with approval, and his D minor solo sonata in particular became well known. Rust's compositions received some publicity in the late 19th century: his grandson, (3) Wilhelm Rust, edited a selection of his sonatas, hailing him as a strikingly original genius who boldly anticipated certain aspects of Romanticism. This claim aroused considerable interest in the composer, particularly in France. But Neufeldt, who examined the original manuscripts of the sonatas, showed that they had been completely rewritten and updated in style by Wilhelm, and Calvocoressi called the affair 'one of the most striking hoaxes to be found in the whole history of musical erudition'.

WORKS
(all MSS in D-Bds; for works ed. W. Rust, see Prieger, 1894)
Edition: *F. W. Rust: Werke für Klavier und Streichinstrumente*, ed. R. Czach, EDM, 2nd ser., *Mitteldeutschland*, i (1939) [C]

INSTRUMENTAL
(numbers in parentheses refer to thematic index in Czach, 1927)
Chamber: Serenade, str qt (108); 2 sonatas, pf, 2 vn, vc, 1775 (109–10); Qt, nail vn, 2 vn, b, 1787 (111), ed. in C; 2 sonatas, va, 2 hn, vc (84, 94); Trio, 2 fl, va d'amore, c1785 (105), ed. in C; Trio, 2 vn, bc (106); Sonata, vn, va, vc (107); 25 sonatas, pf, vn obbl (26–50), 1 ed. in C; 24 vn sonatas, pf acc. (51–71, 73–5); Air varié, vn, pf (72); 3 sonatas, vn solo (80–81, 83), 1 with vn acc. (Leipzig, ?1818), 1 ed. in C as Partite; 2 vn solos (79, 82); 7 vn duets (76–8), 2 ed. in C; 2 va sonatas (89, 91); 6 va d'amore sonatas (85–8, 92–3); Air with variations, va d'amore (90); Sonata, vc, bc (95); 5 lute sonatas (96–100), 3 with vn, 1 with va; 4 harp sonatas (101–4), 1 with vn, 1 with vn, vc
Solo kbd: 6 sonatas (7), pubd in Leipzig according to *GerberL*; 18 sonatas (8–25), 1 for 4 hands, 1 pubd (Leipzig, ?1770), 2 ed. in C; Suite (6); 24 variations on 'Blühe liebes Veilchen' (Dessau, 1782) (3); Allegretto con variazioni, hpd (Berlin, c1791) (1); Andantino with 12

variations, 1791 (5); 12 variations on 'Blühe liebes Veilchen', 1794 (4), ed. in C; variations on 'Ich schlief, da träumte mir' (2); fugue, org (112)

VOCAL

Dramatic: Inkle und Yariko (duodrama, 2, Schink), Dessau, 28 July 1777; Der blaue Montag (operetta, T. Berger), Dessau, 1777; Colma (monodrama, after Ossian), c1780; Korylas und Lalage (pastoral), ?1786; incidental music: Fingal, Inamorulla, Dessau, 1782

Other vocal: Herr Gott dich loben wir; Allgnädiger in allen Höhen, 1784; Gross ist der Herr, 1791; Gott ist die Liebe, 1792; Gott unser Vater, 1794: all sacred cantatas, solo vv, chorus, orch; Ich will den Herrn loben (Ps xxxiv), solo vv, chorus, orch; 2 occasional secular cantatas, 1769, 1773; settings of lieder by Goethe in Die Muse (Leipzig, 1776–7); Oden und Lieder, i (Dessau and Leipzig, 1784), ii (Leipzig, 1796); further choral works, lieder, arias and works pubd in anthologies and periodicals (1779–99)

(2) Wilhelm Karl Rust (*b* Dessau, 29 April 1787; *d* Dessau, 18 April 1855). Pianist, organist and teacher, son of (1) Friedrich Wilhelm Rust. He became well known as a child prodigy, studying with his father until 1805, when he went to Halle to study philosophy. There he was a pupil of Türk. After two years he moved to Vienna, where Beethoven praised his playing, particularly of Bach, and recommended him as a piano teacher. In 1819–27 he was organist of the Protestant church in Vienna, after which he returned to Dessau.

(3) Wilhelm Rust (*b* Dessau, 15 Aug 1822; *d* Leipzig, 2 May 1892). Editor, composer, organist and pianist, grandson of (1) Friedrich Wilhelm Rust. He studied the piano and organ with his uncle, (2) Wilhelm Karl Rust, and in 1840–43 studied composition under Friedrich Schneider. In 1849 he settled in Berlin as a teacher of the piano, singing and composition, and joined the Singakademie and the Bach Society, which he directed from 1862 to 1875. In 1861 he became organist of the church of St Luke, and in 1870 composition teacher at the Stern Conservatory. Meanwhile he was active as a composer and editor. In 1853 he was appointed Berlin representative of the Leipzig Bach-Gesellschaft and in 1858 chief editor of *Johann Sebastian Bachs Werke*. In 1878 he moved to Leipzig as organist of the Thomaskirche and teacher at the conservatory and in 1880 succeeded E. F. Richter as Kantor of the Thomasschule.

Rust's compositions, totalling about 50, are largely forgotten. They consist mostly of sacred songs with piano or organ accompaniment, choral or solo songs, and organ or piano works. He is chiefly remembered as a Bach editor, and the 26 volumes he edited for the Bach-Gesellschaft (1855–81; Jg.v, vii, ix–xiii, xv–xxiii, xxv, xxviii, suppl. Jg.iii, additions to Jg.iv, viii) were long regarded as models of their kind. His numerous prefaces to volumes in the edition contain useful discussions of performing practice and editorial technique.

BIBLIOGRAPHY

EitnerQ; *GerberL*; *GerberNL*

H. Mendel and A. Reissmann: *Musikalisches Conversations-Lexikon*, viii (Berlin, 1877) [incl. list of works for (3) Wilhelm Rust]

F. W. Hosaeus: *Friedrich Wilhelm Rust und das Dessauer Musikleben 1766–1796* (Dessau, 1882)

E. Prieger: *Friedrich Wilhelm Rust: ein Vorgänger Beethovens* (Cologne, 1894)

H. Kretzschmar: 'Bericht über die Bach-Gesellschaft', *Johann Sebastian Bachs Werke*, Jg.xlvi (Leipzig, 1899), p.xlv

E. Prieger: 'Rustiana', *Die Musik*, xii (1912–13), 269 [see also E. Neufeldt, ibid, 339]

V. d'Indy: 'Le cas Rust', *BSIM*, ix/4 (1913), 47 [see also E. Neufeldt, ibid, ix/12 (1913), 14, and d'Indy, ibid, ix/12 (1913), 21]

M. D. Calvocoressi: 'Friedrich Rust, his Editors and his Critics', *MT*, lv (1914), 14

——: 'The Rust Case: its Ending and its Moral', *MT*, lv (1914), 89

R. Czach: *Friedrich Wilhelm Rust* (Essen, 1927)

G. Folker and G. von Dadelsen: 'Rust', *MGG*

E. Forbes, ed.: *Thayer's Life of Beethoven* (Princeton, 1964, 2/1967), 439f, 466

RICHARD JONES

Rust [Rusti], Giacomo (*b* Rome, 1741; *d* Barcelona, 1786). Italian composer. He was perhaps of German descent, but was not related to F. W. Rust. He studied in Naples at the Turchini Conservatory and later in Rome under Rinaldo di Capua. From 1763 to 1777 he worked in Venice, where he brought out his first opera, *La contadina in corte* (1763). Between 1772 and 1776 he produced 14 more (two in collaboration). It was probably the popularity of these works in Italy that led the Archbishop of Salzburg to engage him for his court *cappella*, offering him 1000 gulden, an unusually high salary for Salzburg. Rust was appointed court Kapellmeister on 12 June 1777, but at the end of the year he asked to be relieved of his post, because the bad weather had affected his health. His plea was granted, but his ill-health allowed him to leave only in February 1778. Just before his departure he set Metastasio's *Il Parnaso confuso* for the consecration of the Archbishop of Olmütz. In Rust's absence the performance was conducted by Michael Haydn. Although Rust had been offered the post of *maestro di cappella* at Orvieto Cathedral, he returned to Venice and resumed his operatic career. In 1783 he became *maestro di cappella* at Barcelona Cathedral, where he remained until his death.

WORKS

OPERAS

VM – *Venice, Teatro S Moisè* VS – *Venice, Teatro S Samuele*

La contadina in corte (? G. Gozzi), VM, carn. 1763–4, *P-La*; La finta semplice (P. Mililotti), Bologna, Formagliari, spr. 1772, collab. G. Insanguine; L'isola d'Alcina (G. Bertati), Bologna, Formagliari, spr. 1772; L'avaro deluso (Bertati), Bologna, Formagliari, 1773, collab. G. Gazzaniga; L'idolo cinese (G. B. Lorenzi), VS, 28 Dec 1773, *I-MOe*, *P-La*; Il conte Baccellone (M. Coltellini, after Goldoni: La contessina), VM, aut. 1774; Li cavalieri lunatici, Venice, S Cassiano, aut. 1774

L'amor bizzaro (Bertati), VM, carn. 1775; Li due amanti in inganno, Venice, S Cassiano, carn. 1775, Act 2 by M. Rauzzini; Alessandro nelle Indie (Metastasio), VS, Ascension 1775; Il Baron di Terra Asciuta, VS, 26 Dec 1775; Il Socrate immaginario (Lorenzi), VS, carn. 1776; Calliroe (M. Verazi), Padua, Nuovo, June 1776, 1 aria *I-Pca*; Il Giove di Creta, Venice, S Cassiano, aut. 1776, Gi(l); Li due protetti (P, A. Bagliacca), VM, 26 Dec 1776

Il Parnaso confuso (serenata, Metastasio), Salzburg, Court, 17 May 1778; Vologeso re de' Parti (Zeno), Venice, S Benedetto, 28 Dec 1778, *P-La*; Il talismano (Goldoni), Milan, Canobbiana, Sept 1779, Act 1 by Salieri, *I-Fc*; L'isola capricciosa (C. Mazzolà), VS, carn. 1780, *F-Pc*; Gli antiquari in Palmira (G. Carpani), Milan, La Scala, aut. 1780, *F-Pc*; Demofoonte (Metastasio), Florence, Pergola, aut. 1780, 1 aria *I-Gi(l)*; Il castello deluso, Parma, Ducale, carn. 1781

Artaserse (Metastasio), Perugia, Civico, aut. 1781; Adriano in Siria (Metastasio), Turin, Regio, 26 Dec 1781, *P-La*; L'incognita fortunata (G. Ciliberti), Naples, Fondo, sum. 1782; La caccia di Enrico IV (A. Dian), VM, aut. 1783; L'incontri inaspettati, Rome, Capranica, Feb 1783; Il marito indolente (Mazzolà), Vienna, Court, 1784; Berenice (J. Durandi), Parma, carn. 1785–6, scena and aria pubd

Miscellaneous arias and ovs.: *A-Wgm*, *B-Br*, *D-Bds*, Dlb, Mbs, *E-Mn*, *I-Bc*, Mc, MOe

BIBLIOGRAPHY

EitnerQ; *FétisB*; *LaMusicaD*

E. Anderson, ed.: *The Letters of Mozart and his Family* (London, 1938, 2/1966)

E. Hintermaier: *Die Salzburger Hofkapelle von 1700 bis 1806: Organisation und Personal* (diss., U. of Salzburg, 1972), 343ff

ERNST HINTERMAIER

Rutge, Daniel. German musician, possibly identifiable with DANIEL SPEER.

Ruthenfranz, Robert (*b* Witten, 3 Sept 1905; *d* Witten, 29 Nov 1970). German composer, conductor and administrator. He studied at the Dortmund

Conservatory (1925–8) and also had instruction from Hindemith and Max Trapp. Although he travelled all over Europe on concert tours, he gave much of his energy to developing musical life in his home town, where he established the Musikverein, a chamber choir, the Ruhr Chamber Orchestra, the conservatory and, in 1936, the Wittener Tage für Neue Kammermusik (*see* WITTEN). Deeply attached to the theatre, he founded a Kammerstudio for performing new stage works, and he considered his principal work to have been the ballet *Die olympische Hochzeit*. Among his other compositions are the opera *Die Fischerin* after Goethe, *Evokationen auf Beckett* for cello (intended for performance as a prelude to *Krapp's Last Tape*), other stage music, orchestral pieces, chamber music and vocal works.   HERTA RUTHENFRANZ

Ruthström, (Bror Olof) Julius (*b* Stugun, Jämtland, 30 Dec 1877; *d* Stockholm, 2 April 1944). Swedish violinist. His father, Gustaf Adolf Ruthström (*b* Strömstad, 8 Feb 1860; *d* *c*1903), was a military musician and for some time a member of the Hovkapellet in Stockholm. With the aid of a scholarship from King Oskar II, Julius studied at the Musikhochschule in Berlin under Burmester, Moser and Joachim (1901–3), where he was awarded the Joachim Prize. He gave Reger's solo violin sonata op.42 no.1 its first performance in 1904, and was thereafter frequently engaged as a soloist throughout Germany. He also appeared as a soloist in Göteborg with W. Stenhammar, and made frequent tours of Sweden and other Scandinavian and European countries. He was an active chamber musician and had his own string quartet for about 20 years. As director of the Mellersta Sveriges Kammarmusik-Förening (1928–35), he did much to further the performance of chamber music in Sweden.

Ruthström was a persuasive advocate of Swedish music and an influential teacher. His repertory was unusually large, and he was famed for his performances of Reger, Sibelius's concerto and a variety of contemporary music. He wrote a number of technical studies for the violin.

PEDAGOGICAL WORKS

Technische Studien für die Violine (Stockholm, 1914)
Stråkföringens konst [The art of bowing] (Stockholm, 1922)
Doppeltonstudien für Violine (Stockholm, 1923)
Violonskola för nybörjare [Beginners' school of violin playing] (Stockholm, 1929)

BIBLIOGRAPHY

A. Moser: *Geschichte des Violinspiels* (Berlin, 1923, rev., enlarged 2/1966–7)
E. van der Straeten: *The History of the Violin* (London, 1933)
                    ROBERT LAYTON

Rutini, Ferdinando (*b* *c*1764; *d* Terracina, 13 Nov 1827). Italian composer. A son of Giovanni Marco Rutini, he was born probably in a city where his father had a temporary professional engagement. He was raised and educated in the family home at Florence, where he mainly spent the first part of his career. The *Gazzetta toscana* announced the publication of his *Tre sonate per cembalo-pianoforte*, called his 'first youthful work', in Florence in 1785. Three more sonatas, op.2, were published in 1785. The Florence Conservatory has the manuscript of a harpsichord capriccio, dated June 1788, and a trio for harpsichord, violin and cello, dated August 1788. According to Gervasoni, he composed a cantata for a wedding in Florence in 1789 and also sang

the principal solo part. His first opera, *I vendemmiatori*, was also performed there that year; by 1803 he had written 32, all of them comic and all but five first performed in Florence. In 1804 he became *maestro di cappella* in Ancona and from 1812 to 1816 held that post in Macerata. In 1817 he again attempted to write opera, producing three works in Rome, but without success. According to Cametti, he was *maestro di cappella* in Aquapendente from 1820 to 1825 and then, until his death, in Terracina.

BIBLIOGRAPHY

C. Gervasoni: *Nuova teoria di musica* (Parma, 1812)
A. Cametti: 'Un poeta melodrammatico romano: appunti e notizie in gran parte inedite sopra Jacopo Ferretti', *Gazzetta musicale di Milano*, lii (1897), esp. 341f; also pubd separately
M. Fabbri: 'Incontro con Ferdinando Rutini, il dimenticato figlio musicista del "primo maestro di Mozart"', *Le celebrazioni del 1963 e alcune nuove indagini sulla musica italiana del XVIII e XIX secolo*, Chigiana, xx (1963), 195

                    GIORGIO PESTELLI

Rutini, Giovanni Marco [Giovanni Maria, Giovanni Placido] (*b* Florence, 25 April 1723; *d* Florence, 22 Dec 1797). Italian composer. In April 1739 he was admitted to the Conservatorio della Pietà dei Turchini in Naples, where he studied composition with Leo, the harpsichord with F. N. Fago and the violin with V. A. Pagliarulo. He probably finished his studies in 1744, but remained for a few years as *maestrino* before returning to Florence. In 1748 he was at Prague, where he signed the dedication of the *Sonate per cembalo* op.1 on 15 July, and again in 1753, when his first opera *Semiramide* was performed there. A letter to Padre Martini reveals that during his time in Prague he was under the protection of the Electress of Saxony, Maria Antonia, who wrote the text of his cantata *Lavinia e Turno* (Leipzig, 1756). In Prague he also composed the sets of sonatas opp.2 and 3, the latter dedicated to his pupil the Countess of Nostitz and Rhyeneck.

Between 1754 and 1756 Rutini seems to have visited Dresden and Berlin, but at the beginning of 1758 he was in St Petersburg. According to Mooser he was related to the transfer from Prague to St Petersburg of the impresario G. B. Locatelli's company, which performed Rutini's *Il negligente* in the summer of 1758. The sonatas opp.5 and 6 were produced in St Petersburg (but published by Haffner in Nuremberg), as was his setting of Metastasio's *Grazie a gl'inganni tuoi* (Leipzig, 1758). Rutini won appreciation in St Petersburg high society, becoming harpsichord teacher to the Grand Duchess Fyodorovich (later Catherine II) and living with Count Sheremetev, whose private orchestra he conducted.

From 1761 Rutini was in Florence, where he married on 2 April. In 1762 he began a correspondence with Martini, which lasted until 1780 through more than 40 letters (in *I-Bc*), useful for biographical information and documenting Rutini's desire to train himself in counterpoint. (He also began a translation from the French of Marpurg's *Traité de la fugue*, MS in *I-Bc*.) From 1762 to 1777 Rutini composed at least 14 operas. In January 1762 his *Il caffè de campagna* was performed in Bologna and in March he was received into the Accademia Filarmonica there. Especially successful were *I matrimoni in maschera*, which in 1763 alone was performed in Cremona, Bologna and Florence and then in Madrid, Dresden and Copenhagen, and *L'olandese in Italia*, given between 1765 and 1770 in the principal theatres of central north Italy. In 1769 the favourable reception accorded to his *Nitteti* brought him the appointment of *maestro di cappella* to the Duke of Modena, but Rutini did not give up residence in Florence, perhaps hoping to become *maestro di cappella* to the Grand Duke Leopold (to whom he dedicated the Sonatas op.8 in 1774). Rutini continued to publish harpsichord music in Florence and Bologna until the closing years of his life. From 1780 he also devoted himself to sacred music (a Kyrie and a Gloria for four voices are in manuscript in Berlin), and the *Gazzetta toscana* also gives the titles of some oratorios not mentioned elsewhere.

The historical importance of Rutini's production for harpsichord is remarkable. The Rutini sonata, typical of the age of the transition from the harpsichord to the piano, has a variable number of movements, sometimes having two quick ones together and often ending with a minuet. Its thematic incisiveness and expressive *chiaroscuro* give it an important place in the development of the Classical style. The interest that Mozart took in Rutini is demonstrated by a letter from Leopold, who on 18 August 1771 asked his son to send him some 'good sonatas by Rutini' (Torrefranca thought they could be identified as nos.2 and 6 of op.6), but even more obvious is the stylistic inheritance that Rutini left in the first of Haydn's piano compositions. His sonatas can be divided into two groups: the first, comprising opp.1–6, attracted the attention of Torrefranca, who emphasized Rutini's position as a forerunner of Mozart and even of Beethoven. It is true that many of these sonatas are permeated by a pre-Romantic vein that surfaces in improvisatory passages in the minor mode and in delicate and tender chromaticisms (the fifth sonata of op.5, in F minor, almost a harbinger of 'Sturm und Drang', is the culminating point of this tendency). Many of the dramatic contrasts that Torrefranca related to Beethoven's style (for example, in considering the first sonata of op.1) seem to be derived from theatrical gestures; these may be serious in character, as in the pathetic interruptions on arpeggios of the diminished 7th, or 'recitatives', in the second sonata of op.1, or they may be comic or *affettuoso*, as in the broken phrasing that recalls the languors and caprices of Pergolesi's *La serva padrona* and thus looks back to Rutini's Neapolitan training. Archaisms are not entirely lacking, such as the toccata that opens the first sonata of op.3, but pages given over entirely to insipid Alberti basses (as in op.3 no.2 and op.5 no.3) are rare.

Expressive tension is less frequent beginning with op.7, which inaugurated a simple, linear style of writing ('I have attempted to avoid all complexity', wrote the author in the preface, with satisfaction that 'a young lady of ten' could play all the sonatas without difficulty). These new sonatas are introduced by a brief 'tuning-up' prelude and often end with a simple *balletto*, thus taking on the outward appearance of sonatinas, forerunners of Clementi's. The last sonata of op.8 ends with an arietta 'Clori amabile', to be sung by the player. All these late works have been regarded as the worn-out product of concessions to the hedonistic taste of the period, in spite of the fact that it is in these sonatas (particularly in opp.7–9) that, by renouncing abundant Rococo ornamentation, progress was made towards a style better suited to the piano, and sometimes towards a supple effectiveness that was more mature than the expressiveness of many earlier works.

Rutini's operas still await detailed study. In connec-

tion with *I matrimoni in maschera* Della Corte drew attention not only to the grace of the arias but also to the variety of moods, from the comic to the tender. In general Rutini's comic style was always favourably received by his contemporaries.

WORKS

VOCAL

Operas: Semiramide, Prague, 1753, *D-Dlb*; Il negligente, St Petersburg, 1758; Il caffè di campagna, Bologna, 1762; Ezio, Florence, 1763; I matrimoni in maschera, Cremona, 1763, *P-La* (Acts 1, 3), also perf. as Gli sposi in maschera, *D-Dlb*, *F-Pc*, *I-Fc*; L'olandese in Italia, Florence, 1765, *Bc*, *Fc*; L'amore industrioso, Venice, 1765, *P-La*; Il contadino incivilito, Florence, 1766; Le contese domestiche, Florence, 1767, *I-Fc*; L'amor tra l'armi, Siena, 1768; La Nitteti, Modena, 1769; L'amor per rigiro, Cajano, 1773, *Fc*; Vologeso, Florence, 1775, *Nc*, *P-La*; Il finto amante, Pistoia, 1776; Sicotencal, Turin, 1776; Zulima, Florence, Pergola, 1777; Gli sponsali di Faloppa, *I-Fc*

Oratorios: Giobbe, 1780; Giuseppe venduto, 1783; La liberazione d'Israele, 1793: lost, mentioned in *Gazzetta toscana*

Cantatas: No, non turbati o Nice, 1v, str, 1754 (Nuremberg, n.d.); Lavinia e Turno (Maria Antonia, Electress of Saxony), 1v, str (Leipzig, 1756); Grazie a gl'inganni tuoi (Metastasio), 1v, str (Leipzig, 1758); Genii gloria virtù, 1764, Genoa, private collection

Others: Kyrie–Gloria, 4vv, insts, *D-B*; antiphon, 4vv, 1762, *I-Baf*

KEYBOARD

Hpd sonatas: 6, op.1 (n.p., 1748), 6, op.2 (Nuremberg, *c*1754–7), 6, op.3 (Nuremberg, *c*1756–8), 6, op.5 (Nuremberg, *c*1758–9), 6, op.6 (Nuremberg, *c*1759–60, rev. 2/1765), 6, op.6bis (Florence, ?1762), 6, op.7 (Nuremberg, 1770), 6, op.8 (Florence, 1774), 6, op.9 (Florence, 1774), 6, with vn ad lib, op.10 (Florence, 1776), 6, with vn, op.11 (Florence, 1778), 6, op.12 (Florence, 1780), 6, op.13 (Florence, 1782), 3, with vn, op.14 (Florence, 1786), 5 in Raccolta musicale ... d'altretanti celebri compositori italiani, i–v (Nuremberg, 1756–65)

12 divertimenti facili e brevi, (hpd 4 hands)/(harp, hpd), op.18 (n.p., 1793); Rondò, pf solo/orch acc., op.19 (n.p., 1797)

BIBLIOGRAPHY

A. Della Corte: *L'opera comica italiana del '700* (Bari, 1923)
F. Torrefranca: *Le origini italiane del romanticismo musicale* (Turin, 1930)
——: 'Il primo maestro di W. A. Mozart', *RMI*, xl (1936), 239
R. A. Mooser: *Annales de la musique et des musiciens en Russie au XVIIIe siècle* (Geneva, 1948–51)
L. F. Tagliavini: 'Rutini, Giovanni Marco', *ES*
—— : 'Rutini, Giovanni Marco', *MGG*
W. S. Newman: *The Sonata in the Classic Era* (Chapel Hill, 1963, rev. 2/1972)
G. Balducci: *La figura e l'opera di G. M. Rutini* (diss., U. of Florence, 1964)
G. Meinero: *Le sonate di G. M. Rutini* (diss., U. of Turin, 1975)
G. Pestelli: 'Mozart e Rutini', *AnMc*, no.18 (1978), 290

GIORGIO PESTELLI

Rutkowski, Antoni Wincenty (*b* Warsaw, 21 Jan 1859; *d* Warsaw, 14 Dec 1886). Polish composer, pianist and teacher. He began studying music in 1869 at the Warsaw Institute of Music, where he was a pupil of Moniuszko (harmony), Żeleński (counterpoint), Janothy (piano) and Wecke (horn). After graduating in 1876 he became a piano teacher at the institute, also working as a pianist and composer. From 1881 to 1883 he studied with Noskowski. In ten years of intensive work as a composer, he concentrated on instrumental music; his compositions include sets of piano variations, a Violin Sonata op.5, a Piano Trio op.13 and a set of variations for string quartet. He also composed five solo songs and three choral pieces.

TADEUSZ PRZYBYLSKI

Rutkowski, Bronisław (*b* Komaje, nr. Vilnius, 27 Feb 1898; *d* Leipzig, 1 June 1964). Polish organist, teacher, conductor, composer, and writer on music. He studied music at the St Petersburg Conservatory with Handschin (organ), Kalafati and Vītols (theory). From 1921 he studied at the Warsaw Conservatory with

Surzyński (organ), Rytel and Statkowski (theory) and Melcer (conducting), graduating in 1924 with distinction. From 1924 to 1926 he continued his studies in Paris with Vierne (organ) and Pirro (aesthetics), and from 1926 to 1939 he taught the organ at the Warsaw Conservatory. He also directed music theatre, edited *Muzyka polska*, broadcast on Polish radio, and was organist at Warsaw Cathedral. From 1946 he lived in Kraków, where he taught the organ and from 1955 to 1964 was rector of the State Music High School. As an organist he gave concerts in many countries in Europe. He wrote many organ and choral works.

BIBLIOGRAPHY

S. Kisielewski: 'O Bronisławie Rutkowskim', *Ruch muzyczny* (1964), no.14

BOGUSŁAW SCHÄFFER

Ruttis [Ructis], **Ar. de** (*fl* 1420). Composer. *Prevalet simplicitas*, a three-voice setting of a moralizing text over a much slower textless tenor, is ascribed to him in *GB-Ob* 213 and (lacking the tenor) in *I-Bc* Q15.

BIBLIOGRAPHY

C. van den Borren, ed.: *Polyphonia sacra: a Continental Miscellany of the Fifteenth Century* (London, 1932), 278

TOM R. WARD

Ruuli, Rinaldo. Italian music printer, in partnership with Michel'angelo FEI.

Ruutha, Didrik Persson. See THEODORICUS PETRI NYLANDENSIS.

Ruvo, Giulio (*fl* 1703–7). Italian composer. His extant works, in MS in Milan Conservatory Library, consist of five sonatas for cello and continuo, nine cantatas for solo voice and continuo and two serenatas for three voices and instruments. All were written between 1703 and 1707. Ruvo's obvious familiarity with the style and technique of the cello suggests that he was himself a cellist. The sonatas are stylistically close to those of Vivaldi; they are harmonically quite adventurous and more brilliant in their use of the solo cello.

NONA PYRON

Ruwet, Nicolas (*b* Saive, 31 Dec 1932). French linguist, literary critic and musical analyst, of Belgian birth. He studied Romance philology at the University of Liège; he was a pupil of Lévi-Strauss and Benveniste at the Ecole Pratique de Hautes Etudes, Paris, and of Jakobson and Chomsky at the department of linguistics at the Massachusetts Institute of Technology. In addition, he studied music privately. In 1968 he was appointed professor of linguistics at the University of Paris at Vincennes. Though not primarily a musicologist, he has been the most fundamental thinker in the field of the SEMIOLOGY of music, contributing a series of formative articles (notably 'Méthodes d'analyse en musicologie'), five of which have since been published collectively in *Langage, musique, poésie* (Paris, 1972).

For discussion of his research and publications, see ANALYSIS, §§II, 8; III, 7 and bibliography.

Ruymonte, Pedro. See RIMONTE, PEDRO.

Ruyneman, Daniel (*b* Amsterdam, 8 Aug 1886; *d* Amsterdam, 25 July 1963). Dutch composer and administrator. While still a student at the Amsterdam Conservatory, where his teachers included De Jong (piano) and Zweers (composition), he enjoyed an inter-

national reputation as one of the most adventurous Dutch composers. With Dresden, Vermeulen and Zagwijn he founded in 1918 the Nederlandsche Vereeniging voor Moderne Scheppende Toonkunst, which in 1922 became the Dutch section of the ISCM. In Vienna he founded with Hans Pless the Foundation for International Exchange Concerts, an organization to promote performances of new music in many European capitals and in the USA. He was also co-founder of the Dutch Society for Contemporary Music (1930), of which he remained musical director until 1962, and founder (1931) and editor-in-chief of the society's organ *Maandblad voor hedendaagsche muziek*. From 1947 to 1951 he was general secretary of the ISCM. In 1950 he initiated a series of highly original concerts at the Amsterdam Stedelijk Museum, where works by Schoenberg, Berg, Webern, Stravinsky, Stockhausen, Boulez, Nono and Berio were heard in the Netherlands for the first time.

Ruyneman's compositions reflected contemporary trends. His exploring attitude is evident in two works of 1918: the *Hiëroglyphen* and *De roep*, a choral piece in which the voices are treated instrumentally (Ruyneman returned to this technique for the Sonata of 1931). In about 1925 he began to temper this imaginativeness with a neo-classical emphasis on line, the wind quintet *Nightingales* being the best example. Then from 1950 the influences of newer methods became increasingly great.

WORKS
(selective list)

Operas: De gebroeders Karamasoff, 1928; Le mariage (after Gogol), 1930

Orch: Pf Conc., 1939; Vn Conc., 1940; Amphitryon, ov., 1943; Partita, str, 1943; Sym., 1953; Amatarasu, 1956; Gilgamesj, 1963

Choral: De roep, 1918; Sonata, 1931

Solo vocal: Tagore songs, 1917; Die Weise von Liebe und Tod (Rilke), speaker, orch, 1951; 3 chansons des maquisards condamnés, 1951–7; many other songs

Chamber: Hiëroglyphen, 3 fl, cel, harp, pf, 2 mand, 2 gui, bells, 1918; Sonata, vn, 1925; Divertimento, wind, va, pf, 1927; 4 tempi, 4 vc, 1937; Sonata, fl, pf, 1942; 5 Nocturnes, pf, 1949; Nightingales, wind qnt, 1949; Sonata, vn, pf, 1956; Réflexions I–IV, various insts, 1958–61

Principal publisher: Donemus

BIBLIOGRAPHY

A. Petronio: *Daniel Ruyneman et son oeuvre* (Liège, 1922)

W. Paap: 'Nederlandse componisten van deze tijd: XIII Daniel Ruyneman', *Mens en melodie*, v (1950), 75

J. Wouters: 'Daniel Ruyneman', *Sonorum speculum* (1962), no.11, p.1

E. A. G. Brautigam: 'In memoriam Daniel Ruyneman', *Sonorum speculum* (1963), no.16, p.24

ROGIER STARREVELD

Ruzante. Stage name of ANGELO BEOLCO.

Ruzicka, Peter (*b* Düsseldorf, 3 July 1948). German composer. He attended the Hamburg Conservatory (1963–8), studied jurisprudence and musicology at the universities of Munich and Hamburg, and concerned himself with questions of authors' rights. Among the awards he has received have been a Förderpreis from the City of Stuttgart (1969), a prize in the Bartók Composition Competition (Budapest, 1970), a UNESCO prize (Paris, 1971) and a stipend from the Hamburg Bach Prize Foundation (1972).

Ruzicka belongs with those German composers of the postwar generation who came to attention in the early 1970s for their non-speculative works, often for large orchestra, combining free with strict procedures. He feels himself allied with Henze and Hans Otte, though without any obvious influence or dependence. Apart from composing he is active as a conductor and performer of his own music and that of colleagues.

WORKS
(*selective list*)

Orch: Antifone – Strofe, 25 str, perc, 1970; Metastrofe, 1971; In processo di tempo, 26 insts, vc, 1971; Outside – Inside, 1972; Feedback, 1972; Torso, 1973; Etym, 1974; Befragung, 1975

Vocal: Esta noche, A/T, 2 wind, 2 str, 1967; Todesfuge (Celan), A, ens, 1968; Elis, ob, Mez, orch, 1969; Sinfonia, 25 str, 16 solo vv, perc, 1970–71

Ens and inst: 3 Szenen, cl, 1967; Ausgeweidet die Zeit, pf, 1969; Sonata, vc, 1969; Introspezione, str qt, 1969–70; Movimenti, hpd, 1969–70; . . . fragment . . ., str qt, 1970; DE . . ./Musac, text composition, 1971; Stress, 8 perc groups, 1972

Tape: Bewegung, 1972

Principal publisher: Sikorski

HANSPETER KRELLMANN

Růžičková, Zuzana (*b* Plzeň, 14 Jan 1928). Czech harpsichordist. She was trained at the Prague Academy (where she joined the teaching staff in 1962), and first attracted attention by winning the Munich international competition in 1956. She has performed in several European countries, made a number of gramophone records (including the complete keyboard works of J. S. Bach, characterized by musicality but rather free registration and heavy pointing of structure), and won a Grand Prix du Disque in 1961 (for Benda's G minor Concerto) and the Supraphon Grand Prix in 1968 and 1972. She was made Artist of Merit in 1969. A cofounder with Václav Neumann of the Prague Chamber Soloists, she played in it from 1962 to 1967, and in 1963 she formed a duo with the violinist Josef Suk. She is married to the composer Viktor Kalabis.

BIBLIOGRAPHY

J. Berkovec: *Zuzana Růžičková* (Prague, 1972) [includes discography and list of repertory]

J. Loudová: 'Se Zuzanou Růžičkovou o barokní hudbě' [Růžičková on Baroque music], *HRo*, xxv (1972), 282

LIONEL SALTER

Ruziski, Jacek. *See* RÓŻYCKI, JACEK.

Ruzitska, György (*b* Vienna, 1789; *d* Kolozsvár [now Cluj-Napoca, Romania], 2 Dec 1869). Hungarian composer and teacher, of Austrian birth. The son of Wenzel Ruzitska, an english horn player at the Burgtheater in Vienna, he began studying music at the age of ten, taking piano lessons with Wenzel Müller, the organ with Pater Placidus, and composition with Josef Gelinek in Vienna. In 1810 he travelled to Transylvania as a music teacher to the family of Baron János Bánffy, but in 1819 he moved to Kolozsvár, where he remained until his death. He soon became a prominent personality in the town's musical life (in 1832, for instance, the young people of Kolozsvár organized a public demonstration against 'the piano teacher Ruzitska'). In the 1830s he became friendly with Ferenc Erkel. Ruzitska conducted the New Society of Music in Kolozsvár until 1835 and again from 1837. His name is also associated with the reorganization of the conservatory; he was its director from 1835 until his death, and in 1838 he published a singing manual for the students of the conservatory.

Among Ruzitska's more notable works are his three-act opera *Alonso*, performed in Pest in 1829, and the overture *Zrinyi* (*c*1830). In addition he wrote five masses, a requiem (1829, performed 1835), a *Te Deum* (1850), a symphony (1833), four string quartets and three string quintets. His Violin Sonata op.3 was published in Vienna in 1814, while the two Piano Trios op.4 and a Fantasy-sonata for piano op.6 appeared in Pest. In 1848, the year of the Hungarian Revolution, Ruzitska composed a setting of Petőfi's poem *Nemzeti dal* ('National song'). Other works in the Hungarian style are *Introduction et variations brillantes sur un thème hongrois* for cello and piano, and *Phantasie und Variationen über ein ungarisches Thema* for piano trio (1837).

BIBLIOGRAPHY

ZL

K. Isoz: 'Ruzitska György', *Jelentés a Magyar nemzeti múzeum 1912. évi állapotáról* (Budapest, 1913), 392

I. Lakatos: *A muzsikus Ruzitskák Erdélyben* [The Ruzitskas as musicians in Transylvania] (Cluj, 1939)

L. Ruzitska: 'A kolozsvári zeneckonzervatórium és Ruzitska György: képek Kolozsvár zenei életéből a XIX. században' [The Kolozsvár Conservatory and Ruzitska: sketches from the musical life of Kolozsvár in the 19th century], *Zenetudományi tanulmányok*, i (1953), 601

I. Lakatos: 'A Kolozsvári Dalkör tiszteletbeli tagjai: Mosonyi, Erkel, Ábrányi, Ruzitska és Liszt' [The Kolozsvár Singing Circle's Honorary Members: Mosonyi, Erkel, Ábrányi, Ruzitska and Liszt], *Magyar zenetörténeti tanulmányok*, iii (1973), 79

I. Lakatos, ed.: 'G. Ruzitska: Vázlatok életemből' [Sketches from my life], *Kolozsvári magyar muzsikusok eszmevilága* (Bucharest, 1973)

FERENC BÓNIS

Ruzitska, Ignác (*b* Bazin, 18 April 1777; *d* Veszprém, buried 18 Feb 1833). Hungarian music editor and composer. The son of the *regens chori* in Bazin, József Ruzitska, he began his musical career in the 1780s, first as choirboy in Pressburg Cathedral and later as *musicus dominalis* to Count Mihály Viczay in Hédervár. About 1800 he was engaged as an orchestral player in the cathedral chapter orchestra in Veszprém; he was appointed Kapellmeister there in 1827. He also took part in the secular musical activities of Veszprém. A friend of the *verbunkos* composers Bihari and Csermák, he wrote down the Rákóczy March from Bihari's playing of it on the violin, and he was entrusted with Csermák's unpublished compositions shortly before the latter's death. His most significant achievement was the compilation of the *Magyar nóták Veszprém vármegyéből* ('Hungarian tunes from County Veszprém'), a 15-volume collection comprising 135 Hungarian dances for piano by contemporary composers (including Ruzitska himself), which was the most important contemporary collection of *verbunkos* music in the first third of the 19th century and still serves as one of its most important sources.

BIBLIOGRAPHY

F. Brodszky: *A Veszprémmegyei Zenetársaság 1823–1832* [The music society of County Veszprém 1823–32] (Veszprém, 1941)

B. Szabolcsi: *A magyar zenetörténet kézikönyve* (Budapest, 1947, 3/1978; Eng. trans., 1964, as *A Concise History of Hungarian Music*)

——: *A XIX. század magyar romantikus zenéje* [Hungarian Romantic music of the 19th century] (Budapest, 1951)

F. Bónis: *Magyar táncgyűjtemény az 1820-as évekből* [A collection of Hungarian dances from *c*1820] (Budapest, 1953)

P. P. Domokos: 'A pannonhalmi magyar táncgyűjtemény' [The Pannonhalma collection of Hungarian dances], *Magyar zenetörténeti tanulmányok*, iii (1973)

FERENC BÓNIS

Ruzitska, József (*b* ?Pápa, *c*1775; *d* after 1823). Hungarian conductor and composer. About 1820 he was Kapellmeister of the Josephregiment in Nagyenyed. In 1821 he composed the music to the second part of the Singspiel *Arany idők* ('Golden ages') for the theatre in Debrecen. He lived in Nagyvárad (now Oradea, Romania) as a theatre musician (1821) and in Kolozsvár (Klausenburg; now Cluj-Napoca, Romania) as Kapellmeister of the Hungarian theatre (1822–3). In the Christmas season of 1822 his two operas *Béla futása* ('Béla's escape') and *Kemény Simon avagy dicsőség a hazáért meghalni* ('Simon Kemény, or It is glorious to die for the fatherland') were performed for the first time at the theatre in Kolozsvár. After 1823, when he made a journey to Italy, no details about his life are known.

Despite the apparent brevity of his career, Ruzitska is a significant figure in Hungarian music history. His two operas were among the earliest attempts at original operatic art in Hungary. In these works he used elements of contemporary Italian and German opera, as well as those of popular national Hungarian dance music (*verbunkos*). The Hungarian parts of his operas show the influence of Bihari's music. With his topical historical themes and his endeavour to combine current international with popular national forms of musical expression, Ruzitska paved the way for Hungarian opera in the 19th century.

BIBLIOGRAPHY

I. Bartalus: 'Az első magyar dalmű költője [The composer of the first Hungarian opera], *Hölgyfutár*, xiii (1861)

Z. Ferenczi: *A kolozsvári színészet és színház története* [History of theatrical art and the theatre in Kolozsvár] (Kolozsvár, 1897)

I. Lakatos: 'Az első magyar dalmű [The first Hungarian opera], *Erdélyi helikon*, xii (1939)

B. Szabolcsi: *A magyar zenetörténet kézikönyve* (Budapest, 1947, 3/1978; Eng. trans., 1964, as *A Concise History of Hungarian Music*)

——: *A XIX. század magyar romantikus zenéje* [Hungarian Romantic music of the 19th century] (Budapest, 1951)

M. Pándi: *Száz esztendő magyar zenekritikája* [100 years of Hungarian music criticism] (Budapest, 1967)

FERENC BÓNIS

Ruzsch, Conrad. *See* RUPSCH, CONRAD.

Rwanda. Republic in central Africa. Although it is only 26,338 sq km in area, it is inhabited by three peoples with different origins and cultures, the Hutu, Tutsi and Twa. The Hutu, a Bantu people culturally related to peoples of east Zaïre, are mainly agricultural and form about 90% of the population. They were dominated by Tutsi dynasties from the 16th century but seized power in the years 1959–61. The Tutsi are a people with Nilotic characteristics, primarily cattle-breeders, who came to Rwanda from the north around the 16th century. They conquered the area and founded a feudal kingdom, wielding absolute power over the other population groups although they represented only about 15% of the total population. After the revolution of 1959–61 they formed only 9% and nearly all traditional elements relating to their reign disappeared. The rulers were called *bami* (singular *mwami*); they had a strictly hierarchic court and constantly tried to extend their territory using a well-organized army. The *ingabe* (dynastic drums) were among the symbols of power; the magic power of the *mwami* was symbolized by ritual drums.

The Twa, a pygmoid people, are dominated by the other groups, as in other regions of Africa. In Rwanda they are either hunters, living in the forests and volcanic regions of the north, or farmers and professional potters in central Rwanda. They form about 1% of the population. In addition to these three main groups, there are some small groups of Kiga and Hima (from Uganda) in the north, and a group of Nyambo (from Tanzania) in the south-east.

The Rwandese do not live in villages; each family occupies a hill or part of a hill which is cultivated or used for pasture. Agriculture and cattle-raising form the basis of the economy and there is almost no industry.

1. Instrumental music. 2. Vocal genres. 3. Dance. 4. Musical characteristics.

1. INSTRUMENTAL MUSIC. Musical instruments are few in Rwanda in comparison with other central African regions, possibly because the Rwandese show a marked preference for vocal genres. Nearly all instruments are played exclusively by men.

The flutes of the *insengo* ensemble are cylindrical and made of wood wrapped with skin from a bull's throat. The herdsmen's notched flute, *umwirongi*, has two to

1. Amakondera ensemble of side-blown trumpets and ingaraba drum (cylindrical drum, 2nd from right) accompanying intore dancers

four finger-holes and is played while herding cattle, or at night to pass the time. It is made from reed, bamboo or wood, and measures 30 to 50 cm. The *ihembe*, a side-blown antelope horn, is used as a signalling instrument for hunting and communal work; the trumpets used in the *amakondera* ensemble are side-blown and made of bamboo (fig.1).

There are two main types of membranophone: the cylindrical single-headed *ingaraba* drum of the Twa *amakondera* ensemble (fig.1), and the *iñgoma* drum with two skins laced together (fig.3). The latter name refers to both the ensemble and the drum itself, which is played to accompany the girls' dance *imbyino*.

Chordophones are the most common instruments in Rwanda. The *inanga* (a trough zither; fig.4), with seven or eight strings, is used to accompany epic and historical songs sung in praise of the *mwami*. Yuki III Mazimpaka, who reigned in the first half of the 18th century, was considered a remarkable poet-composer of *inanga* songs depicting the rise of the Tutsi kingdom and his own heroic deeds. Most of the *inanga* songs have been transmitted orally, with little variation, from generation to generation and are thus an important source of information for the early history of the Rwandan kingdom. The *inanga* was formerly played only by professional musicians but has subsequently become free to be played by anyone; as a result the traditional themes of the *inanga* songs have been supplanted by accounts of everyday events and contemporary political personalities.

The *iningiti* (a single-string fiddle derived from Uganda; see fig.2) occurs particularly in the north and is used to accompany songs about persons and events in a less elevated and more improvisatory style than the *inanga*. The singer generally sings falsetto. The large *umuduli* or *umunahi* (musical bow) is played by the Hutu, and like the *iningiti* accompanies songs commenting on everyday events. It is played in the same way as in Uganda: while playing the string the musician beats a basic rhythm on the gourd resonator with a rattle.

The *ikembe* is a lamellaphone which spread from Zaïre to Rwanda through Burundi and is found mostly in south Rwanda; it has 11 to 13 metal keys, played with both thumbs. Various types of rattle exist, such as the *ikinyuguri* gourd rattles, used for the cult of Lyangombe, the chief spirit; the *amayugi* bells attached to the necks of dogs while hunting; and the *inzogera* ankle rattles (fig.5), worn by the *intore* and *imbyino* dancers (see §3 below) to stress the rhythm.

The three main instrumental groups are the *iñgoma*, the *amakondera* and the *insengo*. The *iñgoma* ensemble (fig.3) consists of seven to nine large drums, each with a specific name and pitch. The most important, the *ishakwe* or *ishaako*, is the solo drum, the others providing a uniform basic rhythm; all of them are beaten with *umulishyo* (drumsticks). The most common names for the individual drums are *ishakwe*, *indahura*, *indamutsa* and *igihumulizo*. Although ensembles of this type originated at the court of the *mwami*, they occur in various regions where they perform on festive occasions. Their repertory consists of up to 30 pieces, each with its own rhythmic organization. The main rhythms are the *igihubi* (important in ritual centring on the *mwami*) and the *ikimanuka*, in which the leader of the group plays all the drums himself. Ex.1 shows some of the patterns of the rhythm *umunyuramatwe*.

Ex.1 *Umunyuramatwe* rhythms, *iñgoma* drums; rec. and transcr. J. Gansemans

The *amakondera* ensemble (see fig.1) of Twa musicians consists of six to eight bamboo trumpets, an *ingaraba* drum and a *ruharage* drum. Each trumpet has its own melodic ostinato pattern (ex.2); these are combined in performance. The most usual names for the trumpets are *inkanka*, *urugunda*, *insengo* and *inshuragane*. This ensemble accompanies the *intore* dancers.

Ex.2 *Amakondera* ensemble, ostinato patterns, side-blown trumpets; rec. and transcr. J. Gansemans

The *insengo* ensemble, consisting of five or six flutes, had a ritual significance for the Tutsi dynasties and occurs only in the north. The individual names of the flutes partly correspond to the *iñgoma* drum names, for example *ishakwe*, *igihumulizo* and *indahura*. At court, only members of the Abasindi clan were allowed to play them.

2. VOCAL GENRES. Solo, group and choral singing are all heard in Rwanda, performed by both men and women. The *ibihozo* (lullaby), sung by women or young girls, is a solo genre. Antiphonal songs, in which the two singers have equal parts, include the different types of cattle song (*amahamba*, *kubangulira*, *gushora*, *imyoma*, etc); in the *ibisigo* (sung dynastic poetry) various soloists alternate although exceptionally the parts may overlap. In another important type of solo performance the singer accompanies himself on an instrument such as the *inanga*, *iningiti* or *umuduli*. Eloquence is an envied quality expressed in singing, hence the considerable amount of parlando and recitative in the songs.

Responsorial solo and choral songs form the most important stylistic group and have many functions: the

3

4

5

2. *Iningiti (single-string fiddle)*
3. *Iñgoma ensemble of double-headed drums*
4. *Inanga (trough zither)*
5. *Inzogera (ankle rattles) worn by intore dancers*

imbyino, ikinimba and *ibyishongoro* songs accompany dancing; others are related to the spirit cults or are performed during the *amahigi* (hunting ritual); *amasare* are sung to keep time when rowing and *kwidoga* during agricultural work in the fields; the *indilimbo* and *ibitaramo* songs are sung at night for entertainment. The accompanying instrument, if any, is generally the *ikinyuguri* in the Lyangombe cult, or an *iñgoma* drum in the *imbyino* dance; nearly all songs can also be accompanied by rhythmic hand-clapping.

The Twa vocal style is distinct from that of the neighbouring Hutu and Tutsi: it is based entirely on the yodel technique, with an individual polyphonic structure. This yodel style is also characteristic of other Twa peoples of central Africa, which indicates that the Twa have retained their own traditional music styles despite their contact with Bantu and other peoples.

3. DANCE. Dancing is collective in Rwanda; there is no solo dancing. Men and women have their own dances and dance together only during the Lyangombe cult ceremonies. Rwandan dancing tends to be more expressive than that of other parts of central Africa; both men's and women's dances involve violent movements of the arms and the upper part of the body, with high leaps and stamping of feet.

The best-trained and organized dancers from Rwanda are the *intore*. They originated at the court of the *mwami*, where children of noblemen, as future leaders, were taught the arts of eloquence and fighting, as well as local traditions and dances. The *intore* dancers are now merely picturesque additions to celebrations.

The *inkaranka*, *ikinimba* and *ikinyemera* are war dances found chiefly in the north. The *imbyino* and *ururengo* are typical women's and girls' dances, intended for entertainment. The *imbyino* is performed throughout the country at every celebration by groups of six to eight young girls, accompanied by a chorus with two soloists and an *iňgoma* drum; its modernized musical style shows traces of Western influence. The true traditional *imbyino* dance and song is performed by older women; it has a graceful style, a rich polyphonic structure and a flowing melodic line.

Although these dances are performed mainly by the Hutu and Tutsi, the Twa are generally considered the best dancers. While most other dancers perform in a state of frenzy, the Twa perform the same dances in a more supple and graceful style. In certain rhythms of the *intore* there are traces of a similarly gentle style, probably due to the frequent participation of Twa performers.

4. MUSICAL CHARACTERISTICS. Hutu music clearly shows Bantu elements found in most areas of central Africa. Their melodies are built mainly on anhemitonic pentatonic scales, sometimes extended to hexa- and heptatonic; the use of the 3rd within a curved melodic line is particularly characteristic (see ex.3). Hutu songs generally have a responsorial structure with sporadic overlapping of solo and chorus and occasional use of drone and ostinato.

Ex.3 Melodic structure of a Hutu song (Günther, 1964)

Tutsi music reveals Arab influences, chiefly in the use of melisma, ornamentation and thematic variations, in diatonic as well as chromatic scales; parlando style and repeated notes are prevalent. In their group songs heterophonic structures are common; a general descending contour characterizes *inanga* music.

Twa music contrasts sharply with Hutu and Tutsi music in that it is characterized by melodic yodel, movement in parallel 4ths and 5ths, and frequent use of syncopation and hemiola.

In 1973 C. Nieuwenhuysen and J. Gansemans began an ethnomusicological investigation of Rwanda, commissioned by the Royal Museum for Central Africa, Tervuren (Belgium), and by the National Institute for Scientific Research, Butare (Rwanda), which collects and analyses cultural and anthropological data.

BIBLIOGRAPHY
R. Günther: *Musik in Rwanda* (Tervuren, 1964)
R. Barbaglia: 'Musique africaine du Burundi', CLVLX 296 [disc notes]
D. Hiernaux-L'Hoest: 'Music from Rwanda', BM 30 L 2302 [disc notes]
H. Tracey: 'The Sound of Africa: Rwanda', AMA TR 57–8 [disc notes]
L. A. Verwilghen: 'Songs of the Watutsi', FE 4428 [disc notes]
                                                    J. GANSEMANS

Rwtha, Didrik Persson. See THEODORICUS PETRI NYLANDENSIS.

Ryba [Poisson, Peace, Ryballandini, Rybaville], **Jakub (Šimon) Jan** (*b* Přeštice, nr. Klatovy, 26 Oct 1765; *d* Rožmitál pod Třemšínem, 8 April 1815). Czech teacher, composer, choirmaster and writer on music. He was the son of a cantor and organist who was probably also a composer. After studying singing, thoroughbass, the piano, organ and violin with his father at Nepomuk, he attended the Piarist Gymnasium in Prague (1781–4), where he continued to teach himself (the cello, organ and theory) and began to compose. He returned to Nepomuk and assisted his ailing father, and from 1786 worked as an assistant teacher at Mníšek. On 11 February 1788 he was appointed assistant teacher and on 23 May 1788 cantor (schoolmaster) and church choirmaster at Rožmitál. He held these posts until his death by suicide.

Artistically, Ryba was one of the most prominent 18th-century Czech cantors; though he devoted himself assiduously to his teaching duties (see his school diary), he wrote a large number of compositions (at first under various pseudonyms), of which the sacred ones survive far more completely than the secular. They develop the pre-Classical and early Classical church idiom of J. L. Oehlschlägel and F. X. Brixi; from about the early 1790s a strong Mozartian influence becomes apparent. Ryba's Solemn Mass in Eb (Němeček's catalogue no.378) circulated under the name of Joseph Haydn; his Czech Mass, *Hej, mistře*, is his best-known work. His point of departure as a composer of instrumental music was the keyboard and chamber works of Haydn, C. P. E. Bach, Leopold Kozeluch, J. B. Vanhal, Mysliveček and others. The numerous Czech pastorellas are undoubtedly the most vivid part of his output, with a highly individual amalgamation of Czech folksong elements and a simplified Classical texture. Ryba was one of the earliest composers to introduce Czech into solo art song. In his theoretical treatise he attempted to establish Czech musical terminology; though his terms were not accepted into common use, the treatise is notable as the second of its kind printed in Czech (after Jan Blahoslav's *Musica*, 1558). He also wrote hymn texts, didactic poetry and prose, occasional and gratulatory poems, and translated Latin and Greek works into Czech.

WORKS

A thematic catalogue with sources and editions is in Němeček (1963); a list of works to 1801 compiled by Ryba for Dlabač (MS, CS-Ps D.A.III.36 op.6) is included in I. Janáčková: *J. J. Ryba o svém hudebním životě* (Prague, 1946).

SACRED

Thematic list, 1782–96, compiled by Ryba, in *Pnm* XIV F 94; MSS mainly *Pnm*
*c*90 masses, incl.: 2 in Cz.; 2 [?4] in Cz. and Lat.; some in sets, incl. Cursus sacro-harmonicus, i, 1808, iv, 1814; Hej, mistře [Hail, master!] (Ryba), Cz. pastoral mass, 1796, ed. J. Hercl (Prague and Hamburg, 1973); Missa tono pietatis festis mediocribus accommodata, Eb (Prague, 1814)
Other liturgical: 7 Requiem; over 100 Lat. graduals, motets (offertories), some in sets, incl. Cursus sacro-harmonicus, ii, 1811, iii, 1812–14, v, 1814
Cz. songs, choruses (Ryba): Oktáv neb osmidenní pobožnost k svatému Janu Nepomuckému [Octave, or the eight-day feast of St Jan Nepomuk], 8 songs (Prague, 1803); Svatohorský kůr [The Svatá Hora choir], 8 songs (Prague, 1804); [21] Pohřební písně [Funeral songs] (Prague, 1805); others
Other sacred: 3 Stabat mater, incl. 2 in Cz.; Chvalozpěv k sv. Janu Nepomuckému [Eulogy to St Jan Nepomuk] (Ryba), 1803; Soudný den [Judgment day] (Ryba), 1801, lost; *c*50 arias, several duets, incl. 8 ariae et duetto (Prague, 1808); over 50 pastorellas (pastoral motets, offertories), arias, mostly in Cz. (Ryba)

SECULAR

6 Singspiels and pantomimes, before 1801, incl.: Veselé živobytí neb vandrovní muzikanti [A merry life, or wandering musicians] (Singspiel), lib, 1794, music lost; Das Denkmal in Arkadien (operetta), 1800, music lost except 1 aria, T, arr. as sacred aria Exaudi, Domine
Cz. songs, 1v, pf: 12 böhmische Lieder (Prague, 1800); [12] Neue böhmische Lieder (Prague, 1808); Lenka (V. Nejedlý) (Prague, 1808); Průvod dobré Bětolinky [Procession of good Bětolinka]

(Nejedlý) (Prague, 1808); Dar pilné mládeži [The gift to industrious youth], 12 children's songs (Prague, 1829)
Herzensergiessung der Rossmittaler, gratulatory cantata, 1803

INSTRUMENTAL

c1150 listed in Dlabacž, incl. over 650 dances, 130 variations, 87 sonatas, 72 qts, 56 duos, 48 trios, 38 concs., 35 syms., 35 serenatas and notturnos, 7 qnts etc

(only those extant)

Orch: Sym., C; Cassatio, C; Vc Conc., C, 1800; Vn Conc., d, 1801; Hn Conc., d, inc. (doubtful)
Chamber: 2 str qts, a, d, 1801; Canon, F, str qt; 2 qts, C, F, fl, vn, va, vc, 1811; 3 sonatas, B♭, G, F, vn, vc; 2 duos, a, C, hpd/pf, vn; Canon, d, 2 vn
Org: Novae et liberae cogitationes per [1] toccatas, phantasias, [2] fugas et [2] praeludia exprassae, inc., 1798

WRITINGS

Schultagebuch (MS, Rožmitál pod Třemšínem, municipal museum, 1788–1815); Cz. trans., ed. J. Němeček, as Školní deníky J. J. Ryby (Prague, 1957)
Mein musikalischer Lebenslauf (MS, CS-Ps D.A.III.36 op.6, 1801); Cz. trans., ed. I. Janáčková, as J. J. Ryba o svém hudebním životě (Prague, 1946)
Kancionálek pro českou školní mládež [Little hymnbook for Czech schoolchildren] (Prague, 1808)
Denik [Diary] (MS, CS-Ppp heritage no.605a, 1811; Pnm IB6, 2/1813), 1st version ed. in Slavík (1888)
Počáteční a všeobecní základové ke všemu umění hudebnímu [First and general principles of the whole art of music] (Prague, 1817)
Nábožný kancionál [Pious hymnbook] (Jihlava, n.d.)

BIBLIOGRAPHY

ČSHS
G. J. Dlabacž: Allgemeines historisches Künstler-Lexikon, ii (Prague, 1815/R1973), 610ff
J. E. Ryba: 'Jakob Johann Ryba: Schullehrer in Rožmital', Jb für Lehrer, Aeltern und Erzieher (Leitmeritz [now Litoměřice], 1842), 35
F. A. Slavík: Život a působení Jakuba Jana Ryby [Ryba's life and work] (Prague, 1888)
A. Cmíral: 'J. J. Rybův Kancionálek pro českou školní mládež' [Ryba's little hymnbook for Czech schoolchildren], Cyril, lxii (1916), 110
——: 'J. J. Ryby Počáteční a všeobecní základové ke všemu umění hudebnímu' [Ryba's First and General Principles of the Whole Art of Music], HR, ix (1916), 1, 67
J. Němeček: Světské skladby J. J. Ryby [Ryba's secular works] (diss., U. of Prague, 1945)
T. Straková: 'Pastorely J. J. Ryby: Příspěvek k problematice české pastorální melodiky 18. století' [Ryba's pastorellas: 18th-century Czech pastorella melodies], Acta musaei moraviae, xxxix (1954), 135–81
J. Němeček: Jakub Jan Ryba: Život a dílo [Ryba: life and works] (Prague, 1963) [with thematic catalogue, list of writings and bibliography]
C. Schoenbaum: Review of Němeček, 1963, Mf, xix (1966), 464
J. Němeček: 'Životní osudy a názory J. J. Ryby' [Life history and opinions of Ryba], Vlastivědný sborník Podbrdska, iii (1969), 104

MILAN POŠTOLKA

Rybarič, Richard (b Bratislava, 19 Feb 1930). Slovak musicologist. He studied the piano and music theory, and musicology with Kresánek and Hudec at Bratislava University (1948–53), taking the doctorate there in 1953 with a dissertation on Slovak neumes and nota choralis in the time of church feudalism. Subsequently he was a research assistant at the Slovak Academy of Sciences, Bratislava, and from 1973 a research fellow and head of the music history department of its Arts History Institute, while also working as a part-time lecturer in notation and Slovak music history at Bratislava University (from 1958). His chief area of research is Slovak music history, particularly medieval, Renaissance and Baroque; he has written several studies of individual composers of those periods (Schimbraczky, Capricornus), and on song collections of the 17th and 18th centuries. His other main interest is musical palaeography, and he is on the editorial board of Musicologica slovaca.

WRITINGS

Slovenská neuma a nota choralis v období cirkevnom feudalizmu [Slovak neumes and nota choralis in the time of church feudalism] (diss., U. of Bratislava, 1953; extracts in Hudobnovedné štúdie, i (1955), 151)
'Počiatky hudby na Slovensku v predfeudálnom období' [The beginnings of music in Slovakia in the pre-feudal era]; 'Cirkevná a svetská hudba v období feudalizmu' [Sacred and secular music in the feudal era], Dejiny slovenskej hudby (Bratislava, 1957), 15; 29
'Sekvencie spišského graduálu Juraja z Kežmarku' [Sequences in the Spiš Gradual of Juraj z Kežmarku], Hudobnovedné štúdie, iv (1960), 100
'K otázke genezy elektronickej hudby' [The question of the genesis of electronic music], K problematike súčasnej hudby (Bratislava, 1963), 88
'Sekvencia–legenda–epos', Hudobnovedné štúdie, vi (1963), 194
'Počiatky latinského spevu na Slovensku' [The beginnings of Latin singing in Slovakia], SH, ix (1965), 57
'Slovenská hudba 17–18. storočia vo svetle novoobjavených prameňov' [Slovak music of the 17th and 18th centuries in the light of newly discovered sources], Sborník prací filosofické fakulty brněnské university, F9 (1965), 227
'Die Hauptquellen und Probleme der slowakischen Musikgeschichte bis Ende des 18. Jahrhunderts', Musica antiqua Europae orientalis I: Bydgoszcz 1966, 97
'Osudy slovenskej hudby' [The fates of Slovak music], SH, x (1966), 447
'Z problematiky "oponickej" zbierky piesní a tancov (1730)' [Some problems of the 'Oponice' collection of songs and dances], Hudobnovedné štúdie, vii (1966), 49–86
'Zur Frage der Tabulatur-Partitur im 17. Jahrhundert', Musica antiqua: Brno II 1967, 106
'Ján Šimbracký v rokoch 1635–1642: príspevok k poznaniu diela' [Schimbraczky in the years 1635 to 1642: a contribution to the knowledge of his works], Musicologica slovaca, i (1969), 91
'Johann Šimbracký und die Zipser Musikkultur', Sagittarius, ii (Kassel, 1969), 63
'Primitívna polyfónia a gregoriánsky chorál' [Primitive polyphony and Gregorian chant], Musicologica slovaca, i (1969), 283
'O problematike polyfonnej tradície na Slovensku v 15–17. storočí' [Problems of polyphonic traditions in Slovakia from the 15th century to the 17th], SH, xiv (1970), 81
'Judicium Salomonis – Samuel Capricornus a Giacomo Carissimi', Musicologica slovaca, iii (1971), 161
'Samuel Capricornus v Bratislave', SH, xiv (1970), 253; Ger. version in Musica antiqua Europae orientalis III: Bydgoszcz 1972, 107
'Ján Šimbracký – spišský polyfonik 17. storočia' [Schimbraczky – Spiš polyphonic composer of the 17th century], Musicologica slovaca, iv (1973), 7–83
'Opus musicum Samuela Capricorna', Musicologica slovaca, v (1974), 7–49
'Stredoveké mesto ako hudobnokultúrny organizmus' [The medieval town as a music-cultural organism], Historické štúdie, xix (1974), 181
'Zacharias Zarewutius organista Bartphae (1625–1664)', Nové obzory, xvi (1974), 261
'Zur Polyphonie in der Slowakei bis zum Ende des 17. Jahrhunderts', De musica disputationes pragenses, ii (1974), 56

EDITIONS

with L. Burlas: J. Šimbracký: Congregati sunt inimici nostri (Prague, 1965)
Tance zo Slovenska zo 17. a 18. storočia [Dances from Slovakia in the 17th and 18th centuries] (Prague, 1971)

Rybaville, Jakub Jan. See RYBA, JAKUB JAN.

Rybnický (z Chřenovic), Jakub Kryštof [Ribniczki, Jacobo Christophoro] (b Roudnice, c1600; d Řezno, 2 Aug 1639). Czech composer and Benedictine monk. He took his first vows at Kladruby monastery, near Stříbro, on 15 August 1623, was ordained in the following year and became abbot of the same monastery on 8 March 1627. He died while on a visitation. His only known work, an eight-part Missa concertata . . . super Exultabo Domine (MS at CS-RO), which opens with a sinfonia and lacks a Benedictus, is one of the earliest Czech works in the concertato manner.

BIBLIOGRAPHY

E. Trolda: 'Česká cirkevní hudba v období generalbasu' [Czech church music in the figured bass period], Cyril, lx (1934), 49
A. Buchner: Hudební sbírka Emiliána Troldy [Emilián Trolda's music collection] (Prague, 1954)

JOHN CLAPHAM

Rycardt. *See* RUCKERS family.

Rycefort, Jean. *See* RICHAFORT, JEAN.

Rychlík, Jan (*b* Prague, 27 April 1916; *d* Prague, 20 Jan 1964). Czech composer and writer on music. After studies at the Prague School of Commerce he was a composition pupil of Řídký at the conservatory (1939–45) and in master classes (1945–6). At this time he composed light pieces and swing dance music and also gave music lessons. Throughout his life he was greatly concerned with film music, a field in which he made technical experiments later exploited in concert works. His spontaneous musical gifts were balanced by an unusually broad knowledge of music history and theory, folk music, mathematics and the natural sciences; this wide scope was reflected in his compositions, always inventive and economical. He took an analytic and critical attitude to other music, using any influence in an original way; his approach to post-war developments, with which he came into contact in the late 1950s and early 1960s, was characteristic: Rychlík's later works are among the most significant Czech results from this encounter. He was one of the earliest jazz scholars and also made a study of organs; his essays on instrumentation are valuable.

WORKS
(selective list)
Orch: Symfonická předehra [Sym. ov], 1944; Koncertní předehra, 1947; Partita giocosa, wind, 1947; Prodromi, chamber orch, 1963
Vocal: Vstávejte, pastušci [Awake, shepherds] (trad.), cantata-carol, 1946; Šibeniční madrigaly [Gallows madrigals] (Morgenstern), 1961
Inst: Etudy, eng hn, 1952; 4 studi, fl, 1954; Komorní suita [Chamber suite] (Partita da camera), str qt, 1954; Hommagi clavicembalistici, hpd, 1960; Wind Qnt, 1960; Africký cyklus, 9 insts, 1961; Relazioni, a fl, eng hn, bn, 1963
Film scores, dance music, songs
Principal publishers: Český hudební fond, Orbis, Panton, Supraphon, Svoboda

WRITINGS
'Henry Purcell', *Tempo*, xviii (Prague, 1946), 125
'Jazz', *Tempo*, xix (Prague, 1946), 71, 149
'Bicí nástroje v soudobém orchestru' [Percussion in the contemporary orchestra], *Tempo*, xx (Prague, 1947)
'Claude Debussy, Rusko a Anglie', *Tempo*, xx (Prague, 1947), 185
'Úvahy o orchestraci' [Paper on orchestration], *HRo*, i (1948), 71, 94, 137
Pověry a problémy jazzu [Prejudices and problems of jazz] (Prague, 1959)
Moderní instrumentace (Prague, 1959–63)
'Prvky nových skladebných technik v hudbě minulosti, v hudbě exotické a lidové' [Elements of new techniques of composition in past, exotic and folk music], *Nové cesty hudby* (1964), no.1, p.54

BIBLIOGRAPHY
V. Lébl and L. Mokrý: 'O současném stavu nových skladebných směrů u nás', *Nové cesty hudby* (1964), no.1, p.22
K. Šrom: 'Bez Jana Rychlíka', *HRo*, xvii (1964), 99
V. Lébl: 'Čtyři vzpomínky na Jana Rychlíka', *HRo*, xix (1966), 230
K. Šrom: 'Jan Rychlík: Africký cyklus I–V', *HRo*, xix (1966), 54
JOSEF BEK

Rycke, Antonius. *See* DIVITIS, ANTONIUS.

Rydman, Kari (*b* Helsinki, 15 Oct 1936). Finnish composer. He studied musicology at Helsinki University and is self-taught as a composer. Between 1955 and 1964 he contributed music criticism to many newspapers, also working as sub-editor of the music journal *Rondo*. Subsequently he took teaching appointments at a secondary school and at the Institute of Industrial Art, and he has edited many popular books on music. His compositional interests are wide and eclectic. He has an unusual sympathy with pop music, which he has incor-porated into such works as the *Symphony of the Modern Worlds*, for an orchestra including a tenor saxophone and two electric guitars. In the string quartets and other pieces he has made effective use of stylistic collage.

WORKS
(selective list)
Stage: Poikkeus ja sääntö [Exception and rule] (incidental music, Brecht), 1965; Slottsmordet [Murder in the castle] (comic opera for children, 1), 1974
Orch: Composition, perc, str, 1961; Sérénade à Djamila Boupacha, 1963; Syrinx, 1964; Khoros 2, 1966; Dance Suite, 1966; Rondeaux des nuits blanches d'été, 1966; Sym. of the Modern Worlds, 1968; DNA, 1970
Choral: Sancta Maria ora pro nobis, 1957; Dona nobis pacem, 1963; O crux ave spes unica, 1963
Solo vocal: 3 Songs (Diktonius), 1v, pf, 1957; Miten yksinäisyys minusta leviää [How the solitude spreads from me] (E.-L. Manner), 1v, pf, 1957; Bitte und Marienlied (Hesse), 1v, pf, 1957; Declamatory Songs, narrator, tape, 1961; Suite (T. Anhava), narrator, 11 insts, 1971
Chamber: Composition, pf, 1959; 4 str qts, 1959, 1963, 1964, 1964; Pf Qnt, 1960; Etude sur l'évolution tonale, pf, 1960; Trio, vn, vc, perc, 1961; Sonata no.1, 3 vn, va, vc, pf, perc, 1962; Sonata no.2, vn, va, gui, perc, 1962; Sonata no.4, cl, gui, perc, vn, 1963; Khoros 1, 11 insts, 1964; Sonata no.6, vc, perc ad lib, 1964; Sonata no.9, ens, 1971
ERIK WAHLSTRÖM

Rypdal, Terje (*b* Oslo, 23 Aug 1947). Norwegian jazz guitarist and composer. He received a classical training as a pianist and taught himself the guitar. Later he took a music course at Oslo University, studied composition with Finn Mortensen and learnt the 'Lydian chromatic concept of tonal organization' from its originator George Russell, in whose sextet and big band he played. From the late 1960s he was a member of Jan Garbarek's 'free jazz' group, and first achieved recognition outside Norway at the Free Jazz Festival in Baden-Baden (1969), where he also presented some of his own compositions. In 1972 he formed his own group, Odyssey, with which he has recorded and with which he visited London and the USA. Widely regarded as the most important electric guitarist in Europe, Rypdal developed an independent and individual style by incorporating elements of rock and modern concert music and achieving novel sonorities (e.g. tone clusters produced on the guitar with a violin bow). He is also one of Norway's most important young composers; besides works for his own jazz groups he has written *Eternal Circulation* for symphony orchestra and jazz ensemble (1972), an opera on the Orpheus legend (1972), a symphony and double bass concerto (both 1973) and stage music.
RANDI HULTIN

Rysanek, Leonie (*b* Vienna, 12 Nov 1926). Austrian soprano. She studied at the Vienna Conservatory with Alfred Jerger and later with Rudolf Grossmann. She made her début at Innsbruck in 1949 as Agathe in *Der Freischütz*, and from 1950 to 1952 was at Saarbrücken, where her roles included Arabella, Donna Anna, Tosca, Senta, Sieglinde, and Leonora in *La forza del destino*. At the first postwar Bayreuth Festival in 1951 her Sieglinde created a sensation, and the following year she joined the Bavarian Staatsoper in Munich, where she soon established herself as one of the outstanding young singers of the postwar period. Her rich, opulent voice, with its thrilling upper register, and her dramatic temperament have been heard and seen to advantage in the title roles of Strauss's *Der Liebe der Danae*, *Die aegyptische Helena* and *Salome*, as the Empress in his *Die Frau ohne Schatten* and Chrysothemis in *Elektra*, and as Lady Macbeth, Turandot and Tosca.

Rysanek was first heard in London during the Munich company's season at Covent Garden in September 1953 when she sang Danae; during the next two years she appeared there as Chrysothemis and Sieglinde (her performance in the latter role was generally considered the most womanly since Lotte Lehmann's). Her American début was at San Francisco in 1956 where she sang Senta and Sieglinde. In 1958 she returned to Bayreuth as Elsa in a new production of *Lohengrin*, and in 1959 made her début at the Metropolitan Opera, replacing Callas as Lady Macbeth in a new production. She then appeared regularly at the Metropolitan in the Italian and the German repertories, sharing most of her time between New York and the Vienna Staatsoper, with guest appearances in other leading European houses.

BIBLIOGRAPHY

G. Gualerzi: 'Rysanek, Leonie', *Le grandi voci* (Rome, 1964) [with opera discography by R. Vegeto]

H. Rosenthal: 'Leonie Rysanek', *Great Singers of Today* (London, 1966)

HAROLD ROSENTHAL

Ryse, Philipp. *See* RHYS, PHILIP AP.

Rytel, Piotr (*b* Vilnius, 20 Sept 1884; *d* Warsaw, 2 Jan 1970). Polish teacher and composer. After piano studies in Vilnius with Kulesza, he attended the Warsaw Conservatory as a pupil of Noskowski (composition), Roguski (harmony), Statkowski (instrumentation) and Michałowski (piano). He graduated with diplomas in piano and composition in 1908, and in 1918 he returned as professor of piano and harmony, later becoming professor of composition; his pupils included Baird, Kotoński, Panufnik and Tansman. From 1956 to 1961 he directed the Sopot State College of Music; he was also active as a critic (from 1911). He composed romantic music lacking an individual style. The City of Gdańsk Prize was awarded to him for his work.

WORKS
(selective list)

Operas: Ijola (Rytel, after J. Żuławski), 1928; Krzyżowcy (Rytel), 1942; Andrzej z Chełmna (Rytel), 1944
Ballets: Faun i Psyche, ballet, 1, Warsaw, 1931; Śląski pierścień [Silesian ring], ballet, 6 scenes, H. Tomaszewski, W. Pomorski, 1956
Orch: Sym. no.1, 1909; Sym. no.2 'Mickiewiczowska' (Mickiewicz), T, chorus, orch, 1949; Vn Conc., 1950; Sym. no.3 (J. Słowacki), T, orch, 1951; Symfonia koncertujaca (Sym. no.4), fl, cl, hn, harp, orch, 1960; sym. poems
Other works: cantatas incl. Stalin (S. R. Dobrowolski), 1949; songs, pf pieces

Principal publisher: Polskie Wydawnictwo Muzyczne

BIBLIOGRAPHY

M. Idzikowski: 'W 80 rocznicę urodzin Piotra Rytla', *Ruch muzyczny* (1964), no.23, p.16

BOGUSŁAW SCHÄFFER

Rythme (Fr.). RHYTHM. The term was used by A. Reicha and others to denote a small unit of melodic construction; *see* ANALYSIS, §II, 2.

Rywacka-Morozewicz, Ludwika (*b* Warsaw, 19 April 1817; *d* 19 Feb 1858). Polish soprano. She studied at the Warsaw School of Dramatic Singing, and from 1828 gave concerts in various Polish towns. She sang in *Il turco in Italia* in Italy (1841–2). She first appeared at the Wielki Theatre in 1837, and until 1852 she took leading parts in operas by Meyerbeer, Rossini, Mozart and Verdi. Later she moved to Lwów and founded a school of singing. In 1856 she gave concerts in Zhitomir and Kiev; she died on the way from Kiev to Warsaw, where she was buried.

BIBLIOGRAPHY

SMP

A. Sowiński: *Słownik muzyków polskich dawnych i nowoczesnych* [Dictionary of Polish musicians past and present] (Paris, 1874)

IRENA PONIATOWSKA

Rzepko, Adolf (*b* Prague, 3 April 1825; *d* Warsaw, 31 March 1892). Polish pianist, oboist, conductor and composer, who performed under the name R. Adolf. In 1843 he completed his oboe studies at the Prague Conservatory; he also studied the piano and organ under Tomášek and (before 1842) under Divis Weber. From 1846 he worked in Warsaw, Radom, Piotrków and Kalisz as a teacher, performer and choral and orchestral conductor. In 1869 he settled in Warsaw, where for many years he was principal oboe of the Wielki Theatre orchestra and was also widely in demand as a piano and singing teacher and as a conductor of church choirs. He wrote two teaching manuals, *Zasady muzyki* ('The principles of music', Warsaw, 1869) and *Szkoła na fortepian* ('A piano tutor', Warsaw, n.d.).

WORKS
(all MSS in private collection of Jan Fabijański, Warsaw)

Maria (incidental music, A. Malczewski), *c*1850
Vocal: Missa solemnis, 4vv, orch, 1842; Requiem polskie, 4vv, str orch, org, 1868; Msza [Mass], 1v, org (Warsaw, 1880); Stabat mater, 4 male vv, *c*1890; Puszczyk (B. Zaleski), song, 1v, pf, in *Echo muzyczne, teatralne i artystyczne*, i (1884), 31
Kbd: 26 morceaux faciles et mélodiques précédés chacun d'un prélude composé pour les élèves, pf, op.7 (Warsaw, *c*1860); Souvenir de Varsovie, 20 morceaux agréables, pf, op.17 (Warsaw, n.d.); Récréations instructives, 13 morceaux faciles et mélodiques composées pour les élèves, pf, op.18 (Warsaw, n.d.); 12 nowych melodii kolędowych [12 new Christmas songs], harmonium/org/pf (Warsaw, 1891)

BIBLIOGRAPHY

SMP

'Śp. Adolf Rzepko', *Tygodnik ilustrowany*, v (1892), 269

S. Orgelbrand: *Encyklopedia powszechna z ilustracjami i mapami* (Warsaw, 1898–1904)

BARBARA CHMARA-ŻACZKIEWICZ

Rzepko, Władysław (*b* Piórków, nr. Sandomierz, 21 April 1854; *d* Warsaw, 19 April 1932). Polish violist, composer and teacher, son of Adolf Rzepko, and father of the cellist and composer Karol Rzepko (*b* Warsaw, 30 Oct 1882; *d* Kraków, 14 Nov 1944). After lessons from his father he studied the violin under Apolinary Kątski, theory under Karol Studziński and composition under Moniuszko at the Warsaw Music Institute (1869–73). From 1870 to 1873 he played the violin at the Wielki Theatre and studied conducting privately with Castagnieri. From 1875 he studied further with Emil Stiller (viola), Jan Quattrini (singing), and from 1881 composition with Zygmunt Noskowski. At this time he also played the viola in the string quartet of the Warsaw Music Society and taught the violin, piano and organ. From 1885 he taught choral singing and music theory in the music school of the Warsaw Music Society, as well as music in secondary schools and teacher training colleges. He was co-founder, and from 1887 until his death deputy director, of the Lutnia singing society. He published articles on music in a number of journals, including *Echo muzyczne, teatralne i artystyczne* and *Nowości muzyczne*, and wrote several teaching works: *Szkoła na melodykon lub fisharmonię* ('A harmonium or melodicon tutor', Warsaw, 1893), *Zasady nauki śpiewu oparte na podstawie fizjologii* ('The principles of learning to sing on the basis of physiology', Warsaw,

1903) and *Podręcznik gry skrzypcowej* ('A violin manual', Warsaw, 1910–12). He compiled songbooks and arranged and transcribed Polish and foreign music. He also undertook editorial work for the Warsaw Music Society, publishing numerous works by Moniuszko, including his last *Śpiewniki domowe*.

WORKS
(all MSS in private collection of Jan Fabijański, Warsaw)
VOCAL
Sacred: Missa brevis, 4 male vv (Warsaw, 1888); 30 dawnych kolęd [30 old carols], SATB (Warsaw, 1893); Stabat mater, 4 male vv (Warsaw, 1903); Requiem, B, T, chorus, org, 1905 (Warsaw, 1906)
Secular: Żniwa na Podolu, cantata, solo vv, chorus, orch, 1898; Legenda o św. Jerzym, cantata, solo vv, chorus, orch, 1902; Treny, cantata, solo vv, chorus, orch, 1910; Rok w pieśni [A year in songs], 13 songs, 1v, vc, pf, 1919

INSTRUMENTAL
Orch: 2 suites, no.1, C, str orch, 1896, no.2, F, str orch, 1903; 3 vc concs., no.1, C, 1908, no.2, C, 1923, no.3, D, 1929
Chamber: Variations, c, str qt, 1882; Sonata, c, va, pf, 1883; 2 str qts, no.1, B♭, 1884, no.2, A, 1889; Polska suita, D, vn, pf, 1899; Sonata, C, vc, pf, 1901; Pf Trio, F, 1904; Str Trio no.3, C, 1912; 2 str qnts, no.1, C, 1926, no.2, C, 1927; Str Sextet, G, 1927

BIBLIOGRAPHY
SMP
P. Maszyński: 'Władysław Rzepko: wspomnienie pośmiertne' [Obituary], *Śpiewak* (1932), 71
T. L. Błaszczyk: *Dyrygenci polscy i obcy w Polsce działający w XIX i XX wieku* [Polish and foreign conductors working in Poland in the 19th and 20th centuries] (Kraków, 1964)
W. Poźniak: 'Muzyka kameralna i skrzypcowa XIX wieku' [Violin and chamber music of the 19th century], *Z dziejów polskiej kultury muzycznej*, ii, ed. A. Nowak-Romanowicz and others (Kraków, 1966), 490
I. Chomik: 'Warszawskie towarzystwo śpiewacze Lutnia w latach 1886–1914' [The Warsaw Lutnia Song Society in the years 1886–1914], *Szkice o kulturze muzycznej XIX wieku*, ed. Z. Chechlińska (Warsaw, 1971), 163

BARBARA CHMARA-ŻACZKIEWICZ

Rzewski, Frederic (Anthony) (*b* Westfield, Mass., 13 April 1938). American composer and pianist. He studied with Thompson (counterpoint) and Spies (orchestration) at Harvard University (1954–8) and with Wagner and Strunk at Princeton University (1958–60), where he also attended courses in philosophy and Greek. Throughout most of the 1960s he was active as a pianist and teacher in Europe: he took part in the first performances of Stockhausen's *Klavierstück X* (1962) and *Plus–Minus* (1964), and he taught at the Cologne Courses for New Music (1963, 1964 and 1970). In 1966 he was a founder-member of the live electronic ensemble Musica Elettronica Viva (MEV) in Rome, where he lived until his return to New York in 1971. With MEV, on which he had a strong influence, he explored collective improvisation (in *Work Songs*), and this led to the socialist political concerns expressed in such works as *Coming Together*, composed to the text of a letter from an Attica State Prison inmate. Works from all phases of his career have a characteristic drive and intensity.

WORKS
(selective list)
Preludes, pf, 1957; Poem, pf, 1959; Sonata, 2 pf, 1960; Study, pf, 1960; Dreams, pf, 1961; Octet, fl, cl, tpt, trbn, pf, harp, vn, db, 1961–2; For Violin, 1962; Requiem, chorus, ens, 1963–7; Composition for 2, any 2 insts, 1964; Self-portrait, solo performer, 1964; Speculum Dianae, any 8 insts, 1964; Nature morte, small orch, 1965; Zoologischer Garten, tape, 1965; Impersonation, 2 solo vv, 4 tape rec, mixer, 1966
Projector-piece, 2 groups, dancers, slide projectors, 1966; Portrait, actor, lights, slides, film, photoresistors, 6 tapes, 1967; Work Songs, text compositions, 1967–9; Les moutons de Panurge, any ens, 1969; Last Judgement, trbn, 1969; Jefferson, 1v, pf, 1970; Old Maid, S, chorus, 1970; Falling Music, pf, tape, 1971; Coming Together, speaker, bass insts, ens, 1972; No Progress without Struggle, songs, 1973; Variations on No Place to Go but Around, pf, 1974; The People United will Never be Defeated, pf, 1975

WRITINGS
'Performance: Indeterminate Performance', 'Prose Music', *Dictionary of Contemporary Music*, ed. J. Vinton (New York, 1973)

EDWARD MURRAY

S

Sa'adya Gaon. 10th-century Jewish music theorist; *see* JEWISH MUSIC, §I, 13(iii).

Saar, Louis Victor (Franz) (*b* Rotterdam, 10 Dec 1868; *d* St Louis, 23 Nov 1937). Dutch-American teacher and composer. A graduate of the Strasbourg Gymnasium and later of the Munich Conservatory, he went to New York in 1894 as accompanist at the Metropolitan Opera House; later he taught theory at various institutions in that city and elsewhere in the USA. His compositions include *Psalm cxxviii* for solo, chorus and orchestra, and other choral pieces; an orchestral suite, *From the Kingdom of the Great North-west*, *Three Silhouettes* and other orchestral pieces; chamber music, violin and piano pieces and songs.

WARREN STOREY SMITH

Saar, Mart (*b* Vastemõisa, Livonia, 16 Sept 1882; *d* Tallinn, 28 Oct 1963). Estonian composer. He studied at the St Petersburg Conservatory with Louis Homilius, Rimsky-Korsakov and Lyadov (1901–11). He early became interested in folksong, and in 1905 and 1907 undertook journeys to collect Estonian folk material. From 1908 he was a critic and teacher in Dorpat (now Tartu) and from the early 1920s in Reval (Tallinn) and Hüpassare. He taught composition at the Tallinn Conservatory in 1943–56, and in 1952 was named People's Artist of the Estonian SSR. While Saar's early piano music is indebted to Chopin and Skryabin, the harmonic and melodic colours and even the performing practices of Estonian folk music increasingly influenced his later works. From the refrain structures, recitative-like idiom, rhythms and colours of folksong, combined with his formal musical training, he synthesized a strongly characteristic style that made him one of the foremost Estonian nationalist composers.

WORKS
(selective list)

Vocal: Õhtu mõtted [Evening thoughts], chorus, orch, 1929; Ilo tüterile [To the daughters of Beauty], chorus, orch, 1939; Julgelt edasi [Bravely forward] (H. Toming), Bar, chorus, orch, 1940; choral cantatas; c300 unacc. choral pieces, incl. Lastekoorid [Children's choruses], 2 vols. (1921), Segakoorid [Mixed choruses], 5 vols. (1933–5), Meeskoorid [Men's choruses], 3 vols. (1935); c150 solo songs, duets

Inst: 3 Estonian Suites, pf, 1939, 1941, 1948 (1948–59); Estonian Fantasia, pf, 1946; c40 preludes, pf; c40 other pf pieces; Fantasia and Fugue, org, 1915; orch works, 1918–28

BIBLIOGRAPHY
K. Leichter: *Mart Saar* (Tallinn, 1964)
A. Vahter and others: *Eesti muusika* (Tallinn, 1968–75), i, 205ff, 215ff, 229ff; ii, 65ff, 360ff, 438ff
H. Olt: *Modern Estonian Composers* (Tallinn, 1972)
V. Rumessen, ed.: *Mart Saar sõnas ja pildis* [Mart Saar in words and pictures] (Tallinn, 1973)

SVEN HANSELL

Sá Bacon, José Pereira de. See SANT'ANNA, JOSÉ PEREIRA DE.

Sabadini [Sabatini], **Bernardo** (*b* ?Venice; *d* Parma, 26 Nov 1718). Italian composer and organist. He was a member of the clergy. According to the libretto of his oratorio *I disegni della divina sapienza*, as quoted by the revisers of Allacci, he was a Venetian. He may be identical with the Don Bernardino Sabatini who in December 1673 was a singer at Urbino Cathedral. From 1 July 1681 he was organist at the Farnese court at Parma and on 1 March 1689 became *maestro di cappella* there; he was organist and 'resident' of the ducal church, S Maria della Steccata, from February 1689 and *maestro di cappella* from 1692. In January 1711 he received a benefice attached to that church. As court composer he was, from 1686 to 1700, responsible for the musical preparation of operas performed at the Novissimo Teatro Ducale, Parma, and the Nuovo Teatro Ducale, Piacenza (the second capital of the state), in collaboration with the court poets: Lotto Lotti until 1687, then Aurelio Aureli until 1694 and finally Giovanni Tamagni. Ferdinando Galli-Bibiena designed the scenography, Federico Crivelli the dances and Gasparo Torelli the costumes. With this team Ranuccio II Farnese raised the court operatic spectacles, until then episodic and somewhat provincial, to a level competitive with that of the major Italian theatre cities – Venice, Bologna, Rome and Naples. Aureli supplied a repertory consisting in large part of Venetian imports; later, operas of Neapolitan origin appeared. Sabadini, 'heroic composer of our times', often supplied only new arias. In the later years the success of the Farnese theatrical policy gained for him some productions outside the duchy, at Turin, Rome, Genoa and Pavia. The highpoint of his production, however, was the festivities for the marriage of Odoardo II Farnese and Dorothea Sophia of Neuburg-Pfalz in 1690. These Olympian and sumptuous spectacles reaped European fame for the

Bibiena family but even at the time provoked criticism from Italian intellectuals for the degradation that the dignity of the drama and the music supposedly underwent. A Gasparo Sabadini was court organist from 1696 to 1707.

WORKS
OPERAS
(music lost unless otherwise stated)

Furio Camillo (L. Lotti), Piacenza, 1686
Didio Giuliano (Lotti, from a Sp. orig.), Piacenza, 1687
Zenone il tiranno (Lotti), Piacenza, 1687, arias *I-MOe*
Olimpia placata (A. Aureli), Parma, 1687, rev. of Olimpia vendicata, Venice, 1682, music by D. Freschi
L'Ercole trionfante (G. A. Moniglia, twice rev. Aureli), Piacenza, 1688, rev. of Ercole in Tebe, Venice, 1671, music by G. A. Boretti; arias by Sabadini, *MOe*
Teseo in Atene (Aureli), Parma, 1688, rev. of Medea in Atene, Venice, 1676, music by Antonio Giannettini; arias *MOe*
Hierone tiranno di Siracusa (Aureli), Piacenza, 1688
Amor spesso inganna (Aureli), Piacenza, 1689, ?with some of A. Sartorio's music for orig. version as Orfeo, Venice, 1673
Teodora clemente (A. Morselli, Aureli), Piacenza, 1689, rev. of Teodora Augusta, Venice, 1686, music by Domenico Gabrielli; arias by ?Sabadini, *MOe*
Il Vespesiano (G. C. Corradi, rev. Aureli), Parma, 26 Dec 1689, rev. of orig., Venice, 1678, music by Carlo Pallavicino
La gloria d'Amore (Aureli), Parma, garden of Palazzo Ducale, 24 May 1690
Il favore degli dei (Aureli), Parma, 25 May 1690
Pompeo continente (Aureli), Piacenza, 1690
Diomede punito da Alcide (Aureli), Piacenza, 1691
La pace fra Tolomeo e Seleuco (Morselli, rev. Aureli), Piacenza, 1691, rev. of orig., Venice, 1691, music by C. F. Pollarolo; arias by ?Sabadini, *MOe*
Circe abbandonata da Ulisse (Aureli), Piacenza, 1692, arias, *MOe*
Il Massimino (Aureli), Parma, 1692, ? with some of Carlo Pallavicino's music for orig. version as Massimo Puppieno, Venice, 1685
Talestri innamorata d'Alessandro Magno (Aureli), Piacenza, 1693
Il riso nato fra il pianto (Aureli), Turin, Teatro Regio, 1694, *F-Pn*
Demetrio tiranno (Aureli), Piacenza, 1694
Furio Camillo (M. Noris), Parma, 1697, rev. of orig., Venice, 1692, music by G. A. Perti
La virtù trionfante dell'inganno (G. C. Godi), Piacenza, 1697, orig. perf. as Eraclea, Venice, 1696, music by an unknown composer
L'Aiace (A. d'Averara), Rome, Teatro Capranica, 1697, ?with some of the orig. music by C. A. Lonati, Paolo Magni and Francesco Ballarotti; arias by Sabadini, *GB-Lbm*
L'Eusonia, overo La dama stravagante ('Signori M. N. P. C.'), Rome, Teatro Capranica, 1697, ?rev. of Licinio imperatore (Noris), Venice, 1684, orig. music by Carlo Pallavicino, in which case 'P. C.' may be the reviser's initials; arias by Sabadini, *Lbm, Ob*
L'Alarico, Genoa, 1698
Il Domizio (G. C. Corradi), Genoa, 1698, ?with some of M. A. Ziani's music for orig. version, Venice, 1696
Il Ruggiero (G. Tamagni), Parma, 1699
L'Eraclea (S. Stampiglia), Parma, 1700, with some of Alessandro Scarlatti's music for orig. version, Naples, 1700
Il Meleagro, Pavia, 1705, with A. F. Martinenghi and Paolo Magni
Alessandro amante eroe, Genoa, 1706, arias *E-Mn*
Annibale, Genoa, 1706, arias *Mn*
La virtù coronata, o sia Il Fernando, Parma, 1714, attrib. Sabadini by Balestrieri

OTHER WORKS

I sogni regolati d'Amore, serenata, Parma, 1693, music lost
Italia consolata (G. Tamagni), introduzione al balletto, Parma, Teatrino di corte, 1696, music lost
I disegni della divina sapienza (C. F. Badia), oratorio, Venice, S Maria della Fava, 1698, music lost
Gl' amori d'Apollo e Dafne (G. Tamagni), introduzione al balletto, Parma, Teatrino di corte, 1699, music lost
Po, Imeneo, e Citerea, serenata, 3vv, vn, ob, *I-Bc*
Cantatas, *Fc*
Arias, *B-Bc* (according to Eitner), *GB-Lbm, Ob, I-BGc, Rvat*
Duet, *D-Bs*, wrongly attrib. Sabadini by Eitner
Fuga, *I-Bc*, ed. in AMI, iii (1907/*R*)

BIBLIOGRAPHY

EitnerQ; *FétisB*; *GerberL*; *SchmidlD*
L. Allacci: *Drammaturgia* (Venice, enlarged 2/1755/*R*1961)
G. Gaspari: *Catalogo della biblioteca del Liceo musicale di Bologna*, i–iv (Bologna, 1890–1905/*R*1961); v, ed. U. Sesini (Bologna, 1943/*R*1970)
L. Balestrieri: *Feste e spettacoli alla corte dei Farnesi: contributo alla storia del melodramma* (Parma, 1909)
O. G. T. Sonneck: *Library of Congress: Catalogue of Opera Librettos Printed before 1800* (Washington, 1914)
B. Ligi: 'La cappella musicale del duomo d'Urbino', *NA*, ii (1925), 116
N. Pelicelli: 'Musicisti in Parma nel secolo XVII', *NA*, ix (1932), 221, 245; x (1933), 44, 122, 316
A. Yorke-Long: *Music at Court* (London, 1954), 8ff
B. Becherini: 'Sabadini, Bernardo', *ES*
W. Dürr: 'Sabadino, Bernardo', *MGG*
L. Bianconi: 'L'Ercole in Rialto', *Venezia e il melodramma nel Seicento: Venezia 1972*, 259
C. Sartori: 'Bernardo Sabadini smascherato', *NRMI*, xi (1977), 44

LORENZO BIANCONI

Sabaneyev, Leonid Leonidovich (*b* Moscow, 1 Oct 1881; *d* Antibes, 3 May 1968). Russian musicologist and composer. He studied mathematics and physics, and in his early 20s entered the Moscow Conservatory, where he studied the piano with Zverev and P. J. Shlotsen, and composition with Taneyev. From 1906 he devoted himself wholly to music – to composition and particularly to musicology. He was always an ardent follower of contemporary trends. His writings are among the first to promote the music of Skryabin and extend his influence to the young. Within a short time he became the music critic and correspondent of many Russian and foreign periodicals: *Golos Moskvï*, *Russkoye slovo*, *Utro Rossii*, *Muzïka*, *Apollon*, *Muzïkalnïy sovremennik*, *Melos*, *Der blaue Ritter*, among others. His mathematical training led him to probe the more scientific aspects of music; his early writings include an influential series of theoretical works on harmony, rhythm, pitch, and the relationship between colour and sound. Much of his time was devoted to musical social work. He founded the Moscow Institute of Musicology, became chairman of the music section of the Russian Academy of Fine Arts, and was on the governing boards of numerous important teaching institutes.

Sabaneyev's views were highly respected in the first years of the new Soviet government. He became music editor of *Pravda* and *Izvestiya*, and was president of the forward-looking Association of Contemporary Music. After 1926 he lived abroad, in Germany, France, Britain and the USA. He settled for many years in Villeneuve-Laubet, then eventually in Nice. His historic study *Modern Russian Composers* (1927/*R*1975) has become an English-language classic. Among his compositions are the ballet *L'aviatrice* (Paris, Théâtre des Champs Elysées, 1928), a symphonic poem *Flots d'azur* (1936), an oratorio *The Revelation* (1940), a chaconne for organ and orchestra, two piano trios (1907, 1924), a violin sonata (1924), songs and many piano pieces.

WRITINGS

Evolyutsiya garmonicheskovo sozertsaniya [The evolution of the harmonic idea] (Petrograd, 1915)
Skryabin (Moscow, 1916, 2/1923)
Skryabin i yavleniye tsvetnovo slukha v svyazi so svetovoy simfoniyey 'Prometeya' [Skryabin and the phenomenon of sound colour in connection with his colour symphony *Prometheus*] (Petrograd, 1916)
'Ritm', *Melos*, i (Petrograd, 1917), 35–72
A. N. Skryabin (Moscow, 1922)
Klod Debyussi (Moscow, 1922)
Muzïka rechi: esteticheskoye issledovaniye [The music of speech: an aesthetic investigation] (Moscow, 1923)
ed.: *Pis'ma A. N. Skryabina* [Skryabin's letters] (Moscow, 1923)
'Psikhologiya muzïkal'no-tvorcheskovo protsessa' [The psychology of the process of musical composition], *Iskusstvo* (1923), no.1
Evreyskaya natsional'naya shkola v muzïke [The Jewish national school of music] (Moscow, 1924; Ger. trans., 1927)
Istoriya russkoy muzïki [History of Russian music] (Moscow, 1924; Ger. trans., 1926)
Moris Ravel': kharakteristika evo tvorcheskoy deyatel'nosti i ocherk evo zhizni [Ravel: a description of his creative activity and a sketch of his life] (Moscow, 1924)
Chto takoye muzïka [What music is] (Moscow, 1925, 2/1928)
Vospominaniya o Skryabina [Reminiscences of Skryabin] (Moscow, 1925)
Vseobshchaya istoriya muzïki [General history of music] (Moscow, 1925)
Muzïka posle Oktyabrya [Music after October] (Moscow, 1926)

Muzïka v klube: posobiye dlya klubnïkh rabotnikov [Music in the club: a textbook for workers' clubs] (Moscow, 1926)
Modern Russian Composers (New York, 1927/*R*1975)
Alexander Abramovich Kreyn (Moscow, 1928)
'The Jewish National School in Music', *MQ*, xv (1929), 448
'Musical Tendencies in Contemporary Russia', *MQ*, xvi (1930), 469
S. I. Taneyev: mïsli o tvorchestve i vospominaniya o zhizne [Taneyev: thoughts on his work and reminiscences of his life] (Paris, 1930)
Music for the Films (London, 1935)

RITA McALLISTER

Sabata, Victor de. *See* DE SABATA, VICTOR.

Sabatini, Bernardo. *See* SABADINI, BERNARDO.

Sabatino [Sabbatino, Sabatini], **Nicola** (*b* Naples, *c*1708; *d* Naples, 4 April 1796). Italian composer, son of Giovanni (Sebastiano) Sabatino (*b* Chieti, 1667; *d* Naples, 29 April 1742), a violinist in the Neapolitan royal chapel under Alessandro Scarlatti from 1691. Nicola attended the conservatory S Onofrio, where he studied the violin with Barbella and composition with Feo and Ignazio Prota. He then established himself as a composer of sacred and secular vocal music whose works were in demand in Naples and beyond; existing autograph manuscripts and performance dates attest to his creative activity between 1726 and 1774. In July 1742 he petitioned the King of Naples for the position as violinist in the royal chapel which his father had held until his death, but the post was given to Constantino Roberto, who had served the chapel for several years. In the 1750s Sabatino tried his hand at opera, writing *Cleante* for Rome and *Arsace* for Naples. In 1758 he succeeded G. Maraucci as *maestro di cappella* of the S Giacomo degli Spagnoli church in Naples, and in 1763 was appointed *maestro* at the Oratorio dei Filippini (Gerolamini), where he served until retiring in 1788.

Sabatino's contemporaries considered him a worthy composer. On Jommelli's death (25 August 1774), he was chosen from among the musicians of Naples to compose and conduct the music for the public funeral service. He was honoured by Padre Martini, who requested Sabatino's portrait for his collection, now in the Bologna Conservatory; it carries the inscription 'Nicolaus Sabbatino Napolitanus in sue civitatis oratorio aliisque principibus ecclesiis musici concentus magister'.

His brother Gioacchino (*b* Naples, *c*1718; *d* Naples, 16 June 1800) was a violinist in the royal chapel from 1756 until his death; a *Tota pulchra* for three voices (*I-Nc*) is attributed to him. Another brother, Francesco (*d* Naples, 6 May 1769), was also a violinist, and a priest.

WORKS
OPERAS
Cleante (opera seria), Rome, Argentina, 1752, score lost, several arias in *F-Pc*, *GB-Lbm*
Arsace (opera seria, A. Salvi), Naples, S Carlo, 30 May 1754

OTHER SECULAR VOCAL
(cantatas unless otherwise stated)
Deh, non turbarti o Nice, S, vns, *A-Wgm*, *D-MÜs*; Ma tu tremi, S, bc; Pieta vi suplico dolce Signore (Atto di contrizione), T, T, bc, *A-Wgm*; No, perdonami, o colri, S, vns, *I-Gi(l)*
Il giudizio del re Salomone, Foligno, 1746
La Natività del Santo Bambino, Naples, 1749, *I-Nc* [autograph score]
Endimione (serenata), Dublin, 1758
Several arias: *F-Pc*, *GB-Lbm*, *I-Mc*, *Nc*

ORATORIOS
Jaele, Genoa, 1740
L'aurora foriera della pace fra Giacobbe ed Esaú, Palermo, Congregazione dell'Oratorio, 1757
Debora e Sisaro, part i, *I-Nc*

SACRED VOCAL
5 masses (Ky–Gl) with insts: 4vv, 1726; 5vv, 1728; 9vv, *I-Nc* [autograph], *Mc*; 5vv, 1739, *D-MÜs*; 5vv, 1749, *GB-Lbm* [autograph]

Dixit Dominus, 5vv, insts, 1749 [autograph]; Dixit Dominus, 5vv, insts; De profundis, 2vv, vns; Domine ad adiuvandum; Magnificat, 5vv, insts, 1745 [autograph]; Magnificat, 5vv, insts: all *I-Nc*
5 motets [all autograph]: Letamini fideles, A, vns, bc; Nova luce, 5vv, insts; Ridet, S, insts; Salve coeli, 5vv, insts; Vola turtur de nido, S, insts, 1729; 2 Te Deum, 2vv, 5vv, insts: all *I-Nc*
Alma Redemptoris; Ave maris stella, 5vv, insts; Beati omnes, 4vv, insts; Christus e Miserere, 4vv, 5vv, org [also *Mc*, *Nc*]; Compieta, 4vv, vns; Graduale per S Filippo Neri; Hymn for 3rd Sunday in Sept, 4vv; In convertendo; 2 Inni; Jube Domine, S, insts; 7 lessons for Holy Week [2, 1740; 1, 1741]; Mottetto per l'elevazione, 4vv, bc; O oriens; O sapientia; Pange lingua; 4 Psalms [Credidi, Confitebor, Laudate pueri, Beatus vir]: all *I-Nf* [many autograph]
Qui tollis, B, vns [autograph]; 16 Tantum ergo with org/insts: all *I-Mc*
Atto di contrizione, T, insts, *A-Wgm*

INSTRUMENTAL
Sonata, vc, 2 vn, bc, *A-Wgm*; arr. fl, 2 vn, bc, lost, formerly *D-DS*

BIBLIOGRAPHY
BurneyH
C. A. de Rosa, Marchese di Villarosa: *Memorie di compositori di musica del regno di Napoli* (Naples, 1840)
S. Di Giacomo: 'La casa della musica: i Filippini di Napoli', *Napoli nobilissima*, new ser., ii (1921)
G. Sorge: *I teatri di Palermo* (Palermo, 1926)
U. Prota-Giurleo: *La grande orchestra del R. Teatro San Carlo nel Settecento* (Naples, 1927)
——: *Il teatro di corte del palazzo reale di Napoli* (Naples, 1952)

HANNS-BERTOLD DIETZ

Sabbatini, Galeazzo (*b* ?Pesaro, 1597; *d* Pesaro, 6 Dec 1662). Italian composer. It is not known whether he was related to P. P. Sabbatini. He studied with Vincenzo Pellegrini when the latter was a canon of Pesaro Cathedral and was himself elected to this position in 1626, remaining in it until 1630. From then until 1639 he was *maestro di cappella* at the court of the Duke of Mirandola, and from 1641 he was again a canon at Pesaro Cathedral. In the interim he may have lived at Bergamo, for in 1639 there was a plan to have him appointed to the vacant choirmastership at S Maria Maggiore there; this was, however, rejected by the church authorities. He visited Rome in 1652–3 and 1657–9.

In his sacred music, which consists mainly of motets, Sabbatini shows a preference for small concertato textures, and his last collection is of solo pieces. Most of the *Sacrae laudes* of 1626 are duet and trio motets with continuo; the four- and five-part pieces are somewhat fragmentary in texture and humdrum in contrapuntal procedure. Whereas Sabbatini seems to have been uninterested in structural refrains and did not follow the fashionable trend towards triple time, his bass lines are interesting and mainly slow-moving, and his melodies vary between simple utterance and declamatory ornamentation, often flowering into a climax at the close of a piece. In his madrigals too he shows a preference for smaller textures. The last two collections include some pieces with string parts, most of them belonging to the genre of the strophic canzonet. One of these (1630) is prefaced by a sonata that is also intended as a ritornello; another (1636) is founded on a popular ground bass. The madrigals proper contain elaborate vocal lines of the kind encountered in Sabbatini's motets.

Sabbatini was also something of a theorist: he published a manual on continuo playing and was praised by Kircher for his scientific knowledge of music; this was with reference to a tuning method he had devised in which the tone was divided into five.

WORKS
(all published in Venice)
SACRED
Sacrae laudes, 2–5vv, bc (org), liber 1, op.3 (1626)
Sacrarum laudum, 3–5vv, bc (org), liber II, op.7 (1637)

Deiparae virginis laudes, 3–6vv, op.8 (1638)
Sacrae lodi: concerti, 1v, bc, op.9 (1640)
Motets in 1628³, 1638¹, 1641³, 1642⁴, 1646², 1646³, 1646⁴, 1 motet
and 1 mass in R. Scarselli, Sacrarum modulationum . . . liber I, 2–
4vv, bc (org) (Venice, 1637)
Motet, D-Bds

SECULAR

Il primo libro di madrigali . . . concertati, 2–4vv, op.1 (1625)
Il secondo libro di madrigali concertati, 2–4vv . . . 2 vn, op.2 (1626)
Madrigali concertati, 5vv, con alcuni canzoni concertati con sinfonie e
ritornelli, libro III, op.4 (1627)
Madrigali concertati, 2–5vv, con alcuni canzoni, libro IV, op.5 (1630)
Madrigali concertati, 2–4vv, con alcune canzonette concertate, libro V,
op.6 (1636)
1 madrigal, 1653⁴; 1 madrigal, S-Uu

THEORETICAL WORKS

Regola facile e breve per sonare sopra il basso continuo nell'organo,
manacordo o altro simile stromento (Venice, 1628)

BIBLIOGRAPHY

EitnerQ
A. Kircher: Musurgia universalis (Rome, 1650/R1970)
F. T. Arnold: The Art of Accompaniment from a Thorough-bass
(London, 1931/R1965)

JEROME ROCHE

Sabbatini, Luigi Antonio (*b* Albano Laziale, nr. Rome,
?1732; *d* Padua, 29 Jan 1809). Italian theorist and
composer. His earliest dated work, *Benedictus sit Deus*
for two voices and continuo (in *D-MÜs*), was composed
in his 13th year and indicates that he had received a
strong grounding in music before he became a pupil of
Martini in Bologna. It is generally supposed that his
studies with Martini coincided with his eight years'
residence at the monastery of St Francis in Bologna.
Eitner claimed that he became a Franciscan around
1759, but most other lexicographers state that he joined
the order in the early 1750s. 202 letters to Martini
(autographs in *I-Bc*) written between 2 June 1764 and
17 March 1784 reveal that by 1764 he was no longer
Martini's pupil. They do not substantiate the claim that
he later studied with F. A. Vallotti in Padua (further
letters are in *I-Baf, Bsf, Pca*).

On 28 November 1767 Sabbatini became *maestro di
cappella* at the basilica of S Barnaba in Marino, near his
birth place; his friendship with the Franciscan Cardinal
Ganganelli, later Pope Clement XIV, may have helped
him to obtain this post, as well as one at the Franciscan
basilica of the Twelve Holy Apostles in Rome, to which
he was appointed on 20 April 1772. Late in life Vallotti
is supposed to have named Sabbatini his successor as
maestro di cappella at the basilica of S Antonio, Padua.
But after Vallotti's death Sabbatini recommended
Agostino Ricci, who served from 1780 to 1786. Sabbatini was then invited again to become *maestro*; he was
nominated unanimously on 22 April 1786 and served
from 18 June until his death. In May 1807 he was
elected a member of the music group of the Accademia
Italiana.

All Sabbatini's known music is sacred; much of it is
in the orchestrally accompanied style of the day, but
some is in a learned style using cantus firmus or strict
contrapuntal devices such as canon and fugue. Of his
own musical works only the short *Atto di contrizione*
for two sopranos and continuo was published in his
lifetime, but in 1803 he published an edition of
Benedetto Marcello's psalm settings *Estro poetico-
armonico*. His several published treatises on music place
him beside F. A. Calegari, Vallotti and Tartini as an
important theorist of the Paduan school and reflect his
interest in their work. His manuscript *Trattato di contrappunto* explains Tartini's *terzo suono* and Calegari's

and Vallotti's theory of chord inversion (he made a copy,
in *I-Pn*, of Calegari's *Ampla dimostrazione degli
armoniali musicali tuoni*). His study of Vallotti resulted
in a biographical sketch published in 1780, and in his
most important treatise, *Trattato sopra le fughe
musicali*, in which he analysed Vallotti's so-called real,
tonal and imitative fugues with the aid of two-, three-
and four-part music examples. Musicians in Padua and
Venice praised the work, and the governing board of S
Antonio awarded Sabbatini a gold medal and named
him Vallotti's true successor. Unlike the other Paduan
theorists, he had an interest in the elementary instruction of children in music. In 1781 he endorsed Gennaro
Catalisano's *Grammatica armonica, fisico-matematica
. . . per uso della gioventù studiosa*, and in 1789 and
1790 he published his *Elementi teorici della musica*
with numerous duets and trios, with and without bass,
for teaching beginners. Although Tebaldini considered
his method of setting simple precepts to music childish,
his contemporaries approved, and the book was
reprinted in 1795; the music examples were published
separately as *Solfèges ou leçons élémentaires de
musique* in Paris in 1810 and 1834.

WRITINGS

Notizie sopra la vita e le opere del rev. P. F. A. Vallotti (Padua, 1780)
Elementi teorici della musica colla pratica dei medesimi, in duetti e
terzetti a canone accompagnati dal basso (Rome, 1789–90)
'Brevi memorie intorno alla vita e agli studi del P. Francesco Antonio
Vallotti', in F. Fanzago: Elogi di tre uomini illustri Tartini, Vallotti, e
Gozzi (Padua, 1792), 96
La vera idea delle musicali numeriche segnature diretta al giovane
studioso dell'armonia (Venice, 1799)
Trattato sopra le fughe musicali di L. A. Sabbatini corredato da copiosi
saggi del suo antecessore F. A. Vallotti (Venice, 1802)
Solfèges ou leçons élémentaires de musique (Paris, 1810, 2/1834) [con-
sists chiefly of music examples from Elementi teorici]

Studi di contrappunto fatti alla scuola del Padre Martini (MS, I-Bc)
Esame d'uno scolaro del Padre L. A. Sabbatini (MS, I-Bc)
Trattato di contrappunto (inc. MSS, I-Pca, Vnm)
Canoni sui principi elementari (2 MSS, I-Mc)
Trascritto ad litteram nell'anno 1791 dal P. L. A. Sabbatini (MS, A-
Wn)

WORKS

(* – incl. autograph)

Masses: 5, 4vv, org, A-Wn, I-VId; 1, 8vv, org, Pca; 1 for Palm Sunday
and Good Friday, 4vv, Pca; 1 for Holy Week, 4vv, Pca (Kyrie–
Sanctus–Agnus Dei)
Messe brevi: 6, 4vv, org, D-Mbs, *I-Pca (2 inc.); 4, 4vv, str, org, Pca; 1,
4vv, 2 vc, 2 db, 2 org, Ac; 1, 8vv, str, org, Pca; 1, 4vv, *Bc
Mass movements: Kyrie–Gloria, 4vv, org, Pca; 21 Kyrie, 4vv, str, org,
Pca; 5 Kyrie, 1, 4vv, str, bc, *Bc, *Bsf, Pca; 10 Gloria, 4vv, str, 8
with org, *Bc, Pca; 20 Credo, 4vv, str, org, Bc, Pca, Vnm; Credo
breve, 4vv, str, 2 org, Ac; 5 other mass movts, 4vv, str, org, Bc, *Bsf,
Pca
2 requiems, 4vv, org, Pca; 2 Messe pei defunti, 8vv, str, 2 org, Pca; 4
requiem movts, 4vv, str, org, Pca
Introits: 29 for Advent, Lent, 4vv, org; 47, 4vv, org, 1 with str, 1
unacc.; 6 (inc.): Pca
Graduals, mostly 4vv, 3 with str; tracts for Advent, Lent, Palm
Sunday, 4vv; Stabat mater, 4vv, org: Pca
Responses: for Holy Thursday, Good Friday, 4vv; 3 Si quaeris, 4vv,
org; 2 Si quaeris, 8vv, 2 org (ad lib): Pca
Offertories: for Advent, Lent, Good Friday, Palm Sunday, 4vv, Pca; 19
Domine ad adjuvandum, 4, 8vv, str, org, *Bc, Pca; Benedictus sit
Deus, 2vv, bc (org), D-MÜs; offertory, 4vv, I-Vnm
3 communions for Advent, Good Friday, Ember Days, 4vv, Pca
Antiphons: 4 Alma Redemptoris, 1, 4, 8vv, str, 1 with org; 3 Ave
regina, 1, 4, 8vv, str, 1 with org, Pca; 3 Regina coeli, 4, 8vv, str,
1 with org, Pca; 3 Salve regina, 4, 8vv, str, org, Pca; 7 vesper antiphons, 1–4, 8vv, 4 with str, Pca; 4 for BVM, 4vv, str, org, Pca; 9 others,
1–4, 8vv, str, org, Pca
35 hymns, 1–4, 8vv, org, 6 with str, Ac, *Bc, Pca; compline hymns with
antiphons, 4vv, str, org, Pca
Canticles: 9 Magnificat, 4, 5, 8vv, str, org, Pca; 3 Magnificat, 8vv, str, 2
hn, org, Pca; Magnificat breve, 4vv, *Bc; Nunc dimittis, 4vv, str, *Bc
Psalms: 81, 1–4, 8vv, insts, org, *Bc, Pc, Pca; Salmi per tutto l'anno,
4vv, org, VId; for Terce, 4vv, orch, org, Pc, Pca, VId; for Vespers, 3,

4vv, str, org, *Pca*, *Vnm*; for Compline, 4, 8vv, str, org, *Pca*; others, 4vv, str, org, *BGc*, *Vnm*
Atto di contrizione: Pietà di supplico, 2vv, bc (n.p., n.d.)
Other sacred vocal works, incl. 19 fugues, 2–4, 8vv, org, 2 with str, *D-MÜs*, *I-Ac*, *Bc*, **Bsf*, *Mc*, *Pc*, *Pca*, *Vnm*
ed.: B. Marcello: Estro poetico-armonico (Venice, 1803)

BIBLIOGRAPHY

EitnerQ; *FétisB*; *GerberNL*; *SchmidlD*
G. Della Valle: *Memorie storiche di P. M. Giambattista Martini* (Naples, 1785), 123
'Miscellen', *AMZ*, vi (1804), 391
C. Gervasoni: *Nuova teoria di musica* (Parma, 1812), 258ff
P. Lichtenthal: *Dizionario* (Milan, 1826), iv, 113, 262, 366
M. Balbi, ed.: *Trattato del sistema armonico di Antonio Calegari* (Padua, 1829)
G. Gonzati: *La basilica di S Antonio di Padova descritta ed illustrata* (Padua, 1853), ii, 453
A. Isnenghi: *La cappella musicale della basilica di S Antonio* (Padua, 1854), 456
A. de la Fage: *Essais de diphthérographie, ou Notices, descriptions, analyses, extraits* (Paris, 1864/*R*1964), 95ff
A. Capanna: *Cenni cronologici dei maestri di musica Minori Conventuali che dal 1487 fino all'anno 1874 ... nelle varie cappelle di Assisi, Padova, Bologna* (MS, *I-Bsf*)
E. Colombani: *Catalogo della collezione d'autografi lasciata alla R. Accademia filarmonica di Bologna* (Bologna, 1881/*R*1969), 355f
L. Busi: *Il padre G. B. Martini* (Bologna, 1891/*R*1961), 304ff, 311
G. Tebaldini: *L'archivio musicale della Cappella Antoniana di Padova* (Padua, 1895), 80ff, 111ff, 147
D. Sparacio: 'Musicisti minori conventuali', *Miscellanea francescana*, xxv (1925), 100
C. Stainer: 'Sabbatini, Luigi Antonio', *Grove 5*
U. Prota-Giurleo: 'Sabbatini, Luigi Antonio', *MGG*
R. Schaal, ed.: *Die Tonkünstler-Porträts der Wiener Musiksammlung von Aloys Fuchs* (Wilhelmshaven, 1970), 45

SVEN HANSELL

Sabbatini, Pietro Paolo (*b* Rome, *c*1600; *d* Rome, after 1657). Italian composer and teacher. It is not known whether he was related to Galeazzo Sabbatini. He appears to have spent his life in Rome. In his youth he was probably a chorister there and in 1614 appeared in the allegorical role of the 'Età dell'Oro' ('Golden Age') in the opera *L'Amor pudico*, performed at the Palazzo della Cancelleria. In 1628 he was choirmaster of the Arciconfraternità della Morte et Orazione. He held a similar position at S Luigi dei Francesi in 1630 and until no later than 1 May 1631, when Vincenzo Ugolini was appointed to it. His later publications give no clear indication of his subsequent career, although he seems to have derived at least part of his income from teaching: in his 1650 book, which includes instruction in continuo playing for beginners, he styled himself 'professore di musica'; the music of *Il quarto de villanelle* was collected for publication by one of his pupils, Pietro Simi, and dedicated to another, Girolamo Cosci; his 1641 book includes a trio by another pupil, Giovanni Domenico Rutulini; and Dante Anodaro and Simon Corsi, who are each represented by one song in *Il terzo*, may also have been pupils. He composed quite a large amount of music, much of which is lost; several of his books were reprinted during his lifetime. His surviving output consists mainly of short strophic songs, spiritual as well as secular, some of which are moderately attractive. His 1630 book, by contrast, contains music for double choir and organ. The *Intermedii spirituali*, a set of three dialogues for soloists and chorus, were probably written for performance at the Oratorio della Morte.

WORKS

(all printed works published in Rome unless otherwise stated)

SACRED

Intermedii spirituali ... libro primo, op.9 (1628)
Psalmi, Magnificat cum 4 antiphonis ad Vespera, cum letaniis B. vir-
ginis, liber primus, 8vv, bc (org), op.12 (1630); 3 ed. J. A. Latrobe, *A Selection of Sacred Music* (London, 1806–26)
Canzoni spirituali ... libro secondo, 1–3vv, bc, op.13 (1640)
Villanelle spirituali, in diversi stili ... libro quarto, 1, 2vv, bc, op.20 (1657)
Ariette spirituali, in diversi stili ... libro quinto, 1–3vv, bc, op.21 (1657)
Linguae ardentes, motet, *GB-Lcm*

SECULAR

Il sesto [libro], 1–3vv, op.8 (Bracciano, 1628)
Il terzo [libro de villanelle], 1–3vv (1631[5])
Il quarto [libro] de villanelle, 1–3vv (1631)
Varii caprici: canzonette ... con l'alfabeto della chitarra spagnola ... libro settimo, 1, 3vv, op.14 (1641) [incl. 1 piece by G. D. Rutulini]
Prima scelta di villanelle, delli dieci libri ... con l'alfabeto della chitarra spagnola, 1v (1652) [possibly not 1st edn.; incl. reprs. of pieces from above and lost vols.]
Seconda scelta di villanelle, delli dieci libri ... con l'alfabeto della chitarra spagnola, 1v (1652) [possibly not 1st edn.; incl. reprs. of pieces from above and lost vols.]
Prima scelta di villanelle ... con le lettere accomodate alla chitarra spagnola (1652) [incl. some reprs.]
1 piece, 1v, bc, 1622[11]

THEORETICAL WORKS

Toni ecclesiastici colle sue intonationi, all'uso romano: modo per sonare il basso continuo, chiavi corrispondenti all'altre chiavi generali, et ordinarie ... libro primo, op.18 (1650)

BIBLIOGRAPHY

G. O. Pitoni: *Notitia de contrapuntisti e de compositori di musica* (MS, *I-Rvat* C.G., I/1–2, *c*1725)
D. Alaleona: *Studi su la storia dell'oratorio musicale in Italia* (Turin, 1908, 2/1945 as *Storia dell'oratorio musicale in Italia*), 158f
R. Lunelli: 'Le opere di Orlando di Lasso nel Trentino', *NA*, iii (1926), 209

JOHN WHENHAM

Sabbatino, Nicola. *See* SABATINO, NICOLA.

Sabine, Wallace C(lement Ware) (*b* Richwood, Ohio, 13 June 1868; *d* Cambridge, Mass., 10 Jan 1919). American acoustician. He studied at Ohio State University and Harvard, where he taught physics from 1890; between 1895 and 1919 he laid the foundations of architectural acoustics on the basic principles of engineering design. Charles William Eliot, president of Harvard, prevailed on Sabine to try to correct the serious problem of reverberation in the lecture hall of the Fogg Art Museum, his first acoustical project. At Eliot's urging he also served as consultant for the Boston Music Hall: his outstanding success there illustrated the effects that could be achieved when acoustical engineering design preceded construction. Sabine's discovery of the relation among reverberation time, absorbent capacity and the volume of an auditorium was a fundamental and new contribution; he earned a lasting reputation for the scope and perception of his work. It is indeed appropriate that the unit of sound-absorbing power is named the 'sabine'. His *Collected Papers on Acoustics* was published posthumously (Cambridge, Mass., 1922/*R*1964).

See also ACOUSTICS, §I, 11.

JAMES F. BELL

Sabini, Ippolito. *See* SABINO, IPPOLITO.

Sabini [Sabino], **Nicola** (*b* ?Naples, *c*1675; *d* Naples, 1705). Italian composer. He was an important figure in the early development of Neapolitan *opera buffa*. After studying with Angelo Durante at the Conservatory of S Onofrio, he succeeded Durante in May 1699 as first *maestro di cappella* there, with a monthly salary of six ducats. He left this position in 1702, perhaps because of illness; he died of tuberculosis.

Sabini's historically most interesting work was his

scherzo drammatico, *Il mondo abbatuto* (text, S. de Falco), written in 1701 for the Feast of S Casimiro and performed for the Congregazione de Musici, of which he was a member, in the Church of S Giorgio Maggiore of the Pii Operarii Fathers. This comedy, of which the music has been lost, adumbrates later developments of the Neapolitan commercial comic theatre, with its mixture of Tuscan and Neapolitan dialect. Another dialect work, 'Cantata in lingua napoletana' *Non cchiù Ciccillo mio*, is in *I-Nc*. He also wrote a sacred opera, *Innocenza trionfale* (S. Stampiglia, 1704; music lost), and *Canzone a voce sola per la Purificazione della Vergine* (1696, *I-Nf*).

BIBLIOGRAPHY
S. Di Giacomo: *I quattro antichi conservatorii musicali di Napoli* i, (Milan and Naples, 1924), 70f, 134, 146
U. Prota-Giurleo: 'L'Eco del Parnasso', *Francesco Durante* (Naples, 1955), 17

JAMES L. JACKMAN

Sabinina, Marina Dmitriyevna (*b* Petrograd, 10 Sept 1917). Soviet musicologist. She graduated in 1948 from the faculty of theory and composition at Moscow Conservatory, and in 1951 completed her postgraduate studies there under R. I. Gruber. From 1952 to 1957 she was in charge of a section of the journal *Sovetskaya muzïka*, and in 1960 became a senior research fellow at the Institute for the History of the Arts. In 1974 she was awarded a doctorate for her published works on Shostakovich. Sabinina's writings are devoted mainly to Soviet music and particularly to the works of Prokofiev and Shostakovich.

WRITINGS
Sergey Prokof'yev (Moscow, 1958)
Dmitry Shostakovich (Moscow, 1959)
'Ob opernom stile Prokof'yeva' [Prokofiev's opera style], *Sergey Prokof'yev: stat'i i materialï*, ed. I. V. Nest'yev and G. Ya. Edel'man (Moscow, 1962), 54–93
'Semyon Kotko' i problemï opernoy dramaturgii Prokof'yeva [*Semyon Kotko* and the problems of Prokofiev's dramatic writing] (Moscow, 1963)
Simfonizm Shostakovicha: put' k zrelosti [Shostakovich's symphonies: his path to maturity] (Moscow, 1965)
'Voyna i mir' S. Prokof'yeva i evo tvorchestvo poslednikh let' [Prokofiev's *War and Peace* and the works of his later years], *Sovetskaya muzïka: stat'i i materialï*, ed. M. A. Grinberg and others (Moscow, 1965), 29
'Zametki ob opere *Katerina Izmaylova*' [Notes on the opera *Katerina Izmaylova*], *Dmitry Shostakovich*, ed. G. Sh. Ordzhonikidze (Moscow, 1967), 132–65
'Zametki o 14-y simfonii Shostakovicha' [Notes on Shostakovich's 14th symphony], *SovM* (1970), no.9, p.22
'RSFSR: tvorchestvo russkikh kompozitorov: opera, balet, operetta' [Russian opera, ballet and operetta], *Istoriya muzïki narodov SSSR*, ii, ed. Yu. V. Keldïsh (Moscow, 1970), 33–95
'Russkaya opera', *Istoriya muzïki narodov SSSR*, iii, ed. Yu. V. Keldïsh (Moscow, 1972), 200–34
'Operetta', *Istoriya muzïki narodov SSSR*, iv, ed. Yu. V. Keldïsh (Moscow, 1973), 157
Shostakovich – simfonist: dramaturgiya, estetika, stil' [Shostakovich the symphonist: dramatic qualities, aesthetic and style] (Moscow, 1976)

YURY KELDÏSH

Sabino. Italian family of musicians.

(1) Giovanni Maria Sabino (*b* Turi, nr. Bari, late 16th century; *d* Naples, April 1649). Composer, organist and teacher. He received his musical education from Prospero Testa in Naples, where he settled permanently and was ordained priest. On 4 September 1622 he became a teacher of music and singing at the Conservatorio di S Maria della Pietà dei Turchini, a post that he held until the end of 1626. In the following year he became *maestro di cappella* of the royal church of S Barbara in Castelnuovo. He next was organist to the Congregazione Filippina at the church of the Gerolamini from 1630 to 1634. From the latter year until his death he was *maestro di cappella* of the church of the Annunziata; he also played the organ there. He was a notable teacher of music; Gregorio Strozzi, Giovanni Salvatore and Francesco Provenzale were among the numerous pupils at his school.

WORKS
(*all printed works published in Naples*)
Salmi di compieta, 4vv (1620)
Il secondo libro delli mottetti, 2–4vv (1626) [sic], according to *EitnerQ*
Il primo libro delli mottetti, 2vv (1627)
Psalmi de vespere, 4vv (1627)

1 motet in 1624³
4 motets, 1v, bc, in 1625?
Cantatas; 1 galliard, 4vv: ?*I-Na*

(2) Antonino [Antonio] **Sabino** (*b* ?Naples, late 16th or early 17th century; *d* Naples, July 1650). Composer, organist and teacher, brother of (1) Giovanni Maria Sabino. He was a priest and spent his life in Naples. In October 1635 he was appointed organist of the church of the Annunziata, where his brother (1) Giovanni Maria Sabino was *maestro di cappella*. From May 1642 he held the additional appointment of *maestro di cappella* of the Conservatorio dei Poveri di Gesù Cristo, where he taught music and singing. As a composer, he is known only by an eight-part mass and Vespers for two choirs and organ and a *Salve regina* for eight voices with instruments (possibly in the Archivio dell'Annunziata, Naples).

(3) Francesco Sabino (*b* ?Naples, early 17th century). Teacher, brother of (1) Giovanni Maria Sabino. He lived for a long time in Naples, where he achieved wide fame as an excellent teacher, particularly of singing, which he always taught privately.

BIBLIOGRAPHY
S. Di Giacomo: *I quattro antichi conservatorii musicali di Napoli* (Milan and Naples, 1924–8), i, 188, 204, 299, 310; ii, 145, 150, 154
Registro delle conclusioni for 1635, 1649 and 1650 (MS, *I-Na*)

ARGIA BERTINI

Sabino, Giovanni Francesco. Italian musician, son of IPPOLITO SABINO.

Sabino [Sabini], **Ippolito** (*b* Lanciano, *c*1550; *d* Lanciano, 25 Aug 1593). Italian composer; Giovanni Maria Sabino was probably related to him. Although he published 14 volumes of music, and single pieces by him appeared in about 30 collections between 1566 and 1619, very little is known about his career. He seems to have lived at his birthplace. The dedication of his *Magnificat* settings of 1587 to the canons and chapter of the church at Lanciano led Eitner to conclude that he was probably *maestro di cappella* there. This is plausible, though Sabino referred to himself simply as 'musician of Lanciano'. He addressed most of his dedications from Lanciano to local noblemen. His first published pieces – *Pietosi miei lamenti* and *I' piango ed ella*, the second a setting of the *commiato* of Petrarch's canzone *Quando il soave* (a poem that he later set in its entirety) – appeared in Rore's fifth book of five-part madrigals. Both pieces belong to the polyphonic tradition, frequently employing double points of imitation and relying on skilful contrapuntal craftsmanship rather than on the chromatic writing characteristic of Rore. Sabino continued to write within the same tradition. He preferred six- and seven-part contrapuntal writing to lighter sonorities, but his later madrigals show an increasing use of chordal declamation for contrast. His harmonic language remained diatonic and unaffected by mannerist tendencies. In the preface to the second book of six-part madrigals (1581), Oratio Crisci indicated that he was a pupil of Sabino and that he wished to show his esteem for him by editing a selection of both his own and his teacher's works. The relationship between the two must have continued, for further madrigals by Crisci appeared in Sabino's volumes of 1587 and 1589[16]. His son Giovanni Francesco Sabino is represented by four madrigals in the same books.

WORKS
(all published in Venice)

SACRED VOCAL
Misse sex, 4vv (1575)
Hymni per totum annum, 4vv (1582)
Canticum divae Mariae, liber secundus, 4vv (1583)
Liber secundus missarum, 4vv (1584)
Magnificat omnitonum . . . liber primus, 5vv (1587)

SECULAR VOCAL
Il primo libro de madrigali, 5vv (1570)
Madrigali . . . libro primo, 6vv (1579)
Madrigali . . . libro secondo, 5vv (1580)
Il secondo libro de madrigali, 6vv (1581[11])
Il terzo libro de madrigali, 5, 6vv (1582)
Il quarto libro de madrigali, 4–8vv (1585)
Il quinto libro de madrigali, 5, 6vv (1586)
Il sesto libro de madrigali, 5, 6vv (1587[13])
Il settimo libro de madrigali, 5, 6vv (1589[16])
Further sacred and secular vocal works, 1566[17], 1568[19], 1582[15], 1583[14], 1585[19], 1586[9], 1589[8], 1590[11], 1590[17], 1591[10], 1592[11], 1592[15], 1593[4], 1596[8], 1597[6], 1597[13], 1598[8], 1598[15], 1600[5a], 1600[8], 1601[5], 1601[18], 1605[9], 1606[5], 1606[8], 1609[15], 1610[10], 1612[13], 1619[16]
Several madrigals, D-As, Mbs, PL-WRu

BIBLIOGRAPHY
EitnerQ
A. Einstein: *The Italian Madrigal* (Princeton, 1949/R1971)

PATRICIA ANN MYERS

Sabino, Nicola. *See* SABINI, NICOLA.

Sabkha. Ancient Jewish musical instrument, mentioned in *Daniel*; see JEWISH MUSIC, §I, 4(iv).

Sable, Antoine de la. *See* ARENA, ANTONIUS DE.

Sablières, Jean Granouilhet [Grenouillet], Sieur de (*b* Languedoc, 1627; *d* Paris, *c*1700). French composer. In 1652 he entered the service of Philippe, Duke of Orleans, whose *Maître et intendant de la musique de chambre* he became in 1669. In 1671, to a libretto by Henry Guichard, he composed a pastoral opera, *Les amours de Diane et d'Endymion*, which was revived at St Germain-en-Laye in 1672 under the title *Le triomphe de l'amour*; the music is lost. Also in 1671 he formed an association with Pierre Perrin to exploit with the collaboration of Guichard a share of the privilege that the king had granted Perrin for opera performances. But in 1672 Lully bought back from Perrin the entire privilege for the direction of the Académie Royale de Musique, and Sablières had thus to abandon this activity. In 1679 he was summoned to Languedoc to direct the music that formed part of the festivities organized at Pézenas and Montpellier to mark the signing of the peace treaty with Spain. He produced there 'a very pleasing sort of opera', an aristocratic divertissement celebrating the two nations, to a text by M. de Bray, given under the auspices of Cardinal de Bonsy, Archbishop of Narbonne. The music for this too is lost, as also are several songs by him to poems by Perrin. In fact his only extant pieces are six solo *airs de cour* in *F-Pn* Vm[a] 854 and others for two voices and continuo in the anthology *IIe livre d'airs de différents autheurs . . .* (Paris, 1659[4]); they include songs for 'Madame' (the Duchess of Orleans) and drinking-songs.

BIBLIOGRAPHY
A. Pougin: *Les vrais créateurs de l'opéra français* (Paris, 1881)
C. Nuitter and E. Thoinan: *Les origines de l'opéra français* (Paris, 1886/R)

MARCELLE BENOIT

Saboly, Nicolas (*b* Monteux, baptized 31 Jan 1614; *d* Avignon, 25 July 1675). Provençal poet and composer. In 1628 he joined the Congregation of the Annunciation at the Jesuit College at Carpentras and in 1630 received the first tonsure. From 1628 to 1634 he studied at Avignon University. He was ordained priest in 1635. He was *maître de chapelle* at Carpentras Cathedral from 1639 to 1643, at Arles from 1643 to 1646, at Aix from 1652 to 1655, at Nîmes from 1659 and at St Pierre, Avignon, from 1668 to his death. He was awarded the degree of bachelor of laws by Avignon University in 1658. His reputation in Provence rests on his noëls, which he published (at first anonymously) in a series of booklets from 1668 to 1674. These include 62 in Provençal (two of which are described as 'Noé viei') and seven in French. They were designed to be sung to secular *airs* popular at the time, some of which are taken from Lully's operas. At the present day some of the noëls are sung to tunes other than those that Saboly prescribed. A complete edition of the Provençal noëls was published in 1699. Their liveliness, combined with a certain amount of local colour, has ensured their survival. Two motets and two masses are attributed to Saboly, but he is not otherwise known as a composer.

BIBLIOGRAPHY
J. A. Westrup: 'Nicolas Saboly and his "Noëls Provençaux" ', *ML*, xxi (1940), 34

JACK WESTRUP

Ṣabrá, Wadí' (*b* Beirut, 23 Feb 1876; *d* Beirut, 11 April 1952). Lebanese composer, organist and theoretician. He studied at the Syrian Protestant College in Beirut and from 1893 at the Paris Conservatoire, where he was a pupil of Lavignac (harmony), Lenepveu (composition), Widor and Guilmant (organ) and Bourgault-Ducoudray (history). After working as an organist at several churches in Paris (1893–1900) and at St Esprit (1902–10) he left for Istanbul to present his Turkish national hymn to the sultan. Later in 1910 he returned to Beirut, where he founded the Dār al-Mūsīqā (school of music). He went back to Paris after World War I and there collaborated with Gustave Lyon in studies of the Arabian scale, the ultimate aim being the construction of a piano according to their plans. The instrument was made and introduced into the Lebanon by Ṣabrá in 1922; the firm of Pleyel produced an electric model. After residing in Egypt for some time, Ṣabrá was recalled to the Lebanon as director of the National Conservatory (1925). He received from the French government the Palmes Académiques and the Rosette d'Officier de l'Instruction Publique, and in 1948 he was made a Chevalier de la Légion d'honneur.

Through his work in reforming scales, Western as well as Arabian, Ṣabrá sought to unite the oriental homophonic with the European harmonic system. In 1944 he convened a Universal Musical Congress in Beirut, at which he demonstrated the value of a system which, he claimed, 'opens a new era in musical science'. He composed three operas: *The Shepherds of Canaan* (the first opera in Turkish, text by Halide Edib Hanun), *The Two Kings* (the first opera in Arabic, text by Marun Ghusn) and *L'émigré* (in French). His other works include the oratorio *Le chant de Moïse*, the cantata *Les voix de Noël*, 20 Lebanese folksong arrangements and the national anthem of Lebanon.

WRITINGS
Congrès de musique arabe du Caire: considérations et conclusions (Beirut, 1932)
Nouvelle unité de mesure des intervalles musicaux: gamme universelle (Beirut, 1936)
'Le procès de la gamme mineure', *Revue d'acoustique*, v (1936)
Exposé d'un nouveau système perfectionné de partage des 12 demi-tons de l'octave (Beirut, 1940)
La musique arabe: base de l'art occidental (Beirut, 1941)
Congrès musical universel (Beirut, 1944)
Tonalités en usage sous la dynastie abbasside et recherches des orientalistes sur la matière (Beirut, 1947)

H. G. FARMER/R

Sacabuche (Old Sp.). TROMBONE.

Sacadas [Sakadas] **of Argos** (*fl* *c*580 BC). Greek aulos player and poet. He wrote lyric and elegiac poems, but none has survived. He provided his elegiac verses with musical settings (during the central classical period elegy had no accompaniment). According to Plutarch (*De musica*, chap.8, p.1134*a–b*; ix, 1134*c*; xii, 1135*c*) he was a skilled aulete who three times carried off the prize at the Pythian games, beginning in 586 BC. The reawakening of musical culture at Sparta, after Terpander's great initial changes, was ascribed to Sacadas and a few others who kept the exalted Terpandrian manner but introduced new rhythms.

Pausanias's *Description of Greece* (ii, chap.22, §8f; iv, 27, 7; vi, 14, 9f; ix, 30, 2; x, 7, 4) contains the additional point that Sacadas was the first to perform the 'Pythian aulos tune' at Delphi. This was not an aulodic *nomos* but an auletic one: that is, the piper played without any singer. In some way he portrayed the victorious combat of Apollo with the serpent, the Python, though a date of 580 BC seems much too early for such 'programme music'; perhaps the piping accompanied and formalized pantomimic dancing (Wegner). In his *Onomasticon* (iv, chaps.78, 84) the late lexicographer Pollux also attributed the *nomos Pythikos* to Sacadas and described its musical divisions.

The aulos *nomoi* of Sacadas were still popular more than two centuries later: in 369 BC, at the founding of Messene, the builders worked to the accompaniment of his Boeotian melodies and those composed by the Theban aulete Pronomus (Pausanias, iv, 27, 7). The range and brilliance of his accomplishments made him the outstanding musical performer of the 6th century BC; Pindar composed a prelude (prooimion) in his honour (Pausanias, ix, 30, 2 = Pindar, frag.282*a*, ed. Bowra).

See also GREECE, §I, 4.

BIBLIOGRAPHY
H. Abert: 'Sakadas', *Pauly's Real-Encyclopädie der classischen Altertumswissenschaft*, i/A/2 (Stuttgart, 1920), 1768
J. M. Edmonds, ed. and trans.: *Lyra graeca*, ii (London and Cambridge, Mass., 1924, 5/1964), 4ff
H. Grieser: *Nomos: ein Beitrag zur griechischen Musikgeschichte* (Heidelberg, 1937), 69f
M. Wegner: *Das Musikleben der Griechen* (Berlin, 1949), 146
G. Wille: 'Musik', *Lexikon der alten Welt* (Zurich and Stuttgart, 1965), 2008

WARREN ANDERSON

Saccadé (Fr.: 'jerked'). A kind of sharply accented bowing.

Sacchetti, Franco (*b* Ragusa, between 1332 and 1334; *d* San Miniato, 1400). Italian writer and poet, the son of a Florentine merchant in Ragusa (now Dubrovnik). The family moved to Florence and Franco began writing love lyrics while in his early twenties, modelling his works after Dante and Boccaccio. In 1363 he launched an active career in politics and travelled widely as a *podestà* and merchant. A political upheaval, the death of his wife (1377) and his brother, Giannozzo (beheaded on 17 October 1379), were tragic events, the sadness of which is reflected in his writings.

His major works are: *Battaglia delle belle donne*, begun 1352, *Sposizioni di Vangeli*, begun in 1381, *Trecento novelle*, begun in 1385 and *Libro delle rime* (modern edn. by A. Chiari; Bari, 1936), begun in 1363. In addition he wrote 14 madrigals, 18 ballatas and two cacce, some of which he himself set to music. Others were set by Francesco Landini, Niccolò da Perugia, Giovannes Gherardelli, Jacobus frater Gherardelli, Lorenzo da Firenze, Gherardello da Firenze, Donato da Firenze, Ottolino de Brixia, Guilielmus de Francia and Luca Marenzio, although many of the compositions are lost.

BIBLIOGRAPHY
E. Li Gotti and N. Pirrotta: *Il Sacchetti e la tecnica musicale* (Florence, 1935)

W. THOMAS MARROCCO

Sacchetti [Sakketti], **Liberio Antonovich** (*b* Kenzar, Tambov govt., 30 Aug 1852; *d* Petrograd, 10 March 1916). Russian musicologist. He was the son of an Italian music teacher who had settled in Russia in the late 1840s. He studied at the St Petersburg Conservatory, graduating from Davïdov's cello class in 1874 and Rimsky-Korsakov's composition class in 1878. In 1886 he was appointed to the newly founded chair in music history and aesthetics at the St Petersburg Conservatory. His lectures were so popular that in 1889 he was asked to give a similar series at the Academy of Fine Arts. From 1895 he worked with Stasov at the Imperial Library in St Petersburg. He was the official delegate of the Russian Musical Society at Bologna (1888) and also at Paris (1900), where he presented a paper on Russian church music. He wrote several useful textbooks and histories of music, and his writings on aesthetics were highly regarded by his contemporaries.

WRITINGS
Ocherk vseobshchey istorii muzïki [An outline of the general history of music] (St Petersburg, 1883, 4/1912)
Iz oblasti estetiki i muzïki [From the realms of aesthetics and music] (St Petersburg, 1896)
Kratkaya istoricheskaya muzïkal'naya khrestomatiya s drevneyskikh vremyon do XVII veka vklyuchitel'no [A short historical anthology of music from ancient times up to and including the 17th century] (St Petersburg, 1896, 2/1900)
Kratkoye rukovodstvo k teorii muzïki: elementarnaya teoriya, garmonïya, kontrapunkt, formï instrumental'noy i vokal'noy muzïki [A short guide to music theory: elementary theory, harmony, counterpoint, forms of instrumental and vocal music] (St Petersburg, 1896, 3/1909)
Estetika v obshchedostupnom izlozhenii [A popular account of aesthetics] (St Petersburg, 1905–17)
Istoriya muzïki vsekh vremyon i narodov [The history of music of all periods and peoples] (St Petersburg, 1913)

BIBLIOGRAPHY
Nik. F. [Findeyzen]: 'Liberiy Antonovich Sakketti: biograficheskiy ocherk' [Biographical essay], *RMG* (1898)
N. Bernshteyn: *Kratkiy ocherk zhizni i deyatel'nosti professora L. A.*

Sakketti [A short essay on the life and work of Professor Sacchetti] (St Petersburg, 1903)
Br. [E. M. Braudo]: Obituary, *MS khronika* (1915–16), no.19, p.50
P. A. Vul'fius, ed.: *Iz istorii Leningradskoy konservatorii: materialï i dokumentï 1862–1917* (Leningrad, 1964)

JENNIFER SPENCER

Sacchi, Giovenale (*b* Barzio, nr. Como, 22 Nov 1726; *d* Milan, 27 Sept 1789). Italian mathematician, music theorist and writer. He studied with the Barnabites and entered their order. He taught rhetoric at Lodi and, from 1749, eloquence at the Collegio dei Nobili in Milan. He was in contact with Padre Martini, who encouraged his musical writings, and was also acquainted with Pietro Verri, Parini, Stanislao Mattei, Riccati, Giulini and Gerbert. In 1761 he published the first of several theoretical treatises on music, in 1778 a work on ancient Greek music and in the 1780s biographies of Farinelli and Benedetto Marcello. Fétis praised his erudition and science, but held that his views reflected a lack of intimate knowledge of music, criticizing his *Della divisione del tempo nella musica, nel ballo e nella poesia* (Milan, 1770) for its vagueness. Sacchi's *Delle quinte successive nel contrappunto e delle regole degli accompagnamenti* (Milan, 1780) contains an attack on Rameau's fundamental bass and his concept of inversions.

BIBLIOGRAPHY
EitnerQ; *FétisB* [incl. annotated list of writings]; *GerberL*; *GerberNL*
G. Bertini: *Dizionario storico-critico degli scrittori di musica*, iv (Palermo, 1815) [incl. annotated list of writings]

FERRUCCIO TAMMARO

Sacchini, Antonio (Maria Gasparo Gioacchino) (*b* Florence, 14 June 1730; *d* Paris, 6 Oct 1786). Italian composer, a leading figure in serious opera of the late 18th century.

1. LIFE. When Antonio was four, his father Gaetano, a cook, attached himself to the retinue of the Infante Don Carlos and accompanied him to Naples. At the age of ten he entered the Conservatorio S Maria di Loreto to study the violin with Nicola Fiorenza. He also studied singing with Gennaro Manna, and the harpsichord, organ and composition with Durante, who esteemed him highly and predicted that he would be 'the composer of the century'. He was asked to serve as *mastricello* in 1756, the same year that his first theatrical work, the intermezzo *Fra Donato*, was performed by the students at the conservatory and in various houses throughout the city and province. The success of *Fra Donato* and of *Il giocatore*, a second intermezzo written for the conservatory in 1757, brought invitations to compose comic works for two Neapolitan theatres – the Teatro Nuovo and the Teatro dei Fiorentini. In January 1758 he was nominated *maestro di cappella straordinario* at the conservatory, an unpaid post in which he assisted Manna, the *primo maestro*, and Pierantonio Gallo, the *secondo maestro*. When Manna retired in May 1761, Gallo became *primo maestro* and Sacchini *secondo maestro*. In the same month *Andromaca*, his first *opera seria*, was performed at the Teatro S Carlo, Naples. On 12 October 1762 he was granted leave to go to Venice, where he composed *Alessandro Severo* for the Teatro S Benedetto and *Alessandro nell'Indie* for the Teatro S Salvatore. Neglecting to return to his duties in Naples, he proceeded to Padua, where on 9 July 1763 his *Olimpiade* was such an overwhelming success that it was performed throughout Italy. Further triumphs in Rome, Naples and Florence led him to abandon his post at the conservatory for a career as an opera composer.

For the next few years Sacchini lived in Rome, where he composed a number of comic works for the Teatro Valle that achieved fame throughout Europe, including *Il finto pazzo per amore* (1765), *La contadina in corte* (1766) and *L'isola d'amore* (1766). In 1768 he moved to Venice, where he became director of the Conservatorio dell'Ospedaletto. He quickly gained a reputation as an excellent singing teacher (Laura Conti, Adriana Gabrieli and Nancy Storace were among his pupils). He composed several oratorios for the conservatory and numerous sacred pieces for Venetian churches. In spring 1770 he visited Germany to compose operas for Munich and Stuttgart, and then returned to his post in Venice, where for the next two years he combined his teaching with the composing of successful operas for the major Italian theatres.

In 1772 Sacchini moved to London, where he remained for nearly ten years. Burney described *Il Cid* (January 1773) and *Tamerlano* (May 1773), his first operas for the English capital, as

equal, if not superior, to any musical dramas I had heard in any part of Europe. The airs of Millico, the first man, were wholly written in the delicate and pathetic style of that singer; as the first woman's part was in the spirited and nervous style of Girelli. And he cherished the talents of the inferior singers in so judicious a manner, that all their defects were constantly disguised or concealed.

When Traetta arrived in London in 1776 his opera failed miserably because, according to Burney, 'Sacchini had already taken possession of our hearts, and so firmly established himself in the public favour, that he was not to be supplanted by a composer in the same style'. But Sacchini's dissolute life created many enemies and eventually brought financial ruin. His former friend, the singer Rauzzini, went so far as to claim many of the composer's most famous arias as his own.

Faced with the threat of imprisonment, Sacchini left England in 1781 and went to Paris. He was already famous there because of performances of his *La colonie* (a French version of *L'isola d'amore*) in 1775 and *Olimpiade* in 1777. The success of these works had delighted the Piccinni supporters, who attempted to draw Sacchini to Paris as an ally in their struggle with the Gluck supporters. In autumn 1781 the composer appeared at Versailles, where he was presented to Marie Antoinette and received with enthusiasm. Joseph II of Austria was also visiting the French court at that time and, being particularly fond of Italian opera, he recommended Sacchini to his sister's protection. Determined to keep the composer in France, the queen persuaded the directors of the Opéra to accept his demand for 10,000 francs for each of three operas.

From the very first, Sacchini found himself the object of intrigue and illwill. M. de la Ferté, *l'intendant des Menus-Plaisirs*, contrived to stall the performance of his first opera for Paris, *Renaud*, and to draw attention to the queen's preference for foreign composers, while the Gluck supporters attempted to estrange the composer from his Piccinnist supporters. When *Renaud* was finally performed on 28 February 1783 it was not well received. The Piccinni faction asserted that the score (an adaptation of his *Armida* of 1772) was influenced by Gluck, while the Gluck supporters condemned the work for lacking dramatic power and originality. Sacchini's next opera, *Chimène* (also an adaptation of an earlier work), was performed at Fontainebleau on 18 November

1783 in an atmosphere of open rivalry with Piccinni, whose *Didon* had been performed two days earlier and proclaimed a masterpiece. Although *Chimène* suffered in comparison, receiving only one performance while *Didon* received three, both composers were presented to the king (Sacchini by the queen herself) and given a large pension. *Chimène* was first performed at the Opéra on 9 February 1784 and received 16 performances. The *Mercure de France* found the work full of musical beauty but dramatically weak because of unnecessary arias and ritornellos. The music for Sacchini's next opera, *Dardanus*, was completely original, and with this opera and those that followed, he attempted to create works that conformed to the ideals of French music drama. The failure of *Dardanus* can be attributed in part to an undramatic libretto and an inadequate staging brought about by his enemies at the Opéra. In autumn 1785 the queen had *Dardanus* given at Fontainebleau in a revised version, which proved a success. In the same year Sacchini completed his *Oedipe à Colone*, which the queen had promised would be the first opera to be performed at Fontainebleau during the court's forthcoming stay there, but mounting criticism of her preference for foreigners forced her to revoke her pledge and to cede the honoured place to the French composer Lemoine. Sacchini's beloved pupil, Henri Berton, asserted that this disappointment contributed greatly to the composer's death, which occurred shortly afterwards on 6 October 1786, although Sacchini had been suffering many years from gout and the effects of dissipation. *Oedipe* was performed at the Opéra on 1 February 1787 and hailed as his masterpiece. The work formed a standard part of the repertory until 1830, and achieved 583 performances. *Arvire et Evelina*, Sacchini's last opera, was completed by Rey, the conductor of the Opéra orchestra, and given its première in Paris on 29 April 1788. Although it did not gain the popularity of *Oedipe*, it was heard in Paris until 1827 and had 95 performances.

2. WORKS. The high esteem that Sacchini enjoyed in the judgments of his contemporaries must certainly be modified and put into perspective from a present-day vantage point. In 1770 Burney considered him one of the four greatest composers of Italy, along with Jommelli, Galuppi and Piccinni. While he placed Piccinni supreme in the comic style, he nominated Sacchini 'the most promising composer in the serious'. He described Sacchini's *Il Cid* and *Tamerlano* as 'so entire, so masterly, yet so new and natural, that there was nothing left for criticism to censure, though innumerable beauties to point out and admire'. A critic of the next generation, Giuseppe Carpani, hailed Sacchini as the world's greatest melodist. Indeed, his serious operas display an exceptional gift for melody, and although these melodies are not strikingly original, they are immediately appealing and encompass a wide range of emotional expression. On the other hand, the melodies in his comic works are often similar in character and tend to be monotonous. In general, his style is typical of the late Classical era with its simplicity of texture and balanced phrase structure. At times, however, the Mozartian melodic line gives way to expansive phrases that bring to mind the lyric style of the 19th century. Sacchini's harmony tends to be richer than that of most of his contemporary Italian opera composers, and especially effective is his judicious use of diminished

7ths, dominants of degrees of the scale other than the tonic, and augmented 6ths. He often achieved dramatic tension through the use of changing harmonies over a tonic pedal point or with a sudden change from major to minor. The instrumental accompaniment is employed in such a way that it enhances but never detracts from the vocal line. As Burney observed, 'his accompaniments, though always rich and ingenious, never call off attention from the voice, but, by a constant transparency, the principal melody is rendered distinguishable through all the contrivances of imitative and picturesque design in the instruments'. The virtuoso character of the violin parts in many of the ritornellos and the care with which he notated the accompanimental figures reflect a thorough mastery of this instrument.

Sacchini employed a variety of aria forms. Only rarely did he adhere to the complete da capo form, but he often made use of altered versions of this basic plan. He also made frequent use of a cavatina-like two-part aria that approximates to the *A* portion of the da capo form, and of the vocal rondò, in both comic and serious works. Through-composed arias are occasionally found in his comic operas, while in the French works one finds the cavatina–cabaletta combination that was to become so popular in the 19th century. Sacchini's accompanied recitatives are characterized by exceptional dramatic power and often combine with the following aria to form a unified musical scene through the use of common motivic material. Transitional portions of the aria itself are frequently written in the manner of accompanied recitative.

In his ensembles Sacchini was only partly successful in his attempt to define musically the various characters.

1. Antonio Sacchini: engraving by L. Rados after G. B. Bosio

2. The opening of Act 1 scene i from Sacchini's 'Oedipe a Colonne', from the first edition of the score (Paris: Imbault, 1787)

In the comic works the action continues through the ensemble and is reflected by quick changes of tempo and musical character, although the key centre is generally constant. The chorus remained insignificant in his operas until his London period. Burney reported that Sacchini,

finding how fond the English were of Handel's oratorio choruses, introduced solemn and elaborate choruses into some of his operas; but though excellent in their kind, they never had a good effect: the mixture of English singers with the Italian, as well as the awkward figure they cut, as actors, joined to the difficulty of getting their parts by heart, rendered those compositions ridiculous, which in still life would have been admirable.

Especially effective, however, are the impressive choral scenes in the French operas in which the chorus alternates with soloists in rondo fashion. Indeed, the many choruses and scenes of spectacle in his last operas not only show the strong influence of Gluck but also point the way to the grand opera of Spontini. *Dardanus* and *Oedipe* emerge as true lyric dramas from which all unnecessary ritornellos and airs have been shorn. The great fluidity in combining accompanied recitative, arioso and aria and the variety and attention to detail in the orchestration are used to excellent effect to mirror the changing emotions of the text. With his masterpiece, *Oedipe*, Sacchini admirably achieved a synthesis of Italian melodic style and Gluckian principles within a French dramatic framework.

WORKS

OPERAS

(opere serie unless otherwise stated)

NC – *Naples, Teatro S Carlo*
RV – *Rome, Teatro Valle*
LK – *London, King's Theatre*

Fra Donato (intermezzo, ? P. Trinchera), Naples, Conservatorio S Maria di Loreto, 1756
Il giocatore (intermezzo), Naples, Conservatorio S Maria di Loreto, 1757

Olimpia tradita (commedia), Naples, Fiorentini, 1758
Il copista burlato (commedia, G. A. Federico), Naples, Nuovo, aut. 1759
Il testaccio (opera buffa), Rome, Capranica, 1760
La vendemmia (intermezzo, Goldoni), Rome, Capranica, carn. 1760
I due fratelli beffati (commedia), Naples, Nuovo, aut. 1760
Andromaca (A. Salvi), NC, 30 May 1761
La finta contessa (farsetta), Rome, Capranica, 1761
Li due bari (opera buffa), Naples, Fiorentini, 1762
L'amore in campo (dramma giocoso), RV, 1762
Alessandro Severo (Zeno), Venice, S Benedetto, carn. 1763
Alessandro nell'Indie (Metastasio), Venice, S Salvatore, Ascension 1763; rev. Naples, 1768
Olimpiade (Metastasio), Padua, Nuovo, 9 July 1763; rev. in Fr., Paris, 2 Oct 1777 (Paris, 1777)
Semiramide riconosciuta (Metastasio), Rome, Argentina, carn. 1764
Eumene (Zeno), Florence, Pergola, carn. 1764
Il gran Cidde (G. Pizzi), Rome, Argentina, 1764; rev. as Il Cid (G. Bottarelli), LK, 19 Jan 1773, Favourite Songs (London, 1773); rev. in Fr. as Chimène (N. P. Guillard), Fontainebleau, 18 Nov 1783 (Paris, *c*1784)
Lucio Vero (Zeno), NC, 4 Nov 1764; as pasticcio, London, 1773, Favourite Songs (London, 1773)
Il finto pazzo per amore (intermezzo, T. Mariani), RV, spr. 1765
Il Creso (Pizzi), NC, 4 Nov 1765; rev. LK, 1774, Favourite Songs (London, 1774), as Euriso, LK, 1781
La contadina in corte (intermezzo), RV, carn. 1766, Favourite Songs (London, 1782); in Ger., Vienna, 1767
L'isola d'amore (dramma giocoso, A. Gori), RV, carn. 1766; rev. LK, 1776 (London, 1776); in Fr. as La colonie, Paris, Comédie-Italienne, 16 Aug 1775 (Paris, 1776)
Le contadine bizzarre (dramma giocoso, G. Petrosellini), Milan, Regio Ducale, 1766
Artaserse (Metastasio), Rome, Argentina, carn. 1768
Nicoraste (B. Vitturi), Venice, S Benedetto, Ascension 1769
Scipione in Cartagena (E. Giunti), Munich, Court, 8 Jan 1770
Calliroe (M. Verazi), Stuttgart, Residenz, 11 Feb 1770
L'eroe cinese (Metastasio), Munich, Court, 27 April 1770
Adriano in Siria (Metastasio), Venice, S Benedetto, Ascension 1771
Ezio (Metastasio), NC, 4 Nov 1771
Armida (G. de Gamerra), Milan, Regio Ducale, carn. 1772; rev. as Rinaldo, LK, 22 April 1780, Favourite Songs (London, 1780); rev. in Fr. as Renaud (J. Leboeuf and S. Pellegrin), Paris, Opéra, 28 Feb 1783 (Paris, 1783)
Vologeso (Zeno), Parma, Ducale, 1772
Tamerlano (A. Piovene), LK, 6 May 1773, Favourite Songs (London, 1773)
Perseo (A. Aureli), LK, 29 Jan 1774, Favourite Songs (London, 1774)
Nitteti (Metastasio), LK, 19 April 1774, Favourite Songs (London, 1774)
Motezuma (Botarelli), LK, 7 Feb 1775, Favourite Songs (London, 1775)
Didone abbandonata (Metastasio), LK, 11 Nov 1775, pasticcio
Erifile (De Gamerra), LK, 7 Feb 1778, Favourite Songs (London, 1778)
L'amore soldato (dramma giocoso, N. Tassi), LK, 4 May 1778 (London, 1778)
L'avaro deluso, o Don Calandrino (dramma giocoso, G. Bertati), LK, 24 Nov 1778
Enea e Lavinia (Botarelli), LK, 25 March 1779, Favourite Songs (London, 1779)
Mitridate (Zeno), LK, 23 Jan 1781, Favourite Songs (London, 1781)
Dardanus (tragédie, Guillard), Versailles, Trianon, 18 Sept 1784 (Paris, 1784)
Oedipe à Colone (tragédie lyrique, Guillard), Versailles, Court, 4 Jan 1786 (Paris, 1787)
Arvire et Evelina (tragédie lyrique, Guillard), Paris, Opéra, 29 April 1788 (Paris, 1788); completed by J.-B. Rey

OTHER WORKS

Oratorios: Gesù presentato al tempio, 1761; L'abbandono delle richezze di San Filippo Neri, Bologna, 1766; Machabaeorum mater, Venice, 1770; Jeptes sacrificium, Venice, 1771; Nuptiae Ruth, Venice, 1772; Il popolo di Giuda, liberato dalla morte per intercessione della Regina Ester, Rome, 1777; Juditta, Paris, 1786; L'umiltà esaltata

Sacred: numerous masses, mass movts., motets, psalms etc, *A-Wgm*, *D-Bds*, *MÜs*, *GB-Lbm*, *Lcm*, *T*, *I-Bc*, *Fc*, *Nc*, *Mc*, *Pca*, *PAc*, *PS*

Other vocal: 9 Duets (London, *c*1775); Solfèges (Paris, ?1760); cantatas, arias

Inst: 2 syms. (Paris, 1767); Periodical Ov. no.49, 8 pts. (London, 1776); 6 Trio Sonatas, op.1 (London, *c*1775); 6 Str Qts, op.2 (London, 1778); 6 Sonatas, hpd/pf, vn, op.3 (London, 1779); A Second Set of 6 Favorite Lessons, hpd/pf, vn, op.4 (London, *c*1780)

BIBLIOGRAPHY

BurneyH
C. Burney: *The Present State of Music in France and Italy* (London,

1771, 2/1773); ed. P. Scholes as *Dr. Burney's Musical Tours* (London, 1959)

F. de Villars: 'Oedipe à Colone et Sacchini', *Art musical*, iii (1863), 345, 361

A. L. Nohl: *Lettres de Gluck et de Weber* (Paris, 1870)

A. Jullien: *La cour et l'opéra sous Louis XVI* (Paris, 1878)

F. Florimo: 'Antonio Sacchini', *La scuola musicale di Napoli e i suoi conservatorii*, ii (Naples, 1882), 358

Onoranze a G. B. Pergolesi e Antonio Sacchini (Iesi, 1890)

J. G. Prod'homme: 'L'héritage di Sacchini', *RMI*, xv (1908), 23

——: *Ecrits de musiciens* (Paris, 1912)

G. de Saint-Foix: 'Les maîtres de l'opéra bouffe dans la musique de chambre, à Londres', *RMI*, xxxi (1924), 507

J. G. Prod'homme: 'Un musicien napolitain à la cour de Louis XVI: les dernières années de Gasparo Sacchini', *Le ménestrel*, lxxxvii (1925), 505, 517

V. Morelli: 'Antonio Sacchini fra i Gluckisti e i briganti di Londra', *Vita musicale italiana*, vii–viii (1926)

U. Prota-Giurleo: 'La vera patria di Antonio Sacchini', *Giornale d'Italia* (8 Sept 1928)

A. Pompeati: 'Il Parini e la musica', *RMI*, xxxvi (1929), 556

U. Prota-Giurleo: *Sacchini non nacque a Pozzuoli* (Naples, 1952)

F. Schlitzer: *Antonio Sacchini: schede e appunti per una sua storia teatrale* (Siena, 1955)

U. Prota-Giurleo: *Sacchini a Napoli* (Naples, 1956)

——: *Sacchini fra Piccinisti e Gluckisti* (Naples, 1957)

W. S. Newman: *The Sonata in the Classic Era* (Chapel Hill, 1963, rev. 2/1972)

E. A. Thierstein: *Five French Operas of Sacchini* (diss., U. of Cincinnati, 1974)

DAVID DI CHIERA

Sacconi, (Simone) Fernando (*b* Rome, 30 May 1895; *d* Point Lookout, Long Island, New York, 26 June 1973). Italian maker and restorer of violins. He worked in Rome and New York, and was renowned as an expert on and revolutionized the techniques of instrument repair. He was the son of Gasparo Sacconi, a tailor who was also a good violinist. While still at school he became a workshop assistant to Giuseppe Rossi, a pupil of Degani, and he also studied drawing and sculpture at the Institute of Fine Arts in Rome.

By the time he was 16, Sacconi was already an experienced violin maker with his own clientèle, and with particular ability as a copyist. He had copied the 'Berthier' Stradivari of Franz von Vecsey, and several other instruments, but the outline of his first cello was from an enlargement of a photograph, as he had not then seen a Stradivari cello. He travelled to Monte Carlo and then to Nice, where the violin maker Bianchi could not believe that Sacconi's copy of a Januarius Gagliano violin was anything but an original.

In World War I Sacconi served in the artillery, but he resumed his career immediately afterwards, with increasing success. In 1925 he married Teresita Pacini, the daughter of an opera singer. In 1927 he had his first opportunity to examine the interior of a Stradivari when he was commissioned to repair the 'Piatti' cello of 1720, and to make a copy of it. The copy was presented to Gaspar Cassadó, who used it as a solo instrument for many years. By that time he had made copies of many other instruments, including the 'Paganini' Stradivari viola, and had also become familiar, through the aging violin maker Fiorini, whom he helped, with the moulds, patterns and tools of Stradivari.

In 1931 the dealer Emil Herrmann persuaded Sacconi to go to New York to work for him. He continued to make new instruments – and even an occasional bow – but his time there was mainly taken up with repairs and restoration work. In this field he had no equal: 'good', in his eye, was a repair which could not be seen, new edges indistinguishable from the original, a new piece that could not be detected, a crack which had ceased to exist except on his chart of the instrument. In

what is supposed to be a dying craft it is often taken for granted that the traditional way of doing things is the best. Sacconi, more or less self-taught, saw the vandalism that had been committed and set out to discover a better way. He restored a Stradivari of the best period, virtually destroyed in an accident in 1948, which now shows no sign of having suffered. In the imitation of old Italian varnish he excelled all rivals.

In 1950 Herrmann retired, and Sacconi went with his pupil Dario d'Attili to work for Rembert Wurlitzer. A first-class workshop was built up, and many of the best American repairers were trained in it. The personalities and expertise of Wurlitzer and Sacconi complemented each other, and the reputation of the firm rose to new heights. In his last few years he spent much time teaching young violin makers in Cremona and published *I segreti di Stradivari* (Cremona, 1972), setting out in detail the working methods of the great Cremonese maker. He was made an honorary citizen of Cremona in 1972.

CHARLES BEARE

SACEM. Société des Auteurs, Compositeurs et Editeurs de Musique; *see* COPYRIGHT COLLECTING SOCIETIES, §§I and V, 5(i).

Sacerdote, David [Sacerdoti, Davit de] (*b* Rovere, *fl* *c*1575). Italian composer. His first and only recorded work, *Il primo libro de madrigali a sei voci* (Venice, 1575), is prefaced by an encomiastic sonnet by the composer by Cavaliere Nuvolone, a prominent member of the Accademia degli Invaghiti, founded in Mantua by Cesare Gonzaga in 1562. The volume is dated from Casale on 25 January 1575, and is dedicated to the Marchese del Vasto who seems to have been Sacerdote's patron. It includes settings of one sonnet by Ariosto, and four from Petrarch's *Canzoniere*. Individual madrigals are dedicated to the Duke of Mantua, the Marchese del Vasto, the Prior of Barletta (who was usually a Gonzaga), and to various ladies from distinguished Mantuan families, including Isabella Madrucci. One of the Petrarch texts, *Lieti fiori e felici*, was also set in the anonymous *Madrigali a cinque voci* (Venice, 1583[13]) which can be ascribed to Duke Guglielmo Gonzaga of Mantua.

BIBLIOGRAPHY
G. Tiraboschi: *Storia della letteratura italiana* (Modena, 1772)

IAIN FENLON

Sacher, Paul (*b* Basle, 28 April 1906). Swiss conductor. He studied at the Basle Conservatory with Weingartner and was trained in musicology by Karl Nef at the university there. In 1926 he founded the Basle Chamber Orchestra, to which a chamber choir was affiliated in 1928. Sacher had realized that music from Mozart to Debussy was already amply cultivated, but that pre-Classical and contemporary music were not taken sufficiently into consideration. So in concerts with his own orchestra he included a significant proportion of works in both these categories.

Sacher commissioned or gave the first performances of more than 80 works, among the most important being Bartók's Music for Strings, Percussion and Celesta, Divertimento and the Violin Concerto of 1907–8, Hindemith's *Die Harmonie der Welt*, Honegger's Second and Fourth Symphonies, Martin's *Petite symphonie concertante*, Strauss's *Metamorphosen*, Stravinsky's Concerto in D and *A Sermon, a Narrative, and a*

Paul Sacher

Prayer, and works by Beck, Britten, Burkhard, Fortner, Henze, Malipiero, Tippett and Veress.

From 1941 Sacher also conducted the Collegium Musicum of Zurich, with which he presented similar programmes with many first performances, and included some of the works listed above. He conducts regularly all over Europe, and at such festivals as Lucerne (where his Mozart serenade concerts are a feature), Glyndebourne, Edinburgh and Aix-en-Provence.

Sacher has also taken an active part in music education. In 1933 he founded the Schola Cantorum Basiliensis, an institute for research into early music and its authentic performance. In 1954 he brought together this Schola, the Musikschule and the conservatory to form the Musikakademie der Stadt Basel, of which he was principal until 1969. He became a member of the managing committee of the Association of Swiss Composers in 1931; he was its director from 1946 to 1955 and then honorary president. He was president of the Swiss section of the ISCM, 1935–46. Among his honours are the Schoenberg Medal (1953), the Salzburg Mozart Medal (1956) and an honorary doctorate from Basle University (1957).

BIBLIOGRAPHY

10 Jahre Collegium Musicum Zürich, Leitung Paul Sacher (Zurich, 1951)

Alte und neue Musik, i: Das Basler Kammerorchester unter Leitung von Paul Sacher 1926–1951, ii: 50 Jahre Basler Kammerorchester (Zurich, 1952–77)

E. Mohr: 'Dirigentenporträt: Paul Sacher', *Musica*, vi (1952), 128

K. Blaukopf: 'Paul Sacher', *Grosse Dirigenten* (Teufen, 2/1957)

E. Mohr: 'Sacher, Paul', *MGG*

20 Jahre Collegium Musicum Zürich, Leitung Paul Sacher (Zurich, 1962)

S. Borris: 'Paul Sachers Orchester zur Pflege alter und neuer Musik', *Die grossen Orchester* (Hamburg, 1969)

A. Rosenthal: 'Music Manuscripts in Basle', *MT*, cxvi (1975), 534

E. Lichtenhahn and T. Seebass, eds.: *Musikhandschriften aus der Sammlung Paul Sacher: Festschrift zu Paul Sachers siebzigstem Geburtstag* (Basle, 1976)

M. Rostropovich, ed.: *Dank an Paul Sacher* (Zurich, 1976)

'Paul Sacher zum 70. Geburtstag', *SMz*, cxvi (1976), 95

JÜRG STENZL

Sachs, Curt (*b* Berlin, 29 June 1881; *d* New York, 5 Feb 1959). American musicologist of German birth. He attended the Französisches Gymnasium in his native city while at the same time taking lessons in piano, music theory and composition with Leo Schrattenholz. He then went to Berlin University and though he also studied music history with Fleischer, Kretzschmar and Wolf, it was in the history of art that he took his doctorate (1904) with a dissertation on Verrocchio's sculpture. He then pursued a career as an art historian, helping to edit the *Monatshefte für kunstwissenschaftliche Literatur* and working at the Kunstgewerbe Museum in Berlin. In 1909, however, he began to devote himself wholly to music. After military service in World War I, Sachs returned to Berlin and in 1919 was appointed director of the Staatliche Instrumentensammlung, a distinguished collection of musical instruments which he completely reorganized, having many of the instruments restored so that they could be heard. At the same time he was a *Privatdozent* at the university, becoming reader in 1921 and professor in 1928; he also taught at the Staatliche Hochschule für Musik and the Akademie für Kirchen- und Schulmusik. In addition he held various advisory posts in German museums and in the official educational establishment. In 1930 and 1932, for example, he was invited to Cairo by the Egyptian government to serve as a consultant on oriental music.

Being Jewish, Sachs was deprived of all his academic positions in 1933; he went to Paris, where he worked with André Schaeffner at the ethnological museum, the Musée de l'Homme (then Musée du Trocadéro), and taught at the Sorbonne. In 1934 he began the series of historical recordings, *L'Anthologie Sonore*, which provided an introduction to the sound of early music for several generations of students. In 1937 he emigrated to the USA; from 1937 to 1953 he was professor of music at New York University. Besides being a consultant at the New York Public Library, and serving as visiting professor from time to time at various American universities (Harvard, Northwestern, and Michigan), Sachs also lectured regularly at Columbia University in New York, where he was made adjunct professor from 1953 until his death. In the last decade of his life he received various honorary degrees, including honorary doctorates from Hebrew Union College and from the Free University of Berlin; the West German government appointed him an *Ordinarius emeritus*; the Deutsche Gesellschaft für Musikforschung made him an honorary member; he was president of the American Musicological Society (1950–52) and honorary president of the American Society for Ethnomusicology.

Curt Sachs was a giant among musicologists, as much because of his astounding mastery of a number of subjects as because of his ability to present a comprehensive view of a vast panorama. This latter talent made him a generalist or popularizer in the best sense of the word, a qualification which should not obscure the fact that he developed new fields of inquiry. Indeed his achievement in synthesizing countless facts into a comprehensible whole is all the more impressive since he often dealt with previously unexplored areas. Sachs was one of the founders of modern organology, the study of musical instruments; he not only devised (together with Erich von Hornbostel) the classification scheme for instruments that has gained universal acceptance, but he also wrote the standard dictionary (the *Real-Lexikon*), the best history of instruments and a model catalogue of one of the world's great collections. Through instruments Sachs became interested in the music of non-Western culture, and hence a pioneer ethnomusicologist. His studies in the music of the ancient world produced several standard surveys of the field as well as a number of provocative essays. His fascination with the nature of the musical experience led him to an important study of rhythm and tempo, and his concern with the relationship between music and the other arts inspired his world history of the dance and his major cultural historical study, *The Commonwealth of Art*. Not least among his many talents, Sachs was a great teacher and a warm and vital person, beloved by his many students. He was filled to overflowing with ideas and with energy; the amount of work he produced in his busy life was prodigious.

WRITINGS

Musikgeschichte der Stadt Berlin bis zum Jahre 1800 (Berlin, 1908)
Die Briefe Beethovens (Berlin, 1909)
Musik und Oper am kurbrandenburgischen Hof (Berlin, 1910/*R*1977)
Die Briefe Mozarts (Berlin, 1911)
Real-Lexikon der Musikinstrumente, zugleich ein Polyglossar für das gesamte Instrumentengebiet (Berlin, 1913/*R*1962)
with E. M. von Hornbostel: 'Systematik der Musikinstrumente', *Zeitschrift für Ethnologie*, xlvi (1914), 553–90 [Eng. trans. in *GSJ*, xiv (1961), 3]
Die Musikinstrumente Indiens und Indonesiens (Berlin, 1915, 2/1923)
Handbuch der Musikinstrumentenkunde (Leipzig, 1920, 2/1930)
Die Musikinstrumente des alten Ägyptens (Berlin, 1921)
Sammlung alter Musikinstrumente bei der Staatlichen Hochschule für Musik zu Berlin (Berlin, 1922)
Das Klavier (Berlin, 1923)
Die modernen Musikinstrumente (Berlin, 1923)
Die Musikinstrumente (Breslau, 1923)
Musik des Altertums (Breslau, 1924)
Die Musik der Antike (Wildpark-Potsdam, 1928)
Geist und Werden der Musikinstrumente (Berlin, 1929/*R*1975)
Vergleichende Musikwissenschaft in ihren Grundzügen (Leipzig, 1930)
Eine Weltgeschichte des Tanzes (Berlin, 1933; Eng. trans., 1937/*R*1963)
Les instruments de musique de Madagascar (Paris, 1938)
The History of Musical Instruments (New York, 1940)
The Rise of Music in the Ancient World: East and West (New York, 1943)

Hans Sachs: engraving (1576) by Jost Amman

The Commonwealth of Art: Style in the Fine Arts, Music and the Dance (New York, 1946)
Our Musical Heritage (New York, 1948, 2/1955)
Rhythm and Tempo: a Study in Music History (New York, 1953)
'The Lore of non-Western Music', A. Mendel, C. Sachs and C. C. Pratt: *Some Aspects of Musicology* (New York, 1957), 19–48
ed. J. Kunst: *The Wellsprings of Music: an Introduction to Ethnomusicology* (Leiden and The Hague, 1962/*R*1977)

BIBLIOGRAPHY

E. Hertzmann: 'Alfred Einstein and Curt Sachs', *MQ*, xxvii (1941), 263 [with selective bibliography]
K. Hahn: 'Verzeichnis der wissenschaftlichen Arbeiten von Curt Sachs', *AcM*, xxix (1957), 94
E. Hertzmann: 'Curt Sachs (1881–1959): a Memorial Address', *JAMS*, xi (1958), 1
C. S. Smith: 'Curt Sachs', *AcM*, xxxi (1959), 45
G. Reese and R. Brandel, eds.: *The Commonwealth of Music, in Honor of Curt Sachs* (New York, 1965) [incl. L. Schrade: 'Curt Sachs as Historian', 1]

HOWARD MAYER BROWN

Sachs, Hans (*b* Nuremberg, 5 Nov 1494; *d* Nuremberg, 19 Jan 1576). German poet and Meistersinger. From 1501 to 1509 he attended the grammar school in Nuremberg, and thereafter learnt the trade of shoemaking. The years 1511 to 1516 were his apprentice years, during which he travelled the length and breadth of Germany. After his return to Nuremberg he became a master shoemaker in 1520. He led a settled life of increasing wealth and hardly ever left Nuremberg again.

Sachs was born at a time when the imperial city of Nuremberg was at the height of its economic and cultural development. As early as 1509–11 he joined the Meistersinger guild that had existed in Nuremberg since the 15th century. His teacher was the linen weaver Linhard Nunnenbeck. It was through Sachs that the MEISTERGESANG was brought into the service of the Reformation from 1520 onwards, and the Meistersinger guild at Nuremberg became the model for similar guilds in many German cities including Augsburg, Ulm, Breslau, Colmar and Strasbourg.

Sachs's massive artistic output, totalling over 6000 poetic works, comprises Meisterlieder, satirical and didactic poems in rhyming couplets (*Spruchgedichte*), prose dialogues, Shrovetide plays, comedies and tragedies. He created 13 *Meistertöne* (*see* TON (i)), and composed melodies for them all. The most famous of these is his *Silberweise*. In his works Sachs tried above all to make religious and secular knowledge of the period available as fully as possible to his middle- and lower-class audience. His posthumous fame was assured above all by Goethe's *Erklärung eines alten Holzschnittes, vorstellend Hans Sachsens poetische Sendung* (1776) and by Wagner's *Die Meistersinger von Nürnberg* (1868).

WORKS

Editions: *Hans Sachs*, ed. A. von Keller and E. Goetze (Stuttgart, 1870–1908) [26 vols.; no music]
    Hans Sachs: Sämtliche Fabeln und Schwänke, ed. E. Goetze and C. Drescher (Halle, 1893–1913)
        Der Meistergesang in Geschichte und Kunst, ed. C. Mey (Karlsruhe, 1892, Leipzig, 2/1901) [Me]
        Das Singebuch des Adam Puschman, ed. G. Münzer (Leipzig, 1906) [Mu]
           The Early Meisterlieder of Hans Sachs, ed. F. H. Ellis (Bloomington, 1974)

1513: 'Silberweise' (composed in Braunau), Me 209, Mu 81; 'Goldener Ton' (composed in Ried), Me 214, Mu 79
1516: 'Hohe Bergweise' (composed in Frankfurt), Me 219, Mu 72
1518: '(Hohe) Morgenweise' (Nuremberg), Me 225, Mu 75; 'Gesangweise' (Nuremberg), Me 229, Mu 77
1519: 'Kurzer Ton' (Landshut), Me 234, Mu 82
1520: 'Langer Ton' (Nuremberg), Me 236, Mu 73
1521: 'Neuer Ton' (Nuremberg), Me 242, Mu 76; 'Bewährter Ton' (Nuremberg), Me 247, Mu 78

1527: 'Rosenton' (Nuremberg), Me 258, Mu 82; 'Klingender Ton' (Nuremberg), Me 262, Mu 80; 'Spruchweise' (Nuremberg), Me 264, Mu 81
1529: 'Überlanger Ton' (Nuremberg), Me 252, Mu 70

BIBLIOGRAPHY

H. Brunner: 'Hans Sachs', *Fränkische Klassiker*, ed. W. Buhl (Nuremberg, 1971)
B. Könneker: *Hans Sachs* (Stuttgart, 1971) [with extensive bibliography]
G. Pfeiffer: *Nürnberg: Geschichte einer europäischen Stadt* (Munich, 1971)
H. Brunner, G. Hirschmann and F. Schnelbögl, eds.: *Hans Sachs und Nürnberg: Hans Sachs zum 400. Todestag* (Nuremberg, 1976)
N. Holzberg: *Hans-Sachs-Bibliographie* (Nuremberg, 1976)
K. Wedler: *Hans Sachs* (Leipzig, 1976)
For further bibliography *see* MEISTERGESANG.

HORST BRUNNER

Sachs, Klaus-Jürgen (*b* Kiel, 29 Jan 1929). German musicologist. He studied Protestant church music at the Staatliche Hochschule für Musik, Leipzig, under Karl Straube, Robert Köbler and Paul Schenk (1947–50) and then became choirmaster and organist in Bautzen and lecturer at the Protestant School of Church Music, Görlitz (1951–60). While a music teacher at Erlangen University (1960–62), he also studied musicology, philosophy, educational theory and Italian, continuing under H. H. Eggebrecht at Freiburg, where he took the doctorate in 1967 with a work on 14th- and 15th-century counterpoint. From 1967 to 1969 he was research assistant at the Walcker-Stiftung für Orgelwissenschaftliche Forschung, Freiburg; in 1969 he was appointed lecturer in the department of musicology at Erlangen University. His areas of research have been the history of composition theory, medieval music theory and organology. His aim is to establish, interpret and arrange historical sources in the context of music history.

WRITINGS

Der Contrapunctus im 14. und 15. Jahrhundert: Untersuchungen zum Terminus, zur Lehre und zu den Quellen (diss., U. of Freiburg, 1967; *AMw*, xiii (1974), suppl.)
'Bericht über die Arbeiten an den Pfeifenmensurtraktaten des Mittelalters', *Orgel und Orgelmusik heute: Walcker-Stiftung für orgelwissenschaftliche Forschung: Thurner 1968*, 18
Mensura fistularum: die Mensurierung der Orgelpfeifen im Mittelalter (Stuttgart, 1970–)
'Zur Tradition der Klangschritt-Lehre: die Texte mit der Formel "Si cantus ascendit . . ." und ihre Verwandten', *AMw*, xxviii (1971), 233–70
'Gerbertus cognomento musicus: zur musikgeschichtlichen Stellung des Gerbert von Reims (nachmaligen Papstes Silvester II.)', *AMw*, xxix (1972), 257
'Remarks on the Relationship between Pipe-measurements and Organ-building in the Middle Ages', *Organ Yearbook*, iv (1973), 87
with K.-W. Gümpel: 'Der anonyme Contrapunctus-Traktat aus Ms. Vich 208', *AMw*, xxxi (1974), 87
'Punctus', *HMT*
'Counterpoint', §1, *Grove 6*

HANS HEINRICH EGGEBRECHT

Sack, Johann Philipp (*b* Harzgerode, 11 Nov 1722; *d* Berlin, 14 Sept 1763). German composer. He moved to Magdeburg in 1742 and later became instructor at the orphanage there. In 1747 he obtained a similar position at the Berlin Cathedral School, and in 1749 he and several other musicians founded the Musikübende Gesellschaft, an organization that sponsored private and public concerts. He was appointed organist at Berlin Cathedral in 1756. Sack's compositions consist primarily of simple strophic lieder and short keyboard pieces. However, the three exceptionally fine lieder published in *Kleine Clavierstücke nebst einigen Oden* (1760) have a cantata-like structure with an independent accompaniment, and are among the first to be written on three staves.

WORKS
(published in Berlin unless otherwise stated)

Lieder: 1 in Neue Lieder zum Singen beym Clavier, ed. F. W. Marpurg (1756); 6 in Berlinische Oden und Lieder (Leipzig, 1756–63); 1 in Geistliche moralische und weltliche Oden (1758); 1 in Geistliche Oden in Melodien gesetzt (1758); 2 in Kritische Briefe über die Tonkunst, ed. F. W. Marpurg (1760–64); 3 in Kleine Clavierstücke nebst einigen Oden (1760); 1 in Musikalisches Allerley (1761)
Inst: 5 hpd pieces in Raccolta delle più nuove composizioni, ed. F. W. Marpurg (Leipzig, 1756–7); Polonaise, D, kbd, fl ad lib, in Musikalisches Allerley (1761)

BIBLIOGRAPHY

GerberL
F. W. Marpurg: 'Entwurf einer ausführlichen Nachricht von der Musikübenden Gesellschaft in Berlin', *Historisch-kritische Beyträge zur Aufnahme der Musik*, i (1754–5/*R*1970)
E. O. Lindner: *Geschichte des deutschen Liedes im 18. Jahrhundert*, ed. L. Erk (Leipzig, 1871/*R*1968)
M. Friedlaender: *Das deutsche Lied im 18. Jahrhundert* (Stuttgart and Berlin, 1902/*R*1970)
H. Kretzschmar: *Geschichte des neuen deutschen Liedes*, i: *Von Albert bis Zelter* (Leipzig, 1911/*R*1966)
E. Schmitz: *Geschichte der weltlichen Solokantate* (Leipzig, 1914/*R*1966, rev. 2/1955)
S. Loewenthal: *Die Musikübende Gesellschaft zu Berlin und die Mitglieder Joh. Philipp Sack, Fr. Wilh. Riedt und Joh. Gabr. Seyffarth* (Berne, 1928) [incl. thematic catalogue]

DAVID OSSENKOP

Sackbut. (1) English term used up to the 18th century for TROMBONE.

(2) An ORGAN STOP.

Sackpfeife (Ger.). BAGPIPE.

Sacramentary (from Lat. *sacramentarium*). The liturgical book of the Western Christian Church for the use of the celebrant (bishop or priest etc) at Mass. Essentially it contains Proper prayers (collect, secret and post-Communion), Preface and Canon, usually with a few other formulae, benedictions and so on. Sacramentaries appear to have been used since the 5th century. Important early Roman types were the Leonine (oldest surviving source *I-VEcap* 85, 7th-century), named ostensibly after Leo I (*d* 461); the Gelasian (after Gelasius I, *d* 496); and the Gregorian sacramentary (after Gregory the Great, *d* 604). Other European centres used books partly independent of these. Gamber has given a summary of interrelationships and groupings of sacramentaries (*Sakramentartypen*, Texte und Arbeiten, 1st ser., xlix–1, Beuron, 1958). From the 10th century sacramentaries are found with chant text incipits, or complete chants, included beside the prayers, a development that eventually resulted in the modern MISSAL.

See also LITURGY AND LITURGICAL BOOKS.

Sacramento, Lucino (Tinio) (*b* Licab, Nueva Ecija, 30 June 1908). Filipino composer and teacher. He studied composition with Abelardo at the University of the Philippines Conservatory, where he graduated in 1934. In 1945 he was made head of the composition department at the Cosmopolitan Academy of Music, becoming executive secretary and then director there. He has also taught at the Valencia Academy of Music, Laperal Piano School, the University of Santo Tomas Conservatory, St Scholastica's College, the Centro Escolar University Conservatory (from 1947) and Santa Isabel College; and he was music consultant to the Philippine Normal College.

WORKS
(selective list)

Operas: Pagmamahalan [About love], 1969; Florante at Laura, 3, 1973
Orch: Concert Ov., 1934; Tayo na sa langit, sym. poem, 1939; Cradle
    Conc., pf, orch, 1967; Festival Ov., 1967; Vn Conc., e, 1969; Sym.,
    d, 1972; Maharlika [Royalty] Conc., pf, orch, 1973
Chamber: Souvenir, vn, pf, 1934; Andante and Caprice, 2 vn, pf, 1938;
    Tu es Petrus, 2 vn, pf, 1957; Capriccio sarcastico, vn, 1960; Petite
    suite, 1967; 3 Philippine Vistas, 1969; Balintataw [Fantasy], 1970
Other works: songs, pf pieces

LUCRECIA R. KASILAG

Sacra rappresentazione. *See* RAPPRESENTAZIONE
SACRA.

Sacrati, Francesco (*b* Parma, baptized 17 Sept 1605; *d*
?Modena, 20 May 1650). Italian composer. The name
Paulo [Paolin] that has generally followed 'Francesco'
in references to him seems to have been an invention of
Ivanovich; it was the name of Sacrati's son. Sacrati was
active in Venice as a composer of opera during the early
1640s, always in collaboration with the scenographer
Giacomo Torelli. About 1642 he declined the offer of a
position at St Mark's as unworthy of a person of his
reputation. He may subsequently have belonged to the
Accademici Discordati, an itinerant troupe which performed one of his operas in Bologna and possibly elsewhere. He was *maestro di cappella* of the 'commedia a li
musici' who in March 1648 were invited to perform
operas in Reggio Emilia. Sacrati spent part of that year
at the Villa Malvasia at Panzano near Bologna, where he
composed *L'isola di Alcina*. On 3 June 1649 Francesco
I d'Este appointed him *maestro di cappella* of Modena
Cathedral.

Sacrati was highly esteemed by his contemporaries.
Prince Mattias de' Medici, a close acquaintance, called
him 'one of the best composers around', and the librettist Giacomo Badoaro in *L'Ulisse errante* likened him to
Monteverdi as the moon to the sun. *La finta pazza*,
taken to Paris in 1645 by Torelli and the ballet-master
G. B. Balbi, was one of the first Italian operas to be
performed in France; how much of Sacrati's music
remained in this version, which was only partly sung, is
not certain. None of his works is known to survive.

For a scene from *La finta pazza*, see OPERA, fig.2.

WORKS
(all lost)

OPERAS
(known only from librettos)

La finta pazza (G. Strozzi), Venice, Teatro Novissimo, 1641
Bellerofonte (V. Nolfi), Venice, Teatro Novissimo, 1642
Venere gelosa (N. E. Bartolini), Venice, Teatro Novissimo, 1643 (attrib.
    Sacrati by Ivanovich)
L'Ulisse errante (G. Badoaro), Venice, Teatro SS Giovanni e Paolo,
    1644 [a Reprezantação del Ulisse errante . . . a 1 & 2, in the library
    of John IV of Portugal, may have been a printed version or excerpts]
La Semiramide in India (M. Bisaccioni), Venice, Teatro S Cassiano,
    1648 (attrib. Sacrati by Ivanovich)
L'isola di Alcina (F. Testi), Bologna, 1648
Ergasto (Venice, 1650); cited in *WaltherML* and in *Indice*; ? identical
    with 'Lecasto consecrate Ital. for 1 voice', sold in London, 1691

OTHER WORKS

Arie . . . a 1, 2, 3, listed in *Indice*
Arie . . . liber quarto, listed in *Indice*
Madrigali . . . libro primo, 2–4vv, listed in *Indice*
Madrigais, 1–4vv, lib.1, obra 2, listed in *Primeira parte* [perhaps
    identical with Madrigali . . . libro primo]

BIBLIOGRAPHY

EitnerQ; *FétisB*; *WaltherML*
Indice di tutte le opere di musica che si trovano nella Stampa della
    Pigna di Alessandro Vincenti in Venetia (Venice, 1619–49); repr. in
    MMg, xiv–xv (1882–3/R), suppl.
Primeira parte do index da livraria de musica do muyto alto, e poderoso
    Rey Dom João o IV. nosso senhor (Lisbon, 1649/R1967); ed. J. de
    Vasconcellos (Oporto, 1874–6)

C. Ivanovich: *Minerva al tavolino* (Venice, 1681)
A. Ademollo: *I primi fasti della musica italiana a Parigi* (Milan, 1884)
    [incl. several letters of Sacrati]
H. Prunières: *L'opéra italien en France avant Lully* (Paris, 1913)
O. Rombaldi: 'Profilo della storia del teatro in Reggio Emilia, dal 1568
    al 1857', *Il teatro a Reggio Emilia* (Reggio Emilia, 1957), 77
N. Pirrotta: 'Sacrati, Francesco Paolo', *ES*
C. Sartori: 'Un fantomatico compositore per un'opera che forse non era
    un'opera', *NRMI*, v (1971), 788
L. F. Coral: *Music in English Auction Sales, 1676–1750* (diss., U. of
    London, 1974)

THOMAS WALKER

Sacred Harmonic Society. London amateur choral
society founded in London in 1832; *see* LONDON, §VI,
3(i).

Sacred Harp singing. A 19th- and 20th-century
American vocal tradition using the *Sacred Harp*, a
shape-note tunebook first published in 1844; *see* SHAPE-
NOTE HYMNODY, §2.

Sacred Music Society. New York choral society
founded in 1823, merged in 1849 with the Musical
Institute to form the New York Harmonic Society; *see*
NEW YORK, §7.

Sacro Buscho. *See* JOHANNES DE SACROBOSCO.

Sadai [Sidi], Yizhak (*b* Sofia, 13 May 1935). Israeli
composer of Bulgarian birth. He moved to Israel with
his parents in 1949, and in 1956 graduated from the Tel-
Aviv Academy under Boskovich. The works he composed between 1954 and 1960 show two forces working
almost simultaneously: a striving to integrate *maqāmāt*
with Bergian expressionism, and an attempt at emancipation from Eastern influences. These concerns are
best shown in the plaintive chamber cantata *Ecclesiastes*
and in the *Ricercar symphonique* respectively. Newer
European techniques – suggested by Haubenstock-
Ramati, with whom Sadai studied in 1957 – brought
about the satiric cantata *Psychoanalysis*, and the expressive serial keyboard variations *Impressions d'un chorale*, which was performed at the 1964 ISCM Festival.
Psychoanalysis has complexities of irregular rhythmic
division and *Klangfarbenmelodie* textures. But oriental
melodic shapes are still present in the somewhat simpler
textures of the later Biblical cantata *Hazvi Israel*. Beginning with the *Interpolations variées* for string quartet
and harpsichord or piano (1965), a piece of delicate
Webernian clarity, Sadai embarked on a post-Webern
impressionist style. He holds that phenomenology has
played a major part in his approach to composition and
analysis after 1966, when he met Pierre Schaeffer and
found himself in accord with his humanist views. A later
influence which he has claimed is that of Chomsky's
linguistic structuralism. Sadai is a senior lecturer at
the Jerusalem and Tel-Aviv music academies. He published *Metodologia shel hateoria hamusikalit* ('A
methodological approach to music theory'; Jerusalem,
1964).

WORKS
(selective list)

Ecclesiastes, chamber cantata, 1956; Ricercar symphonique, 1957, rev.
    1964; Psychoanalysis (cantata, Sadai), 1959; Impressions d'un chor-
    ale, hpd/pf, 1960; Hazvi Israel (cantata, Bible), 1960; Interpolations
    variées, str qt, hpd/pf, 1965; Nuances, chamber orch, 1965; Aria da
    capo, 6 insts, tape, 1966; Prélude à Jerusalem, 3 reciters, chorus,
    orch, tape, 1968; Rencontres, tape, 1971; Song into the Night, tape,
    1971; From the Diary of a Percussionist, perc, tape, 1972; Anagram,
    chamber orch, tape, 1973; 9 pieces, pf, 1975; La prière interrompue,
    tape, 1975

Principal publishers: Israeli Music Publications, Israel Music Institute

BIBLIOGRAPHY
A. L. Ringer: 'Musical Composition in Modern Israel', *MQ*, li (1965), 282
Y. W. Cohen: *Werden und Entwicklung der Musik in Israel* (Kassel, 1976) [pt.ii of rev. edn. of M. Brod: *Die Musik Israels*]
W. Y. Elias: *The Music of Israel* (in preparation) [bibliography]

NATHAN MISHORI

Sádecký, Zdeněk (*b* Dvůr Králové nad Labem, 2 June 1925; *d* Prague, 28 Dec 1971). Czech musicologist. From 1945 he studied music education at the Prague Conservatory and musicology at Prague University, where he took the doctorate in 1951 with a dissertation on the part played by songs in the Czech revival. He was assistant lecturer and later lecturer at the music department of Prague Academy, where he lectured in music aesthetics. He obtained the CSc in 1966 with a work on lyricism in Suk's compositions. In his methodological approach he was influenced by the Czech aesthetician Jan Mukařovský and in particular by Antonín Sychra, with whom he worked on the integration of structuralist principles and a Marxist music aesthetic. From the early 1960s he began to concentrate his interest as a scholar on the aesthetics and theory of 19th- and 20th-century Czech music. In a number of analytical studies he increased understanding of the musical means of expression in the works of Smetana, Dvořák, Janáček and in particular Suk.

WRITINGS
Boj za demokratickou píseň v obrození [The struggle for democratic song in the Czech revival] (diss., U. of Prague, 1951; Prague, 1952)
'Josef Suk, velký pokračovatel v díle klasiků české hudby' [Suk, a leading composer in the Czech classical tradition], *HRo*, vii (1954), 11
'O hudební řeči našich masových písní' [The musical speech of Czech songs for the masses], *HRo*, viii (1955), 889
O některých otázkách estetiky O. Hostinského [On some questions of Hostinský's aesthetics] (Prague, 1955)
'Otakar Hostinský hovoří k dnešku' [Hostinský speaks to us today], *HRo*, xiii (1960), 14
'Celotónový charakter hudební řeči v Janáčkově Lišce Bystroušce' [The whole-tone character of the musical speech in Janáček's *Cunning Little Vixen*], *Živá hudba*, ii (1962), 95
Lyrismus v tvorbě Josefa Suka [Lyricism in Suk's works] (diss., U. of Prague, 1966; Prague, 1966)
'Výstavba dialogu a monologu v Janáčkově Její pastorkyni' [Dialogue and monologue construction in Janáček's *Jenůfa*], *Živá hudba*, iv (1968), 73
'Tématické vztahy v Janáčkově klavírním díle' [Thematic relationships in Janáček's piano works], *HV*, vi (1969), 26
'Dvořákova tónina dur a moll' [Dvořák's major and minor keys], *HV*, viii (1971), 152, 318

BIBLIOGRAPHY
J. Smolka: 'In memoriam Zdeňka Sádeckého', *HV*, ix (1972), 92

JOSEF BEK

Sadelar, Johan (*b* Brussels, 1550; *d* Venice, 1610). Flemish copperplate engraver. His works include a number of devotional music publications (1584–90; some ed. in Organum, 1st ser., xix–xx, Leipzig, 1930). These show angels or biblical figures singing and playing from partbooks and were probably intended as religious propaganda for the Counter-Reformation cause (see illustration). The compositions are complete and legible; they are the earliest examples of music engraving, antedating Verovio's first publication by two years.

BIBLIOGRAPHY
M. Seiffert: 'Bildniszeugnisse des 16. Jahrhunderts für die instrumentale Begleitung des Gesanges und den Ursprung des Musikkupferstichs', *AMw*, i (1918–19), 49
P. Bergmans: *La typographie musicale en Belgique au XVIe siècle* (Brussels, 1929)
A. H. King: *Four Hundred Years of Music Printing* (London, 1964)
S. Bain: *Music Printing in the Low Countries in the Sixteenth Century* (diss., U. of Cambridge, 1974)

SUSAN BAIN

Sadie, Stanley (John) (*b* London, 30 Oct 1930). English musicologist, critic and editor. He read music at Gonville and Caius College, Cambridge, from 1950 (BA and MusB 1953, MA 1957), studying with Thurston Dart, Charles Cudworth and Patrick Hadley, and took the PhD there in 1958 with a dissertation on mid-18th-century British chamber music. After teaching at Trinity College of Music (1957–65), he became a music critic on *The Times* in 1964, editor of the *Musical Times* in 1967, and general editor of the Master Musicians series in 1976. In 1970 he was appointed editor of this dictionary. He was for many years a regular broadcaster, chiefly on 17th- and 18th-century music; he has also prepared many critical editions, notably of music by J. C. Bach, Boyce (the trio sonatas), Boccherini and Handel (including the violin sonatas) and of the piano sonatas of Mozart (from 1971). He has written illustrated studies of Handel, Mozart and Beethoven, and a guide to Handel's concertos. In 1978 he married the cellist, bass viol player and musicologist Julie Anne Vertrees (*b* Eugene, Oregon, 26 Jan 1948), author of *The Bass Viol in French Baroque Chamber Music* (Ann Arbor, 1981).

Sadie's reviews in *The Times* and the *Gramophone*, though often expressed with a dry wit, show a sharp but sympathetic insight into the performer's task and a firm commitment to the claims of scholarship. As an editor he has ensured that the *Musical Times*, while keeping abreast of contemporary music-making, has also found room for a wide range of articles presenting the fruits of musicological research. His conviction that scholarship need not be confined to the ivory tower nor performance to the market place is not unique, but only an exceptional energy and range of sympathy could have enabled him to put it into practice in so many ways.

WRITINGS
'The Wind Music of J. C. Bach', *ML*, xxxvii (1956), 107
British Chamber Music, 1720–1790 (diss., U. of Cambridge, 1958)
'Concert Life in Eighteenth Century England', *PRMA*, lxxxv (1958–9), 17
'The Chamber Music of Boyce and Arne', *MQ*, xlvi (1960), 425
Handel (London, 1962)
'F. E. Fisher', *MT*, civ (1963), 864
with A. Jacobs: *The Opera Guide* (London, 1964; as *The Pan Book of Opera*, 1964, rev. 2/1969, 3/1971; as *Opera: a Modern Guide*, 1971)
Mozart (London, 1966)
Beethoven (London, 1967, 2/1974)
Handel (London, 1968, 2/1976)
Handel Concertos (London, 1972)
'Music in the Home, 1760–1800', *Athlone History of Music in Britain*, iv: *The Eighteenth Century*, ed. R. Fiske (in preparation)
'Boccherini, Luigi', 'Mozart', (3) Wolfgang Amadeus, 'Opera', §I, 1 and §II, 3, *Grove 6*
Other articles in *MMR*, *ML*, *MT* and *Opera*

JEREMY NOBLE

Sadler's Wells. London pleasure garden, from 1684 to about 1879; *see* LONDON, §V. Entertainment was provided at the Music House there, later converted into Sadler's Wells Theatre, opened in 1765. The theatre was reconstructed in 1931, partly for the performance of opera. The Sadler's Wells Opera company developed from the Vic-Wells Opera after 1935, when the Sadler's Wells Theatre became its exclusive home. It moved to the Coliseum in 1968 and in 1974 became the English National Opera. See LONDON, §IV, 2–3.

Sádlo [Zátvrzský], **Miloš** (*b* Prague, 13 April 1912). Czech cellist. He studied the violin, taught himself the cello, but then learnt bookbinding until advised by the

Devotional print showing the Virgin and Child with St Anne, and the four-part motet 'Ave gratia plena' by Cornelis Verdonck, engraved by Johan Sadelar after Martin de Vos (Antwerp, 1584)

teacher K. P. Sádlo (whose name he adopted) to make music his career. Though he was active as a soloist from 1929 and made his débuts in Vienna in 1934 and London in 1937, he studied with Sádlo at the Prague Conservatory (1938–40) and with Casals (1955). He was a member of the Prague Quartet (1931–3), the Czech Trio (1940–56, again from 1973), the Suk Trio (1957–60) and the Prague Trio (1966–73). In 1950 he began to teach at the Prague Academy; he has also given courses in the USA and at Weimar. His splendid technique, wonderful tone and full-blooded musicality are admired in classical and contemporary Czech works. He gave the première of Khachaturian's concerto and the modern premières of Dvořák's A major Concerto and Haydn's C major Concerto. He plays a Gagliano of 1750. He was appointed soloist with the Czech PO in 1949 and made Artist of Merit in 1962.

BIBLIOGRAPHY
ČSHS
B. Urie: Čeští violoncellisté XVIII.–XX. století [Czech cellists from the 18th century to the 20th] (Prague, 1946), 217ff
Pa-: 'Miloš Sádlo', HRo, v/4 (1952), 27
B. Karásek: 'S Milošem Sádlo' [With Miloš Sádlo], HRo, xii (1959), 60
K. P. Sádlo: 'Miloši Sádlovi k padesátinám' [To Miloš Sádlo on his 50th birthday], HRo, xv (1962), 294
J. Kozák: Českoslovenští koncertní umělci a komorní soubory [Czechoslovak concert artists and chamber ensembles] (Prague, 1964), 152f
ALENA NĚMCOVÁ

Sadze, Christianus (*fl* 1450). Flemish theorist. His only surviving treatise, *Tractatus modi, temporis et prolationis* (*CS*, iii, 264), is a partial commentary and expansion of early sections of Jehan des Murs' *Libellus cantus mensurabilis* (*CS*, iii, 46) – those dealing with the fundamentals of mensural notation. The treatise begins with traditional definitions of the five types of proportion, drawn from Boethius, and includes a table showing these ratios in numbers. The second part takes up the four levels of mensuration defined by Jehan; the commentary takes the form of adding charts which show pictorially the note shapes and their numbers included at each level of mensuration in the various combinations of triple and duple. The treatise goes no deeper than this and gives no discussion of the complications of alteration, imperfection, etc; there is no mention, for example, of rests. The work is designed for the rank beginner and emphasis is placed on the graphic depiction of mensural relationships.

ALBERT SEAY

Sá e Costa, Helena. Portuguese musician, daughter of Luis Costa; *see* COSTA (i), (18) Luis.

Sá e Costa, Leonilde Moreira. Portuguese pianist, wife of Luis Costa; *see* COSTA (i), (18) Luis.

Sá e Costa, Madalena. Portuguese cellist, daughter of Luis Costa; *see* COSTA (i), (18) Luis.

Saedén, Erik (*b* Vänersborg, Stockholm, 3 Sept 1924). Swedish baritone. Educated in Stockholm at the Royal College of Music, he entered the Royal Opera there in 1952. He has made many appearances abroad, at Bayreuth (1958), Edinburgh (1959 and 1974), Covent Garden (1960), Montreal (1967), Munich, and Berlin, where he created the title role in Dallapiccola's *Ulisse* (1968), but his long and distinguished career has centred on Stockholm, where he sings in the repertory operas of Mozart, Verdi, Wagner, Strauss and Puccini. His roles also include Wozzeck, Nick Shadow, the title role in Dallapiccola's *Il prigioniero*, Eugene Onegin,

Busoni's *Faust*, Baron Prus in Janáček's *The Makropulos Affair*, the Vicar in Britten's *Albert Herring* and Tovey in Bennett's *The Mines of Sulphur*. He created the Mimarobe in Blomdahl's *Aniara* (1959), Julien in Lars-Johann Werle's *Drömmen om Thérèse* (1964), St Phar in Berwald's *Drottningen av Golconda* (1968) and sang in the première of Hilding Rosenberg's *Huset med dubbel ingång* (1970). Made Court Singer in 1966, he is the dedicatee of Leif Thybo's *Dialog*, which he sang at its first performance in Copenhagen (1968). Although his voice has no special beauty of timbre, his outstanding musicality and dramatic conviction combine to make him an artist of exceptional interest.

ELIZABETH FORBES

Saenz, Pedro (*b* Buenos Aires, 4 May 1915). Argentine composer and pianist. He studied at the National Conservatory in Buenos Aires (piano with Alberto Williams, theory with Arturo Palma) and in Paris with Honegger, Milhaud and Rivier. He returned to Buenos Aires and taught at the National Conservatory (1950–63), the Conservatorio Municipal Manuel de Falla (director, 1955–63) and the Catholic University (1963–5). He has given piano and harpsichord recitals in South America and Europe.

WORKS
(selective list)
Orch: Movimentos sinfónicos, 1963; 3 pinturas de Fragonard, 1969
Chamber: Pf Qnt, 1942; Str Trio, 1955; Divertimento, ob, cl, 1959; Capriccio, hpd, str qt, 1966; Sonata, vn, pf
Pf: 3 piezas epigramáticas, 1938; Juguetes; Variaciones sobre un tema original, 1947; Capriccio, 2 pf, 1965; Policromias; 6 piezas, hpd; Dieciochesca
Songs, 1v, pf: 3 canciones; 5 canciones; 5 poemas de Alberti

BIBLIOGRAPHY
Compositores de América/Composers of the Americas, ed. Pan American Union, xii (Washington, DC, 1960), 146

Saeta (Sp.: 'arrow', 'spontaneous outburst'). A devotional song genre, one of the Andalusian categories of CANTE HONDO ('deep song'). The *saeta* has long been associated with Holy Week in Seville: it is sung along the extended route of the all-night street processions in an atmosphere of fervour and vitality, intermixed with deep reverence and joy. The *pasos* ('statue-bearing floats') carried throughout the processions by the various *cofradias* ('brotherhoods') depict scenes from the Passion. The texts of the *saeta* deal with themes of the Passion, and they are sung in *coplas* ('stanzas') comprising four to six octosyllabic hemistichs. They are invocations to the Virgin Mary, who is the central figure in commemorating the Passion. *Saetas* can be heard at any point along the route, from a balcony or window, as a spontaneous rendering offered to a particular *paso*, usually the Virgin Mary or Christ, at which time the procession is halted until the song is completed. An example of a *saeta* collected in Seville is shown in Larrea Palacín.

The origin of the *saeta*, like many other types of *cante hondo*, is uncertain. Its musical foundation has been sought in the Moorish atmosphere of Andalusia, the Byzantine liturgy, synagogue chant and among the gypsy populace, who may have brought it from Hindustan. Larrea Palacín surmised that the *saeta* as a musical form derived from a remote fertility rite, which, when later christianized, lost its earlier sacrificial ideology in the course of centuries. Caffarena suggested that the *saeta*, as known in the 20th century, originated from the liturgical music of the early Christians, and that it was later 'gypsified', perhaps like the *toná*, *mar-*

tinete or the *siguiriya*. Rossy distinguished between the ancient 'sung oration' and the classical *saeta* that came into prominence during the first decades of the 20th century, which was gaining acceptance as a popular song. Kahn linked it to the orations of the Jewish converts. Caballero Bonald and others have expressed a hypothesis that has gained much acceptance, that the *saeta* derived from the *toná*, being a corruption of Catholic liturgical psalmodies, and that *saetas* were first sung only at the end of the 18th century.

See FLAMENCO.

BIBLIOGRAPHY
A. Aguilar y Tejera: *Saetas populares recogidas, ordenadas y anotadas* (Madrid, 1928)
A. Rodríguez González: *Colección de 500 saetas originales* (Seville, 1930)
M. J. Kahn: 'Chant populaire andalou et musique synagogale', *Cahiers d'art*, xiv (1939), 155; Eng. trans. pubd separately (New York, 1956)
B. Jarnes: 'La saeta, canto judio', *Judaica*, x (1943), 443
D. de Valencia: *Historia documentada de la saeta* (Seville, 1947)
A. de Larrea Palacín: 'La saeta', *AnM*, iv (1949), 105
A. Salazar: 'La saeta', *Nuestra música*, vi (1951), 29
A. Caffarena: *Cante jondo* (Madrid, 1955)
J. M. Caballero Bonald: *El cante andaluz* (Madrid, 1956)
H. Rossy: *Teoría del Cante jondo* (Barcelona, 1966)
G. Diego: 'Las saetas: devoción, poesía y música', *Estafeta literaria*, no.147 (1969), 4

ISRAEL J. KATZ

Saeverud, Harald (Sigurd Johan) (*b* Bergen, 17 April 1897). Norwegian composer. He studied with Holmsen at the Bergen Conservatory (1915–20) and with Koch at the Berlin Musikhochschule (1920–21). In the Norwegian Composers' Association he was a member of the executive committee (1946–8) and of the expert council (1946–54, 1961–2). From 1953 he received a state artist's pension. His independence and strength as a composer were already apparent in the first part of the Symphony no.1, performed in Oslo in 1920. The first three symphonies are intense, late Romantic works; Saeverud then developed from this style to the atonal expressionism of the Piano Suite and the Cello Concerto (1931). In the immediately following orchestral pieces, opp.8 and 9, a neo-classical influence became evident, and the variation technique introduced in them was to remain of great importance. The mature works are freely tonal, with extensive polyphony and thematic material that often grows by degrees from concentrated motifs. Saeverud's rhythm is powerful and his orchestration sometimes unconventional or humorous, but always refined; the general effect is one of lucidity. With the German invasion of 1940 Saeverud became more prolific and more nationalist in his expression. In 1948 he composed the incidental music for an anti-romantic production of *Peer Gynt*; the score caused comment for its contrast with Grieg's. Although Saeverud is primarily a symphonic composer, some of his finest work is in the piano pieces *Slåtter og stev fra Siljustøl*; they are romantic character-pieces, but outside the Grieg tradition. However, Saeverud shares with Grieg a fruitful dependence on the folk music of Norway.

Saeverud's son Ketil (*b* 1939), also a composer, studied in Bergen, Stockholm and Copenhagen; he has written concertos for trumpet (1968–9) and double bass (1973) as well as much chamber and instrumental music.

WORKS
(*selective list*)
ORCHESTRAL
Sym. no.1, op.2, 1916–19; Sym. no.2, c, op.4, 1922, rev. 1934; Sym. no.3, B♭, op.5, 1925–6; Vc Conc., op.7, 1931; 50 variazioni piccole,

op.8, 1931; Canto ostinato, op.9, 1934, rev. 1961; Lucretia-suite, op.10 [from incidental music for The Rape of Lucretia, 1935], 1936; Sym. no.4, op.11, 1937; Ob Conc., op.12, 1938; Divertimento no.1, op.13, fl, str, 1939; Bukken og gjetene, op.14a (1941); Syljetone, op.14a/2 [from pf piece], 1939; Rondo amoroso, op.14a/7 [from pf piece], 1940; Gjaetlevise-variasjoner, op.15, 1941
Sym. no.5 'Quasi una fantasia', op.16, 1941; Siljuslåtten, op.17a [from pf piece], 1942; Småfuglvals [Little bird's waltz], op.18a/2 [from pf piece], 1941; Sinfonia dolorosa, op.19, 1942; Galdreslåtten, op.20, 1942, rev. 1955; Siljustølmarsj, op.21a/5 [from pf piece], 1943; Kvernslått, op.22a/2 [from pf piece], 1943; Den siste bå'nlåt, op.22a/3 [from pf piece], 1943; Kjempeviseslåtten, op.22a/5 [from pf piece], 1943; Romanza, op.23, vn, orch, 1942, arr. vn, pf (1946); Salme symfoni, op.27, 1944–5
Peer Gynt, op.28, incidental music and 2 suites, 1947; Olav og Kari, op.29 (incidental music, S. Bugge), 1948; Pf Conc., op.31, 1948–50; Havråtunet, op.33, film score, 1954; Kejser og Galilaeer, op.34 (incidental music, Ibsen), perf. 1951; Vn Conc., op.37, 1956; Vade mors, op.38, 1955, rev. 1956; Allegria (Sinfonia concertante), op.39, 1957; Minnesota Sym., op.40, 1958; Entrata regale, op.41, 1960; Ridder Blåskjeggs mareritt, op.42, ballet and suite, 1960; Håkonshallen, op.43, 1961; Bn Conc., op.44, 1963; Sym. no.9, op.45, 1966; Marcia solenne, op.46, c1967; Sonata jubilata, op.47, 1969; Fanfare and Hymn, op.48, 1970; Mozart-Motto-Sinfonietta, op.50, 1972

OTHER WORKS
Pf: Huldredans Jonsonknatt, perf. 1915; 5 capricci, op.1, 1918–19; Sonata, g, op.3, 1921; Suite, op.6, 1931; Lette stykker, op.14, 1939; Siljuslåtten, op.17, 1942; Småfuglvals, op.18, 1940; Slåtter og stev fra Siljustøl, opp.21–2, 24–6, 5 suites, 1942–c1946; Peer Gynt, op.28 [from incidental music], 11 pieces, 1947; 6 sonatiner, op.30, 1948–50; Bukken og gjetene, n.d.
Chamber: 20 små fiolinduetter, op.32, 1951, arr. 3 wind, n.d.
Choral: Sjå soli på Anaripigg, op.35, 1952

Principal publisher: Norsk Musikkforlag

BIBLIOGRAPHY
K. Egge: 'Saeveruds Siljustlåtten', *Norsk musikkliv* (1943), no.6
S. Lind: 'Harald Saeverud', *Nordisk musikkultur* (1952), no.4, p.167
T. Fischer: 'Motstand: gjennombrudd', *Nordisk musikkultur* (1956), no.3, p.71
M. Pergament: 'Harald Saeverud', *Nordens tidning* (1957), no.1
Harald Saeverud (Oslo, 1967) [Festschrift]
N. Grinde: *Norsk musikkhistorie* (Oslo, 1971)
C. Baden: *Harald Saeverud 80 år* (Oslo, 1977)

KARI MICHELSEN

Safī al-Dīn ['Abd al-Mu'min ibn Yūsuf ibn Kākhir al-Urmawī al-Baghdādī] (*d* Baghdad, 1294). Arab theorist. He was a prominent court musician under the last 'Abbāsid caliph, al-Musta'sim (1242–58), having first attracted attention for his skill as a calligrapher. Surviving the sack of Baghdad in 1258, he entered the service of the Mongol Īl-Khāns and became attached to the powerful Juwaynī family; after their fall (1284) he lost favour, and was to die imprisoned for debt.

Safī al-Dīn was one of the most important figures in the history of music theory in the Islamic Middle East, and the first great theorist since Ibn Sīnā (980–1037) and Ibn Zayla (*d* 1048) whose works are extant. His two treatises on music, the *Kitāb al-adwār* ('Book of cycles') and *Al-risāla al-sharafiyya* ('The Sharafian treatise'), present a synthesis of elements found in the earlier theoretical tradition which dominated the thinking of all the more important theorists of the following two centuries. His most significant and influential contribution was a scale system derived from a tetrachord division given by al-Fārābī as a fretting on the *ṭunbūr khurāsānī* (long-necked lute); the scale system integrated the 'irrational' neutral intervals found in practice (and previously defined empirically on the lute) within a rigidly symmetrical extension of the Pythagorean scale, thereby enabling them to be approximated to just-intonation intervals. It divided the octave into 17 intervals: the octave into two tetrachords and a whole tone (above); the tetrachords into two

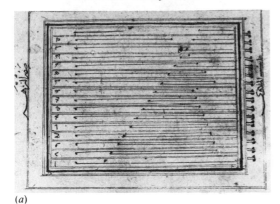

(a)

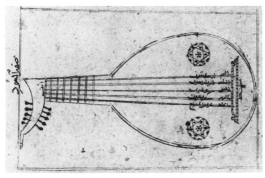

(b)

*1. Drawings from the 'Kitāb al-adwār' ('Book of cycles')
of Ṣafī al-Dīn (GB-Ob Marsh 521, ff.158r and 157v): (a)
nuzha (rectangular psaltery); (b) mughnī (archlute)*

whole tones and a limma (above); and the whole tones
into two limmas and a comma (above). This constitutes
essentially an elegant solution to an analytical problem,
and its relationship to the intervallic system used in
practice is in some respects oblique. Nevertheless, the
use Ṣafī al-Dīn made of it to provide information
about the intervallic outlines of the most important
modes is of inestimable value; apart from being the first
since Ibn Sīnā's his account is much fuller and affords
the earliest opportunity to examine the modal system (or
at least the scale structures) of Islamic art music in any
detail: he supplied a complete list of the two main sets of
modes – the 12 *shudūd* and the six *āwāzāt* – and
noted two further modes derived from two of the
shudūd. Certain aspects of the system are ignored,
however, presumably because the modes concerned
could not readily be expressed in terms of this standard
octave scale structure.

Ṣafī al-Dīn also ignored some of the general topics
dealt with by both earlier and later theorists, and his
range is thus rather narrow. He said nothing about
form, for example, nor about instruments (apart from
the traditional use of the lute as an adjunct to theoretical
demonstration), despite his being credited with the
invention of two instruments: the *nuzha* (a rectangular
psaltery; fig.1*a*) and the *mughnī* (a kind of archlute;
fig.1*b*).

Ṣafī al-Dīn's instructive, if all too brief, examples of
notation afford some slight insight into features of
melodic articulation, but are hardly representative. The
system of notation uses letters for pitch and numerals
for duration, and thus also gives some indication of

rhythmic structure. Ṣafī al-Dīn's general treatment of
rhythm, while perhaps not as original as his analysis of
scale, is clear and informative. The rhythmic cycles,
some with variant forms, are defined in terms derived
from prosody and in such a way as to specify the
various internal divisions and accentual patterns (*see*
ARAB MUSIC, Table 4).

WRITINGS

Al-risāla al-sharafiyya fī al-nisab al-ta'līfiyya [The Sharafian treatise on
  musical proportion] (MS, *GB-Ob* Marsh 521); ed. R. d'Erlanger: *La
  musique arabe*, iii (Paris, 1938), 3–182; ed. Carra de Vaux: *Le traité
  des rapports musicaux* (Paris, 1891)
Kitāb al-adwār [Book of cycles] (MS, *Lbm* Oriental 136, *Ob*
  Marsh 521); ed. R. d'Erlanger: *La musique arabe*, iii (Paris, 1938),
  185–565

BIBLIOGRAPHY

[H. G. Farmer]: 'Mūsīkī', *The Encyclopaedia of Islām* (Leiden and
  London, 1913–38, rev. 2/1960–)
——: 'Ṣafī al-Dīn', *The Encyclopaedia of Islām* (Leiden and London,
  1913–38, rev. 2/1960–)
——: *A History of Arabian Music* (London, 1929/R1973), 227f
L. Manik: *Das arabische Tonsystem im Mittelalter* (Leiden, 1969), 52ff,
  63–121
E. Neubauer: 'Musik zur Mongolzeit in Iran und den angrenzenden
  Ländern', *Der Islam*, xlv (1969), 233
L. Manik: 'Zwei Fassungen einer von Ṣafī al-Dīn notierten Melodie',
  Baessler-Archiv, new ser., xxiii/1 (1975), 145
O. Wright: *The Modal System of Arab and Persian Music, A.D. 1250–
  1300* (London, 1978)
                                                    O. WRIGHT

Safonov, Vasily Il'ich (*b* Cossack settlement, nr. Its-
yursk, Terek, Caucasus, 6 Feb 1852; *d* Kislovodsk,
Caucasus, 27 Feb 1918). Russian conductor, pianist
and teacher. His father was a Cossack general who left
the Caucasus in 1862 to settle in St Petersburg, where
his son attended the Alexander Lyceum and took piano
lessons with Leschetizky. Safonov entered the civil
service in 1872, but resigned in 1879 to enrol in
Zaremba's theory class and Brassin's piano class at
the St Petersburg Conservatory. He made excellent
progress, and graduated in 1880 with a gold medal. In
the same year he made his début as a pianist at one of
the concerts of the Russian Musical Society. He then
embarked on a concert tour with the cellist Karl
Davïdov, travelling extensively throughout western
Europe.

Safonov taught at the St Petersburg Conservatory
until 1885, when he became a professor at the conservatory in Moscow. He devoted himself to his new duties
with great enthusiasm, and in 1889 he was appointed to
the directorship of the conservatory in succession to
S. I. Taneyev. During his time in office sufficient money
was raised to enable the conservatory to move into new
buildings and, thanks to his energetic concern, the standard of teaching improved considerably. He placed particular emphasis on the study of composition, though his
own reputation as a pianist drew piano students of
calibre to the conservatory. His political convictions
tended towards the conservative, and he felt obliged to
resign after the period of student unrest in 1905.

From 1889 to 1905, and again from 1909 to 1911,
he was principal conductor of the Moscow branch of the
Russian Musical Society. He also organized several
seasons of popular concerts in Moscow. In his later
years he conducted without a baton. He prophesied that,
within a few years, all conductors would dispense with
their batons; his example was not widely followed,
though the novelty of the 'batonless conductor' was
much enjoyed by audiences and critics in Russia and
elsewhere. He made occasional appearances with foreign orchestras and, after being invited to New York as
guest conductor of the Philharmonic Society Orchestra

in 1904, he returned to become its sole conductor from 1906 to 1909. At the same time he was appointed director of the National Conservatory of Music in New York. In 1906 he conducted the LSO in a series of concerts, and in 1909 he appeared at the Newcastle Festival. His thoughtful and sensitive approach to music, and his tactful but firm handling of the orchestra were much admired. An American critic commented that 'Russia lost a great general when Safonov became a conductor!' He introduced the music of his Russian contemporaries to European and American audiences, conducting the first foreign performances of works by Tchaikovsky, Glazunov, Skryabin and Rakhmaninov.

On his return to Russia in 1909 he resumed his concert work and also played in chamber ensembles. He was an outstanding solo pianist whose interpretative ability and technical control were frequently commended. He was interested in the physiological and psychological aspects of piano playing, and was much sought after as a teacher; his pupils included Skryabin and Metner. He wrote a book on piano technique, *Novaya formula* (Moscow, 1916; Eng. trans., 1916).

BIBLIOGRAPHY

R. Newmarch: 'Wassily Safonoff', *MT*, lvii (1916), 9
S. Vasilenko: 'Moy vospominaniya o dirizhorakh' [My reminiscences of conductors], *SovM* (1949), no.1, p.92
Ya. Ravicher: 'V. I. Safonov: k 100-letiyu so dnya rozhdeniya' [On the centenary of his birth], *SovM* (1952), no.2, p.85
——: *V. I. Safonov* (Moscow, 1959)
K. Parlow: 'Student Days in Russia', *Canadian Music Journal*, vi (1961), no.1, p.13
E. N. Alexeyev and others: *Vospominaniya o moskovskoy konservatorii* [Reminiscences of the Moscow Conservatory] (Moscow, 1966)
JENNIFER SPENCER

Sagan Keyboard Manuscript (*PL-WRu* I. Q. 438). *See* SOURCES OF KEYBOARD MUSIC TO 1660, §2(iii).

Sagau, Jayme de la Té y. *See* TÉ Y SAGAU, JAYME DE LA.

Sagbut. Early English name for TROMBONE.

Säger, Johann Baptista. *See* SERRANUS, JOHANN BAPTISTA.

Saggion [Saggione]. *See* FEDELI family.

Sagittarius, Henricus. *See* SCHÜTZ, HEINRICH.

Saguer, Louis (*b* Charlottenburg, Germany, 26 March 1907). French composer of German descent. He is extremely secretive about his life; it is believed that he studied with a pupil of Busoni, and that some of his pieces were corrected by Hindemith, Honegger and Milhaud. His music presents a wide range of feeling which is communicated with directness.

WORKS
(*selective list*)

Lili Merveille (opera, after J. L. Bory), n.d.; Mariana Pinéda (opera, after Lorca), 1967
Orch works incl. Suite Sefardi, 1935; Musique d'après-midi, 1942; Musique d'été, 1944; Mouvement 60, str, 1963; Messages, 1964; Musique en sol, vn, orch, 1965
Musique à 3, 1943; Musique pour un, vn, 1960; Quadrilles, 1964; other chamber pieces; Quanta belle Giovinezza, cantata, 1972; many songs

Principal publisher: Editions Françaises de Musique
ANNE GIRARDOT

Sahak I (*b* 387; *d* 439). Catholicos and possibly a hymnographer of the Armenian Church; *see* ARMENIAN RITE, MUSIC OF THE.

Saibe. *See* SAYVE family.

Saikkola, Lauri (*b* Viipuri, 31 May 1906). Finnish composer. He studied the violin at the Viipuri Music Institute (1919–28) and played the viola in the Helsinki orchestra (1934–65). His symphonies show a craftsmanlike orchestration, but his most individual achievement is perhaps the opera *Ristin*, a work of definite Lapp colour.

WORKS
(*selective list*)

Operas: Ristin, 1957–8; Mästarens snusdosa, 1970
Orch: Sinfonia campale, 1938; Sinfonia tragica, 1946; Sym. no.3, 1949; Sym. no.4, 1951; Vn Conc., 1952; Conc. di miniatura, vc, chamber orch, 1953; Sym. no.5, 1958; Cl Conc., 1969; Raseborg, 1971
Chamber: 4 str qts, 1931, 1937, rev. 1973, 1968, 1968

Principal publisher: Finnish Broadcasting Corporation
HANNU ILARI LAMPILA

Sailer [Seyler], **Leonard** (*b* Ulm, 4 Nov 1656; *d* ?Basle, after 1696). German composer and organist. He may have studied with the Ulm Cathedral organist S. A. Scherer. He became composer and organist to Margrave Friedrich Magnus of Baden-Durlach. In 1689 he accompanied the margrave into exile at Basle where he also became involved with the collegium musicum. His only printed collection of music is *Cantiones sacrae* (Basle, 1696), which contains 16 motets and cantatas for one to four voices with organ and either two violins or, in five pieces, viols. Most begin with a sinfonia or sonata, no.2 has a ritornello used twice, no.6 has echo effects, and in no.13, *Das neugeborne Kindelein* – the only one to use a German text – the chorale melody *Vom Himmel hoch* is used and a violin motif in the sinfonia reappears in the first three verses. The pieces are not unlike certain works by Buxtehude. There are three other comparable works by Sailer in the Staatsbibliothek, Berlin: *Vertere in luctum cithara*, for tenor, three obbligato instruments and organ (the end of which is marked *ppp*), *Jesu, liebster Schatz*, for four voices, four instruments and organ, and *O benignissime Jesu* for bass solo, two violins and organ: two others (in *D-W* and *GB-Och* respectively) are doubtful.

BIBLIOGRAPHY

K. Nef: 'Die Musik in Basel von den Anfängen in 9. bis zur Mitte des 19. Jahrhunderts', *SIMG*, x (1908–9), 532–63
F. Refardt: *Historisch-biographisches Musiklexikon der Schweiz* (Leipzig and Zurich, 1928)
H. P. Schanzlin: 'Leonard Sailer und seine Cantiones sacrae', *Musik und Gottesdienst*, ix (1955), 109
F. Baser: *Musikheimat Baden-Württemberg* (Freiburg, 1963)
HORACE FISHBACK

Sailer, Sebastian [Johann Valentin] (*b* Weissenhorn, 12 Feb 1714; *d* Ober Marchtal, 7 March 1777). Swabian poet and writer of Singspiel texts. He was the son of Johann Sailer, clerk to Count Fugger, and entered the Premonstratensian monastery at Ober Marchtal. After completing his studies he was ordained and immediately became professor of canonic studies there. He was subsequently pastor at the abbey's parishes of Reutlingendorf (1748–9, 1754–7) and Dieterskirch (1757–73). The humour of his sermons carried his fame beyond the borders of Swabia into Franconia, Bavaria, Moravia and Switzerland. After preaching at the court church in Vienna in 1767 he was honoured by the Empress Maria Theresia.

In addition to his sermons, addresses and poems, some of them published in his lifetime, Sailer wrote the texts for a number of religious Singspiels, of which *Die Schöpfung des ersten Menschen, der Sündenfall und dessen Strafe* (Schussenried, 10 November 1743) became famous. They were not printed until 1819, however, when they appeared in an edition by Sixt Bachmann. Sailer may also have composed music to these works: in the preface Bachmann, who had known Sailer at Ober Marchtal, recounted that Sailer used to perform his Swabian plays on his own, accompanying himself with a fiddle in the airs, which he sang 'after his own composition'. Lach (1916) maintained that the earliest, rather amateurish manuscript copy of *Die Schöpfung* (in Latin translation, *D-KA* 777) was probably Sailer's, but was later carefully redone by a professional musician (*A-Wn* Cod.Suppl.mus.211). The work was also published with music in 1783 as *Adams und Evens Erschaffung . . . aus dem Schwäbischen ins Österreichische versetzt*, and under this title was set by the Benedictine father Meingosus Gaelle in 1796.

BIBLIOGRAPHY
P. Beck: 'Sebastian Sailer', *Alemannia*, v (1877), 104 [with list of works]
——: 'Sebastian Sailer, Kanzelredner, schwäbischer Humorist, Volks- und Dialektdichter', *Württembergische Vierteljahrshefte für Landesgeschichte*, new ser., iii (1894), 236
R. Lach: 'Sebastian Sailers "Schöpfung" in der Musik: ein Beitrag zur Geschichte des deutschen Singspieles um die Mitte und in der ersten Hälfte des 18. Jahrhunderts', *Kaiserliche Akademie der Wissenschaften in Wien: philosophisch-historische Klasse*, lx (1916)
L. Wills: *Zur Geschichte der Musik an den oberschwäbischen Klöstern im 18. Jahrhundert* (Stuttgart, 1925)

EBERHARD STIEFEL

Sainct-Gelays, Mellin de. *See* SAINT-GELAIS, MELLIN DE.

Sainete (Sp.: 'farce', 'titbit'). A type of one-act dramatic vignette which from the mid-18th century was often played at the end of Spanish theatrical entertainments. Similar to the *entremés* (performed between acts) the *sainete* was of comic and popular character, drawing upon incidents and situations of everyday life. Music formed an important element. Included were *seguidillas* and other dances, songs, vocal quartets and choruses; instrumental pieces were performed with whatever instrumentation was available, ranging from a single guitar to an orchestra. The *sainete* is particularly associated with the name of Ramón de la Cruz, but Antonio Soler, Blas de Laserna and most of the *tonadilla escénica* composers contributed to its repertory. In the second half of the 18th century some 500 examples were performed in Madrid alone; later the form developed (e.g. in Bretón's *Verbena de la Paloma*) into the *género chico* of the ZARZUELA. (The term was also used by Massenet for his *Bérangère et Anatole*, 1876.)

BIBLIOGRAPHY
E. Cotarelo y Mori: *Don Ramón de la Cruz y sus obras* (Madrid, 1899)
J. Subirá: *Historia de la música teatral en España* (Barcelona, 1945), 139
J. A. Montes: 'Sainete', *ES*
J. Subirá: 'La musica nel sainete', *ES*

LIONEL SALTER

Sainne. *See* SAYVE family.

Sainne [Sayne], Lambert de (*b* Rouen, *c*1500; *d* after 1564). French composer. He was a chorister at Rouen Cathedral, where his father, Rodolphe de Sainne, was organist from 1499 until 1514. He later sang in the choir of the imperial chapel at Vienna, and according to Fétis he was still there when Ferdinand I died in 1564.

Two motets by de Sainne survive in *RISM* 1568⁴: a four-part work, *Herodes rex iratus* with the expressive sequel *Vox in rama*, and a five-part work, *Hic est Martinus*, the conclusion of whose second section effectively repeats the closing text and music of the first. There is another five-part motet, *Ecce sacerdos magnus*, less distinctive thematically than the others, in *RISM* 1568⁵.

The slightly emended spelling in the attribution of *Hic est Martinus* in the quintus partbook to 'Lambert de Saievve' encourages further confusion between de Sainne and the later 16th-century composer, Lambert de Sayve.

RICHARD MARLOW

Sainsbury, John H. (*fl* London, 1821–44). English publisher and bookseller. He is known almost solely for *A Dictionary of Musicians*, which he compiled and issued anonymously in 1824, with a reissue in 1825 (*R*1966) and a further edition in 1827. The author's avowed intention was to publicize the merits of British musicians, whom he considered to have been unjustly neglected in the recent foreign dictionaries of Choron and Fayolle (1810–11) and Gerber (1812–14). He relied heavily on these works (large portions of Choron and Fayolle were merely translated) as well as on the histories of Burney, Hawkins and others; but in 1823 he also wrote to many musicians for information about themselves which he incorporated into the work. About 100 of their replies are in the Euing Library at Glasgow University, and many contain interesting facts not printed in the dictionary. Although the book fills gaps in knowledge of Georgian musicians, the information in either edition is not always reliable, and must be used with considerable caution.

BIBLIOGRAPHY
H. G. Farmer: 'British Musicians a Century Ago', *ML*, xii (1931), 384
——: 'Unknown Birthdays of Some Georgian Musicians', *ML*, xx (1939), 299

PETER WARD JONES

St Albans International Organ Festival. Biennial festival founded in 1963 by PETER HURFORD.

Saint-Amans [Saint-Amand, Saint-Amant], Louis Joseph (Claude) (*b* Marseilles, 26 June 1749; *d* Paris, *c*1820). French composer. He abandoned his law studies to play accompaniments for a troupe of Italian singers appearing in southern France. As tutor to the children of a Swiss baron, he spent three years in Italy, where he studied the music of leading Neapolitan composers. In 1769 he went to Paris and had a solo motet, *Cantate Domino*, performed successfully at the Concert Spirituel. During the following years he wrote numerous stage works; although *La coquette du village* and *Le poirier* were well received, most of his works for the Opéra were never produced. In 1778 he was appointed conductor of a theatre in Brussels, where during a six-year stay he presented a number of his own operas. He returned to Paris as a professor of singing at the Ecole Royale de Chant. He taught singing at the Conservatoire from 1798 but was relieved of his duties after the reform of 1800. He lived in Brest for several years, composing chamber music and religious works, including a *Te Deum* for Napoleon's birthday celebration in 1807. He wrote more than 25 stage works, sacred and secular vocal works and instrumental music, little of which was published.

WORKS

STAGE

(lost unless otherwise indicated)

Alvar et Mancia, ou Le captif de retour (comedy with ariettes, 3, A. G. Cailly), Paris, Théâtre-Italien, 13 June 1770

La coquette du village, ou Le baiser pris et rendu (comedy with ariettes, 2, L. Anseaume), Paris, Théâtre-Italien, 19 Sept 1771

Le poirier (opéra comique, 1, Anseaume), Paris, Théâtre-Italien, 20 June 1772 [rev. version of an opera by Vadé], (Paris, 1772)

Le médecin de l'amour (opéra comique, 1, Anseaume), Paris, Théâtre-Italien, 1773 [rev. version of an opera by J. L. Laruette]

Oroès (tragédie lyrique, 5), 1776, unperf., *F-Po*

La mort de Didon (ballet, 3, M. Gardel), Paris, Théâtre de la Cour, 1776 or 1777

Daphnis et Thémire (pastoral), Brussels, 1778

L'occasion (opéra bouffe, 1, ? P. F. Biancolleli), Brussels, 1778 or 1780

La fausse veuve (opéra comique, 2), Brussels, Monnaie, 1778

Psyché et l'Amour (pastoral, C. H. F. de Voisenon), Brussels, Monnaie, 1778

La rosière de Salency (opera, 3, C. S. Favart), Brussels, Monnaie, 1778

La fête de Flore (opera, 1, J.P.A.R. de Saint-Marc), Paris, Opéra, 1784

Le prix de l'arc (opéra comique, 1, A.N.P. La Salle d'Offrémont), Paris, Théâtre de la Cour, 1785

Laurence (opera, 1), Strasbourg, 1790, MS score cited by Eitner

Ninette à la cour, ou Le caprice amoureux (comedy with ariettes, 2, Favart), Paris, Théâtre-Italien, 12 Feb 1785 (Paris, n.d.)

L'heureux démenti (opéra comique, 2), ? Tours, 1794

Aspasie (opera, 2), Paris, 1795

Le pauvre homme (opéra comique, 1), Paris, Théâtre des Jeunes Artistes, 1797

La tireuse de cartes (opéra comique, 1), Paris, Théâtre des Jeunes Artistes, 1799

L'isle déserte (opéra comique, 2), Paris, Théâtre des Jeunes Artistes, 1801

Chacun à son plan (opéra comique, 1), Paris, Théâtre de la Porte-Saint-Martin, 1802

Lost, unperf.: La forêt enchantée, 1774; Le faux vieillard, 1774; Emirène, before 1780; La fée Urgèle, 1788; Scène d'Alcyone, 1789; La leçon littéraire, 1807

Many airs from Saint-Amans' operas in contemporary anthologies

OTHER WORKS

Sacred vocal: Laudate pueri Dominum, motet, 3vv, insts, *F-Pn*; Te Deum, chorus, orch, Paris, 15 Aug 1807, *Pn*; other works, unpubd, lost

Oratorios: David et Goliath, 1777, lost; La destruction de Jéricho, 1804, lost; Oratorio maçonnique, 1806, lost

Inst: Quartetto, hpd 4 hands (Paris, 1773); L'abbé mis au pas par les braves sans-culottes, potpourri, pf (Paris, c1790); Récréation lyrique, air with variations (Paris, after 1800); Conc., hpd/pf, b (Paris, n.d.); other works, lost

Pedagogical: Table élémentaire des accords (Paris, 1802)

BIBLIOGRAPHY

EitnerQ; *FétisB*

C. Burney: *The Present State of Music in France and Italy* (London, 1771, 2/1773); ed. P. Scholes as *Dr. Burney's Musical Tours* (London, 1959)

J. B. de La Borde: *Essai sur la musique ancienne et moderne*, iii (Paris, 1780/*R*1972), 484

A. Choron and F. Fayolle: *Dictionnaire historique des musiciens* (Paris, 1810–11/*R*1971)

C. Pierre: *Le Conservatoire national de musique et de déclamation: documents historiques et administratifs* (Paris, 1900)

C. D. Brenner: *A Bibliographical List of Plays in the French Language 1700–1789* (Berkeley, 1947)

U. Manferrari: *Dizionario universale delle opere melodrammatiche* (Florence, 1954–5)

M. Briquet: 'Saint-Amans, Louis-Joseph-Claude', *MGG*

FRÉDÉRIC ROBERT

Saint Circ, Uc de. See UC DE SAINT CIRC.

Saint-Cyr. Village west of Versailles where in 1686 Mme de Maintenon established the Maison Royale Saint-Louis de Saint-Cyr; see PARIS, §V, 3.

St Denis. Benedictine abbey north of Paris. It is one of the most ancient and influential French abbeys, at which nearly all the French kings are buried, and it played an important part in the Carolingian reform of the ecclesiastical chant.

The earliest evidence of a place of worship at St Denis derives from Gregory of Tours, who stated that secular clergy were living near the tomb of the martyr Dionysius (Denis, Denys), first Bishop of Paris (*fl* 3rd century). Under Dagobert (*d* 638), the first French king to be buried at St Denis, the monument marking the tomb was rebuilt. (The St Denis liturgy was later characterized by a commemoration on 19 January of Dagobert and his wife Nantilde; see Hesbert, 1965, p.14.) The basilica was rebuilt in 775, enlarged by Abbot Suger in the 12th century and again rebuilt by Abbot Mathieu de Vendôme (1231–81).

In 754, at the invitation of Pepin the Short, Pope Stephen II together with his singers visited St Denis. This musical contact with Rome occurred just at the time of the Carolingian liturgy and chant reform (*see* GREGORIAN AND OLD ROMAN CHANT), a reform that relied for its effectiveness on the great abbeys like St Denis and Corbie, and monasteries (e.g. St Corneille de Compiègne) to the north-east of Paris which were visited in turn by the itinerant Carolingian court.

Three abbots were of particular importance for the development of the liturgy at St Denis: Hilduin, Guillaume de Gap and Suger. Hilduin, a notable figure in the first Carolingian reform, knew Greek, and this won him a great reputation in the eyes of the emperor. He translated the works of Dionysius the pseudo-Areopagite from Greek into Latin; they are in a manuscript written in uncial script (*F-Pn* grcc. 437) and given by Louis the Pious to the abbey in 827. Hilduin was also a hagiographer and the author of the Office of SS Cornelius and Cyprian (see Huglo, 1971, p.125), and he altered the Office of St Denis, before 835, to the form found in antiphoners from Paris (see Hesbert, 1965, no.114). He may have translated the Byzantine akathistos hymn into Latin (see Huglo, 1951, pp.27–61), and probably introduced the chanting of the Gloria, Credo and Sanctus in Greek. These chants make up the *Missa greca* in St Denis manuscripts (*Pn* lat.2290, f.7v, 9th century; lat.9436, f.1v, 11th century; *LA* 118, f.156v, 10th century). Finally, Hilduin was probably responsible for the Latin translation of the chêroubikon, which occurs in an 11th-century gradual with neumes (*Pm* 384, f.153); this was still sung at St Denis in the 13th century.

This Greek cult of St Denis – thought to be of authentic Greek origin – is reflected in the chanting of the Gospel in Greek on his feast day, 9 October; but this practice was adopted also at the principal festivals of the year, as is attested by an evangeliary whose Greek text is given a notation resembling the Greek lectionary (ekphonetic) notation (*Pn* lat.9387, f.157v). Guillaume de Gap became abbot in 1173. He was formerly a physician and in 1167 had brought Greek manuscripts from the East. He had the troparia of the Byzantine Office of St Dionysius translated into Latin, although the translations were probably not sung in choir at the abbey, since a later, 13th-century manuscript containing them (*Pn* nouv.acq.lat.1509) lacks musical notation (see J. Handschin, *AnnM*, ii, 1954, p.48).

The power and cultural influence of St Denis reached their climax under the abbacy of Suger (1122–51), adviser to Louis VI the Fat (1132–7), and Regent of France under Louis VII during the Second Crusade

(1147–9). He was a historiographer, an architect and master of works, the signatory of many letters and the author of the *Sancti Dionysii liber* (ed. E. Panofsky, Princeton, 1946). It was probably at this time that a magnificent antiphoner was copied (*Pn* lat.17296; described by Hesbert, 1965, pp.xi–xv and pl.ix); the musical notation is on a dry-line staff, and represents some of the best surviving evidence of the melodies of the Divine Office.

Two surviving 13th-century ordinals (*Pn* lat.976 and *Pm* 526) from St Denis, of similar date, testify that the *Missa greca* was still sung at this period. They contain a list of tropes and sequences found in noted missals of the same or a later date: *Pn* lat.1107, of the second half of the 13th century (see Leroquais, ii, 1924, p.140, no.332; *Le graduel romain*, ii, p.98); *Pn* lat.10505 (Leroquais, ii, p.292, no.469; *Le graduel romain*, ii, p.103); and *GB-Lva* 1346, a noted missal of the mid-14th century (*Le graduel romain*, ii, p.65).

There is evidence of the study of music theory at St Denis. In the late 9th century the modes of introits and communions were indicated with letters: this practice is seen in three graduals without musical notation (*Pn* lat.12050, written after 853; an early 10th-century manuscript in private ownership in Paris, ed. in PalMus, xvi, 1955; and *LA* 118, of the 10th century, whose tonary is published in Huglo, 1971, pp.94–101). There exist copies of treatises by Martianus Capella (*Pn* lat.7200, of the 9th century; *Pn* lat.13026, a 9th-century manuscript of Parisian origin which also at one time belonged to St Germain-des-Près, where Hilduin was abbot from 819) and by Boethius (*Pn* lat.7181 and 7199, both of the 10th or 11th centuries).

Nevertheless, the earliest theorist actually to work at St Denis seems to have been an early 14th-century monk, Guy, the author of a tonary (see Huglo, 1971, pp.336f) surviving in a unique manuscript (*GB-Lbm* Harl.281, f.58*v*) probably copied from a French model. Guy's treatise, however, only discusses plainchant; it would seem that mensural music was not cultivated at St Denis (*see* GUY DE ST DENIS).

The ancient liturgical traditions of St Denis managed to survive even the centralizing tendencies of its affiliation to Cluny in the 12th century, but they were abolished after 1633 when the abbey was incorporated into the congregation of the Benedictines of St Maur.

Under Bédos de Celles in the 18th century the abbey became an important centre for organ building. After the Revolution it was turned into a Collège des Jeunes Filles de la Légion d'honneur by Napoleon. It is now a parish church.

BIBLIOGRAPHY
J. Doublet: *Histoire de l'abbaye de St. Denis-en-France* (Paris, 1625)
M. Félibien: *Histoire de l'abbaye de St. Denis* (Paris, 1766)
F. d'Ayzac: *Histoire de l'abbaye de St. Denis* (Paris, 1860–61)
A. Gastoué: *Histoire du chant liturgique à Paris* (Paris, 1902)
H. Leclercq: 'Abbaye de St. Denis', *Dictionnaire d'archéologie chrétienne et de liturgie*, iv/1 (Paris, 1920), 588–642
V. Leroquais: *Les sacramentaires et les missels manuscrits des bibliothèques publiques de France* (Paris, 1924)
S. M. Crosby: *The Abbey of St. Denis, 475–1122* (New Haven, Conn., 1942)
E. Panofsky, ed. and trans.: *Abbot Suger on the Abbey Church of St. Denis and its Art Treasures* (Princeton, 1946)
M. Huglo: 'L'ancienne version latine de l'Hymne acathiste', *Le muséon*, lxiv (1951), 27–61
L. C. Mohlberg, ed.: *Missale Francorum: Cod.vat.Reg.lat.257*, Rerum ecclesiasticarum documenta, ser. maior, fontes, ii (Rome, 1957)
Le graduel romain, ii (Solesmes, 1957)
J. Formigé: *L'abbaye royale de St. Denis: recherches nouvelles* (Paris, 1960)
G. Hugo: *Über die mittelalterliche Beziehungen des Klosters St. Denys zum Klettau, Hettau und Thirgau* (Schnaittenbach, 1961)
R. J. Hesbert, ed.: *Corpus antiphonalium officii*, ii: *Manuscriptus 'cursus monasticus'*, Rerum ecclesiasticarum documenta, ser. maior, fontes, viii (Paris, 1965)
M. Huglo: *Les tonaires: inventaire, analyse, comparaison* (Paris, 1971)
                                                    MICHEL HUGLO

St Denis, Ruth (1877–1968). American dancer; *see* DANCE, §VII, 2.

Sainte-Colombe (*d* ?Paris, 1691–1701). French bass violist and composer. His first name is unknown; he was always known as 'Monsieur de Sainte-Colombe'. He probably came from a well-to-do family and may have been of independent means. He lived in Paris and was one of the outstanding bass viol virtuosos of the last third of the 17th century. He studied with Hotman and taught Marais, Danoville and Jean Rousseau. He is known to have been alive in 1691, but he must have died before 1701, since Marais included a 'Tombeau pour Monsieur de Sainte-Colombe' in his second volume of *Pièces de violes* published in that year. Danoville and Rousseau credited him with establishing the seven-string bass viol with overspun strings and with developing a fluent left-hand technique and a singing instrumental style. Titon du Tillet praised him as a performer but was critical of his compositions, by which he may have meant the 67 *Concerts à deux violes esgales* (*F-Pn*; ed. in PSFM, i/20, 1973). In instrumental style and musical maturity, they are an important link between the experimental pieces of Hotman and Du Buisson and the fully developed works of Marais and Forqueray. There are also a few pieces for one bass viol (possibly another part is missing) in a privately owned manuscript.

Sainte-Colombe had a son, who was known as 'Monsieur de Sainte Colombe le fils'. He was in London in 1713, when a benefit concert for him took place on 14 May. Some bass viol pieces by him are in a manuscript at Durham Cathedral (there is no continuo part).

BIBLIOGRAPHY
FétisB
Danoville: *L'art de toucher le dessus et basse de viole* (Paris, 1687)
J. Rousseau: *Traité de la viole* (Paris, 1687/R1975)
E. Titon du Tillet: *Le Parnasse françois* (Paris, 1732/R1971)
M. Tilmouth: 'A Calendar of References to Music in Newspapers Published in London and the Provinces (1660–1719)', *RMARC*, i (1961/R1968), 85
M. Urquhart: *Style and Technique in the 'Pièces de violes' of Marin Marais* (diss., U. of Edinburgh, 1970)
J. A. Sadie: *The Bass Viol in French Baroque Chamber Music* (Ann Arbor, 1981)
                                           CLYDE H. THOMPSON

St Emmeram. Benedictine abbey founded at Regensburg in the late 7th century; important centre of musical activity in the Middle Ages.

The abbey was founded in honour of the itinerant Frankish bishop and saint Emmeram, martyred *c*685, who was buried on the *mons martyrum* outside Regensburg. In the following century his burial place became an important centre of pilgrimage. In 975 the monastery became independent of the bishopric of Regensburg. At that time St Emmeram was the centre of Cluniac reform in Bavaria.

In the 11th and 12th centuries the monastery school became an important source of didactic and speculative works on music: in 1030 the abbot placed Othlo in charge of it, and among the names associated with it are Otkerus (author of *Mensura quadripartitae figurae*), WILHELM OF HIRSAU and ARIBO. After 1731 the abbey enjoyed baronial status and once again became a great cultural centre (this time in painting and science) until it came under the control of the principality of Regensburg in 1803; with the dissolution of the monastery in 1810, it passed to Bavaria.

The library was extensive; in about 1500, it contained over 600 MSS. In the early 19th century it passed to the Bavarian State Library in Munich. Of the medieval MSS, a 9th-century MS, two 11th-century cantatoria, part of an early patristic MS, a 12th-century troper and a 15th-century mensural MS are of interest to historians of music. The MS *D-Mbs* Clm.9543, written between 817 and 847 probably by the cleric Engyldeo, contains an alleluia melody provided with text throughout (*Psalle modulamina*, to the alleluia with the verse *Christus resurgens ex mortuis*); this is an early example, with neumes, of the practice of providing texts for the melismas in Roman plainsong. The two cantatoria (Clm.14322, written between 1024 and 1026, and Clm.14083, written between 1031 and 1037) contain, besides the responsorial chants of the Mass, an abundance of troped chants of the Ordinary and the Proper of the Mass and some east Frankish sequences, written in German neumes. The patristic MS (Clm.14843), whose date lies between the 9th and 11th centuries, contains in its supplement (ff.97–104) liturgical tropes, sequences and hymns without neumes. The original flyleaves (ff.1–14) of the 12th-century troper (Clm.14845) contain tropes, sequences, alleluia verses, etc, with neumes. The mensural MS Clm.14274 (olim mus.3232*a*) is a major source of 15th-century music; it is a quarto manuscript of Bavarian origin containing mostly three-voice sacred and secular works mainly by northern French composers from the period around 1400.

BIBLIOGRAPHY

K. Dèzes: 'Der Mensuralkodex des Benediktinerklosters St. Emmerami', *ZMw*, x (1927–8), 65
B. Stäblein: 'Die zwei St. Emmeramer Kantatorien aus dem 11. Jahrhundert', *13. Jahresbericht des Vereins zur Erforschung der Regensburger Diözesangeschichte* (Metten, 1939), 239
B. Bischoff: *Die südostdeutschen Schreibschulen und Bibliotheken in der Karolingerzeit*, i (Leipzig, 1940, rev. 2/1960)
M. Piendl: *Quellen und Forschungen zur Geschichte des ehemaligen Reichsstiftes St Emmeram in Regensburg* (Kallmünz, 1961)
B. Stäblein: 'Zwei Textierungen des Alleluia *Christus resurgens* in St Emmeram, Regensburg', *Organicae voces: Festschrift Joseph Smits van Waesberghe* (Amsterdam, 1963), 157

KARLHEINZ SCHLAGER

Saint-Evremond, Charles de Saint-Denis, Seigneur de (baptized St Denis-le-Gast, Manche, 5 Jan 1614; *d* London, 29 Sept 1703). French man of letters. After studies at the Jesuit college in Paris, he entered military service, rising to the rank of *maréchal de camp* in 1652. During the Fronde he was disgraced by his *Lettre sur la Paix des Pyrénées* (1661) and was obliged to seek exile outside France. He fled to Holland and in 1670 to England, where he was received by Charles II and pensioned. His home in London became a centre of intellectual and social activity as well as of court amusements, all of which is reflected in his literary production.

In his writings on music Saint-Evremond expressed decided views on opera. He was generally opposed to dramatic works sung entirely from beginning to end. To him music was a useful ornament to spoken drama, of which only certain features, such as prayers, oaths and expressions of love or sorrow, were suitable for musical setting. He excepted the works of Lully from this stricture and showed a clear preference for French style over Italian in matters of taste and vocal performance. All told, his musical writings constitute a notable contribution to the development of aesthetics and a philosophy of opera during the late 17th and early 18th centuries.

WRITINGS

Essays and letters on music, some first appearing in *Oeuvres meslées*, vii, xi (Paris, 1684), and others added to later edns. by P. des Maizeaux (1705–; Eng. trans., London, 1728): *Sur les opéra*; *Les opéra, comédie*; *Idylle en musique*; *Observations sur le goût et le discernement des françois*; *Parodie d'une scène de l'opéra de Roland*; *Eclaircissement sur ce qu'on a dit de la musique des italiens*; *A M. Lully*; also 2 short dramatic scenes in verse and a verse/prol., all intended for musical setting.

BIBLIOGRAPHY

C. Gildon: *The Life of Mr. Thomas Betterton . . . With the Judgment of de St. Evremond, upon the Italian and French Music and Opera's* (London, 1710/*R*1970)
I. Lowens: 'St. Evremond, Dryden, and the Theory of Opera', *Criticism*, i (1959), 226
R. Ternois: 'Saint-Evremond, gentilhomme normand', *Annales de Normandie* (1960), 3
——: *Oeuvres en prose de Saint-Evremond*, ed. R. Ternois (Paris, 1962–6)

ALBERT COHEN

St Florian. Monastery near Linz, Austria, founded about 1071 by Augustinian canons. Manuscripts in the monastery library provide evidence of early vocal music in the abbey church; the neumatic notation is similar to that of the St Gall school and dates from the 9th century. The monastery school, where music was taught in addition to the liberal arts, provided regular church music. Polyphony was first performed in the first half of the 14th century, and in 1475 one of the monks achieved fame as an organist. Instrumental music was played, both in the church and the monastery, from the 16th century onwards. An inventory of 1612 lists a regal, two 'double instruments' and 46 string and woodwind instruments in addition to the main organ. There have been composers at St Florian throughout its existence. Among those recorded in the 17th century were Josef Haug, J. K. Merkl, Melchior Kämpfel and Stefan Vogl. The most famous *regens chori* of the 18th century was F. J. Aumann. David Fuhrmann initiated the reconstruction of the monastery in Baroque style (1686–1750), and F. X. Chrismann was commissioned to build the organ in the rebuilt church. This famous instrument originally had three manuals, 59 registers and 5230 pipes, and has since been enlarged to four manuals, 103 registers and 7343 pipes. It is known as the 'Bruckner Organ' in memory of St Florian's greatest musician.

Bruckner, born near St Florian in 1824, was a choirboy at the monastery where he was taught music by the monks. Later he himself taught in the surrounding parishes and in St Florian itself. He was also organist at the monastery in 1848–56; he subsequently lived in Linz and Vienna but often visited St Florian for short periods and is buried there. In 1906–24 F. X. Müller (1870–1948) was director of music at the monastery, where he wrote his *Augustinus-Messe* (1911) and other works. In 1924 he moved to Linz, where he became Kapellmeister of the cathedral.

The monastery's music archives must once have been among the richest in Austria; however, through the rebuilding in the 18th century and inept administration in the mid-19th century much material was lost. Nevertheless, the library contains about 121,000 printed volumes and 800 manuscripts.

BIBLIOGRAPHY

A. Czerny: *Kunst und Kunstgewerbe im Stift St Florian* (Linz, 1886)
J. Hollensteiner: *Das Stift St Florian und Anton Bruckner* (Leipzig, 1940)

St Florian: the church, and organ by F. X. Chrismann known as the 'Bruckner Organ'

L. Hager: *Die Brucknerorgel im Stift St Florian* (Leipzig, 1951)
A. Kellner: '[St] Florian', *MGG*
O. Wutzel: *Das Chorherrenstift St Florian* (Linz, 1971)
W. Pass: 'Studie über Bruckners ersten St Florianer Aufenthalt', *Bruckner-Studien*, ed. O. Wessely (Vienna, 1975), 11–53

ALTMAN KELLNER

Saint-Foix, (Marie-Olivier-)Georges (Poulain), Comte de (*b* Paris, 2 March 1874; *d* Aix-en-Provence, 26 May 1954). French musicologist. While studying law at the Sorbonne he was a pupil of d'Indy at the Paris Schola Cantorum, where he studied the violin (diploma 1906) and music theory, also becoming an able quartet player. From 1900, encouraged by Théodore de Wyzewa, he devoted himself to musicology and became a leading authority on 18th-century music, especially that of Mozart. With Wyzewa and Adolphe Boschot he founded the Société Mozart in 1901. As a member of the Aix-en-Provence Académie des Arts et Sciences he contributed greatly to the artistic direction of the festival there. He was also a founder-member of the Société Française de Musicologie, where he twice served as president, and a member of the Académie des Beaux Arts and the Accademia di S Cecilia, Rome; he received awards from the Austrian government and the Salzburg Mozarteum as well as an honorary doctorate from Edinburgh University.

Saint-Foix's major work was his five-volume study of Mozart's life and works, of which the first two volumes (to 1777) were written with Wyzewa. It shows unprecedentedly minute analysis and chronological classification of Mozart's works based on their style; while modern source research has revealed errors in the chronology and shown this treatment to be too narrowly schematic, the book remains a fundamental study and particularly valuable for its detailed accounts of Mozart's forerunners and contemporaries in relation to his style. This topic, and the corresponding one of Mozart's influence on his successors (especially Beethoven and Schubert), forms a central interest of Saint-Foix's other writings, such as the articles on Schobert, Gluck, Sammartini, J. C. Bach and French symphonists around 1750 and his revision of Picquot's book on Boccherini.

WRITINGS

with T. Wyzewa: 'Un maître inconnu de Mozart' [Schobert], *ZIMG*, x (1908–9), 35; see also p.139
with L. de La Laurencie: 'Contribution à l'histoire de la symphonie française vers 1750', *Année musicale*, i (1911), 1–123
Wolfgang-Amédée Mozart, sa vie musicale et son oeuvre, de l'enfance à la pleine maturité, i–ii (Paris, 1912, 2/1936) [with T. Wyzewa]; iii–v (Paris, 1936–46)
'Chronologie de l'oeuvre instrumentale de Jean-Baptiste Sammartini', *SIMG*, xv (1913–14), 308
'Les débuts milanais de Gluck', *Gluck-Jb*, i (1913), 28
'Mozart et le jeune Beethoven', *RMI*, xxvii (1920), 85
'Mozart on Ferlendis', *RMI*, xxvii (1920), 543
'Les premiers pianistes parisiens', *ReM*, iii/10 (1922), 121 [Schobert]; iv/6 (1923), 93 [N.-J. Hüllmandel]; v/8 (1924), 187 [J.-F. Edelmann]; v/8 (1924), 192 [H.-J. Rigel]; vii/4 (1926), 102 [Boieldieu]
'Nouvelle contribution à l'étude des oeuvres inconnues de la jeunesse de Beethoven', *RMI*, xxx (1923), 177
'Les maîtres de l'opéra bouffe dans la musique de chambre, à Londres', *RMI*, xxxi (1924), 507
'Les symphonies de Clementi', *RdM*, v (1924), 1; also in *RMI*, xxxi (1924), 1
'A propos de Jean-Chrétien Bach', *RdM*, vii (1926), 83
'Un ami de Mozart: Joseph Mysliweczek', *ReM*, ix/5 (1928), 124
'L'éducation instrumentale de Schubert: les premières symphonies', *RdM*, x (1929), 79
Boccherini (Paris, 1930) [rev., enlarged version of L. Picquot: *Notice*

sur la vie et les ouvrages de Luigi Boccherini (Paris, 1851)]
'Cherubini, Maria Luigi Carlo Zenobio Salvatore', Cobbett's Cyclopedic Survey of Chamber Music, ii (London, 1930, 2/1963), 270
'Le dernier quatuor de Mozart', Studien zur Musikgeschichte: Festschrift für Guido Adler (Vienna, 1930/R1971), 168
'Sonate et symphonie', EMDC, II/v (1930), 3130
'Clementi, Forerunner of Beethoven', MQ, xvii (1931), 84
'Histoire de deux trios ignorés de Michel Haydn', RdM, xii (1931), 81
Les symphonies de Mozart (Paris, 1932, 2/1948; Eng. trans., 1947/R1968)
'Le symphoniste Franz Beck et le piano-forte', RdM, xiii (1932), 24
'Les éditions françaises de Mozart, 1765–1801', Mélanges de musicologie offerts à M. Lionel de la Laurencie (Paris, 1933), 247
'Un fonds inconnu de compositions pour mandoline (XVIIIe siècle)', RdM, xiv (1933), 129
'Pergolesi (1710–1736)', RMI, xli (1937), 24
'A Musical Traveller: Giacomo Gotifredo Ferrari (1759–1842)', MQ, xxv (1939), 455
'Sammartini et les chanteurs de son temps', RMI, xliii (1939), 357
'Autour de Paisiello', RMI, xlvii (1946), 243
'La musique instrumentale aux XVIIe et XVIIIe siècles'; 'Haydn et Mozart', La musique des origines à nos jours, ed. N. Dufourcq (Paris, 1946, rev., enlarged 3/1959), 231; 249
'Le problème de la Fantasie en ut mineur de Mozart (Koechel 396)', RBM, iii (1949), 219
'La jeunesse de Mozart: 1771: les diverses orientations de la symphonie', MJb 1950, 14
'Considérations nouvelles sur quelques caractères ou éléments de l'art italien', RdM, xxxvi (1954), 99

EDITIONS
Oeuvres inédites de Beethoven, PSFM, ii (1926)

BIBLIOGRAPHY
Obituary: C. van den Borren, RBM, viii (1954), 3; E. Müller von Asow, ZfM, Jg.115 (1954), 405; M. Pincherle, RdM, xxxvi (1954), 95; W. Richter, Acta mozartiana, i (1954), 50; E. Schenk, Die Mozart-Gemeinde, xxii (1954) [also in Musikerziehung, viii (1954), 104]; E. Schenk, ÖMz, ix (1954), 244
M. Gay: Discours de réception à l'Académie des sciences et arts d'Aix-en-Provence, 15.5.1956 (Aix-en-Provence, 1956)

St Gall [St Gallen]. Benedictine monastery in Switzerland, and one of the most important musical and literary centres during the Carolingian and Ottonian periods; also the city of the same name.

1. History to 1300. 2. 1300 to the present. 3. The chant tradition. 4. The city.

1. HISTORY TO 1300. The origins of St Gall go back to a hermitage established in 612 near the river Steinach by the Irish saint Gallus (c550–c627). Gallus had accompanied St Columbanus to the Continent. Exiled from Luxeuil by Theodoric II (595–613), Columbanus went to Zurich and later to Bobbio. Gallus, however, fell ill and stayed at Zurich, founding his hermitage nearby, where he was joined by a small community. In 720 St Othmar (c689–759) took charge of the hermitage and founded the cloister. The house followed the Irish (Celtic) rule until 760, when it became dependent on the bishopric of Konstanz and adopted the Benedictine rule. Louis the Pious (814–40) made St Gall an independent royal abbey.

With the 9th century, under Abbot Gozbert (816–36) the monastery entered its period of greatest prosperity, both economic and artistic. Rebuilding began in 830, following a plan still extant in the library. The learned and powerful abbots Grimald (841–72) and Salomo (892–920) enlarged the cloister's holdings and encouraged its intellectual life. Scholars, poets, and musicians flourished under them, notably Hartman II (d 864), the Irishman Moengal (d 869), Iso (d 871), Ratpert (d 890), Notker 'Balbulus' (d 912) and Tuotilo (d 915). Their output comprised chronicles, hymns, antiphons, tropes, versus and versus ad sequentias, including Notker's Liber hymnorum, an extraordinary

cycle of versus ad sequentias inspired by the primitive proses in an antiphoner brought to St Gall by a monk from Jumièges c860.

The achievements of the Carolingian school at St Gall were mainly literary, although it is likely that Hartmann, Ratpert and perhaps Notker wrote melodies for some of their works. It is almost certain that Tuotilo, a poet, instrumentalist and sculptor, composed the melodies of his tropes (e.g. Hodie cantandus). The outstanding achievement, however, remains Notker's development of the fully-fledged east Frankish versus ad sequentiam from the primitive models of Jumièges (see Crocker).

The community was also concerned with the preservation of liturgical chant. The monks regarded St Gall and Metz as the main centres of the authentic Roman tradition. From this belief there rose the legend that the Roman cantors Petrus and Romanus, bound for Metz, had arrived at St Gall, that Romanus had fallen ill and remained there, and that he had taught the authentic Roman tradition to the abbey's schola and introduced the use of the Romanian letters. The source for the legend is Ekkehard IV's Casus monasterii Sancti Galli. No earlier document, including the earlier Casus, mentions it.

The artistic traditions of the monastery continued until the early 11th century (albeit without the concentration of talent prevalent in the 9th) through the works of Ekkehard I (d 973), Hartker (d 1011), Notker Labeo (or 'Teutonicus'; d 1022), translator of Boethius and of Martianus Capella and writer of the earliest German music treatise, and Ekkehard IV (d 1060). Nevertheless, the 10th century brought a decline in royal support; there were invasions by the Hungarians in 925 and Saracens in 954. Emperor Conrad II (1024–39) in 1034 ordered the adoption at St Gall of the Cluniac reforms, which further constricted artistic activity. The Annales ceased in 1044 and the Casus in the early 13th century. It is significant that when the Casus was resumed in 1335 in German by Christian Küchemcister, he should have been a townsman, not a monk.

2. 1300 TO THE PRESENT. By the 14th century St Gall had lost its strong intellectual tradition. Abbot Heinrich von Gundelfingen (1411–17) allowed the members of the Council of Konstanz (1414–18) to remove hundreds of manuscripts, most of which were never returned. Similar depredations occurred during the Council of Basle (1431–49).

The early 16th century brought a revival of music at the monastery. Joachim Cuontz copied MS 546, the last of the St Gall tropers, in 1507. Fridolin Sicher (1490–1546) became organist in 1515 and contributed a songbook and a tablature to the library (MSS 461, 530). Part-singing began in 1531, but instrumental music was not admitted until 1692 despite an attempt to introduce it in 1645. Two songbooks, the Heer Liederbuch (MS 462) and the Tschudi Liederbuch (MS 463), came to the monastery from the historian Egidius Tschudi (1505–72).

The Reformation clashes did not spare St Gall. It was occupied by the Protestants (1529–31) and sacked by Berne and Zurich in 1712, when the church's paintings were destroyed and the library looted. Most of the books taken to Berne were returned; those in Zurich were sold and some eventually entered the Zentralbibliothek. The 17th and 18th centuries were musically undistinguished at St Gall.

The monastery was dissolved in 1805, but the library remained in the custody of some of the former monks, notably the historian Idelfons von Arx (1750–1833). In 1844 St Gall was made a bishopric; the conventual church became the cathedral and the library is now the capitular library. It remains among the most important monastic libraries still *in situ*, with some fundamental sources for the history of plainsong. The liturgical and musical manuscripts comprise nos.337*b*–547, including 339 (PalMus, 1st ser., i), a 10th-century gradual; 359 (PalMus, 2nd ser., ii), a 9th-century cantatorium; 390–91 (PalMus, 2nd ser., i), the 10th-century antiphoner of Hartker; and a group of 10th- and 11th-century tropers: 378, 380, 381 and 484. The tropers are particularly important as sources for the works of the St Gall school of the 9th and 10th centuries.

3. THE CHANT TRADITION. The manuscripts mentioned above reflect the rise of the cloister's musical scriptorium in the 9th and 10th centuries. They are notated in a fine neumatic script different from German neumes, which appears in some other Swiss and south German scriptoria (e.g. Einsiedeln and St Emmeram). They transmit a distinct tradition of chant characterized mainly by numerous *episemata* and Romanian letters. Few manuscripts are as rich in rhythmic signs as these: although rhythmic notation was used in manuscripts from nearly every region, it predominates in east Frankish and Messine sources.

The notation in the early St Gall manuscripts is not diastematic, but shows traits that suggest the melodic versions that Peter Wagner called the 'German plainsong dialect' (Wagner, 1930–32, ii, pp.v–xxxvi). The influence of the monastery was perhaps overstressed by the monks of Solesmes in their restoration of the chant, and some scholars now think St Gall peripheral to the main tradition of plainsong. The lasting influence and popularity of the Carolingian and Ottonian poet-musicians of the abbey, however, is attested by the wide diffusion of their works. (*See also* NEUMATIC NOTATIONS, §III, 1–2.)

4. THE CITY. St Gall grew around the cloister in Carolingian times; until the 14th century it was ruled by the abbots, but it became independent in 1353 and a royal town in 1450. Joachim von Watt (Vadianus) (1484–1551), a Reformation leader, founded the Stadtsbibliothek Vadiana with his own library. Dominicus Zyli published a German hymnal in the city in or before 1553, and in 1682 Christian Huber (*d* 1694) published his influential *Geistliche Seelenmusik* there. One of his descendants, Ferdinand Huber (1791–1863), became a prominent composer of lieder. A collegium musicum was founded in 1620 and evolved into the Städtsingerverein, as it is known today. The city has a symphony orchestra, founded by Albert Meyer (1847–1933), and another choir, the St Galler Kammerchor, founded in 1937.

BIBLIOGRAPHY
A. Schubiger: *Die Sängerschule St. Gallens vom 8. bis 12. Jahrhundert* (Einsiedeln and New York, 1858)

A. Mocquereau and J. Gajard, eds.: Paléographie musicale (Solesmes and Tournai, 1889–)

P. Wagner: *Einführung in die gregorianischen Melodien*, i (Leipzig, 1901, 3/1911/R1970; Eng. trans., 1907); ii (Leipzig, 1905, rev. and enlarged 2/1912/R1970); iii (Leipzig, 1921/R1970)

O. Marxer: *Zur spätmittelalterliche Choralgeschichte St. Gallens*, Veröffentlichungen der gregorianischen Akademie zu Freiburg in der Schweiz, iii (St Gall, 1908)

R. van Doren: *Etude sur l'influence musicale de l'abbaye de Saint Gall* (*VIIIᵉ au IXᵉ siècle*) (Brussels, 1925)

J. M. Clark: *The Abbey of St. Gall as a Centre of Literature and Art* (Cambridge, 1926) [with extensive bibliography]

P. Wagner, ed.: *Das Graduale der St. Thomaskirche zu Leipzig* (*14. Jahrhundert*), Publikationen älterer Musik, v, vii (Leipzig, 1930–32)

A. Scheiwiler: *Das Kloster St. Gallen: die Geschichte eines Kulturzentrums* (Einsiedeln and Cologne, 1938) [with extensive bibliography]

W. von den Steinen: *Notker der Dichter und seine geistige Welt* (Berne, 1948)

M. Cocheril: 'Saint Gall', *Encyclopédie de la musique*, ed. F. Michel, iii (Paris, 1961), 615 [with extensive bibliography]

D. J. Rittmeyer-Iselin: 'Sankt Gallen', *MGG*

B. Stäblein: 'Sequenz (Gesang)', *MGG*

——: 'Tropus', *MGG*

R. L. Crocker: 'Some Ninth-century Sequences', *JAMS*, xx (1967), 367–402

ALEJANDRO ENRIQUE PLANCHART

Saint-Gelais [Sainct-Gelays], **Mellin** [Merlin] **de** (*b* Angoulême, 1491; *d* Paris, 1558). French poet. He was the son or nephew of Octavien de Saint-Gelais, a rhetorical poet and Bishop of Angoulême from 1495. From 1508 to 1517 he studied law at the universities of Bologna and Padua. He was among the first to import the spirit of the Italian Renaissance; his light and *galant* verse, influenced by such Italian forms as the sonnet, *capitolo, madrigale* and *villanesca*, made him the most fêted poet at the court of François I, whom he served as almoner and librarian. Although pirated editions of his poetry appeared at Lyons in 1547 and 1574, he followed the example of the strambottists Cariteo, Il Tebaldeo and Serafino by avoiding publication and winning fame by his declamatory improvisation.

His musical talents were extolled by contemporaries, including Tyard, who compared his lute playing with that of Alberto da Ripa, and Barthélemy Aneau, who described him as a poet 'who writes, better indeed than all others, lyrical verses, sets them to music, sings them, plays and performs them on instruments; I know and declare that he can do it. . . . And in that respect he comprises divers persons, being poet [and] musician, [both] vocal and instrumental' (B. Aneau: *Le Quintil Horatien*, Lyons, 1556, included in J. Du Bellay, *La deffence et illustration de la langue françoyse*, ed. E. Parson, Versailles, 1878, p. 205, with attribution to Charles Fontaine).

No musical compositions specifically attributed to Saint-Gelais survive. However, the popularity of his strophic poetry in the *voix-de-ville* repertory of the mid-16th century suggests that his music may have been based on existing dance tunes. The 1547 edition of his verse includes an amorous *complainte* in *capitolo* form (11 three-line stanzas), *Hélas mon Dieu y'a il en ce monde*, with the instruction: 'Pour dire au luth en chant italien'. In later editions this is changed to '. . . sur la chanson des nègres sur la guyterre, *Se lo commo non me dan*'. He exploited the usual lyrical metaphors; one piece is entitled 'Sur un luth', another 'Pour la guiterre' and a third humorously suggests that the latch of a lady's boudoir makes sweeter music than either spinet, flute or lute.

Saint-Gelais figures more prominently than any other poet in musical collections printed during the decade between the death of Clement Marot in 1543 and the publication of Ronsard's *Amours* in 1552. More than 70 of his poems were set between 1529 and 1590 by 54 composers, including Arcadelt, Certon, Crecquillon, Janequin, Lassus, Le Roy, Manchicourt, Sandrin and Sermisy.

BIBLIOGRAPHY

P. Blanchemain, ed.: *Melin de Sainct-Gelays: Oeuvres complètes* (Paris, 1873–4)

C. Marty-Laveaux, ed.: *Gaspart Pontus de Thyard: Les oeuvres poétiques* (Paris, 1875/R1965)

H. J. Molinier: *Mellin de Saint-Gelays (1490–1558)* (Paris, 1910)

P. A. Becker: *Mellin de Saint-Gelais* (Vienna and Leipzig, 1924)

D. Heartz: 'Les goûts réunis', *Chanson and Madrigal 1480–1530: Isham Memorial Library 1961*, 88–138

C. Robbin, ed.: *P. Berés: Autographes et documents évocateurs de cinq siècles d'histoire* (Paris, 1969)

FRANK DOBBINS

Saint-Georges [Saint-George], **Joseph Boulogne, Chevalier de** (*b* nr. Basse Terre, Guadeloupe, *c*1739; *d* Paris, 9 or 10 June 1799). French composer and violinist. He was the son of a former councillor in the Parlement at Metz and a negress from Guadeloupe. Beauvoir indicated that the family moved from Guadeloupe to an estate on St Domingue (now Haiti). In about 1749 they settled in Paris.

At the age of 13 Saint-Georges became a pupil of La Boëssière, a master of arms, with whom his later military rival Thomas-Alexandre Dumas Davy de la Pailleterie also studied. He also had riding lessons with Dugast at the Tuileries. On 8 September 1766 he participated in his first public fencing match in Paris with Giuseppe Gianfaldoni (*b* 1739); Gianfaldoni won, but predicted correctly that Joseph would become the finest swordsman in Europe. Besides his expertise in fencing and riding, he excelled in dancing, swimming and skating.

Little is known of Saint-Georges' musical training either as a violinist or composer. He is reputed to have had some violin lessons with his father's plantation manager Platon on St Domingue, and it has also been suggested that he studied the violin with Leclair and composition with Gossec in France. While none of this

Joseph Boulogne Saint-Georges: engraving by W. Ward after Mather Brown

has been proved, it is unlikely that he was a musical autodidact, especially in view of his long, close association with Gossec. Because the six years he spent in La Boëssière's establishment were devoted exclusively to physical training and academic studies, it is presumed that most of his musical education was accomplished between about 1758 (when he left La Boëssière) and 1769, the year of his first professional engagement, as orchestral violinist under Gossec in the Concert des Amateurs at the Hôtel de Soubise.

Saint-Georges made his public début as a violinist with the Amateurs in 1772, performing his first two violin concertos op.2. These concertos, like all his others, seem to have been written to demonstrate his prowess as a violinist to the greatest advantage. The solo parts reveal much about his capabilities; they make extensive use of the highest positions and require phenomenal agility in crossing the strings and in multiple stopping, often in the quickest of tempos. But the virtuoso surface tissue was not an end in itself. His friend Louise Fusil wrote: 'The expressivity of his performance was his principal merit'. When Gossec became a director of the Concert Spirituel in 1773, Saint-Georges advanced to musical director and leader of the Amateurs, which rapidly became one of the best orchestras in France. La Borde reported that, under Saint-Georges' direction, they played 'with great precision and [fine] nuances'.

Between 1772 and 1779 Saint-Georges published most of his instrumental music: quartets for strings and continuo, violin concertos, *symphonies concertantes* and a pair of symphonies. His reputation as a composer rests primarily on these works. The quartets and *symphonies concertantes* generally have only two movements, a sonata–allegro and a minuet or rondo; the concertos and symphonies have three, fast–slow–fast.

In 1777 Saint-Georges made his début as an opera composer with *Ernestine* at the Comédie-Italienne. In spite of the dramatic flair evident in his concertos and *symphonies concertantes*, he seems to have been unsuited to the theatre. The critics Bachaumont and Grimm noted that, although there are lovely musical moments in his operas, he could not sustain the weak librettos he set. In about 1777 Saint-Georges became affiliated to the private theatre and concerts of Mme de Montesson, secretly married to the Duke of Orleans; the duke put Saint-Georges in charge of his hunting retinue at his seat in Le Raincy.

In January 1781 the Amateurs were disbanded, probably because of financial reverses. Soon thereafter Saint-Georges founded the Concert de la Loge Olympique. As its fame increased, the orchestra moved to the prestigious Salle des Gardes in the Tuileries. It was for this ensemble that the Count of Ogny commissioned Haydn's Paris symphonies, with Saint-Georges as intermediary.

On the death of the Duke of Orleans in 1785, Saint-Georges lost his position in that household and went to London, where he gave exhibition fencing matches at Angelo's Academy before the Prince of Wales and other notables. In London he sat for a portrait by Mather Brown, a young painter from Boston. After the last sitting Saint-Georges reported that it was a frighteningly good likeness. Returning to Paris in 1787, he composed and produced his moderately successful comedy *La fille-garçon* and resumed work with the Loge Olympique.

In December 1789, six months after the outbreak of the Revolution, the Loge Olympique was dissolved and Saint-Georges again went to England, this time in the company of the young Duke of Orleans, Philippe-Egalité. Again there were fencing matches at Angelo's Academy, and at the Royal Pavilion, Brighton, before the Prince of Wales. Saint-Georges returned to Paris in 1790 and, disheartened by the state of affairs there and bereft of his orchestra, he undertook a tour of northern France with the actress Louise Fusil and the horn player Lamothe. He took up official residence in Lille in 1791 where he became captain of the National Guard. Wishing to take a more active part in the Revolution, he formed a corps of light troops in late summer 1792, which was planned to comprise 1000 blacks; among them was the mulatto Thomas-Alexandre Dumas. Known as the Légion National du Midi, the corps had little military success; Saint-Georges was finally relieved of command, and incarcerated for 18 months in a house at Houdainville, near Clermont, Oise. On his release he was forbidden to live in the vicinity of his former comrades.

Unemployed again, Saint-Georges embarked on a vagabond life with Lamothe; they lived for a time on St Domingue. In about 1797 he returned to Paris, where he served briefly as director of a new musical organization, the Cercle de l'Harmonie, in the former residence of the Orleans family. La Laurencie's biographical account (1922–4) remains the most thorough.

WORKS
(*printed works published in Paris unless otherwise stated*)

STAGE
Ernestine (opéra comique, 3, P. Choderlos, after Mme Riccoboni), Paris, Comédie-Italienne, 19 July 1777, excerpts pubd
La chasse (opéra comique, 3, Desfontaines), Paris, Comédie-Italienne, 12 Oct 1778, lost
L'amant anonyme (comédie with ballets, 2, ? after Mme de Genlis), Paris, 8 March 1780, *F-Pc*
Le droit de Seigneur (? Saint-Georges, ? after Beaumarchais), ? perf. privately; 1 aria pubd as no.3 in Journal de Harpe, 1784
La fille-garçon (opéra comique, 2, Desmaillot), Paris, Comédie-Italienne, 18 Aug 1787, lost
Le marchand de marrons (opéra comique, 2), Paris, Beaujolais, 1788, lost
Guillaume tout coeur, 1790, lost, mentioned by La Laurencie (1922–4)
Excerpts in Recueil d'airs et duos, *Pc* 4077 [incl. 4 from Ernestine]; Auprès de vous mon coeur soupire, duo, *Pc* 4142

OTHER WORKS
Orchestral: 2 vn concs., op.2 (1773); 2 vn concs., op.3 (1774); Vn Conc., op.4 (1774); Vn Conc. (1774), also pubd as no.1, and as no.10 (1777); 2 vn concs., op.5 (1775); 2 symphonies concertantes, 2 vn, op.6 (1775); Vn Conc., no.11 (1777); 2 symphonies concertantes, 2 vn, op.9 (1777); Symphonie concertante, 2 vn, op.12 (1777); 2 sinfonies concertantes, 2 vn, va, op.10 (1779); 2 sinfonies, op.11 (1779) [no.2, ov. to L'amant anonyme]; Vn Conc., op.8 (*c*1781); 2 vn concs., op.7 (1782); Symphonie concertante, 2 vn, no.13 (1782); Vn Conc., D (*c*1799); Vn Conc., D (Geneva, n.d.); Vn Conc., *Pn*; Vn Conc., G, solo pt., *US-AA*; Symphonie concertante, D, 2 vn, *CH-Bu* (cited in Brook, 1961)
Chamber: [4] Qts, 2 vn, va, bc, op.1 (*c*1772), pubd in 6 Qts, op.1 (1773); 6 quartetto concertans (1777); 3 sonates, hpd/pf, vn obbl (1781); 6 quatuors, op.14 (1785); 6 sonates, vn, vn acc., 3 pubd (*c*1800); Sonata, E♭, harp, fl acc., *F-Pn*; Recueil de pièces, pf, vn, *Pc*; others in contemporary anthologies, periodicals, MSS
Vocal: L'autre jour à l'ombrage (Saint-Georges), romance, v, gui, *GB-Lbm*; others in contemporary anthologies, periodicals, MSS
Lost: Bn Conc., perf. 1782; Symphonie concertante, 3 solo vn, perf. 1784 [? one of op.10]; Sym., G, Rondo refrain cited by Grétry; Symphonie concertante, G, incipits in L. Sarasin, thematic catalogue *CH-Bu*; 6 airs variés, vn, vn acc. (*c*1799); Les amours et la mort du pauvre oiseau, vn, mentioned by Fusil
?Spurious: Sym., D, arr. pf, 6 It. canzonettas by 'Sigr. St. Georgio' (London, *c*1795), ? by the singing master St Giorgio; see Kelly

BIBLIOGRAPHY
EitnerQ; *FétisB*; *GerberNL*

L. Petit de Bachaumont: *Mémoires secrets* (London, 1777–89, many later edns.)
J.-B. de La Borde: *Essai sur la musique ancienne et moderne* (Paris, 1780/*R*1972)
Tablettes de renommée des musiciens (Paris, 1785)
A. E. Grétry: *Mémoires, ou Essais sur la musique* (Paris, 1789, 2/1797, repr. 1924–5)
A. Choron and F. Fayolle: *Dictionnaire historique des musiciens* (Paris, 1810–11/*R*1971)
F. M. von Grimm, D. Diderot and others: *Correspondance littéraire, philosophique et critique* (Paris, 1812–14) [original version censored; complete version, ed. M. Tourneux, 1877–82]
La Boëssière: 'Notice historique sur Saint-Georges', *Traité de l'art des armes* (Paris, 1818)
M. Kelly: *Reminiscences* (London, 1826, 2/1826/*R*1968)
H. Angelo: *Angelo's Pic Nic* (London, 1834, enlarged 1905)
L. Vigée-Lebrun: *Souvenirs* (Paris, 1835–7, many later edns.; Eng. trans., 1879)
R. Beauvoir: *Le chevalier de Saint-Georges* (Paris, 1840) [novel]
L. Fusil: *Souvenirs d'une actrice* (Paris, 1841)
P. Descaves: *Historique du 13me régiment de chasseurs, 1792–1871* (Béziers, 1891–2)
M. Brenet: *Les concerts en France sous l'ancien régime* (Paris, 1900/*R*1969)
L. de La Laurencie: 'The Chevalier de Saint-George: Violinist', *MQ*, v (1919), 74
——: *L'école française de violon de Lully à Viotti* (Paris, 1922–4/*R*1971)
B. S. Brook: 'The Symphonie Concertante: an Interim Report', *MQ*, xlvii (1961), 493
——: *La symphonie française dans la seconde moitié du XVIIIe siècle* (Paris, 1962)
——: 'Saint-Georges, Joseph Boulogne, Chevalier de', *MGG* [incl. fuller bibliography]
——: *Thematic Catalogues in Music* (Hillsdale, 1972)
E. Derr: *Joseph Boulogne, Chevalier de Saint-Georges: Black Musician and Athlete in Galant Paris* (Ann Arbor, 1972)

ELLWOOD DERR

Saint Germain, Count of (*d* Eckernförde, 27 Feb 1784). Courtier, adventurer, amateur scientist, inventor and dilettante musician. He purposely concealed his background and identity, and used such pseudonyms as Count Welldone, Prince Ragotzy, Count Bellamare and Count Surmont on his wide travels throughout Europe. Further confusion has arisen with the like-named French general Claude Louis de Saint Germain and with Robert-François Quesnay de Saint Germain, an ardent occultist who may have written the essays *La très sainte Trinosofie* and *La magie sainte* (still used by Freemasons) that are attributed to the count. Gerber, alone among the many commentators on Saint Germain's life (which has many times been made the subject of fiction, by Georges Sand and Bulwer-Lytton for instance), maintained that he was identical with an obscure violinist and composer in Berlin named GIOVANNINI, but this is improbable. Saint Germain was most likely either the son of Franz Leopold Rakoczy, exiled Prince of Transylvania, or the illegitimate son of Marie-Ann de Neubourg, widow of Charles II of Spain. In his youth he was probably a protégé of the Grand Duke Gian Gastone (the last of the Medicis) and may have studied at Siena University. He appeared in London society from about 1743, and in 1758 was in Paris, where he became a favourite of Mme de Pompadour and Louis XV. After an embarrassing affair as an unofficial political agent in The Hague (1760) he returned briefly to England. Further travels took him to Russia, Germany and Italy; he visited Berlin at the invitation of Friedrich August of Brunswick, and in 1779 Prince Karl of Hesse, his last patron, gave him a building for his scientific experiments. He claimed to have made several discoveries applicable to manufacturing processes and was associated with industries in the Low Countries.

Most of Saint Germain's musical activities were associated with his visits to England, although his talent was also praised by the French courtiers. According to Burney, the 'celebrated and mysterious' Count Saint Germain contributed several songs to the pasticcio *L'incostanza delusa* (1745) and attended its rehearsals with Prince Lobkowitz (to whom the libretto was dedicated); his 'Per pietà bell' idol mio' was encored nightly, but Burney considered the other songs in the published score insipid. Horace Walpole, who claimed that the count had been in England for about two years by December 1745, described him as follows: 'He sings, plays on the violin wonderfully, composes, is mad and not very sensible'. He published in London several sentimental English songs, a collection of 42 Italian arias (*Musique raisonnée*) and a book each of trio sonatas and solo violin sonatas. The aria collection includes the three from *L'incostanza delusa*; texts and music range from unpretentious idylls to intense dramas, all with considerable emphasis on accurate text rendering. His trio sonatas combine polyphonic and homophonic styles, but the violin sonatas are more Rococo in character.

WORKS
Vocal: Gentle love this hour befriend me, song (London, *c*1745); 3 arias for L'incostanza delusa (pasticcio), London, 1745, in Favourite Songs (London, *c*1745); The maid that's made for love and me, song, in *London Magazine* (1747), 46 [also pubd as Oh wouldst thou know what kind of charms, *Gentleman's Magazine*, xvii (1747), 441, and with new text in The Summer's Tale (pasticcio) (London, 1765)]; Jove, when he saw my Fanny's face, song, in *Gentleman's Magazine*, xviii (1748); Musique raisonnée selon le bon sens aux dames angloises qui aiment le vrai goût en cet art, insts (London, *c*1750); The Self Banish'd, song (London, ?1750)
Inst: 6 Sonatas, 2 vn, bc (London, *c*1750); 7 Solos, vn, bc (London, *c*1760)

BIBLIOGRAPHY
*Burney*H; *Gerber*NL
E. M. Oettinger: *Graf St. Germain* (Leipzig, 1846)
L. Wraxall: *Remarkable Adventurers and Unrevealed Mysteries* (London, 1863)
P. Toynbee, ed.: *The Letters of Horace Walpole, Fourth Earl of Orford*, ii (Oxford, 1903), 161
I. C. Oakley: *The Comte de St.-Germain: the Secret of Kings* (Milan, 1912, 2/1927)
G. B. Volz: *Der Graf von Saint Germain* (Dresden, 1923)
A. E. Waite: 'Comte de Saint-Germain as an Historical Personality', *Occult Review*, xxxvii (1923), 219
P. Chacornac: *Le Comte de Saint-Germain* (Paris, 1947)
J. Franco: 'The Count of St. Germain', *MQ*, xxxvi (1950), 540
J. H. Calmeyer: 'The Count of Saint Germain or Giovannini: a Case of Mistaken Identity', *ML*, xlviii (1967), 4
                                              J. H. CALMEYER

St Germain-des-Prés Chansonnier (*F-Pn* fr.20050). *See* SOURCES, MS, §III, 4.

Saint-Huberty [Huberti], Mme de [Clavel, Antoinette Cécile] (*b* Strasbourg, 15 Dec 1756; *d* London, 22 July 1812). French soprano. Her professional name derives from the assumed name of her first husband. She studied in Warsaw with J. B. Lemoyne and, after a period in Strasbourg, eventually reached Paris where she sang Melissa in Gluck's *Armide* (1777). Although of unremarkable appearance, she became a fine actress and for a short time was the mistress of the Opéra, eclipsing Rosalie Levasseur and Marie Joséphine Laguerre to take over such roles as Gluck's Alcestis and Piccinni's Angélique (in *Roland*) and Sangaride (contributing to the success of the 1783 revival of *Atys*). Her greatest triumph was in Piccinni's *Didon* (1783); she also created Hypermnestra in Salieri's *Les Danaïdes* and the title roles in Sacchini's *Chimène*, Edelmann's *Ariane* and Lemoyne's *Phèdre*. Unreliable in attendance at the

Opéra, she forfeited her place to Mlle Maillard. During the Revolution she emigrated with the Count of Antraigues. They were married in 1790, but the marriage was not announced until 1797, when he was imprisoned by Napoleon in Italy; she assisted in his rescue. They ended their lives in exile in London, where they were assassinated by a servant.

BIBLIOGRAPHY
G. Le Brisoys Desnoiresterres: *La musique française au XVIIIᵉ siècle: Gluck et Piccinni* (Paris, 1872, 2/1875)
A. Jullien: *L'opéra secret au XVIIIᵉ siècle* (Paris, 1880)
E. de Goncourt: *La Saint-Huberty d'après sa correspondance et ses papiers de famille* (Paris, 1882, 2/1885)
H. Sutherland Edwards: *Idols of the French Stage* (London, 1889)
F. Serpa: 'Saint-Huberty, Mme', *ES*
                                              JULIAN RUSHTON

St James's Hall. London concert hall built in 1858; *see* LONDON, §VI, 5(iii).

St John's, Smith Square. London church built between 1713 and 1728 and converted into a concert hall in 1969; *see* LONDON, §VI, 5 (i).

Saint-Lambert, ?Michel de (*fl c*1700). French harpsichordist and composer. Nothing is known of his life except that 'some years' before the *Principes* was written he was called to the provinces to teach some persons of quality who wanted a Parisian master. The only source for the name Michel is Fétis. As far as can be judged from his two didactic works, Saint-Lambert seems to have been a competent player and teacher of the harpsichord, with a good method of teaching and a very open mind, more cultivated than that of the majority of musicians of the time. A set of well-turned verses by him in praise of Marchand, at the beginning of that composer's second book of harpsichord pieces, suggests that the two men were friends.

In his *Principes* he set out the rudiments of music and a method of playing the harpsichord which is apt and well directed. His chapters on ornaments are particularly useful. His examples are drawn from books of harpsichord pieces by Chambonnières, Lebègue and D'Anglebert. He explained the *aspiration* as a kind of *Nachschlag*, a short auxiliary borrowed from the end of the value of the first of two repeated notes and indicated by an upward- or downward-pointing caret. This contrasts with François Couperin's use of the term for a detached note.

His treatise on accompaniment is also remarkably clear. The harmonic theory of the period is set out more simply than by Dandrieu. Because of the precision of his commentaries, Saint-Lambert remains as valuable for musical historians as he was for students of accompaniment in his own day. He made two sensible proposals towards the logical reform of notation. One, explained in his *Principes* (and adopted by Montéclair), is for a reduction in the number of clefs to three, with G always on the first line of the staff but in different octaves. The other proposition, which he expounded in the preface to his *Traité*, passed into practice. Saint-Lambert noticed that signatures for minor keys often showed one flat less than they should. He stated (and offered an example in his book) that 'in every minor key the sixth degree is essentially minor', and that he would 'put the flat in the signature, not in the musical text like an accidental, as is normally done. [The old way] is a great mistake, which has not been recognized up to now.'

WRITINGS

Les principes du clavecin, contenant une explication exacte de tout ce qui concerne la tablature et le clavier (Paris, 1702)

Nouveau traité de l'accompagnement du clavecin, de l'orgue et des autres instruments (Paris, 1707)

ANDRÉ TESSIER/DAVID FULLER

Saint-Léon [Michel], **(Charles Victor) Arthur** (*b* Paris, 17 Sept 1821; *d* Paris, 2 Sept 1870). French violinist, dancer, choreographer and composer. His real surname was Michel. He studied ballet with his father, a ballet-master at the royal theatre in Stuttgart, and studied the violin with Paganini and Mayseder. He made his début as a violinist in Stuttgart in 1834 and as a dancer in Munich in 1835, when he adopted the name Saint-Léon. In 1837–8 he studied ballet with F. D. Albert at the Paris Opéra. From 1838 he toured Europe as a dancer and in 1843 he created the ballet *La vivandiera ed il postiglione* (music by Roland) in Rome. He married the ballerina Fanny Cerrito (1817–1909) in 1845; they danced together frequently until their separation in 1851. Meanwhile he became famous as a choreographer. In the early 1850s he was *premier maître de ballet* at the Opéra. He appeared as choreographer, dancer and violinist in *Le lutin de la vallée* at the Théâtre Lyrique (1853). He produced numerous ballets in Lisbon (1854–6), was intermittently *premier maître de ballet* at the St Petersburg Imperial Theatre from 1859 to 1869 and directed the premières of *La source* (1866) and *Coppélia* (1870) at the Paris Opéra.

Although Saint-Léon was a talented (if superficial) violinist, he was best known as a dancer and choreographer. He astonished audiences by his high leaps and spectacular *pirouettes en l'air*. His virile choreography emphasized dance for its own sake and in many cases paid little heed to the story. He wrote mainly for solo dancers (often at the expense of the *corps de ballet*) and usually for particular performers. He developed many new effects, liked to include singers or a violinist (himself) on stage, and was among the first choreographers to display an interest in popular dance. His creations include *La fille de marbre* (1847), *Tartini il violinista* (1848) and *Stella* (1850) (the music for these by Pugni), *Pâquerette* (1851, music by Benoist) and about 30 other works. He composed a violin concerto (1845), numerous salon pieces for the violin and ballet music for *Saltarello* (1854) and, probably, other works.

BIBLIOGRAPHY

T. Gautier: *Histoire de l'art dramatique en France* (Paris, 1858–9)

S. Lifar: *Histoire du ballet russe* (Paris, 1950; Eng. trans., 1954)

I. Guest: *The Ballet of the Second Empire* (London, 1953–5)

——: *Fanny Cerrito: the Life of a Romantic Ballerina* (London, 1956)

M.-F. Christout: 'Saint-Léon, Arthur', *ES* [incl. detailed list of works]

J. G. PROD'HOMME/R

St Louis. American city, in the state of Missouri. It was founded in 1764; its first settlers were French-Canadians, followed by Anglo-Americans in 1803 and Germans after 1830. St Louis University was established in 1818, and an orchestra, the Philharmonic, was started in 1838. The St Louis Musical Fund Society was organized in the same year with William George Wells as director. It was succeeded by the St Louis Musical Society Polyhymnia, which gave its first concert on 27 November 1845, under William Robyn. This, in turn, was succeeded by the St Louis Philharmonic Society (1860) with Eduard Sobolewski as its first conductor. It lasted ten seasons, giving 62 concerts between 18 October 1860 and 21 April 1870.

On 24 March and 26 April 1881 the St Louis Choral Society gave two concerts, conducted by Joseph Otten. In the same year the St Louis Musical Union was organized and gave its first concert on 17 November with August Waldauer as director. In 1890 it was absorbed by the choral society, adopting the name St Louis Choral Symphony Society. Otten resigned in 1894 and was succeeded by the German Alfred Ernst. Ernst conducted 13 seasons, and under his successor Max Zach, previously an assistant conductor of the Boston SO, the personnel was increased to 64 and the name changed to St Louis Symphony Society. Zach improved the orchestra, introduced many American works and performed works by many contemporary composers. In 1909–10 he gave a Beethoven cycle of six concerts. Zach died in 1921 and was succeeded by Rudolph Ganz, who resigned in 1927. Several seasons under guest conductors followed, among them Enrique Arbos, Eugene Goossens, Bernardino Molinari, Emil Oberhoffer, Carl Schuricht and George Szell. Vladimir Golschmann was permanent conductor from 1931–2 to 1958 and was succeeded by Edouard Van Remoortel. Another series of guest conductors followed after 1961, from whom Eleazar Carvalho was selected as permanent conductor in 1963–4. He resigned in 1968 and was succeeded by Walter Susskind who retired in 1974 and was succeeded in turn by Georg Semkow. The orchestra comprises 100 musicians; since 1968 it has had its own auditorium, Powell Symphony Hall. The St Louis SO is the second oldest orchestra in the USA, with a history dating back to the first concert (24 March 1881) of the St Louis Choral Society. An offshoot, the Little SO, was founded by Igor Geffen in 1935. It has given summer seasons of six concerts in the quadrangle of Washington University since 26 July 1935.

The organization of the Musicians' Mutual Benefit Association on 13 September 1885 altered the personnel of orchestras, barring amateur players from professional groups. The St Louis Amateur Orchestra was organized at the Beethoven Conservatory of Music in 1893. In 1909 it became the St Louis Orchestra Club, then adopted the name Philharmonic Society of St Louis in 1923, the third orchestra to carry that name. It has had numerous conductors, of whom Frank Gecks (1909–29) was the most influential. Other amateur orchestras in the city are the Kirkwood, Webster Groves, Maplewood–Richmond Heights, University City, Jewish Community Centers and Gateway Festival orchestras.

In 1807 Joseph Philipson took from Philadelphia three Piano Trios op.32 by Paul Wranitzky; their performance may have been the first chamber music produced in St Louis. When Charles Balmer went to St Louis in 1839, he took chamber music scores that he had copied in Germany and, with John Fallon, a violinist, and William Robyn, a cellist, he performed Beethoven's Piano Trio op.70 no.1 on 15 January 1840. This appears to have been only the third performance of a Beethoven chamber work in the USA. Chamber music in St Louis eventually assumed formal status in the Balatka Quintet Club, which gave concerts in 1877–8, the Philharmonic Quintet Club (1878–97) and the Mendelssohn Quintet Club (1882–99). Local string quartets have always flourished. The Kneisel Quartet gave annual performances from 1885 to 1917 and the Flonzaley Quartet from 1905 to 1927. Since the 1930–31 season the St Louis Ethical Society has sponsored annual seasons of four concerts in which many contemporary chamber music groups have appeared. In 1971–2 the Fine Arts, the Allegri and the Amadeus quartets and the Warsaw Quintet all visited St Louis.

When Johann Heinrich Weber went to St Louis in 1834, he took an extensive collection of choral music, and it was probably due to his urgings that the St Louis Sacred Music Society was founded; it gave its first concert on 8 December 1840. In 1846 Charles Balmer organized the St Louis Oratorio Society, which remained active for many years. The St Louis Choral Society, mentioned above, was originally a choral organization but ceased performing choral music in 1907. The Pageant Choral Society was an offshoot of the Pageant and Masque given in Forest Park in 1914, and was directed by Frederick Fischer. The Choral Art Society was founded by James T. Quarles and specialized in music of the Romantic period. The St Louis A Cappella Choir was established by William B. Heyne in 1929 and devoted itself to the Baroque. On 10 May 1941 it gave Bach's Mass in B minor; the unqualified success of that performance led to the formation of the Bach Society of St Louis, which gave a second festival on 8–9 May 1942. The *St Matthew Passion, St John Passion*, the *Christmas Oratorio* and many cantatas, other choral works and instrumental works have been performed by the Bach Society.

The first musical play to be performed in St Louis was the ballad opera *The Agreeable Surprise* (16 January 1817). The English opera *Children in the Wood* by Samuel Arnold was staged on 24 April 1818. The earliest production of a 'grand opera' was on 21 July 1830 when Auber's *Masaniello*, possibly given in T. S. Cooke's English version, was performed by a theatrical stock company. The Seguins produced a week of opera in English in 1843; Luigi Arditi and his company gave four weeks of Italian opera in 1853; and the Grover Opera Company performed a week of German opera in 1865. During the second half of the 19th century there was a veritable flood of opera, and many travelling companies played in St Louis. The Metropolitan Opera appeared many times between 1884 and 1965–6. Its first production in St Louis of Wagner's *Der Ring des Nibelungen* (1889) was notable; it was next given in 1930, by a German opera company. In 1905 Henry Savage and the Castle Square Opera Company gave a week of *Parsifal* in English, and also performed *Madama Butterfly* in 1907. An event of particular significance was the production in the summer of 1914 of the Pageant and Masque of St Louis, celebrating the 150th anniversary of the founding of the city. With a cast of 7000 and an attendance of 500,000, this colossal drama proved the possibilities of community collaboration. It led to the formation of the St Louis Municipal Opera Association, which has given a summer season of operettas and musical comedies in Forest Park since 16 June 1919. The centennial drama *Missouri One Hundred Years Ago*, celebrating the admission of Missouri to the USA in 1821, was given five performances in 1921.

St Louis is noted for composers who have specialized in educational music for the piano – the so-called 'teaching piece' and piano methods for beginners. Among them were Jessie Lovell Gaynor (1863–1921), Dorothy Gaynor Blake (1893–1967) and Carl Wilhelm Kern (1874–1945). Other important St Louis composers are Samuel Bollinger (1871–1946), Ernest Richard Kroeger (1862–1934), Alfred George Robyn (1860–

1935), Walter Stockhoff (1876–1968), Albert Stoessel (1894–1943), J. Roy Terry (*b* 1899), Paul Tietjens (1877–1943), Gerald Tyler (1879–1938) and Ben Weber (*b* 1916).

St Louis is particularly important for music publishing in the Midwest. Nathaniel Phillips published the *St Louis Grand March* in 1839. Other notable St Louis publishers have included Balmer & Weber (1848–1907), Kunkel Brothers (1868–1934), Adam and Oliver Shattinger (1876–1958), the Art Publication Society (founded 1912) and Mel Bay (founded 1948). The Gaylord Music Library, built in 1960, was a notable addition to the music department of Washington University. Other active music departments are at St Louis University, Webster College, Font Bonne College, Concordia Seminary and Eden Seminary.

BIBLIOGRAPHY

W. G. B. Carson: *St. Louis Goes to the Opera* (St Louis, 1946)
E. C. Krohn: 'Music in the Vatican Film Library at Saint Louis University', *Notes*, xiv (1956–7), 317
M. E. Holderness: *Curtain Time at Forest Park* (St Louis, 1958)
L. B. Spiess: 'A New Music Library in St. Louis', *Notes*, xix (1961–2), 39
C. V. Clifford: *St. Louis' Fabulous Municipal Theatre* (St Louis, 1970)
E. C. Krohn: *Missouri Music* (New York, 1971)
——: *Music Publishing in the Middle Western States before the Civil War* (Detroit, 1972)

ERNST C. KROHN

Saint-Luc, Jacques de (*b* Ath, 19 Sept 1616; *d* in or after 1684). South Netherlands lutenist, theorbo player and composer, father of Laurent (or Jacques-Alexandre) de Saint-Luc. He was lutenist and theorbo player from 1639 at the court at Brussels and at the royal chapel there from 1673 to 1684, during which period he took part in the first opera performed at the royal palace. Constantijn Huygens, with whom he exchanged letters, praised his compositions but they are not now known to exist. His portrait by Gérard Seghers is in the town hall at Ath.

BIBLIOGRAPHY

E. vander Straeten: *La musique aux Pays-Bas avant le XIXe siècle* (Brussels, 1867–88/*R*1969)
W. J. A. Jonckbloet and J. P. N. Land, eds.: *Musique et musiciens au XVIIe siècle: correspondance et oeuvres musicales de Constantin Huygens* (Leiden, 1882)

JOËL DUGOT

Saint-Luc, Laurent [Jacques-Alexandre] **de** (*b* Brussels, 1663; *d* after 1700). South Netherlands composer, lutenist, theorbo player and guitarist, resident in France and Vienna, son of Jacques de Saint-Luc. He was a pupil of his father. He spent some time at the court of Louis XIV as a lutenist in the *chambre du roi*. In 1700 he went to Vienna in the service of Prince Eugène of Savoy, who held him in high esteem. On 6 June that year he took part with great success in the celebrations organized in Berlin in honour of the wedding of Princess Louise Dorothea Sophie of Brandenburg and Prince Friedrich of Hessen-Kassel. His music is in general light and conventional. Some of his lute pieces are arranged in suites.

WORKS

2 books of pieces, lute (vn/fl, bc ad lib) (Amsterdam, n.d.)
2 books of pieces, lute, fl/ob, bc (Amsterdam, n.d.)

2 books of concertos, lute, vn, bc (172 pieces), *CS-Pu*; 5, incl. 1 suite, ed. in DTÖ, l, Jg.xxv/2 (1918/*R*)
86 pieces, lute, *Pu*; 3 ed. in DTÖ, l, Jg.xxv/2 (1918/*R*)
174 pieces, lute, *A-Wn*
1 minuet, gui, *F-Pn*

Other lute pieces mentioned in Lacoste catalogue, Amsterdam

BIBLIOGRAPHY

A. Koczirz: 'Österreichische Lauten-Musik zwischen 1650 und 1720': introduction to DTÖ, l, Jg.xxv/2 (1918/R); also in SMw, v (1918), 49

JOËL DUGOT

St Martial. Monastery at Limoges (Aquitaine) in southwest France with which an important repertory of medieval music, monophonic and polyphonic, has become associated. Many scholars prefer the adjective 'Aquitanian' to describe the repertory and its manuscripts. (For map see NEUMATIC NOTATIONS, §IV, 5.)

I. General. II. Monophony. III. Polyphony.

I. General

1. History. 2. The manuscripts.

1. HISTORY. Among the French abbeys that were centres of musical and poetic activity from the 9th century to the 12th, none has left so rich a store of musical material as St Martial de Limoges, founded in 848 at the site of the tomb of St Martial, first Bishop of Limoges (3rd century). In the late 10th century, there grew up a legend claiming the saint's apostolicity; fervently supported by the monastery's chronicler, Adémar de Chabannes (*d* 1034), the apostolicity was proclaimed by the councils of Limoges (1028) and Bourges (1031), thus greatly increasing the abbey's prestige. Two significant factors mark the 200 years surrounding this period (930–1130): the flowering of the Aquitanian school of poets and composers, and, towards the end of the period, the rise of Aquitanian polyphony. From the early 13th century a long decline ensued, despite the efforts of a few exceptional men including the historian Bernard Itier (*d* 1224). In 1535 the monastery was secularized; it was dissolved in 1791 and demolished in 1792.

Beyond its actual artistic production, the abbey's importance for music history owes much to historical accident. Over the centuries the monastic library was fortunate to suffer fewer depredations and sacks than those of the great northern French abbeys, and also, during its most prosperous period, to have been in the care of several librarians with a rare collecting zeal. Thus the abbey became a repository of southern French liturgical manuscripts. The manuscripts were sold in 1730 to the Bibliothèque Royale, thus escaping dispersal and destruction during the French Revolution.

2. THE MANUSCRIPTS. The St Martial manuscripts contain the richest surviving collection of west Frankish tropes, proses, sequences, prosulas and verse-songs (*versus*). The list below presents them together with the other surviving Aquitanian tropers in approximate chronological order. Those marked with an asterisk are not from the monastery library. Concerning the dates and places of origin (shown in parentheses) it should be remembered that many are composite manuscripts, which received subsequent additions at different times and places. The decisions about St Martial's apostolicity (1028–31) provide a useful basis for dating: earlier manuscripts or sources from outside St Martial have the Mass *Statuit* for the feast of the saint; after 1028 the Mass *Probavit* was instituted. Older sources, whether from St Martial or elsewhere, were often altered to conform to the new liturgy, and these show erasures and cancellations. A few manuscripts remained unaltered, either because they were no longer in use in the service, or because they were acquired purely as library items.

F-Pn lat.1154 (9th–10th century; ?Limoges, St Martin); lat.1240 (923–34, 10th–12th-century additions; St Martial); lat.1084 (late 10th century, 11th-century additions; ?St Géraud d'Aurillac/St Martial); lat.1118 (987–96, 11th-century additions; Spanish border region); lat.1120 (*c*1000; ?St Martial); lat.1121 (*c*1000; St Martial); lat.1834 (troper fragment in guard folios; ?*c*1000; ?St Martial); lat.903 (1st half of 11th century; St Yrieix); lat.887 (before 1031; ?Limoges, St Martin); lat.1138 (originally a single MS) and 1338 (before 1031; S.W. France)

lat.909 (1025–30; date uncertain as revisions involved recopying of selected fascicles; ?St Martial); lat.1119 (1030; St Martial); lat.1134–6 (mid-11th century; Limoges); *n.a lat 1871 (late 11th century; Moissac, St Pierre); *APT* 17(5) (mid-11th century; Apt); *Pn* lat.1132 (late 11th century; ?St Martial); lat.779 (late 11th century; Limoges); *n.a.lat.1177; (late 11th century; place unknown); lat.1139 (polyphonic source; 1096–1100, 13th-century additions; Limoges, ?St Martial); lat.1133 (late 11th century; Limoges); lat.1137 (*c*1030; Limoges, St Martial); lat.778 (12th century; Narbonne); lat.1086 (12th–13th century; Limoges, St Léonard); lat.3549 (polyphonic source; 12th century; ?Limoges); lat.3719 (polyphonic source; 12th century; ?Limoges); *GB-Lbm* Add.36881 (polyphonic source; late 12th century; region of Apt)

Apart from two graduals (*F-Pn* 903 and 1132), an orational (*Pn* 1154) and the four manuscripts with polyphonic verse-songs these sources contain, besides tropes, proses, sequences and prosulas, a number of other chants including most often Mass Ordinary chants, acclamations, processional and fraction antiphons, the Holy Week offices, and the solo chants of the Mass (inventories in Chailley, 1957; Spanke, 1930–32; Emerson, 1962). Their notation ranges from the primitive neumes of *F-Pn* 1154 (see illustration) and 1240 to the fully developed Aquitanian point notation of the 11th century and an incipient square notation in the 12th (*see* STAFF, fig.2). The breaking of neumes into separate points led at an early stage to reasonably good diastematy, so that even late 10th-century sources often have transcribable melodies. Successive notation of polyphonic parts in *Pn* 1139 (*see* NEUMATIC NOTATIONS, fig.17) has obscured the number of monophonic pieces in this manuscript and led some scholars to assume that the notation may represent monophonic arrangements of polyphonic works. This has been shown to be incorrect by Fuller (1971).

See also NEUMATIC NOTATIONS, §IV, 5; SOURCES, MS, §II.

II. Monophony

1. Trope, prose, sequence, prosula. 2. Verse-songs. 3. Mass and Office chants, processional antiphons.

1. TROPE, PROSE, SEQUENCE, PROSULA. The main corpus of the earliest St Martial troper (*Pn* 1240) already contained a well-developed cycle of Proper tropes, a collection of Gloria tropes, prosulas to the alleluia and offertory, and an incipient proser. No other Ordinary tropes and no sequences appear in the original redaction. The troper included every category of Proper trope found in the later Aquitanian manuscripts. The proses, all of which show wide concordances in later sources, are fully developed works of the typical double-versicle structure, with some assonance as well as musical rhyme (the ending of all versicles with the same cadence), and often with a single versicle at the beginning and end of the piece. There is evidence that part of this repertory, particularly the Proper tropes, came to St Martial from the north (Evans: 'Northern French Elements', 1970). The Gloria tropes also represent an international repertory, but they already show the characteristics of extreme centonization and wandering versicles typical of later Aquitanian versions.

The late 10th- and early 11th-century sources indicate an enormous increase in the repertory. Sequentiaries, sometimes coordinated with a proser (*Pn* 887), made their appearance, together with systematic collec-

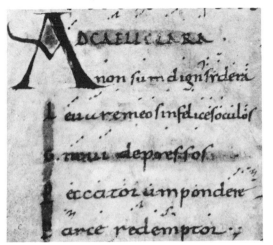

'Song of confession: the penitent's lament', notated in early Aquitanian neumes, in an orational (9th–10th century) from ?Limoges (F-Pn lat.1154, f.99v)

tions of Kyrie prosulas, Sanctus and Agnus tropes, and prosulas to the *Regnum tuum solidum* and the *Fabricae mundi* melismas, as well as a few purely melodic elaborations of the introits or their doxologies, usually connected with textual tropes. In the case of the proses, the writing of new texts for old tunes was responsible for much of the increase. A few of the sequences included short kernel verses which were kept even when the rest of the words in the sequentiaries were left out (see Stäblein, 1961); in these cases the new proses incorporated the kernel verses within their text. A different process obtained in the Proper tropes, where some older texts were provided with new melodies. Often the replaced melodies seem to have been non-Aquitanian, for they survive in northern tropers or in some of the Aquitanian manuscripts that show conflationary contamination or northern influences (e.g. *Pn* 1240, 1118, n a lat.1871 and *APT* 17(5)). It is noteworthy that the later tropers from St Martial itself show the least amount of non-Aquitanian influence within this repertory.

Although the liturgical changes in the feast of St Martial gave rise to a few new pieces around 1031, the repertory had become stagnant by this date. The late 11th-century additions formed a wholly different repertory, mostly of verse-songs, rhymed tropes to the *Benedicamus Domino* closely related in style to the verse-songs, a few Kyrie, Sanctus and Agnus tropes, and new-style proses including, at a later date, some by Adam of St Victor.

See also PROSULA; SEQUENCE (i); TROPE (i).

2. VERSE-SONGS. The early Aquitanian repertory of *versus* or verse-songs (also called conductus or planctus) has an international rather than a Limousin character. The collection in *Pn* 1154 includes *metra* from Boethius's *De consolatione philosophiae*, poems by Gottschalk and Paulinus of Aquileia as well as anonymous works of Spanish (*Versus de die iudicii*, f.121) and possibly north Italian (*Planctus karoli*, f.132) origin. The only certain Limousin piece is the prose *Concelebremus sacram* (f.142v). Although not all pieces are notated, *Pn* 1154 often has the only or the earliest notated version of several of them. Poetically they range

from simple abecedary hymns to verse-songs with one or two refrains. Musical settings are often strophic, so that only the first stanza and the refrain are provided with neumes.

Although such pieces as Theodulf of Orleans's *Gloria laus et honor* or the *Improperia* for Good Friday were often labelled *versus* in the tropers (*Pn* 1240, f.21v, *Pn* 1120, f.15v), the true verse-song repertory of the late 10th century and the early 11th consists of a few works scattered throughout the manuscripts. Notable among them is the *Versus de Sancto Martyrio* (*Pn* 909, f.5), which goes beyond the double-versicle structure of the proses and has a four-versicle pattern, in effect rendering it a sacred lai. A few secular lyrics also found their way into the tropers as late additions (*Pn* 1118, ff. 246–7). In contrast to the international repertory of *Pn* 1154, the late 10th- and early 11th-century Aquitanian verse-songs appear to have been a purely local repertory.

Both prose-like works and strophic verse-songs are present in the late Limousin manuscripts. Though frequently set polyphonically, they are poetically similar to the pieces of *Pn* 1154. The most important difference lies in the use of rhythmic and rhymed verse, and in the presence in several of the texts of Provençal elements. The *sponsus* play in *Pn* 1139 (f.53) is essentially a dramatic cycle of verse-songs. The influence of this repertory upon later secular music has been rightly emphasized by Handschin (1929, 1930). The tropes to the *Benedicamus Domino* in the late Aquitanian sources show no essential difference from the other verse-songs except for the incorporation of the liturgical formula within their text.

See also CONDUCTUS; LAI; PLANCTUS; VERSUS.

3. MASS AND OFFICE CHANTS, PROCESSIONAL ANTIPHONS. Except for the publication of the St Yrieix Gradual (*Pn* 903: PalMus, xiii, 1925), the study of tropes and proses had taken preference over that of mass and Office chants in the St Martial sources. Recent studies of Aquitanian graduals reveal a substantial number of newly composed chants for the older as well as the new feasts. Particularly notable is the large collection of new alleluias in *Pn* 903 which, structurally, form a very homogeneous group. Some graduals also contain a considerable number of old Gallican survivals (see B. Stäblein: 'Gallikanische Liturgie', *MGG*).

The apostolicity proclamations (1028–31) gave rise to new Offices not only for St Martial, but also for his companions, Valeria and Austriclinianus, some of which were written by Adémar de Chabannes (see Emerson, 1965). The processional antiphon repertory also shows traces of an indigenous Aquitanian tradition (see Roederer, 1974). Curiously, about 1000 the Aquitanian versions of the antiphons began to be replaced by more widespread (?'Roman') versions. The growth of the new versions is traceable to sources originating at St Martial itself (*Pn* 1120 and 1121). There is, therefore, an apparent contradiction presented by the abbey's liturgical repertory in the early 11th century: on the one hand there existed a relatively restricted repertory of tropes and proses, almost completely devoid of the non-Aquitanian influences found in the earlier troper *Pn* 1240, or in some of the manuscripts from other Aquitanian houses; on the other hand, in the processional antiphons and other chant repertories (outside the music for the abbey's own local saints)

Aquitanian versions were gradually rejected in favour of more widespread versions. No satisfactory explanation of these cross-currents has yet been advocated.

III. Polyphony

1. The repertory. 2. Style and form. 3. Interpretation.

1. THE REPERTORY. A repertory of two-part music from the earlier 12th century is preserved in *F-Pn* 1139, 3549 and 3719 and *GB-Lbm* Add.36881. A more accurate designation would be Aquitanian polyphony, for there is no actual evidence that any of the surviving repertory originated at the monastery of St Martial at Limoges. The oldest layer of this polyphony, contained in *F-Pn* 1139 (*see* NEUMATIC NOTATIONS, fig.17) and in certain fascicles of *Pn* 3719, was copied about 1100. The latest layer (*GB-Lbm* Add.36881) dates from the second half of the 12th century.

The total corpus of Aquitanian polyphony consists of some 70 pieces: 49 *versus* (see §II, 2), 12 proses (sequences), 2 *prosae* to responds, 3 plain *Benedicamus Domino* versicles, 2 prayers, a hymn and one epistle. The *versus*, which constitute over two-thirds of the repertory, subdivide into one group of ordinary *versus* (29 pieces) and another of *Benedicamus Domino versus* (20 pieces). The latter typically conclude with the versicle *Benedicamus Domino*, or some variant of it. Apart from this difference, the two kinds of *versus* share a common musical and poetic style.

Ex.1(a) *F-Pn* lat. 3719, f. 67

(b) Reduction of (a)

2. STYLE AND FORM. The Aquitanian composers appear to have been the first among the early writers of polyphony to move from note-against-note texture to a developed style of florid counterpoint in which several notes in one voice, the upper, are matched against only one or two notes in the other (see ex.1a). This florid style, though dramatically more ornate than earlier known polyphony, still does not approach the spacious melismas of the Notre Dame organum style. Florid and note-against-note styles may stand side by side in one piece. The contrast is often used to articulate some structural feature of the text or to emphasize the end of a poetic line or strophe in the *versus*. Some of the shorter *versus* are entirely note-against-note, or discantal, in texture, whereas others are florid throughout. The older proses and the *prosae* to responds

Ex.2 *GB-Lbm* Add. 36881, f. 11*v*

[De·us]quam brevis est vi-ta morta-li — — — —

— — — — um su-o pe-rit ag-men — -to

maintain a quite florid texture, but those with new-style rhymed poetic texts are more discantal in setting.

The *versus* exhibit considerable variety in musical form, a reflection of the multiplicity of possible poetic structures. Some are strophic, some are through-composed. Some are set in repeated phrases, sequence-style; others exhibit sporadic, unsystematic phrase repetition. The main phrases or divisions of a *versus* often conclude with an expansive melisma in both voices (see ex.2). Such terminal melismas serve to clarify poetic structure and bear an obvious resemblance to the caudas of the Parisian conductus.

Contrapuntally, the two voices in Aquitanian polyphony are governed by general, but not entirely systematic, principles of contrary motion and perfect consonance. These two principles are most evident when the voices move note-against-note (see ex.2) but also operate within florid style. A basic succession of octaves, 5ths, unisons or 4ths characteristically links the ornate upper voice of a florid passage with the lower voice (see ex.1*b*).

Certain stock contrapuntal figures permeate the Aquitanian repertory. These involve expansion or contraction from one perfect interval to another, as well as voice-crossing within the module of a 5th. Such figures are particularly prominent in terminal melismas where they often appear juxtaposed in a mosaic-like manner (see ex.3). Figures in which the voices are clearly interdependent suggest simultaneous, rather than successive, conception of the parts.

Both musically and textually the polyphonic Aquitanian *versus* appears to be the precursor of the polyphonic Parisian conductus. Like the conductus, its texts are rhymed, strophic, accentual poetry and deal predominantly with themes of the Incarnation and Virgin Birth appropriate to Christmastide. Similarly, its two parts are governed by principles of discant and may break into expansive melismas during the course of a piece. Two compositions, one the frequently printed *Stirps Jesse*, superficially resemble the motet in their combination of an active upper voice presenting a long poetic text with a slower lower voice that is a liturgical *Benedicamus Domino* melody. However, the nature and

Ex.3 *Per partum virginis*, *F-Pn* lat. 3719, f. 64

fe — — — — — — — —

— — de — — ra

○ = lower voice; ● = upper voice

context of these pieces indicate that they are experimental *Benedicamus Domino versus* that have no historical connection with the motet either in procedure or in influence.

3. INTERPRETATION. The classic argument over Aquitanian polyphony concerns rhythmic interpretation. Lack of demonstrable rhythmic meaning in the Aquitanian neumes, coupled with the need for coordinating neumes of unequal numbers of notes between voices, raises critical problems for modern performance or transcription of the music. Some scholars argue for a metric interpretation according to the rules of the rhythmic modes, others claim textual accent as principal guide, while still others prefer a free, improvisatory rendition that cannot be fixed in specific note values. Several factors – such as variants between readings, the appearance of division lines in the latest sources, uncertainty over the advent of modal rhythm (even in Parisian circles) – support a free, non-metric interpretation, but the matter remains controversial.

BIBLIOGRAPHY

MONOPHONY

E. de Coussemaker: *Histoire de l'harmonie au moyen âge* (Paris, 1852–67)
L. Delisle: *Le cabinet des manuscrits de la Bibliothèque impériale* (Paris, 1868–81)
L. Gautier: *Histoire de la poésie liturgique au moyen âge: les tropes, i* (Paris, 1886)
G. M. Dreves, C. Blume and H. M. Bannister, eds.: Analecta hymnica medii aevi, vii (Leipzig, 1889); xlvii (Leipzig, 1905); xlix (Leipzig, 1906); liii (Leipzig, 1911)
W. H. Frere, ed.: *The Winchester Troper*, Henry Bradshaw Society, viii (London, 1894)
L. Delisle: 'Les manuscrits de Saint-Martial de Limoges', *Bulletin de la Société archéologique et historique du Limousin*, xliii (1895), 1–60
——: *Notice sur les manuscrits originaux d'Adémar de Chabannes* (Paris, 1896)
C. de Lasteyrie du Saillant: *L'Abbaye de Saint-Martial de Limoges* (Paris, 1901)
A. Mocquereau, ed.: *Le codex 903 de la Bibliothèque nationale de Paris (XIe siècle), graduel de Saint-Yrieix*, PalMus, xiii (1925)
J. Handschin: 'Über Estampie und Sequenz', ZMw, xii (1929), 1; xiii (1930), 113
H. Spanke: 'St. Martial-Studien: ein Beitrag zur frühromanischen Metrik', *Zeitschrift für französische Sprache und Literatur*, liv (1930–31), 282–317; lvi (1932), 450
A. Hughes, ed.: *Anglo-French Sequelae, Edited from the Papers of the Late Dr. Henry Marriott Bannister* (London, 1934)
H. Spanke: *Deutsche und französische Dichtung des Mittelalters* (Strasbourg, 1943)
P. Hooreman: 'Saint-Martial de Limoges au temps de l'abbé Odolric (1025–1040): essai sur une pièce oubliée du répertoire Limousin', *RBM*, iii (1949), 5–36
S. Corbin: 'Le Cantus Sybillae, origine et premiers textes', *RdM*, xxxi (1952), 1
B. Stäblein: 'Gallikanische Liturgie', MGG
J. Chailley: 'Les anciens tropaires et séquentiaires de l'école de Saint-Martial de Limoges (Xe–XIe siècle)', *Etudes grégoriennes*, ii (1957), 163
R. L. Crocker: *The Repertoire of Proses at Saint-Martial de Limoges (10th and 11th Centuries)* (diss., Yale U., 1957)
——: 'The Repertory of Proses at Saint Martial de Limoges in the 10th Century', *JAMS*, xl (1958), 149
J. Chailley: *L'école musicale de Saint-Martial de Limoges jusqu'à la fin du XIe siècle* (Paris, 1960)
B. Stäblein: 'Zur Frühgeschichte der Sequenz', *AMw*, xviii (1961), 1–33
J. A. Emerson: 'Fragments of a Troper from Saint-Martial de Limoges', *Scriptorium*, xvi (1962), 369
H. Husmann: *Tropen- und Sequenzenhandschriften*, RISM, B/V/1 (Munich and Duisburg, 1964)
J. A. Emerson: 'Two Newly Identified Offices for Saints Valeria and Austriclinianus by Adémar de Chabannes (MS Paris, Bibl. Nat., Latin 909, fols. 79–85v)', *Speculum*, xl (1965), 31
B. Stäblein: 'Sequenz (Gesang)', MGG
R. L. Crocker: 'The Troping Hypothesis', *MQ*, lii (1966), 183
B. Stäblein: 'Tropus', MGG
——: 'Versus', MGG
A. M. Herzo: *Five Aquitanian Graduals: their Mass Propers and Alleluia Cycles* (diss., U. of Southern California, 1967)

K. Rönnau: *Die Tropen zum Gloria in Excelsis Deo, unter besonderes Berücksichtigung des Repertoires der St. Martialhandschriften* (Wiesbaden, 1967)
L. Treitler: *The Aquitanian Repertory of Sacred Monody in the Eleventh and Twelfth Centuries* (diss., Princeton U., 1967)
G. de Poerck: 'Le MS Paris, B. N. lat. 1139, étude codicologique d'un recueil factice de pièces paraliturgiques (XIe–XIIIe siècle)', *Scriptorium*, xxiii (1969), 298
A. Burt: *The Alleluias in the Manuscript Paris, Bibliothèque Nationale, f. lat. 903* (diss., Catholic U. of America, 1969)
R. Steiner: 'The Prosulas of the MS Paris, Bibliothèque Nationale, f. lat. 1118', *JAMS*, xxii (1969), 367
P. Evans: *The Early Trope Repertory of Saint Martial de Limoges*, Princeton Studies in Music, ii (Princeton, 1970)
——: 'Northern French Elements in an Early Aquitainian Troper', *Speculum musicae artis: Festgabe für Heinrich Husmann* (Munich, 1970), 103
G. Weiss, ed.: *Introitus-Tropen; I. Das Repertoire der sudfranzösischen Handschriften des 10. und 11. Jahrhunderts*, Monumenta monodica medii aevi, iii (Kassel, 1970)
S. A. Fuller: 'Hidden Polyphony – a Reappraisal', *JAMS*, xxiv (1971), 169
C. W. Brockett jr: 'Unpublished Antiphons and Antiphon Series found in the Gradual of St. Yrieix', *MD*, xxvi (1972), 5–35
C. Roederer: 'Can we Identify an Aquitanian Chant Style?', *JAMS*, xxvii (1974), 75

POLYPHONY

H. Anglès: 'La música del Ms. de Londres Brit. Museum Add. 36881', *Butlleti de la Biblioteca de Catalunya*, viii (1928–32), 301
H. Spanke: 'Die Londoner St. Martial Conductushandschrift', *Butlleti de la Biblioteca de Catalunya*, viii (1928–32), 280
——: 'St. Martial-Studien', *Zeitschrift für französische Sprache und Literatur*, liv (1930–31), 282–317, 385–422; lvi (1932), 450
F. Ludwig: 'Die geistliche nichtliturgische weltliche einstimmige und die mehrstimmige Musik des Mittelalters', *Handbuch der Musikgeschichte*, ed. G. Adler, i (Berlin, 2/1930), 157–295
W. Krüger: 'Jubilemus, exultemus', *Musica*, vi (1952), 491
W. Apel: 'Bemerkungen zu den Organa von St. Martial', *Miscelánea en homenaje a Monseñor Higinio Anglés*, i (Barcelona, 1958), 61
J. Marshall: 'Hidden Polyphony in a Manuscript from St. Martial de Limoges', *JAMS*, xv (1962), 131
G. Schmidt: 'Strukturprobleme der Mehrstimmigkeit im Repertoire von St. Martial', *Mf*, xv (1962), 11, 205
B. Stäblein: 'Modale Rhythmen im Saint-Martial-Repertoire?', *Festschrift Friedrich Blume* (Kassel, 1963), 340
L. Treitler: 'The Polyphony of St. Martial', *JAMS*, xvii (1964), 29
T. Karp: 'St. Martial and Santiago de Compostela: an Analytical Speculation', *AcM*, xxxix (1967), 144
S. A. Fuller: 'Hidden Polyphony – a Reappraisal', *JAMS*, xxiv (1971), 169

ALEJANDRO ENRIQUE PLANCHART (I, II),
SARAH FULLER (III)

St Martini, Giovanni Battista. See SAMMARTINI, GIOVANNI BATTISTA.

St Martini, Giuseppe. See SAMMARTINI, GIUSEPPE.

Sainton, Prosper (Philippe Catherine) (*b* Toulouse, 5 June 1813; *d* London, 17 Oct 1890). French violinist and composer. He was educated in Toulouse and, from December 1831, at the Paris Conservatoire, where he studied the violin under Habeneck and won a *premier prix* in 1834. For the next two years he played in the orchestras of the Société des Concerts and the Opéra. He then made an extended tour through Italy, Germany, Austria, Russia, Finland, Sweden, Denmark and Spain, with great success. In 1840 he was appointed violin professor at the Toulouse Conservatoire. Having visited England in 1844 he returned in 1845 to settle in London and take up an appointment as professor at the RAM.

He took part in performances of the Beethoven Quartet Society, the Musical Union, the Quartet Association (which he helped to found in 1852) and the Popular Concerts; and he led the orchestras of the Philharmonic Society (1846–54), the Royal Italian Opera at Covent Garden (1847–71), Her Majesty's

Theatre (1871–80) and the Sacred Harmonic Society (from 1848), sometimes acting as deputy conductor to Costa. From 1848 to 1855 he was conductor of the state band and violin soloist to the Queen. For many years he was leader in provincial performances, including those of the Birmingham Festivals. At the opening of the 1862 International Exhibition Sainton conducted the performance of Sterndale Bennett's *Ode*. His farewell concert took place at the Albert Hall on 25 June 1883.

Among his many pupils were Weist-Hill, Amor, A. C. Mackenzie, Burnett, Gabrielle Vaillant and Sutton. His compositions (including two violin concertos) are primarily virtuoso showpieces. In 1860 he married Charlotte Dolby.

BIBLIOGRAPHY
Obituary, *MT*, xxxi (1890), 665
R. H. Legge: 'Sainton, Prosper', *DNB*
GEORGE GROVE/R. J. PASCALL

Sainton-Dolby [née Dolby]**, Charlotte (Helen)** (*b* London, 17 May 1821; *d* London, 18 Feb 1885). English contralto, teacher and composer. She studied from 1832 at the RAM under J. Bennett, Elliot and Crivelli, and made her first appearance at the Philharmonic in a quartet (14 June 1841) and as soloist (14 April 1842). Mendelssohn, impressed by her singing, obtained an engagement for her during the winter of 1845–6 at the Leipzig Gewandhaus Concerts (where she first appeared on 25 October 1845), dedicated the English edition of his Six Songs (op.57) to her, and wrote the contralto part of *Elijah* with her in mind. Following her Leipzig success she toured in France and Holland. In 1860 she married Prosper Sainton and ten years later retired from public life. In 1872 she opened her Vocal Academy; her most famous pupil was Fanny Moody.

She composed the cantatas *The Legend of St Dorothea* (produced London, 1876), *The Story of the Faithful Soul* (produced London, 1879), *Florimel* (1885) and *Thalassa*, and many songs; she also wrote *Madame Sainton-Dolby's Tutor for the English Singer*. Shortly after her death the RAM founded a scholarship in her memory.

BIBLIOGRAPHY
Obituary, *MT*, xxvi (1885), 145
R. H. Legge: 'Sainton, Prosper', *DNB*
WILLIAM BARCLAY SQUIRE/R. J. PASCALL

St Pancras Festival. London festival held annually from 1954; it became the Camden Festival in 1965; *see* LONDON, §VI, 6(iii).

St Paul, Minnesota. *See* MINNEAPOLIS AND ST PAUL.

St Petersburg. *See* LENINGRAD.

Saint-Saëns, (Charles) Camille (*b* Paris, 9 Oct 1835; *d* Algiers, 16 Dec 1921). French composer, pianist, organist and writer. A gifted, fluent and prolific composer, he embodied in his works many of the essential French qualities, above all clarity and order, and impressed a whole generation with his intellectual mastery of the art and his lucid interpretations at the keyboard.

1. LIFE. His ancestors came from the village of St Saëns (Sanctus Sidonius). His father, Jacques Joseph Victor Saint-Saëns (*b* nr. Dieppe, 19 March 1798), an audit clerk at the Ministry of the Interior in Paris, was the son of a smallholder. Victor married Clémence Françoise

Collin (*b* 27 March 1809), a carpenter's daughter, in 1834. He died the following year at the age of 37, a few months after the birth of his son at 3 rue du Jardinet in the Latin Quarter. The child was frail and tubercular. Mme Saint-Saëns, an amateur artist, brought him up with the aid of her aunt, Charlotte Masson, who started teaching him the piano when he was two and a half years old. He had perfect pitch and showed Mozartian precocity by composing his first piano piece a little after his third birthday. More lessons followed with Camille Stamaty, a former pupil of Frédéric Kalkbrenner and Mendelssohn. At the age of seven he went on to study composition with Pierre Maleden and organ playing with Alexandre-Pierre Boëly. The child prodigy was already appearing in public and delighting audiences with his elegant performance of Bach, Handel and Mozart. In 1846, aged ten, he made his formal début at the Salle Pleyel with a programme that included Beethoven and Mozart piano concertos. As an encore he offered to play any one of Beethoven's piano sonatas from memory.

Saint-Saëns showed the same quickness in his general education. Having soon worked through the French classics, he speedily learnt Latin under a private tutor. It was a matter of lifelong regret to him that he never carried out an elaborate scheme he prepared to study Greek. At the same time his curiosity was aroused by mathematics and the natural sciences. He never lost his interest in astronomy, archaeology and philosophy, subjects on which he was later to write with enthusiasm. As a boy he often went out to the stone quarries at Meudon, where, armed with a geologist's hammer, he chipped out fossil shells for his collection. In later life royalties from a set of harmonium pieces financed the purchase of a telescope made to his own specification as a replacement for the opera glasses which, until then, he had used for surveying the heavens.

At the Paris Conservatoire, which he entered in 1848, Saint-Saëns attended organ classes given by the veteran François Benoist. Winner of a *second prix* in 1849 and of a brilliant *premier prix* in 1851, he then began composition lessons with the sympathetic Halévy. Like Ravel, he failed to win the Prix de Rome, although his *Ode à Sainte-Cécile* gained first prize in a competition organized by a Paris musical society and was performed in 1852. At about this time he wrote two symphonies, in A and F respectively, neither of which has been published although both have been recorded. The first of his symphonies to appear in print, the E♭, was composed when he was 18 and given in 1855. The second, in A minor, he wrote at the age of 24.

Saint-Saëns' dazzling gifts early won him the friendship and encouraging patronage of Pauline Viardot, Gounod, Rossini and Berlioz; Berlioz said of him: 'He knows everything but lacks inexperience'. Liszt also was much impressed by him as pianist and composer. In 1853, after a few months as organist at the church of St Séverin, Saint-Saëns took a similar post at St Merry, leaving it in 1857 for the Madeleine, where he remained until 1876; it was there that Liszt heard him improvising and hailed him as the greatest organist in the world. In his youth Saint-Saëns adopted a number of pioneering causes. He was one of the earliest to appreciate Wagner and defended both *Tannhäuser* and *Lohengrin* against the attacks of his elders. Schumann was another modern composer whom he persisted in playing despite the disapproval of conservative opinion. At his own expense he organized and conducted concerts of music by Liszt, whose symphonic poems he was the first to play in France. His own ventures in the form – *Le rouet d'Omphale* (1872), *Phaéton* (1873), *Danse macabre* (1874) and *La jeunesse d'Hercule* (1877) – popularized what was then a novelty and influenced subsequent developments in French music. Old music as well as new attracted his inquiring mind. He helped to revive interest in Bach (even converting his sceptical friend Berlioz to the cause) and did much to restore Mozart to his rightful place. Handel, little known then to French audiences, was the inspiration for Saint-Saëns' own oratorios, among them *Le déluge* (1875) and *The Promised Land* (1913). Gluck was an enthusiasm he shared with Berlioz. One of his most ambitious undertakings was to edit the complete works of Rameau, in those days a much neglected composer whose work he regularly included in his recitals.

The early 1860s were perhaps the most contented and successful years of Saint-Saëns' life. At home he was cocooned in loving comfort by his mother and great-aunt. In public he enjoyed a formidable reputation as composer and virtuoso pianist. His lisp, his parrot-like nose, his short stature and his birdlike strutting walk were made famous by caricaturists. 'I live in music like a fish in water', he remarked. Composing was a natural function, and he produced music, he said, 'as an apple tree produces apples'. He could orchestrate happily for 12 hours at a time and keep up a lively conversation the while. His popular Second Piano Concerto in G minor (1868) took him 17 days to write, and its boulevardier nonchalance was warmly praised by Liszt.

This period also included the only professional teaching appointment Saint-Saëns held. From 1861 to 1865 he taught at the Ecole Niedermeyer, an institution founded by Louis Niedermeyer to improve musical standards in French churches. Saint-Saëns' pupils there included André Messager and Gabriel Fauré, the latter then a boy of 16. Both became close friends, especially Fauré. Although strict about purely technical matters, Saint-Saëns was an inspiring teacher, and his students remembered him with gratitude for the intellectual excitement he stimulated with his revelation of modern music and the arts in general. A more far-reaching result of his activities was the Société Nationale de Musique, which he founded with his colleague Romain Bussine in 1871. The motto 'Ars Gallica' underlined its purpose of encouraging and performing new music by French composers. They, at the time, had few outlets in their own country where concert programmes were largely dominated by the German classics. The secretary was Alexis de Castillon. Committee members included Fauré, César Franck and Edouard Lalo. The Société Nationale was in due course to give many important premières of works by Saint-Saëns, Chabrier, Debussy, Dukas and Ravel, besides music by Fauré, Franck and other original members.

In 1875, then on the verge of 40, Saint-Saëns married the 19-year-old Marie Laure Emilie Truffot. The marriage was not a success. Saint-Saëns' mother disapproved, and her son, irritable, highly strung and capricious, was difficult to live with. Two sons were born and died within six weeks of each other, one (aged two and a half) by falling out of a fourth-floor window, the second of a childhood malady. Saint-Saëns blamed his wife and, in 1881, while on holiday with her, suddenly vanished. A legal separation followed and she

1. Camille Saint-Saëns

never saw him again. She died in 1950 at Cauderan, near Bordeaux, in her 95th year. To a certain extent Saint-Saëns found an outlet for his affection and frustrated paternal instincts in a close relationship with Fauré. Indeed, as the years went by he tended to regard the latter's growing family as his own, and while he did all he could to further his protégé's career he became, for Fauré's wife and children, a benevolent uncle.

The death of his mother in 1888 (his great-aunt had died in 1872) left Saint-Saëns with a crushing sense of loss. He had loved her with passion. For a time he thought of suicide. From then on he became a lonely nomad with only his pet dogs and his faithful manservant Gabriel to keep him company. He travelled ceaselessly and widely, either on long concert tours or on holiday. Algeria and Egypt were favourite resorts and gave him the exotic source of the *Suite algérienne* (1880), *Africa* (1891) and the Fifth Piano Concerto (1896), nicknamed 'Egyptian'. His wanderings took him to Spain, Portugal, Italy, Greece, Uruguay (for which he wrote a national anthem), the Canary Islands and Scandinavia. In Russia he gained the friendship of Tchaikovsky, with whom, on one memorable occasion, he danced an impromptu ballet to the piano accompaniment of Nikolay Rubinstein. He brought back with him a score of Musorgsky's *Boris Godunov*, which he had heard in Russia. Thus, against his will, for he believed Musorgsky to be quite insane, he was responsible for introducing a new element into French music.

Long after his popularity in France had begun to wane Saint-Saëns continued to be regarded in England and America as the greatest living French composer. His visit to America in 1915 was a personal triumph. As early as 1871 he had made the first of many trips to England where he could always be assured of a flattering welcome. He played before Queen Victoria and spent much time studying Handel manuscripts in the library at Buckingham Palace. In 1886 he was commissioned by the Philharmonic Society to write his grandiose Third Symphony, whose first performance he conducted in London. He was awarded honorary doctorates by the universities of Cambridge (1893) and Oxford, and made a Commander of the Victorian Order, having composed a march for the coronation of Edward VII. His last appearance in England was in 1913 when he conducted *The Promised Land*, which had been commissioned by the Gloucester Festival.

Although the prolific Saint-Saëns left few genres untouched – he was, for example, the first established composer to write film music (*L'assassinat du Duc de Guise* in 1908) – he did not succeed as well in the theatre as he did in the concert hall. Of his 13 operas (beginning with *La princesse jaune*, 1872, and including two commissioned by Monte Carlo), only *Samson et Dalila* remains in the repertory. Even this had a struggle to be heard at first, as impresarios fought shy of a biblical subject. Liszt encouraged him to finish it and sponsored the première at Weimar in 1877. It did not reach the Paris Opéra until 1891, although it quickly became established in the repertory.

As a virtuoso pianist of the highest order Saint-Saëns was favourably placed to urge the claims of his own works. (He excelled in Mozart and gave a memorable series of performances in London when he played all the concertos. Purity, grace and sobriety were the hallmarks of his playing, and were praised by Proust.) His material success and his sarcastic tongue made him many enemies. Gounod described him as 'the French Beethoven' (see Bonnerot, p.126), but in old age he was vilified and mocked as 'the composer of the *Wedding Cake* waltz'. During World War I he demanded the suppression of all German music. The vendetta he pursued against the young Debussy was one of several inspired by his dislike of modernity. The first performance of *The Rite of Spring* left him speechless with horror. Yet although he seemed a reactionary to his younger colleagues, in his time he served French music well. The perspective of history shows him as a neo-classicist and as the embodiment of certain traditional French qualities – neat proportions, clarity, polished expression, elegant line and a not unattractive vein of disenchantment.

Saint-Saëns was a prolific writer – of books, articles, prefaces and letters; his published writings on music display vigour and lucidity. He enjoyed polemic and relished lively arguments with his opponents, notably d'Indy. Less controversial were his publications on the décor of ancient Roman theatres, on the instruments depicted in murals at Pompeii and Naples, and on philosophical problems. He also wrote poetry and several plays, one of which was performed with some success. From time to time he sent communications to learned bodies treating of astronomy and acoustics. Such was his scientific curiosity that he would eagerly desert rehearsals or arrange concert tours so that he could observe phenomena like Etna in eruption or an eclipse of the sun.

Saint-Saëns cared deeply about his reputation. That is why, except for 'Le cygne', he forbade performance during his lifetime of *Le carnaval des animaux* (1886), a private joke dashed off in a few days while on holiday. It would have caused him the bitterest annoyance had he known that this witty extravaganza was to become his most popular work. Even so, he was too clear-eyed and experienced a musician not to realize that admirers who called him a second Mozart were exaggerating. At the other end of the scale were detractors who saw him as the composer of 'la mauvaise musique bien écrite'.

2. WORKS. Saint-Saëns wrote in every 19th-century musical genre, but his most successful works are those based on traditional Viennese models, namely sonatas, chamber music, symphonies and concertos. Well schooled in the works of Bach and Beethoven, he was influenced at an early age by Mendelssohn and Schumann. His essentially Viennese upbringing was coloured by the French musical tradition of his day, and salon pieces, operas, and Spanish and exotic compositions survive in abundance. Moreover, his keen historical sense led him to revive many 17th-century French dance forms (bourrées, gavottes, menuets etc) and his feelings of national loyalty are reflected in numerous marches and patriotic choruses. Towards the end of his life, he developed an austere style comparable to Fauré's. Throughout his career his art was one of amalgamation and adaption rather than that of pursuing new and original paths; and this led Debussy to epitomize him as 'the musician of tradition'.

Saint-Saëns' musical language is generally conservative. Although some of his melodies are supple and pliable, many are formal and rigid. They are usually built in well-defined phrases of three or four bars, and the phrase pattern *AABB* is characteristic. The most distinctive aspect of his music is his harmony, in which he was influenced by the theories of Gottfried Weber. Modulations by 3rds are typical, and while most chordal progressions are simple and direct, the many digressions and alterations lend nobility or charm to the music. He had a tendency to repeat rhythmic patterns, not only in his dance music, but as a general aspect of style or to create an exotic atmosphere. He preferred ordinary duple, triple or compound metres (3/4 is often designated as 3) and the use of unusual or free metres is rare (though a 5/4 passage occurs in the Piano Trio op.92, one in 7/4 in the Polonaise for two pianos op.77 and one in free metre in the *Caprice andalous* op.122). Cross-accents are frequent (the Second Symphony op.55 and the Second Violin Sonata op.102), as are changes of metre within a movement or phrase (First Violin Sonata op.75). Although he was a competent orchestrator, he achieved his sense of colour more by harmonic means rather than by purely orchestral effects. Throughout his career he was a master of counterpoint, which he learnt from Cherubini's manual in use at the Conservatoire. His mastery of this aspect of his art is evident in his three sets of keyboard fugues (opp.99, 109, 161), but his contrapuntal craft is a general characteristic of his style and pervades most of his works. He adhered to traditional forms in his neo-classical and sonata-orientated compositions, but allowed himself more formal freedom in descriptive pieces.

Most of Saint-Saëns' juvenile works remain unpublished, as do a great number of unfinished cantatas, choruses, songs and symphonies written before 1850. The only composition of the period to achieve publication (in 1913) was an *Ouverture d'un opéra comique inachevé*, although the most ambitious work of these early years was the Symphony in A (c1850). With the appearance of the Symphony no.1 (1853) and the Piano Quintet op.14 (1855), Saint-Saëns entered a new phase of composition. These are serious and ambitious works written on a large scale, showing the influence of Schumann. The quintet is one of his earliest cyclic compositions and the piano writing is thick and heavy, a texture that is also in evidence in the 'Urbs Roma' Symphony and in those pieces from the period which combine piano and harmonium (e.g. op.8).

Not all the works written in the 1850s and 1860s are so ponderous, however: the First Piano Trio op.18 has moments of extreme delicacy (the ostinato in the second movement is characteristic) and the Symphony no.2 is a prime example of orchestral economy, fugal severity and cyclic unity. The first three piano concertos (also from the 1850s and 1860s) are notable as early examples of the piano concerto in France. The second, still in the repertory, has a first movement that deviates from the typical sonata-form pattern; all three have frivolous finales which capture the prevailing mood of the Second Empire. The First Cello Concerto op.33 is a far more serious work. Its stormy opening movement has an *allegro appassionato* character, more so than the two later works which actually bear this title (opp.43, 70). Saint-Saëns' willingness to experiment with the traditional form of the concerto is evident here and elsewhere, and his first works of descriptive music also date from the 1860s. In the Introduction and Rondo Capriccioso for violin and orchestra he used idiomatic Spanish rhythms, and in later works of this type (the *Havanaise* and *Caprice andalous*) he alternated raised and lowered 7ths to create a wistful mood. *La princesse jaune*, his first opera (1872), employs pentatonic melodies, used earlier in the march *Orient et occident*. His other exotic works (the *Nuit persane*, *Suite algérienne*, *Africa*, the Fifth Piano Concerto and *Souvenir d'Ismaïlia*) are frequently in the minor mode with the 6th and 7th degrees raised, also showing a variety of other techniques. The *Rapsodie d'Auvergne* and the *Caprice sur des airs danois et russes* are based on European folksongs, as are portions of several other works. In the 1870s Saint-Saëns composed four symphonic poems (*Le rouet d'Omphale*, *Phaéton*, *Danse macabre* and *La jeunesse d'Hercule*) in which he experimented with orchestration and thematic transformation. *La jeunesse d'Hercule* is modelled closely on Liszt, but the others concentrate on some physical movement – spinning, riding, dancing – which is described in musical terms. He had previously experimented with thematic transformation in his programmatic overture *Spartacus* and later used it in his Fourth Piano Concerto and the 'Organ' Symphony (no.3).

Some of Saint-Saëns' best and most characteristic compositions date from the 1870s and 1880s. These include the Fourth Piano Concerto, Third Violin Concerto, 'Organ' Symphony, *Samson et Dalila*, *Le déluge*, the Piano Quartet op.41, the First Violin Sonata, First Cello Sonata, Variations on a Theme of Beethoven and *Le carnaval des animaux*. Characteristic of many works written at this time is the use of repeated rhythmic motifs or of chorale melodies, combined in the second movement of the op.41 quartet. Both the Fourth Piano Concerto and the 'Organ' Symphony begin in C minor and end in C major, both employ thematic transformation and a chorale melody, and (as are those of the First Violin Sonata) the four movements are arranged in an interlocking pattern of two plus two. Saint-Saëns worked on *Le carnaval des animaux* concurrently with the 'Organ' Symphony and it remains his most brilliant comic work, parodying Offenbach, Berlioz,

Mendelssohn, Rossini, his own *Danse macabre* and several popular tunes. The Third Violin Concerto (1880) is more rewarding musically and less demanding technically than the two earlier violin concertos; the chorale-like passage in B major near the end may have been influenced by his own Fourth Piano Concerto. A *Morceau de concert* for violin, written in the same year as the concerto, shares a number of affinities with the concerto. Unlike his other *Morceaux de concert* (opp.94, 154), this piece is essentially a concerto first movement.

Samson et Dalila also dates from the 1870s. As an opera composer Saint-Saëns had an unerring sense for accurate declamation; he also retained the identity of aria and ensemble, welding the whole work together with solid musical craftsmanship. Among his other operas, *Etienne Marcel*, *Henry VIII* (which has a principal theme based on a traditional English melody that Saint-Saëns found in the Buckingham Palace library) and *Ascanio* merit study and revival. The subjects he chose call for the flamboyant expertise of a Meyerbeer, and though the operas contain much agreeable and skilfully shaped music, they are deficient in theatrical effect. The success of *Samson et Dalila* can be attributed not least to its having originally been conceived as an oratorio, thereby enabling the composer to concentrate on purely musical aspects.

Much of Saint-Saëns' piano music was written after 1870. Most of it is salon music (mazurkas, waltzes, albumleaves, souvenirs etc); but the three sets of Etudes (opp.52, 111, 135) and the Variations on a Theme of Beethoven op.35 (piano duo) rank with the concertos. The Septet op.65 (1881) is, like the suites (opp.16, 49, 90), a neo-classical work that revives 17th-century

2. Camille Saint-Saëns: caricature by his pupil Gabriel Fauré

French dance forms. Although these dances are rigid and less original than the pavanes and *menuets antiques* of Debussy and Ravel, they reflect Saint-Saëns' interest in the rediscovery and revival of the forgotten French musical tradition of the 17th century (his editions of Lully, Charpentier and Rameau date from this period).

Beginning with the Second Violin Sonata (1896), a stylistic change is noticeable in much of Saint-Saëns' music. The piano writing is generally more linear and less heavy, and there is a growing preference for the thin sonorities of the harp (as in the *Fantaisie* op.95 for harp, the *Fantaisie* op.124 for violin and harp and the *Morceau de concert* op.154 for harp and orchestra) and woodwind (as in *Odelette* op.162 for flute and orchestra and the solo sonatas for oboe, clarinet and bassoon opp.166–8). The two string quartets (opp.112, 153) mark the first elimination of the piano in his chamber works. Remote chord progressions and modal cadences become increasingly apparent and the subjects of his stage works are almost exclusively Greek. This austere tendency is, of course, typical of many composers after World War I, but it serves to emphasize the classical aspect of Saint-Saëns' nature which, latent earlier, had seldom been displayed in such rarefied form. Saint-Saëns' oeuvre, although somewhat uneven as a whole, is diverse and multi-faceted. Both his great reputation and subsequent neglect have been exaggerated, but there is little doubt that his prolific production best represents the conservative tradition in 19th-century France.

Saint-Saëns' writings attest to his wide tolerance on many musical issues and to his concern for order, clarity and precision. Like the Parnassian poets, he was a proponent of 'art for art's sake', and his views on expression and passion in art conflicted with the prevailing Romantic aesthetic. In his memoirs, *Ecole buissonnière*, he wrote:

Music is something besides a source of sensuous pleasure and keen emotion, and this resource, precious as it is, is only a chance corner in the wide realm of musical art. He who does not get absolute pleasure from a simple series of well-constructed chords, beautiful only in their arrangement, is not really fond of music.

Although Saint-Saëns' writings are remarkably consistent, it cannot be said that he evolved a distinctive musical style. He was a master craftsman and designed his works with consummate skill, but his music often lacks those personal details of style which disclose a major creative talent. It was perhaps his aesthetic, rather than his music, which most influenced his pupil Fauré and, later, Ravel.

WORKS

Catalogue: *Catalogue général et thématique des oeuvres de Saint-Saëns*, ed. Durand & Cie (Paris, 1897, rev. 1908)

(*printed works published in Paris unless otherwise stated*)

OPERAS

(*first performed in Paris unless otherwise stated*)

La princesse jaune (opéra comique, 1, L. Gallet), Opéra-Comique, 12 June 1872, op.30 (1872)
Le timbre d'argent (drame lyrique, 4, J. Barbier, M. Carré), National-Lyrique, 23 Feb 1877 (1877)
Samson et Dalila (opera, 3, F. Lemaire), Weimar, Hoftheater, 2 Dec 1877, op.47 (1877)
Etienne Marcel (opera, 4, Gallet), Lyons, Grand Théâtre, 8 Feb 1879 (1879)
Henry VIII (opera, 4, L. Détroyat, A. Silvestre), Opéra, 5 March 1883 (1883)
Proserpine (drame lyrique, 4, Gallet, after A. Vacquerie), Opéra-Comique, 14 March 1887 (1887)
Ascanio (opera, 5, Gallet, after P. Meurice), Opéra, 21 March 1890 (1890)
Phryné (opéra comique, 2, L. Augé de Lassus), Opéra-Comique, 24 May 1893 (1893)

Frédégonde (drame lyrique, 5, Gallet), Opéra, 18 Dec 1895 (1895), collab. E. Guiraud
Les barbares (tragédie lyrique, 3, V. Sardou, P. B. Gheusi), Opéra, 23 Oct 1901 (1901)
Hélène (poème lyrique, 1, C. Saint-Saëns), Monte Carlo, 18 Feb 1904, (1903)
L'ancêtre (drame lyrique, 3, Augé de Lassus), Monte Carlo, 24 Feb 1906 (1905)
Déjanire (drame lyrique, 4, Saint-Saëns, after Gallet), Monte Carlo, 14 March 1911 (1911)

OTHER STAGE WORKS

Antigone (incidental music, Meurice and Vacquerie, after Sophocles), Paris, Comédie Française, 21 Nov 1894 (1893)
Déjanire (incidental music, 4, Gallet), Béziers, 28 Aug 1892 (1898); rev. 1911 as drame lyrique
Javotte (ballet, 1, J. L. Croze), Lyons, 3 Dec 1896 (1896)
Parysatis (incidental music, 3, J. Dieulafoy), Béziers, 17 Aug 1902 (1902)
Andromaque (incidental music, 4, Racine), Paris, Sarah-Bernhardt, 7 Feb 1903 (1903)
L'assassinat du Duc de Guise, op.128 (film score, H. Lavedan), Paris, Salle Charras, 16 Nov 1908
La foi, op.130 (incidental music, E. Brieux), Monte Carlo, 10 April 1909; 3 tableaux (?1909)
On ne badine pas avec l'amour (incidental music, A. de Musset), Paris, Odéon, 8 Feb 1917

SACRED

Moïse sauvé des eux, c1851, *F-Pn*
Mass, solo vv, chorus, orch, org, op.4, 1855 (1857)
Tantum ergo, chorus, org, op.5, 1856 (1868)
Oratorio de Noël, solo vv, chorus, str qt, harp, org, op.12, 1858 (1863)
Veni Creator, C, chorus, org ad lib, 1858 (1866)
O salutaris, B♭, S, A, Bar, org, 1858 (1866)
Ave Maria, B♭, S, org, c1859 (1866)
Ave Maria, E, Bar, org, c1859 (1865)
Ave Maria, A, 2 A, org, c1860 (1865)
Ave verum, E♭, S, A, T, B, org, c1860 (1865)
O salutaris, A, A solo, org, c1860 (1865)
Sub tuum, f, S, A, org, c1860 (1865)
Tantum ergo, E♭, 2 S, A, org, ad lib chorus, c1860 (1866)
Ave verum, b, S, A, org, c1863 (1865)
Coeli enarrant (Ps xviii), solo vv, chorus, orch, op.42, 1865 (1875)
Ave Maria, A, S/T, org, 1865 (1865)
Inviolata, D, A solo, org, 1865 (1867)
O salutaris, A♭, S, A, Bar, org, 1869 (1869)
Le déluge, oratorio, solo vv, chorus, orch, op.45, 1875 (1876)
O salutaris, E♭, S, org, 1875 (1875)
Requiem, solo vv, chorus, orch, op.54, 1878 (1878)
O salutaris, E, T, Bar, org, 1884 (1884)
O salutaris, E♭, A solo, org, 1884 (1884)
Deus Abraham, F, A solo, org, 1885 (1885)
Pie Jesu, c, B solo, org, 1885 (1885)
Panis angelicus, F, T/S, str qnt/org, 1898 (1898)
Offertoire pour la Toussaint, F, chorus, org, ad lib vc, db, 1904 (1904)
Praise ye the Lord (Ps cl), double choir, orch, org, op.127 (New York, 1908)
The Promised Land (H. Klein), oratorio, solo vv, chorus, orch, 1913 (?1913)
Ave Maria, chorus, op.145, 1914 (n.d.)
Tu es Petrus, 4 male vv, org, op.147, 1914 (n.d.)
Quam dilecta, 1v, org, op.148, 1915 (n.d.)
Laudate Dominum, chorus, op.149, 1916 (n.d.)
Litanies à la Sainte Vierge, 1v, org, 1917, *Pn*
Ave verum, D, 4 female vv, org, hn obbl (n.d.)
6 choeurs religieux, *Pn*
9 chants religieux latins, acc., *Pn*
Super flumina Babylonis (Ps cxxxvi), chorus, *Pn*
Canticles: A Saint Joseph, c1844, *Pn*; Dans ce beau moi, c1844, *Pn*; Nous qu'en ces lieux, c1844, *Pn*; Reçois mes hommages, c1844, *Pn*; La madonna col bambino (St Alphonsus Liguori), F, A solo, pf, c1855 (1868); Heureux qui du coeur de Marie, A, A solo/chorus, pf, c1860 (1865); O Saint Autel, D, 3 A, chorus, pf, c1860 (1865); Pour vous bénir, Seigneur (A. Cuinet), E, 3 A, chorus, pf, c1860 (1866); Reine des cieux, A♭, A solo/chorus, pf, c1860 (1866)

SECULAR CHORAL

op.
— Imagine, cantata, c1848, *Pn*
— Les Israélites sur la montagne d'Oreb, oratorio, c1848, frag., *Pn*
— Télétille, cantata, c1848, *Pn*
— Cantata (A. Tastu), c1849, *Pn*
— Antigone (prol), with solo vv, orch, c1850, *Pn*
— Les djinns (V. Hugo), c1850, frag., *Pn*
— La rose, c1850, *Pn*
— Cantata, 3vv, with orch, 1852, *Pn*
— Les cloches, symphonic ode, 1852, *Pn*

— Fugue and chorus, 1852, *Pn*
— Ode à Sainte-Cécile, with solo vv, orch, 1852, *Pn*
— Le retour de Virginie, 1852, *Pn*
— Toilette de la Marquise de Présalé, grande scène lyrique, 1857, MS, Musée de Dieppe
— Macbeth, scène, with orch, 1858, MS, Musée de Dieppe
19 Les noces de Prométhée (R. Cornut), with solo vv, orch, 1867 (1867)
— Sérénade d'hiver (H. Cazalis), 4 male vv, 1867 (1868)
— Le nuage, 1875, *Pn*
46 Les soldats de Gédéon (Gallet), 4 male vv, 1876 (1876)
53 Deux choeurs (Hugo), 1878 (1878): Chanson de grand-père, Chanson d'ancêtre
57 La lyre et la harpe (Hugo), with solo vv, orch, 1879 (1879)
69 Hymne à Victor Hugo, orch, chorus ad lib, 1881 (1884)
68 Deux choeurs, with pf ad lib, 1882 (1883): Calme des nuits, Les fleurs et les arbres
71 Deux choeurs (T. Saint-Félix), 1884 (1884): Les marins de Kermor, Les Titans
74 Saltarelle (E. Deschamps), 4 male vv, 1885 (1885)
84 Les guerriers (G. Audigier), 4 male vv, 1888 (1888)
26bis Nuit persane (A. Renaud), with solo vv, orch, 1891 (1892)
113 Chants d'automne (S. Sicard), 4 male vv, 1899 (1899)
114 La nuit (Audigier), female vv, with S, orch, 1900 (1900)
115 Le feu céleste (Silvestre), with narrator, S, orch, org, 1900 (1900)
121 A la France (J. Combarieu), 4 male vv, mixed vv ad lib, 1903 (1904)
— Ode d'Horace (trans. Saint-Saëns), 4 male vv, 1905 (1905)
126 La gloire de Corneille, 1906 (?1908)
129 Le matin, 4 male vv (n.d.)
131 La gloire, with solo vv, pf, 1911 (n.d.)
134 Aux aviateurs (J. Bonnerot), 4 male vv, 1911 (?1912)
137 Aux mineurs, 4 male vv, 1912 (n.d.)
138 Hymne au printemps, 1912 (n.d.)
141 Deux choeurs, 1913 (n.d.): Des pas dans l'allée, Trinquons
142 Hymne au travail, 4 male vv, 1914 (n.d.)
151 Troix choeurs, 3 female vv, 1917 (?1917): Chanson des aiguilles (Bonnerot), Salut au chevalier (P. Fournier), Le sourire (J. Mirval)
164 Aux conquérants de l'air, 2vv (n.d.)
165 Le printemps, 2vv (n.d.)
— Hymne à Jeanne d'Arc, with org, 1920, *Pn*
— Canon, 2 female vv, *US-Wc*

SONGS
(for 1v, pf unless otherwise stated)
26 Mélodies persanes (A. Renaud), 1870 (1872): 1 La brise, 2 La splendeur vide, 3 La solitaire, 4 Sabre en main, 5 Au cimetière, 6 Tournoiement
146 La cendre rouge (J. Ducquois), 1914. 1 Prélude, 2 Ame triste, 3 Douceur, 4 Silence, 5 Pâques, 6 Jour de pluie, 7 Amoroso, 8 Mai, 9 Petite main, 10 Reviens
— Cinq poèmes de Ronsard (P. de Ronsard), 1921 (1921): 1 L'amour oyseau (1907), 2 L'amour blessé, 3 A Saint-Blaise, 4 Grasselette et Maigrelette (1920), 5 L'amant malheureux
— Vieilles chansons, 1921 (1921): 1 Temps nouveau (C. d'Orléans), 2 Avril (R. Belleau), 3 Villanelle (V. de la Fresnaye)
Ariel, 1841, *F-Pn*; Le soir (Desbordes-Valmore), 1841, *Pn*; La maman (Tastu), *Pn*; Tandis que sur vos ans, 1841, *Pn*; Le Golfe de Baya (Lamartine), c1847, *Pn*; Télesille (Tastu), 1849, *Pn*; Bergeronnette (F. Lombard), 1850, *Pn*; Lamento (Gautier), 1850, *Pn*; Le lac (Lamartine), 1850 (c1856); Guitare (Hugo), 1851 (1870); Le poète mourant (Lamartine), 1851, *Pn*; Le rendezvous (E. Fiéffé), 1851, *Pn*; Rêverie (Hugo), acc. orch, 1851 (1852) Idylle (Deschoulières), 1852, *Pn*; L'automne (Lamartine), c1852, *Pn*
Le pas d'armes du Roi Jean (Hugo), acc. orch, 1852 (1855); Mélodie (Lamartine), acc. orch, 1852, *Pn*; Le feuille de peuplier (Tastu), acc. orch, 1853 (1854); Ruhethal (L. Uhland), 1854, *Pn*; La chasse du burgrave, c1854, ?lost; La porta dell'inferno (Dante), c1854, *Pn*; La cloche (Hugo), c1855 (1856); L'attente (Hugo), acc. orch, c1855 (1856); Le lever de la lune (Ossian), 1855 (1870); Le sommeil des fleurs (G. de Penmarch), 1855 (1856); Plainte (Tastu), acc. orch, c1855 (1856); A la lune, 1856, *Pn*
La mort d'Ophélie (E. Legouvé), c1857 (1858); Pourquoi t'exiler, c1858, *Pn*; Souvenances (F. Lemaire), c1858 (1859); Alla riva del Tebro, c1860 (1870); Etoil du matin (C. Distel), c1860 (1869); Extase (Hugo), c1860 (1864); Soirée en mer (Hugo), 1862 (1864); Canzonetta toscana, c1863 (1870); Le matin (Hugo), c1864 (1866); Claire de lune (C. Mendès), c1865 (1866); Heures passées (A. Lenfaut), 1865, *Pn*; L'enlèvement (Hugo), acc. orch, 1865 (1866); Le chant de ceux qui s'en vont sur la mer (Hugo), 1868 (1870)
La coccinelle (Hugo), 1868 (1896); Maria Lucrezia (Legouvé), 1868 (1870); Tristesse (Lemaire), 1868 (1877); A quoi bon entendre (Hugo), c1869 (1870); Marquise, vous souvenez-vous? (F. Coppée), c1869 (1870); Si vous n'avez rien à me dire (Hugo), 1870 (1896); A

Voice by the Cedar Tree (Tennyson), 1871 (London, 1871); Désir de l'orient (Saint-Saëns), 1871 (1895); My Land (T. Davis), 1871 (1871); Dans ton coeur (H. Cazalis), 1872 (1884); Danse macabre (Cazalis), acc. orch, 1872 (1873); Vogue, vogue la galère (J. Alcard), harmonium ad lib, c1877 (1877)
Night Song to Preciosa (I. Ginner), 1879 (1879); Dans les coins bleus (C. Sainte-Beuve), 1880 (1884); Chanson à boire du vieux temps (N. Boileau), 1885 (1885); Ronde (Coppée), 1885, *Pn*; Une flûte invisible (Hugo), with fl, 1885 (1885); La fiancée du timbalier (Hugo), acc. orch, op.82, 1887 (1888); Suzette et Suzon (Hugo), 1888 (1889); Guitares et mandolines (Saint-Saëns), 1890 (1890); Présage de la croix (S. Bordèse), 1891 (1892); Aimons-nous (Banville), acc. orch, 1891 (1892); Amour viril (G. Boyer), 1891 (1891)
Là-bas (Croze), 1892 (1892); Les fées (Banville), acc. orch, 1892 (1892); Les fleurs (V. de Collerville), 1892, *Pn*; Le rossignol (Banville), 1892 (1892); Madeleine (A. Tranchant), 1892 (1892); Romance (E. Bergerat), acc. harp, 1892, *Pn*; Fière beauté (A. Mahot), acc. orch, 1893 (1893); La sérénité (M. Barbier), 1893 (1895); Peut-être (Croze), 1893 (1894); Primavera (P. Stuart), 1893 (1893); Vive Paris, vive la France (Tranchant), 1893 (1894); La libellule (Saint-Saëns), acc. orch, 1894 (1894); Pallas Athéné (Croze), acc. orch, op.98, 1894 (1894)
Pourquoi rester seulette (Croze), 1894 (1895); Madrigal (J. Molière), 1897 (1897); Alla riva del Tebro, 1898 (1899) [arr. of madrigal by Palestrina]; Les vendanges (Sicard), acc. orch, 1898 (1898); Lever de soleil sur le Nil (Saint-Saëns), acc. orch, 1898 (1898); Si je l'osais (Tranchant), 1898 (1898); Sonnet (Saint-Saëns), 1898 (1898); Les cloches de la mer (Saint-Saëns), 1900 (1900); Lola (Bordèse), acc. orch, op.116, 1900 (1900); Nocturne (J. Quinault), 1900 (1900); Thème varié (Saint-Saëns), 1900 (1900); Désir d'amour (F. Perpiñan), 1901 (1901)
Elle (C. Lecocq), 1901 (1901); L'arbre (J. Moréas), 1903 (1903); Soeur Anne (A. Pressat), 1903 (1903); Le fleuve (G. Audigier), 1906 (1906); L'étoile (Haïdar-Pacha), 1907 (1907); Soir romantique (Comtesse de Noailles), 1907 (1907); Violons dans le soir (Comtesse de Noailles), with vn, 1907 (1907); Fomicacicadéide, 1908, *DI*; Le vent dans la plaine (P. Verlaine), 1912 (1913); Les sapins (P. Martin), 1914 (1914); Vive la France (Fournier), 1914 (1915); La française (M. Zamacoïs), 1915, in *Le petit parisien*
Ne l'oubliez pas (F. Regnault), c1915 (1915); S'il est un charmant gazon (Hugo), 1915 (1915); Honneur à l'Amérique (Fournier), 1917 (1917); Angélus (Aguétant), acc. orch, 1918 (1918); Où nous avons aimé (Aguétant), acc. orch, 1918 (1918); Papillons (R. de Leche), acc. orch, 1918 (1918); Victoire (Fournier), 1918 (1918); Hymne à la paix (J. Faure), op.159, 1919 (1920)
Antwort (Uhland), *Pn*; Chanson de Fortunio (Musset), *Pn*; La cigal et la fourmi (J. de Lafontaine) (Cologne, 1958); L'echo de la harpe, *Pn*; God Save the King [Fr trans. with pf acc.]; Primavera (C. d'Orléans), *Pn*; Sérénade (L. Mangeot), acc. orch (c1866); Toi (E. St Chaffray) (c1856)
Duos: Pastorale (Destouches), 1855 (1856); Viens (Hugo), c1855 (1856); Le soir descend sur la colline, 1857 (1858); Scène d'Horace (P. Corneille), acc. orch, op.10, 1860 (1861); El desdichado, acc. orch, 1871 (1884); Les cygnes (Renaud), acc. orch, chorus ad lib, from op.26bis, 1891 (1892); Vénus (Saint-Saëns), 1896 (1896)
Romance du soir (Croze), S, A, T, B, 1902 (1902?)

op.

(without solo instruments)
— Symphony, B♭, c1848, frag., *Pn*
— Symphony, D, c1850, frag., *Pn*
— Comic opera overture, e, c1850, *Pn*
— Scherzo, small orch, A, c1850, *Pn*
— Symphony, A, c1850, *Pn*
2 Symphony no.1, E♭, 1853 (1855)
140 Ouverture d'un opéra comique inachevé, G, 1854 (1913)
— Symphony, c, 1854, frag., *Pn*
— Symphony 'Urbs Roma', F, 1856
55 Symphony no.2, a, 1859 (1878)
49 Suite, D, 1863 (1877)
— Spartacus Overture, E♭, 1863, MS, private collection, Mme Fauré-Fremiet
34 Marche héroïque, E♭, 1871 (1871)
31 Le rouet d'Omphale, A, 1872 (1872)
39 Phaéton, C, 1873 (1875)
40 Danse macabre, g, 1874 (1875)
50 La jeunesse d'Hercule, E♭, 1877 (1877)
60 Suite algérienne, C, 1880 (1881)
63 Une nuit à Lisbonne, E♭, 1880 (1881)
64 Jota aragonese, a, 1880 (1881)
78 Symphony no.3 'Organ', c, 1886 (1886)
7bis Rapsodie bretonne, F, 1891 (1892)
93 Sarabande et rigaudon, E, 1892 (1892)
117 Marche du couronnement, C, c1902 (1902)
130 Trois tableaux symphoniques d'après La foi, 1908 (?1909)

133 Ouverture de fête, F, 1910 (n.d.)

(with solo instruments)

6   Tarentelle, a, solo fl, cl, 1857 (1857)
17   Piano Concerto no.1, D, 1858 (1875)
58   Violin Concerto no.2, C, 1858 (1879)
20   Violin Concerto no.1, A, 1859 (1868)
28   Introduction and Rondo capriccioso, a, solo vn, 1863 (1870)
22   Piano Concerto no.2, g, 1868 (1868)
29   Piano Concerto no.3, Eb, 1869 (1875)
37   Romance, solo fl/vn, Db, 1871 (1874)
33   Cello Concerto no.1, a, 1872 (1873)
36   Romance, solo hn/vc, F, 1874 (1874)
48   Romance, solo vn, C, 1874 (1876)
44   Piano Concerto no.4, c, 1875 (1877)
61   Violin Concerto no.3, b, 1880 (1881)
62   Morceau de concert, G, solo vn, 1880 (1880)
73   Rapsodie d'Auvergne, C, solo pf, 1884 (1884)
76   Wedding Cake, Ab, solo pf, 1885 (1886)
—   Le carnaval des animaux, see 'Chamber'
83   Havanaise, E, solo vn, 1887 (1888)
94   Morceau de concert, f, solo hn, 1887 (1893)
89   Africa, g, solo pf, 1891 (1891)
103 Piano Concerto no.5 'Egyptian', F, 1896 (1896)
119 Cello Concerto no.2, d, 1902 (1902)
122 Caprice andalous, G, solo vn, 1904 (1904)
154 Morceau de concert, G, solo harp, 1918 (?1919)
156 Cyprès et Lauriers, d, solo org, 1919 (?1919)
162 Odelette, D, solo fl, 1920 (?1920)

MILITARY BAND

25   Orient et occident, 1869 (1870), also arr. with orch
—   Hymne franco-espagnol, 1900 (1901)
125 Sur les bords du Nil (n.d.)
—   Hail California, with orch, org. 1915 (?1915)

CHAMBER

—   Violin Sonata, c1850, frag., *Pn*
—   Piano Quartet, Eb, 1853, *Pn*
14   Piano Quintet, a, 1855 (1865)
—   Caprice brillant, pf, vn, 1859, *US-R*
16   Suite, pf, vc, 1862 (1866)
18   Piano Trio no.1, F, 1863 (1867)
15   Sérénade, Eb (pf, org, vn, va/vc)/orch, 1866 (1868)
27   Romance, Bb, pf, org, vn, 1868 (1868)
—   Les odeurs de Paris, 2 tpt, harp, pf, str, c1870, *F-Pn*
38   Berceuse, Bb, pf, vn, 1871 (1874)
32   Cello Sonata no.1, c, 1872 (1873)
41   Piano Quartet, Bb, 1875 (1875)
43   Allegro appassionato, b, vc, pf/orch, 1875 (1875)
51   Romance, D, pf, vc, 1877 (1877)
65   Septet, Eb, pf, tpt, 2 vn, va, vc, db, 1881 (1881)
67   Romance, E, pf, hn, 1885 (1885)
75   Violin Sonata no.1, d, 1885 (1885)
—   Le carnaval des animaux, 2 pf, 2 vn, va, vc, db, fl, cl, glock, xyl, 1886 (1922)
79   Caprice sur des airs danois et russes, pf, fl, ob, cl, 1887 (1887)
91   Chant saphique, pf, vc, 1892 (1892)
92   Piano Trio no.2, e, 1892 (1892)
95   Fantaisie, harp, 1893 (1893)
102 Violin Sonata no.2, Eb, 1896 (1896)
108 Barcarolle, F, vn, vc, org, pf, 1897 (1898)
112 String Quartet no.1, e, 1899 (1899)
123 Cello Sonata no.2, F, 1905 (1905)
124 Fantaisie, vn, harp, 1907 (1907)
132 La muse et le poète, vn, vc, pf/orch, 1910 (?1910)
136 Tryptique, pf, vn, 1912 (?1912)
143 Elégie, pf, vn, 1915 (?1915)
144 Cavatine, pf, trbn, 1915 (?1915)
153 String Quartet no.2, G, 1918 (?1919)
—   L'air de la pendule, pf, vn, c1918,
158 Prière, org, vn/vc, 1919 (?1919)
160 Elégie, pf, vn, 1920 (?1920)
166 Oboe Sonata, D, 1921 (?1921)
167 Clarinet Sonata, Eb, 1921 (?1921)
168 Bassoon Sonata, G, 1921 (?1921)
—   Gavotte, g, vc, pf/orch, *Pn*
—   Adagio, Eb, pf, hn, *Pn*

PIANO

(for pf 2 hands unless otherwise stated)

Valse, c1843, *Pn*
Variations sur le choeur de Judas Maccabée, 4 hands, c1850, *Pn*
3   Six bagatelles, 1855 (1856)
11   Duettino, G, 4 hands, 1855 (1855)
21   Mazurka no.1, g, 1862 (1868)
23   Gavotte, c, 1871 (1872), orchd
24   Mazurka no.2, g, 1871 (1872)

—   Romance sans paroles, b, 1871 (1872)
35   Variations on a Theme of Beethoven, 2 pf, 1874 (1874)
70   Allegro appassionato, c#, orch ad lib, 1874 (1874)
52   Six études, 1877 (1877)
56   Menuet et valse, 1878 (1878)
59   König Harald Harfagar, 4 hands, 1880 (Berlin, 1880)
66   Mazurka no.3, b, 1882 (1883)
72   Album, 1884 (1884)
—   Andantino, 1884, *Pn*
96   Caprice arabe, 2 pf, 1884 (1884)
—   Improvisation, 1885 (1885)
77   Polonaise, f, 2 pf, 1886 (1886)
80   Souvenir d'Italie, G, 1887 (1887)
81   Feuillet d'album, Bb, 4 hands, 1887 (1887)
86   Pas redoublé, Bb, 4 hands, 1887 (1890)
85   Les cloches du soir, Eb, 1889 (1889)
87   Scherzo, 2 pf, 1889 (1890)
88   Valse canariote, a, 1890 (1890)
90   Suite, F, 1891 (1892)
97   Thème varié, 1894 (1894)
100 Souvenir d'Ismaïlia, 1895 (1895)
104 Valse mignonne, Eb, 1896 (1896)
105 Berceuse, E, 4 hands, 1896 (1896)
8bis Duos, 2 pf, 1898 (n.d.)
106 Caprice héroïque, 2 pf, 1898 (1898)
110 Valse nonchalante, Db, 1898 (1898), orchd
—   Quatre morceaux, c1898 (1898)
111 Six études, 1899 (1899)
120 Valse langoureuse, 1903 (1903)
—   Fueillet d'album, 1909, MS, Musée de Dieppe
135 Six études, left hand, 1912 (?1912)
139 Valse gaie, 1913 (?1913)
152 Vers la victoire, 4 hands (?1918)
155 Marche interalliée, 4 hands, 1918 (?1919)
161 Six Fugues, 1920 (?1920)
163 Marche dédiée aux étudiants d'Alger, 4 hands, chorus ad lib, 1921 (n.d.)
169 Feuillets d'album, 1921 (?1921)
—   Les heurs, pf, narrator, MS, Musée de Dieppe

OTHER KEYBOARD

1   Trois morceaux, harmonium, 1852 (1858)
—   Deux pièces, org, c1853, *Pn*
—   Fantaisie, Eb, org, 1857 (1857)
8   Six duos, harmonium, pf, 1858 (1858)
9   Bénédiction nuptiale, org, 1859 (1866)
13   Elévation, ou Communion, org/harmonium, 1865 (1865)
7   Trois rapsodies sur des cantiques bretons, org, 1866 (1866)
99   Trois préludes et fugues, org, 1894 (1894)
101 Fantaisie, Db, org, 1895 (1895)
107 Marche religieuse, org, 1897 (1898)
109 Trois préludes et fugues, org, 1898 (1898)
150 Sept improvisations, org, 1917 (n.d.)
157 Fantaisie no.3, org, 1919 (?1919)
—   Cinq morceaux, org/harmonium, *Pn*
—   Morceau, org, *Pn*
—   Prélude, org, F, *Pn*,

CADENZAS, TRANSCRIPTIONS AND ARRANGEMENTS

Cadenzas for Beethoven, Pf Conc. no.4, c1878; Beethoven, Vn Conc., 1900; Mozart, Pf Conc. K482; Mozart, Pf Conc. K491

Many transcrs. and arrs. of works by J. S. Bach, Beethoven, Berlioz, Bizet, Chopin, Duparc, J. Durand, Duvernoy, Gluck, Gounod, J. Haydn, Liszt, Massenet, Mendelssohn, L. de Milan, Mozart, Paladilhe, Reber, Schumann and Wagner

DOUBTFUL WORKS

Stage: Finale of Nina Zombie (opéra bouffe), 1878; Sketch for Gabrieli di Vergi (lyric drama), 1885; Le Sicilien, ou L'amour peintre (incidental music, Molière), 1892; La fille de tourneur d'ivoire (incidental music, H. Ferrare), 1909

Vocal: Ivanhoé (V. Roussy), cantata, 1864; Pour le centenaire de Hoche, cantata, 1868, ?lost; Les chants de guerre, 2 solo vv, chorus, orch, 1870; Tecum principium, motet, 1876; Hommage des enfants à Victor Hugo (M. Carminet), cantata, 1907

Inst: Rêverie orientale, orch, 1879; Fantasie on L'vov's Russian National Anthem; Cadenza for Mozart: Concerto K365/316a, 2 solo pf

WRITINGS

Notice sur Henri Reber (Paris, 1881)
Harmonie et mélodie (Paris, 1885, 9/1923)
Charles Gounod et le 'Don Juan' de Mozart (Paris, 1893)
Problèmes et mystères (Paris, 1894; rev., enlarged 1922 as *Divagations sérieuses*)
Portraits et souvenirs (Paris, 1899, 3/1909)
Essai sur les lyres et cithares antiques (Paris, 1902)
Quelques mots sur 'Proserpine' (Alexandria, 1902)

Ecole buissonnière: notes et souvenirs (Paris, 1913; Eng. trans.,
abridged, 1919/*R*1969)
Notice sur Le timbre d'argent (Brussels, 1914)
On the Execution of Music, and Principally of Ancient Music, ed. H. P.
Bowie (San Francisco, 1915)
Au courant de la vie (Paris, 1916)
Germanophilie (Paris, 1916)
Les idées de M. Vincent d'Indy (Paris, 1919)
'Lyres et cithares', *EMDC*, I/i (1921), 538
Outspoken Essays on Music, trans. F. Rothwell (New York and London,
1922/*R*1970) [selection of Saint-Saëns' writings]

Many MSS and letters in *F-Po*, *Pc*, Musée de Dieppe; some MSS in
GB-Lbm, *Lcm*, *Mcm*, Novello & Co., Durand & Cie; Saint-Saëns'
library in *F-DI*.

BIBLIOGRAPHY
C. Bellaigue: *M. Camille Saint-Saëns* (Paris, 1889)
Catalogue général et thématique des oeuvres de Saint-Saëns, ed. Dur-
and & Cie (Paris, 1897, rev. 1908)
O. Neitzel: *Camille Saint-Saëns* (Berlin, 1899)
E. Baumann: *Les grandes formes de la musique: l'oeuvre de Camille
Saint-Saëns* (Paris, 1905, rev. 1923)
R. Rolland: 'Camille Saint-Saëns', *Musiciens d'aujourd'hui* (Paris,
1908/*R*1946; Eng. trans., 1915/*R*1969)
O. Séré [J. Poueigh]: 'Camille Saint-Saëns', *Musiciens français
d'aujourd'hui* (Paris, 1911, rev. 2/1921)
L. Augé de Lassus: *Saint-Saëns* (Paris, 1914)
J. Bonnerot: *C. Saint-Saëns: sa vie et son oeuvre* (Paris, 1914, rev.
2/1922)
J. Montargis: *Camille Saint-Saëns: l'oeuvre, l'artiste* (Paris, 1919)
C. Debussy: 'Entretien sur le Prix de Rome et M. Saint-Saëns',
Monsieur Croche antidilettante (Paris, 1921; Eng. trans., 1927)
A. Hervey: *Saint-Saëns* (London, 1921)
H. Collet: *Samson et Dalila de C. Saint-Saëns* (Paris, ?1922)
W. Lyle: *Camille Saint-Saëns: his Life and Art* (London, 1923)
G. Servières: *Saint-Saëns* (Paris, 1923, rev. 1930)
A. Cortot: 'Saint-Saëns et le piano', *La musique française de piano*, ii
(Paris, 1930, 3/1948)
J. Handschin: *Camille Saint-Saëns* (Zurich, 1930)
P. Aguétant: *Saint-Saëns par lui-même d'après des lettres reçues* (Paris,
1938)
A. Boschot: 'Saint-Saëns', *Portraits de musiciens*, ii (Paris, 1947)
J. Chantavoine: *Camille Saint-Saëns* (Paris, 1947)
P. Lalo: 'Camille Saint-Saëns', *De Rameau à Ravel* (Paris, 1947)
Mélanges d'histoire littéraire et de bibliographie offerts à Jean Bonnerot
(Paris, 1954)
F. Noske: *La mélodie française de Berlioz à Duparc* (Amsterdam,
1954; Eng. trans., 1970)
M. Proust: *Contre Sainte-Beuve* (Paris, 1954)
J. Harding: *Saint-Saëns and his Circle* (London, 1965)
——: *Massenet* (London, 1970)
J.-M. Nectoux, ed.: 'Correspondance Saint-Saëns Fauré', *RdM*, lviii
(1972), 65, 190–252; lix (1973), 60–98
S. T. Ratner: *The Piano Works of Camille Saint-Saëns* (diss., U. of
Michigan, 1972)
D. M. Fallon: *The Symphonies and Symphonic Poems of Camille Saint-
Saëns* (diss., Yale U., 1973)
J.-M. Nectoux, ed.: *Camille Saint-Saëns et Gabriel Fauré: correspon-
dance: soixante ans d'amitié* (Paris, 1973)
E. Harkins: *The Chamber Music of Saint-Saëns* (diss., New York U.,
1976)
D. Fallon: 'Saint-Saëns and the *Concours de composition musicale* in
Bordeaux', *JAMS*, xxxi (1978), 309
JAMES HARDING (1), DANIEL M. FALLON (2, work-list)

Saint-Sévin. *See* L'ABBÉ family.

Saint-Simonians. Followers of a French social and
philosophical movement, among whom several were
musicians. Saint-Simonism was founded by a handful of
disciples of the social thinker Claude-Henri de Rouvroy,
count of Saint-Simon, shortly after his death in 1825.
The Saint-Simonians preached the elimination of all
hereditary rights, international cooperation for the
peaceful exploitation of the globe, and the reorientation
of social institutions towards 'the moral, intellectual and
physical improvement of the poorest and most
numerous class'.

The Saint-Simonians believed in the apostolic role of
the artist and attempted to enlist writers, artists and

musicians to their cause. In about 1830 or 1831, Liszt,
Ferdinand Hiller and the tenor Adolphe Nourrit were
apparently frequent visitors at the Saint-Simonians' public lectures and soirées in Paris. Berlioz became passion-
ately interested at about the same time; on 28 July
1831 he wrote to the Saint-Simonian leader Charles
Duveyrier that, in spite of certain doubts, 'I am today
convinced that Saint-Simon's plan is the only true and
only complete one, as far as the political reorganization
of Society is concerned'. In late 1831 the movement
suffered a schism and soon took on a more mystical
character, thus alienating many of its former sympath-
izers (including Berlioz and Liszt).

This new, almost religious emphasis on the nobility of
physical labour and on fraternal cooperation attracted
several young musicians to Saint-Simonism. Félicien
David became a member of the communal 'Famille saint-
simonienne' at Menilmontant, where he improvised at
the piano during ceremonies and wrote choruses for the
daily ritual. The amateur singers of the 'Family' were
trained by Dominique Tajan-Rogé, a former cellist at
the Opéra-Comique and a friend of Berlioz. In addition,
a number of Saint-Simonian chansonniers wrote
propagandistic poems to familiar tunes, and the most
well-known, Vinçard aîné, wrote his own melodies.

In 1833, as the result of governmental persecution,
many Saint-Simonians left France for Egypt. (The
departures were celebrated by a new adherent, Henri
Reber, in his 'A l'Orient!'.) The Egyptian mission failed,
thus marking the end of large-scale Saint-Simonian
activity, but David gathered themes there which he later
used in *Le désert* (1844) and other works. Apart from
David, only Tajan-Rogé and Vinçard retained close ties
with the movement's leaders later in life. But the
movement left its mark on those who had attended the
soirées of 1830–31 (not least on Liszt and Berlioz in
their popular choral works) and it retains interest as one
of the earliest social movements to make extensive use
of music to propagate its ideas.

BIBLIOGRAPHY
D. Tajan-Rogé: *Fausses notes* (Paris, 1862)
——: *Mémoires d'un piano* (Paris, 1876)
M. Thibert: *Le rôle social de l'art d'après les Saint-Simoniens* (Paris,
1926)
S. Charléty: *Essai sur l'histoire du Saint-Simonisme: 1825–64* (Paris,
rev. 2/1931)
L. D. Fraser: *Saint-Simonism and Music* (diss., Yale U., 1948)
F. Manuel: *The Prophets of Paris* (Cambridge, Mass., 1956)
RALPH P. LOCKE

Saint Sixt. *See* UC DE SAINT CIRC.

St Thomas Church, music of the. *See* SYRIAN CHURCH
MUSIC.

St Trond, Rudolph of. *See* RUDOLF OF ST TROND.

Saione [Saioni]. *See* FEDELI family.

Saitenhalter (Ger.). TAILPIECE.

Saive. *See* SAYVE family.

Sakač, Branimir (*b* Zagreb, 5 June 1918). Yugoslav
composer. He graduated in music at the Zagreb
Academy in 1941, having studied composition with
Franjo Dugan, and remained on the staff there (1941–
6). Following this, he was conductor of the Radio
Zagreb Orchestra (1946–8), chief of the music division

of Radio Rijeka (1949–50) and professor at the state music school in Zagreb (1951–61). He founded and directs the Zagreb Fonoplastički Atelje-Theater, which works in sound, light, movement and space, and which first performed at the Zagreb Biennale in 1967. In 1971 Sakač was made artistic director of the Annual Review of Yugoslav Music in Opatija, and director of the Zagreb Biennale.

Breaking away from a conventional romantic style, Sakač first attracted attention with his expressionist and sometimes violent *Simfonija o mrtvom vojniku* ('Symphony on a dead soldier', 1951), created from incidental music to the radio play *Without a Title* by Norman Corwin; the work's dramatic content has been realized in a powerful ballet. A number of descriptive orchestral works followed, all showing Sakač's ability to sustain his success in an advanced idiom. His *Three Synthetic Poems* for tape marked a new departure in using *musique concrète* for programmatic purposes, an approach repeated in the vivid *Jahači Apokalipse* ('Horsemen of the Apocalypse'). However, a later work, *Prostori* ('Spaces') dispenses with a programme and successfully combines sound transformations on tape with live orchestra. Fundamental to Sakač's development and his conversion to the avant garde is the outstanding large-scale orchestral work, *Episodes*, which shows the composer's complete command of new instrumental and compositional techniques, including the dramatic use of spatial notation. Another aspect of this enlargement of style is his later interest in novel vocal techniques, notably in *Omaggio* and in *Umbrana*, where the 12 solo singers use the clusters, unusual vocal production techniques and textures familiar in works of the Polish avant garde. Sakač is at his most refined in the smaller chamber instrumental works, such as *Solo I* and *Doppio*, notable for their use of new techniques in a forceful yet sympathetic manner.

WORKS
(selective list)

VOCAL AND ORCHESTRAL
Serenade, str, 1947; Simfonija o mrtvom vojniku [Sym. on a dead soldier], 1951; Preludij i Scherzo, 1952; Komorna simfonija [Chamber sym.], 1953; Sluga Jernej, sym. triptych, 1953; Oluja, sym. poem, 1955; Noć, mjesec i smrt [Night, moon and death], lyric poem, 1958; Kornet, lyric poem, 1958; Episodes, orch, 1963; 7 stavka [7 movts], chorus, 1963; Prostori [Spaces], orch, tape, 1965; Syndrome, chamber orch, 1966; Solo I, vn, chamber orch, 1968; Omaggio – canto della commedia, chorus, vn, perc, 1969; Bellatrix-Alleluia, 1v, chamber orch, 1970; Turm-Musik, 1970; Umbrana, 12 solo vv, 1971; Barasou, 1v, chamber ens, 1971; Matrix Sym., reciters, orch, 1972; Songelu, actor, light projections, chamber ens, 1972

CHAMBER, INSTRUMENTAL AND TAPE
2 Preludes, fl, harp, pf, c1950; Suita, 15 insts, 1952; Sonata, vn, 1953; 3 Synthetic Poems: Massacres, The Hole, The War, tape, 1959; Jahači Apokalipse [Horsemen of the Apocalypse], tape, 1960; Noveletta, pf, c1961; Aleatorički preludij, pf, 1961; 2 Miniatures, fl, harp, perc, 1963; Studija I, pf, perc, 1963; Studija II, pf, 1964; Sonet, ens, 1965; 6 Epigrams, 2 pf, 1966; Koralni kvartet, str qt, 1968; Doppio, str qt, 1968; Vario, vn, c1968; Prizme, pf, c1969; Attitudes, vc, pf, 1969; Ad litteram, pf, 1970; Scene, ens, 1971; A Play, ens, 1973; Synthana, tape, 1973

Principal publishers: Ars Croatica (Zagreb), Udruženje kompozitora Hrvatske (Zagreb)

WRITINGS
'Teorija informacija, slušalac i glasba' [The information theory, the listener and music], *Novi Zvuk*, ed. P. Selem (Zagreb, 1972), 6

BIBLIOGRAPHY
K. Kovačević: 'Branimir Sakač', *Muzička enciklopedija*, i (Zagreb, 1958), 526
——: 'Branimir Sakač', *Hrvatski kompozitori i njihova djela* (Zagreb, 1960), 398
——: *The History of Croatian Music in the Twentieth Century* (Zagreb, 1967)
P. Selem: 'Nova hrvatska glazba' [New Croatian music], *Kolo* (1970), no.12, p.1507; repr. in *Novi Zvuk*, ed P. Selem (Zagreb, 1972), 226
Z. Kučakalić: 'Branimir Sakač, Omaggio–canto della commedia', *Zvuk* (1971), nos.115–16, p.294
J. Andreis: *Music in Croatia* (Zagreb, 1974), 361
NIALL O'LOUGHLIN

Sakadas of Argos. *See* SACADAS OF ARGOS.

Sakketti, Liberio Antonovich. *See* SACCHETTI, LIBERIO ANTONOVICH.

Sala, Giuseppe (*fl* 1676–1715). Italian publisher, printer and bookseller. He was active in Venice, and the most important part of his output appeared between 1685 and 1705. He conducted his business, characterized by the sign of King David playing the harp, at S Giovanni Crisostomo in the house of his financier, the musician Natale Monferrato. Sala's first essay in printing, financed by the composer, was Monferrato's *Salmi concertati a 2 voci con violini e senza* (op.11). At some date before 1684, Sala took a share in the publishing side as a partner and, on Monferrato's death in 1685, he became its sole proprietor. In 1682 he published, anonymously, *L'armonia sonora delle sonate di diversi autori*, an anthology, edited by himself, of 12 sonatas for three instruments by various composers.

An *Indice dell'opere di musica sin hora stampate da Giuseppe Sala in Venezia* (?1714) enumerates his output of psalms, motets, cantatas and sonatas, in particular those of Bassani, Monferrato, Taglietti and Corelli; he published at least 14 editions of Corelli's first five opus numbers. The index also shows that he published psalms by Sartorio, D. F. Rossi, Cazzati and Benedetti, motets by Legrenzi, Allegri, Bonporti, G. M. Bononcini and Gasparini, cantatas by Caldara, Gregori and Albinoni and sonatas by Vitali, Legrenzi, de Castro, Corelli, Torelli, Bernabei and Marcello.

BIBLIOGRAPHY
C. Sartori: *Dizionario degli editori musicali italiani* (Florence, 1958)
——: 'Le origini di una casa editrice veneziana', *FAM*, vii (1960), 57
——: *Un catalogo di G. Sala del 1715* (Florence, 1966)
STEFANO AJANI

Sala, Josquino della (*fl* ?1575, 1585–8). Italian composer. He worked at some time in Rome: an eight-part Missa 'Ave regina' in manuscript ascribed to 'Jusquinus de Sala' survives there (in *I-Rvat* C.S.). His reputation evidently extended to Venice, where three publications of 1585 each included a work by him: the four-part madrigal *Le belle arcate ciglia* (RISM 1585²⁹), the madrigal *Ne si dolce com'hor* (RISM 1585²⁶) and the five-part motet *Benedicite Dominum* (RISM 1585⁴). He later contributed this motet to Gerlach's *Continuatio cantionum sacrarum* (RISM 1588²). It is an effective, lively work in which he handled the polyphonic texture confidently, fashioned strong, rhythmic points of imitation, and introduced a buoyant, contrasting middle section in triple metre. One further surviving composition may be by della Sala: a five-part madrigal *Fuggimi pur crudel*, attributed to 'Josquino Salem', appears in a collection compiled by Bavarian composers and published at Venice (RISM 1575¹¹). The records of the Bavarian court chapel include no reference to any musician named Sala, but only to a lutenist called 'Josquino' who flourished there in about 1575.

RICHARD MARLOW

Sala, Nicola (*b* Tocco-Caudio, nr. Benevento, 7 April 1713; *d* Naples, 31 Aug 1801). Italian teacher and composer. From 1732 to 1740 he was a student at the Pietà dei Turchini Conservatory, Naples, under Nicola Fago and Leo. While still a *maestrino* there, he seems to have composed the opera *Vologeso* (Fétis claimed to have seen a score of it with an indication, otherwise unconfirmed, that it was performed in Rome in 1737). After the death of Leo in 1744 Sala applied unsuccessfully to succeed him as *primo maestro* of the royal chapel (his test piece, the five-part fugue *Protexisti me* dated 21 April 1745, is printed in his *Regole*). In the 1760s he had three operas as well as several prologues and other occasional works performed at the S Carlo. In 1783 the senate of Messina petitioned the king to allow them to appoint Sala *maestro di cappella* at the cathedral there without the usual competition, but the king refused.

Sala was most important as a teacher, providing a formative influence on many Neapolitan composers. Early dates are lacking, but he seems to have taught for most of his life at the Pietà dei Turchini Conservatory, becoming *secondo maestro* in 1787 and *primo maestro* from 1793 until his retirement on 11 October 1799. His monumental *Regole del contrappunto pratico* (Naples, 1794) presents a complete course of theoretical and practical counterpoint from basic principles to complex manifestations. It seems to have been characteristic of Neapolitan teaching to emphasize practical demonstration rather than theoretical explanation, and the *Regole* follows this method by offering almost no written text to accompany its series of musical models. According to Villarosa, the work was published at government expense through Paisiello's influence. During the Revolution of 1799 the plates disappeared (about half of them were rediscovered in 1860 and are now in the Naples Conservatory), and the work became rare and expensive. Perhaps partly because of that, Sala soon acquired an almost legendary reputation for profound contrapuntal knowledge (previously his name had been little known outside Italy). Choron described Sala's work as 'the most considerable and esteemed of all', and reprinted the second and third volumes of it in his *Principes de composition* (Paris, 1809), adding a large number of Sala's *partimenti*, not included in the *Regole*. Later, Fétis harshly attacked Sala's competence, describing his counterpoint as poorly written and in a bad style, and his fugues as lacking in interest, frequently monotonous, sometimes tonally uncertain and confused as to the difference between real and tonal answers.

Sala's compositions, although inconsequential and mostly pedestrian, have been unjustly treated by some modern writers. In particular, Mondolfi's harsh judgment on his operas is almost entirely directed at characteristics of the contemporary *opera seria* as a genre, not of Sala's operas exclusively. His greatest weakness was in lyrical melody; some of his arias in an *agitato* or declamatory style are not ineffective. He was better in his church music in a free style, where he could set off operatic solo writing against textures more highly worked and contrapuntal than in the opera. His *Stabat mater* is a worthy upholder of the Pergolesi tradition.

WORKS

DRAMATIC

Vologeso (opera seria, Zeno), Rome, Argentina, 1737, or Lisbon, Condes, 1739
La Zenobia (opera seria, Metastasio), Naples, S Carlo, 12 Jan 1761,
arias in *GB-Lbm, I-Mc, Nc, P-La*
Demetrio (opera seria, Metastasio), Naples, S Carlo, 12 Dec 1762, *La*
Il giudizio d'Apollo (serenata, G. Fenizia), Naples, S Carlo, 1768
La bella eroina (prol), Naples, S Carlo, 13 Aug 1769, *La*
Merope (opera seria, Zeno), Naples, S Carlo, 13 Aug 1769, *I-Nc, P-La*
Giuditta, ossia La Betulia liberata (oratorio, Metastasio), ? Naples, ? Lent 1780, autograph *I-Nc*

Arias in Jommelli: Attilio Regolo, Naples, S Carlo, ? 23 March 1761, *GB-Lbm, I-Mc, Nc, P-La*
Miscellaneous arias: *B-Bc, D-Bds, DS, E-Mn, I-Mc, Nc*

SACRED

Masses: F, 4vv, orch, *I-Mc*, autograph *Nc*; E, a più voci, *Nc*; 4vv, *F-Pc, GB-T*; Introduzione–Messa, B♭, 4vv, insts, *I-Nc*
Magnificat, 4vv, *D-Bds*; Litany, g, 4vv, vns, bc, autograph *I-Nc*; Litany BVM, a, STB, bc (org), *Nc*; Responsori, mercoledi, giovedi, venerdi santo, 4vv, org, *Nc*; 5 Dixit Dominus: 1, 4vv, *F-Pc*, 2, C, E♭, SSATB, orch, both *I-Mc*, 3, 1, D, 4vv, insts, *Nc*, 1, 5vv, insts, *Nc*; 2, Miserere, double choir; 10, *D-Bds*, 1, *GB-T*, 1, c, 1797, *I-Mc*; Justus ut palma, 4vv unacc., *GB-T, I-Nc*; O quam pulchra, Quem pulchri sunt, Sumunt boni, all Barcelona, Biblioteca musicale de la Diputaciò; In memoriam aeterna, SATB, str, *I-Nc*; Te decet, SATB, str, *Nc*; Stabat mater, 2S, str, bc, *GB-Lcm*; A chi muore per Dio, madrigale, 4vv, 1794, *I-Mc, Nc*

DIDACTIC WORKS

Regole del contrappunto pratico (Naples, 1794); partly repr. in Choron: Principes de composition des écoles d'Italie (Paris, 1809)
Principi di contrappunto . . . per uso di Ercole Paganini, *GB-Lcm*
Elementi per ben suonare il cembalo, *I-Nc*
Disposizione a 3 per introduzione alle fughe di tre parti, *Nc*
Il modo di disporre a tre sopra la scala diatonica, *Nc*
Il modo di fare la fuga a due voci per li studiosi scolari, *Nc*
Fugues: 5, 2vv (3 dated 19 Nov 1792), 1, 3vv, 5, 4vv, all *Nc*; Fuga, 2vv, segue un sonnetto, *Nc*; 75 canons, 2vv, *Nc*; Canone sopra canone, *D-Bds*; Solfeggios: B, 1778, *I-Nc*, S, b, *Nc, Nf*
Disposizioni imitate a soggetto e contrasoggetto, *Mc*
Fughe con soggetto e contrasoggetto a suono plagale, *Mc*

BIBLIOGRAPHY

FétisB
C. A. de Rosa [Marchese di Villarosa]: *Memorie dei compositori di musica del regno di Napoli* (Naples, 1840)
F. Florimo: *La scuola musicale di Napoli e i suoi conservatorii*, iii (Naples, 1883/*R*1969), 42
G. Leo: 'Nicola Sala', *Rivista storica del Sannio*, no.5 (1918)
S. di Giacomo: *I quattro antichi conservatorii musicali di Napoli*, i (Milan and Naples, 1924)
U. Prota-Giurleo: 'Musicisti sanniti', *Samnium*, no.1 (1928)
A. Mondolfi: 'Sala, Nicola', *ES*

DENNIS LIBBY (text),
JAMES L. JACKMAN (work-list)

Salabert. French firm of music publishers. It was founded in Paris between 1878 and 1895 by Edouard Salabert (*b* London, 1 Dec 1838; *d* Paris, 8 Sept 1903); he was paralysed in 1901, and the company was taken over by his son Francis Salabert (*b* Paris, 27 July 1884; *d* nr. Shannon, Ireland, 28 Dec 1946). Salabert was among the first to internationalize popular music; his enterprises were diversified and mostly successful, including music from and for films, recordings, music-hall and concert productions, artist management, and paper publication of arrangements and original versions of the repertories of the most famous composers and interpreters of all varieties of light music – European, Latin American and American. Successes in light music permitted Salabert to expand production of the classics, educational materials and modern art music. He published some compositions of Auric, Honegger, Milhaud and others, and by 1946 had bought the catalogues of 51 other publishers, among them Dufresne (1923), Gaudet (1927), Mathot (1930), Christiné (1937), Rouart-Lerolle (1941) and Deiss (1946).

Under Mme Salabert, Francis's widow, Editions Salabert remains a leading publisher of new works. In 1968 a catalogue of the *Jeune école contemporaine* was initiated; by 1972 it contained 246 compositions by 33 young composers, many of them avant-garde.

BIBLIOGRAPHY
Salabert informations, i (1967); ii (1968)
Jeune école contemporaine (Paris, 1969; suppl. 1972) [Salabert catalogue]
ROBERT S. NICHOLS

Salabue, Ignazio Alessandro Cozio di. *See* COZIO DI SALABUE, IGNAZIO ALESSANDRO.

Salaman, Charles (Kensington) (*b* London, 3 March 1814; *d* London, 23 June 1901). English pianist, conductor, composer and teacher. He studied under S. F. Rimbault, Charles Neate and H. Herz. His first public appearance was at Blackheath in 1828. In 1830 he played his own *Rondo brillant* in London and composed an Ode for the Shakespeare commemoration, which was performed at Stratford (23 April) and repeated in London. During 1833–7 he gave annual orchestral concerts in London; in 1835 he helped found the Concerti da Camera. He lived in Rome in 1846–8, where he conducted the first Rome performance of Beethoven's Symphony no.2 and was made an honorary member of the Accademia di S Cecilia. He founded an amateur choral society in London in 1849, and helped found in 1858 the Musical Society and in 1874 the Musical Association. He wrote over 200 songs (including a very popular setting of Shelley's *I arise from dreams of thee*, 1836), psalms and anthems (almost 100 of them for Jewish liturgical use) and piano pieces; he contributed to several music journals.

BIBLIOGRAPHY
'Pianists of the Past: Personal Recollections by the late Charles Salaman', *Blackwoods Edinburgh Magazine*, clxx (July–Dec 1901), 307
Obituary, *MT*, xlii (1901), 530 [with MS facs.]
J. C. Haddon: 'Salaman, Charles Kensington', *DNB*
GEORGE GROVE/R. J. PASCALL

Salari, Francesco (*b* Bergamo, 1751; *d* Bergamo, 27 Dec 1828). Italian composer. He was probably a boy soprano at the cathedral in Bergamo. He studied under C. Cotumacci and G. Doll at the Conservatory of S Onofrio in Naples, later for five years under N. Piccinni, and from 1776 under G. A. Fioroni in Milan. He then went to Venice, where he gave singing instruction and composed for the theatre. In 1805 he returned to Bergamo to teach singing at the Institute of Music and to serve as second *maestro di cappella* at the church of S Maria Maggiore. He gave singing lessons to Donizetti.

WORKS
Operas, music lost: Ifigenia in Aulide, Casal Monferrato, 1776; Il marchese carbonaro, Venice, S Moisè, carn. 1776; L'amor ramingo, Venice, S Samuele, carn. 1777; Le teste deboli (G. Bertati), Venice, S Moisè, carn. 1780
Sacred works: Rapida flamma, 1785; Heu miser, 1790; Sic me semper: all *I-Vc*; other sacred works, lost

BIBLIOGRAPHY
A. Geddo: *Bergamo e la musica* (Bergamo, 1958)
SIEGFRIED GMEINWIESER

Salas Viú, Vicente (*b* Madrid, 29 Jan 1911; *d* Santiago, Chile, 1967). Chilean musicologist and music critic of Spanish birth. He studied the piano and theory at the Madrid National Conservatory of Music (1928–30), and composition with his brother-in-law, the composer Rodolfo Halffter, and Manuel de Falla. Concurrently he wrote for the Madrid newspaper *El sol*. After settling in Santiago, Chile (1939), he became professor of music history at the National Conservatory, and successively head of publicity, technical secretary (1940–52) and director (appointed 1952) of the Instituto de Extensión

Musical of the University of Chile. He founded (1945) and for several years edited the *Revista musical chilena*, the only Latin American music periodical that has managed to survive. When the Instituto de Investigaciones Musicales was founded in 1947, he was appointed its director. His publications include articles for the Santiago *El mercurio*, numerous scholarly articles on Chilean 20th-century music and a valuable and informative book, *La creación musical en Chile 1900–1950*.

WRITINGS
'Allende y el nacionalismo musical', *Revista musical chilena*, no.5 (1945), 15
'Machado en Halffter: glose a unas sonatas', *Revista musical chilena*, no.16 (1946), 14
'El público y la creación musical', *Revista musical chilena*, no.19 (1947), 11; nos.20–21 (1947), 22; nos.22–3 (1947), 46
'La primera sinfonía de Santa Cruz', *Revista musical chilena*, no.29 (1948), 9
'Enrique Soro en el movimiento musical de Chile', *Revista musical chilena*, no.30 (1948), 10
'Alfonso Leng: espíritu y estilo', *Revista musical chilena*, no.33 (1949), 8
'Raíces del estilo de Juan Sebastián Bach', *Revista musical chilena*, no.38 (1950), 5
'La Egloga para soprano, coro y orquesta de Domingo Santa Cruz', *Revista musical chilena*, no.39 (1950), 19
'Las obras para orquesta de Domingo Santa Cruz', *Revista musical chilena*, no.42 (1951), 11
La creación musical en Chile 1900–1950 (Santiago, 1952)
'En torno a "La Muerte de Alsino" ', *Revista musical chilena*, no.54 (1957), 19
'Los festivales de música chilena ¿Una bella iniciativa en dorrota?', *Revista musical chilena*, no.66 (1959), 6; no.67 (1959), 17
'Federico Chopin en el primer centenario de su muerte', *Revista musical chilena*, no.69 (1960), 20
'Nuestra Revista Musical, su pasado y su presente', *Revista musical chilena*, no.71 (1960), 7
'La afinidad entre las artes', *Revista musical chilena*, no.84 (1963), 37
'Berlioz, paradigma del artista romántico', *Revista musical chilena*, no.89 (1964), 15
'La obra de René Amengual: del nacionalismo al expresionismo', *Revista musical chilena*, no.90 (1964), 62
'Creación musical y música aborigen en la obra de Carlos Isamitt', *Revista musical chilena*, no.97 (1966), 14
'Carlos Lavín y la musicología en Chile', *Revista musical chilena*, no.99 (1967), 8

BIBLIOGRAPHY
A. Letelier Llona: 'Vincente Salas Viú', *Revista musical chilena*, no.102 (1967), 3
J. Orrego Salas: 'In Memoriam Vicente Salas Viú', *Yearbook, Inter-American Institute for Musical Research*, iv (1968), 178
GERARD BÉHAGUE

Salas y Castro, Esteban (*b* Havana, 25 Dec 1725; *d* Santiago de Cuba, 14 July 1803). Cuban composer. The first Cuban composer of art music, he was *maestro de capilla* of Santiago de Cuba Cathedral (1764–1803), establishing a conservatory for singers and instrumentalists attached to the cathedral. Besides composing music for the cathedral, he conducted Cuba's first chamber ensemble, performing symphonies by Haydn, Pleyel and Gossec and sacred works by Paisiello, Porpora and Righini. After being ordained in 1790, he taught philosophy, theology and ethics and wrote sensitive religious pastoral poems. His music is written in a rigorous and transparent Classical style, closely resembling that of Haydn, Pergolesi and Antonio Soler. Well versed in contrapuntal devices, mainly canon, he used varied instrumental forces in his sacred works. Probably his most personal contribution is his series of villancicos (1783–1802), based on 17th- and 18th-century Neapolitan models but developed further; the sections are expanded (there are usually three: Recitativo, Pastorela, Allegro) and often preceded by instrumental preludes resembling the Italian overture form. One of the most ambitious of the villancicos, *Kalenda* (1791), begins with three *coplas* in duet form, followed by a big three-part fugue on a theme of popular character. Another, *Pues la fábrica de un templo* (1783), shows Spanish influence and begins with an instrumental section having the character of a Scarlatti sonata.

WORKS
(*MSS in Santiago de Cuba Cathedral*)

5 masses; 3 requiem; 16 Salve; 2 motets; 5 psalms; 2 litanies; 5 hymns; 12 anthems; 3 canticles; 29 alleluias; 7 sequences; 3 Passions
Tonadillas; Autos sacramentales; Stabat mater, solo vv, vv, org, insts, 1790; Las siete últimas palabras, vv, orch; 30 villancicos, 1–6vv, some with insts

BIBLIOGRAPHY

L. Fuentes: *Las artes en Santiago de Cuba* (Santiago de Cuba, 1893)
A. Carpentier: *La música en Cuba* (Mexico City, 1946), 58ff
P. Hernández Balaguer: *Obras de Esteban Salas* (Santiago de Cuba, 1960)

AURELIO DE LA VEGA

Salaverde, Bartolomé de Selma y. *See* SELMA Y SALAVERDE, BARTOLOMÉ DE.

Salazar, Adolfo (*b* Madrid, 6 March 1890; *d* Mexico City, 27 Sept 1958). Spanish writer on music and literature, and composer. He studied history at Madrid University but abandoned the course to concentrate on music; he was later a pupil of Pérez Casas and Falla in Madrid and Ravel in Paris. He edited the *Revista musical hispano-americana* from 1914 to 1918 and was music critic of the Madrid daily *El sol* from 1918 to 1936. From 1915 to 1922 he was secretary of the Sociedad Nacional de Música (founded to encourage performance of contemporary Spanish chamber music). He was a founder-member of the Société Française de Musicologie and in 1917 he became a member of the executive committee of the IMS at The Hague. In 1918 he was made vice-president of the music section of the Ateneo in Madrid, and in 1923 secretary of the Spanish section of the ISCM. At the Residencia de Estudiantes in Madrid during the 1920s he was one of the influential group that included Falla, Turina, Sainz de la Maza, Lorca, Buñuel and Dalí. He chose exile in 1937 soon after the Civil War began, and settled in Mexico. In the next year he was appointed cultural attaché to the Spanish Republican Embassy in Washington. From 1939 he taught at the Colegio de México and from 1946 at the Mexico National Conservatory. He was a corresponding member of the Hispanic Society of America and of the Instituto Español de Musicología in Spain.

Probably no Spanish writer of the 20th century has left deeper marks on Spanish and Latin American musical life. As a journalist, his famed articles in *El sol* and later his concert notices in Mexican newspapers played a major part in encouraging an appreciation of Spanish and Latin American composers. He was one of the first to champion Falla as the guiding light of a new Spanish 'school' founded on the idea of Spanish popular music extolled by Pedrell and Barbieri. But by 1950 Salazar had come to revalue Pedrell's nationalism as 'theoretical' and misleading, and to reappraise Falla as a 'petit maître' who stood at the end of a blind alley. He proceeded to hail other figures with equal verve, including E. Halffter and Lorca in Spain and Chávez in South America. At the same time he set out to educate public and musicians alike in foreign music; no other Spanish writer on music at that time came so near to transcending the pervasive nationalistic outlook. This is even more apparent in his work as an author. Odriozola listed nearly 100 works by Salazar; allowing for duplication and lost manuscripts, he must be credited with over 30 books and some 20 substantial essays. The fullest exposition of his ideas is in *La música en la sociedad europea*. His essential premise was his view of music as part of an evolving society: he saw the need to search for 'the internal motives (acoustic and aesthetic)' rather than a description of musical works (the 'results') in themselves. He was not primarily a musicologist: relatively few of his essays were written for learned journals; yet many of his pages, such as 'Música, instrumentos y danzas en las obras de Cervantes', 'La guitarra, heredera de la *kithara* clásica', 'Poesía y música ... vulgar y sus antecedentes' and the section on instruments in *La música en la sociedad europea*, seem to be the fruits of original research. *La música de España* is a solid history of Spanish music. He took an active interest in public affairs as, for example, in about 1935 when he put forward ambitious plans for a central, governmental body to sponsor the major aspects of Spain's musical life; he was embittered by the predictably cool reception his plans received.

Salazar's compositions have yet to be properly assessed. They include works for orchestra (*Don Juan, Paisajes, Estampas*), chamber music (*Rubaiyat* for string quartet, *Zarabanda* for flute, viola and bassoon, a violin sonata and three piano preludes) and vocal works (*Trois chansons de Paul Verlaine* for voice and piano, *Cuatro letrillas que se cantan en las obras de Cervantes* for a cappella choir). An impressionist rather than a Spanish style is evident except in pieces such as *Cuatro letrillas*; yet even these four pieces are closer to the modern, 'theoretically' popular style which Salazar accused Pedrell of fostering, than to 17th-century song. The most important part of his work has been seen in his work as a teacher both in formal classes and in conversation; his reputation spread beyond his colleges in Mexico City. From his early days in Madrid, he was primarily an educator who set out to enlighten as well as to inform.

WRITINGS

Teoría y práctica de armonía moderna (Madrid, 1915, 2/1947) [trans. of A. E. Hull: *Modern Harmony: its Explanation and Application*, London, 1914]
La música en Rusia: boceto de historia: Borodín y 'El príncipe Igor', Musorgsky y 'Boris Godúnof (Madrid, 1922)
Música y músicos de hoy (Madrid, 1928)
Sinfonía y ballet: idea y gesto en la música y danzas contemporáneas (Madrid, 1929; partly repr. as *Forma y expresión en la música*, Mexico, 1941)
La música contemporánea en España: examen crítico de la música española en el período contemporáneo y de sus orígenes (Madrid, 1930)
La música actual en Europa y sus problemas (Madrid, 1935)
El siglo romántico: ensayos sobre los grandes compositores de la época romántica (Madrid, 1936, 2/1955)
La música en el siglo XX: ensayo de crítica y de estética desde el punto de vista de su función social (Madrid, 1936, rev. 2/1939 as *Música y sociedad en el siglo XX*)
'Music in the Primitive Spanish Theatre before Lope de Vega', *PAMS 1938*, 94
La rosa de los vientos en la música europea: conceptos fundamentales en la historia del arte musical (Mexico, 1940, enlarged 2/1954 as *Conceptos fundamentales en la historia de la música*)
Las grandes estructuras de la música: la música antes de la historia: en el templo, en la escena, en el pueblo (Mexico, 1940)
Los grandes períodos en la historia de la música: introducción al estudio de la historia musical (Mexico, 1941; repr. in *Síntesis de la historia de la música*, Buenos Aires, 1945)
Introducción a la música actual (Mexico, 1942; repr. in *Síntesis de la*

historia de la música, Buenos Aires, 1945)
La música en la sociedad europea (Mexico, 1942–6)
La música moderna: las corrientes directrices del arte musical contemporáneo (Buenos Aires, 1944; Eng. trans., 1946)
La danza y el ballet: introducción al conocimiento de la danza de arte y del ballet (Mexico, 1949, 3/1955)
La música como proceso histórico de su invención (Mexico, 1950, enlarged 2/1953)
En torno a Juan Sebastián Bach: una introducción a la vida y a la obra del gran músico (Mexico, 1951)
Juan Sebastián Bach: un ensayo (Mexico, 1951)
'La musica en la edad homérica', *AnM*, vi (1951), 106; repr. in *La música en la cultura griega* (Mexico, 1954)
'Sobre algunos instrumentos de música mencionados por Cervantes', *Nueva revista de filología hispánica* (Mexico, 1951), 5
La música de España: la música en la cultura española (Buenos Aires, 1953)
La música en la cultura griega (Mexico, 1954) [vol.i of projected *Teoría y práctica de la música a través de la historia*; part of vol.ii printed as *La era monódica*, 1958]
La música orquestal en el siglo XX (Mexico, ·1956)
La era monódica en Oriente y Occidente, i: *Rome* (Mexico, 1958); ii: *La transformación de la prosodia clásica a expensas del acento* (Mexico, 1958)
'Folk Music: a General Survey: XIII, Spanish Folk Music', 'Zarzuela', *The International Cyclopedia of Music and Musicians*, ed. O. Thompson, N. Slonimsky and R. Sabin (London, 1964)
La música en Cervantes y otros ensayos (Mexico, 1961) [incl. 'Parsifal, en tierras románicas', 37; 'Poesía y musica...vulgar y sus antecedentes en la Edad Media: poesía y música en las primeras formas de versificación rimada en lengua vulgar y sus antecedentes en lengua latina en la Edad Media', 59–126; 'Música, instrumentos y danzas en las obras de Cervantes', 127–275; 'La guitarra, heredera de la *kithara* clásica', 277; 'Los grandes maestros del Renacimiento musical en España', (Morales, F. Guerrero, Victoria), 289–321; 'La saeta: Copla y canto', · 337; 'Genio y figura de José Verdi: in memoriam', 349–78]
Articles in *La enciclopedia Espasa Calpe, Suplementos, Música* and programme notes for Sociedad Nacional de Música and Sociedad de Música de Cámara

BIBLIOGRAPHY
F. Sopeña: *Historia de la música española contemporánea* (Madrid, 1958), esp. 152ff, 179ff, 304ff
A. Salazar: *La música en Cervantes y otros ensayos* (Mexico City, 1961) [incl. A. Odriozola: 'La bibliografía de Adolfo Salazar', p.13 and I. Pope: 'Prólogo' (appreciation of Salazar), p.9]

JACK SAGE

Salazar [Zalazar], **Antonio de** (*b c*1650; *d* Mexico City, before 27 May 1715). Mexican composer of Spanish birth. According to music now in Guatemala he was a prebendary in Seville before going to Mexico, where he was appointed *maestro de capilla* of Puebla Cathedral on 11 July 1679. In 1688 he easily defeated four rivals in a competition for the post of *maestro de capilla* of Mexico City Cathedral, and he was officially appointed on 3 September. He proved to be both skilled and conscientious, organizing the music archives, supervising the testing and installation (in 1695) of a magnificent new organ built in Madrid, and encouraging the development of talented pupils with systematic lessons. His staff included his counterpoint pupil Pérez de Gúzman (later *maestro de capilla* at Oaxaca), FRANCISCO DE ATIENZA Y PINEDA and MANUEL DE ZUMAYA. In January 1710 he stated that he was ill and almost blind, and he was allowed to turn over some of his teaching duties to Zumaya, who was also selected as substitute, and in 1711 as acting, *maestro de capilla*.

In his sacred choral works, some of which are for double choir, Salazar demonstrated a fluent contrapuntal technique; he used little imitation but unified his works with recurring motifs, some derived from plainsong. Even for a Spanish-born composer of sacred music, his style is unusually conservative for his time. The textures are transparent, with broad phrases, open spacing and a quiet, even rhythmic flow. Contrasts are subtle, there are a few touches of word-painting, and harmonic colour is employed sensitively, with slight chromaticism. Some textless treble and bass melodies imply the use of instruments, but, as is usual in the Spanish style of this period, the bass is not figured. Salazar apparently enjoyed a wide reputation as a composer of villancicos and *chanzonetas* for feast days, but comparatively few such works by him are extant. In his day, villancicos were often composed as elaborate cycles in eight or nine sections, employing a wide range of instruments and varied vocal resources; they were generously endowed by wealthy benefactors to ensure a suitably brilliant performance. The poem of one villancico cycle (for the feast of St Peter, 1691), attributed to the celebrated Juana Inés de la Cruz and set to music by Salazar, lists the following typical instrumental groups: clarino, trumpet, cornett, trombone, organ and bassoon; shawm and violin; trumpet marine, bassoon, bass viol, cittern and violin; and tenor shawm, vihuela, rebec, bandora and large harp. Prints of texts from Puebla and Medina's lists for Mexico City indicate that Salazar composed nearly 20 such cycles between 1680 and 1704; these include settings of seven cycles attributed to Juana Inés de la Cruz (1680–92) and four commemorating the 'miraculous appearance of the Virgin of Guadalupe' (1695–7), the earliest compositions glorifying the Mexican national saint.

WORKS

Missa sine nomine, 5vv, Colegio de S Rosa, Morelia, Mexico
Oficio de defuntos, 4vv, Puebla Cathedral, Mexico
Magnificat, 5vv, Puebla Cathedral, Mexico; Magnificat, 12vv, Oaxaca Cathedral, Mexico
Litaniae lauretanae, Colección Sánchez Garza, Mexico City
Salve regina, 8vv, Puebla Cathedral, Mexico
6 hymns, 4, 5vv, Puebla Cathedral, Mexico; 4 hymns, 4vv, Mexico City Cathedral; 1 hymn, 8vv, Tepotzotlán Museum, Mexico City; Hymn to Spanish saints, *E-Sc*
Motet, 8vv, Oaxaca Cathedral, Mexico
6 responsories, 8vv, Mexico City Cathedral, 1 ed. in Spiess and Stanford
15 villancicos, Colección Sánchez Garza, Mexico City, 2 ed. in Stevenson (1974); other villancicos: Mexico City Cathedral, Oaxaca Cathedral, Mexico, and Guatemala City Cathedral; 2 ed. in Saldívar and in Stevenson (1952)

BIBLIOGRAPHY
J. T. Medina: *La imprenta en México (1539–1821)*, iii (Santiago de Chile, 1908/R1962)
G. Saldívar: *Historia de la música en México* (Mexico City, 1934)
A. Méndez Plancarte, ed.: *Obras completas de Sor Juana Inés de la Cruz*, ii (Mexico City, 1952)
R. Stevenson: *Music in Mexico* (New York, 1952/R1971)
——: 'Sixteenth and Seventeenth Century Resources in Mexico', *FAM*, i (1954), 69; ii (1955), 10
——: 'Mexico City Cathedral Music: 1600–1750', *The Americas*, xxi (1964), 111
A. R. Catalyne: 'Music of the Sixteenth through the Eighteenth Centuries in the Cathedral of Puebla, Mexico', *Yearbook, Inter-American Institute for Musical Research*, ii (1966), 75
L. B. Spiess and E. T. Stanford: *Introduction to Certain Mexican Musical Archives*, Detroit Studies in Music Bibliography, xv (Detroit, 1969)
R. Stevenson: *Renaissance and Baroque Musical Sources in the Americas* (Washington, DC, 1970)
——: *Christmas Music from Baroque Mexico* (Berkeley and Los Angeles, 1974)

ALICE RAY CATALYNE

Salazar, Diego José [Joseph] **de** (*d* Seville, 25 June 1709). Spanish composer. After being a choirboy at Seville Cathedral he became *maestro de capilla* at the nearby village of Estepa. He was recalled to Seville on 26 November 1685 to succeed Alonso Xuárez (probably his teacher) as cathedral *maestro de capilla*. He wrote a requiem for Charles II's wife María Luisa de Orléans (*d* 12 February 1689) that was used for many later important funerals. He died of the plague, aged about 50.

When catalogued in 1904 the music archive at Seville Cathedral contained an orchestral mass, a Credo, four motets, Lamentations, 23 folders of miscellaneous works and three books of elaborated accompaniments by Salazar; in addition Choirbook CXV contains his hymn for SS Justus and Pastor, *Appetunt cursus et inde.* At least seven instrumentally accompanied villancicos, for one to eight voices, attesting to his picaresque wit and keen sense of drama, survived in Latin American archives during the late 1960s (see Stevenson).

BIBLIOGRAPHY

S. de la Rosa y López: *Los seises de la Catedral de Sevilla* (Seville, 1904), 327f

R. Stevenson: *Renaissance and Baroque Musical Sources in the Americas* (Washington, DC, 1970), 98, 178, 250

J. E. Ayarra Jarne: *La música en la Catedral de Sevilla* (Seville, 1976), 62

ROBERT STEVENSON

Salbinger [Salblinger], **Sigmund.** *See* SALMINGER, SIGMUND.

Saldívar, Gabriel (*b* Santander-Jiménez, 5 Sept 1909). Mexican historian and music historian. After studying at Ciudad Victoria he moved to Mexico City, where he studied medicine at the National University of Mexico for five years; he was self-taught in music. He worked as a historian for the Ministry of Foreign Relations (1934–5) and the state of Tamaulipas (1937–8), concurrently serving as a research associate at the Instituto de Investigaciones Estéticas of the National University and a lecturer at the Colegio Victoria (1930s); from 1941 he was a press and publicity director of the Ministry of Agriculture. He was a member of the Ateneo Musical Mexicano and of the Mexican Society of Folklore and of History. From his early 20s he studied Mexican music history; his most important writings are studies of pre-Columbian and colonial music history and of the *jarabe*, a Mexican folkdance.

WRITINGS

'Las danzas mexicanas', *Nuestro México*, i (1932), 17

Historia de la música en México (épocas pre-cortesiana y colonial) (Mexico City, 1934)

El jarabe, baile popular mexicano (Mexico City, 1937)

'Música india: semejanza entre una melodía maya y otra otomí', *Investigación lingüística*, v/1–2 (1938), 98

'Una tablatura mexicana', *Revista musical mexicana*, ii/2 (1942), 36

'Mariano Elízaga y las canciones de la Independencia', *Boletín de la Sociedad mexicana de geografía y estadística*, lxiii (1947), 641

GERARD BÉHAGUE

Saldoni, Baltasar (*b* Barcelona, 4 Jan 1807; *d* Madrid, 3 Dec 1889). Spanish composer, musicologist and singing teacher. He was first a chorister at S María del Mar in Barcelona, then a member of the Montserrat choir. In Barcelona he studied the piano and the organ with Mateo Ferrer and composition with Francisco Queralt. In 1829 he moved to Madrid and became a pupil of Ramón Carnicer. When the Madrid Conservatory was founded in 1830, he was appointed professor of voice training and singing, a position he held until his death. His compositions, both theatrical and religious, were much influenced by Italian music of the time. His masterpiece is his four-volume *Diccionario biográfico-bibliográfico de efemérides de músicos españoles.* Despite some deficiencies (though there are fewer of these than is generally stated), it is still indispensable for the biographies of Spanish musicians before 1881. Saldoni realized the importance of this work and abandoned his career as a composer to devote himself entirely to it.

WORKS

It. opere serie, perf. Madrid, Cruz: Saladino e Clotilde, cavatina only, 1833; Ipermestra, 20 Jan 1838; Cleonice, regina di Siria, 24 Jan 1840

Zarzuelas: Boabdil, ultimo rey moro de Granada, 1844, unperf.; El rey y la costurera, 1853, unperf.; Guzmán el Bueno, 1855, unperf.; La corte de Mónaco, Madrid, 16 Feb 1857; Los maredos en las máscaras, Barcelona, 26 Aug 1864

Operettas: El triunfo del amor, Barcelona, private perf., 1826; Los o enredos de un curiosa

Sacred: 3 Misa de gloria, 2 Miserere, 2 Stabat mater, 2 Salve regina, 5 Lamentations, other liturgical pieces; motets, villancicos and other pieces for vv, org/pf

WRITINGS

Reseña histórica de la Escolanía de la Virgen de Montserrat en Cataluña desde 1456 hasta nuestros días (Madrid, 1856)

Efemérides de músicos españoles (Madrid, 1860) [complete list of works, 249ff]

Diccionario biográfico-bibliográfico de efemérides de músicos españoles (Madrid, 1868–81) [vol.i incl. autobiography and list of works, 43]

BIBLIOGRAPHY

FétisB

J. Parada y Barreto: *Diccionario técnico, histórico y biográfico de la música* (Madrid, 1868), 344ff

A. Peña y Goñi: *La ópera española y la música dramática en España* (Madrid, 1881), 175ff

E. Cotarelo y Mori: *Historia de la zarzuela* (Madrid, 1934)

J. Subirá: *Historia de la música española e hispanoamericana* (Barcelona, 1953)

JOSÉ LÓPEZ-CALO

Sale (*fl c*1400). This enigmatic name appears at the head of a three-voice composition with the incipit 'O . . .' in the fragments *NL-Lu* 2720, a Dutch or Flemish MS containing both French and Dutch secular songs in the polyphonic style of the Ars Nova.

BIBLIOGRAPHY

H. Wagenaar-Nolthenius: 'De Leidse Fragmenten', *Renaissance-Muziek 1400–1600: Donum Natalicium René Bernard Lenaerts* (Louvain, 1969), 303

GILBERT REANEY

Salé [Salle], **Adrien Trudo** [Trudon] (*b* St Truiden, Limburg, baptized 6 June 1722; *d* Averbode, Brabant, 19 March 1782). South Netherlands organist and composer. He entered the Premonstratensian monastery of Averbode on 2 February 1745 and was ordained priest there in 1748, later becoming librarian and Kantor; his manuscripts indicate that he was also probably the organist there. A few years later he studied theology at the Premonstratensian college at Louvain, after which he returned to Averbode and became a provisor, later an abbot and finally the vicar-general for the district of Brabant. He was probably better known as a performer than as a composer. He wrote some rather primitive accompaniments to plainsong and may have written only the accompaniments to the other compositions associated with his name, three masses and two motets, all in manuscript at the Abbey of Averbode.

BIBLIOGRAPHY

L. Galesloot: 'François-Xavier Le Mire . . . Trond Salé', *Annales de l'Académie archéologique de Belgique*, xviii (1861), 187

A. Goovaerts: 'Salé . . . (Adrien-Trudon)', *BNB*

R. Vannes: *Dictionnaire des musiciens (compositeurs)* (Brussels, 1947)

JACQUES VAN DEUN

Sale [Salec], **François** [Franz]. *See* SALES, FRANZ.

Sale, Giovanni Battista del (*b* ?before *c*1575; *d* Graz, buried 10 Aug 1615). Italian instrumentalist living in Austria. He received his musical education at the expense of Archduke Ferdinand of Inner Austria. On 1 June 1597 he was appointed instrumentalist at the court of Graz. According to the testimony of P. A. Bianco, the court Kapellmeister at Graz, he was a 'guetter Musicus und in allen Instrumenten universalis'. There is no evidence that he was a composer.

HELLMUT FEDERHOFER

Sales [Sale, Salec, Saletz], **Franz** (*b* Namur, ?*c*1550; *d* Prague, 15 July 1599). Netherlands composer. In his 1589 publication he stated that he was the son of 'Hans Saletz von Namur', and that he left 'Belgia nostra' because of the religious conflicts. There is no proof supporting the suggestion that he was a pupil of Lassus. After two unsuccessful attempts in 1579 and 1580 to obtain an appointment at the court chapel in Stuttgart, he served at the courts of Hechingen and Munich in 1580. By 1 November 1580 he was already employed as a tenor at the court chapel in Innsbruck, where he remained until 1587. From 1587 to 1591 he held the post of Kapellmeister at the collegiate foundation for ladies of noble families at Hall in the Tyrol. Subsequently he served from 1 May 1591 until his death as a tenor in the imperial court of Rudolf II at Prague under P. de Monte.

His compositions, many of which were published, are mainly sacred choral works; sacred and secular songs of his also appeared in printed collections published between 1585 and 1604. His importance lies largely in his writing of Mass Propers. His cyclic treatment of the introit, alleluia and communion, based on the plainsong cantus firmi, constitute, together with works by J. de Cleve, C. Erbach and J. Knöfel, the last great Renaissance collection of Mass Propers in Germany. Like de Cleve, Sales adhered to strictly conservative principles and wrote much music in an intricate and richly polyphonic style. Like de Cleve he also wrote simple 'song' masses. The *Missa 'Exultandi tempus est'* is such a work; it is in triple time throughout, and is based on the composer's own chanson motet of the same name, which has melodic links with the Christmas song *Resonet in laudibus*. Both the model and the mass contain directions setting out the ways in which the versicles are to be divided between the performers. The pastoral mass, of which this is an early example, later became very popular.

WORKS

Edition: *Musique religieuse*, ed. R. J. van Maldeghem, Trésor musical, i–vi (Brussels, 1865–70) [contains several sacred works]

Patrocinium musices: missarum solenniorum . . . primus tomus, 5, 6vv (Munich, 1589)
Sacrarum cantionum . . . liber primus, 5, 6vv (Prague, 1593)
Tripartiti operis officiorum missalium, quibus introitus, alleluia et communiones, 5, 6vv, liber primus (Prague, 1596)
Tripartiti operis officiorum missalium . . . 5, 6vv, liber secundus (Prague, 1594)
Tripartiti operis officiorum missalium . . . 5, 6vv, liber tertius (Prague, 1596)
Patrocinium musices: in natalem . . . mutetum, 'Exultandi tempus est' et missa ad eius imitationem composita, 5vv (Munich, 1598)
Dialogismus de amore Christi sponsi erga ecclesiam sponsam, 8vv (Prague, 1598)
Oratio ad Ss BVM, Wenceslaum, Adalbertum, 6vv (Prague, 1598)
Salutationes ad BVM, 4–8vv (Prague, 1598)
Canzonette, Vilanelle, neapolitane per cantar'et sonare con il liuto et altri simili istromenti, a 3 (Prague, 1598)
Several pieces in 1585[17], 1604[7]
MSS of sacred works, *A-Wn, D-Bds, Kl, Mbs, Z, PL-WRu*

BIBLIOGRAPHY

E. vander Straeten: *La musique aux Pays-Bas avant le XIXe siècle* (Brussels, 1867–88/*R*1969)
G. Bossert: 'Die Stuttgarter Hofkantorei unter Herzog Ludwig', *Württembergische Vierteljahrshefte für Landesgeschichte*, new ser., vii (1898), 140; ix (1900), 262; xix (1910), 340
P. Wagner: *Geschichte der Messe* (Leipzig, 1913)

W. Senn: *Musik, Schule und Theater der Stadt Hall in Tirol* (Innsbruck, 1938)
W. Lipphardt: *Die Geschichte des mehrstimmigen Proprium Missae* (Heidelberg, 1950)
W. Senn: *Musik und Theater am Hof zu Innsbruck* (Innsbruck, 1954)

HELLMUT FEDERHOFER

Sales, Nikolaus (*b* ?Namur, before 1550; *d* Stuttgart, 5 April 1606). Netherlands singer and composer, brother of Franz Sales. He served first as an alto and then as a tenor in the court chapel in Stuttgart from the end of 1565 until his death, with only one short interruption in 1581. There is evidence that he was employed for part of that year in the court chapel at Innsbruck. His only known work is a *Komposition des Gesangs wider den Türken*, but this has not survived.

For bibliography *see* SALES, FRANZ.

HELLMUT FEDERHOFER

Sales [de Sala], **Pietro Pompeo** (*b* Brescia, *c*1729; *d* Hanau, 21 Nov 1797). Italian composer. After the early death of his parents in an earthquake and after studies at Innsbruck University, he became conductor of an Italian opera troupe, with which he visited Cologne, Brussels, Lille and other cities. In 1756 he took charge of the court chapel of Prince-Bishop Joseph, Landgrave of Hessen-Darmstadt, in Augsburg and Dillingen an der Donau. He travelled widely as a performer and composer, becoming a member of the Bologna Accademia Filarmonica (1758) and composing an oratorio for Mannheim (1762) and operas for Munich (1765) and Padua (1767). After the landgrave's death in 1768, Sales, taking with him some of the Augsburg musicians, moved to the court of the Trier Elector Clemens Wenzeslaus (who had succeeded to the title of Prince-Bishop of Augsburg) at Ehrenbreitstein am Rhein. There he headed the court chapel, one of the largest in Germany, while maintaining his connection with the Munich court with new operas in 1769 and 1774. In 1776 he appeared in London as a viol player (according to Choron and Fayolle, this was his second visit), and in 1777 he performed a Passion in Frankfurt am Main. In 1786 he moved with the elector's court to the newly built castle at Koblenz, which the court had to abandon twice during the wars of the French Revolution. In 1797 he again had to flee the French and died before he could return.

Sales was a versatile composer in the current Italian style who wrote sacred and chamber music, as well as operas and oratorios. He was considered a great master by his contemporaries, his oratorio *Betulia liberata* being regarded as his masterpiece. Schubart called him a thorough and agreeable composer and a charming man.

WORKS

Stage: Massanissa, oder Die obsiegende Treu (Jesuit drama), Innsbruck 1752; Le cinesi (componimento drammatico, Metastasio), Augsburg, 1757; L'isola disabitata (Singspiel, Metastasio), Augsburg, 1758, *D-Rtt*; Le nozze di Amore e di Norizia (opera, Giunti), Munich, 1765, *Mbs*; Antigona in Tebe (opera), Padua, 1767; L'Antigono (opera, Metastasio), Munich, 1769, *Mbs, F-Pc*; Achille in Sciro (opera, Metastasio), Munich, 1774, *D-Mbs, F-Pc*; Il re pastore (opera, Metastasio), *D-Dlb*
Oratorios: Oratorio per la festa del Santo Natale (Metastasio), Augsburg, 1756, *D-As*; Giefte (M. Verazi), Mannheim, 1762; Passion, Ehrenbreitstein, 1772, Frankfurt, 1777, ?*D-F*; Giuseppe riconosciuto, Ehrenbreitstein, 1780, *Mbs*; Gioas re di Giuda (Metastasio), Ehrenbreitstein, 1781, *Mbs*; La Betulia liberata (Metastasio), Ehrenbreitstein, 1783; Affectus amantis, Ehrenbreitstein, 1784; Sant'Elena (Metastasio), Koblenz, 1791
Sacred: Mass, 4vv, insts, *D-Bds*; Mass, 4vv, insts, *I-MOe*; Ave maris stella, 4vv, bc, 1758, *I-Bc*; Offertory, D, 1765, *D-HR*; 2 Alma Redemptoris mater, 2–4vv, insts, *I-MOe*

Orch: Sym., D, *D-Rtt*, 2 syms., *DS*; Serenade, 2 fl, 2 hn, str, bc, *GB-Lbm*; Conc., D, *D-Rtt*; 2 Concs., F, D, *Mbs*; Hpd Conc., *HR*
Other works: Hpd Sonata, in Raccolta musicale, op.3 (Nuremberg, n.d.), ed. G. Benvenuti in Cembalisti italiani del Settecento, x (Milan, 1926); arias, *D-Dlb*, *DS*, *EB*, *HR*, *Mbs*, *I-MOe*; 2 duets, S, A, insts, 2 S, bc, *D-Dlb*

BIBLIOGRAPHY
EitnerQ; *GerberL*; *GerberNL*
'Nachricht', *AMZ*, ii (1799), col.377
C. F. D. Schubart: *Ideen zu einer Ästhetik der Tonkunst* (Vienna, 1806/*R*1969)
A. Choron and F. Fayolle: *Dictionnaire historique des musiciens* (Paris, 1810–11/*R*1971)
F. Walter: *Geschichte des Theaters und der Musik am kurpfälzischen Hofe* (Leipzig, 1898/*R*1968), 184f
F. Collignon: *Pietro Pompeo Sales* (diss., U. of Bonn, 1923)
ADOLF LAYER

Saletz, Franz. See SALES, FRANZ.

Saléza, Albert (*b* Bruges, Pyrénées, 28 Oct 1867; *d* Paris, 26 Nov 1916). French tenor. He studied with Bax and Obin at the Paris Conservatoire, and made his début at the Opéra-Comique on 19 July 1888 as Mylio in Lalo's *Le roi d'Ys*. After singing at Rouen, Bordeaux and Nice, he was first heard at the Paris Opéra on 16 May 1892 as Mathôs in Reyer's *Salammbô*. At Monte Carlo in 1894 he appeared in the first performance of Franck's posthumous opera *Hulda* (4 March) and in Berlioz's *La damnation de Faust*. At the Opéra that year he sang in the première of Lefebvre's *Djelma* (25 May) and the first Paris performance of Verdi's *Otello* (10 October). He made his Covent Garden début on 10 May 1898 in Gounod's *Roméo et Juliette*; his Metropolitan début, again as Romeo, was on 2 December 1898, and he sang Rodolfo at the first Metropolitan performance of Puccini's *La bohème* on 26 December 1900, evoking 'a frenzy of enthusiasm' (Krehbiel). His repertory included Siegmund, Tannhäuser, Gounod's Faust, Raoul (*Les Huguenots*), Edgardo (*Lucia di Lammermoor*), John of Leyden (*Le prophète*), Masaniello, and the Duke in *Rigoletto*. He made a final appearance at the Opéra-Comique in 1910 as Don José. Doomed to suffer comparison with Jean de Reszke in many of his roles, he had, according to Henderson, 'a pure, mellow tenor voice of admirable quality . . . elegant diction . . . [and] the finish of the Gallic school' in his phrasing.

BIBLIOGRAPHY
H. E. Krehbiel: *Chapters of Opera* (New York, 1909)
W. J. Henderson: *The Art of Singing* (New York, 1938)
I. Kolodin: *The Story of the Metropolitan Opera* (New York, 1953)
S. Wolff: *L'opéra au Palais Garnier (1875–1962)* (Paris, 1962)
ELIZABETH FORBES

Salicet. An ORGAN STOP.

Salicional. An ORGAN STOP (*Salicet*).

Salicus (from Lat. *salire*: 'to leap'). A neume signifying three notes, of which the second is an ORISCUS. Usually the first and second notes were of the same pitch and the third was higher; but sometimes it was understood that the three notes were of different pitches, in ascending order. As with all neumes that include the *oriscus*, there is doubt as to its exact significance. The fact that the *salicus* usually ends on F, B♭ or C has led to the suggestion that it served to orientate a melody tonally (Lipphardt). Wagner did not see the second note as an *oriscus*, and interpreted its shape to mean an extra dip of a semitone before the final step upwards (four notes in all); he also suggested that the *salicus* ending on other degrees of the scale was suppressed when the change to staff notation was made and the interval of a semitone between second and final note essential to the *salicus* was no longer, theoretically, available. Lipphardt saw the central element of the *salicus* in *F-LA* 239 as a letter 'a' (= *altius*), a belief not shared by other writers (for illustration *see* NEUMATIC NOTATIONS, Table 1).

BIBLIOGRAPHY
P. Wagner: *Einführung in die gregorianischen Melodien*, ii: *Neumenkunde: Paläographie des liturgischen Gesanges* (Leipzig, 1905, rev., enlarged 2/1913/*R*1962)
H. M. Bannister: *Codices e vaticanis selecti, phototypice expressi. Monumenti vaticani di paleografia musicale latina*, xii (Leipzig, 1913/*R*1969)
G. M. Suñol: *Introducció a la paleografia musical gregoriana* (Montserrat, 1925; Fr. trans., rev., enlarged 2/1935)
M. Huglo: 'Les noms des neumes et leur origine', *Etudes grégoriennes*, i (1954), 53
W. Lipphardt: 'Notation', *MGG*
E. Jammers: *Tafeln zur Neumenkunde* (Tutzing, 1965)
E. Cardine: 'Sémiologie grégorienne', *Etudes grégoriennes*, xi (1970), 1–158
R. Ponchelet: 'Le salicus en composition dans le codex Saint Gall 359', *Etudes grégoriennes*, xiv (1973), 7

Salieri, Antonio (*b* Legnago, 18 Aug 1750; *d* Vienna, 7 May 1825). Italian composer, mainly resident in Vienna. He can be seen as a bridge between several musical generations: he succeeded to the Viennese heritage of Fux, Gassmann and Gluck, witnessed the phenomenon of Mozart, dominated Parisian opera from 1784 to 1788, had dealings with many artists and scholars of the late 18th and early 19th centuries, and was the teacher of a large number of musicians born between 1770 and 1810. From 1775 his influence was felt in every aspect of Viennese musical life.

1. LIFE. Salieri was the fifth son of the merchant Antonio Salieri and his wife, née Scachi. He was first taught the violin and the harpsichord by his elder brother Francesco, who was a pupil of Tartini, and in the early 1760s began having violin lessons from the organist of Legnago, Giuseppe Simoni, a pupil of Padre Martini. Salieri was orphaned in 1765, and Giovanni Mocenigo, a friend of his father, took him to Venice, where he studied thoroughbass with Giovanni Pescetti, deputy *maestro di cappella* at St Mark's and a pupil of Antonio Lotti, and singing with Ferdinando Pacini, a tenor at St Mark's. Florian Gassmann, who visited Venice in 1766, took Salieri with him to Vienna (arriving there on 16 June 1766) and directed his further education. He learnt Latin and the art of Italian poetry under Pietro Tommasi, German, French, thoroughbass, reading and playing from score, and the violin; Gassmann himself taught him counterpoint and soon introduced him at the chamber concerts of Joseph II. In 1767 Salieri met Metastasio at the house of Martinez, and with his guidance trained himself in the art of declamation. By the end of 1769 he had met Gluck, who was to become his patron and lifelong friend.

Salieri's first surviving comic opera, *Le donne letterate*, was staged in January 1770 at the Vienna Burgtheater (Gluck remarked that it 'succeeded in pleasing the public'), and his first major operatic achievement came 18 months later, with *Armida*. After Gassmann's death (20 January 1774) Salieri succeeded him as court composer and conductor of the Italian opera; thus at the age of 24 he held one of the most important musical positions in Europe. In 1788 he became in addition court Kapellmeister on the death of Giuseppe Bonno, Gassmann's successor in the post.

1. Antonio Salieri: portrait by an unknown artist in the Gesellschaft der Musikfreunde, Vienna

On 10 October 1775 Salieri married Theresia Helferstorfer (1755–1807), who bore him eight children. In the summer of 1778 he received a commission from Italy, and was granted two years' leave of absence by Joseph II. Gluck was to have written a serious opera, *L'Europa riconosciuta*, for the opening of La Scala, Milan, but declined because of his obligations in Paris, and evidently sent Salieri in his place. La Scala opened with Salieri's opera on 3 August 1778, and he moved on to Venice, where *La scuola de' gelosi* was performed on 27 December. Other Italian cities he visited included Rome, where *La partenza inaspettata* was staged (22 December 1779), and Naples. On his return to Vienna he wrote *Der Rauchfangkehrer* (first performed on 30 April 1781) in response to a commission for the National Singspiel Theatre, the German opera established by Joseph II in 1778.

Salieri achieved his greatest triumphs at the Paris Opéra, where he succeeded Gluck. As a result of a good deal of obfuscation on the part of Gluck and the directorate of the Opéra his first work for Paris, *Les Danaides* (26 April 1784), was originally attributed to Gluck himself. Salieri's second Paris opera, *Les Horaces* (1786), was a failure, but *Tarare* (1787) was his greatest operatic success. He subsequently had Beaumarchais' libretto translated and adapted for Vienna by Da Ponte (Salieri's preference for Da Ponte as his librettist from 1783 led to the latter's collaboration with Mozart); the opera was then produced in a completely recomposed version at the Burgtheater on the occasion of the Archduke Franz's marriage to the Princess of Württemberg (8 January 1788) under the title *Axur, Re d'Ormus*.

With the death of Gluck (15 November 1787) Salieri lost not only a patron, but his spiritual father. Between 1788 and 1804 he wrote 16 operas of which three were never performed and one remained unfinished. But from this late period only *Palmira, Regina di Persia* achieved international success. The death of Joseph II (20 February 1790) deprived Salieri of his patron at court who had made him the 'musical pope' of Vienna during the 1780s. His relationship with Leopold II was less cordial, and in autumn 1790 he petitioned the emperor for his release from the direction of the opera. This was granted, subject to his continuing to compose a new opera each year for the court theatre. The appointment of his pupil Joseph Weigl to succeed him was intended, according to Leopold II, 'to honour the master in the pupil'. Salieri gave his own reason for composing no more dramatic works after 1804: 'From this period on I observed that taste in music was gradually changing to a sort completely contrary to that of my own times. Extravagance and confusion of styles replaced rationality and majestic simplicity'. Despite his disagreement with modern trends he did not resign as court Kapellmeister, but encouraged new endeavours as best he could. His few subsequent compositions were mostly entertainment pieces such as canons or *divertimenti musicali*. His Requiem of 1804 was intended to mark his withdrawal from public life as a composer; the autograph is headed 'Picciolo Requiem composto da me Ant. Salieri, picciolissima creatura'. His funeral at the Matzleinsdorf cemetery on 10 May 1825 was attended by the entire complement of musicians at court and by numerous other leading musical figures, including Mosel, Eybler, Treitschke and Gyrowetz.

Salieri had served the Viennese court for more than 50 years, 36 of them (1 March 1788 to 1 March 1824) as court Kapellmeister. His notable achievements in this position included his exemplary administration of the musical establishment and its archives, his concern for the social welfare of the musicians and his encouragement of the rising generation. He was an active supporter of the Vienna Tonkünstler-Sozietät, the musicians' benevolent society founded by his teacher Gassmann; from 1788 to 1795 he was the society's president and subsequently vice-president, composed works to celebrate its 25th anniversary in 1796 and its 50th in 1821, and contributed generously to its funds. Between 1810 and 1820 he drew up the statutes of the Imperial State Conservatory in Vienna, served on the building and founding committee of the Gesellschaft der Musikfreunde and prepared and directed the musical programme of the Congress of Vienna. He held the Gold Medallion and Chain of the City of Vienna, was a Chevalier of the Légion d'honneur and a member of the French National Institute, the Paris Conservatoire and the Swedish Royal Musical Society. He was also important as a teacher, and continued to teach even after his virtual retirement as a composer; Beethoven, Schubert, Czerny, Hummel, Liszt, Moscheles, W. A. Mozart jr, Sechter, Süssmayr, Weigl and Winter were among his pupils, and he was the singing master of Catarina Cavalieri, M. A. Fux-Gassmann, Anna Milder-Hauptmann and others.

It remains to mention the supposed enmity with Mozart, which has traditionally damaged Salieri's posthumous reputation. Even if Salieri did not go out of his

2. Autograph score of the opening of the Sinfonia from Salieri's 'La grotta di Trofonio', first performed at the Vienna Burgtheater on 12 October 1785 (A-Wn); below are some of the composer's comments on the opera written into the score

way to help Mozart, there is little evidence for the intrigues that are frequently attributed to him, nor is any derogatory remark against the younger composer recorded. Mozart himself (letter of 14 October 1791) reported Salieri's warm reception of *Die Zauberflöte*. And the rumour that Salieri poisoned Mozart is without foundation.

2. WORKS. Salieri was at heart an Italian opera composer of the old (and by his later years old-fashioned) school. Although his work reveals various influences, his means of expression remained essentially the human voice; cantabile melody is his hallmark, and it is the shape of the vocal line that delineates his characters. Yet as early as the first major landmark of his operatic career, *Armida* (1771), he began to break away from conventional *opera seria* and turn towards the dramatic ideals of Gluck. Salieri's own description of *Armida* in his autograph score was 'opera di stile magico-eroico-amorosa toccante il tragico' – that is, one combining several different styles, genres and techniques. (The manuscript commentaries appended to many of Salieri's autographs constitute important evidence of his views on opera; see Angermüller, *Antonio Salieri*, iii.) In every scene that contributes to the forward movement of the drama the recitative is orchestrally accompanied, and the chorus is no longer merely passive, but plays an essential part in the dramatic action. His first French opera, *Les Danaides* (1784), still has something of an Italian cast about it, but *Tarare* (1787), which the librettist Beaumarchais intended to open a new chapter in operatic history, most nearly approaches the Gluckian conception of the *tragédie lyrique* and features the sort of psychological insight that is found in Gluck's Paris operas. In all his stage works Salieri is particularly concerned to capture the mood of each scene; key schemes are simple but effective; as in Gluck, counterpoint is little used; the orchestration is carefully tailored to the dramatic situation and never heavy. As a disciple of Gluck he strictly followed the rhythm and word accent of the text. But he was neither Gluck's imitator nor his successor: he maintained the declamatory style only in his French operas, and his works for Vienna betray his Italian origins. Whereas the French critic Laharpe could say that the music of *Tarare* was 'well adapted to the words', the recitative 'expressive and rapid', the opposite is true of its Viennese revision as *Axur, Re d'Ormus*: the scheme is conventional, and the music dominates the text. The innovations of *Tarare* had no sequel. *Palmira, Regina di Persia* is a mixture, containing scenes in the declamatory manner of *Tarare*, others reminiscent of Mozart's *buffa* scenes, and arias that have elements of *opera seria*. But, as their lack of success demonstrates and as Salieri himself was clearly aware, the works from 1788 onwards had little relevance to the history of opera in the late 18th and early 19th centuries.

Apart from a few youthful works and occasional pieces, Salieri's church music dates from after his appointment as court Kapellmeister in 1788. While the early works are indebted to the late Venetian style and Fux (the style that was dominant in Vienna almost up to the middle of the 18th century) his later sacred music is typical of its time, with its roots in the late Neapolitan operatic style but displaying some influence from modern symphonic techniques. His oratorios too adhere to the Italian tradition, though by the time of *Gesù al limbo* (1803) Vienna, largely under the influence of Haydn's *Schöpfung*, had mainly gone over to German oratorio.

Salieri's other works include the charming and whimsical vocal pieces (duets, trios, canons etc) intended for domestic entertainment. Among his small instrumental output the two piano concertos in C and B♭ (1773) stand out. But the attractiveness of Salieri's instrumental music lies in the mixture and juxtaposition of various stylistic elements: Classical triadic material, *galant* melodies, even an occasional touch of *Sturm und Drang*.

In his teaching, as in his compositions, Salieri had most to offer in vocal music. Some 20 works with Italian texts survive which Beethoven submitted to him from time to time, apparently from about 1798 to 1801, and which Salieri corrected in respect of the word-setting (see Nottebohm). Schubert's tuition was on a more formal basis; he was a regular pupil of Salieri between 1812 and 1817 and a number of pieces, especially in 1812–13, originated as exercises. He also dedicated several works to Salieri.

WORKS

hol. – *holograph*

OPERAS

All MS and in *A-Wn* unless otherwise stated; full catalogue in Angermüller, *Antonio Salieri*.

La vestale, Vienna, 1768, lost

Le donne letterate (dramma giocoso, 3, G. Boccherini), Vienna, Burgtheater, Jan 1770

L'amore innocente (pastorale, 2, Boccherini), Vienna, Burgtheater, 1770, hol.

Don Chisciotte alle nozze di Gamace (divertimento teatrale, 1, Boccherini), Vienna, Burgtheater, 1770, hol., inc.

La moda, ossia I scompigli domestici (opera, 2, P. Cipretti), Vienna, 1771, only pt. of Act 2 extant, hol.

Armida (opera seria, 3, M. Coltellini), Vienna, Burgtheater, 2 June 1771 (Leipzig, 1783), hol.

La fiera di Venezia (opera buffa, 3, Boccherini), Vienna, Burgtheater, 29 Jan 1772, hol.

Il barone di Rocca antica (dramma musicale, 1, G. Petrosellini), Vienna, Burgtheater, 12 May 1772, hol.

La secchia rapita (opera buffa, 3, Boccherini), Vienna, Burgtheater, 21 Oct 1772, hol.

La locandiera (opera buffa, 3, D. Poggi, after C. Goldini), Vienna, Burgtheater, 8 June 1773, hol.

La calamità de' cuori (opera buffa, 3, G. Gamerra), Vienna, Burgtheater, 11 Oct 1774, hol.

La finta scema (opera buffa, 3, Gamerra), Vienna, Burgtheater, 9 Sept 1775, hol.

Daliso e Delmita (opera pastorale seria, 2, Gamerra), Vienna, Burgtheater, 29 July 1776, hol.

L'Europa riconosciuta (dramma serio, 2, M. Verazi), Milan, Scala, 3 Aug 1778, hol., inc.

La scuola de' gelosi (opera buffa, 2, C. Mazzolà), Venice, S Moisè, 27 Dec 1778, hol.

Il talismano (opera buffa, 3, Goldoni), Milan, Cannobiana, 21 Aug 1779, Acts 2, 3 by G. Rust

La partenza inaspettata (opera, 2, Petrosellini), Rome, Valle, 22 Dec 1779, hol.

La dama pastorella (opera, 1, Petrosellini), Rome, Valle, 1780, hol.

Der Rauchfangkehrer, oder Die unentbehrlichen Verräther ihrer Herrschaften aus Eigennutz (Lustspiel, 3, T. Auenbrugger), Vienna, Burgtheater, 30 April 1781, hol.

Semiramide (opera seria, 1, Metastasio), Munich, court, 1782, hol.

Les Danaides (tragédie lyrique, 5, Du Roullet and Tschudi), Paris, Opéra, 26 April 1784 (Paris, 1784), hol.

Il ricco d'un giorno (opera buffa, 3, Da Ponte), Vienna, Burgtheater, 6 Dec 1784, hol.

La grotta di Trofonio (opera, 2, G. B. Casti), Vienna, Burgtheater, 12 Oct 1785 (Vienna, 1786), hol.

Prima la musica e poi le parole (operetta, 1, Casti), Schönbrunn Orangerie, 7 Feb 1786, hol.

Les Horaces (tragédie lyrique, 3, N. F. Guillard), Paris, Opéra, 7 Dec 1786, hol.

Tarare (opera, prol, 5, Beaumarchais), Paris, Opéra, 8 June 1787 (Paris, 1787), hol., inc.; ed. R. Angermüller (Munich and Duisburg, 1978)

Axur, Re d'Ormus (opera tragicomica, 4, Da Ponte), Vienna, Burgtheater, 8 Jan 1788 (Bonn and Paris, 1803), hol. [rev. version of Tarare]

Cublai, gran kan de Tartari (opera eroicomica, 2, Casti), 1788, unperf., hol.

Il talismano (opera buffa, 3, Da Ponte), Vienna, Burgtheater, 10 Sept 1788, hol.

Il pastor fido (opera pastorale, 4, Da Ponte), Vienna, Burgtheater, 11 Feb 1789, hol.

La cifra (opera buffa, 2, Da Ponte), Vienna, Burgtheater, 11 Dec 1789, hol.

Catilina (opera, 2, Casti), Vienna, 1792, unperf., hol.

Il mondo alla rovescia (opera buffa, 2, Mazzolà), Vienna, Burgtheater, 13 Jan 1795, hol.

Eraclito e Democrito (opera filosofico-buffa, 2, Gamerra), Vienna, Burgtheater, 13 Aug 1795, hol.

Palmira, Regina di Persia (opera, 2, Gamerra), Vienna, Kärntnertor, 14 Oct 1795, hol.

Il moro (opera buffa, 2, Gamerra), Vienna, Burgtheater, 7 Aug 1796, hol.

I tre filosofo, 2, 1797, unfinished, hol.

Falstaff ossia Le tre burle (opera comica, 2, C. P. Defranceschi), Vienna, Kärntnertor, 3 Jan 1799, hol.

Cesare in Farmacusa (opera eroico-comica, 2, Defranceschi), Vienna, Kärntnertor, 2 June 1800, hol.

L'Angiolina, ossia Il matrimonio per sussurro (opera buffa, 2, Defranceschi), Vienna, Kärntnertor, 22 Oct 1800, hol.

Annibale in Capua (dramma per musica, A. S. Sografi), Trieste, Nuovo, April 1801

La bella selvaggia (opera buffa, 2, G. Bertati), Vienna, 1802, unperf., hol.

Die Hussiten vor Naumberg (Schauspiel, 5, Kotzebue), Vienna, court. 1803, 9 choruses, hol.; ov. and Kinder-Tanz (Vienna, c1808)

Die Neger (opera, 2, F. Treitschke), Vienna, Theater an der Wien, 10 Nov 1804, hol.

Die Generalprobe, frag., lost

Das Posthaus, frag., lost

SACRED

All MS, mostly A-KN, KR, Wgm, Wn; D-B, Bds, LEt, ROu, SWl; DK-Kk; I-Bc; thematic catalogue in Nützlader (1924), 112ff

Oratorios: La sconfitta di Borea, Vienna, 1774, A-Wgm; La passione di Gesù Cristo (Metastasio), Vienna, 1776, Wgm; Gesù al limbo, Vienna, 1803, CS-Bm; Il trionfo della gloria e della virtù, 1774, A-Wgm; Davidde, frag., hol., Wgm; Saulle, frag., lost

Masses: Missa a cappella, C, Vienna, 12 Aug 1767, Missa, D, Vienna, ?1788; Missa, C, Vienna, ?1799; Missa pro defunctis, c, Vienna, Aug 1804; Missa, d, Baden, nr. Vienna, July 1805; Missa, Bb, Vienna, 11 May 1809, Kyric, C, Vienna, 22 Sept 1812; Missa pro defunctis, Vienna, unfinished

Graduals: Ad te levavi animam meam; A solis ortu, Vienna, July 1810; Benedicamus Dominum; Confirma hoc Deus; Improperium; Justorum animae; Liberasti nos Domine, Vienna, 1799; Magna opera Domini, Vienna, 28 May 1810; Spiritus meus, Vienna, 20 Aug 1820; Tres sunt qui testimonium dant; Veni Sancte Spiritus, Bb, Vienna, 25 Jan 1800; Veni Sancte Spiritus, Bb, Vienna, Dec 1805; Venite gentes; Vox tua, mi Jesu, Vienna, 1774

Offertories: Assumpta est Maria; Audite vocem, Vienna, June 1809; Beatus vir qui non abiit; 2 Benedixisti Domine; Bonum est (with all); Cantate Domino; Desiderium animae; Deum corde pio; Domine, Dominus noster, Vienna, 1812; Excelsus super omnes, Vienna, Jan 1806; Gloria et honor, Vienna, July 1809; Jubilate Deo; Justus ut palma; Lauda Sion, Vienna, July 1805; Laudate Dominum, Vienna, Oct 1809; Magna et mirabilia; Magna opera Domini, Brül, Vienna, 12 Sept 1812; Miserere nostri, g, Vienna, Dec 1805; Miserere nostri, Eb; O altitudo divitiarum, Vienna, July 1809; O quam bonus; Populi timete, Vienna, 1778; Salve regina, D, Nikolsburg, 3 Nov 1815; 2 Salve regina; Salvum fac populum; Si ambulavero, Vienna, May 1809; Sub tuum praesidium; 2 Tui sunt coeli

Introits: A vertisti captivitatem Jacob; Beati immaculati; Concupiscit et deficit; Dico ego; Domine exaudi vocem meam; Et justitiam tuam; Et psallere; In civitate; Indutus est Dominus; In mandatis ejus; 2 Jubilate Deo; Laetentur insulae; Ne quando taceas; Neque celaveris; Quam admirabilia; Tu cognovisti

Psalms: Beatus vir; Confitebor tibi Domine; De profundis, g, Vienna, Dec 1805; De profundis, f; Dixit Dominus; Lauda Jerusalem Dominum, Nikolsburg, Nov 1815; Laudate pueri Dominum

Others: Litania de BMV; Litania de Sabbato Sancto; Te Deum, C, Vienna, July 1819; Te Deum de incoronazione, Vienna; Te Deum, D; 2 Mag; Coelestis urbs, hymn; Genitori, hymn; Tantum ergo, C; Tantum ergo, F, Vienna, 1768; Audimus Dei verbum, motet; Cor meum conturbatum, motet; Magna est virtus, motet; Quae

est illa, motet; Tu es spes mea, motet; In te Domine speravi, fuga a 3; Ecce enim veritatem

SECULAR VOCAL

Cantatas: Le jugement dernier, Paris, 1787, F-Pc; La riconoscenza, Vienna, 1796, lost; Der Tyroler Landsturm (J. F. Ratschky), Vienna, 23 May 1799, hol., A-Wn (Vienna, 1799); La riconoscenza de' Tirolesi, Vienna, 1800, Wgm; L'oracolo, Vienna, 1803, lost; Habsburg, Vienna, 1805, Wgm; Die vier Tageszeiten, Vienna, Sept 1819, hol., Wgm; Du, dieses Bundes Fels, hol., Wgm; Lasset uns nahen alle, hol., CS-Bm; Wie eine purpur Blume, F-Pc

Choruses, 3–4vv, pf/insts: An den erwünschten Frieden, 1814, CS-Bm; An die Religion, 1814, hol., A-Wgm (pubd); Bei Gelegenheit des Friedens, 1800, CS-Bm; Beyde reichen dir die Hand, frag., A-Wgm; Del redentor lo scempio, hol., S-Skma; Dio serva Francesco, I-Vs; Do re mi fa, Vienna, 19 April 1818, hol., A-Wgm; Es schallen die Töne, Wgm; Friede reich am Heil, hol., CS-Bm; Die Fuge gut zu singen, A-KR; Geführt von liebevollen Händen, Wgm; Hinab in [den] Schoss der Amphitrite, hol., Wgm; Il piacer la gioja, Wgm; In te Domine speravi, D-DT; Non impedias musicam, DT; O care selve, o cara felice, hol., A-Wgm, in 28 divertimenti vocali (Vienna, 1803); Ogni bosco, ogni pendice, Wgm; Schweb herab o holder Seraph Friede, Wgm; Schwer lag auf unserm Vaterlande, 1813, Wgm; Der Vorsicht Gunst beschütze beglücktes Österreich, Vienna, 1814, hol., Wn (Vienna, 1814)

Over 180 canons, 2 frags., 2–4vv, mostly 1800–1819, incl. 25 in Scherzi armonici vocali, 3vv (Vienna, 1795), 15 for 3vv in Continuazione de' Scherzi armonici (Vienna, n.d.), others mostly A-Wgm, Ssp, Wst

7 qnts, 5vv, unacc., A-Wgm, Wn, F-Lm

15 qts, 4vv, unacc./pf, incl. Herzliche Empfindung bei dem so lange ersehnten und nun hergestellten Frieden (Vienna, 1813), Volle Verschwiegenheit, in Rochus Pumpernickel (Bonn, 1811), others mostly A-Wgm, Wn, SF

Over 80 trios, 3vv, unacc., incl. 4 in 28 divertimenti vocali (Vienna, 1803), Questi suon canoni, in Continuazione de' Scherzi armonici (Vienna, n.d.), others mostly A-Wgm, Wn, Wst

Over 60 duets, 2vv, unacc./pf/insts, incl. 9 in 28 divertimenti vocali (Vienna, 1803), Saper vorrei, se m'ami (Vienna, 1825), others mostly A-Wgm, Wn, M; D-Rp, Dlb, MÜs

Over 90 arias, 3 frags., 1v, pf/insts, some with chorus, incl. Padrona bella per non più penare, in Recueil d'airs françois et italiens (London, n.d.), others mostly A-Wgm, Wn, Wst; B-Bc; D-Bs, Dlb, MÜs; F-Pc; GB-Lbm

Over 70 songs, 1v, pf/insts, incl. 14 in 28 divertimenti vocali (Vienna, 1803), Adieu au bon pays de Pannonie (Vienna, 1806), An die zukünftige Geliebte, in 3 Gedichte (Leipzig, n.d.), Ich denke dein (pubd), Il genio degli stati (Vienna, 1798), La tontananza (Vienna, n.d.), Maylied, in 3 Gedichte (Leipzig, n.d.), Meine höchste Wonne, in 3 Gedichte (Leipzig, n.d.), Der Zufriedene, in 6 deutsche Lieder (Vienna, 1816), others mostly A-Wgm, Wn, Wst; D-Cv; F-Pc

Others, incl. 12 in Continuazione de' Scherzi armonici, 2–4vv (Vienna, n.d.), others mostly A-Wgm, Wn, SF; CH-Bu; CS-Bm; D-HVl, MÜs, Bs; F-Pc

INSTRUMENTAL

Orch: Sinfonia 'Il giorno onomastico', D, chamber orch, ed. R. Sabatini (Milan, 1961); conc., C, vn, ob, vc, orch, Vienna, 1770, hol., A-Wn, ed. J. Wojeiechowski (Berlin, 1964); conc., C, fl, ob, orch, Vienna, 1774, hol., Wn, ed. J. Wojeiechowski (Frankfurt am Main, 1962); fl conc., Vienna, 1777; org conc., acc. 2 ob, 2 tpt, 2 vn, b, Vienna, 1773, hol., Wn; pf conc., C, Vienna, 1773, hol., Wn; pf conc., Bb, Vienna, 1773, Wn; 41 pieces of ballet music, 2 ob, 2 hn, bn, str, some with 2 fl, hol., Wn; 24 variations on 'La folia di Spagnia', Dec 1815, hol., Wn

Chamber: Cassazione, C, 2 ob, 2 eng hn, 2 hn da caccia, 2 bn, Wgm; Armonia per un tempio della notte, Eb, 2 ob, 2 cl, 2 hn, 2 bn, hol., inc., Wn; 2 serenatas, F, C, 2 fl, 2 ob, bn, 2 hn, vle, D-Rtt; Serenade, Bb, 2 cl, 2 hn, bn, vle opt., hol., A-Wn; Qnt, Bb, 2 ob, 2 hn, bn, hol., F-Pc; 3 menuetti, Bb, G, D, 2 ob, 2 hn, str, hol., A-Wn; Fuge, str qt, hol., Wn, ed. R. Sabatini (Vienna, 1963); pf sonata, C, hol., Wn (Vienna, ?1783); Concertino, fl, str, 1777, hol., Wn; Parade Marsch für Harmoniemusik, hol., Wn; Marsch für der Landwehre (n.p.), 1809); 6 petites pièces, gui (Vienna, 1801); 11 marches, ww, brass, perc, some with str, hol., Wn

PEDAGOGICAL WORKS

Libro di partimenti di varia specie per profitto della gioventù, lost
Scuola di canto, in versi, e i versi in musica, 4vv, bc, hol., Wgm

BIBLIOGRAPHY

F. Rochlitz: 'Antonio Salieri', Nekrolog: allgemeine Theaterzeitung und Unterhaltungsblatt für Freunde der Kunst, Literatur und des geselligen Lebens, xviii/99 (1825), 405

I. F. E. von Mosel: Über das Leben und die Werke des A. Salieri (Vienna, 1827)

W. Neumann: A. Salieri (Kassel, 1855)

G. Nottebohm: Beethoven's Unterricht bei J. Haydn, Albrechtsberger *und Salieri*, Beethoven's Studien (Leipzig and Winterthur, 1873/R1971)

A. Jullien: 'Salieri: sa carrière en France (1782–1787)', *Revue et gazette musicale de Paris*, xlii (1875), 58, 65, 74, 81, 89, 97, 113, 121, 129, 145, 155, 161, 169, 177

A. von Hermann: *A. Salieri: eine Studie zur Geschichte seines künstlerischen Wirkens* (Vienna, 1897)

R. Nützlader: *Salieri als Kirchenmusiker* (diss., U. of Vienna, 1924)

A. Della Corte: 'Salieri e suoi contemporanei', *Il pianoforte*, vi (1925), 173, 210

C. Serini: 'Antonio Salieri', *RIM*, xxxii (1925), 412

A. Bonaventura: 'Gli scherzi armonici di Antonio Salieri', *Vita musicale italiana*, xiii (1926), 4

R. Nützlader: 'Salieri als Kirchenmusiker', *SMw*, xiv (1927), 160

G. Magnani: *Antonio Salieri: musicista legnaghese* (Legnago, 1934)

A. Della Corte: *Un italiano all'estero: Antonio Salieri*, appx by I. F. von Mosel: 'Della vita e delle opere', appx trans. B. Allason (Turin and Milan, 1937)

W. Bollert: 'Antonio Salieri und die italienische Oper', *Aufsätze zur Musikgeschichte* (Bottrop, 1938), 43–128

——: 'Antonio Salieri e l'opera tedesca', *Musica d'oggi*, xx (1938), 122

W. Nohl: 'Ist Mozart von Salieri vergiftet worden? Neues Material zu einer alten Frage', *Die Musik*, xxxi (1938–9), 389

F. Schröder: 'Antonio Salieri: ein Lehrer Beethovens', *Das Musikleben*, v (1952), 78

R. Haas: 'Antonio Salieris vergessene Familie', *Festschrift Max Schneider* (Leipzig, 1955), 191

O. E. Deutsch: 'Carpanis Verteidigung Salieris: zur Legende von Mozarts Vergiftung', *SMz*, xcvii (1957), 8

M. J. E. Brown: 'Schubert and Salieri', *MMR*, lxxxviii (1958), 211

K. M. Pisarowitz: 'Salieriana: eine streiflichtende Dokumentarstudie', *Mitteilungen der Internationalen Stiftung Mozarteum*, ix/3–4 (1960), 11

A. Damerini and G. Roncaglia: *Volti musicali di Falstaff, Chigiana*, xviii (Siena, 1961), 23

E. Schenk: 'Salieris "Landsturm"-Kantate von 1799 in ihren Beziehungen zu Beethovens "Fidelio" ', *Colloquium amicorum: Joseph Schmidt-Görg zum 70. Geburtstag* (Bonn, 1967), 338

R. Angermüller: *Antonio Salieri: sein Leben und seine weltlichen Werke unter besonderer Berücksichtigung seiner 'grossen' Opern* (diss., U. of Salzburg, 1970; Munich, 1971–) [with full bibliography]

——: 'Salieri als Hofkapellmeister', *ÖMz*, xxv (1970), 305

——: 'Antonio Salieri und seine "Scuola di Canto" ', *Beethoven-Studien*, ed. E. Schenk (Vienna, 1970), 37

——: 'Beaumarchais und Salieri', *GfMKB, Bonn 1970*, 325

E. E. Swenson: ' "Prima la musica e poi le parole": an Eighteenth-century Satire', *AnMc*, no.9 (1970), 112

R. Angermüller: 'Aus der Frühgeschichte des Metronoms: die Beziehungen zwischen Mälzel und Salieri', *ÖMz*, xxvi (1971), 134

R. Angermüller and R. Ofner: 'Aspekte Salierischer Kirchenmusik', *Mitteilungen der Internationalen Stiftung Mozarteum*, xxi/1–2 (1973), 1

J. Heinzelmann: ' "Prima la musica, poi le parole": zu Salieris Wiener Opernparodie', *ÖMz*, xxviii (1973), 19

R. Angermüller: 'Salieris Gesellschaftsmusik', *AnMc*, no.17 (1976), 146

J. Rushton: 'Salieri's *Les Horaces*: a Study of an Operatic Failure', *MR*, xxxvii (1976), 266

R. Angermüller: 'Salieris Vorbermerkungen zu seinen Opern', *Mitteilungen der Internationalen Stiftung Mozarteum*, xxv/3–4 (1977), 15

——: 'Bemerkungen zur Familie Salieri', *Wiener Figaro*, xliv (1977), Oct, 18

RUDOLPH ANGERMÜLLER

Salii (Lat.: 'dancers'). Company (*sodalitas*) of priests in ancient Rome and other Italian cities responsible for certain rites, especially those of Mars. Two such companies existed at Rome, the Salii Palatini and Salii Collini, each with 12 members. On certain prescribed days in March and October they held a procession, with stations at which they performed *tripudia* (ritual dances characterized by threefold stamping) and sang the *carmen saliare* or *axamenta* probably in responsorial fashion. It was an archaic ritual hymn, unintelligible even in Republican times. Fragments of its text survive but do not permit a reconstruction of the original.

BIBLIOGRAPHY

G. Fleischhauer: *Etrurien und Rom*, Musikgeschichte in Bildern, ii/5 (Leipzig, 1964), 48f

G. Wille: *Musica romana* (Amsterdam, 1967), 43ff

GEOFFREY CHEW

Salimbene de Adam [Salimbene da Parma] (*b* Parma, 1221; *d* 1288). Italian chronicler. A Franciscan, he lived at various places in central Italy and made several journeys to France. His *Chronicle* narrates historical events from 1167 to 1287 in lively style, and also contains autobiographical details, some of which are of particular interest for the history of music in Italy in the mid-13th century. Salimbene had been taught singing by two brother friars, Fra Enrico da Pisa and Fra Vita da Lucca. He quoted the first lines of many poems written and set to music by Fra Enrico, and recalled Fra Vita's skill in adapting a *contracantus* to a *cantus* – i.e. in composing polyphonic music. In the course of the work he mentioned the musical talent of a number of people, e.g. Emperor Frederick II, of whom he said that he could sing and compose *cantilene* and *cantiones*, and Fra Guidolinus Ianuarius da Parma, who he said sang secular songs very well. There are also descriptions of musical performances. During Carnival at Reggio people sang and danced in the street ('in strata publica choreiçando cantabant'). A group of young people performed in a courtyard at Pisa: 'Both the men and the women held *vielle* and *cythare* and other sorts of instruments in their hands, and they made sweet melody ['modulos'] with them and made appropriate gestures. There was no noise, and no one spoke; all listened in silence. The song they sang was very unusual and beautiful, both in its words and in the variety of voices and the way of singing, so that our hearts were exceedingly delighted'.

BIBLIOGRAPHY

O. Holder-Egger, ed.: *Cronica fratris Salimbene de Adam ordinis minorum*, Monumenta Germaniae historica, *Scriptores*, xxxii (Hanover, 1905–13/R1963)

G. Scalia, ed.: *Cronica*, Scrittori d'Italia, ccxxxii (Bari, 1966)

F. A. Gallo: 'Cantus planus binatim: polifonia primitava in fonti tardive', *Quadrivium*, vii (1966), 79

F. ALBERTO GALLO

Salinas, Francisco de (*b* Burgos, 1 March 1513; *d* Salamanca, 13 Jan 1590). Spanish theorist and organist. His father, Juan de Salinas, was a royal treasury official. When Francisco became blind at about the age of ten, his parents arranged for organ lessons. He soon became proficient and gave organ instruction to a young woman in exchange for Latin lessons. He studied philosophy and classical languages at Salamanca University, but failed to take a degree. On leaving Salamanca he joined the retinue of Pedro Sarmiento de Salinas, who was named Archbishop of Santiago de Compostela in 1536, and cardinal on 18 October 1538.

Salinas accompanied him to Rome for the ceremony of investiture; there he studied Greek music treatises at the Vatican library and had others copied from the library of St Mark's, Venice. Pope Paul III recommended his ordination as priest despite his blindness, and awarded him an annual pension of 40 ducats, payable from revenues of a church in the Jaén diocese in Spain. To this was added in May 1546 an absentee benefice in the Burgos diocese, and later the abbacy of St Pancras in the Spanish-ruled kingdom of Naples. Salinas used the title 'abbot' for the rest of his life.

From 1553 to 1558 Salinas was organist at the viceregal chapel at Naples, where Diego Ortiz was *maestro de capilla*. On 2 January 1559 he was appointed organist at Sigüenza Cathedral, and was excused from attending any services other than those accompanied by the organ in order to memorize all the required music. He took occasional leave of absence; in 1560 he was part of the entourage which welcomed Elisabeth of Valois, Philip II's third wife. In 1561 he visited Toledo and Alcalá, and in 1563, Valladolid and Burgos. His next post as organist was at León Cathedral, where he received the substantial annual salary of 300 ducats. In June 1567 he resigned to accept the chair of music at Salamanca University, where he remained until his death. The German Gaspar Stocker, a colleague of Salinas at the university, wrote a Latin treatise on text underlay, and probably edited and indexed Salinas's own treatise. Salinas received an honorary Master of Arts degree from Salamanca in November 1569. On 17 January 1573 he testified before the Inquisition on behalf of Luis de León, whose later *Oda a Salinas* is still regarded as a monument of Spanish literature. Salinas retired in 1587. Vicente Espinel described him (1618) as 'that prince of music . . . who revived the enharmonic genus . . . I have seen him playing his specially tuned instrument [19 keys to the octave] in Salamanca. On it he performed miracles with his hands'.

The *De musica libri septem*, dedicated to the Bishop of Zamora, was first published in Salamanca in 1577 and reprinted with only a change of title-page in 1592. Preliminary drafts of the four books which deal with acoustics are in the Madrid Biblioteca Nacional. The treatise opens with a discussion of proportions and of consonant and dissonant intervals. Salinas then detailed the diatonic, chromatic (16 notes in the octave) and enharmonic (25 notes to the octave) genera, revealing an accurate grasp of the ancient theorists. Although he himself had designed an instrument capable of differentiating between large and small whole tones, he recognized the impracticality of dividing the octave into the 31 pitches called for by Nicola Vicentino. One of the octave divisions he proposed was the equal temperament of the vihuela and other fretted string instruments. Although he approved of the 12 modes specified by Glarean, he regretted the confusion of 'mode' with 'tone'. The section ends with a brief survey of the major theorists from antiquity to Gaffurius and Zarlino. The final three books of the treatise deal with metrics, drawing heavily on Augustine's *De musica*. All the possible metrical combinations are illustrated with music examples, including 57 Spanish and Italian folk melodies. Among these are the purportedly Moorish *Qualbi bi qualbi* and the Montserrat pilgrim song *Yo me iba mi madre*. Hawkins was one of the first to recognize the value of Salinas's treatise; he wrote that 'a greater degree of credit is due to it than to almost any other of the kind, the production of modern times'.

BIBLIOGRAPHY

HawkinsH

V. Espinel: *Vida del escudero Marcos de Obregón* (Madrid, 1618)

M. Salvá and P. Sáinz de Baranda: *Colección de documentos inéditos para la historia de España*, xi (Madrid, 1847), 302f

R. Espinosa Maeso: 'El abad Francisco Salinas organista de la Catedral de León', *Boletín de la Real academia española*, xiii (1926), 186

J. B. Trend: 'Salinas: a Sixteenth-century Collector of Folk-songs', *ML*, viii (1927), 13

A. Daniels: *The De musica libri VII of Franciscus de Salinas* (diss., U. of Southern California, 1962)

E. Lowinsky: 'A Treatise on Text Underlay by a German Disciple of Francisco de Salinas', *Festschrift Heinrich Besseler* (Leipzig, 1962), 231f

F. Tello: *Estudios de historia de la teoría musical* (Madrid, 1962), 539f, 687f

E. Lowinsky: 'Gasparus Stoquerus and Franciscus de Salinas', *JAMS*, xvi (1963), 241

J. Álvarez Pérez: 'El organista Francisco Salinas: nuevos datos para su biografía', *AnM*, xviii (1963), 21

M. García Matos: 'Pervivencia en la tradición actual de canciones populares recogidas en el siglo XVI por Salinas en su tratado "De musica libri septem" ', *AnM*, xviii (1963), 67

ROBERT STEVENSON

Salinis, Hymbert [Huberty] **de.** *See* HYMBERT DE SALINIS.

Salisbury. English cathedral city. 'The Quire of Salisbury Cathedral', wrote the 17th-century antiquary John Aubrey, 'hath produced as many able musicians if not more, than any Quire in this nation.' Until the Reformation, the form of liturgy in the cathedral was known as Sarum Use and was widely adopted throughout England. Among post-Reformation organists may be mentioned the John Farrants, elder and younger, and Michael Wise, and there are local connections with the Lawes family and Adrian Batten. It was to hear music that George Herbert between 1630 and 1633 walked twice weekly into Salisbury and afterwards took part in private music meetings. The 'Society of Lovers of Musick' celebrated St Cecilia's Day in the cathedral in 1700 and probably annually, 1726 and 1727 being recorded.

In 1740 the society subscribed to Handel's 'Twelve Grand Concertos' op.6, and on 27 November St Cecilia's Day was celebrated 'as usual' with a concert at the Assembly Room in New Street (replaced in 1750 by one in the High Street). A *Te Deum* and two anthems by Handel were performed in the morning in the cathedral. Thereafter, the festivals, two days from 1748 and three from 1768, took place annually until 1789 when the closure of the cathedral led to their suspension until 1792. Further festivals took place in 1800, 1804, 1807, 1810, 1813, 1818, 1821, 1824, and a four-day festival in 1828 terminated this event.

The Musical Society also subscribed to regular concerts throughout the year, when musicians from London appeared and the newest music was performed. Mainly owing to its director James Harris, it was the finest society outside London, and performers included Mr Charles, the first named performer on the clarinet in Britain (1743), Signora Avoglio (1746), Abel (1759), Elizabeth Linley (from 1769), Nancy Storace (first in 1773, aged seven), J. C. Bach (1773), Crotch (aged eight, 1783) and Bridgetower (1794). Handel's librettist Thomas Morell was probably present at a performance of *Jephtha* in 1760, 'never play'd before out of London'. One or two Handel oratorios were given at virtually every festival from 1748.

Salisbury musicians contributed a great deal to the concerts, providing first-class singers from the cathedral, and in 1784 the orchestra was said to be 'filled from this city alone'. William Mahon was first violin from c1786 until 1816.

The society declined after the deaths in 1780 of both James Harris and the cathedral organist John Stephens, and disputing factions, supporting his successor Robert Parry and the society's elected conductor, Joseph Corfe, disrupted musical life in the city. The end of the festivals also marked the end of the Musical Society.

Benjamin Banks, the eminent maker of string instruments, worked in Catherine Street from c1757; his sons James, Henry and William, Benjamin Collins, Collins & Johnson, and Edward Easton published some music.

Salisbury remains a minor regional music centre and makes much of its own music. It has however no concert hall. Together with Winchester and Chichester, Salisbury has taken part since 1904 in the Southern Cathedrals Festivals.

BIBLIOGRAPHY

W. H. Husk: *An Account of the Musical Celebrations on St. Cecilia's Day* (London, 1857)

D. Robertson: *Sarum Close* (London, 1938, 2/1969)

R. Sietz: 'Die Cathedrale von Salisbury und ihr Chor', *Cäcilienvereinsorgan*, lxxi (1951), 249

B. Matthews: *The Organs and Organists of Salisbury Cathedral* (Salisbury, 1961, rev. 2/1972)

——: 'Benjamin Banks', *The Strad*, lxxvi (1965), 230

D. Reid and B. Pritchard: 'Some Festival Programmes of the 18th and 19th Centuries', *RMARC*, v (1965), 51; addenda and corrigenda by B. Matthews, viii (1970), 23

B. Matthews: 'J. C. Bach in the West Country', *MT*, cviii (1967), 702

——: 'The Childhood of Nancy Storace', *MT*, cx (1969), 733

R. Findlater: 'A Tale of Two Cities', *Bulletin* (of the Arts Council of Great Britain), v (1971)

M. Foster: *The Music of Salisbury Cathedral* (London, 1974)

BETTY MATTHEWS

Sallantin [Sallentin], **François (Alexandre)** (*b* Paris, 13 Feb 1755; *d* Paris, after 1 Jan 1816). French oboist, teacher and composer. Because numerous members of Sallantin's family were musicians, Fétis (and consequently several later dictionaries) confused his forename, listing it as Antoine. He began playing in the Paris Opéra orchestra in 1770 and retained the post until 1812. In 1785–6 he took a year's leave of absence, which he probably spent in London studying with the oboist J. C. Fischer. During the 1780s he often performed at the Concert Spirituel and other concerts in Paris. He played an oboe concerto of his own composition on at least two of these occasions, but this music was never published. Having joined the National Guard in 1793, he then taught the oboe at the Paris Conservatoire from its establishment in 1795 until his retirement on 1 January 1816. In this capacity he significantly raised the level of oboe playing in France, particularly by influencing his students to develop a more refined tone.

BIBLIOGRAPHY

FétisB

C. Pierre: *Le Conservatoire national de musique et de déclamation: documents historiques et administratifs* (Paris, 1900)

SHERWOOD DUDLEY

Salle, Adrien Trudo. See SALÉ, ADRIEN TRUDO.

Sallé, Marie (*b* Paris, 1707; *d* Paris, 27 July 1756). French dancer. A pupil of the famous virtuoso dancer Françoise Prévost, she made her Paris début at the Foire St Laurent in 1718, in *La princesse de Carisme* (Lesage and Lafont); on 10 July 1721 she appeared at the Opéra in a revival of Campra's *Les fêtes vénitiennes*. In 1725 John Rich engaged five French dancers, including Sallé and her brother, to appear in a season at the Lincoln's Inn Fields Theatre in London: the programme included a comedy called *Love's Last Shift, or The Fool in Fashion* (23 October 1725) and J.-F. Rebel's choreographic divertissement *Les caractères de la danse* (25 November). In April 1727 the Sallés returned to Paris, where Marie made her official début at the Opéra on 14 September 1727 in the third entrée of *Les amours des dieux* (text by Fuzelier, music by Mouret). The *Mercure* for that month reported that she danced (as a shepherdess) and was 'fort goûtée'. In June 1728 she danced a pas de trois with her great rival La Camargo and Mlle Petit in *Hypermnestre* (Lafont and Gervais); she and Camargo subsequently appeared together in numerous performances. On 17 February 1729 she created a sen-

sation by partnering Laval in *Les caractères de la danse* 'tous deux en habits de ville et sans masque'. The abandonment of the traditional mask was the first of a number of her important technical and stylistic innovations which were to make her one of the most important figures in 18th-century dance (*see* DANCE, fig.15).

The early years of her career at the Opéra were interrupted by frequent seasons in England, where she was much impressed by Garrick's acting. During the 1733–4 season she created and danced in two ballets which were to prove highlights of her career and of 18th-century dance. On 14 February 1734 the London correspondent of the *Mercure* reported a performance of the ballet *Pygmalion* at Drury Lane Theatre, in which Sallé 'dared to appear ... without a pannier, skirt or bodice, and with her hair down; she did not wear a single ornament on her head. Apart from her corset and petticoat, she wore only a simple muslin robe, draped round her after the fashion of a Greek statue'. Her triumph in *Pygmalion* was followed on 26 February by *Bacchus and Ariadne*, in which she effectively portrayed, through her attitudes and gestures, 'the sentiments of the most profound sorrow, despair, fury and weakness' (*Mercure*). *Pygmalion* represented the first time that a dancer had dared to abandon the cumbersome and often inappropriate regalia of Baroque stage costume for a simpler style of dress allowing greater freedom; in *Bacchus and Ariadne* Sallé demonstrated her talent for expressive mime through gesture and facial expression, an important step towards the ideal union of music, dance and drama in the *ballet en action* towards which choreographers and composers were working. On 8 November 1734 Sallé appeared with Rich's troupe at Covent Garden, as Terpsichore in the prologue of Handel's *Il pastor fido*, another role that afforded opportunity for expression. She subsequently danced in Handel's *Oreste* (18 December 1734), *Ariodante* (8 January 1735) and *Alcina* (16 April 1735): in the last she appeared dressed as a man, to the disapproval of the audience. By 1735 the theatrical rivalries prompted hostile press notices and she returned to France. Between then and her retirement in 1740 she created three of the four examples of early 18th-century *ballets en action* cited by Noverre: the entrée 'Les fleurs' in Rameau's *Les indes galantes* (1735); the Turkish divertissement in the fifth entrée of *L'Europe galante* (1736; Cahusac described the ingenious 'action épisodique' in which she played a 'jeune odalisque' who desires to win the heart of the sultan but is repulsed – 'Her dance was composed of all the attitudes which could best depict such a passion'), and Hébé's entrée in Act 2 of Rameau's *Castor et Pollux* (1737). Her last important creation before her retirement on 15 June 1740 was the third entrée of Rameau's *Les fêtes d'Hébé*, in which she played Terpsichore.

Unlike Camargo, Sallé never exploited virtuosity for its own sake, but developed an expressive style of dancing appropriate to the *ballet en action*. A typical report (*Mercure*, January 1732) contrasts the nobility, grace and intelligence of her style with the brilliant technical feats of Camargo:

De ta danse active et légère,
J'admire, Camargo, le brillant caractère,
Mais que ta rivale a d'appas
Le grâce au sentiment unie
Exprime en toi, Sallé, l'éloquent harmonie
Du regard, du gest et des pas!

Noverre, who admired her and many of whose ideas (set out in his *Lettres sur la danse*, 1760) she anticipated by nearly 30 years, wrote:

I was enchanted by her dancing; she possessed neither the brilliance nor the technical feats common to dancing nowadays; but for glitter she substituted simple and touching grace; free from affectation, her face was noble, expressive and intelligent. Her voluptuous dance was conceived with as much finesse as lightness, it was not by leaps and frolics that she went to your heart.

See also DANCE, §V, 1.

BIBLIOGRAPHY

L. de Cahusac: *La danse ancienne et moderne* (The Hague, 1754)
J.-G. Noverre: *Lettrẽs sur la danse et sur les ballets* (Lyons, 1760)
E. Dacier: *Une danseuse de l'Opéra sous Louis XV: Mademoiselle Sallé* (Paris, 1909)
C. W. Beaumont: *Three French Dancers of the XVIIIth Century* (London, 1934)
M.-F. Christout: 'Sallé, Marie', *ES*

WENDY THOMPSON

Sallentin, François. *See* SALLANTIN, FRANÇOIS.

Sallinen, Aulis (*b* Salmi, 9 April 1935). Finnish composer. He studied under Merikanto and Kokkonen at the Sibelius Academy, Helsinki (1955–60), where he returned to teach theory and composition after a period as superintendent of the Finnish Radio SO (1960–70). From 1971 to 1974 he was chairman of the Society of Finnish Composers, and in 1971 his *Chorali* was performed at the ISCM Festival. He began his work as a composer in a meditative and lyrical freely serial style, and a certain contemplative quality has remained a feature of his music. In the later 1960s he developed an individual technique in which triads and other tonal elements are used together with new structural principles. A characteristic example is the Third Quartet, a set of variations treating an old Finnish folktune with different modern procedures: the approach is neither traditionally folkloristic nor Bartókian. Symphony no.1, which won the competition held by the city of Helsinki to mark the opening of the Finlandia Hall, begins and ends with an F♯ minor chord and contains clearly tonal themes and motifs, but these are combined with clusters and other effects comparable with those in the orchestral music of, for example, Ligeti. This work, soon followed by a Second Symphony in the form of a dialogue for percussion solo and orchestra, suggested that Sallinen was to take the path of Sibelius, whose influence is very clear in *Chorali*. However, the appearance of his first opera, *Ratsumies* ('The horseman'), in 1975 excited new expectations, for this work, based on a poetic drama of a heavily symbolical character and meandering shape, showed an unusual talent for creating large spans of coherent dramatic music. In his second opera, *Punainen viiva* ('The red line'), Sallinen had the advantage of a plainer libretto, concerning the unchanging lot of the Finnish poor despite the coming of universal suffrage in the last century, and again he created a work of strong continuity embracing scenes of Janáček-like vividness. The principal characters are now fully delineated individuals, which is not the case with the allegorical *Horseman*, and they are placed in a world where icy harmony, tuned percussion and slow motivic growth portray the flat, deep cold of northern Finland.

WORKS
(*selective list*)

Stage: Variations sur Mallarmé (ballet, P. Karhunmaa), 1967; Ratsumies [The horseman] (opera, 3, P. Haavikko), 1973–4; Punainen viiva [The red line] (opera, after I. Kianto), 1977–8
Orch: Kaksi myytillistä kuvaa [2 mythical scenes], 1956; Conc., chamber orch, 1959; Variations, vc, orch, 1961; Mauermusik, 1962;

Juventas, 14 variations, youth orch, 1963; Metamorphoses, pf, chamber orch, 1964; Vn Conc., 1968; Chorali, 32 wind, 2 perc, harp, cel, 1970; Sym. no.1, 1970–71; Sym. Dialogue (Sym. no.2), perc, orch, 1972; Sym. no.3, 1974–5; Chamber Music I, str, 1975; Chamber Music II, a fl, str, 1975–6; Vc Conc., 1976; Sym. no.4, 1979
Vocal: Kolme lyyristä laulua kuolemasta [3 lyrical songs about death] (ancient Finnish), Bar, male vv, orch, 1962–5; Suite grammaticale, youth chorus, youth orch, 1972; Dies irae, S, B, male vv, orch, 1978
Inst: Str Qt no.1, 1958; Str Qt no.2 'Canzona', 1960; Elegy for Sebastian Knight, vc, 1964; Str Qt no.3 'Aspekteja Peltoniemen Hintrikin surumarssista' [Aspects of Peltoniemi Hintrik's funeral march], 1969; Sonata, vc, 1971; Str Qt no.4 'Quiet Songs', 1971; Metamorfora, vc, pf, 1974

Principal publishers: Fazer, Novello

BIBLIOGRAPHY

E. Salmenhaara, ed.: *Miten sävellykseni ovat syntyneet* [Origin of my works] (Helsinki, 1976), 141ff [incl. work-list and discography]
E. Tawaststjerna: 'Sallinen helleeninen sinfonia' [Sallinen's Hellenic symphony], *Esseitä ja arvosteluja* [Essays and criticism] (Helsinki, 1976), 205

ERKKI SALMENHAARA, PAUL GRIFFITHS

Salmanov, Vadim Nikolayevich (*b* St Petersburg, 4 Nov 1912). Russian composer. He began to play the piano when he was six, at first under the guidance of his father. By the age of 18 he had been prepared for entry to the conservatory but was suddenly attracted to geology, which he studied and practised before returning to music in 1935. He then began to compose and in 1936, after preparation under Arseny Gladkovsky, he entered the composition department of the Leningrad Conservatory. There he studied with Gnesin. A developing career as a composer was interrupted by military service in World War II, from which Salmanov returned in 1945 to work with enthusiasm. He produced his First Quartet, a Violin Sonata, a Trio, a Piano Quartet and songs to poems of Blok and Esenin, all containing many pages marked by impressions of the war. In the late 1940s he took up orchestral writing again, producing an important landmark in the First Symphony, in which he used Slav folk melodies. One of his most interesting works, the symphonic suite *Poeticheskiye kartinki* ('Poetic pictures') on stories by Andersen, appeared in 1955; its distinctive subtlety of sonority and gentle lyricism are characteristic of Salmanov's work at this time. And the oratorio-poem *Dvenadtsat'* ('The twelve'), an expansive piece in lush evocative colours, was an apotheosis of this largely illustrative style.

Subsequently Salmanov directed his attention mainly to 'pure' instrumental music, and any remaining programmatic features are of a conventional character (as in the Second Symphony). It is these later works that have established Salmanov's reputation. The six quartets are models of laconic and disciplined thought, strictly linear, sharply expressive and containing a wealth of device within crystal-clear forms. The three symphonies, together with the Violin Concerto and the Sonata for piano and strings, show a gravitation towards compression and an endeavour to give new meaning to sonata and symphonic form. But choral music occupies an important place in Salmanov's output, and the romance genre has been a consistent enthusiasm. Here his highest achievements have been settings of Lorca, Neruda and Rushevich, with melodic lines following speech intonation and accompaniments of richly varied harmony. His choral works are distinguished by a subtle mastery that can achieve great effects with slender resources, as in the cycle ... *No b'yotsya serdtse* ('... But the heart is beating'). Work on choral pieces reawakened his interest in folk melodies, and this interest found clear expression in the choral concerto

Lebyodushka ('The hen swan'), which won a Glinka State Prize. Among his many appointments Salmanov was secretary of the RSFSR Composers' Union and held the chair in composition at the Leningrad Conservatory.

WORKS
(selective list)

Orch: Les [The forest], sym. picture, 1948; Russkoye kaprichchio, 1950; 3 syms., 1952, 1959, 1963; Slavyanskiy khorovod [Slavonic round-dance], 1954; Poeticheskiye kartinki [Poetic pictures], sym. suite, after Andersen, 1955; Privetstvennaya oda [Greeting ode], 1961; Detskaya simfoniya [Children's sym.], 1962; Sonata, str, pf, 1962; Vn Conc., 1964; Nochi bol'shovo goroda [Nights in a big city], vn, chamber orch, 1969; Velichal'naya [Welcome song], 1972

Vocal orch: Zoya, 1949; Dvenadtsat' [The twelve] (oratorio-poem, Blok), 1957; Oda Leninu [Ode to Lenin] (Neruda), 1969

Choral: Lebyodushka [The hen swan] (Russ. trad.), choral conc. no.1; Dobrïy molodets [A good lad], choral conc. no.2, chorus, eng hn, accordion; In memoriam, De profundis, S, chorus, org, 1973; many a cappella pieces (Pushkin, Tyutchev, Esenin, etc)

Chamber: 6 str qts, 1945, 1958, 1961, 1963, 1968, 1971; 2 vn sonatas, 1945, 1962; 2 trios, 1946, 1949; Pf Qt, 1947; Vc Sonata, 1963; Monolog, vc, 1970

Songs: Vityaz' [Hero] (cycle, P. Katenin), 1957; Ispaniya v serdtse [Spain in the heart] (cycle, Lorca, Neruda), 1960; Ochishcheniye [Purification] (cycle, Rushevich), 1966; Pesni ob odinochestve [Songs about loneliness] (cycle, Lorca), 1967; romances (Blok, Fet, Tyutchev, Esenin, etc)

Ballet: Chelovek [Man], after E. Mezhelaytis, Leningrad, 1966

BIBLIOGRAPHY

M. Aranovsky: 'Obrazï Andersena' [Andersen's images], *SovM* (1956), no.6, p.16

——: *Poeticheskiye kartinki V. Salmanova* (Leningrad, 1958)

A. Chernov: 'Tvorchestvo V. Salmanova' [Salmanov's work], *SovM* (1958), no.10, p.16

Yu. Vaynkop: *Dvenadtsat'* (Leningrad, 1958)

M. Aranovsky: *V. N. Salmanov* (Leningrad, 1961)

P. Vul'fius: 'Vadim Salmanov: pervaya simfonia', *55 sovetskikh simfoniy*, ed. B. A. Arapov and others (Leningrad, 1961), 212

M. Aranovsky: 'Vtoraya simfoniya' [Second Symphony], *Sovetskaya simfoniya za 50 let* (Leningrad, 1967)

M. ARANOVSKY

Salmen, Walter (*b* Paderborn, 20 Sept 1926). German musicologist. After attending the Gymnasium at Werl, Westphalia (1944–8), he studied musicology at Heidelberg University under Heinrich Besseler with philosophy and history as subsidiary subjects; he also had lessons in organ and composition from H. Poppen, W. Fortner and W. Petersen. In 1949 he received the doctorate from Münster University with a dissertation on the German Tenorlied. A research assistant at the Deutsches Volksliedarchiv in Freiburg from 1950, he held a scholarship from the Deutsche Forschungsgemeinschaft from 1955 to 1958. In 1958 he completed his *Habilitation* in musicology at Saarbrücken University with a dissertation on the itinerant musician in medieval Europe. He was appointed *ausserplanmässiger Professor* at Saarbrücken in 1963 and research fellow in 1964. In 1966 he became full professor and director of the musicology institute of Kiel University and in 1969 was visiting professor at the University of Illinois in Urbana. He took up the chair of musicology at Innsbruck University in 1973.

Salmen is the editor of the Kieler Schriften zur Musikwissenschaft (Kassel, 1967–), the Müller-Blattau Festschrift (Saarbrücken, 1960), *Beiträge zur Musikanschauung im 19. Jahrhundert* (Regensburg, 1965) and of *Der Sozialstatus des Berufsmusikers vom 17. biz 19. Jahrhundert* (Kassel, 1971). His musicological research concentrates on ethnology, social history and iconography. He has devoted many articles to music in the eastern parts of central Europe (e.g. Westphalia and Schleswig-Holstein) as well as the

status, practices and repertory of the itinerant musician in the Middle Ages and the history of song, folksong, domestic music and chamber music.

WRITINGS

Das deutsche Tenorlied bis zum Lochamer Liederbuch (diss., U. of Münster, 1949)

Das Lochamer Liederbuch (Leipzig, 1951)

Die Schichtung der mittelalterlichen Musikkultur in der ostdeutschen Grenzlage (Kassel, 1954)

Das Erbe des ostdeutschen Volksgesanges: Geschichte und Verzeichnis seiner Quellen und Sammlungen (Würzburg, 1956)

'Bemerkungen zum mehrstimmigen Musizieren der Spielleute im Mittelalter', *RBM*, xi (1957), 17

Der fahrende Musiker im europäischen Mittelalter (Habilitationsschrift, U. of Saarbrücken, 1958; Kassel, 1960)

'Die Beteiligung Englands am internationalen Musikantenverkehr des Mittelalters', *Mf*, xi (1958), 315

'European Song (1300–1530)', *NOHM*, iii (1960), 349–80

'Herder und Reichardt', *Herder-Studien* (Würzburg, 1960), 95

'Johann Gottfried Müthel, der Letzte Schüler Bachs', *Festschrift Heinrich Besseler* (Leipzig, 1961), 351

Johann Friedrich Reichardt (Freiburg, 1963)

Geschichte der Musik in Westfalen (Kassel, 1963–7)

'Goethe und Reichardt', *Jb der Sammlung Kippenberg*, new ser., i (1963), 52

Geschichte der Rhapsodie (Freiburg, 1966)

'Zur Gestaltung der "Thèmes russes" in Beethovens op.59', *Festschrift für Walter Wiora* (Kassel, 1967), 397

' "Alte Töne" und Volksmusik in Kompositionen Paul Hindemiths', *YIFMC*, i (1969), 89–122

'Beiträge Spaniens und Portugals zur Musikentwicklung in Mitteleuropa', *SM*, xi (1969), 371

Haus- und Kammermusik: privates Musizieren im gesellschaftlichen Wandel zwischen 1600 und 1900, Musikgeschichte in Bildern, iv/3 (Leipzig, 1969)

'Die soziale Verpflichtung von Komponisten im 19. Jahrhundert', *Musica bohemica et europea: Brno V 1970*, 289

Musikgeschichte Schleswig-Holsteins in Bildern (Neumünster, 1971)

'Neue Bildquellen zur Praxis von Haus- und Kammermusik im 16. Jahrhundert', *Musica cameralis: Brno VI 1971*, 37

Musikgeschichte Schleswig-Holsteins von der Frühzeit bis zur Reformation (Neumünster, 1972)

'Russische Musik und Musiker in Deutschland vor 1700', *Mf*, xxvi (1973), 167

'Zur Geschichte der Bärentreiber und der Tanzbären', *Studia instrumentorum musicae popularis*, iii, ed. E. Stockmann (Stockholm, 1974), 203

'Das gemachte "neue Lied" im Spätmittelalter', *Handbuch des Volksliedes*, ii (1975), 407

'Ikonographie eines Stammbuchblattes von 1590', *Opernstudien: Anna Amalie Abert zum 65. Geburtstag* (Tutzing, 1975), 221

'Komponist und Musicus im Renaissance-Zeitalter', *ÖMz*, xxx (1975), 569

Musikleben im 16. Jahrhundert, Musikgeschichte in Bildern, iii/9 (Leipzig, 1976)

'Venedig und die Barkarole in Oper und Operette', *Das Lokalkolorit in der Oper des 19. Jahrhunderts*, ed. H. Becker (Regensburg, 1976), 257

'Vom Musizieren zur Zeit der Babenberger', *ÖMz*, xxxi (1976), 265

EDITIONS

with I. Koepp: *Liederbuch der Anna von Köln um 1500*, DRM, iv (1954)

with M. Lang: *Ostdeutscher Minnesang*, Schriften des Kopernikuskreises, iii (Konstanz, 1958)

Music appendix to *Die Lieder Oswalds von Wolkenstein*, ed. K. Klein, Altdeutsche Textbibliothek, lv (Tübingen, 1962)

Bartold Capp (†1636): die Werke der Werler Komponisten (Münster, 1964)

J. F. Reichardt: Goethes Lieder, Oden, Balladen und Romanzen, EDM, 1st ser., lviii–lix (1964–70)

Das Lochamer Liederbuch, DTB, new ser., Sonderband ii (1972)

HANS HEINRICH EGGEBRECHT

Salmenhaara, Erkki (Olavi) (*b* Helsinki, 12 March 1941). Finnish composer and musicologist. He studied composition at the Sibelius Academy, Helsinki, with Kokkonen (diploma 1963) and, in the autumn of 1963, in Vienna with Ligeti, on whose works he wrote his musicology dissertation (1969) for the University of Helsinki, where his teacher was Tawaststjerna. From 1963 to 1973 he was music critic for the daily paper *Helsingin Sanomat*, and in 1963 he was appointed to teach music theory at Helsinki University, becoming assistant professor there in 1975. He was made vice-president of the Finnish Musicological Society in 1969, president of the Society of the Symphony Orchestras of Finland in 1974, and president of the Composers of Finland Society, also in 1974.

Salmenhaara's first mature compositions date from the beginning of the 1960s. At this time he had gone through a period of experiment, following the iconoclastic tendencies of the international avant garde: aleatory music, 'happenings' and so on. These influences proved, however, not to be lasting. The Symphony no.1 'Crescendi' (1960) found him striving towards a synthesis of the great symphonic tradition with new structural methods, and this was to be the principal aim of subsequent works. The Second Symphony (1963, revised 1966) opens with a slowly moving polyphonic texture which gradually develops into a static field, evidently suggested by similar structures in Ligeti's *Atmosphères*. Some have characterized the work as spiritually closer to Sibelius's Fourth Symphony than any other post-Sibelian Finnish composition. Salmenhaara's chamber works of this period, notably the *Elegia 2* for two string quartets (1963), also show influences from Ligeti.

Le bateau ivre for orchestra (1966) marked a stylistic change. It takes the imagery and symbolism of Rimbaud's poem as its point of departure, but is not programmatic or illustrative in the conventional sense, for Salmenhaara's objective was to achieve with musical means what Rimbaud had done with words. Three triads, on consecutive notes, form the basic material. They are used to generate melodic shapes, layered chords or clusters, and fields of definite harmonic 'colour'. Ligetian features are still present, but more important is the return to tonal elements, from this time an essential part of Salmenhaara's language. The orchestration of *Le bateau ivre*, with its rich use of celesta and harpsichord, creates an aqueous, marine sound.

In later works – from the Piano Sonata no.1 (1966) through the *Requiem profanum* and the Fourth Symphony to the opera *Portugalin nainen* ('The Portugese woman', 1972) – Salmenhaara was attempting to establish an expressive language with simple means, often penetrated by historical associations. These works have some technical features in common with neo-classicism (the use of triadic material, bitonality, square rhythms, etc), but the impression is quite different, perhaps because Salmenhaara's attitude is fundamentally romantic rather than anti-romantic. Though his style in these pieces has been severely criticized for its simplicity, it is able to express a powerful individuality. Later compositions, such as the orchestral *Canzona* (1974), have seen an increasing complexity, but without any abandonment of the principles previously established.

WORKS
(selective list)

Opera: Portugalin nainen [The Portugese woman] (3, Salmenhaara, after R. Musil), 1972; Helsinki, 4 Feb 1976
Orch: Sym. no.1 'Crescendi', 1960; Sym. no.2, 1963, rev. 1966; Sym. no.3, 1964; Le bateau ivre, after Rimbaud, 1966; Suomi-Finland, unsym. poem, 1966; La fille en minijupe, 1967; BFK-83, 1967; Illuminations, 1971; Sym. no.4 'Nel mezzo del cammin di nostra vita', 1971; Horn Conc., 1973; Canzona, 1974
Vocal: Requiem profanum (Baudelaire, Espriu, Declaration of Human Rights), S, A, Bar, org, pf, str, 1968–9; 2 choral song cycles, 4 solo song cycles
Inst: Sonata, vc, pf, 1960; Elegia 1, 3 fl, 2 tpt, db, 1963; Elegia 2, 2 str

qts, 1963; Wind Qnt, 1964; Elegia 3, vc, 1965; Toccata, org, 1965; 3 pf sonatas, 1966, 1973, 1975; Elegia 4, va, 1967; Etude, hpd, 1969; 3 scènes de nuit, vn, pf, 1970; Quartetto, fl, str trio, 1971; Sonatina, 2 vn, 1972
Tape: Information Explosion, 1967
Principal publishers: Fazer, Finnish Broadcasting Co.

WRITINGS
'Joonas Kokkonen, romantisoituva klassikko', *Suomen musiikin vuosikirja 1967–68*, ed. I. Oramo (Lahti, 1968), 68
Sointuanalyysi [Harmonic analysis] (Helsinki, 1968)
Vuosisatamme musiiki [The music of our century] (Keuruu, 1968)
Das musikalische Material und seine Behandlung in den Werken Apparitions, Atmosphères, Aventures und Requiem von György Ligeti (diss., U. of Helsinki, 1969; Helskini and Regensburg, 1969)
'The Beatles – viihdettä vai taidetta?' [The Beatles – entertainment or art?], *Suomen musiikin vuosikirja 1968–69*, ed. I. Oramo (Forssa, 1970), 46
Soinnutus [Harmony] (Helsinki, 1970)
Tapiola: sinfoninen runo Tapiola Sibeliuksen myöhäistyylin edustajana [Tapiola: the symphonic poem Tapiola as representative of Sibelius's late style] (Karkkila, 1970)

BIBLIOGRAPHY
P. Helistö: 'Nuorin säveltäjäpolvemme' [Our youngest generation of composers], *Suomen säveltäjiä*, ed. E. Marvia, ii (Borgå, 2/1966), 531

ILKKA ORAMO

Salmhofer, Franz (*b* Vienna, 22 Jan 1900; *d* Vienna, 22 Sept 1975). Austrian composer and conductor. He received his earliest musical training as a choirboy at the monastery of Admont in Styria. He studied composition at the Vienna Academy with Schreker and Franz Schmidt and musicology with Adler at the university. In 1923 he married the pianist Margit Gál. He was conductor at the Burgtheater (1929–39), for which he wrote music for over 300 stage works, then director of the Staatsoper (1945–55) and of the Volksoper (1955–63). He received many awards and honours both for his compositions and for his contribution to Viennese musical life. Salmhofer's music is firmly rooted in the tradition of the Viennese Romantics; it shows a vigorous invention and a sure instinct for dramatic effect undoubtedly resulting from his long connection with the theatre.

WORKS
(selective list)

STAGE
(all performed at Vienna, Staatsoper, unless otherwise stated)
Operas: Dame in Traum, 1935; Iwan Tarassenko, 1938; Das Werkbekleid, Salzburg, Landestheater, 1943; Dreikönig, 1945, Vienna, Volksoper, 1970
Ballets: Das lockende Phantom, 1927; Der Taugenichts in Wien, 1930; Österreichische Bauernhochzeit, 1933; Weihnachtsmärchen (after Johann and Josef Strauss), 1933
Incidental music to c300 plays, incl. Goethe: Faust, pts.i–ii, Shakespeare: King Lear, Merry Wives of Windsor, Othello, Romeo and Juliet, Tempest, perf. Burgtheater; film scores

OTHER
Orch: Der Ackermann und der Tod (sym. ov., after J. von Saaz), 1922; Tpt Conc., 1922; Chamber Suite, 1923; Der geheimnisvolle Trompeter (sym. poem, after Whitman), narrator, orch, 1924; Vc Conc., 1927; 2 syms., 1948, 1955; Vn Conc., 1950; Sym. Prol., 1966
Chamber: 6 str qts; Pf Qt; Str Trio; Sonata, vc, pf; Sonata, va, pf; 4 Charakterstücke, vn, pf; pf pieces
Songs to poems by Eichendorff, Heine, Schaukal

BIBLIOGRAPHY
H. Ullrich: *Fortschritt und Tradition* (Vienna, 1956), 156ff, 328ff

Salminger [Salbinger, Salblinger], **Sigmund** (*b* Munich, *c*1500; *d* Augsburg, 1553 or 1554). German Reform leader, teacher and music editor. Originally a Franciscan monk in Munich, Salminger left the order under the influence of the Reformation, married Anna Hallerin and in 1526 moved to Augsburg. There, both he and his wife joined the Anabaptist movement and were baptized by Hans Hutt in March 1527. Soon afterwards Salminger was chosen by lot to lead the Augsburg group. Imprisoned in September 1527 for his religious beliefs, he remained in gaol throughout the following years of persecution; finally he renounced his ties with the Anabaptist sect in a public confession dated 17 December 1530. After his release he was ordered to leave the city in March 1531, but he petitioned to remain because of ill-health and penury. His activities during the next few years are not known, but by 1537 he had apparently achieved full reinstatement in Augsburg, where he was allowed to teach and even enjoyed the patronage of the powerful FUGGER family. On 4 October 1539 he was granted an imperial copyright for his forthcoming publications.

Salminger's importance in the field of music stems less from his authorship of several hymns and of a treatise on music than from his activities as editor for the printers MELCHIOR KRIESSTEIN and PHILIPP ULHART. His publications include the first complete German psalter with melodies and four collections of motets, important for their many *unica* and first editions of works by leading German and Netherlands composers, both for the Reformed and for Catholic use.

MUSIC EDITIONS
(selective list; publisher's name follows date of publication)

G. Breuning: Dreü gar nützliche und fruchtbare Lieder, im Ton 'Maria Zart' (Augsburg, c1526; Ulhart)
Der gantz Psalter . . . in gsangweiss gestelt (Augsburg, 1537, 2/1538 as Der new Gesang Psalter; Ulhart)
Selectissimae nec non familiarissime cantiones ultra centum (Augsburg, 1540[7]; Kriesstein)
Concentus, 4, 5, 6, 8vv (Augsburg, 1545[2]; Ulhart)
Cantiones, 5–7vv (Augsburg, 1545[3]; Kriesstein)
Cantiones selectissimae, 4vv . . . liber primus [–secundus] (Augsburg, 1548[2]–1549[11]; Ulhart)
Gradatio sive scala principiorum artis musicae (Augsburg, c1545; Ulhart)

BIBLIOGRAPHY
A. Schmid: *Ottaviano dei Petrucci . . . und seine Nachfolger im sechzehnten Jahrhunderte* (Vienna, 1845/R1968), 162
P. Wackernagel: *Das deutsche Kirchenlied* (Leipzig, 1864–77/R1964), i, 407; iii, 807 [incl. text of Salminger's hymns]
H. M. Schletterer: 'Sigmund Salminger', *MMg*, xxi (1899), 177
K. Schottenloher: *Philipp Ulhart, ein Augsburger Winkeldrucker und Helfershelfer der 'Schwärmer' und Wiedertäufer (1523–1529)* (Munich, 1921/R1967), 81
C. Hege: 'Salminger, Sigmund', *The Mennonite Encyclopedia*, iv (Scottdale, Penn., 1959), 408
F. Krautwurst: 'Salminger, Sigmund', *MGG*
C. P. Clasen: *Anabaptism: a Social History, 1525–1618* (Ithaca, NY, 1972)

MARIE LOUISE GÖLLNER

Salmo (Sp.). TAMBOURIN DE BÉARN.

Salmon [née Munday], **Eliza** (*b* Oxford, 1787; *d* Chelsea, 5 June 1849). English singer. Her mother was a member of a leading musical family, the Mahons. A pupil of John Ashley, she made her Covent Garden début in the Lenten Oratorios on 4 March 1803. Gifted with a beautiful voice, a charming manner and a face 'of dazzling fairness', she had immediate success; but her attempts to embellish her solo singing were criticized. In 1806 she married James Salmon, organist of St Peter's Church, Liverpool, but she continued to appear from time to time in London and at the Three Choirs Festival, finding great popularity. In 1823 her husband, in financial difficulties, joined the army and was posted to the West Indies, where he died. Mrs Salmon remained in constant demand, and her professional income in 1823 is said to have reached £5000. But during one of the Concerts of Ancient Music in May 1825 her

voice suddenly collapsed. She never resumed public appearances, and was unable to find pupils. Although she may have remarried, she was destitute in her last years.

Mrs Salmon was a high soprano (she could sing *f′′′* with ease) and had great vocal agility. But the magic of her voice lay in its tone, likened by some to the glass harmonica, by others to the clarinet. However perfectly drilled, she was no musician and gave no character to anything she sang. Her singing was compared with the more florid manner of Catalani.

F. G. RENDALL/R

Salmon, Jacques (*b* Picardy, c1545; *fl* 1571–86). French composer and singer. In 1571 he served among the chamber musicians of François, Duke of Anjou, as a singer. In 1575 he was described as 'chantre et vallet de chambre' to Henri III, the duke's brother, when his chanson *Je meurs pensant en ta douceur* (now lost) won the silver lute prize at the St Cecilia competition at Évreux. He collaborated with Beaulieu in providing music for Beaujoyeulx's *Balet comique de la Royne* (Paris, 1582/R1965; ed. in MSD, xxv, 1971) and in organizing its performance for the wedding of the Duke of Joyeuse on 15 October 1581. He was still in the royal service in 1583 when two of his *airs* were published (in *RISM* 1583[9]). A 'Salmon' was listed as a member of the Congrégation de l'Oratoire de Notre-Dame de Vie Saine, established by Henri III at Vincennes in 1584; the statutes required two musicians as 'confrères'. Nothing is known of him after January 1586 when he rented a room at the Sainte-Chapelle for four months; he may have retired to a canonry he held at St Vulfran in Abbeville. Both his surviving *airs* are in two sections, for four and five voices respectively; both use melodies harmonized by other contemporary composers (Pierre Bonnet, 1585, and Guillaume Tessier, 1582), and introduce the free declamatory rhythm of the new *air de cour*. One of them also appeared in an arrangement for voice and lute by Gabriel Bataille in 1608 (*RISM* 1608[10]; ed. A. Verchaly, *Airs de cour pour voix et luth*, Paris, 1961).

No connection has been established between Jacques Salmon and René Saman.

FRANK DOBBINS

Salmon [Salomon], **Karel** [Karl] (*b* Heidelberg, 13 Nov 1897; *d* Beit Zayit, nr. Jerusalem, 15 Jan 1974). Israeli composer, singer, conductor and pianist of German birth. He studied in Strauss's master classes at the Berlin Academy of Arts, and worked as a répétiteur at the Berlin Stadtsoper, conductor in Baden-Baden, baritone at the Hamburg Opera and double bass player; he also played an active part in the Handel revival, editing *Rodelinda*. In 1933 he emigrated to Palestine where he became active in pioneering musical activities: on the establishment of the Jerusalem radio station in 1936 he was appointed its music director and in 1938 he founded the Israel RSO. In 1944 he organized a Bach and Handel festival in Jerusalem, and from 1948 to 1957 he directed the music department of Israel radio. As a composer he was influenced by Mediterranean and oriental folklore, incorporating eastern instruments in the dance rhapsody *Dalya*. A striking expression of his approach was the *Symphonic Suite on Greek Themes* in which he stressed the affinity between Greek and

Palestinian folktunes. The Second Symphony is an impressionistically coloured, romantic impression of nocturnal Canaan. Most of Salmon's works are in conventional – frequently variation – forms.

WORKS
(selective list)

Operas: David and Goliath (marionette opera, A. Baer), 1930, rev. 1956; Nedarim [The vows] (Salmon), 1954–5; Viermal Methusalem (Salmon), 1965–6

Orch: Ali be'er [Strike up, well], 1937; Sym. Suite on Greek Themes, arr. pf/2 pf, 1943; Pf Conc., 1947; Yerushalayim, carillon, orch, 1948; Sym. no.2 'Leilot K'na'an' [Nights of Canaan], 1949; Israeli Youth Sym., 1950; Dalya, dance rhapsody, 1954; concertante pieces, suites

Choral music, liturgical works, piano pieces, songs

Principal publishers: Israel Music Institute, Israeli Music Publications

BENJAMIN BAR-AM

Salmon, Thomas (*b* Hackney, London, 24 June 1648; *d* Mepsal [now Meppershall], Bedfordshire, buried 16 Aug 1706). English clergyman, musical theorist and amateur musician. He entered Trinity College, Oxford, as a commoner on 8 April 1664, mainly to study mathematics. After graduating MA he became rector of Mepsal, a position he held for the rest of his life.

Salmon was 24 when his *Essay to the Advancement of Musick* appeared. In it he proposed certain changes in notation which he thought would make music more readily understood by doing away with obsolete complexities. Simple letter names would replace names of notes deriving from the hexachordal system; instead of the multiplicity of clefs then in use a four-line staff would be employed, its bottom line always representing G and its pitch level shown by a prefixed symbol: B (bass), M (mean) or T (treble); lute and other tablatures would be replaced by the new staff notation, and any system of variable tuning (viol tunings, for example) would be replaced by a simpler and constant one.

The *Essay* initiated the most celebrated musical pamphlet war of the 17th century. Matthew Locke defended traditional systems in his *Observations upon a Late Book* of 1672. Salmon countered this with his *Vindication*, which in 1673 elicited Locke's *Present Practice of Musick Vindicated*. The dispute was conducted with unbridled abuse and even obscenity, particularly by Locke, but this was typical of the polemics of the time and has been unduly emphasized. Locke, who was joined by John Playford and Milton's nephew John Phillips, objected to the proposals because they offered a less precise means of naming notes and did not, with the three prefixes, reduce the clefs or their equivalents but rather made frequent changes of prefix necessary, particularly with a four-line staff. He considered tablature more suitable for complex lute writing, and he censured the reduction in viol tunings since it would greatly restrict the playing of chords.

Certain aspects of notation did change along the lines that Salmon proposed (though he was hardly responsible for the abandonment of hexachordal names, which were falling into disuse anyway). It has been argued that Playford, the most moderate of the disputants, to some extent adopted one of Salmon's principles when he used the treble clef for both soprano and tenor parts in choral music; this became a distinctive feature of subsequent English notation of vocal music and by the use of super- or subscript octave signs attached to a clef was further rationalized and extended to instrumental notation in the 20th century.

The controversy was much discussed. Salmon's proposals were supported by Anthony Wood, John Wallis, Alexander Malcolm and Burney; the Royal Society recommended their adoption; and the theorist J. B. de la Fond reiterated them without acknowledgment in 1725. They were opposed by Roger North and Hawkins.

Salmon's later work on temperament stemmed from his interest in mathematical acoustics and contributed valuably to investigations made at the time by Wallis and other members of the Royal Society. It was by no means purely theoretical, however: Salmon persuaded the viol players Frederick and Christian Steffkin to fret their instruments so as to produce just intonation by following his mathematical principles. He also became interested in the problem of elucidating ancient Greek enharmonic music but had no time to conduct researches before he died.

WRITINGS

An Essay to the Advancement of Musick, by Casting away the Perplexities of Different Cliffs. And uniting all sorts of Musick . . . in one Universal Character (London, 1672/*R*1966)

A Vindication of an Essay to the Advancement of Musick from Mr. Matthew Lock's Observations (London, 1672)

A Proposal to perform Musick in Perfect & Mathematical Proportions (London, 1688)

'The Theory of Musick Reduced to Arithmetical and Geometrical Proportion', *Philosophical Transactions of the Royal Society*, xxiv (1705), 2077

Letter to Sir Hans Sloane concerning researches into the Greek enharmonic system, *GB-Lbm* Sloane 4040

BIBLIOGRAPHY

BurneyH; *DNB*; *HawkinsH*

A. Malcolm: *A Treatise of Musick* (Edinburgh, 1721), 378ff

J. B. de la Fond: *A New System of Music* (London, 1725)

J. Pulver: *A Biographical Dictionary of Old English Music* (London, 1927)

D. Silbert: 'The C Clef in the Seventeenth Century', *MMR*, lxvii (1937), 169

J. Wilson, ed.: *Roger North on Music* (London, 1959)

L. M. Ruff: 'Thomas Salmon's "Essay to the Advancement of Musick" ', *The Consort*, xxi (1964), 266

O. Baldwin and T. Wilson: 'Musick Advanced and Vindicated', *MT*, cxl (1970), 148

MICHAEL TILMOUTH

A page from Thomas Salmon's 'A Vindication of an Essay to the Advancement of Musick from Mr. Matthew Lock's Observations' (1672)

[4]

Augur-hole, or behind the Wanſcot; but I was afraid even to do that too: for if you obſerv'd how archly he tranſpoſes and perverts my words, (*p* 8.)you would take him for a *living Mouſe-trap.*

However, having timely apprehenſions of his coming, I was not out of all hopes to eſcape, did there not go before him a terrible fellow in Buff, an Epigrammatical Poetaſter; this man, Sir, (one would think) dealt only with Pen, Ink, and Paper; but alas! he was arm'd with all the Inſtruments of Cruelty; and heated with ſuch an implacable Malice, that he ſentences me; firſt, To have my Hide taw'd till it was tender; then to have the foreſaid intimate Garment, my Skin, to be fley'd off whilſt I yet remain'd alive: nay further, could he have got a Rime for *defunct* (which it ſeems was the word he deſigned) I muſt alſo have been eaten alive with Pepper and Salt, three days after I had been *defunct.*

But 'twas well for us, his *Pegaſus* was jaded; and ſo, farewel him. Next comes the *Obſerver* himſelf, whoſe remarques were fitter to be contemn'd than

Salmond, Felix (Adrian Norman) (*b* London, 19 Nov 1888; *d* New York, 19 Feb 1952). English cellist. The son of the singer Norman Salmond, he studied with

Whitehouse at the RCM (1905–9), also taking private lessons with Edouard Jacobs in Brussels. He made his début in October 1909, at the Bechstein Hall, accompanied by his mother. For several years he toured Britain, giving solo recitals and appearing with the Queen's Hall, London Symphony, Hallé and Royal Albert Hall orchestras. On 21 May 1919 he played at the Wigmore Hall in the public premières of Elgar's Quartet in E minor and Piano Quintet in A minor in an ensemble led by Albert Sammons. On 27 October that year Salmond gave the première of Elgar's Cello Concerto at the Queen's Hall, with the LSO conducted by the composer; the disastrous performance was due not to the soloist but to inadequate rehearsal time. Between 1919 and 1921 Salmond was cellist of the Chamber Music Players, but in 1922 he went to the USA, making his début at the Aeolian Hall, New York, on 29 March; he settled there and made many tours of North America. He visited England several times (last in 1947) and also toured in Europe in 1930. He earned great appreciation in America, not only as a fine musician and technician but also as a teacher; he was appointed to the Juilliard graduate school on its inception in 1924, and was head of the cello department of the Curtis Institute, Philadelphia, from 1925 until 1942. His many notable pupils included Orlando Cole, Bernard Greenhouse, Leonard Rose and Daniel Saidenberg. Salmond's repertory showed catholic taste and included works by contemporary composers like Barber, Bloch, Bridge and Enescu.

MARTHA KINGDON WARD/LYNDA LLOYD REES

Salò, Gasparo da. See GASPARO DA SALÒ.

Salomon, Johann Peter (*b* Bonn, baptized 20 Feb 1745; *d* London, 28 Nov 1815). German violinist, impresario and composer, later resident in England. He was the second son of Philipp Salomon, a member of the oboe band and subsequently a court musician in Bonn. On 30 August 1758, at the age of only 13, he was appointed to a salaried position as a musician at the Bonn court. In 1761 or 1762 he went on tour, at first retaining his salary since his father deputized for him. Probably Salomon was trying to gain a footing in Dresden, which at that time was the seat of government of Saxony and Poland. By summer 1764 he was at Rheinsberg as musical director to Prince Heinrich of Prussia. At the prince's second household in Berlin Salomon met C. P. E. Bach, and through him became familiar with J. S. Bach's solo violin sonatas and partitas, which he is said to have still performed in exemplary fashion during his years in London. He left Rheinsberg probably in 1780 and went via Paris to London, where he made his first public appearance at Covent Garden on 23 March 1781. Apart from journeys on the Continent, including repeated visits to Bonn, he remained in England for the rest of his life.

Salomon played a leading part in English musical life, not only in London but in the provinces as well. Having made his name as a brilliant violinist, he made progressively fewer solo appearances and turned his attention to conducting and especially promoting concerts. He mounted subscription concerts from 1783, featuring such international artists as the soprano Mara, and his greatest triumph was to secure Haydn's visits to London in 1790–91 and 1794–5, for which the two sets of six 'Salomon' or 'London' symphonies (HI:93–104) were

Johann Peter Salomon: portrait (c1791) by Thomas Hardy in the Royal College of Music, London

written. Haydn's esteem for his impresario and orchestral leader can sometimes be seen in the symphonies (for example, the phrase marked 'Salomon solo ma piano' in the trio of no.97, and the florid violin part of no.103, second movement); the Concertante in B♭ (HI:105) was composed for Salomon, who played the solo violin part; and the six string quartets opp.71 and 74 (HI:69–74), written between the two London visits in 1793, though dedicated to Count Apponyi, were clearly designed for the public performances that Salomon's quartet gave in London. Salomon is also said to have had a hand in providing Haydn with the original model for the text of *The Creation*. He was one of the founder-members of the Philharmonic Society and led the orchestra at its first concert on 8 March 1813. He died as a result of a riding accident and was buried in the cloisters of Westminster Abbey.

On 28 February 1816 Beethoven, who had had business dealings with Salomon, wrote to Ferdinand Ries: 'I am greatly distressed at the death of Salomon, for he was a noble-minded man whom I well remember since my childhood'. And Rochlitz in his obituary in the *Allgemeine musikalische Zeitung* remarked: 'Among all purely executant musicians of this age none has had so wide, so decisive and so beneficent an influence as he'. Rochlitz's tribute is a qualification of Salomon's merits as well as an appreciation, however, for it explicitly takes no account of his compositions. As the author of a substantial number of works he is virtually forgotten despite his gift for imaginative and attractive tunes, perhaps because of his limited ability in developing his material.

WORKS
THEATRICAL

Les recruteurs (lyric comedy, 1), Rheinsberg, 1771
Le séjour du bonheur (comedy, 1), Berlin, 5 March 1773
Titus, Rheinsberg, 1774
La reine de Golconde, Rheinsberg, 1776; aria (Leipzig, 1790)
Windsor Castle, or The Fair Maid of Kent (opera, 2, W. Pearce), London, Covent Garden, 6 April 1795, collab. R. Spofforth; vocal score (London, 1795)
Scene in Pizarro (R. B. Sheridan) (London, c1800)

OTHER WORKS

Vocal: Hiskias (Blum), oratorio, 1779, *D-Bds*; Kantate zur Ehrung der Zarin Katharina, lost; Grosser Chor zur Feier der Genesung des Königs, 1789; 6 English Canzonets, 1v, pf (London, 1801); A Second Set of [6] English canzonets, S/T, pf (London, 1804); 6 Chansons, S, pf (London); glees and songs, 3–4vv, pf, pubd separately (London, 1803–6)

Inst: Vn Conc., D, arr. kbd by G. Masi (London, 1805); 2 caprices, vn, *c*1780, *US-NYp*; 6 sonates, vn, vc (Paris, 1783), as 6 Solos, op.1 (London, ?1783); Sonata, vn, vc, 1780–90, *B-Bc*; 6 Favorite Airs with Variations, vn, vc/pf, ?*c*1800 (London, 1806); Romance, vn, str orch, ?1810, *F-Pn*, ed. in Diletto musicale, cdlxxi (1971); 6 Variationen in Kirnberger: *Vermischte Musikalien* (Berlin, 1769); vn concs., str trios, str qts, Sonata a 4 for glass harmonica, all lost

Arrs.: J. Haydn: 12 London syms. (HI:93–104) for pf trio (London, n.d.), for fl, str qt, pf ad lib (London, ?1801); 9 other syms. (HI:48, 64, 73, 80, 82, 83, 88, 90, 92) for fl, str qt, pf ad lib; G. B. Viotti: 3 str trios, rev. Salomon (London, 1810)

BIBLIOGRAPHY

F. Rochlitz: 'Johann Peter Salomon', *AMZ*, xviii (1816), col.132
——: *Für Freunde der Tonkunst*, iii (Leipzig, 1830), 187ff
[P. Ayrton]: 'Memoir of Johann Peter Salomon', *The Harmonicon* (1830), 45
C. F. Pohl: *Mozart und Haydn in London* (Vienna, 1867/*R*1970)
C. F. Pohl and H. Botstiber: *Joseph Haydn* (Leipzig, 1875–1927/*R*)
H. C. R. Landon: *The Symphonies of Joseph Haydn* (London, 1955), esp. chap.12
——: *The Collected Correspondence and London Notebooks of Joseph Haydn* (London, 1959)
H. Unverricht: 'Die Simrock-Drucke von Haydns Londoner Sinfonien', *Studien zur Musikgeschichte des Rheinlandes*, ii, ed. H. Drux and others (Cologne, 1962), 235
A. Tyson: 'Salomon's Will', *Studien zur Musikgeschichte des Rheinlandes*, iii, ed. U. Eckart-Bäcker (Cologne, 1965), 43
H. Unverricht: 'Die Kompositionen Johann Peter Salomons: ein Überblick', *Studien zur Musikgeschichte des Rheinlandes*, iii, ed. U. Eckart-Bäcker (Cologne, 1965), 35
M. Braubach: 'Die Mitglieder der Hofmusik unter den vier letzten Kurfürsten von Köln', *Colloquium amicorum: Joseph Schmidt-Görg zum 70. Geburtstag* (Bonn, 1967), 52
H. Unverricht: 'Ein Notenbuch des Sir William Hamilton?', *Musicae scientiae collectanea: Festschrift Karl Gustav Fellerer* (Cologne, 1973), 604

HUBERT UNVERRICHT

Salomon, Joseph-François (*b* Toulon, baptized 3 April 1649; *d* Versailles, 5 March 1732). French composer and organist. According to La Borde he was a master of the viola da gamba and a pupil of Sainte-Colombe. He received his early musical training at the metropolitan church of St Sauveur in Aix-en-Provence, where he was a chorister from 1657 and later sub-deacon (1666) and organist (1669) when G. Poitevin was *maître de chapelle*. He abandoned his ecclesiastical career in 1671 and left Aix-en-Provence. From 1679 or 1680 he was at court in Paris as harpsichordist and organist to Queen Marie Thérèse and violist in the king's chamber music from 1713 (perhaps from 1706). In 1683 he entered the competition held by Louis XIV to replace Du Mont and Robert as *sous-maître de chapelle* of the royal chapel and got through to the second round. His operas, *Medée et Jason* and *Théonoé*, are in the tradition of Lully and Campra, while his published motets show the influence of Bernier's Italianate style.

A Salomon was *maître de chapelle* of Cahors Cathedral in 1750; a *Magnificat* and a motet by him survive (*F-Pn*), and he may also be the composer of a *De profundis* and an *In te Domine speravi* (*F-LYm*) usually ascribed to Joseph-François.

WORKS

Motets, 1–3vv, 2 vn, bc (Paris, 1703)
Medée et Jason (tragédie en musique, prol, 5, LaRoque), Paris, Opéra, 24 April 1713 (Paris, 1713)
Théonoé (tragédie en musique, prol, 5, LaRoque), Paris, Opéra, 13 Dec 1715 (Paris, 1715)
Motet attrib. Salomon: O quam suavis, 2vv, bc, *F-Pn*

BIBLIOGRAPHY

EitnerQ
Nouveau mercure galant (April 1683)
J.-B. Durey de Noinville and L.-A. Travenol: *Histoire du théâtre de l'Académie royale de musique* (Paris, 1757)
J.-B. de La Borde: *Essai sur la musique ancienne et moderne*, iii (Paris, 1780/*R*1972)
A. Gouirand: *La musique en Provence et le Conservatoire de Marseille* (Marseilles, 1908)
H.-A. Durand: 'Salomon, Joseph-François', *MGG*
M. Benoit: *Versailles et les musiciens du roi* (Paris, 1971)

Salomon, Jules Auguste. *See* GARCIN, JULES AUGUSTE.

Salomon, Karel. *See* SALMON, KAREL.

Salomon, (Naphtali) Siegfried (*b* Copenhagen, 3 Aug 1885; *d* Copenhagen, 29 Oct 1962). Danish cellist and composer. He studied with Rüdinger, Malling and Bondesen at the Copenhagen Conservatory (1899–1902), with Klengel in Leipzig and with Le Flem in Paris. In 1903 he joined the Tivoli Orchestra as solo cellist, and from 1907 he played in the Royal Orchestra, from 1924 as second solo cellist. He appeared as a soloist in Copenhagen, Paris and Stockholm, gave orchestral concerts with his own compositions in Copenhagen in 1916 and 1922, and took part in concerts of old music as a viol player. From 1937 he was chairman of the Private Chamber Music Society. His greatest success as a composer and conductor was with the opera *Leonora Christina*, a success due to the work's popular style and to the performance of the soprano Tenna Frederiksen Kraft in the title role.

WORKS
(*selective list*)

Operas: Leonora Christina (A. Barfoed), Copenhagen, Royal Theatre, 1926; 2 others
Orch: 2 syms., 1916, 1920; Vn Conc., 1916; 2 vc concs., 1922, 1958; Pf Conc., 1947; 2 suites, other pieces
Other works: 6 str qts, other chamber music, pf pieces, songs

TORBEN SCHOUSBOE

Salomon Orchestra. London amateur orchestra founded in 1963; *see* LONDON, §VI, 2(iii).

Salonen, Sulo (Nikolai) (*b* Pyhtää, 27 Feb 1899). Finnish composer. He studied the violin and the organ at the Helsinki Church Music Institute, graduating in 1929, and composition at the Helsinki Conservatory (1917–22, 1926–9). Thereafter he was singing master at the lyceum and organist in Jacobstad (now Pietarsaari) (1929–48) and then organist in Sibbo (now Sipoo) (1952–64). His strictly polyphonic music is almost exclusively for the church. One of the best works is the *Missa a cappella*, the first complete mass setting made in Finland and a piece that has been compared with the work of Distler, Pepping and Heiller. The Requiem successfully suits both concert and liturgy; although it occasionally approaches Stravinsky or Orff, Salonen's individuality dominates.

WORKS
(*selective list*)

Sacred choral: Passionskantat, 1942; Missa a cappella, 1957; Viisauden ylistys [In praise of wisdom], cantata, 1961; Requiem, solo vv, chorus, orch, 1962; 7 other cantatas, 29 short motets, 53 gospel motets, other pieces
Secular choruses, 8 solo songs, org pieces

Principal publisher: Fazer

HANNU ILARI LAMPILA

Salonica (Gk. Thessaloniki). City in Greece, the country's second musical centre after Athens; *see* GREECE, §III, 2.

Salpinx. A trumpet-like instrument of the ancient Greeks, consisting of a straight bronze tube of small diameter, shorter than the Roman tuba (*see* TUBA (ii)), with a bone mouthpiece and ending in a bell whose shape was variable.

It was altogether less frequently encountered in Greek musical life than was the tuba in Etruscan and Roman musical life: it was mentioned only twice by Homer and did not become at all common in Greek literature and art until the classical period. It was then depicted on a number of vases, usually being played by a soldier. In some cases the *phorbeia*, a headband often employed by AULOS players, was represented (see illustration). The 5th-century tragedians described the salpinx as *Tyrrhenos* (Etruscan) on several occasions. Bronze instruments were certainly important among the Etruscans, but these references cannot be taken as proof of the Etruscan origins of the instrument, since there are scattered references to it before the Greeks had contact with the Etruscans. The 5th-century authors also associated it with war, an area in which the instrument came to occupy a position second only to the aulos.

BIBLIOGRAPHY
C. Sachs: *The History Of Musical Instruments* (New York, 1940)
M. Wegner: *Griechenland*, Musikgeschichte in Bildern, ii/4 (Leipzig, 1963)

JAMES W. Mc KINNON

Salpinx player: detail from a Greek pottery vessel (c520 BC) (Museo Gregoriano Etrusco, Rome)

Salsa. A popular music style of Cuban origin. It evolved in the 1940s, drawing on elements of the *conjuntos*, dance bands of voices and trumpets (often in call-and-response) against a background of conga and bongo drums, and of the *charangas* in which flutes and fiddles played melodies of European derived dances such as the *danzón*. During the 1940s and 1950s salsa musicians moved to the eastern USA, particularly New York, where the style partly merged with jazz. It acquired a big-band swing style, and 'Latin jazz' developed as a combination of jazz structures and salsa rhythms. In the 1960s and 1970s salsa resumed a more basic Cuban style, as performers blended *conjunto* and *charanga* instrumentation, and replaced trumpets by trombones in *conjuntos*. Puerto Rican and later South American elements were also introduced. Salsa rhythms are based on Afro-American dances such as the bolero, cha cha cha, *guaguancó, guaracha, mambo* and *son montuno*. Layered polymetres and hemiolas are common, but the

Ex.1 *Clave*

distinctive feature underlying the whole structure is the two-bar *clave* (see ex.1). Each piece of music has three sections: a head (melodic) section; a *montuno* in which the lead singer improvises against a repeated vocal refrain; and a *mambo* section of contrasting riffs.

BIBLIOGRAPHY
A. Leon: *Musica folklorica Cubana* (Havana, 1964)
J. S. Roberts: 'Salsa', *Stereo Review* (March 1975)

JOHN STORM ROBERTS

Saltando (It.). SAUTILLÉ.

Saltarello (It.: 'little hop'; Fr. *pas de Brabant*; Ger. *Hopper Tanz, Hupfer Tanz*; Sp. *alta, alta danza*). A generic term for moderately rapid Italian dances, usually in triple metre and involving jumping movements.

The earliest known use of the term saltarello occurs in a Tuscan manuscript from the late 14th or early 15th century (*GB-Lbm* Add.29987, facs. in MSD, xiii, 1965), in which 15 textless monophonic pieces are included under the general heading 'Istampitta'. The last seven items of the group include four pieces labelled 'saltarello', along with a 'trotto' and the comparatively well-known dances *La Manfredina* and *Lamento di Tristano*. Like the *estampies* that precede them (*see* ESTAMPIE, §§1 and 2), the saltarellos consist of several repeated strains, each with a first and second ending (marked 'aperto' and 'chiuso' in the manuscript). Intriguingly the saltarellos do not share a common metre: two may be transcribed in 6/8 (ex.1), one in 3/4, and one in 4/4, leading Sachs (*Eine Weltgeschichte des Tanzes*, 1933; Eng. trans., 1937) to conclude that only the first three were true saltarellos, the last being assumed an example of the 15th-century duple-metre *quarternaria*, sometimes called 'saltarello tedesco'. His conclusion suggests a link between these four dances and the court dances of the 15th and 16th centuries that, however, has yet to be proved; as no choreographies from before the 1430s are known to survive, there is little evidence that these dances had anything in common with later saltarellos.

Ex.1 Saltarello, *GB-Lbm* Add.29987

In the 15th century the name 'saltarello' was applied to one of the dances of the bassadanza family (*see* BASSE DANSE), the most serious and elegant of contemporary Italian court dances. A number of Italian dancing-masters, including Domenico da Piacenza, Antonio Cornazano and Guglielmo Ebreo, described a method of deriving four progressively faster and more athletic dances from a single bassadanza cantus firmus; generally, the cantus firmus was written in either black breves or white semibreves, which had no mensural significance, and the musicians accompanying the dance were to 'rhythm' them according to the kind of dance required. For the bassadanza itself each cantus firmus note would be a perfect long, for the *quarternaria* or *saltarello tedesco* each would be an imperfect long, for the saltarello each would be a perfect breve, and for the PIVA each would be an imperfect breve. Ex.2 shows the application of these successive rhythms to the popular basse danse tune *La Spagna*. It is thought that accompanying musicians improvised two or more parts around the bassadanza tenor, but no corroborating sets of polyphonic 'rhythmed' bassadanzas are known to survive.

Ex.2 *La Spagna*

Little is known about the actual movements of the 15th-century saltarello. Saltarello movements were included in many 15th-century balli (*see* BALLO) as well as in the bassadanza itself, however, and it is from the extant choreographies for these pantomimic theatrical dances that our knowledge of them comes. Domenico da Piacenza's ballo choreography 'Verçeppe' (c1420), for example, includes a series of saltarello steps at the beginning and end, as well as interspersed elsewhere in the main part of the dance (ex.3).

Ex.3 Domenico da Piacenza: *Verçeppe* (*F-Pn*, fonds it. 972, 13)

As early as 1465 Cornazano had explained the mensural relationships of the bassadanza in reverse, using the saltarello as his point of reference; by the early 16th century, in fact, both extremes of the family had fallen into disuse, so that the most common dance group was some variant of the inner *quarternaria*–saltarello pair (*see* NACHTANZ). Although some saltarellos appeared as independent pieces in the growing number of instrumental music collections printed in the 16th century, most surviving examples are afterdances to *paduane*, as in Joan Ambrosio Dalza's *Intabulatura de lauto* of 1508 (*see* PAVAN) or passamezzos (*see* PASSAMEZZO). As afterdances saltarellos usually derived both melodic and harmonic material from their duple-metre partners, depending on them to such an extent that a musical saltarello was often little more than a metrical transformation of its pavan or passamezzo; the resulting dance had regular four-bar phrases and a clear sense of har-

monic direction. An important characteristic of the 16th-century saltarello was an ambiguity of metre such that a piece often seems in transcription to alternate between 6/8 and 3/4. Ex.4 shows the beginnings of a passamezzo and its saltarello. Performers should take care to note that all 16th-century saltarellos were intended to be played in triple metre, although many seem to be in duple in the original prints because of the use of *tactus* barring and a mensuration of ₵ (see Heartz's preface to CEKM, viii, 1965).

Ex.4 Passamezzo and saltarello
      from Giacomo Gorzanis: *Intabolatura di liuto*, ii (1561)
(a) pass'e mezo moderno

(b) saltarello del ditto

Both musically and choreographically there seems to have been little difference between the 16th-century saltarello and the French afterdance for the pavan, the GALLIARD. Both Thoinot Arbeau (*Orchésographie*, 1588) and Thomas Morley (*A Plaine and Easie Introduction to Practicall Musicke*, 1597) described the saltarello as an Italian galliard, Arbeau adding that in the Italian dance the feet were kept closer to the ground, so that the dance could be executed at a faster tempo. Indeed, pieces called saltarellos in Italian sources often appeared in French, Flemish and English sources as galliards (in German prints they were likely to be called *Hupfertanz*, *Spryngertanz*, *Proportz* or simply *Nachtanz*). Arbeau's description of the galliard's basic steps may be taken as partly applicable to the contemporary saltarello: the dance consisted of five steps taken to six crotchets; the first four steps were *grues* (the dancer springs on one foot while raising the other forward 'as if . . . to kick someone'), each ornamented by a *petit saut* ('little hop') on the weight-bearing foot, a *saut majeur* ('leap'), and a *posture* or rest. Although Arbeau suggested that each pattern began on a downbeat, it has been suggested elsewhere that the movements of both saltarellos and galliards actually began on an upbeat of a crotchet, so that the physical accent of the *saut majeur* would coincide with a metrical accent. Fabritio Caroso (*Il ballarino*, 1581, and *La nobiltà di dame*, 1600) included passages 'in saltarello' in certain of his ballettos, but here, too, the steps seem indistinguishable from those of the galliard. (*See also* CINQUE-PAS.)

The courtly saltarello waned in popularity in the 17th century, although some stylized versions have survived, such as Peter Philips's variation 'in saltarello' included among the ten divisions of the *Galiarda passamezzo* in the Fitzwilliam Virginal Book (ed. J. A. Fuller Maitland and W. Barclay Squire, Leipzig, 1899/*R*1963, i, 306) and Giovanni Picchi's saltarellos in *Intavolatura di balli d'arpicordo* (Venice, 2/1621). In 1703, Brossard (*Dictionnaire de musique*) described it as 'a kind of movement that is always jumping, which is almost always made in triple metre with a dotted note at the beginning of every bar'. He went on to say that the FORLANA, the SICILIANA and the English jig (*see* GIGUE (i)) were often said to be written 'in saltarello', apparently because of the prevalence of dotted patterns in their characteristic rhythms.

Towards the end of the 18th century, a popular folk-dance called the saltarello began to gain favour, first in Rome, then in the Italian regions of Ciociara (part of Latium), Romagna, Abruzzi and the Marches. This dance in 3/4 or 6/8 was generally danced alone or by one couple, and consisted of increasingly rapid hopping steps around an imaginary semicircle, accompanied by 'violent' arm movements; musical accompaniment was provided by guitars, tambourines, and often by the singing of onlookers (see 'Saltarello', *ES*). The two saltarellos included by Mendelssohn in the last movement in his Italian Symphony were probably based on tunes for the 19th-century folkdance, as were the saltarellos included in J. Perrot's ballet *Catarina ou La fille du bandit* (London, 1846) and in Arthur Saint-Leon's *Il saltarello* (Lisbon, 1854–6).

BIBLIOGRAPHY

BrownI
J. Wolf: 'Die Tänze des Mittelalters', *AMw*, i (1918–19), 38
O. Gombosi: 'About Dance and Dance Music in the Late Middle Ages', *MQ*, xxvii (1941), 289
M. Bukofzer: 'A Polyphonic Basse Dance of the Renaissance', *Studies in Medieval and Renaissance Music* (New York, 1950), esp. 191
L. Moe: *Dance Music in Printed Italian Lute Tablatures (1507–1611)* (diss., Harvard U., 1956)
G. Reaney: 'The Manuscript British Museum, Additional 29987 (Lo)', *MD*, xii (1958), 67
O. Kinkeldey: 'Dance Tunes of the Fifteenth Century', *Instrumental Music*, ed. D. G. Hughes (Cambridge, Mass., 1959), 3, 89–152
L. Moe: 'Saltarello', 'Piva', *MGG*
W. Apel: *Geschichte der Orgel- und Klaviermusik bis 1700* (Kassel, 1967; Eng. trans., rev. 1972)
I. Brainard: 'Bassedanse, Bassedanza and Ballo in the 15th Century', *Dance History Research*, ed. J. Kealiinohomoku (New York, 1970), 64
——: *Three Court Dances of the Early Renaissance* (New York, 1971) [incl. transcr. of 'Verçeppe']
——: 'Fifteenth- and Early Sixteenth-century Court Dances', *Institute of Court Dances*, ed. J. de Laban (New York, 1972), 1
MEREDITH ELLIS LITTLE

Saltarello Choir. London choir founded in 1965; *see* LONDON, §VI, 3(ii).

Saltato (It.). SAUTILLÉ.

Saltellando (It.: 'skipping along'). A rarely used term; it is found in a treatise of Francesco Rognoni Taeggio (*Selva*, 1620), and may mean a species of slurred staccato, but it is not clear whether the bow leaves the string or stays on it.

Salter, Humphrey (*fl* 1683–1718). English music publisher, editor and composer. His chief claim to fame is as the author of *The Genteel Companion; Being exact Directions for the Recorder with a Collection of the Best and Newest Tunes and Grounds Extant* which was published in London in 1683 by Richard Hunt and Humphrey Salter 'at the Lute in St. Pauls Church-Yard'. The title-page tells us that the music was 'carefully composed and gathered by Humphry Salter'.

As a publisher Salter's name appears in association with John Walsh, Henry Playford and others. The *Daily Courant* for 20 March 1718 carried an advertisement for 'a consort for the benefit of Mr. Salter' at the Academy in Chancery Lane the following day.

EDGAR HUNT

Salter, Lionel (Paul) (*b* London, 8 Sept 1914). English harpsichordist, pianist, conductor, writer on music and administrator. He first studied under Yorke Trotter and Stanley Chapple (1923–31). After a year at the RCM he went to Cambridge, where he studied under Edward Dent and Boris Ord (1932–5; BA 1935, MusB 1936); he then had a further year's study at the RCM. He was a pupil of Constant Lambert for conducting and James Ching and Arthur Benjamin for the piano. He then became known as a performer, especially on the radio, and also worked as a music assistant in BBC television. During war service he was guest conductor (1943–4) of the Radio France SO; returning to the BBC in 1945, he became assistant conductor of the BBC Theatre Orchestra and in 1948 music supervisor of the BBC European Service. After holding various other posts, he moved in 1956 to television as head of music, where he did much to stimulate the television presentation of opera, ballet and concerts and was influential, internationally as well as in Britain, in the establishment of techniques for music programmes. In 1963 he became head of opera (responsible for both sound and television) and in 1967 became assistant controller of music. He retired from the BBC in 1974, and from 1972 to 1976 was opera coordinator and producer for the European Broadcasting Union.

Besides his administrative work, Salter is active as a harpsichordist (he has made several records with the Vienna Capella Academica and other ensembles) and writer: his field of knowledge is wide, with Iberian and Latin American music and keyboard music representing his special studies. He has contributed chapters to many collective works and writes regularly in periodicals (including, since 1948, the *Gramophone*), earning respect for his clear, strongly argued views. He has also been active as a conductor (particularly for films and television), lecturer, adjudicator, broadcaster, and composer and arranger (notably of music for radio plays). Salter has also made many opera translations, for publication and for performance, and has prepared performing editions of many Baroque works, among them Cavalli's *Erismena*, Lully's *Alceste* and sonatas by various composers.

WRITINGS

Going to a Concert (London, 1950)
Going to the Opera (London, 1955)
The Musician and his World (London, 1963)
with J. Bornoff: *Music and the 20th-century Media* (Florence, 1972)
STANLEY SADIE

Saltere (Fr.). PSALTERY.

Salterello (It.). JACK.

Salterio. (1) (It., Sp.) PSALTERY; *see also* DULCIMER.

(2) A name used in Aragon for the TAMBOURIN DE BÉARN.

Saltzmann-Stevens, Minnie (*b* Bloomington, Ill., 17 March 1874; *d* Milan, 25 Jan 1950). American soprano. After singing as a contralto in Chicago churches she went to Paris to study with Jean De Reszke (1905–9). He recommended her to Covent Garden, where she made her début in January 1909 as Brünnhilde in the English *Ring* conducted by Richter. Her intelligence of gesture, declamation, and the general smoothness and finish of her singing created a highly satisfactory impression. She sang at Covent Garden (1910–13) as Sieglinde, Brünnhilde and Isolde; at Bayreuth in 1911 and 1913 as Kundry and Sieglinde; and in Chicago (1911–14). Her highly promising career came to a premature close through illness.

HERMAN KLEIN/HAROLD ROSENTHAL

Salut (Fr.). BENEDICTION.

Salva, Tadeáš (*b* Lúčky pri Ružomberku, north Slovakia, 22 Oct 1937). Slovak composer. He studied at the Žilina Conservatory (1953–8), the Bratislava High School for Music and the Państwowej Wyższej Szkoły Muzycznej in Katowice. Appointments followed as head of music broadcasting for Košice radio (1965) and as producer for Czech television in Bratislava (1968). His style was decisively influenced by the Polish school (he was a pupil of Szabelski and Lutosławski), so timbral and rhythmic elements are to the fore. He works with blocks of characteristic interval structure, density and timbre, also employing aleatory and polymetric techniques. In his vocal writing song is combined with rhythmic recitation.

WORKS
(selective list)

Orch: Ideae, chamber orch, 1964; Symfónia lásky [Sym. of love], 1966; Musica per archi, 1970; Pf Conc., 1970, Burlesca, vn, orch, 1970
Vocal: Canticum Zachariae, S, chamber orch, 1964; Conc., cl, reciter, 4 solo vv, perc, 1965; Requiem aeternam, reciter, chorus, 1967; Litaniae lauretanae, chorus, 1968; Mša glagolskaja, 1969; Óda 70, 1970; Margita a Besná, television opera, 1971; Svadobná balada [Wedding ballad], 1v, chorus, insts, 1972; 2 Italian Madrigals, 1972; Vojna a svet [War and world] (Mayakovsky), 1972; Elegies, speaker, S, chorus, chamber orch, 1974
Inst: 7 Pf Pieces, 1959; 3 str qts, 1961, 1962, 1970; Canti lineae, ens, 1963; Rhapsody, org, 1966; Ballad, 2 cl, 1974
Tape: Alikvoty, 1970

Principal publishers: Opus, Slovenský Hudobný Fond

LADISLAV BURLAS

Salvador [Bahia]. Brazilian city, capital of the state of Bahia. Officially named Salvador da Bahia de todos os Santos, but commonly known as Bahia, it was the capital of the Portuguese colony until 1763, when Rio de Janeiro became the colonial administrative centre. It was the landing place of Álvares Cabral in 1500, the first capital, the first episcopal see and the most active centre of the slave trade, and its importance is paramount for early Brazilian music history. It became a see in 1550 and an archbishopric in 1676. Music at the cathedral occupied a prominent place on special occasions as well as in the regular services. The position of *mestre de capela* was created in 1559 and held by Bartolomeu Pires (*c*1560–86), Francisco Borges da Cunha (1608–*c*1660), Joaquim Corrêa (1661–*c*1665), Antonio de Lima Carseres (1666–9), João de Lima (1670s), Frei Agostinho de Santa Mônica (*c*1683–*c*1703) and Caetano de Mello de Jesus (early 18th century). Mello Jesus wrote a recitative and aria for soprano and strings, dated 2 July 1759, the earliest known Brazilian art-music composition. The vernacular text and the non-religious character of the piece suggest that cathedral musicians participated in secular musical life, as occurred in Spanish America. The post of organist at the Bahia cathedral was established in 1559, first held by Pedro da Fonseca (1560). Many other organists were active in the various churches and convents of Bahia by the end of the 16th century, particularly the Benedictine monks of the Mosteiro de S Bento. Nicolau de Miranda was organist at the church of Misericordia and the Santa Casa de Misericordia in the early 18th century.

Among the native musicians of the 17th century, several priests are praised in Barbosa Machado's *Biblioteca lusitana* (Lisbon, 1747), including Eusébio da Soledade de Matos (1629–92), brother of the famous poet Gregório de Matos. Church music reached its peak at Bahia during the 18th century. The St Cecilia brotherhood (a union of musicians) was established there in 1785 and was active into the next century; among its members were the native composers Damião Barbosa de Araújo (1778–1856) and José Pereira Rebouças (1789–1843).

The first opera houses in Bahia appeared in the early 18th century. The short-lived Teatro da Câmara Municipal (1728) was followed by the Casa da Opera da Praia (1760) and the Teatro do Guadalupe. During the first half of the 19th century the Teatro São João (inaugurated in 1812) became the most important centre for visiting artists and lyric companies. Other lesser theatres opened during the 19th century, such as Ginásio Bonfim (1867) and Politeama Baiano (1882). The São João theatre was burnt down in 1922 and was not replaced until the 1950s, when the Teatro Castro Alves was built.

Although music was taught in the Bahia area from the early 17th century, it was only in 1818 that King João VI, then resident at Rio de Janeiro, created a chair of music to which he appointed José J. de Souza Negrão. He was succeeded in 1832 by Domingos da Rocha Mussurunga, who proposed the first local conservatory of music. With the foundation of the Academia de Belas Artes (1877) music instruction came under the supervision of the state of Bahia. The official conservatory opened in 1897, was reorganized a year later by Silvio Deolindo Fróes, and a few years later became the Instituto de Música da Bahia. It remained the main educational institution until 1934, when the Escola Normal de Música (Escola de Música da Bahia from 1951) was founded under Petro Jatobá. The music educationist Zulmira Silvany contributed to the institute's excellence. The third important music school, called Seminários Livres de Música, was founded in 1954 at the University of Bahia. Under the direction of the German composer Hans J. Koellreutter (1954–63) it became a dynamic centre for new music during the 1960s; the Grupo de Compositores da Bahia was organized there in 1966 through the efforts of Ernt Widmer, and included young composers such as Jamary Oliveira and Lindembergue Cardoso.

The first symphony orchestra in Salvador was organized in 1944 by Father Luiz Gonzaga Mariz and lasted until about 1952. Several instrumental and vocal ensembles as well as a symphony orchestra are active at the Federal University of Bahia.

Concert-promoting associations have included the

Sociedade de Cultura Artística da Bahia (SCAB), founded in 1945, and the Cruzada da Boa Vontade (1956), both merged into the Associação Baiana de Arte in 1958.

BIBLIOGRAPHY

G. de Melo: *A música no Brasil* (Rio de Janeiro, 1908)

R. Almeida: *História da música brasileira* (Rio de Janeiro, 1942)

R. Duprat: 'A música na Bahia colonial', *Revista de história*, lxi (1965), 93

C. Xavier: *A música em 50 anos* (Salvador, 1965)

R. Stevenson: 'Some Portuguese Sources for Early Brazilian Music History', *Yearbook, Inter-American Institute for Musical Research*, iv (1968), 1

H. Machado Brasil: *A música na cidade do Salvador* (Salvador, 1969)

GERARD BÉHAGUE

Salvador-Daniel. *See* DANIEL, FRANCISCO SALVADOR.

Salvadori, Andrea (*b* 1591; *d* Florence, 1635). Poet of the Tuscan court. He wrote librettos from 1616 to 1634 for entertainments set to music by such composers as Peri and Marco da Gagliano. His best-known text is that for Gagliano's opera *La flora*, first performed at the celebrations for the wedding of Margherita de' Medici and Odoardo Farnese in 1628. Domenica Costantini, wife of the Italian comic actor Costantino Costantini, later translated this libretto into French for performances by his troupe of actors in Paris; the translation was printed in 1669. The Italian theatrical company I Comici took Salvadori's libretto for the opera *Lo sposalizio di Medoro e di Angelica*, set by Peri and Gagliano in 1619, and performed it as a play in 1616. Francesca Caccini, a leading composer in Florence, asked him to write the libretto for her opera *La liberazione di Ruggiero* (1625), but he refused in such a way as to lead to a professional feud with her, which, Andrea Cavalcanti reported in his *Memorie*, diminished Salvadori's reputation at the Medici court. Martin Opitz published a German translation of the *Istoria di Iudit* that Salvadori wrote in 1626 for Gagliano (*Judith*, Breslau, 1635).

BIBLIOGRAPHY

A. Solerti: *Musica, ballo e drammatica alla corte medicea dal 1600 al 1637* (Florence, 1905/R1968)

CAROLYN RANEY

Salvadori, Angelo (*fl* 1618–28). Italian music printer. He does not appear to be related to the contemporary librettist of the same name. He worked in Vicenza and is most important for Sabbatini's *Regola facile* (1628), Monte's *Vago fior* (probably printed in the mid-1620s) and for a series of five volumes of canzonettas (*RISM* 1618[17], 1620[22], 1622[20], 1623[11], c1625[12]) of which at least three went into second editions.

STANLEY BOORMAN

Salvai, Maria Maddalena (*fl* 1716–28). Italian soprano. In 1716 she was in the service of the Landgrave of Kassel at a salary of 1250 thalers. She sang at Darmstadt in the winter of 1718–19, and the following spring was engaged for Dresden at 2000 thalers. In March 1720 Senesino wrote to Riva in London, 'she has a most beautiful voice, a good figure and enough talent for the purpose, on which you could obtain more exact advice from Mr Handel'. She joined the Royal Academy in London as second soprano to Durastanti in September 1720, at the same time as Senesino and Berselli, and remained for two seasons, making her King's Theatre début as Polissena (with new arias) in the revival of Handel's *Radamisto* on 28 December. She sang in Amadei's arrangement of Orlandini's *Arsace*, the pasticcio *Odio ed amore*, and the first performances of the composite *Muzio Scevola* (Fidalma), Handel's *Floridante* (Rossane) and Bononcini's *Crispo* and *Griselda*, as well as a number of concerts, at one of which she took part in a cantata by A. Scarlatti. She had a high tessitura and a compass of *e'* to *b♭''*, but seems not to have been an exceptional singer. She appeared in two operas at Venice in 1722–3, three at Naples (including Vinci's *Ernelinda* and Hasse's *Sesostrate*) in 1726–7, and two at Florence in 1727–8. There is a caricature of her by A. M. Zanetti in the Cini collection (*I-Vgc*).

WINTON DEAN

Salvatore, Giovanni (*b* Castelvenere, nr. Benevento, early 17th century; *d* probably Naples, ?1688). Italian composer and organist. He was almost certainly a pupil of Giovanni Maria Sabino and Erasmo Bartoli ('Padre Raimo') at the Conservatorio della Pietà dei Turchini at Naples. Later he became a priest. In 1641 he was organist at S Severino, Naples, and later organist and *maestro di cappella* at S Lorenzo. From 1662 to 1673 he taught at the Conservatorio della Pietà dei Turchini. During his last years he was rector and *maestro di cappella* at the Conservatorio dei Poveri di Gesù Cristo; as his successor was appointed in 1688 he probably died in that year. It was once thought that he taught Alessandro Scarlatti but this is unlikely to be true.

According to Liberati and Pitoni, Salvatore was greatly esteemed during his lifetime. Liberati even placed him above Frescobaldi on the grounds that he could compose fine vocal works without confusing their style with organ music. The vocal music has not yet been critically investigated. The organ works in the *Ricercari*, written in open score, demonstrate much technical skill. They are in the southern Italian tradition of the early 17th century as represented by Mayone, Trabaci and Frescobaldi, and though they do not radically depart from it in style or form, they are more tonal, close-knit and concisely organized. Salvatore occasionally used *durezze* and *ligature* (chromaticism, sharp dissonances and striking harmonic progressions) and the unpredictable, virtuoso, rhapsodic style associated with the Neapolitans and the Romans. The volume contains eight contrapuntally interesting ricercares, one on each of the eight tones, with two, three or four subjects and their permutations. In no.4 the four subjects, having been treated at length in their original forms, appear in turn in traditional cantus firmus settings; in no.8 the hymn *Iste confessor* is presented as a cantus firmus in each voice. Despite its title the volume also includes other music. In three canzonas the opening section is repeated at the end; a fourth is a set of contrapuntal variations on the *bergamasca* melody, reaching a brilliant concluding virtuoso climax. Three organ masses include Kyrie settings based on the melodies *Orbis factor*, *Cunctipotens genitor* and *Cum jubilo*; brief versets in imitative or toccata style are intended for alternation with a choir.

WORKS

Edition: *G. Salvatore: Collected Keyboard Works*, ed. B. Hudson, CEKM, iii (1964) [H]

(*principal sources I-Nc, Nf, many autograph*)

VOCAL

2 psalms, 5vv, 1645[1]

Missa defunctorum, 4vv, org

Mass and Vespers, 4vv

3 masses, 1 dated 1640, 4vv, 2 vn, org
Introits, 4 choirs
Magnificat, 5vv, 2 vn
2 litanies, 5vv, 2 choirs
Audite coeli, 4 choirs; Beati omnes, 5vv; Canticum trium puerorum, 4 choirs, 2 vn, 1657; Confitebor, 2 choirs; Credidi, 4 choirs; Expurgat Deus, 6vv; In monte Oliveti; Laudate pueri, 5vv, vns; Nisi Dominus, 5vv; O quam dulcis, 3vv, org; Portae coeli, 9vv, insts; Salve regina, 5vv, 2 vn; Stabat mater dolorosa, 5vv, org
Other masses, introits, responsories, motets, psalms, hymns

2 secular arias, 1v, bc

KEYBOARD
Ricercari a 4 voci, canzoni francesi, toccate e versi per rispondere nelle messe con l'organo al choro, libro I (Naples, 1641); H
2 ricercari a 2, 1665[5]
Capriccio del primo tono, 2 correnti, durezze e ligature, 2 toccate; H

BIBLIOGRAPHY
A. Liberati: *Lettera in risposta . . . ad una del Sig. Ovidi Persapegi* (Rome, 1685)
G. O. Pitoni: *Notitia de contrapuntisti e de compositori di musica* (MS, *I-Rvat*)
W. Apel: 'Die süditalienische Clavierschule des 17. Jahrhunderts', *AcM*, xxxiv (1962), 128
U. Prota-Giurleo: 'Due campioni della scuola musicale napoletana del XVII secolo', *L'organo*, iii (1962), 115
W. Apel: *Geschichte der Orgel- und Klaviermusik bis 1700* (Kassel, 1967; Eng. trans., rev. 1972)

BARTON HUDSON

Salvayre, (Gervais Bernard) [Gaston] (*b* Toulouse, 24 June 1847; *d* St-Ague, nr. Toulouse, 17 May 1916). French composer and critic. He was a pupil at the Toulouse Conservatory and later the Paris Conservatoire, where he studied with Marmontel (piano), Benoist (organ), Bazin (harmony) and Thomas (composition). He won the *premier prix* for organ in 1868 and, after five unsuccessful attempts, the Prix de Rome in 1872 with *Calypso*. His subsequent stay in Rome was quite productive; on his return to Paris he presented an *Ouverture symphonique* (1874), ballet music for the revival of Grisar's *Les amours du diable* (1874) and the *symphonie biblique La résurrection* (1876, retitled *La vallée de Josaphat* in 1882). In 1877 he was appointed chorus master of the Opéra-Populaire at the Théâtre du Châtelet; in the same year he made an inauspicious operatic début with *Le bravo* and presented a ballet, *Fandango*. Later stage works, including *Richard III* (1883), *Egmont* (1886) and Dumas' *La dame de Monsoreau* (commissioned by the Opéra, 1888), did little to advance his reputation as an opera composer, yet he composed several more dramatic pieces. His other compositions include major choral works, such as the *Stabat mater* (1877) and his last work, the *fresque musicale Sainte-Geneviève* (performed posthumously at Monte Carlo, 1919), as well as numerous songs and some chamber and piano music. Salvayre was a music critic for *Gil Blas* for many years. In 1880 he was made a Chevalier of the Légion d'honneur.

WORKS
(printed works published in Paris unless otherwise indicated)

STAGE
(first performed in Paris, unless otherwise indicated)
Calypso (dramatic scene, V. Roussy), 1872 (1872)
Ballet music for A. Grisar: Les amours du diable, rev. version, Théâtre du Châtelet, 18 Nov 1874
Le bravo (opera, 4, E. Blavet), Théâtre-Lyrique, 18 April 1877, vocal score (1877), excerpts pubd separately
Fandango (ballet, 1), Opéra, 26 Nov 1877, arr. pf (1878)
Richard III (opera, 4, Blavet, after Shakespeare), St Petersburg, Théâtre Marie, 21 Dec 1883, in It. as Riccardo III; original version, Nice, 29 Jan 1891 (1883)
Egmont (drame lyrique, 4, A. Wolff, A. Millaud, after Goethe), Opéra-Comique, 6 Dec 1886, vocal score (1886), excerpts pubd separately

La dame de Monsoreau (opera, 5, A. Maquet, after A. Dumas), Opéra, 30 Jan 1888, vocal score (1888)
Solange (opéra comique, 3, A. Aderer), Opéra-Comique, 10 March 1909 (1909)
?4 other stage works, unpubd

OTHER WORKS
Sacred: La résurrection, symphonie biblique, 1876, retitled La vallée de Josaphat, 1882 (1882); Stabat mater, solo vv, choir, orch (1877); 2 psalms, solo vv, choir, orch: Super flumina Babylonis, vocal score (?n.d.), In exitu Israel, unpubd; other works
Other vocal: Sainte-Geneviève (Aderer), fresque musicale, perf. 1919 (1921); c85 songs
Orch: Ouverture symphonique, 1874; other works
Chamber and pf works, some pubd

JOHN TREVITT

Salve regina (Lat.: 'Hail, queen'). One of the four Marian antiphons. It is now sung at the end of Compline from Trinity Sunday to the Saturday before the first Sunday of Advent. The earliest manuscript source of the antiphon (*D-KA*, Cod. Augiensis LV, f.42*v*, col.1) is believed to date from the 11th century. Although Bernard of Clairvaux, Peter the Venerable and Hermannus Contractus have at various times been cited as its author, both the text and melody were probably composed by Adhemar of Pui. One of its earliest liturgical uses was as a processional chant, as decreed by Peter the Venerable in Cluny in 1135. After 1218 the Cistercians adopted it as a daily processional chant, and from 1230 it was sung each day after Compline by Dominican orders.

During the Renaissance, the immense popularity of the *Salve regina* influenced the development of lay religious societies dedicated to the worship of the Virgin. One of the most brilliant of these *Salve* confraternities was the Marian brotherhood in Antwerp. According to their charter of 1482, the confraternity was organized to celebrate a daily devotional service between five and six o'clock in the evening. This *Salve* service employed four singers, 12 choirboys, a choirmaster, an organist and a priest, and was preceded by the ringing of the church bells. The confraternity included among its members Obrecht and Noel Bauldeweyn. Dufay was a member of the *Salve* chapel of St Géry at Cambrai, and Pierre de La Rue of the Marian brotherhood at 's-Hertogenbosch.

The importance of *Salve regina* within the *Salve* service is mirrored in the great number of polyphonic settings of the antiphon from the Renaissance. English composers of the 15th century wrote numerous settings, as did those 16th-century Spanish composers who were influenced by the Netherlands court of Charles V. More than 127 polyphonic settings can be attributed to Netherlands composers active between 1425 and 1550. All these exhibit a strong dependence on the cantus firmus, and their structural divisions generally reflect the textual divisions. A number of polyphonic compositions for voices set only the even-numbered verses (i.e. *Vita dulcedo*; *Ad te suspiramus*; *Et Jesum*; *O pia*), leaving the odd-numbered verses to be sung in plainchant. The reverse is true of the compositions for organ, which usually include only the odd-numbered verses (*Salve regina*; *Ad te clamamus*; *Eia ergo*; *O clemens*; *O dulcis*). Netherlands composers represented by vocal settings include Alexander Agricola (three), Gombert (four), La Rue (six), Josquin (two), Obrecht (three) and Ockeghem (two). Composers of settings for organ include Paul Hofhaimer, Hans Kotter (two) and Arnolt Schlick.

See also ANTIPHON and MOTET, §II.

BIBLIOGRAPHY

S. Beissel: *Geschichte der Marienverehrung während des Mittelalters* (Freiburg, 1909)

J. de Valois: 'En marge d'une antienne: le Salve Regina', *Tribune de Saint-Gervais*, xvii (1911), 25

——: 'Les auteurs présumés du Salve Regina', *Tribune de Saint-Gervais*, xvii–xviii (1911–12), 226

J. Maier: *Studien zur Geschichte der Marienantiphon Salve Regina* (Regensburg, 1939)

J. Ingram: *The Polyphonic Salve Regina, 1425–1550* (diss., U. of North Carolina, 1973)

JEANNINE S. INGRAM

Salvi, Antonio (*d* Florence, 1742). Italian librettist. He was the last of the important group of Florentine physician-librettists which included G. A. Cicognini. His role in the creation of *opera seria* is not generally recognized.

Salvi's earliest recorded libretto was performed in Florence in 1696, and three years later he replaced G. C. Villifranchi as physician and librettist to Ferdinando de' Medici. From 1701 to 1710 he provided texts for most of the *opere serie* performed at Pratolino; premières of his works are also recorded at the Cocomero Theatre, Florence, up to 1715. Thereafter they occurred primarily in Venice, suggesting that he moved; his last recorded libretto was written for Venice in 1727.

Salvi wrote some 25 librettos, mainly tragedies, many of them drawn from French classical drama by Corneille, Racine, Capistron and others. He also wrote at least seven intermezzos. His works were set by leading Italian composers of the era, including A. Scarlatti, Perti, Vivaldi and Galuppi. The two most often used were *Amore e maesta* (1715; sometimes set as *Arsace*) and *Astiannate* (1701; *Andromaca*).

BIBLIOGRAPHY

R. L. and N. W. Weaver: *A Chronology of Florentine Theater 1590–1750* (Detroit, 1976)

ROBERT LAMAR WEAVER

Salvi, Victor (*b* Chicago, 4 March 1921). American harp maker of Italian descent. He was the youngest son of the immigrant Venetian instrument maker Rudolfo Salvi (1865–1943). Three of Rudolfo's children became professional harpists, including Victor, who began his career in 1938. After service in the US Navy, he opened a harp repair shop in Chicago, moving to New York in 1949. In 1955, he moved to Italy, where he established a harp factory first in Genoa, and later in larger premises at Vignole, Borghera. In 1969 he opened a shop in London for repairs and world-wide distribution of his harps.

The traditional Italian skills in carving and veneering are used to excellent effect on Salvi's seven styles of harps. 43 separate layers of wood, laminated and compressed by a special process, give the neck of the harp the exceptional strength and rigidity necessary to maintain stability of pitch under different climatic conditions. Salvi attributes the even sonority of his instruments to the unique single-shell construction of their bodies. The use of materials such as stainless steel for the linkage system and nylon bearings for the rotating studs ensures a mechanism which is not subject to corrosion and which does not need lubrication. In 1970 Victor Salvi was awarded the first prize at the exhibition of Italian craftsmanship (Mostra del Artigianato) held in Florence.

ANN GRIFFITHS

Salvini-Donatelli, Fanny [Lucchi, Francesca] (*b* Florence, ?1815; *d* Milan, June 1891). Italian soprano. She made her début at the Teatro Apollo, Venice, in 1839 in *Il barbiere di Siviglia*. Engaged in Vienna 1842–3, she sang in *Nabucco* under Verdi's supervision. She created the role of Violetta in *La traviata* at La Fenice, Venice (6 March 1853), and was blamed indirectly for the work's failure, supposedly because she weighed 'precisely 130 kilograms'. After engagements throughout Europe, she sang in Paris and at Drury Lane in London in 1858. She retired the following year but made further appearances in 1865. Berlioz and the London critics esteemed her voice, which was expressive, flexible and lyric and which accommodated itself to dramatic roles.

BIBLIOGRAPHY

N. Bazzetta di Vemenia: *Le cantanti italiane dell'ottocento* (Novara, 1945), 120

CHARLES A. JAHANT

Salviucci, Giovanni (*b* Rome, 26 Oct 1907; *d* Rome, 4 Sept 1937). Italian composer. A pupil of Respighi and Casella, he also read law at Rome University. Subsequently he taught counterpoint and fugue at the Istituto M. Clementi in Rome, and wrote music criticism for the *Rassegna nazionale*. His early death cut short a career so promising that some believe he would have ranked with Dallapiccola and Petrassi. The earliest important works bear the imprints of both Salviucci's teachers (for example, the opening theme of the *Sinfonia italiana*'s Allegro recalls Respighi's *Concerto gregoriano*); yet they already have a lyrical spontaneity which is his own. In the *Sinfonia da camera*, the most successful of these early works, he achieved a lithe, springy, neo-madrigalian exuberance, deploying his instrumental forces with a mastery not found in all his compositions.

The two orchestral pieces of 1934, though perhaps less perfectly realized, branch out in a new direction – they are fiercer, more chromatic, more rugged in rhythm. Salviucci now revealed a growing affinity with the more tense, involuted aspects of Casella's art that also influenced the young Petrassi. Several passages (e.g. the extraordinary end to the 'Introduzione' of the *Introduzione, passacaglia e finale*, with jagged melodic fragments set against a hypnotically reiterated G on the strings) have the visionary uniqueness of genius. It is, however, in his last two works that Salviucci gave the fullest indication of his potential. *Alcesti* is a choral piece comparable in stature with Petrassi's *Psalm ix* or Dallapiccola's *Cori di Michelangelo*, without resembling either. The firmly linear, dissonant yet still basically diatonic fabric retains certain similarities to Casella, but the many incidental chromatic inflections, often producing poignant false relations, are unlike anything else, and ideally suited to the text. Even more original, though lighter, is the Serenata, whose debt to Casella is limited to a few component melodic and rhythmic details, and to the medium, clearly suggested by the older composer's work of the same title. The result is wholly personal – not least in the first movement, abundant in its outpouring of unpredictable yet logical images and textures, and with a nervous energy which carries all before it.

WORKS
(selective list)

Ov., c♯, 1932; Sinfonia italiana, 1932; Str Qt, 1932, unpubd; Salmo di Davide, S/T, pf, 1933, arr. S/T, small orch, 1934; Sinfonia da camera, 17 insts, 1933; Introduzione, orch, 1934; Introduzione,

passacaglia e finale, orch, 1934; Alcesti (after Euripides), chorus, orch, 1936; Serenata, ww qt, tpt, str qt, 1937
Early works: several songs, chamber pieces, sym. poems, etc

Principal publishers: Carisch, Ricordi

BIBLIOGRAPHY
'Voci aggiunti a un dizionario dei musicisti italiani contemporanei: G. Salviucci', *RaM*, ix (1936), 286 [incl. list of works to 1936]
F. Ballo: 'Musicisti del nostro tempo: Giovanni Salviucci', *RaM*, x (1937), 7
A. Casella: 'Giovanni Salviucci', *RMI*, xli (1937), 610
G. Gavazzeni: 'Cronache musicali', *Letteratura*, iii/2 (Florence, 1939), 184 [on *Alcesti*]
M. Rinaldi: 'L'ideale artistico di Giovanni Salviucci', *All'ombra dell' Augusteo* (Rome, 1944), 207
F. d'Amico: 'Giovanni Salviucci vent'anni dopo', *I casi della musica* (Milan, 1962), 171
G. Arledler: *Prospettive critiche su Giovanni Salviucci* (diss., U. of Bologna, 1974)

JOHN C. G. WATERHOUSE

Salway, Thomas (*b* c1706; *d* London, 6 April 1743). English tenor and actor. He received his musical education as a treble at Cannons. He was a popular singer, mainly in Rich's company at Lincoln's Inn Fields and Covent Garden, from 1724 until shortly before his death. He sang between the acts, in ballad operas and afterpieces, burlesques and pantomimes and had a number of acting roles in them. He created the title role in Gay's ballad opera *Achilles*, in which he was disguised as a woman, and also had other petticoat roles. He played the hero Moore of Moore Hall in Lampe's burlesque opera *The Dragon of Wantley*. In March 1731 he was Damon in the first public performance of Handel's *Acis and Galatea*, and repeated this part at Oxford in 1733.

OLIVE BALDWIN, THELMA WILSON

Salzburg. Austrian city. It grew up around an 8th-century Benedictine monastery, and from then until 1806 it was the seat of a series of prince-archbishops, whose court was the centre of the city's musical life. It is specially noted in the 20th century for its festival.

1. To 1500. 2. 16th century. 3. 17th and 18th centuries. 4. 19th and 20th centuries. 5. The Salzburg Festival.

1. TO 1500. The two most important centres for the development of liturgical chant in Salzburg and its missionary districts were the Abbey of St Peter, founded by St Rupert, and the cathedral, founded by St Virgil in 774; the cathedral and its school soon became the centre of the diocese. Under the first archbishop of Salzburg, Arno, the cathedral school, then the 'nucleus of spiritual life in southern Germany' (Spies, 1938), enjoyed its first period of excellence. The numerous manuscripts written in Salzburg (probably 150) certainly included liturgical books; the earliest musical sources from St Peter's, of which only fragments survive, are in St Gall notation, while those of the cathedral follow the Messine tradition. In 798 Archbishop Arno, who was a friend of Alcuin, laid down in his *Instructio pastoralis* for the cathedral that services were to be held 'following the tradition of the Romans'. According to the evidence of the Salzburg statutes of 799, congregational hymns were permitted in addition to the psalm settings and songs sung by the monks. There is no evidence of an independent school of musical theory and of the practice of polyphony until the late Middle Ages. Isolated records from the 14th, 15th and early 16th centuries survive (*RISM* B IV/2–3), mostly on the inside of the covers of bound liturgical manuscripts. The presence in the city of resident instrument makers, bell founders and

musicians indicates a lively and varied musical life in the 12th and 13th centuries. In 1223 Archbishop Eberhard II, who held office from 1200 to 1246, created the position of Kantor for one of the cathedral canons, who became responsible for teaching singing. Although 'her bischof Eberhart' is addressed in the 'Winter songs' of Neidhart von Reuental, there is no definite record of the latter's engagement at his court, although this has often been assumed; the same applies to the Minnesingers Hartwig von Rute, Pleier and Ulrich von Etzenbach.

A mid-12th-century breviary (*A-Smi* MII6) provides a particularly interesting record of the practice of congregational hymn-singing, which had originated in Carolingian times. To the monks' 'Surrexit enim sicut dixit' the people would reply with the German Easter chant 'Christ ist entstanden'. Furthermore, in Salzburg both Easter and Christmas were occasions for sacred non-liturgical or quasi-liturgical performances, often in dramatic form. One of the earliest of such liturgical plays was the 'Bishop's play' for children, peculiar to Salzburg and performed on the Feast of the Holy Innocents (28 December), a tradition that continued until the time of Michael Haydn.

Archbishop Pilgrim von Puchheim ruled from 1365 to 1396, a 'more worldly than spiritual lord, witty, splendour-loving, enthralled by the arts' (Klein). In 1393 he founded the Pilgrimskapelle in the cathedral, where exceptionally festive and musically magnificent services were performed by up to 12 musicians and a 'beautiful and artful organ', dismantled only at the end of the 16th century. The most interesting figure of the circle around the archbishop was undoubtedly the Monk of Salzburg, the first poet–musician to write in German; his work as creator of secular and sacred songs in Latin and German, both solo and polyphonic, some original and some in translation, is characterized by the introduction of liturgical (Gregorian), non-liturgical and popular elements in his melodies. His exceptionally fine polyphonic German songs are in the earliest part of the Mondsee-Wiener Liederhandschrift (*A-Wn* 2856); they were often performed at Schloss Freisaal, a castle south of Salzburg.

In the 15th century, musical foundations, especially for training choirboys (1432) and for preparing music for major feasts (1445), proliferated in Salzburg and neighbouring towns, such as Hofgastein and Radstadt. The cathedral, St Peter's and the Stadtpfarrkirche (now the Franziskanerkirche) employed their own Kantors, and the Mondsee-Wiener Liederhandschrift bears witness to the lavish musical life in the houses of wealthy citizens (the manuscript was owned by the Salzburg goldsmith Peter Spörl from at least 1472). Beside their 'trumetterey' (trumpets and drums) the archbishops employed musicians from the city and beyond, at the end of the 15th century, for instance, the lutenist Georg Gerlach.

2. 16TH CENTURY. With the spread of humanism the court of the Salzburg princes became a centre of south German Renaissance art. Cardinal Matthäus Lang (1519–40), a cultured archbishop and leading statesman, succeeded in attracting to his Hofkapelle such famous musicians as Heinrich Finck (from 1524) and the organist Paul Hofhaimer. Hofhaimer settled in Salzburg in 1522; in addition to him Nicolaus Lescalier (1512–31) and Gregor Peschin (1527–39) were engaged as court organists. Hofhaimer was succeeded in

1. *Interior of Salzburg Cathedral during the celebrations to mark the 1100th anniversary of the founding of the Archbishopric of Salzburg: engraving (1682) by Melchior Küsel*

1537 by Caspar Glanner. The Hofkapelle was directed by Wilhelm Waldner until 1544. The court chamberlain's records show that there were seven discantists in the choir in 1534 and eight in 1537. Kaspar Bockh, who succeeded Glanner, was also a prominent organ builder, and in 1581 worked on the cathedral's small organ, which was built on a balcony 'on which the musicians might stand to execute their music on high feasts'. The music of the cathedral was clearly held in high esteem, for among others Lassus dedicated compositions to the cathedral chapter (1587, 1589). One Salzburg composer of that period was Sebastian Hasenknopf, whose 27 *Sacrae cantiones* for five, six and eight voices were published in Munich in 1588. The first recorded printed music in Salzburg is a 1605 missal from the court printing press, founded in 1598 by Georg Kürner; he was succeeded by Christoph Katzenberger and in 1680 by J. B. Mayer.

A Kantor and ten prebendaries from the Lateinschule were responsible for all music at St Peter's apart from the monks' Gregorian chant. It was in the face of this competition that Johannes Stomius successfully established in 1530 his so-called 'poets' school', for which he compiled an important theoretical work, *Prima ad musicen instructio* (Nuremberg, 1536). In 1617 the Lateinschule and the Rupertsschule (as the cathedral school was known) were closed, and the place of the former was taken first by a Benedictine Gymnasium on the pattern of the Jesuit schools and later by the Academic Gymnasium.

The high standard of organ building is evident from Hofhaimer's recommendations for the organ in St Peter's built by Christian Taler of Wasserburg in 1505; two *positiv* organs were available for the music in the chapels. The cathedral also had three organs (the great organ over the main entrance, dated 1399, a choir organ and the organ of the Pilgrimskapelle), as did the Nonnberg monastery. One of them survives, a 'wonderful positive with a regal'. Other valuable instruments, lutes, violins, wind and folk instruments, especially of the 17th and 18th centuries, are in the Carolino Augusteum Museum in Salzburg.

Musical life was further stimulated during the reign of Archbishop Wolf Dietrich (1587–1612). He bequeathed to his successors the outline for future building projects and thus may rank as the creator of modern Salzburg. Inspired by the neighbouring courts of Innsbruck, Munich, Graz and Vienna and the famous *cappella* of his uncle Marcus Sitticus Altems in Rome, Wolf Dietrich inaugurated the Hofkapelle in 1591 and in 1597 reorganized the cathedral choir, thereby establishing the basis for the practice of music for the following 300 years. Tiburtio Massaino was summoned from Cremona to become the first Kapellmeister, and until secularization the 'prince-bishop's music' was divided into four groups, nominally under separate administration: the court music itself; the court and army trumpeters and drummers; the cathedral music (choral deacons and choristers); and the choirboys. They were directly controlled by the archbishop, who regulated their various tasks, numbers and remuneration. A 1612 list of musicians mentions 24 at court, eight boy discantists, ten trumpeters and a drummer, as well as 20 choral deacons, eight choristers and eight choirboys for the choral music in the minster – a total of 79. There were frequent changes of Kapellmeister; the incumbents were ungenerously treated by their master, although

they included such prominent musicians as Jacobus Flori (1597–9), Johann Stadlmayr (1604–7) and the Netherlander Mathias de Sayve (i) (1607–8). Wolf Dietrich's last Kapellmeister was Peter Guetfreund (1608–25).

At the end of 1589 the Romanesque cathedral burnt down and the organs were dismantled; services were held in the old Stadtpfarrkirche until rebuilding was finished. Not until 1703 did the new cathedral acquire a great organ, built by Joseph Christoph Egedacher; the instrument was enlarged in 1704–6 and again in 1718 by his son Johann Christoph, rebuilt by Ludwig Moser in 1842, enlarged again by Matthias Mauracher (ii) between 1880 and 1883, extensively modernized and expanded by Matthäus Mauracher (i) in 1914, and in 1958–9 given its present form by Dreher & Reinisch. Virtually all the old cathedral's musical treasures were destroyed in the fire of 1589 and only a few presentation volumes survive, together with Josua Pock's claviorgan of 1591 (a combination of spinet, Flute 4′ and Regal 8′), restored in 1973 and on display in the cathedral museum.

3. 17TH AND 18TH CENTURIES. Wolf Dietrich's successor, Archbishop Marcus Sitticus von Hohenems (1612–19), was half Italian and a nephew of S Carlo Borromeo. As a result he cultivated substantial economic and cultural links with Italy, and during his reign Salzburg enjoyed the first flowering of the Baroque. On his instigation monody and opera were introduced, their earliest appearance north of the Alps; in the first year of his reign the famous exponent of the monodic style, Francesco Rasi, a member of the Florence *camerata* and a leading opera singer, visited Salzburg on a journey through Austria and there dedicated a manuscript collection of monody to the archbishop. In 1614 a stage on the Italian model was erected in the archbishop's residence and inaugurated on 10 February with an Italian 'Hoftragicomedia', the first opera performance outside Italy. The imaginative prince then created another, most remarkable, setting for the new artistic import: the Steintheater in the park at Hellbrunn (his summer residence just outside Salzburg, built in 1615), the oldest surviving garden theatre in the German-speaking world. Guest performers from Italy probably joined local artists for the first Salzburg opera performances; the monodist Camillo Orlandi, for instance, was employed there in 1616. In 1617 the Benedictine Gymnasium was founded and with the university (1622) subsequently formed one of the most important centres for drama and music in Salzburg. The Benedictine drama performed there developed during the 17th century into a Baroque 'Gesamtkunstwerk', and increasingly came to resemble opera.

Archbishop Paris Lodron, a skilful politician, reigned from 1619 to 1653, a period notable for the completion of the cathedral and the attendant celebrations in 1628. For the consecration of the cathedral on 24 September that year a 12-chorus *Te Deum* by Hofkapellmeister Stefano Bernardi was sung. (The 53-part *Missa salisburgensis*, formerly thought to have been written for this event by Orazio Benevoli, is now known to date from later in the century; it may have been composed by Biber and was probably performed in Salzburg in 1682.) Also during Paris Lodron's reign Abraham Megerle (an uncle of the famous preacher Abraham a Sancta Clara), who mainly wrote church music, worked in Salzburg (1640–51). During the second half of the

17th century three Bohemian–Austrian prince-bishops left a decisive mark on Salzburg cultural life: Guidobald Thun (1654–68), Max Gandolf von Kuenburg (1668–87) and Johann Ernst von Thun (1687–1709). They were excellent diplomats and succeeded in furthering the policy of neutrality started by Paris Lodron while creating the financial basis for magnificent cultural activity through circumspect commercial management. They were thus able to secure the services, simultaneously and for relatively lengthy periods, of two established composers: the Alsatian Georg Muffat (1678–90) and the Bohemian H. I. F. von Biber (from 1670–71), as well as the equally worthy local composer Andreas Hofer (from 1653). All three wrote church music, while Biber, a great violin virtuoso, and Muffat, a noted exponent of the new French and Italian styles, also wrote instrumental works which became famous far beyond Salzburg. All three also composed dramatic music, which enjoyed new prominence, principally during the rule of Johann Ernst von Thun, for whose enthronement (1687) Muffat's opera *Le fatali felicità di Plutone* was performed. Only the librettos of this work and of Biber's opera *Alessandro in Pietra* (1689) have survived. The single surviving operatic score from this important period in the city's musical history is that of Biber's *Chi la dura la vince*. Hofer, Muffat and particularly Biber also set to music a large number of Benedictine Schuldramen, which at that time already closely resembled opera.

The favourable financial situation also enabled Johann Ernst to found the carillon (1702, still operational), and to have the great cathedral organ built above the main entrance (1703). At the beginning of the 18th century the most prolific composer of Benedictine drama was Matthias Sigismund Biechteler von Greiffenthal, in the service of the court from 1688, while Carl Heinrich von Biber, deputy Kapellmeister from 1714, devoted himself almost exclusively to church music. During the reign of Franz Anton von Harrach (1709–27) the Viennese deputy Hofkapellmeister Antonio Caldara came to Salzburg to compose operas, and between 1716 and 1727 at least 19 of his operas and staged oratorios were performed there. His *Dafne*, a *dramma pastorale*, probably opened the Heckentheater in the present Mirabellgarten in 1719. The transition to the Rococo took place under J. E. Eberlin, who became court organist in 1726 and Hofkapellmeister in 1749; he was preceded in the former post by J. B. Samber and Matthäus Gugl, both more famous as musical theorists. Eberlin's compositions greatly influenced a series of Salzburg court musicians, among them Leopold Mozart (court violinist from 1743 and deputy Hofkapellmeister from 1763), A. C. Adlgasser (court organist from 1750) and Joseph Meissner, (a court bass from 1747). Several of Eberlin's liturgical works were also valued by W. A. Mozart, who was Konzertmeister from 1769 to 1777 and court organist from 1779 to 1781.

Archbishop Siegmund Christoph, Count of Schrattenbach (1753–71), the last Baroque-minded prince, was succeeded by a man of the Enlightenment, Hieronymus, Count of Colloredo (1772–1803). His spiritual princedom was no longer rich enough for him to maintain a magnificent and luxurious court, but though court music was affected by rigorous economic measures Hieronymus, himself a good violinist, managed to engage accomplished musicians. Apart from some unpleasant experiences with Italians due to his too

frequent blind trust in vaunted ability, the level of vocal and orchestral music remained relatively good until about 1796. His best musicians were the Kapellmeisters Domenico Fischietti (1772–5), Giacomo Rust (1777–8) and Luigi Gatti (1782-1817), the oboist Joseph Fiala (1778–85) and the Konzertmeister F. J. Otter (1789–1809). In 1775, on the initiative of the archbishop but at the city's expense, the Ballhaus was converted into the prince-archbishops' Hoftheater, where for the most part travelling companies (at least 18) played, including those of Wahr, Schikaneder, Böhm and Weber. Among the reforms introduced by Hieronymus into church music were the obligatory inclusion of German hymns in all church services (except at the cathedral and the monasteries) and the shortening of liturgical mass settings; Michael Haydn was decisively involved in these reforms. Unlike Mozart, he was content with life in Salzburg; he entered the archbishop's service in 1763 and remained there, esteemed primarily as a composer of church music, for the rest of his life.

Salzburg's musical life enjoyed a last moment of prosperity during the brief reign of Archduke Ferdinand of Tuscany (1803–5). In 1803 the spiritual princedoms of Passau and Eichstädt had come under Salzburg's rule and their court musicians swelled the ranks of the electoral Kammer- und Hofkapellmusik, which served at the Hoftheater, the cathedral and the court itself. When the court was abolished in 1806 the best musicians transferred to the Vienna Hofmusikkapelle, leaving only a modest remnant behind to provide music for church services.

4. 19TH AND 20TH CENTURIES. In 1816 political stability was restored in Austria, and the city changed from an episcopal seat to a provincial town with a stagnant cultural life. Reorganization of cathedral music was hampered by the reluctance of the new state bureaucracy to proffer financial support. Only the Kaiserliches Königliches Nationaltheater (the Hoftheater until 1806) survived, thanks to the Salzburg public's love of the theatre. Singspiels by Weigl, Dittersdorf and Wenzel Müller and operas by Rossini, Cherubini, Mozart and Weber (*Der Freischütz*, 1825) offered a varied musical fare, but with the departure of Michael Haydn's most gifted pupils – Weber, Neukomm, Wölfl, Diabelli and Ignaz Assmayr – the city lost its urgently needed musical impulse.

However, the reactivation and reorganization of local musical forces led to the foundation, on the initiative of Franz von Hilleprandt, of the Dommusikverein und Mozarteum (1841), an artistic institution for 'the promotion of all branches of music, but especially church music'. Its first director was Alois Taux, the most important musician in mid-19th-century Salzburg; he was followed in 1861 by Hans Schläger and in 1868 by Otto Bach (Bruckner applied in vain for this post on both occasions). For the unveiling of the Mozart memorial in 1842 the society held its first music festival. In 1847 the Salzburger Liedertafel was formed from a male-voice choral society and simultaneously a private singing association became the Singakademie; the participation of these two bodies in the so-called Mozarteum Concerts resulted in a broadening of the repertory. In addition to singing festivals a Mozart celebration was held in 1852 and the great Mozart Centenary Festival in 1856 (when Carl Mozart presented valuable Mozartiana to the Mozarteum); both memorial celebrations were

2. Salzburg Hofplatz (now Residenzplatz), with the cathedral (centre), and prince-archbishop's residence (right): engraving (late 18th century) by F. Müller after August Franz Heinrich Naumann

characterized by the participation of 600 singers from numerous Austrian and foreign choral societies, directed by Taux. The latter was appointed to the Nationaltheater in 1839; his term as opera Kapellmeister coincided with the theatre's heyday. Besides his leading role in the Dommusikverein and the Liedertafel, and his composing, he was responsible for giving the cult of Mozart's music a new and decisive impetus. Other composers active during this period were Johann Schnaubelt, Carl Santner and Peter Singer, the last two continuing the line of music theorists into the 19th century.

In 1870 Karl Freiherr von Sterneck (1813–93) effected a necessary reform in local musical life by founding the Internationale Mozart-Stiftung, whose broad initial programme included supporting and encouraging musicians and music students, promoting concerts, building up a library and archive, and organizing and administering periodic conventions of musicians. In 1875 it started the first complete edition of Mozart's works and in 1877 and 1879 held music festivals, at which the orchestra of the Vienna Hofoper (Vienna PO) was conducted by Otto Dessoff and Hans Richter respectively. In 1880 a museum was opened in the house where Mozart was born and in the same year Sterneck succeeded in freeing the Mozarteum from its administrative association with the Dommusikverein and united it with the Internationale Mozart-Stiftung to form the Internationale Stiftung Mozarteum. As a public music school its first director was Joseph Friedrich Hummel; it later became a conservatory (1914; state controlled from 1922), a Reichshochschule für Musik (1939–45), a Musikakademie (1953) and the Hochschule für Musik und darstellende Kunst (1971). Outstanding directors such as Bernhard Paumgartner (1917–38 and 1945–59), Clemens Krauss (1938–45)

and Eberhard Preussner (1959–64) enhanced its function as a centre of musical learning. Composers such as J. N. David, Hindemith and Henze have taught there; others who settled in Salzburg include Cesar Bresgen, Friedrich Doppelbauer, Helmut Eder and Gerhard Wimberger.

Concurrent with the 19th-century Mozart movement there was a trend towards reform of church music, supported by Archbishop Johannes Katschthaler (1832–1914) and put into practice by the cathedral Kapellmeisters Hermann Spies (1892–1920) and particularly Joseph Messner (1926–69). From 1970 Anton Dawidowicz attempted to revive the old choral traditions.

Through the Internationale Stiftung Mozarteum the Internationale Gesellschaft für Neue Musik (ISCM) was founded in 1922 by Rudolph Réti, followed by the Zentralinstitut für Mozartforschung in 1931. In 1966 the Institut für Musikwissenschaft was opened within the university (rebuilt 1962); it is directed by Gerhard Croll.

In addition to the annual Salzburg Festival (Salzburger Theater- und Musik-Sommer) held from the end of July to the end of August (see §5 below) there are other musical events in the city. For the bicentenary of Mozart's birth in 1956 the Internationale Stiftung Mozarteum initiated an annual series of concerts held at the end of January, the Salzburg Mozart Week (Salzburger Mozart-Woche), at which the Vienna PO and other famous interpreters of Mozart's music give concerts of his orchestral, solo, chamber and church music. In 1967 Herbert von Karajan initiated a ten-day Easter Festival (Osterfestspiele), organized by the Osterfestspiele-Gesellschaft (founded 1966), and normally comprising a new opera production, orchestral concerts and an oratorio, all produced and conducted by

Karajan. Opera productions have included the *Ring* (1967–70), *Fidelio* (1971), *Tristan und Isolde* (1972), *Die Meistersinger von Nürnberg* (1974), *La bohème* (1975, produced by Zeffirelli), *Lohengrin* (1976) and *Il trovatore* (1977). There are also smaller concert series at other times of the year, and during the winter months operas and operettas are given at the Landestheater (a new, larger theatre replaced the Nationaltheater and opened in 1893 as the Stadttheater with Mozart's *La clemenza di Tito*; it was renamed the Landestheater in 1938 after extensive exterior alterations).

5. THE SALZBURG FESTIVAL. The first important predecessor of the present-day Salzburg Festival was the 1877 music festival held by the Mozart-Stiftung. Subsequent festivals under Richter (1879; 1887, the centenary of *Don Giovanni*), Jahn (1891, centenary of Mozart's death), Hofkapellmeister Joseph Hellmesberger (ii) (1901), Mottl (1904), Strauss and Mahler (1906, including a performance of *Le nozze di Figaro* by the Vienna Hofoper personally subsidized by Emperor Franz Joseph), Nikisch, Schalk and Weingartner (1910) led to the idea of a regular festival; one was planned for summer 1914, but was cancelled on the outbreak of war. In 1917 Friedrich Gehmacher and Heinrich Damisch founded the Salzburger Festspielhaus-Gemeinde in Vienna with a branch in Salzburg for the purpose of establishing an annual festival of drama and music with special emphasis on the works of Mozart; the first festival took place in 1920 with Reinhardt's production of Hofmannsthal's *Jedermann* in the cathedral square, since then a traditional festival event. Reinhardt, Hofmannsthal, Franz Schalk, Richard Strauss and Alfred Roller set the high artistic standards of the festival. Bernhard Paumgartner organized the first series of concerts at the 1921 festival devoted entirely to the works of Mozart comprising orchestral, chamber music and serenade concerts, and a performance of the Requiem. Operas were first given at the 1922 festival in the small Stadttheater: *Don Giovanni* and *Così fan tutte* conducted by Strauss, and *Le nozze di Figaro* and *Die Entführung aus dem Serail* conducted by Schalk. There were no music performances at the 1923 festival, when the first official ISCM festival was held in Salzburg, and the entire festival was cancelled in 1924 because of the general economic crisis. 1925 was an important year, with the opening of the Festspielhaus (the Winterreitschule converted in 1924 into a theatre by Eduard Hütter), the first lieder recital (since then an important part of the festival) and the first radio broadcast of a festival event (*Don Giovanni*, 24 August). The Festspielhaus was rebuilt in 1926 by Clemens Holzmeister to seat 1200, first used for opera in 1927 (*Fidelio*) and was altered in 1937 and 1939. Open-air performances have been given in the Felsenreitschule (Summer Riding School) since 1926; in the same year a contemporary opera, Strauss's *Ariadne auf Naxos*, was for the first time included in the festival events.

The festivals reached a peak in the 1930s when Bruno Walter, Krauss, Toscanini, Furtwängler and Knappertsbusch were the leading conductors and Herbert Graf the producer of many of the operas; during this period the festival's repertory expanded greatly. However, as a result of the Anschluss in 1938, many conductors left (Walter, Toscanini, Kleiber, Busch and Klemperer); events were curtailed during World War II and the 1944 festival was cancelled. The festival,

renamed the Salzburger Theater- und Musik-Sommer in 1943, resumed in 1945; in 1949 the first Mozart Matinées were given by Paumgartner in the Mozarteum and have since become a regular feature. A number of premières have been given at the festival, notably Strauss's *Die Liebe der Danae* (1952) and Henze's *Die Bassariden* (1966), and also productions of rediscovered early Baroque operas such as Cavalieri's *Rappresentatione di Anima, et di Corpo* (1968); in 1957 a festival event was first televised (*Jedermann*).

The three principal halls used for the events of the festival are on the site of the former court stables: the Felsenreitschule, radically altered in 1968–70 by Holzmeister (capacity 1568); the Kleines Festspielhaus (known as the Festspielhaus until 1960), redesigned in 1963 (capacity 1343) by Hans Hofmann and Erich Engels as a theatre intended principally for the performance of plays and small-scale operas; and the Grosses Festspielhaus (capacity 2371), designed by Holzmeister retaining the original façade of the stables and opened in 1960 with a performance of *Der Rosenkavalier* conducted by Karajan. Performances are also given in the Grosser Saal of the Mozarteum, the Residenz courtyard and the Carabinierisaal, the Mirabell palace, the cathedral and its square, St Peter's, the Kollegienkirche and the Landestheater.

The Vienna PO has long been the musical backbone of the festival; it had a close relationship with the city before the festival's first orchestral concerts in 1921, though it did not give concerts using its own name until 1925. In addition to playing for all orchestral concerts, it also served as the opera orchestra, chamber orchestra for the serenade concerts, and for the sacred concerts. The Budapest Philharmonic gave two guest concerts under Dohnányi in 1931; the next guest orchestra was the Berlin PO in 1957, since when it has shared performance responsibilities equally with the Vienna PO. The festival has always attracted first-rank conductors too numerous to mention, but the postwar era has been dominated by Furtwängler, Karajan (musical director of the festival, 1956–60) and Böhm. Guest orchestras have appeared regularly since 1957 and include the Concertgebouw (1958), the Orchestre National de la ORTF (1959, 1972), the New York PO (1959), the Dresden Staatskapelle (1961, 1972, 1976), the Czech PO (1963), the Cleveland Orchestra (1967), the Orchestre de Paris (1969) and the LSO (1973, 1975, 1977). The Austrian radio orchestra made its first guest appearance in 1970 and has since been used regularly for the festival's contemporary music concerts.

For the 50th-anniversary celebrations in 1970, the festival sponsored a three-day festival at Hellbrunn, the summer palace built by Archbishop Marcus Sitticus in 1615, with as many as a dozen simultaneous events at various places in and around the palace. In the same year a 'Strassentheater' appeared in the city which, together with the festival at Hellbrunn, has become an annual feature.

BIBLIOGRAPHY

GENERAL

F. M. Vierthaler: *Geschichte des Schulwesens und der Kultur in Salzburg* (Salzburg, 1804)

B. Pillwein: *Biographische Schilderungen oder Lexicon Salzburgischer theils verstorbener theils lebender Künstler* (Salzburg, 1821)

[G. A. Pichler]: *Biographien salzburgischer Tonkünstler* (Salzburg, 1845)

A. J. Hammerle: *Chronik des Gesanges und der Musik in Salzburg* (Salzburg, 1874–6)

——: *Neue Beiträge für Salzburgische Geschichte, Literatur und Musik* (Salzburg, 1877)

R. Tenschert: 'Salzburgs Stellung in der Musikgeschichte und im Musikleben der Gegenwart', *ZfM*, Jg.98 (1931), 657

C. Schneider: *Geschichte der Musik in Salzburg von den ältesten Zeiten bis zur Gegenwart* (Salzburg, 1935) [incl. extensive bibliography]

——: *Musikwanderung durch Salzburg* (Vienna, 1937)

V. Keldorfer: *Klingendes Salzburg* (Zurich, Leipzig and Vienna, 1951)

B. Paumgartner: *Erinnerungen* (Salzburg, 1969)

G. Croll and others: 'Musikergedenkstätten in Stadt und Land Salzburg', *ÖMz*, xxvi (1971), 409

CHURCH MUSIC

J. Peregrinus [Hupfauf]: *Geschichte der Salzburgischen Dom-Sängerknaben oder schlechthin des Kapellhauses* (Salzburg, 1889)

H. Spies: 'Aus der musikalischen Vergangenheit Salzburgs bis 1634', *Musica divina*, ii (1914), 314–45

K. A. Rosenthal: 'Zur Stilistik der Salzburger Kirchenmusik von 1600–1730', *SMw*, xvii (1930), 77; xix (1932), 3

H. Spies: 'Neue urkundliche Beiträge zur Geschichte des Innenraumes der Salzburger Münsterkirche', *Mitteilungen der Geschichte für Salzburger Landeskunde*, lxx (1930), 129

——: 'Geschichte der Domschule zu Salzburg', *Mitteilungen der Geschichte für Salzburger Landeskunde*, lxxviii (1938), 1–88

——: 'Beiträge zur Geschichte der Kirchenmusik in Salzburg im Spät-Mittelalter und zu Anfang der Renaissancezeit', *Mitteilungen der Geschichte für Salzburger Landeskunde*, xc (1950), 142; xci (1951), 132

K. Picker: *Beiträge zur Kenntnis der Kirchenmusik in Salzburg zwischen 1850 und 1950* (diss., U. of Innsbruck, 1957)

W. Hummel: 'Das Bruderschaftsbüchl der hl. Kreuz-Bruderschaft an der Bürgerspitalskirche in Salzburg', *Jahresschrift des Salzburger Museum Carolino-Augusteum*, v (1960), 205

H. Federhofer: 'Zur Musikpflege im Benediktinerstift Michaelbeuern (Salzburg)', *Festschrift Karl Gustav Fellerer* (Regensburg, 1962), 106

E. Tittel: 'Kardinal Katschthaler, ein Cäcilianer auf dem Salzburger Fürstenthron', *Musicae sacrae ministerium . . . Festgabe für K. G. Fellerer* (Cologne, 1962), 197

E. Hintermaier: *Die Salzburger Hofkapelle von 1700 bis 1806: Organisation und Personal* (diss., U. of Salzburg, 1972)

——: 'Zur Musikpflege in der Wallfahrtsbasilika Maria Plain im 18. Jahrhundert', *Studien und Mitteilungen zur Geschichte des Benediktinerordens*, new ser., lxxxv (1974), 228

R. Angermüller: 'Künstlerisches Personal des "Dom-Musik-Verein und Mozarteum" 1841–1880 und der Dommusik von 1880–1926', *Mitteilungen der Internationalen Stiftung Mozarteum*, xxiv (1976), 3

E. Hintermaier: ' "Missa salisburgensis": neue Erkenntnisse über Entstehung, Autor und Zweckbestimmung', *Musicologica austriaca*, i (1977), 154–96

OPERA

R. von Freisauff: *Zur 100jährigen Jubelfeier des kaiserlich-königlichen Theaters in Salzburgs* (Salzburg, 1875)

H. F. Wagner: 'Theaterwesen in Salzburg', *Mitteilungen der Geschichte für Salzburger Landeskunde*, xxxiii (1893), 247–329

K. O. Wagner: 'Das Salzburger Hoftheater 1775–1805', *Mitteilungen der Geschichte für Salzburger Landeskunde*, 1 (1910), 285–328

A. Kutscher: *Das Salzburger Barocktheater* (Vienna, 1924)

——: *Vom Salzburger Barocktheater zu den Salzburger Festspielen* (Düsseldorf, 1939)

L. Schmidt: 'Die Stoffe der Salzburger Schuldramatik', *Mitteilungen der Geschichte für Salzburger Landeskunde*, lxxix (1939), 133

F. J. Fischer: 'Das Salzburger Theater vom Barock zum Rokoko', *Mitteilungen der Geschichte für Salzburger Landeskunde*, xcv (1955), 141–88

——: 'Englische Komödianten in Salzburg', *Mitteilungen der Geschichte für Salzburger Landeskunde*, xcix (1959), 159

——: 'Wandertruppen des 17. Jahrhunderts in Salzburg', *Mitteilungen der Geschichte für Salzburger Landeskunde*, c (1960), 431–70

L. Welti: 'Die Prechtin, die erste deutsche Opernsängerin', *Theater in Österreich* (Vienna, 1965)

S. Dahms: *Das Musiktheater des Salzburger Hochbarocks*, i: *Das Benediktinerdrama* (diss., U. of Salzburg, 1974)

E. Hintermaier: 'Das Fürsterzbischöfliche Hoftheater zu Salzburg (1775–1803)', *ÖMz*, xxx (1975), 351

S. Dahms: 'Das musikalische Repertoire des Salzburger Fürsterz-bischöflichen Hoftheaters (1775–1803)', *ÖMz*, xxxi (1976), 340

FESTIVAL

H. von Hofmannsthal: *Festspiele in Salzburg* (Vienna, 1938, 3/1952)

F. Martin: 'Das erste Salzburger Musikfest', *Mitteilungen der Geschichte für Salzburger Landeskunde*, lxxii–lxxiii (1942), 89

R. Tenschert: *Salzburg und seine Festspiele* (Vienna, 1947)

H. C. Fischer: *Die Idee der Salzburger Festspiele und ihre Verwirklichung* (diss., U. of Munich, 1954)

F. Hadamowsky and G. Rech, eds.: *Die Salzburger Festspiele, ihre Vorgeschichte und Entwicklung, 1842–1960* (Salzburg, 1960)

J. Kaut: *Festspiele in Salzburg: eine Dokumentation* (Salzburg, 1969)

INSTRUMENTS

H. Spies: *Die Orgeln in der Regierungszeit des Fürsten und Erzbischofs Wolf Dietrich von Raitenau* (Salzburg, 1927)

——: *Die Salzburger grossen Domorgeln* (Augsburg, 1929) [see also E. Schenk: *ZMw*, xvi (1934), 57, 182]

K. Geiringer: *Alte Musik-Instrumente im Museum Carolino-Augusteum Salzburg* (Leipzig, 1932)

A. Jungwirth: 'Die Glocken und Glockengiesser Salzburgs', *Mitteilungen der Geschichte für Salzburger Landeskunde*, lxxv (1935), 11

H. Spies: 'Geschichtliches über das Salzburger Glockenspiel', *Mitteilungen der Geschichte für Salzburger Landeskunde*, lxxxvi–lxxxvii (1946–7), 49

O. Eberstaller: *Orgeln und Orgelbauer in Österreich* (Graz and Cologne, 1955)

K. Birsak: *Die Holzblas Instrumente im Salzburger Museum Carolino Augusteum* (Salzburg, 1973)

G. Croll: 'Das Claviorganum des Josua Pock (1591)', *Alte und moderne Kunst*, xix (1974), 13

——: 'Ein Claviorganum aus der Salzburger "Kunst- u. Wunderkammer" ', *ÖMz*, xxxi (1976), 355

OTHER STUDIES

[?L. Mozart]: 'Nachrichten von dem gegenwärtigen Zustande der Musik . . . des Erzbischoffs zu Salzburg im Jahre 1757', F. W. Marpurg: *Historisch-kritische Beyträge zur Aufnahme der Musik*, iii (Berlin, 1757/R1970), 183

V. M. Süss: *Salzburgische Volkslieder mit ihren Singweisen* (Salzburg, 1865)

J. E. Engl: *Gedenkbuch der Salzburger Liedertafel* (Salzburg, 1872)

H. F. Wagner: 'Mittelalterliche Hofpoesie in Salzburg', *Mitteilungen der Geschichte für Salzburger Landeskunde*, xxxviii (1898), 107–37

K. Adrian: *Salzburger Volksspiele, Aufzüge und Tänze* (Salzburg, 1908)

F. Martin: 'Kleine Beiträge zur Musikgeschichte Salzburgs, insbesondere zur Biographie Michael Haydns', *Mitteilungen der Geschichte für Salzburger Landeskunde*, liii (1913), 355

80 Jahre Salzburger Liedertafel 1847–1927 (Salzburg, 1927)

H. Spies: 'Die Tonkunst in Salzburg in der Regierungszeit des Fürsten und Erzbischofs Wolf Dietrich von Raitenau (1587–1612)', *Mitteilungen der Geschichte für Salzburger Landeskunde*, lxxi (1931), 1–64; lxxii (1932), 65–136

F. Martin: 'Die "Museumgesellschaft", Salzburgs ältester Verein', *Mitteilungen der Geschichte für Salzburger Landeskunde*, lxxv (1935), 119

C. Schneider: 'Musikwanderung durch Salzburg', *Österreichischer Musik- und Sängeralmanach*, ed. H. Damisch (Vienna, 1937), 122

H. Spies: 'Beiträge zur Musikgeschichte Salzburgs im Spät-Mittelalter und zu Anfang der Renaissancezeit', *Mitteilungen der Geschichte für Salzburger Landeskunde*, lxxxi (1941), 41–96

E. J. Luin: 'Die "Liedertafel" ein Hort des musikalischen Salzburgertums', *Mitteilungen der Geschichte für Salzburger Landeskunde*, xc (1950), 1–36

W. Hummel: *Chronik der Internationalen Stiftung Mozarteum in Salzburg* (Salzburg, 1951)

H. Klein: 'Nachrichten zum Musikleben Salzburgs in den Jahren 1764–1766', *Festschrift Alfred Orel* (Vienna and Wiesbaden, 1960), 93

J. Gassner: 'Die Musikaliensammlung im Salzburger Museum Carolino Augusteum', *Jahresschrift des Salzburger Museum Carolino Augusteum*, vii (1961–2), 119–247

W. Hummel: 'Mozart-Gesellschaften', *MGG*

L. Welti: 'Förderung der Barockkultur durch das Hohenemser Grafenhaus', *Maske und Kothurn*, vii (1961), 235

W. Bauer and O. E. Deutsch, eds.: *Mozart: Briefe und Aufzeichnungen* (Kassel, 1962–75)

R. Federhofer-Königs: 'Ein anonymer Musiktraktat aus der 2. Hälfte des 14. Jahrhunderts in der Stiftsbibliothek Michaelbeuern', *KJb*, xlvi (1962), 43

L. Welti: *Graf Kaspar von Hohenembs 1573–1640* (Innsbruck, 1963)

M. H. Schmid: *Die Musikaliensammlung der Erzabtei, St. Peter in Salzburg: Katalog I*, Schriftenreihe der Internationalen Stiftung Mozarteum, iii–iv (Salzburg, 1970)

'Die Musikpflege an der Salzburger Universität im 17. und 18. Jahrhundert', *Universität Salzburg 1622–1962–1972* (Salzburg, 1972), 193

M. H. Schmid: *Mozart und die Salzburger Tradition* (Tutzing, 1976)

G. Croll: 'Die Musikpflege', *Geschichte Salzburgs Stadt und Land, i: Vorgeschichte-Altertum-Mittelalter* (in preparation)

GERHARD CROLL

Salzedo [Salzédo], **Carlos (Léon)** (*b* Arcachon, 6 April 1885; *d* Waterville, Maine, 17 Aug 1961). American harpist and composer of French birth. He was at the Bordeaux Conservatory (1891–4) and graduated in the piano and the harp from the Paris Conservatoire, where his father taught singing, in 1901. He moved to New York in 1909 and was first harpist of the Metropolitan Opera Orchestra (1909–13). In 1913 he founded the Trio de Lutèce with Georges Barrère and Paul Kéfer. He helped to found the International Composers' Guild in 1921 and from 1921 to 1932 edited the *Eolian Review*, later renamed *Eolus: a Review for New Music*. In 1923 he became an American citizen. He inaugurated the harp department at the Curtis Institute in 1924 and in 1931 the Salzedo Harp Colony at Camden, Maine. Honorary doctorates were awarded to him by the Philadelphia Musical Academy (1937) and the Curtis Institute (1949). His pre-World War I harp compositions published in Paris (opp.1–28) are graceful works whose harmonic vocabulary recalls Ravel. In the USA he became more and more astringent, leaving at his death a second harp concerto with numerous parallel triads contrapuntally interwoven in an athletic idiom. He succeeded in bringing harp literature abreast at least of Hindemith.

WORKS
(selective list)

3 morceaux, op.28, harp (1913); The Enchanted Isle, sym. poem, harp, orch, 1918; Bolmimerie, 7 harps, 1919; 3 Poems by Sara Yarrow, S, ob, bn, hn, 6 harps, 1919; 5 Preludes, harp (1924); 3 Poems by Mallarmé, S, harp, pf, 1924; Sonata, harp, pf (1925); Conc. no.1, harp, 7 wind, 1925–6; Pentacle, 2 harps, 1928; Préambule et jeux, harp, chamber orch, 1928–9; Scintillation, harp, 1936; Suite, harp, 1943; Prélude fatidique, harp, 1954; Harp Conc. no.2 (1966), orchestration completed R. R. Bennett

Principal publishers: Composers' Music Corporation, Elkan-Vogel, Leduc, Lyra, G. Schirmer

WRITINGS

Modern Study of the Harp (New York, 1921, 2/1948)
Method for the Harp (New York, 1929)
with L. Lawrence: *The Art of Modulating* (New York, 1950)

BIBLIOGRAPHY

M. Lambertini: 'León Carlos Salzedo', *A arte musical* (15 Jan 1913), 1
Harp News, iii/4 (1961), autumn [special issue]

ROBERT STEVENSON

Salzedo, Leonard (Lopès) (*b* London, 24 Sept 1921). English composer of Portuguese origin. He studied at the RCM (1940–44), his principal teachers being Isolde Menges (violin) and Howells (composition). In 1944 Rambert commissioned him to write the music for her ballet *The Fugitive* and from that time he has been intermittently associated with ballet. His most successful score was *Witch Boy*; Beecham conducted the first performance of the concert suite in 1959 in the Festival Hall, where three years previously he had introduced Salzedo's First Symphony.

WORKS
(selective list)

Ballets: The Fugitive, 1944; Mardi gras, 1946; Witch Boy, 1956; The Travellers, 1963; Agriona, 1964; Realms of Choice, 1965; Hazard, 1967; Ballet 1973, 1973
Orch: Gabble Retchit, sym. poem, perf. 1955; Sym. no.1, perf. 1956; Rendezvous, 1960; Conc. fervido, 1964; Paean to the Sun, 1966; Toccata, 1967; Perc Conc., 1969
7 str qts, other chamber pieces, songs

Principal publisher: Lopès

CHRISTOPHER PALMER

Salzer, Felix (*b* Vienna, 13 June 1904). American musicologist of Austrian birth. He studied music history with Adler in Vienna, where he took the doctorate in 1926 with a dissertation on Schubert; at the same time he studied theory and analysis with Hans Weisse and Heinrich Schenker. He was awarded a diploma in conducting from the Vienna Academy in 1935. In 1937, with Oswald Jonas, he founded *Der Dreiklang*, a

monthly journal that dealt with Schenker's theories. He emigrated to America in 1940 and taught at the Mannes College of Music (1940–56, 1962–4; executive director 1948–55). In 1963 he became professor of music at Queens College of the City University of New York.

Salzer's writings, derived from the theories of Schenker, have had considerable influence on the study of theory and analysis in the USA. He provided a succinct exposition of Schenker's ideas in his introduction (1969) to the *Five Graphic Music Analyses*. Earlier, in *Structural Hearing* (1952), which organized Schenkerian analysis into a systematic course of study, he had extended the application of these principles to embrace tonal music from the Middle Ages to the present. Further, he had made specific distinctions between 'harmonic' and 'contrapuntal' functions of chords, and had developed the concepts of tonal prolongation and tonal structure. In *Counterpoint in Composition* (1969, with Carl Schachter), he emphasized the relationship of Fux's principles of species counterpoint to tonal music of all styles, thus extending the concepts of part-writing evolved in Schenker's later writings. Both pedagogical works are based on Schenker's *Der Freie Satz* and systematize the techniques of foreground and middleground levels of composition. In 1967, with William J. Mitchell, he founded *The Music Forum*, a periodical primarily devoted to studies based on Schenker's approach.

WRITINGS

Die Sonatenform bei Schubert (diss., U. of Vienna, 1926; extracts in *SMw*, xv (1928), 86–125)
'Über die Bedeutung der Ornamentik in Philipp Emanuel Bachs Klavierwerken', *ZMw*, xii (1929–30), 398–428
Sinn und Wesen der abendländischen Mehrstimmigkeit (Vienna, 1935)
Structural Hearing: Tonal Coherence in Music (New York, 1952, 2/1962; Ger. trans., 1957)
'Tonality in Early Medieval Polyphony', *The Music Forum*, i (1967), 35–98
with C. Schachter: *Counterpoint in Composition* (New York, 1969)
Introduction and glossary to H. Schenker: *Five Graphic Music Analyses* (New York, 1969), 13
'Chopin's Nocturne in C♯ Minor, opus 27, no.1', *The Music Forum*, ii (1970), 283
'Chopin's Etude in F Major, opus 25, no.3: the Scope of Tonality', *The Music Forum*, iii (1973), 281
'Haydn's Fantasia from the String Quartet, Opus 76, No.6', *The Music Forum*, iv (1976), 161–94

SAUL NOVACK

Salzilli, Crescentio (*b* Capua, ?1580–85; *d* in or after 1621). Italian composer and lutenist. There is no proof that, as has sometimes been stated, he was raised in the household of the prince of Rocca Romana, Giovanni Tommaso di Capua, but he was in the prince's service when he dedicated his first book of madrigals to him on 6 March 1607. In February 1610 he was hired as an archlute player at the S Casa dell'Annunziata, Naples, at five ducats a month, and he held this post until at least 1621. His madrigals are successful imitations of Gesualdo's late style, with its contrasts of slow dissonant *durezze e ligature*, fast, dense points of imitation, short chordal phrases in triple metre and sudden silences. Over the four books, which comprise more than 80 pieces, the madrigals become progressively longer, less chordal and more imitative and use phrase repetition more and more. Salzilli's two extant books of three-part canzonettas are provided with guitar tablature. Most of them have three stanzas of text, normally without a refrain, and are in triple metre with abundant syncopations and hemiola.

WORKS

Il primo libro de [21] madrigali, 5vv (Naples, 1607)
Secondo libro de [21] madrigali, 5vv (Naples, 1611[17])
Terzo libro de [21] madrigali, 5vv (Naples, 1613)
La sirena: libro secondo delle [21] canzonette, 3vv (Naples, 1616) [incl. gui tablature]
Amarille: libro terzo delle [23] canzonette, 3vv (Naples, 1616) [incl. gui tablature]
Quarto libro de [22] madrigali, 5vv (Naples, 1621)

BIBLIOGRAPHY

L. Bianconi: 'Weitere Ergänzungen zu Emil Vogels "Bibliothek der gedruckten weltlichen Vocalmusik Italiens, aus den Jahren 1500–1700" aus italienischen Bibliotheken', *AnMc*, no.9 (1970), 181

KEITH A. LARSON

Salzman, Eric (*b* New York, 8 Sept 1933). American composer and critic. He studied the violin, theory and composition at the New York High School of Music and Art, then continued his studies under Luening, Ussachevsky, Beeson and Mitchell at Columbia University, and under Sessions and Babbitt at Princeton. A Fulbright Fellowship took him to Europe (1956–8), where he worked with Petrassi in Rome and attended the Darmstadt summer courses. He wrote music criticism for the *New York Times* (1958–62) and the *New York Herald Tribune* (1963–4, 1965–6), and also contributed to record magazines; in 1969 he was joint winner of the Sang Prize for Criticism in the Fine Arts. His other activities have included the music directorship of the New York non-commercial radio station WBAI-FM (1962–3, 1968–71) and teaching at Queens College (1966–7). At the same time his work as a composer flourished. Mixed-media and music-theatre works increasingly engaged his attention, and in 1970 he founded QUOG, an ensemble of singers, dancers and instrumentalists aiming to explore new forms with an emphasis on improvisation. He also established the Free Music Store, an adventurous performance centre that had great success in reaching a new audience. The most important of his works include *Foxes and Hedgehogs*, the first concentrated expression of his ideas about art, technology and cultural change; *The Nude Paper Sermon*, commissioned by Nonesuch Records; *Can Man Survive?*, the sound environment to an ecological exhibit for the centenary of the American Museum of Natural History; *The Peloponnesian War*, a full-evening dance-mime-music piece and *The Electric Ear*, electronic and mixed-media pieces for performance in Greenwich Village, New York.

WORKS

(selective list)

Partita, vn, 1956–8; In Praise of the Owl and the Cuckoo (Shakespeare), S, fl, cl, gui, vn, va, 1963–4; Foxes and Hedgehogs, music-theatre (J. Ashbery), 4 solo vv, 2 ens, elec, 1963–7; Larynx Music, S, 4-track tape, 1966–7; The Peloponnesian War, music-theatre, 1967–8; Feedback, mixed-media, 1968; The Nude Paper Sermon (Ashbury, Stevenson), actor, Renaissance consort, chorus, elec, 1969; Can Man Survive?, mixed-media, 1968–9; Ecologue, 1971; Chamber Music: Mirror, improvisational music-theatre, 1972; The Conjurer, spectacle (with M. Sahl), 1975; Noah, spectacle, 1978

Principal publisher: Quogue

WRITINGS

Twentieth-century Music: an Introduction (Englewood Cliffs, NJ, 1967)
'The Revolution in Music', *Twentieth-century Views of Music History*, ed. Hays (New York, 1972)

MICHAEL STEINBERG

Salzman, Pnina (*b* Tel-Aviv, 24 Feb 1924). Israeli pianist. She learnt the piano at the Shulamit Conservatory, Tel-Aviv, with Lina Hopenko, and was invited by Cortot to study at the Paris Ecole Normale de Musique from which she graduated at the age of 12. She then studied at the Conservatoire with Magda Tagliafero and at 14 won a *premier prix*. She gave recitals from the age of nine in Paris and at 15 made her concerto début playing with the Orchestre Colonne under Paray. From then on she performed with many major orchestras, under such conductors as Sargent, Münch, Giulini, Solti and Koussevitzky. She made a world tour with the Israel PO in 1960 and in 1963 played in the USSR. She has a wide repertory of sonatas, concertos and chamber music, and in 1969 formed a trio with the clarinettist Yona Ettlinger and the cellist Uzi Wiesel. She is considered the first Israel-born pianist to achieve international fame.

WILLIAM Y. ELIAS

Saman [Samand, Samane, Sament], **René** (*fl* 1610–31). French composer and lutenist. A musician to Louis XIII, he also taught boys of the royal chapel. Several courantes by him are included in 17th-century collections of lute music. Of the three in Robert Dowland's *Varietie of Lute-lessons* (*RISM* 1610[23]/*R*1958) one is also found in Robert Ballard's *Premier livre* (1611/*R*1963), another in his *Deuxième livre* (1614/*R*1964) and the third among eight courantes by Saman in Lord Herbert of Cherbury's manuscript lutebook (*c*1640, *GB-Cfm*). A courante by him is also included in Besard's *Vesontini novus partus* (*RISM* 1617[26]).

BIBLIOGRAPHY

T. Dart: 'Lord Herbert of Cherbury's Lute-book', *ML*, xxxviii (1957), 136
L. E. S. J. de Laborde: *Musiciens de Paris, 1535–1792*, ed. Y. de Brossard (Paris, 1965)
M. le Moël: 'La chapelle de musique sous Henri IV et Louis XIII', *RMFC*, vi (1966), 5
C. A. Price: 'An Organizational Peculiarity of Lord Herbert of Cherbury's Lute Book', *LSJ*, ix (1969), 5

ANDREW ASHBEE

Samaras, Spyridon (Filiskos) (*b* Corfu, 29 Nov ?1863; *d* Athens, 7 April 1917). Greek composer. He studied music with Xyndas in Corfu, later with Enrico Stancabiano at the Athens Conservatory (1877–82) and with Delibes at the Paris Conservatoire (from 1882). His early *verismo* opera *Flora mirabilis* (1886, predating Mascagni's *Cavalleria rusticana* by four years) and some of his later operas were so successful that at one point they almost eclipsed Mascagni's, and he was encouraged to live abroad, mainly in Italy. He returned to Greece in 1911 to spend his last years in Athens. The foremost exponent of the Ionian school, he was the first Greek composer to achieve international recognition. His style, similar to that of the Italian *verismo* composers, changed little during his career, even when he introduced elements of Greek folksong into his music (as in *Rhea*, 1908).

WORKS

Operas: Olas (4, Fravassili), 1880–82, unperf., collab. E. Stancabiano; Medgè (4, P. Elzéar), 1883, Rome, 1888; Flora mirabilis (3, F. Fontani), Milan, 1886; Lionella, Milan, 1891; La martyre (Illica), Naples, 1894; La furia domata, Milan, 1895; Istoria d'amore (P. Milliet), Milan, 1903; Mademoiselle de Belle Isle (3, Milliet), Genoa, 1905; La biondinetta, Gotha, 1906; Rhea (Milliet), Florence, 1908; Hi tigris [The tiger] (R. Simone), inc.
Operettas: Polemos en polemo [War in war] (Tsokopoulos, Delikaterinis), Athens, 1914; Pringipissa tis Sasson [The Princess of Sasson] (Laskaris, Dimitrakopoulos), Athens, 1915; Criticopoula [The Cretan girl] (Laskaris, Dimitrakopoulos), Athens, 1916
Other works: Epinikeia [After the victory] (G. Drossinis), 1v, orch; Sinfonia, orch, 1879; Chitarrata, 10 gui, 10 mand, 1885; Vn Sonata, 1880–81; Scènes orientales, pf 4 hands (Milan, 1884); Hymn for the Olympic Games 1896, men's choir, orch, 1896; numerous pf pieces, songs with pf acc

BIBLIOGRAPHY
T. N. Synadinos: *Historia tis neoellinikis mousikis 1824–1919* [History of modern Greek music 1824–1919] (Athens, 1919), 169ff
S. Mocenigo: *Neoelliniki mousiki* [Modern Greek music] (Athens, 1958)

JOHN G. PAPAIOANNOU

Samaritan music. There is a tradition of sacred vocal (synagogue) music current among the Samaritans, a religious community numbering in the mid-1970s about 500, living in Nablus (Shechem) and Holon near Tel-Aviv. They claim descent from the ancient Israelites, and their music has many apparently archaic features; they differ from the Jews in a number of ways, however – for example, they recognize only the Pentateuch as canonical, and regard Mt Gerizim (near Nablus) rather than Jerusalem as the supreme holy place (cf *John* iv.20).

Samaritan music may be divided into two categories: solo songs and songs sung by the whole community. These are sung at services and at religious and social gatherings. The solo songs are usually free, melismatic recitatives, characterized by prominent glissandos and tremolos on certain notes; they are sung by the priest–cantor who leads the service, or, in certain hymns, by a *mashira* (expert in music).

The group songs are more syllabic in style and rhythmically repetitious, and have fewer glissandos and tremolos. They are sometimes sung in unison, but mostly antiphonally, the worshippers being divided into two groups, one on the right-hand side of the synagogue facing Mt Gerizim, the other on the left; the former group is termed the 'right' or 'upper' group, the latter the 'left' or 'lower' group. Alternate groups of verses (drawn from the Pentateuch or from important hymns) are taken by the two groups, beginning with the 'right' group together with the priests; each group begins as the other reaches approximately the midpoint of its verses,

so that there is an almost continuous bitextual performance. All the group songs are characterized by improvised parallel polyphony, in which all the intervals are at times found, and in which there are also usually drones and notes of indefinite pitch (ex.1; cf the similar improvised polyphony resembling parallel organum to be found in Syrian Christian music: *see* SYRIAN CHURCH MUSIC). Among the group songs, the Pentateuch canticles (the Song of the Sea, *Exodus* xv.1–21, performed five times a year at the presentation of the holy scroll in the synagogue; see ex.1), and the Song of Moses, *Deuteronomy* xxxi.30–xxxii.43) are particularly popular, with different melodies for different occasions; they sometimes include sections sung by the priest–cantor. Old Samaritan manuscripts of the Pentateuch contain traditional accents for the reading of the text, but these are ignored today.

The range of most Samaritan melodies does not exceed three notes; the melodies comprise short phrases repeated over and over or combined in pairs of half-verses in the manner of the *parallelismus membrorum* of the Psalms. Some aspects of the style of the music sung outside services suggests a relationship to Arab folk-song; some, such as the organal polyphony and the extensive use of nonsense syllables (ex.1; cf the Byzantine TERETISMATA), may be archaic survivals. Grove, who visited Nablus in 1861, thought Samaritan music archaic, and Lachmann went so far as to ascribe to the Samaritans the greatest antiquity of any liturgical tradition (1974, p.55). The extreme conservatism and religious exclusivism of leading Samaritans may support this hypothesis.

BIBLIOGRAPHY
J. Mills: *Three Months' Residence at Nablus and an Account of the Modern Samaritans* (London, 1864)
F. Grove: *Narrative of an Explorer in Tropical South Africa*, ii (London, 1890), 241ff
J. A. Montgomery: *The Samaritans, the Earliest Jewish Sect: their History, Theology and Literature* (Philadelphia, 1907)
A. E. Cowley, ed.: *The Samaritan Liturgy* (Oxford, 1909)
A. Z. Idelsohn: 'Die Vortragszeichen der Samaritaner', *Monatsschrift für Geschichte und Wissenschaft des Judentums*, lxi (1917), 117
J. E. H. Thomson: *The Samaritans: their Testimony to the Religion of Israel* (Edinburgh, 1919)
M. Gaster: *The Samaritans: their History, Doctrines and Literature* (London, 1925)
Z. Ben-Hayyim: *Ivrit ve-aramit nusah Shomron* [The literary and oral tradition of Hebrew and Aramaic among the Samaritans] (Jerusalem, 1957–67)
D. Cohen and R. T. Katz: 'Explorations in the Music of the Samaritans: an Illustration of the Utility of Graphic Notation', *EM*, iv (1960), 67
J. Macdonald: 'Arabic Musical and Liturgical Terms employed by the Samaritans', *Islamic Quarterly*, vi (1961), 47
M. Ravina: *Organum and the Samaritans* (Tel-Aviv, 1963)
J. Macdonald: *The Theology of the Samaritans* (London, 1964)
J. Spector: 'Samaritan Chant', *JIFMC*, xvi (1964), 66
S. Hofman: ''Arba'ha-'amîdôt bi-qri'at hat-tôrah befîhaš-šomerônîm' [The four differentiae in the Samaritan reading of the law], *4th World Congress of Jewish Studies: Jerusalem 1965*, ii, 385; Eng. summary, 208
J. Spector: 'The Significance of Samaritan Neumes and Contemporary Practice', *SM*, vii (1965), 141
——: 'Written Tradition and Contemporary Practice in the Biblical Cantillation of the Samaritans', *4th World Congress of Jewish Studies: Jerusalem 1965*, ii, 153
E. Gerson-Kiwi: 'Vocal Folk-polyphonies of the Western Orient in Jewish Traditions', *Yuval*, i (Jerusalem, 1968), 169
S. Hofman: 'Qeriat piyyutê Marqah be-sâbbat befî haš-šômerônîm' [The reading of Marka's poems by the Samaritans on the Sabbath], *Yuval*, i (Jerusalem, 1968), 36; Eng. summary, 251
R. Katz: 'The Reliability of Oral Transmission: the Case of Samaritan Music', *Yuval*, iii (Jerusalem, 1974), 109
——: 'On "Nonsense" Syllables as Oral Group Notation', *MQ*, lx (1974), 187
R. Lachmann: 'Orientalische Musik und Antike', *Robert Lachmann: Posthumous Works*, i, ed. E. Gerson-Kiwi (Jerusalem, 1974), 45

AVIGDOR HERZOG

Ex.1 Beginning of the central section of the Song of the Sea (*Exodus* xv. 12–16), performed five times each year at the presentation of the holy scroll in the synagogue, as recorded by the Israel Broadcasting Authority (*c*1952, ?at Holon): nonsense syllables appear in parentheses; transcr. A. Herzog

*from this point song is performed a semitone higher

Samaroff [née Hickenlooper], **Olga** (*b* San Antonio, Texas, 8 Aug 1882; *d* New York, 17 May 1948). American pianist and teacher. She was the first American woman to win a scholarship to the Paris Conservatoire, entering the piano class of Delaborde. She then studied with Jedliczka in Berlin and with Ernest Hutcheson. Following her New York début (1905), she achieved an international reputation as a pianist, appearing with major orchestras and chamber groups. Her playing was admired for tonal colour, warmth and intellectual control. Forced to retire because of an arm injury, she had a remarkable teaching career at both the Philadelphia Conservatory and the Juilliard School (1924–48). Her notable pupils include William Kapell, Eugene List, Rosalyn Tureck and Alexis Weissenberg. She founded the Schubert Memorial to aid young American musicians and the Layman's Music Course to promote intelligent audiences. From 1911 to 1923 she was married to Stokowski.

WRITINGS
The Layman's Music Book (New York, 1935, rev. 2/1947 as *The Listener's Music Book*)
An American Musician's Story (New York, 1939) [autobiography]
JOHN G. DOYLE

Samazeuilh, Gustave (Marie Victor Fernand) (*b* Bordeaux, 2 June 1877; *d* Paris, 4 Aug 1967). French writer on music and composer. After graduating in law at the Ecole des Hautes Etudes, he turned to music, studying with Chausson, d'Indy and Bordes at the Schola Cantorum (1900–06), and also with Dukas. His music is small in quantity, but of a sustained quality; the style reflects the early works of Ravel and Debussy more than the ambience of the Schola Cantorum. His *Fantaisie élégiaque* was written for Thibaud and Cortot and first performed by them. However, Samazeuilh is better known as a critic and translator. He contributed music criticism to numerous newspapers and reviews, both French and foreign, wrote prefaces to several books on music and published some studies himself. His work as a translator included the preparation of French versions of *Tristan und Isolde*, Schumann's *Genoveva* and Strauss's *Capriccio*, and also of the *Wesendonklieder* and songs by Schubert, Liszt and Richard Strauss.

WORKS
(*selective list*)
Divertissement, musette, small orch, 1902; Sym. Study, 1906; Serenade, 1926; Naïades au soir, orch, 1926; Gitanes, orch, 1931; L'appel de la danse, orch, 1944
Fantaisie élégiaque, vn, pf, 1897, rev. 1914; Str Qt, d, 1900; Vn Sonata, b, 1903; Esquisses d'Espagne, fl, pf, 1914; Chant d'Espagne, cl, vc/pf, 1925; Luciole, cl, 1934; Suite en trio, str, 1937; Suite, str qt, 1937; Cantabile e capriccio, str qt, 1948; 2 Pieces, vc, 1948; Lamento e moto perpetuo, vn, n.d.
Suite, g, pf, 1902; Sonata, pf, 1902; Chanson à ma poupée et 3 petites inventions, pf, 1903; Le chant de la mer, pf, 1919; Serenade, pf, 1925; Nocturne, pf, 1938; Esquisse, pf, 1944; Evocation, pf, 1947
L'âme des iris, 1v, pf, 1897; Japonnerie (J. Lahor), 1v, pf, 1900; Feuillage du coeur (Maeterlinck), 1v, pf, 1903; Dans la brûme argentée (Samain), 1v, orch, 1907; Le somneil de Canope (Samain), 1v, orch, 1907; 2 poèmes chantés (Maeterlinck, de Régnier), 1v, orch, 1925; Chant d'Espagne (trad.), 1v, pf/orch, 1925; Le cercle des heures, female chorus, orch, 1933

Principal publisher: Durand

WRITINGS
Paul Dukas (Paris, 1913, 2/1936)
Ernest Chausson: musicien de mon temps (Paris, 1947)
ed.: *Ecrits de Paul Dukas sur la musique* (Paris, 1948)

BIBLIOGRAPHY
A. Cortot: *La musique de piano* (Paris, 1944)
J. Poupard: *Entretiens avec Gustave Samazeuilh* (Paris, 1962)
ANNE GIRARDOT

Samba. An Afro-Brazilian couple-dance and popular musical form. Originally 'samba' was a generic term designating, along with *batuque*, the choreography of certain circle-dances imported to America from Angola and the Congo. A characteristic element of the folk samba is the *umbigada*, an 'invitation to the dance' manifested by the touching of the couple's navels. Singing always accompanies the dancing. Melodic contours are generally descending and melodies isometric. In the *caipira* (i.e. rural São Paulo) folk samba, singing is almost always in parallel 3rds. Mostly in binary metre, samba melodies and accompaniments are highly syncopated: a semiquaver–quaver–semiquaver figure is particularly characteristic. The dance gradually became urbanized by the late 19th century and urban versions differ substantially from rural folk sambas, but both feature responsorial singing between a soloist and chorus who sing alternating stanzas and refrain.

De Andrade, who studied the rural São Paulo samba in the 1930s, held that the samba was defined by its choreography rather than its musical structure. Its short texts, simpler than those of the urban forms, usually dealt with daily activities and followed the traditional seven-syllable verse pattern of Portuguese poetry, although variations of metre might occur as a result of improvisation in most texts. This variety influenced the caesura of the melodic line of the early urban sambas, in which the texts follow a strophic structure. In the rural samba the typical accompanying ensemble includes the *bombo* (a large bass drum), snare drum, tambourine, *cuíca* (friction drum), *reco-reco* (*güiro* type of rattle) and *guaiá* (a shaken rattle). Regional variants with slightly different choreographic organization are the southern *samba de lenço* and *samba-roda*, and the northern *samba-de-roda* and *samba-de-matuto*. Folk versions in Rio de Janeiro are the *partido-alto* and the *pernada-carioca*, the latter influenced by *capoeira*.

The urban samba became standardized during the 1920s, particularly in Rio de Janeiro. The first recognized samba to be recorded was *Pelo telefone*, by Ernesto dos Santos ('Donga') in 1917. Among the most important composers of urban sambas from 1920 to 1950 were José Barbosa da Silva ('Sinhô'), Noel Rosa, Alfredo da Rocha Viana ('Pixinguinha'), Ari Barroso, Lamartine Babo, João de Barros and Ataulfo Alves. Several species of the form appeared from the late 1920s to the mid-1940s including the *samba de morro*, sometimes also referred to as *batucada*, cultivated by people of the *favelas* (hillside slums) of Rio de Janeiro. Its accompaniment was performed predominantly by percussion instruments. In the 1930s the urban samba acquired the character of a sung ballroom dance, with the backing of a colourful orchestra whose percussion section was considerably reduced compared with the concurrent Carnival samba. Other forms include the *samba de breque* (with spoken words interjected at cadences) and the *samba de enredo*, created by composers associated with the samba schools for their annual Carnival parade. *Samba-canção*, *samba-choro* and *samba-fox* were hybrid forms whose lyrics dealt with love and unhappiness, often melodramatically; they were mainly ballroom and later night-club genres. The urban samba remained basically unchanged until the advent of BOSSA-NOVA in the late 1950s.

See also BRAZIL, §II, and LATIN AMERICA, §IV.

BIBLIOGRAPHY

M. de Andrade: 'O samba rural paulista', *Revista do Arquivo municipal de São Paulo*, xli (1937), 37

R. Tavares de Lima: *Melodia e ritmo no folclore de São Paulo* (São Paulo, 1954)

L. Rangel: *Sambistas e chorões* (São Paulo, 1962)

A. Maynard Araújo. *Folclore nactonal*, íl (São Paulo, 1964)

A. Vasconcelos: *Panorama da música popular brasileira* (São Paulo, 1964)

J. Ramos Tinhorão: *O samba agora vai . . . a farsa da música popular no exterior* (Rio de Janeiro, 1969)

——: *Pequena história da música popular* (Petrópolis, 1974)

GERARD BÉHAGUE

Samber, Johann Baptist (*b* Salzburg, baptized 10 May 1654; *d* Salzburg, buried 19 Sept 1717). Austrian theorist, organist and teacher. He was educated in his native city. About 1660 he entered the court chapel school, founded for children of the chapel choir. He studied music with Andreas Hofer, Kapellmeister of Salzburg Cathedral, and later also with Georg Muffat, who became court organist in 1678. In 1668 he entered Salzburg University but left before completing his studies. In 1689 he began to deputize for the infirm organist of Salzburg parish and cathedral, Hans Jacob Raiff; after Raiff's death in 1693, he succeeded him in these positions. In addition he pursued an active career as music teacher and also as instructor at the court chapel school. In his *Manuductio ad organum* (1704) he reported that he had taught 300 students. As Federhofer has shown, his particular historical significance has gone almost entirely unnoticed, even though his three treatises record in considerable detail the musical practices of south Germany and Austria in the late Baroque period. The *Manuductio ad organum* and the *Continuatio ad manuductionem organicam* (published three years later) contain much information about the elementary fundamentals of music, solmization (richly illustrated with 71 pages of examples and explanations) and keyboard instruction, as well as a most valuable thoroughbass method. The latter partly shows the influence of his teacher Georg Muffat, and subsequently it influenced Samber's successor as cathedral organist, Matthäus Gugl, in his thoroughbass manual *Fundamenta partiturae in compendio data* (Salzburg, 1719). The most important section of Samber's *Continuatio* is entitled 'Wie man eine schöne Harmoniam oder liebliche Gesang nach gewissen Praecepten und Regel componiren'. This consists of a restatement of Christoph Bernhard's contrapuntal doctrine appearing in his *Ausführlicher Bericht vom Gebrauche der Con- und Dissonantien,* especially his concept of the *figurae superficiales,* those exceptional dissonance procedures labelled with rhetorical terms such as *superjectio, variatio, multiplicatio, ellipsis, retardatio, quasi transitus* and *abruptio.* Equally significant is the long description of the registers of the Salzburg Cathedral organ as well as the general comments regarding organ registration, which are particularly relevant to the traditions of organ practice in south Germany and Austria in the Baroque period. Samber's final work, *Elucidatio musicae choralis* (1710), is restricted to an explanation of the learning and performance of plainsong. Although his treatises were neither original nor new in outlook, they encompass a comprehensive view of music theory and performing prac-

tice in Salzburg around 1700. Together with his activities as organist and teacher they make him the major Austrian music theorist before Fux.

WRITINGS

Manuductio ad organum, das ist, Gründlich- und sichere Handleitung durch die höchst-nothwendige Solmisation, zu der edlen Schlag-Kunst (Salzburg, 1704)

Continuatio ad manuductionem organicam, das ist, Fortsetzung zu der Manuduction oder Handleitung zum Orgl-Schlagen (Salzburg, 1707)

Elucidatio musicae choralis, das ist, Gründlich und wahre Erläuterung oder Unterweisung, wie die edle und uralte Choral-Music fundamentaliter nach denen wolgegründten Reglen mit leichter Mühe möge erlehrnet werden (Salzburg, 1710)

BIBLIOGRAPHY

H. Federhofer: 'Ein Salzburger Theoretikerkreis', *AcM*, xxxvi (1964), 50–79

GEORGE J. BUELOW

Sambrooke Manuscript (*US-NYp* Drexel 4302). *See* SOURCES OF INSTRUMENTAL ENSEMBLE MUSIC TO 1630, §7.

Sambson, Giovanni. *See* SANSONI, GIOVANNI.

Sambuca (Lat.; Gk. *sambykē*). One of several terms for the Greco-Roman angle harp (*see* TRIGŌNON). It is Eastern in origin: there are cognates in various languages, notably Aramaic (there the word is *sabbeka*, which appears four times in *Daniel*).

The term was also applied to a Roman engine of war resembling the hull of a boat with a ladder standing in it vertically and attached to it with stretched ropes. Descriptions of the engine likened it to the musical instrument and the greater antiquity of the instrument indicates that the engine was named after it rather than vice versa. This presents us with the clearest verbal description we possess of the angle harp and one which corresponds with pictorial representations. In order to achieve a correspondence exact in every detail the engine of war must be imagined turned on its side since the ladder resembles the harp's horizontal pegboard and the boat's hull the vertical soundboard.

Sambucistria is a term designating a female sambuca player. It was used by authors such as Polybius, Plutarch and Livy to create a sense of foreign-inspired decadence.

BIBLIOGRAPHY

G. Wille: *Musica romana* (Amsterdam, 1967)

JAMES W. MC KINNON

Sambuca lincea. An enharmonic harpsichord or ARCICEMBALO, also known as a pentecontachordon, invented by FABIO COLONNA and described by him in 1618.

Sambykē (Gk.). In antiquity, a category of harp; *see* IBYCUS and JEWISH MUSIC, §I, 4(iv).

Samfundet Dansk Kirkesang. Danish society founded in 1922 to promote Thomas Laub's ideas of restoring hymn tunes; *see* DENMARK, §I, 5.

Samfundet til Udgivelse af Dansk Musik. Danish music publishing society. It was founded on 18 December 1871 by Jacob Christian Fabricius (1840–1919) as a private, noncommercial enterprise with the aim of furthering knowledge of Danish music by publishing major Danish works. The catalogue comprises over 300 works by 110 composers of all periods, and includes Mogens

Pedersøn's madrigals (c1620), works by late 18th-century masters such as F. L. Ae. Kunzen and J. A. P. Schulz, works of the 19th century by Weyse, Kuhlau, Hartmann and Gade, the music of Carl Nielsen and his successors, Riisager, Høffding, Weis, Tarp and Holmboe, and later works by N. V. Bentzon, Maegaard, Mogens Winkel Holm and Nørholm, and the succeeding generation. (The society has issued detailed lists of works by Riisager and Høffding.) Works are published in their original form, mainly in full score (and parts); for modern compositions, where necessary, traditional notation and format have been replaced by graphic notation. From the outset historical editions included informative prefatory material; facsimile editions and critical editions by leading scholars have also been produced. In the mid-1960s the society began issuing gramophone records of works in its catalogue. Samfundet til Udgivelse af Dansk Musik is largely financed by subsidies from the state's cultural fund. In accordance with the original noncommercial principle, composers receive full performing fees as well as royalties.

BIBLIOGRAPHY

D. Fog, ed.: Samfundet til udgivelse af dansk musik 1871–1971: Catalogue (Copenhagen, 1972) [in Eng.]

DAN FOG

Samin, Vulfran (fl 1543–59). French singer and composer. He was a chorister of the Confraternité de Notre Dame at Amiens in 1543–4. A mass by him ('Sancti Spiritus') was published with one each by Cadeac and Hérissant (RISM 1558[1]), and 16 of his chansons appeared in collections (4 in 1546[12], 3 in 1546[14], 1 in 1548[3], 4 in 1548[4], 1 in 1549[20], 1 in 1549[22], 2 in 1559[10]).

BIBLIOGRAPHY

F. Lesure and G. Thibault: Bibliographie des éditions d'Adrian Le Roy et Robert Ballard (Paris, 1955)

F. Lesure: 'Some Minor French Composers of the 16th Century', Aspects of Medieval and Renaissance Music: a Birthday Offering to Gustave Reese (New York, 1966), 538

FRANK DOBBINS

Saminsky, Lazare (b Vale-Hotzulovo, nr. Odessa, 8 Nov 1882; d Port Chester, NY, 30 June 1959). American composer, conductor and writer on music of Russian origin. He studied mathematics and philosophy at St Petersburg University (1906–9) and composition and conducting with Lyadov and Rimsky-Korsakov at the conservatories of St Petersburg and Moscow (1906–10). In 1908 he and some other St Petersburg Conservatory students founded the Society for Jewish Folk Music, and in 1913 he took part in the Baron de Guinzburg Ethnological Expedition to collect religious chants of the Transcaucasian Jews. He was active as a conductor in Tbilisi, Paris and London between 1915 and 1920, and in 1917–18 he directed the Tbilisi Conservatory. In 1920 he settled in New York, where he was a founder of the League of Composers (1923) and its director for two decades. He was also music director of Temple Emamu-El, New York (1924–56), where he established (in 1926) and directed the annual Three Choirs Festival. The Jewish folk and liturgical music which he studied was subtly reworked and developed in his compositions, where lyricism and romantic expressiveness are blended with polyphonic and rhythmic ingenuity. He conducted his works frequently with major orchestras in the USA and Europe, and his articles were published internationally.

WORKS
(selective list)

STAGE AND ORCHESTRAL

Opera: Julian, the Apostate Caesar (3), 1933–8
Ballet: The Lament of Rachel (1), 1913, rev. 1920
Opera-ballets: The Vision of Ariel (1), 1915; The Plague's Gagliarda (1), 1924, New York, 1925; Jephtha's Daughter (3 scenes), 1928
Syms.: no.1 'Of the Great Rivers', 1914; no.2 'Of the Summits', 1918; no.3 'Of the Seas', 1924; no.4, 1926; no.5 'Jerusalem, City of Solomon and Christ', chorus, orch, 1932
Other orch works: Vigiliae, sym. triptych, 1910–11; Ausonia, 1930; To a New World, 1932; 3 Shadows, 1935; Pueblo, a Moon Rhapsody, 1936; Stilled Pageant, 1937; East and West, suite, vn, orch, 1943

CHORAL

4 Sacred Choruses, unacc., 1913; Sabbath Eve Service, cantor, chorus, org, 1925, rev. 1947; Sabbath Morning Service, cantor, chorus, org, 1925–8; By the Rivers of Babylon, S, Bar, chorus, 4 insts, 1926; Holiday Service, cantor, chorus, org, 1927–9; The Lord Reigneth, S, Bar, chorus, pf, org, 1933; Newfoundland Air (Thoreau), chorus, pf, 1935; Out of the Deep, T, chorus, org ad lib, c1937; From the American Poets, chorus, pf, perc ad lib, c1946; Requiem, 1v, chorus, orch, c1946; Anthology of Hebrew Sacred and Traditional Songs, cantor, solo vv, chorus, org, 1946; To Zion, choral fanfare, 1948

OTHER WORKS

Solo vocal: Hebrew Song Cycles nos.1–2, 1909, 1913–14; The Songs of the Three Queens, S, pf/chamber orch, 1924; Litanies of Women, Mez, pf/chamber orch, 1925; 6 Songs of the Russian Orient, 1v, pf/chamber orch, 1925–6; Eon Hours, 4vv, 4 insts, 1935; Rye Septet, 1v, 7 insts, 1942; A Sonnet of Petrarch, 3vv, 3 insts, 1947; A Song Treasury of Old Israel, 1v, pf, 1951
Chamber: Hebrew Rhapsody, vn, pf, 1911; Venice, chamber orch, 1927
Pf: 2 Pieces, 1917; 3 Pieces, 1919; 10 Hebrew Folk Songs and Folk Dances, 1922; From Cynthia's Playnook, 1936

Principal publishers: Birchard, Bloch, Chester, Fischer, Presser, Salabert, Universal

WRITINGS

Music of Our Day (New York, 1932, rev., enlarged 2/1939)
Music of the Ghetto and the Bible (New York, 1934)
Living Music of the Americas (New York, 1949)
Physics and Metaphysics of Music and Essays on the Philosophy of Mathematics (The Hague, 1957)
Essentials of Conducting (New York and London, 1958)

BIBLIOGRAPHY

D. de Paoli and others: Lazare Saminsky: Composer and Civic Worker (New York, 1930)

L. Saminsky: Third Leonardo (MS, 1959) [autobiography]

NATHAN BRODER/BARBARA HAMPTON

Samisen. See SHAMISEN; see also JAPAN, §IV, 4.

Samish music. The inhabitants of Lapland prefer to be known as Sames (from Samish sab'me: 'man') rather than Lapps, since this means people who have gone or been driven to the end (lappu or lappi) of the world, and might thus be thought to be rough or barbaric outcasts.

1. Historical background. 2. The current situation.

1. HISTORICAL BACKGROUND. The original homeland of the Sames and the date of their migration to Finno-Scandinavia are in doubt. Modern investigations suggest that they gradually shifted the nucleus of their territory from the White Sea coast to northern Norway, under pressure from stronger peoples. The first Samish groups probably migrated to Finno-Scandinavia in the middle of the 1st century BC. Today the Sames number about 20,000 in Norway, about 8000 in Sweden, about 3000 in Finland and less than 2000 in the USSR. Their language is classed as Finno-Ugric.

The Samish people have for many centuries been subject to colonization and development of their territory by foreign merchants, royal officials and settlers and to conversion to Christianity by missionaries. They have always suffered from being an alien minority with a different appearance, language and culture from the rest of the population. They have lived mainly by hunting, fishing, agriculture, reindeer breeding and (until the 16th century) fur trading.

The Christian influence became stronger in the 16th century. Samish beliefs about nature and natural phenomena were subject to particular attack. In most Samish rituals a *nåide* (shaman) participated in collective singing and drumming: these rituals, and eventually all singing, were prohibited and most shamanic drums were destroyed. Missionaries and travellers between the 17th and 19th centuries provided the first reports of *juoi'gat* ('singing in the Samish way'), but gave conflicting views about it: some thought it was hideous screaming, while others described it more sympathetically. The adverse reaction was probably due to disapproval of ritual song and of its possible effect on other song.

At that time the Samish way of life still depended on the influence and power of the shaman. Singing by both the shaman and the other participants played a central role in shaman meetings. Loud repetitive singing employing voice disguise, with accompanying gestures, must have been an essential feature. Songs played an important role in other social occasions, and the performance style of these songs and shamanic songs probably influenced one another, so that it is not easy to make a strict division between the two. For this reason, and also because according to Samish traditions they learned to sing from the *uldas* (creatures who live in cliffs, woods and lakes), the missionaries' ban on all song was understandable. The influence of ritual song introduced heathen and forbidden elements into other song, besides an unusual performance style. Some early authors con-

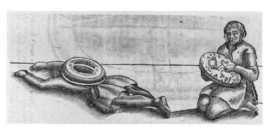

2. Shaman drummers, one of whom is in a state of trance with his drum placed over his head: woodcut from Johannes Schefferus's 'History of Lapland' (1674)

demned all such singing out of hand; others took exception to some aspect of it; and a third group was unprejudiced and enjoyed it.

This ban and the harsh penalties for any infringement was completely successful in abolishing 'heathen' (shamanistic) song, but it is difficult to measure its effect on other singing. *Juoi'gat* almost disappeared from the public scene, but it still exists, even if in schools and at public events it may not be done in 'the Samish way'.

The musical instrument most often mentioned in the source writings is the shamanic drum, commonly of frame or shell type (fig.1). The reindeer hide stretched over the frame or shell was richly painted with symbols and a hammer-shaped piece of reindeer horn served as a drumstick. The drum was used extra-musically to produce a trance and for fortune telling (see fig.2). A few examples are preserved in museums. Apart from other formerly common sound instruments such as rattles and bullroarers, there was one chief melody instrument, the *fadno* (idioglott oboe), made from a fresh stem of *Angelica archangelica*, with three to five finger-holes. This, like other melody instruments (such as the Finnish *kantele*, and the bark trumpet and flutes from Sweden), was probably adopted from neighbouring peoples. Ex.1 shows a typical *fadno* melody, collected before 1942. Although this instrument is no longer played the others are still occasionally used.

1. Samish shaman drum (Museum für Völkerkunde, Staatliche Museen Preussischer Kulturbesitz, Berlin)

Ex.1 *Fadno* (oboe) melody (Tirén, 1942)

2. THE CURRENT SITUATION. *Juoi'gat* (mainly solo singing without instrumental accompaniment) is in the 1970s the sole form of traditional musical expression. Newer musical styles based on traditional *juoi'gat* and retaining some of its features are also found (e.g. the *juoigos* songs with guitar accompaniment by Nils-Aslak Valkeapää of Finland). There is considerable regional variation of meaning of the words *juoigos* or *juoigam*, *luotte* and *vuolle*. In northern Norway the terms *juoigos* and *luotte* mean 'text with melody on persons, animals and things in an appropriate situation' (the word *luotte* is generally found only in this area); in the provinces of northern Sweden both *vuolle* and *juoigos* mean simply 'melody with or without text'. It is risky to draw conclusions from these differences of meaning, although some, such as Ruong, interpret this to mean that the main emphasis is on verbal content in the north and on melodo-rhythmic delivery in the south. But, if the different interpretations are considered together, *juoi'gat* may be taken to mean 'to sing in the Samish way, with a

definite melody, with or without text and on an appropriate occasion'.

The 'Samish way' of singing relates to the vocal technique of the songs and to their structure, which is distinguished by its formal construction, melodic contours and rhythm, and by the way the texts are arranged. The peculiar Samish vocal timbre is marked by frequent use of glottal stops (the strained sound which is caused by rapidly and strongly flexing, and firmly closing, the vocal cords) and, above all, by ornamenting the melody with appoggiaturas, terminal notes and double glides (see ex.2). In these double glides the initial upward glide is caused by an increase in breath pressure: a sudden relaxation follows and the pitch falls again.

Ex.2 Vocal ornaments

A *juoigos* is composed from a definite sequence of two, four, six or more phrases equal in length, but melodically distinct: the melody is repeated at least once, usually three to six times, frequently with added variants. During performance an orderly system of repetition is established to build what Tirén has described as a 'chain song'. Most melodies are based on anhemitonic pentatonic modes and show a preference for disjunct movement. A small category of pentatonic melodies contains clearly emphasized and definitely sounded semitones. There is a variety of rhythmic organization. The basic beat may be divided into two or three with a variety of accentuation and the beats themselves grouped to give simple and compound forms of duple and triple metres or additive metres (see exx.3, 4 and 5).

The *juoigos* repertory can be grouped into four categories according to content. Songs of the first group relate to landscapes and such specific features as lakes, mountains (ex.3), rivers, forests and reindeer pastures,

Ex.3 *Vuolle* (Grundström and Smedeby, 1963)

as well as to transient natural phenomena and impressions (the midnight sun, rainbows, the appearance of the sea). Such songs are common mainly in Sweden (in the region around Piteå and Luleå) and are comparatively rare in other regions. The second group comprises *juoigos* for all the animals of Lapland: animals of the water, land and air (ex.4). The third and largest group of *juoi-*

Ex.4 *Juigos. Haŋgá* (Clangula hyemalis: long-tailed duck) (Lüderwaldt, 1974)

Aaŋgá = sung form of *Haŋgá*, which vaguely characterizes the cry of the bird

gos concerns people (ex.5). The likely subjects are the singer's close relatives and friends, acquaintances and such local characters as priests, officials and merchants. A further and more recent category consists of songs about modern objects and technical achievements. What Ruong has called 'complex joiks' combine themes from different groups and are mainly epic in character. They are typical of Swedish Lapland and the Skolt Sames in north-eastern Finland. The repertory must once have been much more extensive; but after the shaman meetings and rituals disappeared, the music focussed mainly on the three groups described above, although Tirén found 'magic songs' – songs about supernatural creatures, sacrificial songs and incantations – surviving in the 20th century.

Ex.5 *Juigos*, Mikkel P. Sara (Lüderwaldt, 1974)

Syllables and particles form the basis and often the entire text of a *juoigos* melody. In earlier times they were thought to be magical interjections and were believed by the shaman to derive from the language of the spirits. There are many ways in which the texts could be made up from the now 'meaningless' syllables and particles. In many songs only the name of the person or animal concerned is given (exx.4 and 5). But other words or whole phrases may be woven in, or a coherent syntactical text may be used.

There are two main 'appropriate occasions' for singing: work (dealing with reindeer, hunting and fishing – situations which ensure immediate contact with nature) and social activity (particularly any kind of gathering associated with the *sii'da* system). On these occasions the Sames not only sing old and well-known melodies, but also invent and develop new ones. The community plays an important part in disseminating songs. Where the older forms of work, such as reindeer breeding, hunting and fishing, have been replaced by other sources of income and the *sii'da* system has disintegrated, the *juoi'gat* is rare or has disappeared entirely.

Juoi'gat, or 'to sing in the Samish way', can be defined as to sing with the Samish vocal technique and way of constructing and ordering the melody. Turi believed that to sing 'a definite melody with or without text' was to give meaning to a melody and to remember it (Demant). The community provides the 'appropriate occasion', which consolidates the feeling of fellowship. For the Sames *juoi'gat* also means to sing spontaneously, in order to keep their environment in mind and to know that their community is secure. Missionary bans may have outwardly eliminated shaman meetings, drums, shamans and their functions; but they have not prevented spontaneous song, nor have they erased memories or broken up communities.

BIBLIOGRAPHY

O. Donner: *Lieder der Lappen* (Helsinki, 1876)

A. Launis: *Lappische Juoigos-Melodien* (Helsinki, 1908)

——: 'Die Pentatonik in den Melodien der Lappen', *IMusSCR*, iii Vienna 1909, 244

E. Demant, ed.: *J. Turi: Das Buch des Lappen Johan Turi* (Frankfurt, 1912)

T. Lehtisalo: 'Beobachtungen über die Jodler', *Journal de la Société finno-ougrienne*, xlviii/2 (1937), 1–35

E. Manker: *Die lappische Zaubertrommel* (Stockholm, 1938–50)

K. Tirén: *Die lappische Volksmusik* (Stockholm, 1942)

B. Collinder: *The Lapps* (Princeton, 1949)

Å. Campbell: 'Herdsman's Song and Yoik in Northern Sweden', *JIFMC*, iii (1951), 64

R. Graff: 'Music of Norwegian Lapland', *JIFMC*, vi (1954), 29

E. Haeger: 'Om de första jojkningsuppteckningarna i Sverige', *STMf*, xxxvii (1955), 146 [with Eng. summary]

W. Danckert: 'Tonmalerei und Tonsymbolik in der Musik der Lappen', *Mf*, ix (1956), 286

E. Wustmann: *Klingende Wildnis* (Eisenach, 1956)

H. Grundström and A. O. Väisänen: *Lappische Lieder, Texte und Melodien aus Schwedisch-Lappland* (Uppsala, 1958)

E. Lagercrantz, ed.: *Lappische Volksdichtung, iv: Seelappische Gesangsmotive des Varangergebiets* (Helsinki, 1960)

C. G. Widstrand: 'Skolt Lapp Songs of North East Finland', *JIFMC*, xiii (1961), 73

H. Grundström and S. Smedeby: *Lappische Lieder, Texte und Melodien aus Schwedisch-Lappland* (Uppsala, 1963)

E. Emsheimer: *Studia ethnomusicologica eurasiatica* (Stockholm, 1964)

R. Günther: 'Zur Musik der Lappen', *Kölner ethnologische Mitteilungen*, iv (1965), 71

E. Lagercrantz, ed.: *Lappische Volksdichtung, vii: Sonagraphische Untersuchung lyrischer lappischer Volkslieder aus Karasjok und Enontekiö mit Noten und Erklärungen* (Helsinki, 1966)

I. Ruong: *The Lapps in Sweden* (Stockholm, 1967)

M. Arnberg, I. Ruong and H. Unsgaard: *Jojk: Yoik* (Stockholm, 1969) [Swed. and Eng., with 7 discs]

S. Aikio, I. Kecskeméti and Z. Kiss, eds.: *Lappische Joiku-Lieder aus Karasjok gesungen von Anders Ivar Guttorm* (Helsinki, 1972)

G. Szomjas-Schiffert: 'Traditional Singing Style of the Lapps', *YIFMC*, v (1973), 51

A. Lüderwaldt: *Joiken aus Norwegen: Studien zur Charakteristik und gesellschaftlichen Bedeutung des lappischen Gesanges* (diss., Free U. of Berlin, 1974)

ANDREAS LÜDERWALDT

Sammarco, Mario (*b* Palermo, 13 Dec 1868; *d* Milan, 24 Jan 1930). Italian baritone. He studied at Palermo with A. Cantelli and at Milan with F. Emerich, making his début in 1888 at Palermo in *Faust* and then singing in smaller theatres until 1893. In 1894 he appeared at the S Carlo, Naples, in *La damnation de Faust* and in 1895 at the Teatro Real, Madrid, as Thomas' Hamlet, a role he repeated during the 1895–6 season at La Scala, where he also sang Gérard in the first performance of *Andrea Chénier*. He returned to La Scala in 1902, 1905 and 1913, meanwhile singing at Buenos Aires in 1897. His Covent Garden début was in 1904 as Scarpia, and he continued to appear in London until 1914, and then again in 1919. He sang at the Manhattan Opera, New York (1907–10), and at Boston, Philadelphia and Chicago (1909–13). Retiring from the stage in 1919, he later founded a school of singing at Milan, where Paul Schöffler was among his pupils. Sammarco's voice was clear but resonant, rounded and of very extensive range. A most stylish singer, at the beginning of his career he specialized in operas such as *La favorite*, *Ernani*, *Rigoletto*, *Un ballo in maschera*, *Hamlet* and *La gioconda*, but his remarkable theatrical qualities later led him to prefer *verismo* roles, particularly Tonio, Gérard, Scarpia and Wolf-Ferrari's Rafaele, and the parts he created in Leoncavallo's *Zazà* (Teatro Lirico, Milan, 1900) and Franchetti's *Germania* (La Scala, 1902).

BIBLIOGRAPHY

J. Freestone: 'Giuseppe Maria Sammarco', *Gramophone*, xxix (1951), 96 [with discography]

G. Lauri-Volpi: *Voci parallele* (Milan, 1955), 171f

R. Celletti: 'Sammarco, Mario,' *Le grandi voci* (Rome, 1964) [with opera discography by T. Kaufmann]

RODOLFO CELLETTI

Sammartini [St Martini, San Martini, San Martino, Martini, Martino], **Giovanni Battista** (*b* 1700 or 1701; *d* Milan, 15 Jan 1775). Italian composer, brother of Giuseppe Sammartini and a leading figure in the development of the Classical style.

1. Life. 2. Reputation. 3. Style.

1. LIFE. Sammartini was one of eight children of Alexis Saint-Martin, a French oboist who emigrated to Italy, and Girolama de Federici. He was probably born in Milan, the city in which he lived all his life. Since in his death certificate he is said to have been 74, he should have been born in 1700 or the first two weeks of 1701. His earliest musical instruction probably came from his father. In 1720 the 'Sammartini brothers' were listed as oboists in the orchestra of the Teatro Regio Ducal in Milan, a reference to Giuseppe and Giovanni Battista or another brother – Antonio or Carlo. Sammartini's first known composition is an aria (lost) for the oratorio *La calunnia delusa*, performed in 1724, to which Giuseppe and other composers also contributed. His first set of vocal works which is known (also lost) dates from 1725: five cantatas for the Fridays in Lent written for the Congregation of the Ss Entierro, which met in the Jesuit church of S Fedele. Sammartini became *maestro di cappella* of the Congregation in 1728 and continued in that post for most of his life; his last Lenten cantatas are dated 1773.

By 1726, Sammartini was called 'very famous' in his contract as substitute *maestro di cappella* of S Ambrogio (the full appointment came in 1728). Also in 1726 he composed a Christmas oratorio for S Fedele entitled *Gesù bambino adorato dalli pastori*. J. J. Quantz, who visited Milan that year, wrote grudgingly of the music of Sammartini and Francesco Fiorino as 'not bad', though he noted that they were the leading church composers of the city. In his maturity Sammartini became the most active church composer in Milan. The almanac *Milano sacro* for 1761–75 lists him as the *maestro di cappella* of eight churches, while the almanac *La galleria delle stelle* for 1775 lists eleven; these included the ducal chapel S Gottardo, whose director he became in 1768 (there is no evidence to support Burney's statement that he was *maestro di cappella* of the convent of S Maria Maddalena). An excellent organist, Sammartini was praised by Burney as having 'a way peculiar to himself of touching that instrument which was truly masterly and pleasing'.

The 1730s saw a notable stream of symphonies, concertos, sonatas and dramatic works from Sammartini's pen, and recognition of his music outside Italy. His first opera, *Memet*, was performed in Lodi in 1732, and possibly in Vienna the same year. Milan heard his second opera, *L'ambizione superata dalla virtù*, in the Teatro Regio Ducal in 1734, with such noted singers as Vittoria Tesi and the castrato Angelo Maria Monticelli. By the early 1730s he had become the leading figure in the earliest symphonic school in Europe, which included such composers from Milan and nearby as Brioschi, Galimberti, Giulini, Lampugnani and Chiesa. From 1733 there are records of Sammartini's acting as judge in competitions for positions at the cathedral and other churches; in 1762 he sat on one such jury with Padre Martini. Apart from his teaching at the Collegio de' Nobili, where he was appointed in 1730, only two of his no doubt numerous pupils can be identified with any certainty: Count Giorgio Giulini (1716–80), a popular

1. Giovanni Battista Sammartini: copy (1778) by Domenico Riccardi of a lost portrait by an unknown artist, in the Civico Museo Bibliografico Musicale, Bologna

Milanese dilettante composer of symphonies, and Christoph Willibald Gluck, who probably studied with Sammartini from 1737 to 1741. Many of Gluck's early works were influenced by Sammartini, and Gluck borrowed movements from two Sammartini symphonies for his operas *Le nozze d'Ercole e d'Ebe* (1747) and *La contesa dei numi* (1749). Sammartini's last opera, *L'Agrippina, moglie di Tiberio*, was performed in the Teatro Regio Ducal in 1743, with Carestini as Tiberius.

As Milan's most famous composer, Sammartini took a leading role in the life of the city, composing and conducting music for religious and state occasions. In January 1741 he directed a mass of his own composition in S Ambrogio in memory of Cardinal Benedetto Odelscalchi. In 1742 he conducted in the church of S Paolo de' Barnabiti in Vigevano, near Milan. Many other such performances took place in and near Milan. On the birth of Archduke Peter Leopold, Maria Theresia's third son, he composed a secular cantata, *La gara dei geni*, presented in 1747 at the Teatro Regio Ducal by the Lieutenant-governor of Austrian Lombardy, Count Gian-Luca Pallavicini. In 1749 Pallavicini organized concerts on the banks of the moat of the Sforza castle, some of which Sammartini directed. Sammartini presented concerts in 1751 at both the Sforza castle and the ducal palace on the translation of the body of S Carlo Borromeo to Milan Cathedral. For Prince Joseph of Austria's birthday in 1753, Pallavicini commissioned two cantatas jointly composed by Sammartini and Niccolò Jommelli. In 1758 Sammartini became one of the founders of a philharmonic society in Milan, reflecting the city's keen interest in orchestral music.

In 1760 Sammartini published a collection of six of his finest string trios (later issued by Le Clerc as op.7), dedicating the print to Don Filippo, Duke of Parma

(1721–65), one of his most important patrons. During the 1750s and 1760s he came into contact with some of the leading composers of the younger generation, notably J. C. Bach, who lived in Milan from c1754 to 1762, and Luigi Boccherini, who played in orchestras under Sammartini's direction in Pavia and Cremona for the festivities in July 1765 on the visit of Beatrice d'Este, wife of Archduke Leopold. Sammartini is mentioned in Leopold Mozart's letters from Milan in 1770: he heard Wolfgang perform and warmly supported him when there were intrigues against his opera *Mitridate, rè di Ponto*. During 1770 Sammartini also met Charles Burney, who visited Milan in July and left a valuable description of musical life in the city and performances of Sammartini's music. Burney heard a mass, a motet and an 'excellent' symphony by Sammartini. He praised the skilful composition of the orchestral portions of the mass and the beautiful *adagio* aria in the motet; but in the mass he criticized an 'excessive number' of fast movements and the extremely active violins. He observed that despite Sammartini's advanced age 'his fire and invention still remain in their utmost vigour'.

Between April and September 1773 Sammartini composed six string quintets; his last known work, the ballet *Il trionfo d'amore*, was performed in December 1773. That Sammartini's death in January 1775 was unexpected is shown by the schedule of 24 performances in Milanese churches planned for 1775 (published in the almanac *La galleria delle stelle*). The death certificate, dated 17 January 1775, states that Sammartini had died two days earlier and was buried in the church of S Alessandro on the evening of 16 January. Musicians from S Fedele, Milan Cathedral and elsewhere joined in a memorial service on 18 January; the Office and Solemn Mass were sung before a great gathering of people because (as the death certificate states) he was 'a most excellent master and celebrated by a most brilliant renown'. Of Sammartini's family, all that is known is that he was married twice, first to Margherita Benna (5 June 1727; d 13 Nov 1754) and then (on 23 June 1755) to Rosalinda Acquanio, and that his daughter, Marianna Rosa (b 11 Sept 1733), was a singer.

2. REPUTATION. It appears that Sammartini's music was better known outside Italy than in his native land. Many of his works were published in Paris and London, especially by Le Clerc, Venier and Walsh. Vivaldi conducted one of his symphonies in Amsterdam in 1738. Most of his surviving early works are in the Blancheton collection (*F-Pn*), formed in Paris largely between c1740 and c1744. The Concert Spirituel performed a Sammartini symphony in 1751 and his complex ensemble concerto in E♭ (published by Cox in 1756) was played by La Pouplinière's orchestra. His music gained equal popularity in England. It was admired by the Duke of Cumberland, brother of George III, and there is a mention of Sammartini in Sterne's *A Sentimental Journey*. According to Giuseppe Carpani, an early biographer of Haydn, Sammartini's music was introduced in Vienna by Count Harrach, governor of Lombardy from 1747 to 1750. Carpani reported that the music won immediate success and was patronized by such noblemen as Counts Pálffy, Schönborn, Lobkowitz and Clam-Gallas. Though no evidence has been found to support Carpani's assertion that Prince Esterházy commissioned two works a month from Sammartini, a 1759 inventory of the Esterházy collection lists two of his symphonies. There were performances of his music in

Prague as early as 1738, and the library of the Waldstein family (formerly in Doksy, now in Prague) holds the largest of all Sammartini collections.

While Sammartini's influence on Gluck has long been acknowledged, his influence on J. C. Bach and Luigi Boccherini remains to be investigated. His possible influence on Haydn was first mentioned by Carpani, who recounted that the Bohemian composer Josef Mysliveček (1737–81), on hearing some symphonies by Sammartini about 1780, exclaimed: 'I have found the father of Haydn's style'. Though Haydn strongly denied any influence of Sammartini in remarks to his biographer G. A. Griesinger, a study of Sammartini's music shows a marked affinity between the composers in rhythm, structure and even in the province of musical humour.

3. STYLE. Sammartini's music falls into three style periods which reflect the major trends in music between the 1720s and the time of his death. The early period, c1724–39, shows a Baroque–Classical style mixture; the middle period, c1740–58, is early Classical, and the style most characteristic of Sammartini; the late period, c1759–74, points to later Classical developments. Despite these changes, certain basic characteristics can be seen in works of all periods, especially an intense rhythmic drive and continuity of structure; a remarkably varied treatment of sonata form, in which the recapitulation usually contains many changes in the order of ideas and their presentation (variants of the main secondary theme being especially common); and an unusual sensitivity to textural arrangements and contrasts, favouring non-imitative counterpoint with contrasting motifs in the two violin parts. Sammartini com-

2. Opening of the first violin part of a late symphony in D by G. B. Sammartini, op.4 (London: Bremner, 1766)

posed the earliest known dated symphonies, movements from two symphonies used in 1732 as introductions to Acts 2 and 3 of the opera *Memet*. His symphony in G minor, whose finale Gluck borrowed for *La contesa dei numi*, anticipates the *Sturm und Drang* style by more than 20 years. Two ensemble concertos, in E♭ (published in 1756) and A, anticipate the sinfonia concertante in their scoring and two-movement arrangement. In his old age Sammartini produced some of the earliest string quartets (1763–7) and string quintets (1773), the latter scored for the unfamiliar combination of three violins, viola and cello. The few surviving sacred cantatas and liturgical works show a dramatic approach to text setting and an orchestral sophistication of a kind generally associated with the Viennese school. All these examples reveal a composer who was in the vanguard of musical developments throughout his life, and an artist of the greatest integrity and seriousness.

Sammartini's early orchestral music was influenced by the north Italian concerto tradition, especially Vivaldi. The 19 early symphonies have three movements, in the succession fast–slow–fast, some with minuet finales. There is no evidence to support the oft-repeated statement that Sammartini wrote a four-movement symphony in 1734. The only extant four-movement symphony (J–C39) is undated, and the fourth movement is an appended minuet taken from a trio sonata. The symphonies are scored for string orchestra, seven being trio symphonies (most omitting the violas), an important early type. Nearly all the movements have binary division: most of the longer allegros are in sonata form; the slow movements and minuets favour simple binary designs. The movements in sonata form are characterized by well-defined key areas, themes and thematic contrasts, long developments and clear recapitulations, which almost always begin with the opening theme in the tonic key. Multithematic movements are the most common, but some early examples of Classical monothematic sonata form already appear. Though homophony predominates, several movements contain refined textural arrangements and new uses of counterpoint. Sammartini transferred to the symphony the lyrical slow movement of the concerto. He favoured the 2/4 Andante, which became the standard type of Classical slow movement. He preferred the moderate 3/4 to the fast 3/8 minuet, and also wrote long finales in 2/4 and 3/8, some of them in *buffo* style. The main influences in the early symphonies derive from the concerto and the trio sonata rather than the Italian overture. The symphony is already established as an independent genre in these works.

Most of the 37 middle symphonies call for two horns or trumpets as well as strings, and end with minuets, some with trio sections. There are also a few two-movement symphonies (fast–minuet). Movements become longer, harmonic rhythm slower, and almost all movements are in sonata form, including slow movements and minuets. Contrast is intensified in texture, rhythm, dynamics and mood. Many first movements have a motoric character, using themes composed of short modules, half a bar and one bar in length. Melodic continuation by literal or varied repetition and contrast replaces the frequent sequential expansion of the early style. While the development section itself is usually short, developmental interest is supplied by motivic development within themes, thematic derivations and reformulated recapitulations (which act as second developments). The slow movements, often in the minor mode, are among Sammartini's finest creations. Warmly lyrical, concise in form, full in texture and richest in harmony, they contain his most personal expression, ranging from delicate charm to profound melancholy.

In the 12 late symphonies there are independent oboe parts and the cello and bass are often separated. There are longer and more varied periods, a more intense lyricism (which invades even the fast movements) and more complex harmony. The texture resembles the chamber style, with frequent dialogue among all the instruments, and far greater use of imitation, especially in the slow movements. The language in these works often has a Mozartian flavour.

Sammartini's orchestral music has a bright, transparent sound. Rhythmic effects are a prime source of interest and vitality: in the careful variation and contrast of rhythmic patterns and articulations, the deft mixture of regular and irregular phrase lengths, and the carefully calculated changes in rhythmic values. Sammartini avoided large-scale thematic repetitions, preferring understatement to the least possibility of redundancy. The frequent elision of themes and sections produces a strong continuity that is the essence of Sammartini's style.

The remaining works of Sammartini have not yet been carefully studied. Eight of the ten concertos are for solo violin or flute and strings (with wind in two late violin concertos); all but the ensemble concertos mentioned above contain the usual three movements. A wide variety of formal solutions is found; many of them show the influence of binary and sonata form designs on the entire movement as well as the structure of the ritornello. Of the seven orchestral concertinos, four early ones for strings fuse elements of the symphony, concerto and chamber styles, while the middle-period ones are actually short divertimentos in two movements, requiring an orchestra of two flutes or oboes, two horns and strings without violas.

Over 200 chamber and solo works constitute the bulk of Sammartini's extant music: string quintets, flute and string quartets (usually omitting the viola), trios, duets, solo sonatas, and sonatas for keyboard, solo and accompanied. In general the chamber works are more lyrical, more ornamental and more intricate in rhythm than the orchestral music. They are organized in two- and three-movement cycles typical of the early Classical style: slow/fast–minuet/fast, slow–fast–minuet, or fast–slow–minuet. The string trios for two violins and bass form the largest and most important group, and were extremely popular, as the many surviving copies indicate. The relation between the instrumental parts (especially the violins) varies considerably from the complete domination of the first violin to frequent dialogue and imitation, none of the sonatas being consistently imitative in late Baroque fashion. Six late 'sonate notturne' dedicated to his important patron the Duke of Parma reflect the trend towards the elimination of the continuo and achieve an equality of parts within a basic homophonic texture which is close to the ideal of the mature string quartet. Sammartini's most complex chamber works – in texture, harmony, and melody – are his late solo concertinos for string quartet and his quintets.

Sammartini's three operas follow the conventions of *opera seria*. The arias, almost exclusively in da capo form, are carefully written and often intensely expressive, especially in the operas of the 1730s. The few extant sacred works show that Sammartini was a master of the style. The more substantial works, such as the Mass sections, psalm settings and *Magnificat*, synthesize the *galant* and learned styles in large-scale arias, movements in sonata form for solo and choral groups, and concluding fugues. Each of Sammartini's extant Lenten cantatas contains a one-movement overture, three arias prefaced by recitatives, and a concluding 'chorus' of the solo soprano, alto and tenor voices (the 'chorus' of the cantata *Il pianto degli angeli della pace* is also heard twice in the beginning, giving the work a rondo-like structure; this work, dating from 1751, is outstanding among his sacred output). The serious mood of these works is reflected in the use of flat keys and the many minor-key movements. Recitatives make telling use of chromatic and dissonant harmonies, especially diminished 7th chords, and the arias have great lyric beauty and dramatic power. The principal sections of the arias show the same formal ingenuity as the instrumental movements in sonata form. It is in Sammartini's religious works that many of his most dramatic and sophisticated pages are found, as well as a grandeur of effect absent from his other works.

Sammartini's music played a fundamental role in the formation of the Classical style. He was one of the most advanced and experimental composers of the early Classical period, and the first great master of the symphony, preserving his individuality despite the rise of the Viennese and Mannheim schools. Though the extent of Sammartini's influence is still not fully measured, the high quality of his music places him among the leading creative spirits of the 18th century.

WORKS

Principal MS sources *CH-E, CS-Pnm, D-KA, F-Pc, Pn, I-AN, Mc, S-Skma*; detailed information in Jenkins and Churgin (1976)

ORCHESTRAL

Edition: *The Symphonies of G. B. Sammartini*, i: *The Early Symphonies*, ed. B. Churgin (Cambridge, Mass., 1968) [C]

Extant works: 68 syms.; 6 concs., vn, orch; 2 concs., fl, orch; 1 conc., 2 vn, orch; 1 conc., 2 vn, 2 ob, orch; 7 orch concertinos; 4 marches and minuets; lost works: 8 syms.; 2 concs.; 1 orch concertino; printed works listed below

op.
2 Three Concertos (F, D, D), 2 hn, 2 vn, va, b (London, *c*1747) [nos.1, 3 by ? M. Chiesa]
2 XII sonate (F, Bb, D, A, F, Bb, A, F, Bb, Eb, F, Bb), 2/3 vn, b (Paris, 1742); nos.1, 5, 8, 11, ed. in C [nos.2, 6, 10, 12 by A. Brioschi; for others see below]; no.8 also in Six Sonatas . . . by Lampugnani and St. Martini, op.2 (London, 1745); no.11 also in Six Concertos . . . by sigr. Gio. Batt. St. Martini of Milan & sigr. Hasse (London, 1751)
6 [VI] Concerti grossi (G, A, E, A, D, A), 2 vn concertino, 2 vn, va, vc, b/org (London, 1757), arr. by F. Barsanti of a sym., trios and quartets [nos.3–6 from op.5 (Paris, *c*1751) and no.5 from op.5 (London, 1756), see below]
4 An Overture (D) and 2 Grand Concertos (Bb, D), 2 ob, 2 hn, vn solo, 2 vn, va, vc, db (London, 1766)
Conc.: (Eb), 2 ob, 2 hn, 2 solo vn, 2 vn, va, vc/hpd, in Four Overtures & One Quattro . . . by sigr. F. Degiardino and One Concerto . . . by sigr. G. B. St. Martini (London, 1756)
Ovs.: no.4 (A), 2 vn, va, bc, in Sei ouverture . . . da varri autori, op.4 (Paris, *c*1755), same as Quartetto no.2 [see below]; no.1 (A), 2 vn, va, bc, in Sei overture . . . da varri autori, op.7 (Paris, *c*1756); no.4 (g), 2 vn, va, bc, in Sei overture . . . da vari autori (Paris, 1758), also as no.55 in Sinfonies périodiques (Paris, 1763); nos.3 (Eb), 6 (G), 2 hn, 2 vn, va, bc, in Six Favourite Overtures . . . by Galuppi, St Martini & Jomelli (London, 1761) [no.4 by ?Giulini]
Quartet: Quartetto no.2 (A), 2 vn, va, bc, in Six Simphonies . . . Stamitz . . . the Earl of Kelly, and others, op.2 (London, *c*1765) [see Sei ouverture . . . da varri autori, op.4 above]
Sinfonias: no.5 (A), 2 vn, bc, in Sinfonie . . . dei piu celebri autori

d'Italia, bk 1 (Paris, 1747), ed. in C; no.3 (D), 2 vn, va, bc, in
Simphonie novelle . . . Jomelli (Paris, c1748); no.?, in Sei sinfonie . . .
da Jomelli, Wagenseil, Flaminghino, San Martini (Paris, 1756), lost;
no.3 (c), 2 hn, 2 vn, va, bc, in VI sinfonie . . . da vari autori, op.9
(Paris, 1757)
Syms.: nos.3 (F), 5 (B♭), 2 vn, bc, in Six Sonatas . . . by Lampugnani
and St Martini, op.2 (London, 1745), ed. in C [no.1 by ?Brioschi];
no.1 (F), 2 hn, 2 vn, va, bc, in Six Concertos . . . by St Martini and
Hasse (London, 1751)
Arrs. of Sammartini's works pubd in 18th-century anthologies, see
Jenkins and Churgin (1976)

OTHER INSTRUMENTAL

Extant works: 6 quintets, 3 vn, va, b, 1773; 21 quartets (incl. 6 solo
concertinos, 5 dated 1763–7), 3 vn, b, or fl, 2 vn, b, or 2 vn, va, b;
c200 trios, most for 2 vn, bc (some doubtful); 5 sonatas, fl; 11
sonatas, vn; 6 sonatas, hpd, vn; 7 sonatas, vc; c31 sonatas, hpd (some
for org); 23 duets, 2 fl (most doubtful); printed works listed below
1 Six Sonatas (A, E♭, E♭, A, F, D), 2 vn, bc (London, 1744); no.3 by
?Brioschi; no.1 also in Sinfonie . . . dei piu celebri autori (Paris,
1747); no.5 also in Sinfonie . . . dei piu celebri autori d'Italia
(Paris, c1744)
2 XII sonate (Paris, 1742) [see above], nos.3, 4, 7, 9, for 2 vn, bc
4 Sei sonate (B♭, G, B♭, G, F, G), vc, bc (Paris, 1742); no.6 doubtful
— Sonates, fl, bc (Paris, c1750), lost
5 XII sonate (A, C, G, B♭, E, A, D, G, A, G, D, G) (Paris, c1751);
nos.1–8 for 2 vn, bc; nos.9–12 for fl, 2 vn, bc [see op.6 above];
nos.9–12 also in op.9 (London, 1762) [see below]
5 Six Sonatas (A, G, E, E, A, E♭), 2 vn, bc (London, 1756)
— Sonate a 3 instrumenti (B♭, D, C, B♭, A, E), 2 vn, vc (Milan, 1760);
also as 6 trios, op.5 (Paris, 1766), and 6 sonate notturne, op.7
(Paris, c1763–7); ed. B. Churgin, Early Music Monuments, v
(Chapel Hill, 1980)
6 Sei sonate notturne (D, G, E, C, G, D), 2 vn, bc (Paris, c1765)
8 Six Solos (D, G, D, G, G, G), fl/vn, bc (London, 1759); nos.3–4
doubtful
9 Six Sonatas call'd Notturni's (G, D, G, D, C, A), f, 2 vn, bc
(London, 1762), [see op.5 (Paris, c1751) above]
— Six Sonatas (D, G, C, D, G, D), fl, vn, bc (London, 1762)
10 A Third Set of Six Sonatas or Duets (G, D, G, D, G, G), 2 fl/vn
(London, 1763); nos.3–6 doubtful
— Sei sonate (C, D, G, F, B♭, E♭), hpd, vn (London, 1766; Paris,
1766)
Sonata no.4 (G), 2 fl, bc, in Sei sonate . . . di differenti autori (Paris,
c1750), same as no.4 (G), in Six Sonatas . . . by Jomelli (London,
1753); Duet no.4 (D), 2 fl/vn/bn, in Scielta di sei duetti (Paris, n.d.)
Sonatas, hpd: no.7 (D), in XX sonate, op.2 (Paris, 1760); nos.2 (G), 3
(E♭), in A Collection of Lessons . . . by Jozzi, St Martini, Alberti,
Agrell, bk 1 (London, 1761); no.2 (C), 4 (D), in A Second
Collection of Lessons, bk 2 (London, 1762); nos.2 (G), 3 (C), in A
Collection of Lessons, bk 3 (London, 1764); no.5 (F), in Raccolte
musicale, op.5 (Nuremberg, 1765); nos.3 (B♭), 4 (C), 5 (B♭), in Six
Select Sonatas (London, 1769)
Arrs. of Sammartini's works pubd in 18th-century anthologies, see
Jenkins and Churgin (1976)

STAGE

Memet (opera, 3), Lodi, 1732; ov. ed. in C
L'ambizione superata dalla virtù (opera, 3), Milan, Regio Ducal, 26 Dec
1734
L'Agrippina, moglie di Tiberio (opera, 3, G. Riviera), Milan, Regio
Ducal, Jan 1743
La gara dei geni (introduzione e festa da ballo, Riviera), Milan, Regio
Ducal, 28 May 1747; 1 aria extant
Il trionfo d'amore (ballet), Milan, 1773, lost

OTHER SECULAR VOCAL

Cantatas: Paride riconosciuto, Milan, 1750, lost; La reggia de' fati (G.
E. Pascali), Milan, 1753, collab. N. Jommelli, F-Pn [as La Serenata,
acts 1–2]; La pastorale offerta (Pascali), Milan, 1753, collab. Jommelli, F-Pn [as La Serenata, Act 3]; Iride (F. A. Mainoni), Milan,
1772, lost
Arias: Non hà dolor più rio, A, 2 vn, va, bc, B-Bc; Se voi che serva
almen, S, 2 vn, va, bc, Bc; Fieri venti già soffiano, S, 2 tpt, 2 vn, va,
bc, D-KA; Non così rapido scende dal monte, S, 2 tpt, 2 vn, va, bc, F-
Pc; Chiusi i lumi cheto giace, S, 2 vn, va, bc, Pc; Deh spiegate quel
affanno, S, 2 tpt, 2 vn, va, bc, Pc
Perchè si lento il giorno, terzetto, 3 S, 2 tpt, 2 vn, va, bc, Pc
Campane che suona, glee, SAB, ed. T. Warren, A Collection of Catches,
Canons, and Glees, i (London, 1762)

SACRED VOCAL

(most surviving works in CH-E)

Oratorios: Troppo s'avanza, aria, in La calunnia delusa (G. Machio),
Milan, 1724, lost; Gesù bambino adorato dalli pastori, Milan, 11 Jan
1726, 1 aria extant; L'impegno delle virtù, lost
Kyrie–Gloria; Kyrie; Gloria; 2 Credo; 2 litanies; Magnificat; 2 Te
Deum, 1 dated 1771; Beatus vir; 2 Dixit Dominus; 2 Laudate pueri;
Miserere, 1750; Nisi Dominus

8 cantatas for the Fridays in Lent, 5 dated 1751, 2 dated 1759, 1 dated
1760
11 contrafacta; 1 ed. J. Corfe, Sacred Music (London, c1800), Eng. text
Lost works: 36 sacred cantatas; Magnificat, Prague, 1738; Stabat
mater, Milan, 1762

DOUBTFUL WORKS

74 syms. (some spurious); 11 concs. (some spurious); 1 orch concer-
tino; some trios, most for 2 vn, bc; sonata (G), vc; 2 masses; Kyrie–
Gloria–Credo; Kyrie; Gloria–Credo; 2 Credo; 2 litanies; Magnificat;
Miserere; Tantum ergo; printed works listed below
Sonata no.3 (A), 2 vn, bc, in Six Sonatas . . . by Lampugnani and St
Martini, op.1 (London, 1744); same as no.1 in Six Sonatas
(Edinburgh, c1760) [see below]; attrib. Lampugnani (c1745)
Six Sonatas or Duets (G, D, A, G, D, G), 2 fl/vn, op.4 (London, 1748)
A Second Set of Six Sonatas or Duets (G, G, G, D, G, G), 2 fl/vn, op.7
(London, 1757)
Sonatas nos.3–4 in Six Solos, op.8 (London, 1759) [see above]
Sonatas nos.3–6 in A Third Set of Six Sonatas or Duets, op.10 (London,
1763) [see above]
Six Sonatas or Duets (G, G, G, C, G, G), 2 fl/vn, op.7 (London, c1760);
nos.1–3 same as op.7 (1757), nos.1–3
Six Sonatas (A, D, A, G, E, G), 2 vn, bc (Edinburgh, c1760)
Six Easy Solos (G, C, G, D, G, a), fl/vn, bc (London, 1765)
The Lord is righteous (contrafactum), 2 S, ed. J. Corfe, Sacred Music
(London, c1800)

SPURIOUS WORKS

Some syms. and concs., see Jenkins and Churgin (1976); printed works
listed below
Six simphonies . . . del Signor Sans Martini et Briochi (Paris, c1750)
Six Sonatas . . . St Martini, Brioschi & other masters, 2 vn, bc, 3rd set
(London, 1746)

BIBLIOGRAPHY

BurneyH; EitnerQ
J. J. Quantz: 'Lebenslauf', in F. W. Marpurg: Historisch-kritische
Beyträge zur Aufnahme der Musik, i (Berlin, 1754/R1970), 232,
235f
C. Burney: The Present State of Music in France and Italy (London,
1771); ed. P. A. Scholes as Dr. Burney's Musical Tours in Europe
(London, 1959), ii
J.-B. de La Borde: Essai sur la musique ancienne et moderne, iii (Paris,
1780/R1972)
G. A. Griesinger: Biographische Notizen über Joseph Haydn (Leipzig,
1810); ed. F. Grasberger (Vienna, 1954); Eng. trans., ed. V. Gotwals
as Joseph Haydn, Eighteenth-century Gentleman and Genius
(Madison, 1963)
G. Carpani: Le Haydine (Milan, 1812)
P. S. Keller: 'Mittheilungen', MMg, vi (1874), 46
F. Torrefranca: 'Le origini della sinfonia: le Sinfonie dell' imbrattacarte
(G. B. Sanmartini), RMI, xx (1913), 291–346; xxi (1914), 97, 278–
312; xxii (1915), 431
G. de Saint-Foix: 'Les débuts milanais de Gluck', Gluck-Jb, i (1913), 28
——: 'La chronologie de l'oeuvre instrumentale de Jean Baptiste
Sammartini', SIMG, xv (1913–14), 308
G. Cesari: 'Giorgio Giulini, musicista', RMI, xxiv (1917), 1–34, 210–
71
——: 'Sei sonate notturne di G. B. Sanmartini', RMI, xxiv (1917), 479
R. Sondheimer: 'Giovanni Battista Sammartini', ZMw, iii (1920–21),
83
G. de Saint-Foix: 'Découverte de l'acte de décès de Sammartini', RdM, ii
(1921), June, 287
——: 'Histoire musicale: une découverte', RMI, xxviii (1921), 317
G. Roncaglia: 'Una sonata inedita di G. B. Sammartini', RMI, xlii
(1938), 492
——: 'Ancora attorno a una sonata di G. B. Sammartini', RMI, xliii
(1939), 72
G. de Saint-Foix: 'Sammartini et les chanteurs de son temps', RMI, xliii
(1939), 357
H. Mishkin: 'Five Autograph String Quartets by Giovanni Battista
Sammartini', JAMS, vi (1953), 136
G. Barblan: 'Sanmartini e la scuola sinfonica milanese', Musicisti lom-
bardi ed emiliani, Chigiana, xv (1958), 21
——: 'Boccheriniana', RaM, xxix (1959), 123
C. Sartori: 'Giovanni Battista Sammartini e la sua corte', Musica d'oggi,
iii (1960), 3
——: 'Sammartini post-mortem', Hans Albrecht in Memoriam (Kassel,
1962)
G. Barblan: 'Contributo alla biografia di G. B. Sanmartini alla luce dei
documenti', SMw, xxv (1962), 15
B. Churgin: The Symphonies of G. B. Sammartini (diss., Harvard U.,
1963)
W. S. Newman: The Sonata in the Classic Era (Chapel Hill, 1963, rev.
2/1972)
B. Churgin: 'New Facts in Sammartini Biography: the Authentic Print
of the String Trios, Op.7', JAMS, xx (1967), 107

——, ed.: *The Symphonies of G. B. Sammartini*, i: *The Early Symphonies* (Cambridge, Mass., 1968)

M. Donà: 'Notizie sulla famiglia Sammartini', *NRMI*, viii (1974), 3

B. Churgin: 'G. B. Sammartini and the Symphony', *MT*, cxvi (1975), 26

L. Inzaghi: 'Nuova luce sulla biografia di G. B. Sammartini', *NRMI*, ix (1975), 267

——: 'Nozze affrettate di G. B. Sammartini (da un autografo inedito)', *NRMI*, x (1976), 634

N. Jenkins and B. Churgin: *Thematic Catalogue of the Works of Giovanni Battista Sammartini: Orchestral and Vocal Music* (Cambridge, Mass., 1976)

H. Brofsky: 'J. C. Bach, G. B. Sammartini, and Padre Martini: a *Concorso* in Milan in 1762', *A Musical Offering: Essays in Honor of Martin Bernstein* (New York, 1977), 63

N. Jenkins: 'The Vocal Music of Giovanni Battista Sammartini', *Chigiana*, xxiv (1977), 277–309

M. Marley: *The Sacred Cantatas of Giovanni Battista Sammartini* (diss., U. of Cincinnati, 1978)

BATHIA CHURGIN, NEWELL JENKINS

Sammartini [S Martini, St Martini, San Martini, San Martino, Martini, Martino], **Giuseppe** [Gioseffo] **(Francesco Gaspare Melchiorre Baldassare)** (*b* Milan, 6 Jan 1695; *d* London, ? between 17 and 23 Nov 1750). Italian oboist and composer. He was the son of a French oboist, Alexis Saint-Martin, and the elder brother of the composer Giovanni Battista Sammartini. The report of his death (discovered by Evelyn Lance) appeared in the *Whitehall Evening Post* of Saturday, 24 November 1750: 'Last week died at his Royal Highness the Prince of Wales, Signior S. Martini, Musick Master to her Royal Highness and thought to be the finest performer on the hautboy in Europe'.

Sammartini probably studied the oboe with his father, with whom he performed in an orchestra at Novara for a religious ceremony in 1711. In 1720 the 'Sammartini brothers' were listed as oboists in the orchestra of the Teatro Regio Ducal at Milan, a reference to Giuseppe and Giovanni Battista, or to another brother (Antonio or Carlo). An oboe concerto by Giuseppe was published in Amsterdam as early as *c*1717, and in 1724 he contributed an aria and sinfonia for the second part of a Milanese oratorio *La calunnia delusa*. J. J. Quantz, who visited Milan in 1726, regarded Sammartini as the only good wind player in the opera orchestra; when he went to Venice he ranked him with the violinists Vivaldi and Madonis as the outstanding players he had heard.

Sammartini probably left Italy for London in 1728, where his collection of 12 trio sonatas, published by Walsh & Hare, had been announced on 30 September 1727 (he was witness to his sister's marriage in Milan on 13 February 1728). According to Burney, Giuseppe's first appearance in England occurred at a benefit for 'signor Piero' at the Little Theatre in the Haymarket. Sammartini remained in London for the rest of his life, quickly winning recognition as a brilliant performer. In 1730, he played for Maurice Greene at Cambridge when Greene obtained the MusD degree, and also gave a successful benefit concert there. Sammartini appeared at the concerts at Hickford's Room and the Swan and Castle, and he played in the opera orchestra at the King's Theatre. Burney mentioned an aria sung by Farinelli in Porpora's *Polifemo* (1735) that was 'accompanied on the hautbois by the celebrated San Martini'. Though Hawkins said that Sammartini was at first allied with Bononcini, he also played in Handel's orchestra. Dean pointed out that Sammartini's name is attached to many oboe solos in Handel's opera autographs, such as the difficult obbligato for the aria 'Quella fiamme' in *Arminio*, Act 2 (1737). On 14 March 1741 Sammartini performed a solo at a benefit performance of Handel's *Parnasso in Festa*.

Entries in the household accounts of Frederick, Prince of Wales, and his wife Augusta show that Sammartini became the music master of Augusta and her children in 1736, remaining in this post until his death, as noted in the obituary (information from Evelyn Lance). Sammartini dedicated his 12 sonatas op.1 (1736) to Frederick, and his 12 trios op.3 (1743) to Augusta. A set of three ballets exists, with an overture ascribed to Frederick, that Sammartini wrote for the birthday of Frederick's daughter, Lady Augusta. Fiske has suggested that the masque *The Judgment of Paris* performed at Cliveden for Lady Augusta's third birthday in 1740 was actually composed by Sammartini, not Arne, who also wrote a masque to the same text. Hawkins further mentioned a 'musical solemnity' by Sammartini that was publicly performed in the chapel of the Bavarian minister.

Sammartini's music apparently became well known only after his death. Most of the concertos and overtures were published posthumously, becoming so popular that they regularly appeared on the programmes of the Concert of Antient Music well into the 19th century. Some of Sammartini's marches and minuets were performed for the king's birthday as late as 1770–75. Hawkins praised Sammartini as the 'greatest [oboist] that the world had ever known', possessing a remarkable tone that approached the quality of the human voice. He transformed oboe playing in England, and his pupils included the fine English oboist Thomas Vincent. The letters of administration pertaining to Sammartini's estate show that he died a bachelor.

Sammartini was primarily an instrumental composer, and one of the leading writers of concertos and sonatas in England between 1730 and 1750. His printed collections include 24 sonatas for flute and bass, 30 trios for recorders or violins, 24 concerti grossi, four keyboard concertos, an oboe concerto, 16 overtures, and some flute duets and cello sonatas. Hawkins classed Sammartini's instrumental music with that of Corelli and Geminiani. Though his music is rooted in the late Baroque style, it also reflects some later trends. There is considerable variety in the number, succession and type of movements. Most of the solo sonatas are in the more modern three-movement style, sometimes beginning with a slow movement (which Sammartini generally preferred); trios and orchestral works often contain four or five movements, including French overtures, fugal second movements, and transitional slow movements. Sammartini's concerti grossi are scored for strings, with added oboe solos in op.8 nos.4–6, and call for a concertino of either two violins and cello or string quartet. The concertino usually shares and elaborates material of the tutti. The concerto style also greatly influenced the trio sonatas op.3. Many binary fast movements, even in the 1727 collection, have early sonata form designs. Other more Classical features include frequent minuet and rondo finales, fast 2/4 movements, *galant* embellishments and passages in slow harmonic rhythm. Sammartini was a skilled contrapuntist, a fine harmonist with chromatic leanings and a good melodist, the broad lyricism of his slow movements and minuets showing the influence of Handel. His forms are interesting and well organized. Burney and Hawkins much admired Sammartini's music, which Burney praised as being 'full of science, originality, and fire'.

WORKS

(all printed works published in London unless otherwise stated)

ORCHESTRAL

op.
2   6 concerti grossi (A, e, c, B♭, A, D), 2 vn, va and vc concertino, 2 vn, b (1728)
5   [6] Concerti grossi (e, B♭, g, a, c, g), 2 vn, va and vc concertino, 2 vn, b (1747); arr. from trios op.3 nos.2, 3, 5, 9, 10, 12
7–8 8 Overtures (D, E♭, d, A, D, G, D, D), 2 hn, 2 tpt, timp, 2 vn and vc concertino, 2 vn, va, bc (vc, hpd), op.7 and 6 Grand Concertos (g, A, c, C, g, A), ob, 2 vn and vc concertino, 2 vn, va, bc (vc, hpd), op.8 (1752); op.7 no.2 in 6 overture . . . da vari autori, op.1 (Paris, 1755); op.7 no.4, *B-Bc*
9   Giuseppe St. Martini's Concertos (A, F, G, B♭), hpd/org, str (1754)
10   8 Overtures (G, d, A, D, B♭, D, F, E), and 6 Grand Concertos (E, g, A, d, e, B♭) in 7 Parts (1756); 6 concertos as op.11 (*c*1756)
Concerto, F, ob, str, in Concerti a 5 . . . libro primo (Amsterdam, *c*1717)
12 concertos, *GB-Lbm*; ob concerto (E♭), *D-Dlb*; rec concerto (F) and 2 fl concertos (D, A), *S-Skma*; Overtura (G), *CS-Pnm*; minuets, marches, 3 ballets, *GB-Lbm*

OTHER INSTRUMENTAL

—   12 Sonatas (F, F, G, F, F, d, F, F, G, F, F, B♭), 2 fl/vn, bc (1727, lost; 2/*c*1730)
1   [6] Sonate (D, G, C, G, c, b), bk 1, 2 fl, b (1736); [6] Sonate (e, G, A, a, D, A), bk 2, fl, b (*c*1736; Paris, 2/*c*1743 as op.3; 3/1757 as op.12)
2   12 sonate (G, C, e, G, D, a, D, e, G, a, A, D), fl, b (Amsterdam, 1736–7); nos.1–6 as op.2 (*c*1745); nos.7–12 as op.4 (*c*1747)
3   12 sonate (A, e, B♭, G, g, D, e, D, a, c, E, g), 2 vn, vc, hpd ad lib (1743)
6   2 bks, fl, b (Amsterdam, 1742–4), lost
—   6 Sonatas or Duets (D, e, A, G, C, d), 2 fl, bk 1 (*c*1750) [as op.1]
13   Six Solos (G, G, G, G, g, G), fl/vn/ob, bc (*c*1760)

Pieces in 6 Solos for Two Violoncellos (1748), 6 sonate a flauto traverso solo, e violoncello o basso continuo (*c*1762), 6 Solos for a German Flute or Violin . . . compos'd by Sigr Francesco Xaver Richter (1764)
Duets, marches, minuets in contemporary anthologies: see *RISM*
26 ob and fl sonatas, *US-R*; various trios and solos, *B-Bc*, *GB-Lbm*, *Mp*, *US-NYp*; Ob Conc., *GB-Mp*; 9 sonatas, 7 sinfonias, 1 conc., fl, bc, *I-PAc*

VOCAL MUSIC

The Judgment of Paris (pastoral, Congreve), Cliveden, *c*1740, *GB-Lbm*
9 cantatas: In lode della . . . principessa di Gales, S, 2 vn, b, *B-Bc*; Naufraggio vicino, S, 2 vn, va, b, *Bc*; Più non sento, S, 2 vn, b, *Bc*; La rosa (Da procella tempestosa), S, b, *Bc*; L'olmo, S, *Bc*; Da procella tempestosa, S, hpd, *Bc*, *Lbm*; Oh vita, vita, nò, S, hpd, *Lbm*; Ahi qual cruccio, S, hpd, *Lbm*; Solitudine campestra, S, b, *I-Rsc*; Tu piangi, Eurilla mia, S, bc, *Rsc*
Arias: Se fedel, cor mio, tu sei (Metastasio), from the opera Gli orti esperidi; Se a ciascun l'interno affanno: both *GB-Lbm*
Lost aria, Vuoi saper, to pt.1, and sinfonia to pt.2 of La calunnia delusa (oratorio, G. Machio), Milan, 1724

BIBLIOGRAPHY

BurneyH; *HawkinsH*
J. J. Quantz: 'Lebenslauf', in F. W. Marpurg: *Historisch-kritische Beyträge zur Aufnahme der Musik*, i (Berlin, 1754/*R*1970), 232, 235f
G. de Saint-Foix: 'La chronologie de l'oeuvre instrumentale de Jean Baptiste Sammartini', *SIMG*, xv (1913–14), 308
O. E. Deutsch: *Handel: a Documentary Biography* (London, 1955)
C. Sartori: 'Giovanni Battista Sammartini e la sua corte', *Musica d'oggi*, iii (1960), 3
G. Barblan: 'Contributo alla biografia di G. B. Sanmartini alla luce dei documenti', *SMw*, xxv (1962), 15
R. Fiske: 'A Cliveden Setting', *ML*, xlvii (1966), 126
W. Dean: *Handel and the Opera Seria* (Berkeley, 1969)

BATHIA CHURGIN

Sammartini, Pietro. See SANMARTINI, PIETRO.

Sammons, Albert (Edward) (*b* London, 23 Feb 1886; *d* Southdean, Sussex, 24 Aug 1957). English violinist and composer. Apart from a few lessons from his father and others, he was self-taught. He began playing professionally at the age of 11 and led the Earl's Court Exhibition Orchestra when only 13. He made his solo début in 1906. In 1908 Beecham heard him playing Mendelssohn's concerto at the Waldorf Hotel and asked him to lead the Beecham Orchestra, which he did for five years, taking part in over 50 operas and ballets. He was also leader of the Philharmonic Society Orchestra from 1913 and the orchestra of Dyagilev's Ballets Russes from 1911, touring with the latter under Monteux in spring 1913. That year he also appeared as a soloist in Germany. He was the original leader of the London String Quartet (1907–16) and took part in the première of Elgar's Piano Quintet in London, in 1919. Sammons appeared as a soloist with most leading British orchestras and formed a partnership with the pianist William Murdoch which lasted 25 years; they introduced many new violin sonatas by British composers, notably Ireland's Second Sonata in March 1917. Sammons was the dedicatee of Delius's concerto and edited its violin part and that of Delius's Sonata no.2. His complete technical mastery, characteristically large sound and sustained singing tone allied to a tough yet sensitive temperament made him the ideal interpreter of Elgar's concerto, of which he made the first complete recording with Wood in 1929, as well as often performing it under Elgar's direction.

Although his prowess as a soloist was acknowledged by such virtuosos as Kreisler and Heifetz, Sammons seems to have built his reputation solely on performances in England. He composed (notably a Phantasy Quartet for strings which won the Cobbett Prize), was a professor at the RCM, and was made a CBE in 1944. From 1946 his career was hampered and finally terminated by muscular trouble, which even prevented his attending his benefit concert in December 1954. Considered by many to be the outstanding English violinist of his generation, he also had a modest, friendly and humorous personality.

WRITINGS

The Secret of Technique in Violin Playing (London, 1916)
Violin Exercises for Improving the Bowing Technique by Means of the Tone Perfecter (London, 1930)

BIBLIOGRAPHY

G. Tankard and others: 'Albert Sammons', *RCM Magazine*, lii (1956), 94
J. Ireland: 'Albert Sammons: a Tribute', *MT*, xcviii (1957), 548
H. Rutland: Obituary, *MT*, xcviii (1957), 571
H. Howells: 'For Albert Sammons', *MO*, lxxxi (1957), 171
J. Creighton: *Discopaedia of the Violin, 1889–1971* (Toronto, 1974)

LESLIE EAST

Samoa. See POLYNESIA, §6, and PACIFIC ISLANDS.

Samosud, Samuil Abramovich (*b* Tbilisi, 14 May 1884; *d* Moscow, 6 Nov 1964). Soviet conductor. He graduated from the Tbilisi Conservatory as a cellist in 1906, and worked as a cellist with various symphony orchestras for a number of years. From 1917 to 1919 he was a conductor at the Mariinsky Theatre, Petrograd. He was artistic director of the Malïy Theatre, Leningrad (1918–36), of the Bol'shoy Theatre (1936–43), and of the Stanislavsky-Nemirovich-Danchenko Music Theatre, Moscow (1943–50). From 1953 to 1957 he was principal conductor of the Moscow Philharmonia SO and of the All-Union Radio SO. From 1929 to 1936 he taught the orchestra class at the Leningrad Conservatory, where he was made a professor in 1934. He was made People's Artist of the USSR in 1937.

Samosud played a distinguished role as artistic director at the Malïy and Bol'shoy theatres, where his broad artistic perspective, creative initiative and inventiveness, his organizational ability and purposeful determination were given free rein. He championed many new operas by Soviet composers, confirming the Malïy as the 'laboratory of Soviet opera'. He was responsible for the premières there of Shostakovich's *The Nose* in 1930, Dzerzhinsky's *Quiet Flows the Don* in 1935, and the first eight scenes of Prokofiev's *War and Peace* in 1946. At the Bol'shoy Theatre in 1937 he conducted the première of Dzerzhinsky's *Virgin Soil Upturned*, and the original (1947) and revised (1951) versions of Kabalevsky's *The Family of Taras* at the Stanislavsky-Nemirovich-Danchenko Music Theatre. He was also an outstanding symphonic conductor and conducted the première of Prokofiev's Symphony no.7 (1952) in Moscow.

WRITINGS

'Vstrechi s Prokof'yevïm', *Sergey Prokof'yev 1953–63: stat'i i materialï*, ed. I. V. Nest'yev and G. A. Edel'man (Moscow, 2/1962, rev. and enlarged 3/1965), 123–74

'Minuvsheye vstayot peredo mnoyu' [The past stands before me], *SovM* (1965), no.9, p.76

BIBLIOGRAPHY

V. Bogdanov-Berezovsky: 'Molodïye godï: k 80-letiyu S. A. Samosuda' [The early years: for the 80th birthday of Samosud], *SovM* (1964), no.6, p.34

N. Kamarskaya and others: 'S. A. Samosud', *Muzïkal'naya zhizn'* (1964), no.10, p.10

I. Nest'yev: 'S. A. Samosud: pamyati dirizhora' [In memory of the conductor], *Muzïkal'naya zhizn'* (1965), no.2, p.24

I. M. YAMPOL'SKY

Samotulinus, Venceslaus. *See* SZAMOTUŁ, WACŁAW Z.

Sampayo Ribeiro, Mario Luis de (*b* Lisbon, 4 Dec 1898; *d* Lisbon, 13 May 1966). Portuguese musicologist and conductor. He studied music at the Lisbon Conservatory, and then became a teacher. He was an influential force in music organization, being president of the National Musicians' Union and inspector of Portuguese youth choirs. In 1941 he founded the choral group Polyphonia which he conducted for many years, introducing the public to much early Portuguese music. He was also director of *Opera* in which he published numerous articles. In his books and articles he concentrated on the history of Portuguese music, particularly on composers of sacred music and opera, and on Portuguese singers.

WRITINGS

A obra musical do Padre António Pereira de Figueiredo (Lisbon, 1932)

No centenário da morte de M. Portugal (Coimbra, 1933)

Damião de Goes, na Livraria real de música (Lisbon, 1935)

Do justo valor da canção popular (Lisbon, 1935)

A música em Portugal nos séculos XVIII e XIX (Lisbon, 1936)

As guitarras de Alcácer e a guitarra portuguesa (Lisbon, 1936)

A música em Coimbra (Coimbra, 1939)

Utilidades de música através dos tempos (Lisbon, 1940)

Aspectos musicais da exposição de 'Os primitivos portugueses' (Oporto, 1943)

Luísa de Aguiar Todi: cultura artística: estudos diversos (Lisbon, 1943)

O estilo expressivo, raiz de música polifónica portuguesa (Oporto, 1943)

Livraria de música de el Rei Don Joao IV: estudo musical histórico e bibliográfico (Oporto, 1967)

EDITIONS

M. A. de Fonseca Portugal: *Il duca di foix*, PM, ser. B, ix (1964)

JOSÉ LÓPEZ-CALO

Sampion. *See* CHAMPION family.

Samponi, Gioseffo. *See* ZAMPONI, GIOSEFFO.

Sampson [first name unknown] (*d* Eccleshall, Staffs., 25 Sept 1554). ?English composer. Two compositions attributed to 'Mr Sampson' appear in *GB-Lbm* Roy.11.e.xi, dated 1516. One, a very long setting in four parts of *Psallite felices*, is a Latin song in honour of Henry VIII, the other a five-part Marian antiphon: *Quam pulcra es, amica mea*. In his use of declamation,

brief motifs treated in imitation, and general avoidance of lengthy melisma, Sampson showed much greater acquaintance with continental techniques – particularly Flemish – than any other English composer of the period. In view of this it is quite possible that several works ascribed 'Sampson' in German printed collections are by the same composer: a song in 1549[36], a mass cycle on the same song in 1541[1] (both of them strongly retrospective collections) and four motets in 1537[1], 1538[9], 1541[2] and 1546[6].

The only plausible candidate for identification with the composer yet suggested is Richard Sampson, dean of the Chapel Royal from 1523 to 1540. There is nothing in his known biography to suggest that he was in any way a musician, but it is known that he spent the years from 1507 to 1513 studying law in Paris, Perugia and Siena, and was in Antwerp in 1511; between 1514 and 1517 he was Thomas Wolsey's vicar-general in the diocese of Tournai. If he were the composer, these long years abroad could explain the continental style of his writing. Nevertheless, his known career was that of a lawyer, and then a diplomat and trusted official of Cardinal Wolsey and Henry VIII, for whom composition can at best have been no more than a hobby. Among his later benefices were the deaneries of Lichfield, Windsor and St Paul's, and the bishoprics of Chichester (1535–40) and Lichfield (1543–54).

BIBLIOGRAPHY

EitnerS; *FétisB*

F. Ll. Harrison: *Music in Medieval Britain* (London, 1958, 2/1963), 338ff

A. B. Emden: *A Biographical Register of the University of Cambridge to 1500* (Cambridge, 1963), 505f

ROGER BOWERS

Sams, Eric (*b* London, 3 May 1926). English writer on music. He studied modern languages at Cambridge and entered the civil service, becoming a Principal Officer in the Department of Employment in 1953. His musical studies are based on his interest in the relationship between music and language, both in the text settings of the Romantic song composers and in the more general field of aesthetics and inquiry into the nature of musical expression. Much of his work in the field of the lied is concerned with a close analysis of analogues between verbal meaning and musical motif; in his studies of Schumann he has carried this particularly far with his discovery of a cipher system used by the composer. Sams's interest in musical cryptography has also led him to a solution of Elgar's 'enigma'. A penetrating and well-informed reviewer with a witty and allusive style, he has written for the *New Statesman* (1976–8), and in 1977 was visiting professor at McMaster University, Hamilton, Ontario.

WRITINGS

The Songs of Hugo Wolf (London, 1961)

'Did Schumann Use Ciphers?', *MT*, cvi (1965), 584

'Schumann's Year of Song', *MT*, cvi (1965), 105

'The Schumann Ciphers', *MT*, cvii (1966), 392, 1050

'Why Florestan and Eusebius?', *MT*, cvii (1967), 131

The Songs of Robert Schumann (London, 1969, rev. 2/1975)

'The Tonal Analogue in Schumann's Music', *PRMA*, xcvi (1969–70), 113

'A Schumann Primer?', *MT*, cxi (1970), 1096

'Elgar's Cipher Letter to Dorabella', *MT*, cxi (1970), 151

'Elgar's Enigmas', *MT*, cxi (1970), 692

'Variations on an Original Theme (Enigma)', *MT*, cxi (1970), 258

'Brahms and his Musical Love-letters', *MT*, cxii (1971), 329

'Brahms's Clara-themes', *MT*, cxii (1971), 432

'Schumann's Hand Injury', *MT*, cxii (1971), 1156; cxiii (1972), 456

Brahms Songs (London, 1972)

'Schumann and Faust', *MT*, cxiii (1972), 543

'Zwei Brahms-Rätsel', *ÖMz*, xxvii (1972), 83

'The Songs'; 'Schumann and the Tonal Analogue', *Robert Schumann:*

the Man and his Music, ed. A. Walker (London, 1972), 120–61; 390–405
'Notes on a Magic Horn', *MT*, cxv (1974), 556
'Eduard Hanslick, 1825–1904', *MT*, cxvi (1975), 867
'E.T.A. Hoffmann, 1776–1822', *MT*, cxvii (1976), 29
'Schubert's Illness Re-examined', *MT*, cxxi (1980), 15
'The Tonal Analogue in the Songs of Johannes Brahms', *International Brahms Congress: Detroit 1980*

STANLEY SADIE

Samson-François [François, Samson] (*b* Frankfurt, 18 May 1924; *d* Paris, 22 Oct 1970). French pianist and composer. He studied the piano at the Paris Conservatoire (*premier prix* 1940), and in 1943 won the first of what later became the Long–Thibaud competitions. From then on he toured internationally. He was known particularly for his performances of Chopin, Liszt, Debussy, Ravel, Bartók and Prokofiev, and he made many recordings. His own rather rhapsodic piano concerto (1950) is in a composite style sometimes too noticeably indebted to Prokofiev.

DOMINIQUE JAMEUX

Samsony, Giovanni. *See* SANSONI, GIOVANNI.

Samuel, Adolphe(-Abraham) (*b* Liège, 11 July 1824; *d* Ghent, 11 Sept 1898). Belgian composer and critic. He first studied painting in Liège, then took music lessons at the conservatory and soon chose to specialize in music. In 1840 he went with his family to Brussels, where he studied at the conservatory with Michelet (piano), Girschner (organ), Bosselet (harmony) and Fétis (composition). He won the Prix de Rome with his cantata *Vendetta* and later continued his studies with Mendelssohn and Meyerbeer. He became a professor of harmony at the Brussels Conservatory in 1850. He met Berlioz in London in 1853, and maintained a correspondence with him. In 1865 he organized a series of popular concerts, and in 1869 established an annual music festival. He was made director of the Ghent Conservatory in 1871.

As a critic, Samuel contributed to daily newspapers and periodicals. His compositions include operas, symphonic music and sacred and secular vocal music. His seven symphonies clearly show the influence of Berlioz; the last of these, a mystic symphony entitled *Christus*, was written after Samuel's conversion (his family was Jewish) to Catholicism.

WORKS
(*selective list*)

Operas: Giovanni da Procida, op.10, 1848; Madeleine, op.11, 1849; L'heure de la retraite, op.25, 1854
Orch: 7 syms., opp.8, 9, 28, 33, 35, 44, 48 'Christus' [with chorus, org]; ov., 1839; cl conc., 1841; Roland à Roncevaux, sym. poem, 1850
Vocal: Amor lex aeterna, oratorio, 1882; Mass, d, op.53; motets, opp.19 and 51; secular cantatas and choruses, wind, brass, and orch acc.; solo songs
Other instrumental: 2 str qts, opp.5 and 34; piano pieces

WRITINGS
Cours d'accompagnement de la basse chiffrée (Brussels, 1849)
Cours d'harmonie pratique (Brussels, 1861)
Livre de lecture musicale (Paris, 1886)

BIBLIOGRAPHY
C. Bergmans: *Le Conservatoire royal de musique de Gand* (Ghent, 1901), 371ff
E. Mathieu: *Notice sur Adolphe Samuel* (Brussels, 1922) [with complete list of works]
Les concerts populaires de Bruxelles (Brussels, 1927)
C. van den Borren: *Geschiedenis van de muziek in de Nederlanden*, ii (Antwerp, 1951)

ANNE-MARIE RIESSAUW

Samuel, Claude (*b* Paris, 23 June 1931). French music critic. He studied harmony with Maillard-Verger and counterpoint with Lesur at the Schola Cantorum (1955–7) and has written regularly or occasionally in non-specialized papers such as *Paris-presse*, *Valeurs actuelles*, *Réalités*, *Nouveau Candide*, *Le point* and *L'express*. Since 1960 he has also produced broadcasts, mainly of contemporary music, for the ORTF. He was artistic adviser to the Festival International d'Art Contemporain de Royan (1965–72) and in 1973 became artistic director of the Rencontres Internationales d'Art Contemporain de La Rochelle, established in 1972 after a dispute within the Royan committee. He also became artistic adviser to the Rencontres de Musique Contemporaine de Metz on their establishment in 1972.

WRITINGS
Prokofiev (Paris, 1960)
with A. Goléa and A. Hodeir: *Panorama de l'art musical contemporain* (Paris, 1962)
Entretiens avec Olivier Messiaen (Paris, 1964)

CHRISTIANE SPIETH-WEISSENBACHER

Samuel, Gerhard (*b* Bonn, 20 April 1924). American conductor of German birth. He studied conducting with Hermann Gerhard and composition with Howard Hanson at the Eastman School, Rochester. Later he was a composition student of Hindemith's at Yale and worked for two summers with Koussevitzky at Tanglewood. His early experience included orchestral violin playing and conducting in Broadway musicals. He was assistant conductor of the Minneapolis SO (1949–59), then conductor of the Oakland (California) SO (1959–70). During that period he also conducted for Lew Christensen's San Francisco Ballet and was music director of the Cabrillo Festival at Aptos, California. He was associate conductor of the Los Angeles PO (1970–73), then became a freelance conductor. During Samuel's tenure in Oakland, which began just after the orchestra became fully professional, the audience increased greatly. He also instituted a Youth Chamber Orchestra as a training group. He was an advocate of contemporary music, and his Oakland programmes were among the most interesting offered by any orchestra in the USA. He has a most intelligent appreciation of the essentials of orchestral execution, an ability to get his players to listen and respond as though playing chamber music, and an impressive sense of structure. A certain want of lightness and humour might be mentioned. His compositions reflect his sympathy for the avant garde and his interest in mixed media.

MICHAEL STEINBERG

Samuel, Harold (*b* London, 23 May 1879; *d* London, 15 Jan 1937). English pianist. He entered the RCM (where he later taught) at the age of 17 to study the piano with Dannreuther and composition with Stanford. For many years he was known only as an accompanist; but the whole course of his concert career was changed when he gave a week of daily Bach recitals in London in 1921. This series marked the beginning of a widespread demand for Bach's keyboard music in its original form rather than in the currently popular 19th-century arrangements and Samuel was seldom asked to play anything but Bach in England or on his many American tours. He memorized all Bach's keyboard music which he presented with 'extraordinary clarity, sobriety, and sense of shape' (E. Blom, *Grove 5*), and with obvious and infectious enthusiasm. But his repertory was large and his tastes were catholic; he was a fine exponent of Brahms's concertos and an accomplished chamber music player. Samuel's few compositions include music for *As You Like It* (His Majesty's Theatre, 1907), a comic opera, *The Hon'ble Phil*, songs and piano pieces.

BIBLIOGRAPHY
H. Ferguson: 'Harold Samuel', *Recorded Sound* (1962), no.6, p.186 [with discography by H. L. Anderson]
H. C. Schonberg: *The Great Pianists* (London, 1964), 385f
FRANK DAWES

Samuel, Léopold (*b* Brussels, 5 May 1883; *d* Brussels, 10 March 1975). Belgian composer. After studying the cello and theory at the Brussels Conservatory, where his principal teacher was Edgar Tinel, he went to Berlin to complete his education. In 1911 he won the Belgian Prix de Rome for his cantata *Tycho-Brahé*. He was inspector of state musical education from 1920 to 1945, and was elected to the Belgian Royal Academy in 1958. His music is in the tradition of Franck, although there are sometimes impressionist details, as in the *Petite suite fantasque*. His operas are Wagnerian, his chamber works are charmingly written and his songs, notably *Les heures de l'après-midi*, give full expression to his romantic nature.

WORKS
(*selective list*)

Operas: Ilka (4, P. Demeny), 1919; La sirène au pays des hommes (5 scenes, Samuel, after Andersen), 1937
Orch: Morceau de concert, vc, orch (1908); Petite suite fantasque, 1945; 2 tableaux symphoniques, male chorus, orch, 1957
Chamber: Str Qnt (1909); Pf Trio (1920); 3 str qts, 1941, 1942, 1948; Pièce à 5, fl, str trio, harp, 1954; Invocation, vc, pf, 1959; Suite, ww qt, n.d.; Divertimento, vn, pf, n.d.; Octet, ww qt, str qt, n.d.
Songs: Les heures de l'après-midi (Verhaeren), 1v, pf/chamber orch (1910); 3 mélodies (A. van Hasselt, T. Louant) (1922); Les sentiers du silence (E. Polak) (1961)

Principal publisher: Samuel

HENRI VANHULST

Samuel-Holeman, Eugène (*b* Schaerbeek, Brussels, 3 Nov 1863; *d* Etterbeek, Brussels, 25 Jan 1942). Belgian composer, pianist and conductor. Son of Adolphe Samuel, he studied the piano and theory at the Ghent Conservatory, and was, from the first, deeply interested in literature. His career as a pianist and conductor was spent principally in France. A composer of originality, he was concerned with atonality, although his music can appear somewhat artificial, particularly in its romantic outpourings. The monodrama *La jeune fille à la fenêtre* has an economy of means and a refined novelty that bring it close to the work of Debussy and Satie. He published a *Simple aperçu sur deux gammes naturelles* (Brussels, 1898).

WORKS
(*selective list*)

Stage: La jeune fille à la fenêtre, Mez, ob, hn, harp, str qt (1904); Un vendredi saint en Zélande, opera, 3, unorchd; 1 other piece
Other works: Sym., n.d.; Harp Conc., n.d.; Une vie, str qt, n.d.; Adagio, pf, n.d.; Te Deum, n.d.; several songs

Principal publishers: Breitkopf & Härtel, Lauweryns

BIBLIOGRAPHY
C. van der Borren: *Geschiedenis van de muziek in de Nederlanden*, ii (Antwerp, 1951), 248
HENRI VANHULST

Samuel-Rousseau [Rousseau], **Marcel (Louis Auguste)** (*b* Paris, 18 Aug 1882; *d* Paris, 11 June 1955). French composer. He studied at the Paris Conservatoire with his father, Samuel Rousseau, and with Lenepveu, taking

the Prix de Rome in 1905 for *Maïa*. Subsequently he held appointments as organist at St Sévérin (1919–22), professor of harmony at the Conservatoire (1919–52), artistic director of the Pathé company (1929–31), vice-president of SACEM (1935–53) and director of the Paris Opéra (1941–4). He was elected to the Institut in 1947 and made an officer of the Légion d'honneur in 1952. The greatest influences on his music were those of Franck, Fauré and his father.

WORKS
(*selective list*)

Operas: Tarass Boulba (drame musical, 5), begun 1908, Paris, Opéra-Comique, 1919; Le Hulla (conte oriental, 4), begun 1920, Paris, Opéra-Comique, 1923; Le bon roi Dagobert (comédie musicale, 4), begun 1924, Paris, Opéra-Comique, 1927; Kerkeb (drame musical, 1), begun 1931, Paris, Opéra, 1951
Ballets: Promenades dans Rome, 1, begun 1934; Paris, Opéra, 1936; Entre deux rondes, 1, Paris, Opéra, 1940
Orch: Noël berrichon, suite pittoresque, 1905; Variations pastorales sur un vieux noël, 1916; Variations à danser, pf, orch, begun 1916; Bérénice, 4 sym. preludes, 1917–18
Songs, pf pieces

Principal publishers: Choudens, Heugel, Leduc

PAUL GRIFFITHS

San, Herman van (*b* Mechelen, 19 March 1929). Belgian composer. He studied classics, received traditional music instruction from Gabriel Minet and read law and philosophy at Brussels University. After composing a number of serial works he began to exploit his own theories for the construction of music on a mathematical basis. He has criticized the approach that seeks to create a mere musical analogy of scientific principles or processes. The works deriving from his ideas are divided into two categories: 'opus instrumentale mathematicum' (O.I.M.) and 'opus electronicum mathematicum' (O.E.M.).

WORKS
(*selective list*)

Inst and vocal: Qnt, fl, ob, cl, 2 bn, 1948; Qnt, wind qnt, 1949; Sextet, wind qnt, pf, 1950; Conc., bn, 2 pf, 1950; Bagatellen, 4 fl, 1950; Sextet, pic, wind qnt, 1951; Mikrostruktuur, 3 pf, 1951; Kantate (R. C. van de Kerckhove), S, A, T, B, str qt, db, 1952; Strukturen, 16 insts, 1952; Primum O I M., 3 vn, 3 vc, 1953; Secundum O.I.M., 6 vn, 6 vc, 1953; Kantate (Joyce), S, A, T, B, 6 vn, 6 vc, 2 drum, 1954
Elec: Primum O.E., 1953; Secundum O.E., 1954; Tertium O.E., 1955; Primum O.E.M., 1956; Geometrische patterns (Secundum O.E.M.), 1957; Axiomata (Tertium O.E.M.), 1958; Quartum O.E.M., 1960, Quintum O.E.M., 1962; Sextum O.E.M., 1964; Septimum O.E.M., 1967; Octavum O.E.M., 1968; Nonum O.E.M., 1970; Decimum O.E.M., 1972–

WRITINGS
'De nieuwe muziek I', *Tijd en mens* (1950), no.7, p.257
'De nieuwe muziek II', *Tijd en mens* (1954), no.21–2, p.80
'Het structuralisme in de muziek', *De vlaamse gids*, xxxix (1955), 603
'Einheitswissenschaft und Musik', *Gravesaner Blätter* (1957), no.7–8, p.39
'Electronische muziek met klare begrippen', *Periskoop* (1959), no.8, p.13
'Sundry Notes Introductory to the Theoretical Mechanics of Mathematical Music', *Interface*, ii/1 (1973), 23

CORNEEL MERTENS

Şanäşel. Ethiopian sistrum used for the accompaniment of liturgical music; *see* ETHIOPIAN RITE, MUSIC OF THE.

Sances [Sancies, Sanci, Sanes], **Giovanni Felice** (*b* Rome, *c*1600; *d* Vienna, buried 12 Nov 1679). Italian composer, singer and teacher, resident largely in Austria. He was a son of the singer Lorenzo Sances and spent his early years in Rome: he was a pupil at the Collegio Germanico from 16 November 1609 to 1 April 1614, sang in the opera *Amor pudico* in February 1614 and then became a musician in the service of

Cardinal Montalto. According to the preface to the second edition of his collection of motets for one to four voices (1642), he also worked at S Petronio, Bologna, and at Venice, though exactly when and in what capacity is not known. Since he dedicated to Pio Enea degli Obizzi his two volumes of cantatas of 1633, he may have been employed by that important patron of the arts, who, moreover, wrote the libretto of his first opera, *Ermiona*, performed at Padua on 11 April 1636 with Sances himself in the role of Cadmus. On 1 December 1636 he was appointed a singer in the chapel of the Emperor Ferdinand III in Vienna. While holding this position he published, among other music, seven collections of sacred works and wrote many occasional works, including the opera *I trionfi d'Amore* for the emperor's second marriage in 1648; he was also busy as a teacher. On 1 October 1649 he was appointed assistant Kapellmeister at the imperial court and on 16 April 1669 succeeded Antonio Bertali as Kapellmeister, a position he held until his death in spite of severe illnesses that afflicted him from 1673 and made him incapable of fulfilling his duties by early 1676. During his period in these higher offices he continued to be very active as a composer, notably of operas and *sepolcri*, and together with Bertali he played an important part in establishing regular performances of Italian dramatic music at court.

Sances cultivated with some success the prevailing monodic, concertato and polyphonic idioms of 17th-century music. His published volumes of secular vocal chamber music are of a generally high quality and well illustrate his talent. Only four such volumes survive, though the first of them, *Cantade . . . libro secondo* (1633), was issued in two parts, the first containing music for solo voice, the second for two. Sances is specially noteworthy as a melodist. This aspect of his musical personality is also reflected in the fact that most of his secular music is scored for one, two or three voices; only the 1657 book contains music for larger vocal ensembles and ensembles of voices and violins. The earlier books contain many short, attractive strophic canzonettas and arias, some of which, like *Pietosi, allontanatevi* (1636), also include recitative sections. As the title-pages of his 1633 volume suggest, Sances was also among the earliest composers to employ the designation 'cantata' extensively, and he was the first to apply it to both through-composed and strophic pieces in a single publication. The cantatas of the 1633 book, for example, range from the through-composed solo recitative and arioso *Risiede più che mai* to strophic variations like *Altre le vie* (both in part i), a *cantata passeggiata* which combines a 'walking' bass with florid vocal writing and *Occhi, sfere vivaci* (part ii), for one and two voices, which is written almost entirely in a suave, triple-time bel canto style. Sances also employed the designation 'cantata' for two sets of strophic variations, *Chi non sa cosa sia Amor* and *Son amante e son fedele*, in his 1649 book. The remaining six cantatas of the 1633 book and the one included in the 1636 book are composites of recitative and arioso sections founded on ostinato basses. The fine cantata *Usurpator tiranno* (1633, i) is the only one to employ the descending tetrachord ostinato. *Misera, hor si ch'il pianto* and *E così dunque, o Lilla'* (both in part i) are founded on freely invented ostinatos, while *Accenti queruli* (part ii), the two-part *Lagrimosa beltà* (1633, ii) and *Non sia chi mi riprendi* (1636) employ the so-called chaconne bass.

The designation 'cantata' was further employed for the lament *Presso l'onde tranquille* (1633, i), a tripartite structure with a central section using the chaconne bass in duple time. The lament of the jealous Proserpina, *Da più profondi orrori* (1636), has a similar structure but with a central section in triple time. In addition to cantatas and arias, Sances's 1633 and 1649 books each contain two dialogue settings. Among them is one of the few monodic settings, and certainly the finest, of Guarini's notorious pastoral *Tirsi morir volea* (1633, ii). Sances here overcame the problem of narration by introducing a third character, Festaurus, as narrator. The narrator of his dialogue of Angelica and Ruggiero, *Già dell'horrido mostro* (1649), a setting of epic verse (though not, as Leichtentritt stated in Ambros, from Tasso's *Gerusalemme liberata*), is designated 'testo', perhaps in emulation of Monteverdi's *Combattimento di Tancredi e Clorinda*.

WORKS

MS works, mostly lost, listed in *Distinta specificatione dell'archivio musicale per il servizio della cappella e camera cesarea* (MS, *A-Wn*) [catalogue of Leopold I's private collection]

OPERAS

Ermiona (P. E. degli Obizzi), Padua, 11 April 1636, lost
I trionfi d'Amore, Prague, 2 July 1648, lost, pubd lib *Wn*
La Roselmina fatte canara (A. Amalteo), Vienna, Feb 1662, lost, pubd lib *Wn*
Mercurio esploratore (Amalteo), Vienna, 21 Feb 1662, *Wn* [prol and intermezzos to G. A. Cicognini: Mariana]
Apollo deluso (A. Draghi), Vienna, 9 June 1669, *Wn*
Aristomene Messenio (N. Minato), Vienna, 22 Dec 1670, *Wn*

SEPOLCRI

Le lachrime di S Pietro (F. Sbarra), Vienna, 23 April 1666, *Wn*
La morte debellata (Draghi), Vienna, 19 April 1669, lost, pubd lib *Gu*
Le sette consolationi di Maria vergine, Vienna, 4 April 1670, *Wn*
Il trionfo della croce (Minato), Vienna, 28 March 1671, *Wn*
Il paradiso aperto per la morte di Christo (Minato), Vienna, 15 April 1672, *Wn*
L'ingiustitia della sentenza di Pilato (Minato), Vienna, 3 April 1676, lost, pubd lib *Wn*

SACRED VOCAL

Motetti, 1v, bc (Venice, 1638)
Motetti, 1–4vv, bc (Venice, 1638)
Antiphonae e letanie della beata vergine, 2–8vv, bc (Venice, 1640)
Motetti, 2–5vv, bc, op.4 ecclesiastica (Venice, 1642)
Salmi concertati, 8vv, bc (Venice, 1643)
Salmi brevi concertati, 4vv (Venice, 1647)
Antiphonae sacrae Beatae Virginis Mariae per totum annum, 1v, bc (Venice, 1648)

7 motets, 1641², 1641³, 1649¹, 1649⁶, 1653¹

54 masses, 3 requiem masses, 29 introits, 6 Vespers, 142 Complines, 25 Magnificat, 7 Te Deum, 19 Proper antiphons, 92 Marian antiphons, 37 litanies, 166 psalms, 56 motets: some lost, extant works in *A-KR*, *Wn*, *CS-KRa*

SECULAR VOCAL

Cantade . . . libro secondo, parte prima, 1v, bc (Venice, 1633)
Cantade . . . libro secondo, parte seconda, 2, 3vv, bc (Venice, 1633)
Arie . . . libro quarto, 1, 2vv, bc (Venice, 1636); 2 ed. K. Jeppesen, La Flora, ii, iii (Copenhagen, 1949)
Capricci poetici, 1–3vv, bc (Venice, 1649)
Trattenimenti musicali per camera . . . libro primo, 2–5vv, vns, bc, op.6 (Venice, 1657)

37 'compositioni morali et spirituali', 1–11vv, some with insts; 22 occasional cantatas, 1–8vv, insts; 273 'compositioni amorosi', 1–6vv, some with insts: some lost, extant works in *A-Wn*

INSTRUMENTAL

5 sonatas in F. Vismarri: L'Orontea, Vienna, 1660, *Wn*

BIBLIOGRAPHY

L. Allacci: *Drammaturgia* (Venice, enlarged 2/1755)
L. von Köchel: *Die kaiserliche Hof-Musikkapelle in Wien von 1543 bis 1867* (Vienna, 1869)
A. von Weilen: *Zur Wiener Theatergeschichte: die vom Jahre 1629 bis zum Jahre 1740 am Wiener Hofe zur Aufführung gelangten Werke theatralischen Charakters und Oratorien* (Vienna, 1901)
A. W. Ambros: *Geschichte der Musik*, iv (Leipzig, rev. 3/1909 by H. Leichtentritt), 849ff, 858

E. Wellesz: 'Die Opern und Oratorien in Wien 1660–1708', *SMw*, vi (1919), 5–138

B. Brunelli: *I teatri di Padova* (Padua, 1921)

P. Nettl: 'Zur Geschichte der kaiserlichen Hofmusikkapelle von 1636–1680', *SMw*, xvi (1929), 70–85; xvii (1930), 95–104; xviii (1931), 25–35; xix (1932), 33–40

N. Fortune: *Italian Secular Song from 1600 to 1635: the Origins and Development of Accompanied Monody* (diss., U. of Cambridge, 1954), 297f, 344, 375f, 381, 390, 421

A. Bauer: *Opern und Operetten in Wien: Verzeichnis ihrer Erstaufführungen in der Zeit von 1629 bis zur Gegenwart* (Graz, 1955)

F. Hadamowsky: 'Barocktheater am Wiener Kaiserhof; mit einem Spielplan (1625–1740)', *Jb der Gesellschaft für Wiener Theaterforschung, 1951–2* (1955)

A. Kellner: *Musikgeschichte des Stiftes Kremsmünster* (Kassel, 1956)

P. Petrobelli: ' "L'Ermiona" di Pio Enea degli Obizzi ed i primi spettacoli d'opera veneziani', *Quaderni della RaM*, iii (1965), 125

P. Webhofer: *Giovanni Felice Sances (ca. 1600–1679): biographisch-bibliographische Untersuchung und Studie über sein Motettenwerk* (Innsbruck, 1965)

P. Petrobelli: 'Francesco Manelli: documenti e osservazioni', *Chigiana*, xxiv (1967), 43

H. Knaus: *Die Musiker im Archivbestand des kaiserlichen Obersthofmeisteramtes (1637–1705)* (Vienna, 1967–9)

E. Raschl: *Die weltlichen Vokalwerke des Giovanni Felice Sances* (diss., U. of Graz, 1968)

I. Bartels: *Die Instrumentalstücke in Oper und Oratorium der früh-venezianischen Zeit* (diss., U. of Vienna, 1970)

T. D. Culley: *Jesuits and Music, i: A Study of the Musicians Connected with the German College in Rome during the 17th Century and of their Activities in Northern Europe* (Rome, 1970)

RUDOLF SCHNITZLER, JOHN WHENHAM

Sánchez de Fuentes, Eduardo (*b* Havana, 3 April 1874; *d* Havana, 7 Sept 1944). Cuban composer and teacher. A lawyer by profession, he studied music with Ignacio Cervantes and Carlos Anckerman. He occupied influential positions in Cuban musical life and was instrumental in developing public school music education. His melodically inventive music was based essentially on 19th-century Romantic models, though with some influence of white Cuban music and, in the opera *Doreya*, of pre-Columbian pentatony (whose discovery he claimed).

WORKS
(selective list)

Operas: El náufrago (after Tennyson: Enoch Arden), Havana, 1901; La dolorosa, Havana, 1910; Doreya, Havana, 1918; El caminante, 1921, Kabelia (after Hindu legend), Havana, 1942

Other works: Temas del patio, sym. prelude; Bocetos cubanos, S, female chorus, orch, 1922; Anacaona, sym. poem, 1928; songs incl. Mírame así and Tú; pf pieces

Principal publishers: Fernández, Marks, Southern
MSS in Biblioteca Nacional, Havana

WRITINGS
El folklore en la música cubana (Havana, 1923)
Folklorismo (Havana, 1928)
Viejos ritmos cubanos (Havana, 1937)

BIBLIOGRAPHY
M. Guiral: *Un gran musicógrafo y compositor cubano: Eduardo Sánchez de Fuentes* (Havana, 1944)

O. Martínez: *Eduardo Sánchez de Fuentes: in memoriam* (Havana, 1944)

AURELIO DE LA VEGA

Sánchez Málaga, Carlos (*b* Arequipa, Peru, 8 Sept 1904). Peruvian composer, teacher and choral conductor. After his initial musical studies in Arequipa, he began his career as a pianist and director of theatrical companies, and this took him to Chile. For several years he lived in La Paz, Bolivia, where he was appointed professor of solfège and choral singing at the National Conservatory, a position that he held for six years. On his return to Peru in 1929 he took up a similar appointment at the Lima National Conservatory, which he directed from 1943 to 1969. He was also professor of piano, and then director, of the Instituto Bach; and he taught in several state schools. From 1955 he was inspector of the army bands.

As a teacher, and for a long time one of the leaders of Peruvian musical life, Sánchez Málaga has had considerable influence. His musical production, although small, is also quite significant. Like most Peruvian artists of his generation, he has been concerned with native Indian traditions. But while other composers drew on the pre-Hispanic tradition ('Inca pentatonicism'), Sánchez Málaga sought greater spontaneity in the *mestizo* folk traditions of present-day Peru, and particularly those of his native city. An example is the musical genre known as *yaraví*, closely connected to the city's history and life. He is almost self-taught, and his works lack technical sophistication, but they exhibit a frank national character in an impressionist idiom of the early 20th century. Good examples are the suggestive piano pieces *Cayma* and *Yanahuara* (named after towns of the Arequipa province). His music opened the way to an authentic and spontaneous *mestizo* expression.

WORKS
(selective list)

Cayma, pf, 1925; Yanahuara, pf, 1925; Algún día . . . (M. Melgar), 1v, pf, 1926; Distancia (H. Vizcarra), 1v, pf, 1928; Huayno (C. G. Marín), 1v, pf, 1928; Pues bien, yo necesito (M. Acuña), chorus, 1936; A las montañas iré (trad.), chorus, 1937; Acuarelas infantiles, pf, 1938; 2 Choruses: Marinera, Pajarillo errante (trad.), 1938
2 Songs: Medrosamente ibas, Te seguiré (L. F. Xammar), 1v, pf, 1941; Palomita de nieve (E. B. Ballivián), 1v, pf, 1943; La noche se ha hecho en mi corazón (M. Wiesse), 1v, pf, 1946; Cantemos, bailemos (trad.), chorus, 1948; Yaraví (M. Melgar), chorus, 1950; Torito del Portalito (trad.), chorus, 1966

Principal publisher: Tritono

CÉSAR ARRÓSPIDE DE LA FLOR

Sancho Marraco, José (*b* La Garriga, Barcelona, 27 Feb 1879; *d* La Garriga, 17 Sept 1960). Spanish composer and choirmaster. He was a boy chorister at Barcelona Cathedral, where he studied with Viñes (piano) and Más y Serracant (organ and composition). At the age of 16 he was appointed organist of San Agustín, Barcelona, and in 1907 choirmaster. He was also music director at the Romea Theatre, Barcelona (1899–1908), conductor of the 'Montserrat' choir (1913–14) and choirmaster at Barcelona Cathedral (from 1923). One of the most enthusiastic supporters of Otaño's movement for the restoration and purification of religious music in Spain, he took an active part in music organizations and congresses; above all, he contributed to the movement most effectively with his own compositions, which were much used throughout Spain. Indeed, he was one of the greatest 20th-century composers of liturgical music in Spain. All his works show perfection of shape and solid, varied craftsmanship; like those of his Spanish contemporaries, it may be said that they lie halfway between the austerities of the German Cecilianist movement and the lyrical melodicism of Perosi.

WORKS
(selective list)

Masses: Missa 'San Juan ante portam latinam', 4vv, orch; Missa 'San José', 4vv; Missa 'Santa Cruz', 4vv, org; Missa 'San Agustín'; Missa a los mártires de la cruzada española; Requiem, 4vv, org, str orch; others

Other sacred music: Te Deum, 3vv, orch; Te Deum, 4vv; Stabat mater, 4vv, orch; Multifariam, cantata, solo vv, chorus, orch; motets, songs, org pieces, etc

Secular: Los reyes de la inocencia (zarzuela); Retorno (opera, 2); many choral works, several pieces for band

BIBLIOGRAPHY
C. Winkler: *50 maestros de la música sagrada* (Barcelona, 1956), 91f

JOSÉ LÓPEZ-CALO

Sancta Maria, Thomas [Tomás] **de.** *See* SANTA MARÍA, TOMÁS DE.

Sanctorale. *See* PROPER OF THE SAINTS.

Sanctus. An acclamation of the Latin Mass, sung by choir or congregation at the conclusion of the Preface, just before the Canon, as the musical item most closely associated with the eucharistic phase of the Mass. Since the text of the Sanctus does not change from day to day it is reckoned among the Ordinary of the Mass. Numerous melodies were composed from the 10th century on; a selection of these is contained in the *Liber usualis*, Masses I to XVIII, together with three ad libitum melodies.

The Sanctus text is the oldest of the acclamations of the Mass, even though it seems to have been added to the eucharistic prayer some time between the 1st century and the 5th. It functions as a conclusion for, and people's response to, the Preface (which is sung by the celebrant), a rehearsal of God's acts with particular emphasis on those for which thanks are to be rendered on a given occasion. In the early centuries (at least until 800), the Sanctus was sung by everyone, clergy and people, as a terrestrial analogue of the celestial praises of Cherubim and Seraphim described in *Isaiah* vi.3 (whence the text comes). In the same context the Sanctus appears in the *Te Deum*, the great prose hymn dating from before the 6th century.

The same Sanctus text is used in Greek in the Eastern liturgies in the same way. There is, however, another 'thrice-holy', the Greek trisagion ('Holy God, holy and mighty, holy and immortal, have mercy upon us') which is a different item with a different liturgical function; it appears in the Roman rite only on Good Friday. (*See* TRISAGION.)

Sanctus melodies appear in Western MSS from the 10th century on. Thannabaur's catalogue lists 230 melodies and even so is not complete. Distribution of the melodies among the sources shows (as for other items of the Ordinary) that a few melodies, largely from the 11th and 12th centuries, were widely known and used, while a much larger number of melodies were purely local products, appearing in only one or a few MSS. Composition of melodies continued throughout the later Middle Ages, especially the 15th century.

Among the early Western MSS a melody is preserved with the Greek text, and is presumed to be a Byzantine import (Huglo); the presumption has been substantiated, at least for the first part of the melody ('Agios, agios, agios') by a Greek melody from the 13th or 14th century that probably represents an earlier Byzantine congregational practice (Levy). The same melody for the three acclamations 'Sanctus, sanctus, sanctus', however, also appears in the melody for the *Te Deum* as contained in Western MSS from the 12th century, and presumed to be much older than that. Levy argued, on these and additional grounds, that some form of the entire Sanctus melody (through the repetition of 'Hosanna in excelsis') was in use from very early times as the only Sanctus melody in both Greek and Latin rites. In spite of the circumstantial nature of most of the evidence, it seems likely that the 'melismatic arches' for 'Sanctus, sanctus, sanctus', at least, represent a 10th–11th-century reminiscence of a – possibly the – much older universal congregational melody.

Many of the melodies preserved in the early Western MSS are different in nature from such a simple, congregational melody; they reflect monastic origin and (presumably) performance by a trained choir or *schola*, although congregational performance of the Sanctus is documented as late as the 12th century in France. The monastic repertory contains melodies with elaborately worked-out construction, both in phrase shapes and motivic detail. In that respect they recall the Kyrie and to a lesser degree the Gloria chants of the same period; but from the distribution in the sources, the Sanctus repertory seems to have been established a century later than the Gloria (10th–11th rather than 9th–10th centuries) and possibly a little later than the Kyrie as well. In addition, Sanctus melodies have their structural and stylistic idiosyncrasies, due partly to the text and partly, it seems, to musical conventions developed during the 11th century.

The Sanctus is usually set as five main phrases: 'Sanctus . . .', 'Pleni . . .', 'Hosanna . . .', 'Benedictus . . .', 'Hosanna . . .', and many of the more elaborate settings use some degree of melodic repetition or parallelism among these five phrases. Often the second 'Hosanna' repeats the music of the first; most interesting are the cases in which the repetition is not exact, but deliberately modified to carry out the motivic system (as in Sanctus VII). And in the highly structured style of the 11th and 12th centuries absence of repetition does not mean absence of carefully controlled structure.

The phrase 'Benedictus . . .' is often set parallel to 'Pleni . . .' using the same basic line adapted to the different text. 'Benedictus' is longer, and tends to break into two subphrases; some melodic settings put these differences to artistic advantage (Sanctus VIII). Sometimes the parallelism is only approximate, but the treatment is such as to suggest that the intent was to depart from a fairly firm convention of parallelism. The net effect of all these repetitions is to cast Sanctus as a whole into an *ABB* plan.

The opening acclamations are parsed variously by different composers: 'Sanctus/sanctus/sanctus Dominus/Deus Sabaoth/' is frequent, but alternates with other, sometimes less determinate arrangements (as in Sanctus XV). The triple 'Sanctus' itself, regardless of the presence or absence of grouping with 'Dominus', is less often set as three similar melodic units (as in Levy's proto-Sanctus), more often in some alternating fashion (*ABA*: Sanctus III) that suggests the antiphonal performance inherent in the scriptural context of the Sanctus: 'And one cried unto another, and said, Holy, holy, holy . . .'. In some cases, however, there is no such plan, three different settings of the word 'Sanctus' being subsumed under an artfully conceived longer line (Sanctus XI).

Elaborate motivic systems that cut across the larger phrase structure are frequent in the Sanctus repertory, and are characteristic of it. Sanctus II uses the same motive at the start of first and third 'Sanctus', 'Pleni', both 'Hosanna', and 'Benedictus'. Sanctus VI, XII and XIV derive subsequent material from the opening phrase in various sophisticated ways. One of the most popular Sanctus chants of the medieval repertory, Sanctus IV, has the effect of cycling through the same material in ever-changing configurations.

Sanctus was provided with tropes; these often took the form of additional epithets interpolated after each 'Sanctus', for example (*GB-Ob* Bod.775, f.72*v*):

> *Sanctus* Deus pater ingenitus;
> *Sanctus* Filius eius unigenitus;

Sanctus dominus Spiritus Sanctus paraclitus
ab utroque procedens Deus Sabaoth (etc)

Such interpolations are entirely different in musical structure and effect from the highly integrated melodies of the more elaborate Kyries with Latin texts. Some Sanctus melodies were provided with extensive settings of 'Hosanna', and these with additional text in rhyming, scanning verses – a typically 11th–12th century product.

BIBLIOGRAPHY

J. A. Jungmann: *Missarum sollemnia* (Vienna, 1948, 5/1962; Eng. trans., 1951)

M. Huglo: 'La tradition occidentale des mélodies byzantines du Sanctus', *Der kultische Gesang*, ed. F. Tack (Cologne, 1950), 40

K. Levy: 'The Byzantine Sanctus and its Modal Tradition in East and West', *AnnM*, vi (1958–63), 7–67

P. J. Thannabaur: *Das einstimmige Sanctus der römischen Messe in der handschriftlichen Uberlieferung des 11. bis 16. Jahrhunderts* (Munich, 1962)

RICHARD L. CROCKER

Sandberger, Adolf (*b* Würzburg, 19 Dec 1864; *d* Munich, 14 Jan 1943). German musicologist and composer. He studied composition in Würzburg and Munich (1881–7) and musicology in Munich and Berlin (1883–7); his teachers included Rheinberger and Spitta. After receiving his doctorate from Würzburg University in 1887 with a dissertation on Cornelius, he undertook study trips in Italy, France, Austria and Russia. In 1889 he was appointed curator of the music department of the Bavarian State Library. Completing his *Habilitation* with a work on Lassus in 1894, he became reader in musicology at the University of Munich in 1900 and full professor in 1904, the first to occupy these posts in what was then a newly autonomous discipline; he retired in 1930. With his reputation for sound scholarship and new methods of research, he became the founder of a Munich school of musicology and came to exert broad influence through the work of his many famous pupils: Kroyer, Einstein, Bücken, Huber, Bernet Kempers, Schenk and Schiedermair. In the 1930s he was involved in a dispute with J. P. Larsen over Haydn authenticity.

Sandberger's primary areas of interest were 16th-century music and the Viennese Classicists; his writings on Lassus are still fundamental to Lassus research. Equally significant were his activities as an editor, publishing the works of Lassus (1894–1927, with F. X. Haberl), the Denkmäler der Tonkunst in Bayern (1900–31) and the *Neues Beethoven-Jahrbuch* (1924–42). As the composer of two operas, songs, choruses and some chamber and instrumental music he tried with some success to assimilate the styles of his contemporaries Cornelius, Reger and Strauss. His membership of many learned societies both in and outside Germany indicates the widespread recognition granted to his scholarly attainments.

WRITINGS

Peter Cornelius (diss., U. of Würzburg, 1887; Leipzig, 1887)

Beiträge zur Geschichte der Bayerischen Hofkapelle unter Orlando di Lasso (Habilitationsschrift, U. of Munich, 1894; Leipzig, 1894–5) [1st and 3rd vols. only]

'Waelrant, Hubert W.', *ADB*

Emmanuel Chabriers Gwendoline (Munich, 1898)

'Biographische Vorbemerkungen [on Johann Pachelbel]', *J. Pachelbel: Klavierwerke*, DTB, ii, Jg.ii/1 (1901)

'Bemerkungen zur Biographie Hans Leo Hasslers und seiner Brüder, sowie zur Musikgeschichte der Städte Nürnberg und Augsburg im 16. und zu Anfang des 17. Jahrhunderts', *H. L. Hassler: Werke II* DTB, viii, Jg. v/1 (1904)

'Über eine Messe in C-moll, angeblich von W. A. Mozart', *Sitzungsberichte der philosophisch-historischen Klasse der Bayerischen Akademie der Wissenschaften* (Munich, 1904), 297

Über zwei ehedem Wolfgang Mozart zugeschriebene Messen (Munich, 1907)

'Zur älteren italienischen Klaviermusik', *JbMP 1918*, 17

'Beiträge zur Beethoven-Forschung', *AMw*, ii (1920), 394

Ausgewählte Aufsätze zur Musikgeschichte (Munich, 1921–4)

'Zur venezianischen Oper', *JbMP 1924*, 61; *JbMP 1925*, 53

'Drottning Kristinas förhållande till italiensk opera och musik, särskilt til M. A. Cesti', *STMf*, vi (1924), 97–123; vii (1925), 25–45; Ger. trans., *Bulletin de la Societé 'Union musicologique'*, v (1925), 121–73

'Zu den historischen Quellen von Richard Wagners "Tannhäuser" ', *Gedenkboek aangeboden aan Dr. D. F. Scheurleer* (The Hague, 1925), 267

'Über einige neu aufgefundene Jugendkompositionen Beethovens und Anderes', *Beethoven-Almanach der deutschen Musikbücherei auf das Jahr 1927*, ed. G. Bosse (Regensburg, 1927), 235

Introduction to facs. edn. of C. Monteverdi: *L'Orfeo* (Augsburg, 1927)

'Neue Haydniana', *JbMP 1934*, 28 [correspondence and repertory]

'Värdesättningen av Josef Haydns konst i Tyskland', *STMf*, vi (1934); Ger. orig., *NBJb*, vi (1935), 5

'Haydn und das "kleine Quartbuch" ', *ZfM*, Jg.102 (1935), 1118; see also *ZfM*, Jg.103 (1936), 1104; Jg.104 (1937), 38, 534; *AcM*, viii (1936), 18, 139; ix (1937), 31

ed.: J. Fröhlich: *Joseph Haydn* (Regensburg, 1936)

'Zu den unbekannten Sinfonien von Joseph Haydn', *NBJb*, vii (1937), 5

'Ein unbekannter Brief von Josef Haydn', *ZfM*, Jg.105 (1938), 1326

'Mozart-Festrede, gehalten anlässlich der Eröffnung des Augsburger Mozartshauses', *NBJb*, viii (1938), 5

'Christoph Willibald Gluck und die Wittelsbacher', *Zeitschrift für bayerische Landesgeschichte*, xii (1939), 209–43

'Einige ungedruckte Musikerbriefe', *JbMP 1939*, 50

'Notenbild und Werktreue', *Festschrift Fritz Stein* (Brunswick, 1939), 183

'Zu Mozarts Münchener und Mannheimer Aufenthalten', *Neues Mozart-Jb*, i (1941), 24

'Ein Lied-Autograf von Josef Haydn', *ZfM*, Jg.109 (1942), 535

EDITIONS

E. F. dall'Abaco: *Ausgewählte Werke*, i, DTB, i, Jg.i/1 (1900); ii, ibid, xvi, Jg.ix/1 (1908)

J. K. Kerll: *Ausgewählte Werke*, DTB, iii, Jg.ii/2 (1901)

with A. Einstein: A. Steffani: *Ausgewählte Werke*, DTB, xi, Jg.vi/2 (1905)

BIBLIOGRAPHY

Festschrift zum 50. Geburtstag Adolf Sandberger (Munich, 1918)

L. Schiedermair: 'Adolf Sandberger', *ZMw*, xvii (1935), 1

——: 'Adolf Sandberger', *AMf*, viii (1943), 65

HORST LEUCHTMANN

Sandby, Hermann (*b* Kundby, nr. Holbaek, 21 March 1881; *d* Copenhagen, 14 Dec 1965). Danish composer and cellist. After early lessons in Copenhagen he went to Frankfurt am Main (1895–1900) to study the cello with Hugo Becker and composition with Iwan Knorr. In 1912 he emigrated to the USA and was first cellist with the Philadelphia Orchestra until 1916. He then embarked on a career as a soloist and conductor, travelling widely in America and Europe. He returned to Denmark in the 1930s to concentrate on composing.

WORKS
(*selective list*)

Orch: Vc Conc., 1916; The Woman and the Fiddler, incidental music; 5 syms., 1930–54; Pastorale d'automne, 1937; Serenade, str orch, 1940; Nordische Rhapsodie, 1954; Vn Conc.; Triple Conc., vn, va, pf, orch

Chamber: 4 str qts, 1907–36; Str Qnt, 1936; Pf Qnt, 1938; Pf Trio, 1940; pf pieces

Stage works, incl. opera, ballet; songs

BIBLIOGRAPHY

S. Erichsen: *Tale ved bisaettelsen* (Copenhagen, 1966)

Sander. German family of music publishers active in the firm of LEUCKART.

Sander, F. [J.] S. (*b* Bohemia, *c*1760; *d* Berlin, 1796). Bohemian composer and keyboard player. At an early age he settled in Breslau, where he supported himself chiefly as a music teacher. Knowledgeable contemporaries, including C. P. E. Bach, D. G. Türk and C. F. Cramer, held his sonatas in high esteem; Gerber wrote:

'His sonatas show good imagination; in the concertos, on the other hand, there is no end to the blustering' (*GerberL*). His published works for the keyboard specify harpsichord or piano but he seems to have preferred the clavichord for his own performances. Indeed, his sonatas make considerable use of *Bebung*, a device exclusive to the clavichord. They are virtuoso works, resembling Clementi's sonatas. Most of them are in three movements (fast–slow–fast), and the slow movements are floridly embellished, affording the performer little opportunity for further elaboration. Sander published a keyboard method, *Kurze und gründliche Anweisung zur Fingersetzung für Clavierspieler* (Breslau, 1791), by which he hoped to help amateurs overcome the technical difficulties in the works of composers like Haydn, Mozart, Hässler and Wolf.

WORKS
(published works printed in Breslau unless otherwise stated)

Stage: Der Triumph der Eintracht (prol), Breslau, 25 Sept 1795, ?lost; Die Regata zu Venedig (Singspiel, S. G. Bürde), Oels [now Oleśnica], 1796, for kbd according to *GerberNL*; Don Silvio von Roslava (Singspiel, Bürde), Oels, 1797

Other vocal: Das Gebeth des Herrn . . . nebst einigen andern Liedern moralischen Inhalts (1786)

Orch: 3 [? or 6] concs., hpd (1783); Sym., D, *D-Bds*

Chamber: [12] Sonatas, kbd, i–ii (Breslau and Leipzig, 1785–7), ii lost; [12] Leichte Sonaten, i–ii (1786–7), ii lost; kbd sonata with vn (1789), lost; 6 sonatas, hpd, acc. vn (1790); 6 sonatas or divertimentos, hpd, acc. vn (1793), lost

BIBLIOGRAPHY

EitnerQ; *FétisB*; *GerberL*; *GerberNL*
J. G. Meusel: *Teutsches Künstlerlexikon* (Lemgo, 2/1808–14/*R*)
C. J. A. Hoffmann: *Die Tonkünstler Schlesiens* (Breslau, 1830/*R*)
C. Auerbach: *Die deutsche Clavichordkunst des 18. Jahrhunderts* (Kassel, 1930)

ELLWOOD DERR

Sanderling, Kurt (*b* Arys, East Prussia, 19 Sept 1912). German conductor. He joined the Berlin Städtische Oper in 1931 as a répétiteur, while studying privately, but in 1936 he was obliged to leave Germany as a refugee. He moved to Moscow and after making his début (1936) with the Moscow Radio SO was the orchestra's conductor until 1941, when he became conductor of the Leningrad PO. He directed the Leningrad orchestra jointly with Mravinsky, raising it to a high international standard in the 20 years he spent there. In 1960 he returned to Berlin as conductor of the East Berlin SO, an orchestra he has also trained to a high level. In addition he was chief conductor of the Dresden Staatskapelle, 1964–7. He has toured widely as a guest conductor, gaining particular success at the Prague, Salzburg, Vienna and Warsaw festivals, and in Britain, where he appeared with the Leipzig Gewandhaus Orchestra in 1970 and with the New Philharmonia Orchestra from 1972. His acute conceptual judgment, creative energy and precise definition of detail are applied to a wide repertory; he is specially distinguished for his blend of intellectual clarity and expressive shading, as well as dramatic impact, in his performances of Mahler, Prokofiev, Shostakovich, Sibelius and Tchaikovsky. He received the Soviet award of Honoured Artist for his work at Leningrad, and the National Prize of the German Democratic Republic in 1962 and 1974.

Sanders, Ernest H(elmut) (*b* Hamburg, 4 Dec 1918). American musicologist of German birth. He began his schooling in Hamburg, then went to the USA where he studied the piano with Irwin Freundlich at the Juilliard School from 1947 to 1950. As a graduate student in musicology at Columbia University he worked with Lang, Hertzmann and William J. Mitchell; he took the MA from Columbia in 1952 and the PhD in 1963. He became a lecturer at Columbia in 1954 and was appointed professor of music there in 1972. His principal area of study has been polyphony of the 12th to 14th centuries, particularly its forms and compositional techniques and the development of tonal concepts. His writings on English medieval polyphony trace the influence of the English composers on their continental contemporaries.

WRITINGS

'*Oberon* and *Zar und Zimmermann*', *MQ*, xl (1954), 521
Medieval English Polyphony and Its Significance for the Continent (diss., Columbia U., 1963)
'Peripheral Polyphony of the 13th century', *JAMS*, xvii (1964), 261
'Form and Content in the Finale of Beethoven's Ninth Symphony', *MQ*, l (1964), 59
'Tonal Aspects of 13th-century English Polyphony', *AcM*, xxxvii (1965), 19
'Cantilena and Discant in 14th-century England', *MD*, xix (1965), 7–52
'Die Rolle der englischen Mehrstimmigkeit des Mittelalters in der Entwicklung von Cantus-firmus-Satz und Tonalitätsstruktur', *AMw*, xxiv (1967), 24
'The Question of Perotin's Oeuvre and Dates', *Festschrift für Walter Wiora* (Kassel, 1967), 241
Review of A. Holschneider: *Die Organa von Winchester* (Hildesheim, 1968), *JAMS*, xxiv (1971), 201
'Polyphony and Secular Monophony: Ninth Century – c. 1300', 'England: from the Beginning to c. 1540', *A History of Western Music*, i, ed. F. Sternfeld (London, 1973), 89–142, 255–313
'The Medieval Motet', *Gattungen der Musik in Einzeldarstellungen: Gedenkschrift für Leo Schrade*, i (Berne and Munich, 1973), 497
'The Medieval Hocket in Practice and Theory', *MQ*, lx (1974), 246
'The Early Motets of Philippe de Vitry', *JAMS*, xxviii (1975), 24
'Discant', §II, 'England: bibliography of music to 1600', §A, 'Motet', §I, 'Sources, MS', §§V, VI, 'Vitry, Philippe de', 'Worcester polyphony', *Grove 6*

EDITIONS

English Music in the Thirteenth and Early Fourteenth Centuries, PMFC, xiv (1979)

PAULA MORGAN

Sanders, Robert Levine (*b* Chicago, 2 July 1906; *d* Delray Beach, Florida, 26 Dec 1974). American composer. He studied at the Bush Conservatory, Chicago, with Edgar Nelson; in Rome under Respighi, Bustini and Dobici; and in Paris with de Lioncourt and Braud. From 1925 until 1929 Sanders held a fellowship at the American Academy in Rome, where compositions of his were performed by the Orchestra dell'Augusteo and other musical societies. After his return to the USA, his orchestral piece *Saturday Night* was widely performed. His Violin Concerto was first played in Rochester by Jacques Gordon, with Howard Hanson conducting. The concert première of his ballet *L'Ag'ya* was given in the Hollywood Bowl, and the same work later became part of *Tropical Review* in the repertory of the Katherine Dunham Dance Company. Sanders himself conducted in Carnegie Hall his Little Symphony no.1 in G, which had received a prize from the New York Philharmonic; and he also directed the Goldman Band in his Symphony for Concert Band. He has held a number of posts as performer, teacher and administrator. He was conductor of the Chicago Conservatory SO, and assistant conductor of the Chicago Civic Orchestra (1933–6). Between 1930 and 1938 he was organist and choirmaster at the First Unitarian Church, Chicago. He taught at the Meadville Theological School and the University of Chicago. He has lectured on hymnology and liturgical music, and is one of the editors of the *Unitarian Hymnal*. In 1938 he became dean of the School of Music at Indiana University. From 1947 until

1954 he was chairman of the music department at Brooklyn College, where he remained as professor of music until his retirement in 1972. Sanders composed in a neo-classical style, using a widened concept of tonality; and his works are carefully structured. He wrote extremely well for brass instruments; the Symphony for Concert Band, the Brass Quintet in B♭ major and the Trombone Sonata are among his most effective works. His sensitivity to the inflections of the English language shows in his vocal compositions, particularly in his large-scale setting of Walt Whitman's *Song of Myself.*

WORKS
VOCAL
The Mystic Trumpeter (Whitman), narrator, Bar, chorus, orch, 1939–41; An American Psalm, 3 vv, org/inst ens, 1945–6; The Hollow Men (Eliot), 4 male vv, pf, 1947–8
Celebration of Life, cantata, S, chorus, chamber orch, 1956
Song of Myself (Whitman), reciter, S, chorus, brass ens, perc, 1966–8
Numerous choruses, hymn tunes, songs

ORCHESTRAL
Suite for Large Orchestra, 1926–8
Saturday Night, 1933; Vn Concerto, 1932–6
Symphony for Band, 1943; L'Ag'ya, ballet, 1944
Symphony, A, 1954–5
Concerto for Brass Insts, 1962
3 Little Symphonies: G, 1936–7; B♭, 1953; D, 1963

CHAMBER AND INSTRUMENTAL
Trio, c♯, pf, vn, vc, 1926
Quintet, brass insts, 1942; Rhapsody, fl, ob, cl, bn, 1945; Suite, brass qt, 1949
Trio, tpt, hn, trbn, 1958
Str Qt, 2 vn sonatas, Vc Sonata, Trbn Sonata, Hn Sonata, Cl Sonata, pf pieces

Principal publishers: Broude Brothers, Fischer, Galaxy, Mercury

SIEGMUND LEVARIE

Sanderson, Sibyl (*b* Sacramento, 7 Dec 1865; *d* Paris, 15 May 1903). American soprano. She was educated at San Francisco and at 19 entered the Paris Conservatoire, where she studied under Sbriglia and Mathilde Marchesi. She made her début in the title role of Massenet's *Manon* in The Hague in 1888. Massenet, much impressed by her voice, with its range of three octaves, wrote *Esclarmonde* and later *Thaïs* for her; in the former she made her first appearance in Paris at the Opéra-Comique in 1889. Although she also sang in Brussels, St Petersburg, Moscow, London and New York, her popularity was mainly confined to Paris. In his memoirs Massenet called her an 'ideal' Manon and an 'unforgettable' Thaïs.

WARREN STOREY SMITH

Sandi, Luis (*b* Mexico City, 22 Feb 1905). Mexican composer, educationist and conductor. At the Mexico City Conservatory he studied the violin with Rocabruna and composition with Mejía. In 1929 Chávez appointed him head of choral activities in the conservatory, and in 1938 he founded the Coro de Madrigalistas, the foremost Mexican chorus. He directed the music department of the Ministry of Education (1946–51) and the music division of the National Institute of Fine Arts (1959–63). As an administrator, teacher, conductor and critic he played a major part in Mexican musical life for four decades. He first made a mark as a composer with the New York première in May 1940 of *Yaqui Music*, an orchestral arrangement of tribal music. His opera *Carlota* concerns the tragedy of the Emperor Maximilian's wife, who went mad; *Bonampak*, a choreographic tribute to the Maya, was the source of a much played suite. Sandi's publications include the *Introducción al estudio de la música: curso completo* (Mexico City, 23/1956), the most widely used secondary school text in Latin America, *De música . . . y otras cosas* (Mexico City, 1969), a valuable anthology of his newspaper articles of the mid-1960s, and *Bitácora de un viaje* (Mexico City, 1968), the perceptive diary of a world tour that took him to 18 countries between 9 April and 18 July 1968.

WORKS
(selective list)
Stage: Carlota, opera, 1, Mexico City, Palace of Fine Arts, 23 Oct 1948; Bonampak, ballet, Mexico City, Palace of Fine Arts, 2 Nov 1951; La señora en su balcón, opera, 1964
Orch: Suite banale, 1937; Yaqui Music, perf. 1940; Norte, 1941; Bonampak, suite (1958); América, sym. poem, 1968
Choral: Quisiera te pedir, Nisida (Cervantes), 1950; Las troyanas, chorus, wind qnt, harp, perc, 1953; Canto de amor y de muerte (R. L. Velarde), 1957
Inst: El venado, Mexican ens, 1938; Fatima, suite galante, gui, 1948; Str Qt, 1951; Aire antiguo, vn, pf, 1961; Hoja de album, vc, pf, 1963
Songs: 10 haikais, 1947; 4 canciones de amor, 1954; Destino, 1967

Principal publisher: Ediciones Mexicanas de Música

BIBLIOGRAPHY
C. Chávez: 'Luis Sandi', *Nuestra música*, iv (1949), July, 175

ROBERT STEVENSON

Sandley. See STANDLEY.

Sandoni, Pietro Giuseppe (*b* Bologna, 1 Aug 1685; *d* Bologna, 16 Aug 1748). Italian composer and harpsichordist. A pupil of Angelo Predieri and Giovanni Bononcini in counterpoint, he was taught the harpsichord by Francesco Salardi. In 1698 he was organist at the Bolognese church of S Giacomo Maggiore. He was admitted to the Accademia Filarmonica in 1700 as organist, and two years later was promoted to the rank of composer. He served as *principe* in 1713, 1714, 1739 and 1745. Known chiefly as a harpsichordist, he travelled to Vienna, Munich and London where his keyboard improvisations were compared with those of Handel. In 1722 Handel sent him to Venice to bring back the famous soprano Francesca Cuzzoni, and on the return journey he married her. In London, he established himself as an eccentric personality and became involved in the controversies between Handel and Bononcini and between his wife and Faustina Bordoni. In 1728 the couple travelled to Vienna and Venice; from 1734 to 1737 they were again in London, where Sandoni's opera *Issipile* was performed in 1735. In 1737–8 he was in Florence, where he was responsible for church music. He worked in Amsterdam *c*1740 as harpsichordist, organist and composer. By 1745 he had returned to Bologna, where ill-health and financial difficulties plagued him until his death.

Of his operas and oratorios only the librettos remain. His keyboard sonatas, published between 1726 and 1728 at the end of his *Cantate da camera*, are the earliest keyboard sonatas published in England. They are in two or three movements, with thin and fluent texture, and include dance movements and free types.

WORKS
Editions: *P. G. Sandoni e Sereni: Sonate*, I classici della musica italiana, xxix, ed. B. Pratella (Milan, 1921) [contains 3 sonatas and 5 sonata movements]
Antichi maestri bolognesi, ii, ed. F. Vatielli (Bologna, ?1941) [contains 1 aria]

OPERAS
(known only from librettos cited in catalogue, I-Bc)
Artaserse (Zeno and Pariati), Verona, 1709
L'olimpiade (Metastasio), Genoa, Nov 1723
Issipile (Metastasio), London, 8 Apr 1735

ORATORIOS
(known only from librettos cited in catalogue, I-Bc)
La pulcella d'Orleans (G. B. Taroni), Bologna, 1701
Gli oracoli della grazia (T. Stanzani), Bologna, March 1704
Il martirio di S Benedetta (F. Magagnoli), Bologna, July 1704
La Giustizia placata (T. Stanzani), Bologna, 1705
L'Italia difesa da Maria (E. Vajani), Bologna, 1705
Il trionfo di Jaele (E. Vajani), Bologna, 1705
Il trionfo della grazia (E. Vajani), Ferrara, 1705
Lo sposalizio di S Gioseffo con Maria Vergine (F. Marmocchi), Bologna, 1706
S Caterina V. e M., Bologna, n.d.

OTHER WORKS
6 cantate da camera e 3 sonate, hpd (London, c1727)
6 Setts of Lessons, hpd (London, c1745)
1 trio sonata, in Corona de dodici fiori armonici (Bologna, 1706)
MSS of kbd sonatas, D-Bds, Dlb, I-Bc

BIBLIOGRAPHY
G. Berenstadt: letter to ?F. A. Pistocchi, London, 19 May 1724 (MS, I-Bc P/141)
G. B. Martini: *Catalogo degli aggregati dell'Accademia filarmonica di Bologna* (MS, I-Baf)
V. Schoelcher: *The Life of Handel* (London, 1857)
G. Gaspari: *Miscellanea storico-musicale*, ii, iii (MS, I-Bc UU/12)
B. Pratella: 'Le sonate per clavicembalo di P. G. Sandoni', *Il pianoforte*, i/8 (1920), 7
C. Sartori: 'Cuzzoni Sandoni', *ES*
O. E. Deutsch: *Handel: a Documentary Biography* (London, 1955)
W. S. Newman: *The Sonata in the Baroque Era* (Chapel Hill, 1959, rev. 2/1966/R1972)

ANNE SCHNOEBELEN

Sándor, György (*b* Budapest, 21 Sept 1912). American pianist of Hungarian birth. He graduated from the Liszt Royal Conservatory, Budapest, where he studied the piano with Bartók and composition with Kodály. He made his début in Budapest in 1930, played in London (Wigmore Hall) in 1937 and settled in the USA in 1939 after his Carnegie Hall début that year. In 1939 he also went to South America for the first time; in 1950 he went to Australia and in 1969 to the Far East. He was taught at the University of Michigan. Sándor's repertory, much of it recorded, extends from Bach to Prokofiev (whose complete solo piano works he recorded in 1967); not surprisingly, however, his name is particularly associated with Bartók (he won the 1965 Grand Prix de Disque with Bartók's solo piano music). On 8 February 1946 Sándor gave the posthumous première of his teacher's Piano Concerto no.3 with Ormandy and the Philadelphia Orchestra, and a month later he gave the first public performance (Carnegie Hall, New York) of the piano version of the Dance Suite. He has edited works of Prokofiev and Khachaturian and made a bravura transcription of *L'apprenti sorcier* by Dukas.

MICHAEL STEINBERG

Sandrin [Regnault, Pierre] (*b* ?St Marcel, nr. Paris, ?c1490; *d* ?Italy, after 1561). French composer. He probably began his artistic career as an actor. He is mentioned in one play from the mid-16th century as a 'badin antien' (that is, an actor no longer on the stage) and he seems to have taken his sobriquet from the farce *Le savetier qui ne respont que chansons*, in which a cobbler named Sandrin answers every question put to him by singing a chanson incipit.

In 1539 he was dean of the chapter of St Florent-de-Roye in Picardy. Soon after that he must have joined the French royal chapel for in 1543 Claude Chappuys in his *Discours de la court* singled out Sandrin and Claudin de Sermisy as two of the most respected musical figures there. Indeed Sandrin is described as 'composeur' in the documents listing the musicians who took part in the

funeral services for Francis I in 1547, the earliest documents yet found from the French court that give such a title to a musician. Sandrin's name is on the rolls of the royal chapel from 1549 to 1560, as *chantre ordinaire et chanoine de la Chapelle du roi* and as a recipient of various benefices, even though he seems to have spent many of those years in Italy as *maestro di cappella* at the court of Ippolito d'Este, Cardinal of Ferrara and France's representative at the Vatican. Sandrin returned to Paris from Italy briefly in 1560, during which time he made his will. The following year he was back in Rome with the cardinal, but after that all trace of him is lost and he may have died there shortly afterwards.

Although he worked in chapel choirs during most of his recorded professional career, Sandrin seems never to have composed sacred music (unless it is all lost). His complete surviving works comprise 50 chansons and one madrigal. All except two were published for the first time between 1538 and 1549, mostly by Pierre Attaingnant in Paris and Jacques Moderne in Lyons; many were then reprinted by those and other publishers. Only two examples of Sandrin's work during his last years survive, the chanson *Amour si haut*, published by Le Roy & Ballard in 1556, and the madrigal *Amor, l'arco e la rete indarno tendi*, which appeared in the fourth book of madrigals by Cipriano de Rore in 1557, attributed to Sandrino. Although Einstein assumed Sandrino to be Alessandro Striggio, the name probably refers to Regnault.

Most of Sandrin's music published before 1543 is written in the typical Parisian chanson style associated especially with the work of Claudin de Sermisy. It is predominantly chordal, although imitation and other contrapuntal detail are prominent. Often the first phrase or two and the last phrase are repeated. And Sandrin's chansons often begin with a characteristic opening motto, the first half-line of text being set to a distinctive melodic fragment and separated from the remainder of the first phrase. While Sandrin continued to publish similar lyric miniatures, between 1543 and 1549 he directed his attention to developing a more flexible rhythmic style, perhaps to avoid the uniformity of his earlier works. Some of these chansons have the characteristic dance rhythms of the frottola, in triple metre with hemiolas. In others Sandrin experiments with ways to integrate duple and triple metre within a single short work, apparently to allow the text to be declaimed in a supple and stylish manner. Thus even a relatively simple chanson like *Reveillez vous mes damoiselles* displays a highly sophisticated rhythmic style. His last published chanson, *Amour si haut*, reveals the influence of his Italian environment; it is more contrapuntal and more chromatic than most of his earlier chansons, and madrigalisms abound. Indeed his only madrigal proves that he was able to assimilate the Italian style completely during his later years.

Although Sandrin is a minor figure, his chansons are superbly elegant examples of this lyric genre. That they were highly esteemed by his contemporaries is demonstrated not only by the number of times they were reprinted and used as models for parody masses, but also by their wide distribution in the instrumental anthologies of the time. Over and over again lutenists and keyboard players chose Sandrin's music to arrange for their instruments. His chanson *Doulce memoire*, for example, was among the most popular compositions of the entire century, to judge from the number of times it was reprinted, arranged for instruments and parodied.

WORKS

Edition: *P. Sandrin: Opera omnia*, ed. A. Seay, CMM, xlvii (1968) [S]

CHANSONS
(*all for 4vv*)

Amour pense que je dorme, S 37; Amour si haut, S 50; Avant l'aymer je l'ay voulu cognoistre, S 33; Celle qui fut de beaulté, S 16; Celle qui m'a le nom d'amy donné, S 23; Ce qui est plus en ce monde, S 24; Ce qui m'est deu et ordonné, S 27; Ce qui souloit en deux se departir, S 3; Comment mes yeulx, aviez vous bien promis, S 19

Dames d'honneur, voyez mon adventure, S 28; De qui plustost maintenant, S 47; De quoy me sert de tenter la fortune, S 42; De ta blancheur qui la neige surpasse, S 34; Deux cueurs voulans par fermeté, S 10; Doulce memoire en plaisir consommée, S 4; En reveillant les damoiselles, S 38; Helas, amy, je congnois bien, S 11

Il ne se trouve en amytié, S 43; J'ay veu que j'estoys franc, S 25; Je ne le croy et le scay, S 5; Je ne puis bonnement penser, S 20; L'amour première en jeunesse innocente, S 12; Las qu'on congneust mon vouloir, S 15; La volunté si longtemps endormye, S 29; Mais pourquoy n'oze l'on prendre, S 30; M'amie est tant honneste, S 49; Montz et vaulx, faictes moy place, S 44

O combien est malheureux le désir, S 21; O vous mes yeulx qui fustes si longtemps, S 17; Pleurez mes yeulx pour la dure deffense, S 18; Puisque de vous je n'ay aultre visaige, S 9; Puisque vivre en servitude, S 45; Quant j'ay congneu en ma pensée, S 13; Quant ung bien par longtemps est attendu, S 26; Quel bien parler ou compter son affaire, S 35; Qui de s'amye a le bien, S 46; Qui souhaitez avoir tout le plaisir, S 48; Qui vouldra scavoir qui je suis, S 6

Reveillez vous mes damoiselles, S 39; Si de beaucoup je suis aymé, S 31; Si j'ay du bien helas, S 40; Si mon travail vous peut donner, S 7; Si pour t'aymer et désirer, S 22; Si vostre amour ne gist qu'en apparance, S 14

Tous les malheurs que j'ay pour l'amour, S 32; Trop plus penser que bien escrire, S 41; Vaincre n'a peu le temps, S 8; Voulant honneur que de vous je m'absente, S 36; Vous usurpez dames injustement, S 1; Voyez le tort d'amour et de fortune, S 2

MADRIGAL

Amor, l'arco e la rete indarno tendi, 4vv S 51

BIBLIOGRAPHY

BrownI

F. Lesure: 'Un musicien d'Hippolyte d'Este: Pierre Sandrin', *CHM*, ii (1957), 247

H. M. Brown: *Music in the French Secular Theater, 1400–1550* (Cambridge, Mass., 1963), 62f

F. Dobbins: 'Doulce memoire: a Study of the Parody Chanson', *PRMA*, xcvi (1969–70), 85

HOWARD MAYER BROWN

Sandström, Sven-David (*b* Motala, 30 Oct 1942). Swedish composer. He studied in Stockholm, first at the university, and then with Lindholm (composition) at the Royal Academy while working there as a composition assistant. He also took lessons with Ligeti and Nørgård. His music exploits the full range of serial and post-serial techniques, as well as microtones and aleatory procedures.

WORKS
(*selective list*)

Orch and large ens: Bilder, perc, orch, 1969; 17 Bildkombinationer, wind, str, perc, 1969; To You, 1970; Around a Line, 1971; Through and Through, 1972; Con tutta forza, 1976

Chamber and small ens: Concertato, cl, trbn, vc, perc, 1969; Str Qt, 1969; In the Meantime, chamber orch, 1970; Jumping Excursions, cl, vc, trbn, cymbal, 1970; Concentration, 8 wind, 4 db, 1971; Lamento, 3 choruses, 4 trbn, 1971; Under the Surface, 4 trbn, 1972; Just a Bit, S, bn, vn, harp, 1973; Utmost, wind qnt, tpt, trbn, tuba, perc, 1975

1–3 insts: Sonata, fl, 1968; Disjointing, trbn, 1970; Mosaic, str trio, 1970; Concentration II, 2 pf, 1972; Closeness, cl, 1972; Convergence, bn, 1973; The Way, org, 1973; Inside, bass trbn, pf, 1974; Effort, vc, 1977

Vocal: Visst?, S, 2 choruses, vns, orch, 1971; Birgitta-music I, vv, dancers, org, orch, 1973; Expression, Mez, vc, pf 4 hands, 1976; Stark sasom (church opera, B. V. Wall), 1977

BIBLIOGRAPHY

G. Bergendal: 'De fryas musik', *Nutida musik*, xii/3 (1968–9), 12

——: 'Sven-David Sandström – "through and through" ', *Nutida musik*, xvii/3 (1973–4), 14

B. E. Johnson: 'Sandström, Sven-David', *Sohlmans musiklexikon* (Stockholm, 2/1975–9)

Sandunga (Sp.: 'gracefulness', 'agility', 'allurement'). A Mexican song and dance genre of the *son istmeño* type from the Isthmus of Tehuantepec region in the south of Oaxaca state, near the town of Tehuantepec. The *son* is properly performed by a *marimba-orquesta* including a double bass, and wind instruments including clarinets, saxophones, trumpets, trombones, euphoniums and other instruments.

E. THOMAS STANFORD

Sandunova [née Fyodorova], **Elizaveta Semyonovna** (*b* St Petersburg, 1772 or 10 Sept 1777; *d* Moscow, 3 Dec 1826). Russian mezzo-soprano. By command of Catherine II she adopted the professional name Uranova after the planet Uranus, which had been discovered in 1781. She received her musical education at the St Petersburg drama school, studying under Martín y Soler, Paisiello and Sarti. Her first stage appearance was in Martín y Soler's opera *Arbore di Diana*, performed at the Hermitage Theatre in 1790, and in the following year she was engaged as a singer in the Imperial Theatres. She was extremely popular as a performer, and, like many young actresses and singers of the day, was admired by Count Alexander Bezborodko, Catherine's notorious Minister of Foreign Affairs. After performing in *Fedul s detmi* ('Fedul and the children') by Martín y Soler and Pashkevich on 22 Feb 1791, she made a dramatic plea to Catherine to use her power to stop the unwelcome attentions she was receiving from the count and to give permission for her to marry the actor Sila Nikolayevich Sandunov. After their marriage in 1794 they travelled to Moscow and worked together in the Petrovsky Theatre. They were divorced in 1810 however, and three years later Sandunova returned to St Petersburg, where, until her retirement in 1823, she performed frequently in the St Petersburg theatres. She was renowned for her wide-ranging and expressive mezzo-soprano voice, and was one of the finest operatic singers of the early years of the 19th century. She established a considerable reputation as a concert artist and took leading roles in countless operas.

BIBLIOGRAPHY

R. A. Mooser: *Annales de la musique et des musiciens en Russie au XVIIIᵐᵉ siècle* (Geneva, 1948–51)

T. Livanova: *Russkaya muzїkal'naya kul'tura XVIII veka*, ii (Moscow, 1953)

A. A. Gozenpud: 'Iz istorii russkovo opernovo teatra kontsa XVIII – nachala XIX veka', *Uchonїye zapiski*, ed. Institut Teatra, Muzїki i Kinematografii (Leningrad, 1958), 255–93

GEOFFREY NORRIS

Sandvik, Ole Mørk (*b* Nes, 9 May 1875; *d* Holmenkollen, nr. Oslo, 5 Aug 1976). Norwegian musicologist. He was trained as a teacher (1895) and while holding a teaching position studied theology (graduated 1902) and music with his father Paul Sandvik and the Oslo violinist Gudbrand Bøhn. After studying in Germany (1913) he taught at the Hegdehaugen School in Oslo (1913–45) as well as church music at the Seminary for Practical Theology of the University of Oslo (1916–45); he and Olav Gurvin gave the first regular lecture courses in music at the university (1937–9) which resulted in the establishment, after the war, of a music faculty.

Sandvik began to collect folk music in 1910 and was able to include about 400 melodies in his first book, *Folkemusikk i Gudbrandsdalen* (1919). He decided that this repertory (from a small district in eastern Norway) contained early elements which could be described as characteristic of Norwegian folk music in general, a view he argued in *Norsk folkemusikk: saerlig Østlandsmusikken* (1921), for which the University of Oslo awarded him the doctorate (1922, the second ever given a musicologist there). Sandvik did extensive fieldwork in different parts of Norway and in Sweden (1924), Ireland and Scotland (1927), where he investigated possible relationships with Norwegian folk music.

Sandvik's other main interest was church music. In 1941 he published *Kingo-tona*, based on L. M. Lindeman's collection (1848) of the tunes sung to hymns of the 17th-century Danish bishop Kingo as they had survived in Norwegian oral tradition. This was followed by a study of Lindeman as a collector of folk music. In his devotion to folk music and church music as the two pillars of national musical life Sandvik had much in common with Lindeman, though in his efforts to bring the two closer together he contradicted his predecessor on some issues. Thus in *Norsk kirkemusikk og dens kilder* (1918) he recommended that folktunes should be adapted as hymn melodies, a view which Lindeman initially held but later rejected. Sandvik was secretary (1923–6) of the committee appointed to revise the Norwegian hymnbook (*Koralbok for den norske kirke*, 1926), and effected the adoption of 37 folk melodies as hymn tunes and the restoration of the traditional rhythmical performance of many of the early melodies which Lindemann had abandoned in favour of a regular and simple chorale form. His *Norsk koralhistorie* (1930) was an important companion to the new hymnbook. Sandvik's efforts on behalf of church music also extended to liturgical matters: he published a *Graduale for den norske kirke* (1925) and a *Vesperale for den norske kirke* (1941), and helped to prepare the liturgical music for the 900th anniversary of the martyrdom of St Olaf (Trondheim, 1930; the medieval liturgy of St Olaf is given special attention in his *Gregoriansk sang*, 1945).

While pursuing these interests Sandvik also edited songbooks for school use, wrote and edited, with the composer Gerhard Schjelderup, a history of Norwegian music (1921–2; for 50 years the only work of its kind), founded the Norwegian Musicological Society and edited all its yearbooks from 1937 (the first issue) to 1972. He championed Norwegian composers, being the first to acclaim Fartein Valen, whose piano sonata he reviewed as early as 1915. He was responsible for the establishment of the Norsk Musikksamling in 1927 as a special division of the Oslo University library, a national music collection with its own reading room, programme of concerts, publications etc. He had a career of almost unique duration: as a young man he observed Grieg's methods of rehearsal and performance, at the age of 97 he published an account of the great hymn-tune controversy and had other projects in hand. He had an excellent memory and though he did not write his memoirs the Norsk Musikksamling made several recordings of his recollections. For his 100th birthday his many friends contributed to the establishment of a fund to be named after him.

WRITINGS

'Ole Bull', *Kirke og kultur*, xvii (1910), 89
'Norsk folkemusik', *Nordmandsforbundet*, iv (1911), 123
'Norsk mandssang', *Nordmandsforbundet*, v (1912), 655
'Folketoner fra nordre Gudbrandsdalen', *Maal og minne* (1913), 131
'Nyere norsk musik', *Nordmandsforbundet*, vi (1913), 557
'Halfdan Kjerulf 17. sept. 1815–17. sept. 1915', *Nordmandsforbundet*, viii (1915), 598

'Halfdan Kjerulf og poesien', *Edda*, iv (1915), 357
'Baansuller og andre barnesanger fra Gudbrandsdalen', *Maal og minne* (1916), 177
'Fra Kjerulfs krets i 40-årene', *Edda*, ix (1918), 81
'Kirkesang, messe, kirkemusikk', *Norsk kirkeblad*, xv (1918), 8, 23
'Melodier til Storms Døleviso', *Maal og minne* (1918), 29
'Nordisk musikforskning', *Samtiden*, xxix (1918), 568
Norsk kirkemusikk og dens kilder (Oslo, 1918)
Folkemusik i Gudbrandsdalen (Oslo, 1919, 2/1948)
with G. Schjelderup: *Norges musikhistorie* (Oslo, 1921–2)
'Det religiose i Griegs musikk', *Tydninger og tegninger: en hilsen til professor dr. Lyder Brun* (Oslo, 1922), 109
'L. M. Lindeman og Edvard Grieg i deres forhold til norsk folkemusik', *Kirke og kultur*, xxix (1922), 371
Norsk folkemusikk: saerlig Østlandsmusikken (Oslo, 1921; diss., U. of Oslo, 1922)
'Musikk-minner fra oldtiden i vår liturgi', *Kirke og kultur*, xxx (1923), 262
'Nogen gammelkirkelige melodier i Hans Thomissøns psalmbog av 1569', *Norvegia sacra* (1923), 30
'Felespillemaend og folkemusik', *Nordmandsforbundet*, xvii (1924), 306
'Forholdet mellem tekst og tone i norsk folkemusikk', *Festskrift tilegnet førstebibliotekar A. Kjaer* (Oslo, 1924), 22
ed.: H. Panum and W. Behrend: *Illustreret musikleksikon* (Copenhagen, 1924–6; new edn., 1940 with P. Hamburger and others)
'Ny norsk musik', *Nordmandsforbundet*, xvii (1924), 112
'Edvard Grieg und die norwegische Volksmusik', *Gedenkboek aangeboden aan Dr. D. F. Scheurleer* (The Hague, 1925), 271
Graduale for den norske kirke (Oslo, 1925, 2/1957)
with J. Gleditsch and others: *Koralbok for den norske kirke* (Oslo, 1926)
'Melismer og rytmiske eiendommeligheter i norsk folkemusikk', *Juhlakirja Ilmari Krohn'ille* (Helsinki, 1927), 112
'Ved 100-årsdagen for Schuberts død', *Samtiden*, xxxix (1928), 540
Liturgisk musikk til minnegudstjenester på 900-års-jubileet Olsok 1930 (Oslo, 1930)
'Musikken under Olavsfesten i høgmellomalderen', *Andr. Seierstad: Olavsdyrking i Nidaros og nord-Europa* (Nidaros, 1930), 53
Norsk koralhistorie (Oslo, 1930)
'Carl Nielsen in memoriam', *Kirke og kultur*, xxxviii (1931), 525
'Den nye musikk', *Kirke og kultur*, xl (1933), 139
'Norsk folkemusikk', *Nordisk kultur*, xxv (1934), 128
'Norwegian Folk Music and its Connection with the Dance', *JEFDSS*, ii (1935), 92
'Salmetone og forsamlingsmelodi', *Kirke og kultur*, xliii (1936), 344
'Ti "Kingo-tona" fra Vang, Valdres', *Norsk musikkgranskning årbok 1938*, 68 [with melodies]
'Über die norwegische Musikforschung', *AMf*, iii (1938), 484
'Kingo-tona fra Vang, Valdres', *Norsk musikkgranskning årbok 1939*, 53 [with melodies]
'Keltiske melodier og norsk folkemusikk', *Norsk musikkgranskning årbok 1940*, 68
Kingo-tona (Oslo, 1941)
Vesperale for den norske kirke (Oslo, 1941)
'Griegs melodikk', *Norsk musikkgranskning årbok 1942*, 8
'De "Fire samler": korkomponisten Grieg', *Norsk musikkliv*, x (1943), no.5, p.23, no.6, p.2
'Melodiene til Draumkvaedet', *Norsk musikkliv*, xi/3 (1944), 6
Gregoriansk sang (Oslo, 1945)
Ludwig M. Lindeman og folkemelodien: ein kilderstudie (Oslo, 1950)
Setesdalsmelodier (Oslo, 1952)
'Folkemusikken og musikkundervisningen', *Nordisk musikkultur*, ii (1953), 80
'Norsk folkmusik', *Musikrevy*, xiv (1959), 78
'Johan Grundt Tanum, 1891 bis 1961', *Norsk musikkgranskning årbok 1959–61*, 90
'Kantaten i Skien Kirke 11. Des. 1811', *Norsk musikkgranskning årbok 1959–61*, 91
'Nytt fra L. M. Lindemans saga', *Norsk musikkgranskning årbok 1959–61*, 166
Norske religiose folketoner (Oslo, 1960–64)
'Original eller variant?', *STMf*, xliii (1961), 283 [with Eng. summary]
'Springleiker' i norske bygder (Oslo, 1967)
ed. with O. Gaukstad: *David Monrad Johansen i skrift og tale* (Oslo, 1968)
'Koralstrid – menighetssang – folketone', *Norsk musikkgranskning årbok 1962–71*, 46

BIBLIOGRAPHY

Festskrift til O. M. Sandvik, 70 års dagen 1875–9. Mai 1945 (Oslo, 1945) [incl. list of writings to 1945; S. Olsen: 'O. M. Sandvik', 9; A. Sandvold: 'O. M. Sandvik i Norsk kirkemusikk', 20]
O. Gurvin: 'Sandvik, Ole Mørk', *NBL*
S. Olsen: 'O. M. Sandvik 90 år', *Norsk musikktidsskrift*, ii (1965), 89
O. Gaukstad: 'O. M. Sandvik 100 år', *Norsk musikktidsskrift*, xii (1975), 41

JOHN BERGSAGEL

Sanelli, Gualtiero (*b* Parma, 14 May 1816; *d* Maranhão, Brazil, 15 Dec 1861). Italian composer and conductor. At a very early age he joined the chorus of the ducal theatre in Parma, then became chorus master and prompter in the opera at Mantua (1835–9). As a member of a touring opera company he visited Milan and other Italian cities, then (1841) Mexico and probably other Central American countries. On his return to Europe, he began seriously to study music in Paris; later he was active in England as conductor of opera seasons organized by Italian impresarios. By 1858 he was resident conductor in Pernambuco, Brazil, where he had gone with an opera company organized by the impresario Mariangeli. From there he moved to Maranhão, where he died insane. Sanelli composed 11 operas, all first performed in Italy between 1838 and 1855 and conducted by him on his tours. Vocal scores of three of them, and excerpts from three others, were published by Ricordi, who also possessed the autograph scores.

BIBLIOGRAPHY

FétisB; *SchmidlD*

GIOVANNI CARLI BALLOLA

Sanes, Giovanni Felice. *See* SANCES, GIOVANNI FELICE.

San Francisco. American city in the state of California. It was established by Franciscan missionaries and remained a sleepy village until 1849 when gold was discovered in the Sierra Nevada 300 km east. With the city's sudden and rapid growth, a gaudy, elaborate artistic life was born.

1. Opera. 2. Orchestras, concert organizations. 3. Educational institutions, libraries.

1. OPERAS. Opera was the city's first musical love. 'Count' Alfred Roncovieri, a French bass, was responsible for the earliest operatic production – Bellini's *La sonnambula* (1851) – and remained in San Francisco for many years, presenting much of the standard French and Italian repertory of his time. This was also the age of plush-and-gaslight concerts in San Francisco with stars such as Jenny Lind, Henri Herz and Louis Moreau Gottschalk.

Opera was established on a firm footing with the founding of the Tivoli Opera House, which for ten years (1890–1900) never closed its doors, presenting grand opera in winter and light opera in summer. Then the Metropolitan Opera Company brought opera to San Francisco until the earthquake and fire of 1906.

The Italian conductor Gaetano Merola founded the present San Francisco Opera Company in 1923 and was its general director until his death 30 years later. Merola worked almost entirely within the framework of standard repertory, from Mozart to Richard Strauss. His productions were unadventurous, and his casts were drawn almost entirely from the Metropolitan; both he and his financial backers were convinced that opera could be successful in San Francisco only if sung by current New York stars. Merola's season was limited to September and October, but included about 30 performances each year in San Francisco and half that number in Los Angeles and other west coast cities. The season was concentrated in this way for two reasons. One was that the Metropolitan singers had to be back in New York for their own season in November; the other was that the San Francisco Opera Company and the San

Francisco SO used the same orchestral players, and according to a tradition lasting to this day, there could be no symphony concerts in San Francisco during the opera season.

After Merola's death, his chorus master and assistant director, Kurt Herbert Adler, took over as general director. He totally transformed the company by drawing his principal artists from all over the world, no longer relying on the Metropolitan. With the help of such European stage directors as Paul Hager, he improved the company's production standards to such an extent that it may now compare with the best abroad. He stopped touring and thereby more than doubled the length of the season in San Francisco. He has ventured extensively into modern opera, with works of Berg, Stravinsky, von Einem, Janáček, Schuller, Shostakovich and others, and he has revived the works of earlier composers such as Berlioz, Cherubini, Meyerbeer, whose works are seldom heard in American opera houses. Adler also established two smaller subordinate opera companies. Spring Opera, begun in 1960, is a kind of laboratory for experiment in opera; it provides intimate performances in a relatively small theatre with young but established singers, many of them members of the big company, and with much innovation in repertory and methods of production. Western Opera Theater, founded in 1967, is a training school for singers and audiences alike, taking young artists, light scenery and reduced production forces to the smaller towns of the Pacific coast.

2. ORCHESTRAS, CONCERT ORGANIZATIONS. Orchestral concerts in San Francisco, as in most American cities, began under the shadow of German choruses. The first was the Germania Singing Society, founded in the 1850s and led successively by Gustav Hinrichs, Oscar Weil and Hermann Brandt. In the 1890s Fritz Scheel, who later founded the Philadelphia Orchestra, led a Symphony Society in San Francisco. The present San Francisco SO goes back, however, to the year 1911. Its first conductor was Henry Hadley, who directed it for four years. Hadley was more gifted as a composer than as a conductor, a fact which San Francisco discovered in 1915, when the Panama-Pacific International Exposition was held in the city and guest orchestras, notably the Boston SO under Karl Muck, played at the fair.

The success of Muck and the Bostonians led to a demand for a reorganization of Hadley's somewhat provincial venture. Alfred Hertz, then conductor of German opera at the Metropolitan, was brought in to conduct the San Francisco SO. He remained at that post until 1929 and was succeeded by Basil Cameron and Issay Dobroven. In 1934, during the Dobroven regime, the Musical Association of San Francisco, which sponsored the orchestra, went bankrupt, and during the season of 1934–5 the orchestra gave no concerts.

The present San Francisco Symphony Association was revived, partly as the result of the passage of an amendment to the city charter which guaranteed the orchestra a municipal subsidy of $100,000 each year. The municipal concerts are managed by the city itself, through its Art Commission, and for many years have taken the form of summer 'pops' under the direction of Arthur Fiedler.

Pierre Monteux became the conductor of the San Francisco SO in 1935 and remained for 17 years, establishing lasting artistic foundations. Monteux retired in 1952, and in 1954 Enrique Jordá was appointed his successor. Jordá brought San Francisco a particularly wide-ranging and adventurous repertory which created much opposition among the more conservative elements in the community. Josef Krips conducted from 1963 to 1969, and was succeeded by Seiji Ozawa, who was in turn succeeded by Edo de Waart in 1977.

The San Francisco SO season lasts from December to the end of May. Both opera and symphony concerts take place at the War Memorial Opera House, a comfortable, now slightly old-fashioned theatre seating 3300, erected by the city in 1932. Since 1973 the orchestra has maintained its own chorus.

The Oakland SO, in the city of Oakland across the bay, has made great progress in recent years and now provides the community with an alternative symphonic organization of great merit and interest. The coming of age of the Oakland SO was largely the achievement of Gerhard Samuel, who resigned in 1970 to become assistant conductor of the Los Angeles PO and was succeeded by Harold Farberman.

The San Francisco Chamber Music Society, dating from 1961, sponsors about a dozen concerts each year, mostly by ad hoc ensembles; chamber music for the traditional string quartet, trio or duo is most often presented in concert series arranged by the area's educational institutions (the University of California, Stanford University, Mills College and San Francisco State University), rather than those given by commercial agencies.

3. EDUCATIONAL INSTITUTIONS, LIBRARIES. The universities and colleges are the area's principal centres of musical creativity. Composers including Bliss, Sessions, Bloch, Randall Thompson and Andrew Imbrie have taught and worked at the University of California at Berkeley. Darius Milhaud taught for 32 years at Mills College, Oakland; this college is also the community's principal centre for electronic music and has attracted composers from many parts of the world. Stanford University in Palo Alto has an important music course and library. There are notable collections of early music in the music library of the University of California, Berkeley, and the library of the San Francisco State University, Frank V. De Bellis Collection (see LIBRARIES).

The most important music college in the area is the San Francisco Conservatory of Music, founded by Ada Clement in 1915. Bloch came to San Francisco to teach there between 1925 and 1930. One of its most interesting activities is the sponsorship of the New Music Ensemble of San Francisco, directed by Howard Hersch and Robert Moran; this organization is devoted to the leading edge of the avant garde and has aroused international interest.

BIBLIOGRAPHY
L. W. Armsby: *Musicians Talk* (New York, 1935)
Writers Project of the Works Project Administration: *History of Opera in San Francisco* (MS, *US-BE*, 1938)
——: *History of Music in San Francisco* (MS, *US-SFp*, 1939)
A. Bloomfield: *Fifty Years of San Francisco Opera* (San Francisco, 1972)

ALFRED FRANKENSTEIN

Sanglot (Fr.: 'sob'). A term used in the 18th century (or in reference to 18th-century music) for a downward-resolving appoggiatura sung to an appropriate word, such as 'ah' or 'hélas'.

San-hsien. A Chinese long-necked, plucked lute with three strings; *see* CHINA, §§III, 2(iv), 3(ii); V, 4(i), 5(ii); JAPAN, §IV, 4(ii); TAIWAN, §3.

Sankey, Ira David (*b* Edinburgh, Penn., 28 Aug 1840; *d* Brooklyn, 13 Aug 1908). American evangelistic singer and song leader, associated with the revivalist Dwight L. Moody. With P. P. Bliss and others he compiled the *Gospel Hymns* series (1875–94). *See* GOSPEL MUSIC, §I.

BIBLIOGRAPHY
H. E. Starr: 'Sankey, Ira David', *DAB*
The Ira D. Sankey Centenary (New Castle, Penn., 1941)
C. Ludwig: *Sankey Still Sings* (Anderson, Indiana, 1947)
R. M. Stevenson: 'Ira D. Sankey and the Growth of "Gospel Hymnody"', *Patterns of Protestant Church Music* (Durham, N. Carolina, 1953), 151
J. C. Pollock: *Moody* (New York, 1963)

Sankovskaya, Ekaterina (1816–78). Russian dancer; *see* DANCE, §VI, 1(ii).

San Martini [San Martino], **Giovanni Battista**. *See* SAMMARTINI, GIOVANNI BATTISTA.

Sanmartini [Sanmartino], **Giuseppe**. *See* SAMMARTINI, GIUSEPPE.

Sanmartini [San Martino, Sammartini], **Pietro** (*b* Florence, 18 Sept 1636; *d* Florence, 1 Jan 1701). Italian composer, harpsichordist, organist and teacher. He was not related to Giuseppe and G. B. Sammartini. He was a pupil at the music school run in Florence by G. B. Comparini and later became a priest. He worked as a musician in several places, among them Rome, Bologna and Arezzo. From 1659 he lived permanently in Florence, first as vice-*maestro di cappella* of the cathedral and from 21 June 1686 until his death as *maestro*. He also served the Medici court as a musician until his death, principally as a keyboard player. From 1692 he was a composing member of the Accademia Filarmonica of Bologna. He was much admired as a teacher. Very little of his considerable output of vocal and instrumental, sacred and secular music has survived. It is enough to show that he was a competent composer. The last in particular of the ten sinfonias that comprise his op.2 is an important milestone in the development of the *sonata da chiesa*; indeed Cordara and others are probably right to regard him as an originator of the form that later grew into the symphony.

WORKS
Partitura de motetti, 1v, bc, op.1 (Florence, 1685)
Sinfonie, 2 vn, lute, va da gamba, bc (org), op.2 (Florence, 1688)

Beatus vir, 5vv, insts, 1692, *I-Baf*
Miserere; 50 psalms: 4vv, *Fd*
Other sacred works, *Fd*

LOST WORKS
7 operas, incl. Le rivalità favorevoli (Florence, 1688); known only from lib
S Cecilia, oratorio (Florence, 1692); known only from lib
Mass 'Veni sponsa Christi', 18vv; Messa bellica, 9vv, tpt
Arie da camera, 3 vols.
Other masses, oratorios, vespers, motets, instrumental works

BIBLIOGRAPHY
C. Cordara: 'I precursori della sinfonia: un altro Sanmartini sinfonista', *Il primato artistico italiano*, ii/4 (1920), 33
A. Parrini: *Dalle ricerche sul liuto ad un sinfonista sconosciuto del '600* (Florence, 1925)
M. Fabbri: 'Due musicisti genovesi alla corte granducale medicea: Giovanni Maria Pagliardi e Martino Bitti', *Musicisti piemontesi e liguri*, Chigiana, xvi (1959), 82
——: 'Gli ultimi anni di vita di Francesco Maria Veracini', *CHM*, iii (1962), 97

ARGIA BERTINI

San Pedro, Lucio (Diestro) (*b* Angono, Rizal, 11 Feb 1913). Filipino composer and conductor. He graduated in composition and band conducting from the University of the Philippines Conservatory (1938) and studied composition with Gianini and Wagenaar at the Juilliard School (1947–8); there he composed the first Filipino violin concerto. While band instructor to the Ateneo de Manila ROTC Band (1939–41) he taught at several music schools in the capital. Eventually he became chairman of the composition and conducting department at the Conservatory of the University of the Philippines. Once music director at the Metropolitan Theatre (1943 5), he is the conductor of several bands and led the Peng Kong Band in tours of Taiwan in 1964 and from 1967 to 1970. Among the awards he has received are a prize in the National Heroes Day Composition Contest of 1936, a Cardinal Spellman silver medal (1956) and a Republic Cultural Heritage Award (1962). His works are strongly romantic with nationalist themes supported by rich harmonies.

WORKS
(selective list)

Orch: Malakas at Maganda [Strong and Beautiful], ov., 1935; The Devil's Bridge, sym. poem, 1937; Prelude and Fugue, d, 1938; Hope and Ambition, sym. poem, 1946; Vn Conc., d, 1947–8; Moon over the Hills, tone poem, 1952; Suite pastorale, 1956; Transfiguration of Christ, sym. poem, female vv, orch, 1959; Lahing kayumanggi [Brown race], sym. poem, 1962; marches and other band music
Choral: Easter Cantata, female vv, orch, 1950; Rizal's Valedictory Poem, female/mixed vv, 1952; Regina coeli, 1953; Mga tulaing pang kalikasan [Poems of nature], 1973
Solo vocal: Lulay, folksong arr., 1943; Sa mahal kong bayan [To my beloved country], female lv, orch, 1950; Leron-leron sinta, folksong arr., 1951; Of long ago, 1953; Sa umaga [In the morning], 1953; Diwata ng Pagibig [Music of love], 1957
Chamber: Romance, vc, pf, 1937; Ww Qt, 1959

LUCRECIA R. KASILAG

Sanquirico, Alessandro (*b* Milan, 27 July 1777; *d* Milan, 12 March 1849). Italian scene painter and designer. He began his career designing scenery and decorating new theatres in conjunction with other leading artists such as P. Landriani, Giovanni Pedroni, Giovanni Perego and Giorgio Fuentes. From 1817 to 1832 he was sole designer and chief scene painter for La Scala. From this powerful position during a rich period of operatic output, he influenced design standards for the works of Bellini, Donizetti, Mozart, Meyerbeer, Rossini and many other later composers until well into the 20th century. Among the hundreds of operas and ballets he designed at La Scala were the premières of Rossini's *La gazza ladra* (1817; see illustration), Bellini's *Norma* (1831) and Donizetti's *Lucrezia Borgia* (1834).

His designs were the foundation of the style commonly associated with 19th-century grand opera. They combined the restrained neo-classicism of his early training with the romantic trait of basing stage fantasy on historical accuracy and sensibility. Vast enough in scale

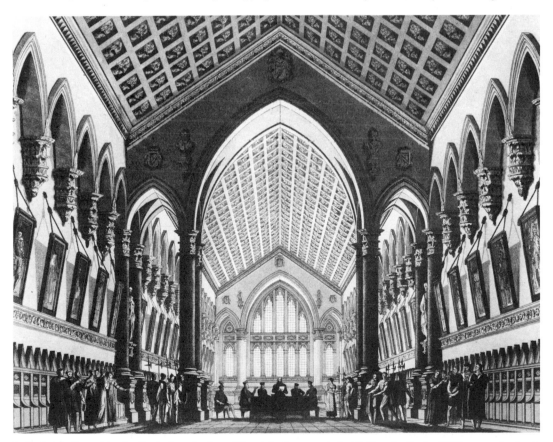

1. Design by Sanquirico for the first production of Rossini's 'La gazza ladra' (Milan, La Scala, 1817): engraving by A. Biasioli from 'Raccolta di varie decorazioni sceniche . . . da Alessandro Sanquirico'

to accommodate the epic quality of lyric drama, they were intimate enough and sufficiently 'realistic' to render human passions credible and reasonably natural. He tended to prefer spacious settings with single perspective, unlike the more intricate plans of the late Baroque period. A typical Sanquirico formula, widely copied and still theoretically valid, was to set a scene in a richly decorated architectural foreground which opened out on to a broad landscape view painted on a backdrop, profound in its simplicity. This solved many technical problems of scale and, at the same time, satisfied the aesthetic needs of romantic audiences for spectacle. The end of his career saw the introduction of gas lighting in theatres, and his painted scenery showed a sensitivity to the nuances of light which later scene painters lost because of advances in lighting control. One reason for Sanquirico's international influence was that portfolios of hand-coloured engravings based on his theatrical and architectural drawings were published and extensively circulated and copied (*Raccolta di scene teatrali eseguite o disegnate dai più celebri pittori scenici di Milano*, 1819–24; *Raccolta di varie decorazioni sceniche inventate ed eseguite per il R. Teatro alla Scala di Milano da Alessandro Sanquirico*, c1827).

See also OPERA, §VIII, 5.

BIBLIOGRAPHY
E. Povoledo: 'Sanquirico, Alessandro', *ES*

PAUL SHEREN

San Rafaele [San Raffaele], **(Carlo Luigi Baldassare) Benvenuto Robbio,** Count of (*b* Chieri, nr. Turin, 25 June 1735; *d* Turin, 27 Feb 1797). Italian author, amateur violinist and composer. Because of the title-page of his sonatas op.2, he is sometimes erroneously called Benevento. He served as royal director of studies for Turin and was an honorary member of the Turin Academy of Painting and Sculpture. Burney called him 'a great performer on the violin, and a good composer', a judgment borne out by his compositions which are technically brilliant and tastefully written. Among a number of poetic and philosophical works, he wrote a short but valuable treatise on the violin and the relative merits of the schools of Corelli, Tartini and Stamitz.

WORKS
6 sonate, hpd solo/vn, b (Paris, c1765); no.5 in Cartier's L'art du violon (Paris, 1798)
6 sonate, vn, b, op.2 (Paris, 1767)
6 duetti, 2 vn (Paris and Lyons, c1770)

WRITINGS
Lettere due sopra l'arte del suono (Vicenzo, 1778; repr. in *Scelta di opuscoli interessanti di Milano*, iii, 1784)

BIBLIOGRAPHY
C. Burney: *The Present State of Music in France and Italy* (London, 1771, 2/1773), 64; ed. P. Scholes as *Dr. Burney's Musical Tours* (London, 1959)
G. Vernazza: 'Notizie intorno a Carlo Benvenuto Robbio, Conte di S. Raffaele', *Giornale della letteratura italiana*, iv (1794), 144
Filandro [pseud. of A. Cerati]: 'Elogio del conte Benvenuto Robbio di San Rafaele', *Opuscoli diversi* (Parma, 1809), ii, 3
P. Lichtenthal: *Dizionario e bibliografie della musica* (Milan, 1826), iv, 186
T. Vallauri: *Storia della poesia in Piemonte* (Turin, 1841), ii, 73ff, 438f

CHAPPELL WHITE

Sanromano, Carlo Giuseppe (*b* Milan, c1630; *d* probably at Milan, after 1680). Italian composer and organist. Almost all the information about his life derives from Picinelli. He started studying music when he was 11 years old; at the age of 12 he became a treble at Milan Cathedral where he stayed for five years. He

studied the organ and counterpoint with A. M. Turati and M. A. Grancini, *maestri di cappella* of the cathedral. At the age of 18 he became organist to the Celestine order. In 1650 he became organist of the collegiate church and teacher of grammar at Casorate, near Milan. In 1655 he returned to Milan as organist of S Babila; soon afterwards he became *maestro di cappella* of S Giovanni in Conca there. Having rejected an appointment as *maestro di cappella* of Vercelli Cathedral, he accepted the positions of organist and *maestro di cappella* of S Maria della Passione, Milan. In 1667 he also took up similar posts at the church of S Maria presso S Celso. The title-page of his last publication shows that he still held his positions at S Maria della Passione in 1680. His compositions, all of them sacred, are written in the concertante style typical of the period. His motets consist of alternating recitatives and arias. Those for two voices include dialogues between Jesus and the soul, and so on, which were popular with Milanese composers at the time.

WORKS
(*all published in Milan*)
La ricchezza schernita (dramma scenico morale, C. Torre) (1658) [collab. other composers]
Cigno sacro, motetti a più voci, op.1 (1668)
Il primo libro de motetti, 1v, op.2 (1670)
Salmi, 2 choirs, Motetti a più voci (?1670); cited in Picinelli
Sirena sacra, motetti, messa, et salmi per li Vesperi … con un Magnificat, Ecce nunc, Pater noster, Veni creator spiritus, Te Deum et le Letanie, 5vv, op.3 (1674)
Armonia sacra, cioè Motetti a più voci, libro II, op.4 (1680)

2 Magnificat, 5, 6vv, org, *I-NOVd*

BIBLIOGRAPHY
F. Picinelli: *Ateneo dei letterati milanesi* (Milan, 1670), 121f

MARIANGELA DONÀ

Sanserre, Pierre. *See* SANTERRE, PIERRE.

Sanseverino, Benedetto (*fl* 1620–22). Italian guitarist, musician and composer. He was a musician at S Ambrosio Maggiore, Milan, when he published *Intavolatura facile delli passacalli* op.3 (Milan, 1620), a book of pieces for five-course Baroque guitar, which reappeared at Milan two years later as *Il primo libro d'intavolatura per la chitarra alla spagnuola*. It contains detailed instructions concerning the *battute* (strummed) style, and accompaniments to popular forms of the period such as the passacaglio, ciaccona, romanesca and saltarello; the 1622 edition also includes six canzonettas for which only the words and accompanimental chords are given. The prescribed tuning is $g/G–c'/c–f/f–a/a–d'$. Sanseverino's opp.1 and 2 have not survived.

BIBLIOGRAPHY
J. Wolf: *Handbuch der Notationskunde*, ii (Leipzig, 1919/R1963), 172f, 177f
R. Hudson: *The Development of Italian Keyboard Variations on the Passacaglio and Ciaccona from Guitar Music in the 17th Century* (diss., U. of California, Los Angeles, 1967), 43ff
S. Murphy: 'Seventeenth-century Guitar Music: Notes on Rasgueado Performance', *GSJ*, xxi (1968), 25
T. Walker: 'Ciaccona and Passacaglia: Remarks on their Origin and Early History', *JAMS*, xxi (1968), 309
W. Kirkendale: *L'Aria di Fiorenza, id est Il ballo del Gran Duca* (Florence, 1972), 23, 43, 59, 65, 75

ROBERT STRIZICH

Sans lenteur (Fr.: 'without slowness'). *See* LENTO.

Sansoni [Samsony, Sambson, Sansone], **Giovanni** (*b* ?Venice, 1593; *d* Vienna, mid-Nov 1648). Italian cornett player and composer. In 1615 Romano Micheli called him 'musicus di Venezia'. In 1613 he became a cornett player at Archduke Ferdinand's court at Graz.

When Ferdinand became emperor Sansoni moved to Vienna with the Graz court and spent the rest of his life there as a respected member of the court orchestra and as a teacher with pupils from outside the court as well. He had connections with John George I of Saxony and with Schütz, who, as Kapellmeister at the Saxon court, sent choirboys to him for instrumental training when their voices broke. In his *Compositioni musicali* (1645) G. A. Bertoli ranked his standing as an authority 'nel Fagotto & nel Cornetto' as equal to that of Francesco Turini on the organ and Antonio Bertali on the violin. In his panegyric of contemporary music of 1647, G. B. Doni mentioned him beside Frescobaldi and M. A. Rossi, but his reputation probably owed more to his ability as a cornett player than to his compositions, of which only fragments survive and which show the influence of Viadana.

WORKS
Ego dormio, 2 A, bc, Ecce quam bonum, 2 B, bc, in Parnassus musicus Ferdinandaeus, ed. G. B. Bonometti (Venice, 1615[13])
Beatus Antonius, con ritornello, 7vv, Laetentur coeli et exultet terra, 8vv (both written in honour of the abbot of Kremsmünster, Anton Wolfradt, *d* 1639), *A-KR* L13

BIBLIOGRAPHY
G. B. Doni: *De praestantia musicae veteris libri 3* (Florence, 1647), ii, 58
H. Federhofer: *Musikpflege und Musiker am Grazer Habsburgerhof der Erzherzöge Karl und Ferdinand von Innerösterreich (1564–1619)* (Mainz, 1967), 208ff

HELLMUT FEDERHOFER

Santa Croce, Francesco (*b* Padua, *c*1487; *d* Loreto, ?1556). Italian composer. The approximate date of his birth may be deduced from that of his ordination in 1512; his birthplace is known from certain documents which refer to him as 'Francesco Patavino'. He is mentioned as a singer at Padua Cathedral in 1511, where he seems to have remained until July 1512, when he was appointed *maestro di cappella* at the convent of S Francesco, Treviso. Documents show that he continued in this post until 1515. Having threatened to leave he was given a stipend increase in July, but this did not prevent him from resigning the following November. In 1520 he was *maestro di cappella* of Treviso Cathedral, where he remained until 1528, when he probably accepted a similar post at Chioggia. In 1531 he went to Udine, which he seems to have left in 1553. He finally returned to his former post at Treviso Cathedral in July 1537 and remained there until 1551. He perhaps may be identified with a canon of Loreto Cathedral who died in 1556.

Santa Croce is of some importance as a composer of church music. He was one of the earliest composers to use *cori spezzati*; he probably learnt double-choir writing from Fra Ruffino in Padua. The ten manuscript psalm settings (in *I-TVca*) show that he was well aware of the possibilities in writing for these forces. Instead of the traditional imitative counterpoint found in many Italian compositions of the early 16th century, Santa Croce used homophonic textures and simple harmonies. His music is particularly interesting for its use of short phrases, with each choir singing only two or three bars before being interrupted by the other. Willaert, who started the vogue for *cori spezzati*, may have known his music and Santa Croce's treatment of the double choir is similar to the technique which was later to form the basis of Andrea Gabrieli's style.

WORKS
10 psalms, double choir, *I-TVca*; 2 ed. in d'Alessi (1952)

O quam suavis, 5vv, *TVca*
Dirigere et sanctificare, 5vv; Domine Deus, 5vv; Magnum mysterium, 5vv: lost
Other psalms, double choir, *VEaf*

BIBLIOGRAPHY
G. d'Alessi: 'Precursors of Adriano Willaert in the Practice of *coro spezzato*', *JAMS*, v (1952), 187
——: *La cappella musicale del duomo di Treviso: 1500–1633* (Treviso, 1954)
A. F. Carver: 'The Psalms of Willaert and his North Italian Contemporaries', *AcM*, xlvii (1975), 270

DENIS ARNOLD

Santa Cruz (Wilson), Domingo (*b* La Cruz, Valparaiso, 5 July 1899). Chilean composer and administrator. He was the leader of Chilean musical life from the early 1920s until the late 1960s.

1. LIFE. He studied composition privately with Soro in Santiago (1917–21) and graduated in law from the University of Chile (1921). While serving as secretary to the Chilean Embassy in Spain (1921–4) he continued private composition studies with del Campo (1922–4). In 1927 he left the diplomatic service to give his attention to music. He had already in 1917 organized a choral group, the Bach Society, which gave the first performance of his *Te Deum* op.4 in 1919, but it was only after his return from Europe in 1924 that the choir entered on the period of intense public activity that lasted until its disbandment in 1932. With this ensemble Santa Cruz introduced to Chilean audiences the repertory of Renaissance polyphony and also such major works as Bach's *Weihnachtsoratorium* (in 1925). The society was active not only in the field of performance: they opened their own conservatory, initiated the music magazine *Marsyas* (1927) and took a leading role in the reorganization and advancement of musical life in Chile.

In 1928 Santa Cruz was asked by the Secretary of Education to take part in the reform of the National Conservatory, which he then joined as professor of history and analysis, a post he retained until 1953. He established the faculty of fine arts in 1930, thus transferring control of the conservatory from the Ministry of Education to the University of Chile. Appointed acting dean of the faculty in 1932, he was elected dean in 1933 and successively re-elected to the post until 1951 (in 1948 the faculty had been split, so that Santa Cruz had charge only of the music department); he was again dean from 1962 to 1968. His achievements during these years were considerable: he founded the Asociación Nacional de Conciertos Sinfónicos under the direction of Carvajal (1931–8), the Institute of Secondary Education to provide an arts training for all faculty students (1933), the *Revista de arte* (1934–42), the National Association of Composers (1936, from 1948 the Chilean section of the ISCM), the Departamento de Extensión Artística at the University of Chile (1939), the Instituto de Extensión Musical (1941, Santa Cruz was its director until 1953), the *Revista musical chilena* (1945), the Institute of Musical Research (1946), the Chilean music festivals and competitions (1948), the Chilean section of the IMC (1953), the Inter-American Institute for Music Education (1960), the Chilean Music Council (1963), the radio station IEM (1967) and the Academy of Fine Arts of the Instituto Chile (1967). As senior dean in 1944 he was appointed vice-rector of the University of Chile.

Apart from thus taking a leading role in the develop-

Domingo Santa Cruz

ment of Chilean culture, Santa Cruz has been active internationally as a conference member, administrator and adjudicator. He was elected vice-president (1953) and president (1955) of the ISME, president of the IMC (1956) and president of the Inter-American Music Council (1963), and in 1964 he was appointed to the Council of Higher Education in the American Republics. In 1960 he taught as Mellon Distinguished Professor at the Carnegie Institute of Technology in Pittsburgh. Among the awards he has received are honorary membership and the title of professor emeritus in the music faculty of the University of Chile (1953), the decoration of officer of the Légion d'honneur (1958) and membership of the Argentinian Academy of Fine Arts. He held a Rockefeller Scholarship (1956–7) and a Guggenheim Fellowship (1970–71), and he has received numerous prizes and commissions.

2. WORKS. Santa Cruz's activity as a composer began in 1917, but little is known of the music he composed before 1925. The *Viñetas* op.8 for piano (1925–7) and the *Cantos de soledad* op.10 (1928) already show certain stylistic features which, in spite of the significant evolution that followed, have remained characteristic. These include a leaning towards a very terse and dramatic harmonic idiom, a highly chromatic linearity, luxuriant counterpoint and textural density. There is also in his music a lack of concern for instrumental colour, and he has avoided virtuoso writing for instruments. To a large extent his work is rooted in the music of the 16th-century contrapuntists and in the fugal style of Bach, yet an important place is left for melodic and rhythmic traits that are purely Spanish in origin and are equally evident in choral pieces, string

quartets and orchestral works. The linear chromaticism of his music links him with Hindemith, yet his Latin background is consistently affirmed.

WORKS
(selective list)

VOCAL

Acc. choral: Te Deum, op.4, solo vv, male vv, org, str, 1919; Cantata de los rios de Chile, op.19 (Santa Cruz), SATB, orch, 1941; Egloga, op.26 (de Vega), S, SATB, orch, 1949; Alabanzas de adviento, op.30 (liturgy), children's vv, org, 1952; Oratio Ieremiae prophetae, op.37 (Bible), SSATTB, orch, 1970
Unacc. choral: 2 Songs, op.7 (Jara, Mistral), SATB, 1926; 5 Songs, op.16 (Santa Cruz), SATB, 1940; 3 Madrigals, op.17 (Santa Cruz), SSATB, 1940; 3 Songs, op.18, TTBB, 1941; Cantares de pascua, op.27 (Santa Cruz), SSA/SSAA, 1949; 6 canciones de primavera, op.28 (Santa Cruz), SATB, 1950
Solo vocal: Endechas, op.32, T, 7 insts, 1960
Songs for 1v, pf: 4 Poems, op.9 (Mistral), 1927; Cantos de soledad, op.10 (Santa Cruz), 1928; Canciones del mar, op.29 (Santa Cruz), 1952

INSTRUMENTAL

Orch: 5 Pieces, op.14, str, 1937; Variations in 3 Movts, op.20, pf, orch, 1943; Sinfonia concertante, op.21, fl, orch, 1945; Sym. no.1, op.22, 1945–6, rev. 1970; Preludios dramáticos, op.23, 1946; Sym. no.2, op.25, str, 1948; Sym. no.3, op.34 (Mistral), A, orch, 1965; Sym. no.4, op.35, 1968
Chamber: 3 str qts, op.12, 1930, op.24, 1946–7, op.31, 1959; 3 Pieces, op.15, vn, pf, 1937; Wind Qnt, op.33, 1960
Pf: Viñetas, op.8, 1925–7; Poemas trágicos, op.11, 1929; Imágenes infantiles, op.13, 1932
Principal publisher: Instituto de Extensión Musical

WRITINGS

'Mis recuerdos sobre la Sociedad Bach', *Revista musical chilena*, vi/40 (1950), 8–62
'Transcendental aniversario en la vida musical chilena: la facultad de bellas artes de 1929', *Revista musical chilena*, xiii/67 (1959), 5
'Antepasados de la *Revista musical chilena*', *Revista musical chilena*, xiv/71 (1960), 17
'¿Crisis en nuestro sistema de estímulo a la composición musical?', *Revista musical chilena*, xiv/69 (1960), 12
'El Instituto de Extensión Musical, su origen, fisonomía y objeto', *Revista musical chilena*, xiv/73 (1960), 7–38
'El compositor Alfonso Letelier', *Revista musical chilena*, xxi/100 (1967), 8

BIBLIOGRAPHY

Revista musical chilena, viii/42 (1952) [Santa Cruz issue]
Compositores de América/Composers of the Americas, ed. Pan American Union, i (Washington, DC, 1955), 69
R. Stevenson: 'Chilean Music in the Santa Cruz Epoch', *Inter-American Music Bulletin* (1968), no.68, p.1

JUAN A. ORREGO-SALAS

Santa Fe Opera Company. An organization founded in New Mexico in 1957 which gives a summer opera season. Under its founder and general director, JOHN CROSBY, the company presents a repertory of familiar works, revivals of rarely performed operas, an annual Mozart production and contemporary works. It has given premières of Marvin David Levy's *The Tower* (1957), Carlisle Floyd's *Wuthering Heights* (1958), Berio's *Opera* (1970), Villa-Lobos's *Yerma* (1971) and American premières of operas by Berg, Henze, Hindemith, Menotti, Penderecki, Reimann, Schoenberg and Shostakovich. Many of the singers are American and the orchestra is drawn from major symphony orchestras in the USA. Operas are staged in an open-air theatre designed in the architectural style of the American Southwest. Apprentice artists (young people selected by national auditions) fill minor roles and sing in the chorus, and a technicians' intern programme allows students to participate in production and stage management.

RITA H. MEAD

Sant'Agata, Tommaso da (*fl* 1636). Italian composer. He was a Franciscan friar of the Observant order. In

1617 he was vicar-general and procurator of his order for the duchy of Urbino. After the last member of the ruling Della Rovere family had died and Urbino had been annexed to the church, he moved, in about 1636, to Rome, where he held similar positions. He published *Motecta . . . liber primus* (Rome, 1636) for one to three voices, the volume also including a three-part mass. Eight further solo motets by him are in *RISM* 1636³. His monodic motets, which form the bulk of his output, are in an expressive arioso style. According to Fétis he also published *Regulae breves et faciles cantus ecclesiastici* (Urbino, 1617), but there is no trace of it now.

ARGIA BERTINI

Santa María, Jorge de (*fl* 1578). Spanish composer. During Andrés de Torrentes's third term as *maestro de capilla* of Toledo Cathedral (1571–80), Jorge de Santa María boarded and instructed the *seises*. He was given six dozen chickens for composing the villancicos for Christmas 1578. His only surviving works are two four-part turba settings from the Passion according to SS Mark and Luke, *Non in die festo* and *Ubi vis parimus* (in *E-Tc* 22).

BIBLIOGRAPHY
R. Stevenson: 'The Toledo Manuscript Polyphonic Choirbooks', *FAM*, iii (1973), 103

ROBERT STEVENSON

Santa Maria, Salvatore (*fl* 1620–28). Italian composer. A Benedictine monk, he received holy orders at the monastery of S Giustino, Padua, and was working at Este, near Padua, in the years in which his main publications appeared. These were two volumes of motets: *Sacrorum concentuum . . . libro primo*, for one to five voices and organ (Venice, 1620), also including a four-part mass, and *Sacrorum concentuum . . . libro secondo*, for one to four and six voices with organ (Venice, 1628), also including four-part litanies. Both are written in the modern concertato style that had become well established in northern Italy. The motets of 1620 have interesting bass lines over which extended vocal melodies are unfolded: in the four-part *Domine exaudi* they are decorated by specified *trillo* ornaments and combine to produce curiously dissonant partwriting of a kind associated with English Restoration church music. The mass, unlike many that were still in the old polyphonic style at this date, is also in the concertato idiom, though it is undistinguished. There are also two motets by Santa Maria in *RISM* 1629⁵.

BIBLIOGRAPHY
J. L. A. Roche: *North Italian Liturgical Music in the Early 17th Century* (diss., U. of Cambridge, 1968)

JEROME ROCHE

Santa María, Tomás de [Sancta Maria, Thomas de] (*b* Madrid; *d* Ribadavia, northwest Spain, 1570). Spanish theorist and composer. He became a friar in the Dominican order at S María de Atocha, Madrid, on 11 March 1536 and served as organist in various Dominican monasteries in Castilla, principally S Pablo in Valladolid, a favourite resort of the Habsburg monarchs; there he may have met the royal organists Antonio and Juan de Cabezón, with whom he conferred in preparing *Arte de tañer fantasía*.

Apparently begun in 1541, this work was first licensed in 1557; however, its publication was delayed by a paper shortage. It was re-licensed in 1563 and was finally published in Valladolid in 1565 (facsimile edition

with introduction by D. Stevens, London, 1972). Concerned mainly with the clavichord, its aim was to teach the playing of fantasias (i.e. how to improvise pieces in fugal style). Part i presents the rudiments of music (in the first 12 chapters) and keyboard technique; part ii the harmonic, contrapuntal and structural procedures. Chapters 13–19 constitute the earliest detailed treatment of keyboard technique, including hand position, touch, articulation, fingering (a surprisingly progressive approach using all five fingers), the two ornaments, *redoble* and *quiebro*, and the use of 'pointed' or dotted style. In chapters 20–23 the performance of composed works and the application of *glosa* or diminution is discussed. Part i concludes with detailed treatment of the eight church modes, both natural and transposed, the 'seculorums' (psalm tones) and the cadence types.

Chapters 1–30 of part ii constitute a systematic approach to harmony. After a brief treatment of dissonances, Santa María concentrated on 'consonancias', meaning not only intervals but also four-note chords. He classified them according to outer and internal intervals, and degrees of sonority, systematically applying them to the harmonization of various note values and melodic progressions, including the *fabordónes*. In chapters 31–51 he gave procedures for constructing four-part imitative pieces, with emphasis on Josquin's voice-pairing technique. The work concludes with advice to beginners, and instructions for tuning the clavichord and vihuela. There are many music examples throughout in a type of vocal notation in which each part has its own staff and clef without barring or alignment. The examples range from brief progressions to complete pieces of 40 to 75 bars (called 'exemplos', not 'fantasías') featuring imitative polyphony in a simple style resembling Cabezón's tientos, but considerably less varied.

Santa María's text is filled with pedantic repetition and elaboration on the obvious – doubtless the product of a scholastic education – but the work is masterful for its clarity and systematic organization. Although clearly within the Spanish theoretical tradition, it is practical in aim and seems wholly original. Later theorists rarely mentioned Santa María, but several, including Artufel, Cerone and Lorente, extensively plagiarized his work.

EDITIONS
F. Pedrell, ed.: *Psalmodia modulata (vulgo fabordones) a diversus auctoribus*, Hispaniae schola musica sacra, vi (Barcelona, 1897/*R*1971) [fabordónes]
L. Villalba Muñoz, ed.: *Antología de organistas clásicos, siglos XVI–XVII* (Madrid, 1914, 2/1971) [23 pieces]
M. S. Kastner, ed.: *Hommage à l'Empereur Charles-Quint* (Barcelona, 1954) [5 pieces]
P. Froidebise, ed.: *Anthologie de l'orgue des primitifs à la renaissance* (Paris, 1957) [8 fantasias]
——: *T. de Santa María: oeuvres transcrites de l'Arte de tañer fantasía*, Orgue et liturgie, xlix (Paris, 1961) [26 fantasias]
J. y. L. Azpiazu, ed.: *T. de Santa María: Veinticinco fantasías del Arte de tañer fantasia* (Madrid, 1965) [25 fantasias]

BIBLIOGRAPHY
J. de Marieta: *Historia eclesiástica de todos los santos de España* (Cuenca, 1596)
O. Kinkeldey: *Orgel und Klavier in der Musik des 16. Jahrhunderts* (Leipzig, 1910/*R*1968)
E. Harich-Schneider and R. Boadella: 'Zum Klavichordspiel bei Tomás de Santa María', *AMf*, ii (1937), 243
E. Ferand: *Die Improvisation in der Musik* (Zurich, 1938)
S. Kastner: *Contribución al estudio de la música española y portuguesa* (Lisbon, 1941)
S. Rubio: *La polifonía clásica* (El Escorial, 1956; Eng. trans., 1972)
C. Jacobs: *La interpretación de la música española del siglo XVI para instrumentos de teclado* (Madrid, 1959)
——: *The Performance Practice of Spanish Renaissance Keyboard Music* (diss., New York U., 1962)

W. Young: 'Keyboard Music to 1600, II', *MD*, xvii (1963), 163
W. E. Hultberg: *Sancta Maria's 'Libro llamado Arte de tañer fantasia':
  a Critical Evaluation* (diss., U. of Southern California, 1964)
A. Howell: 'Paired Imitation in 16th-century Spanish Keyboard Music',
  MQ, liii (1967), 377
H. Lange: 'A Tutor by Santa Maria', *Dolmetsch Foundation Bulletin*,
  xiv (1968), 5
D. Poulton: *'How to Play with Good Style'* by Thomas de Sancta Maria',
  LSJ, xii (1970), 23

ALMONTE HOWELL

Sant'Anna [Sá Bacon], **José Pereira de** (*b* Rio de Janeiro,
4 Feb 1696; *d* Salvaterra, Portugal, 31 Jan 1759).
Portuguese writer on music. Before becoming a calced
Carmelite his name was José Pereira de Sá Bacon. He
studied at Olinda (Brazil) and at Coimbra, there obtaining the doctorate in theology on 17 May 1725. After
several years as sub-prior at Olinda he returned to
Coimbra as a professor and royal family confessor. An
excellent singer and composer of sacred music, he
included important data on the history of Carmelite
music in Portugal in his two-volume *Chronica dos
Carmelitas* (Lisbon, 1745–51) and *Dissertação
apologetica* (Lisbon, 1751).

BIBLIOGRAPHY
R. Stevenson: *Portugaliae musica* (Lima, 1967), 17f

ROBERT STEVENSON

Sante, Sophia (Maria Christina) van (*b* Zaandam, 11
Aug 1925). Dutch mezzo-soprano. She studied at the
Amsterdam Muzieklyceum with To van der Sluys and
Ruth Horna, took the opera course at the Amsterdam
Conservatory, and further studies with, among others,
Marietta Amstad in Italy, where she gave concerts and
recitals. She is a regular soloist with the Netherlands
Opera. Her strong dramatic temperament makes her
particularly suitable for roles like Marie in *Wozzeck*
and the Woman in *Erwartung*. She took part in the first
performances of Ton de Leeuw's *De droom*,
Paccagnini's *Vento nel vento* and Zimmermann's *Omnia
tempus habent*, and in the Dutch premières of
Dallapiccola's *Il prigioniero* and Henze's *Der junge
Lord*. Sante gives lieder recitals and has appeared as
a soloist with the Berlin PO and the Concertgebouw
Orchestra. She teaches at The Hague Conservatory.

TRUUS DE LEUR

Santerre [Sanserre, Senterre, Senserre], **Pierre** (*d*
Poitiers, before 1567). French composer. In 1555 he
served as cathedral organist in Poitiers, and his major
work, a collection of settings for four voices of the 150
Psalms, appeared there in 1567. In a prefatory note, the
printer Nicolas Logerois pointed out that the publication was posthumous. Although one partbook of this
collection was known in the 19th century, there is no
trace of it today.

Eight four-voice chansons by Santerre survive in
anthologies printed by Attaingnant, Du Chemin and Le
Roy & Ballard. Several are designated 'chansons
poitevines', suggesting that they may reflect local
colour. Measured against the norm of Parisian chanson
style, Santerre's music seems somewhat eccentric. In
place of the continuity of phrase structure characteristic
of the Parisian chanson, he provided a choppy, spas-
modic design, in which short motifs interact with one
another. The texts are set syllabically to sprightly
rhythms and animated melodies with extensive use of
repeated notes. The pieces designated 'poitevine' are
long, rambling compositions; one, in particular, the
Procès de Tallebot, uses a Poitiers poetic dialect.

WORKS
(*all 4vv*)

Les CL psalmes de David . . . plus la psalme CXIX diversifé de musique
  . . . selon la lettre alphabetique (Poitiers, 1567), lost

Faict-elle pas bien d'aymer que luy donne, 1536[4]; Hé, que faictes-vous,
  laissez moy, 1545[10–11], *I-Bc* Q26; Or regardez dy quou vilain,
  1556[14]; Procès de Tallebot, 1556[16]; Quand la bergere va aux champs,
  1556[14]; Si vous eussiés seulement dit ouy, 1557[12]; Thenot estoit en
  son cloz resjouy, attrib. Fresneau in 1544[9], attrib. Santerre in
  1545[10–11], 1549[28], 1551[6], *Bc* Q26; Ung laboureux sa journée com-
  mançoit assez matin, attrib. Fresnau in 1544[9], attrib. Santerre in
  1545[10–11], *Bc* Q26

BIBLIOGRAPHY
P. Pidoux: *Le psautier huguenot du XVIe siècle* (Basle, 1962)
F. Lesure: 'Some Minor French Composers of the 16th Century',
  *Aspects of Medieval and Renaissance Music: a Birthday Offering to
  Gustave Reese* (New York, 1966), 538

LAWRENCE F. BERNSTEIN

Santiago. Capital of Chile. From the early colonial
period churches held festivities honouring the Virgin
and saints, in which a mixture of folk music (Negro,
Indian and Spanish) and Spanish religious songs
alternated with the use of plainchant. By the mid-18th
century the former had been forbidden and art music by
the Spaniards Soler and Pons and by the Italians
Porpora, Pergolesi and Paisiello prevailed. French
influence grew during the 18th century. Certain genres
of salon dances were popular, but church music was
also cultivated with distinction by such appointees to the
Metropolitan Cathedral as the Spaniards Cristóbal
Ajuria and José Campderros, and later the Peruvian
José B. Alzedo y Larrain.

Independence completely changed the city's cultural
life. Secular music widened its repertory from earlier
imitations of French salon dances to copies of European
display pieces, accomplished by a host of native composers of very basic skills. By far the most popular form
was opera; musical life was dominated by the influences
of Rossini, Donizetti, Bellini, Mercadante and later of
Verdi and the most italianate French composers. The
first attempts to present an opera season, in 1830,
developed into regular seasons in 1844 at the Teatro de
la Universidad, the auditorium of the Royal University
of S Felipe (founded 1744). In 1853 the opera moved to
the Teatro de la República, remaining there until the
new Teatro Municipal was inaugurated in 1857 with
Verdi's *Ernani*. From that time opera seasons have
alternated there with zarzuelas, ballets, orchestral concerts, and recitals by Chilean and visiting performers.
However, the first permanent ensembles were not established in this house until the 1950s, the best-known
being the Orquesta Filarmónica founded in 1955 by
Juan Matteucci, its permanent conductor until 1963,
and the Ballet Municipal (1955).

In 1819 a pioneering attempt to develop chamber
music beyond the private circles of the upper class,
instigated by the Danish amateur cellist Carlos
Dretwetcke, led to the establishment of the Sociedad
Filarmónica (1827–95), the Sociedad de Música
Clásica (1879–83) and the Sociedad del Cuarteto
(1886–90). Their public concerts were supplemented by
those of the National Conservatory of Music (1849),
which maintained a small orchestra and chorus. First
performances of Verdi's *Requiem* (1890) and Handel's
Messiah (1896) were given in Santiago. The Sociedad
Orquestal (1912–14), in spite of the success of its first
presentation of Beethoven's nine symphonies under
Nino Marcelli in 1913, did not continue after its conductor's departure for Europe. Many efforts to organize

continued concert seasons were finally realized in the 1920s by the Sociedad Bach (1917–32), which emerged as a powerful force for change in Santiago's musical life. It promoted the reform of specialized education in music and its incorporation into the university (*see* CHILE), and laid the groundwork for a regular concert life. The Asociación Nacional de Conciertos Sinfónicos (1931–8) led to the establishment of the Orquesta Sinfónica de Chile (1941) by Armando Carvajal, its artistic director until 1947, when he was succeeded by Victor Tevah. The Instituto de Extensión Musical (1941), part of the University of Chile, sponsors this orchestra and many other ensembles which have raised the standard and quantity of events of Santiago's musical life to a level comparable to that of the most important cities of Latin America.

Choral singing has developed extensively since the establishment of the Orfeo Catalá (1913). The universities have several proficient groups, such as those of the Universidad Católica (1938), the Universidad de Chile (1945) and the Universidad Técnica (1952), as do individual communities, such as the German Singkreis (1942). The work of the universities in training performers and raising musical standards has been supplemented effectively by various private academies; among the best is the Escuela Moderna de Música (1940). Similarly many organizations have shared with the University of Chile and the Municipal Theatre the maintaining of a high level of concert activity in Santiago. In the field of contemporary music the Sociedad Nueva Música (1946–8), the Associación Nacional de Compositores (1950–58) and the Agrupación Tonus (1954–9) have offered representative seasons. The Catholic University maintains the Orquesta de Cámara (1961), conducted by its artistic director Fernando Rosas and guest conductor Juan Pablo Izquierdo; the Cuarteto Santiago was founded in 1956. Other concert-promoting bodies include the Sociedad Mozart (1947–54), the bi-national cultural centres, particularly the Goethe Institute (since 1955) and the Mozarteum (1968). The Ancient Instruments Ensemble (1954) has given consistently good performances of pre-Baroque and Ibero-American colonial music.

Festivals in Santiago are the biennial Chilean Music Festivals (from 1948), the Choral Festivals sponsored by the Music Educators Association (from 1950) and the Contemporary Music Festivals of the Catholic University (from 1968).

BIBLIOGRAPHY
D. Quiroga: 'Aspectos de la opera en Chile en el siglo XIX', *Revista musical chilena* (1947), nos.25–6, p.6
D. Santa Cruz: 'Primer centenario del Conservatorio nacional de Música', *Revista musical chilena* (1949), nos.35–6, p.3
——: 'Mis recuerdos de la Sociedad Bach', *Revista musical chilena* (1950–51), no.40, p.8
E. Pereira Salas: *Historia de la música en Chile* (Santiago, 1957)
——: 'El Centenario del Teatro municipal', *Revista musical chilena* (1957), no.52, p.30
D. Santa Cruz: 'El Instituto de extensión musical, su origen fisonomia y objeto', *Revista musical chilena* (1960), no.73, pp.7–38
JUAN A. ORREGO-SALAS

Santiago, Francisco (*b* Santa Maria, Bulacan, 29 Jan 1889; *d* Manila, 28 Sept 1947). Filipino composer, conductor and pianist. Showing precocious musical talent, he was taken to Manila at the age of ten to train at the Colegio de Tiples of the Cathedral. He studied the piano with Echegoyen, Villacorta and Calzada, and then entered the S Juan de Letran College and later the University of the Philippines Conservatory, where he took teacher's diplomas in the piano (1921) and composition (1922). For a while he taught at the university and composed: he had written his first song in the *kundiman* genre, *Ako'y anak ng dalita* ('I'm a poor child'), in 1917, and he produced the harmonizations for *Filipino Folk Songs* (Manila, 1921, 2/1950), a collection made by Emilia S. Cavan. Santiago then continued his education in Chicago at the American Conservatory (MMus 1924) and the Musical College (DMus 1924). On his return to Manila he was appointed assistant professor of piano and composition at the Conservatory of the University of the Philippines, and he became its first native Filipino director in 1931, holding that post until the outbreak of World War II. As a composer he was a classicist and a great melodist; the Piano Concerto has passages of Lisztian bravura, but the songs are full of a pastoral simplicity of sentiment.

WORKS
(*selective list*)

Orch: Pf Conc., b♭, 1924; Sym. 'Taga-ilog', D, 1938
Sacred vocal: Ave Maria, 1919; Eucharistic Congress Hymn, 1937
Kundiman: Ako'y anak ng dalita [I'm a poor child], 1917; Sakali man, [Perhaps], 1917; Pakiusap [Plea], 1921; Ang pag-ibig [Love], 1922; Ay kalisud [O sorrowful], 1937; Ano kaya ang kapalaran [What may fate bring], 1938
Inst: Str Qt with Fugue, 1921; Sonata filipina, D♭, pf, 1922; Str Qt, G, 1924; Rondo, 2 vn, pf, 1935; Rhapsody, vn, pf; other pf pieces

Principal publisher: Presser

BIBLIOGRAPHY
R. C. Bañas: *The Music and Theater of the Filipino People* (Manila, 1924)
E. A. Manuel: *Dictionary of Philippine Biography*, ii (Quezon City, 1970)
LUCRECIA R. KASILAG

Santiago, Francisco de [Veiga, Vega] (*b* Lisbon, *c*1578; *d* Seville, 5 Oct 1644). Portuguese composer, resident in Spain. Under his family name, Veiga, he was engaged as *maestro de capilla* of Plasencia Cathedral on 16 February 1596, when he was apparently 18. In March he was rebuked for starting motets too soon at festal Masses, and on 15 July, having incurred the displeasure of an important canon, he was dismissed. In 1601, however, the cathedral chapter invited him to take part in special Holy Week services. By 14 May of that year he had joined the calced Carmelites at Madrid and thereafter was known as Francisco de Santiago. He may have studied with Nicolas Dupont in Madrid, for his *Missa 'Ego flos campi'* is based on a motet of that composer. From 1601 to 1617 he was *maestro de capilla* of the rich and influential calced Carmelite house at Madrid. On 11 January 1617 the Seville Cathedral chapter invited him to become *maestro de capilla*, and he assumed the post on 5 April.

Santiago was the first to bring castratos to Seville; they joined an already rich establishment of singers and players. According to the chronicler Castro Palacios, 'Santiago in his humble white friar's habit made a strange sight conducting all this lavish panoply'. From 1619 to 1623 and from 9 February 1628 to 31 December 1635 he was responsible, in addition to his other duties, for the instruction of the cathedral *seises*, who were employed in principal roles in the *coloquios* or musical playlets, given each year at Corpus Christi. He was allowed a long leave every five years to visit Lisbon. In 1640 he was given two months' leave in order to visit the baths at Caldas da Rainha for his sciatica; the cure was paid for by his patron the Duke of Bragança, who that year became King John IV.

Santiago's eight-part responsories remained in use at Seville Cathedral until at least 1772, but it was his villancicos which enjoyed the greatest popularity at Seville and also in Spanish America.

WORKS

Missa, 8vv, *E-Zac*
Conceptio tua, 9vv; Regina coeli laetare, 12vv; Responsoria tene-brarum, 8vv; 3 hymns, 4–5vv: *Sc*
5 villancicos, *Zac*; 2 villancicos, *CO-B*; 1 villancico, Colección J. Sánchez Garza, Mexico City
Lost works: 4 masses, 2 Magnificat, 18 motets, 14 psalms, 11 other sacred works, 538 villancicos; listed in *Primeira parte do index da livraria de musica do muyto alto, e poderoso Rey Dom João IV. nosso senhor* (Lisbon, 1649/*R*1967); ed. J. de Vasconcellos (Oporto, 1874–6)

BIBLIOGRAPHY

S. de la Rosa y López: *Los seises de la Catedral de Sevilla* (Seville, 1904), 131, 137, 145, 152
H. Anglès: 'La música conservada en la Biblioteca Colombina y en la Catedral de Sevilla', *AnM*, ii (1947), 37
P. Becquart: *Musiciens néerlandais à la cour de Madrid: Philippe Rogier et son école* (*1560–1647*) (Brussels, 1967), 139, 183
R. Stevenson: *Renaissance and Baroque Musical Sources in the Americas* (Washington, 1970), 25, 178
——: 'Santiago, fray Francisco de (born *ca*.1578 at Lisbon; died October 5, 1644, at Seville)', *AnM*, xxv (1970), 37
J. E. Ayarra Jarne: *La música en la Catedral de Sevilla* (Seville, 1976), 45ff

ROBERT STEVENSON

Santiago de Compostela. Cathedral city in north-west Spain. Santiago Cathedral was one of the most important shrines for pilgrimage during the Middle Ages. Built over the grave of St James, patron saint of Spain, the present structure was begun in 1078 and represents classic Spanish romanesque architecture. The pilgrimages left their mark on the music of the cathedral and, according to the 12th-century Calixtinus manuscript (*E-SC*; *see* SOURCES, MS, §IV),

it is a source of wonder and gladness to see the choirs of pilgrims in perpetual vigil by the venerable altar of Santiago: Teutons in one place, Franks in another, Italians in another. . . . Some play the cittern, others lyres, kettledrums, flutes, flageolets, trumpets, harps, violins, British or Welsh crwths, some singing with citterns, others accompanied of divers instruments.

It is the only surviving document of medieval music there; further documentation of musical life appears only in the 16th century.

The first *maestro de capilla*, Lorenzo Durán, was appointed in 1526 and the musical chapel, which employed professional singers and boy choristers, dates from that time. Four *ministriles* (reed players) became permanent members of the chapel consort from 1539. The most important *maestros de capilla* in the 16th century were Alonso Ordoñez, Francisco Logroño and Andrés de Villalar.

The number of singers and *ministriles* greatly increased during the 17th century when polychoral music became predominant. This development culminated in the works of José de Vaquedano who frequently wrote for 12 voices (three choruses) and sometimes for 16 or more voices. Other important *maestros de capilla* in the 17th century were Jerónimo Vicente, Diego Pontac and Diego Verdugo.

During the 18th century polychoral styles and counterpoint gave way to the Italian style; this is seen most clearly in the works of Buono Chiodi, an Italian who was formerly *maestro di cappella* at Bergamo and who came to Santiago Cathedral in 1769. Other notable 18th-century *maestros de capilla* were Antonio de Yanguas, Diego de las Muelas, Pedro Rodrigo and Pedro Cifuentes. Even before Chiodi's time some of the best cathedral singers in Santiago were Italian. Two splendid 18th-century organs still stand, though much restored, on either side of the choir. Chiodi's successor was Melchor López Jiménez, whose 38 years as *maestro de capilla* saw a steady evolution towards Classicism, and whose works are models of correctness and religious inspiration. During his tenure the cathedral orchestra reached full size, while the vocal complement remained a double chorus (eight voices) with frequent recourse to solos, duos etc.

The 19th-century *maestros de capilla* were Ramón Palacio, Juan Trallero, José Alfonso and Santiago Tafall Abad, all of them composers, as were some of the organists of this period. After the government's confiscation of church property in the mid-19th century, musical activity in the cathedral began to decline, but a small chorus and orchestra were kept until the mid-20th century, when the orchestra was reorganized. 20th-century *maestros de capilla* have included Manuel Soler, Mariano Pérez Gutiérrez and Nemesio García Carril. The *chirimías* (Spanish shawms) still accompany the solemn processions, and Santiago is the only place where these ancient precursors of the oboe can be heard.

Santiago University library contains Fernando I's mozarabic manuscript (1055). A summer course, given annually from mid-August to mid-September, was founded by Andres Segovia and José Miguel Ruiz Morales in 1958, and offers instruction in performance and composition.

BIBLIOGRAPHY

S. Tafall Abad: 'La capilla de música de la catedral de Santiago', *Boletín de la Real academia Gallega* (La Coruña, 1931)
H. Anglès: *La música a Catalunya fins al segle xiii* (Barcelona, 1935), 156ff
G. Prado Moralejo and W. M. Whitehill: *Liber sancti Jacobi: Codex Calixtinus* (Santiago de Compostela, 1944)
J. López-Calo: 'Fray José de Vaquedano, maestro de capilla de la catedral de Santiago (1681–1711)', *AnM*, x (1955), 191
H. Anglès: 'Die Mehrstimmigkeit des Calixtinus von Compostela und seine Rhythmik', *Festschrift Heinrich Besseler* (Leipzig, 1961)
G. Bourligueux: 'El compositor don Ramón Cuéllar Altarriba, organista de la catedral de Santiago de Compostela', *Compostellanum*, xv (1970), 155
J. López-Calo: *Catálogo musical del archivo de la santa iglesia catedral de Santiago* (Cuenca, 1972)

JOSÉ LÓPEZ-CALO

Santiago de Cuba. City on the southern coast of Cuba. Its cathedral was founded in 1522, and in 1544 the mestizo Miguel Velázquez was *maestro de capilla*. Because of French privateers in 1553, assault by British troops in 1662 and an earthquake in 1675, no early sources of music from Santiago survive. Domingo de Flores was appointed cathedral music director when the *capilla* was re-established in 1682; among his successors the most important composers were the Havanaborn Esteban Salas (1725–1803; *maestro* 1764–1803) and the Santiago-born Cratilio Guerra (1834–96; *maestro* 1866–69 and 1875–78). The first Santiago imprint was the text of the Christmas villancicos set by Salas in 1793; in 1961 the cathedral music archive of 158 works still contained 46 of his festive vernacular works dated between 1783 and 1800. He also composed an extensive Latin repertory. Juan Nicolás de Villavicencio was cathedral organist from 1759 to 1779; his successor, Diego Hierrezuelo, was trained by Salas. In 1812 Juan París (1759–1845) from Barcelona succeeded Salas.

In the 1790s French planters who had fled from Santo Domingo (now the Dominican Republic) founded the first theatre for opera production in the Calle de Santo Tomás; Grétry's *Zémire et Azor* was produced there on 19 March 1800, followed by other operas from the contemporary French repertory. The Coliseo de Marina y Barracones served as the town theatre from 1823 to 1844. In 1851 the Teatro de la Reina opened, with a season including *Norma*, *Lucia di Lammermoor* and *Ernani*; in the same year Mozart's Requiem was sung in the cathedral for the first time, with an orchestra of 60 and a chorus of 42.

The Sociedad Filarmónica de Isabel II, active from 1832 to 1844, was succeeded in 1845 by the more prestigious Sociedad Filarmónica de Cuba. Laureano Fuentes Matons (1825–98), the leading 19th-century composer and music historian born in Santiago, played the *Carnaval de Venecia* at the inaugural concert of the latter society on 5 August 1846. His one-act opera *La hija de Jefté* (to a libretto by Antonio Arnao), first performed at the Teatro de la Reina by a visiting Spanish zarzuela troupe on 16 May 1871, was the first opera by a native Cuban performed in Cuba.

Gottschalk gave five triumphant concerts at Santiago in 1854, cooperating, as was his custom in Latin America, with leading local artists. In that same year a Spanish touring company gave five zarzuelas, beginning with Hernando's *El duende* on 18 July. Gottschalk returned with Adelina Patti in 1857. José White, the leading Cuban violin virtuoso of the 19th century, gave his first Santiago recital on 5 March 1860, and returned to play in the Teatro Principal on 20 February 1875 and 9 January 1879.

Apart from those already named, the main local composers in Santiago before 1940 were Francisco Hierrezuclo (1763–1824), Silvano Boudet (1825–63), Rafael Salcedo (1844–1917), Ramón Figueroa (1862–1928) and Rodolfo Hernández (1856–1937). In 1961 works by all of these were available for study in the Museo Municipal 'Emilio Bacardí Moreau', founded in 1899 by the magnate Bacardí (1844–1922). Among Santiago-born composers active during Castro's epoch, Harold Gramatges (*b* 1918) studied at Tanglewood with Copland, served in 1961–5 as Cuban ambassador in France, and in 1966 organized the music section of the Casa de las Américas. From 1962 Santiago was the seat of the annual Festival Nacional de Coros.

BIBLIOGRAPHY
L. Fuentes Matons: *Las artes en Santiago de Cuba* (Santiago de Cuba, 1893)
E. T. Tolón and J. A. González: *Óperas cubanas y sus autores* (Havana, 1943), 67–119
P. Hernández Balaguer: *Catálogo de música de los archivos de la catedral de Santiago de Cuba y del Museo Barcardí* (Havana, 1961)
——: 'La capilla de música de la catedral de Santiago de Cuba', *Revista musical chilena* (1964), no.90, p.14–61
E. Martín: *Panorama histórico de la música en Cuba* (Havana, 1971), 85f, 139ff

ROBERT STEVENSON

Santini, Fortunato (*b* Rome, 5 Jan 1778; *d* Rome, 14 Sept 1861). Italian bibliophile and composer. He grew up in an orphanage and studied counterpoint with Jannacconi, who continued to teach him when he entered the Collegio Salviati; he left this on 31 July 1798. He studied the organ with Guidi and in 1801 was ordained priest. He had already begun to cultivate an interest in traditional Italian polyphony, both sacred and secular, and in 1796 undertook a massive task of collecting,

copying, collating and scoring which lasted for more than 50 years. He thus created a music library of enormous interest and carried on exchanges with the leading musicologists of Europe, freely offering his advice and loans from his collection, as Mendelssohn described in 1830 in his *Reisebriefe aus Rom*.

In 1820 Santini had already published a catalogue of more than 1000 items in his collection, and manuscript versions of it of varying dates are also in existence. The collection's importance lies in the fact that he managed to make use of the rich holdings of Roman libraries, then generally inaccessible. He made copies of much old music which has otherwise disappeared, and scored music which had been handed down only in performing parts. He also promoted the knowledge of German music in Italy by making versions of works by Bach and Handel and encouraging their performance. (This is also the case with Graun, the text of whose *Tod Jesu* he translated into Italian.)

On the death of his sister Santini retired into a monastery, relinquishing his library in return for his living and for access to it for the rest of his life. The collection, of about 4500 manuscripts and 1100 printed items, was first housed in the German college in Rome, then in the Diocesan Museum at Münster and finally, after other adventures, in the Episcopal Seminary in Münster. Santini was also a composer of modest gifts, and manuscripts of his music, which was mostly sacred, are to be found in Münster, in the library of the Bologna Conservatory and in the Berlin Singakademie. He was a member of numerous European musical academies.

WRITINGS
Catalogo della musica esistente presso Fortunato Santini in Roma nel palazzo de' principi Odescalchi incontro la chiesa de' SS. XII. Apostoli (Rome, 1820)
MS catalogues *B-Bc*, *D-MÜs*, *F-Pc*, *I-Bc*, *Mc*; references to other copies in Grove 5, SchmidlD

BIBLIOGRAPHY
EitnerQ; *FétisB*
F. S. Kandler: 'Über den Musikzustand von Rom', *Münchener allgemeine Musik-Zeitung* (1828), 411
W. Stassoff: *L'Abbé Santini et sa collection musicale à Rome* (Florence, 1854)
J. Killing: *Kirchenmusikalische Schätze der Bibliothek des Abbate Fortunato Santini* (Düsseldorf, 1910)
H. Jansen: 'Die Musikbibliothek des Abbate Santini', *Hochland*, xxiii (1926), 762
F. Smend: 'Zur Kenntnis des Musikers Fortunato Santini', *Westfälische Studien . . . Alois Bömer zum 60. Geburtstag* (Leipzig, 1928), 90
K. G. Fellerer: 'Fortunato Santini als Sammler und Bearbeiter Händelscher Werke', *HJb 1929*, 25
——: *Die musikalische Schätze der Santinischen Sammlungen: Führer durch die Ausstellung* (Münster, 1929)
——: 'Verzeichnis der kirchenmusikalischen Werke der Santinischen Sammlung', *KJb*, xxvi (1931), 111; xxvii (1932), 157; xxviii (1933), 143; xxix (1934), 125; xxx (1935), 149; xxxi (1936–8), 95 [inc.]
F. Gehring: 'Santini, Fortunato', *Grove 5*
K. G. Fellerer: 'Bachs Johannes-Passion in der lateinischen Fassung Fortunato Santinis', *Festschrift Max Schneider* (Leipzig, 1955), 139
V. Fédorov: 'A propos de quelques lettres de Santini à Bottée de Toulmon', *Festschrift Karl Gustav Fellerer* (Regensburg, 1962), 128
——: 'V. V. Stasov chez l'abb. F. Santini à Rome', *Anthony van Hoboken: Festschrift zum 75. Geburtstag* (Mainz, 1962), 55
R. Ewerhart: 'Die Bischöfliche Santini-Bibliothek', *Das schöne Münster*, xxxv (1962)
——: 'Santini, Fortunato', *MGG*

SERGIO LATTES

Santini, Gabriele (*b* Perugia, 20 Jan 1886; *d* Rome, 13 Nov 1964). Italian conductor. After studying at the Morlacchi School of Music, Perugia, and at the Bologna Conservatory (composition), he began his career as an opera conductor. His first engagement at the Costanzi Theatre (later the Royal Opera) in Rome was followed by a period in South America, where he conducted for eight seasons at the Teatro Colón, Buenos Aires, and at the Municipal Theatre, Rio de Janeiro. From 1925 to 1929 he assisted Toscanini at La Scala. From Milan he returned to the Rome Opera, where he remained until 1933, and became artistic director, 1944–7. He conducted at leading Italian theatres and with the Naples San Carlo company at Paris in 1951. Santini kept the lyric tradition alive both by his much-admired performances of the general repertory and by introducing new works like Giordano's *Il re* (Milan and Rome, 1930), and Alfano's *Dottor Antonio* (Rome, 1949). He also conducted the Italian premières of Ravel's *L'heure espagnole* (Milan, 1929) and Milhaud's *Christophe Colomb* (Rome, 1954). His records include *La traviata* (with Callas) and a much admired *Gianni Schicchi* (with Gobbi).

CLAUDIO CASINI

Santini, Prospero (*fl* Rome, 1591–1614). Italian composer. He was *maestro di cappella* of the Congregazione dei Preti dell'Oratorio. He was principally a composer of *laude* and *canzonette spirituali*, eight of which appeared in Roman anthologies (*RISM* 1591[13], 1592[5], 1599[6], 1600[5]) and three in a German collection (*RISM* 1604[12]). His only known work on a larger scale, the eight-voice motet *Angelus Domini descendit* for two choirs (*RISM* 1614[3]) is in the Venetian polychoral style; it was reprinted, and copied into the Pelplin Tablature (in *PL-PE*; ed. in Musica sacra, xxv, Berlin, 1884; facs. in AMP, vi, 1965).

MIROSŁAW PERZ

Santino. See GARSI, SANTINO.

Santley, Sir Charles (*b* Liverpool, 28 Feb 1834; *d* London, 22 Sept 1922). English baritone. Son of William Santley, a music teacher, he was a chorister and an amateur singer before he went to Milan in 1855 to study with Gaetano Nava. He made his début at Pavia in 1857 as Dr Grenville in *La traviata*, and after appearing in several other small roles returned to England for further study with Manuel García. His first professional English appearance was at St Martin's Hall, London (16 November 1857), singing Adam in Haydn's *Creation*. During the next two years he was heard in many concert and oratorio performances, and on 1 October 1859 made his English stage début, as Hoël in Meyerbeer's *Dinorah*, with the Pyne–Harrison Company at Covent Garden. He remained with the company until 1863, creating the Rhine King in Wallace's *Lurline* (1860), Clifford in Balfe's *The Puritan's Daughter* (1861), Don Sallust in Glover's *Ruy Blas* (1861), Danny Man in Benedict's *The Lily of Killarney* (1862) and Fabio in Balfe's *The Armourer of Nantes* (1863).

In 1862 Santley sang the Count of Luna during the Royal Italian Opera season at Covent Garden and later that year joined Mapleson's company at Her Majesty's Theatre, appearing as the Count in *Le nozze di Figaro* and Nevers in *Les Huguenots*. In 1863 he sang Valentine with such success in the first performance of *Faust* in England that Gounod wrote 'Even bravest heart' especially for him and for the production in England the following year. He remained with Mapleson's company until 1870, singing the Dutchman in Italian in the first production of a Wagner opera in

Charles Santley, probably as Valentine in Gounod's 'Faust'

England. After a season with an English company at the Gaiety Theatre, London, and a year (1871) in concert, he toured the USA. Having sung there under Carl Rosa, he was invited by him to join the newly formed Carl Rosa Opera in 1875, appearing as Figaro (Mozart) on the opening night of the company's first London season (11 September 1875). After 1877 he was heard only in concert and oratorio, including Gounod's *Rédemption* (Birmingham, 1882) and Mendelssohn's *Elijah* (Birmingham, 1885). At the Albert Hall on 1 May 1907 he celebrated his jubilee as a singer and later that year was knighted. On 23 May 1911 he made his farewell appearance at Covent Garden in a benefit matinée, singing Tom Tug Dibdin's *The Waterman*. He emerged from retirement in 1915 to sing at the Mansion House, London, in a concert in aid of Belgian refugees. It was generally agreed that although not possessing a naturally beautiful voice, he sang with great expression and was an especially dramatic actor.

Santley wrote a number of religious works for the Roman Catholic Church, and was made Commander of the Order of St Gregory by Pope Leo XIII in 1887; he also composed several songs under the pseudonym of Ralph Betterton.

WRITINGS
Student and Singer (London, 1892)
The Singing Master (London, 1900)
The Art of Singing and Vocal Declamation (London, 1908)
Reminiscences of my Life (London, 1909/R1977)

BIBLIOGRAPHY
J. J. Mewburn Levien: *Sir Charles Santley* (London, 1930)
HAROLD ROSENTHAL

Santo Domingo. *See* DOMINICAN REPUBLIC.

Santoliquido, Francesco (*b* S Giorgio a Cremano, Naples, 6 Aug 1883; *d* Anacapri, 26 Aug 1971). Italian composer. After gaining a diploma at the Liceo di S Cecilia, Rome (1908) he lived mostly as a freelance composer. From 1912 to 1921 he was in Tunisia, mainly in the village of Hammamet; and, though he then moved to Rome, he continued to spend much time in Tunis, where he founded a concert society and in 1927 a music school, which later became a conservatory. In 1933 he settled in Anacapri.

Santoliquido's early works, such as *L'ultima visione di Cassandra* and *Crepuscolo sul mare*, reveal a sensitive but basically unoriginal talent, influenced by both Wagner and Debussy. His residence in Tunisia led him to give several pieces a local colouring; but such features as the augmented 2nds of *Il profumo delle oasi sahariane*, *Ferhuda* and comparable works are never more than picturesque. Nor did his idiom change substantially as time went on, though his best inter-war compositions, such as *Una lauda medievale* (in which Wagner's influence for the time being disappears and Debussy's is modified by wayward progressions of mild dissonances recalling Satie and faintly foreshadowing Messiaen), show that he could sometimes write with real dramatic force. In the triumphal sections of *Alba di gloria sul passo Uarièu*, however, he lapsed into a naive fanfaring bombast all too relatable to his notorious contributions to the fascist press, where he claimed that, among other things, 'modern music' was to be shunned as an invention of the Jews.

WORKS
(selective list)
Stage: La favola di Helga (opera, 1, Santoliquido), Milan, 1910; La bajadera dalla maschera gialla (ballet, 1, Santoliquido), 1917, Rome, 1923; Ferhuda (opera, Santoliquido), 1918, Tunis, 1919; L'ignota (opera, Santoliquido), 1921, unperf.; La porta verde (opera, Santoliquido), Bergamo, 1953; incidental music
Orch: La mort de Tintagiles, prelude, 1907; Crepuscolo sul mare, 1909; Voci d'autunno, 1909; La notte sahariana, La danzatrice araba arr. 2 acquaforti tunisine, pf, 1912; Acquarelli, 1914; Il profumo delle oasi sahariane, 1915; Sym. no.1, F, 1916; La sagra dei morti, 1920; Grotte di Capri, 1925, rev. 1943; Sym. no.2, D, before 1928; Preludio e burlesca, str, 1938; Alba di gloria sul passo Uarièu, 1939; Santuari asiatici, 1951; other pieces
Choral: L'ultima visione di Cassandra, cantata, S, chorus, orch, 1908; Messa facile, chorus, org, 1925
Solo vocal: Meriggio d'estate, 1v, vn, pf, 1900–04; Harmonie du soir, S, small orch, 1906; I canti della sera, 1v, pf, 1907; I poemi del sole, 1v, pf, 1910; 3 poesie persiane, 1v, pf, 1914; Una lirica giapponese, 1v, pf, 1919; Petits poèmes japonais, 1v, pf, 1919; many other songs
Chamber: Sonata, vn, pf, 1924; Str Qt (1931); smaller pieces
Pf: Notturno, Piccola ballata, 1905; 2 acqueforti tunisine, 1912; Ex humo ad sidera, 1920; Una lauda medievale (1927); Giardini notturni (1932); other pieces
Principal publishers: Chester, Forlivesi (Florence), Mignani (Florence), Ricordi

WRITINGS
Ex humo ad sidera (Rome, 1907) [poems]
Il dopo-Wagner: Debussy e Strauss (Rome, 1909, 2/1922)
Nell'ombra del marabutto di Sidi-bu-Yahia (Tunis, 1917); repr. as *I giardini del fuoco* (Rome, 1920) [diary of Arab life]
'Rhythm and Colour in Arab Folk Music', *The Chesterian*, new ser., iii (1921–2), 202

BIBLIOGRAPHY
Miniature Essays: Francesco Santoliquido (London, 1925)
A. de Angelis: *L'Italia musicale di oggi: dizionario dei musicisti* (Rome, 3/1928), pt.i, 440f; pt.ii, 164 [incl. list of works]
F. Bonura and others: *Cronistoria della prima rappresentazione dell' opera 'Ferhuda'* (Rome, 1936)
H. Amano: *Gendai itaria ongaku* [Contemporary Italian music] (Tokyo, 1939), 190ff [list of works, p.357ff]
                    JOHN C. G. WATERHOUSE

Santoliquido [née Puliti], **Ornella** (*b* Florence, 4 Sept 1906; *d* Florence, 11 Nov 1977). Italian pianist. She studied with Brugnoli, obtaining her diploma at the Florence Conservatory, and then took postgraduate courses with Casella in Rome and with Cortot in Paris. At her concerts in Italy and abroad she gave the first performances of many works dedicated to her by contemporary Italian composers, including Casella and Bettinelli. After World War II she was for four years associated with the chamber orchestra I Virtuosi di Roma, and played in duo with the cellist Massimo Amfiteatrov, in trio with Amfiteatrov and Arrigo Pelliccia (violin), and in the Quartetto di Roma with Amfiteatrov, Pelliccia and the viola player Bruno Giuranna. From 1939 to 1971 she taught at the Rome Conservatory. She was the third wife of the composer Francesco Santoliquido.

PIERO RATTALINO

Sant Omer. Name (possibly referring to the town situated between Lille and Calais) appearing at the head of a three-voice Sanctus, archaic in style, in the 14th–15th-century fragment *I-Pu* 1475 (no.1) from Padua.

BIBLIOGRAPHY
B. J. Layton: *Italian Music for the Ordinary of the Mass 1350–1450* (diss., Harvard U., 1960), 116f   KURT VON FISCHER

Santorini, Lorenz (*fl* 1699–1764). Italian tenor and composer active in Germany. He is said to have come from Venice (Marpurg) and was a tenor in the service of Elector Johann Wilhelm in Düsseldorf from 1699 to 1716. With the accession of Elector Karl Philipp of Heidelberg the Düsseldorf court chapel was merged with the elector's, bringing Santorini in 1718 to Heidelberg and in 1720 to Mannheim. During Karl Philipp's reign (until 1742) he was appointed secretary, poet and composer to the court with a large salary, enabling him to buy a house in Mannheim in 1735. He was listed in the court records until 1764, although he had retired by 1756.

At the performance of C. P. Grua's festival opera *Meride* for the inauguration of the Mannheim opera house (1742) Santorini appeared as Cambise. His only known compositions are the mythological serenatas *Il concilio de pianeti* and *Componimento per musica* (librettos at the Reiss Museum, Mannheim), both performed at Heidelberg court festivals in 1721; he made them works of homage to his patron in the Baroque manner. He wrote the texts for C. P. Grua's oratorios *La conversione di Sant Ignazio* (1740) and *Jaele* (1741).

BIBLIOGRAPHY
F. Marpurg: *Historisch-kritische Beyträge zur Aufnahme der Musik*, ii (Berlin, 1756/R1970), 570
F. Walter: *Geschichte des Theaters und der Musik am kurpfälzischen Hofe* (Leipzig, 1898/R1968)
                    ROLAND WÜRTZ

Santoro, Cláudio (*b* Manaus, Amazonas, 23 Nov 1919). Brazilian composer, conductor and violinist. He studied the violin and theory at the Conservatório de Música do Distrito Federal, Rio de Janeiro, graduating in 1936. After making some first attempts at composition in 1938, he became a pupil of Koellreutter, who introduced 12-note techniques to him. He co-founded and played the violin in the Brazilian SO (1941–7), and in 1946 he was awarded a Guggenheim Fellowship, but, unable to secure a visa for the USA, he travelled instead to Paris under a French government fellowship. There he studied with Boulanger and was a conducting pupil of Bigot at the Conservatoire. In 1948 he was the Brazilian delegate to the Prague Congress of Progressive Composers, and the meeting's condemnation of dodecaphony as 'bourgeois decadence' influenced his development. Back in Brazil he worked as music director of the Radio Club do Brasil in Rio (1951–3), professor of composition at the Santos School of Music (1953–4), chief conductor of the Brazilian SO and artistic director of Radio Ministério da Educação e Cultura (1956). In 1962 he was appointed professor and coordinator of music at the University of Brasília, and director of the music section of the Federal Cultural Foundation. He also taught composition at the Pro Arte seminars in Rio and Teresópolis. In 1967 he was invited by the West German government to assist in the organization of the Information and Diffusion Centre for Latin American Music within the Institut für Vergleichende Musikstudien und Dokumentation. After a period as music director of the Teatro Novo, Rio (1968–9), he returned to Germany as professor of composition and conducting at the Heidelberg–Mannheim Hochschule für Musik (1970). He is a member of the Brazilian Academy of Music and of the Brazilian Academy of Arts, and he has received numerous prizes and commissions.

Santoro's early music, that written between early 1939 and about 1947, was orientated towards atonality, evolving under Koellreutter's influence into a pragmatic 12-note technique and from this to a freer, more flexible serial style. One exception to the abstract work of this period is the semi-programmatic *Impressões de uma fundição de aço* for orchestra (1942). Some pieces of the years 1945–7 anticipate a second phase in Santoro's music: the Symphony no.2, the *Música para cordas*, the 6 *peças* for piano and the Trumpet Sonata are all more subjective and lyrical, more spontaneously nationalist. Santoro began serious studies of Brazilian folk and popular music in 1949–50, and he embraced a nationalist style during the period 1948–60 approximately. His socialist views at this time had an effect on his music – there was some affinity with Prokofiev's Soviet phase and with the symphonic writing of Shostakovich. *Canto de amor e paz* for string orchestra (1950) received the International Peace Prize of the World Peace Council in Vienna (1952); the Symphony no.4 (1953) was recorded by the USSR State SO and praised by Soviet critics and composers. Although this latter work calls for Brazilian percussion instruments, it has no other nationalist character, but rather resembles Prokofiev in its rhythmic drive. At the same time Santoro was writing overtly nationalist pieces, such as the Third Quartet and *Ponteio*, and this tendency prevailed in the Symphony no.5. In the next two symphonies he tried to transcend his previously direct folk and popular style, developing a somewhat subjective nationalism in the late 1950s.

In the mid-1960s Santoro returned to a qualified serialism and went on to use aleatory and other new techniques. The Symphony no.8 (1963) was a major turning point in the return, and a clear indication of his concern to free his materials from the restrictions of folk rhythmic and other formulae. Characteristic of what Santoro termed a 'universal form and language' are the Quartets nos.6 and 7 and *Interações assintóticas*, which shows 'a detachment from conventional orchestral writing, compounded by micro-tuning mixed with impassive static blocks of tone and random "noise" of scraping instruments' (London). His use of aleatory methods and graphic notation began in 1966. *Intermitências II*, for example, includes random percussive elements and limited improvisation, as well as new performing techniques in the solo piano part; and the *Cantata elegíaca*, commissioned by the Gulbenkian Foundation, has improvised choral and instrumental passages.

WORKS

ORCHESTRAL

Sym. no.1, 2 str orchs, 1940; Adagio, str, 1942; Impressões de uma fundição de aço, 1942; Divertimento, 1943; Música 1944, pf, orch, 1944; Sym. no.2, 1945; Variações, 1945; Música para cordas 1946, 1946; Sym. no.3, 1947–8; Canto de amor e paz, str, 1950; Pf Conc. no.1, 1951; Ponteio, str, 1953; Sym. no.4 'Da paz', 1953; Brasiliana, 1954; Sym. no.5, 1955; Sym. no.6, 1957; Vn Conc. no.2, 1958 Icamiabas, ballet, 1958–9; Recitativo e variações, chamber orch, 1959; Sym. no.7 'Brasília', 1959–60; Pf Conc. no.3, 1960; Zuimaaluti, ballet, 1960; Vc Conc. no.1, 1961; Introdução e allegro, str, 1962–3; Sym. no.8, 1963; 5 esboços, 1964–5; 3 abstrações, str, 1966; In Tele tonos visionem, str, 1967; Intermitências II, pf, chamber orch, 1967; Intermitências III, pf, orch/pf solo, 1967; Interações assintóticas, 1969

CHAMBER AND INSTRUMENTAL

Sonata, vn, 1940; Sonata, fl, pf, 1941; Str Trio, 1941; 4 epigramas, fl, 1942; Wind Qnt, 1942; Sonatina a 3, fl, va, vc, 1942; Sonatina, ob, pf, 1943; Str Qt no.1, 1943; Música de câmera, fl, cl, b cl, pf, vn, vc, 1944; 3 peças, cl, 1944; Coral, org, 1945; Duo, vn, bn, 1945; Variações miniatura, cl, vn, va, vc, 1945; Adagio, vc, pf, 1946; Sonata, tpt, pf, 1946; Str Qt no.2, 1946–7; Sonata no.3, vn, pf, 1947; Sonata no.2, vc, pf, 1947; Sonata no.4, vn, pf, 1950; Sonata no.3, vc, pf, 1951; Str Qt no.3, 1953 Str Qt no.4, 1955; Sonata no.5, vn, pf, 1957; Sonata no.4, vc, pf, 1963; Str Qt no.6, 1963; Str Qt no.7, 1965; Agrupamento in 10, fl, trbn, perc, pf, xyl, vib, vn, va, db, 1966; Diagramas ciclicos, pf, perc, 1966; 3 espaços, va, pf, 1966; Mutationem I, hpd, tape, 1968, II, vc, tape, 1970, III, pf, tape, 1971, IV, va, tape, 1972, V, vn, tape, 1972, VI, vn, tape, 1972; Pf Trio, 1973

VOCAL

Cantata elegíaca (Camões), chorus, orch, 1970
A menina bôba (O. Alvarenga), 1944; 60 corais infantis, 1951; Irremediável canção (A. de Andrade), 1953; Canção da fuga impossivel (Andrade), 1953; A uma mulher (C. Brant), 1956; Levavas a madrugada (Andrade), 1956; Amor em lágrimas (V. de Morais), 1957; 12 canções de amor (Morais), 1958–9; No meio fio da rua (J. Alimonda), 1960; Tu vais ao mar (Santoro), 1961; Canção (textless), 1961; Canção (textless), 1962; Eu não sei (R. da Costa), 1966; Canção (textless), 1966

PIANO

Pequena toccata, 1942; 4 peças, 1943; Sonata no.1, 1945; Sonatina infantil, 1946; 6 peças, 1946; Preludios nos.1–4, 1946–8; Sonatina no.1, 1948; Sonata no.2, 1948; Preludio no.5, 1950; 2 danças brasileiras, 1951; 9 peças infantis, 1952; Frevo, 1953; 7 paulistanas, 1953; Toccata, 1954; Sonata no.3, 1955; Sonata no.4 'fantasia', 1957; Estudos nos.1–2, 1959–60; Preludios nos.1–25, 1957–63; Sonatina no.2, 1964; Intermitências I, 1967; Duo, 1972

WITHDRAWN WORKS

Orch: Sinfonia de câmera, 1941; 3 pequenos divertimentos, 1942; Conc., vn, chamber orch, 1943; Abertura, 1947; Ballet simples, 1947; A fábrica, ballet, 1947; Anticocos, ballet, 1951; Vn Conc. no.1, 1951; O café, ballet suite, 1953; Chôro, t sax, orch, 1953; Entoando tristemente, 1953; O alegre dia vai nascer, 1956; Abertura trágica, 1958, lost; Pf Conc. no.2, 1958–9; Toada triste, str, 1959
Chamber: Sonata no.1, va, pf, 1940; Divertimento, 7 insts, 1941; Sonata no.2, vn, pf, 1941; Sonata no.1, vc, pf, 1942–3; Sonata, va, pf, 1943; Peça, vn, pf, 1944; Trio, fl, cl, bn, 1946; Trio, cl, tpt, vc, 1946; Trio, ob, cl, bn, 1947; Peça, vn, pf, 1948; Na serra da Mantiqueira, vn, pf, 1949; Introdução e dança, vc, pf, 1951; Str Qt no.5, 1957
Vocal: Ode a Stalingrado, chorus, orch, 1947; Berlin, 13 de agôsto, narrator, chorus, orch, 1961–2
Pf: 4 pequenas invenções a 2 vozes, 1942; Sonata 1942, 1942; Batucada, 1948; Dança, 1950; Miniatura, 1950; Para Joe Gisèle brincarem a 4 mãos, 1973

Principal publishers: Jobert, Ricordi, Southern, Tonos

BIBLIOGRAPHY

V. Mariz: *A canção brasileira* (Rio de Janeiro, 1959)
Compositores de América/Composers of the Americas, ed. Pan American Union, ix (Washington, DC, 1963), 126f

E. London: 'Four Scores by Santoro', *Yearbook for Inter-American Musical Research*, vii (1971), 51

GERARD BÉHAGUE

Santórsola, Guido (*b* Canosa, 18 Nov 1904). Uruguayan composer, string player and conductor of Italian birth. His music studies began in São Paulo, where he had theory lessons from his father before entering the conservatory to study with Autuori (violin) and Cantú (harmony and counterpoint). After further training with Baldi, he went to Europe on a Brazilian Government scholarship to pursue violin studies with Fusella in Naples and with Mitowsky at Trinity College, London. On his return to Brazil in 1925 he joined the Paulista Quartet as violist. He founded the Brazilian Musical Institute, where he directed a chamber music course, and was first viola in the orchestra of the Rio de Janeiro Teatro Municipal, also appearing as a soloist on the viola and the viola d'amore. Thereafter he served as professor of violin, viola and harmony at the São Paulo Conservatory before settling in Montevideo as a violist in the radio symphony orchestra (OSSODRE). In 1943 he led an official mission from the institute of musicology on a tour of Brazilian cities, and in 1948 he reorganized the orchestra of Belo Horizonte, where he conducted a series of concerts. He also founded and conducted the orchestra of the Uruguayan Cultural Association and formed the Kleiber Quartet of Montevideo. In addition he has taught at the Montevideo Conservatory as professor of harmony, aesthetics and composition. His early works are based on the motifs and structures of the folk music of Brazil, and then of Uruguay; later he experimented with 12-note music and explored diverse contemporary techniques.

WORKS
(selective list)

Orch: Va Conc., 1933; Pf Conc., 1938–9; Gui Conc., 1942; Sym. no.1, 1957; Cantata a Artigas, 1965; 2 Gui Conc., 1966; 4 Hn Conc., 1967; 22 other works

Vocal: Os tres misteiros da noite, speaker, A, orch, 1966; choral works, songs

10 chamber pieces; 8 works for vn, pf; 12 gui pieces; 12 pf pieces; many arrs.

BIBLIOGRAPHY

Compositores de América/Composers of the Americas, ed. Pan American Union, viii (Washington, DC, 1962)

SUSANA SALGADO

Santos, (José Manuel) Joly Braga. *See* BRAGA SANTOS, JOLY.

Santos, José Joaquim dos (*b* Senhor da Pedra, nr. Óbidos, *c*1747; *d* Lisbon, 1801). Portuguese composer. He entered the Seminário Patriarcal on 24 June 1754 and after graduating on 1 January 1763 was hired at a yearly salary of 40,000 réis to teach solfège. He remained at the seminary as instructor of harmony, counterpoint and composition until his death. Santos composed convincingly in the vigorous idiom of his teacher David Perez. Two shepherd eclogues by him were sung in 1786 and 1787 at the Lisbon Academia Real das Ciências at its annual celebration of the Feast of the Immaculate Conception (8 December), but his extant works are all sacred.

WORKS

P-La: Te Deum, 8vv, org, 1779; Credo, 8vv, vc, org, 1787; 7 vesper psalms; Magnificat, 4vv, org; Miserere breve, 4vv, vc

P-Lf, 1774–93, various accs.: 5 masses; 25 psalms; 15 motets; 3 Te Deum; Stabat mater; Miserere

P-Ln: Responsório, 1768; Holy Week res, 4vv, org; 2 Miserere; 2 Stabat mater, 1 for 3vv, orch (Lisbon, 1792), 1 for 3vv, 2 va, vc;

Hymnos ad nonam, 4vv, orchd A. L. Miró; Setenário de Nossa Senhora das Dores, 4vv, orch

Rio de Janeiro Cathedral: matins for Holy Week, SATB, orch/org, 1859

BIBLIOGRAPHY

DBP, ii, 274ff

M. A. Machado Santos: *Biblioteca da Ajuda: catálogo de música manuscrita*, v (Lisbon, 1962), 78ff

R. Stevenson: *Renaissance and Baroque Musical Sources in the Americas* (Washington, DC, 1970), 313

ROBERT STEVENSON

Santos, Luciano Xavier dos (*b* Lisbon, 1734; *d* Lisbon, 2 Feb 1808). Portuguese composer. He studied with the Venetian Giovanni Giorgi in the school of religious music established by John V at S Caterina de Ribamar and passed the examination for entrance to the Lisbon Brotherhood of S Cecilia on 20 May 1756. From then until his death he served as first organist and *mestre* of the Bemposta royal chapel, Lisbon. Besides a large quantity of sacred music, he composed several operas and other stage pieces, many to texts by Metastasio, which were performed at Queluz or Ajuda theatres, usually for royal birthday festivities. As a composer he ranks with Sousa Carvalho and Leal Moreira, showing a fine instinct for melody, dramatic contrast, structural tightness and climax.

WORKS
(MSS in P-La unless otherwise stated)

Stage: Le grazie vendicate (azione teatrale, Metastasio), 1762; Gli orti esperide (azione teatrale, Metastasio), 1764, lost; La danza (cantata, Metastasio), 1766; Il Palladio conservato (azione teatrale, Metastasio), 1771; Alcide al bivio (festa teatrale, Metastasio), 1778; Ati e Sangaride (serenata, G. Martinelli), 1779; Palmira di Tebe (serenata, Martinelli), 1781; Esione (serenata), 1784; La Galatea (?opera), 1784; Ercole sul Tago (dramma per musica, V. A. Cigna), 1785; Il re pastore (opera, Metastasio), 1797; ?Clemenza di Tito (Metastasio)

Sacred, mostly 4vv, org: Passione di Gesu Christo (?Metastasio), oratorio, 1783; 79 Lat. compositions, incl. 2 masses, 1773, 1784, 11 Matins, Lamentations, Magnificat; 2 masses, 1760, 1791, Benedictus, 1804, Stabat mater, ps, *Lf*; Te Deum, 4vv, orch, Rio de Janeiro Cathedral

BIBLIOGRAPHY

DBP, ii, 276

O. G. T. Sonneck: *Catalogue of Opera Librettos* (Washington, DC, 1914), 181, 447, 839, 844f

M. A. Machado Santos: *Biblioteca da Ajuda: catálogo de música manuscrita*, v (Lisbon, 1962), 81ff; ix (Lisbon, 1967–8), lxvi, 111

ROBERT STEVENSON

Santos, Ramon Pagayon (*b* Pasig, Rizal, 25 Feb 1941). Filipino composer and teacher. He studied at the University of the Philippines (BMus in composition and conducting 1965), Indiana University (MMus 1969), the State University of New York at Buffalo (PhD in composition 1972) and the Darmstadt summer courses (1974). His university teachers included Thomas Beversdorf, Roque Cordero, Ramon Fuller, William Kothe, Gehlhaar, Anhalt and Perle. In 1973 Santos became chairman of the composition and conducting department at the University of the Philippines College of Music.

WORKS
(selective list)

Stage: Ang hardin ni ligaya [The garden of happiness] (opera, 2, Santos), 1965; Ang puting waling-waling [The white orchids] (music drama, 3, Santos), 1972

Orch: 4 Movts, chamber orch, 1968; Concertino Variations, 1969; The Chant, sym. poem, 1973

Choral: Sa kapurihan at kapalaran [To integrity and fate], sym. ode, A, chorus, orch, 1963; Missa brevis, chorus, chamber orch, 1964; Magnificat, 1969; Ding-ding nga diyawa (Muslim liturgy), chorus, western and oriental perc, 1970; Mass of the Resurrection, 1970

LUCRECIA R. KASILAG

Santos, Rosendo (Ejercito) (*b* Cavite City, 3 Sept 1922). Filipino composer and conductor. He studied at the University of the Philippines (BMus 1950), the Catholic University of America (MMus 1962) and the University of West Virginia (PhD 1964). As a teacher he has been on the staff of the University of the Philippines (1950–61), the Catholic University of America (assistant professor 1961–4), the University of West Virginia (1964–5), Howard University (1965–8) and Wilkes College (head of theory and percussion from 1968). At the same time he has pursued a career as a church musician, serving at St John, Morgantown, West Virginia (1964–5), Chevy Chase Catholic Church (1965–8), Henson Valley Christian Church (1965–8) and Wilkes-Barre United Methodist Church (from 1968). In 1972 he was appointed timpanist and principal percussionist of the Northeastern Pennsylvania Philharmonic Society.

WORKS
(*selective list*)
Orch: Pf Conc. no.1, G, 1948; Lakeside Suite, 1956; Pf Conc. no.2, 1956; Mindoro Sketches, 1961; 4 syms., 1961–5
Vocal: Mapulang Bituin [The red star], zarzuela, 1960; Mass of St Pascual, 1964; Mass of St Peter, 1965; Dawn of Hope, chorus, orch, 1972
Inst: Wind Qt, 1961; Sonata, str, bn, 1963; Hn Suite, 1964; Sonata no.2, cl, pf, 1965; Percussion Heritage, perc ens, 1970; pf works
Principal publisher: Gregorian Institute of America [masses]
LUCRECIA R. KASILAG

Santos Ocampo, Amada (Galvez) (*b* Manila, 23 June 1925). Filipina composer. She studied at St Paul College, Manila (music teacher's diploma), the Centro Escolar University Conservatory (BMus), DePauw University, Indiana (MMus) and the University of Indiana at Bloomington. Among her composition teachers were Molina, Buenaventura and San Pedro in the Philippines, and Harris, White, Heiden and Orrego Salas in the USA. In addition, she had advanced piano lessons with Glen Sherman and Sidney Fosters, and she has toured the Philippines and the USA as a composer-pianist. She taught at Centro Escolar University (1955–8, 1964–7) and Stella Maris College (1965–7) before returning to the USA to take up a post as pianist and assistant professor at the Pennsylvania State University College of Health, Physical Education and Recreation.

WORKS
(*selective list*)
Orch: Tone Poem, 1956; Pf Conc., 1957; Variations, 1960; 2 syms., 1964
Chamber: Sonata, cl, pf, 1960; Concert Piece, 2 pf, 1962; Sonata, vn, pf, 1965
Choral pieces, pf music, orch songs, music for dance and gymnastics
LUCRECIA R. KASILAG

Santos Pinto, Francisco António Norberto dos. *See* PINTO, FRANCISCO ANTÓNIO NORBERTO DOS SANTOS.

Santucci, Marco (*b* Camaiore, Tuscany, 4 July 1762; *d* Lucca, 29 Nov 1843). Italian composer. After appearing at the age of 13 as the prima donna in Sacchini's *La contadina in corte* and having done some composition, he studied at the Conservatorio di Loreto in Naples from 1779. In 1790 he moved to Lucca, where he was ordained in 1794; in 1797 he succeeded Anfossi as *maestro di cappella* at St John Lateran, Rome. He contributed to a cantata *Marco Curzio* (1791) for the Luccan dramatic festival known as the *tasche*, and in 1806 he won the Accademia Napoleone prize for a 16-part motet for four choirs: the novelty of this was much praised by the judges, but was then sharply contested by Baini. He became a canon of Lucca Cathedral in 1808, and was also one of the eight members of the music section of the Società Italiana founded by Napoleon. His many pupils included, briefly and at an early age, Michele Puccini, father of Giacomo. He also wrote a short treatise *Sulla melodia, sull'armonia e sul metro* (Lucca, 1828), dismissed by Fétis as unimportant. His compositions include much church music and some secular choral and instrumental works.

BIBLIOGRAPHY
FétisB
G. Baini: *Lettera sopra il motetto a quattro cori del Sig. Marco Santucci* (Rome, 1806)
G. B. Rinuccini: *Biografia di Marco Santucci* (Massa, 1851)
L. Nerici: *Storia della musica in Lucca* (Lucca, 1879/R1969)
U. Rolandi: *Spettacoli musicali per la funzione delle 'Tasche' in Lucca* (Milan, 1932)
JOHN WARRACK

Santūr [Santur, sant'ur]. A DULCIMER of Turkey and Iran with related forms elsewhere in the Near East; *see also* BURMA, §2(iii); HUNGARY, §II, 5(iii); INDIA, SUBCONTINENT OF, §I, 2(i); IRAN, §I, 5; IRAQ, §5; KASHMIR; MODE, §V, 2(i); TURKEY, §4(ii); UNION OF SOVIET SOCIALIST REPUBLICS, §I, 2(vi–vii).

Sanuti Pellicani, Giovanni Battista (*b* Bologna, 1632–3; *d* Bologna, 7 Aug 1697). Italian lawyer and composer. He was a doctor of laws and a professor at Bologna University. As a member of the Bolognese Accademia dei Gelati he wrote a discourse on a musical subject: 'Perche nelle cantilene si adopri la quinta diminuita, e la quarta superflua; e non questa diminuita, e quella super-flua', printed in *Prose de' Signori Accademici Gelati di Bologna* (Bologna, 1671), 133ff. Cazzati's *Sonate* op.55 (1670) is dedicated to him. His own surviving music amounts to three secular pieces for solo voice and continuo, two in *RISM* 1670[3] and one in 1685[1].

BIBLIOGRAPHY
G. Gaspari: *Catalogo della Biblioteca musicale G. B. Martini di Bologna*, i (Bologna, 1890/R1961), 289
E. Schmitz: *Geschichte der weltlichen Solokantate* (Leipzig, 1914, rev. 2/1955), 133
JOHN WHENHAM

Sanz, Gaspar (*b* Calanda, Aragon, mid-17th century; *d* early 18th century). Spanish guitarist, composer and priest. Early in his life he received a Bachelor of Theology degree from the University of Salamanca and later travelled to Italy, where he studied music under Cristoforo Caresana, Orazio Benevoli, Pietro Andrea Ziani and Lelio Colista. On returning to Spain he published not only his *Instrucción de música sobre la guitarra española* but also two literary works: a Spanish translation of Daniello Bartoli's *L'uomo de lettere* (Madrid, 1678) and a eulogy in praise of Pope Innocent XI entitled *Ecos sagrados* (Madrid, 1681).

Sanz's *Instrucción de música* is the most comprehensive guitar treatise of its time. Comprising three books, it contains 90 pieces written for a five-course instrument tuned *a/a–d'/d'–g/g–b/b–e'*, the majority of which are based on dance forms, such as the *folia*, *canario* and *españoleta*, typical of the late 17th-century Spanish Baroque style. The first book includes a detailed introductory tutor with instructions for stringing, fretting and tuning and an explanation of both the *rasgueado* (strummed) and *punteado* (plucked) styles; it also contains a long essay on figured bass accompaniment for the guitar. While many of its pieces are intended for beginners, those in the second and third books are longer, broader in scope and more demanding.

Sanz's work was very popular in Spain and initiated a series of similar works, such as those of Ruiz de Ribayaz and Guerau. Various pieces from it and parts of the text appear in six publications and MSS, French as well as Spanish, up to 1763.

WORKS

Edition: *The Complete Guitar Works of Gaspar Sanz*, ed. R. Strizich (in preparation)

Instrucción de música sobre la guitarra española y método de sus primeros rudimentos hasta tañerla con destreza (Saragossa, 1674, 8/1697); facs. edns. (Madrid, 1951, Saragossa, 1966) [the latter with introduction and notes by L. García-Abrines]

BIBLIOGRAPHY

R. Hudson: 'Further Remarks on the Passacaglia and Ciaccona', *JAMS*, xxiii (1970), 304

S. Murphy: 'The Tuning of the Five-course Guitar', *GSJ*, xxiii (1970), 52ff, 57, 60

W. Kirkendale: *L'aria di Fiorenza, id est Il ballo del Gran Duca* (Florence, 1972)

R. Strizich: 'Ornamentation in Spanish Baroque Guitar Music', *Journal of the Lute Society of America*, v (1972), 18

R. de Zayas: 'Gaspar Sanz: A Transcription of his Complete Works for the Guitar', *The Consort*, xxxi (1975), 132

ROBERT STRIZICH

Sanza. A term used frequently in the generic sense for several types of African lamellaphone; *see* LAMELLA-PHONE, introduction and §4; GABON, §3.

Sanzogno, Nino (*b* Venice, 13 April 1911). Italian conductor and composer. He studied the violin with de Guarneri and composition with Agostini at the Venice Liceo Musicale (graduating in 1932), and took postgraduate studies with Malipiero in Venice and with Scherchen in Brussels, where he won the 1935 Henry de Beuf International Competition and began a career distinguished by his work for contemporary music. He directed the Gruppo Strumentale Italiano in concerts at home and abroad, and became resident conductor at the Teatro La Fenice, Venice, in 1937, and of the Milan RSO soon afterwards. He first conducted at La Scala in 1939; in 1955 he inaugurated La Piccola Scala with *Il matrimonio segreto* and appeared with this company at the 1957 Edinburgh Festival with Cimarosa's opera and *L'elisir d'amore*. During these years he was responsible for many premières, including Poulenc's *Dialogues des Carmélites* at La Scala (1957), Milhaud's *David* and Malipiero's *L'allegra brigata*; he also conducted the first Italian productions of Walton's *Troilus and Cressida* at La Scala in 1956, and of *Lulu*, *A Midsummer Night's Dream*, *The Fiery Angel* and Shostakovich's *Lady Macbeth of Mtsensk*, mainly at successive Venice Festivals. He has toured widely as a guest conductor, including concerts with the BBC SO with which he introduced to Britain Dallapiccola's *Job* and works by Malipiero, Petrassi and others; he also conducted a double bill of Dallapiccola and Malipiero operas from the Maggio Musicale Fiorentino at the 1969 Edinburgh Festival. At La Piccola Scala and elsewhere his extensive repertory was widened by a developing interest in Classical and early music, and he was resident conductor at La Scala, 1962–5. British audiences were impressed by his quiet, subtle control, Latin precision and deep musical knowledge, and by his firm discipline masked by outward elegance and charm. He has taught conducting at Darmstadt, and his compositions, all written early in his career, include two symphonic poems, *I quattro cavalieri dell'Apocalisse* (1930) and *Vanitas*

(1931), concertos for viola (1935) and cello (1937) and works for chamber ensembles.

LEONARDO PINZAUTI

São Paulo. Brazilian city founded in 1554. The first documented musical references date from 1611 when the cathedral was established; from its foundation it maintained a *mestre de capela*, whose duties included musical composition and teaching; Manoel Pais Linhares, Vieira de Barros and Lopes de Siqueira were *mestres* in the 17th century and Manoel Lopes de Siqueira and Angelo de Siqueira in the 18th. They and their pupils contributed to the development of religious brotherhoods initiated by the Portuguese metropolis. When São Paulo was raised to a diocese in 1745 the *mestre de capela* was Matias Alvares Torres; he was replaced in 1774 by André da Silva Gomes (*b* Lisbon, 1752), who occupied the post for 50 years, concurrently teaching Latin in the city. Some 200 of his sacred compositions in the cathedral archives are the oldest known musical documents of São Paulo. In the 19th and 20th centuries the cathedral continued to be a centre for the cultivation of sacred music, from Antonio José de Almeida, who succeeded da Silva Gomes, to Furio Franceschini (*b* 1876), appointed in 1908.

Within the state of São Paulo several communities developed intense musical activity, evident from the many works of 18th-century *mestres de capela*, of whom the most important included André da Silva Moura (1725–1809) in Santos, Manoel Gonçalves Franco (1740–1814) in Guará, José Ribeiro de Siqueira (1700–72) in Parnaíba, Manoel Julião da Silva Ramos (1763–1824) in Atibaia, Jesuíno do Monte Carmelo (1764–1819) in Itú, Pedro de Alcântara (1722–96) and his son Antonio do Rosário (*b* 1759) in Sorocaba.

In the 18th century in South America 'opera' was a generic term for theatrical performance. By 1750 São Paulo had a Casa da Ópera, under the direction in 1774 of the Bahian musician Antonio Manso da Mota; the Teatro da Ópera in the Pátio do Colégio was also established in the 18th century. Travellers reported local performances of opera excerpts, particularly on the occasion of the acclamation of the first Emperor of Brazil in 1822. Augusta Candiani was the first important European opera singer to perform in São Paulo (1847), and she was followed a few years later by many European artists presenting the standard Italian operatic repertory; in 1860 the Companhia Buffa Francesa presented the music of Offenbach and Delibes. In the following year the Teatro da Ópera produced Fortunato G. P. Andrade's comic opera *Palavra de Rei*, strongly influenced by Donizetti, and at about that time Brazilian opera emerged, with the first presentations at the Rio de Janeiro of works by Elias A. Lobo and Carlos Gomes, both born in São Paulo. The Teatro São José in the Largo São Gonçalo was inaugurated in 1864, preceding by ten years the city's first well-organized lyric company, that of José Ferri. With the inauguration of the Teatro Santana and the Teatro Municipal (1911) regular annual music drama seasons began.

Concert life started in the 1850s, when visiting soloists appeared with the first local orchestras. After 1880 a substantial Italian colony grew up in São Paulo; in that year Luigi Chiaffarelli (1850–1923), founder of the city's piano school and teacher of Guiomar Novais, Antonieta Rudge and others, settled there. He initiated regular concert life in his famous musical soirées (continued later by Agostino Cantù); at one of these in 1899 he presented Henrique Oswald's Quartet in G, in the presence of Saint-Saëns. In 1883 the Clube Haydn was founded under the direction of the composer Alexandre Levy (1864–92), organizing chamber music and symphonic concerts until 1887; it was succeeded by the Clube Mendelssohn, mostly dedicated to choral music. The Sociedade de Cultura Artística (1912) and the Sociedade de Concertos Sinfônicos de São Paulo (1921) reflected the development of concert life in the city. The short-lived Sociedade Sinfônica de São Paulo (1930–31) had Heitor Villa-Lobos and Lamberto Baldi as its conductors.

The Sociedade Bach, under Martin Braunwieser, the Seminários de Música da Pro-Arte, under Hans J. Koellreutter, and the Orquestra Sinfônica de Amadores were founded in the 1940s. The sphere of professional activity widened with the creation of the Orquestra Sinfônica da Rádio Gazeta, the Orquestra de Câmara do Angelicum do Brasil (1951) under Mario Rossini, the Orquestra Sinfônica Estadual de São Paulo (1952) and the Associação Paulista de Música (1956) with its chamber orchestra under the direction of Olivier Toni, its string quartet and Coral Piratininga under Eunice Catunda. The movement of Juventude Musical Brasileira (Brazilian Musical Youth) was also initiated in the 1950s. The Manifesto de Música Nova (1963) brought together avant-garde musicians, including Damiano Cozzella, Rogério Duprat, Régis Duprat, Gilberto Mendes and Willy Corrêa de Oliveira, who advocated and presented concerts of new music. The state educational television (Anchieta Foundation) emerged concurrently with the Movimento Villa-Lobos, which sponsored the creation of mixed choral groups throughout the state, such as the distinguished Coral da Universidade de São Paulo under Benito Juarez.

One of the most far-reaching accomplishments in the city's music history was Mário de Andrade's organization of the Departamento Municipal de Cultura during the 1930s. He initiated regular symphony concerts, which became possible with the founding of the Orquestra Sinfônica Municipal, and founded the Coral Paulistano, the Quarteto Municipal and the Discoteca Municipal. Under his supervision composition contests were instituted and monographs published.

The Conservatório Dramático e Musical de São Paulo (1906), which developed from piano teaching in the city, soon became a centre of musical studies and composition; its teachers included Chiaffarelli, Cantù, João Gomes Araujo, Alférïo Mignone, Samuel Arcanjo, Francisco Casabona and Savino de Beneditis. Among its students were Francisco Mignone, Artur Pereira, Camargo Guarnieri and Frutuoso Viana. The Academia Paulista de Música was founded in the 1960s. In 1928 João Gomes jr, Francisco Casabona, Félix Otero and João Julião organized the Instituto Musical de São Paulo, which underwent considerable reforms in 1971 under the direction of Neide Rodrigues Gomes. In 1970 the department of music of São Paulo University was established at the Escola de Communicações e Artes with a staff of 17 under the direction of Olivier Toni. It offers degree courses in composition, conducting and instrumentation.

The existence of the conservatory prompted the establishment of the Edições Ricordi, which published Italian didactic works and Brazilian works. Publishing ventures expanded with the founding of the Editora

Casa Vitali. Musical periodicals published in São Paulo have included the *Gazeta musical* (1893–5), the review *Música* (1896), the *Gazeta artística* (1909–14), *Ariel* (1923–5) and *Resenha musical* (1938–45). From the early 20th century daily newspapers such as the *Estado de São Paulo*, the *Diário de São Paulo* and the *Diário popular* had regular music columns. A regional council of the Ordem dos Músicos do Brasil (National Musicians' Union) was established in 1960.

BIBLIOGRAPHY

M. de Andrade: *Pequena história da música* (São Paulo, 1942)
C. Penteado de Rezende: *Um século de ópera em São Paulo* (São Paulo, n.d.)
L. H. Corrêa de Azevedo: *150 anos de música no Brasil (1800–1950)* (Rio de Janeiro, 1956)
R. Duprat: 'Música na matriz de São Paulo colonial', *Revista de história*, lxxv (1968), 85
R. Stevenson: 'Some Portuguese sources for early Brazilian music history', *Yearbook, Inter-American Institute for Musical Research*, iv (1968), 1–43

RÉGIS DUPRAT

Saorgin, René (*b* Cannes, 31 Oct 1928). French organist and authority on organs. He studied with Duruflé and Gallon at the Paris Conservatoire, where he received the *premier prix* in counterpoint. In 1958 he won the Bach Prize at the organ competition in Ghent. He is organ professor at the Nice Conservatory, where he is also organist of St Jean-Baptiste, and is an advisory member for historic organs on the Paris Commission Supérieure des Monuments Historiques. Saorgin was one of the founders of the organ academy in St Maximin. In 1972 and 1973 he was professor of French organ music at the organ academy in Haarlem. He is preparing a study of historical Italian organs from the region of Nice and built by Serassi, Lingiardi, Agati, Grinda and Valoncini. Saorgin has undertaken recital tours both in his own country and in Italy, Switzerland, Austria, Belgium and the USA. He specializes in Italian and north German music of the 17th and 18th centuries; among his recordings are the complete works of Buxtehude, pieces by Frescobaldi, and a first performance of 'Musique Militaire et Théatrale' from the 19th century, a recording which won the Grand Prix du Disque.

GERHARD WIENKE

Saporiti [Codecasa], **Teresa** (*b* 1763; *d* Milan, 17 March 1869). Italian soprano. As a member of Pasquale Bondini's company she sang, with her sister, in Leipzig, Dresden and Prague. A report in the *Litteratur und Theater Zeitung* of summer 1782 refers to 'both Demoiselles Saporiti' being engaged for Bondini's company:

The elder, Antonia, had been a concert singer in Leipzig. She sings the most difficult passages with considerable ease; it is a pity that her voice is somewhat small and that she neglects expression in recitatives. Her younger sister is half a beginner as an actress and singer, and is acclaimed only because of her figure. . . . Four men against six women is too few for a theatre; the younger Demoiselle Saporiti has therefore often to appear in man's costume and take over the role of a castrato, which she does poorly and with a bad grace.

In 1785 Trögen reported:

The elder and younger Saporiti have humiliated themselves through their bad performances in Leipzig; particularly so the younger one, who had a liaison with a shopkeeper's apprentice who had stolen 1500 thalers' worth of goods, which he gave her as a reward for her favours. Her mother, who understands only a little German, was so deceived that I feel sorry for her, because they often used the church for their secret meetings, a fact of which the mother knew nothing.

Antonia, Teresa's elder sister, abandoned her career

because of ill-health and took up teaching; she died on 13 October 1787.

In view of these unpromising reviews it is surprising that Mozart thought well enough of Saporiti to write such elaborate and demanding music for her when she created the role of Donna Anna in *Don Giovanni* (Prague, 29 October 1787). She appeared in Venice in Pietro Guglielmi's *Arsace* (26 December 1788) and his *Rinaldo* (28 January 1789). On 20 April 1789 she sang in Bianchi's *Nitteti* at La Scala, Milan, and she later sang in Bologna, Parma and Modena. In 1795 she was designated the *prima buffa assoluta* in a company at St Petersburg; she achieved a personal success in Cimarosa's *Italiana in Londra* and Paisiello's *Il barbiere di Siviglia* (1796). She composed two arias, 'Dormivo in mezzo al prato' and 'Caro mio ben, deh senti', which appeared in a collection by J-B. Hanglaise, *Journal d'airs ... avec accompagnement de guittare* (1796).

Her granddaughter Luisa Codecasa, a well-known artist in Milan, drew attention to the association with *Don Giovanni* when her grandmother died at the age of 105 or 106.

BIBLIOGRAPHY
K. H. Trögen: *Freie Bemerkungen über Berlin, Leipzig und Prag* (Copenhagen, 1785)
O. Teuber: *Geschichte des Prager Theaters*, ii (Prague, 1885)
Bohemia, no.304 (4 Nov 1887)
O. Michtner: *Das alte Burgtheater als Opernbühne* (Vienna, 1970)
CHRISTOPHER RAEBURN

Sapp, Allen Dwight (*b* Philadelphia, 10 Dec 1922). American composer. He was educated at Harvard University and also took lessons from Copland and Boulanger (1942–3); his university career (interrupted by war service as a cryptographer) continued with postgraduate studies under, among others, Piston, Davison and Randall Thompson. In 1949 he joined the faculty of Harvard, and began to compose in earnest – most of his works were written during the next 15 years. He was director jointly with Lukas Foss of the Center for the Creative and Performing Arts at the State University of New York, Buffalo, between 1964 and 1968. His works include two orchestral suites, *Colloquies* for piano and orchestra, chamber music, piano sonatas, and choral pieces to texts by Blake and Eliot.

Sappho (*b* Lesbos, *c*612 BC). Greek lyric poetess. A younger contemporary of Alcaeus, she devoted much of her mature life to leading and training a group of well-born young girls of Mitylene, a chief city of Lesbos, in the performance of ritual and music dedicated chiefly to Aphrodite, the Graces and the MUSES. Men had no part in the life of this group; loyalties and passions were intense. To express her own powerful moods of love, jealousy and disappointment, Sappho employed the new form of lyric monody and the stanza since called by her name. (*See also* ALCAEUS.) Of her choral compositions for cult use, only scattered lines remain. We possess more extensive fragments of her *epithalamia* (wedding songs). Divided choirs of young men and girls, it seems, performed these antiphonally.

Twice (Edmonds, frag.45, l.3; frag.59) Sappho mentioned the *pēktis*, usually identified as a harp-like Lydian instrument. She used the term 'chelys', the specific Greek name for the true lyre, just once (Edmonds, frag. 80, l.1). This is presumably a generic usage; the string instrument regularly associated with her is the barbiton.

Later claims (e.g. in Athenaeus, xiv.635e) that she first brought into use the *pēktis* (alternatively, the *plēktron* or plectrum, the similar Greek terms having been confused) lack any serious basis.

WRITINGS
In *Lyra graeca*, ed. and trans. J. M. Edmonds (London and New York, 1922–7, 2/1928–40)
In *Poetarum lesbiorum fragmenta*, ed. E. Lobel and D. L. Page (Oxford, 1955)
BIBLIOGRAPHY
U. von Wilamowitz-Moellendorff: *Sappho und Simonides* (Berlin, 1913)
C. M. Bowra: *Greek Lyric Poetry* (Oxford, 1936, rev. 2/1967), 176–240
D. L. Page: *Sappho and Alcaeus* (Oxford, 1955)
M. Treu: 'Sappho', *Paulys Real-Encyclopädie* (Stuttgart, 1968)
D. L. Page, ed.: *Lyrica graeca selecta* (Oxford, 1968), 97–129
G. M. Kirkwood: *Early Greek Monody: the History of a Poetic Type* (London and Ithaca, 1974), 100–49
For further bibliography *see* GREECE, §I.
WARREN ANDERSON

Ṣaprā. Office of the Syrian Churches corresponding to Lauds; *see* SYRIAN CHURCH MUSIC.

Saqueboute. A French term used up to the 18th century for TROMBONE.

Sarabande. One of the most popular of Baroque instrumental dances and a standard movement, along with the allemande, courante and gigue, of the suite. It originated during the 16th century as a sung dance in Latin America and Spain. It came to Italy early in the 17th century, as part of the repertory of the Spanish five-course guitar. During the first half of the century various instrumental types developed in France and Italy, at first based on harmonic schemes, later on characteristics of rhythm and tempo. A fast and slow type finally emerged, the former preferred in Italy, England and Spain, the latter in France and Germany.

The French spelling 'sarabande' was also used in Germany and sometimes in England, where 'saraband' was often, however, preferred; the Italian usage is 'sarabanda', the Spanish 'zarabanda'.

1. Early development to *c*1640. 2. The later sarabande: (i) Italy, Spain and England (ii) France and Germany (iii) 19th and 20th centuries.

1. EARLY DEVELOPMENT TO *c*1640. The earliest literary references to the *zarabanda* come from Latin America, the name first appearing in a poem by Fernando Guzmán Mexía in a manuscript from Panama dated 1539, according to B. J. Gallardo (*Ensayo de una biblioteca española de libros raros y curiosos*, Madrid, 1888–9, iv, 1528). A *zarabanda* text by Pedro de Trejo was performed in 1569 in Mexico and Diego Durán mentioned the dance in his *Historia de las Indias de Nueva-España* (1579). The *zarabanda* was banned in Spain in 1583 for its extraordinary obscenity, but literary references to it continued throughout the early 17th century in the works of such writers as Cervantes and Lope de Vega. From about 1580 to 1610 it seems to have been the most popular of the wild and energetic Spanish *bailes*, superseded finally by the *chacona* (see CHACONNE), with which it is frequently mentioned. The dance was accompanied by the guitar, castanets and possibly other percussion instruments, and by a text with refrain.

Most surviving examples of the early *zarabanda* occur in Italian tablatures for the Spanish guitar, beginning in 1606 with Girolamo Montesardo's *Nuova inventione d'intavolatura*. Ex.1 shows a reconstruction of the

Ex.1 The early *zarabanda*

musical scheme that would usually have been repeated for each line of the text, alternating with and without an anacrusis. The top staff shows the melodic framework, which could be varied, and the lower staff (from one of Montesardo's guitar examples) represents major triads to be strummed, the stems showing the direction in which the hand is to move. The refrain text comes from an example in Luis de Briçeño's *Método mui facilissimo* (Paris, 1626). The I–IV–I–V harmonic progression was a constant feature of the early *zarabanda* and can be found also in the later guitar books of Benedetto Sanseverino (see ex.2), G. A. Colonna (1620), Fabrizio Costanzo (1627), G. P. Foscarini (1629), and Antonio Carbonchi (1640 and 1643), as well as in the guitar works of Spanish composers as late as Lucas Ruiz de Ribayaz in 1677. Although the dance seems to have been performed without a text in Italy, the musical scheme of the *zarabanda* was sometimes indicated for the singing of poetry (in *I-Fr* 2774, 2793, 2804, 2849 and 2951).

Ex.2 Sanseverino: *zarabanda* for guitar (1620)

Although ostinato repetition of the single phrase of ex.1 was most usual in Italy, a two-phrase structure occasionally occurred. In Briçeño's two examples entitled *La çaravanda española muy façil*, the first line of the refrain has a harmonic pattern like ex.1, but in the second line the IV chord in the first bar is replaced by V. The same structure appears in pieces by Gaspar Sanz (1674) and Ruiz de Ribayaz (1677), but a different two-phrase plan occurs in the *Aria di saravanda in varie partite* for lute by Piccinini (1623). Its opening phrase is similar to that shown in ex.1, but without the hemiola rhythm; the second phrase begins on a minor sub-mediant chord and bears little resemblance to ex.1.

In Italy and Spain both the single phrases of ex.1 and longer double-phrase structures beginning like ex.1 were often called *zarabanda spagnola* to distinguish them from different types that were developing elsewhere. In France the sarabande usually had no text. Its musical structure, like that of most French Baroque dances, was freely sectional, with two (or sometimes more) repeated sections of varying length. The sarabande appeared early in the 17th century in the *ballet de cour*, as seen in Praetorius's *Terpsichore* (1612). He included examples for each of two types of sarabande, a *courrant* sarabande, made up of repeated sections, and a non-sectional sarabande, which sometimes begins with the pattern shown in ex.1. Ex.3 shows one of the latter, with its metre, barring and note values altered to facilitate comparison with ex.1.

Around 1620 a new type of sarabande called the *zarabanda francese* appeared in Spanish and Italian

Ex.3 Praetorius: *La sarabande* (1612), outer voices

guitar books as well as in the Bentivoglio lutebook of 1615 (*US-SFsc*). The name seems to refer to a non-texted dance with a sectional structure. A *zarabanda francese* by G. A. Colonna (1637) has a harmonic scheme identical to that of ex.3, but its second section (beginning in the fifth bar) is marked for repetition. Briçeño's *Método mui facilissimo* includes an untexted *çaravanda françesa y buena* in addition to texted Spanish examples. Antonio Carbonchi, in 1643, entitled single phrases like ex.1 *serabanda spagnuola* and sectional pieces *serabanda franzese*. Unlike the original Spanish type the Italian *zarabanda francese* could be in either mode. Those in the major tended at first to begin with a phrase like ex.1; those in the minor were often based on the chordal scheme later associated with the FOLIA (chords in brackets indicate those that were sometimes added; upper- or lower-case Roman numerals indicate major or minor triads): i–V–i–(VI)–VII–III–(VI–VII–III)–VII–i–V–(i). Three or five of the opening chords (i–V–i or i–V–i–VII–III) could appear in the first phrase, and the entire scheme could occur either once (with the first half ending on III) or twice (cadencing on V and i). After 1650, however, the *zarabanda francese* seldom displayed any particular harmonic scheme.

During the 1630s rhythm began to become a distinguishing feature of the dance. The sarabandes of François de Chancy, Jacques de Belleville, T. Chevallier and Bouvier contained in Pierre Ballard's *Tablature de luth de differens autheurs* (Paris, 1631) emphasize the rhythm shown in ex.4a. Mersenne (*Harmonie universelle*, 1636) printed two sarabandes, one by 'Mr. Martin' that uses the rhythm of ex.4a, and another that begins like ex.4b. The latter rhythm occurs in a sarabande for trumpet and continuo (1638) by Girolamo Fantini (ex.5 shows the opening statement, which is followed by two variations). He notated it in 3/8, presumably to indicate

Ex.4 Sarabande rhythms

Ex.5 Girolamo Fantini: *Sarabanda detta del Zozzi*, from *Modo per imparare a sonare di tromba* (Frankfurt, 1638).

Ex.6 G. M. Bononcini: *Arie, correnti, sarabande, gighe, & allemande* (Bologna, 1671)

(a) *Sarabanda in stil francese*

(b) *Sarabanda*

a faster tempo than in his saltarellos or *gagliarde*, which he wrote in 3/2, or some of his correntes in 3/4 or 6/4. The same rhythm appeared in later Italian guitar sarabandas (incorporating by this time single notes as well as chords), starting with Francesco Corbetta in 1639. G. M. Bononcini (*Arie, correnti, sarabande, gighe & allemande*, 1671) used the rhythm of ex.4*a* in a piece for violin and continuo called *Sarabanda in stil francese* (ex.6*a*), and the rhythm of ex.4*b* in a *Sarabanda* (ex.6*b*). The first was notated in 3/4, the second in 6/4, suggesting that the rhythm of ex.4*a*, preferred in France, implied a slower tempo with three substantial beats per bar, while that of ex.4*b*, more common in Italy, implied a faster tempo and a compound metre with one accent for each triple group.

Thus there seems to have been a preference, particularly strong among French lute and harpsichord composers, for an increasingly slow and deliberate kind of sarabande, in which (as in French versions of the allemande and the courante) the idiomatic and contrapuntal possibilities of those instruments might be most fully exploited.

2. THE LATER SARABANDE.

(*i*) *Italy, Spain and England.* Italian sarabandas occurred mainly in solo music for guitar and in continuo chamber music. Most sarabandas for guitar from 1640 to 1692 used the rhythm of ex.4*b*, notably the earlier ones of G. P. Foscarini (*c*1640), Antonio Carbonchi, A. M. Bartolotti (1640), Domenico Pellegrini (1650), and G. B. Granata (1651). Corbetta included some sarabandas that began with ex.4*a*, others that used ex.4*b*, in his *Varii capricii per la ghittara spagnuola* (1643). In *La guitarre royalle*, dedicated by Corbetta in 1671 to Charles II of England, two sarabandes with dotted second beats were notated in 3/2 rather than the usual 3/4 metre; one of them, *Sarabande de tombeau de Madame*, has both French and Italian texts. Such titles as *Saravanda alla francese* (Carbonchi, 1640) and *Sarabanda francese per B mole* (Granata, 1646) continued to refer in guitar books simply to the sectional sarabanda as distinct from the original dance music as shown in ex.1. The guitar sarabanda was joined with other dances beginning in A. M. Bartolotti's book (1640) in which it is six times preceded by an allemanda

and two correntes. Corbetta's *Varii capricii* (1643) has allemanda–corrente–sarabanda groups; G. B. Granata (*Nuova scielta di capricci armonici*, 1651) and Ludovico Roncalli (1692) preceded this group with a *preludio* or toccata and sometimes added other dances as well. Ricci, a conservative composer who in 1677 still indicated only strummed chords, wrote that 'in the correnti, sarabande and ciacconne one is to play fast'.

In Italian ensemble music tempos are more explicitly marked. The preferred faster type, often characterized by the rhythm of ex.4*b*, was indicated by the marking 'allegro' or 'presto' in works of P. C. C. Albergati (1682), Domenico Gabrielli (1684), Torelli (1686), Salvatore Mazzella (1689), Giorgio Buoni (1693), and G. B. Brevi (1693). B. G. Laurenti (1691) and T. A. Vitali (1701) marked their sarabandas 'largo', Vivaldi wrote a *Sarabanda andante*, and Corelli used *vivace*, *adagio* and *largo* tempo markings for sarabandas (see

HAM, no.253, for the latter). Dances are usually grouped together in these sources, opening with an allemanda or balletto (preceded sometimes by an introductory movement), followed by a corrente or *giga* or both, and concluding with a sarabanda. Italian sarabandas usually have two repeated sections of variable length, and show a special concern with the tonal and melodic design of each. Buoni in 1693, for example, sometimes repeated the opening melody at the end of the second section, creating a rounded binary form.

The saraband was mentioned in England as early as 1616 in plays of Ben Jonson. Numerous examples began to appear around the mid-17th century, often as the concluding movement in a suite; they include works by William Lawes, John Jenkins, Matthew Locke, Charles Coleman, Simon Ives (i), Mace, Blow, Purcell, Croft and others. Mace described sarabands as being of the 'shortest triple-time' (*Musick's Monument*, London, 1676/*R*1958, p.129), which corresponds with Ricci's suggestion for the tempo of Italian sarabandas. The slower French type, however, also became popular in England and was perhaps introduced by the Italian guitarist Corbetta, who was in France by 1656 and in England by 1662. One of his sarabands played a prominent role in a scandalous adventure and was so popular that all the guitarists at the English court were playing it (Anthony Hamilton's memoirs of Count Gramont). An English keyboard manuscript from the late Baroque period (*F-Pc* Rés.1186*bis*) included some sarabandes entitled 'slow sar.'. Tomlinson (*The Art of Dancing*, London, 1735/*R*1970, i) showed a saraband in 3/4 marked 'slow' (see illustration) and one in 3/2 marked 'very slow' (pl.6). Grassineau's dictionary of 1740 describes the motions of the saraband as slow and serious.

Sarabandes are not numerous in Spanish sources. Gaspar Sanz and Lucas Ruiz de Ribayaz continued the guitar tradition, with the title *zarabanda francese* probably having the same meaning it had for Italian guitar composers. French influence is seen in a keyboard piece, *Zarabanda francesa despacio*, in Martín y Coll's collection (*E-Mn* 1357); similarly, Santiago de Murcia (1714) labelled a guitar composition *Zarabanda despacio*.

(ii) France and Germany. French sarabandes were usually solo instrumental pieces or orchestral accompaniments for stage dancing. There are solo sarabandes for lute (by Ennemond and Denis Gaultier, and Jacques Gallot (ii)), clavecin (Pinel, René Mésangeau, Chambonnières, Louis Couperin, Lebègue, d'Anglebert, Louis Marchand, François Couperin, Rameau), viol (Marais), and guitar (de Visée, François Campion), and orchestral sarabandes occur in the manuscript collection at Kassel (transcr. Ecorcheville, *Vingt suites d'orchestre du xviie siècle français 1640–1670*, Paris and Berlin, 1906/*R*1970), and in ballets and operas by Lully, Lalande, Collasse, La Coste, Campra, Destouches and Rameau. A slow tempo and the rhythm of ex.4*a* were generally favoured, but several other types existed, both slow and fast. French sarabandes could be marked 'grave' (Marais, 1701, or François Couperin), 'adagio' (an operatic example from 1743 in *F-Pn* Vm⁷3644), or 'lentement' (d'Anglebert, 1689, pr. in HAM, no.232), 'tendrement' (La Coste, in *F-Pn* Vm⁷3644), 'doux' or 'gracieusement' (Rameau), 'légèrement' (Lalande orchestral suites of 1727 in *F-Pn* Vm⁷3077), and even *Sarabande en canarie* (presumably fast) (*F-Pn* Vm⁶5). Feuillet (*Recueil de dances*, 1700/*R*1968) has a *Sarabande pour femme* or *pour homme* in 3/4 metre and a *Sarabande espagnole pour homme* in 6/4. The rhythm of ex.4*b* also occurred, but in France it may not necessarily have implied a fast tempo. The *Sarabande italienne* from *Vingt suites d'orchestre* begins with this rhythm plus a two-beat anacrusis (in contrast to the dotted second-beat beginnings of most of the sarabandes in the collection), but is notated in 3/2 instead of the usual 3/4.

French sarabandes are usually in two sections, with a wide variety in the number of bars in each. Many, however, have eight bars in the opening section, 12 or 16 in the second. Often a *petite reprise* occurs at the end, an exact or slightly varied repetition of the last four bars of the piece (sometimes marked 'piano' in German and Italian sources). Occasionally a rondeau form exists (*F-Pn* Vm⁷675, 6296, 3077) and in a few cases a text is present (*F-Pn* Vm⁷675, 3077). Although often occurring at the end of a large group of pieces in the same key, French sarabandes are not associated closely with other dances in suites. Sometimes one is immediately followed by a *double* incorporating more intricate instrumental figuration (see GMB, no.218). The grand type of late French Baroque sarabande is illustrated by ex.7 (which comes, however, from a manuscript that uses Italian titles). The same heavily accented second beats and majestic rhythm are customary also in the contemporary French CHACONNE, *passacaille* (see PASSACAGLIA) and folia. Another Paris manuscript (*F-Pn* Vm⁷ 3555, dated 1712) includes *Les folies d'Espagne en sarabande*, and Taubert in *Rechtschaffener Tanzmeister* (1717) described the folia tune as 'the most

Melody, and choreography in dance notation, for a slow saraband from 'The Art of Dancing' (1735) by Kellom Tomlinson

Ex.7 *Sarabanda*, opening section, *F-Pn* Vm⁷ 741

famous of all sarabande melodies'.

Although earlier German sarabandes of Hammer-schmidt (1636) and Rosenmüller (1654) seem to be the faster type, most later 17th- and early 18th-century German sarabandes were performed slowly and gravely, as described by Walther (*WaltherML*). Sarabandes occur as solo instrumental works for keyboard, violin or lute, or as continuo chamber pieces. Some of the composers are Alessandro Poglietti, J. E. Kindermann, J. C. Kerll, Froberger (see GMB, no.205), Kuhnau, J. C. F. Fischer, Matthias Weckmann, the Muffats, J. A. Reincken, the Schmelzers, Biber, Esias Reusner (see GMB, no.216), J. C. Pezel, Hieronymus Gradenthaler, Jakob Scheiffelhut, R. I. Mayr, J. J. Walther (see GMB, no.239), Böhm, Pachelbel (see HAM, no.250), Handel and J. S. and J. C. Bach. The German sarabande was almost always incorporated into a unified suite, which emerged during the late years of the Baroque period with the standard order of movements: allemande, courante, sarabande and gigue.

(*iii*) *19th and 20th centuries.* Auber included a sarabande in his opera *Les diamants de la couronne* (1841). In the late 19th and early 20th centuries, the form gained in popularity, appearing in instrumental works by Debussy (*Pour le piano*, *Images*, i: 'Hommage à Rameau'), Satie (*Trois sarabandes*), Busoni (*Sarabande und Cortège* op.51), Saint-Saëns, Reynaldo Hahn, Albert Roussel, Germaine Tailleferre and Henry Brant (*Two Sarabandes for Keyboard*, 1931).

BIBLIOGRAPHY

R. Stevenson: 'The First Dated Mention of the Sarabande', *JAMS*, v (1951), 29

D. Devoto: 'La folle sarabande', *RdM*, xlv–xlvi (1960), 3–43, 145–80; see also *RdM*, xlvii (1961), 113

R. Stevenson: 'The Sarabande: a Dance of American Descent', *Inter-American Music Bulletin*, xxx (1962), 1

——: 'The Mexican Origins of the Sarabande', *Inter-American Music Bulletin*, xxxiii (1963), 7

——: 'Sarabande', *MGG*

——: 'Communication', *JAMS*, xvi (1963), 110

D. Devoto: 'Encore sur "la" sarabande', *RdM*, l (1964), 175–207

——: '¿Qué es la zarabanda?', *Boletín interamericano de música* (1965), no.45, p.8; (1966), no.51, p.3

——: 'De la zarabanda à la sarabande', *RMFC*, vi (1966), 27–72

K. H. Taubert: *Höfische Tänze* (Mainz, 1968)

R. Hudson: 'The *Zarabanda* and *Zarabanda Francese* in Italian Guitar Music of the Early 17th Century', *MD*, xxiv (1970), 125

RICHARD HUDSON

Saraceni, Francesco Maria (*b* Rome, 19 April 1911; *d* Cologne, 15 Jan 1961). Italian choral conductor and composer. He was a composition pupil of Di Donato and Casella at the Conservatorio di S Cecilia, also studying the piano, viola and organ at the Accademia. Afterwards he studied early music and Gregorian chant at the Pontificio Istituto di Musica Sacra, Rome, in which city he became organist of the National Argentinian Church, of the Cappella Farnesiana and of the Jesuit church. In addition he was in charge of the second choir and organ for important ceremonies at St Peter's. In 1950 he conducted at the Farnesiana a series of concerts of 14th- to 16th-century music, and after this he founded the Complesso Madrigalistico Luca Marenzio. He made international tours with this group and in 1953 they won a Grand Prix du Disque for a programme of late Renaissance Italian madrigals. In 1951 he founded a Rome university choir which, under the later direction of Razzi and Agostini, took the name of its founder. His works include a requiem and other liturgical works, some of them published by De Santis.

GIANCARLO ROSTIROLLA

Saracinelli, Ferdinando (*b* Orvieto, *c*1590; *d* ?Florence, *c*1640). Italian poet and opera librettist. He was a Knight of Volterra, a member of the Knights of St Stephen and confidential steward of Cosimo II and Ferdinando II, Grand Dukes of Tuscany. He was superintendent of court music and wrote the librettos for two stage works by Francesca Caccini, the *Ballo delle zigane* (1615; music lost, but the text survives) and the opera *La liberazione di Ruggiero* (1625). He also wrote the texts of madrigals, ballettos, *invenzioni* and other theatrical entertainments set to music by Peri and Lorenzo Allegri. Cesare Tinghi, the Florentine court diarist, reported in 1614 that Saracinelli danced in a work whose text he had written. Tinghi also named him as the musical overseer of the 1624 performances of Marco da Gagliano's opera *La Regina Sant'Orsola*.

BIBLIOGRAPHY

A. Solerti: *Musica, ballo e drammatica alla corte medicea dal 1600 al 1637* (Florence, 1905/R1968)

CAROLYN RANEY

Saracini, Claudio (*b* Siena, 1 July 1586; *d* ?Siena, after 1649). Italian composer, singer and lutenist. He was of noble birth and came of a musical family, one of the most distinguished in Siena. He was also called 'Il Palusi', which was probably the name by which he was known in an academy, though which academy he belonged to is not known. In the dedication of his *Seconde musiche* (1620) he stated that from his youth he had travelled through many foreign countries: since he dedicated a song in his *Musiche* (1614) to the Duchess of Brunswick it may be assumed that Germany was one of these countries, and since some of his strophic songs seem to have been influenced by Balkan folk music, countries in south-east Europe may have been among the others. He knew aristocratic and other eminent figures in Italy: for example, dedicating his *Quinte musiche* (1624) to the Archbishop of Bologna, he explained how he wrote its contents at the archbishop's residence at Frascati and that they had often been sung by order of the archbishop's sister, the Duchess of Ruffano, and he dedicated his *Seste musiche* (1624) to Prince Alfonso d'Este of Modena. Among several individual songs in the first three books of *musiche* inscribed to other dedicatees is a fine madrigal at the head of the second book, *Udite, lagrimosi spirti d'Averno*, dedicated to Monteverdi, whom he may also have met.

Saracini is an outstanding example of the cultivated nobleman who had no need to fear comparison with professionals in practising his chosen art. Given the size, range and quality of his output, he may be ranked with Sigismondo d'India as one of the two finest composers of monody in Italy in the heyday of the genre in the early 17th century. Except for three duets and three theorbo pieces in his 1614 book and a brief three-part 'chorus' at the end of his *Sospirava e spargea* [*Lamento della madonna*] all his surviving music is monodic; including the lament, 129 solo songs are extant and all of them except the Latin *Stabat mater* are settings of Italian words, ranging from famous texts of the time such as *Udite, lagrimosi* to simple little poems that are otherwise unknown and may have been written specially for him. He embraced every kind of solo song of his day, from long recitatives and ariosos (the *Lamento della madonna, Stabat mater* and *Lassa, chi mi consola*) through madrigals, both chromatic (*Cruda mia Filli*) and diatonic (*O chiome erranti*), and settings of sonnets and ottavas to little strophic songs, both relatively serious (*Crudel, tu vuoi partire*) and artlessly charming (*Pallidetta qual viola*). There are excellent pieces in every group. He was a master of declamation, responding at his best at once expressively and scrupulously to the text, and he supported his flexible vocal line with bold harmony and a strong bass. Such music may well owe something to Monteverdi; the madrigal dedicated to Monteverdi and the three long recitatives, in which interest is sustained in masterly fashion, are fine examples. Ex.1, from the opening of *Cruda mia Filli*,

Ex.1

demonstrates in extreme form Saracini's penchant for wayward tonality, unusual intervals and surprising juxtapositions of chords (which are not always obvious from the almost unfigured basses); the effect, as perhaps here, is sometimes one of bizarre wilfulness betraying the hand of the dilettante, but there can be no doubt in such passages of his intense response to emotive words. *Tu parti, ahi lasso* is another remarkable song of this type, with no central tonality but with much detailed word-painting; a sense of overall form is sacrificed to the expression of the individual moment. It is no accident that the madrigal poet whom he seems to have set most often was Marino, whose erotic and highly charged verses allowed him to indulge his evident passion for such settings.

On the other hand there can be no gainsaying the success and charm of several of Saracini's strophic songs, which show a very different side of his talent: two contrasting representative pieces are *Più lieto il guardo*, with its strong tonal feeling and sense of form, and *Pallidetta qual viola*, which, though barred in duple time, in effect consists simply of four symmetrical phrases in 5/4 time; this is a good example of the songs of Saracini that were possibly influenced by folk music and is perhaps the most engaging of all his strophic pieces.

WORKS

Le musiche … madrigali & arie, 1–2vv, bc (Venice, 1614); also includes 3 pieces for theorbo [i]
Le seconde musiche, 1v, bc (Venice, 1620/R1933) [ii]
Le terze musiche, 1v, bc (Venice, 1620) [iii]
Le quatre musiche, lost
Le quinte musiche, 1v, bc (Venice, 1624) [v]
Le seste musiche, 1v, bc (Venice, 1624) [vi]

NON-STROPHIC SONGS
(all for 1v, bc)

A Dio, Lidia, a Dio (F. Hondedei), v; Ahi, che veggio, ahi, che sento (Hondedei), vi; Ahi, chi mi fà languire, vi; Ahi, trista e dura sorte ('Ardito Accademico Felice'), vi; Alma afflitta, che fai (Marino), iii; Al partir del mio sole, iii; Ama ch'i t'amo, ò Filli, iii; Amorose dolcezze, vi; Andianne a premer latte (Marino), iii; Anime pellegrine che bramate, iii; Ardo mia vita (Hondedei), vi; Aspra fu la ferita, ii
Ben mio, dammi il tuo core, ii; Canto dolce e soave (P. Capello), i; Come esser può che senza vita, iii; Come viver poss'io, iii; Cor mio, deh non languire (Guarini), ii; Cor mio, deh non piangete, ii; Crud'Amarilli (Guarini), i; Cruda mia Filli, iii
Da te parto, cor mio, ii; Deh, come invan chiedete (Guarini), i; Deh, rimirate, amanti, vi; Dolce de miei desiri, v; Dolcissimo tesoro, ii; Dono, Licori, a batto, i; Ecco l'hora, v; Ecco misero core, vi; Egra langue colei, v
Ferite, feritemi, donna (Hondedei), v; Feritevi, ferite, viperette mordaci, i; Ferma, le piante, i; Filli, un bacio ti chiesi, vi; Fuggi, fuggi, ò mio core (Marino), iii; Già mi rubasti il core, i; Giunto è par, Lidia (Marino), ii; Habbi musica bella, v; Hor che morir ti miro, iii
In quel gelato core (Marino), vi; Intenerite voi, donne e donzelle, ii; Io moro, ecco ch'io moro (Marino), i; Io parto, ahi dipartita, v; Io parto, sì, ma parte meco (Marino), vi; Io senze fede, vi; Ite, amari sospiri, ii; La mia donna, il mio sole (Hondedei), v; Lamento della madonna [see Sospirava e spargea]; Langue a'l vostro languir (Guarini), v; Lassa, chi mi consola, v; Lasso, perche mi fuggi, ii, transcr. in Haas; Legami il core, iii; Lidia, ti lasso, iii
Messaggier di speranza, i; Mi sento, oimè, morire, i; Mori, mi dice, v; O carta avventurosa, iii; Occhi della mia vita, iii; Occhi specchi del core, vi; O chiome erranti (Marino), iii; O Laurinda, v; O quante volte, o quante, i; O rimembranza amara (F. Rasi), i; O vita, ò cara vita, vi
Pallidetto mio sole (Marino), vi; Pargoletta è colei ch'accende, i; Partire, oime, partire, v; Parto ò non parto, i; Perche credi, ò mio core, iii; Per questa vita giuro, iii; Poiche l'alma ne gita, vi; Poi che mori dicesti, v
Se la doglia e'l martire (Marino), ii; Se tu mi lasci, perfida, iii; S'io non ti toglio un bacio, vi; Sono rose e viole, v; Sospirava e spargea [Lamento della madonna], ii, with 3vv; Sospir che del bel petto (Marino), v; Spenta è la fè, iii; Stabat mater, iii
Tacerò si, ben mio, i; Tempesta di dolcezza (Marino), i; Tornate, o cari baci (Marino), vi; Tornate, pur, tornate, v; Tra le pompe di morte, ii; Troppo è ver che il mio cor, v; Tu brami, o bella Clori, v; Tu mi distrigni il core, vi; Tu parti ahi lasso (Marino), vi, transcr. in Ambros (every f'♮ in vocal line should be f'♯); Tu parti, anima mia, vi; Tu parti a pena giunto (Guarini), ii; Tutti à l'armi d'amore, iii
Udite, lagrimosi spirti d'Averno (Guarini), ii, transcr. in Haas; Udite, ò ninfe, vi; Vita mia, di te privo, iii; Voi che l'anima mia, i

STROPHIC SONGS
(all for 1v, bc, unless otherwise indicated)

Ahi, serpentella, iii; A'la luce, a la mia candida Aurora, vi; Ama pur, ninfa gradita, iii; Angioletta Leggiadretta, v, transcr. in Ambros; Bellissima Dori, ii; Care gioie, Che le noie, iii; Cedea la notte ai matuttini albori, i; Con guancia intenerita, iii; Correte voi, lacci e catene, vi; Crudel, tu vuoi partire, ii
Damigella Tutta bella (Chiabrera), 2vv, bc, i; Dispiegate, Guancie amate (A. Cebà), 2vv, bc, i; Gioite di mille tormenti, vi; Giovinetta Vezzosetta, i; Hormai la nott'in giro, ii; Ingrata, lusinghera, v; Leggiadra pastorella, iii; Non fuggir, Fillide bella, i; Non più strali pungenti, vi; Non vuoi ch'io t'ami (A. Ginori), vi
O donzella Tutta bella, i; Pallidetta qual viola (G. F. Ferranti), vi; Perfido amore, iii; Più lieto il guardo, iii; Poiche vol'amor, vi; Questa mia Aurora, 2vv, bc, i; Quest'amore, ii; S'altr'in amar, vi; Se pietade in te, vi; Sorgendo l'alba, iii; Sprezzami, bionda (Ferranti), v; Strane guise d'amar, iii

Tu mi lasci, cruda (Bonardo), vi; Vaga e lucente, ii; Vaghi rai, lucenti stelle (Rinuccini), i; Vezzosa pargoletta, ii, transcr. in Ambros; Voglio il mio duol scoprir (Ferranti), v; Vio mi dite ch'io non v'ami, vi

BIBLIOGRAPHY
R. Morrocchi: *La musica in Siena* (Siena, 1886/R1969), 97
A. W. Ambros: *Geschichte der Musik*, iv (Leipzig, rev. 3/1909 by H. Leichtentritt), 816ff
B. Szabolcsi: *Benedetti und Saracini: Beiträge zur Geschichte der Monodie* (diss., U. of Leipzig, 1923)
R. Haas: *Die Musik des Barocks* (Potsdam, 1928), 50, 53ff
S. A. Luciani: 'Claudio Saracini', *Musica d'oggi*, xv (1933), 348
——: *La musica in Siena* (Siena, 1942), 51ff
M. F. Bukofzer: *Music in the Baroque Era* (New York, 1947), 29ff, 66
B. Szabolcsi: *A melódia története* (Budapest, 1950; Eng. trans., 1966 as *A History of Melody*), chap.5
N. Fortune: 'Italian Secular Monody from 1600 to 1635: an Introductory Survey', *MQ*, xxxix (1953), 171
——: *Italian Secular Song from 1600 to 1635: the Origins and Development of Accompanied Monody* (diss., U. of Cambridge, 1954)
J. Racek: *Stilprobleme der italienischen Monodie* (Prague, 1965)
N. Fortune: 'Solo Song and Cantata', *NOHM*, iv (1968), 160, 175, 183, 201, 212
D. Arnold and N. Fortune, eds.: *The Monteverdi Companion* (London, 1968), 120, 194, 204
J. Racek: 'Die dramatisierende Funktion der Pause in der italienischen Vokal- und dramatischen Musik des 17. Jahrhunderts', *Musicae scientiae collectanea: Festschrift Karl Gustav Fellerer* (Cologne, 1973), 463

NIGEL FORTUNE

Saradzhev [Saradzhian], Konstantin (*b* Derbent, 8 Oct 1877; *d* Erevan, 22 July 1954). Armenian conductor and violinist. He graduated from Hřimalý's violin class at the Moscow Conservatory in 1898, then taught the violin at the Moscow Synodal School and gave solo recitals. In 1900 he had lessons with Ševčík in Prague. From 1901 he was conductor of the Moscow Opera Lovers' Club and at the same time he formed a string quartet. Having decided to devote himself to conducting, he studied with Nikisch in Leipzig (1904–8). After his return to Moscow, he conducted the Sokolniki summer symphony concerts in 1908 and 1910–11. He proved to be a persuasive advocate of new music by young composers; he conducted the first performances of Myaskovsky's symphonic poem *Silence* and of Prokofiev's *Autumn Sketches* and Piano Concerto no.1 (with the composer as soloist). In 1909 Saradzhev was one of the founders of the Evenings of Contemporary Music, and in 1923 he organized the chamber concerts of the Association for Contemporary Music. Saradzhev had an excellent conducting technique, with a clear beat, and the ability to imbue the orchestra with his own artistic ideals. He was professor of the conducting class at Moscow Conservatory (1922–35) and then returned to Armenia as musical director and principal conductor of the Erevan Opera and Ballet Theatre. As principal conductor of the Armenia Philharmonia (1941–4) he popularized the works of young Armenian composers. From 1939 to his death he was director of Erevan Conservatory, where he taught the orchestra, opera and conducting classes. He was made a People's Artist of the Armenian SSR in 1945; a volume of his collected articles and reminiscences was published in Moscow in 1962.

I. M. YAMPOL'SKY

Sárai, Tibor (*b* Budapest, 10 May 1919). Hungarian composer. He studied composition with Pál Kadosa and has held appointments as secretary-general of the Hungarian Musicians' Union (1948), head of the music department at the Ministry of Culture (1949), head of the Hungarian Radio music department (1950–53), teacher at the Budapest Conservatory (1953–9), professor at the Budapest Academy of Music (from 1959) and secretary-general of the Association of Hungarian Musicians (from 1959). In addition, he is on the executive committee of the International Music Council. He received the Erkel Prize in 1959 and the Kossuth Prize in 1975.

Sárai has done important work not only as a composer but as a leader of Hungarian musical life. For a long time he devoted his energies to teaching and administration, and it was only at the end of the 1950s that he found an individual style, which has since crystallized. The First String Quartet (1958) and, even more, the oratorio *Változatok a béke témájára* ('Variations on the theme of peace', 1961–4) were turning-points in his development away from an earlier folkloristic tendency. These and later works show a striking professionalism of finish and, in the case of the oratorios, a humanist attitude. The Symphony no.2 is interesting for its 'inverse' scheme: the four-movement work is in variation form, but the theme is disclosed only at the end in a soprano solo. Another outstanding later work is *Musica per 45 corde*, in which Sárai, a former violinist, explored string sounds with great plasticity and intensity.

WORKS
(*selective list*)

Orch: Serenade, str, 1946; Tavaszi Conc. [Spring conc.], 1955; 2 syms., 1965–7, 1972–3; Musica per 45 corde, 1970–71; Sym. no.2, S, orch, 1972–3
Choral: Falrairók [Party workers], unacc., 1958; Változatok a béke témájára [Variations on the theme of peace], oratorio, 1961–4; Októberi magyar hangok – 1917 [Hungarian voices in October – 1917], male vv, 1966–7; Jövőt faggató ének [Future questioning], A, Bar, male vv, orch, 1971
Solo vocal: De profundis, cantata, T, wind qnt, 1968; Diagnosis '69, T, orch, 1969
Chamber: Humoresque, va, pf, 1953; 2 str qts, 1958, 1971; Lassú és friss [Slow and quick], vn, pf, 1958; Qt, fl, str trio, 1961–2; Studio, fl, pf, 1964
Pf: Rondoletto, 1941; Sonatina, 1959; 8 Little Pieces, 1965

Principal publisher: Editio Musica

ANTAL BORONKAY

Sarajevo. City in Yugoslavia, capital of Bosnia and Hercegovina. The beginnings of organized musical life in Sarajevo coincided with the entry of the Austro-Hungarian troops into Bosnia and Hercegovina in 1878; previously, under Turkish occupation, the whole region had had a long period of cultural stagnation. The establishment of the Austro-Hungarian administration meant that musical links with the rest of the empire were initiated and that local talent was given new opportunities. The first attempt to create a choral society was made in 1879 and the first opera production took place in 1882, when the company of the Deutsches Sommer-Theater in Sarajevo gave a performance of Flotow's *Stradella*. After that opera performances were given mainly by visiting companies from Zagreb and Osijek.

Musical life intensified after World War I. The present building of the National Theatre was opened in 1921 (capacity 600); a permanent resident opera company was established in 1946 with an affiliated ballet company. The Sarajevska Filharmonija (Sarajevo Philharmonic Society), a concert-promoting organization, maintained a semi-professional orchestra between 1923 and 1941. In 1948 a fully professional state orchestra was formed, renamed Sarajevska Filharmonija in 1953. Radio Sarajevo, which started broadcasting in 1942 and was reconstituted in 1945, maintains its own symphony orchestra and a choir. The first private music school was opened in 1900. The regional music school, a recognized educational institution, was founded in 1920 and reconstituted in 1945; the academy of music was founded in 1955. As one of the federal capitals, Sarajevo is the seat of the Bosnian-Hercegovinian branch of the League of Yugoslav Composers and of the Association of Performing Artists.

BOJAN BUJIĆ

Sāraṅgī. A bowed chordophone occurring in a number of forms in the Indian subcontinent. It has a waisted body, a wide neck without frets and is usually carved from a single block of wood; in addition to its three or four playing strings it has one or two sets of sympathetic strings. The *sāraṅgī* originated as a folk instrument but has been used increasingly in classical music.

For a further discussion *see* INDIA, SUBCONTINENT OF, §§II, 6(i), VI, 1.

Sarasate (y Navascuéz), Pablo (Martín Melitón) de (*b* Pamplona, 10 March 1844; *d* Biarritz, 20 Sept 1908). Spanish violinist and composer. The son of a military bandmaster, he began to play the violin at the age of five and gave his first public performance when he was eight. His precocity aroused such interest that he received a private scholarship to study in Madrid with M. R. Sáez. Aided by Queen Isabella, the boy was sent to Paris in 1856 to study at the Conservatoire with Delphin Alard. He arrived well prepared and won the *premier prix* in violin and solfège the following year (1857); continuing his studies, he was awarded a prize in harmony in 1859. That year he began the concert tours which made his name famous in every country of Europe as well as in North and South America (1867–71 and 1889–90). His first appearance in London in 1861 did not attract much attention, but he returned in 1874, playing at a Philharmonic concert and at the Musical Union; other visits followed in 1877 (Crystal Palace) and 1878 (Philharmonic) and frequently afterwards. In 1885 and 1886 he performed at orchestral concerts conducted by Cusins and at the Birmingham Festival of 1885 he played the concerto written for him by Alexander Mackenzie. Sarasate attracted the admiration and friendship of many other famous composers who dedicated their works to him, including Bruch (Violin Concerto no.2 and *Scottish Fantasy*), Saint-Saëns (Concertos nos.1 and 3; *Introduction et Rondo capriccioso*), Lalo (Concerto in F minor and *Symphonie espagnole*), Joachim (Variations for violin and orchestra), Wieniawski (Concerto no.2), and Dvořák (*Mazurek* op.49). Sarasate incorporated all these works into his repertory and played them superbly. His success in the German-speaking countries, which began with his début in Vienna in 1876, was all the more remarkable since his style differed so radically from that of Joachim, Germany's undisputed master violinist. Occasionally, Sarasate's interpretation of the Beethoven concerto was compared unflatteringly with Joachim's (as in Berlin in the 1880s) which angered him greatly. In spite of his virtuoso inclinations, he was also a keen string quartet player, both privately and in public chamber music performances. He liked to play Brahms's string quartets but declined to perform his violin concerto.

Sarasate's playing was distinguished by a tone of unsurpassed sweetness and purity, coloured by a vibrato somewhat broader than usual at that time and produced with a 'frictionless' bow stroke. It was observed, however,

that his tone, while unfailingly beautiful, had little dynamic and emotional shading. His technique was superb, his intonation was perfect, especially in high positions, and his whole manner of playing was so effortless as to appear casual. In his *Memoirs*, Carl Flesch characterized Sarasate's playing by 'aesthetic moderation, euphony, and technical perfection . . . he represented a completely new type of violinist', though he might be criticized for a certain lack of emotional involvement. Sarasate also achieved some fame as a composer of virtuoso violin music. Best known among his 54 opus numbers are the *Zigeunerweisen* op.20 (1878), still an indispensable item in the virtuoso repertory, and the four books of *Spanische Tänze* (opp.21, 22, 23, 26) which make use of folk tunes in elegant arrangements. His fantasy on *Carmen* is ingenious and technically difficult, but his limits as an original composer are shown in such superficial pieces as the

'Arrangement in Black: Pablo de Sarasate': portrait (1884) by James Abbott McNeill Whistler in the Museum of Art, Carnegie Institute, Pittsburgh, Pennsylvania

Introduction et Tarantelle op.43. Sarasate bequeathed his two Stradivari violins to museums: his favourite (dated 1724) to the Paris Conservatoire and the other, the so-called 'Boissier' (1713), to the Madrid Conservatory.

WORKS

(selective list; all for vn, pf unless otherwise stated, several also orchd)

Prière et berceuse, op.17 (Paris, 1870); Zigeunerweisen, op.20 (Leipzig, 1878); Spanische Tänze, op.21 (Berlin, 1878), op.22 (Berlin, 1879), op.23 (Berlin, 1880), op.26 (Berlin, 1882); Caprice basque, op.24 (Leipzig, 1881); Jota aragonesa, op.27 (Leipzig, 1883); Sérénade andalouse, op.28 (Berlin, 1883); El canto del ruiseñor, op.29 (Berlin, 1885); Boléro, op.30 (Berlin, 1885); Muiñiera, op.32 (Leipzig, 1885); Navarra, 2 vn, pf, op.33 (Berlin, 1889); Airs écossais, op.34 (Berlin, 1892); Peteneras, op.35 (Berlin, 1894)

Jota de San Fermín, op.36 (Berlin, 1894); Adiós montañas mias, op.37 (Mainz, 1896); Viva Sevilla!, op.38 (Berlin, 1896); Zortzico, op.39 (Berlin, 1898); Introduction et fandango, op.40 (Berlin, 1898); Introduction et caprice-jota, op.41 (Leipzig, 1899); Miramar, op.42 (Leipzig, 1899); Introduction et tarantelle, op.43 (Leipzig, 1899); La chasse, vn, orch, op.44 (Leipzig, 1901); Nocturne-sérénade, vn, orch, op.45 (Leipzig, 1901); Barcarolle vénitienne, op.46 (Leipzig, c1902); Mélodie roumaine, op.47 (Berlin, 1901); Jota de Pamplona, op.50 (Leipzig, 1904); Rêve, op.53 (Leipzig, 1909)

Concert fantasies on Carmen, op.25 (Paris, ?1883); Der Freischütz (Paris, 1874); Don Giovanni; Faust (Paris, 1874); La forza del destino; Martha (Paris, 1876); Mireille; Roméo et Juliette; Zampa

BIBLIOGRAPHY

A. Moser: *Geschichte des Violinspiels* (Berlin, 1923, rev., enlarged 2/1966–7)

L. Zárate [pseud. of Y. Bourget]: *Sarasate* (Barcelona, 1945)

G. Woolley: 'Pablo de Sarasate: his Historical Significance', *ML*, xxxvi (1955), 237

A. Sagardia: *Pablo Sarasate* (Plasencia, 1956)

C. Flesch: *Memoirs* (London, 1957, 3/1974; Ger. orig., Freiburg, 1960, 2/1961)

BORIS SCHWARZ

Sardana (Sp., possibly from *cerdana*: 'native of Cerdana'). The national dance of Catalonia: an elegant and solemnly executed circle-dance performed to the music of the *cobla*, an ensemble traditionally consisting of *flaviol* and *tambor* (one-handed flute and drum), *tiple* and *tenora* (shawms), but now with more varied instrumentation including two cornets, *fiscorno* (flugelhorn), other brass instruments and string bass. Stylistically the music resembles that of Provence rather than other Spanish music. *See* SPAIN, §II, 7 (vii).

VÉRONIQUE NELSON

Sardena, Orazio (*b* c1550; *d* probably in Vienna, July 1638). Italian trumpeter and composer. He served as a brass player and in particular as a trumpeter first at the archducal court at Graz from 1569 to 1572, then for a short time in the household of Archbishop Wolf Dietrich at Salzburg and again from 1595 onwards at the court at Graz. In 1602 he wrote a *Magnificat*, now lost, for 33 voices. When in 1619 Archduke Ferdinand was elected emperor as Ferdinand II, Sardena followed him to Vienna with the rest of the Graz household. He was still named as a member of the Emperor Ferdinand III's court band in 1637, even though he had been granted a pension in 1622. He was a pupil of Simone Gatto, Kapellmeister of the Graz court, and a colleague of Annibale Perini; after their deaths he published a collection of 52 of their works, all but one of them motets (Venice, 1604, inc.).

BIBLIOGRAPHY

H. Federhofer: 'Graz Court Musicians and their Contributions to the *Parnassus musicus Ferdinandaeus* (1615)', *MD*, ix (1955), 170

——: *Musikpflege und Musiker am Grazer Habsburgerhof der Erzherzöge Karl und Ferdinand von Innerösterreich (1564–1619)* (Mainz, 1967)

HELLMUT FEDERHOFER

Sardi, Dorothea. *See* BUSSANI, DOROTHEA.

Sardi, Giuseppe. *See* SARTI, GIUSEPPE.

Sardinero, Vicente [Vincenzo] (*b* Barcelona, 12 Jan 1937). Spanish baritone. He studied at Barcelona and made his début there in 1964 as Escamillo in *Carmen*. In 1966 he won the international Verdi contest at Busseto, and the following year sang Ashton in *Lucia di Lammermoor* at La Scala. He then appeared at the Vienna Staatsoper and in 1969 sang with the American Opera Society, New York, as Valdeburgo (*La straniera*) and the London Opera Society, at Drury Lane, as Ernesto (*Il pirata*). He sings at the major opera houses of Europe and North and South America, and his repertory includes Mozart's and Rossini's Figaros, Sir Richard (*I puritani*), Alphonse XI (*La favorite*), Nottingham (*Roberto Devereux*) and several Verdi roles: Di Luna, Germont, Renato and Posa. He also sings Valentin (*Faust*), Albert (*Werther*) and Marcello (*La bohème*), his début role at Covent Garden (1976), though his smoothly produced, lightweight baritone is best suited to the music of Bellini and Donizetti.

ELIZABETH FORBES

Sardonius, Jean (*fl* 1607–29). South Netherlands composer and musician. He was succentor of the collegiate church of Notre Dame, Maastricht, on 27 June 1607 and may have been appointed as early as 30 October 1602. He was dismissed on 19 March 1608 'after various remarks and for other reasons'. He may have moved to Ste Gudule, Brussels: certainly a musician of this name was a bassoonist there between 1609 and 1614. According to Vannes, Sardonius became a musician at St Bavon, Ghent, on 15 November 1619. He published a collection of motets (now lost) for two to four voices and continuo, *Angelica musica pro praecipius festis totius anni et communi sanctorum* (Douai, 1629), and according to vander Straeten a lost six-part requiem and five-part mass were recorded in an inventory at Ste Walburge, Oudenaarde.

BIBLIOGRAPHY

E. vander Straeten: *La musique aux Pays-Bas avant le XIXe siècle*, i (Brussels, 1867/R1969), 218

A. Auda: *La musique et les musiciens de l'ancien pays de Liège* (Liège, 1930)

R. Vannes: *Dictionnaire des musiciens (compositeurs)* (Brussels, 1947)

JOSÉ QUITIN

Sardou, Victorien (*b* Paris, 5 Sept 1831; *d* Paris, 8 Nov 1908). French dramatist. The son of an impoverished schoolmaster, he started to train as a doctor but abandoned his studies and devoted himself to writing. Managers rejected his earliest plays, historical dramas in verse in the Romantic manner. His first success was *Les premières armes de Figaro* (1859), a *comédie-vaudeville* owing as much to Scribe as to Beaumarchais. It was with 'well-made' comedies such as *Pattes de mouche* (1860) that he established his reputation. He wrote many gay satirical comedies, e.g. *Famille Benoîton* (1865) and, in collaboration with Najac, *Divorçons* (1880); a staunch conservative, he also pilloried contemporary developments of which he disapproved, and certain political leaders of the day, e.g. in *Les femmes fortes* (1860) and *Rabagas* (1872). Probably inspired by the revivals of Hugo's dramas in the 1860s, Sardou turned in middle age to historical melodramas: *Patrie!* (1869), *La haine* (1874), *Théodora* (1884) and *La Tosca* (1887). In these plays he presented tense, tragic tales of human passion, usually set against the background of a war against an invader or of a popular rebellion, lavish in setting and archaeologically accurate. Some of his melodramas have modern settings, but exotic elements are usually incorporated; in *Fédora* (1882), for example, he presented a beautiful Russian princess involved in a wildly improbable conspiracy. Throughout his career he took pains to create roles for such stars as Virginie Déjazet and Sarah Bernhardt. He was one of the most regularly successful dramatists of his time, and his plays were popular in London as well as in Paris: *Robespierre* (1899) and *Dante* (1903) were written expressly for Irving. Sardou was elected to the Académie Française in 1878.

With his *comédies-vaudevilles* and later his 'well-made' comedies, Sardou may fairly be regarded as Scribe's natural successor. But unlike Scribe, he was not called on to write many librettos, and he achieved no real success as a librettist except in *Le roi Carotte* (1872), written for Offenbach. He took considerable interest in music, however, and was painstaking in his collaboration with Saint-Saëns on *Les barbares* (1901). Most of Sardou's plays required either songs or incidental music, sometimes on a lavish scale, and numerous composers wrote for them, including X. Leroux and Massenet (*Théodora*, 1884).

Composers were immediately attracted by the possibility of making operas of Sardou's melodramas. *Patrie!*, a stirring tale of the Dutch revolt against Spain, appealed to Verdi for a time. *Madame Sans-Gêne* (1893, written in collaboration with E. Moreau) was adapted to form the basis of an *opéra comique* by Giordano (1915) and of I. Caryll's operetta *The Duchess of Dantzic* (1903). Sardou collaborated with Illica and Giacosa on the indifferent rewriting of *La Tosca* for Puccini's *Tosca* (1900), and Colautti fashioned an eventful libretto out of *Fédora* for Giordano in 1898. Sardou's reputation as a dramatist was short-lived, and, like Scribe, he is now remembered mainly for his contribution to opera.

WORKS SET TO MUSIC
(*produced in Paris unless otherwise indicated*)

Piccolino (comedy, 1861; lib, 1869, collab. Lauzières; lib, 1876, collab. C. Nuitter): opera by Mme Frandval, 1869; Karneval in Rom, operetta by J. Strauss (ii), Vienna, 1873; opera by Guiraud, 1876
Les Prés-St-Gervais (vaudeville, 1862; lib, 1874, collab. P. Gille): opéra comique by Lecocq, 1874
La bataille d'amour (lib, 1863, collab. K. Daclin): opéra comique by Vaucorbeil, 1863
Don Quichotte (play, 1864; rev. 1895, collab. Nuitter): incidental music by A. Renaud, 1895
Le capitaine Henriot (lib, 1864, collab. G. Vaëz): opéra comique by Gevaert, 1864
Patrie! (drama, 1869; lib, 1874, d'Arenzio; lib, 1886, collab. L. Gallet): La contessa di Mons, opera by L. Rossi, Turin, 1874; opera by Paladilhe, 1886
Grisélidis: unfinished comic opera by Bizet, 1870–71
Le roi Carotte (lib, 1872): opéra bouffe by Offenbach, 1872
Les merveilleuses (comedy, 1873; lib, 1914, collab. P. Ferrier): operetta by H. Félix, 1914
La haine (drama, 1874): incidental music by Offenbach, 1874; Kordeliya, opera by N. Solov'yov, St Petersburg, 1885
Les noces de Fernande (lib, 1878, collab. Najac): opéra comique by Deffès, 1878; Der Bettelstudent, operetta by Millöcker
Fédora (drama, 1882): opera by Giordano, Milan, 1898
Théodora (drama, 1884; musical drama, 1907, collab. Ferrier): incidental music by Massenet, 1884; music by X. Leroux, Monte Carlo, 1907
Le crocodile (play, 1886): incidental music by Massenet, 1886
La Tosca (drama, 1887; lib, 1900, collab. Illica and Giacosa): opera by Puccini, Rome, 1900, and Paris, 1903
Cléopâtre (drama, 1890, collab. E. Moreau): incidental music by X. Leroux, 1890
Madame Sans-Gêne (comedy, 1893, collab. Moreau): The Duchess of Dantzic, operetta by I. Caryll, London, 1903; opera by Giordano,

New York, 1915; opera by E. Dłuski, c1920, not perf.; La maréchale Sans-Gêne, operetta by P. Petit, 1947; film music by Lavignano, 1962
Gismonda (drama, 1894): opera by H. Fevrier, Chicago, 1919
La fille de Tabarin (lib, 1901, collab. Ferrier): comédie lyrique by Pierné, 1901
Les barbares (lib, 1901, collab. P. Gheusi): operetta by Saint-Saëns, 1901
La sorcière (drama, 1903): incidental music by X. Leroux, 1903; opera by Frlanger, 1912
Fiorella (lib, 1905, collab. Gheusi): operetta by A. Webber, London, 1905

BIBLIOGRAPHY
J. A. Hart: *Sardou and the Sardou Plays* (Philadelphia, 1913)
G. Mouly: *La vie prodigieuse de Sardou* (Paris, 1931)
——, ed.: *Les papiers de V. Sardou: notes et souvenirs* (Paris, 1934)
P. Smith: *The Tenth Muse* (New York, 1970)

C. N. SMITH

Sargent, Sir (Harold) Malcolm (Watts) (*b* Ashford, Kent, 29 April 1895; *d* London, 3 Oct 1967). English conductor. His father, a coal merchant at Stamford, Lincolnshire, was also an organist and choirmaster. Sargent spent his youth in this typical English country town, absorbing Gilbert and Sullivan, learning the piano and the organ, and singing in his father's choir. He was hardworking as well as precocious; amateur music-making went hand in hand with a grounding in church musicianship. At the age of 16 he took the ARCO and became articled pupil to the organist at Peterborough Cathedral. He was appointed parish organist at Melton Mowbray in 1914, took the BMus (Durham) in the same year and a doctorate, after brief army service, in 1919.

The breakthrough to more than local celebrity came in 1921 with an invitation to conduct his own *Impression on a Windy Day* with Henry Wood's Queen's Hall Orchestra, first at Leicester, then at a Promenade Concert in London. With Wood's encouragement he began to concentrate on conducting. He joined the teaching staff of the RCM in 1923, and settled in London the following year. He became chief conductor of the Robert Mayer children's concerts in 1924, and musical director of the Courtauld–Sargent concerts in 1929. A serious illness in 1933–4 proved only a temporary interruption. He was involved from the beginning with the LPO which Beecham founded in 1932, and later toured with it during the Blitz. He was chief conductor of the Hallé Orchestra from 1939 to 1942, and of the Liverpool PO for six years after that. From 1950 to 1957 he was conductor of the BBC SO. He was chief conductor of the Promenade Concerts from 1948 until his death (though illness robbed him of what would have been his 21st season in 1967).

Orchestral work did not deflect him from the tradition on which he had been reared. Sargent was the outstanding British choral conductor of his time, unrivalled in his control of the customary massive forces. Choral singers gave him the unstinted devotion not always forthcoming from professional orchestral players, and he showed deeper involvement in the choral than in the instrumental works of the great Classical masters. He conducted the Royal Choral Society (including several seasons of the Albert Hall staging of Coleridge-Taylor's *Hiawatha*) for nearly a quarter of a century, and the Huddersfield Choral Society for even longer. He was much in demand in the north of England: at the Leeds Festival of 1931 he gave the first performance of Walton's *Belshazzar's Feast*. His prowess with large choirs is commemorated in many recordings.

Malcolm Sargent

Sargent's sporadic operatic experience included the first performances of three operas by Vaughan Williams, *Hugh the Drover* (British National Opera Company, 1924), *Sir John in Love* (1929) and *Riders to the Sea* (1937), both for the RCM, and one by Holst – *At the Boar's Head* (BNOC, 1925). At Covent Garden in 1954 he gave the première of Walton's *Troilus and Cressida*. He was an assistant conductor for the 1927 and 1928 London seasons of Dyagilev's Ballets Russes. His longest theatrical attachment was to the D'Oyly Carte company, which he conducted on several occasions from 1926 and with which he made a number of recordings of Sullivan's operettas.

Sargent made numerous tours overseas, as a guest conductor or at the head of British orchestras or choirs, in Europe, the USA, the USSR, the Near and Far East, South Africa and Australasia. He was content to be described as 'Britain's ambassador of music', and it is possibly as a supremely efficient and energetic populariver of music for listeners on many levels (children, Promenaders, the solid provincial audiences with which he never lost touch, crowned heads and gala assemblies at home or abroad), that he will be chiefly remembered. The personality – good looks, immaculate grooming, trim figure, punctilious attention to detail – was ideal for the job. He remained doggedly faithful to the standard Classics, to certain late Romantics (Dvořák and Sibelius among them), to Elgar, Vaughan Williams, Holst and Walton. In later years his interest in contemporary music hardly went further than Britten and Shostakovich, yet considering the radical nature of the changes, he adapted himself to the new Proms with considerable aplomb. Sargent was a fluent talker and a popular member of the wartime BBC Brains Trust. He was knighted in 1947, and received the gold medal of the Royal Philharmonic Society in 1959.

BIBLIOGRAPHY
T. Russell: *Philharmonic Decade* (London, 1945)
C. Reid: *Malcolm Sargent: a Biography* (London, 1968)
RONALD CRICHTON

Sárközy, István (*b* Pesterzsébet, 26 Nov 1920). Hungarian composer. He was a piano pupil of Lula Földessy-Hermann and from 1938 studied composition at the Budapest Academy of Music with Kodály, Farkas,

Szatmári and Viski. During the same period (1938–44) he earned his living as a statistician. In 1945 he became artistic leader of the youth organization at the academy, in 1947 secretary of the Bartók College and in 1950 music critic of the daily paper *Népszava*. He was a founder-member of the Hungarian Musicians' Association (1951) and in 1954 he was appointed artistic adviser to the National Philharmonic Concert Bureau and the Hungarian Recording Company. In 1957 he was made general editor of Editio Musica and in 1959 he was appointed to teach theory at the Budapest Academy of Music, subsequently teaching composition there.

Sárközy's first work of lasting value was the Concerto grosso of 1943, though during that decade his attention was directed mainly to songs and folksong arrangements. In the early 1950s music for the stage dominated his creative activity; his successful musical play *Szelistyei asszonyok* ('The women of Szelistye') received the Erkel Prize in 1952, and the next year he was awarded it again for his mass songs. The crowning work of this period was the chamber cantata *Júlia énekek* ('Julia songs', 1958), after which he composed little, until, in 1963, the Sinfonia concertante for clarinet and strings initiated a succession of major works. In 1975 Sárközy received the title Merited Artist of the Hungarian People's Republic.

WORKS
(selective list)

STAGE
Az új traktorállomás [The new tractor station] (dance play), 1949; Liliomfi (musical play, E. Szigligeti, D. Mészöly), 1950, rev. for television 1967; Szelistyei asszonyok [The women of Szelistye] (musical play, K. Mikszáth, A. Benedek, J. Semsey, E. Innocent Vincze), 1951; Pettyes (musical comedy, Gy. Sós), 1955; A cigány [The gypsy] (musical play, Szigligeti), 1958
Incidental music, film scores, folkdance plays

VOCAL
Choral: Óda Sztálinhoz (G. Képes), cantata, 1949; Ifjúság [Youth] (E. Sárközy), suite, 1952; Júlia énekek [Julia songs] (B. Balassi), cantata, T, vv, 4 insts, 1958; Reng már a föld [The earthquake approaches] (I. Raics), cantata, Bar, vv, 1958; Aki szegény [Who is poor] (József), rappresentazione profana, S, vv, 1967; Ypszilon-háború [Y war] (M. Vörösmarty), comedy in oratorio form, solo vv, 5vv, 8 insts, 1971
Songs with orch: Egy ismeretlen istennek [For a god unknown] (Steinbeck, trans. M. Benedik), B, orch, 1946; Munkások [Workers] (Rilke, trans. E. Várhelyi), B, orch, 1947; Vörös Rébék [Red Rebecca] (J. Arany), Mez, orch, 1947; Szivárvány havassán [On the snow-capped mountain], 17 folksong arrs., 1948; 2 Romanian, 2 Greek, 2 Bosnian and 2 Macedonian Folksongs, 1949; 12 Balkan Folksongs, S, chamber orch, 1949
Songs with pf: 3 Songs (Verlaine, trans. Z. Szabó, Richepin, Baudelaire, trans. M. Babits), 1947; 2 Hungarian Folksongs, 1953; 4 Hungarian Folksongs, 1955; 2 Songs (Walther von der Vogelweide, Blake, trans. Babits), 1956; 4 Songs (József), 1957; Színészdal [Actor's song] (Petőfi), 1963; Ballad and 3 Songs (A. Mezei), 1968; Sok gondom közt [In all my worries] (József), 21 songs, 1972
Songs with gui: 5 Songs (G. Hajnal), 1974

INSTRUMENTAL
Orch: Conc. grosso, 1943, rev. as Ricordanze I, 1969; Little Suite, 1951; Bulgarian Dance, children's orch, 1951; Fantasy and Dance, gypsy orch, 1952; Az if júsághoz [To youth], ov., 1953; Sinfonia concertante, cl, 24 str, 1963, 2nd version, cl, 24 str, 12 wind, 1964; Conc. semplice (Ricordanze II), A, vn, orch, 1973
Chamber: Sonata da camera, fl, pf, 1964; Ciaccona, vc, 1967; Chamber Sonata, cl, pf, 1969; Wind Qt (Psaume et jeu), 1970; 4 Etudes, cl, 1972; Ricordanze III, str qt, 1977
Pf: 12 Variations, 1945; 2 Pieces, 1947; Sonatina, 4 hands, 1950

Principal publisher: Editio Musica
For fuller list see *Contemporary Hungarian Composers* (Budapest, 3/1974), 137ff

MÁRIA PÁRKAI-ECKHARDT

Sarod. An Indian unfretted plucked lute derived from the west Asian RABĀB. It is smaller than the SITAR and has two resonating chambers, the larger usually covered with goatskin and the smaller with metal. There are six wire playing strings, which are plucked with a coconut-shell plectrum, and 12 to 15 *tarab* (sympathetic strings), which lie below the main strings. The performing practice is similar to that of the sitar. The *sarod* was introduced to the Western concert stage by the Indian artist and composer ALI AKBAR KHAN (*b* 1922).

For illustration *see* INDIA, SUBCONTINENT OF, fig.9.

Saron. A trough-resonated bronze metallophone; *see* INDONESIA, §§I, 2(ii); II, 1(i); III, 1(iii); and SOUTH-EAST ASIA, §II, 4(iii).

Sárosi, Bálint (*b* Csikrákos, 1 Jan 1925). Hungarian ethnomusicologist. He completed his education in Csikszereda (now Mercurea Ciuc, Romania), and took a doctorate in Hungarian and Romanian philology at Budapest (1948) and diplomas in musicology (1956) and composition (1958) at the Budapest Academy, where his teachers included Kodály, Bartha, Szabolcsi and Szervánszky. After working from 1958 in Kodály's group for folk music research at the Hungarian Academy of Sciences he became director (1974) of the folk music department of the Institute for Musicology at that academy. He did fieldwork also in Ethiopia (1965) and Armenia (1972) and has lectured at many international conferences; he has done outstandingly important research in instrumental folk music.

WRITINGS

Die Volksmusikinstrumente Ungarns, Handbuch der europaischen Volksinstrumente, ed. E. Emsheimer and E. Stockmann, I/i (Leipzig, 1967)
'The Music of Ethiopian Peoples', *SM*, ix (1967), 9
'Gypsy Musicians and Hungarian Peasant Music', *YIFMC*, ii (1970), 8
Cigányzene [Gypsy music] (Budapest, 1971; Eng. trans., rev., 1978; Ger. trans., 1977)
'Instrumentalensembles in Ungarn', *Studia instrumentorum musicae popularis*, ed. E. Stockmann, ii (Stockholm, 1972), 116
Zenei anyanyelvünk [Our own musical vernacular] (Budapest, 1973)
'Instrumentale Volksmusik in Ungarn', *Studia instrumentorum musicae popularis*, ed. E. Stockmann, iv (Stockholm, 1976), 115

LUJZA M. TARI

Sarrette, Bernard (*b* Bordeaux, 27 Dec 1765; *d* Paris, 11 April 1858). French musical administrator, founder of the Paris Conservatoire. He held various administrative posts in the French Guards, and was later made a captain in the National Guard (13 July 1789), where he was responsible for the training of musicians. This new body of military musicians took part in various public ceremonies until 4 May 1790, when it was taken over by the city of Paris; it then took part in the first great civic festivities, particularly in the transference of Voltaire's ashes to the Panthéon (11 July 1791). In order to produce new recruits for the band and to increase its size, Sarrette drew up a plan for a school of military music, which was put into effect on 9 June 1792. 120 pupils, sons of soldiers serving in the National Guard, were granted free tuition; in return, the pupils and their teachers were called on to 'provide music for the National Guard and at public festivities'. Thus the first school for wind instrument players was established in France. A decree of 8 November 1793 transformed it into the Institut National de Musique; as such it participated still more fully in public festivities.

From 25 March to 10 May 1794 Sarrette was in prison because of an unreliable denunciation; in 1795 he was in trouble with the Committee of Public Safety. In the meantime the Institut was growing, admitting more pupils, offering more subjects and, for the first time, being given an administrative framework. This provided the basis for the founding of the Conservatoire, officially set up by a decree of 3 August 1795, a few days after a speech by Marie-Joseph Chénier; Sarrette was entrusted with its organization on 23 October. He set up the library and museum of the Conservatoire in 1798. Until the second Restoration, Sarrette's life was very unsettled. He repeatedly offered to relinquish his post, but was confirmed in it until finally he resigned in 1816.

BIBLIOGRAPHY

C. Pierre: *B. Sarrette et les origines du Conservatoire National de Musique* (Paris, 1895)
J. Tiersot: 'Les origines du Conservatoire', *Le ménestrel*, lxi (1895), 31

FRÉDÉRIC ROBERT

Sarro [Sarri], Domenico Natale (*b* Trani, Apulia, 24 Dec 1679; *d* Naples, 25 Jan 1744). Italian composer. His marriage contract dated 6 February 1705 states that he came to Naples between the ages of six and seven, that he had studied at the Neapolitan conservatory S Onofrio, and that he had not been outside the city since. His first known composition is a sacred opera, *L'opera d'amore*, performed in 1702 at the Arciconfraternità della Ss Trinità de' Pellegrini. In 1703 he took part in a public competition (the other competitors being Gaetano Veneziano, Cristoforo Caresana and Francesco Mancini) for the vacant post of court *maestro di cappella*. Veneziano obtained the post, but on 26 December 1704 Sarro was appointed *vicemaestro di cappella*.

During 1706 and 1707 Sarro composed several operas for the Neapolitan public theatres. Between 1708 and 1718, however, he wrote few works of this kind: this may partly have been because of changed circumstances at court. In mid-1707 the Austrians captured Naples and drove out the Spanish regime to which Sarro had pledged allegiance. Both he and Veneziano lost their court appointments on 31 August 1707. There is no evidence from Neapolitan sources that the new Austrian government put Sarro back on its payroll before 1720, so the statement in the Venetian libretto of his intermezzo *Barilotto*, performed in Venice in 1712, that he was 'Maestro nella Real Cappella di Napoli' is almost certainly false.

Sarro's promise as a dramatic composer began fully to materialize in 1718. Between this date and 1741 he composed many operas, of which the earlier ones (i.e. those produced between 1718 and c1725) constitute perhaps his most significant contribution to music. *Didone abbandonata* (Naples, 1724) is particularly important because it is the first setting of Metastasio's first major libretto. In 1720 Sarro was promised two important musical posts when they became vacant. The first was that of *maestro di cappella* to the city of Naples, which he obtained in 1728 on the death of the holder, Gaetano Greco. The second was that of *vicemaestro di cappella* to the court; to help the composer until he actually occupied this post, the viceroy awarded him a salary of 22½ ducats a month. He became *vicemaestro*, with a stipend of 30 ducats a month, in late October 1725, and he remained in the service of the court for the rest of his life. In 1735 he took over the duties, though not the title, of *maestro di cappella* at court when the holder of the post, Mancini, fell ill. When Mancini died in September 1737, Sarro was appointed his successor with a monthly salary of 35 ducats. One of his first tasks was to compose the opera for the official opening of the Teatro S Carlo, newly erected by order of Charles III. The opera was *Achille in Sciro*, given on 4 November 1737, Charles's name day. After 1741, the year of the production of his final opera, *Ezio*, he composed nothing of importance.

Sarro was one of the first prominent composers to emerge from the Neapolitan conservatories during the 18th century. By choosing to confine his activities largely to Naples, he acquired only moderate fame abroad during his lifetime. Commentators have since tended to regard him as a transitional composer in between more important generations of Neapolitans represented on the one hand by the much older Alessandro Scarlatti and on the other by Porpora, Vinci, Leo, and other composers slightly younger than himself. His personal contribution to the important changes in musical style and technique that became apparent in Italian vocal music about 1720 has usually been underrated. Describing these changes in his *General History of Music* (1789), Burney gave credit for them to Vinci, mentioning Sarro only briefly in this context. J. J. Quantz, after hearing Sarro's opera *Tito Sempronio Gracco* in Naples in 1725, declared that the composer was copying Vinci's style. Because of statements like these, Sarro has usually been considered an imitator rather than innovator.

Sarro's earliest music is in the quasi-contrapuntal style associated with Alessandro Scarlatti, though it lacks the nervous energy characteristic of Scarlatti's best work. By 1718, however, Sarro was feeling his way toward a new manner of writing. His musical textures had become less contrapuntal and his melodies more shapely as regards phrase structure and pitch. By about the time of his *Valdemaro* (1726) he had developed a style in which all the musical interest is in the top melodic part and the lower parts of the texture are reduced to mere accompaniment. These are the changes in compositional method with which Burney credited Vinci. Sarro's relationship to Vinci has yet to be fully examined, but there is no present evidence that Vinci was more progressive than Sarro during the period 1718–23 when Sarro was the fashionable composer in Naples. By about 1726, however, Vinci had become prominent, and Sarro's period of greatest success was over. It thus seems that the period around 1720 was the one when Sarro made his most constructive contribution. Very few of his works written after 1730 survive. Those that do lack signs of major technical advance; they lack too the freshness that had made some of his earlier music attractive. By the end of the 1730s his music was generally thought dull and unfashionable. Charles de Brosses, who heard the 1739 Neapolitan revival of his opera *Partenope* (1722), called him 'knowledgeable but cold and sad'. The Minister Ulloa, responsible for recommending the revival of *Partenope* to the king, who did not like the work, afterwards had to excuse himself: 'The composer Sarro has always been a most celebrated man. It is true however that he flourished in a bygone age'. He promised the king to see to it that the composer's next work, a *festa teatrale* called *Le nozze di Teti e Peleo* (1739), had music better suited 'to the grandeur of the joyous day and to good modern taste'.

WORKS

STAGE

(*all heroic operas; first performed in Naples, unless otherwise stated*)
Add. arias in T. Albinoni's La Griselda (Zeno, rev. C. de Petris), S

Bartolomeo, sum. 1706
Candaule Re di Lidia (A. Morselli), Fiorentini, Oct 1706
Le gare generose tra Cesare e Pompeo, S Bartolomeo, ?1706, *I-Mc*, *Nc*, *US-Wc*
Il Vespasiano (G. C. Corradi, rev. de Petris), S Bartolomeo, 1707, *I-Nc*
Amore fra gli impossibili (G. Gigli), Fiorentini, 1707
Barilotto (intermezzi, F. Salvi), Venice, S Angelo, aut. 1712
I gemelli rivalli (N. Serino), Fiorentini, 13 Feb 1713, ?*Me*
Il comando non inteso ed ubbidito (N. Giuvo), Fiorentini, 15 May 1713
Armida al campo (F. Silvani), S Bartolomeo, 13 Feb 1718, *D-ROu*, modern copy *US-Wc*
La fede ne' tradimenti (Gigli), S Bartolomeo, 15 May 1718
Arsace (A. Salvi), S Bartolomeo, 10 Dec 1718, *I-Mc*, *Nc*
Alessandro Severo (Zeno), S Bartolomeo, 14 May 1719
Ginevra Principessa di Scozia (A. Salvi), S Bartolomeo, 20 Jan 1720, *Nc*
Lucio Vero (Zeno rev.), S Bartolomeo, Jan 1722, *Nc*
La Partenope (S. Stampiglia), S Bartolomeo, Dec 1722, with Eurillo e Beltrammo (intermezzi), *A-Wgm*, *I-Nc*, modern copy *US-Wc*
Didone abbandonata (Metastasio), S Bartolomeo, 1 Feb 1724, with Dorina e Nibbio (intermezzi), *I-Nc*; rev. Venice, S Giovanni Grisostomo, aut. 1730, *Nc*
Tito Sempronio Gracco (Stampiglia), S Bartolomeo, Jan 1725, *Nc*
Il Valdemaro, Rome, Delle Dame, carn. 1726, *Nc*
Siroe Re di Persia (Metastasio), S Bartolomeo, 25 Jan 1727, with Moschetta e Grullo (intermezzi), *Nc*
Artemisia (G. Migliavacca), S Bartolomeo, 7 Jan 1731, with La furba e lo sciocco (intermezzi), *Nc*
Berenice, Rome, Argentina, carn. 1732, *Nc*
La finta pellegrina (comic, F. Lucano Cinnéo), Nuovo, carn. 1734, collab. A. Orefice
Demofoonte (Metastasio), S Bartolomeo, Jan 1735, Act 1 only; collab. F. Mancini and L. Leo, intermezzi by G. Sellitto
Gli amanti generosi (comic, T. Mariani), Fiorentini, 15 May 1735
Fingere per godere (comic, Mariani), Nuovo, spr. 1736
Alessandro nell'Indie (Metastasio), S Bartolomeo, 4 Nov 1736
La Rosaura (comic, G. A. Federico), Fiorentini, wint. 1736
Achille in Scio (Metastasio), S Carlo, 4 Nov 1737, *Nc*
Intermezzo for wedding of Infante Filippo, Madrid, 1739
Ezio (Metastasio), S Carlo, 4 Nov 1741

OTHER WORKS

Sacred operas and oratorios: L'opera d'amore, Naples, Arciconfraternità della Ss Trinità de' Pellegrini, 1702; Partenope liberata per patrocinio della Vergine Addolorata (N. Giuvo), Naples, Sept 1704; Il fonte delle grazie, Naples, Congregazione dei dottori, Chiesa dei Gerolamini, 20 Nov 1706; L'andata di Gesù al Calvario (G. B. Caputo), Naples, oratory of S Gaetano, Chiesa di S Paolo, 1708; Oratorio per la festività di S Gaetano, Naples, Congregazione degli orefici, Chiesa di S Paolo, 1712; Ester reparatrice, Naples, Congregazione di S Maria del Rimedio, Chiesa della Ss Trinità degli Spagnuoli, 1724; S Ermenegildo, Rome, Seminario Romano, 1725; Gesù adorato dei re magi, Genoa, 1737, collab. F. Feo, lib in Collegio Rolandi, Rome; La Passione di Gesù Cristo Signor nostro (Metastasio), Bologna, Congregazione di S Filippo Neri, 1738
Occasional works, all perf. in Naples: Serenata a 3vv [characters Amore, Eco, Narciso], palace of the Duke d'Alvito, 8 Sept 1708, on the conquest of Sardinia; Serenata a 3vv [characters Giunone, Imeneo, la Notte], May 1709, on wedding of D. d'Andrea; Serenata a 3vv (G. G. Alberghetti), 21 Jan 1716, on wedding of Prince of Montaguto; Il gran giorno d'Arcadia (serenata), Royal Palace, May 1716, on birth of Archduke Leopold, ?same as Rida il mar (serenata), *GB-Lbm*, *Lcm*; La gara della Virtù e della Bellezza (cantata), 3vv, 1718, on wedding of Duke of Seminara; Serenata a 4vv, Royal Palace, 1718, for Contessa Daun Viceregina; Scherzo festivo fra le ninfe di Partenope (D. Gentile), Royal Palace, 28 Aug 1720, on birthday of the Empress; Serenata a 6vv, 28 Jan 1721, on wedding of Prince della Rocca; Endimione (serenata, Metastasio), 4vv, 30 May 1721, on wedding of Prince of Belmonte; Il Florindo (favola boschereccia), 1725, on wedding of Duke of Canzaro; Le nozze di Teti e Peleo (serenata, Giuvo), Royal Palace, 20 Dec 1739, on marriage of Infante Filippo in Madrid; Serenata, Oct 1741, on visit of Ottoman Ambassador; Serenata, 1742 [not perf.], on birth of Princess Maria Giuseppa of Naples, collab. L. Leo; Cantata a 3vv [characters Deliso, Eurilla, Fileno], n.d., for wedding of Marchese d'Arena, *I-Nc*; Serenata a 3vv [characters Niso, Egle, Eurilla], n.d., *Nc*
5 choruses in Massimini (tragedy, A. Marchese), 1v, insts (Naples, 1729)
Mass, *D-B*; 3 Kyrie-Gloria, *Dlb*; Lyra sonus et cithera, motet, *GB-Ob*; Te Deum, *I-Nf*; Gradual, 4vv, *Nf*
Concerto, fl, insts, *Nc*

BIBLIOGRAPHY

BurneyH
C. A. De Rosa (Marchese di Villarosa): *Memorie dei compositori del regno di Napoli* (Naples, 1840)
F. Florimo: *La scuola musicale di Napoli e i suoi conservatorii*, iii (Naples, 1883)

502   Sarrusophone

B. Croce: *I teatri di Napoli* (Naples, 1891)
U. Prota-Giurleo: *Breve storia del teatro di corte e della musica a Napoli nei secoli xvii–xviii* (Naples, 1952)
H. Hucke: 'La "Didone Abbandonata" di Domenico Sarri nella stesura del 1724 e nella revisione del 1730', *Gazzetta Musicale di Napoli*, ii (Nov–Dec 1956), 180; Ger. trans., 'Die beiden Fassungen der Oper "Didone Abbandonata" von Domenico Sarri', *GfMKB, Hamburg 1956*, 113
U. Prota-Giurleo: 'Domenico Sarro', *Archivi*, xxvi (1959), 73
H. Hucke: 'Die neapolitanische Tradition in der Oper', *IMSCR, viii New York 1961*, 253
M. F. Robinson: *Naples and Neapolitan Opera* (Oxford, 1972)
MICHAEL F. ROBINSON

Sarrusophone. A brass instrument of conical bore, played with a double reed. It was designed in 1856 by Sarrus, a bandmaster in the French army, and initially manufactured by the Paris firm of Gautrot. The inventor's scheme comprised instruments ranging in pitch from soprano to contrabass, although his contrabass models were to some extent anticipated by Stehle of Vienna in 1835, who brought out a contrabassoon in brass with simple fingering; Stehle's model had been further developed by Červený of Hradec Králové and Mahillon of Brussels and came to be generally known as the *contrabasse-à-anche*. But to Sarrus belongs the credit of designing a whole family of double-reed instruments as possible substitutes for the oboes and bassoons in military bands. The objection that has been raised to them is that they fail to produce the delicate and distinctive qualities of the wooden double-reed instruments; their tone, in fact, somewhat resembles that of the saxophones, though it is a little thinner and more incisive.

The complete family of sarrusophones comprises the sopranino in E♭, soprano in B♭, alto in E♭, tenor in B♭, baritone in E♭ (see illustration), bass in B♭, contrabass in E♭, and also contrabasses in C and B♭. All these have a compass from a whole tone below the pitch note to a 6th above its double octave, just like the saxophones. Like the latter they are transposing instruments, so that this compass is written in each case in the treble clef, from b♭ to g′′′; the C contrabass sarrusophone is an exception, its part being written an octave higher than actual pitch, like double-bass parts. In keywork and fingering as well, they all closely resemble the saxophone. The tube of all but the two smallest sizes is bent back upon itself to reduce it to a convenient length. On the bass and contrabasses the tube is bent back three times; even so the contrabass in B♭ stands 132 cm tall. The reeds resemble bassoon reeds and vary in size according to each instrument's pitch; that of the contrabass has blades over 4 cm long and 2·5 cm wide across the tip.

The only sarrusophone used in the orchestra is the contrabass, which made its first appearance at the Exposition Universelle (Paris, 1867), when no contrabassoon could be procured for Saint-Saëns' *Les noces de Prométhée*. The composer was impressed with the new instrument and afterwards used it in many of his works, though the scores and parts retain the traditional heading 'contrebasson'. Massenet used it in his *Esclarmonde* (1889), and was so pleased with it that (according to Pierre) he increased its part for future performances. Gounod and Widor both wrote testimonials for the contrabass sarrusophone in the trade catalogue of Couesnon & Cie (Gautrot's successors). After that it had a long spell of employment in various Paris (and Spanish) orchestras, though it has since lost ground to

contrabassoons built on Heckel's model. Its long use in Paris accounts for its occasional appearance in the scores of Delius (e.g. *Eventyr*) and of Ravel (e.g. *Rapsodie espagnole*). Some French players use a single-reed mouthpiece of the saxophone type with the contrabass sarrusophone.

Military bands tried out the entire family of sarrusophones at the time of its novelty, but soon began to dispense with the smaller members. Sir Thomas Beecham used a bass as well as a contrabass in his experimental wind orchestra (his 1944 book immortalized the sarrusophone with an account of its participation in his 1908 performance of Holbrooke's *Apollo*

Baritone sarrusophone in E♭ by Gautrot, Paris, late 19th century (Spencer Collection, Brighton Museum)

and the Seaman). In the USA E♭ contrabass sarruso-phones were manufactured by C. G. Conn Ltd (Elkhart, Indiana) and were used by some American bands during the 1940s. In Italy, baritone, bass and contrabass sarrusophones figured in band arrangements published by Ricordi in 1927, and some of these instruments may still be seen in the larger municipal bands. In Paris the Garde Républicaine has used a contrabass in C with an enlarged bore. One of the last bands to employ the smaller sizes was the Fanfare la Sirène of Paris, a brass band. About 1925 it included nearly every member of the family; later it included soprano, alto and contra-bass, the first two being allotted the oboe and cor anglais solos in transcriptions of orchestral scores.

BIBLIOGRAPHY

C. Pierre: La facture instrumentale à l'Exposition universelle de 1889 (Paris, 1890)

Occasional Notes, MT, liii (1912), 715

R. Leruste: 'Le sarrusophone', EMDC, II/iii (1927), 1665

T. Beecham: A Mingled Chime: Leaves from an Autobiography (London, 1944)

D. J. BLAIKLEY/ANTHONY C. BAINES

Sarti, Giovanni Vincenzo (b S Agata, ? nr. Urbino; fl 1643–55). Italian composer. He was director of music at Forlì Cathedral in 1643; in 1648 he occupied a similar post at Ravenna Cathedral but had returned to his former one at Forlì in 1655. His output consisted of sacred music, with a leaning typical of its date towards small-scale textures with few voices and continuo. His first four collections of motets are all lost. The last one (1655) shows how the style of motets for few voices had matured by the mid-17th century. There is a wider range of keys and a more definite feeling of modulation; continuo parts are more profusely figured with 6-3 chords and 7–6 and 7–6–5 progressions rather than with the ubiquitous 4–3 suspensions of earlier years. The gradually increasing distinction between recitative and aria in opera is paralleled in his motets, which have recitative-like 4/4 sections and triple-time arioso with varied rhythms.

WORKS

(all published in Venice)

[17] Concerti sacri, 2, 4, 6vv, bc (org), libro V, op.8 (1643)

Letanie, 8vv, bc (org), op.9 (n.d.)

[12] Salmi, 3vv, con un Dixit, Magnificat, e messa, 4vv, bc (org), op.10 (1648)

Concerti sacri, 2, 3vv, bc (org), con 2 litanie della beata virgine, 4vv, bc (org) ... libro VI, op.11 (1655)

Salmi vespertini, F-Pn

BIBLIOGRAPHY

J. L. A. Roche: North Italian Liturgical Music in the Early 17th Century (diss., U. of Cambridge, 1968)

JEROME ROCHE

Sarti [Sardi], Giuseppe (b Faenza, baptized 1 Dec 1729; d Berlin, 28 July 1802). Italian composer. He was a leading figure in late 18th-century opera.

1. LIFE. He was the seventh of 11 children of a jeweller who was also a violinist. He began his musical education with Valotti in Padua and, at the age of ten, went to study with Padre Martini in Bologna. He was organist of Faenza Cathedral from 1748 to 1752, when he accepted the directorship of the theatre in Faenza, for which he wrote his first opera, Pompeo in Armenia. Its success resulted in a commission for an opera to be performed at Carnival 1753 at the Teatro S Moisè, Venice; this work, Il re pastore, was also a triumph.

Late in 1753 Sarti conducted Pietro Mingotti's opera troupe when it visited Copenhagen. His talent and per-

Giuseppe Sarti: portrait by an unknown artist in the Civico Museo Bibliografico Musicale, Bologna

sonality won him the admiration of King Frederik V, who in 1755 nominated him to succeed Scalabrini as court Kapellmeister. Later he became director of the Italian Opera at Copenhagen. He continued to compose opere serie and may also have written a Danish opera (Gram og signe, 1757). When in 1763 the Italian Opera was closed Sarti became director of court music; in this position he had the opportunity to compose instrumental works. In 1765 the king sent Sarti back to Italy to engage singers for the proposed reopening of the Opera; but the king died, and Sarti remained in Italy for the next three years. From 19 May 1766 to 11 September 1767 he was maestro di coro at the Pietà conservatory in Venice. During this time he composed several serious works as well as his first comic opera, La giardiniera brillante. On his return to Copenhagen in 1768 he resumed the post of director of the royal chapel and became the new king's singing teacher. From 1770 to 20 May 1775 he directed the court theatre for which he wrote both Italian and Danish works. While in Copenhagen he married Camilla Passi, by whom he had two daughters. In 1775 he was dismissed after siding with the wrong party in a series of political intrigues, and returned to Italy.

In 1779 he entered a competition (against, among others, Paisiello) to become maestro di cappella of Milan Cathedral. His victory and the success of his Le gelosie villane at La Scala greatly increased his reputation and won him many pupils, including Cherubini. During these years Sarti created a series of works that were extremely popular throughout Europe and brought his fame to its zenith; these included, besides Le gelosie villane (1776), the comic opera Fra i due litiganti (1782) and the opere serie Medonte (1777) and Giulio Sabino (1781). In 1782 the Grand Duke Paul of Russia heard his *Alessandro e Timoteo* at Parma and suggested to Catherine II that he might succeed Paisiello as director of the imperial chapel. The empress extended the invitation and in 1784 he left Italy for St Petersburg, stopping in Vienna where he was graciously received by Joseph II and given the proceeds of a performance of *Fra i due litiganti* which had gained great favour there. He met Mozart who played to him and spoke of him as an honest, good man. Mozart later quoted the theme of 'Come un agnello' from *Fra i due litiganti* in *Don Giovanni* and based a set of keyboard variations on it (though their authenticity has been questioned). Sarti seemed unable to understand Mozart's quartets dedicated to Haydn and in his *Esame acustico fatto sopra due frammenti di Mozart* he pointed out numerous 'barbarisms' and concluded with Rousseau's words 'de la musique pour faire boucher les oreilles'.

In St Petersburg Sarti was showered with honours and under his direction the Italian Opera reached an artistic peak. His outstanding works of this period were the comic opera *I finti eredi* (1785) and the *opera seria Armida e Rinaldo* (1786). He also wrote French and German works and even collaborated with Pashkevich and Canobbio on a Russian opera, *Nachal'noye upravleniye Olega* ('The early reign of Oleg', 1790). This work, which was the sensational event of the season and remained in the repertory for the next five years, was based on a libretto by Catherine II, who supervised the production herself. For the empress's choir Sarti composed two Russian oratorios, a *Te Deum* to celebrate the taking of Ochakov by Potemkin and a requiem in memory of Louis XVI. Court intrigue involving the famous mezzo-soprano Todi sent Sarti into seclusion in a village in the Ukraine given him by Prince Potemkin. There he founded a singing school which later produced some important singers. In 1793 the empress restored him to favour and appointed him director of a conservatory modelled on those in Italy, a position he retained for the rest of his stay in Russia. While there he invented a machine for counting the vibrations of sounds, and thereafter he established a pitch standard for the St Petersburg orchestras ($a' = 436$). In 1801, after the death of the emperor, he decided to return to Italy. He broke his journey at Berlin to visit one of his daughters who was married to the queen mother's Kapellmeister, Natale Mussini. He died there and was buried in the Hedwigkirche.

2. WORKS. The quality of Sarti's theatre works does not justify the popularity they enjoyed. Technical skill and musical inventiveness are evident, but these features rarely coincide with dramatic inspiration. In his arias the melodic style is often pedestrian, and the harmonies are for the most part conventional and slow-moving. He was progressive in his use of form, and the da capo aria appears seldom in his works; in his serious operas he sometimes used written-out *ABA* forms or a short binary form corresponding to the *A* section of the da capo, but he preferred a composite slow–fast structure in which the second section takes on the character of a cabaletta. The through-composed arias that abound in the comic operas, and are sometimes found in the *opere serie*, also frequently end with a fast section. Sarti was at his best in accompanied recitative. Some of these, such as the prison scene in *Giulio Sabino*, are highly developed and involve several characters in dramatic action: the harmonies are rich, the instruments comment

with expressive solo passages, and the string tremolo is used with an emotional significance anticipating Romantic orchestral usage. In general, Sarti's orchestration is flexible and effective. Ensembles and choruses are rare in the serious works, except *Alessandro e Timoteo*, written in 1782 for the court of Parma, which was traditionally French in its taste. On the other hand, very varied ensembles abound in the comic works which are musically fluid and inventive though the music does not always conform with the sense of the words. Della Corte accurately evaluated the music of *Fra i due litiganti* when he described it as 'merely linear, instrumental and rhythmic; it does not correspond to the situation'.

Probably the most curious of Sarti's works is his Russian opera *The Early Reign of Oleg*, in which he attempted to imitate the style of the ancient Greeks. The fifth act, in which the Greek emperor entertains Oleg at Constantinople with a performance of Euripides' *Alcestis*, is a play within a play. The long introduction (probably written by the famous actor and Greek scholar Nicholas Luov) describes how Sarti set the choruses to Greek modes and rhythms, with the accompaniment of flute to represent the tibia; he left the solo passages to be declaimed with interjections by harp and pizzicato violins representing the lyre of the ancients. While his interest in Greek music neither appeared again in his own works nor influenced other composers of the time, the use of Russian subject matter and folk music in this opera foreshadows the later Russian national opera. Sarti also wrote a considerable amount of sacred music which reflects an admirable technical mastery in its effective combination of contrapuntal church style with the dramatic devices of the opera.

For a scene from *Giulio Sabino*, see OPERA, fig.3.

WORKS
STAGE

CC – *Copenhagen, Christiansborg Court*
CK – *Copenhagen, theatre on Kongens Nytorv, later Kongelige Danske Skueplads (1771) and Kongelige Teater (1772)*
PH – *St Petersburg, Hermitage Theatre*
VS – *Venice, S Samuele*
dg – *dramma giocoso*
dm – *dramma per musica*

Pompeo in Armenia (dm, 3, ? B. Vitturi), Faenza, Accademia dei Rimoti, carn. 1752
Il re pastore (dm, 3, Metastasio), Venice, S Moisè, carn. 1753
Vologeso (dm, 3, Zeno: Lucio Vero), CK, carn. 1754; rev. or reset, Venice, 1765, *P-La*
Antigono (dm, 3, Metastasio), CK, 14 Oct 1754, with some arias by others; rev. or reset, Verona, 1765, *La*
Ciro riconosciuto (dm, 3, Metastasio), CK, 21 Dec 1754; pubd without recit. (Copenhagen, 1756)
Arianna e Teseo (dm, ? P. Pariati), CK, carn. 1756
Anagilda (dm, G. Gigli), CK, aut. 1758, *S-Skma*
Armida abbandonata (dm, L. de Villati), CK, 1759
Achille in Sciro (dm, 3, Metastasio), CK, 1759
Andromaca (dm, 3, Zeno), CK, aut. 1759/60
Filindo (pastorale eroica, 3, P. d'Averara), CK, 1760
Astrea placata (festa teatrale, 1, Metastasio), CK, 17 Oct 1760
Nitteti (dm, 3, Metastasio), CK, 12 Oct 1760; rev. or reset, Venice, 1765, *A-Wn*, *P-La*, excerpts *GB-Lbm*
Issipile (dm, 3, Metastasio), CK, aut. 1760/1
Alessandro nell'Indie (dm, 3, Metastasio), CK, 1761; rev. or reset, Padua, 1766, *P-La* (2 copies)
Semiramide (dm, 3, Metastasio), CK, aut. 1762; rev. or reset, Venice, 1768, *La* (2 copies)
Didone abbandonata (dm, 3, Metastasio), CK, wint. 1762, MS in Royal Theatre Archives, Copenhagen
Narciso (dramma pastorale, 3, Zeno), CK, carn. 1763
Cesare in Egitto (dm, 3, G. Bussani), CK, aut. 1763, *D-Bds*
Il naufragio di Cipro (dramma pastorale, 3, P. A. Ziani), CK, Jan/spr. 1764
Il gran Tamerlano (tragedia per musica, 3, A. Piovene), CK, early 1764
Ipermestra (dm, 3, Metastasio), Rome, Argentina, carn. 1766; *GB-Lbm*
La giardiniera brillante (intermezzo, 2 pts.), Rome, Valle, 3 Jan 1768, *I-*

Gi(l)
L'asile de l'amour (dramatic cantata, Deschamps, after Metastasio), CC, 22 July 1769 [perf. before La double méprise]
La double méprise, ou, Carlile et Fany (comédie mêlée d'ariettes, 1, Deschamps), CC, 22 July 1769
Soliman den Anden [Soliman II] (syngespil, 3, C. D. Biehl, after Favart), CK, 8 Oct 1770, DK-Kk (2 copies)
Le bal (opéra comique, Deschamps), CC, 1770
Il tempio d'eternità (festa teatrale, 1, Metastasio), CK, 1771
Demofoonte (dm, 3, Metastasio), CK, 30 Jan 1771, Kk
Tronfølgen i Sidon [The succession to the throne in Sidonia] (lyrisk tragi-comedia [syngespil], 2, N. K. Bredal, after Metastasio: Il re pastore), CK, 4 April 1771; rev., not by Sarti, 1778, Kk
Il re pastore (dm, 3, Metastasio), CK, 1771 [not 1753 work of same name]
La clemenza di Tito (dm, 3, Metastasio), Padua, Obizzi, June 1771
Deucalion og Pyrrha (syngespil, 1, C. A. Thielo and Bredal, after G. F. Pouillain de Saint Foix), CK, 19 March 1772
Aglae, eller Støtten [Aglae, or The column] (syngespil, 1, C. Fasting and A. G. Carstens, after L. Poinsinet de Sivry), CC, 16 Feb 1774
Kierlighedsbrevene [Love letters] (syngespil, 3, Biehl, after Boissy), CC, 22 March 1775
Farnace (dm, 3, A. M. Lucchini), VS, Ascension 1776
Le gelosie villane [Il feudatario] (dg, 3, T. Grandi), VS, Nov 1776, A-Wgm, D-Bds, F-Pn (2 copies), GB-Lcm, I-Fc; rev. in 2 acts, St Petersburg, 1785, USSR-Ltob
Ifigenia (dm, 3), Rome, Argentina, carn. 1777, F-Pn, I-Bc, P-La
Medonte Re di Epiro (dm, 3, G. de Gammerra), Florence, Pergola, 8 Sept 1777, GB-Lbm, P-La; Naples, 1783, F-Pn, I-Nc, P-La, US-Bp; Naples, 1792, GB-Lcm; also A-Wgm (2 acts), I-Fc (2 acts), Mc
Il militare bizzarro (dg, 2, Grandi), VS, 27 Dec 1777, F-Pc, US-Wc
Olimpiade (dm, 3, Metastasio), Florence, 1778, P-La
Scipione (dm, E. Giunti), Mestre, Casa Balbi, aut. 1778, F-Pn, I-Fc, P-La (2 different settings)
I contratempi (dg, N. Porta), VS, Nov 1778, F-Pn, I-Fc, US-Wc; rev., not by Sarti, as Die Zwischenfälle, Dresden, 1782; as Gli equivoci svelati, Vicenza, 1786
Adriano in Siria (dm, 3, Metastasio), Rome, Argentina, 26 Dec 1778, F-Pn (Act 1), USSR-Ltob
L'ambizione delusa (intermezzo, 2 pts.), Rome, Capranica, Feb 1779
Mitridate a Sinope (dm, 3), Florence, Palla a Corda, aut. 1779, F-Pn
Achille in Sciro (dm, 3, Metastasio), Florence, Pergola, aut. 1779, I-Fc (2 acts)
Siroe (dm, 3, Metastasio), Turin, Regio, 26 Dec 1779, duet, 3 arias GB-Lbm
Giulio Sabino (dm, 3, P. Giovannini: Epponina), Venice, S Benedetto, Jan 1781 (Vienna, c1781); also perf. as Epponina, in 2 acts
Demofoonte (dm, 3, Metastasio), Rome, Argentina, carn. 1782 [not 1771 work of same name]
Didone abbandonata (dm, 3, Metastasio), Padua, Obizzi, June 1782, F-Pn, I-Gi(l), P-La [not 1762 work of same name]
Alessandro e Timoteo (dm, 3, G. della Torre di Rezzonico), Parma, Court, 6 April 1782, B-Bc, D-SWl, F-Pn (2 copies), I-Bc, Nc, PAc
Fra i due litiganti il terzo gode (dg, Goldoni: Le nozze), Milan, La Scala, 14 Sept 1782, A-Wn, F-Pn (autograph), I-Fc, PAc, P-La (2 acts); also as I pretendenti delusi (2), Venice, 1782, USSR-Ltob; as Im Trüben ist gut Fischen, Hamburg, 1785, D-Bds; as Le nozze di Dorina, Naples, 1784; as I rivali delusi, London, 1784; as Dorina contrastata, I-Nc; in Fr., Paris, n.d.
Attalo Re di Bitinia (dm, 3, A. Salvi), Venice, S Benedetto, 26 Dec 1782
Idalide (dm, 3, F. Moretti), Milan, La Scala, 8 Jan 1783, D-SWl, F-Pn; also as La vergine del sole, Pisa, 1792
Erifile (dm, 2), Pavia, carn. 1783, F-Pn
Il trionfo della pace (dm, 2, C. Oliveri), Mantua, Ducale, 10 May 1783
Olimpiade (dm, 3, Metastasio), Rome, Dame, 1783, GB-Lbm (Acts 1, 2), US-Wc [not 1778 work of same name]
Gli amanti consolati (dg, 2), St Petersburg, 1784; D-SWl, F-Pn, GB-Lbm, I-Fc, FZc (autograph), USSR-Ltob
I finti eredi (opera comica, 2, G. Bertati), St Petersburg, Kamennïy, 30 Oct 1785, A-Wn, ?D-Dlb, F-Pn, I-Mr, USSR-Ltob (autograph)
Armida e Rinaldo (dm, 2, ? M. Coltellini), PH, 26 Jan 1786, A-Wgm, Wn, B-Bc (Act 2), F-Pn (2 copies), D-SWl, I-Fc, Nc, USSR-Ltob (autograph)
Castore e Polluce (dm, 2, Moretti, after P. J. Gentil-Bernard), PH, 3 Oct 1786, F-Pn
Zenoclea (azione teatrale, 2 pts., Moretti), 1786, not perf.
Alessandro nell'Indie (dm, Metastasio), Palermo, S Cecilia, wint. 1787 [not 1761 work of same name]
Cleomene (dm, 3, De Gamerra), Bologna, Zagnoni, 27 Dec 1788
Nachal'noye upravleniye Olega [The early reign of Oleg] (Russ. opera, 5, Catherine II), PH, 26 Oct 1790; collab. V. Pashkevich and C. Canobbio
Il trionfo d'Atalanta (occasional work), 1791, no known perf.
Andromeda (dm, Moretti), PH, 4 Nov 1798, I-Fc, FZc (Act 1, auto-

graph)
Enea nel Lazio (dm, 2, Moretti), St Petersburg, Kamennïy, 26 Oct 1799, FZc (autograph)
La famille indienne en Angleterre (opera, 3, Marchese di Castelnau, after Kotzebue), St Petersburg, Kamennïy, 1799, FZc (autograph), USSR-Ltob
Les amours de Flore et de Zéphire (ballet anacréontique, 2, P. Chevalier), Gatchina, 19 Sept 1800

(doubtful)
Gram og signe (Bredal), Copenhagen, 1757 [uses arias by Sarti]; La figlia ricoperata [La buona figliuola putta], 1765, D-Bds; Mitridate, Parma, 1765 [cited only in Fétis]; La calzolaia di Strasburgo, ? Modena, 1769; La contadina fedele, Vienna, 1772 [also attrib. Dittersdorf]; L'avaro, Faenza, 1777, or Mantua, 1791; Amore e matrimonio, ?PH, ?1786 [unknown to Mooser]; Lo stravagante inglese, Ancona, 1792; Les indiens et l'anglaise, 1794 [not by Sarti, a confusion with La famille indienne en Angleterre, 1799]

OTHER SECULAR VOCAL
I dei del mare, cantata, 3vv, 1776, D-Mbs
L'amor della patria figurato nella partenza d'Ulisse dall'isola di Calisso, 3vv, Padua, April 1779, I-Fc
Cantata pel giubileo dell'Arcivescovo Conte Nazari di Calabiana, 1779, I-Md
Adieux de la reine de France à sa prison du Temple, 1v, pf, FZc
Inno, 6 solo vv, orch, D, for coronation festivities of Paul I, 1797, FZc (autograph)
Il genio della Russia (Moretti), cantata, 5 solo vv, chorus 4vv, orch, for coronation festivities of Paul I, 1797, FZc (autograph)
Coro per l'incoronazione, 1v, chorus, orch, 1798
Epitalamio, 4 solo vv, orch, 1799, FZc (autograph)
Cantata, 3 solo vv [Giove, la Gloria, Marte], chorus 4vv, 2 orchs, Russ. hns, cannons, FZc (autograph)
Cantata, 3 solo vv [Doride, Nereo, Glauco], orch, FZc (pt.1)

SACRED VOCAL
Masses: 1, GB-T; 8vv, for Milan competition, 1779, I-Md; 4vv, Fc; 2, 4vv, orch, D-Mbs; Messa votiva, 4vv, d, 1783, I-Md; 2 messe brevi, 4vv, org, Md, 3vv, org, G, FZc (autograph)
Mass movements: Kyrie (fugue), 8vv (Leipzig, 1806); 2 Kyrie–Gloria, 4vv, insts, D-Bds (autograph); 8vv, org, A-Wgm; 3 Kyrie 2 choirs, orch, c, 2 choirs, 2 orch, g, 2 choirs, 2 orch, 2 org, G, all I-FZc (autograph); 13 Gloria, I-Md; 3 Gloria, 5vv, orch, Fc, 3vv, F-Pc, 4vv, orch, G, I-FZc (autograph); Credo pieno e breve, 8vv, G, Md; Credo, 4vv, insts, A-Wn, I-Nc
Requiem: 4vv, orch, FZc (autograph); 4 solo vv, chorus 4, 5vv, orch, org, for Louis XVI, 1793; for the Grand Duke of Württemberg, 1798; Missa pro defunctis, 5vv, F, unacc., FZc; Dies irae, 4vv, orch, FZc (autograph), Fc
Magnificat: C, d, 4vv, FZc; 3, 8vv, Md; 2 choirs, insts, 2 org, D, FZc (autograph); 2 choirs, org, a, FZc (autograph)
Miserere: 4vv, 3 va, vc, db, bc, f (Leipzig, n.d.), MS copies, incl., GB-Lbm, I-FZc (autograph); 5, 6vv, orch, g, FZc (autograph); 4vv, org, A-Wn; 4vv, orch, CH-E, I-Fc; 4vv, str, I-PAc
Te Deum: 4vv, orch, I-Fc, Gi(l); 2 choirs, D, 1781, Md; 2 choirs, orch, CH-E, Russ. Te Deum [Tebe Bohu Sualim], 2 choirs, orch, Russ. hns, bells, cannons, D, for taking of Ochakov, 1789, I-Fc, FZc (autograph), USSR-Lsc; Lat. Te Deum, 4vv, chorus 4vv, orch, D, for taking of Kelia, 1790, I-FZc (autograph), ed. in Jones
Slava v vyschnich Bohu [Gloria in excelsis], 2 choirs, 2 orchs, Russ. hns, bells, cannons, fireworks, for peace of Iaşi, 1792, I-FZc, Leningrad, Historical Musical Museum (autograph, see Mooser)
Complete Russ. Liturgy, 2 choirs unacc., Leningrad, Historical Musical Museum (see Mooser); Russ. Christmas hymn, 8vv, orch, I-FZc (autograph)
Russ. oratorio, 2 choirs, orch, 1785, FZc (autograph)
Motets, psalms, Lamentations, hymns, antiphons, introits etc, CH-E, D-Bds, LEt, Mbs, GB-Lcm, I-Bc, Fc, FZc, Md (many in autograph)

INSTRUMENTAL
Sonatas: 3, hpd, vn/fl, D, G, G (Amsterdam, c1765); 3, hpd, G, C, G (London, 1768 or 1769); 6, fl, bc (Paris, 1782); Giulio Sabino ed Epponina, sonata caratteristica, hpd/pf, vn, E, op.1 (Vienna, 1785); Intreccio di diverse idee d'opere favorite, ossia Sonata, hpd, vn, Eb, op.2 (Vienna, ?1787); 3, hpd/pf, vn, C, D, Bb, op.3 (Vienna, 1786); 3, hpd/pf, vn, G, a-A, F, op.4 (Vienna, 1788); 6 sonate dell'opera Fra i due litiganti, hpd, vn, ?D-Dlb; 1, hpd, vn, Mbs; 1, vn, bc, B-Bc; hpd sonatas, B-Bc, F-Pc, I-Nc
3 concertone, Eb, I-Fc; many symphonies

WRITINGS
Trattato del basso generale (MS, B-Bc, I-Bc)
Regole (MS, D-Bds)
Eclaircissement sur la musique composée pour Oleg, in G. Pasolini Zanelli: G. Sarti (Faenza, 1883), 113
Esame acustico fatto sopra due frammenti di Mozart, summarized in AMZ, xxxiv (1832), 373
Sur le moyen de compter les vibrations des sons et d'en comparer la

célérité avec la mesure du tems, read to St Petersburg Academy of Sciences, 23 May 1796
Théorie de l'harmonie simultanée et successive, mentioned in *AMZ*, xxvi (1824), 540

BIBLIOGRAPHY

BurneyH; *FétisB*

T. Overskou: *Den Danske Skueplads in dens historie* (Copenhagen, 1854), ii-iii

G. Pasolini: *Giuseppe Sarti* (Faenza, 1883)

H. Müller: 'Wilhelm Heinse als Musikschriftsteller', *VMw*, iii (1887), 561–605

C. Thrane: 'Sarti in Kopenhagen', *SIMG*, iii (1901–2), 528

A. Untersteiner: 'Giuseppe Sarti', *Gazzetta musicale di Milano*, lvii (1902), 490

H. Abert: *W. A. Mozart* (Leipzig, 1919), i, 254, 442, 840; ii, 53, 171, 262, 641

A. Della Corte: *L'opera comica italiana nel '700* (Bari, 1923), ii, 69

C. Rivalta: *Giuseppe Sarti, musicista faentino del sec. XVIII* (Faenza, 1928)

F. Samory: *A Giuseppe Sarti nel 2° centenario di sua nascita* (Faenza, 1929)

R. A. Mooser: *Annales de la musique et des musiciens en Russie au XVIIIe siècle*, ii (Geneva, 1951)

D. Lehmann: 'Zwischen Sarti und Rasumowski, Mozart im russischen Musikleben des 18. Jahrhunderts', *Acta Mozartiana*, ii/2–3 (1955), 43

H. O'Douwes: 'De russische jaren van Giuseppe Sarti', *Mens en melodie*, xii (1957), 146

E. O. D. Downes: *The Operas of Johann Christian Bach as a Reflection of the Dominant Trends in Opera Seria 1750–1780* (diss., Harvard U., 1958)

M. S. Selden: 'Laurels for Catherine the Great (The Early Reign of Oleg)', *Opera News*, xxiii/20 (1959), 14, 30

F. Mompellio: 'La cappella del duomo dal 1714 ai primi decenni del '900', *Storia di Milano*, xvi (Milan, 1962)

R. Jones: *A Performing Edition and Discussion of G. Sarti's Te Deum in D* (diss., Stanford U., 1966)

W. J. Mitchell: 'Giuseppe Sarti and Mozart's Quartet K421', *CMc* (1969), no.9, p.147

S. Hansell: 'Sacred Music at the "Incurabili" in Venice at the Time of J. A. Hasse', *JAMS*, xxiii (1970), 282, 505

DAVID DiCHIERA (text, bibliography)
DENNIS LIBBY(work-list)

Sarto, Johannes de. *See* JOHANNES DE SARTO.

Sartori, Claudio (*b* Brescia, 1 April 1913). Italian musicologist and music bibliographer. After taking an arts degree with a thesis in music history supervised by Giusto Zampieri at the University of Pavia (1934), he studied with Gérold at the University of Strasbourg and with Franco Vittadini at Pavia Conservatory. He was assistant librarian at the Bologna Conservatory (1938–42), where he became professor of Italian literature (1943), a post he held later at the Milan Conservatory (1967).

Sartori is an outstanding bibliographer in the tradition of Eitner, Vogel and Einstein, and has done equally important work. While conceding that bibliography is only 'a means of arriving at a deeper and surer knowledge of music itself', he realized the lack of such tools in his early music research and with great zeal set about providing them. His first publication dealing specifically with bibliography appeared in 1940, in the form of additions to a Scarlatti opera catalogue. He next published material uncovered during work in the Bologna Conservatory library, but his first significant publication was *Bibliografia delle opere musicali stampate da Ottaviano Petrucci* (1948), a subject to which he added in 1953. His reputation as a leading bibliographer was established with *Bibliografia della musica strumentale italiana stampata in Italia fino al 1700* (1952). In this difficult undertaking, accomplished in spite of postwar chaos, he was advised and assisted by Einstein. The organization of the catalogue was based on Eitner's bibliography for secular music; corrections, additions

and new indices appeared in the second volume (1968). It is a standard reference work and an invaluable handbook for all research on Italian instrumental music.

To compile the catalogue Sartori applied to all libraries in the West, and discovered that many important libraries had incomplete or inaccurate lists of holdings. He then began to exhort individual libraries to make catalogues, and published various general lists of collections of printed music (in *FAM*, from 1955) and more particular lists of important manuscript collections (e.g. at the Lucca seminary, the cathedrals of Piacenza, Vercelli etc). In 1965 he eventually obtained financial support for his work and established the Ufficio Ricerche Musicali, of which he is director. The bureau aims to catalogue all manuscripts and printed music in Italy up to 1900, all printed Italian librettos up to 1800 (including operas, oratorios, serenatas, cantatas and balli) and all literature on music in Italy. This enormous project demands the cooperation of diligent research assistants as well as Sartori's own dedication, and its importance to musicology is evident in the huge quantity of requests (from everywhere in the world) that the centre handles. Another companion bibliographical tool, the list of Italian music publishers, appeared in 1958. In 1962 Sartori began a Cherubini catalogue and in the 1960s a revision of Vogel (published 1978). He has always pursued subjects of general musicological interest, his outstanding work being on Josquin at Milan and on 16th- and 18th-century Milanese music. With Benvenuti he edited Classici Musicali Italiani (1941–3). He is a member of the RISM commission; from 1956 to 1971 he was on the editorial board of *Acta musicologica*, and he edits the series Bibliotheca Musica.

WRITINGS

'Antonio Bazzini negli ultimi anni', *Brescia*, xiv (1936), 17

'Una redazione inedita del Tractatus practice cantus mensurabilis ad modum italicorum di Prosdocimo de Beldemandis', *Archivium romanicum*, xx/3–4 (1936), 1; as *La notazione italiana del Trecento in una redazione inedita del Tractatus practice cantus mensurabilis di Prosdocimo de Beldemandis* (Florence, 1938)

'Ancora due parole su E. Montazio', *Musica d'oggi*, xix (1937), 408

'Uno studio del musicista Chimeri sul musicista Quaranta', *Commentari dell'Ateneo di Brescia, 1936* (Brescia, 1937), 69 [with music exx.]

'Rocester, la prima opera di Verdi', *RMI*, xliii (1939), 97

'Adolescenza ardente di Ferruccio Busoni e un suo primo ignorato progetto lirico', *RaM*, xiii (1940), 183

'Contributo a un catalogo delle opere teatrali di Alessandro Scarlatti', *Gli Scarlatti (Alessandro–Francesco–Pietro–Domenico–Giuseppe): note e documenti sulla vita e sulle opere*, Chigiana, ii (1940), 63

'Dori e Arione . . . di A. Scarlatti', *NA*, xviii (1941), 35

'Il Dafni di Alessandro Scarlatti', *RMI*, xlv (1941), 1

ed. with G. Benvenuti: *Classici musicali italiani* (Milan, 1941–3)

'Soirées musicales'; Dagli Archivi del Liceo Musicale di Bologna', *Rossiniana* (Bologna, 1942), 40; 43

'Gli Scarlatti a Napoli: nuovi contributi', *RMI*, xlvi (1942), 374

Il R. Conservatorio di Musica G. B. Martini di Bologna (Florence, 1942)

'Una lettera inedita di G. Rossini', *RMI*, xlvi (1942), 218

'A Little Known Petrucci Publication', *MQ*, xxxiv (1948), 234

Bibliografia delle opere musicali stampate da Ottaviano Petrucci (Florence, 1948); continued as 'Nuove conclusive aggiunte alla "Bibliografia del Petrucci"', *CHM*, i (1953), 175

'Una Arianna misconosciuta: La Laodice di A. Scarlatti', *La Scala* (1956), no.79, p.41

Bibliografia della musica strumentale italiana stampata in Italia fino al 1700 [*SartoriB*], i (Florence, 1952; ii (1968) [with corrections and addns]

'Monteverdiana', *MQ*, xxxviii (1952), 399

'Il quarto Codice di Gaffurio non è del tutto scomparso', *CHM*, i (1953), 25

'Le quarantaquattro edizioni italiane delle sei opere di Corelli', *RMI*, lv (1953), 28

Monteverdi (Brescia, 1953)

'Pietro Nardini, violinista dell'amore', *Musicisti toscani*, i, Chigiana, xii (1955), 60

'Josquin Des Prés, cantore del Duomo di Milano (1459–1472)', *AnnM*, iv (1956), 55

'Matteo da Perugia e Bertrand Feragut, i due primi maestri di cappella del Duomo di Milano', *AcM*, xxviii (1956), 12

'Una dinastia di editori musicali: documenti inediti sui Gardano e i loro congiunti Stefano Bindoni e Alessandro Raverii', *Bibliofilia*, lviii (1956), 176

Catalogo delle musiche della Cappella del Duomo di Milano (Milan, 1957)

'Organs, Organ-builders, and Organists in Milan', *MQ*, xliii (1957), 57

Riccardo Malipiero (Milan, 1957); repr. in C. Sartori and P. Santi: *Due tempi di Riccardo Malipiero* (Milan, 1964)

Casa Ricordi 1808–1958 (Milan, 1958)

Dizionario degli editori musicali italiani (Florence, 1958)

Giacomo Puccini a Monza (Monza, 1958)

Puccini (Milan, 1958)

ed. with F. Broussard and others: *Dizionario Ricordi della musica e dei musicisti* (Milan, 1959)

with R. Allorto: 'La musicologia italiana dal 1945 a oggi', *AcM*, xxxi (1959), 9

ed.: *Puccini Symposium* (Milan, 1959)

'Giovanni Battista Sammartini e la sua corte', *Musica d'oggi*, new ser., iii (1960), 3

'La musica nel duomo e alla corte sino alla seconda metà del '500', *Storia di Milano*, ix (Milan, 1961), 723

Assisi: la Cappella della Basilica di S. Francesco: catalogo del fondo musicale nella Biblioteca comunale di Assisi (Milan, 1962)

'Henricus Isaac o Isacco Argiruopulo?', *CHM*, iii (1962), 177

with F. Lesure: 'Tentativo di un catalogo della produzione di Luigi Cherubini', *Luigi Cherubini nel II centenario della nascita* (Florence, 1962), 135

ed.: *L'enciclopedia della musica* (Milan, 1963–4)

Commemorazione di Ottaviano de' Petrucci (Fossombrone, 1966)

'Bibliotechemusicali', 'GiuseppeVerdi', 'Stampamusicale', *LaMusicaE*

'Giulio Cesare Monteverde a Salò: nuovi documenti inediti', *NRMI*, i (1967), 685

'La prima diva della lirica italiana: Anna Renzi', *NRMI*, ii (1968), 430

'Orazio Vecchi e Tiburzio Massaino a Salò: nuovi documenti inediti', *Renaissance-muziek 1400–1600: donum natalicium René Bernard Lenaerts* (Louvain, 1969), 233

'La Strepponi e Verdi a Parigi nella morsa quarantottesca', *NRMI*, viii (1974), 3

'Quisquilie pucciniane e intuizioni bazziniane', *NRMI*, viii (1974), 366

Giacomo Carissimi: catalogo delle opere attribuite (Milan, 1975)

ed., with F. Lesure: *Bibliografia della musica italiana vocale profana pubblicata dal 1500 al 1700* (?Geneva, 1978) [rev. of *VogelB*]

Concerto a più strumenti obbligati in Milano ottocentesca (in preparation) [letters of G. Verdi, C. Maffei, G. Strepponi, C. Tenca]

Articles in *FAM* on various Italian music collections

CAROLYN M. GIANTURCO

Sartorio [Sertorio], **Antonio** (*b* Venice, 1630; *d* Venice, 30 Dec 1680). Italian composer partly resident in Germany. He was a leading composer of operas for Venice in the 1660s and 1670s.

1. LIFE. Sartorio is first heard of with the production of his first opera, *Gl'amori infruttuosi di Pirro*, at the Teatro SS Giovanni e Paolo, Venice, on 4 January 1661. His next opera, *Seleuco*, was first performed on 16 January 1666 in the Teatro S Salvatore, popularly called S Luca, where most of his later operas were also produced. By then he had been named Kapellmeister to Duke Johann Friedrich of Brunswick-Lüneburg, who reigned from 1665 and resided at Hanover. This highly educated sovereign, who formed an alliance with Louis XIV in 1672 and also visited Italy four times and lent the republic of Venice substantial military aid against the Turks, had been converted to Catholicism in 1651, and on inheriting the dukedom he introduced the Catholic rite to his court. Sartorio took up his duties as Kapellmeister on Trinity Sunday 1666. The court Kapelle consisted of seven or eight singers and six instrumentalists, many of them Italian. Their repertory, part of which was discovered in 1958 in an organ bellows in the village of Hüpede, included masses, motets and psalms by Du Mont, Bonifazio Graziani and Orazio Tarditi. Sartorio was paid 103 thalers in 1667 for bringing books of music from Italy, and he composed for the Kapelle a *missa brevis* and several vesper

Autograph of the opening of Act 2 scene i of Sartorio's opera 'L'Adelaide', first performed at S Salvatore, Venice, on 19 February 1672 (D-HVl IV.410)

psalms and cantatas in both the *stile antico* and the *stile moderno*.

During his Hanover years, 1666–75, Sartorio often travelled to Venice in the winter, both to compose operas for Carnival and to enlist musicians for service at court. His first such journey was in 1666–7. On 15 January and 3 February 1667 his remarkable double opera, *La prosperità d'Elio Seiano* and *La caduta d'Elio Seiano*, was produced; the librettist, Nicolò Minato, originally intended the two operas to be given on successive nights, but it appears that Sartorio and the singers overruled him. Sartorio spent the winter of 1668–9 in Hanover, but he was in Venice again for the carnival of 1669–70, during which his next opera, *L'Ermengarda Regina de' Longobardi*, was performed. The librettist, Pietro Dolfin, a friend of both Sartorio and Duke Johann Friedrich, administered the duke's theatre loges and corresponded regularly with him between 1669 and 1678; his unpublished letters (in Staatsarchiv, Hanover) are a valuable source of information about Venetian opera performances. Sartorio's next stay in Venice lasted an entire year, from January or February 1672 to Carnival 1672–3. On 19 February 1672 his best-known opera, *L'Adelaide*, was given for the first time. The libretto is again by Dolfin, who reworked some of Gissilla's arias into a cantata by adding recitatives. Sartorio seems to have responded to Dolfin's wish to have the recitatives set, for a *Cantata di Gissilla* is extant; it was apparently conceived for a pupil of Dolfin's named Lucretia, who had sung a role in the opera, probably that of Gissilla.

Poor health, but also the invitation to write one of two operas for S Luca in the coming carnival, prevented Sartorio from returning to Hanover that spring. The lengthy correspondence on this subject shows that Dolfin was finally able to persuade the duke to let Sartorio remain because of the peril of the journey and because of the honour of having been asked to write the opera, the other being by no less a composer than Cavalli. In the event Sartorio wrote both operas for S Luca. *L'Orfeo* was first given on 14 December 1672. Although the Florentine emissary, Marco Antonio Altoviti, reported on 14 January (in a document in *I-Fas*) that Carnival was 'proceeding . . . with not much applause for these first operas' and Dolfin found the scenery and costumes merely ordinary and Aurelio Aureli's libretto 'very bad', both Sartorio's music and the singing of Tonina Coresi, who came specially from Rome to sing the part of Eurydice, were highly praised. Dolfin's objections could have had to do with the fact that Aureli, catering for the fashion of the day, had added to the intricacy of the plot by making Orpheus a jealous husband and by adding fictitious minor episodes that jarred more than usually with the main plot. The other opera at S Luca in this carnival was to have been Cavalli's *Massenzio*. It went into rehearsal, but there it was decided that it would not do, 'for lack of spirited ariettas' (Dolfin). Brusquely, the theatre managers turned the entire project over to Sartorio. No incident could better illustrate the difference between the old school and the new, between Cavalli, the dramatist trained in the school of Monteverdi and using the arioso as his vehicle for dramatic exposition, and Sartorio, for whom opera was first and foremost a brilliant spectacle and the aria the chief means of moving the listener. Sartorio wrote his *Massenzio* in only 13 days, and it was performed from 25 January 1673. It contains no

fewer than 78 arias and duets, a typical number for his operas.

Sartorio spent the following two years at Hanover and then left Duke Johann Friedrich's employ for good in April 1675, receiving a parting gift of 50 thalers and a golden chain. He remained on good terms with the duke, corresponded regularly with him about negotiations with singers or visits on his behalf to cloistered ladies, and continued to call himself a court composer in his remaining operas. He settled in Venice, in the quarter of S Giovanni Grisostomo. On 7 May 1676 he was appointed vice-*maestro di cappella* of St Mark's, defeating Carlo Grossi by three votes. On 17 December, his *Giulio Cesare in Egitto* received its first performance and was particularly successful. Four further operas succeeded it in 1677–9. On 18 December 1679 Duke Johann Friedrich died at Augsburg at the start of his fifth journey to Italy. 1680 saw the appearance of Sartorio's only printed volume of music, a set of eight-part psalms for two choirs. Towards the end of the year he began to compose another opera, *La Flora*, but he died before he could finish it, after seven months of illness; it was finished by M. A. Ziani and performed at the Teatro S Angelo as the first opera of the new carnival season. Sartorio was succeeded at St Mark's by Legrenzi.

According to his epitaph in S Giovanni Grisostomo, Venice, he died at the age of 50. GASPARO SARTORIO was his brother. Another brother, Girolamo [Hieronymo], also had connections with the theatre, as an architect.

2. WORKS. Sartorio's operas, like those of his Venetian contemporaries, deal with heroic themes. In some of them – *La caduta d'Elio Seiano*, *Massenzio* and *Antonino e Pompeiano* – true Senecan tragedy is evoked as death comes to a tyrant. Sejanus committed suicide, wishing the universe to be plunged into chaos, and Antonino was assassinated on stage by the liberators of Rome. Sartorio's greatness as a composer lay in discovering the variety and, more important, the depth of the passions expressed by his librettists. His talent for writing many different kinds of aria was fully developed even in his first opera, *Gl'amori infruttuosi di Pirro* (produced in 1661), which set the pattern for his subsequent operas in containing a large number of arias – several have more than 70. Some of the most noteworthy arias in this work, which recur in similar form in later operas, are Circea's rage aria 'Son tradita' (in Act 3 scene xi), with its florid coloratura ascending to b'', and her aria in 3/2 time, 'Le promesse de gl'amanti' (Act 1 scene viii), in which the inconstancy of lovers' promises is shown by the incessantly wandering crotchets of the bass line.

Sartorio is at his best in two types of aria, the lament and the trumpet aria. The laments are usually written in 3/2 time over an ostinato bass, which is often chromatic. Sartorio was very fond of ostinatos. Some of his most moving laments are Oreste's 'Hermiona, qual sventura' (*Gl'amori infruttuosi di Pirro*, Act 3 scene vi), Adalberto's 'Qual colpa mi date' (*L'Adelaide*, Act 2 scene vii) and Orpheus's 'E morta Euridice' (*L'Orfeo*, Act 3 scene iii), the beginning of which is shown in ex.1. This example also shows how the strings invariably accompany the voice when they are employed in an aria. This is in the manner of an echo: voice and strings rarely participate in more than a few notes simultaneously (although 'Qual colpa mi date' is an exception to this rule). Sartorio also reveals here his penchant for harmonic harshness. In this example such clashes (in which the notes in question are indicated by crosses) can be explained by the affection of extreme suffering. For expressive purposes he reduced the string body on occasion to four violas (preceding Orpheus's aria 'D'un amante, che sospira' in *L'Orfeo*, Act 3 scene iii) or even two (in Antioco's aria 'Per pietà, datemi morte' in *Seleuco*, Act 3 scene viii).

Ex.1 *L'Orfeo*, Act 3 scene iii

Sartorio wrote many trumpet arias. He turned to this instrument to express more adequately the heroic affection pertaining to the grand personages depicted in his operas. He first wrote for trumpet – two in D – in 1672, in the sinfonia to *L'Adelaide*. Although certain of Cavalli's operas – *Le nozze di Teti e di Peleo* (1639), *La Rosinda* (1651) and *L'Elena* (1659) – as well as Boretti's *Marcello* (1670) and Sartorio's own *Gl'amori infruttuosi di Pirro* (1661) make some mention of the trumpet in their texts and even feature imitations of trumpet fanfares in their string writing (as many other operas do), *L'Adelaide* appears to be the first in a long line of Venetian operas to call specifically for the trumpet. Sartorio wrote for a solo trumpet in D in *Massenzio* (an aria of Fame), *Antonino e Pompeiano* (two sinfonias, and arias of Fame and Antonino), *Giulio Cesare in Egitto* (four arias, two sinfonias and a 'tocco di

Tromba'), *L'Anacreonte tiranno* (a sinfonia, and two arias of Oronte) and *La Flora* (three sinfonias, an aria of Flora and two arias of Geminio). In these arias the trumpet alternates with the voice, just as the strings do in arias with strings (see ex.2 for the beginning of Fame's aria in *Massenzio*).

Ex.2 *Massenzio*, Act 3 scene vi

Another mark of Sartorio's style is the juxtaposition of the heroic and the base. Comic figures – usually an old nurse, sung by a tenor – sing arias whose melodies consist of short phrases moving chiefly in quavers, either on one pitch or stepwise. This popular element has appeared to some commentators as a sign of artistic impoverishment, but it should rather be seen in the context of the whole range of Baroque affections.

WORKS

OPERAS

Gl'amori infruttuosi di Pirro (A. Aureli), Venice, SS Giovanni e Paolo, 4 Jan 1661, *I-Vmc* Martinengo 49–70, no.53B (30 arias)

Seleuco (N. Minato), Venice, S Salvatore, 16 Jan 1666, *Vnm* Marc.It.IV.454 (= 9978)

La prosperità d'Elio Seiano (Minato), Venice, S Salvatore, 15 Jan 1667, *Nc* 32.3.19, *Rvat* Chigiano Q.V.63 (as Il Seiano)

La caduta d'Elio Seiano (Minato), Venice, S Salvatore, 3 Feb 1667, *Vnm* Marc.It.IV.397 (= 9921)

L'Ermengarda Regina de' Longobardi (P. Dolfin), Venice, SS Giovanni e Paolo, 26 Dec 1669, lost

L'Adelaide (Dolfin), Venice, S Salvatore, 19 Feb 1672, *D-HVl* IV.410 (autograph), *Mbs* (inc., see Gissilla unica figlia), *I-Vnm* Marc.It.IV.380 (= 9904) (with different opening sinfonia)

L'Orfeo (Aureli), Venice, S Salvatore, 14 Dec 1672, *A-Wn* 17940 (with autograph corrections), *I-Nc* 32.2.25, *Vnm* Marc.It.IV.443 (= 9967)

Massenzio (G. F. Bussani), Venice, S Salvatore, 25 Jan 1673, *Nc* 33.5.17 (9 arias), 32.3.23, *S-Uu* vok.mus.i/165 (autograph, inc.)

Alcina (Dolfin), Venice, intended for Carn. 1674–5 but not perf., lost

Giulio Cesare in Egitto (Bussani), Venice, S Salvatore, 17 Dec 1676, *I-Nc* 33.5.36 (arias), 33.6.29, *Vqs* Cl.VIII Cod.IV (43 arias)

Antonino e Pompeiano (Bussani), Venice, S Salvatore, [Jan] 1677, *D-HVl* IV.414 (with autograph corrections), *I-Vqs* Cl.VIII Cod.IV (36 arias)

L'Anacreonte tiranno (Bussani), Venice, S Salvatore [Dec] 1677, *D-MÜp* Santini 3954 (erroneously attrib. A. Scarlatti), *I-Nc* 33.5.36 (15 arias), *Vqs* Cl.VIII Cod.V (23 arias)

Ercole su'l Termodonte (Bussani), Venice, S Salvatore [Jan–Feb] 1678, *Vqs* Cl.VIII Cod.V (13 arias)

I duo tiranni al soglio (M. Noris), Venice, S Salvatore, 15 Jan 1679, lost

La Flora (N. Bonis), Venice, S Angelo [Dec 1680], *Bca* A.462 (12 arias), *Vnm* Marc.It.IV.423 (= 9947) [music completed by M. A. Ziani]

CANTATAS

Cantata di Gissilla (see Gissilla unica figlia); Carosello (Dolfin), Venice, Jan/Feb 1673, lost; Dite quando volete [Fate quando sapete], *D-Kl*; Entro d'un'antro ombroso, *Kl*; E tiranna la speranza, *Kl*; Già sorgeva la luce, *I-Vmc*; Gissilla unica figlia, *D-Mbs* [incl. arias from L'Adelaide]; Io v'intendo i luci altere, *D-Kl*; Mentre l'humane genti dalle fatiche sue, *Kl*; Mio cor, non amar più, *I-MOe*; O ch'humore stravagante, *Fn*

ARIAS

Chi su l'altrui ruvine, *Vmc*; Dite un sì, labri adorati, 2vv, *Vqs* (inc.); Farmi vivere sempre in pene, *D-Kl*; Gran' tiranna è la speranza, *I-Vmc*; Io non presto fede alcuna, *Vmc*; La fortuna dispettosa, *Vmc*; Lucide faci ch'in cielo splendete, *Vmc*; Non cessate, stelle irate, *Vmc*; Pazzi amanti, *Vmc*; Perchè quando apersi, *Vmc*; Quanti sono d'oggidi, *Vmc*; Quel ch'altrui rassembra, *Vmc*; S'amor tolse l'aurea fila, *Vmc;* Se li chiome tempo avaro, *Vmc*; Selve amiche, *Vmc*; Se non fosse per penare, *D-Kl*; Se potesse il cor cessar, *I-Vmc*; S'in odio m'havete, *Vmc*; Su la rota de la sorte, *Vmc*; Ti flagellino mentitor, *Vmc*; Vive sempre un huom che regna, *Vmc*; Volete così, mie nemiche deità, *Vmc*

SACRED VOCAL

[23] Salmi a due chori ma accomodati all'uso della serenissima capella ducale di S Marco, 8vv, op.1 (Venice, 1680)

Ad tantum triumphum, 1v, insts, bc, 1695[1]

Kyrie eleison, Gloria, Credo; Confitebor tibi Domine; De profundis clamavi ad te; Dixit Dominus Domino meo; Laudate pueri Dominum; Levavi oculos meos; Regina coeli laetare; Salve mi Jesu, ed. E. H. Tarr (Stuttgart, 1976): *D-Bds*

Tu m'assisti, e mi reggi, aria, *I-Vmc*

Surrexit non est hic, March 1672, lost

DOUBTFUL WORKS

(all 3vv unless otherwise stated)

Amanti, ardire; Colui che partesi; Deh, perche non m'uccidete; Ecco l'alba luminosa; Hor che notturna pace; L'alba in ciel; Mio core impara; Navicella, che carca; Oh voi, ch'intorno; Sventurata navicella, 4vv; Un cor che chiede: *D-HVl*

BIBLIOGRAPHY

P. Dolfin, A. Sartorio: various letters (in Staatsarchiv, Hanover)

G. C. Bonlini: *Le glorie della poesia, e della musica* (Venice, 1730)

F. Caffi: *Storia della musica sacra nella già cappella ducale di San Marco in Venezia dal 1318 al 1797* (Venice, 1854–5, repr. 1931)

E. Bodemann: *Die Handschriften der königlichen öffentlichen Bibliothek zu Hannover* (Hanover, 1867)

L. N. Galvani [pseud. of G. Salvioli]: *I teatri musicali di Venezia nel secolo xvii (1637–1700): memorie storiche e bibliografiche* (Milan, 1878)

A. Ademollo: *I teatri di Roma nel secolo decimosettimo* (Rome, 1888/R1969)

T. Wiel: *I codici musicali contariniani del secolo XVII nella R. Biblioteca di San Marco in Venezia* (Venice, 1888)

H. Kretzschmar: 'Die venezianische Oper und die Werke Cavalli's und Cesti's', *VMw*, viii (1892), 99ff

G. Fischer: *Musik in Hannover* (Hanover and Leipzig, 1903)

F. Schuster: 'Kunst und Künstler in Hannover zur Zeit des Kurfürsten Ernst August', *Hannoversche Geschichtsblätter*, vii (1904), 1–11, 49–86, 97–114, 145–240

B. G. Dolfin: *I Dolfin (Delfino), patrizi veneziani sulla storia di Venezia dall'anno 452 al 1910* (Belluno, 1912)

F. Berend: *Nicolaus Adam Strungk, 1640–1700: sein Leben und seine Werke* (Freiburg, 1915)

A. Lorenz: *Alessandro Scarlattis Jugendoper* (Augsburg, 1927)

T. Abbetmeyer: *Über Geschichte der Musik am Hofe in Hannover vor Agostino Steffani 1636–1689* (diss., U. of Göttingen, 1931)

H. C. Wolff: *Die Venezianische Oper in der zweiten Hälfte des 17. Jahrhunderts* (Berlin, 1937)

A. Cametti: *Il Teatro di Tordinona poi di Apollo* (Tivoli, 1938)

S. T. Worsthorne: *Venetian Opera in the Seventeenth Century* (Oxford, 1954/R1968)

G. Schnath: 'Die Geschichte des Leineschlosses 1636–1943', *Hannoversche Geschichtsblätter*, new ser., ix/4 (1956), 19–205

M. Massinis: 'Sartorio, Antonio', *ES*

H. Sievers: *Die Musik in Hannover* (Hanover, 1961)

L. Schrade: *Tragedy in the Art of Music* (Cambridge, Mass., 1964)

Å. Davidsson: 'En "Christina-Opera" på Carolina Rediviva', *Nordisk tidskrift för bok- och biblioteksväsen*, liv (1967), 9

C. M. Gianturco: 'The Revisions of Alessandro Stradella's *Forza*

dell'amor paterno', *JAMS*, xxv (1972), 407

E. Rosand: '*L'Orfeo*: la metamorfosi d'un mito musicale', *La biennale di Venezia: catalogo* (Venice, in preparation); Eng. trans., *Israel Studies in Musicology*, ii (in preparation)

EDWARD H. TARR

Sartorio [Sertorio], Gasparo (*b* Venice, between 18 Oct 1625 and 17 Oct 1626; *d* Venice, 17 Oct 1680). Italian composer and organist, brother of Antonio Sartorio. In 1650 his opera *Orithia*, to a libretto by Count Maiolino Bisaccioni, was performed at the Teatro Ss Apostoli, and his *L'Erginda*, to the first libretto written by Aurelio Aureli, was given at the same theatre in 1652. He composed the third act of *Iphide greca* (1671; *I-Vnm* IV-421, = 9945), the music for Acts 1 and 2 being by Gian Domenico Partenio and Domenico Freschi respectively. The opera *Armidoro*, performed at the Teatro S Cassiano on 20 January 1651, is attributed to Sartorio by Ivanovich, but to Cavalli in other sources; the music is now lost. In January 1673 he failed to obtain the position of organist at S Cassiano. On 16 October 1676 he and Antonio Sartorio were godfathers at the baptism of Girolamo Sartorio's son, Casparus Antonius, at St Clemens, Hanover. According to his epitaph in S Fosca, Venice, he died at the age of 54.

BIBLIOGRAPHY

C. Ivanovich: *Minerva al tavolino* (Venice, 1681, 2/1688)

T. Walker: 'Gli errori di "Minerva al tavolino": osservazioni sulla cronologia delle prime opere veneziane', *Venezia e il melodramma nel Seicento: Venezia 1972*, 7

EDWARD H. TARR

Sartorius, Christian (*b* Querfurt; buried Kulmbach, 14 April 1676). German composer and administrator. From 1626 he was musician and personal servant to Margrave Christian of Brandenburg-Kulmbach at Bayreuth. In 1646 he became 'resident official with special responsibility for music' and in 1647 steward of the religious foundation at Himmelkron, near Bayreuth; he remained there until 1671 at the latest. He wrote the music for the funeral of Margrave Christian in 1655, and it was published in the same year as *Fürstliche Ruhm- und Leich-Text*; it is for ten voices and continuo. His other, more important music is a set of sacred concertos in one to eight parts with continuo, *Unterschiedlicher teutscher nach der Himmelcron Zielender hoher Fest- und Danck-Andachten Zusammenstimmung* (Nuremberg, 1658). His music is wholly in keeping with the practices of the time in the choice of texts, in the ordering of the devotional pieces of 1658 according to the church calendar and in the manner of composition. A vocal combination dominated by the interplay of pairs of voices moving in parallel 3rds and 6ths is supported by a continuo bass which is almost always harmonically conceived and leans heavily on 5-3 chords. The contrast is heightened by a clear differentiation between the nature of the vocal and instrumental writing. That the style is fundamentally monodic is apparent from the frequency with which the melody lies in the top part; following a tendency heralded in earlier works with continuo, the alto voice is no longer represented. On the other hand there are deficiencies which, although Schütz had warned of them in the preface to his *Geistliche Chor-Music* of 1648, Sartorius passed off as peculiarities of the new style. The harmonies are at once stiff and jerky, and false relations and parallel 5ths and octaves are frequent. It is thus precisely in his use of new stylistic means that Sartorius gave a dilettantish impression, more so in the funeral music than in the concertos. It is in the presentation of his music that he most clearly demonstrated his familiarity with contemporary publications; for example, he treated the use of obbligato instruments as normal and provided two continuo parts, one for the organ and one for the violone. His music could be performed by whatever forces happened to be available.

LARS ULRICH ABRAHAM

Sartorius, Erasmus (*b* Schleswig, 1577; *d* Hamburg, 17 Oct 1637). German writer on music and composer. In 1586 he was a choirboy at the Gottorf court. Duke Johann Adolf, who ruled from 1590, allowed him to attend the school at Bordesholm. He later studied at Rostock, where in 1603 or 1604 he was appointed Kantor of St Marien. From 1 November 1605 until his death he was Kantor of the Johanneum, Hamburg. Although he was also required to teach subjects other than music, he succeeded in increasing considerably the amount of polyphonic music performed in Hamburg. The municipal musicians were obliged to give him regular support. In 1607 he performed a festive polychoral work. From 1609, performances of Passions are recorded in which, from 1612, instrumentalists participated. Also from 1612 Sartorius received compensation from the four main Hamburg churches for the performance of polyphonic music.

Sartorius published two theoretical works. *Belligerasmus, id est Historia belli exorti in regno musico* (Hamburg, 1622, 3/1639 ed. P. Lauremberg as *Musomachia, id est Bellum musicale*) is in the form of a fable describing the struggle between Bisthon and Orpheus, the would-be successors to Apollo and the leaders of monodic and polyphonic music respectively. In speeches and reports of the deployment of the armies and the benefits and effects of music, arguments for and against polyphony and details of the theory of *musica choralis* and *figuralis* are expounded. Sartorius did not refer to the more extended *Bellum musicale* (1563) of Claudius Sebastiani, which he possibly did not know, but to similar discourses written for other disciplines. His other theoretical work is *Institutionum musicarum tractatio nova et brevis* (Hamburg, 1635). The preface illustrates the tendency to give more weight to the evidence of the Old Testament on the origins of music than to the Greek sources. In the chapter on solmization Sartorius mentioned the reforms introduced by Calvisius, Hitzler and Puteanus, yet recommended adherence to the old system. Following his Rostock colleague Burmeister, he traced the different characters of the modes to the relative positions of the semitones within them. The composers whose works are most often cited in the discussion of the modes are Lassus (42 works) and Hieronymus Praetorius (39); three works by Clemens non Papa are still mentioned. Sartorius again followed Gengenbach in ending his treatise with a section giving explanations of foreign musical terms, and there is an appendix containing two eight-part canons.

Sartorius probably intended his *Fugae aliquot* (Hamburg, 1635; 12 ed. in F. Jöde, *Der Kanon*, i, Wolfenbüttel, 1943), in two, three, four and eight parts, as a musical supplement to his *Institutionum musicarum tractatio*. He also published a wedding song (Hamburg, 1606). According to Seiffert there were two motets –

one for four voices, one for a solo voice, and both with instruments – ascribed simply to 'Sartorius' in the library of St Michaelis, Lüneburg.

BIBLIOGRAPHY

J. Mattheson: *Grundlage einer Ehren-Pforte* (Hamburg, 1740); ed. M. Schneider (Berlin, 1910/R1969)
J. Sittard: *Geschichte des Musik- und Concertwesens in Hamburg* (Altona and Leipzig, 1890)
E. Praetorius: 'Mitteilungen aus norddeutschen Archiven', *SIMG*, vii (1905–6), 243
M. Seiffert: 'Die Chorbibliothek der St. Michaelisschule in Lüneburg zu Seb. Bachs Zeit', *SIMG*, ix (1907–8), 616
L. Krüger: *Die Hamburgische Musikorganisation im 17. Jahrhundert* (Strasbourg, 1933)

reprinted from *MGG* (xi, 1420) by permission of Bärenreiter
MARTIN RUHNKE

Sartorius [Schneider, Schneickher], **Paul** (*b* Nuremberg, baptized 16 Nov 1569; *d* Innsbruck, 28 Feb 1609). German composer and organist. He was originally called Schneider. In his native city he attended the grammar school of St Lorenz, where one of his teachers was Leonhard Lechner. Then, he explained in the preface to his *Neue teutsche Liedlein*, he went to Italy to study with some of the famous composers of the day. He probably stayed for quite some time in Rome in circles frequented by Palestrina and his pupils; one composer he probably got to know well was Ruggiero Giovannelli, on whose motet *Jubilate Deo omnis terra* he wrote a parody mass. By 1594 at the latest he became organist in the Hofkapelle of Archduke Maximilian II of Austria, and he held this post until his death. The archduke lived at Mergentheim, Franconia, until 1602 and thereafter at Innsbruck, and thus Sartorius must have lived principally at these two places. In 1599 he sent one of his eight-part masses to Duke Maximilian I of Bavaria at Munich and at about the same time sent his eight six-part *Magnificat* settings and some motets to Archbishop Wolf Dietrich von Raitenau at Salzburg. It is out of the question that his permanent home was at Nuremberg, as Eitner supposed, and Eitner and some later authorities wrongly identified him with the Nuremberg pastor Paul Sartorius (1561–1623); nor was he related to the Nuremberg music publisher Johann Friedrich Sartorius (*c*1595–after 1649).

For a German composer of his generation, which was that of Hans Leo Hassler, Sartorius was, as a composer of sacred vocal works, very much up-to-date in his knowledge of Italian music. He was influenced less by Lassus or Hassler than he was by Palestrina. This is particularly evident in the eight six-part *Magnificat* settings, in which he made use not only of single motifs, but even here and there of whole passages taken from *Magnificat* settings by Palestrina. He set only the even-numbered verses, beginning with 'Et exsultavit', and created the impression of a real eight-part double choir by the use of contrasting groups of four voices from the full choir. His German songs are almost entirely in duple time and mainly use pavane and allemande rhythms, with primarily imitative textures and much sequential writing. In form and content they are midway between the sophisticated art of the canzonet and the simple dance-song.

WORKS

Missae tres, 8vv (Munich, 1599)
Madrigali libro primo, 5vv (Venice, 1600)
Neue teutsche Liedlein, nach Art der welschen Canzonette, 4vv (Nuremberg, 1601); 1 ed. in Chor- und Hausmusik aus alter Zeit, ii (Berlin, 1927)

Sonetti spirituali, 6vv (Nuremberg, 1601)
Sacrae cantiones sive motecta, 6–8, 10, 12vv (Nuremberg, 1602)
2 motets, 5vv, 1600², 1604⁷

Missa super 'Jubilate Deo omnis terra', 8vv, *D-Z*, formerly also in
    Breslau Stadtbibliothek, now *?PL-WRu*
8 Magnificat, 6vv, *A-Sd*
3 antiphons, 6, 8vv, *Sd*, *D-Mbs* (org score)
2 hymns, 4, 8vv, *Bds*, *Mbs* (org score)
5 motets, 8vv, *Mbs* (org score)

Litanies, Magnificat, falsobordoni: lost (see Waldner)

BIBLIOGRAPHY

EitnerQ

F. Waldner: 'Zwei Inventarien aus dem 16. und 17. Jahrhundert', *SMw*,
    iv (1916), 128
K. A. Rosenthal: 'Sartorius – Megerle – Biechteler: Komponisten oder
    Bearbeiter?', *ZMw*, xv (1932–3), 145
L. Hübsch-Pfleger: *Das Nürnberger Lied im Stilwandel um 1600* (diss.,
    U. of Heidelberg, 1944), 99ff
W. Senn: *Musik und Theater am Hof zu Innsbruck* (Innsbruck, 1954)
F. Krautwurst: 'Sartorius, Paul', *MGG* [incl. fuller bibliography]

                                        FRANZ KRAUTWURST

Sartory, Eugène (*b* Mirecourt, 22 Sept 1871; *d* Paris, 5
March 1946). French bow maker. He received his first
training from his father. He went to Paris to work first
for Charles Peccatte and then for Alfred Lamy before
setting up on his own account in 1893. He worked first
at 12 boulevard Bonne Nouvelle, moving to 13 rue du
Faubourg Poissonnière and finally to 3 Cité Trévise.
His work was much influenced by Voirin and Lamy but
has marginally more strength, both in the hand and to
the eye. The bows' heads are small and the sticks most
often round; the best are dark brown. The cello bows
usually depart from the Voirin tradition, having more
weight and a broader head. At the beginning of the 20th
century Sartory's bows retailed in London at two
guineas, less than an inferior brand from Dresden. He
was soon better appreciated, however, and among his
patrons was Ysaÿe, who had several presentation bows
made. His bows are very popular today; the brand-
mark, 'E. Sartory à Paris', appears on the handle and also
often under the lapping.

BIBLIOGRAPHY

J. Roda: *Bows for Musical Instruments of the Violin Family* (Chicago,
    1959)

                                        CHARLES BEARE

Sarum rite, music of the. A local medieval modification
of the Roman rite used by the secular (i.e. non-monastic)
chapter of the Cathedral Church of Salisbury ('Sarum'
being a misreading of the conventional Latin abbreviation for Sarisburia). It was in use there between the 13th
century and the Reformation. During that time it
became increasingly popular all over England until it
practically ousted other local rites such as those of
York, Lincoln, Hereford and Bangor. Its influence
spread to Scotland, to Ireland and even to Portugal. The
rite was also adopted by a number of religious houses.

1. History and liturgy. 2. Sources. 3. Music.

1. HISTORY AND LITURGY. The see of Salisbury can be
traced back to the founding by St Birinus in 634 of the
see of Dorchester in Oxfordshire. Dorchester was the
parent church of Sherborne and Ramsbury, which were
united in 1058 by Bishop Herman. The new see was
transferred to Old Sarum in 1075 and it was the work of
Herman's successor, Osmund, to complete the building
there of a cathedral and to draw up a first constitution
for a chapter of secular canons. At the Norman
Conquest English cathedral life was largely reorganized
along continental lines, and in 1090 bishops Thomas of
Bayeux and Remigius of Fécamp established secular

chapters in their respective sees of York and Lincoln.
When Osmund's *Institution* for Salisbury appeared a
few months later, it followed the same general pattern in
its definition of the duties and offices of the various
members of the newly constituted chapter.

In 1218 Bishop Richard Poore transferred the see to
New Sarum, or Salisbury, and two years later laid the
foundation stone of the present cathedral, which was
completed in 1266. It was probably Poore himself who,
with the aid of Edmund Rich, was responsible for a
more fully developed document than the *Institution*, the
consuetudinary (*c*1210), which, together with the
ordinal, is the principal surviving source of information
about the Sarum rite. It deals with three main aspects of
the life of the cathedral clergy: the organization of its
members, the ritual texts of the cathedral services, and
the ceremonial.

The ordinal, dating from the early 13th century and
probably also the work of Richard Poore, sets out day-
to-day instructions for the celebration of Mass and the
Divine Office. It was frequently revised to take account
of changes in ceremonial, and constantly supplemented
as new feasts were added to the calendar. By about 1350
the time was ripe for a complete revision, and this came
to be referred to by contemporaries as the 'New Use'. In
spite of Wyclif's powerful attacks, churchmen showed
increasing concern for correctness of use and the new
ordinal was much in demand. The most noteworthy
subsequent revision was Clement Maydestone's
Directorium sacerdotum. Caxton's printed version of
the simplified rules, commonly known as the 'Pica', or
'Pie', appeared in 1487. The preface to the 1549 Book
of Common Prayer condemns 'the number and
hardness' of its rules; the streamlined prayer book nonetheless owed a considerable debt to its direct ancestor,
the Sarum rite. After a brief revival during the reign
of Mary Tudor, the Sarum rite was officially abolished
by Royal Injunctions of 1559, but was still followed by
members of the English College at Douai until 1577.

'The Church of Salisbury', wrote Bishop Giles of
Bridport about 1256, 'shines as a sun in its orb among
the churches of the whole world in its divine services
and those who minister in it'. Sarum practice did indeed
become known and admired abroad through the travels
of English royal and ducal chapels, particularly at the
time of the Hundred Years War. When Philippa of
Lancaster, daughter of John of Gaunt, married John I of
Portugal, she introduced the Sarum rite in Braga in
1385; some elements of it survived to the 20th century
(see Corbin, 1952, pp.302ff).

2. SOURCES. The following list cites the more important
sources of music for the Sarum rite from before about
1500. For a brief description of those marked with an
asterisk *see* SOURCES, MS:

(i) *Missals.* *F-Pa* 135 (13th century, ?London, ?Canterbury); *GB-Cu*
    Kk.ii.6 (13th century, Hanley Castle, Worcs.); *I-Bu* 2565 (13th
    century)
(ii) *Graduals.* *GB-SB* 149 (12th century, without music); *Lbm* 12194
    (early 13th century, facs. in Frere, 1894); *Ob* Rawl.lit.d.3 (early 13th
    century, inc.); *Llp* 7 (14th century); *I-PAc* 98 (14th century, with
    tonary); *GB-Lbm* 17001 (late 14th century, part facs. in Frere,
    1894); *Ob* Hatton 3 (early 15th century); *Lbm* Lansdowne 462 (15th
    century, part facs. in Frere, 1894); *Cqc* 16 (15th century); *Lbm* Nero
    E viii (late 15th century)
(iii) *Troper.* *Cu* Add.710 (14th century, Dublin, with Sarum con-
    suetudinary, part facs. in Hesbert, 1970)
(iv) *Breviaries. En* 18.2.13B (13th–14th century, Sprouston,
    Roxburgh); *Ob* e Mus.7 (14th century, Salisbury); *SB* 152 (*c*1460,
    'Erlyngham Breviary', part facs. in Frere, 1901–24)

(v) *Antiphoners*. *Cu* Mm.ii.9 (13th century, Barnwell, Cambridge, facs. in Frere, 1901–24); *Cu* Add.2602 (13th century, Springfield, Essex); *En* 18.2.13A (13th–14th century, with tonary); *Ob* Bodley 948 (14th–15th century, St Mary-Axe, London); *Ob* Laud misc.299 (15th century, Langton, Lincs.)

(vi) *Hymnaries*. *Ob* Laud lat.19 (12th–13th century, with collectar); Liverpool City Museum 12016 (14th century, Cardington, Beds., with tonary and psalter); *Llp* 558 (14th–15th century, Canterbury, with psalter); *Ojc* 60 (late 15th century, Thame, Oxford)

(vii) *Processionals*. *Ob* Bodley 637 (14th century, ?Winchester); *Cjc* 268 (14th century); Stonyhurst College 41 (early 15th century, signed by 'Rychard Wylkey of Mouche Wenloke'); *Llp* 438 (15th century); *Lbm* Harl.2945 (15th century); *SB* 148 (15th century); *Ob* Rawl.lit.d.4 (15th century, Dublin); *En* 18.5.20 (15th century)

(viii) *Tonaries* (*apart from several included above*). *Ob* CCC44 (14th century, with Sarum ordinal); *SB* 175 (late 14th century, with Sarum ordinal); *Lbm* Arundel 130 (15th century, with Sarum ordinal)

(ix) *Manuscripts containing polyphonic music*. *Lbm* 57950 (early 15th century, 'OLD HALL MS'); *Ob* Selden B.26 (mid-15th century); *Lbm* Eg.3307 (mid-15th century); *Cmc* Pepys 1236 (2nd half of 15th century); *Lbm* 5665 (late 15th century)

Printed Sarum books include three editions of the gradual (Paris, 1527, 1528 and 1532), Sampson's original and corrected editions of the antiphoner in two volumes (Paris, 1519, 1520) and innumerable editions of the hymnal and the processional, running to at least eight of the former and 25 of the latter within the space of half a century.

3. MUSIC. The melodies of the Sarum rite contain essentially the same music as their counterparts in the Roman rite, although there are points of detail in which they seem to differ fairly regularly. The calendar, though basically Roman, reflected local interest by including such additions as the feasts of St Osmund (after 1456) and St Cuthburga, and the Sarum Feast of Relics (15 September in the oldest sources, or the Sunday after the Translation of St Thomas in sources later than 1220). Certain prayers, including the Secret 'Ut tibi grata' for the second Sunday after Epiphany and the Postcommunion 'Deus qui nos sacramenti' for the fifth, occur regularly in Sarum sources but not elsewhere. Sarum had its own selection of nine farsed Kyries and one farsed Gloria and it shared many of its 94 sequences with other rites. It also had its own series of richly festive processions before Mass and at Evensong, designed to suit the layout of Salisbury Cathedral and the position of its 19 altars (see plan in Harrison, 1958, p.89); other churches adopting the rite had to make modifications to suit their own needs. A feature of the Sarum processional proses for the days following Christmas is the jubilant repetition by the choir of each of the soloists' phrases, vocalized on A, O or E according to the vowel sound of the last syllable. At the ceremony of the Good Friday Sepulchre the choice of pieces sung at Sarum was shared with Bayeux from the 13th century.

The Sarum rite has provided the liturgical setting, the ritual texts and many of the plainsong themes for much English polyphony, including votive antiphons, *alternatim* hymn settings, responsories, festal masses, settings of the Lamentations of Jeremiah and florid festal *Magnificat* settings.

BIBLIOGRAPHY
EDITIONS OF MUSIC
W. H. Frere, ed.: *Graduale sarisburiense* (London, 1894/*R*1966)
——: *Antiphonale sarisburiense* (London, 1901–24/*R*1966)
R.-J. Hesbert, ed.: *Le tropaire-prosaire de Dublin*, Monumenta musicae sacrae, iv (Rouen, 1970)
EDITIONS OF TEXTS
F. Proctor and C. Wordsworth, eds.: *Breviarum ad usum Sarum* (Cambridge, 1879–86)
F. D. Matthew, ed.: *John Wyclif: Of Feigned Contemplative Life* (London, 1880)
W. G. Henderson, ed.: *Processionale ad usum insignis ac praeclarae ecclesiae Sarum* (Leeds, 1882)
W. H. Frere, ed.: *The Use of Sarum* (Cambridge, 1898, 1900) [incl. edn. of tonary]
C. Wordsworth, ed.: *Ceremonies and Processions of the Cathedral Church of Salisbury* (Cambridge, 1901)
W. Cooke and C. Wordsworth, eds.: *Clement Maydestone's Directorium sacerdotum* (London, 1901–2)
J. Wickham Legg, ed.: *The Sarum Missal* (Oxford, 1916/*R*1969)
A. Jefferies Collins, ed.: *Manuale ad usum percelebris ecclesie sarisburiensis* (London, 1960)
STUDIES
E. Bishop: *Liturgica historica* (Oxford, 1918, 2/1962)
K. Edwards: *The English Secular Cathedrals in the Middle Ages* (Manchester, 1949, rev. 2/1967)
D. Stevens: 'Pre-Reformation Organ Music in England', *PRMA*, lxxviii (1951–2), 1
S. Corbin: *Essai sur la musique religieuse portugaise au moyen âge* (Paris, 1952)
D. Stevens: 'A Unique Tudor Organ Mass', *MD*, vi (1952), 167
——: 'Processional Psalms in Faburden', *MD*, ix (1955), 105
F. Ll. Harrison: *Music in Medieval Britain* (London, 1958, 2/1963)
——: 'Music for the Sarum Rite', *AnnM*, xi (1958–63), 99–144
D. Knowles: 'The Twelfth and Thirteenth Centuries', *The English Church and the Continent*, ed. C. R. Dodwell (London, 1959, 2/1963)
S. Corbin: *La déposition liturgique du Christ au vendredi saint* (Paris and Lisbon, 1960)
C. Vogel: *Introduction aux sources de l'histoire du culte chrétien au moyen âge* (Spoleto, 1966)
M. Huglo: *Les tonaires: inventaire, analyse, comparaison* (Paris, 1971)
See also ENGLAND: BIBLIOGRAPHY OF MUSIC TO 1600.

MARY BERRY

Sáry, László (*b* Györ, 1 Jan 1940). Hungarian composer. He was a pupil of Szervánszky at the Budapest Academy of Music (1961–6). After an early phase under the influence of Bartók, his interests turned towards Boulez's music and in about 1970 he became acquainted with Stockhausen's theories. At that time he formed a performing ensemble with Jeney and Vidovszky to experiment with group improvisation; these experiences gave rise to ideas that were later exploited in chamber pieces of excellent formal control. In 1972 Sáry attended the Darmstadt summer courses. He was already acquainted with Cage's work, but the lectures given there by Wolff stimulated him to a rethinking of his musical ideas and this resulted in *Pentagram*, composed for the centenary of Budapest. The works of this later period are free in the number and nature of instruments, are concerned with very simple material and involve accidental combinations of sounds.

WORKS
(selective list)

Variations, cl, pf, 1966; Catacoustics, 2 pf, 1967; Cantata, 1967–8; Versetti, org, 1966–9; Fluttuazioni, vn, pf, 1968–9; Canzone solenne, orch, 1969; Incanto, 5 solo vv, 1969; Sonanti: no.1, hpd, 1969, no.2, fl, perc, 1970, no.3, cimb, 1970; Immaginario no.1, orch, 1970; Hommage aux ancêtres, cantata, 1969–72; Psalmus, S, 2 zithers, 1972; Pentagram, solo vv, ens, 1972; Sounds, solo/ens, 1972; Sunflower, at least 3 performers, 1973; Quadratic, at least 8 performers, 1973; The Flowers of the Sky, solo/ens, 1973; Qt, 1v, fl, cimb, vn, 1974; Drop by drop, str orch, rev. for 2 prepared pf, 1975; Hommage à Olivier Messiaen, orch, 1977

Principal publisher: Editio Musica

F. ANDRÁS WILHEIM

Saryan, Ghazar (*b* Rostov-na-Donu, 30 Sept 1920). Armenian composer and teacher. He studied in the composition classes of Shostakovich and Alexandrov at the Moscow Conservatory from 1945 to 1950, when he was appointed professor of composition at the Erevan Conservatory. In 1960 he was made rector there, and he was chairman of the Armenian Composers' Union in 1955–6. Influenced both by his Moscow training and by his Armenian background, he has concentrated his compositional activity on orchestral music distinguished by clarity of line and tasteful orchestration, together with a national colouring and a pictorial quality. The *Simfonick panno Hayastan* ('Symphonic canvas Armenia'), based on paintings by his father, Martiros Saryan, shows the introduction of a Bartókian neoclassicism, developed in the Violin Concerto. This work's first movement is a set of variations on the interval of a 7th; the second consists of polyphonic variations on a 12-note theme.

WORKS
(selective list)

Orch: Sym. Poem, 1950; Sym. Pictures, 1955; Festival Ov., 1957; Adagio and Dance, str, 1957; Serenada, 1959; Simfonick panno Hayastan [Sym. canvas Armenia], 1966; Vn Conc., 1973

Vocal orchestral: Khaghaghut'yan or [Day of peace] (A. Poghosyan), 1953

Film scores, inst pieces, songs

BIBLIOGRAPHY

T. Mansuryan: 'Iskusstvo radosti' [The art of joy], *SovM* (1970), no.2, p.25

G. Geodakyan: 'Dva tvorcheskikh portreta' [Two creative portraits], *Sovetakan arvest* (1971), no.1, p.33

SVETLANA SARKISIAN

Sas (Orchassal), Andrés (*b* Paris, 6 April 1900; *d* Lima, 26 Aug 1967). Peruvian musicologist and composer of Belgian–French origin. When he was five the family moved to Brussels, where until 1919, under parental pressure, he studied to be a chemical engineer. But in 1920 he completed a course in harmony at the Anderlecht Academy, Brussels, and he then studied at the Brussels Conservatory with Marchot (violin, 1920), Miry (chamber music, 1923) and Closson (history), taking private lessons in counterpoint and fugue under Imbert. After a year of teaching at the Forest Music School, Brussels, he was in 1924 appointed to teach the violin and chamber music at the Lima Academy. He was back in Belgium to direct the municipal music school in Ninove (1928–9), and then returned to Lima, where, with his wife, the pianist Lily Rosay, he founded the Sas–Rosay Academy of Music (1930). Also in that year he collaborated with María Wiesse de Sabogal in founding *Antara*, a short-lived Lima music journal named after the Inca syrinx. Stimulated by the work of Max Uhle, Sas was the first Peruvian to make a scientific study of the clay syrinxes of the Nazca, a pre-Inca coastal tribe, and he established the microtonal nature of their music. He co-edited three further journals: *El correo de insula* (1946), *Anacrusa* (1956) and *Música* (1957). Although none of these lasted more than a few months, Sas's articles on colonial music established him as the leading historian of Peruvian music in Lima. He directed the conservatory there in 1951, continuing to teach composition and theory sporadically until 1966. His pupils included Garrido-Lecca, Iturriaga, Pinilla, Pulgar Vidal and Edgard Valcárcel. As a composer himself he treated Peruvian materials in a Debussian manner, producing salon pieces based on the pentatonic highland melodies.

WORKS
(selective list)

Choral: Ollantai, op.20 (1949)

Chamber: Recuerdos, op.7, vn, pf, 1927; Sonata-fantasía, op.21, fl, pf (1954); Cantos del Perú, op.29, vn, pf (1935)

Songs: 2 melodías indianas, op.11, 1v, fl, harp (1930); Melodías I–II, op.14 (D. Castañeda), 1v, pf (1931); 2 canciones románticas peruanas, op.17, nos.2–3, 1v, pf (1941)

Pf: Aires y danzas indios del Perú, op.13 (1934); Suite peruana, op.16 (1935); Himno y danza, op.22 (1942); Arrulo y tondero, op.31 (1948); Preludio y toccata, op.39 (1952)

Unpubd orch works: Rapsodia peruana, op.9, vn, small orch, 1928; Poema indio, op.30, 1941; Sueño de Zamba, op.32, ballet, 1943; La

patrona del pueblo, op.36, ballet, 1945; Las seis edades de la tía Conchita, op.42, ballet, 1947; La leyenda de la isla de San Lorenzo, op.44, ballet, 1949; Fantasía romántica, op.45, tpt, harp, str, 1950

Principal publishers: Elkan-Vogel, Lemoine, Senart

WRITINGS

'Aperçu sur la musique inca', *AcM*, vi (1934), 1

'Ensayo sobre la música inca', *Boletín latino-americano de música*, i (1935), 71

'Ensayo sobre la música nazca', *Revista del Museo Nacional*, viii/1 (Lima, 1939), 123

'Los primeros músicos indo-peruanos de cultura europea, en el siglo xvi', *Música*, i/1 (1957), 3

'Tomás de Torrejón y Velasco (1644–1728)', *Música*, i/3 (1957), 3

'Una familia de músicos peruanos en el siglo xvii: los Cervantes del Águila', *Música*, i/2 (1957), 2

'La vida musical en la Catedral de Lima durante la colonia', *Revista musical chilena* (1962), nos.81–2, pp.8–53

La música en la Catedral de Lima: historia general; diccionario biografico (Lima, 1970–72)

BIBLIOGRAPHY

'Nuevo director del conservatorio', *Boletín del Conservatorio nacional de musica*, viii/26 (1951), 1

Compositores de América/Composers of the Americas, ed. Pan American Union, ii (Washington, DC, 1956), 116

'Andrés Sas (1900–1967)', *Revista musical chilena* (1967), no.101, p.123

ROBERT STEVENSON

Sass, Sylvia (*b* Budapest, 21 July 1951). Hungarian soprano. She studied at the Liszt Academy in Budapest and after graduating in 1972 joined the company of the Budapest State Opera as a principal. Her début that year was as Gutrune. In 1973 she appeared as Giselda in the Budapest Opera's new production of *I lombardi*, and subsequently made her Covent Garden début in that part in the same production (1976). She had already made her British début, and something of a sensation, as Desdemona in the Scottish Opera *Otello* (1975). She has since appeared at the Bol'shoy and throughout east and west Europe. Her Metropolitan début came in 1977, as Tosca, and in 1976 she appeared at the Aix Festival as Violetta, one of her most noted roles. She is an unpredictable singer, full of temperament and vocal allure. She boasts a refined *pianissimo*, used sometimes to telling, sometimes to selfconscious effect. In *forte* the tone, employed unstintingly, tends to harshness. She has an undoubted dramatic presence, but her acting has been criticized as lacking in spontaneity. She is undoubtedly an artist who commands attention, whatever she is doing on the stage or on the concert platform. Her repertory includes Poppaea, Fiordiligi, Norma, Elisabetta, Violetta, Lady Macbeth, Desdemona and Tosca. On record, at least, she has indicated that her talents may be best suited to the Wagnerian repertory.

ALAN BLYTH

Sassanid Empire, music of the. *See* PERSIA.

Sasse, Konrad (*b* Wernigerode, 3 Oct 1926). German musicologist. He studied musicology at the University of Halle with Max Schneider and Walter Siegmund-Schultze (1948–54), taking the doctorate there in 1962 with a dissertation on Robert Franz. After working as secretary to the Halle Handel Festivals (1954–6), he was appointed director of the Handel House in Halle (1956) and in 1959 joined the committee of the Händel-Gesellschaft. His principal publications are studies of Handel, and include a catalogue of the collections in the Handel House, a Handel bibliography and several studies of the performing aspects of the operas; he is a holder of the Handel Prize. Within the Gesellschaft für

Musikforschung he directs the East German study group on instruments.

WRITINGS

'Die Texte der Londoner Opern Händels in ihren gesellschaftlichen Beziehungen', *Wissenschaftliche Zeitschrift der Martin-Luther-Universität: Gesellschaft- und Sprachwissenschaftliche Reihe*, iv (1955), 627

'Zur Anwendung der Stanislawski-Methode auf die Darstellung der Opern Händels', *Festschrift der Händelfestspiele 1955*, 64

'Neue Daten zu Johann Christoph Schmidt', *HJb 1957*, 115

Das Händel-Haus in Halle: Geburtshaus Georg Friedrich Händels: Geschichte und Führer durch die Ausstellungen (Halle, 1958)

'Händels Stellung zu den gesellschaftlichen Problemen in England', *Händel-Ehrung der Deutschen Demokratischen Republik: Halle 1959*, 81

ed.: 'Opera Register from 1712 to 1734 (Colman-Register)', *HJb 1959*, 199

Katalog zu den Sammlungen des Händel-Hauses in Halle (Halle, 1961–)

Beiträge zur Forschung über Robert Franz unter besonderer Berücksichtigung seiner gesellschaftlichen Stellung und der Erschliessung dokumentarischen Materials (diss., U. of Halle, 1962)

'Probleme der Beispiele in Vorträgen über Musik', *Wissenschaftliche Zeitschrift der Martin-Luther-Universität: Gesellschaft- und Sprachwissenschaftliche Reihe*, xi (1962), 51

'Bemerkungen zur musikalischen Bearbeitungs- und Aufführungspraxis für Händels Opernwerke unter Berücksichtigung der Informationstheorie', *HJb 1963*, 85

'Bibliographie: Habilitationsschriften, Dissertationen und Diplomarbeiten am Institut für Musikwissenschaft: wissenschaftliche und künstlerische Veröffentlichungen der jetzigen Mitglieder des Instituts für Musikwissenschaft', *Traditionen und Aufgaben der Hallischen Musikwissenschaft: Wissenschaftliche Zeitschrift der Martin-Luther-Universität* (1963), suppl., 149

'Gedanken zu einigen Aufgaben und Methoden der Rezeptionsforschung', *Wissenschaftliche Zeitschrift der Martin-Luther-Universität: Gesellschaft- und Sprachwissenschaftliche Reihe*, xii (1963), 647

'Chronologisches Verzeichnis zum Briefwechsel von Robert Franz', *DJbM*, viii (1963), 96

Händel-Bibliographie (Leipzig, 1963, 2/1967 with appx for 1962–5)

'Hinweise zur Bedeutung des Werkes von William Hogarth für die Händel-Forschung', *13. Händelfestspiele Halle 1964*, 49

'Beispiele zu musikalisch-dramaturgischen Problemen der Da-capo-Gestaltung in Händels Opernarien', *HJb 1966*, 32

Halle an der Saale: Musik (Halle, 1968)

'Bemerkungen zur Berücksichtigung des Klanges historischer Hammerflügel für die Interpretation Beethovenscher Klavierwerke auf modernen Instrumenten', *Internationaler Beethoven-Kongress· Berlin 1970*, 559

'Der Beitrag von Robert Franz zur Händel-Rezeption im 19. Jahrhundert', *Funktion und Wirkung der Musik Georg Friedrich Händels in Vergangheit und Gegenwart* (Halle, 1976), 56

HORST SEEGER

Sassetti. Portuguese firm of music publishers and retailers. It was founded in Lisbon in 1848 as Sassetti & Co. by João Baptista Sassetti (1817–89), and published educational works, classical choral and piano music and works by Portuguese composers (e.g. João Arroio, Luís de Freitas Branco, Cláudio Carneyro, Rui Coelho, Rey Colaço, Armando José Fernandes, Frederico de Freitas, Víctor Hussla, Alfredo Keil and José Vianna da Motta). In 1973 Sassetti & Co. started a new company, Sassetti–Sociedade Portuguese de Música e Som, which is involved in the manufacture of records and music, also handling its own sales; it specializes in records, and its programme includes the systematic recording of works by major Portuguese composers (e.g. Carlos Seixas, João Domingos Bomtempo, Fernando Lopes Graça, Jorge Peixinho and Emanuel Nunes). Sassetti & Co. continues as an independent retail business.

CARLOS DE PONTES LEÇA

Sassofone (It.). SAXOPHONE.

Satanowski, Robert (*b* Łódź, 20 June 1928). Polish conductor and composer. He studied conducting in Łódź under Bohdan Wodiczko and gained his diploma in 1951; that year he became conductor of the Lublin PO. From 1954 to 1958 he was conductor and artistic director of the State PO in Bydgoszcz and in 1960 was appointed artistic director of the city theatre and conductor of opera and operetta in Karl-Marx-Stadt. From 1961 to 1963 he was conductor, artistic director and director of the Poznań PO. He founded the Poznań Chamber Orchestra and was conductor of the Poznań Opera, 1963–5. From 1969 to 1976 he was artistic director of the Vereinigte Städtische Bühnen of Krefeld and Mönchengladbach. In 1975 he became conductor and artistic director of the Municipal Music Theatre in Kraków. Among Satanowski's compositions are an *Allegro symfoniczne*, a string quartet, piano and choral works, songs and dramatic music.

MIECZYSŁAWA HANUSZEWSKA

Satchmo. See ARMSTRONG, LOUIS.

Satie, Erik [Eric] **(Alfred Leslie)** (*b* Honfleur, 17 May 1866; *d* Paris, 1 July 1925). French composer. He is best remembered as the composer of music which is deliberately modest and inconsequential, and of bizarre titles. However, he was a harmonic innovator in his earlier pieces, where unusual progressions are presented with quasi-archaic simplicity; much of his music contains a highly purified poetry that is more than merely factitious. Although his work may have been severely restricted in scope, he had an important influence on composers as various as Debussy, Ravel, Poulenc and Cage.

1. LIFE. He was the son of Alfred Satie, a French ship broker, and his Scottish wife. After the 1870 war the family moved to Paris, but two years later Satie's mother died and he was sent back to live with his grandparents. In 1878 his grandmother also died and he was returned once more to Paris where his father organized an informal education for him. If this gave him any joy it was short-lived, for in 1878 Alfred Satie married Eugénie Barnetsche, a pianist and mediocre Romantic composer whom the child disliked.

In 1879 Satie entered the Paris Conservatoire. Records show him as gifted, exceptionally lazy and often absent; in 1882 he was dismissed for failing to reach the required standard, but he spent a year attending Taudou's harmony class, and in 1885 was just accepted into the piano class of Mathias, who assessed him thus: 'Nothing. Three months to learn a piece. Incapable of sight-reading'. His greatest friend of the time, Contamine de Latour, stated that he persisted with his wearisome studies to qualify for the one-year *volontariat* in place of five years' military service. In November 1886 he duly joined the 33rd Infantry, but by April of the next year he had contracted bronchitis and he spent several months convalescing.

Alfred Satie was now trying to establish a music publishing business and brought out five songs by Satie and de Latour. Meanwhile Chabrier's *Le roi malgré lui* had had its first performance and shortly afterwards Satie wrote his three Sarabandes (1887), which owe a debt to Chabrier, and in their turn probably influenced the Sarabande of Debussy's *Pour le piano*. In the following year he produced his *Gymnopédies*, and in 1890, in the wake of the Paris exposition of 1889, his orientally tinged *Gnossiennes*.

Satie, always a keen reader, had by now developed an absorbing interest in mystical religion, Gregorian chant,

Gothic art and the lives of the saints. He had also begun, with de Latour, to frequent Montmartre where, when the *Gymnopédies* were still little known, Vital-Hocquet introduced him to Rudolph Salis's café Chat Noir as 'Erik Satie, gymnopédiste!'. His narrow, bourgeois upbringing had left him shy, discreet, reserved, elegant and well mannered. The Chat Noir was a revelation; under the influence of its camaraderie, escapades and endless revolutionary artistic debates, his character began to evolve. Relations with his family grew strained and he moved to Montmartre with 1600 francs in his pocket, going to smaller and smaller lodgings as his money ran out. His religious interests led him, in the early 1890s, to join the flamboyant Joséphin Péladan, 'Sâr Merodack' of the 'Rose + Croix' artistic movement for which Satie became the official composer. Péladan was an avid Wagnerian. Satie, however, wrote him scores that were hieratic and aloof, notably *Le fils des étoiles* (1891), justly called a 'static sound décor'. During the composition of it he first met the man who for some 25 years was to be perhaps his greatest friend, Debussy. The two were strongly drawn to each other, but it was not a simple relationship. Debussy was prepared to make his superiority felt; Satie became the jester to hide his humiliation.

In doing so Satie could be said to be adopting his most characteristic role. He knew his technique was severely limited; but pride and determination, coupled with great sensitivity, led him to try to bypass his deficiencies with intricate technical systems of his own devising. It also made him allow his natural humour to develop into a protective cloak. This conflict, together with the opposing pulls of nature and upbringing, not only shaped his fascinating, complex, prickly character; it also moulded much of his music, giving it sometimes incongruous traits that are part of its individual charm.

During the Montmartre period Satie's humour was often fashionably exhibitionist. He announced his break with Péladan in 1892 in a flowery, pseudo-archaic letter to *Gil blas*. In the same year he and de Latour wrote *Uspud*, a 'Christian ballet' that they presented to the director of the Opéra (following Péladan's custom), winning an interview only by issuing a duel challenge. Three times Satie applied for the supreme honour of a seat in the Academy. He had a stormy love affair with Utrillo's mother, the painter and one-time circus performer Suzanne Valadon. He formed his own 'Eglise Métropolitaine d'Art de Jésus Conducteur' and, with the help of a legacy of 7000 francs, published a broadsheet, *Le cartulaire*, a mixture of ecclesiastical fantasy and Péladan-style polemics against such figures as Colette's husband Willy, with whom he finally came to blows at one of the Colonne Concerts. With the same legacy he bought his famous 12 identical grey velvet suits. But his generosity was as marked as his appearance and he was soon as poor as before. Two *Gymnopédies* were published in 1895, seemingly on the recommendation of Debussy, who also orchestrated a pair in the following year (not, as Cocteau and others have claimed, misunderstanding and blurring them, but closely following Satie's own orchestral practice of the time).

By now Montmartre was changing. It was losing its rustic, village character and a new generation was coming in. In 1898 Satie packed his belongings into a handcart and moved to his last home, in the southern suburb of Arcueil-Cachan. He cut his long hair, dropped his bohemian trappings and reverted to his respectable, gentlemanly self. It was the start of his most unhappy period. He was forced to earn a living as a *café-concert* pianist, which he considered 'a great lowering', and as a composer of music-hall songs and incidental music. He walked the several kilometres to Montmartre to work each day and walked back in the middle of the night. The main monument to these 15 sad years is the set of *Trois morceaux en forme de poire*, written between 1890 and 1903 and consisting for the most part of arrangements of cabaret melodies.

From 1905 to 1908 Satie became a student again and studied counterpoint, fugue and orchestration under d'Indy and Roussel at the Schola Cantorum. He won a diploma, but his surviving exercises show that he was not by any means exceptional. Nor did this step bear any quick fruit. His output remained low and much of it was a series of attempts to fuse his new contrapuntal skill into a personal style.

When the tide finally turned at the beginning of 1911, it was because Ravel played the Sarabandes at a concert of the Société Musicale Indépendante. It is clear from the programme note that the chief attraction was their prophetic nature and Satie's position as a 'precursor'. Two months later Debussy conducted a performance of his *Gymnopédie* orchestrations and was woundingly surprised at their success. The following years saw the first performances of Roland-Manuel's orchestration of the *Prélude de la porte héroïque du ciel*, and of Ravel's of an excerpt from *Le fils des étoiles*. Articles were published by Jules Ecorcheville, Calvocoressi and Roland-Manuel. In 1913 Ricardo Viñes, one of Satie's most faithful and persistent interpreters, first included his music in a recital, and for once it was a recent composition, the *Quatre préludes flasques*. This attention meant that publishers suddenly began to demand his music. Several of his old pieces were brought out and printed, and he quickly responded with a whole series of 'humorous' piano pieces, with eccentric titles and bizarre commentaries (rewards for the player and on no account to be read out).

Though the outbreak of war interrupted the steadily increasing number of Satie performances, in April 1915 he had his greatest single stroke of fortune when a performance he gave with Viñes of the *Trois morceaux* was heard by the young Cocteau. Satie's meteoric rise to fame after the war was entirely Cocteau's doing. He used his entrée in élite and wealthy circles to win commissions, he persuaded virtuosos – such as the pianist and concert promoter Jean Wiener – to give Satie performances, he wrote and lectured about Satie (particularly in *Le coq et l'arlequin*, March 1918, and *La jeunesse et le scandale*, c1920) and he contributed introductory notes and talks at concert performances. Most important of all, he collaborated with Satie, notably in the Dyagilev–Massin–Picasso ballet *Parade*.

The opening of *Parade* in May 1917 caused a scandal, and established Satie once and for all. The authors were called 'boches' (a legal offence at the time), and Satie was given an eight-day prison sentence and a heavy fine for sending a rude postcard to a critic, but the penalty was suspended, thanks to Roland-Manuel's father-in-law. In the wake of all this, a group of young composers formed around Satie under the banner 'Les Nouveaux Jeunes'. The personnel was finally fixed in 1920 when the journalist Henri Collet somewhat arbitrarily defined Les Six.

Meanwhile, early in 1917 or possibly even before,

Satie had started to work on what is often considered his masterpiece, the cantata *Socrate*. He prepared the text himself by drastically pruning Victor Cousin's translation of Plato's *Dialogues*. He was intent from the outset on writing a work that should be 'white and pure like antiquity'. The result was a creation in which his restricted means came into perfect focus and balance. It was not publicly performed until 1920, but after a private hearing in mid-1919 Stravinsky is reputed to have remarked 'French music is Bizet, Chabrier and Satie'. Satie was now enjoying fame and success and the social life they brought. In 1920 there were two festivals of his music, and in this final period his output was far more varied than before. With Milhaud he produced *Musique d'ameublement* ('furniture music') as a background for the intervals in a concert. He also wrote songs, piano music and ballet scores, culminating, in 1924, in *Mercure* (Massin and Picasso) and *Relâche* (designed by Picabia with a filmed entr'acte by René Clair). Both were scandals, *Relâche* living up to its title ('theatre closed') on the opening night, owing to the illness of the principal dancer, Jean Borlin.

In 1923, prompted by Milhaud, another group of young composers formed around him. They took the title 'L'Ecole d'Arcueil' and consisted of Cliquet-Pleyel, Desormière, Jacob and Sauguet. But Satie's health was beginning to deteriorate. For some years he had drunk quite heavily and become more and more unsociable. After *Relâche* he declined rapidly. He lost what had once been a prodigious appetite, and when he went into Paris to visit, he would sit for hours silently in front of the fire in his hat and coat, with the inevitable umbrella. His friends set him up in hotels to spare him the journey to Arcueil, and he spent his days, still dressed up, sitting in an armchair staring at his reflection, working the light and the door from where he sat with an elaborate string device. Eventually he had to move to hospital, and on 1 July 1925 he died of sclerosis of the liver. When his brother, Milhaud and one or two others went to Arcueil and finally entered the room he had lived in for nearly 30 years without admitting even the concierge, they were astounded by its bareness: a bed, chair and table, a half-empty cupboard with the 12 velvet suits piled on top, an old unused piano whose pedals worked by string, and little else. But he had kept most of his manuscript notebooks, dating back to the early 1890s, and a large quantity of documents. Most of the latter were destroyed in a fire, but thanks to Milhaud the music was saved.

2. WORKS. Satie's output divides itself conveniently into the decades of his life. In his 20s he wrote first the early piano works then the Rose + Croix music, in his 30s mainly cabaret music, in his 40s – after his time at the Schola – the 'humorous' piano music and in his 50s a suddenly far more varied output including the three main ballets, *Socrate*, songs and piano music.

Satie's earliest surviving piece is a ten-bar Allegro of 1884 pointing ahead to the idiom of the more tender *café-concert* melodies. The first published works, the *Valse-ballet* and *Fantaisie-valse* of 1885, bear the hallmarks of his stepmother and are probably not his unaided work. His first significant pieces were the *Ogives* of 1886. They have quasi-plainsong melodies and triadic harmonies (related, typically, by the logic of the top part rather than the bass), and they form the seed from which the remarkable Rose + Croix works blossomed. But before that he wrote his five early songs, said by de

1. Erik Satie

Latour to be inspired by Massenet. They again look forward to the tender cabaret melodies, but with unexpected and delightful twists that clearly show the harmonic ear that was one of his chief gifts.

The Sarabandes of 1887 became famous for their prophetic harmony, particularly their unresolved 9th chords. Though probably stimulated by Chabrier, Satie went considerably further. These pieces also contain the first hint of buffoonery in the form of awkward enharmonic chord spellings. The *Gymnopédies* are in a different world: the textures are simple, with monodies riding over plain, delicately modal accompaniments. They are gentle but stately, calm but just lilting. These pieces are said to have been suggested by Flaubert's *Salammbô*, which Satie particularly admired, and one can detect something of the spirit of *Socrate* in them. The *Gnossiennes* are somewhat similar, but their mode and melodic ornamentation give them an oriental flavour. Bizarre annotations appear for the first time, at this stage only to replace the normal Italian ones.

The Rose + Croix works of 1891–5 form, with the *Ogives*, a fascinating collection. Underlying them is an intense search for a compositional system or method, whose details are at times immensely intricate. On the surface they share a quality of quasi-mystical detachment, sometimes larded over with a buffoonery that finds its peak in *Uspud* and the 840-times repeated passage of *Vexations*. The frequent use of the term 'impressionistic' to describe the harmony of this music is totally mistaken. Satie's use of parallel 9ths and higher extensions is no more like Debussy's than that of a swing band. Some of the Rose + Croix pieces were more successful than others; few reveal their merits casually. Perhaps the most perfect miniature is the *Prélude d'Eginhard*, and the most eccentric *Salut drapeau!* in which a melody in the ancient Greek chromatic mode is accompanied by a non-tonal series of 6-3 chords.

Satie's second creative decade started with a return to the *Gnossienne* style. This he developed, through a series of transitional sketches, into the idiom of the first and third 'Airs à faire fuir' from *Pièces froides*. The 'Danses de travers' introduce a broken-chord left-hand figuration that points ahead to his clearest and most economical piano style. This decade was spent mainly in writing *café-concert* music, much of it of a high quality. The most considerable pieces were *Jack-in-the-box* and *Geneviève de Brabant*, both thought lost but found behind his piano after his death; also the *Angora Ox* (part of which found its way into the *Redite* of the *Trois morceaux*; incomplete versions also exist for piano and orchestra), *California Legend* (which was incorporated into *La belle excentrique*) and *The Dreamy Fish* (music for a story by 'Lord Cheminot', alias de Latour).

The best-known work of this period is the set of *Trois morceaux en forme de poire*. Of the seven sections only the first and the first page of the third appear to have been specially composed; the rest is an anthology of music written between 1890 and 1903. The story that Debussy criticized Satie's form and Satie replied with the *Trois morceaux* three weeks later is disproved by their correspondence. The music in the *café-concert* idiom is not idealized as has been claimed; it is in fact the real thing.

In his output of the Schola period, at the start of his next decade, he appears to have been groping for a new serious style, something that had eluded him for ten years or so. It may be regretted that several pieces from this period have recently been published, since Satie, when he had the opportunity, understandably chose not to release them. Even the *Aperçus désagréables* and *En habit de cheval*, which he did have published, are concerned with rather literal ways of assimilating his new contrapuntal skills. They are full of fugues and chorales (about which he was to say: 'My chorales equal those of Bach with the difference that they are more rare and less pretentious').

Success, when it came, stimulated him far more than study. In his late 40s he produced not only over a dozen sets of humorous piano pieces, but also his notorious play and self-portrait *Le piège de Méduse*, with its incidental music, and *Cinq grimaces* for a projected production by Cocteau of *A Midsummer Night's Dream*. With the piano pieces his style suddenly crystallized. The writing tends to be lean, often in two parts. The form is usually like a string of beads, each a bar or two of some sharply defined texture, a technique that harks back to the Rose + Croix works. Sharp contrasts between one of these 'motifs', to use his own word, and the next, suggest orchestral colours, and in a sense this style culminates in some of the movements of *Parade*. In another sense its apotheosis is in the *Sports et divertissements*, published in a de luxe facsimile with illustrations by Charles Martin. In these 20 miniatures Satie's eccentric annotations, which he had often written apart from the music before, and his beautiful calligraphy, are finally fused into the conception of the work. No element can be left out, and the result is a private art that tends to resist public performance.

Satie's last decade started with *Parade*, famous for the typewriter, siren etc called for in the score. In fact the writing is an orchestral translation of his current piano styles, including a tiny fugato prelude and epilogue. He said of these: 'I like this genre, slightly pompous and feignedly naive'.

Socrate broaches very different territory. For once there are no defences, which has been ascribed to the fact that Debussy was no longer alive, although Satie started work on it at least 15 months before his friend's death and probably even before their final estrangement. In a sense the music harks back to the ideals of the Rose + Croix days, providing again a 'static sound décor' against which the words, unforced and uninflated, can emerge in their own time and create their own effect. By stripping the music of all rhetoric Satie forces the listener to sharpen his responses, to concentrate and focus his sensitivity until the slightest shift becomes significant. And to those who can meet this challenge, the death of Socrates, set to what now becomes an actual plainsong line with a bare ostinato accompaniment, is intensely moving.

There are three sets of songs from the last decade. Their contents vary from a bitter *Elégie* in memory of Debussy to an *allegretto* ('genre Gounod') setting of a poem about the Mad Hatter. To some extent they are less individual than the earlier *Trois poèmes d'amour* (1914) in which Satie's own tiny poems poke fun at the vocalized mute 'e' in sung French. (Singers who attempted to play this down infuriated him.)

Of the piano pieces, the *Sonatine bureaucratique* is interesting in that it paraphrases Clementi, thereby anticipating (and possibly influencing) Stravinsky's use of old material. But undoubtedly the most significant are the five Nocturnes. In their way some of his most serious and successful compositions, these pieces are once

2. *Picasso's design for the French Manager in Satie's 'Parade', first performed by the Ballets Russes in 1917*

again the fruit of a highly calculated system. No.2, for instance, is an exercise in harmony in 2nds, 4ths, 5ths and 7ths; no.5, by contrast, is all in 3rds and 6ths. The final ballets, *Mercure* and *Relâche*, return to his music-hall idiom in varying degrees of stylization.

Satie has three main claims to fame: his possible influence on Debussy, who was certainly not above 'borrowing', and his acknowledged influence on Ravel; his more interesting and far-reaching influence on the current avant garde, via Varèse and particularly Cage; and his intrinsic merit. The last is the most important, and although the initial dispute has passed into history, it has remained a source of considerable disagreement. The reason for this is that Satie represents an extreme – an important special case in music aesthetics. The hallmark of a certain type of sophistication, of what might be called the connoisseur mentality, is to prefer small, exquisitely wrought nuances to anything more effusive which, by contrast, seems tasteless and gross. Satie's most eminent and discriminating admirers have always tended to praise, above all, his clarity, restraint, purity of style and lack of rhetoric or frills. This clearly denies many of music's most potent resources, and while some can accept it readily, many others find the sacrifices too great. More interestingly, because it is essentially a cultivated taste, still others can be educated to it, either directly or through the cultural ethos. The taste for Satie is therefore particularly susceptible to fashion.

It has also been argued that Satie's particular extreme suits some other arts better than it does music. It is no coincidence that Cocteau's description of his own role as a poet exactly parallels his views on Satie. 'True tears', he wrote, 'are not shed over a sad page, but over the miracle of a word in exactly the right place. Few are worthy to weep such tears'. Painters too, at about the time of World War I, were led to see Satie as a 'Picasso of music' who would lead it away from impressionism. *Parade* has often been described as 'Cubist'. So it is not surprising that most of Satie's last works are concerned with some sort of programme, whether it be a song lyric, or a ballet scenario, or the intricate amalgam of *Sports et divertissements*. Even *Socrate* owes its effect essentially to the relationship between words and music, and few works would suffer more from one's not being able to hear or understand the text.

There was a considerable revival of interest in Satie during the early 1970s, especially in the USA, partly, perhaps, a matter of fashion. But it could well be that the man Ravel called a 'precursor both brilliant and clumsy' will eventually be seen to have been far further ahead of his time and of greater genius than his illustrious disciple ever imagined.

WORKS

The published output falls into three categories: works published during Satie's lifetime, works issued shortly after his death under the direction of Milhaud, and works printed much later under the direction of Robert Caby. This list includes all pieces in the first two groups as well as the more important Caby publications. Some lesser works edited by Caby are given in the appendix.

DRAMATIC

Le fils des étoiles (pastorale kaldéenne, Sâr Péladan), 3 preludes ? for fls and harps, 1891; pf score survives
Deux préludes du Nazaréen (incidental music, H. Mazel), pf, 1892
Uspud (ballet chrétien, 3, J. P. Contamine de Latour), 1892; pf score survives with annotations for fls, harps and str
Prélude d'Eginhard (incidental music), pf, 1893
Prélude de la porte héroïque du ciel (drame ésotérique, J. Bois), pf, 1894
Jack-in-the-box (pantomime, J. Depaquit), pf, 1899; as ballet (Balanchine), Paris, Sarah Bernhardt, 3 July 1926
Geneviève de Brabant (miniature marionette opera), vv, pf, 1899

Pousse l'amour (Coco chéri) (parts of operetta), c1905; Monte Carlo, 1913; lost
Le piège de Méduse (play with music, Satie), 7 dances, pf/insts, 1913
Cinq grimaces pour 'Le songe d'une nuit d'été' (incidental music, Shakespeare), orch, 1914
Parade (ballet réaliste, Cocteau, Massin), orch, 1917; Paris, Châtelet, 18 May 1917
La belle excentrique (fantaisie sérieuse for dance) [incl. California Legend, c1902], music-hall orch, pf 2/4 hands, c1902–1920
Recitatives for Gounod: Le médecin malgré lui, 1923; Monte Carlo, 1924
Mercure (ballet, Massin), orch, 1924; Paris, La Cigale, 15 June 1924
Relâche (ballet, Picabia, Börlin), orch, 1924; Paris, Champs-Elysées, 6 Dec 1924

VOCAL
(large-scale works)

Messe des pauvres (Lat. Mass and psalms), chorus, org/pf, c1893–5
Socrate (drame symphonique, Plato, trans. V. Cousin), 1 or more vv, pf/chamber orch, 1918

(songs)

Elégie (Contamine de Latour), 1887; 3 mélodies (Contamine de Latour), 1887; Chanson (Contamine de Latour), 1887; Salut drapeau! (Hymne au drapeau) (Sâr Péladan), 1891; Bonjour Biqui!, 1893; 3 poèmes d'amour (Satie), 1914; 3 mélodies (Fargue, M. Godebska, Chalupt), 1916; 4 petites mélodies (Lamartine, Cocteau, 18th century, Radiguet), 1920; Ludions (Fargue), 1923
Café-concert songs, c1900, incl. Tendrement (V. Hyspa), Je te veux (H. Pacory), La diva de l'empire (D. Bonnaud, N. Blès)

INSTRUMENTAL
(other than for pf solo)

Danse, fl, ob, 2 cl, bn, timp, harp, 1890, arr. pf 4 hands in 3 morceaux en forme de poire; 3 sonneries de la Rose + Croix, tpts, harps, 1892, pf score survives; 3 morceaux en forme de poire, pf 4 hands, 1890–1903; En habit de cheval, pf 4 hands/orch, 1911; Aperçus désagréables, pf 4 hands, 1908–12; Choses vues à droite et à gauche (sans lunettes), vn, pf, 1914; 3 petites pièces montées, orch/pf 4 hands, c1920; Musique d'ameublement, pf, 3 cl, trbn, 1920, collab. Milhaud; Sonnerie pour réveiller le bon gros Roi des Singes, 2 tpt, 1921

(pf solo)

Allegro, 1884; Valse-ballet, 1885; Fantaisie-valse, 1885; 4 ogives, 1886; 3 sarabandes, 1887; 3 gymnopédies, 1888; 3 gnossiennes, 1890; Première pensée Rose + Croix, 1891; Fête donnée par des Chevaliers Normands en l'honneur d'une jeune demoiselle, 1892; Vexations, c1893; Danses gothiques, 1893; Modéré, 1893; Pièces froides, 1897; Poudre d'or, c1901; Le Piccadilly, c1904; Prélude en tapisserie, 1906; Passacaille, 1906; Nouvelles pièces froides, 1906–10; 4 préludes flasques (pour un chien), 1912; 3 véritables préludes flasques (pour un chien), 1912; Descriptions automatiques, 1913; Embryons desséchés, 1913; Croquis et agaceries d'un gros bonhomme en bois, 1913; Chapitres tournés en tous sens, 1913; Vieux sequins et vieilles cuirasses, 1913; Menus propos enfantins, 1913; Enfantillages pittoresques, 1913; Peccadilles importunes, 1913; Les pantins dansent, 1913; Sports et divertissements, 1914; Heures séculaires et instantanées, 1914; Les 3 valses du précieux dégoûté, 1914; Avant-dernières pensées, 1915; Sonatine bureaucratique, 1917; 5 nocturnes, 1919; Rêverie de l'enfance de Pantagruel, c1920; Premier menuet, 1920

APPENDIX
(lesser works ed. Caby)

Song: Chanson médiévale (Mendès)
Pf: Arrière propos, Caresse, Désespoir agréable, 2 rêveries nocturnes, 12 petits chorals, Effronterie, Exercices, The Dreamy Fish, Fâcheux exemple, Froide songerie, Gambades, Gnossiennes nos.4–6; Le grand singe, Harmonies [2 sets], Nouvelles pièces enfantines, Petite ouverture à danser, Poésie, Prélude canin, Prélude de la mort de M Mouche, Prière, Le prisonnier moussade, Profondeur, Songe creux
Also Rêverie du pauvre, pf acc. to missing melody, probably not by Satie

Principal publishers: Salabert
MSS in *F-Pn*

WRITINGS

Many in MSS; articles in *L'avenir d'Arcueil-Cachan* (1909–10), *Feuilles libres* (1922–4), *BSIM*, viii–x (1912–14), *391* (1921–4).
L'esprit musical (Liège, 1950)
ed. G. Charbonnier: 'Humour poétique', *La nef* (1950–51), nos.71–2
Cahiers d'un mammifère (Liège, 1951)
Mémoires d'un amnésique (Liège, 1953)
Propos à propos (Liège, 1954)
Léger comme un oeuf (Paris, 1957)
Oui: lettres d'Erik Satie adressées à Pierre de Massot (Alès, 1960)
'Mémoires d'un amnésique', 'Chronique musicale', *Approdo musicale* (1965), nos.19–20
ed. T. Winkfield: *Dried Embryos* (London, 1972)

ed. N. Wilkins: 'The Writings of Erik Satie: Miscellaneous Fragments', *ML*, lvi (1975), 288
ed. O. Voltà: *D'Esoterik Satie à Satierik (textes et correspondance)* (Paris, 1976)
ed. N. Wilkins: *The Writings of Erik Satie* (London, 1976)
ed. O. Voltà: *Ecrits* (Paris, 1977–)

BIBLIOGRAPHY
MONOGRAPHS
Roland-Manuel: *Erik Satie* (Paris, 1916)
P. D. Templier: *Erik Satie* (Paris, 1932; Eng trans., 1969)
R. Myers: *Erik Satie* (London, 1948)
ReM (1952), no.214 [special number]
Y. Gérard: *Introduction à l'oeuvre d'Erik Satie* (diss., Paris Conservatoire, 1958)
F. Lesure, ed.: *Erik Satie: exposition* (Paris, 1966)
B. Hill: *Characteristics of the Music of Erik Satie that Suggest the 'Id'* (diss., U. of Colorado, 1967)
A. Gillmor: *Erik Satie and the Concept of the Avant-garde* (diss., U. of Toronto, 1972)
A. Rey: *Erik Satie* (Paris, 1974)
G. Wehmeyer: *Erik Satie* (Regensburg, 1974)
J. Harding: *Erik Satie* (London, 1975)

OTHER LITERATURE
J. Cocteau: *Le coq et l'arlequin: notes autour de la musique* (Paris, 1918)
H. Collet: 'Un livre de Rimsky et un livre de Cocteau – les cinq russes, les six français et Erik Satie', *Comoedia* (16 and 23 Jan 1920)
W. Roberts: 'The Problem of Satie', *ML*, iv (1923), 313
C. Koechlin: 'Erik Satie', *ReM*, v/2 (1924), 193
J. Cocteau: 'Fragments d'une conférence sur Eric Satie', *ReM*, v/2 (1924), 217 [from *La jeunesse et le scandale, Oeuvres complètes de Jean Cocteau*, ix (Geneva, 1950)]
J. P. C. de Latour: 'Erik Satie intime', *Comoedia* (3, 5, 6 Aug 1925)
J. Cocteau: *Rappel à l'ordre* (Paris, 1926)
W. Danckert: 'Der Klassizismus Erik Saties und seine geistliche Stellung', *ZMw*, xii (1929–30), 105
W. Mellers: *Studies in Contemporary Music* (London, 1947), 16ff
D. Milhaud: *Notes sans musique* (Paris, 1949; Eng. trans., 1952), 176ff
R. Shattuck: *The Banquet Years* (London, 1955), 88–145
F. Poulenc: *Moi et mes amis* (Paris, 1963), 81ff
P. Gowers: *Erik Satie: his Studies, Notebooks and Critics* (diss., U. of Cambridge, 1966)
——: 'Satie's Rose Croix Music (1891–1895)', *PRMA*, xcii (1965–6), 1
P. Santi: 'Il "point de départ" di Satie', *Chigiana*, xxiii (1966), 183
P. Dickinson: 'Erik Satie (1866–1925)', *MR*, xxviii (1967), 139
G. Wehmeyer: 'Saties Instanteisuns', *Musicae scientiae collectanea: Festschrift Karl Gustav Fellerer* (Cologne, 1973), 626
H. H. Stuckenschmidt: *Die Musik eines halben Jahrhunderts: 1925–1975* (Munich, 1976)

PATRICK GOWERS (text, work-list),
NIGEL WILKINS (writings, bibliography)

Satō, Eishi. *See* KIKKAWA, EISHI.

Satoh, Toyohiko (*b* Hiroshima, 4 Nov 1943). Japanese lutenist. He studied at Rikkio University, Tokyo, and with Eugen Dombois at the Schola Cantorum Basiliensis. He made his début in 1969 in Basle, and though he has since made a special study of Baroque music (lightly-strung Baroque lute, chitarrone and theorbo) he also plays 16th-century music (lute and vihuela). Satoh played at the Vienna Festival in 1971 (with the Concentus Musicus) and at the Holland Festival in 1972, and has made some admired and influential recordings of Baroque music. He teaches at The Hague Royal Conservatory.

DAVID SCOTT

Sattel (Ger.). NUT.

Sättler, Lisbeth. *See* RETHBERG, ELISABETH.

Satz (Ger.). Originally, a musical setting or the act of polyphonic composition; under the influence of the grammar of spoken language, it has come to mean theme, period and especially movement (of a sonata, suite etc), as well as style and texture.

The most general definition, 'musical setting', is based on the derivation of *Satz* from *setzen*, 'to set', which appeared in musical writings in the 16th and 17th centuries in the forms *absetzen*, 'to put into tablature', and *aussetzen*, 'to realize figures in a bass part'. *Satz*, or *Tonsatz*, first appeared in the 18th century, when it referred to a musical setting or the technique used therein. J. G. Walther (*Musicalisches Lexicon*, 1732) defined *Thema* as 'ein Satz zu einer Fuge, oder andern Ausarbeitung', thus making *Satz* equivalent to theme. H. C. Koch (*Musikalisches Lexicon*, 1802) gave four definitions, expanding its meaning while preserving the old notion of musical setting: (1) 'that single element of a piece of music which, in and of itself, expresses a complete thought' – Koch noted both the larger division of a section of a piece into *Hauptsatz* (or *Thema*) and *Nebensätze* (main theme and subsidiary themes) and the smaller division of a theme into *Absatz* and *Schlusssatz* (the modern notion of a period as the sum of two phrases, the first of which arrives at a half-cadence, the second of which completes the musical thought); (2) 'the connection of several individual elements in a main part of the whole', i.e. the modern concept of 'theme group'; (3) movement, i.e. an independent section of a cyclic composition; and (4) 'the grammatical construction of a piece of music', i.e. harmony and counterpoint.

Related to the last of these definitions is the idea of *Satzlehre* or *Setzkunst*. For Koch, *Setzkunst* and *Komposition* were synonyms. Later, *Satzlehre* is distinguished from *Kompositionslehre* in that it teaches one not to compose but merely to understand and be familiar with those occurrences which are typical features of polyphonic music.

By itself and in compounds *Satz* takes on several other musical meanings, such as texture (e.g. *Klaviersatz*) and style (e.g. *Kantilenensatz* versus *Chansonsatz*); one also encounters the terms *Fingersatz*, 'fingering', and (*Instrumenten-*)*satz*, 'consort'. *See also* ANALYSIS, §II, 2.

WILLIAM DRABKIN

Sätzl [Sätzel, Satzl], **Christoph** (*b* Brixen [now Bressanone]; *d* Hall [now Solbad Hall], 13 April 1655). Austrian composer. He studied at the grammar school at Freiburg and was then employed as a schoolmaster. By 1621 he had become Kapellmeister at Brixen Cathedral. From 1632 until his death he held a similar post in the convent at Hall, whose chapel was modelled on that at the Innsbruck court: it had won a high reputation for the standard of its music, the constitution laying down that the Kapellmeister should be able both to compose and to instruct the choristers in the singing of contrapuntal music.

Sätzl's output consists of Latin church music mostly with continuo and occasionally with other instruments. The influence of up-to-date Italian sacred music is strong in his work, due probably as much to the wide dissemination in south Germany and Austria of compositions by Monteverdi, Alessandro Grandi (i) and others as to the music of Italian composers in nearby Innsbruck. His liking for the solo medium is particularly interesting: the 1646 masses include two for solo voice, which may well be unique examples of the genre in early 17th-century Germany and Austria. Sätzl did not merely imitate the Italian style: the masses are undoubtedly northern in idiom. They show a feeling for the expressive possibilities of the medium without undue emphasis on ornamental writing. Unity is achieved by subtle use of repetition and sequence, while a conjunction of syllabic and gently florid word-setting lends variety, as does the continual change of tonal centre. Sätzl's other works display imaginative word-setting and subtle use of contrapuntal devices, especially in two and three parts. Passages in parallel 3rds are common; there are several instances of rondo form, a consciousness of key relationships and a definite tendency to treat the crotchet, not the minim, as the basic pulse.

WORKS

(all except anthologies published in Innsbruck)

Ecclesiastici concentus, 2–5vv, 2 insts, liber I (1621)
Hortus pensilis, qualis apud Babylonios fieri consuevit, Danieli ad recreandos, 2–6vv, bc (1628); 26 pieces
Bethlemitischer Jubel, 5vv (1640)
Certamen musicum (1641); 20 motets
Oesterlicher Jubel, 5–6vv (1641) [not 1642 as on title-page]
Cantiones genethliacae ad Christi cunas addita missa, 5vv, bc (1644)
[9] Missae novae singulis, 1–5vv, bc (1646)
Jubilus Davidicus seu psalmi, 2,3vv, mixto chelium binario modulandi (1653)
Missae 4 novae, 4,5vv, bc (1661)
12 motets in 1627[1]; 7 in 1624[1], 1626[2], 1627[2], 1629[1], *A-Wn*

BIBLIOGRAPHY

W. Senn: *Musik, Schule und Theater der Stadt Hall in Tirol* (Innsbruck, 1938), 684

A. LINDSEY KIRWAN

Saudi Arabia. A Near-Eastern kingdom on the Arabian Peninsula; *see* ARAB MUSIC and ARABIAN GULF.

Sauer. Austrian firm of music publishers. Its founder Ignaz Sauer (*b* Bohemia, 1 April 1759; *d* Vienna, 2 Dec 1833) began his activities in the art and music business as a partner in Joseph Eder's firm (founded 1794); Sauer terminated this relationship at the end of 1797. On 17 January 1798 he advertised his own 'Kunstverlag zu den sieben Schwestern'; this name refers to his seven daughters by his first marriage and appears in the plate inscriptions of his publications, which always bore an 'S.S.' in front of the number. His publications were initially commissioned to Kozeluch and Traeg. In March 1801 he became the Viennese agent for the firm of André in Offenbach. In a large advertisement in the *Wiener Zeitung* of 25 July 1801 (two years before Senefelder's firm was founded) he announced the first attempt at stoneplate printing in Austria with an edition of 12 ländler by Pechatschek. The confusion of war in

Title-page of Vanhal's 'Die grosse Seeschlacht bei Abukir' for keyboard, first published by Sauer in 1800

1805 and 1809 caused a financial decline, and on 25 November 1813 Sauer was obliged to give his stock-in-trade on commission to H. F. Müller.

On 9 December 1822 Sauer was joined by Marcus (Maximilian Josef) Leidesdorf (1787–1840), the son of a Jewish merchant, and as Sauer & Leidesdorf the firm revived, producing about 750 numbers in the next five years. Sauer relinquished his art dealer's licence on 30 April 1826, possibly because of his advanced age. On 9 May 1826 the firm was renamed M. J. Leidesdorf and continued to prosper until 18 July 1832, when Leidesdorf left for Italy and the licence was kept in abeyance until 15 May 1834, when Anton Berka took over the firm. On 4 September 1835 it passed to Diabelli & Co.

Ignaz Sauer's firm, while interesting for the history of publishing, was musically less significant; apart from issuing single works by Asioli, Clementi, Eybler, Mederitsch and Pasterwiz, it published many of Vanhal's late works and some of Sauer's own compositions. But as Sauer & Leidesdorf its calibre improved greatly; Leidesdorf's compositions were superficial fashionable pieces, but under his guidance the company published music by Beethoven and Weber, 49 works by Schubert (many of them first editions, including *Die schöne Müllerin*) and piano reductions of many of Rossini's operas with notable title decorations by Moritz von Schwind.

BIBLIOGRAPHY

J. Jureczek: 'Die Kaiserliche Privatbibliothek im Jahre 1809', *Die Kultur*, ix (1908), 187
'P. Beda Planks Fluchtreise 1800 bis 1801', *63. Programm des k.k. Obergymnasiums zu Kremsmünster* (Linz, 1913), 35ff
F. Gräffer: *Kleine Wiener Memoiren*, ed. A. Schlosser and G. Gugitz (Munich, 1918)
G. Gugitz: 'Alt-Wiener Kunsthändler', *Von Leuten und Zeiten im alten Wien* (Vienna and Leipzig, 1922)
O. E. Deutsch: *Music Publishers' Numbers* (London, 1946; Ger. trans., rev. 1961), 21

ALEXANDER WEINMANN

Sauer, Emil von (*b* Hamburg, 8 Oct 1862; *d* Vienna, 27 April 1942). German pianist. He was a pupil of Nikolay Rubinstein at the Moscow Conservatory (1879–81) and subsequently studied under Liszt and Deppe. From 1882 he made frequent and successful tours as a virtuoso pianist, and his long concert career lasted until 1936. In 1901 he was appointed head of the Meisterschule für Klavierspiel at the Vienna Academy, a post that he gave up in April 1907 but resumed in 1915. He had an admirable technique and his playing, though occasionally wanting in breadth, was always elegant and beautifully finished. His compositions are of minor importance. He edited the complete piano works of Brahms and a number of teaching works by Pischna, Plaidy and Kullak, among others, and published *Meine Welt* (Stuttgart, 1901). He was ennobled with the prefix 'von'.

BIBLIOGRAPHY

W. Niemann: *Meister des Klaviers* (Berlin, 1919), 29f

RONALD KINLOCH ANDERSON

Sauguet [Poupard], Henri(-Pierre) (*b* Bordeaux, 18 May 1901). French composer. Attracted towards music from an early age, he studied the piano and became an enthusiastic admirer of Bizet, Schumann and Debussy. After organ lessons with Paul Combes, he took a modest appointment as organist at a church in the Bordeaux suburbs and studied composition with J. P. Vaubourgoin and Joseph Canteloube. Apart from the

Classical masters, it was the music of Stravinsky and Satie that excited his intense interest; he read Cocteau's *Le coq et l'arlequin* and, following the example of Les Six, he founded a Bordeaux counterpart, 'Les Trois', with the composer J. M. Lizotte and the poet Louis Emié. Sauguet exchanged letters with Milhaud, who asked to see some of his compositions, and it was in response to this request that he wrote a first collection of *Trois françaises* (1923) for piano, spontaneous and serious pieces with clear and supple lines and an atmosphere of tender emotion. These were his first major achievements, affirming the direction of his future output even though his music was to become technically stronger and acquire new means. Milhaud encouraged him to move to Paris, and there introduced him to Koechlin and Satie. From 1923 Sauguet associated with Cliquet-Pleyel, Jacob and Desormière in forming the Ecole d'Arcueil; their inaugural concert at the Sorbonne was presided over by Cocteau, while Satie presented the musicians. This first success brought Sauguet a commission from Mme Bériza for a stage piece, and he wrote both text and music for *Le plumet du colonel*, an impulsive, sometimes comic piece which contains a worthwhile 'Berceuse créole' although the whole is technically flawed, chiefly in its orchestration. A second commission, again resulting from a concert given by the group, opened up the field in which Sauguet was to excel: the ballet. *Les roses* (1924) marked the beginning of his public career.

In the ensuing years this career proceeded smoothly and harmoniously; Sauguet had good friends and his works were successful. Indeed the life was the reflection of the man – equable, courteous, balancing his charm with intelligence – and of his calm, refined music. His second ballet was *La chatte* (1927; Balanchin), one of Dyagilev's successes, and it furthered Sauguet's reputation, although the score does not indicate the full measure of his talent. It was quickly followed by *David*, written for Ida Rubinstein, and *La nuit*, staged in London in 1930 with a scenario by Kochno, choreography by Lifar and scenery by Bérard. The consummation of Sauguet's work for the ballet came in 1945, when *Les forains* was performed by Petit's company. The music – vivacious, playful in the manner of Chabrier and original in its orchestration – completely captures the melancholy of bands of strolling players who, dressed in their gaudy finery of tarnished tinsel, remain sustained by hope.

Just as important as the ballets are Sauguet's operatic works, since he has always been drawn towards writing for the voice. In this sphere his best piece is *La chartreuse de Parme*, an opera in number form including a ballet, although some passages are closer in conception to Wagnerian music drama. While the work has been criticized as somewhat featureless, it is direct in style and freely melodic, and closes with a moving farewell scene at the summit of a continuous progression. He has also composed music for films, television programmes and plays; the incidental music for Giraudoux's *Ondine* is one of the highpoints of his work.

The concert works include four numbered symphonies, of which the first, 'Expiatoire', is a lament in memory of the innocent victims of World War II. Sauguet's concertos display the spontaneous ease of his music, and some are based on poetic ideas: the *Concerto d'Orphée*, with solo violin, evokes the mythic musician, while the Piano Concerto no.3, also called *Concert des mondes souterrains*, was suggested by the dripping water and strange lights of an underground grotto. Although he has made experiments in *musique concrète* and in expanded tonality, Sauguet has remained opposed to particular systems and his music has evolved little. For him the essentials are melody, harmony and rhythm, and he develops his tonal or modal ideas in smooth curves, producing an art of clarity, simplicity and restraint.

Sauguet was elected to the Académie des Beaux-Arts in 1975.

WORKS

DRAMATIC

Operas: Le plumet du colonel (opéra bouffe, 1, Sauguet), 1924; La contrebasse (opéra bouffe, 2, H. Troyat, after Chekhov), 1930; La chartreuse de Parme (opera, 4, A. Lunel, after Stendhal), 1927–36, rev. 1968; La gageure imprévue (opéra comique, 1, P. Bertin, after Sedaine), 1942; Les caprices de Marianne (opera, 2, J. P. Grédy, after Musset), 1954; Le pain des autres (opera, 2, E. Kinds, after Turgenev), 1967–74

Ballets: Les roses (O. Métra: La valse), 1924, lost; La chatte (after Kochno), 1927; David (after Doderet), 1928; Près du bal, 1929; La nuit (after Kochno), 1929; Fastes, 1933; Cartes postales, 1941; La cigale et la fourmi (after J. Chernais), 1941; Les mirages (after Cassandre, Lifar), 1943; Image à Paul et Virginie, 1944; Les forains (after Kochno), 1945; La rencontre (after Kochno), 1948; Pas de deux classique, 1951, lost; Les saisons, 1951; Cordelia (after Sauguet), 1952; Trésor et magie, 1952, lost; Le cardinal aux chats (Bal April in Paris) (after Sauguet), 1952; Le caméléopard (A. Vigot, after Poe), 1956; Les 5 étages (after Béranger), 1957; La dame aux camélias (T. Gsovsky, after Dumas), 1957, rev. 1960; La solitude (after Sauguet), 1958; L'as de cœur (after C. Aveline), 1960; Plus loin que la nuit et le jour (cantata-ballet, L. Emié), T, chorus, 1960; Pâris (after Kochno), 1964; Le prince et le mendiant (ballet-mimodrame, after Kochno), 1965

Much incidental music for the theatre, cinema, radio and television

ORCHESTRAL

Pf Conc. no.1, 1934; Symphonie de la montagne, 1944; Sym. no.1 'Expiatoire', 1945; Stèle symphonique, 1948; Pf Conc. no.2 (Rêverie concertante) [from film score Les amoureux sont seuls au monde], 1948; Sym. no.2 'Allégorique' (Les saisons), S, chorus, children's chorus, orch, 1949; Tableaux de Paris, sym. suite, 1950; Variations sur un thème de Campra, 1952, collab. others; Conc. d'Orphée, vn, orch, 1953; Les 3 lys, 1954

Sym. no.3 'I N R', 1955; Variation en forme de berceuse, 1956, collab. others; La solitude, 1958; Pf Conc. no.3 (Concert des mondes souterrains), 1961–3; Mélodie concertante, vc, orch, 1963; 2 mouvements, str, 1964; Symphonie de marches, 1966; The Garden's Conc., harmonica, chamber orch, 1970; Sym. no.4 'Du troisième âge', 1971

CHAMBER AND INSTRUMENTAL

3 françaises, pf, 1923; Sonatine, fl, pf, 1923; 3 nouvelles françaises, pf, 1925; Vines aux mains de fée, pf duet, 1925, collab. Jacob; Sonata, D, pf, 1926; Romance, C, pf, 1929; 3 feuillets d'album, pf, 1929; Près du bal, cl, bn, pf, 1929; Chant nuptial, org, 1930; Divertissement de chambre, fl, cl, bn, va, pf, 1931; Les jeux de l'amour et du hasard, 2 pf, 1932; Pièces poétiques pour enfants, 2 sets, pf, 1933–4; Suite, cl, pf, 1935; Barcarolle (bn, harp)/(vc, pf), 1936; Nuit coloniale, pf, 1937; Prélude de septembre, pf, 1940; Str Qt no.1, 1941

5 images pour St Louis, fl, ob, hpd, 1941; 6 interludes, org, gui, tambourine, 1942; Trio, ob, cl, bn, 1946; Str Qt no.2, 1948; Bocages, 10 insts, 1949; Plainte, musical saw, pf, 1949; Valse brève, 2 pf, 1949; Sonata, vc, 1956; Le chant de l'oiseau qui n'existe pas, fl, 1957; Soliloque, gui, 1958; Ballade, vc, pf, 1960; Suite royale, hpd, 1962; Golden Suite, brass qnt, 1963; Sonatine bucolique, a sax, pf, 1964; Le bestiaire du petit Noë, 10 Easy pieces, pf, 1965–6; 6 fanfares, 2 tpt, 4 trbn, 1969; 3 Preludes, gui, 1970; Sonatine aux bois, ob, pf, 1971; Un soir à Saint-Emilion, bn, pf, 1971; Sonatine en 2 chants, cl, pf, 1972; Choral varié, accordion, 1973; Petite valse du grand échiquier, pf, 1973; 6 pièces faciles, fl, gui, 1975; Alentours saxophoniques, a sax, wind insts, pf, 1976; Oraisons, 4 sax, org, 1976

CHORAL AND VOCAL

Petite messe pastorale, chorus, org, 1931; Enigme (Heine), S, orch, 1932; La voyante (Sauguet), cantata, female v, 11 insts, 1932; Les ombres du jardin (J. Weterings), cantata, S, T, Bar, B, male chorus 4vv, wind insts, 1938; Cantique à St Vincent, chorus 3vv, org, 1940; Madrigal (J. Aubry), S, fl, str trio, harp, 1942; Beauté, retirez-vous (G. Couturier), S, fl, va, vc, harp, 1943; Ma belle forêt (G. Pajot), chorus, 1943; Je vous salue, Marie, chorus, org, 1943; Les 4 saisons, [from Sym. no.2], children's chorus, 1949; La cornette (Rilke), B/Bar, orch, 1951; Mouton-blanc (Princess Bibesco), chorus, 1952

Requiem aeternam, chorus, org, 1954; Pie Jesu Domine, chorus, org, 1957; Requiem aeternam [from film score Tu es Petrus], chorus 4vv, 1959; Plus loin que la nuit et le jour (Emié), cantata, T, chorus, 1960; L'oiseau a vu tout cela (J. Cayrol), cantata, Bar, str, 1960; Ecce homo, chorus, 1965; Chant pour une vieille meurtrie (M. A. Monfet), oratorio, 6 solo vv, chorus, orch, 1967; 3 chants de contemplation (Lao-Tsen), A, B, rec ens, 1971; Cantate sylvestre (L. Desnoues), female chorus, va, pf, 1972; Au cyprès que j'ai fait planter là-bas, Mez/Bar, va, pf, 1972; Elisabethe de Belgique, la reine aux cheveux d'or (M. Carême), 1v, 6 insts, 1976

SONGS
(for 1v, pf, unless otherwise stated)
Cycles: Les animaux et leurs hommes (P. Eluard), 1921; Plumes (G. Gabory), 1922; Cirque (A. Copperie), 1925; 6 sonnets (L. Labé), 1927; 4 poèmes (Schiller), 1928; 2 poèmes (Shakespeare), 1929; 2 mélodies romantiques sur la rose (Gautier, Lamartine), 1930; Polymètres (Jean-Paul), 1931; 5 poèmes (Hölderlin), 1933; 2 poèmes (Tagore, trans. Gide), 1937; 6 mélodies sur les poèmes symbolistes (Mallarmé, Laforgue, Baudelaire), 1938; 3 duos (Comtesse Murat), S, T, pf, 1939; Les bonnes occasions (G. Courteline), S/A, T, pf, 1940; Neiges (A. d'Harcourt), 1942; 3 mélodies (Guichard), 1943; Force et faiblesse (Eluard), 1943; Le chèvrefeuille (G. Huguet), 1944; 5 poèmes (Les pénitents en maillot rose) (Jacob), 1944; 6 poèmes (A. de Richaud), 1946; 3 mélodies lyriques (J. Fernandez, Mallarmé, anon.), 1947; Visions infernales (Jacob), 1948; Mouvements de coeur (L. de Vilmorin), B, pf, 1949; 2 poèmes (R. Gaillard), 1958; Mon bien (G. E. Clancier), 1958; 3 élégies (M. Desbordes-Valmore), 1959; Vie des campagnes (J. Follain), 1961; L'espace du dedans (Michaux), B, 1965; 3 innocentines (Obaldia), 1969; 3 chants d'ombre (H. Jacqueton), B, pf, 1969; Les jours se suivent (J. Baron), B, pf, 1970; Je sais qu'il existe (Carême), B, pf, 1973
Separate songs: Amour et sommeil (Swinburne), 1929; Herbst (Rilke), 1932; Les ondines (Heine), 1932; Aria d'Eduardo Poeta (ed. James), 1934; Bêtes et méchants (Eluard), 1944; Le bois amical (P. Valéry), 1945; Cinq mars (A. Salmon), 1953; Image (Carême), 1956; Celui qui dort (Eluard), 1963; 2 sonnets (Shakespeare), 1964; 'Le souvenir . . . déjà' (Gacon), 2vv, 1966; Chant de feu (L. Senghor), T, pf, 1976

Principal publishers: Heugel, Jobert, Lemoine, Rouart–Lerolle

BIBLIOGRAPHY
M. Schneider: *Henri Sauguet* (Paris, 1959)
F.-Y. Bril: *Henri Sauguet* (Paris, 1967)

ARTHUR HOÉRÉE

Saumell Robredo, Manuel (*b* Havana, 1817; *d* Havana, 14 Aug 1870). Cuban composer. From a poor family, he received his musical education in Havana. He was the first Cuban composer to cultivate musical nationalism. Reflecting the early 19th-century Romantic style, his music is characterized by Cuban rhythmic patterns derived from Spanish folk material but developed with local characteristics. Several established Cuban dance patterns are first found in his piano contradanzas, the habanera in *La amistad*, the danzón in *La tedezco*, the guajira in *La Matilde*, the clave in *La Celestina*, the criolla in *La nené*, and the Cuban song in *Recuerdos tristes*. In 1839 Saumell conceived a Romantic national opera based on J. A. Echevarría's novel *Antonelli*, set in Havana in 1590. Indians and black slaves were to sing and take part in the action, but the music was never written.

WORKS
(most MSS in CU-Hn)
Conc., vc, pf; Plegaria, S, org; Ave Maria, S, orch; Melopea (after F. Blanchié), orch; Idilio, vn, vc, pf
58 contradanzas, pf, incl. Los ojos de Pepa, La suavecita, Sopla que quema, Lamentos de amor y soledad, Los chismes, La paila, La María
Principal publishers: Edelman, Havana; Ediciones de la Biblioteca Nacional, Havana

BIBLIOGRAPHY
S. Ramírez: *La Habana artística* (Havana, 1891)
A. Carpentier: 'Saumell y el nacionalismo', *La música en Cuba* (Mexico City, 1946), 140
H. González: 'Manuel Saumell, meditaciones con motivo del premer centenario de su muerte', *Música*, xxx (Havana, 1972), 2

AURELIO DE LA VEGA

Saùng-gauk. The classical Burmese arched harp; *see* BURMA, §5.

Saupe, Christian Gottlob (*b* Wechselburg, 1 June 1763; *d* Glauchau, 8 Jan 1819). German organist and composer. He was a friend of Daniel Gottlob Türk and was probably his pupil. In 1782 he moved from Dresden to Glauchau, where the counts of Schönburg appointed him court and municipal organist (unlike his predecessors, however, he had no political function within the community); he held this office until his death.

Saupe performed on Glauchau's Silbermann organ and was reputedly an excellent virtuoso. He composed two large-scale sacred works, some liturgical pieces, songs and keyboard sonatas in a highly personal style with considerable melodic invention and feeling for form. He carefully selected and admirably interpreted the texts to his lieder, which in some respects foreshadow Schubert; his historical romance *Das Razberger Mädchen* influenced Loewe's ballad style. His piano works are in the idiom of Mozart and Clementi, but contain bold harmonic progressions and other effects of an individual character which point towards Beethoven.

WORKS
Sacred: Die siegreiche Auferstehung Jesu, oratorio, solo vv, chorus, orch, org obbl, *D-B*; Osterkantate, S, B, chorus, orch, org, *B*; Mass, Eb, *Dlb*; Mass, D, *WAB*; 2 Gloria, solo vv, chorus, org, arr. J. D. Jacob with orch acc., *WAB*; psalm, chorus, lost
Other: 3 Sonaten und 6 Sonatinen (Glauchau, 1786); [5] Deutsche Gesänge beim Klavier zu singen nebst einem Anhang von Sonatinen zu 2 und 4 Händen (Leipzig, 1791); Der Abend (F. Matthisson), 1v, chorus, hpd/pf (Gera, n.d.)

BIBLIOGRAPHY
GerberL; *GerberNL*
E. Eckardt: *Chronik von Glauchau* (Glauchau, 1882)
W. Hüttel: 'Christian Gottlob Saupe, Leben und Werk', *Mf*, xxiii (1970), 311
——: *Musikgeschichte von Glauchau* (in preparation)

WALTER HÜTTEL

Saupicquet. The name by which VERJUS was known in St Quentin.

Sauret, Emile (*b* Dun-le-Roi, 22 May 1852; *d* London, 12 Feb 1920). French violinist and composer. A child prodigy, he made his début before 1862 and performed in the major cities of Italy, in Vienna, London and especially in France where he was invited to play on many occasions at the court of Napoleon III. There is no record of his having studied at the Paris Conservatoire, though some of his biographers state that he did so. It is not even certain that he was a pupil at the Brussels Conservatory, in spite of the fact that he is considered to have been Charles de Bériot's best pupil. If the dedication of the fourth part of his method *Gradus ad Parnassum du violoniste* can be believed he was also taught by Vieuxtemps and Wieniawski. He was called to the colours on the outbreak of war in 1870, but two years later he was able to resume his career as an international virtuoso. He first made a major tour of the USA in 1872, with such success that he returned several times between 1874 and 1906; in 1876 he met Hans von Bülow and Anton Rubinstein in New York. Back in Europe, he performed for the first time in the Leipzig Gewandhaus in May 1876, playing the Mendelssohn concerto. During the periods between his tours of the major European cities he was active as a teacher in Berlin. He married the Venezuelan pianist Teresa Carreño in 1873; a few years later they were divorced. After his second marriage in 1879, he gave many concerts in Sweden and elsewhere in Scandinavia and in 1892 was admitted to the Kungliga Musikaliska Akademien in Stockholm. He settled in London in 1890 and succeeded Prosper Sainton as professor at the Royal Academy of Music; he resigned his post in 1903 when he left for Chicago to teach in the Musical College. He also devoted a large amount of time to the trio he formed with the pianist Ganz and the cellist Steindl. On returning to Europe in 1906 he divided his time between Geneva and Berlin and was followed by many private pupils, especially Americans. In 1908 he resettled in London to take up an appointment as professor at Trinity College of Music.

Sauret was one of the most characteristic representatives of the Franco-Belgian school of violin playing. He possessed a transcendental technique, rich tone and an individual, expressive vibrato. His repertory included the classics and the works of many of his outstanding contemporaries, including Bruch, Dvořák, Busoni and Moszkowski as well as Mendelssohn. He composed himself, mainly under the influence of Jadassohn, whom he had known at Leipzig, though he wrote little but violin music, notably two *Rhapsodies* (*suédoise* and *russe*) with orchestra and a fine Concerto in D minor; a sonata was dedicated to Emil Sjögren. Sauret also wrote various pieces with piano accompaniment and transcribed selections from Wagner, Mendelssohn and Rubinstein. He left some valuable teaching works, *Gradus ad Parnassum du violiniste* the violin method mentioned above, and many collections of studies. He published editions of classical studies by Gaviniès, Vieuxtemps and Paganini.

BIBLIOGRAPHY

H. C. Lahee: *Famous Violinists of To-day and Yesterday* (London and Boston, 1902)
A. Moser: *Geschichte des Violinspiels* (Berlin, 1923, rev., enlarged 2/1966–7)
E. van der Straeten: *The History of the Violin* (London, 1933/R1968)
C. Flesch: *The Memoirs of Carl Flesch* (London, 1957, 2/1958; Ger. orig., Freiburg, 1960, 2/1961)

ROGER COTTE

Ṣaurīndramohana Ṭhākura. See TAGORE, SOURINDRO MOHUN.

Saursbi. See SOURSBY.

Sautereau (Fr.). JACK.

Sauterie (Fr.). PSALTERY.

Sautillé (Fr.; Ger. *Springbogen*; It. *saltando, saltato*). A bowstroke played rapidly in the middle of the bow, one bowstroke per note, so that the bow bounces very slightly off the string of its own accord. It is not indicated in any consistent manner: sometimes dots are placed above or below the notes, sometimes arrow-head strokes, and sometimes the stroke is simply left to the performer's discretion. The term 'sautillé' was used as early as 1712 (Piani: Solo Violin Sonatas), but it is not clear whether or not Piani meant a bouncing stroke as described above. 'Spiccato' and 'sautillé' are often used as synonyms, but SPICCATO has an additional meaning. *See* BOW, §II, 3 (v–vi).

DAVID D. BOYDEN

Sauveur, Joseph (*b* La Flèche, 24 March 1653; *d* Paris, 9 July 1716). French acoustician. In 1670 he went to Paris, where he attended the lectures of the Cartesian physicist Rohault; his works do not display the knowledge of advanced mathematics that characterizes the scientific progress of the age of Newton, although he held a chair of mathematics for a decade. He was elected to membership of the Académie des Sciences (1696), which left him free to develop his interest in acoustics. He thoroughly mastered the idea of frequency and was the first to interpret beats correctly. He also introduced the terms 'acoustics', 'harmonic sound' (overtone), 'node' and 'loop'. His papers, though not so original as he may have thought them, were fairly clear and descriptive; they were very widely read, and certainly they had great effect upon the centrally important work of Daniel Bernoulli a quarter of a century later. Much has been made of Sauveur's desire to standardize some particular absolute pitch, but nobody has ever given a reason why such a standard should be important to music. He suffered from a speech defect and is said to have had no ear for music. His works include *Principes d'acoustique et de musique* (Paris, 1701/R1973). His papers were published in the *Mémoires* (incorporated in the *Histoire*) *de l'Académie royale des sciences* [*1701–13*] (Paris, 1704–16) and his work is described in the *Histoires* for those years.

See also PHYSICS OF MUSIC, §2.

BIBLIOGRAPHY
S. Dostrovsky: 'Sauveur, Joseph', *Dictionary of Scientific Biography* (New York, 1970–)

C. TRUESDELL

Sauzay, (Charles) Eugène (*b* Paris, 14 July 1809; *d* Paris, 24 Jan 1901). French violinist. He entered the Paris Conservatoire and studied under Baillot from 1824; in 1827 he won the *premier prix* for violin. At the first concert of Habeneck's Société des Concerts du Conservatoire (9 March 1828) he replaced his indisposed teacher in the performance of a Rode concerto and thereafter regularly appeared as a soloist with the Conservatoire orchestra.

Sauzay played the second violin and afterwards the viola in Baillot's string quartet before its dissolution in 1840. He then formed his own group for chamber music with his wife (Baillot's daughter), Boëly, and later, Franchomme. In demand as a teacher as well as a performer, he taught a Conservatoire class from 1860 to 1892. Sauzay wrote studies and other pieces for the violin, also songs and two trios; some of the manuscripts are at the Conservatoire. His ballet music to Molière's *Le sicilien* (1881) is a Lullian pastiche. His *Etudes sur les quatuors de Haydn, Mozart et Beethoven* was published in 1861, *L'école d'accompagnement* in 1869 (R1972) and *Le violon harmonique* in 1889.

BIBLIOGRAPHY
FétisB
A. Lavignac: *La musique et les musiciens* (Paris, 1896)
A. Bachmann: *An Encyclopedia of the Violin* (London, 1925)
E. van der Straeten: *The History of the Violin* (London, 1933/R1968), ii, 179f
B. François-Sappey: 'La vie musicale à Paris à travers les *Mémoires* d'Eugène Sauzay (1809–1901)', *RdM*, lx (1974), 159
F. Raugel: 'Autour de Sauzay, de Boëly et de Reber', *RMFC*, xv (1975), 146

DAVID CHARLTON

Savage, Jane (*fl c*1780–90). English composer, daughter of William Savage. She was a virtuoso keyboard player and an accomplished composer of keyboard music and songs. Her music is in the typically untaxing *galant* style of the late 18th century, and was quite popular in its time.

WORKS
(all published in London)

op.
2 6 Easy Lessons, hpd/pf (1783)
3 6 Rondos, hpd/pf (c1790)
4 Strephan and Flavia, cantata, 1v, kbd (c1790)
5 Hall the Woodman, a Favourite Song, 1v, kbd (c1790)
6 A Favorite Duett, pf/hpd (1789)
7 2 Duetts for Voices, 2vv, bc (c1790)
8 God Save the King, adapted as a Double Lesson, hpd/pf (c1790)

For bibliography *see* SAVAGE, WILLIAM.

CHARLES CUDWORTH

Savage, William (*b* ?London, 1720; *d* London, 27 July 1789). English composer, organist and bass singer. He came of a good family, believed to be a distant branch of the Rivers family. Although said by Burney to have been educated as a boy in the Chapel Royal, which was doubted by R. J. S. Stevens, he was later taught by Pepusch and Geminiani. That he was favoured by Handel is fairly certain, and he first appears as a boy soprano in *Alcina* (1735). He sang as an alto in the operas *Giustino* (1737) and *Faramondo* (1738), in the latter of which he also sang tenor in the choruses, and in English works: *Athalia* (1735), *Acis and Galatea* (1736) and probably *Esther* (1736). From 1740 he sang as a bass in the operas *Imeneo* (1740) and *Deidamia* (1741), in *L'Allegro ed il Penseroso* (probably 1740, 1741 and 1743), and in the oratorios *Saul* (1741), *Samson* (1743) and *Messiah* (1743).

Around 1740 he was organist at Finchley church, Middlesex, and his name appears among the subscribers to Greene's *Forty Select Anthems* (1743). He was admitted a Gentleman-in-Ordinary in the Chapel Royal as a bass in 1744 and succeeded Charles King as vicar-choral, almoner and master of the choristers at St Paul's on 17 March 1747 or 1748. Because of ill-health he resigned the last two posts to Robert Hudson in 1773 and the first to Richard Bellamy in 1777, both of whom were his pupils, as were many other distinguished musicians of the period, including Battishill, Samuel Long, Samuel Porter, C. F. Reinhold, Joseph Vernon, Stephen Paxton, John Percy and R. J. S. Stevens, the last-named having recorded many useful details of the life of his teacher. Savage was a professional member of the Noblemen and Gentlemen's Catch Club and the Beef Steak Club, and an active participant in the Academy of Ancient Music.

Burney said that Savage was 'a powerful and not unpleasant bass', but Stevens insisted that he had 'a pleasant voice of two octaves' and had 'a clear articulation, perfect intonation, great volubility of voice, and chaste and good expression'. The latter also related that he was 'a very good organ player, and vocal composer', as well as being 'an excellent teacher of the science of music in all its branches'; he was especially noted as a teacher of singing.

In the sphere of composition Stevens mentioned two penitential psalms, *O rebuke me not* and *Hearken unto my voice*, as being 'not unworthy even of a Purcell'. A considerable number of his works survive to show that his best work compares favourably with that of his contemporaries Boyce, Battishill, Nares and Kent. Stevens testified that Savage was held 'in much estimation by his contemporaries for his abilities and ingenuity in his profession'. He was one of Handel's intimate friends and until his death treasured a ring given to him at Handel's funeral.

WORKS
(complete list in Farmer)

40 anthems in *GB-Ge* and *Lbm*, incl. Praise the Lord, 27 Sept 1765, and O rebuke me not, 17 May 1767: both in R. J. S. Stevens, *Sacred Music* (London, c1802)
2 Kyrie–Gloria; 1 Sanctus; 1 Credo; 1 Te Deum and Jubilate; 1 Magnificat and Nunc dimittis; 2 Requiescat in pace: in *Ge, Lbm, Lcm*
2 single chants, 1 in S. Arnold, *Cathedral Music* (London, 1790), and Stevens, *Sacred Music* (London, c1802); 20 psalms, 4 in Stevens, *Sacred Music* (London, c1802): in *Ge, Lbm*
My fair is beautiful as love, song (London, c1740); 7 songs in *Lbm*; c18 catches, rounds and canons, many pubd in 18th-century anthologies, others in *Ge, Lbm*
8 short pieces for vn, *Lbm*

BIBLIOGRAPHY
R. J. S. Stevens: *Life of Mr William Savage* (MS, *GB-Ge*); repr. in Farmer, 190
——: *Diaries and Memoirs* (MSS, *GB-Cp*)
C. Burney: articles in *Rees's Cyclopaedia* (London, 1819); cited in P. Scholes, *The Great Dr Burney* (London, 1948)
H. G. Farmer: 'A Forgotten Composer of Anthems', *ML*, xvii (1936), 188
W. Dean: *Handel's Dramatic Masques and Oratorios* (London, 1959)
C. L. Cudworth: 'Two Handelian Anecdotes', *Festschrift Otto Erich Deutsch* (Kassel, 1963), 49

H. G. FARMER/CHARLES CUDWORTH

Savagnone, Giuseppe (*b* Palermo, 27 Nov 1902). Italian composer. After studies in Palermo he worked as a choirmaster and teacher at the conservatories of Rome and Palermo. He evolved an individual harmonic system, described in his book *Prismatismo musicale* (Palermo, 1956, 2/1966). His compositions include the opera *Millesima seconda* (libretto by C. Meano, staged at Palermo in 1949), the ballet *L'attesa* (staged at Turin in 1961) and orchestral, vocal orchestral and chamber pieces.

ALBERTO PIRONTI

Savart, Félix (*b* Mézières, 30 June 1791; *d* Paris, 16 March 1841). French scientist. He was trained at Strasbourg in medicine, taking a degree in 1816. He had long been interested in acoustics when, in 1816, he abandoned medicine and went to Paris, where he came under the guidance of Biot. He became a professor of natural philosophy in 1820 and was elected to the Académie in 1827, also obtaining an appointment at the Collège de France. He is known mainly for the Biot–Savart Law of Electrodynamics. His chief interest, indicated by the titles of his 27 papers (mostly published in the *Annales de chimie et de physique*), was in the study of vibrating bodies. These included important and often ingenious measurements of air, cords, bars, membranes, plates, solids of revolution and, particularly, vocal cords. He proposed theories of the vocal sounds of men and animals. His repetition and extension of Chladni's experiments with sand figures on vibrating plates and longitudinal bars led in the early 19th century to controversy over the velocity of sound in solids. He produced in 1830 a toothed-wheel siren, based on Robert Hooke's, for tone generation at controllable frequencies. His name is also associated with the measuring of intervals, 303·03 savarts being equivalent to an octave.

See also PHYSICS OF MUSIC, §4.

BIBLIOGRAPHY
S. Dostrovsky: 'Savart, Félix', *Dictionary of Scientific Biography* (New York, 1970–)

JAMES F. BELL, R. W. B. STEPHENS

Savary, Jean Nicolas (*b* Guise, Aisne, Sept 1786; *d* Paris, 9 Feb 1853). French bassoon maker. His father was the Paris woodwind maker known as Savary *père* (*fl* c1778–c1827); few of his instruments survive. An elder brother was also active there as a maker from about 1822 to 1833. As younger son he styled himself 'Savary jeune' and first trained as bassoonist under Delcambre at the Paris Conservatoire, winning a *premier prix* in 1808 and later becoming principal at the Théâtre des Italiens. He probably started making bassoons in association with his father; by 1823 he had his own workshop and was 'fournisseur de la maison du Roi, de l'Académie et de l'école royale'. His background as an excellent performer was undoubtedly of great practical value and helped him subsequently to become the best maker of his time of the French type of bassoon. His instruments were unequalled for the sweetness and singing quality of their tone and remained in use and sought after by professionals, especially in England, for almost a century; Day called him the Stradivari of the bassoon. In addition to bassoons with from ten to 14 keys, Savary's output included tenoroons in F and E♭ and an octave bassoon. He did not participate in any of the Paris exhibitions. His last known instrument is dated 1852 and according to Pierre his stock was bought by Galander.

BIBLIOGRAPHY
C. R. Day: *Catalogue of the Royal Military Exhibition* (London, 1891)
C. Pierre: *Les facteurs des instruments de musique* (Paris, 1893/R1971)
L. Letellier and S. Flament: 'Le Basson', *EMDC*, II/iii (1927), 1556–96
L. G. Langwill: *An Index of Musical Wind-instrument Makers* (Edinburgh, 1960, rev. 4/1977)
——: *The Bassoon and Contrabassoon* (London, 1965)
WILLIAM WATERHOUSE

Savetta, Antonio (*b* Lodi; *fl* 1600–41). Italian composer. He was a pupil of Tiburtio Massaino and succeeded him as *maestro di cappella* at Lodi Cathedral in 1609 (a year earlier he was described as 'presbyter'). He probably occupied this post for the rest of his life, though there was apparently an interruption in 1629–30, when it was held by Ignazio Donati. His output, apart from one volume of madrigals, consists of sacred music, the majority of it for the Mass and Offices. He did not adopt the new small-scale concertato style popular in northern Italy in the early 17th century, partly because masses and psalm settings tended to preserve larger scorings and partly because composers in the area around Milan, which includes Lodi, were comparatively impervious to the new style. Thus a fair proportion of his output is for double choir (there was some lost music by him for as many as 24 voices).

WORKS
Magnificat per omnes tonos, 7, 8vv, bc (org), liber I (Venice, 1608); contains 1 motet, 8 Magnificat
Motectorum, 5–12vv, bc (org), liber II (Venice, 1608)
Primus liber missarum, 5vv, bc, op.4 (Venice, 1609)
[16] Madrigali, 5, 7, 8vv, libro I, op.5 (Venice, 1610)
II messe, 12vv, op.6 (Venice, 1616)
Psalmi ad Vesperas in totius anni, 5vv, bc, liber I, op.7 (Venice, 1620)
Salmi concertati, 8vv, libro II, op.11 (Venice, 1635)
Messe concertate, 8vv, op.12 (Venice, 1636)
Salmi ariosi e brevi, 8vv, bc (org), op.14 (Venice, 1636)
Missa e salmi (Venice, 1638), lost
Messa e salmi, 9vv (Venice, 1639), lost
Corona stellata di letanie con le 4 antifone, 8vv (Venice, 1639), lost
Litanie ed antifone, 8vv (Venice, 1641), lost; ?2nd edn. of preceding
Motetti, 4–24vv, lost
12 motets, 5–8vv, in 1600¹, 1612³, 1613², 1617¹, 1621²
Motet, 8vv, *D-Bds*

BIBLIOGRAPHY
H. Wessely-Kropik: 'Mitteilungen aus dem Archiv der arciconfraternità di San Giovanni dei Fiorentini, detta della Pietà in Rom', *SMw*, xxiv (1960), 52
JEROME ROCHE

Savile, Jeremy (*fl* 1651–65). English composer. John Playford listed him among 'many excellent and able Masters' as a teacher 'For the Voyce or Viole' in his *Musicall Banquet* (1651). He was a member of the Old-Jewry Musick Society after the Restoration, though Playford did not list him as such in *The Musical Companion* (1667), possibly because he was by then dead. In addition to glees printed in *The Musical Companion* (1667, 2/1673) and elsewhere, a few of his ayres were included in *Select Musicall Ayres and Dialogues* (1653); they range in style from the charming triple-time setting of Stanley's *I will not trust thy tempting graces*, printed in *English Songs, 1625–1660*, MB, xxxiii (1971), to the rather rambling declamation for Carew's *No more, blind boy*. His most celebrated song is *Here's a health unto his majesty*.

IAN SPINK

Savinio, Alberto [Chirico, Andrea de] (*b* Athens, 25 Aug 1891; *d* Rome, 6 May 1956). Italian composer, writer and visual artist. A brother of the painter Giorgio de Chirico, he studied the piano and composition in Athens, and then, from 1906, he was a pupil of Reger in Munich. After a lengthy stay in Paris he settled in Italy while maintaining, through tours and meetings, the international contacts which were important to his artistic activities. He was particularly influenced by Parisian neo-classicism, which he developed in his compositions, all of them dramatic, with a free detachment, restless fantasy and persistent lively, bitter irony. The same characteristics are displayed in his surrealist visual output, quite close in style to that of his brother but more lucid and precise.

WORKS
(selective list)
Operas: Il tesoro del Rampsenita (Calvocoressi), inc.; Carmela (Savinio), 1906, Rome, 1950; Orfeo vedovo (Savinio), Rome, 1950
Radio operas: Agenzia Fix (Savinio), RAI, 1950; Cristoforo Colombo, RAI, 1952
Ballets: Perseo (Fokin), New York, 1924; Due amori nella notte (Savinio), unperf.; Ballata delle stagioni (Savinio), Venice, 1925; La morte di Niobe (Savinio), Rome, 1925; Vita dell'uomo (Savinio), Milan, 1951

Principal publisher: Ricordi

WRITINGS
Scatola sonora (Milan, 1955)
with B. Barilli: *Alfredo Casella* (Milan, 1957)

PIERO SANTI

Savio, Johann Baptist (*fl* 1760s). Austro-Bohemian composer. He became music director to Joseph von Brunian's theatre company some time before the latter took over the Kotce Theatre, Prague, in 1764. Savio's name does not occur after 1768, though his inclusion in J. J. Stankovský's novel *Vlastencové Bondy* ('Patriots at the Bonda Theatre') (1878), where he figures as Brunian's second in a duel, shows that he was not entirely forgotten. The earliest record of Savio as a composer names him as author of the music to the arias of *Le diable à quatre, ou La double métamorphose* (*Der Teufel in allen Ecken, oder Die zweyfache Verwandlung*), an *opéra comique* translated from the French by C. L. Reuling and performed by Brunian's company (libretto, Prague, 1760, in *CS-Pu*). This work may have been performed in Vienna in the previous year. Garnier also named Savio as the composer of *Die Zigeuner, oder Der von List und Liebe besiegte Geiz* (libretto, Graz, 1766), Erdmann's *Philint und Cleone*, Nuth's *Die doppelte Ehe*, Unger's *Der nach sieben*

Jahren beglückte Bräutigam, Kurz-Bernardon's *Der vergötterte Bernardon* (1764) and F. W. Weisskern's version of *Bastien und Bastienne*, first performed at the Kärntnertor Theatre, Vienna, on 5 May 1764. Felix Berner's company included all these works in its repertory in the early 1770s. Although Savio's Singspiels were quite widely performed in the 1760s and 1770s (Prague, Vienna, Brno, Graz and probably elsewhere), no score is known to survive. Despite his Italianate name it is more likely that his music was Austro-German in style, since Brunian strove to regenerate the Prague theatre and Berner also put the emphasis on native works.

BIBLIOGRAPHY

F. X. Garnier: *Nachricht von der im Jahre 1758 von Herrn Felix Berner errichteten jungen Schauspieler-Gesellschaft* (Vienna, 1786)
O. Teuber: *Geschichte des Prager Theaters*, ii (Prague, 1885), 475f
F. Bischoff: 'Zur Geschichte des Theaters in Graz', *Mitteilungen des historischen Vereins für Steiermark* (Graz, 1892), 132
A. Loewenberg: ' "Bastien and Bastienne" once more', *ML*, xxv (1944), 176
W. Senn: 'Mozarts "Zaide" und der Verfasser der vermutlichen Textvorlage', *Festschrift Alfred Orel* (Vienna, 1960), 173

PETER BRANSCOMBE

Savioli, Alessandro (*b* Parma, 12 Aug 1544; *d* after 1623). Italian composer. He was born in the parish of S Maria borgo Taschieri. He apparently spent his early years in Parma, since his first book of five-voice madrigals is dedicated from there and his earliest known published work, the canzonetta *Mentre campò contento l'arso core*, was in the first book of *Canzonette alla napolitana* (*RISM* 1591²²) of his fellow Parmesan G. B. Massarengo. From the title-pages of his second and third madrigal books it can be assumed that he was *maestro di cappella* at S Alessandro, Bergamo, from at least 28 August 1597 to 8 February 1600. Between 1614 and 1616 he was *maestro di cappella* at Salò, where he was responsible for reorganizing the choir and increasing the number of salaried singers.

WORKS

(*published in Venice*)

Salmi intieri, 5vv (1597)
Madrigali . . . libro primo, 5vv (1595)
Madrigali . . . libro secondo, 5vv (1597)
Madrigali . . . libro terzo, 5vv (1600)
5 canzonettas, 3, 4vv, 2 madrigals, 5vv, 1591²², 1596¹¹, 1615¹⁷, 1616¹⁰

BIBLIOGRAPHY

P. Guerrini: 'La cappella musicale del duomo di Salò', *RMI*, xxix (1922), 106
N. Pelicelli: 'Musicisti in Parma nei secoli XV–XVI', *NA*, ix (1932), 123
C. Sartori: 'Giulio Cesare Monteverde a Salò: nuovi documenti inediti', *NRMI*, i (1967), 690

IAIN FENLON

Savion. *See* FEDELI family.

Savioni, Mario (*b* Rome, 1608; *d* Rome, 22 April 1685). Italian composer and teacher. He spent his life in Rome. As a boy he sang the role of Dorino in Filippo Vitali's opera *L'Aretusa* on 8 February 1620. He was a chorister in the Cappella Giulia at St Peter's from 1621 to 1623. His voice then broke, but he remained there as a contralto until 1626, during which time he studied with Vincenzo Ugolini. In 1626 or shortly after he may have begun to study at Virgilio Mazzocchi's school of music (see Bontempi). Although there is no information about his career during the next 15 years, his reputation as a composer must have been growing, for 23 of his cantatas appeared in an important manuscript in 1641 (if Prunières' dating of the source, *F-Pn* Rés.Vm⁷, is

correct). In February 1642 he sang the part of Alcestis in Luigi Rossi's opera *Il palazzo incantato*. The next month he became a singer in the papal choir, and he was its director from 1659 to 1668. He also won a reputation as a teacher. From 1652 a number of his madrigals, motets and cantatas appeared in various publications, four of them devoted solely to his music, the others anthologies. During this period he probably belonged to the circle of musicians, poets and artists surrounding Queen Christina of Sweden in Rome.

Savioni's music was highly regarded within the fairly small, sophisticated circle for which it was intended. He was one of the more important Italian cantata composers. His numerous cantatas (which are designated as concertos in the two prints containing them and occasionally as arias in manuscripts) embrace the entire range of mid-17th-century Italian cantatas, from single bipartite arias, with or without recitatives and often with the familiar *ABB*¹ structure in the first part, through strophic variations, through-composed arias and da capo arias (all of which show consistent rhyme scheme, in which the final syllable of *B* rhymes with the final syllable of the first line of *A*) to large composite works with several arias and extensive recitatives. The significance of the words is often intensified through melismatic or specially lyrical writing. Most of the texts are anonymous. In their use of recitatives and sometimes elaborate vocal lines Savioni's solo motets are similar in style to his larger solo cantatas, but they are on the whole more conservative in structure, partly because of the nature of the texts. His madrigals, for three to five voices, frequently include large-scale repetitions or reprises of material. The vocal lines are obviously for solo voices, and the outer parts are strongly polarized; the continuo line is seldom more than a *basso seguente*.

WORKS

(*printed works published in Rome unless otherwise stated*)

Concerti morali e spirituali, 3vv (1660)
Madrigali morali e spirituali, 5vv (1668); 5 ed. in Cw, cxiii (1972)
Madrigali e concerti, 3vv (1672)
Motetti, 1v (1676); 13 ed. in SCMA, xvi (1972)
Works in 1652³, 1659¹, 1663¹, 1664¹, 1667¹, 1672¹, 1675³, Recueil des meilleurs airs italiens qui ont été publiés depuis quelques années, III. recueil (n.p., n.d.); 6 ed. I. Eisley, Series of Early Music, iii (Bryn Mawr, Penn., 1970)
Cantatas, 1–3vv, *B-Bc*, *Br*, *F-Pn*, Pthibault, *GB-Lbm*, *Och*, *I-Bc*, *MOe*, *Nc*, *Rc*, *Rvat*
Caduta di Vasti and Assedio di Samaria, oratorios; lost, cited in Mischiati, 144, 150

167 cantatas listed in WECIS, ii (1964) [inaccurate], 9 possible attributions in WECIS, iii/b (1965), v (1966); for full accurate list see Eisley: *The Secular Cantatas* (1964)

BIBLIOGRAPHY

A. Berardi: *Ragionamenti musicali* (Bologna, 1681)
G. A. Bontempi: *Historia musica* (Perugia, 1695)
A. Adami: *Osservazioni per ben regolare il coro dei cantori della cappella pontificia* (Rome, 1711)
L. Torchi: 'Canzoni ed arie italiane a una voce nel secolo XVII', *RMI*, i (1894), 581–656
E. Schmitz: 'Zur Geschichte des italienischen Continuo-Madrigals im 17. Jahrhundert', *SIMG*, xi (1909–10), 509
H. Prunières: 'Les représentations du Palazzo d'Atlante à Rome en 1642', *SIMG*, xiv (1912–13), 2
C. Schoenbaum: *Beiträge zur solistischen katholischen Kirchenmusik im Hochbarock* (diss., U. of Vienna, 1951)
——: 'Die *Opella ecclesiastica* des Joseph Anton Planicky (1691?–1732): eine Studie zur Geschichte der katholischen Solomotette im Mittel- und Hochbarock', *AcM*, xxv (1953), 39–79
R. B. Morris: *A Study of the Italian Solo Cantata before 1750* (diss., Indiana U., 1955)
O. Mischiati: 'Per la storia dell'Oratorio a Bologna: tre inventari del 1620, 1622 e 1682', *CHM*, iii (1958), 131–70, esp. 144, 150
P. Kast: 'Antimo Liberati: eine biographische Skizze', *KJb*, xliii (1959), 64

G. Rose: *The Cantatas of Giacomo Carissimi* (diss., Yale U., 1959)

P. Kast: 'Biographische Notizen zu römischen Musikern des 17. Jahrhunderts', *AnMc*, no.1 (1963), 38–69

I. Eisley: *Mario Savioni*, WECIS, ii (1964) [thematic index of Savioni's cantatas]

——: *The Secular Cantatas of Mario Savioni* (diss., U. of California, Los Angeles, 1964)

E. Caluori: *Luigi Rossi*, WECIS, iii/b (1965) [thematic index of Rossi's cantatas, b: unreliable attributions]

G. Rose: *Giacomo Carissimi*, WECIS, v (1966) [thematic index of Carissimi's cantatas]

IRVING EISLEY

Savonese, Il. *See* CHIABRERA, GABRIELLO.

Savoy. A mountainous area in south-east France which once included parts of present-day Italy, France and Switzerland (see map). The house of Savoy assumed power in 1003 and held the Italian crown from 1860 to 1946. The court took a leading part in the European development of music during the second quarter of the 15th century, sharing with nearby Burgundy a critical role in the early development of Renaissance styles.

Medieval and Renaissance music of the region illustrates both Franco-Burgundian and Italian characteristics. Numerous Provençal troubadours (e.g. Elias de Barjols, Arnaut Catalan and Aimeric de Belenoi) were connected with the Savoyard court in the 13th century, and poems by Savoyards (e.g. Tommaso II di Savoia, Albertet de Savoia and Nicoletto da Torino) show that they quickly adopted the new art. Minstrelsy flourished during the 14th and 15th centuries, its vestiges probably contained in some Piedmontese folksongs of later collections. The local language also appears in 15th-century *laude, canzoni* and *sacre rappresentazioni*. Medieval chant and music theory manuscripts survive at Aosta, Chambéry, Asti, Ivrea, Novara, Turin and Vercelli.

Amadeus VIII (1391–1451), first Duke of Savoy, extended his territory and was a lavish patron of the arts in the manner of the Burgundian dukes. He himself played the organ, and the court enjoyed extravagant tournaments, banquets and festivals, such as that at Chambéry in 1434 when Amadeus's son, Louis, married Anne of Cyprus. The courts of Burgundy and Savoy were both present; Dufay was *maître de chapelle*, and it was probably on this occasion that he met Binchois, a meeting recorded by Martin Le Franc, poet and secretary to Amadeus. Amadeus left minor court duties to Louis in 1434, when he retired to a hermitage. Dufay returned to Savoy and is listed on the register of Louis' musicians from 1437 to 1439. In 1439 Duke Amadeus was elected Antipope Felix V by the Council of Basle. Although Dufay temporarily severed his ties with Savoy, many other musicians, including Brassart and Nicolas Merques, were associated with the council. Large sections of two manuscripts (*I-AO* A¹D19 and *I-TRmn* 92) were apparently copied at Basle while the antipope was there; these manuscripts, among the most prized collections of Burgundian repertory, contain much music by Dufay and are the two most important surviving sources for Binchois' sacred works. Felix V abdicated in 1449; Dufay visited Savoy again in 1450, and served Duke Louis there (1450–56).

Louis (*d* 1465) and Anne continued the splendour of earlier court life, maintaining a chapel with ten to 23 adult singers, six to eight boys, and several chaplains, priests and organists; this was also the pattern for subsequent generations. The Chansonnier Cordiforme (*F-Pn* 2973), probably copied in the 1470s, was made locally and contains numerous chansons by leading composers of that period; its special value lies in anonymous *unica* which illustrate two local stylistic practices, Franco-Burgundian and Italian. Musical patronage was particularly vigorous at the turn of the century, during the rule of Duke Philibert II and his wife, Margaret of Austria. One of Margaret's celebrated chansonniers (*B-Br* 11239) most probably originated at the Savoyard court; another local manuscript (*I-Tn* I.27) includes chansons and sacred Latin pieces. Composers brought to the court at this time included Brumel, Févin, Therache, Longueval and Lodovico Fogliani.

After the death of Philibert II (1504) and the departure of Margaret (1507) the prosperity of the duchy declined, although the chapel survived and regained much of its splendour by the end of the Renaissance. Instrumentalists also continued to perform at the court, and violinists are known to have played there as early as 1523. Violin making and solo and ensemble playing later became specialities of the region. If the bassadanza roll dated 1517 (Archivi Biscaretti, Turin, Mazzo 4, no.14) was made locally, it anticipates the area's significant achievements in dance during later centuries. The court settled at Turin in 1563; its rich patronage of music, theatre and dance was thereafter connected with that city.

See also BURGUNDY and TURIN.

BIBLIOGRAPHY

A. Dufour and F. Rabut: 'Les musiciens, la musique et les instruments de musique en Savoie du XIII au XIX siècle', *Mémoires et documents de la Société savoisienne d'histoire et d'archéologie*, xvii (1878), 5–225

G. Bertoni: *I trovatori d'Italia* (Modena, 1915)

S. Cordero di Pamparato: 'Emanuele Filiberto di Savoia, protettore dei musici', *RMI*, xxxiv (1927), 229, 555; xxxv (1928), 29

M. Tegen: 'Baselkonciliet och kyrkomusiken omkr. 1440', *STMf*, xxxix (1957), 126

H. Ménabréa: *Histoire de la Savoie* (Chambéry, 1958)

R. Hoppin, ed.: *The Cypriot–French Repertory in the Manuscript Torino, Biblioteca Nazionale, J.II.9*, CMM, xxi (1960)

E. Kottick: *The Music of the Chansonnier Cordiforme, Paris, Bibliothèque Nationale, Rothschild 2973* (diss., U. of North Carolina, 1962)

M. Picker: *The Chanson Albums of Marguerite of Austria* (Berkeley, 1965)

E. Kottick, ed.: *The Unica in the Chansonnier Cordiforme*, CMM, xlii

Savoy in the 15th century

(1967)
C. Brero and R. Gandolfo: *La letteratura in Piemontese* (Turin, 1967)
M. Bouquet: 'La cappella musicale dei duchi di Savoia dal 1450 al
1500', *RIM*, iii (1968), 233–85
——: 'La cappella musicale dei duchi di Savoia dal 1504 al 1550',
RIM, iv (1970), 3–36
C. Wright: 'Dufay at Cambrai: Discoveries and Revisions', *JAMS*, xxviii
(1975), 175–229
M. Cobin: *The Aosta MS: a Central Source of Fifteenth-century
Sacred Polyphony* (diss., New York U., 1976)

DAVID CRAWFORD

Savoy Orpheans. English dance band. Formed under the
leadership of Debroy Somers in 1923, it played at the
Savoy Hotel, London; it succeeded the Savoy Quartette
(1916–20) and survived the Savoy Havana Band
(1922–7) into the 1930s, being entirely reconstituted
several times. The early members included Cyril
Newton, who briefly assumed the leadership in 1926,
Carroll Gibbons, who became musical director in 1927,
Rudy Vallee, Billy Thorburn and Reg Batten. The New
Savoy Orpheans under Batten and the Original Savoy
Orpheans under Gibbons and Teddy Sinclair were disbanded after less than a year (1928); other groups were
formed with the same name, but independent of the
hotel, until Gibbons began another engagement there
with the Savoy Hotel Orpheans (1931). The hotel
discouraged outside engagements but the Orpheans and
the Havana made over 300 records between 1922 and
1927. The Orpheans were among the most popular
British dance bands of the period and had a pioneering
role in radio broadcasting. Their repertory was largely
functional dance music with a few 'hot' jazz numbers.

BIBLIOGRAPHY

A. McCarthy: *The Dance Band Era* (London, 1971)

Savoy Theatre. London theatre built in 1881 by
Richard D'Oyly Carte for Gilbert and Sullivan operas;
see LONDON, §IV, 3.

Saw, musical (Fr. *lame musicale*; Ger. *singende Säge*).
A folk instrument of mid-19th-century origin that
gained popularity as a novelty on the music-hall and
vaudeville stages. It consists of a long, flexible handsaw
played by drawing a fiddle bow across the straight edge
of the blade or striking the blade with a soft mallet. The
player sits with the saw handle firmly between his knees
or thighs and with his free hand grasps the tip of the
blade, controlling the pitch frequency of the fundamental mode of vibration by flexing the blade to a greater or
lesser degree. Vibrato is produced either by the hand or
by a quivering of the leg. In the 1920s saws of extra
length (up to 81 cm, some providing a three-octave
range) were manufactured specially for musical use, but
these did not displace the carpentry saw, selected at the
factory for its musical properties; the two types are not
always distinguishable. At least seven makes of musical
saw have been sold in the USA, two each in England and
Germany, and one in Sweden. The instrument's tendency
to portamento was exploited by Henri Sauguet in his
Plainte (1949) for *lame musicale* and piano.

GRAHAM JOHNSON

Sawallisch, Wolfgang (*b* Munich, 26 Aug 1923). German conductor and pianist. He took piano lessons from
childhood and began studies in theory and composition
at school. After training at the Munich Academy he was
engaged in 1947 as a répétiteur at Augsburg, where he
made his conducting début in *Hänsel und Gretel* and
became first conductor. With the violinist Gerhard Seitz

he won first prize for duos at the 1949 Geneva
International Competition, and began to conduct as a
guest in Germany. He became general music director at
Aachen (1953–8), Wiesbaden (1958–60) and Cologne
(1960–63), where he also directed the conductors' class
at the academy. He opened the 1957 Bayreuth Festival
with *Tristan und Isolde* – the youngest conductor then
engaged there – and made two London débuts the same
year, first as the pianist in a lieder programme with
Elisabeth Schwarzkopf, and later as a conductor with
the Philharmonia. He was concurrently principal conductor of the Vienna SO from 1960 and the Hamburg
PO from 1961. His American début was on a tour with
the Vienna SO in 1964, and in 1971 he was appointed
general music director of the Bavarian Staatsoper,
Munich, with which he made his Covent Garden début
during its 1972 London season.

Sawallisch has continued to play as a pianist in lieder
programmes, establishing a close rapport with singers
such as Schwarzkopf, Fischer-Dieskau and Prey. He
occasionally performs as a concerto soloist, usually in
Mozart and early Beethoven, directing from the keyboard. His conducting is distinguished by a concentration on the work's integral musical qualities, sometimes
at the expense of feeling, but in the opera house he
successfully balances restraint of expression with
vitality of spirit. His gramophone records include the
first complete album of Strauss's *Capriccio*
(Philharmonia) and the complete Schubert symphonies
(Dresden SO). He is editing Mendelssohn's complete
symphonic works for publication, and he has recorded
several of them.

NOËL GOODWIN

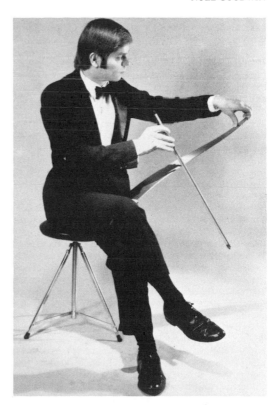

Graham Johnson demonstrating the musical saw

Sawerthal. *See* ZAVRTAL family.

Sawtry. *See* PSALTERY.

Sax. Belgian family of wind instrument makers, of whom the second in line was probably the most remarkable innovator ever to enter the trade.

(1) Charles-Joseph Sax [Sax *père*] (*b* Dinant [now in Belgium], 1 Feb 1791; *d* Paris, 26 April 1865). Some years before 1815 he established a factory for brass and woodwind instruments in Dinant. He was a skilled workman and his products soon attracted notice. In 1815 he received a court appointment and was entrusted with supplying instruments for certain Belgian Army regiments then in course of formation. In the same year the business was transferred to Brussels, where it continued until after his death. Instruments bearing his mark figured at the Paris Exhibition of 1867. In addition to producing the standard instruments of his period, and a clarinet with the 'spectacle' *b/f* key designed by (2) Adolphe Sax, Charles-Joseph Sax devised a valveless 'cor omnitonique' in 1824, and patented an improved version in 1846. He also obtained Belgian protection for an improved system of 'cylinders' applied to the ophicleide. According to Pontécoulant (*Organographie*, Paris, 1861, ii, p.369) Sax's 'omnitonique' idea of 1824 was patented in France in 1832 in the name of Stuckens (presumably a patent agent), and two years later its originality was challenged by Meifred and Deshays, thus foreshadowing the mass of litigation that was later to bedevil the life of his son.

(2) Adolphe [Antoine-Joseph] **Sax** (*b* Dinant, 6 Nov 1814; *d* Paris, 4 Feb 1894). Son of (1) Charles-Joseph Sax. He made his first acquaintance with musical instruments in his father's workshop, and soon acquired exceptional skill. As a student at the Brussels Conservatory (flute and clarinet), he added the player's experience to that of the instrument maker. His inventive talent was tremendous; his business acumen perhaps less so. A great deal has been written of him, both during his lifetime and since, much of it unreliable and contradictory, for he attracted both violent partisans and bitter enemies. It seems that he was of a somewhat quarrelsome, certainly litigious temperament, and through excessive self-esteem may have brought on himself some of the troubles that marked his later years. Nevertheless, he had much to be proud of, and in several directions his influence was profound.

The first of his recorded instruments are flutes and ivory clarinets, shown at the Brussels Industrial Exhibition of 1830, and a clarinet with no fewer than 24 keys made in 1834, which he played and exhibited in 1835. In 1838 he patented a bass clarinet which surpassed any then extant, and it was probably about this time that he began the work which led finally to the saxophone. Feeling the need of a wider scope than he found in Belgium, distressed by family bereavements, and disgusted by the withdrawal on a specious pretext of a major award at the 1841 Brussels Exhibition Sax decided to go abroad. Having declined offers from London and St Petersburg, he moved to Paris in 1842, where he lost no time in seeking influential contacts, first among them Berlioz, who did much to recommend the young man and his ideas. Others who assisted him were Rossini, Halévy, Meyerbeer and Fétis.

Once settled in a modest workshop, Sax began to manufacture standard instruments of superb quality, but very shortly he introduced improvements of his own, as well as devising new instruments. The range of this work is illustrated by the French patent records of the next ten years: the families of saxhorns (1845) and saxotrombas (1845); the saxophones (1846); an adjustable rotary valve for the clarion (1849); a bassoon on 'rational' lines (1840, 1851); an improved trombone (1852) and an original system of six independent valves for brass instruments (1852). To demonstrate his various instruments Sax formed a small band of competent musicians. The independent valve system, however, has not commended itself generally, except perhaps in Belgium where at the Brussels Opéra trombones on this principle were in use about the turn of this century. The design was pirated by at least two rival manufacturers.

Of Sax's major inventions only the saxhorn and saxophone are used today, the former in the brass band, largely through the great influence of the Distin family, and in military circles. The saxophone seems to have been appreciated from the very first by both civil and military musicians, and instruction in this instrument under the direction of the inventor himself was added to the syllabus of the Paris Conservatoire in 1858. The class was suspended in 1871 on financial grounds. It seems unlikely that Sax could have imagined the popularity that was to come to his invention in the 20th century through the commercialization of Afro-American jazz.

Sax also devised, perhaps less happily, timpani with open frames in place of the customary shells, and studied concert-room acoustics.

By 1845 the central authority was showing concern about the declining standards of French army music, and early in that year Sax addressed himself to the Minister of War, Count Rumigny, with proposals for reform incorporating the use of his own instruments, some designed expressly for service conditions. A commission of enquiry was set up under the presidency of the minister which resulted in a public contest on 22 April between a band of 38 directed by Sax and a much larger military band of the traditional constitution. The judgment of a large and representative jury resulted in the official adoption of Sax's instruments and gave him what was virtually a concealed monopoly in French military music.

The début of a young, active and ambitious foreign rival was not well received by the older established instrument makers in France, and almost at once Sax found his activities obstructed by them. Certainly he was not above producing his own version of other men's ideas. Quite early he adopted the 'Berliner Pumpen' of WILHELM WIEPRECHT and Moritz, for example. Nevertheless, extreme measures were taken by some of the Paris makers. Sax was subjected to vicious press campaigns; his best workers were tempted away by higher salaries; a mysterious fire destroyed part of his factory; he was even attacked physically. It was not long before the law was invoked, and suits for nullity of his patents were preferred. For the remainder of his life he was involved in a series of lawsuits, some initiated by him in retaliation, and on his death some remained unsettled. One such was that instituted by the Lyons maker Rivet, probably instigated by others. Here nullity was claimed on the grounds that in the saxhorns the bore dimensions had been established in previous instruments, the principle of the piston valve had been worked out by

Blühmel (*see* VALVE (i)) and the general shape of the instruments had already been adopted by other makers. Sax won this case, but lost many others. The lawsuits ruined him (he was declared bankrupt in 1856 and again in 1873 though he persisted in his work with great fortitude), and several of his attackers. It is said that Sax's military achievements, for which he was decorated by France and several other countries, deprived some renowned makers of their principal outlet, among them Raoux, Labbaye, Halary and Besson, and led to the premature closure of their businesses. After Sax's death his sons continued the business under more peaceful conditions, and one of them, Adolphe Sax (ii), became director of the stage band at the Opéra, a post which his father held from 1858 until his death.

(3) **Alphonse** [?Antoine] **Sax** (*b* Brussels, 9 May 1822; *d* Paris, 26 June 1874). Son of (1) Charles-Joseph Sax. He began a musical career as flute lauréat at the Brussels Conservatory. After a short period in business in that city he joined his brother in Paris in 1844. In 1860 he set up independently, but after a quarrel with Adolphe over 'ascending pistons' at the 1862 London Exhibition his business seems to have declined. After 1867 his name disappears from the lists of Paris makers and the records become obscure.

BIBLIOGRAPHY

G. Kastner: *Manuel général de musique militaire* (Paris, 1848/*R*1973 4)
C. Pierre: *La facture instrumentale à l'Exposition universelle de 1889* (Paris, 1890)
——: *Les facteurs d'instruments de musique* (Paris, 1893), 319, 333, 349, 359
E. Closson: *La facture des instruments de musique à Bruxelles* (Brussels, 1935)
P. Gilson: *Les géniales inventions d'Adolphe Sax* (Brussels, 1939)
A. Remy: *La vie tourmentée d'Adolphe Sax* (Brussels, 1939)
M. Haine: *Adolphe Sax: sa vie, son oeuvre, ses instruments de musique* (Brussels, 1980)

PHILIP BATE

Saxhorn. A homogeneous family of valved brass instruments evolved by Adolphe Sax in the period 1842–5; it was patented by him in France in 1845. The validity of the patent, at least in so far as whether it protected a genuine new invention, has been questioned at different times, and indeed was fiercely challenged in Sax's lifetime by certain long-established French instrument makers. Nevertheless it is certain that Sax at least deserves credit for bringing a degree of consistency to a class of instruments which had hitherto shown little uniformity either of proportion or tonal character. Intended primarily for army use, the saxhorn has revolutionized military, and in particular brass, bands.

The terminology of the larger brass instruments is still very confused since they appeared in many different countries at different times in the early 19th century; hence classification on any but very general lines is difficult. Different makers adopted the proportions which seemed best to each, and gave their products fanciful names. Only in France is the term 'saxhorn' still applied to the entire group, while in England, where the instruments are widely used, only the tenor and baritone sizes are correctly named. Even in England they are often abbreviated to tenor or baritone horn, and elsewhere the name has either gone completely out of use or is so loosely applied as to have no definite significance. Sax himself, at least in his early years in Paris, did not even use the term to describe his inventions.

1. General. 2. History.

1. GENERAL. Saxhorns have a tapered bore (except through the valves and ancillary passages which are necessarily cylindrical) with a fairly rapid expansion in the last section, leading to a bell of only moderate flare. (In the hands of American makers, the bell has been considerably enlarged.) The main tube has a fairly large bore relative to its length, together with many of the proportions associated with the French type of bugle (which some authorities regard as the parent instrument of the type); indeed this similarity was one of the bases on which legal appeals against Sax's patent were founded. The scale of the bore is not quite so large as that generally recognized as definitive of the tuba group (*see* TUBA (i)).

When blown with a rather deep cup mouthpiece saxhorns easily sound their harmonics, from the 2nd to the 8th or higher, and this is generally regarded as their practical compass. On most of them their fundamental (or pedal) note can be sounded, but it is often uncertain and of poor quality. This has led some writers to make the distinction (which is of little use) between 'whole-tube' and 'half-tube' instruments. The need for the complete pedal octave on deeper saxhorns seems to have been felt quite early, and very shortly after their introduction Sax enlarged the bore of the larger members to improve that part of their compass. In so doing he sacrificed some measure of tonal homogeneity in the group but gained other advantages. Since the usual three valves, semitone, tone and minor 3rd, can together only bridge the gap between the fundamental and the 2nd harmonic to the extent of a diminished 5th, an additional valve and tubing for two and a half tones was called for, which Sax soon provided. The result was a complete family, soprano to contrabass, pitched alternately in B♭ and E♭, the three lowest having a complete chromatic scale from the pedal note upwards, while the practical range of the others began a 4th higher.

The tonal distinction between the euphonium (tenor tuba) and the baritone horn, both used in brass bands and standing in the same nominal pitch, has tended to be less pronounced in some parts of the world. American makers and their followers are now building euphoniums to a rather narrower scale than that favoured in England and France. Brass basses are also now being built on the Continent with up to six valves and of such proportions as to make their ultimate parentage, tuba or saxhorn, very difficult to determine.

Saxhorns, in common with all other valved instruments, suffer from two acoustic defects. The unavoidable use of a proportion of cylindrical tubing in the valve slides disturbs the regular taper of the bore to an extent dependent on the number of valves in use at any one time; this modifies the harmonic content of the sound to a variable degree. The effect is minimized by placing the valves as near to the mouthpipe as possible, as in this area the relative disturbance is least. In the first saxhorns the ancillary valve tubing was coiled in circles, a feature that was said to be acoustically advantageous, but it prevented the use of telescopic tuning-slides or the disposal of condensed moisture. The second and more serious defect is an increasing sharpness when two or more valves are used together; for though the extra tube added by one valve may be sufficient to lower the open notes of the main tube by the required amount, it will be insufficient to produce the same degree of lowering if the main tube has already been lengthened by another valve. On smaller saxhorns, as on trumpets or cornets, this trouble can be corrected by the player's lip technique, but on the longer instruments some form of mechanical compensation is desirable. This is supplied automatically by such valve systems as Blaikley's, or (at the discretion of the player) by special supplementary valves bringing in short extra lengths of tubing. Mechanisms have also been designed by which valve slides may be pulled out against the bias of return-springs whenever two or more pistons are depressed together, but these seem to have been short-lived. About 1850 Sax sought to apply to the saxhorn his system of six 'pistons à tubes indépendants'. The effect of this ingenious but technically complicated arrangement is that the valves, which could only be used one at a time, successively shortened the air column in semitone ratios. Thus by using the open tube or any one of the valves the player had at his disposal seven different harmonic series spaced a semitone apart and eliminating the need for the compensation inherent in any 'additive' valve system. In practice this seems to have been something of a disappointment, probably because the large proportion of cylindrical tubing involved would tend to destroy the characteristic tone of an instrument of tapered design. With the basically cylindrical trombone the system achieved a considerable degree of success.

In general shape and appearance, most modern saxhorns, wherever made, present a strong family likeness. The tubing is usually folded in the manner of a large trumpet set on end, and the mouthpipe projects more or less at a right angle. In Germanic instruments the coiling is more strictly elliptical. The bell stands vertical, but in some recent American designs it is tilted sharply forward from the plane of coiling. According to Carse, Sax originally planned his whole group with forward-directed bells, but very shortly changed to the upright form as depicted in Kastner (see illustration). Later, however, he reverted to the more familiar horizontal trumpet shape for the soprano and alto members. Saxhorns have either piston or rotary valves, and both seem equally efficient.

2. HISTORY. The achievement in the second and third decades of the 19th century of a fairly satisfactory valve mechanism had a profound effect on the manufacture of brass instruments. An alternative to the side-hole system, with its large padded key cups and somewhat vulnerable levers, was now possible. In many parts of Europe between 1830 and 1850 makers devoted themselves to applying valves to conically bored instruments of all sizes. Some attempted to add them to tubes of bugle or ophicleide proportions, but others designed entirely new instruments. This resulted in many novelties which are now difficult to classify except in a very general way. The classic ophicleide, however, held its own for some time against these innovations. It had served well for many years as both orchestral and military wind bass, and its characteristic rather dry tone and potential for agility in skilled hands were much admired. The respect accorded to this instrument is indicated by the fact that some early valve bass brass instruments were called ophicleide by their makers although they resembled it in no aspect except pitch.

In 1842 Sax, formerly associated with his father's factory in Brussels, came to Paris and set up a modest establishment as a maker of both brass and woodwind.

With the support of a few notable patrons, in particular Berlioz, he was soon a successful maker, to the annoyance of a number of long-established Parisian firms. A man of great ambition and inventive capacity, Sax secured a large number of patents, but it is now difficult to assess the true value of some of his ideas.

On settling in Paris one of Sax's first activities was to design the saxhorn. The principle involved was not entirely new, having been utilized in the French CLAVICOR and various German types of horn some years earlier. The proportions adopted by Sax, however, undoubtedly made his instrument superior. In 1845 the saxhorn family was patented, and in that year Sax wrote to the Minister of War, Count Rumigny, drawing his attention to them. At that period French military music in general was in decline and long due for reorganization. As a result of the deliberations of a commission headed by Count Rumigny himself, and after a public contest between an established military band and a smaller group of Sax's instruments directed by the inventor, the latter were officially adopted. Thus Sax secured what was virtually a concealed monopoly as supplier to the French army. At that time the saxhorn group ranged from soprano to bass, but within a year or so a sopranino and a contrabass in Bb had been added, as well as some intermediate sizes in unusual keys. Provision was also made for the use of detachable transposing crooks as was still the custom with the cornet. By 1855 a giant contrabass or 'bourdon' in Eb had been constructed; this monster is now in the Musée des Arts et Métiers in Paris.

Sax's claim that his products were something entirely new in the field of music was hotly contested by a number of other manufacturers who denied strongly that they embodied anything in the nature of a protectable invention. Powerful representations were made to the government for the annulment of the *brevets* of 1845. The result was a long series of lawsuits and counter-suits which contributed to the ruin of several famous houses and of Sax himself. He was twice declared bankrupt, yet with incredible fortitude he remained in business. The evidence suggests that Sax's claims were extravagant, even arrogant, but against this must be set his achievement in bringing order to a class of instruments which was developing elsewhere in a hopelessly irregular manner. The standards of workmanship he introduced were beyond reproach.

The earliest saxhorn illustrations we have are those given by Kastner (1848, reproduced here) and from these it seems that the first valves were of the stout 'Berliner Pumpen' type. These were designed by Wieprecht in Berlin and first made there by Moritz; it was the former's contention that Sax's valves were based on those of certain instruments that he or his father had purchased from Moritz. The two men met in 1845 and as a result Wieprecht concluded that it would not be worth his while to try to obtain legal redress. Although Sax does not seem to have been above producing his own version of other men's ideas it must be remembered that in his day, and for many years after, international recognition of patent rights hardly existed. Later saxhorns were provided with the slender 'Perinet' valves and some surviving examples even show a form of the rotary valve.

Sax was particularly fortunate in the artists who first played his instruments publicly. In 1844 the Distin family's brass quintet visited Paris on a concert tour

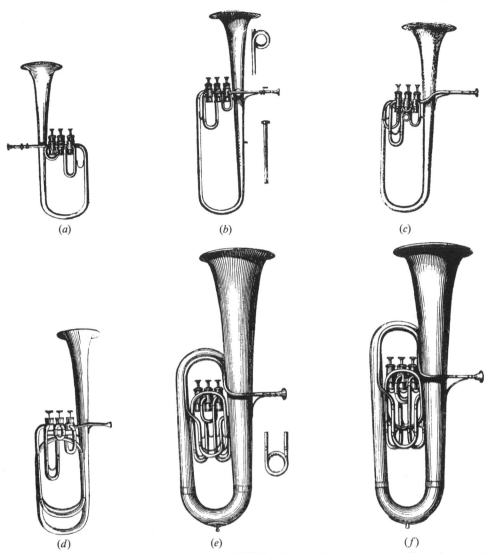

Saxhorns from 'Manuel général de musique militaire' (1848) by Kastner: (a) saxhorn in E♭, (b) saxhorn in B♭, (c) saxhorn in A♭, (d) saxhorn in E♭, (e) saxhorn in F and E♭, (f) saxhorn in E♭

during which their attention was drawn to the first experimental saxhorns. Their admiration was unbounded and resulted in a commission for a set of instruments which was completed in the same year. Those instruments became the regular equipment of the group. There are conflicting accounts of the relationship between the Distins and Sax, but it seems probable that Henry Distin's version given to Enderby Jackson, the historian of brass bands, in 1895 is accurate. It is quoted at length by Russell and Elliot. The influence of the Distins on the fast-growing brass band movement in England was tremendous and their adoption of saxhorns the finest possible advertisement. From 1845 saxhorns began to appear in workmen's bands, though the expense must have been a considerable drain on their small resources. It seems likely that Mossley Temperance Band was the first in England to be completely equipped with saxhorns and their great success at the Belle Vue Contest of 1853 was another striking

recommendation for Sax's work. All the instruments imported for this band were of the upright form, including even the cornets, which Sax also supplied. They were pitched mainly in A♭, which later caused difficulties when B♭ and E♭ became the standard pitches in contests. The Mossley instruments were obtained through Henry Distin who later became a manufacturer in London although he retained the Sax agency for a number of years.

In spite of his championship of saxhorns in Great Britain, Distin must bear some of the blame for the confusion between them and the large-bore tubas. An old page of advertisements forming the back cover to some sheet music sold by his firm depicts a number of instruments, soprano to bass, all labelled 'tuba'. Even allowing for poor commercial engraving, these, by their proportions and by comparison with Kastner's figures, can only have been saxhorns. They are all of the upright type and the same sheet also shows examples of the trumpet shape, soprano to baritone, all correctly named. It has been suggested that this plate indicates an effort on Distin's part to regularize nomenclature by reserving the term saxhorn for horizontal types and calling all upright instruments tubas, but there is no evidence in support of this hypothesis.

BIBLIOGRAPHY

J.-G. Kastner: *Traité général d'instrumentation* (Paris, 1837)
H. Berlioz: 'Les instruments de musique d'Adolphe Sax', *Journal des débats* (12 Jan 1842)
——: 'De la réorganisation du musique militaire', *Journal des débats* (1 April 1845)
——: 'Nouvelle salle de concerts d'Ad. Sax', *Journal des débats* (24 Feb 1847)
——: 'Sax et ses instruments', *Journal des débats* (12 Oct 1847)
G. Kastner: *Manuel général de musique militaire* (Paris, 1848/*R*1973–4)
H. Berlioz: 'Le saxophone', *Journal des débats* (13 April 1851)
A. Sax: *Méthode pour saxhorn* (Paris, ?1851–2) [advertised in *Journal des débats*, 22 Nov 1851]
O. Comettant: *Histoire d'un inventeur du XIXe siècle* (Paris, 1860)
H. Berlioz: 'M. Sax, ses procès, ses procédés pour ses ennemis vaincus', *Monde illustré* (24 Nov 1860)
L. Pontécoulant: *Organographie* (Paris, 1861)
T. Lajarte: *Les instruments de Sax* (Paris, 1867)
O. Comettant: *Les instruments de musique chez les différents peuples: archive de l'exposition de Paris 1867* (Paris, 1869)
H. Berlioz: *Mémoires* (Paris, 1870; ed. and Eng. trans. by D. Cairns, 1969, 2/1970); ed. P. Citron (Paris, 1969)
V. C. Mahillon: *Les éléments d'acoustique musicale et instrumentale* (Brussels, 1874)
——: *Catalogue descriptif et analytique du Musée instrumental du Conservatoire royal de musique de Bruxelles* (Ghent, 1880–1922; i, 2/1893; ii, 2/1909)
F.-A. Gevaert: *Traité d'instrumentation* (Paris, ?1889)
C. Pierre: *La facture instrumentale à l'Exposition universelle de 1889* (Paris, 1890)
J. Brousse: 'Tuba', *EMDC*, II/iii (1927), 1675
M.-A. Soyer: 'Des instruments à vent', *EMDC*, II/iii (1927), 1401–82
I. Blangenois: *Manuel de musique militaire* (Brussels, ?1932)
E. Closson: *La facture des instruments de musique à Bruxelles* (Brussels, 1935)
J. F. Russell and J. H. Elliot: *The Brass Band Movement* (London, 1936)
A. Carse: *Musical Wind Instruments* (London, 1939/*R*1965)
P. Gilson: *Les géniales inventions d'Adolphe Sax* (Brussels, 1939)
A. Remy: *La vie tourmentée d'Adolphe Sax* (Brussels, 1939)
A. Baines: *Brass Instruments and their History* (London, 1974)

PHILIP BATE

Saxhorn-basse (Fr.). The tenor tuba in Bb; *see* TUBA (i).

Saxon, Christian Karl. *See* HARTMANN, CHRISTIAN KARL.

Saxophone (Fr. *saxophone*; Ger. *Saxophon*; It. *sassofone*). An orchestral and military band reed instrument invented by the Belgian-born maker Adolphe Sax (*see* SAX family) *c*1840, and granted a 15-year patent in 1846, four years after he had established an instrument making business in Paris. The saxophones, combining a single-reed mouthpiece with a wide-bore conical tube of metal, form (together with the soprano and sopranino heckel-clarinas) a category of their own. Acoustically, however, they behave as do other cone-bodied reed instruments and 'overblow' at the octave to yield a second register.

1. General description. 2. Compass. 3. Technique. 4. History. 5. Manufacture. 6. Use.

1. GENERAL DESCRIPTION. The body of the saxophone is a fairly wide conical tube of thin metal, commonly brass, expanded at the open end into a small flare. At calculated intervals along the tube is placed a series of 18 to 21 note-holes of graduated size, large in relation to the bore, while towards the mouthpiece end are two very small octave or 'speaker' holes which assist in the sounding of the upper register. Throughout the instrument all holes are controlled by keys, some open, others closed when at rest, according to a system of fingering which in the original design seems to have combined that of the simple oboe with the Boehm arrangement for the right hand. The modifications which have been made to this basic plan over the years are discussed in §3. Each hole is surrounded by a ring or collar which provides a level seating upon which the associated key-pad makes an airtight closure. (*See* BOEHM, THEOBALD.)

As the larger saxophones are of some considerable length they have from the beginning been made more manageable by introducing a U-bend, usually in the region of the third lowest hole and tilting the bell slightly forward, while the section above the main note-holes is made as a detachable crook gently curved through nearly a right angle. From the baritone size downwards, further shortening is secured by double folding at the upper end and though this encroaches on the length occupied by the note-holes it has caused no difficulty since the mechanics of keywork were quite advanced by the time of Sax's invention. This folding has often been regarded as a characteristic and attractive feature of the instrument to the extent that for uniformity both the soprano and sopranino sizes have sometimes been so made. Conversely, tenors and even baritones have occasionally been built straight.

The mouthpiece of the saxophone, originally made of wood but now commonly of ebonite and sometimes of

1. Saxophone: engraving of the instrument patented by Adolphe Sax in 1846

2. The Weintraubs in 1933, with (left to right) bass, baritone, tenor (2), alto (2) and soprano saxophones

metal or even of glass or plastic, is basically similar to that of the clarinet though with different relative proportions and interior configuration. The slightly curved table on which the reed is placed is by comparison wider and a little shorter than in the clarinet, while the slot which communicates with the interior is again relatively wider and usually rounded at the lower end instead of being cut straight across. Internally the saxophone mouthpiece is usually somewhat excavated to form a so-called 'tone chamber' instead of accurately matching the bore at the top of the body tube. Traditionally saxophone mouthpieces are made to slide over the end of the mouthpipe which is lapped with thin cork sheet to make an airtight joint, and the small amount of in-and-out movement this allows serves for fine tuning. Occasionally expensive mouthpieces are made with a metal telescopic section adjusted by a screwed and knurled ring. The small amount of cylindrical tube thus introduced seems to have no adverse tonal effect.

2. COMPASS. The full set of saxophones as originally conceived and covered by the French patent included in all 14 instruments. These were divided into an orchestral group and a military band group each extending from sopranino to contrabass. Inside these groups the instruments stood alternately in F and C, or E♭ and B♭, the orchestral soprano being the only one to sound at written pitch and all others requiring transpositions. With the exception of the C tenor, often called the 'melody' saxophone, and the soprano above it, which have had some vogue on account of their convenience for domestic music, the orchestral group does not seem to have lived long, though in the 1930s the American firm of Conn was listing a revived F alto under the title of mezzo-soprano.

When Adolphe Sax designed his instruments he fixed on a compass of (written) b to f''' for all of them, but soon after the expiry of the initial patent certain French makers extended the tube downwards and added a key for b♭. Indeed it is thought by some that Sax may have done this himself first. Today the accepted lowest note on all standard saxophones is b♭, though some military instruments may still be in use which do not have it, and

on the other hand many makers today list instruments down to a as normal. According to Thiels three full octaves from b were possible on the earliest saxophones, but Sax himself would not admit the extreme high notes which were then somewhat poor and uncertain. (Sounding compasses of the saxophone family are shown in

TABLE 1

Military group		Original orchestral group	
soprano in E♭	d♭′ – a♭′′′	sopranino in F	e♭′ – b♭′′′
soprano in B♭	a♭ – e′′′	soprano in C	b♭ – f′′′
alto in E♭	d♭ – b♭′′	alto in F ('mezzo-soprano')	e♭ – c♭′′′
tenor in B♭	A♭ – f′′	tenor in C ('melody')	B♭ g′′
baritone in E♭	C – b♭′	baritone in F	E♭ c′′
bass in B♭	A♭′ – e♭′	bass in C	B♭′ – d♭′
contrabass in E♭	D♭′ – b♭	contrabass in F	E♭′ – c′

Table 1.) In addition to what we may now call 'normal' extended saxophones, a number of instruments of exceptional range have been built to the requirements of certain virtuoso players. B. Manton-Myatt, for many years chief designer and tuner to Boosey & Hawkes, recalled in particular two such. The first, built in the early 1900s by Couesnon of Paris for Dupaquier of the Garde Républicaine, had a chromatic scale of three octaves from g, while the other, made by Selmer for the Argentinian de Ladario c1920, had a compass of no less than four octaves from a. The upper register was extended by special fingerings assisted by a third 'speaker' key. Finally we should notice here that a sub-contrabass or saxophone-bourdon in B♭ has been constructed though it falls outside Sax's original concept.

3. TECHNIQUE. Compared with the majority of reed instruments the technique of the saxophone is usually regarded as simple and fairly easy. The first register, b to c′′, consists of fundamental sounds; the second, d′′ to c′′′, follows as octave harmonics with a repeat of fingering, plus a slight increase of lip pressure assisted by one or other of the octave keys. The four highest semitones are produced by special keys near the top of the instrument and are also octave harmonics though their fundamentals are rarely used since these notes are duplicated and

a

b

c

d

sound better as the first four semitones of the second register. Special extended saxophones are mentioned above, so it is only necessary to say here that certain specially gifted players can extend the range of the ordinary instrument by superoctave harmonics specially fingered to d'''' or even f''''. Not all saxophones, however, are responsive to such use. Among the facilities now expected by all players is a mechanism by which a single touch-piece for the left thumb operates both octave keys, the selection of the one required being made automatically according to the note fingered. Many designs for such mechanism have been evolved and the best of them are absolutely reliable. The Dupaquier system saxophone appeared for a short time in the Couesnon catalogue, but there is little evidence of its extensive use.

In spite of the simplicity and directness of Sax's original arrangement it soon became evident that the fingering of certain tied or arpeggio passages was very awkward, and once the field became open a number of instrument makers set themselves to this problem. Some merely applied additional touch-pieces giving alternative fingerings, while others went so far as to add supplementary note-holes. Among the most important inno-

vators were Goumas, the Association des Ouvriers, Evette & Schaeffer, Millereau, Lecomte and Fontaine-Besson, all of Paris. The number of these improvers testifies to the growing esteem for the instrument in its own right, and details of their individual contributions can be found in Constant Pierre's report on the Universal Exhibition of 1889. The latest and perhaps most radical revision of the saxophone was introduced as recently as the 1950s by M. Houvenaghel of Leblanc, Paris, and offers quite remarkable technical facilities. This saxophone, termed 'le Rationnel', seems at first sight to differ little from any other except that all but the supplementary top keys stand open at rest. The mechanism is, however, quite different. Its particular virtue lies in the fact that simply dropping the right middle finger lowers by a semitone a whole series of notes $c\sharp$, b, a, g, f and $e\flat$, so that a chromatic passage over two octaves may be played with the normal diatonic fingering plus the alternate raising and lowering of the one digit. It is still perhaps early to assess the impact of this very ingenious innovation.

The production of a good full tone on the saxophone calls for a fair amount of wind and a much looser 'lip'

3. *Saxophones:* (*a*) *sop-ranino in E♭,* (*b*) *soprano in B♭,* (*c*) *alto in E♭,* (*d*) *tenor in B♭,* (*e*) *baritone in E♭,* (*f*) *bass in B♭;* (*b*)–(*d*) *have top F♯ keys,* (*e*) *has a low A key*

than is desirable on the clarinet. For this reason the instrument is not really an easy 'double' for the clarinettist although this is a common practice in dance band circles. Orchestral saxophone players tend to be very much specialists. The characteristic embouchure of the saxophone allows of considerable flexibility of intonation which has commended the instrument to players concerned with natural rather than tempered scales. In the full orchestra it is valuable in sostenuto and cantabile playing and has remarkable dynamic range in the lower and middle registers; nevertheless it does tend to be 'covered up' unless carefully scored for. Its curiously vocal quality commends its discreet use as a solo voice (Bizet: *L'arlésienne*) and it has also considerable agility and is effective in bravura passages. On the saxophone, tongued staccato playing is possible and was at one time

4. The London Saxophone Quartet

much exploited by dance band musicians who developed the almost explosive 'slap tonguing'. Vibrato is also possible and remains purely a matter of taste. A practice not now common and of questionable value is muting. This can be applied to the saxophone by inserting a sort of metal bobbin in the mouthpipe and a padded ring in the bell. The effect is to alter the distribution of partials in the overall complex tone rather than to reduce the volume of sound which can in any case be readily controlled.

4. HISTORY. The initial experiments which led to the fully practical saxophone were undertaken in the years 1840 and 1841 while Sax was still associated with his father's instrument business in Brussels. After moving to Paris in 1842 the young Sax continued his work and had virtually completed it by 1845, when, according to Kastner, some of the new instruments were taken up by certain French infantry regiment bands. The covering patent for the whole family was granted in 1846. Sax's original intention in working out his new instrument remains a matter of debate. It has been suggested that he arrived at his first conception fortuitously in a quest after that recurring pipe-dream, a clarinet that will overblow at the octave. More probable, however, is the suggestion that he deliberately set out to devise a good tonal link between clarinets and tenor brasses in military bands, an area that contemporary band-lists show to have been at least unsatisfactory. Moreover, success in this direction would support his later ideas of supplanting the military woodwinds entirely with a more powerful group. We must remember that Sax, while not always well advised, was a visionary and a man of indefatigable energy.

A single beating reed associated with a conical body tube cannot be regarded as an idea original to Sax. The combination had been used by the Scotsman William Meikle about 1830 in his alto bassoon, of which a number of examples are still to be seen. An even earlier essay by one Desfontenelles of Lisieux is also often suggested as the source of Sax's inspiration. This rather crude wooden instrument (now Paris Conservatoire, no.1136), is mainly of conical bore, but when tested by Jaap Kool *c*1930 it proved to overblow in 12ths and therefore must be regarded as a clarinet type.

How Sax arrived at the shape in which he finally embodied his ideas is also a matter of much speculation. As an experienced woodwind man he must have been aware of the acoustic behaviour of single and double reeds allied to conical and cylindrical tubes, and he may

well have started from first principles. An octave-speaking clarinet would have inevitably demanded a conical tube. It seems more likely, however, that Sax envisaged his new instrument as something in the nature of an ophicleide furnished with a reed mouthpiece, and recent experiments have shown this to be a promising combination. Certainly some of his early patent drawings support this view and we note that the medium to large members of the family came first. As we have already remarked, the exigencies of keywork can hardly have influenced the overall shape of the instrument since by Sax's day this aspect of the trade was well understood and sound mechanical principles were in use. Today nearly all manufacturers have their own variations of saxophone keywork which, with such exceptions as described above, have little effect on the actual fingering or handling of the instrument.

5. MANUFACTURE. The extreme popularity of the saxophone since the first quarter of the 20th century has made its manufacture and marketing one of the most highly commercialized branches of the music industry. It is probably the commonest of all wind instruments in the layman's eyes and, as with motor cars, most of the larger makers have, year by year brought out new models differing only in minor points which might form the basis of a commercial campaign. This great market has, however, justified the installation of expensive machinery at a tremendous initial cost. For the first saxophones the established brass instrument techniques of tube-drawing, hard soldering and hand-hammering were used, and instruments well made on these lines have proved satisfactory and long-lasting. Some Sax-made instruments imported into this country first by the Distins and then by Rudall, Rose, Carte & Co., while the original patent was still in force, survive to bear witness. By the older method the collars of the note-holes were soldered in place and the heat required for this tended to reduce the work-hardening of the main tube in these areas and introduce some weakness. Today the collars are drawn up from the body metal, while the bows and bell blanks are produced from closed tubes by a hydraulic expansion process which ensures great hardness, uniformity to pattern and high finish. In some second-class continental instruments (*c*1900) the bows were produced by placing two stamped-out U-shaped shells face to face and soft-soldering the edges together: plating concealed this very weak construction. Finally we have had in recent years 'plastic' saxophones in which all but the keys and mountings are moulded from synthetic materials. These do not seem to have made much impact in serious professional circles.

6. USE. Since its first try-out in French infantry music over a century ago the saxophone has steadily gained favour in military bands, except those directly under German influence. In Germany the instrument was studiously ignored for many years and one wonders to what extent this may have been due to personal friction between Sax and the very influential WILHELM WIEPRECHT. It is naturally in France and Belgium that military saxophones are most fully exploited and most bands carry at least a quartet of them which yield a warm full harmony rather reminiscent of organ diapason and very characteristic. In Britain two saxophones only, alto and tenor, form the usual military complement, though both there and in America the tendency is to increase the number and extend the range.

In civilian music there is little doubt that from about 1890 onwards the superb wind bands of J. P. Sousa and his one or two rivals did much to make the saxophone familiar to American concert audiences and to launch it on its later wave of popularity in that country. Its English début took place about 1850 at one of Jullien's concerts. The saxophone is today readily available in the symphony orchestra and in the hands of specialists; a far cry from 1904 when Richard Strauss found it almost impossible to recruit a quartet for his *Symphonia domestica*. In the field of opera, French composers particularly, as one might expect, were attracted by the new instrument and as early as 1845 Kastner used it in his now little-known *Le dernier roi de Juda*. Thereafter Meyerbeer, Bizet, Massenet and A. Thomas all made effective use of it mainly in 'tone-colour' solo passages which are quoted in almost every textbook. As support to choral singing the saxophone has occasionally proved valuable, unobtrusively supporting the singers' intonation and fusing with the general tonal mass. From time to time unaccompanied saxophone quartets, soprano to baritone, have appeared on the concert platform in repertories ranging from light pieces to direct transcriptions of familiar classics and more recently to specially composed chamber music of high quality. In this field a pattern of artistry has been set by Marcel Mule and the Quatuor des Saxophones de Paris; in London the Michael Krein Quartet was formerly notable, and in the early 1970s a new London Saxophone Quartet of quite young players was formed to play advanced chamber music. For solo saxophone with larger or smaller orchestras the concert repertory now contains much music of merit, while earlier works include Debussy's *Rhapsody*, Ibert's *Concertino da camera* and Glazunov's *Concerto in E♭*.

In orchestral and theatre music, the saxophone has been used by Ravel (*Bolero*, orchestration of Musorgsky's *Pictures at an Exhibition*), Vaughan Williams (*Job*, Sixth Symphony), Prokofiev (*Lieutenant Kije, Romeo and Juliet*) and Britten (*Billy Budd*); mostly they have used the alto and tenor instruments, and occasionally the soprano, but some recent composers (including Stockhausen and Penderecki) have used the baritone, and Schoenberg (*Von heute auf morgen*) calls for the long-obsolete bass saxophone in C. In America, particularly, the long dominance of the alto and tenor no longer obtains. The pioneer of the American school was Sigurd Rascher, whose work on extending the natural harmonic range of the instrument to over an octave above the conventional *f‴* has been taken up by avant-garde composers.

Finally we must consider the use of the saxophone in the modern dance band. In the 1930s it was often said that the instrument had been vulgarized in the hands of jazz musicians, and said without any understanding of the true meaning of jazz in terms of style and idiom, or of its social connotation. In fact the saxophone was virtually unknown to the Negro marching bands and the small New Orleans dance bands who were the progenitors of the true jazz. Their instruments were trumpet, clarinet and trombone, paralleling as it were the high, medium and low human voice which was at first the only expressive instrument that the Afro-American Negro had. Occasionally in the years just before 1917 the tenor and soprano saxophones did find a supplementary place in the rather larger and more organized bands on the Mississippi river boats, but it was not until 1920 when social conditions forced the majority of coloured

musicians to seek a wider field in Chicago that these instruments became important among them. Then certain band-leaders, both white and black, began to develop large bands with a commercial style in dance music that had little in common with the New Orleans small band style. At this stage saxophones began to form a 'melody' group usually of soprano, two altos and a tenor, balanced by a corresponding weight of brass. A short step farther led to the ever larger show band, and it was here that 'slap tonguing' was most exploited as well as such grotesqueries as the 'smear' and the 'laugh' which a loose embouchure permits. Today these things are gone and the contemporary jazz saxophonist, though far from the original idiom, is a very serious musician.

BIBLIOGRAPHY

G. Kastner: *Manuel général de musique militaire* (Paris, 1848/*R*1973–4)
C. Pierre: *La facture instrumentale à l'Exposition universelle de 1889* (Paris, 1890)
V. Thiels: 'Le saxophone', *EMDC*, II/iii (1927), 1660
F. G. Rendall: 'The Saxophone before Sax', *MT*, lxxiii (1932), 1077
S. Rascher: *Top Tones for the Saxophone* (New York, 1941, rev. 2/1962)
A. Carse: 'Adolphe Sax and the Distin Family', *MR*, vi (1945), 193
Anon.: 'Hydraulic Forming Techniques', *Machinery*, lxxxii (1953), 1089
M. Perrin: *Le saxophone: son histoire, sa technique et son utilisation dans l'orchestre* (Paris, 1955/*R*1977)
J.-M. Londeix: *125 ans de musique pour saxophone* (Paris, 1971)
M. Haine: *Adolphe Sax: sa vie, son oeuvre, ses instruments de musique* (Brussels, 1980)
PHILIP BATE

Saxotromba. A group of valved brass instruments devised principally for the use of mounted military bands by Adolphe SAX and patented in 1845. These instruments had a mainly conical bore, but the 'scale' was considerably narrower than in the corresponding SAXHORN, the idea being to produce a tone-colour somewhat allied to that of the trumpet and trombone. The group was pitched alternately in B♭ and E♭, with an additional member in F designed to replace the french horn in military bands. Saxotrombas did not survive long, and had disappeared from the inventories of French cavalry bands by 1867.

PHILIP BATE

Sayão, Bidú [Balduina] (**de Oliveira**) (*b* Rio de Janeiro, 11 May 1902). Brazilian soprano. After early study in Rio de Janeiro she became a pupil of Jean de Reszke in Nice. Returning to Rio de Janeiro in 1925 she made her concert début and a year later sang Rosina at the Teatro Municipal, repeating the role at the Teatro Costanzi, Rome. After appearances at both Paris houses (1931), the Teatro Colón, Buenos Aires, and in Italy, she made her North American début in a New York Town Hall recital (1935). Two years later she enjoyed a tremendous success as Massenet's Manon on her début at the Metropolitan Opera (13 February 1937), initiating a New York career that lasted until 1951, in lyric and coloratura soprano roles such as Gilda, Rosina, Gounod's Juliet, Mélisande, Violetta, Mimì, Norina, Adina, Zerlina, and – perhaps most memorably – Susanna. She exuded feminine charm, warmth and refinement on stage, singing with pure, silvery tone and enlivening soubrette roles without recourse to soubrette mannerisms. In addition to concert appearances (many with Toscanini), she gave frequent recitals and made numerous recordings. She retired from the stage after farewell performances (1958) in Rio de Janeiro. Her second husband, the baritone Giuseppe Danise, was her manager.

BIBLIOGRAPHY

J. A. Léon and A. Ribeiro Guimaries: 'Bidú Sayão', *Record Collector*, xiii (1960), 125 [with discography]

R. Celletti: 'Sayão, Bidú', *Le grandi voci* (Rome, 1964) [with opera discography by J. P. Kenyon]

MARTIN BERNHEIMER

Saygun, Ahmet Adnan (*b* Izmir, 7 Sept 1907). Turkish composer, conductor and ethnomusicologist. He began his musical career by singing in the chorus of his elementary school and he took piano lessons from the age of 13. In 1925 he became a music teacher in elementary schools, and from the next year he taught in high schools. Having won a contest organized by the Ministry of Education, he left for Paris in 1928 to study music.

Saygun's first teacher at the Paris Conservatoire was Eugène Borrel; later he attended Vincent d'Indy's composition classes at the Schola Cantorum. In 1931 Saygun returned to Turkey and began to teach counterpoint at the Music Teachers School. In 1934 he became conductor of the Ankara Presidential SO, but he had to resign because of his failing hearing. From 1936 to 1939 he taught at the Istanbul Municipal Conservatory. In 1939 he was appointed inspector of Halkevis (cultural institutions), an appointment which enabled him to travel throughout Turkey and to conduct extensive research into Turkish folk music; in this work he collaborated with Bartók (his study *Béla Bartók's Folk Music Research in Turkey* was published, ed. L. Vikár, in Budapest in 1976). From 1946 Saygun taught composition at the Ankara State Conservatory, and he is a member of the Turkish Radio and Television Organization Executive Board.

Saygun is the most prominent figure of the group known as the Turkish Five. He is considered an important authority on folklore, but parallel with this scholarship he has maintained a rich creative inspiration; thus he is equally notable for his compositions and for his scientific research on music. He is a member of the executive board of the International Folk Music Council and he has received several medals from abroad for his research work; he contributed the article 'La musique turque' to the *Encyclopédie de la Pléiade*. His compositions reflect an expression which is a blend of Romanticism and impressionism, but in his later works he tried to apply more recent developments.

Saygun was the first Turkish composer to write operas after the foundation of the republic, but the work that brought him fame was the oratorio, *Yunus Emre*, which illustrates lines by the 13th-century Turkish mystical poet Yunus Emre. The work was completed in 1946 and was performed that year in Ankara, in 1947 in Paris and in 1958 in New York, under the direction of Leopold Stokowski. The majority of Saygun's works have been published by foreign houses and some have been recorded. His opera *Köroğlu* is often performed by the Istanbul State Opera.

WORKS
(*selective list*)

Operas: Özsoy, 1934; Tasbebek, 1934; Kerem, 1947; Köroğlu, 1973

Vocal: Yunus Emre, oratorio, 1946

Orch: 4 syms, 1953, 1958, 1960, 1976; Pf Conc., 1958; Vn Conc., 1967; Suite, 1934; Zeybek, Interlude and Horon, national dances, 1951

Chamber: Vc Sonata, 1935; Pf Sonatina, 1938; Vn Sonata, 1941; 3 str qts, 1947, 1958, 1967

Principal publisher: Southern Music

FARUK YENER

Sayne, Lambert de. *See* SAINNE, LAMBERT DE.

Sayve [Saive, Saibe, Sainne, Sayfe, Seave, Seef, Seyve], **de.** Flemish family of musicians and clerics. The first member known is Raskin de Seave, a burgher of Liège, whose two sons were musicians.

(1) **Mathias** [Mathieu] **de Sayve (i)** (*b* ?Liège, *c*1540–50; *d* ? Bohemia, 1619). Singer and composer, elder son of Raskin de Seave. He was appointed second succentor at the collegiate church of St Martin-en-Mont, Liège, on 9 July 1571, and held the post until at least 1588. By 1 January 1590 he was an alto in the chapel of Emperor Rudolf II in Vienna, and in 1593 was Monte's deputy as choirmaster. According to Vannes he was choirmaster in Salzburg from 1606 to 1608, after which he rejoined the imperial chapel until 30 September 1617. It seems likely he died in Bohemia late in 1619. He published his five-voice *Liber primus motectorum* in Prague in 1595 and one motet and two odes by him appeared in collections (*RISM* 1604[7], 1610[18]).

(2) **Lambert** [Lampertus] **de Sayve** (*b* ? nr. Liège, 1548 or 1549; *d* Linz, 16–28 Feb 1614). Composer and singer, second son of Raskin de Seave, and the most important member of the family. Fétis confused him with Lambert de Sainne. He entered the imperial chapel in Vienna as a choirboy in 1562, and an early indication of his talents was the publication of three motets in books 3 and 4 of Giovannelli's *Novi atque catholici thesauri musici* (*RISM* 1568[4–5]). Emperor Maximilian II made him singing master of Melk Abbey, Lower Austria, in 1569. In 1570–71 he accompanied the Archduchess Anna-Maria on her journey to Spain for her marriage to Philip II; after the marriage he returned to Melk. By February 1577 and until the end of December 1582 he was tutor to the choirboys in the chapel of the Archduke Karl in Graz, and in 1583 he became choirmaster in the chapel of Archduke Matthias of Austria (the brother of the Emperor Rudolf II). In 1584 he was joined in Vienna by his nephew Carl (and possibly Libert), sons of (1) Mathias de Sayve (i); (4) Arnold de Sayve may have joined him later. When Matthias succeeded his brother as emperor in 1612 he took his chapel musicians with him, and Lambert de Sayve became master of the imperial chapel.

De Sayve's *Sacrae symphoniae* (1612) was dedicated to the emperor on his coronation. It is an extensive collection of liturgically ordered motets and contains music written over many years. The contents range from traditional four-part settings in the manner of his teacher Monte, to eight-, 12- and 16-part polychoral works (with instruments) in the Venetian style. The publication includes a portrait of the composer, then aged 63. The fluency and resourcefulness shown in the motets is equally evident in the less ambitious but more consistently successful *Teutsche Liedlein*, reminiscent of Regnart (two of whose lieder are in the same publication). In these short, attractive, strophic songs – canzonets in style and structure, scored for higher and middle-range voices only – de Sayve devised points and textures of surprising variety and interest, coupled with compelling if straightforward harmonies. Praetorius, who referred to de Sayve with glowing enthusiasm in his *Syntagma musicum*, thought well enough of these lieder to reissue the complete set at Wolfenbüttel in 1611.

WORKS
SACRED

Sacrae symphoniae, 4–13vv, 15–16vv (Klosterbruck, 1612); 4 ed. in Cw, lxxxvi (1960)

Maria rein mit dein Sohn gmein, 5vv, 1604[7]
Crucifixus, 1605[1]
3 motets, 3–4vv, 1568[4–5]
2 motets, D-Rp (according to Eitner)
7 masses: Dominus regnavit, 16vv; Omnes gentes, 14vv; Lyram pulset, 5vv, ed. in DTÖ, xc (1954); 1 untitled, 15vv; 3 inc.: A-Wn, Gu, PL-WRu, YU-Lu
De confessoribus, motet, 5vv, A-Wn (according to Eitner)
Missa 'Lauda anima mea', PL-WRu (according to Eitner)
Adorans Daniel Deum, motet, WRu (according to Eitner)
Magnificat, 8vv, YU-Lu (according to MGG)

SECULAR
Primo libro delle [24] canzoni a la napolitana, 5vv (Vienna, 1582); 3 ed. in DTÖ, lxxvii, Jg.xli (1934)
[22] Teutsche Liedlein, 4vv, 1602[11]; ed. in Cw, li (1938/R)
2 chansons in J. Lindemann: Amorum filii Dei (Erfurt, 1598) (according to Vannes)

(3) Erasme [Raso] de Sayve (b c1563; d 1631 or 1632). Singer and composer, son of (1) Mathias de Sayve (i). From 1573 to 1577 he was *duodenus* in the collegiate church of St Martin-en-Mont, Liège, and on 22 February 1587 the chapter of St Martin appointed 'Raso de Sayve, filius succentoris' to the altar of St John the Baptist, an appointment usually reserved for young musicians. Some time after this de Sayve took leave of absence from Liège to study in Vienna; on 29 January 1588 this leave was extended. He entered the service of Archduke Matthias, and on 1 September 1613 was appointed deputy choirmaster in the imperial chapel, thus becoming for a while assistant to his uncle, (2) Lambert de Sayve. Erasme de Sayve apparently left this post in 1617 to become *Burggraf* at the imperial court of Matthias and Ferdinand II; he certainly held that position in October 1631. In December 1632 his widow was awarded an annual pension of 100 thalers.

WORKS
[18] Melodie spirituali, 3vv (Nuremberg, 1614) (according to Eitner; see Vannes)
Salve regina, 6vv, A-Gu
7 motets, 4vv, formerly Biblioteca Rudolfina, Liegnitz (according to Eitner), now ?PL-WRu
Exaudi, Domine, 6vv; 1 motet, org score: D-Bds (according to Eitner)

(4) Arnold de Sayve (b c1574; d 15 July 1618). Singer, son of (1) Mathias de Sayve (i). He entered the choir of St Martin-en-Mont, Liège, on 6 July 1584. According to Bragard he served for the last time as a boy chorister in the imperial chapel at Vienna in 1592; he may then have followed his brother Carl (and possibly Libert), who joined their uncle (2) Lambert de Sayve in Vienna in 1584. On 1 February 1602 he was re-engaged as an alto and remained in the choir until 1617.

(5) Mathias de Sayve (ii) (b c1576–80; d c1616). Singer and ?composer. He was a chorister in the imperial chapel, Vienna from 1590 to 1595, and a tenor in the choir from 1 August 1603 to 1616. Eitner and Vannes referred to masses by him for six and nine voices in Breslau, but these may be by (2) Lambert de Sayve.

BIBLIOGRAPHY
EitnerQ; FétisB
E. vander Straeten: *La musique aux Pays-Bas avant le XIXᵉ siècle*, v (1880/R1969)
P. Magnette: 'Essai sur la musique et les musiciens au pays de Liège', *RMI*, xxviii (1921), 217
A. Auda: *La musique et les musiciens de l'ancien pays de Liège* (Brussels, 1930)
R. Bragard: *Lambert de Sayve: étude biographique et bibliographique* (Liège, 1934)
A. Einstein: 'Italienische Musik und italienische Musiker am Kaiserhof und an den erzherzoglichen Höfen in Innsbruck und Graz', *SMw*, xxi (1934), 3–52
H. Osthoff: *Die Niederländer und das deutsche Lied* (Berlin, 1938)
R. Vannes: *Dictionnaire des musiciens (compositeurs)* (Brussels, 1947)
H. Federhofer: 'Lambert de Sayve an der Grazer Hofkapelle', *RBM*, iii (1949), 213
R. John: Foreword to DTÖ, xc (1954), pp.v–xlii

A. Kellner: *Musikgeschichtes des Stiftes Kremsmünster* (Kassel, 1956)
G. Rebscher: *Lambert de Sayve als Motettenkomponist* (diss., U. of Frankfurt am Main, 1959)
E. Schenk: 'Zur Lebens- und Familiengeschichte von Lambert de Sayve', *Festschrift Helmuth Osthoff* (Tutzing, 1961), 103
J. Quitin: 'A propos de trois musiciens liégeois du 16e siècle: Petit Jean de Latre, Johannes Mangon et Mathieu de Sayve', *Musicae scientiae collectanea: Festschrift Karl Gustav Fellerer* (Cologne, 1973), 451
JOSÉ QUITIN (1, 3–5),
RICHARD MARLOW, JOSÉ QUITIN (2)

Sazandarian, Tatevik (Tigranovna) (b Zangezur, 2 Sept 1916). Armenian mezzo-soprano. She graduated in 1937 from the opera studio of the Moscow House of Armenian Culture, and in 1960 from the Erevan Conservatory. She began giving concerts in 1933 and in 1937 joined the Erevan Opera. She is a distinguished representative of Armenian opera, combining some characteristic elements of her national folksinging with contemporary operatic style. Her voice is opulent and passionate, and she has given fine, convincing performances of leading roles in Armenian operas by Chukhadjian, Tigranyan, Step'anyan and Spendiaryan, as well as of the Russian and Soviet repertory; her Western roles include Stravinsky's Jocasta. Sazandarian has toured Iran, Lebanon, Syria, Greece, Belgium, Czechoslovakia and France. In 1961 she was appointed to teach at the Erevan Conservatory. She was made People's Artist of the USSR in 1956.

BIBLIOGRAPHY
V. Harutyunian: 'Tatevik Sazandarian', *SovM* (1956), no.6, p.107
K. Simonian and V. Harutyunian: *Tatevik Sazandarian* (Erevan, 1959)
I. M. YAMPOL'SKY

Sbara. See BARRIERA.

Sbarra, Francesco (b Lucca, 19 Feb 1611; d Vienna, 20 March 1668). Italian poet and librettist partly resident in Austria. His family belonged to the aristocracy of Lucca, and its head held the title of Marquis of Lombrici (Leombria), which appears on the printed libretto to *Venere cacciatrice* (Innsbruck, 1659). From 1633 he was a member of the Accademia degli Oscuri at Lucca and later of the Accademia degli Accesi, for which he produced the opera *Psiche* (text by F. di Poggio; music by Tomaso Breni) at the Palazzo de' Borghi in 1645. After the death of his wife in that year he entered the priesthood and was twice elected a canon of Lucca Cathedral. On several occasions from 1636 he composed poetry for musical celebrations of government ceremonies (see Rolandi, 1932); he also wrote several sets of *intermedi* during the 1640s.

Sbarra's most original works were a series of musical dramas and *intermedi*, tragic as well as comic, with moralizing intent and using symbolic figures; these include *La verità raminga* (1650), *La moda* (1652), *La corte* (1657) and *La tirannide dell'Interesse* (1653). In the last of these, a five-act 'tragedia politicomorale', Interest kills Intellect, enslaves Desire and with the help of Hypocrisy and Adulation makes himself absolute tyrant of the Isle of Free Will. Although only locally performed, these works saw many editions, were in wide circulation and weathered anti-Seicento Italian literary criticism unusually well (see, for example, Belloni). His most performed work, *Alessandro vincitor di se stesso* (Venice, Teatro SS Giovanni e Paolo, 1651, music by Cesti), owes much to G. A. Cicognini in its verse forms and handling of comedy and even in some details of plot, but has declared allegorical intent as well.

Sbarra had contacts with the archdukes of Austria

from the early 1650s (*Alessandro vincitor di se stesso* is dedicated to Leopold Wilhelm) and with the court of Ferdinand Karl at Innsbruck by 1654 (see Senn). From 1659 he was in residence there as counsellor and court poet, probably as successor to G. F. Apolloni and possibly through the offices of Cesti. For Innsbruck he produced librettos and eulogistic poetry for music, such as the idyll *Il tributo degli elementi* for the new sovereign, Siegmund Franz, in 1663. After the extinction of the Tyrolese line in 1665 he obtained a similar position at the Viennese court, where his compositions included texts for *sepolcri* (e.g. *L'inferno deluso nella morte di Gesù Cristo*, 1665, music by Bertali), further moralizing entertainments (*Le disgrazie d'Amore*, 1667, music by Cesti), ballets and the large-scale festive drama *Il pomo d'oro* (libretto published 1668, music by Cesti), intended for the marriage celebration of Emperor Leopold I.

BIBLIOGRAPHY

LaMusicaD; RicordiE; RiemannL 12
G. Malatesta Garuffi: *L'Italia accademica* (Rimini, 1688)
L. Allacci: *Drammaturgia* (Venice, enlarged 2/1755/R1961)
C. Lucchesini: *Della storia letteraria del ducato lucchese*, ii (Lucca, 1831) [incl. extensive list of writings]
G. Sforza: *F. M. Fiorentini ed i suoi contemporanei lucchesi* (Florence, 1879), 398
A. Bertacchi: *Storia dell'Accademia Lucchese*, i (Lucca, 1881)
G. Sforza: 'Francesco Sbarra ed i suoi melodrammi per musica', *Gazzetta letteraria*, xiv (1890), 34
A. Belloni: *Il seicento* (Milan, 1900)
O. G. T. Sonneck: *Library of Congress: Catalogue of Opera Librettos Printed before 1800* (Washington, 1914)
U. Rolandi: *Spettacoli musicali per la funzione delle 'Tasche' in Lucca* (Milan, 1932)
F. Hadamowsky: 'Barocktheater am Wiener Kaiserhof, mit einem Spielplan (1625–1740)', *Jb der Gesellschaft für Wiener Theaterforschung 1951–2*, 7–117
——: *Il libretto per musica attraverso i tempi* (Rome, 1951)
W. Senn: *Musik und Theater am Hof zu Innsbruck* (Innsbruck, 1954)
W. Osthoff: 'Antonio Cestis "Alessandro vincitor di se stesso" ', *SMw*, xxiv (1960), 13–43

THOMAS WALKER

Scabazzi, Petronio Maria Pio. See SGABAZZI, PETRONIO MARIA PIO.

Scabellum (Lat.; Gk. *kroupezion*). Ancient percussion instrument consisting of foot-activated clappers. It took the form of a sandal with a thick wooden sole hinged to a similarly shaped block of wood on the ground. To each of the wooden parts hollowed clappers of varying materials were attached.

The instrument was comparatively rare in Greece but became relatively prominent in Rome with the general expansion of instrumental usage there. Normally it was played by a tibia player serving as leader of a theatrical instrumental ensemble. He was called the *scabillarius*, and the Roman organization of theatrical musicians was called after him the *collegium scabillariorum*. The scabellum appears also with some frequency in Roman representations of cult music (*see* ROME, fig.5).

BIBLIOGRAPHY

G. Fleischhauer: *Etrurien und Rom*, Musikgeschichte in Bildern, ii/5 (Leipzig, 1964)
G. Wille: *Musica romana* (Amsterdam, 1967)

JAMES W. McKINNON

Scacarum (Lat.). CHEKKER.

Scacchi, Marco (*b* Gallese, nr. Viterbo, *c*1600; *d* Gallese, between 1681 and 1687). Italian composer and writer on music. He is remembered chiefly for his defence of modern music against the conservative PAUL SIEFERT but deserves to be recognized as a highly original thinker about music.

Satyr with scabellum and cymbals: Hellenistic statue (3rd century BC) from the group 'Invitation to the Dance' in the Galleria degli Uffizi, Florence

1. Life. 2. Music and polemical and theoretical writings.

1. LIFE. Scacchi was protégé and disciple of Giovanni Francesco Anerio, who probably took him to Warsaw when he became choirmaster at the court of King Sigismund III in the mid-1620s. In 1626 he was a royal musician and in 1628 was named choirmaster. He remained in this position during the reign of Władisław IV (1632–48) and the first months of Jan Kazimierz II's. Poor health led him to retire to Gallese in March 1649, but he continued to teach; among his pupils was Angelo Berardi, who cited him extensively and printed two of his works in *Documenti armonici* (1687).

2. MUSIC AND POLEMICAL AND THEORETICAL WRITINGS. Scacchi was a versatile composer whose oeuvre included *stile antico* masses, madrigals with continuo, sacred concertos and operas. He believed that each of these genres demanded a distinct style, each of which should have certain standards of compositional technique of its own. It consequently irritated him to find Siefert mixing genres in his *Psalmen Davids, nach französischer Melodey* (Danzig, 1640); or at least this gave him a pretext for answering slanderous statements that Siefert had made about Italian music. These were occasioned by a long-standing quarrel in Danzig between Siefert and the elder Kaspar Förster, respectively organist and choirmaster of the Marienkirche. In his *Cribrum musicum ad triticum Syfertcum* ('Musical sieve for the Syfert wheat', 1643) Scacchi enumerated and discussed 151 errors that he accused Siefert of

perpetrating in his psalms, among them excursions from the mode, parallel 5ths and octaves, incorrect fugal answers and misuse of the thoroughbass. He appended some models of good composition in the various genres: several mass movements, two continuo madrigals for four voices, a continuo motet for five voices, a four-part motet and a duet in 'mixed recitative style', all of which he wrote himself, and 50 learned pieces, mostly canons, by Polish, Italian and other composers resident in Poland, under the rubric *Xenia apollinea* ('Apollonian gifts').

Siefert replied with *Anticribratio musica ad avenam Schachianam hoc est, Ocularis demonstratio crassisssimorum [sic] errorum, quos Marchus Schachius quem Cribrum musicum ad triticum Syferticum baptizavit, passim in eo commisit* (Danzig, 1645). He pleaded that he followed the 'Belgian' and not the 'Italian' school, and he cited his teacher Sweelinck and Giovanni Valentini (who worked in Poland and Vienna) as precedents for some of the practices that Scacchi had criticized. He responded to Scacchi's critique point by point and then went on to enumerate the faults he purported to find in Scacchi's model compositions and offered one of his own canons to add to the *Xenia apollinea*.

Rather than respond directly in print, Scacchi collected letters supporting him from eminent composers, the last dated 4 January 1649, and had them printed in a volume entitled *Judicium cribri musici*. They were written by Schütz, Stobaeus, Starck, Michael, Ducius, Cracowitta, Werner, Triben, Krinkovius and Profe. Schütz, who contributed two letters (on 7 September 1646 and in 1648; nos.59 and 69 in Müller von Asow), diplomatically declined to side with either party in the dispute, praising both of them and urging Scacchi to complete the treatise on counterpoint that he had promised, 'for it would certainly greatly profit our German nation first of all and would bring immortal fame to himself and glory to his name'. Without naming Scacchi, Schütz apparently again referred to this same treatise in the preface to his *Geistliche Chor-Musik* (1648), a reference that was once thought to apply to Christoph Bernhard. Schütz there counselled musicians to find the right road to counterpoint by studying the excellent works of many composers, both Italians and others, in the old and concertato styles, and he added (Neue Ausgabe sämtlicher Werke, v, p.vii):

In this regard I still entertain the hope, indeed I have already reports, that a musician well known to me, highly accomplished in both theory and practice, will soon bring to light an entire treatise. This could be very salutary and profitable, especially for us Germans.

Scacchi did state in his *Lettera per maggiore informatione* that he would produce a brief counterpoint treatise, but there is only a long manuscript letter to Christoph Werner and the *Breve discorso sopra la musica moderna* (1649).

The *Breve discorso* is a plea for the acceptance of a multiplicity of styles. It was written partly to counter the slurs of Siefert (who, however, is not named) against the modern Italian style of church music and partly to shrug off the support of Romano Micheli, whom Scacchi scorned as a decadent contriver of puzzle canons. He admitted that there were fine composers who followed 'the very learned Palestrina', but he saw no reason why everyone should be reduced to the poverty of one style. Every liberal art feeds upon innovation, and so should music. Whereas the older composers built the first practice on the principle 'ut harmonia sit domina

orationis', the moderns build on the second practice, 'ut oratio sit domina harmoniae' (the phrases are the famous ones of G. C. Monteverdi in the Latin of *Cribrum musicum*).

In the letter to Werner, Scacchi made a comprehensive classification of musical styles, all of which he felt were accessible to, and viable for, composers of the time, but for different purposes. There were three main classes: church (*ecclesiasticus*), chamber (*cubicularis*) and scenic or theatrical (*scenicus seu theatralis*). He divided the church style into four types: masses, motets and other vocal pieces without organ for four to eight voices; the same with organ or with several choruses; similar vocal music *in concerto*, that is with instruments; and motets or *concerti* in the modern style, that is (as explained in *Breve discorso*) in *stile misto* or *recitativo imbastardito* ('hybrid recitative'), in which the recitative is interrupted by ornate and melodious passages or sacred songs in aria style. The chamber style had three components: madrigals without instruments (*da tavolino*), vocal pieces with continuo, and vocal pieces with instruments such as violins, violas 'majores', theorbos, lutes and recorders. The theatrical style is a single style of 'speech perfected by song, or song by speech'. The letter also contains valuable suggestions about writing in the polychoral and concerted sacred styles.

Scacchi's classification of styles was further developed by Bernhard in his *Tractatus compositionis augmentatus* and by Berardi in *Ragionamenti musicali* (1681) and *Miscellanea musicale* (1689); it is also the basis of the divisions of musical genres given by Fux in *Gradus ad Parnassum* (1725) and by Mattheson in *Der vollkommene Capellmeister* (1739).

WORKS

Edition: J. Mattheson: *Der vollkommene Capellmeister* (Hamburg, 1739/R1954)

[4] Missarum liber 1, 4vv (Rome, 1633)
[15] Madrigali, 5vv, bc (Venice, 1634)
Cantilenae et lacrimae sepulchrales J. Stobaei, 5vv, bc (Venice, 1647)
1 work, 1646³; 3 motets, 1646⁴

16 Ger. contrafacta of It. madrigals, 2 masses, 3 Magnificat, 5 sacred vocal works: PL-WRu
Missa omnium tonorum, 1664, D-Dds; other works, S Uu; other works, USSR-KA, according to EitnerQ

LOST WORKS

Narciso trasformato (V. Puccitelli)
10 operas, Warsaw, 1628–49
La Santa Cecilia, dramma musicale (V. Puccitelli)

WRITINGS

Cribrum musicum ad triticum Syferticum, seu Examinatio succinta psalmorum (Venice, 1643); contains anthology *Xenia apollinea*, comprising works by Scacchi and the following composers: Walentyn Adamecki, Andrea Baldassini, Bandino de Bandini, Adeodato Barrocchi, Jan Bischoff, Giovanni Maria Brancarini, Hieronymus Caesaris, Francesco Coppola, Pietro Coppola, Alexander Delicki, Laurentius Deykowski, Piotr Elert, Augustinus Eutitius, Baldassare Ferri, Marco Antonio Ferrucci, the younger Kaspar Förster, Angelo Gagliardi, Antoine Gallot, Mathias Gasnicki, Giovanni Battista Gisleni, Adam Gobiatus, Johann Gomer, Jacopo Grandi, Grzegorz Graniczny, Giovanni Guiducci, Pietro Leonardo Guiducci, Michael Hayworth, Giovanni Battista Jacobelli, Adam Jarzębski, Jan Baltazar Karczewski, Michael Kobylecki, Valentin Kotakowski, Simone de Ligoris, Marcin Mielczewski, Alessandro Paradisi, Bartłomiej Pękiel, Paul Pielaszkowski, Antonio Pratogaggi, Nicola Rosa, Paweł Roszkowicz, Giovanni Maria Scalona, Vincenzo Scapitta, Johann Schmidt, Georg Simonides, Samuel Stokrocki, Jan Strzyżewski, Nicola Valdi, Bartłomiej Wardeński, Tomasz Włodawski
Lettera per maggiore informatione a chi leggerà il mio 'Cribrum' (Venice, 1644) [lost, MS transcr. in D-B copy of *Cribrum* and I-Bc, dated 22 Sept 1745]
Epistola ad Excellentissimum Dn. CS. Wernerum, c1648; ed. in Katz, 83ff
Judicium cribri musici (Warsaw, c1649) [lost, MS transcr., I-Bc]

Breve discorso sopra la musica moderna (Warsaw, 1649; Eng. trans. in Palisca, 194ff)

BIBLIOGRAPHY
EitnerQ; *HawkinsH*
P. Syfert [Siefert]: *Anticribratio musica ad avenam Scacchianam* (Danzig, 1645)
R. Micheli: *Avviso inviato . . . col foglio reale del canone musicale 'Fons signatus'* (Rome, 1650)
A. Berardi: *Documenti armonici* (Bologna, 1687) [incl. edns. of 2 works]
M. Seiffert: 'Paul Siefert (1586–1666): biographische Skizze', *VMw*, vii (1891), 397–428
E. Katz: *Die musikalischen Stilbegriffe des 17. Jahrhunderts* (Freiburg, 1926)
H. Feicht: 'Przyczynki do dziejów kapeli królewskiej w Warszawie za rządów kapelmistrzowskich Marka Scacchiego' [Notes towards a history of the royal chapel in Warsaw during Marco Scacchi's period as director of music], *KM*, i (1928–9), 20, 125
E. H. Müller von Asow, ed.: *Heinrich Schütz: gesammelte Briefe und Schriften* (Regensburg, 1931)
H. J. Moser: *Heinrich Schütz* (Kassel, 1936, rev. 2/1954; Eng. trans., 1959)
W. Kmicic-Mieleszyński: *Z dziejów kanonu w Polsce w pierwszej połowie XVII* [Canonic technique in Poland in the first half of the 17th century] (Poznań, 1950)
——: 'Geneza "Cribrum musicum"' [The genesis of the 'Cribrum musicum'], *Muzyka*, ii/3 (1957), 3
H. Federhofer: 'Scacchis "Cribrum musicum" (1643) und die Kompositions-Lehre von Christoph Bernhard', *Festschrift Hans Engel* (Kassel, 1964), 76
C. Dahlhaus: 'Christoph Bernhard und die Theorie der modalen Imitation', *AMw*, xxi (1964), 45
Z. M. Szweykowski: '"Ah dolente partita": Monteverdi–Scacchi', *Quadrivium*, xii (1971), 59
C. V. Palisca: 'Marco Scacchi's Defense of Modern Music (1649)', *Words and Music: the Scholar's View . . . in Honor of A. Tillman Merritt* (Cambridge, Mass., 1972), 189–235 [incl. edns. of 3 works]
Z. M. Szweykowski: 'Poglądy Scacchiego na muzykę jako sztukę' [Scacchi's conception of music as art], *Pagine* (1972), 17
W. Hilse: 'The Treatises of Christoph Bernhard', *Music Forum*, iii (1973), 1–196 [incl. trans. of 3 works]
M. Perz: 'Missarum quattuor vocibus liber primus Marci Scacchii Romani', *Pagine* (1974), 217
Z. M. Szweykowski: '*Stile imbastardito* i *stile rappresentativo* w systemie teoretycznym Marka Scacchiego', *Muzyka*, xix/1 (1974), 11
——: *Musica moderna w ujęciu Marka Scacchiego: z dziejów teorii muzyki w XVII wieku* [*Musica moderna* as conceived by Marco Scacchi: a historical study of 17th-century music theory] (Kraków, 1977)
                                          CLAUDE V. PALISCA

Scaccia, Angelo Maria (*b* Milan, *c*1690; *d* Milan, 29 Sept 1761). Italian violinist and composer. As a youth he was called 'Scaccino' to distinguish him from his violinist father Carlo Federico Scaccia. He was an occasional player in the Milanese ducal theatre and chapel by 1711. On 31 March 1719 he became a supernumerary member of the ducal orchestra, taking his father's regular position on 16 January 1751. For his outstanding ability he was the first to receive the ducal *patente di violinista*.

Scaccia's concertos belong to the tradition of Vivaldi but the lighter texture, delicate ornamentation, more frequent alternation of solo and tutti, broader harmonic plateaux and influence of symphonic form mark them as later productions. On 31 March 1744 St Dutés in Paris received a general privilege to print 12 overtures by Scaccia, but there appears to be no trace of these pieces.

WORKS
[6] Concerti con violino obbligato, 2 vn, va, bc, op.1 (Amsterdam, *c*1730)
[Concerto I] in VI concerti a cinque stromenti a violino principale . . . libro secondo (Amsterdam, *c*1736)
[6] Concerti a 4, due violini, violetta e basso, 26 July 1730, *I-Nc*
4 concertos: A, B♭, A, F, *F-Pc*
3 concertos, vn, insts, *GB-Mp*
2 concertos: C, E♭, D-*Dlb*
Concerto, F, *D-B*
Non sarà la mia sventura, aria from La calunnia delusa (Milan, 1724), ascribed to Scaccia, *I-Mc*

BIBLIOGRAPHY
V. Fedeli, ed.: *Le cappelle musicali di Novara*, IMi, iii (1933), 30
G. Barblan: 'La musica strumentale e cameristica a Milano nel '700', *Storia di Milano*, xvi (1962), 619–60
                                          JOHN WALTER HILL

Scacordum (Lat.). CHEKKER.

Scaffen, Henricus. *See* SCHAFFEN, HENRI.

Scala. London theatre built in 1905; *see* LONDON, §IV, 3.

Scala, Paulus. *See* SKALIĆ, PAVAO.

Scalabrini, Paolo (*b* 1713; *d* Lucca, 1803 or 28 Feb 1806). Italian composer. He was music director for the Mingotti opera company from at least 1742, when it was at Graz. He travelled with it through Germany and parts of the Austrian empire, composing and arranging many operas for it and going in 1747 to Copenhagen, where the company performed every year until 1756. In 1748 J. A. Scheibe was dismissed as court *maestro di cappella* there and Scalabrini given his place, which he held until 1753; he was replaced by Sarti. Scalabrini remained in Copenhagen, composing several intermezzos and Danish Singspiels. He then travelled for some years, but returned to Copenhagen in 1768 as music director of an opera company that he had assembled in Italy. When Sarti left in 1775, Scalabrini again became court *maestro di cappella*, until, after the death of his first wife in 1781, he returned finally to Italy. According to Schmidl he died on 28 February 1806.

WORKS
Operas: numerous It. operas, composed or arr., lost except 1 ov., *DK-Kk*, arias, *A-Wn*, *B-Bc*, *DK-Kk*, *I-PAc*; several Danish operas, lost except Den forliebte Skildrer, 1756, *DK-Kk*; Koerlighed uden Strømper, 1773, *Kk*, vocal score in Samfundet til Udgivelse af Dansk Musik, ii/27 (1909); Oraklet, 1776, *Kk*
Other works: Giuseppe riconosciuto, oratorio, Bologna, 1750; 6 sinfonie, *B-Bc*

BIBLIOGRAPHY
SchmidlD
E. H. Müller von Asow: *Die Mingottischen Opernunternehmungen 1732–1756* (Dresden, 1915) [incl. thematic catalogue of works]
T. Krogh: *Zur Geschichte des dänischen Singspiels im 18. Jahrhundert* (Copenhagen, 1924)

Scalchi, Sofia (*b* Turin, 29 Nov 1850; *d* Rome, 22 Aug 1922). Italian contralto. She studied with Boccabadati and made her début in 1866 at Mantua as Ulrica in *Un ballo in maschera*. On 5 November 1868 she sang Azucena in *Il trovatore* at Covent Garden, where she returned virtually every year until 1889; she was also active in St Petersburg from 1872 to 1881 and in 1889–90. Her repertory included many travesty roles as well as Maddalena (*Rigoletto*), Amneris (*Aida*), Leonore (*La favorite*), Fidès (*Le prophète*) and Ortrud (*Lohengrin*). In 1882 she appeared at Buenos Aires, Rio de Janeiro and at New York, where she made her début on 20 December at the Academy of Music as Arsaces (*Semiramide*). At the opening night of the Metropolitan (22 October 1883) she sang Siebel in *Faust*; after appearing in *La Cenerentola* at Florence (1886) and singing Vanya in the first London performance of Glinka's *A Life for the Tsar* at Covent Garden (12 July 1887), she returned to New York to sing Emilia in the first American performance of Verdi's *Otello* at the Academy of Music (16 April 1888). During her last seasons at the Metropolitan she sang Gluck's *Orfeo*

(1893), Beppe in *L'amico Fritz* (1894) and Mistress Quickly in the American première of *Falstaff* (4 February 1895). She retired in 1896.

BIBLIOGRAPHY
W. H. Seltsam: *Metropolitan Opera Annals* (New York, 1949)
H. Rosenthal: *Two Centuries of Opera at Covent Garden* (London, 1958)

ELIZABETH FORBES

Scalcotas, Nikolaos. *See* SKALKOTTAS, NIKOLAOS.

Scale (Fr. *gamme*; Ger. *Tonleiter*; It. *gamma*). A sequence of notes in ascending or descending order of pitch. As a musicological concept, a scale is long enough to define unambiguously a mode, tonality, or some special linear construction, and that begins and ends (where appropriate) on the fundamental note of the tonality or mode; a scale, therefore, is usually thought of as having the compass of one or more octaves. The following discussion is limited to the scales of European musical theory.

A scale is DIATONIC if the sequence of notes is based on a particular species of octave consisting of five tones (t) and two semitones (s). The white notes of the piano perhaps offer the simplest illustration of diatonic scales; see Table 1. The scales on D, E, F and G as given are the most common of the four authentic church modes (*see* MODE). The 'Locrian' scale, given on B in Table 1, is almost never used, since the unstable interval of a tritone occurs between the two most important degrees, the first and fifth (*see* HYPERAEOLIAN). The remaining scales are those of the major and minor mode without any key signature.

TABLE 1

C D E F G A B C	Major scale (Ionian)
t t s t t t s	
D E F G A B C D	Dorian scale
t s t t t s t	
E F G A B C D E	Phrygian scale
s t t t s t t	
F G A B C D E F	Lydian scale
t t t s t t s	
G A B C D E F G	Mixolydian scale
t t s t t s t	
A B C D E F G A	Minor scale (Aeolian)
t s t t s t t	
B C D E F G A B	'Locrian' scale (Hyperaeolian)
s t t s t t t	

Transposition, the raising or lowering of every note by the same interval, affects the name of a diatonic scale only insofar as it changes its starting note. For instance, if the notes in Table 1 were transposed a semitone up, they would yield scales in D♭ major (D♭–E♭–F–G♭–A♭–B♭–C–D♭), E♭ Dorian (E♭–F–G♭–A♭–B♭–C–D♭–E♭), F Phrygian and so on.

There are three ways of conceiving the minor scale in tonal theory. The natural minor (ex.1) consists simply of the ascending or descending sequence of tones and semitones given under the scale from A to A in Table 1. The melodic minor (ex.2) has raised sixth and seventh degrees ascending, but is the same as the natural minor descending. This scale can be abstracted from the characteristic movement of minor key melodies where the raised seventh acts as a leading note in the ascending direction (the sixth is raised to avoid an augmented interval between the sixth and seventh degrees). The

harmonic minor scale has a raised seventh in both directions, but the sixth is left unaltered. In this way it becomes the product of the three primary harmonic functions, being generated from the triads of the tonic, subdominant, and dominant (with raised third), as illustrated in ex.3.

Ex.1 Natural minor scale

Ex.2 Melodic minor scale

Ex.3 Harmonic minor scale

Ex.4 Ascending chromatic scale
(a)

(b)

Among non-diatonic scales, the chromatic scale proceeds entirely by semitones; it can be spelt either in such a way that every note makes a diatonic interval with the starting note (minor 2nd, major 2nd, minor 3rd etc), as in ex.4a, or so that a minimum number of accidentals are used, as in ex.4b. The WHOLE-TONE SCALE proceeds entirely by whole tones (i.e. C–D–E–F♯–G♯–A♯(B♭) C or D♭–E♭–F–G–A–B–C♯(D♭). Certain European PENTATONIC scales are occasionally described as being 'gapped', as if implying that they are incomplete in comparison with diatonic scales.

WILLIAM DRABKIN

Scaletta, Orazio (*b* Crema, province of Cremona, *c*1550; *d* Padua, 1630). Italian composer. According to his *Madrigali* of 1585, he was then a *maestro di cappella* in Milan. The dedication of the *Vilanelle alla romana* (1590) suggests that he was then living in Venice, and had been for some time, since it acknowledges the influence of Giovanni Gabrieli, 'honoratissimo nella nostra professione'. In the same year he was *maestro* at Lodi, and in 1595 was, according to the dedication of the *Effetti d'amore*, living in Bergamo. Between 1601 and 1609 he was *maestro di cappella* at Crema, and subsequently *maestro* at the Chiesa Maggiore, Salò, until 1611. By 1615 he had moved to S Maria Maggiore, Bergamo, where he was *maestro di cappella*. Although the Duke of Mantua ordered a gold coin to be minted in Scaletta's honour during his time at Crema, and Louis XIII later presented him with a gold crown in Paris and granted him permission to reproduce the *fleur de lys* in his publications, his position at Bergamo does not seem to have been particularly important. Indeed, by 1617 the choir was at a low point with just three altos, two tenors and two basses, and is reported as extremely ill-disciplined, a situation that was also characteristic of his period at Salò. By 1620 he had been replaced by Cavaccio. Towards the end of his life Scaletta may have been at St Anthony in Padua, where he apparently died of the plague.

Scaletta is principally known as the author of two treatises, of which the more popular, *Scala di musica*, was reprinted 14 times before 1647 and appears in a revised version as late as 1685. In both books he dealt with simple didactic matters in a straightforward manner. According to Lederer they demonstrate freedom from Zarlino's strict teachings (unusual for their early dates), and by concentrating on practical issues they suggest that theorists had begun to appreciate the developing *seconda prattica*.

WORKS
(all printed works published in Venice unless otherwise stated)

SECULAR VOCAL
Madrigali, 5vv (1585)
Amorosi pensieri: il secondo libro de madrigaletti, 5vv . . . con una canzone francese, 4vv, et uno dialogo, 7vv (1590[25])
Vilanelle alla romana . . . libro primo, 3vv (1590)
Diletto musicale: primo libro de madrigali, 4vv (1593[7])
Effetti d'amore, canzonette . . . con una mascherata . . . libro primo, 4vv (1595[11])
Affettuosi affetti: madrigali, 6vv (1604[19])

SACRED VOCAL
Sacra armonia, 4–8vv, org (1610[9])
Timpano celeste, 1–4vv, bc (1611)
Messa et il vespro, 3vv, org (Milan, 1615)

Mass, 2 motets, 1622[2], 1628[2]
Motets, *D-Rtt*

INSTRUMENTAL
Partitura della cetra spirituale, org (Milan, 1605)

THEORETICAL
Scala di musica molto necessaria per principianti (1585/*R*1976)
Primo scalino della scala di contrapunto (Milan, 1622)

BIBLIOGRAPHY
P. D. Calvi: *Scena letteraria degli scrittori bergamaschi*, i (Bergamo, 1664), 330
A. Geddo: *Bergamo e la musica* (Bergamo, 1958), 52
J. Roche: 'Music at S Maria Maggiore, Bergamo, 1614–1643', *ML*, xlvii (1966), 302
C. Sartori: 'Giulio Cesare Monteverde a Salò: nuovi documenti inediti', *NRMI*, i (1967), 685
J. H. Lederer: *Lorenzo Penna und seine Kontrapunkttheorie* (diss., U. of Graz, 1970), 69ff
W. Dürr: 'Scaletta, Orazio', *MGG*

IAIN FENLON

Scalichius, Paulus. *See* SKALIĆ, PAVAO.

Scaling (Fr. *diapason*; Ger. *Mensur*). In organ pipes, the relationship between the width of a pipe and its length. Narrow-scaled pipes produce a sound that is richer in overtones and more penetrating than that produced by wide-scaled pipes. Moreover, while a flue pipe sounding an octave below another will be twice its sounding length, the difference in diameter will be somewhat less, the precise increment being determined by the relation of timbre to pitch intended by the builder within each rank.

In string keyboard instruments, the term refers to the sounding length of the strings in relation to their intended pitch. Given constant tension and diameter, a string sounding an octave below another will be twice its length, but for practicability the scaling is normally shortened in the bass, as even in a harpsichord with generally short scaling (25 cm for c'' instead of perhaps 35 cm) the maintenance of 'just' scaling in the bass would oblige the sounding length of the C-string to exceed two metres. Most early clavichords, harpsi-

chords and pianos retain a 'just' scaling for at least the upper half of their compass, and begin to shorten the scaling in the tenor range, the reduction in relative string length being compensated for by increases in diameter and, in many instances, by the use of a heavier substance for the bass strings. In the modern piano the scaling is gradually shortened throughout the range from treble to bass, one aim of this 'tapered' scaling being to achieve a smooth gradation of string tension and timbre throughout the instrument's compass.

EDWIN M. RIPIN, DEREK ADLAM

Scalitz, Paulus. *See* SKALIĆ, PAVAO.

Scalzi, Carlo [Cichion] (*fl* 1719–38). Italian soprano castrato. He was born at Voghera in Lombardy and is first heard of in 1719–21 at Venice, where he sang in five operas by A. Pollarolo, G. Porta and Orlandini. He appeared at Reggio and Modena in 1720, Genoa in 1722–3, Venice again in 1724–5 (four operas, two by Vinci), Parma in 1725, Naples in 1726–7 (Vinci's *Ernelinda*, Hasse's *Sesostrate* and other operas) and 1730 (when he created the title role in Hasse's *Ezio*), and Rome in 1728–9 and 1731–2. Metastasio heard him there in 1731 in Vinci's *Artaserse* and bracketed him with Farinelli as 'incomparable'. Scalzi sang again at Genoa in 1733. Handel engaged him for the London season of 1733–4; he made his début in the pasticcio *Semiramide riconosciuta* on 30 October; between 1729 and 1733 his voice had dropped so much in pitch that Handel had to transpose his arias in *Semiramide* down by between a tone and a 3rd. He subsequently sang in revivals of *Ottone* (Adalberto, an alto part altered), *Sosarme* (Argone, much expanded), *Acis and Galatea* (Dorindo) and *Il pastor fido* (Silvio, May 1734) and in the first productions of *Arianna in Creta* (Alceste) and *Il Parnasso in festa* (Orpheus) as well as two more pastic-

Carlo Scalzi: portrait by Charles-Joseph Flipart (1721–93) in the Wadsworth Atheneum, Hartford, Connecticut

cios. Strictly the only part Handel composed for him was Alceste, since Orpheus consists entirely of old music; but the numerous transpositions and alterations in other parts give us a clear idea of Scalzi's voice, a high soprano with a compass from c' to $b\flat''$; in *Il pastor fido* a Faustina aria was put up a tone for him. He seems to have made little impression in London, but was placed in the front rank on the Continent. He sang in four more operas at Venice in 1737–8, including Porpora's *Rosbale* and Hasse's *Alessandro nell'Indie*. On retiring from the stage he entered the Congregazione dell'Oratorio at Genoa. There is a caricature of him by A. M. Zanetti in the Cini collection (*I-Vgc*) and a striking oil painting, reproduced here, by Charles-Joseph Flipart at the Wadsworth Atheneum, Hartford, Connecticut, showing him in costume as Rosbale in 1737.

WINTON DEAN

Scampion. *See* CHAMPION family.

Scandello, Antonio [Scandellus, Antonius] (*b* Bergamo, 17 Jan 1517; *d* Dresden, 18 Jan 1580). Italian composer. He was descended from a long-established noble family of the north of Italy. His music teacher was probably Gaspar de Albertis, *maestro di cappella* at S Maria Maggiore in Bergamo where Scandello is mentioned as a cornettist in 1541. In 1547 he entered the service of Cardinal Christoph Madruzzi in Trent. Two years later Elector Moritz of Saxony engaged him and five other instrumentalists as cornettists and sackbut players in his Dresden chapel, paying him 228 florins with free board and lodging. On the death of the elector in the battle of Sievershausen, 9 July 1553, Scandello wrote the splendid *Missa sex vocum super epitaphium illustrissimi principis Mauritii*. He was converted to Protestantism and in 1562 received the citizenship of Dresden. In 1566 he became assistant to the ailing Kapellmeister, Le Maistre, taking over most of his duties. Two years later on the latter's retirement he was made Kapellmeister with a salary of 400 florins. He made several private journeys to Italy and went with the chapel to Augsburg (1566), Regensburg (1575) and many other German cities. The Breslau engraver Tobias Wolff made a medallion of him in 1577 which shows the serious, resolute features of the composer with his high forehead and deep-set eyes. The manuscript of his last motet, *Christus vere languores*, bears the date of his death and the remark 'Cygnea cantio' (swan song).

There are three reasons for Scandello's great fame: he was an outstanding instrumentalist, a gifted Kapellmeister and an above-average composer. His reputation as a cornettist and sackbut player was such that musicians came from far and wide for tuition. Although he did not take over the chapel until he was past middle age, it achieved such renown under his leadership that it could claim to be the second best in Germany after Lassus's chapel in Munich. There were, however, more Italians than Germans in the Dresden chapel. Friction between the more gifted (and more highly-paid) foreigners and the Germans, particularly the older musicians, was bound to arise, but apparently Scandello managed to smooth over these difficulties. His authority was unquestioned, and even two generations later when Schütz was Kapellmeister, Scandello was still remembered.

Scandello apparently did not start composing until quite late. His first motets date from no earlier than 1551. In the great memorial mass on the death of the elector he clearly established a link with the rich sound of late Netherlands models in the manner of Gombert and Willaert. The work, a parody mass based on his own motet *Mauritius cedidit*, is characterized by a solemn, sublime grandeur and employs a characteristic motif as its ostinato cantus firmus. More church compositions followed at regular intervals, almost all of them parody masses. He was also at home in the particular musical tradition of Dresden exemplified in the Lutheran-inspired works of his predecessors, Walter and Le Maistre. Although a foreigner, Scandello became quite involved in Protestant music. The *St John Passion* of 1561 and the *Auferstehungshistorie* show a mixture of Italian and German influences, and combine chorale and motet styles in Germany for the first time. Even the sections in direct speech are set polyphonically, revealing the influence of Alberti, who composed three Passions with this feature before 1541. Scandello's two works are distinguished by a wealth of imagery, a direct expression of the text and a liturgical correctness, and the editions of Besler and Harnisch prove that they were in the standard repertory until well into the 17th century. His numerous collections of sacred and secular songs had the greatest influence on his contemporaries. In the *Newe teutsche Liedlein* and *Newe schöne ausserlesene geistliche deudsche Lieder* the majority of the pieces are song motets with descant and tenor cantus firmi, together with simple choral settings. All belong to the purely German tradition. Some of the texts had already been set by Walter and Le Maistre. Scandello's *Neapolitanische Kanzonen* of 1566, the first exclusively Italian song collection in Germany, imported the delicate art of the villanella from southern Italy. His most famous compositions are the *Newe und lustige weltliche deudsche Liedlein*, which synthesized the Italian madrigal and villanella styles with the older German cantus firmus technique, yet at the same time respected the fashionable lied. Their simple movement and smooth style can stand comparison with the corresponding works of Lassus. Some of these pieces, for example the *Hennenlied* and the six-voice *Trinklied*, are still performed today.

Scandello's son, August (*b* Dresden, 1570; *d* Dresden, 1609) also became a musician. He was a choirboy in Dresden and was appointed instrumentalist there after studying in Schulpforta. He is supposed to have spent some years at the court in Wolfenbüttel before he returned to Dresden in 1596 as a musician in the royal household.

WORKS

(selective list)

Mauritius cedidit bellam Germania plange (Nuremberg, 1553)
Missa sex vocum super epitaphium illustrissimi principis Mauritii ducis et electoris Saxoniae (Nuremberg, 1558); ed. in Cw, lxv (1958)
Il primo libro delle canzoni napolitane, 4vv (Nuremberg, 1566)
Newe teutsche Liedlein, 4vv (Nuremberg, 1568)
Newe und lustige weltliche deudsche Liedlein, 4–6vv (Dresden, 1570)
Newe schöne ausserlesene geistliche deudsche Lieder, 5–6vv (Dresden, 1575)
Missae sex, 5–6vv (Munich, 1576)
Gaudii paschalis Jesu Christi, ed. S. Besler (Breslau, 1612); ed. K. Ameln and others, *Handbuch der deutschen evangelischen Kirchenmusik*, i/3 (Göttingen, 1937); Geistliche Chormusik, 2nd ser., viii (Stuttgart, 1960)
Passio: Das Leyden unsers Herrn Jesu Christi nach dem H. Evangelisten Johanne, ed. S. Besler (Breslau, 1621); ed. in O. Kade
Masses, Magnificat settings, motets, single lieder in 1564[2], 1568[21], 1571[17], 1572[12], 1575[17], 1578[1], 1585[37], 1590[5], 1591[21]; Corollarium cantionum sacrarum (Nuremberg, 1591); 1597[7], 1607[12a], 1609[28], 1619[16]; Quodlibetum novum latinum, 5vv (Leipzig, 1620); Cantionale sacrum, das ist, Geistliche Lieder ... unterschiedlicher

Autorum, I–II (Gotha, 1646–55); J. G. Ebeling: Pauli Gerhardi geistliche Andachten (Berlin, 1667); some also in MSS in *A-Wn*; *D-As, Bds, Dlb, LEu, Mbs, Rp, Z*; *GB-Lbm*; *PL-WRu*; *S-Uu*

BIBLIOGRAPHY
O. Kade: *Die ältere Passions-Komposition bis zum Jahre 1631* (Gütersloh, 1893)
R. Kade: 'Antonius Scandellus', *SIMG*, xv (1913–14), 535
R. Velten: *Das deutsche Gesellschaftslied unter dem Einfluss der italienischen Musik* (Heidelberg, 1914)
R. Gerber: *Das Passions-Rezitativ bei H. Schütz und seine stilgeschichtlichen Grundlagen* (Gütersloh, 1929)
H. Engel: *Deutschland und Italien in ihren musikgeschichtlichen Beziehungen* (Regensburg, 1944)
I. Becker-Glauch: *Die Bedeutung der Musik für die Dresdner Hoffeste* (Kassel, 1951)
G. Reese: *Music in the Renaissance* (New York, 1954, rev. 2/1959)
K. von Fischer: 'Zur Geschichte der Passionskomposition des 16. Jahrhunderts in Italien', *AMw*, xi (1954), 189
H. J. Moser: *Die evangelische Kirchenmusik in Deutschland* (Berlin and Darmstadt, 1954)
D. Härtwig: 'Scandello, Antonio', *MGG*
B. Smallman: *The Background of Passion Music* (London, 1957, rev., enlarged, 2/1970)
F. Blume: *Geschichte der evangelischen Kirchenmusik* (Kassel, 2/1965; Eng. trans., enlarged, 1974 as *Protestant Church Music: a History*)
LOTHAR HOFFMANN-ERBRECHT

Scandicus (from Lat. *scandere*: 'to ascend'). A neume signifying three notes in ascending order (for illustration *see* NEUMATIC NOTATIONS, Table 1; Table 2 shows the *scandicus* in notations of different regions).

BIBLIOGRAPHY
M. Huglo: 'Les noms des neumes et leur origine', *Etudes grégoriennes*, i (1954), 53

Scapitta [Scapita]**, Vincenzo** (*b* Valenza del Po; *d* Vienna, 1 Aug 1656). Italian composer and Franciscan friar. From 1621 to 1633 he was chaplain and tenor at the court of Archduke Leopold V of the Tyrol at Innsbruck. In 1633 Leopold's wife recommended him to Cardinal Ernst von Harrach in Prague, who then apparently arranged for him to enter the service of Cardinal Franz Dietrichstein, Bishop of Olomouc and governor of Moravia. However, he died in 1636, whereupon Scapitta moved to Warsaw, where he became chaplain and tenor at the court of King Władisław IV and in 1645 was given permission to found a minorite friary, of which he became prior. He also acted as Provincial for the order in Transylvania and as its Commissioner for Poland and Russia. The Swedish invasion of Poland in 1655 drove him out of Warsaw, via Lemberg (now L'vóv) to Vienna, where he died in the minorite friary. The friary's necrology describes him as 'Capellae Magister' at the Polish court, but this office was held by Marco Scacchi until 1649 and then by Bartłomiej Pękiel.

Two printed volumes of music by Scapitta survive. His *Vaghi fiori di Maria Vergine . . . con le Litaniae . . . e un 'Laudate Dominum, omnes gentes'*, for two to four voices, op.2 (Venice, 1628), contains sacred works in the style of Viadana's *Cento concerti ecclesiastici*; 18 are by Scapitta and four by other composers, including one by Johann Stadlmayr, Kapellmeister at the court at Innsbruck. Scapitta's *Missae* op.3 (Venice, 1629) contains two five-part masses with instruments, '*La Scarmigliona*' and '*Altro non è il mio cor*', and two eight-part masses, '*La lottiera*' and '*Tota pulchra es*'. Since he was praised in Scacchi's *Cribrum musicum* (Venice, 1643) as a leading musician at the Polish court, he may also have made his mark as a composer in Poland, but the only known pieces of his from this period are the two canons published in Scacchi's collection. His lost op.1 may have been published in Augsburg in 1623, and *Musica di camera* (Venice, 1630) is mentioned in J. G. Walther's *Musicalisches Lexicon* (1732).

BIBLIOGRAPHY
J. Surzyński: 'Ueber alte polnische Kirchenkomponisten und deren Werke', *KJb*, v (1890), 78
H. Feicht: 'Przyczynki do dziejów kapeli królewskiej w Warszawie za rządów kapelmistrzowskich Marka Scacchiego' [Notes towards a history of the royal chapel in Warsaw during Marco Scacchi's period as director of music], *KM*, i (1928–9), 131
W. Senn: *Musik und Theater am Hof zu Innsbruck* (Innsbruck, 1954), 435
F. W. Riedel: 'Die Wiener Minoriten und ihre Musikpflege', *Singende Kirche*, xvi (1968–9), 161
J. Sehnal: 'Hudba na dvoře Olomouckých biskupů od 13. do poloviny 17. stol.' [Music at the courts of the bishops of Olomouc from the 13th to the mid-17th centuries], *Časopis vlastivědné společnosti muzejní v Olomouci* (1970), 73
HELLMUT FEDERHOFER

Scappamento (It.). ESCAPEMENT.

Scarabelli [Scarabeus]**, Damiano** (*b* Bologna; *d* ?Milan, ?1598). Italian composer. He was a priest. He studied in Bologna with Andrea Rota, to whom he expressed his debt in the dedication of the reprint of Rota's *Motectorum liber primus* (Milan, 1588). He is recorded as *vicemaestro* in the cathedral chapel in Milan between 28 March 1589 and 19 March 1598, an office which brought him a quarterly salary of 96 lire, rising to 132 lire in 1597. His successor was appointed on 15 September 1598, so Scarabelli may have died in that year.

WORKS
Liber primus motectorum (Venice, 1592)
[10] Magnificat, 4–12vv (Venice, 1596)
Works in 1590[13], 1598[2], 1600[1], 1600[2], 1609[1], 1619[3], 1619[4]

BIBLIOGRAPHY
Indice di tutte le opere di musica che si trovano nella Stampa della Pigna di Alessandro Vincenti in Venetia (Venice, 1621); repr. in *MMg*, xiv–xv (1882–3/R), suppl.
G. Gaspari: *Miscellanea musicale* (MS, *I-Bc* UU.12), iii, 122
F. Mompellio: 'La cappella del duomo di Milano dal 1573 al 1714', *Storia di Milano*, xvi (1962), 512, 514, 515
PIER PAOLO SCATTOLIN

Scarabelli, Diamante Maria (*fl* 1695–1718). Italian soprano. A native of Bologna, she is first heard of at Venice in 1695 in two operas by C. F. Pollarolo, and reappeared there in 1703, 1707–12 and 1714–16, singing in at least 23 operas, most of them by C. F. Pollarolo, Lotti and Caldara, but including Handel's *Agrippina* (26 December 1709), in which she played Poppaea. She sang frequently in her native city (1696–7, 1699, 1700, 1708–9, 1718) and won a spectacular success in the pasticcio *Perseo* in June 1697. This inspired a volume of encomiastic verse, published at Modena, with the punning title *La miniera del 'Diamante'*. Scarabelli also sang at Milan (1699), Mantua (1703), Pavia (1705), Genoa (1705), Ferrara (1715) and Padua (1718). She was at various times in the service of the Duke of Mantua (1697–1708), Cardinal Grimani Viceroy of Naples (1709) and the Duke of Modena (1715). A portrait print was issued to celebrate her triumph in Orlandini's *Lucio Papirio* at Padua in 1718; the scrolls surrounding it record that she sang at Crema, Lodi, Livorno and Turin in addition to the cities already mentioned. Scarabelli was one of the most celebrated sopranos of her age; the part of Poppaea, which requires a flexible virtuoso technique and a compass of c' to $b♭''$, bears witness to her powers.
WINTON DEAN

Scaramella, Bernardino (*fl* 1591). Italian composer. He is known only by his *Primo libro de madrigali a cinque voci*, published in Venice in 1591. He is identified on the title-page as being from Palena, a town north of Naples. His musical style is typical of his time, involving pairing of voices, melismatic passages in 3rds, alternation of chordal with canonic textures and use of cyclic form.

RUTH T. WATANABE

Scaramuccia, Filisteo (*b* Capua; *fl* *c*1580). Italian composer. His only known work is a book of madrigals for four, five and six voices, published in Venice in 1580. The title-page of the print describes the composer as a member of the order of the Knights of St John of Malta, and the volume is dedicated to Jean l'Evêque de la Cassière, Grand Master of the order from 1572 to 1581. The book reflects the strong influence of the canzonetta, and many of the settings are in a largely homophonic style with vigorous rhythms and contrasting triple-time sections. A typical example is the setting of Ariosto's popular *Non rumor di tamburi*. The collection opens with a complete setting of Petrarch's sestina *A la dolce ombra*, a text which had previously appealed to a number of composers, including Animuccia, Berchem and Rore.

IAIN FENLON

Scarani, Giuseppe (*fl* 1628–42). Italian composer, organist and singer. A monk of the Carmelite order, he was organist at the Carmelite church in Mantua in 1628. In January 1629 he went as a singer to St Mark's Basilica, Venice. In 1641 he was court organist in Mantua. He composed two volumes of two-part madrigals by 1628, a volume of *Sonate concertate* for two and three instruments (op.1, 1630), a volume of *Concerti ecclesiastici* (op.2, 1641) and some motets. His sonatas, which are less progressive than their title suggests, embrace both church and chamber styles.

BIBLIOGRAPHY
E. Selfridge-Field: 'Addenda to some Baroque Biographies', *JAMS*, xxv (1972), 236
——: *Venetian Instrumental Music from Gabrieli to Vivaldi* (Oxford, 1975)

ELEANOR SELFRIDGE-FIELD

Scaria, Emil (*b* Graz, 18 Sept 1838; *d* Blasewitz, nr. Dresden, 22 July 1886). Austrian bass. He studied at the Vienna Conservatory and made his début in 1860 at Budapest as St Bris in *Les Huguenots* with little success. After further study with García in London, he made a second début at Dessau, and in 1863 he was engaged at Leipzig and in 1865 at Dresden. His repertory in these early years included Dulcamara in *L'elisir d'amore*, Falstaff in Nicolai's *Die lustigen Weiber von Windsor* and Peter the Great in Lortzing's *Zar und Zimmermann*. Although his powerful voice had the dark colouring of a true bass, its enormous range allowed him to sing baritone roles with equal success. From May 1873 until his death Scaria was engaged at the Vienna Court Opera. He sang Wotan in the first Berlin *Ring* cycle, given by Angelo Neumann's company at the Victoria Theatre, in May 1881, and also in the first London cycle at Her Majesty's Theatre, again presented by Neumann, in May 1882. During Act 3 of *Die Walküre* in London he suffered a breakdown and loss of memory, and, though he got through *Siegfried* two nights later, his place was

taken by Reichmann in the second and third cycles. After a rest, Scaria was able to sing Gurnemanz in the first performance of *Parsifal* at Bayreuth on 26 July 1882, and to rejoin Neumann's touring Wagner company through Germany, Belgium, Holland and Italy, singing Wotan and Rocco in *Fidelio*. During 1883 he sang King Marke in *Tristan und Isolde* at both Berlin and Vienna, and returned to Bayreuth to sing Gurnemanz and to produce *Parsifal* at the first festival held after Wagner's death. The following year he toured the USA in Wagner concerts with Materna and Winkelmann, and also sang Gurnemanz in the first concert performance of *Parsifal* in London, at the Albert Hall on 10 November 1884. Early in 1886 he again suffered a mental breakdown and died insane a few months later.

BIBLIOGRAPHY
H. Klein: *Thirty Years of Musical Life in London* (London, 1903)
A. Neumann: *Erinnerungen an Richard Wagner* (Leipzig, 1907; Eng. trans., 1909)
E. Newman: *The Life of Richard Wagner* (London, 1933–47)
W. Beetz: *Das Wiener Opernhaus 1869 bis 1945* (Vienna, 1949)
E. Pirchan, A. Witeschnik and O. Fritz: *300 Jahre Wiener Operntheater* (Vienna, 1953)
G. Skelton: *Wagner at Bayreuth* (London, 1965)

ELIZABETH FORBES

Scarlatti. Italian family of musicians. The name, in various spellings (Scarlata, Sgarlata etc), was common in Sicily in the early 18th century and there were several fairly distinguished Scarlatti families in Rome and north Italy. Little is known about the parents of (1) Alessandro; the earliest documentary evidence shows that Pietro Scarlatti married Eleonora d'Amato in 1658 in Palermo and that their first child, Anna Maria Antonia Diana, was born in 1659 and died a few months later. Of their eight children five were noted musicians; and of Alessandro's ten children two were musicians (besides Flaminia, a singer in private circles): see family tree, fig.1.

BIBLIOGRAPHY
Memoir of the Scarlatti family, *The Harmonicon*, v (1827), 237
P. Flenga: 'La véritable patrie et la famille d'Alessandro Scarlatti', *ReM*, x/3 (1929), 227
Gli Scarlatti (Alessandro – Francesco – Pietro – Domenico – Giuseppe): note e documenti sulla vita e sulle opere, Chigiana, ii (1940), 63
O. Tiby: 'La famiglia Scarlatti', *JRBM*, i (1947), 275
F. Walker: 'Some Notes on the Scarlattis', *MR*, xii (1951), 185

(1) (Pietro) Alessandro (Gaspare) Scarlatti (*b* Palermo, 2 May 1660; *d* Naples, 24 Oct 1725). Italian composer, noted especially for operas and cantatas; reputed founder of the Neapolitan school of 18th-century opera.

1. Early years. 2. At Naples. 3. The late years. 4. The operas. 5. Serenatas, oratorios, church music. 6. The cantatas. 7. Instrumental music. 8. Teacher and theorist. 9. Historical position.

1. EARLY YEARS. Alessandro was the second of eight children of Pietro Scarlatti. When he was 12, in June 1672, he was sent to Rome with his two sisters, possibly to be cared for by relatives. Conditions of famine and turmoil in Palermo may have influenced the decision; but it was not uncommon for poor parents of large families to place talented children in surroundings where their gifts could develop (Pasquini had also gone to Rome at the age of 12).

Nothing is known about Scarlatti's early musical education. The conservatory at Palermo, founded in 1618, apparently did not offer musical training until towards the end of the century. Scarlatti may have been instructed by his father or some other relative, or by a

1. The Scarlatti family tree

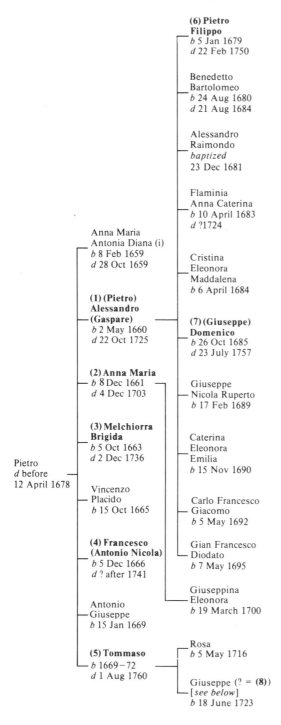

Pietro
d before
12 April 1678

Anna Maria
Antonia Diana (i)
b 8 Feb 1659
d 28 Oct 1659

**(1) (Pietro)
Alessandro
(Gaspare)**
b 2 May 1660
d 22 Oct 1725

(2) Anna Maria
b 8 Dec 1661
d 4 Dec 1703

**(3) Melchiorra
Brigida**
b 5 Oct 1663
d 2 Dec 1736

Vincenzo
Placido
b 15 Oct 1665

**(4) Francesco
(Antonio Nicola)**
b 5 Dec 1666
d ? after 1741

Antonio
Giuseppe
b 15 Jan 1669

(5) Tommaso
b 1669–72
d 1 Aug 1760

**(6) Pietro
Filippo**
b 5 Jan 1679
d 22 Feb 1750

Benedetto
Bartolomeo
b 24 Aug 1680
d 21 Aug 1684

Alessandro
Raimondo
baptized
23 Dec 1681

Flaminia
Anna Caterina
b 10 April 1683
d ?1724

Cristina
Eleonora
Maddalena
b 6 April 1684

**(7) (Giuseppe)
Domenico**
b 26 Oct 1685
d 23 July 1757

Giuseppe
Nicola Ruperto
b 17 Feb 1689

Caterina
Eleonora
Emilia
b 15 Nov 1690

Carlo Francesco
Giacomo
b 5 May 1692

Gian Francesco
Diodato
b 7 May 1695

Giuseppina
Eleonora
b 19 March 1700

Rosa
b 5 May 1716

Giuseppe (? = **(8)**)
[*see below*]
b 18 June 1723

[relationship uncertain (?son of (5) Tommaso, or ?nephew
of (7) Domenico): **(8) Giuseppe** *b* c1718 (or 18 June 1723);
d 17 Aug 1777]

friendly priest. There is a tradition that he had lessons in
Rome with Carissimi; that is not improbable, but no
firm evidence exists and in any case the lessons would
have been cut short by Carissimi's death in January
1674. Possibly Scarlatti attended one of the choir
schools connected with some large church or seminary.
Whatever formal discipline he may have had, at least as
important to his education was the flourishing musical
life to which he was exposed, and in which he certainly
took part, during his formative years at Rome. There he
attracted the attention of patrons on whose continuing
favour his success depended, and with whom he carefully maintained connections all his life. In the private
theatres, the two public opera houses, the numerous
oratorios, churches and academies of Rome, Scarlatti
could have heard music by Cesti, Stradella, Pasquini,
Sartorio and their contemporaries, performed under the
best possible auspices. These years must have given him
a comprehensive acquaintance with the music of his
time and an initiation into the nature of a professional
musical career.

The earliest known Roman document relating to
Scarlatti is the record of his marriage, on 12 April
1678, to Antonia Anzalone, a native of Rome (though
the surname was common in Sicily). They had seven
sons and three daughters, but apparently only five children survived to maturity; provision for his offspring
became one of his constant cares.

Scarlatti is first heard of as a composer early in 1679
when the Arciconfraternità del Ss Crocifisso commissioned him to write an oratorio, probably the one performed for them on 24 February. His earliest known
opera *Gli equivoci nel sembiante* was a resounding
success. Given repeatedly at Rome in 1679, it was soon
produced at Bologna, then at Naples, Monte Filottrano
and Linz (Carnival 1681) and subsequently Ravenna
and Palermo. Scarlatti was probably in Austria in 1681,
and may also have visited Munich.

One of Scarlatti's first patrons was Queen Christina
of Sweden, an important patron of arts and letters in
Rome since 1655; she had founded at her palace two
academies, one later to become the famous Arcadia.
Stradella, Pasquini and Corelli were among her
protégés. In the libretto of his second opera, *L'honestà
negli amori* (1680), Scarlatti is described as her *maestro
di cappella*, a position he held until his departure for
Naples in 1684. At least four more operas and six
oratorios, as well as many cantatas, date from Scarlatti's
first Roman period. Among his influential protectors
were two cardinals, Benedetto Pamphili and Pietro
Ottoboni, both munificent patrons of the arts who maintained theatres in their palaces. Their virtual rivalry in
promoting music was especially fortunate for opera,
since the reigning Pope Innocent XI discouraged public
theatrical spectacles.

2. AT NAPLES. Among the notables at Rome who knew
of Scarlatti and had heard his music was the Marquis
del Carpio, Spanish ambassador to the Vatican. He
became Viceroy of Naples in 1683; influenced probably
by his friend the Duke of Maddaloni, he promptly
invited Scarlatti to become his *maestro di cappella*. It is
not clear why Scarlatti, who, in addition to the favour he
enjoyed from his patrons, was also music director at S
Gerolamo della Carità, chose to leave Rome: one reason
may have been the alleged marriage of one of his sisters
with an ecclesiastic, which had brought the family under

2. *Alessandro Scarlatti: portrait by Lorenzo Vaccaro (1655–1706) in the Biblioteca del Conservatorio di Musica S Pietro a Majella, Naples*

the disfavour of the papal authorities. A still more notorious scandal erupted at Naples. Scarlatti received his appointment from the viceroy in February 1684 on the death of P. A. Ziani; at the same time his brother (4) Francesco Scarlatti, who had come to Naples as a child about ten years before, was named first violinist of the vice-regal chapel. Provenzale, honorary head of the chapel since 1680, had expected to succeed Ziani; on Scarlatti's appointment he resigned, and six singers left in sympathy. It was alleged that the Scarlattis owed their appointments to the intrigues of one of their sisters (apparently (3) Melchiorra Brigida Scarlatti) with two court officials. The officials were discharged and the sister sent to a convent, but the brothers retained their posts; Alessandro remained head of the viceroy's musical establishment until 1702.

In the 1680s Naples was far from being the famous musical and operatic centre that it was soon to become. Opera had begun there with performances by a visiting troupe in 1650; at first the repertory was mainly Venetian, but there were also original operas by Neapolitan composers, including Provenzale. Scarlatti's *Gli equivoci nel sembiante* had been heard there in 1680; *Il Pompeo*, first given in Rome in 1683, was repeated at Naples in January 1684 under the composer's direction. For the next two decades over half the new operas heard in the city were by Scarlatti.

The principal patrons of opera were the viceroys, who maintained theatres in their palace and their summer residence at Posillipo and took an effective interest in the public theatres. Chief among these was the S Bartolomeo, where operas had been given since 1654; destroyed by fire in 1681, it was rebuilt two years later and provided with a permanent company of nine singers, five instrumentalists and a copyist, with Scarlatti as director. In 1696 the Duke of Medinaceli, the penultimate Spanish viceroy, enlarged S Bartolomeo to make room for more and bigger operatic 'machines'. As a rule, a new cantata or serenata would be performed privately for the viceroy and his guests; operas would be given first at the palace and then transferred to S Bartolomeo for the public.

Scarlatti's 18 years at Naples were a time of incessant labour. If *Lucio Manlio* (1705) was really, as he claimed, his 88th stage work, then the 40-odd known operas of 1684–1702 represent less than half his total output for those years. Seven serenatas, nine oratorios and 65 cantatas, figures again far below the actual total, are also datable from those years. Nor was Scarlatti's activity confined to Naples. In 1686 he was at the Palazzo Doria Pamphili in Rome for his new opera *La Rosmene*, and he often went to the city to superintend performances of his new cantatas and oratorios. One opera, *La Statira*, on a libretto by Cardinal Ottoboni, marked the reopening of the Tordinona Theatre there in 1690; in December the same year *Gli equivoci in amore* was performed at the Palazzo della Cancelleria on a double marriage in the families of three of Scarlatti's patrons.

Serenatas and operas for Naples itself came from Scarlatti's pen at an increasing rate in the 1690s; many of the operas quickly made their way to other Italian cities and even abroad. One of the best and most successful, *Il Pirro e Demetrio*, given at S Bartolomeo in 1694, was repeated within a few years at Rome, Siena, Florence, Milan, Brunswick (first in Italian and later in a German version) and probably Mantua and Leipzig. Florence heard it again as late as 1711, Fano in 1716; from 1708 to 1717 it ran for over 60 performances in London, with the words partly in English translation (his only opera given in England during his lifetime). Such international success was rare in Scarlatti's day. Almost equally widespread was the success of *La caduta de' Decemviri* (1697). This acclaim, however gratifying, brought no extra payment to composer or librettist.

By the late 1690s Scarlatti must have felt overwhelmed by the requirements of his Naples position: two or three new operas each year to be composed, rehearsed and conducted (at least at the first one or two performances), and repeated demands from the viceroy and other patrons for new serenatas, oratorios and cantatas; and, with all this, continuing anxiety about arrears of salary and the support of his family. Further, he was becoming discontented with the frivolous musical taste of the Neapolitans; every serious opera coming from Venice to Naples had to be decked out with comic scenes. Finally, by the turn of the century political unrest consequent upon the War of the Spanish Succession was beginning to undermine the privileged status of the nobility at Naples, rendering Scarlatti's situation precarious. In June 1702, having obtained a four-month leave of absence, he departed for Florence with his son (7) Domenico.

3. THE LATE YEARS. Prince Ferdinando de' Medici, son of the Grand Duke Cosimo III of Tuscany, was a distinguished patron of music in the years 1680–1710 and had already promoted a dozen of Scarlatti's operas at Siena, Livorno and Florence and in his own villa at Pratolino. Scarlatti had hoped, and continued to hope, for an appointment in the prince's service; but as that was not forthcoming he left Florence in October 1702, going briefly to Naples and Rome. During the next six years he sent Prince Ferdinando oratorios, church music (including one set of Lamentations and one of responsories) and at least four new operas. Of these last none of the music survives, or only doubtful fragments – a particularly unfortunate loss, since from Scarlatti's letters it is evident that he took special pains, explaining his ideas of composition and trying to adapt his style to the prince's requirements. Meanwhile, at the end of 1703 he had accepted a position in Rome as assistant music director at S Maria Maggiore and, probably at the same time, entered the service of his earlier patron Cardinal Ottoboni. His post at Naples was declared vacant in October 1704.

Prospects at Rome did not look favourable. Shortly after his arrival Scarlatti wrote to Prince Ferdinando: 'Rome has no shelter for Music, which lives here as a beggar'. His complaint was exaggerated, but it accurately reflected the situation as far as opera was concerned. The public theatres had been closed since 1700; private performances were few. Scarlatti's operatic output during these years was limited to the works he sent to Prince Ferdinando and two new operas which he supervised in Venice in 1707. The score of one, *Il Mitridate Eupatore*, is extant; although it is one of Scarlatti's greatest works, the Venetians did not like it and a cruel satirical poem was published about the composer. On his return journey to Rome Scarlatti spent nearly five months at Urbino, where his eldest son (6) Pietro was music director at the cathedral.

The last years at Naples and those at Rome, especially 1704–6, were marked by a great efflorescence of cantatas, serenatas and oratorios, written for cardinals Ottoboni and Pamphili and other patrons, including Prince Francesco Maria Ruspoli, for whose palace concerts Scarlatti furnished oratorios and other works. His high professional standing was recognized by his election in 1706 to the Arcadian Academy, along with Pasquini and Corelli. In the following year he was promoted to *maestro di cappella* at S Maria Maggiore. The situation at Rome, however, could not be borne indefinitely. There may have been difficulties with Ottoboni; there was certainly a financial crisis in Scarlatti's affairs around 1707, when he appealed for help to Prince Ferdinando, who replied with a gift of money and a recommendation to the petitioner to commit himself to the care of divine providence. At the end of 1708 Scarlatti accepted an invitation from Cardinal Grimani, the new Austrian Viceroy of Naples, to resume his former position there.

Scarlatti remained in Naples for ten years, assiduously maintaining contact with his Roman friends. A patent of nobility from Pope Clement XI in 1716 enabled him to sign his compositions with the title 'Cavaliere'. Of his 11 known operas for Naples in these years the most famous was *Il Tigrane*, first performed at S Bartolomeo in 1715, repeated at Innsbruck in the same year and at Livorno and Lucca in 1716. His last opera for Naples was *Il Cambise*, staged at S Bartolomeo in 1719; the composer was not present.

Two new musical interests were now entering Scarlatti's life. Comic operas, or farces in Neapolitan dialect with music in popular style by obscure local composers, had begun to flourish in the smaller theatres of Naples by 1706. Scarlatti apparently tried his hand at a dialect cantata and in 1711, anonymously, at some arias in a comic opera written by his brother Francesco. His only acknowledged comic opera was *Il trionfo dell'onore*, staged at Naples in 1718; but he also wrote comic intermezzos for two of his operas in 1714 and one in 1716. His other new interest was instrumental composition. The set of 12 *Sinfonie di concerto grosso* was begun in June 1715; probably much of his other orchestral and keyboard music dates from about the same period. Possibly this turn to instrumental music was a symptom of a psychological crisis. He had reached the height of his success and popularity in the 1690s. The collapse of his hopes with Prince Ferdinando, his failure at Venice, his discouragement at Rome, could all have been seen as signs pointing along a downward road. He was 55, an old man as such things were then reckoned. He may have felt unwilling, or unable, to adapt his style to the rising fashion for livelier, simpler, more superficially cheerful operatic music. He was subsiding into the status of an old master, admired and respected but unable to compete with younger composers in meeting new demands.

Once more Scarlatti obtained leave of absence from Naples. The 1718 carnival season found him at Rome to conduct his new opera *Telemaco* at the Capranica, a theatre of which Ruspoli was probably a supporting patron. On the same stage in 1719 came *Marco Attilio Regolo*, followed by revivals of two earlier works with revisions, and in 1721 *La Griselda*, Scarlatti's last surviving opera. These final operas were made possible by Scarlatti's loyal Roman patrons; they had no acclaim comparable to that which had greeted many of his earlier works. An oratorio, three masses and several cantatas are among the other compositions of this time.

Scarlatti's last years at Naples (1722–5) seem to have passed in tranquil retirement. The only compositions certainly from those years are four cantatas, a serenata for a royal marriage in 1723 and a set of sonatas for flute and strings (possibly a result of the composer's meeting with J. J. Quantz in 1724). Scarlatti was buried in the Cecilia chapel at S Maria di Montesanto. The affectionate though conventionally fulsome Latin epitaph on his tomb, attributed to Ottoboni, calls him the greatest 'restorer' or 'renewer' of music of all ages.

4. THE OPERAS. The operas and cantatas are Scarlatti's most numerous and most characteristic compositions. These are the forms in which his genius spontaneously expressed itself and in which the traits of his musical style and the changes it underwent during his 40 years

3. Engraving after a stage design by Filippo Juvarra for 'Il Ciro', first performed at the Palazzo della Cancelleria, Rome, in 1712

as a composer can best be observed.

The commonest designation in the librettos of Scarlatti's operas is *dramma per musica*, a term standing for a well-defined type of opera with a serious action and a happy ending. Personages are divided into rulers, their confidants and servants; the action deals with the rulers' love affairs, with all their attendant deceptions, jealousies and misunderstandings. With such librettos it is obvious that the 'dramma' exists only as a frame for the 'musica'. Credible motivation and characterization are exceptional among Scarlatti's works. One of his best dramas is *Il Mitridate Eupatore*, called significantly a *tragedia per musica* and in five acts instead of the usual three. There are a few comedies (including Scarlatti's first three operas at Rome and the *commedia in musica* entitled *Il trionfo dell'onore*) and a few pastoral operas, some of them so designated. Unlike many Venetian operas of the middle and later 17th century, Scarlatti's *drammi per musica* seldom introduce mythological personages or call for elaborate stage machines. The characters, whether ostensibly historical or invented, are stylized. They have no inner life; not luminous in themselves, they may glow by reflection as the spotlight of a particular situation is turned on them, in the arias and duets, where action is suspended and music reigns supreme, but while the action goes on, in recitative, musical interest is minimal.

Scarlatti's style, already well established in *Gli equivoci nel sembiante* (1679), remained essentially consistent throughout his operas. It is misleading to think of the changes that took place between 1679 and 1721 in terms of 'progress'. Changes do of course occur; they involve dropping some of the early formal schemes, expanding the dimensions and clarifying the tonal plan of arias, enlarging the role of the orchestra, sharpening the pictorial outlines and (in exceptional instances) strengthening the dramatic impact. But the consistency and continuity are basic. In its way, *Gli equivoci nel sembiante* is as fine as any of the later operas. They vary in quality according to the circumstances under which the composer had to work. Like Mozart, Scarlatti had both readiness of musical invention to meet day-to-day requirements and the capacity to rise to great occasions.

Scarlatti inherited a tradition of opera which called for a large number of short arias distinctly set off from the recitatives. The performing time of an opera would have been little more than three hours. Allowing for the recitatives, overture, ballets, intermezzos and so on, and the fact that the score could include from 40 to 60 arias or other musical items, it is clear that many of the arias were very short. This is especially true of Scarlatti's early Roman operas and of many of those he wrote for Naples before 1702.

Some of the earliest arias rely for their structure on ostinato or quasi-ostinato bass patterns rather than on a clearly articulated design in the melody itself. A few show a fairly clear bipartite pattern, either *AB* or (less frequently) the 'seicento' form *ABB'*, with modifications. Much more common however are arias in which the first part is repeated, either entire or shortened, after a more or less contrasting middle section: when the first part returns complete the contrasting section is in the dominant (in major arias) or the relative major (in minor ones); when the reprise is shortened, the keys are more often the mediant minor and the dominant minor. A melody in any of the above forms may be repeated identically for a second strophe of text, usually with a short orchestral ritornello played between the strophes and possibly at the beginning or the end. Strophic arias disappeared only gradually from Scarlatti's operas; *Pirro e Demetrio* (1694) and *Massimo Puppieno* (1695) still have them. From the late 1690s onwards, however, the predominant, almost exclusive form is the full da capo aria *ABA* with *B* between a third and a half the length of *A*, similar to it in tempo and material but perhaps more lightly accompanied, modulating more widely and cadencing as a rule so as to define a tonal relationship with *A* of tonic major to mediant minor or tonic minor to dominant minor (or relative major).

The melodic range of an aria seldom exceeds a 9th or 10th. Prevailing movement is by step; wider intervals occur most often at the beginning of a phrase or section and towards the end, where leaps of a 3rd, a 4th, or more, commonly signal the approach of a cadence. The basic rhythm is quickly established, and there is considerable variety of motivic detail, overriding breaks in the vocal line. After an opening phrase or two with periodic structure the melody spins out in phrases of irregular length embodying sequential patterns. In an aria of any length, part *A* will be in two sections, the first cadencing in a closely related key, the second longer and touching on other keys.

Immediate literal repetition of small units, a particular feature of Scarlatti's melody, occurs typically at the beginning of an aria where a concise subject is announced two or three times alternately in voice and accompaniment (not to be confused with the 'motto' or 'Devise', found for the most part only in Scarlatti's late operas, an isolated short phrase for the voice which may even precede the instrumental introduction and may or may not be thematically related to the aria's first phrase). Another common place for repetition is at the end, where the closing phrase may be repeated as a gesture of finality. This device occurs most often in short arias in the early operas; in the longer later arias, the farewell gesture more often takes the form of a distinct, strongly dominant–tonic cadential figure in the voice, preceded usually by a fermata.

Another characteristic of Scarlatti's melody is chromatic inflection of the line at the approach to an important cadence, especially common in slow arias where the text has even the slightest hint of pathetic shading. In major keys the 3rd, and perhaps the 6th, may be made minor at such places, while in minor keys the 2nd may be lowered by a semitone, thus producing a 'Neapolitan 6th' in the harmony. Equally typical are melismatic passages, which even in short and otherwise simply syllabic arias may blossom out in the course of sequential development and lead decisively into a cadence. In longer arias, above all those expressing anger, resolution or martial ardour, the coloraturas are a natural projection of the mood and often motivated by some word or image in the text. They are also an

4. Autograph MS of the opening of Act 1 scene v from Alessandro Scarlatti's opera 'La Griselda', first performed at the Teatro Capranica, Rome, 1721 (GB-Lbm Add.14168, f.18r)

important element of structure, being graduated in length and brilliance to correspond to the different levels of climax in the aria. Such passages call for a high degree of virtuosity, but their difficulties are essentially vocal; Scarlatti never made the awkward demands that Bach sometimes did. His is 'singers' music' in the best sense, and he took care to adapt his style to the capacities of particular performers.

In the early operas most arias have only continuo accompaniment. The relation between air and bass is essentially contrapuntal; the bass is an active line, not merely a foundation for the harmony, as it tended to become later, so that the harmonic rhythm is diversified and comparatively rapid. Orchestral accompaniments supply harmonic (but contrapuntally conceived) support, brief interjections or melodic echoes at pauses in the voice, and general thematic and rhythmic continuity. In the later operas, which have no continuo arias, the accompaniments are fuller and more diversified. The relation of instruments to voice in a Scarlatti aria is like that of ripieno to solo in a Baroque concerto. Sometimes, especially in the early operas, the orchestra participates only at the ritornellos; in others, it plays throughout the aria but with reduced instrumentation or the indication 'piano' while the voice is singing.

The string ensemble was basic, and on occasion Scarlatti called for other instruments, for example trumpets or horns for ceremonial scenes or martial arias, lutes for accompaniment, and (in the later operas) oboes. Obbligato horn parts appear in *Tigrane*, *Telemaco* and *Marco Attilio Regolo*; less common are obbligato parts for flutes, as in *Cambise* and *Griselda*.

Scarlatti's overtures have no thematic or other particular connection with the opera to follow. After about 1695 they settled into the standard three-movement Italian sinfonia form: a brilliant Allegro, often in D, for full orchestra; a short, tentative, transitional slow movement for reduced orchestra; and a bipartite finale in homophonic style and dance rhythm. Apart from the overtures the only orchestral numbers are short sinfonias, used typically to introduce scenes of splendour.

The extraordinary variety among the arias in Scarlatti's operas is the product of an inexhaustible flow of melodic invention coupled with great sensitivity to the rhythm, mood and imagery of a text. Variety is encouraged by the nature of the libretto. A dramatic situation may be implausible, a personage's reaction improbable or inconsistent, but none of these things matters; every aria is a self-contained world, psychologically as well as musically. There is a division into 'big' and 'little' arias: the former longer, more amply developed, usually with fuller orchestral accompaniment, apt to occur at points of strong conflict, and mostly assigned to the principal characters; the latter shorter, simpler in both thematic ideas and development, and apt to be pictorial or reflective. There are a few recurrent types of aria associated with certain keys: the martial-triumphal arias with trumpets (or trumpet-like figures in the strings), nearly always in D; a *deciso* type expressive of abrupt firm resolution, in C (or B♭); a great number of arias simply placid or cheerful, in G; arias typically assigned to the secondary lovers or to pastoral or other situations where no conflict is involved, in G or A (rarely D or E); and arias of sorrow, ranging from simple melancholy to wrenching grief, most often in C minor but for special intensity sometimes in F minor. In serious arias of any type

5. *Alessandro Scarlatti: anonymous portrait in the Civico Museo Bibliografico Musicale, Bologna*

Scarlatti's imagination may seize on some visual image to generate an accompaniment figure that envelops the vocal melody in a nimbus of descriptive coloration. There are also comic arias and duets, lightly orchestrated, almost always in major keys, with rollicking tunes, and subject to sudden changes of mood and movement for quarrelsome outbursts, satirical interjections or parody.

Duets are few, short, and in the same style and form as arias; they are commonly designated 'aria à 2'. In many duets the voices, expressing congenial if not identical sentiments, will alternate before joining in parallel 3rds or 6ths at the cadences. Ensembles for more than two voices are uncommon until the late Roman operas, and even in these the trios and quartets are still essentially no more than da capo arias; they embody no marked contrast of personalities and do not advance the action. Larger ensembles and choruses are extremely rare (the 'septet' in *Eraclea* is merely a tiny three-section aria sung by seven singers in turn). Only at the close of an opera do all the singers and orchestra unite in a brief, perfunctory closing number, usually in D or C.

Scarlatti's recitative differs in no salient respects from that in the operas of his contemporaries. In his early operas, in accordance with 17th-century practice, the *secco* style often shades into melodic arioso passages, particularly at the end of a recitative, thus forming a transition to the following aria. Some recitatives are accompanied by the full string orchestra *senza cembalo* (so marked, though occasionally continuo figures are written below the bass notes in the score); the upper string parts are written sometimes as long sustained notes, sometimes as full chords with the direction 'arpeggio'. Accompanied recitatives appear in operas from Scarlatti's first Neapolitan period; the earliest ones seem to be used mainly to establish atmosphere in nocturnal or dream scenes, a suggestion of the supernatural perhaps analogous to the use of string accompaniment for the Voice of God in Scarlatti's oratorio *Cain overo Il primo omicidio* or for the words of Christ in his *St John Passion*. In the operas from *La Statira* (1690) onwards, and notably in the late Neapolitan and Roman ones, accompanied recitative serves to bring into relief moments of high emotional tension, as in the closing scene of *Griselda*. In such recitatives the orchestra, as well as accompanying the voice, may intervene with interjections between the vocal phrases, as in *Marco Attilio Regolo*, Act 2 scene iv, or *Telemaco*, Act 1 scene xi.

By Scarlatti's time it was customary to end each scene with an aria followed by the exit of the singer; but the later 18th-century stereotype whereby a scene consisted simply of recitative and aria is not always valid for his operas. Not every scene has an aria; a short one may come at the beginning of a scene (especially if it is a solo scene), or in the middle of a scene between two sections of recitative. But the important arias come at the end, rounding off the scene with a quasi-independent musical entity having no thematic or (necessarily) tonal connection with other similar entities in the opera. The principal personages, hence the most important artists, naturally have the most arias, and Scarlatti paid due attention to variety in the type and placing of arias within each act; but attempts to find a tonal plan operating throughout a Scarlatti opera will be successful only in the seeker's imagination.

5. SERENATAS, ORATORIOS, CHURCH MUSIC. The serenatas, unlike the operas, were written to order for celebration of special events in the households of Scarlatti's patrons. The mythological–pastoral texts, in two acts, consist mainly of alternating recitatives and arias. The effect as a whole is that of a picture or a design rather than of a drama; everything is stately and formal. Because of this, and because special performing resources were sometimes available, a good deal of the music in the serenatas is more elaborate than that in the operas. Recitatives, not being obliged to push ahead with a plot, are more leisurely and likely to expand into arioso or even coloratura. Most arias are in the usual da capo form, although strophic arias linger in the serenatas long after the type had disappeared from the operas. There are more duets and ensembles, a trio or quartet often being placed at both the beginning and end of a scene. The orchestra, especially in the later serenatas, is much more conspicuous than in the operas, and the writing includes unusual features such as concerto–ripieno distribution as well as considerable diversity of obbligato instruments and their combination in the accompaniments.

Most of Scarlatti's oratorios were written for Rome where they were performed either in one of the oratories or colleges or in the palaces of his patrons. Subjects include biblical stories, episodes from the lives of saints and allegorical actions or dialogues. The treatment ranges from the opera-like version of the combat between David and Goliath (Scarlatti's only extant Latin oratorio) to the purely internal drama of St Philip Neri's dying conversation with the personified figures of Faith, Hope and Charity. In their musical elements and general style the oratorios resemble the operas but, since the librettos are less stereotyped and not bound by requirements of stage scenery and action, the arias,

recitatives and ensembles are combined more freely and Scarlatti could make more uniform use of all the voice ranges instead of principally sopranos. The 'coro' in these oratorios is not a chorus in the modern sense but an ensemble of all the soloists.

Scarlatti's liturgical music comprises motets and masses in both the so-called Palestrina style and the newer, 18th-century concertato style. Examples of the former are the two masses written for Pope Clement XI (1705, 1716); among the latter the St Cecilia Mass (1720) for five soloists, chorus and orchestra is an imposing large work of external splendour. One of Scarlatti's best liturgical works is the *St John Passion* (c1680), an austere, moving setting of the scriptural text. Roger of Amsterdam printed a collection of miscellaneous *Concerti sacri* (1707–8), brilliant in style; three motets for double choir, *Tu es Petrus*, *O magnum mysterium* and *Volo Pater* (c1707), are broad and dignified, and the little *Laetatus sum* for four voices is a model of counterpoint in Leo's manner.

6. THE CANTATAS. Scarlatti's chamber cantatas reveal perhaps more strikingly than any other class of his works his unbroken continuity with preceding phases of the Baroque era and his separation from the following period. With more than 600 known cantatas for which his authorship is reasonably certain and well over 100 others less reliably attributed to him he is clearly the most prolific composer of cantatas. These works crown the history of a genre which throughout more than a century of vigorous growth held a rank second only to opera; indeed contemporaries generally placed it above opera in refinement and regarded it as the supreme challenge to a composer's artistry. Scarlatti was among the last to contribute significantly to its literature.

A decisive majority of Scarlatti's cantatas are for solo voice, most for soprano but some for alto and a few for bass. A few are for two voices: two sopranos, soprano and alto, or soprano and bass. 90% are accompanied by continuo alone; the remainder, reflecting a contemporary trend, enlist various instrumental ensembles in addition to continuo, mostly strings but occasionally recorders or trumpet. They deal almost exclusively with love; heroic, comic or devotional subjects appear less often than in the past.

The most characteristic text is lyric, presenting in some imagined protagonist's monologue a series of contrasting reflections centred on some unifying thought. In most cantatas for two voices there is dialogue or an alternation between dialogue and lyric monologue. The protagonist is usually a shepherd or nymph, or may be drawn from mythology or history. Occasionally the monologue is introduced by an explicatory narrative or descriptive passage, and further narrative passages may thread the reflections together. The changes are normally paralleled by changes of poetic metre and rhyme pattern, and reflected too in changes in musical metre, tempo, rhythmic and melodic material, harmonic character, texture and the entire constellation of stylistic elements.

The cantata repertory in Rome in the 1670s included works not only by younger composers, such as Stradella, Pasquini and P. S. Agostini, but by composers of older generations too, including Cesti, Savioni, Carissimi and even Luigi Rossi (d 1653). Scarlatti drew comprehensively on this stylistic inheritance. The retrospective characteristics in his cantatas composed before about 1705 are striking. Musical refrains continue to appear as reflections of textual ones, either with periodic regularity or at irregular intervals. Exact or modified musical repetitions – occasionally only loose, imprecise correspondences – with new words reflect strophes in the texts. Not infrequently, however, a second strophe in the text is set to new music, preserving only a structural parallelism with that of the first; and a second strophe may be separated from the first by intervening sections. Responsiveness to his texts according to such procedures sometimes gives rise to forms that had flourished in earlier decades but had, it seems, been laid aside by Scarlatti's immediate predecessors, Pasquini and Agostini.

O dolce servitù, the verse of which is in part strophic, resembles in structure many cantatas of around the 1640s (like Rossi's *Da perfida speranza*): the first strophe consists of a 4/4 section in aria style, a short recitative and a 3/2 arioso. This entire complex is repeated, in part exactly, with the second strophe of the text. Sometimes only the first strophe's bass is repeated (only its pitches, its rhythm having been substantially altered) while the vocal line is in part newly composed: here Scarlatti reached back to the strophic variation, a structure prominent in the cantata's earliest history. An arrangement characteristic of the mid-century cantata survives in *Chi vedesse la ferita*: *ABCAB'C'A*, where *A* is a refrain in music and text while *B'C'* is a musical repetition of *BC* with a second strophe of its text (a similar arrangement is found in Carissimi's *Bel tempo per me*).

In most of Scarlatti's cantatas, late as well as early, diversification is especially conspicuous in composite structures comprising more or less discrete recitatives, arias and ariosos. In works composed before about 1705 they appear in the limitlessly varied combinations seen in the past, reflecting long, complicated poetic structures in which sections in various metres and rhyme patterns follow one another in unruly, wayward succession; these in turn reflect unruly successions of contrasting passions. Such arias continue to show the formal variety found in the past, including *ABB'* and related patterns (as old as Monteverdi), *AB*, ostinato arias, and the increasingly popular *ABA* and *ABA'*. Most have two strophes. In cantatas with instrumental ensemble many are continuo arias with ritornellos, resembling forms in contemporary operas. Recitatives continue to incorporate lyrical, expressive arioso, with refrains and other organizing devices. The integration of declamatory and aria-like elements often survives in Scarlatti's cantata recitatives. The 'curious mixture of air and recitative' with which *Solitudini amene, bersaglio* (1705) begins did not escape Burney's notice (*BurneyH*, ii, 630, 634).

A more orderly form, perhaps manifesting the spirit of the Age of Reason, became increasingly prominent in Scarlatti's cantatas in the 1690s: two (sometimes three) da capo arias contrasting in tempo and expressive character, each preceded by a recitative. Second strophes and refrains were laid aside. In his cantatas after 1704 significant deviations from this pattern are exceptional. A search for increased intensity of expression often gave rise to chromaticism, which is especially characteristic of recitatives, as is illustrated in the celebrated *Andate, o miei sospiri* ('Con idea inhumana', 1712). Notes in the most authoritative copies of this work suggest that Francesco Gasparini had presented Scarlatti with his setting as a token of friendship and that Scarlatti responded with two settings of his own, the first 'Con idea humana' and the second 'Con idea inhumana, ma in regolato Cromatico, non è per ogni Professore'. Both typify his mature style at its most beautiful, and the recitatives of the second are further distinguished by unusually daring chromaticisms.

Already singular in his time, Scarlatti's recitative frequently became even more alien through bold chromaticism, to a degree that his contemporaries could no longer accept. In 1728 J. D. Heinichen censured Scarlatti's 'extravagant and irregular harmony . . . as revealed in the vast production of his cantatas' (*Der General-Bass in der Composition*). Encumbrance with chromaticism, he protested, prevented their attaining the quality of 'rapid recitative'. His strictures reveal that a new conception of recitative had established itself, the rapid parlando, often characterized further by expressive impoverishment and flatness. Regarding this later conception as the norm, Heinichen rejected the impassioned Scarlattian form as 'unnatural and violent'. In the decade when the 'Neapolitan' style triumphantly conquered the European repertory, a contemporary saw Scarlatti not as the founder of any school but as a lonely eccentric, followed by no one except perhaps d'Astorga.

Scarlatti's cantatas for two voices appear in various forms. Most are composite structures. Usually a singer delivers on each entry a recitative followed by an aria. Some recitatives engage both singers in rapid dialogue. The concluding member is usually a duet aria or arioso, and most cantatas include additional duet arias. Some open with a duet aria and close with a repetition of it or with a repetition of its music set to the words of a second strophe; in some all members are duets. The duet arias rely chiefly on the trio texture developed by Monteverdi and basic to musical style throughout the Baroque era. The bass functions harmonically, but it is nevertheless active and melodically defined; it holds consistently apart, however, from the melody, imitations and parallels of the upper pair.

7. INSTRUMENTAL MUSIC. Scarlatti seems to have taken little or no interest in purely instrumental composition before 1715, the year in which he began his 12 *Sinfonie di concerto grosso*. Within ten years he produced other concerti grossi and chamber sonatas and a considerable number of toccatas and short harpsichord pieces. None of these shows him at his best. The orchestral and chamber works are conservative in form and style and singularly unexciting compared with those of his contemporary Corelli or the younger Vivaldi. Scarlatti's best and historically most important orchestral music is found in the overtures and ritornellos of his operas and serenatas. The keyboard toccatas, most in several short movements, show good feeling for the qualities of the instrument but are otherwise unremarkable except for one fine set of variations on the folia.

8. TEACHER AND THEORIST. The legend that made Scarlatti the teacher of a whole generation of Neapolitan composers has no evidence to support it. The only official teaching post he held was at the Conservatory of S Maria di Loreto for two months in spring 1689. No doubt he initiated Domenico, and presumably his other children, in the rudiments of music and it may be supposed that from time to time he assisted other young composers with advice or informal instruction. Hasse claimed to have been his pupil from 1722, but our only information comes from Hasse's conversations with Burney, 50 years later, and old men are apt to gild the recollections of their youth. The principal documents

bearing on Scarlatti as teacher are the *Regole per principianti* prefixed to some manuscripts of his toccatas, which deal partly with fingering but chiefly with rules for the realization of figured basses; in neither respect are they literally 'for beginners'. More important for Scarlatti as theorist is the *Discorso sopra un caso particolare* (1717, but extant only in German translation in Kirnberger's *Die Kunst des reinen Satzes*, 1776–9), a detailed, tactfully worded but firm defence of principles governing the treatment of dissonance in strict counterpoint, with thoughtful observations on the relation of tradition to individual freedom in musical composition.

9. HISTORICAL POSITION. There is a curious anomaly about Scarlatti's reputation in the 18th century. The numerous copies of his operas, cantatas and arias in European libraries testify to an esteem more widespread than the limited success of most of his later operas would indicate; but his contemporaries towards the end of his life, while respecting his achievements, regarded him as an out-of-date composer. One senses this even in the words of his admirers Hasse, Quantz and Jommelli as reported by Burney. In the few 18th-century writings on music that mention Scarlatti he looms as a shadowy father-figure in the background of Vinci, Leo, Pergolesi and their successors of the 'Neapolitan school'. After the middle of the 19th century he is occasionally cited as the arch-villain whose bad example began the 'decline' of dramatic music, as in Emil Naumann's *Illustrierte Musikgeschichte* (1885) and more markedly in Romain Rolland's history of European opera (1895). Modern Scarlatti scholarship, with appreciation of his true qualities and historical position, began in 1905 with Edward J. Dent's *Alessandro Scarlatti*, followed in 1927 by Alfred Lorenz's studies of the early operas. Progress since then, except in details of biography and bibliography, and except for the beginning of publication of the operas and oratorios, has been hampered by the lack of modern editions of cantatas of Scarlatti himself, his predecessors and contemporaries.

From the present viewpoint it seems most accurate to regard Scarlatti as the outstanding composer of the late Italian Baroque period whose work marks the historical consummation of the era of Monteverdi, Cavalli, Cesti, Carissimi and Stradella. Typical for this orientation is Scarlatti's concentration on vocal composition in the forms of the *dramma per musica* and the cantata. Also typical are the stylistic features: the spun-out melodic lines, the basically contrapuntal texture, the sophisticated interplay of voice and orchestra and the characteristically Baroque relationship between drama and music in the operas. In many respects, and particularly in regard to those features of his music that can be most readily described in words, Scarlatti was a man of his time. He surpassed his contemporaries by virtue of superior genius and skill in the handling of a common musical language. He was no more a conscious innovator than Bach. As Bach worked in the comparative isolation of Lutheran Leipzig, so did Scarlatti in the intense but narrow worlds of the Neapolitan and Roman aristocracy; it is significant that Ottoboni lauded him as a 'friend of nobles and princes'. His music had no demonstrable direct influence on later 18th-century composers, Neapolitan or other (even Handel, for whom it has been claimed); but Dent was undeniably right in naming Mozart as his spiritual descendant.

WORKS
* – doubtful; † – autograph
OPERAS
(3 acts unless otherwise stated; source information refers to complete scores unless otherwise stated)
Edition: *The Operas of Alessandro Scarlatti*, ed. D. J. Grout, HPM, ix (1974–) [G]

DP –	*Rome, Palazzo Doria Pamphili*	SB –	*Naples, Teatro S Bartolomeo*
PR –	*Naples, Palazzo Reale*	VM –	*Pratolino, Villa Medicea*
SGG –	*Venice, Teatro S Giovanni Grisostomo*		
TC –	*Rome, Teatro Capranica*		

Title, Genre	Libretto	First Performances, Remarks	Sources, Edn.
Gli equivoci nel sembiante, dramma	D. F. Contini	TC, 5 Feb 1679 (after private performances at the Casa Contini and Collegio Clementino, Rome, 1679); as L'errore innocente, Bologna, 1679; as L'amor non vuole inganni, Linz, carn. 1681	*A-Wn* (Act 1 only), *B-Bc, I-Bc, MOe, Rsc, Vnm*
L'honestà negli amori, dramma	F. Parnasso [?=G. F. Bernini]	Rome, Palazzo Bernini, 6 Feb 1680	*MOe, Rc*
Tutto il mal non vien per nuocere, commedia	G. D. de Totis	Rome, Palazzo Rospigliosi, 1681; as Dal male il bene, Naples, 1687	*D-Bds, I-MC* (partly autograph), *Nc*
*Il Lisimaco, dramma	G. Sinibaldi	Rome, Palazzo Bernini, 1681	—
Il Pompeo, dramma	N. Minato	Rome, Teatro Colonna, 25 Jan 1683	*B-Br*
La guerriera costante	F. Orsini	Rome, palace of Duchess of Bracciano, carn. 1683	*I-Rvat*
L'Aldimiro o vero Favor per favore, dramma	de Totis	PR, 6 Nov 1683	arias *GB-Lbm, Och, I-Bc, Rvat*
La Psiche o vero Amore innamorato, dramma	de Totis	PR, 21 Dec 1683	recit and aria *PAVu*
*Il Fetonte, dramma	de Totis	PR, 22 Nov 1685	—
Olimpia vendicata, dramma	A. Aureli	PR, 23 Dec 1685	*F-Pn, GB-Lbm, I-Vnm*
*L'Etio, dramma	A. Morselli	PR, carn. 1686	aria *MC, Nc*
La Rosmene o vero L'infedeltà fedele, melodramma	de Totis	DP, carn. 1686	*D-BD, MÜs, F-Pn, I-Fc* (Acts 1 and 2)
Clearco in Negroponte, dramma	A. Arcoleo	PR, 21 Dec 1686	*MOe*
La santa Dinna, commedia	B. Pamphili	DP, carn. 1687, Act 1 by Alessandro Melani, Act 2 by B. Pasquini, Act 3 by Scarlatti	
Il Flavio, dramma	M. Noris	PR, ?14 Nov 1688	arias *GB-Och, I-Fc, MOe, Nc*
*La Dori, dramma	A. Apolloni	PR, 18 Jan 1689	arias *MOe, Nc*
L'Anacreonte tiranno, melodramma	G. F. Bussani	SB, 9 Feb 1689	aria *Nc*
*La serva favorita, dramma	C. Villifranchi	VM, 1689	
L'Amazzone corsara [guerriera] o vero L'Alvilda, dramma	G. C. Corradi	PR, 6 Nov 1689	*D-Mbs, I-MC*
La Statira, dramma	P. Ottoboni	Rome, Teatro Tordinona, 5 Jan 1690	*B-Bc, D-Dlb, Mbs, GB-CDp, Lbm, I-MOe*
Gli equivoci in amore o vero La Rosaura, melodramma	G. B. Lucini	Rome, Palazzo della Cancelleria, Dec 1690; as La Rosaura, ?Florence, 1692	*A-Wn, D-WD, F-Pc* (Acts 1 and 2). *GB-Lbm*

Title, Genre	Libretto	First Performances, Remarks	Sources, Edn.
L'humanità nelle fiere o vero Il Lucullo, dramma		SB, 25 Feb 1691	—
La Teodora augusta, dramma	Morselli	PR, 6 Nov 1692	Och, I-Fc
Gerone tiranno di Siracusa, dramma	Aureli	PR, 22 Dec 1692	GB-Och
L'amante doppio o vero Il Ceccobimbi, melodramma		PR, April 1693	—
Il Pirro e Demetrio, dramma	Morselli	SB, 28 Jan 1694; as La forza della fedeltà, Florence, carn. 1712	B-Br, I-Nc
Il Bassiano o vero Il maggior impossibile, melodramma	Noris	SB, spr. 1694	—
La santa Genuinda, o vero L'innocenza difesa dall'inganno, dramma sacro	Pamphili	DP, 1694, Act 1 by G. L. Lulier, Act 2 by Scarlatti, Act 3 by C. F. Cesarini (or C. F. Pollarolo)	D-Mbs, F-Pc, GB-Lbm
Le nozze con l'inimico o vero L'Analinda, melodramma		SB, 1695; as L'Analinda overo Le nozze col nemico, Florence, carn. 1702	F-Pn
Nerone fatto Cesare, melodramma	Noris	PR, 6 Nov 1695	arias and duets I-Nc
Massimo Puppieno, melodramma	Aureli	SB, 26 Dec 1695	MC
Penelope la casta, dramma	Noris	SB, ?23 Feb 1696; ? perf. Palermo, 1694	arias Nc
La Didone delirante, opera drammatica	F. M. Paglia, after A. Franceschi	SB, 28 May 1696	arias Bc, Bsp, Nc, Os, Rvat
Comodo Antonino, dramma	Paglia, after Bussani	SB, 18 Nov 1696	arias F-Pthibault
L'Emireno o vero Il consiglio dell'ombra, opera drammatica	Paglia	SB, 2 Feb 1697	A-Wn, I-Nc
La caduta de' Decemviri, dramma	S. Stampiglia	SB, 15 Dec 1697	B-Br, C-Mc, D-Dl, GB-Lbm, I-Nc, US-I, PO
La donna ancora è fedele, dramma	Contini (rev.)	SB, 1698	I-Nc
Il prigioniero fortunato, dramma	Paglia	SB, 14 Dec 1698	GB-Lbm, I-Nc
Gl'inganni felici, dramma	A. Zeno	PR, 6 Nov 1699; as L'Agarista ovvero Gl'inganni felici, with intermezzi Brenno e Tisbe, Florence, carn. 1706	arias Nc; comic scenes D-Dlb
L'Eraclea, dramma	Stampiglia	SB, 30 Jan 1700	items in A-Wn, B-Br, D-Dlb, F-Pn, GB-Cfm, Lbm, I-Nc; ed. in G i
Odoardo (with intermezzi Adolfo e Lesbina), dramma	Zeno	SB, 5 May 1700	arias F-Pc, I-Nc; comic scenes D-Dlb
Dafni, favola boschereccia	Paglia, after E. Manfredi	Naples, Casino del Vicerè a Posillipo, 5 Aug 1700; as L'amore non viene dal caso, Iesi, carn. 1715	GB-Cfm
Laodicea e Berenice, dramma	Noris (adapted)	SB, April 1701	F-Pn
Il pastor[e] di Corinto, favola boschereccia	Paglia	Naples, Casino del Vicerè a Posillipo, 5 Aug 1701	B-Br
Tito Sempronio Gracco (with intermezzi Bireno e Dorilla), dramma	Stampiglia	SB, ?carn. 1702	arias D-MÜs, F-Pc, I-Nc; comic scenes D-Dlb
Tiberio imperatore d'Oriente, dramma	G. D. Pallavicino	PR, 8 May 1702	arias F-Pc, I-Fc, Nc
Il Flavio Cuniberto, dramma	Noris	VM, Sept 1702 (? not 1st perf.)	GB-Och
Arminio, dramma	A. Salvi	VM, Sept 1703	—
Turno Aricino, dramma	Stampiglia	VM, Sept 1704	—
Lucio Manlio l'imperioso, dramma	Stampiglia	VM, Sept 1705	—
Il gran Tamerlano, dramma	Salvi, after N. Pradon	VM, Sept 1706	—
Il Mitridate Eupatore, tragedia (5 acts)	G. Frigimelica Roberti	SGG, carn. 1707	B-Br, D-Bds, F-Pn
Il trionfo della libertà, tragedia (5 acts)	Frigimelica Roberti	SGG, carn. 1707	arias A-Wn, B-Br, I-Rvat
Il Teodosio, dramma	? V. Grimani	SB, 27 Jan 1709	—
L'amor volubile e tiranno, dramma	G. D. Pioli, G. Papis	SB, 25 May 1709; as La Dorisbe ó L'amor volubile e tiranno, Rome, carn. 1711; as La Dorisbe, Genoa, aut. 1713	B-Bc, D-Dlb
La principessa fedele, dramma	A. Piovene (rev. ? D. A. Parrino)	SB, 8 Feb 1710	B-Br (inc.); ed. in G iv
La fede riconosciuta, dramma pastorale	? B. Marcello	SB, 14 Oct 1710	†GB-Cfm
Giunio Bruto o vero La caduta dei Tarquini, dramma	?Sinibaldi	planned for Vienna, 1711, perf. cancelled; Act 1 by C. F. Cesarini, Act 2 by A. Caldara, Act 3 by Scarlatti	A-Wn
Il Ciro, dramma	Ottoboni	Rome, Palazzo della Cancelleria, carn. 1712	†B-Bc
Scipione nelle Spagne (with intermezzi Pericca e Varrone), dramma	Zeno, N. Serino; intermezzi by ?Salvi	SB, 21 Jan 1714; intermezzi perf. as La dama spagnola ed il cavalier romano, Bologna, carn. 1730	Br, GB-Lbm, I-Bu, MC (Act 1 and intermezzi)
L'amor generoso (with intermezzi Despina e Niso), dramma	Papis, Stampiglia	PR, 1 Oct 1714	GB-Lbm
Il Tigrane o vero L'egual impegno d'amore e di fede, dramma	D. Lalli	SB, 16 Feb 1715	Bu, Lbm, I-Fc, Nc; ed. in G v
Carlo re d'Allemagna (with intermezzi *Palandrana e Zamberlucco), dramma	F. Silvani	SB, 30 Jan 1716	GB-Bu
La virtù trionfante dell'odio e dell'amore, dramma	Silvani	PR, 3 May 1716	—
Telemaco, dramma	C. S. Capece	TC, carn. 1718	†A-Wn, D-MÜs, F-Pc
Il trionfo dell'onore, commedia	F. A. Tullio	Naples, Teatro dei Fiorentini, 26 Nov 1718	†GB-Lbm, US-Wc
Il Cambise, dramma	Lalli	SB, 4 Feb 1719	†I-Nc
Marco Attilio Regolo (with intermezzi Leonzio e Eurilla), dramma		TC, carn. 1719	†GB-Lbm; ed. in G ii
La Griselda, dramma	after Zeno	TC, Jan 1721	B-Bc, D-Bds, MÜs, †GB-Lbm (Acts 1 and 3); ed. in G iii; ed. D. Drechsler (Kassel, 1960)

CONTRIBUTIONS TO OTHER COMPOSERS' OPERAS

DP – *Rome, Palazzo Doria Pamphili*   PR – *Naples, Palazzo Reale*   SB – *Naples, Teatro S Bartolomeo*

Title (genre, libretto)	Composer(s)	Performance	Scarlatti's contribution	Sources
L'Idalma o vero Chi la dura la vince (dramma, G. D. de Totis)	B. Pasquini	DP, 1682	reworking of Act 1	—
Il Giustino (dramma, N. Beregan)	G. Legrenzi	PR, 6 Nov 1684	?prol	—
L'Odoacre (dramma, N. Bonis)	G. Varischino	SB, 5 Jan 1694	arias	—
L'Arione (dramma, O. d'Arles)	C. Valtolina, D. Erba and 25 others	Milan, 9 June 1694	aria, Mio povero core	—
Il figlio delle selve (dramma, C. S. Capece)	C. Bani	?1698	?arias	—
*La forza della virtù (dramma, D. David)	C. F. Pollarolo and others	before 1699; rev. as Creonte tiranno di Tebe, SB, spr. 1699	arias	—
La Semiramide (dramma, F. M. Paglia)	G. Aldrovandini	PR, 19 Dec 1701	?prol, arias	I-Nc
L'Ariovisto (dramma)	G. A. Perti, Magni, Ballarotti	Florence, aut. 1702	arias	arias D-MÜs
La pastorella (opera pastorale)	C. F. Cesarini, G. L. Lulier, G. Bononcini	Rome, Palazzo Venezia, 1705; as Love's Triumph, London, 1708	arias	arias GB-Lbm; pubd (London, 1709)
Thomyris Queen of Scythia (opera, P. A. Motteux)	[pasticcio]	London, Drury Lane, 1 April 1707	arias	arias Lbm; pubd (London, 1707)
La Clotilda (dramma)	F. B. Conti	London, Haymarket, 2 March 1709	arias	arias Lbm; pubd (London, 1709)
Lo Petracchio scremmetore (opera comica, A. Capis)	F. Scarlatti	Aversa, 1711	?15 arias	—
Il Porsenna (dramma, A. Piovene)	A. Lotti	SB, 19 Nov 1713	arias	Lbm, I-MC (Act 2)
Giove in Argo (A. M. Luchini)	Lotti	Dresden, Schlosstheater, 25 Oct 1717	intermezzi: Vespetta e Milo	—

SERENATAS

CV – *Naples, Casino del Viceré a Posillipo*   PR – *Naples, Palazzo Reale*
DP – *Rome, Palazzo Doria Pamphili*   TC – *Rome, Teatro Capranica*

Title (incipit)	Libretto	Scoring	Performance	Sources
Diana ed Endimione (Voi solitarie piante)		2vv, insts	c1680–85	F-Pn, I-MC
Serenata in honour of James II of England			DP, 1688	—
*La sirena consolata	A. Perrucci		?PR, 1692	
Il genio di Partenope, la gloria del Sebeto, il piacere di Mergellina (Venticelli soavi che con ali)			PR, Jan 1696	MC
Venere, Adone e Amore (Dal giardin del piacere)	F. M. Paglia	3vv, insts	CV, 15 July 1696; rev. Rome, 1706	D-MÜs, E-Mn, GB-Och, I-MC
Il trionfo delle stagioni	Paglia		PR, 26 July 1696	
Venere ed Amore (Del mar Tirreno in su l'amena sponda)		2vv, insts	?CV, c1695–1700	B-Br
Clori, Lidia e Filli (Già compito il suo giro)		3vv, insts	c1700	Bc
Clori, Dorino e Amore (Cari lidi, amene sponde)		3vv, insts	PR, 2 May 1702	D-Bds, MÜs
Venere e Adone: Il giardino d'amore (Care selve, amati orrori)		2vv, insts	c1700–05	?B-Br, D-Bds, MÜs, GB-Och
Endimione e Cintia (Sento un'aura che dolce)		2vv, insts	Rome, 1705	D-Bds, MÜs
Amore e Virtù ossia Il trionfo della virtù (No, che non voglio più)		2vv, insts	Rome, 1706	Bds, MÜs
Clori e Zeffiro (Vaga, auretta soave)		2vv, insts	?Rome, 1706	Bds, MÜs
Fileno, Niso e Doralbo: Serenata a Filli (Tacete, aure, tacete)		3vv, insts	?Rome, 1706	MÜs
Sole, Urania e Clio: Le muse Urania e Clio lodano le bellezze di Filli (O mie figlie canore)		3vv, insts	?Rome, 1706	MÜs
Venere, Amore e Ragione: Il ballo delle ninfe: Venere, havendo perso Amore, lo ritrova fra le ninfe e i pastori dei Sette Colli (Cerco Amore, Amor che fa?)	S. Stampiglia	3vv, insts	Rome, 1706	Bds, MÜs
Cupido e Onestà: Il trionfo dell'Onestà (Puote si poco)		2vv, insts	Rome, Sept 1706	MÜs
Le glorie della Bellezza del Corpo e dell'Anima, for the birthday of Queen Elizabeth of Spain	G. Papis	4vv, insts	PR, 28 Aug 1709	—
Pace, Amore e Provvidenza (Al fragor di lieta tromba)	Papis	3vv, 4 choirs, insts	PR, 4 Nov 1711	Bds, MÜs
Il genio austriaco			PR, 21 June 1712	—

Title (incipit)	Libretto	Scoring	Performance	Sources
Il genio austriaco: Zefiro, Flora, il Sole, Partenope e il Sebeto	Papis		PR, 28 Aug 1713	—
Serenata in honour of the vicereine, Donna Barbara d'Erbenstein			PR, 4 Dec 1715	
La gloria di Primavera: Primavera, Estate, Autunno, Inverno e Giove (Nato è già l'Austriaco Sole)	N. Giovo	5vv, insts	? Vienna, April 1716; Naples, Palazzo di Nicola Gaetano d'Aragona e Aurora Sanseverino, ?19 May 1716	A-Wn, D-Mbs, GB-Lbm, I-Nc
Partenope, Teti, Nettuno, Proteo e Glauco (Chi al vasto ondoso)			PR, 1716	—
Filli, Clori e Tirsi (Dalle fiorite arene)			PR, ?1718	D-Bds, MÜs
La virtù negli amori: La Notte, il Sole, Lanso, Lisa, Toante e Agave (Dolce sonno, oblo dei mali)	G. Lamer		TC, 16 Nov 1721	
Erminia, Tancredi, Polidoro e Pastore (Ove smarrita e sola), for the wedding of the Prince of Stigliano		4vv, insts	Naples, Palazzo Stigliano, 13 June 1723	GB-Lcm, I-MC (Part I), Nc (Part I)
Diana, Amore, Venere (Bel piacere ch'è la caccia)		3vv, insts	—	†Mc

ORATORIOS, LARGE SACRED WORKS
(Italian oratorios unless otherwise stated)
Edition: *Gli oratorii di Alessandro Scarlatti*, ed. L. Bianchi (Rome, 1964–) [B]

Title (genre)	Text	Scoring	Performance	Sources, Edn.
?(Lat. oratorio)			Rome, Oratorio del Ss Crocifisso, 24 Feb 1679	—
?(Lat. oratorio)			Rome, Oratorio del Ss Crocifisso, 12 April 1680	—
Passio Domini Nostri Jesu Christi secundum Joannem (Lat. Passion)	Bible	A, B, SATB, str, bc	c1680	I-Nc, Nf; ed. E. Hanley (New Haven, 1955); ed. O. Deffner (Stuttgart, 1966)
?(Lat. oratorio)			Rome, Oratorio del Ss Crocifisso, 20 Feb 1682	
Agar et Ismaele esiliati	G. D. de Totis	3S, A, B, str, bc	Rome, ?Palazzo Pamphili, 1683; as L'Abramo, Palermo, 1691; as Ismaele soccorso dall'angelo, Rome and Florence, 1695; as Il sacrificio di Abramo, Rome, 1703	A-Wn; ed. in B ii
Il trionfo della gratia	B. Pamphili	2S, A, str, bc	Rome, 1685; as La Maddalena pentita, Modena, 1686; as La conversione di S Maria Maddalena, Florence, 1693	D-Dlb, GB-Cfm, I-MOe, Rw
Il martirio di S Teodosia		S, A, T, B, str, bc	Modena, 1685; as S Teodosia vergine e martire, Florence, 1693	A-Wn, B-Br, F-Pn, I-MOe
I dolori di Maria sempre vergine		S, A, T, B, str, bc	Naples, S Luigi di Palazzo, 1693; in Lat. as La concettione della beata vergine, Rome, 1703	F-Pn
La Giuditta (i)	Pamphili	2S, A, T, B, str, tpt, trbns, 2 fl, bc	Naples, 1693	I-Nc, St Elizabeth College, Morristown, NJ, USA; ed. in B i
Samson vindicatus (Lat. oratorio)	Pamphili		Rome, Oratorio del Ss Crocifisso, 25 March 1695	
Cantata . . . per la notte di natale	?P. Ottoboni	4vv	Rome, Palazzo Apostolico, 24 Dec 1695	—
Il martirio di S Orsola		2S, A, T, B, str, tpt, lute, bc	?Lyons, c1695–1700	F-LYm
Davidis pugna et victoria (Lat. oratorio)		2S, A, T, B, SATB, SATB, str, bc	Rome, Oratorio del Ss Crocifisso, 5 March 1700 (probably not 1st perf.)	LYm; ed. in B v
La Giuditta (ii)	A. Ottoboni	S, A, T, str, bc	1700	GB-Ckc; ed. in B iii
L'assunzione della Beata Vergine Maria	P. Ottoboni	2S, 2A, str, bc	Rome, Collegio Clementino, 1703; as Il regno di Maria assunta in cielo, Rome, 23 Aug 1705; as La sposa dei sacri cantici, Naples, 1710	A-Wn, D-MÜs, F-Pc, US-STu
S Michaelis Arcangeli cum Lucifer pugna et victoria (Lat. oratorio)	?Pullioni		Rome, Oratorio del Ss Crocifisso, 3 April 1705	—
S Casimiro, Re di Polonia		3S, A, T, str, bc	Florence, Compagnia della Purificazione di Maria Vergine e di S Zenobi detta di S Marco, 1705	A-Wgm, Wn, F-Mn
S Maria Maddalena de' pazzi	Pamphili		Rome, Collegio Clementino, 1705	—
S Filippo Neri		S, 2A, T, str, tpt, lute, bc	Rome, Collegio Clementino, 1705	B-Br, D-MÜs; ed. R. Giazotto and G. Piccioli (Milan, 1960)
Qual di lieti concenti (Christmas cantata)			Rome, ?Palazzo Apostolico, c1705	MÜs
Il Sedecia, Re di Gerusalemme	F. O. Fabbri	2S, A, T, B, chorus, str, 2 ob, 2 tpt, timp, lute, bc	?Urbino, 1705	A-Wn, B-Bc, D-B, Dlb, Hs, Mbs, I-Rc; ed. G. Guerini (Milan, 1961)

Title (genre)	Text	Scoring	Performance	Sources, Edn.
Abramo il tuo sembiante (Christmas cantata)		2S, A, T, B, chorus, str, 2 ob, bc	Rome, Palazzo Apostolico, 24 Dec 1705	D-MÜs
Il trionfo della Ss Vergine assunta in cielo	P. Ottoboni	2S, 2A, str, fl, 2 ob, tpt, lute, bc	Florence, Compagnia della Purificazione di Maria Vergine e di S Zenobi detta di S Marco, 1706	MÜs
S Francesco di Paola			Urbino, Chiesa della Communità, 1706	—
Humanità e Lucifero		S, T, str, tpt, pic, bc	?1706	MÜs
Il martirio di S Susanna	S. Stampiglia		Florence, Chiesa dei Filippini, 1706	—
Alcone, ove per queste (Christmas cantata)	Fabbri	3vv, ?insts	Rome, Palazzo Apostolico, 24 Dec 1706	—
Cain overo Il primo omicidio		2S, 2A, T, B, str, bc	Venice, Lent 1707	†US-SFsc; ed. in B iv
Il giardino di rose: La Ss Vergine del Rosario		2S, A, T, B, str, 2 tpt, 2 fl, 2 ob, bn, lute, bc	Rome, 24 April 1707	D-MÜs
Serafini al nostro canto (Christmas cantata)	M. S. Mirandolano	3vv, ?insts	Rome, Palazzo Apostolico, 24 Dec 1707	—
Il martirio di S Cecilia			Rome, Lent, 1708	—
La Ss Annunziata		3S, A, T, str, bc	Rome, Palazzo Ruspoli, 25 March 1708 (possibly not 1st perf.)	B-Br, D-MÜs
Oratorio per la Passione di Nostro Signore Gesù Cristo (Passion oratorio)	P. Ottoboni	2S, A, str, 4 tpt, trbn, timp, bc	Rome, Palazzo della Cancelleria, 4 April 1708; in Lat. as Culpa, Poenitentia et Gratia, Rome, 1725	Dlb, WD
La vittoria della fede	C. S. Capece		Rome, Palazzo Zuccari, 12 Sept 1708	—
Il trionfo del valore		5vv, ?insts	Naples, Palazzo Reale, 19 March 1709	—
La Ss Trinità			Naples, May 1715	Fondazione Bravi, Brescia; ed. G. Piccioli (Bologna, 1953)
[La vergine addolorata]		2S, A, T, str, fl, ob, tpt, bc	Rome, 1717	B-Bc, GB-Lwa, I-Nf
La gloriosa gara tra la Santità e la Sapienza		3vv	Rome, 13 June 1720	

Also arias in pasticcio oratorios: I trionfi di Giosuè (G. P. Berzini), Florence, Compagnia di S Marco, 1703, and as Giosuè in Gabaon, Florence; Sara in Egitto (D. Canavese), Florence, Compagnia di S Marco, 1708

CANTATAS

Arranged alphabetically by incipit, titles given in parentheses; for S, bc, unless otherwise stated; for sources see Hanley, 1963, and Pagano, Bianchi and Rostirolla, 1972

A battaglia, pensieri, S, A, 2 vn, vc, db, tpt, mandola, bc, 1699; Abbandonar Fileno dovea, S/A, bc; Abbandonato e solo (Il Nerone), S/A, bc; *A chi t'inganna, bella tiranna, S/A, bc; Ad altro uso serbate; Agitato mio core, dove ti volgi?, 1704; Agitato sen cade (La Sofonisba); Ah ben lo vedi, o core; Ah che pur troppo è vero; Ah crudele, che ti pose tanto foco; Ah fuggi, sì, mio core; Ahi che sarà di me? (Floro e Tirsi), 2S, bc, 2 Sept 1707; Ah Mitilde vezzosa, 29 July 1712; Alba che neghittosa; *Al fin diviene amante
*Al fine, o Clori amata; Al fin m'ucciderete, S/A, bc, 20 July 1705; Alle troiane antenne (Didone abbandonata), 18 Sept 1705; Allor che stanco il sole, S, 2 vn, bc; Allor ch'il Dio di Delo (La Gelosia), 26 Feb 1705; Allor ch'il fier leone; Al mare, al bosco, al rio; Alma, tu che dal cielo (D. A. Ottoboni), S, 2 vn, bc, 12 Sept 1709; Alme voi che provaste; *Al mormorio d'un vago ruscelletto; Al pensiero, miei sguardi, July 1706; Al seren di sì bel giorno, 26 Oct 1704; Al voler del bene amato (Devesi amare per servire); *Amai, dolce mia vita, A, bc; Amanti, anch'io son preso, S, 2 vn, bc
Amica, hora che Aprile (Filli e Clori), 2S, 2 vn, bc, ?1694; Amici s'è vinto (Amor perduto e ritornato) (D. A. Ottoboni), before 1710; Ammore brutto figlio de pottana, T, bc; Amo e godo d'amare; *Amo, e negar nol posso, Dec 1704; Amo, ma l'idol mio, A/S, bc, 9 June 1701; Amo, peno, e languisco, Mez, bc; Amo, peno, gioisco (Amante timido di spiegarsi alla sua dama); *Amor che fia di noi (Cantata grave); Amor con l'idol mio, 3 April 1702; Amore, o mi togli le fiamme; Amor, fabro ingegnoso; Amor, Mitilde è morta (La morte di Mitilde); Amor, o crudo amor, sempre in tormenti; Amor, tu che sì bella fiamma accendesti
Andate, o miei sospiri (i), 1712; Andate, o miei sospiri (ii), 1712; A piè d'un faggio ombroso; A piè d'un verde colle; *Api industri che volate (Paragone amoroso); *A placar la mia bella, T, bc; Appena chiudo gl'occhi (Il sogno), S, vn, bc; Appena giunse al forte campo (Oloferne), B, 2 vn, bc (inc.); A privarmi del bel; Ardea per Coridone Clori; Arder per due pupille (Bella dama contenta), 1704; Ardo d'amore e impatiente; *Ardo e del nobil foco, April ?1696; Ardo, è ver, per te d'amore, S, fl, bc (inc.); Ardo tacito amante, S/A, bc, 30 Aug 1706; Arse felice un tempo; A soffrire impara, o core
Assiso in verde prato; A te, Lisa gentile, A, bc; Augelletti semplicetti che girate (La rete d'amore); Augellino prigioniero, ferma oh Dio; Augellin, sospendi i vanni (i) (B. Pamphili), S, 2 vn, bc; Augellin,

sospendi i vanni (ii) (Pamphili); Augellin vago e canoro, S, 2 fl, bc, 16 June 1699; Aure io son di voi geloso, S/A, bc; A voi che l'accendeste (F. M. Paglia), c1692; Balze alpestri e romite (Amante che gode la beatitudine alpestre); Barbara ingrata Fille, S/A, bc, 18 Sept 1706; Bei prati, freschi rivi (Il disperato); Bei prati, verdi colli, 5 Nov 1704; Bel Dorino–Amata Clori, S, B, 2 vn, bc
Bella, dunque n'andrai; *Bella madre dei fiori, S, 2 vn, bc; Bella onda che mormori, S, ?2 vn, bc, 1694, lost; Bella, per te d'amore, S/A, bc; Bella quanto crudel spietata Irene, June 1717; Bella rosa adorata (La rosa), Sept 1704; Bella se quella face; *Belle faci del cielo, A, 2 vn, tpt, bc; *Belle pupille care, e chi (attrib. Francesco Scarlatti in GB-Mp, Q544 Bk51); Benché o sirena bella; Benché porti nel volto; Benché vezzosa Irene; Ben folle e chi non parte; Ben mio quel verme alato (Paglia), S, 2 vn, bc; Biondi crini ch'in fronte; Boschi amati che cingete col silenzio
Cara sempre agl'occhi miei; *Care pupille belle, belle se mi lasciate; *Care selve, a voi ritorno; Care selve gradite; Caro amor, quant'è gradita; Caro Fileno mio, quanto mi spiace; Caro laccio, dolce nodo, S/A, bc, 1695; Celinda è la mia vita; Cerca nel cor di Mille, A/S, bc, 10 Aug 1706; Cerco, né so trovar beltà fedel; Che fai, mio cor?, S/A, bc; Che le dolcezze estreme, before 1698; Che mai sarà di me?; Che più farai, arciero Amor? (Clori e Dorino), S, B, bc; *Che più tardi, o ninfa bella?; Che pretendi, o tiranna?; Che rispetti, che, mondo?; *Che Sisifo infelice, 25 July 1706
*Chi batte al mio core? (F. Melosio); Chi m'insegna ov'è quel bene?; Chi m'insegna un tetto?; *Chi mi toglie a riposi?; Ch'io da te mi divida, A, bc; *Ch'io scopri il mio affetto, before 1694; *Ch'io ti manchi di fede; *Chiudea presso d'un fonte; Chiudetevi per sempre e di pianger cessate; Chiusa tra fosche bende; Chi vedesse la ferita; Chi vidde mai o chi provò?; Cinta dei più bei fiori; *Cinta di rai splendea; *Cleopatra la bella, la Venere d'Egitto (Lamento di Cleopatra); Cleopatra, mia reina (Marc'Antonio e Cleopatra), S, A, bc; *Clori, adorata Clori, o quante pene; Clori, allor ch'io ti vidi, 17 April 1701
Clori bell'idol mio, Clori mia vita; Clori, bell'idol mio, sai tu qual è il desio?, 1 July 1705; Clori, io tacqui a bastanza; Clori, mia cara Clori, moro; Clori mia, Clori bella, ah non più, S, fl, bc, 18 June 1699; Clori mia–Dorino caro (Dorino e Clori), S, B, bc; *Clori mia, se t'amo (Risoluzione di Tirsi) (Paglia), lost; Clori, mi sento al seno; Clorinda [Mitilde] è bella e sempre è più vivace; Clori spietata, mio crudel tesoro; Clori superba, e come mai?; Clori vezzosa e bella, A, bc; Colui che fisso mira, S/A, bc, April ?1696; Come il foco alla sua sfera; *Come potesti mai; Come può non esser bella?, 15 Feb 1701
Come volubil gira la ruota; *Con la speme di godere; Con non inteso affanno; Contentati mio core, A, bc; Con trasparente velo, 13 Dec 1702; Cor di Bruto, e che risolvi?, B, bc; Coronate il bel crine; Correa nel seno amato, S, 2 vn, bc, before 1694; Cruda Filli spietata;

*Crudelissimo amore, A, bc (probably by Albinoni); *Crudel, mira quest'occhi; Crudel, perchè privarmi?, 2S, bc; Crudo Amor, che vuoi da me?; Crudo Amor, empie stelle, iniqua sorte, before 1702; Crudo Amor, empie stelle, Irene ingrata; Crudo Amor, saper vorrei; Da che Tirsi mirai; Dagli strali d'amore, 3 Sept 1701; *Da l'arco d'un bel ciglio, A, bc (published in Albinoni's op.4, 1702)

Dal bel volto d'Irene, 4 Jan 1705; Dal colle al pian discesa; *Dal crudele Daliso (published in G. B. Bassani's op.3, 1682); Dal dì ch'Amor m'accese; Dal dì che l'empio fato; *Dal giorno fortunato ch'io vidi (Paglia); Dal grato mormorio; *Dalisa, e come mai, A, bc; Dalla fida compagna abbandonata; Dalla nativa sfera scese, 5 Oct 1704; Dalla speme deluso (Paglia); Dalle pene amorose; Dalle tirrene sponde parti Filli; Dall'oscura magion dell'arsa Dite (L'Orfeo), S, 2 vn, bc; Dammi, amore, un altro cor; Da qual parte celeste, 20 Oct 1701; Da quel dì che Mitilde; Da quell'hora fatale (i); Da quell'hora fatale (ii), 1716

Da sventura a sventura, ?1690; Da turbini di pene; *Da voi parto, amati rai, B, bc; *Deh, per mercè l'ignudo Dio; Deh torna, amico sonno (Il sonno); Del faretrato nume amor tiranno; Del lagrimoso lido (Euridice dall'Inferno), 17 June 1699; Della spietata Irene fur l'accese pupille; Delle patrie contrade; Del mio seno la costanza, S/A, bc; Del Tebro in su le sponde; Del Tirreno a le sponde (Cantata di lontananza); Del Tirreno sul lido, A, bc, Dec 1697; Dentro il sen della mia Irene; Dentro un orrido speco; *Di che havete paura?; Di cipresso funesto (Querele e morto di Tirsi per Clori ingrata), before 1694; *Di colore de' cieli (Occhi azzurri); *Di due vaghe pupille nere

Diedi a Fileno il core (Amor corrisposto), A/S, bc, 1705; Di me che sarà?; Dimmi che pensi, o Amore, before 1702; Dimmi, Clori superba (Clori superba), S/A, bc, 1704; *Dimmi, crudel, e quando, S, A, bc; Dimmi, mio ben, perchè; Dipende da te solo la pace, 1v, bc; Di pensiero in pensier, A, bc; Disperate pupille, hor, sì, piangete (Disperazione amorosa), S, B, bc; Dispettoso pensiero; *Dolci istinti d'amore; Dopo lungo penar (i); Dopo lungo penar (ii), B, bc; Dorisbe, i miei lamenti (Eurillo sdegnato); Dormono l'aure estive, S/A, bc, 10 Jan 1705; Dove alfin mi traeste? (L'Arianna); Dov'è Filli, dov'è? Dove fuggi, o bella Clori? (i), S, A, bc; Dove fuggi, o bella Clori? (ii) (Lidio e Clori), S, A, 2 vn, bc; Dove fuggo, a che penso?, S, vn, bc; Dove l'eneta Dori alla reggia; Dove una quercia annosa (Beltà bruna) (Paglia); Dove xestu, cor mio?, lost; Dov'io mi volga o vada; Due nemici tiranni, 1722; D'un platano frondoso; Dunque ingrato spergiuro, S, A, bc; Dunque perchè lontano; Dunque sperar non lice; Ebra d'amor fuggia (L'Arianna), S, 2 vn, bc; Ecco ch'a voi ritorno (after F. de Lemene), 2 versions; E come, oh Dio, lontana?, before 1707; *E come, o Dio, tacito e fido?; E come, ohime, poss'io?, 11 Feb 1714

E con qual core, oh Dio (i); *E con qual core, oh Dio (ii); E con qual core, oh Dio (iii), S, 2 vn, bc; *E gran pena t'amare; E con speme un desio tormentoso, 16 Oct 1704; Elitropio d'amor, S/Mez, bc, 1694; E penar degg'io ancora, S/A, bc; E pure il gran tormento, S/A, bc; *E pur è vero che alletti; E pur odo e non moro; E pur tenti il ritorno (G. Monaci); E pur vuole il cielo e amore (D. Benigni), S, A, bc, before 1706; E quando, ingrata Nice?; E quando mai cessate?; Era già l'alba e in cielo (Europa rapita da Giove in forma di toro)

Era giunta quell'ora, 29 Nov 1704; Era l'oscura notte e d'ogni intorno di fosco ammanto, S, A, bc; Era l'oscura notte e d'ogni intorno le tremolanti stelle; E satio ancor non sei; E sia pur vero, S/A, bc; E sino a quando, Amor?; E sino a quando, o stelle?; *Essere innamorato e non poterlo dir; Eurilla all'or che sei cinta; Eurilla, amata Eurilla, before 1698; Eurilla, io parto, a Dio; Eurilla, oh Dio, nel seno palpita; *E viva al diletto la mia rimembranza; Facile sembra a un core l'amar; Farfalla che s'aggira (La pazzia, overo La stravaganza), 11 Aug 1706; Farfalletta innocente se correndo

Fatto d'amor seguace, S/A, bc; Ferma omai, fugace e bella, A, 2 vn, va, bc, Dec 1724; Fiamma ch'avvampa; Fida compagna, del tuo alato amante (Lontananza), S, 2 vn, bc; Fiero acerbo destin dell'alma mia; Filen, mio caro bene (Filli che esprime la sua fede a Fileno), A, 2 vn, fl, bc; Fileno, oh Dio, Fileno, di quest'anima amante, S, 2 vn, bc; Fileno, ove t'en vai? (Clori abbandonata), 11 Oct 1704; Fileno, quel Fileno, tutto fe', S, 2 vn, bc; Filla mia, perchè piangi?; Fille, dolente Fille; Fille, mia cara Fille, 18 Nov 1701; Fille, tu parti, oh Dio, S/A, bc, 12 March 1722

Filli adorata, ah ben comprendo (Chiese Fileno come stasse in gratia di Fille: ella rispose, 'ne ben, ne male'); Filli adorata e cara, Filli che fosti, 23 April 1705; Filli adorata e cara, io parto (Partenza: Fileno giura fedeltà a Filli), 22 Sept 1706; Filli altera e spietata; *Filli che del mio core, May 1700; Filli che fra gl'orrori (Cantata . . . notturna), S, 2 vn, bc, 1706; Filli crudel, dunque tu parti?; Filli, di questo cor parte più cara; Filli, già volge l'anno; *Filli, la lontananza homicida, 1695; Filli, la tua bellezza, 27 June 1702; Filli mia, Filli cara (Descrittore di bella donna), 15 Jan 1702

*Filli mia, tu mi consoli; Filli, mio ben, mia vita, May 1704; *Filli, sei bella, è ver; Filli, tu sai s'io t'amo (Sconsolato rusignolo), S, 2 fl, bc, April 1701; Fiumicel che del mio pianto; *Fiumicel cui l'onde chiare, A, bc; *Flagellava nel cielo (Il Narciso); Fonte d'ogni dolcezza, 12 March 1709; Fonti amiche, erbe care; Forse di Sirio ardente; Fra liete danze; Fra mille semplicetti augei canori, 14 Aug ?1701; Frangi

l'arco e lo stral, 27 Aug 1706; Fra tante pene, e tante, 23 June 1706; Fu d'oro il primo dardo; *Fuori di sua capanna, S, vn/fl, bc

Giacea d'un mirto all'ombra; Giacea presso alla sponda; Già di trionfi onusto (Il Germanico) (Pamphili), before Oct 1691; Già per lunga stagion bersaglio (Lo strale d'amore); Già sepolto è fra l'onda, S, 2 vn, va, vada gamba, bc; Già sorge l'alba (Dorisbe cacciatrice); Già sul carro dorato (Occhi neri); Già vicina è quell'ora, S/A, bc, 15 June 1699; Giù di Vulcan nella fucina eterna, A, bc, 1698; Giunto è il fatal momento (Partenza), 1705; Goderai sempre crudele, 1695 (inc.); Ha l'umore stravagante; Ho una pena intorno al core; I celesti zaffiri, 19 Aug 1701, lost; Il centro del mio core

Il ciel seren, le fresche aurette (La primavera: Clori e Lisa compagne), 2S, bc; *Il cor che vive oppresso; Il fulgido splendor d'un ciglio arciero, 14 March 1705; Il genio di Mitilde, S/A, bc; Il mio sol non è più meco, 31 Oct 1704; Il più misero amante, A, bc; Il rosignolo se scioglie il volo (i), A/S, bc, 19 Dec 1698; Il rosignolo se scioglie il volo (ii), A/S, bc, 26 Aug 1700; Il timido mio core (Immagini d'orrore); Imagini d'orrore, B, 2 vn, bc, 16 July 1710; In amorosi ardori; In bel sonno profondo; In che giammai t'offesi?, 8 Aug 1706; In due vaghe pupille; Infelice mio core, che ti valse?

Infelice mio core, giunse alfin; *In fra notturni orrori (published in A. Marcello, 12 cantate a voce sola, 1708); Ingiustissimo amor, tu che sovvente; In placida sembianza; In questa lacrimosa orrida valle (Tantalo sitibondo); In solitaria soglia; *In traccia del suo bene (published in G. B. Bassani's op.2, 1680); In vano, amor tiranno tenta; Io ben so che siete arciere, 1704; Io che ad un tronco; *Io che con aurea luce; Io che dal cor di Fille, S/A, bc; Io credei che felice; Io m'accendo a poco a poco; Io morirei contento; Io non v'intendo, o stelle; *Io per Dori mi struggo, before 1694

Io son Neron l'imperator del mondo (Il Nerone), 1698; Io son pur solo; *Io t'amerò e nel mio petto; Io ti vuò dir, Dorisbe, Aug 1700; Io vengo, o Filli, 20 Sept 1704; Irene, idolo mio, in questo a me, 12 July 1705; Irene, idolo mio, se per te vivo; La beltà ch'io sospiro (Pamphili), 16 Aug ?1701; La cagion delle mie pene; Là dell'Arno su l'onde; Là dove al sonno in braccio (Paglia), 1v, insts, lost; Là dove al vivo argento; Là dove a Mergellina, 1725; La face d'amore ch'il core m'arde (D. A. Ottoboni), before 1710; La fortuna di Roma (Il Coriolano) (Pamphili), S/A, bc, ?1694; La gran madre d'amore (Innamoramento di Venere et Adone)

La gratia, la sembianza della tua pastorella, 22 Feb 1702; *Lagrime dolorose dagl'occhi miei, T, 2 vn, bc; Là nel ben sen della regal Sirena; Là nel campo de fiori (inc.); Là nell'arcadie spiagie, 1700; Langue Clori vezzosa; L'armi crudeli e fiere, A, bc; Lascia, deh lascia al fine; Lascia di tormentarmi, amor tiranno, 1709; Lasciami alquanto piangere, May 1716; Lasciami sospirar, io voglio piangere (Dorindo e Fileno), S, B, bc; Lascia omai di tormentarmi, o memoria; Lascia più di tormentarmi, rimembranza, 1688; Lasciate ch'io v'adori (Preghiera amorosa), 19 Oct 1705; Lasciate, homai lasciate di tormentarmi più; Lasciato havea l'adultero superbo (Lucretia Romana) (Pamphili), before 1691; La speranza che lusinga (A. Colombi)

*L'augellin che sciogle il volo, A, bc; La vezzosa Celinda; Leandro, anima mia (Ero e Leandro), A/S, bc; *Leggi, de' leggi, o Clori, A, bc; L'empio mio destin brama la morte, 2 vv, bc; Le vaghe tue pupille (Bella donna crudele); *L'huom che segue una speranza (Tormento della Speranza e della Fortuna), A, bc; Libertà del mio core; Lidio, in van mi condanni (Bella donna rimproverata a torto nel partire del suo vago così risponde); Liete, placide e belle acque, 1709; Licti boschi, ombre amiche, A, bc, 18 Aug 1704; *Lilla, mi parto, addio, S/A, bc; Lisa, del foco mio (Clori e Lisa compagne), 2S, bc, 28 Feb 1706

Lontananza, che fai?, 27 Nov 1701; Lontananza crudele, deh perchè? (Lontananza), 4 Oct 1713; Lontananza crudele, tu mi trafiggi, before 1694; Lontananza non risana, A, bc; Lontananza tiranna che da te mi divide; Lontan da la sua Clori; Lontan dall'idol mio, S/A, bc, 1699; Lontan dal suo tesor; Lontan dal tuo bel viso (Paglia), S/A, bc; Lontano dal suo bene; Lo sa il ciel, sallo amore; Lo so ben io; Luci care al mondo sole; *Luci, siete pur quelle, S/A, bc; Lumi ch'in fronte (Ama e non spera godere), 4 Dec 1703; Lumi, dolenti lumi, chiudetevi, S/A, bc; Lunga stagion dolente, 3 June 1706; Lungi dal ben ch'adoro

Lungi dalla cagion per cui sospiro (Lontananza), 20 Dec 1704; Lungi dall'idol mio, A, bc; *Mal fondati sospetti, 1685; Mal sicuro è il fior nel prato (D. A. Ottoboni), before 1710; Mentre affidan al mar di Cupido; Mentre al sonno chiudea; *Mentre Clori la bella presso un ruscel, S, 2 vn, bc; Mentre Clori la bella sotto l'ombre d'un mirto, S, 2 fl, bc; Mentre da questo monte; Mentre Eurillo fedele [infelice], before 1694; *Mentre in un dolce oblio; Mentre mesto e piangente, A, bc; Mentre sul carro aurato (Clori e Mirtillo), S, A, bc; Mentre un zeffiro altero; Mentre un zeffiro arguto, S/B, 2 vn, bc, ?before 1694

Mesto, lasso e ramingo, June 1704; M'ha divisa il cor dal core (D. A. Ottoboni), A, bc, before 1710; *Mia bella Clori, ascolta; Mia bellissima Clori quando i lumi; Mia Climene adorata se mai occhio, 1710; Mia Dorinda, mia vita, A, bc, 1706; *Mi contento così, T, 2 vn, bc; Mie speranze fallaci; Mi nasce un sospetto (Amante insospettito); *Mio cor, dov'è la bella libertà?, A, vn, bc; Mi parto, Eurilla, a Dio, A, bc; Mira, o Filli, quella rosa (La rosa); Mirtillo, anima mia, già che parti (Partenza), S, 2 vn, bc; Mitilde, addio poichè di nuovo amante; Mitilde, alma mia, se udiste mai, 3 July 1720

Mitilde, anima mia, conforto di mie pene; Mitilde, mio tesor, così veloce; Mitilde, mio tesoro, e dove sei? (Mitilde); Mitilde, oh quanto dolce e lusinghiero; Mi tormenta il pensiero (i), 10 March 1701; Mi tormenta il pensiero (ii) (Amante parlando con il pensiero), A/B, bc; Mondo, non più, lost; Morirei disperato se credessi (Paglia), before 1694; *Mostri, deh non temete; Nacqui a' sospiri e al pianto, S, 2 vn, bc, ? before 1693; Nei languidi respiri; Nel centro oscuro di spelonca; Nel dolce tempo in cui ritorno, 27 May 1712; Nella stagione appunto che il pianeta (Paglia), S, 2 vn, bc

Nella tomba di Gnido (Paglia), S, 2 vn, bc; Nelle arene del Tago, A, bc, 24 July 1698; Nell'estiva stagione; Nel mar che bagna al bel Sebeto il piede, B, bc; Nel mar che bagna a Mergellina il piede; Nel profondo del mio core; Nel sen degl'antri; Nel silentio commune, S, 2 vn, va, bc; Nel suo fido caro nido; Ne' tuoi lumi, o bella Clori (Begl'occhi), 1704; Nice mia, un solo istante; Ninfa crudel, deh vieni, A, bc; Non è come si dice, 20 Aug ?1701; Non è facile ad un core (La catena d'amore), 4 Dec 1704; *Non mi credi, deh perché?; No, non deggio, è troppo cara, 1709; No, non è ver ch'altro amore, 26 Aug 1706

No, non lasciar, canora e bella, 20 Nov 1704; No, non posso fingere (D. A. Ottoboni), before 1710; No, non ti voglio, Cupido, S, A, bc; No, non vorrei vivere fra le catene; Non per pioggia del cielo, 1720; Non più contrasti, no (Amore e rispetto), 6 Oct 1721; Non posso già ne voglio; Non sdegna bella Clori; *Non si parli di ventura; Non so qual più m'ingombra (Cantata pastorale), S, 2 vn, bc, Dec 1716; *Non temo disastri; Non v'è simile al mio core (Paglia), 1v, insts, lost; Notte cara a un cor che langue, 1705; Notte cara, ombre beate, before 1694; Notte ch'in carro d'ombre, S, 2 vn, bc

Notte placida e lieta, 13 Sept 1706; Occhi miei ch'al pianto avvezzi, A, bc; Occhi miei che pagaste, 24 Nov 1705; O che mostro, o che furia (D. A. Ottoboni), 20 July 1709; O che pena è la mia (Fedeltà non creduta), S/A, bc, 1704; *O chi ridir potrebbe?; O Clori, ahi, bella Clori; O come bello con onde chiare (Tirsi e Clori), 2 S, before 1702; O de' pastori diletto stuolo (L'agnellino); O de' regni di Dite Eumenidi spietate; O di fere e d'augelli che ti ricetti; O dolce servitù; *O Fileno, crudele ingrato; O generoso eroe, 17 Dec 1702; Ogni affanno crudele

Oh di Betlemme altera povertà (Cantata pastorale per la nascità di Nostro Signore), S, 2 vn, va, vc, lute; Oh Dio, che viene amore; *Omai dal cielo al più sublime punto; Ombre romite e solitarie piante, S, A, bc; Ombre tacite e sole, S, 2 vn, va, bc, 31 Oct 1716; O Mitilde, fosti meco tiranna, 1711; O Mitilde, o del core, 9 Dec 1708; O pace del mio cor (i), S/A, bc; O pace del mio cor (ii); *O penosa lontananza–O felice lontananza, S, B, bc; Or che a me ritornasti, S/A, bc; Ora che 'l verno riede, A, bc; *Or che barbara sorte; Or ch'in petto d'Eurilla (Eurilla placata)

Or [Hor] che di Febo ascosi, S, 2 vn, bc, 1704; *Or che disciolto è il nodo; Or che di te son privo; Or che di Teti in seno; Or [Hor] che graditi horrori copron del dì (i); Or [Hor] che graditi orrori copron del dì (ii); Or (Hor) che l'aurato Nume, S, 2 vn, bc; Or [Hor] che lungi son io (2 versions); *Or per pietà del mio crudel destino, S, A, bc; O sol degl'occhi miei (D. A. Ottoboni), 31 Dec 1704; O sventurata Olimpia; Ove il fiorito impero mostra; Ove fuor del mio seno (Il sospiro); Ove in grembo a la pace (Desio di solitudine)

Ove placido e cheto; *O v'ingannate a fe'; O voi di queste selve habitatrici, S, 2 vn, bc, 1717; Parla mia pena omai, S/A, bc; Parte da me Cupido; *Pastor d'Arcadia, è morta Clori; Pastorella innamorata; Pastori amici, amiche pastorelle; Peno, e del mio penar (Costanza), 28 Aug 1705; Pensier che in ogni parte, S/A, bc; Pensier che sei inflessibile, 12 Feb 1702; Pensieri, oh Dio, qual pena; Penso che non ho core (Piangi la lontananza della sua donna [bella]), ?1705; *Per celeste bellezza arde il mio cor; Perchè mai, luci amorose?, April 1700; Perchè sospiri, o Niso? (Doralba e Niso), S, A, bc; Perchè tacete, regolati concenti?, A, 2 vn, bc

Perde al vostro confronto, S, 2 vn, bc, ? before 1696; *Per destin d'ingrat' amore, T, bc; Perdono, Amor, perdono (i), A, bc, 6 June ?1702; Perdono, Amor, perdono (ii), 29 Oct 1704; Per farmi amar da tutte (D. A. Ottoboni), before 1710; Perfida Filli ingrata (Costanza), 27 July 1705; *Per formare la bella che adoro (Ritratto di Clori); *Per l'ondoso sentiero, S, 2 vn, bc; Per prova di mia fede, A, bc; Per queste dell'antica Alba famosa; Per saettar un seno (i); Per saettar un seno (ii); Per te, Florida bella, July 1708; Per tormentarmi il core

Per un momento solo (Lo sfortunato), S/A, bc; Per un vago desire (La lezione di musica); *Per un volto di gigli e di rose (probably by Albinoni); Piagge fiorite, ameni prati; Piagge fiorite e amene, io parto, 28 Aug 1716; *Piangea, un dì piangea Fileno, S/A, bc; *Piangete o miei pupille, S, 2 vn, bc; Piangi la tua sventura, 1 July 1706; Piango ogn'ora del mio core; Piango, sospiro, e peno (i); Piango, sospiro, e peno (ii), A, 2 vn, bc, before 1693; Più che penso all'idol mio; Più non risplende, 2S, str, bc, before 1696; Più non si puote amar; Più veggio Lidia e un Tirsi infelice

Poi che cessano al fin; Poi che la bella Clori (Amante schernito), ?1699; *Poi che legge fatal; Poi che l'Ercole argivo (Lisimaco, Re di Traccia); Poi che risceppe Orfeo; *Porto il cor incatenato; Potesse almen, 1v, vn, bc, before 1696, lost; Preparati, o mio core, A, bc; Presso a un limpido fonte (Fileno disingannato), 2 Sept 1706; Presso il balcon dell'incostante Nisa, 15 June 1699; *Pria che desto ai nitriti

spaventati dal ciel; Prima d'esserti infedele (Clori fedele), S, 2 vn, bc; Primavera, sei gentile; Pur al fine la vincesti; Qual bellezza divina?; Quale al gelo s'adugge, 25 Jan 1705

Qualora io veggio la vezzosa Irene, S, 2 vn, bc; *Qualor io vi passeggio; Qualor l'egre pupille; Qualor miro la bella; Qualor tento scoprire (after F. de Lemene), A/B, bc; Quando Amor vuol ferirmi; Quando che ti vedrò; Quando credeva il core, 16 Oct ?1701; *Quando Lidia amorosa; Quando l'umide ninfe, 8 Nov 1704; Quando mai troverò d'Amor nel regno, 7 Jan 1705; Quando satia sarai?; Quando stanche dal pianto; Quando un eroe che s'ama, 2S, bc; Quando veggio un gelsomino; Quante le grazie son, A, bc, 4 June 1703; Quanti affanni ad un core (Pene amorose per lontananza), S/A, bc; Quanto io v'ami o luci, A, bc

*Quanto mi sdegni più; Quanto, o Filli, t'inganni?, 10 March 1701; Quanto piace agl'occhi miei; Quanto vezzosa e quanto adorna; Quel cor ch'a te già diede; Quel Fileno infelice, 24 Sept 1705; Quella che chiudo in sen fiamma amorosa, 25 Feb 1705; Quella pace gradita, S, fl, vn, vc, bc; Quel pastor si gentile, S, 2 vn, bc (inc.); Quel piacer che nell'amarti, 26 Oct 1704; Quel ruscelletto, o Clori; Questa, quest'è la selva, S/A, bc; Questa vermiglia rosa, 30 Jan 1705; Quest'è il giardin felice; Queste torbide e meste onde, 1717; Questo di bei giacinti serto, S/A, bc

Questo silenzio ombroso (Il sonno), S, A, or 2S, bc, 17 Sept 1707; Qui dove alfin m'assido (Il rosignuolo); Qui dove a piè d'un colle; Qui dove aure ed augelli, 15 Jan 1705; *Qui dove in aspre balze, A, bc; Qui vieni, ingrata Fille; *Radamisto, è portento che Zenobia; Regie soglie, alte moli, 18 Oct 1720; *Ritardati momenti, egre dimore (published in G. B. Bassani's op.3, 1682); Rondinella torna al lido (i), 1701; Rondinella torna al lido (ii); S'accinge Eurillo al canto; Sanno, o Filli adorata, 24 Aug 1716; Sarà pur vero, o stelle?; Sarei troppo felice (Pamphili), 30 April ?1701; Sazio di più soffrire, S/B, bc; *Scherza col onda del caro lido; Sciolgo in lagrime amare; Sciolta da freddi amplessi (Marito vecchio, sposa giovane), 1 May 1704

Scompagnata tortorella (La tortorella); Scorgo il fiume e scorgo il rio (La primavera), S/A, bc, 8 June 1704; Scuote di fronte all'Appennin nevoso; *Sdegno fiero ed amore; Se a goder torna il mio core; Se amassi da dovero (L'infedeltà); Se amor con un contento; Se a quel fiero dolor (L'amante non corrisposto lascia d'amare), S/A, bc; *Se credete all'amor mio; *Se dalla cruda Irene, A/S, bc; Se d'Elisa spietate il bel sembiante; Sedeva Eurilla un giorno (Esagerationi d'Eurilla) (Paglia); Se mai Clori gentile; *Se nell'amar Coriste

Senti, bella crudele; Senti, bell'idol mio (Bella donna prega ad essere amata), 1705; *Sentite, o tronchi, o sassi, S/A, bc, before 1715; Sento nel core certo dolore (S'allontana per non innamorarsi), S/A, bc; Senz'alma, senza cor; *Se per amor quest'alma; Serba il mio cor costante; *Se tu parti io morirò (published in G. B. Bassani's op.2, 1680); Se vagheggio nel mattino, 1709; Siamo in contesa la bellezza ed io (Pamphili), 4 May ?1701; Sì, conosco, o Mitilde; Siete unite a tormentarmi, A, 2 vn, bc; Silenzio, aure volanti, S, 2 vn, bc; S'io t'amo, s'io t'adoro, June 1704; Sì, t'intendo, tu vuoi ch'io non pensi (Non può scordarsi della sua dama), S/A, bc

So che non lice, 1v, bc, before 1696, lost; Solitudini amene, apriche collinette, S, fl, bc; Solitudini amene, bersaglio d'empia sorte, 15 April 1705; Solitudini care, in voi spera; Son contenta di soffrire; Son io, barbara donna, A, bc; Son le nere pupillette, A, bc, 12 March 1702; Sono amante e m'arde il core, A, bc, before 1694; Sono un alma tormentata; *Son pur care le catene, S, A, bc; Son quest'ultimi momenti (Cantata di lontananza), S/A, bc, before 1714; Sopra le verdi sponde che la Brenta, before 1694; Sopra le verdi sponde del Sebeto, 2 Feb 1712; Sorge l'alba; Sorta fin da le piume, 8 Jan 1702; Sotto l'ombra d'un faggio, piangente e sospirante, B, vn, bc; Sotto l'ombra d'un faggio, sul margine d'un rivo (Paglia), S, 2 vn, bc; Sovente amor mi chiama, A, bc; Sovra carro stellato, S, 2 vn, bc; Sovra il margine erboso; Sovra questi fecondi ameni colli, 3 Nov 1704; Speranze mie, addio, Mez, bc, 1694; Spero ch'havrò la pace (D. A. Ottoboni), before 1710; *Spesso suol l'alma mia (Amore e gelosia); Spiega l'ali il mio pensiero (Lontananza), ?1702; Splendeano in bel sembiante, B, bc; *Stanca l'afflitta Clori, S/A, bc; Stanco di più soffrire a voi ritorno; Sta presente il mio tesoro

Strali, facelle, amore, A, bc; Stravagante è l'amor (Fileno amante di Clori, Irene, e Nice), 1720; Stravagante non è l'amore, 1720; *Stravaganza d'amore accade in noi (Paglia); Su bel seggio di fiori, 21 May 1705; Su la morbida erbetta, lost; Su la sponda del mare (L'Olimpia), S, 2 vn, va, bc; *Su la sponda fiorita di limpido ruscello, 20 Aug ?1718; Su la sponda fiorita d'un rio pargoleggiante (L'Adone); Su le fiorite sponde di un vago ruscelletto, 2 Aug 1712; Su le rive dell'Elba; Su le sponde d'Abbido (Il Leandro), 1693; Su le sponde del Reno

Su le sponde del Tebro, S, 2 vn, tpt, bc; Sul margine d'un rio dove l'onde fugaci (Elpino tradito), S/A, bc; Sul margine d'un rivo cui facevan ricamo, S, 2 vn, bc; Sul margine fiorito d'un limpido [tumido] ruscello, 4 Dec 1704; *Sul margine fiorito d'un placido torrente; Sul l'ora appunto che col carro d'oro (La fenice), S, 2 vn, bc, 1703; Sventurati miei pensieri; Taccio e tacendo moro, A, bc; Taci, infedele [infelice] amore, 1720; Talor per suo diletto, 28 April ?1718; Tanti affanni e tante pene, April 1697; Tanto strano è l'amor mio, April 1697; Temo d'amarti poco

Tenebrose foreste erme; *The Beautious Melissa; Tiranna ingrata, che far dovrò?, B, 2 vn, bc; *Tiranno di mia fe'; *Tirsi, mentr'io dormiva; Tirsi pastore amante (Pastorello innamorato che va in traccia della sua ninfa), S, 2 vn, bc; Ti vorrei credere speranza; Tormentatemi pur, furie d'amore, S/A, bc; Torna al sen dolce mia pace; Torna il giorno fatale (Anniversario amoroso) (?Pamphili), ?S, bc, June 1710, lost; Tra le pompe fiorite, A, bc; *Tra l'ombre più secrette; Tra queste ombrose piagge, 1709; Tra solitarie balze; Tra speranza e timore, B, vn, bc; Tra verdi piante ombrose

Troppo care, troppo belle (Amante contento); Troppo ingrata Amaranta; Troppo oppressa dal sonno; Tu che una dea rassembri, S, 2 vn, bc; Tu mi chiedi s'io t'amo, 5 Feb 1709; Tu mi lasciasti, o bella, April 1698; Tu parti, idolo amato (i) (Cantata di lontananza), S/A, bc, 1702; Tu parti, idolo amato (ii) (Amante che parte a bella donna che resta), 21 April 1706; Tu resti, o mio bel nume (i), B, 2 vn, bc; Tu resti, o mio bel nume (ii) bc; *Tra l'ombre più secrette; Tra queste resta), 22 April 1706; Tu sei quella che al nome (Bella dama di nome santa), A, 2 vn, fl, bc

*Tutto acceso d'amore, S/A, bc; Udite, o selve, o fiume; Una beltà ch'eguale (Amante sventurato); Un cervello frenetico ch'amò; Un di Tirsi l'amante; Un giorno Amor la benda si disciolse, 1709; Un incredula speranza; Un sol guardo di Clori, A, bc; Un sospiro d'un amante (La luccioletta) (Pamphili); Un spietato destino, A, bc; Un Tantalo assetato; Vaga Elisa, la tua rimembranza, June 1708; Vaghe selve beate (Mitilde ritirata in solitudine); Vaghe tende adorate; Vaghe fonti di luce (Occhi neri); Vago il ciel non saria; Va pur lungi da me, 8 Oct 1704

Vedi, Eurilla, quel fior (Cantata per camera per l'ecc.mo Duca di Maddaloni), S, 2 vn, va, bc, Jan 1725; Vedi, Fille, quel sasso; Veggio l'idolo mio; Venite, amici, e con ghirlande (G. Ansaldi); Venne ad amor desio, 29 April 1705; . . . ver per un diletto ma senza amor (inc.); Vi comanda un cenno solo (D. A. Ottoboni), before 1710; *Viddi un giorno un fiumicello; Vieni, o caro Mirtillo, A, bc, June 1708; *Viva, viva mia libertà, 2S, bc; Voi ben sapete, o di romito bosco

*Voi che dell'alma mia havete il vanto, lost; Voi dell'idolo mio care treccie, A, bc; Voi giungeste, o vaghi fiori (I fiori), A, bc; *Voi mi dite tu sei bella; Vola, Cupido, dal cor mio fido, ? before 1696; *Vo narrando a quel ruscello; Vorrei, Filli adorata, farti palese, S/A, bc, 21 Nov 1705; *Vuoi che mora incenerito; Vuoi ch'io spiri tra i sospiri (Amante desideroso di morire per liberarsi dall'amore), 20 Sept 1699; Vuoi più, Filli crudele? A, bc; *Zeffiretti che spirate, A, bc; Zeffiretto che indrizzi il tuo volo, 14 Dec 1702

MADRIGALS

Arsi un tempo e l'ardore, SSATB, A-Wgm
Cor mio, deh, non languire, SSSSA, D-Bds, Mbs, MÜs, GB-Cfm, Lbm, T, I-Bc, Gi(l), Nc, Rc, USSR-KA
Intenerite voi, lacrime mie (O. Rinuccini), SATTB, GB-Lbm
Mori, mi dici, SSATB, I Nc
O morte, agli altri fosca, a me serena, SSATB, A-Wgm
Or che da te, mio bene, SATB, I-Nc
O selve, o tigre, o ninfa, SSATB, GB-Lbm
Sdegno la fiamma estinse, SSATB, Lbm

MASSES, MASS MOVEMENTS
(complete sources only)

Missa Clementina (i), SSATB, Rome, Dec 1705, A-Wn, B-Br, D-Bds, DS, Mbs, MÜs, SWl, GB-Cfm, Lbm, I Fc, Rvat, USSR-KA
Messa a quattro voci, SATB, Rome, 1706, D-MÜs, F-Pc, GB-Lbm, I-Rf, Rvat
Messa per il natale di Nostro Signore Gesù Cristo, SSATB, SATB, 2 vn, bc, Rome, 1707, lost
Missa Clementina (ii), SSATB, Rome, 1716, D-Bds, Mbs, I-Mc, Nc, Rvat
Missa pro defunctis, SATB, 1717, B-Bc, D-Bds, Mbs, MÜs, F-Pc, †I-BGi
Messa di S Cecilia, S, S, A, T, B, SSATB, 2 vn, va, bc, Rome, Oct 1720, Rc; ed. J. Steele (London, 1968)
Missa ad usum cappellae pontificiae, SATB, 1721, F-Pc, GB-Lbm, I-Rsc
Missa ad canonem, SATB, A-Wn, D-Bds, MÜs, F-Pc, I-Nc
Messa in IV tono, SSATB, org, D-MÜs
Messa tutta in canone di diverse specie, SSATB, A-Wn, D-Bds, F-Pc, GB-Cfm, Lbm, Fc
*Credo, S, A, T, B, SATB, 2 ob, 2 hn, str, org, Nc
*Credo breve, SATB, 2 vn, bc, F-Pn
*Gloria, SATB, 2 vn, va, 2 ob, 2 hn, bc, D-Dkh, Dl

MOTETS

Concerti sacri, motetti . . . e Salve regina, 1–4vv (Amsterdam, 1707–8; Naples, 1702, lost, as Motetti sacri, 1–4vv, vns, op.2) [CS]

Ad amantem cordis, S, 2 vn, bc, I-Nf
Ad Dominum dum tribularer, SATTB, ?1708, Baf, US-U
Adorna thalamum tuum Sion, SATTB, Jan 1708, D-MÜs, GB-Lbm
Ad te Domine levavi, SATTB, ?1708, I-Baf, US-U
Audi filia, et inclina aurem, SSATB, ob, 2 vn, va, org, Oct 1720, †I-Rc; ed. J. Steele (London, 1968)
Ave maris stella, SATB, bc, D-Bds, I-Nc
Ave regina coelorum, SS, bc, 1722, Nc
Beatus vir qui timet, SSATB, org, D-MÜs
Benedicta et venerabilis es, S, SATB, 2 vn, va, bc, 4 July 1720, MÜs

Cantantibus organis Cecilia, S, ob, 2 vn, va, bc, Oct 1720
Caro mea vere est cibus, STB, org, 31 Dec 1707, I-Rvat
Confitebor tibi Domine, SSATB, org, D-MÜs
Constitues eos principes, SAB, org, 1716, MÜs
Date sonum, date cantum, S, bc, 24 Nov 1705, I-Nf
De tenebroso lacu, A, 2 vn, va, bc, GB-Lbm
Dextera Domini fecit virtutem, SSB, org, 1715, A-Wn, D-MÜs, US-U
Diffusa est gratia, SS, org, D-MÜs
Diligam te, SAT, 2 vn, bc, CS
Dixit Dominus (i), SSATB, org, Dl, MÜs
Dixit Dominus (ii), SSATB, ob, 2 vn, va, bc, I-Mc
Dixit Dominus (iii), SSATB, org, D-MÜs
Dixit Dominus (iv), S, A, T, B, SATB, 3 vn, bc, I-Mc
Domine in auxilium meum, SATB, ?1708, Baf, US-U
Domine refugium factus es nobis, SSATB, A-Wn, D-Mbs, MÜs
Domine vivifica me, SATB, ?1708, I-Baf, US-U
Egli è ver che mi consolo, A, bc, 24 Nov 1705, I-Nf
Est dies trophei, SATB, 2 vn, bc, CS
Exaltabo te Domine quoniam, SATB, ?1708, Baf, US-U
Exultate Deo adjutori, SATB, A-Wn, D-Dl, Mbs, MÜs, I-Baf, Nc
Exurge Domine non prevaleat, SATB, ?1708, I-Baf, US-U
Infirmata, vulnerata, A, 2 vn, bc, I-Nf (dated 16 Oct 1702), CS
In hoc mundo inconstante, S, 2 vn, bc, 24 Nov 1705, Nf
Inni e Improperi per la Missa Praesanctificatorum della Parasceve, S, A, SATB, 2 vn, bc, Florence, ?1708: Vexilla regis prodeunt (even-numbered verses); Popule meus; Crux fidelis–Pange lingua gloriosi; Vexilla regis prodeunt (odd-numbered verses): Baf
Intellige clamorem meum, SATB, ?1708, Baf, US-U
Iste est panis, SATB, D-MÜs (inc.)
Jam sole clarior, S, 2 vn, bc, GB-Lcm, CS
Jesu corona virginum, S, A, T, SATB, 2 vn, va, bc, Oct 1720, †I-PLcon, Rsc
Justitiae Domini rectae, SATB, ?1708, Baf, US-U
Laetatus sum (i), SATB, A-Wn, D-Mbs, GB-Lbm
Laetatus sum (ii), SATB, I-Rc (inc.)
Laetatus sum (iii), SATB, 2 vn, bc, 1688, Nf
Laetatus sum (iv), SSATB, 2 vn, va, bc, Aug 1721, †D-Bds
Lamentazioni per la Settimana Santa, Florence, ?1708: Incipit lamentatio Jeremiae prophetae, S, 2 vn, va, bc; Jod–Manum suam misit hostis, S, 2 vn, va, bc; De lamentatione Jeremiae prophetae, S, 2 vn, va, bc; Lamed–Matribus suis dixerunt, S, 2 vn, va, bc; De lamentatione Jeremiae prophetae, S, 2 vn, bc; Aleph–Quomodo obscuratum est, T, 2 vn, bc: I-Baf
Lauda Jerusalem Dominum, SATB, org, D-MÜs
Laudate Dominum omnes gentes, SATTB, 2 vn, 2 va, vc, bc, Bds, MÜs
Laudate Dominum quia benignus, SSB, org, MÜs
Laudate pueri Dominum (i), SSATB, bc, Dl, MÜs
Laudate pueri Dominum (ii), S, SATB, 2 vn, bc, MÜs (inc.)
Magnificat (i), primo tono, SSATB, org, MÜs
Magnificat (ii), D, SSATB, insts, MÜs (inc.)
Memento, Domine, David, SATB, Bds, Dl, Mbs, MÜs, F-Pc, GB-Lbm, T, I-Bc, Mc, †Nc
Miserere mei Deus, miserere, SATB, Baf
Miserere mei Deus, secundum (i), SATB, SSATB, 1680, Rvat
Miserere mei Deus, secundum (ii), e, S, SSATB, 2 vn, va, bc, 1705, D-Bds, MÜs, I-Baf, US-U
Miserere mei Deus, secundum (iii), c, SSATB, 2 vn, va, bc, ?1715, D-Bds, MÜs, I-Baf, US-U
*Miserere mei Deus, secundum (iv), a, SATB, bc, 1721, BE
Mortales non auditis, S, A, 2 vn, bc, CS
Nisi Dominus aedificaverit (i), S, A, SATB, 2 vn, bc, A-Wn, D-Bds, Dl, GB-Lbm
Nisi Dominus aedificaverit (ii), SATB, org, D-MÜs
O magnum mysterium, SATB, SATB, 1707, Dl, MÜs
Properate fideles, SATB, 2 vn, bc, CS
Quae est ista, SAT, 2 vn, bc, CS
[27] Responsori per la Settimana Santa, S, A, T, B, SATB, bc, Florence, ?1708: Aestimatus sum; Amicus meus; Animam meam dilectam; Astiterunt reges terrae; Caligaverunt oculi mei; Ecce quomodo moritur; Ecce vidimus eum; Eram quasi agnus; Ierusalem surge; In Monte Oliveti; Jesum tradidit impius; Judas mercator pessimus; Omnes amici mei; O vos omnes; Plange quasi virgo; Recessit pastor noster; Seniores populi; Sepulto Domino; Sicut ovis; Tamquam ad latronem; Tenebrae factae sunt; Tradiderunt me; Tristis est anima mea; Una hora; Unus ex discipulis; Velum templi; Vinea mea electa: I-Baf
Rorate coeli dulcem, S, 2 vn, bc, GB-Lcm, CS
Sacerdotes Domini incensum et panes, SAT, org, A-Wn, D-MÜs, US-U
Salve regina (i), SA, 2 vn, bc, I-Mc, Nc
Salve regina (ii), SATB, Feb 1703, A-Wn
Salve regina (iii), S, 3 vn, bc, I-Nf
Salve regina (iv), SATB, 2 vn, bc, B-Br, D-Mbs, F-Pn, CS
Salve regina (v), S, 2 vn, va, bc, D-Mbs
Salvum fac populum tuum, SATB, ?1708, I-Baf
Sancti et justi in Domino gaudete, SATB, SATB, D-MÜs (inc.)
Spirate, aure, spirate, A, 2 vn, bc, I-Nf
Stabat mater, SA, 2 vn, bc, Fc, Rsc
Super solium gemmis ornatum, S, 2 vn, bc, Nf

Te Deum, SSATB, 2 ob, 2 vn, va, bc, *Rc*
Totus amore languens, A, 2 vn, bc, *CS*
Tu es Petrus, SATB, SATB, org, *A-Wn*, (?†)*B-Bc*, *D-Bds*, Singakademie, Berlin, *Dl*, *Mbs*, *MÜs*, †*DK-Kk*, *F-Pc*, *GB-Cfm*, *Lbm*, *T*, *I-Bc*, *Mc*, *Nc*, *USSR-KA*
Tui sunt coeli et terra, SSB, org, *A-Wn*, *D-MÜs*, *US-U*
Unam petii a Domino, SATB, ?1708, *I-Baf*
Valerianus in cubiculo, A, ob, 2 vn, va, bc
*Veritas mea et misericordia, SATB, *D-MÜs*
Vexilla regis prodeunt, SS, 2 vn, bc, †*I-MOe*
Volo Pater ut ubi ego sum, SATB, SATB, org, *D-MÜs*

KEYBOARD

Toccate per cembalo, *I-MC*
Dieci partite sopra basso obbligato, 1716, *D-MÜs*, *I-Nc*
Primo e secondo libro di toccate (G, a, G, a, G, d, d, a, G, F), *A-Wn*, *I-Nc*
Due sinfonie per cembalo, 16 June 1699, *D-MÜs*
Toccata per studio di cembalo, 1716, *I-Nc*
Toccata d'intavolatura per cembalo ò pure per organo d'ottava stesa, *PLcon*
Tre toccate, ognuna seguita da fuga e minuetto, 1716, *Nc*
Variations on 'La follia', 1715, *GB-Lbm*
Other keyboard works in *D-MÜs*, *GB-Lbm*, *I-Gi(l)*, *Mc*, *MOe*, *Nc*, *Tn*, *Tci*, *Rsc*, *US-NH*

OTHER INSTRUMENTAL

12 sinfonie di concerto grosso, begun 1 June 1715, †*GB-Lbm*: F, 2 vn, va, vc, 2 fl, bc; D, 2 vn, va, vc, fl, tpt, bc; d, 2 vn, va, vc, fl, bc; e, 2 vn, va, vc, fl, ob/vn, bc; d, 2 vn, va, vc, 2 fl, bc; a, 2 vn, va, vc, fl, bc; g, 2 vn, va, vc, fl, bc; G, 2 vn, va, vc, fl, bc; g, 2 vn, va, vc, fl, bc; a, 2 vn, va, vc, fl, bc; C, 2 vn, va, vc, fl, bc; c, 2 vn, va, vc, fl, bc
VI Concertos in Seven Parts (London, *c*1740) (f, c, F, g, d, E), 2 solo vn, solo vc, 2 vn, va, bc, *D-Bds*, *GB-Cu*, *Ob*, *I-Rsc*, *US-NYp*
*Six Concertos for Keyboard and Orchestra (C, A, e, c, G, E♭), *GB-Lbm* (inc.)
Quattro sonate a quattro (f, c, g, d), 2 vn, va, vc, *D-MÜs*, *F-Pc*
Sette sonate per flauto e archi (D, a, c, a, A, C, g), fl, 2 vn, va, vc, bc, 1725, *I-Nc*
Sonata (F), fl, 2 vn, bc, *D-MÜs*
*Sonata (D), fl, 2 vn, bc, *I-Bc*
Sonata (A), 2 fl, 2 vn, bc, *D-MÜs*
Sonata (F), 3 fl, bc, *MÜs*
Suite (F), fl, bc, 16 June 1699, *MÜs*
Suite (G), fl, bc, June 1699, *MÜs*

THEORETICAL AND PEDAGOGICAL

Regole per principianti, *c*1715, *GB-Lbm*, *I-MC*
Discorso sopra un caso particolare in aprile 1717, lost; Ger. trans. in J. P. Kirnberger, *Die Kunst des reinen Satzes in der Musik* (Berlin and Königsberg, 1776–9), ii, 143
Canons: Tenta la fuga ma la tenta invano, *NT*; Voi sola, 3S, *GB-Y*; Commincio solo, 3S, *Y*; 2 canons a 2, *Lbm*
15 fugues a 2, *I-Nc*, *Ria*
Studio a quattro sulla nota ferma, *GB-Lbm*
Varie partite obligate al basso, *I-MC*
Varie introduttioni per sonare e mettersi in tono delle compositioni, ?1715, *GB-Lbm*

BIBLIOGRAPHY

BurneyH
G. M. Crescimbeni: *L'arcadia*, vii, prosa V (Rome, 1711)
G. Grossi: *Biografia degli uomini illustri del Regno di Napoli* (Naples, 1819)
F. Florimo: *La scuola musicale di Napoli e i suoi conservatorii*, ii (Naples, 1882/*R*1969)
E. J. Dent: 'The Operas of Alessandro Scarlatti', *SIMG*, iv (1902–3), 143
——: 'The Earliest String Quartets', *MMR*, xxxiii (1903), 202
——: 'Alessandro Scarlatti', *PMA*, xxx (1903–4), 77
J. S. Shedlock: 'The Harpsichord Music of Alessandro Scarlatti', *SIMG*, vi (1904–5), 160, 418
E. J. Dent: *Alessandro Scarlatti: his Life and Works* (London, 1905, rev. 2/1960 with additions by F. Walker)
G. Piccini ['Jarro']: 'Alessandro Scarlatti; studio aneddotico su documenti originali', *La lettura*, xiv (1914), 929
H. Junker: 'Zwei Griselda Opern', *Festschrift zum 50. Geburtstag Adolf Sandberger* (Munich, 1918), 51
C. van den Borren: *Alessandro Scarlatti et l'esthétique de l'opéra napolitain* (Brussels and Paris, 1921)
P. Strüver: *Die Cantata da camera Alessandro Scarlattis* (diss., U. of Munich, 1923)
U. Prota-Giurleo: *Alessandro Scarlatti 'il Palermitano'* (Naples, 1926)
A. Lorenz: 'Alessandro Scarlattis Opern und Wien', *ZMw*, ix (1926–7), 86
——: *Alessandro Scarlaitis Jugendoper* (Augsburg, 1927)
A. Bonaventura: 'El Stabat Mater de Alessandro Scarlatti', *Revista de musica*, ii (1928), 145
A. Cametti: 'Carlo Sigismondo Capeci (1652–1728), Alessandro e Domenico Scarlatti e la Regina di Polonia a Roma', *Musica d'oggi*, xiii (1931), 55

P. Dotto: 'Gaspare Alessandro Scarlatti il Palermitano', *Musica d'oggi*, xvii (1935), 383
U. Rolandi: 'Il 'Cain', sconosciuto oratorio di Alessandro Scarlatti', *NA*, xiii (1936), 176
D. de' Paoli: '*Diana ed Endimione* di Alessandro Scarlatti', *RaM*, xiii (1940), 139
C. Sartori: 'Il *Dafni* di Alessandro Scarlatti', *RMI*, xlv (1941), 176
——: '*Dori* e *Arione*, due opere ignorate di Alessandro Scarlatti', *NA*, xviii (1941), 35
E. Zanetti: '*Gli inganni felici* in una sconosciuta raccolta di arie di Alessandro Scarlatti', *RaM*, xiv (1941), 416
C. Sartori: 'Gli Scarlatti a Napoli', *RMI*, xlvi (1942), 374
E. J. Dent: 'A Pastoral Opera by Alessandro Scarlatti', *MR*, xii (1951), 7
U. Prota-Giurleo: 'Breve storia del teatro di corte e della musica a Napoli nei secoli XVII e XVIII', *Il teatro di corte del Palazzo reale di Napoli* (Naples, 1952), 19–146
E. Hanley: 'Current Chronicle', *MQ*, xxxix (1953), 241 [on the *St John Passion*]
R. G. Pauly: 'Alessandro Scarlatti's *Tigrane*', *ML*, xxxv (1954), 339
L. Ronga: 'Motivi critici su Alessandro Scarlatti', *RMI*, lvi (1954), 125
L. Montalto: *Un mecenate in Roma barocca* (Florence, 1955)
J. A. Bank: 'De kerkmuziek van Alessandro Scarlatti', *St Gregoriusblad*, lxxx (1956)
L. Ronga: *Arte e gusto nella musica* (Milan and Naples, 1956), 92–126
C. Sartori: 'Una Arianna misconosciuta: La Laodice di A. Scarlatti', *La Scala* (1956), no.79, p.4
J. Edmunds: 'Chamber Cantatas: the Mastery of Alessandro Scarlatti', *Tempo* (1956–7), no.42, p.24
G. Confalonieri: 'Nota su *Varrone e Pericca* di Alessandro Scarlatti', *Immagini esotiche nella musica italiana*, Chigiana, xiv (1957)
A. Liess: 'Materialien zur römischen Musikgeschichte des Seicento', *AcM*, xxix (1957), 137–71
A. Garbelotto: 'Alessandro Scarlatti', *Archivio storico siciliano*, 3rd ser., x (1959), 239
A. Liess: 'Die Sammlung der Oratorienlibretti (1679–1725) und der restliche Musikbestand des Fondo San Marcello der Biblioteca Vaticana in Rom', *AcM*, xxxi (1959), 63
P. Taylor Lee: *The Keyboard Style of Alessandro Scarlatti* (diss., Yale U., 1959)
M. Fabbri: 'Le musiche di Alessandro Scarlatti "per il tempo di penitenza e di tenebre" ', *I grandi anniversari del 1960 e la musica sinfonica e da camera nell'Ottocento in Italia*, Chigiana, xvii (1960), 17
G. A. Pastore: 'Nuove cantate di Alessandro Scarlatti', *Il San Carlo* (Naples, 1960), 32
Celebrazione del terzo centenario della nascita di Alessandro Scarlatti (n.p., 1960) [RAI publication]
M. Fabbri: *Alessandro Scarlatti e il Principe Ferdinando de' Medici* (Florence, 1961)
R. Pagano: 'Alexander Scarlatti, civitatis Panormi', *Conservatorio di musica Vincenzo Bellini, Palermo, annuario 1960–61* (1962), 11
A. Garbelotto: 'Contributo per un catalogo aggiornato delle opere di Alessandro Scarlatti', *Archivio storico siciliano*, 3rd ser., xiii (1963), 239–344
E. Hanley: *Alessandro Scarlatti's Cantate da Camera: a Bibliographical Study* (diss., Yale U., 1963)
——: 'Scarlatti, Alessandro', *MGG*
O. M. Henry: *The Doctrine of Affections in Selected Solo Cantatas of Alessandro Scarlatti* (diss., Ohio State U., 1963)
C. Terni: 'Stile e armonie di Alessandro Scarlatti per un dramma liturgico', *Le celebrazioni del 1963 e alcune nuove indagini sulla musica italiana del XVIII e XIX secolo*, Chigiana, xx (1963), 115–54
M. Boyd: 'Form and Style in Scarlatti's Chamber Cantatas', *MR*, xxv (1964), 17
C. R. Morey: *The Late Operas of Alessandro Scarlatti* (diss., Indiana U., 1965)
M. Fabbri: 'Torna alla luce la partitura autografa dell'oratorio *Il primo omicidio* di Alessandro Scarlatti', *Chigiana*, xxiii (1966), 245
U. Kirkendale: 'The Ruspoli Documents on Handel', *JAMS*, xx (1967), 222–73
L. Bettarini: 'Appunti critici sulle Sette sonate per flauto e archi di Alessandro Scarlatti', *Chigiana*, xxv (1968), 239
D. J. Grout: 'La *Griselda* di Zeno e il libretto dell'opera di Alessandro Scarlatti', *NRMI*, ii (1968), 207
J. López-Calo: 'L'intervento di Alessandro Scarlatti nella controversia sulla Messa Scala aretina di Francisco Valls', *AnMc*, no.5 (1968), 178
H. J. Marx: 'Die Musik am Hofe Pietro Cardinal Ottobonis unter Arcangelo Corelli', *AnMc*, no.5 (1968), 104–77
D. J. Poultney: *The Oratorios of Alessandro Scarlatti: their Lineage, Milieu, and Style* (diss., U. of Michigan, 1968)
B. Trowell: 'Scarlatti and Griselda', *MT*, cix (1968), 527
J. A. Westrup: 'Alessandro Scarlatti's *Il Mitridate Eupatore* (1707)', *New Looks at Italian Opera: Essays in Honor of Donald J. Grout* (Ithaca, 1968), 133
L. Bianchi: *Carissimi, Stradella, Scarlatti e l'oratorio musicale* (Rome, 1969)

P. Brandvik: *Selected Motets of Alessandro Scarlatti* (diss., U. of Illinois, 1969)

M. Boyd: 'Scarlatti's *La Statira*', *MT*, cxi (1970), 495

J. E. Shaffer: *The Cantus Firmus in Alessandro Scarlatti's Motets* (diss., George Peabody College for Teachers, Nashville, 1970)

P. R. Piersall: *The Bass Cantatas of Alessandro Scarlatti* (diss., U. of Oregon, 1971)

A. Mondolfi Bossarelli: 'Riesumazione di uno sconosciuto Scarlatti', *Conservatorio di musica S. Pietro a Majella, annuario 1965–1971* (Naples, n.d.), 37

R. Pagano, L. Bianchi and G. Rostirolla: *Alessandro Scarlatti* (Turin, 1972) [reviewed by R. Strohm, *RIM*, xi (1976)]

G. Pestelli: 'Haendel e Alessandro Scarlatti: problemi di attribuzione nel MS A.7b.63 della biblioteca del Conservatorio "Nicolo Paganini" di Genova', *RIM*, vii (1972), 103

G. Rose: 'Two Operas by Scarlatti Recovered', *MQ*, lviii (1972), 420

E. H. Alton: 'The Recorder Music of Alessandro Scarlatti (1660–1725)', *Recorder and Music Magazine*, iv (1973), 199

M. Fabbri: 'Il dolore e la morte nelle *voci in solitudine* di Alessandro Scarlatti', *Scritti in onore di Luigi Ronga* (Milan and Naples, 1973), 127

J. Jürgens: 'Die Madrigale Alessandro Scarlattis und ihre Quellen', *Scritti in onore di Luigi Ronga* (Milan and Naples, 1973), 279

E. Krist: 'Alessandro Scarlatti's *Messa di Santa Cecilia*', *American Choral Review*, xv (1973), 3

G. Pestelli: 'Le toccate per strumento a tastiera di Alessandro Scarlatti nei manoscritti napoletani', *AnMc*, no.12 (1973), 169

D. Poultney: 'Alessandro Scarlatti and the Transformation of Oratorio', *MQ*, lix (1973), 584

J. Steele: '*Dixit Dominus*: Alessandro Scarlatti and Handel', *SMA*, vii (1973), 19

E. Badura-Skoda: 'Ein Aufenthalt Alessandro Scarlattis in Wien im Oktober 1681', *Mf*, xxvii (1974), 204

D. J. Grout: 'The Original Version of Alessandro Scarlatti's *Griselda*', *Essays on Opera and English Music in Honour of Sir Jack Westrup* (Oxford, 1975), 103

Colloquium Alessandro Scarlatti: Würzburg 1975

R. Strohm: 'Hasse, Scarlatti, Rolle', *AnMc*, no.15 (1975), 221–57

——: 'Italienische Opernarien des frühen Settecento (1720–1730)', *AnMc*, no.16 (1976) [whole vol.]

M. T. Inkeles: *A Study, Realization, and Performance of Unpublished Cantatas for Soprano and Basso Continuo ca. 1690–1706 of Alessandro Scarlatti* (diss., Columbia U. Teachers College, 1977)

H. E. Smither: *A History of the Oratorio*, i: *The Oratorio in the Baroque Era: Italy, Vienna, Paris* (Chapel Hill, 1977)

D. J. Grout: *Alessandro Scarlatti: an Introduction to his Operas* (Berkeley, 1979)

C. K. Van de Kamp Freund: *Alessandro Scarlatti's Duet Cantatas and Solo Cantatas with Obbligato Instruments* (diss., Northwestern U., Evanston, 1979)

(2) Anna Maria Scarlatti (*b* Palermo, 8 Dec 1661; *d* Naples, 1 Dec 1703). Singer, sister of (1) Alessandro Scarlatti. She went to Rome in June 1672 with Alessandro and her younger sister (3) Melchiorra; both girls became singers. For many years Anna Maria was blamed for causing difficulties for Alessandro, about 1679, through her scandalous life in Rome (the *Avisi di Roma* reported on 15 February 1679 that Alessandro Scarlatti was 'in very bad odour with the court of the Vicar on account of the secret marriage of his sister with an ecclesiastic'); but it is possible (see Walker, *MR*, xii, 1951) that the culprit was Melchiorra. In 1680 Anna Maria was in Venice, where she sang in Agostini's *Il ratto delle sabine*. According to a statement by Alessandro, Anna Maria remained in Rome when he moved to Naples in 1684; she was then married to Paolo Massonio Astro Lusco, who joined the imperial army in 1685 as Uditore and died in a battle against the Turks in Hungary in 1687. In 1699 Anna Maria married the Neapolitan shipowner Nicolo Barbapiccola, who afterwards became impresario of the Teatro S Bartolomeo in Naples (1703–4) and staged (7) Domenico Scarlatti's first operas; their daughter Giuseppina Eleonora (*b* 1700) was an amateur musician and a pupil of Jommelli. In her will, written after her husband's death, Anna Maria authorized Alessandro to take charge of her two children and her belongings, a will which later caused a difficult lawsuit.

(3) Melchiorra Brigida Scarlatti (*b* Palermo, 5 Oct 1663; *d* Naples, 2 Dec 1736). Singer, sister of (1) Alessandro Scarlatti. She went to Rome in June 1672 and was trained as a singer. Though it is not clear whether she caused the scandal in Rome referred to above (see (2) Anna Maria), it is known that she went to Naples in 1682 with other opera singers and actors and probably became the mistress of Don Giovanni de Leone, Secretary of Justice to the viceroy. Through her influence Alessandro was appointed *maestro di cappella* of the royal chapel in February 1684. The Neapolitan chronicler Domenico Conforto reported that the viceroy, on hearing of the affair, dismissed de Leone and two other employees who were involved with 'putane comedianti' and demanded that the ladies either leave Naples or live in a convent, whereupon Melchiorra retired to S Antoniello. In 1688 she married Nicola Pagano (1659–1722), a double bass player at the royal chapel. In May 1708 her husband rented the Teatro dei Fiorentini for six years, but was so unsuccessful that his financial supporters replaced him in 1709 and appointed another impresario.

(4) Francesco (Antonio Nicola) Scarlatti (*b* Palermo, 5 Dec 1666; *d* ?after 1741). Composer, brother of (1) Alessandro Scarlatti. He went to Naples, probably in 1672, to study at one of the conservatories. In 1684, when Alessandro was appointed *maestro di cappella* at the court, Francesco was employed there as a violinist. In 1690 he married Rosalina Albano, and in February 1691 he asked and was granted permission to go to Sicily. In a letter to Emperor Charles VI, in 1715, he said that he had been *maestro di cappella* in Palermo for 26 years, a statement which so far lacks documentation (he is not listed among the musicians employed at the royal chapel in Palermo). In 1710 his oratorio *Israele per foeminane triumphans* was given in Rome, and in 1711 a dialect comedy was given in Aversa near Naples for which he and his brother-in-law Nicola Pagano were responsible. In 1715 he went to Vienna hoping for employment as vice-Kapellmeister and claiming to have lost his position in Palermo because of his Austrian sympathies. His *Miserere* in G minor was performed there, and possibly also a cantata, but his application was turned down although supported by the first Kapellmeister, J. J. Fux. He may have returned to Naples; in February 1719 he drew his stipend from the royal chapel there. The same year he appeared on 1 May at a concert in London, where he apparently settled. His name can be found in concert advertisements in 1720, 1721 and 1724, and as late as 1741 in Dublin a 'Signor Scarlotti' appeared in a concert – more likely Francesco than Domenico or Giuseppe.

WORKS

Cantatas: Il nuovo sole, 2vv, insts, *A-Wn*; O come in un'istante, A, bc, *D-Bds*, *Dlb*; In solitario loco lungi, S, bc, *Dlb*; La dove vegnano, B, bc, *GB-Cfm*; Se lagrimate pupille, S, bc, *Cfm*; Adorna il seno, B, bc, *Cfm*; 2 cantatas, *Mp*

Miserere, g, 5vv, insts, *A-Wn*

Agnus occisus (melodramma sacro), Rome, Oratorio del Ss Crocifisso, 1699, lost

Israele per foeminane triumphans (melodramma sacro), Rome, 1710, lost

Lo Petracchio (comic opera), Aversa, 1711, ?collab. N. Pagano, lost

(5) Tommaso Scarlatti (*b* 1669–72; *d* Naples, 1 Aug 1760). Tenor, brother of (1) Alessandro Scarlatti. He went to Naples so young that he later knew nothing of his infancy in Sicily. He was apparently trained at the Conservatorio S Onofrio. On his marriage in May 1701

he declared that he had lived in Naples since infancy and never left the city. In 1703 he sang in (7) Domenico Scarlatti's *Giustino*, and later in *buffo* operas (appearances are recorded in 1736 and 1740); from 1722 he was employed at the royal chapel. The opera singer Rosa Scarlatti who appeared in Venice in 1747 and later in Vienna may be his daughter of that name (*b* Naples, 5 May 1716). The composer (8) Giuseppe Scarlatti may possibly be his son of that name (*b* Naples, 18 June 1723).

(6) Pietro Filippo Scarlatti (*b* Rome, 5 Jan 1679; *d* Naples, 22 Feb 1750). Composer, son of (1) Alessandro Scarlatti. He probably received his earliest musical training from his father. From 1705 to 1708 he was *maestro di cappella* at Urbino Cathedral, a position he left because (he claimed) his father ordered him to return to Naples. There he was appointed supernumerary organist and in 1712 organist of the royal chapel. Alessandro's further plans for his son's career did not apparently materialize. Not until 1728 did Pietro receive his first commission for an opera, *Clitarco* – probably the only one he wrote. Burney reported that Cotumaccio had called him 'good for nothing'. He had three children (Domenico, Alessandro and Anna); one, Alessandro, must have been a musician because after Pietro's death the children petitioned (unsuccessfully) that their late father's position should be given to him.

WORKS

Clitarco (opera), Naples, S Bartolomeo, 1728, ?lost
Cantatas: Care luci del ben mio, A, 3 insts, bc, *D-Bds*; Scusatemi Signora, S, bc, *Dlb*; Cantate a tre, S, S, A, str, hpd, *I-Mc*
Care luci del ben mio, aria, A, vn, 2 viol, b, *Mc*
3 minuets, vn, *GB-Cfm*; 4 bassi numerati; 21 toccatas, hpd, dated 1739–42: all *I-Mc*

(7) (Giuseppe) Domenico Scarlatti (*b* Naples, 26 Oct 1685; *d* Madrid, 23 July 1757). Composer, keyboard teacher and performer, the sixth of ten children of (1) Alessandro Scarlatti and Antonia Anzalone. Though baptized Giuseppe Domenico, he appears to have used only his second Christian name, which became altered during his years in the Iberian peninsula to Domingo, and the surname to Escarlatti. The lives and works of the Scarlattis constantly intertwine, and he should not be confused with his nephew Giuseppe.

1. Life. 2. Works. 3. Performances, sources, influence.

1. LIFE. It is not known how, where and from whom Scarlatti received his musical training. His name appears on no conservatory roster, and the assertions that Francesco Gasparini, Gaetano Greco, Bernardo Pasquini or any of the elder Scarlattis were his actual teachers are not verifiable (though he learnt a great deal from the compositions of all of those men, among others). On 13 September 1701 he was appointed organist and composer of the Naples royal chapel, of which (1) Alessandro Scarlatti was *maestro*; no compositions from the period of this employment are extant. In the following year, father and son obtained four months' leave to travel to Florence where Alessandro hoped to secure more favourable working conditions in the private theatre of Ferdinando de' Medici. Whether Domenico met the keyboard instrument maker Bartolomeo Cristofori at this time has long been a subject of speculation; it is known that Cristofori supplied Ferdinando's harpsichords and was experimenting with the hammer action of his *gravicembalo col piano e forte*. Scarlatti left his father in Florence and

returned to his post in Naples, probably within the four months allotted to him. He wrote music for two Neapolitan opera productions in 1703 and drastically rewrote Pollarolo's *Irene* for the same stage in 1704. In spring 1705 Alessandro, wielding the full force of parental authority, ordered his son to go from Naples to Venice, through Rome and Florence, in the company of the celebrated castrato Nicolo Grimaldi. It is worth quoting Alessandro's letter of recommendation to Ferdinando de' Medici, where he described his feelings about his son's growing ability with a warmth and precision generally lacking in documents on Domenico's life:

I have forcibly removed him from Naples where, though there was scope for his talent, it was not the kind of talent for such a place. I am removing him from Rome as well, because Rome has no shelter for music, which lives here as a beggar. This son of mine is an eagle whose wings are grown; he must not remain idle in the nest, and I must not hinder his flight. Since the virtuoso Nicolino of Naples is passing through here on the way to Venice, I thought fit to send Domenico with him, escorted only by his own ability. He has advanced much since he was able to be, together with me, in a position to enjoy the honour of serving Your Highness personally, three years ago. He sets forth to meet whatever opportunity may present itself for him to make himself known – opportunity for which one waits in vain in Rome today.

Nothing is known of the four years Scarlatti spent in Venice. In 1709 he entered the service of Maria Casimira in Rome; her renown grew under the patronage of this exiled Polish queen. (A generation earlier his father had enjoyed a similar situation in Rome under the sponsorship of the exiled Swedish Queen Christina.) The private court of Maria Casimira, which had papal permission to present 'decent comedies', was graced by the composition of at least one cantata, one oratorio and six operas by Scarlatti.

An important meeting-place of musical people in Rome during those years was the establishment of Cardinal Pietro Ottoboni, at whose weekly recitals of chamber music (known as the Accademie Poetico-musicali) Scarlatti met virtuosos and composers including Corelli, Handel and a young Englishman, Thomas Roseingrave. Roseingrave became a personal friend and ardent admirer of Scarlatti; from 1718 onwards he was the key figure in the dissemination of Scarlatti's vocal and keyboard music in Britain. At this time Handel and Scarlatti allegedly had a contest in virtuosity at the organ and harpsichord, in which Handel is said to have prevailed on the organ, Scarlatti on the harpsichord; but the only source of this tale is Mainwaring's account in his biography of Handel, written more than a half-century later.

On 22 December 1713 Scarlatti became *maestro di cappella* of the Basilica Giulia; early in 1714, soon after Maria Casimira left Rome, he received a similar appointment with the Marquis de Fontes, Portuguese ambassador to the Vatican. He thus provided music for both sacred and secular employers. But he was still apparently unable to free himself from the interference of a domineering father until legal independence was enforced in a document of 28 January 1717; there are indications that Alessandro continued to exert as much influence over Domenico as he could even after that time.

In August 1719 Scarlatti resigned his positions in Rome and went to Portugal, where he became *mestre* of the increasingly opulent patriarchal chapel in Lisbon. Details about his arrival and sojourn in Lisbon are few; much of the documentation pertaining to his years in Portugal (1719–28) was apparently destroyed in the

6. Engraving by Charles-Joseph Flipart after Jacopo Amiconi's portrait 1752) of King Fernando VI, Maria Barbara and the Spanish royal household; Domenico Scarlatti and Farinelli can be seen front right of the musicians' gallery

earthquake of 1 November 1755 in which the city was nearly obliterated. But we do know from other sources of three visits he made to Italy, apparently on leave from Lisbon. In 1724 he travelled to Rome, meeting Quantz and possibly Farinelli. The following year he went to Naples to pay his final respects to his rapidly failing father; there he probably met the protégé of Alessandro's last years, Hasse. In 1728 he returned to Rome to marry 16-year-old Maria Caterina Gentili, the mother of his first five children. There is no convincing evidence that Domenico ever left the Iberian peninsula after 1728. The Scarlattis who in later years appeared in Austria, France, England or Ireland were other members of this numerous clan.

Scarlatti's duties in Lisbon included the musical education, particularly the training at the keyboard, of King John V's talented daughter, the Infanta Maria Barbara, and his younger brother Don Antonio. With the former Scarlatti formed a lifelong musical symbiosis that resulted in the creation of his most significant work, a body of more than 500 single-movement 'sonatas' in binary form for unaccompanied keyboard. When Maria Barbara married the Spanish Crown Prince Fernando and moved to Madrid in 1728, Scarlatti followed among her retainers; he then spent the last 28 years of his life in the relative obscurity of the Spanish court, performing whatever musical functions Maria Barbara assigned to him, with no record of complaint.

If Scarlatti was musically pre-eminent at the Spanish court from 1729 to 1737, his position must have changed on the arrival of Carlo Broschi, better known

as Farinelli, one of the greatest of all castratos. In Madrid Farinelli's singing was confined to the private chambers of the kings, but he also supervised the productions of theatrical music. Neither the nature of Scarlatti's role at court nor how it related to Farinelli's after 1737 can be ascertained; there are no records of his participation, even as a continuo player, in the festivals that Farinelli directed, but in an official portrait of King Fernando, Maria Barbara and the royal household, painted by Jacopo Amiconi in 1752, Scarlatti and Farinelli are both prominently depicted at the forefront of the lofted gallery of musicians (see fig.6).

On 21 April 1738, at the Capuchin convent of S Antonio del Prado in Madrid, Scarlatti, under the sponsorship of King John V of Portugal, passed initiatory trials to become a Knight of the Order of Santiago. On 6 May 1739 Maria Caterina, his first wife, died; before 1742, he married Anastasia Maxarti Ximenes (orthography varies), the mother of his last four children. None of the four of his nine children who survived infancy became musicians.

Scanty documentation means that little is known about Scarlatti as a man. Stories about his way of life, tastes, and character, especially the oft-repeated account of his passion for gambling, come from indirect and suspect sources. The well-known notion that he grew too fat in his later years to cross his hands at the keyboard has been scotched by the discovery in 1956 of a portrait of him painted by Domingo Antonio de Velasco about 1740 (fig.7); it depicts a newly dubbed knight in full regalia, constitutionally slender, with

7. Domenico Scarlatti: portrait (c1740) by Domingo Antonio de Velasco in the Instituição José Relvas, Alpiarça

prominent cheekbones and forehead, with long thin arms and strong supple hands, well suited to the technical demands of his keyboard music.

2. WORKS. Until 1719, Scarlatti strove to establish a career as a composer in the world of Neapolitan opera over which Alessandro reigned. His musical expressiveness was restricted, however, by a style in which the composer merely provided a blueprint for the castratos or other performers; while others flourished, he languished. Even in the realm of sacred choral music, in which many aspects of his compositional technique ripened, the Neapolitan style's limitations of emotional range and motivic fantasy gave little scope to his latent individuality. An examination of the music of his Italian years shows that the level does not rise above that of professional competence.

After 1720, Scarlatti took advantage of his new freedom to alter his styles of life and composition. Free from the constraints of Neapolitan functional music, he could improvise and compose at the keyboard, exploring whatever path of abstract possibility his fingers could discover. Free from the domineering and critical person of his father, he could make his own mistakes and invest in his own ventures. Free from the unimaginative circles of Italian patronage, he could bask in the encouragement of Maria Barbara and her court. Titil-

lated by the new sounds, sights and customs of Iberia, he could add new elements to his musical language. The resulting hundreds of movements in binary form for keyboard, each simply entitled 'sonata', that he wrote at some time during the last 35 years of his life, raised what Scarlatti himself called 'an ingenious jesting with art' into a uniquely wide-ranging and original corpus of music. These were no mere extensions of the stylized dances of the Baroque suite, but entirely fresh visions of the potentials of binary form; each sonata was an essay in the coordination and control of an unusual problem or problems such as arose from the employment of an eccentric gesture, a peculiar harmony or progression of chords, an irregular phrase or group of phrases, a strange type of motivic development, a tone-colour possible only on a Spanish harpsichord or a Florentine fortepiano, or some other unique problem. Above all, they explore new worlds of virtuoso technique, putting to new musical ends such devices as hand-crossing, rapid repetition of notes, arpeggio figurations rapidly traversing the length of the keyboard, and countless other difficult means of obtaining a devastating brilliance of effect.

The most characteristic of Scarlatti's harmonic mannerisms is the acciaccatura, which he used with greater frequency and variety than any other composer. Attempts to explain this practice in terms of polychords or

Ex.1

(a) K208

(b) K490

(c) K141

other fanciful theoretical constructions are as unsuccessful as they are unnecessary. Gasparini and other 18th-century theorists defined the acciaccatura as a 'simultaneous mordent' (in other words, a lower auxiliary note struck together with its resolution). The difficulty experienced by the listener is that of accepting the dissonant note's immediate resolution back into its progenitor within the chord without requiring further resolution in subsequent chords. The most common acciaccatura resembles the 5–4 dissonance in which the 4th above the bass must resolve downwards to a 3rd; but in all three of the situations cited in ex.1, as well as nearly every other of Scarlatti's acciaccaturas, this 4th has already resolved to the 5th above it and deserves no further part-writing consideration. Whether this use of the acciaccatura is to be linked with the techniques of the guitar music Scarlatti heard in Spain must be a matter for conjecture; writers on his style have however commented on various instrumental imitations in his music, notably the rapid repeated notes or chords that recall the thrumming of the guitar and the fanfare-like passages that hint at the sound of trumpets or horns.

Auxiliary notes in Scarlatti sonatas, even when they resolve properly, manage to discover methods of effecting the process unknown elsewhere. In ex.2, the $c\sharp''$ and the later $b\flat'$ resolve at the last possible instant before the left-hand chord change is articulated, to $d\natural''$ and $c\natural'$ respectively. The resolutions are artfully obscured by the intervening high pedal g''''s restruck throughout the bar. Scarlatti's literal and immediate reiteration of the

Ex.2 K132

phrase is as if to convince the listener that the first playing was not in error.

The other primary source of exceptional harmonic usage in the Scarlatti sonata is what may be called the 'vamp': a section of indeterminate length, normally at the beginning of the second half of a binary movement, sounding like an improvised accompaniment waiting for the entry of an important musical event. It may vary in length from a few bars to a long group of phrases that can occupy two-thirds of the movement's second half. It opens with a figural pattern resembling that of an exploratory solo section in a fast movement of a Vivaldi concerto. But it is tonally much less predictable, teasing the listener, feinting in one direction and then another before reaching a goal different from the one expected. The harmonic rhythm is generally regular within the vamp, but may become extremely irregular towards the end of the longest examples. The part-writing moves clearly and logically, generally by step, but avoids obvious lines of continuation, mostly through the reinterpretation and redirection of leading notes in ways that are complex and difficult to follow. Ex.3 illustrates some of the adventurous techniques of the vamp, combined with a characteristic nagging repetition of a short motif.

Ex.3 K193

Ex.4 illustrates the originality of effect that Scarlatti could bring to the filigree surrounding a fairly straightforward sequence by the use of chromatic notes. The prolongation of an A♭ chord from bar 23 to the downbeat of bar 26 establishes the nature of the section. The sequence progresses up a step to B♭ in bars 26–9 and to C in bars 29–31. Each step is provoked by the substitution of a chromatic note for a diatonic one at exactly that point in the scale where it could not be expected: the a'' in bar 26 replaces the expected $a\flat''$, and the b'' in bar 29 replaces $b\flat''$. The ascending whole-tone-scale fragments, although unusual, are less arresting than the bold stroke that produced them. With this sort of

Ex.4 K106

chromatic substitution established, Scarlatti could substitute e'' for eb'' at the beginning of bar 31 to break the
pattern of the sequence of a bar earlier than expected.

Scarlatti's modulation depends largely on such bold
strokes for its effects. Even when pivot chords effect a
direct transfer from tonic to dominant or relative major,
some attendant feature may be altered by one of these
coups, producing some crooked transfer of register,
chromatically changing part-crossing, common-note
progression, modal alternation between parallel major
and minor, false relation or the like. Each of Scarlatti's
modulations is militantly individual and demands attention. He never wrote modulatory passages merely to
shift from one chord prolongation to another, but tried
to project a strength of purpose and a gestural significance in each one equivalent to that in the statement of a
tonally stable theme or group of themes. The grand tour
becomes an end in itself, with no wasted motion even
when a seemingly circuitous route is chosen.

Scarlatti's binary form, outwardly complex and extremely variable, may be reduced to a useful outline.
The first half begins, in the traditional manner, in the
tonic moving to the dominant (if major) or the relative
major (if minor); the second half continues the motion
either directly or indirectly before circling back to the
tonic. The early music in each half tends to be unstable
in material and tonality, the later music just the opposite. The themes at the end of the first half are almost
always transposed and repeated at the end of the second,
but there is no recapitulation of the movement's opening
in the tonic during the second half, and thus no sonata-
allegro form (save in K159, and that seems to have been
the result of an accident of motivic development).
Unlike the stylized dance movements of the Baroque,
each half of a Scarlatti sonata tends to be sectional, with
many of its phrases coming to full cadences, many
contrasts of material, and frequent shifts of rhythmic
drive, which provide the sense of variety and freshness
in each half that impresses and delights the listener.

The chief objection to this method is that, within each
half, there may have to be so many stops and starts that
momentum will be lost. Rutini, Alberti, Platti and other
composers of this era often failed to solve that problem.
The most characteristic way in which Scarlatti avoided
this pitfall is his technique of phrase elision: for
example, he may write an eight-bar phrase, complete up
to its full cadence, and then repeat it, but at the close of
the repetition the final bar or two may be eliminated in

favour of the smooth early entrance of a new phrase,
and the potential energy left over from the elided bars
speeds the new material on its way. This procedure is
even extended to the junction between the two halves of
the binary form. In more than 100 sonatas, there are
large curved lines above or below (or both) the final bar
or bars of the first half (see ex.5), instructing the performer to omit those bars when playing the first half for
the second time and proceed directly into the opening of
the second half. This notation has long been understood
by scholars, but it is excluded from the editions of the
sonatas by Czerny, von Bülow, Farrenc, Tausig,
Oesterle, Bartók, Buonamici, Georgii, Pauer, Longo,
Granados, Godowsky, Sauer, Gerstenberg, Kirkpatrick
and others, though not from the important edition by
Kenneth Gilbert.

Scarlatti often composed brief passages in imitation
at the 5th or octave. Sometimes he began a piece in a
manner indicating that fugal or some other orderly
method of imitation is to serve as the structural basis,
only to dismiss the idea; the grand Baroque fugal
gesture had lost its potency and interest for him and
became just one more of his contrasting textures. There
are only six pieces that can reasonably be called fugues
(K30, 41, 58, 93, 287 and 417), and each of these is in
some way flighty, overcomposed or grotesque. K315
toys with the principles of fugue in an irrational, almost
taunting manner; its opening motif reappears in a semi-
fugal manner in bars 3, 5, 7, 9 (slightly altered), 11
and frequently thereafter.

Ex.5 K535

3. PERFORMANCE, SOURCES, INFLUENCE. Little information is available about ornamentation in Spanish and
Portuguese music of the 18th century. Most of the
informed guesses about the performance of Scarlatti's
ornaments have been extrapolated from Italian and
German parallels: a reasonable expedient, although the
evidence of the ornamental notation in Iberian pieces
seems to indicate that the practice differs in several
aspects from Baroque norms. Scarlatti's signs are
restricted to small notes (many but not all of which seem
to be best interpreted as appoggiaturas), the usual abbreviations for the trill, and the mysterious tremolo
indications that have occasioned a good deal of concern
and speculation (all one can say at present about this
sign's possible meaning is that, whenever it appears, a
mordent would seem most appropriate musically).

It has long been assumed that all Scarlatti's sonatas
were composed for the harpsichord. A brief flurry of
interest in the clavichord as the possible inspiration for
some of the thinner-textured sonatas had to be put aside
because of the lack of evidence for the existence of
clavichords in Maria Barbara's courts. It is now known

8. Title-page of Scarlatti's 'XLII Suites de pièces pour le clavecin'), i (London: Cooke, 1739), edited by Roseingrave

that at least three pieces (K287, K288 and K328) were meant for organ. Pianos, moreover, were owned and used in each of Maria Barbara's residences. Possibly hundreds of sonatas may have been intended for these delicate, single-escapement hammer-action instruments. Most of the harpsichords for which the sonatas were written were made in Spain after the fashion of Italian builders; Maria Barbara's were largely one-manual, two-register, five-octave instruments with a clean, clear, delicate sound, very different from the Germanic or Flemish instruments favoured today. The fact that some sonatas have frequent hand-crossings while others do not may relate to the nature of the instrument for which particular pieces were written, as well as to the patrons for whom they were written.

The chronology of Scarlatti's sonatas, about which three numerical reckonings have been essayed, still remains uncertain. Before 1910 Alessandro Longo collected, grouped and numbered all the works then known; but his system of cataloguing was arbitrary. In the 1950s Ralph Kirkpatrick formulated a system that carefully followed the order of pieces in what he considered to be the best dated sources; but his calculations are flawed by the fact that no convincing relationship can be demonstrated between the dates of the copying of these sources and the dates of composition – all sources are copyists' manuscripts or printed editions, not directly traceable to the composer, and every autograph is lost. In 1967 Giorgio Pestelli attempted a listing based on stylistic criteria, which however hardly suffice for music so diverse in form, rich in material and intricate in tonality. All these lists of 'keyboard works' in fact include pieces for solo instruments with continuo.

A problem closely related to that of chronology is that of the grouping of movements into larger units. Most of the sonatas seem to be organized in pairs, according to key, at least in the principal sources. But a number of factors, notably the labelling of each movement as a separate sonata (unlike the practice of many contemporaries, notably Rutini and Alberti), the existence of a significant number of single movements among the pairs, and most of all the variant groupings among the best sources, suggest either that the pairs

were an afterthought on the composer's part or the result of the intervention of the scribe or some other person. Kirkpatrick championed the paired movements; Pestelli rejected them. The pairing of movements in 18th-century Italian keyboard sonatas does not seem to conform to any pattern; nor is it usual for there to be any thematic or motivic connection between the pieces. There is thus no touchstone against which to measure the credibility of the pairs, some of which, particularly K347–8, 356–7, 443–4 and 526–7, seem to belong together for clear musical reasons. One may hope that further research will establish a definitive chronology and that the issue of the pairs will be resolved.

The primary sources comprise the following manuscripts: two sets, each of 15 volumes, both copied by the same Spanish scribe, now in the Arrigo Boito Conservatorio library in Parma (AG 31406–20) and the Biblioteca Marciana in Venice (9770–84); later Italian copies include the five thick volumes in the Santini collection, now at Münster (3964–8), and seven volumes, once the property of Brahms, now in the Gesellschaft der Musikfreunde library, Vienna (VII 28011 A–G); further manuscripts recently found in that library (Q 15112–20, Q 11432, Q 15126) may provide new information about the transmission and text of a number of the pieces. There are other, smaller manuscripts with significant textual readings or otherwise unknown sonatas (F-Pa 6, 784, 343; GB-Cfm 32 F 12–13, Lbm Add.31553 and 31589; I-Bc FF232 and KK96, Nc 18–3–11; P-C Mus.58; US-NH Ma 31/Sca 7k/C 11).

Scarlatti's sonatas have had a chequered history in print, which bears heavily on the questions of their authenticity and of the textual accuracy with which they have been transmitted. The first of these publications, of 30 pieces singly called sonatas but collectively entitled *Essercizi per gravicembalo*, appeared in London in 1738, the work of Italian residents in England (possibly contacts of Farinelli), and was immediately pirated by Scarlatti's old acquaintance Thomas Roseingrave; that began a history of pirated or arranged editions which continued throughout the 18th century, particularly in Great Britain, where enthusiasm for the sonatas has never abated. Many notable 18th-century publishers in London, Paris and elsewhere issued collections, including some of arrangements (such as Avison's collection of concerti grossi after Scarlatti sonatas).

Scarlatti exerted considerable influence on the development of keyboard music, particularly in the Iberian peninsula, and also in England, where Burney regarded Joseph Kelway as 'leader of the Scarlatti sect' in London, and the keyboard music of several composers, notably Arne, shows traces of his style. Scarlatti's distinguished Portuguese colleague Carlos Seixas composed, among his many keyboard works, a few that resemble Scarlatti's, but mutual influence between them is still a matter for conjecture. The music of Antonio Soler, on the other hand, reveals strong influence; the two were probably in prolonged contact at the Escorial between 1752 and 1756. The tradition was extended through the next half-century, closing with the keyboard music of Félix Máximo López. An interesting figure among the Iberians influenced by Scarlatti is Sebastián Albero, an organist in the Spanish royal chapel about 1750; 30 of his sonatas in a Venice manuscript alongside Scarlatti's, copied in the same hand, include pieces aping many features of Scarlatti's form, rhetoric and tonal audacity, but never achieving the distinction of his model and thus showing the difficulty, if not impossibility, of isolating the factors contributing to the quality of music.

For the opening of Sonata in A K24 from the *Essercizi, see* FORTIER, B.

WORKS

OPERAS
(lost unless otherwise stated)

Ottavia ristituita al trono (melodramma, G. Convò), Naples, S Bartolomeo, carn. 1703, 31 arias and 2 duets, *I-Nc*
Giustino (dramma per musica, Convò, after N. Beregani), Naples, Palazzo Regio, 19 Dec 1703, collab. Legrenzi, 21 arias and 3 duets, *Nc*
Irene (dramma per musica, adaptation of G. Frigimelica Roberti), Naples, S Bartolomeo, carn. 1704, 33 arias, *Nc* [rev. of orig. by C. F. Pollarolo]
Silvia (dramma pastorale, C. S. Capece), Rome, Palazzo Zuccari, 27 Jan 1710
Tolomeo e Alessandro, ovvero La corona disprezzata (dramma per musica, Capece), Rome, Palazzo Zuccari, 19 Jan 1711, score of Act 1 pubd (Rome, 1711)
Orlando, ovvero La gelosa pazzia (dramma, Capece, after Ariosto), Rome, Palazzo Zuccari, carn. 1711
Tetide in Sciro (dramma per musica, Capece), Rome, Palazzo Zuccari, 10 Jan 1712, full score, Conventuale di S Francesco, Venice
Ifigenia in Aulide (dramma per musica, Capece, after Euripides), Rome, Palazzo Zuccari, 11 Jan 1713
Ifigenia in Tauri (dramma per musica, Capece, after Euripides), Rome, Palazzo Zuccari, 15 Feb 1713
Amor d'un ombra e gelosia d'un'aura (dramma per musica, Capece), Rome, Palazzo Zuccari, 20 Jan 1714; rev. as Narciso (P. A. Rolli after Capece), London, King's, 30 May 1720, with 2 arias and 2 duets added by T. Roseingrave, full score, *D-Hs*; addns pubd (London, 1720)
Ambleto (dramma per musica, Zeno), Rome, Capranica, carn. 1715, Act 1 scene viii, *I-Bc*
La Dirindina (farsetta per musica, G. Gigli), intermezzo for Ambleto, unperf.
Intermedi pastorali, intermezzo in Ambleto, Rome, Capranica, carn. 1715
Berenice, regina d'Egitto, ovvero Le gare d'amore e di politica (dramma per musica, A. Salvi), Rome, Capranica, carn. 1718, collab. N. Porpora
Didone abbandonata (opera, Metastasio), Rome, 1724, doubtful authenticity [? by D. Sarro]

ORATORIOS AND CANTATAS
(lost unless otherwise stated)

La conversione di Clodoveo, re di Francia (oratorio, Capece), Rome, Palazzo Zuccari, carn. 1709
Applauso devoto al nome di Maria Santissima (cantata, Capece), Rome, Palazzo Zuccari, 1712
Applauso Genetliaco (cantata), Rome, Portuguese Embassy, 1714
Cantata da recitarsi . . . la notte del Ss Natale (F. M. Gasparri), Rome, Vatican, 24 Dec 1714

Contesa delle stagioni (serenata), SATB, chorus, 2 tpt, 2 hn. fl, str. Lisbon, Royal Palace, 6 Sept 1720, score of prima parte, *P-Ln*
Cantata pastorale, Lisbon, Royal Palace, 27 Dec 1720
Serenata, Lisbon, 6 Sept 1722
Serenata, Lisbon, 27 Dec 1722
Festeggio armonico, Lisbon, Royal Palace, 11 Jan 1728
Serenata, SSAT, chorus, 2 tpt, 2 hn, fl, str, *I-Vnm*

OTHER SACRED VOCAL

Iste confessor (G), SATB, org, bc, *I-Rvat*; Magnificat (d), SATB, bc, *D-MÜp*; Miserere (e), SATB concertino and ripieno, *I-Rvat*; Miserere (g), SATB concertino and ripieno, *Rvat* [autograph]; Missa quatuor vocum (g), SATB, *E-Mp*; Motetto per l'Ognissanti (D), SATB, *P-Lf*; Salve regina (A), S solo, str, *D-B, MÜp, I-Bc, Nc*, ed. R. Ewerhart (Cologne, 1960); Salve regina (a), SA, org, bc, *I-Bc*; Stabat mater (c), SSATB, SSATB, org, bc, *A-Wn, D-B, MÜp, I-Bc*, ed. in Accademia musicale, xxvii (1973); Te Deum (C), SATB concertino and ripieno, bc, *P-Lf*
Nisi quia Dominus a 4; Mass, 1712: both *I-Rlib*; Memento, Domine, David, *GB-Lbm*; Dixit Dominus and Lauda Jerusalem, both cited in A. Soler, *Llave de la modulación* (Madrid, 1762): all not authenticated

OTHER VOCAL

Miscellaneous cantatas, arias, duets etc, all not authenticated. Principal sources: *A-Wn; B-Bc; D-Dlb, MÜp, SWl; F-Pc, Pn; GB-Lbm, Lcm; I-Bsp, Fc, Nc, PAc, Pca; US-Wc*.
A chi nacque infelice, A, bc; Ah sei troppo infelice, 1v, bc; Al fin diviene amante, 1v, bc; Al fin m'uccidete; Amenissimi prati, B, bc; Bella rosa adorata, S, bc; Belle pupille care, July 1702, S, 2 vn, bc; Che, che pretendi, ò tiranna; Che sarà; Che si peni in amore; Che vidi, o ciel, S, 2 vn, bc; Chi in catene ha il mio core, S, bc; Con qual cor, 1v, bc; Consolati e spera, A, str; Deh che fate o mie pupille, 1v, bc; Dice amor; Di Fille vendicarmi vorrei, 1v, bc; Dir vorrei, S, 2 vn, bc; Dona pace alle sue pene; Dopo lungo servire, 2 July 1702, A, 2 vn, bc; Dorme la rosa, S, bc; E pur per mia sventura, S, bc; Fille già più non parlo, 1v, bc; Gelo avvampo considero; Mi tormenta il pensiero; Ninfe belle e voi pastori, S, bc; Non, non fuggire o Nice, 1v, bc; Nò, nò si può celar; Onde della mia Nera, 1v, bc; O qual meco Nice cangiata, S, 2 vn, bc; O qual meco o Nice; Pende la vita mia, S. bc; Piangete, occhi dolenti, S, 2 vn, bc; Pur nel sonno almen; Pur nel sonno almen tal'ora (Metastasio), S, 2 vn, bc; Qual pensier, 1v bc; Quando miro il vostro foco, 1v, bc; Quando penso, S, bc; Rimirai la rosa un dì, 1v, bc; Ruscelletto ch'è lungi dal mare; Scritte con falso inganno, S, 2 vn, bc; Se dicesse un core, 1v, bc; Se fedele tu m'adori, S, 2 vn, bc; Selve, caverne e monti, S, bc; Se pensi mai, A, str; Se per un sol momento, 2vv, bc; Se sai qual sia la pena, S, bc; Se tu sarai fedel, A, str; Se vuoi ch'io t'ami, A, str; Sono un alma tormentata, S, bc; Sospendi o man per poco, 1v, bc; Stravagante non è l'amor; Stravagante; T'amai, Clori, t'amai, 1v, bc; Tinte a note di sangue, S, 2 vn, bc; Ti ricorda o bella Irene, 1v, bc; Tirsi caro, 2 vv, bc; Tu mi chiedi o mio ben; V'adoro a luci belle, S, bc; Vago il ciel, S, bc; Vedi l'ape

INSTRUMENTAL ENSEMBLE

17 sinfonias, *F-Pn*: A, str, bc; G, fl, ob, str, bc; G, str, bc; D, ob, str, bc; a, 2 vn, bc; Bb, ob, 2 vn, bc; C, str, bc; Bb, ob, str, bc; d, ob, str, bc; G, ob, str, bc; C, ob, str, bc; G, ob, str, bc; Bb, ob, str, bc; G, fl, ob, str, bc; Bb, ob, str, bc; A, ob, str, bc; C, ob, str, bc
1 conc., F, hpd solo, 2 fl, 2 hn, 2 vn, va, bc, *D-B*, ? by G. Scarlatti

SONATAS FOR SOLO KEYBOARD

Catalogues in Longo (1906–8) [L], Kirkpatrick (1953) [K], Pestelli [P]
Editions: *Opere complete per clavicembalo di Domenico Scarlatti,* ed. A. Longo (Milan, 1906–8): i, L1–50; ii, L51–100; iii, L101–50; iv, L151–200; v, L201–50; vi, L251–300; vii, L301–50; viii, L351–400; ix, L401–50; x, L451–500; xi, S1–45
    D. Scarlatti: Sixty Sonatas, ed. R. Kirkpatrick (New York, 1953) [*]
    D. Scarlatti: Complete Keyboard Works in Facsimile, ed. R. Kirkpatrick (New York, 1971–): i, K1–42; ii, K43–68, variants of K8, 31, 33, 37, 41; iii, K69–97, variants of K52, 53; iv, K98–123; v, K124–47; vi, K148–76; vii, K177–205; viii, K206–35; ix, K236–65; x, K266–95; xi, K296–325; xii, K326–57; xiii, K358–87; xiv, K388–417; xv, K418–53; xvi, K454–83; xvii, K484–513; xviii, K514–55
    D. Scarlatti: Sonates, ed. K. Gilbert, Le pupitre (Paris, 1971–): xxxi, K1–52; xxxii, K53–103; xxxiii, K104–55; xxxiv, K156–205; xxxv, K206–55; xxxvi, K256–305; xxxvii, K306–57; xxxviii, K358–407; xxxix, K408–57; xl, K458–506; xli, K507–55
    D. Scarlatti: Sonate per clavicembalo, ed. E. Fadini (Milan, 1978–)

Sources: *Essercizi per gravicembalo* (London, 1738/*R*1967) [E]
    XLII Suites de pièces pour le clavecin, ed. T. Roseingrave (London, 1739) [R]
    Pièces pour le clavecin, 3 vols (Paris, 1742–6, Boivin) [B]
    Domenico Scarlatti: 26 Sonatas ineditas, ed. E. Granados (c1905) [G]

MS Sources: *D-MÜp* 3964–8 [M]
F-Pa 6, 784, 343 [PR]
GB-Cfm Mus.32 F 13 [CF]
GB-Lbm Add.31553, 14248 [LB]
I-PAp AG 31406–20 [PA]
I-Vnm 9770–84 [V]
P-C Mus.58 [C]
US-NH 18, 19 [NH]

K	P	L	Description	Primary source (variant)
1	57	366	d, C, Allegro	E1
2	58	388	G, 3/8, Presto	E2
3	59	378	a, ¢, Presto*	E3
4	60	390	g, C, Allegro	E4
5	61	367	d, 3/8, Allegro	E5
6	62	479	F, 3/8, Allegro	E6
7	63	379	a, 3/8, Presto*	E7
8	64	488	g, 3/4, Allegro	E8 (R1)
9	65	413	d, 6/8, Allegro	E9
10	66	370	d, 3/8, Presto	E10
11	67	352	d, C, —	E11
12	68	489	g, C, Presto	E12
13	69	486	G, 2/4, Presto	E13
14	70	387	G, 12/8, Presto	E14
15	71	374	e, 3/8, Allegro	E15
16	72	397	B♭, ¢, Presto*	E16
17	73	384	F, 3/8, Presto	E17
18	74	416	d, C, Presto*	E18
19	75	383	f, 2/4, Allegro	E19
20	76	375	E, 2/4, Presto	E20
21	77	363	D, 3/8, Allegro	E21
22	78	360	c, 2/4, Allegro	E22
23	79	411	D, C, Allegro	E23
24	80	495	A, C, Presto	E24
25	81	481	f♯, 2/4, Allegro	E25
26	82	368	A, 3/8, Presto	E26
27	83	449	b, 3/4, Allegro	E27
28	84	373	E, 3/8, Presto*	E28
29	85	461	D, C, Presto*	E29
30	86	499	g, 6/8, Moderato	E30
31	19	231	g, 2/4, Allegro	R3
32	14	423	d, 3/8, Aria	R6
33	130	424	D, 3/8, Allegro	V xiv, 43 (R7)
34	15	S7	d, 3/4, Larghetto	R9
35	20	386	g, C, Allegro	R12
36	91	245	a, 3/8, Allegro	V xiv, 25
37	2	406	c, C, Allegro	V xiv, 41
38	97	478	F, 3/8, Allegro	V xiv, 27
39	53	391	A, C, Allegro	R28
40	119	357	c, 3/4, Allegro	R30
41	37	—	d, C, Andante moderato	PA iii, 30 (R42)
42	120	S36	B♭, 3/4, Minuetto	R43
43	133	40	g, 12/8, Allegro assai	PA iii, 7
44	116	432	F, 3/8, Allegro*	PA ii, 20
45	230	265	D, 12/8, Allegro	V xiv, 3
46	179	25	E, ¢, Presto*	PA ii, 15
47	115	46	B♭, C, Presto	PA iii, 11
48	87	157	c, 3/8, Presto	PA ii, 24
49	178	301	C, ¢, Presto	PA iii, 5
50	144	440	f, 3/8, Allegro	PA iii, 22
51	151	20	E♭, C, Allegro	V xiv, 9
52	41	267	d, C, Andante moderato*	V xiv, 10 (V xiv, 61)
53	161	261	D, ¢, Presto	PA vi, 13
54	147	241	a, 12/8, Allegro*	PA iii, 20
55	117	335	G, 3/8, Allegro	PA iii, 1
56	50	356	c, 12/8, Con spirito	PA ii, 25
57	108	S38	B♭, 3/8, Allegro*	PA iii, 12
58	39	158	c, C, Fuga	V xiv, 16
59	22	71	F, C, Allegro	V xiv, 17
60	29	13	g, 3/4, —	V xiv, 19
61	16	136	a, 2/4, —	V xiv, 20
62	49	45	A, 3/8, Allegro	V xiv, 21
63	32	84	G, 2/4, Capriccio: Allegro	V xiv, 23
64	33	58	d, 2/4, Gavota: Allegro	V xiv, 24
65	142	195	A, 3/8, Allegro	V xiv, 26
66	134	496	B♭, C, Allegro	V xiv, 28
67	125	32	f♯, C, Allegro	V xiv, 29
68	7	114	E♭, 3/8, —	V xiv, 30
69	42	382	f, 3/4, —	PA ii, 27
70	21	50	B♭, C, —	V xiv, 34
71	17	81	G, C, Allegro	V xiv, 35
72	1	401	C, C, Allegro	V xiv, 36
74	34	94	A, 2/4, Allegro	V xiv, 38
75	35	53	G, 3/4, Allegro	V xiv, 39
76	23	185	g, 3/8, Presto	V xiv, 40
79	204	80	G, 3/8, Allegrissimo	V xiv, 45a
80	28	—	G, 3/8, Minuet	V xiv, 45b
82	25	30	F, 3/8, —	C2
83	31	S31	A, ¢, —	V xiv, 48
84	45	10	c, 3/4, —*	V xiv, 49
85	24	166	F, C, —	C1
86	122	403	C, C, Andante moderato	V xiv, 51
87	43	33	b, 3/4, —	PA ii, 28
92	44	362	d, 3/4, —	V xiv, 58
93	38	336	g, C, Fuga	V xiv, 60
94	27	—	F, 3/8, Minuet	C4
96	210	465	D, 3/8, Allegro*	PA iii, 29
98	219	325	e, 3/8, Allegrissimo	PA iii, 19
99	135	317	c, 3/4, Allegro	PA iii, 18
100	232	355	C, 12/8, Allegrissimo	PA iii, 28
101	156	494	A, 3/8, Allegro	PA iii, 26
102	88	89	g, 3/8, Allegro	V xv, 4
103	233	233	G, 12/8, Allegrissimo	V xv, 5
104	109	442	G, 3/8, Allegro	PA iii, 2
105	90	204	G, 3/8, Allegro*	PA iii, 24
106	197	437	F, ¢, Allegro	PA iii, 15
107	98	474	F, 3/8, Allegro	PA iii, 16
108	92	249	g, 3/8, Allegro	PA v, 12
109	290	138	a, ¢, Adagio	PA iii, 3
110	129	469	a, 3/8, Allegro	PA iii, 4
111	99	130	g, 12/8, Allegro	PA iii, 17
112	94	298	B♭, 3/8, Allegro	PA iii, 23
113	160	345	A, ¢, Allegro	PA iii, 14
114	141	344	A, 3/8, Con spirito è presto	PA iii, 27
115	100	407	c, 3/4, Allegro*	PA iii, 13
116	111	452	c, 3/8, Allegro*	PA iii, 14
117	181	244	C, ¢, Allegro	V xv, 20
118	266	122	D, ¢, Non presto	PA iii, 9
119	217	415	D, 3/8, Allegro*	PA ii, 17
120	146	215	d, 12/8, Allegrissimo*	PA ii, 16
121	93	181	g, 3/8, Allegrissimo	PA iii, 8
122	118	334	D, 3/8, Allegro	PA iii, 10
123	180	111	E♭, ¢, Allegro	PA iii, 21
124	110	232	G, 3/8, Allegro	PA i, 3
125	152	487	G, 3/8, Vivo	PA ii, 4
126	128	402	c, 3/8, —	PA ii, 26
127	198	186	A♭, ¢, Allegro	PA ii, 21
128	199	296	b♭, ¢, Allegro	PA ii, 29
129	148	460	c, 6/8, Allegro	PA i, 29
130	272	190	A♭, 3/8, Allegro	PA ii, 22
131	154	300	b♭, 3/8, Allegro	PA ii, 30
132	295	457	C, 3/4, Cantabile*	PA v, 5
133	218	284	C, 3/8, Allegro*	PA v, 6
134	143	221	E, 2/4, Allegro	PA ii, 7
135	234	225	E, 6/8, Allegro	PA ii, 8
136	113	377	E, 3/8, Allegro	PA ii, 9
137	231	315	D, 6/8, Allegro	PA ii, 6
138	95	464	d, 3/8, Allegro	PA ii, 5
139	126	6	c, ¢, Presto	PA iii, 6
140	127	107	D, C, Allegro no molto*	PA iii, 25
141	271	422	d, 3/8, Allegro	LB 31553, 41
147	48	376	e, C, —	PR4
148	291	64	a, 3/8, Andante	PA i, 1
149	241	93	a, C, Allegro	PA i, 2
150	205	117	F, 3/8, Allegro	PA i, 3
151	238	330	F, 3/8, Andante Allegro	PA i, 4
152	114	179	G, 3/8, Allegro	PA i, 5
153	235	445	G, 12/8, Vivo	PA i, 6
154	183	96	B♭, ¢, Allegro	PA i, 7
155	208	197	B♭, 3/8, Allegro	PA i, 8
156	248	101	C, C, Allegro	PA i, 9
157	391	405	C, 3/8, Allegro	PA i, 10
158	123	4	c, 3/8, Andante	PA i, 11
159	418	104	C, 6/8, Allegro	PA i, 12
160	131	15	C, 3/8, Allegro	PA i, 14
161	216	417	D, 3/8, Allegro	PA i, 13
162	162	21	E, 3/8, Andante	PA i, 15
163	206	63	E, 3/8, Allegro	PA i, 16
164	274	59	D, 3/4, Andante moderato	PA i, 17
165	292	52	C, 3/4, Andante	PA i, 18
166	190	51	C, ¢, Allegro mà non molto	PA i, 19
167	200	329	F, 3/4, Allegro	PA i, 21
168	182	280	F, ¢, Vivo	PA i, 20
169	247	331	G, C, Allegro con spirito	PA i, 22
170	164	303	C, C, Andante moderato è cantabile	PA i, 23

171	153	77	G, 3/8, Allegro	PA i, 24
172	313	S40	Bb, 6/8, Allegro	PA i, 25
173	51	447	b, 2/4, Allegro	PA i, 26
174	149	410	c, 6/8, Allegro	PA i, 27
175	136	429	a, 2/4, Allegro*	PA i, 28
176	163	163	d, ¢, Cantabile andante	PA i, 30
177	184	364	D, ¢, Andante moderato	V ii, 1
178	392	162	D, 3/8, Vivo	V ii, 2
179	89	177	g, 3/8, Allegro	PA ii, 1
180	192	272	G, ¢, Allegro vivo	PA ii, 2
181	253	194	A, 2/4, —	PA ii, 10
182	207	139	A, 3/8, Allegro	PA ii, 11
183	150	473	f, 2/4, Allegro	PA ii, 12
184	102	189	f, 3/8, Allegro	PA ii, 13
185	121	173	f, ¢, Andante	PA ii, 18
186	46	72	f, 3/8, Allegro	PA ii, 19
187	145	285	f, 3/8, Allegro	PA ii, 23
188	213	239	a, 3/8, Allegro	PA iv, 5
189	257	143	Bb, 3/4, Allegro	PA iv, 10
190	256	250	Bb, 12/8, —	PA iv, 11
191	18	207	d, 3/4, —	PA iv, 15
192	322	216	Eb, ¢, —	PA iv, 16
193	254	142	Eb, 3/8, —	PA iv, 17
194	479	28	F, 3/8, Andante	PA iv, 18
195	185	S18	F, ¢, Vivo	PA iv, 19
196	244	38	g, 2/4, Allegro	PA iv, 4
197	124	147	b, C, Andante	PA iv, 9
198	132	22	e, 3/4, Allegro	PA iv, 20
199	276	253	C, 12/8 Andante moderato	PA vi, 29
200	242	54	C, 2/4, Allegro	PA vi, 30
201	252	129	G, 3/4, Vivo	PA iv, 8
202	173	498	Bb, 3/8, Allegro	PA iv, 12
203	96	380	e, 3/8, Vivo non molto	PA iv, 21
204a	170	—	f, ¢, Allegro	PA iv, 22
204b	255	—	f, 3/8, Allegro	PA iv, 23
205	171	S23	F, ¢, Vivo	PA iv, 24
206	307	257	E, ¢, Andante	PA v, 1
207	140	371	E, 3/8, Allegro	PA v, 2
208	315	238	A, C, Andante è cantabile*	PA i, 1
209	209	428	A, 3/8, Allegro*	PA iv, 2
210	293	123	G, 3/8, Andante	PA iv, 3
211	277	133	A, ¢, Andantino	PA iv, 6
212	155	135	A, 3/8, Allegro molto	PA iv, 7
213	288	108	d, C, Andante	PA iv, 13
214	430	165	D, 12/8, Allegro vivo	PA iv, 14
215	281	323	E, 3/4, Andante*	PA iv, 25
216	320	273	E, 3/4, Allegro*	PA iv, 26
217	287	42	a, 3/4, Andante	PA iv, 27
218	237	392	a, 6/8, Vivo	PA iv, 28
219	278	393	A, ¢, Andante	PA iv, 29
220	309	342	A, 3/8, Allegro	PA iv, 30
221	215	259	A, 3/8, Allegro	PA v, 3
222	236	309	A, 6/8, Vivo	PA v, 4
223	188	214	D, ¢, Allegro	PA v, 7
224	225	268	D, 3/8, Vivo	PA v, 8
225	202	351	C, 3/4, Allegro	PA v, 9
226	101	112	c, 3/8, Allegro	PA v, 10
227	52	347	b, 2/4, Allegro	PA v, 11
228	224	399	Bb, 3/8, Allegro	PA v, 13
229	139	199	Bb, 2/4, Allegro vivo	PA v, 14
230	47	354	c, ¢, Allegro	PA v, 15
231	393	409	C, 3/8, Allegro	PA v, 16
232	317	62	e, ¢, Andante	PA v, 17
233	497	467	e, 3/8, Allegro	PA v, 18
234	286	49	g, 3/4, Andante	PA v, 19
235	172	154	G, 3/8, Allegro	PA v, 20
236	201	161	D, C, Allegro	PA vi, 3
237	446	308	D, 3/8, Allegro	PA vi, 4
238	55	27	f, C, Andante*	PA v, 21
239	56	281	f, 3/4, Allegro*	PA v, 22
240	368	S29	G, ¢, Allegro	PA v, 23
241	431	180	G, 6/8, Allegro	PA v, 24
242	243	202	C, 2/4, Vivo	PA v, 25
243	394	353	C, 3/8, Allegro	PA v, 26
244	298	348	B, 3/8, Allegro	PA v, 27
245	299	450	B, 6/8, Allegro	PA v, 28
246	296	260	c#, ¢, Allegro	PA v, 29
247	297	256	c#, 3/8, Allegro	PA v, 30
248	187	S35	Bb, ¢, Allegro	PA vi, 1
249	424	39	Bb, 3/8, Allegro	PA vi, 2
250	461	174	C, 2/4, Allegro	PA vi, 5
251	314	305	C, 3/8, Allegro	PA vi, 6
252	203	159	Eb, 3/4, Allegro	PA vi, 7
253	239	320	Eb, 12/8, Allegro	PA vi, 8
254	186	219	c, ¢, Andante	PA vi, 9
255	226	439	C, 3/8, Allegro	PA vi, 10
256	480	228	F, 3/4, Andante	PA vi, 11
257	138	169	F, 2/4, Allegro	PA vi, 12
258	494	178	D, 3/4, Andante	PA vi, 14
259	469	103	G, 3/4, Andante*	PA vi, 15
260	304	124	G, 3/4, Allegro*	PA vi, 16
261	300	148	B, 2/4, Allegro	PA vi, 17
262	301	446	B, 12/8, Vivo	PA vi, 18
263	283	321	e, ¢, Andante*	PA vi, 19
264	308	466	E, 3/8, Vivo*	PA vi, 20
265	168	S32	a, C, Allegro	PA vii, 16
266	251	48	Bb, C, Andante	PA vii, 4
267	363	434	Bb, 3/4, Allegro	PA vi, 5
268	369	41	A, ¢, Allegro	PA vi, 21
269	432	307	A, 6/8, Allegro	PA vi, 22
270	481	459	C, ¢, —	PA vi, 23
271	447	155	C, 3/8, Vivo	PA vi, 24
272	518	145	Bb, ¢, Allegro	PA vi, 25
273	174	398	Bb, 3/8, Vivo	PA vi, 26
274	491	297	F, ¢, Andante	PA vii, 1
275	330	328	F, 3/4, Allegro	PA vii, 2
276	433	S20	F, 3/8, Allegro	PA vii, 3
277	275	183	D, ¢, Cantabile andante	PA vii, 6
278	434	S15	D, 6/8, Con velocita	PA vii, 7
279	306	468	A, ¢, Andante	PA vii, 8
280	395	237	A, 3/8, Allegro	PA vii, 9
281	289	56	D, 3/4, Andante	PA vii, 10
282	166	484	D, ¢, Allegro	PA vii, 11
283	482	318	G, ¢, Andante allegro	PA vii, 12
284	169	90	G, 3/8, Allegro	PA vii, 13
285	321	91	A, ¢, Allegro	PA vii, 14
286	410	394	A, 6/8, Allegro	PA vii, 15
287	310	S9	D, C, Andante allegro	PA vii, 17
288	311	57	D, 3/8, Allegro	PA vii, 18
289	249	78	G, 2/4, Allegro	PA vii, 19
290	396	85	G, 3/8, Allegro	PA vii, 20
291	282	61	e, ¢, Andante	PA vii, 21
292	223	24	e, 3/8, Allegro	PA vii, 22
293	157	S44	d, ¢, Allegro	PA vii, 23
294	470	67	d, 3/4, Andante	PA vii, 24
295	211	270	d, 3/8, Allegro	PA vii, 25
296	305	198	F, 3/4, Andante	PA vii, 30
297	448	S19	F, 3/8, Allegro	PA vii, 31
298	194	S6	D, ¢, Allegro	PA vii, 26
299	268	210	D, 3/8, Allegro	PA vii, 27
300	312	92	A, 3/4, Andante	PA vii, 28
301	361	493	A, C, Allegro	PA vii, 29
302	279	7	c, 3/4, Andante	PA viii, 1
303	212	9	c, 3/8, Allegro	PA viii, 2
304	492	88	G, ¢, Andante cantabbile	PA viii, 3
305	397	322	G, 6/8, Allegro	PA viii, 4
306	456	16	Eb, ¢, Allegro	PA viii, 5
307	449	115	Eb, 3/8, Allegro	PA viii, 6
308	318	359	C, ¢, Cantabile*	PA viii, 7
309	333	454	C, ¢, Allegro*	PA viii, 8
310	284	248	Bb, ¢, Andante	PA viii, 9
311	227	144	Bb, 3/8, Allegro	PA viii, 10
312	334	264	D, ¢, Allegro	PA viii, 11
313	398	192	D, 3/8, Allegro	PA viii, 12
314	505	441	G, ¢, Allegro	PA viii, 13
315	54	235	g, 3/8, Allegro	PA viii, 14
316	193	299	F, ¢, Allegro	PA viii, 15
317	258	66	F, 3/4, Allegro	PA viii, 16
318	302	31	F#, ¢, Andante	PA viii, 17
319	303	35	F#, 6/8, Allegro	PA viii, 18
320	335	341	A, ¢, Allegro	PA viii, 19
321	450	258	A, 3/8, Allegro	PA viii, 20
322	360	483	A, ¢, Allegro	PA viii, 21
323	411	95	A, 6/8, Allegro	PA viii, 22
324	285	332	G, ¢, Andante	PA viii, 23
325	451	37	G, 3/8, Allegro	PA viii, 24
326	336	201	C, ¢, Allegro	PA viii, 27
327	399	152	C, 3/8, Allegro	PA viii, 28
328	485	S27	G, 6/8, Andante comodo	PA viii, 25
329	337	S5	C, ¢, Allegro	PA viii, 26
330	222	55	C, 3/8, Allegro	PA ix, 7
331	471	18	Bb, 3/4, Andante	PA viii, 29
332	519	141	Bb, ¢, Allegro	PA viii, 30
333	338	269	D, ¢, Allegro	PA ix, 1
334	412	100	Bb, 6/8, Allegro	PA ix, 2
335	339	S10	D, ¢, Allegro	PA ix, 8
336	262	337	D, 3/8, Allegro	PA ix, 9
337	340	S26	G, ¢, Allegro	PA ix, 10
338	400	87	G, 3/8, Allegro	PA ix, 11
339	189	251	C, ¢, Allegro	PA ix, 12
340	420	105	C, 6/8, Allegro	PA ix, 13
341	103	140	a, 3/8, Allegro	PA ix, 14

342	341	191	A, ¢, Allegro	PA ix, 15
343	495	291	A, C, Allegro andante	PA ix, 16
344	221	295	A, 3/8, Allegro	PA ix, 17
345	342	306	D, ¢, Allegro	PA ix, 18
346	250	60	D, 3/8, Allegro	PA ix, 19
347	294	126	g, ¢, Moderato è cantabbile	PA ix, 20
348	462	127	G, 3/4, Prestissimo	PA ix, 21
349	452	170	F, 3/8, Allegro	PA ix, 22
350	413	230	F, 6/8, Allegro	PA ix, 23
351	165	S34	Bb, ¢, Andante	PA ix, 24
352	343	S13	D, ¢, Allegro	PA ix, 3
353	401	313	D, 3/8, Allegro	PA ix, 4
354	486	68	F, 3/8, Andante	PA ix, 5
355	344	S22	F, ¢, Allegro	PA ix, 6
356	488	443	C, ¢, Con spirito andante	PA ix, 29
357	270	S45	C, 3/8, Allegro	PA ix, 30
358	457	412	D, 3/4, Allegro	PA x, 11
359	425	448	D, 3/8, Allegrissimo	PA x, 12
360	520	400	Bb, ¢, Allegro	PA ix, 25
361	214	247	Bb, 3/8, Allegrissimo	PA ix, 26
362	159	156	c, ¢, Allegro	PA ix, 27
363	104	160	c, 3/8, Presto	PA ix, 28
364	345	436	f, ¢, Allegro	PA x, 1
365	112	480	f, 3/8, Allegro	PA x, 2
366	263	119	F, 2/4, Allegro*	PA x, 6
367	453	172	F, 3/8, Presto*	PA x, 7
368	506	S30	A, ¢, Allegro	PA x, 9
369	259	240	A, 3/8, Allegro	PA x, 10
370	346	316	Eb, ¢, Allegro	PA x, 13
371	264	17	Eb, 3/8, Allegro	PA x, 14
372	402	302	G, 6/8, Allegro	PA x, 15
373	158	98	g, ¢, Presto è fugato	PA x, 16
374	472	76	G, ¢, Andante	PA x, 17
375	414	389	G, 6/8, Allegro	PA x, 18
376	246	34	b, 3/4, Allegro	PA x, 19
377	245	263	b, 2/4, Allegrissimo	PA x, 20
378	347	276	F, ¢, Allegro	PA x, 21
379	107	73	F, 3/8, Minuet	PA x, 22
380	483	23	E, 3/4, Andante commodo	PA x, 23
381	323	225	E, 3/8, Allegro	PA x, 24
382	508	S33	a, ¢, Allegro	PA x, 25
383	269	134	a, 3/8, Allegro	PA x, 26
384	487	2	C, ¢, Cantabbile andante	PA x, 27
385	220	284	C, 3/8, Allegro	PA x, 28
386	137	171	f, ¢, Presto	PA x, 29
387	415	175	f, 6/8, Veloce è fugato	PA x, 30
388	370	414	D, ¢, Presto	PA xi, 3
389	331	482	D, 3/4, Allegro	PA xi, 4
390	348	234	G, ¢, Allegro	PA xi, 1
391	364	79	G, 3/4, Allegro	PA xi, 2
392	371	246	Bb, ¢, Allegro	PA xi, 5
393	326	74	Bb, 3/4, Minuet	PA xi, 6
394	349	275	e, ¢, Allegro*	PA xi, 7
395	273	65	E, 3/8, Allegro*	PA xi, 8
396	435	110	d, ¢, Allegro	PA xi, 9
397	325	208	D, 3/8, Minuet	PA xi, 10
398	493	218	C, 6/8, Andante	PA xi, 11
399	458	274	C, 3/8, Allegro	PA xi, 12
400	228	213	D, 3/8, Allegro	PA xi, 13
401	436	365	D, 6/8, Allegro	PA xi, 14
402	496	427	e, ¢, Andante*	PA xi, 15
403	437	470	E, 6/8, Allegro*	PA xi, 16
404	489	222	A, ¢, Andante	PA xi, 17
405	438	43	A, 6/8, Allegro	PA xi, 18
406	509	5	C, ¢, Allegro	PA xi, 19
407	521	S4	C, 3/8, Allegro	PA xi, 20
408	350	346	b, ¢, Andante	PA xi, 21
409	403	150	b, 3/8, Allegro	PA xi, 22
410	372	S43	Bb, ¢, Allegro	PA xi, 23
411	351	69	Bb, 3/4, Allegro	PA xi, 24
412	463	182	G, 2/4, Allegro	PA xi, 25
413	416	125	G, 6/8, Allegro	PA xi, 26
414	373	310	D, ¢, Allegro	PA x, 3
415	175	S11	D, 12/8, Pastoral; Allegro	PA x, 4
416	454	149	D, 3/8, Presto	PA x, 5
417	40	462	d, ¢, Allegro moderato	PA x, 8
418	510	26	F, ¢, Allegro	PA xi, 27
419	524	279	F, 3/8, Piu tosto presto che allegro	PA xi, 28
420	352	S2	C, ¢, Allegro*	PA xi, 29
421	459	252	C, 3/8, Allegro*	PA xi, 30
422	511	451	C, ¢, Allegro	PA xii, 12
423	455	102	C, 3/8, Presto	PA xii, 13
424	374	289	G, ¢, Allegro	PA xii, 14
425	426	333	G, 3/8, Allegro molto	PA xii, 15
426	500	128	g, 3/8, Andante*	PA xii, 16
427	464	286	G, C, Presto, quanto sia possibbile*	PA xii, 17
428	353	131	A, ¢, Allegro	PA xii, 18
429	439	132	A, 6/8, Allegro	PA xii, 19
430	329	463	D, 3/8, Non presto mà a tempo di ballo	PA xii, 1
431	365	83	G, 3/4, Allegro	PA xii, 2
432	465	288	G, 3/4, Allegro	PA xii, 3
433	440	453	G, 6/8, Vivo	PA xii, 4
434	498	343	d, 3/4, Andante	PA xii, 5
435	466	361	D, C, Allegro	PA xii, 6
436	404	109	D, 3/8, Allegro	PA xii, 7
437	499	278	F, 3/4, Andante commodo	PA xii, 8
438	467	381	F, ¢, Allegro	PA xii, 9
439	473	47	Bb, C, Moderato	PA xii, 10
440	328	97	Bb, 3/4, Minuet	PA xii, 11
441	375	S39	Bb, ¢, Allegro	PA xii, 20
442	229	319	Bb, 3/8, Allegro	PA xii, 21
443	376	418	D, ¢, Allegro	PA xii, 22
444	441	420	d, 6/8, Allegrissimo	PA xii, 23
445	468	385	F, C, Allegro, o presto	PA xii, 24
446	177	433	F, 12/8, Pastorale; Allegrissimo	PA xii, 25
447	191	294	f#, ¢, Allegro	PA xii, 26
448	261	485	f#, 3/8, Allegro	PA xii, 27
449	405	444	G, 3/8, Allegro	PA xii, 28
450	422	338	g, C, Allegrissimo	PA xii, 29
451	366	243	a, 3/4, Allegro	PA xii, 30
452	195	—	A, ¢, Andante allegro	M ii, 51
453	280	—	A, 3/4, Andante	M ii, 52
454	423	184	G, 3/4, Andante spiritoso	PA xiii, 1
455	354	209	G, ¢, Allegro	PA xiii, 2
456	377	491	A, ¢, Allegro	PA xiii, 3
457	442	292	A, 6/8, Allegro	PA xiii, 4
458	260	212	D, 3/4, Allegro	PA xiii, 5
459	167	S14	d, 3/8, Allegro	PA xiii, 6
460	378	324	C, ¢, Allegro*	PA xiii, 7
461	324	8	C, 3/4, Allegro*	PA xiii, 8
462	474	438	f, 3/4, Andante	PA xiii, 9
463	512	471	f, ¢, Multo allegro	PA xiii, 10
464	460	151	C, ¢, Allegro	PA xiii, 11
465	406	242	C, 3/8, Allegro	PA xiii, 12
466	501	118	f, C, Andante moderato	PA xiii, 13
467	513	476	f, 3/4, Allegrissimo	PA xiii, 14
468	507	226	F, 3/4, Allegro	PA xiii, 15
469	514	431	F, C, Allegro molto	PA xiii, 16
470	379	304	G, ¢, Allegro*	PA xiii, 17
471	327	82	G, 3/4, Minuet*	PA xiii, 18
472	475	99	Bb, 3/4, Andante	PA xiii, 19
473	355	229	Bb, ¢, Allegro molto	PA xiii, 20
474	502	203	Eb, 3/4, Andante è cantabbile	PA xiii, 21
475	319	220	Eb, ¢, Allegrissimo	PA xiii, 22
476	427	340	g, 3/8, Allegro	PA xiii, 23
477	419	290	G, 6/8, Allegrissimo	PA xiii, 24
478	503	12	D, 3/4, Andante è cantabbile	PA xiii, 25
479	380	S16	D, ¢, Allegrissimo	PA xiii, 26
480	381	S8	D, ¢, Presto	PA xiii, 30
481	504	187	f, ¢, Andante è cantabbile	PA xiii, 27
482	356	435	F, ¢, Allegrissimo	PA xiii, 28
483	407	472	F, 3/8, Presto	PA xiii, 29
484	428	419	D, 3/8, Allegro	PA xiv, 1
485	490	153	C, ¢, Andante è cantabile	PA xiv, 2
486	515	455	C, ¢, Allegro	PA xiv, 3
487	421	205	C, 3/8, Allegro	PA xiv, 4
488	382	S37	Bb, ¢, Allegro	PA xiv, 5
489	522	S41	Bb, 3/8, Allegro	PA xiv, 6
490	476	206	D, ¢, Cantabile*	PA xiv, 7
491	484	164	D, 3/4, Allegro*	PA xiv, 8
492	443	14	D, 6/8, Presto*	PA xiv, 9
493	383	S24	G, ¢, Allegro*	PA xiv, 10
494	444	287	G, 6/8, Allegro*	PA xiv, 11
495	384	426	E, ¢, Allegro	PA xiv, 12
496	332	372	E, 3/4, Allegro	PA xiv, 13
497	357	146	b, ¢, Allegro	PA xiv, 14
498	367	350	b, 3/4, Allegro	PA xiv, 15
499	477	193	A, ¢, Andante	PA xiv, 16
500	358	492	A, 3/4, Allegro	PA xiv, 17
501	385	137	C, ¢, Allegretto	PA xiv, 18
502	408	3	C, 3/8, Allegro	PA xiv, 19
503	196	196	Bb, ¢, Allegro	PA xiv, 20
504	265	29	Bb, 3/8, Allegro	PA xiv, 21
505	386	326	F, ¢, Allegro non presto	PA xiv, 22
506	409	70	F, 3/8, Allegro	PA xiv, 23

507	478	113	Eb, 2/4, Andantino cantabile	PA xiv, 24	
508	516	19	Eb, 3/4, Allegro	PA xiv, 25	
509	387	311	D, ¢, Allegro	PA xiv, 26	
510	525	277	d, 3/4, Allegro	PA xiv, 27	
511	388	314	D, ¢, Allegro	PA xiv, 28	
512	359	339	D, 3/4, Allegro	PA xiv, 29	
513	176	S3	C, 12/8, Pastorale; Moderato*	PA xiv, 30	
514	389	1	C, ¢, Allegro	PA xv, 1	
515	417	255	C, 3/4, Allegro	PA xv, 2	
516	523	S12	d, 3/8, Allegretto*	PA xv, 3	
517	517	266	d, ¢, Prestissimo*	PA xv, 4	
518	390	116	F, ¢, Allegro*	PA xv, 5	
519	445	475	f, 3/8, Allegro assay*	PA xv, 6	
520	362	86	G, ¢, Allegretto	PA xv, 7	
521	429	408	G, 3/8, Allegro	PA xv, 8	
522	526	S25	G, ¢, Allegro	PA xv, 9	
523	527	490	G, 3/8, Allegro	PA xv, 10	
524	528	283	F, 3/4, Allegro	PA xv, 11	
525	529	188	F, 6/8, Allegro	PA xv, 12	
526	530	456	c, ¢, Allegro comodo	PA xv, 13	
527	531	458	C, 3/4, Allegro assai	PA xv, 14	
528	532	200	Bb, ¢, Allegro	PA xv, 15	
529	533	327	Bb, 3/8, Allegro	PA xv, 16	
530	534	44	E, 3/4, Allegro	PA xv, 17	
531	535	430	E, 6/8, Allegro	PA xv, 18	
532	536	223	a, 3/8, Allegro	PA xv, 19	
533	537	395	A, ¢, Allegro assai	PA xv, 20	
534	538	11	D, ¢, Cantabile	PA xv, 21	
535	539	262	D, 3/4, Allegro	PA xv, 22	
536	540	236	A, ¢, Cantabile	PA xv, 23	
537	541	293	A, 3/4, Prestissimo	PA xv, 24	
538	542	254	G, 3/8, Allegretto	PA xv, 25	
539	543	121	G, ¢, Allegro	PA xv, 26	
540	544	S17	F, ¢, Allegretto	PA xv, 27	
541	545	120	F, 6/8, Allegretto	PA xv, 28	
542	546	167	F, 3/4, Allegretto	PA xv, 29	
543	547	227	F, 6/8, Allegro	PA xv, 30	
544	548	497	Bb, 3/4, Cantabile*	PA xv, 31	
545	549	500	Bb, ¢, Prestissimo*	PA xv, 32	
546	550	312	g, 3/8, Cantabile	PA xv, 33	
547	551	S28	G, ¢, Allegro	PA xv, 34	
548	552	404	C, 3/8, Allegretto	PA xv, 35	
549	553	S1	C, ¢, Allegro	PA xv, 36	
550	554	S42	Bb, ¢, Allegretto	PA xv, 37	
551	555	396	Bb, 3/4, Allegro	PA xv, 38	
552	556	421	d, ¢, Allegretto	PA xv, 39	
553	557	425	d, 3/8, Allegro	PA xv, 40	
554	558	S21	F, ¢, Allegretto	PA xv, 41	
555	559	477	f, 6/8, Allegro	PA xv, 42	

SONATAS FOR SOLO INSTRUMENT AND CONTINUO

73	80	217	c, 3/4, Allegro: C, 3/8, Minuetto	V xiv, 37
77	10	168	d, 3/4, Moderato è cantabile; d, 3/8, Minuet	V xiv, 42
78	26	75	F, 2/4, Gigha; F, 3/8, Minuet	V xiv, 44
81	13	271	e, C, Grave; e, 2/4, Allegro; e, 3/4, Grave; e, 3/8, Allegro	V xiv, 46
88	8	36	g, C, Grave; g, 3/8, Andante moderato; g, 2/4, Allegro; g, 3/8, Minuet	V xiv, 53
89	12	211	d, C, Allegro; d, 3/4, Grave; d, 3/8, Allegro	V xiv, 54
90	9	106	d, C, Grave; d, 2/4, Allegro; d, 12/8, — ; d, 3/8, Allegro	V xiv, 55
91	11	176	G, C, Grave; G, 2/4, Allegro; G, 3/4, Grave; G, 3/8, Allegro	V xiv, 56

DOUBTFUL KEYBOARD SONATAS
(uncertain authenticity, or incomplete or poor texts in the primary sources)

95	—	358	C, 12/8, —	Bp.x, 16
97	5	—	g, 3/8, Allegro	B iii, 6
142	240	—	f#, 12/8, Allegro	LB 31553, 42
143	267	—	C, 3/8, Allegro	LB 31553, 43
144	316	—	G, ¢, Cantabile	LB 31553, 44
145	105	369	D, 3/8, —	CF5
146	106	349	G, 3/8, —	CF7
—	—	—	C, 3/4, Presto	NH18
—	—	—	C, 9/8, Prestissimo	NH19
—	—	—	A, 3/8, —	G10
—	—	—	E, 3/8, —	G13
—	—	—	A, ¢, Allegro; A, 3/8, Spiritoso	LB 14248, f.15v

BIBLIOGRAPHY

BurneyH

A. Longo: Domenico Scarlatti e la sua figura nella storia della musica (Naples, 1913)

W. Gerstenberg: Die Klavier-Kompositionen Domenico Scarlattis (Regensburg, 1933/R1968)

L. Bauer: Die Tätigkeit Domenico Scarlatti und der italienischen Meister in der ersten Hälfte des 18. Jahrhunderts in Spanien (diss., U. of Munich, 1933)

S. Sitwell: A Background for Domenico Scarlatti (London, 1935)

C. Valabrega: Il clavicembalista Domenico Scarlatti, il suo secolo, la sua opera (Modena, 1937, rev. 2/1955)

S. A. Luciani: Domenico Scarlatti (Turin, 1939)

R. Newton: 'The English Cult of Domenico Scarlatti', ML, xx (1939), 138

M. S. Kastner: Contribución al estudio de la música española y portuguesa (Lisbon, 1941)

C. Hopkinson: '18th-century Editions of the Keyboard Compositions of Domenico Scarlatti', Transactions of the Edinburgh Bibliographical Society, iii (1948), 49

R. B. Benton: 'Form in the Sonatas of Domenico Scarlatti', MR, xiii (1952), 264

R. Kirkpatrick: Domenico Scarlatti (Princeton, 1953, rev. 3/1968)

M. Bogianckino: L'arte clavicembalista di Domenico Scarlatti (Rome, 1956)

A. Basso: La formazione storica ed estetica della storia di Domenico Scarlatti (diss., U. of Turin, 1957)

A. Della Corte: 'Tetide in Sciro: l'opera di Domenico Scarlatti ritrovata', RaM, xxvii (1957), 281

H. Keller: Domenico Scarlatti, ein Meister des Klaviers (Leipzig, 1957)

R. Allorto: 'Clementi non ha plagiato Scarlatti', Musica d'oggi, new ser., ii (1959), 66

A. D. McCredie: 'Domenico Scarlatti and his Opera Narcisso', AcM, xxxiii (1961), 19

G. Pestelli: Le sonate di Domenico Scarlatti: proposta di un ordinamento cronologico (Turin, 1967)

P. Williams: 'The Harpsichord Acciacatura: Theory and Practice in Harmony, 1650–1750', MQ, liv (1968), 503

J. L. Sheveloff: The Keyboard Music of Domenico Scarlatti: a Reevaluation of the Present State of Knowledge in the Light of the Sources (diss., Brandeis U., 1970)

L. Hautus: 'Zu dem Domenico Scarlatti zugeschriebenen Capriccio fugato á dodici', Mf, xxiv (1971), 294

——: 'Beitrag zur Datierung der Klavierwerke Domenico Scarlattis', Mf, xxv (1972), 59

S. Choi: Newly Found 18th-century Manuscripts of Domenico Scarlatti's Sonatas and their Relationship to other 18th and Early 19th-century Sources (diss., U. of Wisconsin, Madison, 1974)

(8) **Giuseppe Scarlatti** (b Naples, c1718, or 18 June 1723; d Vienna, 17 Aug 1777). Composer. His date of birth and his relationship to the other Scarlattis remain uncertain, although it is known from various documents and his own statements that (7) Domenico was his uncle. In Vienna in later years he used a title, presumably that conferred on his grandfather (he himself is not known to have been ennobled). Burney and Gerber gave 1718 as his year of birth, but according to the Vienna city archives he was 65 when he died; possibly he was in fact 55 (or in his 55th year). If that is correct, he may be identified as the son Giuseppe of (5) Tommaso Scarlatti, born on 18 June 1723 (in which case it was his sister Rosa whom he brought to Vienna, as a singer, about 1750). Either date of birth, 1718 or 1723, can be reconciled with the fact that his first composition, an oratorio La Ss Vergine Annunziata, was performed in Rome in 1739; the libretto calls Giuseppe 'Maestro di cappella napolitano' (the title is used in an honorific sense, not implying an appointment or seniority). During the following decades Giuseppe Scarlatti was commissioned to write at least 32 operas, most of them for Lucca, Venice or Vienna.

The succession of cities in which Giuseppe Scarlatti's operas were performed implies that from 1739 to 1741 he lived in Rome, and that he moved from there to Florence and Lucca, where he was established by 1744. In 1747 his *Artaserse* was performed in Lucca; a contemporary chronicler reported that after the performance he left the city with his wife, the singer Barbara Stabili. Probably they went to Vienna, where Barbara Scarlatti's name is found in 1748 on the lists of singers at the court theatres; she was one of the *opera buffa* singers, and thus paid only a third of the salary of an *opera seria* singer. Her name also appears in the private court accounts, where it is said that a musician Grigotti was paid for coaching her to take over a role in Wagenseil's *Alessandro nell'Indie* at short notice.

Giuseppe Scarlatti seems to have been unable to find employment in Vienna at this date, which would explain the absence of Barbara's name from the lists of singers the following year. Possibly they lived in Turin or Lucca in 1749–50, where his operas were given and Barbara appeared as a singer. Scarlatti wrote his *Adriano in Siria* for the Venice Carnival of 1752; two more operas were written for Venice that year and one for Padua, and probably the Scarlattis then lived in Venice. It is generally assumed that Giuseppe visited his uncle in Spain before 1755; such a visit would be consistent with the performance of his *L'impostore* at Barcelona in 1752. In 1753 both the Scarlattis were employed in Reggio Emilia. In 1755 Giuseppe returned to Naples, apparently alone; possibly Barbara had died, for she is not known to have appeared after 1753. In 1756 Scarlatti was back in Venice and from 1757 travelling between Vienna and Venice. After his success in two *opere buffe*, Gluck apparently helped him to find employment as a ballet composer at the Vienna Kärntnerthor-Theater. He is noted in Viennese archives as receiving payment, and signed a contract on 1 March 1762 to compose ballet music for which he received 618 florins each season, a salary above the average. He also wrote some operas for Vienna during these years. A letter from Dancourt to Favart in 1762 (see Haas) mentions Giuseppe Scarlatti as receiving the special protection of Gluck, who apparently helped him financially; Dancourt sarcastically remarked that Gluck could afford to be kind to an Italian less rich and less successful than himself, and referred to Scarlatti as a 'virtuoso', possibly indicating his abilities as a harpsichordist (also mentioned by Gerber). Scarlatti's connection with the Viennese court theatres apparently ended in 1764 when Count Durrazzo gave up his position and Gluck's influence had faded. Scarlatti probably went to Italy in 1765 but soon returned to Vienna for the performances of more *opere buffe* and *serie*. In 1766 he may have visited Spain. In the same year he probably married Antonia Lefebure (1744–70); a son was born to them in 1767, and a senior employee of Prince Schwarzenberg stood as godfather. Scarlatti was listed in Viennese documents as 'Herrschaftlicher Kapellmeister' and gave singing lessons to Theresia von Schwarzenberg, so possibly was in the prince's service; that would explain a summer performance of *L'isola disabitata* in Prague in 1767 as well as a remark on the score of the comic intermezzo *Dove è amore è gelosia* ('Posto in musica per commandamento di Sua Altezza il Signor Principe di Schwarzenberg'). At the start of his career, Salieri met Scarlatti; he later reported that Scarlatti looked over part of his first opera, corrected some small mistakes but then praised the music.

Scarlatti had a natural melodic gift, and also a dramatic talent which soon led him to abandon the da capo aria in his *buffo* operas (though a few may be found in his scores) and to handle his texts freely, even those by Metastasio. That enabled him to invent new variations of the *buffo* aria form with multiple sections, or to insert parlando sections in triple time; he was also inclined to avoid slow tempos. His style was distinctive. He could not compete with the expressive range or lyrical quality of Galuppi, or the young Piccinni, but his music compares well with that of the other Italian *buffo* composers working in Vienna in the 1750s and 1760s. By the 1770s the charming but rather simple style of his operas was outdated, and they were superseded by the work of a new generation of *buffo* composers.

Scarlatti was not in the city when Burney visited Vienna in September 1772; possibly he was with the Schwarzenberg family in Bohemia. Burney regretted not meeting him and mentioned him among the important composers. After his second wife's death, in 1770, Scarlatti did not remarry, and he died in 1777 without having made a will, according to the *Wiener Diarium*.

WORKS

STAGE WORKS

(unless otherwise stated, all are operas, ?all lost)

La Ss Vergine Annunziata (oratorio), Rome, 19 March 1739

Componimento per musica (serenata, 2), Rome, ?Palazzo Aquaviva, 1739, *A-Wgm*, according to Eitner

Merope (Zeno), Rome, Capranica, 23 Jan 1740, *I-Bc* (lib), *Nc*, according to Eitner

Dario (G. Baldanza), Rome, Argentina, carn. 1741, lib *I-Bc*, according to Eitner

Arminio in Germania (C. Pasquini), Florence, della Pergola, 24 June 1741, lost

Siroe (Metastasio), Florence, della Pergola, 24 June 1742; rev. Livorno, 1747

Pompeo in Armenia (B. Vitturi), Pisa, Pubblico, carn. 1744

Ezio (Metastasio), Lucca, Civico, aut. 1744; rev. Venice, 1754

Olimpiade (Metastasio), Lucca, ?Pubblico, aut. 1745

Il giocatore, Florence, Cocomero, carn. 1747

Artaserse (dramma musicale, Metastasio), Lucca, 26 Aug 1747, *A-Wn*, *B-Bc*; rev. in Ger. trans. by J. A. Edler von Ghelen with dances by J. Starzer, Vienna, Shrove Tuesday, 1763

Partenope (S. Stampiglia), Turin, Regio, carn. 1749

L'impostore, Barcelona, 1752, collab. G. Cocchi

Adriano in Siria (Metastasio), Venice, S Cassiano, carn. 1752

L'amore della patria (serenata, C. Goldoni), Venice, Accademia dei Nobili, 11 June 1752

Demetrio (Metastasio), Padua, Nuovo, June 1752

I portentosi effetti della madre Natura (Goldoni), Venice, S Samuele, 11 Nov 1752, *A-Wgm*

Alessandro nell'Indie (Metastasio), Reggio Emilia, Pubblico, 12 May 1753, *A-Wgm*

De gustibus non est disputandum (Goldoni), Venice, S Cassiano, carn. 1754, *B-Bc*

Caio Mario (G. Roccaforte), Naples, S Carlo, 20 Jan 1755

La Madamigella (A. Palombo), Naples, Fiorentini, spr. 1755

Antigona (Roccaforte), Milan, Ducale, carn. 1756, lib *I-Rsc*, according to Eitner

Chi tutto abbraccia nulla stringe (Vitturi), Venice, 1756

La clemenza di Tito (Metastasio), Venice, S Moisè, carn. 1757

Il mercato di Malmantile (Goldoni), Venice, 1757; rev. Vienna, Burgtheater, 1758

L'isola disabitata (dramma giocoso, 3, Goldoni), Venice, 1757; rev. Vienna, Burgtheater, 1757, *A-Wgm*, *D-Dlb*; rev. as La cinese smarrita, Genoa, Falconi, sum. 1760

La serva scaltra (opera bernesca, 3), Venice, S Moisè, aut. 1759; rev. Vienna, Burgtheater, 1759, *A-Wn*

L'Issipile (Metastasio), Vienna, Burgtheater, aut. 1760, *D-Bds*

Les aventures de Serail (ballet), Vienna, 1762, *A-Wgm*, according to Eitner

Pelopida (Roccaforte), Turin, Regio, carn. 1763

Bajazet (A. Piovene), Verona, Accademia Filarmonica, carn. 1765

Gli stravaganti (dramma musicale, 'Alcindo Isaurense'), Vienna, Burgtheater, 11 Feb 1765, *Wn*; rev. as La mogile padrona, Vienna, Burgtheater, 1768

Armida (festa teatrale, M. Coltellini), Vienna, Burgtheater, 1767

Dove è amore è gelosia (intermezzo giocoso, Coltellini), Vienna,

Burgtheater, 1768, *Wn*
L'amor geloso, Vienna, ?Schönbrunn, 5 July 1770
Amitie Ontario o I selvaggi (dramma per musica, R. Calzabigi), Vienna, Burgtheater, 1772; lib *Wgm*

OTHER WORKS

Laudate pueri, 3vv, 2 vn, va, bc, *D-Bds, GB-Lbm*
Cantatas: Imeneo, sognando talora, T, bc, *A-Wgm*; I lamenti d'Orfeo, 2vv, orch, *B-Bc*; Amor prigioniero, S, S, insts, *D-Dlb*; all cited by Eitner
Arias (? mainly from operas): *A-Wgm, D-Bds, Dlb, ROu, W*; *GB-Cfm*; *I-Bc, Mc, Nc*, cited by Eitner
Sonata, hpd, in J. U. Haffner, Raccolta musicale, v (Nuremberg, 1765), cited by Eitner

BIBLIOGRAPHY

H. Springer: 'Das Partiturautograph von Giuseppe Scarlattis bisher verschollener "Clemenza di Tito" ', *Beiträge zum Bibliotheks- und Buchwesen: Paul Schenke . . . gewidmet* (Berlin, 1913), 257
R. Haas: *Gluck und Durazzo* (Vienna, 1925)
P. Fienga: 'Giuseppe Scarlatti et son incertaine ascendance directe', *ReM* (1932), no.123, p.113

DONALD J. GROUT (1: text, 1–5, 7–9)
EDWIN HANLEY (1: text, 6)
MALCOLM BOYD (1: work-list, bibliography)
EVA BADURA-SKODA (2–6, 8)
JOEL SHEVELOFF (7)

Scarpini, Pietro (*b* Rome, 6 April 1911). Italian pianist. He studied the piano (Casella), the organ (Germani), composition (Bustini) and conducting (Molinari) at the Accademia di S Cecilia in Rome, and then took advanced composition lessons with Hindemith, and an arts degree at Rome University. Having made his début in Italy in 1937, after the war he performed in Europe and the USA (from 1954), giving recitals and playing with such conductors as Furtwängler, Mitropoulos and Szell. His repertory, which includes music by all the major Classical composers, is especially rich in contemporary works. He gave the first performances of the Sonata for four hands by Hindemith (1938, with the composer), of the *Sonatina canonica* by Dallapiccola, and of many other works by Italian composers in addition to first performances in Italy of compositions by Schoenberg, Skryabin, Rakhmaninov, Bartók and Prokofiev. However, Scarpini plays much Bach: he has given performances of the complete *Kunst der Fuge* (1954) and the '48' (1960). He has taught at the conservatories of Parma, Florence, Naples, Milan and Rome, and has given advanced courses at the Accademia Chigiana in Siena (1948–50 and 1968–71) and in Darmstadt (1950). His compositions include a Piano Quintet (1933), a Piano Concerto (1934) and pieces for piano and for organ.

PIERO RATTALINO

Scarselli, Rinieri [Riniero] (*b* Bologna; *d* after 1 Aug 1642). Italian composer. He was a priest and a canon regular of S Salvatore, Bologna. As a musician he was a pupil of Galeazzo Sabbatini, two of whose compositions, one of them a mass, he included in his earliest publication, *Sacrarum modulationum . . . liber primus* (Venice, 1637), for two to four voices and organ. By 1640 at the latest he had become a member of the Accademia dei Filomusi in Bologna, as is clear from the title-page of his *Il primo libro de' madrigali* op.2, for two to four voices (Venice, 1640; only the bass part survives). His other surviving publication is *Cantate . . . commode da cantarsi in diversi strumenti* (Venice, 1642) for accompanied solo voice. This contains three laments, which according to Fortune are on the whole rather dull; the most interesting is a lament of Andromeda, *Ahi! dolore*, which contains some expressive recitative and a triple-time aria section built on a

passacaglia bass. The volume also includes 11 strophic arias, some of which, such as *Amo bellezza* and *A gran torto fere amate*, are in a madrigalian style. A further publication, *Il primo libro de' madrigali* (Venice, 1642), for five voices, is cited by Fétis but is otherwise unknown.

BIBLIOGRAPHY

FétisB
E. Bohn: *Bibliographie der Musikdruckwerke bis 1700, welche . . . zu Breslau aufbewahrt werden* (Berlin, 1883/R1969), 380f
E. Schmitz: *Geschichte der weltlichen Solokantate* (Leipzig, 1914, rev.2/1955), 25, 81
N. Fortune: *Italian Secular Song from 1600 to 1635: the Origins and Development of Accompanied Monody* (diss., U. of Cambridge, 1954), 443, 446

JOHN WHENHAM

Scastelain, Jean. *See* CHASTELAIN, JEAN.

Scat singing. A technique of jazz singing whereby melodies are sung to onomatopoeic or nonsense syllables. It is said to be derived from the west African practice of singing percussion patterns by assigning fixed syllables to a rhythm, but by the time of the earliest recorded examples of scat singing, notably Louis Armstrong's (e.g. *Hotter than that*, 1927), the technique involved free invention of melodies and syllables with, in Armstrong's case, considerable virtuosity. Armstrong's examples show the application or imitation of many jazz instrumental devices, and as later scat singers, especially Ella Fitzgerald and Sarah Vaughan, incorporated the more advanced techniques of instrumental jazz into their singing, some of their performances rivalled it in complexity. The name 'bebop' and its abbreviated form 'bop' are said to derive from a scat rendition of a common two-note quaver figure in that music. Other notable scat singers include Cab Calloway, probably the model of the scat-singing character Sportin' Life in Gershwin's *Porgy and Bess*, and the trumpeters Dizzy Gillespie and Clark Terry, with his unique 'mumbling' technique. A related practice is the attempt by the jazz singers Jon Hendricks and King Pleasure, among others, to underlay texts to well-known jazz solos, and in the 1960s a form of scat singing was applied by the Swingle Singers to pieces from the classical repertory.

BRADFORD ROBINSON

Sceaux. Château near Paris, used for court entertainments during the reign of Louis XIV; *see* PARIS, §V, 4.

Scellery, Pierre Borjon de. *See* BORJON DE SCELLERY, PIERRE.

Scelsi, Giacinto (*b* La Spezia, 8 Jan 1905). Italian composer. Receiving an education appropriate to his noble birth, he displayed from childhood an exceptional musical sensibility but had no professional training, learning only the rudiments of traditional harmony from Giacinto Sallustio. Lengthy periods abroad kept him from any direct influence of Italian music between the wars; his wanderings took him to Geneva, where he studied under Egon Koehler (a musician whose ideas related to those of Skryabin, and who thus provided Scelsi with a most congenial apprenticeship), and to Vienna, where he worked on 12-note serial technique with Walter Klein (1935–6). In 1951–2 he settled in Rome, where, chiefly as a member of the Nuova Consonanza association, he has occasionally organized concerts of contemporary music, as he had already done in 1934–5. He wrote a number of musical-philosophical essays – mostly unpublished, except for those contributed in 1943–5 to *La Suisse contemporaine* – and three collections of poetry in French, published in Paris in 1949, 1954 and 1962.

Since music is, for Scelsi, an intuitive link with the transcendental and involves the annulment of creative individuality, the countless changes in style contributing to the non-professional features of his vast output should be regarded as pure phenomena, which merely embody a spiritual process substantially unchanging. In surface characteristics his works up to the early 1950s submitted, though with apparent difficulty (as in the simple Violin Sonata of 1934), to the learned tradition of European music. Generally adopting a free atonality, he employed styles ranging from the modish 'machine music' of the 1920s, as in the youthful *Rotative* for ensemble, to the neo-romantic cast of such impromptu-type chamber pieces as the Skryabinesque *Poemi* of 1937 or the struggling *Ballata* of 1945, and from the embryonic serialism emerging in the Variations and Fugue for piano (1941), a partly parodistic homage to Webern, to the eclecticism displayed by the choral cantata *La naissance du Verbe* (1948), which was an attempt at a large form capable of synthesizing opposing tenets of Western music (dodecaphony included) according to a purely metaphysical poetic content.

By the 1950s, as outwardly instanced in his abandonment of conventional for exotic or esoteric titles, Scelsi turned increasingly towards the asceticism of eastern art. Technically this involved a significant modification of the unrelieved motivic procedures previously characterizing his music. Already foreshadowed in the String Quartet no.1 (1944), where he resourcefully stressed the opening harmonic situation in order to develop the tension of the whole work, such a modification reached an extreme point in the intriguing *Quattro pezzi* for orchestra (1959), each piece being based on a single note held throughout, with attention focussed on its smallest variations of rhythm, dynamics or pitch in a manner that suggests comparison with meditative practice. Moreover, the micro-intervallic writing so poignantly exploited in this work – and further developed, chiefly in compositions for strings, such as his last three quartets, *Xnoybis* and *Natura renovatur* – gave way to that inclusion of sound material outside the tempered system which in due course led him to make use even of clusters (*Action Music* for piano) and *musique concrète* (*Prânam* for voice, instruments and tape).

Having broken out of the old-fashioned esoteric attitude underlying his 'first-manner' works (an attitude with antecedents in the theosophical interests of Skryabin and Schoenberg), Scelsi's development in the last 20 years has disclosed an inner sympathy with the anti-rational tendencies of the new music. Hence – ending a lifelong isolation which may help to explain the startling absence of any writing on him – the support eventually provided for his work in radical circles in Italy, and the interest shown in it by foreign composers including Ligeti and Feldman.

WORKS

Selective list; unpublished except for 11 chamber works printed in 1947–9; most dates after 1954 are those of copyright

ORCHESTRAL

Rotative, 3 pf, wind, perc, 1929; Pf Concertino, 1934; Introduction and Fugue, str, 1945; 4 pezzi, 1959; Hurqualja, amp insts, orch, 1960; Chukrum, str, 1963; Nomos, 2 orch, org, 1963; Anagamin, str, 1965; Anahit, vn, 18 insts, 1965; Ohoi, str, 1966; Natura renovatur, str, 1967

VOCAL

Choral: La naissance du Verbe, chorus, orch, 1948; 3 canti popolari, 4vv, 1958; 3 canti sacri, 8vv, 1958; Uaxuctum, chorus, ondes martenot, orch, 1966; Yliam, female vv, 1967; Tkrdg, 6 male vv, amp gui, perc, 1968; Konx-om-pax, chorus, org, orch, 1969; Sauh, 2vv, 1973; Prânam 2, ens, 1974

Solo vocal: 3 canti, 1v, pf, 1932; 3 vocalises sur des mélodies nègres, 1v, 1936; Jamaon, B, 5 insts, 1954–8; Hô, S, 1960; Wo-ma, B, 1960; Khoom, S, 6 insts, 1962; Taiagaru, S, 1962; Ckckc, 1v, mand, 1967; Prânam, 1v, insts, tape, 1971–2

CHAMBER

Chemin du coeur, vn, pf, 1929; Dialogo, vc, pf, 1932; Sonata, vn, pf, 1934; 2 pf trios, 1936, 1939; 4 str qts, 1944, 1961, 1963, 1964, no.1 arr. str orch, 1962; Ballata, vc, pf, 1945; Pwill, fl, 1954; Hyxos, a fl, gong, small bell, 1955; Rucke di guck, pic, ob, 1957; Triphon, vc, 1957; Elegia per Thy, va, vc, 1958; I presagi, 9 insts, 1958; Str Trio, 1958; Kya, cl, 7 insts, 1959; Xnoybis, vn, 1964; Duo, vn, vc, 1965; Ko-lho, fl, cl, 1966

Other works incl. solo pieces for cl, sax, hn, tpt, trbn, gui, va

PIANO

40 preludi, 1930–40; Paralipomeni, 1930–40; Toccata, 1934; Poemi, 1937; Variations, 1940; Variations and Fugue, 1941; Sonata, 1942; 9 suites, 1937–c1946; 15 capricci di Ty, c1938–1950; Suite no.10 'Ka', 1954; Action Music, 1955

Principal publisher: De Santis

CLAUDIO ANNIBALDI

Scena (It.; Fr. *scène*; Ger. *Szene*, formerly *Scene*). The word is derived from the Latin *scaena*, which in turn comes from the Greek *skēnē*, 'tent', 'hut', 'booth' and hence 'stage', 'décor'. It is used in opera, as in drama generally, to mean (1) the stage (e.g. 'sulla scena', on the stage; 'derrière la scène', behind the stage), (2) the scene represented on the stage, (3) a division of an act.

In Italian opera it also has the specific meaning of an episode which has no formal construction but may be made up of diverse elements. The opening of Act 3 of Verdi's *Ernani* (1844) is described as 'Preludio, Scena e Cavatina'. The 'Preludio' is for orchestra. The 'Scena' consists of recitative for the king, with interpolations by his squire. A scena is frequently more extended than this and includes, in addition to recitative, arioso passages and one or more arias, duets, etc. A scena of a particularly dramatic character, often (though not invariably) for a single character, is described as a 'gran scena', e.g. 'Gran scena del sonnambulismo', the sleepwalking scene in Verdi's *Macbeth* (1847, rev. 1865). The word was also used to describe a setting for concert performance of a scene from an opera libretto, e.g. Mozart's *Misera, dove son* K369 (1781), for soprano and orchestra, the text of which is taken from Metastasio's *Ezio*. Spohr's Violin Concerto in A minor op.47 (1816) is subtitled 'In modo di scena cantante'. In French and German opera 'scène' and 'Szene' are used much like 'scena', but generally to describe quite short sections of a work, e.g. no.11bis in Act 2 of Bizet's *La jolie fille de Perth* (1867), which is an accompanied recitative for the duke and Mab.

JACK WESTRUP

Schaal, Richard (*b* Dortmund, 3 Dec 1922). German musicologist. He studied musicology, art history, psychology and historical auxiliary sciences at Marburg University, where he took a doctorate in 1946 with a dissertation on Hugo Kaun. He supplemented his studies with private tuition in music theory with H. Gebhard-Elsass, and conducting with H. W. von Waltershausen; he also attended the library school of the Bavarian State Library, Munich, where in 1956 he passed the senior librarians' examination. As a freelance musicologist Schaal has contributed to *MGG* (about

130 articles), and has drawn up the list of articles for the IMS's *Polyglottes Fachwörterbuch der Musik*. In 1962 he became the musicological adviser in the music department of Bavarian radio. He is editor of the *Quellenkataloge zur Musikgeschichte* (Wilhelmshaven, 1966), the *Taschenbücher zur Musikwissenschaft* (Wilhelmshaven, 1969) and the *Veröffentlichungen zur Musikforschung* (Wilhelmshaven, 1972). Schaal specializes in compiling bibliographies of source materials (manuscripts, prints, inventories and archival collections) for localized music research of the 16th to 19th centuries; he also compiles lexicographies and bibliographies designed for library use.

WRITINGS

Hugo Kaun (diss., U. of Marburg, 1946; Regensburg, 1948)
Das Schrifttum zur musikalischen Lokalgeschichtesforschung (Kassel, 1947)
'Zur Musikpflege in Kollegiatstift St. Moritz zu Augsburg', *Mf*, vii (1954), 1
'Die Musikbibliothek von Raimund Fugger d. J.', *AcM*, xxix (1957), 126
'Stand und Aufgaben der musikalischen Lokalforschung in Deutschland', *Mf*, x (1957), 114
Die vor 1801 gedruckten Libretti des Theatermuseums München (Kassel, 1963)
Verzeichnis deutschsprachiger musikwissenschaftlicher Dissertationen 1861–1960 (Kassel, 1963); *1961–1970* (Kassel, 1974)
'Die Musikinstrumentensammlung von R. Fugger d. J.', *AMw*, xxi (1964), 212
Das Inventar der Kantorei St. Anna in Augsburg (Kassel, 1965)
Quellen und Forschungen zur Wiener Musiksammlung von Aloys Fuchs (Vienna, 1966)
Die Musikhandschriften des Ansbacher Inventars von 1686 (Wilhelmshaven, 1966)
Abkürzungen in der Musikterminologie (Wilhelmshaven, 1969)
'Die Autographen der Wiener Musiksammlung von Aloys Fuchs', *Haydn Yearbook*, vi (1969), 5–191
Die Tonkünstler-Porträts der Wiener Musiksammlung von Aloys Fuchs (Wilhelmshaven, 1970)
'Handschriftenkopien aus der Wiener Musiksammlung von Aloys Fuchs', *Haydn Yearbook*, vii (1970), 225
Fremdwörter-Lexikon Musik: Englisch, Französisch, Italienisch (Wilhelmshaven, 1970)
'Die Berliner Mozart-Abschriften der Sammlung Fuchs-Grasnick', *MJb 1971*, 415
Führer durch deutsche Musikbibliotheken (Wilhelmshaven, 1971)
Musiktitel aus fünf Jahrhunderten (Wilhelmshaven, 1972)
'Dokumente zur Münchner Hofmusik 1740–1753', *Mf*, xxvi (1973), 334
ed.: *Die Kataloge des Augsburger Musikalien-Händlers Kaspar Flurschütz, 1613–1628* (Wilhelmshaven, 1974)
'Ein unbekanntes Inventar der Münchner Hofkapelle aus dem Jahre 1753', *Convivium musicorum: Festschrift Wolfgang Boetticher* (Berlin, 1974), 309
'Ein Brief von Joseph Eybler', *Festschrift Walter Senn* (Munich and Salzburg, 1975), 217
Musiker-Monogramme (Wilhelmshaven, 1976)

HANS HEINRICH EGGEBRECHT

Schaale, Christian Friedrich. *See* SCHALE, CHRISTIAN FRIEDRICH.

Schachinger [Schächinger, Schechinger], **Johann** [Hans] [the elder] (*b* Passau, 1485; *d* ?Munich, *c*1558). German organist and composer. He studied with Paul Hofhaimer in Passau from 1502 to 1506, and his contemporaries considered him one of Hofhaimer's most important pupils. In 1506 he succeeded Hofhaimer as cathedral organist in Passau; he was later appointed court organist to Duke Wilhelm IV in Munich, probably through the intercession of Wilhelm's brother, a member of the chapter in Passau. The first reference to him in Munich is in 1531, and by 1557 he was held in such high regard that he had become the highest-paid member of the court chapel. His capabilities as an organ builder were greatly prized. Schachin-

ger (called 'the elder' to distinguish him from his son Hans, mentioned in the chapel archives from 1551 to 1564) probably died in 1558, because that year a new organist was appointed to the Munich court, and in 1561 Schachinger's widow was granted a pension.

12 four-voice lieder with the initials 'J.S.' in Formenschneider's collection of songs by Heinrich Finck (*RISM* 1536⁹) are undoubtedly Schachinger's. In all except one the cantus firmus appears in the tenor. The works show all the typical formal and melodic characteristics of the 16th-century court song; although their standard varies some are of excellent workmanship and the discant setting *Ach hülf mich Leid* (ed. in Eitner) is outstanding. The folksong setting *Es wollt ein Maidlein Wasser holn* (ed. in EDM, lx, 1969) was attributed to Schachinger by his contemporaries Egenolff (1535¹¹) and Forster (1540²¹), but Johann Ott and several manuscript sources ascribe the work to Ludwig Senfl, whose style of composition it clearly resembles.

BIBLIOGRAPHY

R. Eitner: 'Das alte deutsche mehrstimmige Lied und seine Meister', *MMg*, xxvi (1894), 1–135
A. Sandberger: *Beiträge zur Geschichte der bayerischen Hofkapelle unter Orlando di Lasso*, i (Leipzig, 1894), iii (Leipzig, 1895)
H. J. Moser: *Paul Hofhaimer* (Stuttgart and Berlin, 1929/*R*1966)
W. M. Schmidt: 'Zur Passauer Musikgeschichte', *ZMw*, xiii (1930–31), 289

KURT GUDEWILL

Schacht, Matthias Henriksen (*b* Visby, Gotland, 29 April 1660; *d* Kerteminde, Fyn, 8 Aug 1700). Danish scholar, writer on music, musician and composer. Since the Swedish island of Gotland was under Danish occupation when he was ready to begin his university studies in 1678, he went to the University of Copenhagen. He continued his education at various German universities before in 1682 he was given an appointment at his former school at Visby. The following year the famous Danish bishop Thomas Kingo called him to Odense grammar school as Kantor, and in 1686 he was made rector of the school at Kerteminde. There he served also as town musician and carried on scholarly investigations over a wide range of subjects, including castles in Hungary, the topography of Gotland, and others in such fields as zoology, botany, mathematics and history. He published papers on learned Danish women and on antiquities on the island of Fyn – in connection with which he set up a kind of museum – but very little of his scholarly work appeared in print. Among the manuscripts that he left at his early death was one on music entitled *Musicus danicus eller Danske sangmester*, completed on 1 January 1687 (in *DK-Kk*; ed. G. Skjerne, Copenhagen, 1928). This work, whose four parts cover singing, theory, composition and playing from thoroughbass respectively, is of particular interest for the fact that it begins with a biographical dictionary of musicians, the first known attempt at such a work. It was known to E. L. Gerber (presumably through his Danish collaborator Niels Schiørring, who used it in the preparation of his own *Lexikon* (1790–92), but his theory that Schacht drew on a lost work by Meibom is without foundation. Schacht was also a composer, but none of his music has survived.

BIBLIOGRAPHY

A. Hammerich: *Dansk musikhistorie indtil ca.1700* (Copenhagen, 1921)
G. Skjerne: 'Schacht, Matthias Henriksen', *DBL*

JOHN BERGSAGEL

Schacht, Theodor, Freiherr von (*b* Strasbourg, 1748; *d* Regensburg, 20 June 1823). German composer. From 1756 to 1766 he studied the piano and theory under J. J. Küffner and Riepel at the Thurn and Taxis court in Regensburg, and from 1766 to 1771 he was a pupil of Jommelli at Stuttgart. In 1771 he became a *Hofkavalier* to Prince Carl Anselm of Thurn and Taxis, who in 1773 appointed him intendant of the court's music and commissioned him to set up an Italian opera, which flourished from 1774 to 1778. After the building of a German theatre in 1778 Schacht dedicated himself more to the service of the court. In 1784–6 he again established an Italian opera at the court, and was its leader and Kapellmeister. From 1786 he was the administrator and musical director of the court orchestra. In 1805 he travelled via Salzburg to Vienna, where he won respect as a composer of sacred music. There in 1809 he was asked by Napoleon to compose six solemn masses, and also enjoyed the protection of Archduke Rudolf. He returned to Germany in 1812, lived in the castle of Scheer (in Württemberg) until 1819 and spent his last years in Regensburg.

Schacht's output includes about 200 works, the strongest of which are the theatre pieces in which he cultivated the Italian style of opera. Schacht's church music displays the same theatrical energy, with rich coloratura, homophonic choral movements and a sparing use of fugal sections. His instrumental music was notable less for contrapuntal interest than for its wealth of attractive melodies and harmonies. One of his symphonies was formerly attributed to Haydn (H I:Es12).

WORKS
Stage (all MSS, *D-Rtt*, first performed Regensburg, unless otherwise indicated): Baccocco e Serpilla (intermezzo), spr. 1775; Il marito Giogatore e la moglie Bacchettona (opera), 1775; arr. G. Benda: Romeo und Julie, perf. Feb 1779; Das unterbrochene Fest (opera), 1780; Der betrogene Tormund (opera), 1780; Il tutore deluso (intermezzo), *c*1780; Artaxerxes (opera), 1785; La rosière de Salency (ballet), arr. pf, 2 vn, 2 hn, vc, op.2 (Regensburg, n.d.); Lausus und Lydia (ballet, Albonico), march arr. pf (Regensburg, 1781); Semiramide riconosciuta (opera), 1 aria *Rp*; Gagliarda of a Merry Plague (opera-ballet), New York, spr. 1825, mentioned in Manferrari; others
Other vocal: 6 notturni, S, 2 T, B, hpd/insts, op.1 (Vienna, n.d., 2/1766); 6 terzettini a cantarsi ancora da canoni, hpd/gui (n.p., n.d.); In questa tomba oscura (G. Carpani), arietta, in In questa tomba oscura (Vienna, 1808); 22 sacred works, incl. masses, Requiem, Te Deum, S Elena al Calvario (oratorio, P. Metastasio), *Rtt*; Mass, *A-Wn*; Requiem, Te Deum, Stabat mater, *Wgm*; Die sieben Worte Christi am Kreuze, oratorio, 1818, *D-Rp*; 30 secular cantatas, arias etc, *Rtt*
Inst: XII sonates, hpd, vn, vc (Regensburg, ?*c*1780–85); III Märsche, pf/hpd (Vienna, n.d.); Divertimento del bel sesso nel soggiorno di Baden, 84 canons (n.p., 1811); 25 syms., *D-Rtt*; 6 syms., *Rp*; 2 syms., *Es*; 30 concs., various insts, *Rtt*; 9 concs., various insts, *Bds*; 3 hpd concs., *A-Wgm*; 2 concs., hpd 4 hands, orch, *D-Rp*; cl conc., *Es*; 24 serenades, partitas, divertissements, dances etc, *Rtt*; qnt, vn, ob, hn, va, vc, *Rp*; 5 str qts, *Rtt*; 2 trios, *Rtt*; arr. works by Haydn, orch

BIBLIOGRAPHY
FétisB
G. Schilling, ed.: *Encyclopädie der gesammten musikalischen Wissenschaften oder Universal-Lexikon der Tonkunst* (Stuttgart, 1835–42/R1974)
D. Mettenleiter: *Musikgeschichte der Stadt Regensburg* (Regensburg, 1866)
S. Färber: *Das Regensburger fürstlich Thurn und Taxissche Hoftheater und seine Oper 1760–1786* (Regensburg, 1936)
——: *Der fürstlich Thurn und Taxissche Hofkomponist Theodor von Schacht und seine Opernwerke* (MS)
U. Manferrari: *Dizionario universale delle opere melodrammatiche* (Florence, 1954–5)
J. LaRue: 'A New Figure in the Haydn Masquerade', *ML*, xl (1959), 132

AUGUST SCHARNAGL

Schachtbrett (Ger.). CHEKKER.

Schack [Cziak, Schak, Žák, Ziak], **Benedikt (Emanuel)** (*b* Mirotice, 7 Feb 1758; *d* Munich, 10 Dec 1826). Austrian tenor, composer and flautist of Bohemian origin. He acquired a basic musical and general education from his father, a school teacher, and later studied at Staré Sedlo, Svatá Hora and (from 1773) Prague, where he was a chorister at the cathedral. From 1775 he studied medicine, philosophy and singing (with Karl Frieberth) in Vienna; while a student he wrote some Singspiels and oratorios. In 1780 he was appointed Kapellmeister to Prince Heinrich von Schönaich-Carolath in Silesia. After two years of irregular employment, mostly in Bohemia, he joined Schikaneder's travelling theatrical company (1786); the company settled in Vienna and he became the principal tenor at the Freihaus-Theater auf der Wieden (1789). His fame as a composer was based on the series of Schikaneder's seven 'Anton' Singspiels, mostly written in collaboration with F. X. Gerl. He was a close friend of Mozart, who composed (or assisted with) certain numbers for Schack's theatrical scores (notably the duet 'Nun liebes Weibchen' K625/592*a* for *Der Stein der Weisen*). Mozart also wrote piano variations (K613) on Schack's air 'Ein Weib ist das herrlichste Ding auf der Welt' from *Die verdeckten Sachen*. Schack performed a wide variety of roles: the part of Tamino was written for him (it is to be presumed that he also played Tamino's flute solos), and he was the first German-language Don Gonsalvo (Don Ottavio) and Count Almaviva (Vienna, 1792); he also took the soprano part in an impromptu sing-through of the unfinished Requiem at the composer's bedside on the eve of Mozart's death. His wife Elisabeth (née Weinhold) sang the part of the Third Lady in the première of *Die Zauberflöte*.

In 1793 Schack moved to Graz and in 1796 to Munich, where he was a member of the Hoftheater until about 1814, when he lost his voice and was pensioned. His daughter Antonie (1784–1851) was also a member of the Munich company (1800–06). During his last years he wrote mostly sacred music, including a mass 'with additions by Mozart' (KAnh.C1.02/Anh.235*f*). He died before receiving Constanze Nissen's letter (16 February 1826) asking for help with her husband's biography of Mozart; the letter gives an eloquent if politely exaggerated testimony to the friendship of Schack and Mozart: 'I could think of absolutely no one who knew him better or to whom he was more devoted than you . . . Of great and general interest will be what you can instance of Mozart's few compositions in your operas'. F. L. Schröder commented (May 1791) on Schack as a singer in Wranitzky's *Oberon*: 'Hüon, Schack, a good [*braver*] tenor, but with an Austrian accent and suburban declamation'. Leopold Mozart was more appreciative in a letter to his daughter (26 May 1786): 'He sings excellently, has a beautiful voice, easy and flexible throat, and beautiful method . . . This man sings really very beautifully'.

WORKS
STAGE
All are Singspiels, lost, first performed in Vienna, Freihaus, unless otherwise indicated.

Die Wilden und die Gesitteten (3, Eckartshausen), Vienna, Leopoldstadt, 3 Dec 1784, *D-Mbs*
Don Chisciotto, Vienna, *c*1785, doubtful
Die drei Ringe, oder [Kaspar] Der [lächerliche] Mundkoch (3, Schikaneder), ?Salzburg, 1786; Regensburg, 25 March 1788; pubd lib extant
Der Luftballon (operetta, 3, Schikaneder), Kempten, Sept 1786
Lorenz and Suschen (Schikaneder), Regensburg, ?18 April 1788

Der Krautschneider (4, Schikaneder), Regensburg, ?3 May 1788;
?same as Kaspar der Krautschneider, Vienna, Leopoldstadt, 21 April
1785
Der dumme Gärtner aus dem Gebirge, oder Die zween Anton (2,
Schikaneder), collab. F. X. Gerl, 12 July 1789, vocal score (Bonn,
n.d.) [1st 'Anton' Singspiel]
Jakob und Nannerl, oder Der angenehme Traum (opera, 3,
Schikaneder), 25 July 1789; also attrib. Pecháček, Gerl
Die verdeckten Sachen (2, Schikaneder), collab. Gerl and Lickl, 26 Sept
1789, vocal score I-Fc, songs A-Wgm [2nd 'Anton' Singspiel]
Was macht der Anton im Winter? (2, Schikaneder), 6 Jan 1790, com-
posers uncertain, vocal score I-Fc, songs A-Wgm [3rd 'Anton'
Singspiel]
Der Fall ist noch weit seltner, oder Die geplagten Ehemänner (2,
Schikaneder, sequel to Martín y Soler: Una cosa rara), 10 May 1790;
?same as Lilla, D-Mbs
Der Frühling, oder Der Anton ist noch nicht tot (2, Schikaneder), 18
June 1790, composers uncertain, songs A-Wgm [4th 'Anton'
Singspiel]
Der Stein der Weisen, oder Die Zauberinsel (heroic–comic opera, 2,
Schikaneder), collab. Gerl, Mozart, ?Henneberg, 11 Sept 1790, D-B,
vocal score I-Fc
Die Wiener Zeitung (3, K. L. Gieseke), collab. Gerl, 12 Jan 1791
Anton bei Hofe, oder Das Namensfest (2, Schikaneder), 4 June 1791,
composers uncertain [5th 'Anton' Singspiel]
Das Schlaraffenland (2, Gieseke), collab. Gerl, 23 June 1792
Der Renegat, oder Anton in der Türkei (2, Schikaneder), 15 Sept 1792,
composers uncertain [6th 'Anton' Singspiel]
Die Antwort auf die Frage: Was begehrt das Frauenzimmer? (comic
opera, 3), Vienna, Landstrasse, 16/?18 Dec 1792
Der eifersüchtige Bauer, oder Der Schulmeister im Ofenloch (opera, 2,
Korndorfer), Vienna, Landstrasse, 27/28 Jan 1793
Der beiden Lieschen zweiter Teil, oder Der Schulmeister im Ofenloch
(opera, 2, Korndorfer), Vienna, Landstrasse, 29 Jan 1793; ?same as
Der eifersüchtige Bauer
Der wohltätige Derwisch, oder Die Schellenkappe (3, Schikaneder),
collab. Gerl, Henneberg, ?W. Müller, 10 Sept 1793; as Die
Zaubertrommel, D-MH
Die beiden Nannerln, oder Das chinesische Feuerwerk zu Ehren der
Nannerln (2 acts), 26 July 1794
Frage und Antwort, oder Ein altes Haus [Weib] kann auch was Gutes
stiften, Graz, 1794
Der Zauberbrief (romantic–comic opera, 3), Vienna, Josefstadt, 1 Jan
1795
Das Häuschen im Walde, oder Antons Reise nach seinem Geburtsort
(2, Schikaneder), ?6 Jan 1795, doubtful [7th 'Anton' Singspiel]

OTHER WORKS

Sacred: Missa, 4 male vv, org (Munich, n.d.); Mass, 4vv, orch, ?addns
Mozart (London, 1831); [9] Lamentationen für die Karwoche, 3/4vv,
D-Rp; Wir lagen schaudernd, 4vv chorus, insts, Rp; others, incl. 2
requiems, cantatas, oratorios, mostly lost
Inst (lost): concs., wind, c1780–84; others

BIBLIOGRAPHY

ČSHS; EitnerQ; GerberNL
F. J. Lipowsky: Baierisches Musik-Lexicon (Munich, 1811/R1971),
297ff
F. L. W. Meyer: Friedrich Ludwig Schröder: Beitrag zur Kunde des
Menschen und des Künstlers (Hamburg, 1819)
AMZ, xxix (1827), col.519
C. von Wurzbach: Biographisches Lexikon des Kaiserthums
Oesterreich, xxix (Vienna, 1875), 35
E. Komorzynski: Emanuel Schikaneder (Berlin, 1901, rev. 2/1951)
E. K. Blümml and G. Gugitz: Alt-Wiener Thespiskarren (Vienna, 1925)
O. E. Deutsch: Das Freihaus-Theater auf der Wieden (Vienna, 1937),
30–73
E. Komorzynski: Der Vater der Zauberflöte: Emanuel Schikaneders
Leben (Vienna, 1948)
A. Bauer: Das Theater in der Josefstadt zu Wien (Vienna, 1957)
K. M. Pisarowitz: 'Ein Weib ist das herrlichste Ding auf der Welt',
Mitteilungen der Internationalen Stiftung Mozarteum, vii (1958), 5
W. A. Bauer and O. E. Deutsch, eds.: Mozart: Briefe und
Aufzeichnungen (Kassel, 1962–75)
A. Würz: 'Schak, Benedikt', MGG

PETER BRANSCOMBE

Schadaeus [Schadäus, Schade], **Abraham** (b Senften-
berg, Lusatia, 1566; d Finsterwalde, Lusatia, 10 Oct
1626). German music editor and schoolmaster. He
studied at the university at Frankfurt an der Oder from
1584 and probably received a master's degree there. He
was appointed a teacher at the Fürstenschule at Meissen
in 1588 but because of his active Calvinist leanings was
forced to leave the position in 1592. Later that year he
became Kantor at the Gymnasium and church of St
Petri at Bautzen. After failing to obtain the position of
Konrektor there he became Rektor of the grammar
school at Speyer in 1603. He was dismissed in 1611
and returned to Upper Lusatia in 1613. After serving
for a year as Kantor at Torgau he returned to Bautzen
in 1614, now as Konrektor. In 1615 he became Rektor,
but he resigned in 1617 and went into retirement at
Finsterwalde.

Schadaeus owes his place in music history entirely to
his three-part anthology of motets, *Promptuarium
musicum*, intended for school and church use; a fourth
part was edited by CASPAR VINCENTIUS, who also
provided a continuo part for the first three parts and
performed other functions in connection with the second
and third parts. This anthology differs from the
Florilegium Portense of ERHARD BODENSCHATZ, and
probably influenced the *Promptuarium musicum* of
JOHANN DONFRID, in being ordered according to the
liturgical year and in its emphasis on works 'not yet
published in Germany': hence the predominance of
music by Italian composers. Of the 43 composers
represented in the first part, 33 are Italian, and no fewer
than 45 of the 51 in the second part and 52 of the 61 in
the third are also Italian. Leoni and Bianciardi are
among the most popular composers, but Agazzari,
Giovanni Gabrieli, Marenzio, Massaino and Benedetto
Pallavicino are all well represented. Few German composers appear: eight in the first part, five in the second
and nine in the third. In the first part Vincentius with six
works and Walliser with three are the best represented;
other Germans – Aichinger, Alexius Neander,
Hieronymus Praetorius (with two works) and Ufferer –
are only represented in the third part. Monte and
Luython are the sole representatives of the Netherlands
school. The anthology comprises works for five to eight
voices. It illustrates the then current trend towards
block choral writing, involving double chorus or
dialogues between upper and lower voices: no fewer
than 36 of its composers were leading exponents of the
polychoral style in Italy. That the texts are entirely in
Latin also reflects the Italianate orientation of the
anthology: German motets, which have some place in,
for example, the enlarged 1618 edition of the first part
of Bodenschatz's *Florilegium Portense*, are totally
absent.

EDITIONS

Promptuarii musici sacras harmonias sive motetas . . . pars prima, quae
concentus selectissimos, qui tempore hyemali Ss ecclesiae usui esse
possunt, comprehendit, 5–8vv, bc (org) (Strasbourg, 1611¹)
Promptuarii musici . . . pars altera quae aestivi temporis festivitatibus
dominicisque diebus selectiores concentus Ss ecclesiae usui inser-
vientes continet, 5–8vv, bc (org) (Strasbourg, 1612³)
Promptuarii musici . . . pars tertia quae exhibet concentus varios selec-
tioresque, qui solennioribus sc. Ss Trinitatis, S Joh. Baptistae, B.
Virginis Mariae, Ss Apostolorum . . . per totius anni curriculum
inserviunt, 5–8vv, bc (org) (Strasbourg, 1613²)

Promptuarii musici . . . pars quarta, 5–8vv, bc (org) (Strasbourg,
1617¹), ed. C. Vincentius

BIBLIOGRAPHY

W. Spatz: Reformationsgeschichte der Stadt Speyer oder des evangelis-
chen Speyer, ed. J. M. König (Speyer, 1834)
H. Biehle: Musikgeschichte von Bautzen (Leipzig, 1924)
F. Blume: Die evangelische Kirchenmusik, HMw, x (1931, rev. 2/1965
as Geschichte der evangelischen Kirchenmusik; Eng. trans., enlarged,
1974 as Protestant Church Music: a History)
J. G. Kraner: 'Schadaeus, Abraham', MGG
P. Winter: Der mehrchörige Stil (Frankfurt am Main, 1964)
J. Roche: 'Anthologies and the Dissemination of Early Baroque Italian
Sacred Music', Soundings, iv (1974), 10f

OTTO RIEMER

Schädlich, David. *See* SCHEDLICH, DAVID.

Schaefer, Hansjürgen (*b* Freiburg, Saxony, 7 Oct 1930). German music critic. After working as a primary school teacher in Chemnitz (now Karl-Marx-Stadt), he studied at the Leipzig Musikhochschule (1952–4) and under Meyer and Vetter at the Humboldt University, Berlin (1954–7). He was subsequently critic on the *Berliner Zeitung* (1957–60), editor-in-chief of the periodical *Musik und Gesellschaft* (1960–73) and chief music critic of the newspaper *Neues Deutschland* (from 1960). In 1973 he became artistic director at Deutsche Schallplatten in East Berlin. His main interests are Beethoven and contemporary East German music. He has written a biography of Mendelssohn (Berlin, 1965) and the study *Musik in der sozialistischen Gesellschaft* (Berlin, 1965), and has edited Schiedermair's *Der junge Beethoven* (Berlin, 1971), Rolland's *Beethoven: von der Eroica zur Appassionata* (Berlin, 1970) and a selection of Beethoven's letters. He also brought out a new edition of Schönewolf's *Konzertbuch* (Berlin, 1972–4).

HORST SEEGER

Schaefer, Theodor (*b* Telč, 23 Jan 1904; *d* Brno, 19 March 1969). Czech composer and teacher. He studied composition under Kvapil and conducting under Neumann at the Brno Conservatory (1922–6), completing his composition studies in Novák's master class in Prague (1926–9). He taught at music schools in Kutná Hora (1930–34) and Brno (1934–40); he was then appointed an external teacher, and from 1948 an internal teacher of theory and composition at the Brno Conservatory. In 1959 he moved to the Brno Academy, where he was later made professor. During the 1930s and 1940s he conducted amateur choirs and orchestras in Kutná Hora and Brno; he continued to take an active part in the musical life of Brno, heading the local branch of the Union of Czechoslovak Composers in the 1960s, and directing the newly established International Music Festival there.

His unpublished theoretical studies show that Schaefer thought deeply about composition. He started out from Novák's traditional techniques, but even in the early 1930s he was beginning to broaden his scope under the influence of the western European avant garde, as the stage piece *Julie* (1933–4) demonstrates. The text for this work was used by Martinů four years later. Schaefer extended Novák's tonality by employing modes, and towards the end of his life he began to combine modality with serial principles. In instrumental works he used an original form which he termed 'diathema': subjects are conceived as collections of rearrangeable elements, and recapitulation is replaced by a synthesis of the elements in the subjects exposed. This form is used in the Third String Quartet, *Diathema* for viola and orchestra, *Barbar a růže* ('The barbarian and the rose'), the *Rapsodická reportáž* and the Symphony, Schaefer's principal work.

WORKS
(selective list)

Stage: Julie aneb snář [Juliet or The dreambook] (melodrama, J. Hořejší, after G. Neveux), 1933–4; Legenda o štěstí [Legend of happiness], ballet cycle: prologue, 5 dramas, epilogue, after S. Čech, 1949–54

Orch: Vn Conc., op.4, 1932–3; Pf Conc., op.10, 1937–43; Diathema, op.24, va, orch, 1955–6; Diathema, op.25, 1957–8; Barbar a růže [The barbarian and the rose], op.27, 1957–8; Rapsodická reportáž, 1960; Sym., 1959–62

Inst: Wind Qnt, op.5, 1934–5; 3 str qts, 1944–5, n.d., n.d.; Cigánovy housle [The gypsy's violin], vn, pf, n.d.; 11 pf works

Vocal: 2 song cycles, cantata, choral cycles

BIBLIOGRAPHY
Z. Zouhar: 'Konfese Th. Schaefra posmrtně' [Schaefer's posthumous confession], *OM*, i (1969), 114

JIŘÍ FUKAČ

Schaeffer [Schäffer, Scheffer], **Paul** (*fl* 1617–45). German composer and musician. The title-pages of his surviving prints indicate that between 1617 and 1620 he was an instrumentalist among the municipal musicians at Guhrau, Silesia (now Góra, Poland), and that from 1621 he served the city of Breslau in a similar capacity. A work that he wrote for a wedding on 9 May 1645 shows that he was still working then at Breslau, but no music by him can be dated between 1626 and that year. In 1621 he wrote an *Actus gratulatorius* in honour of the Elector of Saxony, who on 3 November that year, as the emperor's representative, accepted the homage of the Silesian Diet at Breslau, an occasion also celebrated in the *Syncharma musicum* of the elector's Kapellmeister, Schütz. Schaeffer also wrote a work to mark the wedding, on 5 November 1624, of Duke Georg Rudolph of Liegnitz. In 1619 he published Advent and Christmas hymns for solo voice and continuo. His *Cantiones sacrae* of 1621 also comprises Advent and Christmas music, but in the motet style for eight voices; the 13 pieces in this collection were no doubt prompted by the predilection in Breslau for polyphonic settings. As one might expect of a musician in his position, Schaeffer composed a good deal of instrumental music. His *Pratum musicale*, for example, consists of 58 four-part dances with continuo. Here the established dance pair of pavan and galliard is always separated by a canzona and intrada. They are followed by the courante, ballet, volta and branle, all dances that Arbeau had described in detail. An interesting feature is the addition of 'so-called round dances, especially those of Polish origin'. The *Promulsts epuli musicalis*, for only three parts with continuo, also includes the allemande.

WORKS
VOCAL

[24] Melodiarum biblicarum . . . liber I, 5vv/insts (Breslau, 1617)
[25] Melodiarum biblicarum . . . liber II, 6vv/insts (Guhrau, 1618)
De Adventu et Nativitate . . . Jesu Christe, 1v, bc (org) (Guhrau, 1619)
[13] Cantiones sacrae . . . de Adventu et nativitate, 8vv (Guhrau, 1621)
Actus gratulatorius . . . 25 Oct, 8vv (n.p., 1621)
Ego flos campi: Jehova sic disponente . . . 25 Nov, 9vv, tuba, timp, bc (n.p., 1624)
Odae spirituales, 3vv, bc (Jena, 1625)
11 motets, 8–16vv/insts; 2 wedding motets, 8–20vv/insts: *PL-WRu* (see Bohn, 1890)
Hochzeitliche . . . musicalische Concert: Jauchzet dem Herren alle Welt (Ps c), 9 May 1645, 8vv, chorus 16vv, *WRu*
Seelen Lust Gärtlein geistlicher Concerten . . . aus den Psalmen Davids und andern biblischen . . . Sprüchen, 1–3vv, bc (Leipzig, 1636); authenticity doubtful, attrib. P. Schöffer in A. Göhler: *Verzeichnis der in den Frankfurter und Leipziger Messkatalogen der Jahre 1564 bis 1759 angezeigten Musikalien* (Leipzig, 1902/R1965)

INSTRUMENTAL

Intradae et courants . . . cum una canzon, a 6 (Breslau, 1619), ?lost
Pratum musicale . . . padouan. canzon. intrad . . . et choreas quas vocant Polonicas, a 4 (Leipzig, 1622)
Promulsis epuli musicalis continens . . . canzon. padovan. intrad . . . et choreae Polonicae, a 3, bc (n.p., 1626)

BIBLIOGRAPHY
EitnerQ
E. Bohn: *Bibliographie der Musikdruckwerke bis 1700, welche . . . zu Breslau aufbewahrt werden* (Berlin, 1883/R1969)
——: *Die musikalischen Handschriften des 16. und 17. Jahrhunderts in der Stadtbibliothek zu Breslau* (Breslau, 1890), 170, 362

E. H. Meyer: *Die mehrstimmige Spielmusik des 17. Jahrhunderts in Nord- und Mitteleuropa* (Kassel, 1934)
J. G. Kraner: 'Schäffer, Paul', *MGG*

FRITZ FELDMANN

Schaeffer, Pierre (*b* Nancy, 14 Aug 1910). French composer, theorist, writer and teacher. His tape compositions of 1948 originated *musique concrète*. Although his parents were musicians he embarked on a scientific career, entering the Ecole Polytechnique in 1929. In 1934 he began work as a telecommunications engineer in Strasbourg and from 1936 he was a technician with Radiodiffusion Française. Soon he discovered that he was more attracted to literature and philosophy than to technology, and he wrote a number of essays and novels. At this time he developed a taste for communal life, first in scouting, later at Gurdjieff's group meetings. In 1941 he founded 'Jeune France', an interdisciplinary association interested in music, theatre and the visual arts; in the following year he joined Copeau and his pupils in the establishment of the Studio d'Essai, which was to become the centre of the Resistance movement in French radio and later the cradle of *musique concrète*. There he started work on a *Symphonie de bruits*, a project which later materialized as the *Symphonie pour un homme seul*. This led Schaeffer away from simple tricks with disc recordings and towards systematic techniques, soon to be greatly facilitated by the availability of the tape recorder. A composer despite himself, he attracted enough attention to obtain official status for the Groupe de Recherche de Musique Concrète in 1951.

Two years later Schaeffer left the GRMC in the charge of his collaborator Henry in order to direct the foundation and management of Radiodiffusion de la France d'Outre-mer (French overseas broadcasting). He returned to the GRMC in 1958 when, together with Ferrari and Mâche, he re-formed it as the more ambitious Groupe de Recherches Musicales. The investigation of sounds and of new techniques progressed to more general research (which also took in instrumental resources) on the bases of musical perception. Schaeffer stopped composing and gave his attention to increasingly wide theoretical speculations after the establishment in 1960 of the Service de Recherche de la RTF, within which was set up a Groupe de Recherches sur l'Image complementary to the GRM. In 1968 he was appointed associate professor at the Paris Conservatoire to teach electronic composition.

There are difficulties in considering Schaeffer separately as a composer, novelist and essayist, for one of his deepest wishes has been to build bridges between circumscribed fields of thought. Nonetheless, it is through his musical ideas that he has reached a wide public. Schaeffer's musical thought rests on the primacy of the ear over conventional aesthetic considerations. It is his view that recording has placed all sounds – whether music, noises, animal cries or whatever – on an equal footing, since all are experienced in the same manner. They may thus be treated as 'sound objects', distinct from their acoustic and notated sources. Such objects are not categorized in acoustical terms (which are related only complexly to perception) nor for aesthetic qualities, since Schaeffer distrusts both physical measurements without aural relevance and theories of musical structure. He has devoted much effort to a classification of sound objects based on disciplined listening, claiming that this process does not depend on using selected listeners, and that it is a necessary preliminary to further creation.

As a teacher of electronic techniques Schaeffer has been tolerant of his pupils' aesthetic views. His teaching method begins with ear training through carefully directed listening, then proceeds to the synthesis of sound objects having predetermined qualities. Manipulative techniques are next learnt and finally studies are produced through the linking of objects. Schaeffer himself proceeded in this way in composing his last works, notably the *Etude aux objets*, although his earlier pieces had been produced in a more empirical manner. But it is not through his compositions that Schaeffer has exerted most influence: his theories and his development of *musique concrète* have been much more significant. Above all, Schaeffer saw from the outset that electronic techniques were to affect very many aspects of musical thought and practice, that a revolution comparable with that brought about by photography was taking place.

See also ANALYSIS, §II, 8.

WORKS
(all for tape alone)

Etude violette, 1948; Etude au piano, 1948; Etude aux tourniquets, 1948; Etude aux chemins de fer, 1948; Etude pathétique, 1948; Concertino-Diapason, 1948, collab. J. J. Grünewald; Variations sur une flûte mexicaine, 1949; Suite pour 14 insts, 1949; L'oiseau R.A.I., 1950; Bidule en ut, 1950, collab. Henry; Symphonie pour un homme seul, 1950, collab. Henry, rev. 1955; rev. ballet, 1955; La course au kilocycle, radio score, 1950, collab. Henry; Toute la lyre, pantomime, 1951, collab. Henry; Masquerage, film score, dir. M. de Haas, 1952; Orphée 53, opera, 1953, collab. Henry; Sahara d'aujourd'hui (film score, Schwab, Goub), 1957; collab. Henry; Exposition française à Londres, 1958, collab. Ferrari; Continuo, 1958, collab. Ferrari; Etudes aux allures, 1958; Etude aux sons animés, 1958; Etude aux objets, 1959; Phèdre (incidental music, Racine), 1959; Nocturne aux chemins de fer, incidental music, mime by J. Lecocq, 1959; Simultané camerounais, 1959; Phèdre, 1961

WRITINGS ON MUSIC

'Introduction à la musique concrète', *Polyphonie*, vi (1950), 30
A la recherche d'une musique concrète (Paris, 1952)
'Lettre à M. A. Richard', *ReM* (1957), no.236, p.iii
'Vers une musique expérimentale', *ReM* (1957), no.236, p.11
'Le Groupe de recherches musicales', *ReM* (1959), no.244, p.49
'Situation actuelle de la musique expérimentale', *ReM* (1959), no.244, p.10
Traité des objets musicaux (Paris, 1966)
La musique concrète (Paris, 1967)
Le gardien de volcan (Paris, 1969)
L'avenir à reculons (Paris, 1970)
Machines à communiquer, i: *La génèse des simulacres* (Paris, 1970)
'De l'expérience musicale à l'expérience humaine', *ReM* (1971), nos.274–5
Machines à communiquer, ii: *Pouvoir et communication* (Paris, 1972)

BIBLIOGRAPHY

M. Pierret: *Entretiens avec Pierre Schaeffer* (Paris, 1969)
S. Brunet: *Pierre Schaeffer* (Paris, 1970)

FRANÇOIS-BERNARD MÂCHE

Schaeffner, André (*b* Paris, 7 Feb 1895). French musicologist and ethnomusicologist. He studied the piano and harmony with A. Philip, composition with d'Indy at the Schola Cantorum (1921–4), ethnology with M. Mauss at the Institut d'Ethnologie (1932–3) and at the Ecole Pratique des Hautes Etudes (1934–7, diploma in religious science 1940) and archaeology with S. Reinach at the Ecole du Louvre. His career was mainly based at the department of ethnomusicology in the Musée de l'Homme which he founded in 1929 and directed until 1965. Concurrently he worked on the catalogue of the Paris Conservatoire Library (1932–41), and for 24 years (1941–65) at the CNRS as *chargé de recherche* and then *maître de recherche*. He was also artistic secretary of the Paris SO (1929–31) and of the Pléiade Concerts (1943–5), and taught at the Institut d'Ethnologie (1936–43).

Schaeffner's interests extend to both Romantic and modern music; he has written studies of composers (Debussy, Stravinsky), individual works and aesthetics movements (especially music drama) of the 19th and 20th centuries. He has also specialized in European and non-European instruments; in its field his work *Origine des instruments de musique* is authoritative. This led him to study the music of black Africa in its social and religious context; he organized six expeditions to West Africa between 1931 and 1958. Schaeffner edited the third French edition of Riemann's *Musik-Lexikon* and wrote numerous articles in French encyclopedias and in the *Ménestrel*, *Revue musicale*, *Contrepoints*, *Rassegna musicale*, *Revue de musicologie* and *Journal des africanistes*. He has been vice-president (1948–58) and president (1958–61) of the Société Française de Musicologie.

WRITINGS

'Evolution harmonique et fixité tonale dans la musique contemporaine', *Journal de psychologie*, xxiii (1926), 211

with A. Coeuroy: *Le jazz* (Paris, 1926)

'Le clavecin', *EMDC*, II/iii (1927), 2036

Strawinsky (Paris, 1931)

ed.: H. Riemann: *Dictionnaire de la musique* (Paris, 3/1931)

'La sociologie et la vogue du jazz', *Art et littérature dans la société contemporaine*, i, Encyclopédie française, xvi, pt72 (Paris, 1935), 11

Origine des instruments de musique (Paris, 1936/R1967)

'Sur deux instruments de musique des Bata (Nord-Cameroun)', *Journal de la Société des africanistes*, xiii (1943), 123

'Francis Poulenc, musicien français', *Contrepoints* (1946), no.1, p.50

'Halifax R. G. 587', *Contrepoints* (1946), no.5, p.45

ed.: E. T. A. Hoffmann: *Kreisleriana* (Paris, 1949)

'Le lithophone de Ndut Lieng Krak (Vietnam)', *RdM*, xxxiii (1951), 1

Les Kissi: une société noire et ses instruments de musique (Paris, 1951)

'Musique populaire et art musical', *Journal de psychologie*, xliv (1951), 237

'Variations Schoenberg', *Contrepoints* (1951), no.7, p.110

'Timbales et longues trompettes', *Bulletin de l'Institut français d'Afrique noire*, xiv (1952), 1466

'Debussy et ses rapports avec la musique russe', *Musique russe*, i (Paris, 1953), 95

'Ethnologie musicale ou musicologie comparée?', *Cercle international d'études ethno-musicologiques* [*Ethnomusicologie I*]: *Wégimont I 1954*, 18

'L'orgue de Barbarie de Rameau', *Mélanges d'histoire et d'esthétique musicales offerts à Paul-Marie Masson* (Paris, 1955), ii, 135

'Situation des musiciens dans trois sociétés africaines', *Ethno musicologie II: Wégimont 1956*, 33

Introduction and notes to: C. Debussy: *Lettres inédites à André Caplet (1908–1914)*, ed. E. Lockspeiser (Monaco, 1957)

ed.: F. Nietzsche: *Lettres à Peter Gast* (Monaco, 1957)

'Genèse des instruments de musique', *Histoire de la musique*, i, ed. Roland-Manuel (Paris, 1960), 76–117

'Le tambour-sur-cadre quadrangulaire chez les noirs d'Afrique et d'Amérique', *Ethnomusicologie III: Wégimont V 1960*, 229

with A. Joly-Segalen: *Segalen et Claude Debussy* (Monaco, 1961)

'Debussy et ses rapports avec la peinture', *Debussy et l'évolution de la musique au XXᵉ siècle: CNRS Paris 1962*, 151

'Musique et structures sociales (Sociétés d'Afrique noire)', *Revue française de sociologie*, iii/4 (1962), 388

'Claude Debussy', *Histoire de la musique*, ii, ed. Roland-Manuel (Paris, 1963), 909

'Claude Debussy et ses projets shakespeariens', *Revue d'histoire du théâtre*, xvi/4 (1964), 446

'Rituel et pré-théâtre', *Histoire des spectacles* (Paris, 1965)

'Variations sur deux mots: polyphonie, hétérophonie', *RBM*, xx (1966), 43

'Teatro immaginario di Debussy', *NRMI*, i (1967), 303

'Rites agraires, initiatiques et funéraires en Afrique de l'Ouest', *Encyclopédie des musiques sacrées*, i (Paris, 1968), 83

'La musique noire d'un continent à un autre', *La musique dans la vie*, ii (Paris, 1969), 9 [ORTF publication]

'Communications imaginaires ou africaines', *Echanges et communications: Mélanges offerts à Claude Lévi-Strauss* (Paris and The Hague, 1970), 519

'Au fil des esquisses du "Sacre" ', *RdM*, lvii (1971), 179

EDITIONS

F. Couperin: *Musique de chambre I: Concerts royaux, 1722*, Oeuvres complètes, vii (Paris, 1933); *Musique de chambre II: Les goûts-réunis ou Nouveaux concerts, 1724*, ibid, viii (Paris, 1933)

BIBLIOGRAPHY
B. Krader: 'Bibliography: André Schaeffner', *EM*, ii (1958), 27

CHRISTIANE SPIETH-WEISSENBACHER

Schaeuble, Hans (Joachim) (*b* Arosa, canton of Grisons, 29 May 1906). Swiss composer. While a student at Lausanne University he was strongly affected by Ansermet's performances of Stravinsky and of modern French music, and as a result he decided on a musical career. He left the university after a term to study composition with Grabner and the piano with Marthienssen at the Leipzig Hochschule für Musik (1927–31). In addition he took private lessons in Berlin, where his first works were published by Bote & Bock in 1936, and where the *Sinfonische Musik* op.22 received its première under Schuricht in the Philharmonie. He returned to Switzerland in 1939, living in Zurich from 1942 as a freelance composer. Hindemith, Stravinsky, Bartók and later Martin exercised decisive influences on his music; he quickly adopted serial techniques, but chiefly to enrich his part-writing rather than to cloud the tonality. One of his main aims has been to achieve a harmony between content and means, an aim which has led to an increasing clarity and simplicity.

WORKS
(selective list)

Stage: Dagmar, op.2 (opera, after Storm), 1927–8; Fabula aeterna, op.26, ballet, 1943; Dorian Gray, op.32 (opera, after Wilde), 1947–8; Los caprichos, op.36, ballet, 1950–51; Die Rose und die Schatten, op.43, ballet, 1957–8

Orch: 3 pf concs., 1931, 1949, 1967; Toccata, Passacaglia and Finale, op.12, 1932; Musik für 2 Vn und Str, op.18, 1932; Musik für 7 Bläser und Str, op.20, 1937; Sinfonische Musik, op.22, 1937; Va Conc., op.23, 1938–9; Sym., op.25, 1940–42; Sym. 'In memoriam', op.27, str, 1943–4; Hymnus, op.29, 1943; Capriccio, op.30, pf, orch, 1946; Sinfonisch-konzertante Variationen, op.33, str, pf obbl., 1949; Aspects et perspectives (Jeux), op.40, 1954; Vc Conc., op.41, 1959; Musik für Klarinette und Str, op.46, 1961; Conc., pf, str orch, op.50, 1967; Paradise Lost, op.51, 1968

Vocal: Requiem, op.6, chorus, orch, 1929

Chamber: 3 str qts, 1931, 1936, 1950

Principal publisher: Bote & Bock

BIBLIOGRAPHY
H. Schaeuble: 'Nachruf für Hugo Distler', *SMz*, lxxxiii (1943), 10
H. Leeb: 'Hans Schaeuble', *40 Schweizer Komponisten der Gegenwart* (Amriswil, 1956), 160

FRITZ MUGGLER

Schäfer, Dirk (*b* Rotterdam, 25 Nov 1873; *d* Amsterdam, 16 Feb 1931). Dutch pianist and composer. He began his piano studies in 1888 at the Rotterdam Music School, and then studied under a government scholarship at the Cologne Conservatory (1891–4) with Pauer (piano) and Wüllner (composition); in 1892 he won the Mendelssohn Prize of Berlin. After his return to Holland he made many concert tours of Germany, France, Austria and Belgium, though his artistic sensitivity kept him from travelling as an international virtuoso. In 1913–15 he gave a series of 11 concerts surveying the keyboard literature from Byrd to Debussy and Schoenberg; later in life he specialized in Chopin. *Het klavier* (Amsterdam, 1942), compiled from his notes by Ida Schäfer-Dumstorff, sets out his ideas on performance. His compositions show discernment and finesse; particularly in smaller forms he was able to express himself to happy effect in a style that, though related to Chopin and Brahms, has its individuality. He was at his best in writing for the piano, but the two short orchestral pieces show great skill in orchestration.

WORKS
(selective list)

Orch: Suite pastorale, op.8, 1903; Rhapsodie javanaise, op.7, 1904

Chamber: 4 sonatas, vn, pf, op.4, 1901, op.6, 1902, op.11/1, 1904, op.11/2, 1909; Pf Qnt, op.5, 1901; Sonata, op.13, vc, pf, 1909; Str Qt, op.14, 1922

Pf: 8 Etüden, op.3, pf, 1896; Scherzo, pf, 1897, rev. 1917; Valse di bravura, 1897, rev. 1921; 4 petits morceaux, 1894–9; Impromptu, 1899, rev. 1917; 3 Klavierstukken, op.10, 1901; Variationen auf eine Sequenz, 1902; Sonate inaugurale, 1905–11; 6 klavierstukken, op.12, 1893–1915; 8 klavierstukken, op.15, 1921; Interludes, op.17, 1923; Toccata, op.18, 1924; Suite, op.19, 1929; Paraphrase over een wals, 1929

Vocal: 2 Lieder, op.1, chorus, orch, 1894; 2 geistliche Lieder, op.2, chorus, 1895; 4 liederen, op.16, 1894

Principal publishers: Alsbach, Leuckart, Noske

BIBLIOGRAPHY

S. Dresden: *Het muziekleven in Nederland sinds 1880* (Amsterdam, 1923), 94ff

Ter herinnering aan Dirk Schäfer (Amsterdam, 1932)

E. Reeser: *Een eeuw nederlandse muziek* (Amsterdam, 1950), 253ff

JOS WOUTERS

Schafer, R(aymond) Murray (*b* Sarnia, Ont., 18 July 1933). Canadian composer, writer on music and educationist. He studied at the Toronto Conservatory with Guerrero (piano) and Weinzweig (composition). From 1956 to 1961 he worked as a freelance journalist and BBC interviewer in Europe; during this time he edited Pound's opera *Le testament de François Villon* for a BBC performance. In 1961 he founded and became the first president of Ten Centuries Concerts, a Toronto organization for the performance of new and rarely heard music. He was artist-in-residence at

Memorial University, Newfoundland (1963–5), and in 1965 he was appointed to the staff of Simon Fraser University, British Columbia. In 1972 a grant from the Donner Foundation enabled him to undertake research into worldwide acoustic ecology. He has also received Canada Council grants (1961 and 1963), a Fromm Foundation award (1968), the annual medal of the Canadian Music Council (1972) and a Guggenheim fellowship (1974).

The homogeneity of Schafer's mature music defies any attempt to outline a chronological development, while its variety forbids any approach in terms of genre. His work has roots in the major trends of the 1960s – 12-note serialism, indeterminacy, the use of space and of mixed media – but his use of any particular technique has always been free, intuitive and individual. Also, he has often drawn on fields beyond music: the philosophy and literature of many different times and peoples, mythology and symbolism, modern psychology and communication theory. His predilection for texts in dead languages is the result of a wish to emphasize phonetic rather than semantic content, and yet at the same time to illuminate fundamental emotions.

Schafer's originality in the use of language is demonstrated most fully in two substantial works for the stage: *Loving/Toi* (1966) and *Patria* (1972–). The former treats of sexual love and yet is plotless; the participants represent 'attitudes' and not characters. Three female voices stand for Vanity, Ishtar and Modesty; a fourth, in her concluding aria 'The Geography of Eros', fuses the

R. Murray Schafer teaching a class of students

first three. The only male voice also has an alter ego in an offstage recording presenting the Poet. While the women's language is always English, the man uses the vernacular of the country in which the work is performed (in the original version French was used). Through juxtaposing language as sense with language as sound, through modulating from speech to melismatic or electronically manipulated song and through contrasting intelligible words with fragments, Schafer dramatizes states of mind, conscious and subconscious, and forms of love, from the spiritual to the physical.

Patria is planned as a trilogy, to be performed on consecutive nights. The theme of the first two parts is loneliness: the alienation of individuals in hostile environments. As in *Loving/Toi*, there is no straightforward plot. In the first part, *The Characteristics Man*, an immigrant is surrounded by people speaking languages incomprehensible to him; words and sentences from some 40 tongues, some of them invented, are used to establish a frightening atmosphere of non-communication. Again the central figure uses the language of the audience. The second part, *Requiems for the Party Girl*, concerns a schizophrenic girl in a mental hospital where the doctors and nurses communicate in languages incomprehensible to the patients. Only the latter speak in the vernacular, though often incoherently. Ariadne, the principal role, is a synthesis of many characters: sometimes she is a young girl, sometimes a dead soul inspecting her body from another world, sometimes a child. Around her is darkness peopled by voices wishing to help her, but beyond her understanding. The timbres and rhythms of many languages – live and recorded, spoken and sung, singly and chorally – are woven into an intricate web that powerfully suggests the hallucinating schizophrenic mind.

Among Schafer's other works, the orchestral *Son of Heldenleben* (1968) is based on a programme – part satire, part homage – which introduces a new member of the Strauss family. Direct and indirect quotations from the original constitute the material, including two series derived from Strauss's opening melody. In the Five Studies on Texts by Prudentius (1962) the centrally placed soprano is encircled by four flutes in the corners of the hall; the clearly defined spatial movements of the flute canons expose symbolic relationships with the religious texts. Threnody (1966) uses the written memories of children surviving the bombing of Nagasaki, again enhancing the power of words with a discreet but poignant accompaniment of orchestral, choral and taped sounds.

An important part of Schafer's work has been his activity in music education. His music for children is less concerned with theory and skill than with creativity and receptiveness, and his major effort has been in developing awareness of sound in general: his published booklets provide a wealth of ideas directed to this aim. Intense preoccupation with the effects of sound on man has led him to take an active interest in the whole acoustic environment. His inventory of worldwide soundscapes, a project encouraged by UNESCO, has been undertaken with a view to bringing about a new relationship between man and the sounds around him.

WORKS

Concerto, hpd, 8 insts, 1954
3 Contemporaries (Schafer), 1v, pf, 1954–6
Minnelieder, Mez, wind qnt, 1956
Kinderlieder (Brecht), Mez, pf, 1958
Sonatina, fl, hpd/pf, 1958

In memoriam: Alberto Guerrero, str orch, 1959
Protest and Incarceration, Mez, orch, 1960
Brébeuf, Bar, orch, 1961
Canzoni for Prisoners, orch, 1961–2
4 Songs (Tagore), S, Mez, A, SA, 1962
5 Studies on Texts by Prudentius, S, 4 fl, 1962
Untitled Composition for Orchestra, chamber orch, 1963
Statement in Blue, youth orch, 1964
Loving/Toi (music-theatre, Schafer), 1963–6; arrs. of arias: Modesty, Mez, 15 insts, 1963; The Geography of Eros, S, pf, harp, 6 perc, tape, 1964; Air Ishtar, S, pf, cel, 6 perc, tape, 1965; Vanity, Mez, harp, hpd, mand, gui, banjo, perc, vn, vc, 1965
Requiems for the Party Girl (Schafer), Mez, fl + pic, cl + b cl, hn, pf, harp, perc, str trio, 1966 [see also Patria II]
Threnody (Jap. children), 5 child speakers, youth chorus, youth orch, tape, 1966
Gita (Bhagavad Gita), SATB, brass, tape, 1967
Kaleidoscope, multi-track tape, 1967
Epitaph for Moonlight, youth SATB, bells, 1968
Son of Heldenleben, orch, tape, 1968
From the Tibetan Book of the Dead (Bardo Thobel), S, SATB, a fl + pic, cl, tape, 1968
Minimusic, youth ens, 1969
Yeow and Pax (Isaiah xiii.6–13, lx.18–20), SATB, org, tape, 1969
No Longer than Ten Minutes, orch, 1970
Sappho, Mez, harp, pf, gui, perc, 1970
String Quartet, 1970
Enchantress (Sappho), S, fl, 8 vc, 1971
Miniwanka (The Moments of Water), youth SA/SATB, 1971
Okeanos, 4-track tape, 1971
In Search of Zoroaster, male v, SATB, perc, org, 1971
Tehillah (Ps cxlviii), SATB, perc, 1971; rev. 1976 as Psalm
Lustro, vv, orch, tape: Divan i shams i tabriz (Jalal al-Din Rumi), 1969; Music for the Morning of the World (Jalal al-Din Rumi), 1970; Beyond the Great Gate of Light (Tagore), 1971–2
Arcana (Egyptian), 1v, ens/orch, 1972
East, chamber orch, 1972
Patria I: The Characteristics Man (music-theatre, Schafer), 1972
Patria II: Requiems for the Party Girl (music-theatre, Schafer), 1972; study: Dream Passage, Mez, ens, tape, 1969
North White, orch, 1973
String Quartet no.2 'Waves', 1976
Adieu, Robert Schumann, A, orch, 1976
Hymn to Night, S, orch, 1976
Cortège, orch, 1977
Apocalypsis (music-theatre), 1977: John's Vision, soloists, choirs, wind, perc, org; Credo, 12 mixed choirs, tape

Principal publisher: Universal

WRITINGS

'Music and the Iron Curtain', *Queens Quarterly* (1960), Autumn, 407
'Two Musicians in Fiction', *Canadian Music Journal*, iii (1960), Spring, 23
'Ezra Pound and Music', *Canadian Music Journal*, iv (1961), Summer, 15
'Limits of Nationalism in Canadian Music', *Tamarack Review* (1961), Winter, 71
British Composers in Interview (London, 1963)
'Money and Music', *Canadian Forum*, xliv (1964)
The Composer in the Classroom (Toronto, 1965, 3/1972; Ger. trans. as Schöpferisches Musizieren, Vienna, 1971)
Ear Cleaning (Toronto, 1967, 3/1972; Ger. trans. as Schule des Hörens, Vienna, 1972; Fr. trans. as L'oreille pense, Toronto, 1974)
'The Future for Music in Canada', *Transactions of the Royal Society of Canada*, v, series 4 (1967), 37
'The Philosophy of Stereophony', *West Coast Review* (1967), Winter, 4
'A Basic Course', *Source*, v (1969), 45
'A Middle-East Sound Diary', *Focus on Musicology* (1969), no. 1, p.20
The New Soundscape (Toronto, 1969, 3/1972; Ger. trans. as Die Schallwelt in der wir leben, Vienna, 1971; Hung. trans., 1974)
The Book of Noise (Vancouver, 1970, 2/1973)
'Threnody: a Religious Piece for our Time', *Music: Journal of the American Guild of Organists*, iv/5 (1970), 33
When Words Sing (Toronto, 1970, 3/1972; Ger. trans. as ... wenn Wörter klingen, Vienna, 1973; Jap. trans., 1974)
'The World's Soul', *Music Educator's National Magazine* (1970), Oct, 31
Review of *Le bruit* (Montreal, 1970), *Canada Music Book* (1971), no.2, p.181
The Public of the Music Theatre: Louis Riel: a Case Study (London, 1972)
'The Developing Theories of Absolute Rhythm and Great Bass', *Paideuma*, i/3 (1973), 23
'The Music of the Environment', *Cultures*, i/1 (1973), 15–51
'Thoughts on Music Education', *The World of Music*, xv/1 (1973), 4

The Music of Ezra Pound (New York, 1974)
'Notes for the Stage Work "Loving" (1965)', *Canada Music Book* (1974), Spring-Summer, 9
E.T.A. Hoffmann and Music (Toronto, 1975)
ed.: *Ezra Pound and Music: the Complete Criticism* (New York, 1977)
The Tuning of the World (New York, 1977)

BIBLIOGRAPHY

B. Mather: 'Requiems for the Party Girl', *Canada Music Book* (1970), no.1, p.91
K. Potter and J. Shepherd: 'Interview with Murray Schafer', *Contact* (1976), no.13, p.31
J. Rea: 'Richard Wagner and R. Murray Schafer: Two Revolutionary and Religious Poets', *Canada Music Book* (1974), no.8, p.37

UDO KASEMETS

Schaffen [Scaffen], Henri [Henricus, Henrichus, Heinrich] (*b* early 16th century). French or Flemish composer resident in Italy. In his one book of madrigals (1549) he is described as a French nobleman, though the title-page of a collection of his motets refers to his coming from Flanders. His works were issued mainly in Venice from the later 1540s on. They include the above-mentioned book of madrigals, all for four voices under the *note nere* mensuration, and described on the title-page as being 'as new and ravishing a work as any other printed up to now'; 12 madrigals (ten for four voices, two for five) in five anthologies and collections published between 1547 and 1569; two books of motets for five voices (both 1564); and five motets (two for four voices, three for five) in collections from the years 1549–56, two of which were published in Nuremberg.

DON HARRÁN

Schäffer, Bogusław (*b* Lwów, 6 June 1929). Polish composer, theorist and teacher. He studied the violin in Opole and wrote his first atonal chamber piece at the age of 17. Subsequently he studied composition with Malawski at the Kraków Conservatory and in 1952 he was appointed director of the record library of Polish radio in Kraków. The next year he completed his musicological studies under Jachimecki and composed the first Polish 12-note work for orchestra (Music for Strings: Nocturne); this was followed in 1955 by his earliest 'infinitive' compositions, in incomplete notation. He was a music critic between 1953 and 1959, but since then has devoted his time to composition and teaching. In 1963 he was appointed to the staff of the Kraków Conservatory, and in 1965 he began work at the Experimental Studio of Polish radio in Warsaw. The awards he has received include the prize of the Polish Minister of Culture and Art (1971) and a prize for his work in composition teaching (1972). In 1973 concerts of his work were given in Zagreb and Amsterdam.

Schäffer is an unusual figure in Polish music: his prolific creativity and the diversity of his activities are astonishing, but his originality lies in an ability to balance and benefit from the tensions involved in such abundant and multifarious occupations. The theorist supports and sometimes clashes with the composer; the strict, precise analyst contrasts with the intuitive musician of certain works; and a continual dialogue takes place between these and other 'characters' within the single personality. Even when considered solely as a composer, Schäffer appears to contain several isolable creative characters: the composer of music for conventional forces, the electronic composer and the creator of 'happenings'. But these are very often united or intertwined. His career as a composer for traditional instruments and voices began with the piano pieces of 1949–52, yet within this general current he was already

by 1955 elaborating the concept of incompletely composed music, as in his first work of 'instrumental theatre', *TIS MW2* (1963), and later 'happenings'. It was an evolution that took him through Webernian 12-note serialism and then controlled improvisation to a free music transitorily combined with other art forms (painting, sculpture, poetry, theatre etc). This was accompanied by a steady broadening of style and means: thus for a long time he concentrated on instrumental music, then admitted the human voice and finally extended his range to mixed-media forms. Of his instrumental 12-note serial compositions, the most important are *Scultura* (1960) and *Musica ipsa* (1962), both for orchestra. These, like other works of the period, display an individual style, distinct from both post-Webernian pointillism and post-Varèsian brutalism. There is a new approach to the shaping of sound – into heavy, massive blocks in *Scultura*; into carefully modelled and stretched material in *Musica ipsa* – and Schäffer's use of colour, time and space is also quite original. It is significant that he rarely makes use of the same instrumental combination twice.

Throughout his career Schäffer has directed his creative work with a keen analytic sense, responsive to developments in music and in the world at large, so that his work may be seen as impelled by the imperative of protest and the necessity of newness. For him creativity is a constant process of discovery, and also a continuous transformation of things already created: no model or form can be accepted once and for all. His perpetually renewed experiments in composition have embraced theoretical considerations and practice, analysis and polemic. His wide-ranging attitude may be summarized in his own words: 'The potentialities of new music are, for all practical purposes, limitless'. Thus his basic problem has been to find and describe the boundaries of what can be music, a quest introduced by his theoretical treatise *Nowa muzyka* (1958, enlarged 2/1969). This book, which reveals in great depth the situation of the living composer, has had enormous influence in the evolution of modern Polish music, in spite (or perhaps because) of its distance from the assumptions of traditional theory.

It was only after the publication of his book that Schäffer emerged as a leading composer: the decade between its two editions may be regarded as a period when his conception of the nature of music ripened and crystallized. The result was a conception embracing 'de-composition' as well as composition: de-composition understood as creation through negation and destruction. Some of his early piano pieces already show indications of a division into the currents of composition and de-composition, but the latter is subdued, whereas in subsequent years it seems to have gained a position of ascendancy: openness dominates restriction, 'informality' form. Schäffer's early tentatives in this direction, which the piano pieces exemplify, require the performer to supply details (pitches, rhythms etc); the pursuit of such ideas led to 'happenings'. In *TIS MW2*, *Fragment*, *Audiences* and *Comunicazione audiovisiva* there are allusions to the past, and certain tensions are released through the 'absurd' confrontation of 'old' art forms: music, poetry, dance, visual arts etc. But beyond this there are the outlines of a new, synthetic art: works such as these offer intellectual stimulation and show that music is an open domain, inexhaustible in its possibilities.

WORKS

STAGE ETC

TIS MW2, no.69 (K. Irzykowski), 8 performers, 1963
TIS GK, no.78 (Schäffer), ens, 1963
Monodrama, no.113 (radio opera, Ritsos, Seferis, trans. Z. Kubiak, J. Zych), 1968, also television version A Talk with a Young Man
Hommage à Czyżewski, no.153 (T. Czyżewski), ens, 1972
Dreams of Schäffer, no.162 (Ionesco), ens, 1972
Audiovisual music: Visual Music, no.96, 3 actors, pf, vc, 1966; Comunicazione audiovisiva, no.129, 5 performers, 1970; Contract, no.136, S, vc, perc, 1971
Music for actors (Schäffer): Scenario, no.79, actor, 1963; Audiences nos.1–5, no.84, actors, 1964; Qt, no.104, 4 actors, 1966; Fragment, no.117, 2 actors, vc, 1968; Scenario, no.131, 3 actors, 1970; 21 VI 1972, Twilight, no.152, 1972
Action music, happenings, etc: Non-stop, no.51, pf, 1960; Expressive Aspects, no.73, fl, S, 1963; Incident, no.107, audience ens, 1966; Media, no.109, vv, insts, 1967; Reading, no.114, 6 performers, 1968; Creative Act, no.115, 1968; PRSC, no.118, 1968; Simplest Solutions, no.122, ens, 1969; Algorithms, no.128, 7 performers, 1970; Conceptual Music, no.149, 1972; Negative Music, no.154, 1972; ba/vo, no.156, ballerina, S, 1972; o/p, no.158, ens, 1972; Out of Tune, no.163, S, vc, 1972; Polonaise, no.164, 12vv, 1972; Free Form no.1, no.166, 5 insts, 1972; Hommage à Irzykowski, no.171 (Irzykowski), ens, 1973
Incidental music, film scores

ORCHESTRAL AND VOCAL ORCHESTRAL

Vocal orch: Guillaume Apollinaire Poetry, no.15, S, orch, 1949; Cantata (Audiogram), no.95, 60vv, orch, 1966; Howl, no.98 (Ginsberg), 3 actors, chamber orch, 1966
Orch with solo inst: 4 movimenti, no.32, pf, orch, 1957; Tertium datur, no.38, hpd, insts, 1958; Conc. breve, no.42, vc, chamber orch, 1959; Conc. per 6 e 3, no.50, changing solo inst (cl, sax, vn, vc, perc, pf), orch, 1960; Musica, no.56, hpd, insts, 1961; S'alto, no.71 (Dostoyevsky: The Devils), a sax, chamber orch, 1963; Conc., no.72, fl, 3 fl, high insts, 1963; Vn Conc., no.75, 1963; Pf Conc., no.110, 1967; Experimenta, no.144, 2 pf (1 player), orch, 1971; Confrontations, no.148, any solo inst, orch, 1972; Jangwa, db, orch, 1979
Orch: Topofonica, no.48, 40 insts, 1960; Little Sym. 'Scultura', no.55, 1960; Musica ipsa, no.63, low insts, 1962; Sym., no.111, 1967; Texts, no.138, 1971; Sym., no.169, 1973; Tentative Music, no.174, 159 insts, 1973; Warsaw Ov. (Harmonies and Counterpoints I), 1975; Romuald Traugutt (Harmonies and Counterpoints II), 1976
Chamber orch: 3 Short Pieces, no.18, 1951; Equivalenze sonore, no.43, perc, 1960; Codes, no.59, 1961; Collage, no.86, 1964; Gravesono, wind, perc, 1977
Str: Music for Str – Nocturne, no.20, 1953; Monosonata, no.40, 6 str qts, 1959; Joint Constructions, no.52, 1960; Kesukaan, 13 str, 1978

ENSEMBLE

For 6 or more insts: Permutations, no.27, 10 insts, 1956; Extremes, no.29, 10 insts, 1957; Montaggio, no.53, 2 perc, 4 pf, 1960; Azione a 2, no.60, pf, 11 insts, 1961; Imago musicae, no.61, vv, acc., 1961; Decet, no.101, harp, 9 insts, 1966; Mare, no.143, pf, 9 insts, 1971; 19 Micropieces, no.155, vc, 6 performers, 1972; Iranian Set, 1976; Vaniniana, 1978; Heideggeriana, 1979
For 4–5 insts: Qt, no.7, 2 vn, vc, pf, 1947; 2 Short Compositions, no.9, 2 fl, 2 cl, 1948; Little Qt, no.11, tpt, 2 hn, trbn, 1948; Music for Str Qt (Str Qt no.1), no.24, 1954; Str Qt II (Str Qt no.2), no.30, 1957; Conc. (Str Qt no.3), no.44, 1959; Str Qt II (Str Qt no.4), no.85, 1964; Qt, no.90, 2 pf, any 2 performers, 1965; Ob Qt, no.99, 1966; Qt SG, no.112, any 4 performers, 1968; Spectra, no.130, 5 insts, 1970; Str Qt III (Str Qt no.5), no.141, 1971; Variants, no.145, wind qnt, 1971; Sgraffito, no.147, fl, vc/db, hpd, 2 pf, 1971; Str Qt IV (Str Qt no.6), no.173, 1973
For 3 insts: Trio, no.4, 2 vn, vc, 1946; 4 Pieces, no.65, str trio, 1962; Transmission, no.94, vc, 2 pf, 1965; Pf Trio, no.120, 1969; Open Scene, no.123, 1969; Synectics, no.127, any 3 performers, 1970; Estratto (Str Trio no.2), no.139, str trio, 1971; Conc., no.157, 3 pf, 1972; Neues, no.161, 3 vn, 1972

INSTRUMENTAL

For 2 insts: Sonatina, no.2, 2 vn, 1946; 4 Studies, no.6, bn, pf, 1947; Piece, no.10, 2 fl, 1948; Conc., no.17, 2 pf, 1951; 2 Pieces, no.81, vn, pf, 1964; 4H/1P, no.103, pf 4 hands, 1966; Composition, no.105, harp, pf, 1966; 15 Elements, no.142, 2 pf, 1971; Blues III, 2 pf, 1978
For 1 inst: Sonatina, no.3, a sax, 1946; 40 Short Pieces, no.8, vn, 1947–8; Canzona, no.14, vc, 1949; 2 Studies, no.21, fl, 1953; 2 Studies, no.22, a sax, 1954; Sonata, no.25, vn, 1955; Negatives, no.49, fl, 1960; Sound Forms, no.58, a sax, 1961; Constructions, no.68, vib, 1962; Sfumato, no.82, hpd, 1964; 5 Short Pieces, no.88, harp, 1964; 5 Fragments, no.124, gui, 1970; Solo: Conglomeration, no.134, perc, 1970; Variants, no.137, ob, 1971; Interview, no.151,

vn, 1972; Free Form no.2 (Evocazioni), db, 1972; aSa, no.170, amp clvd, 1973; aDieu, no.175, trbn, 1973; Self-expression, vc, 1978
For pf: 3 Short Studies, no.1, 1944–6; Diarium, no.5, 1947; 19 Mazurkas, no.12, 1949; 2 Pieces, no.16, 1949–50; Sonatina, no.19, 1952; Composition, no.23, 1954; Study in Diagram, no.26, 1955–6; Model no.1, no.28, 1956; Model no.2, no.31, 1957; Variations, no.33, 1956–8; 8 Pieces, no.35, 1954–8; Free Composition, no.36, 1958; 3 Studies, no.39, 1958–9; Linear Construction, no.41, 1959; Articulations, no.45, 1959; Configurations, no.46, 1960; Points of Departure, no.47, 1960; Dispositions a, no.54, 1955–60; Model no.3, no.62, 1961; Contours, no.70, 1963; Model no.4, no.77, 1963; Model no.5, no.91, 1965; Dispositions b, no.93, 1960–65; Emotiographs, no.100, 1966; Dispositions c, no.126, 1965–70; Model no.6, no.135, 1970; Model no.7, no.140, 1971; Model no.8, no.150, 1972; Model no.9, 1976

JAZZ

3 Compositions for MJQ, no.57, 1961; Course 'J', no.67, jazz ens, orch, 1962; Music for MI, no.74, vib, 1v, jazz ens, orch, 1963; Collage and Form, no.80, 8 jazz players, orch, 1963; Jazz Conc., no.110, orch, 1969; blueS no.1, no.160, 2 pf, tape, 1972; blueS no.2, no.165, ens, 1972

ELECTRONIC

With live performers: Trio, no.97, fl, harp, va, tape, 1966; Conc., no.121, harp, pf, tape, 1969; Heraclitiana, no.125, 12 alternative solos, tape, 1970; Project, no.132, inst, tape, 1970; Bergsoniana, no.159, S, fl, hn, pf, db, tape, 1972; Blues 1, 2 pf, tape, 1972; Missa elettronica, boys' choir, tape, 1975; Miserere, S, chorus, orch, tape, 1978; Maah, orch, tape, 1979
Tape alone: Sym., no.87, 1964; Assemblages, no.102, 1966; Music for Tape, no.106, 1966; Hommage à Strzemiński, no.108, 1967; Conc., no.116, 1968; Theme, no.133, 1970; Synthistory, no.172, 1973; Poetries, 1978

OTHER WORKS

Songs: 3 Songs, no.13 (Shakespeare, Goethe, Joyce), 1v, pf, 1949
Idea programmes: PR-I no.1, no.34, chorus, 1958; PR-I no.2, no.37, new inst, 1958; PR-I no.3, no.76, chorus, orch, 1963; PR-I no.4, no.83, cquivalent insts, 1964; PR-I no.5, no.89, actors, 1964; PR-I no.6, no.92, chamber chorus, 1965; PR-I no.7, no.146, tape, 1971; PR-I no.8, no.167, any performers, 1972
Designs: Design of an Automatic Musical Composition, no.64, 1962; Design of an Automatic Stage Composition, no.66, 1962

Principal publishers: Ahn & Simrock, Moeck, Modern, Polskie Wydawnictwo Muzyczne

WRITINGS

BOOKS

Almanach polskich kompozytorów współczesnych [Almanac of contemporary Polish composers] (Kraków, 1956, rev. 2/1966)
Mały informator muzyki XX wieku (Kraków, 1958, 3/1974)
Nowa muzyka: problemy współczesnej techniki kompozytorskiej (Kraków, 1958, enlarged 2/1969)
Klasycy dodekafonii (Kraków, 1961–4)
ed., with M. Hanuszewska, A. Trzaskowski and Z. Wachowicz: *Leksykon kompozytorów XX wieku* (Kraków, 1964–6)
Wychowawcze funkcje profesora kompozycji [The educative functions of a composition teacher] (Kraków, 1965)
W kręgu nowej muzyki [In the spheres of new music] (Kraków, 1967)
ed., with M. Karczyńska, Z. Wachowicz and others: *Artur Malawski* (Kraków, 1969)
Dźwięki i znaki [Sounds and signs] (Warsaw, 1969) [introduction to contemporary composition]
Wstęp do kompozycji/Introduction to Composition (Warsaw, 1975) [bilingual]
Historia muzyki – style i twórcy [History of music – styles and composers] (Poznań, 1979)

ARTICLES

'Polskie melodie ludowe w twórczości Witolda Lutosławskiego' [Polish folktunes in Lutosławski's work], *Studia muzykologiczne*, v (1955)
'Nowe drogi muzyki współczesnej' [New ways of contemporary music], *Ruch muzyczny* (1957), nos.1–2
'Perspektywy dydaktyki harmonicznej', *Ruch muzyczny* (1958), nos.9–10
'Präexistente und inexistente Strukturen', *GfMKB: Kassel 1962*, 263
'Muzyka graficzna', *Forum musicum* (1968), no.3
'O dekompozycji', *Forum musicum* (1969), no.4
'Technika kompozytorska', *Forum musicum* (1970), no.8
'Estetyka nowej muzyki', *Forum musicum* (1971), no.12
'Socjologia muzyki współczesnej', *Forum musicum* (1971), no.11
'Super-parametric Composing: its Communicative and Semiological Consequences', *International Symposium on the Problematic of Today's Musical Notation: Rome 1972*
Articles in *Grove 6*, etc

BIBLIOGRAPHY

B. Pociej: 'O twórczości Bogusława Schäffera', *Muzyka*, ix/3–4 (1964), 44; Ger. summary, 137

——: 'Argument for the Existence of Music: B. Schäffer's Work', *Poland* (1966), no.12
'Composer's Workshop: Bogusław Schäffer', *Polish Music*, xii (1969), 16
Z. Mycielski: ' "Scultura" B. Schäffera', *Ruch muzyczny* (1969), no.19
O. Bednarčik: 'Grafický prvek w dile B. Schäffera', *OM*, iii (1971), 179
G. Michalski: *Koncert poświęcony twórczości Bogusława Schäffera* (Warsaw, 1971) [Warsaw National PO publication]
J. Hodor and B. Pociej: *Bogusław Schäffer and his Music* (Glasgow, 1974)
E. Karkoschka: 'Über Boguslaw Schäffer und einige Kriterien musikalischer Qualität', *Melos/NZM*, ii (1976), 197

BOHDAN POCIEJ

Schäffer, Johann Wilhelm. *See* SCHEFFER, JOHANN WILHELM.

Schäffer, Michael (*b* Cologne, 11 Nov 1937; *d* Cologne, 7 Sept 1978). German lutenist. He studied with Walter Gerwig at the Musikhochschule, Cologne, and made his début in Cologne in 1960. His repertory consisted mainly of Baroque music, particularly of the French school, and he made a special study of continuo playing. His performances were firmly based on first-hand knowledge of original and restored 18th-century instruments and of contemporary playing techniques, and as one of the younger generation of German lutenists his influence as a soloist and a teacher (notably at Queekhoven, Netherlands) was considerable.

BIBLIOGRAPHY
E. M. Dombois: 'In Memoriam: Michael Schäffer 1937–1978', *LSJ*, xx (1978), 57

DAVID SCOTT

Schäffer, Paul. *See* SCHAEFFER, PAUL.

Schaffrath [Schafrath, Schafrat], **Christoph** (*b* Hohenstein, nr. Chemnitz, 1709; *d* Berlin, 17 Feb 1763). German harpsichordist, composer and teacher. One of the earliest references to him was in 1733, when he applied for the position of organist at the Sophienkirche, Dresden. In his application he stated that for the past three years he had been 'harpsichordist to the king' and the Polish Prince Sangusko. Although one of three candidates short-listed, Schaffrath was unsuccessful and the post went to Wilhelm Friedemann Bach. By the following year, however, he was in the service of Crown Prince Frederick (later Frederick the Great). He was among those who moved with the prince's establishment from Ruppin to Rheinsberg in 1736, and on Frederick's accession in 1740 was installed as harpsichordist in the court Kapelle at Berlin. In 1741 he was appointed musician to the king's sister, Princess Amalia, a title which appears on contemporary publications of his music and which he was still using in the 1760s. Although he remained at Berlin until his death his name is not included in Marpurg's register of the Kapelle (1754); this implies that he left the orchestra at some point, possibly after the 1741 appointment.

As a composer Schaffrath restricted himself to instrumental music, producing a wide range of chamber and orchestral works. His main interest lay in keyboard music, and various collections of his sonatas (for keyboard alone and keyboard with melody instrument) were published during his lifetime. Almost all the harpsichord sonatas are in three movements with the standard fast–slow–fast arrangement. The first Allegro is usually in sonata form, but the opening part of the exposition is frequently omitted from the recapitulation, and when Schaffrath wrote a full recapitulation he often varied the exposition material by condensing or expanding certain

sections. Schaffrath's keyboard writing in these sonatas is idiomatic yet simple: scale passages and broken-chord figures are employed with good effect but the texture is thin – seldom more than two parts – and the left hand plays a subordinate role. The concertos show the same approach to keyboard writing. Here Schaffrath followed Vivaldian formal methods, using ritornello structure in all three movements and distinguishing clearly between tutti and solo sections.

Stylistically, Schaffrath's music belongs to the transitional era. His works display characteristic *galant* features: tuneful melodies, short phrases, thin texture, slow harmonic rhythm and ubiquitous triplet figures. However, he also had a marked talent for counterpoint, a skill apparent not only in the occasional fugal movement (e.g. op.2 no.6, second movement) but also in the disciplined part-writing of orchestral works and in his frequent use of imitation. Although active in Berlin, Schaffrath was not particularly affected by the 'sensitive' north German style. Exceptional works reveal the influence of C. P. E. Bach in their wide-ranging themes and harmonic asperities, but Schaffrath generally preferred a less emotional style, more in keeping with Hasse's music than with the Empfindsamkeit.

WORKS
6 duetti, vn/fl, hpd obbl, op.1 (Nuremberg, 1746)
6 sonates, hpd, op.2 (Nuremberg, 1749)
6 sonate o trii, 2 fl, b (Leipzig, before 1763), only no.1 extant
1 kbd sonata in XX sonate per cembalo composte da vari autori, ed. G. B. Venier, op.2 no.10 (Paris, 1760); another in Oeuvres mêlées, vii/5 (Nuremberg, 1761)

13 symphonies (see Flueler); at least 6 overtures; Fl Concerto; 2 vn concertos; at least 13 kbd concertos; 2 concertos, 2 kbd, str (see Uldall); 22 duets, vn/ob/va da gamba/fl/lute, kbd; duet, 2 va da gamba; solo, vc, bc; 2 duets, 2 kbd, *c*1750 (see Newman); 17 kbd sonatas (see Stilz); 4 pieces, vn/fl, kbd; many other chamber works for various insts: principal sources *B-Bc*, *D-B*, *DS*, *KA*, *SWl*, *F-Pn* (for details see Stilz and Flueler)
Lost: 5 kbd sonatas, Ob Concerto, 2 bn concertos, advertised by Breitkopf, 1763; other works, possibly identical to the above, listed in Breitkopf catalogues

BIBLIOGRAPHY
F. W. Marpurg: *Historisch-kritische Beyträge zur Aufnahme der Musik* (Berlin, 1754–5/*R*1970), i, 157, 507
R. Eitner: 'Thematischer Katalog der von Thulemeier'schen Musikalien-Sammlung in der Bibliothek des Joachimsthal'schen Gymnasiums zu Berlin', *MMg*, xxxi, suppl. (1899/*R*1960)
M. Flueler: *Die norddeutsche Sinfonie zur Zeit Friedrichs des Grossen* (Berlin, 1908), 55
M. Falck: *Wilhelm Friedemann Bach: sein Leben und seine Werke* (Leipzig, 1913), 13f
H. Mersmann: 'Beiträge zur Aufführungspraxis der vorklassischen Kammermusik in Deutschland', *AMw*, ii (1920/*R*1964), 99–143
H. Uldall: *Das Klavierkonzert der Berliner Schule* (Leipzig, 1928), 69ff
E. Stilz: *Die Berliner Klaviersonate zur Zeit Friedrichs des Grossen* (Berlin, 1930), 23ff
A. Weinmann: *Kataloge Anton Huberty (Wien) und Christoph Toricella*, Beiträge zur Geschichte des Alt-Wiener Musikverlages, 2nd ser., vii (Vienna, 1962), 23, 58
W. S. Newman: *The Sonata in the Classic Era* (Chapel Hill, 1963), 71, 81, 104, 106, 443f
B. S. Brook, ed.: *The Breitkopf Thematic Catalogue, 1762–1787* (New York, 1966)

PIPPA DRUMMOND

Schak, Benedikt. *See* SCHACK, BENEDIKT.

Schale [Schaale, Schall], **Christian Friedrich** (*b* Brandenburg, 10 March 1713; *d* Berlin, 2 March 1800). German organist, cellist and composer. He was a pupil of the organist Christian Rolle, then studied law for a brief period at Halle University (*c*1732). From 1735 he was a member of the orchestra of Prince Heinrich of Prussia until he was appointed to the royal chapel of Frederick the Great in Berlin as cellist and chamber musician (1741). He was also second organist (to J. Philipp Sack) at Berlin Cathedral, and became cathedral organist when Sack died in 1763. He was one of the first members of Sack's Musikübende Gesellschaft, the earliest amateur concert society in Berlin (founded in 1749), and also conducted another group called the Assemblée (made up of members of the royal chapel). Following Sack's death, he merged the two groups; in 1781 Schale and the singer G. C. Concialini used this orchestra to present a series of amateur concerts in Berlin.

Schale composed in a variety of genres, but most of his works were not published. His music is often contrapuntal, and his keyboard works are occasionally quite virtuoso. His lieder are in the folklike style of the first Berlin lied school.

WORKS
Orch: 8 syms., *D-DS*; 4 syms., *Bds*; 1 sym., *B-Bc* [attrib. Schaffrath]; 1 ov., *D-Bds*; 7 kbd concs., *Bds*; 1 kbd conc., *B-Bc*; 3 fl concs. [cited in Biehle]
Other inst: [18] Brevi sonate, hpd (Nuremberg, c1755–c1760); Leichte Vorspiele, org/pf (Berlin, 1794–6); Leichte Nachspiele, org (Berlin, 1795); Allegretto, kbd, 1757, *D-Bds*; sonata, kbd, *B-Bc*; 2 sonatas and 1 trio, kbd, vn [cited in Biehle]; solo, fl, bc, *D-SWl*; other kbd pieces, *Bds*; several inst and kbd pieces in contemporary anthologies
Vocal: Neue Melodien zu G. W. Burmanns [24] kleinen Liedern für kleine Mägdchen (Berlin, 1774); 3 cantatas, 1763–75 [cited in Ledebur]; many other lieder in contemporary anthologies

BIBLIOGRAPHY
EitnerQ; *GerberL*; *GerberNL*
C. von Ledebur: *Tonkünstler-Lexicon Berlin's* (Berlin, 1861/R1965)
M. Flueler: *Die norddeutsche Sinfonie zur Zeit Friedrichs des Grossen* (Berlin, 1908), 56
H. Biehle: 'Christian Friedrich Schale: ein Beitrag zur Berliner Musikgeschichte', *Mitteilungen des Vereins für die Geschichte Berlins*, xl (1923), 17
H. Uldall: *Das Klavierkonzert der Berliner Schule* (Leipzig, 1928)
E. Stilz: *Die Berliner Klaviersonate zur Zeit Friedrichs des Grossen* (Berlin, 1930), 41ff
RAYMOND A. BARR

Schalk, Franz (*b* Vienna, 27 May 1863; *d* Edlach, 3 Sept 1931). Austrian conductor. A pupil of Bruckner at the Vienna Conservatory, he became first conductor at the Vienna Court Opera in 1900, under Mahler's directorship. In 1918 he became director there himself, jointly with Richard Strauss, of whose *Die Frau ohne Schatten* he conducted the first performance in 1919; and on Strauss's resignation in 1924, he was in sole control until 1929. He conducted at the Metropolitan Opera during the 1898–9 season, and at Covent Garden in 1898, 1907 and, when his *Ring* cycles were particularly admired, in 1911. He and his elder brother Josef, who had also studied under Bruckner, were among the earliest champions of their master's symphonies, though they presented them in unauthentic versions prepared by themselves and others. Franz's influence is manifest in the first edition of the revised version of no.3 (1890), and Josef's in the first edition of no.8 (1892); Franz collaborated with Ferdinand Löwe in the spurious first edition of no.4 (1890), and was solely responsible for the equally spurious first edition of no.5 (1896).

BIBLIOGRAPHY
L. Schalk, ed.: *Briefe und Betrachtungen* (Vienna and Leipzig, 1935)
D. Cooke: 'The Bruckner Problem Simplified', *MT*, cx (1969), 20, 142, 362, 479, 828
M. Carner: 'Franz Schalk and Robert Heger', *Recorded Sound* (1970), no.38, p.601 [with discography of Schalk]
DERYCK COOKE

Schall, Claus Nielsen (*b* Copenhagen, 28 April 1757; *d* Copenhagen, 9 Aug 1835). Danish composer, dancer and violinist. In 1772 he joined the Royal Theatre in Copenhagen as a dancer, and in 1775 became a member of the court chapel. The dancer and choreographer Vincenzo Galeotti, recognizing Schall's ability, appointed him répétiteur and director of ballet at the Royal Theatre in 1776; he also engaged Schall to compose music for many of his ballets. After travelling in the late 1780s to Paris, Dresden, Berlin and Prague (where he met Mozart), Schall returned to Copenhagen in 1792 to take Hartmann's place as Konzertmeister at the Opera, working successively under J. A. P. Schulz and F. L. A. Kunzen. In 1795 Schall became composer to the Royal Ballet and in 1818 music director at the Opera, where he remained until 1834; he conducted the première of Weber's *Freischütz* overture there in 1820.

Though self-taught as a composer, Schall was rated highly by his contemporaries, and his experience as a violinist (he played in the court chapel from 1779) and in the theatre gave him an unusually wide scope. His chief importance lies in his collaboration with Galeotti, for whom he wrote about 20 ballets ranging from light divertimentos to full-length tragedies (occasionally with chorus). His models were Gluck and Mozart, but his style is also perceptibly indebted to that of French dramatic music. His other music includes Singspiels, songs and instrumental pieces, of which his chamber works are particularly important, being among the first by a Danish composer.

Schall's brother, Peder Schall (baptized Copenhagen, 30 Dec 1762; *d* Copenhagen, 1 Feb 1820), was a cellist in the court chapel, a guitarist and composer of vocal works with guitar accompaniment.

WORKS
Selective list; all published, in Copenhagen, unless otherwise stated.

STAGE
Unless otherwise stated, all ballets, with librettos and choreography by Galeotti, and all first performed at the Royal Theatre.
Kiaerligheds og mistankens magt, 1780; Lauretta, 1785; Generalen til de tre stjerner, 1786; Claudine von Villa bella (Singspiel, Goethe), 1787, unpubd; Vaskerpigerne og kiedelflikkeren, 1788; Afguden paa Ceilon, 1788; Hververen, 1788; Chinafarerne (Singspiel, P. A. Heinberg), 1792
Aftenen (Singspiel), 1795, unpubd; Den vaegelsindede, 1796; Annette og Lubin, 1797; Lagertha, 1801; Domherren i Milano (Singspiel, N. T. Bruun, after A. Duval), 1802; Ines de Castro, 1804; Rolf Blaaskiaeg, 1808; Romeo og Giulietta, 1811; Dansesygen, 1811; De tre Galninger (Singspiel), 1816, unpubd; Macbeth, 1816; Tycho Brahes Spaadom (Singspiel, J. L. Heiberg), 1819

INSTRUMENTAL
[60] Engelske danse, 2 vn, 2 fl/ob, 2 hn, bc (1787–91) [in 5 vols.]
Arier, viser, sange og andre smaa haandstykker, 2 fl/vn (1791–7)
Cinquième concerto, vn, orch (Paris, n.d.)
6 duos concertants, 2 vn (Hamburg, n.d.) [in 2 vols.]
6 Solos, vn, bc (London, n.d.)
Vn and pf solos, incl. pf arrs. of excerpts from stage works, pubd separately
Concs., *DK-Kk*

VOCAL
Blandede compositioner, 1v, pf (n.d.)
10 chansons (Leonard), 1v, pf (Hamburg, n.d.)
Songs, cantatas, pubd separately

PEDAGOGICAL
Nordens Apollo, udgivet af C. Schall (n.d.) [in several vols., incl. works by Schall]
Etudes de l'archet et du doigter ou 58 exemples, mêlés de caprices, vn (Paris, n.d.)
Suite de l'exercices de l'archet et du doigter ou 58 exemples, mêlés de caprices, vn (Hamburg, n.d.)
Other bowing and fingering exercises, pubd

BIBLIOGRAPHY
T. Krogh: *Zur Geschichte des dänischen Singspiels im 18. Jahrhundert* (Copenhagen, 1924)
J. Friedrich: *Claus Schall als dramatischer Komponist* (diss., U. of Breslau, 1930)

N. M. Jensen: *Der danske romance 1800–50* (Copenhagen, 1964)
K. A. Bruun: *Dansk musiks historie fra Holberg-tiden til Claus Nielsen Schall*, i (Copenhagen, 1969)

based on *MGG* (xi, 1571–2) by permission of Bärenreiter

NILS SCHIØRRING

Schalloch (Ger.). SOUNDHOLE.

Schallstück (Ger.). BELL (ii).

Schalmei (Ger.). (1) [Schalmey] SHAWM.
(2) An ORGAN STOP.

Schamelius [Schamel], **Johann Martin** (*b* Meuselwitz, nr. Altenburg, 5 June 1668; *d* Naumburg, 27 March 1742). German hymnologist. The son of a pastor, he matriculated in 1686 at the University of Leipzig, and obtained a master's degree there in 1689. From 1691 he worked as a private tutor and became a follower of the teachings of A. H. Francke. He resumed his studies in Halle in 1702. In 1703 he became a deacon in Naumburg and a senior pastor in 1708; he lived there until his death. Schamelius published a great number of writings, among which were collections of sermons, a history of the scholars of Naumburg, and several descriptions of monasteries. He is best known for his work in hymnology. His most important publication, the *Evangelischer Lieder-Commentarius*, developed from his *Naumburgisches Gesang-Buch*, which went through several editions. Among his five original hymn texts only *Ich danke Gott in Ewigkeit* became well known.

WRITINGS
(*selective list*)
Naumburgisches Gesang-Buch, i–ii (Naumburg, 1712–14, 5/1735)
Vindiciae cantionum S. ecclesiae evangelicae, i–iii (Leipzig, 1712–18, 2/1719)
Evangelischer Lieder-Commentarius, i–ii (Leipzig, 1724–5, rev. 2/1737)
Weitere Erläuterung derjenigen Stellen, welche bey dem Evangelischen Lieder-Commentario in dem 2. Theil der Lieder-Remarquen Hn. M. Joh. Jacob Gottschalds . . . sind angemercket worden (Leipzig, 1739)

BIBLIOGRAPHY
J. C. Stemler: *Historie und Führung des Lebens Johann Martin Schamelii* (Leipzig, 1743)
E. E. Koch: *Geschichte des Kirchenlieds und Kirchengesangs der christlichen, insbesondere der deutschen evangelischen Kirche*, v (Stuttgart, 3/1868), 526ff

GÜNTER THOMAS

Schamotulinus, Venceslaus. See SZAMOTUŁ, WACŁAW Z.

Schanppecher, Melchior [Malcior de Wormatia] (*b* Worms, *c*1480). German theorist. He studied at Cologne University from 1496 to 1497, and was a member of the 'bursa montana', where later the theorists Cochlaeus, Glarean and Bogentanz also studied. Schanppecher taught Wollick and wrote the third and fourth parts of the latter's treatise, *Opus aurem musicae* (Cologne, 1501).

In 1502 Schanppecher studied in Leipzig, but by 1505 he was back in Cologne, where he obtained the degree of Master of Arts and where, in 1506, he published an elementary treatise on astronomy. Schanppecher's section of Wollick's treatise shows the influence of humanism, which caused practical music to become a subject for university study instead of medieval speculative theory. He discussed the notation of mensural music, and provided rules for composition. This became the first of many textbooks on composition in Germany. The treatise is based on counterpoint, and distinguishes between 'compositio' and 'sortisatio'.

'Compositio' meant the act of musical composition, which is then fixed in musical notation. 'Sortisatio' meant the improvisation of several parts to a Gregorian cantus firmus. According to other sources of about 1500, Schanppecher gathered up contemporary expressions like 'ad sortem cantare' and 'sortisieren' and created out of them a theoretical term used in German theory until well into the 17th century.

BIBLIOGRAPHY
W. Gurlitt: 'Der Begriff der sortisatio in der deutschen Kompositionslehre des 16. Jahrhunderts', *TVNM*, xvi/3 (1942), 206
E. T. Ferand: 'Sodaine and Unexpected Music in the Renaissance', *MQ*, xxxvii (1951), 12
W. Gurlitt: 'Die Kompositionslehre des deutschen 16. und 17. Jahrhunderts', *GfMKB, Bamberg 1953*, 103
K. W. Niemöller: *Nicolaus Wollick und sein Musiktraktat*, Beiträge zur rheinischen Musikgeschichte, 1 (Cologne, 1961)
——: *Die Musica figurativa des Melchior Schanppecher*, Beiträge zur Rheinischen Musikgeschichte, 1 (Cologne, 1961)

KLAUS WOLFGANG NIEMÖLLER

Schantz, Johan Filip von (*b* Ulvila, 17 Jan 1835; *d* Helsinki, 24 July 1865). Finnish conductor and composer. He studied law at Helsinki University and at the same time made a collection of folk melodies. During the Crimean War in 1855 he became involved in a political student demonstration and was obliged to go to Sweden, where he devoted himself to further musical study. There he published some folksongs and a number of his own songs.

He continued his studies at Leipzig from 1857 to 1860 and became conductor at the newly built theatre in Helsinki from 1860 to 1862, but in 1863 went to Stockholm, where a part of the orchestra followed him. He gave many concerts there, also at Göteborg and in Copenhagen. The orchestra then dissolved and Schantz went back to Helsinki. Among his compositions are a large orchestral work, *Kullervo*, based on the *Kalevala*, and many solo and choral songs.

BIBLIOGRAPHY
K. Maasalo: 'Filip von Schantz', *Suomalaisia sävellyksiä*, i (Borgå, 1964), 92

TOIVO HAAPANEN/ILKKA ORAMO

Schanzlin, Hans Peter (*b* Basle, 2 Aug 1916). Swiss musicologist. He studied school music at the Basle Conservatory and musicology with Handschin at Basle University, where he took a doctorate in 1949 with a dissertation on Gletle's motets. He taught music in various schools in Basle (1941–65), and held posts as organist of the French church (1940–50), and as choirmaster at St Matthäus (1949–61). He was responsible for the first cataloguing in Swiss libraries for RISM (1956–65) and worked at the Schola Cantorum Basiliensis (1959–70). In 1965 he took charge of the music section of the Basle University library. He was general secretary of the Schweizerische Musikforschende Gesellschaft (1959–72) and was president of the Basle chapter (1959–71). Schanzlin has written a wide range of publications on Swiss music history, particularly the history of its church music in the 17th century, of which he made a fundamental study in his doctoral dissertation. In 1957 he succeeded Edgar Refardt in collecting the bibliography of 20th-century writings on Swiss music history.

WRITINGS
Johann Melchior Gletles Motetten: ein Beitrag zur schweizerischen Musikgeschichte des 17. Jahrhunderts (diss., U. of Basle, 1949; Berne, 1954)
'Die Cantiones sacrae von Leonhard Sailer', *Musik und Gottesdienst*, ix (1955), 109

'Die Mitarbeit der Schweiz am "Répertoire international des sources musicales" ', *Schweizerische musikforschende Gesellschaft: Mitteilungsblatt* (1956), no.25, p.1
'Vom aargauischen Musikleben im 17. und 18. Jahrhundert', *Jb des Standes Aargau*, iii (1957), 42
'Die Schweizer Kirchenmusik des 17. Jahrhunderts im Ueberblick', *Der Chorwächter*, lxxxii (1957), 132
'Musik-Sammeldrucke in schweizerischen Bibliotheken', *FAM*, iv (1957), 38; vi (1959), 20; viii (1961), 26
'Martin Martinis "Praegustus musicus" von 1697', *KJb*, xlii (1958), 88
'Musikwissenschaft in der Schweiz', *AcM*, xxx (1958), 214
'Zur Geschichte der Litanei im 17. Jahrhundert', *IMSCR, vii Cologne 1958*, 259
'Kirchenmusik in der Stiftsbibliothek zu St. Martin in Rheinfelden (Schweiz)', *KJb*, xliii (1959), 84
Basels private Musikpflege im 19. Jahrhundert (Basle, 1961)
'Briefe des Haydn-Schülers Neukomm an den Schweizer Komponisten Schnyder von Wartensee', *Anthony van Hoboken: Festschrift zum 75. Geburtstag* (Mainz, 1962), 131
'Edgar Refardt: Bibliographie', *Schweizerische musikforschende Gesellschaft: Mitteilungsblatt* (1962), no.33, p.7; (1963), no.34, p.11; (1966), nos.38–9, p.15
ed., with H. Ehinger, P. Meylan and W. Schuh: *Schweizer Musiker-Lexikon* (Zurich, 1964)
'Brahms-Briefe aus Basler Privatbesitz', *Basler Stadtbuch 1966*, 207
ed., with H. Ehinger: M. Walther: *Miszellen zur Musikgeschichte* (Berne, 1967)
'Pionierarbeit auf dem Gebiete der baslerischen und der schweizerischen Musikgeschichte: zum Gedenken an Edgar Refardt (1877–1968)', *Basler Stadtbuch 1969*, 233

EDITIONS

J. M. Gletle: *Ausgewählte Kirchenmusik*, SMd, ii (1959)

JÜRG STENZL

Scharf (Ger.). An ORGAN STOP.

Scharre (Ger.). RATTLE.

Scharrer, Irene (*b* London, 2 Feb 1888; *d* London, 11 Jan 1971). English pianist. She studied at the RAM and with Tobias Matthay. She made her London début at the age of 16 and thereafter appeared regularly before the public until 12 June 1958, when, at a concert at the RAM to commemorate the centenary of Matthay's birth, she played Mozart's two-piano sonata with her cousin Myra Hess, also a pupil of Matthay. She toured Europe and the USA, and in the earlier part of her career played under such distinguished conductors as Richter and Nikisch. A sensitive rather than a powerful pianist, possessed of a beautifully even touch and capable of great refinement of phrasing, she was most happy when playing Romantic music of the 19th century, especially the smaller, more intimate compositions of Chopin.

BIBLIOGRAPHY

Anon.: 'Some Lady Pianists', *Musical Standard* (20 Jan 1917), 47

FRANK DAWES

Scharwenka, (Ludwig) Philipp (*b* Samter [now Szamotuły], 16 Feb 1847; *d* Bad Nauheim, 16 July 1917). Polish–German composer and teacher. His early musical training was at the secondary school in Posen. In 1865 his family moved to Berlin, where he studied composition with Richard Wüerst and Heinrich Dorn at Kullak's New Academy of Music. In 1868 he began his long teaching career as an instructor at the academy. Six years later, his orchestral works began to be performed, and in 1880 he married the violinist Marianne Stresow (*d* 24 Oct 1918). When his younger brother Xaver founded the Scharwenka Conservatory in Berlin (1881) he joined its staff, teaching theory and composition. He became its co-director, with Hugo Goldschmidt, in 1891, when Xaver emigrated temporarily to the USA. Philipp was a competent, dedicated composer and

teacher; his own career, however, was overshadowed by that of his forceful, energetic brother.

WORKS
(selective list from 123 opus numbers)

VOCAL

Roland (opera), *c*1915, unperf.
Sakuntala (C. Witkowsky), solo vv, chorus, orch, vocal score (Leipzig, *c*1884)
Other choral: Dörpertanzweise (V. von Scheffel), chorus, op.35 (Bremen, 1880); Herbstfeier (F. Timpe), solo vv, chorus, orch/pf, op.44, vocal score (Bremen, 1883); Abendfeier in Venedig (E. Geibel), S, female vv, harmonium, pf, op.89 (Leipzig, 1893); 3 Gesänge, male vv, op.90 (Leipzig, 1893)
Songs, incl. op.28 (Berlin, 1878), op.62 (Leipzig, 1886)

INSTRUMENTAL

Orch: Serenade, op.19 (Bremen, 1881), arr. pf 4 hands (Bremen, 1877); 2 polnische Volkstänze, op.20 (Offenbach, 1877); Wald- und Berggeister, intermezzo, op.37 (Leipzig, 1881); Liebesnacht, fantasy piece, op.40 (Bremen, 1882); Festouvertüre, op.43, arr. pf 4 hands (Bremen, 1883); Arkadische Suite, op.76 (Leipzig, 1887); Frühlingswogen, sym. poem, op.87 (Berlin, 1891); Traum und Wirklichkeit, sym. poem, op.92, ?pubd; Vn Conc., op.95 (Leipzig, 1895); 2 syms., opp.96, 115, ?pubd; Dramatische Phantasie, op.108 (Leipzig, 1900)
Chamber: Pf Qnt, op.118 (Leipzig, 1910); 2 str qts, op.117 (Leipzig, 1910), op.120 (Berlin, n.d.); 3 pf trios, op.100 (Leipzig, 1897), op.112 (Leipzig, 1902), op.121 (Leipzig, n.d.); Duo, vn, va, pf acc., op.105 (Leipzig, 1898); Suite, vn, pf, op.99 (Leipzig, n.d.); 2 vn sonatas, op.110 (Leipzig, n.d.), op.114 (Leipzig, 1904); Va Sonata, op.106 (Leipzig, n.d.); Vc Sonata, op.116 (Leipzig, n.d.)
Pf 2 hands: 2 Notturnos, op.16 (Leipzig, *c*1877); 5 Phantasiestücke, op.26 (Bremen, 1878); [5] Albumblätter, op.27 (Leipzig, 1878); In bunter Reihe, op.32 (Leipzig, 1879); Album polonais, op.33 (Berlin, 1880); 3 sonatas, op.61 (Leipzig, 1886); Romantische Episoden, op.65 (Bremen, 1886); Tonbilder, op.69 (Bremen, 1887); 2 Rhapsodien, op.85 (Leipzig, *c*1890)
Pf 4 hands: Tanzsuite, op.21 (Leipzig, 1887); Hochzeitsmarsch, op.23 (Bremen, 1878); All'ongarese, op.30 (Leipzig, 1879); Polnische Tanzweisen, op.38 (Bremen, 1881), orch version (Bremen, 1882); Intermezzi, op.48 (Berlin, 1883); Lieder und Tanzweisen, op.54 (Berlin, 1884); Stimmungsbilder, op.57 (Bremen, 1885); Herbstbilder, op.59 (Leipzig, 1885); 5 Tanzszenen, op.75 (Breslau, 1887)

BIBLIOGRAPHY

H. Wetzel: 'Philipp Scharwenkas Kammermusik', *Die Musik*, x/4 (1910–11), 27
H. Kretzschmar: *Führer durch den Konzertsaal*, i/1 (Leipzig, 4/1913), 422 [syms. and suites]
H. Wetzel: 'Philipp Scharwenkas Klaviermusik', *Der Kunstwart*, xxvii/4 (1914), 376
P. Scharwenka: 'Autobiographische Skizze', *Neue Musik-Zeitung*, xxxviii (1917), 168
H. Leichtentritt: *Das Konservatorium Klindworth–Scharwenka* (Berlin, 1931)

CHARLES SUTTONI

Scharwenka, (Franz) Xaver (*b* Samter [now Szamotuły], 6 Jan 1850; *d* Berlin, 8 Dec 1924). Polish-German pianist, composer, teacher and educationist. Like his elder brother Philipp he received little formal musical training until he was enrolled in the New Academy of Music in Berlin in 1865 where, under Kullak's tutelage, his skill as a pianist developed rapidly. He made his début at the Singakademie in 1869. He then taught at the academy until his military service (1873–4). In December 1874 he began the first of many concert tours that were to take him all over Europe and eventually to the USA and Canada. In 1877 he married Zenaide Gousseff and in the same year gave the first performance of the Piano Concerto in B♭ minor, his most successful and popular work apart from the Polish Dance (op.3 no.1) of 1869.

In the 1880s Scharwenka expanded his activities beyond those of a composer and pianist. In 1881 with Gustav Holländer and Heinrich Grünfeld he organized a very successful annual series of concerts of chamber and solo works at the Singakademie; and in October of

Xaver Scharwenka: engraving by Auguste Weger (1823–92)

PIANO
2 sonatas: no.1, c♯, op.6 (Leipzig, 1872); no.2, E♭, op.36 (Bremen, 1878)
25 Polish dances, opp.3, 9, 29, 34, 40, 47, 58, 61, 66
Pieces, pf 4 hands, opp.21, 24, 39, 44
Technical studies: Beiträge zur Fingerbildung, op.77; Studien im Oktavenspiel, op.78; Meisterschule des Klavier-Spiels
Editions: collected pf works of Schumann and Chopin, 1881–1903

WRITINGS
Methodik des Klavierspiels (Leipzig, 1907)

BIBLIOGRAPHY
A. M. Abell: 'Xaver Scharwenka', *Musical Courier* (27 July 1910), 5
F. X. Scharwenka: *Klänge aus meinem Leben: Erinnerungen eines Musikers* (Leipzig, 1922) [autobiography; incl. complete list of works]
H. Leichtentritt: *Das Konservatorium Klindworth-Scharwenka* (Berlin, 1931)
T. A. Johnson: 'The Pianoforte Music of Xaver Scharwenka', *MO*, lxii (1938–9), 945
C. R. Suttoni: Preface, *Scharwenka Piano Concerto No.1* (New York, 1971)

CHARLES SUTTONI

Schastelain, Jean. See CHASTELAIN, JEAN.

Schat, Peter (*b* Utrecht, 5 June 1935). Dutch composer. He studied composition with Van Baaren at the Utrecht Conservatory (1952–8), took lessons with Seiber for a year in London, and was then a pupil of Boulez in Basle (1960–62). During his student years he established himself as the leading Dutch composer of his generation. His early compositions are influenced by Bartók, Stravinsky and the Second Viennese School; the Septet (1957) brought him to international notice when it was performed at the 1958 ISCM Festival. The 1960 festival included his first orchestral work, *Mozaiken*, which employs an individual 12-note serial technique whereby ever new patterns are assembled from a fixed set of intervals. The following *Concerto da camera* for two clarinets, piano, percussion and strings (1960) is a highly transparent piece in which the ensemble and the separate instruments are handled in a virtuoso, concertante fashion. Here the 12-note series is built from four subsets, and duration relationships are also serial.

With the *Improvisations and Symphonies* for wind quintet (1960) Schat introduced organized improvisation and directed movement by the performers. He was perhaps the first to use the latter technique, which he described as 'the theatrical conquering of space, an obvious consequence of the centrifugal force of antitonal music'. *Entelechie I*, for five separated instrumental groups, was commissioned by South West German Radio for the 1961 Donaueschingen Festival. The work is built from brief ideas which are generally followed by mirror forms, sometimes rhythmically lively, sometimes vague arhythmic heterophonies which Schat terms 'shadow forms'. The five movements are sharply different in formal scheme, but all are built on the principle of 'object – shadow object'. *Clockwise and Anticlockwise* (1967) is a work for 12 wind instruments, placed at the hours of a clock face, and four horns playing music which evolves from the 16th century to the 20th.

The first performance of the opera *Labyrinth* (1961–2) under Maderna in 1966 was a spectacular occasion. Schat had here achieved a complete theatrical work through the independent functioning of music, stage action, film, dance and sets as contradictory or related commentary. Several extracts from the music are available for concert performance, and the orchestration is notable for the lack of violins, the concentration on low instruments and the extensive percussion section. This experiment in music-theatre was followed in 1969 by *Reconstructie*, an opera written collectively by the com-

the same year he opened his own conservatory in Berlin. In 1886 he conducted the first of a series of orchestral concerts devoted chiefly to major works by Liszt, Beethoven and Berlioz; meanwhile he continued to tour extensively and play his works under such men as Richter and Joachim. These multiple activities as a pianist, composer and educator-organizer occupied him for the rest of his long career.

In 1891 Scharwenka made his first tour of the USA. He decided to emigrate and opened a New York branch of his conservatory in October 1891. Seven years later, however, he moved back to Berlin. His conservatory there had merged with that of Karl Klindworth in 1893 but when Scharwenka returned the two men disagreed about policy, and Klindworth withdrew. Scharwenka continued to tour the USA and Canada and by 1914 had crossed the Atlantic 26 times. In Germany Scharwenka took part in founding the Music Teachers' Federation (1900), and was instrumental in establishing the Federation of German Performing Artists (1912). In 1914 he founded yet another music school in Berlin. He published a *Methodik des Klavierspiels* (Leipzig, 1907). He was also one of the foremost pianists of his generation, renowned for his beautiful, sonorous, singing tone and as an interpreter of Chopin's music. His compositions generally have melodic charm and graceful dance-like rhythms.

WORKS
(*selective list*)
STAGE
Mataswintha (3-act opera, E. Koppel, after F. Dahn: Ein Kampf um Rom), Weimar, 4 Oct 1896, vocal score (Leipzig, 1893)

ORCHESTRAL AND CHAMBER
Sym., c, op.60 (Leipzig, 1885)
4 pf concs.: no.1, b♭, op.32 (Bremen, 1876); no.2, c, op.56 (Leipzig, 1881); no.3, c♯, op.80; no.4, f, op.82, pf score (Leipzig, 1908)
Pf Qt, op.37 (Bremen, 1877); 2 pf trios, opp.1, 45; Sonata, vn, pf, op.2 (Leipzig, 1872); Sonata, vc, pf, op.46

posers Schat, Reinbert de Leeuw, Louis Andriessen, Van Vlijmen and Mischa Mengelberg, and the writers Harry Mulisch and Hugo Claus, though Schat was the guiding spirit. Described by its authors as a 'morality', the opera concerns the destructive powers of world imperialism, and the symbolic central character is Don Giovanni (two motifs from the overture to the Mozart opera form the musical point of departure). For the Holland Festival première in 1969 the five composers conducted and the two writers produced.

In 1967 Schat became attached to the Studio voor Electro-Instrumentale Muziek, Amsterdam, a connection which was of importance to his compositions of the early 1970s. Also in 1967 he visited Cuba, and his subsequent compositions are permeated by vehement social criticism. *Thema* for solo oboe, 18 wind, four electric guitars and electric organ (1970) is based on systematic repetitions of various chords and of a basic theme. *To you* (1972) won a prize at the International Rostrum of Composers in Paris in 1973 and enjoyed widespread success. All of the forces involved are treated electronically, and the piece has links with pop music and with the reiterative works of American composers such as Reich and Riley. Mitchell's text is forcefully presented in a socially involved cry of anger and distress. In 1973 Schat established the Amsterdam Electrisch Circus for open-air performances accompanied by slides and films projected onto a huge balloon. It was for this group that he composed *Het vijde seizoen*.

WORKS
Septet, fl, ob, b cl, hn, pf, perc, vc, 1957
Mozaiken, orch, 1959
Cryptogamen (G. Achterberg), Bar, orch, 1959
Inscripties, pf, 1959
Octet, wind qnt, 2 tpt, trbn, 1959
2 pezzi, fl, tpt, perc, vn, 1959
Concerto da camera, 2 cl, pf, perc, str, 1960
Improvisations and Symphonies, wind qnt, 1960
Entelechie I, 5 inst groups, 1961; Entelechie II, 11 insts, 1961
Signalement, 6 perc, dbs, 1961
Labyrinth (opera, L. de Boer, after L. P. Boon), 1961–2; Dansen uit het Labyrinth, orch, 1962; Choirs from the Labyrinth, 1962; Stemmen uit het Labyrinth, 3 solo vv, orch, 1963; Improvisations from the Labyrinth, 3 solo vv, b cl, pf, perc, db, 1964; Scenes uit het Labyrinth, narrator, 3 solo vv, chorus, orch, 1964
Introductie en adagio in oude stijl, str qt, 1965
First Essay on Electrocution, vn, gui, metal perc, 1966
Clockwise and Anticlockwise, 16 wind, 1967
Anathema, pf, 1968
On Escalation, 6 perc, orch, 1968
Hypothema, recs, 1969
Reconstructie (opera, H. Mulisch, H. Claus), 1969, collab. L. Andriessen, R. de Leeuw, M. Mengelberg, J. van Vlijmen
Thema, ob, 18 wind, 4 elec gui, elec org, 1970
To you (A. Mitchell), Mez, 9 elec gui, 4 elec pf, 2 elec org, 6 elec humming tops, 1972
Het vijde seizoen [The fifth season], music-theatre, 1973
Canto general, Mez, vn, pf, 1974
Mei '75: een lied van bevrijding, Mez, Bar, chorus, orch, 1975
Houdini (circus opera, A. Mitchell), 1974–6; Amsterdam, 29 Sept 1977
Houdini symfonie, S, Mez, T, Bar, chorus, orch, 1976
I am Houdini (ballet), T, chorus, 2 pf, 1976
De briefscène, Mez, T, pf, 1976
Kind en kraai (H. Mulisch), S, pf, 1977
Sym. no.1, 1978

Principal publisher: Donemus

BIBLIOGRAPHY
K. van Baaren: 'Entelechie I by Peter Schat', *Sonorum speculum* (1961), no.9, p.8
N. Schuyt: 'Schat's Improvisations and Symphonies', *Sonorum speculum* (1961), no.7, p.12
R. de Leeuw: 'Schat's Labyrinth: an Opera of Sorts', *Sonorum speculum* (1966), no.27, p.19
P. Schat: '*Labyrinth*: a Kind of Opera', *Opera 66*, ed. C. Osborne (London, 1966), 250
E. Vermeulen: 'Compositions by Louis Andriessen and Peter Schat Incorporating Quotations', *Sonorum speculum* (1969), no.35, p.1
P. Schat: *To you* (Hilversum, 1973) [introduction for Paris Rostrum]
JOS WOUTERS

Schattenberg, Thomas (*b* Flensburg, *c*1580; *d* ?Copenhagen, in or after 1622). Danish-German composer and organist. He studied in Hamburg in 1601–2. In 1604 he left Flensburg for Copenhagen, where in the same year he took over the important position of organist of St Nicolai. He published two collections of vocal music: *Jubilus S. Bernardi de nomine Jesu Christi . . . id est Cantiones sacrae* (Copenhagen, 1620), which consists of 39 short four-part motets, and *Flores amoris* (Copenhagen, 1622; inc., possibly lost), containing 24 three-part madrigals.

BIBLIOGRAPHY
A. Pirro: *Dietrich Buxtehude* (Paris, 1913), 10, 41
F. Gundlach: *Des Johs. Reinhusen Annales Flensburgenses, 1558–1604*, Quellen und Forschungen zur Familiengeschichte Schleswig-Holsteins, i (Kiel, 1926)
J. Bolte: *Deutsche Lieder in Dänemark* (Berlin, 1927), 187f
NILS SCHIØRRING

Schechinger, Johann. *See* SCHACHINGER, JOHANN.

Schechner [Schechner-Waagen], **Nanette** [Anna] (*b* Munich, 1806; *d* 29 April 1860). German soprano. She studied with an actor named Weber, and first sang in the chorus of the Munich Opera when she was 15. Chosen from the singing school by Giuseppina Grassini, on a Munich visit, to second her in excerpts from Cimarosa's *Gli Orazi e i Curiazi*, she made a great impression, and won the patronage of the Queen of Bavaria. After being sent to study in Italy from 1822, she reappeared in Munich as a principal, at first in Italian opera (including the role of Mozart's Countess). Moving to Vienna, she made her début as Emmeline in Weigl's *Die Schweizerfamilie* on 22 May 1826. Schubert wrote: 'Mlle Schechner . . . pleased exceedingly. As she looks very much like Milder, she might be good enough for us' (letter of May 1826). In December 1826 she visited Beethoven with the tenor Ludwig Cramolini, to whom she was then engaged, and sang Fidelio to the deaf composer. She turned to German opera conclusively in 1827 on accepting an engagement at Berlin. Fétis recounted how she began her opening performance, as Emmeline, to an almost empty theatre on a fine summer Sunday, but her performance aroused such admiration that word spread in the interval to the neighbouring cafés, and she completed the performance to a full and enthusiastic house. She sang at the Theater an der Wien in 1829, and returning to Munich in 1832 she married the painter Karl Waagen. Her career was interrupted by a chest disease (of nervous origin, according to Fétis) that led to a serious decline and forced her to retire in 1835. When Mendelssohn heard her in Munich in 1830 he wrote: 'Schechner has indeed lost much; the quality of the voice is husky; she often sang out of tune, and yet at times her inner warmth was so touchingly revealed that I was moved to tears' (letter of 6 June 1830). She was described as possessing in her prime an exceptionally rich and full-toned voice, and a natural, unpretentious dramatic talent. Her most successful roles were Fidelio, Donna Anna, Euryanthe, Reiza, the *Tauris* Iphigenia and Spontini's Vestal.

BIBLIOGRAPHY
FétisB
L. Eisenberg: *Grosses biographisches Lexicon der deutschen Bühne im XIX. Jahrhundert* (Leipzig, 1903)
JOHN WARRACK

Scheck, Gustav (Otto) (*b* Munich, 22 Oct 1901). German flautist, recorder player and teacher. He studied musicology with Wilibald Gurlitt and the flute with Richard Roehler. In 1930 he began his distinguished collaboration with the cellist and gambist August Wenzinger and the harpsichordist Fritz Neumayer as a chamber trio, and in a small orchestra, the Kammermusikkreis Scheck-Wenzinger, which used 17th- and 18th-century strings and historic wind instruments. Using new realizations they played a vital part in pioneering the early music revival. In 1934 Scheck became professor of the flute at the Berlin Hochschule für Musik, becoming widely known and continuing his concerts with Wenzinger until the war, when Scheck's anti-Nazi sympathies brought disbandment. He founded the Staatliche Hochschule für Musik at Freiburg in 1946 and directed it until 1962, attracting an international body of students, among them Hans-Martin Linde. In 1950 the University of Freiburg awarded him an honorary doctorate. He has written articles on historic instruments, made many notable recordings, and since 1960 has been principally interested in contemporary experimental flute works. In 1968 he appeared in London for the first time. His recorder playing is marked by clarity of outline in which a spirited approach produces a cool, rather than sensuous tone. The latter he reserves for the Baroque flute, producing a warm, mellow sound. He shows taste and stylishness in his embellishments, which frequently seem uncommonly free and spontaneous. He has written *Die Flöte und ihre Musik* (Mainz, 1975).

BIBLIOGRAPHY
J. M. Thomson: *Recorder Profiles* (London, 1972), 55ff
J. M. THOMSON

Schede, Paul Melissus (*b* Mellrichstadt, Hesse, 20 Dec 1539; *d* Heidelberg, 3 Feb 1602). German musician and poet. Prompted by his mother's name, Ottilie Melisse, he added to his name the symbolic 'Melissus' from Greek mythology. After studying at Würzburg, Erfurt, Zwickau and Jena he became Kantor at Königsberg, Franconia. He was crowned poet in Vienna in 1561, raised to the rank of hereditary nobleman in 1564 and given the titles 'Comes Palatinus', 'Eques Auratus' and 'Civis Romanus' in Italy in October 1579. Meanwhile he went to France in 1567 but had to flee Paris a few years later during the persecution of the Huguenots; he got to know Goudimel at Besançon and became a follower of Calvin at Geneva, and the Elector Friedrich III of Speyer commissioned from him a version of the psalms for the Reformed Church. He travelled in Germany, Italy and France and in 1585 and 1586 was in England, where Elizabeth I, impressed by him as musician and poet, tried to persuade him to stay. But he returned to Germany and lived at Heidelberg until his death.

Schede wrote the poems, in German, Latin and Greek, that he set to music. His settings scrupulously follow the metrical structures of the verses, which are further enhanced by the carefully conceived melodies. They are thus typical of humanist music of the period.

WORKS

Historia de navicula vehente Christum et periclitante in mari, 5vv (Wittenberg, 1564)
Cantionum musicarum, 4–5vv (n.p., 1566)
Di Psalmen Davids in teutsche Gesangreymen nach französischer Melodeien unt sylben Art (Heidelberg, 1572)
Wedding song for Johann Unterholzer (Passau, 1577)

BIBLIOGRAPHY
J. Boissard: *Icones virorum illustrium*, ii (Frankfurt, 1598), 85ff
J. Gutenaecker: *Vita P. M. Schedii a P. Zitter* (Würzburg, 1834)
E. Trunz: 'Die deutschen Übersetzungen des Hugenottenpsalters', *Euphorion*, xxix (1928), 582, n.19 [incl. fuller bibliography]
P. Bergmans: *Deux amis de Rolande de Lassus: les humanistes Ch. Utenhove et P. M. Schede* (Brussels, 1933)
FERDINAND HABERL

Schedel Liederbuch (*D-Mbs* Cgm 810). See SOURCES, MS, §IX, 7, and SOURCES OF INSTRUMENTAL ENSEMBLE MUSIC TO 1630, §4.

Schedlich [Schädlich], David (*b* St Joachimsthal, Bohemia, 1607; *d* Nuremberg, buried 11 Nov 1687). German organist and composer of Bohemian origin. He received his first musical training from his elder brother Jakob, who had studied with Hans Leo Hassler (the Hassler and Schedlich families were related). When Schedlich settled in Nuremberg, probably in the 1620s, the only Hassler musician whom he could have met was Johann Benedikt Hassler, the organist of the Frauenkirche. The first record of Schedlich in Nuremberg is his marriage in 1631 to a daughter of Johann Staden. He thus entered Nuremberg's most influential circle of musicians and was assured of a secure position in the city's musical life. In 1632 he became second organist of the Frauenkirche, and he was organist of the Spitalkirche from 1634 to 1655. His final promotion came in the latter year when he succeeded his brother-in-law S. T. Staden as organist of St Lorenz. Hs reputation appears to have been purely local, though when in 1653 he and Staden were invited to test a new organ at Bayreuth they were referred to there as 'the famous Nurembergers'. Had it not been for two printed collections of instrumental music, *Musikalisches Kleeblatt* and *Musicalisches Stamm-Büchlein*, Schedlich would probably have been ignored by historians; unfortunately neither has survived. His extant music is of little significance. The instrumental works lack technical skill and artistic finesse, though they are really too few for a fair judgment to be made. As with his Nuremberg colleagues, most of his output consists of strophic songs, which as an organist he was often commissioned to write for funerals. His major extant works are the chorale cantata *Nun lob mein Seel den Herren* and his ten settings of *Domine ad adjuvandum* and the *Teutsche Magnificat*. While the chief feature of these works is their concertato style, a striking characteristic is the instrumental nature of the vocal parts. This reflects Schedlich's preoccupation with organ playing, and it is probably as an organist that he chiefly deserves to be remembered.

WORKS
(all printed works published in Nuremberg)

VOCAL

Psalmus LI, 1–10vv, bc (1640); lost (see *SIMG*, vii, 1905–6, 143)
Die mit Threnen säen (Ps cxxvi), funeral motet, 3vv, 2 vn, bc (1656)
Nun lob mein Seel den Herren (Ps ciii), funeral cantata, 3vv, 4 str, bc (1658); ed. in MAM, iii (1955)
15 funeral lieder, 1–4vv, some with 1, 2 vn, bc (1640–77); 3 ed. in MAM, iii (1955)
5 lieder, 1v, bc, in J. C. Arnschwanger: Neue geistliche Lieder (1659)
2 lieder, 1v, bc, in J. Saubert: Nürnbergischer Gesang-Buch (1677); ed. in Zahn i, ii
10 Domine ad adjuvandum, 10 Teutsche Magnificat, 5vv, 1, 2 vn, 1, 2 va, bn, bc, 1681: *D-Nst*
13 liturgical responses, 4, 5vv, *Nla*
Herr Gott dich loben wir, 23vv, perf. 1649; lost (see *SIMG*, vii, 1905–6, 113)

INSTRUMENTAL

Musikalisches Kleeblatt . . . Balletten, Courenten und Sarabanden, 2 vn, violetta (1665); lost, cited in Walther

Musicalisches Stamm-Büchlein, 2 vn, viol (1667); lost, cited in Göhler, probably same work as listed in C. à Beughem: Bibliographia mathematica et artificiosa (Amsterdam, 1688), 365

2 ballette, 2 vn, bc, in J. E. Kindermann: Deliciae studiosorum, i (1640)

3 suite movts, kbd, c1649, A-Wn 18491

1 suite movt, kbd, D-Mbs 4485

BIBLIOGRAPHY

WaltherML

J. Zahn: Die Melodien der deutschen evangelischen Kirchenlieder (Gütersloh, 1889–93/R1963)

A. Göhler: Verzeichnis der in den Frankfurter und Leipziger Messkatalogen der Jahre 1564 bis 1759 angezeigten Musikalien (Leipzig, 1902/R1965), ii, 73, no.1307

R. Wagner: 'Die Organisten der Kirche zum Hl. Geist in Nürnberg', ZMw, xii (1929–30), 458

H. E. Samuel: The Cantata in Nuremberg during the Seventeenth Century (diss., Cornell U., 1963)

HAROLD E. SAMUEL

Scheerer, Theophil. See SCHERER, N.

Scheff, Fritzi (b Vienna, 30 Aug 1879; d New York, 8 April 1954). Austrian soprano. She studied with her mother, the soprano Anna Jaeger, then in Frankfurt and Munich with Schröder-Hanfstängl, making her début at Frankfurt in 1896. She sang at the Munich Hofoper (1897–1900), and from 1900 to 1903 she appeared at both Covent Garden (as Zerlina, Musetta and Nedda) and the Metropolitan Opera (as Elsa, Marzelline, Cherubino, Nedda, Gounod's Marguerite and Juliette, and Asa in Paderewski's Manru). In 1903 she left opera for Broadway, playing in musical comedies by Victor Herbert and others, and later in straight plays, notably Joseph Kesselring's Arsenic and Old Lace.

BIBLIOGRAPHY

'Tales of an Enfant Terrible: Chapters from the Unpublished Memoirs of Fritzi Scheff', Opera News (17 and 24 Jan 1944)

HAROLD ROSENTHAL

Scheffer [Schäffer], Johann Wilhelm (fl 1676–94). German composer and administrator of Swiss origin. In his publication of 1676 he stated that his family came from Koblenz in the Swiss canton of Aargau and that at the time he was a prefect at Illertissen, Bavaria. By 1694 he was an actuary in the service of Count Fürstenberg at Mösskirch, Swabia. His Missae concertatae duabus et tribus vocibus absque instrumentis (Ulm, 1676) contains typical concertato works for a few voices only. He is also known by Chorus Marianus, das ist: Die Melodyen oder Weisen über den Marianischen Reyen sambt beygefügten Ritornellen a 2 Violinen . . . (Überlingen, 1694), which consists of sacred songs characteristic of those written in south Germany at the time; the words are by THEOBALDUS.

AUGUST SCHARNAGL

Scheffer, Paul. See SCHAEFFER, PAUL.

Scheffler, Johannes. See ANGELUS SILESIUS.

Scheibe, Johann (b Saxony, c1680; d Leipzig, 3 Sept 1748). German organ builder, father of Johann Adolf Scheibe. In his capacity as 'Universitätsorgelmacher' at Leipzig, he had all the city's organs in his care. Between 1710 and 1717 he built an organ for the Paulinerkirche (the university church); the scheme (three manuals, 54 stops) was drawn up by A. G. Casparini of Görlitz, and the organ was tested by J. S. Bach. During the years 1721 to 1722 and 1724 to 1725 he enlarged the organs

in the Thomaskirche and Nicolaikirche at Leipzig, originally built by H. Lange of Kamenz in the style of Esaias Beck (both three manuals, 36 stops). He supplied a new organ for the Johanniskirche at Leipzig (two manuals, 22 stops) in 1742 to 1744, and another at Zschorlau, near Delitzsch (one manual, 12 stops), in 1745–6. Scheibe's specifications may perhaps have been influenced by Bach, who tested and praised his organ at the Johanniskirche. He provided Principal choruses – including Tierces – on each manual, but not invariably on the Pedal, where in addition to the usual flue foundation stops he often included reeds at 16', 8', 4' and 2' pitches. Sometimes groups of foundation stops or flute mutations (again with Tierces) appeared on the manuals. He has been described as a man of thoroughly honest principles, and also as a capable writer. Bach gave him good testimonials as an organ builder.

BIBLIOGRAPHY

P. Spitta: Johann Sebastian Bach, ii (Leipzig, 1880, 5/1962; Eng. trans., 1884–99/R1951), 111ff

A. Schering: Johann Sebastian Bachs Leipziger Kirchenmusik (Leipzig, 1936), 90f

——: Musikgeschichte Leipzigs, (Leipzig, 1926–41) ii, 108ff, 257, 317f; iii, 72ff

P. Rubardt: 'Scheibe, Johann', MGG

HANS KLOTZ

Scheibe, Johann Adolph (b Leipzig, 5 May 1708; d Copenhagen, 22 April 1776). German composer and theorist. He was the son of JOHANN SCHEIBE (c1680–1748), a well-known organ builder, greatly respected by J. S. Bach, who tested and specially praised his organ for Leipzig's Johanniskirche. Johann Adolph contributed an autobiography to Mattheson's Grundlage einer Ehren-Pforte, where he recorded the loss of his right eye at the age of six in an accident in his father's shop. At 11 he entered the school at the Nicolaikirche where his education conformed to his father's hopes for him of a career in law. In 1725 he entered Leipzig University to continue studies in jurisprudence, and at this time heard lectures by and became acquainted with Johann Christoph Gottsched, professor of poetry and rhetoric, whose works on the reform of drama and poetry deeply influenced Scheibe's own writings on music theory and aesthetics. However, his university education was abandoned when a family financial crisis forced him to remain at home. Although he said that he had begun to study keyboard instruments at the age of six, it was only at this time that he gave serious thought to music as a career. He read everything he could find written about music, and began to practise the organ with the hope of becoming a professional, to compose music and to study philosophy. Scheibe was therefore largely self-taught as a musician and scholar; his own writings were to reveal his remarkable command of musical knowledge.

In 1729 Scheibe applied for the organ position open at the Nicolaikirche, where Bach was one of the examiners; but J. Schneider secured the post. He also failed in his attempts to gain organ appointments at Prague and Gotha in 1735 as well as Sondershausen and Wolfenbüttel in 1736. In the latter year he moved to Hamburg where he established himself as a music critic and composer, and could count Telemann among his influential friends. In 1737 he initiated the publication, fortnightly throughout 1738 (26 issues), of his Critischer Musikus (title adapted after Gottsched's Versuch einer critischen Dichtkunst), which after a one-year pause was continued as a weekly in 1739–40 (in 78 issues). In addition, according to his autobiography, he composed large quantities of music, now largely lost, including over 150 church pieces, 150 flute concertos, more than 30 violin concertos, and numerous sinfonias, trios, solos, German and Italian cantatas, serenades, Passion oratorios and one opera, *Thusnelde*. The latter, although intended for performance in Hamburg, could not be produced when the opera company closed in 1738. In 1739 Scheibe was named Kapellmeister to Margrave Friedrich Ernst of Brandenburg-Culmbach, the governor of Holstein. In 1740 he went to Christian VI's court in Denmark to direct one of his cantatas at the dedication of the Slotskirke in the Christianborg palace. After other 'test' performances before the Danish king, Scheibe was made Kapellmeister to the Danish court on 1 December, a position he retained until the death of Christian VI in 1747. The new king, Frederik V, retired Scheibe with a meagre pension of 400 talers, replacing him with Paolo Scalabrini, composer with the visiting Mingotti opera troupe. Scheibe moved to Sønderborg (on Als island), where he opened a music school for children, worked on German translations of several Danish classics, wrote a biography of Holberg and continued to compose. Later, he often returned to Copenhagen for performances of his music, and after 1766 resumed a role as a composer for the Danish court.

As a composer Scheibe is totally unknown. Much of his music has been lost, but the remainder has not received the study it surely merits, particularly in view of its potential significance in Danish music history in the critical years of style change between the Baroque and Classical periods.

Most of Scheibe's critical writings are extant, but these too have not received the attention they deserve considering that Scheibe was a major German music theorist and an influential critic during the first half of the 18th century. He has been neglected largely because of his famous criticism of Bach's musical style in the *Critischer Musikus* (no.6). From its publication in 1737, this passage entangled Scheibe in a verbal war with writers who vehemently protested against his attack on J. S. Bach. Although Bach himself never responded, he was defended by J. A. Birnbaum, a teacher of rhetoric in Leipzig, as well as by Lorenz Mizler, C. G. Schröter and others. Subsequently almost every Bach scholar since Spitta has disparaged Scheibe's remarks about Bach, and Scheibe's credibility as a music critic and theorist has in effect been destroyed. The incident, blown up out of all proportion to its significance, has led to a neglect of Scheibe's major theoretical statements, including the bulk of the *Critischer Musikus*. In an anonymous letter Scheibe said of Bach (although without actually naming him) that 'this great man would be the admiration of whole nations if he had more amenity, if he did not take away the natural element in his pieces by giving them a bombastic [*schwülstig*] and confused style, and if he did not darken their beauty by an excess of art' (see David and Mendel). He continued by suggesting that Bach's instrumental and vocal style posed exceedingly difficult problems of performance because Bach wrote his music as if it were all meant to be played on the keyboard. He chided him for writing out all the ornamentation (often left by other composers to realization in performance), which Scheibe thought took away from the beauty of the harmony and obscured the melody. Finally, Bach's bombast, he said, brought his labour into conflict with nature. In the Bach literature Scheibe has been accused of writing with rancour because Bach had prevented his appointment as organist at the Nicolaikirche; there is no evidence to support such a petty view, and it is clear elsewhere in the *Critischer Musikus* that Scheibe had a genuine admiration and respect for Bach. If Scheibe's critics had examined the rest of his theoretical works, they would have found that his negative reaction to Bach's style was not heretical, but rather a natural and predictable conclusion in the light of his own carefully developed concepts about the nature of musical style. Scheibe believed the best music of his day was represented by the works of Telemann, Hasse and Graun. As a critic in the forefront of the Enlightenment, who argued for a return to simplicity, to an imitation of nature and to an emphasis on persuasive melody, Scheibe could not but find Bach's music open to some mild criticism.

A fresh evaluation of Scheibe's ideas is now needed. Beginning with his youthful treatise in manuscript, *Compendium musices theoretico-practicum* (published as a supplement to Benary), and throughout several other publications, there is consistent evidence of his originality and progressiveness as a music theorist. In the *Critischer Musikus* particularly, the major thrust of his musical criticism is to prove that Italian music must not serve as a basis for German composers, and that musical styles are to be conceived in rational concepts based largely on a close analogy to rhetorical principles of style. These views, as well as numerous others, were undoubtedly the result of Gottsched's persuasive influence, as was Scheibe's search for a new rationalism in music generally. He developed at considerable length concepts such as 'good taste', melodic composition, musical invention (which he believed was inborn, not learnt), and the imitation of nature (which 'is the true essence of music as well as of rhetoric and poetry'). The *Critischer Musikus*, like his other theoretical documents, is infused with principles of musical thought characteristic of the developing Classical style in music. With a grasp of Scheibe's total musical philosophy, one can understand why the music of Bach, in 1737, was open to criticism for being 'bombastic and confused', and why these remarks accurately symbolize the end of the Baroque age in German music.

WORKS

3 Sonate, hpd, vn, op.1 (Nuremberg, n.d.)

Neue Freymäurer-Lieder mit bequemen Melodien (Copenhagen, 1749)

Kleine Lieder fürs Klavier (Flensburg, 1766)

Vollständiges Liederbuch der Freymaurer (Copenhagen, 1776)

Die Auferstehung und Himmelfahrt Jesu (cantata, C. W. Ramler), 4vv, insts; Der wundervolle Tod des Welt-Erlösers (oratorio, Scheibe); 2 Magnificat, Ps cxvii, 4vv, insts; Die Patrioten (Cramer): all formerly *D-Bds*, according to *EitnerQ*

Several masses, *A-KR*; 2 cantatas [Wer sich rühmen will; Der Engel des Herrn], *D-LEm*; Sinfonia à 16, 2 tpt, 2 hn, timp, 2 fl, 2 ob, 2 vn, va, bc, hpd, *SWl*; Fl Conc., B♭, *B-Bc*: all according to *EitnerQ*

3 organ trios; 3 sonatas, hpd, vn; 6 pieces, hpd; Partie, D, hpd; *Bc*

2 sonatas, kbd, in J. U. Haffner, Oeuvres mêlées, iii (Nuremberg, 1757)

Songs pubd in 18th-century anthologies

LOST WORKS

c150 church works, 150 fl concs., c30 vn concs., numerous sinfonias, trios, German and Italian cantatas, serenades, Passion oratorios: all lost, cited in Scheibe's autobiography

Thusnelde (Singspiel, ?Scheibe), unperf., music lost; lib (Leipzig and Copenhagen, 1749)

[2] Tragische Kantaten für eine oder zwo Singstimmen und das Clavier [Ariadne auf Naxos (Gerstenberg), Prokris und Cephalus (J. E. Schlegel)], music lost, lib pubd (Copenhagen and Leipzig, 1765, 2/1779)

WRITINGS

Compendium musices theoretico-practicum, das ist Kurzer Begriff derer nötigsten Compositions-Regeln (MS, *D-LEm*, c1730); pubd as suppl. to Benary (1961)

Der critische Musikus, i (Hamburg, 1738), ii (Hamburg, 1740) [complete, Leipzig, 1745/R1970]

Beantwortung der unparteiischen Anmerkungen über eine bedenkliche Stelle in dem sechsten Stücke des critischen Musicus (Hamburg, 1738); repr. with commentary in *Der critische Musikus* (Leipzig, 1745)

'Sendschreibung', in J. Mattheson: *Gültige Zeugnisse über die jüngste Matthesonisch-musicalische Kern-Schrifft* (Hamburg, 1738)

Eine Abhandlung von den musicalischen Intervallen und Geschlechtern (Hamburg, 1739)

'Lebenslauf, von ihm selbst entworfen', in J. Mattheson: *Grundlage einer Ehren-Pforte* (Hamburg, 1740)

Thusnelde, ein Singspiel in vier Aufzügen, mit einem Vorbericht von der Möglichkeit und Beschaffenheit guter Singspiele begleitet (Leipzig and Copenhagen, 1749)

Abhandlung vom Ursprunge und Alter der Musik, insonderheit der Vokalmusik (Altona and Flensburg, 1754)

'Abhandlung über das Rezitativ', *Bibliothek der schönen Wissenschaften und freien Künste*, xi (1764), 209; xii (1765), 217

'Sendschreiben, worinnen vom Recitativ überhaupt und von diesen Kantaten insonderheit geredet wird', *Tragische Kantaten für eine oder zwo Singestimmen und das Clavier* (Copenhagen and Leipzig, 1765, 2/1779)

Über die musikalische Composition, erster Theil: Die Theorie der Melodie und Harmonie (Leipzig, 1773) [no other parts pubd]

BIBLIOGRAPHY

L. Mizler: *Neu eröffnete musikalische Bibliothek* (Leipzig, 1739–54/R1966)

J. Mattheson: *Grundlage einer Ehren-Pforte* (Hamburg, 1740); ed. M. Schneider (Berlin, 1910/R1969)

J. Adlung: *Anleitung zu der musikalischen Gelahrtheit* (Erfurt, 1758/R1953, 2/1783)

V. C. Ravn: *Koncerter og musikalske selskaber i seldre tid* (Copenhagen, 1886)

E. Reichel: 'Gottsched und Scheibe', *SIMG*, ii (1900–01), 654

C. Thrane: *Fra hofviolonernes tid: skildringer af det kongelige kapels historie 1648–1848* (Copenhagen, 1908)

K. A. Storch: *Scheibes Anschauungen von der musikalischen Historie, Wissenschaft und Kunst* (diss., U. of Leipzig, 1923)

E. Rosenkaimer: *J. A. Scheibe als Verfasser des Critischen Musikus* (Bonn, 1929)

H. T. David and A. Mendel: *The Bach Reader* (New York, 1945, rev. 2/1966), 238ff

P. Benary: 'Scheibes Compendium Musices', *Mf*, x (1957), 508

——: *Die deutsche Kompositionslehre des 18. Jahrhunderts* (Leipzig, 1961) [incl. complete edn. of Scheibe's *Compendium musices theoretico-practicum*]

M. Ruhnke: 'Telemann im Schatten von Bach?', *Hans Albrecht in memoriam* (Kassel, 1962), 143

I. Willheim: *Johann Adolph Scheibe: German Musical Thought in Transition* (diss., U. of Illinois, 1963)

G. J. Skapski: *The Recitative in Johann Adolph Scheibe's Literary and Musical Work* (diss., U. of Texas, 1963)

H. Keller: 'Johann Adolph Scheibe und Johann Sebastian Bach', *Musik und Verlag: Karl Vötterle zum 65. Geburtstag* (Kassel, 1968), 383

G. J. Buelow: 'In Defence of J. A. Scheibe against J. S. Bach', *PRMA*, ci (1974–5), 85

GEORGE J. BUELOW

Scheibel, Gottfried Ephraim (*b* Breslau, 1696; *d* Breslau, 1759). German theologian. According to Eitner, he studied theology in Leipzig and became a teacher at Breslau's Elisabeth-Gymnasium in 1736. He had previously lived in Oels, Silesia, where he wrote his most important music treatise, *Zufällige Gedancken von der Kirchenmusic* (1721). This significant book presents a clear statement on the value of music in the Protestant church service at that time, particularly its role in moving the emotions of the congregation in harmony with the word of God. Scheibel defended the place of music in the church against the attacks of those he called 'Zwingelianer'. He was one of the first to suggest that women deserved admission to church choirs, and that the ever-growing scarcity of good boy sopranos made the need for women critical. He also supported the parody practice, giving examples showing the sub-stitution of sacred texts for secular ones used in opera arias by Telemann. He urged that the theatrical style be used to enliven church music, adding: 'I do not understand why the opera alone should have the privilege to move us to tears, and why this is also not appropriate to the church'. Scheibel's work was warmly praised by Mattheson in *Critica musica* (Hamburg, 1722), and there seems to have been a close professional relationship between the two. Scheibel dedicated his *Musicalisch-poetische andächtige Betrachtungen* to Mattheson, and the latter reciprocated by dedicating *Der neue Göttingische. . . Ephorus* (Hamburg, 1727) to Scheibel.

WRITINGS

Zufällige Gedancken von der Kirchenmusic, wie sie heutiges Tages beschaffen ist (Frankfurt and Leipzig, 1721)

Musicalisch-poetische andächtige Betrachtungen über alle Sonn- und Fest-Tags Evangelien durchs gantze Jahr (Breslau, 1726, 2/1738)

Die Geschichte der Kirchen-Music alter und neuer Zeiten (Breslau, 1738)

GEORGE J. BUELOW

Scheibler, Johann Heinrich (*b* Montjoie [now Monschau], 11 Nov 1777; *d* Krefeld, 20 Nov 1837). German theorist. He was a silk manufacturer in Krefeld and had a lifelong interest in tuning and equal temperament. He studied with J. N. Wolff, and played many instruments at a professional standard. Although he had no scientific training, he endeavoured to build an equally tempered scale by pragmatic means, by the use of beats (first mentioned by Rameau in his *Génération harmonique*, 1737). He built a tonometer of 52 tuning-forks per octave (now lost); another tonometer, of 56 forks, still exists. A reconstruction, with 105 tuning-forks, is now in the Science Museum, London. The particulars of Scheibler's experiments may be found in his *Der physikalische und musikalische Tonmesser* (Essen, 1834). In his attempt at the impossible, he was obviously unaware of the work of the Swiss mathematician Leonhard Euler (*d* 1783), who had solved the problem mathematically by finding the 12th root of the number two $(1 \cdot 05946 +)$, an irrational number; nor did he know that the problem was insoluble because all powers of the numbers two (representing the octave), three (representing the 5th), and five (representing the major 3rd) are infinitely incommensurable.

In 1834 at Stuttgart Scheibler proposed the pitch $a' = 440$, which has consequently been called 'the Stuttgart pitch'. In 1816 he invented the 'Aura', which was in fact the first mouth harmonica. This was commended by Hofmann von Fallersleben (*d* 1874). Töpfer (1842) produced a simpler variant of Scheibler's tuning methods, as did A. J. H. Vincent (1849) and LeComte (1856).

WRITINGS

Anleitung, die Orgel vermittelst der Stösse . . . und des Metronoms correct gleichschwebend zu stimmen (Krefeld, 1834)

Über mathematische Stimmung, Temperaturen und Orgelbaustimmung nach Vibrationsdifferenzen oder Stossen (Krefeld, 1835)

Mitteilung über das Wesentliche der musikalischen und physikalischen Tonmessers (Krefeld, 1836)

MARK HOFFMAN

Scheidemann, David. German organist and composer, father of HEINRICH SCHEIDEMANN.

Scheidemann, Heinrich (*b* Wöhrden, Holstein, c1595, *d* Hamburg, early 1663). German composer, organist and teacher. A founder of the north German organ school, he was one of the leading organ composers of the 17th century, notable above all for his chorale-based works.

1. LIFE. Scheidemann's father, David Scheidemann, organist at Wöhrden from 1594, moved to a similar post at the Catharinenkirche, Hamburg, by 1604, when, like Hieronymus Praetorius, Jacob Praetorius (ii) and Joachim Decker, he contributed some pieces to the Hamburg *Melodeyen Gesangbuch*. From November 1611 to November 1614 Heinrich Scheidemann studied at Amsterdam with Sweelinck who dedicated to him, when he left, a canon 'Ter eeren des vromen Jonghmans Henderich Scheijtman, van Hamborgh' (facs. in *J. P. Sweelinck: Werken*, ix, Leipzig, 1901, no.14, p.77). The next surviving contemporary notice of him records him as occupying his father's former position as organist at the Catharinenkirche, Hamburg, in 1629; according to Gerber he took up the post in 1625, but this cannot now be substantiated. He retained it until his death and was also clerk of the church from 1633. He died of the plague.

As organist of the Catharinenkirche, Scheidemann not only held an important and remunerative position but was working in a city that enjoyed a flourishing musical life and offered many opportunities for fruitful friendship and collaboration with musicians and other artists, for instance with the Kantor Thomas Selle, with organist colleagues such as Jacob Praetorius (ii) and later Matthias Weckmann, with the leader of the Hamburg city musicians, Johann Schop (i), and with the poet Johann Rist. The organ at the Catharinenkirche moreover was an excellent instrument, which Scheidemann had enlarged by Gottfried Fritzsche in the mid-1630s to 56 stops (four manuals and pedals). He was highly esteemed as organist, organ expert, composer and teacher. Apart from J. A. Reincken – his assistant from 1658 and successor after his death – his pupils included Werner Fabricius, Wolfgang Wessnitzer of Celle and Wolfgang Druckenmüller of Schwäbisch Hall. As both organist and organ composer Scheidemann exerted an influence on Weckmann, who had been a pupil of Jacob Praetorius (ii) and according to Mattheson strove 'to temper the gravity of Praetorius with the sweetness of Scheidemann'.

2. WORKS. Of Sweelinck's many well-known north German pupils, it is Scheidemann whose organ music survives in the largest number of sources. This is due not only to the chance survival of manuscripts but also to the fact that contemporary north German organists esteemed and disseminated his works. He concentrated almost exclusively on the single genre of organ music, where he was an important innovator. His organ works date from the early years of the north German organ school and represent its first peak; most of them came to light only when Gustav Fock discovered the organ tablatures at Clausthal-Zellerfeld in 1955 and 1960. Scheidemann's harpsichord pieces, on the other hand, are generally insignificant, though one or two notable ones, such as the *Gaillarda ex D* and the *Englische Mascarata*, have survived. He also published several continuo songs to texts by Rist, less, no doubt, from a love of the genre than from his friendship with the poet.

Scheidemann's style was forged in the first instance through his response to the keyboard works of his teacher Sweelinck, which are a blend of the style of the English virginalists – essentially conceived for the keyboard, with virtuoso figuration – and classical Italian

and Spanish vocal polyphony of the second half of the 16th century. His most important achievement as a composer lies largely in his extension of Sweelinck's keyboard style into a specifically organ idiom by harnessing the musical and technical resources of the north German Baroque organ. His finest and most important works are his chorale arrangements, and a series of four-movement *Magnificat* settings, which form a unified group by virtue of his complete exploration of the eight *Magnificat* tones and the use in each setting of a cyclic construction. Though Sweelinck's influence can be seen in all his instrumental writing, it is nowhere more apparent than in the technique of his organ chorale arrangements. Virtually all of Sweelinck's arrangements are of the same type, involving a single, continuous, almost unembellished presentation of the cantus firmus in one part, and it was natural for Scheidemann to follow him in this procedure. But Samuel Scheidt, a somewhat older pupil of Sweelinck, seems also to have inspired him through his *Tabulatura nova* (1624), especially its *Magnificat* arrangements, which adopt the form of the chorale ricercare frequently found in the third part of the volume. To these borrowed techniques Scheidemann added two forms that he himself helped to develop: the monodic organ chorale – embellished cantus firmus in the descant on the *Rückpositiv*, harmonically complementary inner parts on an accompanying manual, bass in the pedals – which can be seen as a transcription for organ of the solo song with continuo; and the virtuoso, musically sophisticated chorale fantasia either on two manuals or on two manuals and pedals. The latter is the north German chorale form *par excellence*, and Scheidemann sometimes extended it to over 200 bars. His influence on the younger composers of the north German organ school rested largely on these two modern forms conceived specifically in terms of the organ.

In his organ music without cantus firmus Scheidemann, unlike Scheidt in his *Tabulatura nova*, did not develop Sweelinck's form of the grand fantasia but cultivated instead the more modest form of the 'praeambulum', which developed from the short improvised introit. His praeambula are historically important. Their fugal middle sections, in which he sometimes referred to Sweelinck's echo fantasias and toccatas, are sometimes so long that they become the main part of the work, and since the final section is occasionally much curtailed, these works seem to approach the two-movement form of prelude and fugue. Of his other freely structured organ compositions the largest and most important is the Toccata in G (for manuals), in which he combined Sweelinck's formal ideas with up-to-date, typically north German treatment of the organ with more than one manual. Besides his original organ works he left arrangements of 12 embellished motets, almost all of them by Lassus or H. L. Hassler, in which he sometimes used musical and technical methods similar to those found in the chorale fantasias. These pieces probably replaced choral performances: it is known from the trial recital Weckmann had to give at the Jacobikirche, Hamburg, in 1655 that extemporization of such works was still part of an organist's duties after the middle of the century.

WORKS

Editions: *H. Scheidemann: Fünfzehn Praeludien und Fugen für Orgel*, ed. M. Seiffert, Organum, iv/1 (Leipzig, n.d.) [S]
 Die Lüneburger Orgeltabulatur KN208¹, ed. M. Reimann, EDM, 1st ser., xxxvi (1957) [R]

H. Scheidemann: Orgelwerke, ed. G. Fock and W. Breig (1967–71) [O]

KEYBOARD

For fuller details see Breig (1967); all for organ unless otherwise stated.

17 chorales, *D-Bds*, *CZ*, *Lr*, O i, 3 in R; 12 motet arrangements, *CZ*, *Lr* (on H. L. Hassler, Lassus, H. Praetorius), 1 in R; 7 Magnificat, *CZ*, *Lr*, O ii; 2 Kyrie, *CZ*, O i; 2 O lux beata Trinitas, *A-Wm*, *D-CZ* (1 frag.), 1 in O i; Te Deum laudamus, *CZ* (frag.)

12 praeambula, C, 6 in d, 2 in e, 2 in F, g, *Bds*, *Lr*, *S-Uu*, O iii, 11 in S, 1 in R; canzona, F, *D-Lr*, O iii, S; Fugue, d, *Lr*, O iii, S; toccata, G, *Bds*, *CZ*, *Lr*, *W*, O iii, R

Hpd: allemande, d; ballett, d; 2 courantes, d; galliard, D; mascherata, C; 12 other dances, some with variations: *CZ*, *Lr*, Wessnitz Tablature, Celle, *DK-Kk*, *NL-Avnm*, *S-Uu*; ballett ed. in MMN, ii (1959), 3 ed. W. Breig, *Lied- und Tanzvariationen der Sweelinck-Schule* (Mainz, 1970)

(*anon., probably by Scheidemann*)

12 chorales, *A-Wm*, *D-CZ*, *Lr*, 11 in O i, 1 in R; 2 Magnificat, *CZ*, O ii; Victimae paschali laudes, *CZ*, O i

2 praeambula, C, G, *Lr*, O iii, ed. in Organum, iv/10 (Leipzig, n.d.); canzona, G, *Bds*, *Lr*, O iii

(*doubtful, attrib. 'H.S.'*)

7 chorales, *PL-PE*, 3 in O i and R; 3 fantasias, C, d, G, *D-Bds*, *Lr*, *USSR-Lan*, O iii; fugue, *D-Lr*, O iii, S, R; toccata, C, *S-Uu*, O iii

SACRED SONGS

34 melodies, 1v, bc, in J. Rist: Neue himlische Lieder sonderbahres Buch (Lüneburg, 1651); J. Rist: Die verschmähte Eitelkeit (Lüneburg, 1658); J. Rist: Die verlangete Seligkeit (Lüneburg, 1658); some ed. J. Zahn, *Die Melodien der deutschen evangelischen Kirchenlieder* (Gütersloh, 1889–93/*R*1963)

BIBLIOGRAPHY

FitnerQ; *GerberL*

J. Mattheson: *Grundlage einer Ehren-Pforte* (Hamburg, 1740); ed. M. Schneider (Berlin, 1910/*R*1969)

M. Seiffert: 'J. P. Sweelinck und seine direkten deutschen Schüler', *VMw*, vii (1891), esp. 227ff

H. Kretzschmar: *Geschichte des neuen deutschen Liedes* (Leipzig, 1911/*R*1966), 49ff

F. Dietrich: *Geschichte des deutschen Orgelchorals im 17. Jahrhundert* (Kassel, 1932), 39ff

G. Frotscher: *Geschichte des Orgel-Spiels und der Orgel-Komposition*, i (Berlin, 1935, enlarged 3/1966)

M. Reimann: 'Pasticcios und Parodien in norddeutschen Klaviertabulaturen', *Mf*, viii (1955), 265

L. Schierning: *Die Überlieferung der deutschen Orgel- und Klaviermusik aus der ersten Hälfte des 17. Jahrhunderts* (Kassel, 1961)

A. Sutkowski and O. Mischiati: 'Una preziosa fonte manoscritta di musica strumentale: l'intavolatura di Pelplin', *L'organo*, ii (1961), 53

W. Breig: 'Über das Verhältnis von Komposition und Ausführung in der norddeutschen Orgel-Choralbearbeitung des 17. Jahrhunderts', *Norddeutsche und nordeuropäische Musik* (Kassel, 1965), 71

J. H. Schmidt: 'Eine unbekannte Quelle zur Klaviermusik des 17. Jahrhunderts', *AMw*, xxii (1965), 1

W. Apel: *Geschichte der Orgel- und Klaviermusik bis 1700* (Kassel, 1967; Eng. trans., rev., 1972)

W. Breig: *Die Orgelwerke von Heinrich Scheidemann* (Wiesbaden, 1967) [incl. complete list of organ works]

WERNER BREIG

Scheidemantel, Karl (*b* Weimar, 21 Jan 1859; *d* Weimar, 26 June 1923). German baritone. He studied with B. Borchers and Julius Stockhausen, making his début in 1878 as Wolfram in *Tannhäuser* at Weimar, where he was engaged until 1886. He then sang at Dresden until 1911. After a guest appearance in Munich (1882) as Wolfram, he made his London début at Covent Garden in the same role (14 June 1884), and that season also sang Pizarro in *Fidelio*, Telramund in *Lohengrin*, Kurwenal in *Tristan und Isolde* and Rucello in Stanford's *Savonarola*; he returned in 1899 to sing Hans Sachs in *Die Meistersinger*. He appeared at every Bayreuth festival from 1886 to 1892, alternating as Klingsor and Amfortas in *Parsifal*, and singing Kurwenal, Hans Sachs and Wolfram, a part he also sang in Vienna (1890) and at La Scala, Milan (1892). A stylish singer with a fine, well-placed voice, he was as successful in Italian as in German roles; at Dresden, he

Karl Scheidemantel as Hans Sachs in Wagner's 'Die Meistersinger'

sang Alfio in *Cavalleria rusticana* (1891), David in *L'amico Fritz* (1892) and Scarpia in *Tosca* (1902), all first local performances. He created two Richard Strauss roles, Kunrad in *Feuersnot* (21 November 1901) and Faninal in *Der Rosenkavalier* (26 January 1911). After his retirement he taught at the Weimar Conservatory until 1920, and then directed the Landestheater, Dresden for two years.

BIBLIOGRAPHY

H. Rosenthal: *Two Centuries of Opera at Covent Garden* (London, 1958)

K. Neupert, ed.: *Die Besetzung der Bayreuther Festspiele* (Bayreuth, 1961)

N. Del Mar: *Richard Strauss* (London, 1962–72)

G. Skelton: *Wagner at Bayreuth* (London, 1965)

ELIZABETH FORBES

Scheidler, Johann David (*b* 1748; *d* Gotha, 20 Oct 1802). German cellist and composer. He was a pupil of the cellist H. B. Preysing and a member of the court orchestra at Gotha. He married his teacher's daughter Sophie Elisabeth Preysing, herself a distinguished singer; their daughter Dorette, a noted harpist, married Louis Spohr in 1806. Scheidler took an active interest in the philanthropic school founded by C. G. Salzmann in nearby Schnepfenthal, and often performed there with the students. For his own work as a teacher he published in Gotha a *Sammlung kleiner Klavierstücke für Liebhaber* (1779, rev. 2/1781) and a second collection of *Kleine Klavier- und Singstücke* (1787), as well as a song *Die Hand der Geliebten* (1783), all in a Classical style approaching the Rococo. Some works by him also appeared in anthologies, and Eitner listed several in manuscript.

BIBLIOGRAPHY
EitnerQ
G. Kraft: 'Scheidler, Johann David', *MGG*

G. KRAFT

Scheidt, Gottfried (*b* Halle, 20 Sept 1593; *d* Altenburg, 1661, buried 3 June). German composer and organist, younger brother of Samuel Scheidt. Like his brother, he studied with Sweelinck in Amsterdam; he was there from 1611 to 1615. He continued to study on returning to Halle, where his brother was among his teachers. In 1617 he became organist to the ducal court at Altenburg. In 1622 he applied – at the instance of his brother, who had refused it – for the post of principal organist at St Marien, Danzig; he had to remain there until 1623 for the applicants' tests, in which he was passed over in favour of Paul Siefert. He thereupon resumed his position at Altenburg and held it until he retired, because of increasing age and infirmity, on 5 May 1658. He was much respected as an organist and was on excellent terms with the ruling family, who encouraged music even during the Thirty Years War; they gradually built up a small Hofkapelle, which he directed. Apart from his contributions to the set of variations on *Allein Gott in der Höh sei Ehr* composed jointly by Sweelinck and others in 1614, no organ music by him is known. His other known works are all vocal; they are probably all occasional pieces and are of little interest.

WORKS

Pia vota et hortulanae devotionis amicor, wedding aria (n.p., 1646); MS copy with Ger. title, Lass sich andere lieblich und schöne seyn dünken, Stadtbibliothek, Zwickau

Selig sind die Toten, funeral music for Sophie Elisabeth, Duchess of Saxony (Leipzig, 1650)

Funeral work, 8vv, 1620[8]; ed. G. Harms, *S. Scheidt: Gesamtausgabe*, iv (Klecken, 1933)

2 works, 4, 6vv, Cantionale sacrum, iii (Gotha, 1648); ed. L. Schoeberlein: *Schatz des liturgischen Chor- und Gemeindegesangs*, iii (Göttingen, 1872)

Allein Gott in der Höh sei Ehr, org, 1614 (incl. 6 variations, 3 by Scheidt, 3 anon., perhaps by Scheidt), *D-Bds* [collab. J. P. Sweelinck and others]; ed. H. J. Moser (Kassel, 1953); ed. G. Gerdes, *46 Choräle für Orgel von J. P. Sweelinck und seinen deutschen Schülern* (Mainz, 1957)

Der Gerechte, ob er gleich zu zeitlich stürbet, 8vv, bc, lost, formerly *Bds*

BIBLIOGRAPHY
K. Gabler: *Sammelband biographischer Notizen über Altenburger Musiker* (*D-ALa* Z.584)
M. Seiffert: 'J. P. Sweelinck und seine direkten deutschen Schüler', *VMw*, vii (1891), 186
——: 'Ueber Sweelinck und seine deutschen Schüler', *TVNM*, iv/1 (1892)
A. Werner: 'Samuel und Gottfried Scheidt', *SIMG*, i (1899–1900), 401–45
——: 'Neue Beiträge zur Scheidt-Biographie', *SIMG*, xiii (1911–12), 297
C. Mahrenholz: *Samuel Scheidt: sein Leben und Werk* (Leipzig, 1924/R1968)
W. Serauky: *Musikgeschichte der Stadt Halle*, ii/1 (Halle and Berlin, 1939/R1970), 8, 21, 46, 108
C. Mahrenholz: 'Scheidt', *MGG*

NIGEL FORTUNE

Scheidt, Samuel (*b* Halle, baptized 3 Nov 1587; *d* Halle, 24 March 1654). German composer and organist. An important member of the first generation of Baroque composers in Germany, he distinguished himself in both keyboard and sacred vocal music, combining traditional counterpoint with the new Italian concerto style.

1. Life. 2. Instrumental works. 3. Canons. 4. Vocal works. 5. Conclusion.

1. LIFE. Scheidt was the eldest surviving son of Konrad Scheidt, municipal beer and wine steward and later superintendent of water for the city of Halle, and his wife Anna, daughter of Simon Achtmann, a baker. Although there were no known musicians among his forebears, the family counted the organists Wolff Eisentraut and Salomon Kramer and the organ builder Heinrich Compenius (ii) as close friends. Two younger sons also became organists, Gottfried (*see* SCHEIDT, GOTTFRIED) and Christian (who was born in 1600 and worked at Eisleben, Alsleben and Frankenhausen).

Scheidt attended the local Gymnasium, where he was probably instructed in music by the Kantor, Matthäus Birkner, and his successor, Georg Schetz. By December 1604 – quite possibly by 1603 – he had become organist at the Moritzkirche, one of the three city churches; his tenure of this post is documented up to April 1607 and may have extended to 1608. It must have been about this time that he went to Amsterdam for a period of study with Sweelinck, which is mentioned by Mattheson and attested to by many similarities in keyboard style as well as by Scheidt's announcement in 1630 of a forthcoming edition by him of Sweelinck fantasias. He was back at Halle by the end of 1609 as court organist to the new administrator, Margrave Christian Wilhelm of Brandenburg. His duties included playing the organ for services at the castle chapel or the cathedral as well as providing secular keyboard music. Among the other court musicians were the lutenist Valentin Strobel (i) and the English violist William Brade, who was briefly Kapellmeister. The Kapellmeister *in absentia* was Michael Praetorius, who himself directed the festive music for the baptism of Christian Wilhelm's first child in April 1616. In 1618 Scheidt again had the opportunity to work with Praetorius, and also with Schütz, since all three were asked to provide special music in the concerted style for Magdeburg Cathedral. Both Praetorius and Schütz were present, together with Johann Staden, when Scheidt gave the dedicatory recital for the new organ at the Stadtkirche, Bayreuth, on 15 August 1619. With Brade's departure, Scheidt was appointed court Kapellmeister in late 1619 or early 1620; he retained his post as organist. The years 1620–25 were extremely productive and probably the happiest of his career. He built up the court musical establishment so that in 1621 it numbered ten instrumentalists and five vocal soloists. He published in quick succession a collection of motets (*Cantiones sacrae*, 1620), three volumes of instrumental ensemble music (*Ludi musici*, 1621, 1622, 1624), a volume of large-scale vocal concertos (*Concertus sacri*, 1622) and his three-volume magnum opus of organ music, the *Tabulatura nova* (1624). In 1624 he also supervised the rebuilding by his friend Johann Heinrich Compenius of the Moritzkirche organ; he himself drew up the specifications (listed in *Werke*, vii, 25). He was recognized as an expert in organ construction and was called upon throughout his life to inspect new organs.

Scheidt's flourishing life at court came to an abrupt end in 1625, when Christian Wilhelm left to join King Christian IV of Denmark to do battle on the Protestant side in the Thirty Years War. Although Scheidt retained his title he received no salary, and most of his musicians obtained employment elsewhere. Halle suffered severely during the war; it changed hands several times and by the end had lost fully half of its population. Yet through the trials of war and the great decline in his professional prestige, Scheidt remained remarkably loyal to Halle, and on 15 April 1627 he married, even though he was unemployed. He was paid that year for some compositions that he had sent to the Stuttgart court, and then and later he must also have derived income from his teaching. Of his many pupils the most famous was Adam Krieger. In 1628 the city created a new post for him, *director musices*, with responsibility for the music in the most important church, the Marktkirche. He immediately set to work purchasing new music, supervising the rebuilding of the organ, strengthening the city's instrumental ensemble and composing many large vocal works in the concerted style. But this second flourishing period also came to an abrupt end, because of a dispute between him and Christian Gueinz, Rektor of the Gymnasium. Both claimed jurisdiction over the choirboys, all of whom were also pupils at the Gymnasium. The situation came to a total impasse on Easter Sunday 1630, when there was no vocal music at all in the church. Gueinz proved the more eloquent, and Scheidt was forced to give up his position. He continued to provide music on commission for weddings, however, and this led to a complaint in 1634 by the Marktkirche organist, Johannes Zahn, that he was impinging on his prerogatives. A compromise was found whereby Scheidt could continue but would have to give part of his income to Zahn. The lowpoint in his life was reached in 1636, when the plague hit Halle, carrying away all four of his surviving children within a month. During these years he nevertheless continued to publish music. The final volume of the *Ludi musici* appeared in 1627, and between 1631 and 1640 he published four volumes of *Geistliche Concerte*, which were probably reduced versions of larger works he had composed earlier for the court and the Marktkirche. Two further volumes were projected but did not appear.

In 1638 peace returned to Halle; the new administrator, Duke August of Saxony, was able to move there, and Scheidt could once again enjoy his position as court Kapellmeister in fact as well as in name. The duke's arrival was celebrated by a service at the cathedral for which Scheidt composed the music, including a polychoral *Te Deum* (which is lost). He and his wife also began a new family. Although the music at court did not regain its pre-war level during his lifetime, he continued to compose and publish music. In 1642 he offered to Duke August of Brunswick a set of over 100 sacred madrigals for five voices and a set of instrumental sinfonias for use as preludes to vocal music. The madrigals are lost, but the sinfonias appeared in print two years later, dedicated to his own duke and thanking him for listening to his music 'with particularly diligent attention and most gracious approval'. (The duke was probably more interested in opera, however, and he built an opera house at Halle soon after Scheidt's death.) Scheidt's final publication was the so-called Görlitzer Tabulatur-Buch of 1650, a collection of 100 chorales for organ, harmonized in four parts. In 1647 he was conveyed in great honour and style to Gera by their town council to inspect a new organ, but his last surviving letters, from 1652, show him ignored by the burgomaster of Bittersfeld, who was a former pupil. His wife died on 5 May 1652, a second edition of the Görlitzer Tabulatur-Buch planned for 1653 did not appear, and he died on Good Friday 1654.

Printz singled out Schütz, Schein and Scheidt as the

1. Samuel Scheidt, with the canon 'In te Domine speravi': woodcut

three best German composers of their time. They were all born between 1585 and 1587, worked in close geographical proximity and knew one another; Schein chose Scheidt as godfather to his daughter Susanna in 1623. Of the three, Scheidt was the only one to distinguish himself as an instrumental performer and the only one whose fame now rests on his instrumental music. He was also the one most devoted to the German chorale and the least adventurous, both in his personal life and in his compositional style.

2. INSTRUMENTAL WORKS.

(*i*) *Keyboard music.* The most important source for Scheidt's keyboard music is the three-volume *Tabulatura nova* (1624). Its title signifies that it was the first German publication of keyboard music to appear in open score rather than in the letter notation of German organ tablature or the two six-line staves used in England and the Netherlands. This format emphasizes the contrapuntal and pedagogical nature of the music, beginning a tradition that persisted up to Bach's *Musicalisches Opfer*. Far from being simply an intellectual exercise, however, this mostly unsystematic assortment of sacred and secular music clearly originated in the practical demands of Scheidt's work as court organist, and he expected organists to copy it back into tablature for use in performance. In each of the first two volumes, variation sets predominate; the tunes on which they are based are almost equally divided between sacred and secular. Scheidt's variation technique is somewhat different for the two types. The eight sacred sets are all based on 16th-century Lutheran chorales, with the cantus firmus set apart in one voice, usually unornamented. Scheidt specified that on an organ with two manuals and pedal this voice should be played on the *Rückpositiv*, 'with a piercing sound, so that the chorale can be heard more distinctly', or on the pedal, using a 4′ stop if the chorale is in the alto. Within each set of variations there is great variety in the number of voices (from two to four), placing of the cantus firmus and treatment of the other voices. These are in free counterpoint, sometimes related to the chorale, and use many types of idiomatic keyboard figuration, often subjecting short motifs to extensive sequential repetition. There is always a fine sense of structure, sometimes resulting in a symmetrical arrangement of the individual variations. The seven secular variation sets are based on dances and songs from the Netherlands, France and England. Here the cantus firmus is more often decorated, and even when it is not it is absorbed into the surrounding texture, suitable for performance on a one-manual instrument, such as a positive organ, harpsichord or clavichord. The melody is more often in the upper voice, the texture more often homophonic, and while the types of figuration are similar to those in the sacred variations there is a greater use of small note values. The remaining pieces in these two volumes are for the most part freely contrapuntal. The third volume differs from the other two both in its systematic organization and in its total exclusion of secular music. It contains precisely those parts of the liturgy that an organist in Halle was required to play, either throughout the year or for a liturgical season, namely the Kyrie, Gloria, Credo and communion hymn (*Jesus Christus unser Heiland*) for Mass and the seasonal Latin hymns, *Magnificat* and *Benedicamus* for Vespers. The hymn settings are variation sets similar to those in the preceding volumes, with the addition of another method of cantus firmus treatment, in which each phrase of the chorale is treated imitatively in all voices. Scheidt used this method systematically for the first variation, and it is the vehicle for some of his best chorale settings. Canonic counterpoint in the free voices also appears only in the third volume. Although all of these techniques appear in the *Magnificat* settings (one for each of the nine tones), they are not strictly speaking variation sets but *alternatim* settings of the even verses. The Kyrie, Gloria and Credo are settings of an entire cantus firmus, while the *Benedicamus* and a similar piece, *Modus ludendi*, are short pieces designed to end the service with the full organ in six parts with double pedal. Scheidt also specified double pedal as one method of playing the tenor and bass voices of a sacred variation with cantus firmus in the alto, an indication of his own high skill as a performer.

The first volume of the *Tabulatura nova* was dedicated to Duke Johann Georg of Saxony, and the other two to the councils of several cities; Schütz at Dresden was consulted as to its value, as was Johann Staden at Nuremberg, and both commended it. Widespread manuscript copies, particularly in southern Germany, further attest to its good reception, yet Scheidt published no further organ music until 1650. The *Tabulatur-Buch hundert geistlicher Lieder und Psalmen* published at Görlitz is also in open score but is entirely different in that it comprises quite simple four-part settings of German chorales. These settings are clearly related to the four-part vocal harmonizations found in hymnals of the time, especially Schein's *Cantional* of 1627. All but 13 of Scheidt's chorales are

2. *A page from Scheidt's 'Tabulatura nova', i (Hamburg: Michael Hering, 1624)*

found in Schein's collection in much the same order, arranged according to the church year and Luther's catechism. But Scheidt's settings were explicitly for organ; they are more contrapuntal, and he stated in the foreword that they were 'for organists to play with Christian congregations' (in alternation, according to Mahrenholz, and not as accompaniment). The organ pieces by Scheidt surviving in manuscript do not add significantly to his published work.

Scheidt inherited many of his stylistic traits from Sweelinck, especially his cultivation of variation form, his preference for contrapuntal writing and many of the motifs in his keyboard figuration. He has often been grouped (most recently by Apel) with Sweelinck's other German pupils, such as Andreas Düben, Jacob Praetorius (ii), Scheidemann and their followers, as a member of the so-called north German school of organ composition. But this is to overlook the fact that some striking features of their music – expressively ornamented chorale melodies, strong textural contrasts, cultivation of virtuosity in the toccata and prelude and above all a love of fantasy that is bold and often daring – are conspicuously absent from Scheidt's much more rationally conceived keyboard music. His great strength lay in the contrapuntal treatment of the chorale, and his music is much more akin to the chorale fugue cultivated in central Germany and ultimately to Bach's canonic variations on *Vom Himmel hoch*. See also CHORALE SETTINGS, §II, 2.

(*ii*) *Ensemble music.* Little of Scheidt's music for instrumental ensemble is extant. Of the four volumes of *Ludi musici*, only the first (1621) survives complete; two partbooks of Part ii (1622) and one of Part iv (1627) are extant, while Part iii has disappeared completely, its title known only from the Fair catalogues of 1625. These subsequent volumes seem to be similar in content to the first, which contains a varied assortment of pavanes, galliards, allemandes, courantes and canzonas and one intrada, all scored for four or five instruments with a continuo part extracted from the instrumental bass. Scheidt indicated that they were composed for viols but allowed the use of other instruments; at least one canzona (no.18) is scored for cornetts, and the Galliard battaglia is dedicated to the court cornettist. The presence of a continuo part makes them more forward-looking than Schein's *Banchetto musicale* (1617); they are not, however, arranged in suites like Schein's collection, and the keys of the individual dances allow for only occasional pairing. The texture is more often homophonic than contrapuntal, although there is a high degree of motivic interplay between the parts; the five-part pieces often approximate to a polychoral texture through alternation of the top two parts. Six canzonas based on secular tunes are of particular interest, for they show a different aspect of Scheidt's variation technique whereby he used the theme as a point of departure rather than as a cantus firmus. He obviously composed the *Ludi musici* as dinner music and light entertainment in his capacity as court Kapellmeister. His only other instrumental publication, *LXX Symphonien* (1644), is also incomplete; the second cantus part is missing, and the one appearing in *Werke*, xiii, was written by the editors. Scheidt did not intend these short pieces in trio texture to be performed as independent instrumental music but offered them instead as introductions or ritornellos for vocal concertos; he had probably composed them as part of his unpublished large vocal concertos.

3. CANONS. Scheidt's canons are on the borderline between instrumental and vocal music. The 12 canons in the first part of the *Tabulatura nova* were probably included more for pedagogical purposes than as pieces for performance; all but one are based on sacred tunes, and some seem intended for voices rather than organ. No.10 was also printed at the beginning, beneath Scheidt's portrait, with the text 'In te Domine speravi, non confundar in aeternum' (see illustration). This must have been a personal motto, for he set it several times. Other canons by him survive in manuscript sources, including one, *Laudate Dominum in chordis et organo*, which formed part of the decoration of the rebuilt Moritzkirche organ. Scheidt is one of a long tradition of German composers, among them Schlick, Buxtehude, Theile and Bach, who cultivated these musical–intellectual puzzles. His favourite canonic techniques are contrary motion and close canon against a cantus firmus; the latter type is also integrated into his organ and vocal music.

4. VOCAL WORKS. Scheidt published seven collections of vocal music between 1620 and 1640, all of it sacred. Three different genres are represented: the motet, the large polychoral concerto with instruments and the small concerto for a few voices and continuo. The concerto principle pervades even the motets, and there is a remarkable similarity of compositional technique in all three types.

Scheidt's first publication of any sort was the *Cantiones sacrae* (1620), a collection of motets for eight voices. As with Schein's *Cymbalum Sionium* (1615), this collection appeared at the time of his appointment as court Kapellmeister; the dedication to Christian Wilhelm of Brandenburg and the title-pages of the soprano and bass parts describe Scheidt only as court organist, while the other parts include his position as Kapellmeister. Again like *Cymbalum Sionium* it is a collection of polychoral motets without continuo, with both Latin and German texts, and, as first publications of sacred music, both probably contain works composed over a number of years. In Scheidt's case, all but one of the motets are scored for a double choir, either two groups of soprano, alto, tenor and bass or two sopranos, alto and tenor, and alto, tenor and two basses. While only one motet specifies instruments (two clarinos in *In dulci jubilo*) and all eight voices are texted, it does not necessarily follow that Scheidt intended these pieces for purely vocal performance. Some of the bass parts lie too low for the human voice (e.g. in *Surrexit pastor bonus*), and it is quite likely that Scheidt envisaged further instrumental participation in the form both of an organ accompaniment derived from the lowest voice of each choir and of substitution or doubling by instruments. The style of Scheidt's motets is a lively mixture of traditional German elements, the Netherlands influence of his teacher Sweelinck (whose own *Cantiones sacrae* had appeared in 1619), and the Italian concerto style as mediated by Michael Praetorius, with whom he had worked in 1616 and 1618. Nearly half of the collection is devoted to settings of German chorales. These are typically restricted to one stanza, beginning with two motet-style expositions of the first phrase, one for each choir, and proceeding to a much closer interchange between choirs, often echoing very short motifs. Two settings *per omnes versus* (*Christe der du bist Tag und Licht* and *Vater unser in Himmelreich*) are similar for the first stanza but continue through the following verses in the manner of the organ variations: two to four voices, strictly contrapuntal, with the cantus firmus in long notes restricted to one voice. There are clear similarities between these two motets and Scheidt's organ settings of the same chorales in the *Tabulatura nova*. The fact that the organ pieces were published four years later does not necessarily mean that they were also composed later; the reverse is perhaps more likely. The final stanza in each motet restores all eight voices, homophonically and in triple time, a practice reminiscent of the final section of the keyboard variations on secular tunes. The texts of the other German motets are all taken from Luther's translation of the Bible and include five complete psalms. The style is similar to that of the single-verse chorale settings, but without a cantus firmus Scheidt could give greater attention to details of text-setting; he used both word-painting and sectional contrast of metre and texture to express the meaning of the text. He wrote *Zion spricht* for the funeral of his father, who died on 15 August 1618 (his brother Gottfried's setting of the same text is also included in this collection as no.35). One third of the collection is devoted to settings of Latin texts, all liturgical antiphons and responsories with the exception of *O Domine Jesu Christe*, a devotional text taken from Andreas Musculus's *Precationes* that had also been set by Giovanni Gabrieli (1597) and H. L. Hassler (1601); Erhard Bodenschatz had included Gabrieli's motet in his *Florilegium Portense* (1603), and Scheidt was undoubtedly familiar with both earlier settings. The other Latin pieces include many concerto-like elements, especially *Quaerite primum regnum Dei*, where the same verse (*Luke* xii.31) is stated five times, the second half as a refrain, homophonic and in triple time, the first half different each time in a highly contrasting florid and contrapuntal style.

The possibilities for concerto-style performance latent in the *Cantiones sacrae* are made explicit and expanded in Scheidt's next publication, *Pars prima concertuum sacrorum* (1622). Two of the 12 concertos are in fact reworkings of motets from the *Cantiones sacrae*, and the revisions are not extensive: addition of a continuo and instrumental sinfonias at the beginning and in the middle and instrumental doublings specified for the tutti passages. In the newly composed concertos the duet and trio writing, already present in the *Cantiones sacrae*, increases in both extent and virtuosity, and the instrumental participation includes obbligato parts as well as sinfonias and doublings. There is a marked shift in content compared with the *Cantiones sacrae*: there are no chorale settings, and the only German text is the psalm *Herr unser Herrscher*, which is the model for the *Missa brevis* that follows it.

Scheidt intended to publish further volumes of large concertos, but he apparently never found a publisher for them. The four volumes entitled *Geistliche Concerte* that he did publish (between 1631 and 1640) are all scored for a few voices (mostly three) and accompanied only by continuo. They also differ in content from the 1622 volume, with only a handful of Latin texts and the chief emphasis on the German chorale. Even so their compositional technique is similar to that of the large concertos. Once again there are two arrangements of works published in the earlier collection, *Herr unser Herrscher* and *Hodie completi sunt*. The reduction is one of length as well as number of voices, and instrumental sinfonias and doublings are omitted. The solo section of the large concerto can be taken over virtually intact, sometimes with a slight reduction in virtuosity, but the tutti sections are cut extensively. The solo–tutti effect is nevertheless maintained by the contrast between counterpoint and homophony that appears in many of the small concertos.

In the second part (1634) Scheidt published an index of all six projected volumes of small concertos, at the end of which he said:

The above sacred concertos, which can be performed thus with a few vocal parts, have also been composed by me in other volumes, namely with eight and 12 voices, two, three and four choruses, with symphonies and all sorts of instruments. . . . Whoever would like to publish and print them, to the glory of God, can get them from me at any time.

Mahrenholz interpreted this to mean that the original form of all the small concertos was a large concerto, a theory disputed by Gessner (pp.80ff). While there are some small concertos that do suggest that they are in their original form, reduction seems more likely in most of them, and five of the titles listed for Part v are also in the 1622 volume of large concertos.

A number of the small concertos are based on the same chorales as appeared in the *Cantiones sacrae*, but there is very little similarity between the two settings. This can be explained by the fact that it is the tutti sections of the large concertos that the motets most closely resemble – precisely those sections that must be cut to form the small concertos. Moreover, the eight voices of the motets most often form only two distinct bodies of sound, whereas the small concertos usually work with three bodies of sound (each a solo voice), supported by continuo; they are much more contrapuntal and tightly constructed. The texts of Parts i–ii and iv of the *Geistliche Concerte* are a mixture of chorales

and biblical passages, most of them rather general in nature. By contrast, Part iii is made up almost entirely of chorale settings, arranged systematically according to the church year. There are also *Magnificat* settings for Christmas, Easter and Pentecost, with German interpolations appropriate to the season between the even verses. Braun has shown that some of these interpolations, as well as other concertos here, are parodies of older motets by other composers. Many of the chorale concertos are settings of more than one stanza of the chorale and are divided into two or three parts, with individual stanzas distinguished by scoring and compositional technique (e.g. *Nun komm der Heiden Heiland*). They are thus reminiscent of the variation cycles in the *Tabulatura nova*, with the cantus firmus treated less rigidly, but they also look ahead to the later chorale cantata.

The *Liebliche Krafft-Blümlein* (1635) is an early example of the numerous 17th-century prints bearing flowery titles. All 12 concertos are scored for two voices and continuo; they are generally shorter and more intimate than those in the *Geistliche Concerte*. All but one are based on short Old Testament texts; the exception is the chorale *Herzlich tut mich erfreuen*. This, together with the setting in Part iv of the *Geistliche Concerte*, may be a reduction from a lost large concerto, but the others appear to be in their original form. *See also* CHORALE SETTINGS, §I, 3.

5. CONCLUSION. Scheidt shared with Handel a propensity to rework musical material, both his own and that of other composers. No genre of his compositions is totally independent: dances from the *Ludi musici* turn up in the *Tabulatura nova*, similar chorale settings and canons are found in both the organ and vocal music, and the distinctions between motet, large concerto and small concerto are blurred. He wrote idiomatically for both voices and instruments, however, a feature particularly evident in his keyboard music. Nevertheless certain stylistic elements unify the entire corpus of his music: a love of variation, particularly of the German chorale, a strong sense of structure, his skilful cultivation of counterpoint, especially in sacred music, and above all the interchange of short motifs, derived from the concerto, which pervades all his music, whether contrapuntal or homophonic, instrumental or vocal.

WORKS

Edition: *S. Scheidt: Werke*, ed. G. Harms and C. Mahrenholz, i–xiii (Hamburg, 1923–62), xiv–xvi (Leipzig, 1971–) [S]

SACRED VOCAL

Cantiones sacrae, 8vv (Hamburg, 1620) [1620]
Pars prima concertuum sacrorum, adiectis symphoniis et choris instrumentalibus, 2–5, 8, 12vv, bc (Hamburg, 1622) [1622]
Newe geistliche Concerten . . . prima pars, 2, 3vv, bc (Halle, 1631) [1631]
Geistliche Concerten . . . ander Theil, 2–6vv, bc (Halle, 1634) [1634]
Geistlicher Concerten . . . dritter Theil, 2–6vv, bc (Halle, 1635) [1635a]
Liebliche Krafft-Blümlein aus des Heyligen Geistes Lustgarten abgebrochen und zum Vorschmack dess ewigen Lebens im zweystimmichten Himmels-Chor versetzet, 2vv, bc (Halle, 1635) [1635b]
Geistlicher Concerten . . . vierter Theil, 2–6vv, bc (Halle, 1640) [1640]
Geistlicher Concerten [pts. v, vi], lost; facs. of projected contents in S ix, p.xi

(German)

Ach Gott tu dich erbarmen, STB, bc, 1640; S xii, 105
Ach Gott und Herr, wie gross und schwer, STB, bc, 1634; S ix, 74
Ach Gott vom Himmel sieh darein, STB, bc, 1640; S xii, 109
Ach mein herzliebes Jesulein, SSTTB, bc, 1635a; S x, 24
Allein Gott in der Höh sei Ehr, STB, bc, 1635a; S xi, 80
Allein nach dir, Herr Jesu Christ, STB, bc, 1634; S ix, 15
Allein zu dir, Herr Jesu Christ, STB, 1634; S ix, 55
Alleluja! Lobet ihr Himmel den Herren, SSATTB, bc, 1634; S ix, 37

Aller Augen warte auf dich, ATB, bc, 1634; S ix, 141
Also heilig ist der Tag, STB, bc, 1635a; S xi, 4
Also sehr jammerts Gott, SATB, bc, 1640; S xii, 76
An Wasserflüssen Babylon, STB, bc, 1631; S viii, 66
Auf meinen lieben Gott, STB, bc, 1634; S ix, 1
Aus meines Herzens Grunde, STB, bc, 1640; S xii, 102
Aus tiefer Not schrei ich zu dir, STB, bc, 1634; S ix, 64
Aus tiefer Not schrei ich zu dir, STB, bc, 1640; S xii, 113
Bleib bei uns Herr, SATB, bc, 1640; S xii, 80
Christ, der du bist der helle Tag, SATB, bc, 1634; S iv, 96
Christe der du bist Tag und Licht, SATB, bc, 1620; S iv, 87
Christe, der du bist Tag und Licht, STB, bc, 1634; S ix, 67
Christ ist erstanden von der Marter, STB, bc, 1635a; S xi, 21
Christ lag in Todesbanden, SATB, SATB, 1620; S iv, 103
Christ lag in Todesbanden, STB, bc, 1635a; S xi, 1
Christo dem Osterlämmelein, 5vv, 5 insts; S xvi
Christum wir sollen loben schon, STB, bc, 1635a; S x, 40
Christ unser Herr zum Jordan kam, STB, bc, 1635a; S xi, 87
Christus, der uns selig macht, STB, bc, 1634; S ix, 83
Da Jesus an dem Kreuze stund, STB, bc, 1634; S ix, 81
Danket dem Herrn, denn er ist freundlich, STB, bc, 1631; S viii, 40
Danket dem Herrn, denn er ist freundlich, ATB, bc, 1631; S viii, 90
Danket dem Herrn heut und allezeit, STB, bc, 1640; S xii, 38
Dank sagen wir alle, STB, bc, 1635a; S x, 36
Das alte Jahr vergangen ist, SATB, SATB, 1620; S iv, 65
Das alte Jahr vergangen ist, STB, bc, 1635a; S x, 102
Der Gerechte, ob er gleich zu zeitlich stirbt, SSB, pubd separately (Halle, 1635); S xvi
Der Tag vertreibt die finstre Nacht, SSATTB, bc, 1640; S xii, 83
Deutsches Magnificat, SATB, bc, 1640; S xii, 4
Die Güte des Herren ist, ST, bc, 1635b; S xvi
Dies sind die heilgen zehn Gebot, STB, bc, 1640; S xii, 116
Drey schöne Ding sind, SATTB, bc, pubd separately (Leipzig, 1641) (inc.); S xvi
Durch Adams Fall ist ganz verderbt, STB, bc, 1640; S xii, 119
Durch Wortes Kraft ... mit Dank wir sollen loben, SSB, bc, 1631; S viii, 30
Ein feste Burg ist unser Gott, SATB, SATB, 1620; S iv, 76
Ein feste Burg ist unser Gott, STB, SS/TT, bc, 1631; S viii, 75
Ein Kindelein so löbelich, SATB, bc, 1635a; S x, 69
Ein Kind geborn zu Bethlehem, SSATTB, bc, 1635a; S x, 49
Erbarm dich mein o Herre Gott, STB, bc, 1634; S ix, 61
Erhalt uns, Herr, bei deinem Wort, STB, bc, 1631; S viii, 61
Es gingen drei heilige Frauen, SATB, bc, 1635a; S x, 14
Es ist das Heil uns kommen her, STB, bc, 1640; S xii, 122
Es spricht der Unweisen Mund wohl, STB, bc, 1640; S xii, 125
Es war einmal ein reicher Mann, STB, bc, 1640; S xii, 128
Es wird schier der letzte Tag herkommen, STB, bc, 1640; S xii, 131
Frewe dich des Weibes deiner Jugend, STB, chorus, insts, pubd separately (Leipzig, 1628); (inc.); S xvi
Gelobet seist du Jesu Christ, SATB, bc, 1635a; S x, 16
Gelobet seystu Jesu Christ, SATB, SATB, 1620; S iv, 52
Gen Himmel zu dem Vater mein, STB, bc, 1635a; S x, 43
Gib Fried, o frommer, treuer Gott, SATB, bc, 1640; S xii, 53
Gott der Vater wohn uns bei, STB, bc, 1635a; S xi, 75
Gott der Vater wohn uns bei, SATB, SATB, 1620; S iv, 81
Gott ist mein Licht und Seligkeit, SATB, bc, 1640; S xii, 71
Helft mir Gotts Güte preisen, STB, bc, 1635a; S x, 99
Herr Gott, dich loben alle wir, STB, bc, 1635a; S xi, 94
Herr Jesu Christ, meins Lebens Licht, STTB, bc, 1640; S xii, 60
Herr Jesu Christ, wahr Mensch und Gott, STB, bc, 1634; S ix, 88
Herr, lehre uns bedenken, ST, bc, 1635b; S xvi
Herr unser Herrscher, SATB, SATB, insts, bc, 1622; S xv, 63
Herr unser Herrscher, SSTB, bc, 1634; S ix, 7
Herr, wenn ich nur dich habe, ST, bc, 1635b; S xvi
Herr, wer wird wohnen in deiner Hütten, STB, bc, 1634; S ix, 132
Herr, wo dein Wort nicht mein Trost gewest wäre, ST, bc, 79
Herzlich lieb hab ich dich, o Herr, SATB, SATB, 1620; S iv, 131
Herzlich lieb hab ich dich, o Herr, S[S]T[T]B, bc, 1634; S ix, 25
Herzlich tut mich erfreuen, ST, bc, 1635b; S xvi
Herzlich tut mich erfreuen, SSTTB, bc, 1640; S xii, 134
Herzlich tut mich verlangen, STB, bc, 1640; S xii, 43
Ich bin die Auferstehung und das Leben, SSATB; S xvi
Ich dank dir lieber Herre, STB, bc, 1640; S xii, 98
Ich freue mich über deinem Wort, ST, bc, 1635b; S xvi
Ich hab mein Sach Gott heimgestellt, STTB, bc, 1631; S viii, 82
Ich hebe meine Augen auff, SSAT, ATBB, 1620; S iv, 23
Ich ruf zu dir, Herr Jesu Christ, STB, bc, 1631; S viii, 57
Ich weiss, dass mein Erlöser lebt, SATB, bc, 1635a; S xi, 7
In dich hab ich gehoffet Herr, STB, bc, 1631; S viii, 79
In meinem Herzen hab ich mir gesetzet für, STB, bc, 1631; S viii, 36
Ist nicht Ephraim mein teurer Sohn, TTB, bc, 1634; S ix, 127
Ist nicht Ephraim mein teurer Sohn, 7vv, bc; S xvi
Jauchzet Gott alle Land!, SSATB, bc, 1634; S ix, 107
Jesu wollst uns weisen, SATB, bc, 1640; S xii, 46

Komm heiliger Geist, Herre Gott, SATB, SATB, 1620; S iv, 39
Komm heiliger Geist, Herre Gott, STB, bc, 1635a; S xi, 46
Komm heiliger Geist, Herre Gott, SS, 2 insts, 1620; S iv, 195
Komm heiliger Geist, Herre Gott, SS, 2 trbn, 1635a; S xi, 50
Kommt vor ihr Gesegneten meines Vaters, dialogue, SATTB, 1634; S ix, 20
Lasst singen und Gott loben, SATB, bc, 1640; S xii, 31
Lobe den Herren meine Seele, ST, bc, 1635b; S xvi
Lobet den Herren alle Heiden, SSATTB, bc, 1640; S xii, 13
Lobet den Herren, denn er ist sehr freundlich, SSAT, ATBB, 1620; S iv, 126
Lobet den Herren, denn er ist sehr freundlich, S[S]T[T]B, bc, 1631; S viii, 71
Lobet den Herren in seinem Heiligtum, echo, SATB, SATB, 1620; S iv, 187
Lobet ihr Himmel den Herren, echo, SATB, SATB, 1620; S iv, 177
Machet die Tore weit, ST, bc, 1635b; S xvi
Mag ich Unglück nicht widerstahn, S[S]T[T]B, bc, 1634, S ix, 121
Mein Hüter und mein Hirt, STB, bc, 1635a; S xi, 94
Mein Trost und Hilf ist Gott allein, SATB, bc, 1640; S xii, 64
Mit Fried und Freud ich fahr dahin, STB, bc, 1635a; S x, 107
Nun danket alle Gott, SSAT, ATBB, 1620; S iv, 137
Nun danket alle Gott, STB, bc, 1635a; S xi, 135
Nun danket alle Gott, STB, bc, 1640; S xii, 19
Nun danket alle Gott, der grosse Dinge tut, 12vv, insts, bc; S xvi
Nun ist es Zeit zu singen hell, STB, bc, 1635a; S x, 74
Nun komm der Heiden Heiland, SATB, SATB, 1620; S iv, 56
Nun komm der Heiden Heiland, STB, bc, 1635a; S x, 5
Nun lasst uns Gott den Herren, STB, bc, 1634; S ix, 142
Nun lob mein Seel den Herren, STB, bc, 1631; S viii, 46
Nun lob mein Seel den Herren, 8vv, insts, bc; S viii, 97
O Jesu süss, wer dein gedenkt, TTB, bc, 1640; S xii, 1
O Jesu süss, wer dein gedenkt, STB, bc, 1640; S xii, 2
O Lamm Gottes unschuldig, SS/TT, bc, 1634; S ix, 86
Richte mich Gott, SSAT, ATBB, 1620; S iv, 112
Rufe getrost, schone nicht, ST, bc, 1635b; S xvi
Schaffe in mir, Gott, ein rein Herz, ST, bc, 1635b; S xvi
Siehe, wie fein und lieblich ist's, TTB, bc, 1634; S ix, 130
Singen wir aus Herzensgrund, STB, bc, 1631; S viii, 88
Singet dem Herren ein neues Lied, ST, bc, 1635b; S xvi
Vater unser im Himmelreich, SATB, SATB, 1620; S iv, 144
Vater unser im Himmelreich, STB, bc, 1631; S viii, 5
Vater unser/Christ unser Herr/Ich ruf zu dir, quodlibet, STB, bc, 1631; S viii, 8
Vom Himmel hoch da komm ich her, SSTB, bc, 1635a; S x, 43
Von Gott will ich nicht lassen, S[S]T[T]B, bc, 1631; S viii, 26
Warum betrübst du dich mein Herz, S[S]T[T]B, bc, 1631; S viii, 52
Warum betrübst du dich mein Herz, SATB, SATB, bc; S xvi
Was mein Gott will, das g'sheh allzeit, SATB, bc, 1640; S xii, 27
Wendet euch um, STB, bc, 1634; S ix, 94
Wenn wir in höchsten Nöten sein, STB, bc, 1634; S ix, 49
Wer Gott vertraut, hat wohl gebaut, STB, bc, 1640; S xii, 24
Wie schön leuchtet der Morgenstern, S[S]T[T]B, 1631; S viii, 10
Wie schön leuchtet der Morgenstern, 8vv [insts, bc]; S viii, 95
Wies Gott gefällt, so g'fällt mirs auch, STB, bc, 1631; S viii, 16
Wirf dein Anliegen auf den Herren, ST, bc, 1635b; S xvi
Wir glauben all an einen Gott, STB, bc, 1631; S viii, 1
Wo Gott der Herr nicht bei uns hält, STB, bc, 1634; S ix, 116
Wohl dem, der in Gotts Furchten steht, SATB, bc, 1640; S xii, 90
Wolan, so kommet her ihr frommen, SATB, pubd separately (Bremen, 1646)
Zion spricht, der Herr hat mich verlassen, SSAT, ATBB, 1620; S iv, 158
Zion spricht, der Herr hat mich verlassen, STB, bc, 1634; S ix, 33

(Latin)

Missa [brevis] super 'Herr unser Herrscher', SATB, SATB, insts, bc, 1622; S xv, 99
Missa super 'Nun danket alle Gott', 8vv, bc, pubd separately (Erfurt, 1638); S xvi

Magnificat (Tone 1), SSATB, bc, 1635a [with Ger. interpolations for Pentecost]; S xi, 55
Magnificat (Tone 2), SSATB, bc, 1635a [with Ger. interpolations for Easter]; S xi, 24
Magnificat (Tone 4), T, SATB, T, insts, bc, 1622; S xv, 97
Magnificat (Tone 5), S[S]AT[T]B, bc, 1635a [with Ger. interpolations for Christmas]; S x, 78
Magnificat (Tone 8), SATB, SATB, insts, bc, 1622; S xv, 37
Magnificat (Tone 9), STB, chorus, insts, 1622; S xiv, 51

Angelus ad pastores ait, SATB, SATB, 1620; S iv, 60
Angelus ad pastores ait, 8vv, insts, bc, 1622; S xiv, 83
Ascendo ad patrem, SATB, SATB, 1620; S iv, 43
Benedicamus Domino, SSATB, bc, 1634; S ix, 138
Cantate Domino, SATTB, insts, bc, 1622; S xiv, 37
Duo seraphim, SSAT, ATBB, 1620; S iv, 47

Hodie completi sunt, 8vv, insts, bc, 1622; S xiv, 61
Hodie completi sunt, SATB, bc, 1635a; S xi, 70
Hosianna filio David, SSATB, bc, 1635a; S x, 1
In dulci jubilo, 8vv, 2 clarinos, 1620; S iv, 70
In dulci jubilo, SSATTB, bc, 1635a; S x, 59
Laudate Dominum, TT, chorus, insts, 1622; S xiv, 3
Laudate Dominum in sanctis, 6vv, insts, bc, 1622; S xiv, 15
Miserere mei Deus, ST, 4 va da gamba, bc, 1634; S ix, 30
O Domine Jesu Christe, SSAT, ATBB, 1620; S iv, 32
O lux beata Trinitas, STB, bc, 1635a; S xi, 83
Psallite unigenito, SATB, SATB (inc.); S xvi
Puer natus in Bethlehem, S, SAATTBB, 1620; S iv, 86
Quaerite primum regnum Dei, SSAT, ATBB, 1620; S iv, 164
Repleatur os meum, SATTB, bc, 1635a; S xi, 100
Resonet in laudibus, SSTB, bc, 1635a; S x, 29
Sic Deus dilexit mundum, SSAT, ATBB, 1620; S iv, 122
Surrexit pastor bonus, SSAT, ATBB, 1620; S iv, 107
Tulerunt Dominum, echo, 8vv, insts, bc, 1622; S xv
Tulerunt Dominum, SATB, SATB, 1620; S iv, 96
Tulerunt Dominum, SATB, SATB, insts, bc, 1622; S xv, 3
Tulerunt Dominum, echo, SATB, SATB, bc, 1622; S xv, 19
Veni Sancte Spiritus . . . reple, SATB, SATB, 1620; S iv, 35

KEYBOARD

Tabulatura nova continens variationes aliquot psalmorum, fantasiarum, cantilenarum, passamezzo et canones (Hamburg, 1624) [1624a]
Pars secunda tabulaturae continens fugarum, psalmorum, cantionum et echus, tocatae, variationes varias omnimodas pro quorumvis organistarum captu et modulo (Hamburg, 1624) [1624b]
III. et ultima pars tabulaturae continens Kyrie Dominicale, Credo in unum Deum, Psalmum de Coena Domini sub communione, hymnos praecipuorum festorum totius anni, Magnificat . . . & Benedicamus (Hamburg, 1624) [1624c]
Tabulatur-Buch hundert geistlicher Lieder und Psalmen (Görlitz, 1650) [1650]

(chorales)

Ach Gott, tu dich erbarmen, 1650; S i, 35
Ach Gott und Herr, 1650; S i, 33
Ach Gott, vom Himmel sieh darein, 1650; S i, 21
Allein Gott in der Höh sei Ehr, 1650; S i, 10
Allein Gott in der Höh sei Ehr; S v, 24
Allein zu dir, Herr Jesu Christ, 1650; S i, 14
Also heilig ist der Tag, 1650; S i, 9
An Wasserflüssen Babylon, 1650; S i, 26
An Wasserflüssen Babylon [arr. of lost vocal work]; S xvi
Auf meinen lieben Gott, 1650; S i, 32
Aus tiefer Not schrei ich zu dir, 1650; S i, 25
Aus tiefer Not schrei ich zu dir, 1650; S i, 26
Christ, der du bist der helle Tag, 1650; S i, 18
Christe, der du bist Tag und Licht (2 versions), 1650; S i, 6
Christ ist erstanden, 1650; S i, 9
Christ lag in Todesbanden, 1624b; S vi/2, 28
Christ lag in Todesbanden (2 versions), 1650; S i, 7
Christum wir sollen loben schon, 1650; S i, 2
Christ unser Herr zum Jordan kam, 1650; S i, 14
Christus der ist mein Leben, 1650; S i, 34
Christus der uns selig macht, 1650; S i, 6
Da Jesus an dem Kreuze stund, 1624a; S vi/1, 102
Da Jesus an dem Kreuze stund, 1650; S i, 5
Dank sagen wir alle Gott, 1650; S i, 5
Dankt dem Herrn heut und allezeit, 1650; S i, 18
Der du bist drei in Einigkeit, 1650; S i, 11
Der Tag hat sich geneiget, 1650; S i, 36
Der Tag vertreibt die finstre Nacht, 1650; S i, 17
Dies sind die heil'gen zehn Gebot, 1650; S i, 12
Durch Adams Fall ist ganz verderbt, 1650; S i, 18
Ein feste Burg ist unser Gott, 1650; S i, 23
Ein Kindelein so löbelich, 1650; S i, 4
Erbarm dich mein, o Herre Gott, 1650; S i, 23
Erhalt uns Herr bei deinem Wort, 1650; S i, 28
Erschienen ist der herrlich Tag, 1650; S i, 8
Esaia dem Propheten das geschah, 1650; S i, 15
Es ist das Heil uns kommen her, 1650; S i, 19
Es spricht der Unweisen Mund wohl, 1650; S i, 22
Es war einmal ein reicher Mann, 1650; S i, 21
Es wird schier der letzte Tag herkommen, 1650; S i, 34
Es woll uns Gott genädig sein, 1650; S i, 23
Gelobet seist du, Jesu Christ, 1624b; S vi/2, 60
Gelobet seist du, Jesu Christ (2 versions), 1650; S i, 1
Gib Fried, o frommer, treuer Gott, 1650; S i, 36
Gott der Vater, wohn uns bei, 1650; S i, 11
Gott hat das Evangelium, 1650; S i, 34
Gott sei gelobet und gebenedeiet, 1650; S i, 16
Gott Vater, der du deine Sonn, 1650; S i, 18
Hats Gott versehn, wer will, 1650; S i, 37
Helft mir Gotts Güte preisen, 1650; S i, 4
Helft mir Gotts Güte preisen (doubtful); S v, 27

Herr Christ, der einig Gotts Sohn, 1650; S i, 19
Herr Gott, dich loben alle wir, 1650; S i, 12
Herr Gott, dich loben wir [Te Deum], 1650; S i, 38
Herr Gott, dich loben wir [Te Deum] (doubtful); S v, 26
Herr Jesu Christ, du höchstes Gut . . . sieh doch (2 versions), 1650; S i, 35
Herr Jesu Christ, ich weiss gar wohl, 1650; S i, 32
Herr Jesu Christ, meins Lebens Licht, 1650; S i, 34
Herr Jesu Christ, wahr Mensch und Gott, 1650; S i, 32
Herzlich lieb hab ich dich, o Herr, 1624b; S vi/2, 22
Herzlich tut mich erfreuen, 1650; S i, 34
Herzlich tut mich verlangen, 1650; S i, 31
Herzlich vertrau du deinem Gott, 1650; S i, 28
Ich dank dir, lieber Herre, 1650; S i, 17
Ich hab mein Sach Gott heimgestellt, 1650; S i, 32
Ich ruf zu dir, Herr Jesu Christ (2 versions), 1650; S i, 20
In dich hab ich gehoffet, Herr, 1650; S i, 22
In dulci jubilo, 1650; S i, 3
Jesus Christus, unser Heiland, der den Tod (2 versions), 1650; S i, 8
Jesus Christus, unser Heiland, der von uns (2 versions), 1650; S i, 16
Jesus Christus, unser Heiland, der von uns [Psalmus sub Communione], 1624c; S vii, 10
Komm, Heiliger Geist, Herre Gott, 1650; S i, 10
Kommt her zu mir, spricht Gottes Sohn, 1650; S i, 21
Lobt Gott, ihr Christen all zugleich, 1650; S i, 4
Mag ich Unglück nicht widerstahn, 1650; S i, 27
Mensch, willst du leben seliglich, 1650; S i, 12
Mit Fried und Freud ich fahr dahin, 1650; S i, 5
Mitten wir im Leben sind, 1650; S i, 33
Nun bitten wir den Heiligen Geist, 1650; S i, 37
Nun freut euch, lieben Christen gmein, 1650; S i, 19
Nun höret zu, ihr Christenleut, 1650; S i, 20
Nun komm, der Heiden Heiland (2 versions), 1650; S i, 1
Nun lasst uns Gott dem Herren, 1650; S i, 17
Nun lob, mein Seel, den Herren, 1650; S i, 24
O Christe, Morgensterne, 1650; S i, 17
O grosser Gott von Macht, 1650; S i, 36
O Herre Gott, dein göttlich Wort, 1650; S i, 29
O Jesulein süss, o Jesulein mild (2 versions), 1650; S i, 2
O Lamm Gottes, unschuldig, 1650; S i, 6
Puer natus in Bethlehem, 1650; S i, 3
Sie ist mir lieb, die werte Magd, 1650; S i, 30
Singen wir aus Herzensgrund, 1650; S i, 18
Vater unser im Himmelreich, 1624a; S vi/1, 19
Vater unser im Himmelreich, 1650; S i, 13
Verzage nicht, o frommer Christ, 1650; S i, 28
Vom Himmel hoch da komm ich her (2 versions), 1650; S i, 2
Von Gott will ich nicht lassen, 1650; S i, 30
Wachet auf, ruft uns die Stimme, 1650; S i, 36
Wär Gott nicht mit uns diese Zeit, 1650; S i, 24
Warum betrübst du dich, mein Herz, 1624a; S vi/1, 48
Warum betrübst du dich, mein Herz (3 versions), 1650; S i, 26
Was Gott tut, das ist wohlgetan, kein einig, 1650; S i, 37
Wenn dich Unglück tut greifen an, 1650; S i, 28
Wenn mein Stündlein vorhanden ist, 1650; S i, 31
Wenn wir in höchsten Nöten sein, 1650; S i, 27
Wie schön leuchtet der Morgenstern; S v, 16
Wie schön leuchtet der Morgenstern, 1650; S i, 31
Wir glauben all an einen Gott, 1624a; S vi/1, 2
Wir glauben all an einen Gott, 1650; S i, 12
Wir glauben all en einen Gott [Credo in unum Deum], 1624c; S vii, 8
Wo der Herr nicht bei uns hält, 1650; S i, 25
Wo Gott zum Haus nicht gibt sein Gunst, 1650; S i, 25
Zion, die werte Gottesstadt, 1650; S i, 37

(other sacred)

A solis ortus cardine, 1624c; S vii, 23
Benedicamus Domino, a 6, modus pleno organo pedaliter, 1624c; S vii, 107
Christe, qui lux es et dies, 1624b; S vi/2, 47
Christe, qui lux es et dies, 1624c; S vii, 29
Credo: see Wir glauben all
Kyrie dominicale in tone 4, cum Gloria, 1624c; S vii, 1
Magnificat (Tone 1), 1624c; S vii, 54
Magnificat (Tone 2), 1624c; S vii, 59
Magnificat (Tone 3), 1624c; S vii, 64
Magnificat (Tone 4), 1624c; S vii, 71
Magnificat (Tone 5), 1624c; S vii, 76
Magnificat (Tone 6), 1624c; S vii, 81
Magnificat (Tone 7), 1624c; S vii, 87
Magnificat (Tone 8), 1624c; S vii, 93
Magnificat (Tone 9, tonus peregrinus), 1624c; S vii, 101
Modus ludendi pleno organo pedaliter, a 6, 1624c; S vii, 106
O lux beata Trinitas, 1624c; S vii, 46
Psalmus sub Communione: see Jesus Christus, unser Heiland
Surrexit Christus hodie, 1650; S i, 8
Veni Creator Spiritus, 1624c; S vii, 42

Veni Redemptor gentium, 1624c; S vii, 18
Vita sanctorum, decus angelorum, 1624c; S vii, 36
Fantasia 'Ich ruf zu dir, Herr Jesu Christ', a 4, 1624a; S vi/1, 107
Toccata 'In te Domine speravi', 1624b; S vi/2, 85

(secular)

Ach du feiner Reiter [Cantio belgica], 1624a; S vi/1, 85
Also gehts, also stehts, allemande, 1624b; S vi/2, 78
Est-ce Mars [Cantio gallica], 1624a; S vi/1, 93
Fortune my foe [Cantilena anglica], 1624b; S vi/2, 56
Soll es sein, allemande, 1624b; S vi/2, 69
Weh, Windchen, weh [Cantio belgica], 1624a; S vi/1, 75
Windecken daer het bosch af drilt (authenticity questioned); S v, 41

Alamanda; ed. O. Mischiati (Mainz, 1967)
Bergamasca; S v, 28
Courante, a 4, 1624a; S vi/1, 83
Courante, a 4, 1624a; S vi/1, 82
Echo ad manuale duplex forte & lene, a 4, 1624b; S vi/2, 10
Fantasia, a 3, 1624b; S vi/2, 40
Fantasia 'Io son ferito lasso', fuga quadruplici, a 4, 1624a; S vi/1, 12
Fantasia 'Ut re mi fa sol la', a 2–4, 1624a; S vi/1, 33
Fuga, a 4, 1624b; S vi/2, 15
Fuga contraria, a 4, 1624b; S vi/2, 1
Galliarda (J. Dowland); S v, 31
Galliarda; S v, 35
Galliarda; S v, 37
Paduana Hispanica (with Sweelinck); S v, 47
Passamezzo, 1624a; S vi/1, 58
Toccata, a 3, C; S v, 15
Toccata, a 4, d; S v, 13
Toccata, a 4, g; S v, 12

OTHER INSTRUMENTAL

Paduana, galliarda, courante, alemande, intrada, canzonetto, ut vocant, in gratiam musices studiosorum, potissimum violistarum, a 4, 5, bc (Hamburg, 1621) [1621]
Ludorum musicorum secunda pars continens paduan, galliard, alemand, canzon, et intrad, a 4, 5, 7, bc (Hamburg, 1622) (inc.)
Ludorum musicorum tertia pars continens paduanas, cour. et canzon., a 3, 4, 7, 8, bc (Hamburg, 1624); lost (cited in Göhler)
Ludorum musicorum quarta pars, a 3, 4, bc (Hamburg, 1627) (inc.)
LXX Symphonien auff Concerten manir: vornemlich auff Violinen zu gebrauchen durch die gewöhnliche Tonos, und die 7 Claves, a 2, bc (Leipzig, 1644) (inc.) [1644]

Alamande, a 4, bc, 1621; S ii–iii, 20
Alamande super Courant belg., a 4, bc, 1621; S ii–iii, 20
Alamande, a 4, bc, 1621; S ii–iii, 20
Canzon ad imitationem Bergam. angl., a 5, bc, 1621; S ii–iii, 36
Canzon cornetto, 4 cornetts, 1621; S ii–iii, 21
Canzon 'Est-ce Mars', a 5, bc, 1621; S ii–iii, 54
Canzon 'J'aime un racomodement', a 5, bc, 1621; S ii–iii, 42
Canzon 'O Nachbar Roland', a 5, bc, 1621; S ii–iii, 47
Canzon 'Windecken daer het bosch af drilt', a 5, bc, 1621; S ii–iii, 66
Canzon super Intrad. Aechiop., a 5, bc, 1621; S ii–iii, 60
Courant, a 4, bc, 1621; S ii–iii, 16
Courant, a 4, bc, 1621; S ii–iii, 17
Courant, a 4, bc, 1621; S ii–iii, 18
Courant, a 4, bc, 1621; S ii–iii, 19
Courant, a 4, bc, 1621; S ii–iii, 21
Courant ad imitationem courant 17, a 5, bc, 1621; S ii–iii, 71
Courant, a 4, bc, 1621; S ii–iii, 25
Courant, a 5, bc, 1621; S ii–iii, 26
Courant, a 5, bc, 1621; S ii–iii, 32
Courant dolorosa, a 4, bc, 1621; S ii–iii, 16
Galliard, a 4, bc, 1621; S ii–iii, 14
Galliard ad imitationem cantus VII, a 5, bc, 1621; S ii–iii, 33
Galliard, a 4, bc, 1621; S ii–iii, 14
Galliard battaglia, a 5, bc, 1621; S ii–iii, 27
Galliard, a 4, bc, 1621; S ii–iii, 34
Intrada, a 5, bc, 1621; S ii–iii, 30
Paduan, a 4, bc, 1621; S ii–iii, 1
Paduan, a 4, bc, 1621; S ii–iii, 3
Paduan, a 4, bc, 1621; S ii–iii, 5
Paduan dolorosa, a 4, bc, 1621; S ii–iii, 7
Paduan, a 4, bc, 1621; S ii–iii, 9
Paduan, a 4, bc, 1621; S ii–iii, 11
Paduana, a 4; S xvi
70 symphoniae, a 2, bc, 1644 (10 each in C, d, e, F, g, G, a); S xiii

CANONS

Tabulatura nova continens variationes aliquot psalmorum, fantasiarum, cantilenarum, passamezzo et canones (Hamburg, 1624) [1624a]

Ach mein herzliebes Jesulein, a 5; S vi/1, 123
Canon 'Ut, re, mi, fa, sol, la', a 3, 1624a; S vi/1, 114
Christum lieb haben ist viel besser, a 5; S vi/1, 124
[Das alte Jahr vergangen ist], a 4, 1624a; S vi/1, 113

Der Herr ist mein Hirt, a 4; S vi/1, 123
Dic nobis Maria, a 3 (anon.); S vi/1, 125
Eia wärn wir da, a 4; S vi/1, 124
Ein hörend Ohr und sehend Auge, a 4 (anon.); S vi/1, 125
[Es spricht der Unweisen Mund wohl], a 3, 1624a; S vi/1, 115
Gott der Vater wohn uns bei, a 4 (anon.); S vi/1, 124
[Gott der Vater wohn uns bei], a 4, 1624a; S vi/1, 112
Ich hielt mich nicht dafür, a 5; S vi/1, 124
In te Domine speravi, a 4, 1624a; S vi/1, 118
In te Domine speravi, a 3; S vi/1, 120
In te Domine speravi, a 3; S vi/1, 121
Laudate Dominum in chordis et organo, a 5 [painted on the case of the Moritzkirche organ, Halle]; S vi/1, 122
Lieblich und schöne sein ist nichts, a 4; S vi/1, 125
Magnificat (Tone 8), a 3, 1624a; S vi/1, 117
Magnificat (Tone 8), a 3, 1624a; S vi/1, 117
Meine Schafe hören meine Stimme und ich kenne sie, a 4; S vi/1, 123
O lux [beata Trinitas], a 3, 1624a; S vi/1, 119
[Vater unser im Himmelreich], a 3, 1624a; S vi/1, 119
[Vater unser im Himmelreich], a 3, 1624a; S vi/1, 116
[Vater unser im Himmelreich], a 4, 1624a; S vi/1, 112
[Wer Gott vertraut hab wohl gebaut], a 3, 1624a; S vi/1, 113

For lost works see *MGG*

BIBLIOGRAPHY

W. C. Printz: *Historische Beschreibung der edlen Sing- und Klingkunst* (Dresden, 1690)
J. Mattheson: *Grundlage einer Ehren-Pforte* (Hamburg, 1740); ed. M. Schneider (Berlin, 1910/R1969)
A. Göhler: *Verzeichnis der in den Frankfurter und Leipziger Messkatalogen der Jahre 1564 bis 1759 angezeigten Musikalien* (Leipzig, 1902/R1965)
K. Nef: *Geschichte der Sinfonie und Suite* (Leipzig, 1921/R1970)
C. Mahrenholz: *Samuel Scheidt: sein Leben und sein Werk* (Leipzig, 1924/R1968)
F. Blume: *Das monodische Prinzip in der protestantischen Kirchenmusik* (Leipzig, 1925/R1975)
——: *Die evangelische Kirchenmusik*, HMw, x (1931, rev. 2/1965 as *Geschichte der evangelischen Kirchenmusik*; Eng. trans., enlarged, 1974 as *Protestant Church Music: a History*)
R. Hünicken: *Samuel Scheidt: ein althallischer Musikus* (Halle, 1934)
A. A. Abert: *Die stilistischen Voraussetzungen der 'Cantiones Sacrae' von Heinrich Schütz* (Wolfenbüttel, 1935)
A. Adrio: *Die Anfänge des geistlichen Konzerts* (Berlin, 1935)
W. Serauky: *Samuel Scheidt in seinen Briefen* (Halle, 1937)
——: *Musikgeschichte der Stadt Halle*, ii/1 (Halle and Berlin, 1939/R1970)
C. Mahrenholz: 'Der 3. Band von Samuel Scheidts Tabulatura Nova 1624 und die Gottesdienstordnung der Stadt Halle', *Mf*, i (1948), 32
A. Adrio: 'Zu Samuel Scheidts Vokalmusik', *Musik und Kirche*, xxiv (1954), 145
M. Reimann: 'Samuel Scheidt in Stuttgart', *Mf*, vii (1954), 341
C. Mahrenholz: 'Samuel Scheidt und die Orgel', *Musik und Kirche*, xxv (1955), 38
W. Gurlitt: 'Canon sine pausis', *Mélanges d'histoire et d'esthétique musicales offerts à Paul-Marie Masson*, i (Paris, 1955), 117
F. Muller: 'La technique de la réalisation variée dans la Tablature de Goerlitz (1650) de Samuel Scheidt', *IMSCR, vii Cologne 1958*, 196
F. W. Riedel: *Quellenkundliche Beiträge zur Geschichte der Musik für Tasteninstrumente in der 2. Hälfte des 17. Jahrhunderts* (Kassel, 1960)
E. Gessner: *Samuel Scheidts geistliche Konzerte: ein Beitrag zur Geschichte der Gattung* (Berlin, 1961)
L. Schierning: *Die Überlieferung der deutschen Orgel- und Klaviermusik aus der ersten Hälfte des 17. Jahrhunderts* (Kassel, 1961)
W. Braun: 'Samuel Scheidts Bearbeitungen alter Motetten', *AMw*, xix–xx (1962–3), 56
O. Mischiati: 'L'intavolatura d'organo tedesca della Biblioteca Nazionale di Torino', *L'organo*, iv (1963), 1–154
F. W. Riedel: *Das Musikarchiv im Minoritenkonvent zu Wien* (Kassel, 1963)
H. Gruss: 'Über Notation und Tempo einiger Werke Samuel Scheidts und Michael Praetorius', *DJbM*, xi (1966), 72
W. Apel: *Geschichte der Orgel- und Klaviermusik bis 1700* (Kassel, 1967; Eng. trans., 1972)
W. Breig: 'Zu den handschriftlich überlieferten Liedvariationen von Samuel Scheidt', *Mf*, xxii (1969), 318
A. Curtis: *Sweelinck's Keyboard Music: a Study of English Elements in Seventeenth-century Dutch Composition* (Leiden and Oxford, 1969, 2/1972)
A. Adrio: 'Samuel Scheidts Cantiones Sacrae Octo Vocum von 1620: Beobachtungen und Anmerkungen', *Kerygma und Melos: Christhard Mahrenholz 70 Jahre* (Kassel, 1970), 210
F. Krummacher: *Die Choralbearbeitung in der protestantischen Figuralmusik zwischen Praetorius und Bach* (Kassel, 1978)

KERALA JOHNSON SNYDER

Scheiffelhut [Scheiffelhuet], **Jakob** [Jacob] (*b* Augsburg, baptized 19 May 1647; *d* Augsburg, 2 July 1709). German composer and instrumentalist. He received his musical education in Augsburg at the choir school attached to St Anna, the leading Protestant church there, and from a Stadtpfeifer called Franck. He was for many years a member of the Augsburg guild of Stadtpfeifer and played at weddings and other festivities. In 1673 he was appointed to play both wind and string instruments at the St Anna choir school, to give instrumental lessons and to compose occasional works. In 1694 he was appointed assistant to the director of music there, Georg Schmezer, after whose death in July 1697 he applied unsuccessfully to succeed him. Instead he became choirmaster of the Barfüsserkirche and remained there until his death. He was much admired as a teacher. His reputation as a composer rests mainly on his instrumental works. These comprise suites which reflect the pronounced French influence cultivated in music at Augsburg at the time, and they were performed far beyond Augsburg too. Scheiffelhut's most important religious music is contained in his volume of 1682, which consists entirely of settings of texts by Narziss Rauner.

WORKS

(all printed works published in Augsburg)

SACRED

Heiliger Jesus und Sonntags-Freud erster und Winter-Theil (30 pieces), 2vv, 2 vn, vle, bc (1682)
Heiliger Jesus und Sonntags-Freud . . . Sommer-Theil (28 pieces), ?5vv/ insts, bc (1684)
7 funeral motets (1678–93)

INSTRUMENTAL

Musikalischer Gemüths-Ergötzungen erstes Werck . . . [48] Sonaten, Allemanden, Couranten, Balletten, Sarabanden und Giquen, 2 vn, vle, bc (1681)
Lieblicher Frülings-Anfang oder Musicalischer Seyten-Klang . . . [56] Praeludien, Allemanden, Couranten, Ballo, Sarabanden, Arien und Giquen, 2 vn, va, vle, bc (1685); 1 suite ed. in Musikschätze der Vergangenheit (Berlin); 1 prelude ed. in *Beihefte der Internationalen Musikgesellschaft*, 1st ser., v (Leipzig, 1902)
Musicalisches Klee-Blat . . . [72] Preludien, Entréen, Rondeau, Bourréen, Arien, March, Canarien, Giquen . . . auf . . . frantzösische Art, 2 vn, vle (1707)

BIBLIOGRAPHY

EitnerQ
K. Nef: *Geschichte der Sinfonie und Suite* (Leipzig, 1921), 66
L. Gerheuser: 'Jacob Scheiffelhut und seine Instrumental-Musik', *Zeitschrift des historischen Vereins für Schwaben und Neuburg*, xlix (1933), 1–92
A. Layer: *Augsburger Musik im Barock* (Augsburg, 1968)

ADOLF LAYER

Schein, Johann Hermann (*b* Grünhain, nr. Annaberg [now Annaberg-Bucholz], 20 Jan 1586; *d* Leipzig, 19 Nov 1630). German composer and poet. He was an important predecessor of Bach, both as Leipzig Thomaskantor and as a gifted composer. He was one of the first composers to graft the style of the Italian madrigal, monody and concerto on to the traditional elements of Lutheran church music.

1. Life. 2. Vocal works. 3. Instrumental works.

1. LIFE. After the death of his father, a pastor and former schoolmaster, in 1593, Schein's family moved to Dresden, whence they had originally come. There, at the age of 13, he was taken into the Hofkapelle of the Elector of Saxony as a soprano. Already grounded in the principles of music, he received further instruction in both theoretical and practical music from the Kapellmeister, Rogier Michael, and became acquainted with an extensive repertory of both secular and sacred

1. Johann Hermann Schein: portrait, artist unknown, in the Musikinstrumenten-Museum, Karl-Marx-Universität, Leipzig

choral music in Latin, German and Italian. He distinguished himself not only in music but in his other studies as well, and following a brief matriculation at the University of Leipzig he was admitted on 18 May 1603 to Schulpforta, an electoral school near Naumburg that specialized in music and the humanities. He arrived there just after Erhard Bodenschatz had ceased to be its Kantor. Bodenschatz had compiled his famous motet collection *Florilegium Portense* (1618[1]–1621[2]; the first part appeared in a different form and with a different title, 1603[1]) for the edification of the students, who sang the motets before and after meals. Schein must have been thoroughly familiar with this repertory, though he was actually taught music by Bodenschatz's successors, first Bartholomäus Scheer and then, from 1606, Martin Roth. He left Schulpforta on 26 April 1607, returned to Dresden and in 1608 enrolled at the University of Leipzig, with an electoral scholarship, to study law and the liberal arts; he remained there for four years. The Thomaskantor at this time was Sethus Calvisius, who had preceded Bodenschatz as Kantor at Schulpforta. Schein's first publication, *Venus Kräntzlein*, appeared in 1609.

In 1613 Schein went to Weissenfels to become house music director and tutor to the children of Gottfried von Wolffersdorff, a friend from his Schulpforta days who soon recommended him for his first purely musical position, as Kapellmeister to Duke Johann Ernst the Younger at Weimar. He took up this post on 21 May 1615. On 12 February 1616 he married Sidonia Hösel, also a native of Grünhain who had moved to Dresden; she must have been a childhood sweetheart, for the two families had long been acquainted, and three of Schein's poems for the *Venus Kräntzlein* have acrostics spelling her name. Of the five children of this marriage only the elder son survived into adulthood. Schein's tenure at Weimar was happy but short. On 19 August 1616 he was called to Leipzig to audition for the position of Thomaskantor, which had been vacant since the death of Calvisius the previous November. He was accepted, began work in late September or early October and was immediately plunged into a dispute with the Konrektor, who was jealous of the Kantor's prestige and salary and especially of the extra income he received for wedding and funeral music. In addition to his responsibilities of directing the choral music in the Thomaskirche and the Nicolaikirche, Schein was required to teach 14 hours a week in the Thomasschule – ten hours of Latin grammar and syntax and four of singing. His most illustrious pupils were the poet Paul Fleming and the composer Heinrich Albert, whose continuo arias show the influence of his *Musica boscareccia*.

Schein's wife died in childbirth and was buried on 2 July 1624. He remarried on 22 February 1625; his new bride was Elizabeth von der Perre, daughter of a painter who had worked on the decoration of the organ in the Nicolaikirche. At least four of the five children of this marriage also died in infancy. In addition to the sorrows in his family life Schein suffered from poor health: he was afflicted with tuberculosis, gout, scurvy and kidney stones. Illness forced him to cancel the performance of a large work composed for the Reformation Jubilee of 1617 and postponed the publication of the first part of *Opella nova*; it also appears to have sapped his creative energy from about 1626. Two visits to the springs at Carlsbad were of no avail, and he died at the age of 44. Johann Höpner, pastor of the Nicolaikirche, preached at his funeral, and the sermon (reprinted in Spitta) includes an account of his life that provides valuable biographical information. His successor as Thomaskantor was Tobias Michael, son of Rogier Michael, his teacher at Dresden.

Printz singled out Schütz, Schein and Scheidt as the three best German composers of their time. They were all born between 1585 and 1587, worked in close geographical proximity and knew one another. The closest friendship was between Schein and Schütz; Schütz visited Schein on his deathbed and at his request composed a motet on the text *Das ist je gewisslich wahr* (1648). There are many parallels in the early careers of these two composers, born within four months and 80 km of each other. They both began as choirboys with a talent that attracted the attention of a nobleman who supported their education, both studied law and, as composers, both distinguished themselves through the expressive setting of Luther's biblical language for a few voices with instrumental accompaniment. Three obvious differences help to account for the greater importance that history has accorded Schütz: his periods of study in Italy, better health and much longer life.

2. VOCAL WORKS. Schein was first and foremost a composer for the voice, and he was equally devoted to sacred and secular music. In the foreword to the *Banchetto musicale* (1617) he announced his intention to publish music for worship and for social gatherings in regular alternation, and he maintained this practice throughout the productive years that followed. The stylistic categories of his music cut across the boundary between sacred and secular: in each case there is an early choral work without continuo (*Cymbalum Sionium* and *Venus Kräntzlein*), and several collections of concertos for a few voices and continuo (*Opella nova* and *Musica boscareccia*) framing a collection of continuo madrigals (*Israelis Brünlein* and *Diletti pastorali*). Although the sacred works are much the more intense, the musical techniques are similar.

(i) *Sacred music*. Schein sent his first collection of sacred music, *Cymbalum Sionium*, to the publisher in April 1615, just before he took up his duties as Kapellmeister at Weimar. The texts of these 30 motets are mostly biblical and are evenly divided between Latin and German. The music shows a greater stylistic variety than any of Schein's other collections, suggesting that he had written them over a period of perhaps ten years, as far back as his student days at Schulpforta. A number of them are closely related stylistically to motets by Bodenschatz, Calvisius, Handl and Lassus contained in the *Florilegium Portense*. Others, particularly those to German texts, are in a more progressive style, less contrapuntal and with closer attention to details of word-setting. The scoring ranges from five vocal parts (two sopranos, alto, tenor and bass) to polychoral works in eight and 12 parts.

The publication of the first part of *Opella nova* in 1618 marked a decisive turning-point in Schein's style. It was his first collection of sacred concertos with continuo, and it is one of the most important early examples of the genre in Germany. The contents are modelled to some extent on Viadana's *Cento concerti ecclesiastici* (1602), which had been printed in Germany in 1609 and was perhaps even more influential there than in Italy. Schein referred the continuo player to Viadana for instructions in realizing the bass. His concertos, however, depart significantly from Viadana's in that most of them are based on Lutheran chorales. In most cases the cantus firmus is fragmented and tossed back and forth between two sopranos over an instrumental bass; five concertos for major feasts have a tenor part with the chorale in complete phrases and longer notes. Although Schein's introduction states that the bass may be played either with a bass instrument (trombone, bassoon, viola grossa) or a harmony instrument (organ, harpsichord, theorbo), there are two separate bass parts, and it is quite clear that the concertos were conceived with realization of the bass in mind. In the preface to the second part of *Opella nova* (1626) he noted that where only one voice is singing it is best to have two realizing instruments, a plucked instrument in addition to the organ. The second part differs noticeably from the first in both content and scoring. Only a third of the pieces are based on chorales, in settings generally similar to those of the first book; the majority are now biblical texts set in a variety of ways, including solo voice with obbligato instruments and solo–tutti contrasts. The concertos are longer, more richly scored, and much more expressive of the text. The Annunciation dialogue *Maria, gegrüsset seist du, Holdselige* is among the finest examples of early Baroque biblical monody in Germany.

Schein had already risen to expressive heights in sacred music with the 1623 publication of *Fontana d'Israel* or *Israelis Brünlein*, a collection of pieces composed 'in a special, graceful Italian madrigal manner'. The texts are mostly from the Old Testament, and all but one are set for five voices (two sopranos, alto, tenor and bass) and continuo. The title-page states that they can be performed 'either alone with singers and

instruments or with organ or harpsichord'. The continuo is not really necessary: it is a *basso seguente* doubling the lowest sounding part, and there are seldom fewer than three voices singing. The 'madrigal manner' refers to the particular care with which each phrase of text is set, though this is done more with the musical-rhetorical figures of the *musica poetica* of German humanism than with the extreme word-painting of the Italian madrigal. Schein's madrigals are also less contrapuntal than classical Italian madrigals, and on numerous occasions he split the voices into two groups, with the alto participating in both. His use of unusual intervals and dissonant harmonic figures, especially the diminished 4th, is more frequent in this collection than any other. It ranks with Schütz's *Geistliche Chor-Musik* as one of the masterpieces of early Baroque choral music in Germany.

Schein's last collection of sacred music was the *Cantional*. The tradition of arranging Lutheran hymns in four-part harmony with the melody in the soprano had begun with Lucas Osiander in 1586 and had flourished in the meantime. Schein's collection superseded the one that Calvisius, his predecessor as Thomaskantor, brought out in 1597. It was the largest to date and included most of the hymns in use in Leipzig at the time, arranged according to liturgical usage. He was the first to introduce continuo figures into the bass part for the use of 'organists, instrumentalists and lutenists'. In assembling the *Cantional* he assumed various

different roles: editor, arranger, author or composer. For most of the hymns he wrote new harmonizations, sometimes making minor changes (often chromatic) in the melody, sometimes replacing an existing melody with a new one of his own. In addition there are 41 hymns with text, melody and setting by Schein himself. Most of them are either psalm paraphrases or funeral hymns, five (nos.245–9) for members of his own family. In 1645 Tobias Michael, Schein's successor as Thomaskantor, prepared a second edition of the *Cantional*, adding 22 more funeral pieces by Schein and four of his own. Although many of Schein's hymns were taken into later hymnals in the 17th and 18th centuries, only one is still in general use, *Mach's mit mir Gott nach deiner Güt*, based on an earlier melody and first published with Schein's text as a funeral piece in 1628. *See also* CHORALE SETTINGS, §I, 3.

(*ii*) *Secular music.* Schein wrote his own texts for all of his secular music. His first collection, *Venus Kräntzlein*, was published while he was still a student at Leipzig University and certainly reflects the informal music-making of the students. The 17 vocal pieces mainly follow in the tradition of the German folksong in both text and music. All but one are in five parts (two sopranos, alto, tenor and bass) and in a simple homophonic style with the melody in the top voice. They are short, syllabic settings in binary form with little text repetition, stylistically indebted to Hans Leo Hassler's

Lustgarten (1601) and with scarcely a hint of the individuality of Schein's later works.

Musica boscareccia or *Wald-Liederlein* appeared in three parts (in 1621, 1626 and 1628), which are all similar in style. These were by far the most popular of Schein's collections, appearing in numerous reprints up to 1643 and finally in the form of sacred contrafacta by Eckhardt Leichner under the title *Musica boscareccia sacra* (1644–51). The texts represent a great change from the *Venus Kräntzlein* in both content and style. The poems are populated by a cast of characters taken from the Italian pastoral tradition: the shepherds and shepherdesses Corydon and Phyllis, Mirtillo and Delia, and the deities Amor or Cupid, Phoebus, Pan and Venus. The literary style is dominated by rhetorical figures such as exclamation, repetition and metaphor, frequently combined with a corresponding musical figure. The settings are all for two sopranos and a bass that is both texted and figured. In his preface Schein outlined six ways of performing them, ranging from three singers without continuo through various vocal and instrumental combinations to one soprano accompanied only by continuo. They thus belong to two traditions, the late Italian villanella, as Schein acknowledged on the title-page, and the few-voiced concerto. The same scoring for two sopranos and bass is found frequently in the first part of *Opella nova*; the two soprano parts are treated in much the same way in both collections, but the bass part in *Musica boscareccia* is more vocal in character and more closely linked motivically with the upper voices, often in parallel 3rds or 10ths.

Schein's *Diletti pastorali* or *Hirten Lust* (1624) is the first published collection of German continuo madrigals, the secular counterpart to *Israelis Brünlein*, which had appeared the previous year. The poetry is similar to that of *Musica boscareccia* but with an even closer reliance on the Italian pastoral tradition, extending to a close imitation of actual metrical and rhyme schemes used by Tasso and Guarini. The music is naturally much lighter than that of *Israelis Brünlein* but is similar in texture; the madrigals are scored for five voices (two sopranos, alto, tenor and bass) and continuo, and, though Schein gave no instructions as to performance, the continuo is equally dispensable. The most important change compared with *Musica boscareccia* is the abandonment of strophic form; this enabled him to set each phrase of a text specifically, without having to worry about how the music would fit succeeding strophes. Poet and composer are more completely integrated here than in any of his other collections, and Rauhe has catalogued a large number of both rhetorical and musical figures that relate to one another in a variety of ways.

The *Studenten-Schmauss* (1626) interrupts the regular alternation of secular and sacred collections and represents a reversion to the style of the *Venus Kräntzlein*. It consists of five simple and delightful drinking-songs for five voices (two sopranos, alto, tenor and bass), with the vocal bass figured. In their earthiness they serve to underline the degree to which the sacred and the secular were intertwined in Schein's work.

(iii) Occasional music. Schein was commissioned to compose music for numerous occasions, mainly weddings and funerals. Following the custom of the time these pieces were published separately in a small edition, and a number of these prints, which extend from 1617 to 1630, still survive, although many catalogued by Prüfer and Eitner were lost in World War II. In many cases the piece was later published in one of the collections, perhaps in revised form: surviving concordances indicate that the funeral music was mainly taken into the *Cantional* and the wedding music into *Musica boscareccia* or *Diletti pastorali*. The wedding pieces could be either sacred or secular. Although most of them are secular trios similar to *Musica boscareccia*, there are large polychoral settings of psalm texts as well. Schein stated in the preface to *Israelis Brünlein* that many of its contents were originally occasional works; although none has survived in a separate print, many of the texts are suitable for a wedding or a funeral. The same can be said of *Cymbalum Sionium*. The earliest surviving funeral piece, *Ich will schweigen*, composed in 1617 for the funeral of Dorothea, Duchess of Saxony, anticipates the style of *Israelis Brünlein*. Schein also composed music for other occasions, such as the yearly inauguration of the new town council. One such piece, *Exaudiat te, Dominus*, was composed for the inauguration of the new Rektor of the university in 1624 and was taken into the second part of *Opella nova*.

3. INSTRUMENTAL WORKS. Instrumental music accounts for only a small portion of Schein's output. Nevertheless, his one instrumental collection, the *Banchetto musicale* (1617), marks a highpoint in the history of the variation suite. Though he did not call them suites, there are 20 numbered groups of 'pavanes, galliards, courantes and allemandes, which are arranged so that they correspond to one another in both mode and invention', to quote Schein's own description. There is also a tripla following each allemande, but it is clear from both the title and the layout of the page that Schein did not consider this a separate movement. Variation takes place on two levels in these suites. The tripla is a strict *proportio* to the allemande, a simple reworking of the same music in triple time. The other three movements also share musical motifs with the allemande, but here the relationship is much freer and there is no bar-for-bar correspondence. Although the immediate predecessor of Schein's collection was Paul Peuerl's *Newe Padouan, Intrada, Däntz unnd Galliarda* (1611), both are clearly rooted in the duple–triple dance pairs of the 16th century. Schein's suites are actually the combination of two such pairs, pavan–galliard and allemande–tripla, separated by a single courante. The allemande and tripla are close to actual dance music, four-part, homophonic and folklike in style; the pavan and galliard are in five parts, stylized and contrapuntal; the courante holds an intermediate position, in 6/4 but with little of the hemiola that was to characterize this dance later. The suites could be played 'on any instruments but preferably on viols' and were probably composed for dinner music at Weissenfels and Weimar. With its lack of a continuo part, the *Banchetto musicale* is the last of Schein's collections in the style of the *prima prattica*; the harmonic boldness of his later style is, however, already apparent, and he announced here that his next publication (*Opella nova*, i) would contain a 'basso continuo ad organum'.

Schein's only other instrumental pieces are appended to his earlier vocal collections. The three canzonas, especially the one in *Cymbalum Sionium*, are comparable with those of Giovanni Gabrieli and are fine early examples of German instrumental fugal art.

WORKS

Editions: *J. H. Schein: Neue Ausgabe sämtlicher Werke*, ed. A. Adrio (Kassel, 1963–) [A]

    J. H. Schein: Sämtliche Werke, i–vii, ed. A. Prüfer (Leipzig, 1901–23/*R*) [P]

Where there is no separate continuo part, but a figured vocal bass, the bc is given in square brackets.

SACRED VOCAL

Monophonic settings and works by other composers in Cantional are not listed.

Cymbalum Sionium sive Cantiones sacrae, 5–12vv (Leipzig, 1615) [1615]

Opella nova, geistlicher Concerten . . . auff italiänische Invention componirt, 3–5vv, bc (Leipzig, 1618, 2/1626) [1618]

Fontana d'Israel, Israelis Brünlein, auserlesener Krafft-Sprüchlin altes und newen Testaments . . . auf einer . . . Italian madrigalische Manier, 5, 6vv, bc (Leipzig, 1623, 2/1651) [1623]

Opella nova, ander Theil, geistlicher Concerten, 3–6vv/insts, bc (Leipzig, 1626) [1626]

Cantional oder Gesangbuch Augspurgischer Confession, 4–6vv (Leipzig, 1627, enlarged 2/1645) [1627 or 1645]

Ach Gott, dass du uns hast so mild, SATB [bc], 1627; A ii/1, 112
Ach Gott, tu dich erbarmen, SATB [bc], 1627; A ii/2, 101
Ach Gott und Herr, SATB [bc], 1627; A ii/2, 75
Ach Gott vom Himmel sieh darein, SATB [bc], 1627; A ii/1, 135
Ach Gott vom Himmel sieh darein, SS, bc, 1618; A iv, 98, P v, 82
Ach Herr, ach meiner schone, SSATB, bc, 1623; A i, 125
Ach Herr, erzeige Gnade mir (funeral motet), SSATB [bc], 1645; pubd separately (Leipzig, 1625); A ii/2, 121
Ach Herr, nach dir verlanget mich (Ps xxv; funeral motet), SATB [bc], 1627; pubd separately (Leipzig, 1623); A ii/1, 140
Ach Herr, wie ist der Feinde mein, SATB [bc], 1627; A ii/1, 132
Ach lob den Herrn, o Seele mein, SATB [bc], 1627; A ii/2, 28
Ach wie elend ist unser Zeit, SATB [bc], 1627; A ii/2, 63
A Domino factum est istud, SSAT, ATBB, 1615; P iv/1, 35
Allein Gott in der Höh sei Ehr, SATB [bc], 1627; A ii/1, 72
Allein Gott in der Höh sei Ehr, SST, 6v, 1626; P vi, 18
Allein nach dir, Herr Jesu Christ, SATB [bc], 1627; A ii/2, 65
Allein zu dir, Herr Jesu Christ, SATB [bc], 1627; A ii/1, 89
Alleluia: Ich danke den Herren, SSAATTBB, 1615; P iv/2, 71
Alleluia: Lobet ihr Knechte des Herrn, SSATB, 1615; P iv/1, 35
Alleluia: Wohl dem, der den Herren fürchtet, SSAT, ATTB, 1615; P iv/2, 81
Alleluia: Wohl dem, der den Herren fürchtet (wedding motet), SATB, SATB, bc (Leipzig, 1618)
Als anfangs im dem Paradeis (funeral motet), SATB [bc], 1645; pubd separately (Leipzig, 1628); A ii/2, 134
Also heilig ist der Tag, SATB [bc], 1627; A ii/1, 50
Also heilig ist der Tag, T, 4 insts, bc, 1626; P vi, 120
An Wasserflüssen Babylon, SATB [bc], 1627; A ii/2, 27
An Wasserflüssen Babylon, SS, bc, 1618; A iv, 120, P v, 100
A solis ortus cardine, SATB [bc], 1627; A ii/1, 11
Aufer immensum Deus, SATB [bc], 1627; A ii/2, 110
Auf meinen lieben Gott, SATB [bc], 1627; A ii/2, 61
Aus meines Herzen Grunde, SATB [bc], 1627; A ii/1, 98
Aus tiefer Not schrei ich zu dir, SATB [bc], 1627; A ii/2, 25
Aus tiefer Not schrei ich zu dir, SS, bc, 1618; A iv, 75, P v, 64
Beati omnes qui timent Dominum (wedding motet), SATB, SATB, bc (Leipzig, 1620)
Benedicam Domino, SSATTB, 1615; P iv/1, 114
Christ, der du bist der helle Tag, SATB [bc], 1627; A ii/1, 103
Christe, der du bist Tag und Licht, SATB [bc], 1627; A ii/1, 102
Christe, der du bist Tag und Licht, SS, bc, 1618; A iv, 16, P v, 15
Christe Jesu Gottes Sohn (funeral motet), SSATB [bc], 1645; pubd separately (Leipzig, 1629); A ii/2, 130
Christe, qui lux es et dies, SATB [bc], 1627; A ii/1, 101
Christe vernantis Iuvenum catervae, SATB [bc], 1627; A ii/2, 109
Christ fuhr gen Himmel, SATB [bc], 1627; A ii/1, 53
Christ ist erstanden, SATB [bc], 1627; A ii/1, 45
Christ lag in Todesbanden, SATB [bc], 1627; A ii/1, 41
Christ lag in Todesbanden, SSATB [bc], 1627; A ii/1, 42
Christ lag in Todesbanden, SST, bc, 1618; A iv, 28, P v, 24
Christum wir sollen loben schon, SATB [bc], 1627; A ii/1, 12
Christ unser Herr zum Jordan kam, SATB [bc], 1627; A ii/1, 88
Christ unser Herr zum Jordan kam, SS, 2 insts, bc, 1618; A iv, 65, P v, 56
Christus, der uns selig macht, SATB [bc], 1627; A ii/1, 35
Da Jakob vollendet hatte, SSATB, bc, 1623; A i, 62
Da Jesus an dem Kreuze stund, SATB [bc], 1627; A ii/1, 32
Da Jesus an dem Kreuze stund, SSATB [bc], 1627; A ii/1, 33
Da Jesus an dem Kreuze stund, SS, bc, 1618; A iv, 21, P v, 18
Dank sagen wir alle, SATB [bc], 1627; A ii/1, 29
Dankt dem Herrn heut und allezeit, SATB [bc], 1627; A ii/1, 109
Da pacem Domine (occasional work, Feb 1630), 10vv, bc (Leipzig, 1630)
Das alte Jahr vergangen ist, SATB [bc], 1627; A ii/1, 27

Das ist meine Freude (funeral motet), SSATB [bc] (Leipzig, 1628)
Das ist mir lieb (Ps cxvi), SSATB (Jena, 1623[14]); ed. in Cw, xxxvi (1935)
Dass noch viel Menschen werden, SATB [bc], 1627; A ii/2, 112
Dennoch bleibe ich stets an dir, SSATB, bc, 1623; A i, 27
Der Gerechte wird grünen, T, vn, bc, 1626; P vii, 100
Der Herr denket an uns, SSATB, bc, 1623; A i, 54
Der Herr, der ist mein Hirt (funeral motet), SATB [bc], 1627; pubd separately (Leipzig, 1623); A ii/1, 139
Der Herr der ist mit mir (funeral motet), SATB (Jena, 1617)
Der Tag der ist so freudenreich, SATB [bc]; A ii/1, 15
Der Tag vertreibt die finstre Nacht, SATB [bc], 1627; A ii/1, 100
Dich für dein Wohltat preise ich (funeral motet), SATB [bc], 1627; pubd separately (Leipzig, 1624); A ii/1, 141
Dicimus grates tibi, SATB [bc], 1627; A ii/1, 75
Die mit Tränen säen, SSATB, bc, 1623; ed. in A i, 15, and Cw, xiv (1931)
Die Nacht ist kommen, SATB [bc], 1627; A ii/1, 104
Dies sind die heilgen zehn Gebot, SATB [bc], 1627; A ii/1, 81
Dies sind die heilgen zehn Gebot, SS, 6v, 1618; A iv, 56, P v, 49
Die Teutsche Litaney, S, SATB [bc], 1627; A ii/1, 103
Die Zeit nunmehr vorhanden ist (funeral motet), SATB [bc], 1627; pubd separately, 5vv (Leipzig, 1622); A ii/2, 87
Drei schöne Ding sind, SSATB, bc, 1623; A i, 130
Drei Ständ hat Gott der Herr, SATB [bc], 1627; A ii/2, 115
Durch Adams Fall ist ganz verderbt, SATB [bc], 1627; A ii/1, 115
Durch Adams Fall ist ganz verderbt, SS, bc, 1618; A iv, 130, P v, 107
Du Sündrin, willt du mit?, SATB [bc], 1627; A ii/1, 128
Ehr sei Gott in der Höh allein, SSAT, SAATTB, 1615; P iv/2, 91
Ein feste Burg ist unser Gott, SATB [bc], 1627; A ii/1, 146
Ein feste Burg ist unser Gott, SS, bc, 1618; A iv, 107, P v, 89
Ein müd und mattes Hirschelein (funeral motet), SATB [bc], 1627; pubd separately, 5vv (Leipzig, 1623); A ii/1, 144
Ein neues Lied wir heben an, SATB [bc], 1627; A ii/2, 39
Erbarm dich mein, O Herre Gott, SATB [bc], 1627; A ii/2, 3
Erbarm dich mein, O Herre Gott, SS, bc, 1618; A iv, 80, P v, 67
Erhalt uns, Herr, bei deinem Wort, SATB [bc], 1627; A ii/2, 42
Erschienen ist der herrliche Tag, SS/TT, 6v, 1626; P vii, 115
Erschienen ist der herrlich Tag, SATB [bc], 1627; A ii/1, 49
Erstanden ist der heilge Christ, SATB [bc], 1627; A ii/1, 48
Es ist das Heil uns kommen her, SATB [bc], 1627; A ii/1, 116
Es ist das Heil uns kommen her, SS, bc, 1618; A iv, 134, P v, 110
Es kränkt ein Vatr- und Mutterherz, SSATB [bc], 1645; A ii/2, 142
Es spricht der Unweisen Mund wohl, SATB [bc], 1627; A ii/1, 137
Es spricht der Unweisen Mund wohl, SS, bc, 1618; A iv, 103, P v, 86
Es war ein gottfürchtiges . . . Jungfräulein, SATB [bc], 1627; A ii/2, 40
Es war einmal ein reicher Mann, SATB [bc], 1627; A ii/1, 125
Es wird schier der letzte Tag herkommen, SATB [bc], 1627; A ii/2, 98
Es wollt uns Gott genädig sein, SATB [bc], 1627; A ii/2, 6
Eva durch ihr begangen Schuld (funeral motet), SATB [bc], 1627; pubd separately, 5vv (Leipzig, 1621); A ii/2, 94
Exaudiat te, Dominus, SSATTB, 1615; P iv/1, 102
Exaudiat te, Dominus (2p. Tribuat tibi), ST, bc, 1626; pubd separately (Leipzig, 1624); P vii, 1
Ex legis observantia, SATB [bc], 1627; A ii/1, 31
Festum nunc celebre magnaque gaudia, SATB [bc], 1627; A ii/1, 54
Freue dich des Weibes deiner Jugend, SSATB, bc, 1623; A i, 8
Freut euch, ihr lieben Christen, SATB [bc], 1627; A ii/1, 21
Freut euch, ihr lieben Kinderlein, SATB [bc], 1627; A ii/2, 84
Frisch auf, mein Seel, verzage nicht, SATB [bc], 1627; A ii/2, 34
Fröhlich wollen wir Alleluja singen, SATB [bc], 1627; A ii/2, 18
Führwahr, er trug unsere Krankheit, T, vn, va da gamba, bc, 1626; P vi, 71
Fürwahr, es ist ein köstlich Ding, SATB [bc],1627; A ii/2, 11
Geborn ist uns der Herre Christ, SATB [bc], 1627; A ii/1, 20
Gehe hin, bis das End komme, SSATB, 1615; P iv/1, 45
Gehet hin in alle Welt, T, 2 vn, bc, 1626; P vii, 35
Geliebten Freund, was tut ihr so verzagen, SATB [bc], 1627; A ii/2, 95
Gelobet sei der Herr, SATB [bc], 1627; A ii/1, 73
Gelobet seist du, Jesu Christ, SATB [bc], 1627; A ii/1, 14
Gelobet seist du, Jesu Christ, SST, 6v, 1618; A iv, 7, P v, 5
Gelobet und gepreist, SATB [bc], 1627; A ii/2, 116
Gib unserm Fürsten und aller Obrigkeit, SATB [bc], 1627; A ii/2, 44
Gott der Vater wohn uns bei, SATB [bc], 1627; A ii/1, 67
Gott der Vater wohn uns bei, SSATB [bc], 1627; A ii/1, 68
Gott der Vater wohn uns bei, SS, bc, 1618; A iv, 50, P v, 44
Gottes Sohn ist kommen, SATB [bc], 1627; A ii/1, 127
Gott hat das Evangelium, SATB [bc], 1627; A ii/2, 100
Gott sei gelobet und gebenedeiet, SATB [bc], 1627; A ii/1, 94
Gott sei gelobet und gebenedeiet (2p.. Herr, durch deinen heiligen Leichnam), SST, bc, 1626; P vi, 104
Gott sei mir gnädig, SSATTB, 1615; P iv/1, 127
Gott sei mir gnädig und barmherzig, SATB [bc], 1627; A ii/2, 52
Gott Vater, der du deine Sonn, SATB [bc], 1627; A ii/1, 114
Haec est dies, SSATB, 1615; P iv/1, 31
Helft mir Gotts Güte preisen, SATB [bc], 1627; A ii/1, 25
Helft mir Gotts Güte preisen, SS, bc, 1626; P vi, 35

O quam metuendus est locus iste (2p. Orantibus in loco isto), SS/TT, bc, 1626; P vi, 153

O Welt, ich muss dich lassen, SATB [bc], 1627; A ii/2, 69

O wie wohl ist dem immer doch (funeral motet), SATB [bc], 1627; pubd separately, 5vv (Leipzig, 1626); A ii/2, 15

Puer natus in Bethlehem, SATB [bc], 1627; A ii/1, 16

Quem pastores laudavere, SATB [bc], 1627; A ii/1, 18

Quem quaeris, Magdalena?, 12vv, 1615; P iv/2, 117

Quem vidistis pastores, SSAT, ATBB, 1615; P iv/2, 1

Referre nil putatur, SATB [bc], 1627; A ii/2, 108

Rex Christe, factor omnium, SATB [bc], 1627; A ii/1, 35

Sankt Paulus die Korinthier, SATB [bc], 1627; A ii/2, 97

Sei fröhlich, meine Seele (funeral motet), SSATB [bc], 1627; A ii/2, 78

Sei gnädig, Herr, SSATB [bc], 1645; A ii/2, 140

Seligkeit, Fried, Freud und Ruh (funeral motet), SSATB [bc], 1627; pubd separately (Leipzig, 1623); A ii/2, 81

Selig sind, die da geistlich arm sind, SSATB, bc, 1626; P vii, 74

Sic Deus dilexit mundum, SSAT, ATBB, 1615; P iv/2, 28

Siehe, also wird gesegnet der Mann, SSATB, 1615; P iv/1, 51

Siehe an die Werk Gottes, SSATB, bc, 1623; A i, 83

Siehe, das ist mein Knecht, T, 2 insts, bc, 1626; P vi, 1

Siehe, nach Trost war mir sehr bange, SSATB, bc, 1623; A i, 118

Sie ist mir lieb, die werte Magd, SATB [bc], 1627; A ii/2, 48

Singen wir aus Herzensgrund, SATB [bc], 1627; A ii/1, 108

Singet fröhlich Gotte, SSATB, 1615; P iv/1, 61

So fahr ich hin mit Freuden (funeral motet), SSATB [bc], 1627; A ii/2, 80

So freue dich, Jüngling, in deiner Jugend, SSATTB, 1615; P iv/1, 96

Spiritus sancti gratia, SATB [bc], 1627; A ii/1, 64

Stellt ein eur Klag und Weinen (funeral motet), SSATB [bc], 1645; pubd separately (Leipzig, 1628); A ii/2, 126

Surge, illuminare Jerusalem, SSAT, ATBB, 1615; P iv/2, 21

Surrexit Christus hodie, SATB [bc], 1627; A ii/1, 47

Trau deinem lieben Gott (funeral motet), SATB [bc], 1627; pubd separately (Leipzig, 1626); A ii/2, 86

Unser Leben währet siebnzig Jahr, SSATB, bc, 1623; A i, 97

Uns ist ein Kind geboren, T, 3 insts, bc, 1626; P vi, 24

Vater unser, der du bist im Himmel, SATB [bc], 1627; A ii/1, 87

Vater unser, der du bist im Himmel, AT, 5vv, insts, bc, 1626; P vi, 138

Vater unser im Himmelreich, SATB [bc], 1627; A ii/1, 86

Vater unser im Himmelreich, SS, bc, 1618; A iv, 60, P v, 52

Veni Creator Spiritus, SATB [bc], 1627; A ii/1, 65

Veni Redemptor gentium, SATB [bc], 1627; A ii/1, 6

Venite, exultemus Domino, 12vv, 1615; P iv/2, 142

Verbum caro factum est, SSATTB, 1615; P iv/1, 70

Verleih uns Frieden gnädiglich, SATB [bc], 1627; A ii/2, 43

Verzage nicht, o frommer Christ, SATB [bc], 1627; A ii/2, 35

Vita sanctorum, SATB [bc], 1627; A ii/1, 44

Vom Himmel hoch da komm ich her, SATB [bc], 1627; A ii/1, 8

Vom Himmel hoch da komm ich her, SSATB [bc], 1627; A ii/1, 9

Vom Himmel hoch da komm ich her, SST, bc, 1618; A iv, 12, P v, 10

Von Gott will ich nicht lassen, SATB [bc], 1627; A ii/2, 47

Vos ad se pueri, SATB [bc], 1627; A ii/2, 107

Wär Gott nicht mit uns diese Zeit, SATB [bc], 1627; A ii/2, 21

Warum betrübst du dich, mein Herz, SATB [bc], 1627; A ii/2, 29

Warum betrübst du dich, mein Herz, SST, bc, 1626; P vii, 84

Warum tobn die Heiden doch, SATB [bc], 1627; A ii/1, 131

Was betrübst du dich, meine Seele, SSATB, bc, 1623; A i, 139

Was fürchst du, Feind Herodes, sehr, SATB [bc], 1627; A ii/1, 28

Was mein Gott will, das gscheh allzeit, SATB [bc], 1627; A ii/2, 55

Was weinet ihr?, SATB (Rostock, 1650)

Wem ein tugendsam Weib bescheret ist, SSATB, bc, 1623; A i, 145

Wende dich, Herr, und sei mir gnädig, SSATB, bc, 1623; ed. in A i, 32, and Cw, xii (1931)

Wenn dich Unglück tut greifen an, SATB [bc], 1627; A ii/2, 36

Wenn dich Unglück tut greifen an, SSATB [bc], 1627; A ii/2, 37

Wenn Gott der Herr Zion erlösen wird (funeral motet), SATB [bc], 1627; pubd separately (Leipzig, 1624); A ii/2, 23

Wenn mein Stündlein vorhanden ist, SATB [bc], 1627; A ii/2, 59

Wer unter dem Schirm, SSAATB, 1615; P iv/1, 150

Wie lieblich sind deine Wohnunge (funeral motet), SATB [bc] (Leipzig, 1628)

Wie lieblich sind die Wohnung dein, SATB [bc], 1627; A ii/2, 8

Wie schön leuchtet der Morgenstern, SATB [bc], 1627; A ii/1, 62

Wir Christenleut habn itzund Freud, SATB [bc], 1627; A ii/1, 24

Wir gläuben all an einen Gott, SATB [bc], 1627; A ii/1, 84

Wir gläuben all an einen Gott, SST, bc, 1626; P vii, 32

Wo Gott der Herr nicht bei uns hält, SATB [bc], 1627; A ii/2, 22

Wo Gott der Herr nicht bei uns hält, SS, bc, 1618; A iv, 112, P v, 93

Wo Gott zum Haus nicht gibt sein Gunst, SATB [bc], 1627; A ii/2, 24

Wo Gott zum Haus nicht gibt sein Gunst, SS, bc, 1618; A iv, 116, P v, 96

Wohl dem, der nicht im Rat der Gottlosen, SATB [bc], 1627; A ii/1, 129

Wohl mir, das ist mir lieb (funeral motet), SATB [bc], 1627; pubd separately, 5vv (Leipzig, 1622); A ii/2, 16

Wo ist dein Freund hingangen, SSA, ATB, 1615; P iv/1, 89

Zion spricht, der Herr hat mich verlassen, SSATB, bc, 1623; ed. in A i, 40, and Cw, xii (1931)

Zion spricht, der Herr hat mich verlassen [Lamentatio ecclesiae], 9/14vv, bc (Leipzig, 1629)

Zwing dich, o liebe Seele mein (funeral motet), SSATB [bc], 1645; pubd separately (Leipzig, 1629), A ii/2, 129

5 motets, 2, 3vv, bc, 1637[3], 1638[5], from 1618

18 chorales, 1641[4], from 1627

1 chorale, 5vv, bc, 1646[5], from 1627

For single prints, now lost, see Prüfer (1895) and *MGG*

SECULAR VOCAL
(*all texts by Schein*)

Venus Kräntzlein . . . oder Newe weltliche Lieder, 5vv, neben etzlichen Intraden, Gagliarden und Canzonen (Wittenberg, 1609) [1609]

Musica boscareccia, oder Wald-Liederlein auff italian-villanellische Invention. . .mit lebendiger Stimm. . .auch auff musicalischen Instrumenten zu spielen, 3vv (Leipzig, 1621, 6/1643) [1621]; Ander Theil (Leipzig, 1626, 6/1641) [1626a]; Dritter Theil (Leipzig, 1628, 5/1643) [1628]; also pubd with altered text as Musica boscareccia sacra, i–iii (Erfurt, 1644–51)

Diletti pastorali, Hirten Lust, 5vv, bc, auff Madrigal-Manier componirt (Leipzig, 1624) [1624]

Studenten-Schmauss a 5: einer löblichen Compagni de la Vinobiera (Leipzig, 1626) [1626b]

Ach, Amor, du Liebesgott (wedding song), SSB [bc] (Leipzig, 1625); P ii, 153

Ach Äsculapi wohl erfahrn (wedding song), SSB [bc] (Leipzig, 1624); P ii, 141

Ach edles Bild, SSATB, 1609; A vi, 16, P i, 18

Ach Filli, Schäfrin zart, SSB [bc], 1626a; P ii, 50

Ach weh, bin ich Amor?, SSB [bc], 1626a; P ii, 56

All wilden Tier im grünen Wald, SSATB, bc, 1624; A viii, 22, P iii, 25

Als Filli schön und fromm, SSATB, bc, 1624; A viii, 60, P iii, 68

Als Filli zart einst etwas dürstig ward, SSB [bc], 1626a; P ii, 60

Amor, das blinde Göttelein, SSB [bc], 1621; P ii, 24

Amor, das liebe Räuberlein, SSATB, bc, 1624; A viii, 91, P iii, 105

Amor heut triumphieret, SSB [bc], 1621; P ii, 35

Amor, wie ist dein Lieblichkeit, SSATB, 1609; A vi, 22, P i, 24

Aurora schön mit ihrem Haar, SSATB, bc, 1624; A viii, 81, P iii, 93

Concordia zu jeder Zeit (wedding song), SSB [bc], 1628; pubd separately (Leipzig, 1626); P ii, 91

Cupido blind, das Venuskind (wedding song), SSATB, bc, 1624; pubd separately (Leipzig, 1622); A viii, 38, P iii, 42

Cupido klein, das Göttlein blind, SSB [bc], 1626a; P ii, 68

Cupido von eim Bienenstich (wedding song), SSB [bc] (Leipzig, 1623); P ii, 137

Der edle Schäfer Coridon, SSB [bc], 1621; P ii, 31

Der Hirte Coridon, SSB [bc], 1621; P ii, 37

Der Hirte Coridon (wedding song), SSATTB, bc (inc.) (Leipzig, 1618); P iii, 131

Der kühle Maien, SSB [bc], 1628; P ii, 114

Die Myrtensträuch und Wälder grün, SSB [bc], 1626a; P ii, 64

Die Vöglein singen, SSATB, bc, 1624; A viii, 32, P iii, 36

Einsmals ich ein Jungfräulein, SSATB, 1609; A vi, 18, P i, 20

Einsmals von einem Bienelein, SSB [bc], 1628; P ii, 118

Einsmals wett Coridon, SSB [bc], 1628; P ii, 104

Filli, deine lieb Äuglein klar, SSB [bc], 1621; P ii, 12

Filli, die schöne Schäferin, SSB [bc], 1621; P ii, 29

Frau Nachtigall mit süssem Schall, SSB [bc], 1621; P ii, 10

Frau Venus in ihr Gärtelein (wedding song), SSB [bc] (Leipzig, 1625); P ii, 149

Frau Venus und ihr blinder Sohn, SSB [bc], 1626a; P ii, 73

Freu dich, mein lieber Coridon (wedding song), SSB [bc] (Leipzig, 1623); P ii, 22

Freut euch, ihr Hirten mein, SSB [bc], 1621; P ii, 22

Frischauf, du edle Musikkunst, SSATB, 1609; A vi, 2, P i, 2

Frischauf, ihr Klosterbrüder mein, SSATB, 1626b; A vi, 58, P iii, 142

Fürwahr, Cupido Klein (wedding song), SSB [bc] (Leipzig, 1625); P ii, 157

Gleichwie ein armes Hirschelein, SSB [bc], 1621; P ii, 42

Gleichwie ein kleines Vöglein, SSATB, 1609; A vi, 13, P i, 14

Gott Febo mit den Strahlen sein (wedding song), SSB [bc] (Leipzig, 1625); P ii, 145

Gott grüss euch, Schäfr und Schäferin, SSB [bc], 1626a; P ii, 54

Herbei, wer lustig sein will hier, SSATB, 1609; A vi, 21, P i, 23

Heulen und schmerzlichs Weinen, SSATB, 1609; A vi, 10, P i, 10

Holla, gut Gsell, SSATB [bc], 1626b; A vi, 67, P iii, 148

Hört Wunder, hört, SSB [bc], 1621; P ii, 96

Ich bin ein Bergmann wohlgemut, SSB [bc], 1626a; P ii, 77

Ich will nun fröhlich singen, SSAA, TTBB, 1609; A vi, 28, P i, 30

Ihr Brüder, lieben Brüder mein, SSATB [bc], 1626b; A vi, 70, P iii, 150

In Filli schönen Äugelein (wedding song), SSATB, bc, 1624; pubd separately (Leipzig, 1622); A viii, 16, P iii, 17
In grosser Traurigkeit, SSB [bc], 1621; P ii, 16
Itzund ich mich vergleiche, SSATB, 1609; A vi, 26, P i, 28
Juch holla, freut euch mit mir (wedding song), SSB [bc], 1626a; pubd separately (Leipzig, 1625); P ii, 58
Kickehihi, kakakanei, SSB [bc], 1628; P ii, 121
Mein Schifflein lief im wilden Meer, SSATB, bc, 1624; A viii, 52, P iii, 59
Mirtillo gut in einem Wald (wedding song), SSB [bc] (Leipzig, 1619); P ii, 125
Mirtillo hat ein Schäfelein (wedding song), T, bc (Leipzig, 1622); P ii, 129
Mirtillo hat ein Schäfelein, SSATB, bc, 1624; A viii, 66, P iii, 76
Mirtillo mein, dein Delia (wedding song), SSB [bc], 1621; pubd separately (Leipzig, 1620); P ii, 27
Mit Freuden, mit Schertzen (wedding song), SSB [bc], 1628; pubd separately (Leipzig, 1627); P ii, 102
Mit Lust zu tragen mir gefällt, SSATB, 1609; A vi, 6, P i, 6
Nun hat sich's Blättlein umgewendt, SSB [bc], 1626a; P ii, 66
O Amarilli, schönste Zier, SSATB, bc, 1624; A viii, 3, P iii, 1
O Amarilli zart (wedding song), SSATB, bc, 1624; pubd separately (Leipzig, 1623); A viii, 72, P iii, 83
O Berg und Tal, ihr Felsen all, SSB [bc], 1626a; P ii, 71
O brennende Äugelein, SSB [bc], 1628; P ii, 84
O Coridon, heut blüht dein Glück, SSB [bc], 1621; P ii, 33
O Coridon, lass dein Schalmei, SSB [bc], 1621; P ii, 19
O Filli, schönste Zier, SSB [bc], 1628; P ii, 111
O Filli, schön und subtil, SSB [bc], 1621; P ii, 5
O Filli, wärt Ihr mein, SSB [bc], 1628; P ii, 109
O Fortun, SSAAT, 1609; A vi, 8, P i, 8
O Kanarivögelein, SSB [bc], 1628; P ii, 116
O Luft, du edles Element, SSB [bc], 1628; P ii, 82
O Schäferin, o Filli mein, SSB [bc], 1626a; P ii, 48
O Scheiden, o bitter Scheiden, SSB [bc], 1621; P ii, 39
O schönste Filli mein, SSB [bc], 1626a; P ii, 75
O seidene Härelein, SSB [bc], 1628; P ii, 86
O Sternenäugelein, SSB [bc], 1628; P ii, 88
O Tirsi, Tirsi, freu dich sehr (wedding song), SSB [bc], 1628; pubd separately (Leipzig, 1627); P ii, 93
O Venus und Cupido blind, SSATB, bc, 1624; A viii, 8, P iii, 6
Post Martinum bonum vinum [Lasst uns freuen], SATTB, 1609; A vi, 54, P i, 57
Relation von Filli und von Coridon, SSB [bc], 1626a; P ii, 52
Ringstum mich schwebet Traurigkeit, SSATB, 1609; A vi, 12, P i, 12
Sieh da, mein lieber Coridon, SSB [bc], 1621; P ii, 14
Sieh da, sieh da, ihr lieben Herrn, SSATB [bc], 1626b; A vi, 64, P iii, 146
So da, mein liebes Brüderlein, SSATB [bc], 1626b; A vi, 61, P iii, 144
Soll ann so mein Herz, SSATB, 1609; A vi, 24, P i, 26
Soll es denn nun nicht anders sein, SSATB, 1609; A vi, 20, P i, 22
Sollt ich mein Freud verschweigen, SSATB, 1609; A vi, 4, P i, 4
Tret't heran, ihr Hirten all, SSB [bc], 1628; P ii, 107
Unlängst dem blinden Göttelein, SSATB, bc, 1624; A viii, 99, P iii, 115
Unverhofft kommet oft, SSB [bc], 1628; P ii, 98
Vergiss aller der Traurigkeit, SSAAT, 1609; A vi, 14, P i, 16
Viel schöner Blümelein (wedding song), SSB [bc], 1626a; pubd separately (Leipzig, 1623); P ii, 62
Wenn Filli ihre Liebesstrahl, SSATB, bc, 1624; A viii, 27, P iii, 30
Wenn ich durch Ach mein Liebesqual, SSB [bc], 1628; P ii, 100
Wie kömmt's, o zarte Filli mein, SSATB, bc, 1624; A viii, 45, P iii, 50
Wohlauf, du edle Lyr, SSB [bc], 1626a; P ii, 46

For single prints, now lost, see Prüfer (1895) and *MGG*

INSTRUMENTAL

All suites in four movements: Padouana, Gagliarda, Courente, Allemande–Tripla

Venus Kräntzlein . . . oder Newe weltliche Lieder [5vv] neben etzlichen Intraden, Gagliarden und Canzonen (Wittenberg, 1609) [1609]
Cymbalum Sionium sive Cantiones sacrae, 5–12vv (Leipzig, 1615) [1615]
Banchetto musicale newer . . . Padouanen, Gagliarden, Courenten und Allemanden a 5, auff allerley Instrumenten (Leipzig, 1617) [1617]

Canzon: Corollarium, a 5, a, 1615; P i, 60
Canzon, a 5, a, 1609; A vi, 39, P i, 41
Canzon, a 6, a, 1609; A vi, 46, P i, 46
Galliarda, a 5, G, 1609; A vi, 37, P i, 39
Galliarda, a 5, d, 1609; A vi, 38, P i, 40
Intrada, a 5, d, 1609; A vi, 32, P i, 33
Intrada, a 5, G, 1609; A vi, 33, P i, 34
Intrada, a 5, a, 1609; A vi, 34, P i, 35
Intrada, a 5, G, 1609; A vi, 35, P i, 37
Intrada, 'Zinck, Viglin, Flödt, Basso', d, 1617; A ix, 145, P i, 198
Padouana, 4 crumhorns, d, 1617; A ix, 147, P i, 201

[Suite] no.1, a 4, 5, d, 1617; A ix, 3, P i, 67
[Suite] no.2, a 4, 5, d, 1617; A ix, 10, P i, 74
[Suite] no.3, a 4, 5, e, 1617; A ix, 18, P i, 81
[Suite] no.4, a 4, 5, G, 1617; ed. in A ix, 25, P i, 87, and Mw, xxvi (1964), 108
[Suite] no.5, a 4, 5, G, 1617; A ix, 33, P i, 94
[Suite] no.6, a 4, 5, a, 1617; A ix, 41, P i, 102
[Suite] no.7, a 4, 5, a, 1617; A ix, 49, P i, 109
[Suite] no.8, a 4, 5, C, 1617; A ix, 56, P i, 115
[Suite] no.9, a 4, 5, d, 1617; A ix, 63, P i, 121
[Suite] no.10, a 4, 5, d, 1617; A ix, 70, P i, 128
[Suite] no.11, a 4, 5, d, 1617; A ix, 77, P i, 135
[Suite] no.12, a 4, 5, d, 1617; A ix, 84, P i, 140
[Suite] no.13, a 4, 5, g, 1617; A ix, 91, P i, 146
[Suite] no.14, a 4, 5, G, 1617; A ix, 98, P i, 153
[Suite] no.15, a 4, 5, G, 1617; A ix, 104, P i, 159
[Suite] no.16, a 4, 5, a, 1617; A ix, 110, P i, 165
[Suite] no.17, a 4, 5, a, 1617; A ix, 117, P i, 172
[Suite] no.18, a 4, 5, C, 1617; A ix, 125, P i, 179
[Suite] no.19, a 4, 5, d, 1617; A ix, 132, P i, 185
[Suite] no.20, a 4, 5, e, 1617; A ix, 139, P i, 192
4 works in Allegrezza musicale, ed. D. Oberndörffer (Frankfurt am Main, 1620)
1 pavan in Amoenitatum musicalium hortulus (Leipzig, 1622)

BIBLIOGRAPHY

EitnerQ
P. Spitta: 'Leichensermone auf Musiker des XVI. und XVII. Jahrhunderts', *MMg*, iii (1871), 24 [incl. repr. of sermon by J. Höpner preached at Schein's funeral (1630)]
A. Prüfer: *Johann Hermann Schein* (Leipzig, 1895)
——: 'Zur Familiengeschichte des Leipziger Thomas-Kantors Johann Hermann Schein', *MMg*, xxx (1898), 141
——: *Johann Hermann Schein und das weltliche deutsche Lied des 17. Jahrhunderts* (Leipzig, 1908)
R. Wustmann: *Musikgeschichte Leipzigs*, i: *bis zur Mitte des 17. Jahrhunderts* (Leipzig, 1909)
F. Blume: *Das monodische Prinzip in der protestantischen Kirchenmusik* (Leipzig, 1925)
——: *Die evangelische Kirchenmusik*, HMw, x (1931, rev. 2/1965 as *Geschichte der evangelischen Kirchenmusik*; Eng. trans., enlarged, 1974 as *Protestant Church Music: a History*)
A. Adrio: *Die Anfänge des geistlichen Konzerts* (Berlin, 1935)
W. Brauer: 'Jakob Regnart, J. H. Schein und die Anfänge der deutschen Barocklyrik', *Deutsche Vierteljahrsschrift für Literaturwissenschaft und Geistesgeschichte*, xvii (1939), 371–404
I. Hueck: *Die künstlerische Entwicklung Johann Hermann Scheins, dargestellt an seinen geistlichen Werken* (diss., U. of Freiburg, 1945)
H. F. Redlich: 'Schein and the German Madrigal', *The Listener*, liii (1955), 681
H. Rauhe: *Dichtung und Musik im weltlichen Vokalwerk Johann Hermann Scheins* (diss., U. of Hamburg, 1959)
W. Reckziegel: *Das Cantional von Johann Hermann Schein: seine geschichtlichen Grundlagen* (Berlin, 1963)
R. H. Thomas: *Poetry and Song in the German Baroque: a Study of the Continuo Lied* (Oxford, 1963)
F. E. Peterson: *Johann Hermann Schein's Cymbalum Sionium: a Liturgico-musical Study* (diss., Harvard U., 1966)
A. Adrio: 'Die Drucker und Verleger der musikalischen Werke Johann Hermann Scheins', *Musik und Verlag: Karl Vötterle zum 65. Geburtstag* (Kassel, 1968), 128
E.-O. Göring: 'Schein, ein hoher Mann, Schein, ein hoher Nam'', *Credo musicale: Festgabe . . . zum 80. Geburtstag . . . Rudolf Mauersberger* (Kassel, 1969), 33
S. Sorensen: 'Johann Hermann Scheins *Opella nova*', *Renaissancemuziek 1400–1600: donum natalicium René Bernard Lenaerts* (Louvain, 1969), 275
H. Glahn: 'J. H. Scheins Kantional "in die Tabulatur transponiert von J. Vockerodt, Mühlhausen 1649" ', *Festskrift Jens Peter Larsen* (Copenhagen, 1972), 47
D. L. Paisey: 'Some Occasional Aspects of Johann Hermann Schein', *British Library Journal*, i (1975), 171
F. Krummacher: *Die Choralbearbeitung in der protestantischen Figuralmusik zwischen Praetorius und Bach* (Kassel, 1978)

KERALA JOHNSON SNYDER

Scheinpflug, Paul (*b* Loschwitz, nr. Dresden, 10 Sept 1875; *d* Memel [now Klaipėda, Lithuania], 11 March 1937). German conductor and composer. He studied music at the Dresden Conservatory. For two years (1897–8) he was music master and violinist in the home of a Russian noble in Kiev, and from 1898 he served as leader and choral director of the Bremen SO. From

1909 to 1914 he was director of the Musikverein orchestra in Königsberg and concurrently conductor of the choruses at the music academy. He was city music director in Duisburg in the 1920s and then served as conductor of the Dresden PO (1929–33). In his later years he enjoyed a good deal of popularity as a guest conductor with many orchestras. Scheinpflug's compositions stand in the mainstream of German music; Brahms was, apparently, often his model, as is particularly evident in the first movement of the Violin Sonata op.13.

WORKS
(selective list)

Opera: Das Hofkonzert, op.24, perf. 1922
Orch: Frühling, op.8 (1906); Lustspiel-Ouvertüre, op.15 (1909); Bundes-Ouvertüre, op.20 (1918); Serenade, op.26, vc, eng hn/va, harp, str (1937); Ein Sommertagebuch, op.27 (1938); Nokturno, op.28 (1938); other works, incl. film scores
Chamber: Pf Qt, E, op.4 (1903); Sonata, F, op.13, vn, pf (1908); Str Qt, c, op.16 (1912); Str Trio, G, op.19 (1912); Prelude and Fugue, op.21, pf/chamber orch (c1918); Notturno, D, vn, pf (n.d.)
Vocal: Rosa Zenock, op.23, reader, S, A, female chorus, orch (1918); over 30 lieder, male choruses

Principal publisher: Heinrichshofen

BIBLIOGRAPHY

F. Dubitzky: 'Paul Scheinpflug', Monographien moderner Musiker, ii (Leipzig, 1907), 231
E. Kroll: 'Scheinpflug, Paul', MGG

WILLIAM D. GUDGER

Scheitholt [Scheitholz] (Ger.: 'log-wood'; Dutch *noordse balk*; Fr. *bûche, bûche de Meuse*; Flemish *vlier*; Swiss-Ger. *Hexenscheit*). A strummed zither of Germany and the Alpine areas. *See* ZITHER.

Schelb, Josef (*b* Bad Krozingen, nr. Freiburg, 14 March 1894). German composer. He studied theory in Basle under Hans Huber, harmony, counterpoint and composition under Barblan and the piano under Stavenhagen in Geneva. As accompanist to the violinist Juan Manén he made concert tours of Europe and South America. In 1924 he was appointed to teach the piano at the Karlsruhe Conservatory (later Musikhochschule), where he also taught orchestration and composition, eventually becoming professor (1932–59). He retired to Baden-Baden. In his music he was strongly influenced by Reger and by French impressionism, though he also used 12-note techniques.

WORKS
(selective list)

Stage: Notturno (ballet, 1, A. von Grolmann), Mannheim, 1941; Charlotte Corday (opera, prologue, 3, epilogue, F. Baser), unperf.; Die schöne Lau (ballet, 3 scenes), Saarbrücken, 1952
Orch: Chamber Sym., 1929; 7 syms., 1930–62; 3 concs. for orch, 1941–5; Sym. Vorspiel, 1959; many concs.
Chamber: Sextet, fl, cl, str qt; Wind Qnt; Cl Qnt; 3 str qts; Ob Qt; Qt, cl, va, vc, pf; Hn Qt; 2 str trios; 2 pf trios; Trio, fl, va, harp; Trio, fl, vn, pf; Trio, cl, vn, pf; Trio, fl, vc, pf; many duo sonatas; pf solos and duets
Vocal: 3 Sonette (Michelangelo), male chorus, pf (1920); De Sancta Trinitate, solo vv, chorus, chamber orch (1930); Kindheit (Rilke), S, str qt, 1949; many solo lieder, motets, secular choruses

Principal publisher: Müller

BIBLIOGRAPHY

H. Schorn: 'Komponist Josef Schelb', Ekkhart, xvi (Karlsruhe, 1935), 102
F. Baser: 'Der badische Komponist Josef Schelb 60 Jahre', Badische Heimat, xxxiv (Freiburg, 1954), 16
W. Zentner: 'Ein Musiker vom Oberrhein', ZfM, cxv (1954), 216
——: 'Josef Schelb 65 Jahre', Baden-Württemberg (Stuttgart, 1959), no.2, p.33
F. Baser: Grosse Musiker in Baden-Baden (Tutzing, 1973)

FRIEDRICH BASER

Schelble, Johann Nepomuk (*b* Hüfingen, 16 May 1789; *d* Hüfingen, 6 Aug 1837). German singer, conductor and teacher. He was a choirboy at Obermarchtal, moving in 1803 to the Donaueschingen Gymnasium. His singing career from 1808 to 1814 centred on the Stuttgart court and opera house, where he sang tenor and baritone roles. From 1812 he also taught at the Stuttgart Royal Musical Institute, and in 1814 went to tour in German opera houses and in Vienna. The Frankfurt am Main theatre engaged him from 1817 to 1819; he left because of ill-health. In 1818 he founded the Frankfurt Cäcilienverein. Built on the lines of the Berlin Singakademie, it performed numerous choral works by Mozart, Handel, Palestrina, Scarlatti and others, and was highly regarded by critics. Schelble participated in the Bach revival, conducting the St Matthew Passion on 2 May 1829: unlike Mendelssohn, Schelble rewrote the recitatives in more 'polished' style. He conducted the Cäcilienverein up to the year of his death. Schelble developed a system of teaching young musicians rudiments and sight-singing that was later adapted by Lanz, Widmann and F. W. Rühle. His compositions chiefly comprise choral and vocal works, some chamber music and various teaching exercises.

BIBLIOGRAPHY

K. Lang: Die Gehörsentwicklung-Methode von Schelble (Brunswick, 1873)
O. Bormann: J. N. Schelble 1789–1837 (diss., U. of Frankfurt am Main, 1926)
R. Sietz: Aus F. Hillers Briefwechsel (Cologne, 1958)
G. Feder: 'J. N. Schelbles Bearbeitung der Matthäuspassion J. S. Bachs', Mf, xii (1959), 201

DAVID CHARLTON

Schellbecken (Ger.). CYMBALS.

Schelle, Johann (*b* Geising, Thuringia, baptized 6 Sept 1648; *d* Leipzig, 10 March 1701). German composer. As Kantor of the Thomaskirche, Leipzig, he held one of the leading musical posts in Germany, and he was an important composer of sacred cantatas to German texts.

1. LIFE. Schelle was born into a respected musical family, his father being Kantor and schoolmaster at Geising. In 1655 he entered the choir of the Dresden electoral chapel under Schütz; two years later he was sent on to the ducal court at Wolfenbüttel, where Schütz was Kapellmeister *in absentia* at the time. He acquitted himself well there and, when his voice broke, continued his education in Leipzig, entering the Thomasschule under Knüpfer in 1665 and later attending the university. In October 1670 he took up the post of Kantor at nearby Eilenburg, having been recommended by Knüpfer as an accomplished performer, especially on the keyboard, with experience in teaching and composition. Schelle remained on friendly terms with Knüpfer (who was godfather to one of his children) and eventually succeeded him as Kantor of the Thomaskirche, Leipzig, on 31 January 1677. The post carried with it the office of *Director chori musici* for the city, responsibility for the music at the Nicolaikirche and also, after 1679, at the Paulinerkirche (on academic occasions), as well as teaching duties at the Thomasschule in music, Latin and catechism.

Schelle's appointment was made against the wishes of the mayor, L. von Adlershelm, who had supported Georg Bleyer, one of the 11 rival candidates, and who remained antagonistic to Schelle and to the changes he introduced into the musical content of services at the

Thomaskirche. Matters came to a head when Schelle replaced the Latin compositions written by Italian masters, which were customarily performed after the morning Gospel, by music to German texts; the latter would often take the form of a cantata based on the Gospel reading, with the insertion of appropriate lied verses or other rhymed texts. Adlershelm instructed the Kantor to restore the Latin settings for the Christmas season of 1683, but his wish was overruled by the city council, who decided in favour of Schelle. The continuation of this practice being thus made possible, it became one of Schelle's most important achievements: he introduced into the Protestant liturgy in Leipzig not only the Gospel cantata to German texts but later the chorale cantata too. The chorale cantata was similarly intended to expound the teaching of the Gospel and was performed immediately after it; the sermon then took place, after which the same chorale would be sung by the whole congregation. This procedure was established through the joint efforts of Schelle and the pastor of the Thomaskirche, J. B. Carpsow. Schelle's setting of *Vom Himmel kam der Engel Schar* was probably intended for this kind of performance, since the chorale is kept intact and would have been easily recognizable by the congregation. He seems to have played little part in the fierce theological controversies that took place at Leipzig in the 1680s between the orthodox Lutherans, led by Carpsow, and the Pietists, although he did reveal his sympathies with the latter by writing some of the melodies for *Der andächtige Student*, a collection of devotional hymns and prayers compiled by JOACHIM FELLER. At the time of his death, the morale of the Thomasschule was in decline, undermined by a spirit of discontent and lack of discipline; while he was by no means solely responsible for this state of affairs, he did not leave an easy task for his successor and cousin, Johann Kuhnau. The university Rector read his funeral oration, and Kuhnau composed an obituary in his memory; both documents survive and contain valuable biographical information (see Richter 1902).

2. WORKS. Schelle's compositions consist almost entirely of sacred works, most of them to German texts. Of the 167 titles listed by Schering (in DDT), relatively few survive and only a handful were published in his lifetime. The importance of his work lies in his development of the sacred cantata as he took it over from Knüpfer, and particularly in the establishment of the Gospel cantata as an independent form and in the consolidation of the types of chorale cantata (see §1). The basic, commonest setting was for five-part choir (SSATB) accompanied by two violins, two violas and bassoon with continuo, but there are many examples of more elaborate scorings with as many as five vocal and instrumental groups, representing the magnificent fullness of sound that was one of the features of the Leipzig festival cantata. Schelle adopted Knüpfer's formal plan – introductory sinfonia, opening chorus and alternation of choral, solo and instrumental episodes – but included more often the repeat of the first chorus at the close; the central episodes sometimes consist of lied verses sung by each voice in turn and described as 'arias'. Although Schelle was capable of writing deeply sensitive, poetically inspired melodies, the closed form of solo aria does not appear in these works, and the use of the solo voice is limited either to these lied settings or to passages in freely constructed arioso style. In affec-

tive and powerful text interpretation he went further than his predecessor; his themes are also broader and flow with a livelier rhythm, while the chorale melody is treated not so much as a basis for counterpoint as in its entirety, stressing its function as a congregational hymn.

While the chorale cantatas are among Schelle's most brilliant and impressive works, it is the settings of Bible texts – mainly from the psalms and Gospels – that represent his most individual and profound achievements. Very few of the Gospel cantatas are extant, and whether he ever completed an entire cycle of such works is not known; of the psalm settings, the most elaborate is the 26-part *Lobe den Herrn*, presumably written for some important event in Leipzig. Set for three instrumental and two vocal groups (marked 'concertino' and 'da cappella'), the brilliance of sound is heightened by the use of a clarino quartet and two cornettinos. The introductory sonata is quite long and is constructed on the pattern of a French overture; then follows a continuously unfolding succession of contrasts: in tempos, dynamics, rhythms, textures and scoring. The choral writing reveals both contrapuntal mastery and a delight in massed, homophonic effects, often on a very simple harmonic basis. The impressively developed climaxes and the broad structure of the final fugue (a particular feature of Schelle) are effectively balanced by delicate and pictorial writing in the solo episodes. The structure of chorale cantatas such as *Vom Himmel kam der Engel Schar*, with its individual treatment of each verse, distinctive instrumental style, preservation of the chorale as a whole, and solo decoration of the melody, may well have influenced Bach in his later treatment of the form. Schelle also shared with Bach a deep awareness of the significance of the Bible text and a conscious desire to give it the fullest possible expression in his music.

WORKS
(all MSS in D-Dlb formerly in GMl)

SACRED VOCAL

Ach mein herzliebes Jesulein, 2vv, bc, *D-Dlb*; ed. in DDT, lviii–lix (1918/*R*)

Actus musicus auf Weyh-Nachten, 6vv, ripieno 5vv, 2 vn, 2 va, fl, schreier, cornett, trbn, bn, bc, *LUC*

Alleluja man singet mit Freuden, 5vv, 2 vn, 2 va, 2 cornetts, bn, bc, *Dlb*

Also hat Gott die Welt geliebet, 5vv, 2 vn, 2 va, 2 clarinos, bn, timp, bc, *B*

Aus der Tiefen rufe ich, Herr, zu dir, 4vv, 2 vn, 2 va, bn, bc, *B*

Barmherzig und gnädig ist der Herr, 5vv, 2 vn, 2 va, bn, bc, *Dlb*; ed. in DDT, lviii–lix (1918/*R*)

Beatus vir qui timet, 5vv, ripieno 5vv, 3 vn, ripieno 3 vn, vc, bc, *Dlb*

Christus, der ist mein Leben, 5vv, 4 vn, 4 va, bn, bc, *B*

Christus ist des Gesetzes Ende, funeral motet, a 8, 13 July 1684 (n.p., ?1684), *GOl, Z*; ed. K. Straube: Ausgewählte Gesänge des Thomanerchores, ii (Leipzig, 1929)

Das ist mir lieb, 5vv, 2 vn, 2 va, bn, bc, *B*

Der Abgrund thut sich auf, 5vv, 2 vn, 2 va, bn, bc, *B*

Der Gerechte, ob er gleich, a 8, *Bds*, formerly Michaelisschule, Erfurt

Der Segen des Herrn machet reich, 5vv, 2 vn, 2 va, bn, bc, *B*

Die auf den Herren hoffen, 5vv, 2 vn, 2 va, bn, bc, *B*

Die Güte des Herrn ists, 5vv, 2 vn, 2 va, bc, *B*

Die Liebe Gottes ist ausgegossen, 5vv, 2 vn, 3 va, bn, bc, *B*

Ehre sei Gott in der Höhe, 5vv, ripieno 5vv, 2 vn, 2 clarinos, 3 trbn, timp, bc, *Dlb*

Erkenne deine Missethat, 6S, 5 va, vle, bc, *Dlb*

Eructavit cor meum (Ps xlv), 10vv, 2 vn, 2 va, 2 cornettinos, 3 trbn, bn/vle, bc, *Dlb*

Es ist genug, mein matter Sinn, 2vv, 3 violettas, 3 bn, vle, org, *B*

Gesegnet ist der Mann, 3vv, 2 vn, 3 va da gamba, bn, bc, *B*

Gott segne dies vertraute Paar, 5vv, 2 vn, 3 clarinos, 2 va/trbn, vle/trbn, bn, timp, org, *B*

Gott sei mir gnädig, 2vv, 2 vn, 2 va, clarino, bn, bc, *B*

Gott sende dein Licht (Ps xliii), 4vv, 2 vn, 2 va, bc, *B, Dlb* (incl. ripieno 4vv, bn)

Hemmt eure Thränenflut, 5vv, 2 vn, 2 va, 4 clarinos, b, bc, *B*

Herr, deine Augen sehen nach dem Glauben, 5vv, 2 vn, 2 cornettinos, 3 trbn, bc, *B*

Herr, lehre uns bedenken (Ps xc), 3vv, vn, violetta, va da gamba, bc, *Dlb*
Herr, wie lange wiltu mein sogar vergessen, 1v, 5 insts, *RUl*
Heut triumphieret Gottes Sohn, 5vv, ripieno 5vv, 2 vn, 2 va, vle, bc, *Bds*, formerly Michaelisschule, Erfurt
Ich hielte mich nicht dafür, 5vv, 4 insts (? 2 vn, 2 va), bc, *B*
Ich lebe, und ihr sollt auch leben, B solo, 2 vn, 2 cornettinos, 2 clarinos, 2 fl, bc, *Dlb*
Ihr Christen freuet euch, 2vv, 2 vn, 2 va, bn, bc, *Dlb*
In dich hab ich gehoffet, 5vv, 2 vn, 2 va, 2 clarinos, bc, *B*
Lobe den Herren meine Seele, double choir 10vv, 2 vn, 2 violettas, 2 cornettinos, 4 clarinos, 3 trbn, bn, timp, org, *B*; ed. in DDT, lviii–lix (1918/R)
Machet die Thore weit, 4vv, ripieno 4vv, 2 vn, 2 va, 2 clarinos, bn, tamburi, bc, *Dlb*
Nun danket alle Gott, ?1681, 5vv, 2 vn, 2 clarinos, bc, *B*
Nun giebst du, Gott, einen gnädigen Regen, 5vv, 5 insts (? 2 vn, 2 va, bn), bc, *B*
Schaffe in mir Gott, 4vv, 2 vn, 2 vn piccolo/2 cornettinos, 2 violettas, clarino, vc, org, *B*
Siehe, es hat uberwünden, 4vv, ripieno 4vv, 2 vn, 2 va, 4 tpt, bn, tamburi, bc, *Dlb*
Und da die Tage ihrer Reinigung, 5vv, 2 vn, 2 va, 2 clarinos, 4 va da gamba, bn, vle, bc, *Bds*, formerly Michaelisschule, Erfurt
Uns ist ein Kind geboren, 5vv, 2 vn, 2 clarinos, 2 trbn, org, *B*
Uns ist ein Kind geboren, 3vv, 2 ob/vn, bn, bc, *MÜG*
Vom Himmel kam der Engel Schar, 5vv, 2 vn, 2 violettas, 2 clarinos, 2 cornetts, 2 trbn, timp, org, *B*; ed. in DDT, lviii–lix (1918/R)
Was du thust, so bedenke, 4vv, vn, 2 va da gamba, bn, bc, *Bds*, formerly Michaelisschule, Erfurt
Wohl dem, der den Herren fürchtet, double choir 10vv, 2 vn, 2 clarinos, 3 trbn, bc, *B*
Wohl dem, der den Herren fürchtet, A solo, 2 vn, 2 va, bn, bc, *B*

Triumph-Lied: Mein Leben war ein Streit, 5vv, in G. Vopelius: Neu Leipziger Gesangbuch (Leipzig, 1682); MS, *Bds*
30 melodies with bc by Schelle and J. C. Pezel in J. Feller: *Devotus studiosus oder Der andächtige Student* (Leipzig, 1682) [exact number of works by each composer not specified]
Nun komm der Heiden Heiland, canon a 6, *Bds*
5 motets, B solo, 2 vn, bc, by 'Johann Schell', see Dürr

LOST WORKS

(for list of titles see DDT, lviii–lix (1918/R))
Missa, a 24; 3 Magnificat, a 19–21; Nunc dimittis, a 20; 2 Latin motets, 3vv and a 8; Passion mit Instrumenten (vn part, *USSR-KAu*); 113 German motets, a 2–30; 6 secular vocal works, incl. Kantate . . . zur Einführung W. von Ryssels als Schulvorsteher, 2 April 1684: mostly cited in lists of works bought by Leipzig council, 1686, 1712

BIBLIOGRAPHY
B. F. Richter: 'Zwei Funeralprogramme auf die Thomaskantoren Sebastian Knüpfer und Joh. Schelle', *MMg*, xxxiii (1901), 205; xxxiv (1902), 9
——: 'Stadtpfeifer und Alumnen der Thomasschule in Leipzig zu Bachs Zeit', *BJb*, iv (1907), 32
M. Seiffert: 'Die Chorbibliothek der St Michaelisschule in Lüneburg zu Seb. Bachs Zeit', *SIMG*, ix (1907–8), 593
R. Sachse, ed.: *Acta Nicolaitana et Thomana: Aufzeichnungen von J. Thomasius während seines Rektorats an der Nikolai- und Thomasschule zu Leipzig, 1670–1684* (Leipzig, 1912)
A. Schering: 'Über die Kirchenkantaten vorbachischer Thomaskantoren', *BJb*, ix (1912), 86–123
——: introduction to DDT, lviii–lix (1918/R)
——: 'Die alte Chorbibliothek der Thomasschule in Leipzig', *AMw*, i (1918–19), 275
——: *Musikgeschichte Leipzigs, ii: von 1650 bis 1723* (Leipzig, 1926)
F. Graupner: *Das Werk des Thomaskantors Johann Schelle* (Berlin, 1929)
M. Geck: 'Die Authentizität des Vokalwerks Dietrich Buxtehudes in quellenkritischer Sicht', *Mf*, xiv (1961), 393
F. Krummacher: 'Zur Sammlung Jacobi der ehemaligen Fürstenschule Grimma', *Mf*, xvi (1963), 324
A. Dürr: 'Eine Handschriftensammlung des 18. Jahrhunderts in Göttingen', *AMw*, xxv (1968), 308
R. A. Murray: *The German Church Music of Johann Schelle* (diss., U. of Michigan, 1971)

A. LINDSEY KIRWAN

Schellen (Ger.). JINGLES.

Schellenbaum (Ger.). TURKISH CRESCENT.

Schellendorf, Hans Bronsart von. *See* BRONSART VON SCHELLENDORF, HANS.

Schellenreif [Schellentrommel] (Ger.). TAMBOURINE.

Schelling, Ernest (*b* Belvidere, NJ, 26 July 1876; *d* New York, 8 Dec 1939). American pianist, conductor and composer. Having made his début as a pianist in Philadelphia at the age of four, he studied in 1882–5 with Mathias at the Paris Conservatoire and later with Moszkowski, Bruckner, Leschetizky, Huber, Barth and Paderewski. He gave recitals throughout Europe and South America as well as in the USA, and also played with most of the leading orchestras and with various chamber groups. From 1935 to 1937 he was conductor of the Baltimore SO, and he frequently appeared with other orchestras, both American and foreign, as pianist and as conductor. From 1924 he gave lectures for young people on the music and instruments of the orchestra.

WORKS
(selective list)
Orch: Sym., c♯; Légende symphonique, 1904; Suite fantastique, pf, orch, 1905; Impressions from an Artist's Life, sym. variations, pf, orch, 1913; Vn Conc. (1924); A Victory Ball, sym. poem, after Noyes (1925); Morocco, sym. tableau, perf. 1927
Other works: Thème et variations, pf, 1904; 6 Compositions, pf, 1904; 3 Poems (T. N. Page), 1v, pf, 1907; Vn Sonata; Divertimenti, pf qnt, 1925

Principal publisher: Leuckart

NATHAN BRODER

Schelling, F(riedrich) W(ilhelm) J(oseph von) (*b* Leonberg, 27 Jan 1775; *d* Ragaz, 20 Aug 1854). German philosopher. He was the characteristic philosopher of German Romanticism, and had an unmatched influence on creative artists among his contemporaries. The composer most notably influenced by him was Weber, who was also a friend, as were Goethe, Hölderlin, Novalis and other outstanding figures of the German Romantic movement. It was Schelling who coined the aphorism that architecture is frozen music.

Because he was precocious and long-lived, his philosophy developed through various distinguishable phases. The most influential was his 'philosophy of nature', which he was propounding at the turn of the century. In it he pictured the world as an endlessly evolving organism, to be understood only in terms of its aim, which is the achievement of self-awareness. Man's emergence from nature is part of this process, so it is an error to think of spirit as being in direct opposition to nature; the two are basically one: nature is visible spirit, spirit invisible nature. Most importantly, the creative process is the same in both. The only difference between nature bringing forth an organism and a genius bringing forth a work of art (which is also to be seen as an organism, and to be understood teleologically) is that the latter acts consciously. However, this means that in great art spirit's awareness of itself and to its identity with nature (and therefore the self-awareness of the world as such) is achieved and manifested, and thus the ultimate purpose of the world's existence accomplished.

This philosophy was embraced by Romantic artists for two of its aspects: its identification of man with nature, the human spirit with natural forces; and its portrayal of art as the highest of all human activities.

WRITINGS
Über das Verhältniss der bildenden Künste zur Natur (Munich, 1807; Eng. trans., 1845)
ed. M. Schröter: *Werke* (Munich, 1927–56)

BRYAN MAGEE

Schemelli [Schemmel], **Georg Christian** (*b* Herzberg, *c*1676; *d* Zeitz, 5 March 1762). German musician.

After singing in the court Kapelle at Dresden, he went to the Thomasschule, Leipzig (1695–1700), was Kantor at Treuenbrietzen from 1707 and court Kantor at Zeitz from 30 January 1727 until 1758, when he was succeeded by his son Christian Friedrich (1713–61). His only known publication, the *Musicalisches Gesangbuch* (Leipzig, 1736), contains 954 hymns, of which 69 have tunes with figured bass; for these see C. S. Terry, *The Four-part Chorals of J. S. Bach* (London, 1929, 2/1964). The book was unsuccessful; by 1760, copies were being sold off at 12 groschen. Dogmatically, the hymns compromise between orthodox Lutheranism and the Pietism of the Freylinghausen collection. As for the tunes, the preface and the Easter fair catalogue imply that all 69 were composed or improved by Bach. His chief task must, however, have been to supply or improve the figured basses; for only three tunes can now be attributed to him: *Vergiss mein nicht* (headed 'di S. Bach D.M. Lips.'); *Dir, dir, Jehova* (autograph in Anna's Notebook of 1725); and *Komm, süsser Tod* (for stylistic reasons). All three (BWV505, 452, 478) are arias rather than chorales.

Schemelli probably made contact with Bach through his son, who was at the Thomasschule from 1731 to 1734. The son is said to have been a good-for-nothing; but in 1740 Bach testified that he had worked hard and had been a useful soprano.

BIBLIOGRAPHY

A. Schering: 'Bach und das Schemellische Gesangbuch', *BJb*, xxi (1924), 105
F. Hamel: 'Die Kompositionen J. S. Bachs im Schemellischen Gesangbuch', *ZMw*, xii (1929–30), 232
G. Kinsky: *Die Originalausgaben der Werke Johann Sebastian Bachs* (Vienna, 1937)
W. Neumann and H.-J. Schulze, eds.: *Bach-Dokumente* (Kassel and Leipzig, 1963–9)

WALTER EMERY

Schenck [Schenk], **Johannes** [Johann, Joan, Jan] (*b* Amsterdam, baptized 3 June 1660; *d* in or after 1712). German composer and viola da gamba player of Dutch birth. He was not, as has been erroneously assumed, a brother of the engraver Peter Schenk of Elberfeld, who did, however, engrave a portrait of him (see illustration). Probably because of his extraordinary prowess on the viola da gamba, the Elector Palatine Johann Wilhelm I, whose residence was at Düsseldorf, appointed him a chamber musician at his court, apparently at the beginning of 1696. He held a respected position there as a *Kammerdiener* and, from about 1710 probably until the elector's death in 1716, as court chamber councillor. His playing was extolled in numerous reports and poems. Although nothing is known of his teachers, it may be concluded from the virtuoso demands of his works for viola da gamba that he was strongly influenced by a technique developed before him by such Englishmen as Daniel Norcombe (ii), Henry Butler and William Young, to which no composer on the Continent had previously aspired; he thus made remarkable advances in the development of viol playing. His earlier works are still in the German–Dutch Baroque tradition, but a later work such as op.10 displays Italian influences. His achievement 'not only stimulated Dutch instrumental music but also fostered a brief flowering of Dutch national opera' (Pauls).

WORKS

Edition: *Gambenkompositionen von Johannes Schenk und Conrad Höffler*, ed. K. H. Pauls, EDM, 1st ser., lxvii (1973)

Johannes Schenck with a viola da gamba: engraving by Peter Schenk

INSTRUMENTAL

Uitgevondene tyd en konst-oeffeningen (15 suites), va da gamba, bc, op.2 (Amsterdam, ?1688)
Il giardino armonico, 2 vn, va da gamba, bc, op.3 (Amsterdam, 1691); lost
Scherzi musicali (101 pieces in 14 suites), va da gamba, bc (ad lib), op.6 (Amsterdam, n.d.); ed. H. Leichtentritt (Leipzig, 1906)
[18] Suonate, vn, vle/hpd, op.7 (Amsterdam, n.d.)
Le nymphe di Rheno (12 suites), 2 va da gamba, op.8 (Amsterdam, n.d.); repr. as Select Lessons for the Bass Viol of Two Parts collected . . . out of the Works of . . . Giovanni Schenk (London, n.d.); orig. version ed. in EDM, 1st ser., xliv (1956)
L'echo du Danube (6 sonatas), va da gamba, some with bc, op.9 (Amsterdam, before 1706)
Les fantaisies bisarres de la goutte, va da gamba, bc, op.10 (Amsterdam, n.d.); lost, MS copy of bc, *D-Bds*
2 sonatas, va da gamba, *A-Wn*

VOCAL

[27] Eenige gezangen, uit de opera von Bacchus, Ceres en Venus, 1v, bc, op.1 (Amsterdam, 1687)
C. van Eekes koninklyke harpliederen, 2vv, 2 va da gamba, bc, op.4 (Amsterdam, 1693 or 1694)
[63] Zangswyze uitbreiding over 't Hooglied van Salomon, 1v, bc, op.5 (Amsterdam, 1697)

BIBLIOGRAPHY

K. H. Pauls: 'Der kurpfälzische Kammermusikus Johannes Schenck', *Mf*, xv (1962), 157 [incl. full bibliography]; *Mf*, xix (1966), 288
——: 'Schenck, Johannes', *MGG*

ERNST HINTERMAIER

Schenk, Erich (*b* Salzburg, 5 May 1902; *d* Vienna, 11 Oct 1974). Austrian musicologist. He studied theory and the piano at the Salzburg Mozarteum (and later at the Munich Academy), and musicology with Sandberger at the University of Munich, where he took the doctorate in 1925 with a dissertation on Paganelli. He then went on a study trip to Italy, returning to further training in musicology with Adler and Lach in Vienna, and with Wolf and Schering in Berlin. After a short period as a teacher and librarian at the Salzburg Mozarteum (1925–6) and as press officer to the Salzburg Festival (1927), he completed his *Habilitation* in 1929 at Rostock University with a work on the trio sonata in Germany after Corelli. In 1936 he founded, and until 1940 directed, the musicology department at Rostock. In 1940 he was appointed successor to Lach at Vienna University, where in 1950–51 he was dean of the philosophy faculty and in 1957–8 the first musicologist to become rector of the university. As director of the musicology institute for more than 30 years (until 1971) he greatly improved study conditions, arranging new teaching space and building up the library, and worked consistently towards the creation and dissemination of a view of the whole of musical life based on historical style, while at the same time not neglecting more specialized source study.

Schenk's main field of work was musical history from the 17th century to the 19th, chiefly the Baroque and Classical eras. His reputation rests particularly on his work for Denkmäler der Tonkunst in Österreich, which he revived very soon after World War II (1947) with vol.lxxxv (Fux's keyboard works). He was responsible for the publication of this series until vol.cxxiv (1972), and also initiated the systematic reprinting of all previous volumes. He revived *Studien zur Musikwissenschaft* (1955), founded the series of books Wiener Beiträge zur Musikwissenschaft (1955) and became a member of the Austrian Academy of Sciences in 1944. In 1946 he became chairman of the academy's commission for music research and directed its publications, the *Mitteilungen der Kommission für Musikforschung* (founded 1955), the *Veröffentlichungen* (founded 1947) and the Tabulae Musicae Austriacae (founded 1964). With the Academy of Sciences, the Gesellschaft zur Herausgabe der Denkmäler der Tonkunst in Österreich (of which Schenk was president), arranged the Vienna international musicological Mozart conference in 1956 and international Beethoven symposium in 1970. Schenk held honorary doctorates from the universities of Rostock and Brno and some of the highest international and national awards.

WRITINGS

Giuseppe Antonio Paganelli: sein Leben und seine Werke (diss., U. of Munich, 1925; Salzburg, 1928)
'Barock bei Beethoven', *Beethoven und die Gegenwart: Ludwig Schiedermair zum 50. Geburtstag* (Berlin and Bonn, 1927), 177–219
'Mozarts Salzburger Vorfahren', *Mozart-Jb*, iii (1929), 81
Studien zur Triosonate in Deutschland nach Corelli (Habilitationsschrift, U. of Rostock, 1929)
'Über Begriff und Wesen des musikalischen Barock', *ZMw*, xvii (1935), 377
Johann Strauss (Potsdam, 1940)
950 Jahre Musik in Österreich (Vienna, 1946)
Kleine Wiener Musikgeschichte (Vienna, 1946)
'Ein unbekannter Brief Leopold Mozarts', *Sitzungsbericht der Österreichischen Akademie der Wissenschaften* (1947), no.225, p.1
'Breitkopfs Musik zum Leipziger Liederbuch', *Wiener Goethe-Festschrift: Chronik des Wiener Goethe-Vereins*, lii–liii (1949), 14
'Osservazioni sulla scuola modenese nel Seicento', *Atti e memorie dell'Accademia di scienze* (Modena, 1952), 1–30
'Das musikalische Opfer von J. S. Bach', *Anzeiger der Österreichischen Akademie der Wissenschaften: philosophisch-historische Klasse*, xc (1953), 51
'Mozart in Mantua', *SMw*, xxii (1955), 1
W. A. Mozart: eine Biographie (Zurich, Vienna and Leipzig, 1955, 2/1975 as *Mozart: sein Leben, seine Welt*; Eng. trans., 1960, as *Mozart and his Time*)
'Halbjahr der Erwartung: der Aufenthalt Robert Schumanns in Wien

1838–39', *Robert Schumann: aus Anlass seines 100. Todestages* (Leipzig, 1956), 12
'Das Weltbild Joseph Haydns', *Almanach der Österreichischen Akademie der Wissenschaften*, cix (1959), 245
'Ist der Göttweiger Rorate-Messe ein Werk Joseph Haydns?', *SMw*, xxiv (1960), 87
'Ein unbekanntes Klavierübungsstück Mozarts', *Anzeiger der Österreichischen Akademie der Wissenschaften: philosophisch-historische Klasse*, xcix (1962), 98
'Zur Aufführungspraxis des Tremolo bei Gluck', *Anthony van Hoboken: Festschrift zum 75. Geburtstag* (Mainz, 1962), 137
Ausgewählte Aufsätze: Reden und Vorträge (Graz and Vienna, 1967)
'Salieri's "Landsturm"-Kantate von 1709 in ihrer Beziehung zu "Fidelio" ', *Colloquium amicorum: Joseph Schmidt-Görg zum 70. Geburtstag* (Bonn, 1967), 338
'Berlioz in Wien', *ÖMz*, xxiv (1969), 217
'Das Geburtshaus Franz Liszts in Raiding', *ÖMz*, xxv (1970), 229
'Ein "Singfundament" von Heinrich Ignaz Franz Biber', *Speculum musicae artis: Festgabe für Heinrich Husmann* (Munich, 1970), 277
ed.: *Beethoven-Studien* (Vienna, 1970) [incl. 'Über Tonsymbolik in Beethovens "Fidelio" ', 230]
'Zur Beethovenforschung der letzten zehn Jahre', *AcM*, xlii (1970), 83
with G. Gruber: ' "Das ganzen Studien": zu Josef Vockners Theorieunterricht bei Anton Bruckner', *Bruckner-Studien*, ed. O. Wessely (Vienna, 1975), 349–78
'Zur Genese der emphatischen None', *Beiträge zur Musikdokumentation: Franz Grasberger zum 60. Geburtstag* (Tutzing, 1975), 405
'Das musikalische Kunstwerk: zwei Studien zum Problem des Schöpferischen', *Anzeiger der Österreichischen Akademie der Wissenschaften: philosophisch-historische Klasse*, cxiv (1977)
Further articles in *Mecklenburger Monatshefte*, *ZMw*, *Musikerziehung*, *ÖMz*, *Die Musik*, *SMw*, publications of the Österreichischen Akademie der Wissenschaften and in Festschriften for Besseler (1961), Osthoff (1961), Fellerer (Regensburg, 1962), Kodály (1962), Feicht (1967), Schering (1967)

EDITIONS

D. Friderici: Ausgewählter geistlicher Gesang, EDM, 2nd ser., *Mecklenburg and Pommern*, ii (1942)
J. J. Fux: Werke für Tasteninstrumente, DTÖ, lxxxv (1947); *Triosuiten*, *Sämtliche Werke*, vi/3 (in preparation)
Salzburger Triosonate, Hausmusik, xcv (1950)
G. Muffat: Armonico tributo (1682), *Exquisitioris harmoniae instrumentalis grave-jucundae selectus primus* (1701), *Concerti grossi II*, DTÖ, lxxxix (1953)
Die italienische Triosonate, Mw, vii (1955; Eng. trans., 1962)
J. H. Schmelzer: Sonate unarum fidium (1664), DTÖ, xciii (1958); *Duodena selectarum sonatarum* (1659), DTÖ, cv (1963)
H. I. F. von Biber: Mensa sonora seu musica instrumentalis: sonatis aliquot liberius sonantibus ad mensam (1680), DTÖ, xcvi (1960); *Fidicinium sacro-profanum: tam choro, quam foro pluribus fibibus concinnatum et concini aptum* (1683), DTÖ, xcvii (1960); *Sonatae tam aris quam aulis servientes* (1676), DTÖ, cv (1963)
Die ausseritalienische Triosonate, Mw, xxxv (1970; Eng. trans., 1970)
L. Tomasini: Ausgewählte Instrumentalwerke, DTÖ, cxxiv (1972)

BIBLIOGRAPHY

SMw, xxv (1962) [Festschrift for Erich Schenk; incl. preface by O. Wessely and list of publications]
E. H. Müller von Asow: 'Erich Schenk zum 70. Geburtstag', *ÖMz*, xvii (1962), 242
W. Szmolyan: 'Erich Schenk zum 70. Geburtstag', *ÖMz*, xxvii (1972), 293
T. Antonicek, R. Flotzinger and O. Wessely, eds.: *De ratione in musica: Festschrift Erich Schenk zum 5. Mai 1972* (Kassel, 1975)
O. Wessely: 'Erich Schenk (1902–1974)', *Mf*, xxviii (1975), 2
RUDOLF KLEIN

Schenk, Johann Baptist (*b* Wiener Neustadt, 30 Nov 1753; *d* Vienna, 29 Dec 1836). Austrian composer and music teacher. According to his autobiographical sketch he was born on 30 November 1761, a date taken over by Eitner and others. The son of an employee at the Wiener Neustadt military academy, he was instructed in the rudiments of music before studying with Anton Stoll, choirmaster at Baden and later a friend of Mozart's. He wrote songs, dances and symphonies while still a boy, became a proficient violinist and keyboard and wind player, and in 1773 was taken to Vienna, where he became Wagenseil's pupil for counterpoint and composition (the works of Handel, to which Wagenseil

Johann Baptist Schenk: portrait by an unknown artist in the Gesellschaft der Musikfreunde, Vienna

introduced him, made a deep impression on him). By the time of Wagenseil's death in 1777 he had advanced sufficiently to be able to undertake various large-scale compositions: Leopold Hofmann performed a mass by him at St Stephen's Cathedral in 1778, in 1779 his *Stabat mater* was performed four times around Easter, and in 1780 he began to compose for the theatre. Although his incidental music to Blumauer's tragedy *Erwine von Steinheim* (1780) was successful, he did not press for performance of five early Singspiels; even the pronounced success of the two works he wrote anonymously for Marinelli's Leopoldstadt Theatre in the mid-1780s (*Die Weinlese*, 1785; *Die Weihnacht auf dem Lande*, 1786) did not diminish his diffidence towards popular acclaim. These two Singspiels, with their important roles for the comic character Kasperl (played by La Roche) were followed by works written for the Kärntnerthortheater and Schikaneder's Freihaus-Theater auf der Wieden. In the late 1780s Schenk also met with success as an instrumental composer: six of his symphonies were performed at F. B. von Keess's concerts, and Schenk remarked in his autobiography on Haydn's complimentary and encouraging comments about them.

It was the mid-1790s before Schenk established himself at the court theatres. His Singspiel *Achmet und Almanzine* had five performances in 1795, and brought him in an honorarium of 225 gulden. Some commentators imply that it was still more successful, confusing it with *Achmet und Zenide*, a play by Iffland that was performed four times in 1796–7. A more widespread and serious confusion surrounds an operetta (Singspiel) *Der Bettelstudent, oder Das Donnerwetter*, which is held to have been performed at the Kärntnerthortheater on 9 February 1796 with music by Schenk and text by Paul Weidmann. Weidmann's comedy of this name had

been performed frequently since its Burgtheater première on 6 October 1776 (it was first seen at the Kärntnerthor in 1773), and it was also produced in three other Viennese theatres. As a Singspiel with music by Winter it had been given at Munich on 2 February 1785, and in Vienna's Theater in der Leopoldstadt on 19 July 1785 (Huber and Wenzel Müller rearranged it for that theatre in 1800). But the court theatre playbills for 1796 invariably refer to *Der Bettelstudent* merely as a comedy ('Lustspiel'), and it was not performed on 4 March 1796, the date usually given as the première of Schenk's 'Singspiel'. There is no record of Schenk's receiving payment for a *Bettelstudent*, and no trace of a score, and it must be considered highly doubtful if Schenk ever did write this work.

With *Der Dorfbarbier* (autumn 1796), Schenk's masterpiece, the ground is firmer, though even here the date of the first performance is uncertain. In 1799 a new Schenk Singspiel, *Die Jagd*, was given with limited success. His last, *Der Fassbinder* (1802), is sometimes attributed to Ignaz Umlauf (who had died six and a half years earlier), or held to be a ballet, or assumed to be identical with the original Audinot–Gossec *Le tonnelier*, which as *Der Fassbinder* had often been heard in Vienna since 1776. Although the 1802 version remains close to the original French story, there is no doubt that the score for the 1802 production is a new and original work by Schenk, and that the (anonymous) libretto is different from the earlier text. Schenk's *Der Fassbinder* had 43 performances in the court theatres until 1810, and was also staged at Eisenstadt in 1805 and in the Theater in der Leopoldstadt in 1812. It is a charming piece, not markedly below *Der Dorfbarbier* in musical (or dramatic) quality. Schenk stated in his autobiographical sketch that he also began to write a grand opera in the manner of Gluck at the turn of the century, but was obliged to abandon it owing to lack of progress and ill-health. For the rest of his long life he lived in the shadow of *Der Dorfbarbier*, an undisputed masterpiece. Indeed, after 1802 he wrote no further works for the stage, though at the time of his death he was revising *Die Jagd* with the help of his friend, the dramatist and poet Eduard von Bauernfeld. His later years were spent mainly in teaching and in writing a small quantity of vocal and choral works, including two cantatas, given at the Redoutensaal in 1819 (*Die Huldigung*, 28 February, and *Der Mai*, 7 May). He himself referred in his interesting but factually unreliable autobiographical sketch to his preference for 'a peaceful and withdrawn private life'; although in the mid-1790s he was Kapellmeister to Prince Auersperg, he did not relish regular employment and responsibilities such as a Kapellmeister's position would have offered.

Schenk is frequently mentioned in Beethoven literature as the man who, at Abbé Josef Gelinek's introduction, aided Beethoven in 1793 with his counterpoint and composition exercises, which Haydn was presumably too preoccupied to correct. Among Schenk's other pupils were Bauernfeld (who mentioned in his memoirs that Schenk introduced him to Schubert with happy results) and Joseph Weigl's daughter. To Weigl himself Schenk bequeathed his music (the collection later passed to the keeping of the Gesellschaft der Musikfreunde, Vienna). His friendly relationship with Mozart is attested in Schenk's well-known statement that Mozart responded to his admiration for the overture of *Die Zauberflöte* at its première by stroking his cheek and smiling, while continuing to conduct with the other hand.

Der Dorfbarbier was for some 25 years one of the most popular and successful of operas. At the Vienna court theatres alone it was given 318 times until 1819; it was mounted at the Leopoldstadt Theatre in 1821 and achieved nearly 50 performances there up to 1858. It was also given in most German opera houses and in many foreign lands (Moscow, 1819; New York, 1847), and even in the 20th century it has quite often been revived. The play on which it is based, Paul Weidmann's comedy of the same name, had been in the repertory of the Burgtheater since 1785 without achieving more than ten performances, and when it was refashioned as a Singspiel (mainly by Paul Weidmann, though his brother Joseph apparently suggested the adaptation), it was at first not a success. Even the date of the première is a matter for dispute. The playbills for the Kärntnerthortheater and Burgtheater respectively give 30 October ('zum ersten mal') and 7 November ('zum zweytenmal') 1796 as the dates of the first two performances; Schenk named 6 November as the date of the première (though the year he gave, 1798, is definitely wrong). The box-office records, perhaps the most reliable source, indicate 6 November 1796 as the date. As the work was given anonymously at first, and there is no record of when – if at all – Schenk received his honorarium, it may be assumed that at the time of the première anything but a popular success was expected. Following one or two performances in the autumn of 1796 *Der Dorfbarbier* disappeared from the repertory for ten months, and it was 1798 before it began to be given regularly. Its success was certainly due in part to a succession of famous singing actors (Joseph Weidmann, Hasenhut and later J. N. Nestroy) and opera singers (Weinmüller, Friedrich Baumann, Magdalena Willmann, Johann Michael Vogl, Maria Anna Gassmann) in its leading roles; yet Schenk's music is an excellent example of the Viennese Singspiel at its best, with charming melodies, well developed and neatly orchestrated; abundant variety between solo numbers of various kinds and duets or larger ensembles; and a well-constructed, witty yet affecting libretto. Many anecdotes testify to its hold on audiences and performers, and in the 1840s it could not have seemed particularly surprising to find Beethoven's librettist G. F. Treitschke writing an article entitled 'Die Zauberflöte, Der Dorfbarbier, Fidelio' (*Orpheus*, ii, 1841, p.239). Weber, who conducted *Der Dorfbarbier* at Prague in 1816, seems to have recalled Suschen's Polacca, 'Mädchen kann man leicht betören', when writing Ännchen's music in *Der Freischütz* a few years later; and Lortzing knew and appreciated it.

WORKS

* – autograph in A-Wgm

STAGE

(all Singspiels, first performed in Vienna, unless otherwise stated)
Der Schatzgräber (opera), 1780, not perf., *
Erwine von Steinheim (incidental music, A. Blumauer), Burg, 18 Dec 1780,* [Schenk's music possibly not used at 1st perf.]
Die Weinlese (3, Wiest), Leopoldstadt, 12 Oct 1785; frags. *A-Wgm*
Die Weihnacht auf dem Lande (3, Wiest), Leopoldstadt, 14 Dec 1786, *
Im Finstern ist nicht gut tappen (2, L. Hiesberger), Kärntnerthor, 12 Oct 1789, * 1787, copy *Wn*
Das unvermutete (unterbrochene) Seefest (3), Freihaus, 9 Dec 1789, *
Das Singspiel ohne Titel (operetta, 3, Hiesberger), Freihaus, 4 Nov 1790, *, autograph *Wn*
Der Erntekranz (Ärndtekranz), oder Das Schnitterfest (2, ? K. Mayer, after C. F. Weisse), Freihaus, ?9 July 1791; frags. *Wgm*
Achmet und Almanzine (2, after Lesage and d'Ormeville), Kärntnerthor, 17 July 1795, *, copy *Wn*
Der Bettelstudent, oder Das Donnerwetter (operetta, 2, P. Weidmann),

Kärntnerthor, ? 9 Feb 1796 [doubtful]
Der Dorfbarbier (1, P. and J. Weidmann), Kärntnerthor, 30 Oct 1796, or Burg, 6 or 7 Nov 1796; vocal score (Hamburg, 1798), *, many MS copies; ed. R. Haas, DTÖ, lxvi, Jg.xxxiv (1927/*R*)
Pantomime and Singspiel, for Empress Maria Theresia's name day, Laxenburg, 15 Oct 1798, *
Die Jagd (2, after Weisse), Kärntnerthor, 7 May 1799, *; inc. rev., 1836, *
Der Fassbinder (1, after Audinot), Kärntnerthor, 18 (? or 17) Dec 1802, *, copy *Wn*
Others: 4 Singspiels, 1780–85, not perf., lost; 2 Singspiels, perf. privately at Prince Karl von Auersperg's estate, sum. and aut., 1794, lost; single arias and lieder from stage works, *Gk*, *Wgm*, *Wn*, some pubd

OTHER VOCAL

Cantatas: Die Schäferstunde, 3 solo vv, insts, 1779; Das traute Stündchen der Liebe, 3 solo vv, insts, 1779; Die Huldigung (Hölty), composed 1818, Vienna, Redoutensaal, 28 Feb 1819; Der Mai, solo vv, chorus, orch, Vienna, Redoutensaal, 7 May 1819: all *; Ariadne auf Naxos (Gerstenberg, *c*1820)
Sacred: Mass, D; Mass (Ky–Gl–Cr), 4vv, 2 vn, 2 cl, org, autograph *D-Bds*; Asperges me, autograph *Bds*; Benedictus, B♭, 1831, *; 3 litanies, C, *A-KR*; litany, B♭, *KN*; Litany, d, 1778, *; Miserere, E♭, *KR*; Stabat mater, E♭, 1779, *
Others: [7] Nocturns, 4vv, acc. wind insts, *; 13 Canons nebst Coda, 3vv, 1812, *; 2 canons, 3vv, kbd, *Wgm*; choruses, lieder, some with inst acc., * [list in Eitner]; songs in contemporary periodicals

INSTRUMENTAL

Orch: 10 syms., *; ov., *; Concertante, E♭, cl, vn, acc. 2 va, 2 hn, vc, b, *; 3 concs., pedal harp, 1784–8, *; conc., cl and hn, *; Andante, cl, orch, *; kbd conc., 1796, * [arr. of Clementi sonata]; minuets, lost [cited in autobiography]
Chamber: 6 trios, 2 vn, vc, 1776, *; 5 str qts, *Wgm*; Qt, F, fl, 2 eng hn, bn, *, ed. H. Steinbeck (Vienna, 1968); Caprice, clvd, 1823, autograph *Wn*; pieces from Cimarosa's Il matrimonio segreto, *, 12 arr. ob, vn, va, vc, April 1792, 8, inc., arr. cl, va, vc, Aug 1792; kbd variation on a theme by Diabelli in *Vaterländischer Kunstlerverein*, ii (Vienna, *c*1824); pf arrs. from Martín y Soler's Una cosa rara and L'arbore di Diana, *Wn*

WRITINGS

Grundsätze des Generalbasses in Beispielen (MS, 1816, autograph *A-Wgm*)
Autobiographische Skizze (MS, 28 July 1830, *GÖ*; repr. in *SMw*, xi, 1924, 75) [written for Aloys Fuchs; mentions early works now lost]

BIBLIOGRAPHY

EitnerQ
Obituary, *AMZ*, xxxix (1837), col.165
E. Bauernfeld: 'Johann Schenk, eine biographische Skizze', *Wiener Zeitschrift für Kunst, Literatur, Theater und Mode* (Vienna, 1837), nos.5–7
C. von Wurzbach: *Biographisches Lexikon des Kaiserthums Oesterreich*, xxix (Vienna, 1875), 198ff
H. M. Schletterer: 'Schenk, Johann', *ADB*
E. Hanslick: 'Der Dorfbarbier von Schenk', *Aus dem Tagebuch eines Musikers* (Berlin, 1892), 122ff
F. Staub: *J. B. Schenk, eine Skizze seines Lebens* (Wiener Neustadt, 1900)
E. Mandyczewski: *Zusatz-band zur Geschichte der kais. kgl. Gesellschaft der Musikfreunde in Wien* (Vienna, 1912), 114f [incl. list of Schenk autographs]
E. Rosenfeld[-Roemer]: *Johann Baptist Schenk als Opernkomponist* (diss., U. of Vienna, 1921)
T. Frimmel: *Beethoven-Handbuch*, ii (Leipzig, 1926), 101ff
F. Hadamowsky: *Das Theater in der Wiener Leopoldstadt* (Vienna, 1934)
F. K. Rieger: *Johann Schenk, ein Altmeister des deutschen Singspiels* (St Pölten, 1944)
A. Bauer: *Opern und Operetten in Wien* (Graz and Cologne, 1955)
A. Loewenberg: *Annals of Opera* (Geneva, 2/1955)
H. Oberhofer: 'Schenk, Johann Baptist', *MGG*
K. Adel: 'Paul Weidmann', *Jb der Gesellschaft für Wiener Theaterforschung*, xv–xvi (1966), 127–78
F. Hadamowsky: *Die Wiener Hoftheater (Staatstheater), 1776–1966*, i (Vienna, 1966)

PETER BRANSCOMBE

Schenk, Johannes. See SCHENCK, JOHANNES.

Schenk, Otto (*b* Vienna, 12 June 1930). Austrian producer and actor. He studied acting at the Reinhardt Seminar and production at the University of Vienna. He entered the theatre as an actor, later moving to producing. His first opera production was *Die Zauberflöte* for the Salzburg Landestheater in 1957: making a virtue of the limitations of a small stage and a provincial company, he demonstrated that it could succeed as a small theatre piece rather than a pantomime-like spectacle. He emerged as a leading opera producer in 1963 with Vienna Festival productions of Einem's *Dantons Tod* and Berg's *Lulu*, as well as a new Salzburg Festival version of *Die Zauberflöte*, and *Der Rosenkavalier* and *Otello* for Frankfurt and Stuttgart respectively. In 1964 he staged *L'heure espagnole* at the Vienna Volksoper and *Jenůfa* at the Staatsoper. Since then he has worked with regular success not only at the Vienna Staatsoper, where he was appointed *Oberspielleiter* in 1965, but also at Salzburg and in leading German opera houses, notably Munich, Berlin, Stuttgart and Frankfurt. He made his Metropolitan Opera début with *Fidelio* (1970), his La Scala début with *Le nozze di Figaro* (1974) and his Covent Garden début with *Un ballo in maschera* (1975), designed by Jürgen Rose, with whom he has worked in his most successful productions.

Schenk is a sensitive and tasteful man of the theatre, unencumbered by loyalties to opera-house tradition or to modern theatrical trickery. He claims to prefer 'people to concepts' and has stated 'You have to seek truth through human behaviour, human passions'. His finest productions are generally marked by convincing delineations of character and high standards of acting. The producer's hand is nearly always unobtrusive; idiosyncratic devices and production ideas are subtly and inoffensively applied. Schenk collaborates closely with his designers and builds his productions around the original singers, disliking the opera-house convention of revivals with new casts. His *Der Freischütz* (Vienna, 1972), which stressed the simplicity and naivety of the story rather than 19th-century pyrotechnics, provoked many into reassessing the opera. His Vienna production of Verdi's *Macbeth* responded to the Italian character in the music rather than the Scottish or Shakespearean factors in the libretto, and the result was a thrilling if melodramatic tragedy. His version of *Der Rosenkavalier* (Munich, 1975) was a theatrical tour de force, an active production full of comic detail and vivid characterizations. The Covent Garden *Un ballo in maschera*, in the Swedish setting, was cold and sombre. Along with his operatic work he has maintained a distinguished career in films, theatre and television.

PAUL SHEREN

Schenker, Friedrich (*b* Zeulenrode, 23 Dec 1942). German trombonist and composer. At the Eisler Hochschule für Musik in Berlin (1961–3) he studied the trombone and composition under Kochan. He joined the Leipzig RSO in 1964, and in 1969 he passed the state composition examination at the Leizpig Hochschule für Musik, where his examiner was Geissler. His studies were completed in Dessau's master class at the German Academy of Arts (1973). Schenker's music shows a pronounced propensity for experiment.

WORKS
(*selective list*)
Ob Conc., 1966; Monolog, ob, 1969; Sonata, vc, 1970; Triple Conc., ob, bn, pf, orch, 1971; Sym., 1971; Stück für Virtuosen, 1971; Chamber Sym., 1971; Str Qt, 1971; Hörstück mit Ob, 1972; Db Conc., 1972; Conc. espressivo e scherzando, 1972; Electrization, beatgroup, orch, 1973; Kammerspiel I, 1974; Landschaften, orch, 1976
Principal publishers: Deutscher Verlag für Musik, Peters (Leipzig)

Schenker, Heinrich (*b* Wisniowczyki, Galicia, 19 June 1868; *d* Vienna, 13 Jan 1935). Austrian theorist of Polish birth. His musical talent was evident at an early age, and as a young man he was awarded an imperial scholarship that enabled him to travel to Vienna, where he studied under Bruckner at the conservatory and took a degree in jurisprudence at the university. He became prominent in Vienna as a lied accompanist, chamber music performer, critic and editor. Brahms was impressed by his compositions and recommended him to his publisher, Simrock. He never taught at a music school or university, but his reputation as a private teacher of piano and theory increased rapidly, and he had as pupils a number of eminent musicians, including John Petri Dunn, Wilhelm Furtwängler, Anthony van Hoboken, Oswald Jonas, Felix Salzer, Otto Vrieslander and Hans Weisse. His theoretical work has been, and remains, particularly influential in the USA.

Schenker's deep interest in musical masterworks and in the creative processes exemplified by great composers provided the motivation both for his general theoretical formulations and for his innovatory editorial work. Among his editions, perhaps the most significant are the 'Erläuterungsausgaben' of the last five sonatas of Beethoven (1913–21), for which he used early editions and autograph manuscripts (op.106 was not completed because the composer's autograph is not extant). At his instigation the Vienna Photogramm-Archiv für Musikalische Meisterhandschriften was established in 1927 under the direction of O. E. Deutsch, with funds provided by Anthony van Hoboken (it is now in *A-Wn*).

With the publication in 1906 of his *Harmonielehre*, the first volume of *Neue musikalische Theorien und Phantasien*, Schenker began the documentation of his theoretical concepts. This continued through his further pedagogical writings in the same series, through the issues of his periodical *Der Tonwille* (1921–4) and its successor *Das Meisterwerk in der Musik* (1925–30), and it culminated in *Der freie Satz* (1935).

Schenker's theory of tonal music developed from certain insights concerning the nature of harmony and counterpoint. With respect to harmony, his most significant concept was that of the *Stufe* or harmonic scale-step. This is a harmony of larger scope and is not necessarily identical with a single chord, especially one that may simply be the result of linear motions and have no longer-range implications; the harmonic scale-step may, for example, comprise several chords. When such a scale-step is supplied with its own dominant, it can itself become a temporary tonic (the process of *Tonikalisierung*, 'tonicization'). The concept of the scale-step within the tonality replaces, in Schenker's view, the notion of arbitrary 'keys' other than the tonic within one composition; the tonal composition is thus always within a single tonality, within which the process of tonicization serves to form coherent and organic surface features that interact with the deeper musical structure.

For Schenker, counterpoint represented an aspect of music more elemental than harmony – a view substantiated by the historical development of music. He believed that the true significance of counterpoint (and counterpoint pedagogy) had gone unrecognized for years and sought to restore the proper perspective. His exposition of counterpoint (in *Kontrapunkt*, 1910–22) constitutes a systematic explication of the traditional species method of Fux. Through the study of the species, he maintained, one comes to understand the simplest and most fundamental intervallic relations between moving voices and the essential nature of the passing note and the auxiliary note, as well as elementary rhythmic phenomena. Counterpoint, in this sense, was explicitly divorced from harmonic events so that the student would more readily understand the interaction of harmony and counterpoint in the complete tonal work (*freier Satz*, 'free composition'), as distinct from the exercise.

Certain aspects of Schenker's view of harmony and counterpoint are traditional and are more or less clearly set forth in treatises by Kirnberger, Heinichen, C.P.E. Bach and other 18th-century writers. The most innovatory (hence most controversial) features of his view of tonal music have to do with the concept of large-scale structure, a concept that developed logically from the notion of the extended scale-step together with the notion of the passing note as a fundamental linear phenomenon capable of being prolonged by subordinate musical events. The chronological development of this concept of large-scale structure is quite clearly delineated in his published works and can be described in terms of the *Urlinie* (fundamental melodic line), the *Ursatz* (fundamental composition) and, finally, the most general concept, that of *Schichten* (structural layers: background, middleground and foreground).

Schenker first mentioned the *Urlinie* in his edition of Beethoven's op.101 (1920). Initially, he defined this melodic structure as a diatonic line derived by analytical reduction when the upper-voice elaborations were removed; the *Urlinie* might thus consist of a succession of short fundamental melodic progressions each spanning several bars, subsuming the 'motif' and other such traditional formations, since it represented a more fundamental structural component.

In the subsequent development of Schenker's ideas the *Urlinie* was extended to span, in effect, the upper voice of the entire composition and, at the same time, was coordinated with the large-scale structural *Bassbrechung* ('bass arpeggiation'), ascending from tonic to dominant and returning to tonic. The resulting contrapuntal structure was named the *Ursatz*. Thus harmony and counterpoint are combined at the deepest level of structure where the *Ursatz* represents the large-scale *Auskomponierung* ('composing out') of the fundamental harmony, the tonic triad. More specifically, the *Urlinie* descends by step within a triadic interval, while the bass is arpeggiated from the tonic to the 5th of the triad.

In a series of remarkable analyses of large works (notably those of the Mozart G minor Symphony K550 and the Beethoven 'Eroica' Symphony in *Das Meisterwerk in der Musik*, ii and iii), Schenker demonstrated the profound implications of his concepts for the study of a musical work of art. The analyses are presented primarily in the form of *Urlinie-Tafeln*, analytical graphs employing both ordinary musical notation and special symbols. This novel graphic method made possible the precise communication of structural content and greatly facilitated the task of prose description.

The general concept of structural levels provides for a hierarchical differentiation of musical components, which, in turn, establishes a basis for describing and interpreting relations among the elements of any composition, from the moment-to-moment events at the surface of the music to the connections of longer range that ensure continuity and coherence over the span of the entire composition. It should be emphasized that in Schenker's view the total work at all levels, not only at the background level, is the object of study and aesthetic perception. Indeed, the greater part of *Der freie Satz*, his culminating statement, is devoted to the consideration of foreground details and the meaning that they derive from the other structural levels.

See also ANALYSIS, §§II, 5–6, III, 2, and figs.12, 16–17, 20–22; ARPEGGIATION; AUSFALTUNG; AUSKOMPONIERUNG; HÖHERLEGUNG; KOPPELUNG; LAYER; OBLIGATE LAGE; PROLONGATION; TEILER; TIEFERLEGUNG; ÜBERGREIFEN; UNTERBRECHUNG; UNTERGREIFEN; URLINIE; URSATZ; ZUG (i).

WRITINGS

Ein Beitrag zur Ornamentik als Einführung zu Ph. E. Bachs Klavierwerke (Vienna, 1904, rev. 2/1908/*R*1954; Eng. trans. in *Music Forum*, iv, 1976, 1–140)

Neue musikalische Theorien und Phantasien, i: *Harmonielehre* (Stuttgart, 1906; Eng. trans., 1954/*R*1973, ed. O. Jonas); ii/1: *Kontrapunkt* (Vienna, 1910); ii/2: *Kontrapunkt* (Vienna, 1922); iii: *Der freie Satz* (Vienna, 1935, rev. 2/1956 by O. Jonas; Eng. trans., 1979, ed. E. Oster)

Beethovens Neunte Sinfonie (Vienna, 1912/*R*1969)

Der Tonwille (Vienna, 1921–4)

Beethovens Fünfte Sinfonie (Vienna, 1925/*R*1969) [orig. pubd serially in *Der Tonwille*]

Das Meisterwerk in der Musik (Vienna, 1925–30/*R*1974) [Eng. trans. of essay on Largo of J. S. Bach's Violin Sonata no.3 BWV1005 in *Music Forum*, iv (1976), 141]

Fünf Urlinie-Tafeln (Vienna, 1932, rev. 2/1969 by F. Salzer as *Five Graphic Music Analyses*)

J. Brahms: Oktaven und Quinten u.a. (Vienna, 1933) [facs. edn. and commentary on a MS with notations and remarks on consecutive 5ths and octaves]

EDITIONS

C. P. E. Bach: Klavierwerke (Vienna, 1902–3)

G. F. Handel: Sechs Orgelkonzerte (Vienna, 1904)

J. S. Bach: Chromatische Phantasie und Fuge (Vienna, 1910)

L. van Beethoven: Die letzten [fünf] Sonaten von Beethoven: kritische Ausgabe mit Einführung und Erläuterung (Vienna, 1913–21), rev. O. Jonas, 1971–2 as *Beethoven: Die letzten Sonaten; Sonate, Op. 27 Nr. 2* (Vienna, 1927) [facs. edn. of autograph and 3 sketch leaves]; *Sämtliche Klaviersonaten* (Vienna, 1934/*R*1975, rev. 1947 by E. Ratz)

BIBLIOGRAPHY

O. Jonas: *Das Wesen des musikalischen Kunstwerks: eine Einführung in die Lehre Heinrich Schenkers* (Vienna, 1934, rev. 2/1972)

A. T. Katz: *Challenge to Musical Tradition: a New Concept of Tonality* (New York, 1945)

H. Federhofer: *Beiträge zur musikalischen Gestaltanalyse* (Graz, 1950)

M. Mann: 'Schenker's Contribution to Music Theory', *MR*, x (1949), 3

F. Salzer: *Structural Hearing: Tonal Coherence in Music* (New York, 1952, rev. 2/1962; Ger. trans., 1957)

O. Jonas: Introduction to Eng. trans. of H. Schenker: *Harmonielehre* (Chicago, 1954)

H. Federhofer: 'Die Funktionstheorie Hugo Riemanns und Die Schichtenlehre Heinrich Schenkers', *Kongressbericht: Wien Mozartjahr 1956*, 183

A. Forte: 'Schenker's Conception of Musical Structure', *JMT*, iii (1959), 1–30

E. Oster: 'Register and the Large-scale Connection', *JMT*, v (1961), 54

H. Federhofer: 'Heinrich Schenker', *Anthony van Hoboken: Festschrift zum 75. Geburtstag* (Mainz, 1962), 63

H. Kaufmann: 'Fortschritt und Reaktion in der Lehre Heinrich Schenkers', *NZM*, Jg.126 (1965), 5

Music Forum (1967–) [incl. many exx. of Schenkerian analysis]

S. Slatin: *The Theories of Heinrich Schenker in Perspective* (diss., Columbia U., 1967)

D. Beach: 'A Schenker Bibliography', *JMT*, xiii (1969), 1037

F. Salzer and C. Schachter: *Counterpoint in Composition: the Study of Voice Leading* (New York, 1969)

J. Rothgeb: 'Design as a Key to Structure in Tonal Music', *JMT*, xv (1971), 230

C. Dahlhaus: 'Schoenberg and Schenker', *PRMA*, c (1973–4), 209

W. Drabkin: 'The New *Erläuterungsausgabe*', *PNM*, xii/1–2 (1973–4), 319

E. Narmour: *Beyond Schenkerism: the Need for Alternatives in Music Analysis* (Chicago, 1977)

M. Yeston, ed.: *Readings in Schenker Analysis and other Approaches* (New Haven, Conn., 1977)

L. Laskowski: *Heinrich Schenker: an Annotated Index to Analyses of Musical Works* (New York, 1978)

ALLEN FORTE
(with WILLIAM DRABKIN, bibliography)

Schentzer, Johannes [Hans]. German organ builder. His name appears on the taxation roll of Stuttgart for 1508. In 1511 he entered into a contract to build an organ at the Abbey of St Gall (two manuals, 27 stops). In 1514–15 he enlarged the organ at St Thomas, Strasbourg. In 1515 he repaired the small organ in Konstanz Minster, and in 1516–20 he built the large organ there (two manuals, c30 stops). He built organs for St Thomas, Strasbourg (1522–3), Meersburg, Lake Konstanz (1517–26), and Bischofszell (1519–23). In 1525 he became a citizen of Meersburg, and in 1529 and 1540–41 he repaired the organs in Speyer Cathedral and Strasbourg Minster. It was Hans Buchner who recommended him for the work at Konstanz and Speyer. Schentzer also collaborated on Fridolin Sicher's composition, *Resonet in laudibus*.

The period about 1500 was a highpoint for organ building in the south-west part of the German-speaking regions. Schentzer was associated with this development, together with such masters of the craft as H. Tugi, W. and R. Eckstetter, M. Affolterer, J. Sager and K. Reuter. It was in this region, during this period, that several types of organ stop originated: the narrow-scaled Schwegel (later known as Viola da gamba) and Schellenpfeife (later Quintaden); 'Horn mixtures' containing tierces (still of Principal scale and counting as mixtures proper); and reeds with full-length resonators (Posaune, Trompete, Krummhorn and Zink). The designs of this group of organ builders were the most richly varied of the time, corresponding to a golden age for organ music in south-west Germany. Organs had two manuals, with ranges *F* to *a''* (pedals *F* to *c'*) with complete Principal choruses of at least three stops and often up to five or more. Other stops included the Regal and the wide-scaled Gedackt, Hohlflöte and Gemshorn, as well as the narrow-scaled stops and full-length reeds already mentioned. Schentzer's organs represented this type in its most highly developed form.

BIBLIOGRAPHY
M. Praetorius: *Syntagma musicum*, ii (Wolfenbüttel, 1618, 2/1619/R1958)
M. Vogeleis: *Quellen und Bausteine zu einer Geschichte der Musik und des Theaters im Elsass 1500 bis 1800* (Strasbourg, 1911)
H. Klotz: *Über die Orgelkunst der Gotik, der Renaissance und des Barock* (Kassel, 1934, 2/1975) 61ff, 86ff
W. R. Nef: 'Der Sankt Galler Organist Fridolin Sicher und seine Orgeltabulatur', *Schweizerisches Jb für Musikwissenschaft*, vii (1938)
I. Rücker: *Die deutsche Orgel am Oberrhein um 1500* (Freiburg, 1940)
M. Schuler: 'Der Orgelmacher Hans Schentzer: zur Geschichte des deutschen Orgelbaus im frühen 16. Jahrhundert', *Musik und Kirche*, xxxii (1962), 123
——: 'Schentzer', *MGG*

HANS KLOTZ

Scherbaum, Adolf (*b* Eger, 23 Aug 1909). German trumpeter of Austrian birth. He studied at the Prague Conservatory from 1923 to 1929, and then obtained his first professional position in a spa orchestra in Moravia. In 1929 he was appointed first trumpet in the orchestra of the Brno Opera, and subsequently became principal trumpet in orchestras in Prague (1939–41), Berlin (1941–5), Bratislava (1946–51) and Hamburg (1951–66). In 1966 he was appointed professor at the Musikhochschule in Saarbrücken.

Scherbaum was already well known as a soloist before World War II. By rigorous training he developed unusually strong diaphragm and cheek muscles for sustained playing in the high register. Thus equipped, he played a leading part in the European revival of the trumpet as a solo instrument in Baroque music, and he

was the first to use a piccolo B♭ trumpet for D trumpet parts. He has toured throughout the world, as a soloist and with his own Baroque ensemble, and has made many gramophone records, including several of Bach's Brandenburg Concerto no.2 (which he has performed more than 400 times). In 1971, with the firm of Scherbaum & Göttner, he started making trumpets with detachable bells, and mouthpieces in three parts, to allow great flexibility of timbre and pitch.

EDWARD H. TARR

Scherchen, Hermann (*b* Berlin, 21 June 1891; *d* Florence, 12 June 1966). German conductor. He was mainly self-taught as a musician, and from the age of 16 was a violist in the Blüthner Orchestra and the Berlin PO, 1907–10. In 1911 he worked with Schoenberg in

Hermann Scherchen

preparing *Pierrot lunaire* for performance, and made his début as a conductor during the German tour that followed the work's Berlin première, showing the support for new musical trends that characterized most of his later work. He became conductor of the Riga SO in 1914, but was interned by the Russians when war broke out. On his return to Berlin in 1918 he founded the Neue Musikgesellschaft, the Scherchen Quartet and, in 1919, the militant musical journal *Melos*. At this time he also lectured at the Musikhochschule, directed a workingmen's choir, and in 1921 became conductor of the Leipzig Konzertverein's Grotrian-Steinweg Orchestra. He succeeded Furtwängler as director of the Frankfurt Museumskonzerte in 1922, and in the same year began an association with the Winterthur Musikkollegium in Switzerland that continued intermittently until 1947. He was also actively involved with the ISCM from its foundation in 1923, and was frequently the principal conductor at its festivals, both before and after World War II. During the 1920s and 1930s he toured widely in Europe, making regular appearances in London, and among the many new works whose premières he gave were the Three Fragments from *Wozzeck* at Frankfurt in 1924 (the year before the opera was first staged under Kleiber), and Hába's *Matka* at Munich (1930). He was appointed Generalmusikdirektor at Königsberg in 1928 and chief conductor of the East German RO, but in 1933 he left Germany to settle in Switzerland, where he became musical director of the Zurich RO and later at Beromünster. He edited *Musica viva*, a journal for new music published in Brussels (1933–6), and gave regular courses in conducting which became an annual summer school in Switzerland in 1939. That year he formed the Ars Viva Orchestra, with which he often toured, and in 1943 at Winterthur he conducted the première of Webern's Variations for Orchestra op.30, with the composer present.

After the war Scherchen resumed his varied activities on a wider scale. He held master classes in conducting at the Venice Biennale and at Darmstadt; founded the Ars Viva edition (for the publication of new music) at Zurich in 1950; and, with the support of UNESCO, opened a studio for electro-acoustic research in 1954 at Gravesano, the Swiss village where he lived; its scientific results were published in the *Gravesaner Blätter*. At the same time he brought fresh vigour to the propagation of new music, conducting the premières of such works as Dallapiccola's *Il prigioniero* (Florence, 1950), Dessau's *Das Verhör des Lukullus* (Berlin, 1951), and the original version of Henze's *König Hirsch* (Berlin, 1956). His Darmstadt performance in 1951 of the 'Dance round the Golden Calf' from *Moses und Aron* was the first music to be heard from Schoenberg's opera. He edited the score for the opera's Hamburg radio première under Rosbaud in 1954, and he conducted the 1959 production at the Berlin Städtische Oper that was regarded as decisive for the work's wider success. His début in the USA was not until 1964, when he appeared first at Philadelphia and later in New York.

Scherchen was one of the 20th century's outstanding musical pioneers, and his career was principally dedicated to the better understanding of contemporary music. He refused to limit his interest to accepted styles and was open to all forms of musical experiment, thereby influencing a generation of younger practitioners by his example and his teaching. His conducting, which usually disdained the use of a baton, was functional, clear and scholarly, but it combined knowledge of detail with vitality of spirit. He wrote a practical and informative textbook on his approach and method. Many of his performances were regarded as model interpretations, especially of works of the Second Viennese School, and of Busoni, Dallapiccola, Hindemith, Prokofiev and Stravinsky. They formed a point of reference for those who followed him, but surprisingly few were recorded. He composed a string quartet, piano trio and songs (*Heine-Lieder*). His work continued until four days before his death, when he had a heart attack during a performance of Malipiero's *Orfeide* at Florence.

WRITINGS
Lehrbuch des Dirigierens (Leipzig, 1929; Eng. trans., 1933, as *Handbook of Conducting*)
Das moderne Musikempfinden, i: *Vom Wesen der Musik* (Zurich, 1946; Eng. trans., 1950, as *The Nature of Music*)
Musik für jedermann (Winterthur, 1950)

BIBLIOGRAPHY
W. Reich: 'Hermann Scherchen', *The Chesterian*, xvii (1936), 176
——: 'Hermann Scherchen und "Melos": zum 60. Geburtstag des Dirigenten am 21. Juni', *Melos*, xviii (1951), 188
F. Herzfeld: 'Hermann Scherchen', *Magie des Taktstocks* (Berlin, 1953, rev. 3/1967)
H. Searle: 'Hermann Scherchen', *Gramophone Record Review* (1957), no.44, p.68 [with discography by F. F. Clough and G. J. Cuming]
H. Curjel: 'Gedenkrede', *Generalprogramm des Musikkollegiums Winterthur* (1967–8)

GERHARD BRUNNER

Scherchen-Hsiao, Tona (*b* Neuchâtel, 12 March 1938). Swiss composer. The daughter of the conductor Hermann Scherchen and the composer Hsiao Shu-sien, she was brought up in Switzerland and then, from 1949, in China, where her maternal grandfather initiated her into classical Chinese culture. She learnt to play the *p'i-p'a* (Chinese lute) and also studied Chinese music at the Peking Conservatory and the Shanghai Music Academy. In 1960 she returned to Europe and completed her education with composition studies under Henze at the Salzburg Mozarteum (1961–3), Messiaen at the Paris Conservatoire (1963–5) and Ligeti in Vienna (1966–7). Her works include a great many with Chinese titles, but she has never made any direct use of Chinese music; her orientalism is, rather, a matter of exquisite gestures placed on unmeasured canvases of time, somewhat as in the music of Takemitsu, whose leanings towards contemporary French music she shares.

WORKS
(*selective list*)
Orch: Khouang, 1966; Vague T'ao, 1974–5; 'S . . .', 1975; L'invitation au voyage, chamber orch, 1976–7; Oeil de chat, 1976–7; Lô, trbn, 12 str, 1978–9
Vocal: Wai, Mez, str qt, 1966; Tzi, 16 solo vv, 1969–70
Chamber: Shen, 6 perc/perc orch, 1968; Hsun, ob + eng hn, tpt, trbn, perc, 2 vc, 1968; Tzoue, fl/cl, hpd, vc/db, 1970; Yun-yu, vn/va, vib, 1972; Bien, 12 insts, 1972–3; Lien, va, 1973; Tjao-huen, fl, ob, cl, trbn, 3 perc, va, vc, 1973; Yi, 2 mar, 1973; Ziguidor, wind qnt, 1977
Principal publishers: Boosey & Hawkes, Universal

PAUL GRIFFITHS

Scherer (i). German family of organ builders. Jakob Scherer (*d* Hamburg, 1574 or later), took over the business of Jakob Iversand (*d* Hamburg, 1537), who had built organs (with Open Diapason 24′) for St Jakobi and St Petri, Hamburg (1512–16 and earlier). Scherer was active from 1538 to 1570; he built new organs for Ratzeburg Cathedral (1551–63; one manual, 11 stops), St Marien, Stettin (1557–60), St Jakobi, Stettin (1564–6), and St Jakobi, Magdeburg (1568), and he carried out major alterations at St Nikolai, Mölln (1555–8; one manual, 14 stops), and St Nikolai, Kiel (1564; two manuals, 22 stops). He built a new *Rückpositiv* for the Totentanzorgel at St Marien, Lübeck, 1557–8, and a new *Brustwerk* for the large organ there, 1560–61. He was repeatedly engaged at St Katharinen and St Jakobi, Hamburg, where he was assisted for some of the time by his son-in-law Dirk Hoyer. Hans Scherer the elder (*d* Hamburg, 1611) is known to have been assisting his father as early as 1541. His organs include those at St Marien, Bernau (1572–3; two manuals, 29 stops), the Liebfrauenkirche, Stendal (1580; two manuals, 29 stops), St Nikolai, Lüneburg (1594), Meldorf Cathedral (1596–7), Brake Castle (1600; two manuals, 20 stops), St Georg, Hildesheim (1601–5), St Gertrud, Hamburg (1605–7), and Rotenburg Castle, Hanover (1608). He also carried out important alterations and enlargements at St Katharinen, St Petri and St Jakobi (enlarged to three manuals, 54 stops), Hamburg, and elsewhere.

Organs built by Hans the younger (*fl c*1600–31) include three at Kassel: the Schlosskirche (1607–9; two manuals, 20 stops), the Brüderkirche (*c*1610; two manuals, 25 stops), and St Martini (1600–12; three manuals, 33 stops), and other instruments at St Stephani, Tangermünde (the casework and some stops survive), St Ägidien, Lübeck (1624–5; three manuals,

36 stops; the casework survives), and Minden Cathedral (1625–6).

The Scherer family, particularly Hans the elder, played a significant part in the development of the Hamburg Baroque style, which was to reach its final stage with Gottfried Fritzsche. They combined into a coherent whole three distinct organ types: the splendid, though relatively undeveloped, organ of early Hamburg (as built by Iversand); the Brabant organ (see NIEHOFF); and the organ of central Germany (see BECK). In contrast to the central German style, the Scherers introduced full-length resonators for Posaune, Trompete, Schalmei, Krummhorn and Zink, and divided the *Hauptwerk* into two parts: *Prinzipalwerk* and *Oberpositiv*. But in contrast to the Brabant organ they retained the use of slider-chests and made the Pedal fully independent.

Pupils of Hans the elder include Hans Bockelmann (organs at Hemme, 1598, and Marne, 1609–10) and Anton Wilde (organs at Lüdingworth, 1598–9, and Wöhrden, 1593–5; both survive in an altered form). His most important pupil was his son, Hans the younger, who was responsible for the most mature examples of the famous 'Hamburg organ front' (introduced by the Scherer family at St Jakobi, Hamburg, in 1576), examples of which can still be seen at Tangermünde and Lübeck.

BIBLIOGRAPHY
M. Praetorius: *Syntagma musicum*, ii (Wolfenbüttel, 1618, 2/1619/*R*1958)
H. Kellinghusen: 'Die Hamburgischen Orgelbauer Hans Scherer, Vater und Sohn', *Mitteilungen des Vereins für Hamburgische Geschichte* (1912), 72
P. Rubardt: 'Einige Nachrichten über die Orgelbauerfamilie Scherer', *Musik und Kirche*, ii (1930) 111
W. Stahl: *Geschichte der Kirchenmusik in Lübeck bis zum Anfang des 19. Jahrhunderts* (Kassel, 1931)
G. Fock: 'Hamburgs Anteil am Orgelbau im niederdeutschen Kulturgebiet', *Zeitschrift des Vereins für Hamburgische Geschichte*, xxxviii (1939), 289–373
——: 'Scherer', *MGG*
——: *Arp Schnitger und seine Schule* (Kassel, 1974)
HANS KLOTZ

Scherer (ii) (*fl* ?1764). Maker of woodwind instruments, probably in France. Although he was one of the most prolific woodwind instrument makers of his day, Scherer left few traces of his place of work and activities behind him. The only contemporary reference to him, an advertisement which appeared in the Lyons *Les affiches* on 15 February 1764, merely concerns the sale of 'a very good bassoon of Scherer'. Zimmermann speculated that Scherer was of Alsatian ancestry because of the prevalence of the name there, and he also suggested that because Scherer used typical French makers' marks, the rearing lion and the fleur-de-lis, he worked in France.

Scherer's instruments are found today in most of the major instrument collections (Berlin, Brussels, Leipzig, Dayton C. Miller, Paris, The Hague and Zurich) as well as numerous smaller ones. They include examples of a *flûte à la tierce*, numerous flutes of standard pitch, flutes d'amore, an alto flute in G and a stock flute; oboes, oboes d'amore and oboes da caccia; clarinets; bassoons and fagottini; and a bass recorder. Many of the flutes as well as some of the clarinets and oboes are made of ivory. Scherer's most famous instruments are a pair of flutes which were made for Frederick the Great; they are now in the Staatliches Institut für Musikforschung at Berlin. Each flute originally comprised a head joint, four

upper middle joints of different lengths including one of d'amore pitch, a lower middle joint and a foot joint; some of these joints are now missing and others had additional keys added to them around 1800. One of the original head joints, which was lost during World War II, bore the king's monogram.

BIBLIOGRAPHY
L. Vallas: *Un siècle de musique et de théâtre à Lyon 1688–1789* (Lyons, 1932), 373
J. Zimmermann: 'Die Flötenmacher Friedrichs des Grossen', *ZI*, xl (1940), 141, 160
F. G. Rendall: *The Clarinet* (London, 1954, rev. 3/1971), 13, 16, 69, 71
L. G. Langwill: *An Index of Musical Wind-instrument Makers* (Edinburgh, 1960, rev. 3/1972), 141
——: *The Bassoon and Contrabassoon* (London, 1965), 29
JANE M. BOWERS

Scherer, Michael. See TONSOR, MICHAEL.

Scherer [Scherrer, Scheerer], **N.** [?Theophil] (*fl* Geneva, *c*1770–90). German harpsichordist, organist and composer. He taught the piano in Geneva to Prince Friedrich Franz of Mecklenburg-Schwerin, to whom he dedicated his first publication, *6 sonates mises en trio* op.1 for harpsichord, violin and cello (as the prince became Grand Duke of Mecklenburg-Schwerin in 1785, the sonatas must have been printed before then). His other extant works made their way to Schwerin through his connection with the prince and probably date from the same period. They include three sets of three sonatas for harpsichord with obbligato violin (opp.3, 4 and 8), two sets of six sonatas for cello and continuo (opp.5 and 9), *6 simphonies* for eight instruments (op.6) and a *Symphonie périodique* for eight instruments. They were all published in Geneva and are concise, pleasant pieces of chamber music in the style of Haydn. The Landesbibliothek, Schwerin, also has a manuscript march for keyboard by him.

BIBLIOGRAPHY
EitnerQ; *GerberL*
H. Mendel and A. Reissmann: *Musikalisches Conversations-Lexikon* (Berlin, 1870–79, suppl. 1880)
C. Meyer: *Geschichte der Mecklenburg-Schweriner Hofkapelle* (Schwerin, 1913)
DIETER HÄRTWIG

Scherer, Sebastian Anton (*b* Ulm, 3 Oct 1631; *d* Ulm, 26 Aug 1712). German composer and organist. He spent almost the whole of his life in his native town. He probably studied with Tobias Eberlin, organist of Ulm Cathedral, whom he succeeded on 22 December 1671 and whose daughter he married. He had been elected a town musician at Ulm on 17 June 1653, and it was probably about this time or shortly afterwards that he became assistant to Eberlin. In 1668 he became director of music at the college in Ulm and taught the cathedral choristers. According to Eitner he was appointed organist of St Thomas's Church, Strasbourg, on 4 November 1684, but, as André Pirro suggested, he only acted as consultant in connection with the organ there: he was in fact organist of Ulm Cathedral for over 40 years up to his death.

Several pieces in Scherer's op.1 reveal a sensitive and imaginative approach to word-setting. He dedicated his op.2 to the collegium musicum at nearby Memmingen, where he may have had family connections and musical associates. The plan of the publication, half of which is in tablature and half in score, owes much to Frescobaldi's *Fiori musicali* (1635), and the last intonation uses the *bergamasca* theme that Merulo and

Frescobaldi had popularized. The volume is not, then, a *livre d'orgue* in the French manner but a fine collection of sturdy organ music in the Italian manner, full of ingenuity and invention. Some of the trio sonatas of 1680 are of fine quality, and the slow movements anticipate the restrained beauty of Corelli's sonatas.

WORKS

Musica sacra . . . missae, psalmi, et motetti, 3–5vv, insts, bc (org), op.1 (Ulm, 1657)
Operum musicorum secundum, distinctum in libros 2: tabulaturam, hpd/org, intonationum brevium per 8 tonos et partituram 8 toccatarum usui aptam cum vel sine pedali (Ulm, 1664); ed. A. Guilmant and A. Pirro, Archives des maîtres de l'orgue, viii (Paris, 1907)
Traur- und Klaggesang, 5vv, bc (Ulm, 1664)
Jubilate Deo and O quam mirabilis, *S-Uu*

[14] Sonatae, 2 vn, va da gamba/bn, bc, op.3 (Ulm, 1680)
Suites, lute (Augsburg, n.d.), lost

BIBLIOGRAPHY

EitnerQ; WaltherML
K. Blessinger: *Studien zur Ulmer Musikgeschichte im 17. Jahrhundert insbesondere über Leben und Werk S. A. Scherers* (Ulm, 1913)
G. Frotscher: *Geschichte des Orgel-Spiels und der Orgel-Komposition* (Berlin, 1935–6, enlarged 3/1966)
W. Apel: *Geschichte der Orgel- und Klaviermusik bis 1700* (Kassel, 1967; Eng. trans., rev. 1972)

GWILYM BEECHEY

Scherffenstein, Martin Kinner von. *See* KINNER VON SCHERFFENSTEIN, MARTIN.

Scherffer von Scherffenstein, Wenzel [Wencel, Wenceslaus] (*b* Leobschütz, Upper Silesia [now Głubczyce, Poland], 1603; *d* Brieg, Silesia [now Brzeg, Poland], 27 Aug 1674). German poet, translator, composer and organist. His life and work were closely connected with his native Silesia and its ducal family, the Piasten. He has been described as their 'court poet' (see Drechsler) for having chronicled in his poetry both major and minor events in their lives and reign. From the early 1630s he was court organist at Brieg for about 40 years. He is more important as a poet and translator than as a musician, and he was crowned poet laureate in 1653. In his poetry he supported the reform efforts of his fellow Silesian MARTIN OPITZ regarding prosody and the purity of the German language. Yet he opposed Opitz's precepts by using the Silesian dialect and thus retained an earthy flavour reminiscent of the German Renaissance which is particularly evident in a raucous comic work, the expanded and updated translation into Alexandrine verse of Fridericus Dedekind's satirical Latin *Grobianus* ('The boor') of 1552–4. His wide-ranging output includes an elaborate eulogy of music, *Der Music Lob*, which is regarded as his finest work.

Scherffer received his musical training from his friend Matthäus Apelles von Löwenstern. His stature as a composer can no longer be assessed, since of four occasional sacred and secular works that survived into the 20th century (see list in *MGG*) only one – *Psalmus CXXXIII: Siehe wie fein und lieblich ist* (Brieg, 1636) – escaped destruction in World War II.

BIBLIOGRAPHY

EitnerQ
P. Drechsler: *Wencel Scherffer von Scherffenstein* (Breslau, 1886)
C. von Faber du Faur: *German Baroque Literature* (New Haven, Conn., 1958), 70f

TRAUTE MAASS MARSHALL

Schering, Arnold (*b* Breslau, 2 April 1877; *d* Berlin, 7 March 1941). German musicologist. He studied the violin at an early age and in 1896 went to Berlin to study under Joachim with a view to becoming a violin virtuoso. Two years later, however, he decided on an academic career and at Berlin University read history of music with Fleischer and psychology of music with Stumpf. In 1902, after one term at Munich with Sandberger, he took the PhD at Leipzig University under Kretzschmar with a thesis on the early violin concerto; he later published this in an extended form as *Die Geschichte des Instrumental-Konzerts bis auf die Gegenwart*.

Schering soon became associated with several music journals; he was editor of the *Neue Zeitschrift für Musik* (1903–5) and of the *Bach-Jahrbuch* (1904–39). In 1907 he completed his *Habilitation* at Leipzig University with a dissertation on the rise of the oratorio, and in 1915 he became professor there in the history and aesthetics of music. From 1909 he also taught music history at the Leipzig Conservatory. In 1920 Schering succeeded Abert as professor of music at Halle, and in 1928 he moved to Berlin, where he held the chair of musicology until his death.

Schering had a deep love for the music of the past; this music he sought to revive and make relevant to modern times. With this end in view, he inaugurated two serial publications, Perlen Alter Kammermusik and Perlen Alter Gesangsmusik, covering the field of both chamber and vocal music. Other new editions appeared in Denkmäler Deutscher Tonkunst, among them works by Hasse, Kuhnau and Schütz (whose *Christmas Story* he had rediscovered at Uppsala in 1908). His greatest contribution to the study of musicology is probably his *Geschichte der Musik in Beispielen* (1931), outstanding in both the scope and the scholarship of its 300 music examples. He wrote the second and third volumes of a general musical history of Leipzig, the second volume of which includes a detailed discussion of Bach.

One of Schering's main interests was the interpretation of Bach's music. In his attempt to rediscover the key to Bach's art of textual interpretation he brought to light what theorists from the 16th to the 18th centuries had called the *ars inveniendi*; its musical counterpart he saw in the *musica poetica* of the Baroque period. His research into the revival of old music found its culmination in the important *Aufführungspraxis alter Musik* (1931); he was also the first to question the generally accepted theory that all sacred music up to the 16th century was performed *a cappella*.

Schering tended increasingly to approach musicology from an aesthetic and even psychological point of view. To him music was a poetic composition in sound stemming from a non-musical source. He expounded these ideas in his book *Das Symbol in der Musik* (1941). He reached the final point of his search for meaning when he turned to Beethoven. Here, applying his ideas of symbolic interpretation, he saw a veiled synthesis of music and poetry. A chance remark of Beethoven's led him to seek in Shakespeare's dramas as well as in Schiller's the hidden inspiration behind certain of Beethoven's string quartets and piano sonatas. In the introduction to *Beethoven und die Dichtung* (1936) he presented this thesis persuasively, even though he overreached himself in his attempt, much criticized at the time, to prove the validity of his conclusions.

See also ANALYSIS, §II, 5, and figs. 9–10.

WRITINGS

Bachs Textbehandlung (Leipzig, 1900)
Geschichte des Instrumental-(Violin-)Konzerts bis A. Vivaldi (diss., U. of Leipzig, 1902; Leipzig, 1905, 2/1927/*R*1965)
Die Anfänge des Oratoriums (Habilitationsschrift, U. of Leipzig, 1907; Leipzig, 1911/*R*1966 as *Geschichte des Oratoriums*)

Musikalische Bildung und Erziehung zum musikalischen Hören
(Leipzig, 1911, 4/1924)
Deutsche Haus- und Kirchenmusik im 16. Jahrhundert (Langensalza, 1912)
Die niederländische Orgelmesse im Zeitalter des Josquin (Leipzig, 1912/R1971)
ed. A. von Dommer: *Handbuch der Musikgeschichte* (Leipzig, 3/1914/R1976, 4–6/1923/R1970)
Studien zur Musikgeschichte der Frührenaissance (Leipzig, 1914)
Tabellen der Musikgeschichte (Leipzig, 1914, 5/1962 ed. H. J. Moser)
Deutsche Musikgeschichte im Umriss (Leipzig, 1917)
Beethoven und der deutsche Idealismus (Leipzig, 1921)
Gegenwarts- und Zukunftsaufgaben unserer Kirchenmusik (Halle, 1922)
Die metrisch-rhythmische Grundgestalt unserer Choralmelodien (Halle, 1924)
Musikgeschichte Leipzigs, ii: Von 1650 bis 1723 (Leipzig, 1926)
Aufführungspraxis alter Musik (Leipzig, 1931/R1969)
Geschichte der Musik in Beispielen (Leipzig, 1931, 2/1954/R1972; Eng. trans., 1950)
Beethoven in neuer Deutung (Leipzig, 1934)
Beethoven und die Dichtung (Berlin, 1936/R1973)
Johann Sebastian Bachs Leipziger Kirchenmusik (Leipzig, 1936/R1968, 2/1954)
Zur Erkenntnis Beethovens (Würzburg, 1938)
Franz Schuberts Symphonie in H-moll und ihr Geheimnis (Würzburg, 1939)
Von grossen Meistern der Musik (Leipzig, 1940)
ed. W. Gurlitt: *Das Symbol in der Musik* (Leipzig, 1941)
J. S. Bach und das Musikleben in Leipzig im 18. Jahrhundert (Leipzig, 1941)
ed. F. Blume: *Über Kantaten J. S. Bachs* (Leipzig, 1942, 2/1950)
——: *Vom musikalischen Kunstwerk* (Leipzig, 1949, 2/1951) [articles 1937–41]
Humor, Heldentum, Tragik bei Beethoven (Strasbourg, 1955)
ed. K. M. Komma: *Vom Wesen der Musik* (Stuttgart, 1974)

EDITIONS

J. A. Hasse: La conversione di Sant'Agostino, DDT, xx (1905/R)
Instrumentalkonzerte deutscher Meister, DDT, xxix–xxx (1905/R)
H. Schütz: Historia von der Geburt Jesu Christi, Sämtliche Werke, xvii (Leipzig, 1909)
Ausgewählte Kirchenkantaten, DDT, lviii–lix (1918/R)
J. Pezel: Turmmusik und Suiten, DDT, lxiii (1928/R)

BIBLIOGRAPHY

M. Schneider: 'Arnold Schering zum 60. Geburtstag', *JbMP 1936*, 9
H. Osthoff, ed.: *Festschrift Arnold Schering* (Berlin, 1937) [contains extensive list of writings]
W. Serauky: 'Arnold Schering zum 60. Geburtstag', *ZfM*, Jg.104 (1937), 371
E. Blom: 'Lurid Lights on Beethoven', *Beethoven's Pianoforte Sonatas Discussed* (London, 1938), 155
W. Gurlitt: 'Arnold Schering', *Musik und Kirche*, xiii (1941), 90
——: 'Nachwort', in A. Schering: *Das Symbol in der Musik* (Leipzig, 1941), 173
H. Osthoff: 'Arnold Schering', *AMf*, vi (1941), 66 [obituary]
——: 'Schering, Arnold', *MGG* [with list of writings incl. articles]
A. Forchert: 'Scherings Beethovendeutungen und ihre methodischen Voraussetzungen', *Beiträge zur musikalischen Hermeneutik* (Regensburg, 1975), 41
EDITH B. SCHNAPPER

Scherley, Joseph. *See* SHERLY, JOSEPH.

Scherman, Thomas (Kielty) (*b* New York, 12 Feb 1917; *d* New York, 14 May 1979). American conductor. He graduated at Columbia University in 1937, then studied the piano with Vengerova, theory with Weisse, and conducting with Carl Bamberger and Max Rudolf. After wartime army service he gained valuable experience in 1947 as assistant conductor at the National Opera in Mexico City. The same year he organized the Little Orchestra Society, whose inaugural series of eight concerts at Town Hall, New York, was successful enough to be followed by an expansion to embrace opera and oratorio, the addition of concerts outside the city, and the inception in 1948 of a series of children's concerts at Hunter College. Dedicated principally to the championing of new and unfamiliar music, and benefiting from Scherman's imaginative programme planning, the society has been one of the longest-lived and most im-portant of several such organizations. Scherman's performances, though affected by the insufficient rehearsal that often bedevils the non-standard repertory, were on occasion, such as a 1967 presentation of Delius's *A Mass of Life*, as memorable in execution as they were bold in conception.
BERNARD JACOBSON

Schermerhorn, Kenneth (de Witt) (*b* Schenectady, NY, 20 Nov 1929). American conductor. He played the trumpet, and was trained as a conductor at the New England Conservatory, Boston, under Richard Burgin, and at the Berkshire Music Center, Tanglewood, where he won the Koussevitzky Prize. He gained important experience as conductor of the 7th US Army SO in Germany, 1954–5. He was music director of the American Ballet Theatre, 1957–67 (he married the company's principal ballerina, Lupe Serrano), assistant conductor of the New York PO, 1960–61, and music director of the New Jersey SO, 1963–8. In 1968 he became music director of the Milwaukee SO.

In part because of his ballet theatre experience, Schermerhorn is one of the most versatile, dependable American conductors of his generation. It was under him that the New Jersey orchestra began to improve considerably, and he has been responsible for the growth of musical life in Milwaukee. A thoughtful, responsible musician, Schermerhorn has paid special attention to the educational functions of a conductor.
MICHAEL STEINBERG

Scherndorp, Philipp. *See* SCHOENDORFF, PHILIPP.

Scherp (Dutch). An ORGAN STOP (*Scharf*).

Scherrer, N. [? Theophil]. *See* SCHERER, N.

Scherzando (It.: 'playfully'; gerund of *scherzare*, to joke, jest). A mark of expression also found in the forms *scherzevole* (adjective from *scherzare*) and *scherzoso* (adjective from *scherzo*: 'joke'). The third movement of Beethoven's Eighth Symphony marked *allegretto scherzando* is perhaps the most famous use of the word and is fully characteristic, as is the same marking on the second movement ('Giuoco delle coppie') of Bartók's Concerto for Orchestra.

For bibliography *see* TEMPO AND EXPRESSION MARKS.
DAVID FALLOWS

Scherzer. German firm of brass instrument manufacturers. It was founded in 1933 by Kurt Scherzer (*b* Markneukirchen, Feb 1895; *d* Augsburg, May 1962), who learnt the trade from his father in Markneukirchen. Hermann Sandner (*b* Graslitz, 23 April 1933), who entered the firm in 1949 and became a Meister in 1953, took over the business in 1961. The firm produces over 70 different models of brass instruments, including trumpets from B♭ to piccolo B♭ (the B♭ and D trumpets are particularly praised), bass trumpets, cornets, horns, trombones from soprano to contrabass, Wagner tubas, tubas in F, E♭, C and B♭, and signal instruments.
EDWARD H. TARR

Scherzetto, scherzino. A short or very slight piece in the character of a scherzo. Schumann used the term in his *Albumblätter* op.124, and 'The Little Bells', from Elgar's Suite no.2, *The Wand of Youth* (1908), is subtitled 'Scherzino'.

Scherzevole. *See* SCHERZANDO.

Scherzo (It.: 'joke'). A classic movement-type, generally swift and light in character and commonly in triple time. The term first appeared in Italy at the beginning of the 17th century as one of the innumerable fanciful names used to describe a vocal madrigal of the balletto type. Monteverdi's *Scherzi musicali* of 1607 are frivolous in tone and unambitious in scope; those in his second book (1632) are more substantial and varied. We also find vocal *scherzi* by Antonio Brunelli, Antonio Cifra (including *Scherzi sacri*, 1616), and Biagio Marini. Troilo's *Sinfonie, scherzi* (etc) of 1608 are instrumental pieces, and it is to instrumental music that the term applies when it occurs, albeit rarely, in the period 1650–1750. Rubert's *Sinfonie, scherzi* (etc; 1650, now lost) are for two violins and continuo; J. J. Walther's *Scherzi* (1676) are for solo violin and continuo; Johannes Schenk's *Scherzi musicali* (c1698) are suites for viola da gamba and continuo. There is a single scherzo in Bach's works, the penultimate movement of the A minor Partita, light rather than frivolous in tone. Bach's use of the term may derive from his knowledge of F. A. Bonporti's *Invenzioni* (c1713), where it occurs several times.

Haydn marked the finale of one of his piano sonatas (F major, HXVI:9, before 1766) 'scherzo', and the marking 'scherzando' appears in C. P. E. Bach's flute sonatas of 1770 (WQ82). The fifth movement of Stephen Storace's Piano Quintet op.2 no.2 (1784) is a scherzo. The scherzo's decisive admission to the canon of movements in regular Classical usage dates from Haydn's quartets op.33 (1781), sometimes known as 'Gli scherzi' since the movement that would then conventionally have been a minuet is headed either 'scherzando' or 'scherzo'. Haydn's intention with this unusual title is not clear, since the movements are not, as a body, lighter or more humorous than his usual type of minuet, and one (no.3) is decidedly serious, even sombre, in colour. Playfulness and jocularity are frequent enough in Haydn's music, but instead of concentrating these qualities into a regular alternative to the minuet in his sonatas and symphonies, he preferred to exploit the scherzo spirit in his finales, as for instance in two of the piano sonatas (HXVI:50 and 51) written in London in 1794.

It was Beethoven who established the scherzo as a regular alternative to the minuet and as a classic movement-type. From his earliest works the scherzo appears regularly in place of the minuet, and he took the term literally by giving the movement a light and often humorous tone. His scherzos are generally, too, very swift. His need for variety at this juncture was all the greater since he presumed from the beginning, unlike Haydn and Mozart, that piano sonatas and the smaller chamber combinations might embrace the full four-movement design, like symphonies and quartets. As early as op.10 he was having doubts about this and four movements ceased to be a regular quota in such works. Schindler recorded that towards the end of his life Beethoven was contemplating revising some of his earlier works and removing the scherzos.

The wind octet of 1792, published posthumously as op.103, is his first true scherzo, anticipating that of the Septet op.20. The scherzo of the Piano Trio op.1 no.1 is very fast and brittle, with a touch of humour and a clear sense of one pulse to a bar, quite foreign to the minuet. The second Trio of op.1 also has a scherzo, this time

employing cross-accents, another favourite feature of Beethoven's scherzos that reaches an extreme point in the string quartets op.18 no.6 and op.135. With his highly sophisticated sense of musical humour, Beethoven often invested his scherzos with elements of surprise or caprice. The Quartet op.18 no.2 has a scherzo with very short, flippant phrases in rapid exchange and some Haydnesque surprises. The most unashamedly capricious of his scherzos is that in the 'Spring' Sonata op.24, where the violin and piano seem constantly out of step with one another. The Violin Sonata op.30 no.2 in C minor is similarly whimsical, and the Cello Sonata in A op.69 has a scherzo of teasing syncopations.

It was Beethoven's introduction of the scherzo into the symphony that was to have the most far-reaching effect. The First Symphony's third movement is marked 'Menuetto' (this is surprising when he had already given the title 'scherzo' to less scherzo-like pieces; though some scherzos are found marked as minuets in the sketchbooks); its pace marks it as something altogether different from the Classical minuet. Thereafter all his symphonies contain scherzos except the Eighth, where the movement is marked 'Tempo di menuetto'. The title 'scherzo' is in fact found only in the Second and Third. In his symphonic scherzos Beethoven generated great forward momentum by a combination of pace and rapidly alternating textures, and he maintained the Classical tradition of offering a different speed or character, or both, in his trios. The symphonies, too, show the broadest expansion of form in scherzo movements, beginning with the 'Eroica' with its tripartite trio and its written-out da capo, this time *pianissimo* and leading to a forceful coda. With second and fourth movements grown to so large a scale, the scherzo's form expanded correspondingly. The Fifth Symphony's scherzo is linked to the finale, during which it reappears. In the Fourth and Seventh Symphonies the trios appear twice, and in the Seventh there is a further brief reference to the trio before the coda. The scherzo of the Ninth, which comes second in order rather than in the more traditional (but by no means invariable) third place, is both humorous in its unpredictable opening and sophisticated in its rapid fugal textures, and is developed on a scale to match that of the whole symphony.

In his middle and late periods Beethoven did not always give titles to movements of scherzo-like character; and by the time of the late quartets he introduced movements in 2/4 or 4/4 where the effect of a scherzo is obviously intended. The Presto movements of op.127 and op.131 illustrate this clearly, even though scherzos in time signatures other than 3/4 are found much earlier. In the String Trio op.9 no.3 the scherzo is in 6/8. The finale of the Piano Sonata op.14 no.2, entitled 'Scherzo', is an extended movement in 3/8, and the Piano Sonatas op.31 no.3 and op.110 both have scherzos in 2/4. Beethoven often used the terms 'scherzando' and 'scherzoso', not so much of true scherzos but as an indication of character and pace, especially in his jog-trot Allegretto movements such as the second movement of op.18 no.4. In the String Quartet op.127 the Andante con moto is marked 'poco scherzoso'.

In the wake of Beethoven the scherzo can be said to be normal in Schubert's sonatas and symphonies, where the two halves of the outer section have grown from the simple binary pattern of the Classical minuet into an expanded movement, often, as in the 'Great' C major

Symphony, in full sonata form. His trios provide lyrical contrast, generally with a change of key and character. In Spohr's output minuets and scherzos are equally common, and in Hummel's Septet op.74 a movement is headed 'minuet or scherzo'. A new and dazzling aspect of the scherzo was revealed by Mendelssohn's brilliant studies in fleetness of foot, known best in the scherzos of the Octet (1825) and of the music to *A Midsummer Night's Dream* (1842). Mendelssohn's fairy-like touch extends to other movements besides scherzos, as for example the last movements of the 'Italian' Symphony and the Violin Concerto, and the scherzos, many of them in duple time, are unfailingly light; the delicate *pianissimo* ending is almost a mannerism. Other fine examples are found in the String Quintet in A op.18, the String Quartet in E minor op.44 no.2 and the Piano Trios opp.49 and 66. Some of his scherzos dispense with a trio.

Berlioz's 'Queen Mab' scherzo in *Roméo et Juliette* (1839), a tour de force of gossamer orchestration, owes something to Mendelssohn's model, and so do a number of Schumann examples, including that in the Piano Quartet op.47. But Schumann and Brahms, especially the latter, were generally content to build scherzos after Beethoven's pattern. Schumann particularly favoured the alternation with more than one trio. Because Brahms avoided the conventional scherzo in his symphonies it has been said that the scherzo was not congenial to him, but this was by no means true, and he is to be credited with introducing a scherzo into the Piano Concerto in B♭ op.83 as an additional movement, an idea that was originally put forward by Schumann and put into practice by Litolff in his 'concerto-symphonies'. In Brahms's First and Third Symphonies the scherzo is replaced by a lyrical movement of moderate tempo, but neither light nor jocular in tone. In the Second Symphony the scherzo and trio are seemingly inverted as well as being thematically linked. The Fourth Symphony contains, in Tovey's words, 'the greatest scherzo since Beethoven', a 2/4 movement of intense seriousness and energy. Mendelssohn's delicacy and Beethoven's humour are absent from Brahms's scherzos, but they can be swift, as in the C major Piano Trio op.87, or rhythmically teasing, as in the *Sonatensatz* for violin and piano. Furthermore Brahms was fond of combining slow movement and scherzo in a single movement, as in the A major Violin Sonata op.100 – an idea which goes back to Beethoven's Serenade op.8 and which was also fruitfully taken up by Lalo in his Cello Concerto.

While in the later 19th century the scherzo was sometimes replaced by a dance movement of national character, as by Dvořák with the furiant, or by a balletic movement, as by Tchaikovsky with the waltz, its standing as a symphonic movement has remained essentially unchallenged, indeed strengthened by its wholehearted acceptance by all major symphonists from Bruckner to Shostakovich. Bruckner's range of scherzos is somewhat narrow, since he favoured a heavy scherzo of great rhythmic impetus with much emphasis on the regular bar-line. The trios normally offer quiet contrast, with ländler-type sections in the earlier symphonies. In the last two symphonies the scherzo is placed second, not third, following the example of Beethoven's Ninth Symphony. Mahler too adopted the ländler, as for example in his First, Fifth and Ninth Symphonies, but he could also give the scherzo a touch of grotesquerie, as in the Fourth Symphony with its scordatura violin, and even horror, as in the Sixth and Seventh

Symphonies. The grotesque is more evident than the jocular in the scherzos of Prokofiev and Shostakovich; Vaughan Williams has a scherzo of pure diablerie in his Sixth Symphony, while Walton marked the scherzo of his First Symphony 'Presto, con malizia'. It is significant that in Holst's *The Planets* it is Uranus the Magician that evokes a scherzo, not Jupiter the Bringer of Jollity; and in Bartók's Concerto for Orchestra the second movement is entitled 'Giuoco delle coppie': though it is a joke, it is not a scherzo.

As an independent movement, detached from the frame of sonata or symphony, the scherzo came vigorously to life with Chopin's four scherzos, all of which are extended works, broadly ternary in structure (except for the Scherzo in C sharp minor) and presto in 3/4 time. Brahms's Scherzo op.4 is of the same kind, with two trios. Smaller unattached scherzos are found in Schumann, including the tiny 'Scherzino' in the *Albumblätter* op.124; a 'Scherzettino' is found among Alkan's *48 Motifs* op.63. Independent orchestral movements of a scherzo type followed, and a number of symphonic poems exploited the scherzo's attributes of grotesquerie, delicacy, or speed. Saint-Saëns' *Danse macabre* is a scherzo in diabolic vein, and Dukas' *L'apprenti sorcier*, subtitled 'scherzo', is both swift and jocular. Strauss's *Burleske* for piano and orchestra was originally entitled 'Scherzo', and his *Till Eulenspiegel* is a scherzo in all but name. With models like Stravinsky's *Scherzo fantastique* and *Scherzo à la Russe*, scherzos for orchestra or other instruments, even for voices, have been common in the present century.

BIBLIOGRAPHY

G. Becking: *Studien zu Beethovens Personalstil: das Scherzothema* (Leipzig, 1921)
A. Adrio: 'Menuett und Scherzo', *Der Musikerzieher*, xxxvi (1940), 115
B. Motylewska: 'Scherzo w okresie przedklasycznym', *Muzyka*, iv (1959), 72
J. Gmeiner: *Menuett und Scherzo: ein Beitrag zur Entwicklungsgeschichte und Soziologie des Tanzsatzes in der Wiener Klassik* (Tutzing, 1979)

HUGH MACDONALD

Scherzoso. *See* SCHERZANDO.

Schetky [Shetky], **J(ohn) George** (*b* Edinburgh, 1 June 1776; *d* Philadelphia, 11 Dec 1831). American cellist, teacher, composer and music publisher of Scottish birth. He was the son of the Edinburgh cellist and composer J. G. C. Schetky and a nephew of Alexander Reinagle. Schetky emigrated to the USA in 1787 and became active as a performer and music teacher in Philadelphia, where he lived with the musicians Benjamin Carr and Joseph C. Taws. With Carr he was co-editor of *The Musical Journal for the Piano Forte* (vols.iii–v) and published music from about 1802 to 1811. Between 1812 and 1818 he apparently visited Britain, for he published piano compositions by his father and himself in London and Edinburgh. He was a co-founder in 1820 of the Musical Fund Society in Philadelphia, which owns a portrait of him.

WORKS

Vocal (1v, pf, unless otherwise stated): The Sails Are Bent, in The Musical Journal for the Piano Forte, iii/51 (1801–2); Haste Ye, in The Musical Journal for the Piano Forte, iii/63 (1801–2); Rondeau chasse, collab. B. Carr, in The Musical Journal for the Piano Forte, iv/91 (1802–3); Largo, in *Masses, Vespers, Litanies*, ed. B. Carr (Philadelphia, 1805); Scena de camera (T. Moore: Lalla Rookh), 2vv, pf (Philadelphia, *c*1821–4); arr. T. Smith: The Welch Harper, 1v, pf/harp (Philadelphia, 1816–17)

Inst: A Favorite Minuet, arr. pf by A. Reinagle, in *12 Favorite Pieces* (Philadelphia, ?1789); Air, pf (Philadelphia, *c*1807–11); arr. Earl

Moira's Welcome to Scotland, rondo, pf (Philadelphia, ?1823); Young Roscius's Strathspey, with variations, pf (Philadelphia, ?1823), arr. F. Koczwara: The Battle of Prague, military band, lost

BIBLIOGRAPHY

L. C. Madeira: *Music in Philadelphia and the Musical Fund Society* (Philadelphia, 1896), 53ff

O. G. Sonneck: *A Bibliography of Early Secular American Music* (Washington, DC, 1905; rev. 2/1945, ed. W. T. Upton; 3/1964)

——: *Early Concert-life in America* (Leipzig, 1907/R1969)

J. Campbell: 'Old Philadelphia Music', *Philadelphia History*, ii (1926), 181

L. O. Schetky: *The Schetky Family: A Compilation of Letters, Memoirs and Historical Data* (Portland, Oregon, 1942)

R. J. Wolfe: *Secular Music in America, 1801–1825: a Bibliography* (New York, 1964)

ANNE SHAPIRO

Schetky, Johann Georg Christoph (*b* Darmstadt, 19 Aug 1737; *d* Edinburgh, 30 Nov 1824). German cellist and composer, father of J. George Schetky. He was born and brought up at the court of Hessen-Darmstadt, where his father, Ernst Gottlieb Schetky (1716–67), was secretary and musician in the service of Landgrave Ludwig VIII. He is said to have studied law at Jena University. At 15 he applied for the post of principal cellist in the Darmstadt orchestra, and he was on the court musicians' payroll from 1758. He studied composition with Endler, the court vice-Kapellmeister, and cello with Anton Filtz, who was in service at nearby Mannheim. With his entire family (his brother Georg Carl Jacob, two sisters Charlotta Louise Dorothea and Ludomilla, and his father), he went to Hamburg in 1763 to give concerts; Schetky's aria *Conservati fidele pensa* for soprano, obbligato cello and strings dates from this time. The concerts were so successful that his father wrote to Darmstadt asking for the family's release from court employment, but was refused. Schetky remained a Darmstadt musician until 1768, though able to travel and give freelance concerts at other courts. He then returned to Hamburg (1768–9) and went to London (early 1772), where he was persuaded by the publisher and agent Robert Bremner to accept the post of principal cellist to the Edinburgh Musical Society.

Schetky at first intended to spend only one year in Edinburgh; but he married Maria Theresa Reinagle, eldest daughter of an émigré Austrian musical family, in 1774, had 11 children, and stayed there the rest of his life. In addition to a certain musical fame achieved by his son J. George Schetky, another son, John Christian Schetky (*b* 1778), was Marine Painter-in-Ordinary to George IV, William IV and Queen Victoria. Schetky easily won a place in fashionable Edinburgh society. He was present at Burns's installation at the Kilwinning masonic lodge (1787); entertained the young Hummel during his Edinburgh visit (1788); set Burns's lyric *Clarinda, Mistress of my Soul* (probably on 24 January 1788, during a heavy evening's drinking with the poet; ironically, this is Schetky's only composition that is remembered in Scotland); and directed the music at the foundation of Edinburgh University's Old Quadrangle (16 November 1789). He entertained Louis XVIII in exile at Holyrood Palace (1793), conducted the band of a famous amateur civil defence regiment, the Gentlemen Volunteers (1794), and set three of Walter Scott's lyrics, with the poet's approval (around 1810). He came out of retirement at 76 to play the cello in the first Edinburgh Musical Festival in 1815.

Schetky's career as a composer stretched from the 1760s to the second decade of the 19th century. His earliest works seem mainly to have been a means of publicizing his abilities as a cellist: they include sonatas, variations and concertos, as well as trios and even vocal works with cello obbligato, and only the three symphonies do not give the cello a prominent role. Other works often ascribed to his early period, an oratorio (actually by Graupner) and a flute trio probably by his brother, are misattributed. The youthful works are weak and dependent on cliché and sequence; the symphonies are pedestrian imitations of works by such Mannheim composers as Filtz.

Most of the compositions from Schetky's Scottish period are considerably more polished. The published chamber pieces, which form the bulk of them, often show a composer of genuine talent and, along with the works of the Earl of Kelly, represent a high point in serious composition in 18th-century Scotland. His only known quartets, op.6 (1777), are outstanding, with rhythmic vitality (often sustained through an orchestral overlapping of phrases), fluent and expressive harmonic language and attractive melodic material. Easily his most popular works, however, were the published ones for cello, which appeared even in continental publishers' catalogues from the late 1770s to about 1800. Like the earlier cello sonatas (described as 'the despair of ... amateurs' in articles on Schetky in *Allgemeine musikalische Zeitung*, ii, 1799–1800, cols.33, 81), these later pieces require an accomplished performer, with their heavy reliance on wide intervals, *bariolage* effects, extended arpeggio passages and much use of multiple stops. Schetky also produced a number of solo keyboard works, including some banal marches and dances, and a few songs in an inconsequential yet charming parlour style. There are also large ensemble works for wind band and orchestra, among which the lost symphonies

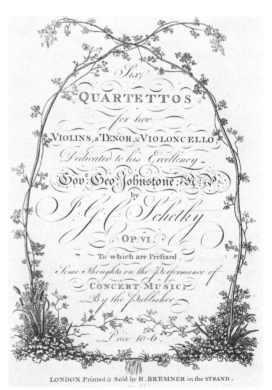

Title-page of Schetky's 'Six Quartettos' op.6 (London: Bremner, 1777)

and cello concertos composed for the Edinburgh Musical Society probably represent an important part of his activities. His didactic writings comprise *Some Observations on, and Rules for Violoncello Playing* (in his op.7, *c*1780), giving basic tenets for the aspiring cellist, and *Practical and Progressive Lessons for the Violoncello* (London, 1811), providing interesting remarks on recitative accompaniment as well as copious advice on elementary technical matters.

WORKS
ORCHESTRAL

Concerto, kbd, 2 vn, 2 fl, bc, in A Select Collection of Choice Music for the Harpsichord or Pianoforte (Edinburgh, *c*1790)
A Collection of Scottish Music, Consisting of 12 Slow Airs and 12 Reels and Strathspeys, 2 cl, 2 fl, 2 hn, (London, *c*1800)
A Collection of Marches, Quicksteps, Slow and Lively Scotch Airs for 2 fifes, piccolo fl, 1/2 bugles (Edinburgh, *c*1806)
3 symphonies, (D, C, C) *D-DS*; other symphonies, lost
4 concertos (C, D, D, D), vc, orch, *D-B*; other vc concertos, incl. 1 listed in Breitkopf catalogue, 1770, lost

CHAMBER, KEYBOARD
(all printed works published in London unless otherwise stated)
6 Trios, 2 vn, vc, op.1 (1773)
6 Duetts, vn, vc, op.2 (1775)
6 Sonatas, hpd/pf, opt. acc. vn, vc, op.3 (1775)
6 Solos, vc, op.4 (1776)
6 Duets, 2 fl, op.5 (1776–7)
6 Quartettos . . . to which are Prefixed some Thoughts on the Performance of Concert-Music, 2 vn, va, vc, op.6 (1777)
12 Duetts . . . with Some Observations on, and Rules for Violoncello Playing, 2 vc, op.7 (*c*1780)
6 Sonatas, hpd/pf, acc. vn, op.8 (*c*1780)
3 Sonatas, hpd/pf, op.9 (Edinburgh, *c*1785)
3 Sonatas, hpd/pf, op.10 (Edinburgh, *c*1785)
3 Sonatas, hpd/pf, acc. vn, va, op.11 (Edinburgh, *c*1785)
6 Solos, vc, b, op.13 (*c*1795)
Sonata, pf, op.15 (Edinburgh, *c*1800)
3 Duets, vn, vc, op.24 (*c*1808)
Other kbd works pubd singly and in 18th-century anthologies
Sonata, A, vc, bc, *D-Bds*; 6 solos, vc, bc, *SWl*; Rondo, kbd, *GB-En*; Sonata, D, vc, bc, *I-Mc*
2 trios, obbl vc, vn, b, listed in Breitkopf catalogue, 1771, Variations on 'Vetter Michel', vc, b, listed in Breitkopf catalogue, 1778; 3 trios, obbl vc, va, b, listed in *AMZ*, ii (1799–1800), col.33: all lost

OTHER WORKS

Conservati fidele pensa, S, obbl vc, str, *c*1763, *D-ROu*
Clarinda, Mistress of my Soul, in J. Johnson, ed., The Scots Musical Museum (Edinburgh, 1787–1803)
6 Canzonets, 1v, pf (Edinburgh, *c*1790)
6 Songs (Edinburgh, *c*1790)
The Bee that Roves (Edinburgh, *c*1800)
3 Songs with Words by Walter Scott (*c*1810)
Pastorale on the Nativity, listed in Edinburgh Musical Society programmes, 1783, 1785; Nacht, A, obbl vc, 2 fl, 2 hn, 2 va, listed in *AMZ*, ii (1799–1800), col.33: Melange containing Scotch Airs, op.30, advertised in N. Gow: Select Collection of Original Dances (Edinburgh, 1815): all lost

BIBLIOGRAPHY
EitnerQ; *GerberL*; *GerberNL*
S. F. L. Schetky: *Ninety Years of Work and Play* (Edinburgh, 1877)
J. Sittard: *Geschichte des Musik- und Concertwesens in Hamburg* (Leipzig, 1890/*R*1971)
D. Fraser-Harris: *St Cecilia's Hall in the Niddry Wynd* (Edinburgh, 1899)
W. Nagel: 'Zur Geschichte der Musik am Hofe von Darmstadt', *MMg*, xxxii (1900), 1, 21, 41, 59, 79
L. O. Schetky: *The Schetky Family: a Compilation of Letters, Memoirs and Historical Data* (Portland, Oregon, 1942)
W. S. Newman: *The Sonata in the Classic Era* (Chapel Hill, 1963, 2/1972)
E. Noack: *Musikgeschichte Darmstadts von Mittelalter bis zur Goethezeit* (Mainz, 1967)
D. Johnson: *Music and Society in Lowland Scotland in the Eighteenth Century* (London, 1972)
G. Beechey: 'J. G. C. Schetky and his "Observations" on Playing the Cello', *MQ*, lx (1974), 451
DAVID JOHNSON, ROGER LARSSON

Scheuenstuhl, Michael (*b* Guttenstetten, Franconia, 3 March 1705; *d* Hof, 26 July 1770). German composer and organist. Apart from the few details recorded

in Mattheson's *Grundlage*, little is known of Scheuenstuhl's life. On 7 May 1722, when only 17, he became organist at the Hohenlohe residence in Wilhelmsdorf. Seven years later he moved to Hof, where he was organist at St Michael's Church from 29 October 1729 until his death. From 1752 onwards he held an additional appointment as a schoolmaster at the local girls' school. Although an organist by profession, Scheuenstuhl was known primarily for his harpsichord pieces, several of which were published by Balthasar Schmidt of Nuremberg during the 1730s and 1740s. These unpretentious works were designed for the growing amateur market, and their lighthearted tone and *galant* style assured success. Scheuenstuhl was among those who contributed to the literature of the *murky*, a species of keyboard music cultivated in Germany from about 1730 to 1800, whose chief characteristic (apart from the tuneful quality of its melodies) was the presence of broken-octave figuration in the left hand. His only large-scale compositions were the keyboard concertos. Originally Scheuenstuhl intended to bring out six concertos, but only three seem to have been published. The G minor concerto for unaccompanied keyboard has been compared with Bach's Italian Concerto; Spitta thought that Scheuenstuhl's work was directly inspired by Bach's, but although both concertos are written in the Italian manner there is nothing to suggest any closer relationship between the two.

WORKS

Sonata, kbd (Hof, 1736), cited by Mattheson, lost
Sechs ganz Neue Galanterie-Stück (Nuremberg, 1737)
Conc., d, kbd, orch (Nuremberg, *c*1738)
Conc., A, kbd, orch (Nuremberg, *c*1738)
Conc., g, kbd (Nuremberg, *c*1740)
Gemüths- und Ohr-ergötzende Clavier-Übung, bestehend in VI . . . Galanterie-Parthien, i (Nuremberg, *c*1743, 2/1747)
Gemüths- und Ohr-ergötzende Clavier-Übung, bestehend in III. grössen . . . Galanterie-Parthien, ii (Nuremberg, *c*1744)
Die beschäftigte Muse Clio . . . und Ohrs eingerichtete III. Galanterie-Suiten auf das Clavier, Neuer Teil (Nuremberg, 1745–6)

BIBLIOGRAPHY
J. Mattheson: *Grundlage einer Ehren-Pforte* (Hamburg, 1740), ed. M. Schneider (Berlin, 1910/*R*1969), 316f
P. Spitta: *Johann Sebastian Bach* (Leipzig, 1873–80, 5/1962; Eng. trans., 1884–99/*R*1951), iii, 151
M. Seiffert: *Geschichte der Klaviermusik* (Leipzig, 1899), 329f
A. Schering: *Die Geschichte des Instrumental-Konzerts* (Leipzig, 1905, 2/1927/*R*1965), 131
H. Daffner: *Die Entwicklung des Klavierkonzerts bis Mozart* (Leipzig, 1906), 6ff
E. Stilz: *Die Berliner Klaviersonate zur Zeit Friedrichs des Grossen* (Berlin, 1930), 14f
E. Dietlein: *Chronik der Stadt Hof*, iv (Hof, 1955), 487f
PIPPA DRUMMOND

Scheuermann, Georg Caspar. *See* SCHÜRMANN, GEORG CASPAR.

Scheurleer, Daniel François (*b* The Hague, 13 Nov 1855; *d* The Hague, 6 Feb 1927). Dutch banker and musicologist. He had many amateur historical interests and paid particular attention to the study of music and its history. He devoted years to the collection of musical source materials and European and non-European instruments, which he then housed in his private museum. After his death his instrument collection and the larger part of his personal library went to the Gemeentemuseum of The Hague, and his source material for the history of Dutch monophonic song to the Royal Library of The Hague. His accomplishments as an administrator were no less important; he served on the boards of directors of the Vereeniging voor Nederlandse Muziekgeschiedenis and the Union

Musicologique, which he founded in 1921 to help re-establish international scholarly contacts broken by World War I. He was granted an honorary doctorate by the University of Leiden in 1920 and was named honorary president of the 1924 musicological congress in Basle.

Scheurleer's foremost importance, apart from his administrative work, lies in his activities as a collector. The Netherlands is indebted to him for its splendid instrument museum, and his studies and compilations of the sources of 18th-century Dutch music history and Dutch monophonic song of the Renaissance are of high scholarly merit.

WRITINGS
De Souterliedekens (Leiden, 1898)
Mozartiana (The Hague, 1903)
Het muziekleven in Nederland in de tweede helft der 18ᵉ eeuw in verband met Mozart's verblijf aldaar (The Hague, 1909)
Het muziekleven van Amsterdam in de 17de eeuw (The Hague, 1911)
Het muziekleven te 's-Gravenhage in de tweede helft der 18ᵉ eeuw (The Hague, 1911)
Catalogus der muziekbibliotheek van D. F. Scheurleer (The Hague, 1893–1910, enlarged 2/1923–5)
Nederlandse liedboeken (The Hague, 1912–23)

EDITIONS
Een devoot ende profitelyck boecxken (The Hague, 1889)
Jan Fruytiers Ecclesiasticus (Amsterdam, 1898)

BIBLIOGRAPHY
Gedenkboek Scheurleer (The Hague, 1925) [contains biography and complete list of writings]
A. Smijers: 'In memoriam', *De muziek*, i (1927), 253
A. Averkamp: 'In memoriam Dr. D. F. Scheurleer (1855–1927)', *TVNM*, xii/2 (1927), 69
E. Reeser: *De Verenging voor Nederlandse muziekgeschiedenis 1868–1943* (Amsterdam, 1943)
M. H. Charbon: 'Daniel François Scheurleer, stichter van het muziekmuseum Scheurleer', *Mededelingen Gemeentemuseum van den Haag*, x (1955), no.2, p.76   ALBERT DUNNING

Scheveningen. See HAGUE, THE.

Schiassi, Gaetano Maria (*b* Bologna, 10 March 1698; *d* Lisbon, 1754). Italian composer. Born of Bolognese parents, Carl Antonio Schiassi and Catterina Minghetti, he was a member of the Accademia Filarmonica as a *suonatore*, and a violinist among the virtuosos at the ducal court of Alderano Cybo Malaspina, to whom he dedicated his *Trattenimenti per camera* in 1724. About three years later he was employed by the Landgrave of Darmstadt. During this period several of his operas and oratorios were performed on Italian stages; Barilli noted that his setting of *Didone abbandonata* was extremely successful ('incontrò a meraviglia'). Of special interest is his comedy *La Zanina finta contessa*, partly written in Bolognese dialect in the manner of G. M. Buini.

From at least the end of 1734 he lived in Lisbon, where he served in the royal chapel and founded the Academia de Música de Trinidade. His letters from Lisbon to Padre Giambattista Martini from 3 January 1735 to 30 September 1753 (now in *I-Bc*) reveal his activities there as composer, teacher and singer. He was asked to compose oratorios based on texts by Metastasio, for which he enlisted Martini's help in supplying fugues for the choruses. The letters also reveal several insights into performing practice and taste in 18th-century Lisbon, where the king refused to allow women to take roles in operas and prohibited all kinds of entertainment during his illness except for oratorios and church festivals. Schiassi also obtained several important books for Martini's library, including a copy of Cerone's rare *El melopeo*.

Schiassi's training as a violinist is reflected in his instrumental writing, which often demands a high level of virtuosity and reflects a good understanding of the instrument. Forms include sonatas, sinfonias, concertos and dance pieces for combinations of one to four instruments with continuo. The vocal music is often written in a pastoral style similar to that of Bolognese composers like G. A. Perti in the first half of the 18th century.

WORKS
OPERAS
(*music lost unless otherwise stated*)
La Rosinda, Cento, Vicini, Sept 1726
La Zanina finta contessa, Modena, Molza, carn. 1728
Stratonica (A. Salvi), Ravenna, Teatro di Ravenna, spr. 1732
Il Demetrio (Metastasio), Milan, Ducale, birth of Elisabetta Cristina, 1732
L'amor fra' nemici (P. A. Bernardoni), Bologna, Marsigli-Rossi, carn. 1732
La fede ne'tradimenti (G. Gigli), Bologna, Marsigli-Rossi, carn. 1732
Alessandro nelle Indie (Metastasio), Bologna, Formagliari, carn. 1734 [aria, Digli ch'io son fedele, *D-Dlb*]
Il Demofoonte (Metastasio), Venice, Grimani, carn. 1735, score, *B-Bc*
Didone abbandonata (Metastasio), Bologna, Formagliari, spr. 1735
Le vicende amorose o L'enigma disciolto (Metastasio), Bologna, Angelelli, 4 Feb 1736
Artaserse (Metastasio), Lisbon, 1737
Arias, in *D-Dlb*: Spero se che la speranza; Mio ben ricordati

ORATORIOS
(*only librettos extant*)
Geremia in Egitto, Bologna, Oratorio Filippini, 1727
Maria vergine al Calvario (M. A. Boccardi), Bologna, Arciconfraternità di S Maria della Morte, Good Friday 1735
4 oratorios cited in letters to G. B. Martini, all libs by Metastasio, all perf. Lisbon: Il sacrificio d'Isaac; Giuseppe riconosciuto; La Passione di Gesù; Gioas rè di Giuda

OTHER WORKS
[12] Sonate, vn, bc (Bologna, 1724)
[10] Trattenimenti musicali per camera, vn, vc/hpd (Bologna, 1724)
XII concerti, vn solo, 2 vn, vc, hpd (Amsterdam, 1729)
Divertimenti da camera, 2 vn, vc, bc; 2 sinfonie, 2 vn, vc, bc: Vienna, Hofburg, cited by Haas; 3 vn concs., *D-Dlb*; several arias and dance movts in Raccolta fatta da diversi autori di gravi, arie e minuetti . . . ad'uso di Petronio Francesco Rampionesi, 1736, *I-Bc*; Pastorale per il Ss Natale, *S-Uu*, ed. W. Upmeyer, *Musikschätze der Vergangenheit* (Berlin, 1928)

BIBLIOGRAPHY
A. Barilli: *Zibaldone* (MS, *I-Bu*)
C. Ricci: *I teatri di Bologna nei secoli XVII e XVIII* (Bologna, 1888/R1965)
R. Haas: *Die estensischen Musikalien: thematisches Verzeichnis mit Einleitung*, i (Regensburg, 1925)
                               ANNE SCHNOEBELEN

Schiavetto [Schiavetti], Giulio [Skjavetić, Julije] (*b* Šibenik; *d* in or after 1564–5). Croatian composer. For many years he was in the service of Girolamo Savorgnano, Bishop of Šibenik from 1557 to 1573, and he was with him at Trent during the closing stages of the Council of Trent. He was a musician of great literary sensibility. His work ranges from simple, artless *greghesche* to contrapuntally sophisticated madrigals and motets; he may be counted the most important Croatian composer of his time.

WORKS
[30] Madrigali, nuovamente composti, 4, 5vv (Venice, 1563)
[18] Motetti, 5, 6vv (Venice, 1564 or 1565), lost, Pater noster pr. in Plamenac (1939); ed. in Spomenici hrvatske glazbene prošlosti, i (Zagreb, 1970)
2 madrigals, 1562⁶; ed. in Spomenici hrvatske glazbene prošlosti, ii (Zagreb, 1971)
2 greghesche, 1564¹⁰; ed. in Spomenici hrvatske glazbene prošlosti, i (Zagreb, 1970)

BIBLIOGRAPHY
D. Plamenac: 'O hrvatskoj muzici u vrijeme renesanse' [Croatian music up to the Renaissance], *Hrvatska revija*, ix (1936), 145
——: 'Music of the 16th and 17th centuries in Dalmatia', *PAMS 1939*, 35
L. Županović: 'La musique croate du XVIᵉ siècle', *Musica antiqua*

Europae orientalis II: Bydgoszcz 1969, 79–126
——: Introductions to Spomenici hrvatske glazbene prošlosti, i–ii
(Zagreb, 1970–71)

LOVRO ŽUPANOVIĆ

Schibler, Armin (*b* Kreuzlingen, Lake Constance, 20
Nov 1920). Swiss composer. He studied the piano and
composition in Zurich with Müller, Frey and Burkhard,
and in England with Rubbra and Tippett (1946). His
work was also decisively influenced by the Darmstadt
summer courses (1949–53) given by Fortner,
Leibowitz, Krenek and Adorno. From 1944 he taught
music at the Zurich cantonal school. As a young man he
was one of Switzerland's best-known composers, writing
in a style dominated by that of Burkhard. In about 1950
he turned to 12-note techniques; this interest continued
for some years, although Schibler was never completely
won over to the method. *Die Füsse im Feuer* is the main
work from this rather expressionist period. The following years were influenced by Stravinskian rhythm and
by a ballet course directed by Harald Kreuzberg. Schibler's lively interest in all contemporary music led him
to an involvement with jazz in connection with dance,
notably in the burlesque *Blackwood & Co.* Through
Adorno he became aware of the sociological implications of music, and this brought about his use of
melodramatic techniques in drawing reciprocal relationships between words and music. In this respect his
collaboration with the writer Alfred Goldmann was
of importance, leading to the total music-theatre of
Gilgamesch and to the incorporation of elements from
pop music in *Antworten, bitte.*

WORKS
(selective list)
Stage: Der spanische Rosenstock, opera, 1947–50; Der Teufel im
Winterpalais, opera, 1953; Die späte Sühne, opera, 1953–4; Der
Raub des Feuers, ballet, 1954; Die Füsse im Feuer, opera, 1955;
Blackwood & Co, dance burlesque, 1955–8; Urs und Flurina, youth
opera, 1956–60; Orpheus, music-theatre, 1968; Gilgamesch: Die
Mauer von Uruk, music-theatre, c1970; other dance works
Choral: Wessobrunner Kantate, 1945; Media in vita, oratorio, 1956;
Enkidus Tod, T, B, 3 speakers, speaking chorus, orch, 1972
Vocal: Antworten, bitte, speaker, ens, 1970; In unserer Sache, speaker,
ens, 1971; ... später als du denkst, 2 speakers, 1v, elec, 1972;
Der Weg des Menschen, 2 speakers, ens, 1973; Epitaph auf einen
Machtigen, 16vv, 2 pf, 1974, many songs
Inst: 3 syms., concs., other orch pieces, 4 str qts, pf works
Educational music, film scores

Principal publishers: Ahn & Simrock, Schibler

WRITINGS
Neue Musik in dritter Generation (Amriswil, 1953)
'Selbstporträt', *Musik der Zeit* (1953), no.10
Zum Werk Gustav Mahlers (Lindau, 1955)
Zur Oper der Gegenwart (Amriswil, 1956)

BIBLIOGRAPHY
K. H. Wörner: *Armin Schibler* (Amriswil, 1953)
P. Mieg: 'Armin Schibler', *40 Schweizer Komponisten der Gegenwart*
(Amriswil, 1956)

FRITZ MUGGLER

Schichart, Johann Christian. See SCHICKHARDT,
JOHANN CHRISTIAN.

Schicht (Ger.). LAYER; *see also* ANALYSIS, §§II, 6; III,
2.

Schicht, Johann Gottfried (*b* Reichenau, nr. Zittau, 29
Sept 1753; *d* Leipzig, 16 Feb 1823). German conductor, keyboard player and composer. He was brought up
by his uncle at Zittau, where he was first taught to play
keyboard instruments by the organist Johann Trier.
From 1776, when he went to Leipzig University to
study law, he played in the concerts at the inn 'Zu den

drei Schwänen' (the 'Grosses Concert') under the direction of Hiller. Abandoning the law, he also played under
Hiller in the Musikübende Gesellschaft and from 1781
played the violin in the Gewandhaus concerts. In 1785
he succeeded Hiller as musical director of the
Gewandhaus concerts and subsequently of the
Neukirche. He founded the Leipzig Singakademie in
1802, directed it until 1807 and became the university's
musical director in 1808. In 1810 he succeeded August
Müller as Kantor of the Thomasschule in Leipzig, where
he attained a high standard of performance. His wife,
the Italian singer Costanza Valdesturla, sang at the
Gewandhaus concerts for many years before her death
in 1809.

Schicht is remembered more for his *Allgemeine
Choralbuch* (Leipzig, 1819) than for his sacred vocal
works (motets, oratorios, masses, Te Deum settings and
cantatas etc) or his secular vocal or instrumental works.
Formally and stylistically, his compositions are indistinguishable from those of many of his contemporaries and
present nothing new. Schicht paid careful attention,
however, to text declamation: his unaccompanied vocal
works are superior to those with functional orchestral
accompaniments. Important as an early editor of chorale preludes, a mass, and five motets by Bach, he also
wrote a treatise on harmony (1812) and translated
pedagogical works by Clementi, Pleyel and Pellegrini-
Celloni. Among his students were Marschner, Reissiger
and Zöllner.

WRITINGS
Grundregeln der Harmonie nach dem Verwechslungssystem (Leipzig,
1812)
'Über das Aussprechen des Deutschen im Gesang', *AMZ*, xvii (1815),
686

BIBLIOGRAPHY
EitnerQ; GerberNL
Review of Schicht's *Grundregeln der Harmonie, AMZ*, xiv (1812), 254,
403
G. Schilling, ed.: *Encyclopädie der gesammten musikalischen
Wissenschaften* (Stuttgart, 1835–8/*R*1973)
H. Mendel and A. Reissmann: *Musikalisches Conversations-Lexikon*
(Berlin, 1870–79, 2/1880–83)
J. Zahn: *Die Melodien der deutschen evangelischen Kirchenlieder*
(Gütersloh, 1889–93/*R*1963)
R. Eitner: 'Schicht, Johann Gottfried', *ADB*
H. J. Nösselt: *Das Gewandhausorchester* (Leipzig, 1943)
P. M. Young: *The Concert Tradition* (London, 1965), 161

GAYNOR G. JONES

Schick, Ernst (J. Christoph) (*b* The Hague, Oct 1756; *d*
Berlin, 10 Dec 1815). Dutch violinist and composer.
His father brought him to Amsterdam, intending him to
follow his own career of dancing-master. The boy's
musical talent was discovered by Kreusser, who taught
him the violin; he soon became a virtuoso player,
emulating the style of Karl Esser and Lolli. In 1774 he
became chamber musician in the electoral chapel at
Mainz. In 1791 he married the singer Margarete
Hamel. He was appointed violinist in the Berlin royal
chapel in 1793, and leader in 1813. In 1804 with K. M.
Bohrer he organized subscription concerts at which
lesser-known Classical works were heard; at one of
these, Beethoven's Second Symphony was performed.
His compositions – six violin concertos and masonic
songs – were never widely known.

BIBLIOGRAPHY
Announcement and review of Schick's and Bohrer's benefit concerts,
AMZ, vii (1804), 112, 144
G. Schilling, ed.: *Encyclopädie der gesammten musikalischen
Wissenschaften* (Stuttgart, 1835–8/*R*1973)
C. Ledebur: *Tonkünstler-Lexicon Berlins* (Berlin, 1861/*R*1965)

GAYNOR G. JONES

Schick [née Hamel], **Margarete (Luise)** (*b* Mainz, 26 April 1773; *d* Berlin, 29 April 1809). German opera singer, wife of Ernst Schick. The daughter of a bassoonist, J. N. Hamel, she received keyboard and vocal instruction before going to Würzburg; there the elector paid for her to study singing for five years with Dominicus Steffani. Subsequently she sang at the elector's court in Mainz and studied with Righini. In 1790 she sang at Leopold II's coronation at Frankfurt under the direction of Mozart, who was greatly impressed by her performance. In 1791, the year of her stage début, she married and joined her husband on a concert tour of Holland. After a guest appearance at Hamburg in 1793 she became chamber and theatre singer at the Berlin court; from 1794 she also sang at the National Theatre. She was renowned for her expressive performances of Gluck and Mozart. Her most famous role was Iphigenia in Gluck's *Iphigénie en Tauride*. Both her daughter Julie and granddaughter Pauline von Schätzel were famous opera singers, and her son Friedrich was a clarinettist.

BIBLIOGRAPHY

K. von Levezow: *Leben und Kunst der Frau Margarete Luise Schick, gebornen Hamel* (Berlin, 1809)

G. Schilling, ed.: *Encyclopädie der gesammten musikalischen Wissenschaften* (Stuttgart, 1835–8/R1973)

C. von Ledebur: *Tonkünstler-Lexicon Berlin's* (Berlin, 1861/R1965)

H. Welti: 'Schick, Margarete', *ADB*　　GAYNOR G. JONES

Schickaneder. See SCHIKANEDER family.

Schickele, Peter (*b* Ames, Iowa, 17 July 1935). American composer and humorist. He studied music at Swarthmore College (BA 1957) and composition with Vincent Persichetti at the Juilliard School of Music (MS 1960); he has held teaching positions there and at the music school of Aspen, Colorado. In addition to producing a large number of works in a wide variety of genres and styles (from atonality to pseudo-Baroque), he has composed film and television scores, made arrangements for Joan Baez and other popular singers, and contributed music and lyrics to the musical *Oh! Calcutta!* He has received awards and commissions from the Ford Foundation (1960–61), Smith College (1960, 1961), the Philadelphia Art Alliance (1965) and the St Louis SO (1970, 1972) among others. He is best known for lecture-concerts (from 1965) and recordings featuring his creation 'P. D. Q. Bach' ('the last and least of the sons of J. S. Bach'; these are in the tradition of Gerard Hoffnung's musical spoofs, but both broader and more musicologically orientated. He published *The Definitive Biography of P. D. Q. Bach (1807–1742?)* (New York, 1976).

WORKS
(selective list)

Orch: Serenade, 1959

Choral: Mass, BBB, acc. ad lib, 1956; After Spring Sunset, SATB, 1961

Solo vocal: The Flow of Memory, Mez, fl, b cl, vn, pf, 1963; Hornsmoke, narrator, tpt, cornet, hn, trbn, tuba, 1975

Chamber and inst: Sequiturs, vc, 1959; Str Trio, 1960; Presents (2 bks), pf, 1960, 1972

as P. D. Q. Bach: Concerto for Horn and Hardart, hn, hardart, str; Iphigenia in Brooklyn, cantata, Bargain Ct, 3 double reeds, tpt mouthpiece, wine bottle, str qt, hpd; Pervertimento, bagpipes, bicycle, balloons, str; The Seasonings, oratorio, S, A, T, B, chorus, 2 slide whistles, 2 kazoos, tromboon, windbreaker, shower hose, foghorn, 2 tpt, timp, str; The Stoned Guest (opera, ⅓), Off-coloratura S, Mezzanine S, Bargain Ct, Basso blotto, Dog, fl, ob, bn, hn, tpt, trbn, str, hpd; Toot Suite, calliope 4 hands/org

as Prof. Schickele: Quodlibet, orch

Principal publisher: Presser

THOMAS WALKER

Schickhardt [Schickhard, Schickhart, Schikardt, Schichart, Schikhart, Schickard], **Johann Christian** (*b* Brunswick, *c*1682; *d* Leiden, before 26 March 1762). German composer and instrumentalist. He received his musical training at the ducal court in Brunswick. The early part of his career was spent in the Netherlands in the service of Friedrich of Hessen-Kassel, Henriette Amalia of Anhalt-Dessau, and Johan Willem Friso, Prince of Orange. By 1712 he was in Hamburg, a city with which he was associated by Walther (1732) and Hawkins (1776), and in which it has hitherto been assumed that he spent most of his life. But by 1717 he had connections with Johann Friedrich, Count of Kastel-Rudenhausen, and around 1719 with Ernst August of Saxe-Weimar and Prince Leopold of Anhalt-Cöthen. In the early 1720s he was probably in Scandinavia. In 1735 he published a collection of 24 sonatas in all the keys, at which date he may have been back in the Netherlands. He was attached to the University of Leiden in 1745; the *Album studiosorum* for that year gives his age as 63. After his death Schickhardt's daughter applied to the university authorities for assistance with burial expenses and from the subsequent act of Senate (26 March 1762) it is seen that he had been 'a master of musical arts and a member of the Academy.' He may have spent some time in France since Forkel (1792) described him as a German musician at Paris, but this has not been supported elsewhere.

Schickhardt had close associations with Estienne Roger, the Amsterdam publisher, and his successors, Jeanne Roger and Michel-Charles Le Cène. Not only did he provide the firm with a constant stream of original compositions, but he also acted as the firm's Hamburg agent around 1712 and undertook occasional editorial projects such as the arrangement of Corelli's op.6 for two recorders and continuo. A woodwind player himself, Schickhardt produced instruction manuals for both the recorder and oboe. But he was known primarily through his chamber music. His sonatas, although written in a conventional, post-Corellian idiom, reveal fine melodic gifts, striking harmonic touches, and a Handelian directness of expression. The widespread popularity of these works in the early 18th century is attested both by the flood of publications from Amsterdam and by the speed with which they were pirated in London. Dart's suggestion that Schickhardt was related to the London instrument maker J.-J. Schuchart appears doubtful.

WORKS
(published in Amsterdam unless otherwise stated)

Solo sonatas with bc: 6 [7] as op.1, rec (1709/10); 6 [7] as op.2, ob/vn (1709/10); 6 [7] as op.3, rec (1709/10); 6 as op.8, ob/vn (1710); 12 as op.17, rec (*c*1712–15); 6 as op.20 no.1, fl/ob/vn (1715); 12 as op.23, rec (*c*1719–20); 6 as op.20 no.2, fl/ob/vn (*c*1723); 6 as op.24, rec (*c*1723–4); 6 as op.25, vn (*c*1723–4); 24 as L'alphabet de la musique, op.30, rec/fl/vn (London, *c*1735), ed. F. Brüggen and W. Bergmann (London, 1978–9)

Other sonatas with bc: Sonates, 2 rec, op.4 (1710); 6 as op.5, rec, 2 ob/vn, va da gamba (1710); 6 as op.6, 2 rec (1710); 12 as op.7, 2 ob/vn (1710); 6 as op.9, 2 rec, bc ad lib (*c*1710–12); 6 as op.10, 2 fl/ob/vn, bc ad lib (*c*1710–12); 6 as op.14, rec, ob/vn, va da gamba (*c*1710–12); 12 as op.16, 2 rec (*c*1710–12); 6 as op.22, 2 rec, ob (*c*1717–18)

Other works: Recueil de menuets, tr inst/ob, bc, op.11 (*c*1710–12); Principes de la flûte . . . avec 42 airs à 2 flûtes, op.12 (*c*1710–12); 6 concerts, 2 vn, 2 ob/vn, bc, op.13 (*c*1710–12); Principes du hautbois, contenant airs à 2 hautbois sans basse, op.15 (*c*1710–12); Recueil d'airs choisis, rec, op.18 no.1 (*c*1712–15); 6 concerts, 4 rec, bc, op.19 (*c*1713–15); Airs spirituels des Luthériens, 2 rec, bc, op.21 (1715); Recueil d'airs de mouvement, rec, op.18 no.2 (*c*1718–19); 6

sonates, 2 fl, arr. rec, op.26 (1727)
Inst works incl. in: The Compleat Tutor to the Hautboy (London, c1715); The Complete Flute Master (London, c1760); G. Visconti: Airs, 2 rec (2/1710) [enlarged with works by Schickhardt]
MSS of concertos, suite, solo and trio sonatas, *D-ROu*, *SWl*, *W*, *GB-DRc*, *Lbm*, *S-K*, *L*, *Uu*

BIBLIOGRAPHY
HawkinsH; *WaltherML*
J. N. Forkel: *Allgemeine Litteratur der Musik* (Leipzig, 1792/*R*1962), 322
G. Du Rieu, ed.: *Album studiosorum academiae lugudno batavae* (The Hague, 1875)
P. C. Molhuysen, ed.: *Bronnen tot de geschiedenis der Leidsche Universiteit* (The Hague, 1921), v, 462f
T. Dart: 'Bressan and Schickhardt', *GSJ*, x (1957), 85
W. S. Newman: *The Sonata in the Baroque Era* (Chapel Hill, 1959, rev. 2/1966), 285, 296f
H. Engel, ed.: *Das Concerto Grosso*, Mw, xxiii (1962; Eng. trans., 1964), 26
D. Lasocki: 'Johann Christian Schickhardt (c1682–1762): a Contribution to his Biography and a Catalogue of his Works', *TVNM* (in preparation)

PIPPA DRUMMOND, DAVID LASOCKI

Schidlowsky, León (*b* Santiago, 21 July 1931). Israeli composer of Chilean birth. He studied at the Santiago National Conservatory (1940–47) and at the University of Chile (1948–52), where he read philosophy and psychology. During his student years he had lessons with Allende-Blin for harmony and counterpoint (1948–50) and with Focke for composition (1950–52), continuing his studies between 1952 and 1954 at the Detmold Music Academy and under Jelinck in Barsbüttel. He returned to Chile in 1955 and became an active member (from 1957 director) of the Agrupación Tonus. He also taught at the Santiago Music Institute (1955–63) and served as secretary of the National Association of Composers (from 1961). In 1961 he was appointed head of the archive at the Instituto de Extensión Musical, which he directed from 1962 to 1966, and he was professor of composition at the University of Chile from 1962 to 1968. He spent 1968 in Germany on a Guggenheim Fellowship and also visited Israel. The next year he settled in Tel-Aviv as senior lecturer in composition and theory at the Rubin Academy of the university, where he was made professor in 1970.

Schidlowsky has progressed from free atonality through 12-note serialism, total serialism and aleatory writing to graphic composition, on which he concentrated from 1969. Whatever the style or means, however, he has always been powerfully influenced by contemporary events, and in particular the Jewish massacre of World War II, the subject of his choral symphony *La noche de cristal*, *Kaddish* for cello and orchestra, and *Invocación* for soprano, narrator, strings and percussion.

WORKS
(selective list)
Stage: Die Menschen (opera, W. Hasenclever), 1969; Vera la morte (monodrama, C. Pavese), singer-actress, perc, 1972; Anna Blüme (stage-divertimento, K. Schwitters), S, A, B (singer-actors), 1973; Dadayamasong (W. Mehring), 1v, 5 performers, conductor, 1975
Orch: Triptico, 1959; New York, 1965; Kaddish, vc, orch, 1967; Epitaph for Scherchen, 1967; Serenade, chamber orch, 1970; Constellation, str, perc, 1971; Babi yar, chamber orch, 1972; Monumentum, 1973; In eius memoriam, 1973
Choral: Caupolicán (Neruda), Bar, SATB, 2 pf, cel, perc, 1958; Sym. 'La noche de cristal', T, male vv, orch, 1961; De profundis, SAT, 9 insts, 1963; Monumento a Bolivar (Asturias, Neruda), reciter, SATB, orch, 1966; Deutsches Tagebuch (Brecht, anon.), narrator, chorus, orch, 1966; 3 Hebraic Songs (Pss), SATB, 1966; Jeremiah, 8 solo vv, str, 1966; Requiem, 12 solo vv, 1968; Eli, eli, lama azavtani, SATB, 1970; Massada (R. Freier), 3 choruses, orch, 1972; Akiva ben Yosef (Freier), S, T, Bar, children's vv, SATB, orch, 1972;

Hommage à Neruda (Schidlowsky), chorus, orch, 1975; Ich komme (Mayakovsky), chorus, 1975; Golem, 7 solo vv, tape, 1975
Solo vocal: Requiem (Rilke), S, orch, 1954; 2 Psalme (Trakl), A, cl, vn, vc, 1954; Cantata negra (Cendrars), A, perc, 1957; Amatorias (Huidobro), T, 9 insts, 1962; Invocación (Schidlowsky), S, narrator, perc, str orch, 1964; Memento (Heraud), reciter, orch, 1966; Espergesia, 1v, perc, 1968; Lyric (Chin. verse), 1v, 5 perc, 1969; In memoriam, Bar, fl, ob, cl, perc, 1971; 11 Tombstones, 1972
Inst: Miniatures, pf, 1952; Cuarteto mixto, fl, cl, vn, vc, 1956; Conc., 6 insts, 1957; Soliloquies, 8 insts, 1961; Eclosión, 9 insts, 1967; Str Qt, 1967; Hexáforos, perc, 1968; Sextet, fl, cl, pf, perc, vn, vc, 1970; Sonora, 1–4 perc, 1970; Koloth [Voices], harp, 1971; Meshulash [Triangle], pf trio, 1971; Actions, pf, 1972; Invention, fl, pf, 1975
Tape: Birth, 1966

Principal publishers: Instituto de Extensión Musical, Israel Music Institute

BIBLIOGRAPHY
Compositores de América/Composers of the Americas, ed. Pan American Union, x (Washington, DC, 1965), 106
M. E. Grebe: 'León Schidlowsky', *Revista musical chilena*, nos.104–5 (1968), 7–52
Y. W. Cohen: *Werden und Entwicklung der Musik in Israel* (Kassel, 1976) [pt.ii of rev. edn. of M. Brod: *Die Musik Israels*]
W. Y. Elias: *León Schidlowsky* (Tel-Aviv, 1978)
——: *The Music of Israel* (in preparation) [bibliography]

WILLIAM Y. ELIAS

Schiedermair, Ludwig (*b* Regensburg, 7 Dec 1876; *d* Bensberg, nr. Cologne, 30 April 1957). German musicologist. He spent his school and university years at Munich where, in addition to history and German literature, he studied musicology under Sandberger and composition and music theory with Beer-Walbrunn. In 1901 he took his doctorate in Erlangen with a thesis on cultural life at the court of Elector Ferdinand Maria of Bavaria. After teaching history, geography and German at Würzburg (1903) he returned to musicology, first at Leipzig University, where he worked under Riemann, and then at Berlin, under Kretzschmar. Following extensive travels in Italy, he became lecturer in the history of music at Marburg University in 1906, submitting for this post a *Habilitationsschrift* on Mayr's operas. In 1911 he left Marburg for Bonn where, in 1915, he was appointed reader in music, and from 1920 until his retirement in 1945 he held the chair of music.

It was due to Schiedermair's active interest in Beethoven that in 1927 (the centenary year of Beethoven's death) the important Beethoven Archives came into being. With Schiedermair as founder and director this institute became the international centre for Beethoven research, gathering under one roof, either in the original or in photographic copies, not only the various editions of Beethoven's works but also his MSS and sketches scattered all over the world. In 1929, in connection with the Beethoven Archives, Schiedermair founded a department exclusively concerned with the musical history of the Rhineland, to which, in 1933, he added a publication department (now part of Cologne University music faculty). In recognition of his outstanding contributions to music bibliography and history, Schiedermair was elected president of the Deutsche Gesellschaft für Musikwissenschaft in 1937 and in 1940 chairman of the music section of the Deutsche Akademie.

Schiedermair's main interests were Mozart and Beethoven. He was the first to attempt a complete edition of Mozart's letters, and *Die Briefe Mozarts und seiner Familie* (1914) was published in four volumes, with a fifth volume of pictures relating to Mozart and his time. This edition formed the basis of Emily Anderson's English translation of the letters. Other standard works were his *Mozart: sein Leben und seine Werke* (1922), *Der junge Beethoven* (1925) and *Die deutsche Oper* (1930).

Schiedermair was a versatile scholar, an outstanding organizer and bibliographer and a gifted teacher.

WRITINGS
Die künstlerischen Bestrebungen am Hofe des Kurfürsten Ferdinand Maria zu Bayern (diss., U. of Erlangen, 1901)
Simon Mayr: Beiträge zur Geschichte der Oper um die Wende des 18. und 19. Jahrhunderts (Habilitationsschrift, U. of Marburg, 1906; Leipzig, 1907–10/R1973)
Bayreuther Festspiele im Zeitalter des Absolutismus (Leipzig, 1908)
Die Briefe Mozarts und seiner Familie (Leipzig, 1914)
Einführung in das Studium der Musikgeschichte (Munich, 1918, 3/1930/R1947)
W. A. Mozarts Handschrift in zeitlich geordneten Nachbildungen (Bückeburg, 1919)
ed.: *Veröffentlichungen des Beethoven Hauses* (Leipzig, 1920–34)
Mozart: sein Leben und seine Werke (Munich, 1922, 2/1948)
Der junge Beethoven (Leipzig, 1925/R1972, 4/1970)
Die deutsche Oper: Grundzüge ihres Werdens und Wesens (Leipzig, 1930/R1971, 3/1943)
Musik am Rheinstrom (Cologne, 1947)

BIBLIOGRAPHY
A. Schmitz: *Beethoven und die Gegenwart: . . . Ludwig Schiedermair zum 60. Geburtstag* (Berlin, 1937)
W. Kahl, H. Lemacher and J. Schmidt-Görg, eds.: *Studien zur Musikgeschichte des Rheinlandes: Festschrift zum 80. Geburtstag von Ludwig Schiedermair* (Cologne, 1956) [contains full list of writings and compositions]
L. Schmidt-Görg: 'Ludwig Schiedermair zum Gedächtnis' [obituary], *Mf*, x (1957), 381
K. Stephenson: 'Ludwig Schiedermair', *Rheinische Musiker*, 4th ser. (1966), 137 [contains extensive bibliography]
K. R. Brachtel: 'Ein Bayerischer Musikgelehrter', *Bayerland*, lxix (1967), no.12, p.59
S. Kross: 'Ludwig Schiedermair', *Bonner Gelehrte* (1968), 449
EDITH B. SCHNAPPER

Schiedmayer. The name of two German firms of piano makers. The first was set up in 1809 by Johann Lorenz Schiedmayer (*b* Erlangen, 2 Dec 1786; *d* Stuttgart, 3 April 1860) and his partner Carl Dieudonné (*d* 1825) in Stuttgart. Johann's grandfather, Balthasar Schiedmayer, and father, Johann David Schiedmayer (*b* Erlangen, 20 April 1753; *d* Nuremberg, 24 March 1805), had both been well-established piano makers, the latter working with J. A. Stein at Augsburg from 1778 to 1781. Johann Lorenz soon became a well-known maker nationally, competing successfully with imports from Vienna, Paris and London. Upright pianos were produced as early as 1842. The business became Schiedmayer & Söhne in 1845 when his sons, Adolf (*b* Stuttgart, 1820; *d* Stuttgart, 1890) and Hermann (*b* Stuttgart, 1821; *d* Stuttgart, 1861), joined in partnership. The firm has made concert and domestic instruments, winning many prizes, notably a gold medal at the London Great Exhibition of 1851. The firm continued into the 1950s.

A second, independent firm was founded in 1853 by the younger sons of Johann Lorenz Schiedmayer, Julius (*b* Stuttgart, 17 Feb 1822; *d* Stuttgart, Feb 1878) and Paul (*b* Kissingen, 1829; *d* Stuttgart, 18 June 1890). Paul had studied instrument making with Debain and Alexander in Paris, and this experience enabled him and his brother to make harmoniums as J. & P. Schiedmayer. By the time their father died in 1860, the upright piano was superseding the harmonium, so they started making pianos. This competition with the older firm resulted in the production of good instruments by both. The newer firm had a larger output than the older one, and it subsequently developed a better reputation. Julius established a family tradition by acting as juror at important exhibitions, from the 1862 London Exhibition on. J. & P. Schiedmayer itself won the Grand Prix at the Paris exhibition of 1900. The firm continued making pianos into the 1960s, when it was known as Schiedmayer Pianofortefabrik.

BIBLIOGRAPHY
A. Eisenmann: *Schiedmayer und Söhne* (Stuttgart, 1909)
M. Rupprecht: *Die Klavierbauerfamilie Schiedmayer* (diss., U. of Erlangen, 1954)
150 Jahre Schiedmayer und Söhne (Stuttgart, 1959)
M. Rupprecht: 'Schiedmayer', *MGG*
C. Ehrlich: *The Piano: a History* (London, 1976)
MARGARET CRANMER

Schieferdecker [Schiefferdecker], **Johann Christian** (*b* Teuchern, nr. Weissenfels, 10 Nov 1679; *d* Lübeck, 5 April 1732). German organist and composer. The son of Christian Schieferdecker, Kantor, organist and teacher at Teuchern, he came of a long line of ministers and church musicians active in Weissenfels and Zeitz from the middle of the 17th century. He attended the Leipzig Thomasschule, 1692–7; later, while a university student in Leipzig, two of his operas were staged. In 1702 he became accompanist to the Hamburg Opera, where three more of his operas were given. On 23 January 1707 Schieferdecker succeeded Buxtehude as organist and parish clerk of the Marienkirche, Lübeck, after acting as his deputy for a year. In accordance with local custom, he married his predecessor's daughter, Anna Margarethe (his senior by four years), on 5 September 1707.

Since Lübeck's importance lay in the cultivation of sacred music, Schieferdecker focussed his attention on the church. He continued the Marienkirche tradition inaugurated by Tunder of providing sacred music for the annual series of concerts (Abendmusiken) given around Advent. To the existing modest resources of one violist and one lutenist the authorities in 1709 allowed Schieferdecker to add another violist. For each season from 1707 to 1729 he wrote a cantata comprising recitatives, solos, choruses and a chorale sung by the congregation with a concluding hymn either in praise of the ruler or of intercession for the city's well-being. No Abendmusiken are recorded for 1731 or 1732. According to Moller, Schieferdecker also wrote a series of *Geistliche Cantaten nach Ordnung der Sonn- und festtäglichen Evangelien*.

WORKS
VOCAL
Heilig ist der Herr Zebaoth, 4vv, str, bc, *D-B*; ed. B. Grusnick (Kassel, 1959)
2 wedding arias, both for T, insts: Keuscher Flammen Liebesfeuer (Lübeck, 1707); Glück zu euren Hochzeitshertzen (Lübeck, 1707)
Missa brevis (Ky–Gl), 4vv, str; In te speravi, T, vn; In te Domine speravi, T, vn, bc [copied by G. Österreich from the Bokemeyer collection, 1704]: all *D-B*
3 cantatas, B, vn, bc, all *B-Bc*: Auf, auf, mein Herz; Weicht ihr schwarzen Trauer-Wolken; Triumpf! Beliel ist nun erleget
Operas, music lost: Justinus, Leipzig, 1700; Medea, Leipzig, 1700; Alarich, Hamburg, 1702; Viktor, Hamburg, 1702; Der königliche Printz Regnerus, Weissenfels, 1701
22 Abendmusiken, texts and music lost, incl.: Die Historia der ersten Eltern (A. Lange), 1708; Der streitbare und siegende Gideon (C. Brandenburg), 1716; Der geduldige Kreutzträger Hiob (J. F. Holten), 1720
Geistliche Cantaten nach Ordnung der Sonn- und festtäglichen Evangelien; texts and music lost, see Moller (1744)

INSTRUMENTAL
Meine Seele erhebet den Herren, org, *D-LÜh*, ed. in EDM, 1st ser. ix (1937/*R*)
XII musikalische Concerte, bestehend in auserlesenen Ouverturen nebst einigen schönen Suiten und Sonaten, 3 vn, 3 ob, b, bc (Hamburg, 1715)

Org pieces, formerly in Berlin-Grünewald, Bibliothek Wolffheim, cited in *EitnerQ*

BIBLIOGRAPHY

GerberNL; *WaltherML*

J. Moller: *Cimbria literata*, ii (Copenhagen, 1744)

C. Stiehl: 'Die Organisten an der St. Marienkirche und die Abendmusiken zu Lübeck', *Zeitschrift des Vereins für Lübeckische Geschichte und Alterthumskunde*, v (1886–8), 167–203

A. Werner: *Städtische und fürstliche Musikpflege in Weissenfels* (Leipzig, 1911)

A. Pirro: *Dietrich Buxtehude* (Paris, 1913)

J. Hennings and W. Stahl: *Musikgeschichte Lübecks* (Kassel, 1952)

H. C. Wolff: *Die Barockoper in Hamburg, 1678–1738* (Wolfenbüttel, 1957)

G. B. SHARP

Schierbeck, Poul (Julius Ouscher) (*b* Copenhagen, 8 June 1888; *d* Copenhagen, 9 Feb 1949). Danish composer. Although in 1906 he was engaged in law studies, he began composition lessons with Nielsen and Laub; he was also a pupil of the organist Paul Hellmuth, the pianist Henrik Knudsen and the conductor Frank van der Stucken. He served as an artillery lieutenant from 1914 to 1918, but at the same time he continued to pursue his musical interests: in 1916 he was appointed organist of Skovshoved Church, a post he held until his death. Appointed to the staff of the Copenhagen Conservatory in 1931, he became an influential teacher of composition and instrumentation. Among the honours he received were the Anckerske Legat (1919), the Lange-Müller Aeresstipendium (1926) and membership of the Royal Swedish Academy of Music (1947).

Schierbeck made a most important contribution to the literature of Danish song. His early style was less attuned to the new folklike idiom of Nielsen and Laub than to the more romantic manner of Lange-Müller, but the later songs, such as the collection *Alverden gaar omkring* ('The world goes round'), op.42, are closer to the former two composers. In addition to the art songs, he composed valuable material for Danish children's songbooks. Among the occasional pieces, which he was always ready to provide, the *Kantate ved Københavns Universitets Immatrikulationsfest* op.16 has become a traditional part of the university's annual ceremonies. The immediately preceding Symphony was first conducted by Nielsen at Göteborg in 1922.

From 1923 to 1930 Schierbeck was at work on the opera *Fête galante*, whose first performance at the Copenhagen Royal Theatre was directed by Schiøler, with Sylvia Larsen, the composer's wife, as Suzon. Although the piece was well applauded, the critics all commented on its excessive length, and it was taken off after six performances. Schierbeck undertook revisions in the expectation of further stagings, but it was not until after his death that a shortened version was broadcast by Danish radio (1949), and there was no complete performance again until the opera returned to the Royal Theatre in 1960; that production met with success, but the work failed to gain a place in the permanent repertory. Disappointed by the problems surrounding his opera, Schierbeck found an outlet for his inclination towards dramatic composition in editing and arranging *The Beggars' Opera*, and in collaborating with the Danish film maker Carl Theodor Dreyer. The most impressive product of this partnership was *Vredens dag* ('Day of wrath'), whose score employs a cantus firmus treatment of the *Dies irae* chant. After Schierbeck's death Dreyer made use of his music in the soundtrack for *Ordet* ('The word').

WORKS

DRAMATIC AND CHORAL

op.

16 Kantate ved Københavns Universitets Immatrikulationsfest (H. H. S. Pedersen), male chorus, str, pf, 1922; perf. with Akademiske festmusik, 1922

19 Julekantate [Christmas cantata] (Bible), SATB, 1922

25 Fête galante (opera, M. Lobedanz), 1923–30; Copenhagen, 1931

36 Tiggerens opera [after Gay and Pepusch: The Beggars' Opera], 1936; Danish radio, 1936

38 Hverdagskantate [Everyday cantata] (A. Garff), SATB, orch, 1937

52 Lille kirkekantate (Bible), SATB, 1940

60 Mødrehjaelpen [The mother's help], film score, dir. Dreyer, 1942

— Vredens dag [Day of wrath], film score, dir. Dreyer, 1943

17 other cantatas, 110 other choral works

SONGS

1   Fjerne melodier [Strange melodies] (T. Lange), 1v, pf, 1912

10 Den kinesiske fløjte (E. Frank), 1v, pf, 1920, orchd

11 2 jydske viser [2 Jutland songs] (J. Aakjaer), 1v, pf, 1920

14 Nakjaelen (M. Børup), cycle, 1v, pf, 1921

42 Alverden gaar omkring [The world goes round], 33 songs, 1v, pf, 1938

48 Häxa [Sorceress] (Karlfelt), S, org, orch, 1939

Others to total of 148

INSTRUMENTAL

Orch.: Sym., op.15, 1916–21; Natten [The night], op.41, sym. scene, pf, orch, 1938; Andante doloroso, op.57, str, 1942; 8 other pieces

Pf: 2 fantastiske etuder, op.4, 1913–14; Sonata, G, op.5, 1915; 3 Waltzes, op.7, 1915; Sydvest, sweater og shag, op.31, 1932

13 chamber works, 18 org chorale preludes

Principal publishers: Engstrøm Sødring, Hansen, Nordens Musik, Samfundet til Udgivelse af Dansk Musik, Skandinavisk, Skandina visk og Borup

MSS in *DK-Kk*

BIBLIOGRAPHY

C. Rebild: 'Poul Schierbecks sange', *Aarhus stiftstiedende* (28 Jan 1940)

R. Hove: 'Poul Schierbeck', *DBL*

G. Fjelrad: 'Poul Schierbeck in memoriam', *Sanger bladet* (1949), no.3

J. Maegaard: 'Den kinesiske fløjte', *Nordisk musikkultur* (1952), no.2, p.160

——: 'En glemt opera?', *Nordisk musikkultur* (1955), no.4, p.113

F. S. Petersen: 'Poul Schierbeck', *Aschehougs musiklexikon*, ii (Copenhagen, 1958), 364

O. Mathisen: *Poul Schierbeck* (diss., U. of Copenhagen, 1972) [incl. listing and analysis of the songs with bibliography]

WILLIAM H. REYNOLDS

Schieti [Schietti], Cesare (*b* Urbino; *d* Urbino, 8 Jan 1600). Italian composer. He was a priest, and was *maestro di cappella* at Urbino Cathedral between 30 June 1555 and 8 January 1575, except for a brief period at Ravenna in the service of Cardinal Giulio Feltrio della Rovere between October 1566 and February 1567. In November 1575 he was appointed to a canonry at the cathedral and between 1584 and 1593 is recorded as a member of the administrative body. He was *maestro di cappella* there again from 15 January 1593 to 1 October 1596, and between June and December 1598. Four years before his death he instituted the office of *coristaria* at the cathedral with funds inherited from his brother Marc'Antonio; a plaque in the sacristy records the chapter's gratitude for his generosity. The six-voice *Missa 'Lucubratio'* demonstrates his mastery of contrapuntal technique, particularly in the last Agnus Dei constructed on a double canon. In 1599 a volume of motets and psalms (*RISM* 1599[2]) containing works by Felice Anerio, Marenzio, G. M. Nanino and Palestrina was dedicated to him.

WORKS

Missa 'Lucubratio', 6vv, *I-LT*

4 motets, 1567[3], 1599[2]; 8 madrigals, 1562[5], 1567[13], 1568[12], 1568[16]; spiritual madrigal, 1598[6]

BIBLIOGRAPHY

G. Radiciotti: *Contributi alla storia del teatro e della musica in Urbino* (Pesaro, 1899), 39

——: *I musicisti marchigiani dal sec. XVI al sec. XIX* (Rome, 1909), 125

G. Tebaldini: *L'archivio musicale della Cappella lauretana* (Loreto, 1921), 27, 29, 171

B. Ligi: 'La cappella musicale del duomo di Urbino', *NA*, ii (1925), 49, 63, 66, 73, 75

O. Mischiati: 'Schieti, Cesare', *MGG*

PIER PAOLO SCATTOLIN

Schiever, Ernst (*b* Hanover, 23 March 1844; *d* Hanover, 1915). German violinist. He studied under Joachim, 1860–64. In 1868 he joined the Müller Quartet, with which he travelled as leader until its dissolution in the following year, when he became a teacher at the Hochschule für Musik in Berlin and a member of the Joachim Quartet. He remained in Berlin two years, organizing another quartet, which was engaged subsequently by Count Hochberg and became known as the Gräflich Hochberg Quartet of Schloss Rohnstock (near Striegau, Silesia).

In 1878 Schiever went to England, making Liverpool his headquarters and becoming leader of the Richter orchestra, with which he was connected for nearly 30 years. He founded the Schiever Quartet which was long favourably regarded in the north of England.

W. W. COBBETT

Schifrin, Lalo (Boris) (*b* Buenos Aires, 21 June 1932). American composer and jazz musician of Argentine origin. He studied with Juan Carlos Paz and from 1950 with Messiaen in Paris, where in 1955 he represented Argentina at the International Jazz Festival. After forming his own jazz band in Buenos Aires he moved to New York (1958) where he played in and made arrangements for a number of jazz bands, including Dizzy Gillespie's with whom he played from 1960 to 1962. From 1964 he lived in Hollywood where he made a highly successful career as a composer for films and television.

WORKS
(selective list)

Inst: music for jazz band, 1960–62; Gillespiana (ballet), 1961; Suite, tpt, brass, 1961; The Ritual of Sound, 15 insts, 1962; Jazz Faust (ballet), 1963; Pulsations, elec kbd, jazz band, orch, 1971

Vocal: Jazz Suite on Mass Texts, 1965; The Rise and Fall of the Third Reich (oratorio), 1967; Madrigals for the Space Age, narrator, chorus, 1976

Film and television scores, incl. The Liquidator, The Fox, The Cincinnati Kid, Mission: Impossible

Schikaneder [Schickaneder]. Austrian family of German origin.

(1) Urban Schikaneder (*b* Regensburg, 2 Nov 1746; *d* Vienna, 11 April 1818). Actor and singer. As 'Hr. Schikaneder der Ältere' he sang First Priest in the première of *Die Zauberflöte*. For some years either side of this event he was a member of the theatrical company of his brother (2) Emanuel Schikaneder, and during its years of travel also took a share in the administrative responsibilities.

(2) Emanuel (Johann Joseph [Baptist]**) Schikaneder** (*b* Straubing, 1 Sept 1751; *d* Vienna, 21 Sept 1812). Dramatist, theatre director, actor, singer and composer, brother of (1) Urban Schikaneder. Educated at the Jesuit Gymnasium at Regensburg, where he was also a cathedral chorister, Schikaneder may have been a town musician for a brief period before he became an actor with F. J. Moser's troupe in 1773 or 1774. In 1774 he danced in a court ballet at Innsbruck and his Singspiel *Die Lyranten* (of which he wrote both words and music) was performed there in 1775 or 1776. In the latter year

the Innsbruck company (then under A. Schopf and Theresia Schimann) moved to Augsburg, where on 9 February 1777 he married Maria Magdalena (known as Eleonore) Arth (*b* Hermannstadt, 1752; *d* Vienna, 22 June 1821), an actress in the company. In 1777–8 they were in Nuremberg with Moser's company, and in December 1777 Schikaneder made a famous guest appearance at the Munich court theatre as Hamlet, being obliged to encore the final scene. From January 1778 he was director of the troupe, appearing with it at Ulm, Stuttgart, Augsburg, Nuremberg, Rothenburg and elsewhere. In 1780 they went to Ljubljana, Klagenfurt and Linz before beginning a lengthy season at Salzburg in September of that year, during which time Schikaneder became friendly with the Mozarts. Further travels through Austria included a guest appearance in summer 1783 at the Kärntnerthortheater, Vienna.

After a season at Pressburg (Bratislava), he became lessee of the Kärntnerthor in November 1783, remaining there for 15 months. For nearly a year from April 1785 he was a member of the National Theatre, his troupe being run by his wife and Johann Friedel and touring in southern Austria until it moved into the Freihaus-Theater auf der Wieden, Vienna, in November 1788. Schikaneder himself had meanwhile (February 1786) been granted an imperial licence for the building of a suburban theatre in Vienna; in fact he did not make use of it for 15 years, forming instead a new company specializing in Singspiels and operas, which he took to Salzburg, Augsburg and Memmingen. In February 1787 he took over the Prince of Thurn and Taxis's court theatre at Regensburg. When Johann Friedel died at the end of March 1789 Schikaneder became reconciled with his wife and took over the Freihaus-Theater with her, bringing from Regensburg the singer–composers Schack and Gerl. Schikaneder's reign at the Freihaus began on 12 July 1789 with the first performance of his 'Anton' opera *Der dumme Gärtner*, and from this time dates the beginning of his steady series of plays, opera and Singspiel librettos which were the backbone of the repertory of his theatre (but were also frequently performed in other theatres, sometimes with new musical scores).

Schikaneder's years of travel had not surprisingly seen the production of more straight plays than operas; in Vienna he placed the emphasis of his company's activities firmly on opera, and commissioned settings of his own textbooks from Mozart (*Die Zauberflöte*), Süssmayr (*Der Spiegel von Arkadien*), Wölfl (*Der Höllenberg*), Mederitsch and Winter (one act each of *Babylons Pyramiden*; Winter also set *Das Labyrinth*, a sequel to *Die Zauberflöte*). He also received scores from his theatre Kapellmeister Henneberg (*Die Waldmänner*), Haibel (*Der tiroler Wastel*) and Seyfried (*Der Löwenbrunn* and *Der Wundermann am Rheinfall*). As the 1790s advanced, so Schikaneder began to suffer from increasingly serious financial difficulties as he strove to surpass the achievements of his rivals and of his own greatest successes. In 1799 he handed over the management of the theatre to Bartholomäus Zitterbarth, while continuing his artistic direction. Of the 12 greatest successes at the Freihaus, which closed on 12 June 1801, eight – including all the first five – were written by Schikaneder himself.

On 13 June 1801 Schikaneder opened the new Theater an der Wien, making use of the licence he had previously been granted; it was the most lavishly

Emanuel Schikaneder as Papageno: engraving (1791) by Ignaz Alberti

equipped and one of the largest theatres of its age, and it has continued in almost unbroken use. It was opened with Teyber's setting of Schikaneder's own libretto *Alexander*, but change in public taste and a marked decline in Schikaneder's own standards and powers of judgment were influential in the decision to sell the licence to Zitterbarth less than a year after the opening of the theatre; Schikaneder continued to supply it with plays and librettos, and to act, but despite two further periods as artistic director, his fortunes were on the decline. After the sale of the theatre to a consortium of noblemen in late 1806 Schikaneder left Vienna and took over the Brno Theatre. At Easter 1809 he was back in Vienna, but financial ruin and failing mental health darkened his last years. On his way to Budapest to take up an appointment as director of a new German theatre company in 1812 he became mad, returned to Vienna, and died in penury shortly after; a performance of his play *Die Schweden vor Brünn* was given for his benefit at the Theater in der Leopoldstadt on 18 July 1812, an uncommon tribute from a rival theatre, albeit one that had successfully staged Schikaneder plays since the early 1780s and would continue to do so until the 1850s.

Schikaneder was one of the most talented and influential theatre men of his age. Although it is fashionable to decry his plays and librettos, they more than satisfied the demands of their day. Goethe praised Schikaneder's skill at creating strong dramatic situations, and though the verse is often trite, the libretto of *Die Zauberflöte* (Giesecke's claims to the authorship of which were proven false by Komorzynski and more scientifically by Rommel) is by no means unworthy of Mozart's music. Some of Schikaneder's comedies (the 'Anton' plays, *Der tiroler Wastel*, *Das abgebrannte Haus*, *Der Fleischhauer von Ödenburg*, *Die Fiaker in Wien*) continued to be much performed for many years and strongly influenced the later development of the Viennese *Lokalstück* ('local play'). Early in his career Schikaneder wrote two, and perhaps several more, theatre scores: it has long been known that the music as well as the text of *Die Lyranten* was his work; and for the production of his Singspiel *Das Urianische Schloss* (Salzburg, 1786) at the Theater in der Leopoldstadt in November 1787 a score by him is specifically mentioned by Wenzel Müller in his diary ('Opera by Em: Schikaneder, music, and book').

LIBRETTOS
(works first performed in Vienna unless otherwise stated)

Die Lyranten (Das lustige Elend, oder Die drei Bettelstudenten) (operetta, 3, Schikaneder), Innsbruck, 1775/6; Der Müllertomerl, oder Das Bergmädchen (Kaspar der Müller Tomerl) (bucolic opera, Haibel), 1785; Der Luftballon (operetta, 3, Schack), Kempten, 1786; Das Urianische Schloss (Singspiel, Schikaneder), Salzburg, 1786; Die drei Ringe oder [Kaspar] Der lächerliche Mundkoch (Singspiel, Schack), ? Salzburg, 1787; Lorenz und Suschen (Singspiel, Schack), ? Salzburg, 1787; Der Krautschneider (comic Singspiel, 4, Schack), Regensburg, 1788; Jacob und Nannerl, oder Der angenehme Traum (comic opera, 3, Schack), 1789; Der dumme Gärtner aus dem Gebirge, oder Die zween Anton (comic opera, 2, Schack, Gerl), 1789 [= Anton I]

Die verdeckten Sachen (comic opera, 2, Schack, Gerl), 1789 [= Anton II]; Was macht der Anton im Winter? (comic opera, 2, ? Schack, Gerl), 1790 [= Anton III]; Die schöne Isländerin, oder Der Mufti von Samarkanda (magic comedy with songs), 1790; Der Fall ist noch weit seltner, oder Die geplagten Ehemänner (opera, 2, Schack), 1790 [= Una cosa rara II]; Der Frühling, oder Der Anton ist noch nicht tot (comic opera, 2), 1790 [= Anton IV]; Der Stein der Weisen, oder Die Zauberinsel (heroic-comic opera, 2, Schack, Gerl and others), 1790; Anton bei Hofe, oder Das Namensfest (comic opera, 2), 1791 [= Anton V]; Die Zauberflöte (grand opera, 2, Mozart), 1791; Der redliche Landmann (bucolic family scene with music, 5), 1792

Johanna von Weimar (knightly play with music, 5, Henneberg), 1792; Der Renegat, oder Anton in der Türkei (comic opera, 2), 1792 [= Anton VI]; Die Kriegsgesetze, oder Die deutsche Griechin (military scene with songs, 3), 1792; Die Eisen-Königin (magic play with songs, 3, Henneberg), 1793; Der Zauberpfeil, oder Das Kabinett der Wahrheit (grand opera, 2, Lickl), 1793; Der wohltätige Derwisch, oder Die Schellenkappe (Die Zaubertrommel) (magic comedy, 3, Schack, Gerl, ?Henneberg), 1793; Die Waldmänner (comic opera, 3, Henneberg), 1793; Die Hirten am Rhein (magic comic opera, 2), 1794; Der Spiegel von Arkadien (grand heroic-comic opera, 2, Süssmayr), 1794; Das Häuschen im Walde, oder Antons Reise nach seinem Geburtsort (comic opera, 3, ?Schack), 1795 [= Anton VII]

Der Scherenschleifer (carnival opera, 2, Henneberg), 1795; Der Königsohn aus Ithaka (grand heroic-comic opera, 2, Hoffmeister), 1795; Der Höllenberg, oder Prüfung und Lohn (heroic-comic opera, 2, Wölfl), 1795; Der tiroler Wastel (comic opera, 3, Haibel), 1796; Östreichs treue Brüder, oder Die Scharfschützen in Tirol (Der Landsturm) (patriotic Singspiel, 2, Haibel), 1796 [= Der tiroler Wastel II]; Das medizinische Konsilium (comic opera, 2, Haibel), 1797; Der Löwenbrunn (Der Löwenbrunnen) (heroic-comic opera, 2, Seyfried), 1797; Babylons Pyramiden (grand heroic-comic opera, 2, Mederitsch, Winter), 1797; Das Labyrinth, oder Der Kampf mit den Elementen (heroic-comic opera, 2, Winter), 1798 [= Die Zauberflöte II]; Die Ostindier vom Spittelberg (Die Rückkehr aus Ostindien) (comic Singspiel, 2, Seyfried, Stegmayer and others), 1799

Konrad Langbart von Friedburg, oder Der Berggeist (knightly play, with music, 3, Henneberg), 1799; Mina [Minna] und Peru, oder Die Königspflicht (heroic-comic Singspiel, 2, Henneberg and Seyfried), 1799; Der Papagei und die Gans, oder Die zisalpinischen Perücken (bucolic-comic family picture with songs, 3, Haibel), 1799; Der Wundermann am Rheinfall (grand comic opera, 2, Seyfried), 1799; Die Spinnerin am Gatterhölzl oder Der Stock-am-Eisen-Platz (Austrian folk legend with songs, 3), 1800; Amors Schiffchen in der

Brigittenaue (comic opera, 1, Seyfried and others), 1800; Proteus und Arabiens Söhne (magic Singspiel, 3, Seyfried, Stegmayer), 1801; Alexander (grand heroic opera, 2, F. Teyber), 1801
Tsching! Tsching! Tsching! (Singspiel, 3, Haibel), 1802; Die Entlarvten (Singspiel, 3, A. Fischer), 1803 [= Die Waldmänner II]; Pfändung und Personal-Arrest (comic Singspiel, 2, Teyber), 1803; Swetards Zaubertal (grand opera, 2, Fischer), 1805; Vestas Feuer (grand heroic opera, 2, J. Weigl), 1805 [also frag. setting by Beethoven]; Die Kurgäste am Sauerbrunn(en) (original Singspiel, 5, Diabelli), 1806; Das Zaubermädchen im Schreywald (opera), Das Fest der Götter (caricature opera), libs passed by Brno censor Nov 1809
Nearly 50 plays

(3) Anna [Nanny, Nanette] Schikaneder (b 1767; d Regensburg, 1862). Singer, daughter of (1) Urban Schikaneder. She sang First Boy in the première of Die Zauberflöte and later became a member of the Theater in der Leopoldstadt, singing the Queen of Night in that company's first performance of the opera in July 1811. After her retirement she lived for many years at Freising, completely blind.

(4) Karl Schikaneder (b Freising, 1770; d Prague, 25 March 1845). German dramatist, composer, actor, singer and producer, son of (1) Urban Schikaneder. After a period with the Freihaus-Theater company of his uncle, Emanuel Schikaneder, he became a producer at the Theater in the Josefstadt in 1803. He moved to Steyr, Karlsbad and Brno (where he was a member of the company his uncle directed in 1807). In 1811, and again from 1816 to 1819, he was a member of the Theater in der Leopoldstadt, being employed as dramatist, singer and actor. He moved to Prague in 1819, where he was appointed opera producer, retiring in 1834. He was the author of a once-popular series of plays and composed a number of music scores, including at least six to his own texts (others of which were set by Wenzel Müller, Franz Teyber and Franz Volkert).

BIBLIOGRAPHY
Theater-Kalender (Gotha, 1775–98)
J. K. Schikaneder: 'Emanuel Schikaneder', Der Gesellschafter, xviii (Berlin, 1834), nos.71–4
C. von Wurzbach: 'Schikaneder', Biographisches Lexikon des Kaiserthums Oesterreich, xxix (Vienna, 1875), 299ff, 311
A. Sauer: 'Schikaneder, Emanuel', ADB
E. von Komorzynski: Emanuel Schikaneder: ein Beitrag zur Geschichte des deutschen Theaters (Berlin, 1901, rev. 2/1951)
L. Eisenberg: 'Schikaneder', Grosses biographisches Lexikon der deutschen Bühne im 19. Jahrhundert (Leipzig, 1903), 881ff
E. von Komorzynski: 'Schikaneder, Karl', ADB
E. K. Blümml: Aus Mozarts Freundes- und Familienkreis (Vienna, 1923)
O. E. Deutsch: Das Freihaus-Theater auf der Wieden (Vienna, 1937)
F. Hadamowsky: Das Theater in der Wiener Leopoldstadt (Vienna, 1934)
E. Anderson, ed.: The Letters of Mozart and his Family (London, 1938, 2/1966)
H. Endrös: 'E. Schikaneder und das Augsburger Theater', Zeitschrift des Historischen Vereins für Schwaben, lv–lvi (Augsburg, 1942–3), 203–98
E. Komorzynski: Der Vater der Zauberflöte: Emanuel Schikaneders Leben (Vienna, 1948)
K. Goedeke: Grundriss zur Geschichte der deutschen Dichtung, xi/1 (Düsseldorf, 2/1951), 132; xi/2 (Düsseldorf, 2/1953), 376ff, 381ff
A. Bauer: 150 Jahre Theater an der Wien (Vienna, 1952)
H. Pigge: Geschichte und Entwicklung des Regensburger Theaters 1786–1859 (diss., U. of Munich, 1953)
A. Bauer: Opern und Operetten in Wien (Graz and Cologne, 1955)
A. Loewenberg: Annals of Opera (Geneva, 2/1955)
W. Senn: 'Schikaneders Weg zum Theater', Acta mozartiana, ix (1962), 39
F. J. Fischer: 'Emanuel Schikaneder und Salzburg', Jb der Gesellschaft für Wiener Theaterforschung, xv–xvi (1966), 179–216
P. Branscombe: 'Die Zauberflöte: some Textual and Interpretative Problems', PRMA, xcii (1965–6), 45
E. M. Batley: A Preface to The Magic Flute (London, 1969)
W. A. Bauer, O. E. Deutsch and J. H. Eibl, eds.: Mozart: Briefe und Aufzeichnungen (Kassel, 1962–75)

PETER BRANSCOMBE

Schikardt [Schikhart], Johann Christian. See SCHICKHARDT, JOHANN CHRISTIAN.

Schildt, Melchior (b Hanover, 1592–3; d Hanover, 18 May 1667). German composer and organist. He came from a Hanover family, four of whom (his grandfather Gerdt, his father Antonius and his brother Ludolph, as well as himself) were employed over a period of more than 125 years as organists at the three churches in the Old Town of Hanover. After initially being taught music at Hanover by his father and Andreas Crappius, he went in December 1609 to Amsterdam to study with Sweelinck, with whom he remained probably until the end of 1612. No documents have survived relating to his activities over the next ten years, but from 1623 to 1626 he was organist at the Hauptkirche in Wolfenbüttel and from 1626 to 1629 was court organist to King Christian IV in Copenhagen. After his father's death in 1629, he succeeded him as organist of the Marktkirche, Hanover, and held this post until his death.

Of the north German organists of Schütz's generation, the pupils of Sweelinck who founded the so-called north German organ school in the first half of the 17th century, Schildt, together with Scheidemann and Jacob Praetorius (ii), is one of those whose extant works mark them out as composers with distinctive personalities. Except for a single vocal work, all of his surviving music is for keyboard, and as with Sweelinck's other pupils, most of it consists of chorale-based organ works. Of his pieces in this genre, the five-verse cycle Herr Christ, der einig Gotts Sohn is stylistically still quite close to Sweelinck, but in the Magnificat I. modi, his most distinguished and important organ work, which is also in five separate sections, the modern north German forms of chorale fantasia and ricercare are clearly visible. This work was probably one of a now lost series of Magnificat settings by Schildt comparable with the cycles of Scheidt, Praetorius and Scheidemann. Of his other keyboard works, the Paduana Lachrymae is specially fine. It is one of many keyboard arrangements by English and continental composers of the first piece in Dowland's Lachrymae (1604) and is notable for its particularly expressive colouring. Schildt's one extant vocal work is the chorale concerto Ach mein herzliebes Jesulein. It is a masterly example of the sacred concerto for voices and instruments. As such it is indebted to Schütz's Symphoniae sacrae, but the way in which Schildt applied this style to the treatment of a chorale in order to provide a subjective interpretation of the content and emotional impact of the chorale text was without precedent. The quality and originality of this piece make the loss of a further nine vocal works by him, known only by their titles, particularly regrettable.

WORKS

VOCAL

Ach mein herzliebes Jesulein, 1v, 2 vn, bn, bc, 21 Jan 1657, S-Uu; ed. W. Breig (Kassel, 1964)
9 further works formerly in D-Lm, now lost, see Seiffert (1907–8)

KEYBOARD

Chorale settings: Allein Gott in der Höh sei Ehr; Herr Christ, der einig Gotts Sohn; Herzlich lieb hab ich dich, O Herr; Magnificat I. modi: ed. in Die Orgel, ii/24 (Cologne, 1968)
Variations: Gleich wie das Feuer; Paduana Lachrymae: ed. W. Breig, Lied- und Tanzvariationen der Sweelinck-Schule (Mainz, 1970)
2 Praeambula, ed. in Organum, iv/2 (Leipzig, 1925)
2 further chorale arrangements in G. V. Scharffe, Tabulaturbuch, now lost (see J. P. Sweelinck: Werke, i, ed. M. Seiffert, Leipzig, 1894, IVf)

BIBLIOGRAPHY
M. Seiffert: 'J. P. Sweelinck und seine direkten deutschen Schüler', *VMw*, vii (1891), 145–240

——: 'Die Chorbibliothek der St. Michaelisschule in Lüneburg zu Seb. Bachs Zeit', *SIMG*, ix (1907–8), 616

T. W. Werner: 'Melchior Schildt und seine Familie', *AMw*, ii (1919–20), 356

F. Dietrich: *Geschichte des deutschen Orgelchorals im 17. Jahrhundert* (Kassel, 1932)

T. W. Werner: 'Archivalische Nachrichten und Dokumente zur Kenntnis der Familie Schildt', *Theodor Kroyer: Festschrift zum sechzigsten Geburtstage* (Regensburg, 1933), 130

——: 'Melchior Schildts Testament', *AMf*, ii (1937), 77

W. Apel: *Geschichte der Orgel- und Klaviermusik bis 1700* (Kassel, 1967; Eng. trans., rev., 1972), 372

W. Breig: 'Melchior Schildt', *Musik und Kirche*, xxxvii (1967), 152

WERNER BREIG

Schilke, Renold O(tto) (*b* Green Bay, Wisc., 30 June 1910). American trumpet and mouthpiece manufacturer. He began to study the cornet under Del Wright in 1918; his later teachers were Max Schlossberg, Georges Mager, Edward Llewellyn and Herbert Clarke. He started playing professionally with the Orpheum Vaudeville Circuit in 1921; he also worked at the Holton factory (1921–2). In 1929 he moved to Chicago, beginning an association with the Chicago SO, first as substitute, then as assistant first trumpet (from 1934), first trumpet in 1939, and substitute again from 1940 to 1961. He began to experiment with trumpet making in the 1920s, and helped Elden Benge from 1934 to 1952. In 1956 he opened his own business, specializing in high quality professional instruments. In 1973, 34 employees, all of them musicians, made 59 models. One result of his considerable acoustical research, in which Victor Mahillon was his most important guide, was the introduction in 1968 of the tuning-bell, through which the mouthpipe tuning-slide was abolished; the first prototype of this device was manufactured in 1928. In 1966 Schilke was appointed consultant for Yamaha, and in 1975 he began to make horns.

EDWARD H. TARR

Schiller, (Johann Christoph) Friedrich von (*b* Marbach, 10 Nov 1759; *d* Weimar, 9 May 1805). German dramatist, poet, aesthetician and historian. The son of an army medical officer, Schiller had a rather unsettled childhood, especially during the years he spent as a student (law and medicine) at the Stuttgart Karlsschule (1773–80). At this time he came into contact with Zumsteeg, and wrote *Die Räuber*. Forced to leave Stuttgart in 1782 (shortly after the Mannheim première of *Die Räuber*), he moved to Mannheim and wrote *Fiesko* and *Kabale und Liebe*. C. G. Körner helped him to find more congenial working conditions in Leipzig and Dresden where, between 1785 and 1787, he completed *Don Carlos* and considered writing a libretto for Naumann. From 1787 until 1794 he was frequently on the move, staying in Weimar, Rudolstadt, Jena and in Swabia. From 1789 he held the chair of history at Jena. In 1790 he married Charlotte von Lengefeld, a gifted amateur pianist, and at about the same time he became acquainted with Rochlitz and Reichardt. From 1794 until his death Schiller was on friendly terms with Goethe, living in Weimar from 1799 and developing with him the most famous artistic collaboration in the history of German letters. These last years saw the production of his 'classical' dramas (the *Wallenstein* trilogy, 1798–9; *Maria Stuart*, 1800; *Die Jungfrau von Orleans*, 1801; *Die Braut von Messina*, 1803; and *Wilhelm Tell*, 1804), and the splendid series of ballads. In all of these works the theme to a more or less marked

extent is the search for moral freedom, though political freedom is as much the theme of *Wilhelm Tell* as it had been of the earlier revolutionary plays.

Schiller was no musician, and indeed there is little evidence that he understood or appreciated music to any great extent. Certainly his tastes were even more conservative than those of the older Goethe: Gluck almost alone among his great contemporaries found a ready appreciation from Schiller, whose comments on Mozart and Haydn for instance are embarrassingly naive. But it is not to be doubted that he was being truthful when he stated that 'a certain musical mood (*Gemütsstimmung*)' was for him the precursor of poetic inspiration. Certainly the rhythmic élan of much of Schiller's verse has a kind of musicality, a quality found both in his lyrics and in the shape and balance of his great dramatic monologues and dialogues. Incidental music plays a modest part in most of Schiller's plays, though in one, *Die Braut von Messina*, he strove to re-create the conditions and mood of ancient Greek tragedy, with an important role for the chorus.

However much one may question Schiller's understanding of music, there is no denying the enormous impact his works have made on composers. Beethoven's setting of verses from Schiller's ode 'An die Freude' in the Ninth Symphony, and Rossini's *Guillaume Tell* and Verdi's *Giovanna d'Arco*, *I masnadieri*, *Luisa Miller* and *Don Carlos* are the most famous examples of works based on Schiller. Bruch, Brahms, Fibich, d'Indy, Lalo, Liszt, Mendelssohn, Pfitzner, Rheinberger, Schubert (nearly 50 settings), Schumann, Smetana, Richard Strauss and Tchaikovsky are other prominent composers who have been drawn to his texts.

BIBLIOGRAPHY
F. A. Brandstaeter: *Über Schillers Lyrik im Verhältnis zu ihrer musikalischen Behandlung* (Danzig, 1863)

A. Schaefer: *Historisches und systematisches Verzeichnis sämtlicher Tonwerke zu den Dramen Schillers* (Leipzig, 1886)

K. Goedeke: *Grundriss zur Geschichte der deutschen Dichtung*, v (Dresden, 2/1893), 15–237

A. Bock: *Deutsche Dichter in ihren Beziehungen zur Musik* (Leipzig, 1893)

A. Kohut: *Schiller in seinen Beziehungen zur Musik* (Stuttgart, 1905)

H. A. H. Knudsen: *Schiller und die Musik* (diss., U. of Greifswald, 1908)

W. Witte: *Schiller* (Oxford, 1949)

H. B. Garland: *Schiller* (London, 1949)

E. L. Stahl: *Schiller's Drama: Theory and Practice* (Oxford, 1954)

P. Weigand: 'Schiller's Dramas as Opera Texts', *Monatshefte* [U. of Wisconsin], xlvi (1954), 249

G. Fricke, ed.: *F. Schiller: Briefe* (Munich, 1955)

R. M. Longyear: *Schiller and Music* (Chapel Hill, 1966)

P. J. Branscombe: 'Schiller and Music', *Forum for Modern Language Studies*, iv/4 (1968), 396

G. Fricke and H. G. Göpfert, eds.: *F. Schiller: Sämtliche Werke* (Munich, 5/1973)

PETER BRANSCOMBE

Schiller, Henryk (*b* Poznań, 2 Aug 1931). Polish composer. He studied theory and composition with Wiechowicz at the Kraków Conservatory, also reading musicology at the university; his studies were continued in Austria and at Darmstadt. In 1966 he was appointed to teach theory at the Warsaw Conservatory, and he was general secretary of the Polish Composers' Union from 1969 to 1973. He is a well-known broadcaster, principally on contemporary music. His compositions include a Piano Sonata (1958), Music no.2 for 13 instruments (1960) and the orchestral works *Inwencje* (1961), *Etiuda* (1966) and *Cztery sekwencje* ('Four sequences', 1968).

MIECZYSŁAWA HANUSZEWSKA

Schilling, Bertha Agnès Lisette. *See* BRÉVAL, LUCIENNE.

Schilling, Gustav (*b* Schwiegershausen, 3 Nov 1805; *d* Crete, Nebraska, March 1880). German musicographer and editor. Like others of his generation, Schilling, the son of a pastor, received his education in both music and theology, in the former partly from his father, in the latter from teachers at Göttingen and Halle. From 1830 to 1836 he was director of a music school in Stuttgart founded by Franz Stöpel, but gave it up to become a freelance writer in theology and politics as well as in music. He was founder and secretary of the Deutsche National-Verein für Musik und ihre Wissenschaft and edited its yearbook from 1839 to 1843. Between 1839 and 1850 Schilling published over a score of books on musical subjects including aesthetics, harmony and composers (among these an account of Liszt, 1842), which are generally superficial. His career in Germany came to an end in 1857 when he was prosecuted for debt and fled to America. There he announced his intention of founding a new conservatory in New York, but the plan came to nothing. After spending some further time in that city, he moved on to Montreal and thence to Crete in Nebraska, where he died on his son's farm.

Schilling is remembered today only for his *Encyclopädie der gesammten musikalischen Wissenschaften oder Universal Lexikon der Tonkunst* (6 vols., Stuttgart, 1835–8/*R*1973, 2/1840–42; supplement, 1841–2/*R*1973). The supplement was edited by F. S. Gassner who was also responsible for the one-volume abridgment published in 1849. The contributors included A. B. Marx, Rellstab, Schnyder von Wartensee, Seyfried, G. W. Fink and Gottfried Weber. Schilling seems to have written many unsigned articles, including perhaps the one on himself. The subject articles are of much less interest than those on musicians, especially secondary names of roughly the editor's own time: the latter often contain information which cannot be found elsewhere.

ALEC HYATT KING

Schilling, Hans Ludwig (*b* Mayen, Rhineland, 9 March 1927). German composer. In 1947 he entered the Staatliche Hochschule für Musik, Freiburg, and later studied at the universities of Zurich (1951–2) and Freiburg (1953–5). During these years his teachers included Genzmer, Uetel and Hindemith (composition) and Gurlitt and Zenck (musicology). From 1954 to 1959 he taught at Freiburg University and in 1960 was visiting professor at the Staatliche Hochschule für Musik, Karlsruhe. He returned to Freiburg in 1962 to teach at the Pädagogische Hochschule and, concurrently, at the Hohe Fachschule für Sozialarbeit. Schilling has also been active as a writer on music and was for 15 years reviewer for the *Badische Zeitung* of Freiburg. His early compositions stand within the Brahms–Reger tradition, although the occasional use of modal structures, isorhythm and canon reveals his interest in medieval music. His first dodecaphonic works, written in the early 1950s, retain a harmonic relationship with Hindemith; later, as his employment of serial technique became more strict, the influence of Dallapiccola became evident. Schilling's most individual works were written after 1960, and they show a variety of means of juxtaposing musical materials. Jazz elements, quodlibet

technique and instrumental contrast are all characteristic of his later style.

WORKS
(*selective list*)

Orch: Cl Concertino, n.d.; Variata, 1953–4; Studie 59, 1959; Streicher-Sinfonie, 1964–5; Martin's Consort, wind, 1965; 3 Choräle, wind, 1967; Akrostichon, 1967–72; Ukraina, wind, 1968; Sinfonia, wind, 1969; Houston Org Conc., 1970–72; HGBS-Sound, org, elec org, 3 ww, big band, 1970–72; Adagio in memoriam Max Reger, 15 str/orch, 1973; Sweet-Ouvertüre, wind, 1974; Clarinettissimo, cl, 1970, 1975; Sinfonia quasi partita, 8/4 brass, org, 1975; Conc. giocoso, tpt, orch, 1976; Symposion, 1977

Inst: Metamorphosen über ein altes Liebeslied, 4 ww, 1950–51; Intrada, 3 tpt, 3 trbn, 1951; Suite, s rec, pf, 1953; Conc., piccolo, fl, eng hn, va, pf, 1954; Suite en miniature, vn, bn, 1954; Partita, org, 1954–64; Capriccio armonico alla rondo inverso, brass, perc, 1965; Canzona, tpt, org, 1966; Quintetto 67: Zeacis Hafis, wind, 1967; Akrostichon II, hpd, 1968; Chaconne nouvelle, org, 1968; Antifone 69, tpt, org, brass, perc, 1969; Zyklus, va, org, 1969; Clarinettissimo, cl, 1970; Jam-Cembalo, 1970–71; Carillon, perc, org, 1976; 3 str qts, 2 str trios, 2 str duos

Vocal: Dem König der Ewigkeit, chorus, 11 insts, 1953; Missa unthematica, chorus 4–7vv, 1953; David singt vor Saul (Rilke), A, 9 insts, 1961; Tout le fatras immonde (Picasso), S, ens, 1962; Hebräische Balladen (E. Lasker-Schüler), S, pf/orch, 1965; Die Legende vom Weisen und Zöllner (Brecht), solo vv, chorus, orch, 1968; Klatsch (sozialkritisches Multimedia-Bühnenseminar, K. Thiele-Dohrmann), speaker, 1v, orch, 1968; Saki Nameh (lyric scene, Goethe), 5 solo vv, 7 insts, 1970; Memento (lyric scene, Jacobson), 3 solo vv, 2 speakers, 3 choruses, 2 orch, 1969–71; church music

Principal publishers: Breitkopf & Härtel, Hänssler, Moeck, Moseler, Schott

WRITINGS
Paul Hindemiths Cardillac: Beiträge zu einem Vergleich der beiden Opernfassungen (Würzburg, 1962)
Paul Hindemith: Handwerker, Baumeister, Stilgründer (in preparation)
with A. Schmidt: *Die Orgel von ihren hellenistischen Ursprüngen bis ins 13. Jh.* (in preparation)

BIBLIOGRAPHY
H. E. Bach: 'Hans Ludwig Schillings Orgelschaffen', *Musik und Kirche*, xl (1970), 284
H. L. Schilling: 'Biographische Notizen und Stellungnahme', *Chor im Gesprach* (Remscheid, 1972)
A. Schmidt: *Der Komponist Hans Ludwig Schilling* (Freiburg, 1972)
GEORGE W. LOOMIS

Schillinger, Joseph (Moiseyevich) (*b* Khar'kov, 31 Aug 1895; *d* New York, 23 March 1943). American theorist, teacher, composer and conductor of Ukrainian origin. He studied composition and conducting at the St Petersburg Conservatory (1914–18), receiving the highest prize in composition. From 1918 to 1922 he was head of the music department of the Board of Education in the Ukraine, dean of the State Academy of Music in Khar'kov and conductor of the Ukrainian State SO; and from 1922 to 1928 he was consultant for the Board of Education of Moscow and Leningrad, senior instructor for the State Institute of Musical Education in Leningrad and professor at the State Institute of History of the Arts. In 1927 he made gramophone recordings of the Georgian tribes and organized the first jazz orchestra in Russia. For the celebration of the tenth anniversary of the establishment of the USSR, also in 1927, he received a commission for a symphonic rhapsody for piano and large orchestra, *Oktyabr* op.19, which was selected as the best symphonic work composed during the first decade of the USSR. He emigrated to the USA in 1928, settling in New York. There he taught music, mathematics, art history and his own theory of rhythmic design at the New School for Social Research, New York University and Teachers College of Columbia University. In 1936 he became a citizen of the USA.

Schillinger's training in mathematics led him to formulate a 'system' of music theory which he used to teach numerous American composers, especially composers of commercial music, and most notably Gershwin, who employed Schillinger techniques in composing and orchestrating his opera *Porgy and Bess* and his *Variations on 'I got rhythm'*.

WORKS
(*selective list*)

Orch: March of the Orient, op.11, 1921–4; Oktyabr, op.19, pf, orch, 1927; First Airphonic Suite, op.21, theremin, orch, 1929; North Russian Sym., op.22, 1930

Inst: Sonata, op.9, vn, pf, 1921; 5 Pieces, op.12, pf, 1922; L'excentriade, op.14, pf, 1924; Sonata Rhapsody, op.17, pf, 1925

Principal publisher: Leeds Music

WRITINGS

Kaleidophone: New Resources of Melody and Harmony (New York, 1940/R1967)

ed. L. Dowling and A. Shaw: *The Schillinger System of Musical Composition* (New York, 1941, 3/1946/R1977)

The Mathematical Basis of the Arts (New York, 1948/R1976)

Encyclopedia of Rhythms (New York, 1966/R1976)

BIBLIOGRAPHY

V. Duke: 'Gershwin, Schillinger, Dukelsky: some Reminiscences', *MQ*, xxxiii (1947), 102

F. Schillinger: *Joseph Schillinger: a Memoir* (New York, 1949/R1976)

JAMES M. BURK

Schillings, Max von (*b* Düren, 19 April 1868; *d* Berlin, 24 July 1933). German composer and conductor. He was raised on his parents' estate at Gürzenich and received parental encouragement and direction for his artistic interests. While attending the Gymnasium at Bonn he studied the violin with the Gürzenich Konzertmeister, O. von Königslow, and theory and the piano with K. J. Brambach. From Königslow Schillings received the methods of David and the theory of Hauptmann; through Brambach, he was exposed to the tradition of Hummel and Beethoven, as taught by Hiller. The compositions written during this period were performed in part in Düren, with Schillings participating either as performer or conductor. After leaving the Gymnasium he spent three years studying law, philosophy, literature and art history at the University of Munich. There he became associated with Strauss and others of the Munich School, and under Strauss's influence he resolved to devote himself entirely to music.

From the beginning Schillings's musical career was focussed on opera. In 1892, largely to make himself thoroughly familiar with theatrical procedures, he took an appointment as assistant stage conductor at Bayreuth, where in 1902 he was made chorus master. His first opera, *Ingwelde*, was produced at Karlsruhe under Mottl in 1894. Schillings's work on the tragedy – the poem, by Count Ferdinand von Sporck, was based on a retelling of the Scandinavian *Svarfdälasaga* in Zedlitz's *Altnordische Bilder* – had begun in 1890. Although greeted with critical approval, *Ingwelde* seemed a student copy of Wagner's style in the *Ring*. This was in part, perhaps, unavoidable, since the plot was closely related to the Nibelungen sagas, and its title-role heroine bore an obvious resemblance to Brünnhilde. Schillings's second dramatic work, *Der Pfeifertag*, stands in stark contrast to the gloomy tragedy of his first opera. Here a merry, picturesque, medieval subject forms the basis for the poem, again by Sporck. But again critics discerned a strong reliance on the example of Wagner, albeit here the Wagner of *Die Meistersinger*. *Der Pfeifertag* was produced at Schwerin under Zumpe in 1899.

When Strauss left Munich for Berlin in 1898,

Schillings rapidly became recognized as the leader of the Munich school. And after Strauss assumed the presidency of the Allgemeine Deutsche Musikverein, his inclusion of music by Schillings and others of the 'modern German' persuasion in the organization's annual festivals helped further Schillings's budding reputation. But Schillings also became known as a conductor and teacher, and was in 1903 named Königlicher Professor at Munich; among his pupils were Furtwängler and Heger. Three years later, he completed his third major stage work, *Moloch*. E. Gerhäuser's poem treats the first cultural development of a crude and uncivilized people under religious influence. Despite its obvious references to Wagner's style in *Parsifal*, this was generally accepted as an erudite score, and Korngold reported that it impressed Mahler.

In 1908, having refused flattering offers of appointments at the operas of Munich, Weimar and Schwerin, Schillings finally accepted a post as assistant to the Intendant of the Royal Opera House, Stuttgart. His duties included conducting court orchestra concerts as well as operas. While this began in Schillings's life a period of exemplary service as a conductor, it much reduced his ability to devote himself to composition; most of his own music was composed before his 40th birthday. Since the Baron zu Putlitz, Intendant at Stuttgart, extended Schillings's broad artistic latitude, his ten years in the Stuttgart house – a period which saw 45 first performances – were a time of stimulating operatic enterprise. He was named general music director in 1911. In 1912, on the occasion of the opening of the new opera theatre in Stuttgart, he was elevated to the nobility by the King of Württemberg. Schillings's condensed version of *Les troyens* was produced in the Stuttgart house in 1913, and the world première of his most successful opera, *Mona Lisa*, was given there in 1915. But it was the first performance of the first version of the Strauss–Hofmannsthal *Ariadne auf Naxos* – with Reinhardt managing the stage and Strauss conducting – that made Stuttgart the momentary centre of musical interest in Germany.

World War I brought to an end these years of achievement. On the outbreak of war Schillings volunteered for service as a medical orderly, also finding time for work on *Mona Lisa*. He later confessed that the project – based on a horrific libretto by Beatrice Dovsky quite unlike the texts of his earlier operas – exerted an inexplicable attraction on him; he completed the piece in four and a half weeks. In 1918 he resigned from the Stuttgart house for personal reasons. While negotiating with the Prussian Ministry for Arts and Sciences for the post of director at the Berlin Music Academy, he was called by a unanimous vote of the artists of the Berlin Opera to head that institution as Intendant, a post he retained until 1925. During his tenure numerous important new works were produced at Berlin, including Pfitzner's *Palestrina*, Schreker's *Die Gezeichneten*, Strauss's *Josephslegende* and *Die Frau ohne Schatten*, Busoni's *Turandot* and *Arlecchino*, and Walter Braunfels's *Die Vögel*. In 1923 Schillings married the soprano Barbara Kemp, his second wife. Until her retirement from the stage in 1932 she helped further his reputation through her portrayal of Mona Lisa. The opera, with Kemp and with Schillings conducting, was presented at the Metropolitan Opera in 1922.

Schillings's resignation from his post as General Intendant at Berlin (1925) stemmed from a disagreement with Becker, the Minister of Culture. During the next few years he undertook extended tours as a guest conductor in Europe and the USA, served as director of the Zoppoter Waldoper and was principal conductor at Charlottenburg. He was also active in the recording studio during this period, directing the orchestra of the Berlin Städtische Oper in music by Beethoven, Schubert, Schumann and Wagner, among others, as well as selections from his own works.

Schillings had served from 1910 until 1920 as president of the Allgemeiner Deutscher Musikverein, and in 1911 the universities of Heidelberg and Tübingen had awarded him honorary doctorates. At the end of his life he received additional awards and honours: he became chairman of the Reichsverbandes Deutscher Tonkünstler and of the Genossenschaft Deutscher Tonsetzer, and president of the Prussian Academy of Arts; and he was awarded the Beethoven Prize and the Goethe Medal. Shortly before his death he was named General Intendant of the Städtische Oper, Berlin.

WORKS
(selective list)

STAGE

Operas: Ingwelde (Count F. von Sporck), Karlsruhe, 1894; Der Pfeifertag (Sporck), Schwerin, 1899, rev. 1931; Moloch (E. Gerhäuser, after fragment by F. Hebbel), Dresden, 1906; Mona Lisa (B. Dovsky), Stuttgart, 1915
Operatic arrs.: recitatives for *Mozart: Die Entführung aus dem Serail*, 1910; *Berlioz: Les troyens*, adaptation, Stuttgart, 1913

ORCHESTRAL

2 Phantasiestücke: Dem Andenken seiner Mutter, 1883, Aus dem Jahre 1890, 1890; 2 symphonische Phantasien, op.6: Meergruss, Seemorgen, 1895; Ein Zwiegespräch, op.8, tone poem, vn, vc, orch, 1896; Symphonischer Prolog zu Sophokles Ödipus, op.11, 1900; Musik zu Aeschylos Orestie, op.12, 1901; Musik zu Goethes Faust: pt. i, op.24, 1908, rev. and enlarged 1915; Vn Conc., op.25, 1910; Festlicher Marsch, military band, 1911; Tanz der Blumen, small orch, 1930

CHORAL

Weihechor, female vv, brass, harp, 1900; Dem Verklärten (J. Schiller), Bar, vv, orch, 1905; Hochzeitslied, op.26 (Goethe), S, Bar, vv, orch, 1910; 2 patriotische Gesänge, op.29 (L. Finck, A. Schlegel), male vv, 1913; 2 Chorlieder, op.30 (Arndt, K. Franke), male vv, 1913; Erschaffen und Beleben, op.35 (Goethe), male vv, 1932

SOLO VOCAL

With orch: Abenddämmerung, Mez/Bar, vn, orch, 1880, rev. 1916; Glockenlieder, op.22 (C. Spitteler), 1908; Die Perle, op.33 (Goethe), S, T, orch/pf, 1918; 4 Zwiegesänge aus dem 'West-östlichen Divan', op.34 (Goethe), S, T, orch/pf, 1919
With pf: 4 Lieder aus der Wanderzeit, op.2 (K. Stieler), 1891; 3 Lieder, op.4 (Stieler, Gräfin, Schwerin, N. Lenau), 1895; Letzte Bitte (O. Bierbaum), 1900; 4 Lieder, op.7 (O. Ernst), 1901; 5 Lieder, op.13 (G. Falke, A. Holz, K. Klitscher, Liliencron, J. Schiller), 1901; Lieder des Anakreon, op.14, 1902; Erntelieder, op.16 (F. Evers), 1902; Intermezzo (Grillparzer), 1902; 4 Lieder, op.17 (R. Presber, D. Biel, M. Boelitz), 1903; 4 Lieder, op.19 (Falke), 1903; Ach herzig's Herz (13th-century), 1905; Der Hufschmied, op.23 (Spitteler), 1908; Herbstbild (Hebbel), 1922; Ich weiss wohl (C. Brentano), unpubd; Du armes Blatt (J. Brentano), unpubd; Wiegenlied (C. Brentano), unpubd

CHAMBER AND INSTRUMENTAL

Str Qt, c, op.1b, 1887, rev. 1906; Improvisation, op.5, vn, pf, 1895; 3 schlichte Weisen, op.18, vn, pf, 1903; In stillen Gedanken, vn, pf, unpubd; Pf Qnt, E♭, op.32, 1917; 4 Pf Pieces, op.36, 1932

Principal publishers: Bote & Bock, Peters, Universal

BIBLIOGRAPHY

E. O. Nodnagel: *Jenseits von Wagner und Liszt: Profil und Perspektiven* (Königsberg, 1902)
R. Loos: 'Max Schillings', *Monographien moderner Musiker*, iii (Leipzig, 1909), 1
M. Halperson: 'Max Schillings, a Musical Leader of Modern Germany', *Musical America*, xxxvii/20 (1922), 4
A. Richard: *Max Schillings* (Berlin, 1922)
J. Beck: *Max von Schillings: Gesamtverzeichnis seiner Werke* (Berlin, 1933)
W. Raupp: *Max von Schillings: der Kampf eines deutschen Künstlers* (Hamburg, 1935) [see replies by W. Altmann, *AMZ*, lxiii (1936),

304; B. von Schillings, *AMZ*, lxiii (1936), 346; W. Golther, *ZfM*, Jg.103 (1936), 467]
W. Furtwängler: 'In memoriam Max von Schillings', *Ton und Wort: Aufsätze und Vorträge 1918 bis 1954* (Wiesbaden, 1954, 8/1958), 72
F. von Lepel: *Max von Schillings und seine Oper 'Mona Lisa'* (Berlin, 1954)
D. Satzky: 'Schillings, Max von', *Rheinische Musiker*, iv, ed. K. G. Fellerer (Cologne, 1966), 141
J. Geuenich and K. Strahn, eds.: *Gedenkschrift Max von Schillings zum 100. Geburtstag* (Düren, 1968)
E. F. Kravitt: 'The Joining of Words and Music in Late Romantic Melodrama', *MQ*, lxii (1976), 571

JOHN MORGAN

Schilson, Baron **János** (*b* *c*1750; *d* after 1809). Hungarian statesman and composer. On 13 December 1777 his drama in five acts Die Wilde, with music by Anton Zimmermann, was performed in Pressburg. From 1782 to 1783 he was the royal commissar in Sopron. In 1791 he was commissioned to draw up the budget of the German theatre planned in Pest. He then lived in Surány for a time. His works written between 1800 and 1809 (including Hungarian and German dances, Hungarian, German, French and Italian songs and canons, a melodrama, a trio for flute, violin and bass, sacred and secular choral works, and two pieces entitled Partita Turchese) are at the Széchényi National Library in Budapest. Outstanding in their melodic invention, they show the influence of both Viennese Classicism and the Hungarian verbunkos. His Egy hadi Tisztnek kedves Feleségétől butsúzó Éneke az Tsata előtt ('Farewell song of an officer parting from his beloved wife before the battle') for voice, two violins, two oboes, two horns and double bass is one of the earliest examples of the Hungarian orchestral song.

BIBLIOGRAPHY
ZL
E. Major: 'Fusz János és kora' [János Fusz and his times], *A Zene*, vii (Budapest, 1925)

FERENC BÓNIS

Schimbraczky [Schimrag, Schimrack, Schimrak], **Johannes** [Šimbracký, Ján] (*fl* 1635–48). Slovak composer and organist. He was the organist of Spišské Podhradie between 1635 and 1642, and from 1643 he was the organist at L'ubica (near Poprad) for a period that cannot be determined. While still at Spišské Podhradie he compiled a collection of 204 works, which he transcribed into tablature score of the new German organ type. This contains 40 of his own compositions, together with others by Croce, Handl, Hassler, Lassus, Michael Praetorius, Scheidt, Schein, Schütz, Viadana, Melchior Vulpius and Wert. A few of Schimbraczky's works bear his name, but the majority are identified by the initials J.S.O.W. (J. Schimbraczky, Organista Waraliensis, i.e. of Spišské Podhradie). The initials J.S.O.L'. occur during the L'ubica period. He made a similar collection after going to L'ubica, which includes Scheidt's Concerti sacri (1622) and the whole of Musikalischer Seelenlust (1634–7) by the Leipzig composer Tobias Michael, but this contains none of Schimbraczky's own compositions. Another MS, forming a supplement to this second collection, includes Schütz's Psalmen Davids, but only nine partbooks are extant. Yet another collection contains two of Schimbraczky's compositions, but this was written by another hand. Schimbraczky is known to have composed 52 vocal works (catalogue in Rybarič, 1973), more than half of which are written in eight parts; four further pieces are possibly by him. A few of his works are in 12 parts, and occasionally he wrote in 15, 16 or 20 parts. No compositions in more than 12 parts are known to have survived in complete form.

WORKS
(* = *incomplete*)

MASSES AND CANTICLES
Missa super 'Omnes gentes', Kyrie, Gloria, 8vv, *CS-L* 13992, *H-Bn* 17a-e
*Missa super 'Verbum caro factum est', 15vv, bc, *CS-L* 5161
Officium [Missa brevis]: Kyrie, *Gloria, 11vv, bc, *L* 13994
*Magnificat, 12vv, bc, *L* 5161
Magnificat (German), 8vv, *L* 13992, 14002, *R-Sb* I.J.36
*Benedicite, ?8vv, *CS-L* 14002

MOTETS
*Quem vidistis, pastores, 20vv, bc, *CS-L* 5161
*A Domino factum est istud, 16vv, bc *L* 5161
Factum est silentium in coelo, 12vv, *L* 13992
Gaudent in coelis animae, 12vv, bc, *L* 13992
9 for 8vv, incl. 1 with bc (8 in *L* 13992, 2 also in *H-Bn* 17a-e, *1 (?8vv) in *CS-L* 14002, *1 in *L* 14004)
2 for 7vv (1 in *L* 13992, *1 in 14002)
Alleluia, heutt' triumphiret Gottes Sohn, 3 choirs (6, 4, 4vv), bc, *L* 13992, *R-Sb* I.J.36
Freuet euch in dem Herren, 12vv, *CS-L* 13992
25 for 8vv, incl. 13 with bc (23 in *L* 13992, 1 also in *L* 13994, 1 also in *L* 5161, *3 in *L* 14002)
1 for 7vv, *L* 13992; 1 for 6vv, bc, *L* 13992; *2 for ?3vv, *L* 14004
Unnamed frag., *L* 14004

BIBLIOGRAPHY
A. Hořejš: 'Levočské tabulatúrne sborníky' [Tablature collections from Levoča], *Hudba na Slovensku v XVII. storočí* [Music in Slovakia in the 17th century] (Bratislava, 1954), 108
R. Rybarič: 'K biografii J. Schimbraczkého a Z. Zarewutia', *SH*, x (1966), 108
——: 'Zur Frage der Tabulatur-Partitur im 17. Jahrhundert', *Musica antiqua: Brno II 1967*, 106
——: 'Ján Šimbracký v rokoch 1635–1645: prispevok k poznaniu jeho diela' [. . . a contribution to the knowledge of his works], *Musicologica slovaca*, i (1969), 91
——: 'Johannes Šimbracký und die Zipser Musikkultur des 17. Jahrhunderts', *Sagittarius*, ii (1969), 63
——: 'Ján Šimbracký: spišský polyfonik 17. storočia', *Musicologica slovaca*, iv (1973), 7–83 [incl. thematic index]
JOHN CLAPHAM

Schimmel. German firm of piano makers. Established in 1885 in Leipzig, the firm operated on a small scale, making about 500 pianos a year before World War I. In 1930 it moved to Brunswick, and after World War II expanded vigorously, by 1970 producing about 7000 uprights and 600 grands a year, approximately 40% of the total West German output. More than half of Schimmel's instruments are exported to other European countries, particularly France, where pianos are sold under the Pleyel, Erard and Gaveau labels.
CYRIL EHRLICH

Schimon, Adolf (*b* Vienna, 29 Feb 1820; *d* Leipzig, 21 June 1887). Austrian composer, pianist and singing teacher. The son of a painter well known for his portraits of Beethoven, Weber and Spohr, he entered the Paris Conservatoire at the age of 16, studying the piano, composition (with Berton and Halévy) and singing (with Bordogni and Banderali). In the 1840s he travelled to Italy for further study in singing and in 1846 his opera *Alessandro Stradella* was produced in Florence. From 1850 to 1853 he was in London, acting as *maestro al cembalo* at Her Majesty's Theatre, as well as touring with Balfe, Sims Reeves and Clara Novello. While doing similar work at the Italian Opera in Paris (1854–9), his comedy *List und List* was produced in Schwerin in 1858 under Flotow and became popular in several theatres in north Germany. He taught singing at the Leipzig Conservatory from 1874 to 1877, and then in

Munich until 1886, later returning to Leipzig. As a singing teacher he had a considerable reputation and was also well known as an accompanist. He wrote chamber music, piano music and songs, and made editions of works by A. Scarlatti, Porpora and Paradisi and of other Italian music.

Schimon's wife, Anna Regan (*b* Aich, 18 Sept 1841; *d* Munich, 18 April 1902), whom he married in Florence in 1872, was a singer of some distinction. She studied in Dresden and then worked under her aunt Karoline Unger in Florence. She made her début in Siena and went on to sing at the court theatre in Hanover. As court singer to the Grand Duchess Helena Pavlovna, she sang in St Petersburg under Berlioz; she also appeared in London, being especially successful in performances of lieder. She toured widely until her marriage, when she appeared less frequently; after Schimon's death she taught in Munich.

BIBLIOGRAPHY
'Nachrichten', *AMZ*, xxxix (1837), col.182; xlviii (1846), col.342
E. Badura-Skoda: 'Schimon, Adolph', *MGG*
GEORGE GROVE/JOHN WARRACK

Schimrack [Schimrag, Schimrak], **Johannes.** *See* SCHIMBRACZKY, JOHANNES.

Schindelmeisser, Louis (Alexander Balthasar) (*b* Königsberg, 8 Dec 1811; *d* Darmstadt, 30 March 1864). German conductor and composer. He studied in Berlin under Gährich and Marx, and continued in Leipzig under his stepbrother Heinrich Dorn (1831), later Hofkapellmeister in Berlin and an opponent of Wagner. He became a friend of Wagner in Leipzig, and in 1832 was named Kapellmeister of the theatre in Salzburg. He then occupied similar posts in Innsbruck, Graz and the Königstadt, Berlin (1837). In 1838 he went to the German theatre in Pest, and from 1847 worked successively in Hamburg, Frankfurt and Wiesbaden. From 1853 he was Hofkapellmeister in Darmstadt.

Schindelmeisser was one of the early admirers and enthusiastic partisans of Wagner. It was probably on his recommendation that Wagner was appointed musical director in Riga in 1837. In 1852–3 he arranged for the first performances in Wiesbaden and Darmstadt of *Tannhäuser*, *Rienzi* and *Lohengrin* (the last having been given previously only in Weimar, by Liszt). His high esteem of Wagner is illustrated in a letter Wagner wrote to Uhlig in 1852: 'He [Schindelmeisser] writes that he is "in a state of shock" ["entsetzt"] over this music [*Tannhäuser*], for "rapture" ["Entzücken"] is inadequate to describe the revolution taking place inside him.' In spite of this, there is hardly a trace of Wagner's influence in Schindelmeisser's compositions, not even in his last opera, *Melusine* (1861). They are, rather, in the style of the older Romantic operatic tradition of Weber and Spohr, though frequently their artless conglomeration of naive dramatic effects and routine orchestration testifics to the decaying state of that tradition. His other works, particularly his songs and character pieces for piano, show a particular liking for the intimacy of the smaller forms.

WORKS
STAGE
Peter von Szapáry (opera, 3), Budapest, 8 Aug 1839
Malwina (opera, 5, Uffer), Budapest, 1841
Der Rächer (opera, 3, O. Prechtler, after Corneille: Le Cid), Budapest, 4 April 1846
Melusine (opera, 4, E. Pasqué), Darmstadt, 1861, vocal score (Berlin, n.d.)

Diavolina (ballet, 4, Ambrogio)
Mathilde (opera, C. Pichler), unperf.
Die zehn glücklichen Tage (opera, 4, Schuler), unperf.
Incidental music for numerous plays

OTHER WORKS

Orch: Cl concertino (Leipzig, 1832); Sinfonia concertante, 4 cl, op.2 (Leipzig, 1833); Schleswig-Holstein meerumschlungen, ov., op.24, arr. pf 4 hands (Mainz, 1848); Sinfonie, B♭, lost, perf. Frankfurt am Main, 1851; Rule, Britannia!, ov., op.43 (Mainz, c1860); Loreley, ov., op.44 (Cologne, c1860); Ein illustriertes Studentenlied, fantasia, op.45 (Cologne, c1860)

Songs, 1v, pf (pubd Hamburg, 1833–48, except where otherwise noted): 6 Lieder, op.3; Des Vaters Erbe, A/Bar, pf, op.5; Der Frühling, op.6; 3 Lieder, S/T, pf, op.9; Ob ich dich liebe, op.10; Reue, op.11; 2 Lieder, S/T, pf, op.12; 3 Lieder, op.15; Waldlied, S/T, pf, op.17; Schlummerlied; Vergiss mein nicht; 6 geistliche Lieder, A, pf (Mainz, 1858)

Pf solo (pubd Hamburg, 1833–48, except where otherwise noted): 3 sonatas, opp.8, 23, 40 (Mainz, 1849); 2 Impromptus, opp.4, 7; 6 Characterstücke in Liedform, op.14; 3 Bagatellen, op.22

BIBLIOGRAPHY

Obituary, Niederrheinische Musikzeitung, xii (1864), 127
H. Dorn: Ergebnisse aus Erlebnissen (Berlin, 1877)
W. Weissheimer: Erlebnisse mit Richard Wagner, Franz Liszt und vielen anderen Zeitgenossen nebst deren Briefen (Stuttgart, 1898)
O.Dorn: 'Das Wiesbadener Theater-orchester und seine Dirigenten', Die Musik, ii (1902–3), 179

KLAUS RÖNNAU

Schindler, Anton Felix (b Meedl, Moravia, 13 June 1795; d Bockenheim, nr. Frankfurt, 16 Jan 1864). Moravian violinist, conductor, writer and biographer of Beethoven. He received his early training on the violin from his father. In 1813 he moved to Vienna to study law, and in the following year first met Beethoven. Schindler's involvement in a political demonstration by university students, his flight to Brno and his arrest by the police interested Beethoven, who asked Schindler to meet him at taverns and accompany him on walks.

With the departure of Franz Oliva (1820) Schindler became Beethoven's secretary, errand boy and factotum. This soon developed into his principal activity, and in 1822 he gave up law in favour of music as a profession. Although he had become leader of the violins at the Josephstadttheater, he spent all his spare time working for Beethoven (unpaid) and studying his piano music. An entry in a conversation book (early spring, 1823) reads 'Now I know all your sonatas by heart'. This was a period of great activity: he attended to financial transactions, copyists, proofreading, household shopping, arrangements for Beethoven's summer residence, people asking favours and so on. In one note to him Beethoven wrote, 'Farewell – attend to everything'. However, a breach occurred in May 1824 when Beethoven accused Schindler of cheating over the receipts from the first performance of the Ninth Symphony, which the latter had worked hard to arrange; and in 1825 Schindler's place was taken by Karl Holz. But in December 1826 Schindler resumed his position of amanuensis, and was tireless in attendance at Beethoven's bedside until the end.

Schindler's reward came in the form of the conversation books and letters, MSS and sketches which he acquired partly as secretary and partly at the composer's death. After prolonged negotiations with England and Germany most of this material was sold in 1846 to the Royal Library of Berlin, and Schindler received an annuity for life. On his death, most of the remaining items were given to the library by his sister. Schindler's possessive devotion to his master led to him taking it upon himself to decide what was and what was not proper to be seen by posterity; as a result he destroyed two-thirds of the 400 conversation books. Further,

recent research has demonstrated that a number of significant entries in the conversation books are falsifications, being written by Schindler long after Beethoven's death.

In his writings, as Thayer was to discover, Schindler showed a pronounced bias and notorious inaccuracies of fact. He became a director of music first at Münster (1831) and then at Aachen (1835). In 1840 he wrote out, hastily, his Beethoven *Biographie*. Two trips to Paris (1841–2) resulted in an appendix, 'Beethoven in Paris', for the second edition of 1845. In 1848 he moved to Frankfurt where he spent his final years teaching and writing. As self-appointed champion of the Beethoven tradition of performance, as he had understood it, he wrote a series of articles (1856) against musicians, including Liszt, who seemed to present virtuosity for its own sake. In this year he moved to his last home, Bockenheim near Frankfurt. In 1860 he published the work for which he is best remembered, the third edition of his Beethoven *Biographie*, a completely rewritten and hence much more responsible chronicle of the Beethoven he knew, though still with many inaccuracies.

WRITINGS

Biographie von Ludwig van Beethoven (Münster, 1840, 2/1845 with two supplements: 'Auszüge aus Beethovens Konversationsheften and 'Beethoven in Paris', 3/1860; Eng. trans., 1841); ed. D. W. MacArdle as Beethoven as I Knew him (London, 1966)

BIBLIOGRAPHY

W. Nohl: 'Die Beziehungen Anton Schindlers zu Beethoven', Die Musik, xvii (1925), 441, 497
T. Frimmel: Beethoven-Handbuch, ii (Leipzig, 1926), 106
D. W. MacArdle: 'Anton Felix Schindler, Friend of Beethoven', MR, xxiv (1963), 51
E. Forbes, ed.: Thayer's Life of Beethoven (Princeton, 1964)
E. Doernberg: 'Anton Schindler', MQ, li (1965), 373
D. Beck and G. Herre: 'Einige Zweifel an der Überlieferung der Konversationshefte', Internationaler Beethoven-Kongress: Berlin 1977, 257
P. Stadlen: 'Schindler's Beethoven Forgeries', MT, cxviii (1977), 549
D. Beck and G. Herre: 'Anton Schindlers fingierte Eintragungen in den Konversationsheften', Zu Beethoven: Aufsätze und Annotationen, ed. H. Goldschmidt (Berlin, 1979), 11–89

ELLIOT FORBES

Schindler, Kurt (b Berlin, 17 Feb 1882; d New York, 16 Nov 1935). American composer and conductor of German birth. He attended the universities of Berlin and Munich (1899–1901), studying the piano with C. Ansorge and F. Gernsheim, composition with L. Bussler, C. Taubmann and L. Thuille, and musicology with Stumpf and Friedlaender. Friedlaender's influence proved lasting, for he had introduced Schindler to European folk music, particularly German. An equally important influence was Schindler's participation in a choral society under Gernsheim which performed modern arrangements of traditional songs.

Schindler made his official début as a composer at the Krefeld Music Festival in June 1902, although his songs had already been performed by such artists as Emmy Destinn, L. Wüllner and E. Welt-Herzog. After successful conducting seasons at the Stuttgart Opera (1902) and the Staatstheater in Würzburg (1903), he was asked to assist Mottl and Strauss at the Berlin Opera (1904). In 1905 Conried invited him to New York to join the conducting staff at the Metropolitan Opera House. In 1909, at Mahler's suggestion, Schindler initiated the MacDowell Chorus, which, three years later, became the Schola Cantorum of New York. Under him, it established a reputation as one of the finest choral societies in North America; he resigned in 1926. A close friendship with Natalie Curtis prompted his continued interest in folk music, which became an important part of the choir's varied programmes, particularly in introducing Russian and Spanish folk music to American audiences. For his efforts in promoting Spanish music, he was invited to become a corresponding member of the Hispanic Society of America.

From 1907 Schindler served almost two decades as a reader, editor and critic for the publishers G. Schirmer; he also worked as an editor for Oliver Ditson. He was the musical director for Temple Emanu-El from 1912 to 1925. In autumn 1928, he went to Spain to undertake a systematic investigation of Spanish folk music. During two field trips (1928 to January 1933), he collected more than 1000 traditional melodies, a third on aluminium discs. In 1933 he was appointed the first chairman of music at the newly founded Bennington College, Vermont, but owing to the strenuous duties and his failing health he had to forgo his research. In 1941 the Hispanic Institute of Columbia University, which sponsored his second field trip, published most of his field transcriptions.

WORKS
(selective list)

Stage: The Mummer's Revel, and the Masque of the Apple (B. Talmud, after R. Harris) (1934)

Songs: Sommerliche Fahrt, op.3 (Liliencron), 4 songs (1901); Tanz und Andacht, op.4 (Falke), 4 songs (1901); 5 Songs, op.5 (Hartleben, Busse, Hölty, Brentano); A Romance and 3 Satirical Songs, op.6 (Heine); 3 Songs, op.7 (Verlaine) (1905); 3 Songs, op.8 (Morgenstern, Hartleben) (1907); Old Swiss Lays, op.9 (Keller); 3 Songs, op.11 (Keats) (1908); Paraphrase on 4 Folk-song Themes as Sung in the Provinces of Novgorod and Voronezh, op.12 (1909); Woman and Cat, op.13 (Verlaine) (1909); 3 Sonnets of Mediaeval Italy, op.14 (trans. Rossetti) (1912); 3 English Songs, op.15 (Wilde, Swinburne, Meredith) (1912); 7 other pubd songs; 23 unpubd songs, 1889–1901

Other works, all unpubd: 14 chamber works, up to 1900; 10 pf works, 1890–97

WRITINGS

The Development of Opera: from its Earliest Beginnings to the Masterworks of Gluck (New York, 1913)

' "Boris Godounoff" and the Life of Moussorgsky'; 'Boris Godounoff: a Drama of the Russian People', *North American Review* (1913), 1, 256

Introduction to A. Schoenberg: *Quartet in D minor, op.7* (New York, 1913)

ed.: *Masters of Russian Song* (New York, 1917)

'The Russian Jewish Folk-song', *Menorah Journal*, iii/3 (New York, 1917), 146

Introduction to *Sixty Russian Folk Songs for One Voice* (New York, 1918–19)

'Discurs presidencial', *Revista musical catalana* (1922), no.223, p.139

'Cradle and Cheder Songs of the Eastern Jew', *The Reflex*, iv/2 (Chicago, 1929), 63

FOLKSONG EDITIONS

A Century of Russian Song from Glinka to Rachmaninoff (New York, 1911)

Songs of the Russian People (Boston, 1915)

Sixty Russian Folk Songs for One Voice (New York, 1918–19)

Bayou Ballads: Twelve Folk Songs from Louisiana (*Mina Monroe*) (New York, 1921)

Folk Music and Poetry of Spain and Portugal (New York, 1941); critical edn. by I. Katz (in preparation)

BIBLIOGRAPHY

I. J. Katz: 'Kurt Schindler's Musicological Field Work in Soria, Spain', *American Philosophical Society Yearbook 1973*, 607

ISRAEL J. KATZ

Schindler, Poul Christian (*b* Copenhagen, 1648; *d* Copenhagen, 1740). Danish composer and instrumentalist. He studied the viola da gamba with the gambist A. G. Roberts at the court at Gottorf. After some years in the court orchestra he went to study composition at Dresden in September 1670. On his return in 1674 he became an instrumentalist at the court at Copenhagen and was also active as a composer. He is credited with being the composer of the first Danish opera, *Der vereinigte Götterstreit*, to a text (in German) by P. A. Burchardt. Written to celebrate King Christian V's birthday on 15 April 1689, it was receiving a second performance on 19 April when the opera house caught fire and burnt so rapidly that most of the audience (estimated at nearly 200), including Schindler's wife and daughter, were unable to escape. Nor did the music of the opera – like the rest of Schindler's output – survive, and no attempt was made to repeat the operatic experiment during the remainder of Christian V's reign. It was taken up again by Frederik IV, but his travels in Italy had given him a taste for Italian music, and Schindler was bypassed as a composer by the appointment in 1703 of Bartolomeo Bernardi. By 1705 Schindler had received no rise in salary for 30 years, and he complained to the king that the amount of composing expected of him had imposed a great strain and damaged his sight. He seems not to have succeeded, however, in improving his situation as a musician; instead, in 1707, he was relieved of some of his burden by being given a non-musical appointment while retaining half his musician's salary. He died at the age of 92, leaving a substantial collection of music and instruments.

BIBLIOGRAPHY

C. Thrane: *Fra hofviolonernes tid* (Copenhagen, 1908)

A. Hammerich: *Dansk musikhistorie indtil ca.1700* (Copenhagen, 1921)

JOHN BERGSAGEL

Schinkel, Karl Friedrich (*b* Neuruppin, 13 March 1781; *d* Berlin, 9 Oct 1841). German architect, stage designer and painter. He moved to Berlin in 1794 and studied architecture under David and Friedrich Gilly, completing his studies in Italy and France (1803–5), where he developed his interest in painting. On returning to Berlin, he started to work as a painter of panoramas and dioramas (mainly for the establishment of the Gropius brothers), exhibiting monumental views (e.g. *Die sieben Wunder der Welt*, 1812) with musical accompaniments (by Rungenhagen and Grell), lighting and transparency effects and movable staffage. Count Brühl, Intendant of the Royal Theatre in Berlin, made Schinkel chief designer (1815–28). As architect and assessor to the Prussian Ministry of Public Buildings from 1810, he also had a definitive influence on theatre construction.

Inspired by philosophical idealism and the pathos of the Wars of Liberation against Napoleon, Schinkel aimed at creating a kind of theatre which would educate and purify the public. This didactic end required that the same degree of participation should be experienced by each member of an audience, and that the stage should be visible from all points of the auditorium, which was not possible with the traditional proscenium arch and wings. He envisaged sets consisting of nothing more than a monumental view on a backcloth, like a panorama or diorama, thus reduced to the 'symbolic background' of the action which would take place in the neutral proscenium area. The orchestra pit should be sunk for optical and acoustic reasons. As the architect of the Berlin Schauspielhaus (1817–21), a royal theatre, Schinkel was unable to realize this 'democratic' ideal, but as a designer for the stage, he put it into practice, partly at least, in the historically accurate, formally perfect panoramic sets for *Die Zauberflöte* (1816; see illustration) and more than 40 other operas, ballets and plays. His stage designs, first published in 1819, had an extraordinary influence on the style of operatic production that followed in Germany. His ideas for the reform

Stage design by Karl Friedrich Schinkel for Mozart's opera 'Die Zauberflöte' (Berlin, 1816): coloured aquatint (Institut für Theaterwissenschaft, University of Cologne)

of theatrical construction influenced Gottfried Semper and Wagner.

See also OPERA, §VIII, 5.

BIBLIOGRAPHY

Decorationen auf den beiden Königlichen Theatern in Berlin (Berlin 1819–24, rev. 4/1874)

F. Kugler: 'Die Dekorationsmalerei der Bühne und Schinkels Entwürfe', *Deutsches Kunstblatt*, vi (1855), 111; also in *Zeitschrift für Bauwesen*, xv (1855), 396

A. von Wolzogen: *Aus Schinkel's Nachlass* (Berlin, 1862–4)

P. Mahlberg: *Schinkel's Theaterdekorationen* (diss., U. of Greifswald, 1916)

L. Nusser: *Schinkel und Brückner in ihrer Bedeutung für die Bühnenmalerei im 19. Jahrhundert* (diss., U. of Würzburg, 1922)

F. B. Biermann: *Die Pläne für die Reform des Theaterbaues bei K. F. Schinkel und G. Semper* (Berlin, 1928)

P. O. Rave: *Karl Friedrich Schinkel* (Berlin, 1935) [bibliography]

——: *Schinkel, Berlin I: Bauten für die Kunst, Kirchen, Denkmalpflege* (Berlin, 1941), 79ff

G. Schöne: 'K. F. Schinkel', *ES*

——: 'Trois mises en scène de "La flûte enchantée" de Mozart: Berlin 1816, Weimar 1817 et Munich 1818', *Anatomy of an Illusion: 4th International Congress on Theatre Research: Amsterdam 1965*, 54

M. Boetzkes: 'K. F. Schinkel', *The Age of Neo-Classicism* (London, 1972), 946

H. G. Pundt: *Schinkel's Berlin* (Cambridge, Mass., 1972)

MANFRED BOETZKES

Schinn, Georg Johann (*b* Sinzing, nr. Regensburg, 14 Sept 1768; *d* Munich, 18 Feb 1833). German composer and disciple of Michael Haydn. After studying philosophy and jurisprudence at the University of Dillingen, Schinn was appointed flautist at the court chapel in Eichstätt, where he also received composition lessons from A. Bachschmidt. Before he became director of the court chapel, he went to Salzburg for further studies under Michael Haydn, with whom he developed a close friendship. He published the first biography of Michael Haydn in 1808 and later formed a society for the promotion of Haydn's music in Munich, where he was violist at the court chapel from 1808. Schinn's own work shows the influence of his teacher, both in his church music and in his use of partsongs for male choir. As a teacher, he gained considerable respect both in Munich and in Salzburg.

WORKS

(*MSS mostly in D-Mbs*)

Gebet am Frieden, op. 13, 4vv, org, orch (Munich, n.d.); 2 masses, solo vv, 4vv, org, orch; 1 requiem (Ger.), 4vv, *D-Rp*; other sacred choral music

6 deutsche Gesänge, 4 male vv (Munich, n.d.); 6 christlichen Lieder, 1v, pf acc. (Munich, n.d.); 3 pubd collections of songs, 1v, pf acc.

WRITINGS

with F. J. Otter: *Biographische Skizze von Johann Michael Haydn* (Salzburg, 1808)

BIBLIOGRAPHY

F. J. Lipowsky: *Baierisches Musik-Lexikon* (Munich, 1811/R1971)

O. Ursprung: *Münchens musikalische Vergangenheit* (Munich, 1827)

H. Jancik: *Michael Haydn, ein vergessener Meister* (Vienna, 1952)

ROGER GREEN

Schiørring, Niels (*b* Sabro, 30 June ?1743; *d* Copenhagen, 6 Feb 1798). Danish harpsichordist, composer and music editor. He studied in Copenhagen with J. A. Scheibe and in Hamburg with C. P. E. Bach, whom he befriended. In 1773 he became a harpsichordist at the royal chapel and a teacher at the Royal Opera Academy. He replaced Giuseppe Sarti as chamber musician to the royal court in 1775. For Guldberg's new official psalter (1778) he edited a series of chorale books (1781–3) based on painstaking studies of early sources, to which, with C. P. E. Bach and the Danish musician Raehs as collaborators, he added outstanding harmonizations; these collections introduced mono-rhythmic chorale melodies (in minims) into Danish church song. Schiørring also edited collections of secular music (particularly popular songs from operas, plays and other works) and contributed to Gerber's *Lexicon*.

WORKS
(all published in Copenhagen)

Kirke-melodierne, 4vv (1781); Choral-bog . . . til psalme-bogen af 1778 (1783) [with figured bass]; Choralsange, 4vv (1783) [partbooks]; Sang-bog (1783) [melodies only]; Selskabs-sange med melodier, i–ii (1785–9); Arier og sange, i–ii (1786–9); Blandinger, 1v, kbd (1787); others

BIBLIOGRAPHY
N. Schiørring: 'Schiørring, Niels', *DBL*

NILS SCHIØRRING

Schiørring, Nils (*b* Copenhagen, 8 April 1910). Danish musicologist. He studied musicology with Abrahamsen and Larsen at the University of Copenhagen (MA 1933); at the same time he trained as a cellist under L. Jensen and was an orchestral player for several years. In 1950 Copenhagen University awarded him a doctorate for his fundamental study of Danish secular music in the 16th and 17th centuries. After working at the Copenhagen Music History Museum (1932–53) he became chairman of its board (1954); he was also music critic of the newspaper *Nationaltidende* (1939–49) and subsequently of the *Berlingske tidende*. He was editor of *Dansk musiktidsskrift* (1943–5) and *Dansk årbog for musikforskning* (with Søren Sørensen, from 1961). He began to teach at Copenhagen University in 1950 and in 1954 he was appointed professor; he was also director of the folk music and ethnomusicological section of the Danish Folklore Collection (1953–71).

Schiørring's research has concentrated on Danish music and has covered all aspects of Danish musical life (nearly all the articles on Danish music and musicians in *MGG* are by him), but he has also considered music outside Denmark. An early interest in the French overture resulted in a monograph (1957) which demonstrated its relationship to the allemande, and his familiarity with 20th-century music is apparent in his survey *Musikkens veje*. His work on Danish popular music began in 1935 with his collaboration on the scholarly edition of the melodies for the great collection of Danish folksongs *Danmarks gamle folkeviser* (completed 1976); he published similar musical companions to H. Grüner-Nielsen's *Danske viser* and to the collected works of Kingo.

WRITINGS
'Melodistof til Danske Viser 1530–1630', *Musikhistorisk arkiv*, i (1939), 346–96
Melodies and commentary to T. Kingo: *Samlede skrifter*, iii (Copenhagen, 1939); vii (Copenhagen, 1945)
'Musik og musikliv', *Danmarks kultur ved aar 1940*, viii (1943), 97
Det 16. og 17. århundredes verdslige danske visesang (diss., U. of Copenhagen, 1950; Copenhagen, 1950)
Billeder fra 125 aars musikliv (1827–1952) (Copenhagen, 1952)
'En svensk kilde til belysning af "Les 24 violons du Roi's" repertoire, *STMf*, xxxvi (1954), 26
'Musical Folklore and Ethnomusicology in Denmark', *Ethnomusicologie II: Wégimont III 1956*, 51
Selma Nielsens Viser (Copenhagen, 1956)
Allemande og fransk ouverture (Copenhagen, 1957)
'H. S. Paulli og dansk musikliv i det 19. århundrede', *Fund og forskning*, iv (1957), 98
Musikkens veje (Copenhagen, 1959, 2/1964)
'C. B. Rutström og Rasmus Nyerup', *STMf*, xliii (1961), 287
'The Contribution of Ethnomusicology to Historical Musicology', *IMSCR*, viii *New York 1961*, i, 380
'Nogle håndskrevne dansk-norske Koralbøger fra det 18. århundredes første halvdel', *Natalicia musicologica Knud Jeppesen* (Copenhagen, 1962), 253

'Ambrosius Lobwasser i Danmark', *Fund og forskning*, x (1963), 53
'Nachwirkungen der Lobwasserpsalter in Dänemark', *Norddeutsche und nordeuropäische Musik: Kiel 1963*, 22
'Wiedergefundene Melodien aus der verschollenen Adam-Krieger-Ariensammlung 1657', *Festschrift für Walter Wiora* (Kassel, 1967), 304
'Notater til et par Petter Dass-melodier', *Festskrift til Olav Gurvin* (Drammen and Oslo, 1968), 134
ed. with S. Kragh-Jacobsen: *August Bournonville: lettres à la maison de son enfance* (Copenhagen, 1969–70)
'Flerstemmighed i dansk middelalder', *Festskrift Jens Peter Larsen* (Copenhagen, 1972), 11
with N. M. Jensen: *Deutsch-dänische Begegnungen um 1800: Kunst, Dichtung, Musik* (Copenhagen, 1974)
Musikkens Historie i Danmark (Copenhagen, 1977–8)

FOLKSONG EDITIONS
Danmarks gamle folkeviser (Copenhagen, 1935–76)
with A. Arnholtz and F. Viderø: *Gamle danske viser* (Copenhagen, 1941–2)
with T. Knudsen: *Folkevisen i Danmark* (Copenhagen, 1960–68)

JOHN BERGSAGEL

Schiøtz, Aksel (Hauch) (*b* Roskilde, 1 Sept 1906; *d* Copenhagen, 19 April 1975). Danish tenor. He studied languages at Copenhagen University, and then singing with various teachers, among them John Forsell. After eight years teaching, he made his début in concerts in 1938, and in 1939 at the Royal Opera, Copenhagen, as Mozart's Ferrando; the next year he sang both Faust and Sverkel in Hartmann's *Liden Kirsten*. He refused to sing publicly during the German occupation, but gave recitals in secret for the Resistance workers. In 1945 he toured Sweden and Norway and broadcast for the BBC. He shared the role of Male Chorus with Peter Pears in the first performances of *The Rape of Lucretia* at Glyndebourne (1946). In 1948 he toured North America and the following year appeared at the Edinburgh Festival.

In 1950 a brain tumour brought his career to an abrupt halt. With great fortitude, he learnt to speak and sing once more, and for a while resumed his career, but as a baritone. He was professor of voice at the universities of Minnesota (1955–8), Toronto (1958–61) and Colorado (1961–8). In 1968 he became a professor at the Royal Danish School of Educational Studies. He was knighted in 1947.

Schiøtz was among the foremost Mozart and lieder singers of the early postwar period as his recordings, particularly of *Dichterliebe* and *Die schöne Müllerin*, show. His tenor voice had a natural silvery quality and he used it with elegance and feeling.

WRITINGS
Kunst og kamp: Gerd og Aksel Schiøtz (Copenhagen, 1951)
The Singer and his Art (New York, 1969)

BIBLIOGRAPHY
H. Rosenberg: 'Aksel Schiøtz', *Nationale diskotek katalog* (Copenhagen, 1966), no.6 [discography]

ALAN BLYTH

Schipa, Tito (*b* Lecce, 2 Jan 1888; *d* New York, 16 Dec 1965). Italian tenor, the outstanding *tenore di grazia* of his generation. Having studied with A. Gerunda in Lecce and E. Piccoli in Milan, he made his début in 1910 in *La traviata* at Vercelli. During the next five years he sang in Italian theatres, as well as at Buenos Aires, reaching La Scala (in *Prince Igor* and *Manon*) in the 1915–16 season. Having first embraced both dramatic and lyrical roles, he began to specialize in the latter after a great success as Des Grieux in Rome, and was soon widely recognized as the legitimate successor of de Lucia, Bonci and Anselmi. In 1917 Schipa created the role of Ruggero in Puccini's *La rondine* at

Monte Carlo.

In 1919 he began an association with the Chicago Opera which lasted until 1932, after which he sang for three consecutive seasons at the Metropolitan Opera, and again in 1941. During this time his repertory took its final shape, consisting essentially of Mozart's Don Ottavio and the more graceful tenor roles of Italian opera together with a smaller French group (*Lakmé*, *Mignon*, *Manon*, *Werther*). Until well after World War II Schipa continued to appear frequently in Italy in these and other roles, especially as the shy hero of Mascagni's *L'amico Fritz*. His last role at La Scala was in *Il matrimonio segreto* in 1949; in 1950 and 1952 he made his final appearances (in *Werther* and *Il barbiere di Siviglia*) in Rome, and in 1954 sang once more at the Colón, Buenos Aires, as well as in his native town, Lecce. In 1957 he undertook a successful concert tour in Russia. For some reason he never appeared at Covent Garden, and even his concert appearances in London were mostly during the postwar period, when his vocal powers were in decline.

Schipa's voice was not powerful, but was so well produced as to carry with ease in large theatres, and it was employed with a skill and taste that must be called exquisite. The unmistakable and very attractive timbre, at moments somewhat veiled, was well suited to moods of tenderness, melancholy or nostalgia, yet equally at home in the airy elegance of the Duke of Mantua's 'Questa o quella'. His musical phrasing was refined, his enunciation a model of clarity and sensibility. These qualities are well displayed in his numerous gramophone records, among them a complete *Don Pasquale*. Schipa wrote an autobiography, *Si confessa* (Genoa, 1961), which includes a discography.

Tito Schipa and Gianna Pederzini in A. Thomas' 'Mignon'

BIBLIOGRAPHY

T. Hutchinson and S. Winstanley: 'Tito Schipa', *Record Collector*, xiii (1960), 77–109 [with discography]

DESMOND SHAWE-TAYLOR

Schipper, Emil (Zacharias) (*b* Vienna, 19 Aug 1882; *d* Vienna, 20 July 1957). Austrian baritone. He studied singing in Milan with Guarino, then made his début at the German Theatre, Prague, as Telramund in 1904. After engagements at Linz (1911–12), the Vienna Volksoper (1912–15) and the Vienna Hofoper (1915–16), he joined the Munich Hofoper (now Staatsoper), where he remained until 1922, and then returned to the Vienna Staatsoper until 1938; he was made an Austrian Kammersänger. In Munich he created Meister Florian in the 1920 revised version of Schreker's *Das Spielwerk*, and he sang Barak in the first performances there of *Die Frau ohne Schatten*. He appeared regularly at Covent Garden, 1924–8 (as the Dutchman, Kurwenal, Hans Sachs, Wotan, Telramund, John the Baptist and Amonasro), in Chicago in 1929, and at the Teatro Colón, Buenos Aires, in 1922–3 and 1938. Schipper sang Agamemnon in Gluck's *Iphigénie en Aulide* under Bruno Walter at the 1930 Salzburg Festival and returned there in 1935–6 as Kurwenal. He also made guest appearances in France, the Netherlands, Spain and Belgium. For a time he was married to the mezzo-soprano Maria Olczewska. He had a powerful, dramatic voice, but did not always use it with subtlety.

BIBLIOGRAPHY

'Emil Schipper Discography', *Record News*, ii (Toronto, 1957), 33

HAROLD ROSENTHAL

Schippers, Thomas (*b* Kalamazoo, Mich., 9 March 1930; *d* New York, 16 Dec 1977). American conductor. After studying at the Curtis Institute in Philadelphia and privately with Olga Samaroff, he won second prize in 1948 in a young conductors' contest sponsored by the Philadelphia Orchestra. His professional conducting début was the same year with the Lemonade Opera Company in New York. In 1950 he became conductor of Menotti's *The Consul* shortly after its première, beginning an association with the composer that continued with Schippers's appointment as music director of Menotti's Festival of Two Worlds at Spoleto, where his impassioned but natural, fluent performances became increasingly admired. He joined the staff of the New York City Opera in 1951, and in 1955 made débuts with the New York PO, at the Metropolitan Opera, and at La Scala, Milan. In 1963 he conducted the new production of *Die Meistersinger* at Bayreuth. Having established himself as a young American opera conductor of international stature, he was a natural choice to conduct the première of Barber's *Anthony and Cleopatra* when the Metropolitan opened its new house at Lincoln Center in September 1966. Schippers was probably best known for his operatic work, particularly in the Romantic repertory. He was also music director of the Cincinnati SO from 1970 until his death, and became a professor at the Cincinnati College–Conservatory of Music in 1972.

BERNARD JACOBSON

Schira, Francesco (*b* Malta, 21 Aug 1809; *d* London, 15 Oct 1883). Italian conductor, composer and teacher. He studied under Basili at the Milan Conservatory and, at 23, was commissioned by La Scala to write an opera, *Elena e Malvina*, which was well received at its first production in 1832. He stayed eight years as music director to the S Carlos Theatre in Lisbon, where he was also professor of harmony and counterpoint at the conservatory. His elder brother, Vincenzo Schira (*d* 1857), conductor and ballet composer, succeeded him at the S Carlos Theatre.

After a brief visit to Paris in 1842, Schira was appointed director of music at the newly opened Princess's Theatre in London. In 1843 he conducted a short season under Alfred Bunn's management at Covent Garden, and in the following year joined Bunn at Drury Lane on the resignation of Benedict as conductor. He remained there intermittently until 1847, conducting both foreign adaptations and a number of English operas. The orchestra at the time was said to be indifferent and the *Illustrated London News* was less than impressed with Bunn's parsimony and Schira's conducting ability (27 September 1845). In 1848 Bunn again managed a three-month season at Covent Garden, with Schira conducting and Sims Reeves making his debut at the theatre. Schira's opera *Kenilworth*, after Scott, was rehearsed but not produced, but the Princess's Theatre gave well-received productions of his operas *Mina* in 1849 and *Thérèse, or The Orphan of Geneva* in 1850.

Schira conducted Bunn's 1852 season at Drury Lane, but thereafter he devoted himself to teaching singing, while continuing to compose. His most famous pupil was Louisa Pyne. His opera *Niccolò de' Lappi* was produced at Her Majesty's Theatre in 1863; in 1875 he achieved his greatest success with *Selvaggia* at Venice, but after *Lia* the following year he composed no more. He was much opposed to modern music, and his obituary noted that 'his music suffered mainly from the disadvantage of being out of fashion'. He was awarded the title Commendatore by Humbert I.

WORKS

Elena e Malvina (opera, 3, F. Romani), Milan, Scala, 17 Nov 1832
Il fanatico per la musica (comic opera, 2, G. Rossi), Lisbon, S Carlos, sum. 1835
I cavalieri di Valenza, ossia Isabel de Lara (opera, 2, Rossi), Lisbon, S Carlos, spr. 1837
The Island Nymph (ballet), London, Drury Lane, 12 Feb 1846
Kenilworth (Schira, after Scott), 1848, not produced
Mina (romantic opera, 2, V. Morris, G. Linley), London, Princess's, 3 Dec 1849
Thérèse, or The Orphan of Geneva (romantic opera, 3, C. Jefferys), London, Princess's, 26 April 1850, vocal score (London, 1851)
Niccolò de' Lappi, ossia L'assedio di Firenze (opera, 4, M. Maggioni), London, Her Majesty's, 7 May 1863, vocal score (London, 1863)
Alina (opera, 2), London, St George's Hall, 7 April 1871
The Ear-ring (operetta, 1, D. L. Ryan), London, St George's Hall, 21 May 1872, vocal score (London, 1873)
The Lord of Burleigh (cantata, Ryan, after Tennyson), Birmingham Festival, 1873, vocal score (London, 1873)
Selvaggia (opera, prol, 3, G. T. Cimino), Venice, Fenice, 20 Feb 1875 (Milan, 1875)
Lia (opera, 3, M. M. Marcello), Venice, Fenice, 25 March 1876

Many separate arias, romances, etc

BIBLIOGRAPHY

Obituary, *MT*, xxiv (1883), 612
L. Arditi: *My Reminiscences* (London, 1896)
C. Santley: *Reminiscences of my Life* (London, 1909)
C. E. Pearce: *Sims Reeves* (London, 1924)

KEITH HORNER

Schirmer. American firm of music publishers (G. Schirmer Inc., as distinct from the smaller firm E. C. Schirmer of Boston). One of the largest and most important of its kind in the USA, it began in New York as an outgrowth of the Kerksieg & Bruesing Company (founded 1848), of which Gustav Schirmer (*b* Königsee, Saxony, 19 Sept 1829; *d* Eisenach, 5 Aug 1893) became manager in 1854 (he had gone to New York in

1837). With Bernard Beer, Schirmer took over the business in 1861, and in 1866 he bought out Beer's interest and established the house of G. Schirmer, Music Publishers, Importers and Dealers. As its activities increased and the firm grew in standing it twice moved to new quarters and in 1891 founded its own engraving and printing plant – one of the few maintained by American music publishing houses. After Gustav's death the business was incorporated under the management of his sons: Rudolph Edward (*b* New York, 22 July 1859; *d* Santa Barbara, 19 Aug 1919) was president, and Gustave (*b* New York, 18 Feb 1864; *d* Boston, 15 July 1907) secretary. When Rudolph died, Gustave's son, also named Gustave (*b* Boston, 29 Dec 1890; *d* Palm Beach, Florida, 28 May 1965), succeeded him as president; he was followed in 1921 by W. Rodman Fay, with Oscar G. Sonneck as vice-president. In May 1929 Carl Engel assumed the presidency and held that office until his death in 1944. Gustave Schirmer (grandson of the founder) was again made president and was succeeded in 1957 by Rudolph Tauhert.

In 1891 the Boston Music Company became affiliated with Schirmer, though publishing its own catalogue of works; the Willis Music Company is also an affiliate, while the Associated Music Publishers is a subsidiary (their joint catalogue includes the works of many internationally known composers, and AMP has become one of the largest music publishing houses in the USA). There are also three separately incorporated affiliates, at Cleveland, Los Angeles and New Orleans.

In 1892 the firm began publishing the Library of Musical Classics, noted for careful editing and typographical excellence, and in 1911 the series G. Schirmer's Collection of Opera-Librettos first appeared. These were followed by masses, cantatas and the American Folk Song Series. Schirmer publishes for all media and has represented such composers as Charles T. Griffes, Victor Herbert, Loeffler, Granados, Bloch, Grainger, Schoenberg, Harris, Barber, Schuman, Menotti, Creston, Bernstein and Ives. It also publishes *Baker's Biographical Dictionary of Musicians*. In 1915 the *Musical Quarterly* was founded, with Oscar Sonneck as its first editor (Sonneck became Schirmer's director of publication as well as being vice-president, and was responsible for the issue of many important American works). During his presidency Carl Engel served as editor of the *Musical Quarterly* (and also continued Sonneck's publication policy for Schirmer's). Subsequent editors have been Gustave Reese (1944–5), Paul Henry Lang (1945–73), Christopher Hatch (1973–7) and Joan Peyser (1977–). G. Schirmer established, and for many years maintained, the principal circulating music library in the USA (in 1906 it was transferred to the Institute of Musical Art). The firm is now owned by the Crowell–Collier–Macmillan group.

W. THOMAS MARROCCO, MARK JACOBS

Schirmer, Ernest Charles (*b* Mt Vernon, NY, 15 March 1865; *d* Waban, Mass., 15 Feb 1958). American music publisher. He was employed by his brother, Gustave, a music publisher in New York, but left to accept a managerial appointment with the Boston Music Company and later became a partner; in 1921 he resigned to found his own publishing house in Boston. The E. C. Schirmer catalogue includes the choral repertory of the Harvard University Glee Club, Radcliffe, Vassar and

Wellesley Colleges, the St Dunstan Edition of Sacred Music and books on music theory and appreciation. When Ernest Schirmer died, E. C. Schirmer jr became president and remained the head of the firm until his death on 6 May 1966, when Robert MacWilliams became president. In addition to standard works, Schirmer publishes electronic music. American composers in its catalogue include Jacob Avshalomov, Howard Boatwright, Copland, Felciano, Karl Korte, Donald Martino, Douglas Moore, Alice Parker, Ronald Perera, Piston, Daniel Pinkham, Rorem, Conrad Susa and Randall Thompson. E. C. Schirmer maintains offices in London and Hamburg and represents Foetisch Frères of Switzerland.

W. THOMAS MARROCCO, MARK JACOBS

Schiroli, Gregorio. *See* SCIROLI, GREGORIO.

Schiske, Karl (Hubert Rudolf) (*b* Raab [now Győr, Hungary], 12 Feb 1916; *d* Vienna, 16 June 1969). Austrian composer and teacher. He studied in Vienna at the music academy and the university (DPhil 1942), his teachers including Orel and Schenk for musicology. In 1952 he was appointed professor of composition at the Vienna Music Academy, and in 1966–7 he was visiting professor at the University of California at Riverside. He received the Austrian State Prize in 1967. In his compositions, which bear witness to a formidable technique, he absorbed influences from Schoenberg, Hindemith, Stravinsky and Netherlands polyphony.

WORKS
(*selective list*)
Orch: Pf Conc., op.11, 1938–9; Conc. no.1, op.14, str, 1941; Sym. no.1, op.16, 1942; Conc. no.2, op.21b, str, 1945; Sym. no.2, op.26, 1948; Chamber Conc., op.28, 1949; Sym. no.3, op.31, 1951; Vn Conc., op.33, 1951–2; Sym. no.4, op.44, 1955; Synthese, op.47, 16 insts, 1958; Divertimento, op.49, chamber orch/10 insts, 1963; Sym. no.5, op.50, 1965
Choral: 4 Chöre, op.22, 3vv, 1945; Vom Tode, op.25, oratorio, 4 solo vv, vv, orch, org, 1946; Psalm xc, op.30, vv, 1949; Missa 'Cunctipotens genitor Deus', op.43, vv, org ad lib, 1954; Candida, op.45 (H. Mösslacher), S, vv, 16 insts, 1956
Chamber: Str Qt no.1, e, op.4, 1936; Sextet, op.5, cl, str qt, pf, 1937; Sonata, op.18, vn, pf, 1943–8; Str Qt no.2, op.21a, 1945; Wind Qnt, op.24, 1945; Musik, op.27, cl, tpt, va, 1948; 3 Stücke für Gloria, op.32, vn, 1951
Pf: Thema, 8 Variationen und Doppelfuge, op.2, 1936; Sonata, op.3, 1936; Tanzsuite, op.23, 1945; Sonata, op.29, 4 hands, 1949; 3 Stücke nach Volksweisen, op.35, 1951; Etüdensuite, op.36, 1951; Sonatina, op.42, 1953
Org: Variationen über ein eigenes Thema, op.10, 1938; Toccata, op.38, 1952; Trio Sonata, op.41, org/3 melody insts, 1954; Chorale Partita, op.46, 1957
Songs: op.7, 1938; op.12, 1943; op.19, 1945

Principal publishers: Doblinger, Universal

Schisma. A tiny intervallic quantity. Until the 19th century the term was liable to be used for various intervals, too small to be used melodically, that are encountered in theoretical calculations. According to J. G. Walther's *Musicalisches Lexicon* (Leipzig, 1732), for example, a schisma is taken as half a COMMA. In 19th- and 20th-century writings (for instance, P. Lichtenthal's *Dizionario e bibliografia della musica*, Milan, 1826) it refers to the difference between the Pythagorean and syntonic commas, which is also the difference between a pure major 3rd and a Pythagorean diminished 4th (that is, the amount by which D♯–G is smaller than a pure major 3rd if the 5ths and 4ths G–D–A–E–B–F♯–C♯–G♯–D♯ are pure). This difference, 1·954 cents, is about 1% of a whole tone and is so close to 1/12 of the Pythagorean comma (1/12·008) that the term 'schisma'

may also refer to the amount by which 5ths are tuned smaller than pure in equal temperament.

Schjelderup, Gerhard (Rosenkrone) (*b* Kristiansand, 17 Nov 1859; *d* Bendiktbeuern, 29 July 1933). Norwegian composer. In 1878 he went to Paris, where he studied the cello with Franchomme and composition with Savard and Massenet. Thereafter he was active principally in Germany, serving as a professor in Dresden and Munich. He received a grant from the Norwegian government in 1910. The most decisive influence on him was a performance of the *Ring* at Karlsruhe in 1887. From that time he saw music drama as his life's work, although his stated objectives were different from those of Wagner: 'I am constantly seeking something nearer to us, something more intimate than Wagner's gods and heroes. . . . I will try not only to give the outward appearance of reality, . . . but, so to speak, to open humanity's heart and reveal the riches which often hide behind the simplest exterior'. He had neither Wagner's feeling for drama nor his sense of line; the strength of his operas lies rather in their detailed characterization and fine lyrical atmosphere. Most of them were composed to his own texts, and their principal theme is the victory of ideal love. His harmony is complex and mainly local in its effects; thorough working of motivic material can sometimes make the forms a little obscure; and the instrumentation, while it has many good details, tends to be too full.

WORKS
(*selective list*)

OPERAS
Østenfor sol og vestenfor måne [East of the sun and west of the moon], 1889–90; Act 1 perf. Munich, 1890
Sampo Lappelill, begun 1890; unperf.
Sonntagsmorgen, 1891–2; Munich, 1893
Norwegische Hochzeit (Bruderovet [The abduction]), 1894; Prague, 1900
En hellig aften [A holy evening], 1895; Oslo, 1915
Et folk i nød [A people in need]; unperf.
Vaarnat [Spring night], 1906–7; Dresden, 1908; rev. as Stjernenaetter [Starry nights]
Opal; Dresden, 1915
Die scharlachrote Blume; unperf.
Sturmvögel; Schwerin, 1926

OTHER WORKS
Stage: Offerildene [The sacrificial fires] (incidental music), 1903; König Friedwahn (incidental music), 1904; Wunderhorn (ballet), Oslo, 1905; Christirose (Christmas play); Uveirsnat og morgenrøde [Stormy night and dawn] (dream play); Brand, Act 3 (incidental music, Ibsen)
Orch: 2 syms., 1887, 1924; Christirose, suite, 1898; In Baldurs hain [In Baldur's grove], vn, orch, 1904; Sommernatt på fjorden, 1904; Brand, sym. poem, 1914; Kleine norwegische Suite, 1930; Frühlingsreigen, 1931; Natstemning [Night mood]; Weihnachts-Suite [from En hellig aften]; En soloppgang på Himalaya [Sunrise in the Himalayas] [from Offerildene]
Chamber: 2 str qts; pieces for vn, pf; pieces for vc, pf; etc
Vocal: Høifjeldsliv [Mountain life], chorus, orch, begun 1880; Prometheus, chorus, orch, begun 1880, perf. 1886; choral songs, *c*40 romances

WRITINGS
Edvard Grieg og hans verker (Copenhagen, 1903, 2/1908 with W. Niemann)
Richard Wagner: hans liv og verker (Copenhagen, 1907, 2/1913)
with O. M. Sandvik: *Norges musikhistorie* (Oslo, 1921)

BIBLIOGRAPHY
W. Altmann: 'Gerhard Schjelderup im heutigen Musikbetrieb', *ZfM*, Jg.100 (1933), 317
I. E. Kindem: *Den norske operas historie* (Oslo, 1941)
O. M. Sandvik: 'Gerhard Schelderup', *SMz*, lxxxviii (1948), 385

KARI MICHELSEN

Schjelderup-Ebbe, Dag (*b* Oslo, 10 Dec 1926). Norwegian musicologist and composer. After training at the Oslo

Conservatory he studied musicology at the University of California (Berkeley) with Bukofzer and Boyden (MA 1950) and composition with Elkus; after further study at Freiburg University with Gurlitt (1956–7) and at the University of Oslo with Gurvin he took his doctorate at Oslo in 1965 with a study of Grieg's early years which revealed much new material. He had begun to teach at Oslo University on his return from the USA (1950) and was later appointed senior lecturer (1963) and professor (1973) at the Institute of Musicology. As a music critic he worked for the Oslo paper *Vårt land* (1957–61) before joining the staff of *Verdens gang* (1961). He is a member of the committee preparing a complete edition of Grieg's works; his extensive research for this has provided a valuable background which has considerably expanded the view of national Romanticism in Norway. Schjelderup-Ebbe's compositions include a work for chorus, *The Ship of Youth* (Oslo, 1969), performed at the Bergen International Festival in 1967, a *Suite for Young People* for piano (Oslo, 1972), *Humoreske* for horn and piano (1976) and other chamber works.

WRITINGS
A Study of Grieg's Harmony, with Special Reference to his Contributions to Musical Impressionism (Oslo, 1953)
'Modality in Halfdan Kjerulf's Music', *ML*, xxxviii (1957), 238
'Neue Ansichten über die früheste Periode E. Griegs', *DAM*, i (1961), 61
Purcell's Cadences (Oslo, 1962)
Edvard Grieg 1858–1867, with Special Reference to the Evolution of his Harmonic Style (diss., U. of Oslo, 1965; Oslo and London, 1964)
'Sibelius og Norge', *Suomen musiikin vuosikirja, 1964–65* (Helsinki, 1965), 80
'Et nyfunnet orkesterpartitur med Rikard Nordraaks musikk til Bjørnstjerne Bjørnsons "Maria Stuart i Skotland"', *SMN*, i (1968), 102
'Kjerulfs fem sanger fra "Spanisches Liederbuch"', *Festskrift til Olav Gurvin* (Drammen and Oslo, 1968), 144
with F. Benestad: 'Norske komponister', *Norsk musikk: studier i norge* (1968), 5
'Neuere norwegische musikwissenschaftliche Arbeiten', *AcM*, xliv (1972), 25
'Some Recollections of Norwegian Artists of German Musical Life in the 1850s', *SMN*, ii (1976)

JOHN BERGSAGEL

Schlag (i). German family of organ builders. In 1831 Christian Gottlieb Schlag (*b* Staschwitz, 27 Feb 1803; *d* Schweidnitz [now Świdnica], 10 March 1889) took over the organ-building workshop of Kiesewetter at Jauer, and from 1834 he and his brother Johann Karl (*b* Staschwitz, 30 Nov 1808; *d* Schweidnitz, after 1869) carried on the business at Schweidnitz. In 1869 Christian Gottlieb's sons Theodor (*b* Schweidnitz, 18 April 1847; *d* Schweidnitz, 2 May 1918) and Oskar (*b* Schweidnitz, 16 June 1848; *d* Schweidnitz, 26 Nov 1918) became partners in the firm, which then became known as Schlag & Söhne. The proprietors were appointed official organ builders to the royal court in 1900, and they were joined by Theodor's sons Reinhold (*b* Schweidnitz, 1874; *d* Pomerania, after 1952) and Bruno (*b* Schweidnitz, 1879; *d* Hof, 1952) in 1903.
The Schlags built organs throughout Silesia, in north and central Germany, and in Bohemia. Their work included organs at the Gnadenkirche, Hirschberg (1859; four manuals, 64 stops; rebuilt in 1904; three manuals, 70 stops); St Elisabeth, Breslau (1879; three manuals, 62 stops; rebuilt in 1907; three manuals, 70 stops); Philharmonic Hall, Berlin (1888; three manuals, 50 stops); St Marien, Berlin (three manuals, 54 stops); St Peter and St Paul, Görlitz (1894; three manuals, 53 stops; a rebuild of the 'Sonnenorgel' built by Eugen Casparini starting 1697); Marienkirche, Köslin (1898;

three manuals, 50 stops); St Jakobi, Chemnitz (1903; three manuals, 62 stops); and Friedenskirche, Schweidnitz (1909; three manuals, 57 stops). The firm was dissolved sometime after 1918.
Like other contemporary builders in Germany, the Schlag family laid most emphasis on foundation stops. Their organs had complete Principal choruses on all manuals (Christian Gottlieb had studied the Baroque organs of Hamburg and Lübeck in 1865). Their larger organs consisted of *Hauptwerk* (with reeds represented by Trompete 8'), *Schwellwerk* (with Oboe, Vox humana or Klarinette 8') and Pedal (with Posaune 16' and Trompete 8'); there would also be a Solo Organ with reeds such as Orchestral oboe and Tuba mirabilis on wind pressures of up to 30 cm (Oskar had studied with Henry Willis in London). When rebuilding old organs, they kept as much historic pipework as possible (e.g. 1859, organ by J. M. Röder, *c*60%, and 1893, Joachim Wagner, *c*90%).
After 1870 Johann Karl's sons Karl (*d* Schweidnitz, 1873) and Heinrich (*d* Liegnitz, 1903) founded in Schweidnitz the firm of Gebrüder Schlag, later managed by Christian Gottlieb's nephew, Ernst (*b* Profen, 1852; *d* Schweidnitz, 1941); this firm mainly built small organs in Silesia.

BIBLIOGRAPHY
E. F. Richter: *Katechismus der Orgel* (Leipzig, 1868, 4/1896)
L. Burgemeister: *Der Orgelbau in Schlesien* (Strasbourg, 1925, enlarged 2/1973)
F. Seidel: 'Die Orgelbauerfamilien Schlag-Schweidnitz', *IZ*, xvi (1961–2), 309, 354
——: 'Schlag', *MGG*

HANS KLOTZ

Schlag (ii) (Ger.). BEAT.

Schlägel (Ger.). Drumstick; *see* DRUM.

Schlager, Karlheinz (*b* Bamberg, 8 Oct 1938). German musicologist and music librarian. From 1958 to 1964 he studied musicology with Stäblein and Eggebrecht at the University of Erlangen-Nuremberg, with German philology, theatre history and philosophy as subsidiary subjects. He took his doctorate at Erlangen in 1964 with a dissertation on alleluia melodies in 10th- and 11th-century manuscripts. From 1964 to 1967 he was Stäblein's research assistant in Erlangen and since 1976 he has been research assistant at the musicology institute of the University of Erlangen–Nuremberg. Since 1968 he has been an editor of *RISM* in Kassel, in charge of single prints up to 1800. His own special interests centre on palaeographic research and style criticism of medieval monophonic music.

WRITINGS
Thematischer Katalog der ältesten Alleluia-Melodien aus Handschriften des 10. und 11. Jahrhunderts (diss., U. of Erlangen-Nuremberg, 1964; Munich, 1965)
'Ein beneventanisches Alleluia und seine Prosula', *Festschrift Bruno Stäblein* (Kassel, 1967), 217
'Anmerkungen zu den zweiten Alleluia-Versen', *AMw*, xxiv (1967), 199
'Der Fall Berglinger: Stufen einer romantischen Biographie am Beispiel Wackenroder', *AMw*, xxix (1972), 115
'Wege zur Restauration: Marginalien zur Kirchenmusik zwischen Augustinus und Thibaut', *Traditionen und Reformen in der Kirchenmusik: Festschrift für Konrad Ameln* (Kassel, 1974), 9
'Erstarrte Idylle: Schumanns Eichendorff-Verständnis im Lied op. 39/VII (Auf einer Burg)', *AMw*, xxxiii (1976), 119
'Alleluia', §1, 'Beneventan rite, music of the', *Grove 6*
Articles in *MGG* and in *Geschichte der katholischen Kirchenmusik*, ed. K. G. Fellerer, i (Kassel, 1972)

EDITIONS
Alleluia-Melodien, Monumenta monodica medii aevi, vii (Kassel, 1968); viii (in preparation)

HANS HEINRICH EGGEBRECHT

Schlagfeder (Ger.). PLECTRUM.

Schlagzeug (Ger.). PERCUSSION INSTRUMENTS.

Schlangenrohr (Ger.). SERPENT.

Schlegel. (1) (Ger.) Drumstick; *see* DRUM.
(2) *See* SLEGEL family.

Schlegel, Leander (*b* Oegstgeest, nr. Leiden, 2 Feb 1844; *d* Overveen, nr. Haarlem, 20 Oct 1913). Dutch pianist and composer. He studied the violin at the Leiden music school and the piano and composition at the royal music school (The Hague) and at the Leipzig Conservatory. After completing his education he toured with the violinist Wilhelmj; he became renowned as a Schumann and chamber music pianist. From 1870 to 1898 he directed the Haarlem music school of the Maatschappij tot Bevordering der Toonkunst and conducted its choral society from 1871 to 1881. After 1898 he directed his own music school. Together with the pianist Vink he founded a Wagner Society in Haarlem in 1873. His most important compositions, however, show him to have been less influenced by Wagner than by Brahms. They consist of ballades, a suite, pieces and studies for the piano, rhapsodies for four hands and a passacaglia for two pianos; he gave a recital of his piano works in Vienna in 1912. He also wrote orchestral works including a violin concerto and chamber music, as well as songs having some impressionistic characteristics.

BIBLIOGRAPHY
E. Reeser: *Een eeuw Nederlandse muziek* (Amsterdam, 1950)
J. de Kerk: *Haarlems muziekleven in de loop der tijden* (Haarlem, 1965)
JAN TEN BOKUM

Schleifer (Ger.). *See* SLIDE (1).

Schleppend (Ger.: 'dragging'; present participle of *schleppen*). A word used both as a tempo modification and as an expression mark. But it is far less common than the characteristically Mahlerian instruction *nicht schleppen!* ('do not drag'), which had already been used by Beethoven, whose song *Merkenstein* op.100 is marked *mässig, jedoch nicht schleppend* ('moderate, but not dragging'). The Trio of Bruckner's Fourth Symphony is marked *nicht zu schnell: keinesfalls schleppend* ('not too fast, not under any circumstances dragging').

For bibliography *see* TEMPO AND EXPRESSION MARKS.
DAVID FALLOWS

Schlesinger. German firm of music publishers. Adolph Martin Schlesinger (*b* Sülz, Silesia, 4 Oct 1769; *d* Berlin, 11 Oct 1838) worked before 1795 as a book dealer in Berlin, and later incorporated printed music into his business; he founded the music-publishing house in April 1810. After his eldest son MAURICE SCHLESINGER had established himself in Paris and his second son Carl (1808–31) had died, the youngest son Heinrich (*b* Berlin, 1810; *d* Berlin, 14 Dec 1879) received full control in 1831. After his father's death he directed the business with his mother, Philippine, and alone from 1844. In 1864 he sold the firm to Robert Lienau.

From 1811 Schlesinger did their own printing, originally producing works by local Berlin composers.

They soon established contacts with Spontini, Mendelssohn, Loewe and Weber, and in August 1814 were thus able to secure the rights for Weber's works and became his original publishers. Encouragement from the Prussian royal house resulted in the *Sammlung preussischer Armeemärsche*, which comprised over 200 numbers. In 1819 Maurice Schlesinger established contact with Beethoven in Vienna, which led to the publication of opp.108–112, 132 and 135. Through the efforts of Adolph Bernhard Marx, who edited the *Berliner allgemeine musikalische Zeitung* (formerly the *Zeitung für Theater und Musik*, 1821–3) for Schlesinger from 1824 to 1830, they issued the first edition of Bach's *St Matthew Passion*. With more than 2000 publications issued by 1836, Schlesinger ranked among the most important Prussian music publishers. Under Heinrich Schlesinger the firm acquired works by Berlioz, Cornelius, Liszt and notably Chopin's posthumous works. It concentrated on inexpensive editions of well-known works and, for copyright reasons, revised editions of earlier publications. The periodical *Echo* (1851–65), chiefly edited by Heinrich Schlesinger himself, was designed to revitalize the musical life of Berlin. A certain stagnation in the firm's activities was overcome when Robert Lienau took it over in 1864. A complete catalogue was never published.

BIBLIOGRAPHY
A. B. Marx: *Erinnerungen aus meinem Leben* (Berlin, 1865)
A. Kalischer: *Beethoven und Berlin* (Berlin, 1908)
R. H. Lienau: 'Die Schlesinger'sche Buch- und Musikhandlung in Berlin', *Börsenblatt für den deutschen Buchhandel*, lxxvii (1910), 3891
M. Unger: *Ludwig van Beethoven und seine Verleger* (Berlin, 1921)
For further bibliography *see* LIENAU.

RUDOLF ELVERS

Schlesinger, Maurice [Moritz Adolf] (*b* Berlin, 30 Oct 1798; *d* Baden-Baden, 25 Feb 1871). French music publisher of German descent. He was the eldest son of Adolf Martin Schlesinger, the Berlin publisher (*see* SCHLESINGER). Before settling in Paris, he served in the Prussian army (1814–15) and worked in his father's firm, visiting Beethoven on his behalf during summer 1819; probably later that year he went to Paris, working first for the bookseller Bossange Père. Not later than July 1821 he started his own business there, his first advertisements bearing the address 13 quai Malaquais (probably his residence). By October 1822 he had moved to 107 rue Richelieu and by February 1824 he was at no.97 of the same street, where he remained until his retirement. In 1826 his business survived a fire that destroyed many manuscripts including letters of Beethoven. On 20 November 1842 *La France musicale* announced that Schlesinger was gradually selling the stock of his firm; it was not until January 1846 that he sold the entire business to Brandus. A few years later he retired to Baden-Baden.

Schlesinger's earliest publications include a series of piano–vocal scores of Mozart's operas, with title-page vignettes by Horace Vernet, and the full score of Méhul's *Valentine de Milan* (1823). These were followed by numerous other operatic publications: piano–vocal scores of at least 50 operas and some two dozen full scores, including the first editions of Meyerbeer's *Robert le diable* and *Les Huguenots*, Halévy's *La juive* and at least 11 of his other works, Adam's *Le postillon de Longjumeau* and Donizetti's *La favorite*. Among his employees between 1840 and 1842 was Wagner, who, then quite impoverished, was engaged to make piano (and other) arrangements of *La favorite* and of Halévy's *La reine de Chypre*. Schlesinger published a great deal of instrumental music. In the 1820s he brought out substantial collections of piano music by Moscheles, Weber and Hummel, and early in 1829 he announced complete editions first of Beethoven's piano works and then of his string trios, quartets and quintets. In 1822–3 he published authentic (and simultaneous first) editions of Beethoven's opp.110 and 111 piano sonatas and in 1827 of the opp.130, 132, 133 and 135 string quartets. In the late 1820s and the early 1830s he published early works by Mendelssohn, Liszt and Berlioz; among his Berlioz publications were the first editions of the *Huit scènes de Faust*, Liszt's piano arrangement of the *Symphonie fantastique* and the full scores of the *Requiem*, the *Symphonie fantastique* and the *Symphonie funèbre et triomphale*. He published about 40 of Chopin's works, most of them simultaneous first, authentic editions. In the 1830s and 1840s he also published a vast quantity of piano music by Heller, Thalberg, Lanner, Labitzky and the elder Johann Strauss. In all, about 4500 editions were published, judging by the chronological series of plate numbers.

Schlesinger's most enduring publication was the weekly *Gazette musicale de Paris*, first published on 5 January 1834. From November 1835 (vol.ii/44) it was merged with *Revue musicale* (edited by Fétis), subsequently appearing as *Revue et gazette musicale*; in 1880 it ceased publication. Among the early contributors were Berlioz, Wagner, Liszt and Schumann. It is an invaluable source of information on music and music publishing in Paris.

Title-page of Berlioz's 'Huit scènes de Faust', published by Schlesinger in 1829

Schlesinger was imaginative, reckless, hard in business and a considerable rogue. He is said to be accurately portrayed by Flaubert as Jacques Arnoux in *L'éducation sentimentale*; Madame Arnoux is just as closely modelled on Schlesinger's wife, Elisa, with whom Flaubert was for many years in love. Irascible by nature, Schlesinger not infrequently became entangled with his colleagues in wrangles over publication rights or allegedly defamatory statements; his clashes with Escudier in 1839, with Troupenas in 1841 and with Rossini in 1843 provide three interesting examples documented in *La France musicale* (1839–43). The autographs from his estate were auctioned by Liepmannssohn in Berlin on 4 November 1907.

BIBLIOGRAPHY

FétisB

F. C. Busset: *M. Fétis mis à la portée de tout le monde* (Paris, 1838)

Catalogue générale (Paris, c1846) [Brandus & Cie catalogue listing all works published by Schlesinger to 30 June 1845]

M. Unger: *Ludwig van Beethoven und seine Verleger* (Berlin, 1921)

O. E. Deutsch: *Music Publishers' Numbers* (London, 1946; Ger. trans., rev., 1961), 22

C. Hopkinson: *A Bibliography of the Musical and Literary Works of Hector Berlioz* (Edinburgh, 1951, rev. 2/1980), 195ff

H. Steinhart-Leins: *Flauberts grosse Liebe: Elisa Foucault, das Urbild der Mde. Arnoux* (Baden-Baden, 1951)

C. Hopkinson: *A Dictionary of Parisian Music Publishers 1700–1950* (London, 1954), 109

E. Anderson: *The Letters of Beethoven* (London, 1961), ii–iii

M. Gregor-Dellin, ed.: *Richard Wagner: Mein Leben* (Munich, 1963)

A. Tyson: 'Maurice Schlesinger as a Publisher of Beethoven, 1822–27', *AcM*, xxxv (1963), 182

P. Gossett: *The Operas of Rossini* (diss., Princeton U., 1970), 607ff

RICHARD MACNUTT

Schlick, Arnolt (*b* ?Heidelberg, *c*1460; *d* ?Heidelberg, after 1521). German organist and composer. The assertions that Schlick came from Bavaria, from the Swabian-Alemannic area or from the southern half of Bohemia are not justifiable. According to Pietzsch's investigations, Schlick's use of language reflects that spoken around Heidelberg at the beginning of the 16th century, so he probably came from the Heidelberg area. In 1486 he played at Maximilian I's election to the imperial throne: an eye-witness reported that 'the organ was played by a blind man . . . it was quite nice to hear.' (Schlick's son, Arnolt the younger, confirmed that his father was blind in a foreword added to the *Tabulaturen*.) In 1490–91 Schlick visited the Netherlands, no doubt because of an epidemic of plague in Heidelberg; in 1491 he went to Strasbourg for the inauguration of the cathedral organ, built by Krebs; in 1495 he went to Worms for the Diet, where he was helpful and considerate to his subsequent rival Sebastian Virdung. In the next few years, he tested a number of organs: in 1503 the small choir organ of St Georg in Hagenau, in 1505 the Speyer Cathedral organ, in 1510 the Hagenau organ again (it had presumably been enlarged). In 1509 he received a life appointment at the palatine court. In 1511 Maximilian granted his request for the copyright of his *Spiegel der Orgelmacher und Organisten* and his *Tabulaturen etlicher lobgesang*, which protected him against unauthorized reprinting for ten years. In August 1516 Schlick travelled to Torgau, where he met Hofhaimer at the Saxon court. As an organ consultant he went to Neustadt an der Haardt in 1516 and Hagenau in 1520. It is not known whether he was at the coronation of Charles V in Aachen in October 1520; his reference to it in the dedication to *Ascendo ad Patrem meum* 'so I thought that I would join in the fun' does not necessarily point to his active participation. The last contemporary document to mention Schlick is a bill of 1521, which states that he had 'heard and examined' the renovated great organ of St George, Hagenau. The foreword to the *Tabulaturen* reports that he had 'for many years played the organ in front of emperors, kings, electors, princes and other spiritual and temporal lords', suggesting that he had travelled a great deal and thus won himself acclaim far afield as an exceptional organist and consultant.

In *Spiegel der Orgelmacher und Organisten*, the first work published in German about organ building and organ playing, Schlick gave an accurate insight into the skills of the organ builder. In ten chapters he dealt with the measurements of pipes, the alloying and working of the metal to be used, the choice of registers and the nature of wind-chests, bellows etc, and gave advice on tuning and on the most suitable positions for an organ. In the *Tabulaturen etlicher lobgesang*, the first printed German organ tablatures, Schlick published a number of his own compositions as practical complement to his *Spiegel der Orgelmacher*. In the introduction he discussed the meaning of the notation, defended himself against Virdung's accusations (see Virdung's *Musica getutscht*, Basle, 1511/R1970), and categorized the compositions. The book contains nine works for organ, in three to five parts, 12 lute pieces with 'zwo stimmen zu zwicken und ein zu singen', and three works for lute with 'drei stimmen zu zwicken'. Among the organ works a five-part *Salve regina* is outstanding; long sections use an imitation technique to be found later in, for example, the music of Sweelinck. In particular, the other parts anticipate motifs which appear later in the cantus firmus. Schlick's skilful writing of counterpoint can also be clearly seen in an organ work based on the German hymn *Maria zart*. Almost every phrase of the melody, which is divided into 13 sections, is treated contrapuntally, often in the form of a free canon. Equal in stature to these works are the eight canonic versets based on the sequence *Gaude Dei genitrix* and the ten-part piece on the antiphon *Ascendo ad patrem meum*, found in Trent by Lunelli. In his introduction Schlick wrote of the settings of *Gaude Dei genitrix* that they were 'something new and of a rare skill: some of them unheard . . . no

two alike, but each a different counterpoint'; also that 'for each composition he had found and made its own rule'; that he had written the chorale *Ascendo ad Patrem* for ten parts 'which can be played on the organ with four parts on the pedals and six on the manuals'. These settings show how contrapuntal parts can be woven around a cantus firmus: the melody of the chorale is set against a faster accompaniment, both parts being supported by additional voices a 3rd, 4th or 6th apart. In some ways *Ascendo ad Patrem* is the climax of Schlick's compositional career. Played on the organ, it is unique in the music up to and including the early 16th century. The opening bars (ex.1) may give an impression of the monumental scale of this work.

Thus Schlick's historical importance does not rest only on his achievements as a theorist and on his widespread reputation as a tester of organs and an organist. His achievements as a composer, which until now have remained in the background, must also be included in the overall picture of a musician who left his mark on the history of organ music in the 16th century.

WORKS

Tabulaturen etlicher lobgesang und lidlein uff die orgeln un lauten (Mainz, 1512/R1977); ed. G. Harms (Hamburg, 1924, 2/1957)
Ascendo ad Patrem meum, a 2, org, *I-TRa* tedesca 105
Ascendo ad Patrem meum, a 10, org, ed. M. S. Kastner and M. Querol Gavaldá, *Hommage à l'empereur Charles-Quint* (Barcelona, 1954)
Gaude Dei genitrix, a 3–5, org, *TRa* tedesca 105
2 songs, 4vv, in 1512[1]
Tenor part 'Mimi', *D-HB* X 2 (? from a mass setting)

THEORETICAL WORK

Spiegel der Orgelmacher und Organisten (Speyer, 1511/R1959); ed. E. Flade (Mainz, 1931, 2/1951); facs., incl. Eng. trans., ed. E. B. Barber (Buren, 1978)

BIBLIOGRAPHY

A. Pirro: 'Orgue et organistes de Hagenau de 1491 à 1525 environ', *RdM*, vii (1926), 11
G. Frotscher: *Geschichte des Orgel-Spiels und der Orgel-Komposition*, i (Berlin, 1935, enlarged 3/1966)
R. Kendall: 'Notes on Arnoldt Schlick', *AcM*, xi (1939), 136
R. Lunelli: 'Contributi trentini alle relazioni musicali fra l'Italia e la Germania nel Rinascimento', *AcM*, xxi (1949), 41
S. Kastner: 'Rapports entre Schlick et Cabezón', *La musique instrumentale de la Renaissance: CNRS Paris 1954*, 217
G. Pietzsch: *Quellen und Forschungen zur Geschichte der Musik am kurpfälzischen Hof zu Heidelberg bis 1622* (Mainz, 1963), 104ff

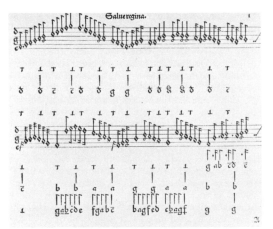

Opening of the 'Salve regina' from Schlick's 'Tabulaturen etlicher lobgesang' (*Mainz: P. Schöffer, 1512*)

W. Apel: *Geschichte der Orgel- und Klaviermusik bis 1700* (Kassel, 1967; Eng. trans., rev., 1972)
H. Husmann: 'Zur Charakteristik der Schlickschen Temperatur', *AMw*, xxiv (1967), 253
W. R. Thomas and J. J. K. Rhodes: 'Schlick, Praetorius and the History of Organ-pitch', *Organ Yearbook*, ii (1971), 58

HANS JOACHIM MARX

Schlick, Rudolf (*b* Meissen; *fl* 1588). German theorist. In the foreword to his treatise he described himself as a doctor of medicine. He was one of several widely educated humanists who had a command of musical theory without being professional musicians. His treatise *Exercitatio, qua musices origo prima, cultus antiquissimus, dignitas maxima et emolumenta ... breviter ac dilucide exponuntur* (Speyer, 1588) deals with the origin, development and uses of music. On the question of origin he quoted on the one hand, as was customary, the testimony of the Bible and the church fathers, and on the other the sayings of classical antiquity. Both sources were considered equally valid; according to Schlick, Greek teaching on the origins of music is distinguished from the Christian only by the fact that the Greeks, through the wiles of the Devil, believed in several gods. The development of music is presented in brief and general terms; in Schlick's opinion music had reached unsurpassable heights in his time, not least because the correct form and method had been discovered for teaching it. He demonstrated the value of music by pointing out its function in church of proclaiming the praise of God, and its influence on the human affections, and stressed the miracles worked by Greek music. He also apparently understood something of the practical music of his own time; he gave no detailed explanation of the modes, but rejected the extension of their number from eight to twelve.

BIBLIOGRAPHY

EitnerQ
J. N. Forkel: *Allgemeine Litteratur der Musik* (Leipzig, 1792/R1962), 505
reprinted from *MGG* (xi, 1823) by permission of Bärenreiter

MARTIN RUHNKE

Schlicker, Herman Leonhard (*b* Hohentrüdingen, Bavaria, 31 Jan 1902; *d* Buffalo, NY, 4 Dec 1974). American organ builder. He was apprenticed to Steinmeyer, and later worked for other European builders, including Marcussen of Denmark. Schlicker came to the USA in 1925, working first for Wurlitzer, then for Tellers of Erie, Pennsylvania. In 1932 he established his own company in Buffalo, New York. He was one of the pioneers in the USA in the move to a more classical style of organ. In 1950 his firm developed an electropneumatic wind-chest with expansion chambers, and in 1963 commenced the building of mechanical-action instruments; ten years later these constituted approximately 45% of the company's output. The work of the Schlicker Organ Co. was continued by his widow, Alice Hagman Schlicker, and his son-in-law, Rolfe Dinwoodie. Among the Schlicker patents are a new slider-chest pallet-valve, and a vacuum-operated drawstop action. The firm's work is found throughout North America, and its important organs include those at Valparaiso University, Indiana (1959), the First Congregational Church, Los Angeles (1969), and the First Methodist Church, Baton Rouge, Louisiana (1972).

BARBARA OWEN

Schlimbach. German family of organ builders. Johann Caspar Schlimbach (1777–1861), after being apprenticed to Anton Walter and Franz Martin Seuffert in Vienna, settled in 1806 in Königshofen im Grabfeld, eastern Franconia, as an organ builder and piano maker. In 1810 he built the aeoline, a keyboard instrument with tuned metal reeds fastened after the fashion of the jew's harp; the instrument was a development of experiments made by his cousin Bernhard Eschenbach (1769–1852). Apart from organ building, Schlimbach was concerned principally with piano making and harmonium building. Of his five sons who became instrument makers, Martin (1811–1901) managed his father's business until the 1880s; Gustav (1818–94) moved in 1845 to Speyer am Rhein, where he was active as an organ builder until at least 1889; and Balthasar (1807–96) moved to Würzburg, where he took over Seuffert's abandoned workshop and set up business under his own name. Balthasar, his son Martin Josef (1841–1914) and his grandson Alfred (1875–1952) developed the firm into the leading organ building establishment of eastern Franconia and built about 260 new organs. This firm, the oldest in eastern Franconia, ceased to exist during World War I.

BIBLIOGRAPHY

O. Kaul: 'Von der Kunst des Orgelbaus in Würzburg', *Die Frankenwarte: Blätter für Heimatkunde* (1938), no.8
F. J. Hirt: *Meisterwerke des Klavierbaus: Geschichte der Saitenklaviere von 1440 bis 1880* (Olten, 1955)
T. Wohnhaas and H. Fischer: 'Johann Philipp Seuffert und seine Nachkommen', *Fränkische Lebensbilder*, ii (1968), 354

THEODOR WOHNHAAS

Schlindel [Schlündl], **Valentin** (*b* ? Hirschfelde, nr. Bautzen, western Bohemia, between 1580 and 1600; *d* Tepl [now Teplá], Bohemia, after 1631). Bohemian composer. He is known by two editions of a hymnal, the second of which states that he came from 'Hirschfeldt auf Pautten'. He intended both for use at the Premonstratensian monastery at Tepl; in the first he referred to himself as secretary of the monastery, and he presumably continued to work there. The first edition appeared as *Hymnodia Catholica, auss underschidlichen von der Catholischen Kirchen approbierten Gesangbüchern, in Processionibus, Bett und Kirchfahrten nutz- und loblich zugebrauchen* (Munich, 1624). It contains 50 hymns with 45 melodies; 27 of these form the tenor parts of simple four-part settings, which according to the preface are by Schlindel himself. He took the contents from such sources as Johannes Leisentrit's hymnal of 1567, the *Obsequiale Ratisbonense* (1570), the Munich hymnal and psalter of 1586, the Neisse hymnal of 1593, the Speyer hymnal (1599) and Conrad Vetter's *Paradeissvogel* (1613). The melodies deviate markedly from the originals, doubtless to make them conform more closely to the Bohemian hymn tradition. Schlindel intended the hymnal not only for the monastery at Tepl but also for the associated convent at Chöttischaw (now Chotěšov). The second edition, which is much extended, appeared under a new title: *Catholisches Gesangbuch, in Kirchen, zu Hauss, in Processionibus und Kirchfahrten gar hailsam; nutzlich, löblich und andächtiglich zugebrauchen* (Munich, 1631). It contains 83 hymns, 62 of which are provided with music: 22 have just a melody, 40 are harmonized settings. About a third of the four-part settings of 1624 are replaced by eight new four-part versions (six with the melody in the treble) and by ten settings for treble and bass, which are the earliest continuo songs in Bohemia. In both types of setting

Schlindel used the four-part settings of the 1628 hymnal of JOHANN DEGEN. His hymnal is a successor to C. Schweher's Prague hymnal of 1581 in that it continued the tradition of the German Catholic hymn in Bohemia; its contents certainly influenced the hymnal published in Prague in 1652.

WALTHER LIPPHARDT

Schlitten-Schellen (Ger). JINGLES.

Schlündel, Valentin. See SCHLINDEL, VALENTIN.

Schlusnus, Heinrich (*b* Braubach, 6 Aug 1888; *d* Frankfurt am Main, 18 June 1952). German baritone. He trained as a postal official but also studied singing and made a successful début at Hamburg in 1915 as the Herald in *Lohengrin*. He was engaged by the Nuremberg Opera between 1915 and 1917 and in 1917 by the Berlin Staatsoper where he remained until 1945, becoming their leading Verdi baritone. In 1918 he made his début as a recitalist after having studied with Louis Blacher in Berlin. As an opera singer he toured extensively, to Amsterdam (1919), Barcelona (1922), Chicago (1927), Bayreuth (1933) and Paris (1937); and in 1949 he undertook a concert tour to South America. His voice, particularly easy in the high register, was steady and smooth, his style economical. Besides excelling in opera he was a lieder singer of outstanding quality. His recordings are extensive.

BIBLIOGRAPHY
E. von Naso and A. Schlusnus: *Heinrich Schlusnus, Mensch und Sänger* (Hamburg, 1957)
E. Csan and A. G. Ross: 'A Schlusnus Discography', *Record News*, iii (1959), 164, 196 [see also ibid, iii (1959), 319, 402; iv (1959), 136]
S. Smolian: 'Heinrich Schlusnus: a Discography', *BIRS Bulletin* (1959), no.14, p.5; (1960), no.15–16, p.16
J. B. Steane: *The Grand Tradition* (London, 1974), 213f
CARL L. BRUUN

Schluss (Ger.). CADENCE.

Schlüsselfidel (Ger.). NYCKELHARPA.

Schmachtend (Ger.: 'yearning', 'longing'). See LANGSAM.

Schmahl. Swabian family of instrument makers. Johann Michael Schmahl (1654–1725) founded the Heilbronn branch of the firm and was succeeded by his son Johann Friedrich (*b* Steinheim, 12 March 1693; *d* Heilbronn, 19 July 1737), who in turn was succeeded by his brother, Johann Adam (*b* Heilbronn, 20 Jan 1704; *d* Heilbronn, 20 June 1757), the most famous organ builder in the family. Georg Friedrich (*b* Heilbronn, 15 Nov 1700; *d* Ulm, 26 Aug 1773), son of Johann Michael, went to Ulm where he founded a second branch, while Leonard Balthasar (1729–79), son of Johann Friedrich, founded a third at Zittau, where he married the daughter of the organ builder J. J. Tamitius. All these members of the family were organ builders, and all made great use of foundation stops (with a preference for Viola da gamba, Gemshorn and Quintadena) and to a lesser extent, reeds (especially Krummhorn, Vox humana and Hautbois), and limited the pedal to stops of 16′ and 8′. They showed considerable variation in their separate uses of the diapason chorus.

Christoph Friedrich Schmahl (*b* Heilbronn, 1739; *d* Regensburg, 15 May 1814), son of Johann Adam, made keyboard instruments other than organs at Regensburg, where he married the daughter of the organ builder

FRANZ JAKOB SPÄTH. He became a partner with his father-in-law in about 1774, continuing the joint firm name after Späth's death in 1786, until 1793. In 1802 Schmahl's son Jacob Friedrich became his partner; a second son Christian Carl took over Schmahl's place on his retirement in 1812. After Christian Carl's early death, the firm was dissolved.

Späth & Schmahl were best known for their production of the keyboard instrument known as the TANGENT PIANO. It is not known whether they were influenced by other 18th-century experiments with tangent action, such as those by Marius (1717), Schröter (1739), Weltmann (1759), Merlin (1774) or Walton (1787).

Signed examples of tangent pianos, all presumably dating from after Späth's death, include those at Berlin, Freiburg, Leipzig and Halle (Späth & Schmahl), and Munich and Nuremberg (C. F. Schmahl). Fortepianos with Viennese action by C. F. Schmahl are in Nuremberg and Halle.

BIBLIOGRAPHY
H. Herrmann: *Die Regensburger Klavierbauer Späth und Schmahl und ihr Tangentenflügel* (Erlangen, 1928)
W. Gurlitt: 'Zur schwäbischen Orgelbaukunst: die Orgelmacherfamilie Schmahl', *Musik und Kirche*, xiii (1941), 11
F. J. Hirt: *Meisterwerke des Klavierbaues* (Olten, 1955), 455
A. Scharnagl: 'Späth und Schmahl', *MGG*
G. Kleemann: 'Die Orgelbauerfamilie Schmahl', *Acta organologica*, vii (1973), 71–106
HANS KLOTZ, MARIBEL MEISEL, PHILIP R. BELT

Schmältzl, Wolfgang. See SCHMELTZL, WOLFGANG.

Schmedes, Erik (*b* Gentofte, nr. Copenhagen, 27 Aug 1866; *d* Vienna, 23 March 1931). Danish tenor. He studied with Rothmühl in Berlin, Ress in Vienna and Padilla in Paris before making a brilliant début as a baritone at Wiesbaden in 1891. As a lyric tenor he made a second début at Nuremberg in 1894, and from 1894 to 1897 was engaged at Dresden. In 1898 he went to Vienna, where he remained through the great Mahler years until 1924, singing the heavier dramatic and Wagnerian parts with great success. In 1899 he sang Siegfried and Parsifal at Bayreuth, returning there for several years, and in 1908 and 1909 he sang at the Metropolitan Opera, New York. He was the first Viennese Cavaradossi, Palestrina (Pfitzner) and Herod. In style rather declamatory, he had a pleasing quality of voice, and was an excellent actor. He recorded extensively from 1902.

BIBLIOGRAPHY
L. Riemens and E. Serpa: 'Schmedes, Erik', *Le grandi voci* (Rome, 1964) [with opera discography by R. Vegeto]
CARL L. BRUUN

Schmeling, Gertrud Elisabeth. See MARA, GERTRUD ELISABETH.

Schmeltzer, Johann Heinrich. See SCHMELZER, JOHANN HEINRICH.

Schmeltzl [Schmältzl], **Wolfgang** (*b* Kemnath, ? between 1500 and 1505; *d* ?St Lorenzen am Steinfeld, Lower Austria, after 1566). German songbook editor and poet. After studying at Vienna University from 1523 he was appointed protestant Kantor in Amberg. By 1540 at the latest he must have become a Catholic for at that time he became schoolmaster in the Schotten monastery in Vienna and singer in St Saviour's Chapel. From 1557 to 1566 he was a priest at St Lorenzen am Steinfeld. He wrote a number of school plays in verse as well as the voluminous *Lobspruch der Stadt Wienn*

(Vienna, 1547), which includes some musical information. His *Der christlich und gewaltig Zug in das Hungerland* (Vienna, 1556) describes the fighting against the Turks in 1556. Schmeltzl edited *Guter seltzamer un kunstreicher teuscher Gesang* (Nuremberg, 1544), the only songbook known to have been compiled in Vienna in the first half of the 16th century. This collection, which may have been intended for musical instruction in the Schotten monastery, contains a selection of German lieder and Italian-influenced settings by Greiter, Matthias, Paminger, Senfl and others, as well as a *battaglia* and another piece by Verdelot. Some of the anonymous pieces may be by Schmeltzl.

BIBLIOGRAPHY
R. Eitner: 'Das deutsche Lied des XV. und XVI. Jahrhunderts', *MMg*, viii (1876/*R*1960), suppl. [incl. edns. of 22 pieces]
W. Crecelius: 'Wolfgang Schmeltzl', *MMg*, xiii (1881/*R*1961), 164
F. Spengler: *Wolfgang Schmeltzl* (Vienna, 1883)
E. Bienenfeld: 'Wolffgang Schmeltzl, sein Liederbuch (1544) und das Quodlibet des XVI. Jahrhunderts', *SIMG*, vi (1904–5), 80–135
OTHMAR WESSELY

Schmelzer [Schmeltzer, Schmelzer von Ehrenruef], **Andreas Anton** (*b* Vienna, baptized 26 Nov 1653; *d* Vienna, 13 Oct 1701). Austrian composer and violinist, eldest son of Johann Heinrich Schmelzer. He was trained by his father and became a full member of the Vienna court orchestra on 16 February 1671. After his father's death in 1680, he assumed the position of official composer of ballet music at court (the decree of appointment is dated 27 February 1681), but ill-health forced him to relinquish it in 1693. He composed some 65 ballet suites (all in *A-Wn*) which, however, do not evince the great variety and musical interest of his father's. He generally reduced the number of movements to three, or even two. Archaic dances such as the trezza, traccanario, folia and *moresca* are rarely found, whereas the gavotte, saraband, bourrée, minuet, aria and intrada appear regularly. Melodic design and harmonic vocabulary are mannered and stylized. A few sonatas and suites (in *S-Uu*, but one sonata in *A-Wm*) are of questionable authenticity.

For bibliography see SCHMELZER, JOHANN HEINRICH.
RUDOLF SCHNITZLER

Schmelzer [Schmeltzer, Schmelzer von Ehrenruef], **Johann Heinrich** (*b* Scheibbs, Lower Austria, *c*1620–23; *d* Prague, between 29 Feb and 20 March 1680). Austrian composer and violinist. He was the leading Austrian composer of instrumental music before Biber and made an influential contribution to the development of the sonata and suite.

1. LIFE. Until recently, descriptions of his background have been based on his petition for ennoblement of 1673, in which he described his father (without mentioning his name) as a career soldier in the service of the Emperor Ferdinand III from about 1616 to 1645. According, however, to the marriage certificate of his sister Eva Rosina, dated May 1645, his father can be identified as Daniel Schmelzer, a baker by profession and burgher of Scheibbs. It is not known when J. H. Schmelzer arrived in Vienna, nor who gave him his musical training, but it seems likely that he studied with one of the mentors of court pupils, Antonio Bertali, Burckhardt Kugler or Giovanni Sansoni. The earliest documentary evidence, relating to his first marriage on 28 June 1643, designates him as an instrumentalist (cornettist) at St Stephen's Cathedral, Vienna. An imperial resolution of 1674, however, indicates that he began his

service in the court chapel as early as 1635–6, probably as a violinist, the capacity in which he enjoyed his greatest fame throughout his life. He was officially appointed a violinist in the court orchestra on 1 October 1649. His position and functions during the next two decades are not entirely clear. The limited information available indicates that he wrote a good deal of music and won increasing fame as violinist and composer. Thus, in 1658 he was included as director of instrumental music in the retinue attending Leopold I at his coronation at Frankfurt am Main. His three major collections of chamber music appeared between 1659 and 1664, and in 1660, in his *Reise-Diarium*, J. J. Müller called him 'the famous and nearly most distinguished violinist in all Europe'. His close relationship with the emperor can be seen not only in his receipt of gifts of money and golden chains (an indication of special favour) but also in the fact that the emperor sought his aid in the preparation of his own compositions.

On 13 April 1671 Schmelzer was appointed vice-Kapellmeister at the imperial court. From about the same time he had to assume an ever increasing share of the responsibilities of the Kapellmeister, the ailing G. F. Sances. There can be little doubt that his efficiency in this position, combined with his previous achievements and rising fame, rather than the supposed military service of his father, prompted Leopold I, in a decree dated 14 June 1673, to accede to his petition for ennoblement, whereupon he added 'von Ehrenruef' to his name; this title was also adopted by his sons. Not, however, until after Sances's death on 24 November 1679 was he officially appointed Kapellmeister. His application for the post, dated 18 December 1679 and submitted to the emperor in Prague, where the court had moved to escape the plague that was raging in Vienna, requested the appointment to be made retrospective to 1 July, but it was granted only as from 1 October. His enjoyment of the position was short-lived. His death from the plague, which had meanwhile reached Prague, must have taken place between 29 February (the date of the first performance of Antonio Draghi's *La patienza di Socrate*, for which he provided the ballet music) and 20 March 1680 (the date of a petition on behalf of his widow and children).

Schmelzer had three sons who became musicians. The eldest was ANDREAS ANTON SCHMELZER; the other two were also trained by him as violinists. About Georg Joseph (*b* Vienna, baptized 7 April 1655; *d* probably at Vienna, before 1701) nothing further is known. Peter Clemens [Clement] (*b* Vienna, baptized 28 June 1672; *d* Vienna, 20 Sept 1746) was accepted into the court orchestra by a decree dated 12 August 1692, but by 1729 he was incapacitated by a finger injury; he retired officially on 30 June 1740. It is questionable whether a *Dialogus musicalis chelycus* by a 'Clemente Mathia ab Ehrenruff' (in *A-Wn*) is by him; it comprises 12 sonatas for lute with organ continuo.

2. WORKS. Together with his older contemporaries Sances and Bertali and his younger contemporary Draghi, Schmelzer was one of the most important musicians at the Habsburg court between about 1655 and 1680. He produced a varied output, but he was influential only as a composer of instrumental music: ballet suites, which he wrote for nearly all performances of secular dramatic music at court from 1665 to 1680, and chamber music.

There was a great demand for ballet music at the

court of Leopold I. Dance suites or individual dances were included in allegorical pageants that had evolved from the jousts and tournaments of earlier times, in disguisings and sleigh rides in which members of the imperial family frequently took part, in the majority of *drammi per musica*, serenatas etc, and even in a number of spoken dramas. The emphasis in most of these presentations was clearly on the visual: nymphs, tritons, centaurs, pages, soldiers, *commedia dell'arte* characters, spirits and even animals appeared in ornate costumes on elaborately decorated sets and carriages. The music composed by the official ballet composers Wolfgang Ebner, Schmelzer and his son Andreas Anton, and J. J. Hoffer is clearly functional and designed to draw attention to the visual spectacle and its allegorical significance and to provide the basis for the execution of the stylized movements of the dancers. Schmelzer's dance suites consist of between two and nine individual dances. Many begin with an intrada (or *aria ad ingressum*) and conclude with a retirada (or *aria ad egressum*). The intervening movements do not adhere to a consistent pattern but are a free alternation of a large number of different types. As with Schmelzer's independent dances, those most often found are the galliard, bourrée, saraband, gigue, gavotte, allemande and courante, interspersed with dances such as the trezza, folia, saltarello, *moresca* and traccanario. Some movements bear programmatic titles, among them *Bauernmädel, Cacciatori, Battaglione, May Blumen, Aria viennense* and *Balletto francese*. The terms 'balletto' and 'aria' are used as general descriptions rather than to indicate a specific type. Within each individual type there is a great deal of melodic and rhythmic variety, which stems mainly from Schmelzer's use of selected elements of Austrian folk music. Short but characteristic motifs, often based on a succession and or alternation of octaves, 5ths, 6ths and major 3rds (which Nettl attributed to an imitation of the sounds of primitive wind instruments found in the folk music of the alpine region), follow one another in quick succession, frequently resulting in irregular phrase lengths. The unity of a suite is usually provided by means of melodic relationships, but here again Schmelzer achieved variety by incorporating movements in tonalities not closely related to its tonal centre. Although most of the ballets in Viennese sources exist only in partial score (highest part and basso continuo), the entire collection at Kroměříž survives in full score and shows Schmelzer's preference for the string quartet (usually violin and soprano, alto and bass violas) or string quintet (with an additional violin or viola), regardless of the scoring of the work for which the ballet music was written. In some notable instances, however, he departed from this practice and included parts marked 'piffari' (probably shawms), 'cornetti', 'clarini', 'trombe', 'trombone' and 'fagotti', in a single or polychoral setting (for example in the ballet suite to Draghi's *Iphide greca*, first performed on 12 July 1670).

In his sonatas Schmelzer favoured both the texture of two melody instruments (two violins or violin and viola da gamba) and continuo (as in *Duodena selectarum sonatarum*) and fuller textures (up to eight parts in *Sacro-profanus concentus musicus*), including polychoral treatment. Historically more important, however, are the six sonatas for violin and continuo forming his *Sonatae unarum fidium* (1664), the earliest publication devoted entirely to this genre in the German-speaking countries. Most of his sonatas rely strongly on the variation principle and consist of a number of short sections in contrasting metres and tempos, but in the solo violin sonatas these sections are extended to allow a greater display of virtuoso technique. Probably influenced by Bertali and Marco Uccellini, Schmelzer included passages of rapid scales and arpeggios, covering the full range of the instrument, but multi-stopping and scordatura tuning are still rare in his sonatas.

In the context of his total output, Schmelzer's secular dramatic music and German songs must be considered peripheral. He seems to have composed his numerous liturgical works (most of them lost) in the 1670s during his period as vice-Kapellmeister. Those that survive display the Venetian influence so prevalent among his Italian contemporaries in Vienna.

Schmelzer is historically significant in two areas: as the major Austrian composer of instrumental music before Biber he influenced the development of the suite as well as the sonata in Austria and south Germany; and his appointment as the first Austrian Kapellmeister at the Habsburg court in the 17th century initiated the ever increasing reliance on native rather than imported talent that was most evident in the first half of the 18th century.

WORKS

DRAMATIC
(first performed at Vienna unless otherwise stated)
L'infinità impicciolita (N. Minato), sepolcro, 16 April 1677, *A-Wn*
Die Stärke der Liebe, sepolcro, 1677, *Wn*
L'urno della sorte, ossequio musicale, 9 June 1677, *Wn* (lib only)
Le memorie dolorose (Minato), sepolcro, 8 April 1678, *Wn*
Le veglie ossequiose (Minato), serenata, 1679, *Wn*
Die sieben Alter stimmen zusammen (J. A. Rudolf), Prague, 18 Jan 1680, *Wn*

SACRED VOCAL
11 masses, introit, 7 offertories, Vespers, Compline, 2 Salve regina: *A-Kr, Wn, CS-KRa*; 1 mass ed. in DTÖ, xlix, Jg.xxv/1 (1918/*R*)
173 sacred works, lost, listed in *Distinta specificatione dell'archivio musicale per il servizio della cappella e camera cesarea*, catalogue of Emperor Leopold I's private collection

SECULAR VOCAL
2 Ger. songs, *CS-KRa*; ed. in DTÖ, lvi, Jg.xxviii/2 (1921/*R*)
3 It. cantatas, 15 madrigals, lost, listed in *Distinta specificatione dell'archivio musicale*, catalogue of Emperor Leopold I's private collection

INSTRUMENTAL
Duodena selectarum [12] sonatarum, 2 vn, va da gamba, bc (Nuremberg, 1659); ed. in DTÖ, cv (1963)
Sacro-profanus concentus musicus (13 sonatas), 2–8 insts, bc (Nuremberg, 1662); ed. in DTÖ, cxi–cxii (1965)
[6] Sonatae unarum fidium, vn, bc (Nuremberg, 1664); ed. in DTÖ, xciii (1958, rev. 2/1960)
Arie per il balletto a cavallo (Vienna, 1667) [ballet music for A. Bertali: Contesa dell'aria e dell'acqua (F. Sbarra)]; extracts ed. in EDM, 1st ser., xiv (1941/*R*1961)

150 ballet suites, 80 sonatas, 2–8 insts, *A-Wn* (inc.), *CS-KRa, D-Bds, F-Pn, GB-DRc, Lbm, S-Uu*; some ed. in DTÖ, lvi, Jg.xxviii/2 (1921/*R*); cv (1963); xciii (1965)

BIBLIOGRAPHY
L. von Köchel: *Die kaiserliche Hof-Musikkapelle in Wien von 1543 bis 1867* (Vienna, 1869)
——: *Johann Josef Fux* (Vienna, 1872/*R*1974)
A. von Weilen: *Zur Wiener Theatergeschichte: die vom Jahre 1629 bis zum Jahre 1740 am Wiener Hofe zur Aufführung gelangten Werke theatralischen Charakters und Oratorien* (Vienna, 1901)
E. Wellesz: *Die Ballett-Suiten von Johann Heinrich und Anton Andreas Schmelzer* (Vienna, 1914)
G. Adler: 'Zur Geschichte der Wiener Messkomposition in der zweiten Hälfte des XVII. Jahrhunderts', *SMw*, iv (1916), 5
G. Beckmann: *Das Violinspiel in Deutschland vor 1700* (Berlin and Leipzig, 1918)
E. Wellesz: 'Die Opern und Oratorien in Wien von 1660–1708', *SMw*, vi (1919), 5–138
P. Nettl: 'Die Wiener Tanzkomposition in der zweiten Hälfte des siebzehnten Jahrhunderts', *SMw*, viii (1921), 45–175
A. Moser: *Geschichte des Violinspiels* (Berlin, 1923, rev., enlarged 2/1966–7)
F. Högler: *Die Kirchensonaten in Kremsier* (diss., U. of Vienna, 1926)
E. H. Meyer: *Die mehrstimmige Spielmusik des 17. Jahrhunderts in*

Nord- und Mitteleuropa (Kassel, 1934)
P. Nettl: *Das Wiener Lied im Zeitalter des Barock* (Vienna, 1934)
F. Hadamowsky: 'Barocktheater am Wiener Kaiserhof; mit einem Spielplan (1625–1740)', *Jb der Gesellschaft für Wiener Theaterforschung, 1951–2*
A. Bauer: *Opern und Operetten in Wien: Verzeichnis ihrer Erstaufführungen in der Zeit von 1629 bis zur Gegenwart* (Graz, 1955)
A. Kellner: *Musikgeschichte des Stiftes Kremsmünster* (Kassel, 1956)
E. H. Meyer: 'Die Bedeutung der Instrumentalmusik am furstbischöf-lichen Hofe zu Olomouc (Olmütz) in Kroměříž (Kremsier)', *Mf*, ix (1956), 388
H. J. Moser: 'Eine Pariser Quelle zur Wiener Triosonate des ausgehen-den 17. Jahrhunderts: der Codex Rost', *Festschrift Wilhelm Fischer* (Innsbruck, 1956), 75
W. S. Newman: *The Sonata in the Baroque Era* (Chapel Hill, 1959, rev. 2/1966/R1972)
F. W. Riedel: *Quellenkundliche Beiträge zur Geschichte der Musik für Tasteninstrumente in der zweiten Hälfte des 17. Jahrhunderts* (Kassel, 1960)
R. Aschmann: *Das deutsche polyphone Violinspiel im 17. Jahrhundert* (diss., U. of Zurich, 1962)
F. W. Riedel: *Das Musikarchiv im Minoritenkonvent zu Wien* (Kassel, 1963)
R. Flotzinger: 'Johann Heinrich Schmelzers Sonata "Lanterly" ', *SMw*, xxvi (1964), 67
A. Koczirz: 'Zur Lebensgeschichte Johann Heinrich Schmelzers', *SMw*, xxvi (1964), 47
J. Sehnal: 'Die Musikkapelle des Olmützer Bischofs Karl Liechtenstein-Castelcorn in Kremsier', *KJb*, li (1967), 79
H. Kraus: *Die Musiker im Archivbestand des kaiserlichen Obersthofmeisteramtes (1637–1705)* (Vienna, 1967–9)
P. Nettl: 'Österreichische Folklore des 17. Jahrhunderts: eine Zusammenfassung', *Musa-mens-musici: im Gedenken an Walther Vetter* (Leipzig, 1969), 75

RUDOLF SCHNITZLER

Schmelzer, Peter Clemens. German instrumentalist and possibly a composer, youngest son of JOHANN HEINRICH SCHMELZER.

Schmelzer von Ehrenruef, Andreas Anton. *See* SCHMEL-ZER, ANDREAS ANTON.

Schmezer [Schmetzer], Georg (*b* Augsburg, 21 March 1642; *d* Augsburg, July 1697). German composer, writer on music and teacher. He received his musical education at the Gymnasium and at the choir school of St Anna, Augsburg, where Jakob Scheiffelhut and Daniel Merck were among his fellow students. After study trips which took him as far as Stockholm he became Kantor and director of music at St Anna (which was the main Protestant church at Augsburg) in 1677 and remained there until his death. In 1690 on the occasion of Joseph I's coronation in Augsburg, he presented a composition to Joseph's father, the Emperor Leopold I. He was a generally respected and proficient musician. Some of his output resulted from his educational work. For example, the school dramas for which he composed music were performed by the pupils at St Anna, and it was no doubt for them that he wrote his two elementary theoretical works: indeed he intended his *Compendium musicae* (1688) as a replacement for Adam Gumpelzhaimer's work of the same name that had been used at St Anna since it was published in 1591.

WORKS
(all published in Augsburg)
Pieris vindicata, oder Die vermeinte Braut-Heimführung, school play (1668), lost
[20] Cantiones sacrae, 2–9vv (1671)
Zuspat eingekommene Klag-, Traur- und Trost-Gedichte (1680)
Davidis polytecni infelix felicitas oder Davids Kinder-Leid und Freud, school play (1687), lost
Sacri concentus latini et partim latino-germanici, 5–17vv (1689)
THEORETICAL WORKS
Methodus musicalis oder musikalisch A.B.C. Täfelein für die Jugend (1678)
Compendium musicae (1688)

BIBLIOGRAPHY
EitnerQ; *GerberL*; *WaltherML*
L. Gerheuser: 'Jacob Scheiffelhut und seine Instrumental-Musik', *Zeitschrift des Historischen Vereins für Schwaben und Neuburg*, xlix (1933), 16ff, 92
A. Layer: *Augsburger Musik im Barock* (Augsburg, 1968)

ADOLF LAYER

Schmicorer, Johann Abraham. *See* SCHMIERER, JOHANN ABRAHAM.

Schmid, Adolf. *See* MÜLLER, ADOLF.

Schmid, Anton (*b* Pihl, nr. Česká Lipa, Bohemia, 30 Jan 1787; *d* Salzburg, 3 July 1857). Austrian musicologist. He was the son of Count Kinsky's brewer, Andreas Schmid, and his wife, Theresia Bergmann. After his initial instruction in singing and piano, he received further musical education after 1798 as a singer in the monastery of the Calced Augustinians in Česká Lipa. From 1804 he lived as a theatre musician and music teacher in Prague where he also began his literary activity. In 1812 he settled as a private teacher in Vienna. He became a drafting probationer for the Viennese court library in 1818, and was made a *Skriptor* in 1819 and a *Kustos* in 1844. At the request of Moritz, Count Dietrichstein, he organized the collec-tion which became the basis for the Austrian Nationalbibliothek, and was its first keeper; his hand-written catalogue is still in use. From this task arose not only his fundamental studies on the history of printing music from movable type, but also his more than 500 supplements and reports appended to C. F. Becker's *Systematisch-chronologische Darstellung der musikal-ischen Literatur* (1839) as well as his 'Beiträge zur Literatur und Geschichte der Tonkunst' which appeared in the Mainz journal *Caecilia* from 1842 to 1848. His other writings on music are concerned with Gluck and with the problems of 18th-century Viennese music his-tory; they appeared in various journals. He also pub-lished a bibliography of chess in 1847.

WRITINGS
Ottaviano dei Petrucci da Fossombrone (Vienna, 1845)
Joseph Haydn und Niccolò Zingarelli (Vienna, 1847)
Christoph Willibald Ritter von Gluck: dessen Leben und tonkünstler-isches Wirken (Leipzig, 1854)
BIBLIOGRAPHY
M. Bermann: 'Zwei österreichische Musikgelehrte: II: Anton Schmid', *Blätter für Musik, Theater und Kunst*, i (1855), 78
'Salzburger Tagesneuigkeiten', *Salzburger Zeitung*, ix (1857), 147
C. von Wurzbach: *Biographisches Lexikon des Kaiserthums Öster-reich*, xxx (Vienna, 1875), 212ff

OTHMAR WESSELY

Schmid [Schmidt], Balthasar (*b* Nuremberg, baptized 20 April 1705; buried 27 Nov 1749). German music printer and composer. He was born into a family of artisans and craftsmen, and continued in the tradition of artistic craftsmanship to become one of the best known music engravers in 18th-century Germany. Church records first mention him as an engraver in 1726, later as a musician and engraver (1734), and again as organ-ist at St Margaretha in Nuremberg (1737). He was highly regarded by Mattheson, who praised him in his *Grundlage einer Ehren-Pforte* (1740) as an organist and fine engraver of musical works; and Ludwig Gerber, writing later in the century, credited Schmid's engraving of some parts of J. S. Bach's *Clavier-Übung* as an impor-tant factor in the renown and distribution of those works.

Schmid devoted his early efforts as a printer to his own compositions, but after 1738 his catalogue included the names of some of the leading musical figures in north Germany: G. P. Telemann (sacred vocal works, portrait, autobiography); G. A. Sorge (organ sonatas, preludes and suites for keyboard); C. Nichelmann (12 keyboard sonatas); J. L. Krebs (sonatas for violin and obbligato keyboard, miscellaneous keyboard works); J. Agrell (at least three keyboard sonatas, sonatas for violin and obbligato keyboard); F. W. Marpurg (six keyboard sonatas); C. F. Schale (six keyboard sonatas); C. P. E. Bach ('Prussian' sonatas, keyboard concertos, trio sonatas, a sinfonia); and J. S. Bach (*Clavier-Übung*, iv: Goldberg Variations and the canonic variations on *Vom Himmel hoch*). Schmid maintained a standard of accuracy and legibility unusual for the time, and it was probably through the high quality of his prints of the Bach keyboard works that he first came to the attention of modern scholars. He was also among the earliest publishers to ascribe numbers to his printed works, a practice which makes it possible for scholars to establish the dates and chronology of compositions. Unfortunately, Schmid's numbering is very erratic in that it includes both Arabic and Roman numerals, as well as a few entries designated with the letter N. An index of his printed works remains (in *A-Wgm* 272/20), and has been reproduced by H. Heussner with probable dates of publication inserted. Schmid's widow, Maria Helena Volland (1710–91), continued the publishing activities after his death; from about 1751 printed works of the firm were identified with 'Balth. Schmids seel. Wittib'.

As a composer Schmid is known primarily by his keyboard works, intended for the growing society of amateurs. Those works which included a flute or violin usually indicated that the additional instrument could be omitted, allowing for solo keyboard performance. His keyboard style derives from patterned diatonic melodies supported by relatively simple chord patterns in the bass, and most works are marked by the form and title of a binary dance movement, traits typical of most keyboard music of the period. Two of his minuets were included in Leopold Mozart's *Notenbuch* for Wolfgang (in fact a forgery). A set of *XII Murki* apparently were so named because of the alternating octave bass in the left hand, an accompaniment pattern common to a rustic dance of that name (*see* MURKY). The *Nürnbergische alte und neue Kirchen-Lieder*, his only venture into vocal music as a composer, consists of 208 chorale melodies set in an open two-part texture with figured bass; the work is a model of the printer's art in its clarity and format.

Schmid's output both as a printer and composer reflects the musical tastes of the time. The preponderance of keyboard music illustrates the increasing popularity of the keyboard as a solo instrument and the influx of the new instrumental style; most works were directed towards the student or musical amateur, and Schmid played a useful role in widening the distribution of music to this public.

Johann Michael Schmidt (1741–93; this spelling appeared on his published works), son of Balthasar, continued the engraving trade and operated the publishing house during the last quarter of the century. He was most active in the realm of vocal music and published many significant lieder collections between 1773 and 1791. His only known compositions are for voice and keyboard, *Kleine Lieder mit Melodien aufs Clavier* (1773); he also brought out a second edition of Balthasar's *Kirchen-Lieder* (1773) to which he added 26 chorale tunes for voice and figured bass.

WORKS

(*all printed works published by Schmid in Nuremberg*)

12 Murkis, kbd (*c*1727)

Menuets, kbd, other inst (fl/vn) ad lib (at least five collections, 1728–55, the last pubd by Schmid's widow)

Divertissement musical, . . . Allemandes, Courantes, Sarabandes, Minueto, Gigues, etc, kbd (1729)

Praeludium und Fuge, C, kbd (1731)

Clavierübung, i–vii (1733–48), allegros, arias, sarabands, minuets, bourrées, vivace

Nürnbergische alte und neue Kirchen-Lieder (1748)

A sinfonia, D, and a minuet and saraband, reported to be in *B-Bc*, are missing.

BIBLIOGRAPHY

J. Mattheson: *Grundlage einer Ehren-Pforte* (Hamburg, 1740); ed. M. Schneider (Berlin, 1910/*R*1969)

Anon.: *Verzeichnis der musicalischen Wercker, welche bey Balthasar Schmid seel Wittib in Nürnberg zu haben sind* (MS, *A-Wgm* 272/20)

C. F. Cramer: *Magazin der Musik*, i (Hamburg, 1783/*R*), 1135; ii (Hamburg, 1784/*R*), 489

W. Barclay Squire: 'Publishers' Numbers', *SIMG*, xv (1913–14), 420

G. Kinsky: *Die Originalausgaben der Werke Johann Sebastian Bachs* (Vienna, 1937)

O. E. Deutsch: *Music Publishers' Numbers, 1710–1900* (London, 1946)

H. Heussner: 'Der Musikdrucker Balthasar Schmid in Nürnberg', *Mf*, xvi (1963), 348

DOUGLAS A. LEE

Schmid [Schmidt, Schmitt, Fabricius], **Bernhard (i)** (*b* ?Strasbourg, 1535; *d* Strasbourg, 1592). Alsatian organist and arranger. His father, also named Bernhard, came from either Maursmünster or Lochweiler and served as administrator for various church and educational institutions; his mother, Prisca Wolfenkinder, held Strasbourg citizenship. Apparently Schmid received his musical training in Strasbourg and married Catharina Klein on 31 October 1552. (Their son BERNHARD SCHMID (ii) was born in 1567.) Schmid was appointed organist in 1562 both of the Thomaskirche and of Strasbourg Cathedral, where he played for Christmas services. In 1578, along with two other organists, he inspected the organ in Ulm Cathedral. Except for this visit and a journey during his youth, Schmid apparently lived his entire life in Strasbourg. He relinquished his cathedral post in 1592, accepted one at Jung St Petrus Kirche, and died before the end of the year. A poem by Schmid, describing a festival shooting contest on 15 May 1590, survives. He may also be the author of an epic poem about Petrus von Stauffenberg.

Schmid's *Zwey Bücher einer neuen kunstlichen Tabulatur . . . allen Organisten und angehenden Instrumentisten zu nutz* was published in Strasbourg in 1577. It employs new German organ tablature notation, and includes keyboard settings of 20 Latin motets (18 by Lassus, one by Crecquillon and one by Richafort) and 28 sacred and secular song arrangements of works by Lassus, Crecquillon, Zirler, Rogier [Pathie], Clemens non Papa, Arcadelt, Berchem, Ferrabosco, Godard, Rore and Meiland. The anthology concludes with five passamezzo–saltarello sets and 13 other dances, several in pairs. Typical keyboard ornamentation (coloration) occurs in all the vocal settings and the voice lines have been adapted for the keyboard. As the full title indicates, Schmid intended his book for all kinds of keyboard instruments. The book serves as an index of the type of keyboard music performed at that time in church and in the home. The ornamentation employed reflects current taste, and is at the root of German Baroque keyboard idioms.

For illustration *see* SOURCES OF KEYBOARD MUSIC TO 1660, fig.5.

BIBLIOGRAPHY

BrownI

W. Merian: *Der Tanz in den deutschen Tabulaturbüchern* (Leipzig,

1927/*R*1968) [includes index, incipits and several complete pieces by Schmid]

C. W. Young: *The Keyboard Tablatures of Bernhard Schmid, Father and Son* (diss., U. of Illinois, 1957)

E. Kraus, ed.: Cantantibus organis, i, vi, vii (Regensburg, 1958–62) [includes three intabulations by Schmid]

C. W. Young: 'Keyboard Music to 1600', *MD*, xvi (1962), 115

CLYDE WILLIAM YOUNG

Schmid, Bernhard (ii) (*b* Strasbourg, baptized 1 April 1567; *d* ?Strasbourg, before 5 Nov 1625). Alsatian organist and arranger. He was the son of Bernhard Schmid the elder, and probably attended local schools, receiving musical training from his father. In 1584 he played the vesper service at St Niklaus, in Undis. From 1589 to 1592 he served as organist at the Thomaskirche, a post held previously by his father. He married first Barbara Stumpff, daughter of the verger of the Thomaskirche on 28 July 1590; and second Maria Mers, a widow, on 24 November 1611. He succeeded his father as organist at Strasbourg Cathedral on 1 April 1592, though he also served as organist and custodian at the Predigerkirche for some time. Like his father he acted as an organ consultant. From 1614 he served as a city councillor. His coat of arms bore the motto:

> Qui non amat musicam
> Plag S. Veitstanz et Podagram.

A new cathedral organist was appointed on 5 November 1625 to replace Schmid.

Schmid's *Tabulatur Buch* (Strasbourg, 1607/*R*1969), in new German tablature, opens with 22 intonations by G. Gabrieli and eight by A. Gabrieli. The following six toccatas come from the works of the two Gabrielis, Diruta and Merulo. For his motet intabulations Schmid chose pieces by Hassler, Massaino, Tresti, Erbach, Bianciardi, Morello, Aichinger, Sambucci, Bonhomio and Weissensee. There follow 16 Italian secular songs, by Hassler, Giovanelli, Quagliati, Soriano, G. Gabrieli, Pozzo, Rore, Marenzio, Orlandini, Orazio Vecchi and Striggio; all the vocal prototypes were 'colored' in the German tradition of the time. Twelve *canzoni alla francese* or *Fugen* by Italians (Malvezzi, Maschera, G. Gabrieli, Mortaro, Bianchieri, Soriano, Brignoli and Orfeo Vecchi) also indicate the addition of keyboard ornamentation. Two *passamezzo–saltarello* sets and 12 galliards end the collection.

In the full title Schmid indicated that he had adapted and ornamented the music he included, and in the forword he stated that the work was intended not for experienced keyboard players but for his own students and other novices. He wrote that rather than reprint his father's book he had decided to produce something new and appropriate to the time. Indeed, this collection shows the strong influence of Italian composers on German music in the early 17th century. Though the German ornamentation which Schmid executed brilliantly remains, the appearance of original keyboard compositions, not based on vocal models, marks an important step in the development of instrumental music. One madrigal intabulation and two motet intabulations appear in Cantantibus organis, vi, vii, xii, ed. E. Kraus (Regensburg, 1961–3).

BIBLIOGRAPHY

Brown1

C. W. Young: *The Keyboard Tablatures of Bernhard Schmid, Father and Son* (diss., U. of Illinois, 1957)

——: 'Keyboard Music to 1600', *MD*, xvi (1962), 115

CLYDE WILLIAM YOUNG

Schmid, Erich (*b* Balsthal, canton of Solothurn, 1 Jan 1907). Swiss conductor and composer. He studied theory and composition with Bernhard Sekles at the Frankfurt Conservatory (1927–30), and in 1928 was awarded the Frankfurt Mozart Prize for composition. After further studies with Schoenberg at the Berlin Academy of Arts (1930–31), he worked for three years with South-west German Radio at Baden-Baden. He then returned to Switzerland and settled in Glarus, where he was music director until 1949. In 1949 he succeeded Andreae as chief conductor of the Tonhalle Orchestra and the mixed choir at Zurich. In 1957 he became principal conductor of the Beromünster RO, and in 1963 director of the Zurich male-voice choir and the conducting classes at the Basle Academy. He has toured elsewhere in Europe, and appeared frequently in London from the 1960s, especially as a conductor of BBC concerts. He became principal guest conductor of the CBSO in 1979. A staunch champion of contemporary music, he was for many years president of the Zurich branch of the ISCM, and published studies of Schoenberg's quartets (*SMz*, lxxiv, 1934, pp.1, 84, 155). His own compositions use a post-Schoenberg idiom and mainly comprise chamber and piano music, songs (including *Rilke-Suite* and *Michelangelo-Gesänge*), unaccompanied choruses and an orchestral arrangement of Debussy's *Six épigraphes antiques*.

BIBLIOGRAPHY

E. Schmid: 'Selbsporträt', *Musik der Zeit*, x (1955), 41

FRITZ MUGGLER

Schmid, Ernst Fritz (*b* Tübingen, 7 March 1904; *d* Augsburg, 20 Jan 1960). German musicologist. After studying biology for a short time, Schmid studied the violin, the viola and the viola d'amore at the Munich Academy (1924–7). He also studied music theory and orchestral conducting privately, and musicology with Sandberger at the University of Munich. After graduating from the academy he was employed as a violist in the Düsseldorf city orchestra (1927–8), and then (1927–9) studied musicology at the universities of Freiburg (with Gurlitt), Tübingen (with Karl Hasse) and Vienna (with Fischer, Haas, Orel and Lach). He took the doctorate at Tübingen in 1929 with a dissertation on C. P. E. Bach and his chamber music. He worked as a freelance conductor and musicologist in Vienna until 1934, when he completed his *Habilitation* as a *Privatdozent* in musicology at Graz University, with a book on the background to Haydn. In 1935 he was appointed a professor at Tübingen University, where he also became conductor of the university orchestra and founded the Schwäbisches Landesmusikarchiv.

In 1937 he left the state system and worked as a private academic in Mainfranken, which became his base for research trips on behalf of the Haydn scholar Anthony van Hoboken. He was also commissioned by the city of Augsburg to do intensive research on the city's music history. After war service he worked as a freelance musicologist and conductor at Ottobeuren and elsewhere (1945–8) and then moved to Augsburg as a music critic. There he founded the Mozartgemeinde (1948) and the German Mozartgesellschaft (1951), of which he was president until 1957, and was a member of the Bavarian Academy of Sciences. In 1954 he was appointed academic director of the Neue Mozart Ausgabe where he was notably successful in clarifying details of source materials and in organizing the Augsburg archives.

His particular interests were Mozart's Swabian fore-runners and the stylistic connections between Viennese Baroque and Classical music (with special reference to the key figure of Gottfried van Swieten). Gerstenberg (1961), writing of Schmid's work in this field, thought his elucidation of these connections was his major achievement as a historian. His Haydn studies were the result of thorough archival research; he also did research on Haydn's predecessor at Eisenstadt, Gregor Joseph Werner. His greatest discovery (1933) was of the private music collection of Emperor Franz II in Graz, a library of 10,000 publications and manuscripts from 18th- and early 19th-century Vienna (now in the Nationalbibliothek, Vienna). Another of Schmid's achievements was to demonstrate conclusively that the so-called 'Kindersymphonie' was written by Leopold Mozart, not Joseph Haydn.

WRITINGS

Carl Philipp Emanuel Bach und seine Kammermusik (diss., U. of Tübingen, 1929; Kassel, 1931)
'Joseph Haydn und die Flötenuhr', ZMw, xiv (1931–2), 193
'Joseph Haydn und C. Ph. E. Bach', ZMw, xiv (1931–2), 299
'Beethovens Bachkenntnis', NBJb, v (1933), 64
Joseph Haydn: ein Buch von Vorfahren und Heimat des Meisters (Habilitationsschrift, U. of Graz, 1934; Kassel, 1934)
Wolfgang Amadeus Mozart (Lübeck, 1934, 3/1955)
Die Orgeln der Abtei Amorbach (Buchen, 1938)
'Hans Leo Hassler und seine Brüder', Zeitschrift des Historischen Vereins für Schwaben, liv (1941), 60–212
'Mozart und das geistliche Augsburg', Zeitschrift des Historischen Vereins für Schwaben, lv–lvi (Augsburg, 1942–3), 40–202
Ein schwäbisches Mozartbuch (Lorch and Stuttgart, 1948)
'Mozarts Urheimat', Merian: das Monatsheft der Städte und Landschaften, i (Augsburg and Hamburg, 1948), 34
'Zu Mozarts Leipziger Bacherlebnis', ZfM, Jg.111 (1950), 297
'Ein neues Autograph zu KV 265', MJb 1950, 10
'Aus Mozarts schwäbischer Sippe', MJb 1950, 90
'Nachkommenliste von David I. Mozart bis auf die Generation Wolfgang Amadeus Mozarts', MJb 1950, 128
'Leopold Mozart und die Kindersinfonie', MJb 1951, 69; MJb 1952, 117
'Der Mozart-Freund Joseph Bullinger', MJb 1952, 17
'Gottfried van Swieten als Komponist', MJb 1953, 15
Musik am Hofe der Fürsten von Löwenstein-Wertheim-Rosenberg 1720–1750 (Würzburg, 1953)
'August Clemens Graf Hatzfeld', MJb 1954, 14
'Leopold Mozart', Lebensbilder aus dem Bayerischen Schwaben, iii (Munich, 1954), 346
'Auf Mozarts Spuren in Italien', MJb 1955, 17–48
'Joseph Haydns Jugendliebe', Festschrift Wilhelm Fischer (Innsbruck, 1956), 109
'Mozart and Haydn', MQ, xlii (1956), 145
'Neue Quellen zu Werken Mozarts', MJb 1956, 35
'Schicksale einer Mozart-Handschrift', MJb 1957, 43
'Mozart und Monsigny', MJb 1957, 57
'Zur Entstehungszeit von Mozarts italienischen Sinfonien', MJb 1958, 71
'Haydns Oratorium Il Ritorno di Tobia', AMw, xvi (1959), 292
Musik an den schwäbischen Zollernhöfen der Renaissance (Kassel, 1962)
'Die Privatmusiksammlung des Kaisers Franz II. und ihre Wiederentdeckung in Graz im Jahre 1933', ÖMz, xxv (1970), 596

EDITIONS

W. A. Mozart: Werke für 2 Klaviere, Neue Ausgabe sämtlicher Werke, ix/24/1 (Kassel, 1955); Quintette mit Bläsern, viii/19/2 (Kassel, 1958)
J. Haydn: Il ritorno di Tobia, Werke, xxviii/1, pts.1–2 (Munich, 1963)

BIBLIOGRAPHY

W. Fischer: Ernst Fritz Schmid zum Gedächtnis, W. A. Mozart: Neue Ausgabe sämtlicher Werke, suppl. vol. (Kassel, 1960)
W. Fischer and others, eds.: In memoriam Ernst Fritz Schmid, 1904–1960: ein Gedenkblatt für seine Angehörigen und Freunde (Recklinghausen, 1961) [incl. tributes by Fischer, W. Gerstenberg and L. Nowak, and list of publications, 23–42]
Obituary: H. F. Deininger, Zeitschrift des Historischen Vereins für Schwaben, lxii–lxiii (1962), 547; J. P. Larsen, Mf, xiii (1960), 129; W. Plath, Musica, xiv (1960), 128

RUDOLF KLEIN

Schmid [Schmidt], Ferdinand (b c1694; d Vienna, 10 Aug 1756). Austrian composer. After his musical train-

ing, probably in Vienna, he became regens chori at the church of St Dorothea, probably as successor to Mathias Timmer, and then at the Augustine church. He was also appointed in 1743 Kapellmeister at the shrine of Maria Pötsch in St Stephen's Cathedral (maestro di cappella della madonna di S Steffano, or second maestro di cappella). Reutter, the first cathedral maestro, wanted to thwart his nomination to this post, but Schmid was nevertheless appointed since the city felt indebted to his family (in 1724 his father-in-law had donated a new organ to the cathedral). As a composer of church music Schmid was not only diligent but also very successful. Innumerable minor sacred works are to be found in the archives of Austrian monasteries and are known to have been performed frequently well into the second half of the 18th century. His church music varies a great deal in style. Many melodic incipits give evidence of a still Baroque training while other works are clearly by a composer well versed in the galant style; on the one side Reutter may have had a strong influence on Schmid, but other works are more in the style of Holzbauer. Of the same generation as such composers as Giessel, Pachschmidt, Werndle and Tuma, he expressed as clearly as they did in his so-called 'Credo masses' (where the repeated exclamation 'Credo' helps create a rounded form) that he belonged to the Viennese school. The fact that he developed many of his melodies in the manner of folk music may have been one reason why Schmid's works so long enjoyed popularity in most parts of Austria. Despite Schmid's industry as composer, teacher and Kapellmeister, he died in poverty.

WORKS

(principal sources A–H, KN, Wd, Wgm, Wn, Wps, Ws, Wsp)
14 masses, C, vv, orch, incl. Sancti Eliae, Sancti Ferdinandi, Rosa mystica
14 requiems
27 Litaniae Lauretanae
2 cantatas: Hirten, lasst die Heerde; Ach Mensch, thu schauen an
12 Regina coeli; 11 Alma Redemptoris; 11 Ave regina; 52 Salve regina; 9 Sub tuum praesidium; 3 Parce mihi Domine [motetti pro defunctis]; 4 Miserere; Motet [recit, Haec est illa; aria, Maria coeli gloria]
Offertorium de Resurrectione
Many Latin motets on diverse texts: Benedicite, Estote, Date, Magna et mirabilia, Te invocamus, Salve sponsa, Pulsate, Eja gentes, Quis non laudet, Laetamini
Vesper psalms: 3 Dixit Dominus; Beatus vir; Confitebor; Lauda Jerusalem; 2 Laetatus sum; Nisi Dominus; Laudate pueri; 2 Magnificat

BIBLIOGRAPHY

EitnerQ; GerberL
C. F. Pohl: Joseph Haydn, i (Berlin, 1875), 40f, 49
C. Rouland: Katalog des Musik-Archiv der St. Peterskirche in Wien (Vienna, 1908), 13
W. Pauker: 'Der Bildhauer und Ing. M. Steinl', Jb des Stiftes Klosterneuburg, ii (Vienna and Leipzig, 1909), 315
R. Haas: Wiener Musiker vor und um Beethoven (Vienna, 1927), 10
G. Reichert: Zur Geschichte der Wiener Messkomposition in der 1. Hälfte des 18. Jahrhunderts (diss., U. of Vienna, 1935)
H. Brunner: Die Kantorei bei St. Stephan in Wien (Vienna, 1948), 19, 55
L. Nowak: Joseph Haydn (Vienna, 1951), 40ff, 538
G. Reichert: 'Mozart's "Credo-Messe" und ihre Vorläufer', MJb 1955, 134

EVA BADURA-SKODA

Schmid, Heinrich Kaspar (b Landau an der Isar, Bavaria, 11 Sept 1874; d Munich, 8 Jan 1953). German composer. He was a choirboy at Regensburg Cathedral from 1884 to 1889; later he studied at the Munich Academy of Music, where he was a pupil of Ludwig Thuille (1899–1903). His first teaching position was at the National Conservatory in Athens. He returned to teach at the Academy in Munich in 1905, and was made professor in 1919. In 1921 he became director of the Karlsruhe Conservatory; he held a similar position at the Augsburg Conservatory from 1924 to 1932. Becoming increasingly blind, Schmid spent the last two decades of his life in the small town of Geiselbullach. Along with August Reuss and others who studied with Thuille, he belonged to the 'Munich School'; his compositions are unabashedly romantic. Between such works as the violin sonatas (no.1, 1920; no.2, 1939) there is little change in musical style and, in these particular works, Brahms is an obvious model. Schmid's compositions are almost exclusively in the smaller genres of vocal and instrumental music. The songs and works for chorus are deliberately simple, after the manner of traditional Bavarian music.

WORKS
(selective list)

Finden und Meiden, op.41 (folksong play, 2 scenes, F. Baumbach)

Choral music incl. Altenglische Schlummerlied, op.6, female chorus, chamber orch; Weihnachtsgesänge, op.14, unison chorus, insts; Lieder eines Dorfpoeten, op.40 (F. P. Küsten), male chorus 4vv; Missa 'Dona nobis pacem', op.63, chorus (1928); Psalter und Harfe, op.65 (after K. J. P. Spitta), female chorus, insts (1928); Mass, d, op.72, chorus, orch, org (1929); Von deutscher Art, op.85, male chorus, pf (1932); Tanzbilder aus unserer Zeit, op.87, male chorus, dance ens; Missa Barbara, D, op.88, chorus, org (1932); Huldigung an Walter von der Vogelweide, chorus, orch

Other vocal works incl. Klang um Klang, op.32a (Eichendorff), S/T, orch; 4 Songs from the Vilsbiburger Marienfestspiel, op.42 (B. Rauch); Abendfeier, op.43, A, fl, cl, bn, hn, pf; 17 song sets

Inst pieces incl. Sonatina, op.3, pf; Variations on 'Will meine junge Aepfel haben', op.5, pf; Waldgang, op.16, pf (1912); Str Qt, G, op.26; Sonata, a, op.27, vn, pf (1920); Wind Qt, B♭, op.28 (1919); Paraphrase on a Theme of Liszt, op.30, 2 pf (1920); 5 Tongedichte, op.34, wind qnt, pf (1920); Pf Trio, d, op.35 (1920); Bayrische Ländler, op.36, pf/pf duet (1921); Sonata, g, op.46, vc, pf; Meditation, op.57, vn, orch; Sonata, op.60, vn, org; Turmmusik, op.105, 6 tpt/3 tpt, 3 trbn, timp ad lib (1940); Sonata, A, op.106, fl/vn, pf (1939); Qt, op.107, 4 rec/str (1942); other pf and org pieces

Principal publishers: Böhm, Breitkopf & Härtel, Schott

BIBLIOGRAPHY

H. Roth: *Heinrich Kaspar Schmid* (Munich, 1921)

A. Würz: ' "Um mich ist Heimat": in memoriam Heinrich Kaspar Schmid', *NZM*, Jg.114 (1953), 85

W. Zentner: 'In memoriam Heinrich Kaspar Schmid', *Musica*, vii (1953), 74

'Schmid, Heinrich Kaspar', *Moser Musik-Lexikon* (Hamburg, 4/1955), ii, 1119

WILLIAM D. GUDGER

Schmid [Schmidt], **Johann Michael** (*b* Pernartitz, Bohemia, *c*1720; *d* Mainz, 19 Dec 1792). German composer. From 1736 to 1740 he was a musician at the Kleinheubach court of Prince Löwenstein-Wertheim-Rosenberg. From 1742 he served as valet and from 1745 as director of the court orchestra for the Prince-Bishop of Augsburg. On 1 April 1756 he succeeded his countryman Zach as court Kapellmeister in Mainz. He gave up this post to Righini in 1787 but remained at full salary, obliged only to take part occasionally in performances of the court orchestra. Haydn and Leopold Mozart were both acquainted with him.

According to contemporary accounts Schmid was an active composer, but few of his works are extant. Two symphonies survive (in *D-HR*), but his output seems to have centred on church music: a mass and nine smaller pieces (all in *MZsch*) show him to have been a skilful composer of average talent whose style developed from post-Baroque to early Classical. These works show a fluent and sometimes even dashing melodic invention which goes beyond the usual method at that time of composing on small motifs. He seems to have given up composition by 1780. His other works, now lost,

included a melodrama *Regina Saba Salomonis hospita* (1753) and the oratorios *Tod und Begräbnis Jesu* (1761), *Die Abnehmung Jesu Christi vom Kreuz* (1766), *Gephte* (1767, 1768), *Die heilige Helena auf dem Calvari Berg* (1769, 1772) and *Das Leiden Jesu Christi* (1775, 1777).

BIBLIOGRAPHY

P. von Stetten: *Kunst-, Gewerb- und Handwerks- Geschichte der Reichs-Stadt Augsburg* (Augsburg, 1779)

F. Collignon: 'Aus dem Leben des kurtrierischen Kapellmeisters Pietro Pompeo Sales', *Festausgabe Coblenzer General-Anzeiger*, cxl (20–21 June 1925), 17

E. F. Schmid: *Musik am Hofe der Fürsten von Löwenstein-Wertheim-Rosenberg* (Würzburg, 1953)

A. Layer: 'Zur Biographie des Augsburger und Mainzer Hofkapellmeister Johann Michael Schmidt', *Mainzer Zeitschrift*, liii (1958), 59

A. Gottron: *Mainzer Musikgeschichte von 1500 bis 1800* (Mainz, 1959)

G. Haberkamp: *Die Musikhandschriften der Fürstlich Oettingen-Wallerstein'schen Bibliothek Schloss Harburg* (Munich, 1976)

HUBERT UNVERRICHT

Schmidl, Carlo (*b* Trieste, 7 Oct 1859; *d* Trieste, 7 Oct 1943). Italian music publisher and writer on music. After beginning to study the violin with his father, an orchestral conductor, he joined the Trieste music publishing firm Vicentini (1872–89) and then founded his own firm (Carlo Schmidl & Co.), which absorbed Vicentini in the following year and was bought by Ricordi in 1902; Schmidl continued to run the Leipzig branch of Ricordi that he had established (1901–6). His firm published a considerable amount of early and contemporary Italian music, including that of Smareglia, Respighi and Busoni, and organized chamber concerts and celebrity recitals (with performances by Ysaÿe, Sarasate and Busoni). Besides two biographies (*Robert Schumann*, Trieste, 1890; *G. S. Mayr*, Trieste, 1901), he wrote the *Dizionario universale dei musicisti* (Milan, 1887–9, suppl. 1938, 3/1938), which remains the best general biographical source for Italian musicians. It gives lists of works (including republications) and dates of first performances, and has particularly valuable articles on Italian literary figures and their relationship to music. Schmidl's collection of music manuscripts and rare editions passed to the Trieste Verdi Museum, which he organized from 1922 to his death.

Schmidlin [Schmidli], **Johannes** (*b* Zurich, 22 May 1722; *d* Wetzikon, 5 Nov 1772). Swiss composer and minister. He trained as a Protestant minister at the Collegium Carolinum in Zurich, where he was a member of the collegium musicum from 1734 and probably studied music under J. C. Bachofen. After being ordained in 1743 he was curate in Dietlikon (1744–54) and minister in Wetzikon-Seegräben (1754–72). In 1755 he founded a choral society in Wetzikon to promote the singing of psalms in church; it lasted until 1825. In 1769 he also established a collegium musicum there. His numerous collections of Pietistic songs, cantatas and odes were a rich source of vocal music for many decades; beginning with his *Singendes und spielendes Vergnügen reiner Andacht* (1752) they were sung both in collegia and in private homes throughout German-speaking Switzerland. Schmidlin also made an important contribution to the development of the solo song, particularly in the patriotic *Schweizerlieder* of 1769; these songs with figured bass show influences of the Berlin lied school in their conscious striving for simplicity, although tempered by an indifferent talent.

Three of his sacred songs are in the present hymnbook of the Evangelical Reformed Church in Switzerland.

WORKS

(all published in Zurich unless otherwise stated)

Lieder collections: [203] Singendes und spielendes Vergnügen reiner Andacht (1752); [85] Geistliche Lieder (1758), suppl. to Singendes und spielendes Vergnügen; Musicalisch-wochentliche Vergnügungen, i–iii (1758–60) [52 pieces in each]; Hrn. Prof. Gellerts [50] geistliche Oden und Lieder (1761); 100 geistliche Lieder (1764); Hrn. Hofprediger Crammers [24] geistliche Oden und Lieder (1767); Geistliche Lieder mit Choral-Melodien (1767, 12/1827); [41] Schweizerlieder mit Melodien, 1–2vv (J. C. Lavater) (Berne, 1769), arr. 4vv by J. H. Egli (1775); J. C. Lavaters christliches Handbüchlein (1769); Lieder zum Gebrauche des Waisenhauses (Lavater) (1772); [52] Musikalisch-wöchentliche Ergetzungen (1773); Musicalisch-wöchentliche Belustigungen in weltliche Liedern (1775)

Other: Hymni oder Lob-Gesänge auf Gott, 2 Tr, A, B, org (1758); Die Tages-Zeiten (F. W. Zachariä), 4 cantatas (1762); Deutliche Anleitung zum gründlichen Singen der Psalmen (1767); Die Psalmen Davids, 4vv (1771); c10 other cantatas and sacred lieder pubd separately

BIBLIOGRAPHY

H. J. Holzhalb: *Supplement zu dem . . . schweizerischen Lexicon*, v (Zug, 1791) [incl. list of works]

F. Meier: *Geschichte der Gemeinde Wetzikon* (Zurich, 1881)

H. Weber: 'J. Schmidlin und seiner geistlicher Volksgesang', *Der evangelische Kirchenchor*, i (1897), 36

A. Nef: *Das Lied in der deutschen Schweiz Ende des 18. und Anfang des 19. Jahrhunderts* (Zurich, 1909)

T. Goldschmid: *Schweizer Gesang-Bücher früherer Zeiten* (Zurich, 1917)

E. Refardt: *Historich-biographisches Musikerlexikon der Schweiz* (Leipzig and Zurich, 1928) [incl. list of works]

JÜRG STENZL

Schmidt, Arthur P. (*b* Altona, Germany, 1 April 1846; *d* Boston, 5 May 1921). American music publisher. He opened a music shop in 1876 in Boston, and began publishing music in that year; after 13 years, he sold his retail business. Schmidt was notable as a supporter of American composers; he was the first American publisher to publish a symphony by a native American (John Knowles Paine's *Spring Symphony*, 1880), and he brought out works by other New England composers such as H. H. A. Beach, George Chadwick and Arthur Foote, as well as almost the entire body of compositions by Edward MacDowell. In 1960 the Arthur P. Schmidt Company was acquired by Summy-Birchard of Chicago.

BIBLIOGRAPHY

H. Dichter and E. Shapiro: *Early American Sheet Music* (New York, 1941)

W. THOMAS MARROCCO, MARK JACOBS

Schmidt, Bernhard. (1) *See* SCHMID, BERNHARD (i).

(2) *See* SMITH, 'FATHER'.

Schmidt, Franz (*b* Pressburg, 22 Dec 1874; *d* Perchtoldsdorf, nr. Vienna, 11 Feb 1939). Austrian composer, conductor, pianist and cellist. He received his first instruction in music in Pressburg (now Bratislava) from Mader, the cathedral organist; as a child he heard Liszt play. In 1888 the Schmidt family moved to Vienna, where financial difficulties forced the boy, by then an excellent pianist, to earn a living in dancing schools. He went to Leschetizky for piano lessons and in 1890 entered the Vienna Conservatory; there he was a pupil of Bruckner and Fuchs for a short while, and he studied the cello with Hellmesberger. From 1896 to 1911 he was a cellist in the Vienna Court Opera orchestra; he also taught the instrument at the conservatory of the Gesellschaft der Musikfreunde (1901–8). In 1914 he was appointed professor of the piano at the Vienna Staatsakademie, where he took over instruction in counterpoint and composition in 1922. He directed the Staatsakademie from 1925 to 1927 and then succeeded Marx as director of the Musikhochschule (1927–31). During the long period he spent as a teacher, organizer and performer, he often showed great strength in overcoming his naturally poor health. On his 60th birthday he received an honorary doctorate from Vienna University. He retired in 1937 and shortly before his death was awarded the Beethoven Prize of the Prussian Academy, Berlin. In 1951 his second wife, Margarethe, founded a Franz Schmidt-Gemeinde.

Schmidt began composing relatively late. He destroyed most of his juvenilia, including two piano sonatas: the surviving three (originally four) *Phantasiestücke nach ungarischen Nationalmelodien* (1892) are scarcely representative. His mature works show sensitive melodic invention, revealing Slovak and Hungarian features alongside Austrian elements, and a rich and original harmonic style. He retained little from his formal training: it is said that he once had his pupils explain the harmonic structure of one of his pieces to establish that he could do without protracted study. His predilection for a very full orchestral sound – as in the stylized gypsy music of the intermezzo to the opera *Notre Dame*, a piece that brought him international fame – is sometimes reminiscent of Bruckner, Liszt, Mahler or Reger. Schmidt was particularly close to Reger in his late chamber and organ music. At the same time he drew from Austrian Baroque style, and his music was influenced peripherally by Schoenberg, Debussy and Hindemith.

It was as a symphonist that Schmidt made his name. He combined the Viennese Classical tradition with Brahmsian variation technique and with Liszt's single-movement form. His handling of variation form is well displayed in the *Variationen über ein Husarenlied*, which, after Reger's cycles, is one of the finest such works of the period. The Fourth Symphony well exemplifies his ramified thematic working. In the chamber music, contemplative, romantic, retrospective and idyllic qualities predominate, although the Second Quartet is more progressive. His solo and concertante works for piano left hand, written for Paul Wittgenstein, were arranged with Schmidt's approval for two hands by his pupil Wührer. Again like Reger, Schmidt composed important pieces for the organ, notably the *Phantasie und Fuge* in D and the Chaconne in C♯ minor. The only vocal works he completed were two operas and an oratorio. The operas are quite uncharacteristic in their *verismo* style; *Notre Dame* had some initial success, but *Fredigundis* failed. On the other hand, *Das Buch mit sieben Siegeln*, a cohesive setting of the Apocalypse, has had a part in sustaining Schmidt's posthumous reputation.

WORKS

VOCAL

Notre Dame (opera, 2, after Hugo), 1902–4
Fredigundis (opera, 3, after F. Dahn), 1916–21
Das Buch mit sieben Siegeln (oratorio, Apocalypse), 1935–7
Deutsche Auferstehung, cantata, 1938–9, inc.

ORCHESTRAL AND CHAMBER

Sym. no.1, E, 1896–9; Sym. no.2, E♭, 1911–13; Konzertante Variationen über ein Thema von Beethoven, pf left hand, orch, 1923; Sym. no.3, A, 1927–8; Variationen über ein Husarenlied, 1930–31; Sym. no.4, C, 1932–3; Pf Conc., E♭, left hand, 1934; Fuga solemnis, 16 wind, org, timp, 1937
3 kleine Phantasiestücke nach ungarischen Nationalmelodien, vc, pf, 1892; Str Qt, A, 1925; Pf Qnt, G, 1926; Str Qt, G, 1929; Qnt, B♭, cl, pf qt, 1932; Qnt, A, cl, pf qt, 1938

KEYBOARD

Org: Variationen und Fuge über ein eigenes Thema, D, n.d.; Königsfanfaren, 1916, 1924, 1925; Phantasie und Fuge, D, 1923–4;

Toccata, C, 1924; Präludium und Fuge, E♭, 1924; Chaconne, c♯, 1925; 4 kleine Choralvorspiele, 1926; Fuge, F, 1927; Präludium und Fuge, E♭, 1927; 4 kleine Präludien und Fugen, 1928; Choralvorspiel zu Haydns 'Gott erhalte', wind ad lib, 1933; Choralvorspiel 'Der Heiland ist erstanden', 1934; Toccata und Fuge, A♭, 1935

Pf: 2 sonatas, c1889–90, destroyed; Toccata, d, left hand, 1938; several arrs.

Principal publishers: Doblinger, Österreichischer Bundesverlag, Universal

BIBLIOGRAPHY

J. Korngold: *Deutsches Opernschaffen der Gegenwart* (Vienna and Leipzig, 1922)
A. Liess: *Franz Schmidt: sein Leben und Schaffen* (Graz, 1951)
C. Nemeth: *Franz Schmidt: ein Meister nach Brahms und Bruckner* (Vienna, 1957)
R. Scholz: *Franz Schmidt als Orgelkomponist* (Vienna, 1971)
N. Tschulik: *Franz Schmidt* (Vienna, 1972)
H. Herrmann: 'Franz Schmidts Harmonik', *ÖMz*, xxix (1974), 534
K. Trötzmüller: 'Editionsprobleme bei Franz Schmidt', *ÖMz*, xxix (1974), 544

HELMUT WIRTH

Schmidt, Gustav (*b* Weimar, 1 Sept 1816; *d* Darmstadt, 11 Feb 1882). German conductor and composer. He studied in Weimar under Hummel, Eberwein and Lobe, and in Leipzig with Mendelssohn. He conducted at the theatre in Brünn (now Brno) from 1841 to 1844, then in Würzburg (1845), Frankfurt (1846), Wiesbaden (1849), Frankfurt (1851–61), Leipzig (1864–76) and Mainz. He finally became court Kapellmeister in Darmstadt in 1876. His operas, for which he wrote his own texts, include the successful *Prinz Eugen* (performed in Frankfurt, 1847), *Weibertreue* (or *Die Weiber von Weinsberg*, Weimar, 1858 under Liszt), and the less popular *La Réole* (Breslau, 1863) and *Alibi* (Weimar, 1880). Much admired as a conductor, he was an early champion of Wagner and introduced *Tannhäuser* and *Lohengrin* to Frankfurt; he also sought to make Berlioz's music better known in Germany. Liszt took an interest in his plan for a conference of Kapellmeisters to increase both their artistic standing in music and at the same time their musical standards. Schmidt also wrote popular songs and choruses.

JOHN WARRACK

Schmidt, Harvey (Lester) (*b* Dallas, 12 Sept 1929). American composer. He studied and wrote revues at the University of Texas, before making his New York début as a composer with *The Fantasticks* (3 May 1960); by the mid-1970s this had become the longest-running American musical. His other stage works include *110 in the Shade* (1963) and *I Do! I Do!* (1971).

See also MUSICAL COMEDY.

Schmidt, Johann Christoph (i) (*b* Hohnstein, nr. Pirna, 6 Aug 1664; *d* Dresden, 13 April 1728). German composer. Son of the Hohnstein Kantor Johann Christian Schmidt (*d* 1690), he became a chorister in 1676 at the court chapel in Dresden where, at the request of the elector Johann Georg III, he was taught by Christoph Bernhard. He later became an instrumentalist in the court orchestra. In 1687 he was appointed master of the choristers and in 1692 second organist. He went to study in Italy in 1694, with support from the elector, and in 1696, on the recommendation of N. A. Strungk, the Dresden court Kapellmeister, became his deputy Kapellmeister and chamber organist. Soon after, Strungk left for Leipzig and Schmidt was appointed principal Kapellmeister on 19 June 1698. During the rule of August the Strong (1694–1733) the court Kapelle served both as the Saxon electoral and Polish royal orchestra, and had extensive duties in Dresden,

Kraków and Warsaw; Schmidt was its director and as Kapellmeister also had responsibility for the Protestant church music at court. In addition, he was director of the Catholic church music until 1717, when he gave that task to J. D. Heinichen. During Schmidt's term as director the Dresden orchestra became one of the most renowned in Europe due to its many distinguished players, who around 1719 included J. B. Volumier, J. G. Pisendel, F. M. Veracini, Christoph Pezold, Pantaleon Hebenstreit, S. L. Weiss, J. D. Zelenka, P. G. Buffardin and J. C. Richter.

In 1719 Schmidt, who had been made Oberkapellmeister in 1717, wrote a French divertissement *Les quatre saisons* in a sequence of recitatives, arias, concerted numbers and choruses, suited to the talents of the dilettantes who performed it on 23 September as part of a Festival of Venus on the marriage of Prince Friedrich August of Saxony to the Archduchess Maria Josepha of Austria. This work, the central event in a typical Dresden court festival of August the Strong's reign, followed the tradition of the 17th-century *opéra-ballet*. Schmidt was noted by Hiller as a solid composer with a good grasp of counterpoint; but although he lacked exceptional artistic gifts he was not a 'dry' or 'infertile' composer, as Hiller wrote. J. S. Bach copied out his motet *Auf Gott hoffe ich*. He ranks as a minor master of his time, clearly handling the musical resources and stylistic conventions of Dresden high Baroque with competence. From 1717 Schmidt and Heinichen ranked equally as Kapellmeisters of church and chamber music respectively, and divided the orchestral work between them; after Schmidt's death Heinichen took over the Protestant church music at the court. Mattheson printed a letter from Schmidt, dated 28 July 1718, in his *Critica musica* (vii, 1722, p.266), dealing with solmization. Schmidt acted as intermediary in the controversy over the old method, suggesting that solmization should be retained for vocal music but advocating the use of the two 'French modes, major and minor' for the 'stylo moderno'. His pupils included C. G. Schröter, C. H. Graun and Melchior Hofmann.

His brother Johann Wolfgang Schmidt (*b* Hohnstein, 20 Nov 1677; *d* Dresden, 5 April 1744) served as copyist at the Dresden court from 1709 and was organist for the Protestant church music there from 1719.

WORKS

SACRED VOCAL

4 masses, D-B, Bds
Motets: Auf Gott hoffe ich, 4vv, 4 tpt, timp, 2 fl, 2 vn, 2 vc, bn, org, theorbo; Bonum est confiteri Domino, A, 2 vn, 2 vc, bn, org, 26 Nov 1696; Wo ist solch ein Gott wie du bist, 10vv, 2 vn, 2 vc, org, 1701; motet, vv: all B
Cantatas: ?lost: Gott, du bleibest doch mein Gott, 4-5vv, insts; Labe mich durch deines Mundes Kuss, S, org, insts; Lobe den Herrn, meine Seele, 4-5vv, insts; Mein Herz ist bereit, T, org, insts; Schwing dich auf zu deinen Gott, 4-5vv, insts; Sie ist fest gegründet auf den heiligen Bergen, 8vv, org, insts; Zion spricht: der Herr hat mich verlassen, T, B, org, str

OTHER WORKS

Les quatre saisons (divertissement, Poisson), solo vv, chorus, 4 tpt, timp, ob, str, bc, Dresden, Grosser Garten, 23 Sept 1719, *Dlb*; airs, *Dlb*
Latona in Delo (opera seria), *Bds*
4 ov.-suites, *Dlb*

BIBLIOGRAPHY

Kurtze, doch ausführliche Beschreibung des sogenannten Venus-Fests (Dresden, 1719)
J. A. Hiller: *Lebensbeschreibungen berühmter Musikgelehrter und Tonkünstler*, i (Leipzig, 1784), 139
M. Fürstenau: *Beiträge zur Geschichte der königlich sächsischen musikalischen Kapelle* (Dresden, 1849)
——: *Zur Geschichte der Musik und des Theaters am Hofe zu Dresden*, i (Dresden, 1861/*R*1971)

R. Eitner: 'Schmidt, Johann Christoph', *ADB*
S. Kümmerle: *Encyklopädie der evangelischen Kirchenmusik*, iii (Gütersloh, 1894/*R*1974)
R. Vollhardt: *Geschichte der Cantoren und Organisten im Königreich Sachsen* (Berlin, 1899)
R. Engländer: 'Die Musik unter August dem Starken', *Dresdner Anzeiger*, x/28 (11 July 1933) [Wissenschaftliche Beilage]
H. Schnoor: *Dresden – 400 Jahre deutsche Musikkultur* (Dresden, 1948)
I. Becker-Glauch: *Die Bedeutung der Musik für die Dresdner Hoffeste* (Kassel and Basle, 1951)

DIETER HÄRTWIG

Schmidt, Johann Christoph (ii). *See* SMITH, JOHN CHRISTOPHER.

Schmidt, Johann Michael (i) (*b* Meiningen, 16 Jan 1728; *d* Marktbreit, Lower Franconia, 8 April 1799). German theologian and writer on music. From 1749 he attended Leipzig University and probably studied music with J. S. Bach. About 1754 he was in Naumburg, and in 1762 he was made rector of the Lateinschule in Marktbreit where in 1788 he became deputy pastor and assessor of the prince's consistory. He published a widely acclaimed *Musico-theologia, oder Erbauliche Anwendung musicalischer Wahrheiten* (Bayreuth and Hof, 1754), directed against certain Enlightenment doctrines; the work is noteworthy for its date in containing several laudatory references to Bach, and reveals an unusual degree of familiarity with his works. Schmidt has also been suggested as the recipient of Bach's seven-part *Faber-Kanon* (BWV1078).

BIBLIOGRAPHY
P. Spitta: *Johann Sebastian Bach*, ii (Leipzig, 1880, 5/1962; Eng. trans., 1899/*R*1951)
H. Besch: *J. S. Bach: Frömmigkeit und Glaube* (Gütersloh, 1938, 2/1950)
F. Hamel: *J. S. Bach: Geistliche Welt* (Göttingen, 1951)
H. J. Schulze: 'J. S. Bachs Kanonwidmungen', *BJb*, liii (1957), 82

Schmidt, Johann Michael (ii) (*b* Nuremberg, 10 or 11 May 1741; *d* Nuremberg, buried 21 March 1793). German music publisher and composer, son of and successor to BALTHASAR SCHMID.

Schmidt, Johann Michael (iii). *See* SCHMID, JOHANN MICHAEL.

Schmidt, Johann Philipp Samuel (*b* Königsberg, 8 Sept 1779; *d* Berlin, 9 May 1853). German composer. He made some early appearances as a pianist, including in his own works, before studying law in Königsberg. He then travelled extensively in Germany, settling briefly in Berlin as a pupil of J. G. Naumann, and eventually returning to Berlin to work in a government post. At the same time he wrote songs for the *Liedertafel* founded there by Zelter and soon resumed his musical career, performing in public and writing essays on music as well as composing operas and other works. Of his operas, which are written in a light and melodically attractive post-Mozartian style, one of the most popular was *Das Fischermädchen* (1818), which was praised by Weber, among other things for its musical characterization, in an essay written before he conducted the Dresden première in 1818. Schmidt also wrote some church music, including two masses, and chamber music, and made many arrangements.

BIBLIOGRAPHY
G. Kaiser, ed.: *Sämtliche Schriften von Carl Maria von Weber* (Berlin and Leipzig, 1908), 305, 396 [incl. Weber's introduction to *Das Fischermädchen*]

D. Härtwig: 'Schmidt, Johann Philipp Samuel', *MGG*
S. Goslich: *Die deutsche romantische Oper* (Tutzing, 1975)

JOHN WARRACK

Schmidt, Nickel. *See* FABER, NICOLAUS (i).

Schmidt, Ole (*b* Copenhagen, 14 July 1928). Danish conductor and composer. After studying at the Royal Conservatory in Copenhagen he went to Kubelik and Celibidache for conducting lessons. He was conductor of the Royal Opera in Copenhagen and of the Hamburg SO (1970–71) before being appointed to the Danish Radio SO in 1971.

WORKS
Orch: 2 syms., 1955, 1958; Conc., pf, str, 1956; Pièce concertante, tpt, trbn, harp, pf, cel, perc, str, 1956; Sym. Fantasy and Fugue, accordion, orch, 1958; Pastel, 1961; Briol, 1962; Conc. no.2, accordion, wind, perc, 1963–4; Horn Conc., 1966; Vn Conc., 1971; Tuba Conc., 1975; Gui Conc., 1976
Chamber: Divertimento, pf qt, 1957; 5 str qts, 1962–77; Improvisation, pf, db, drums, 1961; Painting and Plugging, harp, str, pf, 1963; Rexallo, brass qnt, 1976
Stage works, incl. Feber (ballet), 1957; I det vilde West (ballet), 1961; Hvad en mand har brug for (incidental music, K. Rifbjerg), 1966; Et drommespil (incidental music, Strindberg), 1967; Udstilling (opera, J. Jensen, Rifbjerg), 1968

Schmidt, Peter. *See* FABRICIUS, PETRUS.

Schmidt-Görg, Joseph (*b* Rüdinghausen, Kreis Hörde, Westphalia, 19 March 1897). German musicologist. He studied musicology at Bonn University with Schiedermair and Anton Schmitz with physics and education as subsidiary subjects, took the doctorate at Bonn in 1926 with a dissertation on the masses of Clemens non Papa and in 1927 became an assistant at the newly established Beethoven Archive in Bonn. He completed his *Habilitation* in musical acoustics at Bonn with a dissertation on mean-tone temperament. He then became a lecturer in acoustics at Bonn University. In 1938 his lecturing privileges were extended to the entire faculty of musicology; in the same year he became *ausserplanmässiger Professor*, and from 1948 until his retirement in 1965, he held a full professorship. He became director of the Beethoven Archive in Bonn (1946), and editor of the new series of Veröffentlichungen des Beethovenhauses in Bonn (1951) and of the Beethoven collected edition, all of which posts he held until 1972.

Schmidt-Görg has specialized in musical acoustics and the history of music in the Middle Ages and the Renaissance, together with Gregorian chant and Byzantine music. Beethoven research forms a central feature of his work: by interpreting and cataloguing source materials he has made a notable contribution to biographical knowledge, especially of Beethoven's family.

WRITINGS
Die Messen des Clemens non Papa (diss., U. of Bonn, 1926; extracts in *ZMw*, ix (1926–7), 129)
Unbekannte Manuskripte zu Beethovens weltlicher und geistlicher Gesangsmusik (Bonn, 1928)
Die Mitteltontemperatur (Habilitationsschrift, U. of Bonn, 1930)
'Probleme und Methoden musikalischer Klangfarbenforschung', *ZMw*, xv (1932), 61
Katalog der Handschriften des Beethoven-Hauses und Beethoven-Archivs Bonn (Bonn, 1935)
Nicolas Gombert (Bonn, 1938/*R*1971)
'Die Acta Capitularia der Notre Dame-Kirche zu Kortrijk als musikgeschichtliche Quelle', *Vlaamsch jaarboek voor muziekgeschiedenis*, i (1939), 21–80

Musik der Gotik (Bonn, 1946)
'Musikgeschichtliches aus den ältesten Kapitelakten des Bonner Münsters', *Bonn und sein Münster* (Bonn, 1947), 177
Missa solemnis (Bonn, 1948)
Beethoven: dreizehn unbekannte Briefe an Josephine Gräfin Deym, geboren Brunsvik (Bonn, 1957)
Beethoven: die Geschichte seiner Familie (Bonn, 1964)
'Wasserzeichen in Beethoven-Briefen', *BeJb 1961–2*, 7–74
with H. Schmidt: *Ludwig van Beethoven* (Brunswick, 1969; Eng. trans., 1969–70)
ed.: *Des Bonner Bäckmeisters Gottfried Fischer Aufzeichnung über Beethovens Jugend* (Bonn and Munich, 1971)
'Verleger Verlegenheiten: ein besonderes Kapitel bei Beethoven'. *Festschrift für einen Verleger: Ludwig Strecker* (Mainz, 1973), 135
'Zur Struktur und Rhythmik der frühen Sequenzen', *Musicae scientiae collectanea: Festschrift Karl Gustav Fellerer* (Cologne, 1973), 512
'Die Wichtigkeit der Wasserzeichen für die Datierung von Beethoven-Briefen', *Beiträge zur Musikdokumentation: Franz Grasberger zum 60. Geburtstag* (Tutzing, 1975), 413

EDITIONS
C. *Porta: Missa tertii toni* (*1578*), Musica divina, v (Regensburg, 1950)
N. *Gombert: Opera omnia*, CMM, vi (1951–)
L. van *Beethoven: Drei Skizzenbücher zur Missa solemnis: ein Skizzenbuch aus den Jahren 1819/20*, Veröffentlichungen des Beethovenhauses in Bonn, new ser., i/34–6 (Bonn, 1952–68); *Ein Skizzenbuch zu den Diabelli-Variationen und zur Missa solemnis*, ibid, i/33 (Bonn, 1972); *Variationen für Klavier*, Sämtliche Werke, vii/5 (Munich, 1960); *Kadenzen zu Klavierkonzerten*, ibid, vii/7 (Munich, 1967)
Die Messe, Mw, xxx (1967; Eng. trans., 1968)

BIBLIOGRAPHY
Festschrift Joseph Schmidt-Görg zum 60. Geburtstag: gemeinsam mit seinen Kollegen, Schülern und Freunden im Auftrag des Beethovenhauses herausgegeben von Dagmar Weise (Bonn, 1957)
S. Kross and H. Schmidt, eds.: *Colloquium amicorum: Joseph Schmidt-Görg zum 70. Geburtstag* (Bonn, 1967) [includes complete list of publications]

HANS HEINRICH EGGEBRECHT

Schmidt-Isserstedt, Hans (*b* Berlin, 5 May 1900; *d* Holm-Holstein, nr. Hamburg, 28 May 1973). German conductor and composer. He studied in Berlin at the Musikhochschule and at the university where he wrote a dissertation on the Italian influences on instrumentation in Mozart's early operas. After engagements at various German theatres, he was appointed principal Kapellmeister at the Hamburg Staatsoper in 1935, and in 1943 opera director at the Deutsche Oper in Berlin, where he became general music director in 1944. He acquired a reputation as an exceptional orchestral trainer with the establishment of the North German Radio SO in Hamburg, which he directed from its foundation in 1945 until 1971, when he became its honorary conductor. With this orchestra he went to Paris and Edinburgh, the USSR and the USA. He was also principal conductor of the Stockholm PO (1955–64) and he appeared as a guest conductor with more than 120 orchestras in all the principal musical centres. He conducted memorable performances of *Le nozze di Figaro* at Glyndebourne in 1958, and of *Tristan und Isolde* at Covent Garden in 1962.

Schmidt-Isserstedt aimed at a transparent orchestral texture and strict rhythmic precision, rejecting all superfluous gestures and mannerisms. After World War II he became the advocate of Bartók, Stravinsky and Hindemith, whose music had long been outlawed in Germany. But his chief love was Mozart, whose works he conducted in a remarkably relaxed and delicate way. This is shown particularly by his recordings of *Idomeneo* and *La finta giardiniera*. He also recorded a complete cycle of Beethoven's symphonies. Schmidt-Isserstedt composed orchestral works, chamber music, lieder and dramatic music, including the opera *Hassan gewinnt*, first performed in Rostock in 1928.

HANS CHRISTOPH WORBS

Schmiedeknecht, Johann Matthäus (*b* Ülleben, nr. Gotha, 1660; *d* Gotha, April 1715). German composer and teacher. After working in Ichtershausen he became court Kantor in Gotha in 1685 and was a respected if not specially important music teacher. He had connections with the court Kapellmeisters Wolfgang Mylius and Christian Witt, and with the traditional musical institutions of Gotha, which were linked with the names of Pachelbel, Telemann and, in music education, Andreas Reyher. His *Tyrocinium musices, das ist Erster Anfang zur Singkunst* [or *Fundamente*] (Gotha, 1710) is related to Reyher's *Gothaer Schulmethodus*. Schmiedeknecht was an active representative of these traditions of music theory. His compositions, many of them in the traditional form of the motet for two choirs, show a marked personal touch in their rhythmic and dynamic subtlety. His motets for two choirs include *Da pacem Domine* (eight voices, now in *D-Bds*), *Kommt, ihr Engel und wieget* (six voices, in the Grossenlupnitz Church, Eisenach), *Der Herr segne dich* (two choirs with four voices, Grossenlupnitz Church), and *Ein Diener soll in Freud und Leid* (Gotha, 1696; four voices, with the second choir as an 'echo'). He also wrote many incidental pieces, such as funeral anthems. His compositions were far more widespread than lists in Thuringian Kantoreien suggest. His *Tyrocinium musices* is dedicated, following the model of the textbooks by Schneegass, Dedekind and others, to 'enthusiastic and music-loving youth'.

G. KRAFT

Schmieder, Wolfgang (*b* Bromberg, 29 May 1901). German music librarian. He studied at Heidelberg University under Kroyer and Moser (musicology), F. Panzer and F. von Waldberg (German philology and literature) and C. Neumann (art history); in 1927 he took his doctorate at Heidelberg with a dissertation on melodic construction in the lieder of Neidhart von Reuental. After serving as assistant lecturer in the musicology department at Heidelberg (1927–30), he studied librarianship at the Sächsischen Landesbibliothek, Dresden, under M. Bollert and at the Leipzig University Library under O. Glauning; in 1934 he passed the state examination for administration of specialist libraries in Leipzig, taking an additional examination in the handling of printed music. After acting as librarian at the Technische Hochschule in Dresden (1931–3), he became director of the archives of Breitkopf & Härtel in Leipzig (1933–42). In 1946 he founded the music division of the City and University Library in Frankfurt am Main, which he then directed until 1963. He now lives in retirement in Freiburg.

Schmieder's extensive work in music bibliography and manuscript and source studies is dominated by his *Bach-Werke-Verzeichnis*, a basic tool for Bach research.

WRITINGS
Zur Melodiebildung in Liedern von Neidhart von Reuental (diss., U. of Heidelberg, 1927; extracts in *SMw*, xvii (1930), 3)
ed.: *P. Spitta: J. S. Bach* (Leipzig, 1935, 4/1954; Sp. trans., 1950) [abbreviated edition with notes and appendices]
'Johann Sebastian Bach als Briefschreiber', *BJb*, xxxvii (1940–48), 126
'Musikbibliographie: ein Beitrag zu ihrer Geschichte und ihren Problemen', *AMw*, xii (1944), 239
'Bemerkungen zur Bachquellenforschung', *Die wissenschaftliche Bachtagung der Gesellschaft für Musikforschung: Leipzig 1950*, 219
Thematisch-systematisches Verzeichnis der musikalischen Werke von Johann Sebastian Bach: Bach-Werke-Verzeichnis (Leipzig, 1950, rev. 2/in preparation)
'Das Bach Schrifttum 1945–52', *BJb*, xl (1953), 119

Bibliographie des Musikschrifttums 1950/51–1958/59 (Frankfurt, 1954–64)
'Das Bachschrifttum 1953–1957', *BJb*, xlv (1958), 127
'Werkstatt-Erfahrungen beim Katalogisieren von Musikhandschriften', *FAM*, xiii (1966), 121
with G. Hartwieg: *Kataloge der Herzog-August-Bibliothek Wolfenbüttel*, xii, xiii: *Musik: alte Drucke bis etwa 1750* (Frankfurt am Main, 1967)

EDITIONS
Lieder von Neidhart von Reuental, DTÖ, lxxi, Jg.xxxvii/1 (1930)

BIBLIOGRAPHY
K. Dorfmüller and A. Ott: 'Wolfgang Schmieder: Bibliographie', *FAM*, xiv (1967), 43
K. Dorfmüller and G. von Dadelsen, eds.: *Quellenstudien zur Musik: Wolfgang Schmieder zum 70. Geburtstag* (Frankfurt, 1972)

HANS HEINRICH EGGEBRECHT

Schmiedt, Siegfried (*b* Suhl, Thuringia, *c*1756; *d* Suhl, 1799). German composer and music dealer. From 1786 he was a proofreader for Breitkopf & Härtel in Leipzig, where he dispatched to be printed his own and other composers' works with the greatest care (for which J. A. Hiller thanked him in the foreword to his *Allgemeines Choral Melodienbuch*). He also produced piano arrangements of stage works, including Dittersdorf's *Hieronymus Knicker* (?1787), *Rotkäppchen* (1792) and *Der Schiffspatron* (1793), Mozart's *Der Schauspieldirektor* (1792), *Così fan tutte* (?1794) and *La clemenza di Tito* (?1795) and probably some by Hiller, all published by Breitkopf & Härtel. In 1796 he opened his own music store with Rau in Leipzig, but two years later it had closed and he returned to Suhl.

Schmiedt was praised by his contemporaries as an excellent song composer who combined distinguished learning with his talent as a pianist and composer (*GerberNL*). He was a charming, unassuming figure among the Rococo song and keyboard composers in Leipzig, and his works show the influence of both the Berlin lied school and Hiller's philanthropic, folklike lieder. His settings of Langbein's poems are gay little songs with French ornamentation and Italian coloratura; the clavichord may have been the most suitable accompanying instrument for these delicate pieces and his numerous other lieder. His graceful and fashionable keyboard pieces, likewise music for use in the home, are best played on the clavichord or fortepiano.

WORKS
(published in Leipzig unless otherwise indicated)
Theatrical: Die Feier des 18. Jahrhunderts (melodrama, 1, C. F. Schlenkert), vocal score (1794); Melida (opera), vocal score (1797)
Lieder: pieces in Clavier- und Singstücke, i–ii (1786–8); Auswahl aus Langbeins Gedichten (1790); Fröhliche und gefühlvolle Lieder (1794); Es lebe Freund Bacchus, drinking-song (1796); Lied der Schwermuth (F. von Matthisson), 4vv, inst, *D-Bds*; some songs in contemporary anthologies
Other vocal: Hymne an die Tonkunst (C. F. D. Schubart), 1v, kbd (1792); Gesang am Grabe der unglücklichen Königin Marie Antoinette (U. von Schlippenbach), 1v, kbd (1793); Herr, lass dir unsern Lobgesang, cantata, *GOl*; Die Feyer der Christen bey der Krippe Jesu; 2 psalms; Nun keine Thräne mehr, cantata; Wenn ich, o Schöpfer, cantata; Was kann ich, grosser Gott, ode
Inst: pieces in Clavier- und Singstücke, i–ii (1786–8); 3 Sonaten, hpd/pf (1787); 6 kleine und leichte Sonaten, hpd/pf, i–ii (1788–91); 6 sonatines, op.1, kbd (St Petersburg and Gotha, 1795) [cited in *GerberNL*]; 12 deutsche Tänze, pf 4 hands

BIBLIOGRAPHY
EitnerQ; *GerberNL*
G. Schilling: *Encyclopädie der gesammten musikalischen Wissenschaften oder Universal-Lexikon der Tonkunst* (Stuttgart, 1835–42/*R*1973)
M. Friedlaender: *Das deutsche Lied im 18. Jahrhundert* (Stuttgart and Berlin, 1902/*R*1970)
A. Schering: *Johann Sebastian Bach und das Musikleben Leipzigs im 18. Jahrhundert* (Leipzig, 1941)

DIETER HÄRTWIG

Schmierer [Schmirer, Schmicerer, Schmicorer, Schmikerer], **Johann Abraham** (*b* Augsburg, 1661; *d* Augsburg, 11 June 1719). German composer and administrator. He sang at Augsburg Cathedral until 1680. He then studied at Dillingen University and from 1 November at Salzburg University, eventually graduating as doctor of laws. In 1683 he applied unsuccessfully for the post of Kapellmeister of Augsburg Cathedral but later became director of the Fugger Foundation at Augsburg. As a composer he is known only by *Zodiaci musici in XII Partitas balleticas, veluti sua Signa divisi Pars I* (Augsburg, 1698, ed. in DDT, x, 1902, 2/1958). This first part consists of six suites; the remaining six, which are lost, appear to have been published in 1710. The suites are for four string instruments and continuo; they show the influence of Lully and include French dances such as the bourrée and chaconne.

BIBLIOGRAPHY
K. Nef: *Geschichte der Sinfonie und Suite* (Leipzig, 1921), 85
H. J. Moser: 'Miscellanea, i', *Mf*, xiii (1960), 179
A. Layer: *Augsburger Musik im Barock* (Augsburg, 1968)

ADOLF LAYER

Schmikerer [Schmirer], **Johann Abraham**. *See* SCHMIERER, JOHANN ABRAHAM.

Schmit, Camille (*b* Aubarge, 30 March 1908; *d* Limelette, 11 May 1976). Belgian composer and organist. At the Brussels Conservatory he studied the organ with Malengreau, fugue with L. Jongen and composition with J. Jongen. He was organist at Longwy (1923–39) and at Arlon (1940–48), and then he taught harmony (1947–59) and counterpoint (1959–66) at the Liège Conservatory. From 1966 to 1973 he directed the French section of the Brussels Conservatory. His creative output may be divided into two periods: in the first he was strongly influenced by Stravinsky, but in 1948 he turned, under Souris' influence, to 12-note serialism. He had already written the atonal Woodwind Trio (1945) in furtherance of his wish to compose objective music, although the orchestral *Trois préludes joyeux* (1946) have a discreet touch of irony. The String Quartet (1948), his first serial piece, has little individuality, but the Music for Piano and Orchestra (1949) 'powerfully expresses his vision of the pathos of the world and of art' (Wangermée). In later works the constraints of serial writing did not inhibit Schmit's originality: his Eluard song *La halte des heures* (1958) accords equal importance to the voice and piano parts, the latter bringing out the multiple suggestions of the text. Further works include a Piano Concerto (1955) and other orchestral music, instrumental pieces, *mélodies*, cantatas and choral works. His music is published by CeBeDeM, Leduc and the Société d'Editions Musicales.

BIBLIOGRAPHY
R. Wangermée: *La musique belge contemporaine* (Brussels, 1959)
Music in Belgium (Brussels, 1964) [CeBeDeM publication]

HENRI VANHULST

Schmitt, Bernhard. *See* SCHMID, BERNHARD (i).

Schmitt, Florent (*b* Blamont, Meurthe-et-Moselle, 28 Sept 1870; *d* Neuilly-sur-Seine, Paris, 17 Aug 1958). French composer. On leaving the lycée of his native town at the age of 17, he was admitted to the Nancy Conservatory where he studied the piano with Henry Hess and harmony with Gustave Sandré. When he was 19 he entered the Paris Conservatoire to study harmony with Dubois and then Lavignac, fugue with Gédalge and composition with Massenet, whose advice he valued, and later Fauré. Schmitt did not win the Prix de Rome until his fifth attempt (with *Sémiramis*) in 1900; as a laureate he was able to travel around Europe, and some of his experiences are reflected in the piano duets that were published as *Feuillets de voyage* and *Reflets d'Allemagne*, the latter a suite of eight waltzes evoking various German and Austrian towns. An orchestral suite of the same period, *Musiques de plein air*, may also be related to visual memories (the first movement, 'Procession dans la montagne', was probably suggested by Schmitt's visit to the Benedictines of Monte Cassino). These scores reveal his taste for German Romanticism and his manner of trying to represent landscapes in sound, a quality that brings him close to Debussian impressionism.

Three central works date from early in Schmitt's career; they quickly brought him renown and they pointed the direction that his music would take. The three are Psalm xlvii (1904), *La tragédie de Salomé* (1907) and the Piano Quintet, which was begun in Rome in 1902, continued in Dresden, but not completed until 1908 when Schmitt was staying in Argelès, Pyrénées Orientales. This chamber work caused its composer a great deal of trouble; many sections, including the whole first movement, were thoroughly reworked. It is a solidly crafted work, densely argued and thickly textured in the first movement, while the second, all finesse, shows in more than one detail Schmitt's admiration for Fauré and Debussy. The finale is fiery, its rhythms accented and its themes drawn with vigour. These characteristics are apparent in Psalm xlvii, the last of his 'envois' from Rome and a work that shows Schmitt in full possession of his technical means. Side by side with dreamy atmospheric effects and shimmering sonorities drawn from a rainbow of timbres there are quite contrasted materials: more deeply impressed shapes and a more effusive lyricism. The combination of modern rhythmic and colouristic ideas, romantic exaltation and classical architecture was a reaction against impressionist trends and a presage of neo-classicism. Like many of his contemporaries, Schmitt was attracted by the orient, and his penchant for exoticism is particularly evident in *La tragédie de Salomé*, written for a ballet in 1907 and reorchestrated as a symphonic poem in 1910. The work reveals at once a masterly orchestration and a dynamic power of impressive violence, most notably in the final tableau, 'La danse de l'effroi', whose rhythm and scoring look forward to *The Rite of Spring*. Allowing for the slight early influence of Wagner and the indebtedness to Strauss in the use of orchestral colour, the three works discussed display Schmitt's individual characteristics: melodic arabesque, full but evidently tonal harmony (with distant echoes of Franck), rhythm which may be supple or jagged but always commands a principal position, generally conventional, well-made forms and an orchestration of alternately refined and vigorous eloquence.

Schmitt held appointments as director of the Lyons Conservatory (1922–4) and as music critic of *Le temps* (1929–39). In 1909 he was made a committee member of the Société Musicale Indépendante and in 1938 he became president of the Société Nationale de Musique. He succeeded to Dukas' place at the Institut (1936), held the rank of commander of the Légion d'honneur and received the Grand Prix Musical de Paris (1957).

His later works include a large quantity of piano music, much of which he orchestrated; indeed, the very full keyboard writing seems to call for orchestral treatment. The best of his chamber pieces are the formally novel *Sonate libre en deux parties enchaînées* (1918–19) for violin and piano and the String Quartet (1949), a remarkable work that suggests an evolution towards a sparer style, although in general Schmitt's writing developed very little except for a broadening of his chromaticism. His orchestral work includes many sumptuously brilliant scores, such as *Antoine et Cléopâtre* and *Salammbô*, the latter written for a film version of Flaubert's novel in 1925. Directly opposed to this manner is the sober and moving 'Cippus feralis' for piano, dedicated to the memory of Fauré.

WORKS

ORCHESTRAL

Ballets: La tragédie de Salomé, op.50 (after R. d'Humières), 1907, Paris, 1907, rev. as sym. poem, 1910; Le petit elfe ferme-l'oeil, op.73 (after Andersen), 1912–3, Paris, 1924; Oriane et le prince d'amour, op.83 (after C. Séran), 1933, Paris, 1938
Incidental music: Antoine et Cléopâtre, op.69 (Gide, after Shakespeare), Paris, 1920
Film scores: Salammbô, op.76 (after Flaubert), 1925; Essais de locomotives, op.103, 1943
Concert works: En été, op.10, 1894; Musiques de plein air, op.44, 1897–9; Sélamlik, op.48, 1906; Le palais hanté, op.49 (after Poe), 1900–04; Scherzo vif, op.59, vn, orch, 1903–10; Dionysiaques, op.62, band, 1914–25; Rêves, op.65, 1913–15; Légende, op.66, va/vn/a sax, orch, 1918; Fonctionnaire M.C. XII, op.74, 1924; Danse d'Abisag, op.75, 1925; Final, op.77, vc, orch, 1926; Ronde burlesque, op.78, 1927; Çançunik, op.79, 1929; Kermesse, op.80, waltz, 1903–28; Symphonie concertante, op.82, pf, orch, 1928–31; Enfants, op.91, small orch, 1938; Janian, op.101, str, 1941; Introït, récit et congé, op.113, vc, orch, 1951–2; Scènes de la vie moyenne, op.124, 1950–52; Sym. no.2, op.137, 1958
Orchestrations of pf and chamber works

CHORAL

With orch: Psalm xlvii, op.38, S, chorus, orch, org, 1904; Chansons à 4 voix, op.39, SATB, orch/pf 4 hands, 1903–5; Danses des Devadasis, op.47, S, chorus, orch, 1900–08; Chant de guerre, op.63, T, male vv, orch, 1914; Fête de la lumière, op.88, S, chorus, orch, 1936; L'arbre entre tous, op.95, chorus, orch, 1939; 5 choeurs en 20 minutes, op.117, solo vv, chorus, orch, 1951, Le chant de la nuit, op.120 (Nietzsche), S, A, T, SATB, pf/orch, 1951
With insts: 3 chants en l'honneur d'Auguste Comte, op.71, chorus, 10 wind, 1921; 3 liturgies joyeuses, op.116, 4vv, org ad lib, 1951; Domine, Dominus noster, op.119, 4vv, org ad lib, 1956–8; Quinque cantus – Ad benedictionem sanctissimi sacramenti, op.121, chorus, org ad lib, 1952; Laudate pueri Dominum, op.126, chorus, org ad lib, 1952; Oremus pro pontifice, op.127, chorus, org ad lib, 1952; 5 refrains, op.132, 3vv, pf, 1955–6; Mass, op.138, 4vv, org, 1958
Unacc.: 3 choeurs, op.40, 1896–1913; 5 motets, op.60, 1916–17; Hymne à l'été, op.61 (Silvestre), 1898–1913; 6 choeurs, op.81, female vv, 1930–31; En bonne voix, op.91, 1938; A contre-voix, op.104, 1943; La tête de Kenwarc'h, op.114 (de Lisle), male vv, 1949; Conseil tenu par les rats, op.123 (La Fontaine), male 4vv, 1950; Fables sans morales, op.130 (La Fontaine), 4vv, 1954; De vives voix, op.131, 3vv, 1955–6; Psaume cxii et 2 cantiques, op.135, 4vv, 1956

CHAMBER

For 4 or more insts: Andante et scherzo, op.35, harp, str qt, 1906; Pf Qnt, op.51, 1902–8; Lied et scherzo, op.54, hn/vc, 9 wind, 1910; Suite en rocaille, op.84, fl, str trio, harp, 1934; Hasards, op.96, pf qt, 1939–44; A tour d'anches, op.97, ob, cl, bn, pf, 1939–43; Sax Qt, op.102, 1943–8; Qt, op.106, 4 fl, 1944–9; Qt, op.109, 3 trbn, tuba, 1946; Str Qt, G, 1944–8; Qt, op.112, 1949; Chants alizés, op.125, wind qnt, 1952–5; Sextet, op.128, 6 cl, 1953; Pour presque tous les temps, op.134, fl, pf trio, 1956
For 2–3 insts: Chant du soir, op.7, vn, pf, 1895; Scherzo-pastorale, op.17, fl, pf, 1889–1912; 5 pièces, op.19, vn/vc, pf, 1898–1913; Chant élégiaque, op.24, vc, pf, 1899–1903, orchd 1911; 4 Pieces, op.25, vn, pf, 1901; Sonate libre en 2 parties enchaînées, op.68, vn, pf, 1918–19; Sonatine en trio, op.85, fl, cl, pf/hpd, 1935, arr. pf trio, 1940; Minorités, op.93, fl, vn, pf, 1938; Str Trio, op.105, 1944–6; Suite, op.129, fl, pf, 1954–9, orchd; Suite, op.133, tpt, pf, 1955, orchd

KEYBOARD

For pf solo: 3 Preludes, op.3, 1890–95; Soirs, op.5, 1890–96; Ballade de la neige, op.6, 1896; 2 Pieces, op.12, 1892–9; 3 Little Pieces, op.13, 1902; Musiques intimes, op.16, 1890–1900, op.29, 1898–1904; Nuits romaines, op.23, 1901; 9 Pieces, op.27, 1895–1903; 3 valses nocturnes, op.31, 1901; Petites musiques, op.32, 1906; Pupazzi, op.36, 1907, orchd; 8 Easy Pieces, op.41, 1907–8; Pièces romantiques, op.42, 1908; 4 Pieces, op.46, 1898–1903; Crépuscules, op.56, 1911; 2 Pieces, op.57, 1911; Une semaine du petit elfe ferme-l'oeil, op.58, 1912; Ombres, op.64, 1913–17, orchd; Mirages, op.70, 1920–21, orchd; In memoriam Gabriel Fauré, op.72: Cippus feralis, Scherzo, 1922; 3 danses, op.86, 1935, orchd; Chaîne brisée, op.87, 1935, orchd; Suite sans esprit de suite, op.89, 1937, orchd; 2 Pieces, op.90, 1938; Small Gestures, op.92, 1940; Clavecin obtempérant, op.107, 1945

For pf 4 hands: 7 Pieces, op.15, 1899, 4 orchd; Musiques foraines, op.22, 1895–1902; Feuillets de voyage, op.26, 1903–13, orchd; Reflets d'Allemagne, op.28, 1905, orchd; Sur 5 notes, op.34, 1906; 3 pièces récréatives, op.37, 1907; Humoresques, op.43, 1911

For 2 pf: 3 rapsodies, op.53, 1903–4, orchd

For org: Prière, op.11, 1899; Marche nuptiale, op.108, 1946–51

SOLO VOCAL
(for 1v, pf unless otherwise stated)

O salutaris, op.1, 1891; 2 Songs, op.2, 1890–91; 3 Songs, op.4, 1892–5; Les barques, op.8, 1897, orchd; Soir sur le lac, op.9 (Gautier-Villars), 1898; Sémiramis, op.14 (E. and E. Adenis), lyric scene, 1900; 2 Songs, op.18, 1895–1901; Demande, op.20 (J. Forestier), 1901, orchd; 3 Songs, op.21, 1891–7; Vocalise, op.30, S, pf, 1906; Musique sur l'eau, op.33 (Samain), 1898, orchd; 4 lieds, op.45, 1901–12, orchd; Tristesse au jardin, op.52, 1897–1908, orchd; 2 Songs, op.55, 1892–1911

Kerob-shal, op.67, 1920–24, orchd; 3 chants, op.98, 1943, orchd; 3 trios, op.99, female vv, 1941–2, orchd; 4 poèmes de Ronsard, op.100, 1942, orchd; 4 monocantes, op.115, 1949–50, arr. 1v, 5 insts; 3 poèmes de Ganzo, op.118, 1951–3; 3 duos, op.136, 1957

Principal publisher: Durand

BIBLIOGRAPHY
P. O. Ferroud: *Autour de Florent Schmitt* (Paris, 1927)
Y. Hucher: *Florent Schmitt* (Paris, 1953) [incl. bibliography]
Y. Hucher and M. Raveau: *L'oeuvre de Florent Schmitt* (Paris, 1960) [catalogue, incl. bibliography]

ARTHUR HOÉRÉE

Schmitt, Georgius Adamus Josephus. See SCHMITT, JOSEPH.

Schmitt, Jacqueline. See FONTIJN, JACQUELINE.

Schmitt, Joseph [Georgius Adamus Josephus] (*b* Gernsheim am Rhein, baptized 18 March 1734; *d* Amsterdam, 28 May 1791). German composer and music publisher, active in the Netherlands. His musical education under Carl Friedrich Abel must have taken place in Dresden before 1758, the year Abel left the court chapel there and settled in London. On 2 October 1753 Schmitt took vows at the Cistercian monastery at Eberbach im Rheingau, where he wrote many sacred and secular works. On 9 October 1757 he was ordained priest. From 1763 at the latest the care of the music in the monastery seems to have been entrusted to him as *regens chori*. Before 1767 he established a connection with the music publisher Hummel in Amsterdam, who from this time until 1773 took six luxuriously printed collections of instrumental pieces by Schmitt into his catalogue. In 1771 payments by the monastery for music abruptly ceased, and by 1774 Schmitt had printed his op.7 in Amsterdam under his own imprint. (His setting of the Netherlands *Evangelische gezangen*, 1783, and entry into the Amsterdam Lodge 'La Charité' cannot, in view of the toleration of the Enlightenment, serve as proof that he had renounced his priesthood.)

In Schmitt's early years in the Netherlands he earned his livelihood from his publishing firm (which at first brought out only his own compositions) and perhaps by teaching, as is indicated by his *Principes de la musique dédiés à tous les commençans* and by the violin duos op.8 (printed before 1774) which exhibit a strong didac-

tic bias. When the Felix Meritis Society of Amsterdam opened a new building in 1788, Schmitt was appointed director of the music section. At his death he was succeeded in this post by Bartholomeus Ruloffs, and in his publishing firm by Vincent Springer (a relative of Schmitt's by marriage), a basset-horn player who continued the business until the end of the century.

Joseph Schmitt is hopelessly confused in early literature with Karl Joseph Schmitt, a native of Eltville (Rheingau) who worked as a music director in Amsterdam and Frankfurt. Joseph's importance can be appreciated only from a full consideration of his various activities – as teacher, music director, publisher, and above all as composer. Knowledge of him as a teacher is handicapped by the absence of the violin method ascribed to him (the *Principes de la musique* contains merely elementary information on general music teaching) and of the names of important pupils. As director of the Felix Meritis concerts, however, whose functions were later taken over by the Amsterdam Concertgebouw, Schmitt occupied the most important musical post that Amsterdam could then offer. As a publisher he was in keen competition with Hummel – a catalogue of 1793 cited by Gerber apparently carried over 500 titles. Works published by Schmitt and Springer achieved wide international distribution, particularly in the Scandinavian countries, where they were the primary means of making known the works of the Viennese Classical composers (Schmitt's was principally a reprint firm).

The range of Schmitt's compositions covers church music, symphonies, concertos, chamber music in various combinations and a few sacred songs. As early as 1773 Burney praised 'the boldness, spirit and accuracy' of Schmitt's string trios. Contemporary writers gave prominence to the 'Feuer, Erfindung und Gesang' of his op.1 (J. A. Hiller, *Wöchentliche Nachrichten*, 1767) and expressed the opinion that his works needed no special recommendation because of the author's well-established reputation (C. F. Cramer, *Magazin der Musik*, i, 1783, p.73). The blind flautist Dülon, Schmitt's fellow pupil under Abel, asserted in 1808 that Schmitt's compositions were certainly not the equal of Abel's, but that in 'ardour, boldness and sublimity' they were 'fashioned throughout with the same purity of texture . . . and facility of style' (Wieland). The masses, Requiem and *Te Deum* presumably originated during the Eberbach period, and in view of the ample layout and the instrumentation, which ranged far beyond the resources of the monastery, must have served only for festal occasions. Schmitt's preference for instrumental music is already apparent in the frequently rather meagre treatment of the voice parts, which often had to negotiate unvocal passages in the fugal movements.

The foremost musical influence in Schmitt's youth must have been his teacher Abel, and through him the neighbouring Mannheim symphonists and the Mainz composer Johann Zach. In form and thematic construction, Schmitt's music closely followed the example of Mannheim. Smooth, elegant melodic lines, interlaced with conventional figures in allegro movements, are counterpoised by adagios of a delicate cantabile which even his contemporaries singled out for praise. In his Amsterdam years the influence of his publishing associations with the works of the Viennese Classical composers must have had an effect: the melodic substance becomes more pithy and thoughtful, the groups of themes are formally more broadly devised and are more contrasted, the development gains in significance, slow introductions appear to the first movements, and the instrumentation is extended (see the Sinfonie pastorale op.18). More than a dozen of Schmitt's works have been wrongly attributed to Haydn. The lost vocal compositions of the Felix Meritis concerts, with their bizarre experiments in tone-painting (e.g. the igniting of gunpowder), seem to have appealed to contemporary amateur taste.

WORKS

(printed works published in Amsterdam)

Orch: 2 syms. in 6 pièces de musique, op.1 (before 1767), no.1 in facs. edn. (Leipzig, n.d.); 6 syms., op.6 (1773); Sinfonie à grand orchestre, op.12 (before 1781); 3 Sinfonies à grand orchestre, op.14 (before 1784); Sinfonie pastorale, op.18 (c1793); 6 Sinfonies périodiques (1768–76); Concertino, 2 vn, 2 va, 2 hn, b (before 1775); Concerto grosso, 2 vn, va, vc, insts, bc (before 1778); Conc., 2 fl, op.15 (before 1783); Marche à plusieurs instruments (c1785)

Chamber (thematic catalogue in DTB, xxviii, Jg.xvi, 1915): 6 pièces de musique, op.1 (before 1767) [incl. 2 qnts, 2 qts]; 6 trios, 2 vn, vc, op.2 (1768–9); 6 qts, fl, vn, va, vc, op.3 (1770); 6 sonates, 2 vn, vc, op.4 (1772), no.1 in facs. edn. (Leipzig, n.d.); 6 str qts, op.5 (1773); 6 trios, 2 vn/fl, vc, op.7 (1773–4); 6 duos, 2 vn/(vn, vc), op.8 (1773–4); 3 qts, pf/hpd, fl, vn, vc, op.9 (1776); 6 qts, fl, vn, va, vc, op.10 (before 1778); 6 trios, 2 vn/(vn, va), vc, op.11 (c1778); 6 trios, fl, vn, vc, op.13 (before 1782), no.4 ed. W. Höckner (Copenhagen, n.d.); 3 trios, fl, vn, vc, op.16 (c1784); Potpourri à 4 couleurs, 2 vn, vc (before 1785); Str Qt, op.17 (c1793); 2 qnts, 2 vn, 2 va, vc, 2 hn ad lib; 6 str qts, A-Wn, CS-Bm, D-B, KNh

Vocal: 3 Missa solemnis, EB, F, I-MOe; Mass, D, Augustinerkloster, Münnerstadt; Requiem, D-BAR; Te Deum, 4vv, insts, LEm; Melodijen tot de evangelische gezangen voor Godzoekende Christenen (1783)

For lost works, see Dunning

BIBLIOGRAPHY

EitnerQ; GerberL; GerberNL

C. Burney: *The Present State of Music in Germany, the Netherlands, and the United Provinces* (London, 1773, 2/1775); ed. P. Scholes as *Dr. Burney's Musical Tours* (London, 1959)

C. M. Wieland, ed.: *Dülons des blinden Flötenspielers Leben und Meynungen von ihm selbst bearbeitet* (Zurich, 1806–8)

D. F. Scheurleer: *Het muziekleven in Nederland in de tweede helft der 18e eeuw in verband met Mozart's verblijf aldaar* (The Hague, 1909)

O. Andersson: 'Musikliterarische Fäden zwischen Holland und Finnland am Ende des 18. Jahrhunderts', *Gedenkboek aangeboden aan Dr. D. F. Scheurleer* (The Hague, 1925), 43

J. Saam: *Zur Geschichte des Klavierquartetts bis in die Romantik* (Munich, 1932)

D. J. Balfoort: *Het muziekleven in Nederland in de 17de en 18de eeuw* (Amsterdam, 1938)

A. Dunning: *Joseph Schmitt: Leben und Kompositionen des Eberbacher Zisterziensers und Amsterdamer Musikverlegers (1734–1791)* (Amsterdam, 1962)

A. Gottron: 'Musik in sechs mittelrheinischen Männerklöstern im 18. Jahrhundert', *SMw*, xxv (1962), 214

H. Unverricht: 'Ergänzende Bemerkungen zur Biographie von Joseph Schmitt', *Mitteilungen der Arbeitsgemeinschaft für mittelrheinische Musikgeschichte*, no.18 (1969), June, 174

ALBERT DUNNING

Schmittbaur [Schmittbauer], **Joseph Aloys** (*b* Bamberg, 8 Nov 1718; *d* Karlsruhe, 24 Oct 1809). German composer, conductor and glass harmonica maker. He received his musical education from the organ builder J. P. Seuffert in Würzburg and was a musician at the Rastatt court from about 1753 until its dissolution in 1771. There he was Konzertmeister in 1762 (leading the orchestra from the harpsichord) and Kapellmeister from 1765. In 1772 he became Konzertmeister at the Karlsruhe court, but in 1775 he went to Cologne as Kapellmeister at the cathedral and director of public concerts. Although his stay was brief, he had a lasting influence on Cologne's musical life through his sacred compositions (in particular his mass for the Dreikönigsfest, 1776, published in 1781) and through his introduction of modern orchestral methods in the style of Mannheim. In 1777 he accepted an invitation to return to Karlsruhe as Kapellmeister, and was also active there as a teacher and maker of glass harmonicas, whose range he extended from two octaves to four (*c* to *c''''*). At his retirement in 1804 (he was honoured with the title Oberkapellmeister in 1806) his son, Abbé Ludwig Joseph Schmittbaur (1755–1829), a lieder composer, took his place at court; two other sons, August (*b* 1763), a clarinettist and flautist, and Nepomuk, a violinist, also belonged to the Karlsruhe Hofkapelle, and his daughter Therese was known as a singer and keyboard player in the 1770s.

Schmittbaur's compositions were highly esteemed in the 1780s but his pre-Classical style, for example in his symphonies patterned on the Mannheim school, was soon outdated. His earliest dramatic work, the serenata *L'isola disabitata*, shows the influence of Jommelli, who was in Stuttgart after 1753; his later serenata for the wedding of the Crown Prince Karl Ludwig in 1774, *Endymion*, reflects the opera reforms of Gluck, whom he knew personally. Several of his chamber works were published, including a Paris print of six quartets for flute and strings falsely attributed to Haydn. His most famous pupil was Marianne Kirchgässner, who used a glass harmonica made by Schmittbaur when she improvised for Mozart in 1791.

WORKS

(MSS mainly in A-Wgm, B-Bc, CH-Bu, D-Dl, DS, KA, KNh, SWl)

VOCAL

Stage: L'isola disabitata (serenata, 1, Metastasio), Rastatt, 1762, only pubd lib extant; Lindor und Ismene (Singspiel, F. J. Soden von Sassanfort), Karlsruhe, 1771, D-DS, rev. as Ein Grab in Arkadien, 1779, andantino in Bibliothek der Grazien (Speyer, 1789); Herkules auf dem Oeta (operetta, 1, J. B. Michaelis), Karlsruhe, 1772; Die Insel der Liebe (Singspiel), 1773; Endymion (operetta/serenata), Karlsruhe, 1774, only pubd lib extant; Epilog am Karlstag, ? Karlsruhe, 1788; Betrug aus Liebe (Singspiel, H. F. Möller), 1790

Sacred: Missa, D, 4vv, orch, op.1 (Speyer, 1781) [Dreikönigsmesse]; lied in Die Tochter Sion (Cologne, 1778); 4 masses, 4vv, orch; Passio secundum Matthaeum; Requiem, 4vv, insts; many other pieces, incl. 14 offertories, 4 psalms, litanies etc (see Niemöller, Rheinische Musiker, 1962)

Cantatas: Klagen nach der Abreise der . . . Madame Todi (Bekman), 2 S, insts (Speyer, 1783); 3 for 1v, orch, in Blumenlese für Klavierliebhaber (Speyer, 1782–3); prol, S, orch, 1782; Oster-Cantate, oder Die Freunde am Grabe des Erlösers (J. C. Walz), 1782, D-SWl, aria in Neue Blumenlese für Klavierliebhaber (Speyer, 1784); Die Selbstverläugnung (H. J. Tode), 1783; Auf die Ankunft eines Landesprinzen (Walz), lib (Karlsruhe, 1784); Friedensfeier in der Schlosskirche (Walz), 1806; Die Ur-Eltern im ersten Gewitter (Denis, after painting by van der Werft), 2 S, B, orch

Other vocal: c45 lieder in Blumenlese für Klavierliebhaber (Speyer, 1782–4); other lieder in contemporary collections; 2 It. arias

INSTRUMENTAL

Syms.: 3 à 8, op.2 (Offenbach, before 1777); 2 as op.2 (Berlin and Amsterdam, 1795); 1 for marriage of Elector Maximilian Joseph and Caroline of Baaden (Heilbronn, 1799), lost; Sinfonia hypochondrica, before 1782; many others in MS; 21 advertised by Breitkopf, 1768–75

Concs.: 1 for vn, 1773; 7 for tpt, 1773–4, ? lost; 1 for ob, before 1781; 2 for hn, before 1782; 3 for bn; several for fl

Qts: 6 for fl, 2 vn, vc, op.1 (Mannheim, before 1774; Karlsruhe and Offenbach, n.d.), also arr. as 6 quartetto concertant . . . dal Signor Haydn, op.25 (Paris, 1777); 3 for hpd/pf, fl, vn, b, op.1 (Speyer, before 1781); 4 for hpd/pf, fl, vn, vc, op.1 (Berlin and Amsterdam, 1786); 3 for fl, 2 vn/(vn, va), vc, op.3 (Vienna, before 1787); 3 for hpd, fl, vn, b, op.3 (Offenbach, n.d.); Quartetto périodique no.3, fl, vn, va, vc (Amsterdam, n.d.)

Other chamber: 3 trios, 2 fl, vc (Speyer, 1783); Sonatina, fl, hpd, vc, in Blumenlese für Klavierliebhaber (Speyer, 1782); Vn quatro, 1773; Trio, ob, vn, b, before 1781; 7 divertimentos and partitas, 5–10 wind insts

Kbd: 24 Vor- und Nachspiele, org (Heilbronn, 1797); 5 préludes et 1 rondo, glass harmonica/pf (Vienna, 1803); 35 pieces in Blumenlese für Klavierliebhaber (Speyer, 1782–4); 18 syms., hpd; 2 rondos; Prelude; several pieces in contemporary anthologies

BIBLIOGRAPHY

GerberL; GerberNL

C. L. Junker: *Zwanzig Komponisten* (Berne, 1776)

L. Schiedermair: 'Die Oper an den badischen Höfen des 17. und 18. Jahrhunderts', *SIMG*, xiv (1912–13), 200, 510–50

P. Mies: 'Zur Kirchenmusik der Kölner Domkapellmeister Joseph Aloys Schmittbaur und Franz Ignaz Kaa', *KJb*, xxxvii (1953), 84

K. W. Niemöller: *Kirchenmusik und reichsstädtische Musikpflege im Köln des 18. Jahrhunderts* (Cologne, 1960), 119ff, 290ff

——: 'Joseph Aloys Schmittbaurs Werke und ihre Würdigung im 18. Jahrhundert', *Festschrift Karl Gustav Fellerer* (Regensburg, 1962), 377

——: 'Schmittbaur, Joseph Aloys', *Rheinische Musiker*, ii, ed. K. G. Fellerer (Cologne, 1962), 88

F. Längin: 'J. A. Schmittbaur', *Ekkhart Jb 1969*, 161

KLAUS WOLFGANG NIEMÖLLER

Schmitz, (Franz) Arnold (*b* Sablon, nr. Metz, 11 July 1893). German musicologist. He attended school in Metz and then studied piano with Max van de Sandt and composition with A. Beer-Walbrunn, H. Kaun and F. Bölsche at Cologne. After the war he studied musicology, history and philosophy at the Universities of Bonn, Munich and Berlin, where his teachers included Schiedermair, Sandberger, Kroyer, Wolf and Friedlaender. In 1919 he received his doctorate from Bonn University with a dissertation on the young Schumann's conceptions of musical creation. He served as Klemperer's assistant at Cologne Opera before completing his *Habilitation* at Bonn University in 1921 with a work on the Cologne Jesuit musicians of the 17th century. He taught at Bonn University and, from 1925, at Dortmund Conservatory until 1929, when he became professor at Breslau University and director of the Church Music Institute. After war service he was appointed professor of musicology at the new University of Mainz; he was rector of the university (1953–4 and 1960–61) and retired in 1961.

Schmitz's activities at Bonn naturally led to his research on Beethoven and he became a distinguished but not exclusive specialist in that field. In 1937 he edited the Schiedermair Festschrift *Beethoven und die Gegenwart* and the same year began the series Breslauer Studien zur Musikwissenschaft.

WRITINGS
Untersuchungen über des jungen Schumann Anschauungen vom musikaklischen Schaffen (diss., U. of Bonn, 1919; extracts in *ZMw*, ii (1919–20), 535, iii (1920–21), 111)

Kölner Jesuiten-Musik im 17.Jahrhundert (Habilitationsschrift, U. of Bonn, 1921; extracts in *AMw*, iii (1921), 421–46; *ZMw*, iv (1921–2), 18, 266)

Beethovens 'Zwei Prinzipe' (Berlin and Bonn, 1923)

Beethoven: unbekannte Skizzen und Entwürfe (Bonn, 1924)

'Cherubinis Einfluss auf Beethovens Ouvertüren', *NBJb*, ii (1925), 104

Das romantische Beethovenbild (Berlin and Bonn, 1927)

'Zu Johann Walters Choralpassion', *Festschrift Theodor Siebs* (Breslau, 1933), 445

'Italienische Quellen zur Figuralpassion des 16 Jahrhunderts', *Festschrift Max Schneider* (Halle and Leipzig, 1935), 92

'Musik im mittelalterlich Schlesien', *Geschichte Schlesiens*, i (Breslau, 1938, 3/1961), 593

Die Bildlichkeit der wortgebundenen Musik J. S. Bachs (Mainz, 1950)

'Die oratorische Kunst J. S. Bachs: Grundfragen und Grundlagen', *GfMKB, Lüneburg 1950*, 33

'Die Figurenlehre in den theoretischen Werken J. G. Walthers', *AMw*, ix (1952), 79

'Die Kadenz als Ornamentum musicae', *GfMKB, Bamberg 1953*, 114

'Zur motettischen Passion des 16. Jahrhundert', *AMw*, xvi (1959), 232

'Zum Verständnis des Gloria in Beethovens Missa Solemnis', *Festschrift Friedrich Blume* (Kassel, 1963), 320

'Anton Bruckners Motette "Os justi"', *Epirrhosis*, i (Berlin, 1968), 333

EDITIONS
Oberitalienische Figuralpassionen des 16. Jahrhunderts, Musikalische Denkmäler, i (Mainz, 1955)

KARL GEIRINGER

Schmitz, E. Robert. French pianist, founder of the American society PRO-MUSICA.

Schmitz, Eugen (*b* Neuburg an der Donau, 12 July 1882; *d* Leipzig, 10 July 1959). German musicologist and critic. He studied law and later composition with Anton Beer-Walbrunn and musicology with Sandberger and Kroyer at the University of Munich, where he took the doctorate in 1905 with a dissertation on Johann Staden. He became a music critic for several Munich newspapers and in 1910 he was appointed lecturer at Munich. After serving as the director of the Salzburg Mozarteum (1914–15), he taught musicology at the Technische Hochschule in Dresden (1916–39) and then until his retirement (1953) he was a director of the Peters Edition, Leipzig. Schmitz is principally known for his biographies of great composers intended for amateurs and for his research in the field of 17th-century Italian secular music, notably the chamber cantata.

WRITINGS
'Guitarrentabulaturen', *MMg*, xxxv (1903), 133

'Studien über W. C. Printz als Musikschriftsteller', *MMg*, xxxvi (1904), 100

Max Regers Sinfonietta (Munich, 1905)

Der Nürnberger Organist Johann Staden: Beiträge zur Würdigung seiner musikgeschichtlichen Stellung (diss., U. of Munich, 1905; extracts, Leipzig, 1906; also in DTB, xii, Jg.vii/1, 1906)

Hugo Wolf (Leipzig, 1906)

Richard Strauss als Musikdramatiker: eine ästhetisch-kritische Studie (Munich, 1907)

ed.: *Emil Naumanns illustrierte Musikgeschichte* (Stuttgart, 2/1908, 10/1934)

Beiträge zur Geschichte der italienischen Kammerkantate im 17. Jahrhundert (Habilitationsschrift, U. of Munich, 1909; Leipzig, 1914 as *Geschichte der Kantate und des geistlichen Konzerts I. Theil: Geschichte der weltlichen Solokantate*; 2/1955 as *Geschichte der weltlichen Solokantate*)

Richard Wagner (Leipzig, 1909, 2/1918)

'Das Verhältnis der Musikwissenschaft zur Populärliteratur und Musikkritik', *IMusSCR*, iii *Vienna 1909*, 422

'Zur Geschichte des italienischen Continuo-Madrigals im 17. Jahrhundert', *SIMG*, xi (1909–10), 509

Harmonielehre als Theorie: Aesthetik und Geschichte der musikalischen Harmonik (Munich and Kempten, 1911)

'Zur Frühgeschichte des lyrischen Monodie italiens im 17. Jahrhundert', *JbMP 1911*, 35

Musikästhetik (Leipzig, 1915, 2/1925)

'Zur Geschichte des italienischen Kammerduetts im 17. Jahrhundert', *JbMP 1916*, 43

Klavier, Klaviermusik und Klavierspiel (Leipzig, 1919)

Das Madonnen-Ideal in der Tonkunst (Leipzig, 1920)

'Der Musikkritiker von heute', *JbMP 1930*, 63

Richard Wagner, wie wir ihn heute sehen (Dresden, 1937)

Schuberts Auswirkung auf die deutsche Musik bis zu Hugo Wolf und Bruckner (Leipzig, 1954)

ed.: *Louis Spohr: Selbstbiographie* (Kassel, 1954–5)

'Formgesetze in Mozarts Zauberflöte', *Festschrift Max Schneider* (Leipzig, 1955), 209

Unverwelkter Volksliedstil: J. A. P. Schulz und seine 'Leider im Volkston' (Leipzig, 1956)

EDITIONS
Ausgewählte Werke des Nürnberger Organisten Johann Staden (1581–1634, DTB, xii, Jg.vii/I (1906); xiv, Jg.viii/I (1907)

L. Spohr: Quintett für Klavier und Bläser, op.52, Ausgewählte Werke (Kassel, 1950); *Doppel-Quartett nr.1, D-moll, op.65*, ibid (Kassel and Basle, 1951); *Nonett, op.31*, ibid (Kassel and Basle, 1960)

BIBLIOGRAPHY
H. Grüss: 'Eugen Schmitz zum Gedenken', *Mf*, xiii (1960), 33

M. E. C. BARTLET

Schmölzer, Jakob Eduard (*b* Graz, 9 March 1812; *d* Kindberg, Styria, 9 Jan 1886). Austrian flautist and composer. He played in an orchestra of the Steiermärkische Musikverein at the age of 13, and in 1825 was for a time a pupil of Theobald Boehm. He studied music theory with Hüttenbrenner and Halm, and performed under Kreutzer and the elder Hellmesberger. Late in 1839 he made an extensive and successful concert tour, meeting, among others,

Constanze Mozart, Lindpainter, Mendelssohn and Liszt. Though much admired as a performer, Schmölzer did not regard himself as a professional musician; for he was for many years engaged in administrative work in Styria, and from 1862 was in the service of the Graf Fritz Attems at Oberkindberg. In 1860, at a meeting of a number of distinguished singers, Schmölzer conceived the idea of an all-German *Sängerbund*, and this led to the founding of a music journal, *Die Sängerhalle*.

BIBLIOGRAPHY
H. von Steier: *Jakob Eduard Schmölzer* (Graz, 1891)
G. Gatterer: *Die Verwendung der Querflöte in der Steiermark* (diss., U. of Graz, 1952), 75ff
K. Rappold: *Die Entwicklung des Männerchor-Wesens in der Steiermark* (diss., U. of Graz, 1961)

PHILIP BATE

Schmügel, Johann Christoph (*b* Pritzier, baptized 13 Jan 1727; *d* Mölln, 21 Oct 1798). German organist and composer. He first received instruction from his father, also named Johann Christoph Schmügel (*d* 16 Feb 1771), who was organist of Pritzier. He then went to Hamburg to study with Telemann, who in a letter of recommendation to the Johanniskirche, Lüneburg, described him as one of the best pupils in composition he had ever instructed. In spite of this, Schmügel did not obtain the post of organist at the Johanniskirche until 1758, when the next vacancy arose. During his years in Lüneburg (1758–65) he taught the lied composer J. A. P. Schulz, and maintained his contacts with Hamburg (the dedication of his *Sing- und Spieloden* of 1762 speaks of receiving special encouragement in Hamburg from English merchants, and Gerber cited an *Ode auf das Hamburger Wohl* for 1766). In 1766 he left Lüneburg for an organist's post at the St Nikolai church in Mölln, where in 1784 he also became Kantor. He is best known for his lied collection of 1762, which helped to transmit the Hamburg tradition and was noteworthy for the independence of its keyboard parts in the *Spieloden*.

WORKS
Cantatas: Musicalischer Gluckwünsch (J. F. Kruckenburg), S, B, orch, 1758, *D-Lr*; Friedencantate (C. O. Ebeling), S, S, T, B, 4vv, orch, 1763, *B-Bc*; Feyerlicher Weihnachtsgesang, T/S, 2 female vv, orch, 1768, *Bc*; Du schämst dich nicht, O Gottes Sohn, T, B, orch, *Bc*; Segne, Gott, mit frischem Leben, 3vv, orch, *Bc*
Other vocal: Sing- und Spieloden (Leipzig, 1762), nos.8, 11, 18 ed. in Friedlaender; 4 chorales in J. C. Kühnau: Vierstimmige alte und neue Choralgesänge (Berlin, 1786); chorale book, 4vv, 1790, *D-NM*, 27 ed. in A. Catenhusen: Lauenburgisches vierstimmiges Choralbuch (Hamburg, 1852)
Org: Chorale book, 1766, Mölln, Orgelbibliothek; 24 preludes, *Dlb*; Préludes, fugues et autres pièces, op.1 (Berlin and Amsterdam, 1778)
Other inst: 6 sinfonie da chiesa, 4 insts, *Dlb*; Qt, fl, vn, va, vc, *B-Bc*; Trio, 3 fl, *Bc*; Divertimento, fl, 2 vn, va, vc, *Bc*; Str Qt (Paris, n.d.), lost

BIBLIOGRAPHY
GerberL
M. Friedlaender: *Das deutsche Lied im 18. Jahrhundert* (Stuttgart and Berlin, 1902/*R*1970)
H. Rentzow: *Die mecklenburgischen Liederkomponisten des 18. Jahrhunderts* (Hanover and Berlin, 1938)
G. Karstädt: 'Schmügel, Johann Christoph', *MGG*

GEORG KARSTÄDT

Schnabel, Artur (*b* Lipnik, 17 April 1882; *d* Axenstein, Switzerland, 15 Aug 1951). Austrian pianist and composer later naturalized American. When he was seven his family moved to Vienna, where he studied the piano with Leschetizky and theory with Mandyczewski. Of Leschetizky he once said that his teaching offered no method of any kind, but something infinitely more important: it was 'like a current which sought to release all

Artur Schnabel

latent vitality in the student'. Leschetizky in his turn told Schnabel: 'You will never be a pianist; you are a musician'. And in keeping with this judgment, he allowed Schnabel to ignore Liszt's Hungarian Rhapsodies and encouraged him to work at some of Schubert's sonatas, which at that time were completely neglected. So with his début in 1890 began a career which became more and more devoted only to music which, as Schnabel used to say, 'was better than it could be performed'. He would not have been attracted to a lifetime of piano playing on any other basis. That was the true meaning of Leschetizky's remark: for Schnabel the instrument itself was a medium, not an accomplice.

In 1900 Schnabel went to Berlin, where he lived until a few months after Hitler came to power in 1933. He married the contralto Therese Behr in 1905. She was already a renowned interpreter of Schubert, Schumann and Brahms, and there can be no doubt that she played an important part in Schnabel's artistic development. Their many concerts together culminated in a historic series of Schubert recitals they gave in Berlin in 1928. By then her career was ending, while he was approaching the height of his powers. At various times he also formed ensembles with Flesch and Becker, with Casals, Feuermann, Fournier, Hindemith, Huberman, Szigeti and Primrose. He said, in *My Life and Music*, that the years from 1919 to 1924 were musically the most stimulating and perhaps the happiest he knew. It was then that he made friends with many younger men such as Ernst Krenek and Eduard Erdmann, took part in one of the early performances of *Pierrot lunaire*, and wrote several works, including three string quartets. It was a period when composing, and the search for a new and individual language, filled his thoughts more than ever before. At the same time he 'learned how to play Beethoven' – in other words, evolved his own entirely original readings which have made him justly famous. He was, in fact, a creative virtuoso of the old school; not a Busoni (and he would have been the first to admit that), but a composer of some consequence whose playing belonged to another category from that of even the greatest instrumentalists who were that and nothing more.

In 1925 he entered another phase, devoted to performing and teaching (Clifford Curzon and later Claude Frank were among his pupils). He was invited to take the piano class at the State Academy in Berlin, and for the next five years, until he left, maintained standards that became legendary. In the meantime he had been twice to the USA (the first time in 1921), had returned to England after an absence of 20 years and aroused enthusiasm with his playing of Schubert and Beethoven, which came as a revelation to audiences there; and in 1930 he began making gramophone records of all Beethoven's sonatas, as well as of the concertos and the Diabelli Variations. In 1927, for the centenary year, he had played all the 32 sonatas in Berlin; and between 1932 and 1934 he played them again, first in Berlin and then in London, and these concerts marked the climax of his career. After leaving Berlin he gave summer classes at Tremezzo, on Lake Como, and then, from 1940 to 1945, at the University of Michigan, Ann Arbor. In 1939 he had emigrated to the USA, taking American nationality in 1944. His stature was never as widely recognized there as in Europe. (The agents wanted him to change his programmes and to conform to their convenient patterns of salesmanship; as a result, he dispensed altogether with their services during the last eight years of his life.) There was criticism too that his performances of Beethoven did not admit any difference between the expressive functions of melody and of passage-work; that he made everything equally eloquent. For many musicians, on the other hand, it was precisely his articulation of scale passages, accompaniments, and figurations of every kind, as well as his power of individualizing every strand of the texture, that helped to make his playing unique. It was not the melody that suffered, but the other elements which took on an unheard-of vitality.

It is difficult to define at all briefly the qualities that he brought to his favourite composers. In Schubert he managed to combine lyrical expression with a rhythmic élan and discipline that gave everything a new intensity. In Mozart, to whom he turned only late in life, he tended – perhaps for that reason – to idealize the music and sometimes to adopt very slow tempos; but at his best he showed a deeper understanding than his contemporaries – in many of the concertos, for example, and in the wonderful recording of the Rondo in A minor K511. This also shows to perfection the beauty of his phrasing, and his power of sustaining a long line without ever letting it become dull or lifeless. But despite his incomparable playing of Schubert, Schnabel will probably always be associated above all with Beethoven, and especially with the last sonatas. Here he often achieved a visionary quality in which the piano itself was almost forgotten; and although he allowed himself a remarkable rhythmic freedom at times, his readings were still faithful to the composer's intentions: to the spirit rather than to the letter. The truth is that in playing these great works his own imaginative world found its fullest ex-

pression.

Other things were secondary, but still belonged to his character as a 'creative virtuoso'. Of his books, the most important is *My Life and Music*. His editions of Beethoven's sonatas and of the Diabelli Variations provide an invaluable insight into his modelling of the music and the subtle choice of fingering that went with it. His compositions, few of them published, include three symphonies, five string quartets, a piano concerto written when he was 19, many songs of the same early period, Seven Pieces for piano, a Rhapsody for orchestra, a string trio, and his last work, *Duodecimet* for strings, wind and percussion, a small masterpiece.

WRITINGS

Reflections on Music (Manchester, 1933)
Music and the Line of Most Resistance (Princeton, 1942)
My Life and Music (London, 1961; repr. with *Reflections on Music*, Gerrards Cross, 1970)

BIBLIOGRAPHY

C. Saerchinger: *Artur Schnabel* (London, 1957) [with complete list of works]
R. Stone: 'Artur Schnabel', *Grand baton*, lx/3 (1972), 19 [with discography]
K. Wolff: *The Teaching of Artur Schnabel* (London, 1972)

WILLIAM GLOCK

Schnabel, Joseph Ignaz (*b* Naumburg am Queiss, 24 May 1767; *d* Breslau, 16 June 1831). German church musician and composer. After attracting attention as a rural schoolmaster for the musical attainments of his pupils, he went in 1797 to Breslau where he became organist at St Clara, and violinist at the Vincentiuskirche and in the theatre orchestra, which he also often conducted. His later appointments included Kapellmeister of the cathedral (1805), director of the Richter winter concerts (1806) and the Montags- und Freitagsgesellschaft (1810), director of music at the university (1812), teacher at the Catholic Seminary and director of the Royal Institute of Church Music. At a time when sacred music was at a low ebb in south Germany, Schnabel did much to rejuvenate and improve it; in the secular arena he made an outstanding contribution to Breslau's musical life, introducing not only earlier Classical works but those of contemporaries such as Spohr and Romberg. His own music, including masses, hymns and other sacred and secular vocal works, chamber pieces and military marches, is listed in Guckel.

Other musically active members of Schnabel's family include his brother Michael Schnabel (1775–1842), a piano manufacturer whose instruments were valued by virtuosos such as Liszt and Hummel, and whose sons Julius and Carl (later a composer) continued his business; and his sons Joseph (1791/4–?), an organist and composer, and August (1795–1863) a conductor and music educator who succeeded his father at the Catholic Seminary in Breslau.

BIBLIOGRAPHY

C. J. A. Hoffmann: *Die Tonkünstler Schlesiens* (Breslau, 1830)
H. Mendel and A. Reissmann, eds.: *Musikalisches Conversations-Lexicon* (Berlin, 1870–79, suppl. 1880)
H. E. Guckel: *Katholische Kirchenmusik in Schlesien* (Leipzig, 1912)
A. Schirdewahn: *Domkapellmeister Joseph Schnabel und sein Sohn August als Lehrer am Breslauer Schullehrer-Seminar* (Breslau, 1935)
K. Blum: 'Universität und Musik', *Jb der schlesischen Friedrich-Wilhelms-Universität zu Breslau*, vi (1961)

Schnabel, Karl Ulrich (*b* Berlin, 6 Aug 1909). Austrian pianist, son of Artur Schnabel. He studied with Leonid Kreutzer at the State Academy in Berlin, 1922–6. Faced with his father's achievement in expressing a new vision of the Classical repertory, he still managed to develop an individual style of playing and a poetic insight of his own. He made his début in Berlin in 1926, and gave recitals throughout Europe until leaving for the USA shortly before World War II. There he married the American pianist, Helen Fogel, with whom he played a large repertory of piano duets. In earlier years he had sometimes played for his mother Therese Behr, and the imaginative quality of his accompaniments to the Schubert song cycles is still remembered. He also made distinguished recordings of Schubert piano duets with his father. After the war he became active both as a teacher and a recitalist. He has published *Modern Technique of the Pedal* (New York, 1950).

WILLIAM GLOCK

Schnabelflöte (Ger.). RECORDER.

Schnapper, Edith B(etty) (*b* Frankfurt am Main, 31 Oct 1909). English musicologist of German birth. After receiving private instruction in music, she entered Frankfurt University to study science, but decided to graduate in music. From 1933 to 1934 she studied history of music with Schiedermayr at Bonn and Schering in Berlin, and then with Kurth at Berne University where she took a PhD, with history of art and philosophy as secondary subjects. Settling in Cambridge in 1938, she resumed research under Dent. She worked with Paul Hirsch in his music library (then housed in the University Library) and helped in the preparation of vol. iv of his catalogue. In 1950 Schnapper took over from Deutsch as editor of the *British Union-Catalogue of Early Music*, an undertaking greatly assisted by her musicological training and the experience gained from working in the Hirsch library. Visiting many libraries throughout the British Isles, and often working in conditions of considerable difficulty, she added innumerable new entries to the files and with great pertinacity saw the entire work through to its publication. As a unique, remarkably comprehensive national record of music printed before 1801 it is still invaluable to scholars.

WRITINGS

Die Lieder des jungen Schubert (Berne, 1938)
'The Union Catalogue of Old Music', *Journal of Documentation*, ix (1953), 116
ed.: *The British Union-Catalogue of Early Music, printed before the Year 1801* (London, 1957)

ERIC BLOM/ALEC HYATT KING

Schnarre (Ger.). RATTLE. A *Schnarrtrommel* is a snare drum (*see* DRUM).

Schnarrsaiten (Ger.). SNARES.

Schnarrwerk (Ger.). 17th-century term for the 'rattling stops' or Regals; *see* ORGAN STOP and REED-WORK.

Schnebel, Dieter (*b* Lahr, Baden, 14 March 1930). German composer, writer on music and theologian. He studied in Freiburg at the Musikhochschule (1949–52) and at the university (1952–5), where his subjects were theology, philosophy and musicology. From 1955 to 1963 he was a minister and teacher of religious studies in Kaiserslautern; later he taught religious studies in Frankfurt (1963–70) and in Munich (from 1970). Schnebel's compositional starting-point was the serial

music of Stockhausen, as the choral piece *dt 31₆* shows, though it contains also the seeds for the principal directions that his work was to take. One such direction has been an interest in speech as music, developed in *Glossolalie*, *AMN* and *:!* (*Madrasha 2*). This in turn has led to a concern with the human vocal apparatus in such pieces as *Atemzüge* and *Maulwerke*. The theatrical aspect of *dt 31₆* has been followed up in a use of gesture in many of Schnebel's later works. He took the further step of composing 'music' as a purely visual experience in, for example, *ki-no* and the 'music to read' *mo-no*. Parallel with this 'visible music' Schnebel has also produced, under Cage's influences, a series of projects described as 'Meta-musik': music defined only in verbal terms (e.g. *raum-zeit y*, *Das Urteil*, *Glossolalie* and *Hörfunk 1–2*).

WORKS
(the categorization is that of the composer)
I. Versuche: Analysis, str, perc, 1953; Stücke, str qt, 1954–5; Fragment, 1v, ens, 1955; Compositio, orch, 1955–64
II. für stimmen (. . . missa est); dt 31₆, 12 vocal ens, 1956–8; AMN, 7 vocal ens, 1958–67; :! (Madrasha 2), 3 choruses, 1958–68; Choralvorspiele, org, insts, tape, 1966–9
III. Projekte: raum-zeit y, insts, 1958; Das Urteil, 1959; Glossolalie, speaker, insts, 1959–61
IV. Abfälle 1: réactions, 1 inst, audience, 1960–61; visible music 1, conductor, 1 inst, 1960–62, film adaptation in Kagel: Duo
V. Abfälle 2: stoj, 3 insts, 1964; lectiones, 4 speakers, listeners, 1964
VI. Modelle-Ausarbeitungen: Nostalgie (visible music 2), conductor, 1962, film adaptation in Kagel: Solo; espressivo (visible music 3), pianist, 1961–3; concert sans orchestre (réactions 2, fall-out), pianist, audience, 1964; Passion (réactions 3), singer, audience, 1965; anschläge-ausschläge, 3 insts, 1965–6
VII. Gehörgänge: ki-no, Nachtmusik, projectors, listeners, 1963–7; mo-no, Musik zum Lesen, 1969; Hörfunk 1–2, 1969–72
VIII. Produktionsprozesse: Maulwerke, mouths, elec, 1968; Atemzüge, mouths, elec, 1970–71; Mundstücke, mouths, elec, 1972; Zungenschläge, 1974; Lippenspiel, 1974–
IX. Bearbeitungen: Bach-Bearbeitung [Contrapunctus I from Die Kunst der Fuge], 20vv, hpd, 1973; Webern-Bearbeitung [op.27], chamber orch, 1973; Beethoven-Bearbeitung [op.10 no.3], 1974–; Wagner-Bearbeitung [Good Friday Music from Parsifal], 1974–
X. Schulmusik: Blasmusik, 1973; Gesums, 1973–4; Übungen und Klängen, 1974–

Principal publisher: Schott

WRITINGS AND EDITIONS
Studien zur Dynamik Arnold Schönbergs (diss., U. of Freiburg, 1955)
K. Stockhausen: Texte (Cologne, 1963–71)
Mauricio Kagel (Cologne, 1970)
Denkbare Musik, ed. H. R. Zeller (Cologne, 1971) [incl. collected essays]

BIBLIOGRAPHY
F. C. Reininghaus: *Zwölf Thesen zu Dieter Schnebels Mo-No* (Stuttgart, 1970)
U. Stürzbecher: 'Das grosse Fragezeichen hinter einer gesellschaftspolitischen Funktion der Musik', *Melos*, xxxix (1972), 142
D. Erler: *Textgestalterische Grundzüge in einem Chorwerk Schnebels und dessen Verwendbarkeit zur Werkbetrachtung* (diss., Hanover Musikhochschule, 1973)
C. Gottwald: 'Bausteine zu einer Theorie der neuen Vokalmusik', *Festschrift für einen Verleger: Ludwig Strecker* (Mainz, 1973), 259
C. Henius: 'Fern aller Lust am Untergang', *Melos*, xl (1973), 134
H. R. Zeller: 'Choralbearbeitung als Arbeitsprozess', *Melos*, xl (1973), 97
'Schnebel', *Musique en jeu* (1974), no.16, pp.79–119 [incl. articles, interview and work-list]
E. Karkoschka: 'Schnebels Musik zum Lesen', *Melos*, xli (1974), 350

CLYTUS GOTTWALD

Schneeberger, Hansheinz (*b* Berne, 16 Oct 1926). Swiss violinist. He attended the Berne Conservatory, then studied with Flesch in Lucerne in 1944, and with Boris Kamensky, 1946–7. In 1946 he made his début with the first performance in Switzerland of Bartók's Second Violin Concerto. He taught the violin at the conservatories of Biel (1948–58) and Berne (1952–8). In 1961 he was appointed to teach the violin and chamber music at the Basle Academy of Music. As well as leading the North German RO, Hamburg, he embarked on a solo career, particularly as an interpreter of contemporary music. He gave the first performances of Martin's Violin Concerto in 1952 with Paul Sacher, Bartók's First Violin Concerto in 1958, also with Sacher, and of Huber's Violin Concerto 'Tempora' in 1958 with Francis Travis. His gramophone recordings of Bach's violin and keyboard sonatas reveal his interest in earlier music.

BIBLIOGRAPHY
J. Creighton: *Discopaedia of the Violin, 1889–1971* (Toronto, 1974)
JÜRG STENZL

Schneegass, Cyriacus [Cyriak] (*b* Bufleben, nr. Gotha, 5 Oct 1546; *d* Friedrichroda, nr. Gotha, 23 Oct 1597). German theologian, theorist, editor, composer and poet. He attended the Landeschule at Gotha; the Rektor there was Cyriacus Lindemann, whose daughter he later married. From 1565 he studied theology at the University of Jena, where he came under the influence of Nicolaus Selnecker. He left the university in 1568 with a master's degree, which entitled him to teach at higher institutions of learning. Nevertheless he became a minister, first at Tambach, near Gotha, and then, from 1573 until his death, a few miles away at Friedrichroda. After signing the Concordienformel in 1579 he was given the additional duty of assistant to the Weimar superintendent. Between 1583 and his death he issued some 18 publications, most notably in the disciplines of theology and music, which show the wide range of his intellectual and artistic interests. For example, he edited much important source material for the study of the Reformation, including 66 letters from Philipp Melanchthon to Friedrich Myconius. He wrote both the words and music for many congregational hymns. Many of his prayers and poetic texts arose out of the fear of a Turkish invasion.

In chapter 3 of his *Nova & exquisita monochordi dimensio* Schneegass argued that the ratio of a tempered 5th ought to be 160:107 (a good approximation of a 5th tempered by ¼-comma, as Sethus Calvisius perceived), but prescribed also that the diatonic semitone contain 3¼ 'commas' and the chromatic 2¼. By an ingenious geometrical calculation he applied this rule for the semitones and produced a monochord scheme approximating to ⅔-comma mean-tone temperament (with major 3rds very slightly larger than pure) though Barbour suggested that he may have confused it with ¼-comma mean-tone (with pure major 3rds). His conception of the triad as symbolizing the Trinity clearly anticipates Johannes Lippius's *Synopsis musicae novae* (1612).

WORKS

SACRED VOCAL

Geistliche Lieder und Psalmen für einfältige fromme Hertzen zugerichtet (Erfurt, 1597); ed. F. Fulda, *Des weiland M. Cyriacus Schneegass Geistliche Lieder und Psalmen* (Eskartshaus, 1854)

Texts and melodies in: J. Steuerlein, Epithalamia (1587); J. a Burck, [15] Psalmi graduum (Erfurt, 1595); 40 Weynacht- und Neu-Jahrsmotetten (Erfurt, 1595); Die geistlichen Lieder und Psalmen für einfältige und fromme Herzen (Erfurt, 1597); 1597⁸: many melodies ed. in Wackernagel and Zahn

THEORETICAL

Nova & exquisita monochordi dimensio (Erfurt, 1590)
Isagoges musicae libri duo (Erfurt, 1591)
Isagoges musicae, non ita pridem in lucem editae, methodus (Erfurt, 1591)
Deutsche Musica für die Kinder und andere so nicht sonderlich Latein verstehen (Erfurt, 1592)
Preface to J. Steuerlein: 27 newe geistliche Gesenge (Erfurt, 1588)

BIBLIOGRAPHY
J. C. Wetzel: *Hymnopoeographia . . . III* (Herrnstadt, 1724)
P. Wackernagel: *Das deutsche Kirchenlied von der ältesten Zeit bis zu Anfang des 17. Jahrhunderts* (Leipzig, 1864–77/R1964)
J. Zahn: *Die Melodien der deutschen evangelischen Kirchenlieder* (Gutersloh, 1889–93/R1963)
A. Schumann: 'Schneegass, Cyriacus', *ADB*
T. Schneider: 'Der Friedrichrodaer Pfarrer und Adjunkt M. Cyriacus Schneegass', *Mitteilungen der Vereinigung für Gothaische Geschichte und Altertumsforschung* (1909–10)
J. M. Barbour: *Tuning and Temperament: a Historical Survey* (East Lancing, Mich., 1951, 2/1953)
C. Dahlhaus: 'Der Dreiklang als Symbol', *Musik und Kirche*, xxv (1955), 251
——: 'Musiktheoretisches aus dem Nachlass des Sethus Calvisius', *Mf*, ix (1956), 129
E. FRED FLINDELL

Schnéevoigt, Georg (Lennart) (*b* Viipuri [now Vyborg, USSR], 8 Nov 1872; *d* Malmö, 28 Nov 1947). Finnish conductor and cellist. He studied the cello in Helsinki, Sondershausen (with Schröder), Leipzig (with Klengel), Brussels, Dresden and Vienna (with Robert Fuchs). In 1895–8 and 1899–1903 he was solo cellist with the Helsinki PO and taught the cello at the Helsinki College of Music. After his conducting début in Riga in 1901 he was appointed conductor of the Kaim Orchestra in Munich (1904–8) and of the Kiev SO (1908–9). He founded and conducted a symphony orchestra in Riga (1909–14) and another in Helsinki (1912–14), which combined in 1914 with Kajanus's Helsinki PO to form the Helsinki City Orchestra. Schnéevoigt and Kajanus were joint conductors of the Helsinki City Orchestra from 1916; on Kajanus's retirement in 1932, Schnéevoigt remained as principal conductor until 1941. From 1915 to 1924 he was principal conductor of the Stockholm SO and from 1919 to 1927 conductor of the Oslo PO (which he founded in 1918). He later held posts in Düsseldorf (1924–6), Los Angeles (1927–9) and Malmö (1930–47). Schnéevoigt was a forceful and dynamic personality whose interpretations were sometimes criticized for excess of emotion, especially in the slow movements of Romantic works; but his secure technique as an orchestral trainer, his sharp perception, and deep involvement in music of all periods won him acclaim. In 1907 he married the pianist Sigrid Ingeborg Sundgren (*b* Helsinki, 17 June 1878; *d* Stockholm, 14 Sept 1953) who studied at the Helsinki College of Music, 1886–94, and with Busoni in Berlin, 1894–7; from 1910 she taught at the Helsinki College of Music. She gave recitals and played in orchestral concerts in Europe and the USA, often with her husband conducting.

BIBLIOGRAPHY
S. Ranta: 'Georg Schnéevoigt', *Sävelten taitureita* (Borgå, 1947)
H. Aaltoila: 'Sigridja Georg Schnéevoigt', *Suomalaisia musiikin taitajia* (Helsinki, 1958)
based on *MGG* (xi, 1891–2) by permission of Bärenreiter

Schneickher, Paul. See SARTORIUS, PAUL.

Schneider. German family of musicians.

(1) (Johann Christian) Friedrich Schneider (*b* Alt-Waltersdorf, nr. Zittau, 3 Jan 1786; *d* Dessau, 23 Nov 1853). Composer, conductor and teacher. He learnt the piano from his father, Johann Gottlob Schneider (1753–1840), and began composing at a very early age. In 1798 he entered the Zittau Gymnasium and studied music with Schönfelder and Unger. In 1804 he published his first works, a set of three piano sonatas, and in the following year he entered the University of Leipzig to continue his musical studies. He became organist at the university church in 1807, organist of the

Thomaskirche in 1812 and music director of the city theatre in 1817. His performance of Beethoven's Fifth Piano Concerto in Leipzig on 28 November 1811 is believed to have been the work's première (see *AMZ*, xiv, 1812, col.8).

Schneider became Hofkapellmeister at Anhalt-Dessau, where he contributed much to improve musical life: he founded a Singakademie, a schoolmasters' choral society, a *Liedertafel* and (in 1829) a music school, which was successful for about 15 years and had a number of excellent pupils, among them Robert Franz. Between 1820 and 1851 he directed more than 80 German music and singing festivals, most of which included a performance of one of his oratorios. He belonged to numerous musical societies and received honorary doctorates from the universities of Halle and Leipzig in 1830.

WORKS

Oratorios: Die Höllenfahrt des Messias, 1810; Das Weltgericht (A. Apel), 1819; Totenfeier, 1821; Die Sündflut (E. von Groote), 1823; Das verlorene Paradies (L. de Marées), 1824; Jesu Geburt, 1825; Pharao (A. Brüggemann), 1828; Christus das Kind, 1828–9; Gideon (Brüggemann), 1829; Absalon (Brüggemann), 1831; Das befreite Jerusalem, 1835; Salomonis Tempelbau, 1836; Bonifazius, 1837; Christus der Erlöser, 1838; Gethsemane und Golgotha (W. Schubert), 1838

Other vocal: 7 operas, 1 inc.; 14 masses, 5 a cappella; Gloria settings; TeD; 25 cantatas; 5 hymns; 13 psalm settings; c50 partsongs, mixed chorus; c400 partsongs, male vv; c200 songs, 1v, pf

Instrumental: 23 syms., 20 ovs., 7 pf concs., other smaller orch works; 10 str qts, 3 pf qts, 4 pf trios, 4 vn sonatas, 4 fl sonatas, Vc Sonata; Sonata, 2 pf; 6 sonatas, Polonaise, pf 4 hands; 35 sonatas, various smaller works, pf solo

(2) Johann (Gottlob) Schneider (*b* Alt-Gersdorf, 28 Oct 1789; *d* Dresden, 13 April 1864). Organist, teacher and composer, brother of (1) (Johann Christian) Friedrich Schneider. He also studied music with his father and attended the Zittau Gymnasium. In 1810 he began to study law at the University of Leipzig, but soon gave this up to devote himself to the organ. He became the university church organist in 1812, and by 1820 was recognized as one of the leading living organists. Owing to his splendid playing at a Magdeburg festival in 1825, he was appointed court organist in Dresden, a post he held until his death. In 1861, the 50th year of his artistic career, he was presented with a *Jubel-Album für die Orgel* comprising works of about 30 of his former pupils (including Liszt) and received an honorary doctorate from the University of Leipzig.

As a teacher, Schneider would always end his lessons by playing one of the great organ fugues or chorale preludes of Bach. He had a permanent influence on Schumann, evidenced in the latter's studies for the pedal piano and organ fugues on B–A–C–H, Mendelssohn expressed a like admiration for him.

(3) (Johann) Gottlieb Schneider (*b* Alt-Gersdorf, 19 July 1797; *d* Hirschberg, 4 Aug 1856). Organist and composer, brother of (1) Friedrich Schneider. Like his elder brothers, he studied music with his father and attended the Zittau Gymnasium and the University of Leipzig. From 1825 he lived in Hirschberg, where he gained the reputation of an excellent organist at the Kreuzkirche and composed a number of pieces for the organ and the piano.

(4) Theodor Schneider (*b* Dessau, 14 April 1827; *d* Zittau, 15 June 1909). Cellist and conductor, son of (1) Friedrich Schneider. He began his musical career as a cellist in the Anhalt-Dessau court orchestra, then under his father's direction, and succeeded his father as Kantor and choirmaster of the Schlosskirche in Dessau in 1853. In 1860 he moved to Chemnitz, taking similar church appointments there and directing a Singakademie and a men's choral society.

BIBLIOGRAPHY

W. Neumann: *Friedrich Schneider: eine Biographie*, Die Komponisten der neueren Zeit, iv (Kassel, 1854)

F. Kempe: *Friedrich Schneider als Mensch und Künstler* (Dessau, 1859, 2/1864)

H. M. Schletterer: 'Schneider, F.', 'Schneider, Johann', *ADB*

W. Ketschau: 'Friedrich Schneider: zur 50. Wiederkehr seines Todestages', *NZM*, lxx (1903), 614

A. Lesske: 'Johann Schneider, der Meister im Orgelspiel', *Bunte Bilder aus dem Sachsenlande*, iii (Leipzig, 2/1903), 53

M. Puttmann: 'Friedrich Schneider: ein Gedenkblatt zu seinem 50jährigen Todestage', *AMz*, xxx (1903), no.46

A. Fast: *Friedrich Schneider in seinen Sinfonien und Ouvertüren* (diss., U. of Halle, 1924)

K. Hoede: *Friedrich Schneider und die Zerbster Liedertafel* (Zerbst, 1927)

J. Rammelt: 'Friedrich Schneider', *Mitteldeutsche Lebensbilder*, ii (Magdeburg, 1927), 125

R. Selle: 'Der Dessauer Hofkapellmeister Friedrich Schneider', *Dessauer Kulturspiegel*, iii (1956), 84–383

H. Lomnitzer: *Das musikalische Werk Friedrich Schneiders (1786–1853), insbesondere die Oratorien* (diss., U. of Marburg; Marburg, 1961) [incl. autobiography, list of works, bibliography]

FRANZ GEHRING, E. M. OAKELEY/R

Schneider, (Abraham) Alexander (*b* Vilna, 21 Oct 1908). American violinist and conductor of Russian birth. He entered the Vilna Conservatory at the age of ten and the Hoch Conservatory in Frankfurt when he was 16. Almost at once he became leader of the Frankfurt Museum Orchestra. For several years he worked in Saarbrücken and Hamburg as well as in Frankfurt, as orchestral leader, assistant conductor, solo violinist, and leader of his own quartet.

In 1932 he joined the Budapest Quartet as second violinist, his elder brother, Mischa, having become its cellist two years before. With the Budapest he toured extensively, and settled in the USA in 1939. In 1944 Schneider left the quartet, but he remained active in chamber music, as a member of the Albeneri Trio with Benar Heifetz and Erich Itor Kahn, in the New York Quartet with Mieczysław Horszowski, Milton Katims and Frank Miller, in duos with Ralph Kirkpatrick and Eugene Istomin, and as head of a chamber orchestra. It was he who in 1950 persuaded Casals to come out of retirement and lead a festival at Prades to commemorate the bicentenary of Bach's death, and he continued to be closely associated with Casals, at Prades and Perpignan, at Marlboro, in Israel, and in Puerto Rico, where he organized the Festival Casals in 1957. In 1952 Schneider once again became leader of his own quartet, performing all the Haydn quartets and recording most of them for the Haydn Society. In 1955 he rejoined the Budapest Quartet, staying until its last concerts in 1964. Schneider has also been active as a teacher, as a director of string seminars for young players, as adviser to the Fromm Music Foundation and as an instigator of new concert series (his midnight concerts in Carnegie Hall were especially popular). In 1972 he founded and directed a new chamber ensemble, the Brandenburg Players, and he has since conducted other American orchestras. Schneider is a thoroughly musical, but not always subtle, player, whose performances convey infectious enthusiasm and ebullience. In his middle 60s he was one of the most unquenchably energetic figures in the public musical life of the USA.

BIBLIOGRAPHY

J. Creighton: 'Schneider, Alexander', *Discopaedia of the Violin, 1889–1971* (Toronto, 1974)

MICHAEL STEINBERG

Schneider, Andreas (*b* ?before 1640; buried Höxter, 2 March 1685). German organ builder. He lived in Höxter, but is said to have been a native of Dortmund. The keyboard compass, pipe scaling, wind-chest construction, and formation of the mouths on the show-pipes of his instruments all indicate that he was probably a pupil of one of the Bader family of organ builders. For a time Schneider was an associate of Peter Heinrich Varenholt (with whom he built the organ at St Pauli, Soest, in 1674–6). From 1677 to 1679 Schneider built a small organ in Marienmünster (now in Gehrden); in 1680–82 he repaired the large organ there and in 1681 produced a chancel organ and a west end organ for the church of the Benedictine abbey at Corvey. Both organ cases (in Baroque style) survive, together with four spring-chests of the 'improved' type and a considerable number of the larger organ's pipes. The known specifications of Schneider's organs remain within the style of those of the Bader school and no further independent developments in Westphalian organ building were undertaken by him. He was the first Westphalian builder to make funnel-shaped pipes, which had been known in the Netherlands as early as the beginning of the 17th century. In 1681 Schneider was described by Rhabanus Wernekinck, organist of Münster Cathedral, as 'the best [organ builder] there is at present in Westphalia' (Hans Heinrich Bader had died some time after 1664).

BIBLIOGRAPHY
J. Cordes: 'Über die Orgel des Klosters Corvey', *Mitteilungen des Diözesancäcilienvereins Paderborn*, vii (1906)
J. Linneborn: 'Zur Geschichte der Orgel im ehemaligen Benediktinerkloster Marienmünster', *Cäcilienvereins-Organ*, xlix (1914)
H. Gocke: *Der Orgelbau in den Kreisen Soest und Arnsberg* (Birkeneck, 1936)
H. Böhringer: *Untersuchungen zum Orgelbau im Hochstift Paderborn* (diss., U. of Cologne, 1949)
R. Reuter: *Orgeln in Westfalen* (Kassel, 1965)

HANS KLOTZ

Schneider, Conrad Michael (*b* Ansbach, baptized 28 Aug 1673; *d* Ulm, 23 Nov 1752). German composer and organist. The son of an Ansbach organist, Abdias Schneider, he was a student at Leipzig University in 1695 and was called from that city to Ulm to take up a post at Ulm Cathedral in August 1699. There he assisted and frequently substituted for the cathedral organist S. A. Scherer and, on the latter's death on 26 August 1712, succeeded him. Schneider also directed the collegium musicum in Ulm. During much of his career he was responsible for the care and rebuilding of the cathedral organ. His *Passionsmusik* (lost) was performed in Ulm in June 1725. Schneider's only known works are his six-volume *Clavier-Übung, bestehend in Allemanden, Couranten, Sarabanden, Doubles, Menuets, Trio, Passepieds, Giques* (Augsburg, 1732–41) and a cantata *Du Friedensfürst, Herr Jesu Christ*, for four voices and strings (*F-Sm*, according to *EitnerQ*).

A son, Georg Ludwig (also known as Sartori), was employed in Mannheim in 1747 as a violinist and later as a flautist.

BIBLIOGRAPHY
K. Blessinger: *Studien zur Ulmer Musikgeschichte im 17. Jahrhundert insondere über Leben und Werke Sebastian Anton Scherers* (Ulm, 1913)

GEORGE J. BUELOW

Schneider, Franz (*b* Pulkau, baptized 2 Oct 1737; *d* Melk, 5 Feb 1812). Austrian composer and organist.

After holding a number of minor posts as an organist in Lower Austrian towns, he became a pupil of J. G. Albrechtsberger at Maria Taferl in 1757. He accompanied his teacher to Melk, where he was appointed organist first at the parish church in 1760 and then, as Albrechtsberger's successor, at the Benedictine abbey in January 1766. Performing additional duties as music director after 1787, he remained in the service of the Benedictines in Melk for half a century.

Copies of Schneider's music, particularly the masses, can be found in considerable numbers in provincial Austrian church archives carrying performance dates as late as 1880. Many of his works demonstrate a sound contrapuntal technique, but he did not attempt to follow Albrechtsberger in elevating counterpoint to a central stylistic position. His liking for the use of solo instruments may have been inspired originally by the influential Krems composer J. G. Zechner, but in later works was the result of the limited forces at Melk.

WORKS

Liturgical: 48 masses, 14 requiems, 4 Miserere, 7 Vespers and vesper psalms, 6 Magnificats, 12 litanies, 27 graduals, 8 offertories, 20 Marian antiphons, 2 Te Deum, 11 antiphons and hymns, 2 sequences
Other vocal: 21 Lat. arias, duets and choruses, 2 Ger. arias, 3 Ger. choruses and cantatas
Org: 3 fugues, 14 preludes, 24 versets, *D-Bds*

Principal MS sources: *A-M* (155 works in autograph), *GÖ, KR, Mt, SEI, SF, Wn*

BIBLIOGRAPHY
EitnerQ; *FétisB*
Kurze Lebensbeschreibung des Franz Schneider, Musikmeisters und Schullehrers zu Melk (MS, Melk, Prälaten-Archiv, c1815)
Anon.: 'Bericht über den Musikzustand des löbl. Stiftes Mölk in alter und neuer Zeit', *Wiener allgemeine musikalische Zeitung*, ii (1818), col.366
G. Schilling, ed.: *Encyclopädie der gesammten musikalischen Wissenschaften oder Universal-Lexikon der Tonkunst* (Stuttgart, 1835–42/R1973)
S. Molitor: *Biographische und kunsthistorische Stoffsammlungen zur Musik in Österreich* (MS, *A-Wn*, c1838)
I. F. Keiblinger: *Geschichte des Benediktinerstiftes Melk in Niederösterreich* (Vienna, 1851)
R. N. Freeman: *The Practice of Music at Melk Monastery in the Eighteenth Century* (diss., U. of California, Los Angeles, 1971)
——: *A Thematic Catalogue of the Works of Franz Schneider* (New York, 1979)

ROBERT N. FREEMAN

Schneider, Georg Abraham (*b* Darmstadt, 19 April 1770; *d* Berlin, 19 Jan 1839). German horn player, oboist and composer. He studied several instruments with J. W. Magnold, violinist in the Darmstadt court chapel, and joined the chapel himself at the age of 17. He then learnt theory and composition with J. G. Portmann, whose daughter Karoline, a notable singer, he later married. He left Darmstadt in 1795 to join the court orchestra of Prince Heinrich of Prussia in Rheinsberg, where he composed and published many orchestral and chamber works. In 1803 he joined the royal chapel in Berlin and began to make his name as a horn virtuoso and composer; he founded a series of subscription concerts in 1807 and in 1818 the Musikalische Übungsakademie zur Bildung der Liebhaber. On Kotzebue's invitation he became conductor of his theatre in Reval (now Tallinn) in 1813, retaining his Berlin post and returning to it in 1816. In Berlin his appointments included music director of the Royal Theatre (1820) and Kapellmeister (1825), in which post he devoted himself to the conducting of operas. He also taught at the music school attached to the Royal Theatre and in the Prussian Academy of Arts.

Schneider's large output is unexceptional stylistically,

being marked by all the conventions of the late 18th century; but it is remarkable for the virtuosity of his instrumental writing which proves the extent of his own mastery of many instruments. His theatre music (including many ballets, melodramas and five Singspiels: *Der Orakelspruch, Aucassin und Nicolette, Die Verschworenen, Der Traum, Der Werwolf*) was, like his instrumental works, widely successful during his lifetime.

Schneider's son Louis (*b* Berlin, 29 April 1805; *d* Potsdam, 16 Dec 1878) was a writer and actor, and privy councillor and tutor to Friedrich Wilhelm IV. He is remembered for his *Geschichte der Oper und des königlichen Opernhauses in Berlin* (Berlin, 1852, with suppl. *Geschichte der kurfürstlich Brandenburgischen und königlich Preussischen Kapelle*). He also published three volumes of memoirs as *Aus meinem Leben* (Berlin, 1879).

WORKS

(only published works, all n.d.)

Sym., D, op.9; Ouverture concertante, C; 4 fl concs., G, op.12, a, op.53, e, op.82, F, op.83; Conc., vn, va, D, op.19; Va Conc., B, op.20; Cl Conc., op.84; Bn Conc., op.85; Hn Conc., op.86; Ob Conc., op.87; Sinfonia concertante, fl, ob, op.88; Conc., cl, bn, op.89; Basset hn Conc., op.90

48 duos, 2 fl, 3 as op.18, 3 as op.21, 3 as op.22, 6 as op.24, 3 as op.28, 6 as op.32, 3 as op.36, 3 as op.46, 3 as op.55, 6 as op.56, 6 as op.61, 3 as op.78, op.79, op.91; 3 sonatas, vn, va, op.18; 6 duos, vn, va, op.30, op.44; Duo, va, vc, D, op.15; 3 duos, 2 bn, op.20; 3 trios, fl, vn, vc, op.81; 12 str qts, 3 as op.10, 3 as op.20, 3 as op.65, 3 as op.68; 33 fl qts, 3 as op.40, 3 as op.47, 3 as op.50, 6 as op.51, 3 as op.52, 6 as op.62, 3 as op.69, 3 as op.71, 3 as op.76; 3 qnts, fl, vn, 2 va, vc, op.37, op.49, op.54

BIBLIOGRAPHY

R. Eitner: 'Schneider, Georg Abraham', *ADB*
L. Peckhold: *Louis Schneider, Wesen und Wertung sines Schaffens für das deutsche Theater des 19. Jahrhunderts* (diss., Free U. of Berlin, 1956)
A. Meyer-Hanno: *Georg Abraham Schneider und seine Stellung im Musikleben Berlins* (Berlin, 1965)

Schneider, Hortense (Catherine [Caroline]-**Jeanne)** (*b* Bordeaux, 30 April 1833; *d* Paris, 6 May 1920 or 1922). French soprano. She made her professional début on 15 May 1853 at Agen, as Inès in *La favorite*, and she first appeared in Paris at the Bouffes-Parisiens on 31 August 1855 in a double bill including Offenbach's *Le violoneux*. The following year she sang in *Tromb-al-Cazar* and *La rose de St-Flour* by Offenbach, and *Les pantins de Violette* by Adam. She appeared at the Variétés for two seasons and then from 1858 to 1864 at the Palais-Royal, singing in countless ephemeral comedies, vaudevilles and melodramas. She had decided to leave the stage when Offenbach persuaded her to return to the Variétés for *La belle Hélène* (17 December 1864); her triumphant success as Helen was equalled by her Boulotte in *Barbe-bleue* (5 February 1866) and even surpassed in *La Grande-duchesse de Gérolstein* (12 April 1867), which drew enormous crowds, including nearly every crowned head in Europe, throughout the Exhibition year. A visit to London was followed by *La Périchole* (6 October 1868) and *La diva* (22 March 1869), but the Franco-Prussian War brought an end both to the Second Empire and to the moral climate in which the great Offenbach operettas had flourished. Schneider sang in St Petersburg (1872) and in Paris for a few more years and then retired. Her personal attractions and the scandal of her private life were as important to her success as her voice, which was small though well projected; she also had superb enunciation and genuine talent as an actress.

BIBLIOGRAPHY

L. Schneider: *Offenbach* (Paris, 1923)
M. Rouff and T. Casevitz: *Hortense Schneider: la vie de fête sous le Second Empire* (Paris, 1931)
S. Kracauer: *Jacques Offenbach und die Paris seiner Zeit* (Paris, 1937)

ELIZABETH FORBES

Schneider, Johann (*b* Oberlauter, Coburg, baptized 17 July 1702; *d* Leipzig, 5 Jan 1788). German organist and composer. Schneider's father, a mill owner, gave him an excellent musical education with a local Kantor, with Kapellmeister Reinmann in Saalfeld (*c*1717) and J. S. Bach in Cöthen (1720). As a young man Schneider seems to have been interested in both string instruments and keyboard playing, and studied the violin with J. G. Graun in Merseburg and Johann Graf in Rudolstadt. In 1721 he became organist and Konzertmeister of Saalfeld Castle and five years later moved on to the ducal chapel in Weimar as a professional violinist. It is not certain whether his association with Bach also included organ study in Leipzig in 1723–4, but his former teacher may well have influenced the Nikolaikirche, Leipzig, where he was appointed organist in 1729. Schneider took up this position the following August and remained there for the rest of his career. In Leipzig he also played second violin and harpsichord for the so-called 'Grosse Concert', 1746–8, and may well have directed from the keyboard as well. Mizler said of Schneider's composition or improvisation that 'with the exception of Bach you will not hear anything better in Leipzig'. He may also have been speaking of his playing, for works such as the trio *Mein Gott das Herze bring ich dir*, or the second Fugue in G, demand good technique. It is perhaps more important that his works remain truer to Bach's style than those of other pupils who travelled farther afield. The first Prelude in G is modelled on the 'Dorian' Toccata in D minor BWV538. The Prelude in G minor recalls the rhythm and figuration of the Prelude in E♭ BWV552. Such similarities can be observed in the works of Bach's pupil Krebs, for example, but Schneider's long and close association with the master seems to have shielded him from the more modern influences which Krebs displays.

WORKS

Org: 2 settings of Vater unser im Himmelreich (Leipzig, 1937); Trio, Mein Gott das Herze bring ich dir; Trio, Adagio and (incomplete) Andante; Preludes and Fugues in D, G (two settings), g; Fugue in F (all in *D-B*)
Overture, D, str, *B*
Wedding cantata, B, orch, 1745, mentioned in Schering
Other works ascribed to him in *MGG* are mostly by J. C. F. Schneider (1786–1853) or J. G. Schneider of Dresden (1789–1864).

BIBLIOGRAPHY

P. Spitta: *Johann Sebastian Bach* (Leipzig, 1873–80, 5/1962; Eng. trans., 1884–99/*R*1951)
B. F. Richter: 'Über Seb. Bachs Kantaten mit obligater Orgel', *BJb*, v (1908), 49
C. S. Terry: *Bach: a Biography* (London, 1928, 2/1933)
A. Schering: *Johann Sebastian Bach und das Musikleben Leipzigs im 18. Jahrhundert* (Leipzig, 1941)
H. Löffler: 'Die Schüler Joh. Seb. Bachs', *BJb*, xl (1953), 13
W. Neumann and H.-J. Schulze: *Bach-Dokumente*, ii (Kassel and Leipzig, 1969)

HUGH J. McLEAN

Schneider, Marius (*b* Hagenau, Alsace, 1 July 1903). German musicologist. He studied philology and musicology at the universities of Strasbourg and Paris and the piano with Cortot, taking a doctorate under Wolf at Berlin University (1930) with a dissertation on the 14th-century Ars Nova. He was Hornbostel's assistant at the Berlin Phonogramm-Archiv (1932–4) and in

1934 succeeded him as director. In 1937 the government objected to his *Habilitation* at Berlin University. After military service during World War II he was appointed (1944) founder and director of the department for ethnomusicology at the Spanish Institute of Musicology, Barcelona; later he became a lecturer at the Consejo Superior de Investigaciones Cientificas at Barcelona University (1947–55). In 1955 his *Habilitationsschrift* on the history of polyphony was accepted by University of Cologne, where he taught comparative musicology and ethnomusicology (1955–68); after his retirement he taught at the University of Amsterdam (1968–70).

Schneider was directed to the study of the early Middle Ages by Wolf, and his examination of the origins and history of vocal polyphony led him to various extra-European sources. From a systematic comparison of many music examples from different regions and cultures he derived important conclusions concerning the principles of polyphonic techniques, their worldwide distribution and their historical relationships (see *Geschichte der Mehrstimmigkeit*). He was particularly interested in polyphonic phenomena in the vocal music of Africa and the Caucasus, and also studied the interrelationship between written music in early European manuscripts and surviving folk music traditions, and common traits of different musical cultures in the Mediterranean area including the Near East. Other studies are concerned with the music of specific regions or ethnic groups (Philippines, Mato Grosso, Cameroon, Australia, Assam, Tunisia and especially Spain). His research was always directed to the phenomenology and fundamentals of musical processes; his methodological position in comparative musicology and ethnomusicology was also expressed in basic contributions to handbooks and encyclopedias. In his last years Schneider was increasingly interested in the meaning and function of music in the context of philosophy, mythology and religion throughout the world, and contributed to a deeper understanding of the role of music in the study of symbols and cosmology. His ideas stimulated discussions and controversies among colleagues and students on an international basis, and he greatly influenced the younger generation of his 'Cologne school', which succeeded the 'Berlin school' of Hornbostel.

WRITINGS

Die Ars nova des XIV. Jahrhunderts in Frankreich und Italien (diss., U. of Berlin, 1930; Wolfenbüttel, 1931)
'Zur Satztechnik der Notre-Dame Schule', *ZMw*, xiv (1931–2), 398
Geschichte der Mehrstimmigkeit: historische und phänomenologische Studien, i: *Die Naturvölker*; ii: *Die Anfänge in Europa* (Berlin, 1934–5, 2/1968 with iii: *Die Kompositionsprinzipien und ihre Verbreitung*)
'Ethnologische Musikforschung', in K. T. Preuss: *Lehrbuch der Völkerkunde* (Stuttgart, 1937), 135–71
'Gesänge aus Uganda: ein Beitrag zur musikalischen Formbildung im Wechselgesang', *AMf*, ii (1937), 185–242
'Über die Verbreitung afrikanischer Chorformen', *Zeitschrift für Ethnologie*, lxix (1937), 78
'Die musikalischen Beziehungen zwischen Urkulturen, Altpflanzern und Hirtenvölkern', *Zeitschrift für Ethnologie*, lxx (1938), 287
'Kaukasische Parallelen zur mittelalterlichen Mehrstimmigkeit', *AcM*, xii (1940), 52
'Phonetische und metrische Korrelationen bei gesprochenen und gesungenen Ewe-Texten', *Archiv für Vergleichende Phonetik*, 2nd ser., vii (1943–4), 1
'A propósito del influjo árabe: ensayo de etnografía musical de la España medieval', *AnM*, i (1946), 31–141
El origen musical de los animales-simbolos en la mitología y la escultura antiguas: ensayo histórico-etnográfico sobre le substructura totemística y megalítica de las altas culturas y su supervivencia en el folklore español (Barcelona, 1946)

La danza de espadas y la tarantela: ensayo musicológico, etnográfico y arqueológico sobre los ritos medicinales (Barcelona, 1948)
'Tipología musical y literaria de la canción de cuna en España', *AnM*, iii (1948), 3–58
'Consideraciones acerca del canto gregoriano y la voz humana', *Arbor*, xiv (1949), 367
'Los cantos de Lluvia en España: estudio etnológico comparativo sobre la ideología de los ritos de pluviomagía', *AnM*, iv (1949), 3–57
'La relation entre la mélodie et le langage dans la musique chinoise', *AnM*, v (1950), 62
'Die historischen Grundlagen der musikalischen Symbolik', *Mf*, iv (1951), 113–44
'Ist die vokale Mehrstimmigkeit eine Schöpfung der Altrassen?', *AcM*, xxiii (1951), 40
'Die Bedeutung der Stimme in der alten Kulturen', *Tribus*, ii–iii (1952–3), 9
'Zur Trommelsprache der Duala', *Anthropos*, xlvii (1952), 235
'Arabischer Einfluss in Spanien? Eine Kritik an der rein historizistischen Kriterienbildung', *GfMKB, Bamberg 1953*, 175
'Le verset 94 de la sourate VI du Coran, étudié en une version populaire et en trois nagamât de tradition hispano-musulmane', *AnM*, ix (1954), 80
'Zambomba und Pandero: ein Beitrag zu den spanischen Karnevalsbräuchen', *Spanische Forschungen der Görres-Gesellschaft: gesammelte Aufsätze zur Kulturgeschichte Spaniens*, ix (Münster, 1954), 1
Singende Steine: Rhythmus-Studien an drei katalanischen Kreuzgängen romanischen Stils (Kassel, 1955)
'Entstehung der Tonsysteme', *GfMKB, Hamburg 1956*, 203
'Lieder aus den Naga-Bergen (Assam)', *Ethnomusicologie II: Wégimont III 1956*, 187–295
'Primitive Music', *NOHM*, i (1957), 1–82
'Die Musik der Naturvölker', *Lehrbuch der Völkerkunde*, ed. L. Adam and H. Trimborn (Stuttgart, 3/1958), 82
'Gestaltimitation als Kompositionsprinzip im Cancionero de Palacio', *Mf*, xi (1958), 415
'Prolegomena zu einer Theorie des Rhythmus', *IMSCR, vii Cologne 1958*, 264
'Studien zur Rhythmik im Cancionero de Palacio', *Miscelánea en homenaje a Monseñor Higinio Anglés* (Barcelona, 1958–61), 833
'Lieder der Duala', *DJbM*, iv (1959), 93
'Die musikalischen Grundlagen der Sphärenharmonie', *AcM*, xxxii (1960), 136
'Klagelieder des Volkes in der Kunstmusik der italienischen Ars nova', *AcM*, xxxiii (1961), 162
'Tone and Tune in West African Music', *EM*, v (1961), 204
'Wurzeln und Anfänge der abendländischen Mehrstimmigkeit', *IMSCR, viii New York 1961*, i, 161
'Die Modustransformation in einer spanischen Melodiegestalt', *Festschrift Karl Gustav Fellerer* (Regensburg, 1962), 481
'Das gestalttypologische Verfahren in der Melodik des Francesco Landino', *AcM*, xxxv (1963), 2
Die Natur des Lobgesangs (Basle, 1964)
'Kriterien zur Melodiegestalt', *Festschrift Hans Engel* (Kassel, 1964), 331
'Der Rhythmus als Stilelement im Cancionero de la casa de Medinaceli: ein Beitrag zur Editionstechnik und zum Verhältnis von Musik und Sprache', *Mf*, xviii (1965), 361
'Ein anamitisches Wiegenlied: ein Beitrag zum Verhältnis von Musik und Sprache', *Zum 70.Geburtstag von Joseph Müller-Blattau* (Kassel, 1966), 278
'Pukku und Mikku: ein Beitrag zum Aufbau und zum System der Zahlenmystik des Gilgamesch-Epos', *Antaios*, ix (1967), 262
'Vier Klagelieder aus dem Cancionero de la casa de Medinaceli und ihre Beziehung zur Volksmusik', *Festschrift Bruno Stäblein* (Kassel, 1967), 226
'Zur Metrisierung des altdeutschen Liedes', *Festschrift für Walter Wiora* (Kassel, 1967), 278
'Akul'turaija v muzîke' [Acculturation of music], *Muzîka narodov Azii i Afriki*, ed. V. S. Vinogradov (Moscow, 1969), 285
'Le basi storiche della simbologia musicale', *Conoscenza religiosa*, iii (1969), 267–302
'Über das Wachstum des Rhythmus in der Musik des Volkes des Mittelalters und der Renaissancezeit', *Musik als Gestalt und Erlebnis: Festschrift Walter Graf* (Vienna, 1970)
ed.: *Aussereuropäische Folklore und Kunstmusik* (Cologne, 1972)
'Das Schöpfungswort in der vedischen Kosmologie', *Musicae scientiae collectanea: Festschrift Karl Gustav Fellerer* (Cologne, 1973), 523
'Die Gattung in der Musik der Naturvölker', *Gattungen der Musik in Einzeldarstellungen: Gedenkschrift für Leo Schrade*, i (Berne and Munich, 1973), 95
'Die arabische Komponente im spanischen Volksgesang', *ÖMz*, xxx (1975), 175
ed.: *Studien zur Mittelmeermusik*, i: *Die tunesische Nuba ed Dhil* (Regensburg, n.d.)
Further articles in *MGG*, *RicordiE*, *FasquelleE*, *Die Religion in*

Geschichte und Gegenwart (Tübingen, 3/1960), *Histoire de la musique*, i, ed. Roland-Manuel (Paris, 1960), *Encyclopédie des musiques sacrées*, ed. J. Porte (Paris, 1968)

BIBLIOGRAPHY
R. Günther: 'Special Bibliography: Marius Schneider', *EM*, xiii (1969), 518 [complete list of publications]
Studien zur Phänomenologie der musikalischen Gestaltung: Festschrift für Marius Schneider (Regensburg, 1977)

ROBERT A. GÜNTHER

Schneider, Martin (*b* Silesia, probably at Hirschberg [now Jelenia Góra]; *fl* 1667). German composer and instrumentalist. He is known by a single publication, *Erster Theil neuer geistlicher Lieder, Arietten, Canto solo, cum Sonatella à 5 Violini* (Licgnitz, 1667), in which he called himself an instrumentalist, without stating where he worked, though it was probably at Hirschberg. His volume consists of settings of mystical poems from *Heilige Seelenlust* (1657) by ANGELUS SILESIUS, which were frequently set to music and the original publication of which was furnished with melodies mostly by Georg Joseph. Joseph reflected with some success the restricted metrical range of the poems, as Schneider, not always successfully, also attempted to do; semibreves, minims and crotchets alternate in his settings. The nature of his melodies suggests that he wrote his songs for competent singers, and they were probably confined to a limited circle, possibly the Moravians; they thus cannot really be considered as simple congregational hymns. The Moravians at Hirschberg long practised domestic devotions which demanded such music, and there is also an obvious similarity between Schneider's settings and the *Geistliche Arien* (also 1667) of Christoph Peter, who worked at Guben. Schneider's book contains 40 songs, and each one, except the single secular song (transcribed in Mitjana) is provided with a ritornello, which introduces the melody of the song; this practice shows the influence of the increasingly fashionable operatic aria, and Schneider's use of the term 'arietta' for his pieces is surely no accident. The ariettas themselves are accompanied by continuo alone. Two of them were included in the *Luneburger Choralbuch* (1694) and seven more in the 1695 edition; one of these also appeared in J. B. König's *Harmonischer Liederschatz* (1738).

BIBLIOGRAPHY
WaltherML
J. Zahn: *Die Melodien der deutschen evangelischen Kirchenlieder* (Gütersloh, 1889–93/R1963)
R. Mitjana: *Catalogue critique et descriptif des imprimés de musique des XVIe et XVIIe siècles conservés à la bibliothèque de l'Université d'Upsala* (Uppsala, 1911)

FRIEDRICH BASER

Schneider, Max (*b* Eisleben, 20 Sept 1875; *d* Halle, 5 May 1967). German music historian. He studied musicology with Kretzschmar and Riemann at Leipzig University and composition with Jadassohn. After serving as Kapellmeister in Halle (1897–1901) he resumed his historical studies with Kretzschmar in 1904 at Berlin, where he took his PhD in 1917 with a dissertation on the beginnings of the basso continuo. From 1907 to 1914 he worked as assistant librarian at the Royal Library (now the Deutsche Staatsbibliothek) in Berlin and taught orchestration at the Berlin Church Music Institute, where he was appointed professor in 1913. In 1915 he accepted a professorship at Breslau University, succeeding Otto Kinkeldey. In 1928 he

succeeded Schering as professor of musicology at Halle University. He held this post until he retired from active university service in 1960. Honoured by three Festschriften he was respected as the doyen of German musicology for more than two decades until he died at the age of 92.

Schneider's main field of interest and research, as reflected in his numerous publications, was almost exclusively the history of music from the late 16th century to the mid-18th. Within this area his main concerns were questions of performing practice and problems of sources, printed or manuscript. Of particular significance are his contributions to Bach research which included some major bibliographical, archival and source-material studies as well as exemplary editions. He was co-editor of *Archiv für Musikwissenschaft* (1918–27), co-editor of the *Händel-Jahrbuch* (1955–67) and from 1955 co-editor of the Hallische Händel-Ausgabe.

WRITINGS
'Verzeichnis der bis zum Jahre 1851 gedruckten (und der geschrieben im Händel gewesenen) Werke von J. S. Bach', *BJb*, iii (1906), 84–114
'Thematisches Verzeichnis der musikalischen Werke der Familie Bach', *BJb*, iv (1907), 103–77
'Das sogenannte Orgel-Konzert d-moll von W. F. Bach', *BJb*, viii (1911), 23
'Zur Lukaspassion', *BJb*, viii (1911), 105
'Der Generalbass J. S. Bachs', *JbMP* 1914–15, 21
'Die Begleitung des Secco-Rezitativs um 1750', *Gluck-Jb*, iii (1917), 88
Die Anfänge des Basso continuo und seiner Bezifferung (diss., U. of Berlin, 1917; Leipzig, 1918)
'Die Besetzung der vielstimmigen Musik des 16. und 17. Jahrhunderts', *AMw*, i (1918–19), 205–34
'Zum Weihnachtsoratorium von H. Schütz', *Theodor Kroyer: Festschrift zum sechzigsten Geburtstag* (Regensburg, 1933), 140

EDITIONS
G. P. Telemann: Der Tag des Gerichts; Ino, DDT, xxviii (1907/*R*)
with M. Seiffert: *L. Mozart: Ausgewählte Werke*, DTB, xvii, Jg.ix/2 (1908)
R. Keiser: Der hochmütige, gestürzte und wieder erhabene Croesus, 1730 (1710); Erlesene Sätze aus L'inganno Fedele, 1714, DDT, xxxvii–xxxviii (1912/*R*)
Altbachisches Archiv aus Johann Sebastian Bachs Sammlung von Werken seiner Vorfahren, EDM, 1st ser., i–ii (1935/*R*)
G. P. Telemann: Tre frietti melodiche e tre scherzi, Collegium musicum, lxxiii–lxxv (Leipzig, 1948)
with O. Schröder: *J. Walther: Sämtliche Werke*, i–vi (Kassel and St Louis, Miss., 1953–70)
G. F. Handel: Ezio, Hallische Händel-Ausgabe, ii (Kassel, 1956) [vocal score]
with W. Serauky and S. Flesch: *G. F. Handel: Triosonaten, op.5: 1–7*, Hallische Händel-Ausgabe, iv/10 (Kassel, 1967)
J. S. Bach: Matthäus Passion, Neue Ausgabe sämtlicher Werke, ii/5 (Kassel, 1972)

BIBLIOGRAPHY
H. J. Zingel, ed.: *Festschrift Max Schneider zum 60. Geburtstag* (Halle, 1935) [contains list of writings to 1935]
W. Vetter, ed.: *Festschrift Max Schneider zum 80. Geburtstag* (Leipzig, 1955)
W. Vetter: 'Max Schneider 80 Jahre', *Mf*, viii (1955), 257
W. Siegmund-Schulze, ed.: *Festschrift Max Schneider zum 85. Geburtstag* (Leipzig, 1960)
W. Siegmund-Schulze: 'Max Schneider zum Gedächtnis', *Mf*, xx (1967), 241

CHRISTOPH WOLFF

Schneider, Michael (*b* Weimar, 4 March 1909). German organist and church musician. From 1927 to 1930 he studied church music at the Weimar Musikhochschule and the Leipzig Institute of Church Music, and later musicology at the universities of Jena and Munich. In 1940 he took a doctorate at Cologne University with a dissertation on German organ technique in the early 19th century. He was the town organist and a lecturer at the Musikhochschule at Weimar (1931–4), then until 1936 principal organist and Kantor at the church of St

Matthew in Munich and a lecturer at the Music Academy there. In 1936 he became a professor and head of the department of evangelical church music at the Cologne Musikhochschule. He conducted the Berlin Kantorei, whose performances included cycles of Bach cantatas, and the Berlin Bruckner Choir (1941–5). Schneider then worked in Munich as director of church music at St Mark's, a lecturer at the music academy and conductor of the university chorus. Later he took up posts in Detmold as professor of organ, head of the department of evangelical church music and deputy director at the North-west German Academy of Music. In 1958 he was appointed professor of organ at the Berlin Musikhochschule, and in 1965 returned to the Cologne Musikhochschule. He has given frequent organ concerts in Germany and abroad and is renowned for his dynamic but flexible style. Although well grounded in tradition, Schneider is also a knowledgeable interpreter of contemporary music and has had works dedicated to him by such composers as David, Höller, Max Baumann and Frank Michael Beyer.

BIBLIOGRAPHY
Festschrift für Michael Schneider (Berlin, 1974)
GERHARD WIENKE

Schneider, Paul. See SARTORIUS, PAUL.

Schneiderhan, Wolfgang (Eduard) (*b* Vienna, 28 May 1915). Austrian violinist. He was taught by his mother from the age of three, and when he was five made a public début in Vienna. In 1923 he went to Písek to study with Otakar Ševčík, and later completed his studies with Julius Winkler in Vienna. His international career as a soloist began with a performance of Mendelssohn's concerto in Copenhagen in 1926. For a short period in 1929 he lived in England. He became the first leader of the Vienna SO in 1933, and was appointed to lead the Vienna PO in 1937, the year he formed the Schneiderhan Quartet. In 1951 he left the orchestra and disbanded the quartet to resume his solo career, but continued to play trios with Enrico Mainardi and Edwin Fischer until 1956. He has also been active as a teacher at the Salzburg Mozarteum (1938–56), and at the Vienna Academy of Music (1939–50). In 1949 he succeeded Flesch and Kulenkampf at the Lucerne Conservatory where, in association with his pupil Rudolf Baumgartner, he formed the Lucerne Festival Strings in 1956. He was never a great virtuoso, but his performances are distinguished by his stylistic superiority and sensibly balanced artistry in Viennese works, especially Mozart, Beethoven and Schubert; he has also given fine performances of works by Stravinsky, Martin and Henze. In the 1970s he extended his activities to conducting, giving Franz Schmidt's opera *Notre Dame* at the Vienna Volksoper in 1975. He married the soprano Irmgard Seefried in 1948, and has given many concerts with her.

BIBLIOGRAPHY
F. Fassbind: *Wolfgang Schneiderhan, Irmgard Seefried; eine Künstler-und Lebensgemeinschaft* (Berne, 1960)
J. Creighton: *Discopaedia of the Violin, 1889–1971* (Toronto, 1974)
Wolfgang Schneiderhan zum 60. Geburtstag (Wiesbaden, 1975)
GERHARD BRUNNER

Schneidermann, Dina (*b* Odessa, 28 March 1931). Bulgarian violinist. As a child prodigy she studied at the School of Music in Odessa under Stolyarsky, and in 1956 graduated from the Leningrad Conservatory where she studied under Eidlin. After her marriage in 1956 to the violinist Emil Kamilarov, a professor at the State Academy of Music in Sofia from 1963, she moved to Bulgaria, where with her husband she often arranges concert cycles of violin concertos. She won the 1951 3rd World Youth Festival Competition in Berlin and the 1960 Geneva International Competition. She has appeared in most European countries, as well as in Cuba, Canada, Israel, and elsewhere, with a wide repertory including works by Bulgarian and Soviet composers. An outstanding artistic personality with an expressive temperament, she commands a brilliant technique, a warm tone full of variety and nuance, a lively feeling for musical line, and an individual interpretation.

BIBLIOGRAPHY
J. Creighton: *Discopaedia of the Violin 1889–1971* (Toronto, 1974), 679
LADA BRASHOVANOVA

Schneider-Siemssen, Günther (*b* Augsburg, 7 June 1926). Austrian scene designer of German birth. He was guided by Clemens Krauss to study scene design, and through Kraus gained early experience in scene painting at the Munich State Opera, in addition to other studies in Munich with Ludwig Sievert, Emil Preetorius and Rudolf Hartmann. From 1947 to 1954 he designed for theatres and films in Berlin, Munich and Salzburg. In 1952 he began his 20-year association with the Salzburg Marionettes, eventually revolutionizing the design of the puppet stage and creating several new productions of Mozart operas. In 1954 he was named chief of design at the Bremen State Theatre, where he designed the first of his productions of Wagner's *Ring*. After collaborating with Herbert von Karajan on *Pelléas et Mélisande* at the Vienna Staatsoper in 1960 he became Karajan's personal adviser on production, moving in 1962 to Vienna where he was appointed chief designer for the Staatsoper, the Burgtheater and the Volksoper. He made his Covent Garden début in 1962 designing Peter Ustinov's production of Schoenberg's *Erwartung* and then designed the *Ring*, produced by Hans Hotter and conducted by Georg Solti (1962–4). With Karajan he has worked on numerous productions for the summer and Easter festivals at Salzburg, including *Boris Godunov* (1965), *Don Giovanni* (1967), *Otello* (1969), the *Ring* (1967–70, later given in modified form in New York), *Fidelio* (1971) and *Tristan und Isolde* (1972). He also designed *Le nozze di Figaro* at La Scala in 1973 and *Jenůfa* at the Metropolitan Opera, New York, in 1974.

His designs, particularly for Wagner, are outstanding for the epic, cosmic world they create on stage. Light and projection in sweeping, swirling patterns evoke with powerful symbolism a universe that coincides perfectly with the visions of the producers with whom he has most often worked, Karajan, August Everding and Otto Schenk. The Metropolitan Opera *Tristan und Isolde* (1971) was notable for its superb use of that stage's technical possibilities towards disclosing the lovers' deepest feelings: when they sang of love, the real world disappeared, and vast, spectacular heavens came into view; on King Mark's entry the vegetation of the garden was transformed from lush summer to frosty winter.

BIBLIOGRAPHY
W. Greisenegger: 'Schneider-Siemssen, Günther', *ES*
PAUL SHEREN

Schneider-Trnavský, Mikuláš (*b* Trnava, 24 May 1881; *d* Bratislava, 28 May 1958). Slovak composer and choirmaster. He studied composition at the conservatories of Budapest, Vienna and Prague, where he graduated in 1905. From 1909 until his death he was choirmaster of the Cathedral of St Mikuláš, Trnava, and in 1956 he was made a National Artist of the Czech republic. At first influenced by the turn-of-the-century Prague school, and particularly by the Dvořák tradition, his compositional development was adapted towards the taste of Slovak bourgeois society. He became well known for arrangements of the diatonic Slovak folksongs of modern origin, and his harmonizations of religious songs remain unsurpassed. In art songs he tried to synthesize the German lied tradition with Slovak folksong. A large part of his church music, which is close to the work of Max Filke and W. E. Horák, was written for amateur performance.

WORKS
(selective list)

Operetta: Bellarosa, 1940
Orch: Dumka a tanec, 1909; Pribinov sl'ub [Pribina's vow], 1933; Duhopol, vn, orch, 1954; Sym., e, 1956
Sacred vocal: Jednotný katolícky spevník [Standard Catholic hymnbook], 1v, org, 1937; 24 masses, numerous graduals and offertories
Secular choral: Hľa zlietol orol [Lo, the eagle flew], 1930; Padol kameň [The stone fell], 1930; Na Bradle zádumčivom [On pensive Bradl], Partizánska, 1949
Songs: Drobné kvety [Little flowers], 1907; Slzy a úsmevy [Tears and smiles], 1912; Zo srdca [From the heart], 1921; Slovenské národné piesne [Slovak national songs], 5 vols., 1930; Piesne o matke [Songs about mother], 1940; 50 slowakische Volkslieder, 1943
Inst: Sonata, g, vn, 1905; Slovenská sonatína, pf, 1938; Pestrý rad skladieb [A gay series of compositions], pf, 1944

Principal publishers: Matica Slovenská, Slovenské Hudobné Vydavateľstvo, Spolok Sv. Vojtecha, Jozaf Závodský

BIBLIOGRAPHY
J. Šamko: *Mikuláš Schneider-Trnavský = pohľad na život a dielo* (Bratislava, 1965)

LADISLAV BURLAS

Schneidewind, Hellmut (*b* Grossleiningen, Südharz, 1 Feb 1928). German trumpeter. He received his musical training at the Musikschule Beinroth in Sangerhausen (1942–6) and the conservatory in Sondershausen (1947–50). After playing in the opera orchestras of Wittenberg and Altenburg, he became, in 1953, first trumpeter with the Gewandhaus Orchestra of Leipzig, and, in 1956, first trumpeter of the radio orchestra in Cologne. In 1968 he was appointed trumpet teacher at the North-west German Music Academy in Detmold, where he became professor in 1969. Schneidewind is well known as a soloist, having made many recordings and participated in concert tours with chamber orchestras.

EDWARD H. TARR

Schnell (Ger.: 'rapid', 'swift', 'fast'). A tempo designation. It is the German equivalent of the Italian *presto*. Bruckner gave the finale of his Second Symphony the tempo designation *mehr schnell* ('more fast') at the opening; later it becomes *sehr schnell* ('very fast').

See also TEMPO AND EXPRESSION MARKS.

DAVID FALLOWS

Schnell, Johann Jakob (*b* 1687; *d* Bamberg, 21 Feb 1754). German instrumentalist and composer. From 1714 he was oboist and violinist to the Prince-Bishop of Bamberg, and on 1 July 1727 was appointed by Lothar Franz to direct the court chamber music. With this move began Schnell's effectiveness as representative of the era of the Schönborn family in Franconia. His opp.1 and 8 comprise nine cycles of sacred works and his

other opus numbers are court and chamber music. He described his orchestral masses (a title which indicates that they were innovations) as difficult; they contained concerto-style sonatas to accompany the epistle. The three Vespers op.8 are graded as 'solennes', 'breves' and 'brevissimae' and in the preface three more vespers are promised, though it is not known whether he wrote them. For the Violin Concertos op.3 and the *Neue Parthien* op.9 Schnell used the same small group of instruments as for his church music (strings, with two trumpets or horns). He furnished op.2 with a diagram and fingering for flute and op.3 with a diagram and fingering for the high soloists. Among his works are many flute trios, a genre with which Count Rudolf had become particularly well acquainted during his studies in Rome in 1693, largely owing to his acquaintance with Corelli; Schnell's are fresh and inventive, while his chamber music shows his special mastery of the intimate form. The economies made necessary by the success of the Schönborns' Baroque architecture were turned by Schnell into a virtue, while the majesty of the full-size orchestra was reserved for his successors. In 1738 he also took up publishing.

Other Schnells active in Germany may have been related to Johann Jakob. Judas Thaddäus Schnell (*b* Wangen, before 1550; *d* Füssen, 25 Aug 1619) was a south German choir director and church composer. In the decades before the Thirty Years War he was in charge of musical activities in the Allgäu Benedictine Monastery St Mang in Füssen. Three of his compositions are extant (in *D-Rp* and *Mbs*). Bernhard Schnell (*fl* 1704) was probably the father of Johann Jakob Schnell. He assisted Count Rudolf in Wiesentheid, Lower Franconia, in founding his collection of instruments. Another Johann Jakob (Jean Jacques) Schnell (*b* Vaihingen, Württemberg, 1740) started as a carpenter's apprentice, but by 1760 was making pianos and organs with Gessinger in Rothenburg. He later spent six years with Dulcken in the Netherlands. In 1777 he was in Paris, first making harpsichords for the Countess of Artois and then as court instrument maker for the king. He built an *anemochord* ('wind-piano') which was bought by Marie Antoinette. After five years' military service in France he started a piano shop in Ludwigsburg, and in 1799 demonstrated his *anemochord* in Vienna and sold it to a London surgeon, Robert Robertson, in 1803. Johann Christoph Schnell (*fl* 1788) was either a brother or a son of the later Johann Jakob Schnell. In 1788 he settled in Zweibrücken as a keyboard instrument maker.

WORKS

6 Missae neoeditae, SATB, str, tpt, org, op.1 (Bamberg, 1729)
6 Parthiae trisonae, fl, vn, bc, op.2 (Erlangen, 1731)
6 Concerta commode tractabilia,vn solo, str, bc, op.3 (Erlangen, 1731)
6 Sonatae trisonae, fl/vn/va d'amore, bc, op.4 (n.p., n.d.)
6 Trios, fl, vn, bc, op.5 (n.p., n.d.)
6 Trios, fl, vn, bc, op.7 (n.p., n.d.)
3 Vesperae breves, SATB, 2 vn, 2 tpt/hn, bc, op.8 (Bamberg, 1736)
6 Neue ernst- und schertzhafte Parthien, 2 vn, 2 tpt, bc, op.9 (Bamberg, 1738)
Vn Conc., A, Bavarian Radio Archive, Nuremberg; Sonata, va da gamba, D, *WD*

BIBLIOGRAPHY
FétisBS; *GerberNL*
Leipziger Zeitung, i (1798), 33 [description of an *anemochord*]
G. Schilling, ed.: *Encyclopädie der gesammten musikalischen Wissenschaften* (Stuttgart, 1835–8/*R*1973)
H. Mendel: 'Anemochord', 'Schnell', *Musikalisches Conversations-Lexikon* (Berlin, 1870–79)

HANNS DENNERLEIN

Schneller (Ger.). (1) Faster. A tempo qualification, the comparative of *schnell*.

(2) An unprepared single upper mordent; *see* ORNAMENTS, §III, 8.

Schnetzler, Johann. See SNETZLER, JOHN.

Schnifis, Laurentius von. See LAURENTIUS VON SCHNÜFFIS.

Schnitger. German family of organ builders. Arp Schnitger (*b* Schmalenfleth, Oldenburg, 2 July 1648; *d* 24 July 1719) was apprenticed to his cousin Berendt Huess at Glückstadt in Holstein. From 1669 to 1673 he assisted Huess in building the organ for St Cosmae, Stade (which he enlarged in 1688 and which still exists), and he completed Huess's 43-stop, three-manual and pedal organ at St Wilhadi, Stade, after the latter's death in 1676. His best organ was that at St Nicolai, Hamburg (1682–7). Two of his four sons later assisted him in his work: Johann Georg (Jürgen) (baptized 4 Sept 1690; *d* after 1733) and Franz Caspar (baptized 15 Oct 1693; *d* Netherlands, 1729).

Arp Schnitger achieved fame while quite young; with the aid of his sons and assistants, and a number of privileges giving him virtual monopolies in certain areas, he was able to build some 150 organs of all sizes, firmly establishing his own type of organ in north Germany and the Netherlands. His organs are characterized by well-developed chorus work with adequate mixtures on all manuals and pedals, flutes and reeds at many pitches, including Nasats and Quints at 1⅓ pitch, principal-scaled Sesquialteras and Terzians, normally at least one 16′ stop (and sometimes up to four) on the *Hauptwerk*, often both Gedackt 8′ and Quintation 8′ on even a small *Rückpositiv*, and Pedal organs with mixtures, a solo flute stop and reeds from 16′ to 2′. Cornets and flute Tierces are absent. Very narrow-scale flutes are found, and occasionally string stops. Most of the pipework is metal, the case pipes being sometimes of almost pure tin or overlaid with tin on the front sides. Wooden pipes are rare, but Schnitger occasionally used hard oak for the Gedackts in the *Brustwerk*.

The four-octave compass (*C* to *c′′′*), usually had a short octave on the manuals (omitting the four lowest accidentals, also the lowest one or two accidentals in the pedals), although occasionally the lowest octaves were complete. The pitch was Chorton. Schnitger used sliderchests and normally built his organs against the west wall on the *Werk* principle. His casework was usually designed on the same plan – a central round tower flanked by two-storied flats, the upper being mute, and two triangular towers (the *Rückpositiv* being a smaller version), flanked by two large Pedal towers, sometimes detached from the main case, especially where the height was restricted. The *Brustwerk* in his earlier organs was enclosed behind pierced doors and in his later instruments had its own case pipes.

Besides building new organs, Schnitger enlarged and rebuilt existing ones and often preserved and included good earlier pipework in his reconstructions. Instruments either built or restored by him are at Neuenfelde (1683), Norden, East Friesland (1686–8), Hamburg (Jacobikirche, 1688–93), Noordbroek (1695–6), Dedesdorf (1698), Ganderkesee (1699), Uithuizen (1700–01), Pellworm Island (1711), Cappel, near Cuxhaven (1679–80), Lüdingworth, near Cuxhaven (1682–3), Steinkirchen (1685–7), Groningen (Martinikerk, 1691–2), Stade (St Cosmae, 1688).

After Arp Schnitger's death, Johann Georg and Franz Caspar settled in the Netherlands, where they completed the organ started by their father at the Grote Kerk, Zwolle, and rebuilt the large organ at St Laurents, Alkmaar.

BIBLIOGRAPHY
W. L. Sumner: 'Arp Schnitger and his Organs', *The Organ*, xvii (1938), 139, 193
C. Clutton: 'The Schnitger Organ at Steinkirchen', *The Organ*, xxx (1951), 105
P. Williams: *The European Organ, 1450–1850* (London, 1966)
C. H. Edskes: 'De nagelaten geschriften van de orgelmaker Arp Schnitger', *Bijdragen tot de geschiedenis van het orgelmaken*, ed. S. Meijer (Sneek, 1968)
G. Fock: *Arp Schnitger und seine Schule* (Kassel, 1975)
GUY OLDHAM

Schnittelbach, Nathanael (*b* Danzig, 16 June 1633; *d* Lübeck, 16 Nov 1667). German violinist and composer. His first appointment, not a permanent one, was as viola player at St Marien, Danzig. At the age of 20 he joined the orchestra of Queen Christina of Sweden, but two years later, early in 1655, he returned to Germany as civic musician at Lübeck. He received the freedom of the city on 13 November of the same year and on 11 December married a daughter of the civic musician NICOLAUS BLEYER with whom he studied the violin from 1655 until Bleyer's death in 1658. Gerber called him 'one of the greatest violinists of the seventeenth century'. He was known throughout Germany and in Poland, Denmark, Holland and Sweden and was likewise respected as a teacher; his most famous pupil was Nicolaus Adam Strungk. He became ill while taking part in festivities celebrating a court wedding at Gottorf in October 1667 and died a month later. His only surviving music, two suites for instrumental ensemble in E minor and C minor (*S-Uu*, inc), are typical of civic music of the time and probably date from his years in Lübeck. He is also known to have written a *Magnificat* for five voices and two violins, but it is lost.

BIBLIOGRAPHY
GerberL
A. Moser: *Geschichte des Violinspiels* (Berlin, 1923, rev. 2/1966)
J. Hennings: *Musikgeschichte Lübecks*, i (Kassel, 1951)
GEORG KARSTÄDT

Schnitzer. Two German families of instrument makers, both of Munich origin and active in Nuremberg, with no proved relationship to each other. The members of one were Stadtpfeifers and woodwind instrument makers, the others were brass instrument makers.

The founder of the Stadtpfeifer dynasty was Albrecht Schnitzer the elder (*d* Munich, 1524 or 1525), whose instruments bore the mark 'A'. He started making instruments in Munich in about 1490, and was a Stadtpfeifer from 1493 until his death. He had at least six sons who were musicians. Sigmund Schnitzer the elder (*d* Nuremberg, between 14 March and 13 June 1557) was installed as a Stadtpfeifer in Nuremberg in 1503, becoming a citizen there in 1507. Hans Schnitzer the elder (*b* Munich, *c*1486; *d* Nuremberg, 25 April 1565) was a Stadtpfeifer in Nuremberg between 1506 and 1551. Albrecht Schnitzer the younger was documented in 1521 as a drummer in Nuremberg, where he became a citizen in 1523. Mathes Schnitzer (*d* Nuremberg, 1553) became a Nuremberg Stadtpfeifer in 1522 and a citizen in 1528; he lived in Prague from 1530 until 1532, and in 1534 declined an invitation to go to

Munich as a trombonist, instead becoming senior Stadtpfeifer in Nuremberg in 1535, a position he held until his death. He was also known as a trumpeter and a woodwind instrument maker. Arsazius Schnitzer (*d* Munich, 1557) was a Munich Stadtpfeifer and woodwind instrument maker, and played the trombone. Anton Schnitzer (*d* Munich, in or before 1544) was also a Munich Stadtpfeifer. Sigmund and Arsazius used the mark 'AA' to distinguish their instruments from those of their father and of their brother Hans, who continued to use his father's single 'A'.

Sigmund the elder's son, Sigmund Schnitzer the younger (*d* Nuremberg, 7 Dec 1578), was a Stadtpfeifer in Ulm in 1557, but returned to Nuremberg in the same capacity in 1567. Hans the elder had two sons, Veit Schnitzer (*fl* 1540–55) and Hans Schnitzer the younger (*b* Nuremberg, *c*1515; *d* Kassel, before 22 Nov 1566). Veit was a Nuremberg Stadtpfeifer intermittently from 1540 to 1543, and was apparently also an instrument maker, as he obtained a privilege in 1555 from Emperor Karl V to protect his family's mark, which had often been copied by unauthorized persons; after 1547 he was in the emperor's service as a gentleman-at-arms ('Trabant'). Hans the younger, a cornett player and trumpeter, was a Stadtpfeifer in Nuremberg between 15 May 1537 and August 1538, when he moved to Kassel to become a member of the Hofkapelle. Arsazius also had a son named Hans (*b* Munich, *c*1530; *d* Munich, 1601), who was a Stadtpfeifer and woodwind instrument maker.

Sigmund the elder was perhaps the most important woodwind instrument maker before Denner. He expanded the family of shawms from the single 'tibia tenor' known to Tinctoris and Virdung (and depicted in two of Hans Burgkmair's woodcuts from *The Triumph of Maximilian*, *c*1516) to include seven different sizes. He invented the first 16' bass instrument, the *Doppelquint-Basspommer*. His sons specialized: Mathes built transverse flutes and cornetts, Sigmund the younger recorders and shawms. Hans the younger appears to have made only recorders. Five instruments bearing the mark 'AA' survive: a tenor recorder, two bass recorders and two cornetts. They were made by Sigmund the younger, Arsazius, or perhaps by Mathes. A bass recorder bearing what appears to be a single 'A' is in the Instrument Museum of the Brussels conservatory; it was probably made by Albrecht the elder or Hans the elder.

Erasmus Schnitzer (*d* Nuremberg, 3 Feb 1566), who became a Nuremberg citizen in 1547, is the first Schnitzer known to have made brass instruments; it is not known whether he, too, was a son of Albrecht the elder, nor is his relation to the other Schnitzer brass instrument makers clear. Albrecht the elder's son Anton (see above) was probably the father of Anton Schnitzer the elder (*d* Nuremberg, 28 March 1608), who established the dynasty of brass instrument makers; he took over the NEUSCHEL workshop on the death of his stepfather, Georg Stengel (called Neuschel), in 1557, and became a citizen of Nuremberg in 1558 and a master in 1562. His son Anton Schnitzer the younger (*b* Nuremberg, 20 April 1564) became a master in 1591, and other sons Hans Schnitzer (*b* Nuremberg, 1571; *d* Nuremberg, 1609) and Jobst Schnitzer (*b* Nuremberg, 28 March 1576; *d* Nuremberg, before 1 May 1616) became masters in 1598. Anton the younger's son, Eberhard Schnitzer (*b* Nuremberg, 1600; *d* Nuremberg,

1634), became a master in 1620.

Most of the surviving trumpets and trombones of the Schnitzer family are elaborate ceremonial instruments exhibiting the highest mastery of their trade. Their bells are wide and conical, a type generally characteristic of the late Renaissance. Of the eight surviving instruments, the most significant are: a tenor trombone made in 1551 by Erasmus, the oldest signed and dated trombone in existence (Germanisches Nationalmuseum, Nuremberg; *see* TROMBONE, fig.4*a*); a tenor-bass trombone with a crook like the ones illustrated in Mersenne (v, p.271) and Praetorius (pl.viii), made in 1579 (not 1578) by Anton the elder (Accademia Filarmonica, Verona); a trumpet in modern E♭, silver-plated, with exquisite gold garnishings and elaborate engraving, made in 1581 by Anton the elder (Sammlung alter Musikinstrumente, Kunsthistorisches Museum, Vienna, no.4031; *see* Winternitz); a trumpet in modern E, shaped like a pretzel and containing a medallion with the Bavarian coat of arms in one of the lateral loops of tubing, made in 1585 by Anton the elder and once belonging to the virtuoso Cesare Bendinelli (Verona collection); a trumpet made in 1598 by Anton the elder or younger (no.181 in the Vienna collection) and identical to the 1585 instrument in Verona apart from the lack of a medallion; and a bass trombone made in 1612 by Jobst, the earliest trombone with a double slide (Karl-Marx-Universität collection, Leipzig, no.615).

Anton the elder was doubtless the greatest master of this Schnitzer family, and one of the most productive; the Munich court alone ordered 12, 24 and 18 trumpets from him in 1567, 1590 and 1592 respectively. His 1581 trumpet possesses its original mouthpiece, permanently attached to the mouthpipe. Its bore is an enormous 8·3 mm and marks the instrument for use in the *principale* register. The tubing of the 1585 instrument in Verona is in three parts: mouthpipe, middle section and bell; the joints in the tubing, however, are not covered by the ferrules as was normally the case, but instead are exposed as straight, thin rings – a masterful piece of craftsmanship.

BIBLIOGRAPHY

M. Praetorius: *Theatrum instrumentorum* (Wolfenbüttel, 1620/*R*1958)
M. Mersenne: *Harmonie universelle* (Paris 1636–7/*R*1963; Eng. trans., 1957)
F. Jahn: 'Trompeten- und Posaunenmacher im 16. Jahrhundert', *AMw*, vii (1925), 23
W. Wörthmüller: 'Die Nürnberger Trompeten- und Posaunenmacher des 17. und 18. Jahrhunderts', *Mitteilungen des Vereins für Geschichte der Stadt Nürnberg*, xlv (1954), 208; xlvi (1955), 372
E. Winternitz: *Die schönsten Musikinstrumente* (Munich, 1966; Eng. trans., 1967), frontispiece
E. Nickel: *Der Holzblasinstrumentenbau in der freien Reichsstadt Nürnberg* (Munich, 1971)
E. Tarr: *Die Trompete* (Berne, 1976)

EDWARD H. TARR

Schnitzer [Schnizer], **Franz (Xaver)** (*b* Wurzach, 13 Dec 1740; *d* Ottobeuren, 9 May 1785). German composer. He entered the monastery of Ottobeuren in 1760 and studied music under Placidus Christadler and Benedikt Kraus. He played K. J. Riepp's new organ at the consecration of the monastery's Dreifaltigkeitskirche (1766), and from 1769 served the abbey as *regens chori*, organist and music teacher. Regarded by Lipowsky as a first-rate composer, he wrote much sacred music in the Italian style of his time (in *A-Wn*, *D-FS*, *Mbs*, *OB*) and at least 17 school dramas, now lost, for Ottobeuren (one was also performed in Freising in

1776). He published a set of six keyboard sonatas op.1 (1773) and *Cantus ottoburani monasterii* (1784).

BIBLIOGRAPHY

EitnerQ

F. J. Lipowsky: *Baierisches Musik-Lexikon* (Munich, 1811/*R*1971)
A. Lindner: *Die Schriftsteller und die um Wissenschaft und Kunst verdienten Mitglieder des Benediktiner-Ordens im heutigen Königreich Bayern*, ii (Regensburg, 1880), 83ff; repr. in *Zeitschrift des Historischen Vereins für Schwaben und Neuburg*, xxi (1904), 33
W. Klemm: *Benediktinisches Barocktheater in Südbayern, insbesondere des Reichsstiftes Ottobeuren* (diss., U. of Munich, 1938; *Studien und Mitteilungen zur Geschichte des Benediktiner-Ordens und seiner Zweige*, liv (1936), 95–184, 397–432; lv (1937), 274–304)
U. Siegele: 'Schnitzer, Franz', *MGG*

ADOLF LAYER

Schnitzkius [Schnitzke, Schnitzky], **Gregor** (*b* Danzig, ?*c*1580; *d* after 1627). German composer, singer and teacher. Most of our knowledge of his career derives from his publications. In 1603 he describes himself as 'musicus et scholae ad St. Johann Collega' in Danzig, and by 1607 he had a post at the Marienschule there. At the same time he was a member of the civic choir at the Marienkirche, where he frequently deputized for the aging Kapellmeister, Johann Wanning. He applied for the post of Kapellmeister when it became vacant in 1603, but he and such notable candidates as Philipp Dulichius and the elder Kaspar Förster (who, like Schnitzkius, was already working in Danzig) were passed over in 1607–8 in favour of Andreas Hakenberger, from the chapel of King Sigismund III of Poland. After Hakenberger's death in 1627, Schnitzkius once more applied unsuccessfully; this time Förster was appointed.

Schnitzkius's works reflect his activities in church and school. The *Musices praecepta maxime necessaria latino germanica pro incipientibus illius artis collecta* (Danzig, 1619) is a primer for beginners dealing with the rudiments of music in five sections ('Clavis', 'Vox', 'Cantus', 'Mutatio', 'Figura') in both Latin and German. None of his printed volumes of music survives complete. The three sections of the *Sacri moduli*, which according to the preface were intended for schools and domestic music-making, comprise three-part Latin hymns, and their texts are related symbolically to the number three. *Tibi laus, tibi gloria* from *Sacrarum cantionum* exists complete in MS; it is an eight-part piece for double chorus in which the treatment of the text is rather conventional.

WORKS

(all published in Danzig)

Moduli sacri musicis numeris exornati (1603)
Sacrarum cantionum, 4–12vv, quibus addita est Missa super 'Perchè non debbo', 8vv (1607); 1 piece, Missa super 'Tibi laus gloria', intabulated, *PL-WRu*
Missa super 'Deus noster refugium', et Magnificat, 5, 6vv (1607)
Sacri moduli, omnes ternarium in se continentes, pars I, 3vv (1612); 1 ed. in Rausching
Sacri moduli, pars II (1618)
Sacri moduli, pars III (1625)
All prints inc.; MS copies, *D-Bds, Dlb, PL-WRu*

BIBLIOGRAPHY

GerberNL; *WaltherML*

G. Döring: *Zur Geschichte der Musik in Preussen* (Elbing, 1852)
E. Bohn: *Bibliographie des Musikdruckwerke bis 1700, welche . . . zu Breslau aufbewahrt werden* (Berlin, 1883)
——: *Die musikalischen Handschriften des 16. und 17. Jahrhunderts in der Stadtbibliothek zu Breslau* (Breslau, 1890)
J. Müller-Blattau: *Geschichte der Musik in Ost- und Westpreussen von der Ordenszeit bis zur Gegenwart* (Königsberg, 1931)
H. Rauschning: *Geschichte der Musik und Musikpflege in Danzig* (Danzig, 1931)
E. Schild: *Geschichte der protestantischen Messenkomposition im 17. und 18. Jahrhundert* (Wuppertal, 1934)

JOHANNES GÜNTHER KRANER

Schnizer, Franz. *See* SCHNITZER, FRANZ.

Schnoor, Hans (*b* Neumünster, Holstein, 4 Oct 1893; *d* Bielefeld, 15 Jan 1976). German musicologist and critic. After studies in Geneva and Leipzig, he took the doctorate in 1919 under Riemann (whose last assistant he became) and Schering with a dissertation on the Buxheimer Orgelbuch. From 1922 to 1925 he was music critic for newspapers in Dresden and Leipzig, becoming in 1926 music editor of the *Dresdner Anzeiger*; he also lectured at the Dresden Conservatory. During this period began his lifelong interest in Weber. Having lost his library and musicological materials in the bombing of Dresden, he moved briefly to Berlin, where he substantially helped to reorganize the important Jähns Weber Collection. Renewing his contacts with Weber's descendants, he resumed his Weber research, giving special attention to the diaries and letters.

Though he published many articles and books on general musical subjects, and made a special study of oratorio, it is his work on Weber that has been Schnoor's most important contribution to musicology. The first major product of these studies, *Weber auf dem Welttheater*, concerns itself chiefly with *Der Freischütz* and its career in the opera house. *Weber: Gestalt und Schöpfung* is a more general study, though it places special emphasis on the Dresden period of Weber's life; a larger version, embodying the fruits of all Schnoor's Weber researches, was published in 1974. The thoroughness of his familiarity with his subject and the painstaking nature of his scholarship give his work on Weber a unique authority and value.

WRITINGS

Das Buxheimer Orgelbuch (diss., U. of Leipzig, 1919); extracts in *ZMw*, iv (1921–2), 1
'Geschichte des Oratoriums', *Handbuch der Musikgeschichte*, ed. G. Adler (Frankfurt, 1924, rev. 2/1930/*R*1961); enlarged as 'Oratorium und weltliche Chorwerke', in H. Kretzschmar: *Führer durch den Konzertsaal* (Leipzig, 5/1939)
Musik der germanischen Völker im 19. und 20. Jahrhundert (Breslau, 1926)
with G. Kinsky and R. Haas: *Geschichte der Musik in Bildern* (Leipzig, 1929; Eng. trans., 1930)
'Wie lassen sich Webers Jugendopern aufführen?', *Die Musik*, xxxiv (1941), 3
Weber auf dem Welttheater (Dresden, 1942 [dated 1943], 4/1963)
'Stufen des 19. Jahrhundert', *Karl Straube, zu seinem 70. Geburtstag* (Leipzig, 1943), 233
Dresden: 400 Jahre Musikkultur (Dresden, 1948)
Weber: Gestalt und Schöpfung (Dresden, 1953, rev. 2/1974)
Oper, Operette, Konzert (Gütersloh, 1955)
ed.: *Bilderatlas zur Musikgeschichte* (Brussels, 1960, 2/1963)
Harmonie und Chaos (Munich, 1962)
Musik und Theater – ohne eigene Dach (Hagen, 1969)
Die Stunde des Rosenkavalier (Munich, 1969)
'Oratorische Spiegelbilder', *Ex Deo nascimur: Festschrift. . .Johann Nepomuk David* (Wiesbaden, 1970), 100

JOHN WARRACK

Schnorr von Carolsfeld, Ludwig (*b* Munich, 2 July 1836; *d* Dresden, 21 July 1865). German tenor. The son of the painter Julius Schnorr von Carolsfeld, he studied with Julius Otto and also at the Leipzig Conservatory. While still a student he was engaged by Eduard Devrient for the Karlsruhe opera in 1854, making his first solo appearances in 1855 in *Norma* and *Der Freischütz*. He had already sung smaller roles, including a soldier in *Les Huguenots* with his future wife, Malvina Garrigues, as Valentine in 1854. He became principal tenor of the company in 1858. He and Malvina were engaged in 1857 and married in April 1860, moving in the same year to Dresden. There he quickly made a reputation in lieder, oratorio and opera, especially as Tannhäuser and Lohengrin: his Lohengrin was praised as 'exceptional vocal material . . . played upon by the singer in a musical, cultivated style' (Garrigues, quoting the Dresden *Signale* of 7 June 1860). He began studying Tristan, but his fears and those of his wife about the demands of the role led him to abandon it. Then in 1862 at Biebrich he and Malvina sang Tristan and Isolde to Wagner, who was much moved by Schnorr's singing and praised his artistic sympathy and quickness of understanding. The couple were, with Bülow, largely responsible for the success of the first performance of *Tristan und Isolde* on 10 June 1865, after it had been delayed by Malvina's hoarseness. Schnorr in turn acknowledged that 'I know full well how much is due to me, how small was my part in the success, what driving force Wagner exercised on me. . . . From that day I consider myself dedicated as an artist' (letter to Cosima Wagner, 12 June 1865). It was largely the strain of the experience that caused him to develop a feverish chill. His last public appearance was in Munich as Erik in *Der fliegende Holländer* (9 July 1865), though he sang some excerpts from the *Ring* and *Die Meistersinger* before Ludwig II on 12 July. Returning to Dresden, he rehearsed *Don Giovanni* on the 15th, but on the 16th developed what he termed a 'springende Gicht' (rampant gout) that began in his knee and led to a delirious condition. He burst into song on

his deathbed, calling repeatedly on Wagner's name.

A corpulent, powerfully built man, with baritone colour in his tenor voice, Schnorr was praised for his smoothness of line, his portamento, and his 'elegiac, somewhat veiled' tone (Prölss). Wagner described his voice as 'full, soft and gleaming', and regarded him as inferior vocally to Tichatschek but greatly superior in dramatic power and intelligence. Schnorr's death affected Wagner profoundly, on both personal and artistic grounds: 'In him I lost . . . the great granite block needed to raise my building, and found myself directed to seek his replacement in a pile of bricks'. Schnorr also composed some music and wrote poetry.

His wife Malvina, née Garrigues (*b* Copenhagen, 7 Dec 1825; *d* Karlsruhe, 8 Feb 1904), was the daughter of the Brazilian consul in Copenhagen. She studied in Paris with Garcia and sang in Breslau from 1841 to 1849, making her début in *Robert le diable*, then in Coburg, Gotha, Hamburg and (from 1854) in Karlsruhe. She was praised for her powerful, ringing soprano and her fluent technique. After her husband's death she was unable to continue her career and sank into depression: she took up spiritualism, and in a largely unbalanced state brought various pressures to bear upon Wagner and Cosima at Triebschen. Towards the end of her life she taught in Frankfurt am Main, her pupils including Gudehus. She also wrote songs and published a volume of poems by her husband and herself.

Ludwig Schnorr von Carolsfeld and his wife Malvina as Tristan and Isolde in the first performance of Wagner's opera

BIBLIOGRAPHY
R. Wagner: 'Meine Erinnerungen an Ludwig Schnorr von Carolsfeld', *Gesammelte Schriften und Dichtungen*, viii (Leipzig, 1873, 5/1911), 221; Eng. trans., W. Ashton Ellis, iv (London, 1895)
R. Prölss: *Geschichte des Hoftheaters zu Dresden* (Dresden, 1878)
C. F. Glasenapp: *Das Leben Richard Wagners* (Leipzig, 3/1894–1911, 5/1910–23)
E. Schuré: *Souvenirs sur Richard Wagner: la première de 'Tristan et Iseult'* (Paris, 1900)
L. Eisenberg: *Grosses biographisches Lexicon der deutschen Bühne im XIX Jahrhundert* (Leipzig, 1903)
C. H. N. Garrigues: *Ein ideales Sängerpaar* (Copenhagen, 1937)
E. Newman: *The Life of Richard Wagner*, iii–iv (London, 1945–7)
E. Zuckerman: *The First Hundred Years of Wagner's Tristan* (New York, 1964)
O. Schneider: 'Vor 100 Jahren starb: Ludwig Schnorr von Carolsfeld', *ÖMz*, xx (1965), 378

JOHN WARRACK

Schnüffis [Schnüfis], **Laurentius von.** *See* LAURENTIUS VON SCHNÜFFIS.

Schnyder von Wartensee, (Franz) Xaver (*b* Lucerne, 18 April 1786; *d* Frankfurt am Main, 27 Aug 1868). Swiss composer. He apparently studied the violin as a youth; at 16 he began to study the piano, which he preferred, with P. Heggli. His father, a politician, wanted to train him for a political career. Schnyder became an unsalaried clerk in the department of finance and political science of the Lucerne city government, but soon broke off his career as a civil servant. Having taught himself the double bass, cello, clarinet, viola and timpani, he went to Zurich in 1810. The following year a legacy gave him the opportunity to pursue his musical studies abroad. He went to Vienna and planned to study composition with Beethoven, who did not take him as a pupil but consented to examine and criticize some of Schnyder's compositions; Schnyder studied with J. C. Kienlen instead. He took a lively part in Vienna's musical life and settled in Baden; but a fire in his home destroyed all his possessions, and in 1812 he returned to Switzerland. For two years he lived an independent life in Lucerne, devoting himself to music, poetry, physics and literature. In 1814 he moved into the Schloss Wartensee, which he had inherited; the following year his first songs appeared in print.

In 1816 Schnyder found himself in financial difficulties, and moved to Yverdon to teach singing at Pestalozzi's institute. The next year he went to Frankfurt am Main, where he composed and gave lessons (mostly privately) and where his works were performed. He studied the glass harmonica and gave recitals on this instrument, as well as on the piano. He was an active member of musical unions, and in 1828 he founded the Frankfurt Liederkranz; his oratorio *Zeit und Ewigkeit* was written for the 1838 Frankfurt choral festival. He lived in Lucerne for a while before returning to Frankfurt am Main to spend the last years of his life.

One of Switzerland's most important and versatile musicians of the late Classical and early Romantic periods, Schnyder composed with imagination, wit and feeling, and his works are melodically charming and rich in unusually delicate contrapuntal writing. Beside composing music, he took pleasure in writing essays on musicians and musical events, compiling memoirs and writing his autobiography. In 1847 he founded the Schnyder von Wartensee Foundation in Zurich, which still sets subjects for competitions in various branches of science and supports the publication of scientific and artistic work.

WORKS
(*many unpublished; MSS in CH-Zz*)
Stage: Ubaldo, opera, 1811–12, lost except for 1 chorus; Estelle, oder Leichter Sinn und Liebesmacht, 1825; Fortunat mit dem Säckel und Wünschhütlein, 1827–8, perf. Frankfurt am Main, 2 Oct 1831; Heimweh und Heimkehr, operetta, 1854, perf. Zurich, 14 Dec 1855
Choral with insts: Die Mordnacht von Luzern, 1811; Pestalozzi-Kantate, 1817; Kyrie, 1819; O sacrum convivium, off, 1830; Zeit und Ewigkeit (after Klopstock), 1838; Die Himmelslichter (Zurich, 1841)
Other vocal: *c*25 choruses and songs, male vv; qts; duets; numerous songs, 1v, pf, 4 bks pubd
Inst: 5 syms.; Conc., 2 cl, orch; Variations, pf, orch; other orch works; Vn Sonata; Fantasia, glass harmonica, str qt; Duo, vc, pf; 2 sonatas, inventions, fugues, canons, scherzos, dance pieces, all pf

BIBLIOGRAPHY
F. Hiller: *Erinnerungsblätter* (Cologne, 1868)
G. Keller: 'Erinnerungen an X. Schnyder von Wartensee', *Nachgelassene Schriften* (Berlin, 1893)
P. Spitta: 'X. Schnyder von Wartensee', *Musikgeschichtliche Aufsätze* (Leipzig, 1894)
P. O. Schneider: 'Schnyder von Wartensees musikgeschichtliche Stellung', *SMz*, lxxxiii (1943), 171
M. Herrmann: 'Erinnerungen an Xaver Schnyder von Wartensee in den Erinnerungen eines Südfranzosen', *SMz*, cii (1962), 68

LUISE MARRETTA-SCHÄR

Schoberlechner, Franz (*b* Vienna, 21 July 1797; *d* Berlin, 7 Jan 1843). Austrian pianist and composer. He studied with Hummel and, at his successful début in 1809, played the C major Piano Concerto which his teacher had composed specially for him. He then studied further with E. A. Förster, and in 1814 made a concert tour to Italy. While in Florence he wrote a requiem and *I virtuosi teatrali* (1817), an *opera buffa*. After visits to Rome and Naples he was engaged as Kapellmeister by the Duchess Marie Louise of Lucca, for whom he composed the opera *Gli arabi nelle gallie* (1819). He returned soon afterwards to Vienna, where his operetta *Der junge Onkel* was performed in 1823. Arming himself with letters of introduction (having been refused one by Beethoven), he then set off for Russia. In St Petersburg in 1824 he married the singer Sophie Dall'Occa (*b* St Petersburg, 1807; *d* 1864), a pupil of her father Filippo. After travelling in Russia, Germany and Italy, they returned to St Petersburg, where Sophie sang with great success at the Italian Opera for three years (1827–30), including appearances with Malibran. Her husband wrote his opera *Il barone di Dolzheim* for her (performed 1827). In 1831 they bought an estate near Florence, but continued to make further concert tours. Schoberlechner's last opera, *Rossane*, was performed in Milan in 1839. He died while on tour in Berlin, and Sophie, having retired when her voice began to fail in 1840, was obliged to return to Russia and teach singing. Schoberlechner's operas had some success in their day. His concert works, mostly in virtuoso vein, reflect his own skill as a pianist and his ability to satisfy contemporary taste; they include two piano concertos, three sets of variations for piano and orchestra which show the influence of Hummel, and numerous variations and rondos for piano solo.

BIBLIOGRAPHY
FétisBS; *ME* [incl. Dall'Occa family]
E. Hanslick: *Geschichte des Concertwesens in Wien*, i (Vienna, 1869/*R*1971)
C. von Wurzbach: *Biographisches Lexikon des Kaiserthums Oesterreich* (Vienna, 1876)

JOHN WARRACK

Schobert, Johann [Jean] (*b* ?Silesia, *c*1735; *d* Paris, 28 Aug 1767). Harpsichordist and composer. Grimm's testimony that he was Silesian has been generally accepted. Gerber's *Tonkünstler-lexicon*, however, gives Strasbourg as his place of birth (though the name occurs in no contemporary Alsatian records), and Schubart in his autobiography claimed Schobert as a kinsman, supposedly from Nuremberg. Finally Riemann associated Schobert with the Mannheim school because of stylistic similarities and the dedication of op.3 to 'M. Saum, conseiller du commerce et agent de S.A.S. Mgr le Prince Palatin'. It is possible, however, that Saum exercised his authority from Paris and that Schobert made his acquaintance there; this conjecture is supported by the fact that the records at Mannheim fail to reveal Schobert's name.

Nothing definite is known of his life until his appearance in Paris in 1760 or 1761 and his employment in the service of the Prince of Conti. For several years thereafter he published instrumental music which was engraved at his own expense (and probably in his own home) and distributed to the various Parisian dealers – an arrangement no doubt made possible by his position with the Prince of Conti, which shielded him from the exploitation of publishers. Soon after his arrival in Paris Schobert married a Frenchwoman by whom he had at least two children. In 1765 he made a single, and thoroughly unsuccessful, venture into *opéra comique*, with *La garde-chasse et le braconnier* (he had earlier contributed to a pasticcio). The only remaining information concerning his life is Baron Grimm's account of his gruesome death, along with his wife and one child, as a result of eating poisonous mushrooms.

Grimm's eulogy gives some impression of Schobert's abilities as a performer and composer, and of his personal character:

This musician had a great talent, a brilliant and bewitching technique. He was unequalled in the ease and pure delight in his performance. He did not have as much talent as Eckard, who will always remain the first *maestro* in Paris, but Schobert had more admirers than Eckard, because he was always agreeable . . . Schobert's compositions were charming. He had no valuable ideas to be emulated, but he knew perfectly the effects and magic of harmony and he wrote with great ease.

La Borde, who must have known Schobert personally, described him similarly as having 'manners as gentle and as simple as his talent was extraordinary'. Opposed to these statements is Leopold Mozart's letter of 1 February 1764, which accuses Schobert of 'envy' and 'jealousy', and concludes that 'Schobert is not at all the man he is said to be – he flatters to one's face and is utterly false'. In view of Schobert's influence on the young Mozart and the adaptations of his works which must have been carried out under Leopold's guidance, these remarks seem incongruous; Leopold was probably identifying Schobert with what he regarded as the degenerate Parisian society of the time.

Schobert greatly influenced Mozart, who admired his music warmly. The work which most impressed the seven-year-old composer seems to have been the D major Sonata of op.3; imitation of this sonata and others can be traced in Mozart's subsequent Parisian and English sonatas. Movements from Schobert's sonatas also appear recast in Mozart's earliest piano concertos. His fascination with Schobert's music was not merely fleeting: when Mozart was in Paris in 1778 he taught his pupils Schobert's sonatas, and the A minor Sonata K310, composed in Paris, contains in its Andante an almost literal quotation from a movement of Schobert's op.17 no.1 that Mozart had already arranged years before in a concerto.

Schobert's compositions reveal a skilled and imaginative artist. Several works in their entirety, and several individual movements, possess a spontaneity and freshness of expression that still make an impact. However, many of his works reveal an inability to develop a theme or motif fully: he often resorted to over-extended sequences and occasionally to the empty display of technical virtuosity. This bears out Grimm's remarks that Schobert 'did everything with ease' and that he was content with a less than finished work.

Schobert's significance rests not in the quality of his music but rather in his development of formal and stylistic features which found their complete expression in the closing years of the 18th century and in the opening decade of the 19th. He was one of the few composers who were capable of producing an individual idiom that went beyond the accepted style of the day. In his particular area, that of keyboard music with accompanying instruments (often *ad libitum*), he discovered new forms and means of expression as important as the innovations produced in other European centres between 1750 and 1775.

WORKS

Editions: *J. Schobert: ausgewählte Werke*, ed. H. Riemann, DDT, xxxix (1909/*R*1958) [R]

6 Sinfonien für Cembalo . . . op.9 und op.10, ed. G. Becking and W. Kramolisch, EDM, Sonderreihe, iv (1960) [B]

Printed works published in Paris, 1761–7; see *MGG* for details of later editions

op.
1 [2] Sonates, hpd, vn ad lib; no.2 ed. in Reeser (1939)
2 2 sonates, hpd, vn acc.; no.1 R
3 2 sonates, hpd, vn ad lib; no.1 partly ed. in Saint-Foix (1922)
4 [2] Sonates, hpd
5 2 Sonates, hpd, vn ad lib
6 [3] Sonates en trio, hpd, with vn, vc ad lib; no.1 ed. in NM, cxcvii (1958)
7 [3] Sonates en quatuor, hpd, with 2 vn, vc ad lib, 1764; no.1 R; no.2 ed. in Collegium Musicum, 1 (Leipzig, *c*1925); no.3 ed. in Turrentine (1962)
8 2 sonates, hpd, vn acc. 1764; no.1 part ed. in David (1928)
9 [3] Sinfonies, hpd, with vn, hns ad lib; B; no.2 ed. in NM, cxcix (1962)
10 [3] Sinfonies, hpd, with vn, hns ad lib; B
11 Concerto I, hpd, acc. 2 vn, va, vc, 2 hn ad lib
12 Concerto II, hpd, acc. 2 vn, va, vc, 2 ob, 2 hn ad lib; R
13 Concerto III pastorale, hpd, acc. 2 vn, 2 hn ad lib, va, vc
14 6 sonates, hpd, with vn ad lib, no.1 with vn, va ad lib; nos.1–5 R
15 Concerto IV, hpd, acc. 2 vn, 2 hn ad lib, va, vc
16 4 sonates, hpd, vn acc.; vc; nos.1, 4 R; no.2 ed. in Turrentine (1962); no.4 ed. in NM, cxxxiv (1937)
17 4 sonates, hpd, vn acc.; no.2 ed in Reeser (1939); no.4 ed. in Turrentine (1962)
18 Concerto V, hpd, acc. 2 vn, vc
19 2 sonates, hpd/pf, vn acc. (Paris, 1772; ?spurious; R
20 3 sonates, hpd, vn acc., probably by T. Giordani, see Newman
— Morceau de musique curieux . . . menuet qui peut s'exécuter de différentes façon, hpd, vn, vc; R

Piece(s) in Audinot's Le tonnelier (opéra comique, 1, N.-M. Audinot), Ambigu-Comique, Paris, 28 Sept 1761

Le garde-chasse et le braconnier (opéra comique, 1), Paris, Théâtre-Italien, 18 Jan 1766, lost

BIBLIOGRAPHY

J.-B. de La Borde: *Essai sur la musique ancienne et moderne* (Paris, 1780/*R*1972)

C. F. D. Schubart: *Schubart's Leben und Gesinnungen von ihm selbst, im Kerker aufgesetzt* (Stuttgart, 1791–3)

——: *Ideen zu einer Ästhetik der Tonkunst* (Vienna, 1806/*R*1969)

F. M. von Grimm: *Correspondance littéraire*, ed. M. Tourneux (Paris, 1877–82)

T. de Wyzewa and G. de Saint-Foix: 'Un maître inconnu de Mozart', *ZIMG*, x (1908–9), 35

H. Riemann: Preface to *J. Schobert: ausgewählte Werke*, DDT, xxxix (1909/*R*1958) [with thematic catalogue, and with commentary and historical notes by H. J. Moser]

G. de Saint-Foix: 'Les premiers pianistes parisiens, i: Jean Schobert, vers 1740–1767', *ReM*, iii/10 (1922), 121

H. T. David: *Johann Schobert als Sonatenkomponist* (Leipzig, 1928)

698   Schoeck, Othmar

K. A. Fischer: 'Schobert und Schubart', *ZMw*, xvi (1934), 42
E. Reeser: *De klaviersonate met vioolbegeleiding in het Parijsche muziekleven ten tijde van Mozart* (Rotterdam, 1939)
H. C. Turrentine: *Johann Schobert and French Clavier Music from 1700 to the Revolution* (diss., U. of Iowa, 1962)
E. Reeser: 'Schobert, Johann', *MGG*
H. C. Turrentine: 'The Prince de Conti, a Royal Patron of Music', *MQ*, liv (1968), 309
W. S. Newman: *The Sonata in the Classic Era* (New York, rev. 2/1972)
K. Schalscha: *Zur Würdigung Schoberts* (diss., U. of Munich, 1923) [this work, often cited in Schobert bibliographies, has been lost]
HERBERT C. TURRENTINE

Schoeck, Othmar (*b* Brunnen, canton of Schwyz, 1 Sept 1886; *d* Zurich, 8 March 1957). Swiss composer, conductor and pianist. His early years were spent in his native village in the country near Lake Lucerne. Later he attended the Zurich Industrial College. His father, the painter Alfred Schoeck, wanted his son to take up painting, for which he showed talent, but after a short course of study it was found that his musical gifts were greater. Therefore he was allowed in 1905 to enter the Zurich Conservatory, where his teachers were Attenhofer, Freund, Hegar and Kempter. During his school years he had already written songs and operatic pieces, two genres that he was to favour throughout his life. At the age of 20 he composed a symphonic movement and the Serenade op.1 for student concerts. Following a personal invitation he went to Leipzig to study with Reger (1907–8) who had, however, little direct influence on his work, except perhaps occasionally in the early chamber music, for Schoeck had already developed an individual style in his numerous songs.

In 1908 he returned to Switzerland, where the performance of the Serenade at the Schweizerisches Tonkünstlerfest in Baden brought him considerable recognition. His first songs were published and he began to take his place in the forefront of Swiss musical life as a composer, conductor and accompanist. He was conductor of the Aussersihl Men's Chorus (1909–15), the Harmonie Men's Chorus (1910–11) and the Teachers' Chorus (1911–17), all in Zurich. In 1917, by which time his reputation had spread abroad, he was appointed to conduct the orchestral concerts at St Gall. While still living in Zurich, he did excellent work there until 1944, when a heart complaint forced him to retire. As an accompanist he became renowned in his own and other songs; he gave recitals principally with his wife Hilde Bartscher, the contralto Ilona Durigo, the bass Felix Loeffel and with Stefi Geyer.

The University of Zurich awarded him an honorary doctorate in 1928. Other awards made to him include the Erwin von Steinbach Prize (1936), the music prize of the city of Zurich (1943), the first composer's prize of the Schweizerische Tonkünstlerverein (1945), the Hans Georg Nägeli Medal of the city of Zurich (1956) and the Grand Cross of Merit and Order of Merit of the West German Republic (1956). In spring 1934 he was honoured with a festival week at Berne, and various Swiss towns gave special concerts to celebrate his 50th and 70th birthdays.

With Honegger, Burkhard and Martin, Schoeck was one of the leading Swiss composers of his generation, and of the four he was probably the most typical representative of a specifically Swiss art. His principal achievement was in the domain of song; indeed, he may be regarded as a direct descendant of the lied tradition, perhaps its last great figure. Schoeck's essential links

Othmar Schoeck

with Romanticism are evidenced in his choice of texts for his nearly 400 songs, among them settings of Eichendorff, Lenau, Mörike and Goethe, covering an extremely wide emotional range, from tender reticence to demonic tragedy.

His work up to about 1918 may be considered as that of a first period, a time of youthful and romantic dreaming. A characteristic product is the setting of Lenau's *Der Postillon*. But after World War I Schoeck's music began to reveal a concern with the problems of modern humanity: the *Trommelschläge* op.26 (1915), a short and aggressive work tending towards expressionism, stands out as the first flicker of insight into this other, harsher world. In the *Notturno* and *Lebendig begraben*, for instance, contemporary stresses make themselves heard urgently; the music is not that of a mere belated Romantic. Alive to contemporary advances in compositional technique, he formed a distinct style from Romantic harmony. A work such as the Elegie (1922–3), achieving an astonishing concentration of mood through the simplest of means, stands as one of Schoeck's greatest accomplishments. Also during this period Schoeck came to write for larger accompanying ensembles, though usually including the piano. In these works there are often linking instrumental interludes. Each song is typically built from a basic motif which establishes, usually in the first bar, the elementary material, and which is often continued as an ostinato. During the 1930s, from about op.30, Schoeck reached full maturity, organizing his ideas with subtle and consummate mastery. At the beginning of the period *Das Wandsbecker Liederbuch* was a synthesis of the features of his lyric art; the achievement was repeated two decades later in *Das holde Bescheiden*, a unified cycle like many of Schoeck's collections.

After song the genre to which Schoeck contributed most was opera, the larger form allowing him to generate great dramatic power and emotional tension. His work for the stage developed from the musical play *Erwin und Elmire* through the comic opera *Don Ranudo* to *Venus*, a superb interweaving of youthful romanticism and sinister wizardry, which was produced at the turning point between Schoeck's early and middle periods. But the climax of his dramatic output came in *Penthesilea*, a work whose inner tension is expressed principally in dense harmony, grandiosely orchestrated. This music drama was followed by a dramatic cantata and two conventional operas – *Massimilla Doni* and *Das Schloss Dürande* – which show the psychological refinement of his mature manner at its peak. The few instrumental works display no striking stylistic difference from the songs and stage pieces. After the romantic vividness of the Violin Sonata no.1 and the Violin Concerto, he progressed to the ripeness of the Suite in A♭ major, *Sommernacht* and the Cello Concerto.

Schoeck's style is principally determined by melody, particularly in the earlier works. He was as capable of expressing himself in the most simple tunes, often of an almost folksong type, as in wide chromatic melodic curves. The middle and late period works saw a shift of interest towards harmony, often helping to fix the melody. A combination of leading-note and tonic harmony is particularly characteristic, and may be used both for its expressive tension and for its impressionist-derived colouristic effect. An essential element in Schoeck's vocal works is the correspondence between text and music, attained without superficial word-painting. As Hesse (see Schuh) wrote:

Nowhere in Schoeck's settings is there the slightest misunderstanding of the words, nowhere can we fail to note the most sensitive feeling for light and shade, and everywhere he lays his finger with an almost alarming certainty on the central point where the experience of the poet has become crystallized in a word or in the vibrations between two words. It is this penetration to the germinal cell of each poem which had always been the surest indication of Schoeck's genius for me.

The Othmar Schoeck Gesellschaft, founded in 1959, is dedicated to the propagation of his works.

WORKS

STAGE

op.
— Der Schatz am Silbersee (W. Schoeck), 1901
25 Erwin und Elmire (incidental music and songs, Goethe), 1911–16; Zurich, 11 Nov 1916
27 Don Ranudo de Colibrados (comic opera, A. Rüeger, after Holberg), 1917–18; Zurich, 16 April 1919
28 Das Wandbild (scene and pantomime, Busoni), 1918; Halle, 2 Jan 1921
32 Venus (opera, Rüeger, after Mérimée), 1919–20; Zurich, 10 May 1922
39 Penthesilea (opera, Schoeck, after Kleist), 1924–5; Dresden, Staatsoper, 8 Jan 1927
43 Vom Fischer und syner Fru (dramatic cantata, Schoeck, after P.O. Runge, after Grimm), 1928–30; Dresden, Staatsoper, 3 Oct 1930
50 Massimilla Doni (opera, Rüeger, after Balzac), 1934–5; Dresden, Staatsoper, 2 March 1937
53 Das Schloss Dürande (opera, H. Burte, after Eichendorff), 1938–9; Berlin, Staatsoper, 1 April 1943

CHORAL

— 's Seeli (Lienert), male chorus, 1906–7
— 5 Lieder (Lienert, G. Singer, A. Ritter, Feuchtersleben, Mörike), 1906–15
— Sehnsucht (Eichendorff), male chorus, 1909
18 Der Postillon (Lenau), T, male chorus, pf/orch, 1909
22 Dithyrambe (Goethe), double chorus, orch, 1911
24 Wegelied (Keller), male chorus, pf/orch, 1913

26 Trommelschläge (Whitman, trans. J. Schlaf), chorus, orch, 1915
— Die Drei (Lenau), male chorus, 1930
49 Cantata (Eichendorff), Bar, male chorus, pf/brass, pf, perc, 1933
54 Für ein Gesangfest im Frühling (Keller), male chorus, orch, 1942
— Nachruf (Uhland), SAB, 1943
— Zimmerspruch (Uhland), male chorus, 1947
63 Vision (Keller), male chorus, brass, perc, orch, c1950
67a Maschinenschlacht (Hesse), male chorus, 1953
67b Gestutzte Eiche (Hesse), male chorus, 1953

ORCHESTRAL

— Symphonic movement, 1906, unpubd
1 Serenade, small orch, 1906–7
— Eine Ratcliff-Ouvertüre, after Heine, 1907, unpubd
21 Concerto quasi una fantasia, B♭, vn, orch, 1911–12
48 Praeludium, 1932; for centenary of Zurich University
58 Sommernacht, pastoral intermezzo, after Keller, str, 1945
59 Suite, A♭, str, 1945
61 Cello Concerto, A-a, 1947
64 Festlicher Hymnus, 1951
65 Horn Concerto, 1951

VOCAL WITH ENSEMBLE

36 Elegie (Lenau, Eichendorff), 1v, chamber orch, 1922–3
38 Gaselen (Keller), Bar, fl, ob, b cl, tpt, pf, perc, 1923
40 Lebendig begraben (Keller), Bar, orch, 1926
42 Wandersprüche (Eichendorff), S/T, cl, hn, pf, perc, 1928
47 Notturno (Lenau, Keller), Bar, str qt, 1931–3
66 Befreit Sehnsucht (Eichendorff), 1v, orch, 1952
70 Nachhall (Lenau, Claudius), 1v, orch, 1954–6

SONGS
(for 1v, pf unless otherwise stated)

Farbenkantus, c1901; Das Grab (V. Salis), ?1901; Nachtgesang (Goethe), ?1901; KTV [Kantonsschul-Turnverein] -Kantus (Schoeck), ?1901; Geistergruss (Goethe), ?1902; Kinderliedchen (Blüthgen), 1902; Lieb Seelchen, lass das Fragen sein (Hopfen), 1903; Selbstbetrug (Goethe), 1903; Der Gast (Fontane), 1903; Gleich und gleich (Goethe), 1903; Ueber den Bergen (Busse), 1903; Nun steht der Wald in Blüten, ?1903; Kindergottesdienst (von Gerok), ?1903; Vergangenheit (Lenau), 1904; Wiegenlied (von Fallersleben), ?1904–5

Das Fräulein am Meere (Heine), 1905; Scheideblick (Lenau), 1905; Stummer Abschied, 1905; Lebewohl! (Lenau), 1905; 3 Schilflieder, op.2 (Lenau), 1905; 6 Gedichte, op.3 (Uhland) 1903–7; 3 Lieder, op.4 (Heine), 1904–6; 3 Gedichte, op.5 (Lenau), 1905–7; 6 Lieder, op.6 (Swabian trad., Keller, Meyer, P. Schoeck, Novalis, Verlaine, trans. ?), 1905–7; 3 Lieder, op.7 (Rüeger, Mörike, Shi-King), 1905–7; 4 Gedichte, op.8 (Hesse), 1906–7; 2 Gesänge, op.9 (Michelangelo, trans. ?, Dante, trans. ?), 1907; 3 Gedichte, op.10 (Eichendorff), 1907

3 geistliche Lieder, op.11 (P. Schoeck, Psalm xxiii, Psalm c), 1v, org, 1906–7; Vorwurf (Hesse), 1907; 2 Wanderlieder, op.12 (Eichendorff), 1907–8; 3 Lieder, op.13 (Heine, Busch), 1907; 4 Lieder, op.14 (Mörike, A. Frey, Hebbel), 1907; 6 Lieder, op.15 (H. Leuthold, P. Schoeck, Uhland, Eichendorff, Goethe, Mörike), 1907 8; 8 Lieder, op.17 (Goethe, Uhland, Mörike, Heine, Eichendorff), 1904–9; Mir glänzen die Augen (Keller), ?1910; 8 Lieder, op.19a (Goethe), 1909–14; 13 Lieder, op.19b (Goethe: Westöstlicher Divan), 1906–15

14 Lieder, op.20 (Uhland, Eichendorff), 1905–14; 10 Lieder, op.24a (Lenau, Hebbel, Dehmel, K. Spitteler), 1910–14; 10 Lieder, op.24b (Spitteler, Gamper, Hesse, Keller), 1906–15; 12 Eichendorff-Lieder, op.30, 1917–18; 5 Lieder, op.31 (Michelangelo, trans. ?, Hesse, Anacreon, trans. Mörike, Goethe), 1906–17; 12 Hafis-Lieder, op.33, 1919–20; Der Gott und die Bajadere, op.34 (Goethe), 1921; Die entschwundene (Keller), ?1923; 3 Lieder, op.35 (Keller, Storm, Eichendorff), 1928; 10 Lieder, op.44 (Hesse), 1929

Wanderung in Gebirge, op.45 (Lenau), cycle of 10 songs, 1930; 6 Lieder, op.51 (Eichendorff, Mörike), 1931–43; Das Wandsbecker Liederbuch, op.52 (Claudius), cycle of 17 songs, 1936; Unter Sternen, op.55 (Keller), 23 songs, 1941–2; Canon (Schoeck), 4 solo vv, pf, 1941; Spruch, op.69/1 (Morgenstern), 2 solo vv, pf, 1941; Spielmannsweisen, op.56 (Leuthold), cycle of 6 songs, 1v, pf/harp, 1944; Der Sänger, op.57 (Leuthold), cycle of 26 songs, 1944; Das stille Leuchten, op.60 (Meyer), cycle of 28 songs, 1946; Wiegenlied, 1947; Das holde Bescheiden, op.62 (Mörike), cycle of 36 songs, c1950; Im Nebel (Hesse), 1952; Einkehr, op.69/2 (Uhland), 2 solo vv, pf, 1955

CHAMBER AND INSTRUMENTAL

Minuet and Trio, str qt, 1906 or 1907; Sonata, D, vn, pf, ?1908; Sonata, D, op.16, vn, pf, 1909; Walzer, pf, ?1910; Str Qt no.1, D, op.23, 1912–13; Sonata, G, cl, pf, 1916, 2nd movt only; 2 Pieces, op.29, pf, 1919–20; Str Qt no.2, C, op.37, 1923; Sonata, op.41, b cl, pf, 1927–8; Piano Piece, 1928; Sonata, E, op.46, vn, pf, 1931; 2 Ritornellen und Fughetten, pf, 1952; Ritornelle und Fughetten, op. 68, pf, 1953

Principal publishers: Bärenreiter, Breitkopf & Härtel, Hug, Universal

BIBLIOGRAPHY
P. Pisk: 'Das Profil Othmar Schoecks', *Anbruch*, xvi/5 (1914), 105
H. Corrodi: *Othmar Schoeck* (Zurich, 1919, enlarged 3/1956)
R. Eidenbenz: 'Über Harmonik und tonale Einheit in Othmar Schoeck's "Penthesilea" ', *Schweizerisches Jb für Musikwissenschaft*, iv (1929), 94
H. Hesse: 'Othmar Schoeck', *SMz*, lxxi (1931), 61
H. Corrodi: 'Othmar Schoeck', *Anbruch*, xiv/8 (1932), 164
W. Schuh, ed.: *Othmar Schoeck: Festgabe . . . zum 50. Geburtstag* (Erlenbach and Zurich, 1936)
A. Honegger: 'Souvenirs sur Othmar Schoeck', *SMz*, lxxxvi (1946), 321
W. Schuh: *Schweizer Musik der Gegenwart* (Zurich, 1948)
many writers: 'Othmar Schoeck', *SMz*, xcvi (1956), 337
P. Mieg: 'Othmar Schoeck', *40 Schweizer Komponisten der Gegenwart* (Amriswil, 1956), 172
W. Vogel: *Thematisches Verzeichnis der Werke von Othmar Schoeck* (Zurich, 1956) [incl. bibliography]
T. Vogel: *Othmar Schoeck im Wort: Äusserungen des Komponisten mit einer Auswahl zeitgenössischer Bekenntnisse* (St Gall, 1957)
C. Koenig: 'Der Lyriker Othmar Schoeck', *ÖMz*, xxiv (1969), 141
H. H. Stuckenschmidt: *Twentieth-century Composers, ii: Germany and Central Europe* (New York, 1971)
F. J. Kienberger: *Othmar Schoeck: eine Studie* (Zurich, 1975)
W. Schuh: ' "Trommelschläge": Othmar Schoecks Kriegsvision', *SMz*, cxvi (1976), 376
S. Tiltmann-Fuchs: *Othmar Schoecks Liederzyklen für Singstimme und Orchester* (Regensburg, 1976)
W. Vogel: *Othmar Schoeck: Leben und Schaffen im Spiegel der Selbstzeugnissen und Zeitgenossenberichten* (Zurich, 1976)

KURT VON FISCHER/FRITZ MUGGLER

Schoeffer [Schöfffer], Peter, jr (*b* Mainz, *c*1475–80; *d* Basle, 1547). German printer. He learned the printing trade from his father, Peter Schoeffer, associate of Gutenberg and co-publisher (with Johannes Fust) of the famous Mentzer *Psalterium* (1457). After the elder Schoeffer's death in 1502 or 1503 his son established his own printing business, which he was forced to sell for financial reasons in the summer of 1512. As early as 1518 he began printing in Worms, although he did not move his business there until 1520. In 1529 he became a citizen of Strasbourg through his marriage to Anna Pfintzer and set up his business there, associating himself first with his former typesetter in Worms, Johann Schwintzer, then in 1534 with MATTHIAS APIARIUS, with whom he published only music books. In 1539 he can be traced in Basle and in 1541–2 in Venice, where he published at least seven works before his final return to Basle. His last years appear to have been spent working as a type founder for other printers.

Although the number of his music publications was relatively small (14 out of about 100 works), he is perhaps best known for his superb craftsmanship in this field, producing unusually elegant notation by means of Petrucci's system of multiple impression. His collections of German songs, including works by such composers as Hofhaimer, Schönfelder, Sies and Virdung, represent the repertory of the Stuttgart court chapel under Ulrich of Württemberg.

BIBLIOGRAPHY
A. Schmid: *Ottaviano dei Petrucci . . . und seine Nachfolger im sechzehnten Jahrhunderte* (Vienna, 1845/*R*1968)
J. J. Maier: 'Unbekannte Sammlungen deutscher Lieder des XVI. Jahrhunderts, I: Peter Schöffer's des Jüngeren II. Liederbuch', *MMg*, xii (1880), 6
A. Thürlings: 'Der Musikdruck mit beweglichen Metalltypen im 16. Jahrhundert und die Musikdrucke des Mathias Apiarius in Strassburg und Bern', *VMw*, viii (1892), 389
H. J. Moser: *Paul Hofhaimer* (Stuttgart, 1929, rev.2/1966)
A. Geering: 'Apiarius, Matthias', *MGG*
H. Lehmann-Haupt: *Peter Schoeffer of Gernsheim and Mainz* (Rochester, NY, 1950)
J. Benzing: 'Peter Schöffer der Jüngere, Musikdrucker zu Mainz, Worms, Strassburg und Venedig (tätig 1512–1542)', *Jb für Liturgik*

und Hymnologie, iv (1958–9), 133
K. Meyer-Baer: *Liturgical Music Incunabula: a Descriptive Catalogue* (London, 1962)
J. Benzing: 'Schöffer, Peter', *MGG*

MARIE LOUISE GÖLLNER

Schoelcher, Victor (*b* Paris, 21 July 1804; *d* Houilles, nr. Paris, 24 Dec 1893). French writer on music and politician. He studied at the Collège Louis le Grand, and became known as an ultra-republican. On the accession of Napoleon III he was expelled both from France and Belgium and took refuge in London. He remained in England until 1870, when he returned to Paris just before the September revolution. He was elected to the Assemblée Nationale in 1871 and became a life senator in 1875.

Schoelcher's devotion to the arts was manifested in his articles in *L'artiste* (1832) and the *Revue de Paris* (1833). During his travels he made a collection of non-Western and other folk instruments; he was specially interested in the music of black peoples. His long stay in England led him to develop an enthusiasm for Handel, and he made a large collection of Handel's music as well as books, pamphlets and documents relating to his life and works. He obtained access to the autographs in the Royal Library (then in Buckingham Palace, now in *GB-Lbm*) and the Fitzwilliam Museum, Cambridge, as well as the copies by J. C. Smith formerly in the possession of H. B. Lennard; his book *The Life of Handel* (London, 1857), published a year earlier than the first part of Chrysander's biography, is thus one of the earliest scholarly works on the composer. Schoelcher was assisted by Rophino Lacy, and the book was translated from French by James Lowe. It contains much information beyond that suggested in the title, especially with regard to Italian opera and to English 18th-century musical life. The French manuscript *Haendel et son temps* was handed over to *France musicale*, which began to publish it serially but broke off after the beginning of the fifth chapter, probably for political reasons. It was bought in 1881 for the Conservatoire library, thus completing Schoelcher's gift (1873) of the printed and manuscript scores and documents used in the book's preparation, as well as his collection of instruments. He later added a quantity of music and rare books relating to the history of Italian opera in London and on singing and piano playing in Great Britain. Schoelher also wrote *La modernité de la musique* (Paris, 1881).

GUSTAVE CHOUQUET/R

Schoemaker, Maurice (*b* Anderlecht, Brussels, 27 Dec 1890; *d* Brussels, 24 Aug 1964). Belgian composer. He studied harmony with Ysaÿe, counterpoint with Brusselmans, fugue with Lunssens and composition and orchestration with Gilson. Schoemaker was associated with the 'Synthetistes' group and remained a close follower of Gilson. His *Vuurwerk* was very successful, thanks to outstanding performances by the Belgian Military Guides' Band under Arthur Prévost. The rich orchestration and evocation nature of his orchestral music seek to express something of the Flemish character; the same brilliance of colour is found in his opera *Swane*, a work which embraces the jocular and the tragic.

WORKS
(selective list)

Operas: Swane (E. De Bom, after S. Streuvels), 1933; De toverviool [The magic violin] (A. Van de Velde), 1954; much incidental music
Orch: Vuurwerk, sym. poem, 1922; 2 fantasques, 1924; Brueghelsuite, 1928; Chamber Sym., 1929; De legende van Heer Halewijn, 1930;

Vlaamse rapsodie, 1931; Driekoningen, 1934; Suite in rococostijl, 1936; Sinfonia breve, 1938; Scènes espagnoles, 1943
Inst: Pf Sonata, 1934; Pf Trio, 1934; Suite champêtre, 3 ww, 1940; Pf Qt, 1945
Songs and choral works

Principal publishers: Bosworth (Brussels), Brogneaux, Bruckner, Heinrichshofen, Schott (Brussels), Universal, Vriamont

CORNEEL MERTENS

Schoenbach, Sol(omon Israel) (*b* New York, 15 March 1915). American bassoonist. He began to study the piano at the age of five, and the bassoon five years later. After obtaining his degree at the Juilliard School at 17, he became staff bassoonist with the CBS orchestra. He joined the Philadelphia Orchestra as first bassoonist in 1937, and, apart from two years during World War II, remained there until 1957. He has served on the Pennsylvania Council on the Arts and became executive director of the Settlement Music School in Philadelphia. A frequent performer of chamber music and an active enthusiast for new bassoon music, he was known for a virtuoso technique, a keen musicality and an uncommon beauty of tone.

GEORGE GELLES

Schoenbaum, Camillo (*b* Hohenems, 13 June 1925). Austrian musicologist. He studied musicology under Hutter at Prague University (1945–9) and under Schenk at Vienna University, where he took the doctorate in 1951 with a dissertation on Baroque church music. In 1951 he settled in Denmark, teaching musicology and philosophy at technical colleges (from 1960). His musicological work centres on early Czech music. He has devoted particular attention to subjects connected with his dissertation (especially the work of Plánický), to 18th-century instrumental music (notably the collected instrumental works of Zelenka) and to Czech hymnography of the Reformation and the Baroque period (including a standard work on the Czech origins of the songs of the German Brethren). He also wrote the first substantial postwar synthesizing work on the history of Czech music to 1800 (*Handbuch der Musikgeschichte Böhmens*, MS, 1954–5) and contributed most of the biographical articles on Czech musicians to Honegger's *Dictionnaire de la musique* (Paris, 1970) and Riemann's *Musiklexikon* (12th edition, *Ergänzungsband*). Further, he has reviewed Czech musicological works for German periodicals (*Die Musikforschung, Jahrbuch für Liturgik und Hymnologie*, etc) and edited music in early Austrian sources (in Denkmäler der Tonkunst in Österreich), as well as lecturing on the wider themes of music sociology, music of the 20th century and general music history.

WRITINGS

Beiträge zur solistischen katholischen Kirchenmusik des Hochbarocks, mit besonderer Berücksichtigung J. A. Planitzky's (1691?–1732) (diss., U. of Vienna, 1951)
'Die "Opella ecclesiastica" des Joseph Anton Plánický (1691?–1732)', *AcM*, xxv (1953), 39–79
'Die Kammermusikwerke des Jan Dismas Zelenka (1679–1745)', *Kongressbericht: Wien Mozartjahr 1956*, 552
'Die Weisen des Gesangbuchs der Böhmischen Brüder von 1531', *Jb für Liturgik und Hymnologie*, iii (1957), 44
'Die böhmische Musiker in der Musikgeschichte Wiens vom Barock zur Romantik', *SMw*, xxv (1962), 475
'Threnodia huius temporis', *Sborník prací filosofické fakulty brněnské university*, F9 (1965), 273
'Harmonia pastoralis bohemica', *Festschrift für Walter Wiora* (Kassel, 1967), 348
'Jan Joseph Boz aňs *Slavíček rájský* (Paradiesnachtigall, 1719) und die tschechischen katholischen Gesangbücher des XVII. Jahrhunderts',

Studia Hieronymo Feicht septuagenario dedicata (Kraków, 1967), 252
'Neue Literatur zur slowakischen Musikgeschichte: *Hudobnovedné-štúdie*, v. I–VII', *Mf*, xxi (1968), 327–32
'Über das teilweise Unzureichende einer Edition', *Mf*, xxii (1969), 209–12 [reply to Unverricht's review of Schoenbaum's editon of Zelenka wind sonatas, *Mf*, xxii (1969), 340]
'Bemerkungen zur Methode einer Replïk', *Mf*, xxiii (1970), 184
'Die böhmische Musiker-Emigration, ein Problem', *Musica slavica*, ed. E. Arro and H. H. Eggebrecht (Wiesbaden, 1976)

EDITIONS

J. D. Zelenka: Sonata I F dur, HM, cxxvi (1955, rev. 1969); *Sonata VI c moll*, HM, cxxxii (1955); *Sonata IV g moll*, HM, cxlvii (1957); *Sonata V F dur*, HM, clvii (1959); *Sonata III B dur*, HM, clxxvii (1961); *Composizioni per orchestra*, MAB, lxi (1963); *Sonata II g moll*, HM, clxxxviii (1965)
Geistliche Solomotetten des 18. Jahrhunderts, DTÖ, ci-cii (1962)
J. Mysliveček: Tre ottetti, MAB, lv (1962, 2/1964)
V. Vodička: Sei sonate per violino e basso continuo, MAB, liv (1962, 2/1964)
F. Benda: Sonata e moll per flauto e basso continuo, MAB, lx (1963)
with H. Zeman: *Deutsche Komödienarien 1754–1758*, ii, DTÖ, cxxi (1971)

JAN KOUBA

Schoenberg [Schönberg], **Arnold (Franz Walter)** (*b* Vienna, 13 Sept 1874; *d* Los Angeles, 13 July 1951). Austro-Hungarian composer.

1. Life up to World War I. 2. World War I and after. 3. America. 4. Personality and beliefs. 5. Early tonal works. 6. Expressionist works. 7. Serial and tonal works 1920–36. 8. Later works.

1. LIFE UP TO WORLD WAR I. His father Samuel (1838–90) was born in Szécsény, his mother (née Nachod, 1848–1921) in Prague. They came to Vienna from Pressburg (Bratislava). Schoenberg accordingly inherited Hungarian nationality, which was converted to Czech on the formation of the state of Czechoslovakia in 1918. He became an American citizen in 1941. The family was Jewish, and the three children, Arnold, Ottilie and Heinrich, were brought up in the orthodox faith. Neither parent was particularly musical; Schoenberg remembered his uncle Fritz Nachod, who wrote poetry and taught him French, as the main cultural influence of his childhood. But his sister and brother showed musical talent, and the latter, like their cousin Hans Nachod, became a professional singer. Schoenberg's musical education began when he was eight with violin lessons, and he very soon began composing by the light of nature, imitating the violin duets by such composers as Pleyel and Viotti that he was given to learn, and arranging anything that came his way – operatic melodies or military band music – for the same combination. Somewhat later, having met a schoolfellow who played the viola, he was able to spread his wings to the point of writing trios for two violins and viola.

The family was not well off. In the year after the death of his father, who had kept a shoe shop, Schoenberg was obliged to leave school and take employment as a clerk in a small private bank, where he remained for about five years. Meanwhile he pursued music, literature and philosophy in the evenings, his interest fired by two friends of his own age, David Josef Bach and Oskar Adler. According to his own account Bach taught him the courage to keep his artistic ideals high. Adler was in effect his first music teacher. He was a good violinist, and Schoenberg taught himself the cello, at first using a large viola adapted with zither strings, and then a proper cello which he began by playing with violin fingering. Together they formed an amateur ensemble which permitted Schoenberg to explore the Classical chamber music repertory from the inside and to compose quartets. Adler helped him to educate his ear through playing, and taught him some elementary harmony. For the musical forms he turned to articles in a popular encyclopedia.

Schoenberg and his friends heard very little music except what they could play themselves. Concerts were beyond their means, though they would sometimes stand outside café enclosures to eavesdrop on the band. While he was still working in the bank Schoenberg joined an amateur orchestra, really no more than a handful of string players, conducted by Alexander von Zemlinsky, and the two soon became firm friends. Zemlinsky, the elder by two years, had attended the Vienna Conservatory, where he had distinguished himself. His compositions had attracted Brahms's notice. He was therefore in a position to help Schoenberg with the formal instruction that he had so far missed. Although Schoenberg received encouragement from Josef Labor, to whom he submitted a movement from a string quartet in C in about 1894, and from Richard Heuberger, Zemlinsky was the only regular teacher he ever had. The importance of Zemlinsky's influence is hard to assess. In later life Schoenberg ascribed to him most of his knowledge of the problems and techniques of composing, whereas Zemlinsky merely said that they had shown each other their works. It is difficult to believe that Schoenberg ever needed to be prompted twice about a general principle of composition, but he certainly respected Zemlinsky's advice, and the pattern of their early relationship persisted. At a time when misunder-

standing had taught him to hold himself aloof he still treated Zemlinsky as an equal both as man and musician.

In the autumn of 1897 Schoenberg wrote a string quartet in D major, making various changes in the course of composition in response to Zemlinsky's criticisms. When it was done both felt that it marked a new stage in his work, and Zemlinsky, who was on the committee of the Wiener Tonkünstlerverein, proposed it for performance. It was accepted, played at a concert for members only the following March, and well enough received to be repeated in the next season. It was many years before a new work of Schoenberg's was to meet with comparable success. The Verein turned down his string sextet *Verklärte Nacht* in 1899, and there were protests when songs from opp.1–3 were sung in public in December 1900. From that time on, in his own words, the scandal never stopped. In these early works he had already taken the first steps in the development of chromaticism that was to lead him to abandon triadic harmony and tonality itself by 1908, and each stage in his progress aroused fresh hostility. For the moment, however, little was heard of him. He kept the wolf from the door by conducting small choral societies and orchestrating operettas, and managed between March 1900 and April 1901 to compose the vast *Gurrelieder*.

In October 1901 Schoenberg married Zemlinsky's sister Mathilde (1877–1923). There were two children of the marriage: Gertrud (1902–47), who married Schoenberg's pupil Felix Greissle in 1921 and emigrated to the USA in 1938, and Georg (1906–74). In

1. Fröhliches Quintet, c1895: the cellist is Arnold Schoenberg and the violinist with the moustache Fritz Kreisler

December the young couple moved to Berlin, where Schoenberg had got a job on the musical side of Überbrettl, a kind of cabaret that formed part of Ernst von Wolzogen's Buntes Theater. The idea behind Überbrettl was to use the popular mode to serious ends. Various well-known men of letters, such as Wedekind, Morgenstern and Dehmel, were interested in it. In the summer Schoenberg had tried his hand at setting verses of the Überbrettl type, and at least one song, *Nachtwandler*, was subsequently performed in Berlin, though only once. Schoenberg's employment there lasted only until the following summer, after which he was obliged to interrupt the orchestration of the *Gurrelieder* in order to score operettas. He was saved from further drudgery of this kind by Richard Strauss, to whom he had shown parts of the *Gurrelieder* and his new symphonic poem *Pelleas und Melisande*. Strauss was impressed, and used his influence to obtain for him the Liszt Stipendium and a post as composition teacher at the Stern Conservatory. So he stayed on in Berlin for another year and returned to Vienna in July 1903 with the completed score of *Pelleas*.

That autumn various musical classes were organized in rooms made available at a girls' school founded by Dr Eugenie Schwarzwald. Schoenberg taught harmony and counterpoint there for a single season, and Zemlinsky, in whose house he was living at the time, form and orchestration. When Schoenberg gave up his class some of its members continued to study composition and theory with him privately, among them a number of students of music history under Mahler's friend Guido Adler at the University of Vienna. In the autumn of 1904 this nucleus was joined by two new recruits, Webern (an Adler pupil) and Berg, who were to fulfil their promise as composers through acceptance and individual reinterpretation of the successive steps in their master's development, and bring him the support of their lifelong personal and artistic loyalty.

If private teaching was scarcely lucrative for Schoenberg – he taught Berg free for the first year because his family was not in a position to pay fees – composition was still less so. The Viennese public was conservative in its tastes and reluctant to support new work in any of the arts. Special societies attempted to remedy this situation. To one of them, the Ansorge Verein, Schoenberg owed various early performances, starting with some of his songs early in 1904. At this time he and Zemlinsky were already planning a society of their own, which they launched successfully under the title Vereinigung Schaffender Tonkünstler. For their honorary president they managed to secure Mahler, whose brother-in-law Arnold Rosé had invited him to rehearsals of *Verklärte Nacht* the previous year when Rosé was preparing the quartet that he led for a performance of it. Mahler was deeply impressed and became a staunch supporter of Schoenberg, even though he did not always see eye to eye with him over artistic matters. The new society survived only for the season 1904–5 but succeeded in putting on sizable works by Mahler, Strauss, Zemlinsky and others, and in January the first performance of *Pelleas und Melisande*, conducted by the composer. The orchestra was ill at ease and the reception cool.

The pattern of Schoenberg's life for the next few years was now set. A heavy teaching programme did not save him and his family from material hardship; as late as 1910 he was obliged to borrow from Mahler to pay the rent, and the following year Berg launched an appeal on his behalf, though without his knowledge. The style of his music, which he composed largely in the slacker summer months, became increasingly dissonant; each new work raised a storm. The Rosé quartet gave the first performances of the First Quartet and First Chamber Symphony early in 1907. Mahler stood up for both works in public, and although he privately confessed that he could not fully understand Schoenberg's development he never lost faith in him. His removal from Vienna that spring deprived Schoenberg of a valuable ally, though in the four years that remained to him his concern for Schoenberg's well-being and interest in his work never faltered. Uproar predictably greeted Rosé's first performance of the Second Quartet in December 1908, and when the first freely dissonant works, *Das Buch der hängenden Gärten* and the op.11 piano pieces, were presented in January 1910 they met with almost universal incomprehension.

During these years of crisis for his musical style Schoenberg also turned to painting, and in October 1910 mounted a one-man exhibition. The following January he received a letter from the expressionist painter Kandinsky, whose sympathy for his work extended beyond his painting to his music and ideas. This initiated a lasting friendship. Schoenberg exhibited with the group Der Blaue Reiter founded by Kandinsky, and contributed an essay and a facsimile of *Herzgewächse* to the first and only number of the periodical that bore its name. He showed pictures elsewhere, but, although he continued to paint and draw occasionally in later years, visual means of expression quickly lost the importance that they had briefly held for him.

For some years Schoenberg had kept up a fairly steady output of music, culminating in the extraordinary works of 1909: the op.11 piano pieces, the Five Orchestral Pieces op.16 and *Erwartung*. But now the pace slackened. His spare time in the years 1910–11 was largely devoted to writing the *Harmonielehre* and completing the long-delayed orchestration of the *Gurrelieder*. In 1910 he offered his services to the Royal Academy of Music and Dramatic Art as an external lecturer in theory and composition. His application was successful, but his hopes that this might lead to a professorship were thwarted. A question was asked in parliament, and he was subjected to virulent attacks on racial grounds. By the end of the academic year his circumstances had so far deteriorated that he decided to try his luck once again in Berlin, and moved there with his family in the autumn of 1911.

His arrival was greeted with some extremely unpleasant comment in the press, and his winter lectures at the Stern Conservatory were poorly attended. Nevertheless his fortunes at last began to improve a little. His name at least was now internationally familiar, audiences were beginning to find his earlier music more accessible, and his later work was arousing curiosity. *Pierrot lunaire*, composed in the summer of 1912, was given with considerable success under the composer's direction in October, and then went on tour to 11 German and Austrian cities. Sir Henry Wood had given the first performance of the Orchestral Pieces in London the previous month, and that of the *Gurrelieder* took place in Vienna the following February under Schreker. This was an overwhelming success, but the composer, smarting under years of very different treatment from the Viennese public, refused to acknowledge its applause.

Five weeks later it took its revenge by bringing a concert of music by Schoenberg and his associates to a halt. Meanwhile Schoenberg, relieved of immediate financial worries by the generosity of a rich patron, determined to make a secondary career as a conductor. He lacked experience, but Zemlinsky arranged for him to conduct, early in 1912, a concert including *Pelleas und Melisande*. This set him on the road. By the outbreak of war he had conducted *Pelleas*, the *Gurrelieder* and the Orchestral Pieces in a number of European cities.

2. WORLD WAR I AND AFTER. The war put an end to these developments. Concerts, especially of new music, were less in demand. Many of Schoenberg's pupils were called up, and his teaching ceased entirely. In May 1915 he was himself medically examined in Vienna for the reserve, but to his surprise he was rejected on account of goitre. In September he moved his family back to Vienna, having accepted after some hesitation the offer of a rent-free house from his patron Frau Lieser. Then, after a second medical examination had reversed the decision of the earlier one, he finally joined up in December as a one-year volunteer. Schoenberg's health had, however, never been strong; under the strain of a course of training at Bruck an der Leitha he began to suffer from asthma, to which he was subject all his life, and other ailments. Friends tried to secure his release, which came through quite unexpectedly in October 1916. In the last four years he had written very little music, apart from finishing *Die glückliche Hand* in 1913 and composing the Four Orchestral Songs op.22 at intervals between that year and 1916. But he had been constantly preoccupied with plans for a large-scale religious work. After his return to civilian life he finally decided to embody his ideas in an oratorio. By May 1917 the text of *Die Jakobsleiter* was ready.

2. Arnold Schoenberg

In June he began to compose the music. The time could scarcely have been less favourable. Food and the coal necessary to cook it were becoming desperately short in Vienna; money, at least in the Schoenberg household, was shorter still. Yet in the space of three months Schoenberg set the whole of the first part of the oratorio, though without fully working out the orchestration. During the same period he made known plans for a seminar in composition which would avoid any set course of instruction unrelated to the individual needs of the pupil, and for which each pupil would pay only what he could afford. September brought further difficulties. Schoenberg found himself obliged to leave his house. Potential landlords showed themselves suspicious of his prospects, and for many weeks the family endured the acute discomfort of cheap boarding-houses. On September 17 he was called up again. This time he was given C grading, and, although a transfer away from Vienna remained a possibility until his final discharge in December, his duties were much lighter than before and he was often at home. Consequently he was able to go forward with his seminar at the Schwarzwald school. It prospered, and after his move to Mödling the following April he continued to hold classes there till 1920. But to the oratorio the short spell of military service proved fatal. Despite constant efforts to pick up the thread, he had managed by 1922 to compose only about half of the interlude intended to link the two halves of the work, after which he added nothing more.

A direct outcome of the seminar was the foundation of a Society for Private Musical Performances, the object of which was to give properly rehearsed performances of modern works to a genuinely interested membership. For one class of seat members paid only according to their means. The press was excluded. Details of programmes were not available in advance, and many works were repeated as a point of policy. Orchestral works were given in arrangements for piano or chamber ensemble. In the three years between February 1919 and the end of 1921, when inflation put an end to the society's activities, 353 performances of 154 works were given in 117 concerts. A number of Schoenberg's pupils and ex-pupils helped with the organization of this vast enterprise, but he rehearsed and directed a considerable proportion of the performances himself. Meanwhile peace brought a renewal of international interest in his music. Conducting engagements took him abroad. In Amsterdam he was made president of the International Mahler League, and he returned there for the winter of 1920–21 to take part in a festival of his own works and give a series of lectures on music theory. This was the time of the formulation of serialism. The first three serial works, the op.23 piano pieces, the Serenade and the Piano Suite, were written between 1920 and 1923. The Wind Quintet was completed the next year, which saw the first performances not only of the Serenade and Quintet, but of *Erwartung* (in Prague) and *Die glückliche Hand* (in Vienna).

In October 1923 Mathilde Schoenberg died. Although the marriage had run into difficulties in earlier years Schoenberg's letters written at the time of her death leave no doubt of the depth of his attachment to her. A month later he completed his *Requiem*, a meditation on death the first section of which had been drafted somewhat earlier; he never set it to music. His widowerhood did not, however, last long: at the end of the following August, about a fortnight before his 50th birthday, he married Gertrud Kolisch, the sister of his pupil Rudolf Kolisch. (Kolisch was a violinist and the leader of a string quartet which became the leading exponent of Schoenberg's chamber music in the 1920s and 1930s.) There were three children of this marriage: Nuria (*b* Barcelona, 1932), who married the Italian composer Luigi Nono, Rudolf Ronald (*b* 1937) and Lawrence Adam (*b* 1941).

In 1925 Schoenberg was invited to take charge of the master class in composition at the Prussian Academy of Arts in Berlin, in succession to Busoni, who had died the year before. He accepted, signed the contract in September, and after some delay because of an appendix operation moved in January 1926 from Vienna to Berlin for the third and last time. Some of his pupils, notably Gerhard and Zillig, moved with him, and Eisler, though no longer his pupil, did so independently at about the same time; Skalkottas was to join the class a little later. For the next seven years Schoenberg enjoyed better conditions of work than at any time in his life. He had a say in general questions of policy and administration in the academy, and absolute responsibility for his own courses. Moreover he was required to teach for an average of only six months in the year, and could choose his own times. His creative output increased correspondingly. The Suite op.29, largely written in Vienna, was followed by the Variations for orchestra, the play *Der biblische Weg*, the Third Quartet, *Von heute auf morgen*, the *Begleitmusik zu einer Lichtspielszene*, *Moses und Aron*, the Cello Concerto after Monn, and various smaller pieces. His earlier works continued to gain ground with audiences, and his more recent ones were at least assured of a hearing, if not of approval: the Variations, for instance, had a very mixed reception when Furtwängler introduced them in 1928.

Given that Schoenberg could never hope to make a living from composition, his job at the academy was well adapted to his needs. Perhaps in the long run he would not have stood the climate of Berlin, for in the winter of 1930–31 his asthma grew much worse, and he made so little progress in the summer that he was strongly advised not to risk the next winter in the north. So in October the Schoenbergs went to Barcelona to stay near Gerhard and his wife; various circumstances kept them there until May. However, it was not Schoenberg's health but politics that robbed him of any sense of security in Berlin. Antisemitism had contributed considerably to the hostility towards him in Vienna even before the war. In the early 1920s, when he experienced the grossly insulting behaviour towards Jews that Hitler's agitation was helping to make commonplace, he already foresaw violence as the probable outcome. By 1933 the realization of his fears had begun. It was no surprise when the government's intention to remove Jewish elements from the academy was announced at a meeting of the senate on 1 March, at which Schoenberg was present. He left abruptly, and treated the announcement as his dismissal. This took effect officially from the end of October, in breach of his contract, which should have protected him for another 23 months.

The Schoenbergs left Berlin in May and spent the summer in France. The only work composed at this time was the String Quartet Concerto after Handel. One of Schoenberg's first acts was to return to the Jewish faith, which he had rejected in favour of Lutheranism in 1898. His Christian beliefs had not lasted, but by his own account he was at no time unreligious, let alone anti-religious. By the war years religion had become his sole support. At first he did not attempt to reconcile his beliefs with those of any recognized faith, but with the increase of antisemitism after the war he realized that the faith in which he had been brought up must eventually claim him, and he began to work his way towards his own not entirely orthodox version of it. The ceremony in Paris merely made his reconversion official.

3. AMERICA. Schoenberg's search for employment ended with his acceptance of a teaching post until the next May at the Malkin Conservatory in Boston. The family arrived in the USA at the end of October. The work proved to be on a more elementary level than he had realized. Some of the classes were held in New York, which meant a tiring weekly journey there. As soon as the weather became bad in December his health deteriorated; he fell seriously ill in January and again in March. The summer put him right, but he dared not stay another winter on the east coast and moved to Los Angeles in the autumn of 1934 for the sake of the climate – a decision that probably added several years to his life. He first settled in Hollywood, where he completed the Suite for string orchestra by the end of the year. Private pupils soon began to come to him, and in the academic year 1935–6 he gave lectures at the University of Southern California. In 1936 he accepted a professorship in the University of California at Los Angeles, and moved to a house in Brentwood Park where he lived for the rest of his life. That year saw the composition of the Fourth Quartet and the completion of the Violin Concerto, apparently begun the previous spring or summer.

Though more fortunately placed in his country of exile than many of his fellow refugees, Schoenberg enjoyed little peace of mind. He found much in his alien surroundings hard to accept; few of his pupils were well enough grounded to benefit at all fully from his knowledge and experience; there was no audience for such music as he might write; above all there was the appalling news from Europe and the growing threat to relatives and friends there. His constant efforts on behalf of individual victims of persecution could not ease the sense of helplessness of one who was accustomed to take remedies into his own hands. For once he admitted to depression. In due course, however, he made some kind of truce with his situation. The war disposed in its own way of certain issues. His domestic happiness was a source of strength, and his young American children gave him a certain stake in the country. In the four years after 1936 his only original works had been *Kol nidre*, intended for synagogue use, and the completion of the Second Chamber Symphony, partly composed between 1906 and 1916; but in 1941 he composed the Organ Variations in response to a commission, and three more works had followed by 1943. He also set about recasting material from various unfinished theoretical works in the form of a series of more strictly practical textbooks suitable for his American pupils. Nevertheless, in 1944 he was still thinking of emigrating.

This year was a turning-point in two respects. In February his health began to deteriorate sharply. Diabetes was diagnosed, he suffered from giddiness and fainting, and his asthma grew worse, as did the optical disturbances that had troubled him for some time. On reaching his 70th birthday in September he had to give

3. Arnold Schoenberg with his wife, Gertrud, and three children in Los Angeles

up his professorship. As he had taught in the university for only eight years his pension was very small. Consequently he was obliged to continue giving private lessons, and in 1946 held a course of lectures at the University of Chicago. In August that year he had a heart attack which caused his heart to stop beating; he was resuscitated only by an injection directly into the heart. This experience is in some sense reflected in the String Trio which he composed shortly after his recovery. Although he was well enough in the summer of 1948 to give classes at Santa Barbara, for most of his remaining five years he led the withdrawn existence of an invalid. But he had the satisfaction of seeing the emergence of the state of Israel (he was elected honorary president of the Israel Academy of Music in 1951), and also the upsurge of interest in his music that marked the postwar years. At this time he revised a small selection from his vast accumulation of largely unpublished essays and articles, and published it under the title *Style and Idea*. The few short compositions that he managed to complete were nearly all religious in inspiration. During the last year of his life he worked on a series of meditations which he originally called *Modern Psalms*, and later *Psalmen, Gebete und Gespräche mit und über Gott*; his last composition was an incomplete setting of the first of these.

4. PERSONALITY AND BELIEFS. The scanty recollections of Schoenberg left by those who knew him in early years stress his enthusiasm and resilience. Although such qualities are only to be expected in a young man just finding scope for uncommon gifts, one circumstance behind Schoenberg's growing confidence during the decade before *Verklärte Nacht* claims attention for its fundamental influence on his later outlook and thinking: the fact that he was in all essentials self-taught. Fortune had endowed him not only with prodigious musical aptitude but with the intellectual energy and force of personality to ensure that it triumphed over his very considerable social and educational disadvantages. Naturally he took what steps he could to make up for his lack of formal musical training, but neither his haphazard reading, nor other odd crumbs of instruction

(he is known, for instance, to have heard Bruckner lecture at the academy), nor even Zemlinsky's constant help, could alter his feeling that he never profited from what he was taught unless he had already discovered it for himself; tuition could at best only awaken him to his own knowledge. The process of independent discovery shaped his habits of mind and his spiritual life. His approach to composition, whether in the context of a single work or of his wider development, remained exploratory; he saw life as synonymous with change and religion as a quest.

His early experience is most closely reflected in, and so partly deducible from, his teaching methods. He refused to teach the codified knowledge that he had never learnt, mistrusting mere knowledge as the enemy of understanding. From the earliest stages his pupils were required to create, to derive their simplest exercise from an expressive intention and to remain true to the implications of the initial idea. Their teacher let no inconsequence pass, just as at a deeper level he would detect any transgression against the promptings of their musicality. For many of Schoenberg's pupils, particularly in the earlier years, the kind of moral obligation that he taught them to feel towards the demands of their art found an echo in their whole attitude to life, and they grouped themselves round him like a band of disciples. Their master benefited from the relationship too, for the origin of his lifelong interest in teaching lay in the need constantly to re-enact his own exploration of the resources of music. Just as many composers, himself among them, might exercise their contrapuntal skill in canonic problems, Schoenberg, who habitually thought in terms of processes rather than systems, practised the ability to reach outwards from a given starting-point by helping each pupil to work out his own salvation in accordance with his own personality and musical disposition.

It might be supposed that this approach to teaching would have led to great stylistic freedom, especially in view of his condemnation in the *Harmonielehre* of all academic rules as meaningless abstractions from the practice of a past era. However, he taught strictly within the confines of tonality, and made the principles of traditional grammar live again by demonstrating their functional value for his pupils' work as for that of the great Austrian and German composers, whom he constantly called to witness. His points of departure for technical instruction – Sechter in the *Harmonielehre* and *Structural Functions of Harmony*, Fux in *Preliminary Exercises in Counterpoint*, Classical forms in *Models for Beginners in Composition* and *Fundamentals of Musical Composition* – were relatively unimportant: everything depended on reinterpretation, on exploration through trial and error. His primary aim was to teach logical thinking, and that was best done in a context where theory, which must necessarily lag behind practice, could aid elucidation. Here again his teaching reflects his own position as a composer, which he was at pains to clarify in the *Harmonielehre*. He was convinced that the recent developments in his style, although reached intuitively, were a logical outcome of tradition, and that, while taking no account of rules, they observed fundamental laws which would eventually prove definable. Meanwhile the pupil who felt drawn to similar modes of expression must find his own intuitive path with the aid of self-reliance learnt in better-charted territory, and the listener would need faith.

In the crucial years preceding the *Harmonielehre* Schoenberg's music rarely met with faith or even the modicum of goodwill without which no artistic perception is possible. On the contrary, it was opposed with almost unbelievable persistence and venom. Perhaps no music before or since has encountered such a reception; to the end of his life its author, though internationally famous, had to accept very widespread incomprehension. The price he paid for artistic integrity was proportionately high. It should be remembered that even the sense of outrage that even such a work as *Pelleas und Melisande* aroused at first in the majority of listeners arose not only from unthinking conservatism but from the more positive instinct that its premonitions of a radical disruption in the agreed basis of musical language carried a threat to precision of meaning. Schoenberg, who shared his audience's background and many of its assumptions, understood its fears and so experienced its attack with something like the force of an inner doubt, requiring all the more courage to parry. He felt himself impelled towards the break with tonality almost despite himself, and accomplished it only after considerable hesitation. Since its systematic justification in theory eluded him he looked for some other authority to protect his intuition. He found it eventually in religion.

In the year after Mahler's death in 1911 Schoenberg wrote about him in terms that indicate clearly his preoccupations at that time. He attacked with great bitterness those whose ceaseless denigration of Mahler almost led him to lose faith in his own work, and apostrophized him as saint and martyr. He saw all great music as expressing the longing of the soul for God, and genius as representing man's more spiritual future, so that the uncomprehending present must inevitably persecute the good and promote the bad. His quotation of Mahler's remark that the Eighth Symphony was composed at great speed, almost as though from dictation, is especially significant, for he too composed very quickly,

4. Arnold Schoenberg: self portrait (c1910), in the Arnold Schoenberg Institute, Los Angeles

often with the feeling that however much effort he put into his work something more was given that he could not account for, just as his stylistic development seemed to have been taken out of his hands. It was not only Mahler and his great predecessors whom he had come to see as divinely inspired: his admission that the role of the 'chosen one' in *Die Jakobsleiter* was based on his own experience removes any doubt that he placed himself in their company. (However, Mahler's music never influenced his own at all deeply, and his sympathy for it sometimes wavered – to his discomfort, because he linked entitlement to respect with the ability to accord it.)

Schoenberg's need to understand his artistic role can scarcely have been the only factor in the spiritual crisis that led to his rediscovery of religious faith: it is merely the one to which his work and writings give access. Similarly the ideas embodied in the prose drama *Der biblische Weg* and in *Moses und Aron* cannot fully document the return to Judaism as a result of which religion became his support in racial as in artistic persecution. The decision to make this return official proved a difficult one because it seemed to set the seal on his divorce from the Western tradition which had nurtured him and to which he had contributed so powerfully. In reaction he even spoke at the time of giving up composition and devoting himself to the Jewish national cause. That did not happen, but his personal and racial idealism remained closely intertwined to the end of his life, as a letter written within three months of his death to the Israel Academy of Music shows:

Those who issue from such an institution must be truly priests of art, approaching art in the same spirit of consecration as the priest approaches God's altar. For just as God chose Israel to be the people whose task it is to maintain the pure, true, Mosaic monotheism despite all persecution, despite all affliction, so too it is the task of Israeli musicians to set the world an example of the old kind that can make our souls function again as they must if mankind is to evolve any higher.

The idea of the artist as priest or prophet is often deprecated as inflated, complacent, arrogant or presumptuous. But no reader of *Die Jakobsleiter* and *Moses und Aron* will imagine that Schoenberg looked for cheap self-justification or easy solutions to spiritual or artistic problems. The path that had been pointed out to him was unmarked, to be followed blindfold and often with anguish, in the knowledge that it would be lost the moment faith faltered. Moreover the need to protect the supremacy of faith came into conflict with the urge to rationalize and justify: faith must fear conscious constraints yet needed the support of discipline, which must accordingly in some sense cross the divide between the rational and the intuitive. This ultimately irresoluble tension ran all through Schoenberg's thinking and showed itself in many guises. It lies, for instance, at the heart of serialism, where every note is brought within the law, but in such a way that intuition retains its freedom. And an analogous dichotomy provides the subject of *Moses und Aron*, which concerns the simultaneous duty and impossibility of giving expression to inexpressible truths.

Unhappily Schoenberg's struggle to realize his ideals dominated not only his spiritual but his social life, where the humility belonging to the former too often deserted him. He could not ignore misunderstanding, but fought back. As he said himself in a letter of 1924:

Unfortunately the better sort of people become enemies faster than friends because everything is so serious and important to them that they are perpetually in a defensive position. They are driven to this by the great, indeed ruthless honesty with which they treat themselves and which makes them adopt the same attitude to other people as well. It is very wrong, really, for we human beings are far too much in need of tolerance for any thoroughgoing honesty to be helpful to us. If only we could manage to be wise enough to put people on probation instead of condemning them, if we could only give proven friends such extended credit! – I am speaking of my own defects, knowing very well why I have often been more lonely than could well be pleasant.

Even here he seems to miss the implication of his habitual insistence on his place among 'better' people: to expect respect is to discourage it even in those who recognize that it is due. He did not make life easy for his adherents, regarding interest in modern music beyond that of his own circle as betrayal. No doubt it was true that the contemporary listener or performer prepared to devote himself wholeheartedly to Schoenberg's music would have found it almost as difficult as the composer himself to sympathize with other modes of thought, but he must sometimes have driven away genuine well-wishers along with the opportunists. His enjoyment of his months in Barcelona in 1931–2 arose partly from relief at escaping from the pedestal that he had built for himself in Berlin, and being accepted as an equal by people who knew little about him.

Readers of Schoenberg's posthumously published correspondence, however, discover not only his less accommodating side but much that only the more fortunate of his contemporaries could know: his absolute honesty in all his dealings, his generosity of mind wherever he sensed integrity, his delicacy of feeling where he saw the need to temper his customary directness, his energy in expressing sympathy through practical help, his capacity for gratitude, his loyalty. His critical and aesthetic writings, turning as they invariably do on matters that concern him deeply, reveal his personality no less vividly, displaying the same rather lofty yet compelling idealism, the same irascible pride, the same flashes of humour and warmth, the same justice within the framework of strongly held convictions. His thinking here is at all times a creator's, never that of the historian concerned to give everything its place. He is content to speak as an individual, with a more selfconscious view of his relation to tradition than his predecessors enjoyed, but still with the confidence of one who knows where he stands. Integrity of personality enables limitations in his historical sympathies, and even inconsistencies in the logic on which he naively though not unjustifiably prided himself, to fall into place beside his unique insights into the music that he valued and the musical crisis in which he found himself involved. The special perceptions that distinguish his writing arise directly out of his experience in composition, and so, it would seem, does his manner of presentation, at once direct and cogent yet unexpected and elliptical. And that is hardly surprising, since it is in music that his mind and spirit found their fullest expression.

5. EARLY TONAL WORKS. Schoenberg's music may be divided into four periods, the second and third of which were inaugurated by crises in compositional technique that had important consequences not only for the composer's own work but for music in general. The music of the first period is tonal, or at least employs a tonality as a central point of reference. In 1908 Schoenberg abandoned tonality; he was the first composer to do so. The music of the ensuing second period is often called 'atonal'. Schoenberg considered this term nonsensical,

preferring 'pantonal'. Since either term properly embraces his serial music as well, the period will be referred to here as 'expressionist'. From his work of this time he gradually evolved the principle of serialism, which he first used consistently in 1920; the serial music written between that date and 1936 constitutes the third period. The fourth, less well defined phase may be said to emerge during the 1930s. It is marked by greater stylistic diversity, including occasional returns to tonal composition.

Of the music that Schoenberg is known to have composed in large quantities from childhood to his early 20s not very much survives, and some of that is fragmentary. Unfinished pieces remained with the composer, whereas completed ones were played with friends and usually lost. Songs have fared best, though some of the larger unfinished works contain complete movements. Although Schoenberg had not yet acquired the habit of dating his manuscripts, it should eventually prove possible to trace his early development, at least in outline. At the time of writing, however, only three works antedating his op.1 have been published: two sets of piano pieces, one each for solo and duet dated 1894 and 1896 respectively, and the D major String Quartet of 1897.

The piano pieces scarcely hint at their composer's future stature, but they already display characteristic preoccupations. The solo pieces are fairly ambitious ternary structures, no doubt inspired by Brahms's sets of the previous two years. They show a good grasp of the possibilities offered at the lead-back and coda, but clumsy execution not helped by uncertain feeling for piano textures. Attempts at more original effects – the links between the coda of each piece and the beginning of its successor, and the descant melody in diminution in the third piece – sound distinctly forced. Heuberger, to whom Schoenberg showed some songs at about this time, advised him to write some short pieces in the style of Schubert. The six little duet pieces were the result. Schoenberg clearly took the point that he must learn complete control by testing his every step. He subjugated himself to the same discipline that half a century later he was still advocating in *Models for Beginners in Composition* and *Fundamentals of Musical Composition*. Each melody progresses by drawing on its own motivic resources, which also permeate the accompaniment, and the consequences of every harmony are carefully weighed. The pieces (except no.5) are arranged in ascending order of formal development. The first consists simply of two repeated eight-bar strains. In each subsequent piece there is a little more expansion after the double bar, culminating in tiny contrasting episodes in nos.4 and 6. Only in these two pieces is the slightest deviation from four-bar phraseology admitted. Throughout his life, and especially after 1920, Schoenberg's music drew strength from his acute sensitivity to phrase structure, shifts of emphasis within a regular rhythmic framework and the tensions arising from asymmetry. In the duets he set about sharpening a faculty that the solo pieces show to have been innate.

There is no reason to suppose that these sets of pieces would appear specially important in Schoenberg's output of the mid-1890s if more of it were known. The D major String Quartet, however, marks a huge stride forward, and not only on the available evidence: the composer himself recognized it as a turning-point and remembered it with affection. Brahms is still the dominant influence. The work owes its Classical four-movement layout to his mediation, its structural cogency and clarity derive from him, and so to a large extent does the style, though certain themes speak with a strong Czech accent. Yet there is a freedom of movement, a deftly guided fluency, that does not belong to the older master's closely considered manner, and it is here that Schoenberg's musical personality asserts itself most strikingly. His sheer zest in the making of music is one of his most persistent characteristics: it accounts for the feeling of resilience that accompanies his exploration of even the darkest regions of experience and tempers his findings. If the D major Quartet, delightful though it is, does not seem fully typical of him it is due less to the eclectic idiom than to the absence of another constant factor in his music: the sense of urgency in communicating a particular conception.

This quality, however, begins to make itself felt in the pair of lengthy songs which Schoenberg wrote almost certainly in the following year and eventually selected as his op.1. The effort to match the magniloquent sentiments of the verses called forth better things from the young composer than they deserved. True, the naivety that prompted the choice of text comes through, rather endearingly, in the setting. But although the Wagnerian influence that was to loom so large in the next few years is already perceptible, there is no close model for the firm sonata-influenced forms, the wealth of independent contrapuntal development in the accompaniments or the distinctive breadth and warmth of the asymmetrical melodic lines.

Schoenberg found inspiration for several compositions of 1899 in poems by Dehmel: the songs *Warnung*, *Erwartung*, *Erhebung* and presumably *Schenk mir deinen goldenen Kamm*, and the string sextet *Verklärte Nacht*. (The charming *Waldsonne* of about this time is not a Dehmel song and stands apart.) The desire to give expression to the feelings aroused in him by Dehmel's work considerably influenced the development of his style, as he later confessed to the poet. The songs are shorter and reach out to sharper, less generalized experience than those of op.1, though the main preoccupation is still love. Their concentration of means and mood shows one kind of advance, the expansive textures of *Verklärte Nacht*, in which Wagnerian and Brahmsian modes of thought meet in harmonious accord, a contrasting one. In the Dehmel poem that served as the basis for this symphonic poem a woman confesses to her lover that she is already pregnant by another man, and he replies that through their love the child will be born his own. A knowledge of this unlikely tale is of secondary importance to the listener because the lack of action enables the work to be understood as a single-movement abstract composition. No composer understood better than Schoenberg that music serves its subject best when claiming for itself the greatest possible autonomy.

In March 1900 Schoenberg began setting Jens Peter Jacobsen's *Gurrelieder* as a song cycle for voice and piano, for entry in a competition. In accordance with the ballad-like tone of the verse he built the vocal lines from relatively simple rhythmic elements, a style shared by the songs *Hochzeitslied* and *Freihold* (the first probably and the second certainly dating from the same year), and perhaps suggested by some of Zemlinsky's early songs.

However, Schoenberg soon saw wider possibilities in the text. Having fallen under Wagner's spell he felt the need for subjects that transcended common experience, his first thought being to wring something more from such well-worn themes as love, death and transfiguration. The way lay through mastery and reinterpretation of Wagnerian style, and the *Gurrelieder* offered a far more expansive arena for this important confrontation than *Verklärte Nacht* had done. He therefore decided to connect the songs he had already composed (those in the first two parts of the finished work) with symphonic interludes and set the whole poem as a vast cantata employing several soloists and a huge chorus and orchestra.

The work depicts the love of King Waldemar and Tove under the Tristanesque imminence of death, Waldemar's blasphemous defiance of God after Tove's death, the nightly ride at the head of a ghostly retinue to which the king's restless spirit is subsequently condemned, and its dismissal by the summer wind at the approach of day. Schoenberg encompassed all this in a series of tableaux of extraordinary magnificence. But the poem deals with dramatic events in an undramatic form and so required some kind of interpretative emphasis to bring the great musical design clearly into focus. The opportunity was there, for at some level Schoenberg's choice of the poem must surely have been influenced by Waldemar's rebellion against God and the renewal brought about as the summer wind sweeps away the aftermath of human passion – both themes that border on his religious concerns of a few years later. Yet neither emerges with unifying force, whether because he was unable to commit himself fully to the text or through inexperience in dramatic matters. As late as 1913 he could still write to Zemlinsky that he did not consider himself a dramatic composer in the ordinary sense. In the *Gurrelieder* he tended to fall back on direct reminiscence of Wagner's later operas, especially *Götterdämmerung*, to evoke atmosphere or characterize events. It is significant that after considering an opera on Maeterlinck's *Pelléas et Mélisande* for his next work (he knew nothing of Debussy's opera), he rejected the idea in favour of a symphonic poem on the same subject.

Schoenberg later said that it was Maeterlinck's ability to lend timelessness to perennial human problems that had attracted him to the play. Certainly it was precisely the moments least involved with the action that inspired him to step furthest outside his own chronology towards his stylistic future, for instance in the music associated with Mélisande's first mysterious appearance heard at the outset and again before her death. But such music as Golaud's, and that of the main love scene, is less advanced; it is capable of traditional extension, notably through Wagnerian sequence, and therefore well adapted to carry the narrative. The contrapuntal virtuosity surpasses even that of the *Gurrelieder*, constantly changing the expressive colour of the thematic material in a manner that is entirely individual while paying tribute to Wagner – rather than to Strauss, whose influence appears sporadically on a more superficial level. Yet for all its riches the work contains a structural conflict. The Mélisande and Pelléas themes lose something of their essence as they are drawn into the larger contrapuntal development, a process that may fit the symbolism of the work but also suggests that the composer had not yet mastered the potentialities of his more striking inventions.

Schoenberg now returned to songwriting. The songs of the next three years fall into three groups. Those of the first group, dating from 1903 and the earlier months of 1904, explore various subjects. *Wie Georg von Frundsberg* and *Das Wappenschild*, a fiery showpiece with orchestra, follow the lead of *Freihold* as songs of defiance. They must surely contain the composer's reaction to hostility; perhaps the gloomy *Verlassen* does so too in a different way. *Die Aufgeregten* reflects ironically on human passion, though love remains the theme of some of the most beautiful of these songs. *Geübtes Herz*, *Traumleben* and the orchestral *Natur* cultivate the intense lyrical style first heard in *Schenk mir deinen goldenen Kamm*. *Ghasel* continues this line, but with a change of emphasis in the accompaniment, which involves the voice part in imitation and adopts its even flow. The three Petrarch sonnets from op.8, composed in the later part of 1904 when the D minor String Quartet was already under way, form a distinct group set a little apart from Schoenberg's other songs. Their contrapuntal style derives directly from *Ghasel*, but takes a far more complex form made possible by the orchestral setting.

In the third group, dating from 1905, the vocal lines regain their independence, relying on motifs rather than imitation to relate them to their accompaniments. Except for the slightly earlier orchestral *Sehnsucht* all these songs, which are based on a curious assortment of serious and trivial verses, were composed about the time of the completion of the D minor Quartet, and already show the characteristics of Schoenberg's tonal thinking in its last stages. His early liking for chromatic approaches to diatonic notes, strikingly manifested as early as *Erwartung* (1899), had led to ever-increasing chromatic substitution, especially in the melodic field. This in turn required clarification by correspondingly elaborate harmonization, employing so wide a range of primary and altered degrees within the tonality that modulation lost its force. So his music, which had at no time inclined to constant modulation, became increasingly monotonal. This tendency appears in all the songs, but in two contrasting forms: in *Der Wanderer*, *Am Wegrand* (later quoted in the opera *Erwartung*) and *Mädchenlied*, as in *Verlassen* of 1903, the tonal centre is strongly, sometimes almost obsessively stressed, whereas in *Sehnsucht*, *Alles* and *Lockung* it is scarcely touched on.

The D minor Quartet, Schoenberg's first wholly characteristic and assured large-scale masterpiece, consists, like *Pelleas und Melisande*, of a single vast movement, but naturally without illustrative interludes. A scherzo, slow movement and rondo are interspersed at various points between the first part of the development and the coda of what would normally have been the first movement, and absorbed into it by the use of common material. The general idea for such a form originates in Liszt, whose novel formal concepts Schoenberg admired while finding his attempts to put them into practice schematic and unfelt. But the quartet arose more directly from Schoenberg's fundamental preference for abstract composition reasserting itself and acting upon his recent cultivation of the Straussian symphonic poem. The twin formative influences of Wagner and Brahms once again find an even balance, as they had in *Verklärte Nacht*, but now completely and finally assimilated. Per-

haps the most striking single quality of this work is its extraordinary melodic breadth. As the melodies move away from their initial, firmly tonal contexts, develop, and combine contrapuntally, they form what Schoenberg called vagrant harmonies; the music, though not very dissonant, loses tonal definition. Thus the structure cannot be understood entirely in tonal terms. Its powerful sense of direction is maintained through the composer's exceptional capacity to shape his material in relation to its formal purpose, a capacity that after its abandonment of tonality was to prove strong enough to carry a far heavier structural burden. Late in life he remarked that he had never been content to introduce an idea for structural reasons alone: it must always make a positive contribution to the substance of the work. The D minor Quartet already displays the typical Schoenbergian richness fostered by this habit of mind.

The First Chamber Symphony, completed in July 1906, adopts the quartet's single-movement layout, but in a more concise form; though in no way a slighter work it is barely half as long. Schoenberg aimed here at concentration rather than expansiveness and, as he was so often to do in solving the problems posed by a particular conception, opened up possibilities for the future remote from his immediate artistic concern. In the first place he increased his instrumental forces from four to 15 in order to accommodate the simultaneous presentation of a greater concentration of ideas. Viewed from another angle, however, the increase appears as a reduction: it established the soloistic orchestral writing already found here and there in the *Gurrelieder* and *Pelleas*, and opened the way for the small, strongly differentiated instrumental ensembles appropriate to Schoenberg's later style – and that of many younger composers. But the urge towards concentration affected deeper levels in his musical thought. The two opening themes are based respectively on superimposed perfect 4ths and the whole-tone scale, both of which readily form chordal structures. The distinction between the melodic and harmonic dimensions thus becomes blurred, a process closely bound up with the loss of tonality in Schoenberg's music. However, for the moment the E major frame held.

Although the imminence of change may seem obvious to the listener with hindsight, it was not so to the composer. On completing this exuberant work he felt that he had now arrived at a settled style. The music of the next year or so reflects this conviction. In neither the eight-part chorus *Friede auf Erden*, which he later described as an illusion written when he still thought harmony among men conceivable, nor in the two Ballads op.12, does the threat to tonality grow appreciably. Schoenberg always regretted that he had not had time to follow up all the implications of the style of this period, and 30 years later returned to the task. For the present, however, some inner crisis urged him towards new realms of expression and hastened the inevitable revolution. A change of mood had made itself felt earlier. The songs of 1905, for instance, provide an uneasy, questioning interlude between the confident First Quartet and First Chamber Symphony, and the Second Chamber Symphony, begun immediately after the first, opens in a new spirit of sombre resignation. Despite repeated attempts he was unable to finish this work at the time, perhaps because he could not reconcile the more carefree spirit in which the second movement opens with his changing preoccupations. At all events it was a very intimate, elusive piece, the contemporary first movement of the Second Quartet, that spoke for him now and demanded to be followed up.

6. EXPRESSIONIST WORKS. The new quartet did not, however, occupy his whole attention; it was not finished until the later months of 1908. At the same time he wrote songs and took up painting seriously. This unexpected development apparently arose out of his personal contact with the Viennese painters Oskar Kokoschka and Richard Gerstl. By far the greater part of his work in this sphere belongs to the years 1908–10, when his music underwent its first great crisis. The pictures are mostly portraits or strange, imaginary heads – 'visions' as he called some of them. They are amateurish in execution yet sufficiently skilful to convey the intensity of his imagination, and it seems likely that their importance to him lay in this very opposition. This was a time when artists and writers who were later to be called expressionists sought to obey the promptings of the spirit ever more directly, in some sense bypassing the machinery of artistic tradition in order to reach deeper levels of experience. The relation to tradition remained, of course, the crucial factor: as a painter Schoenberg's amateur status severely limited the scope and quality of his achievement, but allowed him to feel that his hand was guided without his conscious intervention, whereas in music he had to pay for the benefits of mastery by reckoning with its censorship. So for a time his method of painting represented the ideal towards which his real work of composition aspired.

In the winter of 1907–8 Schoenberg interrupted work on the scherzo of the Second Quartet to compose the two songs op.14. They are highly imitative pieces, the second reminiscent of *Ghasel* in texture. As in some of the songs of 1905 tonic harmony scarcely appears until the close and now exerts still less gravitational force. Certain dissonances, notably perfect and altered 4th chords, resolve so tardily and so variously as to weaken expectation of their doing so at all. This process reached its logical conclusion shortly afterwards in songs from *Das Buch der hängenden Gärten*, at least five of which (nos.4, 5, 3, 8, 7) are known to date from March and April 1908. Here dissonance is finally emancipated, that is, it no longer seeks the justification of resolution. Consequently structural harmony disappears, along with its need for measured periods and consistent textures, and so does tonality itself as a central point of reference. By way of compensation motivic work and the tendency to equate the horizontal and vertical dimensions – in fact the essential elements later codified in the serial method – assume greater responsibility. The poems by George that led Schoenberg to explore the untried expressive possibilities of free dissonance describe in rather indirect language the growth of a passion in an exotic setting and the subsequent parting. Neither poet nor composer wishes to arouse sympathy or evoke ecstasy. The songs are predominantly slow and quiet, the lack of tonal or rhythmic propulsion placing them outside time. Each one captures with peculiar vividness the shifts of feeling at a particular moment, but distanced, as though enshrined in the limbo of past experience. There is nothing of Waldemar and Tove here: the summer wind will assuredly soon sweep all

before it. What will be left? Schoenberg gave his answer in the Second Quartet, one of the most personal of all his works.

This quartet consists of four thematically related movements which successively reflect the transformation of his style, but do not further it. The third movement is later but less advanced than the op.14 songs, and the finale, though tonal only in parts, stands in the same relation to the earlier songs of *Das Buch der hängenden Gärten*. The reason for this lies not only in the technical consideration that the later movements could not overstep certain limits set by the enigmatic first movement, which is in F♯ minor: the composer needed to step back in order to see the crisis that had overtaken him clearly. For the crisis was the subject of the work. The trio of the scherzo incorporates the popular melody *O du lieber Augustin*, the words of which end with the tag 'Alles ist hin', as a private reference to his wife's liaison with Gerstl. The two later movements contain settings for soprano voice of George poems, the first a prayer for divine solace after earthly struggles, the second a vision of the spirit's journey to ethereal realms. Although Schoenberg's choice of subject for his next vocal works was to be directed towards human insights, he evidently recognized already that his ultimate aim was religious.

Early in 1909 Schoenberg composed the first two piano pieces of op.11, before completing *Das Buch der hängenden Gärten*. The Five Orchestral Pieces op.16 and the third piece of op.11 followed in the summer. The strange note of resignation that had sounded through the song cycle is still heard in op.11 nos.1 and 2 and op.16 no.2, but the unfamiliar territory of the new style now takes in the explosive turmoil of op.16 nos.1 and 4 and op.11 no.3, and the unique calm of op.16 no.3. Formal expansion does not accompany the extension of expressive range: as Schoenberg later observed, brevity and intensity of expression are interdependent in these pieces. The disintegration of functional harmony appeared at the time to have destroyed the conditions for large-scale form. But other features with roots in traditional practice, in particular fixed points of reference of various kinds (some of them reminiscent of tonality) and thematic or motivic development, survived to assume not only greater responsibility but new guises. These made possible swifter transformations and more abrupt contrasts than music had hitherto known. Moreover dissonance's new independence permitted, at least in an orchestral context, unprecedented simultaneous contrasts. It is not only novelty of expression in itself but the power to bring seemingly irreconcilable elements into relation that gives the music its visionary quality, far beyond that of the painted 'visions'.

For a time Schoenberg believed that by following the dictates of expression he would be able to renounce motivic features as well as tonality. The last two pieces in opp.11 and 16 to be written, the final piece in each set, show the direction of his thinking. The orchestral piece centres on a continuously evolving melodic line with no clear expository stage; the piano piece relies for coherence as much on dynamics and texture as on pattern. From this point two possibilities suggested themselves. One was to devise ideas that were complete in themselves and required no development. This held no lasting attraction for a composer of Schoenberg's imaginative fecundity. He composed two tiny pieces for chamber ensemble and part of a third early in 1910, and the next year six equally minute piano pieces which he published as op.19; thereafter he left this line of thought to Webern. For Schoenberg the way forward lay in the construction of large forms on the basis of a text. This allowed him scope to build on the experience of opp.11 and 16. Immediately after the instrumental pieces he composed in the astonishingly short time of 17 days the half-hour monodrama *Erwartung*.

The single character in this piece is an unnamed woman. Full of fear and apprehension, she is wandering through a forest at night in search of her lover. The only dramatic event, her discovery of his murdered body, occurs at a fairly early stage; the rest of her monologue passes from recollection of their love, through jealousy to a sense of reconciliation born of exhaustion. As the composer remarked, the whole drama may be understood as a nightmare, but the point is immaterial because the reality explored is purely psychological. There is no realistic time scale: past and present co-exist and merge in the woman's mind as terror, desire, jealousy and tenderness cut across one another in confused association. Traditional tonal order could scarcely have met the demands of such a subject: Schoenberg's extraordinary score depends to a considerable extent

upon a rationality beyond conscious control. True, various unifying factors are observable, such as fixed pitch elements that turn upon a vestigial D minor (his favourite key throughout his life, whether in tonal, freely pantonal or serial composition) and a number of motivic figures that recur time and again, especially at the beginning of phrases. But since these are short, widely scattered and quickly submerged in the stream of continuous development their contribution to coherence at surface level is small; the music can scarcely be called athematic, but it goes further in that direction than any other work of Schoenberg. The monologue falls into several lengthy paragraphs which provide the clearest structural feature, but even here divisions are blurred and larger changes of mood disrupted by innumerable contradictory emotions. Beyond a certain point nothing can impinge upon the dreamlike continuum of musical images.

The next year, 1910, Schoenberg wrote the text of *Die glückliche Hand*, and began the music soon after, though he did not finish it for three years. It is a companion-piece to *Erwartung*, in effect another monodrama, centring on an unnamed man. Though shorter it requires more elaborate staging, including an intricate play of coloured lighting synchronized with the action.

5. Autograph MS of the opening of 'Rote Messe' from Schoenberg's 'Pierrot lunaire', composed 1912 (US-Wc)

The subsidiary roles – a woman, a gentleman and some workers – are mimed, since they are merely projections of the man's psyche, but the chorus of 12 soloists, whose commentary opens and closes the drama, reveals through its pity of him that it represents an independent, presumably divine order of existence. At the beginning the chorus asks why he constantly betrays his capacity for the supermundane in a vain quest for earthly happiness. The main action symbolizes this situation. The man loves a woman who deserts him for a rival, but seems to return to him. In the mistaken belief that he has won her he finds strength to withstand his enemies and inspiration for artistic creation. His resulting work is symbolized by a trinket; it excites envy, but he recognizes it as meretricious. The woman plays him false and the cycle is complete. Although the style of the music is close to that of *Erwartung* Schoenberg reintroduces features that he had temporarily set aside, to meet the more varied action and the wider implications of the text. Clear formal divisions reassert themselves: recapitulatory reminiscence plays an important part in the later stages of the action and there are correspondences between the flanking choral scenes, where exact imitation reappears. There is also a new element, barely hinted at in the works of 1909: the use of parody to characterize such situations as the metal working and the woman's fickleness.

Parody assumes a very important role in *Pierrot lunaire*. This work, composed in 1912, before the completion of *Die glückliche Hand*, consists of 21 poems set for speaker and chamber ensemble. Schoenberg had employed melodrama before in the summer wind narrative of the *Gurrelieder*, and the choruses of *Die glückliche Hand* are also partially spoken. His highly stylized use of the speaking voice, for which he notated relative pitches as well as exact rhythms, proved an ideal vehicle for the Pierrot settings, which were conceived in what he described as a light, ironic–satirical tone. The rather modish verses, by turns grotesque, macabre or consciously sentimental, provide the occasion for presenting, with the detachment that the protagonist in *Die glückliche Hand* failed to achieve, human activity as a shadow play in which menace and absurdity are on a level. The focus shifts at random, as in a dream, between the lunatic activities of the clown, impersonal scenes, the poet in the first person and the self-absorbed artist, who is not spared. Within his new style Schoenberg parodies the characteristics of a great range of genre pieces, very often retaining the ghost of their formal layout as well. In music the lines dividing ironic from direct reference are often hard to detect. The peculiar fascination of *Pierrot lunaire* lies in this ambiguity. The nightmare imagery of some of the poems might scarcely be admissible without ironic distancing, yet the music often strikes with authentic horror. Mockery constantly shades into good humour, exaggerated pathos into the genuinely touching. A decade later Schoenberg was to rediscover his sympathy for the world that he was now determined to leave behind him. For the moment, however, he was set on other things.

After *Pierrot* Schoenberg contemplated writing an oratorio based on the vision of Swedenborg's Heaven at the end of Balzac's novel *Séraphita*. This idea was superseded during 1914 by plans for a vast, partly choral symphony of a religious nature, incorporating texts from Dehmel, Tagore and the Old Testament.

Early in 1915 he wrote words for a new final section consisting of two movements entitled *Totentanz der Prinzipien* and *Die Jakobsleiter*, but although he made extensive sketches nothing came to fruition until he decided to make his own statement of faith by turning *Die Jakobsleiter* into an independent oratorio. He began to revise the text in 1916 and composed the first half the next year. At the beginning of the allegory, which owes a good deal to Balzac's *Séraphita*, a host of people approaching death come before the archangel Gabriel, who admonishes and advises them. Six representatives of various philosophical standpoints then come forward to recount their earthly experiences and aspirations, and receive his comments. There is no doubt something of Schoenberg in all of them, and in Gabriel too, but he avowedly identified himself with the 'chosen one', whose spiritual understanding sets him apart and whose word seems doomed to misunderstanding. A central symphonic interlude symbolizing the transition from this world to the hereafter leads to the uncomposed second part in which souls are prepared for reincarnation as the next step in their long spiritual pilgrimage towards ultimate perfection. The chosen one is reluctant to face the world again, once more to stand alone and find himself involuntarily compelled, though receiving no support, to speak and do what he would never have dared to think or take responsibility for. But he is told to remember all that he has in common with the rest of humanity and to accept his prophetic role. At the close Gabriel calls on every soul to seek unity with God through prayer.

The faith and the view of his mission to which Schoenberg gave expression in *Die Jakobsleiter* were to influence the whole course of his later development as a composer. The short score of the first part, however, is more easily seen as a potential culmination to the music composed since 1908 than as a foretaste of that of the 1920s. The closing section of *Die glückliche Hand* provided a model for the big, partly sung, partly spoken choruses. The long paragraphs sung or spoken by the soloists required a more sustained style of writing than that, for instance, of *Erwartung*, where the varying intensity of dissonance breaks continuity of pace and texture. For this Schoenberg was able to turn to the Four Orchestral Songs op.22 (1913–16) and their forerunner *Herzgewächse* (1911), where he had already devised more even textures by maintaining a rather high level of dissonance in six or more parts, with very little octave doubling and a tendency towards symmetrically built chords. Except for *Seraphita* (op.22 no.1) all these songs anticipate the religious preoccupation of *Die Jakobsleiter*. The very high soprano voice that symbolizes prayer in *Herzgewächse* reappears as the soul that ascends heavenward just before the central interlude. In January 1915 Schoenberg wrote to Zemlinsky that his new symphony would be 'worked' ('ein gearbeitetes Werk') in contrast to his many 'purely impressionistic' recent works. He carried this resolve over into the oratorio. His brief exploration of the dream world of free association had permanently enriched his musical language and vision, but he now needed to regain greater formal elaboration and density of meaning. Although *Die Jakobsleiter*, like the monodramas before it, relies primarily on the text for its structure, it employs recurrent themes and melodies, often in contrapuntal combination. Many of these are related through permutations of a hexachord heard at the outset.

At one point in the unfinished central interlude Schoenberg directed that groups of instruments placed at a distance should enter in 'floating' ('schwebend') rhythm not exactly synchronized with that of the main orchestra. The suspension of rhythmic propulsion symbolizes the dissolution of earthly ties on the threshold of the hereafter. How far Schoenberg would have been able to pass beyond this extraordinary conception into the Swedenborgian Heaven of his text had he not been interrupted, it is impossible to say, though the history of *Moses und Aron* suggests that he would not have reached the end. But the 12-note serial method that increasingly occupied him from 1920 provided a continuation of another sort. The omnipresent series sought to establish as principles the equation of the horizontal and vertical aspects of music, and the unity of all ideas in a composition with each other and with their context. Schoenberg expressly compared the unity of musical space to Swedenborg's concept of Heaven where 'there is no absolute down, no right or left, forward or backward'. In a different sense from the symphonic interlude the music must 'float'. The dodecaphonic aspect counteracted the pull of tonal gravity; the only quasi-tonal music in *Die Jakobsleiter* belongs to 'one of the called', who is roundly rebuked for preferring beauty to truth. In June 1922, shortly before he gave up trying to continue the oratorio, but when his foot was already firmly on the serial path, Schoenberg started a new sketchbook by inscribing the cover with the words 'Mit Gott'.

7. SERIAL AND TONAL WORKS 1920–36. Since serialism is a method of composition and does not dictate style Schoenberg might have been expected to find in it the means, if not of completing *Die Jakobsleiter*, at least of continuing in some direction suggested by that work. Instead he evolved a form of neo-classicism. This may not have been his original intention. His first known attempt at consistent serial composition is a dodecaphonic orchestral passacaglia for which he made sketches in March 1920. Its economic textures look forward to the Serenade and Wind Quintet (and he remembered the introduction six years later when he began the Variations for Orchestra), but the structural conception seems to show affinities with the music for 'one who strives' in *Die Jakobsleiter*. The Piano Pieces op.23 nos.1, 2 and 4, written or begun in July 1920, are descendants of the pre-war instrumental pieces, and he began the Piano Suite op.25, exactly a year later, with the only two movements (the Prelude and Intermezzo) that are not dance movements, thinking of the work simply as a second set of pieces. However, the Variations and Dance Scene from the Serenade op.24 had been begun in the later months of 1920, the March followed in September 1921, and by the time all three works were finished in the early part of 1923 movements based on Classical forms predominated. Although every piece in opp.23 and 24 involves serial procedures, only one in each work uses a 12-note series. Both of these postdate the earliest movements of the Suite, which, like the abandoned passacaglia and nearly everything that Schoenberg was to compose in the next ten years, is dodecaphonic throughout.

The reason for Schoenberg's return to Classical forms must be sought in his need to find new scope for his inherently developmental cast of thought. Paradox-

ically, developing variation had brought about, above all in the later works of 1909, a reduction in the conditions for its own exercise. Where every motif is transformed before it can gather associations for the listener there can be no intensification of meaning through development; where no pattern establishes itself only extreme contrasts cheat expectation, and then not for long. If Schoenberg's art of development was to develop further it needed a basis in relative stability, especially in the rhythmic sphere. For him technical needs were inseparable from philosophical ones. It seems likely that he saw his music at this time as initiating a new incarnation analogous to that required of the 'chosen one' in the second part of *Die Jakobsleiter*. In the second turn of the spiral of his musical existence his task was evidently to reinterpret, in accordance with the 'higher and better order' to which he aspired, not his own previous experience, but the course of musical history as he knew and understood it best. His real interest began with Bach. He later declared his teachers to have been in the first place Bach and Mozart, and in the second Beethoven, Wagner and Brahms. Although the last two had appeared as the dominant influences in his tonal music, at least on the surface, the earlier ones now came to the fore. Despite the reluctance of the 'chosen one', like Moses after him, to return to the world and prophesy, Schoenberg was able to write to Hauer in December 1923 that after a 15-year search he had discovered a method of composition that allowed him to compose with a freedom and fantasy such as he had only known in his youth. The next 13 years were remarkably fruitful.

Most of the movements in the Serenade and the Piano Suite draw on late Baroque dance characteristics much as *Pierrot lunaire* had borrowed from the subjects that it parodied. But although the detail of the Serenade often recalls *Pierrot*, as does its humour, six of its seven movements are built on an altogether larger scale, even without the lengthy repeats that Schoenberg adopted from his models. The repeats, here and in the Piano Suite, are the first of any size and almost the last in the whole of his published work. They set him the special problem of canalizing his transforming imagination sufficiently within a given mood and character for a repetition to make sense. The exercise was no doubt an essential step towards establishing strongly differentiated developing characters in the great instrumental and operatic structures of the coming years. But that was incidental: Schoenberg said that he never knew what lay ahead, and his zigzag course towards the crises of 1908 and 1920 bears him out. There is nothing merely preparatory about the early serial masterpieces: his concern was, as ever, with the unique work in hand.

Thus in the marvellous series of instrumental works composed between 1920 and 1936 individuality is not of the limited kind associated with stepping-stones in a stylistic or technical evolution. In each one vigorous expansion within the terms of a particular premise builds a self-sufficient statement of very wide range, yet entirely singular. The next two works, the Wind Quintet and the Suite op.29 for seven instruments, illustrate the point very clearly. Schoenberg turned here to the thematic contrast required by Classical forms and to the traditional four-movement pattern. The first movement of the Quintet follows standard sonata layout, and the finale is a rondo. The first movement of the Suite lacks a regular development section, but despite the dance charac-

6. Arnold Schoenberg

ter of the second and fourth movements consistent symphonic treatment allies it with the Quintet rather than the Serenade. Yet the two works differ radically. The persistent contrapuntal texture of the Quintet looks back to the First String Quartet and First Chamber Symphony (and the emphasis on whole-tone and quartal sonorities is reminiscent of the latter work); the Suite is rooted in a harmonic idea which pervades texture and melody throughout. The divergence affects the music at every level.

In the Variations for orchestra (1926–8) and the Third String Quartet (1927), which are also modelled on Classical forms, Schoenberg avoided these contrapuntal and harmonic extremes for the most part, and finally established the main stylistic characteristics of his serial music; these were to remain fairly constant to the end of his life. The transformations of the series as such cannot, of course, be followed consistently by the ear, and he strongly deprecated any attempt to do so. Although for him the series functioned in the manner of a motif, his themes consist primarily of rhythmic patterns which may carry any serial derivation. The thematic rhythms themselves are not fixed: he showed remarkable skill in varying them without endangering their identity. The interplay of melodic and rhythmic

motif is responsible to a very large extent for the extraordinary richness of the music, bringing about in the course of a work the gradual accumulation of a mass of affinities between disparate elements. It also affects the bar-to-bar texture in an important way. The prodigious contrapuntal combinations so typical of the tonal works lose ground to relatively simple textures in which one or two salient lines predominate. But the rhythmic articulation of accompaniments fashioned out of serial forms in balanced rotation produces a wealth of motivic reference, as well as the play of rhythmic wit which is such a notable feature of Schoenberg's later scores. Thus the superimposition of ideas, with its risk of overloading, gives way to a finely graduated perspective in which the listener discovers with increasing familiarity ever more layers of meaning beyond the clearcut foreground, as his hearing travels towards the inaudible vanishing-point of total serial connection.

At the end of 1928 Schoenberg drafted the first version of the text of *Moses und Aron* (in the form of an oratorio) and composed the one-act comic opera *Von heute auf morgen*. The subjects of both works had been anticipated three years earlier in the two sets of short choral pieces opp.27 and 28. Most of these make considerable use of strict canonic or fugal writing, a feature

7. *Autograph MS of the opening of Schoenberg's Piano Piece op.33a, composed December 1928–April 1929* (*private collection*)

that is taken up on a greatly expanded scale in the ensembles and choruses of the operas. The Three Satires op.28 deride the irresponsibility of modish modernity in music (especially Stravinsky's neo-classicism); *Von heute auf morgen* attacks the same thing in life. This is a comedy of marital strife and reconciliation involving a symmetrical quartet of characters: a wife brings her husband to heel when he takes an interest in an emancipated 'woman of today' by showing that she could play the same game if she wished. The little incident, which Gertrud Schoenberg with her husband's assistance turned into a very serviceable libretto, was suggested by the domestic life of the Schrekers – a source of frequent amusement to the Schoenbergs. The text makes its points bluntly, like most that Schoenberg had a hand in or wrote himself: his musical style is not primarily illustrative and prefers a simple basis for the wealth of comment and interpretation that it provides in its own terms. The opera adopts Classical procedures, but handles them rather freely. Recitative and arioso break into the set pieces, expanding them to accommodate great flexibility of pace and feeling as the bickering characters waver between good sense and self-indulgence. Schoenberg finds no broad comedy in the commonplace and absurd situations, but endless nuances of humour and sentiment which, no less than the extremes of spirituality and depravity in *Moses und Aron*, relate to perennial components in his expressive range.

It was another 18 months before Schoenberg finally began to compose *Moses und Aron*. In the meantime he produced several smaller works in which the relation to

Classical form becomes looser. The first piano piece of op.33 and its slightly later companion (1931) each employ a pair of contrasting themes, but the first, at least, recalls the concentrated manner of op.23. At this time he became interested in the problem of film music. Unwilling to subordinate his music to the requirements of a real film he chose instead to illustrate in his *Begleitmusik zu einer Lichtspielszene* an imaginary and unfilmable sequence of emotions: threatening danger, fear, catastrophe. He employed a kind of free variation form, and thinned out his recent style considerably to suit the programmatic nature of the undertaking. Since 1916 Schoenberg had now and then used tonality in fragmentary sketches and occasional pieces (notably the beautiful *Weihnachtsmusik* of 1921 based on *Es ist ein' Ros' entsprungen*), but never in published works. In 1929, however, he made some folksong settings for a commission, and followed them up with two non-dodecaphonic male choruses, *Glück* and *Verbundenheit*, the second of which centres on D minor. Although the other four choruses that make up op.35 are dodecaphonic, the exceptions show that the urge to return to tonal composition was beginning to gain ground.

Moses und Aron, composed between 1930 and 1932, is Schoenberg's second great profession of faith, a sequel to *Die Jakobsleiter* dealing with the predicament of the chosen one in carrying out his prophetic task. Unlike the oratorio, however, the work is in no real sense unfinished, even though the short third act was never set to music. The reason for this lies in the subject itself. At the beginning of Act 1 God, speaking from the burning bush, assigns to Moses the role of prophet.

Schoenberg had summed up the problems of revelation without distortion in the second chorus from op.27: 'You shall not make an image. For an image confines, limits, grasps what should remain limitless and unimaginable. An image demands a name which you can take only from what is little. You shall not worship the little! You must believe in the spirit, directly, without emotion, selflessly'. Moses complains that he lacks eloquence to express what he understands of God, who accordingly appoints Aaron as his spokesman. Aaron comes to meet Moses; he echoes Moses's thoughts in less uncompromising terms, and this is underlined by the casting of Moses as a speaker and Aaron as a lyrical tenor. They return together to bring the demoralized but expectant Israelites news of the new god who is to deliver them from Egyptian bondage. Moses tells them flatly that the one almighty, invisible and unimaginable God requires no sacrifices of them but complete devotion, and meets with a derision that Aaron can quell only by performing a series of three miracles, thereby substituting an image for the truth.

In Act 2 Aaron is obliged to still the people's doubt when Moses is away praying on the mountain by setting up a real image for them to worship in the form of the golden calf. The healing benefits of a faith so shallowly grounded are soon swept away by an orgy culminating in human sacrifice, suicide, lust and wholesale destruction. When Moses returns the calf vanishes at his word, but Aaron is able to defend his actions by pointing out that he is Moses's interpreter, and not an independent agent. The people are seen following yet another image, this time the pillar of fire, and Moses is left in despair. The uncomposed third act consists of another exchange between the brothers. This time Moses prevails. Aaron, who has been under arrest, is freed but falls dead; with all barriers to spiritual understanding removed the people will at length achieve unity with God. Schoenberg once suggested that Beethoven, Bruckner and Mahler had not been permitted to compose tenth symphonies because they might have revealed something that we are not permitted to know; a ninth seemed to represent a limit beyond which the composer must pass into the hereafter. To have composed music adequate to the idea of unity with God would have been to write a tenth symphony. At some level Schoenberg must have felt this from the outset, for the first two acts of the opera are dramatically and musically complete in themselves. But to remain true to his mission he could not admit that: it was his duty to continue to strive towards the expression of the inexpressible. To the end of his life he still spoke of finishing the work.

In its formal procedures *Moses und Aron* follows *Von heute auf morgen* in striking a balance between Classical number opera and Wagner's continuous symphonic manner, but on a far larger scale incorporating very big choral or orchestral movements. Schoenberg draws on every aspect of his music of the previous decade, and in the partly spoken texture of much of the choral writing looks back further. It is in every way his most comprehensive masterpiece, encompassing the stillness of the purely spiritual glimpsed momentarily in the opening bars, Moses's bitterness and resignation, Aaron's ecstatic eloquence and occasional weakness, and the people's jubilation, instability, mockery, violence and outright savagery. And it is noteworthy that the music interprets the stern morality of the libretto with a breadth of sympathy lacking in the neutral words.

That Schoenberg should now have sought relaxation in a less monumental task is not so surprising as his choice, which took the form of a pair of concertos for cello and for string quartet, based respectively on a keyboard concerto by M. G. Monn for which he had provided a continuo part some 20 years earlier, and Handel's Concerto grosso op.6 no.7 (the only one of the set that lacks separate concertino parts throughout). These works are often mistakenly classified as arrangements. However, whereas in his orchestrations of Bach and Brahms Schoenberg added nothing substantial to the original and never overstepped the style, the concertos are new compositions to almost the same degree as a set of variations on another composer's theme. Thus in each movement of the Cello Concerto he overlaid Monn's exposition with additional counterpoints and harmonies reaching as far forward as Brahms, or even later, and then continued independently in the same style. In the Quartet Concerto he preserved the complete outline of the original first movement and scarcely changed the second; on the other hand he radically recomposed the two remaining movements, taking only a few phrases from Handel in the third. In 1934 he crowned this group of works with a Suite in G for string orchestra in a similar style but based entirely on his own material. By way of indicating their secondary status he did not confer an opus number on any of them, yet they are brilliant compositions that he could certainly not have written earlier. The pressures towards the dissolution of tonality that haunt his older tonal works are entirely absent; the late works accept their terms of reference, and the clarity with which their abundant invention is projected derives directly from the serial works of the previous decade.

The one aspect of Schoenberg's serial music for which *Moses und Aron* had given only restricted opportunity was its abstract symphonic thought. This now became his chief concern again. After his tonal excursion he composed in 1935–6 the Violin Concerto and the Fourth String Quartet, his first 12-note works (apart from the three songs of op.48) since the opera, and with it the culminating productions of this period of his work. They are cast in the respective three- and four-movement moulds traditional in such works, but the individual movements abandon strict Classical layout. The first-movement recapitulations no longer correspond to the measure of the expositions, but are engulfed in the development, which continues unchecked to the close. The forward urge that marks all Schoenberg's music asserts itself so forcefully here that a return to single-movement structure through the breakdown of the divisions between movements might have been foretold. Such a return did indeed take place, but the transition was not a straightforward one.

8. LATER WORKS. Schoenberg's music was once again reaching a turning-point, even if a less acute one than in 1908 or 1920. Since the latter date his progressive reinterpretation of earlier musical principles had led him from Baroque and Classical models to a more fluid formal approach analogous to that of the later 19th century. The next step could only bring him to his own work – not merely to single-movement form but beyond that to the achievement of his expressionist years. But this very achievement was to a considerable degree the basis for his reinterpretation. As though to understand

his situation better he took up, in 1939, the sketches for the Second Chamber Symphony, begun in 1906 on the threshold of the crisis that now, though in a different way, confronted him for the second time. He completed the work in two movements, adding the last 20 bars of the first and about half of the second (from bar 309), but he also rescored and revised the remainder. In the process he increased the emphasis on a technical trait already prominent in the contemporary songs opp.12 and 14. Whereas the harmony of the First Chamber Symphony had been characterized by an abundance of complex suspensions and appoggiaturas, that of the Second tends to progress by stepwise movement in all parts. Schoenberg combined this technique with frequent 4th chords and similar combinations to very austere effect; indeed, the final coda strikes an unequivocally tragic note such as his later style would scarcely have countenanced. Perhaps recognition of this possibility in the material was an additional reason for his returning to it at this difficult period of his life.

In the previous year he had composed a setting of the *Kol nidre* in a tonal style which he hoped would prove acceptable in the synagogue. However, the work was found unsuitable for liturgical use because he had added an introduction and altered the traditional text in an attempt to strengthen its spiritual content. In order to give the main declaration of repentance and dedication 'the dignity of law', in his own phrase, he set it in march-like fashion and reinforced the effect with a harmonic severity that anticipates, in simpler terms, that of the chamber symphony. After finishing the symphony he still felt that his harmonic style just before his first pantonal works offered unused possibilities. He set about exploring them further in the D minor Variations on a Recitative for organ. Here, as in several pieces of the earlier time, harmonic complexity is controlled by unremitting reference to the tonic; there are also, however, serial features. In many ways this work and the next, the setting of Byron's *Ode to Napoleon*, form a complementary pair of opposites. Each is rooted in a special harmonic procedure that gives it a peculiarly individual sound. The D minor work borrows from serialism; the dodecaphonic *Ode* ends in E♭. The Variations respect the integrity of their melodic theme; the series of the *Ode* is freely permuted. The sequence of extraordinarily heterogeneous works starting with the *Kol nidre*, each employing a different technique for a particular end, shows the composer once again moving as though inadvertently towards a definite point, in this case the resumption of serial composition from a rather different angle.

The Piano Concerto of 1942 consists of one movement, less a conflation of several movements like the First Quartet and First Chamber Symphony than an expansion of a single sonata movement to embrace four symphonic characters in traditional sequence. As in the serial works up to 1936 all essential elements derive from the unpermuted series, but there are also strong affinities with the *Ode to Napoleon*. In the first place the music shares to some extent the quasi-tonal leanings of the *Ode*. This leads to more stable textures than are common in the earlier serial works, let alone the expressionist ones, and to symmetrical formal schemes, at least in outline. None of this suggests that Schoenberg was more closely engaged with the crisis of 1908 than he had been in 1936 – rather the reverse. But another legacy from the *Ode* changes the picture. At the very

opening the serial melody is supported by free permutations of itself, its unusual tonal stability achieved through an unstable element. The consequences emerge later: chaos lies in wait at transitional points, above all at the end of each of the middle sections, where the chromatic totality becomes an undifferentiated stack of 4ths which momentarily endanger the work's identity. The abyss had opened before in Schoenberg's music, for instance in *Erwartung*, but never beneath so serene a surface. The effect is correspondingly disturbing.

The following year at the request of his publishers he composed a set of variations in G minor for band. It was intended for wide circulation and so couched in a straightforward tonal idiom, like the G major Suite for Strings, which had been written for college orchestras. It has all the vigour and ebullience of the earlier work, and as there his personality marks every bar no less firmly than in his more dissonant style. After this he wrote nothing for two years owing to deterioration in his health. When he resumed composing approximately one work a year, as he had done fairly regularly since his arrival in America, his bad eyesight obliged him to restrict his scale of activity. He wrote the first work of this last group in response to another commission. He was asked to compose the prelude to a suite for chorus and orchestra by various composers based on selections from the book of *Genesis*. Schoenberg evidently thought of God as creating the world out of divine order rather than primordial chaos, for the core of his compact piece consists of an eight-part double canon followed by two strettos that draw into their orbit the more amorphous elements from the opening. In the works of this last phase (except, of course, the folksong settings op.49), the tonal influence that had still been perceptible in the Piano Concerto recedes, and the language moves somewhat closer to that of the serial works up to 1936.

The longest and most wide-ranging of these late works is the String Trio of 1946. It is cast in a single movement expanded from within by the pressure of continuous and multifarious development. The different musical characters do not group themselves into clear subsidiary sections, as in the Piano Concerto, but alternate with a degree and frequency of contrast that Schoenberg had avoided since his expressionist period. Indeed, with this work he finally overtook his own earlier achievement and absorbed it into his later mode of thought. He divided the score into three 'parts' separated by two 'episodes' of different serial construction. The first part and episode correspond to an exposition, and the second part and episode to a development; the third part contains a truncated but unusually exact recapitulation and a coda. The structure recalls the first movement of the Fourth Quartet in the return early in the development to the codetta of the exposition, before the emergence of an important new melody.

The outpouring of elusive, visionary music held within this framework arose directly from the special circumstances of composition: Schoenberg had just recovered from an almost fatal heart attack, and he confessed that the experience was reflected in the Trio. It is not difficult to guess the direction of his thoughts. Having stood nearer than ever before to the truths that lay beyond man's reach in this world he was under the obligation to reveal what he could. The reinterpretation of expressionism towards which he had been moving suddenly took on a new urgency. Just as, nearly 40 years before, the attempt to lift all constraints from intuition had led to him placing his art in the service of faith, and eventually to a new order in composition, so he might now, from his present level, reach further still. But if the work contains intimations of the hereafter it is also concerned with this world: the melody heard in the second part and again in the coda recalls the music for the woman healed by faith, even though faith in an image, in Act 2 of *Moses und Aron*, and would seem to refer to his precarious recovery. There can be little doubt that the work was intended as a personal and spiritual testament, and it could have closed his life-work worthily.

In the event Schoenberg lived another five years and was able to compose a second testament in 1950. His first work in the interim, *A Survivor from Warsaw*, was wrung from him by a report of an occasion when Jews on their way to the gas chamber found courage in singing the *Shema Yisroel*, the command to love God, who is one lord. Though a short piece it made large demands. The orchestral accompaniment to the witness's spoken narration illustrates a reality more horrible than anything that Schoenberg could have imagined when he wrote his *Begleitmusik*, and his original melody for the Hebrew cantillation is an extraordinary conception, expressing a desperate tenacity that belongs very much to its author. The three folk-songs op.49 are new settings of tunes that he had already arranged in 1929. The two choral settings of *Es gingen zwei Gespielen gut*, the most elaborate in their respective sets, show a revealing shift of emphasis: the 1929 version takes the form of a complex set of canonic variations, that of 1948 is less intricate but allows the original melody to dissolve in the general texture of variation. Schoenberg's last instrumental work is entitled 'Phantasy for violin with piano accompaniment'. The description is exact: the violin part leads throughout, having even been written separately before the accompaniment. Melody accordingly dominates, limiting a tendency towards the sharp contrasts characteristic of the String Trio and checking their more disruptive consequences. This is the key to the work's special quality. It stands close to the Trio in many points of style, including melodic style, and in its subtlety of thematic continuity, but differs more consistent tranquillity.

The three religious choruses for mixed voices of op.50 were conceived at different times for different purposes and have little in common. However, at a time when he still hoped to finish the last one Schoenberg looked forward to their performance as a group. *Dreimal tausend Jahre* is a four-part setting of a short poem looking forward to God's return among the faithful in the new Israel. The close-knit textures and full harmony ally it to the male choruses op.35, whereas the mixture of singing and speech in the more dramatic six-part *De profundis* recalls *Moses und Aron* and throws into relief the varied soloistic phrases expressing repentance and supplication. The third, unfinished piece employs a speaker and an orchestra with the chorus. The text is a meditation on prayer by the composer himself, the first of the series of 'modern psalms' that occupied the last months of his life. Towards the end it speaks of the feeling of unity with God experienced in prayer. The passage is first given to the speaker, and should then have been taken up by the chorus. But at this point the composition breaks off, for it presented Schoenberg with the same task, at once impossible to fulfil yet central to his beliefs, as the third act of *Moses und Aron*: that of

revealing through his music what it is not given to man to know. Although he still entertained the notion of working on *Die Jakobsleiter* and *Moses* until shortly before his death he must really have known that it was out of the question, and that the withdrawal into silence manifested in the *Modern Psalm* represented his final testament.

Since the time of his death Schoenberg's cardinal importance as an innovator has been very widely recognized. As a result most of his works are now assured of at least an occasional hearing. Yet although his idiom is no longer unfamiliar in a general sense, his music remains less easily accessible than that of his eminent pupils and contemporaries. One difficulty has been that musicians who shared his background and artistic assumptions, and might in principle have built up a tradition of performance – men such as Furtwängler, Walter, Kleiber and Klemperer, all of whom worked in Berlin when Schoenberg was there – failed to keep abreast of his development, while the more objective, uncommitted approach cultivated in recent years overlooks too much. But if the scarcity of good performances has not helped to dispel the wider public's indifference, neither does it entirely account for it. There would appear to be more fundamental causes that affect specialist audiences as well.

In 1930 Berg drew attention to the close parallel between Schoenberg's historical position and that of Bach. He showed that a few small changes could make the assessment of the latter in Riemann's encyclopedia apply equally well to Schoenberg, who, like Bach, lived at a time of transition between two musical styles and succeeded in reconciling their opposing characteristics through his genius. Berg did not live to see his comparison further borne out by changes in taste after his teacher's death. Just as Bach's music held no interest for a generation preoccupied with the simpler language of early symphonic music, so the greater part of Schoenberg's work has had limited appeal for ears attuned to the broader effects of new sound resources and aleatory procedures. Its Bach-like density, proliferation and order run counter to the spirit of the age, making exceptional demands on the interpretative discipline of the performer and the sensibility of the listener. In the long run, however, these very qualities are likely to tell no less powerfully in its favour. Perhaps no other composer of the time has so much to offer.

See ANALYSIS, §II, 6 and fig.19.

WORKS

Edition: *A. Schoenberg: Sämtliche Werke* (Mainz, 1966–) [S]

Only a selection of the more considerable of Schoenberg's numerous unfinished compositions is included here. Many more are listed in Rufer (1959), and those up to 1933 are catalogued in greater detail in Maegaard, i (1972). Some fragments are published in Maegaard, iii (1972) [M]. Works without opus numbers are unpublished unless otherwise stated. For more precise details of composition dates see Rufer (1959) and Maegaard (1972).

op.   OPERAS
17   Erwartung (monodrama, 1, M. Pappenheim), Aug–Sept 1909; Prague, Neues Deutsches Theater, 6 June 1924; vocal score by Schoenberg
18   Die glückliche Hand (drama with music, 1, Schoenberg), 1910–Nov 1913; Vienna, Volksoper, 14 Oct 1924
32   Von heute auf morgen (opera, 1, M. Blonda [pseud. of G. Schoenberg]), Oct 1928–Jan 1929; Frankfurt, Opernhaus, 1 Feb 1930; vocal score by Schoenberg; S A/7
—   Moses und Aron (opera, 3, Schoenberg), May 1930–March 1932; Act 3 not composed; Der Tanz um das goldene Kalb perf. Darmstadt, 2 July 1951; Acts 1–2 perf. in concert, Hamburg, 12 March 1954; Acts 1–2 staged, Zurich, Stadttheater, 6 June 1957; (1957)

(fragments)

— Und Pippa tanzt (G. Hauptmann), Aug 1906–March 1907; prelude and recitative, short score, 68 bars

CHORAL

— Ei du Lütte (partsong, K. Groth), early
— Friedlicher Abend senkt sich aufs Gefilde, partsong in canon, early
— Viel tausend Blümlein auf der Au, partsong, early
— Gurrelieder (J. P. Jacobsen, trans. R. F. Arnold), solo vv, choruses, orch, March 1900–March 1901, orchd Aug 1901–1903, July 1910–Nov 1911; (1912)
13 Friede auf Erden (C. F. Meyer), SSAATTBB, insts ad lib, Feb–March 1907, acc. Oct 1911
— Der deutsche Michel (O. Kernstock), male vv, 1914 or 1915
27 Four Pieces, SATB: Unentrinnbar (Schoenberg), Sept 1925; Du sollst nicht, du musst (Schoenberg), Oct 1925; Mond und Menschen (Tschan-Jo-Su, trans. Bethge), Oct 1925; Der Wunsch des Liebhabers (Hung-So-Fan, trans. Bethge), with cl, mand, vn, vc, Nov 1925
28 Three Satires (Schoenberg), SATB: Am Scheideweg, Nov 1925; Vielseitigkeit, Nov–Dec 1925; Der neue Klassizismus, with va, vc, pf, Nov–Dec 1925; pubd with appendix of three canons (see Canons below)
— Three Folksongs, SATB, Jan 1929 (1930): Es gingen zwei Gespielen gut; Herzlieblich Lieb, durch Scheiden; Schein uns, du liebe Sonne
35 Six Pieces (Schoenberg), male vv: Hemmung, Feb 1930; Gesetz, March 1930; Ausdrucksweise, March 1930; Glück, March 1929; Landsknechte, March 1930; Verbundenheit, April 1929
39 Kol nidre (Jewish liturgy in Eng. with alterations and introduction), speaker, chorus, orch, Aug–Sept 1938; S A/19
44 Prelude 'Genesis' (textless), SATB, orch, Sept 1945; S A/19
46 A Survivor from Warsaw (Schoenberg), narrator, male vv, orch, Aug 1947; S A/19
49 Three Folksongs, SATB, June 1948: Es gingen zwei Gespielen gut (Two comely maidens); Der Mai tritt ein mit Freuden (Now May has come with gladness); Mein Herz in steten Treuen (To her I shall be faithful); S A/19
50a Dreimal tausend Jahre (D. D. Runes), SATB, April 1949; S A/19
50b De profundis (Ps cxxx in Heb.), SSATBB, June–July 1950; S A/19
50c Modern Psalm (Der erste Psalm) (Schoenberg), speaker, chorus, orch, Oct 1950, inc.; S A/19

(fragments)

— Wenn weder Mond noch Stern am Himmel stehn (L. Pfau), male vv, wind ens, June 1897; 54 bars
— Darthulas Grabgesang (Goethe), 14vv, orch, April 1903; vocal score, 65 bars
— Symphony with choral movements, 1914–15; sketches; M (extracts)
— Die Jakobsleiter (oratorio, Schoenberg), solo vv, choruses, orch, June 1917–July 1922, rev. begun Oct 1944 and abandoned after bar 104; first half only composed in draft, orchd posthumously by W. Zillig; text pubd 1917 and in *A. Schönberg: Texte* (Vienna, 1926); vocal score, arr. W. Zillig (1975)
— Israel Exists Again (Schoenberg), chorus, orch, March–June 1949; short score, 55 bars; S A/19

ORCHESTRAL

— Adagio, harp, str, early
— Gavotte and Musette (in Olden Style), str, March 1897
4   Verklärte Nacht, arr. str orch 1917, 2nd version 1943
5   Pelleas und Melisande, sym. poem, after Maeterlinck, July 1902–Feb 1903
9   Chamber Symphony no.1, arr. full orch Nov 1922, 2nd version April 1935
10 String Quartet no.2, arr. S, str orch. ?1919
16 Five Orchestral Pieces: no.1 May 1909, nos.2–3 June 1909, no.4 July 1909, no.5 Aug 1909; arr. reduced orch, Sept 1949
31 Variations for Orchestra, May 1926, July–Aug 1928
34 Begleitmusik zu einer Lichtspielszene, Oct 1929–Feb 1930
— Cello Concerto [after Monn: Clavicembalo Concerto in D, 1746], Nov 1932–Jan 1933 (1935); S A/27; red. by Schoenberg for vc, pf; S B/27
— String Quartet Concerto [after Handel: Concerto grosso op.6 no.7], May–Aug 1933 (1963); S A/27
— Suite, G, str, Sept–Dec 1934 (1935)
36 Violin Concerto, 1935–Sept 1936; S A/15
38 Chamber Symphony no.2, Aug 1906–Dec 1916, Aug–Oct 1939; S A,B/11
42 Piano Concerto, July–Dec 1942; S A/15
43a Theme and Variations, band, completed July 1943; arr. orch as op.43b, summer 1943

(fragments)

— Waltz, str, early; 10 sections completed

— Serenade, small orch, 1896; 1st movt completed, 2nd and 3rd inc.
— Frühlings Tod, sym. poem, after Lenau, 1898; 254 bars of which 136 fully scored
— Symphony, G, Feb 1900; Introduction, g, pf score, 73 bars
— Passacaglia, March 1920; sketches; M
— Symphony, Jan–Feb 1937; short score, 30–50 bars of each of the 4 movts
— untitled work, Oct–Nov 1946; short score, 28 bars
— untitled work, April 1948; short score, 25 bars

CHAMBER

— 'Alliance' Walzer, 2 vn, early
— 'Sonnenschein' Polka schnell, 2 vn, early
— 3 Songs without Words, 2 vn, early
— untitled work, d, vn, pf, early
— Presto, C, str qt, early
— String Quartet, D, summer–autumn 1897 (1966)
— Scherzo in F and Trio in a, str qt, July 1897; presumably rejected 2nd movt of preceding
4   Verklärte Nacht, after Dehmel, 2 vn, 2 va, 2 vc, completed Dec 1899
7   String Quartet no.1, d, summer 1904–Sept 1905
9   Chamber Symphony no.1, 15 insts, completed July 1906; S A,B/11
10 String Quartet no.2, with S in movts 3 'Litanei' and 4 'Entrückung' (George), March 1907–Aug 1908
— Three Pieces, wind qnt, org/harmonium, cel, str qt, db, Feb 1910, no.3 inc. (?1970)
— Die eiserne Brigade, march, pf qnt, 1916
24 Serenade, cl, b cl, mand, gui, vn, va, vc, with B in movt 4 'O könnt' ich je der Rach' an ihr genesen' (Petrarch, trans. K. Förster), Aug 1920–April 1923
— Weihnachtsmusik, 2 vn, vc, harmonium, pf, Dec 1921 (1975)
26 Wind Quintet, April 1923–Aug 1924
29 Suite, Eb–cl/fl, cl, b cl/bn, pf, vn, va, vc, Jan 1925–May 1926
30 String Quartet no.3, Jan–March 1927
37 String Quartet no.4, April–July 1936
45 String Trio, Aug–Sept 1946
47 Phantasy, vn, pf, March 1949

(fragments)

— String Quartet, C, early; 41 bars
— Clarinet Quintet, d; 28 bars
— Toter Winkel, after G. Falke, 2 vn, 2 va, 2 vc, ?before op.4; 31 bars
— Chamber Symphony, a, ?before op.9; 22 bars
— Fugue, d, str qt, March 1904; 80 bars
— String Quintet, D, winter 1904–5; 142 bars
— Ein Stelldichein, after Dehmel, ob, cl, pf, vn, vc, Oct 1905; 90 bars
— String Septet, March 1918; 25 bars
— Tempo zwischen langsamem Walzer und Polacca, movt intended for op.24, Aug 1920; 40 bars; M
— Gerpa, F, for Schoenberg's son Georg (hn + vn + pf) and himself (vn + pf + harmonium), Nov 1922; theme and 3 variations completed
— Sonata, vn, pf, Jan–Feb 1928; 43 bars
— String Quartet, June 1949; openings of all 4 movts, 36 complete bars in all

SOLO VOCAL

(for 1v, pf unless otherwise stated)

— Songs, almost all before 1900: Dass gestern eine Wespe Dich; Dass schon die Maienzeit vorüber (A. Christen); Der Pflanze, die dort über dem Abgrund (Pfau); Drüben geht die Sonne scheiden (Schilflied) (Lenau); Du kehrst mir den Rücken (Pfau); Du musst nicht meinen (Mannesbangen) (Dehmel); Duftreich ist die Erde (Ecloge) (W . . .) (1975); Einsam bin ich und alleine (Pfau); Einst hat vor deines Vaters Haus; Es ist ein Flüstern in der Nacht, T, str qt; Es steht sein Bild noch immer da (Gedenken); S A/1; Gott grüss dich Marie (Pfau); Ich grüne wie die Weide grünt (W. Wackernagel); Ich hab' zum Brunnen ein Krüglein gebracht (Das zerbrochene Krüglein) (M. Greif; Im Fliederbusch ein Vöglein sass (R. Reinick); Juble, schöne junge Rose; Klein Vögelein, du zwitscherst fein; Könnt' ich je zu dir mein Licht (Pfau); Lass deine Sichel rauschen (Lied der Schnitterin) (Pfau); Mädel, lass das Stricken (Nicht doch!) (Dehmel); Mein Herz das ist ein tiefer Schacht; Mein Schatz ist wie ein Schneck (Pfau); Nur das thut mir so bitter weh (O. von Redwitz); Sang ein Bettlerpärlein am Schenkentor (Mädchenlied) (P. Heyse); Waldesnacht, du wunderkühle (Heyse); Warum bist Du aufgewacht
— In hellen Träumen hab ich Dich oft geschaut (A. Gold), 1893
— Du kleine bist so lieb und hold (Zweifler) (Pfau), ?1895
— War ein Blümlein wunderfein (Vergissmeinnicht) (Pfau), ?1895
— In meinem Garten die Nelken (Mädchenlied) (E. Geibel), ?1896
— Als mein Auge sie fand (Sehnsucht) (J. C. von Zedlitz), ?1896
— Aprilwind, alle Knospen (Mädchenfrühling) (Dehmel), Sept 1897

1 Two Songs (K. von Levetzow), Bar, pf, ?1898: Dank; Abschied; S A/1

— Sie trug den Becher in der Hand (Die Beiden) (Hofmannsthal), April 1899

2 Four Songs: Erwartung (Dehmel), Aug 1899; Schenk mir deinen goldenen Kamm (Dehmel), ?1899, Erhebung (Dehmel), Nov 1899; Waldsonne (J. Schlaf); S A/1

— Dunkelnd über die See (Gruss in die Ferne) (H. Lingg), Aug 1900

— Lied der Waldtaube [from Gurrelieder], arr. Mez, 17 insts, 1900, arr. Dec 1922 (1923)

— Cabaret songs: Der genügsame Liebhaber (H. Salus), April 1901 (1975); Einfältiges Lied (Salus), April 1901 (1975); Nachtwandler (G. Falke), S, pic, F-tpt, side drum, pf, April 1901 (1969); Jedem das Seine (Colly), June 1901 (1975); Mahnung (G. Hochstetter), July 1901 (1975); Galathea (Wedekind), Sept 1901 (1975); Gigerlette (O. Bierbaum) (1975); Seit ich so viele Weiber sah (Aus dem Spiegel von Arcadia) (Schikaneder) (1975)

— Deinem Blick mich zu bequemen (Goethe), Jan 1903

3 Six Songs, Mez/Bar, pf: Wie Georg von Frundsberg von sich selber sang (Des Knaben Wunderhorn), March 1903; Die Aufgeregten (G. Keller), Nov 1903; Warnung (Dehmel), May 1899; Hochzeitslied (Jacobsen, trans. Arnold), ?1900; Geübtes Herz (Keller), Sept–Nov 1903; Freihold (Lingg), Nov 1900; S A/1

6 Eight Songs: Traumleben (J. Hart), Dec 1903; Alles (Dehmel), Sept 1905; Mädchenlied (P. Remer), Oct 1905; Verlassen (H. Conradi), Dec 1903; Ghasel (Keller), Jan 1904; Am Wegrand (J. H. Mackay), Oct 1905; Lockung (K. Aram), Oct 1905; Der Wanderer (Nietzsche), ?April–Oct 1905; S A/1

8 Six Orchestral Songs: Natur (H. Hart), Dec 1903–March 1904; Das Wappenschild (Des Knaben Wunderhorn), Nov 1903–May 1904; Sehnsucht (Des Knaben Wunderhorn), completed April 1905; Nie ward ich, Herrin, müd' (Petrarch, trans. Förster), June–July 1904; Voll jener Süsse (Petrarch, trans. Förster), completed Nov 1904; Wenn Vöglein klagen (Petrarch, trans. Förster), completed Nov 1904

12 Two Ballads, March–April 1907: Jane Grey (H. Amman), Der verlorene Haufen (V. Klemperer); S A/1

14 Two Songs: Ich darf nicht dankend (George), Dec 1907; In diesen Wintertagen (K. Henckell), Feb 1908; S A/1

15 Das Buch der hängenden Gärten (George), ?March 1908–Feb/May 1909; Unterm Schutz von dichten Blättergründen; Hain in diesen Paradiesen; Als Neuling trat ich ein in dein Gehege, March 1908; Da meine Lippen reglos sind und brennen, March 1908; Saget mir, auf welchem Pfade, March 1908; Jedem Werke bin ich fürder tot; Angst und Hoffen wechselnd mich beklemmen, April 1908; Wenn ich heut nicht deinen Leib berühre, April 1908; Streng ist uns das Glück und Spröde; Das schöne Beet betracht ich mir im Harren; Als wir hinter dem beblühmten Tore; Wenn sich bei heiliger Ruh in tiefen Matten; Du lehnest wider eine Silberweide, Sept 1908; Sprich nicht immer von dem Laub; Wir bevölkerten die abend-düstern Lauben, Feb 1909; S A/1

— Am Strande (?Rilke), Feb 1909, possibly Feb 1908; S A/1

20 Herzgewächse (Maeterlinck, trans. K. L. Ammer and F. von Oppeln-Bronikowski), high S, cel, harp, harmonium, Dec 1911

21 Dreimal sieben Gedichte aus Albert Girauds Pierrot lunaire (trans. O. E. Hartleben), speaker, fl + pic, cl + b cl, vn + va, vc, pf, 1912: Part i: Mondestrunken, April; Colombine, April; Der Dandy, April; Eine blasse Wäscherin, April; Valse de Chopin, May; Madonna, May; Der kranke Mond, April; Part ii: Nacht, May; Gebet an Pierrot, March; Raub, May; Rote Messe, April; Galgenlied, May; Enthauptung, May; Die Kreuze, June (?May)–July; Part iii: Heimweh, May; Gemeinheit, April–June; Parodie, May; Der Mondfleck, May; Serenade, April; Heimfahrt, April–May; O alter Duft, May

22 Four Orchestral Songs: Seraphita (Dowson, trans. George), completed Oct 1913; Alle welche dich suchen (Rilke), Nov–Dec 1914; Mach mich zum Wächter deiner Weiten (Rilke), Dec 1914–Jan 1915; Vorgefühl (Rilke), July 1916

— Allein Gott in der Höh' sei Ehr' (N. Hovesch), chorale arr., A, pf trio, between 1918 and 1925

— Four Folksong Arrangements, Jan 1929 (1930): Der Mai tritt ein mit Freuden; Es gingen zwei Gespielen gut; Mein Herz in steten Treuen; Mein Herz ist mir gemenget; S A/1

41 Ode to Napoleon (Byron), reciter, pf, str qt/str orch, March–June 1942

48 Three Songs (J. Haringer), A/B, pf: Sommermüd, Jan 1933; Tot, Feb 1933; Mädchenlied, Feb 1933; S A/1

(fragments)

— Gethsemane (Dehmel), male 1v, orch, May 1899; vocal score, 88 bars

— Jeduch (H. Löns), ballad intended for op.12, March 1907; 82 bars; M (part)

— Mignon (Kennst du das Land) (Goethe), autumn 1907; 54 bars; M

— Friedensabend (George), intended for op.15, ?April 1908; 27½ bars; M

KEYBOARD

— Six Ländler, pf, early

— Song without Words (Nocturne), pf, early; lost arr. small orch

— Three Piano Pieces, Oct 1894; S A/4

— Six Pieces, pf duet, ?1896; S A/5

9 Chamber Symphony no.1, arr. pf duet before 1912; S A/5

11 Three Piano Pieces, nos.1–2 Feb 1909, no.3 Aug 1909; S A/4

19 Six Little Piano Pieces, nos.1–5 Feb 1911, no.6 June 1911; S A/4

23 Five Piano Pieces, nos.1–2 and beginning of 4, July 1920, rest Feb 1923; S A/4

25 Piano Suite, Prelude and beginning of Intermezzo July 1921, rest Feb–March 1923; S A/4

33a Piano Piece, Dec 1928–April 1929; S A/4

33b Piano Piece, Oct 1931; S A/4

38b Chamber Symphony no.2, arr. 2 pf Dec 1941–Jan 1942; S A/5

40 Variations on a Recitative, org, Aug–Oct 1941; S A/5

(fragments)

— Scherzo, f♯, pf, early; 80 bars; S B/4

— Two Pieces, pf duet, early; no.2 inc.; S B/5

— Piano Piece, c♯, early; 77 bars; S B/4

— Piano Piece, A♭, Dec 1900–Feb 1901; 46 bars; S B/4

— Piano Piece, B♭, winter 1905–6; 26 bars; M; S B/4

— Piano Piece, G, ?spring 1925; 41 bars; S B/4

— Piano Piece, Feb 1931; 35 bars; S B/4

— Piano Piece, C, July 1931; 25½ bars; S B/4

— Phantasy, pf duet, Jan 1937; 25 bars; S A/5

— Piece, 2 pf, Jan 1941; 17 bars; S A/5

— Organ Sonata, Aug 1941; openings of first 2 movts, 50 and 25 bars; S A/5

— Piano Piece, American period; 22 bars; S B/4

— Alla marcia, E♭; complete 2-staff sketch intended for instrumentation, 22 bars

CANONS
(most published in 30 Kanons, ed. J. Rufer, Kassel, 1963)

4-part canon 'O dass der Sinnen doch so viele sind!' (Goethe), ?April 1905

4-part canon 'Wenn der schwer Gedrückte klagt' (Goethe), ?April 1905

'Eyn doppel Spiegel- und Schlüssel-Kanon', 4 parts, Feb 1922

'Ein Spruch und zwei Variationen über ihn: O glaubet nicht, was ihr nicht könnt, sei wertlos', op.28 App.1, 4 parts (Schoenberg), Dec 1925–Jan 1926

Canon for string quartet, op.28 App.2, Feb 1926

'Legitimation als Canon: Wer Ehr erweist, muss selbst davon besitzen', op.28 App.3, 6 parts (Schoenberg), April 1926

3-part canon for D. J. Bach 'Wer mit der Welt laufen will' (Schoenberg), March 1926, July 1934

4-part canon by augmentation and diminution, April 1926

4-part canon for Erwin Stein 'Von meinen Steinen' (Schoenberg), Dec 1926

'Arnold Schönberg beglückwünscht herzlichst Concert Gebouw', 5 parts (Schoenberg), March 1928

Canon in 3 keys for the Genossenschaft deutscher Tonsetzer, 5 parts, April 1928

Mirror canon for string quartet, April 1931

4-part mirror canon, Dec 1931

2-part mirror canon for Herrmann Abraham 'Spiegle Dich im Werk' (Schoenberg), Dec 1931

Mirror canon for string quartet, ?1931

4-part mirror canon for Carl Moll, Dec 1932

3-part puzzle canon for Carl Engel 'Jedem geht es so (No man can escape)' (Schoenberg in Ger. and Eng.), April 1933, text 1943

3-part puzzle canon for Carl Engel 'Mir auch ist es so ergangen (I, too, was not better off)' (Schoenberg in Ger. and Eng.), April 1933, text 1943

4-part perpetual canon, April 1933

4-part mirror canon, April 1933

4-part mirror canon, Dec 1933

3-part puzzle canon, March 1934

4-part puzzle canon by augmentation and diminution, March 1934

4-part puzzle canon, ?March 1934

4-part puzzle canon for Rudolph Ganz 'Es ist so dumm' (Schoenberg), Sept 1934

Canon for Alban Berg on his 50th birthday (Schoenberg), ? Jan 1935, unpubd

4-part mirror canon for Frau Charlotte Dieterle, Nov 1935

4-part mirror canon, Jan 1936

4-part double canon, 1938

4-part canon 'Mr Saunders I owe you thanks' (Schoenberg), Dec 1939

4-part mirror canon, June 1943

4-part canon for Artur Rodzinsky 'I am almost sure, when your nurse will change your diapers' (Schoenberg), March 1945

4-part double canon for Thomas Mann on his 70th birthday, June 1945

4-part canon 'Gravitationszentrum eigenen Sonnensystems' (Schoenberg), Aug 1949

(*fragments*)

'Gutes thu rein aus des Guten Lieben' (Goethe), ?April 1905; coda inc.
'Dümmer ist nichts zu ertragen' (Goethe), ?April 1905; lacking coda
'Wer geboren in bös'sten Tagen' (Goethe), ?April 1905; lacking coda

ARRANGEMENTS

H. Susaneck: Irmen Walzer, 2 vn; *R. Waldman: So wie du*, 2 vn; *Wiener Fiakerlied*, 2 vn; all early
A. Zemlinsky: Sarema, vocal score, summer 1897
H. Schenker: Vier syrische Tänze, orchd 1903
A. Zemlinsky: String Quartet no.2, op.15, pf duet, ?1915
J. S. Bach: Chorale Prelude 'Komm, Gott, Schöpfer, heiliger Geist' BWV 631, orchd April 1922 (1925)
J. S. Bach: Chorale Prelude 'Schmücke dich, O liebe Seele' BWV 654, orchd April–June 1922 (1925)
Johann Strauss (ii): Kaiserwalzer op.437, fl, cl, pf qnt, April 1925 (*c* 1960)
J. S. Bach: Prelude and Fugue, Eb, BWV 552, orchd May–Oct 1928 (1929)
J. Brahms: Piano Quartet, g, op.25, orchd May–Sept 1937; S A/26
Hack-work (in early years Schoenberg scored some 6000 pages of operettas by Zepler and others; the following examples of his hack-work, except for the second, were published): *H. van Eyken: Lied der Walküre* (F. Dahn), orchd ?1901; *B. Zepler: Mädchenreigen*, orchd April 1902; *A. Lortzing: Der Waffenschmied von Worms*, pf duet, ?1903; *G. Rossini: Il barbiere di Siviglia*, pf duet, ?1903; *F. Schubert: Rosamunde: overture, entr'actes and ballet*, pf duet, ?1903
Continuo realizations, 1911 or 1912: *M. G. Monn: Sinfonia a 4, A* (1912); *M. G. Monn: Vc Conc., g* (1912) also arr. vc, pf (1913) and cadenzas, S B 27; *M. G. Monn: Cembalo Conc., D* (1912); *J. C. Monn: Divertimento, D* (1912); *F. Tůma: Sinfonia a 4, e* (1968); *F. Tůma: Partita a 3, A* (1968); *F. Tůma: Partita a 3, c* (1968); *F. Tůma: Partita a 3, G* (1968)
Songs orchd for Julia Culp: *L. van Beethoven: Adelaide op.46*, Feb 1912; *C. Loewe: Der Nöck op.129 no.2*, autumn 1912; *F. Schubert: Three songs*, Sept 1912
Arrs. for the Society for Private Musical Performances (Schoenberg had a hand in various reductions for ensemble of his own and other works, but very few are wholly his, perhaps not even the Busoni arr. listed here; see L. Stein (1966)): *F. Busoni: Berceuse élégiaque*, fl, cl, harmonium, str qt, db, between 1919 and 1921 (1973); *Johann Strauss (ii): Rosen aus dem Süden op.388*, harmonium, pf qnt, May 1921; *Johann Strauss (ii): Lagunenwalzer op.411*, harmonium, pf qnt, May 1921
Instrumentation exercises for teaching purposes, summer 1921: *F. Schubert: Der Lindenbaum D911, no.5*, and *Ständchen D889*, 1v, cl, bn, mand, gui, str qt; *L. Denza: Funiculì, funiculà*, cl, gui, mand, str trio; untitled polka with waltz trio (? original exercise), cl, gui, mand, str trio

Principal publishers: Belmont, Dreililien, Hansen, G. Schirmer, Schott, Universal
MSS in *US-LAusc* (composer's collection), *Wc*, *DN*, Universal Edition (Vienna), Robert Owen Lehman collection (*US-NYpm*)

WRITINGS

TEXTS WITHOUT MUSIC

Totentanz der Prinzipien, Jan 1915 [for Sym. sketched 1914–15]; pubd in *A. Schönberg: Texte* (Vienna, 1926)
Wendepunkt, ? Dec 1916 [for Chamber Sym. no.2 as melodrama]; pubd in Maegaard, i (1972)
Requiem, first section 1920 or 1921, rest Nov 1923; pubd in *A. Schönberg: Texte* (Vienna, 1926)
Der biblische Weg, drama, June 1926–July 1927
Psalmen, Gebete und andere Gespräche mit und über Gott, Sept 1950–July 1951 (Mainz, 1956) [16 pieces, orig. entitled 'Modern Psalms', the last inc., the first partly composed as op.50c]
Fragments: *Aberglaube*, opera lib, early, 2 acts and beginning of 3rd: *Odoaker*, opera lib, early, 3 opening scenes; *Die Schildbürger*, comic opera lib, after G. Schwab, June–July 1901, 2 of 3 acts

THEORETICAL AND PEDAGOGICAL

Harmonielehre, spring 1910–July 1911 (Vienna, 1911, rev. 3/1922; Eng. trans., abridged, 1948, complete, 1978)
Models for Beginners in Composition, completed Sept 1942 (Los Angeles, 1942, enlarged 2/1943, rev. 3/1972 by L. Stein)
Structural Functions of Harmony, completed March 1948, ed. H. Searle (London, 1954, rev. 2/1969 by L. Stein)
Preliminary Exercises in Counterpoint, 1936–50, ed. L. Stein (London, 1963)
Fundamentals of Musical Composition, 1937–48, ed. L. Stein (London, 1967)
Fragments: *Das Komponieren mit selbständigen Stimmen*, June 1911; *Die Lehre von Kontrapunkt*, Oct 1926; *Der musikalische Gedanke und seine Darstellung*, 1925–36, 3 drafts under similar titles

ESSAYS, LETTERS ETC

Style and Idea (New York, 1950) [15 essays]
Briefe, selected and ed. E. Stein (Mainz, 1958; Eng. trans., enlarged, 1964)
Schöpferische Konfessionen, ed. W. Reich (Zurich, 1964)
Testi poetici e drammatici, ed. L. Rognoni (Milan, 1967)
Arnold Schönberg–Franz Schreker: Briefwechsel, ed. F. C. Heller (Tutzing, 1974)
Berliner Tagebuch, ed. J. Rufer (Frankfurt, 1974)
F. Busoni: *Entwurf einer neuen Aesthetik der Tonkunst, mit handschriftlichen Anmerkungen von A. Schönberg* (Frankfurt, 1974)
Style and Idea, ed. L. Stein (London, 1975) [104 essays]
Gesammelte Schriften, i, ed. I. Vojtěch (Frankfurt, 1976)

For list of unpubd writings see Rufer (1959); for bibliography of pubd writings see Brinkmann: *Arnold Schönberg: Drei Klavierstücke Op. 11* (Wiesbaden, 1969)

BIBLIOGRAPHY

MONOGRAPHS

E. Wellesz: *Arnold Schönberg* (Leipzig, 1921; Eng. trans., rev., 1925/R1971)
P. Stefan: *Arnold Schönberg: Wandlung, Legende, Erscheinung, Bedeutung* (Vienna, 1924)
H. Wind: *Die Endkrise der bürgerlichen Musik und die Rolle Arnold Schönbergs* (Vienna, 1935)
R. Leibowitz: *Schönberg et son école* (Paris, 1947; Eng. trans., 1949/R1975)
D. Newlin: *Bruckner, Mahler, Schoenberg* (New York, 1947; Ger. trans., 1954)
R. Leibowitz: *Introduction à la musique de douze sons* (Paris, 1949)
H. Stuckenschmidt: *Arnold Schönberg* (Zurich, 1951, rev. 2/1957; Eng. trans., 1959)
J. Rufer: *Die Komposition mit zwölf Tönen* (Berlin, 1952; Eng. trans., 1954)
L. Rognoni: *Espressionismo e dodecafonia* (Turin, 1954, rev. 2/1966 as *La scuola musicale di Vienna*)
J. Rufer: *Das Werk Arnold Schönbergs* (Kassel, 1959, rev. 2/1975; Eng. trans., rev., 1962)
A. Payne: *Schoenberg* (London, 1968)
W. Reich: *Arnold Schönberg oder der konservative Revolutionär* (Vienna, 1968; Eng. trans., 1971)
R. Leibowitz: *Schoenberg* (Paris, 1969)
J. Maegaard: *Studien zur Entwicklung des dodekaphonen Satzes bei Arnold Schönberg* (Copenhagen, 1972)
E. Freitag: *Arnold Schönberg in Selbstzeugnissen und Bilddokumenten* (Reinbek, 1973)
H. Stuckenschmidt: *Schönberg: Leben, Umwelt, Werk* (Zurich, 1974)
G. Manzoni: *Arnold Schönberg: l'uomo, l'opera, i testi musicati* (Milan, 1975)
C. Rosen: *Arnold Schoenberg* (New York, 1975)
G. Schubert: *Schönbergs frühe Instrumentation* (Baden-Baden, 1975)
M. Macdonald: *Schoenberg* (London, 1976)
J. Maegaard: *Praeludier til musik af Schönberg* (Copenhagen, 1976)
K. Velten: *Schönbergs Instrumentation Bachscher und Brahmsscher Werke als Dokumente seines Traditions-verständhisses* (Regensburg, 1976)
D. Newlin: *Schoenberg Remembered: Diaries and Recollections (1938–76)* (New York, 1980)

COLLECTIONS OF ARTICLES AND ESSAYS

Der Merker, ii/17 (1911) [Schoenberg issue]
Arnold Schönberg: mit Beiträgen von Alban Berg, Paris von Gutersloh [and others] (Munich, 1912)
Arnold Schönberg zum fünfzigsten Geburtstage (Vienna, 1924)
'Schönberg und seine Orchesterwerke', *Pult und Taktstock*, iv (1927), March–April
Arnold Schönberg zum 60. Geburtstag (Vienna, 1934)
M. Armitage, ed.: *Schoenberg* (New York, 1937)
Canon, iii/2 (1949) [Schoenberg issue]
Stimmen (1949), no.16 [Schoenberg issue]
The Score (1952), no.6 [Schoenberg issue]
E. Stein: *Orpheus in New Guises* (London, 1953)
A. Webern: *Der Weg zur neuen Musik* (Vienna, 1960; Eng. trans., 1963)
B. Boretz and E. Cone, eds.: *Perspectives on Schoenberg and Stravinsky* (Princeton, 1968)
'Towards the Schoenberg Centenary', *PNM*, xi–xiii (1972–5)
E. Hilmar, ed.: *Arnold Schönberg, Gedenkausstellung 1974* (Vienna, 1974)
ÖMz, xxix/6 (1974) [Schoenberg issue]
Zeitschrift für Musiktheorie, v/1 (1974) [Schoenberg issue]
Journal of the Arnold Schoenberg Institute (1976–)

SEPARATE ARTICLES

A. Nadel: 'Arnold Schönberg', *Die Musik*, xi/3 (1912), 353
C. Somigli: 'Il modus operandi di Arnold Schönberg', *RMI*, xx (1913), 583

P. Bekker: 'Schönberg', *Melos*, ii (1921), 123

L. Henry: 'Arnold Schönberg', *MO*, xliv (1921), 420, 511

C. Gray: 'Arnold Schönberg, a Critical Study', *ML*, iii (1922), 73

F. Wohlfahrt: 'Arnold Schönbergs Stellung innerhalb der heutigen Musik', *Die Musik*, xvi (1924), 894

R. van den Linden: 'Arnold Schönberg', *ML*, vii (1926), 322; viii (1927), 38

K. Westphal: 'Schönbergs Weg zur Zwölfton-Musik', *Die Musik*, xxi (1929), 491

A. Machabey: 'Schönberg', *Le ménestrel*, xcii (1930), 81, 245, 257

A. Weiss: 'The Lyceum of Schönberg', *MM*, ix (1932), 99

H. Gerigk: 'Eine Lanze für Schönberg', *Die Musik*, xxvii (1934), 87

D. J. Bach: 'A Note on Arnold Schoenberg', *MQ*, xxii (1936), 8

R. Hill: 'Schoenberg's Tone-rows and the Tonal System of the Future', *MQ*, xxii (1936), 14

H. Jalowetz: 'On the Spontaneity of Schoenberg's Music', *MQ*, xxx (1944), 385

D. Milhaud: 'To Arnold Schoenberg on his Seventieth Birthday: Personal Recollections', *MQ*, xxx (1944), 379

R. Sessions: 'Schoenberg in the United States', *Tempo* (1944), no.9, p.2; rev. in *Tempo* (1972), no.103, p.8

D. Newlin: 'Arnold Schoenberg's Debt to Mahler', *Chord and Dischord*, ii/5 (1948), 21

R. Leibowitz: 'Besuch bei Arnold Schönberg', *SMz*, lxxxix (1949), 324

D. Newlin: 'Schoenberg in America', *Music Survey*, i (1949), 128, 185

T. Wiesengrund-Adorno: 'Schönberg und der Fortschritt', *Philosophie der neuen Musik* (Tübingen, 1949; Eng. trans., 1973)

W. Rubsamen: 'Schoenberg in America', *MQ*, xxxvii (1951), 469

R. Vlad: 'L'Ultimo Schönberg', *RaM*, xxi (1951), 106

A. Duhamel: 'Arnold Schoenberg, la critique, et le monde musical contemporain', *ReM* (1952), no.212, p.77

H. Keller: 'Unpublished Schoenberg Letters: Early, Middle and Late', *Music Survey*, iv (1952), 499

G. Perle: 'Schoenberg's Later Style', *MR*, xiii (1952), 274

T. Wiesengrund-Adorno: 'Arnold Schönberg 1874–1951', *Neue Rundschau*, lxiv (1953), 80; repr. in T. Wiesengrund-Adorno: *Prismen* (Munich, 1963), 147

H. Eisler: 'Arnold Schönberg', *Sinn und Form*, vii (1955), 5

W. Reich: 'Alban Berg als Apologet Arnold Schönbergs', *SMz*, xcv (1955), 475

T. Wiesengrund-Adorno: 'Zum Verständnis Schönbergs', *Frankfurter Hefte*, x (1955), 418

J. Birke: 'Richard Dehmel und Arnold Schönberg, ein Briefwechsel', *Mf*, xi (1958), 279; xvii (1964), 60

'Letters of Webern and Schoenberg to Roberto Gerhard', *The Score* (1958), no.24, p.36

H. Stuckenschmidt: 'Stil und Ästhetik Schönbergs', *SMz*, xcviii (1958), 97

P. Gradenwitz: 'Schönbergs religiöse Werke', *Melos*, xxvi (1959), 330; Eng. trans. in *MR* (1960), 19

D. Körner: 'Schönberg als Patient', *Melos*, xxvi (1959), 327

W. Reich: 'Ein unbekannter Brief von Arnold Schonberg an Alban Berg', *ÖMz*, xv (1959), 10

H. Oesch: 'Hauer und Schönberg', *ÖMz*, xv (1960), 157

L. Rognoni: 'Gli scritti e i dipinti di Arnold Schönberg', *L'approdo musicale*, iii (1960), 95

F. Glück: 'Briefe von Arnold Schönberg an Adolf Loos', *ÖMz*, xvi (1961), 8

J. Maegaard: 'A Study in the Chronology of op.23–26 by Arnold Schoenberg', *DAM*, ii (1962), 93

G. Marbach: 'Schlemmers Begegnungen mit Schönberg, Scherchen und Hindemith', *NZM*, Jg.123 (1962), 530

N. Notowicz: 'Eisler und Schönberg', *DJbM*, viii (1963), 8

T. Wiesengrund-Adorno: 'Über einige Arbeiten Arnold Schönbergs', *Forum*, x (1963), 378, 434

R. Nelson: 'Schoenberg's Variation Seminar', *MQ*, l (1964), 141

F. Prieberg: 'Der junge Schönberg und seine Kritiker', *Melos*, xxxi (1964), 264

G. Schuller: 'A Conversation with Steuermann', *PNM*, iii (1964), 22

R. Steiner: 'Der unbekannte Schönberg: aus unveröffentlichten Briefen an Hans Nachod', *SMz*, civ (1964), 284

D. Dille: 'Die Beziehung zwischen Bartók und Schönberg', *Dokumenta bartókiana*, ii (1965), 53

I. Vojtěch: 'Arnold Schönberg, Anton Webern, Alban Berg: unbekannte Briefe an Erwin Schulhoff', *MMC*, xviii (1965), 31

P. Friedheim: 'Rhythmic Structure in Schoenberg's Atonal Compositions', *JAMS*, xix (1966), 59

V. Fuchs: 'Arnold Schönberg als Soldat im ersten Weltkrieg', *Melos*, xxxiii (1966), 178

R. Jung: 'Arnold Schönberg und das Liszt-Stipendium', *BMw*, viii (1966), 56

P. Odegard: 'Schönberg's Variations: an Addendum', *MR*, xxvii (1966), 102

L. Stein: 'The Privataufführungen revisited', *Paul A. Pisk: Essays in his Honor* (Austin, 1966), 203

'Unveröffentlichte Briefe an Alfredo Casella', *Melos*, xxxiv (1967), 45

D. Lewin: 'Inversional Balance as an Organizing Force in Schoenberg's Music and Thought', *PNM*, vi/2 (1968), 1

D. Newlin: 'The Schoenberg–Nachod Collection, a Preliminary Report', *MQ*, liv (1968), 31

E. Klemm: 'Der Briefwechsel zwischen Arnold Schönberg und dem Verlag C. F. Peters', *DJbM*, xv (1970), 5

H. Byrns: 'Meine Begegnung mit Arnold Schönberg', *Melos*, xxxviii (1971), 234

R. Vlad: 'Arnold Schönberg schreibt an Gian Francesco Malipiero', *Melos*, xxxviii (1971), 461

R. Stephan: 'Ein unbekannter Aufsatz Weberns über Schönberg', *ÖMz*, xxvii (1972), 127

V. Lampert: 'Schoenbergs, Bergs und Adornos Briefe an Sándor (Alexander) Jemnitz', *SM*, xv (1973), 355

A. Ringer: 'Schoenbergiana in Jerusalem', *MQ*, lix (1973), 1

F. Glück: 'Briefe von Arnold Schönberg an Claire Loos', *ÖMz*, xxix (1974), 203

K. Hicken: 'Schoenberg's "Atonality": Fused Bitonality?', *Tempo* (1974), no.109, p.28

A. Lessem: 'Schönberg and the Crisis of Expressionism', *ML*, lv (1974), 427

J. Maegaard: 'Schönberg hat Adorno nie leiden können', *Melos*, xli (1974), 262

J. Meggett and R. Moritz: 'The Schoenberg Legacy', *Notes*, xxxi (1974), 30

J. Samson: 'Schoenberg's "Atonal" Music', *Tempo* (1974), no.109, p.16

E. Schmid: 'Ein Jahr bei Schönberg in Berlin', *Melos*, xli (1974), 190

E. Steiner: 'Schoenberg's Quest: Newly Discovered Works from his Early Years', *MQ*, lx (1974), 401

R. Stephan: 'Hába und Schönberg', *Festschrift für Arno Volk* (Cologne, 1974)

W. Szmolyan: 'Schönberg in Mödling', *ÖMz*, xxix (1974), 189

J. Maegaard: 'Zu Th. W. Adornos Rolle im Mann/Schönberg-Streit', *Thomas Mann Gedenkschrift*, Text und Kontext, *Sonderreihe*, ii (Copenhagen, 1975)

A. Dümling: ' "Im Zeichen der Erkenntnis der sozialen Verhältnisse": der junge Schönberg und die Arbeitersängerbewegung', *Zeitschrift für Musiktheorie*, vi (1975), 11

J. Harvey: 'Schönberg: Man or Woman?', *ML*, lvi (1975), 371

J. Maegaard: 'Der geistige Einflussbereich von Schönberg und Zemlinsky in Wien um 1900', *Studien zur Wertungsforschung*, vii (1976)

C. Dahlhaus: 'Schönbergs musikalische Poetik', *AMw*, xxxiii (1976), 81

E. Hilmar: 'Arnold Schönbergs Briefe an den Akademischen Verband für Literatur und Muisk in Wien', *ÖMz*, xxxi (1976), 273

B. Nono-Schoenberg: 'Mon pere Schoenberg', *SMz*, cxvi (1976), 2

W. Szmolyan: 'Schönbergs Wiener Skandalkonzert', *ÖMz*, xxxi (1976), 293

E. Steiner: 'Ein Schönberg-Konzert in Berlin', *ÖMz*, xxxi (1976), 105

J. Maegaard: 'Schönbergs Zwölftonreihen', *Mf*, xxix (1976), 385

STUDIES OF PARTICULAR WORKS
(operas)

H. Keller: 'Schoenberg's "Moses and Aron" ', *The Score* (1957), no.21, p.30

——: 'Schoenberg's Comic Opera', *The Score* (1958), no.23, p.27

K. H. Wörner: *Gotteswort und Magie* (Heidelberg, 1959; Eng. trans., rev., 1963, as *Schoenberg's 'Moses and Aron'*)

T. Wiesengrund-Adorno: 'Sakrales Fragment', *Quasi una fantasia* (Frankfurt, 1963), 306

K. H. Wörner: ' "Die glückliche Hand", Arnold Schönbergs Drama mit Musik', *SMz*, cciv (1964), 274

H. Buchanan: 'A Key to Schoenberg's "Erwartung" ', *JAMS*, xx (1967), 434

K. H. Wörner: 'Schönberg's "Erwartung" und das Ariadne-Thema', *Die Musik in der Geistesgeschichte* (Bonn, 1970), 91

J. Crawford: 'Die glückliche Hand: Schoenberg's Gesamtkunstwerk', *MQ*, lx (1974), 583

(choral works)

A. Berg: *Arnold Schönberg: Gurrelieder Führer* (grosse Ausgabe, Vienna, 1913; kleine Ausgabe, 1914)

G. Strecke: 'Arnold Schönbergs op.XIII', *Melos*, i (1920), 231

S. Günther: 'Das trochäische Prinzip in Arnold Schönbergs op. 13', *ZMw*, vi (1923), 158

H. Nachod: 'The Very First Performance of Schoenberg's "Gurrelieder" ', *Music Survey*, iii/3 (1950), 38

W. Zillig: 'Notes on Arnold Schoenberg's Unfinished Oratorio "Die Jakobsleiter" ', *The Score* (1959), no.25, p.7

H. Pauli: 'Zu Schönbergs "Jakobsleiter" ', *SMz*, cii (1962), 350

R. Lück: 'Arnold Schönberg und das deutsche Volkslied', *NZM*, cxxiv (1963), 86

K. H. Wörner: 'Schönbergs Oratorium "Die Jakobsleiter": Musik zwischen Theologie und Weltanschauung', *SMz*, cv (1965), 250, 333

C. M. Schmidt: 'Schönbergs Kantate "Ein Überlebender aus Warschau" ', *AMw*, xxxiii (1976), 174

(orchestral works)

A. Berg: *Arnold Schönberg: Pelleas und Melisande Op. 5: kurze thematische Analyse* (Vienna, 1920)

C. Dahlhaus: *Schönberg: Variationen für Orchester, op.31* (Munich, 1968)

E. Doflein: 'Schönbergs Opus 16 Nr. 3', *Melos*, xxxvi (1969), 203

P. Förtig: 'Analyse des Opus 16 Nr. 3', *Melos*, xxxvi (1969), 206

J. Rufer: 'Nocheinmal Schönbergs Opus 16', *Melos*, xxxvi (1969), 366

C. Dahlhaus: 'Das obligate Rezitativ', *Melos/NZM*, i (1975), 193

(chamber works)

[A. Berg]: 'Arnold Schönberg fis-moll-Quartett: eine technische Analyse', *Erdgeist*, iv (1909), 225

A. Berg: *Arnold Schönberg: Kammersymphonie Op. 9: thematische Analyse* (Vienna, 1918)

F. Greissle: 'Die formalen Grundlagen des Bläserquintetts von Arnold Schönberg', *Musikblätter des Anbruch*, vii (1925), 63

T. Wiesengrund-Adorno: 'Schönbergs Bläserquintett', *Pult und Taktstock*, v (1928), May–June, 45; repr. in T. Wiesengrund-Adorno: *Moments musicaux* (Frankfurt, 1964), 161

E. Schmid: 'Studie über Schönbergs Streichquartette', *SMz*, lxxiv (1934), 1, 84, 155

P. Gradenwitz: 'The Idiom and Development in Schoenberg's Quartets', *ML*, xxvi (1945), 123

W. Hyamson: 'Schoenberg's String Trio', *MR*, xi (1950), 184

O. Neighbour: 'Dodecaphony in Schoenberg's String Trio', *Music Survey*, iv (1952), 489

——'A Talk on Schoenberg for Composers' Concourse', *The Score* (1956), no.16, p.19 [on op.37]

W. Pfannkuch: 'Zu Thematik und Form in Schönbergs Streichsextett', *Festschrift Friedrich Blume* (Kassel, 1963), 258

E. Klemm: 'Zur Theorie der Reihenstruktur und Reihendisposition in Schönbergs 4. Streichquartett', *BMw*, viii (1966), 27

J. Lester: 'Pitch Structure Articulation in the Variations of Schoenberg's Serenade', *PNM*, vi/2 (1968), 22

E. Staempfli: 'Das Streichtrio Opus 45 von Arnold Schönberg', *Melos*, xxxvii (1970), 35

M. Pfisterer: 'Zur Frage der Satztechnik in den atonalen Werken von Arnold Schönberg', *Zeitschrift für Musiktheorie*, ii/1 (1971), 4 [on op.10]

U. von Rauchhaupt, ed.: *Schoenberg, Berg, Webern: the String Quartets, a Documentary Study* (Hamburg, 1971)

R. Gerlach: 'War Schönberg von Dvořák beeinflusst?', *NZM*, Jg.133 (1972), 122 [on the D major Quartet]

A. Whittall: *Schoenberg Chamber Music* (London, 1972)

——: 'Schoenberg and the "True Tradition": Theme and Form in the String Trio', *MT*, cxv (1974), 739

C. Raab: 'Fantasia quasi una Sonata: Zu Schönbergs "Phantasy for Violin with Piano Accompaniment" op.47', *Melos/NZM*, ii (1976), 191

(solo vocal works)

R. Tenschert: 'Eine Passacaglia von Schönberg', *Die Musik*, xvii (1925), 590 [on op.21 no.8]

K. H. Ehrenforth: *Ausdruck und Form: Schönbergs Durchbruch zur Atonalität* (Bonn, 1963) [on op.15]

——: 'Schönberg und Webern: das XIV. Lied aus Schönbergs Georgelieder op.15', *NZM*, Jg.126 (1965), 102

C. Dahlhaus: 'Schönbergs Lied "Streng ist uns das Glück und spröde" ', *Neue Wege der musikalischen Analyse* (Berlin, 1967), 45

H. Kaufmann: 'Struktur in Schönbergs Georgeliedern', *Neue Wege der musikalischen Analyse* (Berlin, 1967), 53

W. Stroh: 'Schoenberg's Use of the Text: the Text as a Musical Control in the 14th Georgelied, Op. 15', *PNM*, vi/2 (1968), 35

R. Brinkmann: 'Schoenberg und George: Interpretation eines Liedes', *AMw*, xxvi (1969), 1 [on op.15, no.14]

H. Weber: 'Schoenbergs und Zemlinskys Vertonung der Ballade "Jane Gray" von Heinrich Ammann: Untersuchungen zum Spätstadium der Tonalität', *IMSCR*, xi *Copenhagen 1972*, 705

A. Lessem: 'Text and Music in Schoenberg's "Pierrot Lunaire" ', *CMc*, no.19 (1975), 103

(piano works)

L. Welker: 'Arnold Schönbergs Op. 11', *Die Musik*, xii/1 (1912), 109

H. Leichtentritt: 'Arnold Schönberg: opus 11 and opus 19', *Musical Form* (Cambridge, Mass., 1951), 425

T. Tuttle: 'Schoenberg's Compositions for Piano Solo', *MR*, xviii (1957), 300

A. Forte: 'Context and Continuity in an Atonal Work', *PNM*, i/2 (1963), 72 [on op.19]

W. Rogge: *Das Klavierwerke Arnold Schönbergs* (Regensburg, 1964)

R. Travis: 'Directed Motion in Schoenberg and Webern', *PNM*, iv/2 (1966), 85 [on op.19/2]

R. Wille: 'Reihentechnik in Schönbergs opus 19, 2', *Mf*, xix (1966), 42

G. Krieger: *Schönbergs Werke für Klavier* (Göttingen, 1968)

R. Brinkmann: *Arnold Schönberg: Drei Klavierstücke Op. 11* (Wiesbaden, 1969)

J. Graziano: 'Serial Procedures in Schoenberg's Opus 23', *CMc* (1972), no.13, p.58

H. Oesch: 'Schönberg im Vorfeld der Dodekaphonie', *Melos*, xli (1974), 330 [on op.23 no.3]

J. Maegaard: 'Om den kronologiske placering af Schönbergs klaverstykke op.23 nr.3', *Musik en forskning*, ii (1976)

(theoretical works, etc)

E. Stein: *Praktischer Leitfaden zu Schönbergs Harmonielehre* (Vienna, 1923)

R. Lück: 'Die Generalbass-Aussetzungen Arnold Schönbergs', *DJbM*, viii (1963), 26

C. Parmentola: 'La "Harmonielehre" di Schoenberg nella crisi del pensiero moderno', *NRMI*, ii (1968), 81

L. Richter: 'Schönbergs Harmonielehre und die freie Atonalität', *DJbM*, xiii (1968), 43

D. Rexroth: *Arnold Schönberg als Theoretiker der tonalen Harmonik* (Bonn, 1971)

J. Spratt: 'The Speculative Content of Schoenberg's "Harmonielehre" ', *CMc*, no.11 (1971), 83

R. Stephan: Schönbergs Entwurf über "Das Komponieren mit selbständigen Stimmen" ', *AMw*, xxix (1972), 239

C. Dahlhaus: 'Schoenberg and Schenker', *PRMA*, c (1973–4), 209

A. Goehr: 'The Theoretical Writings of Arnold Schoenberg', *PRMA*, c (1973–4), 85

(painting)

J. Rufer: 'Schönberg als Maler, Grenzen und Konvergenzen der Künste', *Aspekte der neuen Musik*, ed. W. Burde (Kassel, 1968)

W. Hofmann: 'Beziehungen zwischen Malerei und Musik', *Schönberg, Webern, Berg: Bilder, Partituren, Dokumente* (Vienna, 1969)

O. W. NEIGHBOUR

Schoenberg Institute. Institute founded in 1974 in LOS ANGELES.

Schoendorff [Schondorpp, Scherndorp], **Philipp** (*b* Liège, 1565–70; *d* in or after 1617). South Netherlands composer, instrumentalist and music editor resident mainly in Bohemia. He was a choirboy at the court of Archduke Matthias. After his voice broke he was sent to continue his education in the household of Jacob Chimarrhaeus, chaplain and later almoner of the imperial court. It was probably on Chimarrheus's recommendation that he was appointed musician and trumpeter at the Prague court of the Emperor Rudolf II, to whom he had already dedicated a mass in 1587; he also taught the pages and choirboys. The Bohemian treasury awarded him an annual pension of 52 florins for life in 1617, after which he is not heard of again. He was one of the lesser Flemish composers who worked in the orbit of Philippe de Monte, Jacob Regnart and Franz Sales and composed only masses, motets and *Magnificat* settings. His *Veni Sancte Spiritus*, which has survived in several sources, is conservative. He edited *Odae suavissimae*, a collection of works, mostly by Habsburg court musicians, in honour of Chimarrhaeus. It is undated and has been assigned to about 1610 in Eitner and *RISM*. But the tenor partbook includes a portrait of Chimarrhaeus dated 1601, showing him at the age of 59. The collection must therefore have been published in 1601 or 1602 for Chimarrhaeus's 60th birthday. Eitner also confused Schoendorff with the imperial violinist Philipp Schoendorffer (*d* c1664–5), who may have been his son.

WORKS

SACRED VOCAL

2 Magnificat, 4, 5vv; 4 motets, 5, 6vv: 1593[1], 1600[1], 1600[2] (incl. Veni Sancte Spiritus), c1610[18] [*recte* 1601 or 1602]

2 masses, 6vv, CS-Pnm, D-Nla

Veni Sancte Spiritus, 5vv (from 1600[2]), PL-Gd, ed. in Musica sacra, xxvii (Regensburg, 1886); PE (intabulation), facs. in AMP, ii (1964), incipit in AMP, i (1963)

EDITIONS

Odae suavissimae in gratiam et honorem admodum reverendi ac illustris Domini D. Jacobi Chimarrhaei, 5, 6vv (n.p., c1610[18] [*recte* 1601 or

1602]) (incl. 2 works by Schoendorff, see above)

BIBLIOGRAPHY

EitnerQ
A. Smijers: 'Die kaiserliche Hofmusik-Kapelle von 1543–1619', *SMw*, ix (1922), 67
G. Pietzsch: 'Zur Musikkapelle Kaiser Rudolfs II', *ZMw*, xvi (1933–4), 172ff
R. Vannes: *Dictionnaire des musiciens (compositeurs)* (Brussels, 1947)
W. H. Rubsamen: 'The International "Catholic" Repertoire of a Lutheran Church in Nürnberg (1574–1597)', *AnnM*, v (1957), 278
K. W. Niemöller: 'Die musikalische Festschrift für den Direktor der Prager Hofkapelle Kaiser Rudolfs II. 1602', *GfMKB, Bonn 1970*, 520
J. Snižková: 'Einige Bemerkungen zur Mehrstimmigkeit in Böhmen', *Mf*, xxiv (1971), 278
——: 'Kutnohorský sborník mší ze sklonku 16. stoleti' [The Kútna Hora collection of masses from the end of the 16th century], *Časopis Národního muzea*, cxli (1972), 49

HELLMUT FEDERHOFER

Schoening, Alwina. *See* VALLERIA, ALWINA.

Schöffer, Peter. *See* SCHOEFFER, PETER.

Schöffler, Paul (*b* Dresden, 15 Sept 1897; *d* Amersham, Bucks., 21 Nov 1977). Austrian bass-baritone of German birth. After studying various aspects of music at the Dresden Conservatory he concentrated on singing, his teachers including Staegemann at Dresden, Grenzebach at Berlin and Sammarco at Milan. He was a member of the Dresden Staatsoper from 1925 to 1937, when he joined the Vienna Staatsoper. He was first heard at Covent Garden in 1934 (Donner, Schwanda), and in the following years London heard him as Gunther, Scarpia, Kurwenal, Figaro, Don Giovanni and Jochanaan, and also as the *Rheingold* Wotan. He sang Hans Sachs at Bayreuth in 1943–4 and the Dutchman in 1956, and during the Vienna Staatsoper 1947 London season he was heard as Don Giovanni, Don Alfonso and Pizarro: he returned in 1953 to sing Hans Sachs. He was invited to the Metropolitan, New York, in 1949, and at Salzburg in 1952 he created the role of Jupiter at the first public performance of Strauss's *Die Liebe der Danae*. He was a notable exponent of Hindemith (Cardillac, Mathis), and among the roles he created was Dunton in Von Einem's *Dantons Tod* (Salzburg, 1947). He continued to be associated with small character parts such as the Music Master (*Ariadne auf Naxos*) and Antonio (*Le nozze di Figaro*) when well over 70.

Schöffler's careful musicianship and fine stage presence were supported by a warm, expressive voice which, though not large, could ride the full orchestra easily and without tiring. Although remembered particularly as an opera singer, he appeared frequently and with success as a concert and recital artist.

BIBLIOGRAPHY
R. Celletti: 'Schöffler, Paul', *Le grandi voci* (Rome, 1964) [with opera discography by R. Vegeto]
H. Christian: *Paul Schöffler: Versuch einer Würdigung* (Vienna, 1967) [with discography]

PETER BRANSCOMBE

Schofield, Bertram (*b* Southport, Lancs., 13 June 1896). English historian and musicologist. As a medieval historian Schofield studied first at Liverpool University, and then from 1919 to 1921 in Paris. He took his PhD at Liverpool in 1921. He began work with the British Museum Department of Manuscripts as an assistant keeper in 1922, was appointed deputy keeper in 1947, and Egerton Librarian and Keeper of Manuscripts in 1956. He retired in 1961. Schofield maintained a special interest in musical MSS. He is particularly known for his part in the controversy over the dating of SUMER IS ICUMEN IN, in which he took issue strongly with Manfred Bukofzer; and also for his work on the so-called 'Windsor MS' or 'Meaux Abbey MS' of the 15th century.

WRITINGS
'Some New Beethoven Letters', *ML*, xx (1939), 235
'A Newly-discovered 15th century MS of the English Chapel Royal', *MQ*, xxxii (1946), 509
'The Provenance and Date of "Sumer is icumen in"', *MR*, ix (1948), 81
'The Adventures of an English Minstrel and his Varlet', *MQ*, xxxv (1949), 351
'The MSS of Tallis's Forty-part Motet', *MQ*, xxxvii (1951), 176
with T. Dart: 'Tregian's Anthology', *ML*, xxxii (1951), 205

IAN D. BENT

Schol, Dirk. *See* SCHOLL, DIRK.

Scholczer, Thomas. *See* STOLTZER, THOMAS.

Scholes, Percy A(lfred) (*b* Headingley, Leeds, 24 July 1877; *d* Vevey, 31 July 1958). English writer on music and encyclopedist. He had little formal schooling and was largely self-taught; he spent some years as a music teacher in Canterbury and South Africa, then as a university extension lecturer on music appreciation at Manchester, meanwhile taking his ARCM, and the BMus degree at Oxford. In 1907 he formed the Home Music Study Union, whose journal the *Music Student* (later the *Music Teacher*) he edited until 1921. In 1912 he moved to London, where he began to make his way as a journalist (*Evening Standard*, 1913–20) and university extension lecturer. During World War I he organized the 'music for the troops' section of the YMCA, work which resulted in his *Listener's Guide to Music* (1919). From 1920 to 1925 he was music critic of *The Observer*, where he became an early champion of broadcasting, the gramophone and the player-piano. He gave fortnightly impromptu radio reviews of musical broadcasts; from 1926 to 1928 he was music editor of the *Radio Times*.

A contract to provide annotations for pianola rolls enabled him to move to Switzerland in 1928. There, while at work simultaneously on several books, he gained the doctorat ès lettres from Lausanne University in 1934 with his thesis (examined in French) on *The Puritans in Music*, which refuted allegations of their unmusicality. He organized Anglo-American conferences of musical educationists in Lausanne in 1929 and 1931. When the pianola market collapsed with the Wall Street crash in 1929, a generous settlement of his contract gave him the means to concentrate on a longer-range project. This was a popular dictionary of music, at first tentatively called 'Everyone's Musical Encyclopedia', which aimed at the practical needs of his particular audience of 'new' listeners. The book appeared in 1938 as the *Oxford Companion to Music*, 'the most extraordinary range of musical knowledge, ingeniously "self-indexed", ever written and assembled between two covers by one man' (*Grove 5*). In this, Scholes's unusual combination of teacher, popularizing lecturer, journalist, critic and scholar was displayed in a way that has remained unrivalled.

In 1940 he made his way to Britain just before the fall of France, and lived at first in Aberystwyth. This was near the wartime home of the British Museum Printroom, and he took the opportunity to procure microfilms of virtually every print of musical interest for his own use. Later he lived in Oxford, where he was elected to the board of the Faculty of Music. He completed his work on Burney, a first-rate source for the history of music in England in the 18th century and a model biography (1948), two further dictionaries and detailed though less significant studies of Hawkins, and *God Save the Queen.*

He had a house built to his own specifications in Clarens, in which he lived for only two years before devaluation of the pound made him move back to Oxford in 1950. Finally, in 1957, he moved once more to Switzerland, and died there the following year. His library is now in the National Library of Canada.

Scholes's awareness of the musical needs of the common man were one aspect of a general humanitarian concern, wide-ranging interests and robust common sense. Oxford awarded him in 1943 an Hon. DMus and in 1950 a DLitt; other distinctions included an Hon. DLitt (Leeds, 1953); he was made an Hon. Fellow and Trustee of St Edmund Hall, Oxford, and an Officer of the Star of Romania (1930); he was an FSA (1938) and in 1957 he was awarded the OBE.

WRITINGS
The Listener's Guide to Music (London, 1919)
The Complete Book of the Great Musicians (London, 1920)
The Listener's History of Music (London, 1923)
The Columbia History of Music (London, 1930–38) [five albums of records with disc notes]
The Puritans and Music (diss., U. of Lausanne, 1934; London, 1934)
Music: the Child and the Masterpiece (London, 1935)
The Oxford Companion to Music (London, 1938, 9/1955, 10/1970 ed. J. O. Ward)
ed.: *The Mirror of Music: 1844–1944* (London, 1947) [selected extracts from *MT*]
The Great Dr Burney (London, 1948)
The Concise Oxford Dictionary of Music (London, 1952, 2/1964 ed. J. O. Ward)
The Life and Activities of Sir John Hawkins (London, 1953)
The Oxford Junior Companion to Music (London, 1954, rev. 2/1979 ed. M. Hurd)
God Save the Queen (London, 1954)
Dr Burney's Musical Tours in Europe (London, 1959) [annotated edn. of Burney's *The Present State of Music in France and Italy* and *The Present State of Music in Germany, the Netherlands, and the United Provinces*, incorporating his unpublished travel diary]

BIBLIOGRAPHY
DNB
P. Cater: 'The Man of a Million Words and Music', *Daily Mail* (9 June 1955)
P. Lewis: 'Let me Introduce Dr Percy Scholes who Wrote a Bestseller', *Yorkshire Evening News* (3 Aug 1958)
'Percy Scholes: Pioneer of Musical Appreciation', *The Times* (2 Aug 1957)
Obituary, *New York Times* (3 Aug 1958)

JOHN OWEN WARD

Scholl [Schol], Dirk (Janszoon) (*b* ?Brielle, nr. Rotterdam, 1641; *d* Delft, 31 March 1727). Dutch organist, carillonist and composer. His first wife was a daughter of the organist and composer Jacobus van Noordt. Scholl was organist and carillonist at Arnhem (St Eusebius, 1661–4) and Delft (Nieuwe Kerk, 1664–1727); in both places he led the local collegium musicum. Of ten volumes he is known to have published, only one survives. It contains simple pieces of chamber music for amateurs, and no doubt his other music was similar in style. He was active as a carillon expert, inspecting instruments all over Holland.

WORKS
(* = *lost*)
*Den spelenden kus-hemel, over 200 compositions for 3 insts, bc (Delft, 1669)
*Olypodrigo ofte mengelmoes (Delft, 1669)
*Delfs engels, bestaende in verscheyde sonaten a 3 instrumenten, 2 vn, va da gamba, bc (Delft, 1671)

Vrede-Triomph ofte Thalia's lust-hoff, opera sexta (Delft, 1678), 6 suites of French dances for 3 scordatura vns (*a–e′–a′–c♯″*), bc (always doubles one of the vns)
*Konincklycke airs a 2, vn, va da gamba, bc, op.8 (Delft, 1684)
*Kermiswerk bestaende in Gigen, Balletten, en Sarbanden, vn, bc, op.9 (Delft, before 1708)
*Vorstelyck snarenspel (before 1708), in at least 3 ptbks or vols.
*D'onnaspeurlyke naspeuring, bestaande in vraag, antwoorden toesang (Delft, 1717)
*Troost in cuderdom . . . en tegenzang voor de jonkheyd, v, bc (Delft, 1717)
* Rouw- en liefde-tranen uitgestort over de smartelyke dood van . . . Maria Stuart, koninginne van Groot-Brittanje, v, bc (Delft, 4/1717) [1st movt in vander Straeten, p.282]

BIBLIOGRAPHY
E. vander Straeten: *La musique aux Pays-Bas avant le XIXe siècle*, iv (Brussels, 1878/*R*1969), 280ff
A. Goovaerts: *Histoire et bibliographie de la typographie musicale dans les anciens Pays-Bas* (Antwerp, 1880/*R*1963), 414, 458f
[J. P.] Heije: 'Muziekwerken van nederlandsche componisten', *Bouwsteenen: JVNM*, iii (1881), 20
W. H. Thijsse: 'Dirk Scholl (1641–1727)', *Mens en melodie*, x (1955), 306
C. C. Vlam and M. A. Vente, eds.: *Bouwstenen voor een geschiedenis der toonkunst in de Nederlanden* (Amsterdam, 1965–71), i, 44f; ii, 271

RANDALL H. TOLLEFSEN

Schollenberger, Kaspar (*b* Höchstädt an der Donau, nr. Donauwörth, 1673; *d* Ulm, 31 Aug 1735). German composer. He attended the school attached to St Ulrich's Church, Augsburg, where he was a choirboy for five years, and then entered a monastery at Wengen bei Ulm. The abbot there, recognizing his unusual ability, arranged for him to study at the University of Dillingen, where he went in 1697. In 1705 he returned to the monastery as philosophy teacher; and in 1713 the first of his three publications appeared.

Schollenberger was one of the few south German composers to publish church music before the 1720s, when the boom in simple liturgical music for parish choirs began. His scoring and style are quite different from that of later publications by composers such as Rathgeber and show that his music was intended only for experienced performers. His orchestra includes an essential viola part, and sometimes also requires oboes and bassoons, as well as the customary violins, trumpets and drums.

Most of Schollenberger's psalms and offertories are divided into six or more separate movements. In his solo arias and duets, he often indulged in elaboration apparently for its own sake; his choral writing is solidly contrapuntal, and since the violins often have independent parts, making six in all, the textures in the choral movements tend to be thick. Schollenberger, though a skilled craftsman, had little gift for melodic or harmonic invention, so his music lacks a sense of purpose, and, however well-constructed, is often dull.

WORKS
Psalmodia ariosa tripartita, op.1, 4vv, 2 vn, vle, org (Augsburg, 1713), 3 Vespers
Thymiama ariosa-ecclesiastica, op.2, 4vv, vn, va, vle, org (Ulm, 1718, 1720, 1723), 38 offertories
Gaudia et luctus, op.3 (Augsburg, 1718), 5 masses, 1 requiem
Lost works: Antiphonarium romanum, 1719, 4vv, bc; Vesperae de Dominica, 4vv, 2 vn, 2 tpt, timp, org; Vesperae de B.V.M., 4vv, 2 vn, 2 ob, org; Confitebor tibi, 4vv, 2 vn, org; Missa S Rainaldi, 1724, 4vv, 2 vn, 2 va, org

ELIZABETH ROCHE

Schollum, Robert (*b* Vienna, 22 Aug 1913). Austrian composer. He studied at the Vienna Music Academy, the New Vienna Conservatory and privately with Marx and Lustgarten for theory and composition, Lafite for the organ and the piano, and Nilius for conducting.

Before the war he worked as a concert organist, pianist and teacher; after 1945 he settled in Linz, where he was city music director in the early 1950s. He was appointed professor at the Vienna Music Academy in 1959. Awards made to him include the Austrian State Prize for composition (1961) and the Prize of the City of Vienna (1971). His compositions are neo-classical in style, though from about 1950 based on a free 12-note serial technique.

WORKS
(selective list)

Operas: Mirandolina (E. Thanner, after Goldoni), 1945–6, unperf.; Oper, op.30, unpubd; Nacht der Verwandlung, op.48 (chamber opera), Linz, 1952

Orch: Vn Conc. no.1, 1944, unpubd; Conc. grosso, op.34, cl, orch, 1948; Serenade, op.39a, 1952; Pf Conc., op.43; Sym. no.1, op.50, 1953–5; Vc Conc., op.52, 1954; 8 Augenblicke, op.54c, 1956–8; Kontraste, op.56, no.1, 1957; Konturen, op.59b, str, 1958; Sym. no.2 'Istrianische', op.60, 1958–9; Gespräche, op.62, chamber orch, 1959; Vn Conc. no.2, op.65, 1961; Sym. no.3, op.67, 1962; Sym. no.4, op.74, 1964; Sym. no.5, op.77, 1969; Spiele, op.82, 1970; Rufe, op.90, 1972

Choral: Im Frühtau zu Berge, vv, orch, 1950; Gesang im brüderlichen Raum (J. L. Stern), cantata, 1953; Gesang aus der Nacht (K. Kleinschmidt), S, vv, orch, 1957; Psalm cxxii, op.58b, vv, orch, 1957; Psalm-Kommentare, op.80, vv, insts, 1969; Chorfantasie, op.86 (after Dante), solo vv, vv, pf, orch, 1971

Chamber and inst: Sonata no.1, op.36, bn, pf, 1949; Sonata no.2, op.38, va d'amore, pf, 1950; Str Qt no.1, op.40, 1949; Sonata no.3, op.42a, cl, pf, 1950; Sonata no.4, op.42b, va, pf, 1950; Sonata no.5, op.42c, vn, pf, 1950; Oktett in 8 Skizzen, op.63, 1959; Str Qt no.2, op.72, 1966; Mosaik, op.75, ob, perc, pf, 1967; 5 Stücke, op.83, wind qnt, 1970; Die Ameisen, op.93, vc, pf, 1974

Other works: songs, kbd works, Spielmusiken

Principal publisher: Doblinger

WRITINGS
Musik in der Volksbildung (Vienna, 1962)
Egon Wellesz, Österreichische Komponisten des XX. Jahrhunderts, ii (Vienna, 1964)
Die Wiener Schule: Entwicklung und Ergebnis (Vienna, 1969)
with J. Fritz and others: *Das kleine Wiener Jazzbuch* (Salzburg, 1970)
Singen als menschliche Kundbegung: Einführung in die Arbeit mit den 'Singblättern zur Musikerziehung' (Vienna, 1970)
'Stilistische Elemente der frühen Webern-Lieder', *5. Internationaler Webern-Kongress: Wien 1972*, 127

BIBLIOGRAPHY
W. Szmolyan: 'Neue Werke von Robert Schollum', *ÖMz*, xxviii (1973), 403

Scholz, Bernhard (*b* Mainz, 30 March 1835; *d* Munich, 26 Dec 1916). German conductor and composer, father of Hans Scholz. He first studied music with Heinrich Esser and Ernst Pauer and, after a trip to Paris to learn lithography at his father's request, took further instruction from S. W. Dehn and Sangiovanni in Milan. He taught theory at the Royal School of Music in Munich from 1856, then conducted the opera in Zurich and Nuremberg before becoming assistant court Kapellmeister to Marschner in Hanover (1859–65). Subsequently he conducted the concerts of the Società Cherubini in Florence (1865–6) before his activity as a conductor in Berlin, where he directed the Philharmonic Concerts and the Cecilia Choir and taught at Kullak's and Stern's conservatories. From 1871 he directed the concerts of the Breslau Orchestral Society. He succeeded Raff as director of Hoch's Conservatory in Frankfurt am Main in 1883, a position he retained until his retirement in 1908. He also conducted the choral union founded by F. W. Rühl (from 1884) and founded a workers' choir (1897). On retirement he went first to Florence and then settled in Munich in 1914. The University of Breslau awarded him an honorary doctorate in 1883.

Scholz belonged to the circle of Brahms, Joachim and Clara Schumann, and was among those who signed the famous manifesto of March 1860 against the New German School. He worked assiduously to promote the works of Brahms, whose influence is most evident in his compositions. His chamber music shows a concern with form and finish in detail without inspired melodic or harmonic traits. His String Quartet in G op.46 won the Florentine Quartet Prize in 1877, and his String Quintet in E minor op.47 was awarded a prize by a St Petersburg society the following year.

WORKS
Operas: Carlo Rosa, Zietensche Husaren, Die vornehmen Wirte, Morgiane, Golo, Der Trompeter von Säckingen, L'ospite di qualità, Gustav Wasa, Hugo, Ingo, Anno 1757, Mirandolina

Orch: 2 syms, pf conc.; Pf Conc.; Capriccio, pf, orch; Capriccio all'ungarese, vc, orch; Wanderung, suite; Im Freien; Iphigenie, ov.

Chamber and pf: Pf Qnt; Str Qnt; Pf Qt; 2 str qts; 2 pf trios; vn and vc sonatas and other works; Pf Sonata; many other pf works, incl. preludes and fugues, variations, sonatinas, ländler, waltzes (4 hands) and variations (2 pf)

Vocal: Requiem; Das Lied von der Glocke, solo vv, chorus, orch; Das Seigesfest; Sylvesterglocken; partsongs and solo songs

WRITINGS
ed.: *S. W. Dehns Lehre vom Contrapunkt, dem Canon und der Fuge* (Berlin, 2/1883)
Wohin treiben wir? (Frankfurt am Main, 1897)
Musikalisches und Persönliches (Stuttgart, 1899)
Die Lehre vom Kontrapunkt und der Nachahmungen (Leipzig, 1904)
Verklungene Weisen (Mainz, 1911)

BIBLIOGRAPHY
E. Segnitz: 'Prof. Bernhard Scholz', *Klavierlehrer*, xxiv (1901), 61
H. Schlemüller: *Neue Musik-Zeitung*, xxiii (1902), 337
H. Hanau: *Dr. Hochs Konservatorium zu Frankfurt am Main* (Frankfurt, 1903)
W. Altmann, ed.: *Johannes Brahms im Briefwechsel mit Karl Reinthaler und ... Bernhard und Luise Scholz* (Berlin, 1908)
A. Moser, ed.: *Briefe von und an Joseph Joachim* (Berlin, 1911–13; Eng. trans., 1914/R1972)
H. Behr: *Denkschrift zum 50 jährigen Bestehen des Breslauer Orchester-Vereins* (Breslau, 1912)
W. Nagel: Obituary, *Neue Musik-Zeitung*, xxxviii (1917), 123
B. Litzmann, ed.: *Clara Schumann, Johannes Brahms: Briefe* (Leipzig, 1927)
S. von der Schulenburg: 'Briefe Wilhelm Diltheys an Bernhard und Hans Scholz', *Sitzungsberichte der Preussischen Akademie* (Berlin, 1933), 416
W. Altmann: *Handbuch für Klavierquartettspieler* (Wolfenbüttel, 1937)
GAYNOR G. JONES

Scholz, Hans (*b* Breslau, 7 March 1879; *d* Munich, 20 Oct 1953). German writer on music, son of Bernhard Scholz. He was enrolled at the Hoch Conservatory before studying musicology at the universities of Berlin and Rostock. In 1910 he completed his studies at Munich University where he also taught theory; later he was active as a music critic in Frankfurt am Main. In 1928 he returned to Munich as a critic for the *Münchner Zeitung*.

WRITINGS
Johann Sigismund Kusser (Cousser): sein Leben und seine Werke (diss., U. of Munich, 1910; Leipzig, 1911)
Lebenserinnerungen (Munich, 1914, 2/1929) [trans. of H. Berlioz: *Mémoires* (Paris, 1870)]
Harmonielehre (Leipzig and Berlin, 1920)
ed.: *Richard Wagner an Mathilde Maier* (Leipzig, 1930)

BIBLIOGRAPHY
S. von der Schulenburg: 'Briefe Wilhelm Diltheys an Bernhard und Hans Scholz', *Sitzungsberichte der Preussischen Akademie* (Berlin, 1933), 416
W. Altmann: *Handbuch für Klavierquartettspieler* (Wolfenbüttel, 1937)
W. Zentner: 'Hans Scholz: 60 Jahre', *NZM*, Jg.106 (1939), 293
A. Würz: 'Abschied von Hans Scholz', *NZM*, Jg.114 (1953), 730
GAYNOR G. JONES

Scholze, Johann Sigismund. See SPERONTES.

Schönbach, Dieter (*b* Stolp, Pomerania, 18 Feb 1931). German composer. After studies in Detmold and Freiburg with Bialas and Fortner (1949–59), he served as music director at the Bochum Schauspielhaus (1959–73). He also worked in theatres in Münster, Westphalia and Basle; he took part in the artistic arrangements for the 1972 Olympic Games in Munich; and he lectured in India and South America for the Goethe Institute. In 1972 he was joint winner of the Stamitz Prize of Stuttgart with Hans Otte and Wolfgang Steffen.

Schönbach is, with Riedl, one of the foremost German exponents of mixed-media composition. Since 1960 he has engaged in collaborative ventures with visual artists, choreographers and film directors, and even in his 'pure' works he makes use of Kandinsky's theory of elements in pictorial form, disposing his materials as 'surfaces', 'points', 'silences' and 'curves'. Many of his pieces require graphic projections, sometimes prepared by other artists. Apart from his self-sufficient compositions, he has worked on advertising films, a multi-vision programme for the tourist office at Cologne and a programme of graphic compositions for underground railways.

WORKS
(selective list)
DRAMATIC AND MIXED MEDIA

Geometrie, Sprache der Formen (film), 1958; Aktionsmusik I, elec rec, audience, 1967, collab. G. Weseler; Die Geschichte von einem Feuer (mixed-media opera, after E. Borchers), 1968, collab. E. Kieselbach, O. Piene, B. Völkle, Weseler; Canzona da sonar 5, S, environment, 1968, collab. Piene; Aktionsmusik II, audience, 1969; Canzona da sonar 5 (film), 1970; Canzona da sonar 6 (mixed-media show with puppets), 1970, collab. Weseler; Hymnus I, speakers, singers, choruses, pop group, tapes, visuals, 1970
Der Sturm (mixed-media show, after Shakespeare), speakers, musicians, tapes, visuals, 1970, collab. Kieselbach; Hysteria—Paradies schwarz (mixed-media opera), 1971, collab. D. Wellershoff, Kieselbach, K. Geldmacher, K. Göhling, P. Brühning, Weseler; Hymnus II—Morgen nach dem Feuer (mixed-media show), speakers, singers, choruses, 3 pop groups, tapes, visuals, 1972; Die chöre des Oedipus (speech composition for radio, after Hölderlin), 1973; Der Sturm (radio scenes, after Shakespeare), 1973; Metro Media, kinetic sound formations for underground railways, 1973
Zum Beispiel Krönungsmesse von Mozart zusammen machen (television film), 1974, collab. E. Schoener and J. Lord; Come S Francesco (chamber opera) [after A. Scarlatti], speakers, singers, dancers, projections, 1975–6

CONVENTIONAL MEDIA

Orch: Conc., D/F-tpt, chamber orch [after A. Scarlatti], 1957; Pf Conc., 1958; Orchesterstück 1 'Farben und Klänge', 1958; Orchesterstück 2 'Ritornelle', 1961; Orchesterstück 3 'Pour Varsovie', 1962; Orchesterstück 4 'Entre', 1963; Canzona da sonar 1, str, 1965
Vocal: Canticum psalmi resurrectionis, S, insts, 1957; Come S Francesco predico agli uccelli, conc., S, insts, 1959; Lyrische Gesänge I (Borchers), S, insts, 1961; Lyrische Gesänge II (Borchers), S, 2 pf, 1962; Canticum psalmi ad laudes, S, insts, 1964, collab. Weseler; Chant liturgique, hommage à Perotin, chorus, orch, 1964, collab. Kieselbach; Canzona da sonar 8 'Birds', S, birdcalls, 1974
Inst: 4 kleine Klavierstücke, 1957; Str Qt, 1957; Kammermusik 1960, 14 insts, 1960; Hoquetus, 8 wind, 1964, collab. Weseler; Canzona da sonar 2, ens, 1966, collab. Weseler; Canzona da sonar 3, tr rec, prepared pf, tape, 1967; Canzona da sonar 7, t sax, pf, tape, 1971

Principal publishers: Moeck, Peters, Süddeutscher Musikverlag

BIBLIOGRAPHY
D. Gojowy: 'Multimedia und graphische Komposition', *Musik und Bildung*, ii (1970), 273
H. Krellmann: 'Die verschmolzenen Melodien', *Musica*, xxiv (1970), 549
G. Weseler: 'Der optische Klang', *Musik und Bildung*, ii (1970), 278
D. Schönbach: 'Neue Aspekte für das totale Theater', *Musik und Bildung*, iii (1971), 525
D. Gojowy: 'Die U-Bahn fährt plötzlich durch Wasser', *Melos*, xli (1974), 10

DETLEF GOJOWY

Schonberg, Harold C(harles) (*b* New York, 29 Nov 1915). American music critic. He was educated at Brooklyn College (BA 1937) and at New York University (MA 1938) and served as music critic and record reviewer for the *American Music Lover* (1939–42), the *Musical Courier* (1948–52) and the *New York*

Sun (1946–50). He became associated with the *New York Times* in 1950, and was the paper's senior music critic, 1960–80. He has also contributed articles to many American magazines. He was the first music critic to be awarded the Pulitzer Prize for criticism (1971), a category established in 1970.

Schonberg's importance in American music criticism lies both in the singular prestige of his forum and the fact that his writings are often syndicated by newspapers throughout the USA. His approach is primarily that of a journalist with musical knowledge. His fields of special interest are piano literature and performance and lesser 19th-century composers.

WRITINGS
Chamber and Solo Instrument Music (New York, 1955)
The Collector's Chopin and Schumann (New York, 1959)
The Great Pianists (New York, 1963)
The Great Conductors (New York, 1967)
Lives of the Great Composers (New York, 1970)

PATRICK J. SMITH

Schönberg, Stig Gustav (*b* Husby, nr. Norrköping, 13 May 1933). Swedish organist and composer. He studied at the Royal Academy of Music in Stockholm (1953–60) with Larsson and Blomdahl, and in Belgium with Peeters. He was a lecturer at the music school in Linköping (1961–2), then assistant organist at the cathedral there (1962–4); in 1965 he became organist of St Göran in Stockholm. He has given recitals in Scandinavia, the Netherlands, Germany and France.

WORKS
(selective list)

Orch: Conc., org, str, 1962; Sinfonia aperta, 1965, rev. 1971; 3 concertinos, str, 1966; Madeleine och Konrad (ballet), 1967, rev. 1972; Concitato, 1968, rev. 1971; Impromptu visionario, 1972; Sym. no.2, 1977
Chamber: Dialoger, fl, cl, 1960; 6 str qts, 1961–72; Partita, cl, pf, 1968; Sonate pastorale, ob, org, 1972; 2 vn sonatas
Solo: Toccata concertante, I–V, org, 1954–77; Lacrimae Domini, org, 1958; Il dolce piano, 10 preludes, pf, 1964; Es sungen drei Engel, 10 chorale variations, org, 1970
Vocal: Rex gloriae, 1v, org, 1969; 5 sånger, 1v, pf, 1971; Regina coeli, S, chorus, org, orch, 1973; Cantata gloriae, 1974

Schondorpp, Philipp. See SCHOENDORFF, PHILIPP.

Schöne, Lotte (*b* Vienna, 15 Dec 1891; *d* Paris, 23 Dec 1977). Austrian soprano, later naturalized French. She studied in Vienna with Johannes Ress and others, and made her début in 1915 at the Volksoper, where she remained for two seasons. She sang at the Vienna Staatsoper, 1917–26, and became a favourite at the Salzburg festivals, 1922–35. Bruno Walter heard her at Salzburg in 1925, and instantly engaged her for the Berlin Städtische Oper, of which she was a member from 1926 to 1933. In Vienna and Berlin she sang a wide range of parts, including operetta, but excelled in such Mozart roles as Cherubino, Susanna, Blonde, Zerlina, Despina, Pamina and Papagena, some of which she also sang at the Munich festivals of that time. Her other parts included Adele in *Die Fledermaus*, Norina in *Don Pasquale*, Gilda and Oscar, Marzelline, Sophie and Zerbinetta, and Musetta, Mimì, Butterfly and especially Liù, which last she sang with marked success at Covent Garden in 1927. Her artistic life was sadly interrupted by the coming to power of the Nazis in 1933. Having established happy relations with France, where her Mélisande was much appreciated, she made her home in Paris after 1933, and appeared in both opera houses there, but was obliged to go into hiding in southern France during the war. Except for a single postwar appearance in Berlin (as Susanna in 1948), her stage career ended in 1938.

A beautiful woman, she had a singularly charming stage presence, of which her light and well-schooled soprano, with its limpid ease of production, seemed the natural counterpart. She made an ideal exponent of the Mozartian soubrette parts, in which her singing and acting were free from the archness that can so easily prove tiresome. The best of her many records are those made in Berlin, 1927–31.

BIBLIOGRAPHY

A. Tubeuf: 'Lotte Schoene', Record Collector, xx (1971), 77 [with discography]

DESMOND SHAWE-TAYLOR

Schoneck. See SCHÖNIG family.

Schonenberger, Georges (b 1808; d Pfäfers, Switzerland, July 1856). French music publisher. His earliest advertisement dates from 10 April 1830; his address, 10 boulevard Poissonnière, Paris, suggests a close connection with, if not actual succession to, Dufaut & Dubois, many of whose publications Schonenberger reissued. The house number was changed, or a move was made, first to no.20 in November or December 1841, and then to no.28 boulevard Poissonnière between December 1842 and January 1843. In the 1860s the name of a successor, Wild, was usually added to or substituted for that of Schonenberger in the imprints, and in June 1875 the business was advertised for sale for 250,000 francs. He died in the St Pirminsberg asylum in the St Gallen canton of Switzerland.

Schonenberger is interesting for his enterprise in publishing full scores and orchestral parts of four Donizetti operas, including La fille du régiment (1840). He put out full scores of some 27 other operas, all but a handful of which were reissues from the plates of other publishers (including Pleyel, Dufaut & Dubois and Bochsa). He published about 50 opera piano–vocal scores, including several little-known works by Rossini and Donizetti. Among his other publications should be noted Berlioz's Grand traité d'instrumentation (1843), piano concertos in parts by Hummel, Mendelssohn and Thalberg, numerous piano works by F. Beyer, J. Herz and Hünten, new editions or reissues of a large proportion of Bochsa's harp music, violin music by Delphin Alard and Paganini, a highly successful piano method by H. Bertini, a certain amount of Spanish music, and translations into Spanish of didactic works published by the firm.

BIBLIOGRAPHY

Catalogue de musique: Schonenberger éditeur (Paris, c1860)

C. Hopkinson: A Dictionary of Parisian Music Publishers 1700–1950 (London, 1954), 110

RICHARD MACNUTT

Schönfeld, Johann Philipp (b Strasbourg, 1742; d Strasbourg, 5 Jan 1790). Alsatian composer and conductor. He attended the Protestant Gymnasium in Strasbourg, studied theology and received his early musical instruction from J. F. Brück. By 1770 he was court steward and tutor to the Münchhausen family in Brunswick. During this period he called himself a musical amateur and published three collections of songs. In August 1777 he became assistant Kapellmeister at the New Church, Strasbourg. The city granted him a leave of absence with a small stipend in 1779 so that he could study in Italy. After his return he was Kapellmeister at the New Church and also concert director for the city from 1781 (assisted by Ignaz Pleyel). His plans of 1787 for the reorganization of the city concerts were abandoned because of the French Revolution. Schubart described Schönfeld as 'a composer of vocal music, who in the most recent times has begun to achieve recognition. He chooses poems by our best poets and often successfully gets at the sense of the poems in his settings; but his taste is too harsh, his shading too brilliant, and the expression of his feelings often too affected'. According to Fétis he left several operas in manuscript, but only one stage work is known.

WORKS

Song collections: Recueil de quelques pièces pour le chant (Nuremberg, c1769); [10] Neue Lieder auf das Clavier, i (Hamburg and Brunswick, c1776); Chansons de franc-maçons (Brunswick, before 1778); [17] Lieder aus der Iris mit 1 Arie mit Begleitung einer Violine zum Singen beym Claviere (Berlin, 1778); lieder, 2–4vv, kbd, B-Bc [perhaps from Lieder aus der Iris]; several pubd in contemporary anthologies and periodicals

Other vocal: Das Milchmädchen und die zween Jäger (comic operetta), D-Bds [incl. arias by Pacini and Duni]; Gelobet seyst du, Herr, cantata, S, chorus, orch, F-Pn; Herr Gott, dich loben wir, cantata, S, B, chorus, orch, Pn; Cantata per il Venerdi Santo, 2 S, 2 choruses, orch, Pc [inc.]; Cantate auf die Feyerliche Einsenkung Grafen Moritz von Sachsen, 1777, lost; other cantatas cited by Vogeleis, lost

BIBLIOGRAPHY

FétisB; GerberL

C. F. D. Schubart: Ideen zu einer Ästhetik der Tonkunst (Vienna, 1806/R1969)

G. Schilling: Encyclopädie der gesammten musikalischen Wissenschaften (Stuttgart, 1835–42/R1973)

M. Friedlaender: Das deutsche Lied im 18. Jahrhundert (Stuttgart and Berlin, 1902/R1970)

M. Vogeleis: Quellen und Bausteine zu einer Geschichte der Musik und des Theaters im Elsass 500–1800 (Strasbourg, 1911)

ELLWOOD DERR

Schönfelder, Gerd (b Köttewitz, nr. Dresden, 27 April 1936). German musicologist. He studied musicology with Vetter, E. H. Meyer and Knepler at the Humboldt University, Berlin (1955–7), modern Chinese at Peking University (1957–9) and Chinese music and drama with Yang Yin Liu and Liao Fu Shu at the Peking Academy of Music (1959–62); from 1962 he continued his studies while teaching at the universities of Berlin and Leipzig. In 1969 he took the doctorate at Leipzig with a transcription, translation, commentary and analysis of a traditional Chinese Peking opera, and in 1972 he took the DSc at Halle with a study of the concept of originality in contemporary music. He became deputy director of teaching and research at the Dresden Hochschule für Musik (1972), where he was later appointed lecturer in musicology (1974). He has served on the council of the East German union of composers and musicologists (from 1969) and the music commission of the East German Cultural Unions council (from 1972). His chief areas of research are Chinese music and music drama, contemporary East German symphonic and chamber music, music of antiquity and 19th-century Romantic music.

WRITINGS

'Chinesische Oper', BMw, iii/3 (1961) [special no.]

'"Die Beschwörung des Ostwinds", eine Peking-Oper', BMw, v (1963), 183

'Die melodische Gerüstgestalt des Örlhuangs und ihre Realisation', GfMKB, Leipzig 1966, 559

'Das ban-Prinzip der Peking-Oper', Jb für musikalische Volks- und Völkerkunde, iv (1968), 98

Die schlagrhythmische und formstrukturelle Gestalt des 'yue mu ci zi' (diss., U. of Leipzig, 1969)

'Zum Gebrauch der Schlaginstrumente im traditionellen chinesischen Theater', SM, xiii (1971), 137

Die Musik der Peking-Oper (Leipzig, 1972)
Untersuchungen zum Begriff des Neuen in der zeitgenössischen Musik: ein Beitrag zur Bestimmung spezifischer inhaltlicher Erscheinungsformen nichtwortgebundener Musik des sozialistischen Realismus (diss., U. of Halle, 1972)
'Zur Frage des Realismus bei Mendelssohn', *BMw*, xiv (1972), 169
'Analyse: Fritz Geisslers "Schöpfer Mensch" ', *Musik und Gesellschaft*, xxiii (1973), 408
'Der sozialistische Realismus in der Sinfonik Fritz Geisslers', *Sammelbände zur Musikgeschichte der Deutschen Demokratischen Republik*, iii (Berlin, 1973), 124
'Analyse: VII. Sinfonie von Fritz Geissler', *Musik und Gesellschaft*, xxiv (1974), 199
Zur Einheit von Rationalem und Emotionalem im musikalischen Schaffens- und Interpretationsprozess (Dresden, 1974)
'Zum Verhältnis von Programmatik, Dramaturgie und Gestalt bei der Analyse nichtwortgebundener Musik', *Musik in der Schule*, xxv (1974), 346
'Entwicklungsmerkmale des Instrumentalschaffens der DDR in den letzten Jahren', *Musik und Gesellschaft*, xxvi (1976), 65
Taschenbuch der Künste: Musikgeschichte (Leipzig, 1977)

Schönfelder, Jorg [Georg, Gregorius] (*b* 2nd half of the 15th century). German composer. The six extant German songs which can be ascribed to him are in Schöffer's *Liederbuch* of 1513 (*RISM* 1513²/*R*1908; 3 ed. in Eitner, 2 ed. in Cw, xxix, *c*1955) in a group of pieces by musicians of the Stuttgart Hofkapelle. This and the style of his songs suggest that he had connections with the Stuttgart Kapelle, although he is not known to have been a member. Of his settings (mainly based on conventional court songs with equally conventional texts) only one became widely known, *Von edler Art*. Its broad melody and style of composition recall the most important songs of Hofhaimer and Adam von Fulda. (Moser in fact claimed that it was by Hofhaimer.) Eitner accurately described Schönfelder's songs as 'deeply personal yet of great simplicity'.

BIBLIOGRAPHY
R. Eitner: 'Das alte deutsche mehrstimmige Lied und seine Meister', *MMg*, xxvi (1894), 1–135
H. J. Moser: *Paul Hofhaimer* (Stuttgart and Berlin, 1929/*R*1966)
HANS-CHRISTIAN MÜLLER

Schönherr, Max (*b* Marburg an der Drau [now Maribor], 23 Nov 1903). Austrian conductor, composer and musicologist. He studied with Hermann Frisch in Marburg and Roderich von Mojsisovics (composition) at the Graz Conservatory. From 1924 to 1928 he was double bass player, répétiteur and conductor at the Municipal Theatre in Graz and then successively conductor of a touring opera company (1928–9), at the Theater an der Wien and Vienna Stadttheater (1929–33) and at the Vienna Volksoper (1933–8). From 1931 to 1968 he conducted for Vienna Radio, giving many concerts with the Vienna SO during the 1930s and founding a radio orchestra in Vienna in 1945; he also made guest appearances on foreign radio stations. He came to specialize in light music, and his radio performances of Viennese operetta and dance music displayed a rare sense of Viennese style. He received the title of professor in 1952, and in 1954 won a Joseph Marx composition prize with his Divertimento. As a composer he relied, even in more serious compositions, on clear melodic lines: his *Bauernmusi' aus Österreich* (1936) and *Tänze aus Österreich* (1937), based on traditional Austrian dances and intended as an Austrian counterpart to the national dances of Brahms, Dvořák, Granados and Grieg, have achieved international popularity in concerts of light Viennese music. His skill as an orchestrator was also employed in many practical editions of classical Viennese dance music, presenting the original orchestration edited for modern performing practice with alternative scoring for various instrumental combinations. After retiring from Vienna Radio he took up musicology and graduated at Vienna University in 1973 with a study of Ziehrer (published in 1974). Here and in his other writings he combined extensive practical experience with a critical judgment and orderly presentation of material unique in studies of popular musical forms.

Schönherr's grandfather Franz (1821–86) and father Max (1873–1955) were military bandmasters and his brother Wilhelm (1902–75) an opera and theatre conductor.

WORKS
(*selective list*)
Ballet: Hotel Sacher (partly after Hellmesberger), Vienna, Staatsoper, 1957
Orch: 4 pieces, str, 1959; Pf Concertino, 1964
Other vocal, orch, inst and theatre compositions, incl. much light music [for fuller list see *La MusicaD*]
Arrs. of music by Strauss family, Lehár, Ziehrer and others
Principal publishers: Bosworth, Doblinger, Ludwig Krenn, Universal

WRITINGS
with K. Reinöhl: *Johann Strauss Vater: ein Werkverzeichnis* (Vienna, 1954)
Various articles on Johann Strauss (ii) in *ÖMZ* (1964–8); list in *ÖMZ*, xxxi (1976), 127
Franz Lehár: Bibliographie zu Leben und Werk (diss., U. of Vienna, 1970); summary in *ÖMZ*, xxv (1970), 330
Carl Michael Ziehrer: sein Werk, sein Leben, seine Zeit (Vienna, 1974)
Kompendium zu Band 1–120 der Denkmäler der Tonkunst in Österreich (Graz, 1974)
'Modelle der Walzerkomposition', *ÖMZ*, xxx (1975), 273
'Ästhetik des Walzers', *ÖMZ*, xxxi (1976), 57
Articles in *MGG*, *RiemannL 12*, *Grove 6*
ANDREW LAMB

Schönig [Schoneck]. German family of printers. Valentin Schönig (*b* Gnodstadt, 1544; *d* Augsburg, 1614) acquired Augsburg citizenship in 1567 through his marriage to Barbara Kriesstein, a daughter of the Augsburg printer Melchior Kriesstein, whose business Schönig probably inherited. With his purchase of Philipp Ulhard's workshop in 1581, he established an efficient printing firm and, in spite of his close adherence to Reformation teaching, continually received commissions from the episcopal court (e.g. to print the last Augsburg diocesan breviary, 1584). The Thirty Years War and unfavourable economic conditions prevented his descendants Hans Ulrich Schönig (1589–1655) and Johann Schönig (1616–80) from extending the firm. Only Johann Jakob Schönig (1657–94), who had married a daughter of the Augsburg music publisher Andreas Erfurt, succeeded in giving it fresh impetus. Valentin Schönig, unlike his predecessors Kriesstein and Ulhard, had restricted himself to printing works of composers active in Augsburg, but Johann Jakob printed mainly Catholic church music. After his early death his widow married J. C. Wagner, who then took over the workshop. In 1710 Johann Jakob's son Johann Matthias Schönig (1685–1753) acquired his own printing business, which published individual prints of songs.

BIBLIOGRAPHY
T. Wohnhaas: 'Die Schönig, eine Augsburger Druckerfamilie', *Archiv für Geschichte des Buchwesens*, v (1964), 5
THEODOR WOHNHAAS

Schonsleder [Schönsleder], **Wolfgang** [Volupius Decorus] (*b* Munich, 21 Oct 1570; *d* Hall, Austria, 17 Dec 1651). German composer, teacher and music theorist.

He became a student at the university in Ingolstadt on 16 October 1587, and he entered the Jesuit order on 14 May 1590. In 1593 he sang under the direction of Lassus in the Kantorei of the court at Munich. From 1596 to 1597 he taught at the University of Dillingen and at the same time became an instructor in rhetoric and ancient languages at the Jesuit college in Munich. The only record of him as a composer is of the *Missa super 'Laudate'* (now lost) that he wrote for the festival of St Ignatius of Loyola held at Dillingen in 1619. After 1628 he went to Wildenau, Upper Pfalz, to join in the establishing of a Jesuit mission. He spent his final years, after 1648, as an instructor in Greek at the Jesuit college at Hall, Austria.

Schonsleder's only surviving work on music is the *Architectonice musices universalis* (Ingolstadt, 1631, 2/1684), which he published under the name of 'Volupius Decorus, Musagetes'. It was not well known to his contemporaries, nor has it become well known in more recent studies of 17th-century German music theory; yet it is an impressive work of great significance in this field. Published in two parts, it was planned as a complete manual for learning the art of vocal composition. It begins by asking the student to learn first how to write chords from the bass, and presents rules for forming chords over both regular and irregular bass progressions. The relationship of these exercises to the typical instructions found in 17th-century thoroughbass manuals is striking. Although Schonsleder never referred to thoroughbass practice it is clear that his approach to composition was similar to the rules of thoroughbass realization, particularly for unfigured basses in which patterns of movement determine chord progressions. The final sections of part i illustrate methods of ornamenting chordal structure with particular emphasis on how the contrapuntal style, in from two to eight parts, should be applied.

Part ii expands on the rules of counterpoint and is profusely illustrated with extensive music examples taken from many well-known composers. Chapter 8, 'De Textu', suggests four categories of words that should receive special musical treatment: (i) words of affect ('to lament', 'to rejoice', 'to weep', 'to fear', 'to smile', etc); (ii) words of motion and place ('to stand', 'to run', 'to jump', 'to ascend', 'to descend', etc); (iii) adverbs of time and number ('fast', 'slow', 'twice', 'thrice', etc); (iv) conditions of man (childhood, youth, old age, etc). This classification did not originate with Schonsleder, who took it from the earlier treatise of Johann Nucius, *Musices poeticae* (Neisse, 1613). However, the importance of this section of Schonsleder's work lies in the many illustrative musical examples showing how other composers have set these words musically, including long excerpts from such composers as Felice Anerio ('laughter'), Binaghi ('rejoicing'), Lassus (childhood and the tedium of old age, among many), Massaino ('jumping') and many more.

GEORGE J. BUELOW

Schönwald, Albert. See SIKLÓS, ALBERT.

Schönzeler, Hans-Hubert (*b* Leipzig, 22 June 1925). British conductor of German birth. His family emigrated to Australia in 1938, and he studied at the New South Wales Conservatorium, Sydney, with Eugene Goossens. Later he won a Paris Conservatoire conductor's diploma, and studied privately with Kubelik; he also received guidance from Furtwängler. Since taking British nationality in 1947, he has conducted several of the leading English, German and Australian orchestras; a great admirer of Furtwängler, he directed the Furtwängler Memorial Concert given in London in 1964. Although he has conducted numerous first British, German and Australian performances of modern works, he is primarily an interpreter of the Austro-German and Slavonic music of the Classical and Romantic periods, especially that of Bruckner, about whom he has written a book (*Bruckner*, London and New York, 1970; Ger. trans., 1974).

DERYCK COOKE

Schoof, Manfred (*b* Magdeburg, 6 April 1936). German jazz trumpeter, composer and band-leader. He attended the Kassel Music Academy (1955–7) and the Musikhochschule in Cologne (1958–63), where he played in various jazz groups and made arrangements for several bands, including Kurt Edelhagen's. In 1964 he founded his own quintet with the pianist Alexander von Schlippenbach; with this group he became the outstanding German proponent of 'free jazz', and a jazz artist of international stature. He combines avant-garde with traditional jazz, and is interested above all in the combination of jazz and modern concert music. His record *Page Two* united his New Jazz Trio with a string quartet. Bernd Alois Zimmermann wrote the jazz part in his opera *Die Soldaten* for Schoof's group and his Trumpet Concerto for Schoof as soloist. Schoof has also appeared with the jazz trombonist Albert Mangelsdorff in Gunther Schuller's *The Visitation*.

JOACHIM E. BERENDT

School of English Church Music. London college founded in 1927 and renamed The Royal School of Church Music in 1945; *see* LONDON, §VII, 4.

School opera. See SCHULOPER.

Schools Music Association. English organization for the promotion of music in education. It was formed in 1938 as a result of the success of non-competitive schools' music festivals that had been held since 1927, initially in Shropshire but later through much of the country, mostly directed by Geoffrey Shaw. The first national festival was held in the Royal Albert Hall, London, in 1938, and its success led to the formation of the association to coordinate the festivals' activities. A leading member was Cyril Winn, inspector of schools for the Board of Education and a pioneer in the development of school music in the 1930s. The administrative decentralization that resulted from the 1944 Education Act resulted in a larger number of local music advisers and thus enlarged the association's activities. In 1946 the National Youth Orchestra was founded by Ruth Railton with the support of Shaw and other members of the association. In 1956 the association founded the British Schools Orchestra, later renamed the British Youth Symphony Orchestra in order to admit a higher age range. In 1968 the British Youth Wind Orchestra was founded.

In 1951 the association's second national festival was held in the Royal Albert Hall as the first musical event of the Festival of Britain; Vaughan Williams's *The Sons of Light* was written for the occasion. National festivals were also held in 1956 and 1959, and subsequently these gave way to regional festivals. Other activities of the association have included the foundation of an advisory and research sub-committee, which has produced numerous reports including, at the request of UNESCO, a survey of music in the United Kingdom; an annual conference on music in schools (1964–) to maintain links with other music education bodies; the publication of the journal *Music* (1966–); national conducting courses; and courses for primary school music teachers. In 1970 it introduced the Suzuki method to Britain by organizing a concert and workshop at the Royal College of Music, London.

Schop. German family of musicians.

(1) Johann Schop (i) (*d* Hamburg, 1667). Composer and instrumentalist. In 1614 Duke Friedrich Ulrich made him a probationary musician in the Hofkapelle at Wolfenbüttel. His performances as a lute, cornett and trombone player and in particular as an excellent violinist led to his being engaged permanently in 1615. Nevertheless, in the same year he responded to a summons to join the flourishing musical establishment of King Christian IV of Denmark in Copenhagen. Here he met the English viol player William Brade, who had earlier been in the service of the city of Hamburg and may have taught him there (at this time there were close connections between English and German musicians). In 1619 Schop and Brade were driven from Copenhagen by the plague. Schop had acquired such a high reputation that he soon obtained a post as Kapellmeister, although it cannot be established where this was. In 1621 he became the leading municipal viol player in Hamburg. The city offered him a substantial income for his participation in the church music and the festivities of the council and citizens, yet allowed him the freedom to undertake journeys to German and foreign courts. In 1634 he travelled to Copenhagen with Schütz and Heinrich Albert for the wedding of Crown Prince Christian: during the splendid festivities he won a contest with the French violinist Jacques Foucart. He had by now become famous, and the Danish king attempted several times to lure him back to his musical establishment, but he stayed in Hamburg until his death.

Schop was a solid and versatile musician in a notable German tradition and showed himself to be a forward-looking player and composer. Through his close contact with the highly accomplished English string players and his encounter with early Italian violin masters, he became the leading exponent of the earliest German violin music: as late as 1740 Mattheson noted in his *Grundlage einer Ehren-Pforte* that one did not often find artists of his calibre in royal or princely establishments. He contributed greatly to the flourishing cultivation of music in Hamburg in the mid-17th century. With his well-loved dance pieces he furthered the composition of suites in Germany between the time of Valentin Haussmann and that of Johann Rosenmüller. His sacred concertos occupy a special place alongside those of Schütz, particularly in their treatment of liturgical melodies. As a composer of solo songs, he was, together with Thomas Selle, the founder of a Hamburg school of songwriting. Many of his melodies to sacred texts by Johann Rist – e.g. *Lasset uns den Herren preisen*, *Werde munter, mein Gemüte* and *O Ewigkeit, du Donnerwort* (in Thomas, p.155) – for long remained in the Lutheran repertory.

WORKS

13 wedding songs to sacred texts, 4–8vv, bc (Hamburg, 1627–52)
Erster Theil newer Paduanen, Galliarden, Allemanden, Balletten, Couranten, Canzonen, a 3–6, bc (Hamburg, 1633)
Zweiter Theil newer Paduanen, Galliarden, Allemanden, Balletten, Couranten, Canzonen, a 3–6, bc (Hamburg, 1635)
Erster Theil geistlicher Concerten, 1–8vv, bc (Hamburg, 1644); [contains composer's portrait]; 1 piece ed. in NM, lxix (1930)
1 suite, a 3 in Hochszeitmusik für D. Penshorn (Hamburg, 1640); 19 dance pieces, 2–3 vn, bc, 1646[11]
Many vocal works in 1642[9]; 1651[5]; 1652[5]/R1974; 1653[5]; Frommer und gottseliger Christen alltägliche Hauszmusik, ed. J. Rist (Lüneburg, 1654); Passion und Bues-Lieder, ed. J. B. Schupp (Hamburg, 1655); Morgen- und Abendlieder, ed. J. B. Schupp (Hamburg, 1655); 1655[3]; Salomonis des Ebreischen Königs geistliche Wohl-Lust, oder hohes Lied, ed. P. von Zesen (Amsterdam, 1657); 1660[3]; Suscitabulum musicum (Greifswald, 1661); 1670[6]

(2) Johann Schop (ii) (*b* Hamburg, baptized 5 Oct 1626; *d* after 1670). Viol player and composer, son of (1) Johann Schop (i). About 1670 he was a viol player at the Schwerin court under Duke Christian Ludwig, in whose entourage he more than once visited Paris and took part in performances of operas. Later he may have gone to England. In addition to a three-part funeral song for his sister (Hamburg, 1654) he also wrote 13 songs published in two collections in Hamburg in 1655–6 (*RISM* 1655[3] and 1656[7]); they are modelled on those of his father.

(3) Albert Schop (*b* Hamburg, baptized 6 July 1632; *d* ?after 1667). Organist and composer, son of (1) Johann Schop (i). He studied with Scheidemann and about 1655 was court organist at Güstrow. Like his brother he wrote a number of songs not unlike those of his father: 29 appeared in collections in Hamburg in 1655–6, others were published at Rostock in 1666. Ten of his psalms for solo voice and continuo appeared in *Exercitia vocis* (Hamburg, 1667); another for three voices and continuo survives in MS.

WORKS

Many songs in Morgen- und Abendlieder, ed. J. B. Schupp (Hamburg, 1655); Passion und Bues-Lieder, ed. J. B. Schupp (Hamburg, 1655); 1656[7]; Erster Theil musikalischer Andachten (Rostock, 1666)
10 psalms, 1v, bc, 1667[7]; 1, 3vv, bc, S-Uu

BIBLIOGRAPHY

W. Krabbe: *Johann Rist und das deutsche Lied* (diss., U. of Berlin, 1910)
A. Moser: 'Johann Schop als Violinkomponist', *Festschrift Hermann Kretzschmar* (Leipzig, 1918), 92
——: *Geschichte des Violinspiels* (Berlin, 1923, rev., enlarged 2/1966–7)
K. Stephenson: *Johann Schop: sein Leben und Wirken* (diss., U. of Halle, 1924)
L. Krüger: *Die Hamburgische Musikorganisation im 17. Jahrhundert* (Strasbourg, 1933)
R. H. Thomas: *Poetry and Music in the German Baroque* (Oxford, 1963), 38, 67ff, 75, 155
D. D. Boyden: *The History of Violin Playing from its Origins to 1761* (London, 1965), 136, 167f

KURT STEPHENSON

Schopenhauer, Arthur (*b* Danzig, 22 Feb 1788; *d* Frankfurt am Main, 21 Sept 1860). German philosopher. His masterpiece, *Die Welt als Wille und Vorstellung* ('The world as will and representation'), was written while he was in his twenties and published in 1818 (dated 1819). It was almost unsold, unreviewed and unread. But he remained convinced that it contained 'the real solution of the enigma of the world' and for the rest of his life continued to work on and develop the ideas contained in it without altering them in any essential. In his last decade he experienced the beginnings of fame. Since his death he has probably had greater influence on more creative artists of the front rank than any other philosopher.

Schopenhauer saw his philosophy as the correction and completion of Kant's. Kant had held that the entire world of experience is a world of appearances only: that objects as they are in themselves, unmediated by our sensory apparatus, are inaccessible to us, and must remain permanently unknown. Schopenhauer's point of departure was the assertion that there is one vital exception to this, one physical object in the world for each man which he has direct access to, and knowledge of, from inside: his own body. This gives him the key to the inner nature of the world. For what is experienced from the outside, like any other piece of matter, through the representations of sense, is experienced from the inside as a will to live. This leads to the insight that matter as such is the embodiment of blind, irrational will to exist, of mindless force. (Schopenhauer would have taken Einstein's demonstration of the equivalence of mass and energy as triumphant corroboration of this on the scientific level.) His whole system is devoted to a many-sided consideration of this one thought: that the world, which is experienced as representation, is, in itself, will.

Schopenhauer took over Plato's doctrine of ideas as the permanent forms of reality underlying phenomena, but saw them as standing between the one will and its differentiated manifestations in the world of sense; so for him they were intermediaries, not ultimates. In his view ideas (in Plato's sense) are manifested in works of art, which is how the arts, with one exception, come to express the unchanging realities below the surface of life. But ideas are the permanent forms behind our representations, and there is one art which is inherently non-representational: music. This is, as it were, a super-art which, without the intermediacy of ideas at all, directly articulates ultimate reality, which is will.

In a language intelligible with absolute directness, yet not capable of translation into that of our faculty of reason, it expresses the innermost nature of all life and existence . . . the composer reveals the innermost nature of the world, and expresses the profoundest wisdom in a language that his reasoning faculty does not understand.

If, per impossibile, we could put what music expresses into concepts, this would be the final revelation in words of reality as it is in itself, independent of all representation, and would thus be the true philosophy.

The philosophers most notably influenced by Schopenhauer were Nietzsche and Wittgenstein; the novelists, Tolstoy, Turgenev, Proust, Mann and Hardy; the composer, above all others, Wagner, who described his having read Die Welt als Wille und Vorstellung in 1854 as the most important event of his life. Everything he did subsequently was influenced by it; from that point his practice as an opera composer departed from the notion of Gesamtkunstwerk in which the various arts were to combine on equal terms, and he accorded music a dominating position (see J. Stein: Richard Wagner and the Synthesis of the Arts, Detroit, 1960). For the rest of his life Wagner's prose works abounded in passages which were little more than paraphrases of Schopenhauer (usually unacknowledged). Most important of all, his next wholly new artistic venture after his reading of Die Welt als Wille und Vorstellung, Tristan und Isolde, is almost an attempt to create the operatic equivalent of that book; Schopenhauer's philosophy is assimilated at every level, not only in the role of the music and in the detailed verbal imagery of the text but in the drama itself, and the whole view of life and death which that presents.

WRITINGS
Die Welt als Wille und Vorstellung (Frankfurt am Main, 3/1859;

Eng. trans., 1958)
A. Hübscher, ed.: Sämtliche Werke (Wiesbaden, 2/1946–50)

BRYAN MAGEE

Schornburg, Heinrich (b Echteld or Tiel, nr. Utrecht, 1533; d Bad Schwalbach, 1596). German theorist, teacher and physician of Netherlands birth. He studied at Kraków and Basle Universities from 1566 to 1569 and went to Cologne in 1570 where in 1575 he received the degree of bachelor of medicine. After several years spent elsewhere he returned to Cologne and in 1583 became professor of medicine at the university, a post he held for the rest of his life. There are indications that he visited France and Italy.

In addition to treatises on logic and astronomy, Schornburg produced a highly unconventional booklet on music, the Elementa musica qualia nunquam antehac ordine, brevitate, perspicuitate, et firmitate visa, cum vera monochordi descriptione, hactenus desiderata, instrumenta musica fabricare volentibus ante omnia cognitu necessaria, published in Cologne in 1582 (ed. A. Friedrich, Beiträge zur rheinischen Musikgeschichte, lxvii, Cologne, 1966). Although this didactic manual is essentially of the musica practica type, presenting the fundamentals of music (notation, solmization and mensuration), there are some important differences. First, topics such as the conventional definition, divisions, uses and inventors of music, normally discussed in treatises of this kind are omitted; second, Schornburg employed his own formulations throughout, rather than borrowing from other treatises as was customary. Finally, and of great significance, about half the treatise is devoted to tuning and temperament, a subject usually reserved for a treatise on musica theorica; the presentation here is in terms of the monochord. Using as a basis the Pythagorean ratios for the different musical intervals, Schornburg, by an individual method of successively and alternately adding and subtracting lengths of the monochord's string in accordance with these ratios, arrived at a two-octave system of 44 notes that avoids the Pythagorean comma. The great variety of intervals involved, however, would have made the practical application of this system problematical.

BIBLIOGRAPHY
H. Hüschen: 'Der Kölner Artzt Heinrich Schornburg und seine Musikabhandlung', Festschrift Friedrich Blume zum 70. Geburtstag (Kassel, 1963), 189

F. E. KIRBY

Schorr, Friedrich (b Nagyvárad, 2 Sept 1888; d Farmington, Conn., 14 Aug 1953). Hungarian bass-baritone, later naturalized American. He studied with Slezak's teacher, Adolf Robinson, and while on holiday in America sang some insignificant roles with the Chicago Opera early in 1912. He made his true début at Graz on 20 June 1912 in the taxing role, for so young a man, of Wotan in Die Walküre; his success and the staying power of his voice testified to his teacher's skill as well as to the abundance of his natural gifts. He remained at Graz until 1916, and then went to Prague for two years. From 1918 to 1923 he was with the Cologne Opera during the Klemperer regime, and was thus a seasoned artist when he was engaged by Erich Kleiber and Leo Blech for the Berlin Staatsoper in 1923. During his seven years in Berlin he sang, besides Wagnerian roles, Strauss's Barak and Altair, Meyerbeer's Nelusko and Busoni's Doktor Faust. But his international fame, which dated from 1924, depended almost wholly on the full range of the

Wagnerian bass-baritone parts: the Dutchman, Wolfram, Telramund, Wotan, Gunther, Kurwenal, Hans Sachs and Amfortas; and it was above all as Hans Sachs and Wotan that he dominated the inter-war operatic scene. From 1925 to 1931 he was the Bayreuth Wotan. His English début took place on 5 May 1924, in *Das Rheingold*; next year he sang his first Covent Garden Hans Sachs, returning regularly until 1933 and singing Strauss's Orestes besides most of his Wagner roles. He became even more of a mainstay at the Metropolitan, making his début there on 14 February 1924, as Wolfram, and returning every season for 19 years until his final *Siegfried* Wanderer of 2 March 1943. During this time, besides all the great Wagnerian parts, he sang Beethoven's Pizarro, Strauss's Orestes and Jokanaan, and – more surprisingly – Faninal, Weinberger's Schwanda, Daniello in Krenek's *Jonny spielt auf*, and even Amonasro and Scarpia.

He was beyond question the outstanding Wagnerian bass-baritone of his day, a worthy successor to Anton van Rooy. His voice had majesty and unfailing beauty, although in later years he had difficulty with the higher notes; he never fell into the notorious 'Bayreuth bark', but maintained a steady legato flow even in declamatory passages. He also commanded an intensity and fire which make a thrilling effect in his recording of Pizarro's vengeance aria with Albert Coates as conductor. A delightful specimen of his art in quite another vein is provided by the song of the 'impatient husband-man' in Haydn's *Die Jahreszeiten*. But the most important part of his recorded legacy consists, naturally, of the extensive excerpts made in his prime from *Der fliegende Holländer*, *Die Meistersinger* and the *Ring*, in which, as it did on the stage, his impeccable enunciation plays an important role in the impression of authority that he conveys. One can believe in the grandeur of a Wotan whose utterances are so commandingly distinct, or in the poetic sensibility of a Sachs to whom words are of such importance.

BIBLIOGRAPHY
A. Frankenstein: 'Friedrich Schorr', *Record Collector*, xix (1971), 245 [with discography by J. Dennis and commentary by B. Semeonoff]
A. F. R. Lawrence, S. Smolian and B. Semeonoff: British Institute of Recorded Sound *Bulletin 8* (1958), 2 [discography, commentary, etc]
DESMOND SHAWE-TAYLOR

Schott. German firm of music publishers. It was founded by Bernhard Schott (*b* Eltville, 10 Aug 1748; *d* Sandhof, nr. Heidesheim, 26 April 1809) in Mainz; Eitner gave 1770 as the year of foundation, and the firm celebrated its bicentenary in 1970, but the publishing house was probably not founded until 1780 when Schott was granted a *privilegium exclusivum* and the title of music engraver to the court of the elector at Mainz. Schott had studied from 1768 to 1771 at the University of Mainz (graduating as magister artium), was clarinettist in a Strasbourg regiment from 1771 to 1773 and travelled in the Netherlands and England; in addition to his musical education, he gained a knowledge of copperplate engraving and particularly of music engraving. He was thus more thoroughly trained for the profession of music publishing than most of his contemporaries. He began his publishing venture with editions of the works of Abbé Vogler and his circle and with the composers for the Hofkapelle at Mainz, especially the works of G. A. Kreusser and F. X. Sterkel. Above all he brought out music for which there was a popular demand, such as piano scores and arrangements of popular operas;

he published the first piano score of Mozart's *Die Entführung aus dem Serail* (1785) and of *Don Giovanni* (1791). He frequently reprinted the works of popular composers, especially Pleyel, and boasted that his own editions were of superior quality. The numerous flute duets and other pieces published in the 1790s are evidence of a marked leaning towards salon music.

Bernhard's sons Johann Andreas (1781–1840) and Johann Joseph (1782–1855), who gave the name 'B. Schott's Söhne' to the firm, enlarged the enterprise both by increasing the scope of the publishing programme and by taking over other publishers. By 1818 they had absorbed partly or completely the firms of Amon of Heilbronn, Falter of Munich and Kreitner of Worms (together with a part interest in Götz of Mannheim and Worms), as well as the firms of Karl Zulehner of Mainz and Georg Zulehner of Eltville. Subsequently the firm established branches in Antwerp (1824, transferred to Brussels in 1843 by Peter Schott, a son of Johann Andreas, where it has been independent from 1889 under the name of Schott Frères), Paris (1826), London (1835; managed by Bernhard's third son Adam Joseph Schott, 1794–1840) and Leipzig (*c*1840). The firm first achieved eminence through the connection it formed with Beethoven in 1824 and through its first publication of such late works as the *Missa solemnis*, the Ninth Symphony and the string quartets opp.127 and 131. The firm continued its tradition of publishing popular works by issuing the compositions of Italian and French opera composers, including Bellini, Donizetti, Rossini, Adam, Auber, Gounod and Halévy. In addition it brought out many works for piano by Ascher, Herz, Hünten, Sydney Smith and Thalberg, and works for violin by Bériot, Dancla and Paganini. From 1824 to 1848 it published the musical periodical *Cäcilia*, edited by Gottfried Weber, which was continued until 1869 as

Title-page of the first edition of the score of Beethoven's Ninth Symphony, published by Schott in 1826

the *Süddeutsche Musikzeitung*, edited by Siegfried Dehn. From 1835 it published, together with the Brussels firm of Leroux, Fétis's *Biographie universelle des musiciens et bibliographie générale de la musique*.

From 1855 until his death Franz Philipp Schott (1811–74), the son of Johann Andreas, carried on the publishing house as sole proprietor. Under him a connection with Wagner was formed in 1859, after which the firm published his music dramas *Der Ring des Nibelungen*, *Die Meistersinger von Nürnberg* and *Parsifal*. Other composers of Wagner's circle turned to Schott, including Liszt, with whom there had already been a slight connection since 1837, as well as Cornelius, Wolf and Humperdinck.

After the death of Franz Philipp Schott the publishing house was bequeathed to Ludwig Strecker (1853–1943) who came from an old Hessian civil service family not related to the Schotts. From 1920 he made his sons Ludwig (1883–1978) and Willy (1884–1958) partners in the publishing house. With the publication of Stravinsky's *Fireworks* (1908) it began to encourage modern music and this is still an important part of the firm's policy. 20th-century composers whose works have been published by Schott include Hindemith, Orff, Fortner, Egk, Françaix, Henze, Schoenberg, Zimmermann, Weill, Ligeti and Penderecki, as well as Goehr and Tippett in association with the English branch of the firm.

In 1907 Willy Strecker assisted MAX ESCHIG in the foundation of his publishing house in Paris, and in 1910 he took over the London firm of Augener; both were expropriated during World War I. Heinz Schneider-Schott, Ludwig Strecker's son-in-law, became a director of the firm in 1952, and in 1974 Arno Volk (the founder of VOLK), who had held a leading position in the firm since 1957, became chairman of the board of directors, the other members being Peter Hanser-Strecker and Günther Schneider-Schott; Volk was succeeded on his retirement in 1977 by Ludolf Freiherr von Canstein.

The more important works of musicology published by Schott since World War II include the 12th edition of the *Riemann Musiklexikon* and the Haydn thematic catalogue edited by Anthony van Hoboken. In addition Schott has undertaken critical editions of the complete works of Wagner, Hindemith and Schoenberg.

The firm has also been much involved in music education. It publishes a number of periodicals including *Melos*, *Neue Zeitschrift für Musik* (these two combined in 1974), *Musik und Bildung* (formerly *Musik im Unterricht*), *Forschung in der Musikerziehung*, *Das Orchester*, *The World of Music* and *Darmstädter Beiträge zur neuen Musik*. In 1953 Schott bought the publishing house of ARS VIVA and in 1971 the gramophone record company of Wergo. It is the German agent for the Richard Strauss edition on behalf of the firm of Fürstner (London). It also cooperates with Universal Edition, Vienna, with which the joint publishing house of Wiener Urtext Edition was formed in 1973. Musifactory, a subsidiary firm which publishes light music, was founded in 1975 and a branch established in the USA in 1977.

The firm survived World War II almost unscathed and is still in possession of its largely complete archives. Some 600 letters of Beethoven and other 19th-century composers were donated by Franz Philipp Schott to the Mainz Stadtbibliothek.

The London branch of the firm was managed, after the death in 1840 of A. J. Schott, by Johann Baptist Wolf, to be followed by Charles G. G. Volkert (1854–1922) who had joined the staff in 1873 and who took over the management in 1881. Under his direction the firm began to develop independently. In 1914 Volkert acquired the firm and it became a limited company in 1924. After his death his son-in-law Max R. B. Steffens took over as joint director with Willy Strecker; Strecker was succeeded on his death by Heinz Schneider-Schott. In 1957 Schott acquired the firm of ERNST EULENBURG. In 1961 Peter W. Makings was appointed managing director, and the firm entered on a period of expansion; additional premises were built at Ashford, Kent, in 1965, to house a new printing works, and the Great Marlborough Street premises were redesigned in 1966 to include a retail shop (a salon was added in 1969 for recitals etc). John S. Harper became managing director in 1980. Though autonomous from 1914 until 1980, when Schott of Mainz resumed control, Schott & Co. kept close links with the parent firm while maintaining a publishing policy of its own: contemporary music is strongly represented (Blomdahl, Peter Maxwell Davies, Fricker, Goehr, Hamilton, Searle, Seiber and Tippett), and educational and school music are an important feature, with an extensive list of recorder music. The firm has taken a special interest in the recorder revival; it both manufactures and sells recorders, and in 1963 established the *Recorder and Music Magazine*.

BIBLIOGRAPHY

EitnerQ

M. Seiffert: 'Das Haus Schott', *AMz*, xx (1893)

E. Istel, ed.: 'Elf ungedruckte Briefe Liszts an Schott', *Die Musik*, v/3 (1905–6), 43

A. Börckel: *Aus der Mainzer Vergangenheit* (Mainz, 1906)

W. Altmann: *Richard Wagners Briefwechsel mit seinen Verlegern*, ii: *Briefwechsel mit B. Schott's Söhnen* (Leipzig, 1911)

H. Schrohe: *Bilder aus der Mainzer Geschichte*, Hessische Volksbücher, xlviii (Friedberg, 1922)

M. Unger: 'Zu Beethovens Briefwechsel mit B. Schott's Söhnen', *NBJb*, iii (1926–51)

B. Ziegler: 'Zur Geschichte des Privilegium exclusivum des Mainzer Musikstechers Bernhard Schott', *Festschrift für Georg Leidinger* (Munich, 1930), 293

K. Schweickert: *Die Musikpflege am Hofe der Kurfürsten von Mainz im 17. und 18. Jahrhundert* (Mainz, 1937)

L. Strecker: *Richard Wagner als Verlagsgefährte* (Mainz, 1951)

A. Gottron: *Mainzer Musikgeschichte 1500–1800*, Beiträge zur Geschichte der Stadt Mainz, xviii (Mainz,1959)

Festschrift für Ludwig Strecker (Mainz, 1973)

H.-C. Müller: *Bernhard Schott, Hofmusikstecher in Mainz: die Frühgeschichte seines Musikverlages bis 1797, mit einen Verzeichnis der Verlagswerke 1779–1797* (Mainz, 1977)

HANS-CHRISTIAN MÜLLER, FRANK DAUNTON

Schott, Georg Balthasar (*b* Schönau, nr. Eisenach, 22 Oct 1686; *d* Gotha, buried 26 March 1736). German organist and composer. His father Burkhard was Kantor and schoolmaster at Schönau, his mother a pastor's daughter. He studied at the Gotha Gymnasium, and the universities of Jena (13 November 1709) and Leipzig (1714). On 1 August 1720 he succeeded J. C. Vogler as organist of the Neukirche, Leipzig, and director of the collegium musicum founded by Telemann in 1702. This student organization, which gave concerts and also played at the Neukirche on feast days, attracted talented players who might otherwise have helped at the Thomaskirche. After Kuhnau's death, Schott applied for the post of Kantor and performed a test piece at the Nikolaikirche on 2 February 1723, but he was unsuccessful. However, in Bach's words, 'the good Lord looked after the worthy Mr Schott', and on 15 February

1729 he became town Kantor and schoolmaster at Gotha; on March 22 the Leipzig Council voted him no less than 24 specie thalers as a leaving present. At Gotha, as at Leipzig, he wrote cantatas for royal occasions, but his music is lost.

Schott often deputized for Bach, and seems to have been friendly with him. Instead of leaving the collegium to his successor at the Neukirche, he offered it to Bach, who needed contact with the students. Bach accepted, and had the Neukirche post given to a young man, C. G. Gerlach, who became his deputy and ran the collegium from 1737 to 1739, when Bach temporarily gave it up.

BIBLIOGRAPHY
A. Schering: *Musikgeschichte Leipzigs*, ii, iii (Leipzig, 1926, 1941)
H. T. David and A. Mendel, eds.: *The Bach Reader* (New York, 1945, rev. 2/1966), 147
W. Neumann: 'Das "Bachische Collegium Musicum" ', *BJb*, xlvii (1960), 5
W. Neumann and H.-J. Schulze, eds.: *Bach-Dokumente* (Kassel and Leipzig, 1963–9)

WALTER EMERY

Schott, Johann Georg (*b* Niederkleen, nr. Butzbach, *c*1548; *d* Butzbach, 9 Jan 1614). German composer. He studied at Marburg, and from 1594 in Heidelberg, probably at the instigation of N. Rosthius, with whom he had lodged for three months late in 1590 and early in 1591. Later he entered the service of the Count of Nassau in Ottweiler (Saar), and rose to the position of an imperial notary and town clerk in Butzbach. In 1610 he described himself as 'Director musices' in charge of the collegium musicum there. Schott's last years coincided with a period when the city was at its most prosperous: in 1609 it became the seat of a branch of the Hessian line, the sole regent of which was Landgrave Philipp (1609–43), an extremely cultured prince.

Schott's only printed work, *Psalmen und Gesangbuch darinnen die geistlichen Lieder D. M. Lutheri und anderer Christen begrieffen, zu 4 Stimmen. Contrapunkts weiss . . . gesetzet*, published in Frankfurt am Main in 1603 belongs, as its title indicates, to the Lutheran chorale book type established by L. Osiander; with its 196 four-voice settings it is one of the largest extant collections. Among the versions of the psalms of Middle and High German origin in the first part, there are 20 rhyming paraphrases from J. Magdeburg's *Der Psalter Davids gesangsweis*. It was only rarely, if ever, that Schott composed new tunes; rather, he created something new out of older melodic material.

Three works by Schott in MS no longer extant: two, for eight voices, were written 'in honorem Ludovici Hassiae Landgraf' – *Paraphrasis brevis et perspicua super psalmum xlv* (a wedding motet), and *Acclamatio musicalis* (cited in J. Steuber: *Catalogi und Nachrichten von der Marpurger und Giesser Bibliothec, D-GI*); the third, *Das neugeborne Kindelein*, is known from an old Butzbach music list.

BIBLIOGRAPHY
J. Zahn: *Die Melodien der deutschen evangelischen Kirchenlieder* (Gütersloh, 1889–93/*R*1963)
S. Kümmerle: *Encyklopädie der evangelischen Kirchenmusik*, iii (Gütersloh, 1894)
K. Dotter: 'J. G. Schott: ein Butzbacher Komponist des 17. Jahrhunderts', *Die Heimat im Bild*, Beilage zum Giessener Anzeiger, l (1926), 200
F. Kaiser: 'Butzbach', *MGG*

WALTER BLANKENBURG

Schottische (Ger.: 'Scottish'). A round dance, like a polka, but slower. Any connection with the écossaise has been denied by some writers, but according to Sachs the schottische arose from the incorporation of waltz-like turns into the écossaise, and after the disappearance of the latter lived on as a waltz in 2/4 time. It was introduced into England in 1848 as the 'German Polka'. The *Schottische bohème*, or *Polka tremblante*, was a particular kind of polka introduced in Paris in the 1840s.

BIBLIOGRAPHY
C. Sachs: *Eine Weltgeschichte des Tanzes* (Berlin, 1933; Eng. trans., 1938/*R*1963)

MICHAEL TILMOUTH

Schousboe, Torben (*b* Copenhagen, 6 Oct 1937). Danish musicologist. He studied the organ with Peter Thomsen and took the organists' examination at the Royal Danish Conservatory of Music in 1960. His début took place with a recital in Odense Cathedral in 1961, after which he became organist at Emdrup Church in Copenhagen. He studied musicology at the University of Copenhagen (MA 1968) and was then appointed lecturer there. His research has been mainly concerned with church music, both pre- and post-Reformation, and with Danish musical history. He has done valuable archival studies of 19th-century concert life in Copenhagen and in particular established himself as an authority on the music of Carl Nielsen. Other posts he has held include secretary of the Danish Carl Nielsen Society (from 1966), chairman of the National Danish RILM Committee (from 1967), and membership of the executive committees of Samfundet Dansk Kirkesang and Selskabet Dansk Tidegaerd.

WRITINGS
with D. Fog: *Carl Nielsen: kompositioner: en bibliografi* (Copenhagen, 1965)
'Koncertforeningen i København', *DAM*, vi (1968–72), 171–209
'Barn af huset – ?', *Dansk kirkesangs årsskrift 1969–70*, 75 [on Carl Nielsen's *Salmer og aandelige sange*]
'Foreningen symfonia – sin tids DUT', *Dansk musiktidsskrift*, xlvi (1970), 156
'Gregoriansk sang på modersmål', *Festskrift Jens Peter Larsen* (Copenhagen, 1972), 401
'Protestant Church Music in Scandinavia', in F. Blume: *Protestant Church Music: a History* (New York, 1974), 609
with I. E. Møller: *Carl Nielsen: dagbøger og korrespondance med Anne Marie Carl-Nielsen* (in preparation)
'Nielsen, Carl', *Grove 6*

JOHN BERGSAGEL

Schrade, Leo (*b* Allenstein, 13 Dec 1903; *d* Spéracèdes, 21 Sept 1964). American musicologist of German birth. From 1923 he studied musicology at the universities of Heidelberg with Halbig (while also taking courses at the Mannheim Conservatory), Munich with Sandberger and Leipzig with Kroyer; he also studied art history, philosophy, literary history, history and economics. He took the doctorate at Leipzig in 1927 with a dissertation on early organ music and then taught in the musicology seminar at Königsberg University, where he completed his *Habilitation* in 1929 with a work on the notation of early instrumental music. From 1932 he taught at Bonn University, being appointed lecturer in the history of medieval music in 1935. After leaving Germany for the USA he taught at Yale University, as assistant professor (1938), associate professor (1943) and professor of music history (1948) and as director of graduate studies in music (1939–58) instituted a course noted for its comprehensive coverage of music history. In 1958 he succeeded Handschin as professor and director of the musicology institute at Basle University; he held these posts until his death. In 1962–3 he was Charles Eliot Norton Professor of Poetry at Harvard, lecturing on

'Tragedy in the Art of Music'. He founded and edited (1947–58) the Yale Studies in the History of Music and the Yale Collegium Musicum series of performing editions; he was also co-editor of the *Journal of Renaissance and Baroque Music* (1946–7), of *Annales musicologiques* (from 1953) and of *Archiv für Musikwissenschaft* (from 1958).

The most prominent characteristic of Schrade's work, manifest equally in his publications and his teaching, was his striving for universality, and in this, rather than in work in any one area, lay his chief importance as a musicologist. While he valued the precision of a specialist, he felt it both a responsibility and an opportunity to be involved in the whole history of music. He was always ready to undertake an important study, irrespective of its period; while refusing to be limited to merely technical issues, he invariably brought specialist attitudes to bear. Concern with the ideas of history and art is evident in such articles as 'Renaissance: the Historical Conception of an Epoch', and in less obvious ways throughout his work. His interest in method and philosophy permeates even the studies in which his specialist involvement was strongest – medieval polyphony (e.g. in 'Political Compositions in French Music of the 12th and 13th Centuries'). And humanist values motivated and illuminated his important critical editions, the series Polyphonic Music of the Fourteenth Century. In his teaching Schrade always complemented awareness of philosophic issues with a clear sense of musical style. He required that a perception of cultural and historical contexts be balanced against a sensitivity to the uniqueness of the individual composer, whether Philippe de Vitry, Monteverdi, Mozart or Stravinsky. His lively enthusiasm for musical performance was particularly evident in the collegium musicum which he fostered and in which he took part.

WRITINGS

Die ältesten Denkmäler der Orgelmusik als Beitrag zu einer Geschichte der Toccata (diss., U. of Leipzig, 1927; Münster, 1928)
'Die Darstellungen der Töne an den Kapitellen der Abteikirche zu Cluni', *Deutsche Vierteljahrsschrift für Literaturwissenschaft und Geistesgeschichte*, vii (1929), 229–66
Die handschriftliche Überlieferung der ältesten Instrumentalmusik (Habilitationsschrift, U. of Königsberg, 1929; Lahr, 1931)
'Das propädeutische Ethos in der Musikanschauung des Boethius', *Zeitschrift für Geschichte der Erziehung und des Unterrichts*, xx (1930), 179–215
'Die Stellung der Musik in der Philosophie des Boethius als Grundlage der ontologischen Musikerziehung', *Archiv für Geschichte der Philosophie*, xli (1932), 368–400
'Studien zu Händels "Alexanderfest" ', *HJb 1932*, 38–114
'Von der "Maniera" der Komposition in der Musik des 16. Jahrhunderts', *ZMw*, xvi (1934), 3, 98, 152
'Die Messe in der Orgelmusik des 15. Jahrhunderts', *AMf*, i (1936), 129–75
Beethoven in France: the Growth of an Idea (New Haven and London, 1942/R1978; Ger. trans. in preparation)
'The Organ in the Mass of the 15th Century', *MQ*, xxviii (1942), 329, 467
'Herder's Conception of Church Music', *The Musical Heritage of the Church*, ii, ed. T. Hoelty-Nickel (Valparaiso, Ind., 1946), 83
Monteverdi: Creator of Modern Music (New York, 1950, 2/1964)
'Das Rätsel des Rhythmus in der Musik', *Melos*, xviii (1951), 304
'Renaissance: the Historical Conception of an Epoch', *IMSCR, v Utrecht 1952*, 19
'Political Compositions in French Music of the 12th and 13th Centuries', *AnnM*, i (1953), 9–63, 409
Bach: the Conflict between the Sacred and the Secular (New York, 1954)
'The Mass of Toulouse', *RBM*, viii (1954), 84
'The Chronology of the Ars Nova in France', *L'ars nova: Wégimont II 1955*, 37
'A Fourteenth Century Parody Mass', *AcM*, xxvii (1955), 13
'Unknown Motets in a Recovered Thirteenth-century Manuscript', *Speculum*, xxx (1955), 393

La représentation d'Edipo Tiranno au Teatro Olimpico (Vicence 1585) (Paris, 1960)
'The Cycle of the Ordinarium Missae', *In memoriam Jacques Handschin* (Strasbourg, 1962), 87
W. A. Mozart (Berne and Munich, 1964)
Tragedy in the Art of Music (Cambridge, Mass., 1964; Ger. trans., 1967 as *Vom Tragischen in der Musik*)
ed. E. Lichtenhahn: *De scientia musicae studia atque orationes* (Berne and Stuttgart, 1967) [articles, incl. ' "Herkules am Scheideweg" – zur neuen Musik der Nachkriegsjahre', 592]
with J. Knapp: *History of Church Music* (New York, in preparation)

EDITIONS
L. de Milán: Libro de musica de vihuela de mano intitulado El maestro, Publikationen älterer Musik, ii (Leipzig, 1927)
The Roman de Fauvel; The Works of Philippe de Vitry (1291–1361); French Cycles of the Ordinarium missae, PMFC, i (1956)
G. de Machaut: Works, PMFC, ii–iii (1956)
F. Landini: Works, PMFC, iv (1958)

BIBLIOGRAPHY
[J. Jacquot]: 'Leo Schrade', *Le lieu théâtral à la renaissance: CNRS Royaumont 1963*, 530
Musik und Geschichte: Leo Schrade zum sechzigsten Geburtstag (Cologne, 1963)
K. von Fischer: 'Leo Schrade (13. Dezember 1903 – 21. September 1964)', *AcM*, xxxvi (1964), 187
——: 'Leo Schrade † 21. September 1964', *AMw*, xxi (1964), 161
D. J. Grout: review of *Tragedy in the Art of Music*, *JAMS*, xviii (1965), 108
E. Lichtenhahn: 'Leo Schrade zum Gedächtnis', *Mf*, xviii (1965), 121
W. G. Waite: 'Leo Schrade', *JAMS*, xviii (1965), 3
Leo Schrade in memoriam (Berne and Munich, 1966) [incl. tributes by R. Stamm, E. Lichtenhahn and A. Schmitz]
ed. E. Lichtenhahn: *Leo Schrade: De scientia musicae studia atque orationes* (Berne and Stuttgart, 1967) [incl. complete list of publications and bibliography to 1965]
W. Arlt and others, eds.: *Gattungen der Musik in Einzeldarstellungen: Gedenkschrift für Leo Schrade* (Berne and Munich, 1973)

RICHARD L. CROCKER

Schradieck, (Carl Franz) Henry [Heinrich] (*b* Hamburg, 29 April 1846; *d* Brooklyn, NY, 25 March 1918). German violinist and teacher. After less than two years' study under his father he appeared in public at the age of five. In 1854 Teresa Milanollo took an interest in him and placed him under Léonard at the Brussels Conservatory, where he gained a *premier prix* in 1858. He then studied under David at Leipzig (1859–61), obtaining his first important solo engagement in the 'Private Concerts' in Bremen in 1864. The next year he was appointed violin professor at the Moscow Conservatory but returned in 1868 to lead the Hamburg Philharmonic Society orchestra. From 1874 to 1882 he worked in Leipzig, leading the Gewandhaus concerts and teaching at the conservatory. He then went to the Cincinnati College of Music as conductor and teacher until 1889, but returned to his former position in Hamburg for the next eight years. In 1898 he moved permanently to the USA, first for a year as principal violin professor at the National Conservatory in New York, then at the South Broad Street Conservatory in Philadelphia from 1899 to 1912, when he returned to New York, to the American Institute of Applied Music.

Schradieck's systematic stress on fingering technique ensured his importance in the founding of modern violin teaching methods. His pedagogical works include 25 Studies op.1 (Leipzig, 1877), *Der junge Violine-Spieler* op.2 (Leipzig, 1882), *The First Position* (New York, 1897) and *Chord Studies* (New York, n.d.); he also edited concertos by Mendelssohn, Spohr, Viotti and Molique, as well as studies by Campagnoli, Polledro and Kreutzer.

BIBLIOGRAPHY
A. Dörffel: *Geschichte der Gewandhausconcerte zu Leipzig* (Leipzig, 1884/R1972)
E. van der Straeten: *The History of the Violin* (London, 1933/R1968)

S. Nelson: *The Violin and Viola* (London, 1972)
W. W. COBBETT/DAVID CHARLTON

Schramm, Johann Jacob (*b* Mülsen St Jacob, 18 Jan 1724; *d* Mülsen St Niclas, 7 June 1808). German organ builder. He lived as a wealthy houseowner in Mülsen St Niclas, and there carried on the tradition of the carpenter Georg Eger (*d* 10 March 1750), who had built small organs at Stenn (1726) and Mülsen St Niclas (1736). Though he studied with Gottfried Silbermann, his instruments possess an individuality of timbre. He favoured narrower pipe-scaling (thereby securing a new type of sound) and tended to tune in equal temperament. A characteristic of his specifications is the inclusion of a 1′ Flageolet on the manual. He was a famed craftsman, whom the Duke of Altenburg wished to appoint court organ builder. The quality of his work shows in solid construction, the use of choice materials, lightness of touch, ease of maintenance, keen voicing, and fresh, silvery tone with tasteful nuances, well balanced between manuals. His organs in Stangengrün (1766–9) and Wechselburg (St Otto, 1774–81; two manuals and pedal, 26 speaking stops, manual and pedal couplers) survive; only the impressive case remains of the organ built in Mülsen St Niclas (1796–1800).

BIBLIOGRAPHY
F. Oehme: *Handbuch über ältere und neuere Orgelwerke im Königreiche Sachsen*, ii (Dresden, n.d.); iii (Dresden, 1897)
P. Rubardt: *Alte Orgeln erklingen wieder!* (Kassel, 1936)
WALTER HÜTTEL

Schramm, Melchior (*b* Münsterberg, Silesia [now Ziębice, Poland], *c*1553; *d* Offenburg, Baden, 6 Sept 1619). German composer and organist. He is first heard of in 1565 as a chorister in the Hofkapelle of Archduke Ferdinand of the Tyrol. He left in 1569 with a three-year scholarship and became a student of the Innsbruck court organist, Servatius Rorif. In 1571 and 1572 he was organist of a convent at Halle. In 1574 he became Kapellmeister and organist of the court at Sigmaringen; from 1594 he was organist only. From 1605 until his death he was civic organist of Offenburg, at the Heilig Kreuz Kirche. Inventories of the period show that his works were widely known, and the appearance of individual pieces in anthologies is a measure of their popularity. As a composer of German madrigals he ranks with Jacob Meiland as one of the most important forerunners of Hans Leo Hassler.

WORKS
Sacrae cantiones, 5, 6vv (Nuremberg, 1576)
Neue auserlesene teutsche Gesäng, 4vv (Frankfurt am Main, 1579)
Cantiones selectae, 5, 6, 8vv (Frankfurt, 1606)
Cantiones selectae pars II (Frankfurt, 1612)

2 masses, 6vv, lost (mentioned in the inventory of Count Eitelfriedrich IV; see Schmid, pp.553ff, 558)
Other works, *A-Wn, D-Rp*

BIBLIOGRAPHY
EitnerQ
W. Senn: *Aus dem Kulturleben einer süddeutschen Kleinstadt: Musik, Schule und Theater der Stadt Hall in Tirol in der Zeit vom 15. bis zum 19. Jahrhundert* (Innsbruck, 1938), 175, 321, 332, 449
——: *Musik und Theater am Hof zu Innsbruck* (Innsbruck, 1954), 67, 89, 96
E. F. Schmid: *Musik an den schwäbischen Zollernhöfen der Renaissance* (Kassel, 1962), 30ff, 41f, 52ff
THEODOR WOHNHAAS

Schrammel, Johann (*b* Neulerchenfeld, nr. Vienna, 22 May 1850, *d* Vienna, 17 June 1893). Austrian violinist and composer. He studied the violin with Ernst Melzer (first violin at the Carltheater in Vienna) and then with Heissler and Hellmesberger at the Vienna Conservatory (1862–6). He played in the Harmonie and Josephstadt theatre orchestras and, after military service (1866–70), in the salon orchestra of K. Margold. In 1878 the Schrammel Trio (later Quartet) was formed, for which he composed many popular dances, marches and songs. His *Wien bleibt Wien* (1887) remains one of the most popular Austrian marches. His brother Joseph Schrammel (*b* Ottakring, nr. Vienna, 3 March 1852; *d* Vienna, 24 Nov 1895), a violinist and composer, was also a pupil of Hellmesberger (1865–7). He was the leader and manager of the Schrammel Trio, which he founded, and composed songs and dances for the ensemble, although these were less successful than his brother's.
ANDREW LAMB

Schrammel Quartet. A quartet of popular instrumentalists that specialized in accompanying popular songs in the *Heurigen* (wine houses) around Vienna. In 1878 the violinist brothers Johann and Joseph Schrammel formed a trio with the bass guitarist Anton Strohmayer to play at inns and private gatherings. After the occasional addition from 1879 of a G clarinet played by Georg Dänzer the ensemble was formalized as a quartet in 1886 and gained wide popularity in Vienna, particularly with musicians such as Brahms, Johann Strauss and Hans Richter. Guest appearances in Berlin (1888) and elsewhere in Germany (1889) were followed by a visit to the Chicago World's Fair (1893), where the Schrammel brothers were replaced because of illness. Dänzer died on the return journey and the G clarinet was replaced by accordion; in this form 'Schrammel quartets' have survived and flourished. In 1964 the Klassische Wiener Schrammelquartett was formed by soloists from the Vienna SO, using the original instrumental combination and original instrumental arrangements. The quartet has made several gramophone recordings and tours. (*See* VIENNA, fig.15.)

BIBLIOGRAPHY
H. Mailler: *Schrammel-Quartett* (Vienna, 1943)
R. A. Moissl: *Die Schrammel-Dynastie* (St Pölten, 1943)
ANDREW LAMB

Schratt, Hans Rauch von (*fl c*1535). German recorder maker. Two of his recorders, one in Munich and another in Salzburg, bear the inscription: 'HANS RAUCH VON SCHRATT'. The latter is also engraved 'IHESUS MARIA ANNA 1535'. Both instruments are marked with trefoils and although not all of the many instruments marked in this way (including one very large recorder in Antwerp) were made by von Schratt, some, notably several column flutes, show very similar marks, design features and quality of workmanship as the instruments bearing his name.

Another recorder maker of similar name may also have been active at this period, for Burney noted that in 1772 there was a set of instruments in Antwerp 'being thirty and forty of the common-flute kind. . . . They were made at Hamburg . . . and are all of one sort of wood and by one maker; 'CASPER RAUCHS SCRATENBACH' was engraved on a brass ring'.

BIBLIOGRAPHY
C. Burney: *The Present State of Music in Germany, the Netherlands and the United Provinces* (London, 1773, 2/1775); ed. P. Scholes as *Dr. Burney's Musical Tours* (London, 1959)

J. Lambrechts-Douillez: 'Een contrabas Blockfluit in het Museum Vleeshuis de Antwerpen', *Miscellanea*, ed. J. Duverges (Ghent, 1965)

FRIEDRICH VON HUENE

Schreiber, Johann Evangelist [Johannes Evangelista] (*b* Arth, baptized 4 April 1716; *d* St Urban, 18 April 1800). Swiss composer and organist. He took his vows at the Cistercian monastery of St Urban in 1738 and was ordained priest in 1741. He is recorded as *capellae magister* at St Urban in 1751, and from 1757 to 1772 was *Instruktor* at the seminary for canon law at Lützel. The solo passages of his masses, as he acknowledged in a preface, are 'often in an Italianate – though not undisciplined – style'. The masses are predominantly homophonic; such contrapuntal writing as does occur is confined to 'regular fugal expositions'. These works conform to the south German Benedictine style of mass composition, which was widespread in Switzerland.

WORKS

Fasciculus ariarum 24 gloriosae virgini Mariae (12 duets, 12 arias), vv, 2 vn, va, bc, op.1 (Fribourg, 1747); Missale cisterciense musicum (6 masses, 2 requiem), solo vv, 4vv, str, 2 tpt/hn, bc (vc, org), op.2 (Fribourg, 1749); Adoratio Dei per 15 offertoria, 4vv, orch, op.3 (St Gall, 1754); [32] Neue Arietten, i (Fribourg, 1761)

MS: Fundamenta pro cantu plano seu chorali cisterciensi, 1780, *CH-Lz*; Pseudo-propheta, Lucerne, 1748, and Sigeric, Zug, 1751; stage works, lost, libs in *Lz*

BIBLIOGRAPHY

EitnerQ

A. Geering: 'Von der Reformation bis zur Romantik', *Schweizer Musikbuch*, ed. W. Schuh (Zurich, 1939), 76f

W. Jerger: 'Die Musikpflege in der ehemaligen Zisterzienserabtei St Urban', *Mf*, vii (1954), 390

H. P. Schanzlin: 'Schreiber, Johannes Evangelista', *MGG*

F. J. Kienberger: *Studien zur Geschichte der Messenkomposition der Schweiz im XVIII. Jahrhundert* (Fribourg, 1968)

WILHELM JERGER

Schreiber, Ottmar (*b* St Goarshausen am Rhein, 16 Feb 1906). German musicologist. He was taught the organ by Heinrich Boell at the Cologne Musikhochschule (1926–9), and by 1928 he was organist at the Protestant church in Cologne-Bayenthal. In 1929 he moved to Munich, where he studied composition and music theory with Gustav Geierhaas at the academy until 1931. He then studied musicology at Berlin, where his lecturers included Schering, Erich Schumann, Sachs and Hornbostel. He took his doctorate at Berlin in 1938 with a dissertation on the German orchestra between 1780 and 1850. From 1931 until his military service in 1941 he taught at various musical institutions in Berlin. In 1947 he was entrusted by Reger's widow Elsa with running and expanding the Max-Reger-Institut, which she had set up in Bonn. After initial difficulties he found a new home for the institute (hitherto housed where Schumann had lived in Bonn-Endenich) at Bonn-Bad Godesberg. As academic director of the institute he has edited its *Mitteilungen* (1954–) and a number of publications, including sketches, letters and the hitherto unpublished original manuscript of the Violin Sonata op.139 and that of the Responsories, originally published in 1914 in Philadelphia. He played a crucial part in Breitkopf & Härtel's complete edition of Reger's works (1950–). Schreiber was also a lecturer at the Musikhochschule in Frankfurt am Main (1960–71).

WRITINGS

Orchester und Orchesterpraxis in Deutschland zwischen 1780 und 1850 (diss., Humboldt U., Berlin, 1938; Berlin, 1938)

'Elsa Reger zum Gedächtnis', *Mitteilungsblatt der Joseph-Haas-Gesellschaft* (1952), no.7, p.12

ed.: *Max Reger: Briefe zwischen der Arbeit* (Bonn, 1956, 1973)

'Max Regers musikalischer Nachlass', *Kongressbericht: Wien Mozartjahr 1956*, 563

'Unbekannte geistliche Reger-Chöre', *Mitteilungen des Max-Reger-Instituts* (1957), no.5, p.8

'Zum Werdegang von Regers Mozart-Variationen', *Mitteilungen des Max-Reger-Instituts* (1957), no.6, p.2

'Ein Symphoniesatz des 17jährigen Reger', 'Ballettsuite und "Pantalon" ', *Programmheft Max-Reger-Fest Dortmund 1960*, 76, 78

' "Freier Jenaischer Stil": Regers Violinsonate op.139 und ihre erste Form', *Mitteilungen des Max-Reger-Instituts* (1962), no.13, p.30

'Max Reger and Contemporary German Musical Life', *Canon*, xvi (Sydney, 1962–3), 81

ed., with G. Sievers: *Max Reger zum 50. Todestag am 11. Mai 1966: eine Gedenkschrift* (Bonn, 1966)

'Max Regers Responsorien', *Musik und Kirche*, xl (1970), 341

'Zur Frage der gültigen Fassung von Regers Orgel-Opus 135b', *Mitteilungen des Max-Reger-Instituts* (1973), no.19, p.34

'Max Reger, einer der unseren', *Musica*, xxvii (1973), 130

ed.: *Sonderheft 1973 zu Max Regers Werk* (Wiesbaden, 1973)

Other articles on Reger in *Mitteilungen des Max-Reger-Instituts*

EDITIONS

M. Reger: *Orchesterwerke*, Sämtliche Werke, v (Wiesbaden, 1958); *Orchesterwerke*, ibid, iv (Wiesbaden, 1962); *Werke für Klavier und Streicher III*, *Werke für Klavier und Bläser*, ibid, xxi (Wiesbaden, 1968); *Sologesänge mit Orchester*, ibid, xxxv (Wiesbaden, 1970); *Streichtrio a-moll op.77b* (Wiesbaden, 1973) [facs. edn.]

BIBLIOGRAPHY

G. Massenkeil and S. Popp, eds.: *Festschrift für Ottmar Schreiber* (Wiesbaden, 1978)

HELMUT WIRTH

Schreider, Christopher. *See* SCHRIDER, CHRISTOPHER.

Schreier, Peter (*b* Meissen, 29 July 1935). German tenor. The son of a Kantor, he became a member of the Dresdner Kreuzchor under Rudolf Mauersberger in 1945, and studied privately with Polster in Leipzig and then with Winkler at the Dresden Musikhochschule from 1956 to 1959. In 1959 he joined the Dresden Staatsoper school and in 1961 made his début as the First Prisoner in *Fidelio*, then went as leading lyric tenor to the Berlin Staatsoper. He sang at Salzburg and the Metropolitan Opera (Tamino, 1967), La Scala and the Teatro Colón (1968), and then in most European centres, appearing regularly in Vienna, Salzburg and Munich in both opera and recitals. By the mid-1960s he was acclaimed as a lively, elegant and accomplished Mozart tenor. His best roles are perhaps Belmonte, Ottavio, Tamino and Ferrando, but he has also sung Fenton, Alfred (*Die Fledermaus*), Rossini's Almaviva, Des Grieux, the Simpleton (*Boris Godunov*), Strauss's Leukippos and Dancing-master, Loge, David, Lensky and the Physicist (Dessau's *Einstein*). In 1970 he made his conducting début with the Berlin Staatskapelle. Among his many honours and awards is the title Kammersänger. Schreier's seamless legato, distinctive tone and fastidious phrasing also make him a notable Evangelist in Bach's Passions; in lieder (especially in Schubert and Schumann) he displays his outstanding ability to shade his enunciation to express details of verbal and musical meaning; yet he never loses the simplicity and sense of proportion that make his art so appealing and distinguished. His extensive concert repertory includes works by Carissimi, Handel, Haydn, Beethoven, Berlioz, Mendelssohn and Orff, many of which he has recorded.

BIBLIOGRAPHY

G. Schmiedel: *Peter Schreier: für Sie porträtiert* (Leipzig, 1976)

Schreierpfeife [Schryari]. A loud straight capped shawm, mentioned by Praetorius (2/1619) and others. *See* WIND-CAP INSTRUMENTS.

Schreker, Franz (*b* Monaco, 23 March 1878; *d* Berlin, 21 March 1934). Austrian composer, teacher and conductor.

1. LIFE. From 1892 to 1900 he studied the violin and composition at the Vienna Conservatory; his composition teacher was Robert Fuchs. His first work to receive a public performance was a piece for string orchestra and harp, *Love Song*, which the orchestra of the Budapest Opera performed in London in July 1896; the manuscript is lost. On 10 July 1900 his *Abiturienarbeit*, a setting for female chorus and orchestra of Psalm cxvi, was performed at the conservatory. It attracted attention and was repeated the following year under Loewe in the Gesellschaftskonzerten. In April 1902 a one-act opera, *Flammen*, was performed in the Bösendorfersaal with the composer playing the orchestral accompaniment on the piano. An Intermezzo for string orchestra was awarded first prize in a competition organized by the Neue Musikalische Presse and received a performance in the Musikverein under Loewe in December 1902. The composition of the opera *Der ferne Klang* was probably begun in or around 1901. At any rate, Acts 1 and 2 were complete in 1903, when, disheartened by the unsympathetic attitude of most of his friends to the libretto, Schreker temporarily abandoned the opera.

In 1908 Schreker's music had its first great success when his ballet *Der Geburtstag der Infantin* was danced by Grete Wiesenthal at the opening of the Kunstschau of the Vienna Secession. In the same year Schreker founded the Philharmonic Choir, which he conducted until 1920 and which was responsible for bringing to performance many modern works, notably Schoenberg's *Gurrelieder*. On 25 November 1909 a successful performance of the Act 3 interlude, or 'Nachtstück', for the as yet unfinished *Der ferne Klang* (by the Wiener Tonkünstlerorchester under Oskar Nedbal) encouraged Schreker to complete the opera. After many difficulties and disappointments *Der ferne Klang* was first performed on 18 August 1912 in Frankfurt am Main under Ludwig Rottenberg; its success immediately established Schreker as one of the leading progressive composers in Germany. On the strength of his growing reputation he was appointed in 1912 to a teaching post in composition at the Music Academy in Vienna.

Schreker's next opera, *Das Spielwerk und die Prinzessin*, was not to enjoy the success accorded its predecessor. With the exception of *Flammen*, it was the only one of Schreker's operas to receive its première in Vienna, at the Hofoper on 15 March 1913, where it caused a scandal; even in Frankfurt am Main, where its first performance took place concurrently, it scored only a moderate success. However, the tremendous acclaim that greeted the operas which followed, *Die Gezeichneten* (25 April 1918, Frankfurt am Main) and especially *Der Schatzgräber* (21 January 1920, Frankfurt am Main), ensured Schreker's pre-eminence among German opera composers.

In 1920 Schreker accepted the directorship of the Berlin Hochschule für Musik, and moved to Berlin, where he was to remain for the rest of his life. For about the next ten years his fame was at its peak. This, however, was due more to his position of prestige at the head of the most important music school in Germany than to his later operas, which never achieved the success of his works up to and including *Der Schatzgräber*. As a Jew

he came under attack in his last years. In 1931 he felt obliged, under threat of Nazi demonstrations, to cancel the première of his seventh opera, *Christophorus*; that of his final opera, *Der Schmied von Gent* (29 October 1932, Berlin), was marred by such demonstrations. In 1932 he was forced to resign from the directorship of the Hochschule; he took over a master class in composition at the Prussian Academy of Arts, from which he was dismissed at the end of 1933. The shock of this event caused a severe heart attack, from which he never recovered.

2. WORKS. Of the three operas on which Schreker's reputation may be said to rest, the first, *Der ferne Klang*, is in many ways the most radical. Its most remarkable characteristic is an almost complete absence of Wagnerian or Straussian influence, apart from the predictable use of the leitmotif technique. The chief influence is that of French impressionism, but even this is put to very individual uses. Apart from a few sections, harmony is entirely non-functional and colouristic. Opposing harmonic complexes are mixed and tonality is often highly ambiguous. In matters of orchestration, *Der ferne Klang* revealed Schreker as a master of every orchestral nuance, from large tuttis to the most delicate chamber effects.

Die Gezeichneten and *Der Schatzgräber* represent a retreat from the more extreme experimentalism of *Der ferne Klang*. A strong Wagnerian element enters the harmonic language, and *Der Schatzgräber* in particular achieves a perfect balance between 'conservative' and 'progressive' elements. Schreker's next opera, *Irrelohe* (1923), is a turning-point in his development. The Wagnerian features of its two predecessors are largely discarded and the 'progressive' characteristics of *Der ferne Klang* and *Das Spielwerk und die Prinzessin* are developed with redoubled vigour. Bitonality and polytonality occur frequently, linear counterpoint is increasingly important, and the resulting harmonic language is of extreme acidity. To a greater extent than its predecessors, *Irrelohe* reveals Schreker as the heir to the more experimental passages in Strauss's *Salome* and *Elektra*.

From *Irrelohe* onwards Schreker turned more and more to the neo-classical ideal. *Der Schmied von Gent* (1932), his final opera, with its harshly dissonant linear counterpoint and its preoccupation with established forms, such as fugue and passacaglia, is far from the sultry eroticism of the earlier works and represents the pathetic attempt of an essentially Romantic composer to write in an up-to-date style to which he was utterly unsuited.

It was Schreker's misfortune to die when his reputation was already declining; the Nazi 'dark age' destroyed that reputation for good. However, *Der Schatzgräber* deserves to live. At all events, Schreker's name will survive through his influence on Alban Berg, who in 1911 made the vocal score of *Der ferne Klang*. Act 2 of Schreker's opera, with its skilful dovetailing of onstage instrumental groups with the main orchestra, was undoubtedly one of the chief progenitors of Act 2 scene iv of *Wozzeck*; the symphonic form of Berg's Act 2 may well have been inspired by the admittedly much looser symphonic structure latent in Act 2 of *Der ferne Klang*.

WORKS

STAGE

Flammen (opera, 1, D. Leen), *c*1900, op.10; concert perf. Vienna, Bösendorfersaal, 24 April 1902

Der Geburtstag der Infantin (pantomime, Schreker, after O. Wilde), str orch, 1908; Vienna, Aug 1908
Der Wind (Tanzallegorie), cl, pf qt, 1908, unpubd
Rokoko (ballet), 1908; rev. as Ein Tanzspiel, 1920
Der ferne Klang (opera, 3, Schreker), c1901–1910; Frankfurt am Main, 18 Aug 1912
Das Spielwerk und die Prinzessin (opera, prol, 2, Schreker), 1909–12; Frankfurt am Main and Vienna, Hofoper, 15 March 1913; rev. in 1 act as Das Spielwerk, 1916, Munich, National, 30 Oct 1920
Die Gezeichneten (opera, 3, Schreker), 1913–15; Frankfurt am Main, 25 April 1918
Der Schatzgräber (opera, prol, 4, epilogue, Schreker), 1915–18; Frankfurt am Main, 21 Jan 1920
Irrelohe (opera, 3, Schreker), 1919–23; Cologne, 27 March 1924
Christophorus, oder Die Vision einer Oper (opera, prol, 2, epilogue, Schreker), 1924–7; unperf.
Der singende Teufel (opera, 4, Schreker), 1924–8; Berlin, Staatsoper, 10 Dec 1928
Der Schmied von Gent (opera, 3, Schreker, after de Coster), 1929–32; Berlin, Deutsches Opernhaus, 29 Oct 1932

ORCHESTRAL

Love Song, str, harp, 1895, unpubd, lost
Intermezzo, op.8, str, 1900; incl. in Romantische Suite
Romantische Suite, 1902, unpubd
Ekkehard, op.12, sym. ov., after V. von Scheffel, 1902
Phantastische Ouvertüre, 1902, unpubd
Festwalzer und Walzerintermezzo, 1908, unpubd
Vorspiel zu einem Drama, 1914; abridged as prelude to Die Gezeichneten
Chamber Symphony, 23 insts, 1916
Suite from 'Der Geburtstag der Infantin', full orch, 1923
Kleine Suite, chamber orch, 1928
Four Little Pieces, 1930
Vorspiel zu einer grossen Oper [for uncomposed 'Memnon'], 1933, unpubd

VOCAL ORCHESTRAL

Der Holdestein (R. Baumbach), S, B, chorus, orch, before 1899, unpubd
Psalm cxvi, op.6, female 3vv, orch, org, 1900
Schwanengesang, op.11 (Leen), chorus, orch, 1902
Fünf Gesänge, A/B, chorus, orch, after 1920 [after song cycle of 1909]
Vom ewigen Leben, 1v, orch, 1927 [after Zwei lyrische Gesänge]
Das Weib des Intaphernes (E. Stucken), speaker, orch, 1930, unpubd

SONGS

Zwei Gesänge, op.2, 1v, pf, before 1899: Sommerfäden (Leen); Stimmen des Tages (Saar)
Fünf Lieder, op.3 (Heyse), 1v, pf, before 1899: In alten, alten Tagen; Im Lenz; Das Glück; Es kommen Blätter; Umsonst
Fünf Lieder, op.4, 1v, pf, before 1899: Unendliche Liebe (Tolstoy); Frühling (Lemayer); Wohl fühl' ich wie das Leben rinnt (Storm); Die Liebe als Recensentin (Sturm), Lenzzauber (Scherenberg)
Zwei Lieder auf den Tod eines Kindes, op.5 (M. Holm), 1v, pf, 1895: O Glocken, böse Glocken; Dass er ganz ein Engel werde
Acht Lieder, 1v, pf, 1898–1900: Wiegenliedchen (Sturm); Späte Reue (Sturm); Traum (Leen); Spuk (Leen); Rosentod (Leen); Ach, noch so jung (Scherenberg); Rosengruss (Scherenberg); Lied des Harfenmädchens (Storm)
Ave Maria, 1v, org, 1902
Entführung (George), 1v, pf, ? 1902
Fünf Gesänge, A/B, pf, 1909: Ich frag' nach dir jedwede Morgensonne (1001 Nights); Dies aber kann mein Sehnen nimmer fassen (E. Ronsperger); Die Dunkelheit sinkt schwer wie Blei (Ronsperger); Sie sind so schön, die milden, sonnenreichen (Ronsperger); Einst gibt ein Tag mir alles Glück zu eigen (Ronsperger)
Zwei lyrische Gesänge (Whitman), 1v, pf, 1924: Wurzeln und Halme sind dies nur; Ein Kind sagte: 'Was ist das Gras?'

OTHER WORKS

Unacc. choral: Versunken (Baumbach), male vv, before 1899, unpubd; Schlehenblüte (Baumbach), male vv, before 1899, unpubd; Auf dem Gottesacker, motet, before 1899, unpubd; Gesang der Armen in Winter (F. von Saar), c1902, unpubd
Inst: Sonata, vn, pf, 1897, unpubd; Zwei Walzerimpromptus, op.9, pf, c1900, unpubd; Adagio, pf, before 1902, unpubd; Melodie, pf, before 1902, unpubd

Principal publisher: Universal

BIBLIOGRAPHY

P. Bekker: Franz Schreker: Studie zur Kritik der modernen Oper (Berlin, 1919)
Musikblätter des Anbruch, ii/1–2 (1920) [special no.]
R. S. Hoffmann: Franz Schreker (Leipzig and Vienna, 1921)
J. Kapp: Franz Schreker: der Mann und sein Werk (Munich, 1921)
Musikblätter des Anbruch, vi/2 (1924) [special no.]
'Franz Schreker zum 50. Geburtstag', Musikblätter des Anbruch, x (1928), 81–118
Schreker-Heft (Berlin, 1959) [pubd by Internationale Franz-Schreker-Gesellschaft]
G. Neuwirth: Franz Schreker (Vienna, 1959)
H. Bures-Schreker: El caso Schreker (Buenos Aires, 1969; Ger. trans., rev., with contributions by H. H. Stuckenschmidt and W. Oehlmann, as Franz Schreker (1970)
G. Neuwirth: Die Harmonik in der Oper 'Der ferne Klang' von Franz Schreker (Regensburg, 1972)
N. Chadwick: 'Franz Schreker's Orchestral Style and its Influence on Alban Berg', MR, xxxv (1974), 29
S. Döhring: 'Franz Schreker und die grosse musiktheatralische Szene', Mf, xxvii (1974), 175
F. C. Heller, ed.: Arnold Schönberg – Franz Schreker: Briefwechsel (Tutzing, 1974)
Franz Schreker in seiner Zeit (Vienna, n.d.) [catalogue of A-Wn exhibition, 1974]
F. C. Heller, ed.: Der Franz-Schreker-Fonds in der Musiksammlung der Österreichischen Nationalbibliothek: Katalog (Vienna, 1975)
R. Blackburn: 'Franz Schreker, 1878–1934', MT, cxix (1978), 224
O. Kolleritsch, ed.: Franz Schreker am Beginn der neuen Musik, Studien zur Wertungsforschung, xi (Graz, 1978)

NICHOLAS CHADWICK

Schreyber, Heinrich. See GRAMMATEUS, HENRICUS.

Schreyer, Gregor (b Kirchenpingarten, nr. Bayreuth, c1720; d Andechs, nr. Munich, 6 June 1768). German composer. In 1740 he entered the Benedictine house at Andechs, one of the most musical German monasteries at the time, where he had ample opportunity to study music, and eventually became choirmaster. He may have spent some time at the monastery of St Emmeram in Regensburg in the early 1750s, but was certainly at Andechs as choirmaster in 1756, the year of his first publication.

Schreyer was one of many composers of church music in the mid-18th century, but unlike most of them he does not seem to have had the needs of the comparatively inexperienced parish choir in mind. The eight masses of his op.1, Jubilus musicus, for four voices, two violins, trumpets, drums and organ (Augsburg, 1756), apparently originally written for the 1000th anniversary celebrations at Andechs, are on a large scale; the Kyrie, Gloria and Credo are each treated as a succession of separate movements, often with difficult solo arias. Moreover, the six masses of Sacrificium matutinum for four voices, two violins and organ, op.2 (Augsburg, 1763), though described as 'breves', are with one exception on an almost equally large scale. His op.3, Sacrificium vespertinum, containing vesper psalms for four voices, two violins and organ, was published at Augsburg in 1766. Almost all Schreyer's arias contain much elaborate coloratura and are heavily ornamented; his violin parts are amongst the most complex to be found in contemporary published church music, making much use of multiple stopping and recurrent demisemiquaver figurations. For the most part, however, Schreyer's ability to devise elaborate vocal and instrumental figuration is not matched by his powers of musical invention, especially in contrapuntal choral movements; but he occasionally shows himself capable of expressive word-painting at appropriate points.

ELIZABETH ROCHE

Schrider [Schreider, Schröder], **Christopher** [Christoph] (buried St Anne's, Soho, London, 31 May 1751). English organ builder of German birth. He settled in London about 1700 and became foreman and son-in-law of Father Smith before the latter's death in February 1708, succeeding then to Smith's business and appointment as organ maker to the royal household.

He broadly followed Father Smith's style of organ building, and his excellent cases are easily recognizable as being in the same German tradition as Smith's later ones. His organs include those at: the Chapel Royal, St James's, London (1710; rebuilt by him in 1732–3); the Chapel Royal, Hampton Court Palace (1710–12; case and some pipework survive); Exeter Cathedral (1713; rebuild); St Mary, Whitechapel, London (1715); St Mary Abbots, Kensington (1716); St Mary the Virgin, Finedon, Northamptonshire (1717; ascribed to Schrider by G. M. Holdich, but to Gerard Smith by Rimbault: twice rebuilt, case and some pipework survive); St Martin-in-the-Fields, London (1724–5; gift from King George I; the organ had pedals; it was moved to Wotton-under-Edge, Gloucestershire, in 1799 where it was given three manuals, and was rebuilt in 1937 with high wind pressure and tubular pneumatic action; said still to contain some original pipework); Westminster Abbey, London (1727–30; his masterpiece, built jointly with Abraham Jordan for the coronation of George II in 1727 and presented by the king to the Abbey where it was opened on 1 August by John Robinson); Henry VII's Chapel, Westminster Abbey (1737; built for the funeral of Queen Caroline, 17 December); St Mary Magdalen, Bermondsey, London (1751; compass Swell added in 1850–51 by J. W. Walker; case survives, and possibly some pipes in Great; rebuilt 1954); Kilkhampton Church, Cornwall (pipework survives; renovated 1958); and St Alkmund's, Whitchurch, Shropshire (case and some pipework survive). Schrider's son Christopher (b ?London; d ?London, 16 Oct 1763), also an organ builder, succeeded his father as organ maker to the king.

BIBLIOGRAPHY
E. J. Hopkins and E. F. Rimbault: The Organ: its History and Construction (London, 1855, 3/1887)
A. Freeman: 'The Organs . . . of St. Martin-in-the-Fields', The Organ, i (1921–2), 1
——: 'The Organs of St. James's Palace', The Organ, iv (1924–5), 194
E. G. Caple: 'The Schrider Organ at Wotton-under-Edge', The Organ, xviii (1938–9), 236

GUY OLDHAM

Schritt (Ger.). STEP.

Schröder. German family of musicians.

(1) Karl Schröder (i) (b Oberbosa, Thuringia, 17 March 1816; d Berlin, 21 April 1890). Violinist and violist. He studied at the Eisleben training college with G. Siebeck and A. B. Marx, becoming first a town musician at Quedlinburg and then music director at Neuhaldensleben. He played the viola until 1866 in the family quartet which included (2) Hermann Schröder, Franz and (3) Karl Schröder (ii).

(2) Hermann Schröder (b Quedlinburg, 28 July 1843; d Berlin, 30 or 31 Jan 1909). Violinist and teacher, son of (1) Karl Schröder (i). He studied music first with his father, then at Magdeburg with W. Sommer and A. G. Ritter. In 1873 he opened a music school in Berlin which he continued to direct after his appointment as violin and harmony teacher at the Institut für Kirchenmusik (1885), of which he later became assistant director. He wrote chamber music for didactic purposes and small works for orchestra; he also published several essays on the physics and aesthetics of sound and a Kunst des Violin-Spiels (Leipzig, 1887).

(3) Karl Schröder (ii) [Carl Schroeder] (b Quedlinburg, 18 Dec 1848; d Bremen, 22 Sept 1935).

Cellist, composer and conductor, son of (1) Karl Schröder (i). He studied with his father, with Karl Drechsler in Dessau and later with Friedrich Kiel and was only 14 when he was appointed to the Sondershausen Hofkapelle. With the family quartet he toured Europe, from Paris to St Petersburg, acquiring a high reputation. In 1872 he was Kapellmeister of the Kroll Opera in Berlin; the quartet was disbanded on his appointment to the Brunswick Hofkapelle in 1873. A year later he became solo cellist of the Leipzig Gewandhaus Orchestra and professor at the conservatory. He returned to Sondershausen in 1881, replacing Max Erdmannsdörffer as Hofkapellmeister and founding a music school; this he sold to A. Schultze in 1886 when he was appointed conductor of the German Opera in Rotterdam. He held similar posts in Berlin (1887) and in Hamburg (1888), where he succeeded Joseph Sucher at the city theatre. His former music school having become a state conservatory, he returned to Sondershausen in 1890 as its director, remaining until 1909. In 1911 he took up his last post, as professor at the Stern Conservatory in Berlin, where he remained for more than a decade before retiring to Bremen. In addition to his compositions and educational works he produced careful editions of Classical cello pieces.

WORKS
Stage and instrumental: 2 operas, 3 syms., 6 vc concs., 2 str qts, Str Trio; numerous didactic works, incl. 2 sets of vc studies
Pedagogical: Führer durch den Violoncell-Unterricht (Leipzig, 1880), Katechismus des Dirigierens (Leipzig, 1889), Katechismus des Violoncell-Spiels (Leipzig, 1890), Katechismus des Violin-Spiels (Leipzig, 1899)

(4) Alwin Schröder (b Neuhaldensleben, Saxony, 15 June 1855; d Boston, 17 Oct 1928). Violist and cellist, son of (1) Karl Schröder (i). He studied the piano with his father and the violin with his brother (2) Hermann Schröder from the age of seven; later he studied at the Berlin Hochschule für Musik with Heinrich de Ahna and Wilhelm Tappert; he was only 11 when he replaced his father as violist in the family quartet. On its dissolution in 1872 he joined Karl Liebig's orchestra. Encouraged by his brother (3) Karl Schröder (ii) he began teaching himself the cello, and when Liebig offered to renew his orchestral contract in 1875 Schröder accepted – with the proviso that he should be a cellist. Liebig suspected a joke, but an audition immediately convinced him and Schröder became principal cellist. After several years in Hamburg he went to Leipzig in 1880 as (2) Karl Schröder (ii)'s deputy, becoming joint principal with Julius Klengel at the Gewandhaus and teacher at the conservatory when his brother left the next year. Ten years later Alwin Schröder settled in Boston where he remained for the rest of his life (apart from short visits to Frankfurt am Main and Geneva) and became an American citizen. He joined the Boston SO, was for a time a member of the Kneisel and Hess quartets and acquired a distinguished reputation both as a performer and as a teacher. He edited Classical works for the cello and published some study material.

BIBLIOGRAPHY
G. Lutze: Die fürstliche Hofkapelle zu Sondershausen von 1801 bis 1901 (Sondershausen, 1901)
F. W. Beinroth: Musikgeschichte der Stadt Sondershausen (Innsbruck, 1943), 140ff

LYNDA LLOYD REES

Schröder, Christopher. See SCHRIDER, CHRISTOPHER.

Schröder, Friedrich (*b* Näfels, 6 Aug 1910). Swiss composer. He was educated at the universities of Münster and Berlin and at the Berlin Hochschule für Musik. From 1934 he was a conductor and arranger at the Metropol Theatre in Berlin, and began to make a name with popular songs, dances and film music. He achieved particular success with the operetta *Hochzeitsnacht in Paradies* (Berlin, 24 September 1942), which has remained a standard work in the German repertory. He was a freelance composer from 1945 and his later operettas include *Nächte in Schanghai* (Berlin, 1947), *Chanel Nr. 5* (1947), *Lucrezia in Stockholm* (Berlin, 1949), *Isabella* (Nuremberg, 1949) and *Das Bad auf der Tenne* (Nuremberg, 1955).

ANDREW LAMB

Schröder, Johannes (*d* Copenhagen, buried 25 Sept 1677). Danish organist and composer, possibly a son of Lorentz Schröder. He became organist of St Petri, the German church at Copenhagen, in 1647, and he was also court organist to King Frederik III. In 1664 he was made deputy director of court music and in *c*1667 he assumed the functions (though apparently not the title) of director abandoned by Kaspar Förster. Among his pupils was Johann Philipp Krieger. Schröder was greatly admired as both performer and composer, but *Adesto virtutum*, for four-part chorus, two violins and bass (at *S-Uu*) is the only piece by him known to survive.

BIBLIOGRAPHY
C. Thrane: *Fra Hofviolonernes Tid* (Copenhagen, 1908)
JOHN BERGSAGEL

Schröder, Lorentz (*d* Copenhagen, before 1647). Danish maker of keyboard instruments, writer on music and organist, of German origin. He was organist of the Helligaandskirken, Copenhagen, but greater interest attaches to his enterprise in two other connections. He established himself as a maker of keyboard instruments, for which in 1632 he received a royal privilege affording him the protection of King Christian IV against possible interference from the guild of master joiners. When this protection was reaffirmed in 1636 it was made clear that his privilege was limited to the making of keyboard instruments and that he was not to undertake other kinds of joinery: hence the making of keyboard instruments was recognized, apparently for the first time in Denmark, as an independent industry. Schröder was the author of *Ein nützliches Tractätlein vom Lobe Gottes, oder Der hertzerfrewenden Musica* (Copenhagen, 1639). This book is a defence of music, which, of the seven liberal arts, was the one that he considered was held in the lowest esteem by the general public in his day. A notable exception, however, was provided by Christian IV, to whom Schröder dedicated his book and of whose musical interests and accomplishments he gave some interesting details, for example that the king was competent personally to audition musicians seeking positions in his employ. He also praised his generosity as a patron of music: he described the lavish musical productions under the direction of Schütz that celebrated the marriage of Prince Christian of Denmark to Princess Magdalena Sibylla of Saxony in 1634. His observation that the lot of church musicians was better in Denmark than in Germany is also interesting.

BIBLIOGRAPHY
A. Hammerich: *Musikken ved Christian den Fjerdes Hof* (Copenhagen, 1892)
JOHN BERGSAGEL

Schröder-Devrient, Wilhelmine (*b* Hamburg, 6 Dec 1804; *d* Coburg, 26 Jan 1860). German soprano. She was the eldest of four children of the baritone Friedrich Schröder (1744–1816), the first German Don Giovanni, and the actress Sophie Schröder, née Bürger (1781–1868). As a child she appeared in ballet in Hamburg, and in Vienna (15 March 1816). In Vienna she further appeared as Aricida in Schiller's *Phädra* (13 October 1819) and as Ophelia at the Hoftheater, being carefully schooled in movement and diction by her mother. She also studied singing with Giuseppe Mozatti. Her first operatic appearance was at the Kärntnertortheater as Pamina (20 January 1821), when the freshness and confidence of her singing made a great impression. She followed this up with Emmeline (Weigl's *Schweizerfamilie*) and Marie (Grétry's *Barbe Bleu*, in German as *Raoul Blaubart*), also singing Agathe on 7 March 1822 under Weber. However, her greatest triumph, and the performance that laid the foundations of her international fame, was as Leonore on 3 November 1822. Also in 1822 she first sang in Dresden, and in 1823 was given a two-year contract to sing at the Hoftheater: she remained associated with Dresden until 1847. There she also had further singing lessons with the chorus master Aloys Mieksch. She married the actor Karl Devrient (1797–1872); they had four children, including the actor Friedrich Devrient (1825–71), but the marriage was dissolved in 1828.

Schröder-Devrient impressed audiences everywhere with the dramatic power of her performances, especially as Donna Anna, Euryanthe, Reiza, Norma, Romeo, Valentine and Desdemona (in Rossini's *Otello*). She had an outstanding success in Berlin in 1828, though she offended Spontini by refusing to sing the title role of *La vestale*; she sang the part a year later in Dresden. In Weimar in 1830 she sang to Goethe, who wrote some lines in her praise. Travelling on to Paris, she triumphed in appearances with Röckel's Germany company (Agathe, 6 May; Leonore, 8 May). She returned to sing Italian opera in 1831 and 1832, appearing with Malibran in *Don Giovanni* and *Otello*. In 1832 she also appeared at the King's Theatre in London ten times monthly during May, June and July, in *Fidelio*, *Don Giovanni* and *Macbeth* (by the season's conductor, Chelard). In the following season she was heard in *Der Freischütz*, *Die Zauberflöte*, *Euryanthe* and *Otello*, less successfully owing to the rival attractions of Taglioni and Fanny Elssler. When, on the death of Malibran in 1836, the English press hailed her as the only artist to take Malibran's place, she was encouraged to return to London in 1837, and sing in *Fidelio*, *La sonnambula* and *Norma*. But her English was poor, her health was failing, and she was paid nothing since the company was found to be bankrupt.

From that time a decline in Schröder-Devrient's vocal powers was noticeable. She seemed tired of the stage and prone to mannerisms, including a tendency to drag the tempo and to declaim rather than sing. Many passing love affairs further dispirited her (the *Memoiren einer Sängerin* (Altona, 1861) attributed to her are a pornographic fabrication). Nevertheless, she continued to have successes in Germany, singing Adriano (*Rienzi*), Senta and Venus for the first time, also singing

Wilhelmine Schröder-Devrient: lithograph (1830) by Henri Grevedon

Gluck's Iphigenia (*Aulide*). Her last appearance was at Riga on 17 December 1847. Her second marriage was to a Saxon officer, Von Döring, with whom she visited St Petersburg and Copenhagen, and who embezzled her earnings. The marriage was dissolved, and in 1850 she married a Livonian baron, Von Bock, who took her to his estate at Trikaten. Having returned to Dresden she was arrested for the sympathy she had publicly expressed with the 1848 revolution; she was banned by a Berlin court from returning to Saxony, and also from re-entering Russia. With difficulty her husband succeeded in overturning these sentences. Her last known concerts were in Germany in 1856.

All accounts agree on the dramatic powers of 'The Queen of Tears', as Schröder-Devrient was dubbed when observed actually to be weeping on stage. In an age when few singers matched their vocal prowess with equal dramatic skill, she impressed audiences especially with her interpretation of Leonore. In this role, Moscheles preferred her to Malibran, and many reports give details of the dramatic effect of her performance. Beethoven, who had rehearsed her, thanked her personally, and promised to write an opera for her. According to Eduard Genast, whose wife accompanied her, she persuaded Goethe of the merits of Schubert's setting of his *Erlkönig* when a poor performance had previously caused him to dismiss it. Weber thought her the best of all Agathes, and to have disclosed more in the part than he had believed was there; however, on hearing her sing Leonore in 1822 he discerned the deficiencies that later (1842) disturbed Berlioz, who deplored her exaggerated acting, her vehement declamation and her failures of style. According to Chorley, 'Her voice was a strong soprano . . . with an inherent expressiveness of tone which made it more attractive on the stage than many a more faultless organ. . . . Her tones were delivered without any care, save to give them due force. Her execution was bad and heavy'. However, he praised her as a marvellous actress, even though she exaggerated her characterization as time went on. It was her Leonore that roused the 16-year-old Wagner to his sense of vocation as a dramatic composer, as he recounted in *Mein Leben*. He dedicated *Über Schauspieler und Sänger* to her memory, and in it gave a moving and detailed critical evaluation of her art, observing that she sang 'more with the soul than with the voice'. Schumann wrote 'Ich grolle nicht' for her; he called her singing of it 'nobly projected' and declared that she was the only singer who could survive with Liszt as an accompanist. Her vocal deficiencies were partly due to erratic training, initially under her mother and insufficiently pursued under other teachers; her inspiration as a singing actress who brought new dramatic powers to the art of opera was influential on the course of German Romantic opera.

BIBLIOGRAPHY
L. Rellstab: 'Wilhelmine Schröder-Devrient', *Gesammelte Schriften*, ix (Leipzig, 1844)

H. Chorley: *Modern German Music* (London, 1854)

——: *Thirty Years' Musical Recollections* (London, 1862, 2/1926, ed. E. Newman)

E. Genast: *Aus dem Tagebuch eines alten Schauspielers* (Leipzig, 1862–6)

C. von Glümer: *Erinnerungen an Wilhelmine Schröder-Devrient* (Leipzig, 1862, 3/1905)

A. von Wolzogen: *Wilhelmine Schröder-Devrient* (Leipzig, 1863)

H. Berlioz: *Mémoires* (Paris, 1870; Eng. trans., 1969)

R. Wagner: 'Über Schauspieler und Sänger', *Gesammelte Schriften*, ix (Leipzig, 1873; Eng. trans., v, 1896)

G. Bonacci: 'Guglielmina Schröder-Devrient e Gasparo Spontini', *Nuova antologia*, no.106 (1903), 306

L. Eisenberg: *Grosses biographisches Lexicon der deutschen Bühne im XIX. Jahrhundert* (Leipzig, 1903)

C. Hagemann: *Wilhelmine Schröder-Devrient* (Berlin, 1904, 2/1947)

J. Bab: *Die Devrients* (Berlin, 1932)

M. Gregor-Dellin, ed.: *Richard Wagner: Mein Leben* (Munich, 1963)

JOHN WARRACK

Schröder-Feinen, Ursula (*b* Gelsenkirchen, 21 July 1936). German soprano. She studied in Gelsenkirchen with Maria Helm, and joined the opera chorus there in 1958. She made her solo début in operetta in 1961, and took the title role in *Aida* later that year. Her repertory at Gelsenkirchen included Handel's Cleopatra, Beethoven's Leonore, Oscar, Chrysothemis, Salome, Turandot and Gershwin's Bess. From 1968 to 1972 she was engaged at the Deutsche Oper am Rhein, Düsseldorf, adding Electra, Kundry and Brünnhilde to her repertory. She has sung at the Metropolitan Opera from 1970, at Bayreuth (as Senta, Ortrud, Kundry and Brünnhilde) from 1971, and at Salzburg (as the Dyer's Wife and Ortrud) from 1975, the year of her British début as Salome at the Edinburgh Festival. Schröder-Feinen is one of the most exciting opera performers to have appeared in the late 1960s and early 1970s, a singer in the great German *hochdramatisch* tradition, with a voice and personality warmer than those of her Scandinavian predecessors in the Wagner and Strauss repertories.

HAROLD ROSENTHAL

Schroeder. *See* SCHRÖTER family.

Schroeder, Hermann (*b* Bernkastel, 26 March 1904). German composer, teacher, organist and choirmaster. On his mother's side he has common ancestry with Beethoven (Hans Peter Schetter, *b* Traben on the

Moselle, 1623, and his wife Eva, née Jonas, who was christened in Cologne in 1625). He studied at the Cologne Musikhochschule (1926–30); teachers who influenced him particularly were Heinrich Lemacher and Walter Braunfels (composition), Hermann Abendroth (conducting) and Hans Bachem (organ). He was a teacher of theory at the Rheinische Musikschule in Cologne (1930–38), was cathedral organist in Trier (1938–45) and from 1940 he was director of the Trier School of Music. In 1946 he started to teach theory at the Cologne Musikhochschule (he became a professor in 1948). Schroeder was also reader at Bonn University (1946–73) and a lecturer at the University of Cologne (1956–61). He was director of Cologne's Bach Society (1947–62) and deputy director of the Cologne Musikhochschule (1958–61). In 1952 he was awarded the Robert Schumann Prize of the City of Düsseldorf, and in 1956 he received an Arts Prize from the state of Rheinland-Pfalz.

Schroeder's importance as a composer is in the sphere of Catholic church music, which he did much to reform. By combining stylistic techniques from the Middle Ages (fauxbourdon, Gregorian modes, etc) and 20th-century polyphony, he did much to break the monopoly of Romantic music in the Catholic Church. The linear, atonal writing of his chamber music has much in common with that of Hindemith. With Heinrich Lemacher, Schroeder has written several textbooks which have gained wide currency in German-speaking countries.

WORKS
(selective list)

SACRED CHORAL
(mixed chorus except where otherwise stated)

Mass, 1927; Mass, 1930; Mass, c, male chorus, 1931; Missa dorica, 1932; Missa brevis, 1935; Missa simplex, male chorus, 1936, rev. mixed chorus, 1957; Pauliner Orgelmesse, 1945; Missa 'Regina caeli', chorus, org, 1950; Requiem, 1952; Marienmesse, female chorus, org ad lib, 1952; Missa psalmodica, 1953; Missa coloniensis, chorus, org, 1954; Missa ambrosiana, 3vv, 1957; Missa gregoriana, 1957 Missa 'Lux et origo', female chorus, 1958; Missa figuralis, chorus, insts, org, 1959; Missa eucharistica, 3vv, 1961; Missa melismatica, 1961; Missa syllabica, 1962; Ordinarium X, chorus, org, 1965; Deutsches Ordinarium, chorus, org, 1965; St Caecilia Mass, chorus, orch, org, 1966; Deutsches Ordinarium no.2, chorus, org, 1966; Lateinisches Ordinarium 1967
Johannes-Passion, 1964; Matthäus-Passion, 1965; many Latin motets; German motets and cantatas

OTHER WORKS
Conc. for str orch, op.23, 1937; vc, op.24, 1937; org, op.25, 1938; ob, op.34, 1955; pf, op.35, 1955; vn, 1956; fl, op.37, 1958; 2 vn, op.41, 1965; va, op.45, 1973; cl, op.47, 1974
Str Trio, e, op.14/1, 1933; Str Qt no.1, c, op.26, 1939; Str Trio, g, op.14/2, 1942; Str Qt no.2, op.30, 1952; Pf Trio no.1, op.33, 1954; Sextet, op.36, pf, wind qnt, 1957; Qt no.3, op.38, ob, vn, va, vc, 1959; Pf Trio no.2, op.40, hn, vn, pf, 1964; Pf Trio no.3, op.43, cl, va, pf, 1967; Concertino, vn, ob, 1968; Conc., ob, org, 1972; Sextet, op.59, wind, 1975
Hero und Leander, opera, 1950
Many secular choral pieces and folksong arrangements
Solo and duo sonatas, pf and org music

Principal publishers: Schwann, Schott, Orbis, Gerig

BIBLIOGRAPHY
K. G. Fellerer: 'Das kirchenmusikalische Schaffen Hermann Schroeders', *Musik und Altar*, vi (1953–4), 66
H. Lemacher: 'Hermann Schroeder 50 Jahre', *Musica sacra*, lxxiv (1954), 110
——: 'Schroeder, Hermann', *Rheinische Musiker*, ii, ed. K. G. Fellerer (Cologne, 1962)
——: 'Schroeder, Hermann', *MGG*
R. Keusen: *Die Orgel- und Vokalwerke Hermann Schroeders* (diss., U. of Bonn, 1972)

RUDOLF LÜCK

Schroeter. See SCHRÖTER family.

Schroeter, Leonhard (*b* Torgau, *c*1532; *d* Magdeburg, *c*1601). German composer. In about 1538 or 1539 he was at school in Torgau where Johannes Walter, a colleague of his father, was one of his teachers. Afterwards he attended school in Annaberg in Erzgebirge until 1545, and then, for at least two years, the ducal school in Meissen. From 1561 (at the latest) to 1576 he was town Kantor in Saalfeld (Thuringia) except for a period of two years between 1571 and 1573 when he was dismissed from his post on account of his sympathy with the Philippists (supporters of the doctrines of Melanchthon), who were not considered sufficiently strict Lutherans. During this period he was librarian at the Wolfenbüttel court. From his first years at Saalfeld he was associated in Mühlhausen with Ludwig Helmbold, probably the most important Protestant poet of his day. Schroeter was Kantor at the Alstadt Lateinschule in Magdeburg from 1576 to 1595, a highly regarded position in view of such eminent predecessors as Martin Agricola and Gallus Dressler.

Schroeter continued the Magdeburg academic tradition representative of mid-German Lutheranism. (This tradition came to an end with Heinrich Grimm in 1631 when Magdeburg was destroyed.) His works comprise mainly chorale settings, both of the traditional type reminiscent of the Reformation polyphonic style (especially in the *Hymni sacri*), and some of a more homophonic variety with closer alliance between music and text. The almost entirely homophonic chorale settings for eight-voice double choir are exceptional. His few psalm settings make an important contribution to the early Protestant motet; an example such as Psalm cxxvii for double choir shows the influence of the Venetian polychoral style.

WORKS
55 geistliche Lieder, 4vv (Wittenberg, 1562) [title-page missing]
Cantiones suavissimae, 4vv, tomus 1 (Erfurt, 1576²)
Der schöne Lobgesang Te Deum laudamus durch D Martin Luther verdeutscht, 8vv (Magdeburg, 1576); ed. O. Kade in A. W. Ambros: *Geschichte der Musik*, v (Leipzig, rev. 3/1911)
Der 12. und 124. Psalm Davids, 4vv (Magdeburg, 1576)
Ein Hochzeitgesang . . . zu Ehren . . . Galli Dressleri, 5vv (Magdeburg, 1577)
Cantiones suavissimae, 4vv, tomus 2 (Erfurt, 1580²)
Canticum sanctorum Ambrosii et Augustini Te Deum laudamus, 8vv, inc. (Magdeburg, 1584)
Newe Weinachtsliedlein, 4, 8vv (Helmstedt, 1586–7); ed. B. Engelke (Leipzig, 1914, 3/1953)
Epithalamii cantilena . . . in honorem nuptiarum . . . Melchioris Papae, 10vv (Magdeburg, 1587)
Hymni sacri, 4–6vv (Erfurt, 1587); 2 ed. Antiqua Chorbuch, i/2 (Mainz, 1951–2), 3 ed. von Winterfeld
Drey Weinachten Lieder (n.p., 1595)
Symbola, lost
6 school songs in Tobias: eine schöne tröstliche Comoedia . . . durch G. Rollenhagen (Magdeburg, 1576); ed. R. von Liliencron, *VMw*, vi (1890), 377
Homo quidam erat dives, 5vv, 1583²⁴
Psalm cxxvii, 8vv, *D-Z*; ed. in Chorarchiv, i (Kassel, 1933, 3/1953)
Sacred works in *A-Wgm, D-Bds, Dlb, Z*

BIBLIOGRAPHY
C. von Winterfeld: *Der evangelische Kirchengesang* (Leipzig 1843–7/R1966) [incl. edn. of 3 hymni sacri]
G. Hofmann: *Leonhart Schroeter: ein lutherischer Kantor zu Magdeburg* (diss., U. of Freiburg, 1932)
——: 'Die freien Kompositionen L. Schroeters', *ZMw*, xvi (1934), 344
O. Riemer: *Musik und Musiker in Magdeburg* (Magdeburg, 1937)
M. Geck: 'Schröter, Leonhart', *MGG*
H. Haase: *Der erste herzogliche Bibliothekar: ein Musiker: Bemerkungen über den Kantor und Komponisten Leonhart Schröter*, Wolfenbütteler Beiträge aus den Schätzen der Herzog August Bibliothek, i (Frankfurt am Main, 1972)

WALTER BLANKENBURG

Schröter [Schroeter, Schroeder]. German family of musicians.

(1) Johann Friedrich Schröter (*b* Eilenburg, 1724; *d* Kassel, 1811). Oboist and teacher. He was an oboist in Count Brühl's regiment when he married at Guben in 1748. The family moved first to Warsaw (*c*1755) and then to Leipzig (*c*1763). His wife died shortly after the birth of their youngest daughter in 1766, but he spared no effort in the development and advancement of his musically gifted children. They all appeared in Leipzig concerts and from 1771 he took them on extended tours to Germany, the Netherlands and England, where the three eldest children appeared in the Bach–Abel concerts on 2 May 1772. His only known publication, six duets for violin and cello, appeared in London about 1772. The family returned to Leipzig in 1773 or 1774. He was subsequently a court musician and teacher at Hanau (1779–86) and Kassel, where he long remained as a pensioner.

(2) Corona Elisabeth Wilhelmine Schröter (*b* Guben, 14 Jan 1751; *d* Ilmenau, 23 Aug 1802). Singer, actress and composer, daughter of (1) Johann Friedrich Schröter. Her earliest instruction was from her father; she studied various instruments, including keyboard and guitar, but she was most successful as a singer. At Leipzig she continued her studies with J. A. Hiller (whose wife was probably her godmother) and from 1765 she appeared in Hiller's Grand Concerts. She became the darling of Leipzig musical audiences, although she shared the limelight with Gertrud Schmeling (later Mme Mara) until 1771. Schröter's voice lacked the strength and Italianate agility of her rival but the purity of sound and her delivery gave her the advantage in the eyes of many admirers. One of these, the young Goethe, summed up her remarkable effect in these terms: 'Because of her beautiful figure, her completely exemplary conduct, and her earnest, graceful delivery, she evoked a general empathy which expressed itself, depending on the individual, in varying degrees of love, respect or adoration'. She was particularly effective in the performance of Hasse's oratorios, according to the momentarily infatuated J. F. Reichardt, among others. After her family returned from London (*c*1774) she became ever more prominent in Leipzig musical circles but also gained acclaim as an actress in amateur theatricals. In 1776 Goethe met her again and arranged her appointment as chamber musician to the Weimar court of Duchess Anna Amalia, where she first performed on 23 November of that year. While she continued to sing at court concerts, she also created many of the leading roles of Goethe's early dramas, often playing opposite the author himself in the amateur court theatre. One of her most heralded portrayals was the title role in *Iphigenia* (1779). In the theatre as in the concert hall Schröter gained much applause because of her peculiar beauty and 'Attic' elegance. She not only created the title role in Goethe's Singspiel *Die Fischerin* (1782) but also composed music for it, including 'Der Erlkönig', which opened the play. This first setting of Goethe's famous ballad is simple, folklike and strophic, and (unlike Schubert's later setting) does not attempt to dramatize the poem's inherent dialogue (see ex.1). In his eulogy 'Auf Miedings Tod' (1782) for the deceased theatre director, Goethe simultaneously immortalized Schröter's great contribution to the Weimar stage and

Ex.1

Etwas langsam und abentheuerlich

Wer reit't so spät durch Nacht und Wind? Es ist der Va-ter mit sein-em Kind

implicitly acknowledged her impact on his own development in drama.

Some biographers place Corona Schröter in the Leipzig concert series again in 1782–4, but the 'Mlle Schröter' in question could plausibly be her young sister (5) Marie Schröter. Corona Schröter continued to sing and teach in Weimar after the court theatre was replaced by a professional company in 1783, but she also devoted herself to poetry, drawing and painting, for which she had a respectable talent. She withdrew from the court altogether by about 1788. During these years she formed a warm friendship with Schiller, some of whose poems she set. About 1801 she went to Ilmenau with her lifelong companion Wilhelmine Probst in the hopes of alleviating a respiratory disease, but she died the following year. Ten of her letters of 1774–1802 survive (in *D-WRgs*)

Schröter composed and published two collections of lieder, the first (including 'Der Erlkönig') in 1786, the second in 1794. The first reflects the strophic simplicity of the folksong revival, but is nevertheless regarded as more effective than the second, which contains more artistically elaborate works, including French and Italian songs. Several other vocal works, among them her settings of Schiller, are lost.

WORKS

Lieder: 25 Lieder in Musik gesetzt, 1v, pf (Weimar, 1786), ed. L. Schmidt (Leipzig, 1907) [facs. edn.]; [16] Gesänge, 1v, pf (Weimar, 1794)

Other vocal: music for Die Fischerin (Goethe), 1782, inc., *D-WRtl*, *WRdn*; further music for stage works, incl. Der Taucher and Die Würde der Frauen (Schiller), lost; anthology of 360 It. arias and duets, cited in *GerberNL*, lost; further single works in contemporary anthologies

(3) Johann Samuel Schroeter (*b* ?Guben, *c*1752; *d* London, 2 Nov 1788). Pianist and composer, brother of (2) Corona Schröter. He received his earliest musical instruction from his father, and studied under Hiller in Leipzig from about 1763. Early chroniclers suggested he studied under C. P. E. Bach, but there is no evidence to support this. He sang in Hiller's concerts until his voice broke, after which he appeared as a pianist (from 1767). When the rest of the family returned from London to Leipzig (*c*1774), Johann Samuel remained behind and published several collections of chamber music in rapid succession, including his opp.1–2, which had already appeared in Amsterdam. He served for some time as organist at the German Chapel in London and found a patron in the musical dilettante Count Brühl (with whom both the Schröter family and Hiller had had previous connections). His sonatas op.1 are dedicated to Brühl and may have served as models for the count's own published sonatas. Through the intervention of J. C. Bach, Schroeter gained the protection and interest of the English court, where he made a great impression. On Bach's death in 1782 he was promptly named music master to Queen Charlotte. His public career was cut short, however, when he eloped to Scotland with one of his students. Her wealthy family, apparently distraught by the marriage, settled a yearly allowance of £500 on Schroeter with the proviso that he abandon his career as a public performer. Nevertheless, he subsequently held an appointment with the Prince of Wales (later George IV), regularly performing in his semi-private concerts, as well as in occasional benefits or concerts of the nobility. Schroeter's health, apparently never robust, deteriorated rapidly so that he lost his voice altogether and died of a lung disease while still young. His widow, Rebecca Schroeter, later became a student and admirer of Haydn during his first London visit. Her affectionate letters were carefully kept by the composer, who dedicated his piano trios H XV:24–6 to her.

Schroeter's importance lies, Burney wrote, in his being 'the first who brought into England the true art of treating [the piano]' (*Rees's Cyclopaedia*). His playing was not without bravura, and he astounded audiences by the graceful ease with which he performed rapid passage-work. His impact was doubtless enhanced by his unique style of performance: 'His touch was extremely light and graceful so that just to watch him play became a pleasure in itself' (*Musikalisches Wochenblatt*). His compositions helped to popularize in England a natural 'singing-allegro' style and his concertos opp.3 and 5, which were among the earliest in England designed specifically for the piano, enjoyed particular success and influence. (Mozart was sufficiently impressed with op.3 to write cadenzas for three of them.) They seem to lack brilliance largely because of their modest ensemble and chamber character, as opposed to the expanded symphonic and dramatic concept of Mozart's works. However, significant affinities with Mozart's concerto style, notably in the handling of keyboard passages, have been traced (see Wolff).

WORKS

(all printed works published in London unless otherwise stated)

Inst (with hpd/pf unless otherwise stated): 6 kbd sonatas, op.1 (Amsterdam, ?1772); 6 sonatas, kbd, acc. vn, vc, op.2 (Amsterdam, ?1773); 12 kbd concs. with str, 6 as op.3 (c1774), as opp.4, 5 (Berlin and Amsterdam), 1 ed. K. Schultz-Hauser (Mainz, 1964), 6 as op.5 (c1777), as op.6 (Paris), as opp.7, 8 (Berlin and Amsterdam); 6 sonatas, kbd, fl/vn, op.4 (c1775), as op.6 (The Hague); 6 sonatas, kbd, vn, vc, op.8 (c1786), as opp.8, 9 (Paris and Mainz); Sonata, B♭, kbd, vn, vc (London, 1788), as op.11 (Paris); 2 sonatas, vn, pf, op.7 (Edinburgh, c1789); 2 qnts, kbd, ob/fl, str, in 3 Quintettos (c1778); La bataille fantasie, pf (Vienna, c1786), also as The Conquest of Belgrade (1789) and The Field of Battle (1797), doubtful

Vocal: 12 Favorite Scotch Songs, 1v, hpd, vn/fl (c1777), as Petits airs d'une exécution facile, arr. hpd, vn/fl ad lib, op.5 (Paris, 1777); Epithalamium, 1v, pf (c1785)

Kbd arrs.: L. Borghi: Vn Conc., 3 sonatas; J. C. Fischer: Ob Conc.; further arrs. of ovs., vocal qts etc

(4) (Johann) Heinrich Schröter (*b* Warsaw, c1760; *d* ?Paris, after 1782). Violinist and composer, brother of (2) Corona Schröter. He played a violin concerto by Dittersdorf in Leipzig in 1770, when his birth year may have been misrepresented by his father to make the prodigy's talents seem more impressive. After the family's successful concert tours he did not remain in London with (3) Johann Samuel Schroeter, contrary to some accounts. He went to Hanau with his father in 1779, and performed with his sister (5) Marie in

Frankfurt (1780) and Leipzig (1782). In the Leipzig concerts he also played the nail violin and is said to have toured France and Germany in the same year playing that instrument. He probably also visited his brother in London, as publications by him appeared there and in Paris before he mysteriously disappeared. In 1805 his aged father complained that he still did not know what had become of Heinrich. His only known compositions are six violin duets (London, c1772), six *Duo concertans* op.1 for two violins (Paris, c1785) and six string trios op.3 (London and Paris, c1786).

(5) Marie Henriette Schröter (*b* Leipzig, 1766; *d* ?Karlsruhe, after 1804). Singer, sister of (2) Corona Schröter. Trained by her father and (probably) J. A. Hiller, she appeared in concerts in Leipzig and with her brother (4) Heinrich Schröter in a concert in Frankfurt (1780). Although only 13 years old, she was included as a music teacher in her father's appointment to the Hanau court. She may have been the 'Mlle Schröter' who regularly sang in Hiller's Grand Concerts during 1782–4. She became a chamber singer to the Darmstadt court, where she married the court official J. J. Rühl in 1788. A letter from her sister Corona in 1794 (see Stümcke) suggests that Marie led a life of quiet domestic tranquillity, but she remained on the court rolls as a singer until 1804.

BIBLIOGRAPHY

EitnerQ; *FétisB*; *GerberL*; *GerberNL*

ABC dario musico (Bath, 1780)

Obituary [Johann Samuel Schroeter], *Gentleman's Magazine*, lviii (1788), 1030

'Nachrichten von Johann Samuel Schröter', *Musikalisches Wochenblatt*, xii (1791), 89 [? Eng. orig., C. Burney]

[C. Burney]: 'Schroeter, John Samuel', *Rees's Cyclopaedia* (London, 1819–20)

R. Keil: *Vor Hundert Jahren*, ii: *Corona Schröter: ein Lebenskizze mit Beiträgen zur Geschichte der Genie-Periode* (Leipzig, 1875)

H. Düntzer: *Charlotte von Stein und Corona Schröter: eine Vertheidigung* (Stuttgart, 1876)

A. Dörffel: *Geschichte der Gewandhausconcerte zu Leipzig* (Leipzig, 1884/R1972)

Mrs V. D. Broughton, ed.: *Court and Private Life in the Time of Queen Charlotte: being the Journals of Mrs Papendiek* (London, 1887)

H. M. Schletterer: 'Schröter, Corona Elise Wilhelmine', *ADB*

H. Burkhardt: 'Das Grabmal der Corona Schroeter in Ilmenau', *Volkslieder*, ed. M. Friedlaender (Ilmenau, 1902)

P. Pasig: *Goethe und Ilmenau mit einer Beigabe: Goethe und Corona Schroeter* (Ilmenau, 1902)

H. Stümcke: *Corona Schroeter* (Bielefeld, 1904, 2/1926)

L. Schmid: 'Nachwort', *25 Lieder* (Leipzig, 1907) [facs. of Corona Schröter's songs]

H. Holle: *Goethes Lyrik in Weisen deutscher Tonsetzer bis zur Gegenwart* (Munich, 1914)

E. Herrmann: *Das Weimarer Lied in der zweiten Hälfte des 18. Jahrhunderts* (diss., U. of Leipzig, 1925), 251ff

K. Wolff: 'Johann Samuel Schroeter', *MQ*, xliv (1958), 338

R. Kidd: *The Sonata for Keyboard with Violin Accompaniment in England: 1750–1790* (diss., Yale U., 1967), 241

RONALD R. KIDD

Schröter, Christoph Gottlieb (*b* Hohnstein, Saxony, 10 Aug 1699; *d* Nordhausen, 20 May 1782). German organist, composer and music theorist.

1. Life. 2. Writings. 3. Piano manufacture.

1. LIFE. After an early training in music from his father, he was sent in 1706 to nearby Dresden, where he joined the royal chapel as soprano and took keyboard lessons from the Kapellmeister, J. C. Schmidt. In 1709 ill-health forced him to live for a while with his godfather Hentschel in Bischofswerda. Returning to Dresden in 1710, on Schmidt's recommendation he was appointed, together with the slightly younger C. H. Graun, *Ratsdiskantist* (town discantist). With his change of

voice he enrolled as a student of the Kreuzschule, where according to his autobiography (see Marpurg) he studied, among other subjects, fugue with Schmidt. He did not say however with whom he studied the organ, although he reported practising on the instruments in the Kreuz- and Sophienkirchen as well as on an organ in the royal residence. In 1717 at his mother's wish he went to Leipzig to study theology, but after her death he returned in 1718 to Dresden, where Schmidt obtained for him the position of music copyist to Antonio Lotti. In 1719, as secretary and musical companion to an unidentified baron, he began five years of travel which took him to the Netherlands and England as well as to many German courts. In 1724 he went to Jena, where he volunteered to give lectures at the university on Mattheson's *Neu-eröffnete Orchestre* (Hamburg, 1713) and the mathematical basis of music theory, and form a collegium musicum: he was one of the first in Germany to reintroduce music to the university curriculum. He became organist at the principal church in Minden in 1726, and in 1732 accepted a similar position in Nordhausen. For the next 50 years he remained in this post, composed sacred music and wrote a large number of theoretical essays and books. In 1739 he was accepted as the fourth member of Mizler's Societät der musikalischen Wissenschaften, a Leipzig corresponding society of music scholars and composers which later included J. S. Bach, Handel and Telemann. On 23 August 1761 the French army occupied Nordhausen, plundered Schröter's home and destroyed his library: among the losses incurred were manuscripts of unpublished works much as a *Historie der Harmonie und Melodie* and the second volume of his thoroughbass treatise. None of Schröter's compositions was published, and practically none seems to survive: a considerable loss since in his autobiography he listed a quantity of works including five cantata cycles (to poetry by Neumeister, Rambach and Scheibel), four Passions, a *Sieben Worte Jesu*, instrumental serenades, concertos, sonatas, fugues etc.

2. WRITINGS. Schröter's most important work is the thoroughbass treatise, *Deutliche Anweisung zum General-Bass* (1772), which had been completed as early as 1754. It remains a valuable mid-18th-century source of information on thoroughbass practice (see Arnold) and is also a manual for composers; Schröter considered the triad as the source of all harmony, an adaptation of Rameau's theory of fundamental harmonies, which had a decisive impact on German theoretical writing after 1730. Like many of his contemporaries, Schröter wrote with a sarcastic, frequently bitter critical tone, and he delighted in attacking those he considered personal enemies or misguided theorists, like G. A. Sorge, who earlier had criticized his theory of equal temperament (which Sorge proved was actually 'unequal'). Schröter also joined the battle over Scheibe's criticism of J. S. Bach's musical style, and his least successful published essays are those (in Mizler's *Musikalische Bibliothek*) attempting to diminish the value of Scheibe's work, *Der critische Musikus*.

As a member of Mizler's corresponding society he contributed a large number of papers on theory to the *Musikalische Bibliothek*. In 1749, at the request of J. S. Bach (who clearly respected his judgment), he agreed to review for publication, under Bach's supervision, Rector Bidermann of Freiburg's *Programma de vita musica*,

which had attacked the use of music in church. Schröter's review appeared in a seriously altered form, and he condemned Bach for sanctioning the changes; but apparently they were made by the printer, not guided by the ailing Bach. Curiously, the Kantor and music director at Frankenhausen, G. F. Einike, who had been Bach's correspondent with Schröter, was credited by an unidentified Dresden reviewer as the author of the revised essay. Einike attempted to unravel this double embarrassment for himself and Bach in their relationship with Schröter by reporting the details of the entire affair in Mattheson's *Gespräche der Weisheit und Musik* (partly reprinted by David and Mendel).

3. PIANO MANUFACTURE. Schröter's letter of 1738 in Mizler's *Bibliothek* (1747, iii/3, 474ff) states that in 1717 he commissioned 'a model of a new keyboard instrument with hammers, partly with and partly without springs' to be built. In Marpurg's *Kritische Briefe* (iii, letters 139–41), he explained that this model of both an up-striking and a down-striking action was presented without result to the Dresden court in 1721 and never returned. This belated claim as the inventor of the piano has been negated by the earlier date of Cristofori's hammer action (of which he was apparently unaware), but he was possibly the first to arrive at the concept independently in Germany. One notable detail of Schröter's drawings in Marpurg, however, is the iron pressure bar serving as a top bridge across the strings, between the nut and the striking point, in both the up-striking action and the tangent action substituted for the less successful down-striking action. No instruments using Schröter's action survive; the illustrations in Harding are from working models in the Stuttgart Landesmuseum. Welcker von Gontershausen attributed to Schröter two actions that seem to have no relation to his drawings. Certain individual features of the up-striking model can be recognized in the pianos of Zumpe, Senft, J. M. Schmahl and Taskin, but evidence is lacking that these makers were directly influenced by Schröter, and there is no certain connection between his and Späth & Schmahl's tangent actions. Schröter himself attributed the difference between his actions and those of his 'second-rate imitators' to their imperfect understanding of his invention. He also invented a device that enabled organists to make sudden changes of dynamics, on manuals and pedals, without altering the registration.

WORKS

Choral-Buch [21 chorales with bc, 4 fugues, and 5 chorale preludes, org], *D-B*
5 cantata cycles to texts by Neumeister, Rambach, Scheibel; 4 Passions; Sieben Worte Jesu; serenades, concs., sonatas, fugues, etc: all lost, all listed in Schröter's autobiography

WRITINGS

Epistola gratulatoria de musica Davidica et Salomonica (Dresden, 1716)
Sendschreiben an Sr. Hoch Edlen, den Herrn Magister Lorenz Mizler, in welchem I. der bevorstehenden Reformation der Musik; II. einer aufgabe wegen der Temperatur; III. einiger nützlicher Erfindungen gedacht; und etliche nöthige Erinnerungen für de Tonkünstler so bescheiden als freymüthig eingeschaltet worden (Nordhausen, 1738); repr. in L. Mizler: *Musikalische Bibliothek*, iii/3 (Leipzig, 1747), 464
Poem in praise of Mizler in L. Mizler: *Musikalische Bibliothek*, i/4 (1738), 87 [under anagram Reschtore]
'Die Nothwendigkeit der Mathematik bey gründlicher Erlernung der musicalischen Composition' [review of J. A. Scheibe: *Der critische Musikus*], in L. Mizler: *Musikalische Bibliothek*, iii/2–3 (Leipzig, 1746–7), 201, 409
'Christliche Beurtheilung des von Herrn M. Bidermann', *Monat Mai des 1749. Jahres edirten Programmatis de vita musica* (n.p., 1749); repr. in J. Mattheson: *Gespräche der Weisheit und Musik . . . als die dritte*

Dosis der Panacea (Hamburg, 1751), 181
'Beurtheilung der zweyten Auflage des critischen Musici' [by Scheibe], in L. Mizler: *Musikalische Bibliothek*, iii/4 (Leipzig, 1752), 726
'Beurtheilung des neuen musikalischen Systems Herrn Telemanns, auf Verlangen aufgesetzet', in L. Mizler: *Musikalische Bibliothek*, iii/4 (Leipzig, 1752), 720
'Der musikalischen Intervallen Anzahl und Sitz', in L. Mizler: *Musikalische Bibliothek*, iii/4 (Leipzig, 1752), 685
'Sendschreiben an die Verfasser der kritischen Briefe', in F. W. Marpurg: *Kritische Briefe über die Tonkunst*, ii (Berlin, 1762), 417
'Herrn C. G. Schröters Bedenken über Herrn Sorges schmähend angefangenen Streit wider Herrn Marpurgs harmonischen Sätze', in F. W. Marpurg: *Kritische Briefe über die Tonkunst*, ii (Berlin, 1762), 448
'Christoph Gottlieb Schröter', in F. W. Marpurg: *Kritische Briefe über die Tonkunst*, ii (Berlin, 1762), 456 [autobiography and work-list]
'C. G. Schröters umständliche Beschreibung seines 1717 erfundenen Clavier-Instrument, auf welchem man stark und schwach spielen kann', in F. W. Marpurg: *Kritische Briefe über die Tonkunst*, iii (Berlin, 1763), 81
Deutliche Anweisung zum General-Bass, in beständiger Veränderung des uns angebohrnen harmonischen Dreyklanges (Halberstadt, 1772)
Christoph Gottlieb Schröters ... Letzte Beschäftigung mit musicalischen Dingen, nebst sechs Temperatur-Plänen und einer Noten-Tafel (Nordhausen, 1782)

LOST

Historie der Harmonie und Melodie [summary in preface to *Deutliche Anweisung zum General-Bass*]
Vom vollstimmigen und unbezifferten General-Bass [part ii of *Deutliche Anweisung zum General-Bass*]
Euclides von der Harmonie aus dem Griechischen übersetzen und mit Beispielen erläutert

BIBLIOGRAPHY

L. Mizler: *Neu eröffnete musikalische Bibliothek* (Leipzig, 1739–54/R1966)
J. Mattheson: *Gespräche der Weisheit und Musik ... als die dritte Dosis der Panacea* (Hamburg, 1751)
J. Adlung: *Anleitung zu der musikalischen Gelahrtheit* (Erfurt, 1758/R1953)
F. W. Marpurg: *Kritische Briefe über die Tonkunst* (Berlin, 1760–64)
H. Welcker von Gontershausen: *Der Flügel* (Frankfurt, 1856), 26f
E. F. Rimbault: *The Pianoforte* (London, 1860), 108ff
O. Paul: *Geschichte des Klaviers* (Leipzig, 1868), 85ff
F. T. Arnold: *The Art of Accompaniment from a Thorough-Bass* (London, 1931/R1965)
R. E. M. Harding: *The Piano-forte: its History Traced to the Great Exhibition of 1851* (Cambridge, 1933, rev. 2/1978), 17ff
H. T. David and A. Mendel: *The Bach Reader* (New York, 1945; rev. 2/1966)
P. Benary: *Die deutsche Kompositionslehre des 18. Jahrhunderts* (Leipzig, 1961)
R.N.: 'Schroeter's Piano Action', *MO*, lxxxvii (1964), 573

GEORGE J. BUELOW (1, 2),
MARIBEL MEISEL, PHILIP R. BELT (3)

Schröter, Johann Georg (*b* Berlstadt, Weimar, 20 Aug 1683; *d* c1750). German organ builder. A citizen of Erfurt, he obtained a monopoly on organ building in the area. He was probably the first organ builder to issue a printed advertising pamphlet (1723). He built only small and medium organs, but these had 8′ Open Diapason, 16′ Quintadena and 8′ Trompete in the Great organ; 8′ Gedackt, 4′ Open Diapason and 8′ Vox humana in the second manual; and 16′ Sub-bass, 8′ Octave and 16′ Posaune in the pedal. The manuals had a wide selection of foundation stops and a complete diapason chorus, except that if mutations were included (an option normally available only on the second manual) the corresponding diapason chorus would be omitted; the pedal had few stops. Schröter's reliability was recognized by Adlung, Bach, J. H. Buttstedt and Walther. Cases and some stops from 11 of his many organs, including that at Andisleben (1737), survive. Among Schröter's pupils were J. N. Ritter of Hof, J. P. Trampeli of Adorf and F. Volckland of Erfurt.

BIBLIOGRAPHY

J. Adlung: *Musica mechanica organoedi* (Berlin, 1768)
W. Wolffheim: 'Ein Orgelattest J. S. Bachs aus Erfurt, 1716', *BJb*, xxv (1928), 172

E. Rupp: *Die Entwicklungsgeschichte der Orgelbaukunst* (Einsiedeln, 1929)

HANS KLOTZ

Schröter, Leonhard. *See* SCHROETER, LEONHARD.

Schryari [*Schreierpfeife*]. A loud straight capped shawm, mentioned by Praetorius (2/1619) and others. *See* WIND-CAP INSTRUMENTS.

Schuba, Konrad Philipp (*b* Radolfzell, 26 Aug 1929). German organist. He studied at the Staatliche Musikhochschule in Stuttgart under Anton Nowakowski (organ), Karl-Heinz Lautner (piano) and Johann Nepomuk David and Karl Marx (composition). In 1957 he won an award for his organ playing at the Munich International Competition. He gained the concert diploma and was the only prizewinner at the West German music colleges' organ competition in Freiburg (1958), and was awarded first prize in the organ improvisation competition in Haarlem (1962). He became organist in 1955 at the minster (basilica) in Konstanz where, in that year, he inaugurated the highly esteemed 'Konstanz organ concerts' given by organists of various nationalities during the summer. In 1968 he was also made permanent organist and choirmaster at the Baroque church at Birnau. He has become internationally known both through his concert tours, which have included Belgium, France, Italy, Austria and Switzerland, and through his many broadcasts and recordings. He is stylistically versatile and a gifted improviser; but his favourite repertory is the music of Bach. He has also made his name as a composer of organ and choral works.

GERHARD WIENKE

Schuback, Jacob (*b* Hamburg, 8 Feb 1726; *d* Hamburg, 15 May 1784). German lawyer and musical amateur. The son of Hamburg's mayor, he attended the Latin school and from 1743 to 1747 the classical school, obtaining at the same time a thorough training in music. He studied law in Göttingen and took up the legal profession on his return to Hamburg in 1750, becoming secretary-archivist of the senate within two years. By 1760 he was trustee of the senate, and from 1771 acted as representative of the Hanseatic Republic to the Reichstag in Regensburg.

Schuback's interest in music certainly exceeded the usual scope of musical amateurism. He composed several large-scale works, some of them to his own texts, and collaborated on an inauguration cantata with C. P. E. Bach, whom he befriended. His choral works are admirable in text-declamation but old-fashioned, his songs sensitive and folklike, his symphonies mediocre. But his importance to music lay primarily in his participation in Hamburg's musical life: he was a skilled choral conductor, directed one of the earliest performances in Hamburg of Handel's *Messiah*, organized public concerts and established a programme of choral music in a local charity school. He also played the keyboard, corresponded with Metastasio on the subject of text-setting, and published anonymously a treatise on musical declamation that gained some currency.

WORKS
(MSS mainly in Hamburg)

Die Grossmuth des Scipio (drama, D. Schiebeler)
Oratorios (perf. Hamburg): *Der für die Sünde der Welt* (Passion oratorio, B. H. Brockes), c1750; *Betrachtung der Leiden unseres Erlösers* (after Metastasio, trans. Schuback), 1763; *Die Rettung*

Bethuliens (after Metastasio, trans. Schuback), 1773; Joas (after Metastasio, trans. Schuback), 1777; Die Jünger zu Emaus (Schuback) (Hamburg, 1778–9)
Other vocal: Vierstimmige gesetzte Kirchenchoräle, biblische Sprüche, geistliche und moralische Lieder für die Rumbaumsche Armenschule (Hamburg, 1779–81); Versuch in Melodien, songs, 1v, kbd (Hamburg, 1779); c12 sacred cantatas, solo vv, chorus, orch; 2 secular It. cantatas; inauguration cantata, 1771, collab. C. P. E. Bach, D-B; other ceremonial music; duets; 2 arias; 2 canons
Inst: 3 syms.

WRITINGS
Von der musikalischen Declamation (Göttingen, 1775); excerpts in J. N. Forkel: *Musikalisch-kritische Bibliothek*, iii (1779/R1964)
Nachricht von dem Singe-Institut bey der Rumbaumschen Armen-Schule (Hamburg, 1780)

BIBLIOGRAPHY
GerberL
C. F. Cramer, ed.: *Magazin der Musik*, ii (1784/R1971–4)
H. Schroeder and A. H. Kellinghusen, eds.: *Lexikon der Hamburgischen Schriftsteller*, iii (Hamburg, 1879)
J. Sittard: *Geschichte des Musik- und Concertwesens in Hamburg* (Altona and Leipzig, 1890/R1971)
K. Stephenson: *Hundert Jahre Philharmonische Geschichte in Hamburg* (Hamburg, 1928)
——: 'Schuback, Jacob', *MGG*

EUGENE HELM

Schubart, Christian Friedrich Daniel (*b* Obersontheim, Swabia, 24 March 1739; *d* Stuttgart, 10 Oct 1791). German poet, journalist, writer on music and composer. Although his literary and musical talents manifested themselves in early youth, his parents decided that he should study theology. He received his preparatory education in Nördlingen and Nuremberg, music instruction from his father and the Nuremberg composer G. W. Gruber, and entered Erlangen University in 1758. At Erlangen he was often in trouble with the university authorities, and in 1760 he returned to his parents' home in Aalen. From 1763 to 1769 he was organist and preceptor in Geisslingen. In 1769 he obtained an organist position in Ludwigsburg, the residence of the Duke of Württemberg, and he was also employed by the court as harpsichordist at the opera house and instructor in music. However, he led a dissolute life, and in 1773 was banished from Württemberg. In 1774 he moved to Augsburg, where he established his *Deutsche* (or *Teutsche*) *Chronik*, a periodical devoted to politics, literature and music. The next year he moved to Ulm, where he successfully continued the venture for three years. However, his criticisms of policies pursued by the Catholic Church and various courts aroused the wrath of the nobility. In 1777 Duke Carl Eugen of Württemberg ordered Schubart's imprisonment at the fortress Hohenasperg, apparently for insulting his mistress (Strauss, 1849, i, 344). Schubart's confinement lasted ten years, during which he wrote several of his most important works: in 1778 and 1779 he dictated his autobiography, *Leben und Gesinnungen, von ihm selbst im Kerker aufgesetzt* (Stuttgart, 1791–3), to a fellow prisoner; and his *Ideen zu einer Ästhetik der Tonkunst* (Vienna, 1806/R1969) dates from 1784–5. Most of his extant compositions were also written during his imprisonment; he published many in *Musicalische Rhapsodien* (Stuttgart, 1786; ed. P. A. Merbach, Leipzig, 1924) and in other collections. On his release in 1787 he was appointed court and theatre poet at Stuttgart. He resumed publishing his periodical (as the *Vaterländische Chronik*, 1787–91), but ill-health caused by his confinement forced him to abandon plans for a collected edition of his poetry and writings on music.

Schubart was a distinguished performer on the organ, harpsichord and clavichord, and many critics, including Burney, praised his virtuosity. He achieved considerable success as a lied composer, and several of his lieder remained popular well into the 19th century. Most are set to his own texts, and strophic form and a folklike melodic idiom predominate. In setting complex poems he occasionally utilized strophic variation techniques, rondo-like patterns and cantata-like structures. Though exhibiting a strong melodic gift, his songs are frequently marred by awkward harmonic progressions and inept part-writing. These same defects are also noticeable in his clavier compositions.

Schubart's *Ideen zu einer Ästhetik der Tonkunst*, his essays on music in the *Chronik*, his prefaces to the *Musicalische Rhapsodien* and his autobiography present vivid accounts of German musical life during the second half of the 18th century and are of considerable value to the music historian. His aesthetic views reflect the proto-Romantic concepts then prevalent in Germany: he considered expression to be the 'golden axle around which the aesthetics of music turn', and emphasized the concept of musical genius. A well-known section in the *Ideen* subjectively describes the characteristics of individual tonalities, expressing the widely held belief that sharp keys portray strong passions and flat keys gentle feelings. Beethoven and Schumann were interested in Schubart's opinions, though they disagreed with him in several respects. Schubart maintained that folksong represents the true musical expression of a people, and he devoted much attention to this subject. His comments on the works of individual composers show an exceptionally keen critical faculty. He praised the profoundly expressive compositions of C. P. E. Bach and his followers and denounced as superficial the *galant* idiom of Piccinni, Paisiello and most of their Italian contemporaries. He also expressed an appreciation of the works of composers of earlier periods and was one of the few writers of his generation to comprehend the true worth of J. S. Bach's works.

Schubart's poetry was frequently set by his contemporaries and by composers of the following generation. The most important of these settings are the four lieder composed by Schubert; two of these, *Die Forelle* and *An mein Klavier*, have achieved a permanent place in the lieder repertory.

WORKS
Lieder: 4 in *Deutsche* [*Teutsche*; *Vaterländische*] *Chronik* (1774–91); 12 in Neue Blumenlese für Klavierliebhaber, ed. H. P. Bossler (Speyer, 1782–5); Die Macht der Tonkunst, cantata, 1v, hpd, in Neue Blumenlese für Klavierliebhaber, ed. H. P. Bossler (Speyer, 1783), repr. in Etwas für Klavier und Gesang von Schubart (Winterthur, 1783); 4 in Schwäbischer Musenalmanach, ed. G. F. Stäudlin (Tübingen, 1783–4); 1 in Zweite Sammlung neuer Klavierstükke mit Gesang für das deutsche Frauenzimmer (Dessau, 1784); 3 in Musikalische Monatschrift für Gesang und Klavier (Stuttgart, 1784); 14 in C. F. D. Schubart: *Musicalische Rhapsodien* (Stuttgart, 1786); 2 Lieder für das nach dem Kap bestimmte von Hügelsche Regiment (Stuttgart, 1787); 1 in Musikalische Real-Zeitung (Speyer, 1789); 3 in Musikalischer Potpourri für Liebhaberinnen und Freunde des Gesangs und Claviers (Stuttgart, 1790); 2 in Vermischte Gedichte von D. E. Friedrich Hübner, mit Klaviermelodien von Schubart und Abeille, ii (Stuttgart, 1791); 57 in Sang und Spiel, 1759–84, D-Sl; 23 in J. J. Wagner's notebooks, Us
Kbd: 2 minuets in Neue Blumenlese für Klavierliebhaber (Speyer, 1782–4); 3 solo sonatas, 1 sonata, kbd 4 hands, in Etwas für Klavier und Gesang von Schubart (Winterthur, 1783); Minuet, Rondo, in C. F. D. Schubart: *Musicalische Rhapsodien* (Stuttgart, 1786); 13 variations (Speyer, 1788); Chorale, Jesus meine Zuversicht, in *Musikalische Korrespondenz der Teutschen filharmonischen Gesellschaft* (1791), Notenblätter, 134

BIBLIOGRAPHY
C. Burney: *The Present State of Music in Germany, the Netherlands, and United Provinces* (London, 1773, 2/1775); ed. P. Scholes as *Dr*

Burney's Musical Tours (London, 1959)

L. Schubart: *Schubarts Karakter* (Erlangen, 1798)

L. Schubart, ed.: *C. F. D. Schubart: Gesammelte Schriften und Schicksale* (Stuttgart, 1839–40/*R*1972)

A. Schindler: *Biographie von Ludwig van Beethoven* (Münster, 1840, rev. 3/1860; Eng. trans., 1966, *as Beethoven as I Knew him*)

D. F. Strauss, ed.: *C. F. D. Schubart's Leben in seinen Briefen* (Berlin, 1849)

——: 'Nachlese zu Schubart', *Gesammelte Schriften* (Bonn, 1876–8), ix, 322

F. Wilkens: 'Dr. Charles Burney on Schubart', *Americana germanica*, ii/4 (1899), 57

M. Friedlaender: *Das deutsche Lied im 18. Jahrhundert* (Stuttgart and Berlin, 1902/*R*1970)

E. Holzer: *Schubart als Musiker* (Stuttgart, 1905) [incl. detailed list of works]

H. Kretzschmar: *Geschichte des neuen deutschen Liedes*, i (Leipzig, 1911/*R*1966)

R. Hammerstein: *Christian Friedrich Daniel Schubart, ein schwäbisch-alemannischer Dichter-Musiker der Goethezeit* (diss., U. of Freiburg, 1943) [with complete list of writings]

H. Eggebrecht: 'Das Ausdrucks-Prinzip im musikalischen Sturm und Drang', *Deutsche Vierteljahrsschrift für Literaturwissenschaft und Geistesgeschichte*, xxix (1955), 323

D. Ossenkop: *Christian Friedrich Daniel Schubart's Writings on Music* (diss., Columbia U., 1960)

L. Plantinga: *Schumann as Critic* (New Haven, 1967)

D. Ossenkop: *The Earliest Settings of German Ballads for Voice and Clavier* (diss., Columbia U., 1968)

R. Harpster: 'Genius in the 18th Century: C. F. D. Schubart's "Vom musikalischen Genie"', *CMc* (1973), no.15, p.73

R. Schollum: 'Schubarts und Schuberts "Forelle"-Vertonungen', *Musikerziehung*, xxviii (1974–5), 19

DAVID OSSENKOP

Schubaur, Johann Lukas (*b* Lechfeld, baptized 23 Dec 1749; *d* Munich, 15 Nov 1815). German doctor and composer. Son of the painter Ignatius Schubaur, he was orphaned at an early age and brought up in the monastery at Zwiefalten. He went to school in Augsburg and attended the theological seminary in Neuburg an der Donau, where he also acquired a comprehensive musical education. While a novice at Wiblingen he grew ill from physical privation and had to give up monastic life. In Vienna he began to study medicine and made a living by giving piano lessons and writing short occasional compositions. After graduating from Ingolstadt, he practised in 1775 at the hospital of the Barmherzige Brüder in Neuburg an der Donau; soon afterwards he settled in Munich and held several important medical posts.

Schubaur's activities as a dilettante composer were linked with the efforts of the Palatine court in Munich to develop an independent German Singspiel alongside Italian and French comic opera. His first effort, *Melide oder Der Schiffer*, translated freely by Schubaur himself from a French model by Falbaire and performed on 24 September 1782 at the Munich National Theatre, failed utterly, and aroused discussion only after the great success of his next Singspiel, *Die Dorfdeputierten*. For this work Schubaur chose a lighter text (by G. E. Heermann, after Goldini's *Il feudatorio*) which had already been set by E. W. Wolf and later appeared in a well-known setting by Dieter and Teyber. It was his greatest artistic and commercial success (largely because of the vocal score, which he published himself) and is said to have received over 100 performances in Munich alone (première at the National Theatre, 8 May 1783) as well as frequent stagings throughout Germany as late as 1813. After the resounding failure of *Das Lustlager* (by F. M. Babo, National Theatre, 1784) and the only moderate success of *Die treuen Köhler* (again by Heermann, National Theatre, 29 September 1786) Schubaur gave up writing for the theatre, though this may also have resulted from the appearance of Mozart's

inimitable *Die Entführung aus dem Serail* in 1785. Among his works only *Die Dorfdeputierten* (manuscript score in *D-MH*; vocal score, Mannheim and Munich, *c*1783) and *Die treuen Köhler* (vocal score, Munich, 1786) are extant; additional works, mentioned by Eitner and Lipowsky, cannot be authenticated as Schubaur's.

BIBLIOGRAPHY

EitnerQ; GerberL; GerberNL

Obituary, *Königliches bayerisches Intelligenzblatt für den Isarkreis* (27 Dec 1815)

F. J. Lipowsky: *Baierisches Musik-Lexikon* (Munich, 1811/*R*1971)

H. Kretzschmar: preface to *I. Holzbauer: Günther von Schwarzburg*, DDT, viii–ix (1902/*R*)

E. Reipschläger: *Schubaur, Danzi und Poissl als Opernkomponisten* (diss., U. of Rostock, 1911; biographical extracts, Berlin-Mariendorf, 1911)

GERHARD ALLROGGEN

Schubert. German family of musicians active in Dresden in the 18th and 19th centuries. Many sources incorrectly give LOUIS SCHUBERT and JOSEPH SCHUBERT as members of this family.

(1) Franz Anton Schubert (*b* Dresden, 20 July 1768; *d* Dresden, 5 March 1827). Double bass player and composer. The younger brother of Anton Schubert (*b* Dresden, 28 June 1766; *d* Dresden, 12 Oct 1853), a double bass player in the Dresden orchestra from 1790 until his retirement in 1840, he became the director of the Italian Opera in 1808 and was appointed royal church composer in 1814. He gave some useful assistance to Weber. He is remembered chiefly for his contemptuous remarks when by mistake a copy of Franz Peter Schubert's *Erlkönig* was sent to him by Breitkopf & Härtel: he retorted, in a letter of 18 April 1817, that the 'cantata' [sic] was not his but that he would retain the copy 'so as to learn if possible who has so impertinently sent you that sort of rubbish and also to discover the fellow who has thus misused my name'. His own numerous works are chiefly liturgical settings.

(2) Franz Schubert (*b* Dresden, 22 July 1808; *d* Dresden, 12 April 1878). Violinist and composer, eldest son of (1) Franz Anton Schubert. He first studied music with his father, then with C. P. Lafont in Paris (where he became a friend of Chopin) before returning to Dresden. In 1861 he succeeded Karol Lipiński as leader of the Dresden orchestra. His music for violin includes some duos with cello, written in collaboration with F. A. Kummer, and a set of 12 bagatelles op.13, of which no.9, *Die Biene*, was once popular. His wife Maschinka (*b* Reval, 25 Aug 1815; *d* Dresden, 20 Sept 1882), the daughter of the Kapellmeister Georg Abraham Schneider (1770–1839) and the singer Caroline Portmann, was a coloratura soprano who studied with her mother and with Giulio Bordogni; she made her début in London in 1832 and was later a valuable, versatile member of the Dresden Opera, her range including soubrette and tragic roles.

(3) Georgine Schubert (*b* Dresden, 28 Oct 1840; *d* Strelitz, 26 Dec 1878). Soprano, daughter of (2) Franz Schubert. She studied first with her mother, then with Jenny Lind and Manuel Garcia. She made her début in *La sonnambula* in Hamburg in 1839, and had a successful international career, including performances at the Monday Popular Concerts in London.

BIBLIOGRAPHY

GerberNL

M. Fürstenau: *Beiträge zur Geschichte der königlich sächsischen musikalischen Kapelle* (Dresden, 1849)

——: *Zur Geschichte der Musik und des Theaters am Hofe zu Dresden*, i (Dresden, 1861/*R*1971)

H. Schnoor: *400 Jahre deutsche Musikkultur* (Dresden, 1948)

JOHN WARRACK

Schubert, Ferdinand (Lukas) (*b* Vienna, 18 Oct 1794; *d* Vienna, 26 Feb 1859). Austrian composer and teacher, brother of Franz Schubert. He received his first music lessons from his father, and after training in the Normalhauptschule in Vienna (1807–8) he became a teacher in his father's school. In 1810 he was appointed assistant teacher at the orphanage in the suburb of Alsergrund and made a full teacher in 1816. He was appointed headmaster at the Normalhauptschule in 1824. Admired in educational circles in Vienna for his efficient service as inspector of schools, he was appointed director of the Normalhauptschule in 1851. He was twice married, first to Anna Schüler (1816) and, after her death, to Therese Spazierer (1832).

A composer of small talent, he frequently drew on his brother's music for help in his daily work, passing it off as his own. The most famous instance of this appropriation is the *Deutsches Requiem* D621, which he submitted to the examiners of the Alt-Lerchenfeld school; & on its strength he was appointed organist and choirmaster (1820). His brother also composed the antiphons for Palm Sunday, D696, for his installation in this post. He wrote vocal music almost exclusively, including two Singspiels, four masses and a requiem. As a custodian of his brother's MSS his record is mixed; he continued to appropriate the lesser, earlier works for school music books and choral test pieces (so that a list of his compositions must be suspect). But he also did all in his power to obtain the publication of Schubert's larger works, and in this task he was more or less successful.

BIBLIOGRAPHY

G. Schilling, ed.: *Encyclopädie der gesammten musikalischen Wissenschaften oder Universal-Lexikon der Tonkunst* (Stuttgart, 1835–8/*R*1973)

O. E. Deutsch: 'Ferdinand Schuberts "Deutsches Requiem" von Franz Schubert', *F. Schubert: Deutsche Trauermesse* (Vienna, 1928) [Ger. and Eng. texts]

O. E. Deutsch with D. R. Wakeling: *Schubert: Thematic Catalogue of all his Works* (London, 1951; Ger. trans., rev., enlarged 2/1978 by W. Dürr, A. Feil, C. Landon and others, Neue Ausgabe sämtlicher Werke, viii/4, as *Franz Schubert: thematisches Verzeichnis seiner Werke*)

F. R. van Hoorickx: 'Schubert's "Pastoral Mass" ', *ML*, xlii (1961), 53

MAURICE J. E. BROWN

Schubert, Franz (Peter) (*b* Vienna, 31 Jan 1797; *d* Vienna, 19 Nov 1828). Austrian composer. He was the only great Viennese master native to the city. His importance lies in many fields of composition, and while it is possibly not true to say (as Sir George Grove did) that he graced every department of music with a masterpiece, he did produce supreme masterpieces in orchestral, piano and chamber music as well as song; and there he is pre-eminent because his rich vein of melody and his expressive harmony reached the heart of the text in a way that music before him had not known.

1. BACKGROUND AND CHILDHOOD. Vienna, in Schubert's day, consisted of an inner city bounded to the north-east by the Danube Canal and enclosed by a rampart; these enclosing walls were to give place to the wide boulevards of the modern Ringstrasse. The real life of the capital was passed in this small and crowded area. Schubert was born in the district of the Himmelpfortgrund, lying to the north-west of the city.

Schubert's father, Franz Theodor Florian, was a schoolmaster. He was a man of probity, a devout Catholic, industrious in his profession and undeniably successful. His ancestors were Moravian peasant farmers: he was born in Neudorf, near Märisch-Schönberg in the Altstadt district of Moravia. He migrated to Vienna to become an assistant to his brother Karl, who had a school in the Leopoldstadt suburb, and in 1785, when he was 25, married Maria Elisabet Katherina Vietz, the composer's mother. We know little of her except that she was born in Zuckmantel, in Austrian Silesia, and before her marriage was in domestic service. Soon after his marriage, Franz Theodor was appointed master of a school in the Himmelpfortgrund district of Vienna and in June 1786 he moved into a house there called 'Zum roten Krebsen'. In the years that followed, no fewer than 12 children were born, of whom only four survived infancy: Ignaz (*b* 1785), Ferdinand (*b* 1794), Karl (*b* 1795) and Franz Peter. A daughter, Maria Theresa (*b* 1801), was the last of the family. The house was later renumbered and the street renamed: it is now 54 Nussdorferstrasse, and since 1912 has been maintained by the city authorities as a Schubert museum. In 1969 it was reopened, after several years, fully restored to its original condition as the boy Schubert knew it.

Soon after the birth of Maria Theresa, the family moved into a new house in the nearby Säulenstrasse (now no.3), which Franz Theodor had bought a few months earlier. It was a smaller house, but more rooms were at his disposal for the growing number of his pupils. We learn from the memoirs of Schubert's father and of his brother, Ferdinand, of his boyhood in the Säulengasse schoolhouse. Franz Theodor's position offered no social standing and was ill-paid. It is not difficult to see that when he induced his sons, as they grew old enough, to become his assistants in the school, the primary aim was to save money. But the relations between father and sons were clearly affectionate, as their extant letters reveal; and Schubert as a boy experienced neither harsh discipline in his training nor exploitation of his obvious musical gifts. His father taught him the violin, his eldest brother Ignaz the piano, and he quickly outstripped them both. Ignaz wryly admitted that the boy told him as much, and that he intended to make his own way in the future. When he was nine or ten his father placed him under the tuition of Michael Holzer, organist at the parish church of Liechtental. Holzer is sketched amusingly by Anton Holzapfel (a schoolfellow of Schubert's) as somewhat bibulous but a sound contrapuntist. In addition to lessons on the piano and violin, young Franz was taught the organ, singing and harmony, and under Holzer's care both his singing and violin playing earned him a local reputation. Holzer said of his pupil: 'If I wished to instruct him in anything fresh, he already knew it. Consequently I gave him no actual tuition but merely conversed with him and watched him with silent astonishment'.

Schubert's extraordinary aptitude for music enabled

him to absorb with ease this elementary instruction, and no further progress was possible on that road. But another lay before him, and was to lead him to an environment which awakened his genius and showed him the full possibilities of self-realization. Towards the end of 1808 he was accepted as a choirboy in the imperial court chapel, and this meant admission as a scholar to the Kaiserlich-königliches Stadtkonvikt (Imperial and Royal City College). His examiners were the court musical directors, Anton Salieri and Josef Eybler, and the choirmaster, Phillip Körner; Schubert also distinguished himself in general subjects. The college was the principal Viennese boarding-school for commoners. The tutors were men in holy orders (although the college was not a religious foundation) and the boarders, about 130 in number, were either scholars at the grammar school or students at the university. Music was a compulsory subject for the choristers, but the principal, Dr Innocenz Lang, was an enthusiastic musical amateur and he encouraged all scholars to practise the art. A young university student, Josef von Spaun, had formed a students' orchestra, which was conducted by a visiting music master, Václav (Wenzel) Růžička, and by the time the young Schubert came to the college, its standard was excellent. Schubert's violin playing greatly impressed Spaun and in a short time he was promoted to be leader of the first violins. The friendship between Schubert and this student, some eight years his senior, was to be one of the happiest things in his life, and it lasted until his death. Schubert was composing in those years, and some of the music has survived (he confessed to Spaun that he was too poor to buy all the music manuscript paper he needed, and Spaun's first act of kindness was to provide it).

When Růžička was absent, Schubert conducted the orchestra – a rare opportunity for a boy such as he to master orchestral techniques. The orchestra played overtures and symphonies by Mozart and Haydn and the first two symphonies of Beethoven. Růžička, like Holzer before him, was nonplussed at the rapidity with which Schubert absorbed his instruction. To him the explanation was simple: 'He has learnt everything from God, that lad'. Eventually Salieri took over the supervision of Schubert's work, a supervision which extended beyond the college years. The association is interesting: it was, indeed, fitting that Salieri, friend of Haydn and rival of Mozart, in a small way a pupil of Gluck and in a smaller way tutor to Beethoven, should have supervised the work of Schubert, the last of these Viennese masters.

The supposition that Schubert neglected other studies to devote himself to music is contradicted by the extant records from Dr Lang of his progress in these years. All subjects are rated 'good' or 'very good' and the comment 'a special musical talent' occurs year after year. Schubert impressed everyone at the college by his musical gifts and an equally deep impression was made by his moral qualities; he was privileged to leave the building for his lessons with Salieri because of his general reliability.

2. EARLY COMPOSITIONS. The compositions which date with certainty from these years are the Fantasie in G for piano duet (D1; 8 April–1 May 1810), the Six Minuets for wind instruments (D2d; 1811, recovered in 1969) and the song *Hagars Klage* (D5; 30 March 1811). It was this song, in Schubert's scena form, which is said to have aroused Salieri's interest. On 8 July 1811, Spaun

took Schubert to his first opera, Weigl's *Die Schweizerfamilie*, at the Kärntnertor-Theater (which was to figure in Schubert's own operatic ventures). His first settings of Schiller date from this time, *Des Mädchens Klage* (D6) and *Leichenfantasie* (D7).

In the following year, on 28 May 1812, Schubert's mother died. That he and his father had quarrelled and were reconciled at her graveside is purely fictitious; so is the assertion that he composed the wind nonet *Eine kleine Trauermusik* (D79) to her memory. The eight undated and incomplete numbers of his first operatic composition, *Der Spiegelritter* (D11), to a text by August von Kotzebue, were completed in 1812. In the summer that year his voice was breaking; after the performance of a mass by Peter von Winter, he scribbled on his part, 'Schubert, Franz, crowed for the last time, 26 July 1812', though he remained a pupil at the college for another year or so. There were two terms in the college year, the main holiday occurring in early autumn. It was during Schubert's holidays that a family string quartet was formed, with the composer playing the viola, his brothers Ignaz and Ferdinand the violins, and his father the cello. For this family quartet the early string quartets of 1811–14 were composed.

The compositions of 1813 are numerous and their variety indicates the wealth of his musical experience. Salieri's tutelage is apparent in the many vocal canons, which are primarily contrapuntal exercises, and in the varied settings of verses by Metastasio. Songs of the year include settings of Schiller, Hölty and Matthisson, and a translation by Herder of Pope's *Vital Spark of Heavenly Flame* (*Verklärung* D59). There are German Dances (*Deutsche*) for strings (D90) and six string quartets. The finest of these, in E♭ (D87), with a finale of true Schubertian quality, was published in 1840 as op.125 no.1.

On 25 April 1813, Schubert's father remarried. His wife, Anna Kleyenböck, was a kindly woman who in later years helped Schubert with loans from her housekeeping money. For his father's name day, 4 October, Schubert wrote the words and music of a trio (D80). The finest of these early works was finished on 28 October, the First Symphony, in D (D82). It is the consummation of those two years of absorption in music at the college and of his vital contact with its orchestra; it was his justification for the future. Two days after its completion he began work on a three-act opera *Des Teufels Lustschloss* (D84), to a libretto by Kotzebue. He is said to have stayed away from his lessons until the opera was finished in the following year, and then to have presented the fully scored work to his astonished master. Salieri's criticisms were heeded, for a revised, second version of the opera is dated five months after the completion of the first.

3. BEGINNING OF CAREER. At the end of 1813, probably late in October, Schubert left the college; unable to withstand family persuasion, he entered a training-school for elementary teachers in the Annagasse, near St Stephen's Cathedral. By autumn 1814 he was teaching in his father's school. It is not true that he adopted the profession of schoolmaster to evade military conscription: assistants, in any case, were not exempt. He was rejected by the military authorities because he was shorter than the minimum height of five feet. His sight was defective, too; by then he was wearing the spectacles familiar from his portraits.

1. *Autograph MS of version a of Schubert's 'Szene aus Goethes Faust'* ('Wie anders, Gretchen, war dirs') D126, *composed December 1814 (F-Pn)*

Although he continued to take lessons with Salieri until the end of 1816, his musical tuition was finished. In those years at the college he was able to draw in abundance on the rich resources of orchestral practice and church choral singing, of piano playing and song and chamber music with his fellows, of string quartet playing in his own home, and of frequent visits to some of the finest opera in Europe. These powerful stimuli were about to produce a staggering result. He was on the threshold of an outburst of composition without parallel in the history of music: the means of self-expression had been acquired and his genius sought utterance.

The early months of 1814, however, produced little work of significance: some string quartet sketches, a few songs, and the arrangement, including a new trio (D96) for the minuet, he made in February of a *Notturno* op.21 by Wenzel Matiegka, for flute, guitar, viola and cello – it is called the 'Guitar' Quartet, and its attribution as a whole to Schubert is unfortunate. Between 17 May and 22 July he composed his first Mass, in F (D105). Another string quartet, in Bb (D112), followed in September. The first movement was written in four and a half hours, as Schubert indicated on the autograph.

This was the period of the Congress of Vienna, and it coincided with the centenary celebrations of the Liechtental Church. Schubert's Mass in F was performed in the church as part of these celebrations on 14 October 1814; Holzer's choir sang, Ferdinand played the organ and Schubert himself conducted. The soprano solos were sung by Therese Grob, a young girl with a

delightful lyric soprano voice. Ten days later the mass was repeated, in the court church of St Augustine, and both performances brought the young composer a welcome public acclaim. But something took place after those ten days more significant than the adulation surrounding the performances of his mass: he had been reading Goethe's *Faust*, and on 19 October 1814 he set the verses now universally known as *Gretchen am Spinnrade* (D118). It was his first masterpiece. The figure in the piano accompaniment represents the spinning-wheel, but as the song proceeds it gathers into itself all Gretchen's changing emotions as she recalls her lover, and the greatest moment is when, under the transported spirit of the suffering girl, the wheel comes to a standstill, falteringly beginning its motion again as she recovers. It is a song which, unlike several others, has never suffered eclipse during the passing years but rather has grown in stature. Another popular song to a Goethe text followed later in the year, *Schäfers Klagelied* (D121). In December, the song *Am See* (D124) was composed to verses by Johann Mayrhofer. Spaun had given the poem to Schubert, and soon afterwards he took him to Mayrhofer's lodgings in the Wipplingerstrasse and introduced him to the poet. There began a friendship that was to affect Schubert deeply. Mayrhofer's poetry reveals the conflict between the idealism of the spirit and the actualities of life; it was, in later years, to evoke noble and profound music from the composer.

Schubert was, in 1815, a schoolmaster, feeling the irksome duties of the classroom as an intolerable barrier between him and the freedom to compose. But he evidently found time to put down on paper the music which, throughout that year, welled ceaselessly in his mind. There can have been scarcely a day when his pen was idle, and no other year in his life approached this one for its sheer volume of work. His Second Symphony, in B♭ (D125), begun the previous December, was finished in March. The Third, in D (D200), was written between 24 May and 19 July. There were numerous dances for piano solo, two sonatas, a set of ten variations on an original theme in F, and a sturdy little string quartet in G minor. Besides much varied choral music of secondary value, there were two masses. The first, in G (D167), was performed in spring 1815, soon after its completion. Depths are sounded in the Agnus Dei unknown to the earlier Mass in F. It is a *lento* movement in E minor, and solo passages for soprano and bass alternate with the chorus quietly intoning 'miserere nobis' to gracious, falling phrases. The violas are used expressively to link these solos and choruses. The second mass of the year, no.3 in B♭ (D324), looks to the later Schubert in page after page. The use of short, lyrical episodes, picturesquely orchestrated, between the vocal phrases foreshadows *Lazarus* of five years later; the use of descant-like melodies in violin or oboe hints at the slow movement of the 'Unfinished' Symphony. Above all, there are bravura passages, for example in the Gloria and Benedictus, which suggest the 'Wanderer' Fantasy and the finale of the 'Great' C major Symphony. This is the most consistently interesting of his four early settings of the Mass. The story put forward by Josef Doppler that the style of this work caused a break between Schubert and Salieri is a fabrication.

In the course of the year, Schubert set four dramatic texts to music. No doubt the successful production of an opera in Vienna appeared to him as the gate to freedom. Since Vienna possessed four theatres at which operas and plays with music were produced, he must have felt confident of eventual success. The four stage works are: *Der vierjährige Posten* (D190), to a one-act play by Theodor Körner, the music composed between 8 and 19 May; *Fernando* (D220), to a one-act play by Albert Stadler, composed 27 June to 9 July; *Claudine von Villa Bella* (D239), to a three-act play by Goethe, which was begun on 26 July, and survives in only an incomplete form, since the manuscript came into the possession of Josef Hüttenbrenner, whose servants, in 1848, unwittingly used the pages of Acts 2 and 3 to light fires; *Die Freunde von Salamanka* (D326), to a two-act play by Mayrhofer, which occupied the composer from 18 November to 31 December. The last of these four is the finest and, although Mayrhofer's text is lost, it is perfectly easy to follow the story from the extant musical numbers and so provide the necessary dialogue.

In addition to these larger musical forms, he composed in 1815 145 songs. The range is tremendous and the accomplishment outstanding. There are tiny songs like *Die Mainacht* (D194) and *Der Traum* (D213) on the one hand, and very long ballads such as *Adelwold und Emma* (D211) on the other. The poets include Schiller, Klopstock, Ossian and Kosegarten. He set 30 poems by Goethe, and some of these are among his finest and most famous songs: *Heidenröslein* (D257), *Erster Verlust* (D226), *Wandrers Nachtlied* (D224) and *Rastlose Liebe* (D138). The last of the Goethe settings, the song by which the year will always be remembered, is *Erlkönig* (D328), composed in late autumn 1815. The story of its composition as told by Spaun and others is full of incredible details; it is, in fact, impossible to separate what is factually correct from subsequent accretions. Spaun called on his friend one afternoon (he wrote) and found him excitedly reading Goethe's ballad. Schubert then wrote the song out in the shortest possible time, and the two of them (possibly with Mayrhofer) hurried to the college and gathered a few congenial spirits to hear the composition. The enthusiasm of the students was tremendous and Růžička justified his pupil's use of the discordant minor 9ths at the cry 'Mein Vater!'. When the song was eventually published, some six years later, it spread Schubert's fame far beyond his native city. In his own lifetime and for generations afterwards it was considered his greatest song. Today, perhaps, some of the more subtle songs of his final years spring to mind before *Erlkönig*, but the wealth of harmonic resource, its masterly structure and the mounting tonal climaxes of the threefold lure will always keep it high among his masterpieces of song.

During the autumn Schubert became acquainted with Franz von Schober, who had come to Vienna to study law. He had heard some of Schubert's songs and now came to seek out their composer. According to his own account, he found Schubert in the classroom correcting pupils' exercises. Of the same age as Schubert, he was a cultured, worldly young man and it was typical of his easy-going nature and wealthy upbringing that he urged Schubert to abandon the drudgery of teaching and devote himself to composition. It was not for another year that the composer could bring himself to make the break, but after his encounter with Schober, the step was inevitable. He attempted to do so in April 1816 by applying, unsuccessfully, for the post of music master in a training school for elementary teachers at Laibach (now Ljubljana), some 65 km north-east of Trieste. In the same month he completed his Fourth Symphony, in C minor (D417); the title 'Tragic' is his own. While he was engaged on this work, Spaun sent to Goethe, at Weimar, a group of Schubert's settings of the poet's verses. It included all the finest of the Goethe songs of the previous two years. The attempt to interest the poet in Schubert's work failed. In musical matters, Goethe was greatly influenced by Zelter. Both men shared the feeling of the north German musical world that in 'true German song' the accompaniment should be subordinate to the vocal part; all extravagances of harmony and modulation were categorized as 'bizarrerie' and eschewed. Schubert's songs were returned, and his appeal for recognition ignored. After Schubert's death, Goethe again heard *Erlkönig*, which was sung to him by Wilhelmine Schröder-Devrient on 24 April 1830; he told her: 'I have heard this composition once before, when it did not appeal to me at all; but sung in this way the whole shapes itself into a visible picture'.

In May 1816 Spaun took lodgings with his friend Josef Witteczek, who later became a devoted Schubertian and amassed a superb collection of Schubert first editions, manuscripts and press cuttings. The house, in the Erdberggasse, was the scene of many of those domestic evening concerts devoted to the music of Schubert which came to be known as *Schubertiade*. They were symptomatic of a new and vigorous social phenomenon, the cultivation of music by the educated middle class; though altogether humbler than the aristocratic employment of quartets and orchestras in the 18th century, its energetic growth is apparent from the ubiquitous piano and the vast mass of suitable music which poured from the publishing houses. A cantata, *Prometheus* (D451), was composed on 17 June for private performance; it was Schubert's first commissioned work and earned him a fee of 40 gulden. The music was given in the garden of the Erdberggasse house on 24 July 1816 and impressed its hearers profoundly. Whether or not this impression was deserved we have no means of knowing, as the score was lost without trace just before Schubert's death. Leopold von Sonnleithner sang in the chorus and thereby made Schubert's acquaintance; the composer was to be fortunate in this contact with so influential and musical a family as the Sonnleithners.

Several pages of a diary which Schubert kept that year have survived. The entries for June have some interest, since they contain references to Mozart and Beethoven. If anything were needed to demonstrate that music was his only medium of self-expression, we have only to turn from the diary pages of September to the work on which he was engaged at this time – the Fifth Symphony, in B♭ (D485), the best and most popular of his six early symphonies. It was finished on 3 October and performed soon afterwards by a private orchestra which had developed from the family string quartet and which met in the house of its conductor, Otto Hatwig.

4. GROWING REPUTATION. Schober returned to Vienna

2. Page from Schubert's diary of 10 June 1816 containing references to Mozart (A-Wgm)

during October 1816, after a four-month visit to his birthplace in Sweden on family matters, and it was then that he persuaded the composer to make a move towards independence. There was no clean break with teaching, but by December Schubert was installed in rooms in the house of Schober's affluent mother – a temporary respite. 1816 had been almost as prolific as the previous year. In addition to the compositions already mentioned there was a further Mass, in C (D452), composed during June and July and published nine years later with a dedication to Michael Holzer. The three sonatas for violin and piano (D384, 385, 408), published by Diabelli in 1836 as 'Sonatinas', and the String Quartet in E (D353) were composed that year. The songs, over 100, include *Der Wanderer* (D489), after *Erlkönig* the most popular of his songs for many years, and masterpieces to poems by Goethe such as the three Harper's Songs from *Wilhelm Meister* (D478–80) and *An Schwager Kronos* (D369). It is one of the enigmas of his music that these songs so richly reveal his personal style, whereas in his contemporary instrumental works it appears only fitfully. A few months after Schubert was installed in his new house, Schober prevailed upon the operatic baritone, Johann Michael Vogl, to visit him and make the acquaintance of the composer and his songs. Vogl was well-to-do, a man of culture with a distinguished, even stately bearing. Schubert was overawed and painfully embarrassed, but the singer, very much at his ease, took the proffered songs: the newly composed *Ganymed* (D544) was one of them. His parting remark was to the effect that, although there was much fine stuff in the songs, it was ill-presented; Schubert, he said, was too little of the charlatan. But he was more impressed than he admitted. Shortly afterwards he revisited the composer and the two men soon became the delight of the Viennese drawing-rooms. Vogl, his days in the theatre nearly over, was not averse to the plaudits of the salons and initially he looked upon the songs as vehicles for his voice. Occasionally he altered them, adding flourishes and introducing wide skips in voice parts. He once embellished a new song of Schubert's, also transposing it to suit his voice, and on presenting the copy a fortnight later was greeted by the composer with 'A good song. Whose is it, then?'. Generations have chuckled over this anecdote, seeing only the 'clairvoyant' genius (Vogl's word) who forgets his own production when the trance is over; they have missed Schubert's implied protest.

An effort was made during the spring of 1817 to publish *Erlkönig*. The song was sent to the Leipzig firm of Breitkopf & Härtel. Knowing only one Franz Schubert, a musician in Dresden, they sent him the manuscript for confirmation. He replied:

With the greatest astonishment I beg to state that this cantata was never composed by me. I shall retain the same in my possession to learn, if possible, who has so impertinently sent you that sort of rubbish and also to discover the fellow who has thus misused my name.

The manuscript was returned to Schubert without comment.

The spring and summer of 1817 were devoted to the composition of piano sonatas. The wide range of piano styles and the use of unusual keys show that Schubert was experimenting in both form and medium during his months of freedom. Three of the sonatas were published posthumously: the one in A minor (D537) as op.164 (*c*1852); the one in E♭ (D568) as op.122 (1829); the one in B (D575) as op.147 (1846). A work in E minor (D566 and 506) has an extraordinary history of publication: each movement appeared separately over the years between 1848 and 1929, and the whole work, edited by Kathleen Dale, was published only in 1948. The Sonata in E♭ (D568) was first planned in the key of D♭; Schubert himself decided on the transposition and he completed the work probably by June 1817. By November he had returned to the parental home and resumed his teaching duties; he had been obliged to vacate his rooms in Schober's house the previous August. The autumn of 1817 saw the composition of the Sonata in A for violin and piano (D574) and the String Trio in B♭ (D581). Both works show clear evidence of the establishment of his style in the growing harmonic complexity, the exuberant melody and (more subtly) in the spontaneity of the modulations and the obvious delight he took in expanding a new rhythmic or melodic idea.

Vienna at that time was in the grip of one of its furores, this time for Rossini, whose operas had been received in the city with frantic enthusiasm. Schubert himself was not unmoved, and signs of the genial Italian's style appear markedly in the work he was then writing, his Sixth Symphony, in C (D589), which was begun in October. It is a transitional work and shows him attempting to express his mature vision, while still using, and being inhibited by, the language of his earlier symphonies. Two overtures 'im italienischen Stile' (D590–91), finished in November, set out to imitate, almost parody, Rossini. They are attractive and tuneful works; Schubert later re-used material from the introduction and the coda of the first in the work now known as the overture to *Rosamunde*. In December, he arranged both overtures for piano duet (D592 and 597). Besides settings of Goethe and Schiller, whose *Gruppe aus dem Tartarus* (D583) evoked one of Schubert's grandest conceptions, there are songs that year to words by his own friends, among them the immortal *An die Musik* (D547) to Schober's text. Two famous songs of 1817 are *Der Tod und das Mädchen* (D531) and *Die Forelle* (D550), which from the first won all hearts. Both melodies later served Schubert as themes for equally beloved instrumental variations. Of the Mayrhofer settings, the finest is *Memnon* (D541); a slighter song is *Erlafsee* (D586), printed in January 1818 as a supplement to a periodical – Schubert's first published work.

In December 1817, Schubert's father was appointed master of a school in the adjoining district of Rossau. The family, augmented by two sons and two daughters of the second marriage, had moved to the new house by early 1818. Schubert remained there as a teacher until the following July. It must have been doubly irksome to him, this resumption of a task he hated after a year of freedom from routine, and a return to the family circle in which he must have felt deep affection but no true kinship after his recent contact with congenial spirits. No wonder he was to say of himself during this period, 'I should have become nothing but a thwarted [*verdorbener*] musician'. His work of that spring reflects his depression. A sonata in C (D613) and a symphony in D (D615) were both left unfinished. Only a little Rondo in D for piano duet from that period (D608) has any sparkle; it was a tribute to his new friend Josef von Gahy, an excellent pianist with whom Schubert loved to play duets. (The title on the first edition, 'Notre amitié est invariable', does not, however, derive from Schubert.) The second 'Italian' overture, in C, was performed in the hall of the Zum römischen Kaiser restaurant on 1 March and again in May – his début in the concert room. These performances secured press notices in Vienna, Dresden and Leipzig.

5. VISIT TO HUNGARY. In July, the opportunity came for him to relinquish his position in the Rossau school. He was offered and accepted the post of music master to the children of Count Johann Esterházy: his pupils were the young princesses Marie and Caroline. The count's summer residence was at Zseliz, then in Hungary, about 480 km east of Vienna. Schubert resigned from his father's school and never returned to teaching.

The first weeks at Zseliz were very happy. On 3 August he wrote to his friends in Vienna:

I am quite well. I live and compose like a god, as though that were as it should be. Mayrhofer's *Einsamkeit* is ready, and I believe it to be the best I have done, for I was without a care . . . Thank God, I live at last, and it was high time . . .

Einsamkeit (D620) is a long, discursive ballad of mixed value, and few people would endorse the composer's opinion of it. Other compositions reveal the fact that he was in charge of two young pianists, for they are almost all for piano duet: a Sonata in B♭ (D617), a set of variations (D624) and a fine but little-known set of polonaises (D599). The variations, on a song called *Reposez-vous, bon chevalier*, were published in 1822 as his op.10 and dedicated to Beethoven 'by his admirer and worshipper, Franz Schubert'. As time passed, Schubert grew discontented with life at Zseliz. He felt that none of the people he met there really cared for music, and his existence began to seem unendurably empty compared with the society he had enjoyed in the capital and the stimulus of his Viennese friendships. He wrote to Schober on 8 September:

At Zseliz I am obliged to rely wholly on myself. I have to be composer, author, audience and goodness knows what else. Not a soul here has any feeling for true art, or at the most the countess now and again (unless I am wrong). So I am alone with my beloved and have to hide her in my room, in my pianoforte and in my bosom. Although this often makes me sad, on the other hand it elevates me the more. Have no fear, then, that I shall stay away longer than is absolutely necessary.

While at Zseliz Schubert composed the *Deutsches Requiem* (D621) for his brother Ferdinand who, possibly to enhance his reputation as a music teacher, passed off the work as his own. In a letter of October he referred to this 'sin of appropriation'. Schubert's reply is one of the most affectionate and sweet-natured letters he wrote: he made nothing of Ferdinand's act, saying only that it was his greatest reward for composing the *Requiem*. It was only with the discovery of this letter by Grove on 26 October 1880, announced in his article 'Schubert' in the first edition of this dictionary, that the true author of the *Deutsches Requiem* was revealed. His Sonata in F minor (D625, ?505) was composed at Zseliz in September 1818; it is not quite complete, and of very different quality from the unfinished and inferior sonata of the previous April. In November the Esterházy family returned to Vienna for the winter, Schubert with them. The association was not broken, however, and he continued to give the children lessons during the winter months. There was no return to school-teaching, although for some years he was officially designated 'school assistant at the Rossau'.

6. VIENNA FRIENDS AND PATRONS, 1819–20. On his return to Vienna, Schubert went to lodge with Mayrhofer in the Wipplingerstrasse. Relations between the two artists were cordial, and even happier was their

association in the songs of that year, for Mayrhofer's verses drew from Schubert a music whose grandeur is surpassed only by his settings of Goethe and Schiller. It is moreover an interesting facet of Schubert's work in lieder to find how the greater Mayrhofer settings often led to even greater Goethe settings – as though Mayrhofer had tapped the springs in Schubert from which Goethe could draw a finer music.

Schubert next began work on Georg von Hofmann's one-act play *Die Zwillingsbrüder* (D647); the overture is dated 19 January 1819. Vogl, for whom the leading roles (the twin brothers) were designed, secured its performance at the Kärntnertor-Theater the following year. On 8 January, a performance of the *Prometheus* cantata was given in the house of Ignaz von Sonnleithner, the father of Schubert's friend Leopold. The elder Sonnleithner was a rich patron of music and in his rooms in the Gundelhof regular and lavish concerts were given. In private circles Schubert's name was becoming widely known, and in public circles, too; an overture of his (probably that in E minor, D648, composed in February 1819), was played at Müllers Hall on 14 March, and a tenor of the Theater an der Wien, Franz Jäger, sang the *Schäfers Klagelied* several times during the spring; the performances received favourable notices in the press, one even in Berlin.

Anselm Hüttenbrenner, who had made Schubert's acquaintance when they were both pupils of Salieri's, had left Vienna for his home in Graz during autumn 1818. Schubert's relationship with him was cordial and his letters very friendly; on 19 May 1819 he wrote: 'In spite of Vogl it is difficult to outwit such *canaille* as Weigl, Treitschke etc. That is why instead of my operetta, they give other rot, enough to make your hair stand on end'. The younger brother, Josef Hüttenbrenner, remained in Vienna and gave Schubert the slavish devotion which frequently provokes snubs; Schubert's earned him the nickname 'The Tyrant'.

The summer of 1819 was one of the happiest periods of Schubert's life. He accompanied Vogl to Steyr at the beginning of July and spent nearly three months in a district which he described as 'inconceivably lovely'. Steyr, some 145 km west of Vienna, was Vogl's birthplace and whenever possible he spent the summer there. The popular 'Trout' Quintet (D667), for piano and strings, was begun there, commissioned by the town's most eminent music patron, Sylvester Paumgartner, a cellist. By the following autumn in Vienna it was finished and despatched to Paumgartner; the variation movement which gives the quintet its nickname owed its inception to Paumgartner's love of the song. It has been well suggested that the Steyr countryside was a secret collaborator in the quintet; it is even fortunate in its nickname, with its suggestion of cool, sun-flecked water.

The friends departed for Vienna in the middle of September. The record of the next six months is a chronicle of composition. Schubert rejoined Mayrhofer and in October set three of his friend's poems, including *Nachtstück* (D672). Two Goethe songs followed: one of them, *Prometheus* (D674), is the finest of his lyrico-dramatic songs. A charming song to verses by Schiller is *Strophe aus Die Götter Griechenlands* (D677, 'Schöne Welt, wo bist du?'), written in November. The fifth mass, in A♭ (D678), was begun in November, but set aside and not completed until September 1822. Another

work, unfortunately, was also left unfinished, and Schubert never returned to this fragmentary score. It is the setting, dated February 1820, of August Niemeyer's sacred poetic drama *Lazarus, oder Die Feier der Auferstehung* (D689). Although a little too full of Schubert's softer, more easy-going lyricism, it is written in a style which is endlessly fascinating; it contains hints of leitmotif, and the orchestral web which forms the accompaniment, colourful and inventive, hints at Wagnerian practice.

Die Zwillingsbrüder was staged on 14 June at the Kärntnertor-Theater with Vogl doubling the roles of the twin brothers. It had only a moderate success and was withdrawn after five further performances. But these performances did bring Schubert's name into greater prominence, and in July he was commissioned by the management of the Theater an der Wien to compose music for a three-act play, *Die Zauberharfe* (D644). It is an extravaganza, full of mechanical stage effects and burdened with a complicated plot. The text was also by Hofmann. Schubert is said to have been as little interested in *Die Zauberharfe* as he had been in *Die Zwillingsbrüder*. The music was composed in a fortnight and the work presented on 19 August 1820. The overture, now known as the *Rosamunde* overture, is Schubert's finest work in this genre and deservedly popular (the reason for its misnaming will be discussed later). The music of *Die Zauberharfe*, entirely unknown to the public, is often very beautiful and had a profound effect on Schubert's development. He was compelled by the nature of the work to write *Melodramen* (i.e. music to accompany spoken words), and for the first time in his operatic pieces was obliged, as it were, to think instrumentally rather than vocally, to develop his themes and thematic figures according to symphonic rather than to lyrical demands. We owe the 'Unfinished' Symphony to *Die Zauberharfe*. That the music was beyond the understanding of the conservative musicians of the day is clear from the words of the critic of the Leipzig *Allgemeine musikalische Zeitung*: 'most of it is much too long, ineffective and fatiguing, the harmonic progressions are too harsh, the orchestration redundant, the choruses dull and feeble'. There were eight performances, the last on 12 October 1820. A poem written by Schubert during September 1820 entitled *Der Geist der Welt* is an enigmatic piece of writing, attacking 'those . . . who with wrangling fill these days'. Many attempts have been made to explain the contemptuous dislike Schubert expressed in these words. Rudolf Klein has convincingly suggested that it was the composer's response to the philistine reception of the music he had written for *Die Zauberharfe*.

Through his association with the Esterházy family, Schubert met Baron von Schönstein in 1820. The possessor of a fine baritone voice, Schönstein was, after Vogl, the most notable interpreter of Schubert's songs during the composer's lifetime, and he later introduced them to Liszt. The poet Matthäus von Collin, a cousin of Spaun, introduced Schubert to Ignaz von Mosel and Count Moritz Dietrichstein, two important officials at the imperial court, and also to Ladislaus Pyrker, Patriarch of Venice. In December 1820, at one of Sonnleithner's concerts, August von Gymnich, accompanied by Anna Fröhlich, sang *Erlkönig*. It was received with overwhelming enthusiasm. The performance was to have far-reaching results. The immediate outcome was

3. Franz Schubert (right) with Anselm Hüttenbrenner and Jenger: drawing by Josef Teltscher (private collection)

that Schubert made the acquaintance of the four Fröhlich sisters, Barbara, Kathi, Josefine and Anna, a cultivated and musical family; through them he met Franz Grillparzer, Austria's most eminent dramatist.

Mayrhofer is the poet of several fine songs written during the autumn of 1820; one is the little-known *Freiwilliges Versinken* (D700), which reveals Schubert's growing power of subtle yet picturesque comment in the accompaniment. The year ends with an outpouring of music of the finest quality. The sketch in C♯ minor of Goethe's *Gesang der Geister über den Wassern* (D705), of superb promise, remained unfinished. Its stormy piano accompaniment, which recalls *Gruppe aus dem Tartarus*, might have been Schubert's finest exposition of this passionate style; the choral work is contrapuntal yet transparently clear. The same exalted mood is recaptured in the extended song *Im Walde* (D708), to words by Friedrich von Schlegel (it is sometimes called *Waldesnacht* to distinguish it from the similarly entitled song of 1825 to words by Ernst Schulze). *Im Walde* is almost impracticable in the concert room, but the Schubertian turns again and again to its outpoured splendour. The setting of Psalm xxiii for female voices (D706) was composed in December 1820 for the singing pupils of Anna Fröhlich, who taught at the Vienna Conservatory. Finally that month there was the first movement of an unfinished String Quartet in C minor, known as the 'Quartettsatz' (D703), in which Schubert achieved the lyrical radiance of the 'Trout' Quintet with

the dramatic intensity of his finest songs. It is the first of the instrumental masterpieces of the 1820s. 41 bars of the slow movement, an Andante in A♭, are extant.

7. EVENTS OF 1821–2. Early in 1821, Schubert left Mayrhofer and moved into a house nearby in the Wipplingerstrasse. He became very friendly with a young painter named Moritz von Schwind, some seven years his junior, who was in after years to paint the most famous of the Schubert pictures: it was called *Schubert-Abend bei Joseph von Spaun* and enshrines for ever the Biedermeier atmosphere of the Schubertiads. The settings of Goethe which he composed that spring have become famous: the songs range from the delicacy and charm of *Geheimes* (D719) to the grandeur of *Grenzen der Menschheit* (D716). A new treatment of *Gesang der Geister* for double male chorus with accompaniment for low strings (D714) was finished in February 1821. The poem held a great attraction for Schubert and this finished setting is a sublime work, though the earlier sketch holds even greater promise. At a public concert in the Kärntnertor-Theater on 7 March 1821, Vogl sang *Erlkönig*; it was a masterly performance which created a profound impression.

The continual performances of Schubert's songs and vocal quartets that year and their enthusiastic reception make it difficult to understand why publishers were so reluctant to issue his work. Songs, string quartets and piano pieces by such people as Anselm Hüttenbrenner,

Benedikt Randhartinger, Franz Volkert, Ignaz von Moscheles and hosts of other minor composers were readily accepted and published, and one has to accept the fact that, at this period in Vienna, fame as a performer was the key to publication, not merit as a composer for one as obscure as Schubert. Leopold von Sonnleithner and other friends took matters into their own hands and determined to issue *Erlkönig* by private subscription. The response was overwhelming; not only was the cost of the song covered, but also that of engraving *Gretchen am Spinnrade*. The firm of Cappi & Diabelli was commissioned to engrave the works. In this manner 20 songs were published, as opp.1–8, by the end of 1821. *Erlkönig* appeared on 31 March, dedicated to Count Dietrichstein, *Gretchen* on 30 April, dedicated to Moritz von Fries. The other songs include *Der Wanderer*, *Heidenröslein*, *Rastlose Liebe* and *Der Tod und das Mädchen*; dedications were offered to Pyrker, Vogl and Salieri. Schubert did very well from some of these carefully directed dedications; he wrote to Spaun at Linz: 'but I must now tell you that my dedications have done their work; that is to say, the Patriarch has forked out 12 ducats, and, through Vogl's intervention, Fries 20, which is a very good thing for me'.

He composed two supplementary numbers, an aria and a duet (D723), for a performance at the Kärntnertor-Theater on 20 June 1821 of Hérold's *Das Zauberglöckchen* (originally *La clochette*). Their almost

symphonic stature is ill-fitting in such a light work, and they made little impression. Soon after this luckless operatic venture, Schubert went to Atzenbrugg with Schober. The property was managed by an uncle of Schober's, and each summer a party of young people met there and spent a holiday together with excursions, concerts, dances and charades. The 1821 visit is the most notable of the three which Schubert made, since it is recorded pictorially by three drawings made by a new friend, the painter Leopold Kupelwieser. Two of these are charming watercolours depicting activities of the holiday party (see fig.4), and the third is a pencil drawing of the composer, signed and dated by him 'July 1821'. The half-dozen waltzes known as the 'Atzenbrugger' Dances (D145 nos.1–3, D365 nos.29–31) were written during this holiday. Back in Vienna he began, in August, the seventh of his symphonies, in E (D729), completing a part of the first movement in score and sketching, sometimes in detail, the remainder of the four movements. No hint of the standard reached in the Quartettsatz can be found in this slender production. The symphony has been 'realized' by J. F. Barnett (1883) and Felix Weingartner (1934) but neither attempt is convincing.

During September 1821 Schubert accompanied Schober to St Pölten; they stayed nearby at the castle of Ochsenburg (owned by the Bishop of St Pölten, a relative of Schober's), seeking in this rural retreat the

4. *Charade at Atzenbrugg: watercolour (1821) by Leopold Kupelwieser in the Schubert-Museum, Vienna; Schubert is seated at the piano with Philipp Karl Hartmann to his left, Schober, Kupelwieser and Jenger (left and right) in the doorway, and Josef von Spaun seated second from the right*

peace and seclusion necessary to embark on the work they were undertaking together, the composition of a full-scale opera, *Alfonso und Estrella* (D732). In later years, Schober wrote that they undertook this opera 'in a state of happy enthusiasm but with great innocence of heart and mind'. The first act was written between 20 September and 16 October. They returned to Vienna towards the end of October, and Schubert finished the second act in November; the opera was completed by 27 February 1822. Schober's libretto has been too readily accepted in the past as the reason for the total neglect of this work. The music is first-rate, full of Schubert's most endearing lyricism and dramatic genius.

The well-known set of waltzes op.9 (D365) was published in November 1821, and shortly after that Schubert began the first of his settings of the poet Rückert, *Sei mir gegrüsst* (D741). From the beginning of 1822 Schubert lodged with Schober in his house in the Spiegelgasse. There Schwind introduced him to Eduard Bauernfeld, later famous as a playwright and translator of Shakespeare and Dickens. Bauernfeld greatly admired Schubert's music and had ardently wished to meet him. These three young men, Schubert, Schwind and Bauernfeld, unlike in character yet united in their artistic ideals and love of music, became inseparable. During February, Schubert met Weber, who was in Vienna to conduct the first full performance in the city of *Der Freischütz* at the Kärntnertor-Theater. The theatre had just come under the management of the famous Italian impresario Domenico Barbaia, who later leased the Theater an der Wien. These moves did not promise particularly well for Schubert's new opera, on which he was placing high hopes. His published songs, however, were making their mark. They were favourably reviewed in January by the Vienna *Allgemeine musikalische Zeitung*, and in March a long, sympathetic and comprehensive criticism by Friedrich von Hentl appeared in the *Zeitschrift für Kunst*. The variations op.10 (D624) were published in April. Schubert himself is supposed to have taken a copy to Beethoven, but the accounts of this event are so contradictory that it is doubtful whether they have any factual foundation. On 3 July Schubert wrote the strange document describing the dream of a quarrel and reconciliation with a father. It is embroidered with sentimental descriptions of a mother's death and burial, and the entombment of a 'gentle maiden'. The title *Mein Traum* was added years later by Ferdinand. Attempts to look upon the tale as autobiographical have given rise to the fiction of a rupture with his father and a reconciliation at his mother's graveside.

A letter from Spaun's brother Anton, written to his wife on 20 July, gives an unpleasant account of Schubert's relations with Schober and Vogl during summer 1822. Schubert seemed to be behaving in a manner at odds with his true nature; he aped the man of the world, became offhand to his friends (discourteously so to Vogl) and extravagant and loose in his way of life. Vogl considered the libretto of *Alfonso und Estrella* to be thoroughly bad; the absence of his backing, together with the fact that Barbaia was engrossed with Rossini, led to its rejection. Apparently Schubert and Vogl were reconciled by the autumn. 12 of his songs were published in Vienna during the year, the three Harper's Songs (op.12, D478–80) and *Geheimes* (op.14, D719) appearing on 13 December. The songs of 1822 include

settings of Mayrhofer, composed in the spring, one of which is the charming *Nachtviolen* (D752); towards the end of the year there were settings of Goethe, not of the stature of *Prometheus*, but containing such sublime specimens of his lyric art as *Der Musensohn* (D764) and *Am Flusse* (D766). The Mass in A♭ (D678) was finished in September, and November saw the first example of his maturity in piano composition, the 'Wanderer' Fantasy (D760).

The outstanding work of that autumn is the eighth of Schubert's symphonies, the 'Unfinished' in B minor (D759). Only one other work among his instrumental compositions up to that time, the Quartettsatz, is not dwarfed by the two movements of the symphony. They were composed during October and the scherzo set aside for the composition of the 'Wanderer' Fantasy.

Many theories have been evolved to account for the fact that Schubert never finished the symphony. That he intended it to be a two-movement work is disposed of by the existence of a substantial part of the third movement. It has been suggested that the symphony was in fact finished: T. C. L. Pritchard put forward the idea in 1942 that Anselm Hüttenbrenner had lost the manuscript of the last two movements, but more recent documentation and discoveries leave no ground for this theory; more recently Gerald Abraham has suggested that the finale of the symphony is the movement used by Schubert as the B minor entr'acte of the *Rosamunde* music, but his arguments are slender and are contrary to the weight of palaeographic evidence. The truth about Schubert's failure to complete the symphony may lie in psychological factors, and particularly in the tragic event which occurred at the end of 1822. He then contracted syphilis, and by the late spring of 1823 he was desperately ill. To a sensitive man like Schubert the association of the composition of his symphony with the events which led to his illness might have made a return to it repugnant. The fate of the manuscript has also been bedevilled by theorizing on scanty facts. The recent disclosure of documents from the Hüttenbrenner family archives shows that Schubert gave the manuscript of the 'Unfinished' Symphony, in its incomplete state, to Josef Hüttenbrenner some time in 1823, to pass it on to his brother Anselm as a private gift (not, as long believed, as an acknowledgment of his election to the Styrian Music Society). This was probably in payment for a debt or an obligation; Anselm had a perfect right to retain the score. It was eventually, in 1865, handed over to the conductor of the orchestra of the Vienna Musikverein and performed in December that year.

8. ILLNESS. The onset of his illness forced Schubert to leave Schober's home. By the end of 1822 he was living in his father's house in the Rossau. In the early weeks of 1823 he was too ill to leave the house, as we learn from a letter which he wrote to Ignaz von Mosel asking him to send *Alfonso und Estrella*, with a letter of recommendation, to Weber at Dresden. On this same day, 24 February, the 'Wanderer' Fantasy was published as op.15.

The pressing need for money forced Schubert into a bad business move that winter. He sold to Cappi & Diabelli, for a lump sum, all his rights in the publication of opp.1–7, and in February offered them the remaining opp.12–14. He suspected the publishers of dishonest dealing with him, and not only in the strict account of sales. He broke with the firm in a letter of 10 April

5. *Autograph sketches for the projected scherzo of Schubert's Symphony no.8 in B minor* D759 *('Unfinished'), composed October 1822 (A-Wgm)*

1823, a letter with an edge which is new in Schubert. His first publication from another house was op.20, issued by Sauer & Leidesdorf; it included *Frühlingsglaube* (D686) and *Sei mir gegrüsst* (D741). His next piano sonata, in A minor (D784), was written in February 1823; it is the first of his mature sonatas, restrained and economical compared with the 'Wanderer' Fantasy, and breaking completely with the graceful, ornamental style of his earlier sonatas. A one-act operetta, *Die Verschworenen* (D787), to a libretto by Ignaz Castelli, was completed in April (in deference to a touchy political censorship the title was changed to *Der häusliche Krieg*). It was not performed in Schubert's lifetime, but has proved to be thoroughly stageworthy, as well as melodious, witty and delightfully scored.

By now, Schubert's condition had grown so serious that he was admitted to the Vienna general hospital. A poem of his, written on 8 May, makes painful reading; it ends:

Take my life, my flesh and blood,
Plunge it all in Lethe's flood,
To a purer, stronger state,
Deign me, Great One, to translate.

Yet during this depressing period the first songs of the *Schöne Müllerin* cycle were composed; they grace this unhappy year, in truth, like 'a sunny archipelago of songs'. The author is Wilhelm Müller, and the story told in the sequence of poems originated in a family charade.

9. STAGE FAILURES. On 25 May Schubert turned once more to the composition of a full-length opera, *Fierabras* (D796). The play has a complicated plot, set in the time of Charlemagne although its ideas and atmosphere are medieval. The libretto was by Josef Kupelwieser, brother of Leopold. Schubert's inability to visualize how ineffective this play would be as a theatrical proposition suggests that there was no genuine theatrical urge behind his repeated operatic ventures. It can never have occurred to him that to earn a living in this way would be as arduous a task as routine classteaching. He spent the weeks from the end of July to mid-September revisiting Linz and Steyr, where he met Spaun, Mayrhofer and Vogl. His life was regular and quiet; that and the summer air of this idyllic countryside restored him somewhat, though even there he suffered a bout of severe illness. He was elected an honorary member of the Linz Musical Society and met the president, Friedrich von Hartmann, whose two sons, Fritz and Franz, later came to Vienna and kept copious diaries which contain many references to Schubert and his friends. *Fierabras* was finished on 26 September, and the overture completed on 2 October. The rejection by Barbaia was inevitable: no discerning manager could

have accepted the play, in spite of the excellence of its music – music which haunts the mind more than that of *Alfonso und Estrella*, which Schubert is supposed to have preferred to all his other operas.

Weber was in Vienna that autumn for the first performance of *Euryanthe* on 25 October. In Schubert's opinion its bad reception was justified, and when he met Weber at the Zur ungarischen Krone inn he told him so, adding that he preferred *Der Freischütz*. Relations between the two men cooled, but there is no trustworthy evidence that this frankness on Schubert's part led to a quarrel between him and Weber. In November Schubert was again seriously ill; but he rallied, and wrote on 30 November to Schober (who was at Breslau attempting to make a name as an actor) that his health seemed to be firmly restored at last. In those days, of course, a cure was out of the question; the disease never again racked him outwardly, but it steadily undermined his central nervous system. His temperament, too, was altering. With his resilient good humour there would always be periods in which he knew no care; but he had also to contend with pain and giddiness which understandably induced fits of irritability and depression. He told Schober that he had composed more *Schöne Müllerin* songs; the cycle was completed soon afterwards. The remaining Rückert songs, including the celebrated *Du bist die Ruh* (D776) and *Dass sie hier gewesen* (D775), were also probably composed that autumn.

In spite of the object-lesson of *Euryanthe*, he accepted in October a commission to write incidental music to a romantic drama by the same author, Helmina von Chézy. The drama, *Rosamunde, Fürstin von Zypern*, is lost, but a synopsis of the plot, surviving in contemporary records, shows its worthlessness. Fortunately most of Schubert's music is instrumental (D797). Produced on 20 December, *Rosamunde* was a failure, and it achieved only two performances. The orchestral parts for the vocal numbers lay in oblivion until 1867, when they were rescued by Grove and Sullivan. Today the entr'actes and ballet music, although written in an incredibly short time, are among Schubert's most popular orchestral works. The fact that he wrote no overture to *Rosamunde* has led to two of his other overtures' being wrongly attributed to the play. For the actual performance he used the overture to *Alfonso und Estrella*, possibly in revised form; it is this work, in D (D732), which was wrongly printed in the Breitkopf & Härtel complete edition at the start of the *Rosamunde* incidental music and so was looked upon as the authentic *Rosamunde* overture. The second misnamed work, now universally performed as the *Rosamunde* overture, is actually the overture composed for the performance of *Die Zauberharfe* in 1820.

Although Schubert never abandoned his ambition to write a successful opera, *Rosamunde* is his last completed dramatic work. He then turned again to purely instrumental forms, and in them achieved masterly success. At the beginning of 1824 he composed his first chamber works for over three years. On 13 February Schwind wrote to Schober: 'Schubert now keeps a fortnight's fast and confinement. He looks much better and is very bright, very comically hungry and writes quartets and German dances and variations without number'. The quartets were the favourite one in A minor (D804), finished in March 1824 (published the following September as op.29 no.1), and the one in D minor

(D810) with variations on the song *Der Tod und das Mädchen* as its slow movement, also finished in March 1824; because of a mistake by Franz Lachner the date 1826 is still often assigned to it. Among the variations mentioned by Schwind is the set for flute and piano (D802) on *Trockne Blumen* from the *Schöne Müllerin* cycle, which Schubert composed for Ferdinand Bogner, professor at the Vienna Conservatory. During February he was also at work on the Octet in F for wind and strings (D803) which had been commissioned by Ferdinand, Count Troyer, a clarinettist and a member of the Archduke Rudolph's musical establishment. The Octet, deservedly popular, was modelled (at Troyer's request) on Beethoven's Septet, and although the work is highly characteristic of Schubert there are links, both obvious and subtle, between the two. The theme of the variation movement is from the duet 'Gelagert unter'm hellen Dach der Bäume' in *Die Freunde von Salamanka*. On 14 March a quartet led by Ignaz Schuppanzigh gave a public performance of the A minor String Quartet; three days later the first part of *Die schöne Müllerin* was published as op.25. Schubert dedicated neither of these works to a rich patron, who might have made some financial return, but instead paid tribute to two fine artists: the first was dedicated to Schuppanzigh, the second to Baron von Schönstein.

10. SCHUBERT'S CIRCLE OF FRIENDS. Letters exchanged in those days between his friends often touch on Schubert or his activities; Schwind wrote to Schober on 6 March: 'If you go to see him during the day, he says, "Hullo, how are you? – Good" and goes on writing'. Reading parties, instituted by Schober in autumn 1822, had become so swollen with new and uncongenial acquaintances that not even custom could prolong their existence. Doblhoff wrote to Schober on 2 April: 'Yesterday our reading circle was formally suspended. It had grown so much that in the end it devoured itself . . . Schubertiads are hardly mentioned any more. Schubert himself cannot sing, and Vogl will sing only in agreeable and respectable society'. Schubert's circle had disintegrated and another one was in the process of forming. While we cannot altogether regret the departure of Schober, it is quite another matter to consider Spaun's absence in Linz, Kupelwieser's departure for Italy and the estrangement of Mayrhofer (which occurred that spring). With Schwind he was on terms of affectionate intimacy, and soon Bauernfeld came into prominence; but in the composer's mind the breaking of his friendships and the wreck of his health became associated, and with almost unbearable misery he wrote to Kupelwieser on 31 March 1824:

In a word, I feel myself to be the most unhappy and wretched creature in the world. Imagine a man whose health will never be right again, and who, in sheer despair over this, ever makes things worse and worse, instead of better; imagine a man, I say, whose most brilliant hopes have perished, to whom the felicity of love and friendship have nothing to offer but pain . . . Thus joyless and friendless I should pass my days, did not Schwind visit me now and again and turn on me a ray of those sweet days of the past.

Schubert went that summer to Zseliz for a second time as music master to the Esterházy family, leaving Vienna on 25 May. It was a grudging move on his part, for he wrote to Schober on 21 September: 'Now I sit here alone in the depths of the Hungarian country whither I unfortunately let myself be enticed a second time without having a single person with whom I could speak a sensible word'. In this letter we again have that aching cry for the past: 'I want to exclaim with Goethe: "Who will bring me back an hour of that sweet time?"' (an allusion to *Erster Verlust*, which he had set in 1815). Family letters survive from 1824 as from 1818. Ferdinand and Franz were always devoted brothers, and the composer's illness had drawn them even closer. On 3 July Ferdinand wrote to his brother that a musical clock in the Zur ungarischen Krone inn had played several of his (Franz's) waltzes, and that hearing them he was moved to ... but he could not finish the sentence. Schubert replied, 'Did all the tears come to your mind which you have seen me weep?'. To Schwind, during August, Schubert wrote:

I am still well, thank goodness, and should be quite comfortable here, if only I had you, Schober and Kupelwieser with me, but as it is, I often long damnably for Vienna, in spite of the certain attractive star. By the end of September, I hope to see you all again. I have composed a grand sonata and variations for four hands, which latter are having a great success here.

Both works mentioned are for piano duet. The 'grand sonata' was composed in June and published posthumously under the title 'Grand Duo' as op.140 (D812). The variations are those in A♭ (D813), published the following spring as op.35. Another piano duet of the period is the famous *Divertissement à l'hongroise* (D818) whose best moments are among the most superb passages in Schubert's music for piano duet. The 'attractive star' of his letter is certainly Caroline

Esterházy, then nearly 20 years old, with whom he was believed to be in love. The vocal quartet *Gebet* (D815) was written for her during one September day, Schubert receiving Fouqué's words after breakfast and presenting the finished composition for rehearsal that evening.

He arrived back in Vienna, with Baron von Schönstein, on 17 September, and once more went to live in the Rossau. He was considerably better for having spent those quiet summer months in Zseliz, and Schwind wrote to Schober on 8 November: 'Schubert is here, well and divinely frivolous, rejuvenated by delight and pain and a pleasant life'. The Sonata in A minor (D821) for piano and arpeggione (a six-string cello-like instrument with frets) was composed in November and played shortly after by the man for whom it was written, Vincenz Schuster; it is a secondary work compared with the giants of the year, but not to be despised. Anna Milder-Hauptmann, whom Schubert in his youth had revered for her operatic singing, wrote to him on 12 December from Berlin. She had come to know and admire his songs, and asked whether she might use her good offices to secure the performance of one of his operas in Berlin. Schubert sent her the score of *Alfonso und Estrella*, but without success.

His growing intimacy with Schwind led him in February 1825 to move into the suburb of Wieden, where he occupied rooms in a house close to Schwind's home. Schubert was fond of the volatile young painter and called him his 'beloved'; Schwind, for his part,

6. Franz Schubert: watercolour portrait (1825) by Wilhelm August Rieder in the Historisches Museum, Vienna

idolized the composer and daily sought his company. In his own sphere as painter and illustrator, Schwind was to achieve notable work, but through Schubert we encounter him in his turbulent youth, and he shows a tiresome strain of adolescent gracelessness, particularly in his childish quarrels. According to Bauernfeld he behaved with studied rudeness to Vogl. Bauernfeld's close friendship with Schubert began during February. It is easy to see how attractive to Schubert was the company of this lighthearted youth, who chaffed him over his love affairs, fraternized with him in taverns and promised him a new operatic libretto.

11. 1825: A PRODUCTIVE YEAR. 1825 saw the steady growth of Schubert's reputation. Songs and vocal quartets were performed in Vienna by the Gesellschaft der Musikfreunde (the Musikverein) and at the Vienna Conservatory. Schubertiads, with Vogl once more supreme, were more popular than ever, taking place in the houses of Witteczek or Weintridt and, on one occasion, in the house of Katherina von Lászny, a former soprano at the Kärntnertor-Theater, courtesan and patron of the arts. To her Schubert dedicated op.36, containing *Der zürnenden Diana* (D707). Another famous singer whom Schubert met that spring was the popular and much loved Sofie Müller. Extracts from her diary tell of frequent visits by Schubert and Vogl to her home in Hietzing, a district which includes the Schönbrunn estate. She herself sang many of his songs, including *Die junge Nonne* (D828) on 3 March 1825, soon after it was composed.

Anna Milder-Hauptmann wrote from Berlin on 8 March and quickly dispelled any hopes Schubert may have had that his opera would be done there. It is evident, reading between the lines, that she had hoped for an opera with a big leading role for herself and had looked upon Schubert as a possible provider of congenial showpieces. At her concert in Berlin on 9 June she included *Erlkönig* and the second Suleika song (D717). The *Berlinische Zeitung* commented appreciatively on the music, and Anna sent the cutting to Schubert, then on holiday in Gmunden. In both Berlin and Dresden, Viennese correspondents reported favourably on his songs. The publications in Vienna during 1825 make an impressive list, both in quantity and in quality. They include, besides such songs as *An Schwager Kronos*, *Ganymed* (both op.19, D369, 544) and *Die junge Nonne* (op.43, D828), the C major Mass (op.48, D452) and the A♭ variations for piano duet (op.35, D813). Quite as interesting is the variety of publishers. Schubert still had no dealings with Diabelli; the works issued by that firm had been acquired before the break in 1823. But Cappi & Co., Sauer & Leidesdorf and Pennauer published his work and before the end of the year Artaria was negotiating with him.

In spring 1825, the fine Piano Sonata in A minor (D845) was composed; but a potentially even finer one in C, known as the 'Reliquie' (D840) was left unfinished. We may regret this the more deeply since the magnificent first movement is accordingly little known. Some of the songs from Scott's *The Lady of the Lake* were composed that month, in a translation by P. Adam Storck; Schubert hoped that the addition of Scott's original text, when the songs were published, would help to make his name known in England.

Towards the end of May he left Vienna for a holiday with Vogl in Upper Austria; the summers of 1824 and 1825 thus parallel the summers of 1818 and 1819. He spent over four months in this district, a supremely happy period in his life; everywhere he found new friends and old admirers of his songs and piano pieces. To facilitate reference, it may be well to list his movements during the period:

Steyr (20 May–4 June; there was a short visit to Linz during this period); Gmunden (4 June–15 July; including a visit to Ebenzweier); Linz (15–25 July; a visit to Steyregg); Steyr (25 July–13 August); Gastein (14 August–4 September; via Werfen and Lake Traun); Gmunden (10–17 September); Steyr (17 September–1 October); Linz to Vienna (1–3 October).

According to a letter of 19 July to Spaun from Anton Ottenwalt, Schubert's host at Linz, the composer 'worked at a symphony at Gmunden'. This is the first mention of the supposedly lost work of 1825, called the 'Gastein' or 'Gmunden–Gastein' Symphony (D849). Interpretations of the documents vary, but certainly a symphony was sketched (Reed, 1972, believed that the work was practically completed), and the sketches probably became the Symphony in C (D944). There is no evidence, however, to connect the 'Gastein' Symphony with the Grand Duo of 1824.

The songs of *The Lady of the Lake*, particularly *Ellens Gesang III* (popularly known as *Ave Maria* D839), frequently featured in the song recitals which Schubert and Vogl gave for their friends that summer. The performance of these two men, playing and singing as if they were one, was something new and unheard of, and they had tremendous success (so Schubert wrote to his brother Ferdinand in September). His letters to his family are long and interesting, coloured as they were by his journeyings through this lovely region, and by the warmth of his reception at the hands of people who were strangers, but who looked upon him, because of his music, as a valued friend. He wrote to his parents on 25 July:

In Upper Austria I find my compositions everywhere, especially at the monasteries of Florian and Kremsmünster, where with the aid of a gallant pianist I produced my four-hand variations and marches with notable success. What pleased especially were the variations in my new sonata for two hands, which I performed alone and not without merit, since several people assured me that the keys became singing voices under my hands.

At Gastein he finished another piano sonata in D (D850), a work full of the overflowing romanticism so typical of that summer; we find it again in two magnificent songs to words by Pyrker, composed in August: *Das Heimweh* (D851) and *Die Allmacht* (D852), Schubert's rapturous creation in music of the summer beauty of the landscape about him, which had so fortified him in spirit and body during these months.

On 3 October Schubert arrived in Vienna, accompanied by Gahy. He found awaiting him not only Bauernfeld and Schwind, but also Schober, returned from Breslau, and Kupelwieser from Italy. Schober quickly assumed his old place in the centre of the stage, and Bauernfeld recorded in his diary that the reunion led to celebrations in inns and coffee houses, often until 2 or 3 a.m. An acknowledgment of Schubert's growing reputation that year is the fact that his portrait was on sale in December at the house of Cappi & Co. An 'extremely good likeness', the firm called it; it is an engraving by J. H. Passini of the best-known portrait, the watercolour by Wilhelm Rieder made from sketches in May 1825 (fig.6).

12. EVENTS OF 1826. In January 1826 Schubert produced the last of his settings of Goethe, the Songs

from *Wilhelm Meister* (D877). All are to lyrics of Mignon which he had set before, but which he now supplemented with more mature if not necessarily more endearing settings. The following month the String Quartet in D minor (D810) was performed at the residence of Josef Barth; it was published posthumously in 1831. The publication, early in 1826, of the A minor Piano Sonata (D845) as op.42 by Pennauer widely established Schubert's status as a composer for the piano; there were favourable notices in Leipzig (1 March) and Frankfurt (26 August). The Zurich publisher Hans Nägeli mentioned Schubert in a series of lectures, purely as a piano composer; he also wrote to Carl Czerny on 18 June saying that the A minor Sonata was a 'capital piece' and asking him to invite Schubert to contribute to a projected series of piano works by contemporary composers. On 4 July Schubert accepted the invitation, but did nothing further in the matter – unless it is to Nägeli's offer that we owe the composition of the Sonata in G major (D894) in the following October.

The publications of the year are more numerous and impressive than those of 1825, and among his publishers Artaria and Thaddeus Weigl make their appearance. The former published the *Lady of the Lake* songs (op.52), the D major Sonata (op.53, D850) dedicated to the pianist Karl von Bocklet, and the *Divertissement à l'hongroise* (op.54, D818). Weigl, in addition to songs, published as op.63 no.1 a Divertissement for piano duet on supposedly French motifs (D823); Schubert intended this to be the first part of a three-section work, the other two parts being an *Andantino varié* and a *Rondeau brillant*. These two, through a mistake, were published as op.84, and the work has remained in this dismembered state ever since. Op.51, from Diabelli in August, contains the favourite *Marche militaire* (D733). On 12 August Schubert wrote to Breitkopf & Härtel and to H. A. Probst, offering to the two Leipzig firms songs and instrumental pieces. Both replied courteously, but there the matter ended. On 7 April 1826, Schubert petitioned the emperor to be appointed as vice-director of the imperial court chapel; it was a move clearly directed by financial need, but equally clearly he genuinely wanted the post and was disappointed when he heard of his failure to secure it.

Bauernfeld spent the summer in Carinthia, and at Villach he wrote *Der Graf von Gleichen* as a libretto for Schubert. Once again we are faced with the extraordinary inability of the composer to assess the merit of opera texts: *Der Graf von Gleichen* (D918) is a lifeless hotch-potch of stock stage situations with, moreover, a bigamous marriage as the central theme. It was prohibited by the censor, but Schubert continued to make sketches, often in considerable detail, for the music. Spaun had returned to Vienna during April and resumed his friendly relations with Schubert; we see the two friends at a new haunt, the inn Zum grünen Anker, near St Stephen's Cathedral. To the composer's closer acquaintance with the poet Johann Seidl we owe a group of songs including *Das Zügenglöcklein* (D871) and the *Vier Refrainlieder* (D866) and two vocal quartets, *Nachthelle* and *Grab und Mond* (D892–3). There was also a fine series of songs in 1826 to poems by Ernst Schulze, among them *Über Wildemann* (D884) and the ever fresh *Im Frühling* (D882). During July, while staying at the Schober house in Währing, he composed the three Shakespeare songs (the German versions were cast

in the original metre, and neither Shakespeare nor Schubert needs to be modified when the songs are sung in English). The well-known story of Schubert's composing *Hark, hark the lark* on the back of a menu card, where a resourceful friend had pencilled staves to accommodate his sudden inspiration, derives from Doppler and is fictional, as are most of his reminiscences of Schubert. If other familiar Schubert anecdotes are missing from these pages, it is because of similar dubious provenance.

His last String Quartet, in G (D887), was finished on 30 June. He had written to Bauernfeld the previous month: 'I am not working at all'; when the period of inactivity passed it was followed by a burst of creation, and the quartet was begun and finished in ten days. In spite of the publications of this year, he had no money for a holiday; a journey with Vogl was out of the question: the aging singer had married on 26 June. Kupelwieser, too, married that year, on 17 September. Schubert improvised dance music during the wedding celebrations; we read that he would not let anyone else go near the piano. A curious sequel to the wedding ceremony has come to light. One of the waltzes he improvised (AI/14) was remembered by the bride, Johanna Lutz. It was handed down in the family, and successive descendants of Johanna learnt the waltz-tune by ear. Eventually, in 1943, it was heard by Richard Strauss, who wrote it down and arranged it for piano.

For a short time in autumn 1826 Schubert lodged with Schober, but at the end of the year was again in rooms of his own. There is an almost day-to-day account of his doings during December in Franz von Hartmann's diary. He was surrounded by his friends, able to meet them at the Zum grünen Anker or Bogner's café, where more often than not they heard the chimes at midnight. There were Schubertiads at Schober's home or at Spaun's, culminating in the imposing event of 15 December. Here, in Spaun's house, a large and distinguished company gathered and heard Vogl, during the course of the evening, sing about 30 songs (Schwind's famous sepia drawing of 1868 was inspired by this concert; see fig.7). On 2 December the overture to *Alfonso und Estrella* was performed at the Kärntnertor-Theater; the performance was reported in the London *Harmonicon* the following June (1827).

13. PERIOD OF 'WINTERREISE'. Schubert and his friends met during 1827 at the inn Zum Schloss Eisenstadt, but he felt himself bound by no social obligations. Schwind, Leopold von Sonnleithner, Anton Ottenwalt and even Schober suffered from his neglect, and the Hartmann brothers recorded that in March Schubert invited them to his rooms at Schober's but never put in an appearance. A hostess, writing to a friend in June, said: '[Schubert] was most amiable and talkative, but escaped suddenly before anyone had an inkling'. Engrossment in the work of composition was frequently the cause of this non-compliance, though not always. According to Bauernfeld, he would fail to keep engagements if an evening walk or the chance of a sociable gathering with his friends tempted him to do so. He heard in January of his failure to secure the court chapel appointment. The successful applicant was Josef Weigl; Schubert's comment was generous: 'Much as I would have liked to receive the appointment, I shall have to make the best of the matter, since it was given to so worthy a man as Weigl'. The first part of the song cycle

7. Schubert Abend bei Joseph von Spaun: sepia drawing by Moritz von Schwind in the Historisches Museum, Vienna; Schubert is at the piano, with Vogl on his right, and Spaun on his left

Winterreise (D911) was composed in February. The poems are by the author of *Die schöne Müllerin* and there is no need for the evidence in letters and memoirs by his friends to make us realize how eagerly Schubert seized this renewed opportunity to treat Müller's picturesque and limpid verses. Soon after the composition of these songs he rejoined Schober, who had moved into a new house, 'Unter den Tuchlauben'. In March of that year, Beethoven, ill and near to death, may have been given some of Schubert's songs to read while on his deathbed. The story is told by Anton Schindler, who related that among the songs were such masterpieces as *Die junge Nonne*, *Die Allmacht* and *Grenzen der Menschheit*, besides the lyrics of *Die schöne Müllerin*. He was impressed by the songs and, if we are to believe the untrustworthy Schindler, said: 'Truly in Schubert there is a divine spark'. Schubert, in the company of the Hüttenbrenner brothers and other friends, visited the dying Beethoven on 19 March, and for the first and last time the two men, who had lived for years as strangers in the same city, met for a brief moment. A week later Beethoven died and was buried in the Währing cemetery. Schubert was one of 36 torch-bearers in the funeral procession.

He resumed negotiations with Diabelli in spring 1827 and the firm published the Mignon songs of 1826 (D877) as op.62 on 2 March. Together with the reappearance of this old name in the list of his publishers is a new one, that of Tobias Haslinger, who published several sets of songs, the *Valses nobles* (op.77, D969; 22

January) and the G major Sonata (op.78, D894; 11 April), dedicated to Spaun. Haslinger gave op.78 the spurious title 'Fantasie, Andante, Menuetto und Allegretto'; the name 'Fantasy' has ever since haunted the work, one of Schubert's noblest essays for the piano.

The Viennese press continued to report on performances of his songs and to review his publications, but there was in 1827 a remarkable and widespread increase in similar reports and reviews in the provincial press of Germany in Frankfurt, Leipzig, Berlin, Mainz and Munich. Not all were favourable, but those that were spoke of the composer with high praise. The Leipzig *Musikalische Zeitung* (26 December) devoted nearly 2000 words to a discussion of op.78; the criticism is still readable and convincing. The numerous press notices belie the 19th-century view of Schubert as a composer with a tragically limited reputation; but their isolation from the context of contemporary documentation produces an equally false view of his fame in Austria and Germany. Its shallowness is proved by the decades of neglect and oblivion which followed his death.

Schubert spent a few weeks in the early summer, possibly with Schober, in the village of Dornbach; he stayed at the inn Zur Kaiserin von Österreich. Vienna was within easy reach, and there were occasional convivial evenings at Zum Schloss Eisenstadt. The only composition known to belong to the period is the lovely *Das Lied im Grünen* (D917), written in June, but probably some of the short piano pieces, later published

8. Title-page of the 'Gesänge aus Wilhelm Meister von Göthe' D877, published by Diabelli on 2 March 1827

as 'Impromptus', were also composed then. His election as a representative to the Vienna Gesellschaft der Musikfreunde was made that month, his own city honouring him as Linz and Graz had already done. An opportunity to visit the latter town in the coming autumn arose through his friendship with Johann Baptist Jenger, which dated from 1825. Jenger was a prominent member of the Styrian Music Society; he and Schubert were invited to spend a few weeks in the home of Dr and Frau Pachler at Graz. Schubert wrote to this lady on 12 June: 'I cannot forbear to accept an invitation whereby I shall not only set eyes at last on much vaunted Graz, but have the privilege, moreover, of making your honour's acquaintance'. The first performance of *Ständchen* (D920), to Grillparzer's words, was given by Anna Fröhlich's pupils on 11 August at Döbling. The occasion was the birthday of one of the pupils, Louise Gosmar, who later married Leopold von Sonnleithner. Anna received the poem from Grillparzer and asked Schubert to set it to music. He did so, for contralto solo and male-voice chorus; the mistake was pointed out to him and he quickly rewrote the chorus parts for female voices. The performance, in the garden of the Gosmar residence on that summer evening, would no doubt have delighted the composer, had he troubled to attend it. The new haunt that summer was the inn called Zum Wolf, der den Gänsen predigt; Schwind's and Bauernfeld's names are missing from the records of the meetings. Both were out of touch with Schubert that year; in fact, Schwind left in August for a visit to Munich, and Bauernfeld wrote in his diary: 'What is to become of us all? Shall we stick together?'.

Schubert and Jenger arrived in Graz on 3 September. Their hostess, Marie Pachler, was an accomplished woman, an excellent pianist, who had known Beethoven. She sought to entertain at her home in Graz any notable artist who was visiting the town. The days were spent in excursions to various places in the lovely neighbourhood of Graz, including the castle of Wildbach. Anselm Hüttenbrenner was an old friend, of course, and he, Jenger and Schubert were responsible for the Schubertiads held in the evenings. Schubert's famous nickname of the period, 'Schwammerl', Viennese dialect for 'little mushroom', is an allusion to his diminutive stature, not to his stoutness (which was denied by Spaun); it may still explain, perhaps, why he preferred to improvise dance music for his friends rather than to dance himself. The dances he composed that holiday were published as the *Grazer Galopp* (D925) and the *Grazer Walzer* (op.91, D924). The two songs of the month, *Heimliches Lieben* (D922) and Herder's translation of the Scottish ballad *Edward* (D923), were both composed at the instigation of Frau Pachler, to whom Schubert dedicated op.106, which contains *An Sylvia* (D891) and settings of the poet Leitner (a personal friend of the Pachlers). Later in the year, their small son, Faust, received from Schubert a *Kindermarsch* for piano duet (D928).

The return to Vienna came on 20 September; in his letter of thanks to Frau Pachler, Schubert wrote of his happiness at Graz, and of his difficulty in settling down to life in Vienna. He was, in fact, in poor health, suffering from severe headaches and frequent suffusions of blood to the head. Both Spaun and Mayrhofer wrote of his depression and drawn looks during October, but they were misguided in associating them with the composition of the concluding songs of *Winterreise*. The sombre depths of these songs are the response of his genius to the moods of Müller's verses, not a reflection of his own sufferings. When Schubert sang the

Winterreise songs to his friends they were nonplussed, and Schober confessed to liking only *Der Lindenbaum*. His preference is illuminating: he cared only for the straightforward, melodious side of Schubert's art, and almost quarrelled with Spaun, earlier in the year, after expressing his dislike of the sonatas opp.42 and 53 (D845 and 850). When Vogl, however, familiarized the friends with *Winterreise*, it was as Schubert had confidently foretold. Their indifference changed to keen admiration. The exact date of composition of the Piano Trio no.1 in B♭ (D898) is not known; it was probably early in 1828. The second, in E♭ (D929), was begun in November 1827. The latter was first performed on 26 December 1827, by Bocklet, Schuppanzigh and Linke. Many years after his death several of Schubert's friends alleged that he had used a Swedish tune in the work; although accounts differ, the tale may have some foundation.

Most of the short piano pieces published under the titles *Impromptus* and *Momens musicals* (sic), as opp.90 and 142, and op.94 respectively, were composed in the autumn of that year. They were in the tradition of Tomášek's similar short lyrics, the 'Eclogues' and 'Dithyrambs', but Schubert owed little to Tomášek; nor has the influence of his own piano pieces of this kind been as great as simplifying historians have claimed. Two pieces from the *Moments musicaux*, D780 nos.3 and 6, belong to earlier years, the first to 1823 and the second to 1824. The last work of 1827 was the Fantasy in C for piano and violin (D934), published in 1850 as op.159. Like the Rondo in B minor of 1826 (D895), for the same combination, it was designed for and played by the Bohemian violinist Josef Slavík. During the course of the Fantasy the song *Sei mir gegrüsst* is used as the basis for virtuoso variations which are not among Schubert's most successful essays in this genre.

14. THE LAST YEAR. The accomplishments of 1828 give to Schubert's death an overwhelmingly tragic aspect. His health was broken, and the feverish rate of production of these unparalleled 11 months before his death undoubtedly exhausted him. The work of 1828 is the *ne plus ultra* of his achievement. At the beginning of the year, and for the last time, his friends were all with him; even Mayrhofer was reconciled and made a brief appearance. The Schubertian circle has occasioned surprised comment on its predominantly non-musical character, but the musicians of that circle were so much less remarkable and articulate than the others that Schubert's quiet friendships with Gahy, Jenger, Lachner and the Hüttenbrenners tend to be overlooked. Under Schober's influence, the reading circles came into existence again, and there in January Schubert made the acquaintance of Heine's *Reisebilder*. Spaun was engaged on 6 January to Franziska Röner; at an evening concert on 28 January to celebrate the occasion – the last Schubertiad to be held at Spaun's house – the B♭ Trio was played by Bocklet, Schuppanzigh and Linke. The marriage took place on 14 April. Schubert's last letter to Anselm Hüttenbrenner, written on 18 January, asks for Anselm's good offices to procure for his brother Karl an appointment as drawing master in the training-school at Graz. He also inquired about two of his songs (*Im Walde* D834 and *Auf der Bruck* D853) which were being lithographed for publication at Graz by Josef Kreiner. They appeared the following May as op.90 (*recte* op.93). In January there were two public performances of his works: Slavík and Bocklet played

the C major Fantasy on 20 January, and four days later, under the auspices of the Gesellschaft der Musikfreunde, the Grillparzer *Ständchen* was given; Schubert was present this time and remarked afterwards to Anna Fröhlich: 'Really, I never thought it was so beautiful'. The plan to give a full-scale public concert consisting solely of his own works, which had been maturing so long in his mind (the first mention of it had been in 1823) was put into effect at the end of March. The use of a room in the house Zum roten Igel, belonging to the Gesellschaft, was petitioned and granted, and on the evening of 26 March the concert was given to a packed and fervently partisan audience. The compositions and their performers were as follows:

1. First movement of a string quartet [? in G]: Böhm, Holz, Weiss and Linke;
2. Songs, *Der Kreuzzug* (D932), *Die Sterne* (D939), *Fischerweise* (D881), *Fragment aus dem Aeschylus* (D450): Vogl, accompanied by Schubert;
3. *Ständchen* (D920b): Josefine Fröhlich and her sister's pupils from the conservatory;
4. Trio in E♭ (D929): Bocklet, Böhm and Linke;
5. *Auf dem Strom* (D943): Ludwig Tietze, with horn obbligato by Josef Lewy;
6. *Die Allmacht* (D852): Vogl and Schubert;
7. *Schlachtlied* (D912): double chorus for male voices.

The event was called 'Franz Schubert's Invitation Concert', and it may be seen from the Deutsch numbers that nearly all the compositions were late ones. The programme gave no key for the string quartet but called it 'new'; the song with horn obbligato was written for the occasion. The concert received hardly a line in the press; it was eclipsed by the advent of Paganini. The great virtuoso threw Vienna into a frenzy greater than that which attended the advent of Rossini a dozen years earlier. Schubert, for a while prosperous (the concert had brought him 320 florins), went to hear Paganini in April and again in May, when he took Bauernfeld.

The 'Great' C major Symphony – probably, as we have seen, the work sketched at Gmunden in 1825 – was finished by March. It is likely that it was finalized for performance by the Gesellschaft der Musikfreunde; Schubert rarely composed without a performance of some sort in mind. The society, it is said, found the work too difficult, whereupon Schubert offered the earlier C major Symphony, no.6 of 1817–18. The manuscript of his last symphony, which came eventually into the possession of the Gesellschaft, shows more signs of revision than is usual in Schubert's fair copies, and all the alterations tend to give greater melodic significance to the work.

A more modest but likable work of the same month is his setting of Grillparzer's *Mirjams Siegesgesang* (D942), for soprano solo and chorus with piano accompaniment; it must originally have been intended for his concert (hence the piano rather than orchestral accompaniment). The repeated requests of his publishers for short and not too difficult piano works, coupled with his desire to find a market in Germany, may be the reason why he produced so many such pieces that year. In April the magnificent F minor Fantasy for piano duet (D940) was finished; it is the only work which he dedicated to the young Countess Caroline Esterházy (tradition has it that he once declared to her that such dedications were unnecessary, since all his work was dedicated to her). Two other piano duets are the sonata movement in A minor (D947), a superb essay, published as op.144 in 1840 and given the absurd, catchpenny title of *Lebensstürme*, and the very attractive Rondo in A (D951), finished in June and published as op.107 in December 1828. The *Drei Klavierstücke* (D946) were composed in the same year, but not published until 1868.

The few publications of 1828 were chiefly songs. Haslinger published the first part of *Winterreise* (D911) as op.89 on 14 January; the second part, beginning with *Die Post*, appeared in December after Schubert's death. Diabelli published on 14 March, as opp. 85 and 86, settings of Andrew MacDonald's *Lied der Anne Lyle* (?1825, D830) and of Walter Scott's *Gesang der Norna* from *The Pirate* (1825, D831) and *Romanze des Richard Löwenherz* from *Ivanhoe* (?1826, D907). On 13 August Weigl announced the publication of *Vier Refrainlieder* (op.95, D866) as a new departure for Schubert: the composer in comic vein (though it is difficult to see how no.2, *Bei dir allein*, fits into this scheme). The *Moments musicaux* were published by Leidesdorf (11 July; op.94, D780).

Both in Berlin (25 June) and Munich (28 July) the *Winterreise* songs received lukewarm comment. Berlin was a stronghold of reaction where songs were concerned: it is a little difficult to see exactly what type of song they considered the 'true German song', but Schubert's did not come into that category and the Berlin journal was derisive in tone. Earlier that year a similar attitude had been adopted towards op.83 (D902), Schubert's three Italian songs dedicated to Luigi Lablache. But as usual the Leipzig *Musikalische Zeitung* was generous in its praise. Johann Rochlitz, the journal's founder, was very favourably disposed towards Schubert, and had written to him on 7 November 1827 proposing his poem *Der erste Ton* as deserving of the composer's attention (it had already been set by Weber); his suggested treatment aroused no response in Schubert. Other letters from distinguished acquaintances, all expressing sincere pleasure in his work, reached the composer in 1828 and must have given him great satisfaction. Johann Schickh, who as editor of the *Wiener Zeitschrift* had initiated a series of song supplements with *Die Forelle* in 1821, wrote on 3 April, in the name of a number of admirers, urging Schubert to repeat his concert. Johann Mosewius, an opera singer and, in 1828, a lecturer in music at Breslau University, sent a glowing appreciation of the songs on 4 June. Later in the month, Karl Brüggemann, a publisher at Halberstadt, asked very deferentially for piano pieces. A letter which would have been of more interest to us than any of these was unfortunately never sent to him: it was written by Robert Schumann, then a boy of 18.

A bulky correspondence survives from 1828 between Schubert and two publishers, H. A. Probst of Leipzig and B. Schott of Mainz. Schubert was clearly doing his utmost to obtain recognition outside Vienna; the steady decline during these last two years in the amount and variety of work issued by the Viennese publishers showed that the market for his music needed some outside stimulus. By a strange coincidence, both publishers wrote to him on the same day, 9 February. Schott asked for piano compositions or songs, pointing out that the firm had an establishment in Paris and publications would be made known there too. Probst, who had already met Schubert in spring 1827, wrote a more personal letter, suggesting that it would be easy 'to disseminate your name throughout the rest of Germany and in the north, in which I will gladly lend a hand,

considering talent like yours'. He replied to Schott on 21 February offering chamber music, impromptus and partsongs; eight days later the publisher expressed interest in several of these works. On 10 April Schubert, elated by the success of his concert, wrote again to both firms. To Schott he offered the E♭ Trio for 100 gulden, the second set of impromptus and a five-part chorus, *Mondenschein* (D875), for 60 gulden each; the same offer was made to Probst, except that the trio was unpriced and the other two works were not specified by name, although the same price was asked for each. It is exasperating to see the subsequent sharp practice of the two publishers, so offhandedly generous in their introductory letters. Schott, for example, accepted the smaller works for 60 gulden (the two); Probst accepted the trio for 60 gulden. The negotiations with Schott came to nothing; the Paris establishment rejected the impromptus as too difficult, and Schubert refused to sell *Mondenschein* for 30 gulden. Under protest, he accepted Probst's offer for the trio, and his two subsequent letters to the publisher (of 10 May and 1 August) are worth quoting:

The cuts indicated in the last movement are to be most scrupulously observed. Be sure to have it performed for the first time by capable people, and most particularly see to a continual uniformity of tempo at the changes of time signature in the last movement. The minuet at a moderate pace and *piano* throughout, the trio, on the other hand, vigorous, except where *p* and *pp* are marked.

The second letter was in reply to Probst's requests for the opus number and a dedication:

The opus number of the trio is 100 . . . This work is to be dedicated to nobody, save those who find pleasure in it. That is the most profitable dedication.

There was no holiday that year; ailing and wretched as he was, a few weeks outside Vienna would have been a godsend. But he had no money. Ferdinand Traweger, his former host at Gmunden, wrote on 19 May offering him a room and board at a nominal price; there was an invitation from Frau Pachler to spend the summer at Graz. Both had to be refused. Jenger, declining the second invitation in his friend's name, mentioned to Frau Pachler that Schubert was 'working diligently at a new mass'. This was the setting in E♭, begun in June (D950). Other church works were composed during the year, all rather superficial in expression and of no great moment. 13 songs of the group known as *Schwanengesang* (D957) were composed in August. The first seven are to poems by Rellstab; there follow six settings of poems by Heine, which Schubert had encountered at the reading circle. Another song, *Die Taubenpost* (D965a), with words by Seidl and composed in October, was added by the publisher. *Schwanengesang* is a rich and masterly epilogue to the long series of his songs: whether purely lyrical as in Rellstab's *Ständchen*, or creating unheard-of atmospheric effects as in *Die Stadt* or *Der Doppelgänger*, Schubert's hand was never more sure nor more powerful.

At the beginning of September he went to live with Ferdinand in the Neue Wieden suburb (the street is known today as the Kettenbrückengasse). His doctor, Ernst Rinna, hoped that his health would benefit from the semi-rural surroundings. He was suffering from acute headaches and giddiness. Unfortunately, the house was damp and unsanitary; far from having the desired beneficial effect, the move hastened the end. The last three sonatas, in C minor, A and B♭ (D958–60), were completed by 26 September; Schubert played from them the next day at the house of Dr Ignaz Menz. He had intended to dedicate them to Hummel, but when Diabelli published them, in 1838, Hummel was dead and they were dedicated to Schumann. His last instrumental work was the Quintet in C for strings (D956), using an extra cello rather than the more common extra viola and thus allowing of a more sonorous effect. The work may be ascribed to autumn 1828, since in a letter to Probst of 2 October Schubert mentioned the sonatas and the Heine songs, and went on to say that he had 'finally turned out' a quintet. As with the songs of *Schwanengesang*, the last instrumental works have a splendour in which there is no sign of decline; no sinking glow as of autumn or sunset lights these vigorous masterpieces. The song with clarinet obbligato *Der Hirt auf dem Felsen* (D965) was composed in October for Anna Milder-Hauptmann and sent to her the following year by Ferdinand. Either this or *Die Taubenpost* is the last song he wrote. Early in October he went on a three-day walking tour with Ferdinand and two acquaintances into Lower Austria, and on as far as Eisenstadt where Haydn was buried. It is doubtful whether, in Schubert's exhausted condition, the excursion was of any value. A cordial letter from Schindler, who was living in Pest, reached him on his return, inviting him to attend the first performance of Lachner's opera *Die Burgschaft* and suggesting that while at Pest he could give a concert of his songs. But by then any such visit was out of the question.

15. ILLNESS AND DEATH. As the month drew to a close, Schubert's condition weakened. It used to be thought that his terminal illness was typhoid, known on the Continent as 'typhus abdominalis'; but it now seems beyond doubt (see Sams, 1980) that syphilis, from which Schubert had suffered since 1822, was the cause of death. Signs of serious deterioration appeared on 31 October, when at the tavern Zum roten Kreuz he tried to eat fish and was nauseated by it. From then until he finally took to his bed he ate nothing. On 4 November he arranged to take lessons in counterpoint from Simon Sechter; whether he had lessons or not is uncertain, but a batch of his exercises was discovered in Vienna in 1969; they had been written for Sechter. A week later he was too ill to leave his room; on 12 November he wrote to Schober: 'I am ill. I have eaten nothing for 11 days and drunk nothing, and I totter feebly and shakily from my chair to my bed and back again. Rinna is treating me. If ever I take anything I bring it up again at once'.

His last occupation was the correction of the proofs of part 2 of *Winterreise*. On 16 November there was a consultation at his sick-bed between two doctors. Josef von Vering and Johann Wisgrill, Rinna himself being ill. There were now professional nurses in attendance, but Ferdinand gave him ceaseless care and Schubert's small stepsister, Josefa, was devotedly attentive to his needs. Randhartinger and Spaun visited him during those days, but Schober, for whatever reason, kept away. His last visitors were Bauernfeld, and Lachner who had returned from Pest. He was delirious, but during a lucid interval talked of Bauernfeld's *Graf von Gleichen*. On Tuesday, 18 November, the delirium persisted; Ferdinand recorded his brother's broken sayings, but no significance can be attached to them. He died the following day, 19 November, at 3 p.m., turning from Ferdinand with the words: 'Here, here is my end'.

9. Schubert's death mask, in the Curtis Institute of Music, Philadelphia

The funeral took place two days later. Schubert's body was borne from the Neue Wieden by a group of young students and laid in St Joseph's Church in the Margareten suburb. A chorus based on the 1817 song *Pax vobiscum* (D551), to new words by Schober, was sung. The interment was in the Währing cemetery, Ferdinand having interpreted Schubert's deathbed utterances as his desire to lie near the body of Beethoven; the graves of the two composers are separated by three others.

In the valuation of his property an item labelled 'some old music' was priced at 10 gulden. This does not refer to his manuscripts, most of which were still with Schober, but to various items of printed music. His effects, as a whole, were assessed at 63 gulden. The expenses of his illness and funeral, and his debts, were together far more than the estimates usually given, amounting in fact to nearly 1000 gulden. All were discharged by the following June through posthumous publication fees.

His death was a blow, not only to his family, but also to his friends and acquaintances; they expressed their grief in diaries and letters. Memorial poems were written by Bauernfeld, Mayrhofer, Baron Schlechta and by many obscure admirers. On 23 December a memorial service was held at St Augustine's Church, at which a requiem by Anselm Hüttenbrenner was sung. A number of his friends, under the guidance of Grillparzer, Jenger and Schober, collected money to erect a monument for him; part of the fund came from a concert given by Anna Fröhlich, on 30 January 1829, at the Musikverein. It included Schubert's *Mirjams Siegesgesang* and the E♭ Trio, and also the first finale from Mozart's *Don Giovanni*. The monument, with Josef Dialer's bust of Schubert in bronze, was erected in the autumn of 1830 and inscribed with Grillparzer's epitaph: 'Die Tonkunst begrub hier einen reichen Besitz, aber noch viel schönere Hoffnungen' ('The art of music here entombed a rich possession, but even fairer hopes').

16. POSTHUMOUS PUBLICATION. The enormous amount of unpublished work which Schubert left at his death eventually came into the possession of Ferdinand, who made unremitting efforts to secure its publication. On 29 November he offered to Diabelli & Co. (later Spina & Co.) a large quantity of manuscripts comprising 'all the songs for solo voice with piano accompaniment', piano music (solo and duet) and chamber works. The offer was accepted. The songs appeared between 1830 and 1851 in 50 instalments under the general title 'Nachgelassene musikalische Dichtungen' (often abbreviated to 'Nachlass'). The masterpieces of chamber music lay unheeded on Diabelli's shelves until the 1850s: the String Quartet in G (D887) appeared as op.161 in 1851; the first three movements of the Octet (D803) as op.166 in 1853; the String Quintet in C (D956) as op.163 in 1853. Diabelli's bulk purchase still left Ferdinand with nearly all his brother's operas, symphonies and masses; the works not in his possession were *Alfonso und Estrella* (the original at Graz, the copy with Anna Milder-Hauptmann in Berlin) and the B minor Symphony in Anselm Hüttenbrenner's possession at Graz. In 1835, he appealed to Schumann, as editor of the *Neue Zeitschrift für Musik*, and on 26 April a paragraph appeared in that journal giving a list of the works available to publishers. There was no immediate result, but a few years later, when Schumann went to Vienna, he visited Ferdinand (on New Year's Day, 1837) and saw the piles of manuscripts for himself. The outcome of this famous visit was a performance, in a heavily cut version, of the 'Great' C major Symphony at the Leipzig Gewandhaus, under Mendelssohn, on 21 March 1839. The Leipzig firm of Breitkopf & Härtel published the work (parts, 1840; score, 1849), paying Ferdinand 180 gulden for it. Projected performances of the symphony in Paris under Habeneck (1842) and in London under Mendelssohn (1844) were brought to nothing by the blank refusal of orchestral players to master its difficulties at rehearsals. There are no records extant of a supposed first performance at Windsor by the private orchestra of Prince Albert. The publication of a complete edition of his works was inspired by the great Schubertian Nicolaus Dumba and carried out by Breitkopf & Härtel between 1884 and 1897. Their Kritisch durchgesehene Gesamtausgabe contained 39 volumes in 21 series, the last a supplementary volume. The operas, the early symphonies, over 200 songs and the smaller, unpublished piano and choral works appeared in print for the first time in three volumes. The editorial commentaries contain all Schubert's sketches then available for instrumental and vocal music; of outstanding interest are those for the 'Unfinished' Symphony of October 1822. In June 1967 the Internationale Schubert-Gesellschaft was founded in Tübingen, with the chief object of preparing the Neue Schubert-Ausgabe, a complete and authentic edition of the composer's work, to be published by Bärenreiter. Like the original Gesamtausgabe of 1884–97, it consists of series of classified works, eight in all, the last (entitled 'Supplement') including fundamental bibliographical works such as O. E. Deutsch's documentary biography and the thematic catalogue. The first volumes appeared in the late 1960s. The Neue Schubert-Ausgabe has been in the care of a group of senior editors, including Walther Dürr, Arnold Feil and Christa Landon, and many Schubert scholars are also responsible for the production.

17. POSTHUMOUS PERFORMANCE. Schubert's fame as a songwriter was firmly established in Austria and Germany, and it soon spread to France and England; for many years it seemed as if it were to be the only reputation allowed him. One recalls Spaun's words to Bauernfeld in 1839: 'For all the admiration I have given the dear departed for years, I still feel that we shall never make a Mozart or a Haydn of him in instrumental and church compositions, whereas in song he is unsurpassed'. This was an opinion which, happily, Spaun abandoned as the years passed and he grew more and more familiar with the instrumental masterpieces as they were published. There were occasional performances of the choral and chamber works in Vienna, chamber music in Berlin (the Eb Piano Trio D929 and the 'Trout' Quintet D667) and in Paris (the Bb Piano Trio D898). Schumann was indefatigable in his praise and propaganda for works for which he had a preference, such as the 'Great' C major Symphony or the Piano Trio in Eb; but even he was strangely unresponsive to the three fine sonatas of 1828, dedicated to him on publication, indeed almost flippant about them. The operas were ignored; the performances of *Alfonso und Estrella* under Liszt at Weimar (24 January 1854) and of *Die Verschworenen* at Frankfurt am Main on 29 August 1861 were travesties, although the latter opera was well received and reviewed. Not until the impact of the Johann Hellmesberger chamber concerts in Vienna in the 1860s, when the Octet and several string quartets were given, and of the performance of the 'Unfinished' Symphony, through Johann Herbeck's enthusiasm, in Vienna in 1865, was the musical world of mid-19th-century Europe forced to the conclusion that in Schubert there was an instrumental master of the front rank. The impression was of slow and by no means unopposed growth; even as late as the 1920s it was possible for a critic to write of the 'dreary passage-work' of the 'Great' C major Symphony. The new respect for Schubert in the 20th century is in part due to the realization that Beethoven's way with sonata form is not the only, Heaven-ordained way, and with that realization Schubert need no longer be considered as a mere offshoot from his great contemporary. It was not until broadcasting extended the orchestral repertory that Schubert's first six symphonies ever reached performance after their initial hearing: they began to be played during the 1930s and no.5, in Bb, quickly became popular. The sonatas were slower in making their way into public esteem. Artur Schnabel's attitude towards, and his performance of, these works proved to be a revelation. Nowadays the last of the sonatas, in Bb (D960), is frequently played and has taken its place with the foremost examples of the Classical sonata. His operas still await discovery, and thus need to be discussed in more detail.

18. MUSIC FOR THE THEATRE. The failure of Schubert's operas to hold the stage, or in some cases even to win a hearing, is usually attributed to his librettos. These are, it is true, with the exception of *Die Verschworenen*, somewhat pedestrian affairs, and their plots are complicated, often requiring elaborate stage machinery. Schubert matched these plays with music which is mainly of secondary value, though frequently, par-

ticularly in the later work, thoroughly characteristic. There is endless resource, and an astounding assurance in his balance of stage mood and movement against the development of his orchestral themes. As we proceed from *Des Teufels Lustschloss* (D84) to the final operas, there is the clear evolution of his own operatic style: the music grows in colour, fluidity and scope. It is unlike the evolution in his songs or instrumental work; it belongs entirely to this unknown sphere of his music. There is an extended use, for example, of richly accompanied recitative, which is quite his own; figuration grows more complex and weaves between voice and orchestra, as in the duets for Florinda and Maragond (*Fierabras*, no.9), or for Alfonso and Estrella (no.12), in a manner quite unlike anything in the songs. The exordia and ritornellos, negligible in early work, achieve the same individuality and importance as in the late songs, until in *Fierabras* there is a movingly sensitive moment where an A major passage, heralding the scene between King Karl and his daughter Emma, is beautifully modified in the orchestra when Fierabras enters and gazes in enraptured silence on the princess.

His handling of the orchestra, competent in *Lustschloss*, grows in skill and boldness until it has the true Schubertian quality, known chiefly from the *Rosamunde* music and the last two symphonies, a quality which was no 'clairvoyant' visitation but the outcome of his endless experimentation and exploration of possibility in the operas. Unlike the orchestra of his early symphonies, which was ordained by college or domestic resources, the orchestra of his operas acknowledged no limitations; he scored for full woodwind and from the first used three trombones. There is much 'nature' music in the operas: winds, storms, floods, birdsong, night and morning scenes, and in all of them the orchestral painting is vivid. *Alfonso* opens in the morning, before daybreak: soft shakes on flute and strings, with phrases on the oboe, depict the scene deliciously. One of the loveliest passages in the whole of his operas closes Act 1 of *Fierabras*: it is night, and Emma appears on a lighted balcony, while Eginhard serenades her from below. The whole of the music is fragrant with the atmosphere of this night in a garden of Spain, with the clarinet breathing its love-song above the plucked strings.

The device, so well known from his songs, whereby a striking word is translated into apt musical figuration for his accompaniments is found in the operas too. For example, the word 'schleiche' ('creep') in Olivia's aria (no.4) from *Die Freunde von Salamanka* D326 is depicted by a slow chromatic rise and fall in the strings, ostinato, a vivid musical suggestion of slow footsteps. To come upon this aria in going through the early operas is like coming upon *Gretchen* among the early songs; it is the first appearance of the authentic voice amid efficient mediocrity. Mayrhofer drew Schubert to finer issues and this two-act Singspiel is full of interesting work; there is even a *Winterreise*-like pathos in the D minor duet for Olivia and Alonso (no.14).

Adrast, also by Mayrhofer, was not finished; of all the dramatic works before 1821 this is the finest. Noteworthy points of orchestration are the use of two cellos to accompany Croesus's air (no.2) and the use of four trombones in the following chorus. Accompanied recitative, characteristically rich in harmonic nuance, pervades the work. *Die Zwillingsbrüder* (D647) and *Die Zauberharfe* (D644) can be seen as transitional works, between the fruitful experimental work of the earlier operas and the individual fulfilment of the later ones. The benefit to Schubert, in the development and perfecting of his own orchestral style, brought about by the particular nature of the libretto for *Die Zauberharfe*, has already been touched upon. The Romance in the Act 2 finale (no.9, 'Was belebt die schöne Welt?') is a marvellously beautiful aria, which should not be allowed to remain in obscurity; it would grace any orchestral concert and repay an enterprising singer. Both works have worthy overtures: the second is famous as the '*Rosamunde* overture', and the other, which uses a theme appearing in the String Quartet in G minor (D173), also deserves revival.

Alfonso und Estrella was said to be Schubert's favourite opera; its period, 1821–2, is sufficient guarantee of its consistently good level, and many of its numbers rise above even that. The music associated with Adolfo, the conventional villain, is the best, his impassioned aria in E♭ minor (Act 2, D732 no.8b) being one of the finest things in the work. One intriguing fact connected with this opera is that six years later Schubert, perhaps unconsciously, took over the melody of Troila's song at the opening of Act 2, 'Das Lied vom Wolkenmädchen' (no.11), as no.19 of *Winterreise* (*Täuschung*). The words of Troila's song clearly show the link:

> Er folgte ihrer Stimme Rufen
> und stieg den rauhen Pfad hinan.
> Sie tanzte über Felsen-stufen
> durch dunkle Schlünde leicht ihm vor.

The words of *Täuschung* which provoked this reminiscence are:

> Ein Licht tanzt freundlich vor mir her
> Ich folg' ihm nach die Kreuz und Quer.

The one-act Singspiel *Die Verschworenen* (D787) is dramatically effective, with music that subtly reflects the atmosphere of this cynical text (based on Aristophanes' *Lysistrata*). A group of ladies, tired of their husbands' insatiable appetite for war-mongering, vow to withhold from them all matrimonial rights until they promise to abandon their exploits. The intrigue, the breaking of vows and the final resolution of the problem are all excellently wrought by the author, Castelli, and Schubert's music is tuneful, witty and colourful as occasion demands. The sad little Romance of Helene (no.2), the ensemble where Udolin tells the knights of their wives' vow (a delicious finger-to-lip quality in this passage), the puzzlement of the ladies (symbolized by a sinuous melody on the violins), and the vivacious play on 'für dich' and 'für mich' in the parallel arias for the Count and Countess – all these warrant an occasional performance of this sparkling operetta.

In *Fierabras*, there is little negligible work: page after page reveals the greater Schubert. One or two of the fine things in the opera have been mentioned. Others are the unaccompanied chorus 'O teures Vaterland' (no.14), also used in the overture, and the outstanding arias for Fierrabras (no.6b) and Florinda (no.13), both of which could find a place in the concert repertory.

His last finished work for the stage, the celebrated *Rosamunde*, is mainly instrumental; had it been otherwise, the feeble libretto would have entombed it, excellent though the music is. The melodies of these ballets and entr'actes, and their poetic orchestration, so completely individual, are additional revelations of the Schubert of the B minor Symphony. Together these works herald the first period of his maturity which culminated in *Winterreise*. One point requires comment. Examination of the score of the B♭ entr'acte (D797 no.5) shows that the interlude in B♭ minor was drawn from an early song, *Der Leidende* (D432a), written as early as May 1816. By some strange chance, the first entr'acte, in B minor, one of the composer's masterpieces, seems to have disappeared from the concert room (Abraham suggested in 1971 that this was the original finale of the 'Unfinished' Symphony, as we have seen).

19. SONGS. One reason for the abiding popularity of Schubert's songs is simple: whatever other elements may or may not be present, the primary essential, the melodic element, or (to put it plainly) an attractive and singable tune, is rarely absent. A second and deeper reason for their appeal is that they are firmly grounded, in idiom and procedure, in the 'Viennese symphonic' period of music, say from 1770 to 1830. One has only to think of such songs as *Halt!* from *Die schöne Müllerin* (D795 no.3), *Auf dem Flusse* from *Winterreise* (D911 no.7), or *Der Zwerg* (D771), with their exposition and development of thematic fragments, to realize that as long as this period remains the most congenial to a large number of listeners, so will his songs with it.

From the first the Schubert song was practically without ancestry; even before *Gretchen am Spinnrade* he was writing passages which have no precedent. Songs there certainly were before his, and in his youth he modelled his own efforts on those of men such as Zumsteeg and Zelter. Many of Beethoven's and Mozart's songs, considered as music, are equal to his own earlier efforts. The miracle he achieved was to match with a reality of music poetry whose depths of human emotion would have appeared to the older composers as rendering it unsuitable for song. Two factors are said to have helped Schubert: the late 18th-century outburst of lyric poetry, whose outstanding exponent is Goethe; and the establishment of the piano accompaniment with its inexhaustible possibilities of picturesque comment. These factors are trifling compared with the power of his genius: otherwise one might ask why Beethoven and Weber, to whom these two possibilities were equally available, composed no masterpieces of song comparable to Schubert's.

The songs, more than 600, fall into four main groups: the simple strophic song in which each verse is sung to the same music; the modified-strophic song in which his endless variety defies classification (examples are *Lachen und Weinen*, D777 and *Das Zügenglöcklein* D871); the *durchkomponiert* (through-composed) song in which various melodies and interpolated recitatives are welded together by the same, basically unchanging accompaniment, like *Die junge Nonne* (D828) and *Auflösung* (D807); and finally the 'scena' type of song, such as *Der Wanderer* (D489) or *Kriegers Ahnung* (D957 no.2), containing separate episodes of different tempo and mood, of which his own scena, Käthe's aria from *Der vierjährige Posten* (D190 no.5), may be cited as a prototype. The poets range from Goethe, Schiller and Heine at one end of the scale to versifying friends like Mayrhofer and Schober at the other. This catholic choice is sometimes taken to indicate that Schubert had

no literary taste; when he chose to set a poem to music, however, he did so not to show his literary judgment but because of its musical possibilities. The ready and sympathetic audience of the Schubertiads must not be overlooked in this connection. Schubert obviously favoured the poem with a 'bite' in the last stanza, even in the last line; as for instance in *Erlkönig*, *Der Wanderer* and *Der Doppelgänger*. The way in which he absorbed the quality of a poem and produced an analogous quality in music can best be appreciated when one turns the pages of his poets – of Goethe or Heine, for example. The swift lyricism and movement of the one, the pith and imagery of the other, are perfectly paralleled in the music.

The refinement of later composers in their attention to the poet's text, and in their balance of interest between voice and piano, is instinctive, but not unconscious, with Schubert. His lyric and harmonic vitality and his spontaneous reaction to the stimulus of the poet's emotional or visual appeal give an almost abandoned quality to the music he poured out. Sometimes, as in *An Schwager Kronos* (D369), the result is overpoweringly convincing; elsewhere, as in *Die Gebüsche* (D646) or in *Fülle der Liebe* (D854), the result is less happy. But always there is the firm grasp of the essential. Schubert's periphery may sweep beyond, or not quite reach out to, that of the poet, but it always encircles the same central point. One perceives it in that quality of his famous songs which can only be called 'atmosphere'. The very first bars of *Im Abendrot* (D799), *An die Musik* (D547) or *Nacht und Träume* (D827) take us to the heart of the poem. Nor need the atmosphere be one of abstraction or rapture: the lighthearted *An die Laute* (D905), or the comfortable *Der Einsame* (D800), illustrate the point equally well.

Schubert's melodies, particularly in his songs, are the most individual and revealing of all the factors in his work. Of infinite variety and grace, they have a quality of pathos, of direct appeal to the listener, which is a reflection of the sweetness and sensitivity of his own nature. They are often based on a juxtaposition of tonic and dominant chords as in *Wohin?* (D795 no.2) and *Der greise Kopf* (D911 no.14). The phrase built on a falling dominant 7th is associated in his mind with weariness or grief, so it is used in *Wandrers Nachtlied* (D224) and in the first of the Harper's Songs (D478). The little figure sung at the start of *Frühlingsglaube* (D686) appears repeatedly in his songs whenever blissful contemplation of nature engrosses both poet and composer. The use of sequence is discreet and flexible, as is shown in *Ungeduld* (D795 no.7) and *An Sylvia* (D891); in the latter song the sequential treatment of the opening phrase is exquisite.

The most familiar characteristic of Schubert's harmony is his passing from minor mode to major and, less frequently, from major to minor; the change may be smooth or abrupt, but it always represents an emotional change. Another characteristic, equally important but insufficiently noticed, is his use of the Neapolitan 6th and relationships based upon it. A third is his fondness for passing, with little or no preparation, into the key a major 3rd below his tonic, as for instance in *Nacht und Träume* (D827; B major to G major). An awareness of these three fundamental processes gives an insight into the masterly way in which he handles his harmonic material, for example in the song *Stimme der Liebe* (D412). This flexible use of harmonic changes had its

10. Autograph MS of the end of 'Am Meer' and beginning of 'Der Doppelgänger' from book 2 of Schubert's 'Schwanengesang', composed August 1828 (US-NYpm)

direct influence on his melody and modulation, but the processes were reversible: melody and modulation affected his harmonic spectrum. In addition to these personal harmonic characteristics, Schubert took over from the normal harmony of his day the augmented 6th (in both the 'German' and 'French' forms) and the diminished 7th, using both chords frequently and often with the most poetic effects: consider the use of the diminished 7th in its form C–E♭–F♯–A throughout the song *Die Stadt* (D957 no.11). Arpeggios based on the chord softly sweep the keyboard to depict Heine's 'feuchter Windzug' and are tenuously resolved at the end of the song by a single held *C* in the bass.

Schubert's accompaniments are celebrated for their graphic reinforcement of the inner meaning of the poem or of the external details of the poet's scene. He seems inexhaustible in contriving graceful pianistic figures to illustrate moving or glinting water or the shimmer of stars. Again and again he devised in his accompaniments a music which derives from both aspects of the poem and achieves thereby a powerful synthesis of which the poetry alone is incapable – the ranging arpeggios of *Auflösung* (D807) or the heartbreak in the gusty diminished 7ths of *Die Stadt* (D957) demonstrate such powers. The preludes of his songs can be remarkably apt: the most beautifully poised entry in them all is in *Ganymed* (D544); how the opening bars depict the glory and contentment of morning! The introductory chords of Goethe's *An den Mond* (D296) cloud the A♭ tonality and prepare the listener for the 'Nebelglanz' of the poet's address to the moon. But the last word has not been said

about the Schubert song when its melody, accompaniment, atmosphere – all the beautiful externals of his music – have been surveyed. There yet remains the ineffable quality of textual illumination to which purpose all these factors are bent. Consider Heine's *Der Doppelgänger* (D957 no.13). 'The night is still', says the poet, 'the streets are deserted', but there needs no ghost to remind him of his anguish on 'so many nights long ago'. Schubert set the opening words to a falling B minor phrase, low in the compass of the voice; the final agony is implicit in this phrase, and it rings out at the end in a florid version an octave higher. Similar examples abound in the mature songs. There is the way in which the pure diatonic harmony at the start of *Du bist die Ruh* (D776) is tinged with colour as the poet turns from 'du bist' to 'ich weihe'. The high opening phrase of *An die Entfernte* (D765) poses a question, 'Have I lost thee?', introduced by an enigmatic diminished 7th; it has an entirely different quality when it recurs later, after a decisive C major chord, to the words 'All my songs cry unto thee'. The refinement by which the main key of *Dass sie hier gewesen* (D775) is held back to coincide with the main statement of each stanza is well known, but this device is just as notably used in *Gruppe aus dem Tartarus* (D583), in which the whole discordant opening prepares for C major and the awesome word 'Eternity', and in *Grenzen der Menschheit* (D716), where the main key of the song is reserved for the declaration of Man's humility. On songs such as these his fame rests; but his stature is as surely revealed in innumerable tiny songs, page-long creations, few without touches of sublimity, where with the most modest means he can encompass greatness in a score of bars.

20. MATURE INSTRUMENTAL MUSIC. The 'Trout' Quintet (D667) is the culmination of Schubert's approach to maturity in instrumental music, and the Quartettsatz (D703) begins the last phase in his work in this sphere. With the solitary exception of the sketched symphony in E of 1821 (D729), the next eight years produced a series of masterpieces marked by an intense lyricism, a chromatic modulation which, for all its spontaneity, moves within an inherent tonal system, an absorbed attention to textural detail and an imagination which moulds its own formal structures. Academic devices such as fugato, elaborately worked canon or invertible counterpoint, all of which can be found dutifully appearing in his early work, are quickly abandoned; but his treatment of subject matter grows more powerful and attains a poetry and an emotion unknown in the years before 1820. As a typical movement, the Quartettsatz stands fittingly at the start of these years. The key scheme of the exposition shows, for the first time, that tonal structure which Schubert was to find so congenial: the C minor and G major tonalities which bracket the section are fairly orthodox, but they enclose a second-subject stretch in A♭ major. His use of the string quartet medium in which cello and first violin have predominant interest is first seen in this movement, and in the demands which are made on the players Schubert is clearly no longer bound by the limitations of the family quartet (particularly in the case of the cello, which was the task of the modestly equipped Schubert père).

The next work of importance is the Symphony in B minor (D759), another unfinished essay. The affinities of the symphony's first movement with that of the quartet are remarkable: in the singing quality, the passionate contrasts and the pathos they are obvious, but two technical points have interest. The first is the withholding of the main theme at the start of the recapitulation, in order to use it with greater force for the coda of the movement; the second is in the choice of key for the second subject. In the case of the 'Unfinished' Symphony this has occasioned much comment, but it has precisely the same relationship with the main key as in the quartet: B minor–G major, C minor–A♭ major; and both are instances of Schubert's favourite shift of a major 3rd downwards.

Between the quartet and the symphony appeared the first important composition for piano, a work of an entirely different character. The 'Wanderer' Fantasy takes its name from the *adagio* section, which is based on a theme from the song *Der Wanderer* (D489), of 1816. It is the first of a series of works in C major which have the epic quality thenceforth associated in his mind with that key, and its massive structure, new to his keyboard writing, is rarely absent from his later compositions for the piano. There is an interesting and deliberate use of cyclic form, one aspect of which derives from the dactylic rhythm of the song theme. This rhythm pervades his mature work and is an indication of

11. *Autograph MS of the first page of Schubert's String Quartet in G* (D887), *composed 20–30 June 1826* (A-Wn)

the profound impression made upon him by the Allegretto from Beethoven's Seventh Symphony. The three chamber works of 1824, the Octet for wind and strings in F (D803) and the string quartets in A minor (D804) and D minor (D810), have much in common. They were written in the short space of only two months, in February and March 1824. They are full of typical melody; all three contain movements based on themes which Schubert had composed for other media from past days, and this fact seems to reflect his mood. In a letter written at this time to Kupelwieser he spoke of a ray of sunlight from past sweet days; the emotion shades from cheerful good humour to pathos, and occasionally, in the D minor String Quartet, to a shuddering terror. Even the cheerful pages, those in the minuet of the Octet, or the finale of the A minor String Quartet, have that characteristic Schubert patina of near-pathos; he was, unlike Haydn or Beethoven, incapable of pure comedy, of Rosalind's 'holiday mood'.

The six piano sonatas (five for solo and one for duet) which belong to the mid-1820s constitute a unified group. To begin with, the main theme of the first movement is invariably the basis of the development section, with supreme effect in the two A minor sonatas (D784 and D845), in the 'Reliquie' Sonata (D840) and in the G major Sonata (D894). The slow movements, with one exception, are in rondo form, the opening songlike theme alternating with dynamic interludes; an attractive example is the Andante of the duet sonata in C (D812). The exception is the slow movement of the Sonata in A minor (D845), a set of variations on an original theme, one of the most successful of his essays in this genre. It contains a delicate use of those chains of suspensions which he had used to good effect in the song *Versunken* (D715) and which are found again in the slow movement of the 'Great' C major Symphony (D944) and in the C minor Impromptu (D899 no.1). The period closes with two magnificent pieces of chamber music. Of the first movement of the String Quartet in G (D887) it is difficult to write without extravagance: the quintessence of every Schubertian virtue is found in its pages. The slow movement (in E minor, though his manuscript shows that it was originally planned in B minor) contains his most daring harmonic adventure, where violin and viola persistently utter a figure in one key, while the music moves more and more remotely from it (bars 52–6, repeated in bars 131–5). The finale is sometimes alleged to show the influence of Rossini; there is as little justification for this as for the so-called 'Hungarian' influence in the finale of the A minor String Quartet.

The Piano Trio in B♭ (D898) nowhere reaches the heights of the G major Quartet, but its humanity (and hence its popular appeal) is greater. The remark that Schubert's lyrical subjects are unsuitable for development is refuted by the first movement of this trio, as indeed it is by the first movement of the G major Sonata; nothing could be more songlike than these themes, yet each forms the basis of a superbly constructed movement. The instrumentation of the trio is admirable, particularly in the controlled use of the piano, which is neither overwhelming nor over-modest in its partnership with the strings. Its soaring flights in the finale are among the most picturesque of Schubert's touches in his chamber music.

Before the next important work, the Piano Trio in E♭ (D929), came the completion of *Winterreise* (D911); and what this meant to Schubert's development can be seen by comparing the temper of the E♭ Trio with that of its predecessor. The music of *Winterreise*, once realized, revealed to the composer newer potentialities in his genius. For the first time in his music we find tragedy, not the wistfulness or luxuriating sadness of previous work but the darkness of the genuine emotion; we find it, numbed, in *Gute Nacht* and *Der Wegweiser*, whose threnodic progressions lead to the slow movements of the 'Great' C major Symphony and the E♭ Trio, despairing and passionate in *Erstarrung* and *Der stürmische Morgen*, whose anguish is found again in the slow movement of the String Quintet (D956). Side by side with this tragic utterance is a profound serenity first voiced in *Der Lindenbaum*, which is so characteristic of his later work, for example in the slow movements of the quintet and in the last sonata (D960). Serenity was no new aspect of Schubert's work but neither *Im Abendrot* (D799) nor *Du bist die Ruh* (D776) has quite the dreamlike quality of the works just cited. Technically his music gained from *Winterreise* a greater harmonic piquancy, a discovery of yet wider and subtler uses of Neapolitan relationships, a newer, one might say a more intellectual, manner with thematic development. This closing period has features of its own which distinguish it from the preceding one. There are signs that Schubert was concerning himself with two sections of his large-scale works which he had hitherto treated somewhat lightheartedly, the trio of the third movement and the finale. Another feature of these final works comes from his changed attitude to the development section of his first movements; no longer invariably based on the opening theme, as was the case in every one of the works between the 'Unfinished' Symphony and the B♭ Trio, they may derive from the introduction (C major Symphony), from subsidiary matter in the exposition (the Quintet) or even from a codetta phrase (E♭ Trio, A major Sonata). In the E♭ Trio, the much maligned finale deserves a kindlier, more informed, judgment; as with other finales, the easy-going start leads on to better and greater things, and the introduction of the theme from the slow movement is a superb moment, and for Schubert a unique one.

We come to what is widely admitted to be his greatest masterpiece, the 'Great' C major Symphony. From any viewpoint the work bears the stamp of greatness, but the chief impression left by a study of it is of tremendous rhythmic vitality. No sketches are extant (this is usually the case with Schubert's finished work) and the manuscript suggests that some of the symphony was composed in full score as fast as the pen could travel. The development section of the first movement displays a remarkable synthesis of elements in the exposition section with the opening bars of the horn theme from the introduction. The Andante con moto can fairly claim to be his loveliest slow movement: in the duet for cellos and oboe, after the big climax; in the soft, repeated notes of the horn (a passage made famous by Schumann's eulogy) which lead to the recapitulation; in the varied string accompaniments to the melody of the A major section: all these have poetry and imagination which he never surpassed and never more ardently expressed. The Scherzo and Finale, the former in full sonata form, have a lively rhythmic energy which sweeps all before it: the first has great lyric beauty, the second a splendour of thematic development. In all four movements the use of the trombones, delicate or authoritative, is perhaps the most notable feature in an orchestration that abounds in felicities.

The last group of works for solo piano consists of eight impromptus, the Three Piano Pieces (D946) and three sonatas. Four of the impromptus (D899) were published as op.90 (nos.1 and 2 in December 1827; no.3, transposed from G♭ to G by the publisher, and no.4 in 1857), and four others (D935) as op.142 by Diabelli in 1839. The Three Piano Pieces appeared in 1868, anonymously edited by Brahms. The 11 pieces are realizations of various moods, dramatic, thoughtful or passionate, and all are supremely lyrical. As the first departure by a major composer from the dominance of the sonata over piano forms, and as the modest forerunners of the Romantic composers' work in this field, they are historically important apart from their own intrinsic worth. But to rank them more highly and to play them more frequently than the sonatas is a folly of which this age is less guilty than the preceding one. And it is ill-informed to consider them as dismembered sonata movements: not only do they, for all their charm, lack the 'grand style' of his sonatas, but a study of their crude transitional passages is convincing of their lesser stature. Schubert's transitions in his sonatas have the vitality and magic which proclaim the master of the form, as may be seen at once in his last three sonatas. This group closes his long series of piano compositions and fittingly contains his finest work. The level of attainment rises in each sonata to the heights in the third, in B♭. In the first movements of all three, the development sections show the features already mentioned; the second subjects are many-sectioned and have picturesque codas. The slow movements are like richly accompanied songs; they have deeply tranquil opening and closing sections with a dramatic interlude which, in the A major Sonata, has an astonishing complexity and vigour. There is point and significance in the trios of the scherzos, and in the finales an extensive and admirable

development of the main theme of the movement. This is especially fine in the finale of the A major Sonata, whose theme is derived, no doubt unconsciously, from the slow movement of the A minor Sonata of 1817 (D537).

Schubert's last great work was the String Quintet in C (D956). It is filled with magnificent moments: the duet for cellos in the first movement; the richness and intriguing instrumentation of the Adagio; the elegiac trio of the third movement (a true pointer to the future); the wonderful rhythmic variants of the finale theme. His subtler blending of the major and minor modes can be seen in the themes of the first and last movements; who, looking at them in isolation, would dream that movements in major keys are being announced? The whole work, as a study of Neapolitan relationships, is without equal.

21. SCHUBERT'S HISTORICAL PLACE. Attempts to look upon Schubert as a herald of the Romantic era are not convincing; in the final count he must be placed among the Classical composers. It is true that formal grace and balance in his compositions are often sacrificed to the exuberance of his imagination, but Romanticism is not the tendency to distort or modify Classical forms, but to dispense with them; and this Schubert was incapable of doing. Except the Fourth Symphony, none of his works bears a title of his own bestowing; none carries a programme, none is labelled with extra-musical hints. On the contrary – and the point has been made – his mature work grows more conventional.

In one respect in which he was a pioneer, in new, far-reaching harmonic and tonal experiments, his innovations had little influence on his successors. By the time his greatest works became known, in the 1860s, music had moved beyond his achievements, and effects which would have been staggering in the 1830s were, 30 years later, the commonplaces of musical utterance.

WORKS

Editions: *F. Schuberts Werke: kritisch durchgeschene Gesamtausgabe*, ed. E. Mandyczewski, J. Brahms and others (Leipzig, 1884–97/R1964–9) [SW, ser./vol., p.]
    F. Schubert: Neue Ausgabe sämtlicher Werke, ed. W. Dürr, A. Feil, C. Landon and others (Kassel, 1964–) [NSA, ser./vol., p.]
Items are ordered by D number as enumerated in W. Dürr, A. Feil, C. Landon and others: *Franz Schubert: thematisches Verzeichnis seiner Werke in chronologischer Folge von Otto Erich Deutsch*, Neue Ausgabe Sämtlicher Werke, viii/4 (Kassel, 1978); where, exceptionally, numbers have been changed in this edition, a cross-reference is given. Numbers in parentheses following a title refer to separate settings of the same text.

THEATRICAL

D	Title	Genre	Text	Composed	First production	Published	SW; NSA
11	Der Spiegelritter	Singspiel, 3, only ov. and 1st act complete	A. von Kotzebue	Dec 1811–1812	Swiss Radio, 11 Dec 1949	1893	xxi, 1, xiv/7, 109; ii/11
84	Des Teufels Lustschloss	opera, 3	Kotzebue			1888	xv/1; ii/1
	version a			30 Oct 1813–15 May 1814	Vienna, Musikvereinsaal,		
	version b			completed 22 Oct 1814	12 Dec 1879 (as pubd in 1888)		
137	Adrast [see ov., 648]	opera 2, unfinished	J. Mayrhofer	?1817–19	Vienna, Redoutensaal, 13 Dec 1868	1893	xv/7, 317; ii/11
190	Der vierjährige Posten	Singspiel, 1	T. Körner	8–19 May 1815	Dresden, 23 Sept 1896	1888	xv/2, 1; ii/2
220	Fernando	Singspiel, 1	A. Stadler	27 June–9 July 1815	Vienna, 13 April 1907	1888	xv/2, 111; ii/2
239	Claudine von Villa Bella	Singspiel, 3, only ov. and 1st act complete	Goethe	begun 26 July 1815	Vienna, Gemeindehaus Wieden, 26 April 1913	1893	xv/7, 1; ii/12
326	Die Freunde von Salamanka	Singspiel, 2	Mayrhofer	18 Nov–31 Dec 1815	Halle, 6 May 1928	1888	xv/2, 171; ii/3

D	Title	Genre	Text	Composed	First production	Published	SW; NSA
435	Die Bürgschaft	opera, 3, 1st and 2nd acts complete	—	begun 2 May 1816	Vienna, 7 March 1908	1893	xv/7, 203; ii/12
644	Die Zauberharfe	melodrama, 3	G. von Hofmann	1820	Vienna, Theater an der Wien, 19 Aug 1820	1891	xv/4, 1; ii/4, 3
647	Die Zwillingsbrüder	Singspiel, 1	Hofmann	Jan 1819	Vienna, Kärntnertor, 14 June 1820	1889	xv/3, 1; ii/5
701	Sakuntala	opera, 3, sketches for 1st and 2nd acts only	J. P. Neumann, after Kalidasa	Oct 1820	Vienna, 12 June 1971	—	—; ii/13
723	Duet and aria for Hérold's Das Zauberglöckchen (La clochette)	—	E. G. M. Théaulon de Lambert, trans. F. Treitsche	spring 1821	Vienna, Kärntnertor, 20 June 1821	1893	xv/7, 365; ii/14
732	Alfonso und Estrella	opera, 3	F. von Schober	20 Sept 1821–27 Feb 1822	Weimar, 24 June 1854	1892	xv/5, 1; ii/6
787	Die Verschworenen (Der häusliche Krieg)	Singspiel, 1	I. F. Castelli, after Aristophanes: Lysistrata	March–April 1823	Vienna, Musikvereinsaal, 1 March 1861	1889	xv/3, 115; ii/7
791	Rüdiger	opera, sketches for nos.1–2 only	?I. von Mosel	begun May 1823	Vienna, Redoutensaal, 5 Jan 1868	1867	—; ii/14
796	Fierabras	opera, 3	J. Kupelwieser	25 May–2 Oct 1823	Karlsruhe, 9 Feb 1897	1886	xv/6, 1; ii/8
797	Rosamunde, Fürstin von Zypern	incidental music to romantic play, 4	H. von Chézy	autumn 1823	Vienna, Theater an der Wien, 20 Dec 1823	1891	xv/4, 345; ii/9
918	Der Graf von Gleichen	opera, 2, sketches only	E. von Bauernfeld	begun 19 June 1827	—	—	—; ii/14
966	[see 11]	orch interlude to 11/3, frag.					
981	Der Minnesänger	Singspiel, unfinished, lost	—	—	—	—	
982	—	opera, sketches, 3 nos. only	—	after 1820	—	—	—; ii/14

SACRED

D	Title	Forces	Composed	Published	SW;NSA
24c	Mass, ?F, frag.	SATB, orch, org	?1812	—	—; i/5
27	Salve regina, F	S, orch, org	28 June 1812	1928	—; i/8
31	Kyrie, d	S, T, SATB, orch, org	25 Sept 1812	1888	xiv, 175; i/5
45	Kyrie, Bb	SATB	1 March 1813	1888	xiv, 226; i/5
49	Kyrie, d	S, A, T, B, SATB, orch	April 1813	1888	xiv, 189; i/5
56	Sanctus, canon with coda, Bb	3vv	21 April 1813	1892	xix, 89; i/8
66	Kyrie, F	SATB, orch, org	12 May 1813	1888	xiv, 203; i/5
71a	Alleluja, F, canon	3vv	?July 1813	1956	—; i/8
105	Mass no.1, F [see also 185]	S, S, A, T, B, SATB, orch, org	17 May–22 July 1814	1856	xiii/1, 1; i/1
106	Salve regina, Bb	T, orch, org	28 June–1 July 1814	1888	xiv, 47; i/8
136	Offertory: Totus in corde langueo, C	S/T, cl/vn, orch, org	?1815	1825, op.46	xiv, 1; i/8
167	Mass no.2, G	S, T, B, SATB, str, org	2–7 March 1815	1846	xiii/1, 121; i/1
175	Stabat mater, g	SATB, orch, org	4–6 April 1815	1888	xiv, 101; i/8
181	Offertory: Tres sunt, a	SATB, orch, org	10–11 April 1815	1888	xiv, 23; i/8
184	Gradual: Benedictus es, Domine, C	SATB, orch, org	15–17 April 1815	c1843, op.150	xiv, 29; i/8
185	Dona nobis pacem, F [alternative movt for 105]	B, SATB, orch, org	25–26 April 1815	1887	xiii/1, 931; i/1
223	Salve regina (Offertorium), F	S, orch, org			—; i/8
	version a		5 July 1815	—	xiv, 9; i/8
	version b		28 Jan 1823	1825, op.47	
324	Mass no.3, Bb	S, A, T, B, SATB, orch, org	begun 11 Nov 1815	c1837, op.141	xiii/1, 157; i/2
379	Deutsches Salve regina (Hymne an die heilige Mutter Gottes), F	SATB, org	21 Feb 1816	1859	xiv, 215; i/8
383	Stabat mater, oratorio, F/f	S, T, B, SATB, orch	begun 28 Feb 1816	1888	xiv, 109; i/7
386	Salve regina, Bb	SATB	early 1816	1833	xiv, 224; i/8
452	Mass no.4, C [see also 961]	S, A, T, B, SATB, orch, org	June–July 1816	1825, op.48	xiii/1, 209; i/2
453	Requiem, c, frag.	SATB, orch	July 1816	—	—; i/5
460	Tantum ergo, C	S, orch, org	Aug 1816	1888	xiv, 39; i/8
461	Tantum ergo, C	S, A, T, B, SATB, orch	Aug 1816	1935	—; i/8
486	Magnificat, C	S, A, T, B, SATB, orch, org	15 Sept 1815	1888	xiv, 77; i/8
488	Auguste jam coelestium, G	S, T, orch	Oct 1816	1888	xiv, 59; i/8
607	Evangelium Johannis VI, E	1v, bc	1818	1920	—; i/8
621	Deutsches Requiem (Deutsche Trauermesse), g	S, A, T, B, SATB, org	Aug 1818	1826	—; i/6
676	Salve regina (Offertorium), A	S, str	Nov 1819	1845, op.153	xiv, 17; i/8

D	Title	Forces	Composed	Published	SW; NSA
678	Mass no.5, A♭	S, A, T, B, SATB, orch, org	Nov 1819–Sept 1822		
	version a			1875	—; i/3
	version b			1887	xiii/2, 1; i/3
696	6 antiphons for Palm Sunday: Hosanna filio David; In monte Oliveti; Sanctus, sanctus, sanctus; Pueri hebraeorum; Cum angelis et pueris; Ingrediente Domino	SATB	March 1820	1829, op.113	xiv, 218; i/8
730	Tantum ergo, B♭	S, A, T, B, SATB, orch, org	16 Aug 1821	1926	—; i/8
739	Tantum ergo, C	SATB, orch, org	1814	1825, op.45	xiv, 37; i/8
750	Tantum ergo, D	SATB, orch, org	20 March 1822	1888	xiv, 43; i/8
755	Kyrie, a, sketch	S, A, T, B, SATB, str, org	May 1822	—	—; i/5
811	Salve regina, C	TTBB	April 1824	1850, op.149	xiv, 220; i/8
872	Deutsche Messe		late summer 1827		
	version a	SATB, org		—	—; i/6
	version b	SATB, orch, org		1870	xiii/2, 325; i/6
	Appx: Das Gebet des Herrn			1845	xiii/2, 340; i/6
950	Mass no.6, E♭	S, A, T, B, SATB, orch	begun June 1828	1865	xiii/2, 167; i/4
961	Benedictus, a [alternative movt for 452]	S, A, T, B, SATB, orch, org	Oct 1828	1829	xiii/1, 247; i/2
962	Tantum ergo, E♭	S, A, T, B, SATB, orch	Oct 1828	1890	xiv, 227, xxi, 269; i/8
963	Offertory: Intende voci, B♭	T, SATB, orch	Oct 1828	1890	xxi, 277; i/8
992	[sketches for 383]				

MIXED VOICES

(NSA nos. refer to vol. in series 3 unless otherwise stated)

D	Title	Forces	Text	Composed	Published	SW; NSA
17	Quell' innocente figlio		Metastasio	c1812		—; viii/2
	version 3	S, A, T			1940	
	version 4	S, A, T, B			1940	
	version 5	S, A, T			1940	
	version 6	S, A, T			1940	
	version 7	S, A, T, B			—	
	version 8	S, A, T, B			1940	
	version 9	S, A, T, B			1940	
33	Entra l'uomo allor che nasce		Metastasio	Sept–Oct 1812	1940	—; viii/2
	version 3	S, A, T				
	version 4	S, A, T, B				
	version 5	S, A, T, B				
	version 6	S, A, T, B				
34	Te solo adoro	S, A, T, B	Metastasio	5 Nov 1812	1940	—; viii/2
35	Serbate, o dei custodi		Metastasio	Oct 1812	1940	—; viii/2
	version 1	S, A, T, B				
	version 2	SATB				
47	Dithyrambe (Der Besuch), frag.	T, B, SATB, pf	Schiller	29 March 1813	—	—; ii
168	Nun lasst uns den Leib begraben (Begräbnislied)	SATB, pf	F. Klopstock	9 March 1815	1872	xvii, 241; ii
168a	Osterlied [formerly 987]	SATB, pf	Klopstock	9 March 1815	1872	xvii, 244; ii
232	Hymne an den Unendlichen	SATB, pf	Schiller	11 July 1815	1829, op.112/3	xvii, 167; ii
294	Namensfeier für Franz Michael Vierthaler (Gratulations Kantate)	S, T, B, STB, orch		27 Sept 1815	1892	xvii, 142; i
329a	Das Grab (1), sketch	SATB	J. Salis-Seewis	?28 Dec 1815	—	—; ii
439	An die Sonne	SATB, pf	J. P. Uz	June 1816	1872	xvii, 218; ii
440	Chor der Engel	SATB	Goethe	June 1816	1839	xvii, 245; ii
451	Prometheus, cantata, lost	S, B, chorus, orch	P. Dräxler von Carin	17 June 1816	—	—
472	Kantate zu Ehren von Josef Spendou	2S, B, SATB, orch	J. Hoheisel	Sept 1816	1830, op.128	xvii, 109; i
609	Die Geselligkeit (Lebenslust)	SATB, pf	J. K. Unger	Jan 1818	1872	xvii, 225; ii
642	Viel tausend Sterne prangen	SATB, pf	A. G. Eberhard	?1812	1937	—; ii
643a	Das Grab (5)	SATB	Salis-Seewis	1819	1972	—; ii
665	Im traulichen Kreise [part of 609]					
666	Kantate zum Geburtstag des Sängers Johann Michael Vogl (Der Frühlingsmorgen)	STB, pf	A. Stadler	10 Aug 1819	1849, op.158	xix, 37; ii
689	Lazarus, oder Die Feier der Auferstehung, oratorio, 3, only 1st act and part of 2nd complete	3S, 2T, B, SATB, orch	A. H. Niemeyer	Feb 1820	1865	xvii, 1; ii/10
748	Am Geburtstag des Kaisers, cantata	S, A, T, B, SATB, orch	J. L. F. von Deinhardstein	Jan 1822	1822; 1849 as op. 157	xvii, 138; ii
763	Des Tages Weihe	SATB, pf		22 Nov 1822	1842, op. 146	xvii, 212; ii
815	Gebet	SATB, pf	Fouqué	Sept 1824	1840, op.139	xvii, 198; ii
826	Der Tanz	SATB, pf	? K. Schnitzer von Mecrau	early 1828	1892	xvii, 228; ii

D	Title	Forces	Text	Composed	Published	SW; NSA
875a	Die Allmacht (2), sketch	SATB, pf	J. L. Pyrker von Felsö-Eör	Jan 1826	—	—; ii
920	Ständchen version a [for version b see 'Female or unspecified voices'] [formerly 921]	A, TTBB, pf	Grillparzer	July 1827	1891	xvi, 108; iii
930	Der Hochzeitsbraten	S, T, B, pf	Schober	Nov 1827	1829, op.104	xix, 14; ii
936	Kantate für Irene Kiesewetter	2T, 2B, SATB, pf 4 hands	anon. It. text	26 Dec 1827	1892	xvii, 231; ii
942	Mirjams Siegesgesang	S, SATB, pf	Grillparzer	March 1828	c1839, op.136	xvii, 170; ii
953	Der 92. Psalm: Lied für den Sabbath	S, A, T, Bar, B, SATB	Heb. text	July 1828	1841	xvii, 247; ii
954	Glaube, Hoffnung und Liebe	2T, 2B, SATB, wind insts/pf	F. Reil	Aug 1828	1828	xvii, 152; i, ii
985	Gott im Ungewitter	SATB, pf	Uz	?1827	1829, op.112/1	xvii, 156; ii
986	Gott der Weltschöpfer	SATB, pf	Uz	?1827	1829, op.112/2	xvii, 164; ii
987	Osterlied [see 168a]					

MALE VOICES

(NSA nos. refer to vol. and p. in series 3)

D	Title	Forces	Text	Composed	Published	SW; NSA
37	Die Advokaten [based on a previous setting by Anton Fischer]	TTB, pf	Baron Engelhart	25–27 Dec 1812	1827, op.74	xix, 2; iii
38	Totengräberlied (1)	TTB	L. C. H. Hölty	?1813	1892	xix, 76; iv, 3
43	Dreifach ist der Schritt der Zeit (1)	TTB	Schiller	8 July 1813	1897	xxi, 337; iv, 4
51	Unendliche Freude (1)	TTB	Schiller	15 April 1813	1897	xxi, 330; iv, 8
53	Vorüber die stöhnende Klage	TTB	Schiller	18 April 1813	1892	xix, 61; iv, 10
54	Unendliche Freude (2), canon	BBB/TTB	Schiller	19 April 1813	1873	xix, 78; iv, 12
55	Selig durch die Liebe	TTB	Schiller	21 April 1813	1892	xix, 67; iv, 14
57	Hier strecket der wallende Pilger	TTB	Schiller	29 April 1813	1897	xxi, 331; iv, 15
58	Dessen Fahne Donnerstürme wallte	TTB	Schiller	May 1813	1892	xix, 63; iv, 18
60	Hier umarmen sich getreue Gatten	TTB	Schiller	3 Oct 1813	1892	xix, 65; iv, 33
62	Thronend auf erhabnem Sitz	TTB	Schiller	9 May 1813	1956	xxi, 334; iv, 22
63	Wer die steile Sternenbahn	TTB	Schiller	10 May 1813	1892	xix, 68; iv, 24
64	Majestätsche Sonnenrosse	TTB	Schiller	10 May 1813	1897	xxi, 335; iv, 26
65	Schmerz verzerret ihr Gesicht, canon, sketch	TTB	Schiller	11 May 1813	1892	xix, 94; iv, 180
67	Frisch atmet des Morgens lebendiger Hauch	TTB	Schiller	15 May 1813	1897	xxi, 335; iv, 27
70	Dreifach ist der Schritt der Zeit ('Ewig still steht die Vergangenheit') (3), canon	TTB	Schiller	8 July 1813	1928	—; iv, 177
71	Die zwei Tugendwege	TTB	Schiller	15 July 1813	1892	xix, 69; iv, 32
75	Trinklied ('Freunde, sammelt euch im Kreise')	B, TTB, pf	F. Schäffer	29 Aug 1813	1850	xvi, 128; iii
80	Zur Namensfeier meines Vaters	TTB, gui	F. Schubert	27 Sept 1813	1892	xix, 48; iii
88	Verschwunden sind die Schmerzen, canon	TTB	Schubert	15 Nov 1813	1892	xix, 77; iv, 35
110	Wer ist gross?	B, TTBB, orch		24–5 July 1814	1891	xvi, 205; i
129	Mailied ('Grüner wird die Au') (1)	TTB	Hölty	c1815	1892	xix, 72; iv, 37
132	Lied beim Rundetanz, 1 part only	? TTB/TTBB	J. von Salis-Seewis	1815 or 1816	1974	—; iv, 177
133	Lied im Freien, 1 part only	? TTB/TTBB	Salis-Seewis	1815 or 1816	1974	—; iv, 178
140	Klage um Ali Bey (1)	TTB, ?pf	M. Claudius	1815	1850	xviii, 32
147	Bardengesang	TTB	Ossian, trans. E. de Harold	20 Jan 1816	1892	xix, 70; iv, 42
148	Trinklied ('Brüder! unser Erdenwallen')	T, TTB, pf	I. F. Castelli	Feb 1815	1830, op.131/2	xix, 59; iii
236	Das Abendrot	TTB, pf	L. Kosegarten	20 July 1815	1892	xix, 57; ii
242	Trinklied im Winter	TTB	Hölty	?Aug 1815	1892	xix, 74; iv, 48
243	Frühlingslied ('Die Luft ist blau') (1)	TTB	Hölty	?Aug 1815	1892	xix, 75; iv, 50
267	Trinklied ('Auf! jeder sei nun froh')	TTBB, pf		25 Aug 1815	1872	xvi, 131; iii
268	Bergknappenlied	TTBB, pf		25 Aug 1815	1872	xvi, 133; iii
269	Das Leben version a [for version b see 'Female or unspecified voices']	TBB, pf	J. C. Wannovius	Aug 1815	—	—; iii
277	Punschlied ('Vier Elemente, innig gesellt')	TTB, pf	Schiller	29 Aug 1815	1892	xix, 58; iii
330	Das Grab (2) version b [for version a see 'Songs']	4 vv, pf	Salis-Seewis	28 Dec 1815	1895	xx/3, 231; iii
331	Der Entfernten (1)	TTBB	Salis-Seewis	c1816	1866	xvi, 194; iv, 56
337	Die Einsiedelei (1)	TTBB	Salis-Seewis	c1816	c1860	xvi, 195; iv, 58

D	Title	Forces	Text	Composed	Published	SW; NSA
338	An den Frühling (2)	TTBB	Schiller	c1816	1891	xvi, 196; iv, 60
339	Amors Macht, 1 part only	? TTB/TTBB	F. von Matthisson	1815 or 1816	1974	—; iv, 178
340	Badelied, T2 only	? TTB/TTBB	Matthisson	1815 or 1816	1974	—; iv, 178
341	Sylphen, T2 only	? TTB/TTBB	Matthisson	1815 or 1816	1974	—; iv, 179
356	Trinklied ('Funkelnd im Becher')	TTBB, lost pf acc.		1816	1844	—; iii
364	Fischerlied (2)	TTBB	Salis-Seewis	c1816–17	1897	xxi, 320; iv, 63
377	Das Grab (3)	TTBB, pf	Salis-Seewis	11 Feb 1816	1872	xx/4, 6; iii
387	Die Schlacht (2), sketch	solo vv, chorus, pf	Schiller	March 1816	1897	xxi, 341; ii
407	Beitrag zur fünfzig jährigen Jubelfeier des Herrn Salieri, [no.1 also in version for TTB, see 441]	T, TTBB, pf	Schubert	by 16 June 1816	1891–2	xvi, 211; iii
422	Naturgenuss (2)	TTBB, pf	Matthisson	?1822	1823, op.16/2	xvi, 76; iii
423	Andenken ('Ich denke dein, wenn durch den Hain') (2)	TTB	Matthisson	May 1816	1927	—; iv, 66
424	Erinnerungen ('Am Seegestad') (2)	TTB	Matthisson	May 1816	1927	—; iv, 68
425	Lebensbild, lost	TTB		May 1816	—	—
426	Trinklied ('Herr Bacchus ist ein braver Mann'), lost	TTB		May 1816	—	—
427	Trinklied im Mai	TTB	Hölty	May 1816	1892	xix, 73; iv, 70
428	Widerhall ('Auf ewig dein')	TTB	Matthisson	May 1816	1927	—; iv, 73
441	[=TTB version of 407/1]	TTB, pf	Schubert	by 16 June 1816	1892	xix, 53; iii
494	Der Geistertanz (4)	TTBBB	Matthisson	Nov 1816	1871	xvi, 173; iv, 77
513	La pastorella al prato (1)	TTBB, pf	C. Goldoni	?1817	1891	xvi, 134; iii
538	Gesang der Geister über den Wassern (2)	TTBB	Goethe	March 1817	1891	xvi, 175; iv, 81
569	Das Grab (4)	unison vv, pf	Salis-Seewis	June 1817	1895	xx/5, 122; iii
572	Lied im Freien	TTBB	Salis-Seewis	July 1817	1872	xvi, 180; iv, 89
598	Das Dörfchen		G. A. Bürger			
	version a, sketch	TTBB		Dec 1817	1891	xvi, 223; iii
	version b [formerly 641]	TTBB, pf		1818	1822, op.11/1	xvi, 41; iii
635	Leise, leise lasst uns singen	TTBB		c1819	1906–7	—; iv, 97
641	Das Dörfchen [see 598]					
656	Sehnsucht ('Nur wer die Sehnsucht kennt') (4)	TTBBB	Goethe	April 1819	1867	xvi, 185; iv, 98
657	Ruhe, schönstes Glück der Erde	TTBB		April 1819	1871	xvi, 187; iv, 102
704	Gesang der Geister über den Wassern [see 714]					
705	Gesang der Geister über den Wassern (3), sketch	TTBB, pf	Goethe	Dec 1820	1897	xxi, 313; iii
709	Frühlingsgesang (1)	TTBB	F. von Schober	before April 1822	1891	xvi, 169; iv, 106
710	Im Gegenwärtigen Vergangenes	TTBB, pf	Goethe	?March 1821	1849	xvi, 119; iii
714	Gesang der Geister über den Wassern (4)		Goethe			
	version a, sketch [formerly 704]	TTTBBBB, 2 va, 2 vc, db		Dec 1820	1891	xvi, 215; i
	version b	TTTBBBB, 2 va, 2 vc, db		Feb 1821	1858, op.167	xvi, 24; i
724	Die Nachtigall	TTBB, pf	J. K. Unger	by April 1821	1822, op.11/2	xvi, 50; iii
740	Frühlingsgesang (2)	TTBB, pf	Schober	Jan–April 1822	1823, op.16/1	xvi, 65; iii
747	Geist der Liebe ('Der Abend schleiert Flur und Hain') (2)	TTBB, pf	Matthisson	Jan 1822	1822, op.11/3	xvi, 59; iii
778b	Ich hab in mich gesogen, sketch	TTBB	Rückert	?1823	1978	—; viii/3
809	Gondelfahrer (2)	TTBB, pf	J. Mayrhofer	March 1824	1824, op.28	xvi, 83; iii
822	Lied eines Kriegers	B, unison vv, pf		31 Dec 1824	1842	xx/8, 32; iii
825	Wehmut	TTBB	H. Hüttenbrenner	before summer 1826	1828, op.64/1	xvi, 141; iv, 121
825a	Ewige Liebe	TTBB	E. Schulze	before summer 1826	1828, op.64/2	xvi, 144; iv, 126
825b	Flucht	TTBB	K. Lappe	by early 1825	1828, op.64/3	xvi, 148; iv, 133
835	Bootgesang	TTBB, pf	Scott, trans. D. A. Storck	1825	1826, op.52/3	xvi, 89; iii
847	Trinklied aus dem 16. Jahrhundert	TTBB	F. Gräffer	July 1825	1849, op.155	xvi, 29; iv, 139
848	Nachtmusik	TTBB	K. S. von Seckendorff	July 1825	1849, op.156	xvi, 166; iv, 143
865	Widerspruch version a [for version b see 'Songs']	TTBB, pf	J. G. Seidl	?1826	1828, op.105/1	xvi, 93; iii
873a	Nachklänge, sketch	TTBB		?Jan 1826	1974	—; iv, 187
875	Mondenschein	TTBBB, pf	Schober	Jan 1826	1831, op.102	xvi, 153; iii
892	Nachthelle	T, TTBB, pf	Seidl	Sept 1826	1839, op.134	xvi, 98; iii
893	Grab und Mond	TTBB	Seidl	Sept 1826	1827	xvi, 197; iv, 148
901	Wein und Liebe	TTBB	J. C. F. Haug	before June 1827	1827	xvi, 190; iv, 150
903	Zur guten Nacht	Bar, TTBB, pf	J. F. Rochlitz	Jan 1827	1827, op.81/3	xvi, 91; iii
912	Schlachtlied (2)	TTBB, TTBB	F. G. Klopstock	28 Feb 1827	1844, op.151	xvi, 157; iv, 156
913	Nachtgesang im Walde	TTBB, 4 hn	Seidl	April 1827	1846, op.139	xvi, 1; i
914	Frühlingslied	TTBB	A. Pollak	April 1827	1897	xxi, 321; iv, 166
916	Das stille Lied, sketch	TTBB	J. G. Seegemund	May 1827	1978	—; iv, 188, viii/3
941	Hymnus an den Heiligen Geist [see 948]					
948	Hymnus an den Heiligen Geist		A. Schmidl	May 1828		
	version a [formerly 941]	2T, 2B, TTBB			1891	xvi, 199; i/8
	version b [formerly 964]	2T, 2B, TTBB, wind insts			1849, op.154	xvi, 11; i/8

D	Title	Forces	Text	Composed	Published	SW; NSA
964	Hymnus an den Heiligen Geist [see 948]					
983	Jünglingswonne	TTBB	Matthisson	?1822	1823, op.17/1	xvi, 137; iv, 112
983a	Liebe	TTBB	Schiller	?1822	1823, op.17/2	xvi, 138; iv, 115
983b	Zum Rundetanz	TTBB	Salis-Seewis	?1822	1823, op.17/3	xvi, 139; iv, 116
983c	Die Nacht	TTBB	? F. W. Krummacher	?1822	1823, op.17/4	xvi, 139; iv, 118
984	Der Wintertag	TTBB, lost pf acc.	?	?	c1865, op.169	—; iii

FEMALE OR UNSPECIFIED VOICES

(*NSA nos. refer to vol. and p. in series 3 unless otherwise stated*)

D	Title	Forces	Text	Composed	Published	SW; NSA
17	Quell' innocente figlio, version 2	2S	Metastasio	c1812	1940	—; viii/2
33	Entra l'uomo allor che nasce, version 2	S, A	Metastasio	Sept–Oct 1812	1940	—; viii/2
61	Ein jugendlicher Maienschwung	3vv	Schiller	8 May 1813	1897	xxi, 333; iv, 20
69	Dreifach ist der Schritt der Zeit (2)	3vv	Schiller	8 July 1813	1892	xix, 80; iv, 30
130	Der Schnee zerrinnt (1), canon	3vv	Hölty	c1815	1892	xix, 82; iv, 38
131	Lacrimoso son io, canon, 2 versions	3vv		?Aug 1815	1892	xix, 87; iv, 40
169	Trinklied vor der Schlacht	2 unison choruses, pf	T. Körner	12 March 1815	1894	xx/2, 68; iii
170	Schwertlied	1v, unison chorus, pf	Körner	12 March 1815	1873	xx/2, 78; iii
183	Trinklied ('Ihr Freunde und du gold'ner Wein')	1v, unison chorus, pf	A. Zettler	12 April 1815	1887	xx/2, 97; iii
189	An die Freude	1v, unison chorus, pf	Schiller	May 1815	1829, op.111/1	xx/2, 102; iii
199	Mailied ('Grüner wird die Au') (2)	2vv/2 hn	Hölty	24 May 1815	1885	xix, 91; iv, 44
202	Mailied ('Der Schnee zerrinnt') (2)	2vv/2 hn	Hölty	26 May 1815	1885	xix, 91; iv, 44
203	Der Morgenstern (2)	2vv/2 hn	Körner	26 May 1815	1892	xix, 92; iv, 45
204	Jägerlied	2vv/2 hn	Körner	26 May 1815	1892	xix, 92; iv, 46
205	Lützows wilde Jagd	2vv/2 hn	Körner	26 May 1815	1892	xix, 93; iv, 46
244	Willkommen, lieber schöner Mai, canon, 2 versions	3vv	Hölty	?Aug 1815	1892	xix, 85; iv, 51
253	Punschlied: im Norden zu singen	2vv	Schiller	18 Aug 1815	1887	xx/3, 30; iv, 54
269	Das Leben version b [for version a see 'Male voices']	SSA, pf	Wannovius	25 Aug 1815	1849	xviii, 31; iii
357	Gold'ner Schein, canon	3vv	Matthisson	May 1816	1892	xix, 81; iv, 64
442	Das grosse Halleluja version b [for version a see 'Songs']	chorus, pf	Klopstock	June 1816	c1847	xx/4, 110; iii
443	Schlachtlied (1) version b [for version a see 'Songs']	chorus, pf	Klopstock	June 1816	1895	xx/4, 112; iii
521	Jagdlied version b [for version a see 'Songs']	unison vv, pf	F. Werner	Jan 1817	1895	xx/5, 3; iii
706	Der 23. Psalm	SSAA, pf	trans. M. Mendelssohn	Dec 1820	1832, op.132	xviii, 3; iii
757	Gott in der Natur	SSAA, pf	E. C. von Kleist	Aug 1822	1839	xviii, 10; iii
836	Coronach (Totengesang der Frauen und Mädchen)	SSA, pf	Scott, trans. Storck	1825	1826, op.52/4	xviii, 1; iii
873	Canon, a sketch	6vv	—	?Jan 1826	1974	—; iv, 187
920	Ständchen [formerly 921] version b [for version a see 'Male voices']	A, SSAA, pf	Grillparzer	July 1827	1840, op.135	xviii, 20; iii
988	Liebe säuseln die Blätter, canon	3vv	Hölty	?1815	1873	xix, 83; iv, 172
988a	—	pf acc. only	—	?after 1820	1969	—; iii

ORCHESTRAL

(*NSA nos. refer to vol. and p. in series 5*)

D	Title	Composed	Published	SW; NSA
2a	Overture, D, frag. [formerly 996]	?1811	—	—; iv
2b	Symphony, D, frag., 1st movt only [formerly 997]	?1811	—	—; iv
4	Overture D, for Albrecht's comedy Der Teufel als Hydraulicus	?1812	1886	ii, 1; iv
12	Overture, D	1811 or 1812	1897	xxi, 23; iv
26	Overture, D	by 26 June 1812	1886	ii, 13; iv
39a	3 minuets and trios, lost	1813	—	—
71c	Orch frag., D [formerly 966a]	Aug/Sept 1813	—	—; v
82	Symphony no.1, D	by 28 Oct 1813	1884	i/1, 1; i, 3
94a	Orch frag., B♭	c1814	—	—; v
125	Symphony no.2, B♭	10 Dec 1814–24 March 1815	1884	i/1, 65; i, 71
200	Symphony no.3, D	24 May–19 July 1815	1884	i/1, 143; i, 153
345	Concerto (Concertstück), D, vn, orch	1816	1897	xxi, 46; iv
417	Symphony no.4, c, 'Tragic'	by 27 April 1816	1884	i/1, 191; ii
438	Rondo, A, vn, str	June 1816	1897	xxi, 73; iv
470	Overture, B♭ [possibly for cantata 472; arr. str qt 601]	Sept 1816	1886	ii, 31; iv

D	Title	Composed	Published	SW; NSA
485	Symphony no.5, Bb	Sept–3 Oct 1816	1885	i/2, 1; ii
556	Overture, D	May 1817	1886	ii, 47; iv
580	Polonaise, Bb, vn, orch	Sept 1817	1928	—; iv
589	Symphony no.6, C	Oct 1817–Feb 1818	1885	i/2, 49; ii
590	Overture, D, 'im italienischen Stile' [arr. pf 4 hands, 592]	Nov 1817	1886	ii, 63; iv
591	Overture, C, 'im italienischen Stile' [arr. pf 4 hands, 597]	Nov 1817	1865, op.170	ii, 83; iv
615	Symphony, D, pf sketches for 2 movts	May 1818	—	—; v
648	Overture, e [possibly for Adrast, 137]	Feb 1819	1886	ii, 101; iv
708a	Symphony, D, sketches	after 1820	—	—; v
729	Symphony [no.7], E, sketched in score	Aug 1821	1934	—; v
759	Symphony [no.7] no.8, b, 'Unfinished'	Oct 1822	1867	i/2, 239; iii
849	'Gmunden–Gastein' Symphony [?identical with 944]	June–Sept 1825	—	—
936a	Symphony, D, sketches	?mid-1828	1978	—; v
944	Symphony [no.8] no.9, C, 'Great'	?1825–8	1840	i/2, 117; iii
966a	Orch frag., D [see 71c]			
966b	Orch sketches, A, frag.	1820 or later	—	—; v
996	Overture [see 2a]			
997	Symphony [see 2b]			

CHAMBER

(NSA nos. refer to vol. and p. in series 6 unless otherwise stated)

D	Title	Forces	Composed	Published	SW; NSA
2c	String Quartet, ?d/F, frag. [formerly 998]	2 vn, va, vc	?1811	1978	—; iii
2d	6 Minuets, C, F, D, C, d, Bb [formerly 995]	2 ob, 2 cl, 2 hn, 2 bn, trbn	1811	1970	—; ix
2f	Trio of a minuet, C, sketch	? wind insts	1811	—	—; ix
3	String Quartet, C, frag.	2 vn, va, vc	?summer 1812	1978	—; iii
8	Overture, c	2 vn, 2 va, vc	29 June 1811	1970	—; ii, 3
8a	Overture, c [arr. of 8]	2 vn, va, vc	after 12 July 1811	1970	—; iii
18	String Quartet, g/Bb	2 vn, va, vc	1810 or 1811	1890	v, 1; iii
19	String Quartet, lost	2 vn, va, vc	1810 or 1811	—	—
19a	String Quartet, lost	2 vn, va, vc	1810 or 1811	—	—
20	Overture, Bb, lost	2 vn, va, vc	1812	—	—
28	Trio (Sonata in 1 movt), Bb	pf, vn, vc	27 July–28 Aug 1812	1923	—; vii, 3
32	String Quartet, C	2 vn, va, vc	Sept–Oct 1812		
	movts, 1, 3			1890	v, 11
	movt 4			1897	Rev. 53
	movts 1–4			1954	—; iii
36	String Quartet, Bb	2 vn, va, vc	19 Nov 1812–21 Feb 1813	1890	v, 19; iii
46	String Quartet, C	2 vn, va, vc	3–7 March 1813	1890	v, 37; iii
68	String Quartet, Bb, 1st movt and finale	2 vn, va, vc	8 June–18 Aug 1813	1890	v, 53; iii
72	Wind octet, F	2 ob, 2 cl, 2 hn, 2 bn	by 18 Aug 1813	1889	iii, 69; i, 3
72a	Allegro, F, unfinished	2 ob, 2 cl, 2 hn, 2 bn	1813	1897	Rev. 41; i, 151
74	String Quartet, D	2 vn, va, vc	22 Aug–Sept 1813	1890	v, 71; iv
79	Wind nonet, eb, 'Franz Schuberts Begräbnis-Feyer' (Eine kleine Trauermusik)	2 cl, 2 bn, dbn, 2 hn, 2 trbn	19 Sept 1813	1889	iii, 81; i, 25
86	Minuet, D	2 vn, va, vc	?Nov 1813	1886	ii, 154; ix
87	String Quartet, Eb	2 vn, va, vc	Nov 1813	1840, op.125/1	v, 147; iv
87a	Andante, C	? 2 vn, va, vc	Nov 1813	—	—; iv
89	5 minuets and 6 trios, C, F, d, G, C	2 vn, va, vc	19 Nov 1813	1886	ii, 141; ix
90	5 Deutsche and 7 trios with coda, C, G, D, F, C	2 vn, va, vc	19 Nov 1813	1886	ii, 147; ix
94	String Quartet, D	2 vn, va, vc	? 1811 or 1812	1871	v, 93; iii
94b	5 minuets and 6 Deutsche with trios, lost	2 vn, va, vc, 2 hn	1814	—	—
96	Trio, G, added to Schubert's arr. of W. Matiegka's Notturno op.21 [replaces orig. 2nd trio]	fl, va, vc, gui	Feb 1814	1926	—; viii/2
103	String Quartet, c, frags., Grave and Allegro	2 vn, va, vc	23 April 1814	1939	—; iv
111a	String Trio, Bb, frag., lost [? sketch for 112]	vn, va, vc	5–13 Sept 1814	—	—
112	String Quartet, Bb	2 vn, va, vc	5–13 Sept 1814	1863, op.168	v, 109; iv
173	String Quartet, g	2 vn, va, vc	25 March–1 April 1815	1871	v, 129; iv
353	String Quartet, E	2 vn, va, vc	1816	1840, op.125/2	v, 165; iv
354	4 komische Ländler, D	2 vn	Jan 1816	1930	—; ix
355	8 Ländler, f♯	?vn	Jan 1816	1928	—; ix
370	9 Ländler, D	?vn	Jan 1816	1930	—; ix
374	11 Ländler, Bb	vn	?Feb 1816	1902	—; ix
384	Sonata (Sonatina), D	vn, pf	March 1816	1836, op.137/1	viii, 26; viii, 3
385	Sonata (Sonatina), a	vn, pf	March 1816	1836, op.137/2	viii, 40; viii, 17
408	Sonata (Sonatina), g	vn, pf	April 1816	1836, op.137/3	viii, 56; viii, 33
471	String Trio, Bb, 1st movt and frag. of 2nd	vn, va, vc	Sept 1816	1890–97	vi, 1, Rev, 84; vi
487	Adagio and Rondo concertante, F	vn, va, vc, pf	Oct 1816	1865	vii/1, 52; vii, 157
574	Sonata (Duo), A	vn, pf	Aug 1817	1851, op.162	viii, 100; viii, 47
581	String Trio, Bb	vn, va, vc	Sept 1817	1897	xxi, 93; vi

D	Title	Forces	Composed	Published	SW;NSA
597a	Variations, A, sketches, lost	vn	Dec 1817	—	—
601	Overture, Bb, frag. [arr. of orch ov. 470]	2 vn, va, vc	c1816	—	—
667	Piano Quintet, A, 'Die Forelle'	pf, vn, va, vc, db	?autumn 1819	1829, op.114	vii/1, 52; vii, 185
703	String Quartet, c (Quartettsatz), with frag. 2nd movt	2 vn, va, vc	Dec 1820	1870–97	v, 183, Rev, 76; v
802	Introduction and variations (on Trockne Blumen from Die schöne Müllerin), e/E	fl, pf	Jan 1824	1850, op.160	viii, 120; viii, 67
803	Octet, F	cl, hn, bn, 2 vn, va, vc, db	Feb–1 March 1824		
	movts 1–3, 6			1853, op.166	—
	movts 1–6			1889	iii, 1; i, 27
804	String Quartet, a	2 vn, va, vc	Feb–March 1824	1824, op.29/1	v, 191; v
810	String Quartet, d, 'Der Tod und das Mädchen'	2 vn, va, vc	March 1824	1831	v, 215; v
821	Sonata, a, 'Arpeggione'	arpeggione, pf	Nov 1824	1871	viii, 142; viii, 89
887	String Quartet, G	2 vn, va, vc	20–30 June 1826	1851, op.161	v, 251; v
895	Rondo, b (Rondo brillant)	vn, pf	Oct 1826	1827, op.70	viii, 1; viii, 107
897	Piano Trio movt, Eb, 'Notturno'	pf, vn, vc	?1828	1846, op.148	vii/2, 106; vii, 143
898	Piano Trio, Bb	pf, vn, vc	?1828	1836, op.99	vii/2, 2; vii, 91
929	Piano Trio, Eb	pf, vn, vc	begun Nov 1827	1828, op.100	vii/2, 46; vii, 17
934	Fantasy, C	vn, pf	Dec 1827	1850, op.159	viii, 70; viii, 131
956	String Quintet, C	2 vn, va, 2 vc	?Sept 1828	1853, op.163	iv, 1; ii, 19
995	6 Minuets [see 2d]				
998	String Quartet [see 2c]				
AI/3	Fugue, C, frag., va part only	? 2 vn, va, vc	?1812	—	—; viii/1

SONATAS, FANTASIES AND SHORTER WORKS FOR PIANO
(NSA nos. refer to vol. in series 7/ii unless otherwise stated)

D	Title and remarks	Composed	Published	SW; NSA
2e	Fantasie, c [formerly 993]	1811	—	—; iv
13	Fugue, d	c1812	—	—; iv
14	Overture, sketch, lost	c1812	—	—
21	6 variations, Eb, lost	1812	—	—
24	7 variations, F, frag., lost	?summer 1812	—	—
24a	Fugue, C, ? for org	?summer 1812	1978	—; iv
24b	Fugue, G, ? for org	?summer 1812	1978	—; iv
24c	Fugue, d, ? for org	?summer 1812	1978	—; iv
24d	Fugue, C, frag.	?summer 1812	1978	—; iv
25c	Fugue, F, frag.	?summer 1812	—	—; viii/2
29	Andante, C [arr. of Str Qt, 3]	9 Sept 1812	1888	xi, 136; iv
37a	fugal sketches, Bb [formerly 967]	?1813	—	—; iv
41a	Fugue, e, frag.	1813	—	—; iv
71b	Fugue, e, frag.	July 1813	—	—; iv
154	Allegro, E [sketch of 157]	11 Feb 1815	1897	xxi, 136; i
156	10 variations, F	15 Feb 1815	1887	xi, 112; iv
157	Sonata, E, inc.	begun Feb 1815	1888	x, 2; i
178	Adagio, G, 2 versions [2nd version frag.]	8 April 1815	1897	xxi, 244; iv
279	Sonata, C [minuet = 277a with alternative trio; ? finale = 346]	Sept 1815	1888	x, 16; i
346	Allegretto, C, frag. [? finale of 279]	?1816	1897	xxi, 222; iv
347	Allegretto moderato, C, frag.	?1813	1897	xxi, 230; iv
348	Andantino, C, frag.	?1816	1897	xxi, 233; iv
349	Adagio, C, frag.	?1816	1897	xxi, 242; iv
459	Sonata, F, frag. (nos.1, 2 of 'Fünf Klavierstücke')	Aug 1816	1843	xi, 170; i
459a	'Fünf Klavierstücke', C, A, F (nos.3–5)	?1816	1843	xi, 178; iv
505	Adagio, Db [orig. slow movt of 625; adapted (? by publisher) as introduction to 506]	?Sept 1818	1897	Rev, 4; iv
506	Rondo, E [? finale of 566]	?June 1817	1848, op.145	xi, 105; iv
537	Sonata, a	March 1817	c1852, op.164	x, 60; i
557	Sonata, Ab	May 1817	1888	x, 30; i
566	Sonata, e [? finale = 506]	June 1817		
	Moderato		1888	x, 40; i
	Allegretto		1907	—; i
	Scherzo		1928–9	—; i
567	Sonata, Db, inc. [1st version of 568]	June 1817	1897	xxi, 140; i
568	Sonata, Eb	?June 1817	1829, op.122	x, 74; i
570	Scherzo, D, Allegro f#, inc. [? intended as movts 3–4 of 571]	?July 1817	1897	xxi, 236; i
571	Sonata, f#, frag. of 1st movt only	July 1817	1897	xxi, 160; i
575	Sonata, B	Aug 1817	1846, op.147	x, 44; i
576	13 variations on a theme by Anselm Hüttenbrenner, a	Aug 1817	1867	xi, 124; iv
593	2 scherzos, Bb, Db	Nov 1817	1871	xi, 190; iv
604	Andante, A [? slow movt of 570/571]	1816 or July 1817	1888	xi, 138; iv
605	Fantasia, C, frag.	1821–3	1897	xxi, 214; iv
605a	Fantasy, C, 'Grazer Fantasie'	?1818	1969	—; iv
606	March, E	?1818	1840	xi, 198; iv
612	Adagio, E [? slow movt of 613]	April 1818	1869	xi, 142; iv
613	Sonata, C, 2 movts, frag. [? slow movt = 612]	April 1818	1897	xxi, 164; ii
625	Sonata, f, 2 movts, frag. [slow movt = 505]	Sept 1818	1897	xxi, 172; ii
655	Sonata, c#, frag. of 1st movt	April 1819	1897	xxi, 186; ii
664	Sonata, A	1819 or 1825	1829, op.120	x, 134; ii

D	Title and remarks	Composed	Published	SW; NSA
718	Variation on a waltz by Diabelli, c	March 1821	1824	xi, 134; iv
759a	Overture to Alfonso und Estrella, D [arr. from 732]	Nov 1822	c1839, op.69	—; iv
760	Fantasy, C, 'Wandererfantasie'	Nov 1822	1823, op.15	xi, 2; v
769a	Sonata, e, frag. [formerly 994]	c1823	1958	—; i
780	6 Momens musicals [sic] C, A♭, f, c♯, f, A♭	1823–8	1828, op.94	xi, 88; v
784	Sonata, a	Feb 1823	1839, op.143	x, 94; ii
817	Ungarische Melodie, b [? 1st version of pf duet, 818]	2 Sept 1824	1928	—; v
840	Sonata, C, 'Reliquie', movts 3–4 inc.	April 1825	1861	xxi, 190; ii
845	Sonata, a	before end May 1825	1826, op.42	x, 110; ii
850	Sonata. D	Aug 1825	1826, op.53	x, 146; ii
894	Sonata, G (formerly known as Fantasie, Andante, Menuetto und Allegretto)	Oct 1826	1827, op.78	x, 178; iii
899	4 Impromptus, c, E♭, G♭, A♭	? summer–autumn 1827		xi, 28; v
	nos.1–2		1827, op.90/1–2	
	nos.3–4		1857, op.90/3–4	
900	Allegretto, c, frag.	? after 1820	1897	xxi, 220; v
915	Allegretto, c	26 April 1827	1870	xi, 146; v
916b	Piano piece, C, sketch	? summer–autumn 1827	1978	—; v
916c	Piano piece, c, sketch	? summer–autumn 1827	1978	—; v
935	4 Impromptus, f, A♭, B♭, f	Dec 1827	1839, op.142	xi, 58; v
946	3 Klavierstücke, e♭, E♭, C	May 1828	1868	xi, 150; v
958	Sonata, c	Sept 1828	1839	x, 204; iii
959	Sonata, A	Sept 1828	1839	x, 232; iii
960	Sonata, B♭	Sept 1828	1839	x, 264; iii
967	fugal sketches [see 37a]			
980f	March, G	?	—	—; vi
993	Fantasie [see 2e]			
994	Sonata [see 769a]			

DANCES FOR PIANO
(*NSA nos. refer to vol. and p. in series 7/ii*)

D	Title and remarks	Composed	Published	SW; NSA
19b	Waltzes and march, lost	? 1812 or 1813	—	—
22	12 minuets with trios, lost	1812	—	—
41	30 minuets with trios, 10 lost	1813	1889	xii, 137; vi
91	2 minuets, D, A, each with 2 trios, 2 other minuets lost	22 Nov 1813	1956	—; vi
128	12 Wiener Deutsche	?1812	1897	xxi, 248: vi
135	Deutscher, E, with trio [see 146]	1815	1930	—; vi
139	Deutscher, C♯, with trio	1815	1930	—; vi
145	12 Waltzes [no.7 = no.2 of 970], 17 Ländler, 9 Ecossaises [no.5 = no.1 of 421; no.6 = no.5 of 697], incl. 3 Atzenbrugger Tänze (nos.1–3)	1815–July 1821	1823, op.18	xii, 14; vii
146	20 Waltzes (Letzte Walzer) [no.3 = 135 with new trio]		1830, op.127	xii, 66; vii
	nos.1, 3–11	1815		
	nos.2, 12–20	Feb 1823		
158	Ecossaise, d/F	21 Feb 1815	1889	xii, 136; vi
277a	Minuet, a [used in Sonata, 279], with trio	?Sept 1815	1925	—; iv
299	12 Ecossaises [no.1 = Ecossaise no.1 from 145]	3 Oct 1815		
	nos.1–8		1897	xxi, 264; vi
	nos.9–12		1912	—; vi
334	Minuet, A, with trio	c1815	1897	xxi, 256; iv
335	Minuet, E, with 2 trios	c1813	1897	xxi, 258; vi
365	36 Originaltänze (Erste Walzer), incl. Trauerwalzer (no.2) and 3 Atzenbrugger Tänze (nos.29–31)	1816–July 1821	1821, op.9	xii, 2; vii
366	17 Ländler [no.17 arr. from 814 no.1]	1816–Nov 1824		xii, 88; vi
	nos.6 and 17		1824	
	nos.1–17		1869	
378	8 Ländler, B♭	13 Feb 1816	1889	xii, 102; vi
380	3 minuets, E, A, C, each with 2 trios, 2nd trio of 3rd minuet lost	22 Feb 1816		
	nos.1 and 2		1897	xxi, 262; vi
	no.3		1956	—; vi
420	12 Deutsche	1816	1871	xii, 94; vii
421	6 Ecossaises, A♭, f, E♭, B♭, E♭, A♭ [no. 1 = Ecossaise no.5 of 145]	May 1816	1889	xii, 132; vi
511	Ecossaise, E♭	c1817	1924	—; vi
529	8 Ecossaises	Feb 1817		
	nos.1–3, 6, 8, D, D, G, D, D		1871	xii, 134; vi
	nos.4, 5, 7, D		1897	xxi, 267; vi
600	Minuet, c♯ [? trio = 610]	?1814	1897	xxi, 261; iv
610	Trio, E [? minuet = 600]	Feb 1818	1889	xii, 157; vi
640	2 dances [see 980a]			
643	Deutscher, c♯, and Ecossaise, D♭	1819	1889	xii, 117; vi
679	2 Ländler [see 980b]			
680	2 Ländler [see 980c]			
681	12 Ländler, nos.1–4 lost	c1815	1930	—; vi
697	6 Ecossaises, A♭	May 1820		
	nos.1–4, 6		1889	xii, 134; vi
	no.5 [= no.6 of 145]		1823	—; vi
722	Deutscher, G♭	8 March 1821	1889	xii, 115; vii
734	16 Ländler and 2 Ecossaises (Wiener-Damen Ländler)	c1822	1826, op.67	xii, 48; vii
735	Galop and 8 Ecossaises	c1822	1825, op.49	xii, 119; vii
769	2 Deutsche			xii, 114; vi
	no.1, A	Jan 1824	1889	
	no.2, D	by Dec 1823	1823	

D	Title and remarks	Composed	Published	SW; NSA
779	34 Valses sentimentales	c1823	1825, op.50	xii, 34; vii
781	12 Ecossaises	Jan 1823		xii, 125; vii
	no.1 [= Ecossaise no.2 of 783]		1825, op.33	
	nos.4, 7		1824	
	nos.2–3, 5–6, 8–12		1889	
782	Ecossaise, D	c1823	1824	—; vii
783	16 Deutsche and 2 Ecossaises [no.2 = no.1 of 781]	Jan 1823–July 1824	1825, op.33	xii, 28; vii
790	12 Deutsche (Ländler)	May 1823	1864, op.171	xii, 82; vi
816	3 Ecossaises, D, D, B♭	Sept 1824	1956	—; vi
820	6 Deutsche, A♭, A♭, A♭, B♭, B♭, B♭	Oct 1824	1931	—; vi
841	2 Deutsche, F, G	April 1825	1930	—; vi
844	Waltz, G (Albumblatt)	16 April 1825	1897	xxi, 268; vi
924	12 Grazer Walzer	?Sept 1827	1828, op.91	xii, 60; vii
925	Grazer Galopp, C	?Sept 1827	1828	xii, 123; vii
944a	Deutscher, lost	1 March 1828	—	—
969	12 Waltzes (Valses nobles)	by end 1826	1827, op.77	xii, 54; vii
970	6 Ländler, E♭, E♭, A♭, A♭, D♭, D♭ [no.2 = no.7 of 145]	?	1889	xii, 106; vii
971	3 Deutsche, a, A, E	by end 1822	1823	xii, 108; vii
972	3 Deutsche, D♭, A♭, A	?	1889	xii, 110; vi
973	3 Deutsche, E, E, A♭	?	1889	xii, 111; vi
974	2 Deutsche, D♭	?	1889	xii, 113; vi
975	Deutscher, D	?	1889	xii, 116; vi
976	Cotillon, E♭	by end 1825	1825	xii, 118; vi
977	8 Ecossaises	?	1889	xii, 129; vi
978	Waltz, A♭	by end 1825	1825	—; vii
979	Waltz, G	by end 1826	1826	—; vii
980	2 waltzes, G, b	by end 1826	1826	—; vii
980a	2 dances, A, E, sketches [formerly 640]	?	1956	—; vi
980b	2 Ländler, E♭ [formerly 679]	?	1925	—; vi
980c	2 Ländler, D♭, frag. [formerly 680]	?	1930	—; vi
980d	Waltz, C	by end 1827	1828	—; vii
980e	2 dances, g, F, sketches [? for pf]	?	—	—; vi

PIANO FOUR HANDS
(NSA nos. refer to vol. and p. in series 7/i)

D	Title and remarks	Composed	Published	SW; NSA
1	Fantasie, G	8 April–1 May 1810	1888	ix/3, 189; i
1b	Fantasie, G, frag.	1810 or 1811	—	—; i
1c	Sonata, F, frag., 1st movt only	1810 or 1811	—	—; i
9	Fantasie, g	20 Sept 1811	1888	ix/3, 224; i
48	Fantasie, c (Grande sonate)	April–10 June 1813		
	1st version [without finale]		1871	ix/3, 234; i
	2nd version [complete]		1888	—; i
592	Overture, D, 'im italienischen Stile' [arr. of orch ov., 590]	Dec 1817	1872	ix/2, 26; v
597	Overture, C, 'im italienischen Stile' [arr. of orch ov., 591]	Nov or Dec 1817	1872	ix/2, 14; v
599	4 polonaises, d, B♭, E, F	July 1818	1827, op.75	ix/3, 160; iv, 126
602	3 marches héroïques, b, C, D	1818 or 1824	1824, op 27	ix/1, 2; iv, 3
603	Introduction, 4 variations on an original theme and finale [see 968a]			
608	Rondo, D			
	version a	Jan 1818	—	—; i
	version b (Notre amitié est invariable)	c1818	1835, op.138	ix/2, 136; i
617	Sonata, B♭	summer–autumn 1818	1823, op.30	ix/2, 40; i
618	Deutscher, G, with 2 trios and 2 Ländler, E	summer–autumn 1818	1909	—; iv, 167
618a	Polonaise and trio, sketch [trio used in 599]	July 1818	1972	—; iv, 180
624	8 variations on a French song, e	Sept 1818	1822, op.10	ix/2, 150; i
668	Overture, g	Oct 1819	1897	xxi, 106; v
675	Overture, F	?Nov 1819	1825, op.34	ix/2, 2; v
733	3 marches militaires, D, G, E♭	? summer–autumn 1818	1826, op.51	ix/1, 56; iv, 20
773	Overture to Alfonso und Estrella [arr. from 732]	1823	1826; 1830 as op.69	—; v
798	Overture to Fierabras [arr. from 796]	late 1823	1897	xxi, 120; v
812	Sonata, C, 'Grand Duo'	June 1824	1838, op.140	ix/2, 66; ii, 5
813	8 variations on an original theme, A♭	summer 1824	1825, op.35	ix/2, 168; ii, 27
814	4 Ländler, E♭, A♭, c, C [no.1 arr. as 366 no.17]	July 1824	1869	ix/3, 172; iv, 176
818	Divertissement à l'hongroise, g	?autumn 1824	1826, op.54	ix/3, 2; ii, 38
819	6 grandes marches, E♭, g, b, D, e♭, E	?autumn 1824	1825, op.40	ix/1, 20; iv, 33
823	Divertissement sur des motifs originaux français, e	c1825		ix/3, 38; ii, 621
	1 Marche brillante		1826, op.63/1	
	2 Andantino varié		1827, op.84/1	
	3 Rondeau brillant		1827, op.84/2	
824	6 polonaises, d, F, B♭, D, A, E	1826	1826, op.61	ix/3, 136; iv, 140
859	Grande marche funèbre, c, on the death of Alexander I of Russia	Dec 1825	1826, op.55	ix/1, 70; iv, 74
885	Grande marche héroïque, a, for the coronation of Nicholas I of Russia	1826	1826, op.66	ix/1, 78; iv, 82
886	2 marches caractéristiques [see 968b]			
908	8 variations on a theme from Hérold's Marie, C	Feb 1827	1827, op.82/1	ix/2, 194; iii
928	March, G, 'Kindermarsch'	12 Oct 1827	1870	ix/1, 116; iv, 124
940	Fantasie, f	Jan–April 1828	1829, op.103	ix/3, 112; iii

D	Title and remarks	Composed	Published	SW; NSA
947	Allegro, a, 'Lebensstürme'	May 1828	1840, op.144	ix/3, 88; iii
951	Rondo, A	June 1828	1828, op.107	ix/2, 118; iii
952	Fugue, e, pf/org	3 June 1828	1848, op.152	ix/3, 176; iii
968	Allegro moderato, C, and Andante, a (Sonatine)	?1818	1888	ix/3, 180; i
968a	Introduction, 4 variations on an original theme and finale, B♭ [formerly 603]	?1824	1860, op.82/2	ix/2, 216; i
968b	2 marches caractéristiques, C [formerly 886]	?1826	1890, op.121	ix/1, 94; i

SONGS

The following list includes duets, melodramas and works for or with unison chorus or incorporating brief passages for four-part chorus; all with pf acc. unless otherwise stated. SW nos. refer to vol. and p. in series 20, and NSA nos. to vol. and p. in series 4, unless otherwise stated. Incipits given where different from title.

D	Title	Incipit	Text	Key	Composed	Published	SW; NSA
1a	Song sketch (no text)	—		c	?1810	1969	—; vi, 157
5	Hagars Klage	Hier am Hügel heissen Sandes	C. A. Schücking	c	30 March 1811	1894	i, 1; vi, 3
6	Des Mädchens Klage (1)	Der Eichwald brauset	Schiller	d	1811 or 1812	1894	i, 16; iii
7	Leichenfantasie	Mit erstorbnem Scheinen	Schiller	d	c1811	1894	i, 22; vi, 22
10	Der Vatermörder	Ein Vater starb von des Sohnes Hand	G. C. Pfeffel	c	26 Dec 1811	1894	i, 40; vi, 46
15	Der Geistertanz (1), frag.	Die bretterne Kammer der Toten erbebt	Matthisson	c	c1812	1895	x, 92; vii, 188
15a	Der Geistertanz (2), frag.	Die bretterne Kammer der Toten erbebt	Matthisson	f	c1812	1895	x, 94; vii, 190
17	Quell' innocente figlio version 1		Metastasio	F	c1812	1940	—; viii/2
23	Klaglied	Meine Ruh' ist dahin	F. Rochlitz	g	1812	1830, op.131/3	i, 52; vi, 56
30	Der Jüngling am Bache (1)	An der Quelle sass der Knabe	Schiller	F	24 Sept 1812	1894	i, 48; iv
33	Entra l'uomo allor che nasce version 1		Metastasio	e	Sept–Oct 1812	1940	—; viii/2
35	Serbate, o dei custodi version 3		Metastasio	C	10 Dec 1812	1940	—; viii/2
39	Lebenstraum	Ich sass an einer Tempelhalle	G. von Baumberg	C	c1810	1969	—; vi, 171
42	Misero pargoletto (1)		Metastasio		?1813		
	version a, inc.			g		1969	—; vi, 180
	version b, inc.			g		1969	—; vi, 181
	Misero pargoletto (2)			g		1895	x, 31; vi, 60
44	Totengräberlied (2)	Grabe, Spaten, grabe!	Hölty	e	19 Jan 1813	1894	i, 54; vi, 64
50	Die Schatten	Freunde, deren Grüfte	Matthisson	A	12 April 1813	1894	i, 58; vi, 68
52	Sehnsucht (1)	Ach, aus dieses Tales Gründen	Schiller	d	15–17 April 1813	1868	i, 62; ii, 241
59	Verklärung	Lebensfunke, vom Himmel ertglüht	A. Pope, trans. J. G. von Herder	a	4 May 1813	1832	i, 68; vi, 73
73	Thekla: eine Geisterstimme (1)	Wo ich sei, und wo mich hingewendet	Schiller	G	22–3 Aug 1813	1868	i, 70; iv
76	Pensa, che questo istante		Metastasio				
	version a			D	7 Sept 1813	1969	—; vi, 184
	version b			D	13 Sept 1813	1871	x, 34; vi, 76
77	Der Taucher	Wer wagt es, Rittersmann	Schiller				
	version a			d	17 Sept 1813–5 April 1814	1831	i, 73; vi, 78
	version b [formerly 111]			d	by 1815	1894	i, 102; vi, 114
78	Son fra l'onde		Metastasio	c	18 Sept 1813	1895	x, 36; vi, 150
81	Auf den Sieg der Deutschen, with 2 vn, vc	Verschwunden sind die Schmerzen	?Schubert	F	autumn 1813	1895	x, 74; xiv
83	Zur Namensfeier des Herrn Andreas Siller, with vn, harp	Des Phöbus Strahlen		G	28 Oct–4 Nov 1813	1895	x, 72; xiv
93	Don Gayseros		F. de la Motte Fouqué		c1815	1894	
	1 Don Gayseros, Don Gayseros			F			i, 132; vii, 167
							i, 137; vii, 173
	2 Nächtens klang die süsse Laute			F			i, 141; vii, 177
	3 An dem jungen Morgenhimmel			E♭			
95	Adelaide	Einsam wandelt dein Freund	Matthisson	A♭	1814	1848	i, 169; vii, 3
97	Trost: an Elisa	Lehnst du deine bleichgehärmte Wange	Matthisson	a	1814	1894	i, 154; vii, 6
98	Erinnerungen (1)	Am Seegestad	Matthisson				
	version a			B♭	autumn 1814	1968	—; vii, 167
	version b			B♭	c1814	1894	i, 166; vii, 8
99	Andenken (1)	Ich denke dein	Matthisson	F	April 1814	1894	i, 144; vii, 11
100	Geisternähe	Der Dämmrung Schein	Matthisson	E♭	April 1814	1894	i, 147; vii, 14
101	Erinnerung	Kein Rosenschimmer leuchtet	Matthisson	e	April 1814	1894	i, 151; vii, 18
102	Die Betende	Laura betet	Matthisson	B	autumn 1814	1840	i, 156; vii, 21
104	Die Befreier Europas in Paris	Sie sind in Paris!	J. C. Mikan				
	version a			G	May 1814	1968	—; vii, 180
	version b			G	May 1814	1968	—; vii, 182
	version c			G	16 May 1814	1895	x, 76; vii, 24

D	Title	Incipit	Text	Key	Composed	Published	SW; NSA
107	Lied aus der Ferne	Wenn in des Abends letztem Scheine	Matthisson				
	version a			E	July 1814	1894	i, 158; vii, 26
	version b			D	?July 1814	1968	—; vii, 29
108	Der Abend	Purpur malt die Tannenhügel	Matthisson	d	July 1814	1894	i, 161; vii, 31
109	Lied der Liebe	Durch Fichten am Hügel	Matthisson	B♭	July 1814	1894	i, 163; vii, 33
111	Der Taucher [see 77]						
113	An Emma	Weit in nebelgrauer Ferne	Schiller				
	version a			F	17 Sept 1814	1894	i, 172; iii
	version b			F	c1814	1821	i, 174; iii
	version c			F	c1814	1826, op.58/2	i, 176; iii
114	Romanze	Ein Fräulein klagt' im finstern Turm	Matthisson				
	version a			g	Sept 1814	1902	—; vii, 36
	version b			g	29 Sept 1814	1868	i, 178; vii, 42
115	An Laura, als sie Klopstocks Auferstehungslied sang	Herzen, die gen Himmel sich erheben	Matthisson	E	2–7 Oct 1814	1840	i, 183; vii, 48
116	Der Geistertanz (3)	Die bretterne Kammer der Toten erbebt	Matthisson	c	14 Oct 1814	1840	i, 186; vii, 52
117	Das Mädchen aus der Fremde (1)	In einem Tal bei armen Hirten	Schiller	A	16 Oct 1814	1894	i, 189; viii
118	Gretchen am Spinnrade	Meine Ruh' ist hin	Goethe	d	19 Oct 1814	1821, op.2	i, 191; i, 10
119	Nachtgesang	O gib vom weichem Pfühle	Goethe	A♭	30 Nov 1814	1850	i, 197; vii, 55
120	Trost in Tränen	Wie kommt's dass du so traurig bist	Goethe	F	30 Nov 1814	1835	i, 198; vii, 56
121	Schäfers Klagelied	Da droben auf jenem Berge	Goethe				
	version a			e	Nov 1814	1894	i, 203; i, 194
	version b			c	30 Nov 1814	1821, op.3/1	i, 200; i, 20
122	Ammenlied	Am hohen, hohen Turm	M. Lubi	g	Dec 1814	1872	i, 224; vii, 59
123	Sehnsucht	Was zieht mir das Herz so?	Goethe	G	3 Dec 1814	1842	i, 206; vii, 60
124	Am See	Sitz' ich im Gras	Mayrhofer				
	version a			g	Dec 1814	1968	—; vii, 194
	version b			g	7 Dec 1814	1885	i, 210; vii, 65
126	Szene aus Goethes Faust (Dom), with 4vv	Wie anders, Gretchen, war dir's	Goethe				
	version a			c	Dec 1814	1873	i, 215; vii, 196
	version b			c	12 Dec 1814	1832	i, 219; vii, 71
134	Ballade	Ein Fräulein schaut vom hohen Turm	J. Kenner	g	c1815	1830, op.126	ii, 198; vii, 77
138	Rastlose Liebe	Dem Schnee, dem Regen	Goethe				
	version a			E	19 May 1815	1821, op.51	iii, 198; i, 35
	version b			D	1821	1970	—; i, 208
141	Der Mondabend	Rein und freundlich lacht der Himmel	J. G. Kumpf	A	1815	1830, op.131/1	ii, 20; vii, 86
142	Geistes-Gruss	Hoch auf dem alten Turme	Goethe		1815 or 1816		
	version a			E♭/G♭		1895	iii, 189; v
	version b			F♭/G♭		1885	iii, 190; v
	version c			D/F		—	—; v
	version d			F♭/G♭		1895	iii, 191; v
	version e			E♭/G♭		—	—; v
	version f			E/G	rev. ?1828	1828, op.92/3	iii, 192; v
143	Genügsamkeit	Dort raget ein Berg	F. von Schober	c♯	1815	1829, op.109/2	iii, 230; vii, 88
144	Romanze, unfinished	In der Väter Hallen ruhte	F. Graf zu Stolberg-Stolberg	E	April 1816	1897	Rev, 46; vii, 201
149	Der Sänger	Was hör' ich draussen vor dem Tor	Goethe				
	version a			D	Feb 1815	1894	ii, 41; vii, 90
	version b			D	1815	1829, op.117	ii, 33; vii, 97
150	Lodas Gespenst	Der bleiche, kalte Mond	Ossian, trans. E. Baron de Harold	g/B♭	17 Jan 1816	1830	ii, 21; vii, 105
151	Auf einen Kirchhof	Sei gegrüsst, geweihte Stille	F. von Schlechta	A	2 Feb 1815	c1850	ii, 1; vii, 119
152	Minona	Wie treiben die Wolken so finster	F. A. Bertrand	a	8 Feb 1815	1894	ii, 6; vii, 124
153	Als ich sie erröten sah	All' mein Wirken	B. A. Ehrlich	G	10 Feb 1815	1845	ii, 15; vii, 135
155	Das Bild	Ein Mädchen ist's	F		11 Feb 1815	1862, op.165/3	ii, 19; vii, 140
159	Die Erwartung	Hör' ich das Pförtchen	Schiller				
	version a			B♭	May 1816	1968	—; vii, 141
	version b			B♭	1816	1829, op.116	ii, 47; vii, 153
160	Am Flusse (1)	Verfliesset, vielgeliebte Lieder	Goethe	d	27 Feb 1815	1894	ii, 58; xiii
161	An Mignon	Über Tal und Fluss getragen	Goethe				
	version a			g♯	27 Feb 1815	1894	ii, 59; i, 249
	version b			g	1815	1825, op.19/2	ii, 60; i, 129

D	Title	Incipit	Text	Key	Composed	Published	SW; NSA
162	Nähe des Geliebten	Ich denke dein	Goethe		27 Feb 1815		
	version a			G♭		1894	ii, 62; i, 276
	version b			G♭		1821, op.5/2	ii, 63; i, 40
163	Sängers Morgenlied (1)	Süsses Licht! aus goldenen Pforten	Körner	G	27 Feb 1815	1894	ii, 64; viii
164	Liebesrausch (1), frag.	. . . Glanz des Guten	Körner	G	March 1815	1928	—; viii
165	Sängers Morgenlied (2)	Süsses Licht! aus goldenen Pforten	Körner	C	1 March 1815	1872	ii, 66; viii
166	Amphiaraos	Vor Thebens siebenfach gähnenden Toren	Körner	g	1 March 1815	1894	ii, 68; viii
169	Trinklied vor der Schlacht, for 2 unison choruses	Schlacht, du brichst an!	Körner	C	12 March 1815	1894	ii, 76; iii/3
170	Schwertlied, with unison chorus	Du Schwert an meiner Linken	Körner	C	12 March 1815	1873	ii, 78; iii/3
171	Gebet während der Schlacht	Vater, ich rufe dich!	Körner	B♭	12 March 1815	1831	ii, 80; viii
172	Der Morgenstern (1), frag.	Stern der Liebe	Körner	G♭	12 March 1815	—	—; viii
174	Das war ich	Jüngst träumte mir	Körner				
	version a			G	26 March 1815	c1842	ii, 84; viii
	version b, frag.			D	cJune 1816	1897	Rev, 16; viii
176	Die Sterne	Was funkelt ihr so mild mich an?	J. G. Fellinger	A♭	6 April 1815	1872	ii, 86; viii
177	Vergebliche Liebe	Ja, ich weiss es	J. K. Bernard	c	6 April 1815	1867, op.173/3	ii, 88; viii
179	Liebesrausch (2)	Dir, Mädchen, schlägt	Körner	G	8 April 1815	1872	ii, 90; viii
180	Sehnsucht der Liebe	Wie die Nacht mit heiligem Beben	Körner				
	version a			G	8 April 1815	1894	ii, 92; viii
	version b, frag., lost			G	July 1815	—	—
182	Die erste Liebe	Die erste Liebe füllt das Herz	Fellinger	C	12 April 1815	1842	ii, 94; viii
183	Trinklied, with unison chorus	Ihr Freunde und du gold'ner Wein	A. Zettler	G	12 April 1815	1887	ii, 97; iii/3
186	Die Sterbende	Heil! dies ist die letzte Zähre	Matthisson	A♭	May 1815	1894	ii, 100; viii
187	Stimme der Liebe (1)	Abendgewölke schweben hell	Matthisson	F	May 1815	1894	ii, 98; viii
188	Naturgenuss (1)	Im Abendschimmer wallt der Quell	Matthisson	B♭	May 1815	1887	ii, 99; viii
189	An die Freude, with unison chorus	Freude, schöner Götterfunken	Schiller	E	May 1815	1829, op.111/1	ii, 102; iii/3
191	Des Mädchens Klage (2)	Der Eichwald brauset	Schiller				
	version a			c	15 May 1815	1894	ii, 104; iii
	version b			c	1815	1826, op.58/3	ii, 106; iii
192	Der Jüngling am Bache (2)	An der Quelle sass der Knabe	Schiller	f	15 May 1815	1887	ii, 108; iv
193	An den Mond	Geuss, lieber Mond	Hölty	f	17 May 1815	1826, op.57/3	ii, 110; iii
194	Die Mainacht	Wann der silberne Mond	Hölty	d	17 May 1815	1894	ii, 112; viii
195	Amalia	Schön wie Engel	Schiller	A	19 May 1815	1867, op.173/1	ii, 113; viii
196	An die Nachtigall	Geuss nicht so laut	Hölty	f♯	22 May 1815	1865, op.172/3	ii, 116; viii
197	An die Apfelbäume, wo ich Julien erblickte	Ein heilig Säuseln	Hölty	A	22 May 1815	1850	ii, 117; viii
198	Seufzer	Die Nachtigall singt überall	Hölty	g	22 May 1815	1894	ii, 120; viii
201	Auf den Tod einer Nachtigall (1), frag.	Sie ist dahin	Hölty	f♯	25 May 1815	1970	—; x
204a	Das Traumbild, lost		Hölty	—	May 1815	—	—
206	Liebeständelei	Süsses Liebchen, komm zu mir!	Körner	E♭	26 May 1815	1872	ii, 122; viii
207	Der Liebende	Beglückt, beglückt, wer dich erblickt	Hölty	B♭	29 May 1815	1894	ii, 123; viii
208	Die Nonne	Es liebt' in Welschland	Hölty				
	version a, frag.			A♭	29 May 1815	1897	Rev, 19; viii
	version b [formerly 212]			A♭	16 June 1815	1895	ii, 124; viii
209	Der Liedler	Gib, Schwester, mir die Harf herab	Kenner	a	Jan 1815	1825, op.38	ii, 184; ii, 144
210	Die Liebe (Klärchens Lied)	Freudvoll und leidvoll	Goethe	B♭	3 June 1815	1838	ii, 130; viii
211	Adelwold und Emma	Hoch, und ehern schier von Dauer	Bertrand	F	5–14 June 1815	1894	ii, 132; viii
212	Die Nonne [see 208]						
213	Der Traum	Mir träumt', ich war ein Vögelein	Hölty	A	17 June 1815	1865, op.172/1	ii, 158; viii
214	Die Laube	Nimmer werd' ich, nimmer dein vergessen	Hölty	A♭	17 June 1815	1865, op.172/2	ii, 159; viii
215	Jägers Abendlied (1)	Im Felde schleich' ich still und wild	Goethe	F	20 June 1815	1907	—; i, 198
215a	Meerestille (1)	Tiefe Stille herrscht im Wasser	Goethe	C	20 June 1815	1952	—; i, 197
216	Meerestille (2)	Tiefe Stille herrscht im Wasser	Goethe	C	21 June 1815	1821, op.3/2	ii, 160; i, 23
217	Kolmas Klage	Rund um mich Nacht	Ossian, trans.	c	22 June 1815	1830	ii, 161; viii
218	Grablied	Er fiel den Tod fürs Vaterland	Kenner	f	24 June 1815	1848	ii, 166; viii
219	Das Finden	Ich hab' ein Mädchen funden	L. Kosegarten	B♭	25 June 1815	1848	ii, 167; viii
221	Der Abend	Der Abend blüht	Kosegarten	B	15 July 1815	1829, op.118/2	ii, 178; viii
222	Lieb Minna	Schwüler Hauch weht mir herüber	A. Stadler	f	2 July 1815	1885	ii, 168; viii

D	Title	Incipit	Text	Key	Composed	Published	SW; NSA
224	Wandrers Nachtlied	Der du von dem Himmel bist	Goethe	G♭	5 July 1815	1821, op.4/3	ii, 170; i, 34
225	Der Fischer	Das Wasser rauscht	Goethe				
	version a			B♭	5 July 1815	1970	—; i, 208
	version b			B♭	c1815	1821, op.5/3	ii, 171; i, 42
226	Erster Verlust	Ach, wer bringt die schönen Tage	Goethe	f	5 July 1815	1821, op.5/4	ii, 172; i, 44
227	Idens Nachtgesang	Vernimm es, Nacht	Kosegarten	B♭	7 July 1815	1885	ii, 173; viii
228	Von Ida	Der Morgen blüht	Kosegarten	f	7 July 1815	1894	ii, 174; viii
229	Die Erscheinung	Ich lag auf grünen Matten	Kosegarten	E	7 July 1815	1829, op.108/3	ii, 175; v
230	Die Täuschung	Im Erlenbusch, im Tannenhain	Kosegarten	E	7 July 1815	1862, op.165/4	ii, 176; viii
231	Das Sehnen	Wehmut, die mich hüllt	Kosegarten	a	8 July 1815	1865, op.172/4	ii, 177; viii
233	Geist der Liebe	Wer bist du, Geist der Liebe	Kosegarten	E	15 July 1815	1829, op.118/1	ii, 180; viii
234	Tischlied	Mich ergreift, ich weiss nicht wie	Goethe	C	15 July 1815	1829, op.118/3	ii, 182; viii
235	Abends unter der Linde (1)	Woher, o namenloses Sehnen	Kosegarten	F	24 July 1815	1894	ii, 204; viii
237	Abends unter der Linde (2)	Woher, o namenloses Sehnen	Kosegarten	F	25 July 1815	1872	ii, 206; viii
238	Die Mondnacht	Siehe, wie die Mondesstrahlen	Kosegarten	F♯	25 July 1815	1894	ii, 208; viii
240	Huldigung	Ganz verloren, ganz versunken	Kosegarten	E	27 July 1815	1894	ii, 210; viii
241	Alles um Liebe	Was ist es, das die Seele füllt?	Kosegarten	E	27 July 1815	1894	ii, 212; viii
245	An den Frühling [see 587b]						
246	Die Bürgschaft	Zu Dionys, dem Tyrannen	Schiller	g	Aug 1815	1830	iii, 11; viii
247	Die Spinnerin	Als ich still und ruhig spann	Goethe	b	Aug 1815	1829, op.118/6	iii, 44; viii
248	Lob des Tokayers	O köstlicher Tokayer	Baumberg	B♭	Aug 1815	1829, op.118/4	iii, 66; viii
249	Die Schlacht (1), frag.		Schiller	b	1 Aug 1815	—	—; iii/2
250	Das Geheimnis (1)	Sie konnte mir kein Wörtchen sagen	Schiller	A♭	7 Aug 1815	1872	iii, 2; xiii
251	Hoffnung (1)	Es reden und träumen die Menschen	Schiller	G♭	7 Aug 1815	1872	iii, 4; iv
252	Das Mädchen aus der Fremde (2)	In einem Tal bei armen Hirten	Schiller	F	12 Aug 1815	1887	iii, 10; viii
253	Punschlied: im Norden zu singen	Auf der Berge freien Höhen	Schiller	B♭	18 Aug 1815	1887	iii, 30; viii
254	Der Gott und die Bajadere	Mahadöh, der Herr der Erde	Goethe	E♭	18 Aug 1815	1887	iii, 32; viii
255	Der Rattenfänger	Ich bin der wohlbekannte Sänger	Goethe	G	19 Aug 1815	c1850	iii, 34; viii
256	Der Schatzgräber	Arm am Beutel, krank am Herzen	Goethe	d	19 Aug 1815	1887	iii, 35; viii
257	Heidenröslein	Sah ein Knab' ein Röslein stehn	Goethe	G	19 Aug 1815	1821, op.3/3	iii, 37; i, 24
258	Bundeslied	In allen guten Stunden	Goethe	B♭	4 or 19 Aug 1815	1887	iii, 38; viii
259	An den Mond (1)	Füllest wieder Busch und Tal	Goethe	E♭	19 Aug 1815	c1850	iii, 40; ix
260	Wonne der Wehmut	Trocknet nicht, trocknet nicht	Goethe	c	20 Aug 1815	1829, op.115/2	iii, 42; viii
261	Wer kauft Liebesgötter?	Von allen schönen Waren	Goethe	C	21 Aug 1815	c1850	iii, 43; viii
262	Die Fröhlichkeit	Wes' Adern leichtes Blut durchspringt	M. J. Prandstetter	F	22 Aug 1815	1895	iii, 64; ix
263	Cora an die Sonne	Nach so vielen trüben Tagen	Baumberg	E♭	22 Aug 1815	1848	iii, 50; ix
264	Der Morgenkuss	Durch eine ganze Nacht	Baumberg				
	version a			E♭	22 Aug 1815	1872	iii, 51; ix
	version b			C	c1815	1850	—; ix
265	Abendständchen: An Lina	Sei sanft wie ihre Seele	Baumberg	B♭	23 Aug 1815	1895	iii, 52; ix
266	Morgenlied	Willkommen, rotes Morgenlicht	Stolberg	F	24 Aug 1815	1895	iii, 54; ix
270	An die Sonne	Sinke, liebe Sonne	Baumberg	E♭	25 Aug 1815	1829, op.118/5	iii, 56; ix
271	Der Weiberfreund	Noch fand von Evens Töchterscharen	A. Cowley, trans. J. F. von Ratschky	A	25 Aug 1815	1895	iii, 57; ix
272	An die Sonne	Königliche Morgensonne	C. A. Tiedge	E♭	25 Aug 1815	1872	iii, 58; ix
273	Lilla an die Morgenröte	Wie schön bist du, du güldne Morgenröte		D	25 Aug 1815	1895	iii, 59; ix
274	Tischlerlied	Mein Handwerk geht durch alle Welt		C	25 Aug 1815	1850	iii, 60; ix
275	Totenkranz für ein Kind	Sanft wehn, im Hauch der Abendluft	Matthisson	g	25 Aug 1815	1895	iii, 61; ix
276	Abendlied	Gross und rotentflammet	Stolberg	A	28 Aug 1815	1895	iii, 62; ix
278	Ossians Lied nach dem Falle Nathos	Beugt euch aus euren Wolken nieder	Ossian, trans. Harold		?Sept 1815		
	version a, frag.			E		1897	Rev, 34; ix
	version b			E		1830	iii, 108; ix
280	Das Rosenband	Im Frühlingsgarten fand ich sie	F. G. Klopstock	A♭	Sept 1815	1837	iii, 72; ix
281	Das Mädchen von Inistore	Mädchen Inistores	Ossian, trans. Harold	c	Sept 1815	1830	iii, 110; ix
282	Cronnan	Ich sitz' bei der moosigten Quelle	Ossian, trans. Harold	c	5 Sept 1815	1830	iv, 21; ix
283	An den Frühling (1)	Willkommen, schöner Jüngling!	Schiller	F	6 Sept 1815	1865, op.172/5	iii, 68; xi

D	Title	Incipit	Text	Key	Composed	Published	SW; NSA
284	Lied	Es ist so angenehm	?Schiller	G	6 Sept 1815	1895	iii, 69; ix
285	Furcht der Geliebten (An Cidli)	Cidli, du weinest	Klopstock				
	version a			Ab	12 Sept 1815	1895	iii, 70; ix
	version b			Ab	c1815	1885	iii, 71; ix
286	Selma und Selmar	Weine du nicht	Klopstock				
	version a			F	c1815	1895	iii, 74; ix
	version b			F	14 Sept 1815	1837	iii, 75; ix
287	Vaterlandslied	Ich bin ein deutsches Mädchen	Klopstock				
	version a			C	14 Sept 1815	1895	iii, 76; ix
	version b			C	c1815	1895	iii, 77; ix
288	An Sie	Zeit, Verkündigerin der besten Freuden	Klopstock	Ab	14 Sept 1815	1895	iii, 78; ix
289	Die Sommernacht	Wenn der Schimmer von dem Monde	Klopstock				
	version a			C	14 Sept 1815	1895	iii, 80; ix
	version b			C	c1815	1895	iii, 82; ix
290	Die frühen Gräber	Willkommen, o silberner Mond	Klopstock	a	14 Sept 1815	1837	iii, 84; ix
291	Dem Unendlichen	Wie erhebt sich das Herz	Klopstock				
	version a			F	15 Sept 1815	1895	iii, 85; ix
	version b			F	c1815	1831	iii, 90; ix
	version c			G	c1815	1895	iii, 95; ix
292	Klage [see 371]						
293	Shilric und Vinvela	Mein Geliebter ist ein Sohn des Hügels	Ossian, trans. Harold	Bb	20 Sept 1815	1830	iii, 100; ix
295	Hoffnung	Schaff, das Tagwerk meiner Hände	Goethe		c1816		
	version a			F		1872	iii, 193; ix
	version b			E		1895	iii, 194; ix
296	An den Mond (2)	Füllest wieder Busch und Tal	Goethe	Ab	c1816	1868	iii, 195; ix
297	Augenlied	Süsse Augen, klare Bronnen!	Mayrhofer		?1817		
	version a			F		1895	iii, 168; ix
	version b			F		1850	—; ix
298	Liane	Hast du Lianen nicht gesehen?	Mayhrofer	C	Oct 1815	1895	iii, 165; ix
300	Der Jüngling an der Quelle	Leise, rieselnder Quell	J. G. von Salis-Seewis	A	c1817	1842	vi, 208; ix
301	Lambertine	O Liebe, die mein Herz erfüllet	J. L. Stoll	Eb	12 Oct 1815	1842	iii, 112; ix
302	Labetrank der Liebe	Wenn im Spiele leiser Töne	Stoll	F	15 Oct 1815	1895	iii, 114; ix
303	An die Geliebte	O, dass ich dir vom stillen Auge	Stoll	G	15 Oct 1815	1887	iii, 116; ix
304	Wiegenlied	Schlumm're sanft!	Körner	F	15 Oct 1815	1895	iii, 117; ix
305	Mein Gruss an den Mai	Sei mir gegrüsst, o Mai	Kumpf	Bb	15 Oct 1815	1895	iii, 118; ix
306	Skolie	Lasst im Morgenstrahl des Mai'n	J. L. von Deinhardstein	Bb	15 Oct 1815	1895	iii, 120; ix
307	Die Sternewelten	Oben drehen sich die grossen	U. Jarnik, trans. Fellinger	F	15 Oct 1815	1895	iii, 121; ix
308	Die Macht der Liebe	Überall, wohin mein Auge blicket	J. N. von Kalchberg	Bb	15 Oct 1815	1895	iii, 123; ix
309	Das gestörte Glück	Ich hab' ein heisses junges Blut	Körner	F	15 Oct 1815	1872	iii, 124; ix
310	Sehnsucht (1)	Nur wer die Sehnsucht kennt	Goethe		18 Oct 1815		
	version a			Ab		1895	iii, 126; iii
	version b			F		1895	iii, 128; iii
311	An den Mond, frag.			A	19 Oct 1815	—	—; ix
312	Hektors Abschied	Will sich Hektor ewig von mir wenden	Schiller				
	version a			f	19 Oct 1815	1895	iii, 130; iii
	version b			f	c1815	1826, op.58/1	iii, 36; iii
313	Die Sterne	Wie wohl ist mir im Dunkeln	Kosegarten	Bb	19 Oct 1815	1895	iii, 142; ix
314	Nachtgesang	Tiefe Feier schauert um die Welt	Kosegarten	Eb	19 Oct 1815	1887	iii, 144; ix
315	An Rosa I	Warum bist du nicht hier	Kosegarten	Ab	19 Oct 1815	1895	iii, 145; ix
316	An Rosa II	Rosa, denkst du an mich?	Kosegarten				
	version a			Ab	19 Oct 1815	1895	iii, 146; ix
	version b			Ab	c1815	1895	iii, 147; ix
317	Idens Schwanenlied	Wie schaust du aus dem Nebelflor	Kosegarten				
	version a			f	19 Oct 1815	—	—; ix
	version b			f	c1815	1895	iii, 148; ix
318	Schwangesang	Endlich stehn die Pforten offen	Kosegarten	f	19 Oct 1815	1895	iii, 150; ix
319	Luisens Antwort	Wohl weinen Gottes Engel	Kosegarten	bb	19 Oct 1815	1895	iii, 152; ix
320	Der Zufriedene	Zwar schuf das Glück hienieden	C. L. Reissig	A	23 Oct 1815	1895	iii, 154; ix
321	Mignon	Kennst du das Land	Goethe	A	23 Oct 1815	1832	iii, 155; ix
322	Hermann und Thusnelda	Ha, dort kömmt er	Klopstock	Eb	27 Oct 1815	1837	iii, 159; ix
323	Klage der Ceres	Ist der holde Lenz erschienen?	Schiller	G	9 Nov 1815– June 1816	1895	iii, 171; ix
325	Harfenspieler (1)	Wer sich der Einsamkeit ergibt	Goethe	a	13 Nov 1815	1895	iii, 187; i, 218
327	Lorma (1), frag.	Lorma sass in der Halle von Aldo	Ossian, trans. Harold	a	28 Nov 1815	1928	—; x
328	Erlkönig	Wer reitet so spät	Goethe				
	version a			g	?Oct 1815	1895	iii, 202; i, 173
	version b			g	1815	1868	iii, 214; i, 180
	version c			g	1815	1895	iii, 208; i, 187

D	Title	Incipit	Text	Key	Composed	Published	SW; NSA
	version d			g	1815	1821, op.1	iii, 219; i, 3
329	Die drei Sänger, frag.	Der König sass beim frohen Mahle	F. Bobrik	A	23 Dec 1815	1895	x, 97; ix
330	Das Grab (2) version a [for version b see 'Male voices']	Das Grab ist tief und stille	Salis-Seewis	c	28 Dec 1815	1895	iii, 231; iii/3
342	An mein Klavier	Sanftes Klavier	C. F. D. Schubart	A	c1816	1885	iv, 138; x
343	Am Tage aller Seelen (Litanei auf das Fest aller Seelen)	Ruhn in Frieden alle Seelen	J. G. Jacobi		Aug 1816		
	version a			Eb		1831	v, 126; x
	version b			Eb		—	—; x
344	Am ersten Maimorgen	Heute will ich fröhlich, fröhlich sein	Claudius	G	c1816	—	—; x
350	Der Entfernten (2)	Wohl denk' ich allenthalben	Salis-Seewis	Eb	?1816	1885	iv, 69; x
351	Fischerlied (1)	Das Fischergewerbe gibt rüstigen Mut!	Salis-Seewis	D	?1816	1895	iv, 70; xi
352	Licht und Liebe (Nachtgesang), S, T	Liebe ist ein süsses Licht	M. von Collin	G	?1816	c1847	iv, 253; iii/2
358	Die Nacht	Du verstörst uns nicht, o Nacht!	J. P. Uz	Ab	1816	c1849	iv, 127; x
359	Sehnsucht (2)	Nur wer die Sehnsucht kennt	Goethe	d	1816	1872	iv, 200; iii
360	Lied eines Schiffers an die Dioskuren	Dioskuren, Zwillingsterne	Mayrhofer	Ab	1816	1826, op.65/1	iv, 221; iii
361	Am Bach im Frühlinge	Du brachst sie nun, die kalte Rinde	Schober	Db	1816	1829, op.109/1	iv, 230; x
362	Zufriedenheit (1)	Ich bin vergnügt	Claudius	A	1815 or 1816	1895	iv, 244; xi
363	An Chloen, frag.	Die Munterkeit ist meinen Wangen	Uz	G	1816	—	—; x
367	Der König in Thule	Es war ein König in Thule	Goethe	d	early 1816	1821, op.5/5	iv, 202; i, 45
368	Jägers Abendlied (2)	Im Felde schleich' ich still und wild	Goethe	Db	?early 1816	1821, op.3/4	iv, 203; i, 25
369	An Schwager Kronos	Spude dich, Kronos!	Goethe	d	1816	1825, op.19/1	iv, 204; i, 121
371	Klage	Trauer umfliesst mein Leben		b	Jan 1816	1872	iv, 5; x
372	An die Natur	Süsse, heilige Natur	Stolberg-Stolberg	F	15 Jan 1816	1895	iv, 2; x
373	Lied	Mutter geht durch ihre Kammern	Fouqué	g	?15 Jan 1816	1895	iv, 3; x
375	Der Tod Oskars	Warum öffnest du wieder	Ossian, trans. Harold	c	Feb 1816	1830	iv, 7; x
376	Lorma (2), frag.	Lorma sass in der Halle von Aldo	Ossian, trans. Harold	a	10 Feb 1816	1895	x, 102; x
381	Morgenlied	Die frohe neubelebte Flur		C	24 Feb 1816	1895	iv, 29; x
382	Abendlied	Sanft glänzt die Abendsonne		F	24 Feb 1816	1895	iv, 30; x
388	Laura am Klavier	Wenn dein Finger durch die Saiten meistert	Schiller			1895	
	version a			E	March 1816		iv, 41; x
	version b			A	c1816		iv, 46; x
389	Des Mädchens Klage (3)	Der Eichwald braust	Schiller	c	March 1816	1873	iv, 52; iii
390	Entzückung an Laura (1)	Laura, über diese Welt	Schiller	A	March 1816	1895	iv, 54; x
391	Die vier Weltalter	Wohl perlet im Glase	Schiller	G	March 1816	1829, op.111/3	iv, 56; x
392	Pflügerlied	Arbeitsam und wacker	Salis-Seewis	C	March 1816	1895	iv, 58; x
393	Die Einsiedelei (2)	Es rieselt, klar und wehend	Salis-Seewis	A	March 1816	c1845	iv, 60; xi
394	An die Harmonie	Schöpferin beseelter Töne!	Salis-Seewis	A	March 1816	1895	iv, 62; x
395	Lebensmelodien	Auf den Wassern wohnt mein stilles Leben	A. W. von Schlegel	G	March 1816	1829, op.111/2	iv, 72; x
396	Gruppe aus dem Tartarus (1), frag.	Horch, wie Murmeln des empörten Meeres	Schiller	c	March 1816	1975	—; ii, 171
397	Ritter Toggenburg	Ritter, treue Schwesterliebe	Schiller	F	13 March 1816	1832	iv, 31; x
398	Frühlingslied (2)	Die Luft ist blau	Hölty	G	13 May 1816	1887	iv, 97; x
399	Auf den Tod einer Nachtigall (2)	Sie ist dahin	Hölty	a	13 May 1816	1895	iv, 98; x
400	Die Knabenzeit	Wie glücklich, wem das Knabenkleid	Hölty	A	13 May 1816	1895	iv, 100; x
401	Winterlied	Keine Blumen blühn	Hölty	a	13 May 1816	1895	iv, 102; x
402	Der Flüchtling	Frisch atmet des Morgens lebendiger Hauch	Schiller	Bb	18 March 1816	1872	iv, 35; x
403	Lied	Ins stille Land	Salis-Seewis				
	version a			g	27 March 1816	1845	iv, 66; x
	version b			a	April 1816	1895	iv, 67; x
	version c			a	March 1816	—	—; x
	version d			a	Aug 1823	—	—; x
404	Die Herbstnacht	Mit leisen Harfentönen	Salis-Seewis	F	March 1816	1885	iv, 61; x
405	Der Herbstabend	Abendglockenhalle zittern	Salis-Seewis				
	version a			f	April 1816	1895	iv, 68; x
	version b			f	1816	—	—; x
406	Abschied von der Harfe	Noch einmal tön, o Harfe	Salis-Seewis	e	March 1816	1887	iv, 80; x
409	Die verfehlte Stunde	Quälend ungestilltes Sehnen	A. W. von Schlegel	f	April 1816	1872	iv, 70; x

D	Title	Incipit	Text	Key	Composed	Published	SW; NSA
410	Sprache der Liebe	Lass dich mit gelinden Schlägen	A. W. von Schlegel	E	April 1816	1829, op.115/3	iv, 78; x
411	Daphne am Bach	Ich hab' ein Bächlein funden	Stolberg-Stolberg	D	April 1816	1887	iv, 81; x
412	Stimme der Liebe	Meine Selinde	Stolberg-Stolberg				
	version a			E	1816	—	—; x
	version b			D	c1816	1838	iv, 82; x
413	Entzückung	Tag voll Himmel	Matthisson	C	April 1816	1895	iv, 84; x
414	Geist der Liebe (1)	Der Abend schleiert Flur und Hain	Matthisson	G	April 1816	1895	iv, 87; x
415	Klage	Die Sonne steigt	Matthisson	C	April 1816	1895	iv, 88; x
416	Lied in der Abwesenheit, frag.	Ach, mir ist das Herz so schwer	Stolberg-Stolberg	b	April 1816	1925	—; x
418	Stimme der Liebe (2)	Abendgewölke schweben hell	Matthisson	G	29 April 1816	1895	iv, 90; x
419	Julius an Theone	Nimmer, nimmer darf ich dir gestehen	Matthisson	g	30 April 1816	1895	iv, 95; x
429	Minnelied	Holder klingt der Vogelsang	Hölty	E	May 1816	1885	iv, 103; x
430	Die frühe Liebe	Schon im bunten Knabenkleide	Hölty				
	version a			E	May 1816	1895	iv, 104; x
	version b, lost			E	c1816	—	—
431	Blumenlied	Es ist ein halbes Himmelreich	Hölty	E	May 1816	1887	iv, 105; x
432	Der Leidende	Nimmer trag' ich länger			May 1816		
	version a			b		1850	iv, 106; x
	version b			b		1895	iv, 107; x
433	Seligkeit	Freuden sonder Zahl	Hölty	E	May 1816	1895	iv, 108; x
434	Erntelied	Sicheln schallen, Ähren fallen	Hölty	E	May 1816	1850	iv, 109; x
436	Klage	Dein Silber schien	Hölty				
	version a			F	12 May 1816	1850	iv, 95; x
	version b [formerly 437]			F	1816	—	—; x
437	Klage [see 436]						
442	Das grosse Halleluja version a [for version b see 'Female or unspecified voices']	Ehre sei dem Hocherhabnen	Klopstock	E	June 1816	c1847	iv, 110; x
443	Schlachtlied (1) version a [for version b see 'Female or unspecified voices']	Mit unserm Arm ist nichts getan	Klopstock	E	June 1816	1895	iv, 112; x
444	Die Gestirne	Es tönet sein Lob	Klopstock	F	June 1816	1831	iv, 114; x
445	Edone	Dein süsses Bild, Edone	Klopstock	Eb	June 1816	1837	iv, 116; x
446	Die Liebesgötter	Cypris, meiner Phyllis gleich	Uz	C	June 1816	1887	iv, 118; x
447	An den Schlaf	Komm, und senke die umflorten Schwingen	A	June 1816		1895	iv, 120; x
448	Gott im Frühlinge	In seinem schimmernden Gewand	Uz				
	version a			E	June 1816	1887	iv, 121; x
	version b			E	cJune 1816	—	—; x
449	Der gute Hirt	Was sorgest du?	Uz	E	June 1816	1872	iv, 124; x
450	Fragment aus dem Aeschylus	So wird der Mann, der sonder Zwang	Aeschylus, trans. Mayrhofer		June 1816		
	version a			Ab		1895	iv, 128; x
	version b			Ab		1832	iv, 131; x
454	Grablied auf einen Soldaten	Zieh hin, du braver Krieger du!	C. F. D. Schubart	c	July 1816	1872	iv, 140; x
455	Freude der Kinderjahre	Freude, die im frühen Lenze	F. von Köpken	C	July 1816	1887	iv, 142; x
456	Das Heimweh	Oft in einsam stillen Stunden	K. G. T. Winkler	F	July 1816	1887	iv, 144; x
457	An die untergehende Sonne	Sonne, du sinkst	Kosegarten	Eb	July 1816– May 1817	1827, op.44	iv, 134; iii
458	Aus Diego Manazares (Ilmerine)	Wo irrst du durch einsame Schatten	F. von Schlechta	Ab	30 July 1816	1872	iv, 146; x
462	An Chloen	Bei der Liebe reinsten Flammen	Jacobi	Ab	Aug 1816	1895	iv, 149; x
463	Hochzeit-Lied	Will singen euch im alten Ton	Jacobi	Eb	Aug 1816	1895	iv, 150; x
464	In der Mitternacht	Todesstille deckt das Tal	Jacobi	c	Aug 1816	1895	iv, 151; x
465	Trauer der Liebe	Wo die Taub in stillen Buchen	Jacobi				
	version a			Ab	Aug 1816	1885	iv, 152; x
	version b			Ab	c1816	—	—; x
466	Die Perle	Es ging ein Mann zur Frühlingszeit	Jacobi	d	Aug 1816	1872	iv, 153; x
467	Pflicht und Liebe	Du, der ewig um mich trauert	F. W. Gotter	c	Aug 1816	1885	x, 104; x
468	An den Mond	Was schauest du so hell und klar	Hölty	A	7 Aug 1816	1895	iv, 148; x
469	Mignon (1), 2 frags.	So lasst mich scheinen	Goethe	Ab	Sept 1816	1897	Rev, 86; iii
473	Liedesend	Auf seinem goldnen Throne	Mayrhofer		Sept 1816		
	version a			c		1895	iv, 154; x
	version b			c		1833	iv, 159; x
474	Lied des Orpheus, als er in die Hölle ging	Wälze dich hinweg	Jacobi				
	version a, inc.			Gb		1895	iv, 164; x
	version b			Gb	1816	1832	iv, 170; x
475	Abschied (nach einer Wallfahrtsarie)	Über die Berge zieht ihr fort	Mayrhofer	G	Sept 1816	1885	iv, 176; xi

D	Title	Incipit	Text	Key	Composed	Published	SW; NSA
476	Rückweg	Zum Donaustrom, zur Kaiserstadt	Mayrhofer	d	Sept 1816	1872	iv, 178; xi
477	Alte Liebe rostet nie		Mayrhofer	B	Sept 1816	1895	iv, 180; xi
478	Harfenspieler I (Gesänge des Harfners no.1) (2)	Wer sich der Einsamkeit ergibt	Goethe				
	version a			a	Sept 1816	1895	iv, 181; i, 220
	version b			a	1822	1822, op.12/1	iv, 189; i, 85
479	Harfenspieler II (Gesänge des Harfners no.3)	An die Türen will ich schleichen	Goethe				
	version a			a	Sept 1816	1895	iv, 184; i, 224
	version b			a	1822	1822, op.12/3	iv, 196; i, 93
480	Harfenspieler III (Gesänge des Harfners no.2) (1, 2, 3)	Wer nie sein Brot mit Tränen ass	Goethe				
	version a			a	Sept 1816	1895	iv, 186; i, 291
	version b			a	Sept 1816	1895	iv, 187; i, 226
	version c			a	1822	1822, op.12/2	iv, 192; i, 89
481	Sehnsucht (3)	Nur wer die Sehnsucht kennt	Goethe	a	Sept 1816	1895	iv, 198; iii
482	Der Sänger am Felsen	Klage, meine Flöte	C. Pichler	e	Sept 1816	1895	iv, 200; xi
483	Lied	Ferne von der grossen Stadt	Pichler	E	Sept 1816	1895	iv, 212; xi
484	Gesang der Geister über den Wassern (1), frag.	. . . dann zur Tiefe nieder	Goethe	G	Sept 1816	1895	x, 594; xi
489	Der Wanderer	Ich komme von Gebirge her	G. P. Schmidt von Lübeck				
	version a			c♯	Oct 1816	1895	iv, 214; i, 200
	version b [formerly 493b]			b	c1816	1970	—; i, 204
	version c [formerly 493a]			c♯	c1816	1821, op.4/1	iv, 217; i, 26
490	Der Hirt	Du Turm! zu meinem Leide	Mayrhofer	F	Oct 1816	1895	iv, 220; xi
491	Geheimnis	Sag an, wer lehrt dich Lieder	Mayrhofer	B♭	Oct 1816	1887	iv, 223; xi
492	Zum Punsche	Woget brausend, Harmonien	Mayrhofer	d	Oct 1816	1849	iv, 226; xi
493	Der Wanderer [see 489b–c]						
495	Abendlied der Fürstin	Der Abend rötet nun das Tal	Mayrhofer	F	Nov 1816	1868	iv, 227; xi
496	Bei dem Grabe meines Vaters	Friede sei um diesen Grabstein	M. Claudius	E♭	Nov 1816	1885	iv, 234; xi
496a	Klage um Ali Bey	Lasst mich! lasst mich! ich will klagen	Claudius	e♭	Nov 1816	1968	—; vii, 84
497	An die Nachtigall	Er liegt und schläft	Claudius	G	Nov 1816	1829, op.98/1	iv, 238; v
498	Wiegenlied	Schlafe, schlafe, holder süsser Knabe		A♭	Nov 1816	1829, op.98/2	iv, 239; v
499	Abendlied	Der Mond ist aufgegangen	Claudius	B♭	Nov 1816	1885	iv, 240; xi
500	Phidile	Ich war erst sechzehn Sommer alt	Claudius	G♭	Nov 1816	1895	iv, 242; xi
501	Zufriedenheit (2)	Ich bin vergnügt	Claudius		Nov 1816		
	version a			E		1895	iv, 246; xi
	version b			G		—	—; xi
502	Herbstlied	Bunt sind schon die Wälder	Salis Seewis	G	Nov 1816	1872	iv, 248; xi
503	Mailied (3)	Grüner wird die Au	Hölty	G	Nov 1816	—	—; xi
504	Am Grabe Anselmos	Dass ich dich verloren habe	Claudius				
	version a			e♭	4 Nov 1816	1821, op.6/3	iv, 236; i, 56
	version b			e♭	c1816	1970	—; i, 216
507	Skolie	Mädchen entsiegelten	Matthisson	G	Dec 1816	1895	iv, 249; xi
508	Lebenslied	Kommen und Scheiden	Matthisson	C	Dec 1816	1845	iv, 250; xi
509	Leiden der Trennung	Vom Meere trennt sich die Welle	Metastasio, trans. H. von Collin		Dec 1816		
	version a, frag.			g		—	—; xi
	version b			g		1872	iv, 251; xi
510	Vedi quanto adoro		Metastasio	E♭	Dec 1816	1895	x, 40; xi
513a	Nur wer die Liebe kennt, sketch		Werner	A♭	?1817	1974	—; xi
514	Die abgeblühte Linde	Wirst du halten, was du schwurst	L. von Széchényi	a	?1817	1821, op.7/1	v, 29; i, 59
515	Der Flug der Zeit	Es floh die Zeit im Wirbelfluge	Széchényi	A	?1817	1821, op.7/2	v, 33; i, 63
516	Sehnsucht	Der Lerche wolkennahe Lieder	Mayrhofer	C	?1816	1822, op.8/2	vi, 386; i, 73
517	Der Schäfer und der Reiter	Ein Schäfer sass im Grünen	Fouqué		April 1817		
	version a			E		1972	—; i, 191
	version b			E		1822, op.13/1	v, 6; i, 95
518	An den Tod	Tod, du Schrecken der Natur	Schubart	B	1816 or 1817	1824	v, 130; v
519	Die Blumensprache	Es deuten die Blumen	? E. Platner	B♭	?1817	1867, op.173/5	v, 25; xi
520	Frohsinn	Ich bin von lockerem Schlage	Castelli				
	version a			F	Jan 1817	1895	v, 2; xi
	version b			F	c1817	1850	—; xi
521	Jagdlied	Trarah! Trarah! wir kehren daheim	Werner	F	Jan 1817	1895	v, 3; xi
	version a [for version b see 'Female and unspecified voices']						

D	Title	Incipit	Text	Key	Composed	Published	SW; NSA
522	Die Liebe	Wo weht der Liebe hoher Geist?	G. Leon	G	Jan 1817	1895	v, 4; xi
523	Trost	Nimmer lange weil' ich hier		c♯	Jan 1817	1885	v, 5; xi
524	Der Alpenjäger	Auf hohen Bergesrücken	Mayrhofer		Jan 1817		
	version a			E		1895	v, 12; i, 233
	version b			D		1970	—; i, 236
	version c			F		1822, op.13/3	v, 16; i, 104
525	Wie Ulfru fischt	Der Angel zuckt	Mayrhofer		Jan 1817		
	version a			d		1970	—; i, 269
	version b			d		1823, op.21/3	v, 18; i, 158
526	Fahrt zum Hades	Der Nachen dröhnt	Mayrhofer	d	Jan 1817	1832	v, 20; xi
527	Schlaflied (Abendlied; Schlummerlied)	Es mahnt der Wald	Mayrhofer		Jan 1817		
	version a			F		1975	—; ii, 193
	version b			F		1823, op.24/2	v, 24; ii, 20
528	La pastorella al prato (2)		C. Goldoni	G	Jan 1817	1872	x, 46; xi
530	An eine Quelle	Du kleine grünumwachs'ne Quelle	Claudius	A	Feb 1817	1829, op.109/3	iv, 232; xi
531	Der Tod und das Mädchen	Vorüber, ach vorüber	Claudius	d	Feb 1817	1821, op.7/3	v, 35; i, 66
532	Das Lied vom Reifen, frag.	Seht meine lieben Bäume an	Claudius	A♭	Feb 1817	1895	v, 36; xi
533	Täglich zu singen	Ich danke Gott und freue mich	Claudius	F	Feb 1817	1895	v, 38; xi
534	Die Nacht	Die Nacht ist dumpfig und finster	Ossian, trans. Harold	g	Feb 1817	1830	v, 39; xi
535	Lied, with small orch	Brüder, schrecklich brennt die Träne		g	Feb 1817	1895	x, 78; iii/1
536	Der Schiffer	Im Winde, im Sturme	Mayrhofer		?March 1817		
	version a			E♭		1970	—; i, 263
	version b			E♭		1823, op.21/2	v, 24; i, 152
539	Am Strome	Ist mir's doch, als sei mein Leben	Mayrhofer	B	March 1817	1822, op.8/4	v, 54; i, 82
540	Philoktet	Da sitz' ich ohne Bogen	Mayrhofer	b	March 1817	1831	v, 56; xi
541	Memnon	Den Tag hindurch nur einmal	Mayrhofer	D♭	March 1817	1821, op.6/1	v, 59; i, 46
542	Antigone und Oedip	Ihr hohen Himmlischen	Mayrhofer	C	March 1817	1821, op.6/2	v, 62; i, 50
543	Auf dem See	Und frische Nahrung	Goethe		March 1817		
	version a			E		1895	v, 66; v
	version b			E♭		1828, op.92/2	v, 70; v
544	Ganymed	Wie im Morgenglanze	Goethe	A♭	March 1817	1825, op.19/3	v, 75; i, 132
545	Der Jüngling und der Tod	Die Sonne sinkt, o könnt ich	J. von Spaun		March 1817		
	version a			c♯		1895	v, 80; xi
	version b			c♯		1872	v, 82; xi
546	Trost im Liede	Braust des Unglücks Sturm empor	Schober	d	March 1817	1827; 1828 as op. 101/3	v, 84; v
547	An die Musik	Du holde Kunst	Schober				
	version a			D	March 1817	1895	v, 86; iv
	version b			D	c1817	1827. op.88/4	v, 87; iv
548	Orest auf Tauris	Ist dies Tauris	Mayrhofer	E♭	March 1817	1831	vi, 118; xi
549	Mahomets Gesang (1), frag.	Seht den Felsenquell	Goethe	c♯	March 1817	1895	x, 110; xiii
550	Die Forelle	In einem Bächlein helle	Schubart				
	version a			D♭	c1817	1895	v, 132; ii, 194
	version b			D♭	c1817	1895	v, 135; ii, 202
	version c			D♭	Feb 1818	1895	v, 138; ii, 198
	version d			D♭	c1820	1820; 1827 as op.32	v, 141; ii, 109
	version e			D♭	Oct 1821	1975	—; ii, 206
551	Pax vobiscum	Der Friede sei mit euch!	Schober	F	April 1817	1831	v, 88; xi
552	Hänflings Liebeswerbung	Ahidi! ich liebe	F. Kind				
	version a			A	April 1817	1970	—; i, 260
	version b			A	c1817	1823, op.20/3	v, 90; i, 145
553	Auf der Donau	Auf der Wellen Spiegel	Mayrhofer	E♭	April 1817	1823, op.21/1	v, 92; i, 148
554	Uraniens Flucht	Lasst uns, ihr Himmlischen	Mayrhofer	D	April 1817	1895	v, 99; xi
555	Song sketch (no text)	—		a	?May 1817	1934	—; xi
558	Liebhaber in allen Gestalten	Ich wollt', ich wär' ein Fisch	Goethe	A	May 1817	1887	iii, 46; xi
559	Schweizerlied	Uf'm Bergli bin i g'sässe	Goethe	F	May 1817	1885	iii, 48; xi
560	Der Goldschmiedsgesell	Es ist doch meine Nachbarin	Goethe	F	May 1817	1850	iii, 49; xi
561	Nach einem Gewitter	Auf den Blumen	Mayrhofer	F	May 1817	1872	v, 116; xi
562	Fischerlied (3)	Das Fischergewerbe gibt rüstigen Mut!	Salis-Seewis	F	May 1817	1895	v, 118; xi

D	Title	Incipit	Text	Key	Composed	Published	SW; NSA
563	Die Einsiedelei (3)	Es rieselt, klar und wehend	Salis-Seewis	C	May 1817	1887	v, 120; xi
564	Gretchen im Zwinger (Gretchen; Gretchens Bitte), frag.	Ach neige; du Schmerzensreiche	Goethe	b♭	May 1817	1838	x, 116; xi
565	Der Strom	Mein Leben wälzt sich murrend fort		d	?June 1817	1876	v, 123; xi
569	Das Grab (4), for unison chorus	Das Grab ist tief und stille	Salis-Seewis	c♯	June 1817	1895	v, 122; iii/3
573	Iphigenia	Blüht denn hier an Tauris Strande	Mayrhofer	G♭	July 1817	1829, op.98/3	v, 127; v
577	Entzückung an Laura (2)		Schiller		Aug 1817		
	frag. a	Laura, Laura, über diese Welt		A		1873	x, 119; x
	frag. b	Amoretten seh ich		D♭		1895	x, 120; x
578	Abschied	Lebe wohl! lebe wohl!	Schubert	b	24 Aug 1817	1838	x, 80; xi
579	Der Knabe in der Wiege (Wiegenlied)	Er schläft so süss	A. Ottenwalt				
	version a			C	autumn 1817	1872	v, 180; xi
	version b, frag.			A♭	Nov 1817	1897	Rev, 70; xi
579a	Vollendung [formerly 989]	Wenn ich einst das Ziel errungen habe	Matthisson	A	?Sept–Oct 1817	1970	—; xi
579b	Die Erde [formerly 989a]	Wenn sanft entzückt	Matthisson	E	?Sept–Oct 1817	1970	—; xi
582	Augenblicke im Elysium [see 990b]						
583	Gruppe aus dem Tartarus (2)	Horch, wie Murmeln des empörten Meeres	Schiller	C	Sept 1817	1823, op.24/1	v, 144; ii, 13
584	Elysium	Vorüber die stöhnende Klage!	Schiller	E	Sept 1817	1830	v, 149; xi
585	Atys	Der Knabe seufzt	Mayrhofer	a	Sept 1817	1833	v, 159; xi
586	Erlafsee	Mir ist so wohl, so weh'	Mayrhofer	F	Sept 1817	1818; 1822 as op.8/3	v, 164; i, 78
587	An den Frühling (3)	Willkommen schöner Jungling!	Schiller				
	version a			A	Oct 1817	1885	iii, 8; xi
	version b [formerly 245]			B♭	c1817	1895	iii, 6; xi
588	Der Alpenjäger	Willst du nicht das Lämmlein huten	Schiller				
	version a, frag.			E♭	Oct 1817	1897	Rev, 66; ii, 236
	version b			C	c1817	1825, op.37/2	v, 168; ii, 138
594	Der Kampf	Nein, länger werd' ich diesen Kampf	Schiller	d	Nov 1817	1829, op.110	v, 171; xi
595	Thekla: eine Geisterstimme (2)	Wo ich sei, und wo mich hingewendet	Schiller				
	version a			c♯	Nov 1817	1895	v, 177; iv
	version b			c	c1817	1827, op.88/2	v, 178; iv
596	Lied eines Kindes, frag.	Lauter Freude fühl' ich		B♭	Nov 1817	1895	x, 122; xi
611	Auf der Riesenkoppe	Hoch auf dem Gipfel deiner Gebirge	Körner	d	March 1818	c1850	v, 184; xii
614	An den Mond in einer Herbstnacht	Freundlich ist dein Antlitz	A. Schreiber	A	April 1818	1832	v, 188; xii
616	Grablied für die Mutter	Hauche milder, Abendluft		b	June 1818	1838	v, 194; xii
619	Vocal exercise, 2vv, figured bass (no text)	—		C	July 1818	1892	ser. xix, 95; viii/2
620	Einsamkeit	Gib mir die Fülle der Einsamkeit!	Mayrhofer	B♭	July 1818	1840	v, 196; xii
622	Der Blumenbrief	Euch Blümlein will ich senden	Schreiber	D	Aug 1818	1833	v, 213; xii
623	Das Marienbild	Sei gegrüsst, du Frau der Huld	Schreiber	C	Aug 1818	1831	v, 214; xii
626	Blondel zu Marien	In düstrer Nacht		e♭	Sept 1818	1842	v, 218; xii
627	Das Abendrot	Du heilig, glühend Abendrot!	Schreiber	E	Nov 1818	1867, op.173/6	v, 220; xii
628	Sonett I	Apollo, lebet noch	Petrarch, trans. A. W. von Schlegel	B♭	Nov 1818	1895	v, 225; xii
629	Sonett II	Allein, nachdenklich, wie gelähmt	Petrarch, trans. A. W. von Schlegel	g	Nov 1818	1895	v, 228; xii
630	Sonett III	Nunmehr, da Himmel, Erde	Petrarch, trans. J. D. Gries	C	Dec 1818	1895	v, 234; xii
631	Blanka (Das Mädchen)	Wenn mich einsam Lüfte fächeln	F. von Schlegel	a	Dec 1818	1885	v, 236; xii
632	Vom Mitleiden Mariä	Als bei dem Kreuz Maria stand	F. von Schlegel	g	Dec 1818	1831	v, 238; xii
633	Der Schmetterling	Wie soll ich nicht tanzen	F. von Schlegel	F	c1819	1826, op.57/1	iii, 225; iii
634	Die Berge	Sieht uns der Blick gehoben	F. von Schlegel	G	c1819	1826, op.57/2	iii, 227; iii
636	Sehnsucht (2)	Ach, aus dieses Tales Gründen	Schiller		c1821		
	version a			b		1975	—; ii, 250
	version b			b		1895	vi, 23; ii, 258
	version c			b		1826, op.39	vi, 29; ii, 165

D	Title	Incipit	Text	Key	Composed	Published	SW; NSA
637	Hoffnung (2)	Es reden und träumen die Menschen	Schiller	B♭	c1819	1827, op.87/2	vi, 36; iv
638	Der Jüngling am Bache (3)	An der Quelle sass der Knabe	Schiller				
	version a			d	April 1819	1895	vi, 40; iv
	version b			c	c1819	1827, op.87/3	vi, 36; iv
639	Widerschein		Schlechta		c1819		
	version a	Fischer harrt am Brückenbogen		D		1820	—; v
	version b [formerly 949]	Tom lehnt harrend auf der Brücke		B♭		1832	ix, 130; v
645	Abend, frag.	Wie ist es denn	L. Tieck	g	?Jan 1819	—	—; xii
646	Die Gebüsche	Es wehet kühl und leise	F. von Schlegel	G	Jan 1819	1885	vi, 1; xii
649	Der Wanderer	Wie deutlich des Mondes Licht	F. von Schlegel	D	Feb 1819	1826, op.65/2	vi, 5; iii
650	Abendbilder	Still beginnt's im Hain zu tauen	J. P. Silbert	a	Feb 1819	1831	vi, 7; xii
651	Himmelsfunken	Der Odem Gottes weht	Silbert	G	Feb 1819	1831	vi, 14; xii
652	Das Mädchen	Wie so innig, möcht ich sagen	F. von Schlegel				
	version a			A	Feb 1819	1842	vi, 16; xii
	version b			A	cFeb 1819	—	—; xii
653	Bertas Lied in der Nacht	Nacht umhüllt mit wehendem Flügel	Grillparzer	e♭	Feb 1819	c1842	vi, 18; xii
654	An die Freunde	Im Wald, im Wald da grabt mich ein	Mayrhofer	a	March 1819	c1842	vi, 20; xii
658	Marie	Ich sehe dich in tausend Bildern	Novalis	D	?May 1819	1895	vi, 53; xii
659	Hymne I	Wenige wissen das Geheimnis	Novalis	a	May 1819	1872	vi, 42; xii
660	Hymne II	Wenn ich ihn nur habe	Novalis	b♭	May 1819	1872	vi, 49; xii
661	Hymne III	Wenn alle untreu werden	Novalis	b♭	May 1819	1872	vi, 50; xii
662	Hymne IV	Ich sag' es jedem	Novalis	A	May 1819	1872	vi, 52; xii
663	Der 13. Psalm, frag.	Ach, Herr, wie lange	trans. M. Mendelssohn	D♭	June 1819	1927	—; xii
669	Beim Winde	Es träumen die Wolken	Mayrhofer	g	Oct 1819	1829	vi, 54; xii
670	Die Sternennächte	In monderhellten Nächten	Mayrhofer	D♭	Oct 1819	1862 op.165/2	vi, 56; xii
671	Trost	Hörnerklagen rufen klagend	Mayrhofer	E♭	Oct 1819	1849	vi, 60; xii
672	Nachtstück		Mayrhofer				
	version a	Wenn über Bergen der Nebel sich breitet		c♯	Oct 1819	1975	—; ii, 225
	version b	Wenn über Berge sich der Nebel breitet		c	c1819	1825, op.36/2	vi, 62; ii, 125
673	Die Liebende schreibt	Ein Blick von deinen Augen	Goethe	B♭	Oct 1819	1832; 1862 as op.165/1	vi, 68; xii
674	Prometheus	Bedecke deinen Himmel, Zeus	Goethe	g	Oct 1819	1850	vi, 70; xii
677	Strophe aus Die Götter Griechenlands	Schöne Welt, wo bist du?	Schiller		Nov 1819		
	version a			a/A		1895	vi, 76; xii
	version b			a/A		1848	vi, 78; xii
682	Über allen Zauber Liebe, frag.	Sie hüpfte mit mir auf grünem Plan	Mayrhofer	G	c1820	1895	x, 123; xii
684	Die Sterne	Du staunest, o Mensch	F. von Schlegel	E♭	1820	1850	vi, 102; xii
685	Morgenlied	Eh' die Sonne früh aufsteht	Werner	a	1820	1821, op.4/2	vi, 104; i, 30
686	Frühlingsglaube	Die linden Lüfte sind erwacht	Uhland				
	version a			B♭	Sept 1820	1970	—; i, 252
	version b			B♭	1820	1970	—; i, 256
	version c			A♭	Nov 1822	1823, op.20/2	vi, 108; i, 141
687	Nachthymne	Hinüber wall' ich	Novalis	D	Jan 1820	1872	vi, 372; xii
688	Vier Canzonen				Jan 1820	1871	
		1 Non t'accostar all'urna	J. A. Vitorelli	C			x, 48; xii
		2 Guarda, che bianca luna	Vitorelli	G			x, 50; xii
		3 Da quel sembiante appresi	Metastasio	B♭			x, 52; xii
		4 Mio ben ricordati	Metastasio	b♭			x, 53; xii
690	Abendröte	Tiefer sinket die Sonne	F. von Schlegel	A	March 1823	1830	vi, 94; xii
691	Die Vögel	Wie lieblich und fröhlich	F. von Schlegel	A	March 1820	1865, op.172/6	vi, 86; xii
692	Der Knabe	Wenn ich nur ein Vöglein wäre	F. von Schlegel	A	March 1820	1872	vi, 88; xii
693	Der Fluss	Wie rein Gesang sich windet	F. von Schlegel	B	March 1820	1872	vi, 91; xii
694	Der Schiffer	Friedlich lieg' ich hingegossen	F. von Schlegel	D	March 1820	1842	vi, 98; xii
695	Namenstagslied	Vater, schenk' mir diese Stunde	A. Stadler	A	March 1820	1895	x, 81; xii
698	Des Fräuleins Liebeslauschen (Liebeslauschen)	Da unten steht ein Ritter	Schlechta	A	Sept 1820	1832	vi, 113; xii
699	Der entsühnte Orest	Zu meinen Füssen brichst du dich	Mayrhofer	C	Sept 1820	1831	vi, 121; xii
700	Freiwilliges Versinken	Wohin? O Helios!	Mayrhofer	d	Sept 1820	1831	vi, 124; xii
702	Der Jüngling auf dem Hügel	Ein Jüngling auf dem Hügel	H. Hüttenbrenner	G	Nov 1820	1822, op.8/1	vi, 126; i, 68
707	Der zürnenden Diana	Ja, spanne nur den Bogen	Mayrhofer		Dec 1820		
	version a			A		1895	vi, 133; ii, 210
	version b			A♭		1825, op.36/1	vi, 141; ii, 113

D	Title	Incipit	Text	Key	Composed	Published	SW; NSA
708	Im Walde (Waldesnacht)	Windes Rauschen, Gottes Flügel	F. von Schlegel	c♯	Dec 1820	1832	vi, 149; xii
711	Lob der Tränen	Laue Lüfte, Blumendüfte	A. W. von Schlegel		1818		
	version a			D		1970	—; i, 229
	version b			D		1822, op.13/2	v, 10; i, 100
712	Die gefangenen Sänger	Hörst du von den Nachtigallen	A. W. von Schlegel	G	Jan 1821	1842	vi, 164; xiii
713	Der Unglückliche	Die Nacht bricht an	Pichler		Jan 1821		
	version a			b		1895	vi, 168; iv
	version b			b		1827, op.87/1	vi, 173; iv
715	Versunken	Voll Locken kraus ein Haupt	Goethe	A♭	Feb 1821	1845	vi, 178; xiii
716	Grenzen der Menschheit	Wenn der uralte heilige Vater	Goethe	E	March 1821	1832	vi, 185; xiii
717	Suleika II	Ach um deine feuchten Schwingen	? M. von Willemer	B♭	?March 1821	1825, op.31	vi, 201; ii, 97
719	Geheimes	Über meines Liebchens Äugeln	Goethe	A♭	March 1821	1822, op.14/2	vi, 183; i, 118
720	Suleika I	Was bedeutet die Bewegung?	?Willemer				
	version a			b	March 1821	1970	—; i, 239
	version b			b	c1821	1822, op.14/1	vi, 194; i, 108
721	Mahomets Gesang (2), frag.	Seht den Felsenquell	Goethe	c♯	March 1821	1895	x, 125; xiii
725	Linde Lüfte wehen, Mez, T, frag.			b	April 1821	1929	—; iii/2
726	Mignon I (1)	Heiss mich nicht reden	Goethe	b	April 1821	1870	vi, 189; iii
727	Mignon II (2)	So lasst mich scheinen	Goethe	b	April 1821	1850	vi, 191; iii
728	Johanna Sebus, frag.	Der Damm zerreisst	Goethe	d	April 1821	1895	x, 128; xiii
731	Der Blumen Schmerz	Wie tönt es mir so schaurig	J. Mayláth	e	Sept 1821	1821; 1867 as op.173/4	vi, 210; v
736	Ihr Grab	Dort ist ihr Grab	K. A. Engelhardt	E♭	?1822	1842	vii, 4; xiii
737	An die Leier	Ich will von Atreus Söhnen	F. S. Ritter von Bruchmann, after Anacreon	E♭	? 1822 or 1823	1826, op.56/2	vii, 42; iii
738	Im Haine	Sonnenstrahlen durch die Tannen	Bruchmann	A	? 1822 or 1823	1826, op.56/3	vii, 46; iii
741	Sei mir gegrüsst	O du Entrissne mir	F. Rückert	B♭	between end 1821 and autumn 1822	1823, op.20/1	vi, 214; i, 137
742	Der Wachtelschlag	Ach! mir schallt's dorten	S. F. Sauter	A	1822	1822; 1827 as op.68	vii, 2; iii
743	Selige Welt	Ich treibe auf des Lebens Meer	J. C. Senn	A♭	?autumn 1822	1823, op.23/2	vii, 14; ii, 6
744	Schwanengesang	Wie klag ich's aus	Senn	A♭	?autumn 1822	1823, op.23/3	vii, 16; ii, 8
745	Die Rose	Es lockte schöne Wärme	F. von Schlegel		1822		
	version a			G		1822; 1827 as op.73	vii, 18; iii
	version b			F		1895	vii, 21; iii
746	Am See	In des Sees Wogenspiele	Bruchmann	E♭	? 1822 or 1823	1831	vii, 74; xiii
749	Herrn Josef Spaun, Assessor in Linz (Sendschreiben an den Assessor Spaun in Linz)	Und nimmer schreibst du?	M. von Collin	c	Jan 1822	1850	x, 84; xiii
751	Die Liebe hat gelogen		A. von Platen-Hallermünde	c	by 17 April 1822	1823, op.23/1	vii, 28; ii, 4
752	Nachtviolen		Mayrhofer	C	April 1822	1872	vii, 6; xiii
753	Heliopolis I	Im kalten rauhen Norden	Mayrhofer	e	April 1822	1826, op.65/3	vii, 10; iii
754	Heliopolis II	Fels auf Felsen hingewälzt	Mayrhofer	c	April 1822	1842	vii, 14; xiii
756	Du liebst mich nicht	Mein Herz ist zerrissen	Platen-Hallermünde		July 1822		
	version a			g♯		1895	vii, 24; iii
	version b			a		1826, op.59/1	vii, 26; iii
758	Todesmusik	In des Todes Feierstunde	Schober	G♭	Sept 1822	1829, op.108/2	vii, 30; v
761	Schatzgräbers Begehr	In tiefster Erde ruht ein alt Gesetz	Schober		Nov 1822		
	version a			d		1823, op.23/4	vii, 35; ii, 10
	version b			d		1895	vii, 187; ii, 189
762	Schwestergruss	Im Mondenschein wall' ich auf und ab	Bruchmann	f♯	Nov 1822	1833	vii, 38; xiii
764	Der Musensohn	Durch Feld und Wald zu schweifen	Goethe				
	version a			A♭	Dec 1822	1895	vii, 48; v
	version b			G	c1822	1828, op.92/1	vii, 51; v

D	Title	Incipit	Text	Key	Composed	Published	SW; NSA
765	An die Entfernte	So hab' ich wirklich dich verloren?	Goethe	G	Dec 1822	1868	vii, 54; xiii
766	Am Flusse (2)	Verfliesset, vielgeliebte Lieder	Goethe	D	Dec 1822	1872	vii, 56; xiii
767	Willkommen und Abschied	Es schlug mein Herz	Goethe				
	version a			D	Dec 1822	1895	vii, 58; iii
	version b			C	c1822	1826, op.56/1	vii, 64; iii
768	Wandrers Nachtlied	Über allen Gipfeln ist Ruh	Goethe	B♭	by July 1824	1827; 1828 as op.96/3	vii, 70; v
770	Drang in die Ferne	Vater, du glaubst es nicht	K. G. von Leitner	a/A	early 1823	1823; 1827 as op.71	vii, 91; iii
771	Der Zwerg	Im trüben Licht verschwinden schon die Berge	M. von Collin	a	? 1822 or 1823	1823, op.22/1	vii, 95; i, 160
772	Wehmut	Wenn ich durch Wald und Fluren geh'	M. von Collin	d	? 1822 or 1823	1823, op.22/2	vii, 102; i, 168
774	Auf dem Wasser zu singen	Mitten im Schimmer der spiegelnden Wellen	Stolberg-Stolberg	A♭	1823	1823; 1827 as op.72	vii, 106; iii
775	Dass sie hier gewesen	Dass der Ostwind Düfte	Rückert	C	?1823	1826, op.59/2	viii, 2; iii
776	Du bist die Ruh		Rückert	E♭	1823	1826, op.59/3	viii, 4; iii
777	Lachen und Weinen		Rückert	A♭	?1823	1826, op.59/4	viii, 7; iii
778	Greisengesang	Der Frost hat mir bereifet	Rückert		by June 1823		
	version a			b		—	—; iii
	version b			b		1826, op.60/1	viii, 10; iii
778a	Die Wallfahrt	Meine Tränen im Bussgewand	Rückert	f	?1823	1969	—; xiii
785	Der zürnende Barde	Wer wagt's, wer wagt's	Bruchmann	g	Feb 1823	1831	vii, 71; xiii
786	Viola	Schneeglöcklein, o Schneeglöcklein	Schober	A♭	March 1823	1830, op.123	vii, 76; xiii
788	Lied (Die Mutter Erde)	Des Lebens Tag ist schwer	Stolberg-Stolberg	a/A	April 1823	1838	vii, 104; xiii
789	Pilgerweise	Ich bin ein Waller auf der Erde	Schober	f♯	April 1823	1832	vii, 108; xiii
792	Vergissmeinnicht	Als der Frühling sich vom Herzen	Schober	A♭	May 1823	1833	vii, 114; xiii
793	Das Geheimnis (2)	Sie konnte mir kein Wörtchen sagen	Schiller	G	May 1823	1867, op.173/2	vii, 125; xiii
794	Der Pilgrim	Noch in meines Lebens Lenze	Schiller				
	version a			E	May 1823	1895	vii, 130; ii, 229
	version b			D	c1823	1825, op.37/1	—; ii, 132
795	Die schöne Müllerin		W. Müller		Oct–Nov 1823	1824, op.25	
	1 Das Wandern	Das Wandern ist des Müllers Lust		B♭			vii, 134; ii, 21
	2 Wohin?	Ich hört' ein Bächlein rauschen		G			vii, 136; ii, 23
	3 Halt!	Eine Mühle seh' ich blinken		C			vii, 140; ii, 29
	4 Danksagung an den Bach	War es also gemeint		G			vii, 143; ii, 34
	5 Am Feierabend	Hätt' ich tausend Arme zu rühren		a			vii, 147; ii, 36
	6 Der Neugierige	Ich frage keine Blume		B			vii, 149; ii, 42
	7 Ungeduld	Ich schnitt es gern in alle Rinden ein		A			vii, 152; ii, 46
	8 Morgengruss	Guten Morgen, schöne Müllerin		C			vii, 154; ii, 50
	9 Des Müllers Blumen	Am Bach viel kleine Blumen stehn		A			vii, 155; ii, 52
	10 Tränenregen	Wir sassen so traulich beisammen		A			vii, 156; ii, 54
	11 Mein!	Bächlein, lass dein Rauschen sein		D			vii, 158; ii, 57
	12 Pause	Meine Laute hab' ich gehängt		B♭			vii, 162; ii, 63
	13 Mit dem grünen Lautenbande	Schad' um das schöne grüne Band		B♭			vii, 165; ii, 68
	14 Der Jäger	Was sucht denn der Jäger		c			vii, 166; ii, 70
	15 Eifersucht und Stolz	Wohin so schnell		g			vii, 168; ii, 72
	16 Die liebe Farbe	In Grün will ich mich kleiden		b			vii, 172; ii, 76
	17 Die böse Farbe	Ich möchte ziehn in die Welt hinaus		B			vii, 174; ii, 78
	18 Trockne Blumen	Ihr Blümlein alle, die sie mir gab		e			vii, 178; ii, 83
	19 Der Müller und der Bach	Wo ein treues Herze in Liebe vergeht		g			vii, 181; ii, 87
	20 Des Baches Wiegenlied	Gute Ruh', gute Ruh'		E			vii, 184; ii, 90
797	Romanze zum Drama Rosamunde (3b)	Der Vollmond strahlt auf Bergeshöhn	H. von Chézy	f	autumn 1823	1824, op.26	—; ii, 94
799	Im Abendrot	O, wie schön ist deine Welt	K. Lappe	A♭	1824 or Feb 1825	1832	viii, 30; xiii
800	Der Einsame	Wann meine Grillen schwirren	Lappe				
	version a			G	early 1825	1825	viii, 36; —
	version b			G	c1825	1827, op.41	viii, 41; ii, 172
801	Dithyrambe	Nimmer, das glaub mir	Schiller	A	by June 1826	1826, op.60/2	viii, 14; iii
805	Der Sieg	O unbewölktes Leben!	Mayrhofer	F	March 1824	1833	viii, 16; iii
806	Abendstern	Was weilst du einsam an dem Himmel	Mayrhofer	a	March 1824	1833	viii, 18; xiii
807	Auflösung	Verbirg dich, Sonne	Mayrhofer	G	March 1824	1842	viii, 20; xiii
808	Gondelfahrer (1)	Es tanzen Mond und Sterne	Mayrhofer	C	March 1824	1872	viii, 26; xiii

D	Title	Incipit	Text	Key	Composed	Published	SW; NSA
822	Lied eines Kriegers, with unison chorus	Des stolzen Männerlebens schönste Zeichen		A	31 Dec 1824	1842	viii, 32; iii/3
827	Nacht und Träume	Heil'ge Nacht, du sinkest nieder	M. von Collin		by June 1823		
	version a			B		1975	—; ii, 267
	version b			B		1825, op.43/2	viii, 32; ii; 184
828	Die junge Nonne	Wie braust durch die Wipfel	J. N. Craigher de Jachelutta	f	early 1825	1825, op.43/1	viii, 62; ii, 178
829	Abschied, melodrama	Leb wohl, du schöne Erde	A. von Pratobevera	F	Feb 1826	1873	x, 136; xiii
830	Lied der Anne Lyle	Wärst du bei mir im Lebenstal	A. MacDonald, trans. ? S. May	c	?early 1825	1828, op.85/1	ix, 78; iv
831	Gesang der Norna	Mich führt mein Weg	Scott, trans. S. H. Spiker	f	early 1825	1828, op.85/2	ix, 82; iv
832	Des Sängers Habe	Schlagt mein ganzes Glück	Schlechta	B♭	Feb 1825	1830	viii, 46; xiii
833	Der blinde Knabe	O sagt, ihr Lieben, mir einmal	C. Cibber, trans. Craigher				
	version a			B♭	April 1825	1895	viii, 54; v
	version b			B♭	April 1825	1827; 1828 as op.101/2	viii, 58; v
834	Im Walde	Ich wandre über Berg und Tal	E. Schulze	g	March 1825	1835, op.93/1	—; v
	version a			b♭	c1825	1828, op.90/1	viii, 96; v
	version b						
837	Ellens Gesang I	Raste, Krieger, Krieg ist aus	Scott, trans. D. A. Storck	D♭	April–July 1825	1826, op.52/1	viii, 70; iii
838	Ellens Gesang II	Jäger, ruhe von der Jagd!	Scott, trans. Storck	E♭	April–July 1825	1826, op.52/2	viii, 78; iii
839	Ellens Gesang III (Hymne an die Jungfrau)	Ave Maria! Jungfrau mild!	Scott, trans. Storck	B♭	April 1825	1826, op.52/6	viii, 90; iii
842	Totengräbers Heimwehe	O Menschheit, o Leben	Craigher	f	April 1825	1833	viii, 50; xiii
843	Lied des gefangenen Jägers	Mein Ross so müd in dem Stalle	Scott, trans. Storck	d	April 1825	1826, op.52/7	viii, 92; iii
846	Normans Gesang	Die Nacht bricht bald herein	Scott, trans. Storck	c	April 1825	1826, op.52/5	viii, 82; iii
851	Das Heimweh	Ach, der Gebirgssohn	J. L. Pyrker von Felsö-Eör		Aug 1825		
	version a			a		1895	viii, 112; iii
	version b			a		1827, op.79/1	viii, 120; iii
852	Die Allmacht (1)	Gross ist Jehovah, der Herr	Pyrker		Aug 1825		
	version a			A		—	—; iii
	version b			C		1827, op.79/2	viii, 120; iii
853	Auf der Bruck	Frisch trabe sonder Ruh	Schulze				
	version a			G	March or Aug 1825	1835, op.93/2	—; iii
	version b			A♭	c1825	1828, op.90/2	viii, 106; iii
854	Fülle der Liebe	Ein sehnend Streben	F. von Schlegel	A♭	Aug 1825	1830	viii, 132; iii
855	Wiedersehn	Der Frühlingssonne holdes Lächeln	A. W. von Schlegel	G	Sept 1825	1842	viii, 136; xiii
856	Abendlied für die Entfernte	Hinaus, mein Blick!	A. W. von Schlegel	F	Sept 1825	1827, op.88/1	viii, 138; iv
857	Zwei Szenen aus dem Schauspiel Lacrimas		C. W. von Schütz		Sept 1825	1829, op.124	
	1 Lied der Delphine	Ach, was soll ich beginnen		A			viii, 146; xiii
	2 Lied des Florio	Nun, da Schatten niedergleiten		E			viii, 143; xiii
860	An mein Herz	O Herz, sei endlich stille	Schulze	a	Dec 1825	1832	viii, 154; xiii
861	Der liebliche Stern	Ihr Sternlein, still in der Höhe	Schulze	G	Dec 1825	1832	viii, 160; xiii
862	Um Mitternacht	Keine Stimme hör ich schallen	Schulze		Dec 1825		
	version a			B♭	Dec 1825	—	—; iv
	version b			B♭	?March 1826	1827, op.88/3	viii, 212; iv
863	An Gott, lost		C. C. Hohlfeld	—	by 1827	—	—
864	Das Totenhemdchen, lost		E. von Bauernfeld	—	after 1824	—	—
865	Widerspruch version b [for version a see 'Male voices']	Wenn ich durch Busch und Zweig	J. G. Seidl	D	?1826	1828, op.105/1	ser. xvi, 93; v
866	Vier Refrainlieder		Seidl		?summer 1828	1828, op.95	
	1 Die Unterscheidung	Die Mutter hat mich jüngst gescholten		G			viii, 240; v
	2 Bei dir allein			A♭			viii, 243; v
	3 Die Männer sind méchant	Du sagtest mir es, Mutter		a			viii, 248; v
	4 Irdisches Glück	So mancher sieht mit finstrer Miene		d			viii, 250; v
867	Wiegenlied	Wie sich der Äuglein kindlicher Himmel	Seidl	A♭	?1826	1828, op.105/2	viii, 252; v
868	Das Echo [see 990c]						
869	Totengräber-Weise	Nicht so düster und so bleich	Schlechta	f♯	1826	1832	viii, 198; xiv

D	Title	Incipit	Text	Key	Composed	Published	SW; NSA
870	Der Wanderer an den Mond	Ich auf der Erd', am Himmel du	Seidl	g/G	1826	1827, op.80/1	viii, 234; iv
871	Das Zügenglöcklein	Kling die Nacht durch, klinge	Seidl		1826		
	version a			A♭		1979	—; iv
	version b			A♭		1827, op.80/2	viii, 237; iv
874	O Quell, was strömst du rasch und wild, frag.		Schulze	G	?Jan 1826	1974	—; xiv
876	Im Jänner 1817 (Tiefes Leid)	Ich bin von aller Ruh geschieden	Schulze	e	Jan 1826	1838	viii, 164; xiv
877	Gesänge aus Wilhelm Meister		Goethe		Jan 1826	1827, op.62	
	1 Mignon und der Harfner (5), S,T	Nur wer die Sehnsucht kennt		b			viii, 166; iii
	2 Lied der Mignon (2)	Heiss mich nicht reden		e			viii, 169; iii
	3 Lied der Mignon (3)	So lasst mich scheinen		B			viii, 172; iii
	4 Lied der Mignon (6)	Nur wer die Sehnsucht kennt		a			viii, 174; iii
878	Am Fenster	Ihr lieben Mauern hold und traut	Seidl	F	March 1826	1828, op.105/3	viii, 176; v
879	Sehnsucht	Die Scheibe friert	Seidl	d	March 1826	1828, op.105/4	viii, 179; v
880	Im Freien	Draussen in der weiten Nacht	Seidl	E♭	March 1826	1827, op.80/3	viii, 184; iv
881	Fischerweise	Den Fischer fechten Sorgen	Schlechta		March 1826		
	version a			D		1895	viii, 190; v
	version b			D		1828, op.96/4	viii, 194; v
882	Im Frühling	Still sitz' ich an des Hügels Hang	Schulze	G	March 1826	1828, op.101/1	viii, 202; v
883	Lebensmut	O wie dringt das junge Leben	Schulze	B♭	March 1826	1832	viii, 206; xiv
884	Über Wildemann	Die Winde sausen am Tannenhang	Schulze	d	March 1826	1829, op.108/1	viii, 216; v
888	Trinklied (Come, thou monarch of the vine)	Bacchus, feister Fürst	Shakespeare, trans. F. M. von Grünbühel and Bauernfeld	C	July 1826	1850	viii, 227; xiv
889	Standchen (Hark, hark the lark)	Horch, horch! die Lerch	Shakespeare, trans. A. W. von Schlegel	C	July 1826	1830	viii, 228; xiv
890	Hippolits Lied	Lasst mich, ob ich auch still verglüh	F. von Gerstenberg	a	July 1826	1830	viii, 230; xiv
891	Gesang (An Sylvia; Who is Sylvia?)	Was ist Silvia	Shakespeare, trans. Bauernfeld	A	July 1826	1828, op.106/4	viii, 232; v
896	Fröhliches Scheiden, sketch	Gar fröhlich kann ich scheiden	Leitner	F	autumn 1827– early 1828	1920	—; xiv
896a	Sie in jedem Liede, sketch	Nehm ich die Harfe	Leitner	B♭	autumn 1827– early 1828	—	—; xiv
896b	Wolke und Quelle, sketch	Auf meinen heimischen Bergen	Leitner	C	autumn 1827– early 1828	—	—; xiv
902	Drei Gesänge				1827	1827, op.83	
	1 L'incanto degli occhi (Die Macht der Augen) (2)	Da voi, cari lumi (Nur euch, schöne Sterne)	Metastasio	C			x, 54; iv
	2 Il traditor deluso (Der getäuschte Verräter) (2)	Ahimè, io tremo! (Weh mir, ich bebe)	Metastasio	e			x, 58; iv
	3 Il modo di prender moglie (Die Art, ein Weib zu nehmen)	Or sù! non ci pensiamo (Wohlan! und ohne Zagen)		C			x, 65; iv
904	Alinde	Die Sonne sinkt ins tiefe Meer	Rochlitz	A	Jan 1827	1827, op.81/1	iv, 257; iv
905	An die Laute	Leiser, leiser, kleine Laute	Rochlitz	D	Jan 1827	1827, op.81/2	iv, 262; iv
906	Der Vater mit dem Kind	Dem Vater liegt das Kind im Arm	Bauernfeld	D	Jan 1827	1832	viii, 261; xiv
907	Romanze des Richard Löwenherz	Grosse Taten tat der Ritter	Scott, trans. K. L. M. Müller		?March 1826		
	version a			b		1979	—; iv
	version b			b		1828, op.86	viii, 220; iv
909	Jägers Liebeslied	Ich schiess' den Hirsch	Schober	D	Feb 1827	1828, op.96/2	viii, 264; v
910	Schiffers Scheidelied	Die Wogen am Gestade schwellen	Schober	e	Feb 1827	1833	viii, 267; xiv
911	Winterreise		Müller		Feb–spring 1827	1828, op.89	
	Book 1:						
	1 Gute Nacht	Fremd bin ich eingezogen		d			ix, 2; iv
	2 Die Wetterfahne	Der Wind spielt mit der Wetterfahne		a			ix, 6; iv

D	Title	Incipit	Text	Key	Composed	Published	SW; NSA
3	Gefrorne Tränen	Gefrorne Tropfen fallen		f			ix, 8; iv
4	Erstarrung	Ich such im Schnee vergebens		c			ix, 10; iv
5	Der Lindenbaum	Am Brunnen vor dem Tore		E			ix, 16; iv
6	Wasserflut	Manche Trän' aus meinen Augen					ix, 20; iv
	version a			f♯			—; iv
	version b			e			ix, 22; iv
7	Auf dem Flusse	Der du so lustig rauschtest		e			ix, 26; iv
8	Rückblick	Es brennt mir unter beiden Sohlen		g			ix, 30; iv
9	Irrlicht	In die tiefsten Felsengründe		b			ix, 32; iv
10	Rast	Nun merk ich erst					
	version a			c			ix, 34; iv
	version b			d		1895	ix, 36; iv
11	Frühlingstraum	Ich träumte von bunten Blumen		A/a			ix, 40; iv
12	Einsamkeit	Wie eine trübe Wolke					
	version a			b			ix, 42; iv
	version b			d		1895	
Book 2:					begun Oct 1827		
13	Die Post	Von der Strasse her ein Posthorn klingt		E♭			ix, 44; iv
14	Der greise Kopf	Der Reif hat einen weissen Schein		c			ix, 48; iv
15	Die Krähe	Eine Krähe war mit mir		c			ix, 50; iv
16	Letzte Hoffnung	Hie und da ist an den Bäumen		E♭			ix, 53; iv
17	Im Dorfe	Es bellen die Hunde		D			ix, 56; iv
18	Der stürmische Morgen	Wie hat der Sturm zerrissen		d			ix, 60; iv
19	Täuschung	Ein Licht tanzt freundlich		A			ix, 62; iv
20	Der Wegweiser	Was vermeid ich denn die Wege		g			ix, 64; iv
21	Das Wirthaus	Auf einen Totenacker		F			ix, 68; iv
22	Mut	Fliegt der Schnee mir ins Gesicht					
	version a			a			—; iv
	version b			g			ix, 70; iv
23	Die Nebensonnen	Drei Sonnen sah ich					
	version a			A			—; iv
	version b			A			ix, 72; iv
24	Der Leiermann	Drüben hinterm Dorfe					
	version a			a		1895	ix, 74; iv
	version b			b			ix, 76; iv
916a	Song sketch (no text)		—	C	?May 1827	—	—; iv
917	Das Lied im Grünen	Ins Grüne, ins Grüne	J. A. F. Reil	A	June 1827	1829, op.115/1	ix,85; xiv
919	Frühlingslied (2)	Geöffnet sind des Winters Riegel	A. Pollak	A♭	?early 1827	1897	ser. xxi, 325; xiv
922	Heimliches Lieben	O du, wenn deine Lippen	K. L. von Klenke				
	version a			B♭	Sept 1827	1895	ix, 92; v
	version b			B♭	c1827	1828, op.106/1	ix, 97; v
923	Eine altschottische Ballade	Dein Schwert, wie ist's von Blut so rot	anon. Eng., trans. Herder				
	version a, 2vv			g	Sept 1827	1862, op.165/5	ix, 104; xiv
	version b			g	c1827	1895	ix, 402; xiv
	version c, 2vv			g	c1827	1971	—, xiv
926	Das Weinen	Gar tröstlich kommt geronnen	Leitner	D	autumn 1827–early 1828	1828, op.106/2	ix, 106; v
927	Vor meiner Wiege	Das also, das ist der enge Schrein	Leitner	b	autumn 1827–early 1828	1828, op.106/3	ix, 108; v
931	Der Wallensteiner Lanzknecht beim Trunk	He! schenket mir im Helme ein!	Leitner	g	Nov 1827	1835	ix, 112; xiv
932	Der Kreuzzug	Ein Münich steht in seiner Zell	Leitner	D	Nov 1827	1832	ix, 114; xiv
933	Des Fischers Liebesglück	Dort blinket durch Weiden	Leitner	a	Nov 1827	1835	ix, 116; xiv
937	Lebensmut, frag.	Fröhlicher Lebensmut	L. Rellstab	B♭	?summer 1828	1872	x, 134; xiv
938	Der Winterabend	Es ist so still	Leitner	B♭	Jan 1828	1835	ix, 118; xiv
939	Die Sterne	Wie blitzen die Sterne	Leitner	E♭	Jan 1828	1828, op.96/1	ix, 125; v
943	Auf dem Strom, with hn/vc obbl	Nimm die letzten Abschiedsküsse	Rellstab	E	March 1828	1829, op.119	x, 2; xiv
945	Herbst	Es rauschen die Winde	Rellstab	e	April 1828	1895	x, 90; xiv
949	Widerschein [see 639b]						
955	Glaube, Hoffnung und Liebe	Glaube, hoffe, liebe!	C. Kuffner	E♭	Aug 1828	1828, op.97	viii, 28; v
957	Schwanengesang				Aug–Oct 1828	1829	
Book 1:							
1	Liebesbotschaft	Rauschendes Bächlein, so silbern	Rellstab	G	Aug 1828		ix, 134; xiv
2	Kriegers Ahnung	In tiefer Ruh liegt um mich her	Rellstab	c			ix, 139, xiv
3	Frühlingssehnsucht	Säuselnde Lüfte wehend so mild	Rellstab	B♭			ix, 144; xiv
4	Ständchen	Leise flehen meine Lieder	Rellstab	d			ix, 148; xiv

D	Title	Incipit	Text	Key	Composed	Published	SW; NSA
5	Aufenthalt	Rauschender Strom, brausender Wald	Rellstab	e			ix, 151; xiv
6	In der Ferne	Wehe dem Fliehenden	Rellstab	b			ix, 156; xiv
	Book 2:						
7	Abschied	Ade! du muntre, du fröhliche Stadt	Rellstab	E♭			ix, 160; xiv
8	Der Atlas	Ich unglückselger Atlas	Heine	g			ix, 167; xiv
9	Ihr Bild	Ich stand in dunklen Träumen	Heine	b♭			ix, 170; xiv
10	Das Fischermädchen	Du schönes Fischermädchen	Heine	A♭			ix, 172; xiv
11	Die Stadt	Am fernen Horizonte	Heine	c			ix, 175; xiv
12	Am Meer	Das Meer erglänzte weit hinaus	Heine	C			ix, 178; xiv
13	Der Doppelgänger	Still ist die Nacht	Heine	b			ix, 180; xiv
14	Die Taubenpost	Ich hab' eine Brieftaub	Seidl	G	Oct 1828		ix, 182; xiv
965	Der Hirt auf dem Felsen, with cl obbl	Wenn auf dem höchsten Fels	Müller, ?H. von Chézy	B♭	Oct 1828	1830, op.129	x, 16; xiv
965a	Die Taubenpost [see 957/14]						
989	Vollendung [see 579a]						
989a	Die Erde [see 579b]						
990	Der Graf von Habsburg	Zu Aachen in seiner Kaiserspracht	Schiller	G	?1815	1853	—; xiv
990a	Kaiser Maximilian auf der Martinswand	Hinauf! hinauf! in Sprung und Lauf	H. von Collin	B♭	?1815	1853	—; xiv
990b	Augenblicke in Elysium, lost [formerly 582]		Schober		?	—	—
990c	Das Echo [formerly 868]	Herzliebe gute Mutter	Castelli	B♭	?	1830, op.130	viii, 258; xiv
990d	Die Schiffende, lost	Sie wankt dahin!	Hölty	—	?	—	—; iv
990e	L'incanto degli occhi (1) ?frag.	Da voi, cari lumi	Metastasio	B♭	?	1933	—; iv
990f	Il traditor deluso (1), ?frag., lost	Ahimè! io tremo!	Metastasio	—	?	—	—
991	[part of 323]						
AI/30	Mein Frieden	Ferne, ferne flammenhelle Sterne	Heine	E♭	?1815	1840	—

INDEX TO THE SONGS

BIBLIOGRAPHY

BIBLIOGRAPHIES

O. E. Deutsch, ed.: *Franz Schubert: die Dokumente seines Lebens und Schaffens*, ii/1: *Die Dokumente seines Lebens* (Munich, 1914, enlarged 2/1964, Neue Ausgabe sämtlicher Werke, viii/5, with a selective list of Deutsch's writings on Schubert, p. 616; Eng. trans., 1946/R1977, as *Schubert: a Documentary Biography*)

W. Kahl: *Verzeichnis des Schrifttums über Franz Schubert: 1828–1928* (Regensburg, 1938)

A. H. King: 'Bibliography', *Schubert: a Symposium*, ed. G. Abraham (London, 1946/R1969, 2/1952)

CATALOGUES

G. Nottebohm: *Thematisches Verzeichnis der im Druck erschienenen Werke von Franz Schubert* (Vienna, 1874)

O. E. Deutsch with D. R. Wakeling: *Schubert: a Thematic Catalogue of his Works* (London, 1951) [preface, p. ix, lists and discusses all previous catalogues; corrections and addns to catalogue in *ML*, xxxiv (1953), 25; Ger. trans., rev., enlarged, by W. Dürr, A. Feil, C. Landon and others, Neue Ausgabe sämtlicher Werke, viii/4, as *Franz Schubert: thematisches Verzeichnis seiner Werke in chronologischer Folge von Otto Erich Deutsch* (Kassel, 1978)

R. van Hoorickx: 'Thematic Catalogue of Schubert's Works: New Additions, Corrections and Notes', *RBM*, xxviii–xxx (1974–6), 136

DOCUMENTS

O. E. Deutsch, ed.: *Franz Schubert: die Dokumente seines Lebens und Schaffens*, ii/1: *Die Dokumente seines Lebens* (Munich, 1914, enlarged 2/1964, Neue Ausgabe sämtlicher Werke, viii/5; Eng. trans., 1946/R1977, as *Schubert: a Documentary Biography*)

——: *Franz Schuberts Briefe und Schriften* (Munich, 1919, 4/1954; Eng. trans., 1928/R1970)

——: *Franz Schuberts Tagebuch* (Vienna, 1928; Eng. trans., 1928) [facs. and transcr.]

H. Werlé, ed.: *Franz Schubert in seinen Briefen und Aufzeichnungen* (Leipzig, 1948, 4/1955)

H. Müller von Asow: 'Unbekannte Briefe der Familie Schubert', *ÖMz*, xiii (1958), 317

R. Klein: *Schubert-Stätten* (Vienna, 1972)

ICONOGRAPHY

A. Trost: 'Franz Schuberts Bildnisse', *Berichte und Mittheilungen des Alterthums-Vereines zu Wien*, xxxiii/2 (1898), 85

O. E. Deutsch, ed.: *Franz Schubert: die Dokumente seines Lebens und Schaffens*, iii: *Sein Leben in Bildern* (Munich, 1913)

O. E. Deutsch: *Die historischen Bildnisse Franz Schuberts in getreuen Nachbildungen* (Vienna, 1922)

A. Orel: *Franz Schubert, 1797–1828: sein Leben in Bildern* (Leipzig, 1939)

R. Petzoldt: *Franz Schubert: sein Leben in Bildern* (Leipzig, 1953)

O. E. Deutsch: 'Rieders Schubert-Bildnis', *ÖMz*, xiv (1959), 1

F. Novotny: 'Zu einem Bildnis Franz Schuberts', *Musica*, xv (1961), 57

E. Hilmar and O. Brusatti, eds.: *Franz Schubert* (Vienna, 1978) [exhibition catalogue]

E. Badura-Skoda: 'A Schubert Life Mask', *MT*, cxx (1979), 575

MANUSCRIPTS, SOURCES

M. Friedlaender: 'Fälschungen in Schuberts Liedern', *VMw*, ix (1893), 166

E. Mandyczewski, ed.: *Revisionsbericht, Franz Schuberts Werke: kritisch durchgesehene Gesamtausgabe* (Leipzig, 1897/R1969)

J. Mantuani: 'Schubertiana: ein Beitrag zur Schubertforschung', *Die Musik*, i (1901–2), 1374 [Schubert autographs found in St Peter's, Vienna]

E. Decsey: 'Aus Josef Hüttenbrenner's Schubert-Nachlass', *Die Musik*, xi (1911–12), 297

R. Lachmann: 'Die Schubert-Autographen der Staatsbibliothek zu Berlin', *ZMw*, xi (1928), 109

J. G. Prod'homme: 'Les manuscrits de Schubert à la Bibliothèque du Conservatoire de Paris', *ReM*, xii (1928), 209

Internationaler Kongress für Schubertforschung: Wien 1928 [contains essays by R. Haas, J. Wolf, G. Kinsky, M. Friedlaender, on Schubert collections and source material]

M. J. E. Brown: 'Recent Schubert Discoveries', *ML*, xxxii (1951), 349

F. Racek: 'Von den Schuberthandschriften der Stadtbibliothek', *Festschrift zum hundertjährigen Bestehen der Wiener Stadtbibliothek, 1856–1956* (Vienna, 1956), 98

M. J. E. Brown: 'New, Old and Rediscovered Schubert Manuscripts', *ML*, xxxvii (1957), 359

——: 'Schubert's Manuscripts: some Chronological Issues', *MR*, xix (1958), 180

——: 'Schubert: Discoveries of the Last Decade', *MQ*, xlvii (1961), 293

W. Suppan: 'Schubert-Autographe im Nachlass Weis-Ostborn', *SM*, vi (1964), 131

M. J. E. Brown: 'Two Schubert Discoveries', *MT*, cix (1968), 801 [Albumleaf, 1821; *Die Wallfahrt* D778a]

A. Feil and W. Dürr: 'Kritisch revidierte Gesamtausgaben von Werken Franz Schuberts im 19. Jahrhundert', *Musik und Verlag: Karl Vötterle zum 65. Geburtstag* (Kassel, 1968), 268

O. E. Deutsch: 'Eine merkwürdige Schubert-Handschrift', *Musamens-musici: im Gedenken an Walther Vetter* (Leipzig, 1969), 283 [Schubert's arr. for voice and orch of Stadler's Psalm viii, AII/4]

A. Feil and W. Dürr: 'Die neue Schubert-Ausgabe: über einige Probleme des Herausgabens von Musik', *ÖMz*, xxiv (1969), 553

R. van Hoorickx: 'About some Early Schubert Manuscripts', *MR*, xxx (1969), 118

I. Kecskeméti: 'Neu entdeckte Schubert-Autographe', *ÖMz*, xxiv (1969), 564

C. Landon: 'Neue Schubert-Funde', *ÖMz*, xxiv (1969), 299; Eng. trans., *MR*, xxxi (1970), 200

A. Orel: 'Schubertiana in Schweden', *Musa-mens–musici: im Gedenken an Walther Vetter* (Leipzig, 1969), 297

R. van Hoorickx: 'Two Essays on Schubert, I: Schubert's Variations, op.10, II: Ferdinand and Franz Schubert', *RBM*, xxiv (1970), 81

M. J. E. Brown: 'Schubert: Discoveries of the Last Decade', *MQ*, lvii (1971), 351

A. Weinmann: 'Zwei neue Schubert-Funde', *ÖMz*, xxvii (1972), 75 [version *a* of *Mut* D911, no.22; 4th setting of *Das Grab* D569 for chorus]

R. van Hoorickx: 'The Schubert Manuscript D.966', *ML*, liv (1973), 385

——: 'A Schubert Manuscript Identified', *MT*, cxv (1974), 127 [D966]

——: 'Un manuscrit inconnu de Schubert', *RBM*, xxviii–xxx (1974–6), 260 [*Über Wildemann* D884]

F. G. Zeileis: 'Bemerkungen zur Erstveröffentlichung einer bisher ungedruckten Komposition aus Franz Schuberts Studienzeit', *Beiträge zur Musikdokumentation: Franz Grasberger zum 60. Geburtstag* (Tutzing, 1975), 493

R. van Hoorickx: 'Some Unknown Schubert Manuscripts', *MT*, cxviii (1977), 1001

E. Hilmar: *Verzeichnis der Schubert-Handschriften in der Musiksammlung der Wiener Stadt- und Landesbibliothek* (Kassel, 1978)

R. Winter: 'Schubert's Undated Works, a New Chronology', *MT*, cxix (1978), 498

CONTEMPORARY ACCOUNTS

R. Bright: *Travels from Vienna through Lower Hungary, with some Remarks on the State of Vienna during the Congress in the year 1814* (Edinburgh, 1818)

J. C. von Zedlitz: 'Nachruf an Schubert', *Wiener Zeitschrift für Kunst und Literatur* (25 Nov 1828)

J. Mayrhofer: 'Erinnerungen an Franz Schubert', *Neues Archiv für Geschichte, Staatenkunde, Literatur und Kunst*, i/16 (1829), 23

L. von Sonnleithner: 'Biographie des Franz Schuberts', *Monatsberichte der Gesellschaft der Musikfreunde des österreichischen Kaiserstaates*, i/2 (1829), 19

J. Mailáth, ed.: *Leben der Sophie Müller* (Vienna, 1832) [diary references]

A. Schindler: 'Erinnerungen an Franz Schubert', *Niederrheinische Musikzeitung für Kunstfreunde und Künstler*, v (1857), 73, 81

H. von Chézy: *Unvergessenes: Denkwürdigkeiten aus dem Leben, von ihr selbst erzählt* (Leipzig, 1858), 259ff

I. F. Castelli: *Memoiren meines Lebens*, iv (Vienna, 1861), 123f

H. Hoffmann von Fallersleben: *Mein Leben: Aufzeichnungen und Erinnerungen*, ii (Hanover, 1868), 50ff

E. von Bauernfeld: 'Einiges von Franz Schubert', *Signale für die musikalische Welt*, xxvii (1869), 977, 993, 1009, 1025; Eng. trans., *Musical World* (15 Jan, 19 Feb 1870)

A. Fareanu: 'Leopold Sonnleithner: Erinnerungen an Franz Schubert', *ZMw*, i (1918–19), 466

J. von Spaun: *Neues um Franz Schubert: einige Bemerkungen über die Biographie Schuberts von Herrn Ritter v. Kreissle-Hellborn* [1865] (Vienna, 1934)

G. Schünemann, ed.: *Erinnerungen an Schubert: Josef von Spauns erste Lebensbeschreibung* [1829] (Berlin and Zurich, 1936)

O. E. Deutsch, ed.: *Schubert: die Erinnerungen seiner Freunde* (Leipzig, 1957, 3/1974; Eng. trans., 1958)

BIOGRAPHY

C. G. von Leitner: *Anselm Hüttenbrenner* (Graz, 1868)

C. von Würzbach: 'Schubert', *Biographisches Lexikon des Kaiserthums Oesterreich*, pt.32 (Vienna, 1876), 30–110

G. Grove: 'Schubert, Franz', *Grove 1*; repr. in *Beethoven, Schubert, Mendelssohn* (London, 1951)

L. Herbeck: *Johann Herbeck: ein Lebensbild von seinem Sohne* (Vienna, 1885), 162ff

M. Friedlaender: *Beiträge zur Biographie Franz Schuberts* (Berlin, 1887; Leipzig, 1928, as *Franz Schubert: Skizze seines Lebens und Wirkens*)

O. E. Deutsch: *Schubert-Brevier* (Berlin, 1905)

M. Vancsa: 'Schubert und seine Verleger', *Jahresbericht des Schubertbundes Vienna, 1905*, 47

E. Mandyczewski: *Geschichte der k. k. Gesellschaft der Musikfreunde*, suppl. (Vienna, 1912)

R. Schmekal: 'Grillparzer und die Gesellschaft der Musikfreunde in Wien', *Der Merker*, v (1915), 447

W. Schweisheimer: 'Der kranke Schubert', *ZMw*, iii (1921), 552

N. Flower: *Franz Schubert: the Man and his Circle* (London, 1928, 2/1949)

K. Kobald: *Franz Schubert und seine Zeit* (Zurich, Leipzig and Vienna, 1928; Eng. trans., 1928)

A. Orel: *Der junge Schubert: aus der Lernzeit des Künstlers* (Vienna, 1940/R1977)

F. Walker: 'Schubert's Last Illness', *MMR*, lxxvii (1947), 232

H. Goldschmidt: *Franz Schubert: ein Lebensbild* (Berlin, 1954, 5/1964)

M. J. E. Brown: *Schubert: a Critical Biography* (London, 1958/R1977, 2/1961; Ger. trans., 1969)

——: 'Schubert and Salieri', *MMR*, lxxxviii (1958), 211

——: 'Schubert's Early Association with the Kärntnertor-Theater', *MT*, c (1959), 261

——: 'Schubert: Discoveries of the Last Decade', *MQ*, xlvii (1961), 293

F. Hüttenbrenner: 'Anselm Hüttenbrenner und Schuberts H-moll Symphonie', *Zeitschrift des Historischen Vereines für Steiermark*, lii (1961), 12

O. E. Deutsch: 'Der "Mutwille" in Hütteldorf', *ÖMz*, xx (1965), 95

——: 'Ein Scherzgedicht aus der Schubertkreis', *ÖMz*, xxi (1966), 49

P. Ronge: 'Franz Schubert: der Mensch, Geschwister, Vorfahren, Lebenslauf: ein Beitrag zur Genealogie', *Genealogie*, xvi (1967), 721; see also xviii (1969), 534

M.-L. Kupelwieser de Brioni: *Une grande amitié: F. Schubert et L. Kupelwieser* (Paris, 1968)

P. Ronge: 'Katarina Laca a Franz Schubert', *SH*, xii (1968), 261

K. Stekl: 'Schuberts Aufenthalt 1827 in Graz', *Mitteilungen des Steirischen Tonkünstlerbundes*, xli (1969), July–Sept, 3

M. J. E. Brown: 'Schubert: Discoveries of the Last Decade', *MQ*, lvii (1971), 351

O. E. Deutsch: 'Schubert und die Königin Hortense', *ÖMz*, xxvii (1973), 121

H. Osterheld: *Franz Schubert: Schicksal und Persönlichkeit* (Stuttgart, 1978)

E. Sams: 'Schubert's Illness Re-examined', *MT*, cxxi (1980), 15

MUSICAL STYLE

G. Abraham, ed.: *Schubert: a Symposium* (London, 1947/R1969)

M. J. E. Brown: *Schubert's Variations* (London, 1954)

H.-W. Berg: *Schuberts Variationswerke* (diss., U. of Freiburg, 1958)

E. G. Porter: 'Schubert's Harmonies', *MR*, xviv (1958), 20

H. Goldschmidt: 'Die Frage der Periodisierung im Schaffen Schuberts', *BMw*, i/2 (1959), p.28

H. Truscott: 'Organic Unity in Schubert's Early Sonata Music', *MMR*, lxxxix (1959), 62

F. Braun: *Studien zur Dynamik in Schuberts Instrumentalmusik* (diss., U. of Tübingen, 1960)

H. Hollander: 'Zur Psychologie des Spätstils in Schuberts Musik', *Musica*, xiv (1960), 565

R. Rhein: *Franz Schuberts Variationswerke* (diss., Saarlandes-U., 1960)

E. Norman-McKay: 'The Interpretation of Schubert's *Decrescendo* and Accent Markings', *MR*, xxii (1961), 108

F. Eibner: 'The Dotted-quaver-and-semiquaver Figure with Triplet Accompaniment in the Works of Schubert', *MR*, xxiii (1962), 281

L. Misch: 'Ein Lieblingsmotiv Schuberts', *Mf*, xv (1962), 146

E. Seidel: *Die Enharmonik in den harmonischen Grossformen Franz Schuberts* (diss., U. of Frankfurt, 1962)

K. P. Bernet Kempers: 'Ganztonreihen bei Schubert', *Organicae voces: Festschrift Joseph Smits van Waesberghe* (Amsterdam, 1963), 7

R. Cox: *Choral Texture in the Music of Franz Schubert* (diss., Northwestern U., 1963)

E. Norman-McKay: 'Rossinis Einfluss auf Schubert', *ÖMz*, xviii (1963), 17

M. Chusid: 'Schubert's Cyclic Compositions of 1824', *AcM*, xxxvi (1964), 37

A. Feil: *Studien zu Schuberts Rhythmik* (Munich, 1966)

W. Riezler: *Schuberts Instrumentalmusik* (Zurich, 1967)

M. Boyd: 'Schubert's Short Cuts', *MR*, xxix (1968), 12

Yu. Khokhlov: *O slednem periode tvorchestva Shuberta* [The works of Schubert's last period] (Moscow, 1968)

M. K. Whaples: 'On Structural Integration in Schubert's Instrumental Works', *AcM*, xl (1968), 186

R. Bruce: 'The Lyrical Element in Schubert's Instrumental Forms', *MR*, xxx (1969), 131

H. Keller: 'Schuberts Verhältnis zur Sonatenform', *Musa–mens–musici: im Gedenken an Walther Vetter* (Leipzig, 1969), 287

A. Whittall: 'The Sonata Crisis: Schubert in 1828', *MR*, xxx (1969), 124

E. T. Cone: 'Schubert's Beethoven', *MQ*, lvi (1970), 779

D. Schnebel: 'Auf die Suche nach die befreiten Zeit: Versuch über Schubert', *NZM*, cxxxi (1970), 498

M. J. E. Brown: 'Schubert and some Folksongs', *ML*, liii (1972), 173

D. Coren: 'Ambiguity in Schubert's Recapitulations', *MQ*, lx (1974), 568

M. K. Whaples: 'Style in Schubert's Piano Music from 1817 to 1818', *MR*, xxxv (1974), 260

W. S. Newman: 'Freedom of Tempo in Schubert's Instrumental Music', *MQ*, lxi (1975), 528

L. M. Griffel: 'A Reappraisal of Schubert's Methods of Composition', *MQ*, lxiii (1977), 186

W. Gray: 'Schubert the Instrumental Composer', *MQ*, lxiv (1978), 483

ORCHESTRAL WORKS

R. Schumann: 'Die 7. Symphonie von Franz Schubert', *NZM*, xii (1840), 81

J. F. Barnett: 'Some Details concerning the Completion and Instrumentation of Schubert's Sketch Symphony in E', *PMA*, xvii (1890–91), 177

F. Weingartner: *Ratschläge fur Aufführungen klassischer Symphonien*, ii (Leipzig, 1919), 1

A. B. Smith: *Schubert*, i: *The Symphonies C major and B minor* (London, 1926)

E. Laaff: *Franz Schuberts Sinfonien* (Wiesbaden, 1933)

O. E. Deutsch: 'The Riddle of Schubert's Unfinished Symphony', *MR*, i (1940), 36

T. C. L. Pritchard: 'The Unfinished Symphony', *MR*, iii (1942), 10

M. J. E. Brown: 'Schubert's Unfinished Symphony in D', *ML*, xxxi (1950), 109 [D615]

O. E. Deutsch: 'The Discovery of Schubert's C major Symphony', *MQ*, xxxviii (1952), 528

A. Carse: 'Editing Schubert's Unfinished Symphony', *MT*, xcv (1954), 143

J. Reed: 'The "Gastein" Symphony Reconsidered', *ML*, xi (1959), 341

E. Laaff: 'Schuberts grosse C-dur-Symphonie: erkennbare Grundlagen ihrer Einheitlichkeit', *Festschrift Friedrich Blume* (Kassel, 1963), 204

M. J. E. Brown: 'Schubert's Italian Overtures', *MR*, xxvi (1965), 303

H. Hollander: 'Die Beethoven-Reflexe in Schuberts grosser C-dur-Symphonie', *NZM*, cxxvi (1965), 183

S. Kunze: *Franz Schubert: Sinfonie h-moll: Unvollendete* (Munich, 1965)

H. Truscott: 'Franz Schubert', *The Symphony*, ed. R. Simpson (Harmondsworth, 1966–7, 2/1972), i, 188

P. Hamburger: 'Schuberts "Ufuldente": kendsgeminger og formodninger' [Schubert's 'Unfinished': facts and assumptions], *Dansk musiktidsskrift*, xl (1967), 37

M. J. E. Brown: *Schubert Symphonies* (London, 1970)

G. Abraham: 'Finishing the Unfinished', *MT*, cxii (1971), 547

R. Weber: *Die Sinfonien Franz Schuberts im Versuch einer Strukturwissenschaftlichen Darstellung und Untersuchungen* (diss., U. of Münster, 1971)

P. Andraschke: 'Die Retuschen Gustav Mahlers an der 7. Symphonie von Franz Schubert', *AMw*, xxxii (1975), 165

J. Reed: 'How the "Great" C major was written', *ML*, lvi (1975), 18

CHAMBER WORKS

A. B. Smith: *Schubert*, ii: *Quartet in D minor and Octet* (London, 1927)

O. E. Deutsch: 'The Chronology of Schubert's String Quartets', *ML*, xxiv (1943), 25

H.-M. Sachse: *Franz Schuberts Streichquartette* (Munich, 1958)

H. Truscott: 'Schubert's D minor String Quartet', *MR*, xix (1958), 27

——: 'Schubert's String Quartet in G major', *MR*, xx (1959), 119

M. Chusid: *The Chamber Music of Franz Schubert* (diss., U. of California, Berkeley, 1961)

A. A. Abert: 'Rhythmus und Klang in Schuberts Streichquintett', *Karl Gustav Fellerer zum 60. Geburtstag* (Cologne, 1962), 1

M. Chusid: 'Schubert's Overture for String Quintet and Cherubini's Overture to *Faniska*', *JAMS*, xv (1962), 78

J. A. Westrup: *Schubert Chamber Music* (London, 1969)

M. J. E. Brown: 'Schubert's D minor Quartet: a Footnote', *MT*, cxi (1970), 985

H. Hollander: 'Stil und poetische Idee in Schuberts d-moll-Streichquartett', *NZM*, cxxxi (1970), 239

R. A. Coolidge: 'Form in the String Quartets of Franz Schubert', *MR*, xxxii (1971), 309

K. Marx: 'Einige Anmerkungen zu Schuberts "Forellenquintett" und Oktet', *MR*, cxxxii (1971), 588

M. Chusid: 'Concerning Orchestral Style in Schubert's Early Chamber Music for Strings', *Zur Aufführungspraxis der Werke Franz Schuberts: Wien 1974*

J. Gillett: 'The Problem of Schubert's G major String Quartet (D.887)', *MR*, xxxv (1974), 281

R. van Hoorickx: 'Schubert's Guitar Quartet', *RBM*, xxxi (1977), 111

M. Willfort: 'Das Urbild des Andante aus Schuberts Klaviertrio Es-dur D.929', *ÖMz*, xxxiii (1978), 277

PIANO WORKS

L. Scheibler: 'Zur Datierung von Schuberts Klaviersonate in A-dur, op.120'; 'Zur Datierung von Schuberts "Letztern Walzer"', op.127', *ZIMG*, viii (1906–7), 485; 487

H. Wetzel: 'Schuberts Werke für Klavier zu vier Hände', *Die Musik*, vi (1906–7), 36

W. Kahl: 'Das lyrische Klavierstück Schuberts und seine Vorgänger seit 1810', *AMw*, iii (1921), 54, 99

H. Költzsch: *Franz Schubert in seinen Klaviersonaten* (Leipzig, 1927/R1976)

M. J. E. Brown: 'An Introduction to Schubert's Sonatas of 1817', *MR*, xii (1951), 35

W. G. Hill: 'The Genesis of Schubert's Posthumous Sonata in B flat major', *MR*, xii (1951), 269

L. Nowak: 'Das Autograph von Schuberts Rondo in D-dur, op.138', *ÖMz*, viii (1953), 325

H. Truscott: 'The Two Versions of Schubert's op.122', *MR*, xiv (1953), 89

P. Mies: 'Der zyklische Charakter der Klaviertänze bei Franz Schubert', *Kongressbericht: Wien Mozartjahr 1956*, 408

H. Truscott: 'Schubert's Unfinished Sonata in C major', *MR*, xviii (1957), 114

A. Weinmann: 'Eine Plagiatsbeschildigung gegen Schubert', *ÖMz*, xii (1957), 19 [Trauerwalzer]

M. J. E. Brown: 'Schubert's "Trauer-Walzer"', *MMR*, xc (1960), 124

P. Mies: 'Die Entwürfe Franz Schuberts zu den letzten drei Klaviersonaten von 1828', *BMw*, ii/3 (1960), 52

P. Badura-Skoda: 'Unbekannter Eigenschriften bekannter Schubert-Werke', *NZM*, cxxii (1961), 502 [4 Impromptus D935]

A. Brendel: 'Die beiden Versionen von Schuberts "Wanderer-Fantasie"', *ÖMz*, xvii (1962), 56

M. J. E. Brown: 'Eine unbekannte Schubert-Handschrift', *NZM*, cxiv (1963), 92

——: 'Schubert: Three Dance-music Manuscripts', *Festschrift Otto Erich Deutsch* (Kassel, 1963), 226

A. L. Hanna: *A Statistical Analysis of some Style Elements in the Solo Piano Sonatas of Franz Schubert* (diss., Indiana U., 1965)

P. Radcliffe: *Schubert Piano Sonatas* (London, 1967)

F. Bisogni: 'Rilievi filologici sulle sonate giovanili di Franz Schubert (1815–17)', *RIM*, ii (1968), 453

M. J. E. Brown: 'Schuberts Fuge in E-moll', *ÖMz*, xxiii (1968), 65

R. van Hoorickx: 'A Schubert Autograph at the Brussels Conservatoire', *RBM*, xxii (1968), 109 [6 Polonaises op.61, D824]

——: 'Two Schubert Dances', *MR*, xxix (1968), 532

M. Hughes, L. Moss and C. Schachter: 'Analysis Symposium', *JMT*, xii (1968), 184–239; see also *JMT*, xiii, (1969), 128, 218 [Moment musical op.94 no.1 D780]

R. Klein: 'Schuberts "Kupelwieser-Walzer": Information zu seiner Überlieferung', *ÖMz*, xxiii (1968), 79

A. Tyson: 'Schubert and Terpsichore', *MT*, cix (1968), 812

D. A. Weekley: *The One-piano, Four-hand Compositions of Franz Schubert: Historical and Interpretative Analysis* (diss., Indiana U., 1968)

K. Stekl: 'Zur Auffindung eines unbekannten Klavierwerkes von Franz Schubert', *Mitteilungen des Steirischen Tonkünstlerbundes*, xxxix (1969), Jan–March, 1 ['Grazer Fantasie' D605a]

W. Dürr: 'Eine unbekannte Fantasia von Schubert', *ÖMz*, xxiv (1969), 569

R. van Hoorickx: 'Franz Schubert (1797–1828): List of the Dances in Chronological order', *RBM*, xxv (1971), 68

K. Stekl: 'Zwei wiederaufgefundene Schubert-Ländler', *Steirische Sängerzeitung*, xli (1971), 1 [D679]

J. P. Vogel: 'Die "Grazer Fantasie" von Franz Schubert', *Mf*, xxiv (1971), 168

K. M. Komma: 'Franz Schuberts Klaviersonate a-moll op.posth. 164 (D537)', *Zeitschrift für Musiktheorie*, iv/2 (1972), 2

K. Musiol: '"Sieben leichte Variationen in G-Dur", ein verschollenes Jugendwerk von Franz Schubert', *Mf*, xxviii (1975), 202

F. Bisogni: 'Rilievi filologici sulle sonate della maturità di Franz Schubert (1817–1828)', *RIM*, xi (1976), 71

W. Dürr: '"Sieben leichte Variationen in G" – von Schubert?' *Mf*, xxix (1976), 175

E. Sams: 'Schubert's Piano Duets', *MT*, cxvii (1976), 120

SACRED WORKS

E. Prout: 'Franz Schubert's Masses', *MMR*, i (1871), 2, 13, 26, 39, 53, 69, 84

O. Wissig: *Franz Schuberts Messen* (Leipzig, 1909)

M. J. E. Brown: 'Schubert's Settings of the "Salve regina"', *ML*, xxxvii (1956), 234

K. Pfannhauser: 'Zur Es-Dur-Messe von Franz Schubert', *NZM*, cxix (1958), 435

A. Bamer: 'Franz Schuberts Messen', *Singende Kirche*, lxxx (1960), 172; also in *Musica sacra*, lxxx (1960), 41

R. van Hoorickx: 'Schubert's "Pastoral" Mass', *ML*, xlii (1961), 53

R. S. Stringham: *The Masses of Franz Schubert* (diss., Cornell U., 1964)

K. J. Nafziger: *The Masses of Haydn and Schubert: a Study in the Rise of Romanticism* (diss., U. of Oregon, 1970)

F. Burkhart: 'Franz Schuberts "Deutsche Messe"', *ÖMz*, xxxi (1976), 565

R. van Hoorickx: 'Schubert and the Bible', *MT*, cxix (1978), 953

STAGE WORKS

F. Liszt: 'Alfonso und Estrella', *Gesammelte Schriften*, iii/1, trans. L. Ramann (Leipzig, 1881), 68

R. Krott: *Die Singspiele Schuberts* (diss., U. of Vienna, 1921)

M. J. E. Brown: 'Schubert's Two Major Operas', *MR*, xx (1959), 104

E. Norman-McKay: 'Schubert's Incidental Music to "Rosamunde"', *MR*, xxi (1960), 8

——: 'Publisher's Errors in Schubert's Overture to "Die Zauberharfe"', *MR*, xxiii (1962), 128

——: *The Stage-works of Schubert, considered in the Framework of Austrian Biedermeier Society* (diss., U. of Oxford, 1962–3)

F. Racek: 'Franz Schuberts Singspiel "Der häusliche Krieg" und seine jetzt aufgefundene Ouvertüre', *Biblos*, xii (1963), 136

E. Norman-McKay: 'Schubert's Music for the Theatre', *PRMA*, xciii (1966–7), 51

M. J. E. Brown: 'Schubert's *Fierrabras*', *MT*, cxii (1971), 338

M. J. Citron: *Schubert's Seven Complete Operas: a Musico-dramatic Study* (diss., U. of North Carolina, 1971)

W. Szmolyan: 'Schubert als Opernkomponist', *ÖMz*, xxvi (1971), 282

G. R. Cunningham: *Franz Schubert als Theaterkomponist* (diss., U. of Freiburg, 1974)

R. van Hoorickx: 'Les opéras de Schubert', *RBM*, xxviii–xxx (1974–6), 238

P. Branscombe: 'Schubert and his Librettists – 1', *MT*, cxix (1978), 943

CHORAL WORKS

V. Keldorfer: 'Schuberts Chorschaffen', *ÖMz*, xiii (1958), 257

P. Mies: 'Interessantes Schubertfragment aufgefunden: "Die Allmacht" für gemischten Chor', *Lied und Chor*, li (1959), 139

A. Niemeyer: 'Franz Schuberts "Lazarus"-Fragment und seine Beziehung zur Textdichtung', *GfMKB, Leipzig 1966*, 300

R. van Hoorickx: 'Schuberts Trio "Die Advokaten"', *RBM*, xxv (1971), 46

A. Weinmann: 'Eine österreichische Volkshymne von Franz Schubert', *ÖMz*, xxvii (1972), 430

SONGS

H. de Curzon: *Les Lieder de Franz Schubert* (Paris, 1899)

L. Scheibler: 'Franz Schuberts einstimmige Lieder nach österreichischen Dichtern', *Musikbuch für Österreich*, v (1908), 3–35

M. Bauer: *Die Lieder Franz Schuberts*, i (Leipzig, 1915) [only 1 vol. pubd]

H. G. Fiedler: 'Schubert's Poets', *ML*, vi (1925), 68

O. E. Deutsch: *Die Originalausgaben von Schuberts Goethe-Liedern* (Vienna, 1926)

R. Capell: *Schubert's Songs* (London, 1928/R1977, rev. 3/1973 by M. Cooper)

P. Mies: *Schubert der Meister des Liedes* (Berlin, 1928)

E. G. Porter: *The Songs of Schubert* (London, 1937)

E. Schnapper: *Die Gesänge des jungen Schubert vor dem Durchbruch des romantischen Liedprinzipes* (Berne and Leipzig, 1937)

E. Schaeffer: 'Schubert's "Winterreise"', *MQ*, xxiv (1938), 39

G. Mackworth-Young: 'Goethe's "Prometheus" and its Settings by Schubert and Wolf', *PRMA*, lxxix (1952–3), 53

M. J. E. Brown: 'Some Unpublished Schubert Songs and Song Fragments', *MR*, xv (1954), 93

T. G. Georgiades: '*Das Wirtshaus* von Schubert und das *Kyrie* aus dem gregorianschen Requiem', *Gegenwart im Geiste: Festschrift für Richard Benz* (Hamburg, 1954), 126

H. Haas: *Über die Bedeutung der Harmonik in den Liedern Franz Schuberts* (Bonn, 1957)

H. Brandenburg: 'Die "Winterreise" als Dichtung: eine Ehrenrettung für Wilhelm Müller', *Aurora*, xviii (1958), 57

M. J. E. Brown: 'Schubert's "Wilhelm Meister"', *MMR*, lxxxviii (1958), 4

A. E. F. Dickinson: 'Fine Points in "The Erl King"', *MMR*, lxxxviii (1958), 141

J. Mainka: *Das Liedschaffen Franz Schuberts in den Jahren 1815 und 1816: Schuberts Auseinandersetzung mit der Liedtradition des 18. Jahrhunderts* (diss., Humboldt U., Berlin, 1958)

J. L. Broeckx: 'Het vraagstuk van de tekstbehandeling in Schuberts Winterreise', *Antwerpen jb 1959*, 51–81

J. Kramarz: *Das Rezitativ im Liedschaffen Franz Schuberts* (diss., Free U. of Berlin, 1959)

E. G. Porter: *Schubert's Song-technique* (London, 1961)

J. Kerman: 'A Romantic Detail in Schubert's *Schwanengesang*', *MQ*, xlviii (1962), 36

V. Levi: 'Le arie e ariette di Schubert su testo italiano', *SMw*, xxv (1962), 307

G. Spies: *Studien zum Liede Franz Schuberts: Vorgeschichte, Eigenart* und *Bedeutung der Strophenvarierung* (diss., U. of Tübingen, 1962)

W. Gerstenberg: 'Schubertiade: Anmerkungen zu einigen Liedern', *Festschrift Otto Erich Deutsch* (Kassel, 1963), 232

P. Hauschild: *Studien zur Liedmelodie Franz Schuberts* (diss., U. of Leipzig, 1963)

A. Holschneider: 'Zu Schuberts "Frühlingsglaube"', *Festschrift Otto Erich Deutsch* (Kassel, 1963), 240

A. C. Bell: *The Songs of Schubert* (Lowestoft, 1964)

M. E. Grebe: 'Estudio analítico de "Der stürmische Morgen": un enfoque metodológico', *Revista musical chilena* (1964), no.18, p.87

M. J. E. Brown: 'Die Handschriften und Frühausgaben von Schuberts "Die Forelle"', *ÖMz*, xx (1965), 578

E. Seidel: 'Ein chromatisches Harmonisierungsmodell in Schuberts "Winterreise"', *GfMKB, Leipzig 1966*, 437; see also *AMw*, xxvi (1965), 285

J. M. Stein: 'Schubert's Heine Songs', *Journal of Aesthetics and Art Criticism*, xxiv (1966), 559

G. Baum: 'Schubert–Müllers *Winterreise* – neu gesehen', *NZM*, cxxviii (1967), 78

M. J. E. Brown: *Schubert Songs* (London, 1967)

T. G. Georgiades: *Schubert: Musik und Lyrik* (Göttingen, 1967)

P. Hamburger: 'Reprisebehandlingen i den Schubert'ske lied', *Dansk musiktidsskrift*, xliii (1967), 163, 196

F. D. Stovall: *Schubert's Heine Songs: a Critical and Analytical Study* (diss., U. of Texas, 1967)

M. J. E. Brown: 'The Therese Grob Collection of Songs by Schubert', *ML*, xlix (1968), 122

R. van Hoorickx: 'Notes on a Collection of Schubert Songs copied from Early Manuscripts around 1821–5', *RBM*, xxii (1968), 86

I. Kecskeméti: 'Eine wieder aufgetauchte Eigenschrift Schuberts', *ÖMz*, xxiii (1968), 70 [*Die Nacht* D534]

D. C. Ossenkop: *The Earliest Setting of German Ballads for Voice and Clavier* (diss., Columbia U., 1968)

L. E. Peake: *The Song Cycle: a Preliminary Inquiry into the Beginnings of the Romantic Song Cycle and the Nature of an Art Form* (diss., Columbia U., 1968)

E. T. Simpson: *A Study, Analysis and Performance of the Schwanengesang of Franz Schubert D.957* (diss., Columbia U., 1968)

D. Berke: 'Zu einigen anonymen Texten Schubertscher Lieder', *Mf*, xxii (1969), 485

J. Chailley: 'Le "Winterreise" et l'énigme de Schubert', *SM*, xi (1969), 107

J. P. Larsen: 'Zu Schuberts Vertonung des Liedes *Nur wer die Sehnsucht kennt*', *Musa–mens–musici: im Gedenken an Walther Vetter* (Leipzig, 1969), 277

E. Schwarmath-Tarján: *Musikalischer Bau und Sprachvertonung in Schuberts Liedern* (Tutzing, 1969)

H. H. Eggebrecht: 'Prinzipien des Schubert-Liedes', *AMw*, xxvii (1970), 89

D. B. Greene: 'Schubert's *Winterreise*: a Study in the Aesthetics of Mixed Media', *Journal of Aesthetics and Art Criticism*, xxix (1970), 181

G. Maier: *Die Lieder Johann Rudolf Zumsteegs und ihr Verhältnis zu Schubert* (diss., U. of Tübingen, 1970)

E. Brody and R. A. Fowkes: *The German Lied and its Poetry* (New York, 1971)

G. Estermann: *Die Klavierbegleitung im Sololied bei Schubert und Schumann* (diss., U. of Innsbruck, 1971)

D. Fischer-Dieskau: *Auf den Spuren der Schubert-Lieder: Werden, Wesen, Wirkung* (Wiesbaden, 1971; Eng trans., 1976)

W. Gray: 'The Classical Nature of Schubert's Lieder', *MQ*, lvii (1971), 62

W. Wiora: *Das Deutsche Lied* (Wolfenbüttel and Zurich, 1971)

W. Gerstenberg: 'Der Rahmen der Tonalität im Liede Schuberts', *Musicae scientiae collectanea: Festschrift Karl Gustav Fellerer* (Cologne, 1973), 147

B. Kinsey: 'Schubert and the Poems of Ossian', *MR*, xxiv (1973), 22

H. Lowen Marshall: 'Symbolism in Schubert's *Winterreise*', *Studies in Romanticism*. xii (1973), 607

S. Sorensen: 'Baek-motiver i Schuberts sange', *Festschrift Gunnar Heerup* (Egtved, 1973), 217

J. H. Thomas: 'Schubert's Modified Strophic Songs with Particular Reference to *Schwanengesang*', *MR*, xxiv (1973), 83

J. Armitage-Smith: 'Schubert's *Winterreise*, Part I: the Sources of the Musical Text', *MQ*, lx (1974), 20

M. Flothuis: 'Franz Schubert's Compositions to Poems from Goethe's *Wilhelm Meisters Lehrjahre*', *Notes on Notes: Selected Essays* (Buren, 1974), 87–138

M. and L. Schochow, eds.: *Franz Schubert: die Texte seiner einstimmig komponierten Lieder und ihre Dichter* (Hildesheim and New York, 1974)

J. Chailley: *Le voyage d'hiver de Schubert* (Paris, 1975)

A. Feil: *Franz Schubert: Die schöne Müllerin, Winterreise* (Stuttgart, 1975)

G. Moore: *The Schubert Song Cycles* (London, 1975; Ger. trans., 1975)

E. Sams: 'Notes on a Magic Flute: the Origins of the Schubertian Lied', *MT*, cxix (1978), 947

R. van Hoorickx: 'A Schubert Song Rediscovered', *MT*, cxxi (1980), 97

GENERAL STUDIES

R. Schumann: *Gesammelte Schriften über Musik und Musiker* (Leipzig, 1854, 5/1914/*R*1969)

H. Kreissle von Hellborn: *Franz Schubert* (Vienna, 1865; Eng. trans., 1869)

A. Reissmann: *Franz Schubert: sein Leben und seine Werke* (Berlin, 1873)

H. F. Frost: *Franz Schubert* (London, 1881, 2/1923)

A. Dvořák: 'Franz Schubert', *Century Magazine*, lxviii (1894), 341

R. Heuberger: *Franz Schubert* (Berlin, 1902, rev. 3/1920 by H. von der Pforten)

W. Klatte: *Franz Schubert* (Berlin, 1907)

W. Dahms: *Schubert* (Berlin, 1912)

O. Bie: *Franz Schubert: sein Leben und sein Werk* (Berlin, 1925; Eng. trans., 1928)

D. F. Tovey: 'Franz Schubert', *The Heritage of Music*, ed. H. J. Foss, i (Oxford, 1927), 82–122

P. Stefan: *Franz Schubert* (Berlin, 1928)

R. Bates: *Schubert* (London, 1934)

W. Vetter: *Franz Schubert* (Potsdam, 1934)

B. Paumgartner: *Franz Schubert* (Zurich, 1943, 2/1947)

A. Hutchings: *Schubert* (London, 1945, rev. 4/1973)

A. Einstein: *Schubert* (London, 1951/*R*1971; Ger. orig., 1952)

W. Vetter: *Der Klassiker Schubert* (Leipzig, 1953)

P. Mies: *Franz Schubert* (Leipzig, 1954)

T. Marek: *Schubert* (Kraków, 1955)

F. Hug: *Franz Schubert: Leben und Werk eines Frühvollendeten* (Frankfurt am Main, 1958)

H. Wagemans: *Schubert* (Haarlem, 1958)

M. Erdelyi: *Franz Schubert* (Budapest, 1962)

L. Kusche: *Franz Schubert: Dichtung und Wahrheit* (Munich, 1962)

J. E. van Ackere: *Schubert en de romantiek* (Antwerp, 1963)

K. Kobald: *Franz Schubert* (Vienna, Munich and Zurich, 1963)

A. Kolb: *Schubert* (Gütersloh, 1964)

J. Bruyr: *Franz Schubert: l'homme et son oeuvre* (Paris, 1965)

F. de Eaubonne and M.-R. Hofmann: *La vie de Schubert* (Paris, 1965)

M. J. E. Brown: *Essays on Schubert* (London, 1966/*R*1977)

W. Marggraf: *Franz Schubert* (Leipzig, 1967)

J. Reed: *Schubert: the Final Years* (London, 1972)

R. van Hoorickx: 'Old and New Schubert Problems', *MR*, xxxv (1974), 76

——: 'Schubert's Reminiscences of his Own Works', *MQ*, lx (1974), 373

COMMEMORATIVE

Die Musik, vi/7–8 (1906–7)

'Die intime Schubert', *Die moderne Welt* (Vienna, 1 Dec 1925) [Schubert suppl.]

Internationaler Kongress für Schubertforschung. Wien 1928

A. Weiss: *Franz Schubert: eine Festgabe* (Vienna, 1928)

MQ, xiv/4 (1928)

ML, ix/4 (1928)

ReM, x/1–3 (1928–9)

Ars (Buenos Aires, 1961), no.92

ÖMz, xxvii/4 (1972) [on Schubert interpretation]

ÖMz, xxxiii/6 (1978)

ÖMz, xxxiii/11 (1978)

MT, cxix (1978)

19th Century Music, iii/2 (1979)

MAURICE J. E. BROWN
(work-list and bibliography with ERIC SAMS)

Schubert, Johann Friedrich (*b* Rudolstadt, 17 Dec 1770; *d* Mülheim an der Ruhr, Oct 1811). German violinist and composer. After studying in his home town, in Frankenhausen (*c*1788) and in Sondershausen his skill on the violin and bassoon impressed E. L. Gerber, who drew him into the court concerts in Sondershausen. In 1791 he joined the orchestra of the Döbbelin Troupe in Berlin as second violinist and moved with it to Stettin (now Szczecin, Poland), where he was appointed director of music after the successful première of his opera *Die nächtliche Erscheinung* (1798). He was director of music at the theatre at Glogau (now Głogów, Poland) from 1801 and in a similar post with a theatrical society in Ballenstedt from 1804. Soon after, he became leader of the concerts of the Cologne Merchant Society in Mülheim.

Schubert's reputation as a composer was based on his opera and a few published works, including a violin concerto, violin duets and keyboard pieces. He was highly esteemed as a violinist, and wrote a voice method (1804) in which he followed Sulzer, Tosi and Hiller in their reliance on a systematic approach and a sound knowledge of literature.

WORKS
(all printed works published in Leipzig)

Die nächtliche Erscheinung (opera, 2), Stettin, 1789

Inst: 3 duos, 2 vn, op.1 (1804); 3 duos, 2 vn, op.2 (n.d.); 24 kleine Stücke, pf, op.3 (n.d.); Symphonie concertante, ob/cl, bn, orch, op.4 (n.d.); Vn Conc. (1805); Cl and Bn Conc., Fantasia, orch, both *A-Wgm*

Pedagogical: Neue Singe-Schule oder gründliche und vollständige Anweisung zur Singkunst in 3 Abtheilungen mit hinlänglichen Uibungsstücken (1804)

BIBLIOGRAPHY

GerberNL

G. Schilling: *Encyclopädie der gesammten musikalischen Wissenschaften oder Universal-Lexikon der Tonkunst* (Stuttgart, 1835–42/*R*1973)

H. Mendel and A. Reissmann: *Musikalisches Conversations-Lexikon* (Berlin, 1870–79, 2/1880–83 with suppl., 3/1890–91/*R*1969)

G. Schünemann: *Geschichte der deutschen Schulmusik*, i (Leipzig, 1928), 299

DIETER HÄRTWIG

Schubert, Joseph (*b* Warnsdorf, 1757; *d* Dresden, 28 July 1837). German violinist, violist and composer. He had his first music lessons from his father, a Kantor, then studied further in Prague and completed his training as a violinist in Berlin. His numerous works include four operas and many instrumental pieces, the latter group praised by Gerber.

JOHN WARRACK

Schubert, Louis (*b* Dessau, 27 Jan 1828; *d* Dresden, 17 Sept 1884). German violinist, singing teacher and composer. He went to St Petersburg in his 17th year and then as leader of the orchestra to Königsberg, where he remained until 1862. He then settled at Dresden, where he enjoyed a great reputation as a teacher of singing. He published a *Gesang-Schule in Liedern*, opp.18, 23–4 (Leipzig, *c*1868) and produced the operettas *Aus Sibirien* (Königsberg, 1856), *Das Rosenmädchen* (Königsberg, 1860), *Die Wahrsagerin* (Dresden, 1864), *Wer ist der Erbe?* (Dresden, 1865), *Die beiden Geizigen* and the opera *Faustina Hasse* (Altenburg, 1879).

GEORGE GROVE/R

Schubert, Manfred (*b* Berlin, 27 April 1937). German composer. He studied music education under Fritz Reuter and Slavonic studies at Berlin University (1955–60), and took part in Wagner-Régeny's master class at the German Academy of Arts in Berlin. In 1962 he was made music critic of the *Berliner Zeitung*. A deep interest in the Second Viennese School resulted in classical 12-note serial works such as the Flute Sonata; in the mid-1960s his interests turned to the music of contemporary Polish composers. Thus the first movement of his Septet is serial, while the second draws its tension from the opposition of serial and aleatory elements.

WORKS
(selective list)

Lieder (Morgenstern, E. Toller, I. Härtelt), Bar, pf/str orch, 1961; 2 pf sonatas, 1961, 1963; 2 str qts, 1963, 1970; 8 Lieder (Brecht), S, pf, 1964; Tanzstudien, orch, 1965; Sonata, fl, 1966; Paean, orch, 1966; Septet, 1967; Moments musicaux, 5 wind, 1967; Nachtstück und Passacaglia, 8 insts, 1968; Capriccieti, str qt, 1969; Divertimento, orch, 1970; Cl Conc., 1971; Konzertante Meditationen (Hommage à

Wagner-Régeny), harp, 13 str, perc, cel, 1972; Canzoni amorosi (J. Bobrowski), Bar, orch, 1973

Principal publisher: Deutscher Verlag für Musik

BIBLIOGRAPHY

E. Schwinger: 'Der andere Schubert', *Musica*, xxix (1974), 243

Schuberth. German family of musicians and music publishers.

(1) **Gottlob Schuberth** (*b* Karsdorf, 11 Aug 1778; *d* Hamburg, 18 Feb 1846). Instrumentalist. He received his musical education at Jena and learnt the violin from Stamitz. In 1804 he went to Magdeburg, where he lived for some years and was distinguished as an excellent clarinettist and oboe player. In 1833 he moved to Hamburg.

(2) **Julius (Ferdinand Georg) Schuberth** (*b* Magdeburg, 14 July 1804; *d* Leipzig, 9 June 1875). Publisher, son of (1) Gottlob Schuberth. He was the founder of the well-known firm of J. Schuberth & Co. at Leipzig and New York. After learning the business of a music publisher at Magdeburg, he started his own firm at Hamburg in 1826. He founded branch establishments at Leipzig (1832) and New York (1850). In 1854 he gave up the Hamburg business to his brother (5) Friedrich Schuberth and devoted himself to the Leipzig and New York branches. He edited a *Musikalisches Fremdwörterbuch* (Hamburg, 1840, 8/1870), a *Musikalisches Conversationslexicon* (Leipzig, 1850, 10/1877; Eng. trans., 1895), the *Kleine Hamburger Musik Zeitung* (1840–50), the New York *Musik Zeitung* (1867) and *Schuberths kleine Musik Zeitung* (1871–2). In 1840 he founded the Norddeutscher Musikverein and received many decorations in recognition of his services to music. In 1874 he settled at Leipzig. His business, which by 1877 had issued over 6000 publications including works by Mendelssohn, Chopin, Schumann and Liszt, was carried on after his death with increasing success by his widow and nephew until 1891, when it was bought by F. Siegel.

(3) **Ludwig Schuberth** (*b* Magdeburg, 18 April 1806; *d* St Petersburg, May 1850). Conductor and composer, son of (1) Gottlob Schuberth. He studied under his father and C. M. von Weber, and at the age of 16 was musical director at the Magdeburg Stadttheater. He was subsequently Hofkapellmeister at Oldenburg, and after living at Riga and Königsberg (1835) became in 1845 conductor of the German Opera in St Petersburg. His compositions include some published chamber music and unpublished operas and symphonies.

(4) **Carl Schuberth** (*b* Magdeburg, 25 Feb 1811; *d* Zurich, 22 July 1863). Cellist, conductor and composer, son of (1) Gottlob Schuberth. He learnt the piano from his father and the cello from L. Hesse. In 1825 he worked under Dotzauer at Dresden and in 1828 made his first concert tour to Ludwigslust and Hamburg. In 1829 he played in Copenhagen and Göteborg, but a series of misfortunes drove him back to Magdeburg, where he occupied the post of first cellist in the theatre orchestra. In 1833 he again played at Hamburg with success and during the next few years gave concerts in all the principal towns of north Germany, Belgium and Holland, besides visiting Paris and London (1835). In the autumn of 1835 he was appointed solo cellist to the tsar. He remained in St Petersburg for 20 years, occupying the posts of musical director at the university, conductor of the imperial court orchestra and inspector

of the Imperial Dramatic College. His compositions include chamber music and cello concertos.

(5) Friedrich (Wilhelm August) Schuberth (*b* Magdeburg, 27 Oct 1817; *d* after 1890). Publisher, son of (1) Gottlob Schuberth. He was the head of the firm of Fritz Schuberth at Hamburg from 1853, and lived in Hamburg at least until 1890.

WILLIAM BARCLAY SQUIRE/R

Schubiger, Anselm (Joseph-Alois) (*b* Uznach, 5 or 9 March 1815; *d* Einsiedeln, 14 March 1888). Swiss music scholar. He entered Einsiedeln monastery in 1835 and served as organist and musical director of the chapel (1842–59), for which he wrote a considerable amount of sacred music; he was ordained in 1839. His study of the choir school of St Gall from the 8th century to the 12th makes extensive use of the primary (but not always trustworthy) chronicle sources associated with St Gall; it includes colour facsimiles of early musical sources from St Gall and Einsiedeln as well as many transcriptions of sequences and other types of medieval chant, some from the earliest readable sources. He transcribed all but one of the larger sequence melodies (i.e. those with couplets) used by Notker, as well as four of the eight smaller, aparallel melodies; he included other sequences from the early repertory, and some by composers after Notker. This was a remarkable study in its time, and the transcriptions were not superseded in later publications. Schubiger's melodic readings, however, necessarily reflect the 12th- and 13th-century sources from which he transcribed; a more comprehensive approach to the sources will produce readings that are closer to Notker's own use, and better musically.

WRITINGS

Die Sängerschule St. Gallens vom achten bis zum zwölften Jahrhundert: ein Beitrag zur Gesanggeschichte des Mittelalters (Einsiedeln, 1858)
'Historische Irrthümer im Fache der Tonkunst', *MMg*, i (1869), 127
'Biographie C. D. Cossoni', *MMg*, iii (1871), 49
'Zur fünf- oder vierstimmigen Passion von J. Reiner', *MMg*, iv (1872), 213
Die Pflege des Kirchengesanges und der Kirchenmusik in der deutschen katholischen Schweiz (Einsiedeln, 1873)
Musikalische Spicilegien über das liturgische Drama, Orgelbau und Orgelspiel, das ausserliturgische Lied und die Instrumentalmusik des Mittelalters (Berlin, 1876)
'System der Lanten', *MMg*, viii (1876), 6
'Ueber Hucbalds Werk "De Musica"', *MMg*, x (1878), 24

RICHARD L. CROCKER

Schuch, Ernst Edler von (*b* Graz, 23 Nov 1846; *d* Kötzschenbroda, nr. Dresden, 10 May 1914). Austrian conductor. While a law student in Graz, he studied music with Eduard Stolz and directed the Graz Musikverein. At the time of his matriculation at Vienna, he was a student of Otto Dessoff. He was appointed music director of Lobe's theatre in Breslau in 1867 and then worked at Würzburg (1868–70), Graz (1870–71) and Basle (1871). In 1872 he was engaged by Pollini in Dresden, where he conducted opera for the first time in March that year. In August he became music director of the Hofoper and in 1873 Kapellmeister, at first sharing conducting duties with Julius Rietz, and from 1879 with Franz Wüllner. In 1882 Schuch assumed sole direction of the opera, and in 1889 became general music director. In spite of many engagements elsewhere in Germany and abroad (Berlin, Munich, Vienna, Paris, Rome, Moscow, St Petersburg, New York etc) he concentrated his activities in Dresden. In 1898 he was ennobled by Franz Joseph.

Schuch was responsible for the growth of the Dresden opera and orchestra to rank among the greatest in the world. During his tenure the Hofoper witnessed 51 world premières as well as the addition of 117 other works to the repertory. He conducted the premières of Strauss's *Feuersnot* (1901), *Salome* (9 December 1905), *Elektra* (25 January 1909) and *Der Rosenkavalier* (26 January 1911), brought Wagner's *Ring*, *Tristan und Isolde* and *Die Meistersinger von Nürnberg* to the Dresden stage, and introduced Puccini's operas and Mascagni's *Cavalleria rusticana* to German audiences; he also gave the first local performances of works by other contemporary composers, including August Bungert, Paderewski, Dohnányi and Wolf-Ferrari. Because he cultivated a particularly close working relationship with his orchestra and singers, it was with reluctance that he moved the rostrum back to the rail from the middle of the orchestra nearer the footlights, a position that had been used in Dresden for many years, during the regimes of Weber, Wagner and others.

Schuch also conducted the concerts of the opera orchestra, the Königliche Kapelle (later Staatskapelle), from 1877. On Palm Sunday 1884 he presented excerpts from *Parsifal*, and his programmes between 1901 and 1914 included, in addition to the Strauss symphonic poems, works by Mahler, Reger, Pfitzner, Debussy, Ravel, Stanford and Elgar, indicating the extent of his support of contemporary music. A man of wide culture and great intelligence, he was a conductor of exceptionally fine technique, taste and inspiration, whose regime of more than a quarter-century was one of the most brilliant periods of the musical history of Dresden.

Schuch was married to the singer CLEMENTINE SCHUCH-PROSKA. Their daughter, Liesel von Schuch, was a coloratura soprano of the Dresden opera.

BIBLIOGRAPHY

P. Sakolowsky: *Ernst von Schuch* (Leipzig, 1901)
A. Seidl: *Moderne Dirigenten* (Berlin, 1902)
F. A. Geissler: 'Ernst von Schuch', *Die Musik*, xi (1911–12), 364
C. Krebs: *Meister des Taktstocks* (Berlin, 1919), 169ff
A. Weissmann: *Der Dirigent im 20. Jahrhundert* (Berlin, 1925)
P. Adolph: *Vom Hof- zum Staatstheater* (Dresden, 1932)
F. Kummer: *Dresden und seine Theaterwelt* (Dresden, 1938)
H. Schnoor: *Dresden: 400 Jahre deutsche Musikkultur* (Dresden, 1948)
F. von Schuch: *Richard Strauss, Ernst von Schuch und Dresdens Oper* (Dresden, 1952, 2/1953)
E. Krause: 'Richard Strauss, Ernst von Schuch und Dresden', *Richard-Strauss-Ehrung*, ed. W. Höntsch (Dresden, 1963–4) [in *Blätter der Staatstheater Dresden*]
G. M. Henneberg and U. Püschel: 'Virtuosentum und Ensemble-gedanke', *300 Jahre Dresdner Staatstheater*, ed. W. Höntsch and U. Püschel (Berlin, 1967)

Schuchardt, Theodor (*b* Weberstedt, nr. Langensalza, 23 March 1601; *d* Eisenach, buried 25 July 1677). German composer and schoolmaster. He studied at Greifswald University, where he matriculated on 4 October 1621, and was then a schoolmaster at two places near his birthplace, first at Merxleben and from 1639 at Thamsbrück. From the beginning of 1644 until his compulsory retirement at the end of 1670 he was Kantor at Eisenach, where by about 1650 he brought the cultivation of church music to an astonishingly high level and where, as teacher of the third form at a school, he published new editions of language textbooks. The church music that he wrote at Eisenach consists of settings of German texts, several for large forces. Unique copies of works by Schütz and Schein transmitted by Schuchardt may indicate that he also had connections with Naumburg. In his own pieces in his principal work, *Threnodia sacra*, homophony and measured declamation of the words are combined with madrigalian characteristics: scoring for a five-part ensemble including two sopranos, division of the voices into contrasting groups, occasional word-painting and a certain amount of animated writing.

WORKS

Der Welt nichtige Vergänglichkcit, 8, 16vv (Erfurt, 1645), lost
Threnodia sacra, 4–6vv (Gotha and Eisenach, 1653)
Christliches Gespräch eines betrübten Vaters (Gotha, 1656)
Christi Blut und Gerechtigkeit, 8vv, inc., *D-WF*
Herr Gott Vater, mein starker Held, 8, 13vv, *BIB*
Herr, nu lässestu deinen Diener, 8vv, *BIB*
Nun danket alle Gott, 8vv, formerly *B*, now inc. *HAh*
Siehe, ich verkündige euch grosse Freude, 8vv, *BIB*
Wie bin ich doch so herzlich froh, 8vv, *BIB*

Several MS arrs. of other composers' works, *BIB*, *WF*

BIBLIOGRAPHY

W. Braun: 'Theodor Schuchardt und die Eisenacher Musikkultur im 17. Jahrhundert', *AMw*, xv (1958), 291
——: 'Das Eisenacher Begräbniskantional aus dem Jahre 1653', *Jb für Liturgik und Hymnologie*, iv (1958–9), 122
W. Steude: 'Neue Schütz-Ermittlungen', *DJbM*, xii (1967), 63

WERNER BRAUN

Schuchart, J(ohan) J(ust) (*b* ?Germany, *c*1695; *d* London, 1758). ?German wind instrument maker. He was living in London in the Savoy precinct by 1721 and very probably worked for Peter Jaillard Bressan. Bressan died in April 1731 and by midsummer of that year Schuchart had set up in Coventry Court, off the Haymarket. He moved subsequently to Panton Street in 1738, to Sherwood Street in 1748 and to Angel Court, Windmill Street, in 1756, where he made his will on 18 February 1757; it was proved on 17 September 1759. His son, Charles Schuchart (1720–65), was at the 'Two Flutes and Hautboy', 20 Chandos Street, in 1754, and was succeeded there by Thomas Collier in 1767 and John Hale, who was active 1785–1804.

A few recorders and an oboe by the elder Schuchart are known; these are marked 'I u I SCHUCHART', with a double-headed spread-eagle. This mark is very similar to that of Bressan. He can also be credited with an early attempt to extend the range of the flute. In 1756, in an advertisement in the *Daily Advertiser*, the flute maker John Mason claimed to have invented a flute descending to *d♭*. Charles Schuchart replied to this in the same paper on 10 and 13 September 1756, stating that his father made a pattern for a flute with an extended foot-joint (i.e. descending below *d*) in about 1726.

Thurston Dart (*GSJ*, x, 1957, p.85) conjectured that Schuchart was related to the composer Christian Schickhart.

BIBLIOGRAPHY

M. Byrne: 'The Church Bard at Swalcliffe', *GSJ*, xvii (1964), 89
——: 'Schuchart and the Extended Foot Joint', *GSJ*, xviii (1965), 7

MAURICE BYRNE

Schuch-Proska [née Procházka], **Clementine** (*b* Sopron, 12 Feb 1850; *d* Kötzschenbroda, nr. Dresden, 8 June 1932). Hungarian soprano. She studied at the Vienna Conservatory with Mathilde Marchesi, and from 1873 to 1904 was engaged at the Hofoper, Dresden, as leading coloratura soprano. In 1875 she married the conductor Ernst von Schuch. She first sang in Vienna in 1879, and made her Covent Garden début on 4 June 1884 as Eva in *Die Meistersinger*. She also appeared as

Aennchen in *Der Freischütz* and sang in Richter's London concerts. In April 1886 she made a guest appearance in Munich, singing Rosina (*Il barbiere di Siviglia*) and Susanna (*Le nozze di Figaro*). At Dresden in 1894 she took part in a revival of Haydn's *Lo speziale* (sung in German as *Der Apotheker*), which was also performed in Vienna the following year. Her repertory included Amina (*La sonnambula*), Blonde (*Die Entführung aus dem Serail*), Zerlina (*Don Giovanni*) and Violetta (*La traviata*); these, along with Eva, were her principal roles. Her voice was light, brilliant and flexible, and she had the impeccable technique of a Marchesi pupil.

BIBLIOGRAPHY

A. Ehrlich: *Berühmte Sängerinnen der Vergangenheit und Gegenwart* (Leipzig, 1895)

ELIZABETH FORBES

Schüchter, Wilhelm (*b* Bonn, 15 Dec 1911; *d* Dortmund, 27 May 1974). German conductor. He studied at the Cologne Hochschule für Musik with Abendroth and Jarnach and made his début in Coburg in 1937 conducting *Cavalleria rusticana* and *Pagliacci*. He held conducting appointments in opera houses in Würzburg (1937–40), Aachen (1940–42), where he worked closely with Karajan, and Berlin (Städtische Oper, 1942–3) and became a conductor for North German Radio, Hamburg, in 1947, as deputy to Schmidt-Isserstedt. He spent three years in Tokyo from 1958 as chief conductor of the NHK SO, returning to Germany in 1962 to become Dortmund's Generalmusikdirektor. His radical improvement of standards in Dortmund drew much attention within Germany and led to his eventual promotion in 1965 to the position of artistic director and general manager of the Dortmund Städtische Oper, which opened its new house in 1966. Schüchter remained at Dortmund until his death. His tenure was not without controversy, but he was generally considered the principal architect of Dortmund's musical advance in the late 1960s. His recordings are remarkable for their opulent and spacious orchestral sound but his interpretations were sometimes considered heavily Wagnerian, although his performances of Wagner's music dramas at Dortmund won warranted acclaim.

BIBLIOGRAPHY

H. Krellmann: 'Im musikalischen Alltag gestählt – Zum Tode des Dirigenten Wilhelm Schüchter', *Musica*, xxviii (1974), 471

LESLIE EAST

Schudi, Burkat. *See* SHUDI, BURKAT.

Schuëcker. American family of musicians of Austrian descent.

(1) Edmund Schuëcker (*b* Vienna, 16 Nov 1860; *d* Bad Kreuznach, 9 Nov 1911). Harpist and composer. He attended the Vienna Conservatory (1871–7), where he studied the harp under Antonio Zamara and graduated with honours. He was solo harpist in the Park Orchestra, Amsterdam (1877–82), the Parlow Orchestra, Hamburg (1882–3) and the Dresden Staatskapelle (1883–4). From 1884 to 1891 he played in the Gewandhaus Orchestra and taught at the Leipzig Conservatory; in 1890 he received the title *Kammervirtuos* from Ernest, Duke of Saxe-Altenberg. He declined an offer from the Boston SO in 1885 in favour of his brother (2) Heinrich Schuëcker, but in 1891 joined Theodore Thomas's newly founded Chicago

SO, returning each summer to direct the Vienna Harp College and give summer courses at Bad Kreuznach. In 1900 Mahler engaged him for the Vienna Court Opera, but he soon resigned because of his health and lived in Bad Kreuznach devoting himself to composition. He joined the Pittsburgh SO (1903–4) and from 1903 to 1906 also made trips to London to be special harpist for the Wagner operas at Covent Garden. From 1904 to 1909 he played with the Philadelphia Orchestra and the following year with the Metropolitan Opera, but over-work brought a complete collapse, and he retired to Bad Kreuznach. In addition to his brilliant Mazurka op.12 which continues to be a popular harp solo, Schuëcker published ten volumes of studies and melodies and seven volumes of orchestral studies selected from the harp parts of operas, symphonies and other works.

WORKS

Selective list; all pieces are for harp solo and, unless otherwise stated, were published in Leipzig without date.

Salon pieces: 2 Phantasiestücke, op.4; Erste Ballade, op.5; Nocturne, op.7; Serenade, op.10; Fantasia de bravura, op.11; Mazurka, op.12; Impromptu, op.13; Phantasie-Caprice, op.14; Am Springbrunnen, op.15; Elegie, op.16; 3 Stücke, op.17; 5 leichte Stücke, op.19 (Chicago, 1892); Legende, op.28 (Bayreuth, 1897); 3 Stücke, op.29; Menuett, op.32; Mazurka no.2, op.33; Fantaisie-appassionato, op.35 (Bayreuth, 1900); Elizabeth-Gavotte, op.37 (Bayreuth, 1900); Barcarolle, op.38 (Bayreuth, 1900); Remembrances of Worcester, op.40 (Bayreuth, n.d.); Henrica, nocturne, op.41 (Bayreuth, 1902); Träumerei, op.44

Studies: Etüden- und Melodien-Album, op.8 (Leipzig, ?1868); Etüden-Schule des Harfenspielers, op.18; 6 Virtuosen-Etuden, op.36 (Bayreuth, 1905); Die bedeutendsten Stellen aus Wagners Ring, Meistersinger und Parsifal (Mainz, n.d.); Orchesterstudien

Transcrs. of works by Berlioz, Jensen, Liszt, Mozart, Weber and others

BIBLIOGRAPHY

M. G. Scimeca: L'arpa nella storia (Bari, 1938), 169
A. N. Schirinzi: L'arpa (Milan, 1961), 138

(2) Heinrich Schuëcker (b Vienna, 25 Nov 1867; d Boston, Mass., 17 April 1913). Harpist, brother of (1) Edmund Schuëcker. He studied the harp under Zamara at the Vienna Conservatory (1878–84). After a season as solo harpist with the Parlow Orchestra he joined the Boston SO in 1885. He also taught at the New England Conservatory, and appeared as a soloist in London and Paris on various occasions. He died of a heart attack during a Boston SO concert.

(3) Joseph E. Schuëcker (b Leipzig, 19 May 1886; d Los Angeles, 9 Dec 1938). Harpist, son of (1) Edmund Schuëcker. He studied with his father and with Alfred Zamara at the Vienna Conservatory, and was solo harp-ist with the Pittsburgh SO during 1904–5 and 1908–9. In 1909 he succeeded his father in the Philadelphia SO and from 1911 to 1913 he was solo harpist with the Savage Opera Company in Boston. He taught and lec-tured on the history of the harp at the Carnegie Institute of Technology in Pittsburgh (1915–20), and in 1926 again joined the Pittsburgh SO, remaining until 1930 when he went to California.

ALICE LAWSON ABER

Schuh, Willi (b Basle, 12 Nov 1900). Swiss music critic and musicologist. He studied music with Eugen Kutschera and Werner Wehrli in Aarau, with Eugen Papst in Berne and with Walter Courvoisier in Munich, where he was also a composition pupil of Anton Beer-Walbrunn. He then studied art history and musicology in Munich with Sandberger (1922–4) and in Berne with Kurth (1924–7). He took his doctorate at Berne in 1927 with a dissertation on Schütz and in 1928 became music critic of the Neue Zürcher Zeitung, of which he

was subsequently also music editor (1944–65). He taught music history and harmony at the Winterthur Music School, the St Gall Handelshochschule and Zurich Conservatory (1930–44) and served as co-editor of the Mitteilungen der Schweizerischen musikfor-schenden Gesellschaft (1934–6) and as editor-in-chief of the Schweizerische Musikzeitung (1941–68). He was a committee member of the Schweizerischer Musikpädagogischer Verband (1931–9) and the IMS (1967–72), and is an honorary member of the Schweizerischer Tonkünstlerverein (1969) and the Schweizerische Musikforschende Gesellschaft (1971). He was awarded the Hans Georg Nägeli medal by the town of Zurich in 1963.

Schuh's work as a music critic for the Neue Zürcher Zeitung was of great importance to Swiss musical life. Building on the work of his predecessor, Ernst Isler, he gave his own stamp to opera and concert criticism. His carefully prepared reviews are of permanent value for their emphasis on the thorough analysis and evaluation of the work performed, particularly in the case of new or rare works. Many of his reviews have been repub-lished in the four volumes of Kritiken und Essays (1947–8, 1955) and in Umgang mit Musik (1970). Schuh's research has centred on the works of Richard Strauss, who chose him as his biographer; they were in continual contact from 1936 to the composer's death, and their correspondence was published in 1969. Schuh has also written on Renoir and Wagner, on the history of French ideas in the late 19th century and on works by Swiss composers, particularly those of Othmar Schoeck.

WRITINGS

Formprobleme bei Heinrich Schütz (diss., U. of Berne, 1927; Leipzig, 1928)
'Der harmonische Stil Othmar Schoecks', Neue Musik-Zeitung, xlix (1928), 466, 657
'Die Sterbegesänge des Meyerschen Totentanzes', Schweizerisches Jb für Musikwissenschaft, v (1931), 127
'Das Volkslied in der Schweiz', Die Schweiz die singt (Zurich, 1932), 25–66
Othmar Schoeck (Zurich, 1934) [speech inaugurating the Schoeck Festival in Berne, 1934]
'Zur Zwölftontechnik bei Ernst Křenck', SMz, lxxiv (1934), 217
'Caspar Diebold (1601–1674): sein Leben und seine Werke', Mitteilungen der Schweizerischen musikforschenden Gesellschaft, iii (1936), 8; also in Volkslied und Hausmusik, iii (1936), 90, 109, 126
ed.: Die Briefe Richard Wagners an Judith Gautier (Zurich, 1936)
ed.: Ferruccio Busoni: Briefe an seine Frau (Zurich, 1936)
Othmar Schoeck: Verzeichnis sämtlicher Werke, Bearbeitungen und Ausgaben (Leipzig, 1936)
ed.: Othmar Schoeck: Festgabe der Freunde zum 50. Geburtstag (Erlenbach, 1936) [incl. 'Zwei Schoeck-Miszellen (die Literarische; die Musiktheoretische)', 120]
'Die Musik in der Schweiz', Confoederatio helveticae, ii (Stuttgart, 1937), 349
ed.: H. von Hofmannsthal: Beethoven (Vienna, 1937, 2/1949)
ed., with H. Ehinger and E. Refardt: Schweizer Musikbuch (Zurich, 1939) [incl. 'Geschichte der Musik in der Schweiz: die neueste Zeit', i, 139–72]
'Idee und Tongestalt in Schoecks "Schloss Dürande" ', SMz, lxxxiii (1943), 74
Kritiken und Essays, i: Über Opern von Richard Strauss (Zurich, 1947)
Kritiken und Essays, ii: Zeitgenössische Musik (Zurich, 1947)
Kritiken und Essays, iii: Schweizer Musik der Gegenwart (Zurich, 1948)
In memoriam Richard Strauss (Zurich, 1949)
ed.: Richard Strauss: Betrachtungen und Erinnerungen (Zurich, 1949, rev. 2/1957; Eng. trans., 1955)
'Zum Melodie- und Harmoniestil der Richard-Strausschen Spät-werke', SMz, lxxxix (1949), 236
'Die Musik in der alemannischen Schweiz 1900–1950', Der Schweizerische Tonkünstlerverein im zweiten Vierteljahrhundert seines Bestehens (Zurich, 1950), 185–248
'Unvollendete Spätwerke von Richard Strauss', SMz, xc (1950), 392
'Die Entstehung des "Rosenkavaliers" ', Trivium, ix (1951), 65

'Richard Strauss' letzte Aufzeichnung', *Gestalt und Gedanke* (Munich, 1951), 32
ed.: *H. von Hofmannsthal: Briefwechsel* (Zurich, 1952, rev. 4/1970; Eng. trans., 1961)
Danae oder die Vernunftheirat (Frankfurt am Main, 1952)
'Kompositionsaufträge', *Alte und neue Musik* (Zurich, 1952), 41–105
'Zur Harmonik Igor Strawinskys', *SMz*, xcii (1952), 243; also in *Internationaler Musikkongress: Wien 1952*, 127
'Der Rosenkavalier: die ursprüngliche Fassung des II. Aktes', *Neue Rundschau*, lxiv (1953), 357–91
'Goethe-Vertonungen', *Goethe-Gedenkausgabe*, ii (Zurich, 1953), 665–739
ed.: *R. Strauss: Briefe an die Eltern* (Zurich, 1954)
ed.: R. Strauss and H. von Bülow: 'Briefwechsel', *Richard Strauss Jb 1954*, 7–88; Eng. trans., 1955
Kritiken und Essays, iv: *Von neuer Musik* (Zurich, 1955)
'Strawinsky und die Tradition', *Melos*, xxiii (1956), 308
ed.: *Igor Strawinsky: Leben und Werk, von ihm selbst* (Zurich and Mainz, 1957)
ed.: *Richard Strauss und Stefan Zweig: Briefwechsel* (Frankfurt am Main, 1957)
Renoir und Wagner (Zurich, 1959)
'Das Szenarium und die musikalischen Skizzen zum Ballett "Kythere" ', *Richard Strauss Jb 1959–60*, 84
'Zu Hofmannsthals "Ariadne": Szenarium und Notizen', *Neue Rundschau*, lxxi (1960), 84
'Richard Wagner und Judith Gautier: neue Dokumente', *SMz*, ciii (1963), 122
ed., with G. K. Kende: *Richard Strauss und Clemens Krauss: Briefwechsel* (Munich, 1963)
Ein paar Erinnerungen an Richard Strauss (Zurich, 1964)
Hugo von Hofmannsthal und Richard Strauss: Legende und Wirklichkeit (Munich, 1964)
with E. Roth: *Richard Strauss: Gesamtverzeichnis* (London, 1964)
ed., with others: *Schweizer Musiker-Lexikon* (Zurich, 1964)
'Musikbilder von Renoir', *Musikkollegium Winterthur: Generalprogramm 1965/66*, 5–41
'Der Sohn im Wort und in der Musik des Vaters', *Festschrift Dr. Franz Strauss* (Tutzing, 1967), 103
'Die Schweiz', *Symposium für Musikkritik: Graz 1967*, 49
Der Rosenkavalier: vier Studien (Olten, 1968)
'Ernest Chabrier, 1833–1881, musicien et poète maudit', *Aspekte der neuen Musik: Professor Hans Heinz Stuckenschmidt zum 65. Geburtstag* (Kassel, 1968), 68
'Marginalien zu Othmar Schoecks Penthesilea-Melodik', *SMz*, cviii (1968), 167
ed.: *Richard Strauss und Willi Schuh: Briefwechsel* (Zurich, 1969)
Umgang mit Musik: über Komponisten, Libretti und Bilder (Zurich, 1970, 2/1971)
'Hugo Wolf im Spiegel eines Tagebuchs: Unbekanntes aus Tagebüchern und Briefen', *SMz*, cxii (1972), 11, 73
'Walter Schulthess' Vertonung eines Distichons von Hugo von Hofmannsthal', *Dreissig Jahre Collegium Musicum Zürich* (Zurich, 1972), 7
'Metamorphosen einer Ariette von Richard Strauss', *Opernstudien: Anna Amalie Abert zum 65. Geburtstag* (Tutzing, 1974), 197
'Hofmannsthals Randnotizen für Richard Strauss zum "Ariadna"-Libretto', *Für Rudolf Hirsch, zum 70. Geburtstag* (Frankfurt, 1975), 224
'Zum Liedwerk Reynaldo Hahns', *Schweizer Beiträge zur Musikwissenschaft*, ii (1975), 103
Richard Strauss: Jugend und frühe Meisterjahre, Lebenschronik 1864–1898 (Zurich, 1976)
' "Trommelschläge": Othmar Schoecks Kriegsvision', *SMz*, cxvi (1976), 376

BIBLIOGRAPHY
SML [with list of writings to 1964]
H. Ehinger, E. Refardt and W. Schuh, eds.: *Schweizer Musikbuch* (Zurich, 1939), ii, 185 [with list of writings to 1939]
A. Briner and P.-A. Gaillard: 'Fünfundzwanzig Jahre Schriftleitung Dr. Willi Schuh', *SMz*, cvi (1966), 196
A. Briner: 'In Beziehung zu Strauss: "Richard Strauss – Briefwechsel mit Willi Schuh" ', *Neue Zürcher Zeitung* (1969), no.169
P. Sacher: 'Dr. Willi Schuh zum Abschied von der "Schweizerischen Musikzeitung" ', *SMz*, cix (1969), 58
[J. Stenzl]: 'Willi Schuh zum 75. Geburtstag', *SMz*, cxv (1975), 340

JÜRG STENZL

Schuijt, Cornelis (Floriszoon). *See* SCHUYT, CORNELIS.

Schuke. German family of organ builders. In 1894 Carl Alexander Schuke (*b* Stepenitz, 14 Aug 1870; *d* Potsdam, 16 Nov 1933) took over the Potsdam organ building business founded in 1820 by Gottlieb Heise

(1785–1848) and directed (until Schuke's acquisition) by Carl Eduard Gesell (1845–94); the firm was then known as Alexander Schuke. Carl Alexander had been a pupil of Gesell and studied also under Otto Dienel; he had worked for the firm of Sauer in Frankfurt an der Oder, and also acquired a first-hand knowledge of the style of German organs of the 17th and 18th centuries. His sons Karl-Ludwig-Alexander (*b* Potsdam, 6 Nov 1906) and Hans-Joachim (*b* Potsdam, 7 Jan 1908) directed the business jointly until 1953, when Hans-Joachim assumed the directorship of the Potsdam works (renamed VEB Potsdamer Schuke-Orgelbau in 1972) and Karl-Ludwig-Alexander that of the Berlin branch established in 1950 (renamed Karl Schuke, Berliner Orgelbauwerkstatt GmbH, in 1972). Karl-Ludwig was appointed to a lectureship at the Hochschule für Musik in Berlin-Charlottenburg in 1955, and to a professorship in 1962.

Organs built by the firm while the brothers directed it in partnership include those for the Ernst-Moritz-Arndt-Kirche, Berlin-Zehlendorf (1934–5; two manuals, 25 stops); Magdeburg Cathedral (the Remter organ, 1949; two manuals, 28 stops) and Schwerin Castle (1951; two manuals, 21 stops). The Schukes also restored historical organs, by Joachim Wagner, Arp Schnitger and Carl August Buchholz, and notably the instrument built by Friedrich Stellwagen in 1653–9 for St Marien, Stralsund (three manuals, 51 stops). Instruments built since 1953 by the Potsdam works include those for Divi Blasii, Mühlhausen (1958; three manuals, 42 stops); the Tchaikovsky Conservatory, Moscow (1959; two manuals, 26 stops); St Margarethen, Gotha (1960–; three manuals, 36 stops); the Philharmonia, Vilnius (from 1962; three manuals, 52 stops); St Michael, Jena (from 1962; three manuals, 51 stops); the Kreuzkirche, Düsseldorf (1966; three manuals, 45 stops); the Thomaskirche, Leipzig (1966; three manuals, 47 stops) and the Bulgaria Concert Hall, Sofia (1974; three manuals, 55 stops). The Berlin branch has built organs for: the Musikhochschule, Berlin (1955; four manuals, 70 stops); the Petrikirche, Mülheim an der Ruhr (1958–; four manuals, 58 stops); St Marien, Wolfenbüttel (1959–; four manuals, 53 stops); Brunswick Cathedral (1962; four manuals, 55 stops); the Kaiser-Wilhelm-Gedächtniskirche, Berlin (1962; four manuals, 63 stops); the Philharmonie, Berlin (1965; four manuals, 84 stops); the Kreuzkirche, Essen (1968; four manuals, 70 stops); the NHK Concert Hall, Tokyo (1973; five manual stops); the National Conservatory, Cologne (1975; three manuals, 36 stops); and Rutgers University, New Brunswick, NJ (1976; three manuals, 42 stops). In 1933 the Schukes abandoned the exhaust wind-chest with pneumatic or electro-pneumatic action in favour of the slider-chest with mechanical action. They are among those German organ builders who have made a particular point of incorporating the advantages of the Baroque organ into their own style of construction.

BIBLIOGRAPHY
T.-M. Langner: 'Schuke', *MGG*
K.-L. Schuke: 'Deutsche Orgellandschaft zwischen Elbe, Stralsund und Görlitz', *Acta organologica*, i (1967), 28

HANS KLOTZ

Schulhoff, Ervín (*b* Prague, 8 June 1894; *d* Wülzbourg, 18 Aug 1942). Czech composer and pianist. On Dvořák's advice he studied with Kaan at the Prague Conservatory (1904–6) and was then a pupil of Thern in Vienna, completing his education at the conservatories of Leipzig (1908–10) and Cologne (1911–14). He also took lessons with Reger and Debussy. In 1913 he won the Mendelssohn Prize for piano, and in 1918 that for composition. After service in World War I he returned to Prague before settling in Germany (1919–23). There he associated with new artistic groups, with Grosz and Klee, Däubler, the German dadaists and many leading young musicians. He planned a ballet with Tzara, but the project foundered. In Dresden (1919–20) he initiated a series of concerts 'Werkstatt der Zeit', providing a platform for works by the Second Viennese School and others. His own *Zehn Themen*, a piano cycle, was written to accompany some cubist-futurist lithographs by Otto Griebel.

Schulhoff returned to Prague to teach the piano; from 1929 to 1931 he also taught instrumentation and score-reading at the conservatory. As a pianist of unusual technical range he gave many recitals with an emphasis on new music: he was the first to play the quarter-tone pieces of Hába and his pupils. From the early 1920s he was active as a jazz pianist, also using jazz idioms in his compositions. He was a member of the Prague Theatre jazz orchestra led by Voskovec and Werich. In 1935–8 he worked for Czech radio in Ostrava and, for a short while, in Brno. He had been a communist from the early 1930s and after the Munich agreement he took Soviet citizenship; his political views and his Jewish origins led to his imprisonment during the German occupation, and to his death in a concentration camp. A versatile composer, Schulhoff readily responded to the trends of the day, from Germanic late Romanticism to impressionism, expressionism, the use of jazz, neo-classicism, socialist realism and Bartókian folklorism.

WORKS
(selective list)

Stage: Ogelala, ballet, K. J. Beneš, after Abbé Brasseur de Bourbourg, 1923; Plameny [The flames] (opera, 2, Beneš), 1927–8; La somnambule, dance grotesque, perf. 1931; incidental music
Orch: Suite, chamber orch, 1920; Pf Conc., 1922; 6 syms. incl. no.1, 1924–5, no.2, 1932, no.6 'Sym. of Freedom', 1941; Double Conc., fl, pf, str, 2 hn, 1927; Conc., str qt, wind, 1930
Vocal: HMS Royal Oak, jazz oratorio, 1930
Inst: 2 str qts, 1924, 1925; Concertino, fl, va, db, 1925; Sonata, vn, 1926; Divertissement, ob, cl, bn, 1926; Sonata, fl, pf, 1927; Sonata, a sax, pf, 1930
Pf: 10 Themen, 1918; 2 sonatas, 1924, 1926; many sets of pieces incl. Etudes de jazz, Esquisses de jazz, Hot music

Principal publishers: Schott, Universal

BIBLIOGRAPHY
E. Steinhard: 'Erwin Schulhoffs Musik zum "Bürger als Edelmann"', *Der Auftakt*, vii (1927), 50
K. B. Jirák: 'Schulhoffova Suita pro levou ruku', *Tempo*, vii (Prague, 1927–8), 256
K. Hába: 'E. Schulhoff: Sonate pour violon seul', *Tempo*, viii (Prague, 1928–9), 228
E. Steinhard: 'Modernmusiker Erwin Schulhoff', *Der Auftakt*, ix (1929), 80
——: 'Erwin Schulhoff: Flammen', *Der Auftakt*, xii (1932), 78
V. Helfert and E. Steinhard: *Die Musik in der Tschechoslowakischen Republik* (Prague, 1938), 177
A. Sychra: 'Dvě hudební vítězství z doby boje proti fašismu', *HRo*, ii (1949), 151
J. Stanislav: 'Ervín Schulhoff', *HRo*, vii (1954), 44
V. Hudec: 'Schulhoffův koncert pro smyčcový kvartet', *HRo*, xi (1958), 84
V. Stara, ed.: *Erwin Schulhoff* (Prague, 1958)
V. Musil: 'Příklad bojovníka', *HRo*, xvi (1963), 141
J. Ludvová: 'Ervín Schulhoff: pianista', *HV*, x (1973), 225 [with Ger. summary]
JOSEF BEK

Schuller, Gunther (*b* New York, 22 Nov 1925). American composer, conductor and teacher. The son of a New York PO violinist, he studied composition, flute and horn at the St Thomas Choir School (1938–42). His progress as a horn player was so rapid that he was soon playing professionally. After one season (1943) with the Ballet Theater Orchestra he was appointed principal in the Cincinnati SO (1943–5) and then in the Metropolitan Opera Orchestra (1945–59). His career as a composer also began early: at Cincinnati he was the soloist in his Horn Concerto (1944) and by 1959, when he gave up horn playing to give more time to composition, he had written over 30 works. Besides being a prolific composer, he has involved himself in work as a conductor, broadcaster, editor, writer, teacher and administrator. His teaching activities began at the Manhattan School of Music (1950–63) and continued at the Yale School of Music (teacher of composition 1964–7) and the New England Conservatory, of which he was president from 1967 to 1977. Under his dynamic leadership the conservatory became an important training establishment for teachers, composers and performers of contemporary and classical music, jazz and ragtime. He has also worked at Tanglewood as a composition teacher (from 1963), head of contemporary music activities (from 1965) and artistic co-director (from 1969).

Schuller's activities as a conductor have included the concert series Twentieth Century Innovations (Carnegie Hall, 1962–5), as well as guest appearances with major orchestras in North America and Europe. In 1970 he received the Ditson Conducting Award for 'his unselfish championship of fellow composers'. As a broadcaster he has made a series of 153 weekly radio programmes for WBAI, New York, on the course of music from 1900 to the 1960s, and in 1973 he wrote and introduced six programmes on contemporary music for Public Television. His writings include books on horn technique and jazz and several articles on contemporary music; the first volume of his two-volume history of jazz is a substantial contribution in an area which has lacked thorough analytical and historical treatment. Moreover, it is an articulate study by a composer–performer who is also a highly critical listener. The focus is on the musical developments observable in the principal styles of jazz, while the larger historical context is always in view. He has also prepared editions of works by Ives, Joplin and Weill.

As a composer Schuller is entirely self-taught. His interests cover the Western tradition as well as modern art and popular forms; but, though he draws on many sources, he is more syncretist than eclectic. His aim appears to be, at least in part, the amalgamation of diverse techniques, styles and aesthetics with a view to evolving hybrids possessing a new viability, adaptability and communicative power. Even his earliest published work, the Suite for wind quintet (1944), indicates a number of his preoccupations: the first movement has an *ABA* form contrasting a Phrygian tune accompanied by chords in sprung rhythm with a brief chromatic fugato; the second is a precisely notated blues fantasy; and the last is a rhythmically asymmetric, harmonically static toccata dominated by a brief diatonic motif. After this piece his development was marked by a protean assimilation of styles and genres, but especially of jazz, an unerring instinct for instrumental technique and orchestration, a decreasing dependence on textures of accompanied melody and a growing freedom in the modelling of sound masses, and the movement from a somewhat selfconscious rhetoric to a fuller integration of powerful gestures into the deeper structure.

Jazz has always been a source of stimulation to Schuller. In the 1950s he associated with jazz musicians who were beginning to incorporate more formal compositional procedures into their music; he worked particularly closely with John Lewis and the Modern Jazz Quartet. The term 'third stream music' was coined by him in 1957 to describe amalgamations of jazz and art music, and has gained wide currency. His own essays in this direction are much concerned with bringing principles of 12-note composition into jazz. At the same time he has derived powerful impulses from visual forms, and several of his works are intended as musical analogues of paintings or sculpture. In the *Seven Studies on Themes of Paul Klee* he sought a 'retranslation into musical terms of the "musical" elements in certain Klee pictures'. Such 'translations' range from close textural and thematic analogies to relationships at the level of structure or character. The first movement of the *American Triptych* 'portrays' a Calder mobile by means of four lines which rotate through four different orchestral 'orbits' or 'tracks' at different speeds, so that the spatial movement of sounds is composed. The work's other movements are a pointillist piece after Pollock's *Out of the West* and a jazz parallel of Davis's *Swing Landscape*.

Schuller has also drawn discriminatingly and creatively on techniques developed by the great composers of the 20th century: on Stravinsky's metrics, Schoenberg's serialism, Webern's orchestration, Varèse's manipulation of planes and volumes, and Babbitt's principles of combinatoriality. His Symphony (1965), in which serial analogues for diatonic functions are derived by combinatorial operations on the source set, is indicative of his radical conservatism in that it revives symphonic procedures that had been regarded as inappropriate to serial music.

WORKS
(selective list)
DRAMATIC

Journey to the Stars (film score), orch, 1962
Yesterday in Fact (film score), jazz qnt, 5 insts, 1963
The Visitation (opera, 3, Schuller, after Kafka), Hamburg, 12 Oct 1966
The Five Senses (television ballet), orch, 1967
The Fisherman and his Wife (children's opera, 1, Updike, after Grimm), Boston, 7 May 1970

ORCHESTRAL

Hn Conc., 1944; Vertige d'Eros, 1945; Sym. Study, 1947–8; Sym., brass, perc, 1950; Dramatic Ov., 1951; Recitative and Rondo, vn, orch, 1953; Sym. Tribute to Duke Ellington, 1955; Little Fantasy, 1957; Contours, 1958; Spectra, 1958; Concertino, jazz qt, 1959; 7 Studies on Themes of Paul Klee, 1959; Capriccio, tuba, orch, 1960; Contrasts, wind qnt, orch, 1960; Variants, jazz qt, orch, 1960; Journey into Jazz, narrator, jazz qnt, orch, 1962; Movts, fl, str, 1962; Pf Conc., 1962; Composition in 3 Parts, 1963; Diptych, brass qnt, band, 1963; Meditation, band, 1963; Threnos, ob, orch, 1963; 5 Bagatelles, 1964; American Triptych, 1965; Sym., 1965; Conc. for Orch 'Gala Music', 1965–6; Study in Textures, band, 1966; 5 Etudes, 1966; Triplum, 1967; Colloquy, 2 pf, orch, 1968; Db Conc., 1968; Fanfare for St Louis, 1968; Shapes and Designs, 1969; Consequents, 1970; Museum Piece, Renaissance ens, orch, 1970; Capriccio stravagante, 1972; 3 Nocturnes, 1973; 4 Soundscapes, 1975; Triplum II, 1975; Vn Conc., 1975–6; Hn Conc., 1977; Deaï, 2 orch, 1978

VOCAL

6 Early Songs (Li-Po), S, pf, 1943–4, orchd 1973; Meditations, 1960; 6 Renaissance Lyrics, T, 7 insts, 1962; 5 Shakespearean Songs, Bar, orch, 1964; Sacred Cantata (Ps xcviii), 1966; 7 Songs, S, pf; The Power within us, oratorio, Bar, narrator, chorus, orch, 1971; Poems of Time and Eternity (E. Dickinson), chorus, 9 insts, 1972

ENSEMBLE AND INSTRUMENTAL

For 8–16 insts: Atonal Jazz Study, 12 insts, 1948; Twelve by Eleven,

10 insts, 1955; Transformation, 11 insts, 1957; Abstraction, 9 insts, 1959; Conversations, jazz qt, str qt, 1959; Lines and Contrasts, 16 hn, 1960; Variants on a Theme of John Lewis, 11 insts, 1960; Variants on a Theme of Thelonious Monk, 13 insts, 1960; Double Qnt, wind qnt, brass qnt, 1961; Fanfare, 4 tpt, 4 trbn, 1962; Conc. da camera, 9 insts, 1971; 3 invenzioni, chamber ens, 1972

For 3–5 insts: Suite, wind qnt, 1944; Qt, 4 db, 1947; Perpetuum mobile, 4 hn, bn/tuba, 1948; Trio, ob, hn, va, 1948; 5 Pieces, 5 hn, 1952; Music, vn, pf, perc, 1957; Str Qt no.1, 1957; Wind Qnt, 1958; Fantasy Qt, 4 vc, 1959; Lifelines, fl, gui, perc, 1960; Music, brass qnt, 1961; Densities no.1, cl, harp, vib, db, 1962; Night Music, jazz qnt (b cl, gui, 2 db, drums), 1962; Little Brass Music, tpt, hn, trbn, tuba, 1963; Str Qt no.2, 1966; Aphorisms, fl, str trio, 1967; 4 Moods, 4 tubas, 1973; Sonata serenata, cl, vn, vc, pf, 1978

For 1–2 insts: Sonata, ob, pf, 1948–51; Duo Sonata, cl, b cl, 1949; Fantasy, vc, 1951; Recitative and Rondo, vn, pf, 1953; Fantasy, harp, 1959; Music, carillon, 1962; Studies, hn, 1962; Episodes, cl, 1964

Principal publishers: Associated, Modern Jazz Quartet, Universal

WRITINGS

Horn Technique (London and New York, 1962)
'American Performance and New Music', *PNM*, i/2 (1963), 1
'Conversation with Steuermann', *PNM*, iii/1 (1964), 22
'Conversation with Varèse', *PNM*, iii/2 (1965), 32
'The Future of Form in Jazz', *The American Composer Speaks*, ed. G. Chase (Baton Rouge, 1966), 216
Early Jazz: its Roots and Musical Development (New York, 1968)
'Composing for Orchestra', *PNM*, x/1 (1971), 185

AUSTIN CLARKSON

Schuloper (Ger.: 'school opera'). A German opera written for didactic use in schools; its suitability for performance by children is a secondary consideration. Early examples, which belong more strictly to the category of 'school drama', derived from 15th-century humanism and concentrated on religious training and the teaching of Latin; music was confined to choruses and short interludes. Although Singspiels were written for children during the 18th and 19th centuries, the *Schuloper* belongs to the 20th century. Interest in the idea was reawakened in the late 1920s through the influential musical Jugendbewegung and through the concern for amateur music shown by leading contemporary composers. The pedagogic content concentrated on the teaching of music, drama and a community spirit. The most important examples are Weill's *Der Jasager* (1930), which also encouraged political thinking, and Hindemith's *Wir bauen eine Stadt* (1930), the latter well suited to performance by children in junior and middle schools.

See also GEBRAUCHSMUSIK.

BIBLIOGRAPHY

RiemannL 12
K.-G. Hartmann and J. Bužga: 'Schuldrama', *MGG*
K. Weill: *Ausgewählte Schriften* (Frankfurt, 1975), 61ff

IAN KEMP

Schultheiss, Benedict (*b* Nuremberg, 20 Sept 1653; *d* Nuremberg, 1 March 1693). German composer and organist. He spent his whole life at Nuremberg. Like his contemporary Pachelbel, he was taught by Heinrich Schwemmer and G. C. Wecker; he also probably studied with Johann Dretzel. By the age of 17 he was playing the organ at services at the Augustinian church. In 1673 he became organist of St Walburg auf der Veste. In 1686 he became organist of the Frauenkirche and from 1687 until his death was organist of St Egidien.

The suites in his two volumes called *Muth- und Geistermunternde Clavierlust* (1679–80) follow the traditions of the Nuremberg school but also foreshadow at a modest technical level certain features typical of the later development of the keyboard suite. Schultheiss was the first German composer to adopt what later became the stereotyped order allemande–courante–sarabande–gigue, to which he added a prelude in the four suites of the 1679 set. He asked that 'the allemandes and sarabandes be played rather slow, and courantes and gigues rather faster and more freshly', so that by the change of tempo the suites might 'please honest feelings'. A variation-like connection between the movements of a suite is sometimes suggested but is not yet a conscious structural device. Schultheiss wrote his suites for a bourgeois circle of amateurs and wished to fill a gap with them 'because so far few such keyboard pieces have been published'. Seiffert's low opinion of them is based on wrong criteria, since he compared them with more ambitious virtuoso works written for professional musicians and aristocratic patrons. The suites are Schultheiss's only known secular music. After he joined, probably about 1680, the group of intellectuals and artists known as the Pegnesische Blumenorden, he was mainly interested in sacred songs, and he contributed 40 melodies with continuo to collections brought out by this circle. These continuo songs are aria-like and the vocal lines move mostly in quavers determined by the rhythm of the words, with occasional semiquaver figuration and sequences. Schultheiss also published in 1682 'orchestral' sacred songs with introductory sinfonias.

WORKS

Muth- und Geist-ermunternde Clavierlust (Nuremberg, 1679); 2 sarabands, gigue, ed. K. Herrmann, Altnürnberger Klavierbüchlein (Mainz, n.d.); 1 suite ed. H. Fischer and F. Oberdörffer, Deutsche Klaviermusik des 17. and 18. Jahrhunderts, ii (Berlin, 1935–6, rev. 2/1960)
Muth- und Geist-ermunternde Clavierlust, ander Theil (Nuremberg, 1680)
Hertz-Brüderlicher Glücks-Zuruff (Nuremberg, 1679), lost, authenticity doubtful
Nun der Kampf ist ausgekämpfet; Wenn Paulus dort brennt von der Gotteslieb: 1v, 1–4 str, bc, in A. Myhldorfer: Neumännischer loeblicher Abzug und lieblicher Einzug (Nuremberg, 1682)
40 sacred lieder, 1v, bc, in S. von Birken: Heiliger Sonntags-Handel und Kirch-Wandel (Nuremberg, 1681), H. Müller: Der geistlichen Erquick-Stunden ... poetischer Andacht-Klang (Nuremberg, 2/1691), W. C. Dessler: Gottgeheiligter Christen nützlich-ergetzende Seelen-Lust (Nuremberg, 1692)
9 melodies (1 with bc), ed. in J. Zahn: Die Melodien der deutschen evangelischen Kirchenlieder (Gütersloh, 1889–93/R1963)

BIBLIOGRAPHY

WaltherML
M. Seiffert: Geschichte der Klaviermusik (Leipzig, 1899), 194ff
E. von Rumohr: Der Nürnberger Tasteninstrumentalstil im 17. Jahrhundert (diss., U. of Münster, 1939), 49ff, 61
F. W. Riedel: Quellenkundliche Beiträge zur Geschichte der Musik für Tasteninstrumente (Kassel, 1960), 60f, 121, 127, 162
LINI HÜBSCH-PFLEGER

Schultheiss, Michael. See PRAETORIUS, MICHAEL.

Schulthesius, Johann Paul (*b* Fechheim, nr. Neustadt, 14 Sept 1748; *d* Livorno, 18 April 1816). German composer, keyboard player and priest. He received his earliest training in music from his father. After studying at the Gymnasium in Coburg (*c*1764–70) he entered Erlangen University where he completed his theological studies; while in Erlangen he also studied music with the organist and composer J. B. Kehl, who acquainted him with the keyboard sonatas of C. P. E. Bach. In 1773 he accepted the pastorship of the Netherlands and German businessmen's congregation in Livorno, where he continued his musical studies with Raniero Checchi and soon became known as an expert keyboard player and fashionable composer. He played a private recital of his own works in 1782 before Grand Duke Leopold of Tuscany and the Duchess of Parma, who turned pages

for him. In 1807 he was elected permanent secretary of the fine arts division of the Società Italiana di Scienze, Lettere ed Arti.

The keyboard figures prominently in Schulthesius's published works, which are chiefly 'characteristic' sets of variations. Of the *Sept variations* op.9 (dedicated to Forkel) a reviewer wrote: 'The theme is well chosen – interesting and clear, so that it is worth the trouble of varying. ... These [variations] are not so much those that one calls *brillant* than well considered; they are placed in good sequence, and knowledgeably composed' (*AMZ*, iii, 1800–01, col.750). Besides his *Memoria sulla musica da chiesa* (Livorno, 1810) he wrote short articles for the *Allgemeine musikalische Zeitung*. The fullest contemporary account of his life (possibly autobiographical) is in Gervasoni's *Nuova teoria di musica*.

WORKS

op.
1 Tre sonate, hpd/pf, acc. vn obbl (Livorno, *c*1780)
2 Sonata a solo, hpd/pf (Livorno, *c*1781)
2 Four Sonatas, hpd/pf, acc. vn obbl (London, *c*1784)
3 Two Quartets, hpd/pf, acc. vn, va, vc (London, *c*1785)
4 Otto variazioni facili, hpd/pf, vn, va, vc (Livorno, 1787), lost
5 Allegretto avec 12 variations, hpd/pf, acc. vn, va, vc (Basle, *c*1792)
6 Allegretto with 12 Variations, hpd/pf (Basle, n.d.), lost
6 Andantino grazioso de Mr Pleyel varié, hpd/pf, acc. vn, vc (Basle and Augsburg, n.d.)
8 Andantino avec 8 variations, hpd/pf (Basle, n.d.) [? pubd as op.7 in Augsburg]
9 Sept variations, pf (Augsburg, 1797)
10 Eight Variations on a Russian Air, hpd/pf (Livorno, n.d.), lost
11 Twelve New Variations on Marlborough's Air, hpd/pf, vn, va, vc (Florence, n.d.), lost
12 Riconciliazione fra due amici [L. Marchesi, Schulthesius] ... variazioni analoghe al soggetto, pf (Augsburg, 1803)
13 L'allegria sopra la suddetta riconciliazione, ?pf (?Livorno), lost
14 Eight Variations on an Original Theme, pf (Livorno, n.d.), lost
15 Variazioni sentimentali sopra tema originale, pf (Leipzig, *c*1812)
16 X variations sur un thème original, pf (Leipzig, *c*1812)
17 IX variazioni sopra tema originale e rondò, pf (Leipzig, 1814)
18 Sonata caratteristica, pf (Leipzig, *c*1816)

For unpublished works, see Gervasoni

BIBLIOGRAPHY

FétisB; GerberL
J. N. Forkel, ed.: Musikalischer Almanach 1784 (Leipzig, 1783/R); 1789 (1788/R)
C. Gervasoni: Nuova teoria di musica (Parma, 1812/R), 68ff
ELLWOOD DERR

Schulthess, Walter (*b* Zurich, 24 July 1894; *d* Zurich, 23 June 1971). Swiss composer and pianist. He was a pupil of Andreae in Zurich, of Courvoisier in Munich and of Ansorge in Berlin. In 1918 he was a conducting trainee at the Vienna Hofoper, and then he settled in Zurich as a concert agent, conductor and pianist, particularly as accompanist to his wife, Steffi Geyer. He founded the Konzertgesellschaft (1928) and the Collegium Musicum Zurich (1941). His small output includes violin pieces for his wife and some Stamm and Morgenstern lieder of intimate expression and transparent accompaniment.

WORKS
(*selective list*)

Vocal: Buddha Gautama, speaker, Bar, male chorus, 2 cl, fl, perc; 6 Lieder (M. Lienert) (1919); 6 Lieder (Hesse); 6 Lieder, op.4 (1920); 2 Gedichte, op.10 (Eichendorff), male chorus, orch (1924); Lieder (Stamm), 1928; 2 Liederzyklen (Morgenstern), 1941, 1943
Orch: Vn Concertino, op.7 (1921); Serenade, op.9 (1921); Symphonische Variationen, op.14, vc, orch (1926)
Inst: Variationen über ein eigenes Thema, op.1, pf (1914); Str Qt, op.5 (1921); Serenade, op.6, str trio (1921); 2 sonatas, vn, pf, op.8, 1921, op.11, 1922; 3 Capricen nach Paganini, vn, pf (1923); 3 Klavierstücke, op.12 (1924); Kleine Fantasiestücke, pf; Passacaglia, 2 vn, pf; Sonatine, vn, pf

Principal publishers: Hug, Schott

BIBLIOGRAPHY

W. Schuh: 'Schulthess' Vertonung eines Distichons von H. v. Hofmannsthal', *Dreissig Jahre Collegium Musicum Zurich* (Zurich, 1972), 7

PETER ROSS

Schultz [Schultze]. *See* PRAETORIUS family.

Schultz, Bartold. *See* PRAETORIUS, BARTHOLOMAEUS.

Schultz, Helmut (*b* Frankfurt am Main, 2 Nov 1904; *d* Waldenburg, Saxony, 19 April 1945). German musicologist. He attended the Leipzig Thomasschule and studied musicology at the university under Kroyer and at Vienna, and took the doctorate at Leipzig in 1928 with a dissertation on Johann Vesque von Püttlingen. In the same year he became an assistant at the musicology institute there and succeeded Kroyer a year later as its director. After completing his *Habilitation* in 1933 with a work on the form of the madrigal he became reader at Leipzig University. He also worked as director of the Heyer collection of musical instruments and the Saxon State Research Institute for Musicology. In addition to his writings about instruments Schultz made numerous performing and scholarly editions, in particular of works by Hugo Wolf and Haydn.

WRITINGS
Johann Vesque von Püttlingen 1803–1883 (diss., U. of Leipzig, 1928; Regensburg, 1931)
Die Karl Straube-Orgel des Musikwissenschaftlichen Instituts (Leipzig, 1929, 2/1930)
Führer durch das Musikwissenschaftliche Instrumenten-Museum der Universität Leipzig (Leipzig, 1929)
Instrumentenkunde (Leipzig, 1931, rev. 2/1954 by R. Eller)
Das Madrigal als Formideal (Habilitationsschrift, U. of Leipzig, 1933; Leipzig, 1939)
ed. with H. Zenck and W. Gerstenberg: *Theodor Kroyer Festschrift zum sechzigsten Geburtstage* (Regensburg, 1933) [incl. 'Das Orchester als Ausleseprinzip', p.169]
'Gesetze der Volksmusik', *JbMP 1934*, 51
Ludwig van Beethoven: sein Leben in Bildern (Leipzig, 1936)
Hugo Wolf (Berlin, 1937)
Giuseppe Verdi: sein Leben in Bildern (Leipzig, 1938)
'Tanzstil und Suite', *JbMP 1939*, 58

EDITIONS
J. Haydn: Symphonien Nr. 41–49, Werke, i/4 (Leipzig, 1908–32); *Symphonies 50–57*, Gesamtausgabe, i/5 (Leipzig, 1952)
with R. Haas: *H. Wolf: Lieder mit Klavierbegleitung*, Nachgelassene Werke, i/1–4 (Vienna and Leipzig, 1935)
Deutsche Bläsermusik vom Barock bis zur Klassik, EDM, 1st ser., xiv (1941)

BIBLIOGRAPHY
W. Gerstenberg: 'Helmut Schultz', *Mf*, ii (1949), 5

ALFRED GRANT GOODMAN

Schultz, Johann Abraham Peter. *See* SCHULZ, JOHANN ABRAHAM PETER.

Schultz, Johannes (*b* Lüneburg, baptized 26 June 1582; *d* Dannenberg, buried 16 Feb 1653). German composer and organist. He probably received his musical education at Lüneburg. However, he is not heard of until 1605: from that year until his death he was organist for the Brunswick-Lüneburg court at Dannenberg. His instrumental dances of 1617 are formally well within the German tradition of such pieces, and the *Thesaurus musicus*, which was planned as part of a year's cycle of motets, likewise owes much to tradition. Schultz turned again to secular music in most of the contents of his *Musicalischer Lüstgarte*, a collection of instrumental pieces, dance-songs, madrigals and motets arranged in ascending order of the number of parts. The older texts here are modelled on those of the songbook printed in 1536 by the younger Peter Schöffer and Matthias Apiarius. The presence of tenor cantus firmus parts even

at this late date – another illustration of Schultz's conservatism – is highlighted by the fact that the title-page of the tenor partbook is printed in red as well as black.

WORKS
40 neuwe ausserlesene schöne liebliche Paduanen, Intraden und Galliard, a 4 [with Passamezzo-Variationen, a 8] (Hamburg, 1617)
Thesaurus musicus continens cantiones sacras, a 3–9, 12, 16 (Lüneburg, 1621)
Musicalischer Lüstgarte, a 2–8 (Lüneburg, 1622); ed. H. Zenck, EDM, 2nd ser., *Niedersachsen*, i (Wolfenbüttel, 1937/*R*)
Epithalamium musicum, wedding motet, 8vv (Lüneburg, 1623)
Glückselig fried und freudenreich musicalisch New Jahres Wunsch, 7 motets, 4, 5, 8vv (Hamburg, 1645)
2 galliards, a 5, 1607²⁸ (? by Jacob Praetorius (ii))
Thesaurus musicus ecclesiasticus (1651), lost; cited in Schmieder
Teutsche Oster Historia, lost; cited in Siebeck, 73

BIBLIOGRAPHY
R. Siebeck: *Johannes Schultz, fürstlich Braunschweig-Lüneburgischer Organist in Dannenberg*, Beihefte der internationalen Musikgesellschaft, 2nd ser., xii (Leipzig, 1913)
B. Delli: *Pavane und Galliarde: zur Geschichte der Instrumentalmusik im 16. und 17. Jahrhundert* (diss., Free U. of Berlin, 1957), 172f, 189, appx
W. Schmieder: *Kataloge der Herzog-August-Bibliothek Wolfenbüttel*, xii (Frankfurt am Main, 1967)
R. Caspari: *Liedtradition im Stilwandel um 1600* (Munich, 1971)

HORST WALTER

Schultz, Svend S(imon) (*b* Nykøbing Falster, 30 Dec 1913). Danish composer. He studied the piano and composition at the Copenhagen Conservatory with Schierbeck and others (1933–8). He has worked as a teacher and as music critic for *Politiken* (1942–9) and was appointed choir conductor and instructor for Danish Radio in 1949. As a pianist and conductor he has toured Scandinavia, Italy and Switzerland with his own works. In his compositions he has concentrated on chamber music and vocal music. Danish chamber music of the 1930s was associated with a popular, entertaining style on a tonal, often neo-classical basis, and Schultz's chamber works have followed that trend. He has expressed more serious moods in the choral work *Job* and the symphonies (especially nos.3 and 4), which appear to be influenced by Sibelius, Prokofiev and Shostakovich. But easily accessible musical expression characterizes both his solo songs and most of his choral music. Through a series of short, often *buffo*-like operas for small ensembles he has continued with public success the Danish conversational opera of Børresen, Schierbeck and Jeppesen.

WORKS
(selective list)

DRAMATIC
Operas: Bag Kulisserne (Schultz), Copenhagen, 1949; Kaffehuset (opera buffa), 1949, withdrawn; Solbadet (Schultz), Århus, 1949; Høst (E. Falk-Rønne), Århus, 1950; Bryllupsrejse (opera buffa, H. Boland), Copenhagen, 1951; Hosekræmmeren, 1955, 1975 (2 versions); Tordenvejret (Falk-Rønne), Århus, 1955; Dommer Lynch, 1959
Operetta: Den kåde donna, Ålborg, 1957
Church drama: Eva (M. Balslev), 1968
Television operas: Hyrdinden og skorstensfejeren (marionette opera), 1953; Marionetterne, 1959; Konen i muddergrøften, 1965; Støv, 1969
School operas: Svinedrengen, 1970; Lykken og forstanden, 1972
Ballet: Sommerdanse, 1970
Pantomime: Det er ganske vist, 1948
Radio fantasies, solo vv, chorus, orch: Sankt Hans Nat, 1953; Prins Karneval, 1955
Incidental music, film scores, other radio music

OTHER WORKS
Orch: Serenade, str, 1940; Sinfonia piccola, 1941; Pf Conc. no.1, 1943; Ouverture champêtre, 1947; Sym. no.2, 1949; Pf Conc. no.2, 1951; Concertino, pf, str, 1953; Sym. no.3, 1955; Festouverture, 1957; Sym. no.4, 1957; Sym. no.5, 1960; Sym. no.6, 1962; Sinfonia piccola no.2, 1973

Vocal: Pan lo, solo vv, chorus, orch, 1944; Stormene suse, solo vv, chorus, orch, 1944; Job, solo vv, chorus, orch, 1945; Hr. Mortens klosterrov, solo vv, chorus, orch, 1958; De fire temperamenter, solo vv, chorus, orch, 1971; 4 madrigaler, chorus, 1971; 4 fragmenta ex Ovidii Ars amandi, chorus, 1972; solo songs

Chamber: Concertino, 4 vn, pf, 1936; Qt, fl, pf trio, 1936; Divertimento, fl, str trio, 1937; 6 str qts, 1939, 1940, 1960, 1961, 1962, 1975; Qnt, fl, str qt, 1944; Une amourette, wind qnt, 1945; Romantisk trio, vn, va, pf, 1960, withdrawn; sonatas, other pieces

Pf: Sonata, 1938; 2 sonatinas, 1940, 1950; Løvspring, suite, 1941; Concert-suite, 1945; Til Søren, suite, 1945; Moments musicaux, 1971

Principal publishers: Enstrøm & Sødring, Hansen

NIELS MARTIN JENSEN

Schultze. See PRAETORIUS family.

Schultze, Christoph (*b* Sorau [now Żary, nr. Wrocław], *c*20 Dec 1606; *d* Delitzsch, 26 Aug 1683). German composer. He himself fully charted the stages of his life: he went to school at Wittenberg (1619–20) and Torgau (1620–25), studied at Leipzig University (where he matriculated in 1627) and was Kantor at Neumarkt, Halle, from Easter 1628 to February 1633 and thereafter at Delitzsch. His worry and distress when his post at Delitzsch was imperilled by war and differences of opinion are reflected in numerous official and personal documents. Like a number of other composers in central Germany, Schultze identified strongly with the generation of composers 25 or so years older than himself who cultivated a more modern kind of church music. As a student at Leipzig he was influenced by Schein's late sacred works, three of which he transmitted in unique copies, and in Halle he was close to Scheidt. He knew the Catholic concertato settings of Latin words from the collected edition of Viadana and from Donfrid's *Promptuarium musicum*, both of which appeared in Germany in the early 1620s. It was typical of composers such as Schultze that the body of his church music, dependent upon earlier models, should, through his pronounced interest in form, show such a full and varied range of sound. In his music for few voices – parts of his sacred concertos, his pedagogical pieces and the 29 tuneful bicinia published in 1659 and 1664 – it must be admitted that intensive counterpoint typical of Scheidt is worked out in a way hardly conducive to a clear enunciation of the words. Schultze's *St Luke Passion* (1653) is the first notable dramatic Passion after Melchior Vulpius's *St Matthew Passion* (1613). It contains several features familiar from Schütz's Passions. The choruses – those early in the work are for four voices, the later ones for six – are generally plain in both texture and harmony. The supple recitatives are still based on the traditional Passion tone.

WORKS

Collegium musicum charitativum, 5vv (Leipzig, 1647)
Geduldig und gar kurze Zeit, 5vv, funeral song, *c* 4 Feb 1647
Anfang und Unterweisung . . . in der Singekunst (Leipzig, 1649) [incl. several pedagogical pieces]
Ich harre des Herren, 5vv, bc (Leipzig, 1650)
Lukaspassion, 4, 6vv (Leipzig, 1653)
11 pieces, 2vv, in B. Praetorius: Jauchzendes Libanon (Leipzig, 1659)
18 pieces, 2vv, in B. Praetorius: Spielende Myrtenaue (Leipzig, 1664)

Melodia cygnaea, 8vv, 1633, inc., *D-DL*
Grosse Hymnus-Buch, after 1635, *D*-Delitzsch, Superintendantut [incl. early version of Anfang und Unterweisung, dated 1638; fugues, *c*1649; 3 canons]
Klingender newes Jahres Wunsch ex psal. cxxxiii, 1662, *DL*
Furcht des Herren, ex. Syrac. xxxiv, motet, 8vv, 1682, *DL*
3 motets, 8vv, *MÜG*, inc.
8 sacred works, 4–6vv; 8 concertos; arrs. of works by other composers: *HAh* Kapell MS

LOST WORKS

Concerten mit Symphonien und Capellen elaboriret, 5vv, 1647, cited in foreword to Collegium musicum
Mutetten und Concerten, 5, 6, 8vv, 1647, cited in foreword to Collegium musicum
1 other sacred work, 1, 2vv, 1649, cited in foreword to Anfang und Unterweisung
Johannespassion, before 1654, cited in Grosse Hymnus-Buch
Kirchen-Zierde, up to 1682, cited in Furcht des Herren [60 pieces in 7 volumes]

BIBLIOGRAPHY

WaltherML
A. Werner: 'Zur Musikgeschichte von Delitzsch', *AMw*, i (1918–19), 537, 546
E. A. Fischer: 'Eine Sammelhandschrift aus dem Anfang des 17. Jahrhunderts', *AMw*, viii (1925–6), 430
W. Schulz: *Studien über das deutsche, protestantische monodische Kirchenlied des 17. Jahrhunderts* (diss., U. of Breslau, 1934), 75f
B. Smallman: *The Background of Passion Music* (London, 1957, rev. and enlarged 2/1970)
W. Braun: 'Der Kantor Christoph Schultze (1606–1683) und die "Neue Musik" in Delitzsch', *Wissenschaftliche Zeitschrift der Martin Luther-Universität Halle-Wittenberg, Gesellschaftswissenschaftlichsprachwissenschaftliche Reihe*, x/4 (1961), 1187–1225
——: 'Das "Grosse Hymnus-Buch" des Kantors Christoph Schultze', *Jb für Liturgik und Hymnologie*, vi (1961), 123

WERNER BRAUN

Schultze, Michael. See PRAETORIUS, MICHAEL.

Schultze, Norbert (*b* Brunswick, 26 Jan 1911). German composer. He studied conducting, composition and the piano at the Staatliche Hochschule für Musik in Cologne, then studied theatre in Cologne and Munich (1931). He was a composer and actor in a students' cabaret in Munich (1931–2), became an opera conductor in Heidelberg (1932–3) and Darmstadt (1933–4), then worked for the Telefunken record company (1934–5). From 1936 he was an independent composer for stage, films and television. In 1938 he composed the song *Lili Marleen* (Hans Leip), published and recorded in 1939 and made famous by Marlene Dietrich, Vera Lynn and others. From 1953 he owned a music publishing firm. Schultze's stage works include the fairy-tale opera *Schwarzer Peter* (Hamburg, 1936), the ballet *Struwwelpeter* (Hamburg, 1937), the musical *Käpt'n Bay-Bay* (Hamburg, 1950) and the operetta *Regen in Paris* (Nuremberg, 1954). For a minor part of his output he used the *noms de plume* Frank Norbert, Peter Kornfeld and Henri Iversen. His principal publishers are Sikorski (Hamburg) and Apollo-Verlag (Berlin and Frankfurt).

ANDREW LAMB

Schulz [Schulze]. See PRAETORIUS family.

Schulz [Schultz], **Johann Abraham Peter** (*b* Lüneburg, 31 March 1747; *d* Schwedt an der Oder, 10 June 1800). German composer and conductor. His father was a baker who planned a religious career for him, so he attended both of Lüneburg's Lateinschulen; but his interests lay chiefly with music, and he frequently appeared as soloist with various school and church choirs in Lüneburg. He studied music with the local organist J. C. Schmügel, who gave him violin, flute, keyboard and theory instruction. At the age of 15 he accompanied his mother to Lüchow for a family wedding, then continued alone to Berlin, where he sought out his musical heroes C. P. E. Bach and Joseph Kirnberger to enlist their help in his musical career. He was persuaded to complete his education in Lüneburg, but when he was 18 he returned to Berlin and Kirnberger accepted him as a pupil. In one of several later autobiographical sketches he complained that his three years of study with Kirnberger consisted almost entirely of the analysis and composition of chorales.

In 1768 Kirnberger recommended Schulz for the position of accompanist and music teacher to Princess Sapieha Woiwodin von Smolensk of Poland. Schulz travelled with the princess throughout Europe for three years, during which time he came into contact with a much wider range of musical ideas than he had known under Kirnberger. He was particularly impressed by Gluck's ideas, and met Grétry and Haydn (according to Reichardt). He also met Johann Reichardt in Danzig (1771) and the two became lifelong friends.

After visiting Poland, Schulz returned to Berlin in 1773. There Kirnberger enlisted his help in writing the music articles for J. G. Sulzer's encyclopedia *Allgemeine Theorie der schönen Künste*. Schulz wrote all the music articles from S to Z as well as assisting with and editing several others. He also assisted Kirnberger in writing *Die wahren Grundsätze zum Gebrauche der Harmonie*, although only the latter's name was credited when it was published in 1773.

In 1776, on Reichardt's recommendation, Schulz was appointed music director of the newly built French theatre in Berlin, and in 1778 he was given a similar position at the private theatre of the Prussian crown princess, Friederike Luise. In April 1780 he was appointed to yet another position with the Prussian royal family, as court composer in Rheinsberg to the king's younger brother Prince Heinrich.

Schulz was a champion of new music, producing French operettas along with operas by Gluck, Piccinni and Sacchini at these courts; this brought him into disfavour with the royal family and led to his resignation after seven years in Rheinsberg (1787). He then accepted an even more important position in the court at Copenhagen as Hofkapellmeister and director of the Royal Danish Theatre. There he reorganized the royal chapel, staged works which reflected society's concern for problems such as land reform, founded a benefit fund for musicians' widows and wrote a treatise on music education, *Gedanken über den Einfluss der Musik auf die Bildung eines Volks* (1790). This much-discussed essay reflected both his own aesthetic of folk-like lieder and the contemporary political and social developments in Copenhagen. As a result of his varied activities, Copenhagen became one of the leading musical centres of Europe.

Schulz was pensioned at an early age in 1795, having contracted tuberculosis. He sailed for Portugal that autumn, but his ship was forced ashore by bad weather at Arendal, on the southern coast of Norway, where he stayed the winter at great detriment to his health. The following spring he visited his birthplace in Lüneburg, then returned to Prussia. For the remainder of his life he divided his time between Berlin and Rheinsberg, with frequent visits to Schwedt for medical reasons.

Apart from a few compositions written while he was studying with Schmügel and Kirnberger, Schulz did not compose seriously until his return to Berlin in 1773. He set a prologue for Frederick the Great's birthday in 1774, but the three-act operetta *Clarissa, oder Das unbekannte Dienstmädchen* (Berlin, 1775) was his first large stage work; it was followed by several others in the next two decades. The 1770s also saw the publication of his only significant keyboard works: six pieces for harpsichord or piano (op.1, 1776) and a harpsichord sonata (op.2, 1778).

It was not until 1779 that he published his first collection of lieder (*Gesänge am Clavier*), the genre of composition for which he is best known and through which he exerted the greatest influence during his lifetime. It comprises folklike lieder in the style of the first Berlin lied school, with optional accompaniments secondary to the vocal line. Choosing texts by leading poets was a cause to which he addressed himself continuously; by using the poetry of outstanding literary figures such as Claudius, Voss, Bürger, Klopstock and Hölty, as well as Metastasio and Beaumarchais, Schulz set a standard of excellence for other lied composers.

His most influential collection was *Lieder im Volkston*. Its first two volumes were composed in Rheinsberg and the third in Copenhagen, but all three were published in Berlin (1782, 1785 and 1790). In the preface to the second volume Schulz outlined his aesthetic of lied composition: he intended to write lieder which would have the 'appearance of familiarity' to the listener on first hearing (thus resembling folk music), and further intended, in using only the work of the best poets, that the musical setting should reflect and enhance the meaning of the text, rather than being independent. This aesthetic, and Schulz's own simple, accessible style, influenced lieder into the 19th century.

Schulz was very influential in Denmark and has been called the pioneer of that country's national music (Gottwaldt and Hahne). His simple melodies and strophic forms remained standard for the songs of his pupil C. E. F. Weyse and other 19th-century Danish lieder composers. His choruses and stage works written there were important as embodiments of political ideas.

WORKS

STAGE

Das Opfer der Nymphen (prol, C. W. Ramler), for birthday of Frederick the Great, 1774; ?lost
Clarissa, oder Das unbekannte Dienstmädchen (operetta, 3, J. C. Bock), Berlin, 1775; 8 songs in Lieder im Volkston
Musique de l'impromptu (comédie avec ariettes, 1), c1779, *B-Bc*
La fée urgèle, ou Ce qui plait aux dames (comédie avec ariettes, 4, C. S. Favart), 1780–81, ?Rheinsberg, 1782; rev. and Ger. trans., Berlin, National, 1789, vocal score, *D-Bds*
La vérité (epilogue, G. de Morveau), Rheinsberg, 1784; ?lost
Panomphée (divertissement), c1785, lost
Athalie (tragedy, 5, J. Racine), Rheinsberg, 1785; rev. Berlin, Corsicascher Konzertsaal, 1786; choruses, songs, in Polyhymnia (Hamburg and Kiel, 1786)
Minona oder Die Angelsachsen (tragic melodrama, 4), Hamburg, 1786; lost
Aline, reine de Golconde (opera, 3, M. Sédaine), Rheinsberg, sum. 1787; vocal score, ed. C. F. Cramer (Copenhagen, 1790)
Indtoget (Singspiel, 2, P. A. Heiberg), 1789–90, Copenhagen, 26 Feb 1793; vocal score (Copenhagen, 1793)
Høstgildet (Singspiel, 1, T. Thaarup), Copenhagen, Royal Theatre, 16 Sept 1790; vocal score (Copenhagen, 1790)
Peters bryllup (Singspiel, 2, T. Thaarup), Copenhagen, 12 Dec 1793; vocal score (Copenhagen, ?1791)
Miscellaneous pieces for stage works, most in collections, incl. 1 for Die Hochzeit des Figaro, 2 for Le barbier de Seville, 1 for Goetz von Berlichingen

LIEDER

[25] Gesänge am Clavier (Berlin and Leipzig, 1779)
[48] Lieder im Volkston, i (Berlin, 1782, 2/1785); ii–iii (Berlin, 1785–90); Dan. trans. as Viser og sange (Copenhagen, 1792)
Johann Peter Uzens lyrische Gedichte religiösen Inhalts (Hamburg, 1784, 2/1794); Dan. trans. as Hellige sange forfattede af de tydske digtere Uz (Copenhagen, 1785)
Religiöse Oden und Lieder aus den besten deutschen Dichtern (Hamburg, 1786, 2/1792)
Gedichte von Friederike Brun, geboren Münter (Zurich, 1795) [incl. 7 set by Schulz]
Many others pubd singly and in 18th-century periodicals and anthologies

OTHER WORKS

Oratorios: Maria og Johannes (J. Ewald), Passion oratorio, 1787–8, vocal score, ed. C. F. Cramer (Copenhagen, 1789), score (Copenhagen, 1791); Christi død (J. Baggesen), Passion oratorio, Christiansborg, 1792, *D-Bds*; Frelserens sidste Stund (V. K. Hjort), Passion oratorio, Copenhagen, March 1794, Ger. trans., *Bds*; Das Lob Gottes, *A-Wn*

Cantatas: Vater, bester lebe, 1v, orch, Berlin, 1774, *D-Bds*; Universitets-kantata til dod af H. v. Stampe (T. Thaarup), Copenhagen, 1789; Kantata til Kronprinds Fredericks formoeling (Schönheyder), Copenhagen, 1790; Sorge-sange da Prindsesse Sophie Frederike bisattes (T. Thaarup), Roskilde, cathedral, 28 Dec 1794; Jesu Minde, Passion cantata, 1794; Der Versöhnungstod, 4vv, orch (Leipzig, 1810) [arr. from slow movts of J. Haydn: syms. H I: 93, 87, 98, 80, 99 and Str Qt H III: 74]; Dank ich Gott an deine Güte, 4vv, orch (Leipzig, 1811) [arr. from 2nd movt of J. Haydn: sym. H I: 104]

Miscellaneous sacred: Vor dir, o Ewiger (C. Lavater), motet, 4vv, in Reichardt: Musikalisches Kunstmagazin (Berlin, 1782); Gott Jehova sey hoch gepreiset (T. Thaarup), hymn, choir, orch, 1790, vocal score (Copenhagen, 1793); Jesu dydens milde lører (T. Thaarup), Passion motet, Copenhagen, 1790; Te Deum (T. Thaarup), Copenhagen, 1792; Gud, du es stor (E. Storm), hymn, 4vv, inst, 1792, *D-Bds*, and Lovsang (J. Baggesen), 1793, *Bds*, vocal scores, pubd together (Copenhagen, c1795); Lysenes vader (C. Friman, after Horace), hymn, 1793, *Bds*; Laudate Dominum omnes gentes, psalm, and Te splendor et virtus patris per vespera S Michaelis archangeli, hymn, both 4vv, inst, *A-Wn*; Zu Zions Höhen, 4vv, lost [formerly in library of the Singakademie, Berlin]; 2 choruses, 4vv, *D-Bds*; others in 18th-century periodicals

Other vocal: Aria de bravura: Moi seule au temple de mémoire, S, orch (Berlin, 1786), lost; Freund, ich achte nicht des Mahles, round, 2 S, T, B (Hamburg, ?1804); Ah, que l'amour est chose jolie, S, inst, and 21 polyphonic songs, *A-Wn*; 4 arias, *D-Bds*; Chansons italiennes (Berlin, 1782), cited in *GerberL*

Instrumental: 6 diverses pièces, hpd/pf, op.1 (Berlin and Amsterdam, 1776); Sonata, hpd, op.2 (Berlin, 1778); Largo, glass harmonica, in *AMZ*, ii (1799–1800), suppl.i; Sonate, kbd, vn, *D-Bds*; Waltzer and Eccossai, kbd, 1800, cited in *MGG*; Entractes, 2 vn, va, b, 2 bn, *B-Bc*; others in contemporary anthologies

WRITINGS

Music articles from S to Z (others collab. Kirnberger) in J. G. Sulzer: *Allgemeine Theorie der schönen Künste* (Leipzig, 1771–4 and later edns.)

with J. P. Kirnberger: *Die wahren Grundsätze zum Gebrauche der Harmonie . . . als Zusatz zu der Kunst des reinen Satzes in der Musik* (Berlin and Königsberg, 1773/R1974, 2/1793)

Entwurf einer neuen und leichtverständlichen Musiktablatur (Berlin, 1786)

Gedanken über den Einfluss der Musik auf die Bildung eines Volks (Copenhagen, 1790; Dan. trans., 1790)

Über den Choral und die ältere Literatur desselben (Erfurt, 2/1872) [1st edn. unknown]

BIBLIOGRAPHY

EitnerQ; GerberL; GerberNL

J. F. Reichardt: Biography, *AMZ*, iii (1800–01), cols.153, 169, 597, 613, 629

C. von Ledebur: *Tonkünstler-Lexicon Berlin's* (Berlin, 1861/R1965)

E. O. Lindner: *Geschichte des deutschen Liedes im XVIII. Jahrhundert*, ed. L. Erk (Leipzig, 1871/R1968)

M. Friedlaender: *Das deutsche Lied im 18. Jahrhundert* (Stuttgart and Berlin, 1902/R1970)

C. Klunger: *J. A. P. Schulz in seinen volkstümlichen Liedern* (Leipzig, 1909)

H. Kretzschmar: *Geschichte des neuen deutschen Liedes* (Leipzig, 1911/R1966)

O. Riess: *Johann Abraham Peter Schulz' Leben* (Leipzig, 1913); also in *SIMG*, xv (1913–14), 169–270

M. Seiffert: 'J. A. P. Schulz' "dänische" Oper', *AMw*, i (1918–19), 422

H. Gottwaldt, ed.: 'Drei Fragmente einer eigenen Lebensbeschreibung', *Lüneburger Blätter*, vi (1955); xi–xii (1961)

E. Schmitz: *Unverwelkter Volkslied-Stil J. A. P. Schulz und seine 'Lieder im Volkston'* (Leipzig, 1956)

G. Hahne, ed.: *Briefwechsel zwischen J. A. P. Schulz und J. H. Voss* (Kassel and Basle, 1960)

G. Hahne and H. Gottwaldt: 'Schulz, Johann Abraham Peter', *MGG*

G. Hahne: 'Johann Heinrich Voss' Versuch einer Gesamtausgabe der Lieder Johann Abraham Peter Schulz', *Mf*, xx (1967), 176

RAYMOND A. BARR

Schulz [Schulze], Johann Philipp Christian (*b* Langensalza, 24 Sept 1773; *d* Leipzig, 30 Jan 1827). German conductor and composer. He attended the Thomasschule in Leipzig and from 1787 appeared as a soprano in the Gewandhaus concerts. In 1793 he began studying theology at Leipzig University, but soon changed to music and became a pupil of the court organist Engel and of J. G. Schicht. In 1800 he was appointed conductor with Franz Seconda's theatre company in Leipzig, for which he also composed stage music. In 1810 he became director of the second Leipzig Singakademie and of the Gewandhaus concerts, where at first he conducted only secular vocal music; in 1816 he took over from Schicht as director of sacred works there as well. His post at the Singakademie connected him with the university, and in 1818 he was appointed music director there.

Schulz was most highly regarded as a singing tutor to amateurs. His few works include a number of quite popular lieder and partsongs, published by G. W. Finck in the *Musikalischer Hausschatz der Deutschen* (Gera, 10/1893) and *Die deutsche Liedertafel* (Leipzig, 1845), as well as in various separate editions; the canon *O wie wohl ist mir am Abend* is still popular. Published orchestral works, such as the Overture op.8 for Klingemann's *Faust*, demonstrate thematic development in the style of Haydn. Schulz also published a *Salvum fac regem* for chorus and orchestra, and Gerber mentioned stage music by him for Schiller's *Die Jungfrau von Orleans* and *Wallenstein*.

BIBLIOGRAPHY

GerberNL

Obituary, *AMZ*, xxix (1827), col.101

A. Dörffel: *Geschichte der Gewandhauskonzerte zu Leipzig* (Leipzig, 1884/R1972)

G. Hempel: *Von der Leipziger Ratsmusik zum Stadt- und Gewandhausorchester* (diss., U. of Leipzig, 1961)

GUNTER HEMPEL

Schulze. German family of organ builders. It comprised the founder Johann Andreas Schulze (c1740–1810), who built about 14 small organs (of which only one, at Kahla, survives); his son Johann Friedrich Schulze (*b* Milbilz, 27 Jan 1793; *d* Paulinzella, 9 Sept 1858), who studied with Ehle in Stadtilm, working independently from 1815 (from 1825 in Paulinzella); and three of the latter's five sons: Heinrich Edmund Schulze (*b* Paulinzella, 26 March 1824; *d* Paulinzella, 13 July 1878), who took over the management of the firm in 1858; Herward Schulze (c1830–1908), who designed and built the cases; and Eduard Schulze (1830–80). The firm worked in central Germany, building organs at St Marien, Mühlhausen (1820, three manuals, 42 stops); Weimar town church (1824–5, three manuals, 47 stops); St Benedikt, Quedlinburg (c1836, three manuals, 45 stops); Halberstadt Cathedral (1838; four manuals, 65 stops) and St Martini, Halberstadt (1838, three manuals, 4 stops); the market church (1840) and St Moritz, Halle (1847). It built organs in other parts of Germany, in Barmen, Berlin, Bremen Cathedral (three manuals, 60 stops), Düsseldorf concert hall, Elberfeld, Lübeck (St Marien; four manuals, 80 stops), Soest, Solingen, Sorau, Stolk, Wismar Cathedral (three manuals, 56 stops) and Verden Cathedral, and in Budapest, New Orleans and Riga. It had particular success in England with a small organ for the Great Exhibition in Hyde Park (1851) and a large organ for Doncaster parish church; it was consequently invited to build a large chamber organ (now in St Bartholomew's, Armley) for T. S. Kennedy's wife; and instruments in St Peter's, Harrogate; St Marylebone, London; Seaton Carew; St Mary's, Tyne Dock and Northampton Town Hall. By 1846 over 100 new organs had been produced by the Schulze firm.

The style of its organs was influenced by the meeting

of Johann Andreas Schulze and JOHANN GOTTLOB TÖP-
FER in 1824–5, during the alterations of Töpfer's organ
at Weimar. Schulze was sympathetic to Töpfer's ideas
on organ design and was prepared to put them into
practice. He subsequently designed his organs to include
a considerable number of 32′ (even on the manuals), 16′,
8′ and 4′ foundation stops, which blended unobtrusively
with the reed and mixture stops. The consequent reduction in importance of the diapason chorus was a decisive
step towards the Romantic ideal of organ sound. J. F.
Schulze's modifications were adopted and introduced
into England by his son Edmund Schulze. The firm's
craftsmanship was supported by considerable technical
knowledge; J. F. Schulze increased the wind pressure up
to a water-column of 120 mm (later reduced by Edmund
Schulze); the pipe's foot-holes were widened; pipes were
cut up higher and their mouths broadened. Broad scales
were preferred in the bass pipes but avoided for acoustical reasons in discant pipes, while flute and string stops
were constructed in a variety of forms. Tin and lead
were replaced by zinc and wood in large pipes. Curved
upper lips, nicks or notches in the languids, constant
scale proportions (Edmund Schulze later reverted to
variable proportions), swell organs, free reeds and
'decorative' pipes were usual, as were the fan-shaped
layout of the pedals, the Barker lever and fixed combinations. As a result of these innovations some contemporaries, notably C. F. G. Wilke, missed the sound of the
older organ; but others praised the 'wonderful mel-
lowness', 'the blending of the various ranks' and 'a very
subtle colouring of deep purple velvetiness' in the
diapasons. The influence of the Schulze firm (which
closed down in 1880) on German and English organ
building was considerable, and the following builders
could be described as belonging to the Schulze school:
J. K. Andrews (Hull), W. Berger (Halberstadt), J. J.
Binns (Leeds), B. J. A. Forster and T. C. Lewis
(London), P. Mehmel (Stralsund), F. Schmidt
(Gagerndorf) and J. Winzer (Rostock).

BIBLIOGRAPHY

J. G. Töpfer: *Die Orgelbaukunst, nach einer neuen Theorie dargestellt* (Weimar, 1833–4)
J. J. Seidel: *Die Orgel und ihr Bau* (Breslau, 1843)
W. Pole: *Musical Instruments in the Great Industrial Exhibition of 1851* (London, 1851)
J. G. Töpfer: *Lehrbuch der Orgelbaukunst nach den besten Methoden älterer und neuerer ... Orgelbaumeister und begründet auf mathematischen und physikalischen Gesetzen* (Weimar, 1855)
H. Sattler: *Die Orgel* (Langensalza, 1858, rev. 5/1873)
H. Jimmerthal: *Beschreibung der St. Marienorgel zu Lübeck* (Erfurt and Leipzig, 1859)
E. F. Richter: *Katechismus der Orgel* (Leipzig, 1864, 4/1896)
R. Spittel: *Die Stolper St. Marienorgel* (Stolp, 1933)
W. Stahl: *Die grosse Orgel der Marienkirche zu Lübeck* (Kassel, 1938)
G. Frotscher: *Deutsche Orgeldispositionen aus fünf Jahrhunderten* (Wolfenbüttel, 1939)
N. A. Bonavia-Hunt: *The Modern British Organ* (London, 1948)
W. L. Sumner: *The Organ: its Development, Principles of Construction and Use* (London, 1952, 4/1973)

HANS KLOTZ

Schulze [Schultze, Schultz, Praetorius], **Christian
Andreas** (*b* Dresden, *c*1660; *d* Meissen, 11 Sept 1699).
German composer. He is first heard of in 1669, when on
4 June he was sent to the Kreuzschule, Dresden. From
the winter term of 1675 he studied at Leipzig
University. He applied unsuccessfully for the post of
Kantor of the Annenkirche, Dresden, on 9 October
1677 and participated at the beginning of 1678 in operatic performances at Dresden. On the recommendation
of the Saxon Elector Johann Georg II he was appointed

Kantor of the municipal church and the municipal
Lateinschule – the Franciscaneum – at Meissen on 22
April 1678, and he also became Kantor of the cathedral
there. He held these positions for the rest of his life,
though probably from economic motives he applied,
unsuccessfully, for other posts as Kantor or teacher – in
1682 at Zittau, in 1694 and 1697 at his old school at
Dresden and in 1699 at Freiberg.

The vast majority of Schulze's surviving works are
sacred concertos for several voices – often tending towards the form of the cantata – or various kinds of early
Protestant church cantata: cantatas on biblical or liturgical texts (concerto cantatas), chorale cantatas and
those to mixed texts. They contain a good deal of fine
writing, in the manner of small-scale sacred concertos,
for one to three solo voices, including solo arias. There
are no recitatives. From the musical point of view the
Protestant chorale is of little importance in them: it is
used as a cantus firmus in only four cantatas.
Instruments play a prominent part. At the beginning of a
work there is always a sinfonia or sonata, and in many
cases arias are surrounded by ritornellos. Sometimes
there are obbligato parts including typically instrumental figuration, as in the virtuoso violin solos in the
cantatas *Delectare in Domino* and *Schaffe in mir*.
Schulze's very interesting *Historia resurrectionis* continued the tradition of such works leading from
Scandello through Schütz and Selle. It is the only extant
work of this kind from the late 17th century. The text is
a compilation from the Gospels by Johann Bugenhagen
that Schütz also used. The work is written in a vivid,
dramatic style without employment of the liturgical
Easter tone. The exordium (which has an introductory
sonata), the chorus of the disciples and the final
movement are concerto-like pieces in several parts. The
part of the Evangelist consists of affective recitative,
while the parts of Christ and the other soloists are in an
aria-like or dramatic style.

To sum up, Schulze's works stem from the motet-like
concertato style of 17th-century German Protestant
church music with its concern for the interpretation and
expression of the text. They hold an honoured place in
this tradition by virtue of their richness of form and
expression, in which elements of psalmody, dialogue and
quodlibet are found and in which the chiefly homophonic textures are enhanced by varied and colourful
harmony often resembling that of Buxtehude.

WORKS

Missa alla breve, 5vv, 2 cornetts, 2 vn, 2 va, bn, bc, *F-Ssp*
Historia resurrectionis Domini nostri Jesu Christi secundum quatuor evangelistas (Ger. text), 1686, 6vv, chorus 5vv, 2 piffari, 2 vn, 2 va/trbn, vle/bn/b trbn, bc, *D-Dlb*
Te Deum, 5vv, 2 tpt, 2 vn, 3 trbn, bn/timp, bc, *F-Ssp*

Animae iustorum in manu Dei sunt, 3vv, 2 vn, bn, bc, *D-Dlb*
Delectare in Domino (Ps xxxvii), 1v, vn, 3 va, vle, bc, *Dlb*
Duo seraphim stabant, 5vv, chorus 5vv, 2 vn, 2 va, bn, 2 cornettinos, 3 trbn, bc, *Dlb*
Laetatus sum (Ps cxxii), 5vv, chorus 5vv, 2 vn, 3 va, 2 piffari, 3 trbn, bc, *Dlb*
Media vita in morte sumus, 2vv, 2 vn, bc, *Dlb*
Omnia flumina currunt ad mare, 2vv, 4 vn, bc, *Dlb*
Quum me pulsat, 3vv, 2 vn, bn, bc, *Dlb*
Tu Christe deficis, 2vv, 2 vn, bc, *Dlb*
Veni Sancte Spiritus, 6vv, chorus 6vv, 2 piffari, 2 vn, 2 va, bn, timp, bc, *F-Ssp*

Aber deine Toten werden leben, 8vv, bc, *D-Dlb*, inc.
Ach Gott und Herr, wie gross und schwer, 7vv, chorus 6vv, 2 vn, va, bn, 4 trbn, bc, *F-Ssp*
Als der Tag der Pfingsten erfüllet war, 3vv, vn, cornett, trbn, bn, bc, *D-Dlb*, inc.
Als der Tag der Pfingsten erfüllet war, 4vv, 4 vn, bc, *Dlb*

Also heilig ist der Tag, 10vv, 2 vn, 2 va, bn, 2 cornetts, 3 trbn, bc, *Dlb*
Bessre dich Jerusalem, 5vv, 4 insts, bc, *Bds*
Das Blut Jesu Christi, 2vv, 3 insts, bc, *Bds*
Das ist meine Freude, 3vv, 6 insts, bc, *Bds*
Das Wort ward Fleisch, 6vv, 2 vn, 3 va, 2 ob, bn, bc, *LUC*
Der Gott Abraham, 5vv, chorus 5vv, 2 vn, 2 va, bn, 2 cornettinos, 3 trbn, bc, *F-Ssp*
Der Tod ist verschlungen in den Sieg, 1v, chorus 5vv, 2 ob, 2 t insts, bn, bc, *D-MÜG*
Es sei denn, dass jemand geboren werde, 5vv, chorus 5vv, 2 vn, 2 va, bn, bc, *F*
Habt nicht lieb die Welt, 6vv, chorus 6vv, 2 vn, 2 va, bn, bc, *F*
Herr Jesu Christ, du höchstes Gut, 5vv, chorus 5vv, 2 vn, 2 va, bn, bc, *F-Ssp*
Heut triumphieret Gottes Sohn, 1v, 2 vn, 2 va, bn, 2 cornettinos, 2 trbn, vle, bc, *D-Dlb*
Ich schreie mit einer Stimme zu Gott (Ps lxxvii), 5vv, 2 vn, 2 va, bn, bc, *F-Ssp*
Kommt all' herzu, ihr Engelein, 2vv, 2 vn, bc, *Dlb*
Meine Lieben und Freunde stehen gegen mir, 5vv, 2 vn, 2 va, bn/vle, bc, *Dlb*
Schaffe in mir, Gott, 1v, 2 vn, bn, bc, *LUC*, inc.
Seid böse ihr Völker, 5vv, chorus 8vv, 2 vn, 2 va, bn, 2 piffari, 3 trbn, bn, timp, bc, *Dlb*
Siehe, eine Jungfrau, 1v, 2 vn, bc, *LUC*, inc.
Singet um einander, 5vv, chorus 5vv, 2 vn, 2 va, bn, bc, *B*
So wahr ich lebe, 5vv, chorus 5vv, 5 insts, bc, *F*, inc.
Warum sollt' ich mich denn grämen, 5vv, chorus 5vv, 2 vn, 2 va, bn, bc, *F-Ssp*
Was du tust, so bedenke das Ende, 5vv, chorus 5vv, 2 vn, 2 va, bn, bc, *D-Dlb*, inc.
Wer mich liebet, 5vv, chorus 5vv, 2 vn, 2 va, bn, bc, *F*
Wie der Hirsch schreiet, 1v, 4 insts, bc, *Bds*

LOST WORKS

1 Magnificat, 2vv, 2 vn, vle, bc; 5 concertos, 1–10vv, 2–10 insts, bc: cited in 1696 inventory *D-Lm*
18 works, 1–10vv, 3–10 insts, bc; cited in inventory *c*1680–90, Fürstenschule, Grimma
1 work, 9vv/insts; cited in 1718 inventory, Ulrichskirche, Halle
1 concerto, 1v, 2 vn, 3 va, bc, cited in Gerber
3 occasional secular works, 1683–95, texts in *Dla*, authenticity doubtful

BIBLIOGRAPHY

EitnerQ; *GerberNL*; *WaltherML*
J. F. Lobstein: *Beiträge zur Geschichte der Musik im Elsass* (Strasbourg, 1840), 68f
H. Kreyssig: 'Verzeichnis der Lehrer an der Lateinschule zu Meissen von 1539 bis 1800', *Mitteilungen des Vereins für Geschichte der Stadt Meissen*, i/4 (1884), 45
H. Wittich: 'Die Erbhuldigung zu Meissen im Jahre 1692', *Mitteilungen des Vereins für Geschichte der Stadt Meissen*, iv (1897), 235
M. Seiffert: 'Die Chorbibliothek der St. Michaelisschule in Lüneburg', *SIMG*, ix (1907–8), 593
M. Seiffert: introduction to DTB, xxx, Jg.xviii (1917), p.xiii
K. Paulke: 'Musikpflege in Luckau', *Niederlausitzer Mitteilungen*, xiv (1918), 145
E. Noack: 'Die Bibliothek der Michaeliskirche zu Erfurt', *AMw*, vii (1925), 65
C. Süss: *Stadtbibliothek Frankfurt am Main: kirchliche Musikhandschriften des XVII. und XVIII. Jahrhunderts: Katalog* (Berlin and Frankfurt, 1926), 58
W. Serauky: *Musikgeschichte der Stadt Halle*: music examples and notes to ii/1 (Halle and Berlin, 1940/*R*1970), 70ff
F. Krummacher: 'Zur Sammlung Jacobi der ehemaligen Fürstenschule Grimma', *Mf*, xvi (1963), 324
——: *Die Überlieferung der Choralbearbeitungen in der frühen evangelischen Kantate* (Berlin, 1965)
B. Baselt: 'Actus musicus und Historie um 1700 in Mitteldeutschland', *Kongressbericht: Leipzig 1966*, 230
H. Kümmerling: *Katalog der Sammlung Bokemeyer* (Kassel, 1970)
PETER KRAUSE

Schulze, Hans-Joachim (*b* Leipzig, 3 Dec 1934). German musicologist. He studied musicology in Leipzig at the Hochschule für Musik (1952–4) and with Eller, Serauky and Besseler at the university (1954–7), where he took a diploma. Subsequently he became a research assistant (1957) and acting director (from 1974) at the Leipzig Bach Archive. His research has been entirely concerned with J. S. Bach; he has concentrated on biography and sources, and besides writing many articles on individual works has produced a documen-

tary biography. He was appointed co-editor of the *Bach-Jahrbuch* (1975) and also edited the fifth volume of *Bach-Studien* (1975). His editions of Bach's works include several facsimiles.

WRITINGS

'Bemerkungen zu einigen Kantatentexten Johann Sebastian Bachs', *BJb*, xlvi (1959), 168
'Marginalien zu einigen Bach-Dokumenten', *BJb*, xlviii (1961), 79
'Zur Identifizierung der anonymen Missa BWV anh. 24', *Mf*, xiv (1961), 328
'Frühe Schriftzeugnisse der beiden jüngsten Bach-Söhne', *BJb*, l (1963–4), 61
ed.: *Bach-Dokumente* (Leipzig and Kassel, 1963–72) [i–ii with W. Neumann]
'Randnotizen zu zwei kleinen Bach-Beiträgen', *Mf*, xvii (1964), 401
'Beiträge zur Bach-Quellenforschung', *GfMKB, Leipzig 1966*, 269
'Wer intavolierte Johann Sebastian Bachs Lautenkompositionen?', *Mf*, xix (1966), 32
'Johann Sebastian Bachs Kanonwidmungen', *BJb*, liii (1967), 82
'Das "Kleine Magnificat" BWV Anh.21 und sein Komponist', *Mf*, xxi (1968), 44
'Ein unbekannter Brief von Silvius Leopold Weiss', *Mf*, xxi (1968), 203
'Johann Sebastian Bach und Christian Gottlob Meissner', *BJb*, liv (1968), 80
'Neuerkenntnisse zu einigen Kantatentexten Bachs auf Grund neuer biographischer Daten', *Bach-Interpretationen: Walter Blankenburg zum 65. Geburtstag* (Göttingen, 1969), 22
'Das c-Moll-Trio BWV 585: eine Orgeltranskription Johann Sebastian Bachs?', *DJbM*, xvi (1971), 150
'Der Schreiber "Anonymus 400": ein Schüler Johann Sebastian Bachs', *BJb*, lviii (1972), 104
'J. S. Bach's Concerto-arrangements for Organ: Studies or Commissioned Works?', *Organ Yearbook*, iii (1972), 4
'Vier unbekannte Quittungen J. S. Bachs und ein Briefauszug Jacob von Stählins', *BJb*, lix (1973), 88
'Johann Sebastian Bachs Konzertübertragungen nach Vivaldi und anderen Studien- oder Auftragswerke?', *DJbM*, xviii (1973–4)
'Wie entstand die Bach-Sammlung Mempell-Preller?', *BJb*, lx (1974), 104
'". . . da man nun die besten nicht bekommen könne": Kontroversen und Kompromisse vor Bachs Leipziger Amtsantritt', *Wissenschaftliche Bach-Konferenz: Leipzig 1975*
'Die Bach-Überlieferung: Plädoyer für ein notwendiges Buch', *BMw*, xvii (1975), 45
'Ein "Drama per musica" als Kirchenmusik: zu Wilhelm Friedemann Bachs Aufführungen der Huldigungskantate BWV 205a', *BJb*, lxi (1975), 133
Johann Sebastian Bach: Leben und Werk in Dokumenten (Leipzig, 1975)
'Johann Sebastian Bach und Georg Gottfried Wagner: neue Dokumente', *Bach-Studien*, v (1975), 147
'Melodiezitate und Mehrtextigkeit in der Bauernkantate und in den Goldberg-Variationen', *BJb*, lxii (1976), 58
Katalog der Sammlung Manfred Gorke: Bachiana und andere Handschriften und Drucke des 18. und frühen 19. Jahrhunderts (Leipzig, in preparation)

Schuman, William (Howard) (*b* New York, 4 Aug 1910). American composer and teacher. After two years of study at the School of Commerce of New York University, he entered the Malkin Conservatory, New York, in 1930 to study harmony with Max Persin and counterpoint and composition with Charles Haubiel. While still a high school student he had organized and performed in jazz bands, and by 1935 he had written more than 150 popular songs, some of them in collaboration with Edwin B. Marks jr and Frank Loesser. Schuman's studies were continued at Teachers College, Columbia University (1933–7), where he received the BS in 1935 and the MA in 1937; during the summer of 1935 he earned a certificate in conducting at the Salzburg Mozarteum. In 1936 he began two years of study with Roy Harris at the Juilliard School; Harris proved to be a dominant and enduring influence on Schuman's music, and he was responsible for bringing Schuman to the attention of Copland and Koussevitzky. The latter performed the Second Symphony with the Boston SO, and conducted the first performances of the

American Festival Overture (1939), the Symphony no.3 (1941, awarded the first New York Critics' Circle Award), *A Free Song* (1943, awarded the first Pulitzer Prize in music) and the Symphony for Strings (1943).

The public and critical success of the Third Symphony established Schuman as one of the leading composers of the USA, and since that time his music has been widely performed. Almost as important as his compositional career has been his work as a teacher and administrator, first at Sarah Lawrence College (1935–45), where he was responsible for introducing the study of music of all periods in theory courses. After serving for four months as director of publications for G. Schirmer, he was appointed president of the Juilliard School in 1945, and by 1948 he had fused the usual theory curriculum into a course on the 'Literature and Materials of Music'. He appointed a number of prominent American composers to the staff, among them Bergsma, Mennin, Persichetti and Weisgall, and an exposition of his approach to music education appeared as *The Juilliard Report* (1953). Another of Schuman's innovations was the formation of the Juilliard Quartet, which became the model for many quartets-in-residence at American colleges.

In 1962 Schuman was made president of the Lincoln Center in New York, a position which gave him great power in the administration of the arts, and which he continued to hold until 1969. He encouraged the commissioning and performance of American works, and the importance he placed on the Center's service to urban communities led to the Lincoln Center Student Program, which instituted concerts in schools and opened the Center's halls for students' concerts. Other new projects were the Lincoln Center Chamber Music Society, the New York PO summer promenade concerts and the summer series of performances by visiting opera companies. Schuman left his post at the Lincoln Center to become chairman of the board of the Videorecord Corporation of America in 1970.

The core of Schuman's output is formed by his orchestral music, of which the symphonies are the most significant part. From Harris he inherited a broad non-repetitive cantilena, non-functional triadic and polytonal harmony, and expansive gestures. But there are also individual features in the vigorous drive, febrile rhythm and bonhomie of the symphonies and the *American Festival Overture*. Schuman writes for a large orchestra, which he generally uses in homogeneous groups, with similar material tossed from one choir to another. He is also inclined to superimpose up to three distinct layers moving at different speeds. For example, his slow movements often present rich successions of triads in the lower register with one or more weaving melodic strands above. In fast sections, principal melodies are frequently accompanied by sharp, rhythmically irregular ideas, and this – like the layered scoring – appears to have been suggested by *The Rite of Spring* and other of Stravinsky's works. Schuman often uses Baroque-like ostinato or fugato procedures, and the subjects of his fugues or passacaglias may undergo substantial change during the course of a movement. Sections frequently begin with canonic statements of characteristic long, legato melodies, as in the Third and Ninth Symphonies. Other typical elements are the timpani solos and the almost apocalyptic finales.

In the Third Symphony the harmonic foundation is the major triad, and in the compact Symphony for Strings it is a polytonal chord, appearing most conspicuously in the second movement. The Sixth Symphony (1948), perhaps Schuman's best achievement, is permeated by the major–minor chord, a sound that has since become the hallmark of Schuman's harmony. 12 years separated the Seventh from the Sixth Symphony, and during this period Schuman composed in diverse styles and for various forces; more probing pieces alternated with the 'baseball opera' *The Mighty Casey* (1951–3) and the popular *New England Triptych* (1956), works that represent his last ventures in Americana. *Credendum* (1955) was the first musical composition commissioned by the US government. In the Seventh Symphony (1960), Schuman continued the new directions first explored in the *Carols of Death* (1958). There are long stretches of harmonic stasis, and dense sonorities are insistently reiterated. Slow, melancholy music predominates, and the march-like dotted rhythms and string adagios recall the later Mahler symphonies. Also like Mahler, Schuman became fascinated by bell sounds. During the 1960s he produced two small concertante works: *A Song of Orpheus*, based on a song Schuman wrote in 1944, formed a reticent bridge to the massive Eighth Symphony; and *To Thee Old Cause* is a bleak 'evocation' in memory of Martin Luther King and Robert Kennedy. The moving Symphony no.9 'Le fosse ardeatine' is the finest of the later works; its dark and solemn mood, unity of form and detail, and slow-fast-slow plan recall the Sixth Symphony.

WORKS

STAGE

Undertow, ballet, 1945; cond. Dorati, New York, 10 April 1945

Night Journey, ballet, 1947; Martha Graham, cond. L. Horst, Cambridge, Mass., 3 May 1947

Judith, ballet, 1949; Graham, cond. R. Whitney, Louisville, 4 Jan 1950

The Mighty Casey (opera, 3 scenes, J. Gury), 1951–3; cond. M. Paranov, Hartford, Conn., 4 May 1953; rev. as cantata, 1976

Voyage for a Theater, ballet, 1953; Graham, cond. S. Sadoff, New York, 17 May 1953

The Witch of Endor, ballet, 1965; Graham, cond. R. Irving, New York, 2 Nov 1965

ORCHESTRAL

Symphony no.1, 18 insts, 1935; cond. J. Werner, New York, 21 Oct 1936; unpubd, withdrawn

Prelude and Fugue, 1937; unpubd, withdrawn

Symphony no.2, 1937; cond. E. Schenkman, New York, 25 May 1938; withdrawn

American Festival Ov., 1939; cond. Koussevitzky, Boston, 6 Oct 1939

Symphony no.3, 1941; cond. Koussevitzky, Boston, 17 Oct 1941

Symphony no.4, 1941; cond. A. Rodzinsky, Cleveland, 22 Jan 1942

Newsreel, in Five Shots, band, 1941; cond. G. Howard, Pennsylvania State College, 1942; version for orch, 1942; cond. A. Smallens, New York, 15 July 1942

Piano Concerto, 1942; R. Tureck, cond. D. Saidenberg, New York, 13 Jan 1943

Prayer in Time of War, 1943; cond. Reiner, Pittsburgh, 26 Feb 1943

Symphony for Strings (Symphony no.5), 1943; cond. Koussevitzky, Boston, 12 Nov 1943

Circus Overture: Side Show, small orch/full orch, 1944; small orch, cond. Abravanel, Philadelphia, 17 Dec 1944; full orch, cond. Reiner, Pittsburgh, 7 Jan 1945

Undertow, choreographic episodes [from ballet], 1945; cond. A. Wallenstein, Los Angeles, 29 Nov 1945

Violin Concerto, 1947; Stern, cond. Munch, Boston, 10 Feb 1950; rev. 1954, Stern, cond. J. Morel, New York, 26 Feb 1956; rev. 1958–9, R. Totenberg, cond. I. Solomon, Aspen, Colorado, 9 Aug 1959

Symphony no.6, 1948; cond. Dorati, Dallas, 27 Feb 1949

George Washington Bridge, band, 1950; Interlocken, Mich., 30 July 1950

Credendum, Article of Faith, 1955; cond. T. Johnson, Cincinnati, 4 Nov 1955

New England Triptych, 1956; cond. Kostelanetz, Miami, 28 Oct 1956

Chester [from New England Triptych], band, 1956; Louisville U., Jan 1957

When Jesus Wept [from New England Triptych], band, 1958; cond. R.

F. Goldman, summer 1958
Symphony no.7, 1960; cond. C. Münch, Boston, 21 Oct 1960
A Song of Orpheus, fantasy, vc, orch, 1961; L. Rose, cond. I. Solomon, Indianapolis, 17 Feb 1962
Symphony no.8, 1962; cond. Bernstein, New York, 4 Oct 1962
Variations on America [arr. of Ives], orch/band, 1963; orch, cond. Kostelanetz, New York, 20 May 1964
The Orchestra Song, 1963; cond. Kostelanetz, Minneapolis, 11 April 1964; arr. band as The Band Song, 1963
Philharmonic Fanfare, 1965; cond. Steinberg, New York, 10 Aug 1965; withdrawn
Dedication Fanfare, band, 1968; St Louis, 4 July 1968
To Thee Old Cause, evocation, ob, brass, timp, pf, str, 1968; H. Gomberg, cond. Bernstein, New York, 3 Oct 1968
Symphony no.9 'Le fosse ardeatine', 1968; cond. Ormandy, Philadelphia, 10 Jan 1969
In Praise of Shahn, 1969; cond. Bernstein, New York, 29 Jan 1970
Voyage, cycle of 5 pieces, 1972; cond. G. Meier, Rochester, New York, 27 Oct 1972
Concerto on old English rounds, va, female chorus, orch, 1974; D. McGinnes, cond. M. T. Thomas, Boston, 29 Nov 1974
Symphony no.10 'American Muse', 1976; Washington, DC, 6 April 1976

VOCAL

God's World, 1v, pf, 1932
4 Canonic Choruses (Chorale Canons) (Millay, Cullen, Sandburg, Tennyson), SATB, 1932–3; cond. C. Gutekunst, New York, 3 May 1935
Pioneers! (Whitman), SSAATTBB, 1937; cond. H. Switten, Princeton, 23 May 1938
Choral Etude, SATB, 1937; cond. L. Engel, New York, 16 March 1938
Prologue (G. Taggard), SATB, orch, 1939; cond. A. Richter, New York, 7 May 1939
The Orchestra Song (Austrian trad., trans. M. Farquhar), 1939
Prelude (Wolfe), female chorus/SATB, 1939; cond. Schuman, New York, 24 April 1940
This is Our Time (Taggard) (Secular Cantata no.1), SATB, orch, 1940; cond. A. Smallens, New York, 4 July 1940
Requiescat, female chorus/SATB, pf, 1942; cond. Schuman, New York, 4 April 1942
Holiday Song (Taggard), SATB, pf, 1942; cond. R. Shaw, New York, 13 Jan 1943
A Free Song (Whitman) (Secular Cantata no.2), 1942; SATB, orch, 1942; cond. Koussevitzky, Boston, 26 March 1943
Orpheus and his Lute (Shakespeare), 1v, pf, 1944
Te Deum, SATB, 1944; cond. G. Wallace Woodworth, Cambridge, Mass., April 1945
Truth Shall Deliver (Chaucer, adapted M. Farquhar), male chorus, 1946; cond. M. Bartholomew, New Haven, 7 Dec 1946
The Lord Has a Child (L. Hughes), SATB, pf, 1956
Four Rounds on Famous Words, 1956
Carols of Death (Whitman), SATB, 1958; Canton, NY, St Lawrence U., 20 March 1959
Deo ac veritati, male chorus, 1963; cond. W. Skelton, Hamilton, NY, Colgate U., 19 April 1963
Declaration Chorale (Whitman), SATB, 1971; cond. R. Shaw, New York, 30 April 1972
Mail Order Madrigals (Sears, Roebuck 1897 catalogue), SATB, 1971; cond. W. D. Pritchard, Ames, Iowa State U., 12 March 1972
To Thy Love, choral fantasy on old English rounds, SSSA, 1973
Casey at the Bak, cantata, S, chorus, orch, 1976 [rev. version of opera]; Washington, DC, 6 April 1976
The Young Dead Soldiers (A. MacLeish), S, hn, ww, str; Washington, DC, 6 April 1976

CHAMBER AND INSTRUMENTAL

Canon and Fugue, pf trio, 1934; unpubd, withdrawn
Choreographic Poem, 7 insts, 1934; unpubd, withdrawn
Str Qt no.1, 1936; New Str Qt, New York, 21 Oct 1936; unpubd, withdrawn
Str Qt no.2, 1937; Forum Str Qt, New York, spring 1938
Quartettino, 4 bn, 1939
Str Qt no.3, 1939; Coolidge Str Qt, New York, 27 Feb 1940
Three-Score Set, pf, 1943; J. de Menasce, 29 Aug 1943
Str Qt no.4, 1950; Hungarian Str Qt, Washington, 28 Oct 1950
Voyage, pf, 1953; L. Steuber, Chicago, 18 Aug 1953
Three Piano Moods, 1958; J. Rosen, Athens, 2 Dec 1958
Amaryllis Variations, str trio, 1964; New York Str Trio, Washington, 31 Oct 1964
Anniversary Fanfare, brass, perc, 1969; cond. Prausnitz, New York, 13 April 1970
Prelude for a Great Occasion, brass, perc, 1974; cond. Dorati, Washington, 1 Oct 1974

Principal publishers: G. Schirmer, Presser

WRITINGS

'Unconventional Case History', MM, xv (1938), 222

'On Teaching the Literature and Materials of Music', MQ, xxxiv (1948), 155
Introduction to The Juilliard Report on Teaching the Literature and Materials of Music, ed. R. F. Goldman (New York, 1953), 7
'The Compleat Musician: Vincent Persichetti and Twentieth Century Harmony', MQ, xlvii (1961), 379

BIBLIOGRAPHY

L. Bernstein: 'William Schuman', MM, xix (1942), 97
N. Broder: 'The Music of William Schuman', MQ, xxxi (1945), 17
R. F. Goldman, ed.: The Juilliard Report (New York, 1953)
F. R. Schreiber and V. Persichetti: William Schuman (New York, 1954) [incl. bibliography]
J. Edmunds and G. Boelzner: Some Twentieth-century American Composers (New York, 1959–60), ii, 42ff
R. F. Goldman: 'Current Chronicle', MQ, xlix (1963), 91
R. Evett: 'Current Chronicle', MQ, li (1965), 408
H. Weisgall: 'Schuman, William', Dictionary of Contemporary Music, ed. J. Vinton (New York, 1974)

BRUCE SAYLOR

Schumann [née Wieck], **Clara (Josephine)** (b Leipzig, 13 Sept 1819; d Frankfurt am Main, 20 May 1896). German pianist and composer. The eldest child of Friedrich and Marianne WIECK, she began to study the piano at the age of five with her father; he had resolved even before her birth to develop the child into a musician of consummate artistry. After several private concerts she made her first public appearance at a concert in the Leipzig Gewandhaus (20 October 1828), where she also gave her first complete recital (8 November 1830). During the concert season 1831–2 her father took her on her first extended concert tour, travelling as far as Paris. After her return to Leipzig she continued to perform extensively, and studied – in addition to the piano – singing, the violin, instrumentation, score reading, counterpoint and composition; during these years she published a number of compositions for piano solo. By 1835 she was acclaimed throughout Europe as a phenomenally talented child prodigy; her admirers included Goethe, Mendelssohn, Chopin, Paganini and Schumann.

In the next few years Clara continued to perform throughout Europe with dazzling success. Liszt considered that she had 'complete technical mastery, depth and sincerity of feeling'; Grillparzer honoured her with a poem, Clara Wieck und Beethoven (F-moll-Sonate) (1838). In 1838 she was appointed k.k. Kammervirtuosin to the Austrian court, an honour rarely bestowed on a foreigner, particularly one so young; later the same year she was elected to the Gesellschaft der Musikfreunde.

These triumphs, however, were embittered by a prolonged conflict with her father. Robert Schumann, who had come to live with the Wiecks in 1830, formally asked Wieck in 1837 for permission to marry Clara, touching off a fierce three-year battle between Wieck and the two lovers. After Wieck's initial efforts to prevent communication between the two and to dampen their devotion proved unsuccessful, his behaviour became more and more irrational, extending to the most spiteful attempts at slander and sabotage, both professional and personal. Clara and Robert were eventually obliged to take their case to court, and after a favourable ruling were eventually married on 12 September 1840.

The Schumanns settled first in Leipzig, moving to Dresden in 1844 and to Düsseldorf in 1850. Married life posed numerous obstacles to Clara's playing and composing, to her great dismay. Robert could not be disturbed while composing, and her time was now additionally occupied with household cares and maternal duties: Marie (b 1841), Elise (b 1843), Julie (b 1845),

Emil (*b* 1846; *d* 1847), Ludwig (*b* 1848), Ferdinand (*b* 1849), Eugenie (*b* 1851) and Felix (*b* 1854). Nonetheless she managed to continue performing, even making concert tours as far as Copenhagen (1842) and Russia (1844). Both Clara and Robert taught at the Leipzig Conservatory, and Clara continued to teach privately in Dresden and Düsseldorf. Her works of this period, though few, reflect her expanding horizons: in addition to piano music, including a set of preludes and fugues (op.16), she composed songs (opp.12 and 13) and chamber music (op.17).

In 1853 the family moved to a new house in Düsseldorf, and finally their rooms were situated so that Clara could practise and compose without disturbing Robert. As soon as the concert season was over, she turned to composition; during June and July she wrote a set of variations (op.20), three piano romances (op. 21), three romances for violin and piano (op.22) and six songs (op.23). In September the young Johannes Brahms made his first appearance in the Schumann household.

These propitious events were tragically overshadowed by the rapidly deteriorating state of Robert's nervous system, culminating in his collapse in 1854 and his commitment in March to the asylum at Endenich, where he remained until his death in 1856 – leaving Clara to care for seven young children. During this difficult time Brahms proved a devoted, invaluable companion; he and Clara formed an extremely close friendship that lasted until her death. The extent of their relationship remains uncertain, as they destroyed a large amount of correspondence and perhaps other material; it is certainly clear that they cared for each other deeply. Johannes wrote to Clara in March 1876: 'I love you better than myself or than anyone or anything in the world'.

Clara performed frequently and extensively for the rest of her life. She made her first concert tour to England shortly before Robert's death, in 1856, returning nearly every year for at least 16 more visits, and made another highly successful tour to Russia in 1864. She became particularly well known as an interpreter of works by her husband and by Brahms, and made every effort to promote them.

In 1857 Clara moved to Berlin, mainly to be with her mother, who had divorced Wieck and married Adolf Bargiel (*d* 1841) in 1825. From 1863 to 1873 she lived in Baden-Baden, and from 1873 to 1878 again lived periodically in Berlin. In the 1870s her family suffered several losses: in 1870 Ludwig was committed to a mental asylum, where he remained until his death in 1899; Julie died in 1872; Friedrich Wieck died in 1873; Felix died of consumption in 1879. In 1878 Clara became principal teacher of piano at the Hoch Conservatory in Frankfurt. In addition to performing and teaching, she was engaged in preparing a complete edition of Robert's music (published 1881–93) and an edition of his letters (1827–40), published as *Jugendbriefe* (Leipzig, 1885). Despite growing hearing problems and rheumatic pains, she continued to lead an active life: she made her last public performance in 1891 (shortly before the death of her son Ferdinand) and continued to teach, play privately, travel and receive friends until her death.

As a pianist Clara Schumann was indisputably of the highest rank. Even as a child appearing on a musical scene dominated by brilliant Paris-trained virtuosos, she was universally praised not only for her technical mas-

Clara Schumann (see also SCHUMANN, ROBERT, *fig.8)*

tery but also for her thoughtful interpretations. Her playing was always characterized by poetic spirit, depth of feeling, a singing tone and strict adherence to the composer's indications. She was noted for her progressive repertory, and was the first in Germany to perform many works of Chopin, Schumann and Brahms.

Widely influential as a teacher and as an interpreter of Schumann and Brahms, Clara Schumann also directly influenced the two composers themselves; the extensive correspondence and diaries show a decidedly two-way flow of music criticism. In particular Brahms, 14 years her junior, set great store by her opinions and took much of her advice to heart.

Clara's musical ideas are most tangibly manifested in her compositions. Her childhood works, modelled on the brilliant virtuoso pieces then in her concert repertory, are imaginative for a child of 11 or 12, but by 1836 her compositions were more serious – even in 1835 Chopin had praised her talent. The *Soirées musicales* op.6 show tendencies also apparent in the music of Mendelssohn and Chopin; the Piano Concerto op.7 is remarkably effective for the work of a 15-year-old, with its dramatic momentum and control of orchestral colour. The compositions of the early 1840s reflect her broadening musical horizons, owing partly to studies undertaken with Robert. The three songs op.12 (published in Robert's op.37) and the six songs op.13 are quiet pieces not without subtle nuances. In the Piano Trio op.17 musical details are placed in a larger context: piquant rhythms, vivid harmonies, flowing melodies and unexpected phrase lengths are brought into relief against a highly cohesive, harmonically directed structure. Her last compositions, dating from summer 1853, show striking originality; in particular, the songs op.23 are spiced with whimsical turns of melody, rhythm and harmony.

In spite of her creative talents and her overwhelming successes in other musical endeavours, Clara Schumann never had serious ambitions as a composer; 19th-century Germany was distinctly inhospitable to any such ambitions in women. She wrote in her diary as early as 1839: 'I once thought that I possessed creative talent, but I have given up this idea; a woman must not desire to compose – not one has been able to do it, and why should I expect to? It would be arrogance, although, indeed, my father led me into it in earlier days'.

WORKS

All printed works were published in Leipzig unless otherwise stated; MSS are in *D-Zsch* and *A-Wgm*.

op.

ORCHESTRAL AND CHAMBER

7 Piano Concerto, a, 1835 or 1836 (1836)
17 Piano Trio, g, by 1846 (1847)
— Piano Concertino, f, 1847
22 Drei Romanzen, vn, pf, 1853 (1855 or 1856)

PIANO

— Variationen über ein Tyroler Lied, 1830
— Variationen über ein Original-Thema, 1830
1 Quatre polonaises, 1828–?1830 (1830)
2 Caprices en forme de valse, by 1833 (1832 or 1833)
3 Romance varié, C, 1831 (1833)
— Rondo, b, 1833
4 Valses romantiques, ?1833 (c1835)
5 Quatre pièces caractéristiques, 1835 or 1836 (1839): Impromptu le sabbat, Caprices à la boleros, Romance, Scène fantastique: le ballet de revenants
6 Soirées musicales, 1835 or 1836 (1836): Toccatina, Ballade, Nocturne, Polonaise, Mazurka, Mazurka
8 Variations de concert sur la cavatine du Pirate de Bellini, by 1834 (Vienna, 1837)
9 Souvenir de Vienne, Impromptu, G, 1837 or 1838 (Vienna, 1838)
10 Scherzo, d, by 1839 (1838 or 1839)
11 Trois romances, 1839 (Vienna, 1839): e♭, g, A♭ [no.2 also pubd separately as Andante and Allegro, *NZM*, vi (1839), suppl.3]
— Sonatina: Allegro and Scherzo, 1841, last movt, 1842
14 Deuxième scherzo, c, by 1845 (1845)
15 Quatre pièces fugitives, by 1845 (1845)
16 Drei Präludien und Fugen, g, B♭, d, by 1845 (1846)
20 Variationen über ein Thema von Robert Schumann, f♯, 1853 (1854)
21 Drei Romanzen, a, F, g, 1853 (1855 or 1856)
— Geburtstagmarsch, E♭, 1879

SONGS

— An Alexis, 1833
— Walzer (Lyser), 1834
12 Three songs (Rückert), 1840 (1841) [pubd as nos.2, 4, 11 of R. Schumann: Gedichte aus Liebesfrühling, op.37]: Er ist gekommen, Liebst du um Schönheit, Warum willst du andre fragen?
— Liebeszauber (E. Geibel), 1842 (n.d.)
— Loreley (Heine), 1843 (n.d.)
13 Sechs Lieder, 1842–3 (c1844): Ich stand in dunklen Träumen (Heine), Sie liebten sich Beide (Heine), Liebesgarten (Geibel), Der Mond kommt still gegangen (Geibel), Ich hab' in deinem Auge (Rückert), Die stille Lotosblume (Geibel)
— Mein Stern (Serre), 1846
— Beim Abschied (Serre),1846
23 Sechs Lieder aus Jucunde (H. Rollet), 1853 (1855 or 1856): Was weinst du, An einem lichten Morgen, Geheimes Flüstern hier und dort, Auf einem grünen Hügel, Das ist ein Tag, O Lust
— Der Traum
— Volkslied (Heine)
— Am Strande (Burns), *NZM*, viii (1841), suppl.2
— Abendstern
— Oh–weh des scheidens (Rückert)

OTHER WORKS

Partsongs: Schwäne kommen gezogen, 1830; 3 partsongs (Geibel); partsongs, 1848 [?identical with Geibel settings]
Cadenzas (n.d.): Beethoven: Pf Conc., c, op.37 [1st movt], Pf Conc., G, op.58 [1st and 3rd movts]; Mozart: Pf Conc., d, κ466 [1st and 3rd movts]

BIBLIOGRAPHY

W. J. von Wasielewski: *Robert Schumann: eine Biographie* (Dresden, 1858, rev., enlarged 2/1906; Eng. trans., c1871/R1975)
A. Meichsner: *Friedrich Wieck und seine beiden Töchter Clara Schumann, geb. Wieck, und Marie Wieck* (Leipzig, 1875)
L. Ramman, ed.: 'Clara Schumann, 1855', F. Liszt: *Gesammelte Schriften*, iv (Leipzig, 1882), 187
A. Kohut: *Friedrich Wieck: ein Lebens- und Künstlerbild* (Dresden, 1888)
W. J. von Wasielewski: *Aus siebzig Jahren: Lebenserinnerungen* (Stuttgart, 1897)
V. Joss: *Der Musikpädagoge Friedrich Wieck und seine Familie* (Leipzig, 1902)
B. Litzmann: *Clara Schumann: eine Künstlerleben*, i (Leipzig, 1902, 8/1925/R1971), ii (1905, 7/1925/R1971), iii (1908, 6/1923/R1971); Eng. trans., abridged (1913/R1972 and 1979)
R. Hohenemser: 'Clara Wieck-Schumann als Komponistin', *Die Musik*, v/4 (1905–6), 113, 166
A. Moser and J. Joachim, eds.: *Briefe von und an Joseph Joachim* (Berlin, 1911–13; Eng. trans., abridged, 1914)
F. May: *The Girlhood of Clara Schumann* (London, 1912)
E. Segnitz: 'Clara Schumann und Johannes Brahms', *AMZ*, xxxix (1912), 1342, 1372
M. Wieck: *Aus dem Kreise Wieck-Schumann* (Dresden, 1912, 2/1914)
F. Schumann: 'Brahms and Clara Schumann', *MQ*, ii (1916), 507 [orig. in *NZM*, lxxxii (1915), 225]
——: 'Erinnerungen an Clara Schumann', *NZM*, lxxiv (1917), 69, 77, 85, 93, 101; Eng. trans., abridged as *Reminiscences of Clara Schumann as found in the Diary of Ferdinand Schumann*, ed. J. Dickinson (New York, 1949/R1973)
M. Kreisig: 'Ein Blick in die Clara-Schumann-Ausstellung im Schumanns Museum zu Zwickau', *NZM*, lxxvi (1919), 229
E. Schumann: *Erinnerungen* (Stuttgart, 1925; Eng. trans., 1927)
B. Litzmann, ed.: *Clara Schumann, Johannes Brahms: Briefe aus den Jahren 1853–1896* (Leipzig, 1927; Eng. trans., abridged, 1927/R1972)
E. Schumann: *Robert Schumann: ein Lebensbild meines Vaters* (Leipzig, 1931)
A. Meuer: 'Clara Schumanns eigenschöpferisches Werk', *NZM*, cvi/1 (1939), 142
J. Burk: *Clara Schumann: a Romantic Biography* (New York, 1940)
A. de Lara: 'Clara Schumann's Teaching', *ML*, xxvi (1945), 143
K.-F. Bernhardt: 'Schumanns Weggefährtin zur musikschöpferischen Emanzipation der Frau', *Musica*, x (Kassel, 1956), 460
L. W. Leven: 'Clara Schumann's First Visit to England', *MT*, xcvii (1956), 190
K. Walch-Schumann, ed.: *Friedrich Wieck: Briefe aus den Jahren 1830–1838* (Cologne, 1968)
K. Stephenson: *Clara Schumann: 1819–1896* (Bonn, 1969)
F. Munte: *Verzeichnis des deutschsprachigen Schrifttums über Robert Schumann 1856–1970* (Hamburg, 1972) [with appx on Clara Schumann literature]
P. Susskind Pettler: 'Johannes Brahms and Clara Schumann: Clara's Influence as Critic, Advisor and Friend', *International Brahms Congress: Detroit 1980*

PAMELA SUSSKIND

Schumann, Elisabeth (*b* Merseburg an der Saale, 13 June 1888; *d* New York, 23 April 1952). German soprano. She studied with Natalie Hänisch in Dresden, with Marie Dietrich in Berlin and with Alma Schadow in Hamburg. She made her début at the Hamburg Stadttheater, as the Shepherd in *Tannhäuser*, in 1909, and she remained a member of the Hamburg company until 1919, in which year Richard Strauss persuaded her to join the Vienna Staatsoper. There she established herself firmly in the hearts of the musical public and in 1937 became an *Ehrenmitglied* of the company. A year later the Nazi annexation of Austria caused her to leave the country.

She was first heard in England in 1924, when she made an enormous success as Sophie in *Der Rosenkavalier*; after that she made many appearances at Covent Garden in this and in Mozartian parts. It is especially with Mozart that she was associated; she had a beautifully controlled high soprano of delicate, ringing timbre and of crystalline purity, and a charming stage presence, especially in demure, mischievous parts. This combination of qualities made her ravishing as Susanna, Blonde, Zerlina and Despina. Strauss's Sophie will also remain inseparably linked with her name; few who heard her in her prime will forget her delivery of those long, soaring *pianissimo* phrases with which Sophie acknowledges the gift of the rose at the beginning of the second act; it seemed as though the composer must have had just such a quality of voice in mind when writing the part. Her Eva in *Die Meistersinger*, though the part taxed her strength, was charmingly youthful and lyrical; her Adele in Bruno Walter's revival of *Die Fledermaus* was a delicious essay in flirtatious gaiety. In the concert hall her popularity was even greater, and Richard Strauss was so delighted by her singing of his songs that he toured the USA with her in 1921. Her emotional range as a lieder singer was to some extent restricted by the light weight and silvery tone of her voice; but within her chosen limits, and especially in the more lyrical, playful or purely decorative songs of Schubert, she was inimitable.

Elisabeth Schumann was made an *Ehrenmitglied* of the Vienna Philharmonic, an Austrian *Kammersängerin* and a Chevalier of the Légion d'honneur. In 1937 she became attached for three months to the vocal department of the Curtis Institute of Music in Philadelphia; in 1938 she made her home in New York, where she had sung Sophie and several other parts at the Metropolitan during the single season of 1914–15. In 1945 she reappeared in Britain at the Albert Hall, and in 1947 took part in the first Edinburgh Festival; and she gave many subsequent recitals, besides teaching and singing at the Bryanston Summer School of Music. The passing years dealt lightly with her voice, and to the end it was rare for her to produce a note which was not of beautiful quality. So perfect a method was ideally suited to the gramophone; and her many records, especially the famous abridged version of *Der Rosenkavalier* and the long series of lieder by Schubert, Schumann and others, are among the most delightful of their kind ever made.

Elisabeth Schumann as Sophie in 'Der Rosenkavalier', Hamburg, 1911

Of Elisabeth Schumann's three marriages the first was to Walther Puritz, an architect in Hamburg; the second to Karl Alwin (1891–1945), a conductor at the Vienna Staatsoper and pianist, who often accompanied her in recitals and recordings; and the third to the Austrian dermatologist Hans Kruegger.

WRITINGS

German Song (London, 1948)

BIBLIOGRAPHY
H. G. Owen and J. Cone: 'Elisabeth Schumann', *Record Collector*, vii (1952), 221 [with discography]
E. Puritz: *The Teaching of Elisabeth Schumann* (London, 1956)
A. Mathis: 'Elisabeth Schumann', *Opera*, xxiv (1973), 672, 783, 968
G. Puritz: [biography] (in preparation)
                                                        DESMOND SHAWE-TAYLOR

Schumann, Frederic Theodor (*fl* London, 1760–80). German guitarist, composer and player of the musical glasses. He appeared in London early in the 1760s (when numerous German musicians were attracted by the court of Queen Charlotte) and performed there on the musical glasses from at least October 1761. The dedication (to the queen) of his harpsichord concertos op.4 (*c*1769) indicates that he had performed on the glasses in court. He may also have played Franklin's new instrument (Pohl listed him as a performer on the glass harmonica), and if so was one of its earliest performers, along with Marianne Davies. His works, several collections of which were reprinted on the Continent, comprise mainly harpsichord sonatas and simple guitar pieces for students and amateurs. The first keyboard sonatas are curious in their fluid, improvisatory character, suggesting at once the composer's orientation to the guitar and the example of C. P. E. Bach's fantasias. Simplification in his next works suggests the influence of Abel's and J. C. Bach's sonatas.

WORKS

(all published in London)

Inst: 38 Lessons with . . . 6 French & Italian Songs, gui, op.1 (1763); A Collection of the Most Celebrated Songs, arr. gui (*c*1763); A 2nd Set of Lessons, gui/2 gui, op.2 (*c*1765); 3 Sonatas, hpd, vn/fl acc., op.3 (*c*1768); A Second Set of English, French and Italian Songs, arr. gui (*c*1768); 4 Concertos, hpd, 2 vn, vc, op.4 (*c*1769); 6 Sonatas, pf/hpd, acc. 2 vn, vc, op.5 (*c*1770); A 2nd Set of 6 Sonatas, hpd/pf, acc. vn, op.7 (*c*1772); 6 Sonatas, 3 for vn, 2 vc, 3 for fl/vn, vn, vc, op.8 (*c*1773), as op.1 (Amsterdam, 1733); A 3rd Set of 6 Sonatas, hpd/pf, vn acc., op.9 (*c*1777)

Songs: The Address (*c*1770); Haughty Strephon (*c*1770)

Gui solos, op.6, and canzonets, op.10, listed by Gerber

BIBLIOGRAPHY
EitnerQ; *GerberL*; *GerberNL*
C. F. Pohl: *Mozart und Haydn in London* (Vienna, 1867/*R*1970)
A. H. King: 'The Musical Glasses and Glass Harmonica', *PRMA*, lxxii (1945–6), 97
P. Bone: *The Guitar and the Mandoline* (London, 2/1954)
R. Kidd: *The Sonata for Keyboard with Violin Accompaniment in England (1750–1790)* (diss., Yale U., 1967), 254
——: 'The Emergence of Chamber Music with Obbligato Keyboard in England', *AcM*, xliv (1972), 138
                                                        RONALD R. KIDD

Schumann, Georg (Alfred) (*b* Königstein, Saxony, 25 Oct 1866; *d* Berlin, 23 May 1952). German composer and conductor. He was taught the violin by his father and the organ by his grandfather, playing in the Königstein orchestra at the age of nine and serving as town organist at 12. After initial piano studies in Dresden, he studied the piano and composition under Reinecke, Jadassohn and Zwintscher at the Leipzig Conservatory (1882–8). He was director of the Danzig Gesangverein (1890–96) and of the Bremen PO and Chorus (1896–9). In 1900 he was appointed director of the Berlin Singakademie with the title of royal professor, and he remained with that organization for 50 years, touring extensively and developing a highly individual style of choral performance. Appointed to the Prussian Academy of Arts in 1907, he became its vice-president (1918) and president (1934), and he led a master class in composition there (1913–45).

WORKS
(selective; for fuller list see Biehle)

Choral orch: Amor und Psyche, op.3; Totenklage, op.33; Sehnsucht, op.40; Ruth, op.50, oratorio; Das Tränenkrüglein, op.57; David und Absalon, Ständchen, op.70, dramatische Burleske

Orch: Zur Karnevalszeit, op.22, suite; Variationen on 'Wer nur den lieben Gott lässt walten', op.24, org, orch; Variationen und Doppelfuge über ein lustiges Thema, op.30; Serenade, op.34; Sym., op.42, f; Variations on 'Gestern Abend war Vetter Michel da', op.77; sym. poems, ovs., other syms.

Chamber: Pf Qnt, e, op.18; Vc Sonata, op.19; Pf Qt, f, op.29

Org: Passacaglia über BACH, op.39; 10 Chorale Preludes, op.77

Lieder, pf pieces

BIBLIOGRAPHY
P. Hielscher: *Georg Schumann*, Monographien moderner Musiker, i (Leipzig, 1906)
H. Biehle: *Georg Schumann* (Münster, 1925)
F. Ohrmann: 'Georg Schumann', *ZfM*, Jg.97–8 (1930), 613

JOSEPH CLARK

Schumann, Robert (Alexander) (*b* Zwickau, Saxony, 8 June 1810; *d* Endenich, nr. Bonn, 29 July 1856). German composer, a central figure of musical Romanticism. In many ways Schumann represents the quintessential Romantic composer, with his emphasis on self-expression, his strong vein of lyricism, and his interest in extra-musical (particularly literary) associations. His contributions are of special importance in the fields of piano music and song.

1. Early years. 2. Leipzig. 3. Heidelberg. 4. Leipzig again. 5. 1832–4. 6. Ernestine and Clara. 7. 1837–8. 8. Towards marriage. 9. The year of song. 10. Orchestral music. 11. Chamber music. 12. Choral music. 13. Dresden. 14. Opera plans. 15. A prolific spell. 16. Last months in Dresden. 17. Düsseldorf. 18. Declining health. 19. Last creative spell. 20. The end. 21. Influences and piano music. 22. Songs. 23. Orchestral and chamber music. 24. Choral and dramatic music. 25. Critical writings.

1. EARLY YEARS. He was the fifth and youngest child of August Schumann, bookseller, publisher and author (*b* 1773, son of a Saxon clergyman), and his wife Johanna Christiana (*b* 1771, daughter of a surgeon named Schnabel). The parents were married in 1795 and lived for more than 11 years at Zeitz; in the spring of 1807 they moved to Zwickau, where Schumann founded a publishing house. In the year of Robert's birth his father was attacked by a 'nervous disorder' which affected his remaining years. The boy's education began in 1816, when he was sent to a local private school, where he showed no special gifts; at about the same time he seems to have had his first piano lessons from J. G. Kuntzsch (1775–1855), organist of St Mary's Church, a somewhat pedantic musician of limited ability. In August 1819 he heard Moscheles play at Karlsbad, and the impression was indelible; the piano style of Moscheles is still easily perceptible in Schumann's earlier published compositions. Either the same year or the year before the boy was taken to hear his first opera, *Die Zauberflöte*, at Leipzig. On 6 November 1821 he took part, at the piano, in Kuntzsch's performance of Friedrich Schneider's oratorio *Weltgericht* in St Mary's and, possibly under the influence of this work, then enormously popular, he composed in January 1822 a setting of Psalm cl for soprano, contralto, piano and orchestra, inscribed 'Oeuv. I' – 26 pages of 13-line score

on plain paper ruled by himself – which was performed by his fellow pupils and other young friends. For them also he composed in the same year an *Ouverture et Chor fürs grosse Orchester, Oeuv. 1/No. 3* – a nine-page overture followed by a brief chorus on words beginning 'Wie reizend ist der schöne Morgen' – apparently suggested by a vocal score of Paer's *Achille* which had fallen into his hands. At Easter 1820 he had entered the Zwickau Lyceum, where he remained for eight years, and the record of his public appearances at the 'evening entertainments' arranged from time to time by the head of the Lyceum shows his considerable ability as a pianist.

At the same time the boy showed equal if not greater literary ability. Side by side with his regular education at the Lyceum he largely educated himself by promiscuous reading in his father's shop and library. This was encouraged by his father, who allowed him at the age of 13 to contribute some short articles to one of his publications, the *Bildergalerie der berühmtesten Menschen aller Völker und Zeiten*. At about the same time the boy compiled an anthology of album-verses, poems (partly his own, including a scene from a five-act tragedy, *Der Geist*) and passages from Schubart's *Ideen zu einer Aesthetik der Tonkunst*: 'Blätter und Blümchen aus der goldenen Aue. Gesammelt und zusammengebunden von Robert Schumann, genannt Skülander. 1823 (November und Dezember)'. A second book, begun in 1825 and continued until 1828, *Allerley aus der Feder Roberts an der Mulde* – Zwickau stands on the river Mulde – consists mainly of his own verses, which reflect the school exercise of making metrical German versions of Latin poems (he collected into a still extant volume his translations of selected odes of Horace). Schumann's love of 'societies' began to show itself in 1825, when he took a leading part in the founding of two schoolboy bodies, a secret 'Schülerverbindung' (founded 19 May) which cultivated fencing, but apparently not politics, and a literary 'Schülerverein' (first meeting 12 December) for the study of German literature. Probably to this period of the Schülerverein belong the beginnings of some further dramatic essays: a comedy, *Coriolan*; *Leonhard und Mantellier*; *Die beiden Montalti* and *Die Brüder Lanzendörfer* (said to be 'horror dramas').

Schumann's father now thought of sending him to study composition with Weber, but that master's death put an end to the plan and, a month or so after Weber, August Schumann himself died (10 August 1826). His 19-year-old daughter Emilie, Robert's only sister, a physical and mental invalid, had died a short time before. Calf-love for two girls whose names have been recorded, Nanni Patsch and Liddy Hempel, provided further emotional experiences which were characteristically worked into an autobiographical story, *Juniusabende und Julitage*, that he described two years later as 'my first work, my truest and my finest; how I wept as I wrote it and yet how happy I was'. Nanni and Liddy were soon partly but not entirely displaced in his affections by Agnes Carus, the young, intelligent and musical wife of a doctor at Colditz. At the end of July 1827, after visiting the Caruses at Colditz, he made a further excursion to Leipzig (where his closest school friends were now at the university), Dresden, Prague and Teplice (where he again met, and parted with, Liddy Hempel). His letters during this holiday refer frequently to champagne drinking, a habit he shook off only years later. Another habit formed in 1827 was that of keeping a diary or commonplace-book; his earliest diary was entitled 'Tage des Jünglinglebens'. From the summer of 1827, too, date his literary enthusiasm for Jean Paul, which had an overwhelming effect on his already flowery prose style, and his musical enthusiasm for Schubert. His notes record 'daily improvisation at the instrument. Attempts to compose without instrument. . . . Beginnings of a piano concerto in F minor'. Four songs dating from 1827 have survived: *Verwandlung* (words by E. Schulze), *Lied für xxx* (to his own poem *Leicht wie gaukelnde Sylphiden*), *Sehnsucht* (also to his own words), written in February and revised in June, and a translation of Byron's *I saw thee weep* (in July); no doubt they were written for Frau Carus, who was a singer.

2. LEIPZIG. On 15 March 1828 Schumann passed his school-leaving examination, winning high praise. In obedience to the wishes of his mother and his guardian he then unwillingly matriculated as a law student in the University of Leipzig (29 March). Some autobiographical notes from a later period record: 'Easter 1828. Night raptures. Constant improvisation daily. Also literary fantasies in Jean Paul's manner. Special enthusiasm for Schubert, Beethoven too, Bach less. Letter to Franz Schubert (not sent)'.

Before settling at Leipzig he and a new acquaintance made there, Gisbert Rosen, set out on an expedition in the latter part of April to Bayreuth, Nuremberg, Augsburg and Munich, where on 8 May they introduced themselves to Heine and then parted – Rosen to study at Heidelberg, Schumann to return by way of Zwickau to Leipzig, where he was to share lodgings with his old school friend Emil Flechsig. He reached Leipzig again on 15 May; his friends the Caruses had now settled there, and at their house he met musicians, including Marschner, and took part in chamber music; otherwise his circle of friends was limited to Flechsig and a few other students. Despite his promises to his mother and guardian that he would devote himself to legal study, he did not attend a single lecture (according to Flechsig), but spent hours daily on his imitations of Jean Paul and in improvisation at the piano. He was already haunted from time to time by fears of insanity. The literary productions of this period, recorded in a new notebook, 'Hottentottiana' (May 1828–June 1830) include notes for a novel, *Selene*, in which his idealized self figures as Gustav, fragments of shorter stories, *Die Harmonika* and *Weltteil*, and the beginning of a book on the aesthetics of music. Admiration for Schubert's *Erlkönig* led directly to the composition of another Goethe ballad, *Der Fischer* (June); it was followed by three settings of poems by Justinus Kerner (29 June–10 July), and these, perhaps with some earlier songs, were on 15 July submitted to the criticism of Gottlob Wiedebein (1779–1854), who then enjoyed some reputation as a song composer. In a second letter to Wiedebein (5 August), Schumann confessed that he was 'neither a connoisseur of harmony and thoroughbass nor a contrapuntist, but purely and simply guided by nature'; he would now set about the proper study of composition. Nevertheless, of four other songs written at this period he was afterwards able to use the musical substance of three (*An Anna II*, *Im Herbste* and *Hirtenknabe*) with little change in mature compositions: the Piano Sonatas op.11 and op.22 and the Intermezzo op.4 no.4. In August he began a course of piano study with the celebrated teacher Friedrich Wieck and consequently made the

acquaintance of Wieck's nine-year-old daughter Clara (Hummel's A minor Concerto was one of the works studied; he told Hummel himself that he worked at it for a year). During August and September Schumann composed a set of *VIII polonaises pour le piano à quatre mains* in imitation of Schubert's duet polonaises; they were numbered op.3, the number 2 having been bestowed on a collection of 11 of the songs. Other compositions of the autumn and winter of 1828 include a set of four-hand variations on a theme by Prince Louis Ferdinand of Prussia, whose chamber music Schumann admired, and (during January–March 1829) a would-be Schubertian Piano Quartet in C minor op.5, which in January 1830 he began to 'cobble into a symphony'. When in November he learnt of Schubert's death, his sobbing was heard by Flechsig all through the night.

1. Robert Schumann: miniature by an unknown artist in the Robert-Schumann-Haus, Zwickau

3. HEIDELBERG. Schumann was constantly hankering for Rosen's society at Heidelberg, where another attraction was one of the law professors, Justus Thibaut, who a few years before had published a book on musical aesthetics (*Über die Reinheit der Tonkunst*, Heidelberg, 1825). He persuaded his mother and guardian to allow him to move to the other university, left Leipzig on 11 May 1829 and, after a detour in the Rhineland which left him temporarily penniless, reached Heidelberg ten days later. He enjoyed life at Heidelberg and, under the influence of Thibaut's lively personality, even attended lectures for a short time. As a musician Thibaut was more enthusiastic than knowledgeable, but he had formed a musical society of students and friends, and in his private music room Schumann made the acquaintance of a considerable range of choral music, mainly Italian, from Palestrina and Victoria to Handel and Bach. The summer term ended on 20 August, and Schumann spent the holiday alone, touring Switzerland and northern Italy, where he got as far as Venice; at Milan he heard Pasta sing in Rossini's *La gazza ladra* at La Scala and for the first time fully appreciated Italian music. He returned to Heidelberg (on 20 October) by way of Augsburg and Stuttgart. Despite assurances to his mother to the contrary, he completely neglected his law studies during the autumn term, and Thibaut seems

to have irritated him even as a musician by his narrow conservatism and dogmatism. He told Wieck (letter of 6 November) that he was studying the last movement of Hummel's F♯ minor Sonata, 'a truly great, epic titan of a work', and asked him to send 'all Schubert's waltzes – only the two-hand ones (I believe there are 10–12 sets), Moscheles's G minor Concerto, Hummel's B minor Concerto' and 'anything *new* by Herz and Czerny'. He excused this last request on the ground that he was invited into family circles, but a later notebook entry suggests that he succumbed for a time to their 'shallow virtuosity' until it was eclipsed by Paganini's; from 1832, when his enthusiasm for Paganini was at its height, dates an unfinished *Phantasie satyrique* (*nach Henri Herz*). In the same letter to Wieck, Schumann spoke of having begun a number of symphonies, none of which he had completed; but it is clear from the context that he had done little more than improvise symphonic daydreams at the piano. At this period he was more concerned with piano playing than with composition, sometimes practising for seven hours a day, and in February 1830 he made a public appearance – his only one at Heidelberg – playing his old favourite, Moscheles's variations on *La marche d'Alexandre*, with a brilliant success that led to invitations to play at Mannheim and Mainz; these he declined. That winter he also led a full social life, attending a number of balls and masquerades.

4. LEIPZIG AGAIN. On Easter Sunday 1830 Schumann heard Paganini play at Frankfurt, an experience which deeply impressed him despite his doubts about Paganini's artistic ideals. His year at Heidelberg had now expired and he was due to return to Leipzig to complete his legal studies; but his guardian allowed him a term's respite. The summer was spent largely in composition; in April Schumann wrote (or perhaps only completed) a set of waltzes for piano, under the obvious influence of Schubert's waltzes, and in May an *Etude fantastique en double-sons* in D, which was afterwards styled 'Toccata' and (after revision and transposition to C in July 1832) published as op.7. In June he wrote a piano piece entitled *Papillote*, based on his song *Im Herbste*, which was later used as the third movement of the Sonata op.22. Later on he resumed work on a Concerto in F for piano and orchestra, of which a part – or perhaps an independent set of variations in the same key, on the lines of Moscheles's *Alexandre* variations for piano and orchestra – was completed in August for piano without orchestra and published in November 1831, as the definitive op.1: *Thème sur le nom 'Abegg' varié pour le pianoforte*, its name being that of a girl whose acquaintance he had made (the theme, 'Abegg-Walzer', dates from February 1830).

At the very time he was writing the 'Abegg' Variations, Schumann was trying desperately to persuade his mother to allow him to abandon law for music as a profession. At his request his mother appealed on 7 August to Friedrich Wieck, who replied two days later that Robert, with his talent and imagination, could in three years be made into one of the foremost living pianists provided he would work hard and steadily at the acquisition of a technique. Wieck made no secret of his doubt of the steadfastness of Schumann's character, of his possessing the resolution not only to work at the mechanics of piano playing, but to study 'dry, cold theory' as well for two years with the Kantor of the

Thomasschule, C. T. Weinlig; he ended by advising Frau Schumann to allow her son a trial period of six months. Robert eagerly accepted the condition (22 August). On 24 September he bade farewell to Heidelberg, going on a Rhine trip nearly as far as the Dutch border, and in October settled at Leipzig once more.

On 20 October he went to live in Wieck's own house (Grimmaische Gasse 36). His promises to reform his way of life – particularly in the matters of cigar smoking and heavy drinking – still seem to have been unfulfilled, for his letters to Zwickau continue to record his penniless condition due to overspending of his allowance. He dreamed of composing an opera on *Hamlet* and resumed his piano study with Wieck, but the latter seems to have been more interested in the formation of his prodigy daughter Clara; he was absent with her on a concert tour from Christmas 1830 until the end of January 1831, and the prospect of a still longer absence from September 1831 onwards obliged Schumann to look elsewhere. Accordingly on 20 August 1831 he wrote to Hummel asking to be accepted as a pupil; nothing came of the idea, but he was still clinging to it in May of the following year. The letter to Hummel voices his dissatisfaction with Wieck's teaching and his diary entries for the summer often record deep despondency concerning his own playing as well as disagreement with Wieck's views of music. Nothing had come of the proposed study of theory with Weinlig; only in June 1831 did he at last approach Heinrich Dorn, then conductor at the Leipzig theatre, who on 12 July began his instruction in thoroughbass (according to Dorn's account to Wasielewski 25 years later, Schumann's first exercise, a four-part chorale, was 'a model of part-writing in defiance of the rules'). In the meantime Schumann had found a new musical idol: Chopin. He was completely captivated by the latter's op.2, the variations on 'Là ci darem', which he unsuccessfully tried to master, and as early as 2 May he made up his mind to write about them.

On 8 June he wrote some poems headed 'Schmetterlinge' and recorded in his diary his decision to give his friends 'more beautiful, more suitable names': Wieck became 'Meister Raro', Clara 'Zilia', Christel (a girl who had just begun to play an important part in his sex life) 'Charitas', Dorn 'The Music Director', and so on. Five days later he had the idea of using them as characters in a novel, *Die Wunderkinder*, in which 'Florestan the *improvisatore*' appeared for the first time and Paganini, under a pseudonym, was to have a leading role. On 1 July, 'entirely new persons enter my diary today – two of my best friends. . . . Florestan and Eusebius', but it was not until 13 October that Florestan became 'my bosom friend; actually in the story he is to be my real self', while Eusebius, Meister Raro and the rest 'have changed their roles and from real persons have become fantasy characters'. Both Florestan and Eusebius appeared in the Chopin article, 'Ein Opus II', which at last sent to the *Allgemeine musikalische Zeitung* on 27 September (two days after the departure of Friedrich and Clara Wieck on their seven-month tour), though it did not appear till 7 December.

Schumann's most ambitious composition of 1831 was a Sonata in B minor, of which the first movement (embodying material from some variations on Paganini's *Rondo à la clochette*) was afterwards published as op.8; on 4 January 1832 he completed a set of variations on an original theme for Clara, and at the same time a set of piano pieces made up partly of the waltzes of the previous year, partly of revised versions of the four-hand polonaises of 1828, partly of new compositions, which he styled *Papillons* and related with incidents at the masked ball in Jean Paul's novel *Flegeljahre*. These were published by Kistner in April as op.2.

5. 1832–4. In April 1832 Dorn refused to go on with the lessons in thoroughbass and counterpoint, and Schumann was left to continue his studies with the help of Marpurg's *Abhandlung von der Fuge* in theory and Bach's *Das wohltemperirte Clavier* as practical models. The Wiecks returned at the beginning of May, but Schumann did not go back to his old quarters in their house, which he had left when they went away, nor apparently was there any resumption of piano lessons. About this time he began to have serious trouble with his fingers. This has often been attributed to his use of a mechanical device as an aid to piano playing. The device has been blamed for maiming one of his fingers, putting an end to his hopes of a career as a virtuoso; but the weakness in the index and middle fingers of the right hand preceded the use of the device, and may well have been an effect of mercury poisoning, induced by treatment for syphilis.

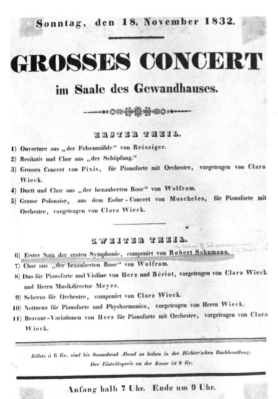

2. *Programme of the concert given by Clara Wieck and her father at the Zwickau Gewandhaus on 18 November 1832*

Compositions of the spring and summer of 1832 include an (apparently lost) *Exercice fantastique* op.5, dedicated to Kuntzsch, sometimes confused with the earlier *Etude fantastique* op.6 (i.e. the Toccata op.7, of which the second version was completed at the same time, July); piano transcriptions of six of Paganini's Caprices for unaccompanied violin: a set of *Pièces phantastiques* (or Intermezzos) for piano, mostly new but embodying portions of earlier compositions; a *Fundango: fantaisie rhapsodique pour le pianoforte, Oeuv. 4*, which was later expanded into the first movement of the F♯ minor Piano Sonata; and a set of 'XII Burlesken (Burle) in the style of the *Papillons*', which Schumann offered, in vain, to Breitkopf & Härtel later in the year, and of which one may survive as op.124 no.12 and possibly others as op.124 nos.1, 3 and 15, and the Intermezzo in the third movement of the F♯ minor Sonata. The Paganini Studies, the Intermezzos and the Toccata were published by Hofmeister of Leipzig. In October Schumann embarked on a much more ambitious work; in July he had confided to his old teacher, Kuntzsch, his intention to study 'score-reading and instrumentation', and on 2 November he approached Gottlieb Müller, Gewandhaus violinist and conductor of the Euterpe concerts, with a request for 'instruction in instrumentation' and 'to go through with you a symphony movement of my own composition' which he had 'worked at almost entirely according to my own ideas and without guidance'. A fortnight or so later he took the score of this movement, in G minor, with him to Zwickau where (and at Schneeberg near by) he spent four months of the winter. Clara Wieck and her father gave a concert there on 18 November, and the movement was performed on the same occasion; as a result Schumann completely rewrote it, and the revised version was played at Schneeberg in February 1833, when it shared the programme with Beethoven's Seventh Symphony, which exercised a marked influence on the second movement of his own work.

In March 1833 Schumann returned to Leipzig, occupying a new apartment in Riedels Garten, and on 29 April the first movement of the G minor Symphony was played at Clara Wieck's 'grand concert' in the Gewandhaus. By his own account it was a success, yet in May he abandoned the symphony in a not quite completed state. Some material from the fugal finale was embodied in the last number of a new composition, originally orchestrated though it survives only as a piano work, a set of so-called 'Impromptus' (really free variations) on the theme of Clara Wieck's *Romance variée* op.3; this was offered to Kistner as 'a second set of *Papillons*' but declined by him and issued at the composer's expense by his brothers' firm at Schneeberg in August. In June he wrote the first and third movements of the Piano Sonata in G minor op.22 and in July completed a second set of Paganini transcriptions, published as op.10. In June, too, Schumann, Wieck and a number of their friends began seriously to consider the desirability of founding a new musical periodical. A draft prospectus was prepared and (ultimately abortive) negotiations were begun with Hofmeister for its publication at the end of October. From July to the autumn (when in September he moved again, to Burgstrasse 21) Schumann suffered from the consequences of a feverish chill; in October he was thrown into a deeply melancholic state by the death of his sister-in-law Rosalie, and on the 'fearful night of the 17th' attempted or contemplated suicide by throwing himself from his fourth-floor window; he was left with a lifelong dread of living in upper storeys and promptly moved to a first-floor flat in the same house. A further blow was given by the death of his brother Julius on 18 November. Perhaps as a result of his mental condition – his diary records his obsession with the fear that he would go mad – he was unable to finish the two works on which he was engaged 'from Michaelmas to Christmas': a set of *Scènes mignonnes* or *Scènes musicales sur un thème connu de Fr. Schubert* (variations on Schubert's so-called *Sehnsuchtswalzer* op.9 no.2) and *Etüden in Form freier Variationen über ein Beethovensches Thema* (the Allegretto of the Seventh Symphony), of which one variation was published years later as op.124 no.2. A new friendship formed in December with the 23-year-old composer Ludwig Schunke, who shared his new flat, did much to rescue Schumann from mental depression. Schunke in turn introduced him in January to a music-loving couple, Karl and Henriette Voigt, to the latter of whom Schumann dedicated his Schubert variations.

In his letters of March 1834 Schumann several times mentioned 'three sonatas'; these were the F♯ minor, the G minor and one in F minor which is quite distinct from that afterwards published as op.14. He continued to work intermittently at this never completed F minor Sonata until February 1837; nor were its companions finished in 1834. From March onwards Schumann's time was almost wholly taken up with the affairs of the new periodical. In February Breitkopf & Härtel had, like Hofmeister, declined to handle it, but a publisher was found at last in C. H. F. Hartmann, and the first number of the *Neue Leipziger Zeitschrift für Musik*, published twice weekly, appeared on 3 April. This at once became the chief field of Schumann's literary activity – articles had previously appeared in *Der Komet* and the *Leipziger Tageblatt*, besides his one contribution to the *Allegemeine musikalische Zeitung* – though in 1840–41 he also contributed to the *Deutsche allgemeine Zeitung*. The first nominal editor of the new periodical was Julius Knorr, but Knorr's illness threw all the work on Schumann who, at the very same time, undertook to write the musical articles for Herlosssohn's *Damenkonversationslexikon*.

6. ERNESTINE AND CLARA. On 21 April 1834 a girl of 17½ years named Ernestine von Fricken came to Leipzig to board with the Wiecks as a piano pupil. She was the illegitimate child of a Captain Baron von Fricken in the little town of Asch. Schumann, who took her to be 'the daughter of a rich Bohemian baron', quickly fell in love with her and by 2 July was telling his mother he would like to marry her. Frau Voigt was their confidante, and the lovers met at the Voigts' house. On 1 September Baron von Fricken, disquieted by reports of the affair, came to Leipzig to take Ernestine away; a day or two before his arrival the lovers became betrothed, though only the Voigts were in the secret. On 5 September the Frickens went to Zwickau to interview Schumann's mother; Schumann himself rushed after them and there was some sort of discussion, but the Frickens left for Asch next day with the engagement still undisclosed. Just a week later Schumann conceived the idea of the set of piano pieces based on the musical letters – *S–C–H–A* – common to his name and to the town of Asch, which he called *Fasching: Schwänke auf vier Noten*, but afterwards renamed *Carnaval: scènes*

mignonnes sur quatre notes; by about 23 September he had written some 'pathetic' variations on a 'Thema quasi marcia funebre' in C♯ minor by the baron, who was an amateur flautist, variations which were later expanded into the work generally known as the *Etudes symphoniques*. Another variation-work of 1834, which cannot be dated more precisely, was a never completed set on Chopin's Nocturne op.15 no.3.

The new friend Schunke was dying of consumption; the Voigts were caring for him, but Schumann, unable to bear the sight, fled to Zwickau (25 October), where a month later he was struggling with a finale to the variations, beginning like the definitive Variation I, in which the funeral march was to be worked up 'gradually into a proud triumphal procession' (Schunke died on 7 December). On 4 December Schumann paid a visit to Asch; even then he did not know the truth about Ernestine's parentage. On 13 December Fricken formally adopted her as his daughter.

On 15 December Schumann was summoned back from Zwickau to Leipzig to negotiate a change of publisher for the *Neue Zeitschrift für Musik*. He and his group were dissatisfied with Hartmann, and from the first number of 1835 the paper was issued by J. A. Barth, with Schumann as the named editor and principal if not sole proprietor. In April 1835 Clara Wieck, now aged 15½, returned to Leipzig after a concert tour that had lasted since the previous November, and until the end of July, when she left for a concert tour, Schumann was with her daily; a marked cooling of his attitude to Ernestine followed and in August, when he had discovered the circumstances of her birth, he began to try to withdraw from his engagement. On 20 October the *Neue Zeitschrift* published the first of 'Eusebius's' *Schwärmbriefe an Chiara*; on 25 November he and Clara exchanged their first kiss; we hear of more kisses at Zwickau in December; on New Year's Day 1836 Ernestine was formally jilted.

Little is known of Schumann's compositions, or his life generally, during 1835; but the F♯ minor Sonata had been completed by the end of August and in October most of the original finale of the G minor Sonata was written (the very end was still unwritten in March 1837). In August Mendelssohn paid a visit to Leipzig preparatory to his permanent settlement at the end of September as director of the Gewandhaus concerts, an event which revolutionized the musical life of the city and gave Schumann a new friend. At the beginning of October he also met two other of his idols at the Wiecks' house, Chopin and Moscheles. From this year, too, dates Schumann's long essay on Berlioz and his *Symphonie fantastique* which appeared in the *Neue Zeitschrift*, nos.33–49 of 1835.

In the middle of January 1836 Wieck took Clara to Dresden, probably to remove her from proximity to Schumann. But the latter was called to Zwickau by his mother's death on 4 February and, taking advantage of Wieck's temporary absence, he was able to see Clara between 7 and 11 February. Wieck, learning of this on his return, was furious with Clara and wrote to Schumann breaking off all relations with him: he may well have suspected that Schumann had contracted syphilis. When at last father and daughter returned to Leipzig on 8 April the lovers were obliged to avoid each other; Clara completely obeyed her father and even showed some leaning towards Carl Banck, whom Wieck engaged to give her singing lessons and who replaced

Schumann as her mentor in composition. For his part, Schumann 'sought out Charitas' again and again, and afterwards noted that this had 'consequences' in January 1837.

When on 8 June the F♯ minor Sonata op.11 ('Dedicated to Clara by Florestan and Eusebius') was published, Schumann sent her a copy; she replied, doubtless under compulsion, by returning all his letters and asking him for hers. On 5 June he completed another sonata, the F minor op.14, originally in five movements, which was published later in the year by Haslinger of Vienna without its two scherzos and under the title 'Concert sans orchestre' (one of the scherzos was restored in 1853, when the second edition was issued as *Troisième grande sonate*; the other was published separately, on Brahms's initiative, in 1866). In the same month he sketched out yet another piano sonata, in C, into which he poured the expression of his desperate resignation, though the work was also intended as a contribution to the proposed Beethoven memorial at Bonn; it was practically completed by the beginning of December and offered on 19 December to Kistner as *Ruinen, Trophäen, Palmen: grosse Sonate für das Pianoforte, für Beethovens Monument, von Florestan und Eusebius*, with the suggestion that 100 copies should be given to the Bonn committee for them to sell; nothing came of this, and the work, particularly the last movement with its concealed reference to Beethoven's Seventh Symphony, underwent considerable revision before it was published as the Phantasie op.17 in April 1839.

Early in August 1836 Schumann was 'thinking of a quintet for strings and piano duet', but nothing came of the project. Then another visit from Chopin on 12 September seems to have sent him back to his *Etudes symphoniques* during the following week; he spent 'the whole day of 18 September at the piano', composing 'études with great gusto and excitement'. The present finale must have been written later still, for the young Mendelssohn disciple, Sterndale Bennett, who was musically saluted with a Marschner quotation in that finale, did not arrive at Leipzig until 29 October. Sterndale Bennett's first visit to Leipzig, during which he formed a warm friendship with Schumann, lasted until June of the following year; he paid a second visit from October 1838 to March 1839.

7. 1837–8. At the beginning of 1837 Schumann seems to have been resigned to the loss of Clara; he was living quietly, reading *Ivanhoe*, *King John* and *Macbeth*, copying out Bach's *Art of Fugue*, studying 'older music', working at the finale of his other, never completed F minor Sonata, thinking of a Symphony in E♭. But in March this mood gave way to one of passionate despair, which he seems to have tried to drown in drink and by such riotous behaviour that his landlady, tolerant as she was, threatened to turn him out of his lodgings. On 3 May Clara Wieck returned to Leipzig after a concert tour of two or three months; a few weeks later Banck, too, fell into disgrace with her father – to her own consternation – and on 19 May Schumann published in his paper an article 'On the Last Art-historical Ball at Editor * *'s' evidently written before Banck's dismissal, in which Banck himself was ridiculed as 'de Knapp' and Clara as 'Ambrosia', the still-loved aspect of Clara being personified as 'Beda'. At this period Schumann's love for Clara was strongly mingled with hatred and,

whether or not with the idea of 'avenging himself on her', as he afterwards said, he contemplated marriage to another Clara whose surname remains unknown. From mid-June to early July he was much in the company of the beautiful 18-year-old Scottish pianist Robena Laidlaw, to whom he dedicated the *Phantasiestücke* op.12, most of which were composed in the period 22 May–4 July.

Then a step towards reconciliation was taken by Clara. Through their common friend E. A. Becker she asked Schumann to return to her the letters she had sent back more than a year before. He replied on 13 August in a letter which Clara justly described as 'cold, serious and yet so beautiful', assuring her she was still 'the dearest in the world' to him; the same day she played in public, in the Börsensaal, three of the *Etudes symphoniques*, and the day after – her letter is misdated 15 August – she formally pledged herself to him. Not until 8 or 9 September were the lovers able to meet, and on 13 September, Clara's birthday, Schumann wrote to her father asking for her hand. Both then and during the next few months Wieck seems to have been coldly and mockingly evasive rather than frankly hostile, and on 15 October he was able to take Clara away on a seven-month concert tour. During that separation the lovers corresponded secretly, but Clara's letters did not always give Schumann unalloyed consolation; for one thing, she was determined not to marry until Robert was in a financial position to assure her comfort. Even before the parting, Schumann's diary for early October shows that he was again contemplating suicide.

Schumann's first compositions after the reconciliation were the *Davidsbündlertänze* (by October), which were published the following year at his own expense through Friese, who in July 1837 had taken over the publication of the *Neue Zeitschrift* (its circulation at the time was between 450 and 500). Throughout October and November he was working 'furiously' at fugue, using Marpurg's textbook, but the first compositions of 1838 show little trace of this preoccupation; they were the *Novelletten* – the eight of op.21 and some of the pieces published later in opp.99 and 124 – and the *Kinderszenen*, the latter nearly all written in February; in March he completed the definitive form of the C major Phantasie op.17, and towards the end of April the *Kreisleriana* 'in four days'. Then on 14 May the Wiecks returned to Leipzig, and before long Clara's proximity – they were able to meet fairly often – had an unfortunate effect on his work. On the other hand, when Clara went to Dresden for a month in July, he had days and nights of fearful depression, and his diary records that one night he was 'within a moment of bearing it no longer'. They had for some time thought of settling together in Vienna, where Clara already enjoyed a high reputation, and persuading Haslinger there to publish the *Neue Zeitschrift*; in order to reconnoitre the position Schumann spent the winter in the Austrian capital, leaving Leipzig on 27 September and travelling by way of Dresden and Prague. The editorial direction of the *Neue Zeitschrift* was left in the hands of Oswald Lorenz.

In Vienna Schumann occupied a first-floor room at Schön Laternengasse 679. There in December he wrote the definitive finale of the G minor Piano Sonata, the Scherzo, Gigue and Romanze op.32, the little piece for Clara (*An C——*, *Gruss zum Heiligen Abend* and *Wunsch*, as it is headed in various manuscripts) afterwards published without title as op.99 no.1, and the Arabeske op.18; in January 1839 the *Blumenstück* op.19, and the first movement of a Piano Concerto in D minor; by about the end of February the *Humoreske* op.20; by the middle of March the beginning of 'a big *romantic sonata*' (possibly the work we now know as the *Faschingsschwank aus Wien*, of which four movements date from this period, though a lost Allegro in C minor may really be the first movement of this sonata), and soon afterwards the earliest of the *Nachtstücke* op.23 (as late as 10 December 1839 the Intermezzo from the *Faschingsschwank* was published as a supplement to the *Neue Zeitschrift* as a 'fragment from the *Nachtstücke* which are to appear shortly').

8. TOWARDS MARRIAGE. Apart from creative work, the year 1839 opened auspiciously with a visit to Schubert's brother in the course of which Schumann unearthed a number of the master's manuscripts, including that of the 'Great' C major Symphony. But Schumann's hopes of Vienna were dashed one by one; he saw it would be impossible to publish the *Neue Zeitschrift* there; and on 30 March he received news of his brother Eduard's serious illness. He returned hurriedly to Leipzig, and after his brother's death on 6 April found himself confronted with a financial crisis in the family affairs; for a time he even contemplated the temporary abandonment of his career as a composer in order to take over the management of the family publishing and bookselling business. He had no sooner learnt that this would not be necessary than he was alarmed by the attitude of Clara, who had been sent to Paris in January and now began to insist again on financial security as a preliminary to marriage. Harmony between the lovers was restored by the middle of May, and after another attempt by Wieck to break the engagement, Clara signed, on 15 June, the formal statement leading to legal proceedings for the setting aside of her father's consent. On 30 June Schumann placed the case in a lawyer's hands and on 15 or 16 July the plea was submitted to the courts, which on the 19th ordered an attempt at arbitration. At this period Schumann contemplated a marriage in Paris, and at the end of July he visited Berlin to enlist Clara's mother, now married to Adolf Bargiel, as an ally.

The course of the legal proceedings obliged Clara to return from Paris. Schumann met her at Altenburg on 19 August, and they spent a few happy days at Schneeberg with his relations, she a few more alone at Zwickau; on the 30th she followed him to Leipzig, staying with Friese. Her mother arrived next day and, in accordance with the court order, Archdeacon Fischer made two attempts to effect an arbitration; but the first time Wieck did not appear at all, the second too late. On 3 September Clara's mother took her away to Berlin. Ten days later Schumann followed her there and on the 17th, as the result of a fresh advance by Wieck, brought her back to Leipzig, where she stayed with maternal relatives. Clara's interviews with her father were abortive, as he imposed impossible financial conditions as the price of his consent to the marriage: on the one hand the sacrifice to him of all Clara's earnings during the last seven years, on the other a settlement on her of two-thirds of Schumann's capital. On 2 October the case came before the court of appeal, but Wieck did not appear, pleading that the previous order for arbitration had not yet been carried out! The result of

3. Robert Schumann: lithograph by Feckert after a portrait by Adolf Menzel (1815–1905)

this manoeuvre was a further postponement until mid-December. The next day Clara returned to Berlin.

This was the most painful period of all for the lovers; Wieck's slanders and annoyances – now directed against Clara herself as well as against Schumann – reached a new height. Schumann's mental health had begun to suffer in September and things became worse during the next two months; the death of his old friend Henriette Voigt on 15 October was a further cause of depression. It is true that in one letter to Clara he speaks of 'about 50 new compositions begun', but there are many more references to 'complete lack of ideas' and 'inability to compose any more'. Indeed the second half of 1839 was almost completely blank as regards creative work. In June Schumann had begun two string quartets, and on 23 July a third, but nothing came of these; the little Fughette in G minor op.32 no.4 dates from the same period. In October he reported to Clara that he has been 'chewing for eight days at a stupid prelude and fugue' which he later condensed into the Präludium op.99 no.10. Only the imminence of Clara's return for the next court hearing seems to have released a fresh burst of activity, of which the principal fruit was the set of three Romanzen op.28.

On 18 December all parties appeared before the court of appeal and Wieck so lost control of himself that he had to be silenced by the president of the court. Judgment was reserved until 4 January 1840, and during the period of waiting the lovers spent Christmas together in Berlin. The decision, when it came, was not completely favourable; the court dismissed all Wieck's objections except one – the charge that Schumann was a heavy drinker. Wieck returned to the legal attack in a *Deductionsschrift*, handed to the court on 26 January, and privately distributed lithographed copies of his

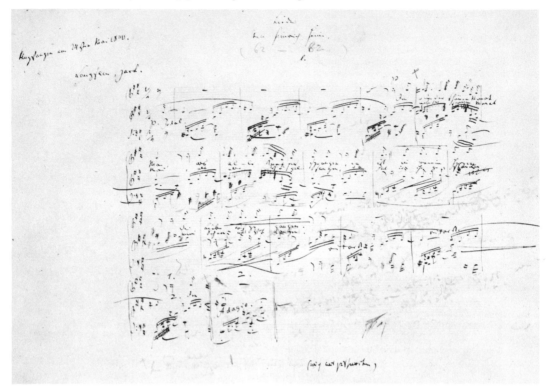

4. Autograph MS of 'Im wunderschönen Monat Mai' from Schumann's 'Dichterliebe', 1840 (D-Bds)

original charges to Schumann's and Clara's friends; Schumann replied to the renewed legal accusation in a *Refutationsschrift* on 13 February, but was advised to take no action against the defamatory lithographs. On 28 March the parties were informed that the higher court of appeal had confirmed the judgment of 4 January; the onus of proving the charge of drunkenness rested with Wieck. In the meantime Schumann had had the idea of strengthening his position by acquiring a doctorate; on 31 January he inquired of Dr G. A. Keferstein the conditions for the granting of a Jena degree, and his friend was soon able to assure him that the university was prepared to make him a Doctor of Philosophy, without thesis or examination, in recognition of his achievements as composer, writer and editor. His curriculum vitae was sent in on 17 February, and he received his diploma 11 days later.

9. THE YEAR OF SONG. The wave of creative energy gained impetus in January; a 'little Sonatina in B♭' was begun, and towards the end of the month the *Faschingsschwank* was taken up again and completed. Far more important: after an interval of 12 years, Schumann returned to the composition of songs. The earliest of the 1840 songs actually dated was the Fool's Song from *Twelfth Night*, op.127 no.5, written on 1 February. In a letter of 16 February, Schumann told Clara of the composition of 'six books of songs, ballads, big and little, and four-part'. Four of the 'sechs Hefte' consist of the songs published in October of the same year as *Myrthen* op.25, though not all of them had been composed when Schumann wrote to Clara. The only

'big ballad' was the setting of Heine's *Belsatzar* (on 7 February), published in 1846 as op.57. The Heine *Liederkreis* op.24 was completed by 24 February. The flow of songs was slowed down in March by preliminary work on an opera, *Doge und Dogaressa*, based on a story in the second part of Hoffmann's *Serapions-Brüder*; Schumann himself sketched out a prose libretto which Julius Becker tried, not very successfully, to versify, and the project was not finally abandoned until May. During March Liszt visited Leipzig and Schumann made his acquaintance.

In the meantime Clara had visited Leipzig again and the pair had spent a blissful fortnight together in Berlin (17–30 April), to which the Eichendorff *Liederkreis* op.39, composed during May, was the immediate sequel. The Eichendorff cycle was immediately followed by a Heine cycle, 20 songs composed between 24 May and 1 June: the *Dichterliebe* op.48 and four other songs (op.127 nos.2 and 3; op.142 nos.2 and 4) originally intended as part of the same set. On 5 June Clara came to Leipzig and songwriting was suspended.

On 7 July the lovers learnt that Wieck had failed to produce his proof of habitual drunkenness. They at once began a search for a dwelling and on the 16th found 'a little apartment in the Inselstrasse'. Legal consent to the marriage was granted on 1 August, and the banns were published on 16 August, Clara seeking distraction during this last nerve-racking period by a short concert tour in Thuringia while Schumann returned to his songwriting. During July he had composed the three Chamisso songs op.31, the five lieder op.40 and the Chamisso cycle *Frauenliebe und -leben* op.42 (on 11–

12 July); now in August he completed the Geibel songs op.30, and the Reinick songs op.36. On 12 September Clara and Robert were married at the village church of Schönefeld near Leipzig.

The first composition after marriage was the vocal duet *Wenn ich ein Vöglein wär* op.43 no.1 (afterwards incorporated in the opera *Genoveva*). Ten days later (13 October) Schumann noted in his *Haushaltbuch*: 'Afternoon symphonic attempts'. A year before Clara had confided to her diary her belief that

it would be best if he composed for orchestra; his imagination cannot find sufficient scope on the piano.... His compositions are all orchestral in feeling.... My highest wish is that he should compose for orchestra – that is his field! May I succeed in bringing him to it.

But the impulse to songwriting was as yet still predominant. After a patriotic potboiler, *Der deutsche Rhein*, for solo voice, chorus and piano, of which 1500 copies were sold in a month or so, came an outpouring of Kerner songs in November and December, most of them published as op.35, others posthumously in opp.127 and 142. Other scattered songs of this prolific year, 1840, were collected in the first volume of *Lieder und Gesänge* op.27 and the first three volumes of *Romanzen und Balladen* opp.45, 49 and 53. Schumann's 'great' song period ended with op.37, the *Gedichte aus 'Liebesfrühling'* by Rückert, to which Clara contributed three numbers (2, 4 and 11); they were begun in January 1841, but not completed until August. Schumann had in the intervening months turned to a very different field.

10. ORCHESTRAL MUSIC. In four days, 23–6 January 1841, to Clara's great joy, he sketched out his symphony, in B♭, op.38, suggested by a poem of Adolph Böttger's and originally entitled 'Spring Symphony'. The orchestration took from 27 January to 20 February; the symphony was rehearsed by Mendelssohn on 28 March and performed under his direction three days later in the Leipzig Gewandhaus at a concert given by Clara on behalf of the orchestra's pension fund. It was well received, though in reality not quite so enthusiastically as the Schumanns imagined. But Schumann felt encouraged to proceed with 'all sorts of other orchestral plans', of which the next was an Overture in E, begun on 12 April and completed in score five days later. Then came a 'scherzo to the overture' and a finale in E, the whole 'Suite' (as it was first called) being finished on 8 May; Schumann a little later spoke of it as 'die Symphonette', but when it was first performed (with the D minor Symphony) on 6 December of the same year, the work was described as 'Overture, Scherzo and Finale'. Next, in little more than a week, came a Fantasie in A minor for piano and orchestra, completed on 20 May, which Clara tried out at a Gewandhaus rehearsal on 13 August; this was the piece we now know as the first movement of the Piano Concerto. (Just over a fortnight later, on 1 September, she gave birth to the first of their eight children, Marie.) Ten days after the completion of the Fantasie, Schumann began a second symphony, in D minor, and at about the same time made some revision of no.1. This Symphony in D minor, which we now know in a different guise as 'no.4', was completed in its original form on 9 September, and within a fortnight Schumann had begun a successor to it; the first movement and scherzo of a Symphony in C minor ('Sinfonie III') were roughed out on 23 September, the Adagio and Rondo

the following day, and by the 26th the sketch was 'practically finished'. But nothing more came of it; only the scherzo was later published as a piano piece, op.99 no.13. The wave of symphonic activity had spent itself; the *Neue Zeitschrift* was still taking up much of Schumann's time, and his thoughts were turning in a fresh direction – to opera. He considered subjects from Calderón and came under the spell of Moore's *Paradise and the Peri*. On 22 August he was working on a 'text to the Peri', presumably in the first place an opera libretto; later in the year he called in Böttger's help, and on 6 January 1842, the 'text' was finished, though possibly not that composed two years later. The only other major work of 1841 was a setting of Heine's *Tragödie* for chorus and orchestra, practically finished on 8 November, but abandoned in this form and finally published for one and two voices with piano as op.64 no.3.

11. CHAMBER MUSIC. In November 1841 the Schumanns had been invited to Weimar, Clara to play, Robert to be present at the performance of his works (the B♭ Symphony and songs). In February 1842 they set out on a similar tour to Bremen, Oldenburg and Hamburg, in the course of which Schumann became unpleasantly conscious of his rather passive part as Clara's shadow. (He had declined an invitation to conduct the symphony, pleading short sight.) Partly because of this, partly because it was difficult to absent himself longer from the *Neue Zeitschrift*, he returned alone to Leipzig on 12 March while Clara went on to Copenhagen, where she stayed for a month (20 March–18 April). Schumann spent this period of separation in deep melancholy, which he tried to drown in 'beer and champagne', unable to compose, working at counter-

5. *Title-page of the first edition of Schumann's 'Phantasiestücke' op.88 (Leipzig: Kistner, 1850)*

(a)

(b)

6. Autograph score of the opening of Schumann's Symphony in D minor: (a) 1841 version (A-Wgm); (b) 1851 version (D-B)

point and fugue, brooding over the possibility of taking Clara to America, while Wieck spread a rumour that the pair had parted. Before setting out in February Schumann had been visited by 'quartet-ish thoughts'; now in his loneliness he returned to the study of Mozart's and Haydn's quartets, then of Beethoven's.

Clara's return on 26 April brought a happier mood. On 2 June he made 'quartet essays'; two days later the A minor Quartet was begun; on the 11th he began a second quartet before the first was finished; and the third quartet of op.41 was written between 8 and 22 July. In the interval between the second and third quartets Schumann turned again on his old enemy Banck, attacking his *Wallfahrt zur heiligen Madonna* in a savage article that he did not reprint when he came to collect his writings in book form years later. At about the same time a libellous onslaught on another foe of some years' standing, Gustav Schilling, earned Schumann a sentence of six days' imprisonment – commuted to a five-thaler fine. After a short holiday at Karlsbad and Marienbad in August, and a successful rehearsal of the three quartets on 8 September, Schumann began a Piano Quintet on 23 September, completing the fair copy on 12 October; and despite the 'constant fearful sleepless nights' a Piano Quartet was begun on 24 October and finished a month later. The last products of this period of preoccupation with chamber music were a Piano Trio in A minor, completed in December 1842, and an Andante and Variations for two pianos, two cellos and horn, completed by the end of January 1843. Neither satisfied him in its original form, but the trio, seven years later, yielded the material for the *Phantasiestücke* op.88, and the variations were recast for pianos only in August and published as op.46 in February 1844; the first variation was now suppressed and the ending extended.

12. CHORAL MUSIC. February 1843 was marked by a good deal of intercourse with Berlioz, who visited Leipzig twice in that month, and by Clara's visit of reconciliation to her father at Dresden. (In the following December Wieck made an embarrassed approach to Schumann himself and an uneasy peace was concluded.) And on the 20th or 23rd (Schumann's own dates are at variance) he also began a composition which had occupied his thoughts for 18 months, a setting of *Das Paradies und die Peri*, not now as an opera but as 'an oratorio not for the oratory'. The text was arranged by himself from a manuscript translation of Moore by his friend Flechsig and the published translation by Theodor Oelckers. The score, which Schumann considered his most important up to that date, was completed on 16 June. During the composition of the *Peri* the Leipzig Conservatory was opened (3 April) with Mendelssohn as its director and Schumann as one of the professors, responsible for 'piano playing, composition and playing from score'. And on 25 April a second daughter, Elise, was born. After the completion of the *Peri*, for which Peters paid 550 thalers, Schumann lay fallow for the rest of the year or struggled with projects that came to nothing. Opera in particular occupied his thoughts. On 1 December Schumann conducted the first orchestral rehearsal of the *Peri* – his début as a conductor – and on the 4th and 11th the actual performances; he himself was satisfied and the Leipzig public were enthusiastic, but it is clear that he was passive and ineffectual as a conductor – as, indeed, he was also as a teacher at the conservatory.

The first five months of 1844 were spent in a concert tour of Russia, long desired by Clara, long dreaded by her husband, who at last allowed himself to be persuaded to go by Mendelssohn. Leaving the children with the relations at Schneeberg, the Schumanns set off on 25 January. They travelled by way of Königsberg, Riga, Mitau and Dorpat (where Schumann had a week's illness), Clara giving concerts in each town, and reached St Petersburg on 4 March. There Clara gave four successful public concerts and played to Nicholas I and the tsaritsa; they were warmly greeted both by foreign musicians, including their old friend Henselt, and by wealthy Russian dilettantes such as A. F. L'vov and Count Michal Wielhorski, whose orchestra played the B♭ Symphony in private under Schumann's direction on 21 March; but the visit did little to introduce Schumann's music to the wider musical public. He met neither Glinka nor Dargomïzhsky, though he and Clara attended a party at which the former was present. On 2 April they left St Petersburg, spent Easter at Tver with Schumann's maternal uncle, who had settled in Russia, and arrived in Moscow on 10 April. Clara's audiences were small, but the aristocracy were amiable and Schumann's Quintet was given at a matinée. They heard *A Life for the Tsar*, of which only the first act won Schumann's praise, and were greatly impressed by the Kremlin, which inspired him to write five poems. On 8 May they left again for St Petersburg and ten days later sailed from Kronstadt for Swinemünde; on 30 May they were back at Leipzig.

Throughout the Russian tour Schumann had been tortured by fits of melancholy, partly physical in origin, partly psychological – the result of consciousness that his part was markedly secondary to Clara's. He was also irritated by the fact that he was wasting time, unable to work at the opera he had been 'burning' to write since November. He took the second part of Goethe's *Faust* with him, selected certain scenes during his illness at Dorpat and even sketched music for the closing scene. Still in ill-health, on returning to Leipzig his first care was to disembarrass himself of another obstacle to creative work, the editorship of the *Neue Zeitschrift für Musik* (in the previous November Dr Härtel had offered him the editorship of the much older *Allgemeine musikalische Zeitung*, but he had declined). He was succeeded at the end of June by Oswald Lorenz, who made way for Franz Brendel at the beginning of the next year. *Faust* was now superseded as an opera subject by Byron's *Corsair*; on 2 July he approached a librettist, and he actually composed a chorus of corsairs and an air for Conrad. But a visit from Hans Andersen on 22 July turned his attention to the poet's *Lykkens Kalosker* which he thought would make 'a fine *Zauberoper*', an idea to which he clung at least until the following April. In August he returned to *Faust* and completed the first three numbers of what we now know as part 3 of *Szenen aus Goethes Faust*, possibly a first draft of the Chorus Mysticus as well; in December he began to think of treating *Faust* as an oratorio instead of an opera, but laid the subject aside for several years.

The rather forced labour on *Faust* had completely exhausted Schumann's nervous energy, and at the end of August he had a very serious breakdown; it became intolerable to listen to music, 'which cut into my nerves as if with knives': in addition he felt slighted by the appointment of Gade to succeed Mendelssohn, who had

7. *Schumann's sketch of the Kremlin (made during the 1844 concert tour of Russia) in the Robert-Schumann-Haus, Zwickau*

left Leipzig, in the direction of the Gewandhaus concerts. A visit to the Harz in mid-September and treatment with Karlsbad salts both left Schumann in a worse state than before.

13. DRESDEN. On 3 October 1844 the Schumanns went to Dresden; the first eight days were terrible – Schumann was sleepless, tortured by fearful imaginings, Clara found him 'swimming in tears' each morning, and even walking was difficult; but then a slight improvement set in, and they came to a decision to move to Dresden altogether. On 17 October they took a flat in the Waisenhausstrasse, no.35, and on 13 December they left Leipzig for their new home.

In the musically rather dull and conservative atmosphere of Dresden a mental convalescence began. In January 1845 Schumann started to teach Clara counterpoint, and on 28 February he himself wrote a fugue in D minor (either no.1 or no.2 of op.72). In April his *Haushaltbuch* begins to record happier moods and 'spring feelings'. On the 7th he began to guide Clara through Cherubini's *Cours de contrepoint* and started writing an organ fugue on B–A–C–H op.60 no.1; a second fugue was completed on the 18th (but the sixth not until 22 November). Later in April he had the idea of composing for the pedal piano – they had just hired a pedal attachment in order to practise organ playing – and the Studies and Sketches opp.56 and 58 were composed in the period 29 April–7 June. They were followed by a more important work, a Rondo for piano and orchestra, which with a middle movement (completed on 16 July) was appended to the Fantasie of 1841 to form the Piano Concerto op.54, which Clara played for the first time at the Leipzig Gewandhaus on 1 January 1846. Schumann's health was by no means fully restored in 1845, and he had to give up the idea of attending the unveiling of the Beethoven memorial at Bonn on 10 August. In October he rewrote the finale of op.52, finishing the score on the 20th. The previous day *Tannhäuser* had been given its first performance, but Schumann, who had formed a poor opinion of the work from the score given him by Wagner, was not present; when he did hear the opera, on 22 November, he radically changed his view. At this period he and Wagner belonged to the same circle, which with Hiller was concerned in founding regular subscription concerts at Dresden on the lines of the Leipzig Gewandhaus series.

A passage in a letter to Mendelssohn dating from the end of September 1845 has been generally interpreted as an indication that the Symphony in C was conceived then, but the earliest hint in the *Haushaltbuch* is dated 12 December; the sketch of the first movement was finished by the 17th and the whole work practically completed in draft by the 28th. But Schumann hesitated long over the orchestration; it was not begun until 12 February 1846 and, owing to aural nerve trouble (continual singing in the ears), even the first movement was not finished until 8 May, the whole work only on 19 October, less than three weeks before the first performance (Gewandhaus, 5 November). Except for a few partsongs, opp.55 and 59, the year 1846 was otherwise completely unproductive. Opera plans were considered, but rejected one after another; so too (in March) was an autobiography (*Biographie eines Davidsbündlers*). The other events of the year included the birth of a fourth child, their first son, Emil (8 February), visits to Maxen (May), to Norderney for sea-bathing (July–August) and a concert-giving expedition to Vienna on which the Schumanns embarked on 24 November. Even Clara's playing failed to arouse much enthusiasm in Vienna, and at the third concert, on 1 January 1847, the Piano Concerto and B♭ Symphony conducted by the composer were very coolly received. The Schumanns left on 21 January, gave a concert at Brno and two in Prague, which were more successful, and returned to Dresden on 4 February. From 11 February to 24 March they were in Berlin, where Clara introduced the Piano Quintet at her concerts on 1 and 17 March and Schumann conducted a rather unsuccessful performance of *Das Paradies und die Peri* by the Singakademie on 17 February; here they were strongly tempted to make their home, for Clara had few close friends at Dresden, and in Berlin she had her mother and Mendelssohn's sister Fanny; but Fanny Hensel's death on 14 May put an end to the plan.

14. OPERA PLANS. Directly after the return from Berlin, at the end of March 1847, Schumann again began serious consideration of opera projects. For a few days he toyed with Słowacki's *Mazeppa*, but on 1 April decided definitely on Hebbel's *Genoveva*, which he had just read, and asked Robert Reinick to work out a libretto in accordance with his ideas. On 5 April he actually completed the first draft of the overture. But he soon became dissatisfied with Reinick's text and on 14 May approached Hebbel himself with a request for help; nothing came of this, though a personal visit from Hebbel in the course of the summer made a deep impression on Schumann. Ultimately the libretto of *Genoveva* was compiled by the composer from Reinick's attempt, Hebbel's play and the play on the same subject by Tieck. While waiting for the *Genoveva* text Schumann took up *Faust* again on 17 April and composed and orchestrated the final chorus by 23 April; however, this failed to satisfy him, and on 22 May he began another version, which he completed by the end of July. The D minor Trio op.63 was written at the same time (3–16 June), and in May two Mörike songs were composed which, with the solo version of the Heine *Tragödie* of 1841, made up the fourth volume of *Romanzen und Balladen* op.64. Notwithstanding the death of their youngest child, Emil, on 22 June, the Schumanns went on 2 July to Zwickau, where for nearly a fortnight the little Saxon town fêted her now famous son with a serenade, a concert of his works and a popular concert at the Burgkeller; on 10 July Schumann conducted the C major Symphony and the choral *Beim Abschied zu singen* op.84, specially written for the occasion. On 14 July he completed a drastic revision of this symphony and in August began yet another trio – the F major op.80 – of which the sketch was completed on 25 October.

On 5 November Schumann was shocked by the news of Mendelssohn's death the previous day. He attended the memorial service at Leipzig on the 7th and on his return, with a view to a long article or even short book, began to note down some 'Reminiscences of Felix Mendelssohn-Bartholdy', published only in 1947. Two days after Mendelssohn's funeral came the farewell dinner for Ferdinand Hiller, who was leaving Dresden for Düsseldorf. Schumann succeeded Hiller as master of the Dresden *Liedertafel* and composed for it the choruses opp.65 (November) and 62 (December); this activity interested him so much that at the end of November he conceived the idea of a parallel society for mixed voices, and accordingly the Verein für Chorgesang met for its first practice on 5 January 1848. He composed *solfeggi*, which have remained unpublished, for both the male-voice *Liedertafel* and the choral society.

On 26 December 1847 Schumann finished the orchestration of his *Genoveva* overture, sketched eight months earlier, and immediately started the composition of the first act; the excitement at once told heavily on his nerves, and he had to wrestle with the remoulding of the libretto in the intervals of composition, each act being completed (in the order of text, composition sketch, score) before the next was begun. Nevertheless the first act was finished in sketch by 3 January 1848, though not played to Clara until 16 days later (on the next day, the 20th, she gave birth to a son, Ludwig). Act 2 was sketched between 21 January and 4 February, and completed in full score on 30 March. In the meantime Schumann had been thrown into great excitement, and

Clara into deep alarm, by the revolutionary outbreaks. On 18 March his *Haushaltbuch* hailed a 'springtime of the peoples' (*Völkerfrühling*), the next day he noted 'the *great* news from Berlin' and during 3–19 April he composed three patriotic and revolutionary songs for men's chorus and wind band, originally numbered op.65 but never published in his lifetime. Act 3 of *Genoveva* was sketched between 24 April and 3 May, and then on 6 May the B♭ major chorus 'Gerettet ist das edle Glied' for *Faust* (part 3 no.4, last section). On 25 June he was able, semi-privately, to try out the whole of the *Faust* music so far written (part 3 of the *Szenen*) with chorus and orchestra – to his great satisfaction, for the last chorus had given him very great trouble. Two days later he finished the composition sketch of the fourth act of *Genoveva* and on 4 August the full score of the whole opera. The very next day he began to sketch some music for Byron's *Manfred*; this work was interrupted by the making of the four-hand arrangement of the C major Symphony and the composition during the fortnight 30 August–14 September of the *Album für die Jugend* op.68, of which the first seven pieces were given to Marie on her birthday (1 September); but the *Manfred* overture was 'practically finished' on 19 October, the whole first act was sketched in a single day (6 November) and the entire score was completed on 23 November.

15. A PROLIFIC SPELL. Schumann was now in full flood of composition. On 25 November he began two very different works, both inspired by the writings of Rückert, the *Adventlied* for chorus and orchestra (completed in sketch on 30 November; orchestrated on 3–19 December) and the *Bilder aus Osten* for piano duet, suggested by Rückert's version of the Arabic *Makamen* of Hariri (completed 26 December). Another piano work of literary inspiration was the set of solo *Waldscenen* op.82, suggested by H. Laube's *Jagdbrevier* (composed 29 December–6 January 1849). The first three and a half months of 1849 were equally productive; works of the most diverse kinds followed in rapid succession – the touching-up of *Genoveva* (January), the *Phantasiestücke* for clarinet and piano (op.73; 11–12 February), the Adagio and Allegro for horn and piano (op.70; 14–17 February), the *Conzertstück* for four horns and orchestra (op.86; sketched 18–20 February, orchestrated by 11 March), a number of *Romanzen und Balladen* for mixed chorus (opp.67, 75 and some at least of those posthumously published as opp.145–6; 6–16 March), two sets of *Romanzen* for women's voices (opp.69, 91; 17–22 March – op.91 no.6 added in August), the *Spanisches Liederspiel*, a cycle of vocal solos, duets and quartets (op.74; sketched 24–8 March). Then the trios in D minor and F were revised for publication, a labour that was completed on 9 April, on which day Schumann lost his last surviving brother, Karl. The 'choral ballads', in which Schumann considered he had discovered a new species, were at once tried out with the Chorverein and met with success. (He had given up the *Liedertafel* the previous year, finding it more trouble than it was worth.) On 13–15 April were written the five *Stücke im Volkston* for cello and piano, and on the 21st Schumann began the *Liederalbum für die Jugend* op.79.

Then came a dramatic interruption. On 3 May the Schumanns returned from a day in the country to find Dresden in revolutionary uproar; alarm bells rang and

8. Robert and Clara Schumann: daguerreotype, 1850

shots were fired. Next day the democrats formed a provisional government, and barricades were thrown up in the streets. Unwilling to take an active part like Wagner, Schumann on 5 May evaded forcible enrolment in the street guard by flight through the garden door with Clara and the seven-year-old Marie, abandoning the younger children; they took a train to Mügeln, then walked to Dohna and finally took refuge with their friend Major Serre at Maxen, where Schumann that evening wrote the *Frühlingslied* op.79 no.18. Clara was anxious to return to fetch the younger children; accompanied by two other women, she set off at three o'clock in the morning, found the children asleep despite the firing, and fetched them safely to Maxen where 'my poor Robert had also spent anxious hours' (at this period she was advanced in another pregnancy, for she gave birth to a third son, Ferdinand, on 16 July). On the afternoon of the 10th they ventured back, the insurrection having been suppressed with Prussian help; Schumann at first waited at Strehla while Clara went into the city and collected things for a longer stay in the country; presently he joined her and they walked through the damaged streets 'swarming with Prussians'. They returned to Maxen in the evening and next morning moved the whole family to Kreischa near by, where they remained until 12 June, devouring the newspapers and gradually recovering their equilibrium. Even this period

was not barren; on 13 May Schumann completed the *Liederalbum für die Jugend* op.79; during 18–21 May he returned to Laube's *Jagdbrevier* and set five numbers – perhaps begun in April before the insurrection – for male voices and four horns; during 23–6 May he made a setting of Rückert's *Verzweifle nicht im Schmerzenstal* op.93, for double men's chorus with an ad libitum organ part, which he orchestrated in May 1852; during 1–5 June (the autograph was, by a slip, misdated 1–5 May) came the *Minnespiel* from Rückert's *Liebesfrühling*, op.101, another cycle for several voices. A period of depression, which darkened Schumann's 39th birthday, then brought a pause and a rather sudden decision to return to Dresden. On the way back, on 12 June, Schumann's democratic emotion welled up to inspire the first of the Four Marches op.76; the other three, with a fifth which, in slightly revised form, was published later as op.99 no.14, were written during the next four days. Schumann at once sent them to the publisher Whistling with an intimation that they were 'republican' and that he wished their content to be suggested by the date '1849' printed large; this was suppressed on more prudent reflection. But they were known in the Schumanns' intimate circle as 'the barricade marches'.

Schumann had included as the last song of the *Liederalbum* op.79 a setting of 'Kennst du das Land' from Goethe's *Wilhelm Meister*. This was written at

Kreischa; now on his return to Dresden, perhaps with the approaching Goethe centenary in mind, he composed Mignon's other songs (also intended at first for op.79), the Harper's ballad and Philine's *Singet nicht in Trauertönen* (18–22 June), sketched the *Requiem für Mignon* which he later worked out for soloists, chorus and orchestra (2–3 July) and finally the Harper's three other songs (6–7 July). The solo songs, including *Kennst du das Land*, were later published as op.98*a*, the *Requiem für Mignon* as op.98*b*. This preoccupation with Goethe not unnaturally led Schumann back to *Faust*; during 13–18 July he composed the three numbers which now constitute the first part of the *Szenen aus Goethes Faust* – and during 24–6 July the sunrise scene with Ariel and the spirits and Faust's awakening; these were all orchestrated in August. On 29 August – the day after the actual centenary – the closing scenes (i.e. the third part of the *Szenen*) were performed in the Grosser Garten at Dresden; they also formed part of the Goethe celebrations at Weimar and Leipzig.

By the end of August Schumann had completed a little set of duets for soprano and tenor, op.78, begun on 25 July. Next, with his little daughter Marie again in mind, he set about the composition of piano duets 'for small and large children', one of which, the Birthday March op.85 no.1, he and Marie played as a birthday surprise for Clara on 13 September; the whole set, op.85, was composed in the periods 10–15 September and 27 September–1 October, the intervening period having been occupied with a more imposing work, the Introduction and Allegro for piano and orchestra op.92 (sketched 18–20 September, score completed on the 26th). During 11–16 October were composed three songs for double chorus which, with a similar setting of Goethe's *Talismane*, were published posthumously as op.141. A setting of Hebbel's *Nachtlied* op.108, was sketched on 4 November and orchestrated on 8–11 November. Later in the month Schumann completed a 'second *Spanisches Liederspiel*', this time with piano duet accompaniment and including at least one number (*Flutenreicher Ebro*) composed in April, presumably for the first set; this second *Liederspiel* was ultimately published, posthumously, as *Spanische Liebeslieder* op.138. December was equally fruitful, especially of experimental works; on 4–5 December three of Byron's *Hebrew Melodies* were set with harp accompaniment, op.95; on the 7th Schumann wrote the first of the three Romances for oboe and piano op.94; on the 22nd, after a week's inaction due to eye trouble, he composed a piano accompaniment for the declamation of Hebbel's *Schön Hedwig* op.106, which the poet himself considered 'extraordinarily beautiful'; at the turn of the year he was appropriately sketching a setting of Rückert's *Neujahrslied* for chorus and orchestra (27 December–3 January 1850).

16. LAST MONTHS IN DRESDEN. The mood of Rückert's poem reflected his own, faced as he was by a serious decision. After five years at Dresden Schumann still had few real friends there and no place in or recognition by the official world; he had even been snubbed – for instance by Lüttichau, the intendant of the Opera, who had refused him the courtesy of complimentary tickets. In July 1849 he had put out feelers for the post of director of the Leipzig Gewandhaus, which he wrongly believed was about to fall vacant (two years earlier he had made similar private inquiries about the direc-

torship of the Vienna Conservatory); and on 17 November he had received from Hiller a proposal that he should succeed the latter as municipal music director at Düsseldorf with a salary of 750 thalers; Schumann had remembered Mendelssohn's disparagement of the Düsseldorf musicians and, though tempted by the suggestion, he had replied by asking Hiller a number of questions about conditions. He was perturbed to learn that Düsseldorf possessed a lunatic asylum, for he disliked everything that reminded him of insanity. The year 1850 began more promisingly with two fairly successful performances of the *Peri* (5 and 12 January) which enhanced his reputation at Dresden; 'some influential people' misguidedly began trying to get him the post of second conductor at the Opera, vacant since Wagner's flight after the May insurrection; and he hoped that a successful production of *Genoveva* at Leipzig, promised for February after a postponement from the previous summer, might improve his position and make a move to Düsseldorf unnecessary. He told Hiller and the Düsseldorf authorities that he could give no definite answer before 1 April.

The Schumanns went to Leipzig in February for the rehearsals of *Genoveva*, only to meet with a sharp disappointment: the production was postponed again, to make way for Meyerbeer's *Le prophète*. Nor was the first performance of the Introduction and Allegro by Clara at the Gewandhaus on the 14th very successful; on the other hand the *Conzertstück* for horns and the *Genoveva* overture, conducted by the composer at the orchestral pension fund concert on the 25th, aroused general enthusiasm. On 3 March the Schumanns left Leipzig for Bremen, where they gave only one concert (7 March), and Hamburg and Altona, where they stayed for more than a fortnight giving a number of concerts – two of them (21 and 23 March) with Jenny Lind – which brought them a clear profit of 800 thalers. After a short pause in Berlin they returned to Dresden on 29 March. Two days later Schumann sent his acceptance of the Düsseldorf post, though still secretly hoping that one less distant would offer itself.

These disturbances made composition impossible; January, February and March were completely unproductive. At the beginning of April Schumann busied himself with 'putting in order many compositions' – op.88 in its published form probably dates from this period – and, a second edition of the *Album für die Jugend* being contemplated, wrote on the 11th (in the blank spaces of the original sketchbook for the *Album*) the *Haus- und Lebensregeln* as an 'instructive appendix' to the *Album für die Jugend*; they first appeared as a supplement to the *Neue Zeitschrift* (no.36 of 1850) and were also published separately. Then the three songs of op.83 were written, and *Aufträge* op.77 no.5, after which Schumann returned yet again to *Faust*, sketching the scenes of the four grey women and Faust's death during 25–8 April and orchestrating them by 10 May. The six settings of poems by 'Wielfried von der Neun' (F. W. T. Schöpff) op.89 were begun on 10 May and completed before the Schumanns' departure for Leipzig on 18 May for the long-delayed production of *Genoveva*. The first rehearsal with the soloists took place on 22 May, with Clara at the piano, the first rehearsal of the orchestra alone on the 29th, the first full rehearsal on 7 June. On 23 June there was an orchestral rehearsal attended by Spohr, Gade, Hiller and Moscheles, among others; next day was the dress rehearsal, and on the 25th the first performance, attended by a great concourse of friends including Liszt. Schumann himself conducted and, owing partly to a mishap on the stage, the success was only moderate. The second performance, on the 29th, went better; the third, on the 30th, conducted by Julius Rietz, went best of all. But the opera was then withdrawn and not heard again until Liszt produced it at Weimar on 9 April 1855. On 10 July the Schumanns returned to Dresden. During this stay at Leipzig Schumann took a leading part, with Otto Jahn, Dr Härtel and others, in founding a 'Bach Society' – Schumann's own use of the English word suggests that the inspiration came from the English Bach Society, founded the previous October – to commemorate the centenary of Bach's death by issuing a complete edition of his works; the first meeting was apparently held on 1 June.

July was marked by songwriting: the whole of op.96, op.77 nos.2 and 3, op.125 nos.1, 2, 3 and 5, and op.127 no.4. The last Dresden composition was op.90, a set of songs by Lenau, begun on 2 August, rounded off by a 'Requiem' translated from a Latin poem attributed to Héloïse. Schumann added this under the impression that Lenau was already dead; by a strange chance the news of the poet's actual death reached him on 25 August, on which day the songs were sung for the first time in a little circle of friends who had gathered to take leave of him and Clara. Early on the morning of 1 September they left Dresden, reaching Düsseldorf on the evening of the following day.

17. DÜSSELDORF. The Rhineland town, which had been paying Schumann's salary since 7 May, now welcomed them warmly. They were met by Hiller and the concert directors, greeted with a serenade from the *Liedertafel* on the evening of arrival and another from the orchestra two days later, and on the 7th they were treated to a concert of Schumann's works, a dinner with official speeches and a ball which (from sheer weariness) they did not attend. Both were exhausted and worried; Schumann was unwell and increasingly irritated by the street noises of their temporary uncomfortable apartments at the corner of the Allee- and Grabenstrassen, which made it almost impossible for him to work. However, he was able to orchestrate the Rückert *Neujahrslied*, and on 29 September they enjoyed a visit to Cologne and were profoundly impressed by the cathedral, where the Cardinal Archbishop Geissel was enthroned the next day. On 10 October Schumann's will to compose returned; he began the Cello Concerto, completing the sketch on the 16th and the full score on the 24th. On the day the concerto was completed Schumann also conducted the first of the ten subscription concerts of the season. He had brought from Leipzig a new leader, W. J. von Wasielewski, afterwards his biographer; he was satisfied with the orchestra; and Clara won her usual success as soloist. Altogether Schumann conducted eight subscription concerts during this season of 1850–51, introducing new works of his own at four of them, the *Requiem für Mignon* (21 November), the *Neujahrslied* (11 January), the Symphony in E♭ (6 February) and the *Nachtlied* and overture to Schiller's *Die Braut von Messina* (both 13 March).

The new symphony had been begun on 2 November 1850, the first movement finished in sketch on the 9th (despite the interruption of another visit to Cologne), the scherzo on 25 November, the whole work in score on 9 December. The overture to *Die Braut von Messina* was sketched on 29–31 December and orchestrated 1–12 January 1851. Richard Pohl had sent Schumann an opera libretto on that subject; he rejected the libretto, after some consideration, but a re-reading of Schiller's tragedy suggested the overture. He then had the idea of writing a series of tragedy overtures, and sketched and orchestrated one to Shakespeare's *Julius Caesar* during 23 January–2 February. Between the two overtures he composed the songs op.107 nos.1, 2, 3 and 6 and op.125 no.4. In March came the four *Märchenbilder* op.113, for viola and piano, some Lenau songs op.117 and the long-unpublished *Frühlingsgrüsse*.

By this time the happy relationships of the first few months at Düsseldorf had begun to cloud over. There were temperamental misunderstandings between the silent, introspective composer and the sociable Rhinelanders, whom he found too talkative and, musically, not serious enough. At the same time the well-drilled chorus and orchestra he had inherited from Hiller soon felt the consequences of his relaxed disci-

9. Playbill for Schumann's opera 'Genoveva', first performed at the Stadttheater, Leipzig, on 25 June 1850

pline and shortcomings as a conductor. At the concert on 13 March the choir sang badly, the new *Braut* overture was coldly received and an article in the Düsseldorf paper was frankly critical of Schumann's direction of the concerts. Four days later the *Haushaltbuch* records 'doubts about staying longer at Düsseldorf'. But the performance of Bach's *St John Passion* on 13 April appears to have been successful.

Schumann's productivity was unabated. A long correspondence with Pohl concerning an oratorio libretto on Luther led to no result, but in April Moritz Horn sent him a poem, *Der Rose Pilgerfahrt*, which attracted him, though he asked Horn to make a number of alterations before setting it; and on 3 May he enlisted Horn's help in altering the end of Uhland's ballad *Der Königssohn*, of which he had nearly completed a setting for soloists, chorus and orchestra. The *Rose* was completed in its original form for solo voices, chorus and piano by 11 May; Schumann's own catalogue of his compositions gives '12 May–1 June' for the bulk of *Der Königssohn*, but the dates cannot be reconciled with those in the *Haushaltbuch* and statements in dated letters, and must have been entered from (faulty) memory. From the end of May date the duets and solo songs to verses by the child poet Elisabeth Kulmann, opp.103 and 104, and two Uhland settings for unaccompanied chorus, op.145 no.3 and op.146 no.1; *Der Königssohn* was finished, with Horn's ending, in June; and on 12 June Schumann returned to a set of piano duets (originally called *Kinderball* but renamed *Ballszenen* op.109), of which four numbers had been written at some earlier date, and completed it during the next few days. At this period Schumann began negotiating with the Elberfeld publisher F. W. Arnold for the publication of numerous oddments for piano, originally 30 or more, to be collectively entitled *Spreu* ('Chaff'); ultimately only 14 were published, as *Bunte Blätter*, the original idea being to issue the pieces separately with wrappers of various colours.

On 6 July *Der Rose Pilgerfahrt* was given a successful private performance in the Schumanns' own house by a little body of 24 picked singers from which in the following autumn Schumann formed a *Singekränzchen* which met fortnightly in private houses to sing Bach motets, Palestrina, Lassus (*Miserere*) and Lotti (*Crucifixus*), though it collapsed in a few months. *Der Königssohn* suggested the idea of a whole series of 'ballads' for chorus and orchestra, and Schumann asked Pohl to interrupt work on *Luther* to adapt Uhland's *Des Sängers Fluch* for musical setting. Then came a relaxation: on 18 or 19 July the Schumanns made a trip up the Rhine to Heidelberg and thence to Baden-Baden, Basle, Geneva, Chamonix and Vevey, returning to Düsseldorf on 5 August. After 11 days, in which Schumann wrote the song op.107 no.5 and the three piano pieces op.111, he set off again, to Antwerp to judge a competition for men's choirs, visiting Brussels at the same time. He returned home on 22 August to find himself quickly confronted with unpleasantness. On 25 August there was a meeting of the Gesangsverein at which Schumann made some sort of outburst, and on 6 September there was a 'storm with Wortmann', the assistant burgomaster who was also secretary of the Musikverein, at the first meeting to discuss the winter concerts; and Schumann was again beset with 'doubts about the future'. According to his own statement to

Wasielewski he composed the Violin Sonata in A minor op.105 (12–16 September) at a time when he was 'very angry with certain people'. It was followed, after the group of Pfarrius songs op.119, by two more chamber works, the G minor Trio op.110 (2–9 October) and the D minor Violin Sonata op.121 (26 October–2 November). Next he busied himself with orchestration: first he scored the piano part of *Der Rose Pilgerfahrt* (7–27 November), a labour, pressed on him by friends, which he considered both unnecessary and uninteresting; then he orchestrated the scherzo of Burgmüller's Second Symphony, of which he had found the manuscript score at Düsseldorf (1 and 2 December), made a piano score of his D minor Symphony, altering many details (3–11 December), and entirely reorchestrated it (12–19 December); the original title-page shows that he thought of calling this revised version – not that of 1841, as is commonly believed – a 'Symphonistische Fantasie', but it ultimately appeared as 'Symphony no.4'. The last composition of 1851 was an overture to an unwritten Singspiel on Goethe's *Hermann und Dorothea* (sketched 19–20 December; orchestration finished 23 December). The idea of such a play with music, with piano accompaniment, had been in Schumann's mind since 1846; now in 1851 Moritz Horn had recalled it, and there was some discussion about the preparation of a libretto; even a year after the composition of the overture Schumann was still debating with Horn the possibility of a 'concert oratorio' on the subject.

The year 1852 opened with the composition of the Uhland–Pohl ballad, *Des Sängers Fluch* op.139, sketched 1–6 January, scored 10–19 January. *Der Rose Pilgerfahrt* was given in its new form on 5 February, 'only tolerably', according to Schumann himself; but his relations with the choir were growing steadily worse. During that winter he had continued his Bach propaganda with portions of the B minor Mass and *St Matthew Passion*, and it is possible that this activity suggested the composition of his own Mass op.147 and Requiem op.148. The Mass was sketched on 13–22 February and orchestrated (and the piano score made) during 24 February–5 March and 24–30 March, the interruption of the scoring being due to a short visit to Leipzig (5–22 March) with Clara when *Rose* and the *Manfred* overture were performed – the latter for the first time – on the 14th. They had hoped also to go to Weimar for Liszt's stage production of *Manfred* and, if possible, a performance of *Lohengrin*; but *Manfred* was postponed until June. The Requiem was sketched on 26 April–8 May; during 9–15 May Schumann orchestrated the organ part of his Rückert motet of 1849 op.93, and during 16–23 May his Requiem. From then until 4 June he busied himself with 'setting in order his old articles' (*Davidsbündlerei*) with a view to their republication in book form; but he had great difficulty in finding a publisher for these *Aufzeichnungen über Musik und Musiker aus den Jahren 1834 bis 1844*, which were offered in turn to Breitkopf & Härtel, to Senff, to Kahnt and to Georg Wigand, the last of whom accepted them in November 1853 and published them as *Gesammelte Schriften über Musik und Musiker* in four volumes in spring 1854.

18. DECLINING HEALTH. At the beginning of April 1852 Schumann had some sort of 'rheumatic attack' (accord-

10. Robert Schumann: chalk drawing (1853) by J. J. B. Laurens in the Musée Duplessis, Carpentras; the artist commented on the abnormal enlargement of the pupils of Schumann's eyes

ing to Clara) with sleeplessness and depression, which grew worse in June and prevented his attending the Weimar production of *Manfred* on 13 June. (At this period he was putting out confidential inquiries about the post of court Kapellmeister at Sondershausen.) On recovering he sketched his setting of Geibel's four ballads *Vom Pagen und der Königstochter* op.140 for soloists, chorus and orchestra, and wrote a piano accompaniment for the recitation of Shelley's *The Fugitives* op.122 no.2. His malady was now beginning to show itself in greater hesitancy of speech and slowness of movement (reflected in his feeling for musical tempos), and in general apathy. From 26 June to 6 July he went to Godesberg for a cure, which only made him worse. On 28 July he began the scoring of the Geibel ballad cycle and on 1–4 August took a small part, smaller than had been intended, in the conducting of a big male-choir festival at Düsseldorf (it was on this occasion that he brought out the *Julius Cäsar* overture). In the middle of August he and Clara went to Scheveningen to try the effect of sea-bathing and remained there until 17 September; this seems to have been beneficial, and the orchestration of *Vom Pagen und der Königstochter* was actually finished in Holland; but Schumann was ordered to avoid all exertion, such as conducting, on his return to Düsseldorf. He occupied himself with the mechanical work of writing vocal scores (*Sängers Fluch*, Requiem, and Part 2 of the *Szenen aus Goethes Faust*), and at his request the first two concerts of the 1852–3 season were directed by Julius Tausch, the deputy. In the middle of October he had a serious attack of giddiness and on 21 November he noted 'remarkable aural symptoms'. He reappeared at the concert on 3 December, when *Vom Pagen und der Königstochter* had its first performance, but he was

coldly received. Moreover, the choir disliked working under him again, after the more efficient Tausch, and the concert directors of the Gesangsverein actually invited him to resign; after a tremendous storm (11–23 December) the three directors resigned instead and the matter was smoothed over, but it was agreed that Tausch should take over all choral rehearsals – Schumann had already asked him to take the preliminary rehearsals of new works – leaving to Schumann only the orchestral rehearsals and public performances. The five *Gedichte der Königin Maria Stuart* op.135 were written during this unhappy period (9–16 December) and a piano duet arrangement of the D minor Symphony was made; the symphony was also played in its revised form at the subscription concert of 30 December.

Another more or less 'mechanical' work began the year 1853. A performance of the Bach violin Chaconne with Mendelssohn's piano accompaniment suggested to Schumann that other of Bach's works for violin solo would reach a wider public if provided with accompaniments; he suggested the idea to Dr Härtel on 4 January and completed the accompaniments to the sonatas on 5 February. After an interval in which he set an adaptation of Uhland's *Das Glück von Edenhall* for solo voices, men's chorus and orchestra (27 February–12 March), he wrote similar accompaniments for Bach's cello sonatas (19 March–10 April), and (15–19 April) a Festival Overture, with final chorus, on the *Rheinweinlied* – already begun the previous summer – specially for the Lower Rhine Music Festival next month. Schumann scored a notable success with the D minor Symphony on the first day of the festival (15 May), which ended two days later with the new overture, but friends who came to Düsseldorf on this occasion were disquieted to find him obsessed with 'magnetic experiments' in the form of table-turning (his first experiment was on 24 April, and on the 27th he wrote an article on the phenomena – unfortunately lost). Later in the summer there were further disturbing physical symptoms, including, on 30 July, an apparent stroke during a visit to Bonn.

19. LAST CREATIVE SPELL. A great deal of work was done that summer: the Overture, Scherzo and Finale arranged for piano solo (20–24 April), the piano score of *Faust* 'put in order' (by 24 May), the seven Fughettas for piano op.126 composed (28 May–9 June), the *Drei Clavier-Sonaten für die Jugend* op.118 (11–24 June), piano solo arrangements of the string quartets op.41 nos.1 and 2 (4–11 August), an overture to *Faust* (13–17 August), an Allegro with Introduction for piano and orchestra op.134 (24–30 August), a Fantasie for violin and orchestra op.131 (2–7 September), a piano accompaniment to the recitation of Hebbel's *Ballade vom Heideknaben* op.122 no.1 (15 September), five pieces for piano duet which, with an earlier *Menuett*, make up the *Kinderball* op.130 (18–20 September) and a Violin Concerto (21 September–3 October).

The violin Fantasie and concerto were both written for the 22-year-old Joachim, whose performance of Beethoven's concerto had deeply impressed Schumann at the Lower Rhine Festival in May and who had revisited Düsseldorf during 28–31 August, and again profoundly impressed him by his 'wonderful' playing (the excitement caused a sudden 'affection of the speech' on 30 August). On 30 September the Schumanns were visited by Joachim's new friend, the 20-year-old

Brahms, who at once made a profound impression on them as composer and pianist; Schumann promptly expressed his enthusiasm in an article (written 9–13 October) entitled 'Neue Bahnen' and published in the *Neue Zeitschrift für Musik* on 28 October. Brahms stayed at Düsseldorf until 3 November, and his visit coincided almost exactly with Schumann's last period of creative activity: the *Märchenerzählungen* op.132 for clarinet, viola and piano were composed 9–11 October and the *Gesänge der Frühe* for piano (also called *An Diotima* after Hölderlin's heroine), which Schumann described to the publisher Arnold as 'characteristic pieces which depict the emotions on the approach and advance of morning, but more as expression of feeling than painting', 15–18 October. On the 21st he returned to the harmonization of unaccompanied string works, this time writing an accompaniment to Paganini's Caprice no.24 (on the theme of which Brahms later composed his variations). Joachim was to come to give the first performance of the violin Fantasie at the first subscription concert of the season on 27 October, and also to hear his own *Hamlet* overture, and Schumann, Brahms and Schumann's disciple Albert Dietrich agreed to collaborate in the composition of a Violin Sonata in A minor on *F–A–E*, the initials of Joachim's motto 'Frei aber einsam'; Schumann's contributions were the second and fourth movements, an intermezzo in F and finale in A minor and major (composed 22–3 October). The collective sonata was duly presented to Joachim the day after the concert and played at sight by him and Clara; next morning (the 29th) Schumann set about the replacement of Dietrich's first movement and Brahms's scherzo with two movements of his own, and on the 31st completed his third violin sonata. During 2–4 November he wrote five Romanzen for cello and piano.

The concert of 27 October was the last conducted by Schumann at Düsseldorf. As the result of a disastrous performance of a mass by Hauptmann at the Maximilian Church on 16 October the choir refused to sing Mendelssohn's *Erste Walpurgisnacht* under Schumann on the 27th, and he had to allow Tausch to conduct it. The rehearsal of Joachim's *Hamlet* on the afternoon of the concert was chaotic. The Musikverein committee was obliged to take some action, and on 7 November the chairman and another member called on Schumann with the committee's unanimous proposal that he should in future conduct only his own compositions, while Tausch should deputize for him on all other occasions; they were seen by Clara, who had completely blinded herself to her husband's condition and ability, and who saw in this suggestion nothing but an 'infamous intrigue' on Tausch's part and an 'insult for Robert'. On the 9th Schumann replied with the assertion that such a proposal – although it was only a proposal – was a breach of contract; he himself actually broke the contract next day by failing to appear at either rehearsal or concert. He thought of leaving Düsseldorf for either Vienna or Berlin. On the 14th the committee replied courteously to Schumann, but at the same time implemented its proposal by a decision to that effect. On 6 December the burgomaster wrote to Schumann offering arbitration, or at least investigation, by a sub-committee of the municipal council (the town continued to pay his salary as municipal director of music until the middle of 1855).

Apparently Schumann never replied to the burgomaster; he and Clara had already left on 24 November for a concert tour in Holland in the course of which Clara played the new Introduction and Allegro op.134 for the first time, at Utrecht on the 26th. They were enthusiastically received there, at The Hague, Rotterdam (where they were honoured with a torchlight serenade) and Amsterdam, Schumann conducting the well-drilled Dutch orchestras in his Second and Third Symphonies, and returned to Düsseldorf on 22 December.

During 19–30 January 1854 the Schumanns visited Hanover, where Joachim played the violin Fantasie and conducted the D minor Symphony, Clara played twice at court, and they again enjoyed the company of Brahms. Before, during and after this expedition to Hanover Schumann was occupied in the compilation of a 'Dichtergarten', an anthology of sayings on music by great writers, and at the beginning of February he wrote a preface to it (now lost). During 6–8 February he was searching through Plato and Homer in the Düsseldorf Municipal Library, to the alarm of Clara, who feared the results of the mental exertion.

20. THE END. On 10 February Schumann recorded 'very strong and painful aural symptoms'; this was repeated the next night and grew worse the following day; he now had the illusion of 'wonderfully beautiful music' constantly sounding in his head, an illusion which, especially in conjunction with his other sufferings, supports the diagnosis of syphilis. There was little respite, and in the night of the 17th he rose and wrote down a theme in E♭ which he said the angels had sung to him (actually an echo of the slow movement of the Violin Concerto); on the 18th and 19th the angels were replaced by devils in the form of tigers and hyenas who threatened him with Hell, though sometimes the angel voices brought comfort. This state lasted for a week, though in lucid intervals he was able to write two business letters and to compose five variations on the E♭ theme. On the evening of the 26th he asked to be taken to a lunatic asylum, but was persuaded by Clara and the doctor to go to bed. Next morning he was making a fair copy of the variations when, being left alone for a few moments, he ran out of the house to the Rhine bridge and threw himself into the river. He was rescued by fishermen and brought home. After being kept at home for several days, during which Clara was not allowed to see him, he was taken on 4 March to Dr Richarz's private asylum at Endenich near Bonn. After a gradual improvement, with many setbacks, Schumann suddenly wished for a letter from Clara and was able to reply rationally on 14 September; then for seven months he was able to correspond with her and with Brahms, Joachim and the publisher Simrock. On 24 December he was visited by Joachim and on 11 January 1855 by Brahms. In March 1855 he asked for the Paganini capriccios and resumed his accompaniment writing, 'not', he wrote, 'in canonically complicated style as with the A minor Variations [i.e. no.24], but simple harmonizations'. Brahms saw him again on 2 April, but these visits agitated him, and he was never allowed to see Clara. There was a speedy relapse. On 5 May he wrote Clara the last letter she received from him, and on 10 September Dr Richarz told her there was no longer hope of a complete recovery. On 8 June 1856, his birthday, Brahms found him making alphabetical lists of towns and countries. On 23 July Clara was summoned to Endenich by telegram, as he was not expected to live; but the crisis passed, and she returned to Düsseldorf still without having seen him, though Brahms did so. The

suspense was unbearable; she returned to Endenich with Brahms on the 27th and saw her husband for the first time after nearly two and a half years. He appeared to recognize her but could not speak intelligibly. She and Brahms were constantly with him or near him on the 28th, and at 4 p.m. on the 29th he died. He was buried two days later in the cemetery by the Sternentor at Bonn.

21. INFLUENCES AND PIANO MUSIC. Schumann's earliest attempts at composition seem to have been attempts to imitate Schubert and Weber, Hummel and Moscheles, Spohr, Prince Louis Ferdinand of Prussia and other minor figures. Despite his unbounded admiration for Beethoven, there are comparatively few traces of Beethoven's influence in his melodic invention or harmonic procedure, and he hardly ever attempted to rival Beethoven's sustained, continuous flights of thought. Chopin, another idol of his younger days, affected his style even less. Bach on the other hand, particularly Bach's fugal themes, did so profoundly in his later years; the sketches for Schumann's later works, and his fugal studies, show that a number of themes – ultimately not treated fugally – were originally conceived as Bachian fugue subjects. Angular themes derived from conventional Bachian shapes, even Bachian passage-work, are fused with 19th-century Romantic harmony and treated on Romantic lines with varying success in such very different works as the *Manfred* and *Faust* overtures, the cathedral scene and the tenor solo, 'Ewiger Wonnebrand', in *Faust*, the Adagio of the E♭ Symphony and 'Verrufene Stelle' in the *Waldszenen*. But in his early days, and to some extent throughout his life, Schumann's musical thoughts were engendered by dance rhythms, particularly the waltz and the polonaise, by the metres of lyrical verse, and above all by dreamy keyboard improvisation; he was for years – and the years in which he created his most individual work – unable to compose except at the piano and, with all his efforts, he never completely emancipated himself; he believed in the advice he gave to young musicians in the *Haus- und Lebensregeln*, 'to make everything in the head', but the things he made in his own head were inferior to the things he found at the keyboard.

Schumann's earliest surviving works are songs, and it is significant that, although he published none of them himself in that form, he used the material of three of them with little alteration in piano works which he did publish. Many of the lyrical melodies of the years between 1828 and 1840, when he devoted himself almost entirely to piano composition, are so square-cut, 'rhyming' and stanzaic as to suggest very strongly that they too were inspired by verse, even if they never existed in an intermediate stage as actual songs. (In 1833 he contemplated writing *Musikalische Gedichte, mit unterlegten Liedern von H. Heine*.) Equally characteristic of the younger Schumann of the piano pieces are the aphoristic themes and figures discovered by his fingers and fitted together, in the manner of a mosaic, into short pieces of the type of Schubert's short lyrical piano pieces, a type that in the 1820s and 1830s became very popular. (cf Tomášek's *Eclogues*, Ludwig Berger's *Etudes*, Wilhelm Taubert's *Minnelieder*, Mendelssohn's *Lieder ohne Worte*). Sometimes a Schumann piece as we have it (e.g. the Intermezzo op.4 no.4) consists of fragments of as many as three different abandoned compositions.

Schumann's short pieces are distinguished from those of his predecessors and contemporaries not only by their intrinsic charm and fantasy but also by their literary and musical allusiveness and by their autobiographical nature. While some of Schumann's early music has its origin (afterwards concealed) in lyrical verse, other of it – purely musical in origin – was given literary or pictorial titles or brought into relationship with some literary idea later. A notable case is the cycle *Papillons*: constructed partly from earlier waltzes and four-hand polonaises written in imitation of Schubert; provided with a programmatic finale suggesting the end of a ball, and related number by number to paragraphs in a chapter of Jean Paul's *Flegeljahre* (though the relationship was never made public); and finally published with an enigmatic title bearing no relation to the work's origin or its acquired connection with Jean Paul and fully significant only to the composer himself ('larvae' and 'butterflies' played important parts in his private world of thought). Such literary connections persisted to the end in Schumann's piano music, though the public was not allowed to know about, for instance, the relationship between the *Waldszenen* and Laube's *Jagdbrevier* or between the *Gesänge der Frühe* and Hölderlin's *Diotima* poems. Sometimes, instead, they were teased with hints and suggestions, with quotations from Goethe (op.4 no.2) or Shakespeare (the Intermezzo of op.21 no.3), with the pretence that Schumann's compositions were the work of his fictional Florestan and Eusebius, with themes that spell out proper names ('Abegg', 'Asch', 'Gade'). His music is full of musical quotations and allusions; he alluded to the *Marseillaise*, to the traditional German *Grossvatertanz*, to Beethoven, to Marschner, to Clara's compositions, to other music of his own sometimes openly but more often under subtle disguises and with a significance often difficult and sometimes impossible to guess (e.g. the reference to the 'Abegg' theme in op.4 no.6). He obviously took pleasure in hiding behind masks, in burying these secrets in his music – doubtless there are a number that have never been discovered – and it is clear that his music meant more to him than it can ever mean to anyone else. All his most individual music is completely introvert, pages from a secret autobiography or, rather, diary; it has been argued that a number of his themes or motifs derive from a private method of musical cryptography, with correspondences between letters and notes (the most pervasive of them involving an encipherment of the name 'Clara'). His sketchbooks make it clear that he often cherished a theme or a harmonic progression not only for its intrinsic musical sake, but because it recalled to him the precise moment and mood in which it was conceived; he dated a theme used in the finale of the Phantasie op.17 '30.11.36. and wallowed blissfully in it when I was sick', or another '29 April 38, since no letter came from you'. He took pleasure less in communicating a mood or emotion than in hugging the secret circumstance of the mood. In many of these respects – love of extra-musical associations, fundamental lyricism, emphasis on self-expression – Schumann is the typical musical Romantic; he is equally so in his earlier technique.

The individual theme or melody being specially valuable for its own sake, its function as structural material tends to be neglected. Indeed with the earlier Schumann structure is merely a framework on which to spread the themes; the parts matter much more than the whole. Consequently the forms are simple, and the simpler the more satisfactory. The material is seldom 'developed' in the Classical sense, but continually remoulded, as if under an improviser's fingers. Schumann's preference for variation writing when he wished to create a larger work is characteristic, as is also the fact that his variations are less often ornamental or Beethovenian in method than plastic remodellings of the theme. The same principle of thematic remodelling is employed in the three piano sonatas for the purpose of giving unity to these larger compositions, but Schumann's static, mosaic-like conception of form and the lack of germinal quality in the themes are here more serious defects than in the short pieces. They are overcome more successfully in the C major Phantasie than in the sonatas; the Phantasie, however, was conceived as a whole, not assembled from heterogeneous earlier compositions. Schumann also experimented with the naive concatenation of a number of simple formal units, contrasted or related, to form long pieces such as the *Humoreske* and *Blumenstück*, but such pieces depend solely on the charm of the separate sections and cannot be said to exist as wholes.

The texture of Schumann's piano music is much more individual and contributes much more to the effect of the separate melodies and aphorisms than the structure. In a criticism dating from 1835 of a piano sonata by Loewe, Schumann asserted his growing conviction that 'the piano expresses itself essentially and peculiarly in three things above all – through richness of part-writing [*Stimmenfülle*] and harmonic change (as in Beethoven and Schubert), through use of the pedal (as in Field), or through volubility (as in Czerny and Herz)'. All three are fully exploited in his own, though the element of volubility becomes less noticeable in the music written after the finger trouble of 1832 (from the same time begins his neglect of the brilliant upper register of the instrument which he had used freely enough in the 'Abegg' Variations, *Papillons* and the Allegro op.8). Rapidly changing, often boldly chromatic harmony; pedal effects novel in the 1830s and passages impossible without pedal; cross-rhythms and syncopation; endless variety of accompaniment figures – chordal, arpeggiated, broken-chordal, counter-melodic, broken-chord figures suggesting counter-melodies that are never explicit – all help to envelop essentially clear and simple melodic ideas in a rich, diffused, Romantic light.

22. SONGS. Schumann's later work is seen in true perspective only when considered in relation to, or contrast with, the piano music of 1831–9. The great outpouring of songs in 1840 is, as Brendel said, a 'continuation of his character-pieces for piano'; but the songs are not only piano pieces with another dimension, an additional tone-colour: they are explicit, whereas the piano pieces are reserved. The lyrical element is set free and its emotional content made precise. Schumann himself acknowledged to Zuccalmaglio (letter of 31 December 1840) that 'the *Myrthen* certainly allow a deeper insight into my inner musical workings'. Moreover the poem (which Schumann nearly always chose with care because it answered to something in himself, and generally chose with good literary taste) acted as a lens for his musical thought, sharpening, concentrating, shaping it. In holding the balance between poem and music and between voice and piano, Schumann generally stands midway between Schubert and Wolf; there are a number of purely lyrical songs, such as *Widmung* op.25 no.1, in which the voice sings and the piano 'accompanies', and there are declamatory songs such as *Auf einer Burg* op.39 no.7 (though in both

these particular cases the bulk of the piano parts is self-contained, embodying the melodic line). But Schumann's most typical songs are those in which the melody is shared by voice and piano either simply as in *Der Nussbaum* op.25 no.3, or more subtly as in *Kommen und Scheiden* op.90 no.3, and those in which some other, non-melodic element in the piano part provides a perfect complement to the vocal part and is equally important to the total effect (e.g. *Im Rhein im heiligen Strome* op.48 no.6; *Der Gärtner* op.107 no.3). Another common feature of Schumann's songs is the piano epilogue, often extensive; this is particularly noticeable in the songs of the *Dichterliebe* cycle and those originally intended to form part of it, such as *Mein Wagen rollet langsam* op.142 no.4, indeed of the Heine songs generally.

It is noteworthy that Schumann was at his happiest with Heine, a poet of double or veiled meanings. He was specially happy, too, with Eichendorff and in his few Mörike songs; Chamisso and Kerner led him on to ground where he was weaker, though he rose superior to Chamisso in the *Frauenliebe und -leben* cycle. Goethe's lyrics seldom drew his best from him, and Schiller he neglected almost entirely. His settings of Burns (in translation) – more successful when solo songs than when he composed them for unaccompanied chorus – and his quasi-*Volkslieder* in German vein include some attractive things (e.g. the *Volksliedchen* op.51 no.2 and *Marienwürmchen* op.79 no.13), but are not specially characteristic. The narrative or quasi-narrative ballad attracted him again and again to experiment not only in the forms of solo song and unaccompanied chorus, but as 'melodrama' (accompanied recitation) and, towards the end of his life, in pieces for soloists, chorus and orchestra. As always with Schumann, the lessening of the personal, subjective element was accompanied by a weakening of inspiration.

Parallel with Schumann's love of 'cycles' of piano pieces, connected by threads of varying tenuity, is his cultivation of the *Liederkreis*, sometimes united only by the circumstance that all the verses come from a single poet, as in the cases of the Heine and Eichendorff cycles actually so called, op.24 and op.39, sometimes adumbrating a story, as in *Frauenliebe und -leben*. Schumann sought to make the latter type a little more dramatic by distributing the songs among four voices, which sometimes unite in duets and quartets, in the two *Liederspiele* on Geibel's translations from the Spanish, opp.74 and 138, and the Rückert *Minnespiel* op.101.

23. ORCHESTRAL AND CHAMBER MUSIC. The great turning-point in Schumann's creative career came in 1841, after his marriage. Encouraged by his wife, he felt the need to strike out in the larger forms and in less limited media; he did not cease to be a Romantic, but his Romantic conception of music first as a medium of self-expression was now modified by the older Classical view of musical composition as a craft to be practised. His first essay in orchestral composition, the never completed G minor Symphony of 1832–3, had been discouraging; and the first completed symphony, the Bb, suffers (though less seriously) from the same principal defect: that it is inflated piano music with mainly routine orchestration. The basic substance of this symphony is similar to that of the short piano pieces; the opening motto theme was probably even verbally inspired (by the line 'Im Tale blüht der Frühling auf ' in the poem by Böttger which suggested the composition of

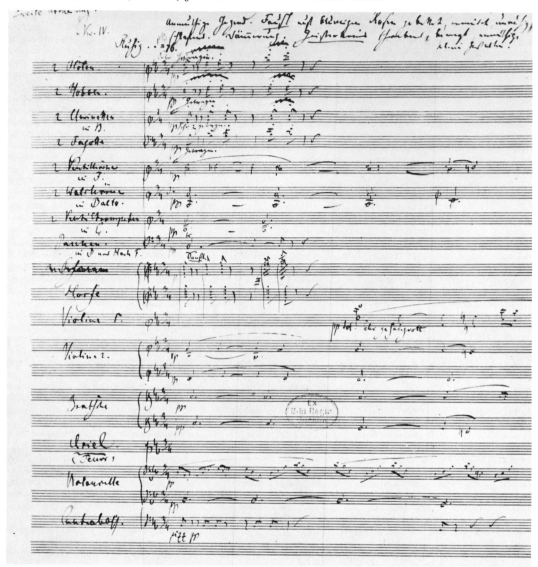

*11. Autograph MS of the beginning of the Sunrise Scene from Part 2 of Schumann's 'Szenen aus Goethes Faust',
composed 1844–53 (D-Bds)*

the symphony in the first place); the four movements originally bore 'characteristic' titles connected with springtime. But Schumann's inability to cover a large canvas with his playful aphorisms and lyrical melodies is as painfully apparent here as in the piano sonatas, and the inventiveness which seldom failed to produce new and interesting piano texture almost dried up when he had at his disposal a medium capable of figuration far richer but not shaped under his fingers. Only in his last symphony, the E♭, did Schumann hit upon at least an opening Allegro theme that was genuinely symphonic in character, capable of expansion; elsewhere in avoiding the lyrical he adopted mere patterns, more like passage-work than true themes, capable of endless manipulation but lifeless and infertile.

The charm of Schumann's symphonies lies in their never long-repressed lyricism, their interest in the devices by which Schumann sought to unify them thematically, to overcome his natural tendency to loose, suite-like structure. In the B♭ Symphony the brass theme of the slow introduction generates the main theme of the following Allegro; slow movement and scherzo are not only played without a break but are thematically related through a trombone passage at the end of the former. Thematic interrelationship is carried much further in the D minor Symphony, especially in its original form, and in the definitive version the movements are directed to be played without a break; indeed the whole work is so closely knit and so novel in structure that, despite its weakness of invention and (in the definitive version) muddy orchestration, it constitutes a landmark in the history of the symphony. The C major Symphony, too, has a slow introduction presenting not only a motto theme on the brass but much of the thematic material of the following Allegro; the finale refers back to this and also to the slow movement. The finale of the C major Symphony is marked by another favourite symphonic device of Schumann's: the introduction of a new, lyrical theme towards the end of a movement (cf the first movement of the B♭ Symphony and the first and last movements of the D minor). In the E♭ Symphony Schumann gave freer rein to his tendency towards the suite; there are five 'picturesque' movements, of which only the finale looks back at moments to the fourth, though here Schumann dispensed with the double trios of the symphonies in B♭ and C.

Schumann's concertos are even farther from the Viennese Classical models than his symphonies. Like Chopin's, his models were Hummel and Moscheles rather than Mozart and Beethoven. It is significant that his first completed essay in this field was the lyrical, essentially monothematic Phantasie for piano and orchestra which he later converted into a full-length concerto by the addition of an intermezzo and finale. All the tonal and thematic subtleties of the Classical concerto are jettisoned: the A minor Concerto is essentially a piano work with a lightly, transparently scored orchestral accompaniment which here and there takes over cantabile melodies from the soloist: as Schumann himself said, 'something between symphony, concerto and grand sonata'. The two later pieces for piano and orchestra adopt the same formula, but with less success. The Cello Concerto, in three connected movements, is (as the composer put it in his own catalogue) really a 'Concert Piece for cello with orchestral accompaniment' (in the slow movement a decidedly pianistic accompaniment). Only in the late Violin Concerto, the second of the two works for violin and orchestra inspired by Joachim's playing, did Schumann return to the Classical concerto model with 'double exposition' in the first movement; even so, he failed to grasp the point of the Classical ritornello, for the tutti simply anticipates the solo exposition.

Of Schumann's other orchestral works, the Manfred overture is outstanding, a 'character study' in which Schumann could be as subjective as he wished, identifying himself with Byron's hero, and where neither crabbed thematic invention nor sombre scoring was out of place. It has affinities, besides identity of key, with that other sombre masterpiece, the fourth movement of the E♭ major Symphony.

Schumann seems hardly ever to have been able to think directly in terms of the orchestra, and his scoring is very often a matter of rather conservative routine; but his earlier orchestral works (e.g. the Symphony in B♭, the original version of the D minor, the Piano Concerto) are free from the thickness, the unnecessary doublings, of (for instance) the second version of the D minor Symphony. The scherzo of the B♭ Symphony has some delightful 'open-work' scoring, and two passages in the finale of the D minor Symphony were actually so thin in the original version that the editor (Franz Wüllner) strengthened them in the published score of that version. Two of Schumann's most delightful passages of orchestration occur in works seldom heard, the Waterfall Scene in Manfred and the Sunrise Scene at the beginning of Part 2 of the Szenen aus Goethes Faust, where he used harp, divided strings and the other apparatus of the Romantic orchestra with great skill (see fig.11).

Schumann's chamber music may, even more than the orchestral, be regarded as an extension of his piano music. The piano is physically present in everything but the three string quartets and even there its spiritual presence is frequently felt in themes and figuration. In the works with piano the strings tend to double it or to be opposed to it as a block (particularly in the Quartet and Quintet). In other respects Schumann's chamber scoring is happier than his orchestral scoring; it presented him with fewer problems, and he was more comfortable in the more intimate media with their opportunities for the complex figuration and harmonic subtlety so characteristic of his thought. Like the symphonies and piano sonatas, the chamber works are often linked internally by unobtrusive thematic references in one movement to another.

24. CHORAL AND DRAMATIC MUSIC. It was in the choral works that Schumann attempted to extend his reach farthest from his fundamental piano style. They date from the period when he was trying to emancipate himself from the habit of composition at the keyboard; the texts generally exclude subjectivity, and the medium makes intimacy impossible. Schumann's choral writing is seldom very enterprising: a large proportion of it (as in his later music generally) is homophonic and rather plainly chordal, square-cut and rhythmically monotonous; and his contrapuntal studies make themselves felt in the shaping of his themes rather than in the flow of his general texture, despite the fairly numerous passages of deliberate (but always essentially harmonic) counterpoint. But his works for soloists, chorus and orchestra were courageously experimental. The first of them, the 'secular oratorio' Das Paradies und die Peri, and its later and weaker companion Der Rose Pilgerfahrt were new of their kind, 'through-composed' in the sense that the numbers are distinct but not separated, with the older type of recitative replaced by a more melodic type of declamation and symphonically accompanied. Elijah had not yet been written in 1843, though Mendelssohn's Erste Walpurgisnacht had just been given in the form in which we know it; but Schumann's models, particularly in the part of the Peri herself, were evidently found rather in the newest German Romantic operas, Marschner's Der Vampyr and Der fliegende Holländer. Much more successful artistically, despite the beautiful lyrical passages of Paradies und die Peri, is the exquisite Requiem für Mignon, intimate and subjective, a work falling into no definite category.

Two other important works stand with one foot in the concert hall and one on the stage: the Manfred music and the Szenen aus Goethes Faust, the former incidental music to a drama not intended for the stage, the latter a collection of compositions spread over nine years and connected only by the circumstance that they are all settings of portions of a drama part of which can be staged and part can only be read. Both contain many fine lyrical pages, and Manfred shows Schumann attempting (as he also attempted with the piano in op.106 and op.122) the never satisfactory species of accompaniment to recitation, while the first two sections of the Faust music consist largely of music that might well be part of an opera and was probably conceived as such.

The lack of genuine dramatic talent revealed in Manfred and Faust is the mortal weakness of Schumann's one opera. The score of Genoveva has many beauties and is written in a convention little less advanced than Wagner's at the same period, with continuous texture and almost complete absence of bare recitative, but suffers from lyrical expansiveness and feeble characterization. *Genoveva* employs thematic reminiscence – particularly in association with the villain Golo – quite as much as *Tannhäuser* or *Lohengrin* (Wagner himself had not yet arrived at the true symphonic leitmotif), but it is characteristic of Schumann's lack of theatre sense that his points are made so unobtrusively that they have often passed unnoticed, whereas Wagner's are driven home with the necessary emphasis.

Harmonically and in melodic contours the Schumann of *Genoveva* (and *Manfred* and other late works) speaks a language strikingly akin to that of Wagner in the 1850s; indeed both spring from many of the same roots. It has been generally agreed that Schumann's later music shows a falling off in inspiration which has been attributed to the deterioration of his mind, to overproduction, to the influence of Mendelssohn and to various other causes. It is certainly true that a number of his late works, particularly those of the last two years, are failures and that even ten years earlier an element of heavy, solemn, sometimes bombastic banality begins to appear and then appears with increasing frequency; but such fairly late works as the E♭ Symphony and the D minor Violin Sonata or, among the miniatures, the delightful setting of Mörike's *Der Gärtner* op.107 no.3 show that the general decline must not be dated too early. Some of the manifestations that have been taken for symptoms of mental decay – melodic and thematic angularity, increased harmonic complication – really betoken nothing more than a normal development of style influenced partly by the *Zeitgeist*, partly by Bach.

25. CRITICAL WRITINGS. From 1831 to 1844 Schumann was active as a musical journalist. He had at his command an exuberant, florid prose style, modelled on that of Jean Paul Richter, and the best of his writing reveals the fantastic, lyrical, aphorism-scattering personality of the composer of the early piano pieces. Here, too, he loved to conceal himself behind the same fictional masks, Florestan and Eusebius, and from his projected novel of 1831 he also took other masks to accompany them, the members of the 'Davidsbund' – 'Meister Raro' and the rest – masks which now concealed real persons such as Friedrich Wieck, now himself, now mere puppets of his imagination. Even his reviews of new music were sometimes dressed in a fantastic fictional garb. As a critic Schumann uttered many acute and often quoted dicta on his contemporaries and on the older masters he adored. But, like that of most creative artists, his judgment was intensely subjective, conditioned almost entirely by affinities with his own creative nature. Thus he was apt to be blind to the merits of important composers whose art had nothing in common with his own, and over-kind to lesser but more congenial men. The fact that his first and his last published writings both hailed the advent of young and still unrecognized geniuses, Chopin and Brahms, has earned him a reputation for unusual perspicacity which he scarcely deserves. Nevertheless the whole corpus of his critical writing is valuable for the light it throws on his own creative personality and on the emotional and intellectual climate of musical Germany in the 1830s, the high noon of Romanticism.

WORKS

Edition: *R. Schumann: Werke*, ed. C. Schumann, J. Brahms and others (Leipzig, 1881–93) [SW]

THEATRICAL

op.	Title	Libretto	Composed	Publication/MS	Production	Remarks	SW
—	Der Corsar, opera	O. Marbach, after Byron	1844	D-Bds	—	unfinished; chorus of corsairs and sketch for Conrad's air only	—
81	Genoveva, opera	R. Reinick, after L. Tieck and C. F. Hebbel, with alterations by Schumann	1847–9	1851	Leipzig, 25 June 1850	in 4 acts; first pubd in piano reduction	ix/2
115	Manfred, incidental music	Byron, trans. K. A. Suckow	1848–9	1853	Leipzig, 13 June 1852	first pubd in piano reduction	ix/4, 1

CHORAL WITH ORCHESTRA

Opp.98b, 108, 112, 116, 139, 140 and 143 are also pubd in vocal score in SW ix/8, and opp.144, 147, 148 and the Szenen aus Goethes Faust in SW ix/9.

op.	Title, forces	Text	Composed	Publication	First performance	Remarks	SW
—	Psalm cl, S, A, pf, orch	biblical	1822	—	—		—
—	Overture and chorus (Chor von Landleuten), chorus, orch	—	1822	—	—		—
—	Tragödie	Heine	1841	—	—	orch version of op.64 no.3	—
50	Das Paradies und die Peri, solo vv, chorus, orch	T. Moore's Lalla Rookh, trans. and adapted	1843	1845	Leipzig, 4 Dec 1843	first contemplated Aug 1841	ix/1, 3
—	Szenen aus Goethes Faust, solo vv, chorus, orch	Goethe	1844–53	1858	Cologne, 13 Jan 1862	first pubd in piano reduction	ix/7
71	Adventlied, S, chorus, orch	F. Rückert	1848	1849	—	first pubd in piano reduction	ix/1, 43
84	Beim Abschied zu singen, chorus, wind insts	E. von Feuchtersleben	1847	1850	—		ix/3, 1
93	Verzweifle nicht im Schmerzenstal, double chorus, orch	Rückert	1852	1893	—	orch version of motet op.93	ix/3, 6
98b	Requiem für Mignon, solo vv, chorus, orch	from Goethe's Wilhelm Meister	1849	1851	Düsseldorf, 21 Nov 1850	see also Songs, op.98a	ix/3, 67

op.	Title, forces	Text	Composed	Publication	First performance	Remarks	SW
108	Nachtlied, chorus, orch	Hebbel	1849	1853	Düsseldorf, 13 March 1851		ix/3, 114
112	Der Rose Pilgerfahrt, solo vv, chorus, orch	M. Horn	1851	1852	Düsseldorf, 5 Feb 1852	first pubd in piano reduction	ix/3, 138
116	Der Königssohn, solo vv, chorus, orch	L. Uhland	1851	1853			ix/4, 101
123	Fest–Ouverture, T, chorus, orch	W. Müller, M. Claudius	1852–3	1857	Düsseldorf, 17 May 1853	on J. André's Rheinweinlied	ii, 145
139	Des Sängers Fluch, solo vv, chorus, orch	R. Pohl, after Uhland	1852	1858	—		ix/4, 184
140	Vom Pagen und der Königstochter, solo vv, chorus, orch	E. Geibel	1852	1857	Düsseldorf, 3 Dec 1852		ix/5, 1
143	Das Glück von Edenhall, solo vv, chorus, orch	L. Hasenclever, after Uhland	1853	1860	—		ix/5, 99
144	Neujahrslied, chorus, orch	Rückert	1849–50	1861	Düsseldorf, 11 Jan 1851		ix/5, 148
147	Mass, chorus, orch	liturgical	1852–3	1862	—	first pubd in piano reduction	ix/9, 2
148	Requiem, chorus, orch	liturgical	1852	1864	—		ix/9, 3

ORCHESTRAL

op.	Title, key, forces	Composed	Publication/MS	First performance	Remarks	SW
—	Pf Concerto, Eb	1828	—	—	unfinished	—
—	Pf Concerto, F	1829–31	—	—	unfinished	—
—	Introduction and Variations on a theme of Paganini	1831	—	—	introduction, theme and sketches for 4 variations; variations 3 and 4 used in opps.4 and 8	—
	Symphony, g	1832–3	1972	Zwickau, 18 Nov 1832 (1st movt only); Schneeberg, 12 Feb 1833 (rev. and completed)	3 movts completed; sketch for 4th movt	—
—	Pf Concerto, d	1839	—	—	1 movt only	—
—	Symphony, c	1840–41	—	—	sketches for 4 movts; scherzo used in Bunte Blätter, pts. of Adagio used in Adagio and finale of Symphony no.2	—
38	Symphony no.1, Bb, 'Spring'	1841	1841	Leipzig, 31 March 1841	movts orig. entitled 1 Frühlingsbeginn, 2 Abend, 3 Frohe Gespielen, 4 Voller Frühling	i, 1
52	Overture, Scherzo and Finale, e–E	1841; last movt rev. 1845	1846	Leipzig, 6 Dec 1841	orig. title Suite, then Symphonette	ii, 1
54	Pf Concerto, a	1st movt 1841; 2nd and 3rd movts 1845	1846	Leipzig, 1 Jan 1846	first movt orig. Fantasie, pf, orch	iii, 146
61	Symphony no.2, C	1845–6	1847	Leipzig, 5 Nov 1846		i, 109
81	Genoveva, ov. to opera, c	1847	1850	Leipzig, 25 June 1850		i, 47
86	Conzertstück, 4 hn, F	1849	1851	Leipzig, 25 Feb 1850		iii, 69
92	Introduction and Allegro appassionato (Concertstück)	1849	1852	Leipzig, 14 Feb 1850		iii, 239
97	Symphony no.3, Eb, 'Rhenish'	1850	1851	Düsseldorf, 6 Feb 1851		i, 243
100	Die Braut von Messina, ov., c	1850–51	1851	Düsseldorf, 13 March 1851	to Schiller's play	ii, 70
115	Manfred, ov., eb	1848–9	1852	Weimar, 14 March 1852	see Theatrical	ii, 104
120	Symphony no.4, d	1841 as no.2; rev. 1851 as no.4	1853	Leipzig, 6 Dec 1841; Düsseldorf, 30 Dec 1852	first version pubd (1891)	i, 310
128	Julius Cäsar, ov., f	1851	1854	Düsseldorf, 3 Aug 1852	to Shakespeare's play	ii, 175
129	Vc Concerto, a	1850	1854	Leipzig, 9 June 1860		iii, 29
131	Fantasie, vn, C	1853	1854	Hanover, Jan 1854		iii, 1
134	Introduction and Allegro, pf, d–D	1853	1855	Utrecht, 26 Nov 1853		ii, 291
136	Hermann und Dorothea, ov., b	1851	1857	—	to Goethe's epic poem	ii, 214
—	Vn Concerto, d	1853	1937	Berlin, 26 Nov 1937		—
—	Szenen aus Goethes Faust, ov., d	1853	1858	Cologne, 13 Jan 1862	see Choral with orchestra	i, 231

CHAMBER

op.	Title, key, forces	Composed	Publication/MS	Remarks	SW
—	Quartet, vn, va, vc, pf, c	1828–30	—	orig. op.5	—
—	Quartet, f	1829	—		—
—	Quartet, vn, va, vc, pf, B	1831–2	—	unfinished	—
—	Quartet	1838	—	lost	—
—	2 string quartets, D, E♭	1839	D-Bds	sketches	—
41	3 string quartets, a, F, A	1842	1843		iv, 1, 22, 41
44	Quintet, 2 vn, va, vc, pf, E♭	1842	1843		v/1, 1
47	Quartet, vn, va, vc, pf, E♭	1842	1845		v/1, 2
—	Andante and variations, 2 pf, 2 vc, hn	1843	1893	orig. version of op.46, see Keyboard	xiv/1, 1
63	Trio no.1, vn, vc, pf, d	1847	1848		v/2, 2
70	Adagio and Allegro, hn (vn/vc ad lib), pf, A♭	1849	1849	orig. title Romanze und Allegro	v/3, 2
73	Phantasiestücke, cl (vn/vc ad lib), pf	1849	1849	orig. title Soiréestücke	v/3, 12
80	Trio no.2, vn, vc, pf, F	1847	1849		v/2, 50
88	Phantasiestücke, vn, vc, pf: 1 Romanze, 2 Humoreske, 3 Duett, 4 Finale	1842	1850		v/2, 124
94	3 Romanzen, ob (vn/cl ad lib), pf	1849	1851		v/3, 100
102	5 Stücke im Volkston, vc (vn ad lib), pf	1849	1851		v/3, 110
105	Sonata no.1, vn, pf, a	1851	1852		v/3, 26
110	Trio no.3, vn, vc, pf, g	1851	1852		v/2, 90
113	Märchenbilder, va (vn ad lib), pf	1851	1852		v/3, 82
121	Sonata no.2, vn, pf, d	1851	1853		v/3, 48
—	Pf acc. to 6 vn sonatas by Bach	1853	1853		—
—	Pf acc. to 6 vc sonatas by Bach	1853	c1870		—
132	Märchenerzählungen, cl (vn ad lib), va, pf	1853	1854		v/2, 148
—	Sonata, vn, pf, 'F.A.E.'	1853	1935	2nd and 4th movts only; 1st and 3rd by Dietrich and Brahms	—
—	Sonata no.3, vn, pf, a	1853	1956	in 4 movts, 2 being those which Schumann wrote for 'F.A.E.' sonata	—
—	5 Romanzen, vc, pf	1853	—	lost	—
—	Pf acc. to Paganini's vn capriccios	1853–5	1941		—

PARTSONGS FOR MIXED VOICES
(SATB, unaccompanied, unless otherwise stated; incipit given only if different from title)

op.	Title, forces	Incipit	Text	Composed	Publication	SW
55	Fünf Lieder:		R. Burns, trans. Gerhard	1846	1847	xii, 1
	1 Das Hochlandmädchen	Nicht Damen tönt von hohem Rang				
	2 Zahnweh	Wie du mit gift'gem Stachel fast				
	3 Mich zieht es nach dem Dörfchen hin					
	4 Die alte, gute Zeit	Wer lenkt nicht gern den heitern Blick				
	5 Hochlandbursch	Schönster Bursch, den je ich traf				
59	Vier Gesänge [orig. pubd as 4, 1, 2, 3; 5 added later]			1846	1848	xii, 11
	1 Nord oder Süd!		K. Lappe			
	2 Am Bodensee	Schwelle die Segel, günstiger Wind!	A. Platen			
	3 Jägerlied	Zierlich ist des Vogels Tritt im Schnee	Mörike			
	4 Gute Nacht	Die gute Nacht, die ich dir sage	Rückert			
	5 Hirtenknaben-Gesang, SSTT	Heloe! Heloe! Komm du auf unsre Heide	A. von Droste-Hülshoff	1846	1930	—
67	Romanzen und Balladen, i:			1849	1849	xii, 20
	1 Der König von Thule	Es war ein König in Thule	Goethe			
	2 Schön-Rohtraut	Wie heisst König Ringangs Töchterlein?	Mörike			
	3 Heidenröslein	Sah ein Knab' ein Röslein steh'n	Goethe			
	4 Ungewitter	Auf hohen Burgeszinnen	Chamisso			
	5 John Anderson	John Anderson, mein Lieb!	Burns, trans. Gerhard			
75	Romanzen und Balladen, ii:			1849	1850	xii, 28
	1 Schnitter Tod	Es ist ein Schnitter, der heisst Tod	Des Knaben Wunderhorn (Brentano)			
	2 Im Walde (2nd setting)	Es zog eine Hochzeit den Berg entlang	Eichendorff			
	3 Der traurige Jäger	Zur ew'gen Ruh' sie sangen die schöne Müllerin	Eichendorff			
	4 Der Rekrut	Sonst kam mein John mir zu	Burns, trans. Gerhard			
	5 Vom verwundeten Knaben	Es wollt' ein Mädchen früh aufsteh'n	Herder's Volkslieder			
141	Vier doppelchörige Gesänge:			1849	1858	xii, 36
	1 An die Sterne	Sterne, in des Himmels Ferne!	Rückert			
	2 Ungewisses Licht	Bahnlos und pfadlos	J. C. von Zedlitz			
	3 Zuversicht	Nach oben musst du blicken	Zedlitz			
	4 Talismane	Gottes ist der Orient!	Goethe			
145	Romanzen und Balladen, iii:			1849–51	1860	xii, 60
	1 Der Schmidt	Ich hör' meinen Schatz	Uhland			
	2 Die Nonne	Sie steht am Zellenfenster	anon.			
	3 Der Sänger	Noch singt den Widerhallen	Uhland			
	4 John Anderson	John Anderson, mein Lieb!	Burns, trans. Gerhard			
	5 Romanze vom Gänsebuben	Helf' mir Gott	O. Malsburg			

op.	Title, forces	Incipit	Text	Composed	Publication	SW
146	Romanzen und Balladen, iv:			1849–51	1860	xii, 68
	1 Brautgesang	Das Haus benedei ich und preis' es laut	Uhland			
	2 Der Bänkelsänger Willie	O Bänkelsänger Willie, du ziehst zum Jahrmarkt aus	Burns, trans. Gerhard			
	3 Der Traum	Im schönsten Garten wallten zwei Buhlen	Uhland			
	4 Sommerlied	Seinen Traum, lind wob	Rückert			
	5 Das Schifflein, fl, hn	Ein Schifflein ziehet leise	Uhland			
—	Des Glockentürmers Töchterlein	Mein hochgebornes Schätzelein	Rückert	1851	—	—
—	Bei Schenkung eines Flügels, pf	Orange und Myrthe hier	Schumann	1853	1942	—

PARTSONGS FOR WOMEN'S VOICES
(*SSAA; incipit given only if different from title*)

op.	Title, accompaniment	Incipit	Text	Composed	Publication	SW
69	Romanzen, i, pf ad lib:			1849	1849	x/2, 16
	1 Tamburinschlägerin	Schwirrend Tamburin	Alvaro de Ameida, trans. Eichendorff			
	2 Waldmädchen	Bin ein Feuer hell	Eichendorff			
	3 Klosterfräulein	Ich armes Klosterfräulein	Kerner			
	4 Soldatenbraut (2nd setting)	Ach, wenn's nur der König auch wüsst	Mörike			
	5 Meerfey	Still bei Nacht fährt manches Schiff	Eichendorff			
	6 Die Kapelle	Droben stehet die Kapelle	Uhland			
91	Romanzen, ii, pf ad lib:			1849	1851	x/2, 32
	1 Rosmarien	Es wollt die Jungfrau früh aufsteh'n	Des Knaben Wunderhorn			
	2 Jäger Wohlgemut	Es jagt' ein Jäger wohlgemut	Des Knaben Wunderhorn			
	3 Der Wassermann	Es war in des Maien mildem Glanz	Kerner			
	4 Das verlassene Mägdelein (2nd setting)	Früh wann die Hähne kräh'n	Mörike			
	5 Der Bleicherin Nachtlied	Bleiche, bleiche weisses Lein	Reinick			
	6 In Meeres Mitten		Rückert			

PARTSONGS FOR MEN'S VOICES
(*TTBB; unaccompanied unless otherwise stated; incipit given only if different from title*)

op.	Title	Incipit	Text	Composed	Publication	SW
33	Sechs Lieder:			1840	1842	xi, 1
	1 Der träumende See	Der See ruht tief im blauen Traum	J. Mosen			
	2 Die Minnesänger	Zu dem Wettgesange schreiten	Heine			
	3 Die Lotosblume (2nd setting)	Die Lotosblume ängstigt	Heine			
	4 Der Zecher als Doktrinär	Was quälte dir dein banges Herz?	Mosen			
	5 Rastlose Liebe	Dem Schnee, dem Regen	Goethe			
	6 Frühlingsglocken	Schneeglöckchen tut läuten	Reinick			
62	Drei Gesänge:			1847	1848	xi, 12
	1 Der Eidgenossen Nachtwache	In stiller Bucht	Eichendorff			
	2 Freiheitslied	Zittr', o Erde dunkle Macht	Rückert			
	3 Schlachtgesang	Mit unserm Arm ist nichts getan	Klopstock			
65	Ritornelle in canonischen Weisen [orig. order 5, 4, 2, 1, 6, 7, 8, 3]:		Rückert	1847	1849	xi, 20
	1 Die Rose stand im Tau, 2 Lasst Lautenspiel und Becherklang, 3 Blüt' oder Schnee!, 4 Gebt mir zu trinken!, 5 Zürne nicht des Herbstes Wind, 6 In Sommertagen rüste den Schlitten, 7 In Meeres Mitten ist ein offener Laden, 8 Hätte zu einem Traubenkerne [pubd 1906]					
—	Zum Anfang	Mache deinem Meister Ehre	Rückert	1847	1928	—
—	Drei Freiheitsgesänge, wind insts ad lib:			1848	1913	—
	1 Zu den Waffen	Vom Angesicht die Mask' herab!	Ullrich			
	2 Schwarz-Rot-Gold	In Kümmernis und Dunkelheit	F. Freiligrath			
	3 Deutscher Freiheitsgesang	Der Sieg ist dein, mein Heldenvolk!	J. Fürst			
93	Verzweifle nicht im Schmerzenstal, motet, double chorus, org ad lib [orchd 1852]		Rückert	1849	1851	—
137	Fünf Gesänge aus H. Laubes Jagdbrevier, 4 hn ad lib [orig. order 1, 2, 3, 5, 4]:		Laube	1849	1857	ix/4, 175
	1 Zur hohen Jagd	Frisch auf zum fröhlichen Jagen				
	2 Habet acht!	Habet Acht auf der Jagd				
	3 Jagdmorgen	O frischer Morgen, frischer Mut				
	4 Frühe	Früh steht der Jäger auf				
	5 Bei der Flasche	Wo gibt es wohl noch Jägerei				

SONGS
(*duets, trios etc and works for vocal declamation with pf acc. and/or other insts ad lib; incipit given only if different from title*)

op.	Title, forces	Incipit	Text	Composed	Publication/MS	SW
—	Verwandlung	Wenn der Winter sonst entschwand	E. Schulze	1827	—	—
—	Lied für xxx	Leicht wie gaukelnde Sylphiden	Schumann	1827	—	—

op.		Title, forces	Incipit	Text	Composed	Publication/MS	SW
—		11 songs:					
	1	Sehnsucht	Sterne der blauen himmlischen Auen	Schumann	1827	1933	—
	2	Die Weinende	Ich sah dich weinen!	Byron, trans.	1827	1933	—
	3	Erinnerung	Glück der Engel!	J. G. Jacobi	1828	1933	—
	4	Kurzes Erwachen	Ich bin im Mai gegangen	Kerner	1828	1933	—
	5	Gesanges Erwachen	Könnt' ich einmal wieder singen	Kerner	1828	1933	—
	6	An Anna I	Lange harrt ich	Kerner	1828	1933	—
	7	An Anna II [used in op.11]	Nicht im Tale	Kerner	1828	1893	xiv/1, 34
	8	Im Herbste [used in op.22]	Zieh' nur, du Sonne	Kerner	1828	1893	xiv/1, 36
	9	Hirtenknabe [used as op.4 no.4]	Bin nur ein armer Hirtenknab	Schumann	1828	1893	xiv/1, 37
	10	Der Fischer	Das Wasser rauscht, das Wasser schwoll	Goethe	1828	1933	—
	11	Klage [lost]		Jacobi	1828		—
—		Vom Reitersmann		Old Ger.	—	D-Zsch	—
—		Maultreiberlied [lost]		—	1838		—
—		Ein Gedanke	Sie schlingt um meinen Nacken	E. Ferrand	1840	1942	—
—		Patriotisches Lied, 1v, chorus, pf	Sie sollen ihn nicht haben	N. Becker	1840	1840	x/2, 168
—		Der Reiter und der Bodensee [frag.]	Der Reiter reitet durchs helle Tal	G. Schwab	1840	1897	—
—		Die nächtliche Heerschau [frag.]	Nachts um die zwölfte Stunde	Zedlitz	1840	1897	—
24		Liederkreis:		Heine	1840	1840	xiii/1, 3
		1 Morgens steh ich auf und frage, 2 Es treibt mich hin, 3 Ich wandelte unter den Bäumen, 4 Lieb Liebchen, 5 Schöne Wiege meiner Leiden, 6 Warte, warte, wilder Schiffmann, 7 Berg und Burgen schaun herunter, 8 Anfangs wolt ich fast verzagen, 9 Mit Myrten und Rosen					
25		Myrthen			1840	1840	xiii/1, 24
	1	Widmung	Du meine Seele, du mein Herz	Rückert			
	2	Freisinn	Lasst mich nur auf meinem Sattel gelten!	Goethe			
	3	Der Nussbaum	Es grünet ein Nussbaum vor dem Haus	Mosen			
	4	Jemand	Mein Herz ist betrübt	Burns, trans. Gerhard			
	5	Lieder aus dem Schenkenbuch im Divan I	Sitz ich allein	Goethe			
	6	Lieder aus dem Schenkenbuch im Divan II	Setze mir nicht	Goethe			
	7	Die Lotosblume	Die Lotosblume ängstigt	Heine			
	8	Talismane	Gottes ist der Orient	Goethe			
	9	Lied der Suleika	Wie mit innigstem Behagen	Goethe, attrib. Marianne von Willemer			
	10	Die Hochländer-Witwe	Ich bin gekommen ins Niederland	Burns, trans. Gerhard			
	11	Lieder der Braut aus dem Liebesfrühling I	Mutter, Mutter! Glaube nicht	Rückert			
	12	Lieder der Braut aus dem Liebesfrühling II	Lass mich ihn am Busen hangen	Rückert			
	13	Hochländers Abschied	Mein Herz ist im Hochland	Burns, trans. Gerhard			
	14	Hochländisches Wiegenlied	Schlafe, süsser kleiner Donald	Burns, trans. Gerhard			
	15	Aus den hebräischen Gesängen	Mein Herz ist schwer!	Byron, trans. J. Körner			
	16	Rätsel	Es flüstert's der Himmel	C. Fanshawe, trans. K. Kannegiesser			
	17	Zwei Venetianische Lieder I	Leis rudern hier	Moore, trans. Freiligrath			
	18	Zwei Venetianische Lieder II	Wenn durch die Piazzetta	Moore, trans. Freiligrath			
	19	Hauptmanns Weib	Hoch zu Pferd!	Burns, trans. Gerhard			
	20	Weit, weit	Wie kann ich froh	Burns, trans. Gerhard			
	21	Was will die einsame Träne?		Heine			
	22	Niemand	Ich hab mein Weib allein	Burns, trans. Gerhard			
	23	Im Westen	Ich schau über Forth hinüber	Burns, trans. Gerhard			
	24	Du bist wie eine Blume		Heine			
	25	Aus den östlichen Rosen	Ich sende einen Gruss	Rückert			
	26	Zum Schluss	Hier in diesen erdbeklommnen Lüften	Rückert			
27		Lieder und Gesänge, i:			1840	1849	xiii/1, 72
	1	Sag an, o lieber Vogel		Hebbel			
	2	Dem roten Röslein		Burns, trans. Gerhard			
	3	Was soll ich sagen?	Mein Aug ist trüb	Chamisso			
	4	Jasminenstrauch	Grün ist der Jasminenstrauch	Rückert			
	5	Nur ein lächelnder Blick		G. W. Zimmermann			
29		Drei Gedichte:		Geibel	1840	1841	x/2, 2
	1	Ländliches Lied, 2 S	Und wenn die Primel schneeweiss blickt				
	2	Lied, 3 S	In meinem Garten die Nelken				

op.	Title, forces	Incipit	Text	Composed	Publication/MS	SW
	3 Zigeunerleben, S, A, T, B, triangle, tambourine ad lib	Im Schatten des Waldes				
30	Drei Gedichte:		Geibel	1840	1840	xiii/1, 80
	1 Der Knabe mit dem Wunderhorn	Ich bin ein lust'ger Geselle				
	2 Der Page	Da ich nun entsagen müssen				
	3 Der Hidalgo	Es ist so süss zu scherzen				
31	Drei Gesänge:			1840	1841	xiii/1, 92
	1 Die Löwenbraut	Mit der Myrte geschmückt	Chamisso			
	2 Die Kartenlegerin	Schlief die Mutter endlich ein	Chamisso, after Béranger			
	3 Die rote Hanne, chorus ad lib	Den Säugling an der Brust	Chamisso, after Béranger			
34	Vier Duette, S, T:			1840	1841	x/1, 2
	1 Liebesgarten	Die Liebe ist ein Rosenstrauch	Reinick			
	2 Liebhabers Ständchen	Wachst du noch, Liebchen, Gruss and Kuss!	Burns, trans. Gerhard			
	3 Unterm Fenster	Wer ist vor meiner Kammertür?	Burns, trans. Gerhard			
	4 Familien-Gemälde	Grossvater und Grossmutter	A. Grün			
35	Zwölf Gedichte:		Kerner	1840	1841	xiii/1, 108
	1 Lust der Sturmnacht	Wenn durch Berg und Tale				
	2 Stirb, Lieb und Freud!	Zu Augsburg steht ein hohes Haus				
	3 Wanderlied	Wohlauf! noch getrunken den funkelnden Wein!				
	4 Erstes Grün	Du junges Grün, du frisches Gras!				
	5 Sehnsucht nach der Waldgegend	Wär ich nie aus euch gegangen				
	6 Auf das Trinkglas eines verstorbenen Freundes	Du herrlich Glas				
	7 Wanderung	Wohlauf und frisch gewandert				
	8 Stille Liebe	Könnt ich dich in Liedern preisen				
	9 Frage	Wärst du nicht, heil'ger Abendschein!				
	10 Stille Tränen	Du bist vom Schlaf erstanden				
	11 Wer machte dich so krank?	Dass du so krank geworden				
	12 Alte Laute	Hörst du den Vogel singen?				
36	Sechs Gedichte:		Reinick	1840	1842	xiii/1, 132
	1 Sonntags am Rhein	Des Sonntags in der Morgenstund				
	2 Ständchen	Komm in die stille Nacht				
	3 Nichts schöneres	Als ich zuerst dich hab gesehn				
	4 An den Sonnenschein	O Sonnenschein!				
	5 Dichters Genesung	Und wieder hatt ich der Schönsten gedacht				
	6 Liebesbotschaft	Wolken, die ihr nach Osten eilt				
37	Zwölf Gedichte aus 'Liebesfrühling' [nos.2, 4, 11, by Clara Schumann]:		Rückert	1840	1841	xiii/2, 2
	1 Der Himmel hat ein Träne geweint, 3 O ihr Herren, 5 Ich hab in mich gesogen, 6 Liebste, was kann denn uns scheiden?, S, T, 7 Schön ist das Fest des Lenzes, S, T, 8 Flügel! Flügel! um zu fliegen, 9 Rose, Meer und Sonne, 10 O Sonn, o Meer, o Rose, 12 So wahr die Sonne scheinet, S, T					
39	Liederkreis (op.77/1 orig. incl. as 1st song, but omitted in 2/1850):		Eichendorff	1840	1842	xiii/2, 28
	1 In der Fremde	Aus der Heimat hinter den Blitzen rot				
	2 Intermezzo	Dein Bildnis wunderselig				
	3 Waldesgespräch	Es ist schon spät				
	4 Die Stille	Es weiss und rät es doch keiner				
	5 Mondnacht	Es war, als hätt der Himmel die Erde still geküsst				
	6 Schöne Fremde	Es rauschen die Wipfel und schauern				
	7 Auf einer Burg	Eingeschlafen auf der Lauer				
	8 In der Fremde	Ich hör die Bächlein rauschen				
	9 Wehmut	Ich kann wohl manchmal singen				
	10 Zwielicht	Dämm'rung will die Flügel spreiten				
	11 Im Walde	Es zog eine Hochzeit den Berg entlang				
	12 Frühlingsnacht	Überm Garten durch die Lüfte				
40	Fünf Lieder:			1840	1842	xiii/2, 50
	1 Märzveilchen	Der Himmel wölbt sich rein und blau	H. C. Andersen, trans. Chamisso			
	2 Muttertraum	Die Mutter betet herzig	Andersen, trans. Chamisso			
	3 Der Soldat	Es geht bei gedämpfter Trommel Klang	Andersen, trans. Chamisso			
	4 Der Spielmann	Im Städtchen gibt es des Jubels viel	Andersen, trans. Chamisso			
	5 Verratene Liebe	Da Nachts wir uns küssten	Chamisso			
42	Frauenliebe und -leben:		Chamisso	1840	1843	xiii/2, 62
	1 Seit ich ihn gesehen, 2 Er, der Herrlichste von allen, 3 Ich kann's nicht fassen, nicht glauben, 4 Du Ring an meinem Finger, 5 Helft mir, ihr Schwestern, 6 Süsser Freund, du blickest, 7 An meinem Herzen, an meiner Brust, 8 Nun hast du mir den ersten Schmerz getan					
43	Drei zweistimmige Lieder:			1840	1844	xi/1, 18
	1 Wenn ich ein Vöglein wär [later incorporated in op.81]		Des Knaben Wunderhorn			
	2 Herbstlied	Das Laub fällt von den Bäumen	S. A. Mahlmann			
	3 Schön Blümelein	Ich bin hinaus gegangen	Reinick			

op.	Title, forces	Incipit	Text	Composed	Publication/MS	SW
45	Romanzen und Balladen, i:			1840	1843	xiii/2, 78
	1 Der Schatzgräber	Wenn alle Wälder schliefen	Eichendorff			
	2 Frühlingsfahrt	Es zogen zwei rüst'ge Gesellen	Eichendorff			
	3 Abends am Strand	Wir sassen am Fischerhause	Heine			
48	Dichterliebe:		Heine	1840	1844	xiii/2, 88
	1 Im wunderschönen Monat Mai, 2 Aus meinen Tränen spriessen, 3 Die Rose, die Lilie, die Taube, die Sonne, 4 Wenn ich in deine Augen seh, 5 Ich will meine Seele tauchen, 6 Im Rhein, im heiligen Strome, 7 Ich grolle nicht, 8 Und wüssten's die Blumen, die kleinen, 9 Das ist ein Flöten und Geigen, 10 Hör ich das Liedchen klingen, 11 Ein Jüngling liebt ein Mädchen, 12 Am leuchtenden Sommermorgen, 13 Ich hab im Traum geweinet, 14 Allnächtlich im Traume, 15 Aus alten Märchen, 16 Die alten, bösen Lieder					
49	Romanzen und Balladen, ii:			1840	1844	xiii/2, 122
	1 Die beiden Grenadiere	Nach Frankreich zogen zwei Grenadier'	Heine			
	2 Die feindlichen Brüder	Oben auf des Berges Spitze	Heine			
	3 Die Nonne	Im Garten steht die Nonne	A. Fröhlich			
51	Lieder und Gesänge, ii:				1850	xiii/2, 132
	1 Sehnsucht	Ich blick in mein Herz	Geibel	1840		
	2 Volksliedchen	Wenn ich früh in den Garten geh	Rückert	1840		
	3 Ich wandre nicht	Warum soll ich denn wandern	C. Christern	1840		
	4 Auf dem Rhein	Auf deinem Grunde haben sie an verborgnem Ort	K. L. Immermann	1846		
	5 Liebeslied	Dir zu eröffnen mein Herz	Goethe	1850		
53	Romanzen und Balladen, iii:			1840	1845	xiii/2, 142
	1 Blondels Lied	Spähend nach dem Eisengitter	J. G. Seidl			
	2 Loreley	Es flüstern und rauschen die Wogen	W. Lorenz			
	3 Der arme Peter	1 Der Hans und die Grete tanzen herum	Heine			
		2 In meiner Brust				
		3 Der arme Peter wankt vorbei				
57	Belsatzar	Die Mitternacht zog näher schon	Heine	1840	1846	xiii/3, 2
64	Romanzen und Balladen, iv:				1847	xiii/3, 10
	1 Die Soldatenbraut	Ach, wenn's nur der König auch wüsst	Mörike	1847		
	2 Das verlassne Mägdelein	Früh wann die Hähne krähn	Mörike	1847		
	3 Tragödie	1 Entflieh mit mir und sei mein Weib	Heine	1841		
		2 Es fiel ein Reif in der Frühlingsnacht				
		3 Auf ihrem Grab, S, T				
74	Spanisches Liederspiel:		Geibel, after Spanish poets	1849	1849	x/2, 46
	1 Erste Begegnung, S, A	Von dem Rosenbusch, o Mutter				
	2 Intermezzo, T, B	Und schläfst du, mein Mädchen, auf!				
	3 Liebesgram, S, A	Dereinst, dereinst, o Gedanke mein				
	4 In der Nacht, S, T	Alle gingen, Herz, zur Ruh'				
	5 Es ist verraten, S, A, T, B	Dass ihr steht in Liebesglut				
	6 Melancholie, S	Wann, wann erscheint der Morgen				
	7 Geständnis, T	Also lieb ich euch				
	8 Botschaft, S, A	Nelken wind ich und Jasmin				
	9 Ich bin geliebt, S, A, T, B	Mögen alle bösen Zungen				
	10 Der Kontrabandiste, Bar	Ich bin der Kontrabandiste				
77	Lieder und Gesänge, iii:				1851	xiii/3, 18
	1 Der frohe Wandersmann	Wem Gott will rechte Gunst erweisen	Eichendorff	1840 (orig. incl. in op.39)		
	2 Mein Garten	Veilchen, Rosmarin, Mimosen	Hoffmann von Fallersleben	1850		
	3 Geisternähe	Was weht um meine Schläfe	A. Halm	1850		
	4 Stiller Vorwurf	In einsamen Stunden drängt Wehmut sich auf	? O. L. Wolff	1840		
	5 Aufträge	Nicht so schnelle	C. L'Egru	1850		
—	Soldatenlied	Ein scheckiges Pferd	Hoffmann von Fallersleben	1844	1845	xiii/4, 122
—	Das Schwert	Zur Schmiede ging ein junger Held	Uhland	1848	—	—
—	Der weisse Hirsch, sketches	Es gingen drei Jäger	Uhland	1848	—	—
—	Die Ammenuhr	Der Mond, der scheint	Des Knaben Wunderhorn	1848	—	—
78	Vier Duette, S, T:			1849	1850	x/1, 28
	1 Tanzlied	Eia, wie flattert der Kranz	Rückert			
	2 Er und Sie	Seh ich in das stille Tal	Kerner			
	3 Ich denke dein		Goethe			
	4 Wiegenlied	Schlaf, Kindlein, schlaf	Hebbel			
—	Sommerruh, duet	Sommerruh, wie schön bist du	C. Schad, altered by Schumann	1849	1850	xiv/1, 38
79	Lieder-Album für die Jugend:			1849	1849	xiii/3, 30
	1 Der Abendstern	Du lieblicher Stern	Hoffmann von Fallersleben			
	2 Schmetterling	O Schmetterling, sprich	Hoffmann von Fallersleben			
	3 Frühlingsbotschaft	Kuckuck, Kuckuck ruft aus dem Wald	Hoffmann von Fallersleben			
	4 Frühlingsgruss	So sei gegrüsst vieltausendmal	Hoffmann von Fallersleben			

op.	Title, forces	Incipit	Text	Composed	Publication/MS	SW
	5 Vom Schlaraffenland	Kommt, wir wollen uns begeben	Hoffmann von Fallersleben			
	6 Sonntag	Der Sonntag ist gekommen	Hoffmann von Fallersleben			
	7 Zigeunerliedchen	1 Unter die Soldaten	Geibel			
		2 Jeden Morgen, in der Frühe	Geibel			
	8 Des Knaben Berglied	Ich bin vom Berg der Hirtenknab	Uhland			
	9 Mailied, duet ad lib	Komm, lieber Mai	C. A. Overbeck			
	10 Das Käuzlein	Ich armes Käuzlein kleine	Des Knaben Wunderhorn			
	11 Hinaus ins Freie!	Wie blüht es im Tale	Hoffmann von Fallersleben			
	12 Der Sandmann	Zwei feine Stieflein hab ich an	H. Kletke			
	13 Marienwürmchen	Marienwürmchen, setze dich	Des Knaben Wunderhorn			
	14 Die Waise	Der Frühling kehret wieder	Hoffmann von Fallersleben			
	15 Das Glück, duet	Vöglein vom Zweig	Hebbel			
	16 Weihnachtslied	Als das Christkind ward zur Welt gebracht	Andersen, trans.			
	17 Die wandelnde Glocke	Es war ein Kind	Goethe			
	18 Frühlingslied, duet ad lib	Schneeglöckchen klingen wieder	Hoffmann von Fallersleben			
	19 Frühlings Ankunft	Nach diesen trüben Tagen	Hoffmann von Fallersleben			
	20 Die Schwalben, duet	Es fliegen zwei Schwalben	Des Knaben Wunderhorn			
	21 Kinderwacht	Wenn fromme Kindlein schlafen gehn	anon.			
	22 Des Sennen Abschied	Ihr Matten, lebt wohl, ihr sonnigen Weiden!	Schiller			
	23 Er ist's	Frühling lässt sein blaues Band	Mörike			
	24 Spinnelied, trio ad lib	Spinn, spinn	anon.			
	25 Des Buben Schützenlied	Mit dem Pfeil, dem Bogen	Schiller			
	26 Schneeglöckchen	Der Schnee, der gestern noch in Flöckchen	Rückert			
	27 Lied Lynceus des Türmers	Zum Sehen geboren	Goethe			
	28 Mignon	Kennst du das Land	Goethe			
83	Drei Gesänge:			1850	1850	xiii/3, 78
	1 Resignation	Lieben, von ganzer Seele lieben	J. Buddeus			
	2 Die Blume der Ergebung	Ich bin die Blum' in Garten	Rückert			
	3 Der Einsiedler	Komm, Trost der Welt	Eichendorff			
87	Der Handschuh	Vor seinem Löwengarten	Schiller	1850	1850	xiii/3, 88
89	Sechs Gesänge:		W. von der Neun [F. W. T. Schöpff]	1850	1850	xiii/3, 94
	1 Es stürmet am Abendhimmel					
	2 Heimliches Verschwinden	Nachts zu unbekannter Stunde				
	3 Herbstlied	Durch die Tannen und die Linden				
	4 Abschied vom Walde	Nun scheidet vom sterbenden Walde				
	5 Ins Freie	Mir ist's so eng allüberall!				
	6 Röselein, Röselein!					
90	Sechs Gedichte:		N. Lenau	1850	1851	xiii/3, 108
	1 Lied eines Schmiedes	Fein Rösslein, ich beschlage dich				
	2 Meine Rose	Dem holden Lenzgeschmeide				
	3 Kommen und Scheiden	So oft sie kam				
	4 Die Sennin	Schöne Sennin, noch einmal singe				
	5 Einsamkeit	Wild verwachs'ne dunkle Fichten				
	6 Der schwere Abend	Die dunklen Wolken hingen				
	7 Requiem	Ruh von schmerzensreichen Mühen aus	anon.			
95	Drei Gesänge:		Byron, trans. Körner	1849	1851	xiii/3, 126
	1 Die Tochter Jephthas	Da die Heimat, o Vater				
	2 An den Mond	Schlaflose Sonne, melanchol'scher Stern!				
	3 Dem Helden	Dein Tag ist aus, dein Ruhm fing an				
96	Lieder und Gesänge, iv:			1850	1851	xiii/3, 136
	1 Nachtlied	Über allen Gipfeln ist Ruh	Goethe			
	2 Schneeglöckchen	Die Sonne sah die Erde an	anon.			
	3 Ihre Stimme	Lass tief in dir mich lesen	Platen			
	4 Gesungen!	Hört ihr im Laube des Regens	Neun [Schöpff]			
	5 Himmel und Erde	Wie der Bäume kühne Wipfel	Neun [Schöpff]			
98a	Lieder und Gesänge aus Wilhelm Meister:		Goethe	1849	1851	xiii/4, 2
	1 Kennst du das Land, 2 Ballade des Harfners ('Was hör ich draussen vor dem Tor'), 3 Nur wer die Sehnsucht kennt, 4 Wer nie sein Brot mit Tränen ass, 5 Heiss mich nicht reden, 6 Wer sich der Einsamkeit ergibt, 7 Singet nicht in Trauertönen, 8 An die Türen will ich schleichen, 9 So lasst mich scheinen					
101	Minnespiel:		Rückert	1849	1852	x/2, 88
	1 Meine Töne still und heiter, T, 2 Liebster, deine Worte stehlen, S, 3 Ich bin dein Baum, A, B, 4 Mein schöner Stern!, T, 5 Schön ist das Fest des Lenzes, S, A, T, B, 6 O Freund, mein Schirm, mein Schutz!, A/S, 7 Die tausend Grüsse, S, T, 8 So wahr die Sonne scheinet, S, A, T, B					

op.	Title, forces	Incipit	Text	Composed	Publication/MS	SW
103	Mädchenlieder, S, A/2S:		E. Kulmann	1851	1851	x/1, 42
	1 Mailied	Pflücket Rosen, um das Haar schön				
	2 Frühlingslied	Der Frühling kehret wieder				
	3 An die Nachtigall	Bleibe hier und singe, liebe Nachtigall!				
	4 An den Abendstern	Schweb empor am Himmel				
104	Sieben Lieder:		Kulmann	1851	1851	xiii/4, 27
	1 Mond, meiner Seele Liebling, 2 Viel Glück zur Reise, Schwalben!, 3 Du nennst mich armes Mädchen, 4 Der Zeisig ('Wir sind ja, Kind, im Maie'), 5 Reich mir die Hand, o Wolke, 6 Die letzten Blumen starben, 7 Gekämpft hat meine Barke					
106	Schön Hedwig, declamation	Im Kreise der Vasallen	Hebbel	1849	1853	xiii/4, 106
107	Sechs Gesänge:			1851–2	1852	xiii/4, 40
	1 Herzeleid	Die Weiden lassen matt die Zweige hangen	Ullrich			
	2 Die Fensterscheibe	Die Fenster klär ich zum Feiertag	Ullrich			
	3 Der Gärtner	Auf ihrem Leibrösslein	Mörike			
	4 Die Spinnerin	Auf dem Dorf in den Spinnstuben	P. Heyse			
	5 Im Wald	Ich zieh so allein in den Wald hinein!	W. Müller			
	6 Abendlied	Es ist so still geworden	G. Kinkel			
114	Drei Lieder, 3 female vv:			1853	1853	x/2, 118
	1 Nänie	Unter den roten Blumen schlummre	L. Bechstein			
	2 Triolett	Senkt die Nacht den sanften Fittig nieder	L'Egru			
	3 Spruch	O blicke, wenn den Sinn dir will die Welt	Rückert			
117	Vier Husarenlieder, Bar:		Lenau	1851	1852	xiii/4, 52
	1 Der Husar, trara!, 2 Der leidige Frieden, 3 Den grünen Zeigern, 4 Da liegt der Feinde gestreckte Schar					
119	Drei Gedichte:		G. Pfarrius	1851	1853	xiii/4, 60
	1 Die Hütte	Im Wald, in grüner Runde				
	2 Warnung	Es geht der Tag zur Neige				
	3 Der Bräutigam und die Birke	Birke, Birke, des Waldes Zier				
122	Zwei Balladen, declamations:			1852–3	1853	xiii/4, 112
	1 Ballade vom Haideknaben	Der Knabe träumt	Hebbel			
	2 Die Flüchtlinge	Der Hagel klirrt nieder	Shelley, trans.			
125	Fünf heitere Gesänge:			1850–51	1853	xiii/4, 68
	1 Die Meerfee	Helle Silberglöcklein klingen	Buddeus			
	2 Husarenabzug	Aus dem dunkeln Tor wallt	C. Candidus			
	3 Jung Volkers Lied [orig. intended for op.107 no.4]	Und die mich trug im Mutterarm	Mörike			
	4 Frühlingslied	Das Körnlein springt	F. Braun			
	5 Frühlingslust	Nun stehen die Rosen in Blüte	Heyse			
127	Fünf Lieder und Gesänge:				1854	xiii/4, 80
	1 Sängers Trost	Weint auch einst kein Liebchen	Kerner	1840		
	2 Dein Angesicht [orig. intended for op.48]		Heine	1840		
	3 Es leuchtet meine Liebe [orig. intended for op.48]		Heine	1840		
	4 Mein altes Ross		Moritz, Graf von Strachwitz	1850		
	5 Schlusslied des Narren	Und als ich ein winzig Bübchen war	Shakespeare, trans. Tieck and A. Schlegel	1840		
—	Frühlingsgrüsse	Nach langem Frost	Lenau	1851	1942	
135	Gedichte der Königin Maria Stuart:		trans. G. Vincke	1852	1855	xiii/4, 90
	1 Abschied von Frankreich	Ich zieh dahin				
	2 Nach der Geburt ihres Sohnes	Herr Jesu Christ				
	3 An die Königin Elisabeth	Nur ein Gedanke				
	4 Abschied von der Welt	Was nützt die mir noch zugemess'ne Zeit?				
	5 Gebet	O Gott, mein Gebieter				
138	Spanische Liebeslieder:		Geibel	1849	1857	x/2, 124
	1 Vorspiel, pf 4 hands, 2 Tief im Herzen trag ich Pein, S, 3 O wie lieblich ist das Mädchen, T, 4 Bedeckt mich mit Blumen, S, A, 5 Flutenreicher Ebro, Bar, 6 Intermezzo, pf 4 hands, 7 Weh, wie zornig ist das Mädchen, T, 8 Hoch, hoch sind die Berge, A, 9 Blaue Augen hat das Mädchen, T, B, 10 Dunkler Lichtglanz, S, A, T, B					
139	From Des Sängers Fluch:		Pohl, after Uhland	1852	1858	—
	4 Provenzalisches Lied	In den Talen der Provence				
	7 Ballade	In der hohen Hall sass König Sifrid				
142	Vier Gesänge:			1840	1858	xiii/4, 98
	1 Trost im Gesang	Der Wandrer, dem verschwunden	Kerner			
	2 Lehn deine Wang [orig. intended for op.48]		Heine			
	3 Mädchen-Schwermut	Kleine Tropfen, seid ihr Tränen	L. Bernhard			
	4 Mein Wagen rollet langsam [orig. intended for op.48]		Heine			

op.	Title, forces	Incipit	Text	Composed	Publication/MS	SW
—	Mailied [duet]			1851	D-Zsch	—
—	Liedchen von Marie und Papa, duet	Gern mach' ich dir	Schumann	1852	1942	—
—	Glockentürmers Töchterlein	Mein hochgebor'nes Schätzelein	Rückert	—	—	—
—	Das Käuzlein [2nd setting]	Ich armes Käuzlein kleine	Des Knaben Wunderhorn	—	Zsch	—
—	Deutscher Blumengarten [duet]		Rückert	—	—	—

bin im Mai gegangen', 1828; 'Ich bin vom Berg der Hirtenknab', op.79 no.8; 'Ich blick in mein Herz', op.51 no.1; 'Ich denke dein', op.78 no.3; 'Ich grolle nicht', op.48 no.7; 'Ich hab im Traum geweinet', op.48 no.13; 'Ich hab in mich gesogen', op.37 no.5; 'Ich hab mein Weib allein', op.25 no.22
'Ich hör die Bächlein rauschen', op.39 no.8; 'Ich kann's nicht fassen, nicht glauben', op.42 no.3; 'Ich kann wohl manchmal singen', op.39 no.9; 'Ich sah dich weinen', 1827; 'Ich schau über Forth hinüber', op.25 no.23; 'Ich sende einen Gruss', op.25 no.25; 'Ich wandelte unter den Bäumen', op.24 no.3; Ich wandre nicht, op.51 no.3; 'Ich will meine Seele tauchen', op.48 no.5; 'Ich zieh dahin', op.135 no.1; 'Ich zieh so allein in den Wald hinein', op.107 no.5; Ihre Stimme, op.96 no.3; 'Ihr Matten, lebt wohl, ihr sonnigen Weiden', op.79 no.22
'Im Garten steht die Nonne', op.49 no.3; Im Herbste, 1828; 'Im Kreise der Vasallen', op.106; 'Im Rhein, im heiligen Strome', op.48 no.6; 'Im Schatten des Waldes', op.29 no.3; 'Im Städtchen gibt es des Jubels viel', op.40 no.4; Im Wald, op.107 no.5; Im Walde, op.39 no.11; 'Im Wald, in grüner Runde', op.119 no.1; Im Westen, op.25 no.23; 'Im wunderschönen Monat Mai', op.48 no.1; 'In den Talen der Provence', op.139 no.4; In der Fremde, op.39 no.1; In der Fremde, op.39 no.8; 'In der hohen Hall sass König Sifrid', op.139 no.7; In der Nacht, op.74 no.4
'In einsamen Stunden drängt Wehmut sich auf', op.77 no.4; 'In meinem Garten die Nelken', op.29 no.2; 'In meiner Brust', op.53 no.3; Ins Freie, op.89 no.5; Intermezzo, op.39 no.2; Intermezzo, op.74 no.2; Jasminenstrauch, op.27 no.4; 'Jeden Morgen, in der Frühe', op.79 no.7; Jemand, op.25 no.4; Jung Volkers Lied, op.125 no.3; 'Kennst du das Land', op.79 no.28; 'Kennst du das Land', op.98a no.1; Kinderwacht, op.79 no.21; Klage, 1828; 'Kleine Tropfen, seid ihr Tränen', op.142 no.3; Kommen und Scheiden, op.90 no.3
'Komm in die stille Nacht', op.36 no.2; 'Komm, lieber Mai', op.79 no.9; 'Komm, Trost der Welt', op.83 no.3; 'Kommt, wir wollen uns begeben', op.79 no.5; 'Könnt ich dich in Liedern preisen', op.35 no.8; 'Könnt' ich einmal wieder singen', 1828; 'Kuckuck, Kuckuck ruft aus dem Wald', op.79 no.3; Kurzes Erwachen, 1828; Ländliches Lied, op.29 no.1; 'Lange harrt ich', 1828; 'Lass mich ihm am Busen hangen', op.25 no.12; 'Lass tief in dir mich lesen', op.96 no.3; 'Lasst mich nur auf meinem Sattel gelten', op.25 no.2; 'Lehn deine Wang', op.142 no.2; 'Leicht wie gaukelnde Sylphiden', 1827; 'Leis rudern hier', op.25 no.17
'Lieben, von ganzer Seele lieben', op.83 no.1; Liebesbotschaft, op.36 no.6; Liebesgarten, op.34 no.1; Liebesgram, op.74 no.3; Liebeslied, op.51 no.5; Liebhabers Ständchen, op.34 no.2; 'Lieb Liebchen', op.24 no.4; 'Liebster, deine Worte stehlen', op.101 no.2; 'Liebste, was kann denn uns scheiden?', op.37 no.6; Lied, op.29 no.2; Liedchen von Marie und Papa, 1852; Lied der Suleika, op.25 no.9; Lied eines Schmiedes, op.90 no.1; Lieder-Album für die Jugend, op.79; Lieder aus dem Schenkenbuch im Divan I, op.25 no.5; Lieder aus dem Schenkenbuch im Divan II, op.25 no.6; Lieder der Braut aus dem Liebesfrühling I, op.25 no.11; Lieder der Braut aus dem Liebesfrühling II, op.25 no.12; Liederkreis, op.24; Liederkreis, op.39
Lied für xxx, 1827; Lied Lynceus des Türmers, op.79 no.27; Loreley, op.53 no.2; Lust der Sturmnacht, op.35 no.1; Mädchenlieder, op.103; Mädchen-Schwermut, op.143 no.3; Mailied, op.79 no.9; Mailied, op.103 no.1; Mailied, after op.142; Marienwürmchen, op.79 no.13; 'Marienwürmchen, setze dich', op.79 no.1; Märzveilchen, op.40 no.1; Maultreiberlied, 1838; 'Mein altes Ross', op.127 no.4; 'Mein Aug ist trüb', op.27 no.3; Meine Rose, op.90 no.2
'Meine Töne still und heiter', op.101 no.1; Mein Garten, op.77 no.2; 'Mein Herz ist betrübt', op.25 no.4; 'Mein Herz ist im Hochland', op.25 no.13; 'Mein Herz ist schwer', op.25 no.15; 'Mein hochgebornes Schätzelein', after op.142; 'Mein schöner Stern', op.101 no.4; 'Mein Wagen rollet langsam', op.142 no.4; Melancholie, op.74 no.6; Mignon, op.79 no.28; Minnespiel, op.101; 'Mir ist's so eng allüberall!', op.89 no.5; 'Mit dem Pfeil, dem Bogen', op.79 no.25; 'Mit der Myrte geschmückt', op.31 no.1; 'Mit Myrten und Rosen', op.24 no.9; 'Mögen alle bösen Zungen', op.79 no.9; 'Mond, meiner Seele Liebling', op.104 no.1
Mondnacht, op.39 no.5; 'Morgens steh ich auf und frage', op.24 no.1; 'Mutter, Mutter glaube nicht', op.25 no.11; Muttertraum, op.40 no.2; Myrthen, op.25; Nach der Geburt ihres Sohnes, op.135 no.2; 'Nach diesen trüben Tagen', op.79 no.19; 'Nach Frankreich zogen zwei Grenadier', op.49 no.1; 'Nach langem Frost', 1851; Nachtlied, op.96 no.1; 'Nachts um die zwölfte Stunde', 1840; 'Nachts zu unbekannter Stunde', op.89 no.2; Nänie, op.114 no.1; 'Nelken wind ich und Jasmin', op.74 no.8; 'Nicht im Tale', 1828; 'Nicht so schnelle', op.77 no.5
Nichts Schöneres, op.36 no.3; Niemand, op.25 no.22; 'Nun hast du mir den ersten Schmerz getan', op.42 no.8; 'Nun scheidet vom sterbenden Walde', op.89 no.4; 'Nun stehen die Rosen in Blüte', op.125 no.5; 'Nur ein Gedanke', op.135 no.2; 'Nur ein lächelnder Blick', op.27 no.5; Nur wer die Sehnsucht kennt, op.98a no.3; 'Oben auf des Berges Spitze', op.49 no.2; 'O blicke, wenn den Sinn dir will die Welt', op.114 no.4; 'O Freund, mein Schirm, mein Schutz, op.101 no.6; 'O Gott, mein Gebieter', op.135 no.5
'O ihr Herren', op.37 no.3; 'O Schmetterling, sprich', op.79 no.2; 'O Sonnenschein!', op.36 no.4; 'O Sonn, o Meer, o Rose', op.37 no.10;

'O wie lieblich ist das Mädchen', op.138 no.3; 'Pflücket Rosen, um das Haar schön', op.103 no.1; Provenzalisches Lied, op.139 no.4; Rätsel, op.25 no.16; 'Reich mir die Hand, o Wolke', op.104 no.5; Requiem, op.90 no.7; Resignation, op.83 no.1; 'Rose, Meer und Sonne', op.37 no.9; Röselein, Röselein!, op.89 no.6; 'Ruh von schmerzensreichen Mühen aus', op.90 no.7
'Sag an, o lieber Vogel mein', op.27 no.1; Sängers Trost, op.127 no.1; 'Schlafe, süsser kleiner Donald', op.25 no.14; 'Schlaf, Kindlein, schlaf', op.78 no.4; 'Schlafe Mutter endlich ein', op.31 no.2; Schlusslied des Narren, op.127 no.5; Schmetterling, op.79 no.2; Schneeglöckchen, op.79 no.26; Schneeglöckchen, op.96 no.2; 'Schneeglöckchen klingen wieder', op.79 no.18; Schön Blümelein, op.43 no.3; Schöne Fremde, op.39 no.6; 'Schöne Sennin, noch einmal singe', op.90 no.4
'Schöne Wiege meiner Leiden', op.24 no.5; Schön Hedwig, op.106; 'Schön ist das Fest des Lenzes', op.37 no.7; 'Schön ist das Fest des Lenzes', op.101 no.5; 'Schweb empor am Himmel', op.103 no.4; 'Seh ich in das stille Tal', op.78 no.2; Sehnsucht, 1827; Sehnsucht, op.51 no.1; 'Sehnsucht nach der Waldgegend', op.35 no.5; 'Seit ich ihn gesehen', op.42 no.1; 'Senkt die Nacht den sanften Fittig nieder', op.114 no.2; 'Setze mir nicht', op.25 no.6; 'Sie schlingt um meinen Nacken', 1840; 'Sie sollen ihn nicht haben', 1840; 'Singet nicht in Trauertönen', op.98a no.7; 'Sitz ich allein', op.25 no.5
'So lasst mich scheinen', op.98a no.9; Soldatenlied, ?1845; Sommerruh, 1849; 'Sommerruh, wie schön bist du', 1849; Sonntag, op.79 no.6; Sonntags am Rhein, op.36 no.1; 'So oft sie kam', op.90 no.3; 'So sei gegrüsst vieltausendmal', op.79 no.4; 'So wahr die Sonne scheinet', op.37 no.12; 'So wahr die Sonne scheinet', op.101 no.8; 'Spähend nach dem Eisengitter', op.53 no.1; Spanische Liebeslieder, op.138; Spanisches Liederspiel, op.74; Spinnelied, op.79 no.24; 'Spinn, spinn', op.79 no.24; Spruch, op.114 no.3; Ständchen, op.36 no.2; 'Sterne der blauen himmlischen Auen', 1827; Stille Liebe, op.35 no.8; Stille Tränen, op.35 no.10; Stiller Vorwurf, op.77 no.4
Stirb, Lieb und Freud!, op.35 no.2; 'Süsser Freund, du blickest', op.42 no.6; Talismane, op.25 no.8; Tanzlied, op.78 no.1; 'Tief im Herzen trag ich Pein', op.138 no.2; Tragödie, op.64 no.3; Triolett, op.114 no.2; Trost im Gesang, op.142 no.1; 'Über allen Gipfeln ist Ruh', op.96 no.1; 'Überm Garten durch die Lüfte', op.39 no.12; 'Und als ich ein winzig Bübchen war', op.127 no.5; 'Und die mich trug im Mutterarm', op.125 no.3; 'Und schläfst du, mein Mädchen, auf', op.74 no.2
'Und wenn die Primel schneeweiss blickt', op.29 no.1; 'Und wieder hatt ich der Schönsten gedacht', op.36 no.5; 'Und wüssten's die Blumen, die kleinen', op.48 no.8; 'Unter den roten Blumen schlummere', op.114 no.1; 'Unter die Soldaten', op.79 no.7; Unterm Fenster, op.34 no.3; 'Veilchen, Rosmarin, Mimosen', op.77 no.2; Verratene Liebe, op.40 no.5; Verwandlung, 1827; 'Viel Glück zur Reise, Schwalben', op.104 no.2; Vier Husarenlieder, op.117; 'Vöglein vom Zweig', op.79 no.15; Volksliedchen, op.51 no.2; Vom Reitersmann, after 1828; Vom Schlaraffenland, op.79 no.5
'Von dem Rosenbusch', op.74 no.1; 'Vor seinem Löwengarten', op.87; 'Wachst du noch, Liebchen, Gruss und Kuss!', op.79 no.2; Waldesgespräch, op.39 no.3; Wanderlust, op.35 no.3; Wanderung, op.35 no.7; 'Wann, wann erscheint der Morgen', op.74 no.6; 'Wär ich nie aus euch gegangen', op.35 no.5; Warnung, op.119 no.2; 'Wärst du nicht, heil'ger Abendschein!', op.35 no.9; 'Warte, warte, wilder Schiffmann', op.24 no.6; 'Warum soll ich denn wandern', op.51 no.3; 'Was hör ich draussen vor dem Tor', op.98a no.2; 'Was nützt die mir noch zugemessne Zeit?', op.135 no.4; Was soll ich sagen?, op.27 no.3
'Was weht um meine Schläfe', op.77 no.3; 'Was will die einsame Träne?', op.25 no.21; Wehmut, op.39 no.9; 'Weh, wie zornig ist das Mädchen', op.138 no.7; Weihnachtslied, op.79 no.16; 'Weint auch einst kein Liebchen', op.127 no.1; Weit, weit, op.25 no.20; 'Wem Gott will rechte Gunst erweisen', op.77 no.1; 'Wenn alle Wälder schliefen', op.45 no.1; 'Wenn der Winter sonst entschwand', 1827; 'Wenn durch Berg und Tale', op.35 no.1; 'Wenn durch die Piazzetta', op.25 no.18
'Wenn fromme Kindlein schlafen gehn', op.79 no.21; 'Wenn ich ein Vöglein wär', op.43 no.1; 'Wenn ich früh in den Garten geh', op.51 no.2; 'Wenn ich in deine Augen seh', op.48 no.4; 'Wer ist vor meiner Kammertür?', op.34 no.3; 'Wer machte dich so krank?', op.35 no.11; 'Wer sein Brot mit Tränen ass', op.98a no.4; 'Wer sich der Einsamkeit ergibt', op.98a no.6; Widmung, op.25 no.1; 'Wie blüht es im Tale', op.79 no.11; 'Wie der Bäume kühne Wipfel', op.96 no.5; Wiegenlied, op.78 no.4
'Wie kann ich froh', op.25 no.20; 'Wie mit innigstem Behagen', op.25 no.9; 'Wild verwachs'ne dunkle Fichten', op.90 no.5; 'Wir sassen am Fischerhause', op.45 no.3; 'Wir sind ja, Kind, im Maie', op.104 no.4; 'Wohlauf! noch getrunken den funkelnden Wein', op.35 no.3; 'Wohlauf und frisch gewandert', op.35 no.7; 'Wolken, die ihr nach Osten eilt', op.6; 'Zieh' nur du Sonne', 1828; Zigeunerleben, op.29 no.3; Zigeunerliedchen, op.79 no.7; 'Zu Augsburg steht ein hohes Haus', no.2
Zum Schluss, op.25 no.26; 'Zum Sehen geboren', op.79 no.27; 'Zur Schmiede ging ein junger Held', 1848; 'Zwei feine Stieflein hab ich an', op.79 no.12; Zwei Venetianische Lieder I, op.25 no.17; Zwei Venetianische Lieder II, op.25 no.18; Zwielicht, op.39 no.10

KEYBOARD
(for solo pf unless otherwise stated)

op.	Title, key	Composed	Publication/MS	Remarks	SW
—	8 polonaises, pf 4 hands	1828	1933	some material used in Papillons, op.2	—
—	Variations on a theme of Prince Louis Ferdinand of Prussia, pf 4 hands	1828	—	—	—
—	Romanze, f	1829	—	unfinished	—
—	6 Walzer	1829–30	—	some material used in Papillons, op.2	—
1	Thème sur le nom Abegg varié pour le pianoforte	1829–30	1831	also orch sketches	vii/1, 2
—	Variations on a theme of Weber	1831	—	on a theme from Preziosa	—
—	Valse, E♭	1831	—	unfinished	—
—	Valse per F. Wieck	1831–2	—	unfinished	—
—	Sonata, A♭	1831–2	—	1st movt and Adagio only	—
—	Andante with variations on an orig. theme, G	1831–2	—	inscribed 'Mit Gott', some material used in op.124 no.2	—
—	Prelude and fugue	1832	–		
2	Papillons	1829–31	1831	includes some material from the 4-hand polonaises (1828) and some used also in 6 Walzer (1829–30)	vii/1, 12
3	6 Studien nach Capricen von Paganini, i	1832	1832	orig. op.2	vii/1, 22
4	6 intermezzos	1832	1833	orig. op.3 and entitled Pièces phantastiques	vii/1, 46
—	Phantasie satyrique	1832	—	on a theme of Henri Herz; fragments only	—
—	Fandango, f♯	1832	—	later used in op.11	—
—	Exercice fantastique	1832	—	orig. op.5; lost	—
—	Rondo, B♭	1832	—	unfinished	—
—	12 Burlesken (Burle)	1832	—	later used in op.124	—
—	Fugue, d	?1832	D-Bds		—
—	Movt in B♭	?1832	S-Skma	sketch	—
—	Fugal piece, b♭ [one of many]	?1832	Skma	sketch	—
—	Canonic piece, A	?1832	Skma	sketch	—
—	Fugue no.3	?1832	—	probably intended as finale of op.5	—
—	5 short pieces:	1832–3	—		—
	1 Notturnino			unfinished	
	2 Ballo				
	3 Burla				
	4 Capriccio			unfinished	
	5 Ecossaise			unfinished	
—	Sehnsuchtswalzer Variationen: scènes musicales sur un thème connu	1832–3	—	also entitled Scènes mignonnes and Scènes musicales sur un thème connu de Fr. Schubert; opening used as opening of Carnaval, op.9	—
5	10 Impromptus über ein Thema von Clara Wieck	1833	1833	last no. includes material from finale of Symphony, g (1832–3); 2nd version of 1850 omits 2 variations but introduces a new variation, no.3	vii/1, 68
—	Etüden in Form freier Variationen über ein Beethovensches Thema	1833	1976	Allegretto of Beethoven's Symphony no.7: one variation pubd as op.124 no.2	—
—	Variations sur un nocturne de Chopin	1834	D-Zsch	Chopin's op.15 no.3, g	—
—	Sonata movt, B♭	1836			—
—	Sonata no.4, f	1836–7		unfinished	—
6	Davidsbündlertänze: 18 character-pieces	1837	1837	title in 2nd edn. (1850–51) Die Davidsbündler	vii/1, 96
7	Toccata, C	1829–32	1834	orig. op.6; orig. title Etude fantastique en double-sons, D	vii/1, 146
8	Allegro, b	1831	1835	1st movt of projected sonata	vii/1, 156
9	Carnaval: scènes mignonnes sur quatre notes:	1833–5	1837	orig. title Fasching: Schwänke auf vier Noten für Pianoforte von Florestan, op.12	vii/2, ?
	1 Préambule, 2 Pierrot, 3 Arlequin, 4 Valse noble, 5 Eusebius, 6 Florestan, 7 Coquette, 8 Réplique, Sphinxes, 9 Papillons, 10 ASCH–SCHA (Lettres dansantes), 11 Chiarina, 12 Chopin, 13 Estrella, 14 Reconnaissance, 15 Pantalon et Colombine, 16 Valse allemande, 17 Intermezzo: Paganini, 18 Aveu, 19 Promenade, 20 Pause, 21 Marche des Davidsbündler contres les Philistins				
10	6 Konzert-Etüden nach Capricen von Paganini, ii	1833	1835	orig. title Capricen für das Pianoforte, auf dem Grund der Violinstimme von Paganini zu Studien frei bearbeitet	vii/2, 30
11	Sonata no.1, f♯	1832–5	1836	on title-page 'Pianoforte-Sonata, Clara zugeignet von Florestan und Eusebius'	vii/2, 52
12	Phantasiestücke:	1837	1838	orig. title Phantasien; no.7 composed not later than 1832	vii/2, 82
	1 Des Abends, 2 Aufschwung, 3 Warum?, 4 Grillen, 5 In der Nacht, 6 Fabel, 7 Traumes Wirren, 8 Ende vom Lied				
—	9***	1837	1935	omitted from op.12	—
13	Symphonische Etüden	1834–7	1837	orig. title Etüden im Orchestercharakter für Pianoforte von Florestan und Eusebius; 2nd version (1852) entitled Etudes en formes de variations; 5 extra variations pubd in 1873 and incl. in SW xiv, 40; variation unpubd	vii/2, 108
14	Concert sans orchestre, f	1835–6	1836	3 movts of orig. 5 pubd 1836; rev. and pubd 1853 as Sonata no.3 with 1 scherzo restored	vii/3
—	Scherzo	1836	1866	rejected movt of op.14	—
15	Kinderszenen:	1838	1839		vii/3
	1 Von fremden Ländern und Menschen, 2 Curiose Geschichte, 3 Hasche-Mann, 4 Bittendes Kind,				

op.	Title, key	Composed	Publication/MS	Remarks	SW
	5 Glückes genug, 6 Wichtige Begebenheit, 7 Träumerei, 8 Am Camin, 9 Ritter vom Steckenpferd, 10 Fast zu ernst, 11 Fürchtenmachen, 12 Kind im Einschlummern, 13 Der Dichter spricht				
16	Kreisleriana: 8 fantasies	1838	1838	rev. 2/1850	vii/3
17	Phantasie, C	1836–8	1839	orig. title Obolen auf Beethovens Monument: Ruinen, Trophäen. Palmen: grosse Sonate für das Pianoforte, für Beethovens Monument, von Florestan und Eusebius, op.12; also entitled Ruine, Siegesbogen und Sternbild	vii/3
18	Arabeske, C	1838	1839		vii/3
19	Blumenstück, D♭	1839	1839	orig. title Guirlande	vii/3
20	Humoreske, B♭	1838	1839	orig. title Grosse Humoreske	vii/4, 2
21	8 Novelletten	1838	1839		vii/4, 28
22	Sonata no.2, g	1833–8	1839	new finale composed 1838	vii/4, 76
—	Presto passionato	?1833	1866	rejected finale of op.22	xiv/1, 53
23	Nachtstücke: 4 pieces	1839	1840	Schumann envisaged the titles: 1 Trauerzug, 2 Kuriose Gesellschaft, 3 Nächtliches Gelage, 4 Rundgesang mit Solostimmen	vii/4, 96
—	Allegro, c	1839	—	lost	—
26	Faschingsschwank aus Wien: Phantasiebilder: 1 Allegro, 2 Romanze, 3 Scherzino, 4 Intermezzo, 5 Finale	1839–40	1841	no.4 pubd separately Dec 1839	vii/4, 110
28	3 Romanzen, b♭, F♯, B	1839	1840		vii/4, 132
32	Klavierstücke: 1 Scherzo, 2 Gigue, 3 Romanze, 4 Fughette	1838–9	1841		vii/4, 146
—	Sonatina, B♭	1840		lost	—
46	Andante and variations, B♭, 2 pf	1843	1844	orig. with 2 vc, hn; see Chamber music	vi, 2
56	Studien für den Pedal-Flügel: 6 pieces in canon, pedal pf	1845	1845		vii/5
58	4 Skizzen für den Pedal-Flügel	1845	1846		vii/5
60	6 Fugues on B–A–C–H, org/pedal pf	1845	1846		vii/1, 2
—	Piece for harmonium, F	1849	—	2 movts only	—
66	Bilder aus Osten: 6 impromptus, pf 4 hands	1848	1849		vi, 24
68	Album für die Jugend	1848	1848	Orig. title Weihnachtsalbum; facs. of autograph (Leipzig, 1956); facs. of sketchbook (London, 1924), with 4 other pf pieces by Schumann, ed. L. Windesperger: Kuckuck im Versteck, Lagune in Venedig, Haschemann, waltz in G; these and 5 other pf pieces from sketchbook, ed. J. Werner (London, c1958): Für ganz Kleine, Puppenschlaffliedchen, Linke Hand soll sich auch zeigen, Auf der Gondel, untitled piece; other unpubd material, ed. J. Demus (Milan, 1973), with 2 further pieces: Rebus, Bärentanz	

Pt. 1, Für Kleinere: 1 Melodie, 2 Soldatenmarsch, 3 Trällerliedchen [orig. Kinderstückchen], 4 Ein Choral, 5 Stückchen, 6 Armes Waisenkind [orig. Armes Bettlerkind], 7 Jägerliedchen, 8 Wilder Reiter, 9 Volksliedchen [orig. Volkslied], 10 Fröhlicher Landmann, von der Arbeit zurückkehrend, 11 Sizilianisch [orig. Zwei Sizilianische], 12 Knecht Ruprecht, 13 Mai, lieber Mai [orig. Mai, schöner Mai], 14 Kleine Studie, 15 Frühlingsgesang, 16 Erster Verlust [orig. Kinderunglück], 17 Kleiner Morgenwanderer, 18 Schnitterliedchen Pt. 2, Für Erwachsenere: 19 Kleine Romanze, 20 Landliches Lied, 21***, 22 Rundgesang, 23 Reiterstück, 24 Ernteliedchen, 25 Nachklänge aus dem Theater, 26***, 27 Canonisches Liedchen [orig. Canon], 28 Erinnerung [orig. Erinnerung an Mendelssohn], 29 Fremder Mann, 30***, 31 Kriegslied, 32 Sheherazade, 33 Weinlesezeit – fröhliche Zeit!, 34 Thema, 35 Mignon, 36 Lied italienischer Marinari [orig. Schifferlied], 37 Matrosenlied, 38 Winterszeit I, 39 Winterszeit II, 40 Kleine Fuge, 41 Nordisches Lied (Gruss an G), 42 Figurierter Choral, 43 Sylversterlied [orig. Zum Schluss]

72	4 fugues, d, d, f, F	1845	1850		vii/5
76	4 marches, E♭, g, B♭ (Lager-Scene), E♭	1849	1849		vii/5
82	Waldscenen: 1 Eintritt, 2 Jäger auf der Lauer [orig. Jägersmann auf der Lauer], 3 Einsame Blumen, 4 Verrufene Stelle [orig. Verrufener Ort], 5 Freundliche Landschaft [orig. Freier Ausblick], 6 Herberge [orig. Jägerhaus], 7 Vogel als Prophet, 8 Jagdlied, 9 Abschied	1848–9	1850		vii/5
85	12 vierhändige Klavierstücke für kleine und grosse Kinder: 1 Geburtstagsmarsch, 2 Bärentanz, 3 Gartenmelodie, 4 Beim Kränzewinden, 5 Kroatenmarsch, 6 Trauer, 7 Turniermarsch, 8 Reigen, 9 Am Springbrunnen, 10 Versteckens, 11 Gespenstermärchen, 12 Abendlied	1849	1850	no.2 from sketches in op.68; no.3 orig. title Gartenlied	vi, 48
99	Bunte Blätter:		1852		vii/6, 2
	Drei Stücklein:				
	1		1838	MS inscribed 'An meine geliebte Braut zum heiligen Abend 1838'	
	2		1839		
	3		1839	orig. title Jagdstück	
	Fünf Albumblätter:				
	4		1841	theme used by Brahms for Variations, op.9	
	5		1838	orig. title Fata Morgana	
	6		1836	rejected from Carnaval, op.9	
	7		1838	orig. title Jugendschmerz	
	8		1838		
	9 Novellette		1838		
	10 Präludium		1839		

op.	Title, key	Composed	Publication/MS	Remarks	SW
	11 Marsch	1843			
	12 Abendmusik	1841			
	13 Scherzo	1841		orig. intended for a projected symphony	
	14 Geschwindmarsch	1849		orig. intended for op.76	
109	Ballszenen, pf 4 hands:	1851	1853	orig. title Kinderball	vi, 94
	1 Préambule, 2 Polonaise, 3 Walzer, 4 Ungarisch, 5 Française, 6 Mazurka, 7 Ecossaise, 8 Walzer, 9 Promenade				
111	Phantasiestücke: 3 pieces, c, Ab, c	1851	1852	orig. title Cyclus für Pianoforte	vii/6, 36
118	Drei Clavier-Sonaten für die Jugend, G, D, C	1853	1853		vii/6, 44
124	Albumblätter:		1854	no.12 perhaps one of the 12 Burlesken offered to Kistner in 1832	vii/6, 78
	1 Impromptu (1832), 2 Leides Ahnung (1832), 3 Scherzino (1832), 4 Walzer (1835), 5 Phantasietanz (1836), 6 Wiegenliedchen (1843), 7 Ländler (1836), 8 Lied ohne Ende (1837), 9 Impromptu (1838), 10 Walzer (1838), 11 Romanze (1835), 12 Burla (1832), 13 Larghetto (1832), 14 Vision (1838), 15 Walzer (1832), 16 Schlummerlied (1841), 17 Elfe (1835) [orig. intended for op.9], 18 Botschaft (1838), 19 Phantasiestück (1839), 20 Canon (1845)				
126	Sieben Klavierstücke in Fughettenform	1853	1854		vii, 102
130	Kinderball, pf 4 hands:	1853	1854		vi, 142
	1 Polonaise, 2 Walzer, 3 Menuett, 4 Ecossaise, 5 Française, 6 Ringelreihe				
133	5 Gesänge der Frühe	1853	1855	MS inscribed 'An Diotima'	vii/6, 114
—	Canon on F. H. Himmel's An Alexis send ich dich, Ab		1859	in Julius Knorr's op.30	—
—	Thema, Eb	1854	1893	theme used by Brahms for Variations for pf duet op.23	xiv/1, 67
—	Variations on an original theme	1854	1939		—

BIBLIOGRAPHY

CATALOGUES

A. Dörffel: *Thematisches Verzeichniss sämmtlicher in Druck erschienenen Werke Robert Schumanns* (Leipzig, 1860, 4/1868/R1966)

G. Eismann: 'Nachweis der internationalen Standorte von Notenautographen Robert Schumanns', *Sammelbände der Robert-Schumann-Gesellschaft*, ii (Leipzig, 1966), 7–37

K. Hofmann: *Die Erstdrucke der Werke von Robert Schumann* (Tutzing, 1979)

BIBLIOGRAPHIES

G. Abraham, ed.: *Schumann: a Symposium* (London, 1952), 301

P. Mies: 'Literatur um Robert Schumann: ein Beitrag zu seinem 100. Todestag', *Musikhandel*, vii (1956), 93

F. Munte: *Verzeichnis des deutschsprachigen Schrifttums über Robert Schumann 1856–1970* (Hamburg, 1972)

A. Walker, ed.: *Robert Schumann: the Man and his Music* (London, 1972, rev. 2/1976), 442

GENEALOGIES

E. Bienenfeld: 'Die Stammtafel der Familie Robert Schumanns: Ahnen und Nachkommen eines Genies', *Archiv für Rassen- und Gesellschaftsbiologie*, xxvi (1932), 57

C. Eismann: 'Bemerkenswertes zur Genealogie Robert Schumanns', *Mf*, xxii (1969), 61

A. Walker: 'Schumann's Family Tree', *Robert Schumann: the Man and his Music* (London, 1972, rev. 2/1976), 418

ICONOGRAPHY

W. Gertler: *Robert Schumann* (Leipzig, 1936)

G. Eismann: *Eine Biographie in Wort und Bild* (Leipzig, 1956, enlarged 2/1964; Eng. trans., 1964)

R. Petzold and E. Crass: *Robert Schumann: sein Leben in Bildern* (Leipzig, 1956)

G. Eismann: 'Das authentische Schumann-Bild', *Sammelbände der Robert-Schumann-Gesellschaft*, i (Leipzig, 1961), 86

DIARIES

R. Schumann: *Tagebücher*, i (*1827–38*) (Leipzig, 1971)

LETTERS

C. Schumann, ed.: *Jugendbriefe von Robert Schumann* (Leipzig, 1885, 4/1910; Eng. trans., 1888)

F. Jansen, ed.: *Robert Schumanns Briefe: neue Folge* (Leipzig, 1886, 2/1904; Eng. trans., 1890)

H. Erler: *Robert Schumanns Leben: aus seinen Briefen geschildert* (Berlin, 1886–7, 3/1927)

J. Gensel: 'Robert Schumanns Briefwechsel mit Henriette Voigt', *Die Grenzboten*, li (1892), 269, 324, 368; enlarged offprint (Leipzig, 1892)

F. Jansen: 'Briefwechsel zwischen Robert Franz und Robert Schumann', *Die Musik*, viii (1908–9), 280, 346

WRITINGS

R. Schumann: *Gesammelte Schriften über Musik und Musiker* (Leipzig,

1854, 4/1891/R1968, 5/1914; Eng. trans., 1877; new Eng. trans. [selection], 1947)

H. Deiters: 'Schumann als Schriftsteller', *AMZ*, iii (1865), 761, 777, 793

F. Liszt: 'Ein Kapitel zur Reform der musikalischen Kritik', *Gesammelte Schriften*, iv (Leipzig, 1882), 115–55

G. Wustmann: 'Die Davidsbündler: ein verloren geglaubter Aufsatz Robert Schumanns', *Die Grenzboten*, xlviii/4 (1889), 23

P. Spitta: 'Ueber Robert Schumanns Schriften', *Musikgeschichtliche Aufsätze* (Berlin, 1894), 383

G. Noren-Herzberg: 'Robert Schumann als Musikschriftsteller', *Die Musik*, v/4 (1905–6), 100

G. Wustmann: 'Zur Entstehungsgeschichte der Schumannschen Zeitschrift für Musik', *ZIMG*, viii (1906), 396

P. Kehm: *Die 'Neue Zeitschrift für Musik' unter Schumanns Redaktion: 1834–44* (diss., U. of Munich, 1943)

G. Eismann, ed.: *R. Schumann: Erinnerungen an Felix Mendelssohn Bartholdy* (Zwickau, 1947, enlarged 2/1948)

I. Forger: *Robert Schumann als Kritiker: ein Beitrag zur Geschichte der musikalischen Kritik und zum Schumann-Problem* (diss., U. of Münster, 1948)

J. Alf: 'Der Kritiker Robert Schumann', *110. Niederrheinisches Musikfest 1956*, 50

H. Homeyer: *Grundbegriffe der Musikanschauung Robert Schumanns: ihr Wesen, ihre Bedeutung und Funktion in seinem literarischen Gesamtwerk* (diss., U. of Münster, 1956)

H. Pleasants: *The Musical World of Robert Schumann* (New York and London, 1965)

K. Laux: 'Was ist ein Musikschriftsteller?: Carl Maria von Weber und Robert Schumann als Vorbild', *Sammelbände der Robert-Schumann-Gesellschaft*, ii (Leipzig, 1966), 38

L. Plantinga: *Schumann as Critic* (New Haven, 1967/R1977)

——: 'Schumann and the "Neue Zeitschrift für Musik"', *Robert Schumann: the Man and his Music*, ed. A. Walker (London, 1972, rev. 2/1976), 162

H. Pleasants: 'Schumann the Critic', *Robert Schumann: the Man and his Music*, ed. A. Walker (London, 1972, rev. 2/1976), 179

DOCUMENTARY COMPILATIONS

F. Kerst: *Schumann-Brevier* (Berlin, 1905)

A. Schumann, ed.: *Der junge Schumann: Dichtungen und Briefe* (Leipzig, 1910)

W. Boetticher: *Robert Schumann in seinen Schriften und Briefen* (Berlin, 1942)

G. Eismann: *Robert Schumann: ein Quellenwerk über sein Leben und Schaffen* (Leipzig, 1956)

R. Münnich: *Aus Robert Schumanns Briefen und Schriften* (Weimar, 1956)

W. Schwarz: 'Robert Schumann und der deutsche Osten: aus unveröffentlichten Tagebuchaufzeichnungen, Briefen und Berichten', *Musik des Ostens*, ii (1963), 193

GENERAL STUDIES

E. Grieg: 'Robert Schumann', *Nyt tidskrift*, new ser., ii (1893–4), 217; also in *Century Magazine*, xlvii (1894), 440

R. Pugno: *Leçons écrites sur Schumann* (Paris, 1914)

W. Boetticher: *Robert Schumann: Einführung in Persönlichkeit und Werk* (Berlin, 1941)

H. Wolff: 'Robert Schumann: der Klassizist', *Musica*, ii (1948), 47

G. Abraham, ed.: *Schumann: a Symposium* (London, 1952)

H. Moser and E. Rebling, eds.: *Robert Schumann: aus Anlass seines 100. Todestages* (Leipzig, 1956)

E. Melkus: 'Schumanns letzte Werke', *ÖMz*, xv (1960), 565

——: 'Zur Revision unseres Schumann-Bildes', *ÖMz*, xv (1960), 182

A. Walker, ed.: *Robert Schumann: the Man and his Music* (London, 1972, rev. 2/1976)

BIOGRAPHY, MEMOIRS

F. Brendel: 'Schumanns Biographie von Wasielewski', *NZM*, xlviii (1858), 113, 125, 137, 157, 169, 181, 193

W. von Wasielewski: *Robert Schumann* (Dresden, 1858, enlarged 2/1906; Eng. trans., 1871/*R*1975)

R. Pohl: 'Erinnerungen an Robert Schumann', *Deutsche Revue*, ii (1878), 169, 306

F. Jansen: *Die Davidsbündler: aus Robert Schumanns Sturm- und Drangperiode* (Leipzig, 1883)

W. von Wasielewski: *Schumanniana* (Bonn, 1883)

——: 'Robert Alexander Schumann', *ADB*

E. Hanslick: *Aus meinem Leben*, i (Berlin, 1894/*R*1971), 66, 105

W. von Wasielewski: 'Robert Schumanns Herzenserlebnisse: ein wichtiger Beitrag zur Schumann-Biographie', *Deutsche Revue*, xxii (1897), 40, 226

E. Hanslick: 'Robert Schumann in Endenich', *Am Ende des Jahrhunderts* (Berlin, 1899), 317

V. Joss: *Der Musikpädagoge Wieck und seine Familie: mit besonderer Berücksichtigung seines Schwiegersohnes R. Schumann* (Dresden, 1902)

B. Litzmann: *Clara Schumann: ein Künstlerleben nach Tagebüchern und Briefen* (Leipzig, 1902–8/*R*1971; Eng. trans., abridged, 1913/*R*1972)

E. van der Straeten: 'Streiflichter auf Mendelssohns und Schumanns Beziehungen zu zeitgenössichen Musikern', *Die Musik*, iv/3 (1904–5), 25, 105

C. Mauclair: *Schumann* (Paris, 1906)

F. May: *The Girlhood of Clara Schumann* (London, 1912)

M. Wieck: *Aus dem Kreise Wieck–Schumann* (Leipzig, 1912, rev. 2/1914)

F. Niecks: *Robert Schumann: a Supplementary and Corrective Biography* (London, 1925)

R. Pitrou: *La vie intérieure de Robert Schumann* (Paris, 1925)

E. Schumann: *Erinnerungen* (Stuttgart, 1925; Eng. trans., 1927)

V. Basch: *Schumann* (Paris, 1926)

——: *La vie douloureuse de Schumann* (Paris, 1928; Eng. trans., 1932)

K. Wagner: *Robert Schumann als Schüler und Abiturient* (Zwickau, 1928)

E. Schumann: *Robert Schumann: ein Lebensbild meines Vaters* (Leipzig, 1931)

P. Sutermeister: *Robert Schumann: sein Leben nach Briefen, Tagebüchern und Erinnerungen des Meisters und seiner Gattin* (Zurich, 1949)

E. Flechsig: 'Erinnerungen an Robert Schumann', *NZM*, Jg.117 (1956), 392

R. Stockhammer: 'Robert Schumann in Wien', *ÖMz*, xv (1960), 177

A. Walker: 'Schumann and his Background', *Robert Schumann: the Man and his Music*, (London, 1972, rev. 2/1976), 1–40

HEALTH

F. Richarz: 'Robert Schumanns Krankheit', *AMZ*, viii (1873), 597

H. Schaafhausen: 'Einige Reliquien berühmter Männer: Robert Schumanns Gehirn- und Gehörsorgane', *Correspondenz-Blatt der Deutschen Gesellschaft für Anthropologie*, xvi (1885), 147

P. Möbius: *Über Robert Schumanns Krankheit* (Halle, 1906)

H. Gruhle: 'Brief über Robert Schumanns Krankheit und P. Möbius', in P. Möbius: *Über Scheffels Krankheit* (Halle, 1907), 25

C. Pascal: 'Les maladies mentales de Robert Schumann', *Journal de psychologie normale et pathologique* (1908), March–April

E. Morselli: *La pazzia di Roberto Schumann e la psicologia supernormale* (Rome, 1909)

R. Bancour: 'La maladie de Schumann', *Chronique médicale* (1910), 481

F. Nussbaum: *Der Streit um Robert Schumanns Krankheit* (diss., U. of Cologne, 1923)

B. Springer: *Die genialen Syphilitiker* (Berlin, 1926), 143

H. MacMaster: *La folie de Robert Schumann* (Paris, 1928)

H. Kleinebreil: *Der kranke Schumann: Untersuchungen über Krankheit und Todesursache Robert Schumanns* (diss., U. of Jena, 1943)

E. Slater and A. Meyer: 'Contributions to a Pathography of the Musicians: I Robert Schumann', *Confinia psychiatrica*, ii (1959), 65

D. Kerner: 'Robert Schumann', *Krankheiten grosser Musiker* (Stuttgart, 1963), 123

H.-J. Rothe: 'Neue Dokumente zur Schumann-Forschung im Stadtarchiv Leipzig', *Arbeitsberichte zur Geschichte der Stadt Leipzig* (Leipzig, 1967), 1

E. Sams: 'Schumann's Hand Injury', *MT*, cxii (1971), 1156; cxiii (1972), 456

E. Slater: 'Schumann's Illness', *Robert Schumann: the Man and his Music*, ed. A. Walker (London, 1972, rev. 2/1976), 406

R. Henson and H. Urich: 'Schumann's Hand Injury', *British Medical Journal* (1978), no.1, p.900

L. Carerj: 'La mano invalida di Robert Schumann', *NRMI*, xiii (1979), 609

LIFE AND WORKS

A. Ambros: 'Robert Schumanns Tage und Werke', *Culturhistorische Bilder aus der Gegenwart* (Leipzig, 1860), 51–96

A. Reissmann: *Robert Schumann: sein Leben und seine Werke* (Berlin, 1865, 2/1871; Eng. trans., 1886)

P. Spitta: 'Schumann, Robert', *Grove 1*

F. Liszt: 'Robert Schumann', *Gesammelte Schriften*, iv (Leipzig, 1882), 103, 156

H. Reimann: *Robert Schumanns Leben und Werke* (Leipzig, 1887)

H. Hadow: 'Robert Schumann and the Romantic Movement in Germany', *Studies in Modern Music*, i (London, 1892), 149–231

H. Abert: *Robert Schumann* (Berlin, 1903)

L. Schneider and M. Mareschal: *Schumann: sa vie et ses oeuvres* (Paris, 1905)

W. Dahms: *Schumann* (Berlin, 1916)

M. Ninck: *Schumann und die Romantik in der Musik* (Heidelberg, 1929)

M. Beaufils: *Schumann* (Paris, 1932)

C. Valabrega: *Schumann* (Modena, 1934)

W. Korte: *Robert Schumann* (Potsdam, 1937)

E. Bücken: *Robert Schumann* (Cologne, 1940)

R. Schauffler: *Florestan: the Life and Work of Robert Schumann* (New York, 1945)

J. Chissell: *Schumann* (London, 1948, rev. 2/1967)

K. Wörner: *Robert Schumann* (Zurich, 1949)

A. Coeuroy: *Robert Schumann* (Paris, 1950)

P. and W. Rehberg: *Robert Schumann: sein Leben und sein Werk* (Zurich, 1954)

M. Brion: *Schumann et l'âme romantique* (Paris, 1954; Eng. trans., 1956)

A. Boucourechliev: *Schumann* (Paris, 1957; Eng. trans., 1959)

E. Lippmann: 'Schumann, Robert', *MGG*

P. Young: *Tragic Muse: the Life and Works of Robert Schumann* (London, 1957, enlarged 2/1961)

I. Porena-Cappelli: 'Robert Schumann', *La MusicaE*

K. Laux: *Robert Schumann* (Leipzig, 1972)

PIANO MUSIC

F. Liszt: 'Robert Schumanns Klavierkompositionen op.5, 11 und 14', *Gesammelte Schriften*, ii (Leipzig, 1881), 99

R. Hohenemser: 'Formale Eigentümlichkeiten in R. Schumanns Klaviermusik', *Festschrift zum 50. Geburtstag Adolf Sandberger* (Munich, 1918), 31

J. Fuller Maitland: *Schumann's Pianoforte Works* (London, 1927)

M. Cohen: *Studien zur Sonataform bei Robert Schumann* (diss., U. of Vienna, 1928)

R. Goldenberg: *Der Klaviersatz bei Schumann* (diss., U. of Vienna, 1930)

W. Gertler: *Robert Schumann in seinen frühen Klavierwerken* (Wolfenbüttel, 1931)

M. Schweiger: *Die Harmonik in den Klavierwerken Robert Schumanns* (diss., U. of Vienna, 1931)

W. Schwarz: *Schumann und die Variation: mit besonderer Berücksichtigung der Klavierwerke* (Kassel, 1932)

K. Geiringer: 'Ein unbekanntes Klavierwerk aus Schumanns Jugendzeit' [Polonaises for piano duet], *Die Musik*, xxv (1932–3), 721

——: 'Ein unbekanntes Blatt aus Schumanns Endenicher Zeit', *Anbruch*, xvii (1935), 273

G. Kinsky: 'Ein unbekanntes Fantasiestück aus Schumanns Jugendzeit', *SMz*, lxxv (1935), 769

D. Tovey: 'Schumann: Carnaval', *Essays in Musical Analysis: Illustrative Music* (London, 1936), 109

W. Georgii: *Klaviermusik* (Zurich, 1941, 2/1950), 301

D. Tovey: 'Schumann: Novelette in F sharp minor op.21 no.8', *Essays in Musical Analysis: Chamber Music* (London, 1944)

G. Abraham: 'Schumann's Opp.II and III', *MMR*, lxxvi (1946), 123, 162, 222; repr. in *Slavonic and Romantic Music* (London, 1968), 261

R. Réti: 'Schumann's Kinderszenen: a Theme with Variations', *The Thematic Process in Music* (New York, 1951, rev. 2/1961), 31

K. Dale: 'The Piano Music', *Schumann: a Symposium*, ed. G. Abraham (London, 1952), 12–97

I. Parrott: 'A Plea for Schumann's Op.11', *ML*, xxxiii (1952), 55

J. Fiske: 'A Schumann Mystery', *MT*, cv (1964), 574 [on *Die Davidsbündlertänze* op.6]

K. Wörner: 'Schumanns "Kreisleriana"', Sammelbände der Robert-Schumann-Gesellschaft, ii (Leipzig, 1966), 58

W. Boetticher: 'Neue textkritische Forschungen an Robert Schumanns Klavierwerk', AMw, xxv (1968), 46–76

J. Chissell: Schumann Piano Music (London, 1972)

Y. Solomon: 'Solo Piano Music: (I) the Sonatas and Fantasie', Robert Schumann: the Man and his Music, ed. A. Walker (London, 1972, rev. 2/1976), 41

B. Vázsonyi: 'Solo Piano Music: (II) the Piano Cycles', Robert Schumann: the Man and his Music, ed. A. Walker (London, 1972, rev. 2/1976), 68

J. Weingarten: 'Interpreting Schumann's Piano Music', Robert Schumann: the Man and his Music, ed. A. Walker (London, 1972, rev. 2/1976), 93

J. L. Kollen: 'Robert Alexander Schumann (1810–1856): Tema, Opus 13', Notations and Editions: a Book in Honor of Louise Cuyler (Dubuque, Iowa, 1974), 163

L. C. Roesner: 'The Autograph of Schumann's Piano Sonata in F minor, opus 14', MQ, lxi (1975)), 98

W. Boetticher: Robert Schumanns Klavierwerke: Entstehung, Urtext, Gestalt: Untersuchungen anhand unveröffentlicher Skizzen und biographischer Documente (Wilhelmshaven, 1976–)

A. Walker: 'Schumann, Liszt and the C major Fantasie, Op.17: a Declining Relationship', ML, lx (1979), 156

SONGS

M. Friedlaender: Textrevision zu Robert Schumanns Liedern (Leipzig, 1887)

V. Wolff: Robert Schumann Lieder in ersten und späteren Fassungen (Leipzig, 1914)

O. Bie: 'Robert Schumann', Das deutsche Lied (Berlin, 1926), 75–124

C. Spitz: 'Schumann's "Mary Stuart Songs"', MMR, lxvii (1937), 153

R. Felber: 'Schumann's Place in German Song', MQ, xxvi (1940), 340

R. Hernried: 'Four Unpublished Compositions by Robert Schumann', MQ, xxviii (1942), 50

G. Abraham: 'Schumann's Opp.II and III', MMR, lxxvi (1946), 123, 162, 222; repr. in Slavonic and Romantic Music (London, 1968), 261

W. Edelmann: Über Text und Musik in Robert Schumanns Sololieder (diss., U. of Münster, 1950)

M. Cooper: 'The Songs', Schumann: a Symposium, ed. G. Abraham (London, 1952), 98–137

E. Sams: 'Schumann's Year of Song', MT, cvi (1965), 105

——: The Songs of Robert Schumann (London, 1969, rev. 2/1975)

S. Walsh: The Lieder of Schumann (London, 1971)

A. Desmond: Schumann Songs (London, 1972)

E. Sams: 'The Songs', Robert Schumann: the Man and his Music, ed. A. Walker (London, 1972, rev. 2/1976), 120

A. Mayeda: 'Das Reich der Nacht in den Liedern Robert Schumanns', De ratione in musica: Festschrift Erich Schenk (Kassel, 1975), 202

K. Schlager: 'Erstarrte Idylle: Schumanns Eichendorff-Verständnis im Lied op.39/VII "Auf einer Burg"', AMw, xxxiii (1976), 119

R. E. Hallmark: The Genesis of Schumann's 'Dichterliebe': a Source Study (Ann Arbor, 1979)

OTHER VOCAL MUSIC

E. Hanslick: 'Szenen aus Goethes Faust von R. Schumann (3. Abteilung)'; 'Schumanns Musik zu Goethes Faust', Aus dem Concert-Saal (Vienna, 1870/R1971, 2/1896), 218; 304

——: 'Manfred von Robert Schumann', Aus dem Concert-Saal (Vienna, 1870/R1971, 2/1896), 190

——: 'Paradies und die Peri', Aus dem Concert-Saal (Vienna, 1870/R1971, 2/1896), 155

——: 'R. Schumann als Opernkomponist', Die moderne Oper (Berlin, 1875/R1971, 3/1911), 256

S. Bagge: 'Schumann und seine Faustszenen', Sammlung musikalischer Vorträge (Leipzig, 1879), no.4, p.121

Graf Waldersee: 'Über Schumanns Manfred', Sammlung musikalischer Vorträge (Leipzig, 1880), no.13, p.3

L. Torchi: 'R. Schumann e le sue "Scene tratte dal Faust di Goethe"', RMI, ii (1895), 381–419, 629–65

R. Heuberger: Robert Schumann: Scenen aus Goethes 'Faust' [Musikführer no.62] (Frankfurt, n.d.)

——: Robert Schumann: Das Paradies und die Peri [Musikführer no.89] (Frankfurt, n.d.)

H. Abert: 'R. Schumanns Genoveva', ZIMG, xi (1909), 277

F. Strich: 'Byrons Manfred in Schumanns Vertonung', Festgabe Samuel Singer (Tübingen, 1930), 167

G. B. Shaw: Music in London 1890–94, iii (London, 1932), 107 [on Genoveva]

G. Abraham: 'The Dramatic Music', Schumann: a Symposium, ed. G. Abraham (London, 1952), 260

J. Horton: 'The Choral Works', Schumann: a Symposium, ed. G. Abraham, (London, 1952), 283

H. Wolff: 'Schumanns "Genoveva" und der Manierismus des 19. Jahrhunderts', Beiträge zur Geschichte der Oper (Regensburg, 1969), 89

F. Cooper: 'Operatic and Dramatic Music', Robert Schumann: the Man and his Music, ed. A. Walker (London, 1972, rev. 2/1976), 324

L. Halsey: 'The Choral Music', Robert Schumann: the Man and his Music, ed. A. Walker (London, 1972, rev. 2/1976), 324

E. Sams: 'Schumann and Faust', MT, cxiii (1972), 543

L. Siegel: 'A Second Look at Schumann's Genoveva', MR, xxxvi (1975), 17

ORCHESTRAL WORKS

P. Tschaikowski: 'Schumann als Symphoniker', Musikalische Erinnerungen und Feuilletons (Berlin, 1899)

F. Weingartner: Ratschläge für die Aufführung klassicher Symphonien, vii (Leipzig, 1918), 30–119

O. Karsten: Die Instrumentation Robert Schumanns (diss., U. of Vienna, 1922)

D. Tovey: 'Schumann', Essays in Musical Analysis: Symphonies (London, 1935), 45

——: 'Schumann: Concerto for Four Horns and Orchestra'; 'Introduction and Allegro appassionato op.92'; 'Piano Concerto in A minor op.54'; 'Violoncello concerto in A minor op.129', Essays in Musical Analysis: Concertos (London, 1936), 182; 184; 188

——: 'Schumann: Overture to Byron's "Manfred"', Essays in Musical Analysis: Illustrative Music (London, 1936), 112

——: 'Schumann: Overture, Scherzo and Finale op.52', Essays in Musical Analysis: Miscellaneous Notes (London, 1939), 40

G. Abraham: 'The Three Scores of Schumann's D minor Symphony', MT, lxxxi (1940), 105; repr. in Slavonic and Romantic Music (London, 1968), 281

M. Carner: 'Mahler's Re-scoring of the Schumann Symphonies', MR, ii (1941), 97; repr. in Of Men and Music (London, 1944), 115

G. Abraham: 'On a Dull Overture by Schumann' [op.136], MMR, lxxvi (1946), 238; repr. in Slavonic and Romantic Music (London, 1968), 288

B. Shore: 'Schumann'; 'Schumann's Symphony in D minor', Sixteen Symphonies (London, 1949), 99; 103

G. Abraham: 'Schumann's "Jugendsinfonie" in G minor', MQ, xxxvii (1951), 45; repr. in Slavonic and Romantic Music (London, 1968), 267

R. Réti: 'Schumann: Symphony in B-flat major', The Thematic Process in Music (New York, 1951, rev.2/1961), 295

M. Carner: 'The Orchestral Music', Schumann: a Symposium, ed. G. Abraham (London, 1952), 176–244

M. Lindsey: 'The Works for Solo Instrument and Orchestra', Schumann: a Symposium, ed. G. Abraham (London, 1952), 245

A. Zlotnik: 'Die beiden Fassungen von Schumanns D-Moll Symphonie', ÖMz, xxi (1966), 271

M. Maniates: 'The D minor Symphony of Robert Schumann', Festschrift für Walter Wiora (Kassel, 1967), 441

A. Gebhardt: Robert Schumann als Symphoniker (Regensburg, 1968)

A. Nieman: 'The Concertos', Robert Schumann: the Man and his Music, ed. A. Walker (London, 1972, rev. 2/1976), 241–76

B. Schlotel: 'The Orchestral Music', Robert Schumann: the Man and his Music, ed. A. Walker (London, 1972, rev. 2/1976), 277

S. Walsh: 'Schumann's Orchestrations: Function and Effect', Musical Newsletter, iii (1972), 3

CHAMBER MUSIC

J. Fuller Maitland: Schumann's Concerted Chamber Music (London, 1929)

F. Davies: 'Some Notes on the Interpretation of Schumann's Chamber Music', Cobbett's Cyclopedic Survey of Chamber Music (London, 1929–30, rev., enlarged 2/1963), 390

G. Wilcke: Tonalität und Modulation in Streichquartetten Schumanns und Mendelssohns (Leipzig, 1933)

D. Tovey: 'Schumann: Quintet in E flat major op.44', Essays in Musical Analysis: Chamber Music (London, 1944), 149

A. Dickinson: 'The Chamber Music', Schumann: a Symposium, ed. G. Abraham (London, 1952), 138–75

O. Neighbour: 'Schumanns dritte Violinesonate', NZM, Jg.117 (1956), 423

A. Molnar: 'Die beiden Klavier-Trios in d-moll von Schumann (op.63) und Mendelssohn (op.49)', Sammelbände der Robert-Schumann-Gesellschaft, i (Leipzig, 1961), 79

J. Gardner: 'The Chamber Music', Robert Schumann: the Man and his Music, ed. A. Walker (London, 1972, rev. 2/1976), 200–240

AESTHETICS

R. Bouyer: 'Schumann et la musique à programme', Le ménestrel (1903), no.37, p.290

H. Kretzschmar: 'Robert Schumann als Ästhetiker', JbMP 1906, 49

A. Schmitz: Untersuchungen über des jüngeren Robert Schumanns Anschauungen vom musikalischen Schaffen (diss., U. of Bonn, 1919); extracts in ZMw, ii (1919–20), 535; iii (1920–21), 111

H. Kötz: Der Einfluss Jean Pauls auf Robert Schumann (Weimar, 1933)

'Robert Schumann': l'esthétique et l'oeuvre, ReM (1935), no.161 [special issue]

R. Jacobs: 'Schumann and Jean Paul', ML, xxx (1949), 250

M. Elssner: *Zum Problem des Verhältnisses von Musik und Wirklichkeit in den musikästhetischen Arbeiten der Schumann-Zeit* (diss., U. of Halle, 1964)

E. Lippmann: 'Theory and Practice in Schumann's Aesthetics', *JAMS*, xvii (1964), 310–45

T. Brown: *The Aesthetics of Robert Schumann* (New York, 1968)

OTHER SPECIAL STUDIES

R. Prochazka: 'Ernestine von Fricken: Robert Schumanns erste Braut', *Arpeggien: Musikalisches aus alten und neuen Tagen* (Dresden, 1897); repr. in *ÖMz*, xi (1956), 216

M. Kalbeck: 'Schumann und Brahms', *Deutsche Rundschau*, cxiv (1903), 232

J. Tiersot: 'Robert Schumann et la Révolution de 1848', *BSIM*, ix (1913), 5

F. Schnapp: *Heinrich Heine und Robert Schumann* (Hamburg, 1924)

P. Frenzel: *Robert Schumann und Goethe* (Leipzig, 1926)

W. Gurlitt: 'Robert Schumann in seinen Skizzen gegenüber Beethoven', *Beethoven-Zentenarfeier: Wien 1927*, 91

W. Boetticher: 'Robert Schumann in seinen Beziehungen zu Johannes Brahms', *Die Musik*, xxix (1936–7), 548

H. Redlich: 'Schumann Discoveries', *MMR*, lxxx (1950), 143, 182, 261; lxxxi (1951), 14

G. von Dadelsen: 'Robert Schumann und die Musik Bachs', *AMw*, xiv (1957), 46

U. Martin: 'Ein unbekanntes Schumann-Autograph aus dem Nachlass E. Krügers' [the copy Schumann made of *Die Kunst der Fuge*, in 1837], *Mf*, xii (1959), 405

R. Fritsch: *Schumanns Vater als Verleger* (Frankfurt, 1960)

O. Alain: 'Schumann und die französische Musik', *Sammelbände der Robert-Schumann-Gesellschaft*, i (Leipzig, 1961), 47

D. Schitormirski: 'Schumann in Russland', *Sammelbände der Robert-Schumann-Gesellschaft*, i (Leipzig, 1961), 19

D. Kämper: 'Zur Frage der Metronombezeichnungen Robert Schumanns', *AMw*, xxi (1964), 141

E. Sams: 'Did Schumann use Ciphers?', *MT*, cvi (1965), 584; see also cvii (1966), 392, 1051

M. Beaufils: 'Mythos und Maske bei Robert Schumann', *Sammelbände der Robert-Schumann-Gesellschaft*, ii (Leipzig, 1966), 66

E. Sams: 'Why Florestan and Eusebius?', *MT*, cviii (1967), 131

W. Boetticher: 'Robert Schumann und seine Verleger', *Musik und Verlag: Karl Vötterle zum 65. Geburtstag* (Kassel, 1968), 168

E. Sams: 'Politics, Literature, People in Schumann's Op.136', *MT*, cix (1968), 25

——: 'The Tonal Analogue in Schumann's Music', *PRMA*, xcvi (1969–70), 103; repr. in *Robert Schumann: the Man and his Music*, ed. A. Walker (London, 1972, rev. 2/1976), 390

——: 'A Schumann Primer?', *MT*, cxi (1970), 1096

B. Schlotel: 'Schumann and the Metronome', *Robert Schumann: the Man and his Music*, ed. A. Walker (London, 1972, rev. 2/1976), 109

GERALD ABRAHAM (text)
ERIC SAMS (work-list, bibliography)

Schumann-Heink, Ernestine [née Rössler] (*b* Lieben, nr. Prague, 15 June 1861; *d* Hollywood, 17 Nov 1936). Austrian contralto and mezzo-soprano, later naturalized American. She learnt singing first from Marietta von Leclair at Graz, and later had instruction from Franz Wüllner, G. B. Lamperti (the younger) and others. Having made her stage début at Dresden as Azucena on 15 October 1878, she remained there for four seasons. After marriage to Ernst Heink, she obtained an engagement at Hamburg, where she stayed as a busy member of the company until the death of its manager, Pollini, in 1897; her big chance came in 1889, when she deputized for the ailing Marie Goetze as Carmen, Fidès (*Le prophète*) and Ortrud. After some Berlin appearances, she accompanied the Hamburg troupe to London in 1892, with the young Mahler as conductor, and was much applauded as Erda, Fricka and Brangäne. In 1893 she divorced her first husband and married the actor Paul Schumann, assuming the familiar hyphenated form of her surname. A long and fruitful relationship with Bayreuth began in 1896 when she sang Erda in five cycles of the *Ring*; she returned there frequently until 1914, undertaking also the First Norn, Waltraute, Magdalena, Mary in *Der fliegende Holländer* and the unseen alto voice in *Parsifal*.

In 1897 Schumann-Heink took part in the first of four consecutive Covent Garden seasons, singing mainly Wagner roles; and on 9 January 1899 (after preliminary appearances with the New York company on tour in Chicago) she sang Ortrud at the Metropolitan in a notable cast that included Nordica, Bispham and the two De Reszkes. From that time her American reputation was secure. Cancelling a contract with the Berlin Opera, she stayed at the Metropolitan until 1903, but subsequently returned only for single seasons, partly because Grau, to whom she was devoted, had been succeeded as manager by Conried, but also because she had begun the series of highly popular and profitable cross-country concert tours that occupied much of the rest of her long career and eventually made her into a national legend. After the death of her second husband, she married in 1905 William Rapp, a Chicago lawyer, and shortly afterwards became a naturalized American citizen. On 25 January 1909 she returned to Dresden to sing the part of Clytemnestra in the première of *Elektra*; it was not an experience that she relished. During World War I, sons by her first two marriages fought in the armed forces on both sides.

Non-Wagnerian roles, such as Fidès, Azucena and the Witch in *Hänsel und Gretel*, rarely came her way at the Metropolitan, and it was in her old part of Erda (*Rheingold* on 26 February 1932, *Siegfried* on 11 March) that she bade farewell to that house at the age of 70, still captivating the audience, as Olin Downes wrote, with 'knowledge and imagination embodied in the tone and in every syllable of the text she delivered so memorably'. These words well describe the effect still produced by her recordings of Erda's Warning and Waltraute's Narration made less than three years before. In general, her numerous records, made over a period of 25 years, although sadly unrepresentative of her serious repertory, give a splendid impression of her powers: of her opulent and flexible tones from low D to high B, the

Ernestine Schumann-Heink as Clytemnestra (left) with Anny Krull in the title role of Strauss's 'Elektra'

amazing fullness and evenness of her shake, her artistic conviction, dramatic temperament and vivid enunciation. Among them should also be mentioned the Brindisi from *Lucrezia Borgia* (several versions, all good), the Prison Scene from *Le prophète*, Sextus's aria from *La clemenza di Tito*, and the duet with Caruso ('Ai nostri monti') from *Il trovatore*.

BIBLIOGRAPHY
M. Lawton: *Schumann-Heink: the Last of the Titans* (New York, 1928/ R1977)
J. McPherson: 'Ernestine Schumann-Heink', *Record Collector*, xvii (1967), nos.5–6, pp.99–144; no.7, p.154 [with discography by W. R. Moran]
DESMOND SHAWE-TAYLOR

Schünemann, Georg (*b* Berlin, 13 March 1884; *d* Berlin, 2 Jan 1945). German musicologist and music educationist. In addition to practical musical training at the Stern Conservatory in Berlin, Schünemann also studied musicology (under Kretzschmar, Fleischer, Friedländer, Stumpf and Wolf), German literature and philosophy at the University of Berlin. He took his doctorate in 1907 with a dissertation on the history of conducting. At first he was an orchestral flautist. During World War I he made a collection of the songs of German colonists in Russian POW camps. From 1919 he taught at Berlin University and in 1920 became deputy director of the Berlin Hochschule für Musik; in 1932 he succeeded Schreker as its director. In 1933 he was dismissed without notice by the Nazi régime, though shortly afterwards he was appointed director of the State Musical Instrument Collections and in 1935 he became director of the music section of the Prussian State Library.

Schünemann was one of the founders of modern German music education. He devoted himself to questions of elementary teaching, started a practical class at the music education department of the Berlin Hochschule für Musik as well as advanced classes for choir conductors and he instigated an orchestral school; in the 1930s he and Leo Kestenberg were involved in reorganizing every aspect of institutional and private music education in Prussia. Almost all his writings are concerned with music teaching and related problems. Through his organizational talents the Berlin Hochschule für Musik became one of the leading institutes in Germany, largely because he was able to secure excellent teachers and carry out far-reaching reforms. His German translations of the librettos of Mozart's *Le nozze di Figaro*, *Don Giovanni* and *Così fan tutte* (Leipzig, 1939–40) became familiar on many German stages.

WRITINGS
Geschichte des Dirigierens (diss., U. of Berlin, 1907; Leipzig, 1913/R1965)
'Beiträge zur Biographie Hammerschmidts', *SIMG*, xii (1910–11), 207
'Neue Attestate J. S. Bachs', *Festschrift . . . Rochus Freiherrn von Liliencron* (Leipzig, 1910), 290
'J. C. Friedrich Bach', *BJb*, xi (1914), 45
'Kasantatarische Lieder', *AMw*, i (1918), 499
Das Lied der deutschen Kolonisten in Russland (Berlin, 1923)
'Mendelssohns Jugendopern', *ZMw*, v (1923), 506
Die Musica des Listhenius (Berlin, 1927)
Geschichte der deutschen Schulmusik (Leipzig, 1928, 2/1931/R1968)
Die Musikerziehung, i: *Die Musik in Kindheit und Jugend, Schule und Volk* (Leipzig, 1930)
C. F. Zelter, der Begründer der Preussischen Musikpflege (Berlin, 1932)
'J. Gottfried Walther und H. Bokemeyer', *BJb*, xxx (1933), 86
Führer durch die Chorliteratur (Wolfenbüttel, 1935–6)
'Die Musikinstrumente der 24 Alten', *AMf*, i (1936), 42
ed.: *Musiker-Handschriften von Bach bis Schumann* [facs.] (Berlin, 1936) [enlarged Eng. trans., 1968, rev. W. Gerstenberg and M. Hürimann]
'Musikinstrumente der Indianer', *AMf*, i (1936), 368, 467
C. F. Zelter, der Mensch und sein Werk (Berlin, 1937)
'Neue Kanons von Beethoven', *Festschrift Arnold Schering* (Berlin, 1937), 207
'Beethovens Studien zur Instrumentation', *NBJb*, viii (1938), 146
'Eine neue Tristan-Handschrift', *AMf*, iii (1938), 129
'Czernys Erinnerungen an Beethoven', *NBJb*, ix (1939), 47
Die Violine (Hamburg, 1940)
Geschichte der Klaviermusik (Hamburg, 1940) [rev. H. Gerigk, 1953, 2/1956]
Die Singakademie zu Berlin (Regensburg, 1941)
ed.: *Ludwig van Beethovens Konversationshefte* (Berlin, 1941–3)
'Carl Maria von Weber in Berlin', *Von deutscher Tonkunst: Festschrift Peter Raabe* (Leipzig, 1942), 78

EDITIONS
J. C. F. Bach: Die Kindheit Jesu, Die Auferweckung Lazarus, DDT, lvi (1917/R1958)
Trompetenfanfaren, Sonaten und Feldstücke des 16.–17. Jahrhunderts, EDM, 1st ser., vii (1936)

BIBLIOGRAPHY
E. Preussner: 'Georg Schünemann', *Mf*, i (1948), 19
LOTHAR HOFFMANN-ERBRECHT

Schuppanzigh, Ignaz (*b* Vienna, 20 Nov 1776; *d* Vienna, 2 March 1830). Austrian violinist and conductor. In about 1793, having previously learnt the viola, Schuppanzigh took up the violin, and adopted music as a profession. He soon became the leader of a string quartet which gave weekly concerts at Prince Lichnowsky's apartments. Beethoven was the prince's guest at this time, and a fruitful relationship developed between the composer and the four young instrumentalists, Schuppanzigh, Sina, Weiss and Kraft. Thayer wrote:

> They enjoyed an advantage known to no other quartet – that of playing the compositions of Haydn and Förster under the eyes of the composers, and being taught by them every effect that the music was intended to produce . . . When Beethoven began to compose quartets he had, therefore, a set of performers schooled to perfection by his great predecessors, and who already had experience in his own music through his trios and sonatas.

The 1794 entry in Beethoven's memorandum book, 'Schupp. 3 times a W.', could refer either to violin lessons with Ignaz or lessons in cultural subjects with his father, who was professor at the Realschule. In 1795 he became the leader, and also, about 1798, the manager of the orchestral concerts at the Augarten. According to Czerny, it was Schuppanzigh who advised Beethoven to place the Quartet in F first in the publication of op.18. Schuppanzigh's obesity was a constant source of amusement to Beethoven (e.g. see his musical joke, *Lob auf den Dicken*).

In the winter of 1804–5 Schuppanzigh formed a quartet including Mayseder, Schreiber and Kraft to give subscription concerts; it was probably this quartet which introduced op.59 three years later. In 1807 Schuppanzigh married Fräulein Kilitzky, sister of the singer Josephine Schulze-Kilitzky. In 1808 Count Razumovsky asked Schuppanzigh to assemble for him 'the finest string quartet in Europe': he chose Linke (cello), Weiss (viola) and Sina for second violin whenever the count did not care to play. Meanwhile his career as a conductor continued. In an expression of thanks to the musicians who had played in the benefit concerts of December 1813, Beethoven cited 'Herr Schuppanzigh, leader of the first violins, who by his fiery and expressive playing swept the orchestra along with him'.

In 1814 Razumovsky's palace burnt down and he became unable to maintain his quartet. Accordingly in 1816 Schuppanzigh decided to travel east and settled in St Petersburg; from here he was able to introduce and spread the fame of Beethoven's music in Russia. His return to Vienna in 1823 provoked a greeting to 'Milord Falstaff', as Beethoven liked to call him, in the form of a canon, *Falstafferel, lass' dich sehen!* He joined the court chapel, in time became the director of the court opera, and resumed quartet meetings with Weiss, Linke and the new second violinist, Karl Holz. Böhm had been their regular leader, but his concert tours enabled Schuppanzigh to take his place in a series of concerts in the spring and autumn of 1823. His participation in these subscription concerts continued until his death.

Schuppanzigh played a major role in introducing Beethoven's music to Vienna. He participated in first performances from the 1790s to 1828 which included opp.16, 20, 59, 95, 97, 125, 127, 130 (both versions), 132 and 135. He also gave first performances of works by Schubert, including the Octet and the Quartet in A minor, which Schubert dedicated to him. His personal relationship with Beethoven varied. In 1824, after the first performance of the Ninth Symphony, Beethoven accused him, along with Schindler and Umlauf, of cheating over the receipts. Again, in 1825, after being given only two weeks to rehearse the E♭ Quartet op.127, he was the subject of Beethoven's wrath and was forced to give way to Böhm in subsequent performances. As he aged, his corpulence and short fingers became an increasing handicap in his playing. But, as Mahaim pointed out, 'Ignaz Schuppanzigh remains the greatest figure among the Beethoven quartet players of that original period, and the most admirable because of his unchangeable devotion to the inspired composer, the most terrible of masters'.

BIBLIOGRAPHY
T. Frimmel: *Beethoven-Handbuch*, ii (Leipzig, 1926), 161
E. Forbes, ed.: *Thayer's Life of Beethoven* (Princeton, 1964, 2/1967)
I. Mahaim: *Beethoven* (Paris, 1964), 40–71
D. W. MacArdle: 'Beethoven and Schuppanzigh', *MR*, xxvi (1965), 3
                                        ELLIOT FORBES

Schürer, Johann Georg (*b* ?Raudnitz [now Roudnice], Bohemia, *c*1720; *d* Dresden, 16 Feb 1786). German composer. He was working in about 1746 as resident composer and music director of an opera troupe that appeared in Dresden with the Mingotti company at the Zwinger; the Dresden repertory had been dominated by Hasse since 1734. On 29 October 1746 they performed Schürer's opera *Astrea placata* (which had been given in Warsaw on 7 October in honour of the king's birthday); it was repeated several times. On 8 November of the same year his *Galatea* was given at Dresden, and repeated with new settings in the presence of the court a week later and again on 28 June 1747, the day before Gluck's festival opera *Le nozze d'Ercole e d'Ebe* was given at Pillnitz. During the 1747 court festivities Schürer's opera *L'Ercole sul Termodonte* and his German Singspiel *Doris* were performed. His last opera was *Calandro*, a comedy, performed on 20 January 1748 in the little Zwinger theatre; thereafter he confined himself to composing sacred music, beginning with the oratorios *Il figliuol prodigo* and *Isacco*. In 1748 he was appointed *Kirchencompositeur* in royal service.

Schürer was thus one of a notable succession of musicians, headed by Hasse, who worked at the Dresden court of August II. Zelenka had died in 1745 and Schürer succeeded him as director of church music, first in the Catholic court chapel at Taschenberg and from 1751 in the newly built Catholic court church, with G. A. Ristori, Tobias Butz and Father M. Breunich

assisting him with the church music, and Porpora employed as Kapellmeister and composer. His principal occupation was composing, which he did with enormous industry, especially in 1757 and 1758. In the former year he wrote a requiem on the death of the Electress Maria Josepha. During the 1763 Carnival his cantata *Donna Augusta perdona* was performed and in the autumn of the same year he wrote the funeral motet for the king, *Manus tuae fecerunt me*. In autumn 1764 the young J. G. Naumann was appointed second church composer, but he soon left for Italy so that all the work was once again Schürer's responsibility (although between 1765 and 1772 Domenico Fischietti was also contributing church music). In 1767 Schürer sold the manuscript parts of his church compositions (978 sheets) to the Saxon court and in 1772, when Friedrich August was elector, he sold them the scores as well (522, dated 1742 to 1770) for 900 thalers. Schürer himself had compiled an index of these works, giving the opening bars and date of composition of each (*Cursus annuus*, MS, 1765, *D-B*). He retired in 1780 and sold a further 68 scores of sacred works written between 1767 and 1772 for 200 thalers in 1782, again with a detailed catalogue. The output of this prolific and indefatigable composer seems to have ceased in his last years in office, which were overshadowed by worry and illness; his pupils Joseph Schuster and Franz Seydelmann were working with him as church composers from 1772.

Although Schürer, according to Reichardt, was a 'very skilful composer', master of his craft and of counterpoint, his music met with only limited appreciation in Dresden because he did not bow to the prevalent neo-Neapolitan taste. Gerber called him one of the most proficient church composers of the 18th century and noted that 'his masses were famed among worthy men outside Dresden'. In fact his six masses dedicated to S Antonio of Padua and his *Litaniae Xaverianae* are distinguished by their structure and their serious, expressive musical cast. His operas and oratorios also exemplify the changing style of his time, combining use of the traditional figured bass with delicate Rococo sentiment. Stylistically his music places him between the mature Telemann and the 12-year-old Mozart; but his melodic ideas are limited and eventually become tedious. The pastorale *Galatea* and the German Singspiel *Doris* have *galant*, Rococo features also found in Mozart's *Bastien und Bastienne*.

WORKS
(all in D-Dlb unless otherwise stated)

OPERAS

Astrea placata ovvero La felicità della terra (dramma per musica, 1, B. Campagnari), Warsaw, 7 Oct 1746, lib *D-B*

La Galatea (componimento drammatico, 2, Metastasio), Dresden, 8 Nov 1746; also 4 arias in Ger.

L'Ercole sul Termodonte (dramma per musica, 3, C. F. Bussani), Dresden, 9 Jan 1747

Doris (Singspiel, 2), Dresden, 13 Feb 1747

Calandro (comedia per musica, 3, S. Pallavicino), Dresden, 20 Jan 1748

ORATORIOS

Il figliuol Prodigo (azione sacra, G. C. Pasquini), solo vv, chorus, orch, Dresden, 1747, lib *D-B*

Isacco figura del Redentore (Metastasio), solo vv, chorus, orch, Dresden, 1748, lib *D-B*

La Passione di Jesu Christo, solo vv, chorus, orch

CANTATAS

Cantata per la nascita di S. A. R. il Principe Carlo, A, insts, 13 July 1753

Cantata per solennizzare il giorno del nome di S. A. R. . . . Principe Xaverio, A, insts, Dresden, 1755

Disgrazia accaduta al Nicolino à Sedlitz, A, insts, Dresden and Friedrichstadt, 1759

Donna Augusta perdona, A, 2 hn, 2 fl, 2 vn, va, bc, Dresden, 1763, *D-B*, *D-Dlb*
Cantata . . . per la nascita di S. P. Carlo, S, A
Nel felicissimo giorno del glorioso Nome . . . di Augusto III [characters Nice, Dorisbe, Filli]
Oggi si che più risplende, A, insts

MASSES, MASS MOVEMENTS

6 Missae ad Sanctum Antonium de Padua, 4vv, 2 ob, 2 vn, va, bc, org, 1758–64
Credo, vv, insts; Gl, 4vv, 2 vn, 2 ob, 2 hn, 2 tpt, timp, org; Gl, 4vv, insts: all *D-B*

OTHER WORKS

Regina coeli, 4vv, insts, org, *A-Wn*
?2 Litaniae Xaverianae, 4vv, insts
Partitura et Directio sacrae noctis in nativitate Domini, Dresden, 1756
2 arias, S, insts: La sventurata adora, Friedrichstadt, 24 Aug 1759; Delude fallace, Friedrichstadt, 19 Aug 1759

LOST WORKS

(*presumed lost; for complete list see Haas*)

Several operas, cantatas, etc; c30 masses; c13 motets; 56 offertories; 3 requiems; 3 Te Deum; 15 Litaniae Lauretanae; 17 Sub tuum; 12 Alma Redemptoris; 12 Ave regina; 12 Regina coeli; 29 Salve regina; 6 Miserere; 152 psalms; 6 Laudate pueri; 6 Magnificat; other sacred works

BIBLIOGRAPHY

EitnerQ; GerberL; GerberNL
J. F. Reichardt: *Briefe eines aufmerksamen Reisenden*, ii (Frankfurt am Main and Breslau, 1776/*R*), 176
G. J. Dlabacž: *Allgemeines historisches Künstler-Lexikon* (Prague, 1815/*R*1973)
G. Schilling, ed.: *Encyclopädie der gesammten musikalischen Wissenschaften* (Stuttgart, 1835–42/*R*1973)
M. Fürstenau: *Beiträge zur Geschichte der königlich sächsischen musikalischen Kapelle* (Dresden, 1849)
——: *Zur Geschichte der Musik und des Theaters am Hofe zu Dresden*, i (Dresden, 1861/*R*1971)
C. Niessen: *Die Kirchenmusik in der katholischen Hofkirche Dresden* (Vienna, 1865)
R. Eitner: 'Schürer, Johann Georg', *ADB*
R. Vollhardt: *Geschichte der Cantoren und Organisten von den Städten im Königreich Sachsen* (Berlin, 1899)
R. Haas: *J. G. Schürer (1720–1786): ein Beitrag zur Geschichte der Musik in Dresden* (Dresden, 1915)
K. Pembaur: *Drei Jahrhunderte Kirchenmusik am sächsischen Hofe* (Dresden, 1920)
O. Schmid: *Musik im alten Dresden*, i (Dresden, 1921)
L. Schiedermair: *Die deutsche Oper* (Leipzig, 1930, 2/1940)
G. Pietzsch: *Sachsen als Musikland* (Dresden, 1938)
H. Schnoor: *Dresden: 400 Jahre deutsche Musikkultur* (Dresden, 1948)
D. Härtwig: 'Schürer, Johann Georg', *MGG*

DIETER HÄRTWIG

Schuricht, Carl (*b* Danzig, 3 July 1880; *d* Corseaux-sur-Vevey, 7 Jan 1967). German conductor and composer. He studied under Humperdinck at the Berlin Hochschule and with Reger in Leipzig. After serving a musical apprenticeship in provincial theatres he was appointed musical director at Wiesbaden in 1911, where he remained until 1944. During this time he organized and conducted regular festivals of contemporary music, becoming a persuasive advocate in Germany for Debussy, Delius, Ravel, Schoenberg and Stravinsky, and conducting choirs in Berlin and Frankfurt. He toured abroad, and for several years conducted annual summer concerts at Scheveningen, Holland, for which he was awarded the Order of Oranje-Nassau in 1938. From 1944 he lived in Switzerland, continuing his career as guest conductor with principal European orchestras, including the BBC SO and LSO.

Schuricht provided a link with the 19th-century German conducting tradition, interpreting the major classics with considerable freedom in expressive phrasing and fluctuations of tempo, but achieving a convincing sense of musical purpose by his firm control of the orchestra. His compositions include orchestral works, piano sonatas and some songs.

BIBLIOGRAPHY

F. Oeser: 'Carl Schuricht', *ZfM*, Jg.101 (1934), 610
B. Gavoty: *Carl Schuricht* (Geneva, 1955)
F. Wohlfahrt: 'Das Porträt – Carl Schuricht', *NZM*, Jg.118 (1957), 226

NOËL GOODWIN

Schürmann [Schurmann, Scheuermann], **Georg Caspar** (*b* Idensen, nr. Hanover, 1672 or 1673; *d* Wolfenbüttel, 25 Feb 1751). German composer. Walther recorded that he was the son of a pastor, identified as Statius Caspar Schürmann (*d* 1678), who went to Idensen in 1666. His son began his career at the age of 20 in Hamburg where he found engagements as a male alto both at the opera and in various churches. During the next six years Schürmann performed in an ideal musical milieu for a young musician, especially at the opera where Conradi, Kusser and Keiser were involved with productions of their works, and the music of Steffani (among other outstanding composers) was often heard. In 1697 he travelled with the Hamburg opera company for a series of guest appearances at the Brunswick court of Duke Anton Ulrich of Brunswick-Lüneburg. Soon after, Duke Anton Ulrich appointed Schürmann as solo alto to the court and also, according to Walther, as a conductor for the opera and court church.

Except for two periods of absence, Schürmann remained at the Brunswick-Wolfenbüttel court until his death 54 years later. He quickly established himself as a gifted composer, and in 1700 his first dramatic work, the Italian pastorale *Endimione*, was performed at the court theatres at Salzthal and Wolfenbüttel. The following year he wrote and produced two sacred operas, *Salomon* and *Daniel*. In late 1701 Duke Anton Ulrich sent him to Venice, no doubt to complete his education in the Italian operatic style. Walther said that he made the acquaintance of the most famous composers and musicians while in Venice, and one can speculate that these would have included Antonio and Carlo Francesco Pollarolo, Tommaso Albinoni, Francesco Gasparini and Francesco Pistocchi. Nothing specific is known of Schürmann's Italian period, and apparently he returned to Germany after only one year to become, on loan from the Duke of Brunswick, Kapellmeister and composer at the court of Meiningen. He remained there until at least 1706 and, in addition to serving as music teacher to the royal family, he wrote several operas and many church cantatas. In 1706 Schürmann went to produce an opera at Naumburg, where each year an important opera festival was maintained at court during the Petri-Pauli fair (beginning on 29 June and lasting eight days).

Walther stated that Schürmann returned permanently to Brunswick-Wolfenbüttel in 1707. Over more than 30 years his productivity was enormous. After 1739 he is not known to have composed operas, but he remained immersed in court musical life as a conductor, producer of operas, and translator and arranger of the Italian operas which had become the mainstay of the theatre. Schürmann rearranged many of his own works, inserting arias by other composers and creating numerous pasticcios. In his final years he continued to compose for the church as well as occasional pieces for special court festivals.

Schürmann, together with Conradi, Kusser, Keiser and Telemann, was an outstanding contributor to the history of German Baroque opera. It is regrettable that of more than the 40 operas he is known to have written only three seem to survive in their entirety and another nine remain in manuscripts of excerpts; and none of these three manuscripts has been published in a complete modern edition. An outstanding study of Schürmann's operas was written by G. F. Schmidt, who examined the music in great detail.

Schürmann's operas demonstrate a successful blending of the operatic style developed in north Germany, especially in Hamburg in the music of Keiser, with the Italian practices he observed in Venice. His operas are aria-orientated, and each aria, in characteristic Baroque fashion, is planned to express a single affection or emotional idealization. Most of the arias have fairly extensive da capo structures, but Schürmann filled these stereotyped forms with richly inventive melodic ideas, strong textural variety (including frequent contrapuntal interplay between the voice and instrumental parts) and colourful solo instrumental writing. The recitatives are in the north German tradition of affective, rhetorical declamation, in which vocal line, harmonic colour (in the continuo part as well as the melody) and dramatic accent add strength and theatrical effectiveness. This is not the recitative of contemporary Italian opera, with its rapid parlando patter, and frequent 'dry' punctuations of cadential harmonic formulae in the accompanying harpsichord continuo realization. For Schürmann, as for the Hamburg opera composers, the recitative was still an important component of the musical drama.

Schürmann's melodic gift, undoubtedly in part the result of his own lengthy career as an operatic singer, makes his works impressively lyrical. The voice parts are never overshadowed by the orchestra, and the instrumental parts generally take on the melodic characteristics of the vocal style – not the reverse procedure, as one finds, for example, in Keiser's operas. Schürmann continued the Hamburg opera composers' proclivity for folklike melodies and for arias based on dance rhythms (especially the siciliano, barcarolle and minuet). The dance is in fact a major part of each work, although for the most part other composers (frequently French ones) supplied the music for such ballet insertions. Although Schürmann gave his soloists ample opportunity to excel in written-out coloratura ornamentation, this kind of vocal virtuosity never dominated his arias, as it did for example in much of Keiser's music.

However, Schürmann's operas move clearly beyond his Hamburg heritage and in many ways remind one of the later works of Handel. While the textures are frequently contrapuntal, the use of counterpoint occurs as an element of variation, not as a basic compositional procedure. Harmonic rhythm, especially in his last surviving opera, *Ludovicus Pius*, is markedly slow, at times static, and often similar to that of the early Classical style in Germany. Bass lines, then, are not generally melodic, and indeed often seem to be in the early Classical mould with their tendency to serve a purely harmonic function. Schürmann's music, in fact, points strongly in the direction of the Classical style and suggests that this composer, who worked with both C. H. Graun and Hasse at Wolfenbüttel, may have played a significant part in the style's development in Germany during the first half of the 18th century.

WORKS

STAGE

(all performed in Brunswick; music lost unless otherwise stated)

Endimione (favola per musica, F. de Lemene), Salzthal, 1700
?Der sich erfreuende Jahrs-Zeiten (ballet), Wolfenbüttel, 1700

Salomon (Singspiel, 3, Duke Anton Ulrich of Brunswick and/or J. C. Knorr von Rosenroth), 1701, *D-SWl*
Daniel (Singspiel, 3, Knorr von Rosenroth), 1701
?Opffer der Zeiten der Wahren Tugend gewidmet (ballet, 5 scenes), Meiningen, 1703
?Eintracht der Tugend, Schönheit und Jugend mit der erlaubten Wollust (ballet), Meiningen, 1703
?Sieg der Liebe (ballet), Meiningen, 1704
Leonilde oder der siegende Beständigkeit (Singspiel, 3, G. Fielder), 1704 or 1705, 4 arias *Bds*
Das verstöhrte Troja (Singspiel, 5, J. C. Frauendorf), 1706, arias and duets *B*
Telemaque (opera, 4, ?Frauendorf), Naumburg, 1706
Giasone, overo Il conquisto del vello d'oro (dramma per musica, 3, F. Parisetti, Ger. trans. Schürmann), 1707, pasticcio incl. music by various It. composers *Bds*
Die schöne Psyche (Singspiel, 3, C. Postel), 1708, ?adaptation or partial recomposition of R. Keiser, Die wunderschöne Psyche
Der erfreuten Ocker-Schäffer angestelltes Fest (Festspiel with ballet, 7 scenes), 1708
?Mario (opera, 3, S. Stampiglia, Ger. trans.), Leipzig, 1709, ?collab. J. D. Heinichen with some music from It. opera by G. B. Bononcini
Issé, oder Die vergnügende Liebe (pastorale, 3, A. Houdart de la Motte, Ger. trans.), Wolfenbüttel, 1710, ?adaptation or partial recomposition of opera by A. Destouches
Procris und Cephalus (Singspiel, 3, F. C. Bressand), 1714, pasticcio incl. music by Keiser, A. Lotti and others
Regnero (dramma per musica, prol, 3, Zeno and Pariati), 1715, ?only prol by Schürmann
Heinrich der Löwe (opera, 3, O. Mauro, Ger. trans. Fiedler), 1716, pasticcio with music largely by A. Steffani
L'amor insanguinato, oder Holofernes (Singspiel, 5, J. Beccau), 1716, pasticcio
Die Plejades oder Das Siebengestirn (Singspiel, 3, Bressand), 1716
Claudio ed Agrippina (dramma per musica, prol, 3), 1717, ?only prol by Schürmann
Atis, oder Der stumme Verliebte (opera, 3, L. von Bostel), 1717
Telemachus und Calypso (opera, 3, Frauendorf), 1717
Porsenna (Clelia) (Singspiel, 5, Bressand), 1718, excerpts *B*
Tiridate ovvero L'amor tirannico (dramma per musica, 3, D. Lalli), 1718
?Herodes (Singspiel, 4, J. S. Müller), Wolfenbüttel or Salzthal, ?1718
Heinrich der Vogler, pt.1 (Singspiel, 3, J. U. König), 1718
?Doppia festa d'Himeneo (favola pastorale, 25 scenes, Mauro, Ger. trans. ?Schürmann), Salzthal, 1718, ?music partly or entirely by Steffani
Die getreue Alceste (opera, 3, König, after P. Quinault), 1719, MS of Hamburg, 1719 perf. *B*
?Cadmus (opera, 3, König), 1720
Heinrich der Vogler, pt.2 (Singspiel, König), 1721
Das eroberte Jerusalem, oder Armida und Rinaldo (Singspiel, 3, Müller, after G. C. Corradi), 1722
Ixion (opera, 3, Fiedler), 1722, excerpts *B*
Orlando furioso (dramma per musica, 3, G. Braccioli, arr. and Ger. trans. Schürmann), 1722, pasticcio
Rudolphus Habspurgicus (opera, 3, 2 'Anreden', Müller), 1723
?Justinus (opera, 3, C. E. Simonetti, after N. Beregani), 1725
Ludovicus Pius, oder Ludewig der Fromme (opera, 3, Simonetti), 1726, incl. some arias by C. H. Graun, baltet music partly from operas by Destouches and Campra, *Bsommer*; partial edn. in PÄMw, xvii (1890)
Hannibal in Capua (opera, 3, Beregani, arr. Schürmann), 1726
?Der beglückte Zeit-wechsel (serenata, König), Wolfenbüttel, 1726
Orpheus (opera, 3, Bressand, ?arr. Schürmann), 1727, ?music by Schürmann and Keiser
Musicalisches Neu-Jahrs-Opfer (serenata), 1728, Wolfenbüttel, ?music by Schürmann and/or C. H. Graun
Der von Londinen zugleich geliebte und ungeliebte Pharasmanes, König von Iberien (Singspiel, 3, J. F. von Uffenbach), ?1729
?Ninus und Semiramis (opera, 3), 1730
Magnus Torquatus (opera, 3, Müller), 1730
Single arias from operas in *Bds*, *SWl*, *W*

OTHER WORKS

Sacred cantatas (autograph *Bds* unless otherwise stated): Aber über das Haus Davids, solo vv, chorus, orch, Meiningen, 27 May 1705; Gnädig und barmherzig ist der Herr, solo vv, chorus, orch, Meiningen, 29 May 1705; Siehe, ich will meiner Herde selbst annehmen, solo vv, chorus, orch, Meiningen, 30 May 1705; Komm, o Tröster, mein Verlangen, A, B, chorus, orch, 1717; Nimm das Opfer unserer Herzen, S, orch, New Year 1720, *B*; Auf, jauchzet, lobsinget dem König der Ehren, solo vv, chorus, orch, ?same as cantata for the dedication of Grauen Hofkapelle, Brunswick, 24 Sept 1724; Es wird ein Stern aus Jacob aufgehen, 4vv, insts; Gott ist unsere Zuversicht und Stärke, solo vv, chorus, orch; Pflüget ein Neues und säet nicht, 4vv, 4 insts; Siehe, eine Jungfrau ist schwanger, 4vv, 4 insts

Lost sacred cantatas: Gott hat alles Wohlgemacht, 1713; Jesu, meiner Seelen Weide, A. ?insts, see Schmidt; Trauermusik on death of Princess Christine Louise, Wolfenbüttel, Schlosskirche, 10 Dec 1747, text Ws; numerous cantatas, many written after 1727 to texts of J. F. von Uffenbach

Instrumental-Suiten zu Tafel-Musicken, according to Walther, lost

BIBLIOGRAPHY

WaltherML

F. Chrysander: 'Geschichte der Braunschweig-Wolfenbüttelschen Capelle und Oper vom 16.–18. Jahrhundert', *Jb für musikalische Wissenschaft*, i (1863), 147–286

H. Sommer: 'Die Oper Ludwig der Fromme von G. C. Schürmann', *MMg*, xiv (1882), 48, 53

G. F. Schmidt: *Die frühdeutsche Oper und die musikdramatische Kunst Georg Caspar Schürmanns* (Regensburg, 1933–4)

E. Rosendahl: 'Wo und wann G. K. Schürmann geboren wurde', *AMf*, vii (1942), 229

G. Croll: 'Schürmann, Georg Caspar', *MGG*

R. Brockpähler: *Handbuch zur Geschichte der Barockoper in Deutschland* (Emsdetten, 1964)

GEORGE J. BUELOW

Schurmann [Schürmann], **(Edward) Gerard** (*b* Kertosono, Indonesia, 19 Jan 1928). British composer of Dutch origin. Although he took private lessons from Rawsthorne at the RCM, he is largely self-taught as a composer. He attracted public attention at an early age and in the early 1940s he received many performances in England and the Netherlands. A slow-working and self-critical composer, he achieves a certain terseness and intensity of expression through complex contrapuntal writing and a highly chromatic harmony. The *Six Studies of Francis Bacon* (1968–9) – a product of close friendship with the painter – are typical, individual in style and temperamentally unstable.

WORKS
(selective list)

Orch: 6 Studies of Francis Bacon, 1968–9; Variants, chamber orch, 1968–70; Attack and Celebration, 1971; Pf Conc., 1972–3; Vn Conc., 1975–8

Vocal: 9 Poems of Blake, 1v, pf, 1955; Carceri, Bar, orch, 1958; Chuench'i, 1v, pf, 1966, orchd 1967; Summer is Coming, chorus, 1970; The Double Heart (Marvell), SATB, 1976; Piers Plowman, opera-cantata, 1979–80

Inst: Wind Qnt, 1963, rev. 1976; Str Qt no.2, 1964; Fantasia, vc, pf, 1963–5; Sonatina, fl, pf, 1968; Serenade, vn, 1969; Contrasts, pf, 1973; Leotaurus, pf, 1974–5

Other works: 2 ballets, 34 film scores, arrs. of music by G. C. Schürmann and others

Principal publisher: Novello

BIBLIOGRAPHY

K. Loveland: 'The Music of Gerard Schurmann', *MT*, cxi (1970), 490

G. Schurmann: 'Variants', *The Listener*, lxxxix (1973), 490

R. Matthew-Walker: 'Gerard Schurmann and Piers Plowman', *MT*, cxxi (1980), 495

RICHARD COOKE

Schuster, Giora [Georg] (*b* Hamburg, 20 Oct 1915). Israeli composer of German origin. He settled in Palestine in 1938 and studied music there privately. In the mid-1950s he undertook further study at the Musikhochschulen of Hamburg and Cologne, and with Fortner in Freiburg. He was later appointed to teach orchestration, acoustics and 20th-century music at the Music Teachers' College, Tel-Aviv, and Haifa University.

WORKS
(selective list)

Vocal: Cantata (Rilke), 1958; 2 Dialogues and Recitative (Eluard), 1v, fl, pf, 1960–65

Inst: Pf Qnt; Intermezzi, 4 brass, 1960; Per duo, vn, pf, 1961; Mimos, pf 4 hands, 1966; Movts, orch, 1967; Arabesque, 5 insts, 1968; Entrata and Passacaglia piccola, org, 1968; 4 Intermezzi, vn, pf, 1974

Principal publishers: Israeli Music Publications, Israel Music Institute

BIBLIOGRAPHY

Y. W. Cohen: *Werden und Entwicklung der Musik in Israel* (Kassel, 1976) [pt.ii of rev. edn. of M. Brod: *Die Musik Israels*]

W. Y. Elias: *The Music of Israel* (Tel-Aviv, in preparation)

WILLIAM Y. ELIAS

Schuster, Ignaz (*b* Vienna, 20 July 1779; *d* Vienna, 6 Nov 1835). Austrian actor, singer and composer. He was a treble, and later a bass, chorister at the Schottenstift in Vienna; Eybler and Franz Volkert were among his music teachers. At about the same time he was offered posts as a bass in the Esterházy musical establishment and at the Theater in der Leopoldstadt in Vienna. He chose the latter, and despite his rather small, misshapen figure he quickly established himself as a comic actor and singer after a successful début in December 1801. From 1804 he began to figure as a composer too (*Baron Barfuss*, by Perinet), supplying some 30 or 40 scores for farces, parodies and pantomimes, some of them enjoying a long and distinguished life. In 1806 he was appointed a solo singer at the Hofkapelle – such was the urbanity of Vienna's cultural life that nothing untoward was felt about the city's leading comic actor (which Schuster had by then become) being also employed as singer in the imperial and royal chapel, and in St Stephen's Cathedral. A notable date in his career was 22 October 1813, when he created the role of Staberl in Bäuerle's *Die Bürger von Wien* and thereby inaugurated the last of the comic *personae* that from Hanswurst via Kasperl formed the principal sources of public delight in the old Viennese popular theatre. He earned special admiration for his brilliant imitation of Borgondio in the Bäuerle–Müller parody of Rossini's *Tancredi* in 1817. On Christmas eve 1818 he appeared in the title role of *Die falsche Primadonna* (the censor had forbidden its original title of *Die falsche Catalani*), for which he also composed the score. This work, the finest of the long line of Krähwinkel plays that followed Kotzebue's *Die deutschen Kleinstädter*, was frequently imitated but never equalled; it was given all over the German-speaking lands, and in the Leopoldstadt alone it was performed 161 times in 40 years.

Despite the rising popularity of Raimund, which provoked jealousy from the older Schuster, he continued to enjoy triumphs as actor, singer and composer. During and after the Congress of Vienna, crowned heads praised and honoured him. In his own theatre he held the offices of chorus director and later senior producer. He was one of the singers who honoured Beethoven's memory with a double quartet on the day of his funeral, before bearing the coffin to the minorite church. From 1828 Schuster was increasingly in demand for guest appearances at home and abroad; he retired in October 1835, less than a month before his death. Apart from his theatre scores, some of which were published in vocal score, and which include such parodies as *Othello, der Mohr in Wien* (1806), *Werthers Leiden* (1806) and *Romeo und Julie* (1808), all to texts by J. F. Kringsteiner, he also wrote a mass that was performed at the Schottenkirche in 1817, and songs. His manuscripts and some printed works are now in the important Vienna libraries.

BIBLIOGRAPHY

Biographical sketch, MS, *A-Wgm* [with incomplete list of works]

C. von Wurzbach: *Biographisches Lexikon des Kaiserthums Oesterreich*, xxxii (Vienna, 1876), 240

L. Eisenberg: *Grosses biographisches Lexikon der deutschen Bühne im*

XIX. Jahrhundert (Leipzig, 1903), 942

E. von Bauernfeld: *Erinnerungen aus Alt-Wien* (Vienna, 1923)

F. Hadamowsky: *Das Theater in der Wiener Leopoldstadt* (Vienna, 1934)

PETER BRANSCOMBE

Schuster, Joseph (*b* Dresden, 11 Aug 1748; *d* Dresden, 24 July 1812). German composer and conductor. The son of a court musician in Dresden, he received his first musical instruction from his father and from the composer J. G. Schürer. He received a scholarship from the elector and, together with Franz Seydelmann, spent the years 1765–8 with J. G. Naumann in Italy, where he studied counterpoint with the Venetian Girolamo Pera. In 1772 both he and Seydelmann were appointed church composers in Dresden. From 1774 to 1777 Schuster again visited Italy, where he studied with Padre Martini in Bologna, composed operas for Naples and Venice and received the honorary title of *maestro di cappella* to the King of Naples. His first *opera seria*, *Didone abbandonata* (Naples, 1776), to a text by Metastasio, established his popularity with the Italian public. New opera contracts brought about his last journey to Italy in 1778–81, when he established closer relations with J. A. Hasse and had further stage successes in Naples and Venice. By this time he was also admired in Germany as a composer of *opera buffa* and Singspiel: his *Der Alchymist oder Der Liebesteufel* (1778), one of the most charming and successful examples of the genre, remained popular in Germany into the 19th century. From 1781 he conducted in the Dresden court church and theatre (alternately with Naumann, Schürer and Seydelmann), and in 1787 he was appointed Kapellmeister to the elector, again simultaneously with Seydelmann.

Schuster had an easy social manner, was attracted by everything fashionable and was a very productive composer. Apart from his work as a conductor, his most important duties at court included managing the elector's chamber music and court concerts, giving music instruction, acquiring new music (primarily from Vienna, including works by Haydn, Mozart and Pleyel) and handling new appointments. He also participated enthusiastically in Dresden's concert life; his role in it during the last two decades of the 18th century was significant, and during the 1780s he was at the height of his creativity and international success, particularly in opera. By 1792 he was recognized throughout Germany as 'one of our most popular composers' (*GerberL*).

Apart from his operas Schuster also composed church music, including oratorios, masses and many smaller sacred works, as well as secular songs, Italian cantatas and instrumental music. The cantata *Lob der Musik*, performed until the mid-19th century, was one of his few published works (1784); its treatment of choir and orchestra is particularly melodious. His initiative is shown in his chamber works, in which, as in *Der Alchymist* and the piano concertos, he consciously approached the Viennese style. The spirited divertimentos for harpsichord and violin of about 1777 are distinguished both by equal treatment of the violin and the keyboard and by originality of form; they were Schuster's introduction to Munich as he passed through on his last trip to Italy. It was in Munich that Mozart came across them and was prompted to efforts in the

same 'gusto' (letter of 6 October 1777), resulting in his sonatas K296, 301–3/293*a–c* and 305/293*d*. The Padua string quartet in C (1780), for some time attributed to Mozart as KAnh.211/Anh.C 20.02, has been proved to be by Schuster (Köchel, 1964). Most of his piano works were composed for the Dresden court and serve as a reminder that he deserves considerable credit as a champion and 'great master' (Schubart, 1806) of the fortepiano; both in Italy and in Dresden he contributed to the popularization of the *Hammerflügel*.

WORKS

STAGE

DKT – *Dresden, Kleines Kurfürstliches Theater*
NC – *Naples, Teatro S Carlo*　　VM – *Venice, Teatro S Moisè*

Addl music in F. L. Gassmann: La contessina, Dresden, 2 Jan 1772
La fedeltà in amore (opera buffa, 2), DKT, 1773, *D-Dlb*
L'idolo cinese (opera buffa, 3, G. Lorenzi), DKT, 1776, *Dlb*
L'amore artigiano (opera buffa, 3, C. Goldoni), VM, 1776, *B-Bc*
La Didone abbandonata (opera seria, 3, P. Metastasio), NC, 1776; *D-Dlb, I-Nc*; 1 song [also attrib. G. Gazzaniga]
Demofoonte (opera seria, 3, Metastasio), Forlì, Teatro Nuovo, 1776, *D-Dlb, F-Pc*
La schiava liberata (opera buffa, 3, G. Martinelli), DKT, 2 Oct 1777; 2 scores and vocal score, *D-Dlb*
Der Alchymist oder Der Liebesteufel (Singspiel, 1, A. G. Meissner), DKT, March 1778, *Dlb*; vocal score, ed. G. Sartorius, *Mbs*; ed. R. Engländer (Kassel, 1958)
Die wüste Insel (Singspiel, 1, Meissner, after Metastasio), Leipzig, Theater am Ranstädter Tor, 1779, *A-Wn, B-D*
Creso in Media (opera seria, 3, G. Pagliuca), NC, 1779, *Dlb, I-Nc*
Amor e Psyche (opera seria, 2, after M. Coltellini), NC, 1780, *D-Dlb, I-Nc*
Il bon ton (opera buffa, 2), VM, 1780, ?lost
Il marito indolente (opera buffa, 2, C. Mazzolà), DKT, 1782, *D-Dlb*; Ger. trans. as Der gleichgültige Ehemann, *Bds*
Il pazzo per forza (opera buffa, 2, Mazzolà), DKT, 1784, *Dlb*
Lo spirito di contradizione (opera buffa, 2, Mazzolà), DKT, 1785, *Dlb*; Ger. trans. as Dr Murner, *Dlb*
Gli avari in troppola (opera buffa, 2, Mazzolà), DKT, 1787, *Dlb*
Rübezahl ossia Il vero amore (opera buffa, 2, Mazzolà), DKT, 14 Feb 1789; score, *Dlb, A-Wgm*
Il servo padrone ossia L'amore perfetto (opera buffa, 2, Mazzolà), DKT, 1793, *D-Dlb*
Osmano dey d'Algeri (opera buffa, 2, ? G. Cinti), DKT, 1800, *Dlb*
Il giorno natalizio (opera buffa, 2, Cinti), pasticcio, DKT, 24 Feb 1802, *Dlb*
Der Schauspieldirector (Singspiel), *DS* [doubtful; cited in *EitnerQ*]

OTHER VOCAL

Oratorios (most for Catholic court chapel, Dresden): La passione di Gesù Cristo (Metastasio), 1778, *A-Wgm, D-Bds, Dlb, Rp*; Ester, Venice, Conservatorio Ospedaletto, 1781 [cited in *GerberNL*]; Mosè riconosciuto (G. A. Migliavacca), 1786, ?lost; La Betulia liberata (Metastasio), 1796, *Bds, Dlb*; Gioas re di Giuda (Metastasio), 1803, *Dlb*; 2, *Dkh*
Masses: 19, *Dkh*; 5 for choir, orch, 1768 and 1777, *Dlb*; 4 for 4vv, orch, *Bds*; 1 for 3vv, orch, *I-Mc*; 1, *A-Wgm*; frags. in *Wn, Wgm, D-Bds, Dlb, LEm*
Musikalische Todenfeier den Manen Leopolds des Weisen geheiligt ([?J. C. R.] Heydenreich), vocal score (Leipzig, 1792)
Other sacred music, incl. Magnificat settings, offertories, psalms, etc, most in *D-Dkh*, others in *A-Wgm, D-Bds, Dlb, LEm, LEt, SWl, I-Bc, USSR-KAu*
Cantatas: Amor prigioniero, 2vv, insts, 1769, *D-Dlb*; Lob der Musik (Meissner), 1v, choir, orch, *Bds, Dlb, SWl*, vocal score (Leipzig, 1784); cantata (Orlandi), 1807, *Dlb*; Il ritorno del sole sull'orizonte, 1808, *Dlb, LEm*; Gesang zur Feyer des Friedens und der sächsischen Königswürde, T, B, pf (Leipzig, n.d.); Per il felice ritorno di Carlsbad, *Dlb*; La sorpresa, *Dlb*; La tempesta (Metastasio), 1v, insts, *Dlb*; Il nome, S, orch, *Dlb* [inc.]
Many arias and songs, *A-Wgm, B-Br, D-Bds, Dlb, DS, LÜh, W, I-Bc, Mc, MC, NL-Avnm, USSR-KAu*
Numerous songs in contemporary anthologies

INSTRUMENTAL

Syms./ovs.: 9, incl. 2 dated 1765, *D-Dlb*; 4, *I-Mc*; 3, 1788, *D-DS*; 2 each, *W, Z*; 1 each, *A-Wgm, D-SWl*; 2, *CS-KRa*
Chamber: Trio, 2 vn, b, c1768, *D-Dlb*; 6 sonatas, hpd, vn, c1776, *I-Nc* [?1 in *Mc*]; 6 divertimenti da camera, hpd, vn, ?1777, *D-Dlb, B*, ed. W. Plath (Kassel, 1971–3); str qt, c1780, *I-Pca*
Many concs. and kbd pieces
3 pieces, mand, *D-Dlb*

BIBLIOGRAPHY

EitnerQ; GerberL; GerberNL

C. F. D. Schubart: *Ideen zu einer Ästhetik der Tonkunst* (Vienna, 1806/*R*1969), 115f

M. Fürstenau: *Beiträge zur Geschichte der königlich sächsischen musikalischen Kapelle* (Dresden, 1849)

R. Engländer: 'Die Opern Joseph Schusters (1748–1812)', *ZMw*, x (1927–8), 257–91

——: 'Les sonates de violon de Mozart et les "Duetti" di Joseph Schuster', *RdM*, xx (1939), 6

——: 'Problem kring Mozarts violinsonat i e-moll K. 304', *STMf*, xxxiii (1951), 127

——: 'Die Echtheitsfrage in Mozarts Violinsonaten KV 55–60', *Mf*, viii (1955), 292

——: 'Die Dresdner Instrumentalmusik in der Zeit der Wiener Klassik', *Uppsala universitets arsskrift 1956*, no.5

——: 'Nochmals Mozart und der Dresdner Joseph Schuster', *STMf*, xxxix (1957), 141

W. S. Newman: *The Sonata in the Classic Era* (Chapel Hill, 1963, rev. 2/1972)

L. von Köchel, ed.: *Chronologisch-thematisches Verzeichnis sämtlicher Tonwerke Wolfgang Amadé Mozarts* (Leipzig, 6/1964)

L. Finscher: 'Mozarts "Mailänder" Streichquartette', *Mf*, xix (1966), 270

DIETER HÄRTWIG

Schusterfleck (Ger.). *See* ROSALIA.

Illustration Acknowledgments

We are grateful to those listed below for permission to reproduce copyright illustrative material, and those contributors who supplied or helped us obtain it. Every effort has been made to contact copyright holders; we apologize to anyone who may have been omitted. Brian and Constance Dear prepared the maps and technical diagrams, and Oxford Illustrators the typographic diagrams (except where otherwise stated). Photographs acknowledged to the following sources are Crown copyright: Her Majesty the Queen, the Victoria and Albert Museum (including the Theatre Museum), the Science Museum and the National Monuments Record. The following forms of acknowledgment are used where the copyright of an illustration is held by a contributor:

photo John Smith – John Smith is contributor and photographer
John Smith – John Smith is contributor and copyright holder
photo John Smith, London – John Smith is a contributor (not of the article concerned) and photographer
John Smith, London – John Smith is a contributor (not of the article concerned) and copyright holder.

Where illustrations are taken from books out of copyright, the full title and place and date of publication are given, unless in the caption.

Riegger, Wallingford Broadcast Music Inc., New York
Rimsky-Korsakov, Nikolay Andreyevich *1* Editions d'Art Lucien Mazenod, Paris: from J. Lacroix, *Les musiciens célèbres* (1948); *2* M. E. Saltïkov-Shchedrin State Public Library, Leningrad
Robinson, Anastasia The Lord Langford, Bodrhyddan
Rococo Metropolitan Museum of Art (Harris Brisbane Dick Fund, 1935), New York
Rodzinski, Artur Chicago Symphony Orchestra
Roger, Estienne British Library, London
Roller, Alfred Institut für Theaterwissenschaft, University of Cologne
Romania *1–6* Institutul de Cercetāri Etnologice şi Dialectologice, Bucharest
Romantic Kunsthalle, Hamburg
Romberg Royal College of Music, London
Rome *1, 4* Mansell Collection, London, and Alinari, Florence; *2* Soprintendenza alle Antichità delle Provincie di Napoli e Caserta, Naples; *5* Monumenti Musei e Gallerie Pontificie, Vatican City; *6* Trustees of the British Museum, London; *7* Museo di Roma; *9* Biblioteca Nazionale, Turin; *10, 11* British Library, London; *12* photo Musées Nationaux, Paris; *13* Conservatorio di Musica Santa Cecilia, Rome
Rondeau *1* Bibliothèque Nationale, Paris; *2* Giraudon, Paris
Rore, Cipriano de *1* Kunsthistorisches Museum, Vienna; *2* Civico Museo Bibliografico Musicale, Bologna
Rosbaud, Hans photo Erich Auerbach, London
Rosenmüller, Johann Bayerische Staatsbibliothek, Munich
Rosenthal, Moriz Music Division, New York Public Library at Lincoln Center, Astor, Lenox and Tilden Foundations
Rossi, Luigi British Library, London
Rossi, Michelangelo British Library, London
Rossi, Salamone British Library, London
Rossini, Gioachino *1* Edward T. Cone, Princeton, New Jersey; *2* Accademia Filarmonica, Bologna; *4* Mansell Collection, London; *5, 6* Richard Macnutt, Tunbridge Wells; *7* British Library, London
Rotte (i) Bayerische Staatsbibliothek, Munich
Rotte (ii) *1* British Library, London; *2a* Trustees of the British Museum, London; *2b* Museum für Vor- und Frühgeschichte, Staatliche Museen Preussischer Kulturbesitz, Berlin; *2c* Römisch-Germanisches Museum, Cologne; *3* Antikvarisk Topografiska Arkivet, Stockholm / photo Sören Hallgren; *4* Norsk Folkemuseum, Oslo; *5* Museo Archeologico Nazionale, Cividale del Friuli; *6* Stiftsbibliothek, St Gall
Rousseau, Jean-Jacques Rowe Music Library, King's College, Cambridge
Roussel, Albert H. Roger-Viollet, Paris / photo Harlingue

Rozhdestvensky, Gennady photo Erich Auerbach, London
Rubbra, Edmund Alfred Lengnick & Co. Ltd, Croydon
Rubini, Giovanni Battista Theatre Museum, Victoria and Albert Museum, London
Rubinstein, Anton Royal College of Music, London
Rubinstein, Artur photo Clive Barda, London
Rubinstein, Nikolay Deutsches Musikgeschichtliches Archiv, Kassel
Ruckers *1* HM the Queen; *2, 3* photo Grant O'Brien
Ruffo, Titta Harold Rosenthal, London
Ruggles, Carl American Music Edition, Carl Fischer Inc., New York
Russian bassoon photo Schweizerisches Landesmuseum, Zurich
Russolo, Luigi Assessorato ai Beni e alle Attività Culturali, Regione Lombardia, Milan: from G. Franco Maffina, *Russolo: l'arte dei rumori 1913–1931* (1978)
Rwanda *1–5* photo Jos Gansemans
Sacchini, Antonio *1* Theatre Museum, Victoria and Albert Museum, London; *2* Rowe Music Library, King's College, Cambridge
Sacher, Paul photo Regula Zimmermann-Meier, Zurich
Sachs, Hans Stadtbibliothek, Porträtsammlung, Nuremberg
Sadeler, Johan Metropolitan Museum of Art (Harris Brisbane Dick Fund, 1953), New York
Safi al-Dīn Bodleian Library, Oxford
St Florian photo Max Eiersebner, Linz
Saint-Georges, Joseph Boulogne British Library, London
St Martial Bibliothèque Nationale, Paris
Saint-Saëns, Camille *1* SPADEM, Archives Photographiques, Paris; *2* James Harding
Salieri, Antonio *1* Gesellschaft der Musikfreunde, Vienna; *2* Österreichische Nationalbibliothek, Vienna
Salmon, Thomas British Library, London
Salomon, Johann Peter Royal College of Music, London
Salpinx Monumenti Musei e Gallerie Pontificie, Vatican City
Salzburg *1, 2* Museum Carolino Augusteum, Salzburg
Samish music *1* Staatliche Museen Preussischer Kulturbesitz, Berlin; *2* British Library, London
Sammartini, Giovanni Battista *1* Civico Museo Bibliografico Musicale, Bologna; *2* Kungliga Biblioteket, Stockholm
Sanquirico, Alessandro Institut für Theaterwissenschaft, University of Cologne
Santa Cruz, Domingo Revista Musical Chilena, Universidad de Chile, Santiago / photo Jean Lemann
Santley, Charles Harold Rosenthal, London
Sarabande British Library, London
Sarasate, Pablo de Museum of Art, Carnegie Institute, Pittsburgh
Sargent, Malcolm BBC, London